IMPORTANT! SAVE THIS CARD!

Your essential study ___ are just a click away.

STEP 1: SIGN IN

Shrink-wrapped to the back of your new copy of *Gardner's Art through the Ages*, you'll find the **ACCESS CODE** to essential resources, including **ArtStudy Online**, the interactive website that will help you save time and ace your exams. Follow the easy "First-Time Registration" instructions on the card.

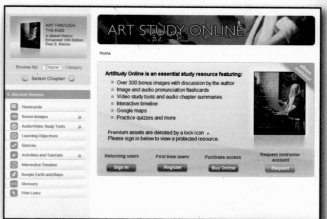

STEP 2: CHOOSE A CHAPTER AND CLICK ON A RESOURCE

After selecting a chapter, simply click on a tool—*Bonus Images, Flashcards, Audio/Video Study Tools, Quizzes,* or any of the other resources listed in the navigation bar.

HUNDREDS OF BONUS IMAGES

Icons in the margins of this book prompt you to click on *Bonus Images* at the website. Each of the hundreds of *Bonus Images* include a zoomable, high-resolution image of the artwork along with the discussion.

Video Study Tools, Audio Chapter Summaries, Image Flashcards, and more help you study and learn.

GARDNER'S
ART
through the
AGES

A GLOBAL HISTORY

ENHANCED THIRTEENTH EDITION

FRED S. KLEINER

WADSWORTH
CENGAGE Learning™

Australia • Brazil • Japan • Korea • Mexico • Singapore • Spain • United Kingdom • United States

WADSWORTH
CENGAGE Learning™

Gardner's Art through the Ages: A Global History,
Enhanced Thirteenth Edition
Fred S. Kleiner

Publisher: Clark Baxter

Senior Development Editor: Sharon Adams Poore

Assistant Editor: Kimberly Apfelbaum

Editorial Assistant: Ashley Bargende

Senior Media Editor: Wendy Constantine

Marketing Manager: Diane Wenckebach

Marketing Coordinator: Loreen Pelletier

Marketing Communications Manager: Heather Baxley

Senior Content Project Manager: Lianne Ames

Senior Art Director: Cate Barr

Print Buyer: Julio Esperas

Production Service/Layout: Joan Keyes, Dovetail Publishing Services

Text Designer: tani hasegawa

Photo Manager: John Hill

Cover Designer: tani hasegawa

Cover Image: *Woman Holding a Balance,* c. 1664 (oil on canvas), VERMEER, JAN (1632–75)/National Gallery of Art, Washington, DC, USA/The Bridgeman Art Library

Compositor: Thompson Type

For product information and technology assistance, contact us at
**Cengage Learning Customer & Sales Support,
1-800-354-9706**
For permission to use material from this text or product,
submit all requests online at **www.cengage.com/permissions.**
Further permissions questions can be emailed to
permissionrequest@cengage.com

Library of Congress Control Number: 2009932089

ISBN-13: 978-0-495-79986-3
ISBN-10: 0-495-79986-6

Wadsworth
20 Channel Center Street
Boston, MA 02210
USA

Cengage Learning is a leading provider of customized learning solutions with office locations around the globe, including Singapore, the United Kingdom, Australia, Mexico, Brazil, and Japan. Locate your local office at: **international.cengage.com/region**

Cengage Learning products are represented in Canada by Nelson Education, Ltd.

For your course and learning solutions, visit
www.cengage.com

Purchase any of our products at your local college store or at our preferred online store **www.ichapters.com**

Printed in the United States of America
2 3 4 5 6 7 13 12 11 10

About the Cover Art

JAN VERMEER, *Woman Holding a Balance, ca.* 1664. Oil on canvas, 1′ 3$\frac{7}{8}$″ × 1′ 2″. National Gallery of Art, Washington, D.C. (Widener Collection).

JAN VERMEER (1632–1675) was the preeminent painter of Dutch domestic interiors. Women figure prominently in Vermeer's paintings, which are idealized depictions that reflect the social values of the 17th-century Dutch middle class. In *Woman Holding a Balance,* a young woman wearing a veil and a fur-trimmed jacket stands before a table on which are spread her most precious possessions—pearl necklaces, gold chains, and gold coins. But neither the woman nor her treasures are the focus of the viewer's attention. Rather, Vermeer drew the viewer's eye to the center of the canvas and the balance for weighing gold that the woman holds in her right hand. The scales, however, are empty—in perfect balance, the way Ignatius of Loyola advised Catholics (Vermeer was a Catholic convert in the Protestant Dutch Republic) to lead a temperate, self-aware life and to balance one's sins with virtuous behavior. The mirror on the wall may refer to self-knowledge, but it may also symbolize the sin of vanity, as do the pearls and gold. Bolstering this interpretation is Vermeer's inclusion of a large framed painting of the *Last Judgment* depicting Christ as weigher of souls. Therefore, this tranquil domestic scene is pregnant with hidden meaning. The woman holds the scales in balance and contemplates the life she must lead—a life free from the temptations of worldly riches—in order to be judged favorably on Judgment Day.

The trio of covers for this enhanced 13th edition of *Art through the Ages* features one work each of painting, sculpture, and architecture, dating from the fourth century BCE to the 1990s, by one man, one woman, and one anonymous artist. The selection mirrors the content of the book as a whole, which surveys the art of all periods from prehistory to the present and worldwide, and examines artworks and buildings of all types, signed and anonymous, in the context of the cultures in which they were created.

CONTENTS

CHAPTER 11
LATE ANTIQUITY 289

CHAPTER 12
BYZANTIUM 311

CHAPTER 13
THE ISLAMIC WORLD 341

CHAPTER 14
NATIVE ARTS OF THE AMERICAS BEFORE 1300 365

CHAPTER 15
AFRICA BEFORE 1800 393

CHAPTER 16
EARLY MEDIEVAL EUROPE 407

PREFACE

THE GARDNER LEGACY IN THE 21ST CENTURY

I take great pleasure in introducing this enhanced version of the 13th edition of *Gardner's Art through the Ages: A Global History,* the first hybrid art history textbook. This innovative new "Gardner" retains all of the best features of traditional books on paper while harnessing 21st-century technology to expand by 25 percent the number of works examined—and, significantly, at no additional cost to students.

When Helen Gardner published the first edition of *Art through the Ages* in 1926, she could not have imagined that more than 80 years later instructors all over the world would still be using her textbook in their classrooms. Indeed, if she were alive today, she would not recognize the book that long ago became—and remains—the most widely read introduction to the history of art and architecture in the English language. During the past half century, successive authors have constantly reinvented Helen Gardner's groundbreaking global survey, always keeping it fresh and current and setting an ever-higher standard in both content and publication quality with each new edition. I am deeply gratified that both professors and students seem to agree that the 13th edition, released in 2008, lives up to that venerable tradition, for they have made it the number-one choice for art history survey courses. I hope they will find the enhanced version of this best-selling book exceeds the high expectations they have for each new Gardner edition.

In addition to the host of new features (described later) in the original 13th edition, the enhanced 13th edition incorporates an important new online component. All new copies of the enhanced edition come with a free access code to a Web site with discussions and illustrations of more than 300 "bonus" works of painting, sculpture, and architecture of all eras, from prehistory to the present, and worldwide, including virtually all of the works that professors have told me they would like to see added to the book. By combining an online component with the traditional book, I have been able to fulfill those requests without increasing either the length or the cost of the 13th edition. I am extremely grateful to Cengage/Wadsworth for making the considerable investment that has made this remarkable new hybrid textbook possible. In this enhanced edition, access is also available to more than 50 new multimedia lectures that focus on specific artworks, comparisons, media, and trends in art history.

To facilitate the use of the new online component of the hybrid Gardner, the margins of the pages of the printed book feature thumbnail photographs and abbreviated captions for every bonus work illustrated and discussed on the accompanying Web site. The thumbnails are situated at precisely the point in the book where those discussions tie in with and amplify the material treated in the original 13th edition. Video icons tie in content with the multimedia lectures. All maps have also been revised to incorporate every new site examined in the online component. Of course, all the ancillary resources (see page xv) for the 13th edition have been updated to reflect the greater number of artworks in the new hybrid text.

Although the original 13th edition and this enhanced version offer much that is fresh and new, some things have not changed since 1926, including the fundamental belief that guided Helen Gardner—namely, that the primary goal of an introductory art history textbook should be to foster an appreciation and understanding of historically significant works of art of all kinds from all periods and from all parts of the globe. Because of the longevity and diversity of the history of art, it is tempting to assign responsibility for telling its story to a large team of specialists. The Gardner publishers themselves took this approach for the first edition prepared after Helen Gardner's death, and it has now become the norm for introductory art history surveys. But students overwhelmingly say that the very complexity of the global history of art makes it all the more important for the story to be told with a consistent voice if they are to master so much diverse material. I think Helen Gardner would be pleased to know that the 13th edition of *Art through the Ages* once again has a single storyteller.

I continue to believe that the most effective way to tell the story of art through the ages, especially to anyone studying art history for the first time, is to organize the vast array of paintings, sculptures, buildings, and other artworks according to the civilizations that produced them and to consider each work in roughly chronological order. This approach has not merely stood the test of time. It is the most appropriate way to narrate the *history* of art. The principle that underlies my approach to every period of art history is that the enormous variation in the form and meaning of the artworks and buildings men and women have produced over the past 30,000 years is largely the result of the constantly changing contexts in which artists and architects worked. A historically based narrative is therefore best suited for a global history of art because it permits the author to situate each work discussed in its historical, social, economic, religious, and cultural context. That is, after all, what distinguishes art *history* from art *appreciation.*

In the 1926 edition of *Art through the Ages,* Helen Gardner discussed Henri Matisse and Pablo Picasso in a chapter entitled "Contemporary Art in Europe and America." Since then many other artists have emerged on the international scene, and the story of art through the ages has grown longer and even more complex. More important, perhaps, the discipline of art history has changed markedly in recent decades, and so too has Helen Gardner's book. The 13th edition fully reflects the latest art historical research emphases while maintaining the traditional strengths that have made previous editions of *Art through the Ages* so popular. While sustaining attention to style, chronology, iconography, and technique, I also ensure that issues of patronage, function, and context loom large in every chapter. I treat artworks not as isolated objects in sterile 21st-century museum settings but with a view toward their purpose and meaning in the society that produced them at the time they were produced. I examine not only the role of the artist or architect in the creation of a work of art or a building but also the role of the individuals or groups who paid the artists and influenced the shape their creations took. Further, I devote more space than previously to the role of women and women artists in societies worldwide over time, especially in this enhanced version of the 13th edition, with its greatly expanded list of works illustrated and discussed. In every chapter, I have tried to choose artworks and buildings that reflect the increasingly wide range of interests of scholars today, while not rejecting the traditional list of "great" works or the very notion of a "canon." Consequently, the selection of works in this edition encompasses every artistic medium and almost every era and culture, and includes many works that until recently art historians would not have considered to be "art" at all.

New to the 13th Edition

For the 13th edition of *Gardner's Art through the Ages: A Global History,* I have retained all of the features that made the 12th edition the best-selling version of the book in its 80-year history. Once again, the book boasts roughly 1,400 photographs, plans, and drawings, nearly all in color and reproduced according to the highest standards of clarity and color fidelity—plus more than 300 additional digital illustrations in the enhanced version (the "bonus images"). In total, there are well over 600 new or upgraded photos in the hybrid edition by a host of new photographers, as well as redesigned maps and plans and an extraordinary new set of architectural drawings prepared exclusively for *Art through the Ages* by John Burge.

The captions to the illustrations in the 13th edition of *Art through the Ages,* as before, contain a wealth of information, including the name of the artist or architect, if known; the formal title (printed in italics), if assigned, description of the work, or name of the building; the provenance or place of production of the object or location of the building; the date; the material(s) used; the size; and the current location if the work is in a museum or private collection. As in previous editions, scales accompany all plans, but for the first time scales now also appear next to each photograph of a painting, statue, or other artwork. The works illustrated vary enormously in size, from colossal sculptures carved into mountain cliffs and paintings that cover entire walls or ceilings to tiny figurines, coins, and jewelry that one can hold in the hand. Although the captions contain the pertinent dimensions, it is hard for students who have never seen the paintings or statues in person to translate those dimensions into an appreciation of the real size of the objects. The new scales provide an effective and direct way to visualize how big or how small a given artwork is and its relative size compared with other objects in the same chapter and throughout the book.

Also new to this edition are the Quick-Review Captions that students report they find invaluable when preparing for examinations. These brief synopses of the most significant aspects of each illustrated artwork or building accompany the captions to all images in the book and all images in the online supplement. The 13th edition offers two other new tools to aid students in reviewing and mastering the material presented. Each chapter now ends with a full-page feature called The Big Picture, which sets forth in bullet-point format the most important characteristics of each period or artistic movement discussed in the chapter. Small illustrations of characteristic works discussed accompany the summary of major points. Finally, I have attempted to tie all of the chapters together by providing with each copy of *Art through the Ages* a poster-size Global Timeline. This too features illustrations of key artworks and buildings of each age and geographical area as well as a brief enumeration of the most important art historical developments during that period. The time-

line has four major horizontal bands corresponding to Europe, the Americas, Asia, and Africa, and 34 vertical columns for the successive chronological periods from 30,000 BCE to the present.

Another pedagogical tool not found in any other introductory art history textbook is the *Before 1300* section that appears at the beginning of the second volume of the paperbound version of the 13th edition. Because many students taking the second half of a yearlong survey course will not have access to volume one, I have provided a special set of concise primers on religion and mythology and on architectural terminology and construction methods in the ancient and medieval worlds—information that is essential for understanding the history of art after 1300, both in the West and the East. The subjects of these special boxes are The Gods and Goddesses of Mount Olympus; Buddhism and Buddhist Iconography; Hinduism and Hindu Iconography; The Life of Jesus in Art; Greco-Roman Temple Design and the Classical Orders; Arches and Vaults; and Medieval Church Design.

Boxed essays once again appear throughout the book as well. This popular feature first appeared in the 11th edition of *Art through the Ages,* which won both the Texty and McGuffey Prizes of the Text and Academic Authors Association for the best college textbook of 2001 in the humanities and social sciences. In this edition the essays are more closely tied to the main text than ever before. Consistent with that greater integration, nearly all the boxes now incorporate photographs of important artworks discussed in the text proper that also illustrate the theme treated in the boxed essays. These essays fall under six broad categories, one of which is new to the 13th edition.

Architectural Basics boxes provide students with a solid foundation for the understanding of architecture. These discussions are concise explanations, with drawings and diagrams, of the major aspects of design and construction. The information included is essential to an understanding of architectural technology and terminology. The boxes address questions of how and why various forms developed; the problems architects confronted; and the solutions they used to resolve them. Topics discussed include how the Egyptians built the pyramids; the orders of classical architecture; Roman concrete construction; and the design and terminology of mosques, stupas, and Gothic cathedrals.

Materials and Techniques essays explain the various media artists employed from prehistoric to modern times. Since materials and techniques often influence the character of artworks, these discussions contain essential information on why paintings, sculptures, and works in other media appear as they do. Hollow-casting bronze statues; fresco painting; Chinese silk; Andean weaving; Islamic tile work; embroidery and tapestry; engraving, etching, and lithography; and daguerreotype and calotype photography are among the many subjects treated.

Religion and Mythology boxes introduce students to the principal elements of the world's great religions, past and present, and to the representation of religious and mythological themes in painting and sculpture of all periods and places. These discussions of belief systems and iconography give readers a richer understanding of some of the greatest artworks ever created. The topics include the gods and goddesses of Egypt, Mesopotamia, Greece, and Rome; the life of Jesus in art; Buddha and Buddhism; Muhammad and Islam; and Aztec religion.

Art and Society essays treat the historical, social, political, cultural, and religious context of art and architecture. In some instances, specific artworks are the basis for a discussion of broader themes, as when the Hegeso stele serves as the springboard for an exploration of the role of women in ancient Greek society. Another essay discusses how people's evaluations today of artworks can differ from those of the society that produced them by examining the problems created by the contemporary market for undocumented archaeological finds. Other subjects include Egyptian mummification; Etruscan women; Byzantine icons and iconoclasm; artistic training in Renaissance Italy; 19th-century academic salons and independent art exhibitions; the Mesoamerican ball game; Japanese court culture; and art and leadership in Africa.

Written Sources boxes present and discuss key historical documents illuminating important works of art and architecture throughout the world. The passages quoted permit voices from the past to speak directly to the reader, providing vivid and unique insights into the creation of artworks in all media. Examples include Bernard of Clairvaux's treatise on sculpture in medieval churches; Giovanni Pietro Bellori's biographies of Annibale Carracci and Caravaggio; Jean François Marmontel's account of 18th-century salon culture; as well as texts that bring the past to life, such as eyewitness accounts of the volcanic eruption that buried Roman Pompeii and of the fire that destroyed Canterbury Cathedral in medieval England.

A new category is *Artists on Art* in which artists and architects throughout history discuss both their theories and individual works. Examples include Sinan the Great's account of the mosque he designed for Selim II; Leonardo da Vinci and Michelangelo debating the relative merits of painting and sculpture; Artemisia Gentileschi reflecting on the special problems she confronted as a woman artist; Jacques-Louis David on Neoclassicism; Gustave Courbet on Realism; Henri Matisse on color; Pablo Picasso on Cubism; Diego Rivera on art for the people; and Judy Chicago on her seminal work *The Dinner Party.*

Instructors familiar with previous editions of *Art through the Ages* will also find that many of the chapters in the 13th edition have been reorganized, especially in volume two. For example, the treatment of European 17th-century art now appears in two discrete chapters, one devoted to Baroque Italy and Spain, the other to Northern Europe. A single chapter is devoted to the 18th century, another to the period from 1800 to 1870, and a third to 1870 to 1900. To assist instructors who end the first semester and begin the second semester at different points, Chapter 19 on Italian art from 1200 to 1400 appears for the first time in both volumes one and two of *Art through the Ages.*

Rounding out the features in the book itself is a Bibliography of books in English, including both general works and a chapter-by-chapter list of more focused studies, and a Glossary containing definitions of all terms introduced in the text in italics. The Glossary at the back of the enhanced 13th edition has been expanded to incorporate all the new terms introduced in the online essays discussing the 300-plus bonus images. I have also taken care to italicize and define in the text all Glossary terms that appear in volume two even if they have been used and defined in volume one, because many students enrolled in the second semester of a yearlong course will not have taken the first semester and will not be familiar with those terms.

A COMPLETE LEARNING PACKAGE

The 13th edition of *Art through the Ages,* even in the enhanced version, is not, however, a stand-alone text. In addition to the Global Timeline, every new copy of the book comes with a password to *Art-Study Online,* a Web site with access to the new bonus images and discussions, video study tools, and a host of multimedia resources that students can employ throughout the entire course, including image flashcards, audio study tools, and more. Instructors have access to a host of teaching tools, including digital images with zoom capabilities, video, and Google Earth™ coordinates. A new e-book is also available with this edition.

ACKNOWLEDGMENTS

A work as extensive as a global history of art could not be undertaken or completed without the counsel of experts in all areas of world art. As with previous editions, Cengage/Wadsworth has enlisted more than a hundred art historians to review every chapter of *Art through the Ages* in order to ensure that the text lived up to the Gardner reputation for accuracy as well as readability. I take great pleasure in acknowledging here the invaluable contributions to the 13th edition made by the following for their critiques of various chapters: Charles M. Adelman, University of Northern Iowa; Kirk Ambrose, University of Colorado–Boulder; Susan Ashbrook, Art Institute of Boston; Zainab Bahrani, Columbia University; Susan Bakewell, University of Texas–Austin; James J. Bloom, Florida State University; Suzaan Boettger, Bergen Community College; Colleen Bolton, Mohawk Valley Community College; Angi Elsea Bourgeois, Mississippi State University; Kimberly Bowes, Fordham University; Lawrence E. Butler, George Mason University; Alexandra Carpino, Northern Arizona University; Jane Carroll, Dartmouth College; Hipolito Rafael Chacon, University of Montana; Catherine M. Chastain, North Georgia College & State University; Violaine Chauvet, Johns Hopkins University; Daniel Connolly, Augustana College; Michael A. Coronel, University of Northern Colorado; Nicole Cox, Rochester Institute of Technology; Jodi Cranston, Boston University; Kathy Curnow, Cleveland State University; Giovanna De Appolonia, Boston University; Marion de Koning, Grossmont College; John J. Dobbins, University of Virginia; Erika Doss, University of Colorado–Boulder; B. Underwood DuRette, Thomas Nelson Community College; Daniel Ehnbom, University of Virginia; Lisa Farber, Pace University; James Farmer, Virginia Commonwealth University; Jerome Feldman, Hawaii Pacific University; Sheila ffolliott, George Mason University; Ferdinanda Florence, Solano Community College; William B. Folkestad, Central Washington University; Jeffery Fontana, Austin College; Mitchell Frank, Carleton University; Sara L. French, Wells College; Norman P. Gambill, South Dakota State University; Elise Goodman, University of Cincinnati; Kim T. Grant, University of Southern Maine; Elizabeth ten Grotenhuis, Silk Road Project; Sandra C. Haynes, Pasadena City College; Valerie Hedquist, University of Montana; Susan Hellman, Northern Virginia Community College; Marian J. Hollinger, Fairmont State University; Cheryl Hughes, Alta High School; Heidrun Hultgren, Kent State University; Joseph M. Hutchinson, Texas A&M University; Julie M. Johnson, Utah State University; Sandra L. Johnson, Citrus College; Deborah Kahn, Boston University; Fusae Kanda, Harvard University; Catherine Karkov, Miami University; Wendy Katz, University of Nebraska–Lincoln; Nita Kehoe-Gadway, Central Wyoming College; Nancy L. Kelker, Middle Tennessee State University; Cathie Kelly, University of Nevada–Las Vegas; Katie Kempton, Ohio University; John F. Kenfield, Rutgers University; Herbert L. Kessler, Johns Hopkins University; Monica Kjellman-Chapin, Emporia State University; Ellen Konowitz, State University of New York–New Paltz; Kathryn E. Kramer, State University of New York–Cortland; Carol Krinsky, New York University; Lydia Lehr, Atlantic Cape Community College; Krist Lien, Shelton State Community College; Ellen Longsworth, Merrimack College; David A. Ludley, Clayton State University; Henry Luttikhuizen, Calvin College; Christina Maranci, University of Wisconsin–Milwaukee; Dominic Marner, University of Guelph; Jack Brent Maxwell, Blinn College; Anne McClanan, Portland State University; Brian McConnell, Florida Atlantic University; Amy McNair, University of Kansas; Patrick McNaughton, Indiana University; Heather McPherson, University of Alabama–Birmingham; Cynthia Millis, Houston Community College–Southwest; Cynthia Taylor Mills, Brookhaven College; Keith N. Morgan, Boston University; Johanna D. Movassat, San Jose State University; Helen Nagy, University of Puget Sound; Heidi Nickisher, Rochester Institute of Technology; Bonnie Noble, University of North Carolina–Charlotte; Abigail Noonan, Rochester Institute of Technology; Marjorie Och, University of Mary Washington; Karen Michelle O'Day, University of Wisconsin–Eau Claire; Edward J. Olszewski, Case Western Reserve University; Allison Lee Palmer, University of Oklahoma; Martin Patrick, Illinois State University; Glenn Peers, University of Texas–Austin; Jane Peters, University of Kentucky; Julie Anne Plax, University of Arizona; Frances Pohl, Pomona College; Virginia C. Raguin, College of the Holy Cross; Donna Karen Reid, Chemeketa Community College; Albert W. Reischuck, Kent State University; Jonathan Ribner, Boston University; Cynthea Riesenberg, Washington Latin School; James G. Rogers Jr., Florida Southern College; Carey Rote, Texas A&M University–Corpus Christi; David J. Roxburgh, Harvard University; Conrad Rudolph, University of California–Riverside; Catherine B. Scallen, Case Western Reserve University; Denise

Schmandt-Besserat, University of Texas–Austin; Natasha Seaman, Berklee College of Music; Malia E. Serrano, Grossmont College; Laura Sommer, Daemen College; Natasha Staller, Amherst College; Nancy Steele-Hamme, Midwestern State University; Andrew Stewart, University of California–Berkeley; John R. Stocking, University of Calgary; Francesca Tronchin, Ohio State University; Frances Van Keuren, University of Georgia; Kelly Wacker, University of Montevallo; Carolynne Whitefeather, Utica College; Nancy L. Wicker, University of Mississippi; Alastair Wright, Princeton University; John G. Younger, University of Kansas; and Michael Zell, Boston University.

I am also happy to have this opportunity to express my gratitude to the extraordinary group of people at Cengage/Wadsworth involved with the editing, production, and distribution of *Art through the Ages*. Some of them I have now worked with on various projects for nearly two decades and feel privileged to count among my friends. The success of the Gardner series in all of its various iterations depends in no small part on the expertise and unflagging commitment of these dedicated professionals: Sean Wakely, president Cengage Arts and Sciences; at Wadsworth Publishing, P. J. Boardman, vice president and editor-in-chief; Clark Baxter, publisher; Sharon Adams Poore, senior development editor; Lianne Ames, senior content project manager; Wendy Constantine, senior media editor; Kimberly Apfelbaum, assistant editor; Ashley Bargende, editorial assistant; Cate Barr, senior art director; Scott Stewart, vice president managing director sales; Diane Wenckebach, senior marketing manager; as well as Heather Baxley, Doug Easton, tani hasegawa, Aimee Alcorn Lewis, Ellen Pettengell, and the incomparable group of local sales representatives who have passed on to me the welcome advice offered by the hundreds of instructors they speak to during their visits to college campuses throughout North America.

I am also deeply grateful to the following for their significant contributions to the success of the 13th edition of *Art through the Ages* and for their work on the enhanced version of the book: Joan Keyes, Dovetail Publishing Services; Ida May B. Norton, copy editor; Pat Lewis and Pete Shanks, proofreaders; Catherine Schnurr and Nancy Tobin, PrePressPMG, photo research; Sarah Evertson and Stephen Forsling, photo researchers; John Pierce, Thompson Type; Don Larson, Mapping Specialists; Mark Stanley, Digital Media Inc., U.S.A; Cindy Geiss, Graphic World; and, of course, John Burge, for his superb architectural drawings. I also wish to acknowledge my debt to Edward Tufte for an illuminating afternoon spent discussing publication design and production issues and for his insightful contribution to the creation of the scales that accompany all reproductions of paintings, sculptures, and other artworks in this edition. I am also deeply grateful to Kathleen Cohen and Yu Bong Ko for their work on the Study Guide and the Advanced Placement Guide, respectively.

Finally, I owe thanks to my colleagues at Boston University and to the thousands of students and the scores of teaching fellows in my art history courses during the past three decades. From them I have learned much that has helped determine the form and content of *Art through the Ages* and made it a much better book than it otherwise might have been.

Fred S. Kleiner

About the Author

FRED S. KLEINER (Ph.D., Columbia University) is the author or co-author of the 1st and 2nd editions of *Art through the Ages: A Concise Western History*, as well as the 10th, 11th, 12th, and 13th editions of *Art through the Ages: A Global History*, and more than a hundred publications on Greek and Roman art and architecture, including *A History of Roman Art*, also published by Wadsworth. He has taught the art history survey course for more than three decades, first at the University of Virginia and, since 1978, at Boston University, where he is currently Professor of Art History and Archaeology and Chair of the Department of the History of Art and Architecture. From 1985 to 1998, he was Editor-in-Chief of the *American Journal of Archaeology*. Long acclaimed for his inspiring lectures and devotion to students, Professor Kleiner won Boston University's Metcalf Award for Excellence in Teaching as well as the College Prize for Undergraduate Advising in the Humanities in 2002, and he is a two-time winner of the Distinguished Teaching Prize in the College of Arts and Sciences Honors Program. In 2007, he was elected a Fellow of the Society of Antiquaries of London, and, in 2009, in recognition of lifetime achievement in publication and teaching, a Fellow of the Text and Academic Authors Association.

Also by Fred Kleiner: *A History of Roman Art* (Wadsworth 2007; ISBN 0534638465), winner of the 2007 Texty Prize as the best new college textbook in the humanities and social sciences. In this authoritative and lavishly illustrated volume, Professor Kleiner traces the development of Roman art and architecture from Romulus' foundation of Rome in the eighth century BCE to the death of Constantine in the fourth century CE, with special chapters devoted to Pompeii and Herculaneum, Ostia, funerary and provincial art and architecture, and the earliest Christian art.

INTRODUCTION: WHAT IS ART HISTORY?

Except when referring to the modern academic discipline, people do not often juxtapose the words "art" and "history." They tend to think of history as the record and interpretation of past human actions, particularly social and political actions. Most think of art, quite correctly, as part of the present—as something people can see and touch. Of course, people cannot see or touch history's vanished human events, but a visible, tangible artwork is a kind of persisting event. One or more artists made it at a certain time and in a specific place, even if no one today knows just who, when, where, or why. Although created in the past, an artwork continues to exist in the present, long surviving its times. The first painters and sculptors died 30,000 years ago, but their works remain, some of them exhibited in glass cases in museums built only a few years ago.

Modern museum visitors can admire these objects from the remote past—and countless others humankind has produced over the millennia—without any knowledge of the circumstances that led to the creation of those works. The beauty or sheer size of an object can impress people, the artist's virtuosity in the handling of ordinary or costly materials can dazzle them, or the subject depicted can move them. Viewers can react to what they see, interpret the work in the light of their own experience, and judge it a success or a failure. These are all valid responses to a work of art. But the enjoyment and appreciation of artworks in museum settings are relatively recent phenomena, as is the creation of artworks solely for museum-going audiences to view.

Today, it is common for artists to work in private studios and to create paintings, sculptures, and other objects commercial art galleries will offer for sale. This is what the American painter CLYFFORD STILL (1904–1980) did when he created large canvases of pure color (FIG. I-1) titled simply with the year of their creation. Usually, someone the artist has never met will purchase the artwork and display it in a setting the artist has never seen. This practice is not a new phenomenon in the history of art—an ancient potter decorating a vase for sale at a village market stall probably did not know who would buy the pot or where it would be housed—but it is not at all typical. In fact, it is exceptional. Throughout history, most artists created paintings, sculptures, and other objects for specific patrons and settings and to fulfill a specific purpose, even if today no one knows the original contexts of most of those works. Museum visitors can appreciate the visual and tactile qualities of these objects, but they cannot understand why they were made or why they appear as they do without knowing the circumstances of their creation. Art *appreciation* does not require knowledge of the historical context of an artwork (or a building). Art *history* does.

Thus, a central aim of art history is to determine the original context of artworks. Art historians seek to achieve a full understanding not only of why these "persisting events" of human history look the way they do but also of why the artistic events happened at all. What unique set of circumstances gave rise to the erection of a particular building or led an individual patron to commission a certain artist to fashion a singular artwork for a specific place? The study of history is therefore vital to art history. And art history is often very important to the study of history. Art objects and buildings are historical documents that can shed light on the peoples who made them and on the times of their creation in a way other historical documents cannot. Furthermore, artists and architects can affect history by reinforcing or challenging cultural values and practices through the objects they create and the structures they build. Thus, the history of art and architecture is inseparable from the study of history, although the two disciplines are not the same.

The following pages introduce some of the distinctive subjects art historians address and the kinds of questions they ask, and explain some of the basic terminology they use when answering these questions. Readers armed with this arsenal of questions and terms will be ready to explore the multifaceted world of art through the ages.

ART HISTORY IN THE 21ST CENTURY

Art historians study the visual and tangible objects humans make and the structures humans build. Scholars traditionally have classified such works as architecture, sculpture, the pictorial arts (painting, drawing, printmaking, and photography), and the craft arts, or arts of design. The craft arts comprise utilitarian objects, such as ceramics, metalwork, textiles, jewelry, and similar accessories of ordinary living. Artists of every age have blurred the boundaries among these categories, but this is especially true today, when multimedia works abound.

From the earliest Greco-Roman art critics on, scholars have studied objects that their makers consciously manufactured as "art" and to which the artists assigned formal titles. But today's art historians also study a vast number of objects that their creators and owners almost certainly did not consider to be "works of art." Few ancient Romans, for example, would have regarded a coin bearing their emperor's portrait as anything but money. Today, an art museum may exhibit that coin in a locked case in a climate-controlled room, and scholars may subject it to the same kind of art historical analysis as a portrait by an acclaimed Renaissance or modern sculptor or painter.

The range of objects art historians study is constantly expanding and now includes, for example, computer-generated images, whereas in the past almost anything produced using a machine would not have been regarded as art. Most people still consider the performing arts—music, drama, and dance—as outside art history's realm because these arts are fleeting, impermanent media. But recently even this distinction between "fine art" and "performance art" has become blurred. Art historians, however, generally ask the same kinds of questions about what they study, whether they employ a restrictive or expansive definition of art.

The Questions Art Historians Ask

HOW OLD IS IT? Before art historians can construct a history of art, they must be sure they know the date of each work they study. Thus, an indispensable subject of art historical inquiry is *chronology,*

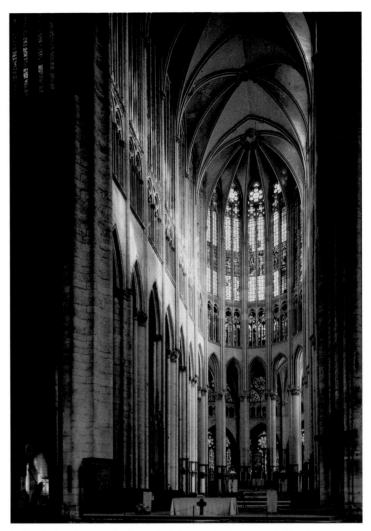

I-2 Choir of Beauvais Cathedral, Beauvais, France, rebuilt after 1284.

The style of an object or building often varies from region to region. This cathedral has towering stone vaults and large stained-glass windows typical of 13th-century French architecture.

the dating of art objects and buildings. If researchers cannot determine a monument's age, they cannot place the work in its historical context. Art historians have developed many ways to establish, or at least approximate, the date of an artwork.

Physical evidence often reliably indicates an object's age. The material used for a statue or painting—bronze, plastic, or oil-based pigment, to name only a few—may not have been invented before a certain time, indicating the earliest possible date someone could have fashioned the work. Or artists may have ceased using certain materials—such as specific kinds of inks and papers for drawings—at a known time, providing the latest possible dates for objects made of those materials. Sometimes the material (or the manufacturing technique) of an object or a building can establish a very precise date of production or construction. Studying tree rings, for instance, usually can help scholars determine within a narrow range the date of a wood statue or a timber roof beam.

Documentary evidence can help pinpoint the date of an object or building when a dated written document mentions the work. For example, official records may note when church officials commissioned a new altarpiece—and how much they paid to which artist.

Internal evidence can play a significant role in dating an artwork. A painter might have depicted an identifiable person or a kind of hairstyle, clothing, or furniture fashionable only at a certain

RESOURCES

FOR FACULTY

PowerLecture DVD with Digital Image Library and JoinIn
ISBN 1439085854

Bring digital images into the classroom with this one-stop lecture- and class-presentation tool that makes it easy to assemble, edit, and present customized lectures for your course using Microsoft® PowerPoint®. Available on DVD, the Digital Image Library provides high-resolution images (maps, diagrams, most of the fine-art images from the text, and all of the 300-plus new bonus images) for lectures, either in an easy-to-use PowerPoint presentation format or in individual file formats compatible with other image-viewing software. A zoom feature allows you to magnify selected portions of an image for more detailed display in class, or you can display images side by side for comparison and contrast. You can easily customize your classroom presentation by adding your personal visuals to those from the text. The PowerLecture also includes a Google Earth™ application that enables you to zoom in on an entire city as well as key monuments and buildings within it. There are links to specific figures for every chapter. The PowerLecture includes an Image Transition Guide, an electronic Instructor's Manual, and a Test Bank with multiple-choice, matching, short-answer, and essay questions in ExamView® computerized format. These text-specific Microsoft® PowerPoint® slides are created for use with JoinIn™ software for classroom personal-response systems ("clickers"). JoinIn™ is the easiest way to turn your lecture into a personal, fully interactive experience for your students. JoinIn™ turns PowerPoint® technology into a powerful audience-response vehicle enabling you to take attendance, poll students, check student comprehension of difficult concepts, and even administer quizzes without collecting papers or grading.

WebTutor on Blackboard or WebCT
WebTutor ISBN: 0495910686
BlackBoard ISBN: 04959106451

This package allows you to assign preformatted, text-specific content that is available as soon as you log on, or to customize the learning environment in any way you choose—from uploading images and other resources to adding Web links to creating your own practice materials. Cartridge content includes Test Bank, practice quizzes, Video Study Tools, and ArtStudy Online.

Contact your Wadsworth representative.

Slides

Contact your Wadsworth representative.

FOR STUDENTS

ArtStudy Online

This tool gives access to the additional bonus images (more than 300) from the 13th enhanced edition together with commentary by the author, as well as the new Video Study Tools (multimedia lectures) and a host of resources including **image flashcards** of artworks in the text that can be magnified with a zoom feature. With the compare-and-contrast feature, two works can be displayed side by side for more in-depth analysis. Additional tools include Interactive Google Maps™ (virtually tour the locations featured in the book); an interactive timeline; audio chapter summaries; architectural basics tutorials; audio study tools; student practice quizzes; a guide to researching art history online; and tips on becoming a successful student of art and art history.

e-Book

A new multimedia e-book offers links within the page to the bonus images and discussions as well as to the new Video Study Tools and Interactive Google Maps™. The e-book also provides search tools, an index, and an audio pronunciation glossary. The e-book pages match the printed book exactly, and can be zoomed to reveal details of high-resolution images. This product is available with ArtStudy Online as a stand-alone textbook solution.

Contact your Wadsworth representative.

Slide Guide

With this lecture companion, students can take notes alongside reprints of the art images shown in class. It features reproductions of the images from the book with full captions, page numbers, and space for note-taking. New to this edition's slide guide are two features—(1) Google Earth™ coordinates to link satellite images of historical sites and images to textual references and (2) end-of-chapter questions incorporating Google Earth™ use and critical thinking to help students gain a more comprehensive understanding of artwork discussed in class.

Study Guide
Volume 1 ISBN: 0495503916
Volume 2 ISBN: 0495503924

This study tool focuses on critical analysis of the subject through a workbook section that includes discussions, maps, timelines, and essay and multiple-choice questions. To enhance student learning and provide more practical application of information, there are three self-quizzes covering each chapter of the text. Test questions include multiple choice, short answer, and image identification. Complete answers and page references are at the end of the guide.

If you are interested in bundling any of the preceding student resources with the text, contact your Wadsworth representative.

To order student editions packaged with the Timeline and ArtStudy Online at no extra cost to students, use the ISBNs listed below:

Gardner's Art through the Ages: A Global History,
13th enhanced edition
ISBN: 0495799866

Gardner's Art through the Ages: A Global History,
13th enhanced edition, Volume I
ISBN: 1439085781

Gardner's Art through the Ages: A Global History,
13th enhanced edition, Volume II
ISBN: 1439085811

1 ft.

I-1 CLYFFORD STILL, *1948-C, PH-15,* 1948. Oil on canvas, 6′ 8$\frac{7}{8}$″ × 5′ 10$\frac{3}{4}$″. Hirshhorn Museum and Sculpture Garden, Smithsonian Institution, Washington, D.C. (purchased with funds of Joseph H. Hirshhorn, 1992).

Clyfford Still painted this abstract composition without knowing who would purchase it or where it would be displayed, but throughout history most artists created works for specific patrons and settings.

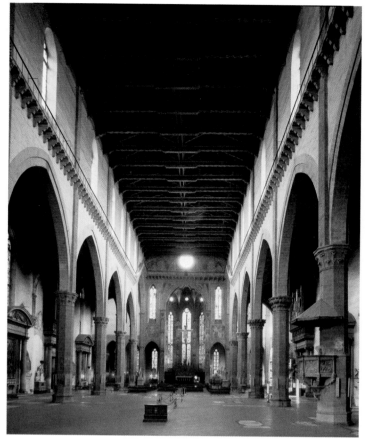

I-3 Interior of Santa Croce, Florence, Italy, begun 1294.

In contrast to Beauvais Cathedral (FIG. I-2), this contemporaneous Florentine church conforms to the quite different regional style of Italy. The building has a low timber roof and small windows.

I-4 GEORGIA O'KEEFFE, *Jack-in-the-Pulpit No. 4,* 1930. Oil on canvas, 3′ 4″ × 2′ 6″. National Gallery of Art, Washington, D.C. (Alfred Stieglitz Collection, bequest of Georgia O'Keeffe).

O'Keeffe's paintings feature close-up views of petals and leaves in which the organic forms become powerful abstract compositions. This approach to painting typifies the artist's distinctive personal style.

time. If so, the art historian can assign a more accurate date to that painting.

Stylistic evidence is also very important. The analysis of *style*—an artist's distinctive manner of producing an object—is the art historian's special sphere. Unfortunately, because it is a subjective assessment, stylistic evidence is by far the most unreliable chronological criterion. Still, art historians find style a very useful tool for establishing chronology.

WHAT IS ITS STYLE? Defining artistic style is one of the key elements of art historical inquiry, although the analysis of artworks solely in terms of style no longer dominates the field as it once did. Art historians speak of several different kinds of artistic styles.

Period style refers to the characteristic artistic manner of a specific time, usually within a distinct culture, such as "Archaic Greek" or "Late Byzantine." But many periods do not manifest any stylistic unity at all. How would someone define the artistic style of the opening decade of the new millennium in North America? Far too many crosscurrents exist in contemporary art for anyone to describe a period style of the early 21st century—even in a single city such as New York.

Regional style is the term art historians use to describe variations in style tied to geography. Like an object's date, its *provenance,* or place of origin, can significantly determine its character. Very often two artworks from the same place made centuries apart are more similar than contemporaneous works from two different regions. To cite one example, usually only an expert can distinguish between an Egyptian statue carved in 2500 BCE and one made in 500 BCE. But no

one would mistake an Egyptian statue of 500 BCE for one of the same date made in Greece or Mexico.

Considerable variations in a given area's style are possible, however, even during a single historical period. In late medieval Europe, French architecture differed significantly from Italian architecture. The interiors of Beauvais Cathedral (FIG. I-2) and the Florentine church of Santa Croce (FIG. I-3) typify the architectural styles of France and Italy, respectively, at the end of the 13th century. The rebuilding of the east end of Beauvais Cathedral began in 1284. Construction commenced on Santa Croce only 10 years later. Both structures employ the *pointed arch* characteristic of this era, yet the two churches differ strikingly. The French church has towering stone ceilings and large expanses of colored windows, whereas the Italian building has a low timber roof and small, widely separated windows. Because the two contemporaneous churches served similar purposes, regional style mainly explains their differing appearance.

Personal style, the distinctive manner of individual artists or architects, often decisively explains stylistic discrepancies among monuments of the same time and place. In 1930 the American painter GEORGIA O'KEEFFE (1887–1986) produced a series of paintings of flowering plants. One of them was *Jack-in-the-Pulpit No. 4* (FIG. I-4), a sharply focused close-up view of petals and leaves. O'Keeffe captured the growing plant's slow, controlled motion while converting

1 ft.

I-5 BEN SHAHN, *The Passion of Sacco and Vanzetti*, 1931–1932. Tempera on canvas, 7' ½" × 4'. Whitney Museum of American Art, New York (gift of Edith and Milton Lowenthal in memory of Juliana Force).

A contemporary of O'Keeffe's, Shahn developed a style of painting that differed markedly from hers. His paintings are often social commentaries on current events and incorporate readily identifiable people.

the plant into a powerful abstract composition of lines, forms, and colors (see the discussion of art historical vocabulary in the next section). Only a year later, another American artist, BEN SHAHN (1898–1969), painted *The Passion of Sacco and Vanzetti* (FIG. I-5), a stinging commentary on social injustice inspired by the trial and execution of two Italian anarchists, Nicola Sacco and Bartolomeo Vanzetti. Many people believed Sacco and Vanzetti had been unjustly convicted of killing two men in a holdup in 1920. Shahn's painting compresses time in a symbolic representation of the trial and its aftermath. The two executed men lie in their coffins. Presiding over them are the three members of the commission (headed by a college president wearing academic cap and gown) that declared the original trial fair and cleared the way for the executions. Behind, on the wall of a stately government building, hangs the framed portrait of the judge who pronounced the

I-6 GISLEBERTUS, The weighing of souls, detail of Last Judgment (FIG. 17-12), west tympanum of Saint-Lazare, Autun, France, ca. 1120–1135.

In this high relief portraying the weighing of souls on Judgment Day, Gislebertus used disproportion and distortion to dehumanize the devilish figure yanking on the scales of justice.

initial sentence. Personal style, not period or regional style, sets Shahn's canvas apart from O'Keeffe's. The contrast is extreme here because of the very different subjects the artists chose. But even when two artists depict the same subject, the results can vary widely. The *way* O'Keeffe painted flowers and the *way* Shahn painted faces are distinctive and unlike the styles of their contemporaries. (See the "Who Made It?" discussion on page 5.)

The different kinds of artistic styles are not mutually exclusive. For example, an artist's personal style may change dramatically during a long career. Art historians then must distinguish among the different period styles of a particular artist, such as the "Blue Period" and the "Cubist Period" of the prolific 20th-century artist Pablo Picasso.

WHAT IS ITS SUBJECT? Another major concern of art historians is, of course, subject matter, encompassing the story, or narrative; the scene presented; the action's time and place; the persons involved; and the environment and its details. Some artworks, such as modern abstract paintings (FIG. I-1), have no subject, not even a setting. The "subject" is the artwork itself. But when artists represent people, places, or actions, viewers must identify these aspects to achieve complete understanding of the work. Art historians traditionally separate pictorial subjects into various categories, such as religious, historical, mythological, *genre* (daily life), portraiture, *landscape* (a depiction of a place), *still life* (an arrangement of inanimate objects), and their numerous subdivisions and combinations.

Iconography—literally the "writing of images"—refers both to the content, or subject of an artwork, and to the study of content in art. By extension, it also includes the study of *symbols*, images that stand for other images or encapsulate ideas. In Christian art, two intersecting

I-7 The four evangelists, folio 14 verso of the *Aachen Gospels*, ca. 810. Ink and tempera on vellum, $1' \times 9\frac{1}{2}''$. Cathedral Treasury, Aachen.

Artists depict figures with attributes in order to identify them for viewers. The authors of the four gospels have distinctive attributes—John an eagle, Luke an ox, Mark a lion, and Matthew a winged man.

I-8 ALBRECHT DÜRER, *The Four Horsemen of the Apocalypse*, ca. 1498. Woodcut, $1'\ 3\frac{1}{4}'' \times 11''$. Metropolitan Museum of Art, New York (gift of Junius S. Morgan, 1919).

Personifications are abstract ideas codified in human form. Here, Albrecht Dürer represented Death, Famine, War, and Pestilence as four men on charging horses, each carrying an identifying attribute.

lines of unequal length or a simple geometric cross can serve as an emblem of the religion as a whole, symbolizing the cross of Jesus Christ's crucifixion. A symbol also can be a familiar object the artist imbued with greater meaning. A balance or scale, for example, may symbolize justice or the weighing of souls on Judgment Day (FIG. I-6).

Artists may depict figures with unique *attributes* identifying them. In Christian art, for example, each of the authors of the New Testament Gospels, the four evangelists (FIG. I-7), has a distinctive attribute. People can recognize Saint John by the eagle associated with him, Luke by the ox, Mark by the lion, and Matthew by the winged man.

Throughout the history of art, artists have used *personifications*—abstract ideas codified in human form. Worldwide, people visualize Liberty as a robed woman with a torch because of the fame of the colossal statue set up in New York City's harbor in the 19th century. *The Four Horsemen of the Apocalypse* (FIG. I-8) is a terrifying late-15th-century depiction of the fateful day at the end of time when, according to the Bible's last book, Death, Famine, War, and Pestilence will annihilate the human race. The German artist ALBRECHT DÜRER (1471–1528) personified Death as an emaciated old man with a pitchfork. Dürer's Famine swings the scales that will weigh human souls (compare FIG. I-6), War wields a sword, and Pestilence draws a bow.

Even without considering style and without knowing a work's maker, informed viewers can determine much about the work's period and provenance by iconographical and subject analysis alone. In *The Passion of Sacco and Vanzetti* (FIG. I-5), for example, the two coffins, the trio headed by an academic, and the robed judge in the background are all pictorial clues revealing the painting's subject. The work's date must be after the trial and execution, probably while the event was still newsworthy. And because the two men's deaths caused the greatest outrage in the United States, the painter–social critic was probably American.

WHO MADE IT? If Ben Shahn had not signed his painting of Sacco and Vanzetti, an art historian could still assign, or *attribute* (make an *attribution* of), the work to him based on knowledge of the artist's personal style. Although signing (and dating) works is quite common (but by no means universal) today, in the history of art countless works exist whose artists remain unknown. Because personal style can play a large role in determining the character of an artwork, art historians often try to attribute anonymous works to known artists. Sometimes they assemble a group of works all thought to be by the same person, even though none of the objects in the group is the known work of an artist with a recorded name. Art historians thus reconstruct the careers of artists such as "the Achilles Painter," the anonymous ancient Greek vase painter whose masterwork is a depiction of the hero Achilles. Scholars base their attributions on internal evidence, such as the distinctive way an artist draws or carves drapery folds, earlobes, or flowers. It requires a keen, highly trained eye and long experience to become a *connoisseur*, an expert in

1 in.

I-9 Augustus wearing the corona civica, early first century CE. Marble, 1′ 5″ high. Glyptothek, Munich.

Patrons frequently dictate the form their portraits will take. The Roman emperor Augustus demanded that he always be portrayed as a young, godlike head of state even though he lived to age 76.

assigning artworks to "the hand" of one artist rather than another. Attribution is subjective, of course, and ever open to doubt. At present, for example, international debate rages over attributions to the famous 17th-century Dutch painter Rembrandt.

Sometimes a group of artists works in the same style at the same time and place. Art historians designate such a group as a *school.* "School" does not mean an educational institution. The term connotes only chronological, stylistic, and geographic similarity. Art historians speak, for example, of the Dutch school of the 17th century and, within it, of subschools such as those of the cities of Haarlem, Utrecht, and Leyden.

WHO PAID FOR IT? The interest many art historians show in attribution reflects their conviction that the identity of an artwork's maker is the major reason the object looks the way it does. For them, personal style is of paramount importance. But in many times and places, artists had little to say about what form their work would take. They toiled in obscurity, doing the bidding of their *patrons,* those who paid them to make individual works or employed them on a continuing basis. The role of patrons in dictating the content and shaping the form of artworks is also an important subject of art historical inquiry.

In the art of portraiture, to name only one category of painting and sculpture, the patron has often played a dominant role in deciding how the artist represented the subject, whether that person was the patron or another individual, such as a spouse, son, or mother. Many Egyptian pharaohs and some Roman emperors, for example, insisted that artists depict them with unlined faces and perfect youthful bodies no matter how old they were when portrayed. In these cases, the state employed the sculptors and painters, and the artists had no choice but to depict their patrons in the officially approved manner. This is why Augustus, who lived to age 76, looks so young in his portraits (FIG. I-9). Although Roman emperor for more than 40 years, Augustus demanded that artists always represent him as a young, godlike head of state.

All modes of artistic production reveal the impact of patronage. Learned monks provided the themes for the sculptural decoration of medieval church portals (FIG. I-6). Renaissance princes and popes dictated the subject, size, and materials of artworks destined for buildings constructed according to their specifications. An art historian could make a very long list of commissioned works, and it would indicate that throughout the history of art, patrons have had diverse tastes and needs and demanded different kinds of art. Whenever a patron contracts an artist or architect to paint, sculpt, or build in a prescribed manner, personal style often becomes a very minor factor in the ultimate appearance of the painting, statue, or building. In these cases, the identity of the patron reveals more to art historians than does the identity of the artist or school. The portrait of Augustus wearing a *corona civica,* or civic crown (FIG. I-9), was the work of a virtuoso sculptor, a master wielder of hammer and chisel. But scores of similar portraits of that emperor exist today. They differ in quality but not in kind from this one. The patron, not the artist, determined the character of these artworks. Augustus's public image never varied.

The Words Art Historians Use

Like all specialists, art historians have their own specialized vocabulary. That vocabulary consists of hundreds of words, but certain basic terms are indispensable for describing artworks and buildings of any time and place. They make up the essential vocabulary of *formal analysis,* the visual analysis of artistic form. Definitions of the most important of these art historical terms follow.

FORM AND COMPOSITION *Form* refers to an object's shape and structure, either in two dimensions (for example, a figure painted on a canvas) or in three dimensions (such as a statue carved from a marble block). Two forms may take the same shape but may differ in their color, texture, and other qualities. *Composition* refers to how an artist organizes (*composes*) forms in an artwork, either by placing shapes on a flat surface or by arranging forms in space.

MATERIAL AND TECHNIQUE To create art forms, artists shape materials (pigment, clay, marble, gold, and many more) with tools (pens, brushes, chisels, and so forth). Each of the materials and tools available has its own potentialities and limitations. Part of all artists' creative activity is to select the *medium* and instrument most suitable to the artists' purpose—or to develop new media and tools, such as bronze and concrete in antiquity and cameras and computers in modern times. The processes artists employ, such as applying paint to canvas with a brush, and the distinctive, personal ways they handle materials constitute their *technique.* Form, material, and technique interrelate and are central to analyzing any work of art.

LINE Among the most important elements defining an artwork's shape or form is *line.* A line can be understood as the path of a point moving in space, an invisible line of sight. More commonly, however, artists and architects make a line tangible by drawing (or chiseling) it on a *plane,* a flat surface. A line may be very thin, wirelike, and delicate. It may be thick and heavy. Or it may alternate quickly from broad to narrow, the strokes jagged or the outline broken. When a continuous line defines an object's outer shape, art historians call it a *contour line.* All of these line qualities are present in Dürer's *Four Horsemen of the Apocalypse* (FIG. I-8). Contour lines define the basic shapes of clouds, human and animal limbs, and weapons. Within the forms, series of short broken lines create shadows and textures. An overall pattern of long parallel strokes suggests the dark sky on the frightening day when the world is about to end.

COLOR Light reveals all colors. Light in the world of the painter and other artists differs from natural light. Natural light, or sunlight, is whole or *additive light.* As the sum of all the wavelengths composing the visible *spectrum,* natural light may be disassembled or fragmented into the individual colors of the spectral band. The painter's light in art—the light reflected from pigments and objects—is *subtractive light.* Paint pigments produce their individual colors by reflecting a segment of the spectrum while absorbing all the rest. Green pigment, for example, subtracts or absorbs all the light in the spectrum except that seen as green.

Hue is the property that gives a color its name. Although the spectrum colors merge into each other, artists usually conceive of their hues as distinct from one another. Color has two basic variables—the apparent amount of light reflected and the apparent purity. A change in one must produce a change in the other. Some terms for these variables are *value,* or *tonality* (the degree of lightness or darkness), and *intensity,* or *saturation* (the purity of a color, or its brightness or dullness).

Artists call the three basic colors—red, yellow, and blue—the *primary colors.* The *secondary colors* result from mixing pairs of primaries: orange (red and yellow), purple (red and blue), and green (yellow and blue). *Complementary colors* represent the pairing of a primary color and the secondary color created from mixing the two other primary colors—red and green, yellow and purple, and blue and orange. They "complement," or complete, each other, one absorbing colors the other reflects.

Artists can manipulate the appearance of colors, however. One artist who made a systematic investigation of the formal aspects of art, especially color, was JOSEF ALBERS (1888–1976), a German-born artist who emigrated to the United States in 1933. In connection with his studies, Albers created the series *Homage to the Square*—hundreds of paintings, most of which are color variations on the same composition of concentric squares, as in the illustrated example (FIG. I-10). The series reflected Albers's belief that art originates in "the discrepancy between physical fact and psychic effect."[1] Because the composition in most of these paintings remains constant, the works succeed in revealing the relativity and instability of color perception. Albers varied the hue, saturation, and value of each square in the paintings in this series. As a result, the sizes of the squares from painting to painting appear to vary (although they remain the same), and the sensations emanating from the paintings range from clashing dissonance to delicate serenity. Albers explained his motivation for focusing on color juxtapositions:

> They [the colors] are juxtaposed for various and changing visual effects.... Such action, reaction, interaction ... is sought in order to make obvious how colors influence and change each other; that the same color, for instance—with different grounds or neighbors—looks different.... Such color deceptions prove that we see colors almost never unrelated to each other.[2]

Albers's quotation is only one example of how artists' comments on their own works are often invaluable to art historians. In *Art through*

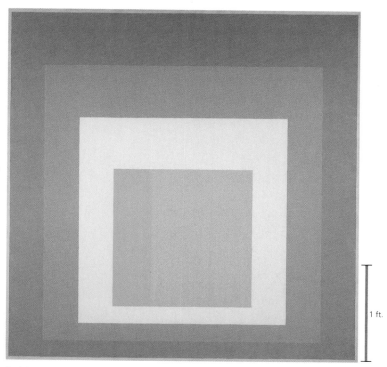

1 ft.

I-10 JOSEF ALBERS, *Homage to the Square: "Ascending,"* 1953. Oil on composition board, 3′ 7½″ × 3′ 7½″. Whitney Museum of American Art, New York.

Josef Albers painted hundreds of canvases with the same composition but employed variations in hue, saturation, and value in order to reveal the relativity and instability of color perception.

the Ages, artist commentaries appear frequently in boxed features called "Artists on Art."

TEXTURE The term *texture* refers to the quality of a surface, such as rough or shiny. Art historians distinguish between true texture, or the tactile quality of the surface, and represented texture, as when painters depict an object as having a certain texture even though the pigment is the true texture. Sometimes artists combine different materials of different textures on a single surface, juxtaposing paint with pieces of wood, newspaper, fabric, and so forth. Art historians refer to this mixed-media technique as *collage.* Texture is, of course, a key determinant of any sculpture's character. A viewer's first impulse is usually to handle a piece of sculpture—even though museum signs often warn "Do not touch!" Sculptors plan for this natural human response, using surfaces varying in texture from rugged coarseness to polished smoothness. Textures are often intrinsic to a material, influencing the type of stone, wood, plastic, clay, or metal sculptors select.

SPACE, MASS, AND VOLUME *Space* is the bounded or boundless "container" of objects. For art historians, space can be the literal three-dimensional space occupied by a statue or a vase or contained within a room or courtyard. Or space can be *illusionistic,* as when painters depict an image (or illusion) of the three-dimensional spatial world on a two-dimensional surface.

Mass and *volume* describe three-dimensional objects and space. In both architecture and sculpture, mass is the bulk, density, and weight of matter in space. Yet the mass need not be solid. It can be the exterior form of enclosed space. Mass can apply to a solid Egyptian pyramid or stone statue, to a church, synagogue, or mosque—architectural shells enclosing sometimes vast spaces—and to a hollow metal statue or baked clay pot. Volume is the space that mass organizes, divides, or encloses. It may be a building's interior spaces, the

I-11 Claude Lorrain, *Embarkation of the Queen of Sheba,* 1648. Oil on canvas, 4′ 10″ × 6′ 4″. National Gallery, London.

To create the illusion of a deep landscape, Claude Lorrain employed perspective, reducing the size of and blurring the most distant forms. Also, all diagonal lines converge on a single point.

1 ft.

intervals between a structure's masses, or the amount of space occupied by three-dimensional objects such as sculpture, pottery, or furniture. Volume and mass describe both the exterior and interior forms of a work of art—the forms of the matter of which it is composed and the spaces immediately around the work and interacting with it.

PERSPECTIVE AND FORESHORTENING *Perspective* is one of the most important pictorial devices for organizing forms in space. Throughout history, artists have used various types of perspective to create an illusion of depth or space on a two-dimensional surface. The French painter CLAUDE LORRAIN (1600–1682) employed several perspectival devices in *Embarkation of the Queen of Sheba* (FIG. **I-11**), a painting of a biblical episode set in a 17th-century European harbor with a Roman ruin in the left foreground. For example, the figures and boats on the shoreline are much larger than those in the distance. Decreasing the size of an object makes it appear farther away. Also, the top and bottom of the port building at the painting's right side are not parallel horizontal lines, as they are

1 ft.

I-12 Ogata Korin, *White and Red Plum Blossoms,* Edo period, ca. 1710–1716. Pair of twofold screens. Ink, color, and gold leaf on paper, each screen 5′ 1⅝″ × 5′ 7⅞″. MOA Art Museum, Shizuoka-ken.

Ogata Korin was more concerned with creating an interesting composition of shapes on a surface than with locating objects in space. Asian artists rarely employed Western perspective.

I-13 PETER PAUL RUBENS, *Lion Hunt,* 1617–1618. Oil on canvas, 8′ 2″ × 12′ 5″. Alte Pinakothek, Munich.

Foreshortening—the representation of a figure or object at an angle to the picture plane—is a common device in Western art for creating the illusion of depth. Foreshortening is a type of perspective.

in an actual building. Instead, the lines converge beyond the structure, leading viewers' eyes toward the hazy, indistinct sun on the horizon. These perspectival devices—the reduction of figure size, the convergence of diagonal lines, and the blurring of distant forms—have been familiar features of Western art since the ancient Greeks. But it is important to note at the outset that all kinds of perspective are only pictorial conventions, even when one or more types of perspective may be so common in a given culture that people accept them as "natural" or as "true" means of representing the natural world.

In *White and Red Plum Blossoms* (FIG. I-12), a Japanese landscape painting on two folding screens, OGATA KORIN (1658–1716) used none of these Western perspective conventions. He showed the two plum trees as seen from a position on the ground, but viewers look down on the stream between them from above. Less concerned with locating the trees and stream in space than with composing shapes on a surface, the painter played the water's gently swelling curves against the jagged contours of the branches and trunks. Neither the French nor the Japanese painting can be said to project "correctly" what viewers "in fact" see. One painting is not a "better" picture of the world than the other. The European and Asian artists simply approached the problem of picture-making differently.

Artists also represent single figures in space in varying ways. When the Flemish artist PETER PAUL RUBENS (1577–1640) painted *Lion Hunt* (FIG. I-13), he used *foreshortening* for all the hunters and animals—that is, he represented their bodies at angles to the picture plane. When in life one views a figure at an angle, the body appears to contract as it extends back in space. Foreshortening is a kind of perspective. It produces the illusion that one part of the body is farther away than another, even though all the forms are on the same surface. Especially noteworthy in *Lion Hunt* are the gray horse at the left, seen from behind with the bottom of its left rear hoof facing viewers and most of its head hidden by its rider's shield, and the fallen hunter at the painting's lower right corner, whose barely visible legs and feet recede into the distance.

The artist who carved the portrait of the ancient Egyptian official Hesire (FIG. I-14) did not employ foreshortening. That artist's purpose was to present the various human body parts as clearly as possible, without overlapping. The lower part of Hesire's body is in profile to give the most complete view of the legs, with both the heels and toes of the foot visible. The frontal torso, however, allows viewers

I-14 Hesire, relief from his tomb at Saqqara, Egypt, Third Dynasty, ca. 2650 BCE. Wood, 3′ 9″ high. Egyptian Museum, Cairo.

Egyptian artists combined frontal and profile views to give a precise picture of the parts of the human body, as opposed to depicting how an individual body appears from a specific viewpoint.

1 in.

I-15 King on horseback with attendants, from Benin, Nigeria, ca. 1550–1680. Bronze, 1′ 7½″ high. Metropolitan Museum of Art, New York (Michael C. Rockefeller Memorial Collection, gift of Nelson A. Rockefeller).

This African artist used hierarchy of scale to distinguish the relative rank of the figures, making the king the largest. The sculptor created the relief by casting (pouring bronze into a mold).

many sculptors devised canons of proportions so strict and all-encompassing that they calculated the size of every body part in advance, even the fingers and toes, according to mathematical ratios.

Proportional systems can differ sharply from period to period, culture to culture, and artist to artist. Part of the task art history students face is to perceive and adjust to these differences. In fact, many artists have used disproportion and distortion deliberately for expressive effect. In the medieval French depiction of the weighing of souls on Judgment Day (FIG. I-6), the devilish figure yanking down on the scale has distorted facial features and stretched, lined limbs with animal-like paws for feet. Disproportion and distortion make him appear "inhuman," precisely as the sculptor intended.

In other cases, artists have used disproportion to focus attention on one body part (often the head) or to single out a group member (usually the leader). These intentional "unnatural" discrepancies in proportion constitute what art historians call *hierarchy of scale,* the enlarging of elements considered the most important. On a bronze plaque from Benin, Nigeria (FIG. I-15), the sculptor enlarged all the heads for emphasis and also varied the size of each figure according to its social status. Central, largest, and therefore most important is the Benin king, mounted on horseback. The horse has been a symbol of power and wealth in many societies from prehistory to the present. That the Benin king is disproportionately larger than his horse, contrary to nature, further aggrandizes him. Two large attendants fan the king. Other figures of smaller size and status at the Benin court stand on the king's left and right and in the plaque's upper corners. One tiny figure next to the horse is almost hidden from view beneath the king's feet.

One problem that students of art history—and professional art historians too—confront when studying illustrations in art history books is that although the relative sizes of figures and objects in a painting or sculpture are easy to discern, it is impossible to determine the absolute size of the works reproduced because they all appear at approximately the same size on the page. Readers of *Art through the Ages* can learn the size of all artworks from the dimensions given in the captions and, more intuitively, from the scales that appear—for the first time in this 13th edition—at the lower left or right corner of the illustration.

to see its full shape, including both shoulders, equal in size, as in nature. (Compare the shoulders of the hunter on the gray horse or those of the fallen hunter in *Lion Hunt*'s left foreground.) The result, an "unnatural" 90-degree twist at the waist, provides a precise picture of human body parts. Rubens and the Egyptian sculptor used very different means of depicting forms in space. Once again, neither is the "correct" manner.

PROPORTION AND SCALE *Proportion* concerns the relationships (in terms of size) of the parts of persons, buildings, or objects. People can judge "correct proportions" intuitively ("that statue's head seems the right size for the body"). Or proportion can be a mathematical relationship between the size of one part of an artwork or building and the other parts within the work. Proportion in art implies using a *module,* or basic unit of measure. When an artist or architect uses a formal system of proportions, all parts of a building, body, or other entity will be fractions or multiples of the module. A module might be a *column*'s diameter, the height of a human head, or any other component whose dimensions can be multiplied or divided to determine the size of the work's other parts.

In certain times and places, artists have formulated *canons,* or systems, of "correct" or "ideal" proportions for representing human figures, constituent parts of buildings, and so forth. In ancient Greece,

CARVING AND CASTING Sculptural technique falls into two basic categories, *subtractive* and *additive. Carving* is a subtractive technique. The final form is a reduction of the original mass of a block of stone, a piece of wood, or another material. Wooden statues were once tree trunks, and stone statues began as blocks pried from mountains. An unfinished marble statue of a bound slave (FIG. I-16) by the Italian artist MICHELANGELO BUONARROTI (1475–1564) clearly reveals the original shape of the stone block. Michelangelo thought of sculpture as a process of "liberating" the statue within the block. All sculptors of stone or wood cut away (subtract) "excess material." When they finish, they "leave behind" the statue—in this example, a twisting nude male form whose head Michelangelo never freed from the stone block.

In additive sculpture, the artist builds up the forms, usually in clay around a framework, or *armature.* Or a sculptor may fashion a *mold,* a hollow form for shaping, or *casting,* a fluid substance such as bronze or plaster. The ancient Greek sculptor who made the bronze statue of a warrior found in the sea near Riace, Italy, cast the head (FIG. I-17), limbs, torso, hands, and feet in separate molds and then *welded* them together (joined them by heating). Finally, the artist added features, such as the pupils of the eyes (now missing), in other materials. The warrior's teeth are silver, and his lower lip is copper.

1 ft.

I-16 MICHELANGELO BUONARROTI, unfinished captive, 1527–1528. Marble, 8′ 7½″ high. Galleria dell'Accademia, Florence.

Carving a freestanding figure from stone or wood is a subtractive process. Michelangelo thought of sculpture as a process of "liberating" the statue within the block of marble.

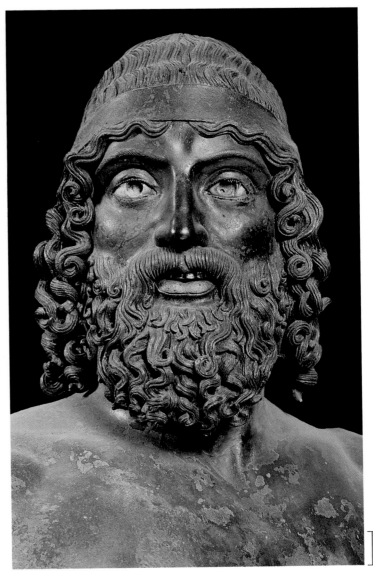

1 in.

I-17 Head of a warrior, detail of a statue (FIG. 5-35) from the sea off Riace, Italy, ca. 460–450 BCE. Bronze, full statue 6′ 6″ high. Museo Nazionale della Magna Grecia, Reggio Calabria.

The sculptor of this life-size statue of a bearded Greek warrior cast the head, limbs, torso, hands, and feet in separate molds, then welded the pieces together and added the eyes in a different material.

RELIEF SCULPTURE *Statues* that exist independent of any architectural frame or setting and that viewers can walk around are *freestanding* sculptures, or *sculptures in the round*, whether the artist produced the piece by carving (FIG. I-9) or casting (FIG. I-17). In *relief* sculpture, the subjects project from the background but remain part of it. In *high-relief* sculpture, the images project boldly. In the medieval weighing-of-souls scene (FIG. I-6), the relief is so high that not only do the forms cast shadows on the background, but some parts are even in the round, which explains why some pieces, for example the arms of the scale, broke off centuries ago. In *low relief*, or *bas-relief*, such as the portrait of Hesire (FIG. I-14), the projection is slight. Relief sculpture, like sculpture in the round, can be produced either by carving or casting. The plaque from Benin (FIG. I-15) is an example of bronze casting in high relief.

ARCHITECTURAL DRAWINGS Buildings are groupings of enclosed spaces and enclosing masses. People experience architecture both visually and by moving through and around it, so they perceive architectural space and mass together. Architects can represent these spaces and masses graphically in several ways, including as plans, sections, elevations, and cutaway drawings.

A *plan*, essentially a map of a floor, shows the placement of a structure's masses and, therefore, the spaces they circumscribe and enclose. A *section*, like a vertical plan, depicts the placement of the masses as if someone cut through the building along a plane. Drawings showing a theoretical slice across a structure's width are *lateral sections*. Those cutting through a building's length are *longitudinal sections*. Illustrated here are the plan and lateral section of Beauvais Cathedral (FIG. I-18), which may be compared to the photograph of the church's *choir* (FIG. I-2). The plan shows not only the choir's shape and the location of the *piers* dividing the *aisles* and supporting the *vaults* above but also the pattern of the crisscrossing vault *ribs*. The lateral section shows both the interior of the choir with its vaults and tall *stained-glass* windows as well as the roof structure and the form of the exterior *flying buttresses* that hold the vaults in place.

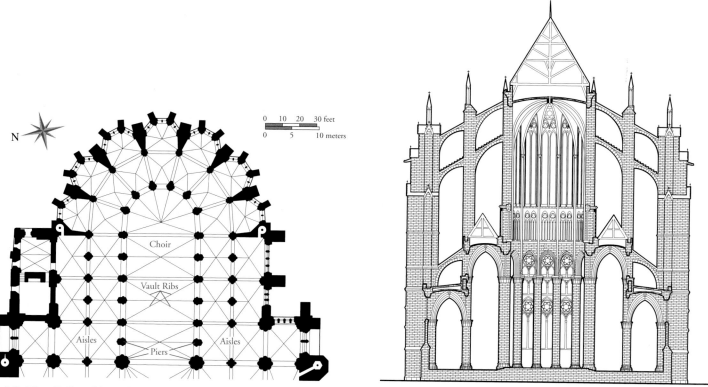

I-18 Plan (*left*) and lateral section (*right*) of Beauvais Cathedral, Beauvais, France, rebuilt after 1284.

Architectural drawings are indispensable aids for the analysis of buildings. Plans are maps of floors, recording the structure's masses. Sections are vertical "slices," across either a building's width or length.

Other types of architectural drawings appear throughout this book. An *elevation* drawing is a head-on view of an external or internal wall. A *cutaway* combines in a single drawing an exterior view with an interior view of part of a building.

This overview of the art historian's vocabulary is not exhaustive, nor have artists used only painting, drawing, sculpture, and architecture as media over the millennia. Ceramics, jewelry, textiles, photography, and computer art are just some of the numerous other arts. All of them involve highly specialized techniques described in distinct vocabularies. As in this introductory chapter, new terms are in *italics* where they first appear. The comprehensive Glossary at the end of the book contains definitions of all italicized terms.

Art History and Other Disciplines

By its very nature, the work of art historians intersects with that of others in many fields of knowledge, not only in the humanities but also in the social and natural sciences. To do their job well today, art historians regularly must go beyond the boundaries of what the public and even professional art historians of previous generations traditionally considered the specialized discipline of art history. In short, art historical research in the 21st century is typically interdisciplinary in nature. To cite one example, in an effort to unlock the secrets of a particular statue, an art historian might conduct archival research hoping to uncover new documents shedding light on who paid for the work and why, who made it and when, where it originally stood, how its contemporaries viewed it, and a host of other questions. Realizing, however, that the authors of the written documents often were not objective recorders of fact but rather observers with their own biases and agendas, the art historian may also use methodologies developed in

such fields as literary criticism, philosophy, sociology, and gender studies to weigh the evidence the documents provide.

At other times, rather than attempt to master many disciplines at once, art historians band together with other specialists in multidisciplinary inquiries. Art historians might call in chemists to date an artwork based on the composition of the materials used or might ask geologists to determine which quarry furnished the stone for a particular statue. X-ray technicians might be enlisted in an attempt to establish whether a painting is a forgery. Of course, art historians often reciprocate by contributing their expertise to the solution of problems in other disciplines. A historian, for example, might ask an art historian to determine—based on style, material, iconography, and other criteria—if any of the portraits of a certain king date to after his death. That would help establish the ruler's continuing prestige during the reigns of his successors. (Some portraits of Augustus, FIG. I-9, the founder of the Roman Empire, postdate his death by decades, even centuries.)

DIFFERENT WAYS OF SEEING

The history of art can be a history of artists and their works, of styles and stylistic change, of materials and techniques, of images and themes and their meanings, and of contexts and cultures and patrons. The best art historians analyze artworks from many viewpoints. But no art historian (or scholar in any other field), no matter how broad-minded in approach and no matter how experienced, can be truly objective. Like artists, art historians are members of a society, participants in its culture. How can scholars (and museum visitors and travelers to foreign locales) comprehend cultures unlike their own? They can try to reconstruct the original cultural contexts of artworks, but they are limited by their distance from the thought

1 in.

I-19 *Left:* JOHN HENRY SYLVESTER, *Portrait of Te Pehi Kupe* (detail), 1826 . Watercolor, $8\frac{1}{4}'' \times 6\frac{1}{4}''$. National Library of Australia, Canberra (Rex Nan Kivell Collection). *Right:* TE PEHI KUPE, *Self-Portrait*, 1826. From Leo Frobenius, *The Childhood of Man* (New York: J. B. Lippincott, 1909).

These strikingly different portraits of the same Maori chief reveal how differently Western and non-Western artists "see" a subject. Understanding the cultural context of artworks is vital to art history.

patterns of the cultures they study and by the obstructions to understanding—the assumptions, presuppositions, and prejudices peculiar to their own culture—their own thought patterns raise. Art historians may reconstruct a distorted picture of the past because of culture-bound blindness.

A single instance underscores how differently people of diverse cultures view the world and how various ways of seeing can cause sharp differences in how artists depict the world. Illustrated here are two contemporaneous portraits of a 19th-century Maori chieftain (FIG. I-19)—one by an Englishman, JOHN SYLVESTER (active early 19th century), and the other by the New Zealand chieftain himself, TE PEHI KUPE (d. 1829). Both reproduce the chieftain's facial tattooing. The European artist (FIG. I-19, *left*) included the head and shoulders and underplayed the tattooing. The tattoo pattern is one aspect of the likeness among many, no more or less important than the chieftain's European attire. Sylvester also recorded his subject's momentary glance toward the right and the play of light on his hair, fleeting aspects that have nothing to do with the figure's identity.

In contrast, Te Pehi Kupe's self-portrait (FIG. I-19, *right*)—made during a trip to Liverpool, England, to obtain European arms to take back to New Zealand—is not a picture of a man situated in space and bathed in light. Rather, it is the chieftain's statement of the supreme importance of the tattoo design that symbolizes his rank among his people. Remarkably, Te Pehi Kupe created the tattoo patterns from memory, without the aid of a mirror. The splendidly composed insignia, presented as a flat design separated from the body and even from the head, is Te Pehi Kupe's image of himself. Only by understanding the cultural context of each portrait can viewers hope to understand why either representation appears as it does.

As noted at the outset, the study of the context of artworks and buildings is one of the central concerns of art historians. *Art through the Ages* seeks to present a history of art and architecture that will help readers understand not only the subjects, styles, and techniques of paintings, sculptures, buildings, and other art forms created in all parts of the world for 30 millennia but also their cultural and historical contexts. That story now begins.

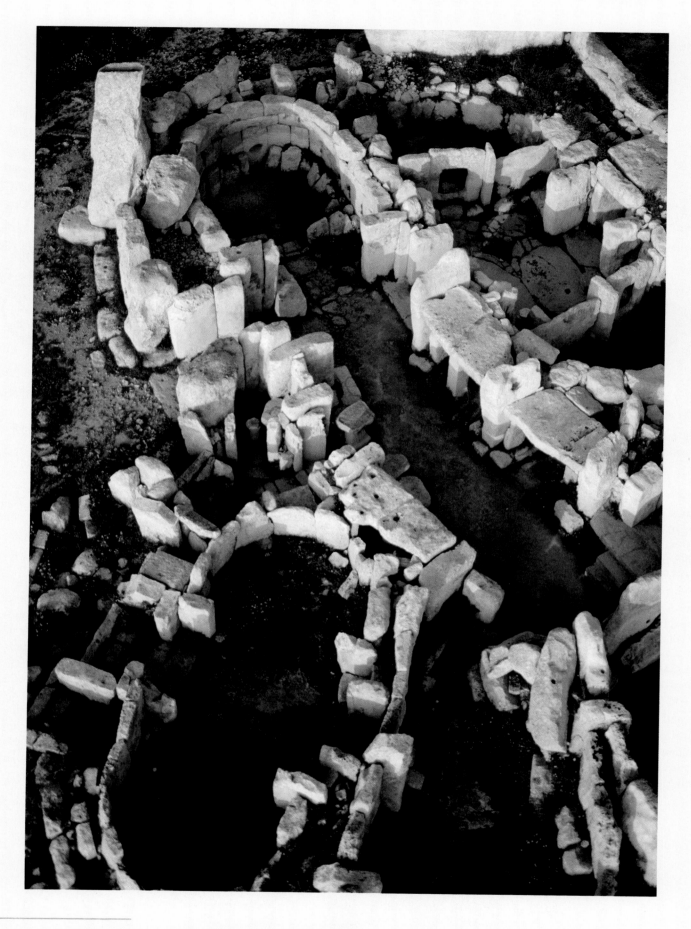

1-1 Aerial view of the ruins of Hagar Qim, Malta, ca. 3200–2500 BCE.

One of the earliest stone temples in the world is on the island of Malta. The 5,000-year-old structure is remarkably sophisticated for its date, especially in the combination of rectilinear and curved forms.

ART BEFORE HISTORY

Humankind seems to have originated in Africa in the very remote past. From that great continent also comes the earliest evidence of human recognition of abstract images in the natural environment, if not the first examples of what people generally call "art." In 1925, explorers of a cave at Makapansgat in South Africa (MAP 15-1) discovered bones of *Australopithecus,* a predecessor of modern humans who lived some three million years ago. Associated with the bones was a waterworn reddish-brown jasperite pebble (FIG. 1-2) that bears an uncanny resemblance to a human face. The nearest known source of this variety of ironstone is 20 miles away from the cave. One of the early humans who took refuge in the rock shelter at Makapansgat must have noticed the pebble in a streambed and, awestruck by the "face" on the stone, brought it back for safekeeping.

Is the Makapansgat pebble art? In modern times, many artists have created works people universally consider art by removing objects from their normal contexts, altering them, and then labeling them. In 1917, for example, Marcel Duchamp took a ceramic urinal, set it on its side, called it *Fountain* (FIG. 35-27), and declared his "ready-made" worthy of exhibition among more conventional artworks. But the artistic environment of the past century cannot be projected into the remote past. For art historians to declare a found object such as the Makapansgat pebble an "artwork," it must have been modified by human intervention beyond mere selection—and it was not. In fact, evidence indicates that, with few exceptions, it was not until three million years later, around 30,000 BCE, when large parts of northern Europe were still covered with glaciers during the Ice Age, that humans intentionally manufactured sculptures and paintings. That is when the story of art through the ages really begins.

PALEOLITHIC ART

The several millennia following 30,000 BCE saw a powerful outburst of creativity. The works produced by the peoples of the Old Stone Age or *Paleolithic* period (from the Greek *paleo,* "old," and *lithos,* "stone") are of an astonishing variety. They range from simple shell necklaces to human and animal forms in ivory, clay, and stone to monumental paintings, engravings, and relief sculptures covering the huge wall surfaces of caves. During the Paleolithic period, humankind went beyond the *recognition* of human and animal

1-3 Animal facing left, from the Apollo 11 Cave, Namibia, ca. 23,000 BCE. Charcoal on stone, $5'' \times 4\frac{1}{4}''$. State Museum of Namibia, Windhoek.

Like most other paintings for thousands of years, this very early example from Africa represents an animal in strict profile so that the head, body, tail, and all four legs are clearly visible.

1-2 Waterworn pebble resembling a human face, from Makapansgat, South Africa, ca. 3,000,000 BCE. Reddish-brown jasperite, $2\frac{3}{8}''$ wide.

Three million years ago someone recognized a face in this pebble and brought it to a rock shelter for safekeeping, but the stone is not an artwork because it was neither manufactured nor modified.

forms in the natural environment to the *representation* (literally, the presenting again—in different and substitute form—of something observed) of humans and animals. The immensity of this achievement cannot be exaggerated.

Africa

Some of the earliest paintings yet discovered come from Africa, and, like the treasured pebble in the form of a face found at Makapansgat, the oldest African paintings were portable objects.

APOLLO 11 CAVE Between 1969 and 1972, scientists working in the Apollo 11 Cave in Namibia (MAP 15-1) found seven fragments of stone plaques with paint on them, including four or five recognizable images of animals. In most cases, including the example illustrated here (FIG. 1-3), the species is uncertain, but the forms are always carefully rendered. One plaque depicts a striped beast, possibly a zebra. The charcoal from the archaeological layer in which the Namibian plaques were found has been dated to around 23,000 BCE.

Like every artist in every age in every medium, the painter of the Apollo 11 plaque had to answer two questions before beginning work: *What* shall be my subject? *How* shall I represent it? In Paleolithic art, the almost universal answer to the first question was an animal—bison, mammoth, ibex, and horse were most common. In fact, Paleolithic painters and sculptors depicted humans infrequently and men almost never. In equally stark contrast to today's world, there was also agreement on the best answer to the second question. Artists presented virtually every animal in every Paleolithic, *Mesolithic* (Middle Stone Age), and *Neolithic* (New Stone Age) painting in the same manner—in strict profile. The profile is the only view of an animal wherein the head, body, tail, and all four legs can be seen. A frontal view would have concealed most of the body, and a three-quarter view would not have shown either the front or side fully. Only the profile view is completely informative about the animal's shape, and this is why the Stone Age painter chose it. A very long time passed before artists placed any pre-

mium on "variety" or "originality," either in subject choice or in representational manner. These are quite modern notions in the history of art. The aim of the earliest painters was to create a convincing image of the subject, a kind of pictorial definition of the animal capturing its very essence, and only the profile view met their needs.

Western Europe

Even older than the Namibian painted plaques are some of the first sculptures and paintings of western Europe (MAP 1-1), although examples of still greater antiquity may yet be found in Africa, bridging the gap between the Makapansgat pebble and the Apollo 11 painted plaques.

MAP 1-1 Prehistoric sites in Europe.

1-4 Human with feline head, from Hohlenstein-Stadel, Germany, ca. 30,000–28,000 BCE. Mammoth ivory, $11\frac{5}{8}''$ high. Ulmer Museum, Ulm.

One of the oldest known sculptures is this large ivory figure of a human with a feline head. It is uncertain whether the work depicts a composite creature or a human wearing an animal mask.

1-5 Nude woman (*Venus of Willendorf*), from Willendorf, Austria, ca. 28,000–25,000 BCE. Limestone, $4\frac{1}{4}''$ high. Naturhistorisches Museum, Vienna. ◼◀

The anatomical exaggerations in this tiny figurine from Willendorf are typical of Paleolithic representations of women, whose child-bearing capabilities ensured the survival of the species.

HOHLENSTEIN-STADEL

One of the earliest sculptures discovered yet is an extraordinary ivory statuette (FIG. **1-4**), which may date back as far as 30,000 BCE. It was found in fragments inside a cave at Hohlenstein-Stadel in Germany and has been meticulously restored. Carved out of mammoth ivory and nearly a foot tall—a truly huge image for its era—the statuette represents something that existed only in the vivid imagination of the unknown sculptor who conceived it. It is a human (whether male or female is debated) with a feline head. Such composite creatures with animal heads and human bodies (and vice versa) were common in the art of the ancient Near East and Egypt (compare, for example, FIGS. **2-10**, *right,* and **3-36**). In those civilizations, surviving texts usually allow historians to name the figures and describe their role in contemporary religion and mythology. But for Stone Age representations, no one knows what their makers had in mind. The animal-headed humans of Paleolithic art sometimes have been called sorcerers and described as magicians wearing masks. Similarly, Paleolithic human-headed animals have been interpreted as humans dressed up as animals. In the absence of any Stone Age written explanations—this is a time before writing, before (or pre-) history—researchers can only speculate on the purpose and function of a statuette such as that from Hohlenstein-Stadel.

Art historians are certain, however, that these statuettes were important to those who created them, because manufacturing an ivory figure, especially one a foot tall, was a complicated process. First, a tusk had to be removed from the dead animal by cutting into the ivory where it joined the head. The sculptor then cut the tusk to the desired size and rubbed it into its approximate final shape with sandstone. Finally, a sharp stone blade was used to carve the body, limbs, and head, and a stone *burin* (a pointed engraving tool) to *incise* (scratch) lines into the surfaces, as on the Hohlenstein-Stadel creature's arms. All this probably required at least several days of skilled work.

1-5A Head of a woman, Brassempouy, ca. 25,000–20,000 BCE.

VENUS OF WILLENDORF The composite feline-human from Germany is exceptional for the Stone Age. The vast majority of prehistoric sculptures depict either animals or humans. In the earliest art, humankind consists almost exclusively of women as opposed to men, and the painters and sculptors almost invariably showed them nude, although scholars generally assume that during the Ice Age both women and men wore garments covering parts of their bodies. When archaeologists first discovered Paleolithic statuettes of women, they dubbed them "Venuses," after the Greco-Roman goddess of beauty and love, whom artists usually depicted nude (FIG. **5-62**). The nickname is inappropriate and misleading. It is doubtful that the Old Stone Age figurines represented deities of any kind.

One of the oldest and the most famous of the prehistoric female figures is the tiny limestone figurine of a woman that long has been known as the *Venus of Willendorf* (FIG. **1-5**) after its *findspot* in Austria. Its cluster of almost ball-like shapes is unusual, the result in part of the sculptor's response to the natural shape of the stone selected for carving. The anatomical exaggeration has suggested to many that this and similar statuettes served as fertility images. But other Paleolithic stone women of far more slender proportions exist, and the meaning of these images is as elusive as everything else about Paleolithic art. Yet the preponderance of female over male figures in the Old Stone Age seems to indicate a preoccupation with women, whose child-bearing capabilities ensured the survival of the species.

One thing at least is clear. The *Venus of Willendorf* sculptor did not aim for naturalism in shape and proportion. As with most Paleolithic figures, the sculptor did not carve any facial features. Here the carver suggested only a mass of curly hair or, as some researchers have recently argued, a hat woven from plant fibers—evidence for the art of textile manufacture at a very early date. In either case, the emphasis is on female anatomy. The breasts of the Willendorf woman are enormous, far larger than the tiny forearms and hands that rest upon them. The carver also took pains to scratch into the stone the outline of the pubic triangle. Sculptors often omitted this detail in other early figurines, leading some scholars to question the nature of these figures as fertility images. Whatever the purpose of these statuettes, the makers' intent seems to have been to represent not a specific woman but the female form.

LAUSSEL Because precision in dating is impossible for the Paleolithic era, art historians usually can be no more specific than assigning a range of several thousand years to each artifact. But probably later in date than the *Venus of Willendorf* is a female figure (FIG. **1-6**) from Laussel in France. The Willendorf and Hohlenstein-Stadel figures were *sculpted in the round* (that is, they are *freestanding sculptures*). The Laussel woman is one of the earliest *relief sculptures* known. The sculptor employed a stone *chisel* to cut into the relatively flat surface of a large rock and create an image that projects from its background.

1 in.

1-6A Reclining woman, La Magdelaine, ca. 12,000 BCE.

Today the Laussel relief is exhibited in a museum, divorced from its original context, a detached piece of what once was a much more imposing monument. When the relief was discovered, the Laussel woman (who is about $1\frac{1}{2}$ feet tall, more than four times larger than the Willendorf statuette) was part of a great stone block that measured about 140 cubic feet. The carved block stood in the open air in front of a Paleolithic rock shelter. Rock shelters were a common type of dwelling for early humans, along with huts and the mouths of caves. The Laussel relief is one of many examples of open-air art in the Old Stone Age. The popular notions that early humans dwelled exclusively in caves and that all Paleolithic art comes from mysterious dark caverns are false.

After chiseling out the female form and incising the details with a sharp burin, the Laussel sculptor applied red ocher, a naturally colored mineral, to the body. (The same color is also preserved on parts of the *Venus of Willendorf*.) Contrary to modern misconceptions about ancient art, stone sculptures were frequently painted in antiquity. The Laussel woman has the same bulbous forms as the earlier Willendorf figurine, with a similar exaggeration of the breasts, abdomen, and hips. The head is once again featureless, but the arms have taken on greater importance. The left arm draws attention to the midsection and pubic area, and the raised right hand holds what most scholars identify as a bison horn. The meaning of the horn is debated.

LE TUC D'AUDOUBERT Paleolithic sculptors sometimes created reliefs by building up forms out of clay rather than by cutting into stone blocks or stone walls. Sometime 12,000 to 17,000 years ago in the low-ceilinged circular space at the end of a succession of cave chambers at Le Tuc d'Audoubert, a master sculptor modeled a pair of bison (FIG. **1-7**) in clay against a large, irregular freestanding rock. The two bison, like the much older painted animal (FIG. **1-3**) from the Apollo 11 Cave, are in strict profile. Each is about two feet long. They are among the largest Paleolithic sculptures known. The sculptor brought the clay from elsewhere in the cave complex and modeled it by hand into the overall shape of the animals. The artist then

1-6 Woman holding a bison horn, from Laussel, France, ca. 25,000–20,000 BCE. Painted limestone, 1′ 6″ high. Musée d'Aquitaine, Bordeaux.

One of the oldest known relief sculptures depicts a woman who holds a bison horn and whose left arm draws attention to her belly. Scholars continue to debate the meaning of the gesture and the horn.

smoothed the surfaces with a spatula-like tool and finally used fingers to shape the eyes, nostrils, mouths, and manes. The cracks in the two animals resulted from the drying process and probably appeared within days of the sculptures' completion.

LA MADELEINE As already noted, sculptors fashioned ivory mammoth tusks into human and animal (FIG. **1-4**) forms from very early times. Prehistoric carvers also used antlers as a sculptural medium, even though it meant they were forced to work on a very small scale. The broken spearthrower (FIG. **1-8**) in the form of a bison found at La Madeleine in France is only four inches long and was carved from reindeer antler. The sculptor incised lines into the bison's mane using a sharp burin. Compared to the bison at Le Tuc d'Audoubert, the engraving is much more detailed and extends to the horns, eye, ear, nostrils, mouth, and the hair on the face. Especially interesting is the engraver's decision to represent the bison with the head turned. The small size of the reindeer horn may have been the motivation for this space-saving device. Whatever the reason, it is noteworthy that the sculptor turned the neck a full 180 degrees to maintain the strict profile Paleolithic sculptors and painters insisted on for the sake of clarity and completeness.

Representations of animals are far more common than of humans in Paleolithic European art. The sculptor built up these clay bison using a stone spatula-like smoothing tool and fingers to shape the details.

1 ft.

ALTAMIRA The works examined here thus far, whether portable or fixed to rocky outcroppings or cave walls, are all small. They are dwarfed by the "herds" of painted animals that roam the cave walls of southern France and northern Spain, where some of the most spectacular prehistoric art has been discovered (see "Paleolithic Cave Painting," page 20). The first examples of cave paintings were found accidentally by an amateur archaeologist in 1879 at Altamira, Spain. Don Marcelino Sanz de Sautuola was exploring a cave where he had already found specimens of flint and carved bone. His little daughter Maria was with him when they reached a chamber some 85 feet from the cave's entrance. Because it was dark and the ceiling of the debris-filled cavern was only a few inches above the father's head, the child was the first to discern, from her lower vantage point, the shadowy forms of painted beasts on the cave roof (FIG. 1-9, a detail of a much

1 in.

1-8 Bison with turned head, fragmentary spearthrower, from La Madeleine, France, ca. 12,000 BCE. Reindeer horn, 4″ long.

This fragment of a spearthrower was carved from reindeer antler. Details were incised with a stone burin. The sculptor turned the bison's head a full 180 degrees to maintain the profile view.

1 ft.

1-9 Bison, detail of a painted ceiling in the cave at Altamira, Spain, ca. 12,000–11,000 BCE. Each bison 5′ long.

As in other Paleolithic caves, the painted ceiling at Altamira has no ground line or indication of setting. The artist's sole concern was representing the animals, not locating them in a specific place.

Paleolithic Cave Painting

The caves of Altamira (FIG. 1-9), Pech-Merle (FIG. 1-10), Lascaux (FIGS. 1-11 and 1-13), and other sites in prehistoric Europe are a few hundred to several thousand feet long. They are often choked, sometimes almost impassably, by deposits, such as stalactites and stalagmites. Far inside these caverns, well removed from the cave mouths early humans often chose for habitation, painters sometimes made pictures on the walls. Examples of Paleolithic painting now have been found at more than 200 sites, but prehistorians still regard painted caves as rare occurrences, because the images in them, even if they number in the hundreds, were created over a period of some 10,000 to 20,000 years.

To illuminate the surfaces while working, the Paleolithic painters used stone lamps filled with marrow or fat, with a wick, perhaps, of moss. For drawing, they used chunks of red and yellow ocher. For painting, they ground these same ochers into powders they mixed with water before applying. Recent analyses of the pigments used show that Paleolithic painters employed many different minerals, attesting to a technical sophistication surprising at so early a date.

Large flat stones served as *palettes*. The painters made brushes from reeds, bristles, or twigs, and may

have used a blowpipe of reeds or hollow bones to spray pigments on out-of-reach surfaces. Some caves have natural ledges on the rock walls upon which the painters could have stood in order to reach the upper surfaces of the naturally formed chambers and corridors. One Lascaux gallery has holes in one of the walls that once probably anchored a scaffold made of saplings lashed together. Despite the difficulty of making the tools and pigments, modern attempts at replicating the techniques of Paleolithic painting have demonstrated that skilled workers could cover large surfaces with images in less than a day.

1-10 Spotted horses and negative hand imprints, wall painting in the cave at Pech-Merle, France, ca. 22,000 BCE. 11′ 2″ long.

The purpose and meaning of Paleolithic art are unknown. Some researchers think the painted hands near the Pech-Merle horses are "signatures" of community members or of individual painters.

1 ft.

larger painting approximately 60 feet long). Sanz de Sautuola was certain the bison painted on the ceiling of the cave on his estate dated back to prehistoric times. Professional archaeologists, however, doubted the authenticity of these works, and at the Lisbon Congress on Prehistoric Archaeology in 1880, they officially dismissed the paintings as forgeries. But by the close of the century, other caves had been discovered with painted walls partially covered by mineral deposits that would have taken thousands of years to accumulate. This finally persuaded skeptics that the first paintings were of an age far more remote than they had ever dreamed.

The bison at Altamira are 13,000 to 14,000 years old, but the painters of Paleolithic Spain approached the problem of representing an animal in essentially the same way as the painter of the Namibian stone plaque (FIG. 1-3), who worked in Africa more than 10,000 years earlier. Every one of the Altamira bison is in profile, whether alive and standing or curled up on the ground (probably dead, although this is disputed; one suggestion is that these bison are giving birth). To maintain the profile in the latter case, the painter had to adopt a viewpoint above the animal, looking down, rather than the view a person standing on the ground would have.

Modern critics often refer to the Altamira animals as a "group" of bison, but that is very likely a misnomer. In FIG. 1-9, the several

bison do not stand on a common *ground line* (a painted or carved baseline on which figures appear to stand in paintings and reliefs), nor do they share a common orientation. They seem almost to float above viewers' heads, like clouds in the sky. And the dead(?) bison are seen in an "aerial view," while the others are seen from a position on the ground. The painting has no setting, no background, no indication of place. The Paleolithic painter was not at all concerned with *where* the animals were or with how they related to one another, if at all. Instead, several *separate* images of a bison adorn the ceiling, perhaps painted at different times, and each is as complete and informative as possible—even if their meaning remains a mystery (see "Art in the Old Stone Age," page 21).

PECH-MERLE That the paintings did have meaning to the Paleolithic peoples who made and observed them cannot, however, be doubted. In fact, signs consisting of checks, dots, squares, or other arrangements of lines often accompany the pictures of animals. Representations of human hands also are common. At Pech-Merle in France, painted hands accompany representations of spotted horses (FIG. 1-10). These and the majority of painted hands at other sites are "negative;" that is, the painter placed one hand against the wall and then brushed or blew or spat pigment around it. Occasionally,

Art in the Old Stone Age

From the moment in 1879 that cave paintings were discovered at Altamira (FIG. 1-9), scholars have wondered why the hunters of the Old Stone Age decided to cover the walls of dark caverns with animal images like those found at Altamira, Pech-Merle (FIG. 1-10), Lascaux (FIGS. 1-11 and 1-13), and Vallon-Pont-d'Arc (FIG. 1-12). Scholars have proposed various theories including that the painted and engraved animals were mere decoration, but this explanation cannot account for the narrow range of subjects or the inaccessibility of many of the representations. In fact, the remoteness and difficulty of access of many of the images, and indications that the caves were used for centuries, are precisely why many researchers have suggested that the prehistoric hunters attributed magical properties to the images they painted and sculpted. According to this argument, by confining animals to the surfaces of their cave walls, the Paleolithic hunters believed they were bringing the beasts under their control. Some prehistorians have even hypothesized that rituals or dances were performed in front of the images and that these rites served to improve the hunters' luck. Still others have stated that the animal representations may have served as teaching tools to instruct new hunters about the character of the various species they would encounter or even to serve as targets for spears.

In contrast, some scholars have argued that the magical purpose of the paintings and reliefs was not to facilitate the *destruction* of bison and other species. Instead, they believe prehistoric painters and sculptors created animal images to assure the *survival* of the herds on which Paleolithic peoples depended for their food supply and for their clothing. A central problem for both the hunting-magic and food-creation theories is that the animals that seem to have been diet staples of Old Stone Age peoples are not those most frequently portrayed. For example, faunal remains show that the Altamirans ate red deer, not bison.

Other scholars have sought to reconstruct an elaborate mythology based on the cave paintings and sculptures, suggesting that Paleolithic humans believed they had animal ancestors. Still others have equated certain species with men and others with women and postulated various meanings for the abstract signs that sometimes accompany the images. Almost all of these theories have been discredited over time, and most prehistorians admit that no one knows the intent of these representations. In fact, a single explanation for all Paleolithic animal images, even ones similar in subject, style, and *composition* (how the motifs are arranged on the surface), is unlikely to apply universally. The works remain an enigma—and always will, because before the invention of writing, no contemporaneous explanations could be recorded.

1-11A "Chinese horse," Lascaux, ca. 15,000–13,000 BCE.

1-11 Hall of the Bulls (left wall) in the cave at Lascaux, France, ca. 15,000–13,000 BCE. Largest bull 11′ 6″ long.

Several species of animals appear together in the Hall of the Bulls. Many are colored silhouettes, but others were created by outline alone—the two basic approaches to painting in the history of art.

The World's Oldest Paintings?

One of the most spectacular archaeological finds of the past century came to light in December 1994 at Vallon-Pont-d'Arc, France, and was announced at a press conference in Paris on January 18, 1995. Unlike some other recent "finds" of prehistoric art that proved to be forgeries, the paintings in the Chauvet Cave (named after the leader of the exploration team, Jean-Marie Chauvet) seemed to be authentic. But no one, including Chauvet and his colleagues, guessed at the time of their discovery that *radiocarbon dating* (a measure of the rate of degeneration of carbon 14 in organic materials) of the paintings might establish that the murals in the cave were more than 15,000 years older than those at Altamira (FIG. 1-9). When the scientific tests were completed, the French archaeologists announced that the Chauvet Cave paintings were the oldest yet found anywhere, datable around 30,000–28,000 BCE.

This new early date immediately caused scholars to reevaluate the scheme of "stylistic development" from simple to more complex forms that had been nearly universally accepted for decades. In the Chauvet Cave, in contrast to Lascaux (FIG. 1-11), the horns of the aurochs (extinct long-horned wild oxen) are shown naturalistically,

one behind the other, not in the twisted perspective thought to be universally characteristic of Paleolithic art. Moreover, the two rhinoceroses at the lower right of FIG. 1-12 appear to confront each other, suggesting to some observers that the artist intended a narrative, another "first" in either painting or sculpture. If the paintings are twice as old as those of Lascaux, Altamira (FIG. 1-9), and Pech-Merle (FIG. 1-10), the assumption that Paleolithic art "evolved" from simple to more sophisticated representations is wrong.

Much research remains to be conducted in the Chauvet Cave, but already the paintings have become the subject of intense controversy. Recently, some archaeologists have contested the early dating of the Chauvet paintings on the grounds that the tested samples were contaminated. If the Chauvet animals were painted later than those at Lascaux, their advanced stylistic features can be more easily explained. The dispute exemplifies the frustration—and the excitement—of studying the art of an age so remote that almost nothing remains and almost every new find causes art historians to reevaluate what had previously been taken for granted.

1-12 Aurochs, horses, and rhinoceroses, wall painting in the Chauvet Cave, Vallon-Pont-d'Arc, France, ca. 30,000–28,000 or ca. 15,000–13,000 BCE.

The date of the Chauvet Cave paintings is the subject of much controversy. If the murals are the oldest paintings known, they exhibit surprisingly advanced features, such as overlapping animal horns.

1 ft.

the painter dipped a hand in the pigment and then pressed it against the wall, leaving a "positive" imprint. These handprints, too, must have had a purpose. Some researchers have considered them "signatures" of cult or community members or, less likely, of individual painters. But like everything else in Paleolithic art, their meaning is unknown.

The *mural* (wall) paintings at Pech-Merle also allow some insight into the reason certain subjects may have been chosen for a specific location. One of the horses (at the right in FIG. 1-10) may have been inspired by the rock formation in the wall surface resembling a horse's head and neck. Old Stone Age painters and sculptors

frequently and skillfully used the caves' naturally irregular surfaces to help give the illusion of real presence to their forms. Many of the Altamira bison (FIG. 1-9), for example, were painted over bulging rock surfaces. In fact, prehistorians have observed that bison and cattle appear almost exclusively on convex surfaces, whereas nearly all horses and hands are painted on concave surfaces. What this signifies has yet to be determined.

LASCAUX Perhaps the best-known Paleolithic cave is that at Lascaux, near Montignac, France. It is extensively decorated, but most of the paintings are hundreds of feet from any entrance, far removed from the daylight. The largest painted area at Lascaux is the so-called Hall of the Bulls (FIG. 1-11), although not all of the animals depicted are bulls. Many are represented using colored silhouettes, as at Altamira (FIG. 1-9) and on the Apollo 11 plaque (FIG. 1-3). Others—such as the great bull at the right in FIG. 1-11—were created by outline alone, as were the Pech-Merle horses (FIG. 1-10). On the walls of the Lascaux cave one sees, side by side, the two basic approaches to drawing and painting found repeatedly in the history of art. These differences in style and technique alone suggest that the animals in the Hall of the Bulls were painted at different times, and the modern impression of a rapidly moving herd of beasts was probably not the original intent. In any case, the "herd" consists of several different kinds of animals of various sizes moving in different directions.

Another feature of the Lascaux paintings deserves attention. The bulls there show a convention of representing horns that has been called *twisted perspective* or a *composite view,* because viewers see the heads in profile but the horns from the front. Thus, the painter's approach is not strictly or consistently optical (seen from a fixed viewpoint). Rather, the approach is descriptive of the fact that cattle have two horns. Two horns are part of the concept "bull." In strict optical-perspective profile, only one horn would be visible, but to paint the animal in that way would amount to an incomplete definition of it. This kind of twisted perspective was the norm in prehistoric painting, but it was not universal. In fact, the recent discovery at Vallon-Pont-d'Arc in France of Paleolithic paintings (FIG. 1-12) in the Chauvet Cave, where the painters represented horns in a more natural way, has caused art historians to rethink many of the assumptions they had made about Paleolithic art (see "The World's Oldest Paintings?" page 22).

Perhaps the most perplexing painting (FIG. 1-13) in the Paleolithic caves of Europe is deep in a well shaft at Lascaux, where man (as opposed to woman) makes one of his earliest appearances in prehistoric art. At the left, and moving to the left, is a rhinoceros, rendered with all the skilled attention to animal detail customarily seen in cave art. Beneath its tail are two rows of three dots of uncertain significance. At the right is a bison, also facing left but more schematically painted, probably by someone else. The second painter nonetheless successfully suggested the bristling rage of the animal, whose bowels are hanging from it in a heavy coil. Between the two beasts is a bird-faced (masked?) man (compare the feline-headed human, FIG. 1-4, from Hohlenstein-Stadel) with outstretched arms and hands with only four fingers. The man is depicted with far less care and detail than either animal, but the painter made the hunter's gender explicit by the prominent penis. The position of the man is ambiguous. Is he wounded or dead or merely tilted back and unharmed? Do the staff(?) with the bird on top and the spear belong to him? Is it he or the rhinoceros who has gravely wounded the bison—or neither? Which animal, if either, has knocked the man down, if indeed he is on the ground? Are these three images related at all? Researchers can be sure of nothing, but if the painter placed the figures beside each other to tell a story, then this is evidence for the creation of complex narrative compositions involving humans and animals at a much earlier date than anyone had imagined only a few generations ago. Yet it is important to remember that even if the artist intended to tell a story, very few people would have been able to "read" it. The painting, in a deep shaft, is very difficult to reach and could have been viewed only in flickering lamplight. Like all Paleolithic art, the scene in the Lascaux well shaft remains enigmatic.

1 ft.

1-13 Rhinoceros, wounded man, and disemboweled bison, painting in the well of the cave at Lascaux, France, ca. 15,000–13,000 BCE. Bison 3′ 8″ long.

If these paintings of two animals and a bird-faced (masked?) man deep in a Lascaux well shaft depict a hunting scene, they constitute the earliest example of narrative art ever discovered.

NEOLITHIC ART

Around 9000 BCE, the ice that covered much of northern Europe during the Paleolithic period melted as the climate grew warmer. The sea level rose more than 300 feet, separating England from continental Europe and Spain from Africa. The reindeer migrated north, and the woolly mammoth disappeared. The Paleolithic gave way to a transitional period, the Mesolithic, and then, for several thousand years at different times in different parts of the globe, a great new age, the Neolithic, dawned.* Human beings began to domesticate plants and animals and to settle in fixed abodes. Their food supply assured, many groups changed from hunters to herders, to farmers, and finally to townspeople. Wandering hunters settled down to organized community living in villages surrounded by cultivated fields.

The basis for the conventional division of prehistory into the Paleolithic, Mesolithic, and Neolithic periods is the development of stone implements. However, a different kind of distinction may be made between an age of food gathering and an age of food production. In this scheme, the Paleolithic period corresponds roughly to the age of food gathering, and the Mesolithic period, the last phase of that age, is marked by intensified food gathering and the taming of the dog. In the Neolithic period, agriculture and stock raising became humankind's major food sources. The transition to the Neolithic occurred first in the ancient Near East.

Ancient Near East

The remains of the oldest known settled communities have been found in the grassy foothills of the Antilebanon, Taurus, and Zagros mountains in present-day Turkey, Syria, Iraq, and Iran (MAP 1-2). These regions provided the necessary preconditions for the development of agriculture. Species of native plants, such as wild wheat and barley, were plentiful, as were herds of animals (goats, sheep, and pigs) that could be domesticated. Sufficient rain occurred for the raising of crops. When village farming life was well developed, some settlers, attracted by the greater fertility of the soil and perhaps also by the need to find more land for their rapidly growing populations, moved into the valleys and deltas of the Tigris and Euphrates rivers.

In addition to systematic agriculture, the new sedentary societies of the Neolithic Age originated weaving, metalworking, pottery, and counting and recording with clay tokens. Soon, these innovations spread with remarkable speed throughout the Near East. Village farming communities such as Jarmo in Iraq and Çatal Höyük in southern Anatolia date back to the mid-seventh millennium BCE. The remarkable fortified town of Jericho, before whose walls the biblical Joshua appeared thousands of years later, is even older. Archaeologists are constantly uncovering surprises, and the discovery and exploration of new sites each year are compelling them to revise their views about the emergence of Neolithic society. But three sites known for some time—Jericho, Ain Ghazal, and Çatal Höyük—offer a fascinating picture of the rapid and exciting transformation of human society and of art during the Neolithic period.

JERICHO By 7000 BCE, agriculture was well established from Anatolia to ancient Palestine and Iran. Its advanced state by this date presupposes a long development. Indeed, the very existence of a major settlement such as Jericho gives strong support to this assumption. The site of Jericho—a plateau in the Jordan River valley with a spring that provided a constant water supply—was occupied by a small village as early as the ninth millennium BCE. This village

*This chapter treats the Neolithic art of Europe and the Near East only. For the Neolithic art of Africa, see Chapter 15; for Asia, see Chapters 6 to 8.

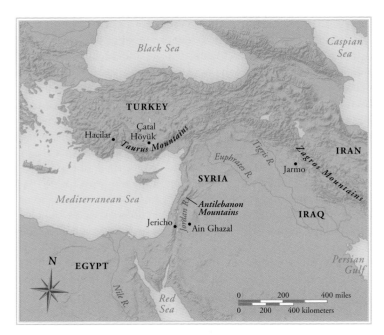

MAP 1-2 Neolithic sites in Anatolia and the Near East.

underwent spectacular development around 8000 BCE, when the inhabitants built a new Neolithic settlement covering about 10 acres. Its mud-brick houses sat on round or oval stone foundations and had roofs of branches covered with earth.

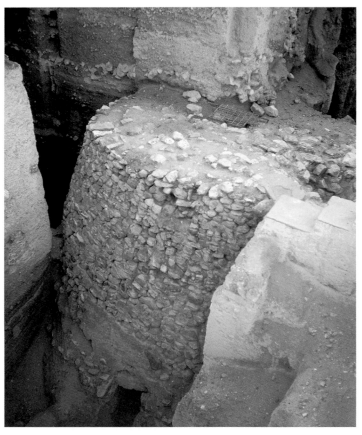

1-14 Great stone tower built into the settlement wall, Jericho, ca. 8000–7000 BCE.

Neolithic Jericho was protected by 5-foot-thick walls and at least one stone tower 30 feet high and 33 feet in diameter—an outstanding achievement that marks the beginning of monumental architecture.

As Jericho's wealth grew, the need for protection against marauding nomads resulted in the first known permanent stone fortifications. By approximately 7500 BCE, a wide rock-cut ditch and a 5-foot-thick wall surrounded the town, estimated to have had a population of more than 2,000 people. Into the circuit wall, which has been preserved to a height of almost 13 feet, was built a great circular tower (FIG. **1-14**) of roughly shaped stones laid without mortar and originally about 30 feet high. Almost 33 feet in diameter at the base, the tower has an inner stairway leading to its summit. (Today, a grate covers the entrance to the stairway.) Not enough of the site has been excavated to determine whether this tower was solitary or one of several similar towers that formed a complete defense system. In either case, a structure as large as this was a tremendous technological achievement and a testimony to the builders' ability to organize a significant workforce. The walls and tower(s) of Jericho mark the beginning of the long history of monumental architecture.

AIN GHAZAL Near Amman, Jordan, the construction of a highway in 1974 revealed another important Neolithic settlement in ancient Palestine at the site of Ain Ghazal, occupied from ca. 7200 to ca. 5000 BCE. The inhabitants built houses of irregularly shaped stones, but carefully plastered and then painted their floors and walls red. The most striking finds at Ain Ghazal, however, are two caches containing three dozen plaster statuettes (FIG. **1-15**) and busts, some with two heads, datable to ca. 6500 BCE. The sculptures appear to have been ritually buried. The figures were fashioned of white plaster, which was built up over a core of reeds and twine. The sculptors used black bitumen, a tarlike substance, to delineate the pupils of the eyes. On some of the later figures painters added clothing. Only rarely did the artists indicate the gender of the figures. Whatever their purpose, by their size (as much as three feet tall) and sophisticated technique, the Ain Ghazal statuettes and busts are distinguished from Paleolithic figurines such as the tiny *Venus of Willendorf* (FIG. **1-5**) and even the foot-tall Hohlenstein-Stadel ivory statuette (FIG. **1-4**). They mark the beginning of monumental sculpture in the ancient Near East.

ÇATAL HÖYÜK Remarkable discoveries also have been made in Anatolia. Excavations at Hacilar, Çatal Höyük, and elsewhere have shown that the central Anatolian plateau was the site of a flourishing Neolithic culture between 7000 and 5000 BCE. Twelve successive building levels excavated at Çatal Höyük between 1961 and 1965 have been dated between 6500 and 5700 BCE. On a single site, it is possible to retrace the evolution of a Neolithic culture over a period of 800 years. An

1-15 Human figure, from Ain Ghazal, Jordan, ca. 6750–6250 BCE. Plaster, painted and inlaid with bitumen, 3′ 5⅜″ high. Louvre, Paris.

The dozens of large white plaster statuettes, some with two heads and with details added in paint, found at Ain Ghazal date to the mid-seventh millennium BCE and are the earliest large sculptures known.

1 ft.

important source of Çatal Höyük's wealth was trade, especially in obsidian, a glasslike volcanic stone Neolithic toolmakers and weapon makers valued highly because it could be chipped into fine cutting edges. Along with Jericho, Çatal Höyük seems to have been one of the first experiments in urban living. The regularity of its plan suggests that the town was built according to some predetermined scheme. A peculiar feature is the settlement's complete lack of streets. The houses adjoin one another and have no doors (FIG. **1-16**). Openings in the roofs provided access to the interiors. The openings also served as chimneys to ventilate the hearth in the combination living room and kitchen that

1-16 Restored view of a section of Level VI, Çatal Höyük, Turkey, ca. 6000–5900 BCE (John Swogger).

Archaeologists have discovered 12 successive building levels at Çatal Höyük. The houses in this early city adjoined one another and had no doors. Openings in the roofs provided access to the interiors.

formed the core of the house. Impractical as such an arrangement may appear today, it did offer some advantages. The attached buildings were more stable than freestanding structures and, at the limits of the town site, formed a defensive perimeter wall. If enemies managed to breach the exterior wall, they would find themselves not inside the town but above the houses with the defenders waiting there on the roof.

The houses, constructed of mud brick strengthened by sturdy timber frames, varied in size but repeated the same basic plan. Walls and floors were plastered and painted, and platforms along walls served as sites for sleeping, working, and eating. The dead were buried beneath the same platforms. A great number of decorated rooms have been found at Çatal Höyük. The excavators called these rooms shrines, but their function is uncertain. Their number suggests that these rooms played an important role in the life of Çatal Höyük's inhabitants.

The "shrines" are distinguished from the house structures by the greater richness of their interior decoration, which consisted of wall paintings, plaster reliefs, animal heads, and *bucrania* (bovine skulls). Bulls' horns, widely thought to be symbols of masculine potency, are the most common motif in these rooms. In some cases they are displayed next to plaster breasts, symbols of female fertility, projecting from the walls. Many statuettes of stone or *terracotta* (baked clay) also have been found at Çatal Höyük. Most are quite small (2 to 8 inches high) and primarily depict female figures. A few reach 12 inches.

Although animal husbandry was well established, hunting continued to play an important part in the early Neolithic economy of Çatal Höyük. The importance of hunting as a food source (until about 5700 BCE) is reflected also in wall paintings, where, in the older decorated rooms, hunting scenes predominate. In style and concept, however, the deer hunt mural (FIG. 1-17) at Çatal Höyük is worlds apart from the wall paintings the hunters of the Paleolithic period produced. Perhaps what is most strikingly new about the Çatal Höyük painting and others like it is the regular appearance of the human figure—not only singly but also in large, coherent groups with a wide variety of poses, subjects, and settings. As noted earlier, humans were unusual in Paleolithic cave paintings, and pictorial narratives have almost never been found. Even the "hunting scene" (FIG. 1-13) in the well at Lascaux is doubtful as a narrative. In Neolithic paintings, human themes and concerns and action scenes with humans dominating animals are central.

In the Çatal Höyük hunt, the group of hunters—and no one doubts it is, indeed, an organized hunting party, not a series of individual figures—shows a tense exaggeration of movement and a rhythmic repetition of basic shapes customary for the period. The painter took care to distinguish important descriptive details—for example, bows, arrows, and garments—and the heads have clearly defined noses, mouths, chins, and hair. The Neolithic painter placed all the heads in profile for the same reason Paleolithic painters universally chose the profile view for representations of animals. Only the side view of the human head shows all its shapes clearly. However, at Çatal Höyük the torsos are presented from the front—again, the most informative viewpoint—whereas the painter chose the profile view for the legs and arms. This composite view of the human body is quite artificial because the human body cannot make an abrupt 90-degree shift at the hips. But it is very descriptive of what a human body is—as opposed to what it looks like from a particular viewpoint. The technique of painting also changed dramatically since Paleolithic times. The pigments were applied with a brush to a white background of dry plaster. The careful preparation of the wall surface is in striking contrast to the direct application of pigment to the irregularly shaped walls and ceilings of caves.

More remarkable still is a painting (FIG. 1-18 is a watercolor copy) in one of the older rooms at Çatal Höyük that art historians generally have acclaimed as the world's first *landscape* (a picture of a natural setting in its own right, without any narrative content). As such, it remained unique for thousands of years. According to radiocarbon dating, the painting was executed around 6150 BCE. The foreground has been interpreted as a town with rectangular houses neatly laid out side by side, probably representing Çatal Höyük itself.

1-17 Deer hunt, detail of a wall painting from Level III, Çatal Höyük, Turkey, ca. 5750 BCE. Museum of Anatolian Civilization, Ankara.

This Neolithic painter depicted human figures as a composite of frontal and profile views, the most descriptive picture of the shape of the human body. This format would become the rule for millennia.

1-18 Landscape with volcanic eruption(?), watercolor copy of a wall painting from Level VII, Çatal Höyük, Turkey, ca. 6150 BCE.

This late-seventh-millennium BCE mural painting may represent Çatal Höyük during a volcanic eruption. It is the first known landscape painting in which neither humans nor animals appear.

Behind the town appears a mountain with two peaks. Many archaeologists think that the dots and lines issuing from the higher of the two cones represent a volcanic eruption, and have suggested that the mountain is the 10,600-foot-high Hasan Dağ. It is located within view of Çatal Höyük and is the only twin-peaked volcano in central Anatolia. The conjectured volcanic eruption shown in the mural does not necessarily depict a specific historical event. If, however, the Çatal Höyük painting relates a story, even a recurring one, then it cannot be considered a pure landscape. Nonetheless, this mural is the first depiction of a place devoid of both humans and animals.

The rich finds at Çatal Höyük give the impression of a prosperous and well-ordered society that practiced a great variety of arts and crafts. In addition to painting and sculpture, weaving and pottery were well established, and even the technique of smelting lead in small quantities was known before 6000 BCE. The conversion to an agricultural economy appears to have been completed by about 5700 BCE.

Western Europe

In western Europe, where Paleolithic paintings and sculptures abound, no comparably developed towns of the time of Çatal Höyük have been found. However, in succeeding millennia, perhaps as early as 4000 BCE, the local Neolithic populations in several areas developed a monumental architecture employing massive rough-cut stones. The very dimensions of the stones, some as high as 17 feet and weighing as much as 50 tons, have prompted historians to call them *megaliths* (great stones) and to designate Neolithic architecture employing megaliths as *megalithic*.

NEWGRANGE One of the most impressive megalithic monuments in Europe is also one of the oldest. The megalithic tomb at Newgrange in Ireland, north of Dublin, may have been constructed as early as 3200 BCE and is one of the oldest burial monuments in Europe. It takes the form of a *passage grave*, that is, a tomb with a long stone corridor (FIG. **1-19**) leading to a burial chamber, all covered by a great *tumulus* (earthen burial mound). Passage graves have been found also in England, France, Spain, and Scandinavia. All attest to the importance of honoring the dead in Neolithic society. Some mounds contain more than one passage grave. The Newgrange

1-19A House 1, Skara Brae, ca. 3100–2500 BCE.

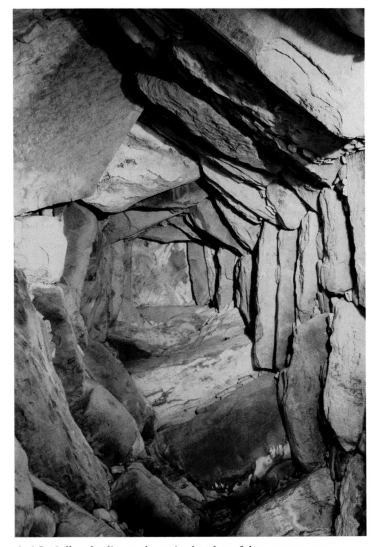

1-19 Gallery leading to the main chamber of the passage grave, Newgrange, Ireland, ca. 3200–2500 BCE.

The Newgrange passage grave is an early example of corbeled vaulting. The megaliths of the corridor leading to the burial chamber beneath the tumulus are held in place by their own weight.

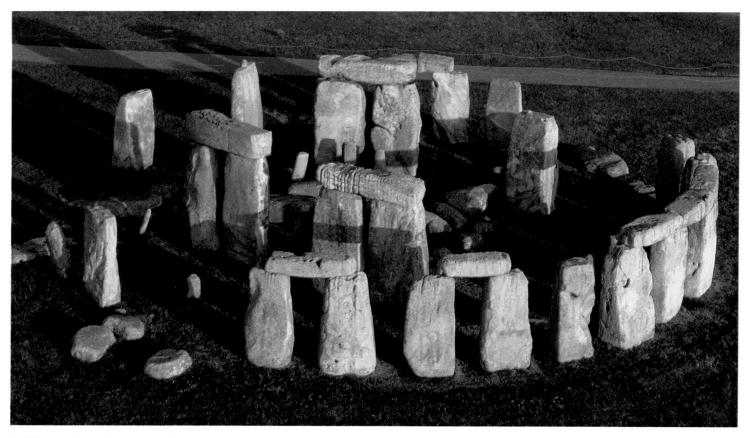

1-20 Aerial view (looking northwest) of Stonehenge, Salisbury Plain, England, ca. 2550–1600 BCE. Circle is 97′ in diameter; trilithons 24′ high.

The circles of trilithons at Stonehenge probably functioned as an astronomical observatory and solar calendar. The sun rises over its "heel stone" at the summer solstice. Some of the megaliths weigh 50 tons.

tumulus is 280 feet in diameter and 44 feet tall. Its passageway is 62 feet long and is an early example of a construction technique used in other later ancient cultures and even today—the *corbeled vault* (FIGS. 4-16 and 4-17*b*). At Newgrange, huge megaliths form the ceiling of the passage and the burial chamber. The stones are held in place by their own weight, those on one side countering the weight of the megaliths on the other side of the passageway. Some of the stones are decorated with incised spirals and other abstract motifs (not visible in FIG. 1-19). A special feature of the Newgrange tomb is that at the winter solstice the sun illuminates the passageway and the burial chamber.

HAGAR QIM Contemporary with Newgrange but on an island far to the south is the megalithic temple (FIG. 1-1) of Hagar Qim, one of many constructed on Malta between 3200 and 2500 BCE and one of the oldest stone temples anywhere in the world. The Maltese builders constructed their temples by piling carefully cut stone blocks in *courses* (stacked horizontal rows). The doorways at Hagar Qim were built using the *post-and-lintel* system (FIG. 4-17*a*) in which two upright stones (posts) support a horizontal beam (*lintel*). The layout of this and other Neolithic Maltese temples is especially noteworthy for the combination of rectilinear and curved forms, including multiple *apses* (semicircular recesses). Inside the Hagar Qim temple archaeologists found altars (hence the identification of the structure as a religious shrine) and several stone statues of headless

nude women, one standing, the others seated. The level of architectural and sculptural sophistication seen on this isolated island at so early a date is extraordinary.

STONEHENGE The most famous megalithic monument in Europe is Stonehenge (FIG. 1-20) on the Salisbury Plain in southern England. A *henge* is an arrangement of megalithic stones in a circle, often surrounded by a ditch. The type is almost entirely limited to Britain. Stonehenge is a complex of rough-cut sarsen (a form of sandstone) stones and smaller "bluestones" (various volcanic rocks) built in several stages over hundreds of years. The final henge took the form of concentric post-and-lintel circles. The outer ring, almost 100 feet in diameter, consists of huge sarsen megaliths. Inside is a ring of bluestones, which in turn encircle a horseshoe (open end facing east) of *trilithons* (three-stone constructions)—five lintel-topped pairs of the largest sarsens, each weighing 45 to 50 tons. Standing apart and to the east (outside the aerial view in FIG. 1-20) is the "heel stone," which, for a person looking outward from the center of the complex, would have marked the point where the sun rose at the summer solstice. Stonehenge seems to have been a kind of astronomical observatory and a remarkably accurate solar calendar.

The megalithic tombs, temples, and henges of Europe are enduring testaments to the rapidly developing intellectual powers of Neolithic humans as well as to their capacity for heroic physical effort.

ART BEFORE HISTORY

PALEOLITHIC (OLD STONE AGE) ART, ca. 30,000–9000 BCE

■ The first sculptures and paintings antedate the invention of writing by tens of thousands of years. Paleolithic humans' decision to represent the world around them initiated an intellectual revolution of enormous consequences.

■ No one knows why humans began to paint and carve images or what role those images played in the lives of Paleolithic hunters. Women were far more common subjects than men, but animals, not humans, dominate Paleolithic art.

■ The works created range in size from tiny figurines like the so-called *Venus of Willendorf* to painted walls and ceilings covered with over-life-size animals, as in the cave at Lascaux.

■ Artists always depicted animals in profile so that the image was complete, including the head, body, tail, and all four legs. This format persisted for millennia.

Nude woman (*Venus of Willendorf*), ca. 28,000–25,000 BCE

Hall of the Bulls, Lascaux, ca. 15,000–13,000 BCE

NEOLITHIC (NEW STONE AGE) ART, ca. 8000–2300 BCE

■ Around 9000 BCE, the ice that had covered much of northern Europe for millennia receded. After a transitional period, the Neolithic Age began, but at different times in different places. It also continued longer in remote places like Stonehenge in England and Hagar Qim on Malta.

■ The Neolithic Age revolutionized human life with the beginning of agriculture and the formation of the first settled communities, like that at Çatal Höyük in Anatolia.

■ In art, the Neolithic period saw the birth of monumental sculpture, notably the painted plaster figurines from Ain Ghazal, and of monumental stone architecture in the walls and tower(s) of Jericho.

■ In painting, coherent narratives became common and artists began to represent human figures as composites of frontal and profile views—another formula that would remain universal for a very long time.

Plaster figurine, Ain Ghazal, ca. 6750–6250 BCE

Stonehenge, Salisbury Plain, ca. 2550–1600 BCE

1 in.

2-1 **Hammurabi and Shamash, detail of the stele of Hammurabi** (FIG. 2-17)**, from Susa, Iran, ca. 1780 BCE.**

The relationship between king and god in the ancient Near East is set out on this Babylonian stele representing the sun god extending to Hammurabi the symbols of his authority to govern and enact laws.

2

THE ANCIENT
NEAR EAST

When humans first gave up the dangerous and uncertain life of the hunter and gatherer for the more predictable and stable life of the farmer and herder, the change in human society was so significant that it justly has been called the Neolithic Revolution. This fundamental change in the nature of daily life first occurred in Mesopotamia—a Greek word that means "the land between the [Tigris and Euphrates] rivers." Mesopotamia is at the core of the region often called the Fertile Crescent, a land mass that forms a huge arc from the mountainous border between Turkey and Syria through Iraq to Iran's Zagros Mountains (MAP 2-1). There, humans first learned how to use the wheel and the plow and how to control floods and construct irrigation canals. The land became a giant oasis, the presumed locale of the biblical Garden of Eden.

2-1A Beaker with animal decoration, Susa, ca. 4000 BCE.

As the region that gave birth to three of the world's great modern faiths—Judaism, Christianity, and Islam—the Near East has long been of interest to historians. But not until the 19th century did systematic excavation open the public's eyes to the extraordinary art and architecture of the ancient land between the rivers. After the first discoveries, the great museums of Europe, consistent with the treasure-hunting spirit of the era, began to acquire Mesopotamian artworks as quickly as possible. The instructions the British Museum gave to Austen Henry Layard, one of the pioneers of Near Eastern archaeology, were typical: Obtain as many well-preserved artworks as you can while spending the least possible amount of time and money doing so. Interest heightened with each new find, and soon North American museums also began to collect Near Eastern art.

The most popular 19th-century acquisitions were the stone reliefs depicting warfare and hunting (FIGS. 2-22 and 2-23) and the colossal statues of monstrous human-headed bulls (FIG. 2-21) from the palaces of the Assyrians, rulers of a northern Mesopotamian empire during the ninth to the seventh centuries BCE. But nothing that emerged from the Near Eastern soil attracted as much attention as the treasures Leonard Woolley discovered in the 1920s at the Royal Cemetery at Ur in southern Mesopotamia. The interest in the lavish third-millennium Sumerian burials he unearthed rivaled the fascination with the 1922 discovery of the tomb of the Egyptian boy-king Tutankhamen (see Chapter 3). The Ur cemetery yielded gold objects, jewelry, artworks, and musical instruments (FIGS. 2-8 to 2-11) of the highest quality.

SUMER

The discovery of the treasures of ancient Ur put the Sumerians once again in a prominent position on the world stage. They had been absent for more than 4,000 years. The Sumerians were the people who in the fourth millennium BCE transformed the vast and previously sparsely inhabited valley between the Tigris and Euphrates into the Fertile Crescent of the ancient world. Ancient Sumer, which roughly corresponds to southern Iraq today, was not a unified nation. Rather, it was made up of a dozen or so independent *city-states*. Each was thought to be under the protection of a different Mesopotamian deity (see "The Gods and Goddesses of Mesopotamia," page 33). The Sumerian rulers were the gods' representatives on earth and the stewards of their earthly treasure.

The rulers and priests directed all communal activities, including canal construction, crop collection, and food distribution. The development of agriculture to the point that only a portion of the population had to produce food meant that some members of the community could specialize in other activities, including manufacturing, trade, and administration. Specialization of labor is a hallmark of the first complex urban societies. In the city-states of ancient Sumer, activities that once had been individually initiated became institutionalized for the first time. The community, rather than the family, assumed functions such as defense against enemies and against the caprices of nature. Whether ruled by a single person or a council chosen from among the leading families, these communities gained permanent identities as discrete cities. The city-state was one of the great Sumerian inventions.

Another was writing. The oldest written documents known are Sumerian records of administrative acts and commercial transactions. At first, around 3400–3200 BCE, the Sumerians made inventories of cattle, food, and other items by scratching *pictographs* (simplified pictures standing for words) into soft clay with a sharp tool, or *stylus*. The clay plaques hardened into breakable, yet nearly indestructible, tablets. Thousands of these plaques dating back nearly five millennia exist today. The Sumerians wrote their pictorial signs from the top down and arranged them in boxes they read from right to left. By 3000–2900 BCE, they had further simplified the pictographic signs by reducing them to a group of wedge-shaped (*cuneiform*) signs

MAP 2-1 The ancient Near East.

(FIG. 2-7 is an early example; see also FIGS. 2-1, 2-16, and 2-17). The development of cuneiform marked the beginning of writing, as historians strictly define it. The surviving cuneiform tablets testify to the far-flung network of Sumerian contacts reaching from southern Mesopotamia eastward to the Iranian plateau, northward to Assyria, and westward to Syria. Trade was essential for the Sumerians, because despite the fertility of their land, it was poor in such vital natural resources as metal, stone, and wood.

The Sumerians also produced great literature. Their most famous work, known from fragmentary cuneiform texts, is the late-third-millennium *Epic of Gilgamesh*, which antedates Homer's *Iliad* and *Odyssey* by some 1,500 years. It recounts the heroic story of Gilgamesh, legendary king of Uruk and slayer of the monster Huwawa. Translations of the Sumerian epic into several other ancient Near Eastern languages attest to the fame of the original version.

2-2 White Temple and ziggurat, Uruk (modern Warka), Iraq, ca. 3200–3000 BCE.

Using only mud bricks, the Sumerians erected temple platforms called ziggurats several centuries before the Egyptians built stone pyramids. The most famous ziggurat was the biblical Tower of Babel.

The Gods and Goddesses of Mesopotamia

The Sumerians and their successors in the ancient Near East worshiped numerous deities, mostly nature gods. Listed here are the Mesopotamian gods and goddesses discussed in this chapter.

- **Anu.** The chief deity of the Sumerians, Anu was the god of the sky and of the city of Uruk. One of the earliest Sumerian temples (FIGS. 2-2 and 2-3) may have been dedicated to his worship.

- **Enlil.** Anu's son, Enlil was the lord of the winds and the earth. He eventually replaced his father as king of the gods.

- **Inanna.** The Sumerian goddess of love and war, Inanna was later known as **Ishtar.** She is the most important female deity in all periods of Mesopotamian history. As early as the fourth millennium BCE, the Sumerians constructed a sanctuary to Inanna at Uruk. Amid the ruins, excavators uncovered fourth-millennium statues and reliefs (FIGS. 2-4 and 2-5) connected with her worship.

- **Nanna.** The moon god, Nanna was also known as **Sin.** He was the chief deity of Ur, where his most important shrine was located.

- **Utu.** The sun god, Utu was known later as **Shamash** and was especially revered at Sippar. On a Babylonian stele (FIG. 2-1) of ca. 1780 BCE, King Hammurabi presents his law code to Shamash, who is depicted with flames radiating from his shoulders.

- **Marduk, Nabu,** and **Adad.** Marduk was the chief god of the Babylonians. His son Nabu was the god of writing and wisdom. Adad was the Babylonian god of storms. Representations of Marduk and Nabu's dragon and Adad's sacred bull adorn the sixth-century BCE Ishtar Gate (FIG. 2-24) at Babylon.

- **Ningirsu.** The local god of Lagash and Girsu, Ningirsu helped Eannatum, one of the early rulers of Lagash, defeat an enemy army. Ningirsu's role in the victory is recorded on the *Stele of the Vultures* (FIG. 2-7) of ca. 2600–2500 BCE. Gudea (FIG. 2-16), one of Eannatum's Neo-Sumerian successors, built a great temple about 2100 BCE in honor of Ningirsu after the god instructed him to do so in a dream.

- **Ashur.** The local deity of Assur, the city that took his name, Ashur became the king of the Assyrian gods. He sometimes is identified with Enlil.

WHITE TEMPLE, URUK The layout of Sumerian cities reflected the central role of the gods in daily life. The main temple to each state's chief god formed the city's monumental nucleus. In fact, the temple complex was a kind of city within a city, where a staff of priests and scribes carried on official administrative and commercial business, as well as oversaw all religious functions.

The outstanding preserved example of early Sumerian temple architecture is the 5,000-year-old White Temple (FIG. 2-2) at Uruk, a city that in the late fourth millennium BCE had a population of about 40,000. Usually only the foundations of early Mesopotamian temples can still be recognized. The White Temple is a rare exception. Sumerian builders did not have access to stone quarries and instead formed mud bricks for the superstructures of their temples and other buildings. Almost all these structures have eroded over the course of time. The fragile nature of the building materials did not, however, prevent the Sumerians from erecting towering works, such as the Uruk temple, several centuries before the Egyptians built their famous stone pyramids. This says a great deal about the Sumerians' desire to provide monumental settings for the worship of their deities.

2-3 Reconstruction drawing of the White Temple and ziggurat, Uruk (modern Warka), Iraq, ca. 3200–3000 BCE.

The White Temple at Uruk was probably dedicated to Anu, the sky god. It has a central hall (cella) with a stepped altar where the Sumerian priests would await the apparition of the deity.

Enough of the Uruk complex remains to permit a fairly reliable reconstruction (FIG. 2-3). The temple (whose whitewashed walls lend it its modern nickname) stands atop a high platform, or *ziggurat,* 40 feet above street level in the city center. A stairway on one side leads to the top but does not end in front of any of the temple doorways, necessitating two or three angular changes in direction. This *bent-axis plan* is the standard arrangement for Sumerian temples, a striking contrast to the linear approach the Egyptians preferred for their temples and tombs (see Chapter 3).

Like other Sumerian temples, the corners of the White Temple are oriented to the cardinal points of the compass. The building, probably dedicated to Anu, the sky god, is of modest proportions (61 × 16 feet). By design, it did not accommodate large throngs of worshipers but only a select few, the priests and perhaps the leading community members. The temple has several chambers. The central hall, or *cella,* was set aside for the divinity and housed a stepped altar. The Sumerians referred to their temples as "waiting rooms," a reflection of their belief that the deity would descend from the heavens to appear before the priests in the cella. Whether the Uruk temple had a roof and, if it did, what kind, are uncertain.

The Sumerian idea that the gods reside above the world of humans is central to most of the world's religions. Moses ascended Mount Sinai to receive the Ten Commandments from the Hebrew God, and the Greeks placed the home of their gods and goddesses on Mount Olympus. The elevated placement of Mesopotamian temples on giant platforms reaching toward the sky is consistent with this widespread religious concept. Eroded ziggurats still dominate most of the ruined cities of Sumer. The loftiness of the great temple platforms made a profound impression on the peoples of the ancient Near East. The tallest ziggurat of all, at Babylon, was about 270 feet high. Known to the Hebrews as the Tower of Babel, it became the centerpiece of a biblical story about the insolent pride of humans (see "Babylon, City of Wonders," page 48).

INANNA A fragmentary white marble female head (FIG. **2-4**) from Uruk is also an extraordinary achievement at so early a date. The head, one of the treasures of the Iraq Museum in Baghdad, disappeared during the Iraq war of 2003 but was later recovered. (FIG. 2-4, which shows the head during its presentation at a press conference after its recovery, gives an excellent idea of its size. Other missing items from the museum that were later recovered, in some cases damaged, include FIGS. 2-5 and 2-12.) The lustrous hard stone used to carve the head had to be brought to Uruk at great cost, and the Sumerians used the stone sparingly. The "head" is actually only a face with a flat back. It has drilled holes for attachment to the rest of the head and the body, which may have been wood. Although found in the sacred precinct of the goddess Inanna, the subject is unknown. Many scholars have suggested that the face is an image of Inanna, but a mortal woman, perhaps a priestess, may be portrayed.

Often the present condition of an artwork can be very misleading, and the Uruk head is a dramatic example. Its original appearance would have been much more vibrant than the pure white fragment preserved today. Colored shell or stone filled the deep recesses for the eyebrows and the large eyes. The deep groove at the top of the head anchored a wig, probably made of gold leaf. The hair strands engraved in the metal fell in waves over the forehead and sides of the face. The bright coloration of the eyes, brows, and hair likely over-

shadowed the soft modeling of the cheeks and mouth. The missing body was probably clothed in expensive fabrics and bedecked with jewels.

WARKA VASE The Sumerians, pioneers in so many areas, also may have been the first to use pictures to tell coherent stories. Sumerian narrative art goes far beyond the Stone Age artists' tentative efforts at storytelling. The so-called *Warka Vase* (FIG. **2-5**) from Uruk (modern Warka) is the first great work of narrative relief

1 ft.

2-5 Presentation of offerings to Inanna (*Warka Vase*), from Uruk (modern Warka), Iraq, ca. 3200–3000 BCE. Alabaster, 3′ ¼″ high. Iraq Museum, Baghdad.

In this oldest known example of Sumerian narrative art, the sculptor divided the tall stone vase's reliefs into registers, a significant break with the haphazard figure placement found in earlier art.

1 in.

2-4 Female head (Inanna?), from Uruk (modern Warka), Iraq, ca. 3200–3000 BCE. Marble, 8″ high. Iraq Museum, Baghdad.

The Sumerians imported the marble for this head at great cost. It may represent the goddess Inanna and originally had inlaid colored shell or stone eyes and brows, and a wig, probably of gold leaf.

sculpture known. Found within the Inanna temple complex, it depicts a religious festival in honor of the goddess.

The sculptor divided the vase's reliefs into several bands (also called *registers* or *friezes*), and the figures stand on a *ground line* (the horizontal base of the composition). This new kind of composition marks a significant break with the haphazard figure placement found in earlier art. The register format for telling a story was to have a very long future. In fact, artists still employ registers today in modified form in comic books.

The lowest band on the *Warka Vase* shows crops above a wavy line representing water. Then comes a register with ewes and rams—in strict profile, consistent with an approach to representing animals that was then some 20,000 years old. The crops and the alternating male and female animals were the staple commodities of the Sumerian economy, but they were also associated with fertility. They underscore that Inanna had blessed Uruk's inhabitants with good crops and increased herds.

A procession of naked men fills the band at the center of the vase. The men carry baskets and jars overflowing with the earth's abundance. They will present their bounty to the goddess as a *votive offering* (gift of gratitude to a deity usually made in fulfillment of a vow) and will deposit it in her temple. The spacing of each figure involves no overlapping. The Uruk men, like the Neolithic deer hunters at Çatal Höyük (FIG. 1-17), are a composite of frontal and profile views, with large staring frontal eyes in profile heads. The artist indicated those human body parts necessary to communicate the human form and avoided positions, attitudes, or views that would conceal the characterizing parts. For example, if the figures were in strict profile, an arm and perhaps a leg would be hidden. The body would appear to have only half its breadth. And the eye would not "read" as an eye at all, because it would not have its distinctive oval shape. Art historians call this characteristic early approach to representation *conceptual* (as opposed to optical) because artists who used it did not record the immediate, fleeting aspect of figures. Instead, they rendered the human body's distinguishing and fixed properties. The fundamental forms of figures, not their accidental appearance, dictated the artist's selection of the composite view as the best way to represent the human body.

In the uppermost (and tallest) band is a female figure with a tall horned headdress next to two large poles that are the sign of the goddess Inanna. (Some scholars think the woman is a priestess and not the goddess herself.) A nude male figure brings a large vessel brimming with offerings to be deposited in the goddess's shrine. At the far right and barely visible in FIG. 2-5 is an only partially preserved clothed man. Near him is the early pictograph for the Sumerian official that is usually, if ambiguously, called a "priest-king," that is, both a religious and secular leader. The greater height of the priest-king and Inanna compared to the offering bearers indicates their greater importance, a convention called *hierarchy of scale*. Some scholars interpret the scene as a symbolic marriage between the priest-king and the goddess, ensuring her continued goodwill—and reaffirming the leader's exalted position in society.

ESHNUNNA STATUETTES Further insight into Sumerian religious beliefs and rituals comes from a cache of sculptures reverently buried beneath the floor of a temple at Eshnunna (modern Tell Asmar) when the structure was remodeled. Carved of soft gypsum and inlaid with shell and black limestone, the statuettes range in size from well under a foot to about 30 inches tall. The two largest figures are shown in FIG. 2-6. All of the statuettes represent mortals, rather than deities, with their hands folded in front of their chests in a gesture of prayer, usually holding the small beakers the Sumerians used in religious rites. Hundreds of similar goblets have been found in the temple complex at Eshnunna. The men wear belts and fringed skirts. Most have beards and shoulder-length hair. The women wear long robes, with the right shoulder bare. Similar figurines from other sites bear inscriptions giving information such as the name of the donor and the god or even specific prayers to the deity on the owner's behalf. With their heads tilted upward, they wait in the Sumerian "waiting room" for the divinity to appear.

The sculptors of the Eshnunna statuettes employed simple forms, primarily cones and cylinders, for the figures. The statuettes are not portraits in the strict sense of the word, but the sculptors did distinguish physical types. At least one child was portrayed—next to the woman in FIG. 2-6 are the remains of two small legs. Most striking is the disproportionate relationship between the inlaid oversized eyes and the tiny hands. Scholars have explained the exaggeration of the eye size in various ways. But because the purpose of these votive figures was to offer constant prayers to the gods on their donors' behalf, the open-eyed stares most likely symbolize the eternal wakefulness necessary to fulfill their duty.

2-6A Urnanshe, from Mari, ca. 2600–2500 BCE.

2-6 Statuettes of two worshipers, from the Square Temple at Eshnunna (modern Tell Asmar), Iraq, ca. 2700 BCE. Gypsum inlaid with shell and black limestone, male figure 2′ 6″ high. Iraq Museum, Baghdad.

The oversized eyes probably symbolized the perpetual wakefulness of these substitute worshipers offering prayers to the deity. The beakers the figures hold were used to pour libations in honor of the gods.

STELE OF THE VULTURES The city-states of ancient Sumer were often at war with one another, and warfare is the theme of the so-called *Stele of the Vultures* (FIG. 2-7) from Girsu. A *stele* is a carved stone slab erected to commemorate a historical event or, in some cultures, to mark a grave. The Girsu stele presents a labeled historical narrative with cuneiform inscriptions filling almost every blank space on the stele. (It is not, however, the first historical representation in the history of art. That honor belongs—at the moment—to an Egyptian relief (FIG. 3-3) carved more than three centuries earlier.) The inscriptions reveal that the *Stele of the Vultures* celebrates the victory of Eannatum, the *ensi* (ruler; king?) of Lagash, over the neighboring city-state of Umma. The stele has reliefs on both sides and takes its nickname from a fragment with a gruesome scene of vultures carrying off the severed heads and arms of the defeated enemy soldiers. Another fragment shows the giant figure of the local god Ningirsu holding tiny enemies in a net and beating one of them on the head with a mace.

The fragment in FIG. 2-7 depicts Eannatum leading an infantry battalion into battle (above) and attacking from a war chariot (below). The foot soldiers are protected behind a wall of shields and trample naked enemies as they advance. (The fragment that shows vultures devouring corpses belongs just to the right in the same register.) Both on foot and in a chariot, Eannatum is larger than anyone else, except Ningirsu on the other side of the stele. The artist presented him as the fearless general who paves the way for his army. Lives were lost, however, and Eannatum himself was wounded in the campaign, but the outcome was never in doubt because Ningirsu fought with the men of Lagash.

Despite its fragmentary state, the *Stele of the Vultures* is an extraordinary document, not only as a very early effort to record historical events in relief but also for the insight it yields about Sumerian society. Through both words and pictures, it provides information about warfare and the special nature of the Sumerian ruler. Eannatum was greater in stature than other men, and Ningirsu watched over him. According to the text, the ensi was born from the god Enlil's semen, which Ningirsu implanted in the womb. When Eannatum was wounded in battle, it says, the god shed tears for him. He was a divinely chosen ruler who presided over all aspects of his city-state, both in war and in peace. This also seems to have been the role of the ensi in the other Sumerian city-states.

STANDARD OF UR Agriculture and trade brought considerable wealth to some of the city-states of ancient Sumer. Nowhere is this clearer than in the so-called Royal Cemetery at Ur, the city that was home to the biblical Abraham. In the third millennium BCE, the leading families of Ur buried their dead in chambers beneath the earth. Scholars still debate whether these deceased were true kings and queens or simply aristocrats and priests, but the Sumerians laid them to rest in regal fashion. Archaeologists exploring the Ur cemetery uncovered gold helmets and daggers with handles of lapis lazuli (a rich azure-blue stone imported from Afghanistan), golden beakers and bowls, jewelry of gold and lapis, musical instruments, chariots, and other luxurious items. Dozens of bodies were also found in the richest tombs. A retinue of musicians, servants, charioteers, and soldiers was sacrificed in order to accompany the "kings and queens" into the afterlife. (Comparable rituals are documented in other societies, for example, in ancient America; see Chapter 14.)

Not the costliest object found in the "royal" graves, but probably the most significant from the viewpoint of the history of art, is the so-called *Standard of Ur* (FIGS. 2-8 and 2-9). This rectangular box of uncertain function has sloping sides inlaid with shell, lapis lazuli, and red limestone. The excavator, Leonard Woolley, thought the object was

2-7 Fragment of the victory stele of Eannatum (*Stele of the Vultures*), from Girsu (modern Telloh), Iraq, ca. 2600–2500 BCE. Limestone, fragment 2′ 6″ high, full stele 5′ 11″ high. Louvre, Paris.

Cuneiform inscriptions on this stele describe the victory of Eannatum of Lagash over the city of Umma. This fragment shows Eannatum leading his army into battle. The artist depicted the king larger than his soldiers.

1 ft.

2-8 War side of the *Standard of Ur*, from tomb 779, Royal Cemetery, Ur (modern Tell Muqayyar), Iraq, ca. 2600 BCE. Wood inlaid with shell, lapis lazuli, and red limestone, 8″ × 1′ 7″. British Museum, London. ◼◂

Using a mosaic-like technique, this Sumerian artist depicted a battlefield victory in three registers. In the top band, soldiers present bound captives to a kinglike figure who is larger than everyone else.

2-9 Peace side of the *Standard of Ur*, from tomb 779, Royal Cemetery, Ur (modern Tell Muqayyar), Iraq, ca. 2600 BCE. Wood inlaid with shell, lapis lazuli, and red limestone, 8″ × 1′ 7″. British Museum, London. ◼◂

The feast on the peace side of the *Standard of Ur* may be a victory celebration. The narrative again reads from bottom to top, and the size of the figures varies with their importance in Sumerian society.

originally mounted on a pole, and he considered it a kind of military standard—hence its nickname. Art historians usually refer to the two long sides of the box as the "war side" and "peace side," but the two sides may represent the first and second parts of a single narrative. The artist divided each into three horizontal bands. The narrative reads from left to right and bottom to top. On the war side (FIG. 2-8), four ass-drawn four-wheeled war chariots mow down enemies, whose bodies appear on the ground in front of and beneath the animals. The gait of the asses accelerates along the band from left to right. Above, foot soldiers gather up and lead away captured foes. In the uppermost register, soldiers present bound captives (who have been stripped naked to degrade them) to a kinglike figure, who has stepped out of his chariot. His central place in the composition and his greater stature (his head breaks through the border at the top) set him apart from all the other figures.

In the lowest band on the peace side (FIG. 2-9), men carry provisions, possibly war booty, on their backs. Above, attendants bring animals, perhaps also spoils of war, and fish for the great banquet depicted in the uppermost register. There, seated dignitaries and a larger-than-life "king" (third from the left) feast, while a lyre player and singer entertain the group. Art historians have interpreted the scene both as a victory celebration and as a banquet in connection with cult ritual. The two are not necessarily incompatible. The absence of an inscription prevents connecting the scenes with a specific event or person, but the *Standard of Ur* undoubtedly is another early example of historical narrative.

BULL-HEADED LYRE From the "King's Grave" at Ur comes a fragmentary lyre (FIG. 2-10) that, when intact, probably resembled the instrument depicted in the feast scene (FIG. 2-9, *top right*) on the *Standard of Ur*. A magnificent bull's head (FIG. 2-10, *left*) caps the instrument's sound box. It is fashioned of gold leaf over a wooden core. The hair, beard, and details are lapis lazuli. The sound box (FIG. 2-10, *right*) also features bearded—but here human-headed—bulls in the uppermost of its four inlaid panels. Imaginary composite creatures are commonplace in the art of the ancient Near East and Egypt. On the Ur lyre, a heroic figure embraces the two man-bulls in a *heraldic composition* (symmetrical on either side of a central figure). His body and that of the scorpion-man in the lowest panel are in composite view. The animals are, equally characteristically, solely in profile: the dog wearing a dagger and carrying a laden table, the lion bringing in the beverage service, the ass playing the lyre, the jackal playing the zither, the bear steadying the lyre (or perhaps dancing), and the gazelle bearing goblets. The banquet animals almost seem to be burlesquing the kind of regal feast reproduced on the peace side of the *Standard of Ur*. The meaning of the sound-box scenes is unclear. Some scholars have suggested, for example, that the creatures inhabit the land of the dead and that the narrative has a funerary significance. In any event, the sound box is a very early specimen of the recurring theme in both literature and art of animals acting as people. Later examples include Aesop's fables in ancient Greece, medieval *bestiaries*, and Walt Disney's cartoon animal actors.

CYLINDER SEALS A banquet is also the subject of a *cylinder seal* (FIG. 2-11) found in the tomb of "Queen" Pu-abi and inscribed with her name. (Many historians prefer to designate her more conservatively and ambiguously as "Lady" Pu-abi.) The seal is typical of the period, consisting of a cylindrical piece of stone engraved to produce a raised impression when rolled over clay (see "Mesopotamian Seals," page 39). In the upper zone, a woman, probably Pu-abi, and a man sit and drink from beakers, attended by servants. Below, male attendants serve two more seated men. Even in miniature and in a medium very different from that of the *Standard of Ur*, the Sumerian artist employed the same figure types and followed the same compositional rules. All the figures are in composite views with large frontal eyes in profile heads, and the seated dignitaries are once again larger in scale to underscore their elevated position in the social hierarchy.

2-10 Bull-headed lyre from tomb 789 ("King's Grave"), Royal Cemetery, Ur (modern Tell Muqayyar), Iraq, ca. 2600 BCE. Lyre (*left*): Gold leaf and lapis lazuli over a wooden core, 5′ 5″ high. Sound box (*right*): Wood with inlaid gold, lapis lazuli, and shell, 1′ 7″ high. University of Pennsylvania Museum of Archaeology and Anthropology, Philadelphia.

This lyre from a royal grave at Ur is adorned with a bearded bull's head of gold leaf and lapis lazuli, and inlaid figures of a Gilgamesh-like hero and animals acting out scenes of uncertain significance.

1 ft.

1 ft.

Mesopotamian Seals

Seals have been unearthed in great numbers at sites throughout Mesopotamia. Generally made of stone, seals of ivory, glass, and other materials also survive. The seals take two forms: flat *stamp seals* and *cylinder seals*. The latter have a hole drilled lengthwise through the center of the cylinder so that they could be strung and worn around the neck or suspended from the wrist. Cylinder seals (FIG. 2-11) were prized possessions, signifying high positions in society, and they frequently were buried with the dead.

The primary function of cylinder seals, however, like the earlier stamp seals, was not to serve as items of adornment. The Sumerians (and other peoples of the Near East) used both stamp and cylinder seals to identify their documents and protect storage jars and doors against unauthorized opening. The oldest seals predate the invention of writing and conveyed their messages with pictographs that ratified ownership. Later seals often bear long cuneiform inscriptions and record the names and titles of rulers, bureaucrats, and deities. Although sealing is increasingly rare, the tradition lives on today whenever a letter is sealed with a lump of wax and then stamped with a monogram or other identifying mark. Customs officials often still seal packages and sacks with official stamps when goods cross national borders.

In the ancient Near East, artists decorated both stamp and cylinder seals with incised designs, producing a raised pattern when the seal was pressed into soft clay. (Cylinder seals largely displaced stamp seals because they could be rolled over the clay and thus cover a greater area more quickly.) FIG. 2-11 shows a cylinder seal from the Royal Cemetery at Ur and a modern impression made from it. Note how cracks in the stone cylinder become raised lines in the impression and how the engraved figures, chairs, and cuneiform characters appear in relief. Continuous rolling of the seal over a clay strip results in a repeating design, as the illustration also demonstrates at the edges.

The miniature reliefs the seals produce are a priceless source of information about Mesopotamian religion and society. Without them, archaeologists would know much less about how Mesopotamians dressed and dined; what their shrines looked like; how they depicted their gods, rulers, and mythological figures; how they fought wars; and what role women played in ancient Near Eastern society. Clay seal impressions excavated in architectural contexts shed a welcome light on the administration and organization of Mesopotamian city-states. Mesopotamian seals are also an invaluable resource for art historians, providing them with thousands of miniature examples of relief sculpture that span roughly 3,000 years.

1 in.

2-11 Banquet scene, cylinder seal (*left*) and its modern impression (*right*), from the tomb of Pu-abi (tomb 800), Royal Cemetery, Ur (modern Tell Muqayyar), Iraq, ca. 2600 BCE. Lapis lazuli, 2″ high. British Museum, London.

Seals were widely used in Mesopotamia to identify and secure goods. Artists incised designs into stone cylinders and then rolled them over clay to produce miniature artworks like this banquet scene.

AKKAD AND THE THIRD DYNASTY OF UR

In 2332 BCE, the loosely linked group of cities known as Sumer came under the domination of a great ruler, Sargon of Akkad (r. 2332–2279 BCE). Archaeologists have yet to locate the specific site of the city of Akkad, but it was in the vicinity of Babylon. The Akkadians were Semitic in origin—that is, they were a Near Eastern people who spoke a language related to Hebrew and Arabic. Their language,

Akkadian, was entirely different from the language of Sumer, but they used the Sumerians' cuneiform characters for their written documents. Under Sargon (whose name means "true king") and his followers, the Akkadians introduced a new concept of royal power based on unswerving loyalty to the king rather than to the city-state. During the rule of Sargon's grandson, Naram-Sin (r. 2254–2218 BCE), governors of cities were considered mere servants of the king, who in turn called himself "King of the Four Quarters"—in effect, ruler of the earth, akin to a god.

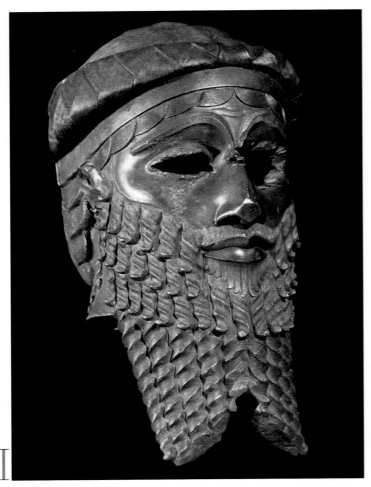

1 in.

2-12 Head of an Akkadian ruler, from Nineveh (modern Kuyunjik), Iraq, ca. 2250–2200 BCE. Copper, 1′ 2⅜″ high. Iraq Museum, Baghdad.

The sculptor of this first known life-size hollow-cast head captured the distinctive features of the ruler while also displaying a keen sense of abstract pattern. The head was vandalized in antiquity.

AKKADIAN PORTRAITURE A magnificent copper head of an Akkadian king (FIG. 2-12) found at Nineveh embodies this new concept of absolute monarchy. The head is all that survives of a statue that was knocked over in antiquity, perhaps when the Medes, a people that occupied the land south of the Caspian Sea (MAP 2-1), sacked Nineveh in 612 BCE. But the damage to the portrait was not due solely to the statue's toppling. There are also signs of deliberate mutilation. To make a political statement, the enemy gouged out the eyes (once inlaid with precious or semiprecious stones), broke off the lower part of the beard, and slashed the ears of the royal portrait. Nonetheless, the king's majestic serenity, dignity, and authority are evident. So, too, is the masterful way the sculptor balanced naturalism and abstract patterning. The artist carefully observed and recorded the man's distinctive features—the profile of the nose and the long, curly beard—and brilliantly communicated the differing textures of flesh and hair, even the contrasting textures of the mustache, beard, and braided hair on the top of the head. The coiffure's triangles, lozenges, and overlapping disks of hair and the great arching eyebrows that give so much character to the portrait reveal that the sculptor was also sensitive to formal pattern.

No less remarkable is the fact this is a life-size, hollow-cast metal sculpture (see "Hollow-Casting Life-Size Bronze Statues," Chapter 5, page 122), one of the earliest known. The head demonstrates the artisan's sophisticated skill in casting and polishing copper and in engraving the details. The portrait is the earliest known great monumental work of hollow-cast sculpture.

1 ft.

2-13 Victory stele of Naram-Sin, from Susa, Iran, 2254–2218 BCE. Pink sandstone, 6′ 7″ high. Louvre, Paris.

To commemorate his conquest of the Lullubi, Naram-Sin set up this stele showing him leading his army up a mountain. The sculptor staggered the figures, abandoning the traditional register format.

NARAM-SIN STELE The godlike sovereignty the kings of Akkad claimed is also evident in the victory stele (FIG. 2-13) Naram-Sin set up at Sippar. The stele commemorates his defeat of the Lullubi, a people of the Iranian mountains to the east. It is inscribed twice, once in honor of Naram-Sin and once by an Elamite king who had captured Sippar in 1157 BCE and taken the stele as booty back to Susa in southwestern Iran (MAP 2-1), where it was found. On the stele, the grandson of Sargon leads his victorious army up the slopes of a wooded mountain. His routed enemies fall, flee, die, or beg for mercy. The king stands alone, far taller than his men, treading on the bodies of two of the fallen Lullubi. He wears the horned helmet signifying divinity—the first time a king appears as a god in Mesopotamian art. At least three favorable stars (the stele is damaged at the top) shine on his triumph.

By storming the mountain, Naram-Sin seems also to be scaling the ladder to the heavens, the same conceit that lies behind the great ziggurat towers of the ancient Near East. His troops march up the mountain behind him in orderly files, suggesting the discipline and organization of the king's forces. The enemy, in contrast, is in disarray, depicted in a great variety of postures—one falls headlong down

Enheduanna, Priestess and Poet

In the man's world of ancient Akkad, one woman stands out prominently—Enheduanna, daughter of King Sargon and priestess of the moon god Nanna at Ur. Her name appears in several inscriptions, and she was the author of a series of hymns in honor of the goddess Inanna. Enheduanna's is the oldest recorded name of a poet, male or female. Indeed, hers is the earliest known name of the author of any literary work in world history.

The most important surviving object associated with Enheduanna is the alabaster disk (FIG. 2-14) found at Ur in several fragments in the residence of the priestess of Nanna. The reverse bears a cuneiform inscription identifying Enheduanna as the "wife of Nanna" and "daughter of Sargon, king of the world" and credits Enheduanna with erecting an altar to Nanna in his temple. The dedication of the relief to the moon god explains its unusual round format, which corresponds to the shape of the full moon. The front of the disk shows four figures approaching a four-story ziggurat. The first figure is a nude man who is either a priest or Enheduanna's assistant. He pours a libation into a plant stand. The second figure, taller than the rest and wearing the headgear of a priestess, is Enheduanna herself. She raises her right hand in a gesture of greeting and respect for the god. Two figures, probably female attendants, follow her.

Artworks created to honor women are rare in Mesopotamia and in the ancient world in general, and Enheduanna's is the oldest known. Enheduanna was, however, a princess and priestess, not a ruler in her own right, and her disk pales in comparison to the monuments erected almost a thousand years later in honor of Queen Hatshepsut of Egypt (see "Hatshepsut," Chapter 3, page 68).

1 in.

2-14 Votive disk of Enheduanna, from Ur (modern Tell Muqayyar), Iraq, ca. 2300–2275 BCE. Alabaster, diameter 10″. University of Pennsylvania Museum of Archaeology and Anthropology, Philadelphia.

Enheduanna, daughter of Sargon of Akkad and priestess of Nanna at Ur, is the first author whose name is known. She is the tallest figure on this disk that she dedicated in honor of the moon god.

the mountainside. The Akkadian artist adhered to older conventions in many details, especially by portraying the king and his soldiers in composite views and by placing a frontal two-horned helmet on Naram-Sin's profile head. But the sculptor showed daring innovation in creating a landscape setting for the story and placing the figures on successive tiers within that landscape. For the first time, an artist rejected the standard way of telling a story in a series of horizontal registers, the compositional formula that had been the rule for a millennium. The traditional frieze format was used, however, for an alabaster disk (FIG. 2-14) that is in other respects one of the

most remarkable discoveries ever made in the ancient Near East (see "Enheduanna, Priestess and Poet," above).

ZIGGURAT, UR Around 2150 BCE, a mountain people, the Gutians, brought Akkadian power to an end. The cities of Sumer, however, soon united in response to the alien presence, drove the Gutians out of Mesopotamia, and established a Neo-Sumerian state ruled by the kings of Ur. This age, which historians call the Third Dynasty of Ur, saw the construction of the ziggurat (FIG. 2-15) at Ur, one of the largest in Mesopotamia. Built about a millennium later than that at

2-15 Ziggurat (northeastern facade with restored stairs), Ur (modern Tell Muqayyar), Iraq, ca. 2100 BCE.

The Ur ziggurat is one of the largest in Mesopotamia. It has three ramplike stairways of a hundred steps each that originally ended at a gateway to a brick temple, which does not survive.

The Piety of Gudea

One of the central figures of the Neo-Sumerian age was Gudea of Lagash. Nearly two dozen portraits of him survive. All stood in temples where they could render perpetual service to the gods and intercede with the divine powers on his behalf. Although a powerful ruler, Gudea rejected the regal trappings of Sargon of Akkad and his successors in favor of a return to the Sumerian votive tradition of the Eshnunna statuettes (FIG. 2-6). Like the earlier examples, many of Gudea's statues are inscribed with messages to the gods of Sumer. One from Girsu says, "I am the shepherd loved by my king [Ningirsu, the god of Girsu]; may my life be prolonged." Another, also from Girsu, as if in answer to the first, says, "Gudea, the builder of the temple, has been given life." Some of the inscriptions help explain why Gudea was portrayed the way he was. For example, his large chest is a sign that the gods have given him fullness of life and his muscular arms reveal his god-given strength. Other inscriptions underscore that his large eyes signify that his gaze is perpetually fixed on the gods (compare FIG. 2-6).

Gudea built or rebuilt, at great cost, all the temples in which he placed his statues. One characteristic portrait (FIG. 2-16) depicts the pious ruler of Lagash seated with his hands clasped in front of him in a gesture of prayer. The head is unfortunately lost, but the statue is of unique interest because Gudea has a temple plan drawn on a tablet on his lap. It is the plan for a new temple dedicated to Ningirsu. Gudea buried accounts of his building enterprises in the temple foundations. The surviving texts describe how the Neo-Sumerians prepared and purified the sites, obtained the materials, and dedicated the completed temples. They also record Gudea's dreams of the gods asking him to erect temples in their honor, promising him prosperity if he fulfilled his duty. In one of these dreams, Ningirsu addresses Gudea:

> When, O faithful shepherd Gudea, thou shalt have started work for me on Erinnu, my royal abode [Ningirsu's new temple], I will call up in heaven a humid wind. It shall bring the abundance from on high. . . . All the great fields will bear for thee; dykes and canals will swell for thee; . . . good weight of wool will be given in thy time.*

*Translated by Thorkild Jacobsen, in Henri Frankfort, *The Art and Architecture of the Ancient Orient*, 5th ed. (New Haven: Yale University Press, 1996), 98.

2-16 Seated statue of Gudea holding temple plan, from Girsu (modern Telloh), Iraq, ca. 2100 BCE. Diorite, 2′ 5″ high. Louvre, Paris.

Gudea of Lagash built or rebuilt many temples and placed statues of himself in all of them. In this seated portrait, Gudea has on his lap a plan of the new temple he erected to Ningirsu.

Uruk (FIGS. 2-2 and 2-3), the Ur ziggurat is much grander. The base is a solid mass of mud brick 50 feet high. The builders used baked bricks laid in bitumen, an asphaltlike substance, for the facing of the entire monument. Three ramplike stairways of a hundred steps each converge on a tower-flanked gateway. From there another flight of steps probably led to the temple proper, which does not survive.

GUDEA OF LAGASH The most conspicuous preserved sculptural monuments of the Neo-Sumerian age portray Gudea, the ensi of Lagash around 2100 BCE (see "The Piety of Gudea," above). His statues (FIG. 2-16) show him seated or standing, hands tightly clasped, head shaven, sometimes wearing a woolen brimmed hat, and always dressed in a long garment that leaves one shoulder and arm exposed. Gudea was zealous in granting the gods their due, and the numerous statues he commissioned are an enduring testimony to his piety—and to his wealth and pride. All his portraits are of polished diorite, a rare and costly dark stone that had to be imported. Diorite is also extremely hard and difficult to carve. The prestige of the material—which in turn lent prestige to Gudea's portraits—is evident from an inscription on one of Gudea's statues: "This statue has not been made from silver nor from lapis lazuli, nor from copper nor from lead, nor yet from bronze; it is made of diorite."

2-16A Gudea holding water jar, Girsu, ca. 2100 BCE.

Hammurabi's Law Code

In the early 18th century BCE, King Hammurabi of Babylon formulated a comprehensive law code for his people. At the time, parts of Europe were still in the Stone Age. Even in Greece, it was not until more than 1,000 years later that Draco provided Athens with its first written set of laws. Two earlier Sumerian law codes survive in part, but Hammurabi's laws are the only ones known in great detail, thanks to the chance survival of a tall black-basalt stele (FIG. 2-17) that was carried off as booty to Susa in 1157 BCE, together with the Naram-Sin stele (FIG. 2-13). At the top (FIG. 2-1) is a representation in high relief of Hammurabi in the presence of Shamash, the flame-shouldered sun god. The king raises his hand in respect. The god extends to Hammurabi the rod and ring that symbolize authority. The symbols derive from builders' tools—measuring rods and coiled rope—and connote the ruler's capacity to build the social order and to measure people's lives, that is, to render judgments and enforce the laws spelled out on the stele. The judicial code, written in Akkadian, was inscribed in 3,500 lines of cuneiform characters. Hammurabi's laws governed all aspects of Babylonian life, from commerce and property to murder and theft to marital fidelity, inheritances, and the treatment of slaves.

Here is a small sample of the infractions described and the penalties imposed (which vary with the person's standing in society):

- If a man puts out the eye of another man, his eye shall be put out.

- If he kills a man's slave, he shall pay one-third of a mina.

- If someone steals property from a temple, he will be put to death, as will the person who receives the stolen goods.

- If a man rents a boat and the boat is wrecked, the renter shall replace the boat with another.

- If a married woman dies before bearing any sons, her dowry shall be repaid to her father, but if she gave birth to sons, the dowry shall belong to them.

- If a man's wife is caught in bed with another man, both will be tied up and thrown in the water.

Hammurabi's stele is noteworthy artistically as well. The sculptor depicted Shamash (FIG. 2-1) in the familiar convention of combined front and side views, but with two important exceptions. His great headdress with its four pairs of horns is in true profile so that only four, not all eight, of the horns are visible. And the artist seems

2-17 Stele with law code of Hammurabi, from Susa, Iran, ca. 1780 BCE. Basalt, 7′ 4″ high. Louvre, Paris.

The stele that records Hammurabi's remarkably early law code also is one of the first examples of an artist employing foreshortening—the representation of a figure or object at an angle (compare FIG. 2-1).

1 ft.

to have tentatively explored the notion of *foreshortening*—a means of suggesting depth by representing a figure or object at an angle, instead of frontally or in profile. Shamash's beard is a series of diagonal rather than horizontal lines, suggesting its recession from the picture plane, and the sculptor represented the side of his throne at an angle.

SECOND MILLENNIUM BCE

The resurgence of Sumer was short-lived. The last of the kings of the Third Dynasty of Ur fell at the hands of the Elamites, who ruled the territory east of the Tigris River. The following two centuries witnessed the reemergence of the traditional Mesopotamian political pattern of several independent city-states existing side by side.

2-17A Investiture of Zimri-Lim, Mari, ca. 1775–1760 BCE.

HAMMURABI Babylon was one of those city-states until its most powerful king, Hammurabi (r. 1792–1750 BCE), reestablished a centralized government in southern Mesopotamia. Perhaps the most renowned king in Mesopotamian history, Hammurabi was famous for his conquests. But he is best known today for his law code (FIGS. 2-1 and 2-17), which prescribed penalties for everything from adultery and murder to the cutting down of a neighbor's trees (see "Hammurabi's Law Code," above).

LION GATE, HATTUSA The Babylonian Empire toppled in the face of an onslaught by the Hittites, an Anatolian people who conquered and sacked Babylon around 1595 BCE. They then retired to their homeland, leaving Babylon in the hands of the Kassites. Remains of the strongly fortified capital city of the Hittites still may be seen at Hattusa near modern Boghazköy, Turkey. Constructed of large blocks

2-18 Lion Gate, Hattusa (modern Boghazköy), Turkey, ca. 1400 BCE.

The Hittites conquered and sacked Babylon around 1595 BCE. Their fortified capital at Boghazköy in Anatolia had seven-foot-tall stone lions guarding the main gateway (compare FIGS. 2-21 and 4-19).

of heavy stone—a striking contrast to the brick architecture of Mesopotamia—the walls and towers of the Hittites effectively protected them from attack. Symbolically guarding the gateway (FIG. 2-18) to the Hattusa citadel are two huge (seven-foot-high) lions. Their simply carved forequarters project from massive stone blocks on either side of the entrance. These Hittite guardian beasts are early examples of a theme that was to be echoed on many Near Eastern gates. Notable are those of Assyria (FIG. 2-21), one of the greatest empires of the ancient world, and of the reborn Babylon (FIG. 2-24) in the first millennium BCE. But the idea of protecting a city, palace, temple, or tomb from evil by placing wild beasts or fantastic monsters before an entranceway was not unique to the Near Eastern world. Examples abound in Egypt, Greece, Italy, and elsewhere.

NAPIR-ASU OF ELAM To the east of Sumer, Akkad, and Babylon was Elam, which appears in the Bible as early as Genesis 10:22. During the second half of the second millennium BCE, Elam reached the height of its political and military power. At this time the Elamites were strong enough to plunder Babylonia and to carry off the stelae of Naram-Sin and Hammurabi (FIGS. 2-13 and 2-17) and display them as war booty at their capital city, Susa.

In the ruins of Susa, archaeologists discovered a life-size bronze-and-copper statue (FIG. 2-19) of Queen Napir-Asu, wife of one of the most powerful Elamite kings, Untash-Napirisha. The statue weighs 3,760 pounds even in its fragmentary and mutilated state, because the sculptor, incredibly, cast the statue with a solid bronze core inside a hollow-cast copper shell. The bronze core increased the cost of the statue enormously, but the queen wished her portrait to be a permanent, immovable votive offering in the temple where it was found. In fact, the Elamite inscription on the queen's skirt explicitly asks the gods to protect the statue:

> He who would seize my statue, who would smash it, who would destroy its inscription, who would erase my name, may he be smitten by the curse of [the gods], that his name shall become extinct, that his offspring be barren. . . . This is Napir-Asu's offering.[1]

Napir-Asu's portrait thus falls within the votive tradition going back to the third-millennium BCE Eshnunna figurines (FIG. 2-6). In the Elamite statue, the Mesopotamian instinct for cylindrical volume is again evident. The tight silhouette, strict frontality, and firmly crossed hands held close to the body are all enduring characteristics common to the Sumerian statuettes. Yet within these rigid conventions of form and pose, the Elamite artist managed to create refinements that must

have come from close observation. The sculptor conveyed the feminine softness of arm and bust, the grace and elegance of the long-fingered hands, the supple and quiet bend of the wrist, the ring and bracelets, and the gown's patterned fabric. The loss of the head is especially unfortunate. The figure presents a portrait of the ideal queen. The hands crossed over the belly may allude to fertility and the queen's role in assuring peaceful dynastic succession.

2-19 Statue of Queen Napir-Asu, from Susa, Iran, ca. 1350–1300 BCE. Bronze and copper, 4' 2¾" high. Louvre, Paris.

This life-size bronze-and-copper statue of the wife of one of the most powerful Elamite kings weighs 3,760 pounds. The queen wanted her portrait to be an immovable votive offering in a temple.

1 ft.

ASSYRIA

During the first half of the first millennium BCE, the fearsome Assyrians vanquished the various warfaring peoples that succeeded the Babylonians and Hittites, including the Elamites, whose capital of Susa they sacked in 641 BCE. The Assyrians took their name from Assur, the city on the Tigris River in northern Iraq named for the god Ashur. At the height of their power, the Assyrians ruled an empire that extended from the Tigris River to the Nile and from the Persian Gulf to Asia Minor.

The royal citadel (FIG. **2-20**) of Sargon II (r. 721–705 BCE) at Dur Sharrukin reveals in its ambitious layout the confidence of the Assyrian kings in their all-conquering might. Its strong defensive walls also reflect a society ever fearful of attack during a period of almost constant warfare. The city measures about a square mile in area. The palace, elevated on a mound 50 feet high, covered some 25 acres and had more than 200 courtyards and rooms. Timber-roofed rectangular halls were grouped around square and rectangular courts. Behind the main courtyard, whose sides each measured 300 feet, were the residential quarters of the king, who received foreign emissaries in the long, high, brightly painted throne room. All visitors entered from another large courtyard, where over-life-size figures of the king and his courtiers lined the walls.

Sargon II regarded his city and palace as an expression of his grandeur. The Assyrians cultivated an image of themselves as merciless to anyone who dared oppose them, although they were forgiving to those who submitted to their will. Sargon, for example, wrote in an inscription, "I built a city with [the labors of] the peoples subdued by my hand, whom Ashur, Nabu, and Marduk had caused to lay themselves at my feet and bear my yoke." And in another text, he proclaimed, "Sargon, King of the World, has built a city. Dur Sharrukin he has named it. A peerless palace he has built within it."

In addition to the complex of courtyards, throne room, state chambers, service quarters, and guard rooms that made up the palace, the citadel included a great ziggurat and six sanctuaries for six different gods. The ziggurat at Dur Sharrukin may have had as many as seven stories. Four remain, each 18 feet high and painted a different color. A continuous ramp spiraled around the building from its base to the temple at its summit. Here, the legacy of the Sumerian bent-axis plan may be seen more than two millennia after the erection of the White Temple (FIG. **2-3**) on the ziggurat at Uruk.

Guarding the gate to Sargon's palace were colossal limestone monsters (FIG. **2-21**), which the Assyrians probably called *lamassu*. These winged, man-headed bulls served to ward off the king's enemies. The task of moving and installing these immense stone sculptures was so daunting that several reliefs in the palace of Sargon's successor celebrate the feat,

2-20 Reconstruction drawing of the citadel of Sargon II, Dur Sharrukin (modern Khorsabad), Iraq, ca. 720–705 BCE (after Charles Altman).

The fortified walls of the vast royal citadel of Sargon II enclosed courtyards, a throne room, service quarters, guard rooms, a great ziggurat, and six sanctuaries for six different gods.

2-21 Lamassu (winged, human-headed bull), from the citadel of Sargon II, Dur Sharrukin (modern Khorsabad), Iraq, ca. 720–705 BCE. Limestone, 13′ 10″ high. Louvre, Paris.

Ancient sculptors insisted on showing complete views of animals. This four-legged Assyrian palace guardian has five legs—two when seen from the front and four in profile view.

2-22 Assyrian archers pursuing enemies, relief from the Northwest Palace of Ashurnasirpal II, Kalhu (modern Nimrud), Iraq, ca. 875–860 BCE. Gypsum, 2′ 10⅝″ high. British Museum, London.

Assyrian palaces were adorned with extensive series of narrative reliefs exalting the king and recounting his great deeds. This one depicts Assyrian archers driving the enemy into the Euphrates River.

showing scores of men dragging lamassu figures with the aid of ropes and sledges. The Assyrian lamassu sculptures are partly in the round, but the sculptor nonetheless conceived them as high reliefs on adjacent sides of a corner. They combine the front view of the animal at rest with the side view of it in motion. Seeking to present a complete picture of the lamassu from both the front and the side, the sculptor gave the monster five legs—two seen from the front, four seen from the side. This sculpture, then, is yet another case of early artists' providing a conceptual picture of an animal or person and of all its important parts, as opposed to an optical view of the lamassu as it actually would stand in space.

PALACE OF ASHURNASIRPAL II For their palace walls the Assyrian kings commissioned extensive series of painted narrative re-

liefs exalting royal power. The degree of documentary detail in the Assyrian reliefs is without parallel in the ancient world before the Roman Empire (see Chapter 10). One of the earliest and most extensive cycles of reliefs comes from the palace of Ashurnasirpal II (r. 883–859 BCE) at Kalhu. Throughout the palace, painted gypsum reliefs sheathed the lower parts of the mud-brick walls below brightly colored plaster. Rich textiles on the floors contributed to the luxurious ambience. Every relief celebrated the king and bore an inscription naming Ashurnasirpal and describing his accomplishments.

2-22A Ashurnasirpal II with attendants, Kalhu, ca. 875–860 BCE.

FIG. 2-22 probably depicts an episode that occurred in 878 BCE when Ashurnasirpal drove his enemy's forces into the Euphrates River. In the relief, two Assyrian archers shoot arrows at the fleeing foe. Three enemy soldiers are in the water. One swims with an arrow in his back. The other two attempt to float to safety by inflating animal

2-23 Ashurbanipal hunting lions, relief from the North Palace of Ashurbanipal, Nineveh (modern Kuyunjik), Iraq, ca. 645–640 BCE. Gypsum, 5′ 4″ high. British Museum, London.

In addition to ceremonial and battle scenes, the hunt was a common subject of Assyrian palace reliefs. The Assyrians considered the hunting and killing of lions manly royal virtues on a par with victory in warfare.

skins. Their destination is a fort where their compatriots await them. The artist showed the fort as if it were in the middle of the river, but it must, of course, have been on land, perhaps at some distance from where the escapees entered the water. The artist's purpose was to tell the story clearly and economically. In art, distances can be compressed and the human actors enlarged so that they stand out from their environment. Literally interpreted, the defenders of the fort are too tall to walk through its archway. (Compare Naram-Sin and his men scaling a mountain, FIG. 2-13.) The sculptor also combined different viewpoints in the same frame, just as the figures are composites of frontal and profile views. The river is seen from above; the men, trees, and fort from the side. The artist also made other adjustments for clarity. The archers' bowstrings are in front of their bodies but behind their heads in order not to hide their faces. The men will snare their own heads in their bows when they launch their arrows! All these liberties with optical reality result, however, in a vivid and easily legible retelling of a decisive moment in the king's victorious campaign. This was the artist's primary goal.

PALACE OF ASHURBANIPAL Two centuries later, sculptors carved hunting reliefs for the Nineveh palace of the conqueror of Elamite Susa, Ashurbanipal (r. 668–627 BCE). The Assyrians, like many other societies before and after, regarded prowess in hunting as a manly virtue on a par with success in warfare. The royal hunt did not take place in the wild, however, but in a controlled environment, ensuring the king's safety and success. In FIG. 2-23, lions released from cages in a large enclosed arena charge the king, who, in his chariot and with his attendants, thrusts a spear into a savage lion. The animal leaps at the king even though it already has two arrows in its body. All around the royal chariot is a pathetic trail of dead and dying animals, pierced by what appear to be far more arrows than needed to kill them. Blood streams from some of the lions, but they refuse to die. The artist brilliantly depicted the straining muscles, the swelling veins, the muzzles' wrinkled skin, and the flattened ears of the powerful and defiant beasts. Modern sympathies make this scene of carnage a kind of heroic tragedy, with the lions as protagonists. It is unlikely, however, that the king's artists had any intention other than to glorify their ruler by showing the king of men pitting himself against and repeatedly conquering the king of beasts. Portraying Ashurbanipal's beastly foes as possessing courage and nobility as well as the power to kill made the king's accomplishments that much grander.

The Assyrian Empire was never very secure, and most of its kings had to fight revolts in large sections of the Near East. Assyria's conquest of Elam in the seventh century BCE and frequent rebellions in Babylonia apparently overextended its resources. During the last years of Ashurbanipal's reign, the empire began to disintegrate. Under his successors, it collapsed from the simultaneous onslaught of the Medes from the east and the resurgent Babylonians from the south. Neo-Babylonian kings held sway over the former Assyrian Empire until the Persian conquest.

NEO-BABYLONIA AND PERSIA

The most renowned of the Neo-Babylonian kings was Nebuchadnezzar II (r. 604–562 BCE), whose exploits the biblical Book of Daniel recounts. Nebuchadnezzar restored Babylon to its rank as one of the great cities of antiquity. The city's famous hanging gardens were among the Seven Wonders of the ancient world, and the Bible immortalized its enormous ziggurat as the Tower of Babel (see "Babylon, City of Wonders," page 48).

ISHTAR GATE, BABYLON Nebuchadnezzar's Babylon was a mud-brick city, but dazzling blue-glazed bricks faced the most important monuments, such as the Ishtar Gate (FIG. 2-24), actually a pair of gates, one of which has been restored and installed in a German museum. The Ishtar Gate consists of a large *arcuated* (*arch*-shaped) opening flanked by towers, and features *glazed* bricks with molded reliefs of animals, real and imaginary. Each Babylonian brick was molded and glazed separately, then set in proper sequence on the wall. On the Ishtar Gate, profile figures of Marduk and Nabu's dragon and Adad's bull alternate. Lining the processional way leading up to the gate were reliefs of Ishtar's sacred lion, glazed in yellow, brown, and red against a blue background.

2-24 Ishtar Gate (restored), Babylon, Iraq, ca. 575 BCE. Glazed brick. Vorderasiatisches Museum, Staatliche Museen zu Berlin, Berlin.

Babylon under King Nebuchadnezzar II was one of the greatest cities of the ancient world. Its arcuated Ishtar Gate featured glazed bricks depicting Marduk and Nabu's dragon and Adad's bull.

Babylon, City of Wonders

The uncontested list of the Seven Wonders of the ancient world was not codified until the 16th century. But already in the second century BCE, Antipater of Sidon, a Greek poet, compiled a roster of seven must-see monuments, including six of the seven later Wonders. All of the Wonders were of colossal size and constructed at great expense. Three of them were of great antiquity: the pyramids of Gizeh (FIG. 3-8), which Antipater described as "man-made mountains," and "the hanging gardens" and "walls of impregnable Babylon."

Babylon was the only site on Antipater's list that could boast two Wonders. Later list makers preferred to distribute the Seven Wonders among seven different cities. Most of these Wonders date to Greek times—the Temple of Artemis at Epheos, with its 60-foot-tall columns; Phidias's colossal gold-and-ivory statue of Zeus at Olympia; the grandiose tomb of Mausolus (the "Mausoleum") at Halikarnassos; the Colossus of Rhodes, a bronze statue of the sun god 110 feet tall; and the lighthouse at Alexandria, perhaps the tallest building in the ancient world. The pyramids are the oldest and the Babylonian gardens the only Wonder in the category of "landscape architecture."

Several ancient texts describe Babylon's gardens. Quintus Curtius Rufus, writing in the mid-first century CE, reported:

> On the top of the citadel are the hanging gardens, a wonder celebrated in the tales of the Greeks. . . . Columns of stone were set up to sustain the whole work, and on these was laid a floor of squared blocks, strong enough to hold the earth which is thrown upon it to a great depth, as well as the water with which they irrigate the soil; and the structure supports trees of such great size that the thickness of their trunks equals a measure of eight cubits [about twelve feet]. They tower to a height of fifty feet, and they yield as much fruit as if they were growing in their native soil. . . . To those who look upon [the trees] from a distance, real woods seem to be overhanging their native mountains.*

Not qualifying as a Wonder, but in some ways no less impressive, was Babylon's Marduk ziggurat, the biblical Tower of Babel. According to the Bible, humankind's arrogant desire to build a tower to Heaven angered God. The Lord put an end to it by causing the workers to speak different languages, preventing them from communicating with one another. The fifth-century BCE Greek historian Herodotus described the Babylonian temple complex:

> In the middle of the sanctuary [of Marduk] has been built a solid tower . . . which supports another tower, which in turn supports another, and so on: there are eight towers in all. A stairway has been constructed to wind its way up the outside of all the towers; halfway up the stairway there is a shelter with benches to rest on, where people making the ascent can sit and catch their breath. In the last tower there is a huge temple. The temple contains a large couch, which is adorned with fine coverings and has a golden table standing beside it, but there are no statues at all standing there. . . . [The Babylonians] say that the god comes in person to the temple [compare the Sumerian notion of the temple as a "waiting room"] and rests on the couch; I do not believe this story myself.†

*Translated by John C. Rolfe, *Quintus Curtius I* (Cambridge, Mass.: Harvard University Press, 1971), 337–339.
†Translated by Robin Waterfield, *Herodotus: The Histories* (New York: Oxford University Press, 1998), 79–80.

THE PERSIAN EMPIRE Although Nebuchadnezzar, "King of Kings" of the biblical Daniel, had boasted that he "caused a mighty wall to circumscribe Babylon . . . so that the enemy who would do evil would not threaten," Cyrus of Persia (r. 559–529 BCE) captured the city in the sixth century. Cyrus, who may have been descended from an Elamite line, was the founder of the Achaemenid dynasty and traced his ancestry back to a mythical King Achaemenes. Babylon was but one of the Persians' conquests. Egypt fell to them in 525 BCE, and by 480 BCE the Persian Empire was the largest the world had yet known, extending from the Indus River in South Asia to the Danube River in northeastern Europe. Only the successful Greek resistance in the fifth century BCE prevented Persia from embracing southeastern Europe as well. The Achaemenid line ended with the death of Darius III in 330 BCE, after his defeat at the hands of Alexander the Great (FIG. 5-70).

PERSEPOLIS The most important source of knowledge about Persian art and architecture is the ceremonial and administrative complex on the citadel at Persepolis (FIG. 2-25), which the successors of Cyrus, Darius I (r. 522–486 BCE) and Xerxes (r. 486–465 BCE), built between 521 and 465 BCE. Situated on a high plateau, the heavily fortified complex of royal buildings stood on a wide platform overlooking the plain. Alexander the Great razed the site in a gesture symbolizing the destruction of Persian imperial power. Some said it was an act of revenge for the Persian sack of the Athenian Acropolis in the early fifth century BCE (see Chapter 5). But even in ruins, the Persepolis citadel is impressive.

The approach to the citadel led through a monumental gateway called the Gate of All Lands, a reference to the harmony among the peoples of the vast Persian Empire. Assyrian-inspired colossal manheaded winged bulls flanked the great entrance. Broad ceremonial stairways provided access to the platform and the royal audience hall, or *apadana*, a huge hall 60 feet high and 217 feet square, containing 36 colossal columns. An audience of thousands could have stood within the hall.

2-25A Capital with bull protomes, Persepolis, ca. 521–465 BCE.

The reliefs (FIG. 2-26) decorating the walls of the terrace and staircases leading to the apadana represent processions of royal guards, Persian nobles and dignitaries, and representatives from 23 subject nations bringing the king tribute. Every one of the emissaries wears his national costume and carries a typical regional gift for the conqueror. The carving of the Persepolis reliefs is technically superb, with subtly modeled surfaces and crisply chiseled details. Traces of color prove that the reliefs were painted, and the original effect must have been even more striking than it is today. Although the Persepolis sculptures may have been inspired by those in Assyrian palaces, they are different in style. The forms are more rounded, and they project more from the background. Some of the details, notably the treatment of drapery folds, echo forms characteristic of Archaic Greek sculpture (see Chapter 5), and Greek influence seems to be one of the many ingredients of Achaemenid style. Persian art testifies to the active exchange of ideas and artists among all the Mediterranean and Near Eastern civilizations at this date. A building inscription at Susa, for example, names Ionian Greeks, Medes, Egyp-

2-26A Gold rhyton, Hamadan, fifth to third century BCE.

2-25 Aerial view (looking west) of Persepolis (apadana in the background), Iran, ca. 521–465 BCE.

The heavily fortified complex of Persian royal buildings on a high plateau at Persepolis contained a royal audience hall, or apadana, 60 feet high and 217 feet square with 36 colossal columns.

tians, and Babylonians among those who built and decorated the palace. Under the single-minded direction of its Persian masters, this heterogeneous workforce, with a widely varied cultural and artistic background, created a new and coherent style that perfectly suited the expression of Persian imperial ambitions.

SASANIAN CTESIPHON Alexander the Great's conquest of Persia in 330 BCE marked the beginning of a long period of first Greek and then Roman rule of large parts of the ancient Near East,

beginning with one of Alexander's former generals, Seleucus I (r. 312–281 BCE), founder of the Seleucid dynasty. In the third century CE, however, a new power rose up in Persia that challenged the Romans and sought to force them out of Asia. The new rulers called themselves Sasanians. They traced their lineage to a legendary figure named Sasan, said to be a direct descendant of the Achaemenid kings. Their New Persian Empire was founded in 224 CE, when the first Sasanian king, Artaxerxes I (r. 211–241), defeated the Parthians (another of Rome's eastern enemies).

2-26 Processional frieze (detail) on the terrace of the apadana, Persepolis, Iran, ca. 521–465 BCE. Limestone, 8′ 4″ high.

The reliefs decorating the walls of the terrace and staircases leading up to the Persepolis apadana included depictions of representatives of 23 subject nations bringing tribute to the Persian king.

1 ft.

Neo-Babylonia and Persia   **49**

2-27 Palace of Shapur I, Ctesiphon, Iraq, ca. 250 CE.

The last great pre-Islamic civilization of the Near East was that of the Sasanians. Their palace at Ctesiphon, near Baghdad, features a brick audience hall (iwan) covered by an enormous pointed vault.

The son and successor of Artaxerxes, Shapur I (r. 241–272), succeeded in further extending Sasanian territory. He also erected a great palace (FIG. **2-27**) at Ctesiphon, the capital his father had established near modern Baghdad in Iraq. The central feature of Shapur's palace was the monumental *iwan,* or brick audience hall, covered by a *vault* (here, a deep arch over an oblong space) that came almost to a point more than 100 feet above the ground. The facade to the left and right of the iwan was divided into a series of horizontal bands made up of *blind arcades,* a series of arches without actual openings, applied as wall decoration. A thousand years later, Islamic architects looked at Shapur's palace and especially its soaring iwan and established it as the standard for judging their own engineering feats (see Chapter 13).

SHAPUR I AND ROME So powerful was the Sasanian army that in 260 CE Shapur I even succeeded in capturing the Roman emperor Valerian near Edessa (Turkey). His victory over Valerian was such a significant event that Shapur commemorated it in a series of rock-cut reliefs in the cliffs of Bishapur in Iran, far from the site of his triumph. FIG. **2-28** reproduces one of the Bishapur reliefs. Shapur appears larger than life, riding in from the right wearing the distinctive tall Sasanian crown, which breaks through the relief 's border and draws attention to the king. At the left, Valerian kneels before Shapur and begs for mercy. Similar scenes of kneeling enemies before triumphant generals are commonplace in Roman art—but at Bishapur the roles are reversed. This appropriation of Roman compositional patterns and motifs in a relief celebrating the Sasanian defeat of the Romans adds another, ironic, level of meaning to the political message in stone.

The New Persian Empire endured more than 400 years, until the Arabs drove the Sasanians out of Mesopotamia in 636 CE, just four years after the death of Muhammad. Thereafter, the greatest artists and architects of Mesopotamia worked in the service of Islam (see Chapter 13).

2-28 Triumph of Shapur I over Valerian, rock-cut relief, Bishapur, Iran, ca. 260 CE.

The Sasanian king Shapur I humiliated the Roman emperor Valerian in 260 CE and commemorated his surrender in over-life-size reliefs cut into the cliffs outside Persepolis.

THE ANCIENT NEAR EAST

SUMERIAN ART, ca. 3500–2332 BCE

▌ The Sumerians founded the world's first city-states in the valley between the Tigris and Euphrates rivers and invented writing in the fourth millennium BCE.

▌ They were also the first to build towering temple platforms, called ziggurats, and to place figures in registers to tell coherent stories.

Standard of Ur, ca. 2600 BCE

AKKADIAN ART, ca. 2332–2150 BCE

▌ The Akkadians were the first Near Eastern rulers to call themselves kings of the world and to assume divine attributes. The earliest recorded name of an author is the Akkadian priestess Enheduanna.

▌ Akkadian artists may have been the first to cast hollow life-size bronze sculptures and to place figures at different levels in a landscape setting.

Portrait of an Akkadian king, ca. 2250–2200 BCE

NEO-SUMERIAN AND BABYLONIAN ART, ca. 2150–1600 BCE

▌ During the Third Dynasty of Ur, the Sumerians rose again to power and constructed one of the largest ziggurats in Mesopotamia at Ur.

▌ Gudea of Lagash (r. ca. 2100 BCE) built numerous temples and placed diorite portraits of himself in all of them as votive offerings to the gods.

▌ Babylon's greatest king, Hammurabi (r. 1792–1750 BCE), established a comprehensive law code for the empire he ruled. Babylonian artists were among the first to experiment with foreshortening.

Stele of Hammurabi, ca. 1780 BCE

ASSYRIAN ART, ca. 900–612 BCE

▌ At the height of their power, the Assyrians ruled an empire that extended from the Persian Gulf to the Nile and Asia Minor.

▌ Assyrian palaces were fortified citadels with gates guarded by monstrous lamassu. Painted reliefs depicting the king in battle and hunting lions decorated the walls of the ceremonial halls.

Lamassu, citadel of Sargon II, Dur Sharrukin, ca. 720–705 BCE

NEO-BABYLONIAN AND PERSIAN ART, ca. 612–330 BCE

▌ In the sixth century BCE, the Babylonians constructed two of the Seven Wonders of the ancient world. The Ishtar Gate, with its colorful glazed brick reliefs, gives an idea of how magnificent Babylon was under Nebuchadnezzar II (r. 604–562 BCE).

▌ The capital of the Achaemenid Persians was at Persepolis, where Darius I (r. 522–486 BCE) and Xerxes (r. 486–465 BCE) built a huge palace complex with an audience hall that could accommodate thousands. Painted reliefs of subject nations bringing tribute decorated the terraces.

▌ Alexander the Great conquered the Persian Empire in 330 BCE.

Ishtar Gate, Babylon, ca. 575 BCE

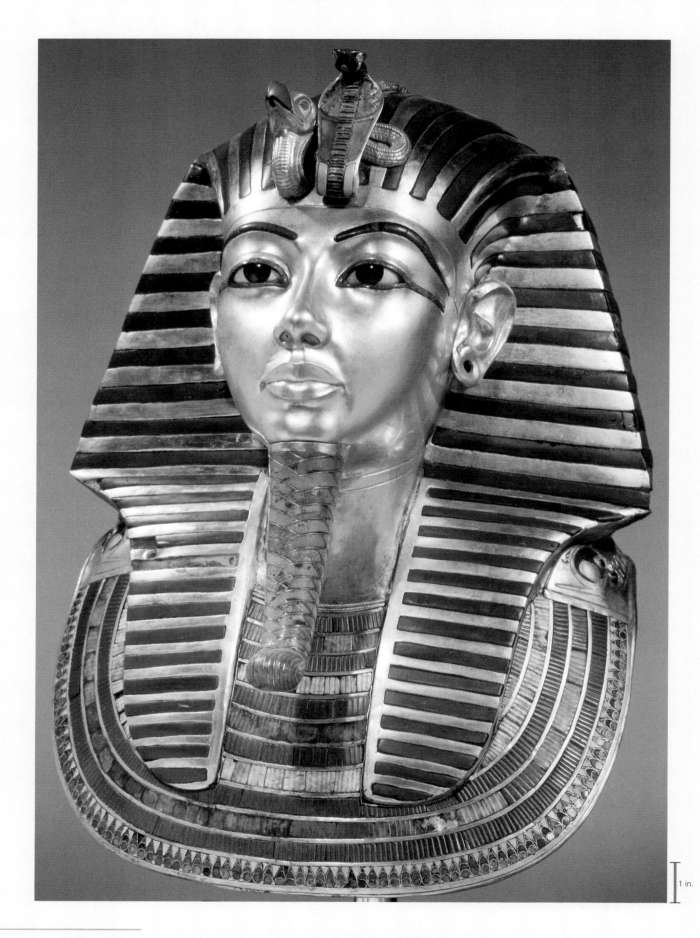

1 in.

3-1 Death mask of Tutankhamen, from the innermost coffin in his tomb at Thebes, Egypt, 18th Dynasty, ca. 1323 BCE. Gold with inlay of semiprecious stones, 1′ 9¼″ high. Egyptian Museum, Cairo.

The extraordinary treasures in the boy-king Tutankhamen's tomb attest to the wealth the Egyptian pharaohs lavished on preparing for the afterlife. Tutankhamen's mask is gold with inlaid gems.

EGYPT UNDER THE PHARAOHS

Nearly 2,500 years ago, the Greek historian Herodotus wrote, "Concerning Egypt itself I shall extend my remarks to a great length, because there is no country that possesses so many wonders, nor any that has such a number of works that defy description."[1] Even today, many would agree with this assessment. The ancient Egyptians left to the world a profusion of spectacular monuments dating across three millennia. From the cliffs of the Libyan and Arabian deserts they cut giant blocks of stone and erected grand temples to their immortal gods (see "The Gods and Goddesses of Egypt," page 54). From the same imperishable material that symbolized the timelessness of their world, the Egyptians set up countless statues of their equally immortal god-kings and built thousands of tombs to serve as eternal houses of the dead. The solemn and ageless art of the Egyptians expresses the unchanging order that, for them, was divinely established.

The backbone of Egypt was, and still is, the Nile River, whose annual floods supported all life in that ancient land (MAP 3-1). Even more than the Tigris and the Euphrates rivers of Mesopotamia, the Nile defined the cultures that developed along its banks. Originating deep in Africa, the world's longest river flows through regions that may not receive a single drop of rainfall in a decade. Yet crops thrive from the rich soil that the Nile brings thousands of miles from the African hills. In the time of the *pharaohs,* the ancient Egyptian kings, the land bordering the Nile consisted of marshes dotted with island ridges. The Egyptians hunted the amphibious animals that swarmed through the tall forests of *papyrus* and rushes in the marshes. Egypt's fertility was famous. When Egypt became a province of the Roman Empire after Queen Cleopatra's death (r. 51–30 BCE), it served as the granary of the Mediterranean world.

Even in the Middle Ages, Egypt's reputation as an ancient land of wonders and mystery lived on. Until the late 18th century, people regarded its undeciphered writing and exotic monuments as treasures of occult wisdom, locked away from any but those initiated in the mystic arts. Scholars knew something of Egypt's history from references in the Old Testament, from Herodotus and other Greco-Roman authors, and from preserved portions of a history of Egypt written in Greek in the third century BCE by an Egyptian high priest named Manetho. Manetho described the succession of pharaohs, dividing them into the still-useful groups called dynasties, but his chronology was inaccurate, and the absolute dates of the pharaohs are still debated. The chronologies scholars have proposed for the earliest Egyptian dynasties

The Gods and Goddesses of Egypt

The worldview of the Egyptians was distinct from those of their neighbors in the ancient Mediterranean and Near Eastern worlds. Egyptians believed that before the beginning of time the primeval waters, called *Nun,* existed alone in the darkness. At the moment of creation, a mound rose out of the limitless waters—just as muddy mounds emerge from the Nile after the annual flood recedes. On this mound the creator god appeared and brought light to the world. In later times, the mound was formalized as a pyramidal stone called the *ben-ben* supporting the supreme god, *Amen,* the god of the sun (*Re*).

The supreme god also created the first of the other gods and goddesses of Egypt. According to one version of the myth, the creator masturbated and produced *Shu* and *Tefnut,* the primary male and female forces in the universe. They coupled to give birth to *Geb* (Earth) and *Nut* (Sky), who bore Osiris, Seth, Isis, and Nephthys. The eldest, *Osiris,* was the god of order and was revered as the king who brought civilization to Egypt. His brother, *Seth,* was his evil opposite, the god of chaos. Seth murdered Osiris and cut him into pieces, which he scattered across Egypt. *Isis,* the sister and consort of Osiris, with the help of *Nephthys,* Seth's wife, succeeded in collecting Osiris's body parts, and with her powerful magic brought him back to life.

The resurrected Osiris fathered a son with Isis—*Horus,* who avenged his father's death and displaced Seth as king of Egypt. Osiris then became the lord of the Underworld. Horus is represented in art either as a falcon, considered the noblest bird of the sky, or as a falcon-headed man. All Egyptian pharaohs were identified with Horus while alive and with Osiris after they died.

Other Egyptian deities included *Mut,* the consort of the sun god Amen, and *Khonsu,* the moon god, who was their son. *Thoth,* another lunar deity and the god of knowledge and writing, appears in art as an ibis, a baboon, or an ibis-headed man crowned with the crescent moon and the moon disk. When Seth tore out Horus's falcon-eye (*wedjat*), Thoth restored it. He, too, was associated with rebirth and the afterlife. *Hathor,* daughter of Re, was a divine mother of the pharaoh, nourishing him with her milk. She appears in Egyptian art as a cow-headed woman or as a woman with a cow's horns. *Anubis,* a jackal or jackal-headed deity, was the god of the Underworld and of mummification. *Maat,* another daughter of Re, was the goddess of truth and justice. Her feather was used to measure the weight of the deceased's heart on Anubis's scales to determine if the *ka* (life force) would be blessed in the afterlife.

---

can vary by as much as two centuries. Exact years cannot be assigned to the reigns of individual pharaohs until 664 BCE (26th Dynasty).[2]

At the end of the 18th century, when Europeans rediscovered Egypt, the land of the Nile became the first subject of archaeological exploration. In 1799, Napoleon Bonaparte, on a military expedition to Egypt, took with him a small troop of scholars, linguists, antiquarians, and artists. The chance discovery of the famed *Rosetta Stone,* now in the British Museum, provided the key to deciphering Egyptian *hieroglyphic* writing. The stone bears an inscription in three sections: one in Greek, which the Frenchmen easily read; one in *demotic* (Late Egyptian); and one in formal hieroglyphic. On the assumption that the text was the same in all three sections, scholars attempted to decipher the two non-Greek sections. Eventually, Jean-François Champollion deduced that the hieroglyphs were not simply pictographs but the signs of a once-spoken language whose traces survived in Coptic, the language of Christian Egypt. The ability to read hieroglyphic inscriptions revolutionized the study of Egyptian civilization and art.

THE PREDYNASTIC AND EARLY DYNASTIC PERIODS

The Predynastic, or prehistoric, beginnings of Egyptian civilization are chronologically vague. But tantalizing remains of tombs, paintings, pottery, and other artifacts attest to the existence of a sophisticated culture on the banks of the Nile around 3500 BCE.

Painting and Sculpture

In Predynastic times, Egypt was divided geographically and politically into Upper Egypt (the southern, upstream part of the Nile Valley), a narrow tract of grassland that encouraged hunting, and Lower (northern) Egypt, where the rich soil of the Nile Delta islands encouraged agriculture and animal husbandry. The major finds of Predynastic art come from Upper Egypt, especially Hierakonpolis.

TOMB 100, HIERAKONPOLIS Archaeologists exploring the Predynastic cemetery at Hierakonpolis found extraordinary mural paintings on three interior walls of tomb 100. The tomb is no longer preserved, but a watercolor copy (FIG. 3-2) of the murals records

MAP 3-1 Ancient Egypt.

3-2 People, boats, and animals, detail of a watercolor copy of a wall painting from tomb 100 at Hierakonpolis, Egypt, Predynastic, ca. 3500–3200 BCE. Paint on plaster, entire painting 16' 4" × 3' 7⅜". Egyptian Museum, Cairo.

The oldest Egyptian mural painting depicts boats, a heraldic group of a human and animals, and a man striking prisoners. The random arrangement of the motifs is characteristic of Neolithic painting.

1 ft.

their original appearance. The paintings formed a frieze running around three adjacent walls of the tomb and represented what seems to be, at least in part, a funerary scene with people, animals, and large boats. The stick figures and their apparently random arrangement recall the Neolithic painted hunters (FIG. 1-17) of Çatal Höyük. One black and five white boats, symbolic of the journey down the river of life and death, carry cargo of uncertain significance. The figures include a heraldic grouping of two animals flanking a human figure (at the lower left) and a man striking three prisoners with a mace (lower left corner). The heraldic group, a compositional type usually associated with Mesopotamian art (FIG. 2-10, *right*), suggests that influences from Mesopotamia not only had reached Egypt by this time but

also already had made the thousand-mile journey up the Nile. The second group, however, is characteristically Egyptian, and the motif was to have a long history in Egyptian painting and sculpture alike.

PALETTE OF KING NARMER The Predynastic period ended with the unification of Upper and Lower Egypt, which until recently scholars thought occurred during the rule of the First Dynasty pharaoh Menes, identified by many Egyptologists with King Narmer. Narmer's image and name appear on both sides of a ceremonial *palette* (stone slab with a circular depression) found at Hierakonpolis. The palette (FIG. 3-3) is one of the earliest historical (versus prehistorical) artworks preserved, but Egyptologists still debate

3-3 Palette of King Narmer (*left,* back; *right,* front), from Hierakonpolis, Egypt, Predynastic, ca. 3000–2920 BCE. Slate, 2' 1" high. Egyptian Museum, Cairo.

These earliest preserved labeled historical reliefs commemorate the unification of Upper and Lower Egypt. Narmer, the largest figure, effortlessly defeats a foe on one side, and on the other surveys the beheaded enemy.

1 in.

The Predynastic and Early Dynastic Periods   **55**

exactly what event is depicted. No longer regarded as commemorating the foundation of the first of Egypt's 31 dynasties around 2920 BCE (the last ended in 332 BCE), the reliefs probably record the unification of the two kingdoms. Scholars now believe this unification occurred over several centuries, but the palette depicts the creation of the "Kingdom of the Two Lands" as a single great event.

Narmer's palette is an elaborate, formalized version of a utilitarian object commonly used in the Predynastic period to prepare eye makeup. (Egyptians used makeup to protect their eyes against irritation and the glare of the sun.) Narmer's palette is important not only as a document marking the transition from the prehistorical to the historical period in ancient Egypt but also as a kind of early blueprint of the formula for figure representation that characterized most Egyptian art for 3,000 years. At the top of each side of the palette are two heads of a cow with a woman's face, usually identified as the goddess Hathor but sometimes as the sky goddess Bat. Between the two heads is a hieroglyph giving Narmer's name (catfish = *nar*; chisel = *mer*) within a frame representing the royal palace, making Narmer's palette the earliest existing labeled work of historical art.

On the back (FIG. 3-3, *left*) of the palette, the king, wearing the high, white, bowling-pin–shaped crown of Upper Egypt and accompanied by an official who carries his sandals, slays an enemy. The motif closely resembles the group at the lower left of the Hierakonpolis mural (FIG. 3-2) and became the standard pictorial formula signifying the inevitable triumph of the Egyptian god-kings over their enemies. Above and to the right, the falcon with human arms is Horus, the king's protector. The falcon-god takes captive a man-headed hieroglyph with a papyrus plant growing from it that stands for the land of Lower Egypt. Below the king are two fallen enemies.

On the front (FIG. 3-3, *right*) of the palette, the elongated necks of two felines form the circular depression that would have held eye makeup in an ordinary palette not made for display. The intertwined necks of the animals (a motif common in Mesopotamian art) may be another pictorial reference to Egypt's unification. In the uppermost register, Narmer, wearing the red crown of Lower Egypt, reviews the beheaded bodies of the enemy. The dead are seen from above, as are the bison (FIG. 1-9) lying on the ground on the ceiling of the Altamira cave. The artist depicted each body with its severed head neatly placed between its legs. By virtue of his superior rank, the king, on both sides of the palette, performs his ritual task alone and towers over his own men and the enemy. The king's superhuman strength is symbolized in the lowest band by a great bull knocking down a rebellious city whose fortress walls also are seen in an "aerial view." Specific historical narrative was not the artist's goal in this work. What was important was the characterization of the king as supreme, isolated from and larger than all ordinary men and solely responsible for the triumph over the enemy. Here, at the very beginning of Egyptian history, is evidence of the state policy that established the pharaoh as a divine ruler.

The artist's portrayal of Narmer on both sides of the palette combines profile views of his head, legs, and arms with front views of his eye and torso—the same composite view of the human figure found in Mesopotamian art and even some Stone Age paintings. Although the proportions of the human figure changed, this composite representation of the body's parts became standard in Egyptian art as well. In the Hierakonpolis painting (FIG. 3-2), the artist scattered the figures across the wall more or less haphazardly. On Narmer's palette, the sculptor subdivided the surface into registers and inserted the pictorial elements into their organized setting in a neat and orderly way. The horizontal lines separating the narratives also define the ground supporting the figures. This too was the preferred mode for narrative art in the ancient Near East. Narmer's palette established it as the norm in Egyptian art for millennia. Egyptian artists who departed from this compositional scheme did so deliberately, usually to express the absence of order, as in a chaotic battle scene (FIG. 3-35).

Architecture

Narmer's palette is exceptional among surviving Egyptian artworks because it is commemorative rather than funerary in nature. Far more typical is the Predynastic mural from Hierakonpolis. In fact, Egyptian tombs provide the principal, if not the exclusive, evidence for the historical reconstruction of Egyptian civilization. The majority of monuments the Egyptians left behind were dedicated to ensuring safety and happiness in the next life (see "Mummification and Immortality," page 57).

The standard tomb type in early Egypt was the *mastaba* (FIG. 3-4). The mastaba (Arabic for "bench") was a rectangular brick or stone structure with sloping sides erected over an underground burial chamber. The form probably developed from earthen mounds that had covered even earlier tombs. Although mastabas originally housed single burials, as in FIG. 3-4, they later accommodated multiple family burials and became increasingly complex. The main feature of the tomb, other than the burial chamber itself, was the

1. Chapel
2. False door
3. Shaft into burial chamber
4. Serdab (chamber for statue of deceased)
5. Burial chamber

3-4 Section (*top*), plan (*center*), and restored view (*bottom*) of typical Egyptian mastaba tombs.

The standard early Egyptian tomb had an underground burial chamber and rooms to house a portrait statue and offerings to the deceased. Scenes of daily life often decorated the interior walls.

Mummification and Immortality

The Egyptians did not make the sharp distinction between body and soul that is basic to many religions. Rather, they believed that from birth a person was accompanied by a kind of other self, the *ka* (life force), which, on the death of the body, could inhabit the corpse and live on. For the ka to live securely, however, the body had to remain as nearly intact as possible. To ensure that it did, the Egyptians developed the technique of embalming (*mummification*) to a high art. Although the Egyptians believed that the god Anubis invented embalming to preserve the body of the murdered Osiris (see "The Gods and Goddesses of Egypt," page 54), they did not practice mummification systematically until the Fourth Dynasty.

The first step in the 70-day process was the surgical removal of the lungs, liver, stomach, and intestines through an incision in the left flank. The Egyptians thought these organs were most subject to decay. The organs were individually wrapped and placed in four containers known as *canopic jars* for eventual deposit in the burial chamber with the corpse. (The jars take their name from the Egyptian port of Canopus, where human-headed jars were worshiped as personifications of Osiris. These jars were not, however, used in embalming.) The brain was extracted through the nostrils and discarded. The Egyptians did not attach any special significance to the brain. But they left in place the heart, necessary for life and regarded as the seat of intelligence.

Next, the body was treated for 40 days with natron, a naturally occurring salt compound that dehydrated the body. Then the corpse was filled with resin-soaked linens, and the embalming incision was closed and covered with a representation of the *wedjat* eye of Horus, a powerful *amulet* (a device to ward off evil and promote rebirth). Finally, the body was treated with lotions and resins and then wrapped tightly with hundreds of yards of linen bandages to maintain its shape. The Egyptians often placed other amulets within the bandages or on the corpse. The most important were heart *scarabs* (gems in the shape of beetles). Spells written on them ensured that the heart would be returned to its owner if it were ever lost. A scroll copy of the *Book of the Dead* (FIG. **3-36**) frequently was placed between the legs of the deceased. It contained some 200 spells intended to protect the mummy and the ka in the afterlife. The mummies of the wealthy had their faces covered with funerary masks (FIG. **3-1**).

The Egyptian practice of mummification endured for thousands of years, even under Greek and Roman rule. Roman mummies with painted portraits (FIG. **10-62**) dating to the first three centuries CE have long been known, but the discovery in 1996 of a cemetery at Bahariya Oasis in the desert southwest of Cairo greatly expanded their number. The site—at least four square miles in size—has come to be called the Valley of the Golden Mummies. The largest tomb found to date contained 32 mummies, but another held 43, some stacked on top of others because the tomb housed several generations of Egyptians and space ran out.

The care with which the Egyptians laid the dead to rest in the Bahariya cemetery varied markedly with the social position and wealth of the deceased. The bodies of the poorer members of the community were carelessly wrapped in linen and have almost completely decayed. The 60 most elaborate mummies, probably those of successful merchants and their families, have gilded *stucco* masks. Some also have gilded chest plates with reliefs depicting Egyptian deities, including Thoth holding Maat's feather (compare the weighing scene in FIG. **3-36**). Others have painted decoration, and some have eyes of white marble with black obsidian irises and copper eyelashes. The excavators believe the cemetery was still in use as late as the fourth or fifth century CE.

Preserving the deceased's body by mummification was only the first requirement for immortality in ancient Egypt. Food and drink also had to be provided, as did clothing, utensils, and furniture. Nothing that had been enjoyed on earth was to be lacking. Statuettes called *ushabtis* (answerers) also were placed in the tomb. These figurines performed any labor required of the deceased in the afterlife, answering whenever his or her name was called.

Beginning in the third millennium BCE, the Egyptians also set up statues of the dead in their tombs. The statues were meant to guarantee the permanence of the person's identity by providing substitute dwelling places for the ka in case the mummy disintegrated. Wall paintings and reliefs recorded the recurring round of human activities. The Egyptians hoped and expected that the images and inventory of life, collected within the protective stone walls of the tomb, would ensure immortality.

---

chapel, which had a false door through which the ka could join the world of the living and partake in the meals placed on an offering table. Some mastabas also had a *serdab*, a small room housing a statue of the deceased.

IMHOTEP AND DJOSER One of the most renowned figures in Egyptian history is IMHOTEP, the builder for King Djoser (r. 2630–2611 BCE) of the Third Dynasty. Imhotep was a man of legendary talent who served also as the pharaoh's chancellor and high priest of the sun god. After his death, the Egyptians revered Imhotep as a god and in time may have inflated the list of his achievements, but his is the first recorded name of an artist in history.

The historian Manetho states that Imhotep designed the Stepped Pyramid of Djoser at Saqqara, the ancient *necropolis* (Greek for "city of the dead") for Memphis, Egypt's capital at the time. Built before 2600 BCE, the pyramid (FIG. **3-5**) is one of the oldest stone structures in Egypt and, in its final form, the first truly grandiose royal tomb. Begun as a large mastaba with each of its faces oriented toward one of the cardinal points of the compass, the tomb was enlarged at least twice before taking on its ultimate shape. About 200 feet high, the Stepped Pyramid seems to be composed of a series of mastabas of diminishing size, stacked one atop another to form a structure that resembles the great Mesopotamian ziggurats (FIGS. **2-15** and **2-20**, *top center*). Unlike the ziggurats, however, Djoser's pyramid is a tomb, not a temple platform, and its dual function was to protect the mummified king and his possessions and to symbolize, by its gigantic presence, his absolute and godlike power. Beneath the pyramid was a network of several hundred underground rooms and galleries cut out of the Saqqara

3-5 Iмнотер, Stepped Pyramid and mortuary precinct of Djoser, Saqqara, Egypt, Third Dynasty, ca. 2630–2611 BCE.

Imhotep, the first artist whose name is recorded, built the first pyramid during the Third Dynasty for King Djoser. Djoser's pyramid resembles a series of stacked mastabas of diminishing size.

3-6 Plan (*top*) and restored view (*bottom*) of the mortuary precinct of Djoser, Saqqara, Egypt, Third Dynasty, ca. 2630–2611 BCE.

Djoser's pyramid was the center-piece of an immense funerary complex that included a mortuary temple, other buildings, and court-yards. Its network of underground galleries resembled a palace.

1. Stepped pyramid
2. Funerary temple of Djoser
3. Court with serdab
4. Large court with altar
5. Entrance portico
6. Heb-Sed court and sham chapels
7. Small temple
8. Court before North Palace
9. North Palace
10. Court before South Palace
11. South Palace
12. South tomb
13. Royal Pavilion
14. Magazines

3-6A Entrance hall, Djoser precinct, Saqqara, ca. 2630–2611 BCE.

bedrock. The vast subterranean complex resembles a palace. It was to be Djoser's new home in the afterlife.

Befitting the god-king's majesty, Djoser's pyramid (FIG. 3-5) stands near the center of an immense (37-acre) rectangular enclosure (FIG. 3-6) surrounded by a 34-foot-high and 5,400-foot-long wall of white limestone. The huge precinct, with its protective walls and tightly regulated access, stands in sharp contrast to the roughly contemporary Sumerian Royal Cemetery at Ur, where no barriers kept people away from the burial area. Nor did the Mesopotamian cemetery have a temple for the worship of the deified dead. At

Saqqara, a funerary temple (FIG. 3-6, no. 2) stands against the northern face of Djoser's pyramid. Priests performed daily rituals at the temple in celebration of the divine pharaoh.

Djoser's funerary temple was but one of many buildings arranged around several courts. Most of the others were dummy structures (FIG. 3-6, no. 6) with stone walls enclosing fills of rubble, sand, or gravel. The buildings imitated in stone masonry various types of temporary structures made of plant stems and mats erected in Upper and Lower Egypt to celebrate the Jubilee Festival, which perpetually reaffirmed the royal existence in the hereafter. The trans-

3-7 Detail of the facade of the North Palace of the mortuary precinct of Djoser, Saqqara, Egypt, Third Dynasty, ca. 2630–2611 BCE.

The earliest known stone columns are in Djoser's funerary precinct. Those on the North Palace facade are engaged (attached) to the walls and have shafts and capitals resembling papyrus stalks and blossoms.

lation into stone of structural forms previously made out of plants may be seen in the *columns* (FIG. 3-7) of the North Palace (FIG. 3-6, no. 9) of Djoser's funerary precinct. The columns end in *capitals* ("heads") that take the form of the papyrus blossoms of Lower Egypt. The column *shafts* resemble papyrus stalks. Djoser's columns are not freestanding, as are most later columns. They are *engaged* (attached) to walls, but are nonetheless the earliest known stone columns in the history of architecture.

THE OLD KINGDOM

The Old Kingdom is the first of the three great periods of Egyptian history, called the Old, Middle, and New Kingdoms, respectively. Many Egyptologists now begin the Old Kingdom with the first pharaoh of the Fourth Dynasty, Sneferu (r. 2575–2551 BCE), although the traditional division of kingdoms places Djoser and the Third Dynasty in the Old Kingdom. It ended with the demise of the Eighth Dynasty around 2134 BCE.

Architecture

The pharaohs of the Old Kingdom amassed great wealth and expended it on grandiose architectural projects, of which the most spectacular were the Great Pyramids of Gizeh, the oldest of the Seven Wonders of the ancient world (see "Babylon, City of Wonders," Chapter 2, page 48). The prerequisites for membership in this elite club were colossal size and enormous cost.

GREAT PYRAMIDS, GIZEH The three pyramids (FIGS. 3-8 and 3-9) of Gizeh were built in the course of about 75 years (see "Building the Great Pyramids," page 60) as the tombs of the Fourth Dynasty pharaohs Khufu (r. 2551–2528 BCE), Khafre (r. 2520–2494 BCE), and Menkaure (r. 2490–2472 BCE). They represent the culmination of an architectural evolution that began with the mastaba, but the classic pyramid form is not simply a refinement of the stepped pyramid. The new tomb shape probably reflects the influence of Heliopolis, the seat of the powerful cult of Re, whose emblem was a pyramidal stone, the *ben-ben* (see "The Gods and

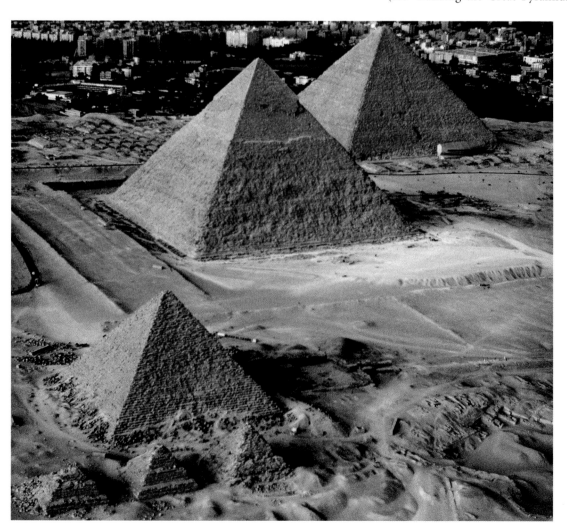

3-8 Great Pyramids, Gizeh, Egypt, Fourth Dynasty. *From bottom:* Pyramids of Menkaure, ca. 2490–2472 BCE; Khafre, ca. 2520–2494 BCE; and Khufu, ca. 2551–2528 BCE.

The Great Pyramids of Gizeh took the shape of the ben-ben, the emblem of the sun, Re. The sun's rays were the ramp the Egyptian pharaohs used to ascend to the heavens after their death and rebirth.

The Old Kingdom **59**

Building the Great Pyramids

The Great Pyramids (FIG. 3-8) across the Nile from modern Cairo attest to the extraordinary engineering and mathematical expertise of the Egyptians of the mid-third millennium BCE. They also are testaments to the Old Kingdom builders' mastery of stone masonry and ability to mobilize, direct, house, and feed a huge workforce engaged in one of the most labor-intensive enterprises ever undertaken. Like all building projects of this type, the process of erecting the pyramids began with the quarrying of stone, in this case primarily the limestone of the Gizeh plateau itself. Teams of skilled workers had to cut into the rock and remove large blocks of roughly equal size using stone or copper chisels and wooden mallets and wedges. Often, the artisans had to cut deep tunnels to find high-quality stone free of cracks and other flaws. To remove a block, the workers cut channels on all sides and partly underneath. Then they pried the stones free from the bedrock with wooden levers.

After workers liberated the stones, the rough blocks had to be transported to the building site and *dressed* (shaped to the exact dimensions required, with smooth faces for a perfect fit). Small blocks could be carried on a man's shoulders or on the back of a donkey, but the massive blocks used to construct the Great Pyramids were moved using wooden rollers and sleds. The artisans dressed the blocks by chiseling and pounding the surfaces and, in the last stage, by rubbing and grinding the surfaces with fine polishing stones. This kind of construction, in which carefully cut and regularly shaped blocks of stone are piled in successive rows, or *courses,* is called *ashlar masonry.*

To set the ashlar blocks in place, workers erected great rubble ramps against the core of the pyramid. Their size and slope were adjusted as work progressed and the tomb grew in height. Scholars debate whether the Egyptians used simple linear ramps inclined at a right angle to one face of the pyramid or zigzag or spiral ramps akin to staircases. Linear ramps would have had the advantage of simplicity and would have left three sides of the pyramid unobstructed. But zigzag ramps placed against one side of the structure or spiral ramps winding around the pyramid would have greatly reduced the slope of the incline and would have made the dragging of the blocks easier. Some scholars also have suggested a combination of straight and spiral ramps.

The Egyptians used ropes, pulleys, and levers both to lift and to lower the stones, guiding each block into its designated place. Finally, the pyramid received a casing of white limestone blocks (FIG. 3-9, no. 1), cut so precisely that the eye could scarcely detect the joints. The reflection of sunlight on the facing would have been dazzling,

underscoring the pyramid's solar symbolism. A few casing stones still can be seen in the cap that covers the Pyramid of Khafre (FIGS. 3-8, *center,* and 3-11, *left*).

Of the three Fourth Dynasty pyramids at Gizeh, the tomb of Khufu (FIGS. 3-9 and 3-10, no. 7) is the oldest and largest. Except for the galleries and burial chamber, it is an almost solid mass of limestone masonry. Some dimensions will suggest the immensity of the Gizeh pyramids: At the base, the length of one side of Khufu's tomb is approximately 775 feet, and its area is some 13 acres. Its present height is about 450 feet (originally 480 feet). The structure contains roughly 2.3 million blocks of stone, each weighing an average of 2.5 tons. Some of the stones at the base weigh about 15 tons. Napoleon's scholars calculated that the blocks in the three Great Pyramids were sufficient to build a wall 1 foot wide and 10 feet high around France.

1. Silhouette with original facing stone
2. Thieves' tunnels
3. Entrance
4. Grand gallery
5. King's chamber
6. So-called Queen's chamber
7. False tomb chamber
8. Relieving blocks
9. Airshafts(?)

3-9 Section of the Pyramid of Khufu, Gizeh, Egypt, Fourth Dynasty, ca. 2551–2528 BCE.

Khufu's pyramid is the largest at Gizeh. Constructed of roughly 2.3 million blocks of stone weighing an average of 2.5 tons, the structure is an almost solid mass of stone quarried from the Gizeh plateau itself.

Goddesses of Egypt," page 54). The Great Pyramids are symbols of the sun. The Pyramid Texts, inscribed on the burial chamber walls of many royal tombs beginning with the Fifth Dynasty Pyramid of Unas (r. 2356–2323 BCE), refer to the sun's rays as the ramp the pharaoh uses to ascend to the heavens. Djoser's Stepped Pyramid (FIG. 3-5) may also have been conceived as a giant stairway. The pyramids were where Egyptian kings were reborn in the afterlife, just as the sun is reborn each day at dawn. As with Djoser's pyramid, the four sides of each of the Great Pyramids are oriented to the cardinal points of the compass. But the funerary temples associated with the three Gizeh pyramids are not placed on the north side, facing

the stars of the northern sky, as was Djoser's temple. The temples sit on the east side, facing the rising sun and underscoring their connection with Re.

From the remains surrounding the Pyramid of Khafre at Gizeh, archaeologists have been able to reconstruct an entire funerary complex (FIG. 3-10). The complex included the pyramid itself with the pharaoh's burial chamber; the *mortuary temple* adjoining the pyramid on the east side, where offerings were made to the dead king, ceremonies performed, and cloth, food, and ceremonial vessels stored; the roofed causeway leading to the mortuary temple; and the *valley temple* at the edge of the floodplain. According to one theory,

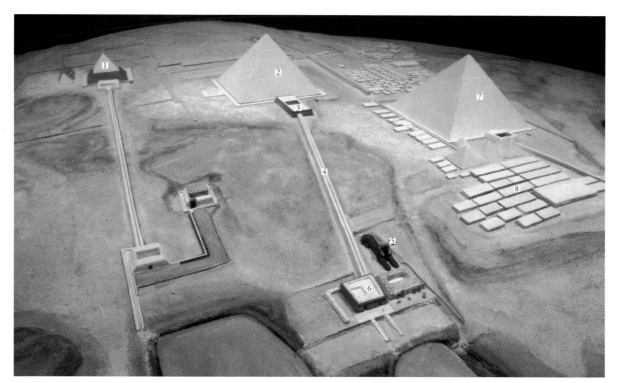

3-10 Model of the Fourth Dynasty pyramid complex, Gizeh, Egypt. Harvard University Semitic Museum, Cambridge. 1) Pyramid of Menkaure, 2) Pyramid of Khafre, 3) mortuary temple of Khafre, 4) causeway, 5) Great Sphinx, 6) valley temple of Khafre, 7) Pyramid of Khufu, 8) pyramids of the royal family and mastabas of nobles.

Like Djoser's pyramid (FIG. 3-5), the Great Pyramids were not isolated tombs but parts of funerary complexes with a valley temple, a covered causeway, and a mortuary temple adjoining the pyramid.

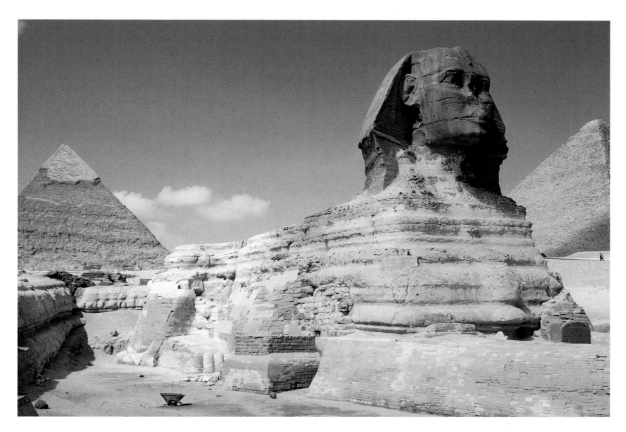

3-11 Great Sphinx (with Pyramid of Khafre in the background at left), Gizeh, Egypt, Fourth Dynasty, ca. 2520–2494 BCE. Sandstone, 65′ × 240′.

Carved out of the Gizeh stone quarry, the Great Sphinx is the largest statue in the Near East. The sphinx is associated with the sun god, and joins the body of a lion with the head of a pharaoh.

the complex served not only as the king's tomb and temple but also as his palace in the afterlife.

GREAT SPHINX Beside the causeway and dominating the valley temple of Khafre rises the Great Sphinx (FIG. 3-11). Carved from a spur of rock in an ancient quarry, the colossal statue—the largest in the ancient Near East—represents a pharaoh, probably Khafre (origi-

nally complete with the pharaoh's ceremonial beard and uraeus headdress), although some scholars believe it portrays Khufu and was carved before construction of Khafre's complex began. Whoever it portrays, the *sphinx*—a lion with a human head—was associated with the sun god and therefore was an appropriate image for a pharaoh. The composite form suggests that the pharaoh combines human intelligence with the immense strength and authority of the king of beasts.

Sculpture

Old Kingdom statues survive in significant numbers because they fulfilled an important function in Egyptian tombs as substitute abodes for the ka (see "Mummification and Immortality," page 57). Although Egyptian sculptors used wood, clay, and other materials, mostly for images of those not of the royal or noble classes, the primary material for funerary statuary was stone.

3-12A Rahotep and Nofret, Maidum, ca. 2575–2550 BCE.

KHAFRE ENTHRONED The seated statue of Khafre (FIG. **3-12**) is one of a series of similar statues carved for the pharaoh's valley temple (FIG. **3-10**, no. 6) near the Great Sphinx. The stone is diorite, an exceptionally hard dark stone brought some 400 miles down the Nile from royal quarries in the south. (The Neo-Sumerian ruler Gudea, FIG. **2-16**, so admired diorite that he imported it to far-away Girsu.) Khafre wears a simple kilt and sits rigidly upright on a throne formed of two stylized lions' bodies. Intertwined lotus and papyrus plants—symbolic of the united Egypt—appear between the throne's legs. The falcon-god Horus extends his protective wings to shelter the pharaoh's head. Khafre has the royal false beard fastened to his chin and wears the royal linen *nemes* headdress with the *uraeus* cobra of kingship on the front. The headdress covers his forehead and falls in pleated folds over his shoulders. (The head of the Great Sphinx is similarly attired.) As befitting a divine ruler, the sculptor portrayed Khafre with a well-developed, flawless body and a perfect face, regardless of his actual age and appearance. The Egyptians considered ideal proportions appropriate for representing their god-kings, and the statue of Khafre is not a true portrait and was not intended to be. The purpose of pharaonic portraiture was not to record individual features or the distinctive shapes of bodies, but rather to proclaim the divine nature of Egyptian kingship.

The enthroned Khafre radiates serenity. The sculptor created this effect, common to Egyptian royal statues, in part by giving the

3-12 Khafre enthroned, from Gizeh, Egypt, Fourth Dynasty, ca. 2520–2494 BCE. Diorite, 5′ 6″ high. Egyptian Museum, Cairo.

This portrait from his pyramid complex depicts Khafre as an enthroned divine ruler with a perfect body. The rigidity of the pose creates the effect of eternal stillness, appropriate for the timeless afterlife.

3-13 Menkaure and Khamerernebty(?), from Gizeh, Egypt, Fourth Dynasty, ca. 2490–2472 BCE. Graywacke, 4′ 6½″ high. Museum of Fine Arts, Boston. ◼◀

The double portrait of Menkaure and his wife displays the conventional postures used for statues designed as substitute homes for the ka. The frozen gestures signify that the man and woman are married.

figure great compactness and solidity, with few projecting, breakable parts. The form manifests the purpose: to last for eternity. Khafre's body is one with the unarticulated slab that forms the back of the king's throne. His arms are held close to the torso and thighs, and his legs are close together. Part of the original stone block still connects the king's legs to his chair. Khafre's pose is frontal, rigid, and *bilaterally symmetrical* (the same on either side of an axis, in this case the vertical axis). The sculptor suppressed all movement and with it the notion of time, creating an eternal stillness.

To produce the statue, the artist first drew the front, back, and two profile views of the pharaoh on the four vertical faces of the stone block. Next, apprentices chiseled away the excess stone on each side, working inward until the planes met at right angles. Finally, the master sculpted the parts of Khafre's body, the falcon, and so forth. The finishing was done by *abrasion* (rubbing or grinding the surface). This *subtractive* method of creating the pharaoh's portrait accounts in large part for the blocklike look of the standard Egyptian statue. Nevertheless, other sculptors, both ancient and modern, with different aims, have transformed stone blocks into dynamic, twisting human forms (for example, FIGS. I-16 and 5-84).

MENKAURE AND KHAMERERNEBTY The seated statue is one of only a small number of basic formulaic types that Old Kingdom sculptors employed to represent the human figure. Another is the image of a person or deity standing, either alone or in a group, for example the double portrait (FIG. **3-13**) of Menkaure and one of his wives, probably Khamerernebty. The statue once stood in the valley temple of Menkaure's pyramid complex at Gizeh. Here, too, the figures remain wedded to the stone block from which they were carved. In fact, the statue could be classified as a high-relief sculpture. Menkaure's pose, which is duplicated in countless other Egyptian statues, is rigidly frontal with the arms hanging straight down and close to his well-built body. His hands are clenched into fists with the thumbs forward. His left leg is slightly advanced, but no shift occurs in the angle of the hips to correspond to the uneven distribution of weight. Khamerernebty stands in a similar position. Her right arm, however, encircles the king's waist, and her left hand gently rests on his left arm. This frozen stereotypical gesture indicates their marital status. The husband and wife show no other sign of affection or emotion and look not at each other but out into space. The artist's aim was not to portray living figures, but to suggest the timeless nature of the stone statue that was designed to provide an eternal substitute home for the ka.

SEATED SCRIBE Traces of paint remain on the portraits of Menkaure and Khamerernebty. Most Egyptian statues were painted, although sometimes the stone was left its natural color, enhancing the sense of abstraction and timelessness. A striking example of painted statuary is the seated portrait (FIG. **3-14**) of a Fourth Dynasty scribe found at Saqqara. Despite the stiff upright posture and the frontality of head and body, the color lends a lifelike quality to the stone statue. The head displays an extraordinary sensitivity. The sculptor conveyed the personality of a sharply intelligent and alert individual with a penetration and sympathy seldom achieved at this early date. The scribe sits directly on the ground, not on a throne or even on a chair. Although he occupied

3-14A Hemiunu, Gizeh, ca. 2550–2530 BCE.

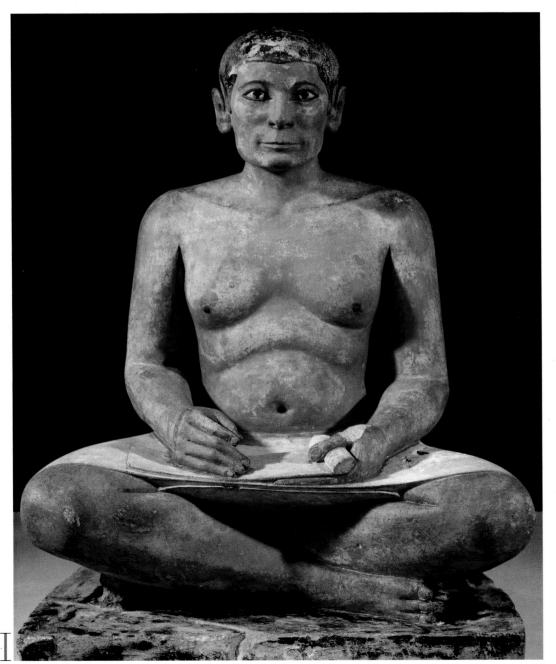

1 in.

3-14 Seated scribe, from Saqqara, Egypt, Fourth Dynasty, ca. 2500 BCE. Painted limestone, 1′ 9″ high. Louvre, Paris.

The idealism that characterizes the portraiture of the Egyptian god-kings did not extend to the portrayal of non-elite individuals. This more realistic painted portrait of a scribe shows clear signs of aging.

Sculptors rk, Chapel khmire, es, ca. BCE.

a position of honor in a largely illiterate society, the scribe was a much lower figure in the Egyptian hierarchy than the pharaoh, whose divinity made him superhuman. In the history of art, especially portraiture, it is almost a rule that as a human subject's importance decreases, formality is relaxed and realism is increased. It is telling that the sculptor portrayed the scribe with sagging chest muscles and a protruding belly. These signs of age would have been disrespectful and wholly inappropriate in a depiction of an Egyptian god-king. But the statue of the scribe is not a true portrait either. Rather, it is a composite of conventional types. Obesity, for example, characterizes many nonroyal Old Kingdom portraits, perhaps because it attested to the comfortable life of the person represented and his relatively high position in society.

3-14B Ka-Aper, Saqqara, ca. 2450–2350 BCE.

TOMB OF TI, SAQQARA In Old Kingdom tombs, images of the deceased also frequently appear in relief sculpture and in mural painting, sometimes alone (FIG. I-14) and sometimes in a narrative context. The painted limestone relief scenes that decorate the walls of the mastaba of a Fifth Dynasty official named Ti typify the subjects Old Kingdom patrons favored for the adornment of their final resting places. Depictions of agriculture and hunting fill Ti's tomb. These activities were associated with the provisioning of the ka in the hereafter, but they also had powerful symbolic overtones. In ancient Egypt, success in the hunt, for example, was a metaphor for triumph over the forces of evil.

On one wall (FIG. 3-15), Ti, his men, and his boats move slowly through the marshes, hunting hippopotami and birds in a dense growth of towering papyrus. The sculptor delineated the reedy stems of the plants with repeated fine grooves that fan out gracefully at the top into a commotion of frightened birds and stalking foxes. The water beneath the boats, signified by a pattern of wavy lines, is crowded with hippopotami and fish. Ti's men seem frantically busy with their spears, while Ti, depicted twice their size, stands aloof. The basic conventions of Egyptian figure representation used a half millennium earlier for the palette of King Narmer (FIG. 3-3) are seen again here. As on the Predynastic palette, the artist exaggerated the size of Ti to announce his rank, and combined frontal and profile views of Ti's body to show its most characteristic parts clearly. This approach to representation was well suited for Egyptian funerary art because it emphasized the essential nature of the deceased, not his accidental appearance. Ti's conventional pose contrasts with the realistically rendered activities of his tiny servants and with the naturalistically carved and painted birds and animals among the papyrus buds. Ti's immobility suggests that he is not an actor in the hunt. He does not *do* anything. He simply *is,* a figure apart from time and an impassive observer of life, like his ka.

The idealized and stiff image of Ti is typical of Egyptian relief sculpture. Egyptian artists regularly ignored the endless variations in body types of real human beings. Painters and sculptors did not sketch their subjects from life but applied a strict *canon,* or system of proportions, to the human figure. They first drew a grid on the wall. Then they placed various human body parts at specific points on the network of squares. The height of a figure, for example, was a fixed number of squares, and the head, shoulders, waist, knees, and other parts of the body also had a predetermined size and place within the scheme. This approach to design lasted for thousands of years. Specific proportions might vary from workshop to workshop and change over time, but the principle of the canon persisted.

On another wall (FIG. 3-16) of Ti's mastaba, the artist represented in two registers goats treading in seeds and cattle fording a canal in the Nile. Once again, the scenes may be interpreted on

1 ft.

3-15 Ti watching a hippopotamus hunt, relief in the mastaba of Ti, Saqqara, Egypt, Fifth Dynasty, ca. 2450–2350 BCE. Painted limestone, 4′ high.

In Egypt, a successful hunt was a metaphor for triumph over evil. In this painted tomb relief, the deceased stands aloof from the hunters busily spearing hippopotami. Ti's size reflects his high rank.

a symbolic as well as a literal level. The fording of the Nile, for example, was a metaphor for the deceased's passage from life to the hereafter. Ti is absent from the scenes, and all the men and animals participate in the narrative. Despite the sculptor's repeated use of similar poses for most of the human and animal figures, the reliefs are full of anecdotal details. Especially charming is the group at the lower right. A youth, depicted in a complex unconventional posture, carries a calf on his back. The animal, not a little afraid, turns its head back a full 180 degrees (compare FIG. 1-8) to seek reassurance from its mother, who returns the calf's gaze. Scenes such as this demonstrate that Egyptian artists could be close observers of daily life. The suppression of the anecdotal (that is, of the time-bound) from their representations of the deceased both in relief and in the round was a deliberate choice. Their primary purpose was to suggest the deceased's eternal existence in the afterlife, not to portray nature.

THE MIDDLE KINGDOM

About 2150 BCE, the Egyptians challenged the pharaohs' power, and for more than a century the land was in a state of civil unrest and near anarchy. But in 2040 BCE, the pharaoh of Upper Egypt, Mentuhotep II (r. 2050–1998 BCE), managed to unite Egypt again under the rule of a single king and established the so-called Middle Kingdom (11th to 14th Dynasties).

The fording of the Nile was a metaphor for the passage to the afterlife. These reliefs combine stereotypical poses for humans and animals with unconventional postures and anecdotal details.

Sculpture

Although in most respects Middle Kingdom sculptors adhered to the conventions established during the Old Kingdom, there were some notable innovations.

SENUSRET III One of Mentuhotep II's successors was Senusret III (r. 1878–1859 BCE), who fought four brutal military campaigns in Nubia (MAP **3-1**). Although Egyptian armies devastated the land and poisoned the wells, Senusret III never fully achieved secure control over the Nubians. In Egypt itself, he attempted, with greater success, to establish a more powerful central government. His portraits (FIG. **3-17**) are of special interest because they represent a sharp break from Old Kingdom practice. Although the king's preserved statues have idealized bodies, the sculptors brought a stunning and unprecedented realism to the rendition of Senusret III's features. His pessimistic expression reflects the dominant mood of the time and is echoed in Middle Kingdom literature. The strong mouth, the drooping lines about the nose and eyes, and the shadowy brows show a determined ruler who had also shared in the cares of the world, sunk in brooding meditation. The portrait is different in kind from the typically impassive faces of the Old Kingdom. It is personal, almost intimate, in its revelation of the mark of anxiety that a troubled age might leave on the soul of a king.

3-17 Fragmentary head of Senusret III, 12th Dynasty, ca. 1860 BCE. Red quartzite, $6\frac{1}{2}''$ high. Metropolitan Museum of Art, New York.

The portraits of Senusret III exhibit an unprecedented realism. The king's brooding expression reflects the dominant mood of the time and contrasts sharply with the impassive faces of Old Kingdom pharaohs.

1 in.

-17A Lady ennuwy, erma, ca. 960–1916 BCE.

Architecture

Senusret III's tomb, at Dashur, is a mud-brick pyramid, but the most characteristic funerary monuments of the Middle Kingdom are rock-cut tombs. These tombs, which also existed during the Old Kingdom, became especially popular during the Middle Kingdom and largely replaced the mastaba as the standard Egyptian tomb type.

BENI HASAN Some of the best-preserved Middle Kingdom tombs are at Beni Hasan. Hollowed out of the cliffs, these tombs (FIG. 3-18) often have a shallow columnar porch, which led into a columned hall and then into a burial chamber. In the 12th Dynasty tomb of Amenemhet, the columns in the hall (FIG. 3-19) serve no supporting function because, like the porch columns, they are continuous parts of the rock fabric. (Note the broken column in the rear suspended from the ceiling like a stalactite.) The column shafts are *fluted* with vertical channels in a manner similar to later Greek columns, and there is no doubt that the Greeks knew about and emulated many aspects of Egyptian architecture (see Chapter 5). Archaeologists believe fluting derived from the dressing of softwood trunks with the rounded cutting edge of the adze. Fluted stone

3-18 Rock-cut tombs BH 3–5, Beni Hasan, Egypt, 12th Dynasty, ca. 1950–1900 BCE.

The tombs of Beni Hasan are characteristic of the Middle Kingdom. Hollowed out of the cliffs, these tombs often have a shallow columnar porch, which leads into a columned hall and burial chamber.

3-19 Interior hall of the rock-cut tomb of Amenemhet (tomb BH 2), Beni Hasan, Egypt, 12th Dynasty, ca. 1950–1900 BCE.

The columnar hall of Amenemhet's tomb was carved out of the living rock, which explains the suspended broken column at the rear. The shafts are fluted in a manner Greek architects later emulated.

columns are yet another case of Egyptian builders' translating perishable natural forms into permanent architecture. Artists decorated the tomb walls with paintings and painted reliefs, as in former times, and placed statues of the deceased in niches.

THE NEW KINGDOM

Like its predecessor, the Middle Kingdom disintegrated, and power passed to the Hyksos, or shepherd kings, who descended on Egypt from the Syrian and Mesopotamian uplands. They brought with them a new and influential culture and that practical animal, the horse. Their innovations in weaponry and war techniques ironically contributed to their own overthrow by native Egyptian kings of the 17th Dynasty around 1600–1550 BCE. Ahmose I (r. 1550–1525 BCE), final conqueror of the Hyksos and first king of the 18th Dynasty, ushered in the New Kingdom, the most brilliant period in Egypt's long history. At this time, Egypt extended its borders by conquest from the Euphrates River in the east deep into Nubia to the south. A new capital—Thebes, in Upper Egypt—became a great and luxurious metropolis with magnificent palaces, tombs, and temples along both banks of the Nile.

Architecture

If the most impressive monuments of the Old Kingdom are its pyramids, those of the New Kingdom are its grandiose temples, often built to honor pharaohs and queens as well as gods. Great pharaonic mortuary temples arose along the Nile in the Thebes district. These shrines provided the rulers with a place for worshiping their patron gods during their lifetime and then served as temples in their own honor after their death. The temples were elaborate and luxuriously decorated, befitting both the pharaohs and the gods.

TEMPLE OF HATSHEPSUT The most majestic of these royal mortuary temples (FIG. **3-20**), at Deir el-Bahri, honored the female pharaoh Hatshepsut, one of the most remarkable women of the ancient world (see "Hatshepsut, the Woman Who Would Be King," page 68). Some have attributed the temple to SENMUT (FIG. **3-27**), Hatshepsut's chancellor and possible lover, who is described in two inscriptions as royal architect. His association with this project is uncertain, however. Hatshepsut's temple rises from the valley floor in three colonnaded terraces connected by ramps on the central axis. It is remarkable how visually well suited the structure is to its natural setting. The long horizontals and verticals of the *colonnades* and their rhythm of light and dark repeat the pattern of the limestone cliffs above. The colonnade *pillars*, which are either simply rectangular or *chamfered* (beveled, or flattened at the edges) into 16 sides, are well proportioned and rhythmically spaced.

In Hatshepsut's day, the terraces were not the barren places they are now but gardens with frankincense trees and rare plants the pharaoh brought from the faraway "land of Punt" on the Red Sea. Her expedition to Punt figures prominently in the poorly preserved

3-20A King and queen of Punt, Hatshepsut temple, ca. 1473–1458 BCE.

3-20 Mortuary temple of Hatshepsut (looking west with the Middle Kingdom mortuary temple of Mentuhotep II at left), Deir el-Bahri, Egypt, 18th Dynasty, ca. 1473–1458 BCE.

Hatshepsut was the first great female monarch whose name is recorded. Painted reliefs recounting her divine birth and significant achievements adorned her immense funerary temple.

Hatshepsut, the Woman Who Would Be King

In 1479 BCE, Thutmose II, the fourth pharaoh of the 18th Dynasty (r. 1492–1479 BCE), died. His principal wife (and half sister), Queen Hatshepsut (r. 1473–1458 BCE), had not given birth to any sons who survived, so the title of king went to Thutmose III, son of Thutmose II by a minor wife. Hatshepsut was named regent for the boy-king. Within a few years, however, the queen proclaimed herself pharaoh and insisted that her father Thutmose I had actually chosen her as his successor during his lifetime. Underscoring her claim, one of the reliefs decorating Hatshepsut's enormous funerary complex (FIG. 3-20) depicts Thutmose I crowning his daughter as king in the presence of the Egyptian gods. Hatshepsut is the first great female monarch whose name has been recorded. (In the 12th Dynasty, Sobekneferu was crowned king of Egypt, but she reigned as pharaoh for only a few years.) Hatshepsut boasted of having made the "Two Lands to labor with bowed back" for her, and for two decades she ruled what was then the most powerful and prosperous empire in the world.

Hatshepsut commissioned numerous building projects, and sculptors produced portraits of the female pharaoh in great numbers for display in those complexes. Unfortunately, Thutmose III (r. 1458–1425 BCE), for reasons still not fully understood, late in his reign ordered Hatshepsut's portraits destroyed. In her surviving portraits, Hatshepsut uniformly wears the costume of the male pharaohs, with royal headdress and kilt, and in some cases (FIG. 3-21) even a false ceremonial beard. Many inscriptions refer to Hatshepsut as "*His* Majesty"! In other statues, however, Hatshepsut has delicate features, a slender frame, and breasts, leaving no doubt that artists also represented her as a woman.

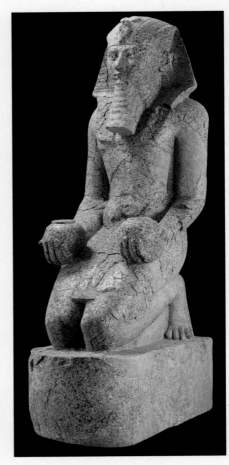

3-21 Hatshepsut with offering jars, from the upper court of her mortuary temple, Deir el-Bahri, Egypt, 18th Dynasty, ca. 1473–1458 BCE. Red granite, 8′ 6″ high. Metropolitan Museum of Art, New York.

Many of Hatshepsut's portraits were destroyed after her death. Conservators reassembled this one, which depicts the queen as a male pharaoh with false beard, consistent with inscriptions calling her "His Majesty."

1 ft.

but once brightly painted low reliefs that cover many walls of the complex. In addition to representing great deeds, the reliefs also show Hatshepsut's coronation and divine birth. She was said to be the daughter of the god Amen-Re, whose sanctuary was situated on the temple's uppermost level. The painted reliefs of Hatshepsut's mortuary temple constituted the first great tribute to a woman's achievements in the history of art. Their defacement after her death is therefore especially unfortunate.

HATSHEPSUT'S PORTRAITS As many as 200 statues in the round depicting Hatshepsut in various guises complemented the extensive relief program. On the lowest terrace, to either side of the processional way, Hatshepsut repeatedly appeared as a sphinx. On the uppermost level, sculptors represented the female pharaoh standing or seated or in the form of a mummy. At least eight colossal kneeling statues in red granite lined the way to the entrance of the Amen-Re sanctuary.

The statue in FIG. 3-21 suffered the same fate as most of Hatshepsut's portraits during the reign of Thutmose III. It was smashed and the pieces were thrown in a dump, but the portrait has been skillfully reassembled. Hatshepsut holds a globular offering jar in each hand as she takes part in a ritual in honor of the sun god. (A king kneeled only before a god, never a mortal.) She wears the royal male nemes headdress (compare FIGS. 3-11 to 3-13) and the pharaoh's ceremonial beard. The agents of Thutmose III hacked off

the uraeus cobra that once adorned the front of the headdress. The figure is also anatomically male, although other surviving portraits of Hatshepsut represent her with a woman's breasts. The male imagery is, however, consistent with the queen's formal assumption of the title of king and with the many inscriptions that address her as a man.

TEMPLE OF RAMSES II The sheer size of Hatshepsut's mortuary temple never fails to impress visitors, and this is no less true of the immense rock-cut temple (FIG. 3-22) of Ramses II (r. 1290–1224 BCE) at Abu Simbel. In 1968, engineers moved the immense Nubian temple nearly 700 feet—an amazing feat in its own right—to save it from submersion in the Aswan High Dam reservoir. Ramses was Egypt's last great warrior pharaoh, and he ruled for two-thirds of a century, an extraordinary accomplishment in an era when life expectancy was far less than it is today. The pharaoh, proud of his many campaigns to restore the empire, proclaimed his greatness by placing four colossal images of himself on the temple *facade*. The portraits are almost eight times as large as Hatshepsut's kneeling statues and, at 65 feet tall, almost a dozen times the height of an ancient Egyptian, even though the pharaoh is seated. Spectacular as they are, the rock-cut statues nonetheless lack the refinement of earlier periods, because much was sacrificed to overwhelming size. This is a characteristic of colossal statuary of every period and every place.

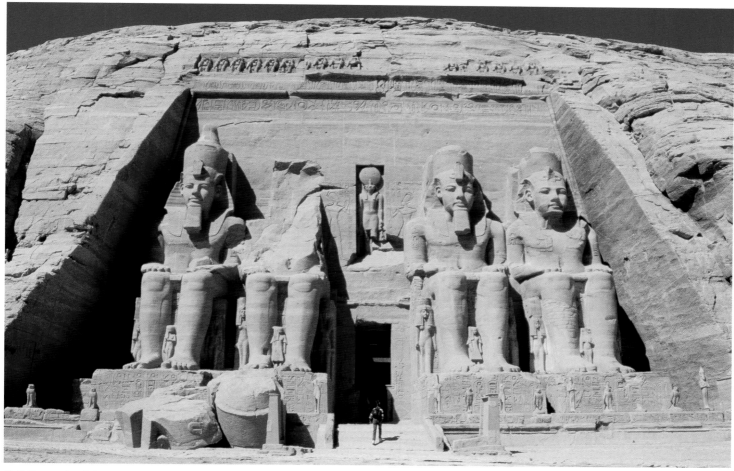

3-22 Façade of the Temple of Ramses II, Abu Simbel, Egypt, 19th Dynasty, ca. 1290–1224 BCE. Sandstone, colossi 65′ high.

Four rock-cut images of Ramses II dominate the facade of his mortuary temple at Abu Simbel in Nubia. The colossal portraits are a dozen times the height of a man, even though the pharaoh is seated.

The rock-cut interior (FIG. 3-23) of the temple is also of colossal size. The distance from the facade to the back wall is an astounding 206 feet. In the main gallery there are 32-foot-tall figures of the king in the guise of Osiris, carved as one with the pillars, facing each other across the narrow corridor. The pillars, carved from the cliff like the pharaoh's facade portraits, have no load-bearing function. In this respect, they resemble the columns in the tombs at Beni Hasan (FIG. 3-19). The statue-column, in its male (*atlantid*) or female (*caryatid*) variants, reappears throughout the history of art. Often, as here, the human figure is attached to a column or pier. At other times the figure replaces the architectural member and forms the sole source of support (FIG. 5-54).

FAMILY OF RAMSES Ramses, like other pharaohs, had many wives, and he fathered scores of sons. The pharaoh honored the most important members of his family with immense monuments

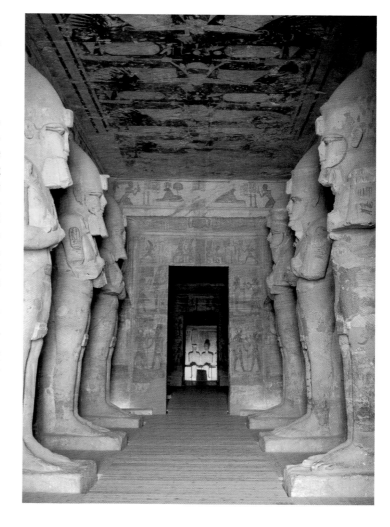

3-23 Interior of the temple of Ramses II, Abu Simbel, Egypt, 19th Dynasty, ca. 1290–1224 BCE. Sandstone, pillar statues 32′ high.

Inside Ramses II's mortuary temple are 32-foot-tall figures of the long-reigning pharaoh in the guise of Osiris, carved as one with the pillars, facing each other across the narrow corridor.

The New Kingdom　**69**

3-24 Restored view of the temple of Amen-Re, Karnak, Egypt, begun 15th century BCE (Jean Claude Golvin).

The vast Karnak temple complex contains an artificial lake associated with the primeval waters of the Egyptian creation myth and a pylon temple with a bilaterally symmetrical axial plan.

of their own. At Abu Simbel, for example, north of his own temple, Ramses ordered the construction of a grand temple for his principal wife, Nefertari. Huge rock-cut statues—four standing images of the king and two of the queen—dominated the temple's facade. For his sons, Ramses constructed a huge underground tomb complex in the Valley of the Kings at Thebes, which an American archaeological team rediscovered in 1987. The tomb, however, was looted within a half century of its construction, but the excavators have yet to find the royal burial chambers themselves, so the tomb may one day yield important artworks.

TEMPLE OF AMEN-RE, KARNAK Distinct from the temples honoring pharaohs and queens are the edifices built to honor one or more of the gods. Successive kings often added to them until they reached gigantic size. The temple of Amen-Re (FIG. **3-24**) at Karnak, for example, was largely the work of the 18th Dynasty pharaohs, including Thutmose I and III and Hatshepsut, but Ramses II (19th Dynasty) and others also contributed sections. Chapels were added to the complex as late as the 26th Dynasty. The artificial sacred lake within the precinct of the Karnak temple is a reference to the primeval waters before creation (see "The Gods and Goddesses of Egypt," page 54). The temple rises from the earth as the original sacred mound rose from the waters at the beginning of time.

The New Kingdom temples all had similar *axial plans*. A typical *pylon temple* (the name derives from the simple and massive gateways, or *pylons*, with sloping walls) is bilaterally symmetrical along a single axis that runs from an approaching avenue through a colonnaded court and hall into a dimly lit sanctuary. Only the pharaohs and the priests could enter the sanctuary. A chosen few were admitted to the great columnar hall. The majority of the people were allowed only as far as the open court, and a high wall shut off the site from the outside world. The central feature of the New Kingdom pylon temple

3-24A Temple of Amen-Re, Luxor, begun early 14th century BCE.

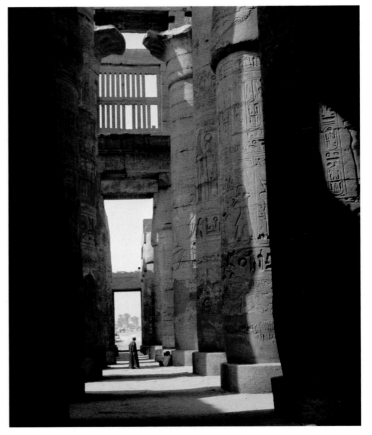

3-25 Hypostyle hall, temple of Amen-Re, Karnak, Egypt, 19th Dynasty, ca. 1290–1224 BCE.

The hypostyle hall of the Amen-Re temple is crowded with columns. The tallest are 66 feet high and have capitals that are 22 feet in diameter. The columns support a roof of stone slabs carried on lintels.

plan—a narrow axial passageway through the complex—is characteristic of much of Egyptian architecture. Axial corridors are also the approaches to the Great Pyramids (FIG. 3-10) and to Hatshepsut's multilevel mortuary temple (FIG. 3-20).

The dominating feature of the statuary-lined approach to a New Kingdom temple was the monumental facade of the pylon, which sculptors routinely covered with reliefs glorifying Egypt's rulers (FIG. 3-38). Inside was an open court with columns on two or more sides, followed by a hall between the court and sanctuary, its long axis placed at right angles to the corridor of the entire building complex. This *hypostyle hall* (one where columns support the roof) was crowded with massive columns, which supported a roof of stone slabs carried on lintels. In Karnak's hypostyle hall (FIGS. 3-25 and 3-26), the columns have bud-cluster or bell-shaped capitals resembling lotus or papyrus, the plants of Upper and Lower Egypt. The central columns are 66 feet high, and the capitals are 22 feet in diameter at the top, large enough to hold a hundred people. The Egyptians, who used no cement, depended on precise cutting of the joints and the weight of the huge stone blocks to hold the columns in place. The two central rows of columns are taller than those at the sides. Raising the roof's central section created a *clerestory*. Openings in the clerestory permitted sunlight to filter into the interior, although the stone grilles (FIG. 3-25) would have blocked much of the light. This method of construction appeared in primitive form in the Old Kingdom valley temple of Khafre at Gizeh. The clerestory is evidently an Egyptian innovation, and its significance hardly can be overstated. Before the invention of the electric light bulb, illuminating a building's interior was always a challenge for architects. The clerestory played a key role in the history of architecture until very recently.

In the hypostyle hall at Karnak, the columns are indispensable structurally, unlike the rock-cut columns of the tombs at Beni Hasan (FIGS. 3-18 and 3-19) and Abu Simbel (FIG. 3-23). But horizontal bands of painted *sunken relief* sculpture almost hide their function as vertical supports. To create these reliefs, the New Kingdom sculptors chiseled deep outlines below the stone's surface, rather than cut back the stone around the figures to make the figures project from the surface. Sunken reliefs preserve the contours of the columns they adorn. Otherwise, the Karnak columns would have had an irregular, wavy profile. Despite this effort to maintain sharp architectural lines, the overwhelming of the surfaces with reliefs indicates that the architects' intention was not to emphasize the functional role of the columns. Instead, they used columns as image- and message-bearing surfaces.

Sculpture and Painting

Although the great temple complexes of the New Kingdom were lavishly decorated with statues and painted reliefs, many of the finest examples of statuary and mural painting were produced for tombs, as in the Old and Middle Kingdoms.

SENMUT AND NEFRURA *Block statues* were extremely popular during the New Kingdom. In these works the idea that the ka could find an eternal home in the cubic stone image of the deceased was expressed in an even more radical simplification of form than was common in Old Kingdom statuary. In the statue (FIG. 3-27) of Senmut and Princess Nefrura, the streamlined design concentrates attention on the heads and treats the two bodies as a single cubic block, given over to inscriptions. Hatshepsut's chancellor holds the pharaoh's daughter by Thutmose II in his "lap" and envelops the

3-27 Senmut with Princess Nefrura, from Thebes, Egypt, 18th Dynasty, ca. 1470–1460 BCE. Granite, 3' $\frac{1}{2}$" high. Ägyptisches Museum, Berlin.

New Kingdom block statues exhibit an even more radical simplification of form than do Old Kingdom statues. Here, Hatshepsut's chancellor holds the queen's daughter in his "lap" and envelops her in his cloak.

3-26 Model of the hypostyle hall, temple of Amen-Re, Karnak, Egypt, 19th Dynasty, ca. 1290–1224 BCE. Metropolitan Museum of Art, New York.

The two central rows of columns of Karnak's hypostyle hall are taller than the rest. Raising the roof's central section created a clerestory that admitted light to the interior through windows with stone grilles.

3-28 Fowling scene, from the tomb of Nebamun, Thebes, Egypt, 18th Dynasty, ca. 1400–1350 BCE. Fresco on dry plaster, 2′ 8″ high. British Museum, London.

Nebamun's wife and daughter—depicted smaller than the deceased—accompany him on his hunt for fowl. A painted inscription states that Nebamun is enjoying recreation in his eternal afterlife.

1 ft.

girl in his cloak. The polished stone shape has its own simple beauty, with the surfaces turning subtly about smoothly rounded corners. The work—one of many surviving statues depicting Senmut with Hatshepsut's daughter—is also a reflection of the power of Egypt's female ruler. The frequent depiction of Senmut with Nefrura was meant to enhance Senmut's stature through his association with the princess (he was her tutor) and, by implication, with Hatshepsut herself.

TOMB OF NEBAMUN Some of the best-preserved mural paintings of the New Kingdom come from the 18th Dynasty Theban tomb of Nebamun, whose official titles were "scribe and counter of grain." On one wall (FIG. 3-28), the painter depicted Nebamun standing in his boat, flushing birds from a papyrus swamp. The hieroglyphic text beneath his left arm says that Nebamun is enjoying recreation in his eternal afterlife. (Here, as elsewhere in Egyptian art, the accompanying text amplifies the message of the picture—and

vice versa.) In contrast to the static pose of Ti watching others hunt hippopotami (FIG. 3-15), the painter showed Nebamun striding forward and vigorously swinging his throwing stick. In his right hand, he holds three birds he has caught. A wild cat, impossibly perched on a papyrus stem just in front of and below him, has caught two more in its claws and is holding the wings of a third in its teeth. Nebamun's wife and daughter accompany him on this hunt and hold the lotuses they have gathered. The artist scaled down their figures in proportion to their rank, as did Old Kingdom artists. And, as in Ti's tomb, the animals show a naturalism based on careful observation.

The painting technique, also employed in earlier Egyptian tombs, is *fresco secco* (dry fresco), whereby artists let the plaster dry

3-29 Musicians and dancers, from the tomb of Nebamun, Thebes, Egypt, 18th Dynasty, ca. 1400–1350 BCE. Fresco on dry plaster, 1′ × 2′ 3″. British Museum, London.

A second fresco in Nebamun's tomb represents a funerary banquet in which the artist experimented with frontal views of faces and bodies— a relaxation of the Old Kingdom's stiff rules of representation.

1 in.

before painting on it. This procedure, in contrast to true fresco painting on wet plaster (see "Fresco Painting," Chapter 19, page 504), permitted slower and more meticulous work than painting on wet plaster, which had to be completed before the plaster dried. Fresco secco, however, is not as durable as true fresco painting, because the colors do not fuse with the wall surface.

Another fresco fragment (FIG. 3-29) from Nebamun's tomb shows four noblewomen watching and apparently participating in a musicale and dance where two nimble and almost nude dancing girls perform at a banquet. When Nebamun was buried, his family must have eaten the customary ceremonial meal at his tomb. They would have returned one day each year to partake in a commemorative banquet for the living to commune with the dead. This fresco represents one of these funerary feasts, with an ample supply of wine jars at the right. It also shows that New Kingdom artists did not always adhere to the old standards for figural representation. This painter carefully recorded the dancers' overlapping figures, their facing in opposite directions, and their rather complicated gyrations, producing a pleasing intertwined motif at the same time. The profile view of the dancers is consistent with their lower stature in the Egyptian hierarchy. The painter still reserved the composite view for Nebamun and his family. Of the four seated women, the artist represented the two at the left conventionally, but the other two face the observer in what is a rarely attempted frontal pose. They clap and beat time to the dance, while one of them plays the reeds. The painter took careful note of the soles of their feet as they sat crosslegged and suggested the movement of the women's heads by the loose arrangement of their hair strands. This informality constituted a relaxation of the Old Kingdom's stiff rules of representation.

The frescoes in Nebamun's tomb testify to the luxurious life of the Egyptian nobility, filled with good food and drink, fine musicians, lithe dancers, and leisure time to hunt and fish in the marshes. But, as in the earlier tomb of Ti, the scenes should be read both literally and allegorically. Although Nebamun is shown enjoying himself in the afterlife, the artist symbolically asked viewers to recall how he got there. Hunting scenes reminded Egyptians of Horus, the son of Osiris, hunting down his father's murderer, Seth, the god of disorder. Successful hunts were metaphors for triumphing over death and disorder, ensuring a happy existence in the afterlife. Music and dance were sacred to Hathor, who aided the dead in their passage to the other world. The sensual women at the banquet are a reference to fertility, rebirth, and regeneration.

Akhenaton and the Amarna Period

Not long after Nebamun was laid to rest in his tomb at Thebes, a revolution occurred in Egyptian society and religion. In the mid-14th century BCE, the pharaoh Amenhotep IV, later known as Akhenaton (r. 1353–1335 BCE), abandoned the worship of most of the Egyptian gods in favor of Aton, identified with the sun disk, whom he declared to be the universal and only god. Akhenaton blotted out the name of Amen from all inscriptions and even from his own name and that of his father, Amenhotep III. He emptied the great temples, enraged the priests, and moved his capital downriver from Thebes to a site he named Akhetaton (after his new god), where he built his own city and shrines. It is now called Amarna. The pharaoh claimed to be both the son and sole prophet of Aton. To him alone could the god make revelation. Moreover, in stark contrast to earlier practice, artists represented Akhenaton's god neither in animal nor in human form but simply as the sun disk emitting life-giving rays. The pharaohs who followed Akhenaton reestablished the cult and priesthood of Amen and restored the temples and the inscriptions. The gigantic temple complex at Karnak (FIG. 3-24), for example, was dedicated to the re-

3-30 Akhenaton, from the temple of Aton, Karnak, Egypt, 18th Dynasty, ca. 1353–1335 BCE. Sandstone, 13′ high. Egyptian Museum, Cairo.

Akhenaton initiated a religious revolution, and his art is also a deliberate reaction against tradition. This curious androgynous image may be an attempt to portray the pharaoh as Aton, the sexless sun disk.

1 ft.

newed worship of the Theban god Amen. Akhenaton's brief religious revolution was soon undone, and his new city was largely abandoned.

During the brief heretical episode of Akhenaton, however, profound changes occurred in Egyptian art. A colossal statue (FIG. 3-30) of Akhenaton from Karnak, toppled and buried after his death, retains the standard frontal pose of canonical pharaonic portraits. But the effeminate body, with its curving contours, and the long face with full lips and heavy-lidded eyes are a far cry indeed from the heroically proportioned figures of the pharaoh's predecessors (compare FIG. 3-13). Akhenaton's body is curiously misshapen, with weak arms, a narrow waist, protruding belly, wide hips, and fatty thighs. Modern doctors have tried to explain his physique by attributing a variety of illnesses to the pharaoh. They cannot agree on a diagnosis, and their premise—that the statue is an accurate depiction of a physical deformity—is probably faulty. Some art historians think that Akhenaton's portrait is a deliberate artistic reaction against the established style, paralleling the suppression of traditional religion. They argue that Akhenaton's artists tried to formulate a new androgynous image of the pharaoh as the manifestation of Aton, the sexless sun disk. But no consensus exists other than that the style was revolutionary and short-lived.

3-31 THUTMOSE, Nefertiti, from Amarna, Egypt, 18th Dynasty, ca. 1353–1335 BCE. Painted limestone, 1′ 8″ high. Ägyptisches Museum, Berlin.

Nefertiti, Akhenaton's influential wife, is portrayed here as an elegant beauty, with a pensive expression and a long, delicately curved neck. The unfinished portrait was found in Thutmose's workshop.

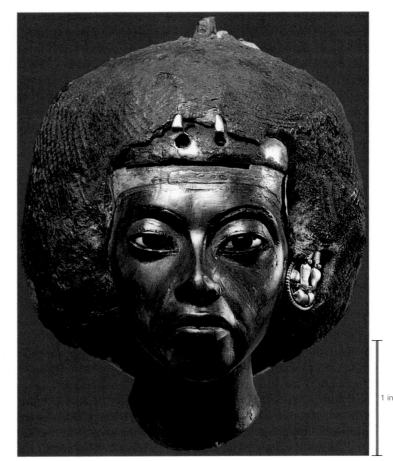

3-32 Tiye, from Ghurab, Egypt, 18th Dynasty, ca. 1353–1335 BCE. Wood, with gold, silver, alabaster, and lapis lazuli, $3\frac{3}{4}$″ high. Ägyptisches Museum, Berlin.

This portrait of Akhenaton's mother is carved of dark yew wood, probably to match the queen's complexion. The head was remodeled during her son's reign to remove all references to traditional deities.

NEFERTITI AND TIYE A painted limestone bust (FIG. 3-31) of Akhenaton's queen, Nefertiti (her name means "The Beautiful One Has Come"), exhibits a similar expression of entranced musing and an almost mannered sensitivity and delicacy of curving contour. The piece was found at Amarna in the workshop of the sculptor THUTMOSE and is a deliberately unfinished model very likely by the master's own hand. The left eye socket still lacks the inlaid eyeball, making the portrait a kind of before-and-after demonstration piece. With this elegant bust, Thutmose may have been alluding to a heavy flower on its slender stalk by exaggerating the weight of the crowned head and the length of the almost serpentine neck. The sculptor seems to have adjusted the actual likeness of his subject to meet the era's standard of spiritual beauty.

A moving portrait of old age is preserved in the miniature head (FIG. 3-32) of Queen Tiye, mother of Akhenaton. Although not of royal birth, Tiye was the daughter of a high-ranking official and became the chief wife of Amenhotep III. Her portrait, carved of dark yew wood, probably to match her complexion, was found at Ghurab

with other objects connected with the funerary cult of Amenhotep III. Another artist probably remodeled the work during her son's reign to eliminate all reference to deities of the old religion. That is when the head acquired the present wig of plaster and linen with small blue beads. Tiye is shown as an older woman with lines and furrows, consistent with the new relaxation of artistic rules in the Amarna age. Her heavy-lidded slanting eyes are inlaid with alabaster and ebony, the lips are painted red, and the earrings (one is hidden by the later wig) are of gold and lapis lazuli. The wig covers what was originally a silver-foil headdress. A gold band still adorns the forehead. Such luxurious materials were common for royal portraits.

Both Nefertiti and Tiye figured prominently in the art and life of the Amarna age. Tiye, for example, regularly appeared in art beside her husband during his reign, and she apparently played an important role in his administration as well as her son's. Letters survive from foreign rulers advising the young Akhenaton to seek his mother's counsel in the conduct of international affairs. Nefertiti too was an influential woman. She frequently appears in the decoration of the Aton temple at Karnak, and she not only equals her husband in size but also sometimes wears pharaonic headgear.

FAMILY PORTRAITURE A sunken relief stele (FIG. 3-33), perhaps from a private shrine, provides a rare look at this royal family. The style is familiar from the colossus of Akhenaton (FIG. 3-30) and the portrait head of Nefertiti (FIG. 3-31). Undulating curves replace rigid lines, and the figures possess the prominent bellies that

In this sunken relief the Amarna artist provided a rare intimate look at the royal family in a domestic setting. Akhenaton, Nefertiti, and three of their daughters bask in the life-giving rays of Aton, the sun disk.

1 in.

characterize figures of the Amarna period. The pharaoh, his wife, and three of their daughters bask in the life-giving rays of Aton, the sun disk. The mood is informal and anecdotal. Akhenaton lifts one of his daughters in order to kiss her. Another daughter sits on Nefertiti's lap and gestures toward her father while the youngest daughter reaches out to touch a pendant on her mother's crown. This kind of intimate portrayal of the pharaoh and his family is unprecedented in Egyptian art. The political and religious revolution under Akhenaton was matched by an equally radical upheaval in art.

The Tomb of Tutankhamen and the Post-Amarna Period

The most famous figure of the Post-Amarna period is Tutankhamen (r. 1333–1323 BCE), who was probably Akhenaton's son by a minor wife. Tutankhamen ruled for a decade and died at age 18. (Although some people speculated foul play, examination of the king's mummy in 2005 ruled out murder.) Tutankhamen was a very minor figure in Egyptian history, however. The public remembers him today solely because in 1922 Howard Carter, a British archaeologist, discovered the boy-king's tomb with its fabulously rich treasure of sculpture, furniture, and jewelry largely intact.

TOMB OF TUTANKHAMEN The principal item that Carter found in Tutankhamen's tomb is the enshrined body of the pharaoh himself. The royal mummy reposed in the innermost of three coffins, nested one within the other. The innermost coffin (FIG. 3-34) was the most luxurious of the three. Made of beaten gold (about a quarter ton of it) and inlaid with semiprecious stones such as lapis lazuli, turquoise, and carnelian, it is a supreme monument to the sculptor's and goldsmith's crafts. The portrait mask (FIG. 3-1), which covered the king's face, is also made of gold with inlaid semiprecious stones. It is a sensitive portrayal of the serene adolescent king dressed in his official regalia, including the nemes headdress and false beard. The general effects of the mask and of the tomb treasures as a whole are of grandeur and richness expressive of Egyptian power, pride, and affluence.

3-34 Innermost coffin of Tutankhamen, from his tomb at Thebes, Egypt, 18th Dynasty, ca. 1323 BCE. Gold with inlay of enamel and semiprecious stones, 6' 1" long. Egyptian Museum, Cairo.

The boy-king Tutankhamen's fame today is due to the discovery of his treasure-laden tomb. His mummy was encased in three nested coffins. The innermost one, made of gold, portrays the pharaoh as Osiris.

1 ft.

3-35 Painted chest, from the tomb of Tutankhamen, Thebes, Egypt, 18th Dynasty, ca. 1333–1323 BCE. Wood, 1′ 8″ long. Egyptian Museum, Cairo.

Tutankhamen is here represented triumphing over Asian enemies. The artist contrasted the orderly registers of Egyptian chariots with the chaotic pile of foreign soldiers who fall before the king.

Although Tutankhamen probably was considered too young to fight, his position as king required that he be represented as a conqueror. He is shown as such in the panels of a painted chest (FIG. 3-35) deposited in his tomb. The lid panel shows the king as a successful hunter pursuing droves of fleeing animals in the desert, and the side panel shows him as a great warrior. From a war chariot pulled by spirited, plumed horses, the pharaoh, shown larger than all other figures on the chest, draws his bow against a cluster of bearded Asian enemies, who fall in confusion before him. (The absence of a ground line in an Egyptian painting or relief implies chaos and death.) Tutankhamen slays the enemy, like game, in great numbers. Behind him are three tiers of undersized war chariots, which serve to magnify the king's figure and to increase the count of his warriors. The themes are traditional, but the fluid, curvilinear forms are features reminiscent of the Amarna style.

3-36 Last judgment of Hu-Nefer, from his tomb at Thebes, Egypt, 19th Dynasty, ca. 1290–1280 BCE. Painted papyrus scroll, 1′ 6″ high. British Museum, London.

The *Book of the Dead* contained spells and prayers. This scroll depicts the weighing of Hu-Nefer's heart against Maat's feather before the deceased can be brought before Osiris, god of the Underworld.

SCROLL OF HU-NEFER Tutankhamen's mummy case (FIG. 3-34) shows the boy-king in the guise of Osiris, god of the dead and king of the Underworld, as well as giver of eternal life. The ritual of the cult of Osiris is recorded in the so-called *Book of the Dead*, a collection of spells and prayers. Illustrated papyrus scrolls, some as long as 70 feet, containing these texts were the essential equipment of the tombs of well-to-do persons (see "Mummification and Immortality," page 57).

The scroll (FIG. 3-36) of Hu-Nefer, the royal scribe and steward of Seti I, was found in his tomb in the Theban necropolis and represents the final judgment of the deceased. At the left, Anubis, the jackal-headed god of embalming, leads Hu-Nefer into the hall of judgment. The god then adjusts the scales to weigh the dead man's heart against the feather of the goddess Maat, protectress of truth and right. A hybrid crocodile-hippopotamus-lion monster, Ammit, devourer of the sinful, awaits the decision of the scales. If the weighing had been unfavorable to the deceased, the monster would have eaten his heart. The ibis-headed god Thoth records the proceedings. Above, the gods of the Egyptian pantheon are arranged as witnesses, while Hu-Nefer kneels in adoration before them. Having been justified by the scales, Hu-Nefer is brought by Osiris's son, the falcon-headed Horus, into the presence of the green-faced Osiris and his sisters Isis and Nephthys to receive the award of eternal life.

In Hu-Nefer's scroll, the figures have all the formality of stance, shape, and attitude of traditional Egyptian art. Abstract figures and hieroglyphs alike are aligned rigidly. Nothing here was painted in the flexible, curvilinear style suggestive of movement that was evident in the art of Amarna and Tutankhamen. The return to conservatism is unmistakable.

FIRST MILLENNIUM BCE

During the first millennium BCE, Egypt lost the commanding role it once had played in the ancient Near East. The empire dwindled away, and foreign powers invaded, occupied, and ruled the land, until it was taken over by Alexander the Great of Macedon and his Greek successors and, eventually, by the emperors of Rome.

Kingdom of Kush

One of those foreign powers was Egypt's gold-rich neighbor to the south, the kingdom of Kush, part of which is in present-day Sudan. Called Nubia by the Romans, perhaps from the Egyptian word for "gold," Kush is mentioned in Egyptian texts as early as the Old Kingdom. During the New Kingdom, the pharaohs colonized Nubia and appointed a viceroy to administer the Kushite kingdom, which included Abu Simbel (FIG. 3-22) and controlled the major trade route between Egypt and sub-Saharan Africa. But in the eighth century BCE, the Nubians conquered Egypt and ruled the land of the Nile as the 25th Dynasty.

TAHARQO Around 680 BCE, the Kushite pharaoh Taharqo (r. 690–664 BCE) constructed a temple at Kawa and placed a portrait of himself in it. Emulating traditional Egyptian types, the sculptor portrayed Taharqo as a sphinx (FIG. 3-37; compare FIG. 3-11) with the ears, mane, and body of a lion but with a human face and a head-dress with two uraeus cobras. The king's name is inscribed on his chest, and his features are distinctly African, although, as in all pharaonic portraiture, they should be considered generic and idealized rather than a specific likeness.

3-37A Mentuemhet, Karnak, ca. 660–650 BCE.

1 in.

3-37 Taharqo as a sphinx, from temple T, Kawa, Sudan, 25th Dynasty, ca. 680 BCE. Granite, 1′ 4″ × 2′ 4¾″. British Museum, London.

Nubian kings ruled Egypt during the 25th Dynasty and adopted traditional Egyptian artistic types, but the sculptor of the Taharqo sphinx reproduced the Kushite pharaoh's distinctly African features.

3-38 Temple of Horus, Edfu, Egypt, ca. 237–47 BCE.

The pylon temple at Edfu is more than a thousand years later than that at Karnak (FIG. 3-24), but it adheres to the same basic architectural scheme. Egyptian artistic forms tended to have very long lives.

After Alexander

Once formulated, Egyptian traditions tended to have very long lives, in architecture as in the other arts—even after Alexander the Great established Greek rule in the land of the Nile.

TEMPLE OF HORUS, EDFU The temple of Horus at Edfu (FIG. 3-38), built during the third, second, and first centuries BCE, after Alexander the Great's conquest of Egypt, still follows the basic pylon temple scheme architects worked out more than a thousand years before (compare the temple of Amen-Re at Karnak, FIG. 3-24). The great entrance pylon at Edfu is especially impressive. The broad sur-

face of its massive facade, with its sloping walls, is broken only by the doorway with its overshadowing *moldings* at the top and sides, deep channels to hold great flagstaffs, and sunken reliefs. The reliefs depict Horus and Hathor witnessing an oversized King Ptolemy XIII (r. 51–47 BCE) smiting undersized enemies. It is a striking monument to the persistence of Egyptian architectural and sculptural types.

Indeed, the exceptional longevity of formal traditions in Egypt is one of the marvels of the history of art. It testifies to the invention of an artistic style so satisfactory that it endured in Egypt for millennia. Everywhere else in the ancient Mediterranean world, stylistic change was the only common denominator.

EGYPT UNDER THE PHARAOHS

PREDYNASTIC AND EARLY DYNASTIC PERIODS, ca. 3500–2575 BCE

▊ The unification of Upper and Lower Egypt into a single kingdom under the rule of a divine pharaoh occurred around 3000–2920 BCE. The event was commemorated on the earliest preserved work of narrative art, the palette of King Narmer, which also established the basic principles of Egyptian representational art for 3,000 years.

▊ Imhotep, the first artist in history whose name is known, established the tradition of monumental stone architecture in Egypt in the funerary complex and Stepped Pyramid he built for King Djoser (r. 2630–2611 BCE) at Saqqara.

Palette of King Narmer,
ca. 3000–2920 BCE

OLD KINGDOM, ca. 2575–2134 BCE

▊ The Old Kingdom was the first golden age of Egyptian art and architecture, the time when three pharaohs of the Fourth Dynasty erected the Great Pyramids at Gizeh, the oldest of the Seven Wonders of the ancient world. The pyramids were emblems of the sun on whose rays the pharaohs ascended to the heavens after their death.

▊ Old Kingdom sculptors created seated and standing statuary types in which all movement was suppressed in order to express the eternal nature of pharaonic kingship. These types would dominate Egyptian art for 2,000 years.

Great Sphinx and Pyramids, Gizeh,
ca. 2550–2475 BCE

MIDDLE KINGDOM, ca. 2040–1640 BCE

▊ After an intermediate period of civil war, Mentuhotep II (r. 2050–1998 BCE) reestablished central rule and founded the Middle Kingdom.

▊ The major artistic innovation of this period was the rock-cut tomb in which both the facade and interior chambers were hewn out of the living rock. The fluted columns in Middle Kingdom tombs closely resemble the columns later used in Greek temples.

Tomb of Amenemhet, Beni Hasan,
ca. 1950–1900 BCE

NEW KINGDOM, ca. 1550–1070 BCE

▊ During the New Kingdom, Egypt extended its borders to the Euphrates River in the east and deep into Nubia in the south.

▊ The most significant architectural innovation of this period was the axially planned pylon temple incorporating an immense gateway, columnar courtyards, and a hypostyle hall with clerestory windows.

▊ Powerful pharaohs such as Hatshepsut (r. 1473–1458 BCE) and Ramses II (r. 1290–1224 BCE) erected gigantic temples in honor of their patron gods and, after their deaths, for their own worship.

▊ Akhenaton (r. 1353–1335 BCE) abandoned the traditional Egyptian religion in favor of Aton, the sun disk, and initiated a short-lived artistic revolution in which undulating curves and anecdotal content replaced the cubic forms and impassive stillness of earlier Egyptian art.

Akhenaton, Nefertiti, and three
daughters, ca. 1353–1335 BCE

FIRST MILLENNIUM BCE

▊ After the demise of the New Kingdom, Egypt's power in the ancient world declined and it came under the control of foreigners, such as the Kushite kings of Nubia and, after 332 BCE, Alexander the Great and his Greek successors. In 30 BCE, Egypt became a province of the Roman Empire.

▊ The traditional forms of Egyptian art and architecture lived on even under foreign rule—for example, in the pylon temple erected at Edfu in honor of Horus.

Temple of Horus, Edfu,
ca. 237–47 BCE

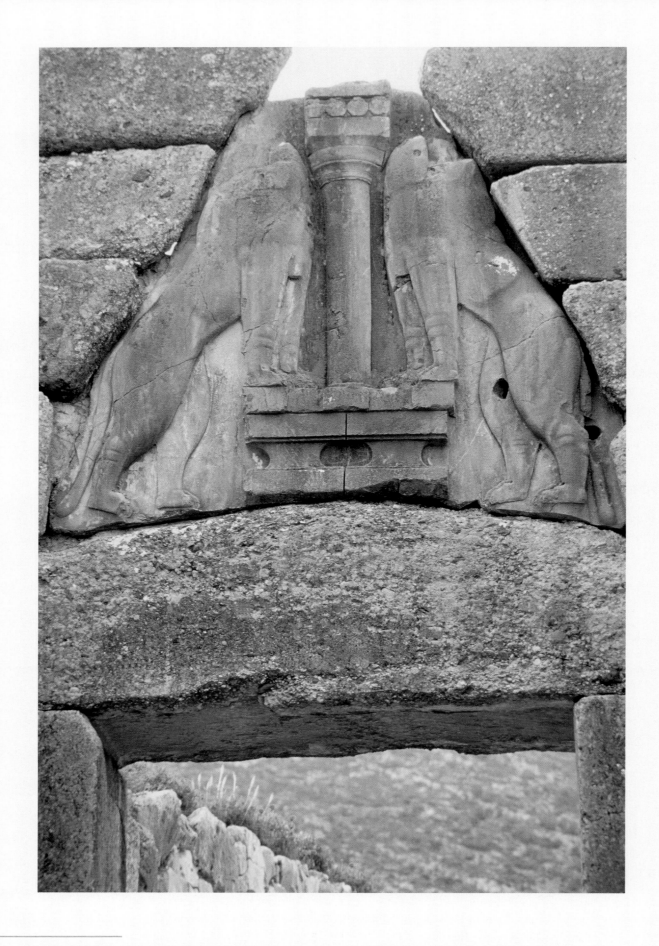

4-1 Relieving triangle with confronting lions, detail of Lion Gate (FIG. 4-19), Mycenae, Greece, ca. 1300–1250 BCE.

The gateway to the citadel of Mycenae, legendary home of King Agamemnon of Homer's *Iliad,* was built of such large stones that the later Greeks believed that giants, not mortals, erected it.

THE PREHISTORIC AEGEAN

In the *Iliad,* Homer describes the might and splendor of the Greek armies poised before the walls of Troy.

> Clan after clan poured out from the ships and huts onto the plain . . . innumerable as the leaves and blossoms in their season . . . the Athenians . . . the men of Argos and Tiryns of the Great Walls . . . troops from the great stronghold of Mycenae, from wealthy Corinth . . . from Knossos . . . Phaistos . . . and the other troops that had their homes in Crete of the Hundred Towns.[1]

The Greeks had come from far and wide, from the mainland and the islands (MAP **4-1**), to seek revenge against Paris, the Trojan prince who had abducted Helen, wife of King Menelaus of Sparta. Composed around 750 BCE, the *Iliad* is the first great work of Greek literature. In fact, until about 1870, Homer's epic poem was generally regarded as pure fiction. Scholars discounted the bard as a historian, attributing the profusion of names and places in his writings to the rich abundance of his imagination. The prehistory of Greece remained shadowy and lost in an impenetrable world of myth.

TROY AND MYCENAE In the late 1800s, however, a wealthy German businessman turned archaeologist proved that scholars had done less than justice to the truth of Homer's account. Between 1870 and his death 20 years later, Heinrich Schliemann (whose methods have sometimes been harshly criticized) uncovered some of the very cities Homer named. In 1870, he began work at Hissarlik on the northwestern coast of Turkey, which a British archaeologist, Frank Calvert, had postulated was the site of Homer's Troy. Schliemann dug into a vast mound and found a number of fortified cities built on the remains of one another. One of them had been destroyed by fire in the 13th century BCE. This, scholars now generally agree, was the Troy of King Priam and his son Paris, the city Homer celebrated some 500 years later.

Schliemann continued his excavations at Mycenae on the Greek mainland, where, he believed, King Agamemnon, Menelaus's brother, had once ruled. Here his finds were even more startling. A massive fortress-palace with a monumental gateway (FIGS. **4-1** and **4-19**); domed tombs beneath earthen mounds (FIGS. **4-20** and **4-21**); quantities of gold jewelry, masks (FIG. **4-22**), and cups; and inlaid bronze weapons

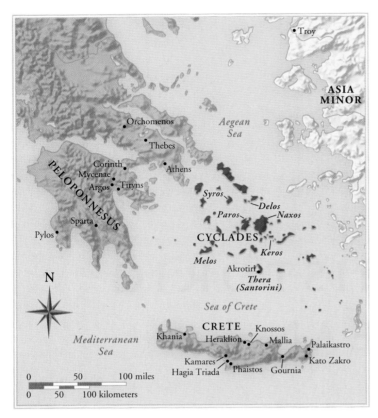

MAP 4-1 The prehistoric Aegean.

(FIG. 4-23) revealed a magnificent civilization far older than the famous vestiges of Classical Greece that had remained visible in Athens and elsewhere. Further discoveries proved that Mycenae had not been the only center of this fabulous civilization.

MINOAN CRETE Another legendary figure was King Minos of Knossos on the island of Crete. He had exacted from Athens a tribute of youths and maidens to be fed to the *Minotaur,* a creature half bull and half man housed in a vast labyrinth. Might this story, too, be based on fact? In 1900, an English archaeologist, Arthur Evans, began work at Knossos, where he uncovered a palace (FIGS. 4-4 and 4-5) that did indeed resemble a maze. Evans named its builders the Minoans, after their mythological king. Further evidence of the Minoans was soon uncovered at Phaistos, Hagia Triada, and other sites, including Gournia, which Harriet Boyd Hawes, an American archaeologist (and one of the first women of any nationality to direct a major excavation), explored between 1901 and 1904.

More recently, important Minoan remains have been excavated at many other locations on Crete, and contemporary sites have been discovered on other islands in the Aegean, most notably on Santorini (ancient Thera). Art historians now have many buildings, paintings, and, to a lesser extent, sculptures that attest to the wealth and sophistication of the people who lived in that once-obscure heroic age celebrated in later Greek mythology.

AEGEAN ARCHAEOLOGY TODAY Less glamorous than the palaces and art objects, but arguably more important for the understanding of Aegean society, are the many documents archaeologists have found written in scripts dubbed Linear A and Linear B. The progress made during the past several decades in deciphering these texts has provided a welcome corrective to the romanticism that characterized the work of Schliemann and Evans. Linear B can now be read as an early form of Greek, and scholars have begun to reconstruct Aegean civilization by referring to contemporaneous records and not just to Homer's heroic account. Archaeologists now also know that humans

inhabited Greece as far back as the late Paleolithic period and that village life was firmly established in Greece and on Crete in Neolithic times. But the heyday of the ancient Aegean was not until the second millennium BCE, well after the emergence of the river valley civilizations of Mesopotamia, Egypt, and South Asia (see Chapters 2, 3, and 6).

The prehistoric Aegean has three geographic areas, and each has its own distinctive artistic identity. *Cycladic* art is the art of the Cycladic Islands (so named because they *circle* around Delos), as well as of the adjacent islands in the Aegean, excluding Crete. *Minoan* art encompasses the art of Crete. *Helladic* art is the art of the Greek mainland (*Hellas* in Greek). Scholars subdivide each area chronologically into early, middle, and late periods, with the art of the Late Helladic period designated Mycenaean after Agamemnon's great citadel of Mycenae.

CYCLADIC ART

Marble was abundantly available in the superb quarries of the Aegean Islands, especially on Naxos and Paros. The sculptors of the Early Cycladic period used that marble to produce statuettes (FIGS. 4-2 and 4-3) that collectors highly admire today (see "Archaeology, Art History, and the Art Market," page 83) because of their striking abstract forms, which call to mind the simple and sleek shapes of some modern sculptures (FIG. 35-20).

WOMAN FROM SYROS Most of the Cycladic sculptures, like many of their Stone Age predecessors in the Aegean, the Near East, and western Europe (FIG. 1-5), represent nude women with their arms folded across their abdomens. They have been found both in graves and in settlements and vary in height from a few inches to almost life-size. The statuette illustrated here (FIG. 4-2) is about a foot and a half tall—but only about a half inch thick—and comes from a grave on the island of Syros. The sculptor rendered the human body in a highly schematic manner. Large simple triangles dominate the form—the head, the body itself (which tapers from exceptionally broad shoulders to tiny feet), and the incised triangular pubis. The feet are too fragile to support the figurine. It must have been placed on its back in the grave—lying down, like the deceased. Whether the Syros statuette and the many other similar Cycladic figurines known

4-2 Figurine of a woman, from Syros (Cyclades), Greece, ca. 2500–2300 BCE. Marble, 1′ 6″ high. National Archaeological Museum, Athens.

Most Cycladic statuettes depict nude women. This one comes from a grave, but whether it represents the deceased is uncertain. The sculptor rendered the female body schematically as a series of large triangles.

1 in.

Archaeology, Art History, and the Art Market

One way the ancient world is fundamentally different from the world today is that ancient art is largely anonymous and undated. No equivalent exists in antiquity for the systematic signing and dating of artworks commonplace in the contemporary world. That is why the role of archaeology in the study of ancient art is so important. Only the scientific excavation of ancient monuments can establish their context. Exquisite and strikingly "modern" sculptures such as the marble Cycladic figurines illustrated in FIGS. 4-2 and 4-3 may be appreciated as masterpieces when displayed in splendid isolation in glass cases in museums or private homes. But to understand the role these or any other artworks played in ancient society—in many cases, even to determine the date and place of origin of an object—the art historian must know where the piece was uncovered. Only when the context of an artwork is known can one go beyond an appreciation of its formal qualities and begin to analyze its place in art history—and in the society that produced it.

The extraordinary popularity of Cycladic figurines in recent decades has had unfortunate consequences. Clandestine treasure hunters, eager to meet the insatiable demands of modern collectors, have plundered many sites and smuggled their finds out of Greece to sell to the highest bidder on the international art market. Entire prehistoric cemeteries and towns have been destroyed because of the high esteem in which these sculptures are now held. Two British scholars have calculated that only about 10 percent of the known Cycladic marble statuettes come from secure archaeological contexts. Many of the rest could be forgeries produced after World War II when developments in modern art fostered a new appreciation of these abstract renditions of human anatomy and created a boom in demand for "Cycladica" among collectors. For some categories of Cycladic sculptures—those of unusual type or size—not a single piece with a documented provenance exists. Those groups may be 20th-century inventions designed to fetch even higher prices due to their rarity. Consequently, most of the conclusions art historians have drawn about chronology, attribution to different workshops, range of types, and how the figurines were used are purely speculative. The importance of the information the original contexts would have provided cannot be overestimated. That information, however, can probably never be recovered.

4-3 Male lyre player, from Keros (Cyclades), Greece, ca. 2700–2500 BCE. Marble, 9″ high. National Archaeological Museum, Athens.

The meaning of all Cycladic figurines is elusive, but this seated musician may be playing for the deceased in the afterlife. The statuette displays the same simple geometric shapes and flat planes as FIG. 4-2.

today represent dead women or fertility figures or goddesses is still debated. In any case, the sculptors took pains to emphasize the breasts as well as the pubic area. In the Syros statuette, a slight swelling of the belly may suggest pregnancy. Traces of paint found on some of the Cycladic figurines indicate that at least parts of these sculptures were colored. The now almost featureless faces would have had painted eyes and mouths in addition to the sculpted noses. Red and blue necklaces and bracelets, as well as painted dots on the cheeks and necks, characterize a number of the surviving figurines.

LYRE PLAYER FROM KEROS Male figures also occur in the Cycladic repertoire. The most elaborate of these take the form of seated musicians, such as the lyre player (FIG. **4-3**) from Keros. Wedged between the echoing shapes of chair and instrument, he may be playing for the deceased in the afterlife, although, again, the meaning of these statuettes remains elusive. The harpist reflects

the same preference for simple geometric shapes and large flat planes as the female figures. Still, the artist showed a keen interest in recording the elegant shape of what must have been a prized possession: the harp with a duck-bill or swan-head ornament at the apex of its sound box. (Animal-headed instruments are well documented in contemporary Mesopotamia [FIG. **2-10**] and Egypt.)

In one instance, figurines of both a musician and a reclining woman were placed in a woman's grave. This suggests that the lyre players are not images of dead men, but it does not prove that the female figurines represent dead women. The man might be entertaining the deceased herself, not her image. Given the absence of written documents in Greece at this date, as everywhere else in prehistoric times, and the lack of information about the provenance of most finds, art historians cannot be sure of the meaning of the Cycladic sculptures. It is likely, in fact, that the same form took on different meanings in different contexts.

MINOAN ART

During the third millennium BCE, both on the Aegean Islands and on the Greek mainland, most settlements were small and consisted only of simple buildings. Only rarely were the dead buried with costly offerings such as the Cycladic statuettes just examined. In contrast, the construction of large palaces marked the opening centuries of the second millennium (the Middle Minoan period on Crete).

Architecture

The first, or Old Palace, period came to an abrupt end around 1700 BCE, when fire destroyed these grand structures, probably following an earthquake. Rebuilding began almost immediately, and the ensu-ing Late Minoan (New Palace) period is the golden age of Crete, an era when the first great Western civilization emerged. The rebuilt palaces were large, comfortable, and handsome, with residential suites for the king and his family and courtyards for pageants, cere-monies, and games. They also had storerooms, offices, and shrines that permitted these huge complexes to serve as the key administra-tive, commercial, and religious centers of Minoan life. The principal palace sites on Crete are at Knossos, Phaistos, Mallia, Kato Zakro, and Khania. All of the complexes were laid out along similar lines. Their size and number, as well as the rich finds they have yielded, at-test to the power and prosperity of the Minoans.

PALACE AT KNOSSOS The largest of the palaces, at Knossos (FIGS. 4-4 and 4-5), was the legendary home of King Minos. Here,

4-4 Aerial view (looking northeast) of the palace at Knossos (Crete), Greece, ca. 1700–1400 BCE.

The Knossos palace is the largest on Crete and was the legendary home of King Minos. Its layout features a large central court, around which all the residential and administrative units were grouped.

4-5 Plan of the palace at Knossos (Crete), Greece, ca. 1700–1400 BCE.

The mazelike plan of the Knossos palace gave rise to the Greek myth of the Cretan labyrinth inhabited by the Minotaur, a half-man half-bull monster that the Athenian king Theseus killed.

Earlier structures { Reconstruction / Existing / Reconstruction

1. West porch
2. Corridor of the procession
3. South propylon
4. Central court
5. "Theater area"
6. North-south corridor
7. Pillar hall
8. Magazines
9. Throne room
10. Palace shrine and lower verandas
11. Stepped porch
12. Grand staircase
13. Light well
14. East-west corridor
15. Hall of the Double Axes (principal reception room)
16. "Queen's Megaron"

0 25 50 75 100 feet
0 10 20 30 meters

the hero Theseus was said to have battled with the bull-man Minotaur. According to the myth, after defeating the monster, Theseus found his way out of the mazelike complex only with the aid of the king's daughter, Ariadne. She had given Theseus a spindle of thread to mark his path through the labyrinth and thus to find his way out safely again. In fact, the English word *labyrinth* derives from the intricate plan and scores of rooms of the Knossos palace. *Labrys* means "double ax," and it is a recurring motif in the Minoan palace, referring to sacrificial slaughter. The labyrinth was the "House of the Double Axes."

The Knossos palace was a rambling structure built against the upper slopes and across the top of a low hill that rises from a fertile plain (FIG. 4-4). All around the palace proper were mansions and villas of the Minoan elite. The great rectangular court (FIG. 4-5, no. 4), with the palace units grouped around it, had been leveled in the time of the old palace. The new layout suggests that the later palace was carefully planned, with the court serving as the major organizing element. A secondary organization of the palace plan involves two long corridors. On the west side of the court, a north-south corridor (FIG. 4-5, no. 6) separates official and ceremonial rooms from the storerooms (no. 8), where wine, grain, oil, and honey were stockpiled in large jars. On the east side of the court, a smaller east-west corridor (no. 14) separates the administrative areas (to the south) from the workrooms (to the north). At the northwest corner of the palace is a theaterlike area (no. 5) with steps on two sides that may have served as seats. This form is a possible forerunner of the later Greek theater (FIG. 5-71). Its purpose is unknown, but it is a feature paralleled in the Phaistos palace.

The Knossos palace was complex in elevation as well as plan. It had as many as three stories around the central court and even more on the south and east sides where the terrain sloped off sharply.

Interior light and air wells with staircases (FIG. 4-6) provided necessary illumination and ventilation. The Minoans also gave thought to issues such as drainage of rainwater. At Knossos, a remarkably efficient system of terracotta pipes underlies the enormous building.

The Cretan palaces were well constructed, with thick walls composed of rough, unshaped fieldstones embedded in clay. The builders used ashlar masonry at corners and around door and window openings. The painted wooden columns (which Evans restored in cement at Knossos) have distinctive capitals and shafts. The bulbous, cushionlike Minoan capitals resemble those of the later Greek Doric order (FIG. 5-14), but the column shafts—essentially stylized inverted tree trunks—taper from a wide top to a narrower base, the opposite of both Egyptian and later Greek columns.

Painting

Mural paintings liberally adorn the palace at Knossos, constituting one of its most striking features. The brightly painted walls and the red shafts and black capitals of the wooden columns provided an extraordinarily rich effect. The paintings depict many aspects of Minoan life (bull-leaping, processions, and ceremonies) and of nature (birds, animals, flowers, and marine life).

LA PARISIENNE From a ceremonial scene of uncertain significance comes the fragment (FIG. 4-7) dubbed *La Parisienne* (The Parisian Woman) on its discovery because of the elegant dress, elaborate coiffure, and full rouged lips of the young woman depicted. Some have argued that she is a priestess taking part in a religious ritual, but because the figure has no arms, it is most likely a statue of a goddess. Although the representation is still convention-bound (note especially the oversized frontal eye in the profile head), the charm and freshness of the mural are undeniable. Unlike the

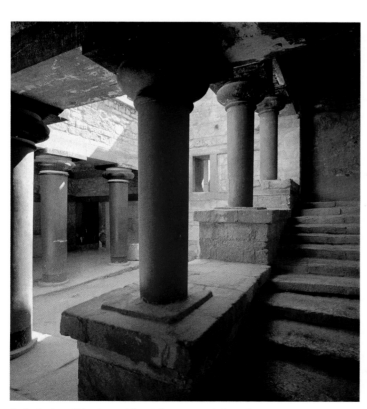

4-6 Stairwell in the residential quarter of the palace at Knossos (Crete), Greece, ca. 1700–1400 BCE.

The Knossos palace was complex in elevation as well as plan. It had at least three stories on all sides of the court. Minoan columns taper from top to bottom, the opposite of Egyptian and Greek columns.

4-7 Minoan woman or goddess (*La Parisienne*), from the palace at Knossos (Crete), Greece, ca. 1450–1400 BCE. Fragment of a fresco, 10″ high. Archaeological Museum, Herakleion.

Frescoes decorated the Knossos palace walls. This fragment depicts a woman or a goddess—perhaps a statue—with a large frontal eye in her profile head, as seen also in Near Eastern and Egyptian art.

1 in.

4-8 Bull-leaping, from the palace at Knossos (Crete), Greece, ca. 1450–1400 BCE. Fresco, 2′ 8″ high, including border. Archaeological Museum, Herakleion. 📹

The subjects of the Knossos frescoes are often ceremonial scenes, like this one of bull-leaping. The women have fair skin and the man has dark skin, a common convention in ancient painting.

1 ft.

Egyptians, who painted in *fresco secco* (dry fresco), the Minoans coated the rough fabric of their rubble walls with a fine white lime plaster and used a true (wet) fresco method in which the pigments are mixed with water and become chemically bound to the plaster after it dries (see "Fresco Painting," Chapter 19, page 504). Consequently, the Minoan painters had to execute their work rapidly while the walls were still wet, in contrast to Egyptian practice.

4-8A Sarcophagus, Hagia Triada, ca. 1450–1400 BCE.

BULL-LEAPING Another fresco (FIG. 4-8) from the palace at Knossos depicts the Minoan ceremony of bull-leaping, in which young men grasped the horns of a bull and vaulted onto its back—a perilous and extremely difficult acrobatic maneuver. Only fragments of the full composition have been recovered (the dark patches are original; the rest is a modern restoration). The Minoan artist painted the young women (with fair skin) and the youth (with dark skin) according to the widely accepted ancient convention for distinguishing male and female. The painter brilliantly suggested the powerful charge of the bull by elongating the animal's shape and using sweeping lines to form a funnel of energy, beginning at the very narrow hindquarters of the bull and culminating in its large, sharp horns and galloping forelegs. The human figures also have stylized shapes, with typically Minoan pinched waists, and are highly animated. Although the profile pose with the full-view eye was a familiar convention in Egypt and Mesopotamia, the elegance of the Cretan figures, with their long, curly hair and proud and self-confident bearing, distinguishes them from all other early figure styles. In contrast to the angularity of the figures in Egyptian wall paintings, the curving lines the Minoan artist employed suggest the elasticity of living and moving beings.

THERA FRESCOES Much better preserved than the Knossos frescoes are those Greek archaeologists discovered in excavations begun in 1967 and still in progress at Akrotiri on the volcanic island of Santorini (ancient Thera) in the Cyclades, some 60 miles north of Crete. In the Late Cycladic period, Thera was artistically, and possibly also politically, within the Minoan orbit. The mural paintings from Akrotiri are invaluable additions to the fragmentary and frequently misrestored frescoes from Crete. The excellent condition of the Theran paintings is due to an enormous seismic explosion on Santorini that buried Akrotiri in volcanic pumice and ash, making it a kind of Pompeii of the prehistoric Aegean (see "The Theran Eruption and the Chronology of Aegean Art," page 87). The Akrotiri frescoes decorated the walls of houses, not the walls of a great palace such as that at Knossos, and therefore the number of painted walls from the site is especially impressive.

4-9A Miniature Ships Fresco, Akrotiri, ca. 1650 BCE.

The almost perfectly preserved mural painting from Akrotiri known as the *Spring Fresco* (FIG. 4-9) is one of the earliest examples of a pure landscape painting (compare FIG. 1-18). The artist's aim, however, was not to render the rocky island terrain realistically but rather to capture the landscape's essence. The irrationally undulating and vividly colored rocks, the graceful lilies swaying in the cool island breezes, and the darting swallows express the vigor of growth, the delicacy of flowering, and the lightness of birdsong and flight. In the lyrical language of curving line, the artist celebrated the rhythms of spring. The *Spring Fresco* represents the polar opposite of the first efforts at mural painting in the caves of Paleolithic Europe (see Chapter 1), where animals (and occasionally humans) appeared as isolated figures without any indication of setting.

4-9B Crocus gatherers, Akrotiri, ca. 1650 BCE.

The Theran Eruption and the Chronology of Aegean Art

Today, ships bound for the beautiful Greek island of Santorini, with its picture-postcard white houses, churches, shops, and restaurants, weigh anchor in a bay beneath steep, crescent-shaped cliffs. Until about 20,000 BCE, however, ancient Thera had a roughly circular shape and gentler slopes. Then, suddenly, a volcanic eruption blew out the center of the island, leaving behind the moon-shaped main island and several lesser islands grouped around a bay that roughly corresponds to the shape of the gigantic ancient volcano. The volcano erupted again, thousands of years later, during the zenith of Aegean civilization.

In that eruption, the site of Akrotiri, which Greek excavators gradually are uncovering, was buried by a layer of pumice more than a yard deep in some areas and by an even larger volume of volcanic ash (*tephra*) that often exceeds five yards in depth, even after nearly 37 centuries of erosion. Tephra filled whole rooms, and boulders the volcano spewed forth pelted the walls of some houses. Closer to the volcano's cone, the tephra is almost 60 yards deep in places. In fact, the force of the eruption was so powerful that sea currents carried the pumice and wind blew the ash throughout the ancient Mediterranean, not only to Crete, Rhodes, and Cyprus but also as far away as Anatolia, Egypt, Syria, and Israel.

Until recently, most scholars embraced the theory formulated decades ago by Spyridon Marinatos, an eminent Greek archaeolo-

gist, that the otherwise unexplained demise of Minoan civilization on Crete around 1500 BCE was the by-product of the volcanic eruption on Thera. According to Marinatos, devastating famine followed the rain of ash that fell on Crete. But archaeologists now know that after the eruption, life went on in Crete, if not on Thera. At one Cretan site, the Minoans collected Theran pumice and deposited it in conical cups on a monumental stairway, possibly as a votive offering.

Teams of researchers, working closely in an impressive and most welcome interdisciplinary effort, have pinpointed 1628 BCE as the date of a major climatic event. They have studied tree rings at sites in Europe and in North America for evidence of retarded growth and have examined ice cores in Greenland for peak acidity layers. Both kinds of evidence testify to a significant disruption in weather patterns in that year. Most scholars now believe the cause of this disruption was the cataclysmic volcanic eruption on Thera. The discovery in 2006 of a datable olive tree in the Santorini tephra brought welcome confirmation for this theory.

The new 17th-century BCE date has profound consequences for the chronology of Aegean art. The Akrotiri frescoes (FIG. 4-9) must be around 150 years older than scholars thought when they were first discovered. The frescoes predate by many decades the Knossos palace murals (FIGS. 4-7 and 4-8).

4-9 Landscape with swallows (*Spring Fresco*), from room Delta 2, Akrotiri, Thera (Cyclades), Greece, ca. 1650 BCE. Fresco, 7′ 6″ high. National Archaeological Museum, Athens.

Aegean muralists painted in wet fresco, which required rapid execution. In this first known pure landscape, the Theran painter used vivid colors and undulating lines to capture the essence of springtime.

1 ft.

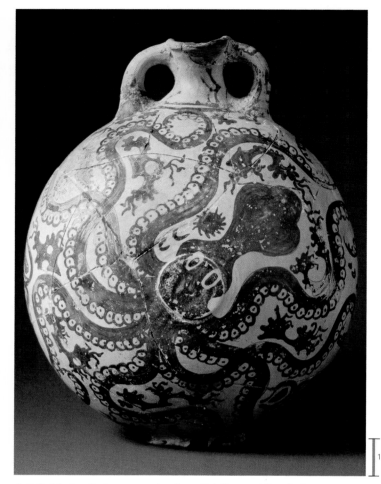

4-10 Kamares-ware jar, from Phaistos (Crete), Greece, ca. 1800–1700 BCE. 1′ 8″ high. Archaeological Museum, Herakleion.

Kamares vases have creamy white and reddish-brown decoration on a black background. This jar combines a fish (and a net?) with curvilinear abstract patterns including spirals and waves.

4-11 Marine Style octopus jar, from Palaikastro (Crete), Greece, ca. 1500 BCE. 11″ high. Archaeological Museum, Herakleion.

Marine Style vases have dark figures on a light ground. On this octopus jar the tentacles of the sea creature reach out over the curving surface of the vessel to fill the shape perfectly.

MINOAN POTTERY The love of nature manifested itself in Crete on the surfaces of painted vases even before the period of the new palaces. During the Middle Minoan period, Cretan potters fashioned sophisticated shapes using newly introduced potters' wheels, and decorated their vases in a distinctive and fully polychromatic style. These Kamares-ware vessels, named for the cave on the slope of Mount Ida where they were first discovered, have been found in quantity at Phaistos and Knossos and at sites throughout the Mediterranean and Near East. On the illustrated jar (FIG. **4-10**), as on other Kamares vases, the painter set creamy white and reddish-brown decoration against a rich black ground. The central motif is a great leaping fish and perhaps a fishnet surrounded by a host of curvilinear abstract patterns including waves and spirals. The swirling lines evoke life in the sea, and both the abstract and the natural forms beautifully complement the shape of the vessel.

The sea and the creatures that inhabit it also inspired the Late Minoan Marine Style octopus jar (FIG. **4-11**) from Palaikastro, which is contemporary with the new palaces at Knossos and elsewhere. The tentacles of the octopus reach out over the curving surfaces of the vessel, embracing the piece and emphasizing its volume. This is a masterful realization of the relationship between the vessel's decoration and its shape, always a problem for the vase painter. This later jar differs markedly from its Kamares-ware predecessor in color. Not only is the octopus vase more muted in tone, but the Late

Minoan artist also reversed the earlier scheme and placed dark silhouettes on a light ground. This dark-on-light format remained the norm for about a millennium in Greece, until about 530 BCE when, albeit in a very different form, light figures and a dark background emerged once again as the preferred manner (compare FIG. 5-22, *left* and *right*).

Sculpture

In contrast to Mesopotamia and Egypt, no temples or monumental statues of gods, kings, or monsters have been found in Minoan Crete. Large wooden images may once have existed—*La Parisienne* (FIG. 4-7) may depict one of them—but what remains of Minoan sculpture is uniformly small in scale.

SNAKE GODDESS One of the most striking finds at the palace at Knossos was the *faience* (low-fired opaque glasslike silicate) statuette popularly known as the *Snake Goddess* (FIG. **4-12**). Reconstructed from many pieces, it is one of several similar figurines that some scholars believe may represent mortal attendants rather than a deity, although the prominently exposed breasts suggest that these figurines stand in the long line of prehistoric fertility images usually considered divinities. The Knossos woman holds snakes in her hands and also supports a leopardlike feline on her head. This implied power over the animal world also seems appropriate for a

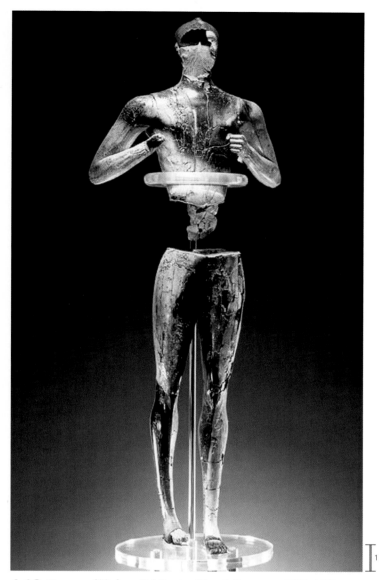

4-12 *Snake Goddess,* from the palace at Knossos (Crete), Greece, ca. 1600 BCE. Faience, $1' 1\frac{1}{2}''$ high. Archaeological Museum, Herakleion.

This figurine may represent a priestess, but it is more likely a bare-breasted goddess. The snakes in her hands and the feline on her head imply that she has power over the animal world.

4-13 Young god(?), from Palaikastro (Crete), Greece, ca. 1500–1475 BCE. Ivory, gold, serpentine, and rock crystal, restored height $1' 7\frac{1}{2}''$. Archaeological Museum, Siteia.

This statuette, probably representing a young god, is a very early example of chryselephantine (gold and ivory) sculpture, a technique later used for the largest and costliest Greek cult statues.

deity. The frontality of the figure is reminiscent of Egyptian and Near Eastern statuary, but the costume, with its open bodice and flounced skirt, is distinctly Minoan. If the statuette represents a goddess, as seems likely, then it is yet another example of how human beings fashion their gods in their own image.

PALAIKASTRO YOUTH British excavations at Palaikastro between 1987 and 1990 yielded fragments of one of the most remarkable objects ever found on Crete. It is a statuette (FIG. **4-13**) nearly 20 inches tall, fashioned from hippopotamus-tusk ivory, gold, serpentine, and rock crystal. The figurine is a very early example of *chryselephantine* (gold and ivory) sculpture, a technique that the Greeks would later use for their largest and costliest cult images (FIG. **5-46**). The ivory and gold were probably imported from Egypt, the source also of the pose with left foot advanced (FIG. **3-13**), but the style and iconography are unmistakably Cretan. The work is the creation of a sculptor of extraordinary ability who delighted in rendering minute details of muscles and veins. The Palaikastro youth (his

coiffure, with shaved head save for a central braid, indicates his age) was displayed alone in a shrine and therefore seems to have been a god rather than a mortal. Archaeologists found the statuette in scattered and blackened fragments, suggesting fire following an act of vandalism in the 15th century BCE.

HARVESTERS VASE The finest surviving example of Minoan relief sculpture is the so-called *Harvesters Vase* (FIG. **4-14**) from Hagia Triada. Only the upper half of the egg-shaped body and neck of the vessel are preserved. Missing are the lower parts of the harvesters (or, as some think, sowers) and the ground on which they stand as well as the gold leaf that originally covered the relief figures. Formulaic scenes of sowing and harvesting were staples of Egyptian funerary art (FIG. **3-16**), but the Minoan artist shunned static repetition in favor of a composition that bursts with the energy of its individually characterized figures. The relief shows a riotous crowd singing and shouting as they go to or return from the fields. The artist vividly captured the forward movement and lusty exuberance of the youths.

4-14 *Harvesters Vase,* from Hagia Triada (Crete), Greece, ca. 1500 BCE. Steatite, originally with gold leaf, greatest diameter 5″. Archaeological Museum, Herakleion.

The relief sculptor of the singing harvesters on this small stone vase was one of the first artists in history to represent the underlying muscular and skeletal structure of the human body.

Although most of the figures conform to the age-old convention of combined profile and frontal views, the sculptor singled out one figure (FIG. **4-14,** *right*) from his companions. He shakes a rattle to beat time, and the artist depicted him in full profile with his lungs so inflated with air that his ribs show. This is one of the first instances in the history of art of a sculptor showing a keen interest in the underlying muscular and skeletal structure of the human body. The artist's painstaking study of human anatomy is a remarkable achievement, especially given the size of the *Harvesters Vase,* barely five inches at its greatest diameter. Equally noteworthy is how the sculptor recorded the tension and relaxation of facial muscles with astonishing exactitude, not just for this figure but for his three closest companions as well. This degree of animation of the human face is without precedent in ancient art.

MINOAN DECLINE Scholars dispute the circumstances ending the Minoan civilization, although they now widely believe that Mycenaeans had already moved onto Crete and established themselves at Knossos at the end of the New Palace period. From the palace at Knossos, these intruders appear to have ruled the island for at least a half century, perhaps much longer. Parts of the palace continued to be occupied until its final destruction around 1200 BCE, but its importance as a cultural center faded soon after 1400 BCE, as the focus of Aegean civilization shifted to the Greek mainland.

MYCENAEAN ART

The origins of the Mycenaean culture are still debated. The only certainty is the presence of these forerunners of the Greeks on the mainland about the time the old palaces were built on Crete—that is, about the beginning of the second millennium BCE. Doubtless, Cretan civilization influenced these people even then, and some believe that the mainland was a Minoan economic dependency for a long time. In any case, Mycenaean power developed on the mainland in the days of the new palaces on Crete, and by 1500 BCE a distinctive Mycenaean culture was flourishing in Greece. Several centuries later, Homer described Mycenae as "rich in gold." The dramatic discoveries of Schliemann and his successors have fully justified this characterization, even if today's archaeologists no longer view the Mycenaeans solely through the eyes of Homer.

4-15 Aerial view of the citadel at Tiryns, Greece, ca. 1400–1200 BCE.

In the *Iliad,* Homer called the fortified citadel of Tiryns the city "of the great walls." Its huge, roughly cut stone blocks are examples of Cyclopean masonry, named after the mythical one-eyed giants.

Architecture

The destruction of the Cretan palaces left the mainland culture supreme. Although this Late Helladic civilization has come to be called Mycenaean, Mycenae was but one of several large palace complexes. Archaeologists have also unearthed Mycenaean remains at Tiryns, Orchomenos, Pylos, and elsewhere, and Mycenaean fortification walls have even been found on the Acropolis of Athens. The best-preserved and most impressive Mycenaean remains are those of the fortified palaces at Tiryns and Mycenae. Both were built beginning about 1400 BCE and burned (along with all the others) between 1250 and 1200 BCE, when the Mycenaeans seem to have been over-run by northern invaders or to have fallen victim to internal warfare.

TIRYNS Homer knew the citadel of Tiryns (FIG. **4-15**), located about 10 miles from Mycenae, as Tiryns of the Great Walls. In the second century CE, when Pausanias, author of an invaluable guidebook to Greece, visited the long-abandoned site, he marveled at the towering fortifications and considered the walls of Tiryns as spectacular as the pyramids of Egypt. Indeed, the Greeks of the historical age believed mere humans could not have erected such edifices and instead attributed the construction of the great Mycenaean citadels to the mythical *Cyclopes*, a race of one-eyed giants. Historians still refer to the huge, roughly cut stone blocks forming the massive fortification walls of Tiryns and other Mycenaean sites as *Cyclopean masonry*.

The heavy walls of Tiryns and Mycenae contrast sharply with the open Cretan palaces (FIG. 4-4) and clearly reveal their defensive character. Those of Tiryns average about 20 feet in thickness, and in one section they house a long gallery (FIG. **4-16**) covered by a corbeled vault (FIG. **4-17b**) similar to that constructed long before at Neolithic Newgrange (FIG. **1-19**). At Tiryns, the builders piled the large, irregular Cyclopean blocks in horizontal courses and then cantilevered them inward until the two walls met in a pointed arch. No mortar was used, and the vault is held in place only by the weight of the blocks (often several tons each), by the smaller stones used as wedges, and by the clay that fills some of the empty spaces. This primitive but effective vaulting scheme possesses an earthy monumentality. It is easy to see how a later

4-16 Corbeled gallery in the walls of the citadel, Tiryns, Greece, ca. 1400–1200 BCE.

The walls of Tiryns contain a long corbel-vaulted gallery in which irregular Cyclopean blocks were piled in horizontal courses and then cantilevered inward until the two walls met in a pointed arch.

4-17
Three methods of spanning a passageway:
(a) post and lintel,
(b) corbeled arch,
(c) arch.

Post-and-lintel construction (**a**) was the norm in ancient Greece, but the Mycenaeans also used corbeled arches (**b**). The round arch (**c**), used already in the Near East, was popular in Rome.

Megaron

Citadel walls

Approach ramp

Main gate

Citadel walls

Outer propylon

N

| 0 | 25 | 50 | 75 | 100 feet |
| 0 | 10 | 20 | 30 meters |

4-18 Plan of the palace and southern part of the citadel, Tiryns, Greece, ca. 1400–1200 BCE.

The king's reception and throne room, or megaron, was the main feature of Mycenaean palaces. Its plan, consisting of a hall with a columnar porch, is similar to that of early Greek temples (FIG. 5-6).

age came to believe that the uncouth Cyclopes were responsible for these massive but unsophisticated fortifications.

Would-be attackers at Tiryns were compelled to approach the palace (FIG. 4-18) within the walls via a long ramp that forced the (usually right-handed, as in FIG. 4-25) soldiers to expose their un-shielded sides to the Mycenaean defenders above. Then—if they got that far—they had to pass through a series of narrow gates that also could be defended easily. Inside, at Tiryns as elsewhere, the most important element in the palace plan was the *megaron*, or reception hall and throne room, of the king. The main room of the megaron had a throne against the right wall and a central hearth bordered by four Minoan-style wooden columns serving as supports for the roof. A vestibule with a columnar facade preceded the throne room. A variation of this plan later formed the core of some of the earliest Greek temple plans (FIG. 5-6), suggesting some architectural continuity between the Mycenaean age and historical Greece.

4-18A Megaron, Palace of Nestor, Pylos, ca. 1300 BCE.

LION GATE, MYCENAE The severity of these fortress-palaces was relieved by frescoes, as in the Cretan palaces, and, at Agamemnon's Mycenae at least, by monumental architectural sculpture. The so-called Lion Gate (FIG. 4-19) is the outer gateway of the stronghold at Mycenae. It is protected on the left by a wall built on a natural rock outcropping and on the right by a projecting bastion of large blocks. Any approaching enemies would have had to enter this 20-foot-wide channel and face Mycenaean defenders above them on both sides. The gate itself consists of two great monoliths capped with a huge lintel (FIG. 4-17*a*). Above the lintel, the masonry courses form a *corbeled arch* (FIG. 4-17*b*), leaving an opening that lightens the weight the lintel carries. Filling this *relieving triangle* (FIG. 4-1) is a great limestone slab where two lions carved in high relief stand on the sides of a Minoan-type column. The whole design admirably matches its triangular space, harmonizing in dignity, strength, and scale with the mas-

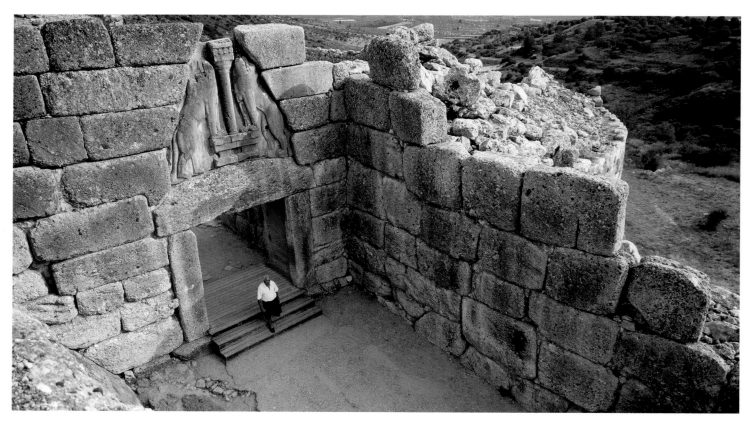

4-19 Lion Gate, Mycenae, Greece, ca. 1300–1250 BCE. Limestone, relief panel 9′ 6″ high. 🎬

The largest sculpture in the prehistoric Aegean is the relief of confronting lions (FIG. 4-1) that fills the relieving triangle of Mycenae's main gate. The gate itself consists of two great monoliths and a huge lintel.

4-20 Treasury of Atreus, Mycenae, Greece, ca. 1300–1250 BCE. ▮◀

The best-preserved Mycenaean tholos tomb is named for Homer's King Atreus. An earthen mound covers the burial chamber, which is accessed through a doorway at the end of a long passageway.

sive stones that form the walls and gate. Similar groups appear in miniature on Cretan seals, but the idea of placing monstrous guardian figures at the entrances to palaces, tombs, and sacred places has its origin in the Near East and Egypt (FIGS. 2-18, 2-21, and 3-11). At Mycenae the animals' heads were fashioned separately and are lost. Some scholars have suggested that the "lions" were actually composite beasts in the Eastern tradition, possibly sphinxes.

TREASURY OF ATREUS The Lion Gate at Mycenae and the towering fortification wall circuit of which it formed a part were constructed a few generations before the presumed date of the Trojan War. At that time, wealthy Mycenaeans were laid to rest outside the citadel walls in beehive-shaped tombs covered by enormous earthen mounds. Nine are preserved at Mycenae and scores more at other sites. The best-preserved of these *tholos tombs* is Mycenae's so-called Treasury of Atreus (FIG. 4-20), which already in antiquity was mistakenly believed to be the repository of the treasure of Atreus, father of Agamemnon and Menelaus. Approached by a long passageway (*dromos*), the tomb chamber was entered through a doorway surmounted by a relieving triangle similar to that employed in the roughly contemporary Lion Gate. (As in the Lion Gate, the open triangle was originally covered. Both the doorway and the relieving triangle also once had engaged columns on each side, preserved in fragments today.) The *tholos* (FIG. 4-21) is composed of a series of

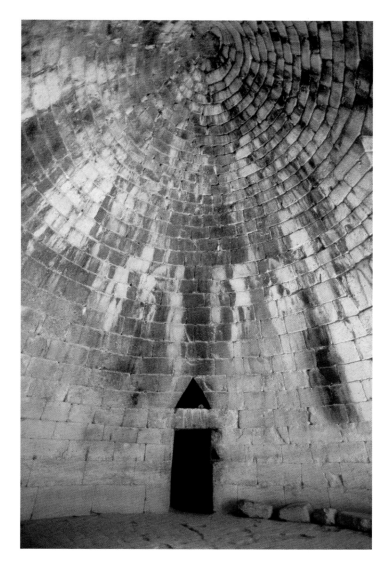

4-21 Vault of the tholos of the Treasury of Atreus, Mycenae, Greece, ca. 1300–1250 BCE.

The beehive-shaped tholos of the Treasury of Atreus is composed of corbeled courses of stone blocks laid on a circular base. The 43-foot-high dome was the largest in the world for almost 1,500 years.

stone corbeled courses laid on a circular base to form a lofty *dome*. The builders probably constructed the vault using rough-hewn blocks. After they set the stones in place, the masons had to finish the surfaces with great precision to make them conform to both the horizontal and vertical curves of the wall. The principle involved is no different from that of the corbeled gallery (FIG. 4-16) of Tiryns. But the problem of constructing a complete dome is much more complicated, and the execution of the vault in the Treasury of Atreus is far more sophisticated than that of the vaulted gallery at Tiryns. About 43 feet high, this was at the time the largest vaulted space without interior supports that had ever been built. The achievement was not surpassed until the Romans constructed the Pantheon (FIG. 10-51) almost 1,500 years later using a new technology—concrete construction—unknown to the Mycenaeans.

Metalwork, Sculpture, and Painting

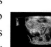

The Treasury of Atreus had been thoroughly looted long before its modern rediscovery, but excavators have found spectacular grave goods elsewhere at Mycenae. Just inside the Lion Gate, Schliemann uncovered what archaeologists now designate as Grave Circle A. It predates the Lion Gate and the walls of Mycenae by some three centuries. Grave Circle A encloses six deep shafts that had served as tombs for kings and their families. The Mycenaeans laid their dead to rest on the floors of these shaft graves with masks covering their faces, recalling the Egyptian funerary practice. They buried women with their jewelry and men with their weapons and golden cups.

4-22A Grave Circle A (looking southeast), Mycenae, 1600–1250 BCE.

MASKS AND DAGGERS Among the most spectacular of Schliemann's finds is a gold mask (FIG. 4-22), one of several from

the royal burial complex. The Mycenaean masks were made using the *repoussé* technique, that is, the goldsmiths hammered the shape from a single sheet of metal and pushed the features out from behind. The mask illustrated here has often been compared to Tutankhamen's gold mummy mask (FIG. 3-1). The treatment of the human face is, of course, more primitive in the Mycenaean mask. But this was one of the first attempts in Greece to render the human face at life-size, whereas Tutankhamen's mask stands in a long line of monumental Egyptian sculptures going back more than a millennium. It is not known whether the Mycenaean masks were intended as portraits, but the goldsmiths recorded different physical types with care. They portrayed youthful faces as well as mature ones. The illustrated example (FIG. 4-22), with its full beard, must depict a mature man, perhaps a king—although not Agamemnon, as Schliemann wished. If Agamemnon was a real king, he lived some 300 years after this mask was fashioned. Clearly the Mycenaeans were "rich in gold" long before Homer's heroes fought at Troy.

Also found in Grave Circle A were several magnificent bronze dagger blades inlaid with gold, silver, and *niello* (a black metallic alloy), again attesting to the wealth of the Mycenaean kings as well as to their warlike nature. The largest and most elaborate of the group is decorated on one side (FIG. 4-23) with a scene of four hunters attacking a lion that has struck down a fifth hunter, while two other lions flee. The other side shows lions attacking deer. The slim-waisted, long-haired figures are Minoan in style, but the artist borrowed the subject from the repertoire of the ancient Near East. It is likely that a Minoan metalworker made the dagger for a Mycenaean patron who admired Minoan art but whose taste in subject matter differed from that of his Cretan counterparts.

4-23A Gold drinking cup, Vapheio, ca. 1600–1500 BC

4-22 Funerary mask, from Grave Circle A, Mycenae, Greece, ca. 1600–1500 BCE. Beaten gold, 1′ high. National Archaeological Museum, Athens. ■◀

Homer described the Mycenaeans as "rich in gold." This beaten gold (repoussé) mask of a bearded man comes from a royal shaft grave. It is one of the first attempts at life-size sculpture in Greece.

1 in.

4-23 Inlaid dagger blade with lion hunt, from Grave Circle A, Mycenae, Greece, ca. 1600–1500 BCE. Bronze, inlaid with gold, silver, and niello, 9″ long. National Archaeological Museum, Athens.

The treasures buried with the Mycenaean kings attest to their wealth. The lion hunters on this bronze dagger are Minoan in style, but the metalworker borrowed the subject from the artistic repertory of the Near East.

4A Two ddesses d a child, cenae, ca. 00–1250 BCE.

PLASTER SCULPTURE Large-scale figural art is very rare on the Greek mainland, as on Crete, other than the Minoan-style paintings that once adorned the walls of Mycenaean palaces. The triangular relief (FIG. 4-1) of the Lion Gate at Mycenae is exceptional, as is the painted plaster head (FIG. 4-24) of a woman, goddess, or, perhaps, sphinx found at Mycenae. The white flesh tone indicates that the head is female. The hair and eyes are dark blue, almost black, and the lips, ears, and headband are red. The artist decorated the cheeks and chin with red circles surrounded by a ring of red dots, recalling the facial paint or tattoos recorded on Early Cycladic figurines of women. Although the large staring eyes give the face a menacing, if not terrifying, expression appropriate for a guardian figure such as a sphinx, the closest parallels to this work in the prehistoric Aegean are terracotta images of goddesses. This head may therefore be a very early example of a monumental cult statue in Greece.

Were it not for this plaster head and a few other exceptional pieces, art historians might have concluded—wrongly—that the Mycenaeans had no monumental freestanding statuary—a reminder that it is

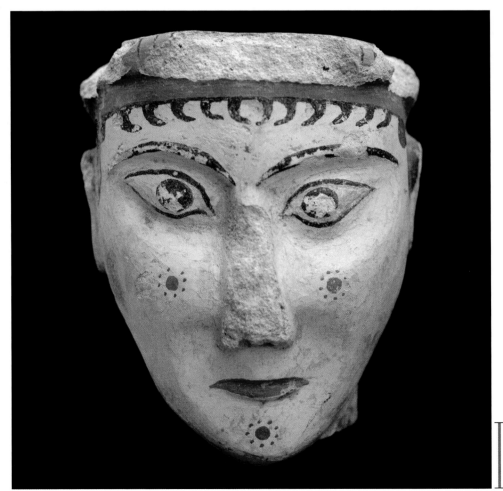

4-24 Female head, from Mycenae, Greece, ca. 1300–1250 BCE. Painted plaster, $6\frac{1}{2}$″ high. National Archaeological Museum, Athens.

This painted white plaster head of a woman with large staring eyes may be a very early example of a monumental statue of a goddess in Greece, but some scholars think it is the head of a sphinx.

4-25 *Warriors Vase,* from Mycenae, Greece, ca. 1200 BCE. 1′ 4″ high. National Archaeological Museum, Athens.

This krater, or mixing bowl, shows a woman bidding farewell to a column of heavily armed Mycenaean warriors depicted using both silhouette and outline and a combination of frontal and profile views.

always dangerous to generalize from the fragmentary remains of an ancient civilization. Nonetheless, life-size Aegean statuary must have been rare. After the collapse of Mycenaean civilization and for the next several hundred years, no attempts at monumental statuary are evident until, after the waning of the so-called Dark Ages, Greek sculptors were exposed to the great sculptural tradition of Egypt (see Chapter 5).

WARRIORS VASE An art form that did continue throughout the period after the downfall of the Mycenaean palaces was vase painting. One of the latest examples of Mycenaean painting is the *krater* (bowl for mixing wine and water) commonly called the *Warriors Vase* (FIG. **4-25**) after its prominent frieze of soldiers marching off to war. At the left a woman bids farewell to the column of heavily

armed warriors moving away from her. The painting on this vase reveals no setting and lacks the landscape elements that characterized earlier Minoan and Mycenaean art. All the soldiers also repeat the same pattern, a far cry from the variety and anecdotal detail of the lively procession of the Minoan *Harvesters Vase* (FIG. 4-14).

This simplification of narrative has parallels in the increasingly schematic and abstract treatment of marine life on other painted vases. The octopus, for example, eventually became a stylized motif composed of concentric circles and spirals that are almost unrecognizable as a sea creature. By Homer's time, the heyday of Aegean civilization was but a distant memory, and the men and women of Crete and Mycenae—Minos and Ariadne, Agamemnon and Helen—had assumed the stature of heroes from a lost golden age.

THE PREHISTORIC AEGEAN

EARLY CYCLADIC ART, ca. 3000–2000 BCE

▌ Marble statuettes are the major surviving artworks of the Cycladic Islands during the third millennium BCE, but little is known about their function.

▌ Many of the Cycladic figurines were buried in graves and may represent the deceased, but others, for example, musicians, almost certainly do not. Whatever their meaning, these statuettes mark the beginning of the long history of marble sculpture in Greece.

Lyre player, Keros,
ca. 2700–2500 BCE

LATE MINOAN ART, ca. 1700–1200 BCE

▌ The so-called Old Palace period (ca. 2000–1700 BCE) on Crete saw the construction of the first palaces on the island, but the golden age of Crete was the Late Minoan period.

▌ The greatest Late Minoan palace was at Knossos. A vast multistory structure arranged around a central court, the Knossos palace was so complex in plan that it gave rise to the myth of the Minotaur in the labyrinth of King Minos.

▌ The largest art form in the Minoan world was fresco painting on walls, usually illustrating palace rituals like bull-leaping.

▌ Vase painting also flourished. Sea motifs, for example, the octopus, were popular subjects.

▌ Minoan sculpture was of small scale, consisting of statuettes of "snake goddesses" and reliefs on stone vases.

Bull-leaping fresco, Knossos,
ca. 1450–1400 BCE

Snake Goddess, Knossos,
ca. 1600 BCE

MYCENAEAN (LATE HELLADIC) ART, ca. 1700–1200 BCE

▌ The Mycenaeans, who with their Greek allies later waged war on Troy, were already by 1600–1500 BCE burying their kings in deep shaft graves with gold funerary masks and bronze daggers inlaid with gold and silver.

▌ By 1450 BCE, the Mycenaeans had occupied Crete, and between 1400 and 1200 BCE, they erected great citadels at Mycenae, Tiryns, and elsewhere with "Cyclopean" walls of huge, irregularly shaped stone blocks.

▌ Masters of corbel vaulting, the Mycenaeans also erected beehive-shaped tholos tombs like the so-called Treasury of Atreus, which had the largest dome in the pre-Roman world.

▌ The oldest preserved monumental sculptures in Greece, most notably Mycenae's Lion Gate, date to the end of the Mycenaean period.

Gold funerary mask, Mycenae,
ca. 1600–1500 BCE

Vault of the Treasury of Atreus,
Mycenae, ca. 1300–1250 BCE

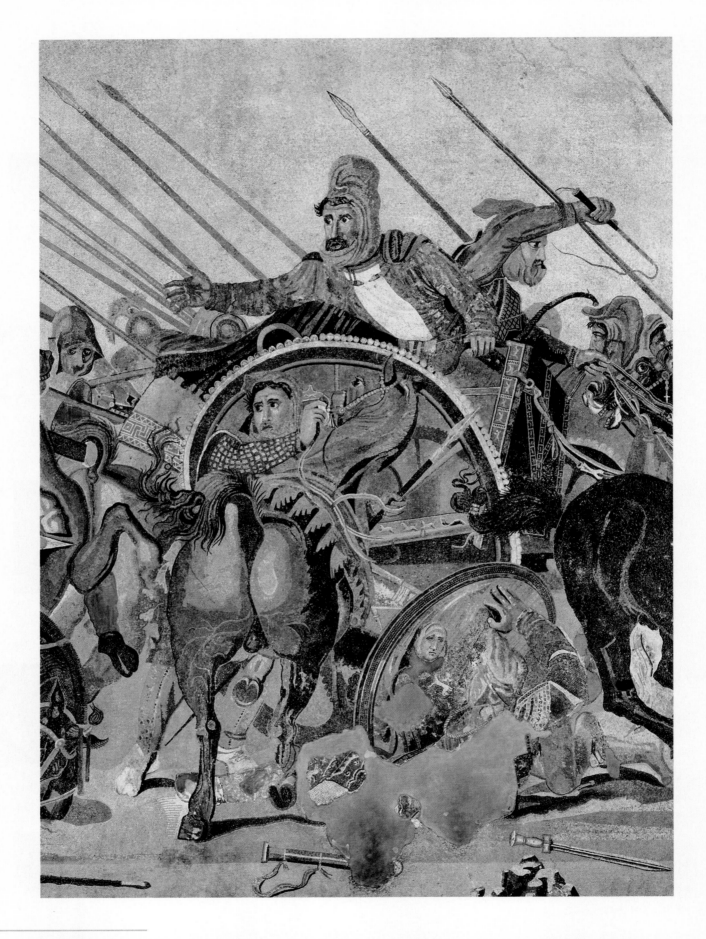

5-1 The Persian king Darius III, detail of Philoxenos of Eretria, *Battle of Issus* (FIG. 5-70), Roman mosaic copy of a painting of ca. 310 BCE. Museo Archeologico Nazionale, Naples. ◼◂

Greek painters were the first to employ foreshortening consistently, to model figures in color, and to depict reflections and shadows—practices that became standard in later painting in the Western world.

5

ANCIENT GREECE

Ancient Greek art occupies a special place in the history of art through the ages. Many of the cultural values of the Greeks, especially the exaltation of humanity as the "measure of all things," remain fundamental tenets of Western civilization. This humanistic worldview led the Greeks to create the concept of democracy (rule by the *demos,* the people) and to make seminal contributions in the fields of art, literature, and science. Ancient Greek ideas are so completely part of modern Western habits of mind that most people are scarcely aware that the concepts originated in Greece more than 2,500 years ago.

The Greeks, or *Hellenes,* as they called themselves, appear to have been the product of an intermingling of Aegean peoples and Indo-European invaders. They never formed a single nation but instead established independent city-states, or *poleis* (singular, *polis*). The Dorians of the north, who many believe brought an end to Mycenaean civilization, settled in the Peloponnesos (MAP **5-1**). The Ionians settled the western coast of Asia Minor (modern Turkey) and the islands of the Aegean Sea. The origin of the Ionians is disputed. Some say the northern invaders forced the Ionians out of Greece and that they then sailed eastward from Athens to their new homes. Others hold that the Ionians developed in Asia Minor between the 11th and 8th centuries BCE out of a mixed stock of settlers.

Whatever the origins of the various regional populations, in 776 BCE the separate Greek-speaking states held their first ceremonial games in common at Olympia. The later Greeks calculated their chronology from these first Olympic Games—the first *Olympiad.* From then on, despite their differences and rivalries, the Greeks regarded themselves as citizens of *Hellas* (the ancient name of Greece), distinct from the surrounding "barbarians" who did not speak Greek.

Even the gods of the Greeks (see "The Gods and Goddesses of Mount Olympus," page 101) differed in kind from those of neighboring civilizations. Unlike Egyptian and Mesopotamian deities, the Greek gods and goddesses differed from human beings only in that they were immortal. It has been said that the Greeks made their gods into humans and their humans into gods. The perfect individual became the Greek ideal—and the portrayal of beautiful humans became the focus of many of the greatest Greek artists.

MAP 5-1 The Greek world.

Although the sculptures, paintings, and buildings discussed in this chapter were made and built all over Greece and in its many colonies abroad (MAP 5-1), Athens, the capital of Greece today, has justifiably become the symbol of ancient Greek culture. Athens is where the great plays of Aeschylus, Sophocles, and Euripides were first performed. And there, in the city's central square (*agora*), covered colonnades (*stoas*), and gymnasiums (*palaestras*), Socrates engaged his fellow citizens in philosophical argument, and Plato formulated his prescription for the ideal form of government in the *Republic*. Complementing the rich intellectual life of ancient Athens was a strong interest in physical exercise, which played a large role in education, as well as in daily life. The Athenian aim of achieving a balance of intellectual and physical discipline, an ideal of humanistic education, is well expressed in the familiar phrase "a sound mind in a sound body."

The distinctiveness and originality of Greek contributions to art, science, and politics should not, however, obscure the enormous debt the Greeks owed to the cultures of Egypt and the Near East. Scholars today increasingly recognize this debt, and the ancient Greeks themselves readily acknowledged borrowing ideas, motifs, conventions, and skills from those older civilizations. Nor should a high estimation of Greek art and culture blind anyone to the realities of Hellenic life and society. Even Athenian "democracy" was a political reality for only one segment of the demos. Slavery was regarded as natural, even beneficial, and was a universal institution among the Greeks. Greek women were in no way the equals of Greek men. Women normally remained secluded in their homes, emerging usually only for weddings, funerals, and religious festivals. They played little part in public or political life. Despite the fame of the poet Sappho, only a handful of female artists' names are known, and none of their works survive. Both the existence of slavery and the exclusion of women from public life are reflected in Greek art. On many occa-

sions freeborn men and women appear with their slaves in monumental sculpture. The *symposium* (a dinner party that only men and prostitutes attended) is a popular subject on painted vases.

Although the Greeks invented and passed on to future generations the concept and practice of democracy, most Greek states, even those constituted as democracies, were dominated by wellborn white males, and the most admired virtues were not wisdom and justice but statecraft and military valor. Greek men were educated in the values of Homer's heroes and in the athletic exercises of the palaestra. War among the city-states was chronic. Fighting among themselves, the Greeks eventually fell victim to the Macedonians and Romans.

GEOMETRIC AND ORIENTALIZING PERIODS

Disintegration of the Bronze Age social order accompanied the destruction of the Mycenaean palaces. The disappearance of powerful kings and their retinues led to the loss of the knowledge of how to cut masonry, to construct citadels and tombs, to paint frescoes, and to sculpt in stone. Even the arts of reading and writing were forgotten. Depopulation, poverty, and an almost total loss of contact with the outside world characterized the succeeding centuries, sometimes called the Dark Age of Greece. Only in the eighth century BCE did economic conditions improve and the population begin to grow again. This era was in its own way a heroic age, a time when the poleis of Classical Greece took shape; when the Greeks broke out of their isolation and once again began to trade with cities both in the east and the west; when Homer's epic poems, formerly memorized and passed down from bard to bard, were recorded in written form; and when the Olympic Games were established.

The Gods and Goddesses of Mount Olympus

The names of scores of Greek gods and goddesses were recorded as early as the eighth century BCE in Homer's epic tales of the war against Troy (*Iliad*) and of the adventures of the Greek hero Odysseus on his long and tortuous journey home (*Odyssey*). Even more are enumerated in the poems of Hesiod, especially his *Theogony* (*Genealogy of the Gods*) composed around 700 BCE.

The Greek deities most often represented in art are all ultimately the offspring of the two key elements of the Greek universe, Earth (*Gaia/Ge*; all names are given in their Greek and Latin, that is, Greek and Roman forms) and Heaven (*Ouranos/Uranus*). Earth and Heaven mated to produce 12 Titans, including Ocean (*Okeanos/Oceanus*) and his youngest brother *Kronos* (*Saturn*). Kronos castrated his father in order to rule in his place, married his sister *Rhea*, and then swallowed all his children as they were born, lest one of them seek in turn to usurp him. When *Zeus* (*Jupiter*) was born, Rhea deceived Kronos by feeding him a stone wrapped in clothes in place of the infant. After growing to manhood, Zeus forced Kronos to vomit up Zeus's siblings. Together they overthrew their father and the other Titans and ruled the world from their home on Mount Olympus, Greece's highest peak.

This cruel and bloody tale of the origin of the Greek gods has parallels in Near Eastern mythology and is clearly pre-Greek in origin, one of many Greek borrowings from the East. The Greek version of the creation myth, however, appears infrequently in painting and sculpture. Instead, the later 12 Olympian gods and goddesses, the chief deities of Greece, figure most prominently in art—not only in Greek, Etruscan, and Roman times but also in the Middle Ages, the Renaissance, and up to the present.

The 12 Olympian deities were

▌ ***Zeus*** (***Jupiter***) King of the gods, Zeus ruled the sky and allotted the sea to his brother Poseidon and the Underworld to his other brother Hades. His weapon was the thunderbolt, and with it he led the other gods to victory over the giants, who had challenged the Olympians for control of the world. Jupiter was also the chief god of the Romans.

▌ ***Hera*** (***Juno***) Wife and sister of Zeus, Hera was the goddess of marriage.

▌ ***Poseidon*** (***Neptune***) Poseidon was one of the three sons of Kronos and Rhea and was lord of the sea. He controlled waves, storms, and earthquakes with his three-pronged pitchfork (*trident*).

▌ ***Hestia*** (***Vesta***) Sister of Zeus, Poseidon, and Hera, Hestia was goddess of the hearth.

▌ ***Demeter*** (***Ceres***) Third sister of Zeus, Demeter was the goddess of grain and agriculture. She taught humans how to sow and plow.

▌ ***Ares*** (***Mars***) God of war, Ares was the son of Zeus and Hera and the lover of Aphrodite. Mars, father of the twin founders of Rome, Romulus and Remus, looms much larger in Roman mythology and religion than Ares does in Greek.

▌ ***Athena*** (***Minerva***) Goddess of wisdom and warfare, Athena was a virgin (*parthenos* in Greek), born not from a woman's womb but from the head of her father, Zeus. She competed with Poseidon for the honor of becoming the patron deity of Athens. She won the contest and the city bears her name.

▌ ***Hephaistos*** (***Vulcan***) God of fire and of metalworking, Hephaistos fashioned the armor Achilles wore in battle against Troy. He also provided Zeus his scepter and Poseidon his trident, and was the "surgeon" who split open Zeus's head when Athena was born. In some accounts, Hephaistos is the son of Hera without a male partner. In others, he is the son of Hera and Zeus. He was born lame and, uncharacteristically for a god, ugly. His wife Aphrodite was unfaithful to him.

▌ ***Apollo*** (***Apollo***) God of light and music, and a great archer, Apollo was the son of Zeus with **Leto/Latona,** daughter of one of the Titans. His epithet *Phoibos* means "radiant," and the young, beautiful Apollo was sometimes identified with the sun (**Helios/Sol**).

▌ ***Artemis*** (***Diana***) Sister of Apollo, Artemis was goddess of the hunt and of wild animals. As Apollo's twin, she was occasionally regarded as the moon (**Selene/Luna**).

▌ ***Aphrodite*** (***Venus***) Daughter of Zeus and **Dione** (daughter of Okeanos and one of the *nymph*s—the goddesses of springs, caves, and woods), Aphrodite was the goddess of love and beauty. In one version of her myth, she was born from the foam (*aphros* in Greek) of the sea. She was the mother of Eros by Ares and of the Trojan hero Aeneas by Anchises.

▌ ***Hermes*** (***Mercury***) Son of Zeus and another nymph, Hermes was the fleet-footed messenger of the gods and possessed winged sandals. He was also the guide of travelers, including the dead journeying to the Underworld. He carried the *caduceus*, a magical herald's rod, and wore a traveler's hat, often also shown with wings.

Other important Greek gods and goddesses were

▌ *Hades* (*Pluto*) One of the children of Kronos who fought with his brothers against the Titans, Hades was equal in stature to the Olympians but never resided on Mount Olympus. Hades was the lord of the Underworld and god of the dead.

▌ *Dionysos* (*Bacchus*) The son of Zeus and a mortal woman, Dionysos was the god of wine. In Roman times, an important mystery religion centered on Dionysos.

▌ *Eros* (*Amor* or *Cupid*) The son of Aphrodite and Ares, Eros was the winged child-god of love. In early representations, he appears as an adolescent, but artists normally depicted him as an infant.

▌ *Asklepios* (*Aesculapius*) The son of Apollo and a mortal woman, Asklepios was the Greek god of healing, whose serpent-entwined staff is the emblem of modern medicine.

Geometric Art

Also during the eighth century BCE, the human figure returned to Greek art—not in monumental statuary, which was exceedingly rare even in Bronze Age Greece, but in small bronze figurines and in paintings on ceramic pots.

DIPYLON KRATER One of the earliest examples of Greek figure painting is a huge krater (FIG. **5-2**) that marked the grave of a man buried around 740 BCE in the Dipylon cemetery of Athens. At well over three feet tall, this vase is a considerable technical achievement and a testament both to the potter's skill and to the wealth and position of the deceased's family in the community. The bottom of the great vessel is open, perhaps to permit visitors to the grave to pour libations in honor of the dead, perhaps simply to provide a drain for rainwater, or both.

The artist covered much of the krater's surface with precisely painted abstract angular motifs in horizontal bands. Especially prominent is the *meander,* or key, pattern around the rim of the krater. Most early Greek painters decorated vases exclusively with abstract motifs. The nature of the ornament has led art historians to designate this formative period of Greek art as *Geometric.* The earliest examples of the Geometric style date to the ninth century BCE.

On this krater, the artist reserved the widest part of the vase for two bands of human figures and horse-drawn chariots rather than for geometric ornament. Befitting the vase's function as a grave marker, the scenes depict the mourning for a man laid out on his bier and the grand chariot procession in his honor. The painter filled every empty surface with circles and M-shaped designs, negating any sense that the mourners or soldiers inhabit open space. The human figures, animals, and furniture are as two-dimensional as the geometric shapes elsewhere on the vessel. For example, in the upper band, the shroud, raised to reveal the corpse, is an abstract checkerboard-like backdrop. The figures are silhouettes constructed of triangular (frontal) torsos with attached profile arms, legs, and heads (with a single large frontal eye in the center), following the age-old convention. To distinguish male from female, the painter added a penis growing out of one of the deceased's thighs. The mourning women, who tear their hair out in grief, have breasts emerging beneath their armpits. In both cases the artist's concern was specifying gender, not anatomical accuracy. Below, the warriors look like walking shields, and in the old conceptual manner, both wheels of the chariots are shown. The horses have the correct number of heads and legs but seem to share a common body, so that there is no sense of overlapping or depth. Despite the highly stylized and conventional manner of representation, this vessel marks a significant turning point in the history of Greek art. Not only was the human figure reintroduced into the painter's repertoire, but the art of storytelling also was revived.

HERAKLES AND NESSOS One of the most impressive surviving Geometric sculptures is a characteristically small solid-cast bronze group (FIG. **5-3**) made up of two schematic figures locked in a hand-to-hand struggle. The man is a hero, probably Herakles (see "Herakles," page 120). His opponent is a *centaur* (a mythological beast that was part man, part horse), possibly Nessos, the centaur who had volunteered to carry the hero's bride across a river and then assaulted her. Whether or not the hero is Herakles and the centaur is Nessos, the mythological nature of the group is certain. The repertoire of the Geometric artist was not limited to scenes inspired by daily life (and death). Composite monsters were enormously popular in the ancient Near East and Egypt, and renewed contact with foreign cultures may have inspired the human-animal monsters of Geometric Greece. The centaur, however, is a purely Greek invention—and one that posed a problem for the artist, who, of course, had never seen such a creature. The Geometric artist conceived the centaur as a man in front and a horse in back, a rather unhappy and unconvincing configuration that results in the forelegs belonging to a different species from the hind legs. In this example, the sculptor rendered the figure of the hero and the human part of the centaur in a similar fashion. Both are bearded and wear helmets, but (contradictory to nature) the man is larger than the horse, probably to suggest that he will be the victor. Like other Geometric male figures, both painted and sculpted, this hero is nude, in contrast to the Near Eastern statuettes that might have inspired the Greek works. Here, at the very beginning of Greek figural art, one can recognize the Hellenic instinct for the natural beauty of the human figure. In fact, Greek athletes exercised without their clothes and even competed nude in the Olympic Games from very early times.

1 ft.

5-2 Geometric krater, from the Dipylon cemetery, Athens, Greece, ca. 740 BCE. 3′ 4½″ high. Metropolitan Museum of Art, New York.

Figure painting reappeared in Greece in the Geometric period, named for the abstract ornamentation on vessels like this krater, which features a mourning scene and procession in honor of the deceased.

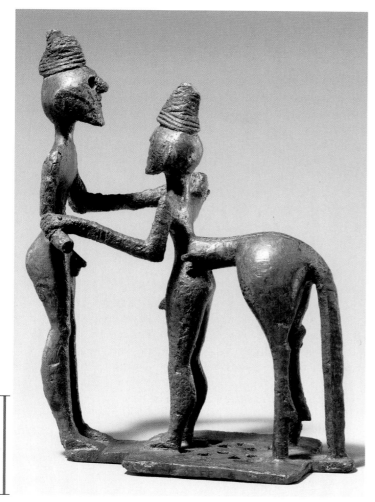

5-3 Hero and centaur (Herakles and Nessos?), from Olympia, Greece, ca. 750–730 BCE. Bronze, $4\frac{1}{2}''$ high. Metropolitan Museum of Art, New York (gift of J. Pierpont).

Sculpture of the Geometric period is small scale, and the figures have simple stylized shapes. This solid-cast bronze statuette depicts a hero battling a centaur—an early example of mythological narrative.

Orientalizing Art

During the 600s BCE, the pace and scope of Greek trade and colonization accelerated and Greek artists became exposed more than ever before to Eastern artworks, especially small portable objects such as Syrian ivory carvings. The closer contact had a profound effect on the development of Greek art. Indeed, so many motifs borrowed from or inspired by Egyptian and Near Eastern art entered the Greek pictorial vocabulary at this time that art historians have dubbed the seventh century BCE the *Orientalizing* period.

MANTIKLOS APOLLO One of the masterworks of the early seventh century BCE is the *Mantiklos Apollo* (FIG. **5-4**), a small bronze statuette dedicated to Apollo at Thebes by an otherwise unknown man named Mantiklos. With characteristic pride in the ability to write, the sculptor (or another) scratched into the thighs of the figure a message from the dedicator to the deity: "Mantiklos dedicated me as a tithe to the far-shooting Lord of the Silver Bow; you, Phoibos [Apollo], might give some pleasing favor in return." Because the Greeks conceived their gods in human form, it is uncertain whether the figure represents the youthful Apollo or Mantiklos

5-4 *Mantiklos Apollo,* statuette of a youth dedicated by Mantiklos to Apollo, from Thebes, Greece, ca. 700–680 BCE. Bronze, 8″ high. Museum of Fine Arts, Boston.

Mantiklos dedicated this statuette to Apollo, and it probably represents the god. The treatment of the body reveals the interest seventh-century BCE Greek artists had in reproducing details of human anatomy.

(or neither). But if the left hand at one time held a bow, then the statuette is certainly an image of the deity. In any case, the purpose of the votive offering is clear. Equally apparent is the increased interest Greek artists at this time had in reproducing details of human anatomy, such as the long hair framing the unnaturally elongated neck, and the pectoral and abdominal muscles, which define the stylized triangular torso. The triangular face has eye sockets that were once inlaid, and the head may have had a separately fashioned helmet on it.

Greek Vase Painting

The techniques Greek ceramists used to shape and decorate fine vases required great skill, which they acquired over many years as apprentices in the workshops of master potters. During the Archaic and Classical periods, when the art of vase painting was at its zenith in Greece, both potters and painters frequently signed their work. These signatures reveal the pride of the artists.

The signatures also might have functioned as "brand names" for a large export market. The products of the workshops in Corinth and Athens in particular were highly prized and have been found all over the Mediterranean world. The Corinthian Orientalizing amphora shown here (FIG. 5-5) was found on Rhodes, an island at the opposite side of the Aegean from mainland Corinth (MAP 5-1). The Etruscans of central Italy (MAP 9-1) were especially good customers. Athenian vases were staples in Etruscan tombs, and all but one of the illustrated examples (FIGS. 5-20 to 5-24, 5-59, and 5-60) came from an Etruscan site. Other painted Athenian pots have been found as far away as France, Russia, and the Sudan.

The first step in manufacturing a Greek vase was to remove any impurities found in the natural clay and then to knead it, like dough, to remove air bubbles and make it flexible. The Greeks used dozens of different kinds and shapes of pots, and most were produced in several parts. Potters formed the vessel's body by placing the clay on a rotating horizontal wheel. While an apprentice turned the wheel by hand, the potter pulled up the clay with the fingers until the desired shape was achieved. The handles were shaped separately and attached to the vase body by applying *slip* (liquefied clay) to the joints.

Then a specialist, the painter, was called in, although many potters decorated their own work. (Today most people tend to regard painters as more elevated artists than potters, but in Greece the potters owned the shops and employed the painters.) Art historians customarily refer to the "pigment" the painter applied to the clay surface as *glaze*, but the black areas on Greek pots are neither pigment nor glaze but a slip of finely sifted clay that originally was of the same rich red-orange color as the clay of the pot. In the three-phase firing process Greek potters used, the first (*oxidizing*) phase turned both pot and slip red. During the second (*reducing*) phase, the potter shut off the oxygen supply into the kiln, and both pot and slip turned black. In the final (*reoxidizing*) phase, the pot's coarser material reabsorbed oxygen and became red again, whereas the smoother, silica-laden slip did not and remained black. After long experiment, Greek potters developed a velvety jet-black "glaze" of this kind, produced in kilns heated to temperatures as high as 950° Celsius (about 1,742° Fahrenheit).

The firing process was the same whether the painter worked in black-figure or in red-figure. In fact, sometimes Greek artists employed both manners on the same vase (FIG. 5-22).

1 in.

5-5 Corinthian black-figure amphora with animal friezes, from Rhodes, Greece, ca. 625–600 BCE. 1′ 2″ high. British Museum, London.

The Corinthians invented the black-figure technique of vase painting in which artists painted black silhouettes and then incised linear details within the forms. This early example features Orientalizing animals.

ORIENTALIZING AMPHORA An elaborate Corinthian *amphora* (FIG. 5-5), or two-handled storage jar, typifies the new Greek fascination with the Orient. In a series of registers recalling the organization of Geometric painted vases, animals such as the native boar appear beside exotic lions and panthers and composite creatures inspired by Eastern monsters such as the sphinx and lamassu. In this instance, the painter prominently displayed a *siren* (part bird, part woman) on the amphora's neck. The wide appeal of such vases was not due solely to their Orientalizing animal friezes. They owed their popularity also to a new ceramic technique the Corinthi-

ans invented. Art historians call this type of vase decoration *black-figure painting* (see "Greek Vase Painting," above). The black-figure painter first put down black silhouettes on the clay surface of the vessel, as in Geometric times, but then used a sharp pointed instrument to incise linear details within the forms, usually adding highlights in white or purplish-red over the black figures before firing the vase. The combination of the weighty black silhouettes with the delicate detailing and the bright polychrome overlay proved to be irresistible, and Athenian painters soon copied the technique the Corinthians pioneered.

5-6 **Plan of Temple A, Prinias, Greece, ca. 625 BCE.**

The first Greek stone temples, like this one at Prinias, were similar in plan to the megarons of Mycenaean palaces, with a porch and a main room with two columns flanking a hearth or sacrificial pit.

1. Cella
2. Hearth or sacrificial pit
3. Doorway with sculptured frieze

5-7 *Lady of Auxerre,* ca. 650–625 BCE. Limestone, 2′ 1½″ high. Louvre, Paris.

Probably from Crete, this kore (maiden) typifies the so-called Daedalic style of the seventh century BCE with its triangular face and hair and lingering Geometric fondness for abstract pattern.

TEMPLE A, PRINIAS The foundation of the Greek trading colony of Naukratis in Egypt (MAP 3-1) before 630 BCE brought the Greeks into direct contact with the monumental stone architecture of the Egyptians. Not long after that, construction began in Greece of the first stone buildings since the fall of the Mycenaean kingdoms. At Prinias on Crete, for example, the Greeks built a stone temple, called Temple A (FIG. 5-6), around 625 BCE to honor an unknown deity. Although the inspiration for the structure may have come from the East, the form resembles that of a typical Mycenaean megaron, such as that at Tiryns (FIG. 4-18), with two interior columns flanking a hearth or sacrificial pit. The facade consisted of three great piers. The roof was probably flat. Temple A at Prinias is the earliest known example of a Greek temple with sculptured decoration. Above the doorway was a huge limestone lintel with a relief frieze of Orientalizing panthers with frontal heads—the same motif as that on the contemporary Corinthian black-figure amphora (FIG. 5-5), underscoring the stylistic unity of Greek art at this time.

LADY OF AUXERRE Probably also originally from Crete is a limestone statuette of a goddess or maiden (*kore;* plural, *korai*) popularly known as the *Lady of Auxerre* (FIG. 5-7) after the French town that is her oldest recorded location. As with the figure Mantiklos dedicated (FIG. 5-4), it is uncertain whether the young woman is a mortal or a deity. She is clothed, as are all Greek goddesses and women of this period, but she does not wear a headdress, as a goddess probably would. Moreover, the placement of the right hand across the chest is probably a gesture of prayer, also indicating that this is a kore. The style is much more naturalistic than in Geometric times, but the love of abstract shapes can still be seen. Note, for example, the triangular flat-topped head framed by long strands of hair that form triangles complementary to the shape of the face, and the decoration of the long skirt with its incised concentric squares, once brightly painted, as were all Greek stone statues. The modern notion that Greco-Roman statuary was pure white is mistaken. The Greeks did not, however, color their statues garishly. The flesh was left in the natural color of the stone, which was waxed and polished, while eyes, lips, hair, and drapery were painted in *encaustic* (see "Iaia of Cyzicus and the Art of Encaustic Painting," Chapter 10, page 275). In this technique, the painter mixed the pigment with hot wax and applied the tinted wax to the statue to produce a durable coloration.

ARCHAIC PERIOD

The *Lady of Auxerre* is the masterpiece of the style that art historians usually refer to as *Daedalic,* after the legendary artist Daedalus, whose name means "the skillful one." In addition to having been a great sculptor, Daedalus was said to have built the labyrinth (FIG. 4-5) in Crete to house the Minotaur and also to have designed a temple at Memphis in Egypt (MAP 3-1). The historical Greeks attributed to him almost all the great achievements in early sculpture and architecture before the names of artists and architects were recorded. The story that Daedalus worked in Egypt reflects the enormous impact of Egyptian art and architecture on the Greeks of the aptly named Orientalizing age of the seventh century, as well as on their offspring in the succeeding *Archaic* period of the sixth century BCE.

Statuary

According to one Greek writer, Daedalus used the same compositional patterns for his statues as the Egyptians used for theirs, and the first truly monumental stone statues of the Greeks follow very closely the canonical Egyptian format.

NEW YORK KOUROS One of the earliest examples (FIG. 5-8) of life-size statuary in Greece is the marble *kouros* ("youth"; plural, *kouroi*) now in New York. The Greek kouros emulates the stance of

1 ft.

5-8 Kouros, ca. 600 BCE. Marble, 6' ½" high. Metropolitan Museum of Art, New York.

The sculptors of the earliest life-size statues of kouroi (young men) adopted the Egyptian pose for standing figures (FIG. 3-13), but the kouroi are nude and liberated from the original block of stone.

Egyptian statues (FIG. 3-13). In both Egypt and Greece, the figure is rigidly frontal with the left foot advanced slightly. The arms are held beside the body, and the fists are clenched with the thumbs forward. The New York kouros, like most Egyptian statues, was also a funerary statue. It stood over a grave in the countryside somewhere near Athens. Statues like this one replaced the huge vases (FIG. 5-2) of Geometric times as the preferred form of grave marker in the sixth century BCE. The Greeks also used kouroi as votive offerings in sanctuaries. The kouros type, because of its generic quality, could be employed in several different contexts.

Despite the adherence to Egyptian prototypes, Greek kouros statues differ from their models in two important ways. First, the Greek sculptors liberated them from their original stone block. The Egyptian obsession with permanence was alien to the Greeks, who were preoccupied with finding ways to represent motion rather than stability in their sculpted figures. Second, the kouroi are nude, and in the absence of identifying attributes, they, like the bronze statuette (FIG. 5-4) Mantiklos dedicated, are formally indistinguishable from Greek images of deities with their perfect bodies exposed for all to see.

The New York kouros shares many traits with the *Mantiklos Apollo* and other Orientalizing works such as the *Lady of Auxerre* (FIG. 5-7), especially the triangular shape of head and hair and the flatness of the face—the hallmarks of the Daedalic style. Eyes, nose, and mouth all sit on the front of the head, and the ears on the sides. The long hair forms a flat backdrop behind the head. The placement of the various anatomical parts is the result of the sculptor's having drawn these features on four independent sides of the marble block, following the same workshop procedure used in Egypt for millennia. The New York kouros also has the slim waist of earlier Greek statues and exhibits the same love of pattern. The pointed arch of the rib cage, for example, echoes the V-shaped ridge of the hips, which suggests but does not accurately reproduce the rounded flesh and muscle of the human body.

CALF BEARER A generation later than the New York kouros is the statue (FIG. 5-9) of a *moschophoros,* or calf bearer, found in fragments on the Athenian Acropolis. Its inscribed base (not visible in the photograph) states that a man named Rhonbos dedicated the statue. Rhonbos is almost certainly the calf bearer himself, bringing an offering to Athena in thanksgiving for his prosperity. He stands in the left-foot-forward manner of the kouroi, but he has a beard and therefore is no longer a youth. He wears a thin cloak (once painted to set it off from the otherwise nude body). No one dressed this way in ancient Athens. The sculptor adhered to the artistic convention of male nudity and attributed to the calf bearer the noble perfection that nudity suggests while also indicating that this mature gentleman is clothed, as any respectable citizen would be in this context. The Archaic sculptor's love of pattern may be seen once again in the handling of the difficult problem of representing man and animal together. The calf's legs and the moschophoros's arms form a bold **X** that unites the two bodies both physically and formally.

The calf bearer's face differs markedly from those of earlier Greek statues (and those of Egypt and the Near East) in one notable way. The man smiles—or at least seems to. From this time on, Archaic Greek statues always smile, even in the most inappropriate contexts (see, for example, FIG. 5-28, where a dying warrior with an arrow piercing his chest grins broadly at the spectator). This so-called *Archaic smile* has been variously interpreted, but it is not to be taken literally. Rather, the smile seems to be the Archaic sculptor's way of indicating that the person portrayed is alive. By adopting this convention, the Greek artist signaled a very different intention from any Egyptian counterpart.

ANAVYSOS KOUROS Sometime around 530 BCE a young man named Kroisos died a hero's death in battle, and his family erected a kouros statue (FIG. 5-10) over his grave at Anavysos, not far from Athens. Fortunately, some of the paint is preserved, giving a better sense of the statue's original appearance. The inscribed base invites visitors to "stay and mourn at the tomb of dead Kroisos, whom raging Ares destroyed one day as he fought in the foremost ranks." The statue, with its distinctive Archaic smile, is no more a portrait of a specific youth than is the New York kouros. But two generations later, without rejecting the Egyptian stance, the Greek sculptor rendered the human body in a far more naturalistic manner. The head is no longer too large for the body, and the face is more rounded, with swelling cheeks replacing the flat planes of the earlier work. The long hair does not form a stiff backdrop to the head but falls naturally over the back. Rounded hips replace the V-shaped ridges of the New York kouros.

5-9 Calf bearer, dedicated by Rhonbos on the Acropolis, Athens, Greece, ca. 560 BCE. Marble, restored height 5′ 5″; fragment 3′ 11½″ high. Acropolis Museum, Athens.

This statue of a bearded man bringing a calf to sacrifice in thanksgiving to Athena is one of the first to employ the so-called Archaic smile, the Archaic Greek sculptor's way of indicating a person is alive.

5-10 Kroisos, from Anavysos, Greece, ca. 530 BCE. Marble, 6′ 4″ high. National Archaeological Museum, Athens. ■◀

This later kouros stood over the grave of Kroisos, a young man who died in battle. The statue displays increased naturalism in its proportions and more rounded modeling of face, torso, and limbs.

PEPLOS KORE A stylistic "sister" to the Anavysos kouros is the statue of a woman traditionally known as the *Peplos Kore* (FIG. 5-11) because until recently scholars thought this kore wore a peplos. A *peplos* is a simple, long, woolen belted garment. Careful examination of the statue has revealed, however, that she wears four different garments, one of which only goddesses wore. The attribute the goddess once held in her left hand would immediately have identified her. Whoever she is, the contrast with the *Lady of Auxerre* (FIG. 5-7) is striking. Although in both cases the drapery conceals the entire body save for head, arms, and feet, the sixth-century BCE sculptor rendered the soft female form much more naturally. This softer treatment of the flesh also sharply differentiates later korai from contemporary kouroi, which have hard, muscular bodies.

Traces of paint are preserved on the *Peplos Kore*. Like the Anavysos kouros, this Athenian statue was buried for more than two millennia. The earthen "grave" protected the painted surface from the destructive effects of exposure to the atmosphere and to bad weather. The *Peplos Kore*—along with the calf bearer (FIG. 5-9) and many other statues—had been knocked over by the Persians during their sack of the Acropolis in 480 BCE (see page 118). Shortly thereafter, the Athenians buried all the damaged Archaic sculptures. Before that time, they stood as votive offerings in Athena's sanctuary.

KORE IN IONIAN DRESS By the late sixth century BCE, the light linen Ionian *chiton*, worn in conjunction with a heavier *himation* (mantle), was the garment of choice for fashionable women. Archaic

1 ft.

1 in.

5-11 *Peplos Kore,* from the Acropolis, Athens, Greece, ca. 530 BCE. Marble, 4′ high. Acropolis Museum, Athens.

Unlike men, women are always clothed in Archaic statuary. This kore is a votive statue of a goddess wearing four garments. She once held her identifying attribute in her missing left hand.

5-12 Kore, from the Acropolis, Athens, Greece, ca. 520–510 BCE. Marble, 1′ 9″ high. Acropolis Museum, Athens.

Archaic sculptors delighted in rendering the intricate asymmetrical patterns created by the cascading folds of garments like the Ionian chiton and himation worn by this smiling Acropolis kore.

Greek Temple Plans

The core of an ancient Greek temple plan (FIG. 5-13) was the *naos*, or *cella*, a room with no windows that usually housed the cult statue of the deity. It was preceded by a *pronaos*, or porch, often with two columns between the *antae*, or extended walls (columns *in antis*). A smaller second room might be placed behind the cella (FIG. 5-16), but in its canonical form, the Greek temple had a porch at the rear (*opisthodomos*) set against the blank back wall of the cella. The purpose was not functional but decorative, satisfying the Greek passion for balance and symmetry. A colonnade could be placed across the front of the temple (*prostyle*; FIG. 5-52), across both front and back (*amphiprostyle*; FIG. 5-55), or, more commonly, all around the cella and its porch(es) to form a *peristyle*, as in FIG. 5-13 (compare FIG. 5-15). Single (*peripteral*) colonnades were the norm, but double (*dipteral*) colonnades were features of especially elaborate temples (FIG. 5-75).

5-13 Plan of a typical Greek peripteral temple.

The basic form of the canonical Greek temple derives from that of the megaron of a Mycenaean palace (FIG. 4-18), but Greek temples housed statues of deities and most were surrounded by columns.

sculptors delighted in rendering the intricate patterns created by the cascading folds of thin, soft material. In another Acropolis kore (FIG. 5-12), the asymmetry of the folds greatly relieves the stiff frontality of the body and makes the figure appear much more life-like than contemporary kouroi. The sculptor achieved added variety by showing the kore grasping part of her chiton in her left hand (unfortunately broken off) to lift it off the ground in order to take a step forward. This is the equivalent of the advanced left foot of the kouroi and became standard for statues of korai. Despite the varied surface treatment of brightly colored garments on the korai, the kore postures are as fixed as those of their male counterparts.

Architecture and Architectural Sculpture

Many of the earliest Greek temples do not survive because they were built of wood and mud brick. Pausanias noted in his second-century CE guidebook to Greece that in the even-then-ancient Temple of Hera at Olympia, one oak column was still in place. (Stone columns had replaced the others.) Archaic and later Greek temples, however, were constructed of more permanent materials—limestone, in many cases, and, where it was available, marble, which was more impressive and durable (and more expensive). In Greece proper, if not in its western colonies, marble was readily at hand. Bluish-white marble came from Hymettus, just east of Athens. Glittering white marble particularly adapted for carving was brought from Pentelicus, northeast of the city, and from the Aegean Islands, especially Paros.

Already in the Orientalizing seventh century BCE, the Greeks had built at Prinias a stone temple (FIG. 5-6) embellished with stone sculptures, but the Cretan temple resembled the megaron of a Mycenaean palace more than anything Greek traders had seen in their travels overseas. In the Archaic age of the sixth century, with the model of Egyptian columnar halls such as that at Karnak (FIG. 3-25) before them, Greek architects began to build the columnar stone temples that became more influential on the later history of architecture in the Western world than any other building type ever devised.

Greek temples differed in function from most later religious shrines. The altar lay outside the temple—at the east end, facing the rising sun—and the Greeks gathered outside, not inside, the building to worship. The temple proper housed the so-called *cult statue* of the deity, the grandest of all votive offerings. Both in its early and mature manifestations, the Greek temple was the house of the god or goddess, not of his or her followers.

TEMPLE PLANS In basic plan (see "Greek Temple Plans," above, and FIG. 5-13), the Greek temple still discloses a close affinity with the Mycenaean megaron (FIG. 4-18), and, even in its most elaborate form, it retains the latter structure's basic simplicity. In all cases, the remarkable order, compactness, and symmetry of the Greek scheme strike the eye first, reflecting the Greeks' sense of proportion and their effort to achieve ideal forms in terms of regular numerical relationships and geometric rules. Whether the plan is simple or more complex, no fundamental change occurs in the nature of the units or of their grouping. Classical Greek architecture, like classical music, has a simple core theme with a series of complex, but always quite intelligible, variations developed from it.

The Greeks' insistence on proportional order guided their experiments with the proportions of temple plans. The earliest temples tended to be long and narrow, with the proportion of the ends to the sides roughly expressible as 1:3. From the sixth century BCE on, plans approached but rarely had a proportion of exactly 1:2. Classical temples tended to be a little longer than twice their width. To the Greek mind, proportion in architecture and sculpture was much the same as harmony in music, reflecting and embodying the cosmic order.

TEMPLE ORNAMENTATION Figural sculpture played a major role in the exterior program of the Greek temple from early times, partly to embellish the god's shrine, partly to tell something about the deity symbolized within, and partly to serve as a votive offering. But the building itself, with its finely carved capitals and moldings, also was conceived as sculpture, abstract in form and possessing the power of sculpture to evoke human responses. The commanding importance of the sculptured temple, its inspiring function in public life, was emphasized in its elevated site, often on a hill above the city (*acropolis* means "high city").

Sculptural ornament was concentrated on the upper part of the building, in the frieze and pediments (see "Doric and Ionic Orders," page 110). Architectural sculpture, like freestanding statuary, was painted (FIG. 5-27, *right*) and usually was placed only in the building parts that had no structural function. This is true particularly of the

Doric and Ionic Orders

Architectural historians describe the elevation (FIG. 5-14) of a Greek temple in terms of the platform, the colonnade, and the superstructure (*entablature*). In the Archaic period, two basic systems evolved for articulating the three units. These are the so-called *orders* of Greek architecture. The orders are differentiated both in the nature of the details and in the relative proportions of the parts. The names of the orders derive from the Greek regions where they were most commonly employed. The *Doric*, formulated on the mainland, remained the preferred manner there and in the western colonies of the Greeks. The *Ionic* was the order of choice in the Aegean Islands and on the western coast of Asia Minor. The geographical distinctions are by no means absolute. The Ionic order, for example, was often used in Athens (where, according to some, the Athenians considered themselves Ionians who never migrated).

In both orders, the columns rest on the *stylobate*, the uppermost course of the platform. Metal clamps held together the stone blocks in each horizontal course, and metal dowels joined vertically the blocks of different courses. The columns have two or three parts, depending on the order: the *shaft*, which is marked with vertical channels (*flutes*); the *capital*; and, in the Ionic order, the *base*. Greek column shafts, in contrast to their Minoan and Mycenaean forebears, taper gradually from bottom to top. They usually are composed of separate *drums*

joined by metal dowels to prevent turning as well as shifting, although instances of *monolithic* (single-piece) columns are known. The capital has two elements. The lower part (the *echinus*) varies with the order. In the Doric, it is convex and cushionlike, similar to the echinus of Minoan (FIG. 4-6) and Mycenaean (FIG. 4-1) capitals. In the Ionic, it is small and supports a bolster ending in scroll-like spirals (the *volutes*). The upper element, present in both orders, is a flat, square block (the *abacus*) that provides the immediate support for the entablature.

The entablature has three parts: the *architrave*, the main weight-bearing and weight-distributing element; the *frieze*; and the *cornice*, a molded horizontal projection that together with two sloping (*raking*) cornices forms a triangle that enframes the *pediment*. In the Ionic order, the architrave is usually subdivided into three horizontal bands. In the Doric order, the frieze is subdivided into *triglyphs* and *metopes*, whereas in the Ionic the frieze is left open to provide a continuous field for relief sculpture.

The Doric order is massive in appearance, its sturdy columns firmly planted on the stylobate. Compared with the weighty and severe Doric, the Ionic order seems light, airy, and much more decorative. Its columns are more slender and rise from molded bases. The most obvious differences between the two orders are, of course, in the capitals—the Doric, severely plain, and the Ionic, highly ornamental.

DORIC ORDER

IONIC ORDER

5-14 Elevations of the Doric and Ionic orders.

The major differences between the Doric and Ionic orders are the form of the capitals and the treatment of the frieze. The Doric frieze is divided into triglyphs and metopes.

5-15 Temple of Hera I ("Basilica"), Paestum, Italy, ca. 550 BCE.

The peristyle of this huge early Doric temple consists of heavy, closely spaced, cigar-shaped columns with bulky, pancakelike capitals, characteristic features of Archaic Greek architecture.

Doric order (FIG. **5-14,** *left*), where decorative sculpture appears only in the metope and pediment "voids." Ionic (FIG. 5-14, *right*) builders, less severe in this respect as well, were willing to decorate the entire frieze and sometimes even the lower column drums. Occasionally, they replaced their columns with female figures (*caryatids;* FIGS. **5-18** and **5-54**). Capitals, decorative moldings, and other architectural elements were also painted. By painting parts of the building, the designer could bring out more clearly the relationships of the structural parts and soften the stone's glitter at specific points, as well as provide a background to set off the figures.

Although the Greeks used color for emphasis and to relieve what might have seemed too bare a simplicity, Greek architecture primarily depended on clarity and balance. To the Greeks, it was unthinkable to use surfaces in the way the Egyptians used their gigantic columns—as fields for complicated ornamentation (FIG. 3-25). The history of Greek temple architecture is the history of Greek architects' unflagging efforts to find the most satisfactory (that is, what they believed were perfect) proportions for each part of the building and for the structure as a whole.

BASILICA, PAESTUM The prime example of early Greek efforts at Doric temple design is not in Greece but in Italy, south of Naples, at Paestum (Greek Poseidonia). The huge (80 × 170 feet) Archaic temple (FIG. **5-15**) erected there around 550 BCE retains its entire peripteral colonnade, but most of the entablature, including the frieze, pediment, and all of the roof, has vanished. Called the "Basilica" after the Roman columnar hall building type (see Chapter 10) that early investigators felt it resembled, the structure was actually a temple of Hera. Scholars refer to it as the Temple of Hera I to distinguish it from its later neighbor, the Temple of Hera II (FIG. 5-30). The misnomer is partly due to the building's plan (FIG. **5-16**), which differs from that of most other Greek temples. The unusual feature, found only in early Archaic temples, is the central row of columns that divides the cella into two aisles. Placing columns underneath the *ridgepole* (the timber beam running the length of the building below the peak of the gabled roof) might seem the logical way to provide interior support for the roof structure, but it resulted in several disadvantages. Among these was that this interior arrangement allowed no place for a central statue of the deity to whom the temple was

1. Cella with central row of columns
2. Pronaos with three columns in antis

5-16 Plan of the Temple of Hera I, Paestum, Italy, ca. 550 BCE.

The Hera temple's plan also reveals its early date. The temple has an odd number of columns on the facade and a single row of columns in the cella, leaving no place for a central cult statue.

dedicated. Also, the peripteral colonnade, in order to correspond with the interior, required an odd number of columns (nine in this case) across the building's facade. At Paestum, the builders also set three columns in antis instead of the standard two, which in turn ruled out a central doorway for viewing the statue. (Some scholars have suggested, however, that this design was well suited for two statues, perhaps of Zeus and Hera.) The architect nonetheless achieved a simple 1:2 ratio of facade and flank columns by erecting 18 columns on each side of the temple.

Another early aspect of the Paestum temple is the shape of its heavy, closely spaced columns (FIG. **5-15**) with their large, bulky, pancakelike Doric capitals, which seem compressed by the overbearing weight of the entablature. The columns have a pronounced swelling (*entasis*) at the middle of the shafts, giving them a profile akin to that of a cigar. If the temple's immense roof were preserved, the columns would seem even more compressed, squatting beneath

1 ft.

5-17 West pediment from the Temple of Artemis, Corfu, Greece, ca. 600–580 BCE. Limestone, greatest height 9′ 4″. Archaeological Museum, Corfu.

The hideous Medusa and two panthers at the center of this early pediment serve as temple guardians. To either side, and much smaller, are scenes from the Trojan War and the battle of gods and giants.

what must have been a high and massive entablature. The columns and capitals thus express in a vivid manner their weight-bearing function. One structural reason, perhaps, for the heaviness of the design and the narrowness of the spans between the columns might be that the Archaic builders were afraid thinner and more widely spaced columns would result in the superstructure's collapse. In later Doric temples (FIGS. 5-25, 5-30, and 5-44), the builders placed the columns farther apart and refined the forms. The shafts became more slender, the entasis subtler, the capitals smaller, and the entablature lighter. Greek architects sought the ideal proportional relationship among the parts of their buildings. The sculptors of Archaic kouroi and korai grappled with similar problems. Architecture and sculpture developed in a parallel manner in the sixth century BCE.

TEMPLE OF ARTEMIS, CORFU Architects and sculptors were also frequently called on to work together, as at Corfu (ancient Corcyra), where the Greeks constructed a great Doric temple dedicated to Artemis in the sixth century BCE. Corfu, an island off the western coast of Greece, was an important stop on the trade route between the mainland and the Greek settlements in Italy (MAP 5-1). Prosperity made possible the erection of one of the earliest stone peripteral temples in Greece, one also lavishly embellished with sculpture. Reliefs (unfortunately very fragmentary today) decorated the metopes, and huge high-relief sculptures (more than nine feet high at the center) filled both pediments. The pediments appear to have been decorated in an identical manner. The west pediment (FIG. 5-17) is better preserved.

Designing figural decoration for a pediment was never an easy task for the Greek sculptor because of the pediment's awkward triangular shape. The central figures had to be of great size. In contrast, as the pediment tapered toward the corners, the available area became increasingly cramped. At the center of the Corfu pediment is the *gorgon* Medusa, a demon with a woman's body and a bird's wings. Medusa also had a hideous face and snake hair, and anyone who gazed at her turned into stone. The sculptor depicted her in the conventional Archaic bent-leg, bent-arm, pinwheel-like posture that signifies running or, for a winged creature, flying. To her left and right are two great felines. Together they serve as temple guardians, repulsing all enemies from the sanctuary of the goddess. Similar panthers

stood sentinel on the lintel of the seventh-century BCE temple at Prinias. The Corfu felines are in the tradition of the guardian lions of the citadel gate (FIG. 4-1) at Mycenae and the beasts that stood guard at the entrances to Near Eastern palaces (FIGS. 2-18 and 2-21). The triad of Medusa and the felines recalls as well Mesopotamian heraldic human-and-animal compositions (FIG. 2-10). The Corfu figures are, in short, still further examples of the Orientalizing manner in early Greek sculpture.

Between Medusa and the two felines are two smaller figures—the human Chrysaor at her left and the winged horse Pegasus at her right (only the rear legs are preserved next to Medusa's right foot). Chrysaor and Pegasus were Medusa's children. According to legend, they sprang from her head when the Greek hero Perseus severed it with his sword. Their presence here on either side of the living Medusa is therefore a chronological impossibility. The Archaic artist had less interest in telling a coherent story than in identifying the central figure by depicting her offspring. Narration was, however, the purpose of the much smaller groups situated in the pediment corners. To the viewer's right is Zeus, brandishing his thunderbolt and slaying a kneeling giant. In the extreme corner (not preserved) was probably a dead giant. The *gigantomachy* (battle of gods and giants) was a popular theme in Greek art from Archaic through Hellenistic times and was a metaphor for the triumph of reason and order over chaos. In the pediment's left corner is one of the Trojan War's climactic events: Achilles' son Neoptolemos kills the enthroned King Priam. The fallen figure to the left of this group may be a dead Trojan.

The master responsible for the Corfu pediments was a pioneer, and the composition shows all the signs of experimentation. The lack of narrative unity and the figures' extraordinary diversity of scale eventually gave way to pedimental designs with freestanding figures in place of reliefs all acting out a single event and appearing the same size. But the Corfu designer already had shown the way, by realizing, for example, that the area beneath the raking cornice could be filled with gods and heroes of similar size if a combination of standing, leaning, kneeling, seated, and prostrate figures were employed in the composition. The Corfu master also discovered that animals could be very useful space fillers because, unlike humans, they have one end taller than the other.

5-18 Reconstruction drawing of the Siphnian Treasury, Delphi, Greece, ca. 530 BCE (John Burge).

Treasuries were storehouses in sanctuaries for a city's votive offerings. The Ionic treasury the Siphnians erected at Delphi featured caryatids in the porch, and sculptures in the pediment and frieze.

Doric columns in the porch and sculptured metopes in the frieze. The Siphnians equally characteristically employed the Ionic order for their Delphic treasury. Wealth from the island's gold and silver mines made the luxurious building possible. In the porch, where one would expect to find fluted Ionic columns, far more elaborate *caryatids* were employed instead. Caryatids are rare, even in Ionic architecture, but they are unknown in Doric architecture, where they would have been discordant elements in that much more severe order. The Siphnian statue-columns resemble contemporary korai dressed in Ionian chitons and himations (FIG. 5-12).

Another Ionic feature of the Siphnian Treasury is the continuous sculptured frieze on all four sides of the building. The north frieze represents the popular theme of the gigantomachy, but the rendition is much more detailed than that in the corner of the Corfu pediment. In the section reproduced here (FIG. 5-19), Apollo and Artemis pursue a fleeing giant at the right, while behind them one of the lions pulling a goddess's chariot attacks a giant and bites into his midsection. Paint originally enlivened the crowded composition, and painted labels identified the various protagonists. Some figures had metal weapons. The effect must have been dazzling. On one of the shields the sculptor inscribed his name (unfortunately lost), a clear indication of pride in accomplishment.

SIPHNIAN TREASURY, DELPHI The sixth century BCE also saw the erection of grandiose Ionic temples on the Aegean Islands and the west coast of Asia Minor. The gem of Archaic Ionic architecture and architectural sculpture, however, is not a temple but a treasury erected by the city of Siphnos in the Sanctuary of Apollo at Delphi. It can be reliably reconstructed (FIG. 5-18) based on the surviving fragments now on display in the Delphi museum. Greek *treasuries* were small buildings set up for the safe storage of votive offerings. At Delphi many poleis expressed their civic pride by erecting these templelike but nonperipteral structures. Athens built one with

5-19 Gigantomachy, detail of the north frieze of the Siphnian Treasury, Delphi, Greece, ca. 530 BCE. Marble, 2′ 1″ high. Archaeological Museum, Delphi.

Greek friezes were brightly painted. As in contemporaneous vase painting, the Siphnian frieze also had painted labels identifying the various gods and giants. Some of the figures held metal weapons.

Vase Painting

Labeled figures and artists' signatures also appear on Archaic painted vases. By the mid-sixth century BCE, the Athenians, having learned the black-figure technique from the Corinthians (FIG. 5-5), had taken over the export market for fine painted ceramics.

FRANÇOIS VASE The masterpiece of early Athenian black-figure painting is the *François Vase* (FIG. 5-20), named for the excavator who uncovered it in an Etruscan tomb at Chiusi. The vase is a new kind of krater with volute-shaped handles, probably inspired by costly metal prototypes. It was signed by both its painter ("KLEITIAS painted me") and potter ("ERGOTIMOS made me"), whose signatures each appear twice among the more than 200 figures in six registers. Labels abound, naming humans and animals alike, even some inanimate objects. The painter devoted only one of the bands to the Orientalizing repertoire of animals and sphinxes. The rest constitute a selective encyclopedia of Greek mythology, focusing on the exploits of Peleus and his son Achilles, the great hero of Homer's *Iliad*, and of Theseus, the legendary king of Athens.

In the detail shown here (FIG. 5-20, *bottom*), Lapiths (a northern Greek tribe) and centaurs battle (*centauromachy*) after a wedding celebration where the man-beasts, who were invited guests, got drunk and attempted to abduct the Lapith maidens and young boys. Theseus, also on the guest list, was prominent among the centaurs' Greek adversaries. Kleitias did not fill the space between his figures with decorative ornament, as did his Geometric predecessors (FIG. 5-2). But his heroes still conform to the age-old composite type (profile heads with frontal eyes, frontal torsos, and profile legs and arms). His centaurs, however, are much more believable than their Geometric counterparts (FIG. 5-3). The man-horse combination is top/bottom rather than front/back. The lower (horse) portion has four legs of uniform type, and the upper part of the monster is fully human. In characteristic fashion, Kleitias painted the animal section of the centaur in strict profile, whereas the human head and torso are a composite of frontal and profile views. (He used a consistent profile for the more adventurous detail of the collapsed centaur at the right.)

EXEKIAS The acknowledged master of the black-figure technique was an Athenian named EXEKIAS, whose vases were not only widely exported but copied as well. Perhaps his greatest work is an amphora (FIG. 5-21), found in an Etruscan tomb at Vulci, that Exekias signed as both painter and potter. Unlike Kleitias, Exekias did not divide the surface of the vase into a series of horizontal bands. Instead, he placed figures of monumental stature in a single large framed panel. At the left is Achilles, fully armed. He plays a dice game with his comrade Ajax. From the lips of Achilles comes the word *tesara* (four). Ajax calls out *tria* (three). Although Ajax has taken off his helmet, both men hold their spears, and their shields are close at hand. Each man is ready for action at a moment's notice. This depiction of "the calm before the storm" is the antithesis of the Archaic preference for dramatic action. The gravity and tension that will characterize much Classical Greek art of the next century, but that are absent in Archaic art, already may be seen in this vase.

Exekias had no equal as a black-figure painter. This is evident in such details as the extraordinarily intricate engraving of the patterns on the heroes' cloaks (highlighted with delicate touches of white) and in the brilliant composition. The arch formed by the backs of the two warriors echoes the shape of the rounded shoulders of the amphora. The shape of the vessel (compare FIG. 5-22) is echoed again in the void between the heads and spears of Achilles and Ajax. Exekias also used the spears to lead the viewer's eyes toward the thrown dice, where the heroes' eyes are fixed. Of course, those eyes

1 ft.

1 in.

5-21A EXEKIAS, *Achilles Killing Penthesilea,* ca. 540–530 BCE

5-20 KLEITIAS and ERGOTIMOS, *François Vase* (Athenian black-figure volute krater), from Chiusi, Italy, ca. 570 BCE. General view (*top*) and detail of centauromachy on other side of vase (*bottom*). 2' 2" high. Museo Archeologico, Florence. ▶

Found in an Etruscan tomb, this huge krater is signed by both the painter and the potter and has more than 200 mythological figures presented in registers, as on Geometric and Orientalizing vases.

5-21 Exekias, Achilles and Ajax playing a dice game (detail from an Athenian black-figure amphora), from Vulci, Italy, ca. 540–530 BCE. Whole vessel 2' high; detail $8\frac{1}{2}$" high. Musei Vaticani, Rome. ◼◀

The dramatic tension, adjustment of figures' poses to the vase's shape, and intricacy of the engraved patterns of the cloaks are hallmarks of Exekias, the greatest master of black-figure painting.

do not really look down at the table but stare out from the profile heads in the old manner. For all his brilliance, Exekias was still wedded to many of the old conventions. True innovation in figure drawing would have to await the invention of a new ceramic painting technique of greater versatility than black-figure, with its dark silhouettes and incised details.

BILINGUAL PAINTING The birth of this new technique came around 530 BCE from an artist known as the ANDOKIDES PAINTER, that is, the anonymous painter who decorated the vases signed by the potter Andokides. The differences between the two techniques can best be studied on a series of experimental vases with the same composition painted on both sides, once in black-figure and once in the new technique, *red-figure*. Such vases, nicknamed *bilingual vases*, were produced for only a short time. An especially interesting example is an amphora (FIG. **5-22**) by the Andokides Painter that features copies of the Achilles and Ajax panel by Exekias, his teacher.

In neither black-figure nor red-figure did the Andokides Painter capture the intensity of the model, and the treatment of details is decidedly inferior. Yet the new red-figure technique had obvious advantages over the old black-figure treatment. Red-figure is the opposite

of black-figure. What was previously black became red, and vice versa. The artist employed the same black glaze but instead of using it to create the silhouettes of figures, the painter outlined the figures and then colored the background black. The artist reserved the red clay for the figures themselves. Interior details were then drawn with a soft brush in place of a stiff metal graver, giving the painter much greater flexibility. The artist could vary the thickness of the lines and even build up the glaze to give relief to curly hair or dilute it to create brown shades, thereby expanding the chromatic range of the Greek vase painter's craft. The Andokides Painter—many think he was the potter Andokides himself—did not yet appreciate the full potential of his invention. But he created a technique that, in the hands of other, more skilled artists, helped revolutionize the art of drawing.

5-22 ANDOKIDES PAINTER, Achilles and Ajax playing a dice game (Athenian bilingual amphora), from Orvieto, Italy, ca. 525–520 BCE. Black-figure side (*left*) and red-figure side (*right*). 1' 9" high. Museum of Fine Arts, Boston. ◼◀

Around 530 BCE, the Andokides Painter invented the red-figure technique. Some of his early vases are "bilingual"—that is, the same scene appears on both sides, one in black-figure and one in red-figure.

5-23 EUPHRONIOS, Herakles wrestling
Antaios (detail of an Athenian red-figure
calyx krater), from Cerveteri, Italy, ca. 510 BCE.
Whole vessel 1′ 7″ high; detail 7¾″ high.
Louvre, Paris.

Euphronios rejected the age-old composite
view for his depiction of Herakles and the
giant Antaios and instead attempted to
reproduce how the human body is seen
from a particular viewpoint.

EUPHRONIOS One of these younger
and more adventurous painters was EU-
PHRONIOS, whose krater depicting the
struggle between Herakles and Antaios
(FIG. 5-23) reveals the exciting possibili-
ties of the new red-figure technique. Antaios was a Libyan giant, a
son of Earth, and he derived his power from contact with the
ground. To defeat him, Herakles had to lift him into the air and
strangle him while no part of the giant's body touched the earth. In
the scene on the krater, the two wrestle on the ground, and Antaios
still possesses enormous strength. Nonetheless, Herakles has the
upper hand. The giant's face is a mask of pain. His eyes roll and his
teeth are bared. His right arm is paralyzed, with the fingers limp.

Euphronios used diluted glaze to show Antaios's unkempt
golden brown hair—intentionally contrasted with the neat coiffure
and carefully trimmed beard of the emotionless Greek hero. The
artist also used thinned glaze to delineate the muscles of both figures. But rendering human anatomy convincingly was not his only
interest. Euphronios also wished to show that his figures occupy
space. He deliberately rejected the conventional composite posture
for the human figure, which communicates so well the specific parts
of the human body, and attempted instead to reproduce how a particular human body is *seen*. He presented, for example, not only Antaios's torso but also his right thigh from the front. The lower leg disappears behind the giant, and one glimpses only part of the right
foot. The viewer must mentally make the connection between the
upper leg and the foot. The red-figure painter did not create a two-
dimensional panel filled with figures in stereotypical postures, as his
Archaic and pre-Greek predecessors always did. His panel is a window onto a mythological world with protagonists moving in three-
dimensional space—a revolutionary new conception of what a picture was supposed to be.

5-24A ONESIMOS,
Girl preparing
to bathe,
ca. 490 BCE.

EUTHYMIDES A preoccupation with the art of drawing per se
may be seen in a remarkable amphora (FIG. 5-24) painted by
EUTHYMIDES, a rival of Euphronios. The subject is appropriate for a
wine storage jar—three tipsy revelers. But the theme was little more
than an excuse for the artist to experiment with the representation of
unusual positions of the human form. It is no coincidence that the
bodies do not overlap, for each is an independent figure study. Euthymides cast aside the conventional frontal and profile composite
views. Instead, he painted torsos that are not two-dimensional surface patterns but are *foreshortened*, that is, drawn in a three-quarter
view. Most noteworthy is the central figure, who is shown from the
rear with a twisting spinal column and buttocks in three-quarter
view. Earlier artists had no interest in attempting such postures because they not only are incomplete but also do not show the "main"

side of the human body. But for Euthymides the challenge of drawing the figure from such an unusual viewpoint was a reward in itself.
With understandable pride he proclaimed his achievement by
adding to the formulaic signature "Euthymides painted me" the
phrase "as never Euphronios [could do!]"

5-24 EUTHYMIDES, Three revelers (Athenian red-figure amphora),
from Vulci, Italy, ca. 510 BCE. 2′ high. Staatliche Antikensammlungen,
Munich. ■◀

Euthymides chose this theme as an excuse to represent bodies in
unusual positions, including a foreshortened three-quarter view from
the rear. He claimed to have surpassed Euphronios as a draftsman.

5-25 Temple of Aphaia, Aegina, Greece, ca. 500–490 BCE.

In this refined early-fifth-century BCE Doric design (compare FIG. 5-15), the columns are more slender and widely spaced, and there are only 6 columns on the facade and 12 on the flanks.

5-26 Model of the Temple of Aphaia, Aegina, Greece, ca. 500–490 BCE, showing internal elevation. Glyptothek, Munich.

Later Doric architects also modified the plan of their temples (compare FIG. 5-16). The Aegina temple's cella has two colonnades of two stories each (originally with a statue of the deity between them).

Aegina and the Transition to the Classical Period

The years just before and after 500 BCE were also a time of dynamic transition in architecture and architectural sculpture. Some of the changes were evolutionary in nature, others revolutionary. Both kinds are evident in the Temple at Aegina dedicated to Aphaia, a local goddess.

TEMPLE OF APHAIA, AEGINA The temple (FIG. 5-25) sits on a prominent ridge with dramatic views out to the sea. The colonnade is 45 × 95 feet and consists of 6 Doric columns on the facade and 12 on the flanks. This is a much more compact structure than the impressive but ungainly Archaic Temple of Hera I (FIG. 5-15) at Paestum, even though the ratio of width to length is similar. Doric architects had learned a great deal in the half century that elapsed between construction of the two temples. The columns

of the Aegina temple are more widely spaced and more slender. The capitals create a smooth transition from the vertical shafts below to the horizontal architrave above. Gone are the Archaic flattened echinuses and bulging shafts of the Paestum columns. The Aegina architect also refined the internal elevation (FIG. 5-26) and plan (FIG. 5-27, *left*). In place of a single row of columns down the center of the cella is a double colonnade—and each row has two stories. This arrangement allowed a statue to be placed on the central axis and also gave worshipers gathered in front of the building an unobstructed view through the pair of columns in the pronaos.

Both pediments featured painted life-size statuary (FIG. 5-27, *right*) in place of the high reliefs characteristic of Archaic temple pediments. The theme of both statuary groups was the battle of Greeks and Trojans, but the sculptors depicted different episodes. The compositions were nonetheless almost identical, with Athena at the center of the bloody combat. She is larger than all the other figures because she is superhuman, but all the mortal heroes are the

5-27 Plan (*left*) and GUILLAUME-ABEL BLOUET'S 1828 restored view of the facade (*right*) of the Temple of Aphaia, Aegina, Greece, ca. 500–490 BCE.

The restored view suggests how colorful Greek temples were. The designer solved the problem of composing figures in a pediment by using the whole range of body postures from upright to prostrate.

5-28 Dying warrior, from the west pediment of the Temple of Aphaia, Aegina, Greece, ca. 490 BCE. Marble, 5′ 2½″ long. Glyptothek, Munich.

The statues of the west pediment of the early-fifth-century BCE temple at Aegina exhibit Archaic features. This fallen warrior still has a rigidly frontal torso and an Archaic smile on his face.

1 ft.

5-29 Dying warrior, from the east pediment of the Temple of Aphaia, Aegina, Greece, ca. 480 BCE. Marble, 6′ 1″ long. Glyptothek, Munich.

The eastern dying warrior already belongs to the Classical era. His posture is more natural, and he exhibits a new self-consciousness. Concerned with his own pain, he does not face the viewer.

1 ft.

same size, regardless of the statue's position in the pediment. Unlike the experimental design at Corfu (FIG. 5-17), the Aegina pediments feature a unified theme and consistent scale. The designer was able to keep the size of the figures constant by using the whole range of body postures from upright (Athena) to leaning, falling, kneeling, and lying (Greeks and Trojans).

The sculptures of the Aegina pediments were probably set in place when the temple was completed around 490 BCE. Many scholars believe the statues at the eastern end were damaged and replaced with a new group a decade or two later, although some think both groups were installed after 480 BCE. Whatever the precise dates of the sculptures, it is very instructive to compare the eastern and western figures. The west pediment's dying warrior (FIG. 5-28) was still conceived in the Archaic mode. His torso is rigidly frontal, and he looks out directly at the spectator—with his face set in an Archaic smile in spite of the bronze arrow that punctures his chest. He is like a mannequin in a store window whose arms and legs have been arranged by someone else for effective display. There is no sense whatsoever of a thinking and feeling human being.

The comparable figure (FIG. 5-29) in the east pediment is radically different. His posture is more natural and more complex, with the torso placed at an angle to the viewer. (He is on a par with the painted figures of Euphronios, FIG. 5-23.) Moreover, he reacts to his wound as a flesh-and-blood human would. He knows that death is inevitable, but he still struggles to rise once again, using his shield for support. And he does not look out at the spectator. He is concerned with his pain, not with the viewer. No more than a decade separates the two statues, but they belong to different eras. The eastern warrior is not a creation of the Archaic world, when sculptors imposed anatomical patterns (and smiles) on statues from without. This statue belongs to the Classical world, where statues move as humans move and

possess the self-consciousness of real men and women. This was a radical change in the conception of what a statue was meant to be. In sculpture, as in painting, the Classical revolution had occurred.

EARLY AND HIGH CLASSICAL PERIODS

Art historians mark the beginning of the Classical* age from a historical event: the defeat of the Persian invaders of Greece by the allied Hellenic city-states. Shortly after the Persians occupied and sacked Athens in 480 BCE, the Greeks won a decisive naval victory over the Persians at Salamis. It had been a difficult war, and at times it had seemed as though Asia would swallow up Greece, and the Persian king Xerxes (see Chapter 2) would rule over all. When the Persians destroyed the Greek city Miletos in 494 BCE, they killed the male inhabitants and sold the women and children into slavery. The narrow escape of the Greeks from domination by Asian "barbarians" nurtured a sense of Hellenic identity so strong that from then on the history of European civilization would be distinct from the civilization of Asia, even though they continued to interact. Typical of the time were the views of the great dramatist Aeschylus, who celebrated, in his *Oresteia* trilogy, the triumph of reason and law over barbarous crimes, blood feuds, and mad vengeance. Himself a veteran of the epic battle of Marathon, Aeschylus repudiated in majestic verse all the slavish and inhuman traits of nature that the Greeks at that time of crisis associated with the Persians.

*Note: In *Art through the Ages,* the adjective "Classical," with uppercase C, refers specifically to the Classical period of ancient Greece, 480–323 BCE. Lowercase "classical" refers to Greco-Roman antiquity in general, that is, the period treated in Chapters 5, 9, and 10.

5-30 Temple of Hera II, Paestum, Italy, ca. 460 BCE.

The second Hera temple at Paestum was modeled on Libon's Temple of Zeus at Olympia. The Paestum temple reflects the Olympia design, but the later building lacks the pedimental sculpture of its model.

Architecture and Architectural Sculpture

The decades following the removal of the Persian threat are universally considered the high point of Greek civilization. This is the era of the dramatists Sophocles and Euripides, as well as Aeschylus; the historian Herodotus; the statesman Pericles; the philosopher Socrates; and many of the most famous Greek architects, sculptors, and painters.

TEMPLE OF ZEUS, OLYMPIA The first great monument of Classical art and architecture is the Temple of Zeus at Olympia, site of the Olympic Games. The temple was begun about 470 BCE and was probably completed by 457 BCE. The architect was Libon of Elis. Today the structure is in ruins, its picturesque tumbled column drums an eloquent reminder of the effect of the passage of time on even the grandest monuments humans have built. A good idea of its original appearance can be gleaned, however, from a slightly later Doric temple modeled closely on the Olympian shrine of Zeus—the second Temple of Hera (FIG. 5-30) at Paestum. The plans and elevations of both temples follow the pattern of the Temple of Aphaia (FIGS. 5-26 and 5-27) at Aegina: an even number of columns (six) on the short ends, two columns in antis, and two rows of columns in two stories inside the cella. But the Temple of Zeus was more lavishly decorated than even the Aphaia temple. Statues filled both pediments, and the six metopes over the doorway in the pronaos and the matching six of the opisthodomos were adorned with reliefs.

The subject of the Temple of Zeus's east pediment (FIG. 5-31) had deep local significance: the chariot race between Pelops (from whom the Peloponnesos takes its name) and King Oinomaos. The story is a sinister one. Oinomaos had one daughter, Hippodameia, and it was foretold that he would die if she married. Consequently, Oinomaos challenged any suitor who wished to make Hippodameia his bride to a chariot race from Olympia to Corinth. If the suitor won, he also won the hand of the king's daughter. But if he lost, he was killed. The outcome of each race was predetermined, because Oinomaos possessed the divine horses of his father Ares. To ensure his victory when all others had failed, Pelops resorted to bribing the king's groom, Myrtilos, to rig the royal chariot so that it would collapse during the race. Oinomaos was killed and Pelops won his bride, but he drowned Myrtilos rather than pay his debt to him. Before he died, Myrtilos brought a curse on Pelops and his descendants. This curse led to the murder of Pelops's son Atreus and to events that figure prominently in some of the greatest Greek tragedies of the Classical era, Aeschylus's three plays known collectively as the *Oresteia:* the sacrifice by Atreus's son Agamemnon of his daughter Iphigeneia; the slaying of Agamemnon by Aegisthus, lover of Agamemnon's wife Clytaemnestra; and the murder of Aegisthus and Clytaemnestra by Orestes, the son of Agamemnon and Clytaemnestra.

Indeed, the pedimental statues (FIG. 5-31), which faced toward the starting point of all Olympic chariot races, are posed as actors on a stage—Zeus in the center, Oinomaos and his wife on one side, Pelops and Hippodameia on the other, and their respective chariots to each side. All are quiet. The horrible events known to every

A West iment, ple of Zeus, npia, ca. -456 BCE.

1 ft.

5-31 East pediment from the Temple of Zeus, Olympia, Greece, ca. 470–456 BCE. Marble, 87' wide. Archaeological Museum, Olympia.

The east pediment of the Zeus temple depicts the chariot race between Pelops and Oinomaos, which began at Olympia. The actors in the pediment faced the starting point of Olympic chariot races.

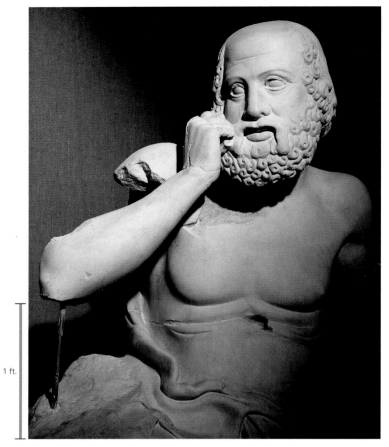

5-32 Seer, from the east pediment of the Temple of Zeus, Olympia, Greece, ca. 470–456 BCE. Marble, full figure 4′ 6″ high; detail 3′ 2½″ high. Archaeological Museum, Olympia.

The balding seer in the Olympia east pediment is a rare depiction of old age in Classical sculpture. He has a shocked expression because he foresees the tragic outcome of the chariot race.

spectator have yet to occur. Only one man reacts—a seer who knows the future (FIG. **5-32**). He is a remarkable figure. Unlike the gods, heroes, and noble youths and maidens who are the almost exclusive subjects of Archaic and Classical Greek statuary, this seer is a rare depiction of old age. He has a balding, wrinkled head and sagging musculature—and a shocked expression on his face. This is a true show of emotion, unlike the stereotypical Archaic smile, without precedent in earlier Greek sculpture and not a regular feature of Greek art until the Hellenistic age.

The metopes of the Zeus temple are also thematically connected with the site, for they depict the 12 labors of Herakles (see "Herakles, Greatest of Greek Heroes," right), the legendary founder of the Olympic Games. In the metope illustrated here (FIG. **5-33**), Herakles holds up the sky (with the aid of the goddess Athena—and a cushion) in place of Atlas, who had undertaken the dangerous journey to fetch the golden apples of the Hesperides for the hero. The load soon will be transferred back to Atlas (at the right, still holding the apples), but now each of the very high relief figures in the metope stands quietly with the same serene dignity as the statues in the Olympia pediment. In both attitude and dress (simple Doric peplos for the women), all the Olympia figures display a severity that contrasts sharply with the smiling and elaborately clad figures of the Late Archaic period. Many art historians call this Early Classical phase of Greek art the *Severe Style*.

Herakles, Greatest of Greek Heroes

Greek heroes were a class of mortals of intermediate status between ordinary humans and the immortal gods. Most often the children of gods, some were great warriors, such as those who fought at Troy and were celebrated in Homer's epic poems. Others pursued one fabulous adventure after another, ridding the world of monsters and generally benefiting humankind. Many heroes were worshiped after their deaths, and the greatest of them were honored with shrines, especially in the cities with which they were most closely associated.

The greatest Greek hero was *Herakles* (the Roman *Hercules*), born in Thebes and the son of Zeus and Alkmene, a mortal woman. Zeus's jealous wife Hera hated Herakles and sent two serpents to attack him in his cradle, but the infant strangled them. Later, Hera caused the hero to go mad and to kill his wife and children. As punishment he was condemned to perform 12 great labors. In the first, he defeated the legendary lion of Nemea and ever after wore its pelt. The lion's skin and his weapon, a club, are Herakles' distinctive attributes (FIG. **5-66**). His last task was to obtain the golden apples Gaia gave to Hera at her marriage (FIG. **5-33**). They grew from a tree in the garden of the Hesperides at the western edge of the ocean, where a dragon guarded them. After completion of the 12 seemingly impossible tasks, Herakles was awarded immortality. Athena, who had watched over him carefully throughout his life and assisted him in performing the labors, introduced him into the realm of the gods on Mount Olympus. According to legend, it was Herakles who established the Olympic Games.

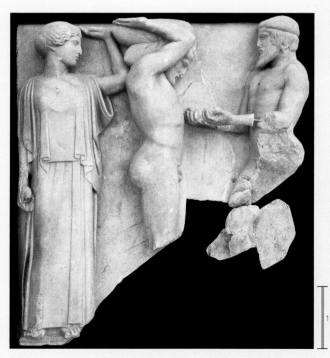

5-33 Athena, Herakles, and Atlas with the apples of the Hesperides, metope from the Temple of Zeus, Olympia, Greece, ca. 470–456 BCE. Marble, 5′ 3″ high. Archaeological Museum, Olympia.

Herakles founded the Olympic Games, and his 12 labors were the subjects of the 12 Doric metopes of the Zeus temple. This one shows the hero holding up the world (with Athena's aid) for Atlas.

Statuary

Early Classical sculptors were also the first to break away from the rigid and unnatural Egyptian-inspired pose of the Archaic *kouroi*. This change is evident in the postures of the Olympia figures, but it occurred even earlier in independent statuary.

KRITIOS BOY Although it is well under life-size, the marble statue known as the *Kritios Boy* (FIG. **5-34**)—so titled because it was once thought the sculptor Kritios carved it—is one of the most important works of Greek sculpture. Never before had a sculptor been concerned with portraying how a human being (as opposed to a stone image) actually stands. Real people do not stand in the stiff-legged pose of the *kouroi* and *korai* or their Egyptian predecessors. Humans shift their weight and the position of the main body parts around the vertical but flexible axis of the spine. When humans move, the body's elastic musculoskeletal structure dictates a harmonious, smooth motion of all its elements. The sculptor of the *Kritios*

Boy was among the first to grasp this fact and to represent it in statuary. The youth has a slight dip to the right hip, indicating the shifting of weight onto his left leg. His right leg is bent, at ease. The head also turns slightly to the right and tilts, breaking the unwritten rule of frontality dictating the form of virtually all earlier statues. This weight shift, which art historians describe as *contrapposto* (counterbalance), separates Classical from Archaic Greek statuary.

RIACE WARRIOR The innovations of the *Kritios Boy* were carried even further in the bronze statue (FIG. **5-35**) of a warrior found in the sea near Riace at the "toe" of the Italian "boot." It is one of a pair of statues divers accidentally discovered in the cargo of a ship that sank in antiquity on its way from Greece probably to Rome, where Greek sculpture was much admired. Known as the Riace Bronzes, they had to undergo several years of cleaning and restoration after nearly two millennia of submersion in salt water, but they are nearly intact. The statue shown here lacks only its shield, spear, and helmet. It is a masterpiece of hollow-casting (see "Hollow-Casting Life-Size Bronze

5-34 *Kritios Boy,* from the Acropolis, Athens, Greece, ca. 480 BCE. Marble, 3′ 10″ high. Acropolis Museum, Athens.

This is the first statue to show how a person naturally stands. The sculptor depicted the shifting of weight from one leg to the other (contrapposto). The head turns slightly, and the Archaic smile is gone.

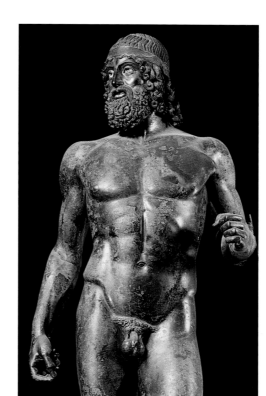

5-35 Warrior, from the sea off Riace, Italy, ca. 460–450 BCE. Bronze, 6′ 6″ high. Museo Archeologico Nazionale, Reggio Calabria.

The bronze Riace warrior statue has inlaid eyes, silver teeth and eyelashes, and copper lips and nipples (FIG. I-17). The contrapposto is more pronounced than in the *Kritios Boy* (FIG. **5-34**).

1 ft.

1 ft.

Hollow-Casting Life-Size Bronze Statues

Monumental bronze statues such as the Riace warrior (FIG. 5-35), the Delphi charioteer (FIG. 5-37), and the Artemision god (FIG. 5-38) required great technical skill to produce. They could not be manufactured using a single simple mold, as were small-scale Geometric and Archaic figures (FIGS. 5-3 and 5-4). Weight, cost, and the tendency of large masses of bronze to distort when cooling made life-size castings in solid bronze impractical, if not impossible. Instead, large statues were hollow-cast by the *cire perdue* (lost-wax) method. The lost-wax process entailed several steps and had to be repeated many times, because monumental statues were typically cast in parts—head, arms, hands, torso, and so forth.

First, the sculptor fashioned a full-size clay model of the intended statue. Then a clay master mold was made around the model and removed in sections. When dry, the various pieces of the master mold were reassembled for each separate body part. Next, a layer of beeswax was applied to the inside of each mold. When the wax cooled, the mold was removed, and the sculptor was left with a hollow wax model in the shape of the original clay model. The artist could then correct or refine details—for example, engrave fingernails on the wax hands or individual locks of hair on the head.

In the next stage, a final clay mold (*investment*) was applied to the exterior of the wax model, and a liquid clay core was poured inside the hollow wax. Metal pins (*chaplets*) were driven through the new mold to connect the investment with the clay core (FIG. 5-36*a*). Then the wax was melted out ("lost") and molten bronze poured into the mold in its place (FIG. 5-36*b*). When the bronze hardened and assumed the shape of the wax model, the investment and as much of the core as possible were removed, and the casting process was complete. Finally, the individually cast pieces were fitted together and soldered, surface imperfections smoothed, eyes inlaid, teeth and eyelashes added, attributes such as spears and wreaths provided, and so forth. Bronze statues were costly to make and highly prized.

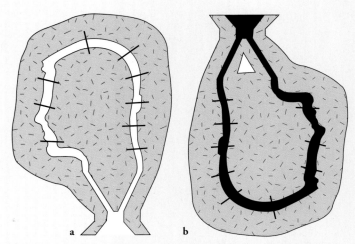

5-36 Two stages of the lost-wax method of bronze casting (after Sean A. Hemingway).

Drawing *a* shows a clay mold (investment), wax model, and clay core connected by chaplets. Drawing *b* shows the wax melted out and the molten bronze poured into the mold to form the cast bronze head.

1 ft.

5-37 Charioteer, from a group dedicated by Polyzalos of Gela in the sanctuary of Apollo, Delphi, Greece, ca. 475 BCE. Bronze, 5′ 11″ high. Archaeological Museum, Delphi.

The charioteer is almost all that remains of a large bronze group that also included a chariot, a team of horses, and a groom, requiring hundreds of individually cast pieces soldered together.

Statues," page 122), and FIG. **5-36**), with inlaid eyes, silver teeth and eyelashes, and copper lips and nipples (FIG. **I-17**). The weight shift is more pronounced than in the *Kritios Boy.* The warrior's head turns more forcefully to the right, his shoulders tilt, his hips swing more markedly, and his arms have been freed from the body. Natural motion in space has replaced Archaic frontality and rigidity.

CHARIOTEER OF DELPHI The high technical quality of the Riace warrior is equaled in another bronze statue set up a decade or two earlier to commemorate the victory of the tyrant Polyzalos of Gela (Sicily) in a chariot race at Delphi. The statue (FIG. **5-37**) is almost all that remains of a large group composed of Polyzalos's driver, the chariot, the team of horses, and a young groom. The charioteer stands in an almost Archaic pose, but the turn of the head and feet in opposite directions as well as a slight twist at the waist are in keeping with the Severe Style. The moment chosen for depiction is not during the frenetic race but after, when the driver quietly and modestly holds his horses still in the winner's circle. He grasps the reins in his outstretched right hand (the lower left arm, cast separately, is missing), and he wears the standard charioteer's garment,

girdled high and held in at the shoulders and the back to keep it from flapping. The folds emphasize both the verticality and calm of the figure and recall the flutes of a Greek column. A band inlaid with silver, tied around the head, confines the hair. Delicate bronze lashes shade the eyes made of glass paste.

ARTEMISION ZEUS The male human form in motion is, in contrast, the subject of another Early Classical bronze statue (FIG. **5-38**), which, like the Riace warrior, divers found in an ancient shipwreck, this time off the coast of Greece itself at Cape Artemision. The bearded god once hurled a weapon held in his right hand, probably a thunderbolt, in which case he is Zeus. A less likely suggestion is that this is Poseidon with his trident. The pose could be employed equally well for a javelin thrower. Both arms are boldly extended, and the right heel is raised off the ground, underscoring the lightness and stability of hollow-cast monumental statues.

MYRON, *DISKOBOLOS* A bronze statue similar to the Artemision Zeus was the renowned *Diskobolos* (*Discus Thrower*) by the Early Classical master MYRON. The original is lost. Only marble copies (FIG. **5-39**) survive, made in Roman times, when demand so

1 ft.

5-38 Zeus (or Poseidon?), from the sea off Cape Artemision, Greece, ca. 460–450 BCE. Bronze, 6′ 10″ high. National Archaeological Museum, Athens.

In this Early Classical statue of Zeus hurling a thunderbolt, both arms are boldly extended and the right heel is raised off the ground, underscoring the lightness and stability of hollow-cast bronze statues.

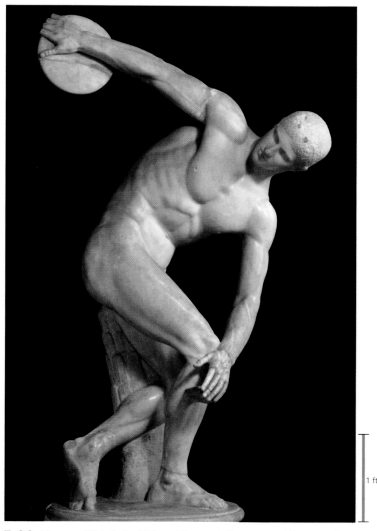

1 ft.

5-39 MYRON, *Diskobolos* (*Discus Thrower*). Roman marble copy of a bronze original of ca. 450 BCE, 5′ 1″ high. Museo Nazionale Romano– Palazzo Massimo alle Terme.

This marble copy of Myron's lost bronze statue captures how the sculptor froze the action of discus throwing and arranged the nude athlete's body and limbs so that they formed two intersecting arcs.

Polykleitos's Prescription for the Perfect Statue

One of the most influential philosophers of the ancient world was Pythagoras of Samos, who lived during the latter part of the sixth century BCE. A famous geometric theorem still bears his name. Pythagoras also is said to have discovered that harmonic chords in music are produced on the strings of a lyre at regular intervals that may be expressed as ratios of whole numbers—2:1, 3:2, 4:3. He and his followers, the Pythagoreans, believed more generally that underlying harmonic proportions could be found in all of nature, determining the form of the cosmos as well as of things on earth, and that beauty resided in harmonious numerical ratios.

By this reasoning, a perfect statue would be one constructed according to an all-encompassing mathematical formula. In the mid-fifth century BCE, the sculptor Polykleitos of Argos set out to make just such a statue (FIG. 5-40). He recorded the principles he followed and the proportions he used in a treatise titled the *Canon* (that is, the standard of perfection). His treatise is unfortunately lost, but Galen, a physician who lived during the second century CE, summarized the sculptor's philosophy as follows:

> [Beauty arises from] the commensurability [*symmetria*] of the parts, such as that of finger to finger, and of all the fingers to the palm and the wrist, and of these to the forearm, and of the forearm to the upper arm, and, in fact, of everything to everything else, just as it is written in the *Canon* of Polykleitos. . . . Polykleitos supported his treatise [by making] a statue according to the tenets of his treatise, and called the statue, like the work, the *Canon*.*

This is why Pliny the Elder, writing in the first century CE, maintained that Polykleitos "alone of men is deemed to have rendered art itself [that is, the theoretical basis of art] in a work of art."[†]

Polykleitos's belief that a successful statue resulted from the precise application of abstract principles is reflected in an anecdote (probably a later invention) told by the Roman historian Aelian:

> Polykleitos made two statues at the same time, one which would be pleasing to the crowd and the other according to the principles of his art. In accordance with the opinion of each person who came into his workshop, he altered something and changed its form, sub-

mitting to the advice of each. Then he put both statues on display. The one was marvelled at by everyone, and the other was laughed at. Thereupon Polykleitos said, "But the one that you find fault with, you made yourselves; while the one that you marvel at, I made."[‡]

5-40 POLYKLEITOS, *Doryphoros* (*Spear Bearer*). Roman marble copy from Pompeii, Italy, after a bronze original of ca. 450–440 BCE, 6′ 11″ high. Museo Archeologico Nazionale, Naples. ■◀

Polykleitos sought to portray the perfect man and to impose order on human movement. He achieved his goals by employing harmonic proportions and a system of cross balance for all parts of the body.

1 ft.

*Galen, *De placitis Hippocratis et Platonis*, 5. Translated by J. J. Pollitt, *The Art of Ancient Greece: Sources and Documents* (New York: Cambridge University Press, 1990), 76.
[†]Pliny the Elder, *Natural History*, 34.55. Translated by Pollitt, 75.
[‡]Aelian, *Varia historia*, 14.8. Translated by Pollitt, 79.

far exceeded the supply of Greek statues that a veritable industry was born to meet the call for Greek statuary to display in public places and private villas alike. The copies usually were made in less costly marble. The change in medium resulted in a different surface appearance. In most cases, the copyist also had to add an intrusive tree trunk to support the great weight of the stone statue and struts between arms and body to strengthen weak points. The copies rarely approach the quality of the originals, and the Roman sculptors sometimes took liberties with their models to conform to their own tastes and needs. Occasionally, for example, a mirror image of the

original was created for a specific setting. Nevertheless, the copies are indispensable today. Without them it would be impossible to reconstruct the history of Greek sculpture after the Archaic period.

Myron's *Diskobolos* is a vigorous action statue, like the Artemision Zeus, but it is composed in an almost Archaic manner, with profile limbs and a nearly frontal chest, suggesting the tension of a coiled spring. Like the arm of a pendulum clock, the right arm of the *Diskobolos* has reached the apex of its arc but has not yet begun to swing down again. Myron froze the action and arranged the body and limbs to form two intersecting arcs (one from the discus to the left hand, one from the head to the right knee), creating the impression of a tightly stretched bow a moment before the string is released. This tension is not, however, mirrored in the athlete's face, which remains expressionless. Once again, as in the warrior statue (FIG. 5-29) from the Aegina temple's east pediment, the head is turned away from the spectator. In contrast to Archaic athlete statues, the Classical *Diskobolos* does not perform for the spectator but concentrates on the task at hand.

POLYKLEITOS, *DORYPHOROS* One of the most frequently copied Greek statues was the *Doryphoros* (*Spear Bearer*) by the sculptor POLYKLEITOS, whose work epitomizes the intellectual rigor of Classical art. The best marble replica (FIG. 5-40) stood in a palaestra at Pompeii, where it served as a model for Roman athletes. The *Doryphoros* was the embodiment of Polykleitos's vision of the ideal statue of a nude male athlete or warrior. In fact, the sculptor made it as a demonstration piece to accompany a treatise on the subject. *Spear Bearer* is a modern descriptive title for the statue. The name Polykleitos assigned to it was *Canon* (see "Polykleitos's Prescription for the Perfect Statue," page 124).

The *Doryphoros* is the culmination of the evolution in Greek statuary from the Archaic kouros to the *Kritios Boy* to the Riace warrior. The contrapposto is more pronounced than ever before in a standing statue, but Polykleitos was not content with simply rendering a figure that stood naturally. His aim was to impose order on human movement, to make it "beautiful," to "perfect" it. He achieved this through a system of cross balance. What appears at first to be a casually natural pose is, in fact, the result of an extremely complex and subtle organization of the figure's various parts. Note, for instance, how the statue's straight-hanging arm echoes the rigid supporting leg, providing the figure's right side with the columnar stability needed to anchor the left side's dynamically flexed limbs. If read anatomically, however, the tensed and relaxed limbs may be seen to oppose each other diagonally—the right arm and the left leg are relaxed, and the tensed supporting leg opposes the flexed arm, which held a spear. In like manner, the head turns to the right while the hips twist slightly to the left. And although the *Doryphoros* seems to take a step forward, the figure does not move. This dynamic asymmetrical balance, this motion while at rest, and the resulting harmony of opposites are the essence of the Polykleitan style.

The Athenian Acropolis

While Polykleitos was formulating his *Canon* in Argos, the Athenians, under the leadership of Pericles, were at work on one of the most ambitious building projects ever undertaken, the reconstruction of the Acropolis after the Persian sack of 480 BCE. Athens, despite the damage it suffered at the hands of the army of Xerxes, emerged from the war with enormous power and prestige. The Athenian commander Themistocles had decisively defeated the Persian navy off the island of Salamis, southwest of Athens, and forced it to retreat to Asia.

In 478 BCE, in the aftermath of the Persians' expulsion from the Aegean, the Greeks formed an alliance for mutual protection against any renewed threat from the east. The new confederacy came to be known as the Delian League, because its headquarters were on the sacred island of Delos, midway between the Greek mainland and the coast of Asia Minor. Although at the outset each league member had an equal vote, Athens was "first among equals," providing the allied fleet commander and determining which cities were to furnish ships and which were instead to pay an annual tribute to the treasury at Delos. Continued fighting against the Persians kept the alliance intact, but Athens gradually assumed a dominant role. In 454 BCE the Delian treasury was transferred to Athens, ostensibly for security rea-

sons. Pericles, who was only in his teens when the Persians laid waste to the Acropolis, was by midcentury the recognized leader of the Athenians, and he succeeded in converting the alliance into an Athenian empire. Tribute continued to be paid, but the surplus reserves were not expended for the common good of the allied Greek states. Instead, Pericles expropriated the money to pay the enormous cost of executing his grand plan to embellish the Acropolis of Athens.

The reaction of the allies—in reality the subjects of Athens—was predictable. Plutarch, who wrote a biography of Pericles in the early second century CE, indicated the wrath the Greek victims of Athenian tyranny felt by recording the protest voiced against Pericles' decision even in the Athenian assembly. Greece, Pericles' enemies said, had been dealt "a terrible, wanton insult" when Athens used the funds contributed out of necessity for a common war effort to "gild and embellish itself with images and extravagant temples, like some pretentious woman decked out with precious stones."[1] The source of funds for the Acropolis building program is important to keep in mind when examining those great and universally admired buildings erected in accordance with Pericles' vision of his polis reborn from the ashes of the Persian sack. They are not the glorious fruits of Athenian democracy but are instead the by-products of tyranny and the abuse of power. Too often art and architectural historians do not ask how a monument was financed. The answer can be very revealing—and very embarrassing.

PORTRAIT OF PERICLES A number of Roman copies are preserved of a famous portrait statue of Pericles by KRESILAS, who was born on Crete but who worked in Athens. The bronze portrait was set up on the Acropolis, probably immediately after the leader's death in 429 BCE, and depicted Pericles in heroic nudity. The statue must have resembled the Riace warrior (FIG. 5-35). The copies, in marble, reproduce the head only, sometimes in the form of a *herm* (a bust on a square pillar, FIG. 5-41), a popular format in Roman times

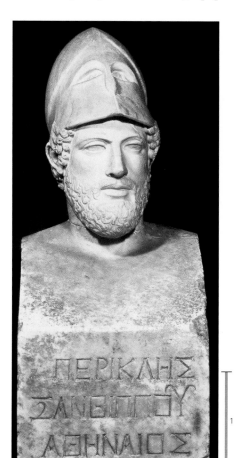

5-41 KRESILAS, Pericles. Roman marble herm copy of a bronze original of ca. 429 BCE. Full herm 6′ high; detail 4′ 6½″ high. Musei Vaticani, Rome.

In his portrait of Pericles, Kresilas was said to have made a noble man appear even nobler. Classical Greek portraits were not likenesses but idealized images in which humans appeared godlike.

1 ft.

for abbreviated copies of famous statues. The herm is inscribed "Pericles, son of Xanthippos, the Athenian," leaving no doubt as to the identification. Pericles wears the helmet of a *strategos* (general), the position he was elected to 15 times. The Athenian leader was said to have had an abnormally elongated skull, and Kresilas recorded this feature (while also concealing it) by providing a glimpse through the helmet's eye slots of the hair at the top of the head. This, together with the unblemished features of Pericles' Classically aloof face and, no doubt, his body's perfect physique, led Pliny to assert that Kresilas had the ability to make noble men appear even more noble in their portraits. This praise was apt because the Pericles herm is not a portrait at all in the modern sense of a record of actual features. Pliny referred to Kresilas's "portrait" as "the Olympian Pericles," for in this image Pericles appeared almost godlike.[2]

PERICLEAN ACROPOLIS The centerpiece of the Periclean building program on the Acropolis (FIG. **5-42**) was the Parthenon (FIG. **5-43**, no. 1), or the Temple of Athena Parthenos, erected in the remarkably short period between 447 and 438 BCE. (Work on the great temple's ambitious sculptural ornamentation continued until 432 BCE.) As soon as the Parthenon was completed, construction commenced on a grand new gateway to the Acropolis from the west (the only accessible side of the natural plateau), the Propylaia (FIG. **5-43**, no. 2). Begun in 437 BCE, it was left unfinished in 431 at the outbreak of the Peloponnesian War between Athens and Sparta. Two later temples, the Erechtheion (FIG. **5-43**, no. 4) and the Temple of Athena Nike (FIG. **5-43**, no. 5), built after Pericles died, were probably also part of the original design. The greatest Athenian architects and sculptors of the Classical period focused their attention on the construction and decoration of these four buildings.

That these fifth-century BCE buildings exist at all today is something of a miracle. In the Middle Ages, the Parthenon, for example, was converted into a Byzantine and later a Roman Catholic church and then, after the Ottoman conquest of Greece, into a mosque. Each time the building was remodeled for a different religion, it was modified structurally. The Christians early on removed the colossal statue of Athena inside. The churches had a great curved *apse* at the east end

housing the altar, and the mosque had a *minaret* (tower used to call Muslims to prayer). In 1687 the Venetians besieged the Acropolis, which at that time was in Turkish hands. Venetian weaponry scored a direct hit on the ammunition depot the Turks had installed in part of the Parthenon. The resultant explosion blew out the building's center. To make matters worse, the Venetians subsequently tried to remove some of the statues from the Parthenon's pediments. In more than one case, they dropped statues, which then smashed on the ground. From 1801 to 1803, Lord Elgin brought most of the surviving sculptures to England. For the past two centuries they have been on exhibit in the British Museum (FIGS. **5-47** to **5-50**), although Greece has appealed many times for the return of the "Elgin Marbles." Today, a uniquely modern blight threatens the Parthenon and the other buildings of the Periclean age. The corrosive emissions of factories and automobiles are decomposing the ancient marbles. A major campaign has been under way for decades to protect the columns and walls from further deterioration. What little original sculpture remained in place when modern restoration began, the Greeks transferred to the Acropolis Museum's climate-controlled rooms.

PARTHENON: ARCHITECTURE Despite the ravages of time and humanity, most of the Parthenon's peripteral colonnade (FIG. **5-44**) is still standing (or has been reerected), and art historians know a great deal about the building and its sculptural program. The architects were IKTINOS and KALLIKRATES. The statue of Athena (FIG. **5-46**) in the cella was the work of PHIDIAS, who was also the overseer of the temple's sculptural decoration. In fact, Plutarch claimed that Phidias was in charge of the entire Acropolis project.

Just as the contemporary *Doryphoros* (FIG. **5-40**) may be seen as the culmination of nearly two centuries of searching for the ideal proportions of the various human body parts, so, too, the Parthenon may be viewed as the ideal solution to the Greek architect's quest for perfect proportions in Doric temple design. Its well-spaced columns, with their slender shafts, and the capitals, with their straight-sided conical echinuses, are the ultimate refinement of the bulging and squat Doric columns and compressed capitals of the Archaic Hera temple at Paestum (FIG. **5-15**). The Parthenon architects and Poly-

5-42 Aerial view of the Acropolis looking southeast, Athens, Greece. ■◄

Under the leadership of Pericles, the Athenians undertook the costly project of reconstructing the Acropolis after the Persian sack of 480 BCE. The funds came from the Delian League treasury.

5-43 Restored view of the Acropolis, Athens, Greece (John Burge). (1) Parthenon, (2) Propylaia, (3) pinakotheke, (4) Erechtheion, (5) Temple of Athena Nike.

Of the four main fifth-century BCE buildings on the Acropolis, the first to be erected was the Parthenon, followed by the Propylaia, the Erechtheion, and the Temple of Athena Nike.

kleitos were kindred spirits in their belief that beautiful proportions resulted from strict adherence to harmonious numerical ratios, whether in a temple more than 200 feet long or a life-size statue of a nude man. For the Parthenon, the controlling ratio for the *symmetria* of the parts may be expressed algebraically as $x = 2y + 1$. Thus, for example, the temple's short ends have 8 columns and the long sides have 17, because $17 = (2 \times 8) + 1$. The stylobate's ratio of length to width is 9:4, because $9 = (2 \times 4) + 1$. This ratio also characterizes the cella's proportion of length to width, the distance between the centers of two adjacent column drums (the *interaxial*) in proportion to the columns' diameter, and so forth.

The Parthenon's harmonious design and the mathematical precision of the sizes of its constituent elements tend to obscure the fact that this temple, as actually constructed, is quite irregular in shape. Throughout the building are pronounced deviations from the strictly horizontal and vertical lines assumed to be the basis of all Greek post-and-lintel structures. The stylobate, for example, curves upward at the center on the sides and both facades, forming a kind of shallow dome, and this curvature is carried up into the entablature. Moreover, the peristyle columns lean inward slightly. Those at the corners have a diagonal inclination and are also about two inches thicker than the rest. If their lines continued, they would meet about 1.5 miles above the temple. These deviations from the norm meant that virtually every Parthenon block and drum had to be carved according to the special set of specifications dictated by its unique place in the structure. This was obviously a daunting task, and a reason must have existed for these so-called refinements in the Parthenon. Some modern observers note, for example, how the curving of horizontal lines and the tilting of vertical ones create a dynamic balance in the building—a kind of architectural contrapposto—and give it a greater sense of life. The oldest recorded explanation, however, may be the most likely. Vitruvius, a Roman architect of the late first century BCE who claimed to have had access to Iktinos's treatise on the Parthenon—again note the kinship with the *Canon* of Polykleitos—maintained that the builders made these adjustments to compensate for optical illusions. Vitruvius noted, for example, that if a stylobate is laid out on a level surface, it will appear to sag at the center, and that the corner columns of a building should be thicker because they are surrounded by light and would otherwise appear thinner than their neighbors.

The Parthenon is "irregular" in other ways as well. One of the ironies of this most famous of all Doric temples is that it is "contaminated" by Ionic elements (FIG. 5-45). Although the cella had a two-story Doric colonnade, the back room (which housed the goddess's treasury and the tribute collected from the Delian League) had four

5-44 IKTINOS and KALLIKRATES, Parthenon (Temple of Athena Parthenos, looking southeast), Acropolis, Athens, Greece, 447–438 BCE. ▮◀

The architects of the Parthenon believed that perfect beauty could be achieved by using harmonic proportions. The ratio for larger and smaller parts was $x = 2y + 1$ (for example, a plan of 17×8 columns).

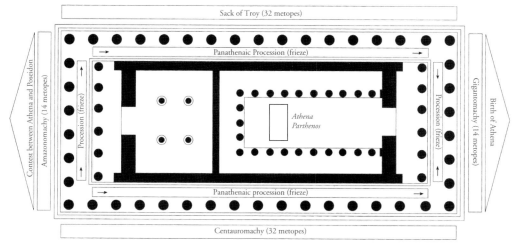

Sack of Troy (32 metopes)

Panathenaic Procession (frieze)

Contest between Athena and Poseidon

Amazonomachy (14 metopes)

Procession (frieze)

Athena Parthenos

Procession (frieze)

Gigantomachy (14 metopes)

Birth of Athena

Panathenaic procession (frieze)

Centauromachy (32 metopes)

N

0 10 20 30 40 50 feet
0   5   10   15 meters

5-45 Plan of the Parthenon, Acropolis, Athens, Greece, with diagram of the sculptural program (after Andrew Stewart), 447–432 BCE.

The Parthenon was lavishly decorated under the direction of Phidias. Statues filled both pediments, and figural reliefs adorned all 92 metopes. There was also an inner 524-foot sculptured Ionic frieze.

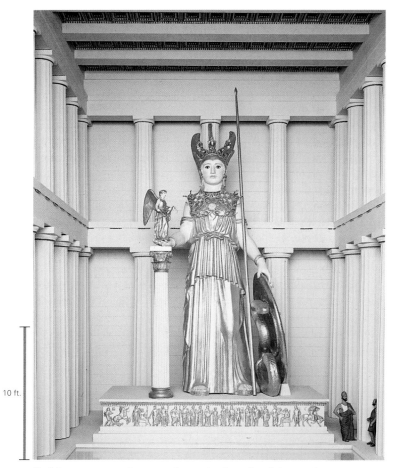

5-46 PHIDIAS, *Athena Parthenos,* in the cella of the Parthenon, Acropolis, Athens, Greece, ca. 438 BCE. Model of the lost chryselephantine statue. Royal Ontario Museum, Toronto.

Inside the cella of the Parthenon was Phidias's 38-foot-tall gold-and-ivory statue of Athena Parthenos (the Virgin), fully armed and holding Nike (Victory) in her extended right hand.

tall and slender Ionic columns as sole supports for the superstructure. And whereas the temple's exterior had a canonical Doric frieze, the inner frieze that ran around the top of the cella wall was Ionic. Perhaps this fusion of Doric and Ionic elements reflects the Athenians' belief that the Ionians of the Aegean Islands and Asia Minor were descended from Athenian settlers and were therefore their kin. Or it may be Pericles' and Iktinos's way of suggesting that Athens was the leader of *all* the Greeks. In any case, a mix of Doric and Ionic features characterizes the fifth-century BCE buildings of the Acropolis as a whole.

ATHENA PARTHENOS The costly decision to incorporate two sculptured friezes in the Parthenon's design is symptomatic. This Pentelic-marble temple was more lavishly adorned than any Greek temple before it, Doric or Ionic. Every one of the 92 Doric metopes was decorated with relief sculpture. So, too, was every inch of the 524-foot-long Ionic frieze. The two pediments were filled with dozens of larger-than-life-size statues. And inside was the most expensive item of all—Phidias's gold-and-ivory (*chryselephantine*) statue of *Athena Parthenos,* the Virgin. Art historians know a great deal about Phidias's lost statue from descriptions by Greek and Latin authors and from Roman copies. A model (FIG. 5-46) gives a good idea of its appearance and setting. Athena stood 38 feet tall, and to a large extent the Parthenon was designed around her. To accommodate the statue's huge size, the cella had to be wider than usual. This,

in turn, dictated the width of the facade—eight columns at a time when six columns were the norm.

Athena was fully armed with shield, spear, and helmet, and she held Nike (the winged female personification of Victory) in her extended right hand. No one doubts that this Nike referred to the victory of 479 BCE. The memory of the Persian sack of the Acropolis was still vivid, and the Athenians were intensely conscious that by driving back the Persians, they were saving their civilization from the eastern "barbarians" who had committed atrocities at Miletos. In fact, the *Athena Parthenos* had multiple allusions to the Persian defeat. On the thick soles of Athena's sandals was a representation of a centauromachy. The exterior of her shield was emblazoned with high reliefs depicting the battle of Greeks and Amazons (*Amazonomachy*), in which Theseus drove the Amazons out of Athens. And Phidias painted a gigantomachy on the shield's interior. Each of these mythological contests was a metaphor for the triumph of order over chaos, of civilization over barbarism, and of Athens over Persia.

PARTHENON: METOPES Phidias took up these same themes again in the Parthenon's Doric metopes (FIG. 5-45). The best-preserved metopes—although the paint on these and all the other Parthenon marbles long ago disappeared—are those of the south side, which depicted the battle of Lapiths and centaurs, a combat in which Theseus of Athens played a major role. On one extraordinary slab (FIG. **5-47**), a triumphant centaur rises up on its hind legs, exulting over the crumpled body of the Greek it has defeated. The relief is so high that parts are fully in the round. Some have broken off. The sculptor knew how to distinguish the vibrant, powerful form of the living beast from the lifeless corpse on the ground. In other metopes the Greeks have the upper

5-47 Lapith versus centaur, metope from the south side of the Parthenon, Acropolis, Athens, Greece, ca. 447–438 BCE. Marble, 4′ 8″ high. British Museum, London. ◼◀

The Parthenon's centauromachy metopes allude to the Greek defeat of the Persians. The sculptor of this metope knew how to distinguish the vibrant living centaur from the lifeless Greek corpse.

hand, but the full set suggests that the battle was a difficult one against a dangerous enemy and that losses as well as victories occurred. The same was true of the war against the Persians.

PARTHENON: PEDIMENTS The subjects of the two pediments were especially appropriate for a temple that celebrated Athena—and the Athenians. The east pediment depicted the birth of the goddess. At the west was the contest between Athena and Poseidon to determine which one would become the city's patron deity. Athena won, giving her name to the polis and its citizens. It is significant that in the story and in the pediment the Athenians are the judges of the relative merits of the two gods. The choice of theme reflects the same arrogance that led to the Athenians' use of Delian League funds to adorn the Acropolis.

The center of the east pediment was damaged when the apse was added to the Parthenon at the time of its conversion into a church. What remains are the spectators to the left and the right who witnessed Athena's birth on Mount Olympus. At the far left (FIG. 5-48) are the head and arms of Helios (the Sun) and his chariot horses rising from the pediment floor. Next to them is a powerful male figure usually identified as Dionysos or possibly Herakles, who entered the realm of the gods on completion of his 12 labors. At the right (FIG.

5-49) are three goddesses, probably Hestia, Dione, and Aphrodite, and either Selene (the Moon) or Nyx (Night) and more horses, this time sinking below the pediment's floor. Here, Phidias, who designed the composition even if his assistants executed it, discovered an entirely new way to deal with the awkward triangular frame of the pediment. Its bottom line is the horizon line, and charioteers and their horses move through it effortlessly. The individual figures, even the animals, are brilliantly characterized. The horses of the Sun, at the beginning of the day, are energetic. Those of the Moon or Night, having labored until dawn, are weary. The reclining figures fill the space beneath the raking cornice beautifully. Dionysos/Herakles and Aphrodite in the lap of her mother Dione are monumental Olympian presences yet totally relaxed organic forms. The sculptors fully understood not only the surface appearance of human anatomy, both male and female, but also the mechanics of how muscles and bones make the body move. The Phidian school also mastered the rendition of clothed forms. In the Dione-Aphrodite group, the thin and heavy folds of the garments alternately reveal and conceal the main and lesser body masses while swirling in a compositional tide that subtly unifies the two figures. The articulation and integration of the bodies produce a wonderful variation of surface and play of light and shade.

5-48 Helios and his horses, and Dionysos (Herakles?), from the east pediment of the Parthenon, Acropolis, Athens, Greece, ca. 438–432 BCE. Marble, greatest height 4′ 3″. British Museum, London.

The east pediment of the Parthenon depicts the birth of Athena. At the left, the horses of Helios (the Sun) emerge from the pediment's floor, suggesting the sun rising above the horizon at dawn.

5-49 Three goddesses (Hestia, Dione, and Aphrodite?), from the east pediment of the Parthenon, Acropolis, Athens, Greece, ca. 438–432 BCE. Marble, greatest height 4′ 5″. British Museum, London.

The statues of Hestia, Dione, and Aphrodite conform perfectly to the sloping right side of the east pediment. The thin and heavy folds of the garments alternately reveal and conceal the body forms.

PARTHENON: IONIC FRIEZE In many ways the most remarkable part of the Parthenon's sculptural program is the inner Ionic frieze (FIG. 5-50). Scholars still debate its subject, but most agree that it represents the Panathenaic Festival procession that took place every four years in Athens. If this identification is correct, the Athenians judged themselves fit for inclusion in the temple's sculptural decoration. It is another example of the extraordinarily high opinion the Athenians had of their own worth.

The procession began at the Dipylon Gate, passed through the agora (central square), and ended on the Acropolis, where the Athenians placed a new peplos on an ancient wooden statue of Athena. That statue (probably similar in general appearance to the *Lady of Auxerre*, FIG. 5-7) was housed in the Archaic temple the Persians razed in 480 BCE. The statue had been removed from the Acropolis before the Persian attack for security reasons, and eventually it was installed in the Erechtheion (FIG. 5-53, no. 1). On the Parthenon frieze the procession begins on the west, that is, at the temple's rear, the side facing the gateway to the Acropolis. It then proceeds in parallel lines down the long north and south sides of the building and ends at the center of the east frieze, over the doorway to the cella housing Phidias's statue of Athena. It is noteworthy that the upper part of the frieze is in higher relief than the lower part so that the more distant and more shaded upper zone is as legible from the ground as the lower part of the frieze. This is another instance of the architects' taking optical effects into consideration.

The frieze vividly communicates the procession's acceleration and deceleration. At the outset, on the west side, marshals gather and youths mount their horses. On the north (FIG. 5-50, *top*) and south, the momentum picks up as the cavalcade moves from the lower town to the Acropolis, accompanied by chariots, musicians, jar carriers, and animals destined for sacrifice. On the east, seated gods and goddesses (FIG. 5-50, *center*), the invited guests, watch the procession slow almost to a halt (FIG. 5-50, *bottom*) as it nears its goal at the shrine of Athena's ancient wooden idol. Most remarkable of all is the role assigned to the Olympian deities. They do not take part in the festival or determine its outcome but are merely spectators. Aphrodite, in fact, extends her left arm to draw her son Eros's attention to the Athenians, just as today a parent at a parade would point out important people to a child. And the Athenian people *were* important—

5-50 Details of the Panathenaic Festival procession frieze, from the Parthenon, Acropolis, Athens, Greece, ca. 447–438 BCE. Marble, 3′ 6″ high. Horsemen of north frieze (*top*), British Museum, London; seated gods and goddesses (Poseidon, Apollo, and Artemis) of east frieze (*center*), Acropolis Museum, Athens; and elders and maidens of east frieze (*bottom*), Louvre, Paris. ◼◀

The Parthenon's Ionic frieze represents the procession of citizens on horseback and on foot that took place every four years under the watchful eyes of the gods. The temple celebrated the Athenians as much as Athena.

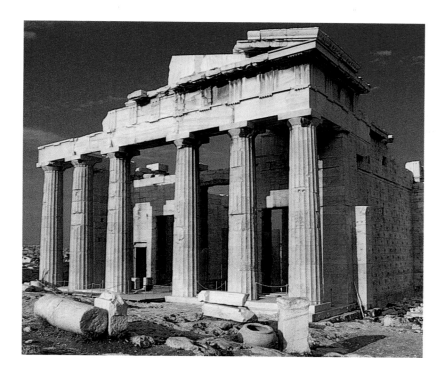

Mnesikles disguised the change of ground level by splitting the Propylaia into eastern and western sections. Each facade resembles a Doric temple but with a wider space between the central columns.

self-important, some might say. They were the masters of an empire, and in Pericles' famous funeral oration he painted a picture of Athens that elevated its citizens almost to the stature of gods. The Parthenon celebrated the greatness of Athens and the Athenians as much as it honored Athena.

PROPYLAIA Even before all the sculpture was in place on the Parthenon, work began on a new monumental entrance to the Acropolis, the Propylaia (FIG. **5-51**). The architect entrusted with this important commission was MNESIKLES. The site was a difficult one, on a steep slope, but Mnesikles succeeded in disguising the change in ground level by splitting the building into eastern and western sections (FIG. **5-43**, no. 2), each one resembling a Doric temple facade. Practical considerations dictated that the space between the central pair of columns on each side be enlarged. This was the path the chariots and animals of the Panathenaic Festival procession took, and they required a wide ramped causeway. To either side of the central ramp were stairs for pedestrian traffic. Inside, tall, slender Ionic columns supported the split-level roof. Once again an Athenian architect mixed the two orders on the Acropolis. But as with the Parthenon, he used the Doric order for the stately exterior and the Ionic only for the interior.

Mnesikles' full plan for the Propylaia was never executed because of a change in the fortunes of Athens after the outbreak of the Peloponnesian War in 431 BCE. Of the side wings that were part of the original project, only the northwest one (FIG. **5-43**, no. 3) was completed. That wing is of special importance in the history of art. In Roman times it housed a *pinakotheke* (picture gallery). In it were displayed paintings on wooden panels by some of the major artists of the fifth century BCE. It is uncertain whether this was the wing's original function. If it was, the Propylaia's pinakotheke is the first recorded structure built for the specific purpose of displaying paintings, and it is the forerunner of modern museums.

ERECHTHEION In 421 BCE work finally began on the temple that was to replace the Archaic Athena temple the Persians had destroyed. The new structure, the Erechtheion (FIGS. **5-52** and

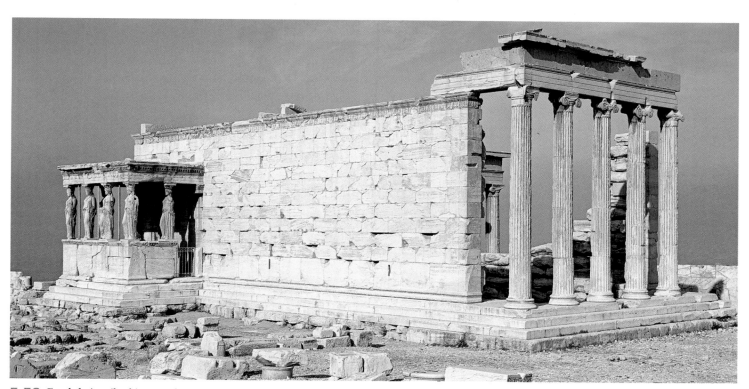

5-52 Erechtheion (looking northwest), Acropolis, Athens, Greece, ca. 421–405 BCE.

The Erechtheion is in many ways the antithesis of the Doric Parthenon directly across from it. An Ionic temple, it has some of the finest decorative details of any ancient Greek building.

1. Shrine housing wooden image of Athena
2. Athena's olive tree
3. Poseidon's trident mark
4. Ruins of Archaic temple

5-53 Plan of the Erechtheion, Acropolis, Athens, Greece, ca. 421–405 BCE.

The asymmetrical form of the Erechtheion is unique for a Greek temple. It reflects the need to incorporate preexisting shrines into the plan, including those of the kings Erechtheus and Kekrops.

1 ft.

5-54 Caryatid from the south porch of the Erechtheion, Acropolis, Athens, Greece, ca. 421–405 BCE. Marble, 7′ 7″ high. British Museum, London.

The south porch of the Erechtheion features caryatids, updated Classical versions with contrapposto stances of the Archaic caryatids of the porch of the Siphnian Treasury (FIG. 5-18) at Delphi.

5-53), built to the north of the old temple's remains, was, however, to be a multiple shrine. It honored Athena and housed the ancient wooden image of the goddess that was the goal of the Panathenaic Festival procession. But it also incorporated shrines to a host of other gods and demigods who loomed large in the city's legendary past. Among these were Erechtheus, an early king of Athens, during whose reign the ancient wooden idol of Athena was said to have fallen from the heavens, and Kekrops, another king of Athens, who served as judge of the contest between Athena and Poseidon. In fact, the site chosen for the new temple was the very spot where that contest occurred. Poseidon had staked his claim to Athens by striking the Acropolis rock with his trident and producing a salt-water spring. The imprint of his trident remained for Athenians of the historical period to see. Nearby, Athena had miraculously caused an olive tree to grow. This tree still stood as a constant reminder of her victory over Poseidon.

The asymmetrical plan (FIG. 5-53) of the Ionic Erechtheion is unique for a Greek temple and the antithesis of the simple and harmoniously balanced plan of the Doric Parthenon across the way. Its irregular form reflected the need to incorporate the tomb of Kekrops and other preexisting shrines, the trident mark, and the olive tree into a single complex. The unknown architect responsible for the building also had to struggle with the problem of uneven terrain. The area could not be made level by terracing because that would disturb the ancient sacred sites. As a result, the Erechtheion has four sides of very different character, and each side rests on a different ground level.

Perhaps to compensate for the awkward character of the building as a whole, the architect took great care with the Erechtheion's decorative details. The frieze, for example, was given special treat-

ment. The stone chosen was the dark-blue limestone of Eleusis to contrast with the white Pentelic marble of the walls and columns and the marble relief figures attached to the dark frieze. But the temple's most striking and famous feature is its south porch, where cary-

5-55 KALLIKRATES, Temple of Athena Nike (looking southwest), Acropolis, Athens, Greece, ca. 427–424 BCE.

The Ionic temple at the entrance to the Acropolis is an unusual amphiprostyle building. It celebrated Athena as bringer of victory, and one of the friezes depicts the Persian defeat at Marathon.

atids (FIG. **5-54**) replaced Ionic columns, as they did a century earlier on the Ionic Siphnian Treasury (FIG. **5-18**) at Delphi. The Delphi caryatids resemble Archaic korai, and their Classical counterparts equally characteristically look like Phidian-era statues. Although they exhibit the weight shift that was standard for the fifth century BCE, the role of the caryatids as architectural supports for the unusual flat roof is underscored by the vertical flutelike drapery folds concealing their stiff, weight-bearing legs. The Classical architect-sculptor successfully balanced the dual and contradictory functions of these female statue-columns. The figures have enough rigidity to suggest the structural column and just the degree of flexibility needed to suggest the living body.

TEMPLE OF ATHENA NIKE Another Ionic building on the Athenian Acropolis is the little Temple of Athena Nike (FIG. **5-55**), designed by Kallikrates, who worked with Iktinos on the Parthenon (and perhaps was responsible for the Ionic elements of that Doric temple). The temple is amphiprostyle with four columns on both the east and west facades. It stands on what used to be a Mycenaean bastion near the Propylaia and greets all visitors entering Athena's great sanctuary. As on the Parthenon, reference was made here to the victory over the Persians—and not just in the temple's name. Part of its frieze was devoted to a representation of the decisive battle at Marathon that turned the tide against the Persians—a human event, as in the Parthenon's Panathenaic Festival procession frieze. But now the sculptors chronicled a specific occasion, not a recurring event involving anonymous citizens.

Around the building, at the bastion's edge, was a *parapet* decorated with exquisite reliefs. The theme of the balustrade matched that of the temple proper—victory. Nike's image was repeated dozens of times, always in different attitudes, sometimes erecting trophies bedecked with Persian spoils and sometimes bringing for-

1 ft.

5-56 Nike adjusting her sandal, from the south side of the parapet of the Temple of Athena Nike, Acropolis, Athens, Greece, ca. 410 BCE. Marble, 3′ 6″ high. Acropolis Museum, Athens.

The image of winged Victory was repeated dozens of times on the parapet around the Athena Nike temple. Here, the sculptor carved a figure whose garments appear almost transparent.

ward sacrificial bulls to Athena. One relief (FIG. **5-56**) shows Nike adjusting her sandal—an awkward posture that the sculptor rendered elegant and graceful. Here, the artist carried the style of the Parthenon pediments (FIG. **5-49**) even further and created a figure whose garments cling so tightly to the body that they seem almost transparent, as if drenched with water. The sculptor was, however, interested in much more than revealing the supple beauty of the young female body. The drapery folds form intricate linear patterns unrelated to the body's anatomical structure and have a life of their own as abstract designs.

HEGESO STELE Although the decoration of the great building projects on the Acropolis must have occupied most of the finest sculptors of Athens in the second half of the fifth century BCE, other

The Hegeso Stele

In Geometric times, huge painted vases (FIG. 5-2) marked the graves of wealthy Athenians. In the Archaic period, kouroi (FIGS. 5-8 and 5-10) and, to a lesser extent, korai were placed over Greek burials, as were grave stelae ornamented with relief depictions of the deceased. The grave stele (FIG. 5-57) of Hegeso is in this tradition. It was erected at the end of the fifth or beginning of the fourth century BCE to commemorate the death of Hegeso, daughter of Proxenos. Both names are inscribed on the cornice of the pediment that crowns the stele. Antae at left and right complete the architectural framework.

Hegeso is the well-dressed woman seated on an elegant chair (with footstool). She examines a piece of jewelry (once rendered in paint, not now visible) selected from a box a servant girl brings to her. The maid's simple unbelted chiton contrasts sharply with the more elaborate attire of her mistress. The garments of both women reveal the body forms beneath them. The faces are serene, without a trace of sadness. Indeed, both mistress and maid are shown in a characteristic shared moment out of daily life. Only the epitaph reveals that Hegeso is the one who has departed.

The simplicity of the scene on the Hegeso stele is deceptive, however. This is not merely a bittersweet scene of tranquil domestic life before an untimely death. The setting itself is significant—the secluded women's quarters of a Greek house, from which Hegeso rarely would have emerged. Contemporary grave stelae of men regularly show them in the public domain, as warriors. And the servant girl is not so much the faithful companion of the deceased in life as she is Hegeso's possession, like the jewelry box. The slave girl may look solicitously at her mistress, but Hegeso has eyes only for her ornaments. Both slave and jewelry attest to the wealth of Hegeso's father, unseen but prominently cited in the epitaph. (It is noteworthy that the mother's name is not mentioned.) Indeed, even the jewelry box carries a deeper significance, for it probably represents the dowry Proxenos would have provided to his daughter's husband when she left her father's home to enter her husband's home. In the patriarchal society of ancient Greece, the dominant position of men is manifest even when only women are depicted.

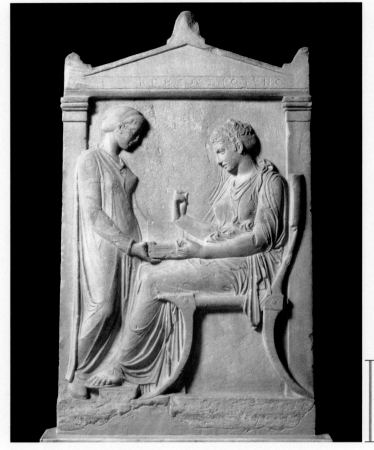

5-57 Grave stele of Hegeso, from the Dipylon cemetery, Athens, Greece, ca. 400 BCE. Marble, 5′ 2″ high. National Archaeological Museum, Athens.

On her tombstone, Hegeso examines jewelry from a box her servant girl holds. Mistress and maid share a serene moment of daily life. Only the epitaph reveals that Hegeso is the one who died.

---

commissions were available in the city, notably in the Dipylon cemetery. There, around 400 BCE, a beautiful and touching grave stele (FIG. 5-57) in the style of the Temple of Athena Nike parapet reliefs was set up in memory of a woman named Hegeso. Its subject—a young woman in her home, attended by her maid (see "The Hegeso Stele," above)—and its composition have close parallels in contemporary vase painting.

Painting

In the Classical period, some of the most renowned artists were the painters of monumental wooden panels displayed in public buildings, both secular and religious. Such works are by nature perishable, and all of the great panels of the masters are unfortunately lost. Nonetheless, one can get some idea of the polychrome nature of those panel paintings by studying Greek vases, especially those painted using the *white-ground* technique, which takes its name from the chalky-white clay slip used to provide a background for the painted figures. Experiments with white-ground painting date back to the Andokides Painter, but the method became popular only toward the middle of the fifth century BCE.

ACHILLES PAINTER One of the masters of white-ground painting was the so-called ACHILLES PAINTER, who decorated the *lekythos* (flask containing perfumed oil) in FIG. 5-58. White-ground is essentially a variation of the red-figure technique. First the painter covered the pot with a slip of very fine white clay, then applied black glaze to outline the figures and colored them with diluted brown, purple, red, and white. Other colors—for example, the yellow chosen for the garments of both figures on the Achilles Painter's lekythos—also could be employed, but these had to be applied after firing because the Greeks did not know how to make them withstand the heat of the kiln. Despite the obvious attractions of the technique, the impermanence of the expanded range of colors discouraged white-ground painting on everyday vessels, such as drinking cups and kraters. In fact, artists explored the full polychrome possibilities of the white-ground technique almost exclusively on lekythoi, which were commonly placed in Greek graves as offerings to the deceased. For vessels designed for short-term use, the fragile nature of white-ground painting was of little concern.

The Achilles Painter's lekythos is decorated with a scene appropriate for its funerary purpose. A youthful warrior takes leave of his

5-58A REED PAINTER, War[rior] seated at his tomb, ca. 410–400 BCE.

5-59 Niobid Painter, Artemis and Apollo slaying the children of Niobe (Athenian red-figure calyx krater), from Orvieto, Italy, ca. 450 BCE. 1′ 9″ high. Louvre, Paris. ◼◀

The placement of figures on different levels in a landscape on this red-figure krater depicting the massacre of Niobe's children reflects the compositions of the lost panel paintings of Polygnotos of Thasos.

5-58 Achilles Painter, Warrior taking leave of his wife (Athenian white-ground lekythos), from Eretria, Greece, ca. 440 BCE. 1′ 5″ high. National Archaeological Museum, Athens. ◼◀

White-ground painters applied the colors after firing because most colored glazes could not withstand the kiln's heat. The Achilles Painter here displayed his mastery at drawing an eye in profile.

wife. The red scarf, mirror, and jug hanging on the wall behind the woman indicate that the setting is the interior of their home. The motif of the seated woman is strikingly similar to that of Hegeso on her grave stele (FIG. 5-57), but here the woman is the survivor. It is her husband, preparing to go to war with helmet, shield, and spear, who will depart, never to return. On his shield is a large painted eye, roughly life-size. Greek shields often were decorated with devices such as the horrific face of snake-haired Medusa, intended to ward off evil spirits and frighten the enemy. This eye undoubtedly was meant to recall this tradition, but it was little more than an excuse for the Achilles Painter to display superior drawing skills. Since the

late sixth century BCE, Greek painters had abandoned the Archaic habit of placing frontal eyes on profile faces and attempted to render the eyes in profile. The Achilles Painter's mastery of this difficult problem in foreshortening is on exhibit here.

POLYGNOTOS The leading painter of the first half of the fifth century BCE was Polygnotos of Thasos, whose works adorned important buildings both in Athens and Delphi. One of these was the pinakotheke of Mnesikles' Propylaia, but the most famous was a portico in the Athenian marketplace that came to be called the Stoa Poikile (Painted Stoa). Descriptions of Polygnotos's paintings make clear that he introduced a revolutionary compositional style. Before Polygnotos, figures stood on a common ground line at the bottom of the picture plane, whether they appeared in horizontal bands or single panels. Polygnotos placed his figures on different levels, staggered in tiers in the manner of Ashurbanipal's lion-hunt relief (FIG. 2-23) of two centuries before. He also incorporated landscape elements into his paintings, making his pictures true "windows onto the world" and not simply surface designs peopled with foreshortened figures. Polygnotos's abandonment of a single ground line was as momentous a break from the past as Early Classical Greek sculptors' rejection of frontality in statuary.

NIOBID PAINTER Polygnotos's influence is evident on a red-figure krater (FIG. 5-59) painted around the middle of the fifth century BCE by the Niobid Painter—so named because one side of the krater depicts the massacre of the Niobids, the children of Niobe. Niobe, who had at least a dozen children, had boasted that she was superior to the goddess Leto, who had only two offspring, Apollo

Phiale Painter, *Hermes bringing the infant Dionysos to Papposilenos* (Athenian white-ground calyx krater), from Vulci, Italy, ca. 440–435 BCE. 1′ 2″ high. Musei Vaticani, Rome.

In the Phiale Painter's white-ground representation of Hermes and the infant Dionysos at Nysa, the use of diluted brown to color and shade the rocks may also reflect the work of Polygnotos.

and Artemis. To punish Niobe's *hubris* (arrogance) and teach the lesson that no mortal could be superior to a god or goddess, Leto sent her two children to slay all of Niobe's many sons and daughters. On the Niobid Painter's krater, the horrible slaughter occurs in a schematic landscape setting of rocks and trees. The figures are disposed on several levels, and they actively interact with their setting. One slain son, for example, not only has fallen upon a rocky outcropping but is partially hidden by it. The Niobid Painter also drew the son's face in a three-quarter view, something that not even Euphronios and Euthymides had attempted.

PHIALE PAINTER Further insight into the appearance of monumental panel painting of the fifth century BCE comes from a white-ground krater (FIG. 5-60) by the so-called PHIALE PAINTER. The subject is Hermes handing over his half brother, the infant Dionysos, to Papposilenos ("grandpa-satyr"). The other figures represent the nymphs in the shady glens of Nysa, where Zeus had sent Dionysos, one of his numerous natural sons, to be raised, safe from the possible wrath of his wife Hera. Unlike the decorators of funerary lekythoi, the Phiale Painter used for this krater only colors that could survive the heat of a Greek kiln—reds, brown, purple, and a special snowy white reserved for the flesh of the nymphs and for such details as the hair, beard, and shaggy body of Papposilenos. The use of diluted brown wash to color and shade the rocks may reflect the coloration of Polygnotos's landscapes. This vase and the Niobid krater together provide a shadowy idea of the character and magnificence of Polygnotos's great paintings.

TOMB OF THE DIVER, PAESTUM Although all of the panel paintings of the masters disappeared long ago, some Greek mural paintings are preserved today. An early example is in the so-called Tomb of the Diver at Paestum. The four walls of this small, coffinlike tomb are decorated with banquet scenes such as appear

5-61 *Youth diving*, painted ceiling of the Tomb of the Diver, Paestum, Italy, ca. 480 BCE. 3′ 4″ high. Museo Archeologico Nazionale, Paestum. ▨

This tomb in Italy is a rare example of Classical mural painting. The diving scene most likely symbolizes the deceased's plunge into the Underworld. The trees resemble those on the Niobid krater (FIG. 5-59).

regularly on Greek vases. On the tomb's ceiling (FIG. 5-61), a youth dives from a stone platform into a body of water. The scene most likely symbolizes the plunge from this life into the next. Trees resembling those on the Niobid krater are included within the decorative frame.

LATE CLASSICAL PERIOD

The Peloponnesian War, which began in 431 BCE, ended in 404 BCE with the complete defeat of a plague-weakened Athens. The victor, Sparta, and then Thebes undertook the leadership of Greece, both unsuccessfully. In the middle of the fourth century BCE, a threat from without caused the rival Greek states to put aside their animosities and unite for their common defense, as they had earlier against the Persians. But at the battle of Chaeronea in 338 BCE, the Greek cities suffered a devastating loss and had to relinquish their independence to the Macedonian king, Philip II. Philip was assassinated in 336, and his son, Alexander III, better known simply as Alexander the Great, succeeded him. In the decade before his death in 323 BCE, Alexander led a powerful army on an extraordinary campaign that overthrew the Persian Empire (the ultimate revenge for the Persian invasion of Greece in the early fifth century BCE), wrested control of Egypt, and even reached India (see Chapter 6).

Sculpture

The fourth century BCE was thus a time of political upheaval in Greece, and the chaos had a profound impact on the psyche of the Greeks and on the art they produced. In the fifth century BCE, Greeks had generally believed that rational human beings could impose order on their environment, create "perfect" statues such as the *Canon* of Polykleitos, and discover the "correct" mathematical formulas for constructing temples such as the Parthenon. The Parthenon frieze celebrated the Athenians as a community of citizens with shared values. The Peloponnesian War and the unceasing strife of the fourth century BCE brought an end to the serene idealism of the previous century. Disillusionment and alienation followed. Greek thought and Greek art began to focus more on the individual and on the real world of appearances rather than on the community and the ideal world of perfect beings and perfect buildings.

PRAXITELES The new approach to art is immediately apparent in the work of PRAXITELES, one of the great masters of the fourth century BCE. Praxiteles did not reject the themes favored by the sculptors of the High Classical period. His Olympian gods and goddesses retained their superhuman beauty, but in his hands they lost some of their solemn grandeur and took on a worldly sensuousness. Nowhere is this new humanizing spirit plainer than in the statue of Aphrodite (FIG. 5-62) that Praxiteles sold to the Knidians after another city had rejected it. The lost original, carved from Parian marble, is known only through copies of Roman date, but Pliny considered it "superior to all the works, not only of Praxiteles, but indeed in the whole world." It made Knidos famous, and many people sailed there just to see the statue in its round temple (compare FIG. 5-72), where "it was possible to view the image of the goddess from every side." According to Pliny, some visitors were "overcome with love for the statue."[3]

The *Aphrodite of Knidos* caused such a sensation in its time because Praxiteles took the unprecedented step of representing the goddess of love completely nude. Female nudity was rare in earlier Greek art and had been confined almost exclusively to paintings on vases designed for household use. The women so depicted also tended to be courtesans or slave girls, not noblewomen or goddesses, and no one had dared place a statue of an unclothed goddess in a

temple. Moreover, Praxiteles' Aphrodite is not a cold and remote image. In fact, the goddess engages in a trivial act out of everyday life. She has removed her garment, draped it over a large *hydria* (water pitcher), and is about to step into the bath.

Although shocking in its day, the *Aphrodite of Knidos* is not openly erotic (the goddess modestly shields her pelvis with her right hand), but she is quite sensuous. Lucian wrote in the second century CE that she had a "welcoming look" and a "slight smile" and that Praxiteles was renowned for his ability to transform marble into soft and radiant flesh. Lucian mentioned, for example, the "dewy quality of Aphrodite's eyes."[4] Unfortunately, the rather mechanical Roman copies do not capture the quality of Praxiteles' modeling of the stone.

Those qualities are evident, however, in a statue once thought to be by the hand of the master himself but now generally considered either a copy of the highest quality or an original work by a son or grandson of Praxiteles. Found in the Temple of Hera at Olympia, the

5-62A Head of a woman, Chios, ca. 320–300 BCE.

1 ft.

5-62 PRAXITELES, *Aphrodite of Knidos.* Roman marble copy of an original of ca. 350–340 BCE, 6′ 8″ high. Musei Vaticani, Rome.

The first nude statue of a goddess caused a sensation in the fourth century BCE. But Praxiteles was also famous for his ability to transform marble into soft and radiant flesh. His Aphrodite had "dewy eyes."

5-63 PRAXITELES(?), Hermes and the infant Dionysos, from the Temple of Hera, Olympia, Greece. Copy of a statue by Praxiteles of ca. 340 BCE or an original work of ca. 330–270 BCE by a son or grandson. Marble, 7′ 1″ high. Archaeological Museum, Olympia.

Praxiteles humanized the Olympian deities. This Hermes is as sensuous as the sculptor's Aphrodite. The god gazes dreamily into space while he dangles grapes as temptation for the infant god of wine.

1 ft.

followers. But other sculptors pursued very different interests. One of these was SKOPAS OF PAROS, and although his work reflects the general trend toward the humanization of the Greek gods and heroes, his hallmark was intense emotionalism. None of Skopas's statues survives, but a grave stele (FIG. 5-64) found near the Ilissos River in Athens exhibits the psychological tension for which the master's works were famous. The stele was originally set into an architectural frame similar to that of the earlier Hegeso stele (FIG. 5-57). A comparison between the two works is very telling. In the Ilissos stele, the relief is much higher, with parts of the figures carved fully in the round. But the major difference is the pronounced change in mood, which reflects the innovations of Skopas. The later work makes a clear distinction between the living and the dead, and depicts overt mourning. The deceased is a young hunter who has the large, deeply set eyes and fleshy overhanging brows that characterized Skopas's sculpted figures. At his feet a small boy, either his servant or perhaps a younger brother, sobs openly. The hunter's dog also droops its head in sorrow. Beside the youth, an old man, undoubtedly his father, leans on a walking stick and, in a gesture reminiscent of that of the Olympia seer (FIG. 5-32), ponders the irony of fate that has taken the life of his powerful son and preserved him in

5-64A Head of Herakles, Temple of Athena Alea, Tegea, ca. 340 BCE.

statue of Hermes and the infant Dionysos (FIG. 5-63) brings to the realm of monumental statuary the theme the Phiale Painter had chosen for a white-ground krater (FIG. 5-60) a century earlier. Hermes has stopped to rest in a forest on his journey to Nysa to entrust the upbringing of Dionysos to Papposilenos and the nymphs. Hermes leans on a tree trunk (here it is an integral part of the composition and not a copyist's addition), and his slender body forms a sinuous, shallow S-curve that is the hallmark of many of Praxiteles' statues. He looks off dreamily into space while he dangles a bunch of grapes (now missing) as a temptation for the infant, who is to become the Greek god of the vine. This is the kind of tender and very human interaction between an adult and a child that is common in real life but that had been absent from Greek statuary before the fourth century BCE.

The quality of the carving is superb. The modeling is deliberately smooth and subtle, producing soft shadows that follow the planes as they flow almost imperceptibly one into another. The delicacy of the marble facial features stands in sharp contrast to the metallic precision of Polykleitos's bronze *Doryphoros* (FIG. 5-40). Even the *Spear Bearer*'s locks of hair were subjected to the fifth-century sculptor's laws of symmetry and do not violate the skull's perfect curve. A comparison of these two statues reveals how broad was the change in artistic attitude and intent from the fifth to the fourth century BCE. In the statues of Praxiteles, the deities of Mount Olympus still possess a beauty mortals can aspire to, although not achieve, but they are no longer remote. Praxiteles' gods have stepped off their fifth-century pedestals and entered the fourth-century BCE world of human experience.

5-63A Artist painting a statue of Herakles, ca. 350–320 BCE.

SKOPAS In the Archaic period and throughout most of the Early and High Classical periods, Greek sculptors generally shared common goals, but in the Late Classical period of the fourth century BCE, distinctive individual styles emerged. The dreamy, beautiful divinities of Praxiteles had enormous appeal, and the master had many

5-64 Grave stele of a young hunter, found near the Ilissos River, Athens, Greece, ca. 340–330 BCE. Marble, 5′ 6″ high. National Archaeological Museum, Athens.

The emotional intensity of this stele representing an old man mourning the loss of his son and the figures' large, deeply set eyes with fleshy overhanging brows reflect the style of Skopas of Paros.

1 ft.

his frail old age. Most remarkable of all, the hunter himself looks out at the viewer, inviting sympathy and creating an emotional bridge between the spectator and the artwork inconceivable in the art of the High Classical period.

LYSIPPOS The third great Late Classical sculptor, Lysippos of Sikyon, won such renown that Alexander the Great selected him to create his official portrait. (Alexander could afford to employ the best. The Macedonian kingdom enjoyed vast wealth. King Philip hired the leading thinker of his age, Aristotle, as the young Alexander's tutor.) Lysippos introduced a new canon of proportions in which the bodies were more slender than those of Polykleitos— whose own canon continued to exert enormous influence—and the heads roughly one-eighth the height of the body rather than one-seventh, as in the previous century. The new proportions are apparent in one of Lysippos's most famous works, a bronze statue of an *apoxyomenos* (an athlete scraping oil from his body after exercising), known, as usual, only from Roman copies in marble (FIG. 5-65). A comparison with Polykleitos's *Doryphoros* (FIG. 5-40) reveals more than a change in physique. A nervous energy, lacking in the balanced form of the *Doryphoros*, runs through Lysippos's *Apoxyomenos*. The *strigil* (scraper) is about to reach the end of the right arm, and at any moment the athlete will switch it to the other hand so that he can

scrape his left arm. At the same time, he will shift his weight and reverse the positions of his legs. Lysippos also began to break down the dominance of the frontal view in statuary and encouraged the observer to look at his athlete from multiple angles. Because Lysippos represented the athlete with his right arm boldly thrust forward, the figure breaks out of the shallow rectangular box that defined the boundaries of earlier statues. To comprehend the action, the observer must move to the side and view Lysippos's work at a three-quarter angle or in full profile.

To grasp the full meaning of another work of Lysippos, a colossal statue (FIG. 5-66) depicting a weary Herakles, the viewer must walk around it. Once again, the original is lost. The most impressive of the surviving marble copies is nearly twice life-size and was exhibited in the Baths of Caracalla in Rome. Like the marble copy of Polykleitos's *Doryphoros* (FIG. 5-40) from the Roman palaestra at

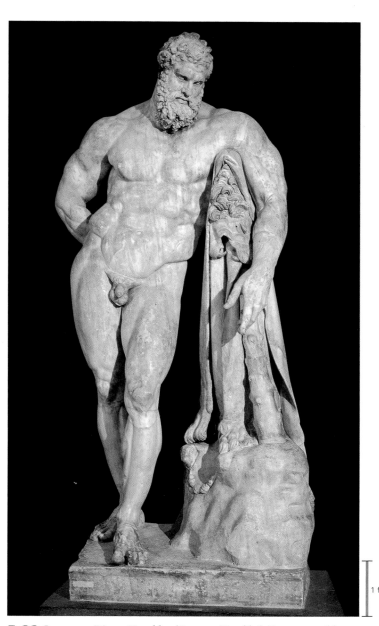

1 ft.

5-66 Lysippos, Weary Herakles (*Farnese Herakles*). Roman marble copy from Rome, Italy, signed by Glykon of Athens, of a bronze original of ca. 320 bce, 10′ 5″ high. Museo Archeologico Nazionale, Naples.

Lysippos's portrayal of Herakles after the hero obtained the golden apples of the Hesperides ironically shows the mythological strong man as so weary that he must lean on his club for support.

Pompeii, Lysippos's muscle-bound Greek hero provided inspiration for Romans who came to the baths to exercise. (The copyist, GLYKON OF ATHENS, signed the statue. Lysippos's name is not mentioned, but the educated Roman public did not need a label to identify the famous work.) In the hands of Lysippos, however, the exaggerated muscular development of Herakles is poignantly ironic, for the sculptor depicted the strong man as so weary that he must lean on his club for support. Without that prop, Herakles would topple over. Lysippos and other fourth-century BCE artists rejected stability and balance as worthy goals for statuary.

Herakles holds the golden apples of the Hesperides in his right hand behind his back—unseen unless the viewer walks around the statue. Lysippos's subject is thus the same as that of the metope (FIG. 5-33) of the Early Classical Temple of Zeus at Olympia, but the fourth-century BCE Herakles is no longer serene. Instead of expressing joy, or at least satisfaction, at having completed one of the impossible 12 labors, he is almost dejected. Exhausted by his physical efforts, he can think only of his pain and weariness, not of the reward of immortality that awaits him. Lysippos's portrayal of Herakles in this statue is an eloquent testimony to Late Classical sculptors' interest in humanizing the great gods and heroes of the Greeks. In this respect, despite their divergent styles, Praxiteles, Skopas, and Lysippos followed a common path.

Alexander the Great and Macedonian Court Art

Alexander the Great's favorite book was the *Iliad,* and his own life was very much like an epic saga, full of heroic battles, exotic places, and unceasing drama. Alexander was a man of singular character, an inspired leader with boundless energy and an almost foolhardy courage. He personally led his army into battle on the back of Bucephalus, the wild and mighty steed only he could tame and ride (FIG. 5-70).

ALEXANDER'S PORTRAITS Ancient sources reveal that Alexander believed only Lysippos had captured his essence in a portrait, and that is why only he was authorized to sculpt the king's image. Lysippos's most famous portrait of the Macedonian king was a full-length heroically nude bronze statue of Alexander holding a lance and turning his head toward the sky. Plutarch reported that an epigram inscribed on the base stated that the statue depicted Alexander gazing at Zeus and proclaiming, "I place the earth under my sway. You, O Zeus, keep Olympus." Plutarch further stated that the portrait had "leonine" hair and a "melting glance."[5] The Lysippan original is lost, and because Alexander was portrayed so many times for centuries after his death, it is very difficult to determine which of the many surviving images is most faithful to the fourth-century BCE portrait. A leading candidate is a third-century BCE marble head (FIG. 5-67) from Pella, the capital of Macedonia and Alexander's birthplace. It has the sharp turn of the head and thick mane of hair that were key ingredients of Lysippos's portrait. The sculptor's treatment of the features also is consistent with the style of the later fourth century BCE. The deep-set eyes and parted lips recall the manner of Skopas, and the delicate handling of the flesh brings to mind the faces of Praxitelean statues. Although not a copy, this head very likely approximates the young king's official portrait and provides insight into Alexander's personality as well as the art of Lysippos.

PELLA MOSAICS Alexander's palace has not been excavated, but the sumptuousness of life at the Macedonian court is evident from the costly objects found in Macedonian graves and from the abundance of mosaics (see "Mosaics," Chapter 11, page 303)

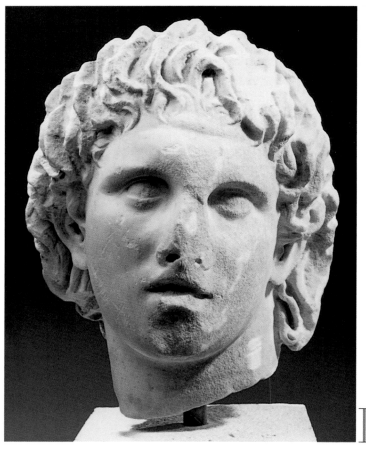

5-67 Head of Alexander the Great, from Pella, Greece, third century BCE. Marble, 1′ high. Archaeological Museum, Pella.

Lysippos was the official portrait sculptor of Alexander the Great. This third-century BCE sculpture has the sharp turn of the head and thick mane of hair of Lysippos's statue of Alexander with a lance.

5-68 GNOSIS, Stag hunt, from Pella, Greece, ca. 300 BCE. Pebble mosaic, figural panel 10′ 2″ high. Archaeological Museum, Pella.

The floor mosaics at the Macedonian capital of Pella are of the early type made with pebbles of various natural colors. This stag hunt by Gnosis bears the earliest known signature of a mosaicist.

uncovered at Pella in the homes of the wealthy. The Pella mosaics are *pebble mosaics*. The floors consist of small stones of various colors collected from beaches and riverbanks and set into a thick coat of cement. The finest pebble mosaic yet to come to light has a stag hunt (FIG. 5-68) as its *emblema* (central framed panel), bordered in turn by an intricate floral pattern and a stylized wave motif (not shown in the illustration). The artist signed his work in the same manner as proud Greek vase painters and potters did: "GNOSIS made it." This is the earliest mosaicist's signature known, and its prominence in the design undoubtedly attests to the artist's reputation. The house owner wanted guests to know that Gnosis himself, and not an imitator, created this floor.

The Pella stag hunt, with its light figures against a dark ground, has much in common with red-figure painting. In the pebble mosaic, however, thin strips of lead or terracotta define most of the contour lines and some of the interior details. Subtle gradations of yellow, brown, and red, as well as black, white, and gray pebbles suggest the interior volumes. The musculature of the hunters, and even their billowing cloaks and the animals' bodies, are modeled by shading. Such use of light and dark to suggest volume is rarely seen on Greek painted vases, although examples do exist. Monumental painters, however, commonly used shading. The Greek term for shading was *skiagraphia* (literally, "shadow painting"), and it was said to have been invented by an Athenian painter of the fifth century BCE named Apollodoros. Gnosis's emblema, with its sparse landscape setting, probably reflects contemporaneous panel painting.

HADES AND PERSEPHONE Recent excavations at Vergina have provided valuable additional information about Macedonian art and about Greek mural painting. One of the most important finds is a painted tomb with a representation of Hades, lord of the Underworld, abducting Persephone, the daughter of Demeter, the goddess of grain. The mural (FIG. 5-69) is remarkable for its intense drama and for the painter's use of foreshortening and shading. Hades holds the terrified seminude Persephone in his left arm and steers his racing chariot with his right as Persephone's garments and hair blow in the wind. The artist depicted the heads of both figures and even the chariot's wheels in three-quarter views. The chariot, in fact, seems to be bursting into the viewer's space. Especially noteworthy is the way the painter used short dark brush strokes to

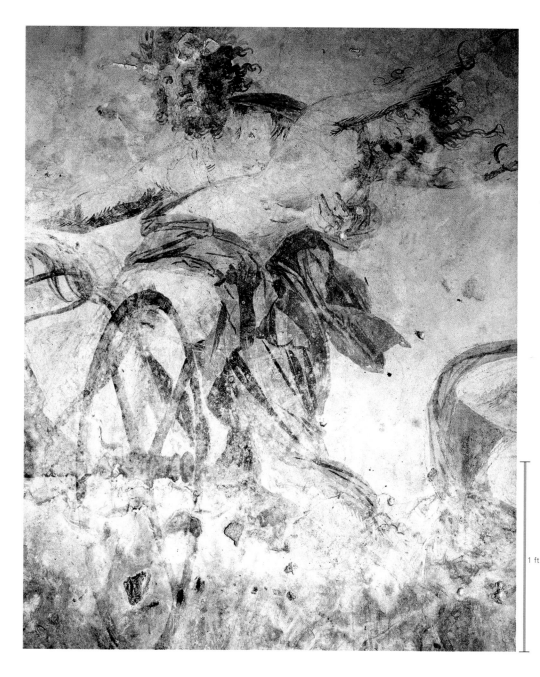

5-69 Hades abducting Persephone, detail of a wall painting in tomb 1, Vergina, Greece, mid-fourth century BCE. 3′ 3½″ high.

The intense drama, three-quarter views, and shading in this representation of the lord of the Underworld kidnapping Demeter's daughter are characteristics of mural painting at the time of Alexander.

1 ft.

5-70 PHILOXENOS OF ERETRIA, *Battle of Issus,* ca. 310 BCE. Roman copy (*Alexander Mosaic*) from the House of the Faun, Pompeii, Italy, late second or early first century BCE. Tessera mosaic, 8′ 10″ × 16′ 9″. Museo Archeologico Nazionale, Naples.

Philoxenos's *Battle of Issus* (see also FIG. 5-1) was considered one of the greatest paintings of antiquity. In it he captured the psychological intensity of the confrontation between the two kings.

suggest shading on the under side of Hades' right arm, on Persephone's torso, and elsewhere. Although fragmentary, the Vergina mural is a precious document of the almost totally lost art of monumental painting in ancient Greece.

BATTLE OF ISSUS Further insight into developments in painting at the time of Alexander comes from a large mosaic that decorated the floor of one room of a lavishly appointed Roman house at Pompeii. In the *Alexander Mosaic* (FIG. 5-70), as it is usually called, the mosaicist employed *tesserae* (tiny stones or pieces of glass cut to the desired size and shape) instead of pebbles (see "Mosaics," Chapter 11, page 303). The subject is a great battle between the armies of Alexander the Great and the Persian king Darius III, probably the battle of Issus in southeastern Turkey, when Darius fled the battlefield in his chariot in humiliating defeat. The mosaic dates to the late second or early first century BCE. It is widely believed to be a reasonably faithful copy of *Battle of Issus,* a famous panel painting of ca. 310 BCE made by PHILOXENOS OF ERETRIA for King Cassander, one of Alexander's successors. Some scholars have proposed, however, that the mosaic is a copy of a painting by one of the few Greek female artists whose name is known, Helen of Egypt.

Battle of Issus is notable for the artist's technical mastery of problems that had long fascinated Greek painters. Even Euthymides would have marveled at the fourth-century BCE painter's depiction of the rearing horse (FIG. 5-1) seen in a three-quarter rear view below Darius. The subtle modulation of the horse's rump through shading in browns and yellows is much more accomplished than the comparable attempts at shading in the Pella mosaic (FIG. 5-68) or the Vergina mural (FIG. 5-69). Other details are even more impres-

sive. The Persian to the right of the rearing horse has fallen to the ground and raises, backward, a dropped Macedonian shield to protect himself from being trampled. Philoxenos recorded the reflection of the man's terrified face on the polished surface of the shield. Everywhere in the scene, men, animals, and weapons cast shadows on the ground. The interest of Greek painters in the reflection of insubstantial light on a shiny surface, and in the absence of light (shadows), was far removed from earlier painters' preoccupation with the clear presentation of weighty figures seen against a blank background. The Greek painter here truly opened a window into a world filled not only with figures, trees, and sky but also with light. This Classical Greek notion of what a painting should be characterizes most of the history of art in the Western world from the Renaissance on.

Most impressive about *Battle of Issus,* however, is the psychological intensity of the drama unfolding before the viewer's eyes. Alexander is on horseback leading his army into battle, recklessly one might say, without even a helmet to protect him. He drives his spear through one of Darius's trusted "Immortals," who were sworn to guard the king's life, while the Persian's horse collapses beneath him. The Macedonian king is only a few yards away from Darius, and Alexander directs his gaze at the Persian king, not at the man impaled on his now-useless spear. Darius has called for retreat. In fact, his charioteer is already whipping the horses and speeding the king to safety. Before he escapes, Darius looks back at Alexander and in a pathetic gesture reaches out toward his brash foe. But victory has slipped from his hands. Pliny said Philoxenos's painting of the battle between Alexander and Darius was "inferior to none."[6] It is easy to see why he reached that conclusion.

5-71 POLYKLEITOS THE YOUNGER, Theater, Epidauros, Greece, ca. 350 BCE.

The Greeks always situated their theaters on hillsides, which supported the cavea of stone seats overlooking the circular orchestra. The Epidauros theater is the finest in Greece. It accommodated 12,000 spectators.

Architecture

In architecture, as in sculpture and painting, the Late Classical period was a time of innovation and experimentation.

A Model of Mausoleum, karnassos, 353–340 BCE.

THEATER OF EPIDAUROS In ancient Greece, plays were not performed repeatedly over months or years as they are today but only during sacred festivals. Greek drama was closely associated with religious rites and was not pure entertainment. At Athens in the fifth century BCE, for example, the great tragedies of Aeschylus, Sophocles, and Euripides were performed at the Dionysos festival in the theater dedicated to the god on the southern slope of the Acropolis. The finest theater in Greece, however, constructed shortly after Alexander the Great was born, is located at Epidauros in the Peloponnesos. The architect was POLYKLEITOS THE YOUNGER, possibly a nephew of the great fifth-century sculptor. His theater (FIG. 5-71) is still used for performances of ancient Greek dramas.

The precursor of the formal Greek theater was a place where ancient rites, songs, and dances were performed. This circular piece of earth with a hard, level surface later became the orchestra of the theater. *Orchestra* literally means "dancing place." The actors and the chorus performed there, and at Epidauros an altar to Dionysos stood at the center of the circle. The spectators sat on a slope overlooking the orchestra—the *theatron*, or "place for seeing." When the Greek theater took architectural shape, the auditorium (*cavea*, Latin for "hollow place, cavity") was always situated on a hillside. The cavea at Epidauros, composed of wedge-shaped sections (*cunei*, singular *cuneus*) of stone benches separated by stairs, is somewhat greater than a semicircle in plan. The auditorium is 387 feet in diameter, and its 55 rows of seats accommodated about 12,000 spectators. They entered the theater via a passageway between the seating area and the scene building (*skene*), which housed dressing rooms for the actors and also formed a backdrop for the plays. The design is simple but perfectly suited to its function. Even in antiquity the Epidauros theater won renown for the harmony of its proportions. Although spectators sitting in some of the seats would have had a poor view of the skene, all had unobstructed views of the orchestra. Because of the open-air cavea's excellent acoustics, everyone could hear the actors and chorus.

CORINTHIAN CAPITALS The theater at Epidauros is situated some 500 yards southeast of the sanctuary of Asklepios, and Polykleitos the Younger worked there as well. He was the architect of the *tholos*, the circular shrine that probably housed the sacred snakes of the healing god. That building lies in ruins today, its architectural fragments removed to the local museum, but an approximate idea of its original appearance can be gleaned from the somewhat earlier and partially reconstructed tholos (FIG. 5-72) at Delphi that THEODOROS OF PHOKAIA designed. Both tholoi had an exterior colonnade of Doric columns. Inside, however, the columns had

5-72 THEODOROS OF PHOKAIA, Tholos, Delphi, Greece, ca. 375 BCE.

Theodoros of Phokaia's tholos at Delphi, although in ruins, is the best-preserved example of a round temple of the Classical period. It had Doric columns on the exterior and Corinthian columns inside.

The Corinthian Capital

The Corinthian capital (FIG. 5-73) is more ornate than either the Doric or Ionic (FIG. 5-14). It consists of a double row of acanthus leaves, from which tendrils and flowers emerge, wrapped around a bell-shaped echinus. Although this capital often is cited as the distinguishing feature of the Corinthian order, in strict terms no such order exists. Architects simply substituted the new capital type for the volute capital in the Ionic order.

The sculptor Kallimachos invented the Corinthian capital during the second half of the fifth century BCE. Vitruvius recorded the circumstances that supposedly led to its creation:

> A maiden who was a citizen of Corinth . . . died. After her funeral, her nurse collected the goblets in which the maiden had taken delight while she was alive, and after putting them together in a basket, she took them to the grave monument and put them on top of it. In order that they should remain in place for a long time, she covered them with a tile. Now it happened that this basket was placed over the root of an acanthus. As time went on the acanthus root, pressed down in the middle by the weight, sent forth, when it was about springtime, leaves and stalks; its stalks growing up along the sides of the basket and being pressed out from the angles because of the weight of the tile, were forced to form volute-like curves at their extremities. At this point, Kallimachos happened to be going by and noticed the basket with this gentle growth of leaves around it. Delighted with the order and the novelty of the form, he made columns using it as his model and established a canon of proportions for it.*

Kallimachos worked on the Acropolis in Pericles' great building program. Many scholars believe that a Corinthian column supported the outstretched right hand of Phidias's *Athena Parthenos* (FIG. 5-46) because some of the Roman copies of the lost statue include a Corinthian column. In any case, the earliest preserved Corinthian capital dates to the time of Kallimachos. The new type was rarely used before the mid-fourth century BCE, however, and did not become popular until Hellenistic and especially Roman times. Later architects favored the Corinthian capital because of its ornate character and because it eliminated certain problems of both the Doric and Ionic orders.

The Ionic capital, unlike the Doric, has two distinct profiles—the front and back (with the volutes) and the sides. The volutes always faced outward on a Greek temple, but architects met with a vexing problem at the corners of their buildings, which had two adjacent "fronts." They solved the problem by placing volutes on both outer faces of the corner capitals (as on the Erechtheion, FIG. 5-52, and the Temple of Athena Nike, FIG. 5-55), but the solution was an awkward one.

Doric design rules also presented problems for Greek architects at the corners of buildings. The Doric frieze was organized according to three supposedly inflexible rules:

- A triglyph must be exactly over the center of each column.
- A triglyph must be over the center of each *intercolumniation* (the space between two columns).
- Triglyphs at the corners of the frieze must meet so that no space is left over.

These rules are contradictory, however. If the corner triglyphs must meet, then they cannot be placed over the center of the corner column (FIGS. 5-25, 5-30, and 5-44).

The Corinthian capital eliminated both problems. Because the capital's four sides have a similar appearance, corner Corinthian capitals do not have to be modified, as do corner Ionic capitals. And because the Ionic frieze is used for the Corinthian "order," architects do not have to contend with metopes or triglyphs.

5-73 POLYKLEITOS THE YOUNGER, Corinthian capital, from the tholos, Epidauros, Greece, ca. 350 BCE. Archaeological Museum, Epidauros.

Corinthian capitals, invented in the fifth century BCE by the sculptor Kallimachos, are more ornate than Doric and Ionic capitals. They feature a double row of acanthus leaves with tendrils and flowers.

*Vitruvius, *De architectura*, 4.1.8–10. Translated by J. J. Pollitt, *The Art of Ancient Greece: Sources and Documents* (New York: Cambridge University Press, 1990), 193–194.

Corinthian capitals (FIG. 5-73; see "The Corinthian Capital," above), an invention of the second half of the fifth century BCE.

Consistent with the extremely conservative nature of Greek temple design, architects did not readily embrace the Corinthian capital. Until the second century BCE, Corinthian capitals were employed, as at Delphi and Epidauros, only for the interiors of sacred buildings. The earliest instance of a Corinthian capital on the exterior of a Greek building is the Choragic Monument of Lysikrates (FIG. 5-74), which is not really a building at all. Lysikrates had sponsored a chorus in a theatrical contest in 334 BCE, and after he won, he erected a monument to commemorate his victory. The monument consists of a cylindrical drum resembling a tholos on a rectangular base. Engaged Corinthian columns adorn the drum of Lysikrates' monument, and a huge Corinthian capital sits atop the roof. The freestanding capital once supported the victor's trophy, a bronze *tripod* (a deep bowl on a tall three-legged stand).

The first known instance of the use of the Corinthian capital on the exterior of a building is the monument Lysikrates erected in Athens to commemorate the victory his chorus won in a theatrical contest.

HELLENISTIC PERIOD

Alexander the Great's conquest of the Near East and Egypt (where the Macedonian king was buried) ushered in a new cultural age that historians and art historians alike call *Hellenistic*. The Hellenistic period opened with the death of Alexander in 323 BCE and lasted nearly three centuries, until the double suicide of Queen Cleopatra of Egypt and her Roman consort Mark Antony in 30 BCE after their

decisive defeat at the battle of Actium by Antony's rival Augustus. That year, Augustus made Egypt a province of the Roman Empire.

The cultural centers of the Hellenistic period were the court cities of the Greek kings who succeeded Alexander and divided his far-flung empire among themselves. Chief among them were Antioch in Syria, Alexandria in Egypt, and Pergamon in Asia Minor. An international culture united the Hellenistic world, and its language was Greek. Hellenistic kings became enormously rich on the spoils of the East, priding themselves on their libraries, art collections, scientific enterprises, and skills as critics and connoisseurs, as well as on the learned men they could assemble at their courts. The world of the small, austere, and heroic city-state passed away, as did the power and prestige of its center, Athens. A cosmopolitan ("citizen of the world," in Greek) civilization, much like today's, replaced it.

Architecture

The greater variety, complexity, and sophistication of Hellenistic culture called for an architecture on an imperial scale and of wide diversity, something far beyond the requirements of the Classical polis, even beyond that of Athens at the height of its power. Building activity shifted from the old centers on the Greek mainland to the opulent cities of the Hellenistic monarchs in the East.

TEMPLE OF APOLLO, DIDYMA Great scale, a theatrical element of surprise, and a willingness to break the rules of canonical temple design characterize one of the most ambitious temple projects of the Hellenistic period, the Temple of Apollo at Didyma. The Hellenistic temple was built to replace the Archaic temple at the site the Persians had burned down in 494 BCE when they sacked nearby Miletos. Construction began in 313 BCE according to the design of two architects who were natives of the area, PAIONIOS OF EPHESOS and DAPHNIS OF MILETOS. So vast was the undertaking, however, that work on the temple continued off and on for more than 500 years—and still the project was never completed.

The temple was dipteral in plan (FIG. **5-75,** *left*) and had an unusually broad facade of 10 huge Ionic columns almost 65 feet tall. The sides had 21 columns, consistent with the Classical formula for

5-75 PAIONIOS OF EPHESOS and DAPHNIS OF MILETOS, Temple of Apollo, Didyma, Turkey, begun 313 BCE. Plan (*left*) and aerial view (*right*).

This unusual Hellenistic temple was hypaethral (open to the sky) and featured a double peripteral (dipteral) colonnade with a smaller temple inside the interior courtyard of the larger temple.

Dipteral colonnade

Inner shrine

Courtyard

Oracular room

0   25   50   75   100 feet
0   5   10   20   30 meters

5-76 Restored view of the city of Priene, Turkey, fourth century BCE and later (John Burge).

Despite its irregular terrain, Priene had a strict grid plan conforming to the principles of Hippodamos of Miletos, whom Aristotle singled out as the father of rational city planning.

perfect proportions used for the Parthenon—21 = (2 × 10) + 1—but nothing else about the design is Classical. One anomaly immediately apparent to anyone who approached the building was that it had no pediment and no roof—it was *hypaethral*, or open to the sky. Also, the grand doorway to what should be the temple's cella was elevated nearly five feet off the ground so that it could not be entered. The explanation for these peculiarities is that the doorway served rather as a kind of stage where the oracle of Apollo could be announced to those assembled in front of the temple. The unroofed dipteral colonnade was really only an elaborate frame for a central courtyard (FIG. 5-75, *right*) with a small prostyle shrine containing a statue of Apollo. Entrance to the interior court was through two smaller doorways to the left and right of the great portal and down two narrow vaulted tunnels that could accommodate only a single file of people. From these dark and mysterious lateral passageways, worshipers emerged into the clear light of the courtyard, which also had a sacred spring and laurel trees in honor of Apollo. Opposite Apollo's inner temple, a stairway some 50 feet wide rose majestically toward three portals leading into the oracular room that also opened onto the front of the temple. This complex spatial planning marked a sharp departure from Classical Greek architecture, which stressed a building's exterior almost as a work of sculpture and left its interior relatively undeveloped.

HIPPODAMOS OF MILETOS When the Persians were finally expelled from Asia Minor in 479 BCE, the Greek cities there were in near ruin. Reconstruction of Miletos began after 466 BCE according to a plan laid out by Hippodamos of Miletos, whom Aristotle singled out as the father of rational city planning. Hippodamos imposed a strict grid plan on the site, regardless of the terrain, so that all streets met at right angles. Such *orthogonal plans* actually predate Hippodamos, not only in Archaic Greece and Etruscan Italy but also in the ancient Near East and Egypt. But Hippodamos was so famous that his name has ever since been synonymous with such urban plans. The so-called *Hippodamian plan* also designated separate quarters for public, private, and religious functions. A "Hippodamian city" was logically as well as regularly planned. This desire to impose order on nature and to assign a proper place in the whole to each of the city's constituent parts was very much in keeping with the philosophical tenets of the fifth century BCE. Hippodamos's formula for the ideal city was another manifestation of the same outlook that produced Polykleitos's *Canon* and Iktinos's Parthenon.

PRIENE Hippodamian planning was still the norm in Late Classical and Hellenistic Greece. The city of Priene (FIG. 5-76), also in Asia Minor, was laid out during the fourth century BCE. It had fewer than 5,000 inhabitants (Hippodamos thought 10,000 was the ideal number). Situated on sloping ground, many of its narrow north-south streets were little more than long stairways. Uniformly sized city blocks, the standard planning unit, were nonetheless imposed on the irregular terrain. More than one unit was reserved for major structures such as the Temple of Athena and the theater. The central agora was allotted six blocks.

STOA OF ATTALOS, ATHENS Priene's agora was bordered by *stoas*. These covered colonnades, or *porticos*, which often housed shops and civic offices, were ideal vehicles for shaping urban spaces, and they were staples of Hellenistic cities. Even the agora of Athens, an ancient city notable for its haphazard, unplanned development, was eventually framed to the east and south by stoas placed at right angles to one another. These new porticos joined the famous Painted Stoa (see page 135), where the Hellenistic philosopher Zeno and his successors taught. The *Stoic* school of Greek philosophy took its name from that building.

The finest of the new Athenian stoas was the Stoa of Attalos II (FIG. 5-77), a gift to the city by a grateful alumnus, the king of Pergamon, who had studied at Athens in his youth. The stoa was meticulously reconstructed under the direction of the American School of Classical Studies at Athens and today has a second life as a museum housing more than seven decades of finds from the Athenian agora, as well as the offices of the American excavation team. The stoa has two stories, each with 21 shops opening onto the colonnade. The facade columns are Doric on the ground level and Ionic on the second story. The mixing of the two orders on a single facade had occurred even in the Late Classical period. But it became increasingly common in the Hellenistic period, when architects showed greatly diminished respect for the old rules of Greek architecture, and a desire for variety and decorative effects often prevailed. Practical considerations also governed the form of the Stoa of Attalos. The columns are far more widely spaced than in Greek temple architecture, to allow for easy access. And the builders left the lower third of every Doric column shaft unfluted to guard against damage from constant traffic.

5-77 Stoa of Attalos II, Agora, Athens, Greece, ca. 150 BCE (with the Acropolis in the background).

The Stoa of Attalos II in the Athenian agora has been meticulously restored. Greek stoas were covered colonnades that housed shops and civic offices. They were also ideal vehicles for shaping urban spaces.

Pergamon

Pergamon, the kingdom of Attalos II (r. 159–138 BCE), was one of those born in the early third century BCE after the breakup of Alexander's empire. Founded by Philetairos, the Pergamene kingdom embraced almost all of western and southern Asia Minor. Upon the death in 133 BCE of its last king, Attalos III (r. 138–133 BCE), Pergamon was bequeathed to Rome, which by then was the greatest power in the Mediterranean world. The Attalids enjoyed immense wealth, and much of it was expended on embellishing their capital city, especially its acropolis. Located there were the royal palace, an arsenal and barracks, a great library and theater, an agora, and the sacred precincts of Athena and Zeus.

ALTAR OF ZEUS, PERGAMON The Altar of Zeus at Pergamon, erected about 175 BCE, is the most famous Hellenistic sculptural ensemble. The monument's west front (FIG. 5-78) has been reconstructed in Berlin. The altar proper was on an elevated platform and framed by an Ionic stoalike colonnade with projecting wings on either side of a broad central staircase. All around the altar platform was a sculpted frieze almost 400 feet long, populated by about a hundred larger-than-life-size figures. The subject is the battle of Zeus and the gods against the giants. It is the most extensive representation Greek artists ever attempted of that epic conflict for control of the world. A similar subject appeared on the shield of Phidias's *Athena Parthenos* and on some of the Parthenon metopes, where the Athenians wished to draw a parallel between the defeat of the giants and the defeat of the Persians. In the third century BCE, King Attalos I (r. 241–197 BCE) had successfully turned back an invasion of the Gauls in Asia Minor. The gigantomachy of the Altar of Zeus alluded to that Pergamene victory over those barbarians.

5-78 Reconstructed west front of the Altar of Zeus, Pergamon, Turkey, ca. 175 BCE. Staatliche Museen, Berlin.

The gigantomachy frieze of Pergamon's monumental Altar of Zeus is almost 400 feet long. The battle of gods and giants alluded to the victory of King Attalos I over the Gauls of Asia Minor.

5-79 Athena battling Alkyoneos, detail of the gigantomachy frieze, from the Altar of Zeus, Pergamon, Turkey, ca. 175 BCE. Marble, 7′ 6″ high. Staatliche Museen, Berlin.

The tumultuous battle scenes of the Pergamon altar have an emotional power unparalleled in earlier Greek art. Violent movement, swirling draperies, and vivid depictions of suffering fill the frieze.

1 ft.

A deliberate connection was also made with Athens, whose earlier defeat of the Persians was by then legendary, and with the Parthenon, which already was recognized as a Classical monument—in both senses of the word. The figure of Athena (FIG. 5-79), for example, is a variation of the Athena from the Parthenon's east pediment. While Ge, the earth goddess and mother of all the giants, emerges from the ground and looks on with horror, Athena grabs the hair of the giant Alkyoneos as Nike flies in to crown her. Zeus himself (not illustrated) was based on the Poseidon of the west pediment. But the Pergamene frieze is not a dry series of borrowed motifs. On the contrary, its tumultuous narrative has an emotional intensity that has no parallel in earlier sculpture. The battle rages everywhere, even up and down the very steps one must ascend to reach Zeus's altar (FIG. 5-78). Violent movement, swirling draperies, and vivid depictions of death and suffering are the norm. Wounded figures writhe in pain, and their faces reveal their anguish. When Zeus hurls his thunderbolt, one can almost hear the thunderclap. Deep carving creates dark shadows. The figures project from the background like bursts of light. These features have been justly termed "baroque" and reappear in 17th-century European sculpture (see Chapter 24). One can hardly imagine a greater contrast than between the Pergamene gigantomachy frieze and that of the Archaic Siphnian Treasury (FIG. 5-19) at Delphi.

DYING GAULS On the Altar of Zeus, sculptors presented the victory of Attalos I over the Gauls in mythological disguise. An earlier Pergamene statuary group explicitly represented the defeat of the barbarians. Roman copies of some of these figures survive. The sculptor carefully studied and reproduced the distinctive features of the foreign Gauls, most notably their long, bushy hair and mustaches and the *torques* (neck bands) they frequently wore. The Pergamene victors were apparently not included in the group. The viewer saw only their foes and their noble and moving response to defeat.

In what was probably the centerpiece of the Attalid group, a heroic Gallic chieftain (FIG. 5-80) defiantly drives a sword into his own chest just below the collarbone, preferring suicide to surrender. He already has taken the life of his wife, who, if captured, would have been sold as a slave. In the best Lysippan tradition, the group can be fully appreci-

5-80 EPIGONOS(?), Gallic chieftain killing himself and his wife. Roman marble copy of a bronze original of ca. 230–220 BCE, 6′ 11″ high. Museo Nazionale Romano–Palazzo Altemps, Rome.

The defeat of the Gauls was also the subject of Pergamene statuary groups. The centerpiece of one group was a Gallic chieftain committing suicide after taking his wife's life. He preferred death to surrender.

1 ft.

The Gauls in the Pergamene victory groups were shown as barbarians with bushy hair, mustaches, and neck bands, but they were also portrayed as noble foes who fought to the end.

ated only by walking around it. From one side, the observer sees the Gaul's intensely expressive face, from another his powerful torso, and from a third the woman's limp and almost lifeless body. The man's twisting posture, the almost theatrical gestures, and the emotional intensity of the suicidal act are hallmarks of the Pergamene baroque style and have close parallels in the later frieze of Zeus's altar.

The third Gaul from this group is a trumpeter (FIG. 5-81) who collapses upon his large oval shield as blood pours from the gash in his chest. He stares at the ground with a pained expression. The Hellenistic figure recalls the dying warrior (FIG. 5-29) from the east pediment of the Temple of Aphaia at Aegina, but the pathos and drama of the suffering Gaul are far more pronounced. As in the suicide group and the gigantomachy frieze, the sculptor rendered the male musculature in an exaggerated manner. Note the tautness of the chest and the bulging veins of the left leg—implying that the unseen Attalid hero who has struck down this noble and savage foe must have been an extraordinary warrior. If this figure is the *tubicen* (trumpeter) Pliny mentioned as the work of the Pergamene master Epigonos, then Epigonos may be the sculptor of the entire group and the creator of the dynamic Hellenistic baroque style.

Sculpture

In different ways, Praxiteles, Skopas, and Lysippos had already taken bold steps in redefining the nature of Greek statuary. But Hellenistic sculptors went still further, both in terms of style and in expanding the range of subjects considered suitable for monumental sculpture.

NIKE OF SAMOTHRACE One of the masterpieces of Hellenistic baroque sculpture was set up in the Sanctuary of the Great Gods on the island of Samothrace. The *Nike of Samothrace* (FIG. 5-82) has just alighted on the prow of a Greek warship. Her missing right arm was once raised high to crown the naval victor, just as Nike placed a wreath on Athena on the Altar of Zeus (FIG. 5-79). But the Pergamene

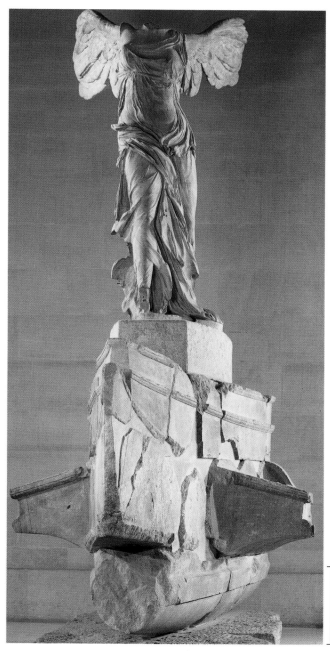

5-82 Nike alighting on a warship (*Nike of Samothrace*), from Samothrace, Greece, ca. 190 BCE. Marble, figure 8' 1" high. Louvre, Paris.

Victory has just landed on a prow to crown a victor at sea. Her wings still beat, and the wind sweeps her drapery. The placement of the statue in a fountain of splashing water heightened the dramatic visual effect.

relief figure seems calm by comparison. The Samothracian Nike's wings still beat, and the wind sweeps her drapery. Her himation bunches in thick folds around her right leg, and her chiton is pulled tightly across her abdomen and left leg.

The statue's setting amplified its theatrical effect. The war galley was displayed in the upper basin of a two-tiered fountain. In the lower basin were large boulders. The fountain's flowing water created the illusion of rushing waves dashing up against the prow of the ship. The statue's reflection in the shimmering water below accentuated the sense of lightness and movement. The sound of splashing water added an aural dimension to the visual drama. Art and nature were here combined in one of the most successful sculptures ever fashioned. In the *Nike of Samothrace* and other works in the Hellenistic baroque manner, sculptors resoundingly rejected the Polykleitan conception of a statue as an ideally proportioned, self-contained entity on a bare pedestal. The Hellenistic statues interact with their environment and appear as living, breathing, and intensely emotive human (or divine) presences.

VENUS DE MILO In the Hellenistic period, sculptors regularly followed Praxiteles' lead in undressing Aphrodite, but they also openly explored the eroticism of the nude female form. The famous *Venus de Milo* (FIG. **5-83**) is a larger-than-life-size marble statue of Aphrodite found on Melos together with its inscribed base (now lost) signed by the sculptor, ALEXANDROS OF ANTIOCH-ON-THE-MEANDER. In this statue, the goddess of love is more modestly draped than the *Aphrodite of Knidos* (FIG. **5-62**) but is more overtly sexual. Her left hand (separately preserved) holds the apple Paris awarded her when he judged her the most beautiful goddess of all. Her right hand may have lightly grasped the edge of her drapery near the left hip in a half-hearted attempt to keep it from slipping farther down her body. The

5-83A
Aphrodite,
Eros, and
Pan, Delos,
ca. 100 BCE.

5-83 ALEXANDROS OF ANTIOCH-ON-THE-MEANDER, Aphrodite (*Venus de Milo*), from Melos, Greece, ca. 150–125 BCE. Marble, 6′ 7″ high. Louvre, Paris.

Displaying the eroticism of many Hellenistic statues, this Aphrodite is more overtly sexual than the Knidian Aphrodite (FIG. **5-62**). The goddess has a slipping garment to tease the spectator.

5-84 Sleeping satyr (*Barberini Faun*), from Rome, Italy, ca. 230–200 BCE. Marble, 7′ 1″ high. Glyptothek, Munich.

In this statue of a restlessly sleeping, drunken satyr, a Hellenistic sculptor portrayed a semihuman in a suspended state of consciousness—the antithesis of the Classical ideals of rationality and discipline.

sculptor intentionally designed the work to tease the spectator, imbuing his partially draped Aphrodite with a sexuality absent from Praxiteles' entirely nude image of the goddess.

BARBERINI FAUN Archaic statues smile at their viewers, and even when Classical statues look away from the viewer they are always awake and alert. Hellenistic sculptors often portrayed sleep. The suspension of consciousness and the entrance into the fantasy world of dreams—the antithesis of the Classical ideals of rationality and discipline—had great appeal for them. This newfound interest can be seen in a statue of a drunken, restlessly sleeping *satyr* (a semi-human follower of Dionysos) known as the *Barberini Faun* (FIG. 5-84) after the Italian cardinal who once owned it. The statue was found in Rome in the 17th century and restored (not entirely accurately) by Gianlorenzo Bernini, the great Italian Baroque sculptor (see Chapter 24). Bernini no doubt felt that this dynamic statue in the Pergamene manner was the work of a kindred spirit. The satyr has consumed too much wine and has thrown down his panther skin on a convenient rock and then fallen into a disturbed, intoxicated sleep. His brows are furrowed, and one can almost hear him snore.

Eroticism also comes to the fore in this statue. Although men had been represented naked in Greek art for hundreds of years, Archaic kouroi and Classical athletes and gods do not exude sexuality. Sensuality surfaced in the works of Praxiteles and his followers in the fourth century BCE. But the dreamy and supremely beautiful Hermes playfully dangling grapes before the infant Dionysos (FIG. 5-63) has nothing of the blatant sexuality of the *Barberini Faun,* whose wantonly spread legs focus attention on his genitals. Homosexuality was common in the man's world of ancient Greece. It is not surprising that when Hellenistic sculptors began to explore the sexuality of the human body, they turned their attention to both men and women.

DEFEATED BOXER Although Hellenistic sculptors tackled an expanded range of subjects, they did not abandon such traditional themes as the Greek athlete. But they often rendered the old subjects in novel ways. This is certainly true of the magnificent bronze statue (FIG. 5-85) of a seated boxer, a Hellenistic original found in Rome and perhaps at one time part of a group. The boxer is not a victorious young athlete with a perfect face and body but a heavily battered, defeated veteran whose upward gaze may have been directed at the man who had just beaten him. Too many punches from powerful hands wrapped in leather thongs—Greek boxers did not use the modern sport's cushioned gloves—have distorted the boxer's face. His nose is broken, as are his teeth. He has smashed, "cauliflower" ears. Inlaid copper blood drips from the cuts on his forehead, nose, and cheeks. How radically different is this rendition of a powerful bearded man from that of the noble warrior from Riace (FIGS. 5-35 and I-17) of the Early Classical period. The Hellenistic sculptor appealed not to the intellect but to the emotions when striving to evoke compassion for the pounded hulk of a once-mighty fighter.

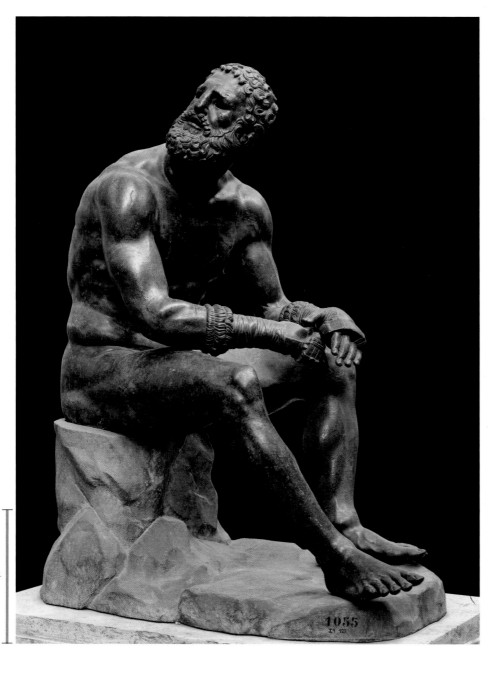

1 ft.

5-85 Seated boxer, from Rome, Italy, ca. 100–50 BCE. Bronze, 4′ 2″ high. Museo Nazionale Romano–Palazzo Massimo alle Terme, Rome.

Even when Hellenistic artists treated traditional themes, they approached them in novel ways. This bronze statue represents an older, defeated boxer with a broken nose and battered ears.

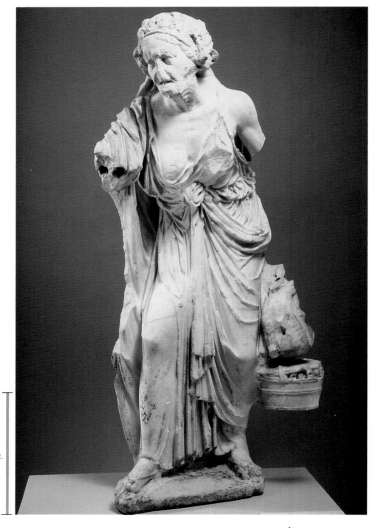

5-86 Old market woman, ca. 150–100 BCE. Marble, 4′ $\frac{1}{2}$″ high. Metropolitan Museum of Art, New York.

Consistent with the realism of much Hellenistic art, many statues portrayed old men and women from the lowest rungs of society. They were never considered suitable subjects in earlier Greek statuary.

OLD MARKET WOMAN The realistic bent of much of Hellenistic sculpture—the very opposite of the Classical period's idealism—is evident above all in a series of statues of old men and women from the lowest rungs of the social order. Shepherds, fishermen, and drunken beggars are common—the kinds of people pictured earlier on red-figure vases but never before thought worthy of monumental statuary. One of the finest preserved statues of this type depicts a haggard old woman (FIG. **5-86**) bringing chickens and a basket of fruits and vegetables to sell in the market. Her face is wrinkled, her body bent with age, and her spirit broken by a lifetime of poverty. She carries on because she must, not because she derives any pleasure from life. No one knows the purpose of these statues, but they attest to an interest in social realism absent in earlier Greek statuary.

Statues of the aged and the ugly are, of course, the polar opposites of the images of the young and the beautiful that dominated Greek art until the Hellenistic age, but they are consistent with the period's changed character. The Hellenistic world was a cosmopolitan place, and the highborn could not help but encounter the poor and a growing number of foreigners (non-Greek "barbarians") on a daily basis. Hellenistic art reflects this different social climate in the depiction of a much wider variety of physical types, including different ethnic types. The sensitive portrayal of Gallic warriors with their

5-87 POLYEUKTOS, Demosthenes. Roman marble copy of a bronze original of ca. 280 BCE, 6′ 7$\frac{1}{2}$″ high. Ny Carlsberg Glyptotek, Copenhagen.

One of the earliest Hellenistic portraits, frequently copied, was Polyeuktos's representation of the great orator Demosthenes as a frail man who possessed great courage and moral conviction.

shaggy hair, strange mustaches, and golden torques (FIG. **5-80** and **5-81**) has already been noted. Africans, Scythians, and others, formerly only the occasional subject of vase painters, also entered the realm of monumental sculpture in Hellenistic art.

DEMOSTHENES These sculptures of foreigners and the urban poor, however realistic, are not portraits. Rather, they are sensitive studies of physical types. But the growing interest in the individual beginning in the Late Classical period did lead in the Hellenistic era to the production of true likenesses of specific persons. In fact, one of the

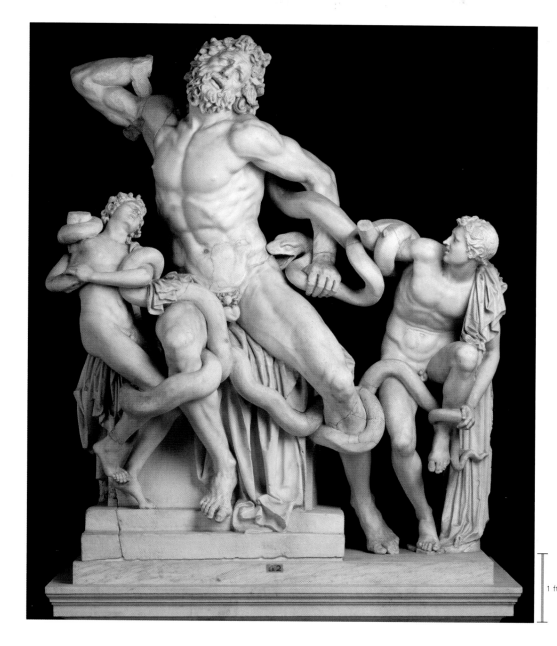

5-88 Athanadoros, Hagesandros, and Polydoros of Rhodes, Laocoön and his sons, from Rome, Italy, early first century CE. Marble, 7' 10½" high. Musei Vaticani, Rome.

Hellenistic style lived on in Rome. Although stylistically akin to Pergamene sculpture, this statue of sea serpents attacking Laocoön and his two sons matches the account given only in the *Aeneid*.

1 ft.

great achievements of Hellenistic artists was the redefinition of portraiture. In the Classical period, Kresilas was admired for having made the noble Pericles appear even nobler in his portrait (FIG. 5-41). But in Hellenistic times sculptors sought not only to record the actual appearance of their subjects in bronze and stone but also to capture the essence of their personalities in likenesses that were at once accurate and moving.

One of the earliest of these, perhaps the finest of the Hellenistic age and frequently copied in Roman times, was a bronze portrait statue of Demosthenes (FIG. 5-87) by POLYEUKTOS. The original was set up in the Athenian agora in 280 BCE, 42 years after the great orator's death. Demosthenes was a frail man and in his youth even suffered from a speech impediment, but he had enormous courage and great moral conviction. A veteran of the disastrous battle against Philip II at Chaeronea, he repeatedly tried to rally opposition to Macedonian imperialism, both before and after Alexander's death. In the end, when it was clear the Macedonians would capture him, he took his own life by drinking poison.

Polyeuktos rejected Kresilas's and Lysippos's notions of the purpose of portraiture and did not attempt to portray a supremely confident leader with a magnificent physique. His Demosthenes has an aged and slightly stooped body. The orator clasps his hands nervously in front of him as he looks downward, deep in thought. His face is lined, his hair is receding, and his expression is one of great sadness. Whatever physical discomfort Demosthenes felt is here joined by an inner pain, his deep sorrow over the tragic demise of democracy at the hands of the Macedonian conquerors.

Hellenistic Art under Roman Patronage

In the opening years of the second century BCE, the Roman general Flamininus defeated the Macedonian army and declared the old poleis of Classical Greece free once again. The city-states never regained their former glory, however. Greece became a Roman province in 146 BCE. When, 60 years later, Athens sided with King Mithridates VI of Pontus (r. 120–63 BCE) in his war against Rome, the general Sulla crushed the Athenians. Thereafter, Athens retained some of its earlier prestige as a center of culture and learning, but politically it was just another city in the ever-expanding Roman Empire. Nonetheless, Greek artists continued to be in great demand, both to furnish the Romans with an endless stream of copies of Classical and Hellenistic masterpieces and to create new statues *à la grecque* (in the Greek style) for Roman patrons.

LAOCOÖN One such work is the famous group (FIG. 5-88) of the Trojan priest Laocoön and his sons, which was unearthed in Rome in

1506 in the presence of the great Italian Renaissance artist Michelangelo. The marble group, long believed an original of the second century BCE, was found in the remains of the palace of the emperor Titus (r. 79–81 CE), exactly where Pliny had seen it more than 14 centuries before. Pliny attributed the statue to three sculptors—ATHANADOROS, HAGESANDROS, and POLYDOROS OF RHODES—whom most art historians now think worked in the early first century CE. They probably based their group on a Hellenistic masterpiece depicting Laocoön and only one son. Their variation on the original added the son at Laocoön's left (note the greater compositional integration of the two other figures) to conform with the Roman poet Vergil's account in the *Aeneid*. Vergil vividly described the strangling of Laocoön and his *two* sons by sea serpents while sacrificing at an altar. The gods who favored the Greeks in the war against Troy had sent the serpents to punish Laocoön, who had tried to warn his compatriots about the danger of bringing the Greeks' wooden horse within the walls of their city.

In Vergil's graphic account, Laocoön suffered in terrible agony, and the sculptors communicated the torment of the priest and his sons in a spectacular fashion in the marble group. The three Trojans writhe in pain as they struggle to free themselves from the death grip of the serpents. One bites into Laocoön's left hip as the priest lets out a ferocious cry. The serpent-entwined figures recall the suffering giants of the great frieze of the Altar of Zeus at Pergamon, and Laocoön himself is strikingly similar to Alkyoneos (FIG. 5-79), Athena's opponent. In fact, many scholars believe that a Pergamene statuary group of the second century BCE was the inspiration for the three Rhodian sculptors.

SPERLONGA That the work seen by Pliny and displayed in the Vatican Museums today was made for Romans rather than Greeks was confirmed in 1957 by the discovery of fragments of several Hellenistic-style groups illustrating scenes from Homer's *Odyssey*. These fragments were found in a grotto that served as the picturesque summer banquet hall of the seaside villa of the Roman emperor Tiberius (r. 14–37 CE) at Sperlonga, some 60 miles south of Rome. One of these groups—depicting the monster Scylla attacking Odysseus's ship—is signed by the same three sculptors Pliny cited as the creators of the Laocoön group. Another of the groups, installed around a central pool in the grotto, depicted the blinding of the Cyclops Polyphemos by Odysseus and his comrades, an incident also set in a cave in the Homeric epic. The head of Odysseus (FIG. 5-89) from this theatrical group is one of the finest sculptures of antiquity. The hero's cap can barely contain his swirling locks of hair. Even Odysseus's beard seems to be swept up in the emotional intensity of the moment. The parted lips and the deep shadows produced by sharp undercutting add drama to the head, which complemented Odysseus's agitated body.

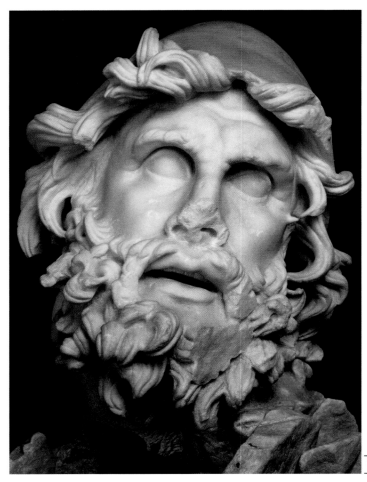

5-89 ATHANADOROS, HAGESANDROS, and POLYDOROS OF RHODES, head of Odysseus, from Sperlonga, Italy, early first century CE. Marble, $2' 1\frac{1}{4}''$ high. Museo Archeologico, Sperlonga.

This emotionally charged depiction of Odysseus was part of a mythological statuary group that the Laocoön sculptors made for a grotto at the emperor Tiberius's seaside villa at Sperlonga.

At Tiberius's villa in Sperlonga and in Titus's palace in Rome, the baroque school of Hellenistic sculpture lived on long after Greece ceased to be a political force. When Rome inherited the Pergamene kingdom from the last of the Attalids in 133 BCE, it also became heir to the Greek artistic legacy, and what Rome adopted from Greece it in turn passed on to the medieval and modern worlds. If Greece was peculiarly the inventor of the European spirit, Rome surely was its propagator and amplifier.

ANCIENT GREECE

GEOMETRIC AND ORIENTALIZING ART, ca. 900–600 BCE

▮ Homer lived during the eighth century BCE, the era when the city-states of Classical Greece took shape, the Olympic Games were founded (776 BCE), and the Greeks began to trade with their neighbors to both east and west.

▮ Also at this time, the human figure returned to Greek art in the form of bronze statuettes and simple silhouettes amid other abstract motifs on Geometric vases.

▮ Increasing contact with the civilizations of the Near East precipitated the so-called Orientalizing phase (ca. 700–600 BCE) of Greek art, when Eastern monsters began to appear on black-figure vases.

Dipylon krater, Athens,
ca. 740 BCE

ARCHAIC ART, ca. 600–480 BCE

▮ Around 600 BCE, the first life-size stone statues appeared in Greece. The earliest kouroi emulated the frontal poses of Egyptian statues, but artists depicted the young men nude, the way Greek athletes competed at Olympia.

▮ During the course of the sixth century BCE, Greek sculptors refined the proportions and added "Archaic smiles" to the faces of their statues to make them seem more lifelike.

▮ The Archaic age also saw the erection of the first stone temples with peripteral colonnades and the codification of the Doric and Ionic orders.

▮ The Andokides Painter invented red-figure vase painting around 530 BCE. Euphronios and Euthymides rejected the age-old composite view for the human figure and experimented with foreshortening.

Kroisos, kouros from Anavysos,
ca. 530 BCE

EARLY AND HIGH CLASSICAL ART, ca. 480–400 BCE

▮ The Classical period opened with the Persian sack of the Athenian Acropolis in 480 BCE and the Greek victory a year later. The fifth century BCE was the golden age of Greece, when Aeschylus, Sophocles, and Euripides wrote their plays, and Herodotus, the "father of history," lived.

▮ During the Early Classical period (480–450 BCE), sculptors revolutionized statuary by introducing contrapposto (weight shift) to their figures.

▮ In the High Classical period (450–400 BCE), Polykleitos developed a canon of proportions for the perfect statue. Iktinos and Kallikrates similarly applied mathematical formulas to temple design in the belief that beauty resulted from the use of harmonic numbers.

▮ Under the patronage of Pericles and the artistic directorship of Phidias, the Athenians rebuilt the Acropolis after 447 BCE. The Parthenon, Phidias's *Athena Parthenos,* and the works of Polykleitos have defined what it means to be "Classical" ever since.

Parthenon, Acropolis, Athens,
447–438 BCE

LATE CLASSICAL ART, ca. 400–323 BCE

▮ In the aftermath of the Peloponnesian War, which ended in 404 BCE, Greek artists, while still adhering to the philosophy that humanity was the "measure of all things," began to focus more on the real world of appearances than on the ideal world of perfect beings.

▮ Late Classical sculptors humanized the remote deities, athletes, and heroes of the fifth century BCE. Praxiteles, for example, caused a sensation when he portrayed Aphrodite undressed. Lysippos depicted Herakles as a strong man so weary that he needed to lean on his club for support.

▮ In architecture, the ornate Corinthian capital became increasingly popular, breaking the monopoly of the Doric and Ionic orders.

▮ The period closed with Alexander the Great, who transformed the Mediterranean world politically and ushered in a new artistic age as well.

Praxiteles, *Aphrodite of Knidos,*
ca. 350–340 BCE

HELLENISTIC ART, ca. 323–30 BCE

▮ The Hellenistic age extends from the death of Alexander until the death of Cleopatra, when Egypt became a province of the Roman Empire. The great cultural centers of the era were no longer the city-states of Archaic and Classical Greece but royal capitals such as Alexandria in Egypt and Pergamon in Asia Minor.

▮ In art, both architects and sculptors broke most of the rules of Classical design. At Didyma, for example, a temple to Apollo was erected that had no roof and contained a smaller temple within it.

▮ Hellenistic sculptors explored new subjects—Gauls with strange mustaches and necklaces, impoverished old women—and treated traditional subjects in new ways—athletes with battered bodies and faces, openly erotic goddesses. Artists delighted in depicting violent movement and unbridled emotion.

Altar of Zeus, Pergamon,
ca. 175 BCE

6-1 Interior of the chaitya hall, Karle, India, ca. 50 CE.

An early example of Buddhist architecture, the chaitya hall at Karle is carved out of the living rock. It has a pillared ambulatory that allows worshipers to circumambulate the stupa in the apse of the cave.

6

SOUTH AND SOUTHEAST ASIA BEFORE 1200

South and Southeast Asia is a vast geographic area comprising, among others, the nations of India, Pakistan, Sri Lanka, Thailand, Vietnam, Cambodia, Bangladesh, and Indonesia (MAP **6-1**). Not surprisingly, the region's inhabitants display tremendous cultural and religious diversity. The people of India alone speak more than 20 different major languages. Those spoken in the north belong to the Indo-European language family, whereas those in the south form a completely separate linguistic family called Dravidian. The art of South and Southeast Asia is equally diverse—and very ancient. When Alexander the Great and his army reached India in 326 BCE, the civilization they encountered was already more than two millennia old. The remains of the first cities in the Indus Valley predate the palaces (FIGS. **4-15** and **4-19**) of Homer's Trojan War heroes by a millennium. Covered in this chapter are the art and architecture of South and Southeast Asia from their beginnings almost five millennia ago through the 12th century. Chapter 26 treats the later art of the region up to the present day.

INDIA AND PAKISTAN

In the third millennium BCE, a great civilization arose over a wide geographic area along the Indus River in Pakistan and extended into India as far south as Gujarat and east beyond Delhi. Archaeologists have dubbed this early South Asian culture the Indus Civilization.

Indus Civilization

The Indus Civilization flourished from about 2600 to 1500 BCE, and evidence indicates there was active trade during this period between the peoples of the Indus Valley and Mesopotamia. The most important excavated Indus sites are Harappa and Mohenjo-daro. These early, fully developed cities featured streets oriented to compass points and multistoried houses built of carefully formed and precisely laid kiln-baked bricks. But in sharp contrast to the contemporaneous civilizations of Mesopotamia and Egypt, no surviving Indus building has yet been identified as a temple or a palace.

MAP 6-1 South and Southeast Asian sites before 1200.

MOHENJO-DARO The Indus cities boasted one of the world's first sophisticated systems of water supply and sewage. Throughout Mohenjo-daro, hundreds of wells provided fresh water to homes that featured some of the oldest recorded private bathing areas and toilet facilities with drainage into public sewers. In the heart of the city stood the so-called Great Bath, a complex of rooms centered on a sunken brick pool (FIG. 6-2) 39 feet long, 23 feet wide, and 8 feet deep. The builders made the pool watertight by sealing the joints between the bricks with bitumen, an asphaltlike material also used in Mesopotamia. The bath probably was not a purely recreational facility but rather a place for ritual bathing of the kind still practiced in the region today.

Excavators have discovered surprisingly little art from the long-lived Indus Civilization, and all of the objects found are small.

6-2 Great Bath, Mohenjo-daro, Pakistan, ca. 2600–1900 BCE.

The Indus cities of the third millennium BCE had sophisticated water-supply and sewage systems, which made possible this brick complex used for ritual bathing of a kind still practiced in South Asia today.

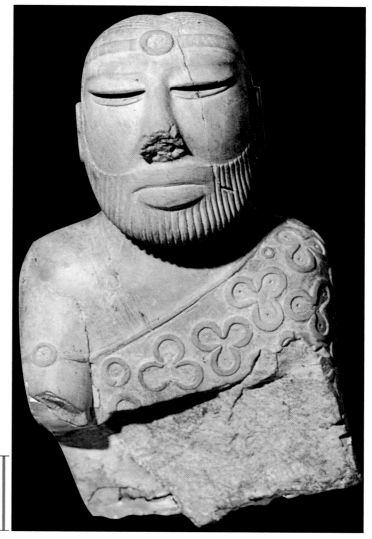

1 in.

6-3 Robed male figure, from Mohenjo-daro, Pakistan, ca. 2000–1900 BCE. Steatite, $6\frac{7}{8}$″ high. National Museum of Pakistan, Karachi.

Little art survives from the Indus Civilization, and all of it is of small scale. This bearded figure, which scholars think represents a priest-king, has iconographic similarities to some Sumerian sculptures.

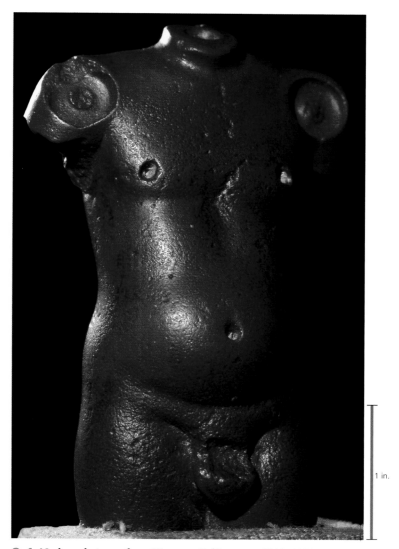

1 in.

6-4 Nude male torso, from Harappa, Pakistan, ca. 2000–1900 BCE. Red sandstone, $3\frac{3}{4}$″ high. National Museum, New Delhi.

This miniature figure, with its emphasis on sensuous polished surfaces and swelling curves, already displays many of the stylistic traits that would characterize South Asian sculpture for thousands of years.

Perhaps the most impressive sculpture discovered is a robed male figure (FIG. 6-3) with half-closed eyes, a low forehead, and a closely trimmed beard with shaved upper lip. He wears a headband with a central circular emblem, matched by a similar armband. Holes on each side of his neck suggest that he also wore a necklace of precious metal. *Trefoils* (cloverlike designs with three stylized leaves) decorate his elegant robe. They, as well as the circles of the head- and arm-bands, originally held red paste and shell inlays, as did the eyes. Art historians often compare the Mohenjo-daro statuette to Sumerian sculptures, in which the trefoil motif appears in sacred contexts, and scholars usually refer to the person portrayed as a "priest-king," the ambiguous term used for some Sumerian leaders. The identity and rank of the Mohenjo-daro figure, however, are uncertain. Nonetheless, the elaborate costume and precious materials make clear that he too was an elite individual.

HARAPPA Quite different in style is the miniature red-sand-stone torso of a nude male figure (FIG. 6-4) found at Harappa. Scholars usually compare this figure, which is less than four inches tall, to Greek statues of much later date, but the treatment of anatomy separates it sharply from the classical tradition. The highly polished surface of the stone and the swelling curves of the abdomen reveal the Indus artist's interest in the fluid movement of a living body, not in the logical anatomical structure of Greek sculpture. This sense of pulsating vigor and the emphasis on sensuous surfaces would continue to be chief characteristics of South Asian sculpture for thousands of years.

INDUS SEALS The most common Indus art objects are steatite seals with incised designs. They are similar in many ways to the stamp seals found at contemporaneous sites in Mesopotamia (see "Meso-potamian Seals," Chapter 2, page 39). Most of the Indus examples have an animal or tiny narrative carved on the face, along with an as-yet-untranslated script. On the back, a *boss* (circular knob) with a hole permitted insertion of a string so that the seal could be worn or hung on a wall. As in the ancient Near East, the Indus peoples some-times used the seals to make impressions on clay, apparently for se-curing trade goods wrapped in textiles. The animals most frequently represented include the humped bull, elephant, rhinoceros, and tiger. Each is portrayed in strict profile, as in the paintings and reliefs of all other early cultures. Some of the narrative seals appear to show that the Indus peoples considered trees sacred, as both Buddhists and

6-5 Seal with seated figure in yogic posture, from Mohenjo-daro, Pakistan, ca. 2300–1750 BCE. Steatite coated with alkali and baked, $1\frac{3}{8}'' \times 1\frac{3}{8}''$. National Museum, New Delhi.

This seal depicting a figure (with three faces?) wearing a horned headdress and seated in a posture used in yoga is evidence that this important Indian meditative practice began as early as the Indus Civilization.

language yet identified in South Asia. Around 1500 BCE, they composed the first of four *Vedas*. These Sanskrit compilations of religious learning (Veda means "knowledge") included hymns intended for priests (called Brahmins) to chant or sing. The Brahmins headed a social hierarchy, perhaps of pre-Aryan origin, that became known as the caste system, which still forms the basis of Indian society today. Below the priests were the warriors, traders, and manual laborers (including artists and architects), respectively. The Aryan religion centered on sacrifice, the ritual enactment of often highly intricate and lengthy ceremonies in which the priests placed materials, such as milk and soma (an intoxicating drink), into a fire that took the sacrifices to the gods in the heavens. If the Brahmins performed these rituals accurately, the gods would fulfill the prayers of those who sponsored the sacrifices. These gods, primarily male, included Indra, Varuna, Surya, and Agni, gods associated, respectively, with the rains, the ocean, the sun, and fire. There is no evidence to indicate the Aryans made images of these deities.

UPANISHADS The next phase of South Asian urban civilization developed east of the Indus heartland, in the Ganges River Valley. Here, from 800 to 500 BCE, religious thinkers composed a variety of texts called the *Upanishads*. Among the innovative ideas of the Upanishads were *samsara, karma,* and *moksha* (or *nirvana*). Samsara is the belief that individuals are born again after death in an almost endless round of rebirths. The type of rebirth can vary. One can be reborn as a human being, an animal, or even a god. An individual's past actions (karma), either good or bad, determine the nature of future rebirths. The ultimate goal of a person's religious life is to escape from the cycle of birth and death by merging the individual self into the vital force of the universe. This escape is called either moksha (liberation, for Hindus) or nirvana (cessation, for Buddhists).

HINDUISM AND BUDDHISM Hinduism and Buddhism, the two major modern religions originating in Asia, developed in the late centuries BCE and the early centuries CE. Hinduism, the dominant religion in India today, discussed in more detail later, has its origins in Aryan religion. The founder of Buddhism was the Buddha, a historical figure who advocated the path of *asceticism,* or self-discipline and self-denial, as the means to free oneself from attachments to people and possessions, thus ending rebirth (see "Buddhism and Buddhist Iconography," page 161). Unlike their predecessors in South Asia, both Hindus and Buddhists use images of gods and holy persons in religious rituals. To judge from surviving works, Buddhism has the older artistic tradition. The earliest Buddhist monuments date to the Maurya period.

Hindus later did. Many historians have suggested religious and ritual continuities between the Indus Civilization and later Indian culture.

One of the most elaborate seals (FIG. 6-5) depicts a male figure with a horned headdress and, perhaps, three faces, seated (with erect penis) among the profile animals that regularly appear alone on other seals. The figure's folded legs with heels pressed together and his arms resting on the knees suggest a yogic posture (compare FIG. 6-12). *Yoga* is a method for controlling the body and relaxing the mind used in later Indian religions to yoke, or unite, the practitioner to the divine. Although most scholars reject the identification of this figure as a prototype of the multiheaded Hindu god Shiva (FIG. 6-18) as Lord of Beasts, the yogic posture argues that this important Indian meditative practice began as early as the Indus Civilization.

Vedic and Upanishadic Period

By 1700 BCE, the urban phase of the Indus Civilization had ended in most areas. The production of sculptures, seals, and script gradually ceased, and village life replaced urban culture. Very little art survives from the next thousand years, but the religious foundations laid during this period helped define most later South and Southeast Asian art.

VEDAS The basis for the new religious ideas were the oral hymns of the Aryans, a mobile herding people from Central Asia who occupied the Punjab, an area of northwestern India, in the second millennium BCE. The Aryans ("Noble Ones") spoke Sanskrit, the earliest

Maurya Dynasty

When Alexander the Great reached the Indus River in 326 BCE, his troops refused to go forward. Reluctantly, Alexander abandoned his dream of conquering India and headed home. After Alexander's death three years later, his generals divided his empire among themselves. One of them, Seleucus Nicator, reinvaded India, but Chandragupta Maurya (r. 323–298 BCE), founder of the Maurya dynasty, defeated him in 305 BCE and eventually consolidated almost all of present-day India under his domain. Chandragupta's capital was Pataliputra (modern Patna) in northeastern India, far from the center of the Indus Civilization. Megasthenes, Seleucus's ambassador to the Maurya court, described Pataliputra in his book on India as a large and wealthy city enclosed within mighty wooden walls so extensive that the circuit had 64 gates and 570 towers.

Buddhism and Buddhist Iconography

THE BUDDHA AND BUDDHISM

The Buddha (Enlightened One) was born around 563 BCE as Prince Siddhartha Gautama, the eldest son of the king of the Shakya clan. A prophecy foretold that he would grow up to be either a world conqueror or a great religious leader. His father preferred the secular role for young Siddhartha and groomed him for kingship by shielding the boy from the hardships of the world. When he was 29, however, the prince rode out of the palace, abandoned his wife and family, and encountered firsthand the pain of old age, sickness, and death. Siddhartha responded to the suffering he witnessed by renouncing his opulent life and becoming a wandering ascetic searching for knowledge through meditation. Six years later, he achieved complete enlightenment, or buddhahood, while meditating beneath a pipal tree (the Bodhi tree) at Bodh Gaya ("place of enlightenment") in eastern India. Known from that day on as Shakyamuni (Wise Man of the Shakya clan), the Buddha preached his first sermon in the Deer Park at Sarnath. There he set in motion the Wheel (*chakra*) of the Law (*dharma*) and expounded the Four Noble Truths that are the core insights of Buddhism: (1) Life is suffering; (2) the cause of suffering is desire; (3) one can overcome and extinguish desire; (4) the way to conquer desire and end suffering is to follow the Buddha's Eightfold Path of right understanding, right thought, right speech, right action, right livelihood, right effort, right mindfulness, and right concentration. The Buddha's path leads to nirvana, the cessation of the endless cycle of painful life, death, and rebirth. The Buddha continued to preach until his death at 80 at Kushinagara. His disciples carried on his teaching and established monasteries where others could follow the Buddha's path to enlightenment and nirvana.

This earliest form of Buddhism is called Theravada (the Path of the Elders) Buddhism. The new religion developed and changed over time as the Buddha's teachings spread from India throughout Asia. The second major school of Buddhist thought, Mahayana (Great Path) Buddhism, emerged around the beginning of the Christian era. Mahayana Buddhists refer to Theravada Buddhism as Hinayana (Lesser Path) Buddhism and believe in a larger goal than nirvana for an individual—namely, buddhahood for all. Mahayana Buddhists also revere *bodhisattvas* ("Buddhas-to-be"), exemplars of compassion who restrain themselves at the threshold of nirvana to aid others in earning merit and achieving buddhahood. Theravada Buddhism became the dominant sect in southern India, Sri Lanka, and mainland Southeast Asia, whereas Mahayana Buddhism took root in northern India and spread to China, Korea, Japan, and Nepal.

A third important Buddhist sect, especially popular in East Asia, venerates the Amitabha Buddha (Amida in Japanese), the Buddha of Infinite Light and Life. The devotees of this Buddha hope to be reborn in the Pure Land Paradise of the West, where the Amitabha resides and can grant them salvation. Pure Land teachings maintain that people have no possibility of attaining enlightenment on their own but can achieve paradise by faith alone.

BUDDHIST ICONOGRAPHY

The earliest (first century CE) depictions of the Buddha in human form show him as a robed monk. Artists distinguished the Enlightened One from monks and bodhisattvas by *lakshanas*, body attributes indicating the Buddha's suprahuman nature. These distinguishing marks include an *urna*, or curl of hair between the eyebrows, shown as a dot; an *ushnisha*, a cranial bump shown as hair on the earliest images (FIGS. 6-10 to 6-12) but later as an actual part of the head (FIG. 6-13); and, less frequently, palms and soles imprinted with a wheel (FIG. 6-12). The Buddha is also recognizable by his elongated ears, the result of wearing heavy royal jewelry in his youth, but the enlightened Shakyamuni is rarely bejeweled, as are many bodhisattvas (FIG. 6-15). Sometimes the Buddha appears with a halo, or sun disk, behind his head (FIGS. 6-10, 6-12, and 6-13).

Representations of the Buddha also feature a repertory of *mudras*, or hand gestures, conveying fixed meanings. These include the *dhyana* (meditation) mudra, with the right hand over the left, palms upward (FIG. 6-10); the *bhumisparsha* (earth-touching) mudra, right hand down reaching to the ground, calling the earth to witness the Buddha's enlightenment (FIG. 6-11*b*); the *dharmachakra* (Wheel of the Law, or teaching) mudra, a two-handed gesture with right thumb and index finger forming a circle (FIG. 6-13); and the *abhaya* (do not fear) mudra, right hand up, palm outward, a gesture of protection or blessing (FIGS. 6-11*c* and 6-12).

Episodes from the Buddha's life are among the most popular subjects in all Buddhist artistic traditions. No single text provides the complete or authoritative narrative of the Buddha's life and death. Thus, numerous versions and variations exist, allowing for a rich artistic repertory. Four of the most important events are his birth at Lumbini from the side of his mother, Queen Maya (FIG. 6-11*a*); his achievement of buddhahood while meditating beneath the Bodhi tree at Bodh Gaya (FIG. 6-11*b*); his first sermon as the Buddha at Sarnath (FIGS. 6-11*c* and 6-13); and his attainment of nirvana when he died (*parinirvana*) at Kushinagara (FIGS. 6-11*d* and 6-26). Buddhists erected monasteries and monuments at the four sites where these key events occurred, although the Buddha himself disapproved of all luxury, including lavish religious shrines with costly figural art. Monks and lay pilgrims from throughout the world continue to visit these places today.

ASHOKA The greatest Maurya ruler was Ashoka (r. 272–231 BCE), who left his imprint on history by converting to Buddhism and spreading the Buddha's teaching throughout and beyond India (see "Ashoka's Conversion to Buddhism," page 162). Ashoka formulated a legal code based on the Buddha's dharma and inscribed his laws on enormous *monolithic* (one-piece stone) columns erected throughout his kingdom. Ashoka's pillars reached 30 to 40 feet high and are the first monumental stone artworks in India. The pillars penetrated deep into the ground, connecting earth and sky, forming an "axis of the universe," a pre-Buddhist concept that became an important motif in Buddhist architecture. The columns stood along pilgrimage routes to sites associated with the Buddha and on the roads leading to Pataliputra. Capping Ashoka's pillars were elaborate capitals, also carved from a single block of stone. The finest of these comes from Sarnath, where the Buddha

6-6A Lion pillar, Lauriya Nandangarh, ca. 245 BCE.

Ashoka's Conversion to Buddhism

The reign of the Maurya king Ashoka marks both the beginning of monumental stone art and architecture (FIG. 6-6) in India and the first official sponsorship of Buddhism. The impact of Ashoka's conversion to Buddhism on the later history of art and religion in Asia cannot be overstated.

An edict carved into a rock at Dhauli in the ancient region of Kalinga (roughly equivalent to the modern state of Orissa on the Bay of Bengal) records Ashoka's embrace of nonviolence and of the teachings of the Buddha after an especially bloody conquest that claimed more than 100,000 lives. The inscription also captures Ashoka's missionary zeal, which spread Buddhism far beyond the boundaries of his kingdom.

> The Beloved of the Gods [Ashoka], conqueror of the Kalingas, is moved to remorse now. For he has felt profound sorrow and regret because the conquest of a people previously unconquered involves slaughter, death, and deportation. . . . [King Ashoka] now thinks that even a person who wrongs him must be forgiven . . . [and he] considers moral conquest [conquest by dharma] the most important conquest. He has achieved this moral conquest repeatedly both here and among the peoples living beyond the borders of his kingdom. . . . Even in countries which [King Ashoka's] envoys have not reached, people have heard about dharma and about [the king's] ordinances and instructions in dharma. . . . This edict on dharma has been inscribed so that my sons and great-grandsons who may come after me should not think new conquests worth achieving. . . . Let them consider moral conquest the only true conquest.*

The story of Ashoka at Kalinga and his renunciation of violent aggression still resonates today. It inspired one of the most important 20th-century Indian sculptors to take up the theme and imbue it with contemporary meaning (FIG. 26-15).

*Rock Edict XIII. Translated by N. A. Nikam and Richard McKeon, *The Edicts of Aśoka* (Chicago: University of Chicago Press, 1959), 27–30.

6-6 Lion capital of the column erected by Ashoka at Sarnath, India, ca. 250 BCE. Polished sandstone, 7' high. Archaeological Museum, Sarnath.

Ashoka formulated a legal code based on the Buddha's teachings and inscribed those laws on columns erected throughout his kingdom. The lions on this capital once supported the Buddha's Wheel of the Law.

1 ft.

6-6B Yakshi holding a fly whisk, Didarganj, mid-third century BCE.

gave his first sermon and set the Wheel of the Law in motion. It is a seven-foot lion capital (FIG. 6-6). Stylistically, Ashoka's capital owes much to the ancient Near East, especially the Achaemenid art of Persepolis (see Chapter 2), but its iconography is Buddhist. Two pairs of back-to-back lions (the Buddha is often referred to as "the lion") stand on a round abacus decorated with four wheels and four animals symbolizing the four quarters of the world. The lions once carried a large stone wheel on their backs. The wheel (chakra) referred to the Wheel of the Law but also indicated Ashoka's stature as a *chakravartin* ("holder of the wheel"), a universal king imbued with divine authority. The open mouths of the four lions that face the four quarters of the world may signify the worldwide announcement of the Buddha's message.

Shunga, Andhra, and Kushan Dynasties

The Maurya dynasty came to an abrupt end when its last ruler was assassinated by one of his generals, who founded a new dynasty in his own name. The Shungas, however, never ruled an empire as extensive as that of the Mauryas. Their realm was confined to central India. They were succeeded by the Andhras, who also controlled the Deccan plateau to the south. By the middle of the first century CE, an even greater empire, the Kushan, rose in northern India. Its most celebrated king was Kanishka, who came to power during the late first or early second century CE and who set up capitals at Peshawar and other sites in Gandhara, a region largely in Pakistan today, close to the Afghanistan border. The Kushans grew rich on trade between China and the west along one of the main caravan routes bringing the luxuries of the Orient to the Roman Empire (see "Silk and the Silk Road," Chapter 7, page 188). Kanishka even struck coins modeled on the imperial coinage of Rome, some featuring Greco-Roman deities, but Kanishka's coins also carried portraits of himself and images of the Buddha and various Hindu deities.

SANCHI The unifying characteristic of this age of regional dynasties in South Asia was the patronage of Buddhism. One of the most important Buddhist monasteries, founded during Ashoka's reign and in use for more than a thousand years, is at Sanchi in central India. It consists of many buildings constructed over the centuries, including *viharas* (celled structures where monks live), large *stupas* (see "The Stupa," page 163), *chaitya halls* (halls with rounded, or *apsidal*, ends for housing smaller stupas), and temples for sheltering images.

The Great Stupa at Sanchi dates originally to Ashoka's reign, but its present form (FIG. 6-7), with its tall stone fence and four gates, dates from ca. 50 BCE to 50 CE. The solid earth-and-rubble dome stands 50 feet high. Worshipers enter through one of the gateways, walk on the lower circumambulation path, then climb the stairs on the south side to circumambulate at the second level. Carved onto the different parts of the Great Stupa are more than 600 brief inscriptions showing that the donations of hundreds of individuals (more than a

The Stupa

An essential element of Buddhist sanctuaries is the *stupa,* a grand circular mound modeled on earlier South Asian burial mounds of a type familiar in many other ancient cultures (FIGS. 4-20 and 9-6). The stupa was not a tomb, however, but a monument housing relics of the Buddha. When the Buddha died, his cremated remains were placed in eight *reliquaries,* or containers, similar in function to the later reliquaries housed in medieval churches at pilgrimage sites throughout the Christian world (see "Pilgrimages and the Cult of Relics," Chapter 17, page 432). But unlike their Western equivalents, which were put on display, the Buddha's relics were buried in solid earthen mounds (stupas) that could not be entered. In the mid-third century BCE, Ashoka opened the original eight stupas and spread the Buddha's relics among thousands of stupas in all corners of his realm. Buddhists venerated the Buddha's remains by *circumambulation,* walking around the stupa in a clockwise direction. The circular movement, echoing the movement of the earth and the sun, brought the devotee

into harmony with the cosmos. Stupas come in many sizes, from tiny handheld objects to huge structures, such as the Great Stupa at Sanchi (FIG. 6-7), constructed originally by Ashoka and later enlarged.

The monumental stupas are three-dimensional *mandalas,* or sacred diagrams of the universe. The domed stupa itself represents the world mountain, with the cardinal points marked by *toranas,* or gateways. The *harmika,* positioned atop the stupa dome, is a stone fence or railing that encloses a square area symbolizing the sacred domain of the gods. At the harmika's center, a *yasti,* or pole, corresponds to the axis of the universe, a motif already present in Ashoka's pillars. Three *chatras,* or stone disks, assigned various meanings, crown the yasti. The yasti rises from the mountain-dome and passes through the harmika, thus uniting this world with the heavenly paradise. A stone fence often encloses the entire structure, clearly separating the sacred space containing the Buddha's relics from the profane world outside.

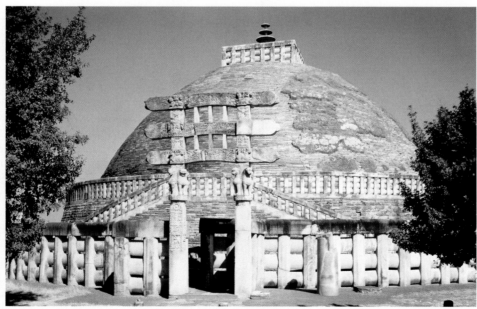

6-7 Diagram (*top*) and view from the south (*bottom*) of the Great Stupa, Sanchi, India, third century BCE to first century CE.

The sanchi stupa is an earthen mound containing relics of the Buddha. Buddhists walk around stupas in a clockwise direction. They believe that the circular movement brings the devotee into harmony with the cosmos.

India and Pakistan **163**

1 ft.

6-8 Yakshi, detail of the east torana, Great Stupa, Sanchi, India, mid-first century BCE to early first century CE. Sandstone, 5′ high.

Yakshis personify fertility and vegetation. The Sanchi yakshis are scantily clad women who make mango trees flower. The yakshis' pose was later used to represent Queen Maya giving birth to the Buddha.

0 10 20 30 40 50 feet
0   5   10   15 meters

6-9 Plan (*top*) and section (*bottom*) of the chaitya hall (FIG. 6-1), Karle, India, ca. 50 CE.

Chaitya halls in Buddhist monasteries house stupas. The form of the rock-cut cave at Karle imitates earlier wooden halls. The massive interior (45 feet tall, 125 feet long) has excellent acoustics for devotional chanting.

6-8A East torana, Great Stupa, Sanchi, ca. 50 BCE to 50 CE.

third of them women) made the monument's construction possible. Veneration of the Buddha was open to all, not just the monks, and most of the dedications were by common laypeople, who hoped to accrue merit for future rebirths with their gifts.

The reliefs on the four toranas at Sanchi depict the story of the Buddha's life and those of his past lives (*jatakas*). In Buddhist belief, everyone has had innumerable past lives, including Siddhartha. During Siddhartha's former lives, as recorded in the jatakas, he accumulated sufficient merit to achieve enlightenment and become the Buddha. In the life stories recounted in the Great Stupa reliefs, however, the Buddha never appears in human form. Instead, the artists used symbols—for example, footprints, a parasol, or an empty seat—to indicate the Buddha's presence. Some scholars regard these symbols as markers of where the Buddha once was, enabling others to follow in his footsteps.

Also carved on the east torana is a scantily clad, sensuous woman called a *yakshi* (FIG. 6-8). These goddesses, worshiped throughout India, personify fertility and vegetation. The Sanchi yakshi reaches up to hold on to a mango tree branch while pressing her left foot against the trunk, an action that has brought the tree to flower. Buddhists later adopted this pose, with its rich associations of procreation and abundance, for representing the Buddha's mother, Maya, giving birth (FIG. 6-11*a*). Thus, the Buddhists adopted pan-Indian symbolism, such as the woman under the tree, and the sensuality of the Indus sculptural tradition (FIG. 6-4) when creating their own Buddhist iconography.

KARLE The chaitya hall (FIGS. 6-1 and 6-9) carved out of the living rock at Karle in imitation of earlier wooden structures is the best early example of a Buddhist stupa hall. Datable around 100 CE, the Karle hall has a pillared *ambulatory* (walking path) that allows worshipers to circumambulate the stupa placed at the back of the sacred cave. The hall also has excellent acoustics for devotional chanting. It is nearly 45 feet high and 125 feet long and surpasses in size even the rock-cut chamber (FIG. 3-23) of the temple of the Egyptian pharaoh Ramses II. Elaborate capitals atop the rock-cut pillars depict men and women riding on elephants. Outside, amorous couples (*mithunas*) flank the entrance. Like the yakshis at Sanchi, these auspicious figures symbolize the creative life force.

GANDHARA The first anthropomorphic representations of the Buddha probably appeared in the first century CE. Scholars still debate what brought about this momentous shift in Buddhist iconography, but one factor may have been the changing perception of the Buddha himself. Originally revered as an enlightened mortal, the Buddha increasingly became regarded as a divinity. Consequently, the Buddha's followers desired images of him to worship.

Many of the early portrayals of the Buddha in human form come from the Gandhara region. A second-century CE statue (FIG. 6-10) carved in gray schist, the local stone, shows the Buddha, with ushnisha and urna, dressed in a monk's robe, seated in a cross-legged yogic posture similar to that of the ancient figure on the Indus seal in FIG. 6-5. The Buddha's hands overlap, palms upward, in the dhyana mudra, the gesture of meditation (see "Buddhism," page 161). This statue (and Gandharan sculpture in general) owes much to Greco-Roman art, both in the treatment of body forms, such as the sharp, arching brows and continuous profile of forehead and nose (FIG. 5-41), and in the draping of the togalike garment (FIG. 10-71).

One of the earliest pictorial narrative cycles in which the Buddha appears in human form also comes from Gandhara. The schist frieze (FIG. 6-11) depicts, in chronological order from left to right, the

6-10A Standing Buddha, Gandhara, second to third century

6-10 Meditating Buddha, from Gandhara, Pakistan, second century CE. Gray schist, 3' 7½" high. National Museums of Scotland, Edinburgh. 🎥

Many of the earliest portrayals of the Buddha in human form come from Gandhara and depict the Enlightened One as a robed monk. The style of this Gandharan Buddha owes much to Greco-Roman art.

Buddha's birth at Lumbini, his enlightenment at Bodh Gaya, his first sermon at Sarnath, and the Buddha's death at Kushinagara. At the left, Queen Maya, in a posture derived from that of earlier South Asian yakshis (FIG. 6-8), gives birth to Prince Siddhartha, who emerges from her right hip, already with his attributes of ushnisha, urna, and halo. Receiving him is the god Indra. Elegantly dressed ladies, one with a fan of peacock feathers, suggest the opulent court life the Buddha left behind. In the next scene, the Buddha sits beneath the Bodhi tree while the soldiers and demons of the evil Mara attempt to distract him from his quest for knowledge. They are unsuccessful, and the Buddha reaches down to touch the earth (bhumisparsha mudra) as witness to his enlightenment. Next, the Buddha preaches the Eightfold Path to nirvana in the Deer Park at Sarnath. The sculptor set the scene by placing two deer and the Wheel of the Law beneath the figure of the Buddha, who raises his right hand (abhaya mudra) to bless the monks and other devotees who have come to hear his first sermon. In the final section of the frieze, the parinirvana, the Buddha lies dying among his devotees, some of whom wail in grief, while one monk, who realizes that the Buddha has been permanently released from suffering, remains tranquil in meditation.

Although the iconography of the frieze is Buddhist, Roman reliefs must have served as stylistic models for the sculptor. For example, the distribution of standing and equestrian figures over the relief ground, with those behind the first row seemingly suspended in the

a

b

c

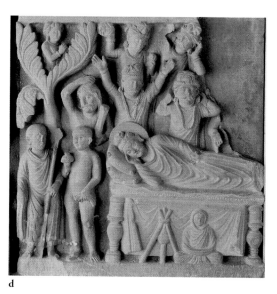

d

6-11 The life and death of the Buddha, frieze from Gandhara, Pakistan, second century CE. Schist, 2' 2⅜" × 9' 6⅛". Freer Gallery of Art, Washington, D.C. (a) birth at Lumbini, (b) enlightenment at Bodh Gaya, (c) first sermon at Sarnath, (d) death at Kushinagara.

This Gandharan frieze is one of the earliest pictorial narrative cycles in which the Buddha appears in human form. It recounts the Buddha's life story from his birth at Lumbini to his death at Kushinagara.

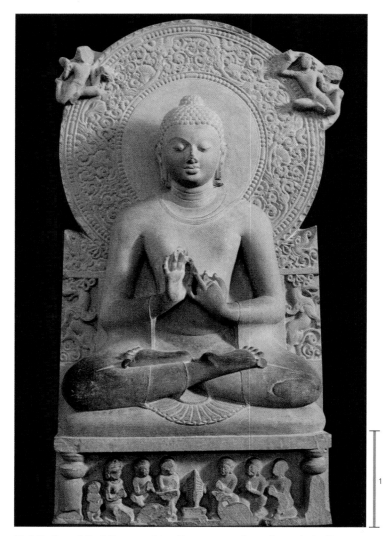

6-12 Buddha seated on lion throne, from Mathura, India, second century CE. Red sandstone, 2′ 3½″ high. Archaeological Museum, Muttra.

Stylistically distinct from the Gandharan Buddhas are those of Mathura, where the Buddha has the body type of a yaksha but wears a monk's robe. This example depicts the Buddha under the Bodhi tree.

6-13 Seated Buddha preaching first sermon, from Sarnath, India, second half of fifth century. Tan sandstone, 5′ 3″ high. Archaeological Museum, Sarnath.

Under the Guptas, artists formulated the canonical image of the Buddha, combining the Gandharan monastic-robe type with the Mathuran type of soft, full-bodied figure attired in clinging garments.

air, is familiar in Roman art of the second and third centuries CE (FIGS. 10-65 and 10-70). The figure of the Buddha on his deathbed finds parallels in the reclining figures on the lids of Roman sarcophagi (FIG. 10-61). The type of hierarchical composition in which a large central figure sits between balanced tiers of smaller onlookers is also common in Roman imperial art (FIG. 10-76).

MATHURA Contemporary to but stylistically distinct from the Gandharan sculptures are the Buddha images of Mathura, a city about 90 miles south of Delhi that was also part of the Kushan Empire. The Mathura statues (for example, FIG. 6-12) are more closely linked to the Indian portrayals of *yakshas,* the male equivalents of the yakshis. Indian artists represented yakshas as robust, powerful males with broad shoulders and open, staring eyes. Mathura Buddhas, carved from red sandstone like the Harappa nude male (FIG. 6-4), retain these characteristics but wear a monk's robe (with right shoulder bare) and lack the jewelry and other signs of wealth of the yakshas. The robe appears almost transparent, revealing the full, fleshy body beneath. In FIG. 6-12, the Buddha sits in a yogic posture on a lion throne under the Bodhi tree, attended by fly-whisk bearers. He raises his right hand palm outward in the abhaya gesture, indicating to worshipers that they need have no fear. His hands and feet bear the mark of the Wheel of the Law.

The Gupta and Post-Gupta Periods

Around 320* a new empire arose in north-central India. The Gupta emperors chose Pataliputra as their capital, deliberately associating themselves with the prestige of the former Maurya Empire. The heyday of this dynasty was under Chandragupta II (r. 375–415), whose very name recalled the first Maurya emperor. The Guptas were great patrons of art and literature.

SARNATH Under the Guptas, artists formulated what became the canonical image of the Buddha, combining the Gandharan monastic robe covering both shoulders with the Mathuran tradition of soft, full-bodied Buddha figures dressed in clinging garments. These disparate styles beautifully merge in a fifth-century statue (FIG. 6-13) of the Buddha from Sarnath. The statue's smooth, unadorned surfaces conform to the Indian notion of perfect body form and emphasize the figure's spirituality. The Buddha's eyes are downcast in meditation, and he holds his hands in front of his body in the Wheel-turning gesture, preaching his first sermon. Below the Buddha is a scene with the Wheel of the Law at the center between two (now partially broken) deer sym-

*From this point on, all dates in this chapter are CE unless otherwise stated.

bolizing the Deer Park at Sarnath. Buddha images such as this one became so popular that temples housing Buddha statues seem largely to have displaced the stupa as the norm in Buddhist sacred architecture.

AJANTA The new popularity of Buddha imagery may be seen in the interior of a chaitya hall (FIG. **6-14**) carved out of the mountainside at Ajanta, northeast of Bombay, at about the same time a Gupta sculptor created the classic seated Buddha at Sarnath. Ajanta had been the site of a small Buddhist monastery for centuries, but royal patrons of the local Vakataka dynasty, allied to the Guptas by marriage, added more than 20 new caves in the second half of the fifth century. The typological similarity of the fifth-century Ajanta chaitya halls to the earlier example at Karle (FIG. 6-1) is immediately evident and consistent with the conservative nature of religious architecture in all cultures. At Ajanta, however, sculptors carved into the front of the stupa an image of the Buddha standing between columns. Ajanta's fame, however, stems from the many caves that retain their painted wall (FIG. **6-15**) and ceiling decoration (see "The Painted Caves of Ajanta," below).

Buddhists and Hindus (and adherents of other faiths) practiced their religions side by side in India, often at the same site. For example, the Hindu Vakataka king Harishena (r. 462–481) and members of his court were the sponsors of new caves at the

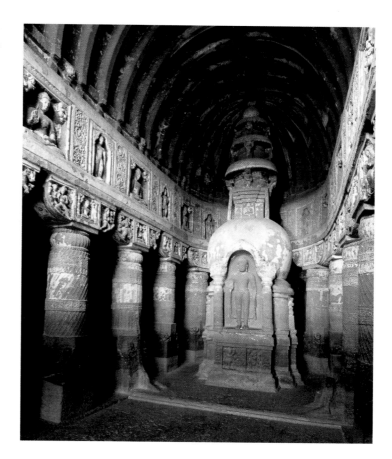

6-14 Interior of cave 19, Ajanta, India, second half of fifth century.

The popularity of Gupta Buddha statues led to a transformation in Indian religious architecture. Cave 19 at Ajanta is a chaitya hall with an image of the Buddha carved on the front of its stupa.

The Painted Caves of Ajanta

Art historians assume India had a rich painting tradition in ancient times, but because early Indian artists often used perishable materials, such as palm leaf and wood, and because of the tropical climate in much of India, nearly all early Indian painting has been lost. At Ajanta in the Deccan, however, paintings cover the walls, pillars, and ceilings of several caves datable to the second half of the fifth century. FIG. **6-15** reproduces a detail of one of the restored murals in cave 1 at Ajanta. The bodhisattva Padmapani sits among a crowd of devotees, both princes and commoners. With long, dark hair hanging below a jeweled crown, he stands holding his attribute, a blue lotus flower, in his right hand. The painter rendered with finesse the sensuous form of the richly attired bodhisattva, gently modeling the figure with gradations of color and delicate highlights and shading, especially evident in the face and neck. The artist also carefully considered the placement of the painting in the cave. The bodhisattva gazes downward at worshipers passing through the entrance to the shrine on their way to the rock-cut Buddha image in a cell at the back of the cave.

To create the Ajanta murals, the painters first applied two layers of clay mixed with straw and other materials to the walls. They then added a third layer of fine white lime plaster. Unlike true fresco painting (see "Fresco Painting," Chapter 19, page 504), in which the painters apply colors to wet plaster, the Indian painters waited for the lime to dry. This method produces less durable results, and the Ajanta murals have suffered water damage over the centuries. The painters next outlined the figures in dark red and then painted in the details of faces, costumes, and jewelry. They used water-soluble colors produced primarily from local minerals, including red and yellow ocher. Blue, used sparingly, came from costly lapis lazuli imported from Afghanistan. The last step was to polish the painted surface with a smooth stone.

6-15 Bodhisattva Padmapani, detail of a wall painting in cave 1, Ajanta, India, second half of fifth century.

In this early example of Indian painting in an Ajanta cave, the artist rendered the sensuous form of the richly attired bodhisattva with gentle gradations of color and delicate highlights and shadows.

Hinduism and Hindu Iconography

Unlike Buddhism (and Christianity, Islam, and other religions), Hinduism recognizes no founder or great prophet. Hinduism also has no simple definition but means "the religion of the Indians." Both "India" and "Hindu" have a common root in the name of the Indus River. The practices and beliefs of Hindus vary tremendously, but the literary origins of Hinduism can be traced to the Vedic period, and some aspects of Hindu practice seem already to have been present in the Indus Civilization of the third millennium BCE. Ritual sacrifice by Brahmin priests is central to Hinduism, as it was to the Aryans. The goal of sacrifice is to please a deity in order to achieve release (moksha, or liberation) from the endless cycle of birth, death, and rebirth (samsara) and become one with the universal spirit.

Not only is Hinduism a religion of many gods, but the Hindu deities have various natures and take many forms. This multiplicity suggests the all-pervasive nature of the Hindu gods. The three most important deities are the gods Shiva and Vishnu and the goddess Devi. Each of the three major sects of Hinduism today considers one of these three to be supreme—Shiva in Shaivism, Vishnu in Vaishnavism, and Devi in Shaktism. (*Shakti* is the female creative force.)

Shiva is the Destroyer, but, consistent with the multiplicity of Hindu belief, he is also a regenerative force and, in the latter role, can be represented in the form of a *linga* (a phallus or cosmic pillar). When Shiva appears in human form in Hindu art, he frequently has multiple limbs and heads (FIGS. **6-17**, **6-18**, and **6-25**), signs of his suprahuman nature, and matted locks piled atop his head, crowned by a crescent moon. Sometimes he wears a serpent scarf and has a third eye on his forehead (the emblem of his all-seeing nature). Shiva rides the bull *Nandi* (FIG. **6-17**) and often carries a *trident*, a three-pronged pitchfork.

Vishnu is the Preserver of the Universe. Artists frequently portray him with four arms (FIGS. **6-20** and **6-29**) holding various attributes, including a conch-shell trumpet and discus. He sometimes reclines on a serpent floating on the waters of the cosmic sea (FIGS. **6-20** and **6-29**). When the evil forces of the universe become too strong, he descends to earth to restore balance and assumes different forms (*avatars*, or incarnations), including a boar (FIG. **6-16**), fish, and tortoise, as well as *Krishna,* the divine lover (FIG. **26-7**), and even the Buddha himself.

Devi is the Great Goddess who takes many forms and has many names. Hindus worship her alone or as a consort of male gods (*Parvati* or *Uma,* wife of Shiva; *Lakshmi,* wife of Vishnu), as well as *Radha,* lover of Krishna (FIG. **26-7**). She has both benign and horrific forms. She both creates and destroys. In one manifestation, she is *Durga,* a multiarmed goddess who often rides a lion. Her son is the elephant-headed *Ganesha* (FIG. **6-17**).

The stationary images of deities in Hindu temples are often made of stone. Hindus periodically remove portable images of their gods, often of bronze (FIG. **6-25**), from the temple, particularly during festivals to enable many worshipers to take *darshan* (seeing the deity and being seen by the deity) at one time. In temples dedicated to Shiva, the stationary form is the linga.

1 ft.

6-16 Boar avatar of Vishnu rescuing the earth, cave 5, Udayagiri, India, early fifth century. Relief 13′ × 22′; Vishnu 12′ 8″ high.

The oldest Hindu cave temples are at Udayagiri, a site that also boasts some of the earliest Hindu stone sculptures, such as this huge relief of Vishnu as the boar Varaha rescuing the earth.

6-17 Dancing Shiva, rock-cut relief in cave temple, Badami, India, late sixth century.

Shiva here dances the cosmic dance and has 18 arms, some holding objects, others forming mudras. Hindu gods often have multiple limbs to indicate their suprahuman nature and divine powers.

6-18 Shiva as Mahadeva, cave 1, Elephanta, India, ca. 550–575. Basalt, Shiva 17′ 10″ high.

This immense rock-cut image of Shiva as Mahadeva ("Great God") emerges out of the depths of the Elephanta cave as worshipers' eyes adjust to the darkness. The god has both male and female faces.

Buddhist monastery at Ajanta. Buddhism and Hinduism are not monotheistic religions, such as Judaism, Christianity, and Islam. Instead, Buddhists and Hindus approach the spiritual through many gods and varying paths, which permits mutually tolerated differences. In fact, in Hinduism, the Buddha was one of the 10 incarnations of Vishnu, one of the three principal Hindu deities (see "Hinduism and Hindu Iconography," page 168).

UDAYAGIRI More early Buddhist than Hindu art has survived in India because the Buddhists constructed large monastic institutions with durable materials such as stone and brick. But in the Gupta period, Hindu stone sculpture and architecture began to rival the great Buddhist monuments of South Asia. The oldest Hindu cave temples are at Udayagiri, near Sanchi. They date to the early fifth century, some 600 years after the first Buddhist examples. Although the Udayagiri temples are architecturally simple and small, the site boasts monumental relief sculptures showing an already fully developed religious iconography. One of these reliefs (FIG. 6-16), carved in a shallow niche of rock, shows a 13-foot-tall Vishnu in his incarnation as the boar Varaha. The avatar has a human body and a boar's head. Vishnu assumed this form when he rescued the earth—personified as the goddess Bhudevi clinging to the boar's tusk—from being carried off to the bottom of the ocean. Vishnu stands with one foot resting on the coils of a snake king (note the multiple hoods behind his human head), who represents the conquered demon that attempted to abduct the earth. Rows of gods and sages form lines to witness the event.

The relief served a political as well as a religious purpose. The patron of the relief was a local king who honored the great Gupta king Chandragupta II in a nearby inscription dated to the year 401. Many scholars believe that the local king wanted viewers to see

Chandragupta (he is known to have visited the site) as saving his kingdom by ridding it of its enemies in much the same way Varaha saved the earth.

BADAMI During the sixth century, the Huns brought down the Gupta Empire, and various regional dynasties rose to power. In the Deccan plateau of central India, the Chalukya kings ruled from their capital at Badami. There, Chalukya sculptors carved a series of reliefs in the walls of halls cut into the cliff above the city. One relief (FIG. 6-17), datable to the late sixth century, shows Shiva dancing the cosmic dance, his 18 arms swinging rhythmically in an arc. Some of the hands hold objects, and others form prescribed mudras. At the lower right, the elephant-headed Ganesha tentatively mimics Shiva. Nandi, Shiva's bull mount, stands at the left. Artists often represented Hindu deities as part human and part animal (FIG. 6-16) or, as in the Badami relief, as figures with multiple body parts. Such composite and multilimbed forms indicate that the subjects are not human but suprahuman gods with supernatural powers.

ELEPHANTA Another portrayal of Shiva as a suprahuman being is found at a third Hindu cave site, on Elephanta, an island in Bombay's harbor that early Portuguese colonizers named after a life-size stone elephant sculpture there. A king of the Kalachuri dynasty that took control of Elephanta in the sixth century may have commissioned the largest of the island's cave temples. Just inside the west entrance to the cave is a shrine housing Shiva's linga, the god's emblem. Deep within the temple, in a niche once closed off with wooden doors, is a nearly 18-foot-high rock-cut image (FIG. 6-18) of Shiva as Mahadeva, the "Great God" or Lord of Lords. Mahadeva appears to emerge out of the depths of the cave as worshipers' eyes become accustomed to the darkness. This image of

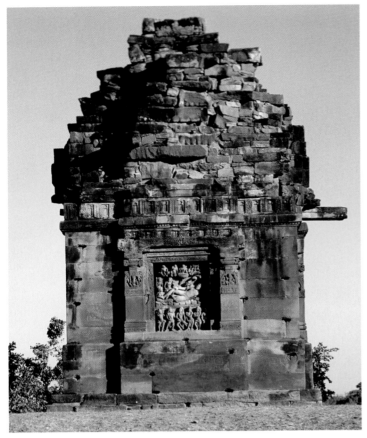

6-19 Vishnu Temple (looking north), Deogarh, India, early sixth century.

One of the first masonry Hindu temples, the Vishnu Temple at Deogarh is a simple square building with a tower. Sculpted guardians protect its entrance. Narrative reliefs adorn the three other sides.

6-20 Vishnu asleep on the serpent Ananta, relief panel on the south facade of the Vishnu Temple, Deogarh, India, early sixth century.

Sculptors carved the reliefs of the Vishnu Temple at Deogarh in classic Gupta style. In this one, the four-armed Vishnu sleeps on the serpent Ananta as he dreams the universe into reality.

Shiva has three faces, each showing a different aspect of the deity. (A fourth, unseen at the back, is implied—the god has not emerged fully from the rock.) The central face expresses Shiva's quiet, balanced demeanor. The clean planes of the face contrast with the richness of the piled hair encrusted with jewels. The two side faces differ significantly. That on the right is female, with framing hair curls. The left face is a grimacing male with a curling mustache who wears a cobra as an earring. The female (Uma) indicates the creative aspect of Shiva. The fierce male (Bhairava) represents Shiva's destructive side. Shiva holds these two opposing forces in check, and the central face expresses their balance. The cyclic destruction and creation of the universe, which the side faces also symbolize, are part of Indian notions of time, matched by the cyclic pattern of death and rebirth (samsara).

DEOGARH The excavated cave shrines just considered are characteristic of early Hindu religious architecture, but temples constructed using quarried stone became more important as Hinduism evolved over the centuries. As they did with the cave temples, the Hindus initially built rather small and simple temples but decorated them with narrative reliefs displaying a fully developed iconography. The Vishnu Temple (FIG. 6-19) at Deogarh in north-central India, erected in the early sixth century, is among the first Hindu temples constructed with stone blocks. A simple square building, it has an elaborately decorated doorway at the front and a relief in a niche on each of the other three sides. Sculpted guardians and mithunas protect the doorway at Deogarh, because it is the transition point be-

tween the dangerous outside and the sacred. The temple culminates in a tower that was originally at least 40 feet tall.

The reliefs in the three niches of the Deogarh temple depict important episodes in the saga of Vishnu. On the south (FIG. 6-20), Vishnu sleeps on the coils of the giant serpent Ananta, whose multiple heads form a kind of umbrella around the god's face. While Lakshmi massages her husband's legs (he has cramps as he gives birth), the four-armed Vishnu dreams the universe into reality. A lotus plant (said to have grown out of Vishnu's navel) supports the four-headed Hindu god of creation, Brahma. Flanking him are other important Hindu divinities, including Shiva on his bull. Below are six figures. The four at the right are personifications of Vishnu's various powers. They will defeat the two armed demons at the left. The sculptor carved all the figures in the classic Gupta style, with smooth bodies and clinging garments (compare FIG. 6-13).

Early Medieval Period

During the several centuries corresponding to the early medieval period in western Europe (see Chapter 16), the early Islamic period in the Near East (see Chapter 13), the Tang and Song dynasties in China (see Chapter 7), and the Nara and Heian periods in Japan (see Chapter 8), regional dynasties ruled parts of India. Among the most important of these kingdoms were the Palas and Chandellas in northern India and the Pallavas and Cholas in the south. Whereas Buddhism spread rapidly throughout eastern Asia, in medieval India it gradually

Indian architects also created temples by sculpting them from the living rock. The seventh-century rathas ("chariots" of the gods) at Mamallapuram were all carved from a single huge granite outcropping.

◀A *Descent he Ganges,* mallapuram, t half of enth tury.

◀B *Durga ying nisha,* mallapuram, enth century.

declined, and the various local kings vied with one another to erect glorious shrines to the Hindu gods.

MAMALLAPURAM In addition to cave temples and masonry temples, Indian architects created a third type of monument: freestanding temples carved out of rocky outcroppings. Sculpted monolithic temples are rare. Some of the earliest and most impressive are at Mamallapuram, south of Madras on the Bay of Bengal, where they are called *rathas,* or "chariots" (that is, vehicles of the gods). In the late seventh century, the Pallava dynasty had five rathas (FIG. **6-21**) carved out of a single huge granite boulder jutting out from the sand. The group is of special interest because it illustrates the variety of temple forms at this period, based on earlier wooden structures, before a standard masonry type of temple became the rule in southern India.

The largest Mamallapuram ratha, the Dharmaraja (FIG. **6-21**, *left*), dedicated to Shiva, is an early example of the typical southern-style temple with stepped-pyramid vimana (see "Hindu Temples," page 172). The tower ascends in pronounced tiers of cornices decorated with miniature shrines. The lower walls include carved columns and figures of deities inside niches. The Bhima ratha to the right, dedicated to Vishnu, has a rectangular plan and a rounded roof; the next ratha, the Arjuna, is a smaller example of the southern Indian type. At the end of the row sits the very small Draupadi ratha, which was modeled on a thatched hut and is dedicated to Durga, a form of the goddess Devi. The two largest temples were never finished.

THANJAVUR Under the Cholas, whose territories extended into part of Sri Lanka and even Java, architects constructed temples of unprecedented size and grandeur in the southern Indian tradition. The Rajarajeshvara Temple (FIG. **6-22**) at Thanjavur, dedicated in 1010 to Shiva as the Lord of Rajaraja, was the largest and tallest temple (210 feet high) in India at its time. The temple stands inside a walled precinct. It consists of a stairway leading to two flat-roofed mandapas, the larger one having 36 pillars, and to the garbha griha in the base of the enormous pyramidal vimana that is as much an emblem of the Cholas' secular power as of their devotion to Shiva. On the exterior walls of the lower stories are numerous reliefs in niches depicting the god in his various forms.

KHAJURAHO At the same time the Cholas were building the Rajarajeshvara Temple at Thanjavur in the south, the Chandella dynasty was constructing temples—in northern style—at Khajuraho. The Vishvanatha Temple (FIG. **6-23**) is one of more than 20 large and elaborate temples at that site. Vishvanatha ("Lord of the World") is another of the many names for Shiva. Dedicated in 1002, the structure has three towers over the mandapas, each rising higher than the preceding one, leading to the tallest tower at the rear, in much the same way the foothills of the Himalayas, Shiva's home, rise to meet their highest peak. The mountain symbolism applies to the interior of the Vishvanatha Temple as well. Under the tallest tower, the shikhara, is the garbha griha, the small and dark inner sanctuary chamber, like a cave, which houses the image of the deity. Thus,

6-22A Kailasanatha Temple, Ellora, second half of eighth century.

Hindu Temples

The Hindu temple is the home of the gods on earth and the place where they make themselves visible to humans. At the core of all Hindu temples is the *garbha griha,* the "womb chamber," which houses images or symbols of the deity—for example, Shiva's linga (see "Hinduism," page 168). Only the Brahmin priests can enter this inner sanctuary to make offerings to the gods. The worshipers can only stand at the threshold and behold the deity as manifest by its image. In the elaborate multi-roomed temples of later Hindu architecture, the worshipers and priests progress through a series of ever more sacred spaces, usually on an east-west axis. Hindu priests and architects attached great importance to each temple's plan and sought to make it conform to the sacred geo-metric diagram (mandala) of the universe.

Architectural historians, following ancient Indian texts, divide Hindu temples into two major typological groups tied to geography. The most important distinguishing feature of the **northern** style of temple (FIG. 6-23) is its bee-hivelike tower or *shikhara* ("mountain peak"), capped by an *amalaka,* a ribbed cushionlike form, derived from the shape of the amala fruit (believed to have medicinal powers). Amalakas appear on the corners of the lower levels of the

shikhara too. Northern temples also have smaller towerlike roofs over the halls (*mandapas*) leading to the garbha griha.

Southern temples (FIG. 6-22) can easily be recognized by the flat roofs of their pillared mandapas and by their shorter towered shrines, called *vimanas,* which lack the curved profile of their northern counterparts and resemble multilevel pyramids.

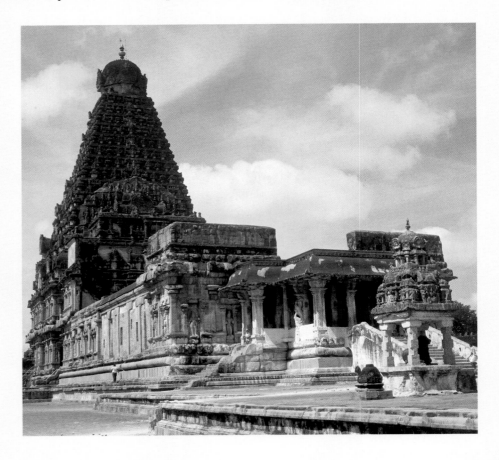

6-22 Rajarajeshvara Temple, Thanjavur, India, ca. 1010.

The Rajarajeshvara Temple at Thanjavur is an example of the southern type of Hindu temple. Two flat-roofed mandapas lead to the garbha griha in the base of its 210-foot-tall pyramidal vimana.

6-23 Vishvanatha Temple (view looking north, *left,* and plan, *above*), Khajuraho, India, ca. 1000.

The Vishvanatha Temple is a northern Hindu temple type. It has four towers, each taller than the preceding one, symbolizing Shiva's mountain home. The largest tower is the beehive-shaped shikara.

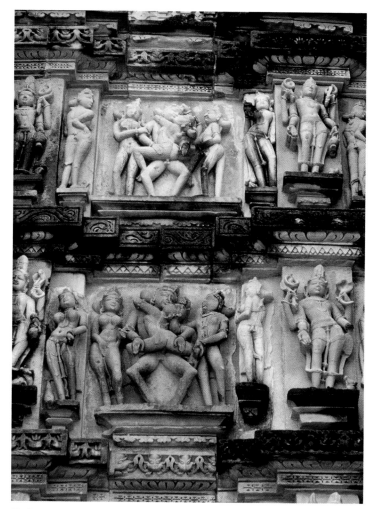

6-24 Mithuna reliefs, detail of the north side of the Vishvanatha Temple, Khajuraho, India, ca. 1000.

Northern Hindu temples are usually decorated with reliefs depicting deities and amorous couples (mithunas). The erotic sculptures suggest the propagation of life and serve as protectors of the sacred precinct.

6-25 Shiva as Nataraja, ca. 1000. Bronze. Naltunai Ishvaram Temple, Punjai.

One of many portable images of the gods used in Hindu worship, this solid-bronze statuette of Shiva as Lord of the Dance depicts the god balancing on one leg atop a dwarf representing ignorance.

temples such as the Vishvanatha symbolize constructed mountains with caves, comparable to the actual cave temples at Elephanta and other Indian sites. In all cases, the deity manifests himself or herself within the cave and takes various forms in sculptures. The temple mountains, however, are not intended to appear natural but rather are perfect mountains designed using ideal mathematical proportions.

The reliefs of Thanjavur's Rajarajeshvara Temple are typical of southern temple decoration, which is generally limited to images of deities. The exterior walls of Khajuraho's Vishvanatha Temple are equally typical of northern temples in the profusion of sculptures (FIG. 6-24) depicting mortals as well as gods, especially pairs of men and women (mithunas) embracing or engaged in sexual intercourse in an extraordinary range of positions. The use of seminude yakshis and amorous couples as motifs on religious buildings in India has a very long history, going back to the earliest architectural traditions, both Hindu and Buddhist (Sanchi, FIG. 6-8, and Karle). As in the earlier examples, the erotic sculptures of Khajuraho suggest fertility and the propagation of life and serve as auspicious protectors of the sacred precinct.

SHIVA AS NATARAJA Portable objects also play an important role in Hinduism. The statuette (FIG. 6-25) of Shiva in the Naltunai Ishvaram Temple in Punjai, cast in solid bronze around 1000, recalls the sixth-century relief (FIG. 6-17) in the Badami cave, but it is one of

many examples of moveable images of deities created under the Chola kings and still used in Hindu rituals today. Here, Shiva dances as Nataraja ("Lord of the Dance") by balancing on one leg atop a dwarf representing ignorance, which the god stamps out as he dances. Shiva extends all four arms, two of them touching the flaming *nimbus* (light of glory) encircling him. These two upper hands also hold a small drum (at right) and a flame (at left). Shiva creates the universe to the drumbeat's rhythm, while the small fire represents destruction. His lower left hand points to his upraised foot, indicating the foot as the place where devotees can find refuge and enlightenment. Shiva's lower right hand, raised in the abhaya mudra, tells worshipers to come forward without fear. As Shiva spins, his matted hair comes loose and spreads like a fan on both sides of his head.

At times, worshipers insert poles into the holes on the base of the Punjai Shiva to carry it, but even when stationary, the statuette would not appear as it does in FIG. 6-25. Rather, when Hindus worship the Shiva Nataraja, they dress the image, cover it with jewels, and garland it with flowers. The only bronze part visible is the face, marked with colored powders and scented pastes. Considered the embodiment of the deity, the image is not a symbol of the god but the god itself. All must treat the image as a living being. Worship of the deity involves taking care of him as if he were an honored person. Bathed, clothed, given foods to eat, and taken for outings, the image also receives such gifts as melodic songs, bright lights (lit oil lamps),

6-26 Death of the Buddha (Parinirvana), Gal Vihara, near Polonnaruwa, Sri Lanka, 11th to 12th century. Granulite, Buddha 46′ long × 10′ high.

The sculptor of this colossal recumbent Sri Lankan Buddha emulated the classic Gupta style of a half millennium earlier in the figure's clinging robe, rounded face, and coiffure.

pleasing aromas (incense), and beautiful flowers—all things the god can enjoy through the senses. The food given to the god is particularly important, as he eats the "essence," leaving the remainder for the worshiper. The food is then *prasada* (grace), sacred because it came in contact with the divine. In an especially religious household, the deity resides as an image and receives the food for each meal before the family eats. When the god resides in a temple, it is then the duty of the priests to feed, clothe, and take care of him.

The Chola dynasty ended in the 13th century, a time of political, religious, and cultural change in South Asia. At this point, Buddhism survived in only some areas of India. It soon died out completely there, although the late form of northern Indian Buddhism continued in Tibet and Nepal. At the same time, Islam, which had arrived in India as early as the eighth century, became a potent political force with the establishment of the Delhi Sultanate in 1206. Hindu and Islamic art assumed preeminent roles in India in the 13th century (see Chapter 26).

SOUTHEAST ASIA

Art historians once considered the art of Southeast Asia an extension of Indian civilization. Because of the Indian character of many Southeast Asian monuments, scholars hypothesized that Indian artists had constructed and decorated them and that Indians had colonized Southeast Asia. Today, researchers have concluded that no Indian colonization occurred. The expansion of Indian culture to Southeast Asia during the first millennium CE was peaceful and non-imperialistic, a by-product of trade. In the early centuries CE, ships bringing trade goods from India and China to Rome passed through Southeast Asia on the monsoon winds. The local tribal chieftains quickly saw an opportunity to participate, mainly with their own forest products, such as aromatic woods, bird feathers, and spices. Accompanying the trade goods from India were Sanskrit, Buddhism, and Hinduism—and Buddhist and Hindu art. But the Southeast Asian peoples soon modified Indian art to make it their own. Art historians now recognize Southeast Asian art and architecture as a distinctive and important tradition.

Sri Lanka

Sri Lanka (formerly Ceylon) is an island located at the very tip of the Indian subcontinent. Theravada Buddhism, the oldest form of Buddhism, stressing worship of the historical Buddha, Shakyamuni

Buddha, arrived in Sri Lanka as early as the third century BCE. From there it spread to other parts of Southeast Asia. With the demise of Buddhism in India in about the 13th century, Sri Lanka now has the longest-lived Buddhist tradition in the world.

GAL VIHARA One of the largest sculptures in Southeast Asia is the 46-foot-long recumbent Buddha (FIG. 6-26) carved out of a rocky outcropping at Gal Vihara in the 11th or 12th century. To the left of the Buddha, much smaller in scale, stands his cousin and chief disciple, Ananda, arms crossed, mourning Shakyamuni's death. Although more than a half millennium later in date, the Sri Lankan representation of the Buddha's parinirvana reveals its sculptor's debt to the classic Gupta sculptures of India, with their clinging garments, rounded faces, and distinctive renditions of hair (compare FIG. 6-13). Other Southeast Asian monuments, in contrast, exhibit a marked independence from Indian models.

6-26A Ananda Temple, Bagan begun 1091.

Java

On the island of Java, part of the modern nation of Indonesia, the period from the 8th to the 10th centuries witnessed the erection of both Hindu and Buddhist monuments.

BOROBUDUR Borobudur (FIG. 6-27), a Buddhist monument unique in both form and meaning, is colossal in size, measuring about 400 feet per side at the base and about 98 feet tall. Built over a small hill on nine terraces accessed by four stairways aligned with the cardinal points, the structure contains literally millions of blocks of volcanic stone. Visitors ascending the massive monument on their way to the summit encounter more than 500 life-size Buddha images, at least 1,000 relief panels, and some 1,500 stupas of various sizes.

Scholars debate the intended meaning of Borobudur. Most think the structure is a constructed cosmic mountain, a three-dimensional mandala where worshipers pass through various realms on their way to ultimate enlightenment. As they circumambulate Borobudur, pilgrims first see reliefs illustrating the karmic effects of various kinds of human behavior, then reliefs depicting jatakas of the Buddha's earlier lives, and, farther up, events from the life of Shakyamuni. On the circular terraces near the summit, each stupa is hollow and houses a statue of the seated Buddha, who has achieved spiritual enlightenment and preaches using the Wheel-turning mudra. At the very top is the largest, sealed stupa. It may once have contained another Buddha image, but some think it was left empty to symbolize the formlessness of true enlightenment. Although

6-27 Aerial view of Borobudur, Java, Indonesia, ca. 800.

Borobudur is a colossal Buddhist monument of unique form. Built on nine terraces with more than 1,500 stupas and 1,500 statues and reliefs, it takes the form of a cosmic mountain, which worshipers circumambulate.

scholars have interpreted the iconographic program in different ways, all agree on two essential points: the dependence of Borobudur on Indian art, literature, and religion, and the fact that nothing comparable exists in India itself. Borobudur's sophistication, complexity, and originality underline how completely Southeast Asians had absorbed, rethought, and reformulated Indian religion and art by 800.

Cambodia

In 802, at about the same time the Javanese built Borobudur, the Khmer King Jayavarman II (r. 802–850) founded the Angkor dynasty, which ruled Cambodia for the next 400 years and sponsored the construction of hundreds of monuments, including gigantic Buddhist monasteries (*wats*). For at least two centuries before the founding of Angkor, the Khmer (the predominant ethnic group in Cambodia) produced Indian-related sculpture of exceptional quality. Images of Vishnu were particularly important during the pre-Angkorian period.

3A
dhisattva
itreya,
khon Chai,
nth to ninth
tury.

HARIHARA A statue of Vishnu (FIG. 6-28) from Prasat Andet shows the Hindu god in his manifestation as Harihara (Shiva-Vishnu). To represent Harihara, the sculptor divided the statue vertically, with Shiva on the god's right side, Vishnu on his left. The tall headgear reflects the division most clearly. The Shiva half, embellished with the winding locks of an ascetic, contrasts with the kingly Vishnu's plain miter. Attributes (now lost) held in the four hands also helped differentiate the two sides. Stylistically, the Cambodian statue, like the Sri Lankan parinirvana group (FIG. 6-26), derives from Indian sculptures (FIG. 6-13) of Gupta style. But unlike almost all stone sculpture in India, carved in relief on slabs or steles, this Khmer image is in the round. The Harihara's broken arms and ankles vividly attest to the vulnerability of this format. The Khmer sculptors, however, wanted their statues to be seen from all sides in the center of the garbha grihas of brick temples.

6-28 Harihara, from Prasat Andet, Cambodia, early seventh century. Stone, 6′ 3″ high. National Museum, Phnom Penh.

Harihara is a composite of Shiva (the god's right side) and Vishnu (on the left). Although stylistically indebted to Gupta sculpture, the Khmer statue is freestanding so that it could be viewed from all sides.

1 ft.

1 ft.

6-29 Vishnu lying on the cosmic ocean, from the Mebon temple on an island in the western baray, Angkor, Cambodia, 11th century. Bronze, 8′ long.

This fragmentary hollow-cast bronze statue was originally more than 20 feet long and inlaid with gold, silver, and jewels. It portrays Vishnu asleep on the cosmic ocean at the moment of the universe's creation.

RECLINING VISHNU The Khmer kings were exceedingly powerful and possessed enormous wealth. A now-fragmentary statue (FIG. 6-29) portraying Vishnu lying on the cosmic ocean testifies to both the luxurious nature of much Khmer art and to the mastery of Khmer bronze casters. The surviving portion is about 8 feet long. In complete form, at well over 20 feet long, the Vishnu statue was among the largest bronzes of the ancient and medieval worlds, surpassed only by such lost wonders as the statue of Athena (FIG. 5-46) in the Parthenon and the 120-foot-tall colossus of the Roman emperor Nero (see "The Golden House of Nero," Chapter 10, page 259). Originally, gold and silver inlays and jewels embellished the image, and the god wore a separate miter on his head. The subject of the gigantic statue is the same as that carved in relief (FIG. 6-20) on the Deogarh Vishnu Temple. Vishnu lies asleep on the cosmic ocean at the moment of the creation of the universe. In the myth, a lotus stem grows from Vishnu's navel, its flower supporting Brahma, the creator god. In this statue, Vishnu probably had a waterspout emerging from his navel, indicating his ability to create the waters as well as to create Brahma and protect the earth. The statue was displayed in an island temple in the western *baray* (reservoir) of Angkor.

ANGKOR WAT For more than four centuries, successive kings worked on the construction of the site of Angkor. Founded by Indravarman (r. 877–889), Angkor is an engineering marvel, a grand complex of temples and palaces within a rectangular grid of canals and reservoirs fed by local rivers. Each of the Khmer kings built a temple mountain at Angkor and installed his personal god—Shiva, Vishnu, or the Buddha—on top and gave the god part of his own royal name, implying that the king was a manifestation of the deity. When the king died, the Khmer believed that the god reabsorbed him, because he had been the earthly portion of the deity during his lifetime, so they worshiped the king's image as the god. This concept of kingship approaches an actual deification of the ruler, familiar in many other societies, such as pharaonic Egypt (see Chapter 3).

Of all the monuments the Khmer kings erected, Angkor Wat (FIG. 6-30) is the most spectacular. Built by Suryavarman II (r. 1113–1150), it is the largest of the many Khmer temple complexes. Angkor Wat rises from a huge rectangle of land delineated by a moat measuring about 5,000 × 4,000 feet. Like the other Khmer temples, its purpose was to associate the king with his personal god, in this case Vishnu. The centerpiece of the complex is a tall stepped tower surrounded by four smaller towers connected by covered galleries. The five towers symbolize the five peaks of Mount Meru, the sacred mountain at the center of the universe. Two more circuit walls with galleries, towers, and gates enclose the central block. Thus, as one progresses inward through the complex, the towers rise ever higher, in similar manner as the towers of Khajuraho's Vishvanatha Temple (FIG. 6-23) but in a more complex sequence and on a much grander scale.

Throughout Angkor Wat, stone reliefs glorify both Vishnu in his various avatars and Suryavarman II. A detail of a relief (FIG. 6-31) on the inner wall of the lowest gallery shows the king holding court. Suryavarman II sits on an elaborate wooden throne, its bronze legs rising as cobra heads. Kneeling retainers, smaller than the king because they are lesser figures in the Khmer hierarchy, hold a forest of umbrellas and fans, emblems of Suryavarman's exalted rank. In the reliefs of Angkor Wat, religion and politics are united.

6-30 Aerial view (looking northeast) of Angkor Wat, Angkor, Cambodia, first half of 12th century.

Angkor Wat, built by Suryavarman II to associate the Khmer king with the god Vishnu, has five towers symbolizing the five peaks of Mount Meru, the sacred mountain at the center of the universe.

6-31 King Suryavarman II holding court, detail of a stone relief, lowest gallery, south side, Angkor Wat, Angkor, Cambodia, first half of 12th century.

The reliefs of Angkor Wat glorify Vishnu in his various avatars, or incarnations, and Suryavarman II, whom the sculptor depicted holding court and surrounded by his attendants, all of smaller scale than the king.

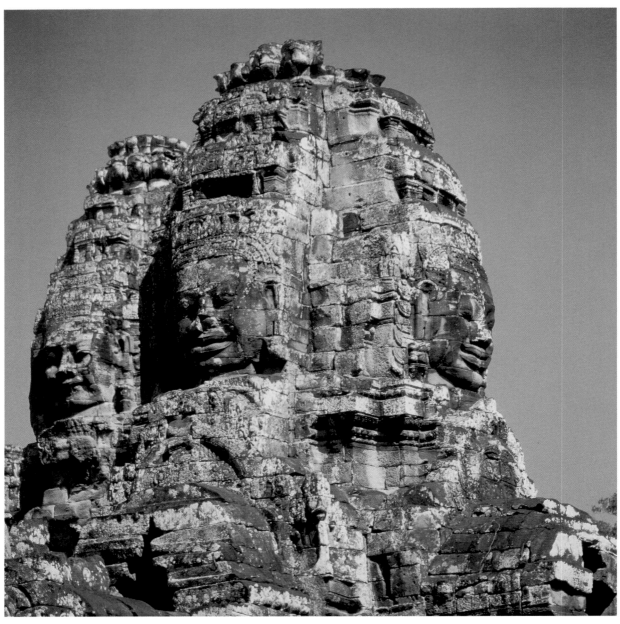

6-32 Towers of the Bayon, Angkor Thom, Cambodia, ca. 1200.

Jayavarman VII embraced Buddhism instead of Hinduism. His most important temple, the Bayon, has towers carved with giant faces that probably depict either the bodhisattva Lokeshvara or the king himself.

BAYON Jayavarman VII (r. 1181–1219), Suryavarman II's son, ruled over much of mainland Southeast Asia and built more during his reign than all the Khmer kings preceding him combined. His most important temple, the Bayon, is a complicated monument constructed with unique circular terraces surmounted by towers carved with giant faces (FIG. 6-32). Jayavarman turned to Buddhism from the Hinduism the earlier Khmer rulers embraced, but he adapted Buddhism so that the Buddha and the bodhisattva Lokeshvara ("Lord of the World") were seen as divine prototypes of the king, in the Khmer tradition. The faces on the Bayon towers perhaps portray Lokeshvara, intended to indicate the watchful compassion emanating in all directions from the capital. Other researchers have proposed that the faces depict Jayavarman himself. The king's great experiment in religion and art was short-lived, but it also marked the point of change in Southeast Asia when Theravada Buddhism began to dominate most of the mainland. Chapter 26 chronicles this important development.

During the first to fourth centuries, Buddhism also spread to other parts of Asia—to China, Korea, and Japan. Although the artistic traditions in these countries differ greatly from one another, they share, along with Southeast Asia, a tradition of Buddhist art and an ultimate tie with India. Chapters 7 and 8 trace the changes Buddhist art underwent in East Asia, along with the region's other rich artistic traditions.

SOUTH AND SOUTHEAST ASIA BEFORE 1200

INDUS CIVILIZATION, ca. 2600–1500 BCE

❚ One of the world's earliest civilizations arose in the Indus Valley in the third millennium BCE. Indus cities had streets oriented to the compass points and sophisticated water-supply and sewage systems.

❚ Little Indus art survives, mainly seals with incised designs and small-scale sculptures like the statue of a "priest-king" from Mohenjo-daro.

Robed male figure, Mohenjo-daro, ca. 2000–1900 BCE

MAURYA DYNASTY, 323–185 BCE

❚ The first Maurya king repelled the Greeks from India in 305 BCE. The greatest Maurya ruler was Ashoka (r. 272–231 BCE), who converted to Buddhism and spread the Buddha's teaching throughout South Asia.

❚ Ashoka's pillars are the first monumental stone artworks in India. Ashoka was also the builder of the original Great Stupa at Sanchi.

Lion capital of Ashoka, Sarnath, ca. 250 BCE

SHUNGA, ANDHRA, AND KUSHAN DYNASTIES, ca. 185 BCE–320 CE

❚ The unifying characteristic of this age of regional dynasties in South Asia was the patronage of Buddhism. In addition to the stupa, the chief early type of Buddhist sacred architecture was the pillared rock-cut chaitya hall.

❚ The first representations of the Buddha in human form probably date to the first century CE. Gandharan Buddha statues owe a strong stylistic debt to Greco-Roman art.

❚ By the second century CE, the iconography of the life of the Buddha from his birth at Lumbini to his death at Kushinagara was well established.

The Buddha's first sermon at Sarnath, Gandhara, second century CE

GUPTA AND POST-GUPTA PERIODS, ca. 320–647

❚ Gupta sculptors established the canonical Buddha image in the fifth century, combining Gandharan iconography with a soft, full-bodied figure in clinging garments.

❚ The Gupta-period Buddhist caves of Ajanta are the best surviving examples of early mural painting in India.

❚ The oldest Hindu monumental stone temples and sculptures date to the fifth and sixth centuries, including the rock-cut reliefs of Udayagiri, Badami, and Elephanta, and the Vishnu Temple at Deogarh.

Bodhisattva Padmapani, Ajanta, second half of fifth century

MEDIEVAL PERIOD, 7th to 12th Centuries

❚ As various dynasties ruled South Asia for several hundred years, distinctive regional styles emerged in Hindu religious architecture. Northern temples, such as the Vishvanatha Temple at Khajuraho, have a series of small towers leading to a tall beehive-shaped tower, or shikhara, over the garbha griha. Southern temples have flat-roofed pillared halls (mandapas) leading to a pyramidal tower (vimana).

❚ Medieval Southeast Asian art and architecture reflect Indian prototypes, but many local styles developed. The most distinctive monuments of the period are Borobudur on Java and the Buddhist temple complexes of the Khmer kings at Angkor in Cambodia.

Vishvanatha Temple, Khajuraho, ca. 1000

1 ft.

7-1 FAN KUAN, *Travelers among Mountains and Streams,* Northern Song period, early 11th century. Hanging scroll, ink and colors on silk, 6′ 7$\frac{1}{4}$″ × 3′ 4$\frac{1}{4}$″. National Palace Museum, Taibei.

Landscape painting was one of the premier art genres in China. Chinese painters, however, did not aim to represent specific places but to capture the essence of nature using brush and ink on silk.

7

CHINA AND KOREA TO 1279

E ast Asia is a vast area, varied in both topography and climate. Dominated by the huge land mass of China, the region also encompasses the peninsula of Korea and the islands of Japan (MAP 7-1). The early arts of China and Korea are discussed in this chapter, and early Japanese art and architecture are treated in Chapter 8. Chapters 27 and 28 examine later developments in China and Korea and in Japan.

CHINA

China's landscape includes sandy plains, mighty rivers, towering mountains, and fertile farmlands. Its political and cultural boundaries have varied over the millennia, and at times its territory has grown to about twice the area of the United States, encompassing Tibet, Chinese Turkestan (Xinjiang), Mongolia, Manchuria, and parts of Korea. China boasts the world's largest population and is ethnically diverse. The spoken language varies so much that speakers of different dialects do not understand one another. However, the written language, which employs *characters* (signs that record spoken words, even if those words are spoken differently in the various dialects), has made possible a shared Chinese literary, philosophic, and religious tradition.

Neolithic Age through Shang Dynasty

China is the only continuing civilization that originated in the ancient world. The Chinese archaeological record, extraordinarily rich, begins in Neolithic times. Discoveries in recent years have expanded the early record enormously and have provided evidence of settled village life as far back as the seventh or early sixth millennium BCE. Excavators have uncovered sites with large multifamily houses constructed of wood, bamboo, wattle, daub, and mud plaster and equipped with hearths. These early villages also had pens for domesticated animals, kilns for pottery production, pits for storage and refuse, and cemeteries for the dead. Chinese Neolithic artisans produced impressive artworks, especially from jade and clay.

YANGSHAO POTTERY Mastery of the art of pottery occurred at a very early date in China. The potters of the Yangshao Culture, which arose along the Yellow River in northeastern China, produced fine

MAP 7-1 China during the Tang dynasty.

decorated *earthenware* bowls (see "Chinese Earthenwares and Stonewares," page 196) even before the invention of the potter's wheel in the fourth millennium BCE. In the third millennium, the Yangshao potters of Gansu Province formed by hand and then painted vessels (FIG. 7-2) of astonishing sophistication. The multiplicity of shapes suggests that the vessels served a wide variety of functions in daily life, but most of the finds come from graves. Decoration is in red and brownish-black on a cream-colored ground. Some pots and bowls include stylized animal motifs, but most feature abstract designs. The painters reveal a highly refined aesthetic sensibility, effectively integrating a variety of angular and curvilinear geometric motifs, including stripes, zigzags, lozenges, circles, spirals, and waves.

SHANG DYNASTY During the past century, archaeologists have begun to confirm China's earliest royal dynasties, long thought to have been mythical. In 1959 excavators found what they believe to be traces of the Xia (ca. 2000–1600 BCE), China's oldest dynasty, at Yanshi in Henan Province. Much better documented, however, is the Shang dynasty (ca. 1600–1050 BCE), the first great Chinese dynasty of

7-2 Yangshao Culture vases, from Gansu Province, China, mid-third millennium BCE.

Neolithic Chinese artists produced vessels of diverse shapes even before the invention of the potter's wheel and decorated them with abstract motifs in red and brownish-black on a cream-colored ground.

Shang Bronze-Casting

Among the finest bronzes of the second millennium BCE are those that Shang artists created using piece molds. The Shang bronze-workers began the process by producing a solid clay model of the desired object. When the model dried to durable hardness, they pressed damp clay around it to form a mold that hardened but remained somewhat flexible. At that point, they carefully cut the mold in pieces, removed the pieces from the model, and baked the pieces in a kiln to form hard earthenware sections. Sculptors then carved the intricate details of the relief decoration into the inner surfaces of the piece molds. Next, the artists shaved the model to reduce its size to form a core for the piece mold. They then reassembled the mold around the model using bronze spacers to preserve a void between the model and the mold—a space equivalent to the layer of wax used in the lost-wax method (see "Hollow-Casting Life-Size Bronze Statues," Chapter 5, page 122). The Shang bronze-casters then added a final clay layer on the outside to hold everything together, leaving open ducts for pouring molten bronze into the space between the model and the mold and to permit gases to escape. Once the mold cooled, they broke it apart, removed the new bronze vessel, and cleaned and polished it.

Shang bronzes show a mastery in casting rivaling that of any other ancient civilization. The great numbers of cast-bronze vessels strongly suggest well-organized workshops. Shang bronzes held wine, water, grain, or meat for sacrificial rites. Each vessel's shape matched its intended purpose. All were highly decorated with abstract and animal motifs. On the guang illustrated here (FIG. 7-3), the multiple designs and their fields of background spirals integrate so closely with the form of the libation-pouring vessel that they are not merely an external embellishment but an integral part of the

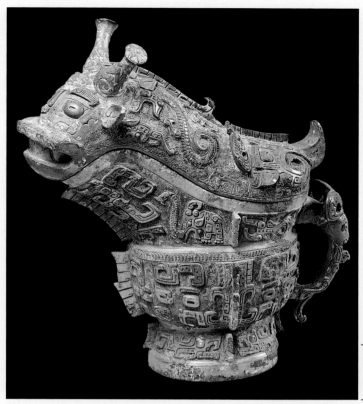

7-3 Guang, probably from Anyang, China, Shang dynasty, 12th or 11th century BCE. Bronze, $6\frac{1}{2}$" high. Asian Art Museum of San Francisco, San Francisco (Avery Brundage Collection).

Shang artists perfected the casting of elaborate bronze vessels decorated with animal motifs. The animal forms, real and imaginary, on this libation guang are probably connected with the world of spirits.

1 in.

sculptural whole. Some motifs on the guang's side may represent the eyes of a tiger and the horns of a ram. A horned animal forms the front of the lid, and at the rear is a horned head with a bird's beak. Another horned head appears on the handle. Fish, birds, elephants, rabbits, and more abstract composite creatures swarm over the surface against a background of spirals. The fabulous animal forms, real and imaginary, on Shang bronzes are unlikely to have been purely decorative. They are probably connected with the world of spirits addressed in the rituals.

the Bronze Age. The Shang kings ruled from a series of royal capitals in the Yellow River valley and vied for power and territory with the rulers of neighboring states. In 1928 excavations at Anyang (ancient Yin) brought to light the last Shang capital. There, archaeologists found a large number of objects—turtle shells, animal bones, and bronze containers—inscribed in the earliest form of the Chinese language. These fragmentary records and the other finds at Anyang provide important information about the Shang kings and their affairs. They reveal a warlike, highly stratified society. Walls of pounded earth protected Shang cities. Servants, captives, and even teams of charioteers with chariots and horses accompanied Shang kings to their tombs, a practice also documented at the Royal Cemetery at Ur (see Chapter 2).

The excavated tomb furnishings include weapons and a great wealth of objects in jade, ivory, lacquer, and bronze. Not only the kings received lavish burials. The tomb of Fu Hao, the wife of Wu Ding (r. ca. 1215–1190 BCE), contained an ivory beaker inlaid with turquoise and more than a thousand jade and bronze objects. Many of the vessels found in Shang tombs, for example, the guang (FIG. 7-3), shaped like a covered gravy boat, were used in sacrifices to ancestors and in funerary ceremonies. In some cases families erected shrines for ancestor worship above the burial places. Shang artists cast their elaborate bronze vessels in piece molds (see "Shang Bronze-Casting," above).

SANXINGDUI Recent excavations in other regions of China have greatly expanded historical understanding of the Bronze Age. They suggest that at the same time Anyang flourished under its Shang rulers in northern China, so did other major centers with distinct aesthetic traditions. In 1986, pits at Sanxingdui, near Chengdu in southwestern China, yielded a treasure of elephant tusks and objects in gold, bronze, jade, and clay of types never before discovered. They attest to an independent kingdom of enormous wealth contemporary with the better-known Shang dynasty.

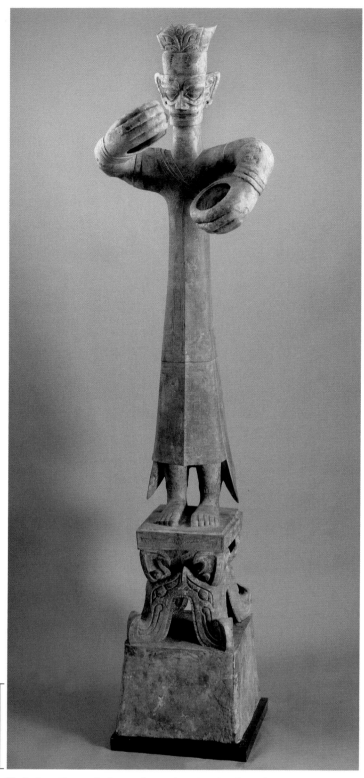

7-4 Standing male figure, from pit 2, Sanxingdui, China, ca. 1200–1050 BCE. Bronze, 8′ 5″ high, including base. Museum, Sanxingdui.

Excavations at Sanxingdui have revealed a Chinese civilization contemporary to the Shang but with a different artistic aesthetic. This huge statue has elongated proportions and large, staring eyes.

The most dramatic find, a bronze statue (FIG. **7-4**) more than eight feet tall, matches anything from Anyang in masterful casting technique. Very different in subject and style from the Shang bronzes, it initially shocked art historians who had formed their ideas about Bronze Age Chinese aesthetics based on Shang material. This figure—of unknown identity—is highly stylized, with elon-

gated proportions and large, staring eyes. It stands on a base composed of four legs formed of fantastic animal heads with horns and trunklike snouts. The statue tapers gently as it rises, and the figure gradually becomes rounder. Just below the neck, great arms branch dramatically outward, ending in oversized hands that once held an object, most likely one of the many elephant tusks buried with the bronze statue. Chinese representations of the human figure on this scale are otherwise unknown at this early date. Surface decoration of squared spirals and hook-pointed curves is all that links this gigantic statue with the intricate Shang piece-mold bronze vessels (FIG. **7-3**). Systematic excavations and chance finds will probably produce more surprises in the future and cause art historians to revise once again their picture of Chinese art in the second half of the second millennium BCE.

Zhou and Qin Dynasties

Around 1050 BCE, the Zhou, former vassals of the Shang, captured Anyang and overthrew their Shang overlords. The Zhou dynasty proved to be the longest lasting in China's history—so long that historians divide the Zhou era into two periods: Western Zhou (ca. 1050–771 BCE) and Eastern Zhou (770–256 BCE). The dividing event is the transfer of the Zhou capital from Chang'an (modern Xi'an) in the west to Luoyang in the east. The closing centuries of Zhou rule include a long period of warfare among competing states (Warring States Period, ca. 475–221 BCE). The Zhou fell to one of these states, the Qin, in 256 BCE.

ZHOU JADE Under the Zhou, the development of markets and the introduction of bronze coinage brought heightened prosperity and a taste for lavish products, such as bronzes inlaid with gold and silver. Late Zhou bronzes featured scenes of hunting, religious rites, and magic practices. These may relate to the subjects and compositions of lost paintings mentioned in Zhou literature. Other materials favored in the late Zhou period were *lacquer*, a varnishlike substance made from the sap of the Asiatic sumac, used to decorate wood furniture and other objects (see "Lacquered Wood," Chapter 27, page 724), and jade (see "Chinese Jade," page 185). The carving of jade objects for burial with the dead, beginning in Neolithic times, reached a peak of technical perfection during the Zhou dynasty. Among the most common finds in tombs of the period are *bi* disks (FIG. **7-5**)—thin, flat circular pieces of jade with a hole in the center, which may have symbolized the circle of Heaven. Bi disks were status symbols in life as well as treasured items the dead took with them to the afterlife. After a battle, for example, the victors forced their defeated foes to surrender their bi disks as symbols of their submission. The disks also had a high monetary value.

THE FIRST EMPEROR During the Warring States Period, China endured more than two centuries of political and social turmoil. This was also a time of intellectual and artistic upheaval, when conflicting schools of philosophy, including Legalism, Daoism, and Confucianism, emerged (see "Daoism and Confucianism," page 186). Order was finally restored when the powerful armies of the ruler of the state of Qin (from which the modern name "China" derives) conquered all rival states. Known to history by his title, Qin Shi Huangdi (the First Emperor of Qin), between 221 and 210 BCE he controlled an area equal to about half of modern China, much larger than the territories of any of the earlier Chinese dynasties. During his reign, Shi Huangdi ordered the linkage of active fortifications along the northern border of his realm to form the famous Great Wall. The wall defended China against the fierce nomadic peoples of the north, especially the Huns, who eventually made their

Chinese Jade

The Chinese first used jade—or, more precisely, nephrite—for artworks and ritual objects in the Neolithic period. Nephrite polishes to a more lustrous, slightly buttery finish than jadeite (the stone Chinese sculptors preferred from the 18th century on), which is quite glassy. Both stones are beautiful and come in colors other than the well-known green and are tough, hard, and heavy. In China, such qualities became metaphors for the fortitude and moral perfection of superior persons. The Chinese also believed jade possessed magical qualities that could protect the dead. In a Han dynasty tomb, for example, archaeologists discovered the bodies of a prince and princess dressed in suits composed of more than 2,000 jade pieces sewn together with gold wire.

Because of its extreme hardness, jade could not be carved with the Neolithic sculptor's stone tools. Researchers can only speculate on how these early artists were able to cut, shape, and incise the nephrite objects found at many Neolithic Chinese sites. The sculptors probably used cords embedded with sand to incise lines into the surfaces. Sand placed in a bamboo tube drill could perforate the hard stone, but the process would have been long and arduous, requiring great patience as well as superior skill.

Even after the invention of bronze tools, Chinese sculptors still had to rely on grinding and abrasion rather than simple drilling and chiseling to produce the intricately shaped, pierced, and engraved works such as the *bi* (FIG. 7-5) said to have come from a royal Eastern Zhou tomb at Jincun. Rows of raised spirals, created by laborious grinding and polishing, decorate the disk itself. Within the inner circle and around the outer edge of the bi are elegant dragons. The Chinese thought dragons inhabited the water and flew between Heaven and Earth, bringing rain, so these animals long have been symbols of good fortune in East Asia. They also symbolized the rulers' power to mediate between Heaven and Earth. To sculpt the dragons on the bi from Jincun required long hours of work to pierce through the hard jade. The bi testifies to the Zhou sculptor's mastery of this difficult material.

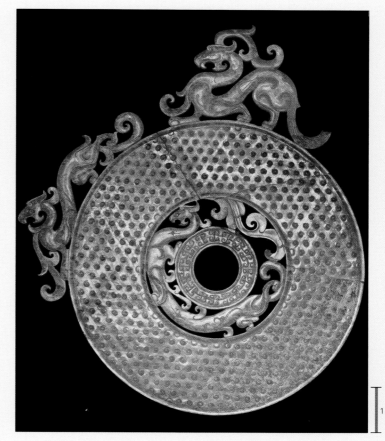

1 in.

7-5 Bi disk with dragons, from Jincun(?), near Luoyang, China, Eastern Zhou dynasty, fourth to third century BCE. Nephrite, $6\frac{1}{2}''$ in diameter. Nelson-Atkins Museum of Art, Kansas City.

This intricately shaped jade bi required long hours of grinding, piercing, engraving, and polishing to produce. The Chinese believed dragons were symbols of good fortune and flew between Heaven and Earth.

way to eastern Europe. By sometimes brutal methods, the First Emperor consolidated rule through a centralized bureaucracy and adopted standardized written language, weights and measures, and coinage. He also repressed schools of thought other than Legalism, which espoused absolute obedience to the state's authority and advocated strict laws and punishments. Chinese historians long have condemned the First Emperor, but the bureaucratic system he put in place had a long-lasting impact. Its success was due in large part to Shi Huangdi's decision to replace the feudal lords with talented salaried administrators and to reward merit rather than favor high birth.

TERRACOTTA ARMY, LINTONG In 1974 excavations started at the site of the immense burial mound of the First Emperor of Qin at Lintong. For its construction, the ruler conscripted more than 700,000 laborers and had the tomb filled with treasure. The project continued after his death. The mound itself remains unexcavated except for some test trenches, but researchers believe it contains a vast underground funerary palace designed to match the fabulous palace the emperor occupied in life. The historian Sima

Qian (136–85 BCE) described both palaces, but scholars did not take his account seriously until the discovery of pits around the tomb filled with more than 6,000 life-size painted terracotta figures (FIG. 7-6) of soldiers and horses, as well as bronze horses and chariots. The terracotta army served as the First Emperor's bodyguard deployed in perpetuity outside his tomb.

The Lintong army, composed of cavalry, chariots, archers, lancers, and hand-to-hand fighters, was one of the 20th century's greatest archaeological discoveries. Lesser versions of Shi Huangdi's army have since been uncovered at other Chinese sites, suggesting that the First Emperor's tomb became the model for many others. The huge assemblage at Lintong testifies to a very high degree of organization in the Qin imperial workshop. Manufacturing this army of statues required a veritable army of sculptors and painters as well as a large number of huge kilns. The First Emperor's artisans could have opted to use the same molds over and over again to produce thousands of identical soldiers standing in strict formation. In fact, they did employ the same molds repeatedly for different parts of the statues but assembled the parts in many different combinations. Consequently, the stances, arm positions, garment folds, equipment,

China **185**

Daoism and Confucianism

Daoism and Confucianism are both philosophies and religions native to China. Both schools of thought attracted wide followings during the Warring States Period (ca. 475–221 BCE), when political turbulence led to social unrest.

Daoism emerged out of the metaphysical teachings attributed to Laozi (604?–531? BCE) and Zhuangzi (370?–301? BCE). It takes its name from Laozi's treatise *Daodejing* (*The Way and Its Power*). Daoist philosophy stresses an intuitive awareness, nurtured by harmonious contact with nature, and shuns everything artificial. Daoists seek to follow the universal path, or principle, called the Dao, whose features cannot be described but only suggested through analogies. For example, the Dao is said to be like water, always yielding but eventually wearing away the hard stone that does not yield. For Daoists, strength comes from flexibility and inaction. Historically, Daoist principles encouraged retreat from society in favor of personal cultivation in nature and the achievement of a perfect balance between *yang*, active masculine energy, and *yin*, passive feminine energy.

Confucius (551–479 BCE) was born in the state of Lu (roughly modern Shandong Province) to an aristocratic family that had fallen on hard times. From an early age, he showed a strong interest in the rites and ceremonies that helped unite people into an orderly society. As he grew older, he developed a deep concern for the suffering the civil conflict of his day caused. Thus, he adopted a philosophy he hoped would lead to order and stability. The *junzi* ("superior person" or "gentleman"), who possesses *ren* ("human-heartedness"), personifies the ideal social order Confucius sought. Although the term *junzi* originally assumed noble birth, in Confucian thought anyone can become a junzi by cultivating the virtues Confucius espoused, especially empathy for suffering, pursuit of morality and justice, respect for ancient ceremonies, and adherence to traditional social relationships, such as those between parent and child, elder and younger sibling, husband and wife, and ruler and subject.

Confucius's disciple Mencius (or Mengzi, 371?–289? BCE) developed the master's ideas further, stressing that the deference to age and rank that is at the heart of the Confucian social order brings a reciprocal responsibility. For example, a king's legitimacy depends on the goodwill of his people. A ruler should share his joys with his subjects and will know his laws are unjust if they bring suffering to the people.

Confucius spent much of his adult life trying to find rulers willing to apply his teachings, but he died in disappointment. However, he and Mencius had a profound impact on Chinese thought and social practice. Chinese traditions of venerating deceased ancestors and outstanding leaders encouraged the development of Confucianism as a religion as well as a philosophic tradition. Eventually, Emperor Wu (r. 140–87 BCE) of the Han dynasty established Confucianism as the state's official doctrine. Thereafter, it became the primary subject of the civil service exams required for admission into and advancement within government service.

"Confucian" and "Daoist" are broad, imprecise terms scholars often use to distinguish aspects of Chinese culture stressing social responsibility and order (Confucian) from those emphasizing cultivation of individuals, often in reclusion (Daoist). But both philosophies share the idea that anyone can cultivate wisdom or ability, regardless of birth.

---

coiffures, and facial features vary, sometimes slightly, sometimes markedly, from statue to statue. Additional hand modeling of the cast body parts before firing permitted the sculptors to differentiate the figures even more. The Qin painters undoubtedly added further variations to the appearance of the terracotta army. The result of these efforts was a brilliant balance of uniformity and individuality.

7-6 Army of the First Emperor of Qin in pits next to his burial mound, Lintong, China, Qin dynasty, ca. 210 BCE. Painted terracotta, average figure 5′ 10⅞″ high. ▪◄

The First Emperor was buried beneath an immense mound guarded by more than 6,000 life-size terracotta soldiers. Although produced from common molds, every figure has an individualized appearance.

Han Dynasty

Soon after the First Emperor's death, the people who had suffered under his reign revolted, assassinated his corrupt and incompetent son, and founded the Han dynasty in 206 BCE. The Han ruled China for four centuries, integrating many of the Qin reforms in a more liberal governing policy. They also extended China's southern and western boundaries, penetrating far into Central Asia (modern Xinjiang). Han merchants even traded indirectly with distant Rome (via the so-called Silk Road (see "Silk and the Silk Road, p. 188).

THE MARQUISE OF DAI In 1972 archaeologists excavated the tomb of the Marquise of Dai at Mawangdui in Hunan Province. The tomb contained a rich array of burial goods used during the funerary ceremonies and to accompany the deceased woman into the afterlife. Among the many finds were decorated lacquer utensils, various textiles, and an astonishingly well-preserved corpse in the innermost of four nested sarcophagi. Most remarkable, however, was the discovery of a painted T-shaped silk banner (FIG. **7-7**) draped over the marquise's coffin. Scholars generally agree that the area within the cross at the top of the T represents Heaven. Most of the vertical section below is the human realm. At the very bottom is the Underworld. In the heavenly realm, dragons and immortal beings appear between and below two orbs—the red sun and its symbol, the raven, on the right, and the silvery moon and its symbol, the toad, on the left. Below, the standing figure on the first white platform near the center of the vertical section is probably the Marquise of Dai herself—one of the first portraits in Chinese art. The woman awaits her ascent to Heaven, where she can attain immortality. Nearer the bottom, the artist depicted her funeral. Between these two sections is a form resembling a bi disk (FIG. **7-5**) with two intertwining dragons. Their tails reach down to the Underworld and their heads point to Heaven, unifying the whole composition.

WU FAMILY SHRINES Even more extensive Han pictorial narratives appear on the walls of the Wu family shrines at Jiaxiang in Shandong Province, dating between 147 and 168 CE. The shrines document the emergence of private, nonaristocratic families as patrons of religious and mythological art with political overtones. Dedicated to deceased male family members, the Wu shrines consist of three low walls and a pitched roof. On the interior surfaces, carved images of flat polished stone stand out against an equally flat,

7-7 Funeral banner, from tomb 1 (tomb of the Marquise of Dai), Mawangdui, China, Han dynasty, ca. 168 BCE. Painted silk, 6' 8¾" × 3' 1¼". Hunan Provincial Museum, Changsha.

This T-shaped silk banner was draped over the coffin of the Marquise of Dai, who is shown at the center awaiting her ascent to immortality in Heaven, the realm of the red sun and silvery moon.

1 ft.

though roughly textured, ground. The historical scenes include a representation of the third-century BCE hero Jing Ke's attempt to assassinate the tyrannical First Emperor of Qin. On the slab shown in FIG. **7-8,** a *rubbing* (an impression made by placing paper over the surface and rubbing with a pencil or crayon) taken from the stone

1 ft.

7-8 The archer Yi(?) and a reception in a mansion, Wu family shrine, Jiaxiang, China, Han dynasty, 147–168 CE. Rubbing of a stone relief, 3' × 5'.

The Wu family shrines depict historical, legendary, and contemporaneous subjects. Here, the hero Yi shoots down suns to save the Earth from scorching. To the right is a ceremonial scene in a Han mansion.

Silk and the Silk Road

Silk is the finest natural fabric ever produced. It comes from the cocoons of caterpillars called silkworms. The manufacture of silk was a well-established industry in China by the second millennium BCE. The basic procedures probably have not changed much since then. Farmers today still raise silkworms from eggs, which they place in trays. The farmers also must grow mulberry trees or purchase mulberry leaves, the silkworms' only food source. Eventually, the silkworms form cocoons out of very fine filaments they extrude as liquid from their bodies. The filaments soon solidify with exposure to air. Before the transformed caterpillars emerge as moths and badly damage the silk, the farmers kill them with steam or high heat. They soften the cocoons in hot water and unwind the filaments onto a reel. The filaments are so fine that workers generally unwind those from five to ten cocoons together to bond into a single strand while the filaments are still soft and sticky. Later, the silkworkers twist several strands together to form a thicker yarn and then weave the yarn on a loom to produce silk cloth. Both the yarn and the cloth can be dyed, and the silk fabric can be decorated by weaving threads of different colors together in special patterns (*brocades*) or by stitching in threads of different colors (*embroidery*). Many Chinese artists painted directly on plain silk.

Greatly admired throughout most of Asia, Chinese silk and the secrets of its production gradually spread throughout the ancient world. The Romans knew of silk as early as the second century BCE and treasured it for garments and hangings. Silk came to the Romans along the ancient fabled Silk Road, a network of caravan tracts across Central Asia linking China and the Mediterranean world (MAP 7-1). The western part, between the Mediterranean region and India, developed first, due largely to the difficult geographic conditions to India's northeast. In Central Asia, the caravans had to skirt the Taklimakan Desert, one of the most inhospitable environments on earth, as well as to climb high, dangerous mountain passes. Very few traders traveled the entire route. Along the way, goods usually passed through the hands of people from many lands, who often only dimly understood the ultimate origins and destinations of what they traded. The Roman passion for silk ultimately led to the modern name for the caravan tracts, but silk was by no means the only product traded along the way. Gold, ivory, gems, glass, lacquer, incense, furs, spices, cotton, linens, exotic animals, and other merchandise precious enough to warrant the risks passed along the Silk Road.

Ideas moved along these trade routes as well. Most important perhaps, travelers on the Silk Road brought Buddhism to China from India in the first century CE, opening up a significant new chapter in both the history of religion and the history of art in China.

---

relief, the archer at the upper left is probably the hero Yi. He saves the Earth from scorching by shooting down the nine extra suns, represented as crows in the Fusang tree. (The small orbs below the sun on the Mawangdui banner, FIG. 7-7, probably allude to the same story.) The lowest zone shows a procession of umbrella-carriages moving to the left. Above, underneath the overhanging eaves of a two-story mansion, robed men bearing gifts pay homage to a central figure of uncertain identity, who is represented as larger and therefore more important. Two men kneel before the larger figure. Women occupy the upper story. Again, one figure, at the center and facing forward, is singled out as the most important. The identities of the individual figures are unknown. Interpretations vary widely, and in the past decade scholars have discovered that some of the Wu reliefs have re-carved inscriptions, leading them to question even the traditional date of the slabs. Nonetheless, these scenes of homage and loyalty are consistent with the Confucian ideals of Han society.

7-8A Flying horse of Governor-General Zhang, late second century CE.

HAN HOUSES AND PALACES No actual remains of Han buildings survive, but ceramic models of houses deposited in Han tombs, together with representations such as those in the Wu family shrines, provide a good idea of Chinese architecture during the early centuries CE. An especially large painted earthenware model (FIG. 7-9) reproduces a Han house with sharply projecting tiled roofs resting on a framework of timber posts, lintels, and brackets. This construction method (FIG. 7-10) typifies much Chinese architecture even today (see "Chinese Wooden Construction," page 189). Descriptions of Han palaces suggest they were grandiose versions of the type of house reproduced in this model but with more luxurious decoration, including walls of lacquered wood and mural paintings.

Period of Disunity

For three and a half centuries, from 220 to 581,* civil strife divided China into competing states. Scholars variously refer to this era as the Period of Disunity or the period of the Six Dynasties or of the Northern and Southern Dynasties. The history of this era is extremely complex, but one development deserves special mention—the occupation of the north by peoples who were not ethnically Han Chinese and who spoke non-Chinese languages. It was in the northern states, connected to India by the desert caravan routes of the Silk Road (see "Silk and the Silk Road," above), that Buddhism first took root in China during the Han dynasty. Certain practices shared with Daoism, such as withdrawal from ordinary society, helped Buddhism gain an initial foothold in the north. But Buddhism's promise of hope beyond the troubles of this world earned it an ever broader audience during the upheavals of the Period of Disunity. In addition, the fully developed Buddhist system of thought attracted intellectuals. Buddhism never fully displaced Confucianism and Daoism, but it did prosper throughout China for centuries and had a profound effect on the further development of the religious forms of those two native traditions.

ZHAO BUDDHA A gilded bronze statuette (FIG. 7-11) of Shakyamuni Buddha, the historical Buddha, bears an inscription giving its date as 338. Although some scholars have questioned whether the inscription is a later addition, many art historians still accept the statuette as the earliest precisely datable Chinese image of the Buddha, created during the Later Zhao dynasty (319–351). The oldest Chinese Buddhist texts describe the Buddha as golden and radiating

---

*From this point on, all dates in this chapter are CE unless otherwise stated.

Chinese Wooden Construction

Although the basic unit of Chinese architecture, the rectangular hall with columns supporting a roof, was common in many ancient civilizations, Chinese buildings are distinguished by the curving silhouettes of their roofs and by their method of construction. The Chinese, like other ancient peoples, used wood to construct their earliest buildings. Although those structures do not survive, scholars believe many of the features giving East Asian architecture its specific character may date to the Zhou dynasty. Even the simple buildings reproduced on Han stone carvings (FIG. 7-8) and in clay models (FIG. 7-9) reveal a style and a method of construction long basic to China.

The typical Chinese hall has a pitched roof with projecting eaves. Wooden columns, lintels, and brackets provide the support. The walls serve no weight-bearing function. They act only as screens separating inside from outside and room from room. The colors of Chinese buildings, predominantly red, black, yellow, and white, are also distinctive. Chinese timber architecture is customarily multi-colored throughout, save for certain parts left in natural color, such as railings made of white marble. The builders usually painted the screen walls and the columns red. Chinese designers often chose dazzling combinations of colors and elaborate patterns for the beams, brackets, eaves, rafters, and ceilings. The builders painted or lacquered the surfaces to protect the timber from rot and wood parasites, as well as to produce an arresting aesthetic effect.

FIG. 7-10 shows the basic construction method of Chinese architecture, with the major components of a Chinese building labeled. The builders laid *beams* (no. 1) between columns, decreasing the length of the beams as the structure rose. The beams supported vertical *struts* (no. 2), which in turn supported higher beams and eventually the *purlins* (no. 3) running the length of the building and carrying the roof's sloping *rafters* (no. 4). Unlike the rigid elements of the triangular trussed timber roof common in the West, which produce flat sloping rooflines, the varying lengths of the Chinese structure's cross beams and the variously placed purlins can create curved profiles. Early Chinese roofs have flat profiles (FIGS. 7-8 and 7-9), but curving rafters (FIGS. 7-10 and 7-23) later became the norm, not only in China but throughout East Asia. The interlocking clusters of brackets were capable of supporting roofs with broad overhanging *eaves* (no. 5), another typical feature of Chinese architecture. Multiplication of the *bays* (spaces between the columns) could extend the building's length to any dimension desired, although each bay could be no wider or longer than the length of a single tree trunk. The proportions of the structural elements could be fixed into modules, allowing for standardization of parts. This enabled rapid construction of a building. Remarkably, the highly skilled Chinese workers fit the parts together without using any adhesive substance, such as mortar or glue.

7-9 Model of a house, Han dynasty, first century CE. Painted earthenware, 4′ 4″ high. Nelson-Atkins Museum of Art, Kansas City.

This model of a Han house provides invaluable information about the form, coloration, and construction methods of Chinese architecture. The flat profile of the rooflines is typical of earlier Chinese buildings.

7-10 Chinese raised-beam construction (after L. Liu).

Chinese walls serve no weight-bearing function. They act only as screens separating inside from outside and room from room. Tang dynasty and later buildings usually have curved rafters and eaves.

China   **189**

Chinese Painting Materials and Formats

Mural paintings in caves (FIG. 7-15) were popular in China, as they were in South Asia (FIG. 6-15), but Chinese artists also employed several distinctive materials and formats for their paintings.

The basic requirements for paintings not on walls were the same as for writing—a round tapered brush, soot-based ink, and either silk or paper. The Chinese were masters of the brush. Sometimes Chinese painters used modulated lines for contours and interior details that elastically thicken and thin to convey depth and mass. In other works, they used *iron-wire lines* (thin, unmodulated lines with a suggestion of tensile strength) to define each individual figure in their paintings.

Chinese painters also used richly colored minerals as pigments, finely ground and suspended in a gluey medium, and watery washes of mineral and vegetable dyes.

The formats of Chinese paintings on silk or paper tend to be personal and intimate, and they are usually best viewed by only one or two people at a time. The most common types are

Hanging scrolls (FIGS. 7-1, 7-25, and 7-26). Chinese painters often mounted pictures on, or painted directly on, unrolled vertical scrolls for display on walls.

Handscrolls (FIGS. 7-12, 7-17, and 7-21). Paintings were also frequently attached to or painted on long, narrow scrolls that the viewer unrolled horizontally, section by section from right to left.

Album leaves (FIGS. 7-24 and 27-14). Many Chinese artists painted small panels on paper leaves, which were collected in albums.

Fans (FIG. 27-13). Stiff round or arched folding fans were also popular painting formats.

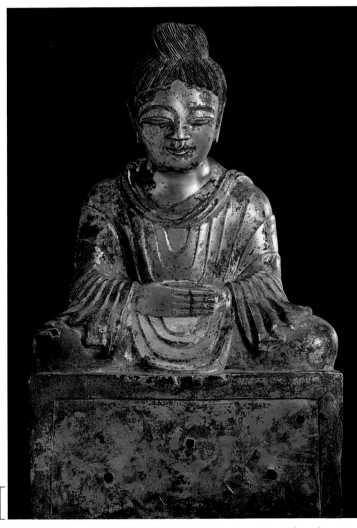

1 in.

7-11 Shakyamuni Buddha, from Hebei Province, Later Zhao dynasty, Period of Disunity, 338. Gilded bronze, 1′ 3½″ high. Asian Art Museum of San Francisco, San Francisco (Avery Brundage Collection).

This earliest datable Chinese Buddha image is stylistically indebted to Gandharan prototypes (FIG. 6-10), but the sculptor, unfamiliar with Buddhist iconography, misrepresented the dhyana mudra.

light, characteristics that no doubt account for the choice of gilded bronze as the sculptor's medium. In both style and iconography, this early Buddha resembles the prototype conceived and developed at Gandhara (FIG. 6-10). The Chinese figure recalls its presumed South Asian models in the flat, relieflike handling of the robe's heavy concentric folds, the ushnisha (cranial bump) on the head, and the cross-legged position. So new were the icon and its meaning, however, that the Chinese sculptor misrepresented the canonical dhyana mudra, or meditation gesture (see "Buddhism and Buddhist Iconography," Chapter 6, page 161). Here, the Buddha clasps his hands across his stomach. In South Asian art, they are turned palms upward, with thumbs barely touching in front of the torso.

LADY FENG'S HEROISM Secular arts also flourished in the Period of Disunity, as rulers sought calligraphers and painters to lend prestige to their courts. The most famous early Chinese painter with whom extant works can be associated was GU KAIZHI (ca. 344–406). Gu was a friend of important members of the Eastern Jin dynasty (317–420) and won renown as a calligrapher, a painter of court portraits, and a pioneer of landscape painting. A *handscroll* (see "Chinese Painting Materials and Formats," above) attributed to Gu Kaizhi in the 11th century is not actually by his hand, but it provides a good idea of the key elements of his art. Called *Admonitions of the Instructress to the Court Ladies,* the horizontal scroll contains painted scenes and accompanying explanatory text. Like all Chinese handscrolls, this one was unrolled and read from right to left, with only a small section exposed for viewing at one time.

The handscroll section illustrated here (FIG. 7-12) records a well-known act of heroism, the Lady Feng saving her emperor's life by placing herself between him and an attacking bear—a perfect model of Confucian behavior. As in many early Chinese paintings, the artist set the figures against a blank background with only a minimal setting for the scene, although in other works Gu provided landscape settings for his narratives. The figures' poses and fluttering drapery ribbons, in concert with individualized facial expressions, convey a clear quality of animation. This style accords well with painting ideals expressed in texts of the time, when representing inner vitality and spirit took precedence over reproducing surface appearances (see "Xie He's Six Canons," page 191).

Xie He's Six Canons

China has a long and rich history of scholarship on painting, preserved today in copies of texts from as far back as the fourth century and in citations to even earlier sources. Few of the first texts on painting survive, but later authors often quoted them, preserving the texts for posterity. Thus, educated Chinese painters and their clients could steep themselves in a rich art historical tradition. Perhaps the most famous subject of later commentary is a set of six "canons," or "laws," of painting that Xie He formulated in the early sixth century. The canons, as translated by James Cahill,* are as follows:

1. Engender a sense of movement through spirit consonance.
2. Use the brush with the bone method.
3. Responding to things, depict their forms.
4. According to kind, describe appearances [with color].
5. Dividing and planning, positioning and arranging.
6. Transmitting and conveying earlier models through copying and transcribing.

Several variant translations have also been proposed, and scholars actively debate the precise meaning of these succinct (Xie He employed only four characters for each) and cryptic laws. Interpreting the canons in connection with existing paintings is often difficult but nonetheless offers valuable insights into what the Chinese valued in painting.

The simplest canons to understand are the third, fourth, and fifth, because they show Chinese painters' concern for accuracy in rendering forms and colors and for care in composition, concerns common in many cultures. However, separating form and color into different laws gives written expression to a distinctive feature of early Chinese painting. Painters such as Gu Kaizhi (FIG. 7-12) and Yan Liben (FIG. 7-17) used an outline-and-color technique. Their brushed-ink outline drawings employ flat applications of color. To suggest volume, they used ink shading along edges, such as drapery folds.

Also noteworthy is the order of the laws, suggesting Chinese painters' primary concern: to convey the vital spirit of their subjects and their own sensitivity to that spirit. Next in importance was the handling of the brush and the careful placement of strokes, especially of ink. The sixth canon also speaks to a standard Chinese painting practice: copying. Chinese painters, like painters in other cultures throughout history, trained by copying the works of their teachers and other painters. In addition, artists often copied famous paintings as sources of forms and ideas for their own works and to preserve great works created using fragile materials. In China, as elsewhere, change and individual development occurred in constant reference to the past, the artists always preserving some elements of it.

*James Cahill, "The Six Laws and How to Read Them," *Ars Orientalis* 4 (1961), 372–381.

7-12 Gu Kaizhi, *Lady Feng and the Bear,* detail of *Admonitions of the Instructress to the Court Ladies,* Period of Disunity, late fourth century. Handscroll, ink and colors on silk, entire scroll 9¾″ × 11′ 4½″. British Museum, London.

Lady Feng's act of heroism to save the life of her emperor was a perfect model of Confucian behavior. In this early Chinese representation of the episode, the painter set the figures against a blank background.

China **191**

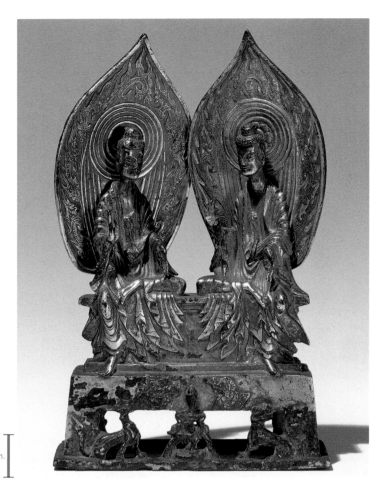

7-13 Shakyamuni and Prabhutaratna, from Hebei Province, Northern Wei dynasty, 518. Gilded bronze, $10\frac{1}{4}$″ high. Musée Guimet, Paris.

The sculptor of this statuette transformed the Gandhara-derived style of earlier Chinese Buddhist art (FIG. 7-11). The bodies have elongated proportions, and the garment folds form sharp ridges.

MEETING OF TWO BUDDHAS A gilded bronze statuette (FIG. **7-13**) shows how the sculptors of the Northern Wei dynasty (386–534) transformed the Gandhara-derived style of earlier Buddhist art in China (FIG. 7-11). Dated 518, the piece was probably made for private devotion in a domestic setting or as a votive offering in a temple. It represents the meeting of Shakyamuni Buddha (at the viewer's right) and Prabhutaratna, the Buddha who had achieved nirvana in the remote past, as recounted in the most famous *sutra*, the *Lotus Sutra*, an encyclopedic collection of Buddhist thought and poetry. When Shakyamuni was preaching on Vulture Peak, Prabhutaratna's stupa miraculously appeared in the sky. Shakyamuni opened it and revealed Prabhutaratna himself, who had promised to be present whenever the Lotus Law was preached. Shakyamuni sat beside him and continued to expound the law. The meeting of the two Buddhas symbolized the continuity of Buddhist thought across the ages.

Behind each Buddha is a flamelike nimbus (*mandorla*). Both figures sit in the *lalitasana* pose—one leg folded and the other hanging down. This standard pose, which indicates relaxation, underscores the ease of communication between the two Buddhas. Their bodies have elongated proportions, and their smiling faces have sharp noses and almond eyes. The folds of the garments drop like a waterfall from their shoulders to their knees and spill over onto the pedestal, where they form sharp ridges resembling the teeth of a saw. The rhythmic sweep and linear elegance of the folds recall the brushwork of contemporaneous painting.

Tang Dynasty

The emperors of the short-lived Sui dynasty (581–618) succeeded in reuniting China and prepared the way for the brilliant Tang dynasty (618–907). Under the Tang emperors, China entered a period of unequaled magnificence (MAP 7-1). Chinese armies marched across Central Asia, prompting an influx of foreign peoples, wealth, and ideas into China. Traders, missionaries, and other travelers journeyed to the cosmopolitan Tang capital at Chang'an, and the Chinese, in turn, ventured westward. Chang'an was laid out on a grid scheme and occupied more than 30 square miles. It was the greatest city in the world during the seventh and eighth centuries.

LONGMEN CAVES In its first century, the new dynasty continued to support Buddhism and to sponsor great monuments for Buddhist worshipers. Cave complexes decorated with reliefs and paintings, modeled on those of India (see Chapter 6), were especially popular. One of the most spectacular Tang Buddhist sculptures is carved into the face of a cliff in the great Longmen Caves complex near Luoyang. Work at Longmen had begun almost two centuries earlier, during the Period of Disunity, under the Northern Wei dynasty (386–534). The site's 2,345 shrines and more than 100,000 statues and 2,800 inscriptions attest to its importance as a Buddhist center.

The colossal relief (FIG. **7-14**) that dominates the Longmen complex features a central figure of the Buddha that is 44 feet tall—seated. An inscription records that the project was completed in 676 when Gaozong (r. 649–683) was the Tang emperor and that in 672 the empress Wu Zetian underwrote a substantial portion of the considerable cost with her private funds. Wu Zetian was an exceptional woman by any standard, and when Gaozong died in 683, she declared herself emperor and ruled until 705, when she was forced to abdicate at age 82.

7-14A Seated Buddha, Cave 20, Yungang, ca. 460–470.

Wu Zetian's Buddha is the Vairocana Buddha, not the historical Buddha of FIGS. 7-11 and 7-13 but the Mahayana Cosmic Buddha, the Buddha of Boundless Space and Time (see "Buddhism," Chapter 6, page 161). Flanking him are two of his monks, attendant bodhisattvas, and guardian figures—all smaller than the Buddha but still of colossal size (shown in FIG. 7-14 are visitors to the site, whose size underscores the scale of the work). The sculptors represented the Buddha in serene majesty. An almost geometric regularity of contour and smoothness of planes emphasize the volume of the massive figure. The folds of his robes fall in a few concentric arcs. The artists suppressed surface detail in the interest of monumental simplicity and dignity.

DUNHUANG GROTTOES The westward expansion of the Tang Empire increased the importance of Dunhuang, the westernmost gateway to China on the Silk Road. Dunhuang long had been a wealthy, cosmopolitan trade center, a Buddhist pilgrimage destination, and home to thriving communities of Buddhist monks and nuns of varied ethnicity, as well as to adherents of other religions. In the course of several centuries, the Chinese cut hundreds of sanctuaries with painted murals into the soft rock of the cliffs near Dunhuang. Known today as the Mogao Grottoes and in antiquity as the Caves of a Thousand Buddhas, the Dunhuang grottoes also contain sculptured images of painted unfired clay and stucco. The earliest recorded cave at Dunhuang was dedicated in 366, but the oldest extant caves date to the early fifth century. The Dunhuang caves are especially important because in 845 the emperor Wuzong instituted a major persecution, destroying 4,600 Buddhist temples and 40,000 shrines and forcing the return of 260,500 monks and nuns to lay life. Wuzong's policies did not affect Dunhuang, then under Tibetan rule, so the site preserves much of the type of art lost elsewhere.

7-14 Vairocana Buddha, disciples, and bodhisattvas, Fengxian Temple, Longmen Caves, Luoyang, China, Tang dynasty, completed 676. Limestone, Buddha 44′ high. ▣◀

Empress Wu Zetian sponsored these colossal rock-cut sculptures. The Tang artists represented the Mahayana Cosmic Buddha in serene majesty, suppressing surface detail in the interest of monumental simplicity.

10 ft.

Paradise of Amitabha (FIG. **7-15**), on the wall of one of the Dunhuang caves, shows how the splendor of the Tang era and religious teachings could come together in a powerful image. Buddhist Pure Land sects, especially those centered on Amitabha, Buddha of the West, had captured the popular imagination in the Period of Disunity under the Six Dynasties and continued to flourish during the Tang dynasty. Pure Land teachings asserted that individuals had no hope of attaining enlightenment through their own power because of the waning of the Buddha's Law. Instead, they could obtain rebirth in a realm free from spiritual corruption simply through faith in Amitabha's promise of salvation. Richly detailed, brilliantly colored pictures steeped in the opulence of the Tang dynasty, such as this one, greatly aided worshipers in gaining faith by visualizing the wonders of the Pure Land Paradise. Amitabha sits in the center of a raised platform, his principal bodhisattvas and lesser divine attendants surrounding him. Before them a celestial dance takes place. Bodhisattvas had strong appeal in East Asia as compassionate beings ready to achieve buddhahood but dedicated to humanity's salvation. Some received direct worship and became the main subjects of sculpture and painting.

7-15A *Bodhisattva Guanyin,* Dunhuang, late ninth or early 10th century.

7-15 *Paradise of Amitabha,* cave 172, Dunhuang, China, Tang dynasty, mid-eighth century. Wall painting 10′ high.

This richly detailed, brilliantly colored mural aided Tang worshipers at Dunhuang in visualizing the wonders of the Pure Land Paradise promised to those who had faith in Amitabha, the Buddha of the West.

1 ft.

A complex grid of beams and purlins and a thicket of interlocking brackets support the 14-foot overhang of the eaves of the timbered and tiled curved roof of this early Chinese Buddhist temple.

MOUNT WUTAI In the Dunhuang mural, Amitabha appears against a backdrop of ornate buildings characteristic of the Tang era. The Tang rulers embellished their empire with extravagant wooden structures, colorfully painted and of colossal size, decorated with furnishings of great luxury and elaborate gold, silver, and bronze ornaments. Unfortunately, few Tang buildings survive. Among them is the Foguang Si (Buddha Radiance Temple) on Mount Wutai, one of the oldest surviving Buddhist temples in China. It lacks the costly embellishment of imperial structures in the capital, but its east main hall (FIG. 7-16) displays the distinctive curved roofline of later Chinese architecture (FIG. 7-10), which was not present in the Han examples (FIGS. 7-8 and 7-9) discussed earlier. A complex grid of beams and purlins and a thicket of interlocking brackets support the overhang of the eaves—some 14 feet out from the column faces—as well as the timbered and tiled roof.

YAN LIBEN The Tang emperors also fostered a brilliant tradition of painting. Although few examples are preserved, many art his-

7-17 Attributed to YAN LIBEN, *Emperor Xuan and Attendants*, detail of *The Thirteen Emperors*, Tang dynasty, ca. 650. Handscroll, ink and colors on silk, detail 1′ 8$\frac{1}{4}$″ × 1′ 5$\frac{1}{2}$″; entire scroll 17′ 5″ long. Museum of Fine Arts, Boston.

This handscroll portrays 13 Chinese rulers as Confucian exemplars of moral and political virtue. Yan Liben, a celebrated Tang painter, was a master of line drawing and colored washes.

torians regard the early Tang dynasty as the golden age of Chinese figure painting. In perfect accord with contemporary and later Chinese poets' and critics' glowing descriptions of Tang painting style are the unrestored portions of *The Thirteen Emperors* (FIG. 7-17), a masterpiece of line drawing and colored washes. The painting has long been attributed to YAN LIBEN (d. 673). Born into an aristocratic family and the son of a famous artist, Yan Liben was prime minister under the emperor Gaozong as well as a celebrated painter. This handscroll depicts 13 Chinese rulers from the Han to the Sui dynasties. Its purpose was to portray these historical figures as exemplars of moral and political virtue, in keeping with the Confucian ideal of learning from the past. Each emperor stands or sits in an undefined space. The emperor's great size relative to his attendants immediately establishes his superior stature. Simple shading in the faces and the robes gives the figures an added semblance of volume and presence.

The detail in FIG. 7-17 represents the emperor Xuan of the Chen dynasty (557–589) seated among his attendants, two of whom carry the ceremonial fans that signify his rank and focus the viewer's attention on him. Xuan stands out from the others also because of his dark robes. His majestic serenity contrasts with his attendants' animated poses, which vary sharply from figure to figure, lending vitality to the composition.

TOMB OF YONGTAI Wall paintings in the tomb of the Tang princess Yongtai (684–701) at Qianxian, near Chang'an, permit an analysis of court painting styles unobscured by problems of authenticity and reconstruction. When she was 17 years old, Yongtai was either murdered or forced to commit suicide by Wu Zetian. Her underground tomb dates to 706, however, because her formal burial had to await Wu Zetian's own death. The detail illustrated here (FIG. 7-18) depicts palace ladies and their attendants, images of pleasant court life to accompany the princess into her afterlife. The figures appear as if on a shallow stage. The artist did not provide any indications of background or setting, but intervals between the two rows and the figures' grouping in an oval suggest a consistent ground plane. The women assume a variety of poses, seen in full-face and in three-quarter views, from the front or the back. The device of paired figures facing into and out of the space of the picture appears often in paintings of this period and effectively conveys depth. Thick, even contour lines describe full-volumed faces and suggest solid forms beneath the drapery, all with the utmost economy. This simplicity of form and line, along with the measured cadence of the poses, creates an air of monumental dignity.

TANG CERAMIC SCULPTURE Tang ceramists also achieved renown and produced thousands of earthenware figures of people, domesticated animals, and fantastic creatures for burial in tombs. These statuettes attest to a demand for ceramic sculpture by a much wider group of patrons than ever before, but terracotta funerary sculpture has a long history in China. The most spectacular example is the ceramic army (FIG. 7-6) of the First Emperor of Qin. The subjects of the Tang figurines are also much more diverse than in earlier periods. The depiction of a broad range of foreigners, including Semitic traders and Central Asian musicians on camels, accurately reflects the cosmopolitanism of Tang China.

7-18 Palace ladies, detail of a wall painting, tomb of Princess Yongtai, Qianxian, China, Tang dynasty, 706. Detail 5′ 10″ high.

The paintings in this Tang princess's tomb depict scenes of pleasant court life. The muralist used thick, even contour lines and did not provide any setting, but the composition effectively conveys depth.

China   195

Chinese Earthenwares and Stonewares

China has no rival in the combined length and richness of its ceramic history. Beginning with the makers of the earliest pots in prehistoric villages, ancient Chinese potters showed a flair for shaping carefully prepared and kneaded clay into diverse, often dramatic and elegant vessel forms. Until Chinese potters developed true *porcelains* (extremely fine, hard, white ceramics; see "Chinese Porcelain," Chapter 27, page 722) in about 1300, they produced only two types of clay vessels or objects—earthenwares and stonewares. For both types, potters used clays colored by mineral impurities, especially iron compounds ranging from yellow to brownish-black.

The clay bodies of *earthenwares* (FIG. 7-2), fired at low temperatures in open pits or simple kilns, remain soft and porous, thus allowing liquids to seep through. Chinese artists also used the low-fire technique to produce terracotta sculptures, even life-size figures of humans and animals (FIG. 7-6). Over time, Chinese potters developed kilns capable of firing clay vessels at much higher temperatures—more than 2,000° Fahrenheit. High temperatures produce *stonewares,* named for their stonelike hardness and density.

Potters in China excelled at the various techniques commonly used to decorate earthenwares and stonewares. Most of these decorative methods depend on changes occurring in the kiln to chemical compounds found in clay as natural impurities. When fired, many compounds change color dramatically, depending on the conditions in the kiln. For example, if little oxygen remains in a hot kiln, iron oxide (rust) turns either gray or brownish-black, whereas an abundance of oxygen produces a reddish hue.

Chinese potters also decorated vessels simply by painting their surfaces. In one of the oldest decorative techniques, the potters applied *slip* (a mixture of clay and water like a fine, thin mud)—by painting, pouring, or dipping—to a clay body not yet fully dry. The natural varieties of clay produced a broad, if not bright, range of colors, as seen in Neolithic vessels (FIG. 7-2). But Chinese potters often added compounds such as iron oxide to the slip to change or intensify the colors. After the vessels had partially dried, the potters could incise lines through the slip down to the clay body to produce designs such as those seen in later Chinese stonewares (FIG. 7-22). Chinese artists also inlaid designs, carving them into plain vessel surfaces and then filling them with slip or soft clay of a contrasting color. These techniques spread throughout East Asia (FIG. 7-29).

To produce a hard, glassy surface after firing, potters coated plain or decorated vessels with a *glaze,* a finely ground mixture of minerals. Clear or highly translucent glazes were often used, but so too were opaque, richly colored glazes. Sometimes the painters allowed the thick glazes to run down the side of a vase or a figurine (FIG. 7-19) to produce dramatic effects.

1 in.

7-19 Neighing horse, Tang dynasty, eighth to ninth century. Glazed earthenware, 1′ 8″ high. Victoria & Albert Museum, London.

Tang ceramists achieved renown for their earthenware figurines decorated with colorful lead glazes that ran in dramatic streams down the sides when a piece was fired, as in this statuette.

The artists painted some figurines with colored slips and decorated others, such as the spirited, handsomely adorned neighing horse in FIG. 7-19, with colorful lead glazes that ran in dramatic streams down the objects' sides when fired (see "Chinese Earthenwares and Stonewares," above). The popularity of the horse as a subject of Chinese art reflects the importance the emperors placed on the quality of their stables. The breed represented here is powerful in build. Its beautifully arched neck terminates in a small, elegant head. Richly harnessed and saddled, the horse testifies to its rider's nobility.

Song Dynasty

The last century of Tang rule brought many popular uprisings and the empire's gradual disintegration. After an interim of internal strife known as the Five Dynasties period (907–960), General Zhao Kuangyin succeeded in consolidating the country once again. He established himself as the first emperor (r. 960–976) of the Song dynasty (960–1279), which ruled China from a capital in the north at Bianliang (modern Kaifeng) during the Northern Song period (960–1127). Under the Song emperors, many of the hereditary privileges of the elite class were curtailed. Political appointments were made on the basis of scores on civil service examinations, and education came to be a more important prerequisite for Song officials than high birth.

The three centuries of Song rule, including the Southern Song period (1127–1279) when the capital was at Lin'an (modern Hangzhou) in southern China, were also a time of extraordinary technological innovation. Under the Song emperors, the Chinese invented the magnetic compass for sea navigation, printing with movable clay type, paper money, and gunpowder. Song China was the most

7-20 FAN KUAN, detail of *Travelers among Mountains and Streams* (FIG. 7-1), Northern Song period, early 11th century. Hanging scroll, ink and colors on silk, entire scroll 6' 7$\frac{1}{4}$" × 3' 4$\frac{1}{4}$"; detail 2' 10$\frac{1}{4}$" high. National Palace Museum, Taibei.

Fan Kuan, a Daoist recluse, spent long days in the mountains studying the effects of light on rock formations and trees. He was one of the first masters at recording light, shade, distance, and texture.

1 ft.

technologically advanced society in the world in the early second millennium.

FAN KUAN For many observers, the Song dynasty also marks the apogee of Chinese landscape painting, which first emerged as a major subject during the Period of Disunity. Although many of the great Northern Song masters worked for the imperial court, FAN KUAN (ca. 960–1030) was a Daoist recluse (see "Daoism and Confucianism," page 186) who shunned the cosmopolitan life of Bianliang. He believed nature was a better teacher than other artists, and he spent long days in the mountains studying configurations of rocks and trees and the effect of sunlight and moonlight on natural forms. Just as centuries later Giorgio Vasari would credit Italian Renaissance painters with the conquest of naturalism (see Chapter 21), so too did Song critics laud Fan Kuan and other leading painters of the day as the first masters of the recording of light, shade, distance, and texture. Yet the comparison with 15th- and 16th-century Italy is misleading. Chinese landscape painters such as Fan Kuan did not aim to produce portraits of specific places. They did not seek to imitate or to reproduce nature. Rather, they sought to capture the essence of nature and of its individual elements using brush and ink on silk. Their paintings are tributes to nature, not representations of individual rock or tree formations.

In *Travelers among Mountains and Streams* (FIG. 7-1), datable to the early 11th century, Fan Kuan painted a vertical landscape of massive mountains rising from the distance. The overwhelming natural forms dwarf the few human and animal figures (for example, the mule train in the lower right corner; FIG. 7-20), which the artist reduced to minute proportions. The nearly seven-foot-long silk hanging scroll cannot contain nature's grandeur, and the landscape

continues in all directions beyond its borders. The painter showed some elements from level ground (for example, the great boulder in the foreground), and others obliquely from the top (the shrubbery on the highest cliff). The shifting perspectives lead the viewer on a journey through the mountains. To appreciate the painted landscape fully, the viewer must focus not only on the larger composition but also on intricate details and on the character of each brush stroke. Numerous "texture strokes" help model massive forms and convey a sense of tactile surfaces. For the face of the mountain, for example, Fan Kuan employed small, pale brush marks, the kind of texture stroke the Chinese call "raindrop strokes."

HUIZONG A century after Fan Kuan painted in the mountains of Shanxi, HUIZONG (1082–1135; r. 1101–1126) assumed the Song throne at Bianliang. Less interested in governing than in the arts, he brought the country to near bankruptcy and lost much of China's territory to the armies of the Tartar Jin dynasty (1115–1234), who captured the Song capital in 1126 and took Huizong prisoner. He died in their hands nine years later. An accomplished poet, calligrapher, and painter, Huizong reorganized the imperial painting academy and required the study of poetry and calligraphy as part of the official training of court painters. *Calligraphy,* or the art of writing, was highly esteemed in China throughout its history, and prominent inscriptions are frequent elements of Chinese paintings (see "Calligraphy and Inscriptions on Chinese Paintings," Chapter 27, page 726). Huizong also promoted the careful study both of nature and of the classical art of earlier periods, and was an avid art collector as well as the sponsor of a comprehensive catalogue of the vast imperial art holdings.

清曉飄凌拂彩霓飛鳴仙禽告瑞忽來儀詩以紀其實

祥瑞故作詩以紀其實

經時不散迤邐歸飛西北陽散感兹

往來都民無不稽首瞻望歎異久之

之端類甚閒適餘皆翱翔如應奏節

飛鳴於空中仰而視之若有歸態

低映端門眾皆仰而視之倏有群鶴

故如正和壬辰上元之次夕忽有祥雲拂鬱

7-21 Attributed to Huizong, *Auspicious Cranes,* Northern Song period, 1112. Section of a handscroll, ink and colors on silk, $1' 8\frac{1}{8}'' \times 4' 6\frac{3}{8}''$. Liaoning Provincial Museum, Shenyang.

The Chinese regarded the 20 white cranes that appeared at Huizong's palace in 1112 as an auspicious sign. This painting of that event is a masterful combination of elegant composition and realistic observation.

A short handscroll (FIG. **7-21**) usually attributed to Huizong is more likely the work of court painters under his direction, but it displays the emperor's style as both calligrapher and painter. Huizong's characters represent one of many styles of Chinese calligraphy. They are made up of thin strokes, and each character is meticulously aligned with its neighbors to form neat vertical rows. The painting depicts cranes flying over the roofs of Bianliang. It is a masterful combination of elegant composition and realistic observation. The painter carefully recorded the black and red feathers of the white cranes and depicted the birds from a variety of viewpoints to suggest they were circling around the roof. Huizong did not, however, choose this subject because of his interest in the anatomy and flight patterns of birds. The painting was a propaganda piece commemorating the appearance of 20 white cranes at the palace gates during a festival in 1112. The Chinese regarded the cranes as an auspicious sign, proof that Heaven had blessed Huizong's rule. Although few would ever have viewed the handscroll, the cranes were also displayed on painted banners on special occasions, where they could be seen by a larger public.

CIZHOU POTTERY Song-era artists also produced superb ceramics. Some reflect their patrons' interests in antiquities and imitate the powerful forms of the Shang and Zhou bronzes. Song ceramics, however, more commonly had elegant shapes with fluid silhouettes. Many featured monochromatic glazes, such as the famous celadon wares, also produced in Korea (FIG. **7-29**). A quite different kind of pottery, loosely classed as Cizhou, emerged

7-22 Meiping vase, from Xiuwi, China, Northern Song period, 12th century. Stoneware, Cizhou type, with sgraffito decoration, $1' 7\frac{1}{2}''$ high. Asian Art Museum of San Francisco, San Francisco (Avery Brundage Collection).

Chinese potters developed the technique of sgraffito (incising the design through a colored slip) during the Northern Song period. This Cizhou vase features vines and flowers created by cutting through a black slip.

7-23 View (*left*) and cross-section (*right;* after L. Liu) of Foguang Si Pagoda, Yingxian, China, Liao dynasty, 1056.

The tallest wooden building in the world is this pagoda in the Yingxian Buddhist temple complex. The nine-story tower shows the Chinese wooden beam-and-bracket construction system at its most ingenious.

in northern China. The example shown (FIG. **7-22**) is a vase of the high-shouldered shape known as *meiping.* Chinese potters developed the subtle techniques of *sgraffito* (incising the design through a colored slip) during the Northern Song period. They achieved the intricate black-and-white design here by cutting through a black slip (see "Chinese Earthenwares and Stonewares," page 196). The tightly twining vine and flower-petal motifs on this vase closely embrace the vessel in a perfect accommodation of surface design to vase shape.

FOGUANG SI PAGODA For two centuries during the Northern Song period, the Liao dynasty (907–1125) ruled part of northern China. In 1056 the Liao rulers built the Foguang Si Pagoda (FIG. **7-23**), the tallest wooden building ever constructed, at Yingxian in Shanxi Province. The *pagoda,* or tower, the building type most often associated with Buddhism in China and other parts of East Asia, is the most eye-catching feature of a Buddhist temple complex. It somewhat resembles the tall towers of Indian temples and their distant ancestor, the Indian stupa (see "The Stupa," Chapter 6, page 163). Like stupas, many early pagodas housed relics and provided a focus for devotion to the Buddha. Later pagodas served other functions, such as housing sacred images and texts. The Chinese and Koreans built both stone and brick pagodas, but wooden pagodas were also common and became the standard in Japan.

The nine-story octagonal pagoda at Yingxian is 216 feet tall and made entirely of wood (see "Chinese Wooden Construction," page

189). Sixty giant four-tiered bracket clusters carry the floor beams and projecting eaves of the five main stories. They rest on two concentric rings of columns at each level. Alternating main stories and windowless mezzanines with cantilevered balconies, set back farther on each story as the tower rises, form an elevation of nine stories altogether. Along with the open veranda on the ground level and the soaring pinnacle, the balconies visually lighten the building's mass. The cross-section (FIG. **7-23**, *right*) shows the symmetrical placement of statues of the Buddha inside, the colossal scale of the ground-floor statue, and the intricacy of the beam-and-bracket system at its most ingenious.

SOUTHERN SONG PERIOD When the Jin captured Bianliang and Emperor Huizong in 1126 and took control of northern China, Gaozong (r. 1127–1162), Huizong's sixth son, escaped and eventually established a new Song capital in the south at Lin'an. From there, he and his successors during the Southern Song period ruled their reduced empire until 1279.

Court sponsorship of painting continued in the new capital, and, as in the Northern Song period, some of the emperors were directly involved with the painters of the imperial painting academy. During the reign of Ningzong (r. 1194–1224), members of the court, including Ningzong himself and Empress Yang, frequently added brief poems to the paintings created under their direction. Some of the painters belonged to families that had worked for the Song emperors for several generations.

The Chinese inscription in the upper right reads (top to bottom, right to left):

觸袖野色多自錄
避人出嶌不成啼

7-24 MA YUAN, *On a Mountain Path in Spring*, Southern Song period, early 13th century. Album leaf, ink and colors on silk, $10\frac{3}{4}'' \times 17''$. National Palace Museum, Taibei.

Unlike Fan Kuan (FIG. 7-1), Ma Yuan reduced the landscape on this silk album leaf to a few elements and confined them to one part of the page. A tall solitary figure gazes out into the infinite distance.

7-24A XIA GUI, *Twelve Views from a Thatched Hut*, ca. 1200–1225.

MA YUAN The most famous Song family of painters was the Ma family, which began working for the Song dynasty during the Northern Song period. MA YUAN (ca. 1160–1225) painted *On a Mountain Path in Spring* (FIG. 7-24), a silk album leaf, for Ningzong in the early 13th century. In his composition, in striking contrast to Fan Kuan's much larger *Travelers among Mountains and Streams* (FIG. 7-1), the landscape is reduced to a few elements and confined to the foreground and left side of the page. A tall solitary figure gazes out into the infinite distance. Framing him are the carefully placed diagonals of willow branches. Near the upper right corner a bird flies toward the couplet that Ningzong added in ink, demonstrating his mastery of both poetry and calligraphy:

> *Brushed by his sleeves, wild flowers dance in the wind;*
> *Fleeing from him, hidden birds cut short their songs.*

Some scholars have suggested that the author of the two-line poem is actually Empress Yang, but the inscription is in Ningzong's hand. In any case, landscape paintings such as this one are perfect embodiments of the Chinese ideals of peace and unity with nature.

LIANG KAI Religious painting was also popular under the Southern Song emperors. Neo-Confucianism, a blend of traditional Chinese thought and selected Buddhist concepts, became the leading philosophy, but many painters still depicted Buddhist themes. Chan Buddhism (see "Chan Buddhism," page 201), which stressed the quest for personal enlightenment through meditation, flourished under the Song dynasty. LIANG KAI (active early 13th century) was a master of an abbreviated, expressive style of ink painting that found great favor among Chan monks in China, Korea, and Japan. He served in the painting academy of the imperial court in Hangzhou, and his early works include poetic landscapes typical of the Southern Song. Later in life, he left the court and concentrated on figure painting, including Chan subjects.

Surviving works attributed to Liang Kai include an ink painting (FIG. 7-25) of the Sixth Chan Patriarch, Huineng, crouching as he chops bamboo. In Chan thought, the performance of even such mundane tasks had the potential to become a spiritual exercise. More specifically, this scene represents the patriarch's "Chan moment," when the sound of the blade striking the bamboo resonates within his spiritually attuned mind to propel him through the final doorway to enlightenment. The scruffy, caricature-like representation of the revered figure suggests that worldly matters, such as physical appearance or signs of social status, do not burden Huineng's mind. Liang Kai used a variety of brushstrokes in the execution of this deceptively simple picture. Most are pale and wet, ranging from the fine lines of Huineng's beard to the broad texture strokes of the tree. A few darker strokes, which define the vine growing around the tree and the patriarch's clothing, offer visual accents in the painting. This kind of quick

Chan Buddhism

Under the Song emperors (960–1279), the new school of *Chan* Buddhism gradually gained importance, until it was second only to Neo-Confucianism.

The Chan school traced its origins through a series of patriarchs (the founder and early leaders, joined in a master–pupil lineage). The First Chan Patriarch was Bodhidharma, a semilegendary sixth-century Indian missionary. By the time of the Sixth Chan Patriarch, Huineng (638–713; FIG. **7-25**), in the early Tang period, the religious forms and practices of the school were already well established.

Although Chan monks adapted many of the rituals and ceremonies of other schools over the course of time, they focused on the cultivation of the mind or spirit of the individual in order to break through the illusions of ordinary reality, especially by means of meditation.

In Chan thought, the means of enlightenment lie within the individual, and direct personal experience with some ultimate reality is the necessary step to its achievement. Meditation is a critical practice. In fact, the word "Chan" is a translation of the Sanskrit word for meditation. Bodhidharma is said to have meditated so long in a cave that his arms and legs withered away.

The "Northern School" of Chan holds that enlightenment comes only gradually after long meditation. The "Southern School" believes that the breakthrough to enlightenment can be sudden and spontaneous.

These beliefs influenced art and aesthetics as they developed in China and spread to Korea and Japan. In Japan, Chan (Japanese *Zen*) had an especially extensive, long-term impact on the arts and remains an important school of Buddhism there today (see "Zen Buddhism," Chapter 28, page 736).

1 in.

7-25 LIANG KAI, *Sixth Chan Patriarch Chopping Bamboo,* **Southern Song period, early 13th century. Hanging scroll, ink on paper, 2′ 5¼″ high. Tokyo National Museum, Tokyo.**

Liang Kai was a master of an expressive style of ink painting. Here, he depicted the Sixth Chan Patriarch's "Chan moment," when the chopping sound of his blade propelled the patriarch to enlightenment.

and seemingly casual execution of paintings has traditionally been interpreted as a sign of a painter's ability to produce compelling pictures spontaneously as a result of superior training and character, or, in the Chan setting, progress toward enlightenment.

ZHOU JICHANG Another leading Southern Song painter of Buddhist themes was ZHOU JICHANG (ca. 1130–1190), who painted *Lohans Giving Alms to Beggars* (FIG. **7-26**) around 1178. The scroll was one in a series of 100 scrolls produced at the southern coastal city of Ningbo for an abbot who invited individual donors to pay for the paintings as offerings in the nearby Buddhist temple. *Lohans* are enlightened disciples of the Buddha who have achieved freedom

from rebirth (nirvana) by suppression of all desire for earthly things. They were charged with protecting the Buddhist Law until the arrival of the Buddha of the Future. In his Ningbo scroll, Zhou Jichang arranged the foreground, middle ground, and background vertically to clarify the lohans' positions relative to one another and to the beggars. The lohans move with slow dignity in a plane above the ragged wretches who scramble miserably for the alms their serene benefactors throw down. The extreme difference in deportment between the two groups distinguishes their status, as do their contrasting features. The lohans' vividly colored attire, flowing draperies, and quiet gestures set them off from the dirt-colored and jagged shapes of the people physically and spiritually beneath them. In this painting,

KOREA

Korea is a northeast Asian peninsula that shares borders with China and Russia and faces the islands of Japan (MAP 7-1). Korea's pivotal location is a key factor in understanding the relationship of its art to that of China and the influence of its art on that of Japan. Ethnically, the Koreans are related to the peoples of eastern Siberia and Mongolia as well as to the Japanese. At first, the Koreans used Chinese characters to write Korean words, but later they invented their own phonetic alphabet. Korean art, although frequently based on Chinese models, is not merely derivative but has, like Korean civilization, a distinct identity.

Three Kingdoms Period

Pottery-producing cultures appeared on the Korean peninsula in the Neolithic period no later than 6000 BCE, and the Korean Bronze Age dates from ca. 1000 BCE. Bronze technology was introduced from the area that is today northeastern China (formerly known as Manchuria). About 100 BCE, during the Han dynasty, the Chinese established outposts in Korea. The most important was Lelang, which became a prosperous commercial center. By the middle of the century, however, three native kingdoms—Koguryo, Paekche, and Silla—controlled most of the Korean peninsula and reigned for more than seven centuries until Silla completed its conquest of its neighbors in 668. During this era, known as the Three Kingdoms period (ca. 57 BCE–688 CE), Korea remained in continuous contact with both China and Japan. Buddhism was introduced into Korea from China in the fourth century CE. The Koreans in turn transmitted it from the peninsula to Japan in the sixth century.

SILLA CROWN Tombs of the Silla kingdom have yielded spectacular artifacts representative of the wealth and power of its rulers. Finds in the region of Kyongju justify the city's ancient name—Kumsong ("City of Gold"). The gold-and-jade crown (FIG. 7-27) from a tomb at Hwangnamdong, near Kyongju, dated to the fifth or sixth century, also attests to the high quality of artisanship among Silla artists. The crown's major elements, the band and the uprights, as well as the myriad spangles adorning them, were cut from sheet gold and embossed along the edges. Gold rivets and wires secure the whole, as do the comma-shaped pieces of jade further embellishing the crown. Archaeologists interpret the uprights as stylized tree and antler forms believed to symbolize life and supernatural power. The Hwangnamdong crown has no counterpart in China, although the technique of working sheet gold may have come to Korea from northeast China.

Unified Silla Kingdom

Aided by China's emperor, the Silla kingdom conquered the Koguryo and Paekche kingdoms and unified Korea in 668. The era of the Unified Silla Kingdom (688–935) is roughly contemporary with the Tang dynasty's brilliant culture in China, and many consider it to be Korea's golden age.

BUDDHIST SOKKURAM The Silla rulers embraced Buddhism both as a source of religious enlightenment and as a protective force. They considered the magnificent Buddhist temples they constructed in and around their capital of Kyongju to be supernatural defenses against external threats as well as places of worship. Unfortunately, none of these temples survived Korea's turbulent history.

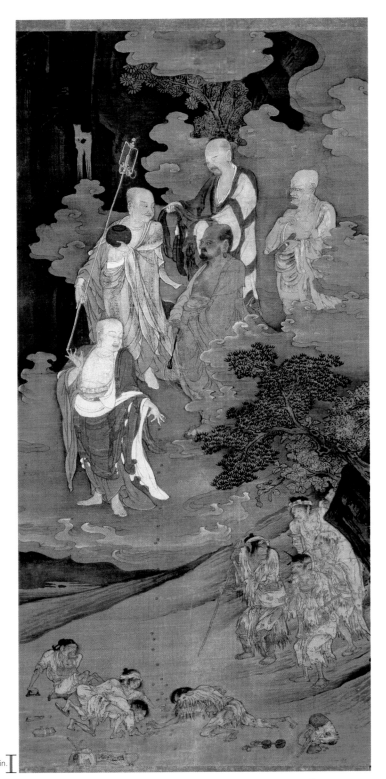

1 in.

7-26 ZHOU JICHANG, *Lohans Giving Alms to Beggars,* Southern Song period, ca. 1178. Hanging scroll, ink and colors on silk, 3′ 7⅞″ × 1′ 8⅞″. Museum of Fine Arts, Boston.

In this hanging scroll made for a Buddhist monastery, Zhou Jichang arranged the fore-, middle-, and background vertically to elevate the lohans in their bright attire above the ragged, dirt-colored beggars.

consistent with Xie He's principles (see "Xie He's Six Canons," page 191), Zhou Jichang used color for symbolic and decorative purposes, not to imitate nature or depict the appearance of individual forms. The composition of the landscape—the cloudy platform and lofty peaks of the lohans and the desertlike setting of the beggars—also distinguishes the two spheres of being.

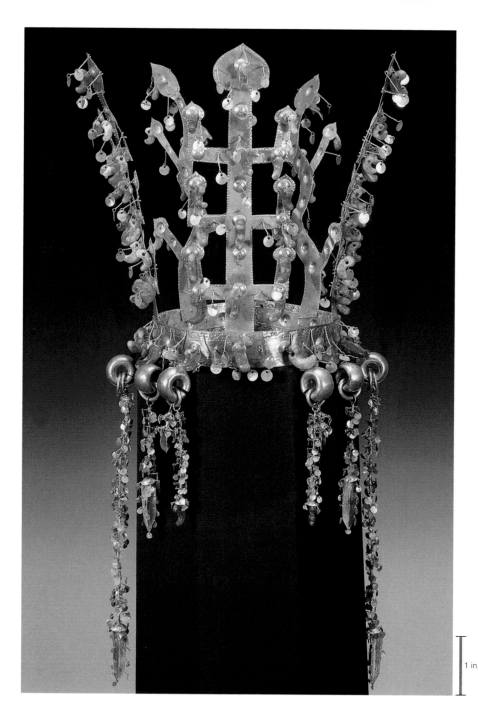

7-27 Crown, from north mound of tomb 98, Hwangnamdong, near Kyongju, Korea, Three Kingdoms period, fifth to sixth century. Gold and jade, $10\frac{3}{4}''$ high. Kyongju National Museum, Kyongju.

This gold-and-jade crown from a Silla tomb attests to the wealth of that kingdom and the skill of its artists. The uprights may be stylized tree and antler forms symbolizing life and supernatural power.

1 in.

However, at Sokkuram, near the summit of Mount Toham, northeast of the city, a splendid granite Buddhist monument is preserved. Scant surviving records suggest that Kim Tae-song, a member of the royal family who served as prime minister, supervised its construction. He initiated the project in 742 to honor his parents in his previous life. Certainly the intimate scale of Sokkuram and the quality of its reliefs and freestanding figures support the idea that the monument was a private chapel for royalty.

The main *rotunda* (circular area under a dome; FIG. **7-28**) measures about 21 feet in diameter. Despite its modest size, the Sokkuram project required substantial resources. Unlike the Chinese Buddhist caves at Longmen (FIG. **7-14**), the interior wall surfaces and sculpture were not cut from the rock in the process of excavation. Instead, workers assembled hundreds of granite pieces of various shapes and sizes, attaching them with stone rivets instead of mortar.

Sculpted images of bodhisattvas, lohans, and guardians line the lower zone of the wall. Above, 10 niches contain miniature statues of seated bodhisattvas and believers. All these figures face inward toward the 11-foot-tall statue of Shakyamuni, the historical Buddha, which dominates the chamber and faces the entrance. Carved from a single block of granite, the image represents the Buddha as he touched the earth to call it to witness the realization of his enlightenment at Bodh Gaya (FIG. **6-11***b*). Although remote in time and place from the Sarnath Buddha (FIG. **6-13**) in India, this majestic image remains faithful to its iconographic prototype. More immediately, the Korean statue draws on the robust, round-faced figures (FIG. **7-14**) of Tang China, and its drapery is a more schematic version of the fluid type found in Tang sculpture. However, the figure has a distinctly broad-shouldered dignity combined with harmonious proportions that are without close precedents. Art historians consider it one of the finest images of the Buddha in East Asia.

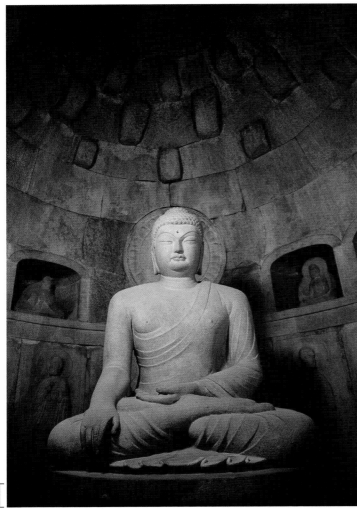

1 ft.

7-28 Shakyamuni Buddha, in the rotunda of the cave temple, Sokkuram, Korea, Unified Silla Kingdom, 751–774. Granite, 11′ high.

Unlike rock-cut Chinese Buddhist shrines, this Korean cave temple was constructed using granite blocks. Dominating the rotunda is a huge statue depicting the Buddha at the moment of his enlightenment.

1 in.

7-29 Maebyong vase, Koryo dynasty, ca. 918–1000. Celadon with inlaid decoration, 1′ 4½″ tall. Kansong Art Museum, Seoul.

Celadon wares feature highly translucent iron-pigmented glazes with incised designs. This green maebyong vase is decorated with engraved cranes highlighted by white and colored slip in the incised lines.

Koryo Dynasty

Although Buddhism was the established religion of Korea, Confucianism, introduced from China during the Silla era, increasingly shaped social and political conventions. In the ninth century, the three old kingdoms began to reemerge as distinct political entities, but by 935 the Koryo (from Koguryo) had taken control, and they dominated for the next three centuries. The Unified Silla and Koryo kingdoms overlap slightly (the period ca. 918–935) because both kingdoms existed during these shifts in power. In 1231 the Mongols, who had invaded China, pushed into Korea, beginning a war lasting 30 years. In the end, the Koryo had to submit to forming an alliance with the Mongols, who eventually conquered all of China (see Chapter 27).

CELADON WARE Koryo potters in the 12th century produced the famous Korean *celadon* wares, admired worldwide. Celadon wares feature highly translucent iron-pigmented glazes, fired in an oxygen-deprived kiln to become gray, pale blue, pale green, or brownish-olive. Incised or engraved designs in the vessel alter the thickness of the glaze to produce elegant tonal variations.

A vase in the shape called *maebyong* in Korean (FIG. 7-29; *meiping* in Chinese, FIG. 7-22) probably dates to the early Koryo period (ca. 918–1000). It is decorated using the inlay technique for which Koryo potters were famous. The artist incised delicate motifs of flying cranes—some flying down and others, in *roundels* (circular frames), flying up—into the clay's surface and then filled the grooves with white and colored slip. Next, the potter covered the incised areas with the celadon green glaze. Variation in the spacing of the motifs shows the potter's sure sense of the dynamic relationship between ornamentation and ceramic volume.

KOREA, CHINA, AND JAPAN China's achievements in virtually every field spread beyond even the boundaries of the vast empires it at various times controlled. Although Buddhism began in India, the Chinese adaptations and transformations of its teachings, religious practices, and artistic forms were those that spread farther east. The cultural debt of China's neighbors to China is immense. Nevertheless, Korea was the crucial artistic, cultural, and religious link between the mainland and the islands of Japan, the subject of Chapter 8.

CHINA AND KOREA TO 1279

SHANG DYNASTY, ca. 1600–1050 BCE

▌ The Shang dynasty was the first great Chinese dynasty of the Bronze Age. The Shang kings ruled from a series of capitals in the Yellow River valley.

▌ Shang bronze-workers were among the best in the ancient world and created a wide variety of elaborately decorated vessels using a sophisticated piece-mold casting process.

Guang, from Anyang,
12th or 11th century BCE

ZHOU AND QIN DYNASTIES, ca. 1050–206 BCE

▌ The Zhou dynasty was the longest in China's history. The Western Zhou kings (ca. 1050–771 BCE) ruled from Chang'an and the Eastern Zhou kings (770–256 BCE) from Luoyang. During the last centuries of Zhou rule, Daoism and Confucianism gained wide followings in China.

▌ Zhou artists produced lavish works in bronze, lacquer, and especially jade.

▌ China's First Emperor founded the short-lived Qin dynasty (221–206 BCE) after defeating the Zhou and all other rival states.

▌ A terracotta army of more than 6,000 soldiers guarded the First Emperor's burial mound at Lintong. The tomb itself remains unexcavated.

Army of the First Emperor of Qin,
Lintong, ca. 210 BCE

HAN DYNASTY AND PERIOD OF DISUNITY, 206 BCE–581 CE

▌ The Han dynasty (206 BCE–220 CE) extended China's boundaries to the south and west and even traded indirectly with Rome via the fabled Silk Road.

▌ Earthenware models found in tombs give a good idea of the appearance and construction methods of Han wooden buildings.

▌ Civil strife divided China into competing states from 220 to 581 CE. The earliest Chinese images of the Buddha and the first paintings that can be associated with an artist whose name was recorded date to this so-called Period of Disunity.

▌ In the early sixth century, Xie He formulated his six canons of Chinese painting.

Model of a Han dynasty house,
first century CE

TANG DYNASTY, 618–907

▌ China enjoyed unequaled prosperity and power under the Tang emperors, whose capital at Chang'an became the greatest and most cosmopolitan city in the world.

▌ The Tang dynasty was the golden age of Chinese figure painting. The few surviving works include Yan Liben's *The Thirteen Emperors* handscroll illustrating historical figures as exemplars of Confucian ideals. The Dunhuang caves provide evidence of the magnificence of Tang Buddhist art, especially mural painting.

▌ Korea also enjoyed an artistic golden age at this time under the Unified Silla Kingdom (688–935).

Yan Liben, *The Thirteen Emperors*,
ca. 650

SONG DYNASTY, 960–1279

▌ Song China (Northern Song, 960–1127, capital at Bianliang; Southern Song, 1127–1279, capital at Lin'an) was the most technologically advanced society in the world in the early second millennium.

▌ In art, the Song era marked the apogee of Chinese landscape painting. Fan Kuan, a Daoist recluse, was a pioneer in recording light, shade, distance, and texture in his hanging scrolls.

▌ For part of this period, the Liao dynasty (907–1125) ruled northern China and erected the tallest wooden building in the world, the Foguang Si Pagoda at Yingxian.

Fan Kuan, *Travelers among Mountains
and Streams*, early 11th century

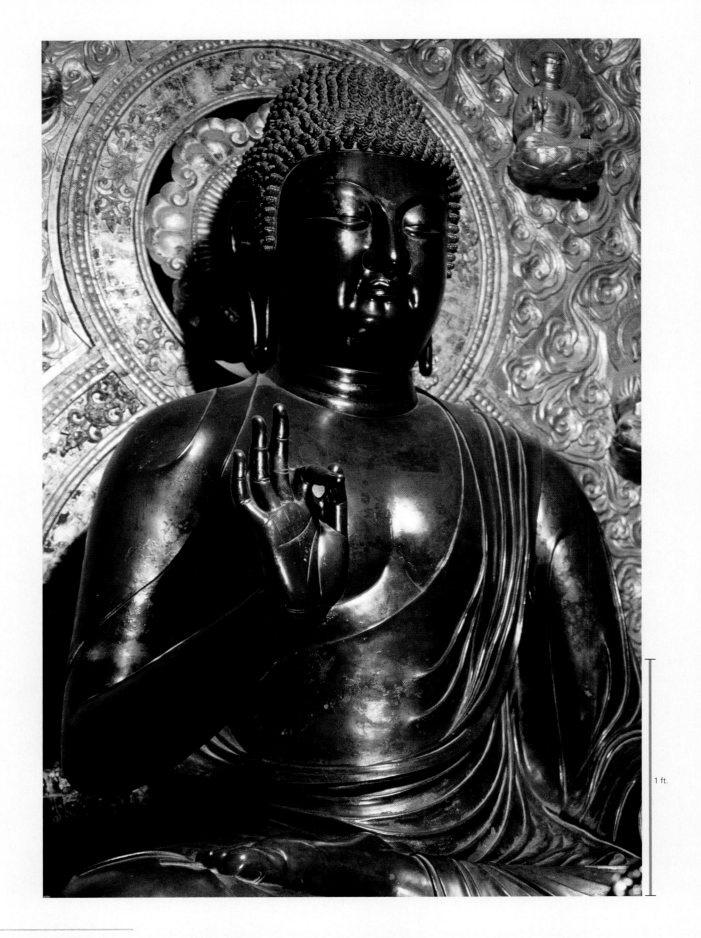

8-1 Detail of Yakushi, Yakushi triad (FIG. 8-8), kondo, Yakushiji, Nara Prefecture, Japan, Nara period, late seventh or early eighth century CE. Bronze, detail 3′ 10″ high.

The introduction of Buddhism in 552 CE profoundly changed the character of Japanese art and architecture. This early masterpiece of Japanese Buddhist sculpture reveals debts to both China and India.

1 ft.

8

JAPAN BEFORE 1333

The Japanese archipelago (MAP **8-1**) consists of four main islands—Hokkaido, Honshu, Shikoku, and Kyushu—and hundreds of smaller ones, a surprising number of them inhabited. Over the centuries, the Japanese have demonstrated a remarkable ability to surmount geographical challenges, such as Japan's mountainous island terrain that makes travel and communication difficult. Japanese culture, however, does not reveal the isolation typical of some island civilizations but rather reflects a responsiveness to imported ideas, such as Buddhism and Chinese writing systems, that filtered in from continental eastern Asia. Acknowledging this responsiveness to mainland influences does not suggest that Japan simply absorbed these imported ideas and practices. Indeed, throughout its history, Japan has developed a truly distinct culture. Ultimately, Japan's close proximity to the continent has promoted extensive exchange with mainland cultures, but the sea has helped protect it from outright invasions and allowed it to develop an individual and unique character.

JAPAN BEFORE BUDDHISM

The introduction of Buddhism to Japan in 552 CE so profoundly changed the character of Japanese art and architecture that art historians traditionally divide the early history of art in Japan into pre-Buddhist and Buddhist eras.

Jomon and Yayoi Periods

Japan's earliest distinct culture, the Jomon (ca. 10,500–300 BCE), emerged roughly 10,000 years before the Buddha's birth. The term *jomon* ("cord markings") refers to the technique Japanese potters of this era used to decorate earthenware vessels. The Jomon people were hunter-gatherers, but unlike most hunter-gatherer societies, which were nomadic, the Jomon enjoyed surprisingly settled lives. Their villages consisted of pit dwellings—shallow round excavations with raised earthen rims and thatched roofs. Their settled existence permitted the Jomon people to develop distinctive ceramic technology, even before their

MAP 8-1 Japan before 1333.

development of agriculture. In fact, archaeologists have dated some ceramic
sherds (pottery fragments) found in
Japan to before 10,000 BCE—older than
sherds from any other area of the world.

MIDDLE JOMON POTTERY
In addition to rope markings, incised
lines and applied coils of clay adorned
Jomon pottery surfaces. The most impressive examples come from the Middle
Jomon period (2500–1500 BCE). Much of
the population then lived in the mountainous inland region, where lo-cal variations in ceramic form and surface treatment flourished. However, all Jomon
potters shared a highly developed feeling
for modeled, rather than painted, ceramic ornament. Jomon pottery displays
such a wealth of applied clay coils,
striped incisions, and sometimes quasi-
figural motifs that the sculptural treatment in certain instances even jeopar-
dizes the basic functionality of the vessel.
Jomon vessels served a wide variety of
purposes, from storage to cooking to
bone burial. Some of the most elaborate
pots may have served ceremonial functions. A dramatic example (FIG. 8-2)
from Miyanomae shows a characteristic,

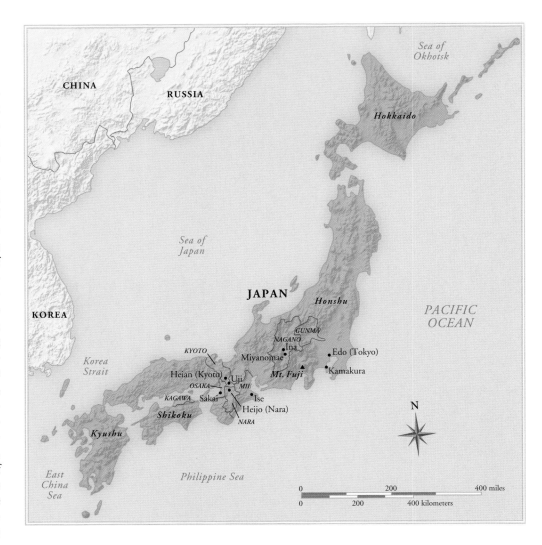

intricately modeled surface and a partially sculpted rim. Jomon pottery
contrasts strikingly with China's most celebrated Neolithic earthenwares (FIG. 7-2) in that the Japanese vessels are extremely thick and
heavy. The harder, thinner, and lighter Neolithic Chinese earthenware
emphasizes basic ceramic form and painted decoration.

YAYOI Jomon culture gradually gave way to Yayoi (ca. 300 BCE–
300 CE). The period takes its name from the Yayoi district of Tokyo,
where evidence of this first post-Jomon civilization was discovered, but
the culture emerged in Kyushu, the southernmost of the main Japanese
islands, and spread northward. Increased interaction with both China
and Korea and immigration from Korea brought dramatic social and
technological transformations during the Yayoi period. People continued to live in pit dwellings, but their villages grew in size, and they developed fortifications, indicating a perceived need for defense. In the
third century CE, Chinese visitors noted that Japan had walled towns,
many small kingdoms, and a highly stratified social structure. Wet-rice
agriculture provided the social and economic foundations for such development. The Yayoi period was a time of tremendous change in Japanese material culture as well. The Yayoi produced pottery that was less
sculptural than Jomon ceramics and sometimes polychrome, and they
developed bronze casting and loom weaving.

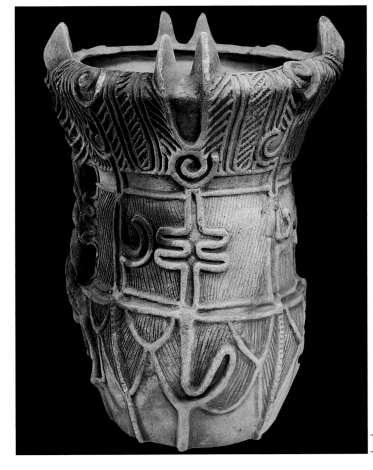

**8-2 Vessel, from Miyanomae, Nagano Prefecture, Japan, Middle Jomon
period, 2500–1500 BCE. Earthenware, 1′ 11$\frac{2}{3}$″ high. Tokyo National
Museum, Tokyo.**

Jomon pottery is the earliest art form of Japan. Characteristic features
are the applied clay coils, striped incisions, and quasi-figural motifs that
in some examples jeopardize the functionality of the vessel.

8-3 Dotaku with incised figural motifs, from Kagawa Prefecture, Japan, late Yayoi period, 100–300 CE. Bronze, 1′ 4⅞″ high. Tokyo National Museum, Tokyo.

Yayoi dotaku were based on Han Chinese bells, but they were ceremonial objects, not musical instruments. They feature geometric decoration and the earliest Japanese images of people and animals.

DOTAKU Among the most intriguing objects Yayoi artisans produced were *dotaku*, or bells. They resemble Han Chinese bell forms, but the Yayoi did not use dotaku as musical instruments. The bells were treasured ceremonial bronzes and the Japanese often deposited them in graves. Cast in clay molds, these bronzes generally featured raised geometric decoration presented in bands or blocks. On some of the hundreds of surviving dotaku, including the example illustrated here (FIG. 8-3), the ornament consists of simple line drawings of people and animals. Scholars have reached no consensus on the meaning of these images. In any case, the dotaku engravings are the earliest extant examples of pictorial art in Japan.

Kofun Period

Historians named the succeeding Kofun period (ca. 300–552)* after the enormous earthen burial mounds, or *tumuli*, that had begun to appear in the third century (*ko* means "old"; *fun* means "tomb"). The tumuli recall the earlier Jomon practice of placing the dead on sacred mountains. The mounds grew dramatically in number and scale in the fourth century.

TOMB OF NINTOKU The largest tumulus (FIG. 8-4) in Japan is at Sakai and is usually identified as the tomb of Emperor Nintoku, although many scholars think the tumulus postdates his death in 399. The central mound, which takes the "keyhole" form standard for tumuli during the Kofun period, is approximately 1,600 feet long and rises to a height of 90 feet. Surrounded by three moats, the entire site covers 458 acres. Numerous objects were placed with the coffin in a stone-walled burial chamber near the summit of the mound to assist in the deceased's transition to the next life. For exalted individuals like Emperor Nintoku, objects buried included important symbolic items and imperial regalia—mirrors, swords, and comma-shaped jewels. Numerous bronze mirrors came from China, but the form of the tombs themselves and many of the burial goods suggest even closer connections with Korea. For example, the comma-shaped jewels are quite similar to those found on Korean Silla crowns (FIG. 7-27), whose simpler gilt bronze counterparts lay in the Japanese tombs.

*From this point on, all dates in this chapter are CE unless otherwise stated.

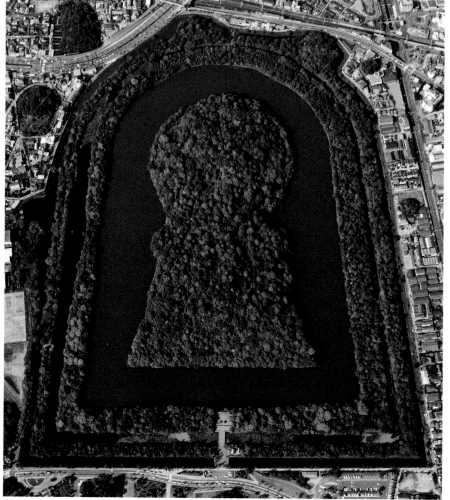

8-4 Tomb of Emperor Nintoku, Sakai, Osaka Prefecture, Japan, Kofun period, late fourth to early fifth century.

The largest Kofun tumulus, attributed to Emperor Nintoku, has a keyhole shape and three surrounding moats. About 20,000 clay haniwa (FIG. 8-5) were originally displayed on the giant earthen mound.

The Japanese of the Kofun period set the statues both in curving rows around the tumulus and in groups around a haniwa house placed directly over the deceased's burial chamber. Presumably, the number of sculptures reflected the stature of the dead person. Emperor Nintoku's tumulus had about 20,000 haniwa statues placed around the mound.

SHRINE OF AMATERASU The religious system the Japanese embraced during the Yayoi and Kofun eras is known as Shinto (see "Shinto," page 211). The Japanese imperial clan traces its origins to the Shinto sun goddess Amaterasu. Her shrine (FIG. **8-6**) at Ise is the most important Shinto religious center. The location, use, and ritual reconstruction of this shrine every 20 years reflect the primary characteristics of Shinto—sacred space, ritual renewal, and purification. The Ise shrine is traditionally dated to the Kofun period. Many scholars now favor a later date, but the shrine still serves as a representative example of sacred architecture in ancient Japan. Although Japanese shrine architecture varies tremendously, scholars believe the Ise shrine preserves some of the very earliest design elements. Yet the Ise shrine is unique. Because of its connection to the Japanese imperial family, no other shrines may be constructed with the identical design. The original source for the form of the Ise complex's main hall appears to be Japanese granaries. Granaries were among the most important buildings in Japan's early agrarian society. Although not every aspect of the Ise shrine is equally ancient, the three main structures of the inner shrine convey some sense of Japanese architecture before the introduction of Buddhism and before the development of more elaborately constructed and adorned buildings.

Aside from the thatched roofs and some metallic decorations, the sole construction material at Ise is wood, fitted together in a *mortise-and-tenon* system, in which the builders slip the wallboards into slots in the pillars. Two massive freestanding posts (once great cypress trunks), one at each end of the main sanctuary, support most of the weight of the *ridgepole,* the beam at the crest of the roof. The golden-hued cypress columns and planks contrast in color and texture with the white gravel covering the sacred grounds. The roof was originally constructed of thatch, which was smoked, sewn into bundles, and then laid in layers. The smooth shearing of the entire surface produced a gently changing contour. Today, cypress bark covers the roof. Decorative elements (originally having a structural function) enhance the roofline and include *chigi*, extensions of the rafters at each end of the roof, and *katsuogi*, wooden logs placed at right angles across the ridgepole to hold the thatch of the roof in place. The Amaterasu shrine highlights the connection, central to Shinto, between nature and spirit. Not only are the construction materials derived from the natural world, but the shrine also stands at a specific location where a kami is believed to have taken up residence.

BUDDHIST JAPAN

In 552, according to traditional interpretation, the ruler of Paekche, one of Korea's Three Kingdoms (see Chapter 7), sent Japan's ruler a gilded bronze statue of the Buddha along with *sutras* (Buddhist scriptures) translated into Chinese, at the time the written language of eastern Asia. This event marked the beginning of the Asuka period (552–645), when Japan's ruling elite embraced major elements of continental Asian culture that had been gradually filtering into Japan. These cultural components became firmly established in Japan and included Chinese writing, Confucianism (see "Daoism and Confucianism," Chapter 7, page 186), and Buddhism (see "Buddhism and Buddhist Iconography," Chapter 6, page 161). In 645 a

1 ft.

8-5 Haniwa warrior, from Gunma Prefecture, Japan, Kofun period, fifth to mid-sixth century. Low-fired clay, 4′ 3¼″ high. Tokyo National Museum, Tokyo. ■◀

During the Kofun period, the Japanese set up cylindrical clay statues (haniwa) of humans, animals, and objects on burial tumuli. They served as a protective spiritual barrier between the living and the dead.

HANIWA The Japanese also placed unglazed ceramic sculptures called *haniwa* on and around the Kofun tumuli. These sculptures, usually several feet in height, as is the warrior shown here (FIG. **8-5**), are distinctly Japanese. Compared with the Chinese terracotta soldiers and horses (FIG. **7-6**) buried with the First Emperor of Qin, these statues appear deceptively whimsical as variations on a cylindrical theme (*hani* means "clay"; *wa* means "circle"). Yet haniwa sculptors skillfully adapted the basic clay cylinder into a host of forms, from abstract shapes to objects, animals (for example, deer, bears, horses, and monkeys), and human figures, such as warriors and female shamans. These artists altered the shapes of the cylinders, emblazoned them with applied ornaments, excised or built up forms, and then painted the haniwa. The variety of figure types suggests that haniwa functioned not as military guards but as a spiritual barrier protecting both the living and the dead from contamination.

Shinto

The early beliefs and practices of pre-Buddhist Japan, which form a part of the belief system later called Shinto ("Way of the Gods"), did not derive from the teachings of any individual founding figure or distinct leader. Formal scriptures, in the strict sense, do not exist for these beliefs and practices either. Shinto developed in Japan in conjunction with the advent of agriculture during the Yayoi period. Shinto thus originally focused on the needs of this agrarian society and included agricultural rites surrounding planting and harvesting. Villagers venerated and prayed to a multitude of local deities or spirits called *kami*. The early Japanese believed kami existed in mountains, waterfalls, trees, and other features of nature, as well as in charismatic people, and they venerated not only the kami themselves but also the places the kami occupy, which are considered sacred.

Each clan (a local group claiming a common ancestor, and the basic societal unit during the Kofun period) had its own protector kami, to whom members offered prayers in the spring for successful planting and in the fall for good harvests. Clan members built shrines consisting of several buildings for the veneration of kami. Priests made offerings of grains and fruits at these shrines and prayed on behalf of the clans. Rituals of divination, water purification, and ceremonial purification at the shrines proliferated. Visitors to the shrine area had to wash before entering in a ritual of spiritual and physical cleansing.

Purity was such a critical aspect of Japanese religious beliefs that people would abandon buildings and even settlements if negative events, such as poor harvests, suggested spiritual defilement. Even the early imperial court moved several times to newly built towns to escape impurity and the trouble it caused. Such purification concepts are also the basis for the cyclical rebuilding of the sanctuaries at grand shrines. The buildings of the inner shrine (FIG. 8-6) at Ise, for example, have been rebuilt every 20 years for more than a millennium with few interruptions. Rebuilding rids the sacred site of physical and spiritual impurities that otherwise might accumulate. During construction, the old shrine remains standing until the carpenters erect an exact duplicate next to it. In this way, the Japanese have preserved ancient forms with great precision.

When Buddhism arrived in Japan from the mainland in the sixth century, Shinto practices changed under its influence. For example, until the introduction of Buddhism, painted or carved images of Shinto deities did not exist. Yet despite the eventual predominance of Buddhism in Japan, Shinto continues to exist as a vital religion for many Japanese, especially those living in rural areas.

8-6 Main hall, Amaterasu shrine, Ise, Mie Prefecture, Japan, Kofun period or later; rebuilt in 1993.

The most important Shinto shrine in Japan is that of the sun goddess Amaterasu at Ise. Constructed of wood with a thatch roof, the shrine reflects the form of early Japanese granaries.

considerable time lag) that surviving Japanese temples have helped greatly in the reconstruction of what was almost completely lost on the continent.

TORI BUSSHI Among the earliest extant examples of Japanese Buddhist sculpture is a bronze *Buddha triad* (Buddha flanked by two bodhisattvas; FIG. 8-7) dated 623. Empress Suiko commissioned the work as a votive offering when Prince Shotoku fell ill in 621. When he died, the empress dedicated the triad to the prince's well-being in his next life and to his hoped-for rebirth in paradise. The central figure in the triad is Shaka (the Indian/Chinese Sakyamuni), the historical Buddha, seated with his right hand raised in the abhaya mudra (fear-not gesture; see "Buddhism and Buddhist Iconography," Chapter 6, page 161). Behind Shaka is a flaming *mandorla* (a lotus-petal-shaped *nimbus*) incorporating small figures of other Buddhas. The sculptor, TORI BUSSHI (*busshi* means "maker of Buddhist images"), was a descendant of a Chinese immigrant. Tori's Buddha triad reflects the style of the early to mid-sixth century in China and Korea and is characterized by elongated heads and elegantly stylized drapery folds that form gravity-defying swirls.

YAKUSHI TRIAD In the early Nara period, Japanese sculptors began to move beyond the style of the Asuka period in favor of new ideas and forms coming out of Tang China and Korea. More direct relations with China also narrowed the time lag between developments there and their transfer to Japan. In the triad of Yakushi (the Indian Bhaisajyaguru, the Buddha of Healing who presides over the Eastern Pure Land; FIG. 8-8) in the Yakushiji temple of the late seventh century in Nara, the sculptor favored greater anatomical definition and shape-revealing drapery (FIG. 8-1) over the dramatic stylizations of Tori Busshi's triad. The statues of the attendant bodhisattvas Nikko and Gakko, especially, reveal the long stylistic trail back through China (FIG. 7-14) to the sensuous fleshiness (FIG. 6-13) and outthrust-hip poses (FIG. 6-8) of Indian sculpture.

HORYUJI KONDO Tori Busshi created his Shaka triad for an Asuka Buddhist temple complex at Horyuji, seven miles south of modern Nara, but fire destroyed the temple. The statue was reinstalled around 680 in the *kondo* (Golden Hall; the main hall for worship that contained statues of the Buddha and the bodhisattvas to whom the temple was dedicated; FIG. 8-9, *left*) of the successor Nara period complex (FIG. 8-9, *right*). Although periodically repaired and somewhat altered (the covered porch is an eighth-century addition; the upper railing dates to the 17th century), the structure retains its graceful but sturdy forms beneath the modifications. The main pillars (not visible in FIG. 8-9, *left*, due to the porch addition) decrease in diameter from bottom to top. The tapering provides an effective transition between the more delicate brackets above and the columns' stout forms. Also somewhat masked by the added porch is the harmonious reduction in scale from the first to the second story. Following Chinese models, the builders used ceramic tiles as roofing material and adopted the distinctive curved roofline of Tang (FIG. 7-16) and later Chinese architecture. Other buildings at the site include a five-story pagoda (FIG. 8-9, *right*) that serves as a reliquary.

Until a disastrous fire in 1949, the interior walls of the Golden Hall at Horyuji preserved some of the finest examples of Buddhist wall painting in eastern Asia. Executed around 710, when Nara became the Japanese capital, these paintings now survive only in color photographs. The most important paintings depicted the Buddhas of the four directions. Like the other three, Amida (Indian

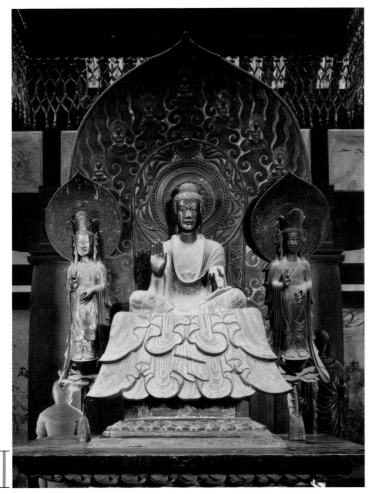

1 ft.

8-7 TORI BUSSHI, Shaka triad, kondo, Horyuji, Nara Prefecture, Japan, Asuka period, 623. Bronze, central figure 5′ 9½″ high.

Tori Busshi's Shaka triad (the historical Buddha and two bodhisattvas) is among the earliest Japanese Buddhist sculptures. The elongated heads and elegant swirling drapery reflect the sculptural style of China.

series of reforms led to the establishment of a centralized government in place of the individual clans that controlled the different regions of Japan. This marked the beginning of the Nara period (645–784), when the Japanese court, ruling from a series of capitals south of modern Kyoto, increasingly adopted the forms and rites of the Chinese court. In 710 the Japanese finally established what they intended as a permanent capital at Heijo (present-day Nara). City planners laid out the new capital on a symmetrical grid closely modeled on the plan of the Chinese capital of Chang'an.

For a half century after 552, Buddhism met with opposition, but by the end of that time, the new religion was established firmly in Japan. Older beliefs and practices (those that came to be known as Shinto) continued to have significance, especially as agricultural rituals and imperial court rites. As time passed, Shinto deities even gained new identities as local manifestations of Buddhist deities.

Asuka and Nara Periods

In the arts associated with Buddhist practices, Japan followed Korean and Chinese prototypes very closely, especially during the Asuka and Nara periods. In fact, early Buddhist architecture in Japan adhered so closely to mainland standards (although generally with a

8-8 Yakushi triad, kondo, Yakushiji, Nara Prefecture, Japan, Nara period, late seventh or early eighth century. Bronze, central figure 8′ 4″ high, including base and mandorla. ▣◀

The sculptor of this Nara Buddha triad favored greater anatomical definition and shape-revealing drapery than the Asuka artist Tori Busshi (FIG. 8-7). The Nara statues display the sensuous fleshiness of Indian sculpture.

8-9 Kondo (*above*) and aerial view of the temple complex (*right*), Horyuji, Nara Prefecture, Japan, Nara period, ca. 680.

The kondo, or Golden Hall, of a Buddhist temple complex housed statues of the Buddha and bodhisattvas. The Horyuji kondo follows Chinese models in its construction method and its curved roofline.

1 ft.

1 ft.

8-10 Amida triad, wall painting formerly in the kondo, Horyuji, Nara Prefecture, Japan, Nara period, ca. 710. Ink and colors, 10′ 3″ × 8′ 6″. Horyuji Treasure House, Nara.

The murals of the Horyuji kondo represented the Buddhas of the four directions. Amida, the Buddha of the Western Pure Land, has red iron-wire lines and reflects Chinese Tang painting style.

designs from paper to wall by piercing holes in the paper and pushing colored powder through the perforations (*pouncing*). As with the Buddha triad (FIG. 8-8) at Yakushiji, the mature Tang style, with its echoes of Indian sensuality, surfaces in this work. The smooth brush lines, thoroughly East Asian, give the figures their substance and life. These lines, often seen in Buddhist painting, are called iron-wire lines because they are thin and of unvarying width with a suggestion of tensile strength. As in many other Buddhist paintings, the lines are red instead of black. The identity of the painters of these pictures is unknown, but some scholars have suggested they were Chinese or Korean rather than Japanese.

DAIBUTSUDEN, TODAIJI At the Todaiji temple complex at Nara, the kondo is known as the Daibutsuden (FIG. 8-11), or Great Buddha Hall. Originally constructed in the eighth century, the Daibutsuden was rebuilt in the early 18th century. The Nara period temple housed a 53-foot bronze image of the Cosmic Buddha, Roshana (Vairocana), inspired by Chinese colossal stone statues (FIG. 7-14) of this type. The commissioning of Todaiji and its Great Buddha statue (Daibutsu) by Emperor Shomu in 743 was historically important as part of an imperial attempt to unify and strengthen the country by using religious authority to reinforce imperial power. The temple served as the administrative center of a network of branch temples built in every province. Thus, the consolidation of imperial authority and thorough penetration of Buddhism throughout the country went hand in hand. The dissemination of a common religion contributed to the eventual disruption of the clan system and the unification of disparate political groups. So important was the erection of both the building and the Daibutsu that court and government officials as well as Buddhist dignitaries from China and India were present at the opening ceremonies in 752. Chinese Buddhist monks also came to Japan in large numbers and were instrumental in spreading Buddhist teachings throughout Japan. Sadly, the current building is significantly smaller than the original. Today the Daibutsuden has 7 bays. The original had 11. Yet even in its diminished size, the Todaiji Great Buddha Hall is the largest wooden building in the world.

Amitabha; FIG. 8-10), the Buddha of immeasurable light and infinite life, ruler of the Western Pure Land, sits enthroned in his paradisical land, attended by bodhisattvas. The exclusive worship of Amida later became a major trend in Japanese Buddhism, and much grander depictions of his paradise appeared, resembling those at Dunhuang (FIG. 7-15) in China. Here, however, the representation is simple and iconic. Although executed on a dry wall, the painting process involved techniques similar to fresco, such as transferring

8-11 Daibutsuden, Todaiji, Nara, Japan, Nara period, 743; rebuilt ca. 1700.

The Great Buddha Hall of the Todaiji temple complex at Nara is the largest wooden building in the world. Constructed by Emperor Shomu in 743, it originally had 11 bays instead of the current 7.

Heian Period

In 784, possibly to escape the power of the Buddhist priests in Nara, the imperial house moved its capital north, eventually relocating in 794 in what became its home until modern times. Originally called Heiankyo ("capital of peace and tranquility"), it is known today as Kyoto. The Heian period (794–1185) of Japanese art takes its name from the new capital. Early in the period, Japan maintained fairly close ties with China, but from the middle of the ninth century on, relations between the two deteriorated so rapidly that court-sponsored contacts had ceased by the end of that century. Japanese culture became much more self-directed than it had been in the preceding few centuries.

ESOTERIC BUDDHISM Among the major developments during the early Heian period was the introduction of Esoteric Buddhism to Japan from China. Esoteric Buddhism is so named because of the secret transmission of its teachings. Two Esoteric sects made their appearance in Japan at the beginning of the Heian period: Tendai in 805 and Shingon in 806. The teachings of Tendai were based on the *Lotus Sutra,* one of the Buddhist scriptural narratives, and Shingon (True Word) teachings on two other sutras. Both Tendai and Shingon Buddhists believe that all individuals possess buddha nature and can achieve enlightenment through meditation rituals and careful living. To aid focus during meditation, Shingon disciples use special hand gestures (mudras) and recite particular words or syllables (*mantras* in Sanskrit, *shingon* in Japanese). Shingon became the primary form of Buddhism in Japan through the mid-10th century.

TAIZOKAI MANDARA Because of the emphasis on ritual and meditation in Shingon, the arts flourished during the early Heian period. Both paintings and sculptures provided followers with visualizations of specific Buddhist deities and allowed them to contemplate the transcendental concepts central to the religion. Of particular importance in Shingon meditation was the *mandara* (*mandala* in Sanskrit), a diagram of the cosmic universe. Among the most famous Japanese mandaras is the Womb World (Taizokai), which usually hung on the wall of a Shingon kondo. The Womb World is composed of 12 zones, each representing one of the various dimensions of buddha nature (for example, universal knowledge, wisdom, achievement, and purity). The mandara illustrated here (FIG. 8-12) is among the oldest and best preserved in Japan and is located at Kyoogokokuji (Toji), the Shingon teaching center established at Kyoto in 823. Many of the figures hold lightning bolts, symbolizing the power of the mind to destroy human passion. The Womb World mandara is one of a pair of paintings. The other depicts the Diamond World (Kongokai). The central motif in the Womb World is the lotus of compassion. In the Diamond World the central motif is the diamond scepter of wisdom. Both of the Toji mandaras reflect Chinese models.

PHOENIX HALL, UJI During the middle and later Heian period, belief in the vow of Amida, the Buddha of the Western Pure Land, to save believers through rebirth in his realm gained great prominence among the Japanese aristocracy. Eventually, the simple message of Pure Land Buddhism—universal salvation—facilitated the spread of Buddhism to all classes of Japanese society. The most

8-12 Taizokai (Womb World) mandara, Kyoogokokuji (Toji), Kyoto, Japan, Heian period, second half of ninth century. Hanging scroll, color on silk, 6′ × 5′ $\frac{5}{8}$″.

The Womb World mandara is a diagram of the cosmic universe, composed of 12 zones, each representing one dimension of Buddha nature. Mandaras played a central role in Esoteric Buddhist rituals and meditation.

1 ft.

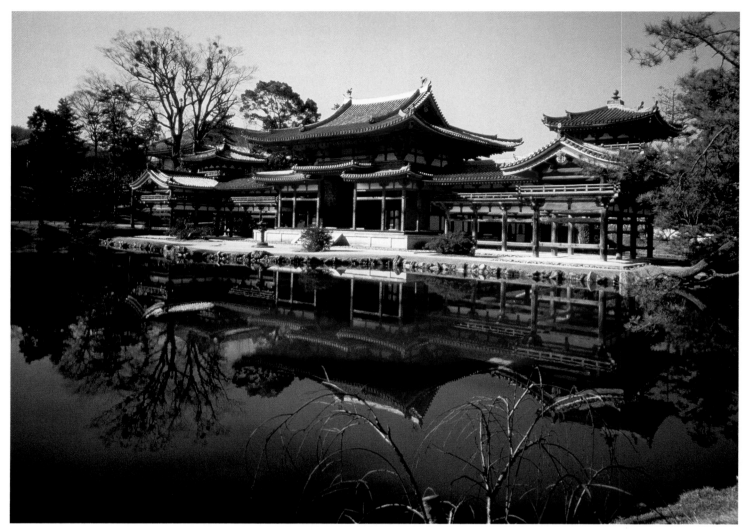

8-13 Phoenix Hall, Byodoin, Uji, Kyoto Prefecture, Japan, Heian period, 1053.

The Phoenix Hall's elaborate winged form evokes images of Amida's palace in the Western Pure Land. Situated on a reflective pond, the temple suggests the floating weightlessness of celestial architecture.

8-13A JOCHO, Seated Amida, Phoenix Hall, Uji, 1053.

important surviving monument in Japan related to Pure Land beliefs is the so-called Phoenix Hall (FIG. 8-13) of the Byodoin. Fujiwara Yorimichi, the powerful regent for three emperors between 1016 and 1068, built the temple in memory of his father, Michinaga, on the grounds of Michinaga's summer villa at Uji. Dedicated in 1053, the Phoenix Hall houses a wooden statue of Amida carved from multiple joined blocks, the predominant wooden sculpture technique by this time. The building's elaborate winged form evokes images of the Buddha's palace in his Pure Land, as depicted in East Asian paintings (FIG. 7-15) in which the architecture reflects the design of Chinese palaces. By placing only light pillars on the exterior, elevating the wings, and situating the whole on a reflective pond, the Phoenix Hall builders suggested the floating weightlessness of celestial architecture. The building's name derives from its overall birdlike shape and from two bronze phoenixes decorating the ridgepole ends. In eastern Asia, these birds were believed to alight on lands properly ruled. Here, they represent imperial might, sometimes associated especially with the empress. The authority of the Fujiwara family derived primarily from the marriage of daughters to the imperial line.

TALE OF GENJI Japan's most admired literary classic is *Tale of Genji,* written around 1000 by Murasaki Shikubu (usually referred to as Lady Murasaki), a lady-in-waiting at the court. Recounting the lives and loves of Prince Genji and his descendants, *Tale of Genji* provides readers with a view of Heian court culture (see "Heian Court Culture," page 217). The oldest extant examples of illustrated copies are fragments from a deluxe set of early-12th-century handscrolls (see "Chinese Painting Materials and Formats," Chapter 7, page 190). From textual and physical evidence, scholars have suggested that the set originally consisted of about 10 handscrolls produced by five teams of artisans. Each team consisted of a nobleman talented in calligraphy, a chief painter who drew the compositions in ink, and assistants who added the color. The script is primarily *hiragana,* a sound-based writing system developed in Japan from Chinese characters. Hiragana originally served the needs of women (who were not taught Chinese) and became the primary script for Japanese court poetry. In these handscrolls, pictures alternate with text, as in Gu Kaizhi's *Admonitions* scrolls (FIG. 7-12). However, the Japanese work focuses on emotionally charged moments in personal relationships rather than on lessons in exemplary behavior.

8-14A FUJIWARA NO SADANOBU, *Ishiyama-gire,* early 12th century.

In the scene illustrated here (FIG. 8-14), Genji meets with his greatest love near the time of her death. The bush-clover in the garden identifies the season as autumn, the season associated with the fading of life and love. A radically upturned ground plane and strong

Heian Court Culture

During the Nara and especially the Heian periods, the Japanese imperial court developed as the center of an elite culture. In a time of peace and prosperity, the aristocracy had the leisure to play musical instruments and write poetry. Exchanging poems became a common social practice and a frequent preoccupation of lovers. Both men and women produced poems as well as paintings and calligraphy that critics generally consider "classical" today. Heian court members, especially those from the great Fujiwara clan that dominated the court for a century and a half and built the Phoenix Hall (FIG. 8-13) at Uji, compiled the first great anthologies of Japanese poetry and wrote Japan's most influential secular prose.

A lady-in-waiting to an empress of the early 11th century wrote the best-known work of literature in Japan, *Tale of Genji*. Known as

Lady Murasaki, the author is one of many important Heian women writers, including especially diarists and poets. Generally considered the world's first lengthy novel (the English translation is almost a thousand pages), *Tale of Genji* tells of the life and loves of Prince Genji and, after his death, of his heirs. The novel and much of Japanese literature consistently display a sensitivity to the sadness in the world caused by the transience of love and life. These human sentiments are often intertwined with the seasonality of nature. For example, the full moon, flying geese, crying deer, and certain plants symbolize autumn, which in turn evokes somber emotions, fading love, and dying. These concrete but evocative images frequently appear in paintings, such as the illustrated scrolls of *Tale of Genji* (FIG. 8-14).

8-14 *Genji Visits Murasaki,* from the Minori chapter, *Tale of Genji,* Heian period, first half of 12th century. Handscroll, ink and color on paper, $8\frac{5}{8}''$ high. Goto Art Museum, Tokyo.

In this handscroll illustrating Lady Murasaki's *Tale of Genji,* the upturned ground plane and diagonal lines suggest three-dimensional space. Flat fields of color emphasize the painting's two-dimensional character.

diagonal lines suggest three-dimensional space. The painter omitted roofs and ceilings to allow a privileged view of the interior spaces where the action takes place. The unusual angles were also intended as metaphors for the emotions of the characters depicted. Flat fields of unshaded color emphasize the painting's two-dimensional character. Rich patterns in the textiles and architectural ornament give a feeling of sumptuousness. The human figures appear constructed of stiff layers of contrasting fabrics, and the artist simplified and generalized the aristocratic faces, using a technique called "a line for the eye and a hook for the nose." This lack of individualization may reflect societal restrictions on looking directly at exalted persons.

Several formal features of the *Genji* illustrations—native subjects, bright mineral pigments, lack of emphasis on strong brushwork, and general flatness—were later considered typical of *yamato-e* (native-style painting; the term *yamato* means "Japan" and is used to describe anything that is characteristically Japanese).

LEGENDS OF MOUNT SHIGI Heian painting was diverse in both style and subject matter. *Legends of Mount Shigi,* painted during the late 12th century, represents a different facet of Heian narrative handscroll painting. The stories belong to a genre of pious Buddhist tales devoted to miraculous events involving virtuous

8-15 The flying storehouse, from *Legends of Mount Shigi*, Heian period, late 12th century. Handscroll, ink and colors on paper, 1′ $\frac{1}{2}$″ high. Chogosonshiji, Nara.

This Heian handscroll is very different from the *Genji* scroll (FIG. 8-14) in both subject and style. The artist exaggerated each feature of the gesticulating and scurrying figures in this Buddhist miracle story.

individuals. Unlike the *Genji* scrolls, short segments of text and pictures do not alternate. Instead, the painters took advantage of the scroll format to present several scenes in a long, unbroken stretch. For example, the first scroll shows the same travelers at several stages of their journey through a continuous landscape.

The *Mount Shigi* scrolls illustrate three miracles associated with a Buddhist monk named Myoren and his mountaintop temple. The first relates the story of the flying storehouse (FIG. 8-15) and depicts Myoren's begging bowl lifting the rice-filled granary of a greedy farmer and carrying it off to the monk's hut in the mountains. The painter depicted the astonished landowner, his attendants, and several onlookers in various poses—some grimacing, others gesticulating wildly and scurrying about in frantic amazement. In striking contrast to the *Genji* scroll figures, the artist exaggerated each feature of the painted figures, but still depicted the actors and architecture seen from above.

Kamakura Period

In the late 12th century, a series of civil wars between rival warrior families led to the end of the Japanese imperial court as a major political and social force. The victors, headed by the Minamoto family, established their *shogunate* (military government) at Kamakura in eastern Japan. The imperial court remained in Kyoto as the theoretical source of political authority, but actual power resided with the *shoguns*. The first shogun was Minamoto Yoritomo, on whom the emperor officially bestowed the title in 1185. The ensuing period of Japanese art is called the Kamakura period (1185–1332), named for

the locale. During the Kamakura shogunate, more frequent and positive contact with China brought with it an appreciation for more recent cultural developments there, ranging from new architectural styles to Zen Buddhism.

SHUNJOBO CHOGEN Rebuilding in Nara after the destruction the civil wars inflicted presented an early opportunity for architectural experimentation. A leading figure in planning and directing the reconstruction efforts was the priest Shunjobo Chogen (1121–1206), who is reputed to have made three trips to China between 1166 and 1176. After learning about contemporary Chinese architecture, he oversaw the rebuilding of Todaiji, among other projects, with generous donations from Minamoto Yoritomo. Chogen's portrait statue (FIG. 8-16) is one of the most striking examples of the high level of naturalism prevalent in the early Kamakura period. Characterized by finely painted details, a powerful rendering of the signs of aging, and the inclusion of such personal attributes as prayer beads, the statue of Chogen exhibits the carving skill and style of the Kei School of sculptors (see "Heian and Kamakura Artistic Workshops," page 219). The Kei School traced its lineage to Jocho, a famous sculptor of the mid-11th century. Its works display fine Heian carving techniques combined with an increased concern for natural volume and detail learned from studying, among other sources, surviving Nara period works and sculptures imported from Song China. Enhancing the natural quality of Japanese portrait statues is the use of inlaid rock crystal for the eyes, a technique found only in Japan.

8-16A UNKEI, Agyo, Todaiji, 1203.

8-16B KOSHO, Kuya preaching early 13th century.

Heian and Kamakura Artistic Workshops

Until the late Heian period, major artistic commissions came almost exclusively from the imperial court or the great temples. As shogun warrior families gained wealth and power, they too became great art patrons—in many cases closely following the aristocrats' precedents in subject and style.

Artists, for the most part, did not work independently but rather were affiliated with workshops. Indeed, until recently, hierarchically organized male workshops produced most Japanese art. Membership in these workshops was often based on familial relationships. Each workshop was dominated by a master, and many of his main assistants and apprentices were relatives. Outsiders of considerable skill sometimes joined workshops, often through marriage or adoption. The eldest son usually inherited the master's position, after rigorous training in the necessary skills from a very young age. Therefore, one meaning of the term "school of art" in Japan is a network of workshops tracing their origins back to the same master, a kind of artistic clan. Inside the workshops, the master and senior assistants handled the most important production stages, but artists of lower rank helped with the more routine work. The Kamakura portrait statue (FIG. 8-16) of Shunjobo Chogen, for example, is the creation of a workshop based on familial ties.

Artistic cooperation also surfaced in court bureaus, an alternative to family workshops. These official bureaus, located at the imperial palace, had emerged by the Heian period. The painting bureau accrued particular fame. Teams of court painters, led by the bureau director, produced pictures such as the scenes in the *Tale of Genji* handscrolls (FIG. 8-14). This system remained vital into the Kamakura period and well beyond. Under the direction of a patron or the patron's representative, the master painter laid out the composition by brushing in the initial outlines and contours. Under his supervision, junior painters applied the colors. The master then completed the work by brushing in fresh contours and details such as facial features. Very junior assistants and apprentices assisted in the process by preparing paper, ink, and pigments. Unlike mastership in hereditarily run workshops, competition among several families determined control of the court painting bureau during the Heian and Kamakura periods.

Not all art was controlled by the bureaus or by family workshops. Priest-artists were trained in temple workshops to produce Buddhist art objects for public viewing as well as images for private priestly meditation. Amateur painting was common among aristocrats of all ranks. As they did for poetry composition and calligraphy, aristocrats frequently held elegant competitions in painting. Both women and men participated in these activities. In fact, court ladies probably played a significant role in developing the painting style seen in the *Genji* scrolls, and a few participated in public projects.

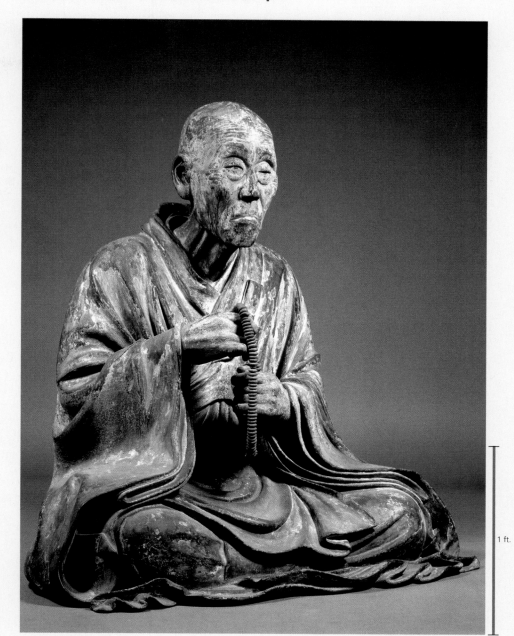

1 ft.

8-16 Portrait statue of the priest Shunjobo Chogen, Todaiji, Nara, Japan, Kamakura period, early 13th century. Painted cypress wood, 2′ 8⅜″ high.

The Kei School's interest in naturalism is seen in this moving portrait of a Kamakura priest. The wooden statue is noteworthy for its finely painted details and powerful rendering of the signs of aging.

The *Heiji* scroll is an example of Japanese historical narrative painting. Staccato brushwork and vivid flashes of color beautifully capture the drama of the night attack and burning of Emperor Goshirakawa's palace.

ATTACK ON SANJO PALACE All the painting types flourishing in the Heian period continued to prosper in the Kamakura period. A striking example of handscroll painting is *Events of the Heiji Period,* which dates to the 13th century and illustrates another facet of Japanese painting—historical narrative. The scroll depicts some of the battles in the civil wars at the end of the Heian period. The section reproduced here (FIG. 8-17) represents the attack on the Sanjo palace in the middle of the night in which the retired emperor Goshirakawa was taken prisoner and his palace burned. Swirling flames and billowing clouds of smoke dominate the composition. Below, soldiers on horseback and on foot do battle. As in other Heian and Kamakura scrolls, the artist represented the buildings seen from above at a sharp angle. Noteworthy here are the painter's staccato brushwork and the vivid flashes of color that beautifully capture the drama of the event.

AMIDA DESCENDING Buddhism and Buddhist painting also remained vital in the Kamakura period, and elite patrons continued to commission major Pure Land artworks. Pure Land Buddhism in Japan stressed the saving power of Amida, who, if called on, hastened to believers at the moment of death and conveyed them to his Pure Land. Pictures of this scene often hung in the presence of a dying person, who recited Amida's name to ensure salvation. In *Amida Descending over the Mountains* (FIG. 8-18), a gigantic Amida rises from behind the mountains against the backdrop of a dark sky. His two main attendant bodhisattvas, Kannon and Seishi, have already descended and are depicted as if addressing the deceased directly. Below, two boys point to the approaching divinities. In contrast to these gesticulating figures, Amida is still and frontal, which gives his image an iconic quality. Particularly striking

is the way in which his halo (nimbus) resembles a rising moon, an image long admired in Japan for its spiritual beauty.

MUROMACHI The Kamakura period ended the way it began—with civil war. After several years of conflict, one shogun emerged supreme and governed Japan from his headquarters in the Muramachi district of Kyoto. The art and architecture of the Muromachi period to the present are the subject of Chapter 28.

Pictures of Amida descending to convey the dead to the Buddhist Pure Land Paradise often hung in the room of a dying person. In this hanging scroll the representation of Amida has an iconic character.

JAPAN BEFORE 1333

JOMON AND YAYOI PERIODS, ca. 10,500 BCE–300 CE

▌ The Jomon (ca. 10,500–300 BCE) is Japan's earliest distinct culture. It takes its name from the applied clay cordlike coil decoration of Jomon pottery.

▌ Archaeologists unearthed the first evidence for the Yayoi culture (ca. 300 BCE–300 CE) in the Yayoi district of Tokyo, but the culture emerged in Kyushu and spread northward. Increasing contact with the East Asian mainland is evident in the form of Yayoi dotaku, which were modeled on Han Chinese bells.

Middle Jomon vessel, ca. 2500–1500 BCE

KOFUN PERIOD, ca. 300–552

▌ Kofun means "old tomb," and great earthen burial mounds are the primary characteristic of the last pre-Buddhist period of Japanese art. The largest tumulus in Japan, attributed to Emperor Nintoku, who died in 399, is at Sakai.

▌ About 20,000 clay cylindrical figures (haniwa) stood around and on top of the Sakai tumulus. Haniwa sculptures represent inanimate objects and animals as well as human figures, including warriors. They formed a protective spiritual barrier between the living and the dead.

Haniwa warrior, fifth to mid-sixth century

ASUKA AND NARA PERIODS, 552–784

▌ Buddhism was introduced to Japan in 552, and the first Japanese Buddhist artworks, such as Tori Busshi's Shaka triad at Horyuji, date to the Asuka period (552–645).

▌ During the Nara period (645–784), a centralized imperial government was established, whose capital was at Nara from 710 to 784.

▌ Nara architecture, for example, the Horyuji kondo, followed Tang Chinese models in the use of ceramic roof tiles and the adoption of a curved roofline. The Daibutsuden constructed at Todaiji in 743 is the largest wooden building in the world.

Kondo, Horyuji, ca. 680

HEIAN PERIOD, 794–1185

▌ In 794 the imperial house moved its capital to Heiankyo (Kyoto). Shortly thereafter, Esoteric Buddhism was introduced to Japan. Painted mandaras of the Womb World and the Diamond World facilitated meditation.

▌ A masterpiece of Heian Buddhist architecture is the Phoenix Hall at Uji, which evokes images of the celestial architecture of the Buddha's Pure Land of the West.

▌ Narrative scroll painting was a major Heian art form. Illustrated scrolls of Lady Murasaki's *Tale of Genji* feature elevated viewpoints that suggest three-dimensional space and flat colors that emphasize the painting's two-dimensional character.

Tale of Genji, first half of 12th century

KAMAKURA PERIOD, 1185–1332

▌ In 1185 power shifted from the Japanese emperor to the first shogun of Kamakura. The shoguns became great patrons of art and architecture.

▌ Kamakura painting is diverse in both subject and style and includes historical narratives, such as *Events of the Heiji Period,* and Buddhist hanging scrolls.

▌ Kamakura wooden portraits—for example, the seated statue of the priest Shunjobo Chogen—are noteworthy for their realism and the use of rock crystal for the eyes.

Shunjobo Chogen, early 13th century

1 ft.

9-1 Double-flute player, detail of a mural painting in the Tomb of the Leopards, Tarquinia, Italy, ca. 480–470 BCE. Detail 3′ 3½″ high.

Although Etruscan art owes an obvious stylistic debt to Greek art, painted murals in monumental tombs such as the Tomb of the Leopards at Tarquinia are unknown in Greece at the same time.

9

THE ETRUSCANS

"The Etruscans, as everyone knows, were the people who occupied the middle of Italy in early Roman days, and whom the Romans, in their usual neighborly fashion, wiped out entirely." So opens D. H. Lawrence's witty and sensitive *Etruscan Places* (1929), one of the earliest modern essays to value Etruscan art highly and treat it as much more than a debased form of the art of the contemporaneous city-states of Greece and southern Italy. ("Most people despise everything B.C. that isn't Greek, for the good reason that it ought to be Greek if it isn't," Lawrence quipped.) Today it is no longer necessary to argue the importance and originality of Etruscan art. Deeply influenced by, yet different from, Greek art, Etruscan sculpture, painting, and architecture not only provided the models for early Roman art and architecture but also had an impact on the art of the Greek colonies in Italy.

The heartland of the Etruscans was the territory between the Arno and Tiber rivers of central Italy (MAP **9-1**). The lush green hills still bear their name—Tuscany, the land of the people the Romans called Tusci, the region centered on Florence, birthplace of Renaissance art. So do the blue waters that splash against the western coastline of the Italian peninsula, for the Greeks referred to the Etruscans as Tyrrhenians and gave that name to the sea off Tuscany. The origin of the Tusci—the enduring "mystery of the Etruscans"—is not clear at all, however. Their language, although written in a Greek-derived script and extant in inscriptions that are still in large part obscure, is unrelated to the Indo-European linguistic family. Ancient authors, as fascinated by the puzzle as modern scholars are, generally felt that the Etruscans emigrated from the east. Herodotus, the fifth-century BCE Greek historian, specifically declared they came from Lydia in Asia Minor and that King Tyrsenos was their leader—hence their Greek name. But Dionysius of Halicarnassus, writing at the end of the first century BCE, maintained the Tusci were native Italians. And some modern researchers have theorized the Etruscans came into Italy from the north.

All these theories are current today, and no doubt some truth exists in each one. The Etruscan people of historical times were very likely the result of a gradual fusion of native and immigrant populations. This mixing of peoples occurred in the early first millennium BCE. At that time the Etruscans emerged as a people with a culture related to but distinct from those of other Italic peoples and from the civilizations of Greece and the Orient.

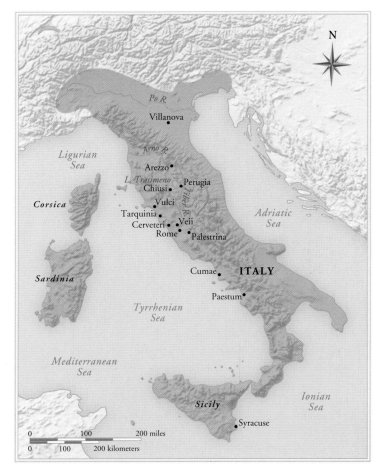

MAP 9-1 Italy in Etruscan times.

During the eighth and seventh centuries BCE, the Etruscans, as highly skilled seafarers, enriched themselves through trade abroad. By the sixth century, they controlled most of northern and central Italy from such strongholds as Tarquinia (ancient Tarquinii), Cerveteri (Caere), Vulci, and Veii. But these cities never united to form a state, so it is inaccurate to speak of an Etruscan "nation" or "kingdom," only of Etruria, the territory the Etruscans occupied. Their cities coexisted, flourishing or fading independently. Any semblance of unity among them was based primarily on common linguistic ties and religious beliefs and practices. This lack of political cohesion eventually made the Etruscans relatively easy prey for the Romans.

EARLY ETRUSCAN ART

Although recognizing the distinctive character of Etruscan painting, sculpture, and architecture, art historians still usually divide the history of Etruscan art into periods mirroring those of Greek art. The seventh century BCE is the Orientalizing period of Etruscan art (followed by Archaic, Classical, and Hellenistic periods).

Orientalizing Art

During the seventh century BCE, the Etruscans successfully mined iron, tin, copper, and silver, creating great mineral wealth that transformed Etruscan society. Villages with agriculturally based econo-

mies gave way to prosperous cities engaged in international commerce. Elite families could afford to acquire foreign goods, and Etruscan aristocrats quickly developed a taste for luxury objects incorporating Eastern motifs. To satisfy the demand, local artisans, inspired by imported goods, produced magnificent objects for both homes and tombs. As in Greece at the same time, the locally produced Orientalizing artifacts cannot be mistaken for their foreign models.

REGOLINI-GALASSI TOMB About 650–640 BCE, a wealthy Etruscan family stocked the so-called Regolini-Galassi Tomb (named for its excavators) at Cerveteri with bronze cauldrons and gold jewelry of Etruscan manufacture and Orientalizing style. The most spectacular of the many luxurious objects in the family tomb is a golden *fibula* (clasp or safety pin; FIG. 9-2) of unique shape used to fasten a woman's gown at the shoulder. The giant fibula is in the Italic tradition, but the five lions that stride across the gold surface are motifs originating in the Orient. The technique, also emulating Eastern imports, is masterful, combining *repoussé* (hammered relief) and *granulation* (the fusing of tiny metal balls, or granules, to a metal surface). The Regolini-Galassi fibula equals or exceeds in quality anything that might have served as a model.

1 in.

9-2 Fibula with Orientalizing lions, from the Regolini-Galassi Tomb, Cerveteri, Italy, ca. 650–640 BCE. Gold, 1' $\frac{1}{2}$" high. Musei Vaticani, Rome.

This huge gold pin found with other Orientalizing jewelry in a Cerveteri tomb combines repoussé and granulation and is the work of an Etruscan artist, but the lions are Near Eastern motifs.

The jewelry from the Regolini-Galassi Tomb also includes a golden *pectoral* that covered a deceased woman's chest, and two gold circlets that may be earrings, although they are large enough to be bracelets. A taste for this kind of ostentatious display is frequently the hallmark of newly acquired wealth, and this was certainly the case in seventh-century BCE Etruria.

Archaic Art and Architecture

Etruscan artists looking eastward for inspiration were also greatly impressed by the art and architecture of Greece. But however eager they may have been to emulate Greek works, the distinctive Etruscan temperament always manifested itself. The vast majority of Archaic Etruscan artworks depart markedly from their prototypes.

ETRUSCAN TEMPLES The design of Etruscan temples superficially owes much to Greece, but the differences far outweigh the similarities. Because of the materials Etruscan architects employed, usually only the foundations of Etruscan temples have survived. These are nonetheless sufficient to reveal the plans of the edifices. Supplementing the archaeological record is the Roman architect Vitruvius's treatise on architecture written near the end of the first century BCE. In it, Vitruvius provided an invaluable chapter on Etruscan temple design.

Archaeologists have constructed a model (FIG. **9-3**) of a typical Archaic Etruscan temple based on Vitruvius's account. The sixth-century BCE Etruscan temple resembled contemporary Greek stone gable-roofed temples (see Chapter 5), but it had wooden columns and a terracotta-tiled wooden roof, and its walls were of sun-dried brick. Entrance was possible only via a narrow staircase at the center of the front of the temple, which sat on a high podium, the only part of the building made of stone. Columns, often three times a man's height or more, also were restricted to the front of the building, creating a deep porch that occupied roughly half the podium and setting off one side of the structure as the main side. In contrast, the front and rear of Greek temples were indistinguishable, and builders placed steps and columns on all sides (FIG. **5-13**). The Etruscan

Etruscan Counterparts of Greco-Roman Gods and Heroes

Etruscan	*Greek*	*Roman*
Tinia	Zeus	Jupiter
Uni	Hera	Juno
Menrva	Athena	Minerva
Apulu	Apollo	Apollo
Artumes	Artemis	Diana
Hercle	Herakles	Hercules

temple was not intended to be viewed as a sculptural mass from the outside and from all directions, as Greek temples were. Instead it functioned primarily as an ornate home for grand statues of Etruscan gods. It was a place of shelter, protected by the wide overhang of its roof.

Etruscan temples differed in other ways from those of Greece. Etruscan (or Tuscan) columns resembled Greek Doric columns (FIG. 5-14, *left*), but *Tuscan columns* were made of wood, were unfluted, and had bases. Because of the lightness of the superstructure they had to support, Tuscan columns were, as a rule, much more widely spaced than Greek columns. Unlike their Greek counterparts, Etruscan temples frequently had three cellas—one for each of their chief gods, Tinia, Uni, and Menrva (see "Etruscan Counterparts of Greco-Roman Gods and Heroes," above). And pedimental statuary was exceedingly rare in Etruria. The Etruscans normally placed life-size narrative statuary—in terracotta instead of stone—on the peaks of their temple roofs.

9-3 Model of a typical sixth-century BCE Etruscan temple as described by Vitruvius. Istituto di Etruscologia e di Antichità Italiche, Università di Roma, Rome.

Etruscan temples resembled Greek temples but had widely spaced unfluted wooden columns only at the front, walls of sun-dried mud brick, and a narrow staircase at the center of the facade.

Etruscan Artists in Rome

In 616 BCE, according to the traditional chronology, Tarquinius Priscus of Tarquinia became Rome's first Etruscan king. He ruled for almost 40 years. His grandson, Tarquinius Superbus ("the Arrogant"), was Rome's last king. Outraged by his tyrannical behavior, the Romans drove him out in 509 BCE. Before his expulsion, however, Tarquinius Superbus embarked on a grand program to embellish the city he ruled.

The king's most ambitious undertaking was the erection of a magnificent temple on the Capitoline Hill for the joint worship of Jupiter, Juno, and Minerva. For this great commission, he summoned architects, sculptors, and workers from all over Etruria. Rome's first great religious shrine was Etruscan in patronage, in manufacture, and in form. The architect's name is unknown, but several sources preserve the identity of the Etruscan sculptor brought in to adorn the temple. His name was Vulca of Veii, and he may also have made a statue of the god Apulu (FIG. 9-4) for his native city. Pliny the Elder described his works as "the finest images of deities of that era . . . more admired than gold."* The Romans entrusted Vulca with making the statue of Jupiter that stood in the central cella of the Capitoline temple's three cellas. He also fashioned the enormous terracotta statuary group of Jupiter in a four-horse chariot, which was mounted on the roof at the highest point directly over the center of the temple facade. The fame of Vulca's red-faced (painted terracotta) portrayal of Jupiter was so great that Roman generals would paint their faces red in emulation of his Jupiter when they paraded in triumph through Rome after a battlefield victory. (The model of a three-cella Etruscan temple in FIG. 9-3 also gives an approximate idea of the appearance of the Capitoline Jupiter temple and of Vulca's roof statue.)

Vulca is the only Etruscan artist any ancient writer names, but the signatures of other Etruscan artists appear on preserved artworks. One of these is Novios Plautios (FIG. 9-13), who also worked in Rome, although a few centuries later. By then the Etruscan kings

9-4 Apulu (Apollo), from the roof of the Portonaccio temple, Veii, Italy, ca. 510–500 BCE. Painted terracotta, 5' 11" high. Museo Nazionale di Villa Giulia, Rome.

The Veii Apulu was part of a statuary group depicting a Greek myth. Distinctly Etruscan, however, are the god's vigorous motion and gesticulating arms and the placement of the statue on a temple roof.

1 ft.

of Rome were a distant memory, and the Romans had captured Veii and annexed its territory.

*Pliny, *Natural History,* 35.157.

APULU OF VEII The finest of these rooftop statues to survive today is the life-size image of Apulu (FIG. 9-4), which displays the energy and excitement that characterize Archaic Etruscan art in general. The statue comes from a temple in the Portonaccio sanctuary at Veii. It is but one of a group of at least four painted terracotta figures that adorned the top of the temple roof and depicted one of the 12 labors of Herakles/Hercles (see "Herakles," Chapter 5, page 120). The god confronts Hercle for possession of the Ceryneian hind, a wondrous beast with golden horns that was sacred to Apulu's sister Artumes. The bright paint and the rippling folds of Apulu's garment call to mind the Archaic korai of the Acropolis in Ionian garb (FIG. 5-12). But Apulu's vigorous striding motion, gesticulating arms, fanlike calf muscles, and animated face are distinctly Etruscan. Some scholars have attributed the Apulu statue to VULCA OF VEII, the most

famous Etruscan sculptor of the time (see "Etruscan Artists in Rome," above). The statue's discovery in 1916 was instrumental in prompting a reevaluation of the originality of Etruscan art.

CERVETERI SARCOPHAGUS Although life-size terracotta statuary was known in Greece, this medium was especially favored in Etruria. Another Archaic Etruscan terracotta masterwork is the sarcophagus (FIG. 9-5) from a Cerveteri tomb in the form of a husband and wife reclining on a banquet couch. The sarcophagus, which was once brightly painted, was cast in four sections and is of monumental size, but it contained only the ashes of the deceased. Cremation was the most common means of disposing of the dead in Italy at this time. This kind of funerary monument had no parallel at this date in Greece, where there were no monumental tombs that

The "Audacity" of Etruscan Women

At the instigation of the emperor Augustus at the end of the first century BCE, Titus Livy wrote a history of Rome from its legendary founding in 753 BCE to his own day. In the first book of his great work, Livy recounted the tale of Tullia, daughter of Servius Tullius, an Etruscan king of Rome in the sixth century BCE. The princess had married the less ambitious of two brothers of the royal Tarquinius family, while her sister had married the bolder of the two princes. Together, Tullia and her brother-in-law, Tarquinius Superbus, arranged for the murder of their spouses. They then married each other and plotted the overthrow and death of Tullia's father. After the king's murder, Tullia ostentatiously drove her carriage over her father's corpse, spraying herself with his blood. (The Roman road where the evil deed occurred is still called the Street of Infamy.) Livy, though condemning Tullia's actions, placed them in the context of the famous "audacity" of Etruscan women.

The independent spirit and relative freedom women enjoyed in Etruscan society similarly horrified (and threatened) other Greco-Roman male authors. The stories the fourth-century BCE Greek historian Theopompus heard about the debauchery of Etruscan women appalled him. They epitomized immorality for Theopompus, but much of what he reported is untrue. Etruscan women did

not, for example, exercise naked alongside Etruscan men. But archaeological evidence confirms the accuracy of at least one of his "slurs": Etruscan women did attend banquets and recline with their husbands on a common couch (FIGS. 9-5 and 9-9). Aristotle also remarked on this custom. It was so foreign to the Greeks that it both shocked and frightened them. Only men, boys, slave girls, and prostitutes attended Greek symposiums. The wives remained at home, excluded from most aspects of public life. In Etruscan Italy, in striking contrast to contemporaneous Greece, women also regularly attended sporting events with men. This, too, is well documented in Etruscan paintings and reliefs.

Etruscan inscriptions also reflect the higher status of women in Etruria as compared with Greece. They often give the names of both the father and mother of the person commemorated (for example, the inscribed portrait of Aule Metele, FIG. 9-16), a practice unheard of in Greece (witness the grave stele of "Hegeso, daughter of Proxenos," FIG. 5-57). Etruscan women, moreover, retained their own names and could legally own property independently of their husbands. The frequent use of inscriptions on Etruscan mirrors and other toiletry items (FIG. 9-13) buried with women seems to attest to a high degree of female literacy as well.

9-5 Sarcophagus with reclining couple, from Cerveteri, Italy, ca. 520 BCE. Painted terracotta, $3' 9\frac{1}{2}'' \times 6' 7''$. Museo Nazionale di Villa Giulia, Rome.

Sarcophagi in the form of a husband and wife on a dining couch have no parallels in Greece. The artist's focus on the upper half of the figures and the emphatic gestures are Etruscan hallmarks.

1 ft.

could house large sarcophagi. The Greeks buried their dead in simple graves marked by a stele or a statue. Moreover, although banquets were common subjects on Greek vases (which, by the late sixth century BCE, the Etruscans imported in great quantities and regularly deposited in their tombs), only men dined at Greek symposiums. The image of a husband and wife sharing the same banquet couch is uniquely Etruscan (see "The 'Audacity' of Etruscan Women," above).

The man and woman on the Cerveteri sarcophagus are as animated as the Veii Apulu (FIG. 9-4), even though they are at rest. They are the antithesis of the stiff and formal figures encountered in Egyptian tomb sculptures (compare FIG. 3-13). Also typically Etruscan, and in striking contrast to contemporaneous Greek statues with their emphasis on proportion and balance, is the manner in which the Cerveteri sculptor rendered the upper and lower parts of each body. The legs were only summarily modeled, and the transition to

9-6 Tumuli in the Banditaccia necropolis, Cerveteri, Italy, seventh to second centuries BCE.

In the Banditaccia necropolis (city of the dead) at Cerveteri, the Etruscans buried several generations of families in multi-chambered rock-cut underground tombs covered by great earthen mounds (tumuli).

the torso at the waist is unnatural. The Etruscan artist's interest focused on the upper half of the figures, especially on the vibrant faces and gesticulating arms. Gestures are still an important ingredient of Italian conversation today, and the Cerveteri banqueters and the Veii Apulu speak to the viewer in a way that Greek statues of similar date, with their closed contours and calm demeanor, never do.

BANDITACCIA NECROPOLIS The exact findspot of the Cerveteri sarcophagus is not known, but the kind of tomb that housed such sarcophagi is well documented. The typical tomb in Cerveteri's Banditaccia necropolis (FIG. **9-6**) took the form of a mound, or *tumulus,* not unlike the Mycenaean Treasury of Atreus (FIG. **4-20**). But whereas the Mycenaean tholos tomb was constructed of masonry blocks and then covered by an earthen mound, each Etruscan tumulus covered one or more subterranean multichambered tombs cut out of the dark local limestone called tufa. These burial mounds sometimes reached colossal size, with diameters in excess of 130 feet. They were arranged in cemeteries in an orderly manner along a network of streets, producing the effect of veritable "cities of the dead" (the literal meaning of the Greek word *necropolis*), and were always located some distance from the cities of the living.

The underground tomb chambers cut into the rock resembled the houses of the living. In the plan (FIG. **9-7**) of the Tomb of the Shields and Chairs, for example, the central entrance and the smaller chambers opening onto a large central space mirror the axial sequence of rooms in Etruscan dwellings of the time. The effect of a domestic interior was enhanced by the beds and grand armchairs with curved backs and footstools (clearly visible on the plan), as well as the ceiling beams, framed doorways, and even windows that the sculptors cut out of the rock. The technique recalls that of rock-cut Egyptian tombs (FIG. **3-19**) and highlights the very different values of the Etruscans and the Greeks. The Etruscans' temples no longer stand because they constructed them of wood and mud brick, but their grand subterranean tombs are as permanent as the bedrock itself. The Greeks employed stone for the shrines of their gods but only rarely built monumental tombs for their dead.

9-7A Tomb of the Shields and Chairs, Cerveteri, ca. 550–500 BCE.

Chairs

Beds

| 0 | 5 | 10 | 15 feet |
| 0 | 1 | 2 | 3 | 4 | 5 meters |

9-7 Plan of the Tomb of the Shields and Chairs, Cerveteri, Italy, second half of the sixth century BCE.

In plan, the subterranean tombs of Cerveteri resemble the houses of the living. Sculptors enhanced the effect of a domestic interior by carving beds, chairs, doors, and ceiling beams out of the bedrock.

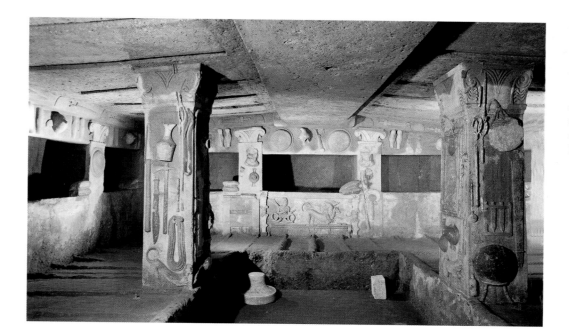

TOMB OF THE RELIEFS The most elaborate of the Cerveteri tombs, in decoration if not in plan, is the so-called Tomb of the Reliefs (FIG. 9-8). Like the much earlier Tomb of the Shields and Chairs, it accommodated several generations of a single family. The walls and piers of this tomb were, as usual, gouged out of the tufa bedrock, but in this instance painted stucco reliefs covered the stone. The stools, mirrors, drinking cups, pitchers, and knives effectively suggest a domestic context, underscoring the connection between Etruscan houses of the dead and those of the living. Other reliefs, such as the helmet and shields over the main funerary couch (the pillows are also shallow reliefs), are signs of the elite status of this Cerveteri family. The three-headed dog Cerberus, guardian of the gate to the Underworld, beneath the same couch is a reference to the passage from this life to the next.

TARQUINIA Large underground burial chambers hewn out of the natural rock were also the norm at Tarquinia. Earthen mounds may once have covered the Tarquinia tombs too, but the tumuli are no longer preserved. In contrast to Cerveteri, the subterranean rooms at Tarquinia do not have carvings imitating the appearance of Etruscan houses. In some cases, however, paintings decorate the walls. Painted tombs are statistically rare, the privilege of only the wealthiest Etruscan families. Nevertheless, archaeologists have discovered many paintings at Tarquinia by using periscopes to explore tomb interiors from the surface before considering time-consuming and costly excavation. Consequently, art historians have an almost unbroken record of monumental painting in Etruria from Archaic to Hellenistic times.

TOMB OF THE LEOPARDS A characteristic example dating to the early fifth century BCE is the Tomb of the Leopards (FIG. 9-9), named for the beasts that guard the interior of the painted chamber from their perch within the pediment of the rear wall. They

9-10 Diving and fishing, detail of a mural painting in the Tomb of Hunting and Fishing, Tarquinia, Italy, ca. 530–520 BCE. Detail, 5′ 6½″ high. ◼◀

Scenes of young men enjoying the pleasures of nature cover the walls of this Tarquinian tomb. The Etruscan diving scene predates a similar landscape painting (FIG. 5-61) in a Greek tomb at Paestum.

9-9A Tomb of the Triclinium, Tarquinia, ca. 480–470 BCE.

are reminiscent of the panthers on each side of Medusa in the pediment (FIG. 5-17) of the Temple of Artemis at Corfu. But mythological figures, whether Greek or Etruscan, are uncommon in Tarquinian murals, and the Tomb of the Leopards has none. Instead, banqueting couples (the men with dark skin, the women with light skin, in conformity with the age-old convention) adorn the walls—painted versions of the terracotta sarcophagus (FIG. 9-5) from Cerveteri. Pitcher- and cup-bearers serve the guests, and musicians entertain them. The banquet takes place in the open air or perhaps in a tent set up for the occasion. In characteristic Etruscan fashion, the banqueters, servants, and entertainers all make exaggerated gestures with unnaturally enlarged hands (FIG. 9-1). The man on the couch at the far right on the rear wall holds up an egg, the symbol of regeneration. The tone is joyful. The painting is a celebration of life, food, wine, music, and dance, rather than a somber contemplation of death.

In stylistic terms, the Etruscan figures are comparable to those on sixth-century Greek vases before Late Archaic painters became preoccupied with the problem of foreshortening. Etruscan painters may be considered somewhat backward in this respect, but in other ways they seem to have outpaced their counterparts in Greece, especially in their interest in rendering nature. In the Tomb of the Leopards, the landscape is but a few trees and shrubs placed between the

entertainers (and leopards) and behind the banquet couches. But elsewhere the natural environment was the chief interest of Tarquinian painters.

TOMB OF HUNTING AND FISHING Scenes of Etruscans enjoying the pleasures of nature decorate all the walls of the main chamber of the aptly named Tomb of Hunting and Fishing at Tarquinia. In the detail reproduced here (FIG. 9-10), a youth dives off a rocky promontory, while others fish from a boat and birds fill the sky all around. On another wall, youthful hunters aim their slingshots at the brightly painted birds. The scenes of hunting and fishing recall the paintings in Egyptian tombs (FIGS. 3-15 and 3-28) and may indicate knowledge of that Eastern funerary tradition. The multicolored rocks resemble those of the Theran *Spring Fresco* (FIG. 4-9), but art historians know of nothing similar in contemporaneous Greek art save the Tomb of the Diver (FIG. 5-61) at Paestum. That exceptional Greek work, however, is from a tomb in Italy dated about a half century later than the Tarquinian tomb. In fact, the Paestum composition probably emulated older Etruscan designs, undermining the now-outdated judgment of art historians that Etruscan art was merely derivative and that Etruscan artists never set the standard for Greek artists.

9-11 *Capitoline Wolf*, from Rome, Italy, ca. 500–480 BCE. Bronze, 2' 7½" high. Musei Capitolini, Rome.

An Etruscan sculptor cast this bronze statue of the she-wolf that nursed the infants Romulus and Remus, founders of Rome. The animal has a tense, gaunt body and an unforgettable psychic intensity.

1 ft.

LATER ETRUSCAN ART

The fifth century BCE was a golden age in Greece but not in Etruria. In 509 BCE the Romans expelled the last of their Etruscan kings, Tarquinius Superbus (see "Etruscan Artists in Rome," page 226), replacing the monarchy with a republican form of government. In 474 BCE an alliance of Cumaean Greeks and Hieron I of Syracuse (Sicily) defeated the Etruscan fleet off Cumae, effectively ending Etruscan dominance of the seas—and with it Etruscan prosperity.

Classical Art

These events had important consequences in the world of art and architecture. The number of Etruscan tombs, for example, decreased sharply, and the quality of the furnishings declined markedly. No longer were tombs filled with golden jewelry and imported Greek vases or decorated with mural paintings of the first rank. But art did not cease in Etruria. Indeed, in specialties in which Etruscan artists excelled, especially the casting of statues in bronze and terracotta,

they continued to produce impressive works, even though fewer in number.

CAPITOLINE WOLF The best-known of these later Etruscan statues—one of the most memorable portrayals of an animal in the history of world art—is the *Capitoline Wolf* (FIG. 9-11). The statue is a somewhat larger than life-size hollow-cast bronze portrayal of the she-wolf that, according to legend, nursed Romulus and Remus after they were abandoned as infants. When the twins grew to adulthood, they quarreled, and Romulus killed his brother. On April 21, 753 BCE, Romulus founded Rome and became the city's king. The statue of the she-wolf seems to have been made, however, for the new Roman Republic after the expulsion of Tarquinius Superbus. The appropriately defiant image became the new government's totem and has remained the emblem of Rome to this day.

The *Capitoline Wolf*, however, is not a work of Roman art, which had not yet developed a distinct identity, but rather is the product of an Etruscan workshop. (The suckling infants are 15th-century additions.) The vitality accorded the human figure in Etruscan art is here concentrated in the tense, watchful animal body of the she-wolf, with her spare flanks, gaunt ribs, and taut, powerful legs. The lowered neck and head, alert ears, glaring eyes, and ferocious muzzle capture the psychic intensity of the fierce and protective beast as danger approaches. Not even the great animal reliefs of Assyria (FIG. 2-23) match this profound characterization of animal temperament.

CHIMERA OF AREZZO Another masterpiece of Etruscan bronze-casting is the *Chimera of Arezzo* (FIG. 9-12), which dates about a century later than the *Capitoline Wolf*. The *chimera* is a monster of Greek invention with a lion's head and body and a serpent's tail (restored in this case). A second head, that of a goat, grows out of the lion's left side. The goat's neck bears the wound the Greek hero Bellerophon inflicted when he hunted

9-12 *Chimera of Arezzo*, from Arezzo, Italy, first half of fourth century BCE. Bronze, 2' 7½" high. Museo Archeologico Nazionale, Florence.

The chimera was a composite monster slain by the Greek hero Bellerophon. In this Etruscan statue, the artist depicted the wounded beast poised to attack and growling ferociously.

1 ft.

9-13 NOVIOS PLAUTIOS, *Ficoroni Cista,* from Palestrina, Italy, late fourth century BCE. Bronze, 2′ 6″ high. Museo Nazionale di Villa Giulia, Rome.

Novios Plautios made this container for a woman's toiletry articles in Rome and engraved it with the myth of the Argonauts. The composition is probably an adaptation of a Greek painting.

and slew the composite beast. As rendered by the Etruscan sculptor, the chimera, although injured and bleeding, is far from defeated. Like the earlier she-wolf statue, the bronze chimera has muscles that are stretched tightly over its rib cage. The monster prepares to attack, and a ferocious cry emanates from its open jaws. Some scholars have postulated that the statue was part of a group that originally included Bellerophon, but the chimera could just as well have stood alone. The menacing gaze upward toward an unseen adversary need not have been answered. In this respect, too, the chimera is in the tradition of the *Capitoline Wolf.*

Etruscan Art and the Rise of Rome

At about the time the *Chimera of Arezzo* was fashioned, Rome began to appropriate Etruscan territory. Veii fell to the Romans in 396 BCE, after a terrible 10-year siege. Peace was concluded with Tarquinia in 351, but by the beginning of the next century, Rome had annexed Tarquinia too, and in 273 BCE the Romans conquered Cerveteri.

FICORONI CISTA Rome's growing power in central Italy is indicated indirectly by the engraved inscription on the *Ficoroni Cista* (FIG. 9-13). Etruscan artists began to produce such *cistae* (cylindrical containers for a woman's toiletry articles), made of sheet bronze with cast handles and feet and elaborately engraved bodies, in large numbers in the fourth century BCE. Along with engraved bronze mirrors, they were popular gifts for both the living and the dead. The center of the Etruscan bronze cista industry was Palestrina (ancient Praeneste), where the *Ficoroni Cista* was found. The inscription on the handle states that Dindia Macolnia, a local noblewoman, gave the bronze container to her daughter and that the artist was NOVIOS PLAUTIOS. According to the inscription, his workshop was not in Palestrina but in Rome, which by this date was becoming an important Italian cultural as well as political center.

The engraved frieze of the *Ficoroni Cista* depicts an episode from the Greek story of the expedition of the Argonauts in search of the Golden Fleece. Scholars generally agree that the composition is an adaptation of a lost Greek panel painting, perhaps one then on display in Rome—additional testimony to the burgeoning wealth and prestige of the city Etruscan kings once ruled. The Greek source for Novios Plautios's engraving is evident in the figures seen entirely

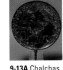

9-13A Chalchas examining a liver, ca. 400–375 BCE.

from behind or in three-quarter view, and in the placement of the protagonists on several levels in the Polygnotan manner (FIG. 5-59).

PORTA MARZIA, PERUGIA In the third century BCE, the Etruscan city of Perugia (ancient Perusia) formed an alliance with Rome and was spared the destruction that Veii, Cerveteri, and other Etruscan towns suffered. Portions of Perugia's ancient walls are still standing, as are some of its gates. One of these, the so-called Porta Marzia (Gate of Mars), was dismantled during the Renaissance, but the upper part of the gate (FIG. 9-14) is preserved, embedded in a later wall. The archway is formed by a series of trapezoidal stone *voussoirs* held in place by the weight of the blocks pressing against one another (FIG. 4-17c). Earlier architects built arches in Greece as well as in Mesopotamia (FIG. 2-24), but in Italy, first under the Etruscans and later under the Romans, *arcuated* (arch-shaped) gateways and freestanding ("triumphal") arches became a major architectural type.

The use of Hellenic-inspired *pilasters* (flat columns) to frame the rounded opening of the Porta Marzia typifies the Etruscan adaptation of Greek motifs. Arches bracketed by engaged columns or

The arch has a long history in ancient architecture, but it was most commonly used in Etruscan and Roman buildings. Often Greek pilasters or engaged columns frame an arcuated opening.

pilasters have a long and distinguished history in Roman and later times. In the Porta Marzia, sculpted half-figures of Jupiter and his sons Castor and Pollux and their steeds look out from between the fluted pilasters. The divine twins had appeared miraculously on a battlefield in 484 BCE to turn the tide in favor of the Romans. The presence of these three deities at the apex of the Porta Marzia may reflect the new Roman practice of erecting triumphal arches with gilded bronze statues on top.

SARCOPHAGUS OF LARS PULENA In Hellenistic Etruria, the counterparts of the magnificent Archaic terracotta sarcophagus (FIG. 9-5) from Cerveteri were made of local stone. The leading production center was Tarquinia, where an Etruscan sculptor fashioned the sarcophagus of Lars Pulena (FIG. 9-15) early in the second century BCE. The scene sculpted on the front of the coffin shows the deceased in the Underworld between two *charuns* (Etruscan death demons) swinging hammers. It signifies that Lars Pulena has successfully made the

9-15A Sarcophagus of Ramtha Visnai and Arnth Tetnies, ca. 350–300 BCE.

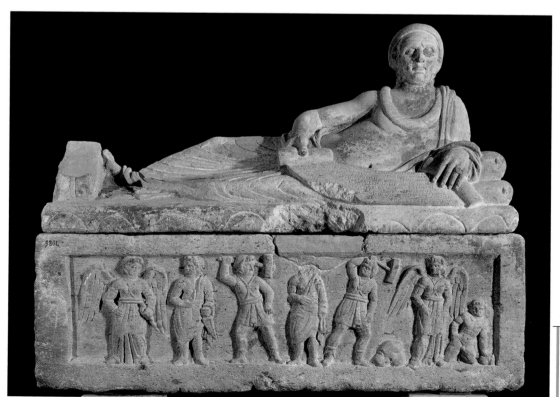

9-15 Sarcophagus of Lars Pulena, from Tarquinia, Italy, early second century BCE. Tufa, 6′ 6″ long. Museo Archeologico Nazionale, Tarquinia.

Images of the deceased on late Etruscan sarcophagi are much more somber than those on Archaic examples (FIG. 9-5), but Lars Pulena proudly displays a list of his life's achievements on an open scroll.

1 ft.

Later Etruscan Art **233**

9-16 Aule Metele (*Arringatore*), from Cortona, near Lake Trasimeno, Italy, early first century BCE. Bronze, 5′ 7″ high. Museo Archeologico Nazionale, Florence.

Inscribed in Etruscan, this bronze statue of an orator is Etruscan in name only. Aule Metele wears the short toga and high boots of a Roman magistrate, and the style of the portrait is also Roman.

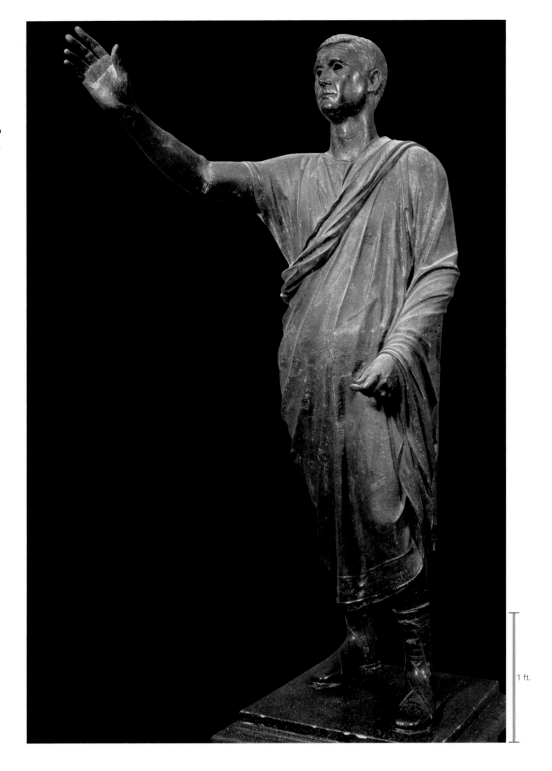

1 ft.

journey to the afterlife. Above, the deceased is shown in a reclining position, but he is not at a festive banquet, and his wife is not present. His somber expression contrasts sharply with the smiling, confident faces of the Archaic era when Etruria enjoyed its greatest prosperity. Similar heads—realistic but generic types, not true portraits—are found on all later Etruscan sarcophagi and in tomb paintings. They are symptomatic of the economic and political decline of the once-mighty Etruscan city-states. Nonetheless, Lars Pulena is a proud man. He wears a wreath around his neck and displays a partially unfurled scroll inscribed with the record of his life's accomplishments.

AULE METELE An even later Etruscan portrait is the statue (FIG. **9-16**) of the magistrate Aule Metele raising his arm to address an assembly—hence his modern nickname *Arringatore* (*Orator*).

This life-size statue proves that Etruscan artists continued to be experts at bronze-casting long after the heyday of Etruscan prosperity. The *Arringatore* was most likely produced at about the time the Romans achieved total hegemony over the Etruscans. The so-called Social War of the early first century BCE ended in 89 BCE with the conferring of Roman citizenship on all of Italy's inhabitants. In fact, Aule Metele—his Etruscan name and his father's and mother's names are inscribed on the hem of his garment—wears the short toga and high laced boots of a Roman magistrate. His head, with its close-cropped hair and signs of age in the face, resembles portraits produced in Rome at the time. This orator is Etruscan in name only. If the origin of the Etruscans remains debatable, the question of their demise has a ready answer. Aule Metele and his compatriots became Romans, and Etruscan art became Roman art.

THE ETRUSCANS

ORIENTALIZING ART, ca. 700–600 BCE

▪ During the early first millennium BCE, the Etruscans emerged as a people with a culture distinct from those of other Italic peoples and the Greeks.

▪ In the seventh century BCE, the Etruscans traded metals from their mines for foreign goods and began to produce jewelry and other luxury objects decorated with motifs modeled on those found on imports from the Near East.

Regolini-Galassi fibula, Cerveteri, ca. 650–640 BCE

ARCHAIC ART, ca. 600–480 BCE

▪ The sixth century BCE was the apex of Etruscan power in Italy. Etruscan kings even ruled Rome until 509 BCE.

▪ The Etruscans admired Greek art and architecture but did not copy Greek works. Etruscan temples were made of wood and mud brick instead of stone and had columns and stairs only at the front. Terracotta statuary decorated the roof.

A typical sixth-century BCE Etruscan temple

▪ Most surviving Etruscan artworks come from underground tomb chambers. At Cerveteri, great earthen mounds (tumuli) covered tombs with interiors sculptured to imitate the houses of the living.

▪ At Tarquinia, painters covered the tomb walls with monumental frescoes, usually depicting funerary banquets attended by both men and women.

Tomb of the Leopards, Tarquinia, ca. 480–470 BCE

CLASSICAL AND HELLENISTIC ART, ca. 480–489 BCE

▪ The Greek defeat of the Etruscan fleet off Cumae in 474 BCE ended Etruscan domination of the sea and marked the beginning of Etruria's decline. Rome destroyed Veii in 396 BCE and conquered Cerveteri in 273 BCE. All of Italy became Romanized by 89 BCE.

▪ A very different, more somber, mood pervades Etruscan art during the fifth through first centuries BCE, as seen, for example, in the sarcophagus of Lars Pulena.

Sarcophagus of Lars Pulena, early second century BCE

▪ Later Etruscan architecture is noteworthy for the widespread use of the stone arch, often framed with Greek pilasters or columns, as on the Porta Marzia at Perugia.

Porta Marzia, Perugia, second century BCE

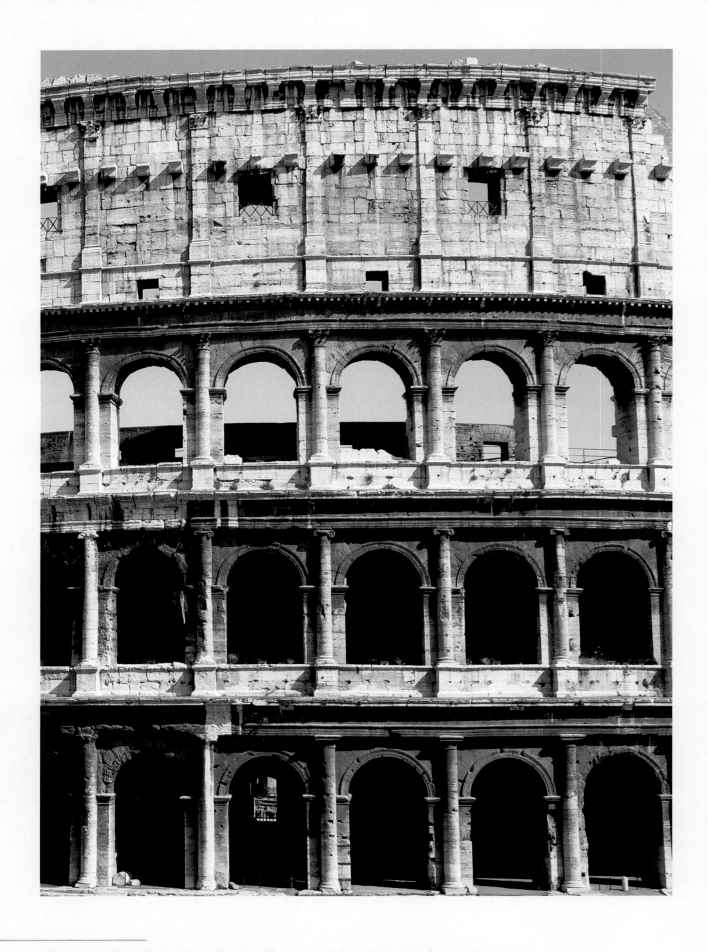

10-1 Detail of the facade of the Colosseum (Flavian Amphitheater), Rome, Italy, ca. 70–80 CE. ▣◀

Rome's most famous landmark (FIG. 10-36) is a prime example of Roman eclecticism. The architect mixed Greek columns and Roman arches on the facade, which masked a skeleton of concrete vaults.

10

THE ROMAN EMPIRE

With the rise and triumph of Rome, a single government ruled, for the first time in history, from the Strait of Gibraltar to the Nile, from the Tigris and Euphrates to the Rhine, Danube, Thames and beyond (MAP 10-1). Within the Roman Empire's borders lived millions of people of numerous races, religions, tongues, and cultures: Britons and Gauls, Greeks and Egyptians, Africans and Syrians, Jews and Christians, to name but a few. Of all the ancient civilizations, the Roman most closely approximated today's world in its multicultural character.

Roman monuments of art and architecture, spread throughout the vast territory the Romans governed, are the most conspicuous and numerous of all the remains of ancient civilization. In Europe, the Middle East, and Africa today, Roman temples and basilicas have an afterlife as churches. The powerful concrete vaults of ancient Roman buildings form the cores of modern houses, stores, restaurants, factories, and museums. Bullfights, sports events, operas, and rock concerts are staged in Roman amphitheaters. Ships dock in what were once Roman ports, and Western Europe's highway system still closely follows the routes of Roman roads.

Ancient Rome also lives on in the Western world in concepts of law and government, in languages, in the calendar—even in the coins used daily. Roman art speaks in a language almost every Western viewer can readily understand. Its diversity and eclecticism foreshadowed the modern world. The Roman use of art, especially portraits and narrative reliefs, to manipulate public opinion is similar to the carefully crafted imagery of contemporary political campaigns. And the Roman mastery of concrete construction began an architectural revolution still felt today.

The center of the far-flung Roman Empire was the city on the Tiber River that, according to legend, Romulus and his twin brother Remus founded on April 21, 753 BCE. Their Rome consisted only of small huts clustered together on the Palatine Hill (FIG. 10-2, no. 3) overlooking what was then uninhabited marshland. In the Archaic period, Rome was essentially an Etruscan city, both politically and culturally. Its greatest shrine, the Temple of Jupiter Optimus Maximus (Best and Greatest) on the Capitoline Hill, was built by an Etruscan king, designed by an Etruscan architect, made of wood and mud brick in the Etruscan manner, and decorated with terracotta statuary created by an Etruscan sculptor (see "Etruscan Artists in Rome," Chapter 9, page 226).

MAP 10-1 The Roman Empire at the death of Trajan in 117 CE.

10-2 Model of the city of Rome during the early fourth century CE. Museo della Civiltà Romana, Rome.
(1) Temple of Portunus,
(2) Circus Maximus,
(3) Palatine Hill, (4) Temple of Jupiter Capitolinus,
(5) Pantheon, (6) Column of Trajan, (7) Forum of Trajan, (8) Markets of Trajan,
(9) Forum of Julius Caesar,
(10) Forum of Augustus,
(11) Forum Romanum,
(12) Basilica Nova, (13) Arch of Titus, (14) Temple of Venus and Roma, (15) Arch of Constantine, (16) Colossus of Nero, (17) Colosseum.

By the time of Constantine, the city of Rome was densely packed with temples, forums, triumphal arches, theaters, baths, racetracks, aqueducts, markets, private homes, and apartment houses.

An Outline of Roman History

MONARCHY (753–509 BCE)

Latin and Etruscan kings ruled Rome from the city's founding by Romulus and Remus until the revolt against Tarquinius Superbus (exact dates of rule unreliable).

REPUBLIC (509–27 BCE)

The Roman Republic lasted from the expulsion of Tarquinius Superbus until the bestowing of the title of Augustus on Octavian, the grandnephew of Julius Caesar and victor over Mark Antony in the civil war that ended the Republic. Some major figures were

- Marcellus, b. 268(?), d. 208 BCE, consul
- Marius, b. 157, d. 86 BCE, consul
- Sulla, b. 138, d. 79 BCE, consul and dictator
- Pompey, b. 106, d. 48 BCE, consul
- Julius Caesar, b. 100, d. 44 BCE, consul and dictator
- Mark Antony, b. 83, d. 30 BCE, consul

EARLY EMPIRE (27 BCE–96 CE)

The Early Empire began with the rule of Augustus and his Julio-Claudian successors and continued until the end of the Flavian dynasty. Selected emperors and their dates of rule (with names of the most influential empresses in parentheses) were

- Augustus (Livia), r. 27 BCE–14 CE
- Tiberius, r. 14–37
- Caligula, r. 37–41
- Claudius (Agrippina the Younger), r. 41–54
- Nero, r. 54–68
- Vespasian, r. 69–79

- Titus, r. 79–81
- Domitian, r. 81–96

HIGH EMPIRE (96–192 CE)

The High Empire began with the rule of Nerva and the Spanish emperors, Trajan and Hadrian, and ended with the last emperor of the Antonine dynasty. The emperors (and empresses) of this period were

- Nerva, r. 96–98
- Trajan (Plotina), r. 98–117
- Hadrian (Sabina), r. 117–138
- Antoninus Pius (Faustina the Elder), r. 138–161
- Marcus Aurelius (Faustina the Younger), r. 161–180
- Lucius Verus, coemperor with Marcus Aurelius, r. 161–169
- Commodus, r. 180–192

LATE EMPIRE (193–337 CE)

The Late Empire began with the Severan dynasty and included the so-called soldier emperors of the third century, the tetrarchs, and Constantine, the first Christian emperor. Selected emperors (and empresses) were

- Septimius Severus (Julia Domna), r. 193–211
- Caracalla (Plautilla), r. 211–217
- Severus Alexander, r. 222–235
- Trajan Decius, r. 249–251
- Trebonianus Gallus, r. 251–253
- Diocletian, r. 284–305
- Constantine I, r. 306–337

REPUBLIC

In 509 BCE the Romans overthrew Tarquinius Superbus, the last of Rome's Etruscan kings, and established a constitutional government (see "An Outline of Roman History," above). The new Roman Republic vested power mainly in a *senate* (literally, "a council of elders," *senior* citizens) and in two elected *consuls*. Under extraordinary circumstances, a *dictator* could be appointed for a specified time and a specific purpose, such as commanding the army during a crisis. All leaders came originally from among the wealthy landowners, or *patricians*, but later also from the *plebeian* class of small farmers, merchants, and freed slaves.

Before long, the descendants of Romulus conquered Rome's neighbors one by one: the Etruscans and the Gauls to the north, the Samnites and the Greek colonists to the south. Even the Carthaginians of North Africa, who under Hannibal's dynamic leadership had annihilated some of Rome's legions and almost brought down the Republic, fell before the mighty Roman armies.

Architecture

The year 211 BCE was a turning point both for Rome and for Roman art. Breaking with precedent, Marcellus, conqueror of the fabulously wealthy Sicilian Greek city of Syracuse, brought back to Rome not only the usual spoils of war—captured arms and armor, gold and silver coins, and the like—but also the city's artistic patrimony. Thus began, in the words of the historian Livy, "the craze for works of Greek art."[1] Exposure to Greek sculpture and painting and to the splendid marble temples of the Greek gods increased as the Romans expanded their conquests beyond Italy. Greece became a Roman province in 146 BCE, and in 133 BCE the last Attalid king of Pergamon willed his kingdom to Rome (see Chapter 5). Nevertheless, although the Romans developed a virtually insatiable taste for Greek "antiques," the Etruscan basis of Roman art and architecture was never forgotten. The buildings and statues of the Roman Republic are highly eclectic, drawing on both Greek and Etruscan traditions.

TEMPLE OF PORTUNUS, ROME Eclecticism is the primary characteristic of the Republican temple on the east bank of the Tiber popularly known as the Temple of Fortuna Virilis (FIGS. 10-2, no. 1, and 10-3). It is actually a temple dedicated to Portunus, the Roman god of harbors. Its plan follows the Etruscan pattern with a high podium and a flight of steps only at the front. Freestanding columns are confined to the deep porch. But the structure is built of stone (local tufa and travertine), overlaid originally with stucco in imitation of Greek marble. The columns are not Tuscan but Ionic, complete with flutes and bases, and there is a matching Ionic frieze (see "Doric and Ionic Orders," Chapter 5, page 110). Moreover, in an effort to approximate a peripteral Greek temple yet maintain the basic Etruscan plan, the architect added a series of engaged Ionic half columns to the sides and back of the cella. The result was a *pseudoperipteral* temple. Although the design combines Etruscan and Greek elements, the resultant mix is uniquely Roman.

10-3 Temple of Portunus (Temple of "Fortuna Virilis"), Rome, Italy, ca. 75 BCE. ◼◀

Republican temples combine Etruscan plans and Greek elevations. This pseudoperipteral stone temple employs the Ionic order, but it has a staircase and freestanding columns only at the front.

10-4 Temple of Vesta(?), Tivoli, Italy, early first century BCE.

The round, or tholos, temple type is unknown in Etruria. The models for the Tivoli temple's builders were in Greece (FIG. 5-72), but the Roman building has a frontal orientation and a concrete cella.

TEMPLE OF VESTA, TIVOLI The Romans' admiration for the Greek temples they encountered in their conquests also led to the importation into Republican Italy of a temple type unknown in Etruscan architecture—the round, or tholos, temple. At Tivoli (ancient Tibur), on a dramatic site overlooking a deep gorge, a Republican architect erected such a Greek-inspired temple (FIG. 10-4) early in the first century BCE. The temple is circular in plan—standard for shrines of Vesta—and has travertine Corinthian columns. The frieze is carved with garlands held up by oxen heads, also in emulation of Greek models. But the high podium can be reached only via a narrow stairway leading to the cella door. This arrangement introduced an axial alignment not found in Greek tholoi (FIG. 5-72), where, as in Greek rectangular temples, steps continue all around the structure. Also in contrast with the Greeks, the Roman builders constructed the cella wall not with masonry blocks but with a new material of recent invention: concrete (see "Roman Concrete Construction," page 241).

SANCTUARY OF FORTUNA, PALESTRINA The most impressive and innovative use of concrete during the Republic was in the Sanctuary of Fortuna Primigenia (FIG. 10-5), the goddess of good fortune, at Palestrina (ancient Praeneste, formerly an Etruscan city). The great complex was constructed in the late second century BCE. Spread out over several terraces leading up the hillside to a tho-

10-5 Restored view of the Sanctuary of Fortuna Primigenia, Palestrina, Italy, late second century BCE (John Burge).

Fortuna's hillside sanctuary at Palestrina was made possible by the use of concrete barrel vaults for terraces, ramps, shops, and porticos spread out over several levels. A tholos temple crowned the complex.

Roman Concrete Construction

The history of Roman architecture would be very different had the Romans been content to use the same building materials as the Greeks, Etruscans, and other ancient peoples. Instead, the Romans developed concrete construction, which revolutionized architectural design. Roman *concrete* was made from a changing recipe of lime mortar, volcanic sand, water, and small stones (*caementa,* from which the English word *cement* derives). Builders placed the mixture in wooden frames and left it to dry. When the concrete hardened completely, they removed the wooden molds, leaving behind a solid mass of great strength, though rough in appearance. The Romans often covered the rough concrete with stucco or with marble *revetment* (facing). Despite this lengthy procedure, concrete walls were much less costly to construct than walls of imported Greek marble or even local tufa and travertine.

The advantages of concrete go well beyond cost, however. It is possible to fashion concrete shapes that masonry construction cannot achieve, especially huge vaulted and domed rooms without internal supports. Concrete enabled Roman builders to think of architecture in revolutionary ways. Roman concrete became a vehicle for shaping architectural space.

The most common types of Roman concrete vaults and domes are

▮ *Barrel Vaults* Also called the *tunnel vault,* the *barrel vault* (FIG. 10-6*a*) is an extension of a simple arch, creating a semicylindrical ceiling over parallel walls. Pre-Roman builders constructed barrel vaults using traditional ashlar masonry (FIG. 2-24), but those earlier vaults were less stable than concrete barrel vaults. If even a single block of a cut-stone vault comes loose, the whole vault may collapse. Also, masonry barrel vaults can be illuminated only by light entering at either end of the tunnel. Using concrete, Roman builders could place windows at any point in a barrel vault, because once the concrete hardens, it forms a seamless sheet of "artificial stone" in which the openings do not lessen the vault's structural integrity. Whether made of stone or concrete, barrel vaults

require *buttressing* (lateral support) of the walls below the vaults to counteract their downward and outward *thrust.*

▮ *Groin Vaults* A *groin* or *cross vault* (FIG. 10-6*b*) is formed by the intersection at right angles of two barrel vaults of equal size. Besides appearing lighter than the barrel vault, the groin vault needs less buttressing. The barrel vault's thrust is concentrated along the entire length of the supporting wall. The groin vault's thrust, however, is concentrated along the *groins,* the lines at the juncture of the two barrel vaults. Buttressing is needed only at the points where the groins meet the vault's vertical supports, usually *piers.* The system leaves the area between the supports open, permitting light to enter. Groin vaults, like barrel vaults, can be built using stone blocks—but with the same structural limitations when compared with concrete vaulting.

When a series of groin vaults covers an interior hall (FIG. 10-6*c;* compare FIG. 10-46), the open lateral arches of the vaults form the equivalent of a *clerestory* of a traditional timber-roofed structure (for example, FIG. 11-10). Such a *fenestrated* (with openings or windows) sequence of groin vaults has a major advantage over wooden clerestories. Concrete vaults are relatively fireproof, always an important consideration given that fires were common occurrences (see "Timber Roofs and Stone Vaults," Chapter 17, page 435).

▮ *Hemispherical Domes* The largest domed space in the ancient world for more than a millennium was the corbeled, beehive-shaped tholos (FIG. 4-21) of the Treasury of Atreus at Mycenae. The Romans were able to surpass the Mycenaeans by using concrete to construct hemispherical *domes* (FIG. 10-6*d*), which usually rested on concrete cylindrical *drums.* If a barrel vault is described as a round arch extended in a line, then a hemispherical dome may be described as a round arch rotated around the full circumference of a circle. Masonry domes, like masonry vaults, cannot accommodate windows without threatening their stability. Concrete domes can be opened up even at their apex with a circular *oculus* ("eye"), allowing much-needed light to reach the vast spaces beneath (FIGS. 10-35 and 10-51).

10-6 Roman concrete construction. (a) barrel vault, (b) groin vault, (c) fenestrated sequence of groin vaults, (d) hemispherical dome with oculus (John Burge).

Concrete domes and vaults of varying designs enabled Roman builders to revolutionize the history of architecture by shaping interior spaces in novel ways.

los at the peak of an ascending triangle, the layout reflects the new Republican familiarity with the terraced sanctuaries of the Hellenistic East. The means of construction, however, was distinctly Roman. The builders used concrete barrel vaults (FIG. 10-6*a*) of enormous strength to support the imposing terraces and to cover the great ramps leading to the grand central staircase, as well as to give shape

to the shops selling food, souvenirs, and the like, aligned on two consecutive levels. In this way, the Romans transformed the entire hillside, subjecting nature itself to human will and rational order. The Palestrina sanctuary is emblematic of the growing dominance of Rome in the Mediterranean world. By the end of the second century BCE, Romulus's village of huts belonged to the legendary past.

Sculpture

Nearly all the builders of Republican temples and sanctuaries were men from old and distinguished families. Often they were victorious generals who used the spoils of war to finance public works. These aristocratic patricians were fiercely proud of their lineage. They kept likenesses (*imagines*) of their ancestors in wooden cupboards in their homes and paraded them at the funerals of prominent relatives. Portraiture was one way the patrician class celebrated its elevated position in society. The case of Marius, a renowned Republican general who lacked a long and distinguished genealogy, underscores the importance of ancestral imagines in elite circles. Marius's patrician colleagues in the Senate ridiculed him as a man who had no portraits in his home.

VERISM The subjects of these portraits were almost exclusively men (and to a lesser extent women) of advanced age, for generally only elders held power in the Republic. These patricians did not ask sculptors to make them appear nobler than they were, as Kresilas portrayed Pericles (FIG. 5-41). Instead, they requested brutally realistic images with distinctive features, in the tradition of the treasured household *imagines*. One of the most striking of these so-called *veristic* (superrealistic) portraits is the head (FIG. 10-7) of an unidentified patrician from Osimo. The sculptor painstakingly recorded each rise and fall, each bulge and fold, of the facial surface, like a mapmaker who did not want to miss the slightest detail of surface change. Scholars debate whether such portraits were truly blunt records of actual features or exaggerated types designed to make a statement about personality: serious, experienced, determined, loyal to family and state—virtues that were much admired during the Republic.

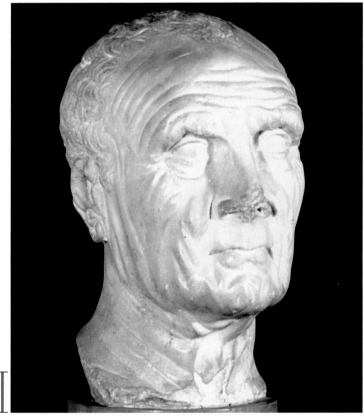

10-7 Head of an old man, from Osimo, mid-first century BCE. Marble, life-size. Palazzo del Municipio, Osimo.

Veristic (superrealistic) portraits of old men from distinguished families were the norm during the Republic. The sculptor of this head painstakingly recorded every detail of the elderly man's face.

10-8 Portrait of a Roman general, from the Sanctuary of Hercules, Tivoli, Italy, ca. 75–50 BCE. Marble, 6′ 2″ high. Museo Nazionale Romano–Palazzo Massimo alle Terme, Rome.

The sculptor based this life-size portrait of a general on idealized Greek statues of heroes and athletes, but the man's head is a veristic likeness. The eclectic combination is typical of Republican art.

1 ft.

TIVOLI GENERAL The Osimo head also illustrates that the Romans believed the head alone was enough to constitute a portrait. The Greeks, in contrast, believed the head and body were inseparable parts of an integral whole, so their portraits were always full length (FIG. 5-87). In fact, in Republican portraiture, veristic heads were often—although incongruously—placed on bodies to which they could not possibly belong. Such is the case in the curious and discordant portrait of a general (FIG. 10-8) found at Tivoli. The *cuirass* (leather breastplate) at his side, which serves as a prop for the heavy marble statue, is the emblem of his rank. But the general does not appear as he would in life. Although he has a typically stern and lined Republican head, it sits atop a powerful, youthful, almost nude body. The sculptor modeled the portrait on the statues of Greek athletes and heroes the Romans admired so much and often copied (see Chapter 5). The incorporation of references to Greek art in these portrait statues evoked the notion of patrician cultural superiority and elevated the person portrayed to heroic status.

NONELITE PORTRAITURE In stark contrast to this elite tradition of publicly displaying portraits, slaves and former slaves could not possess *any* family portraits, because under Roman law, their parents and grandparents were not people but property. Freed slaves, however, often ordered portrait reliefs (FIGS. 10-9 and 10-10) for their tombs to commemorate their new status as Roman citizens (see "Art for Former Slaves," page 243).

Art for Former Slaves

Historians and art historians alike tend to focus on the lives and monuments of famous individuals, but some of the most interesting remains of ancient Roman civilization are the artworks commissioned by ordinary people, especially former slaves, or *freedmen* and *freedwomen*. Slavery was common in the Roman world. Indeed, researchers estimate that Italy at the end of the Republic had some two million slaves, or roughly one slave for every three citizens. The very rich might own hundreds of slaves, but slaves could be found in all but the poorest households. The practice was so much a part of Roman society that even slaves often became slave owners when their former masters freed them. Some gained freedom in return for meritorious service. Others were only freed in their masters' wills. Most slaves died as slaves in service to their original or new owners.

The most noteworthy artworks that Roman freedmen and freedwomen commissioned are the stone reliefs that regularly adorned their tomb facades. One of these reliefs (FIG. 10-9) depicts three people, all named Gessius. At the left is Gessia Fausta, at the right Gessius Primus. Both are the freed slaves of Publius Gessius, the freeborn citizen in the center, shown wearing a general's cuirass and portrayed in the standard Republican veristic fashion (FIGS. 10-7 and 10-8). As slaves this couple had no legal standing. They were the property of Publius Gessius. After they were freed, however, they became people by law. These stern frontal portraits proclaim their new status as legal members of Roman society—and, by including him in the relief, their gratitude to Publius Gessius for granting them that status.

As was the custom, the two former slaves bear their patron's name, but whether they are sister and brother, wife and husband, or unrelated is unclear. The inscriptions on the relief explicitly state that the monument was paid for with funds provided by the will of Gessius Primus and that the work was directed by Gessia Fausta, the only survivor of the three. The relief thus depicts the living and the dead side by side, indistinguishable except by the accompanying message. This theme is common in Roman art and affirms that death does not break bonds formed in life.

More rarely, freed slaves commissioned tomb reliefs that were narrative in character. A relief (FIG. 10-10) from Amiternum depicts the honorary funeral cortege, complete with musicians, professional female mourners who pull their hair in a display of feigned grief, and the deceased's wife and children. The deceased is laid out on a bier with a canopy as a backdrop, much like the figures on Greek Geometric vases (FIG. 5-2). Surprisingly, however, the dead man here props himself up as if still alive, surveying his own funeral. This may be an effigy, like the reclining figures on the lids of Etruscan sarcophagi (FIGS. 9-5 and 9-15), rather than the deceased himself.

Compositionally, the relief is also unexpected. Mourners and musicians stand on floating ground lines, as if on flying carpets. They are not to be viewed as suspended in space, however, but as situated behind the front row of pallbearers and musicians. This sculptor, in striking contrast to the (usually Greek) artists the patrician aristocracy employed, had little regard for the rules of Classical art. The Amiternum artist studiously avoided overlapping and placed the figures wherever they fit, so long as they were clearly visible. This approach to making pictures was characteristic of pre-Classical art, but it had been out of favor for several centuries. There are no similar compositions in the art of the consuls and senators of the Roman Republic. In ancient Rome's cosmopolitan world, as today, stylistic tastes often were tied to a person's political and social status.

10-9 Funerary relief with portraits of the Gessii, from Rome(?), Italy, ca. 30 BCE. Marble, 2′ 1½″ high. Museum of Fine Arts, Boston.

Roman freedmen often placed reliefs depicting themselves and their former owners on the facades of their tombs. The portraits and inscriptions celebrated their freedom and new status as citizens.

10-10 Relief with funerary procession, from Amiternum, Italy, second half of first century BCE. Limestone, 2′ 2″ high. Museo Nazionale d'Abruzzo, L'Aquila.

This depiction of a procession of mourners and musicians in honor of a dead freedman has figures standing on floating ground lines. The sculptor ignored the rules of Classical art that elite patrons favored.

10-11 Denarius with portrait of Julius Caesar, 44 BCE. Silver, diameter $\frac{3}{4}$". American Numismatic Society, New York.

Julius Caesar was the first to place his own portrait on the Roman coinage during his lifetime. This denarius, issued just before his assassination, shows the dictator with a deeply lined face and neck.

10-11A Pompey the Great, ca. 55–50 BCE.

JULIUS CAESAR Beginning early in the first century BCE, the Roman desire to vaunt distinguished ancestry led to the placement of portraits of illustrious forebears on Republican coins. These ancestral portraits supplanted the earlier Roman tradition (based on Greek convention) of using images of divinities on coins. No Roman, however, dared to place his own likeness on a coin until 44 BCE, when Julius Caesar, shortly before his assassination on the Ides of March, issued coins featuring his portrait and his newly acquired title, *dictator perpetuo* (dictator for life). The *denarius* (the standard Roman silver coin, from which the word *penny* ultimately derives) illustrated here (FIG. **10-11**) records Caesar's aging face and receding hairline in conformity with the Republican veristic tradition. But placing the likeness of a living person on a coin violated all the norms of Republican propriety. Henceforth, Roman coins, which circulated throughout the vast territories under Roman control, would be used to mold public opinion in favor of the ruler by announcing his achievements—both real and fictional.

POMPEII AND THE CITIES OF VESUVIUS

On August 24, 79 CE, Mount Vesuvius, a long-dormant volcano, suddenly erupted (see "An Eyewitness Account of the Eruption of Mount Vesuvius," page 245). Many prosperous towns around the Bay of Naples (the ancient Greek city of Neapolis), among them Pompeii, were buried in a single day. This event was a catastrophe for the inhabitants of the Vesuvian cities but became a boon for archaeologists and art historians. When researchers first explored the buried cities in the 18th century, the ruins had been undisturbed for nearly 1,700 years. The Vesuvian sites permit a reconstruction of the art and life of Roman towns of the Late Republic and Early Empire to a degree impossible anywhere else.

The Oscans, one of the many Italic tribes that occupied Italy during the peak of Etruscan culture, were the first to settle at Pompeii. Toward the end of the fifth century BCE, the Samnites, another Italic people, took over the town. Under the influence of their Greek neighbors, the Samnites greatly expanded the original settlement and gave monumental shape to the city center. Pompeii fought with other Italian cities on the losing side against Rome in the so-called Social War that ended in 89 BCE, and in 80 BCE Sulla founded a new Roman colony on the site, with Latin as its official language. The colony's population had grown to between 10,000 and 20,000 when, in February 62 CE, an earthquake shook the city, causing extensive damage. When Mount Vesuvius erupted 17 years later, repairs were still in progress.

Architecture

Walking through Pompeii today is an unforgettable experience. The streets, with their heavy flagstone pavements and sidewalks, are still there, as are the stepping stones that enabled pedestrians to cross the streets without having to step in puddles. Ingeniously, the city planners placed these stones in such a way that vehicle wheels could straddle them, enabling supplies to be brought directly to the shops, taverns, and bakeries. Tourists still can visit the impressive concrete-vaulted rooms of Pompeii's public baths, sit in the seats of its theater and amphitheater, enter the painted bedrooms and statue-filled gardens of private homes, even walk among the tombs outside the city's walls. Pompeii has been called the living city of the dead for good reason.

10-12 Aerial view of the forum (looking northeast), Pompeii, Italy, second century BCE and later. (1) forum, (2) Temple of Jupiter (Capitolium), (3) basilica.

The center of Roman civic life was the forum. At Pompeii, colonnades frame a rectangular plaza with the Capitolium at the northern end. At the southwestern corner is the basilica, Pompeii's law court.

An Eyewitness Account of the Eruption of Mount Vesuvius

Pliny the Elder, whose *Natural History* is one of the most important sources for the history of Greek art, was among those who tried to rescue others from danger when Mount Vesuvius erupted. He was overcome by fumes the volcano spewed forth, and died. His nephew, Pliny the Younger, a government official under the emperor Trajan, left an account of the eruption and his uncle's death:

> [The volcanic cloud's] general appearance can best be expressed as being like a pine . . . for it rose to a great height on a sort of trunk and then split off into branches. . . . Sometimes it looked white, sometimes blotched and dirty, according to the amount of soil and ashes it carried with it. . . . The buildings were now shaking with violent shocks, and seemed to be swaying to and fro as if they were torn from their foundations. Outside, on the other hand, there was the danger of falling pumice-stones, even though these were light and porous. . . . Elsewhere there was daylight, [but around Vesuvius, people] were still in darkness, blacker and denser than any night that ever was. . . . When daylight returned on the 26th—two days after the last day [my uncle] had been seen—his body was found intact and uninjured, still fully clothed and looking more like sleep than death.*

*Betty Radice, trans., *Pliny the Younger: Letters and Panegyricus*, vol. 1 (Cambridge, Mass.: Harvard University Press, 1969), 427–433.

FORUM The center of civic life in any Roman town was its *forum,* or public square, usually located at the city's geographic center at the intersection of the main north-south street, the *cardo,* and the main east-west avenue, the *decumanus* (FIG. 10-42). The forum, however, generally was closed to all but pedestrian traffic. Pompeii's forum (FIG. 10-12) lies in the southwest corner of the expanded Roman city but at the heart of the original town. The forum probably took on monumental form in the second century BCE when the Samnites, inspired by Hellenistic architecture, erected two-story colonnades on three sides of the long and narrow plaza. At the north end they constructed a temple of Jupiter (FIG. 10-12, no. 2). When Pompeii became a Roman colony in 80 BCE, the Romans converted the temple into a *Capitolium*—a triple shrine of Jupiter, Juno, and Minerva, the chief Roman gods. The temple is of standard Republican type, constructed of tufa covered with fine white stucco and combining an Etruscan plan with Corinthian columns. It faces into the civic square, dominating the area. This arrangement contrasts with the siting of Greek temples (FIGS. 5-42 and 5-43), which stood in isolation and could be approached and viewed from all sides, like colossal statues on giant stepped pedestals. The Roman forum, like the Etrusco-Roman temple, has a chief side, a focus of attention.

The area within the porticos of the forum at Pompeii was empty, except for statues portraying local dignitaries and, later, Roman emperors. This is where the citizens conducted daily commerce and held festivities. All around the square, behind the colonnades, were secular and religious structures, including the town's administrative offices. Most noteworthy is the *basilica* (FIG. 10-12, no. 3) at the southwest corner, the earliest well-preserved building of its kind. Constructed during the late second century BCE, the basilica housed the law court of Pompeii and also was used for other official purposes. In plan it resembles the forum itself: long and narrow, with two stories of internal columns dividing the space into a central *nave* and flanking *aisles*. This scheme had a long afterlife in architectural history and will be familiar to anyone who has ever entered a church.

AMPHITHEATER Shortly after the Romans took control of Pompeii, two of the town's wealthiest officials, Quinctius Valgus and Marcus Porcius, used their own funds to erect a large amphitheater (FIG. 10-13) at the southeastern end of town. It is the earliest amphitheater known and could seat some 20,000 spectators—more than the entire population of the town even a century and a half after its construction. The donors would have enjoyed choice reserved seats in the new entertainment center. In fact, seating was assigned by rank, both civic and military, so that the Roman social hierarchy was on display at every event.

The word *amphitheater* means "double theater," and Roman amphitheaters closely resemble two Greek theaters put together. Greek theaters were situated on natural hillsides (FIG. 5-71), but supporting an amphitheater's continuous elliptical *cavea* (seating area) required building an artificial mountain. Only concrete, unknown to the Greeks, could meet that requirement. In the Pompeii amphitheater, a series of shallow concrete barrel vaults forms a giant retaining wall that holds up the earthen mound and stone seats. Barrel vaults

10-13 Aerial view of the amphitheater, Pompeii, Italy, ca. 70 BCE.

Pompeii's amphitheater is the oldest known. It is also an early example of Roman concrete technology. In the arena, bloody gladiatorial combats and wild animal hunts were staged for 20,000 spectators.

10-14 Brawl in the Pompeii amphitheater, wall painting from House I,3,23, Pompeii, Italy, ca. 60–79 CE. Fresco, 5′ 7″ × 6′ 1″. Museo Archeologico Nazionale, Naples.

This mural painting records a brawl that broke out in the Pompeii amphitheater in 59 CE. The painter included the cloth awning that could be rolled down to shield the audience from the sun and rain.

10-15 Atrium of the House of the Vettii, Pompeii, Italy, second century BCE, rebuilt 62–79 CE.

Roman townhouses had a central atrium with an impluvium to collect rainwater. Cubicula (bedrooms) opened onto the atrium, and in Hellenized houses such as this one, builders added a peristyle garden at the rear.

running all the way through the mountain of earth form the tunnels leading to the *arena,* the central area where bloody gladiatorial combats and wild animal hunts (see "Spectacles in the Colosseum," page 260) occurred. (*Arena* is Latin for "sand," which soaked up the blood of the wounded and killed.) The Roman amphitheater stands in sharp contrast, both architecturally and functionally, to the Greek theater, home of refined performances of comedies and tragedies.

A painting (FIG. **10-14**) on the wall of a Pompeian house records an unfortunate incident that occurred in the amphitheater. A brawl broke out between the Pompeians and their neighbors, the Nucerians, during a gladiatorial contest in 59 CE. The fighting left many seriously wounded and led to the closing of the amphitheater for a decade. The painting shows the cloth awning (*velarium*) that could be rolled down from the top of the cavea to shield spectators from sun and rain. It also features the distinctive external double staircases (not visible in FIG. **10-13**) that enabled large numbers of people to enter and exit the cavea in an orderly fashion.

HOUSE OF THE VETTII The evidence from Pompeii regarding Roman domestic architecture (see "The Roman House," page 247) is unparalleled anywhere else and is the most precious byproduct of the catastrophic volcanic eruption of 79 CE. One of the best-preserved houses at Pompeii, partially rebuilt, is the House of the Vettii, an old Pompeian house remodeled and repainted after the 62 CE earthquake. A photograph (FIG. **10-15**) taken in the *fauces* (foyer; see FIG. **10-16**) shows the *impluvium* in the center of the *atrium,* the opening in the roof above, and, in the background, the *peristyle* garden with its marble tables and splendid mural paintings dating to the last years of the Vesuvian city. At that time, two brothers, Aulus Vettius Restitutus and Aulus Vettius Conviva, probably freedmen who had made their fortune as merchants, owned the house. Their wealth enabled them to purchase and furnish the kind of fashionable townhouse that in an earlier era only patricians could have acquired.

10-15A
Peristyle,
House of
the Vettii,
Pompeii,
second
century BCE.

Painting

The houses and villas around Mount Vesuvius have yielded a treasure trove of mural paintings, the most complete record of the changing fashions in interior decoration found anywhere in the ancient world. The sheer quantity of these paintings tells a great deal about both the prosperity and the tastes of the times. How many homes today, even of the very wealthy, have custom-painted murals in nearly every room? Roman wall paintings were true frescoes (see "Fresco Painting," Chapter 19, page 504), with the colors applied while the plaster was still damp. The process was painstaking. First the painter had to prepare the wall by applying the plaster (mixed with marble dust if the patron could afford it) in several layers with a smooth trowel. Only then could painting begin. Finally, when the surface dried, the painter polished the wall to achieve a marblelike finish.

In the early years of exploration at Pompeii and nearby Herculaneum, excavators focused almost exclusively on the figural panels that formed part of the overall mural designs, especially those depicting Greek heroes and famous myths. Workers cut the panels out of the walls and transferred them to the Naples Archaeological Museum. In time, more enlightened archaeologists halted the practice of cutting pieces out of the walls and began to give serious attention to the mural designs as a whole. Toward the end of the 19th century, August Mau, a German art historian, divided the various mural painting schemes into four so-called Pompeian Styles. Mau's classification system, although later refined and modified in detail, still serves as the basis for the study of Roman painting.

The Roman House

The Roman house was more than just a place to live. It played an important role in Roman societal rituals. In the Roman world, individuals were frequently bound to others in a patron-client relationship whereby a wealthier, better-educated, and more powerful *patronus* would protect the interests of a *cliens,* sometimes large numbers of them. The standing of a patron in Roman society often was measured by clientele size. Being seen in public accompanied by a crowd of clients was a badge of honor. In this system, a plebeian might be bound to a patrician, a freed slave to a former owner, or even one patrician to another. Regardless of rank, all clients were obligated to support their patron in political campaigns and to perform specific services on request, as well as to call on and salute the patron at the patron's home.

A client calling on a patron would enter the typical Roman *domus* (private house) through a narrow *fauces* (the "jaws" of the house), which led to a large central reception area, the *atrium*. The rooms flanking the fauces could open onto the atrium, as in FIG. 10-16, or onto the street, in which case they were rented out as shops. The roof over the atrium was partially open to the sky, not only to admit light but also to channel rainwater into a basin (*impluvium*) below. The water could be stored in cisterns for household use. Opening onto the atrium was a series of small bedrooms called *cubicula* (cubicles). At the back were two recessed areas (*alae,* wings) and the patron's *tablinum* or "home office," a dining room (*triclinium*), a kitchen, and sometimes a small garden.

Endless variations of the same basic plan exist, dictated by an owner's personal tastes and means, the size and shape of the lot purchased, and so forth, but all Roman houses of this type were inward-looking in nature. The design shut off the street's noise and dust, and all internal activity focused on the brightly illuminated atrium at the center of the residence. This basic module (only the front half of the typical house in FIG. 10-16) resembles the plan of the typical Etruscan house as reflected in the Tomb of the Shields and Chairs (FIG. 9-7) and other tombs at Cerveteri. Thus, few scholars doubt that the early Roman house, like the early Roman temple, grew out of the Etruscan tradition.

During the second century BCE, when Roman architects were beginning to construct stone temples with Greek columns, the Roman house also took on Greek airs. Builders added a *peristyle* garden behind the Etruscan-style house, providing a second internal source of illumination as well as a pleasant setting for meals served in a summer triclinium. The axial symmetry of the plan meant that on entering the fauces of the house, a visitor could be greeted by a vista through the atrium directly into the peristyle garden (as in FIG. 10-15), which often boasted a fountain or pool, marble statuary, mural paintings, and mosaic floors.

While such private houses were typical of Pompeii and other Italian towns, they were very rare in large cities such as Rome, where the masses lived instead in multistory apartment houses (FIG. 10-54).

10-16 Restored view and plan of a typical Roman house of the Late Republic and Early Empire (John Burge). (1) fauces, (2) atrium, (3) impluvium, (4) cubiculum, (5) ala, (6) tablinum, (7) triclinium, (8) peristyle.

Older Roman houses closely followed Etruscan models and had atriums and small gardens, but during the Late Republic and Early Empire, Roman builders added peristyles with Greek columns.

10-17 First Style wall painting in the fauces of the Samnite House, Herculaneum, Italy, late second century BCE.

In First Style murals, the decorator's aim was to imitate costly marble panels using painted stucco relief. The style is Greek in origin and another example of the Hellenization of Republican architecture.

FIRST STYLE The *First Style* is also called the Masonry Style because the decorator's aim was to imitate costly marble panels using painted stucco relief. The fauces (FIG. **10-17**) of the Samnite House at Herculaneum greets the visitor with a stunning illusion of walls constructed, or at least faced, with marbles imported from quarries all over the Mediterranean. This approach to wall decoration is comparable to the modern practice, employed in private libraries and corporate meeting rooms alike, of using cheaper manufactured materials to approximate the look and shape of genuine wood paneling. The practice is not, however, uniquely Pompeian or Roman. First Style walls are well documented in the Greek world from the late fourth century BCE on. The use of the First Style in Republican houses is yet another example of the Hellenization of Roman architecture.

SECOND STYLE The First Style never went completely out of fashion, but after 80 BCE a new approach to mural design became more popular. The *Second Style* is in most respects the antithesis of the First Style. Some scholars have argued that the Second Style also has precedents in Greece, but most believe it is a Roman invention. Certainly, the Second Style evolved in Italy and was popular until around 15 BCE, when Roman painters introduced the Third Style. Second Style painters did not aim to create the illusion of an elegant marble wall, as First Style painters sought to do. Rather, they wanted to dissolve a room's confining walls and replace them with the illusion of an imaginary three-dimensional world.

VILLA OF THE MYSTERIES An early example of the new style is the room (FIG. **10-18**) that gives its name to the Villa of the Mysteries at Pompeii. Many scholars believe this chamber was used to celebrate, in private, the rites of the Greek god Dionysos (Roman Bacchus). Dionysos was the focus of an unofficial mystery religion popular among women in Italy at this time. The precise nature of the Dionysiac rites is unknown, but the figural cycle in the Villa of the Mysteries, illustrating mortals (all female save for one boy) interacting with mythological figures, probably provides some evidence for the cult's initiation rites. In these rites young women, emulating Ariadne, daughter of King Minos (see Chapter 4), united in marriage with Dionysos.

The backdrop for the nearly life-size figures is a series of painted panels imitating marble revetment, just as in the First Style but without the modeling in relief. In front of this marble wall (but actually on the same two-dimensional surface), the painter created the illusion of a shallow ledge on which the human and divine actors move around the room. Especially striking is the way some of the figures interact across the corners of the room. For example, a seminude winged woman at the far right of the rear wall lashes out with her whip across the space of the room at a kneeling woman with a bare back (the initiate and bride-to-be of Dionysos) on the left end of the right wall. Nothing comparable to this room existed in Hellenistic Greece. Despite the presence of Dionysos, satyrs, and other figures from Greek mythology, this is a Roman design.

VILLA AT BOSCOREALE In the early Second Style Dionysiac mystery frieze, the spatial illusionism is confined to the painted platform that projects into the room. But in mature Second Style designs, Roman painters created a three-dimensional setting that also extends beyond the wall. An example is a cubiculum (FIG. **10-19**) from the Villa of Publius Fannius Synistor at Boscoreale, near Pompeii, decorated between 50 and 40 BCE. The excavators removed the frescoes soon after their discovery, and today they are part of a reconstructed Roman bedroom in the Metropolitan Museum of Art. All around the room the Second Style painter opened up the walls with vistas of Italian towns, marble temples, and colonnaded courtyards. Painted doors and gates invite the viewer to walk through the wall into the magnificent world the painter created.

Although the Boscoreale painter was inconsistent in applying it, this Roman artist, like many others around the Bay of Naples, demonstrated a knowledge of single-point *linear perspective*, often incorrectly said to be an innovation of Italian Renaissance artists (see "Renaissance Perspectival Systems," Chapter 21, page 547). In this kind of perspective, all the receding lines in a composition converge on a single point along the painting's central axis to show depth and distance. Ancient writers noted that Greek painters of the fifth century BCE first used linear perspective for the design of Athenian stage sets (hence its Greek name, *skenographia*, "scene painting"). In the Boscoreale cubiculum, the painter most successfully employed the device in the far corners, where a low gate leads to a

10-18 Dionysiac mystery frieze, Second Style wall paintings in room 5 of the Villa of the Mysteries, Pompeii, Italy, ca. 60–50 BCE. Fresco, frieze 5′ 4″ high.

Second Style painters created the illusion of an imaginary three-dimensional world on the walls of Roman houses. The figures in this room are acting out the initiation rites of the Dionysiac mysteries.

10-19 Second Style wall paintings (general view, *left,* and detail of tholos, *right*) from cubiculum M of the Villa of Publius Fannius Synistor, Boscoreale, Italy, ca. 50–40 BCE. Fresco, 8′ 9″ high. Metropolitan Museum of Art, New York.

In this Second Style bedroom, the painter opened up the walls with vistas of towns, temples, and colonnaded courtyards. The convincing illusionism is due in part to the use of linear perspective.

10-20 Gardenscape, Second Style wall paintings, from the Villa of Livia, Primaporta, Italy, ca. 30–20 BCE. Fresco, 6' 7" high. Museo Nazionale Romano–Palazzo Massimo alle Terme, Rome.

The ultimate example of a Second Style "picture-window" wall is Livia's gardenscape. To suggest recession, the painter used atmospheric perspective, intentionally blurring the most distant forms.

peristyle framing a tholos temple (FIG. 10-19, *right*). Linear perspective was a favored tool of Second Style painters seeking to transform the usually windowless walls of Roman houses into "picture-window" vistas that expanded the apparent space of the rooms.

VILLA OF LIVIA, PRIMAPORTA The ultimate example of a Second Style picture-window mural (FIG. 10-20) comes from the Villa of Livia, wife of the emperor Augustus, at Primaporta, just north of Rome. There, imperial painters decorated all the walls of a vaulted room with lush gardenscapes. The only architectural element is the flimsy fence of the garden itself. To suggest recession, the painter mastered another kind of perspective, *atmospheric perspective*, indicating depth by the increasingly blurred appearance of objects in the distance. At Livia's villa, the artist precisely painted the fence, trees, and birds in the foreground, whereas the details of the dense foliage in the background are indistinct. Among the wall paintings examined so far, only the landscape fresco (FIG. 4-9) from Thera offers a similar wraparound view of nature. But the Aegean fresco's white sky and red, yellow, and blue rock formations do not create a successful illusion of a world filled with air and light just a few steps away.

10-21 Detail of a Third Style wall painting, from cubiculum 15 of the Villa of Agrippa Postumus, Boscotrecase, Italy, ca. 10 BCE. Fresco, 7' 8" high. Metropolitan Museum of Art, New York.

In the Third Style, Roman painters decorated walls with delicate linear fantasies sketched on predominantly monochromatic backgrounds. Here, a tiny floating landscape on a black ground is the central motif.

THIRD STYLE The Primaporta gardenscape is the polar opposite of First Style designs, which reinforce, rather than deny, the heavy presence of confining walls. But tastes changed rapidly in the Roman world, as in society today. Not long after Livia had her villa painted, Roman patrons began to favor mural designs that reasserted the primacy of the wall surface. In the *Third Style* of Pompeian painting, artists no longer attempted to replace the walls with three-dimensional worlds of their own creation. Nor did they seek to imitate the appearance of the marble walls of Hellenistic kings. Instead they decorated walls with delicate linear fantasies sketched on predominantly *monochromatic* (one-color) backgrounds.

VILLA AT BOSCOTRECASE One of the earliest examples of the new style is a cubiculum (FIG. 10-21) in the Villa of Agrippa Postumus at Boscotrecase. The villa was probably painted just before 10 BCE. Nowhere did the artist use illusionistic painting to penetrate the wall. In place of the stately columns of the Second Style are insubstantial and impossibly thin *colonnettes* supporting featherweight canopies barely reminiscent of pediments. In the center of this delicate and elegant architectural frame is a tiny floating landscape painted directly on the jet black ground. It is hard to imagine a sharper contrast with the panoramic gardenscape at Livia's villa. On other Third Style walls, landscapes and mythological scenes appear in frames, like modern canvas paintings hung on walls. Never could these framed panels be mistaken for windows opening onto a world beyond the room.

FOURTH STYLE In the *Fourth Style*, however, a taste for illusionism returned once again. This style became popular in the 50s CE, and it was the preferred manner of mural decoration at Pompeii when the eruption of Vesuvius buried the town in volcanic ash in 79. Some examples of the new style, such as room 78 (FIG. 10-22) in the emperor Nero's Golden House in Rome (see page 259), display a kinship with the Third Style. All the walls are an austere creamy white. In some areas the artist painted sea creatures, birds, and other motifs directly on the monochromatic background, much like the landscape in the Boscotrecase villa (FIG. 10-21). Landscapes appear here too—as framed paintings in the center of each large white subdivision of the wall. Views through the wall are also part of the design, but the Fourth Style architectural vistas are irrational fantasies. The viewer looks out not on cityscapes or round temples set in peristyles but at fragments of buildings—columns supporting half-pediments, double stories of columns supporting nothing at all—painted on the same white ground as the rest of the wall. In the Fourth Style, architecture became just another motif in the painter's ornamental repertoire.

10-22 Fourth Style wall paintings in room 78 of the Domus Aurea (Golden House) of Nero, Rome, Italy, 64–68 CE.

The creamy white walls of this room in Nero's Golden House display a kinship with the Third Style, but views through the wall revealing irrational architectural vistas characterize the new Fourth Style.

10-23 Fourth Style wall paintings in the Ixion Room (triclinium P) of the House of the Vettii, Pompeii, Italy, ca. 70–79 CE.

Late Fourth Style murals are often garishly colored, crowded, and confused compositions with a mixture of architectural views, framed mythological panel paintings, and First and Third Style motifs.

IXION ROOM In the latest Fourth Style designs, Pompeian painters rejected the quiet elegance of the Third Style and early Fourth Style in favor of crowded and confused compositions and sometimes garish color combinations. The Ixion Room (FIG. **10-23**) of the House of the Vettii at Pompeii was decorated in this manner just before the eruption of Mount Vesuvius. The room served as a triclinium in the house the Vettius brothers remodeled after the earthquake. It opened onto the peristyle seen in the background of FIG. **10-15**.

The decor of the Ixion Room serves as a synopsis of all the previous styles, another instance of the eclecticism noted earlier as characteristic of Roman art in general. The lowest zone, for example, is one of the most successful imitations anywhere of costly multicolored imported marbles, despite the fact that the painter created the illusion without recourse to relief, as in the First Style. The large white panels in the corners of the room, with their delicate floral frames and floating central motifs, would fit naturally into the most elegant Third Style design. Unmistakably Fourth Style, however, are the fragmentary architectural vistas of the central and upper zones of the walls. They are unrelated to one another, do not constitute a unified cityscape beyond the wall, and incorporate figures that would tumble into the room if they took a single step forward.

The Ixion Room takes its name from the mythological panel painting at the center of the rear wall (FIG. **10-23**). Ixion had attempted to seduce Hera, and Zeus punished him by binding him to a perpetually spinning wheel. The panels on the two side walls also have Greek myths as subjects. The Ixion Room may be likened to a small private art gallery with paintings decorating the walls, as in many modern homes. Scholars long have believed that these and the many other mythological paintings on Third and Fourth Style walls were based on lost Greek panels. They attest to the Romans' continuing admiration for Greek artworks three centuries after Marcellus brought the treasures of Syracuse to Rome. But few, if any, of these mythological paintings can be described as true copies of "Old Masters," as are the many Roman replicas of famous Greek statues that have been found throughout the Roman world, including Pompeii (FIG. **5-40**).

WALL MOSAICS Mythological figures were on occasion also the subject of Roman mosaics. In the ancient world, mosaics were usually confined to floors (as was the Pompeian *Alexander Mosaic*, FIG. **5-70**), where the tesserae formed a durable as well as decorative surface. In Roman times, however, mosaics also decorated walls and even ceilings, foreshadowing the extensive use of wall and vault mosaics in the Middle Ages (see "Mosaics," Chapter 11, page 303). The mosaic shown in FIG. **10-24** adorns a wall in the House of Neptune and Amphitrite at Herculaneum. The statuesque figures of the sea god and his wife preside over the running water of the fountain in the courtyard in front of them where the home's owners and guests enjoyed outdoor dining in warm weather.

PRIVATE PORTRAITS The subjects chosen for Roman wall paintings and mosaics were diverse. Although mythological themes were immensely popular, Romans commissioned a vast range of other subjects. As noted, landscape paintings frequently appear on Second, Third, and Fourth Style walls. Paintings and mosaics depicting scenes from history include the *Alexander Mosaic* (FIG. **5-70**) and

10-24 Neptune and Amphitrite, wall mosaic in the summer triclinium of the House of Neptune and Amphitrite, Herculaneum, Italy, ca. 62–79 CE.

In the ancient world, mosaics were usually confined to floors, but this example depicting Neptune and Amphitrite decorates the wall of a private house. The sea deities fittingly overlook an elaborate fountain.

1 in.

10-25 Portrait of a husband and wife, wall painting from House VII,2,6, Pompeii, Italy, ca. 70–79 CE. Fresco, 1′ 11″ × 1′ 8$\frac{1}{2}$″. Museo Archeologico Nazionale, Naples.

This husband and wife wished to present themselves to their guests as thoughtful and well-read. The portraits are individualized likenesses, but the poses and attributes they hold are standard types.

the mural painting (FIG. 10-14) of the brawl in the amphitheater of Pompeii. Given the Roman custom of keeping *imagines* of illustrious ancestors in atriums, it is not surprising that painted portraits also appear in Pompeian houses. The portrait of a husband and wife illustrated here (FIG. 10-25) originally formed part of a Fourth Style wall of an *exedra,* or recessed area, opening onto the atrium of a Pompeian house. The man holds a scroll and the woman a *stylus* (writing instrument) and a wax writing tablet, standard attributes in Roman marriage portraits. They suggest the fine education of those depicted—even if, as was sometimes true, the individuals were uneducated or even illiterate. Such portraits were thus the Roman equivalent of modern wedding photographs of the bride and groom posing in rented formal garments that they never wore before or afterward (see "Role Playing in Roman Portraiture," page 254). In contrast, the heads are not standard types but sensitive studies of the couple's individual faces. This is another instance of a realistic portrait placed on a conventional figure type (compare FIG. 10-8), a recurring phenomenon in Roman portraiture.

STILL-LIFE PAINTING The Roman interest in recording the unique appearance of individual people extended to everyday objects. This explains the frequent inclusion of *still-life* paintings (representations of inanimate objects, artfully arranged) in the mural schemes of the Second, Third, and Fourth Styles. A still life with peaches and a carafe (FIG. 10-26), a detail of a painted wall from Herculaneum, demonstrates that Roman painters sought to create illusionistic effects when depicting small objects as well as buildings and landscapes. The artist paid as much attention to shadows and highlights on the fruit, the stem and leaves, and the glass jar as to the objects themselves. Art historians have not found evidence of paintings comparable to these Roman studies of food and other inanimate objects until the Dutch still lifes of the 17th and 18th centuries (FIGS. 25-22 and 25-23).

1 in.

10-26 Still life with peaches, detail of a Fourth Style wall painting, from Herculaneum, Italy, ca. 62–79 CE. Fresco, 1′ 2″ × 1′ 1$\frac{1}{2}$″. Museo Archeologico Nazionale, Naples.

The Roman interest in illusionism explains the popularity of still-life paintings. This painter paid scrupulous attention to the play of light and shadow on different shapes and textures.

Pompeii and the Cities of Vesuvius **253**

Role Playing in Roman Portraiture

In every town throughout the vast Roman Empire, portraits of the emperors and empresses and their families were on display—in forums, basilicas, baths, and markets; in front of temples; atop triumphal arches—anywhere a statue could be placed. The rulers' heads varied little from Britain to Syria. All were replicas of official images, either imported or scrupulously copied by local artists. But the Roman sculptors placed the portrait heads on many types of bodies. The type chosen depended on the position the person held in Roman society or the various fictitious guises members of the imperial family assumed. Portraits of Augustus, for example, show him not only as armed general (FIG. 10-27) but also as recipient of the civic crown for saving the lives of fellow citizens (FIG. I-9). Other statues show him as veiled priest, toga-clad magistrate, traveling commander on horseback, heroically nude warrior, and various Roman gods, including Jupiter, Apollo, and Mercury.

Such role playing was not confined to emperors and princes but extended to their wives, daughters, sisters, and mothers. Portraits of Livia (FIG. 10-28) depict her as many goddesses, including Ceres, Juno, Venus, and Vesta. She also appears as the personification of Health, Justice, and Piety. In fact, it was common for imperial women to appear on Roman coins as goddesses or as embodiments of feminine virtue. Faustina the Younger, for example, the wife of Marcus Aurelius and mother of 13 children, appears as Venus and Fecundity, among many other roles. Julia Domna (FIG. 10-63), Septimius Severus's wife, is Juno, Venus, Peace, or Victory in some portraits.

Ordinary citizens also engaged in role playing. Some assumed literary pretensions, as did a husband and wife (FIG. 10-25) in their Pompeian home. Others equated themselves with Greek heroes (FIG. 10-60) or Roman deities (FIG. 10-61) on their coffins. The common people followed the lead of the emperors and empresses.

10-27 Portrait of Augustus as general, from Primaporta, Italy, early-first-century CE copy of a bronze original of ca. 20 BCE. Marble, 6′ 8″ high. Musei Vaticani, Rome. ◼◀

Augustus's idealized portraits were modeled on Classical Greek statues (FIG. 5-40) and depict him as a never-aging son of a god. This portrait presents the emperor in armor in his role as general.

1 ft.

EARLY EMPIRE

The murder of Julius Caesar on the Ides of March, 44 BCE, plunged the Roman world into a bloody civil war. The fighting lasted until 31 BCE when Octavian (better known as Augustus), Caesar's grandnephew and adopted son, crushed the naval forces of Mark Antony and Queen Cleopatra of Egypt at Actium in northwestern Greece. Antony and Cleopatra committed suicide, and in 30 BCE, Egypt, once the wealthiest and most powerful kingdom of the ancient world, became another province in the ever-expanding Roman Empire.

Historians mark the passage from the Roman Republic to the Roman Empire from the day in 27 BCE when the Senate conferred the majestic title of Augustus (r. 27 BCE–14 CE) on Octavian. The Empire was ostensibly a continuation of the Republic, with the same constitutional offices, but in fact Augustus, whom the Senate recognized as *princeps* (first citizen), occupied all the key positions. He was consul and *imperator* (commander in chief; root of the word *emperor*) and even, after 12 BCE, *pontifex maximus* (chief priest of the state religion). These offices gave Augustus control of all aspects of Roman public life.

PAX ROMANA With powerful armies keeping order on the Empire's frontiers and no opposition at home, Augustus brought peace and prosperity to a war-weary Mediterranean world. Known in his own day as the *Pax Augusta* (Augustan Peace), the peace Augustus established prevailed for two centuries. It came to be called simply the *Pax Romana*. During this time the emperors commissioned a huge number of public works throughout the Empire: roads, bridges, theaters, amphitheaters, and bathing complexes, all on an unprecedented scale. The erection of imperial portrait statues and monuments covered with reliefs recounting the rulers' great

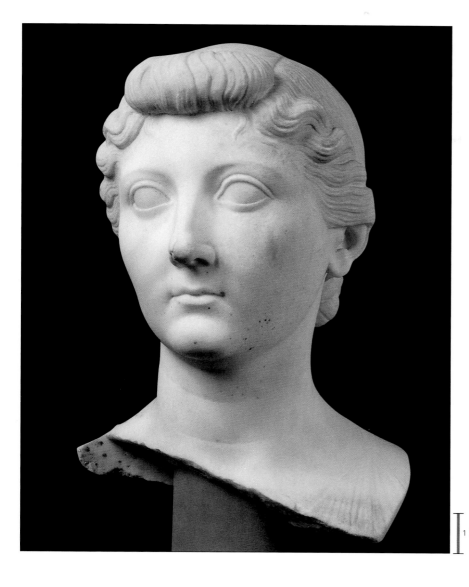

1 in.

deeds reminded people everywhere of the source of this beneficence. These portraits and reliefs often presented a picture of the emperors and their achievements that bore little resemblance to historical fact. Their purpose, however, was not to provide an objective record but to mold public opinion. The Roman emperors and the artists they employed have had few equals in the effective use of art and architecture for propagandistic ends.

Augustus and the Julio-Claudians

When Augustus vanquished Antony and Cleopatra at Actium and became undisputed master of the Mediterranean world, he was not yet 32 years old. The rule by elders that had characterized the Roman Republic for nearly a half millennium came to an abrupt end. Suddenly, Roman portraitists were called on to produce images of a *youthful* head of state. But Augustus was not merely young. Caesar had been made a god after his death, and Augustus, though never claiming to be a god himself, widely advertised himself as the son of a god. His portraits were designed to present the image of a godlike leader who miraculously never aged. Although Augustus lived until 14 CE, even official portraits made near the end of his life show him as a handsome youth (FIG. I-9). Such fictional portraits might seem ridiculous today, when the media circulate pictures of world leaders as they truly appear, but in antiquity few people had actually seen the emperor. His official image was all most knew. It therefore could be manipulated at will.

AUGUSTUS AS IMPERATOR The portraits of Augustus depict him in his many different roles in the Roman state (see "Role Playing in Roman Portraiture," page 254), but the models for many of them were Classical Greek statues. The portrait (FIG. 10-27) of the emperor found at his wife Livia's villa (FIG. 10-20) at Primaporta portrays Augustus as general, standing in the pose of Polykleitos's *Doryphoros* (FIG. 5-40) but with his right arm raised to address his troops in the manner of the orator Aule Metele (FIG. 9-16). Augustus's head, although portraying a recognizable individual, also emulates the idealized head of the Polykleitan spear bearer in its overall shape, the sharp ridges of the brows, and the tight cap of layered hair. Augustus is not a nude athlete, however, and the details of the statue carry political messages. The reliefs on the cuirass advertise an important diplomatic victory—the return of the Roman military standards the Parthians had captured from a Republican general—and the Cupid at Augustus's feet alludes to his divine descent. (Caesar's family, the Julians, traced their ancestry back to Venus. Cupid was the goddess's son.)

LIVIA A marble portrait (FIG. 10-28) of Livia shows that the imperial women of the Augustan age shared the emperor's eternal youthfulness. Although she sports the latest Roman coiffure, with the hair rolled over the forehead and knotted at the nape of the neck, Livia's blemish-free skin and sharply defined features derive from images of Classical Greek goddesses. Livia outlived Augustus by 15 years, dying at age 87. In her portraits, the coiffure changed with the introduction of each new fashion, but her face remained ever young, befitting her exalted position in the Roman state.

10-29 Ara Pacis Augustae (Altar of Augustan Peace; looking northeast), Rome, Italy, 13–9 BCE. 📹

Augustus sought to present his new order as a Golden Age equaling that of Athens under Pericles. The Ara Pacis celebrates the emperor's most important achievement, the establishment of peace.

10-30 Female personification (Tellus?), panel from the east facade of the Ara Pacis Augustae, Rome, Italy, 13–9 BCE. Marble, 5′ 3″ high. 📹

This female personification with two babies on her lap epitomizes the fruits of the Pax Augusta. All around her the bountiful earth is in bloom, and animals of different species live together peacefully.

1 ft.

ARA PACIS AUGUSTAE On Livia's birthday in 9 BCE, Augustus dedicated the Ara Pacis Augustae (Altar of Augustan Peace; FIG. **10-29**), the monument celebrating his most significant achievement, the establishment of peace. Figural reliefs and acanthus tendrils adorn the altar's marble precinct walls. Four panels on the east and west ends depict carefully selected mythological subjects, including (at the right in FIG. 10-29) a relief of Aeneas making a sacrifice. Aeneas was the son of Venus and one of Augustus's forefathers. The connection between the emperor and Aeneas was a key element of Augustus's political ideology for his new Golden Age. It is no coincidence that Vergil wrote the *Aeneid* during the rule of Augustus. The epic poem glorified the young emperor by celebrating the founder of the Julian line.

A second panel (FIG. **10-30**), on the other end of the altar enclosure, depicts a seated matron with two lively babies on her lap. Her identity is uncertain. She is usually called Tellus (Mother Earth), although some scholars have named her Pax (Peace), Ceres (goddess of grain), or even Venus. Whoever she is, she epitomizes the fruits of the Pax Augusta. All around her the bountiful earth is in bloom, and animals of different species live peacefully side by side. Personifications of refreshing breezes (note their windblown drapery) flank her. One

rides a bird, the other a sea creature. Earth, sky, and water are all elements of this picture of peace and fertility in the Augustan cosmos.

Processions of the imperial family (FIG. **10-31**) and other important dignitaries appear on the long north and south sides of the Ara Pacis. These parallel friezes were clearly inspired to some degree by the Panathenaic procession frieze (FIG. **5-50**, *bottom*) of the Parthenon. Augustus sought to present his new order as a Golden Age equaling that of Athens under Pericles in the mid-fifth century BCE. The emulation of Classical models thus made a political statement as well as an artistic one.

Even so, the Roman procession is very different in character from that on the Greek frieze. On the Parthenon, anonymous figures act out an event that recurred every four years. The frieze stands for *all* Panathenaic Festival processions. The Ara Pacis depicts a specific event—possibly the inaugural ceremony of 13 BCE when work on the altar began—and recognizable contemporary figures. Among those

10-31 Procession of the imperial family, detail of the south frieze of the Ara Pacis Augustae, Rome, Italy, 13–9 BCE. Marble, 5′ 3″ high. ◼◀

Although inspired by the Panathenaic procession frieze (FIG. 5-50) of the Parthenon, the Ara Pacis friezes depict recognizable individuals, including children. Augustus promoted marriage and child-bearing.

1 ft.

Luna). Prior to the opening of these quarries in the second half of the first century BCE, marble had to be imported at great cost from abroad, and the Romans used it sparingly. The ready availability of Italian marble under Augustus made possible the emperor's famous boast that he found Rome a city of brick and transformed it into a city of marble.

portrayed are children, who restlessly tug on their elders' garments and talk to one another when they should be quiet on a solemn occasion—in short, children who act like children and not like miniature adults, as they frequently do in the history of art. Their presence lends a great deal of charm to the procession, but that is not why children were included on the Ara Pacis when they had never before appeared on any Greek or Roman state monument. Augustus was concerned about a decline in the birthrate among the Roman nobility, and he enacted a series of laws designed to promote marriage, marital fidelity, and raising children. The portrayal of men with their families on the Altar of Peace served as a moral exemplar. Once again, the emperor used art to further his political and social agendas.

The extensive use of Carrara marble for public monuments (including the Ara Pacis) must be seen as part of Augustus's larger program to make his city the equal of Periclean Athens. In fact, the Forum of Augustus incorporated several explicit references to Classical Athens and to the Acropolis in particular, most notably copies of the caryatids (FIG. 5-54) of the Erechtheion in the upper story of the porticos. The forum also evoked Roman history. The porticos contained dozens of portrait statues, including images of all the major figures of the Julian family going back to Aeneas. Augustus's forum became a kind of public atrium filled with *imagines*. His family history thus became part of the Roman state's official history.

FORUM OF AUGUSTUS Augustus's most ambitious project in the capital was the construction of a new forum (FIG. 10-2, no. 10) next to Julius Caesar's forum (FIG. 10-2, no. 9), which Augustus completed. Both forums featured white marble from Carrara (ancient

NÎMES The Forum of Augustus is in ruins today, but many scholars believe some workers on that project also erected the so-called Maison Carrée (Square House; FIG. 10-32) at Nîmes (ancient

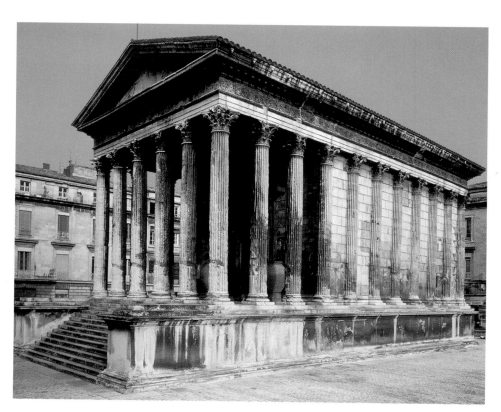

10-32 Maison Carrée, Nîmes, France, ca. 1–10 CE. ◼◀

This exceptionally well preserved Corinthian pseudoperipteral temple in France, modeled on the Temple of Mars Ultor in Rome, exemplifies the conservative Neo-Classical Augustan architectural style.

10-33 Pont-du-Gard, Nîmes, France, ca. 16 BCE. ◼◀

Roman engineers constructed roads and bridges throughout the empire. This aqueduct bridge brought water from a distant mountain spring to Nîmes—about 100 gallons a day for each inhabitant.

Nemausus) in southern France (ancient Gaul). This exceptionally well preserved Corinthian pseudoperipteral temple, which dates to the opening years of the first century CE, is the best surviving example of the Augustan Neo-Classical architectural style.

An earlier Augustan project at Nîmes was the construction of the great aqueduct-bridge known today as the Pont-du-Gard (FIG. 10-33). Beginning in the fourth century BCE, the Romans built aqueducts to carry water from mountain sources to their city on the Tiber River. As Rome's power spread through the Mediterranean world, its architects constructed aqueducts, roads, and bridges to serve colonies throughout the far-flung empire. The Pont-du-Gard demonstrates the skill of Rome's engineers. The aqueduct provided about 100 gallons of water a day for each inhabitant of Nîmes from a source some 30 miles away. The water was carried over the considerable distance by gravity alone, which required channels built with a continuous gradual decline over the entire route from source to city. The three-story bridge at Nîmes maintained the height of the water channel where the water crossed the Gard River. Each large arch spans some 82 feet and is constructed of blocks weighing up to two tons each. The bridge's uppermost level consists of a row of smaller arches, three above each of the large openings below. They carry the water channel itself. Their quickened rhythm and the harmonious proportional relationship between the larger and smaller arches reveal that the Roman engineer had a keen aesthetic as well as practical sense.

PORTA MAGGIORE Many aqueducts were required to meet the demand for water in the capital. Under the emperor Claudius (r. 41–54 CE), a grandiose gate, the Porta Maggiore (FIG. **10-34**), was constructed at the point where two of Rome's water lines (and two intercity trunk roads) converged. Its huge *attic* (uppermost story) bears a wordy dedicatory inscription that conceals the conduits of both aqueducts, one above the other. The gate is the outstanding example of the Roman *rusticated* (rough) masonry style. Instead of using the precisely shaped blocks Greek and Augustan architects preferred, the designer of the Porta Maggiore combined smooth and rusticated surfaces. These created an exciting, if eccen-

tric, facade with crisply carved pediments resting on engaged columns composed of rusticated drums.

NERO'S GOLDEN HOUSE In 64 CE, when Nero (r. 54–68 CE), stepson and successor of Claudius, was emperor, a great fire destroyed large sections of Rome. Architects carried out the rebuilding in accordance with a new code that required greater fireproofing, resulting in the widespread use of concrete, which was both cheap and fire resistant. Increased use of concrete gave Roman builders the opportunity to explore the possibilities opened up by the still relatively new material.

10-34 Porta Maggiore, Rome, Italy, ca. 50 CE.

This double gateway, which supports the water channels of two important aqueducts, is the outstanding example of Roman rusticated (rough) masonry, which was especially popular under Claudius.

The Golden House of Nero

Nero's Domus Aurea (FIG. 10-35), or Golden House, was a vast and notoriously extravagant country villa in the heart of Rome. The second-century CE Roman biographer Suetonius described it vividly:

> The entrance-hall was large enough to contain a huge statue [of Nero in the guise of Sol, the sun god, by Zenodorus; FIG. 10-2, no. 16], 120 feet high; and the pillared arcade ran for a whole mile. An enormous pool, like a sea, was surrounded by buildings made to resemble cities, and by a landscape garden consisting of ploughed fields, vineyards, pastures, and woodlands—where every variety of domestic and wild animal roamed about. Parts of the house were overlaid with gold and studded with precious stones and mother-of-pearl. All the dining-rooms had ceilings of fretted ivory, the panels of which could slide back and let a rain of flowers, or of perfume from hidden sprinklers, shower upon [Nero's] guests. The main dining-room was circular, and its roof revolved, day and night, in time with the sky. Sea water, or sulphur water, was always on tap in the baths. When the palace had been decorated throughout in this lavish style, Nero dedicated it, and condescended to remark: "Good, now I can at last begin to live like a human being!"*

Suetonius's description is a welcome reminder that the Roman ruins tourists flock to see are but a dim reflection of the magnificence of the original structures. Only in rare instances, such as the Pantheon, with its marble-faced walls and floors (FIG. 10-51), can visitors experience anything approaching the architects' intended effects. Even there, much of the marble paneling is of later date, and the gilding is missing from the dome.

*Suetonius, *Nero*, 31. Translated by Robert Graves, *Suetonius: The Twelve Caesars* (New York: Penguin, 1957; illustrated edition, 1980), 197–198.

10-35 SEVERUS and CELER, section (*left*) and plan (*right*) of the octagonal hall of the Domus Aurea (Golden House) of Nero, Rome, Italy, 64–68 CE.

Nero's architects illuminated this octagonal room by placing an oculus in its concrete dome, and ingeniously lit the rooms around it by leaving spaces between their vaults and the dome's exterior.

After the great fire, Nero asked SEVERUS and CELER, two brilliant architect-engineers, to construct a grand new palace for him on a huge confiscated plot of fire-ravaged land near the Forum Romanum (see "The Golden House of Nero," above). Nero's Domus Aurea had scores of rooms, many adorned with frescoes (FIG. 10-22) in the Fourth Style, others with marble paneling or painted and gilded stucco reliefs. Structurally, most of these rooms, although built of concrete, are unremarkable. One octagonal hall (FIG. 10-35), however, stands apart from the rest and testifies to Severus and Celer's entirely new approach to architectural design.

The ceiling of the octagonal room is a dome that modulates from an eight-sided to a hemispherical form as it rises toward the *oculus*—the circular opening that admitted light to the room. Radiating outward from the five inner sides (the other three, directly or indirectly, face the outside) are smaller, rectangular rooms, three covered by barrel vaults, two others (marked by a broken-line X on the plan; FIG. 10-35, *right*) by the earliest known concrete groin vaults. Severus and Celer ingeniously lit these satellite rooms by leaving spaces between their vaulted ceilings and the central dome's exterior. But the most significant aspect of the design is that here, for the first time, the architects appear to have thought of the walls and vaults not as limiting space but as shaping it.

Today, the octagonal hall no longer has its stucco decoration and marble *incrustation* (veneer). The concrete shell stands bare, but this serves to focus the visitor's attention on the design's spatial complexity. Anyone walking through the rooms sees that the central domed octagon is defined not by walls but by eight angled piers. The wide square openings between the piers are so large that the rooms beyond look like extensions of the central hall. The grouping of spatial units of different sizes and proportions under a variety of vaults creates a dynamic three-dimensional composition that is both complex and unified. Nero's architects were not only inventive but also progressive in their recognition of the malleable nature of concrete, a material not limited to the rectilinear forms of traditional architecture.

Early Empire   **259**

Spectacles in the Colosseum

Romans flocked to amphitheaters all over the Empire to see two main kinds of spectacles: gladiatorial combats and animal hunts.

Gladiators were professional fighters, usually slaves who had been purchased to train as hand-to-hand combatants in gladiatorial schools. Their owners, seeking to turn a profit, rented them out for performances. Beginning with Domitian, however, all gladiators who competed in Rome were state-owned to ensure that they could not be used as a private army to overthrow the government. Although every gladiator faced death every time he entered the arena, some had long careers and achieved considerable fame. Others, for example, criminals or captured enemies, were sent into the amphitheater without any training and without any defensive weapons. Those "gladiatorial games" were a form of capital punishment coupled with entertainment for the masses.

Wild animal hunts (*venationes*) were also immensely popular. Many of the hunters were also professionals, but often the hunts, like the gladiatorial games, were executions in thin disguise involving helpless prisoners who were easy prey for the animals. Sometimes no one would enter the arena with the animals. Instead, skilled archers shot the beasts with arrows from positions in the stands. Other times animals would be pitted against other animals—bears versus bulls, lions versus elephants, and such—to the delight of the crowds.

The Colosseum (FIG. 10-36) was the largest and most important amphitheater in the world, and the kinds of spectacles staged there were costlier and more impressive than those held anywhere else. There are even accounts of the Colosseum being flooded so that naval battles could be staged before an audience of tens of thousands, although some scholars have doubted that the arena could be made watertight or that ships could maneuver in the space available.

In the early third century, the historian Dio Cassius described the ceremonies Titus sponsored at the inauguration of the Colosseum in 80.

10-36 Aerial view of the Colosseum (Flavian Amphitheater), Rome, Italy, ca. 70–80 CE. ◀

A complex system of concrete barrel vaults once held up the seats in the world's largest amphitheater, where 50,000 spectators could watch gladiatorial combats and wild animal hunts.

There was a battle between cranes and also between four elephants; animals both tame and wild were slain to the number of nine thousand; and women . . . took part in despatching them. As for the men, several fought in single combat and several groups contended together both in infantry and naval battles. For Titus suddenly filled [the arena] with water and brought in horses and bulls and some other domesticated animals that had been taught to behave in the liquid element just as on land. He also brought in people on ships, who engaged in a sea-fight there. . . . On the first day there was a gladiatorial exhibition and wild-beast hunt. . . . On the second day there was a horse-race, and on the third day a naval battle between three thousand men, followed by an infantry battle. . . . These were the spectacles that were offered, and they continued for a hundred days.*

*Dio Cassius, *Roman History*, 66.25. Translated by Earnest Cary, *Dio's Roman History*, vol. 8 (Cambridge, Mass.: Harvard University Press, 1925), 311, 313.

The Flavians

Because of his outrageous behavior, Nero was forced to commit suicide in 68 CE, bringing the Julio-Claudian dynasty to an end. A year of renewed civil strife followed. The man who emerged triumphant in this brief but bloody conflict was Vespasian (r. 69–79 CE), a general who had served under Claudius and Nero. Vespasian, whose family name was Flavius, had two sons, Titus (r. 79–81 CE) and Domitian (r. 81–96 CE). The Flavian dynasty ruled Rome for more than a quarter century.

COLOSSEUM The Flavians left their mark on the capital in many ways, not the least being the construction of the Colosseum (FIGS. 10-2, no. 17, and 10-36), the monument that, for most people, still represents Rome more than any other building. In the past it was identified so closely with Rome and its empire that in the early Middle Ages there was a saying, "While stands the Colosseum, Rome shall stand; when falls the Colosseum, Rome shall fall; and when Rome falls—the World."[2] The Flavian Amphitheater, as it was known in its day, was one of Vespasian's first undertakings after becoming emperor. The decision to build the Colosseum was very shrewd politically. The site chosen was the artificial lake on the grounds of Nero's Domus Aurea, which engineers drained for the purpose. By building the new amphitheater there, Vespasian reclaimed for the public the land Nero had confiscated for his private pleasure and provided Romans with the largest arena for gladiatorial combats and other lavish spectacles that had ever been constructed. The Colosseum takes its name, however, not from its size—it could

10-37 Portrait of Vespasian, ca. 75–79 CE. Marble, 1′ 4″ high. Ny Carlsberg Glyptotek, Copenhagen.

Vespasian's sculptors revived the veristic tradition of the Republic to underscore the elderly new emperor's Republican values in contrast to Nero's self-indulgence and extravagance.

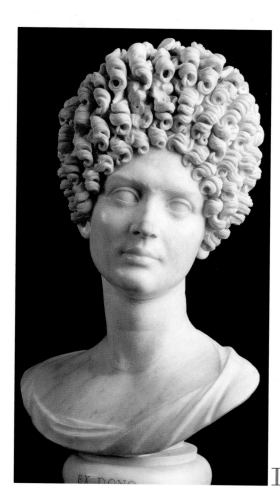

10-38 Portrait bust of a Flavian woman, from Rome, Italy, ca. 90 CE. Marble, 2′ 1″ high. Musei Capitolini, Rome.

The Flavian sculptor reproduced the elaborate coiffure of this elegant woman by drilling deep holes for the corkscrew curls and carved the rest of the hair and the face with hammer and chisel.

hold more than 50,000 spectators—but from its location beside the Colossus of Nero (FIG. 10-2, no. 16), the huge statue at the entrance to his urban villa. Vespasian did not live to see the Colosseum in use. Titus completed and formally dedicated the amphitheater in 80 CE with great fanfare (see "Spectacles in the Colosseum," page 260).

The Colosseum, like the much earlier amphitheater at Pompeii (FIG. 10-13), could not have been built without concrete. A complex system of barrel-vaulted corridors holds up the enormous oval seating area. This concrete "skeleton" is apparent today to anyone who enters the amphitheater (FIG. 10-36). In the centuries following the fall of Rome, the Colosseum served as a convenient quarry for ready-made building materials. Almost all its marble seats were hauled away, exposing the network of vaults below. Hidden in antiquity but visible today are the arena substructures, which in their present form date to the third century. They housed waiting rooms for the gladiators, animal cages, and machinery for raising and lowering stage sets as well as animals and humans. Cleverly designed lifting devices brought beasts from their dark dens into the arena's bright light. Above the seats a great velarium, as at Pompeii (FIG. 10-14), once shielded the spectators. Poles affixed to the Colosseum's facade held up the giant awning.

The exterior travertine shell (FIG. 10-1) is approximately 160 feet high, the height of a modern 16-story building. Numbered entrances led to the cavea, where the spectators sat according to their place in the social hierarchy. The relationship of the 76 gateways to the tiers of seats within was carefully thought out and resembles the systems seen in modern sports stadiums. The decor of the exterior, however, had nothing to do with function. The facade is divided into four bands, with large arched openings piercing the lower three. Ornamental Greek orders frame the arches in the standard Roman sequence for multistoried buildings: from the ground up, Tuscan, Ionic, and then Corinthian. This sequence is based on the proportions of the orders, with the Tuscan viewed as capable of supporting the heaviest load. Corinthian pilasters (and between them the brackets for the wooden poles that held up the velarium) circle the uppermost story.

The use of engaged columns and a lintel to frame the openings in the Colosseum's facade is a variation of the scheme seen on the Etruscan Porta Marzia (FIG. 9-14) at Perugia. The Romans commonly used this scheme from Late Republican times on. Like the pseudoperipteral temple, which is an eclectic mix of Greek orders and Etruscan plan, this manner of decorating a building's facade combined Greek orders with an architectural form foreign to Greek post-and-lintel architecture, namely the arch. The Roman practice of framing an arch with an applied Greek order had no structural purpose, but it added variety to the surface. It also unified a multistoried facade by casting a net of verticals and horizontals over it.

FLAVIAN PORTRAITURE Vespasian was an unpretentious career army officer who desired to distance himself from Nero's extravagant misrule. His portraits (FIG. 10-37) reflect his much simpler tastes. They also made an important political statement. Breaking with the tradition Augustus established of depicting the Roman emperor as an eternally youthful god on earth, Vespasian's sculptors resuscitated the veristic tradition of the Republic, possibly at his specific direction. Although not as brutally descriptive as many Republican likenesses, Vespasian's portraits frankly recorded his receding hairline and aging, leathery skin—proclaiming his traditional Republican values in contrast to Nero's.

Portraits of people of all ages survive from the Flavian period, in contrast to the Republic, when only elders were deemed worthy of depiction. A portrait bust (FIG. 10-38) of a young woman is a case in point. Its purpose was to project not Republican virtues but rather idealized beauty—through contemporary fashion rather than by reference to images of Greek goddesses. The portrait is notable for its elegance and delicacy and for the virtuoso way the sculptor rendered the differing textures of hair and flesh. The elaborate Flavian coiffure,

10-39 Arch of Titus, Rome, Italy, after 81 CE.

Domitian erected this arch on the road leading into the Roman Forum to honor his brother, the emperor Titus, who became a god after his death. Victories fill the spandrels of the arcuated passageway.

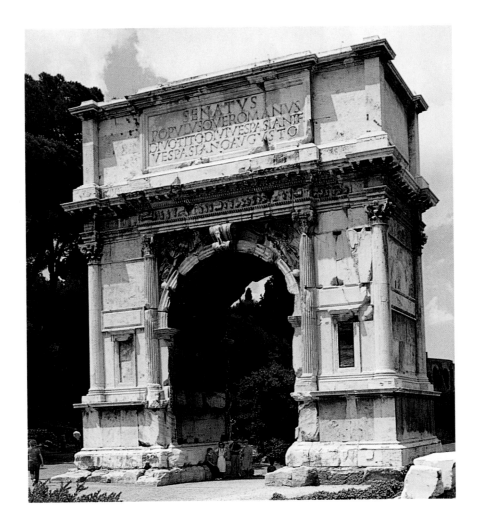

with its corkscrew curls punched out using a drill instead of a chisel, creates a dense mass of light and shadow set off boldly from the softly modeled and highly polished skin of the face and swanlike neck. The drill played an increasing role in Roman sculpture in succeeding periods and in time was used even for portraits of men, when much longer hair and full beards became fashionable.

ARCH OF TITUS When Titus died in 81 CE, only two years after becoming emperor, his younger brother, Domitian, succeeded him. Domitian erected an arch (FIGS. 10-2, no. 13, and 10-39) in Titus's honor on the Sacred Way leading into the Republican Forum Romanum (FIG. 10-2, no. 11). This type of arch, the so-called *triumphal arch*, has a long history in Roman art and architecture, beginning in the second century BCE. The term is something of a misnomer, however, because Roman arches celebrated more than just military victories. Freestanding arches, usually crowned by gilded-bronze statues, commemorated a wide variety of events, ranging from victories abroad to the building of roads and bridges at home.

The Arch of Titus is typical of the early triumphal arch and consists of one passageway only. As on the Colosseum, engaged columns frame the arcuated opening, but their capitals are the *Composite* type, an ornate combination of Ionic volutes and Corinthian acanthus leaves that became popular at about the same time as the Fourth Style in Roman painting. Reliefs depicting personified Victories (winged women, as in Greek art) fill the *spandrels* (the area between the arch's curve and the framing columns and entablature). A dedicatory inscription stating that the arch was erected to honor the god Titus, son of the god Vespasian, dominates the attic. Roman emperors normally were proclaimed gods after they died, unless they ran afoul of the Senate and were damned. The statues of those who suffered *damnatio memoriae* were torn down, and their names were erased from public inscriptions. This was Nero's fate.

Inside the passageway of the Arch of Titus are two great relief panels. They represent the triumphal parade of Titus down the Sacred Way after his return from the conquest of Judaea at the end of the Jewish Wars in 70 CE. One of the reliefs (FIG. 10-40) depicts Roman soldiers carrying the spoils—including the sacred seven-branched candelabrum, the *menorah*—from the Temple in Jerusalem. Despite considerable damage to the relief, the illusion of movement is convincing. The parade moves forward from the left background into the center foreground and disappears through the obliquely placed arch in the right background. The energy and swing of the column of soldiers suggest a rapid march. The sculptor rejected the Classical low-relief style of the Ara Pacis (FIG. 10-31) in favor of extremely deep carving, which produces strong shadows. The heads of the forward figures have broken off because they stood free from the block. Their high relief emphasized their different placement in space compared with the heads in low relief, which are intact. The play of light and shadow across the protruding foreground and receding background figures enhances the sense of movement.

The panel (FIG. 10-41) on the other side of the passageway shows Titus in his triumphal chariot. The seeming historical accuracy of the spoils panel—it closely corresponds to the Jewish historian Josephus's contemporaneous description of Titus's triumph—gave way in this panel to allegory. Victory rides with Titus in the four-horse chariot and places a wreath on his head. Below her is a

10-40 Spoils of Jerusalem, relief panel from the Arch of Titus, Rome, Italy, after 81 CE. Marble, 7′ 10″ high.

The reliefs inside the bay of the Arch of Titus commemorate the emperor's greatest achievement—the conquest of Judaea. Here, Roman soldiers carry the spoils from the Jewish temple in Jerusalem.

10-41 Triumph of Titus, relief panel from the Arch of Titus, Rome, Italy, after 81 CE. Marble, 7′ 10″ high.

Victory crowns Titus in his triumphal chariot. Also present are personifications of Honor and Valor in this first known instance of the intermingling of human and divine figures in a Roman historical relief.

bare-chested youth who is probably a personification of Honor (*Honos*). A female personification of Valor (*Virtus*) leads the horses. These allegorical figures transform the relief from a record of Titus's battlefield success into a celebration of imperial virtues. Such an intermingling of divine and human figures occurs on the Republican Villa of the Mysteries frieze (FIG. 10-18) at Pompeii, but the Arch of Titus panel is the first known instance of divine beings interacting with humans on an official Roman historical relief. (On the Ara Pacis, FIG. 10-29, Aeneas and "Tellus" appear in separate framed panels, carefully segregated from the procession of living Romans.) The Arch of Titus was erected after the emperor's death, and its reliefs were carved when Titus was already a god. Soon afterward, however, this kind of interaction between mortals and immortals became a staple of Roman narrative relief sculpture, even on monuments honoring a living emperor.

HIGH EMPIRE

In the second century CE, under Trajan, Hadrian, and the Antonines, the Roman Empire reached its greatest geographic extent (MAP 10-1) and the height of its power. Rome's might was unchallenged in the Mediterranean world, although the Germanic peoples in Europe, the Berbers in Africa, and the Parthians and Persians in the Near East constantly applied pressure. Within the empire's secure boundaries, the Pax Romana meant unprecedented prosperity for all who came under Roman rule.

Trajan

Domitian's extravagant lifestyle and ego resembled Nero's. He demanded to be addressed as *dominus et deus* (lord and god) and so angered the senators that he was assassinated in 96 CE. The Senate chose the elderly Nerva, one of its own, as emperor. Nerva ruled for only 16 months, but before he died he established a pattern of succession by adoption that lasted for almost a century. Nerva picked Trajan, a capable and popular general born in Italica (Spain), as the next emperor. Trajan was the first non-Italian to rule Rome. Under Trajan, imperial armies brought Roman rule to ever more distant areas (MAP 10-1), and the imperial government took on ever greater responsibility for its people's welfare by instituting a number of farsighted social programs. Trajan was so popular that the Senate granted him the title *Optimus* (the Best), an epithet he shared with Jupiter (who was said to have instructed Nerva to choose Trajan as his successor). In Late Antiquity, Augustus, the founder of the Roman Empire, and Trajan became the yardsticks for success. The goal of new emperors was to be *felicior Augusto, melior Traiano* (luckier than Augustus, better than Trajan).

10-42 Aerial view of Timgad (Thamugadi), Algeria, founded 100 CE.

Timgad, like other new Roman colonies, was planned with great precision. Its strict grid scheme features two main thoroughfares, the cardo and the decumanus, with the forum at their intersection.

TIMGAD In 100 CE, Trajan founded a new colony for army veterans at Timgad, ancient Thamugadi (FIG. **10-42**), in what is today Algeria. Like other colonies, Timgad became the physical embodiment of Roman authority and civilization for the local population and served as a key to the Romanization of the provinces. The town was planned with great precision, its design resembling that of a Roman military encampment or *castrum*. (Scholars still debate which came first. The castrum may have been based on the layout of Roman colonies.) Unlike the sprawling unplanned cities of Rome and Pompeii, Timgad is a square divided into equal quarters by its two main streets, the cardo and the decumanus. They cross at right angles and are bordered by colonnades. Monumental gates once marked the ends of the two avenues. The forum is located at the point where the streets intersect. The quarters are subdivided into square blocks, and the forum and public buildings, such as the theater and baths, occupy areas sized as multiples of these blocks. The Roman plan is a modification of the Hippodamian plan of Greek cities (FIG. **5-76**), though more rigidly ordered.

The fact that most of these colonial settlements were laid out in the same manner, regardless of whether they were in North Africa, Mesopotamia, or England, expresses concretely the unity and centralized power of the Roman Empire at its height. But even the Romans could not regulate human behavior completely. As the aerial view reveals, when the population of Timgad grew sevenfold and burst through the Trajanic colony's walls, rational planning was ignored, and the city and its streets branched out haphazardly.

FORUM OF TRAJAN Trajan completed several major building projects in Rome, including the remodeling of the Circus Maximus (FIG. **10-2**, no. 2), Rome's giant chariot-racing stadium, and the construction of a vast new bathing complex near the Colosseum constructed on top of Nero's Golden House. His most important undertaking, however, was a huge new forum (FIGS. **10-2**, no. 7, and **10-43**), roughly twice the size of the century-old Forum of Augustus (FIG. **10-2**, no. 10)—even excluding the enormous market complex next to the forum. The new forum glorified Trajan's victories in his two wars against the Dacians (who lived in what is now Romania) and was paid for with the spoils of those campaigns. The archi-

10-43 APOLLODORUS OF DAMASCUS, Forum of Trajan, Rome, Italy, dedicated 112 CE (James E. Packer and John Burge). (1) Temple of Trajan, (2) Column of Trajan, (3) libraries, (4) Basilica Ulpia, (5) forum, (6) equestrian statue of Trajan.

With the spoils from two Dacian wars, Trajan built Rome's largest forum. It featured an equestrian statue of the emperor, statues of Dacian captives, two libraries, and a basilica with clerestory lighting.

tect was APOLLODORUS OF DAMASCUS, Trajan's chief military engineer during the Dacian Wars. Apollodorus's plan incorporated the main features of most early forums (FIG. 10-12), except that a huge basilica, not a temple, dominated the colonnaded open square. The temple (completed after the emperor's death and dedicated to the newest god in the Roman pantheon, Trajan himself) was set instead behind the basilica. It stood at the rear end of the forum in its own courtyard, with two libraries and a giant commemorative column, the Column of Trajan (FIGS. 10-43, no. 2, and 10-44).

Entry to Trajan's forum was through an impressive gateway resembling a triumphal arch. Inside the forum were other reminders of Trajan's military prowess. A larger-than-life-size gilded-bronze equestrian statue of the emperor stood at the center of the great court in front of the basilica. Statues of captive Dacians stood above the columns of the forum porticos.

The Basilica Ulpia (Trajan's family name was Ulpius) was a much larger and far more ornate version of the basilica in the forum of Pompeii (FIG. 10-12, no. 3). As shown in FIG. 10-43, no. 4, it had *apses,* or semicircular recesses, on each short end. Two aisles flanked the nave on each side. In contrast to the Pompeian basilica, the entrances were on the long side facing the forum. The building was vast: about 400 feet long (without the apses) and 200 feet wide. Light entered through clerestory windows, made possible by elevating the timber-roofed nave above the colonnaded aisles. In the Republican basilica at Pompeii, light reached the nave only indirectly through aisle windows. The clerestory (used millennia before at Karnak in Egypt, FIG. 3-26) provided much better illumination.

COLUMN OF TRAJAN The Column of Trajan (FIG. 10-44) was probably also the brainchild of Apollodorus of Damascus. The idea of covering the shaft of a colossal freestanding column with a continuous spiral narrative frieze seems to have been invented for this monument, but it was often copied in antiquity, the Middle Ages (FIG. 16-25), and as late as the 19th century. Trajan's column is 128 feet high. It once featured a heroically nude statue of the emperor at the top. (The present statue of Saint Peter dates to the 16th century.) The tall pedestal, decorated with captured Dacian arms and armor, served as Trajan's tomb.

Scholars have likened the 625-foot band that winds around the column to an illustrated scroll of the type housed in the neighboring libraries (and that Lars Pulena holds on his sarcophagus, FIG. 9-15). The reliefs depict Trajan's two successful campaigns against the Dacians. The story unfolds in more than 150 episodes in which some 2,500 figures appear. The band increases in width as it winds to the top of the column, so that it is easier to see the upper portions. Throughout, the relief is very low so as not to distort the contours of the shaft. Paint enhanced the legibility of the figures, but a viewer still would have had difficulty following the narrative from beginning to end.

Much of the spiral frieze is given over to easily recognizable compositions such as those found on coin reverses and on historical relief panels: Trajan addressing his troops, sacrificing to the gods, and so on. The narrative is not a reliable chronological account of the Dacian Wars, as was once thought. The sculptors nonetheless accurately recorded the general character of the campaigns. Notably, battle scenes take up only about a quarter of the frieze. As is true of modern military operations, the Romans spent more time constructing forts, transporting men and equipment, and preparing for battle than fighting. The focus is always on the emperor, who appears throughout the frieze, but the enemy is not belittled. The Romans won because of their superior organization and more powerful army, not because they were inherently superior beings.

44A Spiral
ze, Column
'rajan,
ne, 112 CE.

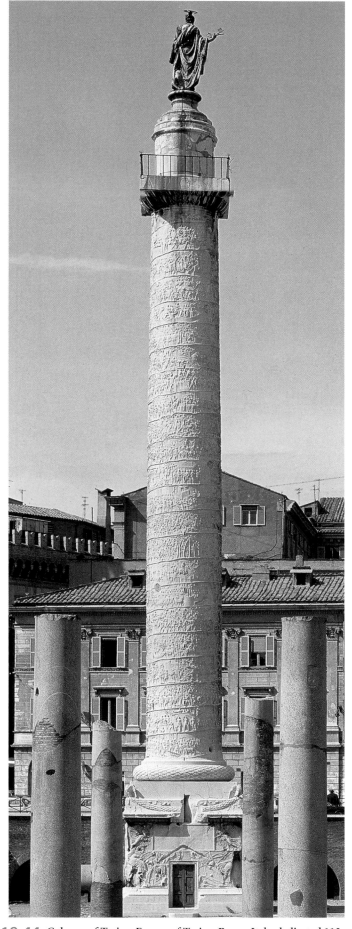

10-44 Column of Trajan, Forum of Trajan, Rome, Italy, dedicated 112 CE. ■◀

The spiral frieze of Trajan's column tells the story of the Dacian Wars in 150 episodes. All aspects of the campaigns were represented, from battles to sacrifices to road and fort construction.

Apollodorus of Damascus used brick-faced concrete to transform the Quirinal Hill overlooking Trajan's forum in Rome into a vast multilevel complex of barrel-vaulted shops and administrative offices.

MARKETS OF TRAJAN On the Quirinal Hill overlooking the forum, Apollodorus built the Markets of Trajan (FIGS. 10-2, no. 8, and 10-45) to house both shops and administrative offices. As earlier at Palestrina (FIG. 10-5), concrete made possible the transformation of a natural slope into a multilevel complex. Trajan's architect was a master of this modern medium as well as of the traditional stone-and-timber post-and-lintel architecture of the forum below. The basic unit was the *taberna*, a single-room shop covered by a barrel vault. Each taberna had a wide doorway, usually with a window above it that allowed light to enter a wooden inner attic used for storage. The shops were on several levels. They opened either onto a hemispherical facade winding around one of the great exedras of Trajan's forum, onto a paved street farther up the hill, or onto a great indoor market hall (FIG. 10-46) resembling a modern shopping mall. The hall housed two floors of shops, with the upper shops set back on each side and lit by skylights. Light from the same sources reached the ground-floor shops through arches beneath the great umbrella-like groin vaults (FIG. 10-6c) covering the hall.

ARCH OF TRAJAN, BENEVENTO In 109 CE, Trajan opened a new road, the Via Traiana, in southern Italy. Several years later the Senate erected a great arch (FIG. 10-47) honoring Trajan at the point where the road entered Benevento (ancient Beneventum). Architecturally, the Arch of Trajan at Benevento is almost identical to Titus's arch (FIG. 10-39) in Rome, but relief panels cover both facades of the Trajanic arch, giving it a billboardlike function. Every inch of the surface heralded the emperor's achievements. In one panel, he enters Rome after a successful military campaign. In another, he distributes largesse to needy children. In still others, he is portrayed as the founder of colonies for army veterans and as the builder of a new port at Ostia, Rome's harbor at the mouth of the Tiber. The reliefs present Trajan as the guarantor of peace and security in the empire, the benefactor of the poor, and the patron of soldiers and merchants alike. In short, the emperor is all things to all people. In several of the panels, Trajan freely intermingles with

10-46 APOLLODORUS OF DAMASCUS, interior of the great hall, Markets of Trajan, Rome, Italy, ca. 100–112 CE.

The great hall of Trajan's markets resembles a modern shopping mall. It housed two floors of shops, with the upper ones set back and lit by skylights. Concrete groin vaults cover the central space.

10-47 Arch of Trajan, Benevento, Italy, ca. 114–118 CE.

Unlike Titus's arch (FIG. 10-39), Trajan's has relief panels covering both facades, transforming it into a kind of advertising billboard featuring the emperor's many achievements on and off the battlefield.

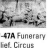

-47A Funerary lief, Circus aximus, . 110–130 CE.

-48A adrianic ndi, Arch Constantine, . 130–138 CE.

divinities, and on the arch's attic (which may have been completed after his death and deification), Jupiter hands his thunderbolt to the emperor, awarding him dominion over Earth. Such scenes, depicting the "first citizen" of Rome as a divinely sanctioned ruler in the company of the gods, henceforth became the norm, not the exception, in official Roman art.

Hadrian

Hadrian, Trajan's chosen successor and fellow Spaniard, was a connoisseur and lover of all the arts as well as an author and architect. He greatly admired Greek culture and traveled widely as emperor, often in the Greek East. Everywhere he went, statues and arches were set up in his honor.

HADRIANIC PORTRAITURE More portraits of Hadrian exist today than of any other emperor except Augustus. Hadrian, who was 41 years old at the time of Trajan's death and who ruled for more than two decades, is always depicted in his portraits as a mature adult who never ages. Hadrian's portraits (FIG. **10-48**) more closely resemble Kresilas's portrait of Pericles (FIG. **5-41**) than those of any Roman emperor before him. Fifth-century BCE statues also provided the prototypes for the idealizing official portraits of Augustus, but the Augustan models were Greek images of young athletes. The models for Hadrian's artists were Classical statues of mature Greek men. Hadrian himself wore a beard—a habit that, in its Roman context, must be viewed as a Greek affectation. Beards then became the norm for all subsequent Roman emperors for more than a century and a half.

PANTHEON Soon after Hadrian became emperor, work began on the Pantheon (FIGS. 10-2, no. 5, and **10-49**), the temple of all the gods, one of the best-preserved buildings of antiquity and most

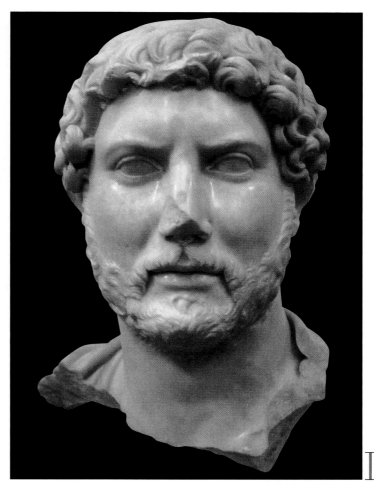

10-48 Portrait bust of Hadrian, from Rome, ca. 117–120 CE. Marble, $1' 4\frac{3}{4}''$ high. Museo Nazionale Romano–Palazzo Massimo alle Terme, Rome.

Hadrian, a lover of all things Greek, was the first Roman emperor to wear a beard. His artists modeled his idealizing official portraits on Classical Greek statues like Kresilas's Pericles (FIG. 5-41).

10-49 Pantheon, Rome, Italy, 118–125 CE.

Originally, the approach to Hadrian's "temple of all gods" in Rome was from a columnar courtyard. Like a temple in a Roman forum (FIG. 10-12), the Pantheon stood at one narrow end of the enclosure.

10-50 Restored cutaway view (*left*) and lateral section (*right*) of the Pantheon, Rome, Italy, 118–125 CE (John Burge).

The Pantheon's traditional facade masked its revolutionary cylindrical drum and its huge hemispherical dome. The interior symbolized both the orb of the earth and the vault of the heavens.

influential designs in architectural history. The Pantheon reveals the full potential of concrete, both as a building material and as a means for shaping architectural space. Originally, visitors approached the Pantheon from a columnar courtyard, and the temple itself, like temples in Roman forums, stood at one narrow end of the enclosure (FIG. **10-50**, *left*). Its facade of eight Corinthian columns—almost all that could be seen from ground level in antiquity—was a bow to tradition. Everything else about the Pantheon was revolutionary. Behind the columnar porch is an immense concrete cylinder covered by a huge hemispherical dome 142 feet in diameter. The dome's top is also 142 feet from the floor (FIG. **10-50**, *right*). The design is thus based on the intersection of two circles (one horizontal, the other vertical) so that the interior space can be imagined as the orb of the earth and the dome as the vault of the heavens.

If the Pantheon's design is simplicity itself, executing that design required all the ingenuity of Hadrian's engineers. They built up the cylindrical drum level by level using concrete of varied composition. Extremely hard and durable basalt went into the mix for the foundations, and the builders gradually modified the "recipe" until, at the top, featherweight pumice replaced stones to lighten the load. The dome's thickness also decreases as it nears the oculus, the circular opening 30 feet in diameter that is the only light source for the interior (FIG. **10-51**). The use of *coffers* (sunken decorative panels) lessened the dome's weight without weakening its structure. The coffers further reduced the dome's mass and also provided a handsome pattern of squares within the vast circle. Renaissance drawings suggest that each coffer once had a glistening gilded-bronze rosette at its center, enhancing the symbolism of the dome as the starry heavens.

Below the dome, much of the original marble veneer of the walls, niches, and floor has survived. In the Pantheon, visitors can get a sense, as almost nowhere else, of how magnificent the interiors of Roman concrete buildings could be. But despite the luxurious skin of the Pantheon's interior, the sense experienced on first entering the structure is not the weight of the enclosing walls but the space they enclose. In pre-Roman architecture, the form of the enclosed space was determined by the placement of the solids, which did not so much shape space as interrupt it. Roman architects were the first to conceive of architecture in terms of units of space that could be

10-51 Interior of the Pantheon, Rome, Italy, 118–125 CE.

The coffered dome of the Pantheon is 142 feet in diameter and 142 feet high. The light entering through its oculus forms a circular beam that moves across the dome as the sun moves across the sky.

Hadrian and Apollodorus of Damascus

Dio Cassius, a third-century CE senator who wrote a history of Rome from its foundation to his own day, recounted a revealing anecdote about Hadrian and Apollodorus of Damascus, architect of the Forum of Trajan (FIG. 10-43):

> Hadrian first drove into exile and then put to death the architect Apollodorus who had carried out several of Trajan's building projects. . . . When Trajan was at one time consulting with Apollodorus about a certain problem connected with his buildings, the architect said to Hadrian, who had interrupted them with some advice, "Go away and draw your pumpkins. You know nothing about these problems." For it so happened that Hadrian was at that time priding himself on some sort of drawing. When he became emperor he remembered this insult and refused to put up with Apollodorus's outspokenness. He sent him [his own] plan for the temple of Venus and Roma [FIG. 10-2, no. 14], in order to demonstrate that it was possible for a great work to be conceived without his [Apollodorus's] help, and asked him if he thought the building was well designed. Apollodorus sent a [very critical] reply. . . . [The emperor did not] attempt to restrain his anger or hide his pain; on the contrary, he had the man slain.*

The story says a great deal both about the absolute power Roman emperors wielded and about how seriously Hadrian took his architectural designs. But perhaps the most interesting detail is the description of Hadrian's drawings of "pumpkins." These must have been drawings of concrete domes like the one in the Serapeum (FIG. 10-52) at Hadrian's Tivoli villa. Such vaults were too adventurous for Apollodorus, or at least for a public building in Trajanic Rome, and Hadrian had to try them out later at home at his own expense.

*Dio Cassius, *Roman History*, 69.4.1–5. Translated by J. J. Pollitt, *The Art of Rome, c. 753 B.C.–A.D. 337: Sources and Documents* (New York: Cambridge University Press, 1983), 175–176.

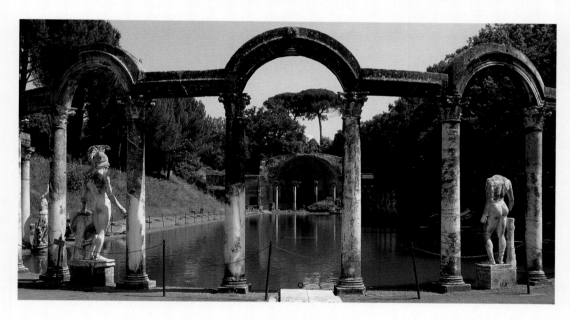

10-52 Canopus and Serapeum, Hadrian's Villa, Tivoli, Italy, ca. 125–128 CE.

Hadrian was an architect and may have personally designed some buildings at his private villa at Tivoli. The Serapeum features the kind of pumpkin-shaped concrete dome the emperor favored.

shaped by the enclosures. The Pantheon's interior is a single unified, self-sufficient whole, uninterrupted by supporting solids. It encloses visitors without imprisoning them, opening through the oculus to the drifting clouds, the blue sky, the sun, and the gods. In this space, the architect used light not merely to illuminate the darkness but to create drama and underscore the interior shape's symbolism. On a sunny day, the light that passes through the oculus forms a circular beam, a disk of light that moves across the coffered dome in the course of the day as the sun moves across the sky itself. Escaping from the noise and torrid heat of a Roman summer day into the Pantheon's cool, calm, and mystical immensity is an experience almost impossible to describe and one that should not be missed.

HADRIAN'S VILLA, TIVOLI Hadrian, the amateur architect, was not the designer of the Pantheon, but the emperor was deeply involved with the construction of his private country villa at Tivoli. One of his projects there was the construction of a pool and an artificial grotto, called the Canopus and Serapeum (FIG. 10-52), respectively. Canopus was an Egyptian city connected to Alexandria by a canal. Its most famous temple was dedicated to the god Serapis. Nothing about the Tivoli design, however, derives from Egyptian architecture. The grotto at the end of the pool is made of concrete and has an unusual pumpkin-shaped dome that Hadrian probably designed himself (see "Hadrian and Apollodorus of Damascus," above). Yet, in keeping with the persistent eclecticism of Roman art and architecture, Greek columns and marble copies of famous Greek statues lined the pool, as would be expected from a lover of Greek art. The Corinthian colonnade at the curved end of the pool, however, is of a type unknown in Classical Greek architecture. The colonnade not only lacks a superstructure but has *arcuated* (curved or arched) lintels, as opposed to traditional Greek horizontal lintels, between alternating pairs of columns. This simultaneous respect for Greek architecture and willingness to break its rules are typical of much Roman architecture of the High and Late Empire.

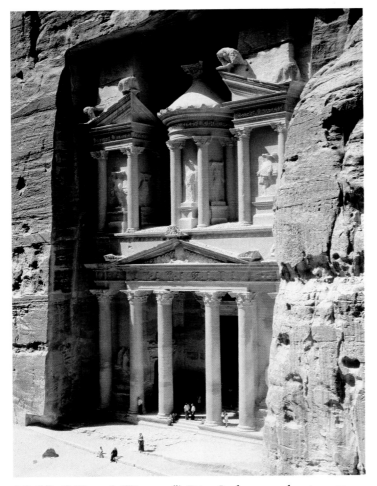

10-53 Al-Khazneh ("Treasury"), Petra, Jordan, second century CE.

This rock-cut tomb facade is a prime example of Roman "baroque" architecture. The designer used Greek architectural elements in a purely ornamental fashion and with a studied disregard for Classical rules.

AL-KHAZNEH, PETRA An even more extreme example of what many scholars have called Roman "baroque" architecture (because of the striking parallels with 17th-century Italian buildings; see Chapter 24) is the second-century CE tomb nicknamed Al-Khazneh, the "Treasury" (FIG. **10-53**), at Petra, Jordan. It is one of the most elaborate of many tomb facades cut into the sheer rock faces of the local rose-colored mountains. As at Hadrian's villa, Greek architectural elements are used here in a purely ornamental fashion and with a studied disregard for Classical rules.

The tomb's facade is more than 130 feet high and consists of two stories. The lower story resembles a temple facade with six columns, but the columns are unevenly spaced and the pediment is only wide enough to cover the four central columns. On the upper level, a temple-within-a-temple sits on top of the lower temple. Here the facade and roof split in half to make room for a central tholoslike cylinder, which contrasts sharply with the rectangles and triangles of the rest of the design. On both levels, the rhythmic alternation of deep projection and indentation creates dynamic patterns of light and shadow. At Petra, as at Tivoli, the architect used the vocabulary of Greek architecture, but the syntax is new and distinctively Roman. In fact, the design recalls some of the architectural fantasies painted on the walls of Roman houses—for example, the tholos seen through columns surmounted by a broken pediment (FIG. **10-19**, *right*) in the Second Style cubiculum from Boscoreale.

Ostia

The average Roman, of course, did not own a luxurious country villa and was not buried in a grand tomb. About 90 percent of Rome's population of close to one million lived in multistory apartment blocks (*insulae*). After the great fire of 64 CE, these were brick-faced concrete buildings. The rents were not cheap, as the law of supply and demand in real estate was just as valid in antiquity as it is today. Juvenal, a Roman satirist of the early second century CE, commented that people willing to give up chariot races and the other diversions Rome had to offer could purchase a fine home in the countryside "for a year's rent in a dark hovel" in a city so noisy that "the sick die mostly from lack of sleep."[3] Conditions were much the same for the inhabitants of Ostia, Rome's harbor city. After its new port opened under Trajan, Ostia's prosperity increased dramatically and so did its population. A burst of building activity began under Trajan and continued under Hadrian and throughout the second century CE.

APARTMENT HOUSES Ostia had many multistory insulae (FIG. **10-54**). Shops occupied the ground floors. Above were up to four floors of apartments. Although many of these were large, they had neither the space nor the light of the typical Pompeian private domus (see "The Roman House," page 247). In place of peristyles, insulae had only narrow light wells or small courtyards. Consequently, instead of looking inward, large numbers of glass windows faced the city's noisy streets. The residents cooked their food in the hallways. Only deluxe apartments had private toilets. Others shared latrines, often on a different floor from the apartment. Still, these insulae were quite similar to modern apartment houses, which also sometimes have shops on the ground floor.

10-54A Insula of the Painted Vaults, Ostia, early third century CE.

10-54 Model of an insula, Ostia, Italy, second century CE. Museo della Civiltà Romana, Rome.

Rome and Ostia were densely populated cities, and most Romans lived in multistory brick-faced concrete insulae (apartment houses) with shops on the ground floor. Private toilet facilities were rare.

10-55 Neptune and creatures of the sea, detail of a floor mosaic in the Baths of Neptune, Ostia, Italy, ca. 140 CE.

Black-and-white floor mosaics were very popular during the second and third centuries. The artists conceived them as surface decorations, not as illusionistic compositions meant to rival paintings.

Another strikingly modern feature of these multifamily residences is their brick facades, which were not concealed by stucco or marble veneers. When a classical motif was desired, builders could add brick pilasters or engaged columns, but always left the brick exposed. Ostia and Rome have many examples of apartment houses, warehouses, and tombs with intricate moldings and contrasting colors of brick. In the second century CE, brick came to be appreciated as attractive in its own right.

BATHS OF NEPTUNE Although the decoration of Ostian insulae tended to be more modest than that of the private houses of Pompeii, the finer apartments had mosaic floors and painted walls and ceilings. The most popular choice for elegant pavements at Ostia in both private and public edifices was the black-and-white mosaic. One of the largest and best-preserved examples is in the so-called Baths of Neptune, named for the grand mosaic floor (FIG. **10-55**) showing four seahorses pulling the Roman god of the sea across the waves. Neptune needs no chariot to support him as he speeds along, his mantle blowing in the strong wind. All about the god are other sea denizens, positioned so that wherever a visitor enters the room, some figures appear right side up. The second-century artist rejected the complex polychrome modeling of figures seen in Pompeian mosaics such as *Battle of Issus* (FIG. **5-70**) and used simple black silhouettes enlivened by white interior lines. Roman artists conceived black-and-white mosaics as surface decorations, not as three-dimensional windows, and thus they were especially appropriate for floors.

ISOLA SACRA The tombs in Ostia's Isola Sacra cemetery were usually constructed of brick-faced concrete, and the facades of these houses of the dead resembled those of the contemporary insulae of the living. These were normally communal tombs, not the final resting places of the very wealthy. Many of them were adorned with small painted terracotta plaques immortalizing the activities of middle-class merchants and professional people. A characteristic example (FIG. **10-56**) depicts a vegetable seller behind a counter. The artist had little interest in the Classical-revival style of contemporary imperial art and tilted the counter forward so that the observer can see the produce clearly. Such scenes of daily life appear on Roman funerary reliefs all over Europe. They were as much a part of the artistic legacy to the later history of Western art as the monuments of the Roman emperors, which until recently were the exclusive interest of art historians.

10-56 Funerary relief of a vegetable vendor, from Ostia, Italy, second half of second century CE. Painted terracotta, 1′ 5″ high. Museo Ostiense, Ostia.

Terracotta plaques illustrating the activities of middle-class merchants frequently adorned Ostian tomb facades. In this relief of a vegetable seller, the artist tilted the counter to display the produce clearly.

The Antonines

Early in 138 CE, Hadrian adopted the 51-year-old Antoninus Pius (r. 138–161 CE). At the same time, he required that Antoninus adopt Marcus Aurelius (r. 161–180 CE) and Lucius Verus (r. 161–169 CE), thereby assuring a peaceful succession for at least another generation. When Hadrian died later in the year, the Senate proclaimed him a god, and Antoninus Pius became emperor. Antoninus ruled the Roman world with distinction for 23 years. After his death and deification, Marcus Aurelius and Lucius Verus became the Roman Empire's first co-emperors.

COLUMN OF ANTONINUS PIUS Shortly after Antoninus Pius's death, Marcus and Lucius erected a memorial column in his honor. Its pedestal has a dedicatory inscription on one side and a relief illustrating the *apotheosis* (FIG. **10-57**), or ascent to Heaven, of Antoninus and his wife Faustina the Elder on the opposite side. On the adjacent sides are two identical representations of the *decursio* (FIG. **10-58**), or ritual circling of the imperial funerary pyre.

The two figural compositions are very different. The apotheosis relief remains firmly in the Classical tradition with its elegant, well-proportioned figures, personifications, and single ground line corresponding to the panel's lower edge. The Campus Martius (Field of Mars), personified as a youth holding the Egyptian obelisk that stood in that area of Rome, reclines at the lower left corner. Roma (Rome personified) leans on a shield decorated with the she-wolf suckling Romulus and Remus (compare FIG. **9-11**). Roma bids

10-57 Apotheosis of Antoninus Pius and Faustina, pedestal of the Column of Antoninus Pius, Rome, Italy, ca. 161 CE. Marble, 8′ 1½″ high. Musei Vaticani, Rome.

This representation of the apotheosis (ascent to Heaven) of Antoninus Pius and Faustina is firmly in the Classical tradition with its elegant, well-proportioned figures, personifications, and single ground line.

1 ft.

10-58 Decursio, pedestal of the Column of Antoninus Pius, Rome, Italy, ca. 161 CE. Marble, 8′ 1½″ high. Musei Vaticani, Rome.

In contrast to FIG. **10-57**, the Antonine decursio reliefs break sharply with Classical art conventions. The ground is the whole surface of the relief, and the figures stand on floating patches of earth.

1 ft.

farewell to the couple being lifted into the realm of the gods on the wings of a personification of uncertain identity. All this was familiar from earlier scenes of apotheosis. New to the imperial repertoire, however, was the fusion of time the joint apotheosis represents. Faustina had died 20 years before Antoninus Pius. By depicting the two as ascending together, the artist wished to suggest that Antoninus had been faithful to his wife for two decades and that now they would be reunited in the afterlife.

The decursio reliefs (FIG. 10-58) break even more strongly with Classical convention. The figures are much stockier than those in the apotheosis relief, and the panel was not conceived as a window onto the world. The ground is the whole surface of the relief, and marching soldiers and galloping horses alike stand on floating patches of earth. This, too, had not occurred before in imperial art, only in plebeian art (FIG. 10-10). After centuries of following the rules of Classical design, elite Roman artists and patrons finally became dissatisfied with them. When seeking a new direction, they adopted some of the non-Classical conventions of the art of the lower classes.

MARCUS AURELIUS Another break with the past occurred in the official portraits of Marcus Aurelius, although his images retain the pompous trappings of imperial iconography. In a larger-than-life-size gilded-bronze equestrian statue (FIG. 10-59), the emperor possesses a superhuman grandeur and is much larger than any normal human would be in relation to his horse. Marcus stretches out his right arm in a gesture that is both a greeting and an offer of clemency. Some evidence suggests that beneath the horse's raised right foreleg an enemy once cowered, begging the emperor for mercy. Marcus's portrait owed its preservation throughout the Middle Ages to the fact that it was mistakenly thought to portray Constantine, the first Christian emperor of Rome. Most ancient bronze statues were melted down for their metal value, because Christians regarded them as impious images from the pagan world. Even today, after centuries of new finds, only a few bronze equestrian statues survive. The type was, however, often used for imperial portraits—an equestrian statue of Trajan stood in the middle of his forum (FIG. 10-43, no. 6). Perhaps more than any other statuary type, the equestrian portrait expresses the Roman emperor's majesty and authority.

This message of supreme confidence is not conveyed, however, by the portrait head of Marcus's equestrian statue or any of the other portraits of the emperor in the years just before his death. Portraits of aged emperors were not new (FIG. 10-37), but Marcus's were the first ones in which a Roman emperor appeared weary, saddened, and even worried. For the first time, the strain of constant warfare on the frontiers and the burden of ruling a worldwide empire show in the emperor's face. The Antonine sculptor ventured beyond Republican verism, exposing the ruler's character, his thoughts, and his soul for all to see, as Marcus revealed them himself in his *Meditations,* a deeply moving philosophical treatise setting forth the emperor's personal worldview. This was a major turning point in the history of ancient art, and, coming as it did when the Classical style was being challenged in relief sculpture (FIG. 10-58), it marked the beginning of the end of Classical art's domination in the Greco-Roman world.

ORESTES SARCOPHAGUS Other profound changes also were taking place in Roman art and society at this time. Beginning under Trajan and Hadrian and especially during the rule of the Antonines, Romans began to favor burial over cremation. This reversal of funerary practices may reflect the influence of Christianity and

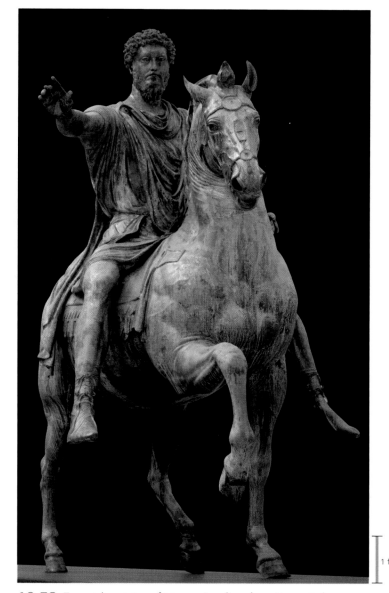

10-59 Equestrian statue of Marcus Aurelius, from Rome, Italy, ca. 175 CE. Bronze, 11′ 6″ high. Musei Capitolini, Rome.

In this equestrian portrait of Marcus Aurelius as omnipotent conqueror, the emperor stretches out his arm in a gesture of clemency. An enemy once cowered beneath the horse's raised foreleg.

other Eastern religions, whose adherents believed in an afterlife for the human body. Although the emperors themselves continued to be cremated in the traditional Roman manner, many private citizens opted for burial. Thus they required larger containers for their remains than the ash urns that were the norm until the second century CE. This in turn led to a sudden demand for sarcophagi, which are more similar to modern coffins than are any other ancient type of burial container.

Greek mythology was one of the most popular subjects for the decoration of these sarcophagi. In many cases, especially in the late second and third centuries CE, the Greek heroes and heroines were given the portrait features of the Roman men and women interred in the marble coffins. These private patrons were following the model of imperial portraiture, where emperors and empresses frequently masqueraded as gods and goddesses and heroes and heroines (see "Role Playing in Roman Portraiture," page 254). An early example of the type (although it lacks any portraits) is the sarcophagus

10-60 Sarcophagus with the myth of Orestes, ca. 140–150 CE. Marble, 2′ 7½″ high. Cleveland Museum of Art, Cleveland.

Under the Antonines, Romans began to favor burial over cremation, and sarcophagi became very popular. Themes from Greek mythology, such as the tragic saga of Orestes, were common subjects.

(FIG. **10-60**) now in Cleveland, one of many decorated with the story of the tragic Greek hero Orestes. All the examples of this type use the same basic composition. Orestes appears more than once in every case. Here, at the center, Orestes slays his mother Clytaemnestra and her lover Aegisthus to avenge their murder of his father Agamemnon, and then, at the right, takes refuge at Apollo's sanctuary at Delphi (symbolized by the god's tripod).

The repetition of sarcophagus compositions indicates that sculptors had access to pattern books. In fact, sarcophagus production was a major industry during the High and Late Empire. Several important regional manufacturing centers existed. The sarcophagi produced in the Latin West, such as the Cleveland Orestes sarcophagus, differ in format from those made in the Greek-speaking East. Western sarcophagi have reliefs only on the front and sides, because they were placed in floor-level niches inside Roman tombs. Eastern sarcophagi have reliefs on all four sides and stood in the center of the burial chamber. This contrast parallels the essential difference between Etrusco-Roman and Greek temples. The former were set against the wall of a forum or sanctuary and approached from the front, whereas the latter could be reached (and viewed) from every side.

MELFI SARCOPHAGUS An elaborate example (FIG. **10-61**) of a sarcophagus of the Eastern type comes from Rapolla, near Melfi in southern Italy. It was manufactured, however, in Asia Minor and

10-61 Asiatic sarcophagus with kline portrait of a woman, from Rapolla, near Melfi, Italy, ca. 165–170 CE. Marble, 5′ 7″ high. Museo Nazionale Archeologico del Melfese, Melfi.

Sarcophagi were produced in several regional centers. Western sarcophagi were decorated only on the front. Eastern sarcophagi, such as this one with a woman's portrait on the lid, have reliefs on all four sides.

Iaia of Cyzicus and the Art of Encaustic Painting

The names of very few Roman artists are known. Those that are tend to be names of artists and architects who directed major imperial building projects (Severus and Celer, Domus Aurea; Apollodorus of Damascus, Forum of Trajan), worked on a gigantic scale (Zenodorus, Colossus of Nero), or made precious objects for famous patrons (Dioscurides, gem cutter for Augustus).

An interesting exception to this rule is Iaia of Cyzicus. Pliny the Elder reported the following about this renowned painter from Asia Minor who worked in Italy during the Republic:

> Iaia of Cyzicus, who remained a virgin all her life, painted at Rome during the time when M. Varro [116–27 BCE; a renowned Republican scholar and author] was a youth, both with a brush and with a cestrum on ivory, specializing mainly in portraits of women; she also painted a large panel in Naples representing an old woman and a portrait of herself done with a mirror. Her hand was quicker than that of any other painter, and her artistry was of such high quality that she commanded much higher prices than the most celebrated painters of the same period.*

The *cestrum* Pliny mentioned is a small spatula used in *encaustic* painting, a technique of mixing colors with hot wax and then applying them to the surface. Pliny knew of encaustic paintings of considerable antiquity, including those of Polygnotos of Thasos (see Chapter 5, page 135). The best evidence for the technique, however, comes from Roman Egypt, where mummies were routinely furnished with portraits painted with encaustic on wooden panels (FIG. 10-62).

Artists applied encaustic to marble as well as to wood. According to Pliny, when Praxiteles was asked which of his statues he preferred, the fourth-century BCE Greek artist, perhaps the ancient world's greatest marble sculptor, replied: "Those that Nikias painted."† This anecdote underscores the importance of coloration in ancient statuary.

*Pliny the Elder, *Natural History*, 35.147–148. Translated by J. J. Pollitt, *The Art of Rome, c. 753 B.C.–A.D. 337: Sources and Documents* (New York: Cambridge University Press, 1983), 87.
†Pliny the Elder, *Natural History*, 35.133.

10-62 Mummy portrait of a priest of Serapis, from Hawara (Faiyum), Egypt, ca. 140–160 CE. Encaustic on wood, 1′ 4¾″ × 8¾″. British Museum, London.

In Roman times, the Egyptians continued to bury their dead in mummy cases, but painted portraits replaced the traditional masks. This portrait was painted in encaustic—colors mixed with hot wax.

attests to the vibrant export market for such luxury items in Antonine times. The decoration of all four sides of the marble box with statuesque images of Greek gods and heroes in architectural frames is distinctively Asiatic. The figures portrayed include Venus and the legendary beauty Helen of Troy. The lid portrait, which carries on the tradition of Etruscan sarcophagi (FIGS. 9-5 and 9-15), is also a feature of the most expensive Western Roman coffins. Here the deceased, a woman, reclines on a *kline* (bed). With her are her faithful little dog (only its forepaws remain at the left end of the lid) and Cupid (at the right). The winged infant-god mournfully holds a down-turned torch, a reference to the death of a woman whose beauty rivaled that of his mother, Venus, and of Homer's Helen.

MUMMY PORTRAITS In Egypt, burial had been practiced for millennia. Even after the Kingdom of the Nile was reduced to a Roman province in 30 BCE, Egyptians continued to bury their dead in mummy

cases (see "Mummification," Chapter 3, page 57). In Roman times, however, painted portraits on wood often replaced the traditional stylized portrait masks (see "Iaia of Cyzicus and the Art of Encaustic Painting," above). Hundreds of Roman mummy portraits have been preserved in the cemeteries of the Faiyum district. One of them (FIG. 10-62) depicts a priest of the Egyptian god Serapis, whose curly hair and beard closely emulate Antoine fashion in Rome. Such portraits, which mostly date to the second and third centuries CE, were probably painted while the subjects were still alive. This one exhibits the painter's refined use of the brush and spatula, mastery of the depiction of varied textures and of the play of light over the soft and delicately modeled face, and sensitive portrayal of the deceased's calm demeanor. Art historians use the Faiyum mummies to trace the evolution of portrait painting after Mount Vesuvius erupted in 79 CE (compare FIG. 10-25).

The Western and Eastern Roman sarcophagi and the mummy cases of Roman Egypt all served the same purpose, despite their

62A Mummy Artemidorus, 100–120 CE.

10-62B Mummy portrait of a young woman, ca. 110–120 CE.

differing shape and character. In an empire as vast as Rome's, regional differences are to be expected. As will be discussed later, geography also played a major role in the Middle Ages, when Western and Eastern Christian art differed sharply.

LATE EMPIRE

By the time of Marcus Aurelius, two centuries after Augustus established the Pax Romana, Roman power was beginning to erode. It was increasingly difficult to keep order on the frontiers, and even within the Empire the authority of Rome was being challenged. Marcus's son Commodus (r. 180–192 CE), who succeeded his father, was assassinated, bringing the Antonine dynasty to an end. The economy was in decline, and the efficient imperial bureaucracy was disintegrating. Even the official state religion was losing ground to Eastern cults, Christianity among them, which were beginning to gain large numbers of converts. The Late Empire was a pivotal era in world history during which the pagan ancient world was gradually transformed into the Christian Middle Ages.

The Severans

Civil conflict followed Commodus's death. When it ended, an African-born general named Septimius Severus (r. 193–211 CE) was master of the Roman world. He succeeded in establishing a new dynasty that ruled the Empire for nearly a half century.

SEVERAN PORTRAITURE Anxious to establish his legitimacy after the civil war, Septimius Severus adopted himself into the Antonine dynasty, declaring that he was Marcus Aurelius's son. It is not surprising, then, that official portraits of the emperor in bronze and marble depict him with the long hair and beard of his Antonine "father"—whatever Severus's true appearance may have been. That is also how he appears in the only preserved painted portrait of an em-

10-64 Portrait of Caracalla, ca. 211–217 CE. Marble, 1′ 2″ high. Metropolitan Museum of Art, New York.

Caracalla's suspicious personality is brilliantly captured in this portrait. The emperor's brow is knotted, and he abruptly turns his head over his left shoulder, as if he suspects danger from behind.

peror. The portrait (FIG. 10-63), discovered in Egypt and painted in *tempera* (pigments in egg yolk) on wood (as were many of the mummy portraits from Faiyum), shows Severus with his wife Julia Domna, the daughter of a Syrian priest, and their two sons, Caracalla and Geta. Painted imperial likenesses must have been quite common all over the empire, but their perishable nature explains their almost total loss.

The Severan family portrait is of special interest for two reasons beyond its survival. Severus's hair is tinged with gray, suggesting that his marble portraits—which, like all marble sculptures in antiquity, were painted—also may have revealed his advancing age in this way. (The same was very likely true of the marble likenesses of the elderly Marcus Aurelius.) The group portrait is also notable because the face of the emperor's younger son, Geta, was erased. When Caracalla (r. 211–217 CE) succeeded his father as emperor, he had his brother murdered and the Senate damn his memory. (Caracalla also ordered the death of his wife Plautilla.) The painted *tondo* (circular format, or *roundel*) portrait from Egypt is an eloquent testimony to that *damnatio memoriae* and to the long arm of Roman authority. This kind of defacement of a political rival's portrait is not new. Thutmose III of Egypt, for example, destroyed Hatshepsut's portraits (FIG. 3-21) after her death. But the Roman government employed damnatio memoriae as a political tool more often and more systematically than did any other civilization.

10-63 Painted portrait of Septimius Severus and his family, from Egypt, ca. 200 CE. Tempera on wood, 1′ 2″ diameter. Staatliche Museen, Berlin.

The only known painted portrait of an emperor shows Septimius Severus with gray hair. With him are his wife Julia Domna and their two sons, but Geta's head was removed after his damnatio memoriae.

CARACALLA In the Severan painted tondo, Caracalla is portrayed as a boy with curly Antonine hair. The portraits of Caracalla as emperor are very different. In the head illustrated here (FIG. 10-64), the sculptor brilliantly suggested the texture of the emperor's short hair and close-cropped beard through deft handling of the chisel and

10-65 Chariot procession of Septimius Severus, relief from the attic of the Arch of Septimius Severus, Lepcis Magna, Libya, 203 CE. Marble, 5′ 6″ high. Castle Museum, Tripoli.

A new non-naturalistic aesthetic emerged in later Roman art. In this relief from a triumphal arch, Septimius Severus and his two sons face the viewer even though their chariot is moving to the right.

incisions into the marble surface. More remarkable, however, is the moving characterization of Caracalla's suspicious nature, a further development from the groundbreaking introspection of the portraits of Marcus Aurelius. Caracalla's brow is knotted, and he abruptly turns his head over his left shoulder, as if he suspects danger from behind. The emperor had reason to be fearful. An assassin's dagger felled him in the sixth year of his rule. Assassination would be the fate of many Roman emperors during the turbulent third century CE.

LEPCIS MAGNA The hometown of the Severans was Lepcis Magna, on the coast of what is now Libya. In the late second and early third centuries CE, the Severans constructed a modern harbor there as well as a new forum, basilica, arch, and other monuments. The Arch of Septimius Severus has been rebuilt. It features friezes on the attic on all four sides. One frieze (FIG. **10-65**) depicts the chariot procession of the emperor and his two sons on the occasion of their homecoming in 203. Unlike the triumph panel (FIG. **10-41**) on the Arch of Titus in Rome, this relief gives no sense of rushing motion. Rather, it has a

stately stillness. The chariot and the horsemen behind it are moving forward, but the emperor and his sons are detached from the procession and face the viewer. Also different is the way the figures in the second row have no connection with the ground and are elevated above the heads of those in the first row so that they can be seen more clearly.

Both the frontality and the floating figures were new to official Roman art in Antonine and Severan times, but both appeared long before in the private art of freed slaves (FIGS. **10-9** and **10-10**). Once sculptors in the emperor's employ embraced these non-Classical elements, they had a long afterlife, largely (although never totally) displacing the Classical style the Romans adopted from Greece. As is often true in the history of art, the emergence of a new aesthetic was a by-product of a period of social, political, and economic upheaval. Art historians call this new non-naturalistic, more abstract style the Late Antique style.

BATHS OF CARACALLA The Severans were also active builders in the capital. The Baths of Caracalla (FIG. **10-66**) in Rome were the greatest in a long line of bathing and recreational complexes

10-66 Plan of the Baths of Caracalla, Rome, Italy, 212–216 CE. (1) natatio, (2) frigidarium, (3) tepidarium, (4) caldarium, (5) palaestra.

Caracalla's baths could accommodate 1,600 bathers. They resembled a modern health spa and included libraries, lecture halls, and exercise courts in addition to bathing rooms and a swimming pool.

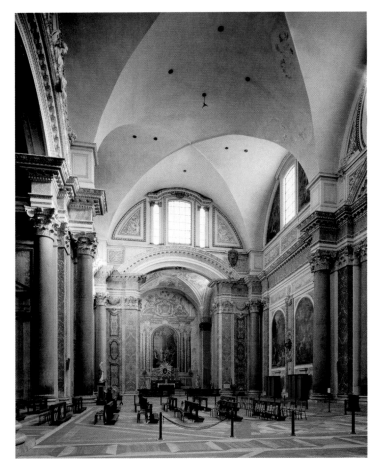

10-67 Frigidarium, Baths of Diocletian, Rome, ca. 298–306 CE (remodeled by MICHELANGELO as the nave of Santa Maria degli Angeli, 1563).

The groin-vaulted nave of the church of Santa Maria degli Angeli in Rome was once the frigidarium of the Baths of Diocletian. It gives an idea of the lavish adornment of imperial Roman baths.

erected with imperial funds to win the public's favor. Made of brick-faced concrete and covered by enormous vaults springing from thick walls up to 140 feet high, Caracalla's baths dwarfed the typical baths of cities and towns such as Ostia and Pompeii. The design was symmetrical along a central axis, facilitating the Roman custom of taking sequential plunges in warm-, hot-, and cold-water baths in, respectively, the *tepidarium, caldarium,* and *frigidarium.* The caldarium (FIG. 10-66, no. 4) was a huge circular chamber with a concrete drum even taller than the Pantheon's (FIGS. 10-49 to 10-51) and a dome almost as large. Caracalla's baths also had landscaped gardens, lecture halls, libraries, colonnaded exercise courts (*palaestras*), and a giant swimming pool (*natatio*). The entire complex covered an area of almost 50 acres. Archaeologists estimate that up to 1,600 bathers at a time could enjoy this Roman equivalent of a modern health spa. A branch of one of the city's major aqueducts supplied water, and furnaces circulated hot air through hollow floors and walls throughout the bathing rooms.

The Baths of Caracalla also featured stuccoed vaults, mosaic floors (both black-and-white and polychrome), marble-faced walls, and marble statuary. One statue on display was the 10-foot-tall copy of Lysippos's Herakles (FIG. 5-66), whose muscular body must have inspired Romans to exercise vigorously. The concrete vaults of the baths collapsed long ago, but visitors can get an excellent idea of what the central bathing hall, the frigidarium, once looked like from the nave (FIG. 10-67) of the church of Santa Maria degli Angeli in Rome, which was once the frigidarium of the later Baths of Diocle-

tian. The Renaissance interior (remodeled in the 18th century) of that church has, of course, many new elements foreign to a Roman bath, including a painted altarpiece. The ancient mosaics and marble revetment are long gone, but the present-day interior with its rich wall treatment, colossal columns with Composite capitals, immense groin vaults, and clerestory lighting gives a better sense of the character of a Roman imperial bathing complex than does any other building in the world. It takes a powerful imagination to visualize the original appearance of Roman concrete buildings from the woeful ruins of brick-faced walls and fallen vaults at ancient sites today, but Santa Maria degli Angeli makes the task much easier.

The Soldier Emperors

The Severan dynasty ended when Severus Alexander (r. 222–235 CE) was murdered. The next half century was one of almost continuous civil war. One general after another was declared emperor by his troops, only to be murdered by another general a few years or even a few months later. (In 238 CE, two co-emperors the Senate chose were dragged from the imperial palace and murdered in public after only three months in office.) In these unstable times, no emperor could begin ambitious architectural projects. The only significant building activity in Rome during the era of the "soldier emperors" occurred under Aurelian (r. 270–275 CE). He constructed a new defensive wall circuit for the capital—a military necessity and a poignant commentary on the decay of Roman power.

TRAJAN DECIUS If architects went hungry in third-century Rome, sculptors and engravers had much to do. The mint produced great quantities of coins (in debased metal) so that the troops could be paid with money stamped with the current emperor's portrait and not with that of his predecessor or rival. Each new ruler set up portrait statues and busts everywhere to assert his authority. The sculpted portraits of the third century CE are among the most moving ever made, as notable for their emotional content as they are for their technical virtuosity. Portraits of Trajan Decius (r. 249–251), such as the marble bust illustrated here (FIG. 10-68), show the emperor, who is best known for persecuting Christians, as an old man with bags under his eyes and a sad expression. In his eyes, which glance away nervously rather than engage the viewer directly, is the anxiety of a man who knows he can do little to restore order to an out-of-control world. The sculptor modeled the marble as if it were pliant clay, compressing the sides of the head at the level of the eyes, etching the hair and beard into the stone, and chiseling deep lines in the forehead and around the mouth. The portrait reveals the anguished soul of the man—and of the times.

10-68A Philip the Arabian, 244–249 CE.

TREBONIANUS GALLUS Decius's successor was Trebonianus Gallus (r. 251–253 CE), another short-lived emperor. In a larger-than-life-size bronze portrait (FIG. 10-69), Trebonianus appears in heroic nudity, as had so many emperors and generals before him. His physique is not, however, that of the strong but graceful Greek athletes Augustus and his successors admired so much. Instead, his is a wrestler's body with massive legs and a swollen trunk. The heavyset body dwarfs his head, with its nervous expression. In this portrait, the Greek ideal of the keen mind in the harmoniously proportioned body gave way to an image of brute force, an image well suited to the age of the soldier emperors.

THIRD-CENTURY SARCOPHAGI By the third century, burial of the dead had become so widespread that even the imperial family was practicing it in place of cremation. Sarcophagi were more popular than ever. An unusually large sarcophagus (FIG. 10-70), discovered in Rome in 1621 and purchased by Cardinal Ludovisi, is

10-68 Portrait bust of Trajan Decius, 249–251 CE. Marble, full bust 2′ 7″ high. Musei Capitolini, Rome.

This portrait of a short-lived "soldier emperor" depicts an older man with bags under his eyes and a sad expression. The eyes glance away nervously, reflecting the anxiety of an insecure ruler.

10-69 Heroic portrait of Trebonianus Gallus, from Rome, Italy, 251–253 CE. Bronze, 7′ 11″ high. Metropolitan Museum of Art, New York.

In this over-life-size heroically nude statue, Trebonianus Gallus projects an image of brute force. He has the massive physique of a powerful wrestler, but his face has a nervous expression.

10-70 Battle of Romans and barbarians (*Ludovisi Battle Sarcophagus*), from Rome, Italy, ca. 250–260 CE. Marble, 5′ high. Museo Nazionale Romano–Palazzo Altemps, Rome.

A chaotic scene of battle between Romans and barbarians decorates the front of this sarcophagus. The sculptor piled up the writhing, emotive figures in an emphatic rejection of Classical perspective.

On many third-century sarcophagi, the deceased appears as a learned intellectual. Here, the seated Roman philosopher is the central frontal figure. His two female muses also have portrait features.

1 ft.

decorated on the front with a chaotic scene of battle between Romans and one of their northern foes, probably the Goths. The sculptor spread the writhing and highly emotive figures evenly across the entire relief, with no illusion of space behind them. This piling of figures is an even more extreme rejection of Classical perspective than was the use of floating ground lines on the pedestal of the Column of Antoninus Pius (FIG. 10-58). It underscores the increasing dissatisfaction Late Antique artists felt with the Classical style.

Within this dense mass of intertwined bodies, the central horseman stands out vividly. He wears no helmet and thrusts out his open right hand to demonstrate that he holds no weapon. Several scholars have identified him as one of the sons of Trajan Decius. In an age when the Roman army was far from invincible and Roman emperors were constantly felled by other Romans, the young general on the Ludovisi battle sarcophagus is boasting that he is a fearless commander assured of victory. His self-assurance may stem from his having embraced one of the increasingly popular Oriental mystery religions. On the youth's forehead is carved the emblem of Mithras, the Persian god of light, truth, and victory over death.

The insecurity of the times led many Romans to seek solace in philosophy. On many third-century sarcophagi, the deceased assumes the role of the learned intellectual. One especially large example (FIG. 10-71) depicts a seated Roman philosopher holding a scroll. Two standing women (also with portrait features) gaze at him from left and right, confirming his importance. In the background are other philosophers, students or colleagues of the central deceased teacher. The two women may be the deceased's wife and daughter, two sisters, or some other combination of family members. The composition, with a frontal central figure and two subordinate flanking figures, is typical of the Late Antique style. This type of sarcophagus became very popular for Christian burials. Sculptors used the wise-man motif not only to portray the deceased (FIG. 11-6) but also Christ flanked by his apostles (FIG. 11-7).

TEMPLE OF VENUS, BAALBEK The decline in respect for Classical art also can be seen in architecture. At Baalbek (ancient Heliopolis) in present-day Lebanon, the architect of the Temple of Venus (FIG. 10-72), following in the "baroque" tradition of the Treasury at Petra (FIG. 10-53), ignored almost every rule of Classical design. Although made of stone, the third-century building, with its circular domed cella set behind a gabled columnar facade, was in many ways a critique of the concrete Pantheon (FIG. 10-49), which by then had achieved the status of a classic. Many features of the Baalbek temple intentionally depart from the norm. The platform, for example, is scalloped all around the cella. The columns—the only known instance of *five*-sided Corinthian capitals with corresponding pentagonal bases—support a matching scalloped entablature (which serves to buttress the shallow stone dome). These concave forms and those of the niches in the cella walls play off against the cella's convex shape. Even the "traditional" facade of the Baalbek temple is eccentric. The unknown architect inserted an arch within the triangular pediment.

Diocletian and the Tetrarchy

In an attempt to restore order to the Roman Empire, Diocletian (r. 284–305 CE), whose troops proclaimed him emperor, decided to share power with his potential rivals. In 293 he established the *tetrarchy* (rule by four) and adopted the title of Augustus of the East. The other three *tetrarchs* were a corresponding Augustus of the West, and Eastern and Western Caesars (whose allegiance to the two Augusti was cemented by marriage to their daughters). Together, the four emperors ruled without strife until Diocletian retired in 305. Without his leadership, the tetrarchic form of government collapsed and renewed civil war followed. The division of the Roman Empire into eastern and western spheres survived, however. It persisted throughout the Middle Ages, setting the Latin West apart from the Byzantine East.

10-73 Portraits of the four tetrarchs, from Constantinople, ca. 305 CE. Porphyry, 4′ 3″ high. Saint Mark's, Venice.

Diocletian established the tetrarchy to bring order to the Roman world. In group portraits, artists always depicted the four co-rulers as nearly identical partners in power, not as distinct individuals.

10-72 Restored view (*top*) and plan (*bottom*) of the Temple of Venus, Baalbek, Lebanon, third century CE.

This "baroque" temple violates almost every rule of Classical design. It has a scalloped platform and entablature, five-sided Corinthian capitals, and a facade with an arch inside the triangular pediment.

TETRARCHIC PORTRAITURE The four tetrarchs often were portrayed together, both on coins and in the round. Artists did not try to capture their individual appearances and personalities but sought instead to represent the nature of the tetrarchy itself—that is, to portray four equal partners in power. In the two pairs of porphyry (purple marble) portraits of the tetrarchs (FIG. **10-73**) that are now embedded in the southwestern corner of Saint Mark's in Venice, it is impossible to name the rulers. Each of the four emperors has lost his identity as an individual and been subsumed into the larger entity of the tetrarchy. All the tetrarchs are identically clad in cuirass and cloak. Each grasps a sheathed sword in the left hand. With their right arms they embrace one another in an overt display of concord. The figures, like those on the decursio relief (FIG. **10-58**) of the Column of Antoninus Pius, have large cubical heads on squat bodies. The drapery is schematic and the bodies are shapeless. The faces are emotionless masks, distinguished only by the beard on two of the

figures (probably the older Augusti, distinguishing them from the younger Caesars). Nonetheless, each pair is as alike as freehand carving can achieve. In this group portrait, carved eight centuries after Greek sculptors first freed the human form from the formal rigidity of the Egyptian-inspired kouros stance, an artist once again conceived the human figure in iconic terms. Idealism, naturalism, individuality, and personality now belonged to the past.

PALACE OF DIOCLETIAN When Diocletian abdicated in 305, he returned to Dalmatia (roughly the area of the former Yugoslavia), where he was born. There he built a palace (FIG. **10-74**) for himself at Split, near ancient Salona on the Adriatic coast of Croatia. Just as Aurelian had felt it necessary to girdle Rome with fortress walls, Diocletian instructed his architects to provide him with a well-fortified suburban palace. The complex, which covers about 10 acres, has the layout of a Roman castrum, complete with watchtowers flanking the gates. It gave the emperor a sense of security in the most insecure of times.

Within the high walls, two avenues (comparable to the cardo and decumanus of a Roman city; FIG. **10-42**) intersected at the palace's center. Where a city's forum would have been situated, Diocletian's palace had a colonnaded court leading to the entrance to the

10-74 Restored view of the palace of Diocletian, Split, Croatia, ca. 298–306.

Diocletian's palace resembled a fortified Roman city (compare FIG. 10-42). Within its high walls, two avenues intersected at the forumlike colonnaded courtyard leading to the emperor's residential quarters.

imperial residence, which had a templelike facade with an arch within its pediment, as in the Temple of Venus (FIG. 10-72) at Baalbek. Diocletian wanted to appear like a god emerging from a temple when he addressed those who gathered in the court to pay homage to him. On one side of the court was a Temple of Jupiter. On the other side was Diocletian's *mausoleum* (FIG. 10-74, *center right*), which towered above all the other structures in the complex. The emperor's huge domed tomb was a type that would become very popular in Early Christian times not only for mausoleums but eventually also for churches, especially in the Byzantine East. In fact, the tomb is a church today.

Constantine

An all-too-familiar period of conflict followed the short-lived concord among the tetrarchs that ended with Diocletian's abdication. This latest war among rival Roman armies lasted two decades. The eventual victor was Constantine I ("the Great"), son of Constantius Chlorus, Diocletian's Caesar of the West. After the death of his father, Constantine invaded Italy. In 312, at the battle of the Milvian Bridge to Rome, he defeated and killed Maxentius and took control of the capital. Constantine attributed his victory to the aid of the Christian god. The next year, he and Licinius, Constantine's co-emperor in the East, issued the Edict of Milan, ending the persecution of Christians.

In time, Constantine and Licinius became foes, and in 324 Constantine defeated and executed Licinius near Byzantium (modern Istanbul, Turkey). Constantine, now unchallenged ruler of the whole Roman Empire, founded a "New Rome" at Byzantium and named it Constantinople ("City of Constantine"). In 325, at the Council of Nicaea, Christianity became the de facto official religion of the Roman Empire. From this point on, paganism declined rapidly. Constantinople was dedicated on May 11, 330, "by the commandment of

God," and in 337 Constantine was baptized on his deathbed. For many scholars, the transfer of the seat of power from Rome to Constantinople and the recognition of Christianity mark the end of antiquity and the beginning of the Middle Ages.

Constantinian art is a mirror of this transition from the classical to the medieval world. In Rome, for example, Constantine was a builder in the grand tradition of the emperors of the first, second, and early third centuries, erecting public baths, a basilica on the road leading into the Roman Forum, and a triumphal arch. But he was also the patron of the city's first churches (see Chapter 11).

ARCH OF CONSTANTINE Between 312 and 315, Constantine erected a great triple-passageway arch (FIGS. 10-2, no. 15, and 10-75) next to the Colosseum to commemorate his defeat of Maxentius. The arch was the largest erected in Rome since the end of the Severan dynasty. Much of the sculptural decoration, however, was taken from earlier monuments of Trajan, Hadrian, and Marcus Aurelius, and all of the columns and other architectural elements date to an earlier era. Sculptors refashioned the second-century reliefs to honor Constantine by recutting the heads of the earlier emperors with the features of the new ruler. They also added labels to the old reliefs, such as *Liberator Urbis* (liberator of the city) and *Fundator Quietus* (bringer of peace), references to the downfall of Maxentius and the end of civil war. The reuse of statues and reliefs on the Arch of Constantine has often been cited as evidence of a decline in creativity and technical skill in the waning years of the pagan Roman Empire. Although such a judgment is in large part deserved, it ignores the fact that the reused sculptures were carefully selected to associate Constantine with the "good emperors" of the second century. That message is underscored in one of the arch's few Constantinian reliefs. It shows Constantine on the speaker's platform in the Roman Forum between statues of Hadrian and Marcus Aurelius.

10-75 Arch of Constantine (south side), Rome, Italy, 312–315 CE.

Much of the sculptural decoration of Constantine's arch came from monuments of Trajan, Hadrian, and Marcus Aurelius. Sculptors recut the heads of the earlier emperors with Constantine's features.

In another Constantinian relief (FIG. 10-76), the emperor distributes largesse to grateful citizens who approach him from right and left. Constantine is a frontal and majestic presence, elevated on a throne above the recipients of his munificence. The figures are squat in proportion, like the tetrarchs (FIG. 10-73). They do not move according to any Classical principle of naturalistic movement but rather have the mechanical and repeated stances and gestures of puppets. The relief is very shallow, the forms are not fully modeled, and the details are incised. The frieze is less a narrative of action than a picture of actors frozen in time so that the viewer can distinguish instantly the all-important imperial donor (at the center on a throne) from his attendants (to the left and right above) and the recipients of the largesse (below and of smaller stature).

This approach to pictorial narrative was once characterized as a "decline of form," and when judged by the standards of Classical art, it was. But the composition's rigid formality, determined by the rank of those portrayed, was consistent with a new set of values. It soon became the preferred mode, supplanting the Classical notion that a picture is a window onto a world of anecdotal action. Comparing this Constantinian relief with a Byzantine icon (FIG. 12-18) reveals that the compositional principles of the Late Antique style are those of the Middle Ages. They were very different from—but not necessarily "better" or "worse" than—those of the Greco-Roman world. The Arch of Constantine is the quintessential monument of its era, exhibiting a respect for the past in its reuse of second-century sculptures while rejecting the norms of Classical design in its frieze, paving the way for the iconic art of the Middle Ages.

1 ft.

10-76 Distribution of largesse, detail of the north frieze of the Arch of Constantine, Rome, Italy, 312–315 CE. Marble, 3′ 4″ high.

This Constantinian frieze is less a narrative of action than a picture of actors frozen in time. The composition's rigid formality reflects the new values that would come to dominate medieval art.

COLOSSUS OF CONSTANTINE After Constantine's victory over Maxentius, his official portraits broke with tetrarchic tradition as well as with the style of the soldier emperors, and resuscitated the Augustan image of an eternally youthful head of state. The most impressive of Constantine's preserved portraits is an eight-and-one-half-foot-tall head (FIG. 10-77), one of several marble fragments of a colossal enthroned statue of the emperor composed of a brick core, a wooden torso covered with bronze, and a head and limbs of marble. Constantine's artist modeled the seminude seated portrait on Roman images of Jupiter. The emperor held an orb (possibly surmounted by the cross of Christ), the symbol of global power, in his extended left hand. The nervous glance of third-century portraits is absent, replaced by a frontal mask with enormous eyes set into the broad and simple planes of the head. The emperor's personality is lost in this immense image of eternal authority. The colossal size, the likening of the emperor to Jupiter, the eyes directed at no person or thing of this world—all combine to produce a formula of overwhelming power appropriate to Constantine's exalted position as absolute ruler.

BASILICA NOVA, ROME Constantine's gigantic portrait sat in the western apse of the Basilica Nova ("New Basilica," FIGS. **10-2**, no. 12, and **10-78**), a project Maxentius had begun and Constantine completed. From its position in the apse, the emperor's image dominated the interior of the basilica in much the same way that enthroned statues of Greco-Roman divinities loomed over awestruck mortals who entered the cellas of pagan temples.

10-78 Restored cutaway view of the Basilica Nova, Rome, Italy, ca. 306–312 CE (John Burge).

The lessons learned in the construction of baths and market halls were applied to the Basilica Nova, where fenestrated concrete groin vaults replaced the clerestory of a traditional stone-and-timber basilica.

10-77 Portrait of Constantine, from the Basilica Nova, Rome, Italy, ca. 315–330 CE. Marble, 8′ 6″ high. Musei Capitolini, Rome.

Constantine's portraits revive the Augustan image of an eternally youthful ruler. This colossal head is one of several fragments of an enthroned Jupiter-like statue of the emperor holding the orb of world power.

1 ft.

The Basilica Nova ruins never fail to impress tourists with their size and mass. The original structure was 300 feet long and 215 feet wide. Brick-faced concrete walls 20 feet thick supported coffered barrel vaults in the aisles. These vaults also buttressed the groin vaults of the nave, which was 115 feet high. The walls and floors were richly marbled and stuccoed. The reconstruction in FIG. 10-78 effectively suggests the immensity of the interior, where the great vaults dwarf even the emperor's colossal portrait. The drawing also clearly reveals the fenestration of the groin vaults, a lighting system akin to the clerestory of a traditional stone-and-timber basilica. Here, Roman builders applied to the Roman basilica the lessons learned in the design and construction of buildings such as Trajan's great market hall (FIG. 10-46) and the Baths of Diocletian (FIG. 10-67).

AULA PALATINA, TRIER At Trier (ancient Augusta Treverorum) on the Moselle River in Germany, the imperial seat of Constantius Chlorus as Caesar of the West, Constantine built a new palace complex. It included a basilica-like audience hall, the Aula Palatina (FIG. 10-79), of traditional form and materials. The Aula Palatina measures about 190 feet long and 95 feet wide and has an austere brick exterior, which was enlivened somewhat by highlighting in grayish white stucco. The use of lead-framed panes of glass for the windows enabled the builders to give life and movement to the blank exterior surfaces.

Inside (FIG. 10-80), the audience hall was also very simple. Its flat, wooden, coffered ceiling is some 95 feet above the floor. The interior has no aisles, only a wide space with two stories of large windows that provide ample light. At the narrow north end, the main hall is divided from the semicircular apse (which also has a flat ceiling) by a so-called *chancel arch.* The Aula Palatina's interior is quite severe, although marble veneer and mosaics originally covered the arch and apse to provide a magnificent environment for the enthroned emperor. The design of both the interior and exterior has close parallels in many Early Christian churches.

10-79 Aula Palatina (exterior), Trier, Germany, early fourth century CE.

The austere brick exterior of Constantine's Aula Palatina at Trier is typical of later Roman architecture. Two stories of windows with lead-framed panes of glass take up most of the surface area.

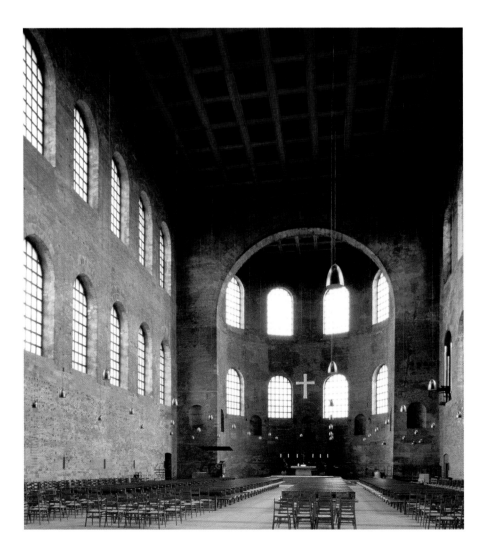

10-80 Aula Palatina (interior), Trier, Germany, early fourth century CE. ■◀

The interior of the audience hall of Constantine's palace complex in Germany resembles a timber-roofed basilica with an apse at one end, but it has no aisles. The large windows provided ample illumination.

CONSTANTINIAN COINS The two portraits of Constantine on the coins in FIG. **10-81** reveal both the essential character of Roman imperial portraiture and the special nature of Constantinian art. The first (FIG. **10-81**, *left*) was issued shortly after the death of Constantine's father, when Constantine was in his early 20s and his position was still insecure. Here, in his official portrait, he appears considerably older, because he adopted the imagery of the tetrarchs. Indeed, were it not for the accompanying label identifying this Caesar as Constantine, it would be impossible to know who was portrayed. Eight years later (FIG. **10-81**, *right*)—after the defeat of Maxentius and the Edict of Milan—Constantine, now the unchallenged Augustus of the West, is clean-shaven and looks his actual 30 years of age, having rejected the mature tetrarchic look in favor of youth. These two coins should dispel any uncertainty about the often fictive nature of imperial portraiture and the ability of Roman emperors to choose any official image that suited their needs. In Roman art, "portrait" is often not synonymous with "likeness."

The later coin is also an eloquent testimony to the dual nature of Constantinian rule. The emperor appears in his important role as imperator, dressed in armor, wearing an ornate helmet, and carrying a shield bearing the enduring emblem of the Roman state—the she-wolf nursing Romulus and Remus (compare FIG. **9-11** and Roma's shield in FIG. **10-57**). Yet he does not carry the scepter of the pagan Roman emperor. Rather, he holds a cross crowned by an orb. In addition, at the crest of his helmet, at the front, just below the grand plume, is a disk containing the *Christogram*, the monogram made up of *chi* (X), *rho* (P), and *iota* (I), the initial letters of Christ's name in Greek (compare the shield one of the soldiers holds in FIG. **12-10**). Constantine was at once portrayed as Roman emperor and as a soldier in the army of the Lord. The coin, like Constantinian art in general, belongs both to the classical and to the medieval world.

10-81 Coins with portraits of Constantine. Nummus (*left*), 307 CE. Billon, diameter 1″. American Numismatic Society, New York. Medallion (*right*), ca. 315 CE. Silver, diameter 1″. Staatliche Münzsammlung, Munich.

These two coins underscore that portraits of Roman emperors are rarely true likenesses. On the earlier coin, Constantine appears as a bearded tetrarch. On the later coin, he appears eternally youthful.

THE ROMAN EMPIRE

MONARCHY AND REPUBLIC, 753–27 BCE

�\ According to legend, Romulus and Remus founded Rome in 753 BCE. In the sixth century, Etruscan kings ruled the city and Roman art was Etruscan in character.

▯ In the centuries following the establishment of the Republic (509–27 BCE), Rome conquered its neighbors in Italy and then moved into Greece, bringing exposure to Greek art and architecture.

▯ Republican temples combined Etruscan plans with the Greek orders, and houses had peristyles with Greek columns. The Romans, however, pioneered the use of concrete as a building material.

▯ The First Style of mural painting derived from Greece, but the illusionism of the Second Style is distinctly Roman.

▯ Republican portraits were usually superrealistic likenesses of elderly patricians and celebrated traditional Roman values.

Villa of the Mysteries, Pompeii,
ca. 60–50 BCE

EARLY EMPIRE, 27 BCE–96 CE

▯ Augustus (r. 27 BCE–14 CE) became the first Roman emperor after defeating Mark Antony and Cleopatra at Actium in 31 BCE.

▯ Augustan art revived the Classical style with frequent references to Periclean Athens. Augustus's ambitious building program made lavish use of marble, and his portraits always depicted him as an idealized youth.

▯ Under the Julio-Claudians (r. 14–68 CE), the full potential of concrete began to be realized in buildings such as the Golden House of Nero.

▯ The Flavian emperors (r. 69–96 CE) erected the Colosseum, Rome's first and largest amphitheater, and arches and other monuments celebrating their victory in Judaea.

▯ Pompeii and Herculaneum were buried in 79 CE during the eruption of Mount Vesuvius. During the last quarter century of the towns' existence, the Third and Fourth Styles were used to decorate the walls of houses.

Augustus as general, Primaporta,
ca. 20 BCE

Arch of Titus, Rome
after 81 CE

HIGH EMPIRE, 96–192 CE

▯ The Roman Empire reached its greatest extent under Trajan (r. 98–117 CE). The emperor's new forum and markets transformed the civic center of Rome. The Column of Trajan commemorated his two campaigns in Dacia in a spiral frieze with thousands of figures.

▯ Hadrian (r. 117–138 CE), emulating Greek statesmen and philosophers, was the first emperor to wear a beard. He built the Pantheon, a triumph of concrete technology.

▯ Under the Antonines (r. 138–192 CE), the dominance of Classical art began to erode, and imperial artists introduced new compositional schemes in relief sculpture and a psychological element in portraiture.

Pantheon, Rome,
118–125 CE

LATE EMPIRE, 193–337 CE

▯ In the art of the Severans (r. 193–235 CE), the Late Antique style took root. Artists represented the emperor as a central frontal figure disengaged from the action around him.

▯ During the chaotic era of the soldier emperors (r. 235–284 CE), artists revealed the anxiety and insecurity of the emperors in moving portraits.

▯ Diocletian (r. 284–305 CE) reestablished order by sharing power. Statues of the tetrarchs portray the four emperors as identical and equal rulers, not as individuals.

▯ Constantine (r. 306–337 CE) restored one-man rule, ended persecution of the Christians, and transferred the capital of the Empire from Rome to Constantinople in 330. The abstract formality of Constantinian art paved the way for the iconic art of the Middle Ages.

Arch of Constantine, Rome,
312–315 CE

11-1 Interior of the Mausoleum of Galla Placidia, Ravenna, Italy, ca. 425.

Before Late Antiquity, mosaics were usually confined to floors. In the so-called Mausoleum of Galla Placidia (FIG. 11-15), mosaics cover every square inch of the interior above the marble-faced walls.

LATE ANTIQUITY

The Roman Empire was home to an extraordinarily diverse population. In Rome alone on any given day, someone walking through the city's various quarters would have encountered people of an astonishing range of social, ethnic, racial, linguistic, and religious backgrounds. The multicultural character of Roman society became even more pronounced as the Romans expanded their territories throughout Europe, Africa, and the Near East (MAP 10-1). The previous chapter focused on the public and private art and architecture of the pagan Roman world. During the third and fourth centuries, a rapidly growing number of Romans rejected *polytheism* (belief in multiple gods) in favor of *monotheism* (the worship of a single all-powerful god)—but they did not stop commissioning works of art. Jewish and Christian art of the Late Antique period is no less Roman than are sarcophagi with mythological scenes. Indeed, the artists may in some cases have been the same. The Jewish and Christian sculptures, paintings, and buildings of Late Antiquity are Roman in style and technique, but they differ in subject and function from contemporaneous Roman secular and religious art and architecture. For that reason, and because these Late Antique artworks and sacred buildings formed the foundation of the art and architecture of the Middle Ages, they are examined separately in this chapter.

DURA-EUROPOS

The powerful religious crosscurrents of Late Antiquity may be seen in microcosm in a distant outpost of the Roman Empire on a promontory overlooking the Euphrates River in Syria (MAP 11-1). Called Europos by the Greeks and Dura by the Romans, the town probably was founded shortly after the death of Alexander the Great by one of his successors. By the end of the second century BCE, Dura-Europos was in the hands of the Parthians. Trajan captured the city in 115,* but Dura reverted to Parthian control shortly thereafter. In 165, under Marcus Aurelius, the Romans retook the city and placed a permanent garrison there. Dura-Europos fell in 256 to Rome's new enemy in the East, the Sasanians, heirs to the Parthian Empire (see Chapter 2). The Sasanian siege of Dura is an important fixed point in the chronology of Late Antiquity because the inhabitants evacuated the town, leaving its buildings largely intact. This "Pompeii of the desert" has revealed the

---

*In this chapter, all dates are CE unless otherwise indicated.

MAP 11-1 The Mediterranean world in Late Antiquity.

remains of more than a dozen different cult buildings, including many shrines of the polytheistic religions of the Mediterranean and Near East. But the excavators also discovered places of worship for the monotheistic creeds of Judaism and Christianity.

SYNAGOGUE PAINTINGS The synagogue at Dura-Europos is remarkable not only for its very existence in a Roman garrison town but also for its extensive cycle of mural paintings (FIG. 11-2) depicting biblical themes. The building, originally a private house with a central courtyard, was converted into a synagogue during the latter part of the second century. The paintings surprised scholars when they were first reported, because they seemed to defy the Bible's Second Commandment prohibiting the making of graven images. The Dura find established that although the Jews of the Roman Empire did not worship idols as did their pagan contemporaries, biblical stories appeared on the painted walls of synagogues and probably also in painted manuscripts, though no illustrated Bible of this period survives. God (YHWH, or Yahweh in the Old Testament), however, never appears in the Dura paintings, except as a hand emerging from the top of the framed panels.

11-2 Interior of the synagogue, Dura-Europos, Syria, with wall paintings of Old Testament themes, ca. 245–256. Tempera on plaster. Reconstruction in National Museum, Damascus.

The Dura-Europos synagogue was a converted private house with a central courtyard. The niche housing the sacred Torah is at the center of one long wall adorned with paintings depicting Old and New Testament scenes.

The Dura murals are mostly devoid of action, even when the subject is a narrative theme. The artists told the stories through stylized gestures, and the figures, which have expressionless features and lack both volume and shadow, tend to stand in frontal rows. The painting of Samuel anointing David (FIG. 11-3) exemplifies this Late Antique style, also seen in the friezes of the Arch of Septimius Severus (FIG. 10-65) at Lepcis Magna and the Arch of Constantine (FIG. 10-76) in Rome. The episode is just to the right of the niche (FIG. 11-2, *center*) that housed the sacred Jewish *Torah* (the scroll containing the *Pentateuch*, the first five books of the Hebrew Scriptures). The prophet anoints the future king of Israel, while David's six older brothers look on. The painter drew attention to Samuel by depicting him larger than all the rest, a familiar convention of Late Antique art. David and his brothers are emotionless and almost disembodied spiritual presences—their bodies do not even have enough feet. The painter, however, distinguished David from his brothers by the purple toga he wears. The color purple was associated with the Roman emperor, and the Dura artist borrowed the imperial toga to signify David's royalty.

CHRISTIAN COMMUNITY HOUSE The meeting house (FIG. 11-4) of the Christian community at Dura-Europos was also a remodeled private residence with a central courtyard (FIG. 11-4, no. 1). Its meeting hall (FIG. 11-4, no. 2)—created by removing the partition between two rooms on the courtyard's south side—could accommodate no more than about 70 people at a time. The hall had a raised platform at one end where the leader of the congregation sat or stood. Another room (FIG. 11-4, no. 3), on the opposite side of the courtyard, had a font for conducting the rite of *baptism*, the all-important ceremony initiating a new convert into the Christian community.

Although the *baptistery* had mural paintings (poorly preserved), the place where Christians gathered to worship at Dura, as elsewhere in the Roman Empire, was a modest secondhand house, in striking contrast to the grand temples of the Roman gods. Because Christian communities could not obtain the approval of the state, they remained small in number. Nonetheless, the emperor Diocletian

11-4 Restored cutaway view of the Christian community house, Dura-Europos, Syria, ca. 240–256 (John Burge). (1) former courtyard of private house, (2) meeting hall, (3) baptistery.

The Christian community at Dura-Europos met in a remodeled private home that could accommodate only about 70 people. The house had a central courtyard, a meeting hall, and a baptistery.

became so concerned by the growing popularity of Christianity in the Roman army ranks that he ordered a fresh round of persecutions in 303 to 305, a half century after the last great persecutions under Trajan Decius. As Christianity's appeal grew, so too did the Roman state's fear of its weakening imperial authority. The Christians refused to pay even token homage to the Roman state's official gods (which included deified emperors as well as the traditional pantheon of gods and goddesses). Persecution ended only in 311, when Galerius issued an edict of toleration, and especially in 313, when Constantine, who believed the Christian god was the source of his power rather than a threat to it (see Chapter 10), issued the Edict of Milan. That declaration established Christianity as a legal religion with equal or superior standing to the traditional Roman cults.

THE CATACOMBS AND FUNERARY ART

Very little is known about the art of the first Christians. When art historians speak about "Early Christian art," they are referring to the earliest preserved artworks having Christian subjects, not the art of Christians at the time of Jesus. Most Early Christian art in Rome dates to the third and fourth centuries and is found in the *catacombs*—vast subterranean networks of galleries (passageways) and chambers designed as cemeteries for burying the Christian dead. The name derives from the Latin *ad catacumbas*, which means "in the hollows." To a much lesser extent, the catacombs also housed the graves of Jews and others. The builders tunneled the catacombs out of the tufa bedrock, much as the Etruscans fashioned the underground tomb chambers in the Cerveteri necropolis (FIG. 9-6). The catacombs are less elaborate than the Etruscan tombs but much more extensive. The known catacombs in Rome (others exist elsewhere) comprise galleries estimated to run for 60 to 90 miles. From the second through the fourth centuries, these burial complexes were in constant use, housing as many as four million bodies.

1 ft.

11-3 Samuel anoints David, detail of the mural paintings in the synagogue, Dura-Europos, Syria, ca. 245–256. Tempera on plaster, 4′ 7″ high.

The figures in the biblical mural paintings in the Dura-Europos synagogue lack volume and shadow, stand in frontal rows, and have stylized gestures—features also of contemporaneous pagan art.

11-5 The Good Shepherd, the story of Jonah, and orants, painted ceiling of a cubiculum in the Catacomb of Saints Peter and Marcellinus, Rome, Italy, early fourth century.

Catacomb paintings mixed Old and New Testament themes. Jonah was a popular subject because he was swallowed by a sea monster and emerged safely after three days, prefiguring Christ's Resurrection.

11-5A Via Dino Compagni Catacomb, Rome, ca. 320–360.

In accordance with Roman custom, Christians had to be buried outside a city's walls on private property, usually purchased by a *confraternity*, or association, of Christian families pooling funds. Each of the catacombs was initially of modest extent. First, the builders dug a gallery three to four feet wide around the perimeter of the burial ground at a convenient level below the surface. In the walls of these galleries, they cut *loculi* (openings to receive the bodies of the dead, one above another, like shelves). Often, small rooms carved out of the rock, called *cubicula* (as in Roman houses of the living), served as mortuary chapels. Once the original perimeter galleries were full of loculi and cubicula, the Christians excavated other galleries at right angles to them. This process continued as long as lateral space permitted, at which point they opened lower levels connected by staircases to those above. Some catacomb systems extended as deep as five levels. When adjacent burial areas belonged to members of the same Christian confraternity, or by gift or purchase fell into the same hands, the owners cut passageways between the respective cemeteries. The galleries thus spread laterally and gradually occupied a vast expanse. After Christianity received official approval, churches rose on the land above the catacombs so that the pious could worship openly at the burial sites of some of the earliest Christian *martyrs* (individuals who chose to die rather than deny their religious beliefs; the Church declared many of them *saints*).

Painting

As already noted, Early Christian art is Roman in style but Christian in subject. The painted ceiling (FIG. **11-5**) of a cubiculum in the Catacomb of Saints Peter and Marcellinus in Rome, for example, is similar in format to the painted vaults of some third-century apartment houses at Ostia that have a circular frame with a central medallion and *lunettes* (semicircular frames) around the circumference. The lunettes in this Early Christian cubiculum contain the key episodes from the Old Testament story of Jonah. The sailors throw him from his ship on the left. He emerges on the right from the "whale." (The Greek word is *ketos*, or sea dragon, and that is how the artist represented the monstrous marine creature that swallowed Jonah; compare the sea creature, FIG. 10-30, *right*.) Safe on land at the bottom, Jonah contemplates the miracle of his salvation and the mercy of God. Jonah was a popu-

lar figure in Early Christian painting and sculpture, especially in funerary contexts. The Christians honored him as a *prefiguration* (prophetic forerunner) of Christ, who rose from death as Jonah had been delivered from the belly of the ketos, also after three days. Old Testament miracles prefiguring Christ's Resurrection abound in the catacombs and in Early Christian art in general (see "Jewish Subjects in Christian Art," page 293).

A man, a woman, and at least one child occupy the compartments between the Jonah lunettes. They are *orants* (praying figures), raising their arms in the ancient attitude of prayer. Together they make up a cross-section of the Christian family seeking a heavenly afterlife. The central medallion shows Christ as the Good Shepherd, whose powers of salvation are underscored by his juxtaposition with Jonah's story. The motif can be traced to Archaic Greek art, but there the pagan calf bearer (FIG. 5-9) offered his animal in sacrifice to Athena. In Early Christian art, Christ is the youthful and loyal protector of the Christian flock, who said to his disciples, "I am the good shepherd; the good shepherd gives his life for the sheep" (John 10:11). In the Christian motif, the sheep on Christ's shoulders is one of the lost sheep he has retrieved, symbolizing a sinner who has strayed and been rescued. Early Christian artists almost invariably represented Christ either as the Good Shepherd or as a teacher. Only after Christianity became the Roman Empire's official religion in 380 did representations of Christ in art take on such imperial attributes as the halo, the purple robe, and the throne, which denoted rulership. Eventually artists depicted Christ with the beard of a mature adult, which has been the standard form for centuries, supplanting the youthful imagery of most Early Christian portrayals of the Savior.

11-5B Catacomb of Commodilla, Rome, ca. 370–385.

Jewish Subjects in Christian Art

From the beginning, the Old Testament played an important role in Christian life and Christian art, in part because Jesus was a Jew and so many of the first Christians were converted Jews, but also because Christians came to view many of the persons and events of the Old Testament as prefigurations of New Testament persons and events. Christ himself established the pattern for this kind of biblical interpretation, called *typology,* when he compared Jonah's three-day stay in the belly of the sea monster (usually translated as "whale" in English) to the comparable time he would be entombed in the earth before his Resurrection (Matt. 12:40). In the fourth century, Saint Augustine (354–430) confirmed the validity of this typological approach to the Old Testament when he stated that "the New Testament is hidden in the Old; the Old is clarified by the New."* Thus the Old Testament figured prominently in Early Christian art in all media. Biblical tales of Jewish faith and salvation were especially common in funerary contexts but appeared also in churches and on household objects.

The following are four of the most popular Old Testament stories depicted in Early Christian art:

▌ *Adam and Eve* Eve, the first woman, tempted by a serpent, ate the forbidden fruit of the tree of knowledge and fed some to Adam, the first man. As punishment, God expelled Adam and Eve from Paradise. This "Original Sin" ultimately led to Christ's sacrifice on the cross so that all humankind could be saved. Christian

theologians often consider Christ the new Adam and his mother, Mary, the new Eve.

▌ *Sacrifice of Isaac* God instructed Abraham, the father of the Hebrew nation, to sacrifice Isaac, his only son, as proof of his faith. When it became clear that Abraham would obey, the Lord sent an angel to restrain him and provided a ram for sacrifice in Isaac's place. Christians view this episode as a prefiguration of the sacrifice of God's only son, Jesus.

▌ *Jonah* The Old Testament prophet Jonah had disobeyed God's command. In his wrath, the Lord caused a storm while Jonah was at sea. Jonah asked the sailors to throw him overboard, and the storm subsided. A sea dragon then swallowed Jonah, but God answered his prayers, and the monster spat out Jonah after three days and nights, foretelling Christ's Resurrection.

▌ *Daniel* When Daniel, one of the most important Jewish prophets, violated a Persian decree against prayer, the Persians threw him into a den of lions. God sent an angel to shut the lions' mouths, and Daniel emerged unharmed. Like Jonah's story, this is an Old Testament salvation tale, a precursor of Christ's triumph over death.

*Augustine, *City of God,* 16.26.

Sculpture

Most Christians rejected cremation, and the wealthiest Christian faithful, like their pagan contemporaries, favored impressive marble sarcophagi for burial. Many of these coffins have survived in catacombs and elsewhere. Predictably, the most common themes painted on the walls and vaults of the Roman subterranean cemeteries were also the subjects that appeared on Early Christian sarcophagi. Often, the decoration of the marble coffins was a collection of significant Christian themes, just as on the painted ceiling (FIG. 11-5) in the Catacomb of Saints Peter and Marcellinus.

SANTA MARIA ANTIQUA SARCOPHAGUS On the front of a sarcophagus (FIG. **11-6**) in Santa Maria Antiqua in Rome, the story of Jonah occupies the left one-third. At the center are an orant and a seated philosopher, the latter a motif borrowed directly from contemporary pagan sarcophagi (FIG. **10-71**). The heads of both the praying woman and the seated man reading from a scroll are unfinished. Roman workshops often produced sarcophagi before knowing who would purchase them. The sculptors added the portraits at the time of burial, if they added them at all. This practice underscores the universal appeal of the themes chosen. At the right

11-6 Sarcophagus with philosopher, orant, and Old and New Testament scenes, ca. 270. Marble, 1' 11¼" × 7' 2". Santa Maria Antiqua, Rome.

This Early Christian sarcophagus depicts the salvation of Jonah, Christ as Good Shepherd, and the baptism of Christ. The two figures with unfinished heads were intended as portraits of the deceased.

11-7 Sarcophagus of Junius Bassus, from Rome, Italy, ca. 359. Marble, 3′ 10½″ × 8′. Museo Storico del Tesoro della Basilica di San Pietro, Rome.

The wealthiest Christians, like the recently converted city prefect Junius Bassus, favored elaborately decorated sarcophagi. Here, biblical episodes from Adam and Eve to Christ before Pilate appear in 10 niches.

are two different, yet linked, representations of Jesus—as the Good Shepherd and as a child receiving baptism in the Jordan River, though he really was baptized at age 30 (see "The Life of Jesus in Art," pages 296–297). The sculptor suggested the future ministry of the baptized Jesus by turning the child's head toward the Good Shepherd and by placing his right hand on one of the sheep. In the early centuries of Christianity, baptism was usually delayed almost to the moment of death because it cleansed the Christian of all sin. One of those who was baptized on his deathbed was the emperor Constantine (see Chapter 10).

JUNIUS BASSUS SARCOPHAGUS Another pagan convert to Christianity was the city prefect of Rome, Junius Bassus, who, according to the inscription on his sarcophagus (FIG. **11-7**), was baptized just before he died in 359. The sarcophagus is of eclectic format—decorated only on three sides in the western Roman manner (see Chapter 10), but divided into two registers of five compartments, each framed by columns in the tradition of Asiatic sarcophagi (FIG. **10-61**). In contrast to the Santa Maria Antiqua sarcophagus (FIG. **11-6**), the deceased does not appear on the body of the coffin. Instead, stories from the Old and New Testaments fill the niches. Christ has pride of place and appears in the central compartment of each register: as a teacher enthroned between his chief

apostles, Saints Peter and Paul (above), and triumphantly entering Jerusalem on a donkey (below). Appropriately, the sculptor placed the scene of Christ's heavenly triumph above that of his earthly triumph. Both compositions owe a great deal to official Roman art. In the center of the upper zone, Christ, like an enthroned Roman emperor, sits above a personification of the sky god holding a billowing mantle over his head, indicating that Christ is ruler of the universe. The scene below derives from portrayals of Roman emperors entering cities on horseback, but Christ's steed and the absence of imperial attributes contrast sharply with the imperial models the sculptor used as compositional sources.

All of the Old Testament scenes on the Junius Bassus sarcophagus are precursors of New Testament events (see "Jewish Subjects in Christian Art," page 293). Adam and Eve, for example, are in the second niche from the left on the lower level. Their Original Sin of eating the apple in the Garden of Eden ultimately necessitated Christ's sacrifice for the salvation of humankind. To the right of the entry into Jerusalem is Daniel, unscathed by flanking lions, saved by his faith. At the upper left, Abraham is about to sacrifice Isaac. Christians believe this Old Testament story was a prefiguration of God's sacrifice of his own son, Jesus.

The Crucifixion itself, however, does not appear on the Junius Bassus sarcophagus. Indeed, the subject was very rare in Early Chris-

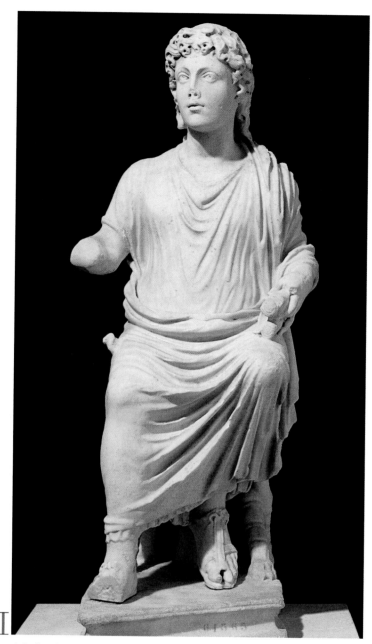

1 in.

11-8 Christ seated, from Civita Latina, Italy, ca. 350–375. Marble, 2′ 4½″ high. Museo Nazionale Romano–Palazzo Massimo alle Terme, Rome.

The earliest representations of Jesus show him as a young man. Statues of Christ are rare during the Early Christian period, however, because of the Second Commandment prohibition of idol worship.

tian art and unknown prior to the fifth century. Artists emphasized Christ's divinity and exemplary life as teacher and miracle worker, not his suffering and death at the hands of the Romans. This sculptor, however, alluded to the Crucifixion in the scenes in the two niches at the upper right depicting Jesus being led before Pontius Pilate for judgment. The Romans condemned Jesus to death, but he triumphantly overcame it. Junius Bassus and other Christians, whether they were converts from paganism or from Judaism, hoped for a similar salvation.

STATUETTE OF CHRIST Apart from the reliefs on privately commissioned sarcophagi, monumental sculpture became increasingly uncommon in the fourth century. The authorities continued to erect portrait statues of Roman emperors and other officials, and

artists still made statues of pagan gods and mythological figures, but the number of statues decreased sharply. In his *Apologia*, Justin Martyr, a second-century philosopher who converted to Christianity and was mindful of the Second Commandment's admonition to shun graven images, accused the pagans of worshiping statues as gods. Christians tended to suspect the freestanding statue, linking it with the false gods of the pagans, so Early Christian houses of worship had no "cult statues." Nor did the first churches have any equivalent of the pedimental statues and relief friezes of Greco-Roman temples.

The Greco-Roman experience, however, was still a living part of the Mediterranean mentality, and many Christians like Junius Bassus were recent converts from paganism who retained some of their classical values. This may account for those rare instances of freestanding Early Christian sculpture, such as the marble statuette (FIG. **11-8**) of Christ seated from Civita Latina. Less than three feet tall, the figure closely resembles the Christ situated between Saints Peter and Paul on the Junius Bassus sarcophagus (FIG. **11-7**, *top center*). As on the relief, Christ's head is that of a long-haired Apollo-like youth, but the Romans employed the statuary type only for bearded philosophers of advanced age. Like those learned men, Christ wears the Roman tunic, toga, and sandals and holds an unopened scroll in his left hand. The piece is unique, and unfortunately its original context and function are unknown. Several third- and fourth-century marble statuettes of Christ as the Good Shepherd and of Jonah also survive, but they too are exceptional.

11-8A Christ as Good Shepherd, ca. 300–350.

ARCHITECTURE AND MOSAICS

Although some Christian ceremonies were held in the catacombs, regular services took place in private community houses of the type found at Dura-Europos (FIG. **11-4**). Once Christianity achieved imperial sponsorship under Constantine, an urgent need suddenly arose to construct churches. The new buildings had to meet the requirements of Christian *liturgy* (the official ritual of public worship), provide a suitably monumental setting for the celebration of the Christian faith, and accommodate the rapidly growing numbers of worshipers.

Constantine was convinced that the Christian god had guided him to victory over Maxentius, and in lifelong gratitude he protected and advanced Christianity throughout the Empire as well as in the obstinately pagan capital city of Rome. As emperor, he was, of course, obliged to safeguard the ancient Roman religion, traditions, and monuments, and, as noted in Chapter 10, he was (for his time) a builder on a grand scale in the heart of the city. But eager to provide buildings to house the Christian rituals and venerated burial places, especially the memorials of founding saints, Constantine also was the first major patron of Christian architecture. He constructed elaborate basilicas, memorials, and mausoleums not only in Rome but also in Constantinople, his "New Rome" in the East, and at sites sacred to Christianity, most notably Bethlehem, the birthplace of Jesus, and Jerusalem, the site of the Crucifixion.

Rome

The major Constantinian churches in Rome stood on sites associated with the graves of Christian martyrs, which, in keeping with Roman custom, were all on the city's outskirts. The decision to erect churches at those sites also permitted Constantine to keep the new Christian shrines out of the city center and to avoid any confrontation between Rome's Christian and pagan populations.

The Life of Jesus in Art

Christians believe that Jesus of Nazareth is the son of God, the *Messiah* (Savior, Christ) of the Jews prophesied in the Old Testament. His life—his miraculous birth from the womb of a virgin mother, his preaching and miracle working, his execution by the Romans and subsequent ascent to Heaven—has been the subject of countless artworks from Roman times through the present day. The primary literary sources for these representations are the Gospels of the New Testament attributed to the Four Evangelists, Saints Matthew, Mark, Luke, and John (see "The Four Evangelists," Chapter 16, page 412); later apocryphal works; and medieval theologians' commentaries on these texts.

The life of Jesus dominated the subject matter of Christian art to a far greater extent than Greco-Roman religion and mythology ever did classical art. Whereas images of athletes, portraits of statesmen and philosophers, narratives of war and peace, genre scenes, and other secular subjects were staples of the classical tradition, Christian iconography held a near-monopoly in the art of the Western world in the Middle Ages.

Although many of the events of Jesus' life were rarely or never depicted during certain periods, the cycle as a whole has been one of the most frequent subjects of Western art, even after the revival of classical and secular themes in the Renaissance. Thus it is useful to summarize the entire cycle of events as they usually appear in the artworks.

INCARNATION AND CHILDHOOD

The first "cycle" of the life of Jesus consists of the events of his conception (Incarnation), birth, infancy, and childhood.

▮ *Annunciation to Mary* The archangel Gabriel announces to the Virgin Mary that she will miraculously conceive and give birth to God's son Jesus. Artists sometimes indicate God's presence at the Incarnation by a dove, the symbol of the Holy Spirit, the third "person" of the *Trinity* with God the Father and Jesus.

▮ *Visitation* The pregnant Mary visits Elizabeth, her older cousin, who is pregnant with the future Saint John the Baptist. Elizabeth is the first to recognize that the baby Mary is bearing is the Son of God, and they rejoice.

▮ *Nativity, Annunciation to the Shepherds,* and *Adoration of the Shepherds* Jesus is born at night in Bethlehem and placed in a basket. Mary and her husband Joseph marvel at the newborn in a stable or, in Byzantine art, in a cave. An angel announces the birth of the Savior to shepherds in the field, who rush to Bethlehem to adore the child.

▮ *Adoration of the Magi* A bright star alerts three wise men (*magi*) in the East that the King of the Jews has been born. They travel 12 days to find the Holy Family and present precious gifts to the infant Jesus.

▮ *Presentation in the Temple* In accordance with Jewish tradition, Mary and Joseph bring their firstborn son to the temple in Jerusalem, where the aged Simeon, who God said would not die until he had seen the Messiah, recognizes Jesus as the prophesied Savior of humankind.

▮ *Massacre of the Innocents* and *Flight into Egypt* King Herod, fearful that a rival king has been born, orders the massacre of all infants in Bethlehem, but an angel warns the Holy Family and they escape to Egypt.

▮ *Dispute in the Temple* Joseph and Mary travel to Jerusalem for the feast of Passover (the celebration of the release of the Jews from bondage to the pharaohs of Egypt). Jesus, only 12 years old at the time, engages in learned debate with astonished Jewish scholars in the temple, foretelling his ministry.

PUBLIC MINISTRY

The public-ministry cycle comprises the teachings of Jesus and the miracles he performed.

▮ *Baptism* The beginning of Jesus' public ministry is marked by his baptism at age 30 by John the Baptist in the Jordan River, where the dove of the Holy Spirit appears and God's voice is heard proclaiming Jesus as his son.

▮ *Calling of Matthew* Jesus summons Matthew, a tax collector, to follow him, and Matthew becomes one of his 12 disciples, or *apostles* (from the Greek for "messenger"), and later the author of one of the four Gospels.

▮ *Miracles* In the course of his teaching and travels, Jesus performs many miracles, revealing his divine nature. These include acts of healing and raising the dead, turning water into wine, walking on water and calming storms, and creating wondrous quantities of food. In the miracle of loaves and fishes, for example, Jesus transforms a few loaves of bread and a handful of fishes into enough food to feed several thousand people.

▮ *Delivery of the Keys to Peter* The fisherman Peter was one of the first men Jesus summoned as a disciple. Jesus chooses Peter (whose name means "rock") as his successor. He declares that Peter is the rock on which his church will be built and symbolically delivers to Peter the keys to the kingdom of Heaven.

▮ *Transfiguration* Jesus scales a high mountain and, in the presence of Peter and two other disciples, James and John the Evangelist, is transformed into radiant light. God, speaking from a cloud, discloses that Jesus is his son.

▮ *Cleansing of the Temple* Jesus returns to Jerusalem, where he finds money changers and merchants conducting business in the temple. He rebukes them and drives them out of the sacred precinct.

PASSION

The Passion (from Latin *passio,* "suffering") cycle includes the events leading to Jesus' death, Resurrection, and ascent to Heaven.

- **Entry into Jerusalem** On the Sunday before his Crucifixion (Palm Sunday), Jesus rides triumphantly into Jerusalem on a donkey, accompanied by disciples. Crowds of people enthusiastically greet Jesus and place palm fronds in his path.

- **Last Supper** and **Washing of the Disciples' Feet** In Jerusalem, Jesus celebrates Passover with his disciples. During this Last Supper, Jesus foretells his imminent betrayal, arrest, and death and invites the disciples to remember him when they eat bread (symbol of his body) and drink wine (his blood). This ritual became the celebration of *Mass* (*Eucharist*) in the Christian Church. At the same meal, Jesus sets an example of humility for his apostles by washing their feet.

- **Agony in the Garden** Jesus goes to the Mount of Olives in the Garden of Gethsemane, where he struggles to overcome his human fear of death by praying for divine strength. The apostles who accompanied him there fall asleep despite his request that they stay awake with him while he prays.

- **Betrayal** and **Arrest** One of the disciples, Judas Iscariot, agrees to betray Jesus to the Jewish authorities in return for 30 pieces of silver. Judas identifies Jesus to the soldiers by kissing him, and Jesus is arrested. Later, a remorseful Judas hangs himself from a tree.

- **Trials of Jesus** and **Denial of Peter** Jesus is brought before Caiaphas, the Jewish high priest, and is interrogated about his claim to be the Messiah. Meanwhile, the disciple Peter thrice denies knowing Jesus, as Jesus predicted he would. Jesus is then brought before the Roman governor of Judaea, Pontius Pilate, on the charge of treason because he had proclaimed himself King of the Jews. Pilate asks the crowd to choose between freeing Jesus or Barabbas, a murderer. The people choose Barabbas, and the judge condemns Jesus to death. Pilate washes his hands, symbolically relieving himself of responsibility for the mob's decision.

- **Flagellation** and **Mocking** The Roman soldiers who hold Jesus captive whip (flagellate) him and mock him by dressing him as King of the Jews and placing a crown of thorns on his head.

- **Carrying of the Cross, Raising of the Cross,** and **Crucifixion** The Romans force Jesus to carry the cross on which he will be crucified from Jerusalem to Mount Calvary (Golgotha, the "place of the skull," where Adam was buried). He falls three times and his robe is stripped off along the way. Soldiers erect the cross and nail his hands and feet to it. Jesus' mother, John the Evangelist, and Mary Magdalene mourn at the foot of the cross, while soldiers torment Jesus. One of them (the centurion Longinus) stabs Jesus in the side with a spear. After suffering great pain, Jesus dies. The Crucifixion occurred on a Friday, and Christians celebrate the day each year as Good Friday.

- **Deposition, Lamentation,** and **Entombment** Two disciples, Joseph of Arimathea and Nicodemus, remove Jesus' body from the cross (the Deposition); sometimes those present at the Crucifixion look on. They take Jesus to the tomb Joseph had purchased for himself, and Joseph, Nicodemus, the Virgin Mary, Saint John the Evangelist, and Mary Magdalene mourn over the dead Jesus (the Lamentation). (When in art the isolated figure of the Virgin Mary cradles her dead son in her lap, it is called a *Pietà*—Italian for "pity.") In portrayals of the Entombment, his followers lower Jesus into a sarcophagus in the tomb.

- **Descent into Limbo** During the three days he spends in the tomb, Jesus (after death, Christ) descends into Hell, or Limbo, and triumphantly frees the souls of the righteous, including Adam, Eve, Moses, David, Solomon, and John the Baptist. In Byzantine art, this episode is often labeled Anastasis (Greek, "resurrection"), although the term refers to events preceding Christ's emergence from the tomb and reappearance on earth.

- **Resurrection** and **Three Marys at the Tomb** On the third day (Easter Sunday), Christ rises from the dead and leaves the tomb while the guards outside are sleeping. The Virgin Mary, Mary Magdalene, and Mary, the mother of James, visit the tomb, find it empty, and learn from an angel that Christ has been resurrected.

- **Noli Me Tangere, Supper at Emmaus,** and **Doubting of Thomas** During the 40 days between Christ's Resurrection and his ascent to Heaven, he appears on several occasions to his followers. Christ warns Mary Magdalene, weeping at his tomb, with the words "Don't touch me" (*Noli me tangere* in Latin), but he tells her to inform the apostles of his return. At Emmaus he eats supper with two of his astonished disciples. Later, Thomas, who cannot believe that Christ has risen, is invited to touch the wound in his side that Longinus inflicted at the Crucifixion.

- **Ascension** On the 40th day, on the Mount of Olives, with his mother and apostles as witnesses, Christ gloriously ascends to Heaven in a cloud.

11-9 Restored cutaway view (*top*) and plan (*bottom*) of Old Saint Peter's, Rome, Italy, begun ca. 319 (John Burge). (1) nave, (2) aisle, (3) apse, (4) transept, (5) narthex, (6) atrium.

Erected by Constantine, the first imperial patron of Christianity, this huge church stood on the spot of Saint Peter's grave. The building's plan and elevation resemble those of Roman basilicas, not pagan temples.

OLD SAINT PETER'S The greatest of Constantine's churches in Rome was Old Saint Peter's (FIG. 11-9), probably begun as early as 319. The present-day church (FIG. 24-4), one of the masterpieces of Italian Renaissance and Baroque architecture, is a replacement for the Constantinian structure. Old Saint Peter's stood on the western side of the Tiber River on the spot where Constantine and Pope Sylvester believed Peter, the first apostle and founder of the Christian community in Rome, had been buried. Excavations in the Roman cemetery beneath the church have in fact revealed a second-century memorial erected in honor of the Christian martyr at his reputed grave. The great Constantinian church, capable of housing 3,000 to 4,000 worshipers at one time, was raised upon a terrace over the ancient cemetery on the irregular slope of the Vatican Hill. It enshrined one of the most hallowed sites in Christendom, second only to the

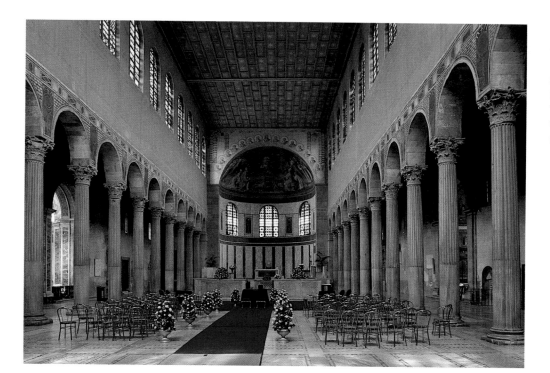

11-10 Interior of Santa Sabina, Rome, Italy, 422–432. ■◀

Early Christian basilican churches like Santa Sabina were timber roofed and illuminated by clerestory windows. The Corinthian columns of the nave focused attention on the apse, which framed the altar.

Holy Sepulchre in Jerusalem, the site of Christ's Resurrection. The project also fulfilled the figurative words Christ himself said to the first disciple: "Thou art Peter, and upon this rock I will build my church" (Matt. 16:18). Peter was Rome's first bishop and also the head of the long line of popes that extends to the present.

The plan and elevation of Old Saint Peter's resemble those of Roman basilicas and audience halls, such as the Basilica Ulpia (FIG. 10-43, no. 4) in the Forum of Trajan and Constantine's own Aula Palatina (FIGS. 10-79 and 10-80) at Trier, rather than the design of any Greco-Roman temple. The Christians, understandably, did not want their houses of worship to mimic the look of pagan shrines, but practical considerations also contributed to their shunning the form of pagan temples. Greco-Roman temples housed only the cult statue of the deity. All rituals took place outside at open-air altars. The classical temple, therefore, could have been adapted only with great difficulty as a building that accommodated large numbers of people within it. The Roman basilica, in contrast, was ideally suited as a place for congregation.

Like Roman basilicas, Old Saint Peter's had a wide central *nave* (FIG. 11-9, no. 1) with flanking *aisles* (FIG. 11-9, no. 2) and an *apse* (FIG. 11-9, no. 3) at the end. But unlike pagan basilicas, which sometimes had doorways on one long side, opening onto an aisle (FIG. 10-43, no. 4), all Early Christian basilicas had a pronounced *longitudinal* axis. Worshipers entered the basilica through a *narthex* (FIG. 11-9, no. 5), or vestibule. When they emerged in the 300-foot-long nave, they had an unobstructed view of the altar in the apse, framed by the *chancel arch* dividing the nave from the transept (FIG. 11-9, no. 4). The *transept*, or transverse aisle, an area perpendicular to the nave between the nave and apse, was a special feature of the Constantinian church. It housed the relics of Saint Peter that hordes of pilgrims came to see. (*Relics* are the body parts, clothing, or objects associated with a saint or Christ himself; see "Pilgrimages and the Cult of Relics," Chapter 17, page 432.) The transept became a standard design element in Western churches only much later, when it also took on, with the nave and apse, the symbolism of the Christian cross. Saint Peter's basilica also had an open colonnaded courtyard in front of the narthex, very much like the forum proper in the Forum of Trajan (FIG. 10-43, no. 5) but called an *atrium* (FIG. 11-9, no. 6), like the central room in a Roman private house (FIG. 10-16, no. 2).

Unlike pagan temples, Old Saint Peter's was not adorned with lavish exterior sculptures. Its brick walls were as austere as those of the Aula Palatina (FIG. 10-79). Inside, however, were frescoes and mosaics, marble columns (taken from pagan buildings, as was customary at the time), and costly ornaments. The *Liber pontificalis*, or *Book of the Pontiffs* (Popes), compiled by an anonymous sixth-century author, lists Constantine's gifts to Old Saint Peter's. They included altars, chandeliers, candlesticks, pitchers, goblets, and plates fashioned of gold and silver and sometimes embellished with jewels and pearls, as well as jeweled altar cloths for use in the Mass and gold foil to sheathe the vault of the apse.[1] A huge marble *baldacchino* (domical canopy over an altar), supported by four spiral porphyry columns, marked the spot of Saint Peter's tomb.

SANTA SABINA Some idea of the character of the timber-roofed interior of Old Saint Peter's can be gleaned from the interior (FIG. 11-10) of Santa Sabina in Rome. Santa Sabina, built a century later, is a basilica church of much more modest proportions, but it still retains its Early Christian character. The Corinthian columns of its *nave arcade* (a series of arches supported by columns separating the nave from the aisles) produce a steady rhythm that focuses all attention on the chancel arch and the apse, which frame the altar. In Santa Sabina, as in Old Saint Peter's, the nave is drenched with light from the *clerestory* windows piercing the thin upper wall beneath the timber roof. The same light would have illuminated the frescoes and mosaics that commonly adorned the nave and apse of Early Christian churches. Outside, Santa Sabina has plain brick walls. They closely resemble the exterior of Trier's Aula Palatina (FIG. 10-79).

11-10A West doors, Santa Sabina, Rome, ca. 432.

SANTA COSTANZA The rectangular basilican church design was long the favorite of the Western Christian world, but Early Christian architects also adopted another classical architectural type: the *central-plan* building. The type is so named because the building's parts are of equal or almost equal dimensions around the center. Roman central-plan buildings were usually round or polygonal domed structures. Byzantine architects developed this form to

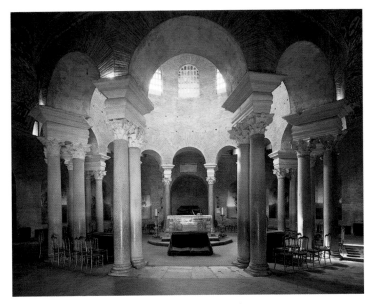

11-11 Interior of Santa Costanza, Rome, Italy, ca. 337–351. ◼◀

Possibly built as the mausoleum of Constantine's daughter, Santa Costanza later became a church. Its central plan, featuring a domed interior, would become the preferred form for Byzantine churches.

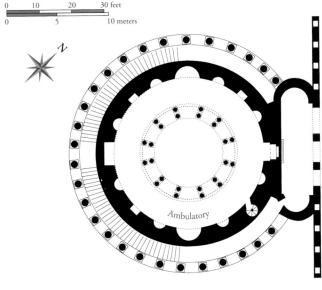

11-12 Plan of Santa Costanza, Rome, Italy, ca. 337–351.

Santa Costanza has antecedents in the domed temples (FIG. 10-51) and mausoleums (FIG. 10-74) of the Romans, but its plan, with 12 pairs of columns and an ambulatory, is unique.

Ambulatory

monumental proportions and amplified its theme in numerous ingenious variations (see Chapter 12). In the West, builders generally used the central plan for structures adjacent to the main basilicas, such as mausoleums, baptisteries, and private chapels, rather than for churches, as in the East.

A highly refined example of the central-plan design is Santa Costanza (FIGS. **11-11** and **11-12**), built on the northern outskirts of Rome in the mid-fourth century, possibly as the mausoleum for Constantina, the emperor Constantine's daughter. Recent excavations have called the traditional identification into question, but Constantina's monumental porphyry sarcophagus stood in the building, even if the structure was not originally her tomb. The mausoleum, later converted into a church, stood next to

the basilican church of Saint Agnes, who was buried in a nearby catacomb. Santa Costanza has antecedents traceable to the tholos tombs (FIGS. 4-20 and 4-21) of the Mycenaeans, but its immediate predecessors were the domed structures of the Romans, such as the Pantheon (FIGS. 10-49 to 10-51) and, especially, imperial mausoleums such as Diocletian's (FIG. 10-74) at Split. At Santa Costanza, the architect modified the interior design of the Roman buildings to accommodate an *ambulatory,* a ringlike barrel-vaulted corridor separated from the central domed cylinder by a dozen pairs of columns.

Like Early Christian basilicas, Santa Costanza has a severe brick exterior. Its interior was once richly adorned with mosaics, although most are lost. Old and New Testament themes appeared side by side, as in the catacombs and on Early Christian sarcophagi. The Santa

11-13 Detail of vault mosaic in the ambulatory of Santa Costanza, Rome, Italy, ca. 337–351.

The vault mosaics of Santa Costanza depict putti harvesting grapes and producing wine, motifs associated with Bacchus, but for a Christian such scenes brought to mind the Eucharist and Christ's blood.

Costanza mosaic program, however, also included subjects common in Roman funerary art, although they were susceptible to a Christian interpretation. In one section (FIG. 11-13) of the mosaic in the ambulatory vault, for example, are scenes of putti harvesting grapes and producing wine. (Similar scenes decorate Constantina's sarcophagus.) A portrait bust is at the center of a rich vine scroll. There is a second bust in another section of the mosaic vault, but both are heavily restored, and the identification of the pair as Constantina and her husband is uncertain. In the Roman world, wine was primarily associated with Bacchus, but for a Christian, the vineyards brought to mind the wine of the Eucharist and the blood of Christ.

SANTA MARIA MAGGIORE Mosaic decoration (see "Mosaics," page 303) played an important role in the interiors of Early Christian buildings of all types. In churches, mosaics not only provided a beautiful setting for the Christian liturgy, but also were vehicles for instructing the congregation about biblical stories and Christian dogma. Old Testament themes are the focus of the extensive fifth-century mosaic cycle in the nave of the basilican church of Santa Maria Maggiore in Rome, the first major church in the West dedicated to the Virgin Mary. Construction of the church began in 432, the year after Mary had been officially designated as the Mother of God (*Theotokos*, "bearer of god" in Greek) at the Council of Ephesus. The council had been convened to debate whether Mary had given birth to the man Jesus or to God as man. It ruled that the divine and human coexisted in Christ and that Mary was indeed the Mother of God.

One of the mosaic panels (FIG. 11-14) in Santa Maria Maggiore dramatically represents the parting of Abraham and his nephew Lot, as set forth in Genesis, the Bible's opening book. Agreeing to disagree, Lot leads his family and followers to the right, toward the city of Sodom, while Abraham heads for Canaan, moving toward a basilica-like building (perhaps symbolizing the Christian Church) on the left. Lot's is the evil choice, and the instruments of the evil (his two daughters) are in front of him. The figure of the yet-unborn Isaac, the instrument of good (and, as noted earlier, a prefiguration of Christ), stands before his father, Abraham.

The cleavage of the two groups is emphatic, and the mosaicist represented each group using a shorthand device that could be called a "head cluster," which had precedents in antiquity and had a long history in Christian art. The figures engage in a sharp dialogue of glance and gesture. The wide eyes turn in their sockets, and the enlarged hands make broad gestures. This kind of simplified motion, which is characteristic of Late Antique narrative art of both Roman and Christian subject matter, has great power to communicate without ambiguity. But the Abraham and Lot mosaic also reflects the heritage of classical art. The town in the background would not be out of place in a Pompeian mural (FIG. 10-19, *left*), and the figures themselves are modeled in light and dark, cast shadows, and still loom with massive solidity. Another century had to pass before Western Christian mosaicists portrayed figures entirely as flat images, rather than as three-dimensional bodies, finally rejecting the norms of classical art in favor of a style better suited for a focus on the spiritual instead of the natural world. Early Christian art, like Late Antique Roman art in general, vacillates between these two stylistic poles.

Ravenna

In the decades after the founding in 324 of Constantinople, the New Rome in the East, and the death of Constantine in 337, the pace of Christianization of the Roman Empire quickened. In 380 the emperor Theodosius I issued an edict finally establishing Christianity as the state religion. In 391 he enacted a ban against pagan worship, and in 394 he abolished the Olympic Games, the enduring symbol of the classical world and its values. Theodosius died in 395, and imperial power passed to his two sons, Arcadius, who became Emperor of the East, and Honorius, Emperor of the West. In 404, when the Visigoths, under their king, Alaric, threatened to overrun Italy from the northwest, Honorius moved his capital from Milan to Ravenna, an ancient Roman city (perhaps founded by the Etruscans) near Italy's Adriatic coast, some 80 miles south of Venice. In 410, Rome fell to Alaric, and in 476, Ravenna fell to Odoacer, the first Germanic king of Italy. Odoacer was overthrown in turn by Theodoric, king of the Ostrogoths, who established his capital at Ravenna in 493. Ravenna fell to the Byzantine emperor Justinian in 539, and the subsequent history of the city belongs with that of Byzantium (see Chapter 12).

11-14 The parting of Abraham and Lot, nave of Santa Maria Maggiore, Rome, Italy, 432–440. Mosaic, 3′ 4″ high.

In this mosaic panel representing the Old Testament parting of Abraham and Lot, the artist included the figure of the yet-unborn Isaac because of his importance as a prefiguration of Christ.

1 ft.

This cruciform chapel with a domed crossing is an early example of the combination of central and longitudinal plans. The unadorned brick shell encloses a rich ensemble of mosaics (FIG. 11-1).

MAUSOLEUM OF GALLA PLACIDIA The so-called Mausoleum of Galla Placidia, Honorius's half-sister, is a rather small *cruciform* (cross-shaped) structure (FIG. 11-15) with barrel-vaulted arms and a tower at the *crossing*. Built shortly after 425, almost a quarter century before Galla Placidia's death in 450, it was probably intended as a chapel to the martyred Saint Lawrence. The building was once thought, however, to be Galla Placidia's tomb, hence its name today. Originally, the chapel adjoined the narthex of the now greatly altered palace-church of Santa Croce (Holy Cross), which was also cruciform in plan. The chapel's cross arms are of unequal length, so that the building has a longitudinal orientation, unlike the centrally planned Santa Costanza (FIGS. 11-11 and 11-12), but since all four arms are very short, the emphasis is on the tall *crossing tower* with its vault resembling a dome. This small, unassuming building thus represents one of the earliest successful fusions of the two basic Late Antique plans—the longitudinal, used for basilican churches, and the central, used primarily for baptisteries and mausoleums. It introduced, on a small scale, a building type that was to have a long history in church architecture: the longitudinally planned building with a vaulted or domed crossing.

The chapel's unadorned brick shell encloses one of the richest mosaic ensembles (FIG. 11-1) in Early Christian art. Mosaics (see "Mosaics," page 303) cover every square inch of the interior surfaces above the marble-faced walls. Garlands and decorative medallions resembling snowflakes on a dark blue ground adorn the barrel vaults of the nave and cross arms. The tower has a large golden cross set against a star-studded sky. Representations of saints and apostles cover the other surfaces. At the end of the nave is a mosaic representing Saint Lawrence next to the gridiron on which he was tortured. The martyred saint carries a cross, suggesting that faith in Christ led to his salvation.

Christ as Good Shepherd is the subject of the lunette (FIG. 11-16) above the entrance. No earlier version of the Good Shepherd is as regal as this one. Instead of carrying a lamb on his shoulders, Jesus sits among his flock, haloed and robed in gold and purple. To his left and right, the sheep are distributed evenly in groups of three. But their arrangement is rather loose and informal, and they

11-16A Orthodox Baptistery, Ravenna, ca. 458.

11-16 Christ as the Good Shepherd, mosaic from the entrance wall of the Mausoleum of Galla Placidia, Ravenna, Italy, ca. 425. ◼◀

Jesus sits among his flock, haloed and robed in gold and purple. The landscape and the figures, with their cast shadows, are the work of a mosaicist still deeply rooted in the naturalistic classical tradition.

Mosaics

As an art form, *mosaic* had a rather simple and utilitarian beginning, seemingly invented primarily to provide an inexpensive and durable flooring. Originally, small beach pebbles were set, unaltered from their natural form and color, into a thick coat of cement. Artisans soon discovered, however, that the stones could be arranged in decorative patterns. At first, these *pebble mosaics* were uncomplicated and were confined to geometric shapes. Generally, the artists used only black and white stones. Examples of this type, dating to the eighth century BCE, have been found at Gordion in Asia Minor. Eventually, artists arranged the stones to form more complex pictorial designs, and by the fourth century BCE, the technique had developed to a high level of sophistication. Mosaicists depicted elaborate figural scenes using a broad range of colors—yellow, brown, and red in addition to black, white, and gray—and shaded the figures, clothing, and setting to suggest volume. Thin strips of lead provided linear definition (FIG. 5-68).

By the middle of the third century BCE, artists had invented a new kind of mosaic that permitted the best mosaicists to create designs more closely approximating true paintings. The new technique employed *tesserae* (Latin for "cubes" or "dice"). These tiny cut stones gave the artist much greater flexibility because their size and shape could be adjusted at will, eliminating the need for lead strips to indicate contours and interior details. Much more gradual gradations of color also became possible (FIG. 5-70), and mosaicists finally could aspire to rival the achievements of painters.

In Early Christian mosaics (FIGS. 11-1, 11-13, 11-14, and 11-16 to 11-18), the tesserae were usually made of glass, which reflects light and makes the surfaces sparkle. Ancient mosaicists occasionally used glass tesserae, but the Romans preferred opaque marble pieces. Mosaics quickly became the standard means of decorating walls and vaults in Early Christian buildings, although mural paintings were also popular. The mosaics caught the light flooding through the windows in vibrant reflection, producing sharp contrasts and concentrations of color that could focus attention on a composition's central, most relevant features. Mosaics worked in the Early Christian manner were not meant to incorporate the subtle tonal changes a naturalistic painter's approach would require. Color was "placed," not blended. Bright, hard, glittering texture, set within a rigorously simplified pattern, became the rule. For mosaics situated high in an apse or ambulatory vault or over the nave colonnade, far above the observer's head, as in the church of Sant'Apollinare Nuovo (FIG. 11-17) in Ravenna, the painstaking use of tiny tesserae seen in Roman floor and wall mosaics (FIGS. 5-70 and 10-24) would be meaningless. Early Christian mosaics, designed to be seen from a distance, employed larger tesserae. The pieces were also set unevenly so that their surfaces could catch and reflect the light. Artists favored simple designs for optimal legibility. For several centuries, mosaic, in the service of Christian theology, was the medium of some of the supreme masterpieces of medieval art.

11-17 Interior of Sant'Apollinare Nuovo, Ravenna, Italy, dedicated 504. ◼◀

Theodoric, king of the Ostrogoths, established his capital at Ravenna in 493. His palace-church features an extensive series of mosaics depicting Old Testament prophets and scenes from the life of Christ.

occupy a carefully described landscape that extends from foreground to background beneath a blue sky. As at Santa Maria Maggiore (FIG. 11-14), all the forms have three-dimensional bulk and are still deeply rooted in the classical tradition.

SANT'APOLLINARE NUOVO Around 504, soon after Theodoric settled in Ravenna, he ordered the construction of his own palace-church, a three-aisled basilica (FIG. 11-17) dedicated to

the Savior. In the ninth century, the relics of Saint Apollinaris were transferred to this church. The building has been known since that time as Sant'Apollinare Nuovo.

The rich mosaic decorations of the nave walls are divided into three zones. Only the upper two date from Theodoric's time. Old Testament patriarchs and prophets stand between the clerestory windows. Above them, scenes from Christ's life alternate with decorative panels.

11-18 Miracle of the loaves and fishes, mosaic from the top register of the nave wall (above the clerestory windows in FIG. 11-17) of Sant'Apollinare Nuovo, Ravenna, Italy, ca. 504.

In contrast to FIG. 11-16, Jesus here faces directly toward the viewer. Blue sky has given way to the otherworldly splendor of heavenly gold, the standard background color for medieval mosaics.

11-18A Hagios Georgios, Thessaloniki, ca. 390–450.

The mosaic depicting the miracle of the loaves and fishes (FIG. 11-18) stands in sharp contrast to the 80-year-earlier mosaics of the Mausoleum of Galla Placidia. Jesus, beardless, in the imperial dress of gold and purple, and now distinguished by the cross-inscribed *nimbus* (halo) that signifies his divinity, faces the viewer directly. With extended arms he instructs his disciples to distribute to the great crowd the miraculously increased supply of bread and fish he has produced. This Ravenna artist made no attempt to supply details of the event. The emphasis is instead on the holy character of it, the spiritual fact that Jesus is performing a miracle by the power of his divinity. The fact of the miracle removes it from the world of time. The presence of almighty power, not anecdotal narrative, is the important aspect of this scene. The mosaicist told the story with the least number of figures necessary to make its meaning explicit, aligning the figures laterally, moving them close to the foreground, and placing them in a shallow picture box. The composition, so different from those in the lunettes of the Mausoleum of Galla Placidia, is similar to that of the Samuel and David mural (FIG. 11-3) in the Dura-Europos synagogue two and a half centuries earlier. This similarity illustrates once again that Early Christian artists inherited both classical naturalism and Late Antique abstraction from Roman art. But the Sant'Apollinare Nuovo mosaic differs from the Dura murals as well as the Galla Placidia mosaics in having a golden background. The landscape setting, which the artist who decorated the Mausoleum of Galla Placidia so explicitly depicted (FIG. 11-16), is here merely a few rocks and bushes that enclose the figure group like parentheses. The blue sky of the physical world has given way to the otherworldly splendor of heavenly gold. The ethereal golden background as well as the weightless figures with their flat, curtainlike garments would soon become the norm in Byzantine art, although even in Byzantium echoes of classical naturalism persisted (see Chapter 12).

LUXURY ARTS

Throughout history, artists have produced so-called "minor arts"—jewelry, metalwork, cameos, ivories, among other "crafts"—alongside the "major arts" of sculpture and painting. Although the terminology seems to suggest a difference in importance or quality, "minor" refers only to size. Indeed, the artists who fashioned jewelry, carved ivories and cameos, and produced gold and silver vessels by casting or hammering (*repoussé*) employed the costliest materials known. Some of them, for example, Dioscurides, official gem cutter of the emperor Augustus, are among the few Roman artists whose names were recorded. In Late Antiquity and the Middle Ages, the minor arts—more appropriately called "luxury arts"—had high status, and they figure prominently in the history of art through the ages.

Illuminated Manuscripts

Although few examples survive, illustrated books were popular in the ancient world. The long tradition of placing pictures in manuscripts began in pharaonic Egypt (FIG. 3-36) and continued in Greek and Roman times.

VATICAN VERGIL The oldest preserved painted Greek or Latin manuscript is the *Vatican Vergil,* which dates from the early fifth century. It originally contained more than 200 pictures illustrating all of Vergil's works. Today only 50 painted pages of the *Aeneid* and *Georgics* survive. The manuscript is important not only because of its age. The *Vatican Vergil* is a prime example of the survival of traditional Roman iconography and of the classical style long after Theodosius banned all pagan cults.

The page illustrated here (FIG. 11-19) includes a section of text from the *Georgics* at the top and a framed illustration below. The poem recounts Vergil's visit to a modest farm near Tarentum (Taranto, in southern Italy) belonging to an old man from Corycus in Asia Minor. In the illustration, the old farmer sits at the left. His rustic farmhouse is in the background, rendered in a three-quarter view. The farmer speaks about the pleasures of the simple life in the country—a recurrent theme in Latin poetry—and on his methods of gardening. His audience is two laborers and, at the far right, Vergil himself in the guise of a farmhand. The style is reminiscent of Pompeian landscapes, with quick touches that suggest space and atmosphere. In fact, the heavy, dark frame has close parallels in the late Pompeian styles of mural painting (FIG. 10-22).

VIENNA GENESIS The oldest well-preserved painted manuscript containing biblical scenes is the early sixth-century *Vienna Genesis,* so called because of its present location. The book is sumptuous. The pages are fine calfskin dyed with rich purple, the same dye used to give imperial cloth its distinctive color. The scribe used silver ink for the Greek text (see "Medieval Manuscript Illumination," page 305).

Folio 7 (FIG. 11-20) of the *Vienna Genesis* illustrates the story of Rebecca and Eliezer (Gen. 24:15–61). When Isaac, Abraham's son, was 40 years old, his parents sent their servant Eliezer to find a wife for him. Eliezer chose Rebecca, because when he stopped at a well, she was the first woman to draw water for him and his camels. The man-

11-20A Story Jacob, *Vienna Genesis,* early sixth century.

Medieval Manuscript Illumination

Rare as medieval books are, they are far more numerous than their ancient predecessors. An important invention during the Early Empire was the *codex,* which greatly aided the dissemination of manuscripts as well as their preservation. A codex is much like a modern book, composed of separate leaves (*folios*) enclosed within a cover and bound together at one side. The new format superseded the long manuscript scroll (*rotulus*) of the Egyptians, Greeks, Etruscans, and Romans. (The Etruscan magistrate Lars Pulena, FIG. 9-15; the philosophers on Roman and Early Christian sarcophagi, FIGS. 10-71 and 11-6; and Christ himself in his role as teacher, FIGS. 11-7 and 11-8, all hold rotuli in their hands.) Much more durable *vellum* (calfskin) and *parchment* (lambskin), which provided better surfaces for painting, also replaced the comparatively brittle *papyrus* used for ancient scrolls. As a result, luxuriousness of ornament became increasingly typical of sacred books in the Middle Ages, and at times the material beauty of the pages with

their illustrations overwhelms the spiritual beauty of the text. Art historians refer to the luxurious painted books produced before the invention of the printing press as *illuminated manuscripts,* from the Latin *illuminare,* meaning "to adorn, ornament, or brighten." The oldest preserved examples (FIGS. 11-19 to 11-21) date to the fifth and sixth centuries.

Illuminated books were costly to produce and involved many steps. Numerous artisans performed very specialized tasks, beginning with the curing and cutting (and sometimes the dyeing) of the animal skin, followed by the sketching of lines to guide the scribe and to set aside spaces for illumination, the lettering of the text, the addition of paintings, and finally the binding of the pages and attachment of covers, buckles, and clasps. The covers could be even more sumptuous than the book itself. Many covers survive that are fashioned of gold and decorated with jewels, ivory carvings, and repoussé reliefs (FIG. 16-16).

11-19 The old farmer of Corycus, folio 7 verso of the *Vatican Vergil,* ca. 400–420. Tempera on parchment, $1'\frac{1}{2}'' \times 1'$. Biblioteca Apostolica Vaticana, Rome.

The earliest surviving painted Latin manuscript is a collection of the poet Vergil's works. This page includes part of the text of the *Georgics* and a pastoral scene reminiscent of Roman landscape murals.

11-20 Rebecca and Eliezer at the well, folio 7 recto of the *Vienna Genesis,* early sixth century. Tempera, gold, and silver on purple vellum, $1'\frac{1}{4}'' \times 9\frac{1}{4}''$. Österreichische Nationalbibliothek, Vienna.

This sumptuously painted book is the oldest well-preserved manuscript containing biblical scenes. Two episodes of the Rebecca story appear in a single setting filled with classical motifs.

uscript painter presented two episodes of the story within a single frame. In the first episode, at the left, Rebecca leaves the city of Nahor to fetch water from the well. In the second episode, she offers water to Eliezer and his camels, while one of them already laps water from the well. The artist painted Nahor as a walled city seen from above, like

the cityscapes in the Santa Maria Maggiore mosaics (FIG. 11-14) and innumerable earlier Roman representations of cities in painting and relief sculpture. Rebecca walks to the well along the colonnaded avenue of a Roman city. A seminude female personification of a spring is the source of the well water. These are further reminders of the persistence of classical motifs and stylistic modes in Early Christian art. Contemporaneous with, but radically different from, the mosaic panels (FIG. 11-17) of Sant'Apollinare Nuovo, the *Vienna Genesis* incorporates many anecdotal details, such as the drinking camel and Rebecca bracing herself with her raised left foot on the rim of the well as she tips up her jug for Eliezer. Nonetheless, the figures are seen against a blank landscape except for the miniature city and the road to the well. As at Ravenna, everything necessary for bare narrative is present and nothing else.

ROSSANO GOSPELS Closely related to the *Vienna Genesis* is another early-sixth-century Greek manuscript, the *Rossano Gospels,* the earliest preserved illuminated book that contains illustrations of the New Testament. By this time a canon of New Testament iconography had been fairly well established. As in the *Vienna Genesis,* the text of the *Rossano Gospels* is in silver on purple vellum. The Rossano artist, however, attempted with considerable success to harmonize the colors with the purple background. The subject of folio 8 (FIG. 11-21) is the appearance of Jesus before Pilate, who asks the Jews to choose between Jesus and Barabbas (Matt. 27: 2–26). The vividly gesturing figures are on two levels separated by a simple ground line. In the upper level, Pilate presides over the tribunal. He sits on an elevated dais, following a long-established pattern in Roman art (FIG. 10-76). The people form an arch around

Pilate (the artist may have based the composition on a painting in an apse) and demand the death of Jesus, while a court scribe records the proceedings. Jesus (here a bearded adult, as soon became the norm for medieval and later depictions of Christ) and the bound Barabbas appear in the lower level. The painter explicitly labeled Barabbas to avoid any possible confusion so that the picture would be as readable as the text. Pilate on his magistrate's dais, flanked by painted imperial portraits, and the haloed Christ needed no further identification.

Ivory Carving

Among the other important luxury arts of Late Antiquity was ivory carving, which has an even longer history in the ancient world than manuscript illustration (see "Ivory Carving," page 307).

CRUCIFIXION OF CHRIST A century before the pages of the *Rossano Gospels* were illuminated with scenes from the Passion cycle, a Roman or northern Italian sculptor produced a series of ivory plaques for a small box that dramatically recount the suffering and triumph of Christ. The narrative on the box begins with Pilate washing his hands, Jesus carrying the cross on the road to Calvary, and Peter denying Jesus, all compressed into a single panel.

The next plaque in the sequence (FIG. 11-22) shows, at the left, Judas hanging from a tree with his open bag of silver dumped on the

11-21 Christ before Pilate, folio 8 verso of the *Rossano Gospels,* early sixth century. Tempera on purple vellum, 11″ × 10¼″. Museo Diocesano d'Arte Sacra, Rossano.

The sources for medieval manuscript illustrations were diverse. The way the people form an arch around Pilate on this page suggests that the composition derives from a painting in a church apse.

Ivory Carving

Ivory has been prized since the earliest times, when Ice Age artists fashioned the tusks of European mammoths into pendants, beads, and other items for body adornment, and, occasionally, statuettes (FIG. 1-4). The primary ivory sources in the historical period have been the elephants of India and especially Africa, where the species is larger than the Asian counterpart and the tusks longer, heavier, and of finer grain. African elephant tusks 5 to 6 feet in length and weighing 10 pounds are common, but tusks of male elephants can be 10 feet long or more and weigh more than 100 pounds. Carved ivories are familiar, if precious, finds at Mesopotamian and Egyptian sites, and ivory objects were manufactured and coveted in the prehistoric Aegean and throughout the classical world. Most frequently employed then for household objects, small votive offerings, and gifts to the deceased, ivory also could be used for grandiose statues such as Phidias's *Athena Parthenos* (FIG. 5-46).

The Greeks and Romans admired ivory both for its beauty and because of its exotic origin. Elephant tusks were costly imports, and Roman generals proudly displayed them in triumphal processions when they paraded the spoils of war before the people. (In FIG. 12-14

a barbarian brings tribute to a Byzantine emperor in the form of an ivory tusk.)

Adding to the expense of the material itself was the fact that only highly skilled artisans were capable of working in ivory. The tusks were very hard and of irregular shape, and the ivory workers needed a full toolbox of saws, chisels, knives, files, and gravers close at hand to cut the tusks into blocks for statuettes or thin plaques decorated with relief figures and ornament.

In Late Antiquity and the early medieval period, ivory was employed most frequently for book covers, chests and boxes (FIG. 11-22), and diptychs (FIGS. 11-23 and 12-15). A *diptych* is a pair of hinged tablets, usually of wood, with a wax layer on the inner sides for writing letters and other documents. (Both the court scribe recording Jesus' trial in the *Rossano Gospels*, FIG. 11-21, and the woman in a painted portrait from Pompeii, FIG. 10-25, hold wooden diptychs.) Diptychs fashioned out of ivory generally were created for ceremonial and official purposes—for example, to announce the election of a consul or a marriage between two wealthy families or to commemorate the death of an elevated member of society.

1 in.

11-22 Suicide of Judas and Crucifixion of Christ, plaque from a box, ca. 420. Ivory, 3″ × 3 7/8″. British Museum, London. ◼◣

This plaque from a luxurious ivory box is the first known representation of the Crucifixion. Christ is a beardless youth who experiences no pain. At the left, Judas, his betrayer, hangs himself.

Woman sacrificing at an altar, right leaf of the diptych of the Nicomachi and the Symmachi, ca. 400. Ivory, $11\frac{3}{4}'' \times 5\frac{1}{2}''$. Victoria & Albert Museum, London.

Even after Theodosius banned all pagan cults in 391, some Roman families still practiced the ancient rites. The sculptor who carved this ivory plaque also carried on the classical artistic style.

1 in.

ground beneath his feet. The Crucifixion is at the right. The Virgin Mary and Joseph of Arimathea are to the left of the cross. On the other side Longinus thrusts his spear into the side of the "King of the Jews" (*REX IVD* is inscribed above Jesus' head). The two remaining panels show two Marys and two soldiers at the open doors of a tomb with an empty coffin within and the doubting Thomas touching the wound of the risen Christ.

The series is one of the oldest cycles of Passion scenes preserved today. The artist who fashioned the ivory box helped establish the iconographical types for medieval narratives of Christ's life. On these plaques, Jesus always appears as a beardless youth. In the Crucifixion (FIG. 11-22), the earliest known rendition of the subject in the history of art, he exhibits a superhuman imperviousness to pain. The Savior is a muscular, nearly nude, heroic figure who appears virtually weightless. He does not *hang* from the cross; he is *displayed* on it, a divine being with open eyes who has conquered death. The striking contrast between the powerful frontal, serenely calm Jesus on the cross and the limp hanging body of his betrayer with his snapped neck is highly effective, both visually and symbolically.

DIPTYCH OF THE SYMMACHI Although after Constantine all the most important architectural projects in Italy were Christian in character, not everyone converted to the new religion, even after Theodosius closed all temples and banned all pagan cults in 391.

An ivory plaque (FIG. 11-23), probably produced in Rome around 400, strikingly exhibits the endurance of pagan themes and patrons and of the classical style. The ivory, one of a pair of leaves of a diptych, may commemorate either the marriage of members of two powerful Roman families of the senatorial class, the Nicomachi and the Symmachi, or the passing within a decade of two prominent male members of the two families. Whether or not the diptych relates to any specific event(s), the Nicomachi and the Symmachi here ostentatiously reaffirmed their faith in the old pagan gods. Certainly, the families favored the aesthetic ideals of the classical past, as exemplified by such works as the stately processional friezes of the Greek Parthenon (FIG. 5-50) and the Roman Ara Pacis (FIG. 10-31).

The leaf inscribed "of the Symmachi" (FIG. 11-23) represents a woman sacrificing at an altar in front of a tree. She wears ivy in her hair and seems to be celebrating the rites of Bacchus, although scholars dispute the identity of the divinity honored. The other diptych panel, inscribed "of the Nicomachi," also shows a woman at an open-air altar. On both panels, the precise yet fluent and graceful lines, the relaxed poses, and the mood of spiritual serenity reveal an artist who practiced within a still-vital classical tradition that idealized human beauty as its central focus. The great senatorial magnates of Rome, who resisted the empire-wide imposition of the Christian faith at the end of the fourth century, probably deliberately sustained the classical tradition.

Despite the widespread adoption during the third and fourth centuries of the new non-naturalistic Late Antique aesthetic featur-ing wafer-thin frontal figures, the classical tradition in art lived on and was never fully extinguished in the Middle Ages. Classical art survived in intermittent revivals, renovations, and restorations side by side and in contrast with the opposing nonclassical medieval styles until it rose to dominance once again in the Renaissance.

LATE ANTIQUITY

THIRD CENTURY CE

▌ Christ was crucified ca. 29, but very little Christian art or architecture survives from the first centuries of Christianity. "Early Christian art" means the earliest art of Christian content, not the art of Christians at the time of Jesus.

▌ The Second Commandment prohibition against graven images once led scholars to think that the Jews of the Roman Empire had no figural art, but the synagogue at Dura-Europos contains biblical mural paintings.

▌ Excavators have also uncovered the remains of a Christian community house of the mid-third century at Dura-Europos.

▌ At about the same time, sarcophagi with a mixture of Old and New Testament scenes began to appear.

Synagogue, Dura-Europos,
ca. 245–256

Sarcophagus with Old and
New Testament scenes, ca. 270

CHRISTIAN ART UNDER CONSTANTINE, 306–337

▌ Constantine's Edict of Milan of 313 granted Christianity legal status equal or superior to paganism. The emperor was the first great patron of Christian art and built the first churches in Rome, including Old Saint Peter's.

▌ In a Christian ceremony, Constantine dedicated Constantinople as the new capital of the Roman Empire in 330. He was baptized on his deathbed in 337.

▌ Early Christian artists produced mural and ceiling paintings in the catacombs and sarcophagi depicting Old and New Testament stories in great numbers.

Catacomb of Saints Peter and Marcellinus,
early fourth century

CHRISTIAN ART, 337–526

▌ The emperor Theodosius I (r. 379–395) proclaimed Christianity the official religion of the Roman Empire in 380 and banned pagan worship in 391.

▌ Honorius (r. 395–423) moved the capital of his Western Roman Empire to Ravenna in 404. Rome fell to the Visigothic king Alaric in 410.

▌ Mosaics became a major vehicle for the depiction of Christian themes in churches. Extensive mosaic cycles are preserved in Santa Maria Maggiore in Rome and in Sant'Apollinare Nuovo in Ravenna.

▌ The first manuscripts with illustrations of the Old and New Testaments, for example, the *Vienna Genesis,* date to the early sixth century. Illuminated manuscripts would become one of the major art forms of the Middle Ages.

Sant' Apollinare Nuovo,
Ravenna, 504

Vienna Genesis,
early sixth century

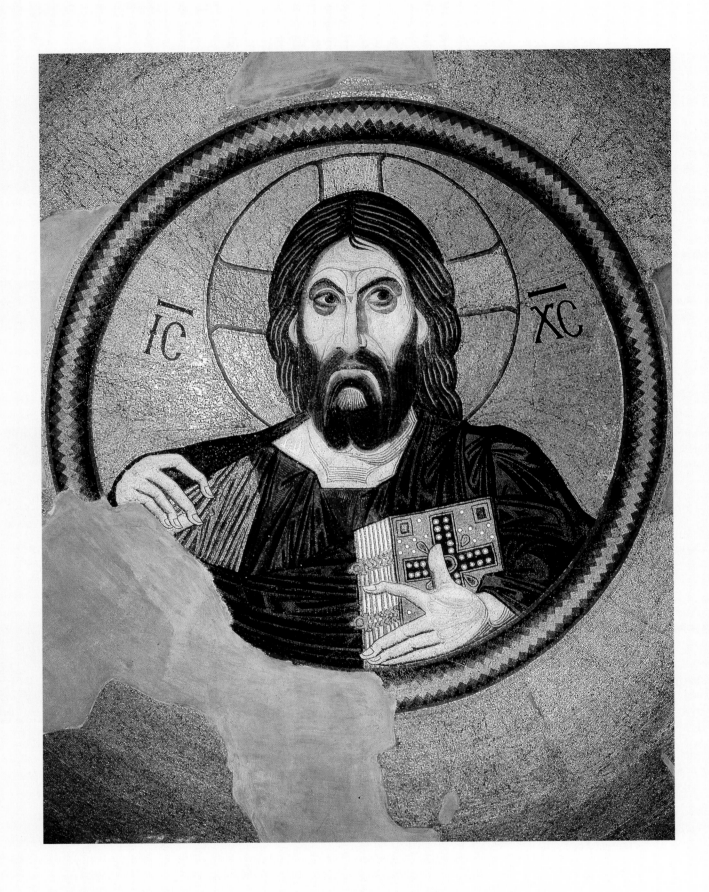

12-1 Christ as Pantokrator, dome mosaic in the Church of the Dormition, Daphni, Greece, ca. 1090–1100.

This dome mosaic of Christ as Last Judge of humankind is like a gigantic Byzantine icon hovering dramatically in space, connecting the awestruck worshiper below with Heaven through Christ.

BYZANTIUM

When Constantine I founded a "New Rome" in the East in 324 on the site of the ancient Greek city of Byzantium and called it Constantinople in honor of himself, he legitimately could claim to be ruler of a united Roman Empire. But when Theodosius I (r. 379–395) died, he bequeathed the Empire to his two sons, Arcadius, the elder, who became Emperor of the East, and Honorius, who became Emperor of the West. The Emperor of the East ruled from Constantinople. After the sack of Rome in 410, Honorius moved the western capital to Milan and later to Ravenna. Though not formally codified, Theodosius's division of the Empire (which paralleled Diocletian's century-earlier division of administrative responsibility) became permanent. Centralized government soon disintegrated in the western half and gave way to warring kingdoms (see Chapter 16). The eastern half of the Roman Empire, only loosely connected by religion to the West and with only minor territorial holdings there, had a long and complex history of its own. Centered at New Rome, the Eastern Christian Empire remained a cultural and political entity for a millennium, until the last of a long line of Eastern Roman emperors, ironically named Constantine XI, died at Constantinople in 1453, defending it in vain against the Ottoman Turks.

Historians refer to that Eastern Christian Roman Empire as Byzantium (MAP **12-1**), employing Constantinople's original name, and use the term *Byzantine* to identify whatever pertains to Byzantium—its territory, its history, and its culture. The Byzantine emperors, however, did not use these terms to define themselves. They called their empire Rome and themselves Romans. Though they spoke Greek and not Latin, the Eastern Roman emperors never relinquished their claim as the legitimate successors to the ancient Roman emperors. During the long course of its history, Byzantium was the Christian buffer against the expansion of Islam into central and northern Europe, and its cultural influence was felt repeatedly in Europe throughout the Middle Ages. Byzantium Christianized the Slavic peoples of the Balkans and of Russia, giving them its Orthodox religion and alphabet, its literary culture, and its art and architecture. Byzantium's collapse in 1453 brought the Ottoman Empire into Europe as far as the Danube River, but Constantinople's fall made an impact even farther to the west. The westward flight of Byzantine scholars from the Rome of the East introduced the study of classical Greek to Italy and helped inspire there the new consciousness of antiquity that historians call the Renaissance.

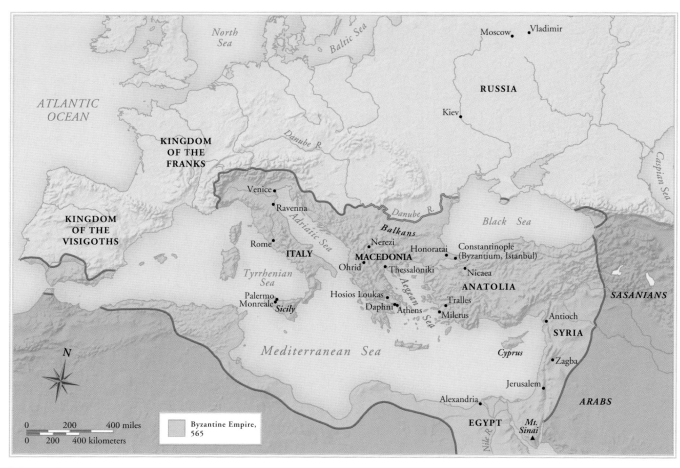

MAP 12-1 The Byzantine Empire at the death of Justinian in 565.

Constantine recognized Christianity at the beginning of the fourth century, Theodosius established it as the Roman Empire's official religion at the end of the fourth century, and Justinian, in the sixth century, proclaimed it New Rome's only lawful religion. By that time it was not simply the Christian religion but the Orthodox Christian doctrine that the Byzantine emperor asserted as the only permissible creed for his subjects. In Orthodox Christianity, the central article of faith is the equality of the three aspects of the Trinity of Father, Son, and Holy Spirit (as stated in Roman Catholic, Protestant, and Eastern Orthodox creeds today). All other versions of Christianity were heresies, especially the Arian, which asserted that the Father and Son were distinct entities and that the Father created the Son and therefore Christ was not equal to God. Also classified as a heresy was the Monophysite view that Christ had only one nature, which was divine, contrary to both the Orthodox and Arian belief that Christ had a dual divine-human nature. Justinian considered it his first duty not only to stamp out the few surviving pagan cults but also to crush all those who professed any Christian doctrine other than the Orthodox.

Art historians divide the history of Byzantine art into the three periods of its greatest glory, sometimes referred to as "golden ages." The first, Early Byzantine, extends from the accession of Justinian in 527 to the onset of *iconoclasm* (the destruction of images used in religious worship) under Leo III in 726. The Middle Byzantine period begins with the renunciation of iconoclasm in 843 and ends with the western Crusaders' occupation of Constantinople in 1204. Late Byzantine corresponds to the two centuries after the Byzantines recaptured Constantinople in 1261 until its final loss in 1453 to the Ottoman Turks and the conversion of many churches to mosques (see Chapter 13).

EARLY BYZANTINE ART

The emperor Justinian (r. 527–565) briefly restored much of the Roman Empire's power and extent (MAP 12-1). His generals, Belisarius and Narses, drove the Ostrogoths out of Italy, expelled the Vandals from the African provinces, routed the Bulgars on the northern frontier, and held the Sasanians at bay on the eastern borders. At home, the emperor quelled a dangerous rebellion in 532 of political and religious factions in the city (the Nika revolt), and Orthodoxy triumphed over the Monophysite heresy. Justinian also supervised the codification of Roman law in a great work known as the *Corpus juris civilis* (*Code of Civil Law*), which became the foundation of the law systems of many modern European nations. Justinian could claim, with considerable justification, to have revived the glory of "Old Rome" in New Rome. Under Justinian, Byzantine art emerged as a recognizably novel and distinctive style, leaving behind the uncertainties and hesitations of Early Christian artistic experiment. Though still reflecting its sources in Late Antique art, it definitively expressed, with a new independence and power of invention, the unique character of the Eastern Christian culture centered at Constantinople.

Architecture and Mosaics

In Constantinople alone, Justinian built or restored more than 30 churches of the Orthodox faith, and his activities as builder extended throughout the Byzantine Empire. The historian of his reign, Procopius, declared that the emperor's ambitious building program was an obsession that cost his subjects dearly in taxation. But his grand monuments defined the Byzantine style in architecture forever after.

12-2 ANTHEMIUS OF TRALLES and ISIDORUS OF MILETUS, aerial view of Hagia Sophia (looking north), Constantinople (Istanbul), Turkey, 532–537. ◼◀

The reign of Justinian marks the beginning of the first golden age of Byzantine art. Hagia Sophia was the most magnificent of the more than 30 churches that Justinian built or restored in Constantinople alone.

HAGIA SOPHIA The most important monument of Early Byzantine art is Hagia Sophia (FIG. 12-2), the Church of Holy Wisdom, in Constantinople. ANTHEMIUS OF TRALLES and ISIDORUS OF MILETUS, a mathematician and a physicist—neither man an architect in the modern sense of the word—designed and built the church for Justinian between 532 and 537. They began work immediately after fire destroyed an earlier church on the site during the Nika riot in January 532. Justinian intended the new church to rival all other churches ever built and even to surpass in scale and magnificence the Temple of Solomon in Jerusalem. The result was Byzantium's grandest building and one of the supreme accomplishments of world architecture.

Hagia Sophia's dimensions are formidable for any structure not built of steel. In plan (FIG. 12-3, *top*), it is about 270 feet long and 240 feet wide. The dome is 108 feet in diameter, and its crown rises some 180 feet above the pavement (FIG. 12-3, *bottom*). (The first dome collapsed in 558. Its replacement required repair in the 9th and 14th centuries. The present dome is greater in height and more

stable than the original.) In scale, Hagia Sophia rivals the architectural wonders of Rome: the Pantheon, the Baths of Caracalla, and the Basilica of Constantine (see Chapter 10). In exterior view (FIG. 12-2), the great dome dominates the structure, but the building's present external aspects are much changed from their original appearance. Huge buttresses were added to the Justinianic design, and after the Ottoman conquest of 1453, when Hagia Sophia became a mosque, the Turks constructed four towering minarets. The building, secularized in the 20th century, is now a museum.

The characteristic Byzantine plainness and unpretentiousness of the exterior (which in this case also disguise the massive scale) scarcely prepare visitors for the building's interior (FIG. 12-4). A poet and member of Justinian's court, Paul the Silentiary (an usher responsible for maintaining silence in the palace), vividly described the original magnificence of Hagia Sophia's interior:

> Who . . . shall sing the marble meadows gathered upon the mighty walls and spreading pavement. . . . [There is stone] from the green flanks of Carystus [and] the speckled Phrygian stone, sometimes rosy mixed with white, sometimes gleaming with purple and silver

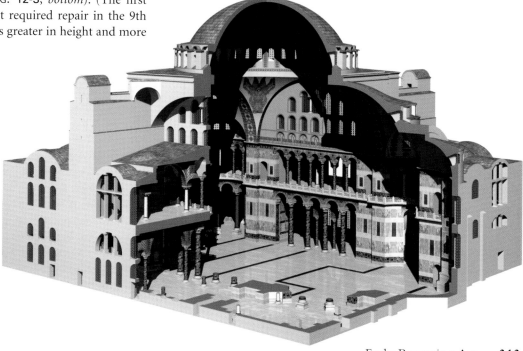

12-3 ANTHEMIUS OF TRALLES and ISIDORUS OF MILETUS, plan (*top*) and restored cutaway view (*bottom*) of Hagia Sophia, Constantinople (Istanbul), Turkey, 532–537 (John Burge). ◼◀

In Hagia Sophia, Justinian's architects succeeded in fusing two previously independent architectural traditions: the vertically oriented central-plan building and the longitudinally oriented basilica.

12-4 ANTHEMIUS OF TRALLES and ISIDORUS OF MILETUS, interior of Hagia Sophia (looking southwest), Constantinople (Istanbul), Turkey, 532–537. ◼◀

Pendentive construction made possible Hagia Sophia's lofty dome, which seems to ride on a halo of light. A contemporary said the dome seemed to be suspended by "a golden chain from Heaven."

flowers. There is a wealth of porphyry stone, too, besprinkled with little bright stars. . . . You may see the bright green stone of Laconia and the glittering marble with wavy veins found in the deep gullies of the Iasian peaks, exhibiting slanting streaks of blood-red and livid white; the pale yellow with swirling red from the Lydian headland; the glittering crocus-like golden stone [of Libya]; . . . glittering [Celtic] black [with] here and there an abundance of milk; the pale onyx with glint of precious metal; and [Thessalian marble] in parts vivid green not unlike emerald. . . . It has spots resembling snow next to flashes of black so that in one stone various beauties mingle.[1]

The feature that distinguishes Hagia Sophia from equally lavish Roman buildings such as the Pantheon (FIG. **10-51**) is the special mystical quality of the light that floods the interior (FIG. **12-4**). The soaring canopy-like dome that dominates the inside as well as the outside of the church rides on a halo of light from windows in the dome's base. Visitors to Hagia Sophia from Justinian's time to today have been struck by the light within the church and its effect on the human spirit. The 40 windows at the base of the dome create the illusion that the dome is resting on the light that pours through them. Procopius, who wrote at the emperor's request a treatise on his ambitious building program, observed that the dome looked as if it were suspended by "a golden chain from Heaven." Said he: "You might say that the space is not illuminated by the sun from the outside, but that the radiance is generated within, so great an abundance of light bathes this shrine all around."[2]

Paul the Silentiary compared the dome to "the firmament which rests on air" and described the vaulting as covered with "gilded tesserae from which a glittering stream of golden rays pours abundantly and strikes men's eyes with irresistible force. It is as if one were gazing at the midday sun in spring."[3] Thus, Hagia Sophia has a vastness of space shot through with light, and a central dome that appears to be supported by the light it admits. Light is the mystical element—light that glitters in the mosaics, shines forth from the marble-clad walls and floors, and pervades and defines spaces that, in themselves, seem to escape definition. Light seems to dissolve material substance and transform it into an abstract spiritual vision. Pseudo-Dionysius, perhaps the most influential mystic philosopher of the age, wrote in *The Divine Names:* "Light comes from the Good and . . . light is the visual image of God."[4]

PENDENTIVES To achieve this illusion of a floating "dome of Heaven," Justinian's architects used *pendentives* (see "Pendentives and Squinches," page 315) to transfer the weight from the great dome to the piers beneath, rather than to the walls. With pendentives (FIG. **12-5**, *left*), not only could the space beneath the dome be unobstructed but scores of windows also could puncture the walls themselves. Pendentives created the impression of a dome suspended above, not held up by, walls. Experts today can explain the technical virtuosity of Anthemius and Isidorus, but it remained a mystery to their contemporaries. Procopius communicated the sense of wonderment experienced by those who entered Justinian's great church: "No matter how much they concentrate their attention on this and that, and examine everything with contracted eyebrows, they are unable to understand the craftsmanship and always depart from there amazed by the perplexing spectacle."[5]

By placing a hemispherical dome on a square base instead of on a circular base, as in the Pantheon, Anthemius and Isidorus succeeded in fusing two previously independent and seemingly mutually exclusive architectural traditions: the vertically oriented central-plan building and the longitudinally oriented basilica. Hagia Sophia is, in essence, a domed basilica (FIG. **12-3**)—a uniquely successful conclusion to several centuries of experimentation in Christian church architecture. However, the thrusts of the pendentive construction at Hagia Sophia made external buttresses necessary, as well as huge internal northern and southern wall piers and eastern and western half-domes (FIG. **12-4**). The semidomes' thrusts descend, in turn, into still smaller half-domes surmounting columned exedrae that give a curving flow to the design.

Pendentives and Squinches

Perhaps the most characteristic feature of Byzantine architecture is the placement of a dome, which is circular at its base, over a square, as in the Justinianic church of Hagia Sophia (FIGS. 12-2 to 12-4) and countless later structures (for example, FIGS. 12-22 and 12-24). Two structural devices that are hallmarks of Byzantine engineering made this feat possible: *pendentives* and *squinches*.

In pendentive construction (from the Latin *pendere*, "to hang") a dome rests on what is, in effect, a second, larger dome (FIG. 12-5, *left*). The top portion and four segments around the rim of the larger dome are omitted so that four curved triangles, or pendentives, are formed. The pendentives join to form a ring and four arches whose planes bound a square. The weight of the dome is thus transferred not to the walls but rather through the pendentives and arches to the four piers from which the arches spring. The first use of pendentives on a monumental scale was in Hagia Sophia (FIG. 12-4) in the mid-sixth century, although Near Eastern architects had experimented with them earlier. In Roman and Early Christian central-plan buildings, such as the Pantheon (FIGS. 10-50 and 10-51) and Santa Costanza (FIG. 11-11), the domes spring directly from the circular top of a cylinder (FIG. 10-6*d*).

The pendentive system is a dynamic solution to the problem of setting a round dome over a square. The device made possible a union of centralized and longitudinal or basilican structures. A similar effect can be achieved using squinches (FIG. 12-5, *right*)—arches, corbels, or lintels—that bridge the corners of the supporting walls

| Pendentives | Squinches |

12-5 Dome on pendentives (*left*) and on squinches (*right*).

Pendentives (triangular sections of a sphere) make it possible to place a dome on a ring over a square. Squinches achieve the same goal by bridging the corners of the square to form an octagonal base.

and form an octagon inscribed within a square (FIG. 12-22). To achieve even greater height, a builder can rest a dome on a cylindrical drum that in turn rests on either pendentives or squinches, but the principle of supporting a dome over a square is the same.

The diverse vistas and screenlike ornamented surfaces mask the structural lines. The columnar arcades of the nave and second-story galleries have no real structural function. Like the walls they pierce, they are only part of a fragile "fill" between the huge piers. Structurally, although Hagia Sophia may seem Roman in its great scale and majesty, it does not have Roman organization of its masses. The very fact that the "walls" in Hagia Sophia are actually concealed (and barely adequate) piers indicates that the architects sought Roman monumentality as an *effect* and did not design the building according to Roman principles. Using brick in place of concrete marked a further departure from Roman practice and characterizes Byzantine architecture as a distinctive structural style. Hagia Sophia's eight great supporting piers are ashlar masonry, but the screen walls are brick, as are the vaults of the aisles and galleries and the dome and semicircular half-domes.

The ingenious design of Hagia Sophia provided the illumination and the setting for the solemn liturgy of the Orthodox faith. Through the large windows along the rim of the great dome, light poured down upon the interior's jeweled splendor, where priests staged the sacred spectacle. Sung by clerical choirs, the Orthodox equivalent of the Latin Mass celebrated the sacrament of the Eucharist at the altar in the apsidal sanctuary, in spiritual reenactment of Jesus' Crucifixion. Processions of chanting priests, accompanying the patriarch (archbishop) of Constantinople, moved slowly to and from the sanctuary and the vast nave. The gorgeous array of their vestments rivaled the interior's polychrome marbles; finely wrought, gleaming candlesticks and candelabra; the illuminated books bound in gold or ivory and inlaid with jewels and enamels; and the crosses, sacred vessels,

and processional banners. Each feature, with its great richness of texture and color, glowing in shafts of light from the dome, contributed to the majestic ambience of Justinian's great church.

The nave of Hagia Sophia was reserved for the clergy. The laity, segregated by sex, were confined to the shadows of the aisles and galleries, restrained in most places by marble parapets. The complex spatial arrangement allowed only partial views of the brilliant ceremony. The emperor was the only layperson privileged to enter the sanctuary. When he participated with the patriarch in the liturgical drama, standing at the pulpit beneath the great dome, his rule was again sanctified and his person exalted. Church and state were symbolically made one. The church building was then the earthly image of the court of Heaven, its light the image of God and God's holy wisdom.

At Hagia Sophia, the intricate logic of Greek theology, the ambitious scale of Rome, the vaulting tradition of the Near East, and the mysticism of Eastern Christianity combined to create a monument that is at once a summation of antiquity and a positive assertion of the triumph of Christian faith.

RAVENNA In 493, Theodoric, the Ostrogoths' greatest king, chose the Italian city of Ravenna as the capital of his kingdom, which encompassed much of the Balkans and all of Italy (see Chapter 11). During the short history of Theodoric's unfortunate successors, the importance of the city declined. But in 539, Justinian's general Belisarius captured Ravenna, initiating the third and most important stage of the city's history. Ravenna remained the Eastern Roman Empire's foothold in Italy for two centuries, until the Lombards and

12-6 Aerial view of San Vitale (looking northwest), Ravenna, Italy, 526–547. ▶

Justinian's general Belisarius captured Ravenna from the Ostrogoths. The city became the seat of Byzantine dominion in Italy. San Vitale honored Saint Vitalis, who was martyred at Ravenna.

0	10	20	30	40	50 feet	
0		5	10		15	20 meters

1. Narthex
2. Domed octagon
3. Apse

12-7 Plan of San Vitale, Ravenna, Italy, 526–547.

Centrally planned like Justinian's churches in Constantinople, San Vitale is unlike any other church in Italy. The design features two concentric octagons. A dome crowns the taller, inner octagon.

then the Franks overtook it. During Justinian's reign, Ravenna enjoyed its greatest cultural and economic prosperity—at a time when repeated sieges, conquests, and sackings threatened the "eternal city" of Rome with extinction. As the seat of Byzantine dominion in Italy, Ravenna and its culture became an extension of Constantinople. Its art, even more than that of the Byzantine capital (where little other than architecture has survived), clearly reveals the transition from the Early Christian to the Byzantine style.

SAN VITALE San Vitale (FIGS. **12-6** and **12-7**), dedicated by Bishop Maximianus in 547 in honor of Saint Vitalis, who was martyred at Ravenna in the second century, is the most spectacular building in Ravenna. The church is an unforgettable experience for all who have entered it and marveled at its intricate design and magnificent golden mosaics. Construction of San Vitale began under Bishop Ecclesius shortly after Theodoric's death in 526. Julianus Argentarius (Julian the Banker) provided the 26,000 gold coins (weighing more than 350 pounds) required to proceed with the work. The church is unlike any of the other sixth-century churches of Ravenna (FIG. **11-17**). Indeed, it is unlike any other church in Italy. San Vitale is not a basilica. It is centrally planned, like Justinian's churches in Constantinople, and it seems, in fact, to have been loosely modeled on the earlier Church of Saints Sergius and Bacchus there.

The design features two concentric octagons. The dome-covered inner octagon rises above the surrounding octagon to provide the interior with clerestory lighting. The central space is defined by eight large piers that alternate with curved, columned exedrae that push outward into the surrounding two-story ambulatory and create, on the plan, an intricate leafed design (FIG. **12-7**). The exedrae closely integrate the inner and outer spaces that otherwise would have existed simply side by side as independent units. A cross-vaulted *choir* preceding the apse interrupts the ambulatory and gives the plan some axial stability. Weakening this effect, however, is the off-axis placement of the narthex, whose odd angle never has been explained fully. (The atrium, which no longer exists, may have paralleled a street that ran in the same direction as the angle of the narthex.)

San Vitale's intricate plan and elevation combine to produce an effect of great complexity. The exterior's octagonal regularity is not readily apparent inside (FIG. **12-8**). A rich diversity of ever-changing perspectives greets visitors walking through the building. Arches looping over arches, curving and flattened spaces, and wall and vault shapes seem to change constantly with the viewer's position. Light filtered through alabaster-paned windows plays over the glittering mosaics and glowing marbles that cover the building's complex surfaces, producing a sumptuous effect.

The mosaics that decorate San Vitale's choir and apse (FIG. **12-9**), like the building itself, must be regarded as among the most climactic achievements of Byzantine art. Completed less than a decade after the Ostrogoths surrendered Ravenna, the apse and choir decorations form a unified composition, whose theme is the holy ratification of Justinian's right to rule.

In the apse vault, Christ, youthful in the Early Christian tradition, holds a scroll with seven seals (Rev. 5:1) and sits on the orb of the world at the time of his Second Coming. The four rivers of Paradise flow beneath him, and rainbow-hued clouds float above. Christ extends the golden martyr's wreath to Vitalis, the patron saint of the church, whom an angel introduces. At Christ's left, another angel presents Bishop Ecclesius, in whose time the church foundations were laid. Ecclesius offers a model of San Vitale to Christ. The arrangement recalls Christ's prophecy of the last days of the world: "And then shall they see the Son

12-8 Interior of San Vitale (looking from the apse into the choir), Ravenna, Italy, 526–547. ◾◀

Light filtered through alabaster-paned windows plays over the glittering mosaics and glowing marbles that cover San Vitale's complex wall and vault shapes, producing a sumptuous effect.

of Man coming in the clouds with great power and glory. And then shall he send his angels, and shall gather together his elect from the four winds, from the uttermost part of Heaven" (Mark 13:26–27).

Images and symbols covering the entire sanctuary express the single idea of Christ's redemption of humanity and the reenactment of it in the Eucharist. Below the apse mosaic (at the right in FIG. 12-8), for example, the lunette mosaic over the two columns of the choir depicts the story of Abraham and the three angels. Sarah, Abraham's wife, was 90 years old and childless when three angels visited Abraham. They announced that Sarah would bear a son, and she later miraculously gave birth to Isaac. Christians believe the Old Testament angels symbolized the Holy Trinity. Immediately to the right in the lunette is the sacrifice of Isaac, a prefiguration of Christ's Crucifixion (see "Jewish Subjects in Christian Art," Chapter 11, page 293).

JUSTINIAN AND THEODORA On the choir wall to the left of the apse mosaic appears Justinian (FIG. 12-10) and on the right wall is his empress, Theodora (FIG. 12-11). Justinian stands on the Savior's right side (FIG. 12-9). The two are united visually and symbolically by the imperial purple they wear and by their halos. A dozen attendants accompany Justinian, paralleling Christ's 12 apostles. Thus, the mosaic program underscores the dual political and religious roles of the Byzantine emperor. The laws of the Eastern Church and the laws of the

state, united in the laws of God, were manifest in the person of the emperor, whose right to rule was God-given.

The positions of the figures are all-important. They express the formulas of precedence and rank. Justinian is at the center, distinguished from the other dignitaries by his purple robe and halo. At his left (at right in the mosaic) is Bishop Maximianus, the man responsible for San Vitale's completion. The mosaicist stressed the bishop's importance by labeling his figure with the only identifying inscription in the composition. Some scholars have identified the figure behind and between Justinian and Maximianus as Julianus Argentarius, the church's benefactor. The artist divided the figures into three groups: the emperor and his staff; the clergy; and the imperial guard, bearing a shield with the *chi-rho-iota* (☧) monogram of Christ.

Each group has a leader whose feet precede (by one foot overlapping) the feet of those who follow. The positions of Justinian and Maximianus are curiously ambiguous. Although the emperor appears to be slightly behind the bishop, the golden *paten* (large shallow bowl or plate for the Eucharist bread) he carries overlaps the bishop's arm. Thus, symbolized by place and gesture, the imperial and churchly powers are in balance. Justinian's paten, Maximianus's cross, and the attendant clerics' book and censer produce a slow forward movement that strikingly modifies the scene's rigid formality. No background is indicated. The artist wished the observer to understand the procession

12-9 Choir and apse of San Vitale with mosaic of Christ between two angels, Saint Vitalis, and Bishop Ecclesius, Ravenna, Italy, 526–547. ◼◀

In the apse vault, a youthful Christ, seated on the orb of the world at the time of his Second Coming, extends the golden martyr's wreath to Saint Vitalis. Bishop Ecclesius offers Christ a model of San Vitale.

12-10 Justinian, Bishop Maximianus, and attendants, mosaic on the north wall of the apse, San Vitale, Ravenna, Italy, ca. 547. ◼◀

San Vitale's mosaics reveal the new Byzantine aesthetic. Justinian is foremost among the weightless and speechless frontal figures hovering before the viewer, their positions in space uncertain.

12-11 Theodora and attendants, mosaic on the south wall of the apse, San Vitale, Ravenna, Italy, ca. 547. ◼◀

Justinian's counterpart on the opposite wall is the empress Theodora, a powerful figure at the Byzantine court. Neither she nor Justinian ever visited Ravenna. San Vitale's mosaics are proxies for the absent sovereigns.

Theodora, a Most Unusual Empress

Theodora (FIG. 12-11), wife of Justinian and empress of Byzantium, was not born into an aristocratic family. Her father, who died when she was a child, was the "keeper of bears" for one of the circus factions (teams distinguished by color) at Constantinople. His responsibility was to prepare these animals for bear fights, bear hunts, and acrobatic performances involving bears in a long tradition rooted in ancient Rome. Theodora's mother was an actress, and after the death of her father the young Theodora took up the same career. Acting was not a profession the highborn held in esteem. At Byzantium, actresses often doubled as prostitutes, and the beautiful Theodora was no exception. In fact, actresses were so low on the Byzantine social ladder that the law prohibited senators from marrying them.

Justinian met Theodora when he was about 40 years old, she only 25. She became his mistress, but before they could wed, as they did in 525, ignoring all the social norms of the day, Justinian's uncle, the emperor Justin, first had to rewrite the law against senatorial

marriages to actresses to permit wedlock with an ex-actress. When Justin died in April 527, the patriarch of Constantinople crowned Justinian emperor, and Theodora became empress of Byzantium, capping what can be fairly described as one of the most remarkable and improbable "success stories" of any age. By all accounts, even of those openly hostile to the imperial couple, Justinian and Theodora remained faithful to each other for the rest of their lives.

It was not Theodora's beauty alone that attracted Justinian. John the Lydian, a civil servant at Constantinople at the time, described her as "surpassing in intelligence all men who ever lived." As her husband's trusted adviser, she repaid him for elevating her from poverty and disgrace to riches and prestige. During the Nika revolt in Constantinople in 532, when all of her husband's ministers counseled flight from the city, Theodora, by the sheer force of her personality, persuaded Justinian and his generals to hold their ground. The revolt was suppressed.

---

as taking place in this very sanctuary. Thus, the emperor appears forever as a participant in the sacred rites and as the proprietor of this royal church and the ruler of the Western Empire.

The procession at San Vitale recalls but contrasts with that of Augustus and his entourage (FIG. 10-31) on the Ara Pacis, erected more than a half millennium earlier in Rome. There the fully modeled marble figures have their feet planted firmly on the ground. The Romans talk among themselves, unaware of the viewer's presence. All is anecdote, all very human and of this world, even if the figures themselves conform to a classical ideal of beauty that cannot be achieved in reality. The frontal figures of the Byzantine mosaic, by comparison, hover before viewers, weightless and speechless, their positions in space uncertain. Tall, spare, angular, and elegant, the figures have lost the rather squat proportions characteristic of much Early Christian work. The garments fall straight, stiff, and thin from the narrow shoulders. The organic body has dematerialized, and, except for the heads, some of which seem to be true portraits, viewers see a procession of solemn spirits gliding silently in the presence of the sacrament. Indeed, the theological basis for this approach to representation was the principle that the divine is invisible and that the purpose of religious art is to stimulate spiritual seeing. Theodulf of Orleans summed up this idea around 790, when he wrote "God is beheld not with the eyes of the flesh but only with the eye of the mind."[6] The mosaics of San Vitale reveal this new Byzantine aesthetic, one very different from that of the classical world but equally compelling. Blue sky has given way to heavenly gold, and matter and material values are disparaged. Byzantine art is an art without solid bodies or cast shadows, with blank golden spaces, and with the perspective of Paradise, which is nowhere and everywhere.

Justinian's counterpart on the opposite wall of the apse is Theodora (FIG. 12-11), one of the most remarkable women of the Middle Ages (see "Theodora, a Most Unusual Empress," above). The empress too is accompanied by her retinue. Both processions move into the apse, Justinian proceeding from left to right and Theodora from right to left, in order to take part in the Eucharist. Justinian carries the paten containing the bread, and Theodora the golden cup

with the wine. The portraits in the Theodora mosaic exhibit the same stylistic traits as those in the Justinian mosaic, but the women are represented within a definite architecture, perhaps the atrium of San Vitale. The empress stands in state beneath an imperial canopy, waiting to follow the emperor's procession. An attendant beckons her to pass through the curtained doorway. The fact that she is outside the sanctuary in a courtyard with a fountain and only about to enter attests that, in the ceremonial protocol, her rank was not quite equal to her consort's. But the very presence of Theodora at San Vitale is significant. Neither she nor Justinian ever visited Ravenna. Their participation in the liturgy at San Vitale is pictorial fiction. The mosaics are proxies for the absent sovereigns. Justinian was represented because he was the head of the Byzantine state, and by his presence he exerted his authority over his territories in Italy. But Theodora's portrayal is more surprising and testifies to her unique position in Justinian's court. Theodora's prominent role in the mosaic program of San Vitale is proof of the power she wielded at Constantinople and, by extension, at Ravenna. In fact, the representation of the three magi on the border of her robe suggests that she belongs in the elevated company of the three monarchs who approached the newborn Jesus bearing gifts.

SANT'APOLLINARE IN CLASSE Until the ninth century, Sant'Apollinare in Classe housed the body of Saint Apollinaris, who suffered his martyrdom in Classe, Ravenna's port. The church itself is Early Christian in type, a basilica with a nave and flanking aisles, like Theodoric's palace-church (FIG. 11-17) dedicated to the same saint in Ravenna. As in the earlier church, the Justinianic building's exterior is plain and unadorned, but sumptuous mosaics decorate the interior, although in this case they are confined to the apse (FIG. 12-12).

The mosaic decorating the semidome above the apse probably was completed by 549, when the church was dedicated. (The mosaics of the framing arch are of later date.) Against a gold ground, a large medallion with a jeweled cross dominates the composition. This may represent the cross Constantine erected on the hill of Calvary to commemorate the martyrdom of Jesus. Visible just above the cross is the hand of God. On either side of the medallion, in the clouds, are the Old Testament prophets Moses and Elijah, who appeared before Jesus during his Transfiguration. Below these two figures are three sheep, symbols of the disciples John, Peter, and Paul, who accompanied Jesus to the foot of the mountain he ascended in order to converse with the prophets. Beneath, amid green fields with trees, flowers, and birds, stands the church's patron saint, Apollinaris. The mosaicist portrayed him in the Early Christian manner as an orant with uplifted arms. Accompanying Apollinaris are 12 sheep, perhaps representing the Christian congregation under the saint's protection, and forming, as they march in regular file across the apse, a wonderfully decorative base.

Comparison of the Early Byzantine Sant'Apollinare in Classe mosaic with the Galla Placidia mosaic (FIG. 11-16) from the Early Christian period at Ravenna shows how the style and artists' approach to the subject changed during the course of a century. Both mosaics portray a human figure and some sheep in a landscape. But in Classe, in the mid-sixth century, the artist did not try to re-create a segment of the physical world, instead telling the story in terms of flat symbols, lined up side by side. The mosaicist carefully avoided overlapping in what must have been an intentional effort to omit all reference to the three-dimensional space of the material world and physical reality. Shapes have lost the volume seen in the earlier mosaic and instead are flat silhouettes with linear details. The effect is that of an extremely rich, flat tapestry without illusionistic devices. This new Byzantine style became the ideal vehicle for conveying the extremely complex symbolism of the fully developed Christian dogma.

The Sant'Apollinare in Classe apse mosaic, for example, carries much more meaning than first meets the eye. The cross symbolizes not only Christ's own death, with its redeeming consequences, but also the death of his martyrs (in this case, Saint Apollinaris). The lamb, also a symbol of martyrdom, appropriately represents the martyred apostles. The whole scene expands above the altar, where the priests celebrated the sacrament of the Eucharist—the miraculous recurrence of the supreme redemptive act. The very altars of Christian churches were, from early times, sanctified by the bones and relics of martyrs (see "Pilgrimages and the Cult of Relics," Chapter 17, page 432). Thus, the mystery and the martyrdom were joined in one concept. The death of the martyr, in imitation of Christ, is a triumph over death that leads to eternal life. The images above the altar present an inspiring vision to the eyes of believers, delivered with overwhelming force. Looming above their eyes is the apparition of a great mystery, ordered to make perfectly simple and clear that humankind's duty is to seek salvation. Even the illiterate, who might not grasp the details of the complex theological program, could understand that the way of the martyr is open to the Christian faithful and that the reward of eternal life is within their reach.

MOUNT SINAI During Justinian's reign, building continued almost incessantly, not only in Constantinople and Ravenna but all over the Byzantine Empire. At about the time mosaicists in Ravenna were completing their work at San Vitale and Sant'Apollinare in Classe, Justinian's builders were reconstructing an important early *monastery* (an enclosed compound for monks) at Mount Sinai in Egypt where Moses received the Ten Commandments from God. Now called Saint Catherine's, the monastery marked the spot at the foot of the mountain where the Bible says God first spoke to the Hebrew prophet from a burning bush.

Monasticism began in Egypt in the third century and spread rapidly to Palestine and Syria in the East and as far as Ireland in the West. It began as a migration to the wilderness by those who sought a more spiritual way of life, far from the burdens, distractions, and temptations of town and city. In desert locations, these refuge seekers lived austerely as hermits, in contemplative isolation, cultivating the soul's perfection. So many thousands fled the cities that the authorities became alarmed—noting the effect on the tax base, military recruitment, and business in general.

12-13 *Transfiguration of Jesus,* apse mosaic, Church of the Virgin, monastery of Saint Catherine, Mount Sinai, Egypt, ca. 548–565.

Unlike the Sant'Apollinare mosaicist, this Mount Sinai artist swept away all traces of landscape for a depthless field of gold. The prophets and disciples cast no shadows even though bathed in divine light.

The origins of the monastic movement are associated with Saint Anthony and Saint Pachomius in Egypt in the fourth century. By the fifth century, regulations governing monastic life began to be codified. Individual monks came together to live according to a rule within a common enclosure, a community under the direction of an abbot (see "Medieval Monasteries and Benedictine Rule," Chapter 16, page 420). The monks typically lived in a walled monastery, an architectural complex that included the monks' residence (an alignment of single cells), an *oratory* (monastic church), a *refectory* (dining hall), a kitchen, storage and service quarters, and a guest house for pilgrims (FIG. 16-19).

Justinian rebuilt the monastery at Mount Sinai between 548 and 565 and erected imposing walls around it. The site had been an important pilgrimage destination since the fourth century, and Justinian's fortress was intended to protect not only the hermit-monks but also the lay pilgrims during their visits. The Mount Sinai church was dedicated to the Virgin Mary, whom the Orthodox Church had officially recognized in the mid-fifth century as the Mother of God (*Theotokos*), putting to rest a controversy about the divine nature of Christ. The church's apse mosaic (FIG. 12-13) depicts the *Transfiguration.* (Other mosaics in the church depict Moses receiving the Law and standing before the burning bush.) Jesus appears in a deep-blue almond-shaped *mandorla* (almond-shaped aureole of light). At his feet are John, Peter, and James. At the left and right are Elijah and Moses. Portrait busts of saints and prophets in medallions frame the whole scene. The artist stressed the intense whiteness of Jesus' transfigured, spiritualized form, from which rays stream down on the disciples. The stately figures of the

prophets and the static frontality of Jesus set off the frantic terror and astonishment of the gesticulating disciples. These characteristics effectively contrast the eternal composure of heavenly beings with the distraught responses of the earthbound.

In this apse the mosaicist swept away all traces of landscape and architectural setting for a depthless field of gold, fixing the figures and their labels in isolation from one another. A rainbow band of colors graduating from yellow to blue bounds the golden field at its base. The figures are ambiguously related to this multicolor ground line. Sometimes they are placed behind it. Sometimes they overlap it. The bodies cast no shadows, even though supernatural light streams over them. This is a world of mystical vision, where the artist subtracted all substance that might suggest the passage of time or motion through physical space. In the absence of such physicality, the devout can contemplate the eternal and motionless world of religious truth.

Ivory Carving and Painting

As in the Early Christian period, ivory carving and manuscript painting were important art forms during the Early Byzantine era. Most of the finest examples date to the sixth century. They feature both secular and religious subjects.

BARBERINI IVORY Carved in five parts (one is lost), the ivory plaque known today as the *Barberini Ivory* (FIG. 12-14)—it was once part of the 17th-century collection of Cardinal Barberini in Rome—shows at the center an emperor, usually identified as Justinian, riding triumphantly on a rearing horse, while a startled, half-

The Emperors of New Rome

Byzantine art is generally, and properly, considered to belong to the Middle Ages rather than to the ancient world, but the emperors of Byzantium, New Rome, considered themselves the direct successors of the emperors of Old Rome. Although the official state religion was Christianity and all pagan cults were suppressed, the political imagery of Byzantine art displays a striking continuity between ancient Rome and medieval Byzantium. Artists continued to portray emperors sitting on thrones holding the orb of the earth in their hands, battling foes while riding on mighty horses, and receiving tribute from defeated enemies. In the Early Byzantine period, official portraits continued to be set up in great numbers throughout the territories Byzantium controlled. But, as was true of the classical world, much of imperial Byzantine statuary is forever lost. Nonetheless, some of the lost portraits of the Byzantine emperors can be visualized from miniature versions of them on ivory reliefs such as the *Barberini Ivory* (FIG. 12-14) and from descriptions in surviving texts.

One especially impressive portrait in the Roman imperial tradition, melted down long ago, depicted the emperor Justinian on horseback atop a grandiose column. Cast in glittering bronze, like the equestrian statue of Marcus Aurelius (FIG. 10-59) set up nearly 400 years earlier, it attested to the continuity between the art of New Rome and Old Rome, where pompous imperial images were commonly displayed at the apex of freestanding columns. (Compare FIG. 10-44 where a statue of Saint Peter has replaced a lost statue of the emperor Trajan.) Procopius, Justinian's official historian, described the equestrian portrait:

> Finest bronze, cast into panels and wreaths, encompasses the stones [of the column] on all sides, both binding them securely together and covering them with adornment. . . . This bronze is in color softer than pure gold, while in value it does not fall much short of an equal weight of silver. At the summit of the column stands a huge bronze horse turned towards the east, a most noteworthy sight. . . . Upon this horse is mounted a bronze image of the Emperor like a colossus. . . . He wears a cuirass in heroic fashion and his head is covered with a helmet . . . and a kind of radiance flashes forth from there. . . . He gazes towards the rising sun, steering his course, I suppose, against the Persians. In his left hand he holds a globe, by which

12-14 Justinian as world conqueror (*Barberini Ivory*), mid-sixth century. Ivory, 1′ 1½″ × 10½″. Louvre, Paris.

Classical style and motifs lived on in Byzantine art in ivories such as this one, where Justinian rides a rearing horse accompanied by personifications of Victory and Earth. Above, Christ blesses the emperor.

1 in.

the sculptor has signified that the whole earth and sea were subject to him, yet he carries neither sword nor spear nor any other weapon, but a cross surmounts his globe, by virtue of which alone he has won the kingship and victory in war. Stretching forth his right hand towards the regions of the East and spreading out his fingers, he commands the barbarians that dwell there to remain at home and not to advance any further.*

Statues such as this are the missing links in an imperial tradition that never really died and that lived on also in the Holy Roman Empire (FIG. 16-12) and in Renaissance Italy (FIGS. 21-15 and 21-16).

*Cyril Mango, trans., *The Art of the Byzantine Empire, 312–1453: Sources and Documents* (reprint of 1972 ed., Toronto: Toronto University Press, 1986), 110–111.

hidden barbarian recoils in fear behind him. The dynamic twisting postures of both horse and rider and the motif of the equestrian emperor thrusting his spears are survivals of the pagan Roman Empire (see "The Emperors of New Rome," above), as are the personifications of bountiful Earth (below the horse) and palm-bearing Victory (flying in to crown the conqueror). Also borrowed from pagan art are the barbarians at the bottom of the plaque bearing tribute and seeking clemency. They are juxtaposed with a lion, an elephant, and a tiger—exotic animals native to Africa and Asia, sites of Justinian's conquests. At the left, a Roman soldier carries a statuette of another Victory, reinforcing the central panel's message. The source of the emperor's strength, however, comes not from his earthly armies but from God. The uppermost panel depicts two angels holding aloft a youthful image of Christ carrying a cross in his left hand. Christ blesses Justinian with a gesture of his right hand, indicating approval of the emperor's rule.

ARCHANGEL MICHAEL IVORY Another ivory panel (FIG. 12-15), created somewhat earlier than the *Barberini Ivory* and likewise carved in the Eastern Christian Empire, perhaps in Constantinople, offers further evidence of the persistence of classical art. The panel, the largest extant Byzantine ivory, is all that is preserved from a hinged diptych in the Early Christian tradition. It depicts Saint Michael the Archangel, patron of the imperial church of Hagia Sophia. The inscription opens with the words "Receive these gifts." The dedication is perhaps a reference to the cross-surmounted orb of power the archangel once offered to a Byzantine emperor depicted on the missing diptych leaf. The prototype of Michael must have been a pagan winged Victory, although Victory was personified as a woman in Greco-Roman art and usually carried a palm branch, as does the Victory on the *Barberini Ivory*. The Christian artist here ingeniously adapted a pagan motif and imbued it with new meaning.

The archangel's flowing drapery, which reveals the body's shape, the delicately incised wings, and the facial type and coiffure are other indications that the artist who carved this ivory was still working in the tradition of classical art. Nonetheless, the Byzantine ivory carver had little concern for the rules of naturalistic representation. The archangel dwarfs the architectural setting. Michael's feet, for example, rest on three steps at once, and his upper body, wings, and arms are in front of the column shafts while his lower body is behind the column bases at the top of the receding staircase. These spatial ambiguities, of course, do not detract from the figure's striking beauty, but they do signify the emergence of the same new aesthetic already noted in the mosaics of Ravenna. Here, as there, the Byzantine artist rejected the goal of most classical artists: to render the three-dimensional world in convincing and consistent fashion and to people that world with fully modeled figures firmly rooted on the ground. Michael seems more to float in front of the architecture than to stand in it.

VIENNA DIOSKORIDES The physical world was the focus, however, of one of the rare secular books to survive from the early Middle Ages, either in Byzantium or the West. In the mid-first century, a Greek physician named Dioskorides compiled an encyclopedia of medicinal herbs called *De materia medica*. An early-sixth-century copy of this manual, nearly a thousand pages in length, is in the Austrian National Library. The *Vienna Dioskorides*, as it is called, was a gift from the people of Honoratai, near Constantinople, to Anicia Juliana, daughter of the short-lived Emperor of the West, Anicias Olybrias (r. 472). Anicia Juliana was a leading patron of the arts and had built a church dedicated to the Virgin Mary at Honoratai in 512. She also provided the funds to erect Saint Polyeuktos in Constantinople between 524 and 527. The excavated ruins of that church indicate that it was a domed basilica—an important forerunner of the pioneering design of Justinian's Hagia Sophia.

The *Vienna Dioskorides* contains 498 illustrations, almost all images of plants rendered with a scientific fidelity to nature that stands in stark contrast to contemporary Byzantine paintings and mosaics of religious subjects. It is likely that the *Vienna Dioskorides*

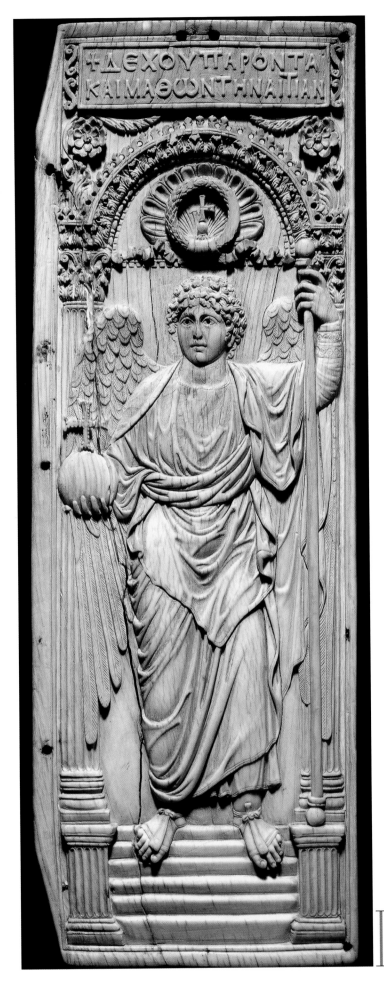

12-15 Saint Michael the Archangel, right leaf of a diptych, early sixth century. Ivory, 1′ 5″ × 5½″. British Museum, London.

The sculptor who carved this largest extant Byzantine ivory panel modeled Saint Michael on a classical winged Victory, but the archangel seems to float in front of the architecture rather than stand in it.

1 in.

12-16 Anicia Juliana between Magnanimity and Prudence, folio 6 verso of the *Vienna Dioskorides*, from Honoratai, near Constantinople (Istanbul), Turkey, ca. 512. Tempera on parchment, 1′ 3″ × 1′ 11″. Österreichische Nationalbibliothek, Vienna.

In gratitude for her generosity, the people of Honoratai presented Anicia Juliana, a great art patron, with a book in which she appears enthroned with personifications of Magnanimity and Prudence.

painters copied the illustrations as well as the text of a classical manuscript. One page, however, cannot be a copy—the dedication page (FIG. 12-16) featuring a portrait of Anicia Juliana in an eight-pointed star and circle frame. This earliest known illustrated dedication page shows Anicia Juliana enthroned between personifications of Magnanimity and Prudence, with a kneeling figure labeled Gratitude of the Arts at her feet. The shading and modeling of the figures, the heads posed at oblique angles, the perspectival rendering of the throne's footstool, and the use of personifications establish that the painter still worked in the classical tradition that most other Byzantine artists by then had rejected.

RABBULA GOSPELS One of the essential Christian beliefs is that following his Crucifixion and entombment, Christ rose from the dead after three days and, on the 40th day, ascended from the Mount of Olives to Heaven. The *Ascension* is the subject of a full-page painting (FIG. 12-17) in a manuscript known as the *Rabbula Gospels*. Written in Syriac by the monk Rabbula at the monastery of Saint John the Evangelist at Zagba, Syria, it dates to the year 586. The composition shows Christ, bearded and surrounded by a mandorla, as in the Mount Sinai *Transfiguration* (FIG. 12-13), but the mandorla is here borne aloft by angels. Below, Mary, other angels, and various apostles look on. The artist set the figures into a mosaic-like frame

(compare FIGS. 12-10 and 12-11), and many art historians think the model for the manuscript page was a mural painting or mosaic in a Byzantine church somewhere in the Eastern Empire.

The account of Christ's Ascension is not part of the accompanying text of the *Rabbula Gospels* but is borrowed from the biblical book of Acts. And even Acts omits mention of the Virgin's presence at the miraculous event. Here, however, the Theotokos occupies a very prominent position, central and directly beneath Christ. It is an early example of the important role the Mother of God played in later medieval art, in both the East and the West. Frontal, with a nimbus, and posed as an orant, Mary stands apart from the commotion all about her and looks out at the viewer. Other details also depart from the Gospel texts. Christ, for example, does not rise in a cloud. Rather, as in the vision of Ezekiel in the book of Revelation, he ascends in a mandorla above a fiery winged chariot. The chariot carries the symbols of the Four Evangelists—the man, lion, ox, and eagle (see "The Four Evangelists," Chapter 16, page 412). This page therefore does not illustrate the Gospels but presents one of the central tenets of Christian faith. Similar compositions appear on pilgrims' flasks from Palestine that were souvenir items reproducing important monuments visited. They reinforce the theory that the *Ascension* page of the *Rabbula Gospels* was based on a lost painting or mosaic in a major church.

12-17 *Ascension of Christ*, folio 13 verso of the *Rabbula Gospels*, from Zagba, Syria, 586. Tempera on parchment, 1′ 1″ × 10½″. Biblioteca Medicea-Laurenziana, Florence.

The Gospels do not mention the Virgin Mary as a witness of Christ's Ascension. Her prominent position in the *Rabbula Gospels* is an early example of the important role Mary played in later medieval art.

Icons and Iconoclasm

Byzantine *icons* ("images" in Greek) are small portable paintings depicting Christ, the Virgin, or saints (or a combination of all three, as in fig. 12-18). Icons survive from as early as the fourth century. From the sixth century on, they became enormously popular in Byzantine worship, both public and private. Eastern Christians considered icons a personal, intimate, and indispensable medium for spiritual transaction with holy figures. Some icons (for example, fig. 12-29) came to be regarded as wonder-working, and believers ascribed miracles and healing powers to them.

Icons were by no means universally accepted, however. From the beginning, many Christians were deeply suspicious of the practice of imaging the divine, whether on portable panels, on the walls of churches, or especially as statues that reminded them of pagan idols. The opponents of Christian figural art had in mind the Old Testament prohibition of images the Lord dictated to Moses in the Second Commandment: "Thou shalt not make unto thee any graven image or any likeness of anything that is in heaven above, or that is in the earth beneath, or that is in the water under the earth. Thou shalt not bow down thyself to them, nor serve them" (Exod. 20:4, 5). For example, early in the fourth century, Constantia, sister of the emperor Constantine, requested an image of Christ from Eusebius, the first great historian of the Christian Church. He rebuked her, referring to the Second Commandment:

> Can it be that you have forgotten that passage in which God lays down the law that no likeness should be made of what is in heaven or in the earth beneath? . . . Are not such things banished and excluded from churches all over the world, and is it not common knowledge that such practices are not permitted to us . . . lest we appear, like idol worshipers, to carry our God around in an image?*

Opposition to icons became especially strong in the eighth century, when the faithful often burned incense and knelt before them in prayer to seek protection or a cure for illness. Although icons were intended only to evoke the presence of the holy figures addressed in prayer, in the minds of many people, icons became identified with the personages represented. Icon veneration became confused with idol worship, and this brought about an imperial ban on the making of icons, followed by the wholesale wreckage of sacred images (*iconoclasm*). The *iconoclasts* (breakers of images) and the *iconophiles* (lovers of images) became bitter and irreconcilable enemies. The anguish of the latter can be gleaned from a graphic description of the deeds of the iconoclasts, written in about 754:

> In every village and town one could witness the weeping and lamentation of the pious, whereas, on the part of the impious, [one saw] sacred things trodden upon, [liturgical] vessels turned to other use, churches scraped down and smeared with ashes because they contained holy images. And wherever there were venerable images of Christ or the Mother of God or the saints, these were consigned to the flames or were gouged out or smeared over.†

1 in.

12-18 Virgin (Theotokos) and Child between Saints Theodore and George, icon, sixth or early seventh century. Encaustic on wood, 2′ 3″ × 1′ 7⅜″. Monastery of Saint Catherine, Mount Sinai, Egypt.

Byzantine icons continued the Roman tradition of painting on wood panels (FIGS. 10-62 and 10-63), but their style as well as the Christian subjects broke sharply from classical models.

The consequences of iconoclasm for the history of Byzantine art are difficult to overstate. For more than a century, not only did the portrayal of Christ, the Virgin, and the saints cease, but the iconoclasts also destroyed countless works from the early centuries of Christendom. Assembling a complete history of Early Byzantine art presents a great challenge to art historians.

---

* Cyril Mango, trans., *The Art of the Byzantine Empire, 312–1453: Sources and Documents* (reprint of 1972 ed., Toronto: University of Toronto Press, 1986), 17–18.
† Ibid., 152.

12-18A Christ blessing, Mount Sinai, sixth century.

ICONS Gospel books such as the *Rabbula Gospels* played an important role in monastic religious life. So, too, did *icons*, which also figured prominently in private devotion (see "Icons and Iconoclasm," page 326). Unfortunately, few early icons survive. Some of the finest early examples come from Saint Catherine's monastery at Mount Sinai. The one illustrated here (FIG. 12-18) was painted in encaustic on wood, continuing a tradition of panel painting in Egypt that, as true of so much else in the Byzantine world, has roots in the Roman Empire (FIGS. 10-62 and 10-63). In a composition reminiscent of the portrait of Anicia Juliana (FIG. 12-16) in the *Vienna Dioskorides,* the Sinai icon painter represented the enthroned Theotokos and Child with Saints Theodore and George. The two guardian saints intercede with the Virgin on the viewer's behalf. Behind them, two angels gaze upward to a shaft of light where the hand of God appears. The foreground figures are strictly frontal and have a solemn demeanor. Background details are few and suppressed. The forward plane of the picture dominates. Space is squeezed out. Traces of the Greco-Roman illusionism noted in the Anicia Juliana portrait remain in the Virgin's rather personalized features, in her sideways glance, and in the posing of the angels' heads. But the painter rendered the saints' bodies in the new Byzantine manner.

ICONOCLASM The preservation of the Early Byzantine icons at the Mount Sinai monastery is fortuitous but ironic, for opposition to icon worship was especially prominent in the Monophysite provinces of Syria and Egypt. There, in the seventh century, a series of calamities erupted, indirectly causing the imperial ban on images. The Sasanians (see Chapter 2), chronically at war with Rome, swept into the eastern provinces early in the seventh century. Between 611 and 617, they captured the great cities of Antioch, Jerusalem, and Alexandria. The Byzantine emperor Heraclius (r. 610–641) had barely defeated them in 627 when a new and overwhelming power appeared unexpectedly on the stage of history. The Arabs, under the banner of the new Islamic religion, conquered not only Byzantium's eastern provinces but also Persia itself, replacing the Sasanians in the age-old balance of power with the Christian West (see Chapter 13). In a few years the Arabs were launching attacks on Constantinople, and Byzantium was fighting for its life.

These were catastrophic years for the Eastern Roman Empire. They terminated once and for all the long story of imperial Rome, closed the Early Byzantine period, and inaugurated the medieval era of Byzantine history. Almost two-thirds of the Byzantine Empire's territory was lost—many cities and much of its population, wealth, and material resources. The shock of these events may have persuaded the emperor Leo III (r. 717–741) that God was punishing the Christian Roman Empire for its idolatrous worship of icons by setting upon it the merciless armies of the infidel—an enemy that, moreover, shunned the representation not only of God but of all living things in holy places (see Chapter 13). Some scholars believe that another motivation for Leo's 726 ban on picturing the divine was to assert the authority of the state over the Church. In any case, for more than a century, Byzantine artists produced little new religious figurative art. In place of images of holy figures, the iconoclasts used symbolic forms already familiar in Early Christian art, for example, the Cross (FIG. 12-12).

MIDDLE BYZANTINE ART

In the ninth century, a powerful reaction against iconoclasm set in. The destruction of images was condemned as a heresy, and restoration of the images began in 843. Shortly thereafter, under a new line of emperors, art, literature, and learning sprang to life once again. In

this great "renovation," as historians have called it, Byzantine culture returned to its ancient Hellenistic sources and accommodated them to the forms inherited from the Justinianic age. Basil I (r. 867–886), head of the new Macedonian dynasty, regarded himself as the restorer of the Roman Empire. He denounced as usurpers the Carolingian monarchs of the West (see Chapter 16) who, since 800, had claimed the title "Roman Empire" for their realm. Basil bluntly reminded their emissary that the only true emperor of Rome reigned in Constantinople. The Carolingians were not Roman emperors but merely "kings of the Germans." Iconoclasm had forced Byzantine artists westward, where doubtless they found employment at the courts of these Germanic kings (see "Theophanu, a Byzantine Princess in Ottonian Germany," Chapter 16, page 428). They strongly influenced the character of Western European art.

Architecture and Mosaics

The triumph of the iconophiles over the iconoclasts meant that Byzantine mural painters, mosaicists, book illuminators, ivory carvers, and metalworkers once again received plentiful commissions. Basil I and his successors also undertook the laborious and costly task of refurbishing the churches the iconoclasts had defaced and neglected.

THEOTOKOS, HAGIA SOPHIA In 867, the Macedonian dynasty dedicated a new mosaic (FIG. 12-19) depicting the enthroned Virgin with the Christ Child in her lap in the apse of the Justinianic church of Hagia Sophia. In the vast space beneath the dome

12-19 Virgin (Theotokos) and Child enthroned, apse mosaic, Hagia Sophia, Constantinople (Istanbul), Turkey, dedicated 867. ◼◀

Shortly after the repeal of iconoclasm, the emperor Basil I dedicated a huge new mosaic in the apse of Hagia Sophia depicting the Virgin and Child enthroned. It replaced one the iconoclasts had destroyed.

12-20 Katholikon, Hosios Loukas, Greece, first quarter of 11th century.

Middle Byzantine churches typically are small and high shouldered, with a central dome on a drum and exterior wall surfaces with decorative patterns, probably reflecting Islamic architecture.

12-21 Plan of the Church of the Theotokos (*top*) and the Katholikon (*bottom*), Hosios Loukas, Greece, second half of 10th and first quarter of 11th centuries. (1) Dome on pendentives, (2) dome on squinches.

The plans of the pair of monastic churches at Hosios Loukas in Greece take the form of a domed square at the center of a cross with four equal-length vaulted arms (the Greek cross).

of the great church, the figures look undersized, but the seated Theotokos is more than 16 feet tall. An accompanying inscription, now fragmentary, announced that "pious emperors" (the Macedonians) had commissioned the mosaic to replace one the "impostors" (the iconoclasts) had destroyed.

The original mosaic's subject is uncertain, but the ninth-century work echoes the style and composition of the Early Byzantine icon (FIG. 12-18) at Mount Sinai of the Theotokos, Christ, and saints. In the mosaic, however, the angular placement of the throne and foot-stool alleviate the strict frontality of Mother and (much older) Child. The mosaicist rendered the furnishings in a perspective that, although imperfect, recalls once more the Greco-Roman roots of Byzantine art. The treatment of the folds of Christ's robes is, by comparison, even more schematic and flatter than in earlier mosaics. These seemingly contradictory stylistic features are not uncommon in Byzantine paintings and mosaics. Most significant about the images in the Hagia Sophia apse is their very existence, marking the end of iconoclasm in the Byzantine Empire.

12-22 Interior of the Katholikon (looking into the dome), Hosios Loukas, Greece, first quarter of 11th century.

The dome of the Katholikon rests on an octagon formed by squinches, which play the same role as pendentives in making the transition from a square base to a round dome but create a different visual effect.

HOSIOS LOUKAS Although the new emperors did not wait long to redecorate the churches of their predecessors, they undertook little new church construction in the decades following the renunciation of iconoclasm in 843. But in the 10th century and through the 12th, a number of monastic churches arose that are the flowers of Middle Byzantine architecture. They feature a brilliant series of variations on the domed central plan. From the exterior, the typical Middle Byzantine church building is a domed cube, with the dome rising above the square on a kind of cylinder or *drum*. The churches are small, vertical, high shouldered, and, unlike earlier Byzantine buildings, have exterior wall surfaces decorated with vivid patterns, probably reflecting Islamic architecture.

The Katholikon (FIGS. **12-20** and **12-21**, *bottom*) at Hosios Loukas (Saint Luke) in Greece, near ancient Delphi, dates to the early 11th century. One of two churches at the site—the other is the Church of the Theotokos (FIG. **12-21**, *top*) built during the second half of the 10th century—the Katholikon exemplifies church design during this second golden age of Byzantine art and architecture. Light stones framed by dark red bricks—the so-called *cloisonné* technique, a term borrowed from enamel work (FIG. **16-3**)—make up the walls. The interplay of arcuated windows, projecting apses, and varying roof lines further enhances this surface dynamism. The plans of both Hosios Loukas churches (FIG. **12-21**) show the form of a domed cross in square with four equal-length, vaulted cross arms

(the *Greek cross*). The dome of the smaller Church of the Theotokos rests on pendentives. In the case of the larger and later Katholikon, the architect placed the dome (FIG. **12-22**) over an octagon inscribed within a square. Forming the octagon are squinches (FIG. **12-5**, *right*), which play the same role as pendentives in making the transition from a square base to a round dome but create a different visual effect on the interior. This arrangement departs from the older designs, such as Santa Costanza's circular plan (FIG. **11-12**), San Vitale's octagonal plan (FIG. **12-7**), and Hagia Sophia's dome on pendentives rising from a square (FIG. **12-3**). The Katholikon's complex core lies within two rectangles. The outer one forms the exterior walls. Thus, in plan from the center out, a circle-octagon-square-oblong series exhibits an intricate interrelationship that is at once complex and unified.

12-22A Saint Sophia, Kiev, begun 1037.

The interior elevation of the Katholikon reflects its involved plan. Like earlier Byzantine buildings, the church creates a mystery out of space, surface, light, and dark. High and narrow, it forces the viewer's gaze to rise and revolve. The eye is drawn upward toward the dome (FIG. **12-22**), but much can distract it in the interplay of flat walls and concave recesses; wide and narrow openings; groin and barrel vaults; single, double, and triple windows; and illuminated and dark spaces. Middle Byzantine architects seem to have aimed for the creation of complex interior spaces with dramatically shifting perspectives.

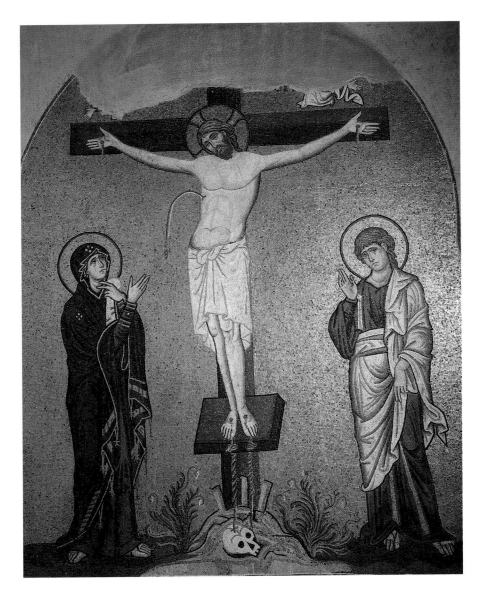

12-23 Crucifixion, mosaic in the Church of the Dormition, Daphni, Greece, ca. 1090–1100.

The Daphni Crucifixion is a subtle blend of Hellenistic style and the more abstract Byzantine manner. The Virgin Mary and Saint John point to Christ on the Cross as if to a devotional object.

DAPHNI Much of the original mosaic decoration of the Hosios Loukas Katholikon does not survive, but at Daphni, near Athens, the mosaics produced during Byzantium's second golden age fared much better. In the Church of the Dormition (from the Latin for "sleep," referring to the ascension of the Virgin Mary to Heaven at the moment of her death), at the Daphni monastery, the main elements of the late-11th-century pictorial program are intact, although the mosaics were restored in the 19th century. Gazing down from on high in the central dome (FIG. 12-1) is the fearsome image of Christ as *Pantokrator* (literally "ruler of all" in Greek but usually applied to Christ in his role as Last Judge of humankind). The dome mosaic is the climax of an elaborate hierarchical pictorial program including several New Testament episodes below. The Daphni Pantokrator is like a gigantic icon hovering dramatically in space. The mosaic serves to connect the awestruck worshiper in the church below with Heaven through Christ. The Pantokrator theme was a common one in churches throughout the Byzantine Empire. There was also a mosaic of the Pantokrator in the dome of the Hosios Loukas Katholikon. Today a painting (FIG. 12-22) replaces it.

On one of the walls below the Daphni dome, beneath the barrel vault of one arm of the Greek cross, an unknown artist depicted Christ's Crucifixion (FIG. 12-23) in a pictorial style characteristic of the posticonoclastic Middle Byzantine period. Like the Pantokrator mosaic in the dome, the Daphni Crucifixion is a subtle blend of the painterly Hellenistic style and the later more abstract and formalistic Byzantine style. The Byzantine artist fully assimilated classicism's simplicity, dignity, and grace into a perfect synthesis with Byzantine piety and pathos. The figures have regained the classical organic structure to a surprising degree, particularly compared with Justinianic figures (FIGS. 12-10 and 12-11). The style is a masterful adaptation of classical statuesque qualities to the linear Byzantine manner.

In quiet sorrow and resignation, the Virgin and Saint John flank the crucified Christ. A skull at the foot of the cross indicates Golgotha, the "place of skulls." The artist needed nothing else to set the scene. Symmetry and closed space combine to produce an effect of the motionless and unchanging aspect of the deepest mystery of the Christian religion, as recalled in the ceremony of the Eucharist. The picture is not a narrative of the historical event of the Crucifixion, the approach taken by the carver of the Early Christian ivory panel (FIG. 11-22) examined in the previous chapter. Nor is Christ a triumphant, beardless youth, oblivious to pain and defiant of the laws of gravity. Rather, he has a tilted head and sagging body, and although the Savior is not overtly in pain, blood and water spurt from the wound Longinus inflicted on him, as recounted in Saint John's gospel. The Virgin and John point to the figure on the cross as if to a devotional object. They act as intercessors between the viewer below and Christ, who, in the dome, appears as the Last Judge of all humans. The mosaic decoration of the church is the perfect complement to Christian liturgy.

SAINT MARK'S, VENICE The revival on a grand scale of church building, featuring vast stretches of mosaic-covered walls, was not confined to the Greek-speaking Byzantine East in the 10th to 12th centuries. A resurgence of religious architecture and of the

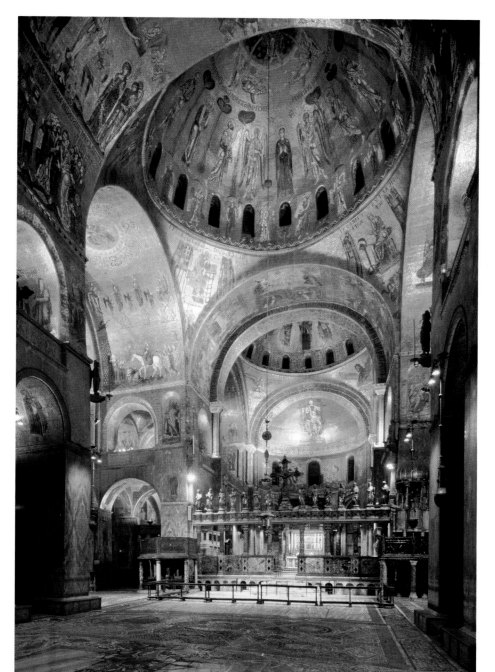

12-24 Interior of Saint Mark's (looking east), Venice, Italy, begun 1063.

Saint Mark's has a central dome over the crossing and four other domes over the four equal arms of the Greek cross. The walls and vaults are covered with 40,000 square feet of dazzling mosaics.

time. That church no longer exists, but its key elements were a cruciform plan with a central dome over the crossing and four other domes over the four equal arms of the Greek cross, as at Saint Mark's. Because of its importance to the city, the doges repeatedly remodeled the 11th-century structure, in time disguising its lower levels with Romanesque and Gothic additions. In 1807, Saint Mark's became the Cathedral of Venice.

The interior (FIG. **12-24**) of Saint Mark's is, like its plan, Byzantine in effect. Light enters through a row of windows at the bases of all five domes, vividly illuminating a rich cycle of mosaics. Both Byzantine and local artists worked on Saint Mark's mosaics over the course of several centuries. Most of the mosaics date to the 12th and 13th centuries. Cleaning and restoration on a grand scale have returned the mosaics to their original splendor, enabling visitors to experience the full radiance of mosaic (some 40,000 square feet of it) as it covers the walls, arches, vaults, and domes, as if it were a gold-brocaded figured fabric.

In the vast central dome, 80 feet above the floor and 42 feet in diameter, Christ ascends to Heaven in the presence of the Virgin Mary and the 12 apostles. The great arch framing the church crossing bears a narrative of the Crucifixion and Resurrection of Christ and of his liberation from death (Anastasis) of Adam and Eve, Saint John the Baptist, and other biblical figures. The mosaics have explanatory labels in both Latin and Greek, reflecting Venice's position as the key link between eastern and western Christendom in the later Middle Ages. The insubstantial figures on the walls, vaults, and domes appear weightless, and they project no farther from their flat field than do the elegant Latin and Greek letters above them. Nothing here reflects on the world of matter, of solids, of light and shade, of perspective space. Rather, the mosaics reveal the mysteries of the Christian faith.

12-24A *Pala d'Oro*, Saint Mark's, Venice, ca. 1105.

12-24B Archangel Michael icon, Venice, ca. 1100.

mosaicist's art also occurred in areas of the former Western Roman Empire where the ties with Constantinople were the strongest. In the Early Byzantine period, Venice, about 80 miles north of Ravenna on the eastern coast of Italy, was a dependency of that Byzantine stronghold. In 751, Ravenna fell to the Lombards, who wrested control of most of northern Italy from Constantinople. Venice, however, became an independent power. Its *doges* (dukes) enriched themselves and the city through seaborne commerce, serving as the crucial link between Byzantium and the West.

Venice had obtained the relics of Saint Mark from Alexandria in Egypt in 829, and the doges constructed the first Venetian shrine dedicated to the evangelist—a palace chapel and *martyrium* (martyr's shrine)—shortly thereafter. Fire destroyed the ninth-century chapel in 976. The Venetians then built a second shrine on the site, but a grandiose new church begun in 1063 by Doge Domenico Contarini (r. 1043–1071) replaced it. This building was modeled on the Church of the Holy Apostles at Constantinople, built in Justinian's

12-25 Pantokrator, Theotokos and Child, angels, and saints, apse mosaic in the cathedral at Monreale (Sicily), Italy, ca. 1180–1190.

In centrally planned Byzantine churches, the image of the Pantokrator usually appears in the main dome, but the Monreale cathedral is a longitudinal basilica and the semidome of the apse is its only vault.

12-25A Cappella Palatina, Palermo, begun 1142.

NORMAN SICILY Venetian success was matched in the western Mediterranean by the Normans, the northern French descendants of the Vikings (see Chapter 16) who, having driven the Arabs from Sicily, set up a powerful kingdom there. Though they were the enemies of Byzantium, the Normans, like the Venetians, assimilated Byzantine culture and even employed Byzantine artisans. The Normans also incorporated in their monuments elements of the Islamic art of the Arabs they had defeated (see Chapter 13). The Normans' Palatine (palace) Chapel at Palermo, with its prismatic (*muqarnas*) ceiling, a characteristic Muslim form (FIG. 13-17), is one example of the rich interplay of Western Christian, Byzantine, and Islamic cultures in Norman Sicily.

The mosaics of the great basilican church of Monreale, not far from Palermo, are striking evidence of Byzantine influence. They rival those of Saint Mark's in both quality and extent. One scholar has estimated that more than 100 million glass and stone tesserae were required for the Monreale mosaics. The Norman king William II paid for them, and he is portrayed twice, continuing the theme of royal presence and patronage of the much earlier Ravenna portraits of Justinian and Theodora (FIGS. 12-10 and 12-11) at San Vitale. In one panel, William, clearly labeled, unlike Justinian or his consort, stands next to the enthroned Christ, who places his hand on William's crown. In the second, the king kneels before the Virgin and presents her with a model of the Monreale church, a role that Bishop Ecclesius (FIG. 12-9), rather than the emperor or empress, played at San Vitale. As in the Ravenna church, the Monreale mosaic program commemorates both the piety and power of the ruler who reigns with divine authority.

The apse mosaics (FIG. 12-25) are especially impressive. The image of Christ as Pantokrator, as ruler and judge of Heaven and Earth, is in the vault. It served also as a colossal allusion to William's kingly power and a challenge to all who would dispute the royal right. In Byzantium proper, the Pantokrator's image usually appears in the main dome of centralized churches such as those at Daphni (FIG. 12-1) and Hosios Loukas (FIG. 12-22), but the Greek churches are monastic churches and were not built for the glorification of monarchs. Monreale, moreover, is a basilica—longitudinally planned in the Western tradition. The semidome of the apse, the only vault in the building and its architectural focus, was the most conspicuous place for the vast image with its political overtones. Below the Pantokrator in rank and dignity, the enthroned Theotokos is flanked by archangels and the 12 apostles, symmetrically arranged in balanced groups. Lower on the wall (and less elevated in the hierarchy) are popes, bishops, and other saints. The artists observed the stern formalities of Byzantine style here, far from Constantinople. The Monreale mosaics, like those at Saint Mark's (FIG. 12-24) in Venice, testify to the stature of Byzantium and of Byzantine art in medieval Italy.

12-26 Christ enthroned with saints (*Harbaville Triptych*), ca. 950. Ivory, central panel $9\frac{1}{2}'' \times 5\frac{1}{2}''$. Louvre, Paris.

In this small three-part shrine with hinged wings used for private devotion, the ivory carver depicted the figures with looser, more classical stances in contrast to the frontal poses of most Byzantine figures.

Ivory Carving and Painting

Costly carved ivories also were produced in large numbers in the Middle Byzantine period, when the three-part *triptych* replaced the earlier diptych as the standard format for ivory panels.

HARBAVILLE TRIPTYCH One example of this type is the *Harbaville Triptych* (FIG. 12-26), a portable shrine with hinged wings used for private devotion. Ivory triptychs were very popular—among people who could afford such luxurious items—and they often replaced icons for use in personal prayer. Carved on the wings of the *Harbaville Triptych*, both inside and out, are four pairs of full-length figures and two pairs of medallions depicting saints. A cross dominates the central panel on the back of the triptych (not illustrated). On the inside is a scene of *Deësis* (supplication). Saint John the Baptist and the Theotokos appear as intercessors, praying on behalf of the viewer to the enthroned Savior. Below them are five apostles.

The formality and solemnity usually associated with Byzantine art, visible in the mosaics of Ravenna and Monreale, yielded here to a softer, more fluid technique. The figures may lack true classical contrapposto, but the looser stances (most stand on bases, like freestanding statues) and three-quarter views of many of the heads relieve the hard austerity of the customary frontal pose. This more natural, classical spirit was a second, equally important, stylistic current of the Middle Byzantine period. It also surfaced in mural painting and book illumination. When the emperors lifted the ban against religious images and again encouraged religious painting at Constantinople, the impact was felt far and wide. The style varied from region to region, but a renewed enthusiasm for picturing the key New Testament figures and events was universal.

NEREZI In 1164, at Nerezi in Macedonia, Byzantine painters embellished Saint Pantaleimon with murals of great emotional power. One of these represents the Lamentation over the dead Christ

12-27 Lamentation over the dead Christ, wall painting, Saint Pantaleimon, Nerezi, Macedonia, 1164.

Working in the Balkans in an alternate Byzantine mode, this painter staged the emotional scene of the Lamentation in a hilly landscape below a blue sky and peopled it with fully modeled figures.

(FIG. **12-27**). It is an image of passionate grief. The artist captured Christ's followers in attitudes, expressions, and gestures of quite human bereavement. Joseph of Arimathea and the disciple Nicodemus kneel at his feet, while Mary presses her cheek against her dead son's face and Saint John clings to Christ's left hand. In the Gospels, neither Mary nor John was present at the entombment of Christ. Their inclusion here, as elsewhere in Middle Byzantine art, intensified for the viewer the emotional impact of Christ's death. Representations such as these parallel the development of liturgical hymns recounting the Virgin's lamenting her son's death on the Cross.

At Nerezi, the painter set the scene in a hilly landscape below a blue sky—a striking contrast to the abstract golden world of the mosaics favored for church walls elsewhere in the Byzantine Empire. The artist strove to make utterly convincing an emotionally charged realization of the theme by staging the Lamentation in a more natural setting and peopling it with fully modeled actors. This alternate representational mode is no less Byzantine than the frontal, flatter figures of Ravenna. In time, this more naturalistic style would also be emulated in Italy (FIG. **19-9**).

PARIS PSALTER Another example of this classical-revival style is a page from a book of the Psalms of David. The so-called *Paris Psalter* (FIG. **12-28**) reasserts the artistic values of the Greco-Roman past

12-28 David composing the Psalms, folio 1 verso of the *Paris Psalter,* ca. 950–970. Tempera on vellum, $1' 2\frac{1}{8}'' \times 10\frac{1}{4}''$. Bibliothèque Nationale, Paris.

During the so-called Macedonian Renaissance, Byzantine painters revived the classical style. David is here portrayed as if a Greek hero and is accompanied by personifications of Melody, Echo, and Bethlehem.

1 in.

with astonishing authority. Art historians believe the manuscript dates from the mid-10th century—the so-called Macedonian Renaissance, a time of enthusiastic and careful study of the language and literature of ancient Greece, and of humanistic reverence for the classical past. It was only natural that artists would once again draw inspiration from the Hellenistic naturalism of the pre-Christian Mediterranean world.

David, the psalmist, surrounded by sheep, goats, and his faithful dog, plays his harp in a rocky landscape with a town in the background. Similar settings appeared frequently in Pompeian murals. Befitting an ancient depiction of Orpheus, the Greek hero who could charm even inanimate objects with his music, allegorical figures accompany the Old Testament harpist. Melody looks over his shoulder, and Echo peers from behind a column. A reclining male figure points to a Greek inscription that identifies him as representing the mountain of Bethlehem. These allegorical figures do not appear in the Bible. They are the stock population of Greco-Roman painting. Apparently, the artist had seen a work from Late Antiquity or perhaps earlier and partly translated it into a Byzantine pictorial idiom. In works such as this, Byzantine artists kept the classical style alive in the Middle Ages.

VLADIMIR VIRGIN Nothing in Middle Byzantine art better demonstrates the rejection of the iconoclastic viewpoint than the painted icon's return to prominence. After the restoration of images, icons multiplied by the thousands to meet public and private demand. In the 11th century, the clergy began to display icons in hierarchical order (Christ, the Theotokos, John the Baptist, and then other saints, as on the *Harbaville Triptych*) in tiers on the *templon*, the low columnar screen separating the sanctuary from the main body of a Byzantine church.

The renowned *Vladimir Virgin* (FIG. **12-29**) is a masterpiece of Middle Byzantine icon painting. Descended from works such as the Mount Sinai icon (FIG. **12-18**), the *Vladimir Virgin* clearly reveals the stylized abstraction resulting from centuries of working and reworking the conventional image. The artist was probably a Constantinopolitan painter, and this icon exhibits all the characteristic Byzantine traits: the Virgin's long, straight nose and small mouth; the golden rays in the infant's drapery; the decorative sweep of the unbroken contour that encloses the two figures; and the flat silhouette against the golden ground. But the *Vladimir Virgin* is a much more tender and personalized image of the Theotokos than that in the Mount Sinai icon. Here Mary appears as the Virgin of Compassion, who presses her cheek against her son's in an intimate portrayal of Mother and Child. The image is also infused with a deep pathos as Mary contemplates the future sacrifice of her son. (The back of the icon bears images of the instruments of Christ's Passion.)

The *Vladimir Virgin*, like most icons, has seen hard service. Placed before or above altars in churches or private chapels, the icon became blackened by the incense and smoke from candles that burned before or below it. It was frequently repainted, often by inferior artists, and only the faces show the original surface. First painted in the late 11th or early 12th century, it was taken to Kiev (Ukraine) in 1131, then to Vladimir (Russia) in 1155 (hence its name), and in 1395, as a wonder-working image, to Moscow to protect that city from the Mongols. The Russians believed that the sacred picture saved the city of Kazan from later Tartar invasions and all of Russia from the Poles in the 17th century. The *Vladimir Virgin* is a historical symbol of Byzantium's religious and cultural mission to the Slavic world.

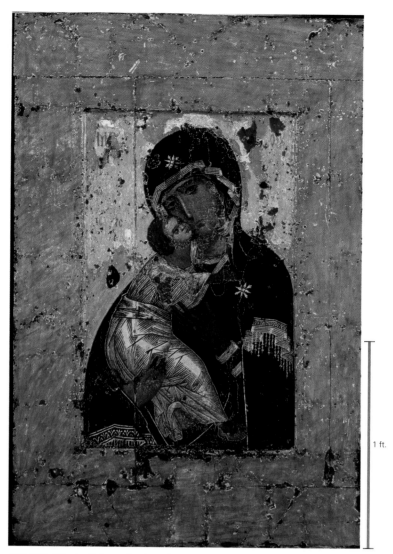

12-29 Virgin (Theotokos) and Child, icon (*Vladimir Virgin*), late 11th to early 12th centuries. Tempera on wood, original panel $2' 6\frac{1}{2}'' \times 1' 9''$. Tretyakov Gallery, Moscow.

In this icon, the artist depicted Mary as the Virgin of Compassion, who presses her cheek against her son's as she contemplates his future. The reverse side shows the instruments of Christ's Passion.

LATE BYZANTINE ART

When rule passed from the Macedonian to the Comnenian dynasty in the later 11th and the 12th centuries, three events of fateful significance changed Byzantium's fortunes for the worse. The Seljuk Turks conquered most of Anatolia. The Byzantine Orthodox Church broke finally with the Church of Rome. And the Crusades brought the Latins (a generic term for the peoples of the West) into Byzantine lands on their way to fight for the Cross against the Saracens (Muslims) in the Holy Land (see "The Crusades," Chapter 17, page 442).

Crusaders had passed through Constantinople many times en route to "smite the infidel" and had marveled at its wealth and magnificence. Envy, greed, religious fanaticism (the Latins called the Greeks "heretics"), and even ethnic enmity motivated the Crusaders when, during the Fourth Crusade in 1203 and 1204, the Venetians persuaded them to divert their expedition against the Muslims in Palestine and to attack Constantinople instead. The Crusaders took the city and sacked it. Nicetas Choniates, a contemporaneous historian, expressed the feelings of the Byzantines toward their attackers: "The accursed Latins would plunder our wealth and wipe out our race. . . . Between us there can be only an unbridgeable gulf of hatred. . . . They bear the Cross of Christ on their shoulders, but even the Saracens are kinder."[7]

The Latins set up kingdoms within Byzantium, notably in Constantinople itself. What remained of Byzantium split into three small states. The Palaeologans ruled one of these, the kingdom of Nicaea. In 1261, Michael VIII Palaeologus (r. 1259–1282) succeeded in recapturing Constantinople. But his empire was no more than a fragment, and even that disintegrated during the next two centuries. Isolated from the Christian West by Muslim conquests in the Balkans and besieged by Muslim Turks to the east, Byzantium sought help from the West. It was not forthcoming. In 1453, the Ottoman Turks, then a formidable power, took Constantinople and brought to an end the long history of Byzantium (see Chapter 13). But despite the state's grim political condition under the Palaeologan dynasty, the arts flourished well into the 14th century.

12-30A Saint Catherine, Thessaloniki, ca. 1280.

Painting

During the 14th and 15th centuries, artists throughout the Byzantine world produced masterpieces of mural and icon painting rivaling those of the earlier periods. Four characteristic examples from the old capital of Constantinople and as far away as Russia can serve to illustrate the range and quality of painting during the Late Byzantine period.

CHRIST IN CHORA A fresco (FIG. **12-30**) in the apse of the *parekklesion* (side chapel, in this instance a funerary chapel) of the Church of Christ in Chora in Constantinople depicts the Anastasis. One of many subsidiary subjects that made up the complex mosaic program of Saint Mark's (FIG. **12-24**) in Venice, the Anastasis is here central to a cycle of pictures portraying the themes of human mortality and redemption by Christ and of the intercession of the Virgin, both appropriate for a funerary chapel. Christ, trampling Satan and all the locks and keys of his prison house of Hell, raises Adam and Eve from their tombs. Looking on are John the Baptist, King David, and King Solomon on the left, and various martyr saints on the right. Christ, central and surrounded by a luminous mandorla, reaches out equally to Adam and Eve. The action is swift and smooth, the supple motions executed with the grace of a ballet. The figures float in a spiritual atmosphere, spaceless and without material mass or shadow-casting volume. This same smoothness and lightness can be seen in the modeling of the figures and the subtly nuanced coloration. The jagged abstractions of drapery found in

12-30 Anastasis, apse fresco in the parekklesion of the Church of Christ in Chora (now the Kariye Museum), Constantinople (Istanbul), Turkey, ca. 1310–1320. ◼◀

In this Late Byzantine funerary chapel, Christ, a white apparition surrounded by a luminous mandorla, raises Adam and Eve from their tombs as John the Baptist and Kings David and Solomon look on.

many earlier Byzantine frescoes and mosaics are gone in a return to the fluid delineation of drapery characteristic of the long tradition of classical illusionism.

Throughout the centuries, Byzantine artists looked back to Greco-Roman illusionism. But unlike classical artists, Byzantine painters and mosaicists were not concerned with the systematic observation of material nature as the source of their representations of the eternal. They drew their images from a persistent and conventionalized vision of a spiritual world unsusceptible to change. That consistent vision is what unites works as distant in time as the sixth-century apse mosaic (FIG. 12-13) at Mount Sinai and the 14th-century fresco in the Church of Christ in Chora.

OHRID ICONS Byzantine spirituality was perhaps most intensely revealed in icon painting. In the Late Byzantine period, the Early Byzantine templon developed into an *iconostasis,* a high screen with doors and tiers of icons. As its name implies, the iconostasis supported tiers of painted devotional images, which began to be produced again in large numbers, both in Constantinople and throughout the diminished Byzantine Empire.

One example (FIG. 12-31), notable for the lavish use of finely etched silver foil to frame the painted figure of Christ as Savior of

Souls, dates to the beginning of the 14th century. It comes from Saint Clement at Ohrid in Macedonia, where many Late Byzantine icons imported from the capital have been preserved. The painter of the Ohrid Christ, in a manner consistent with Byzantine art's conservative nature, adhered to an iconographical and stylistic tradition traceable to the earliest icons from the monastery at Mount Sinai. As elsewhere (for example, FIG. 12-1), the Savior holds a bejeweled Bible in his left hand while he blesses the faithful with his right hand. The style is typical of Byzantine eclecticism. Note especially the juxtaposition of Christ's fully modeled head and neck, which reveal the Byzantine painter's Greco-Roman heritage, with the schematic linear folds of Christ's garment, which do not envelop the figure but rather seem to be placed in front of it.

In the Late Byzantine period, icons often were painted on two sides because they were intended to be carried in processions. When deposited in the church, the icons were not mounted on the iconostasis but were exhibited on stands so worshipers could view both sides. The Ohrid icon of Christ has a painting of the Crucifixion on its reverse. Another double icon from Saint Clement's, also imported from Constantinople, represents the Virgin on the front as Christ's counterpart as Savior of Souls. The Annunciation (FIG. 12-32) appears on the reverse. With a commanding gesture of heavenly

1 ft.

1 ft.

12-31 Christ as Savior of Souls, icon from Saint Clement, Ohrid, Macedonia, early 14th century. Tempera, linen, and silver on wood, $3' \frac{1}{4}'' \times 2' 2\frac{1}{2}''$. Icon Gallery of Saint Clement, Ohrid. ▣

Notable for the lavish use of finely etched silver foil, this icon typifies Byzantine eclecticism. Christ's fully modeled head and neck contrast with the schematic linear folds of his garment.

12-32 Annunciation, reverse of two-sided icon from Saint Clement, Ohrid, Macedonia, early 14th century. Tempera and linen on wood, $3' \frac{1}{4}'' \times 2' 2\frac{3}{4}''$. Icon Gallery of Saint Clement, Ohrid.

Late Byzantine icons often were painted on two sides because they were intended to be carried in processions. On this icon the Virgin Mary appears on the front and this Annunciation scene on the back.

12-33 ANDREI RUBLYEV, Three angels (Old Testament Trinity), ca. 1410. Tempera on wood, 4′ 8″ × 3′ 9″. Tretyakov Gallery, Moscow. ▄◀

This exceptionally large icon, which features subtle lines and intensely vivid colors, is one of the masterworks of Russian painting. It depicts the three angels who appeared to Abraham, prefiguring the Trinity.

1 ft.

authority, the angel Gabriel announces to Mary that she is to be the Mother of God. She responds with a simple gesture conveying both astonishment and acceptance. The gestures and attitudes of the figures are again conventional, as are the highly simplified architectural props. The painter rendered the latter in inconsistent perspective derived from classical prototypes, but set the sturdy three-dimensional forms against an otherworldly gold sky, suggesting the sacred space in which the narrative unfolds. This icon also exemplifies the eclecticism that characterizes Byzantine art throughout its long history.

ANDREI RUBLYEV In Russia, icon painting flourished for centuries, extending the life of the Byzantine painting style well beyond the collapse of the Byzantine Empire in 1453. Russian paintings usually had strong patterns, firm lines, and intense contrasting colors. All served to heighten the legibility of the icons in the wavering candlelight and clouds of incense that worshipers encountered in church interiors. For many art historians, Russian painting reached a climax in the work of ANDREI RUBLYEV (ca. 1370–1430). His nearly five-foot-tall panel (FIG. **12-33**) depicting the three Old Testament angels who appeared to Abraham is a work of great spiritual power. It is also an unsurpassed example of subtle line in union with intensely vivid color. The angels sit about a table, each framed

with a halo and sweeping wings, three nearly identical figures distinguished only by their garment colors. The light linear play of the draperies sets off the tranquil demeanor of the figures. Color defines the forms and becomes more intense by the juxtaposition of complementary hues. The intense blue and green folds of the central figure's cloak, for example, stand out starkly against the deep-red robe and the gilded orange of the wings. In the figure on the left, the highlights of the orange cloak are an opalescent blue green. The unmodulated saturation, brilliance, and purity of the color harmonies are the hallmark of Rublyev's style.

THE THIRD ROME With the fall of Constantinople in 1453, Russia became Byzantium's self-appointed heir, defending Christendom against the infidel. The court of the tsar (the title derives from "Caesar") declared: "Because the Old Rome has fallen, and because the Second Rome, which is Constantinople, is now in the hands of the godless Turks, thy kingdom, O pious Tsar, is the Third Rome. . . . Two Romes have fallen, but the Third stands, and there shall be no more."[8] Rome, Byzantium, Russia—Old Rome, New Rome, and Third Rome—were a continuum, spanning two and a half millennia during which artists and architects produced many of the most significant paintings, sculptures, and buildings in the long history of art through the ages.

12-33A Large sakkos of Photius, ca. 1417.

BYZANTIUM

EARLY BYZANTINE ART, 527–726

Hagia Sophia, Constantinople, 532–537

▌ The reign of Justinian (r. 527–565) opened the first golden age of Byzantine art. Justinian was a great patron of the arts, and in Constantinople alone he built or restored more than 30 churches.

▌ Constructed in only five years, Hagia Sophia, a brilliant fusion of central and longitudinal plans, rivaled the architectural wonders of Rome. Its 180-foot-high dome rests on pendentives but seemed to contemporaries to be suspended "by a golden chain from Heaven."

▌ The seat of Byzantine power in Italy was Ravenna, which enjoyed its greatest prosperity under Justinian. San Vitale is Ravenna's greatest church. Its mosaics, with their weightless, hovering, frontal figures against a gold background, reveal the new Byzantine aesthetic.

San Vitale, Ravenna, 526–547

▌ Justinian also rebuilt the monastery at Mount Sinai in Egypt, where the finest Early Byzantine icons are preserved. In 726, however, Leo III (r. 717–741) enacted a ban against picturing the divine, initiating the era of iconoclasm (726–843).

MIDDLE BYZANTINE ART, 843–1204

Paris Psalter, ca. 950–970

▌ In 867, Basil I (r. 867–886) dedicated a new mosaic depicting the Theotokos (Mother of God) in Hagia Sophia. It marked the triumph of the iconophiles over the iconoclasts.

▌ Middle Byzantine art is stylistically eclectic. Mosaics with otherworldly golden backgrounds were common, but some paintings, for example those in the *Paris Psalter*, revived the naturalism of classical art.

▌ Middle Byzantine churches like those at Hosios Loukas have highly decorative exterior walls and feature domes that rest on drums above the center of a Greek cross. The climax of the interior mosaic programs was often an image of Christ as Pantokrator in the dome.

Katholikon, Hosios Loukas, first quarter of 11th century

LATE BYZANTINE ART, 1261–1453

Andrei Rublyev, Three angels, ca. 1410

▌ In 1204, Latin Crusaders sacked Constantinople, bringing to an end the second golden age of Byzantine art. In 1261, Michael VIII Palaeologus (r. 1259–1282) succeeded in retaking the city. Constantinople remained in Byzantine hands until the Ottoman Turks captured it in 1453.

▌ Important mural paintings of the Late Byzantine period are in the Constantinopolitan Church of Christ in Chora. An extensive picture cycle portrays Christ as Redeemer; in the apse he raises Adam and Eve from their tombs.

▌ Late Byzantine icons were displayed in tiers on an iconostasis or on individual stands so that the paintings on both sides could be seen. The great painting centers during this period were in Constantinople and Russia. The work of Andrei Rublyev is notable for its great spiritual power and intense colors.

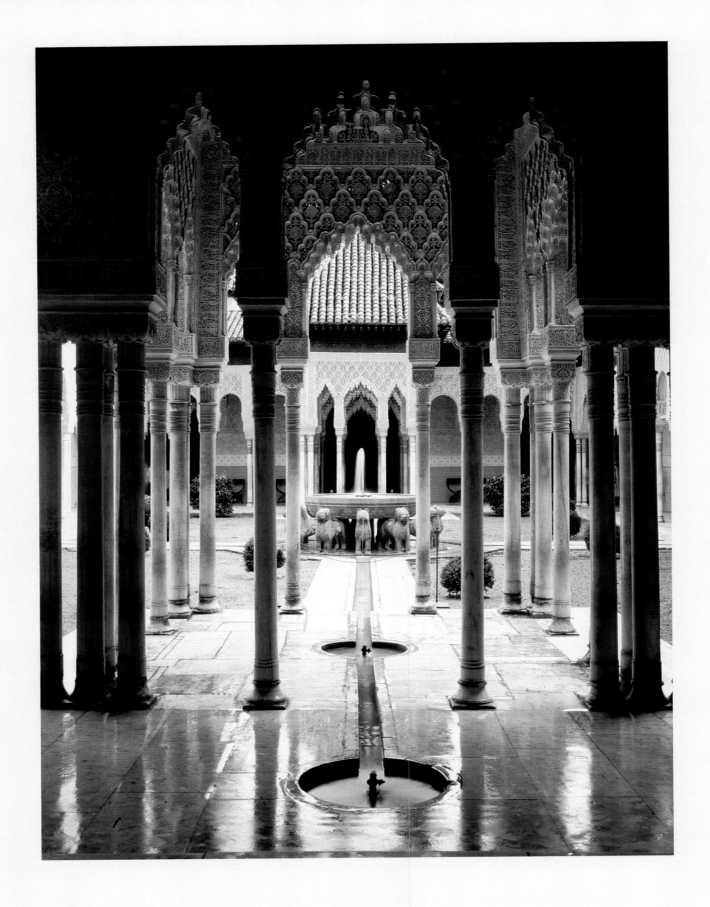

13-1 Court of the Lions, Palace of the Lions, Alhambra, Granada, Spain, 1354–1391.

The Palace of the Lions, named for its fountain's unusual statues, is distinctly Islamic in the use of multilobed pointed arches and the interweaving of Arabic calligraphy and abstract ornament in its stuccoed walls.

THE ISLAMIC WORLD

The religion of Islam (an Arabic word meaning "submission to God") arose among the peoples of the Arabian Peninsula early in the seventh century (see "Muhammad and Islam," page 343). At the time, the Arabs were nomadic herders and caravan merchants traversing the vast Arabian desert and settling and controlling its coasts. They were peripheral to the Byzantine and Persian empires. Yet within little more than a century, the eastern Mediterranean, which Byzantium once ringed and ruled, had become an Islamic lake, and the armies of Islam had subdued the Middle East, long the seat of Persian dominance and influence.

The swiftness of the Islamic advance is among the wonders of world history. By 640, Muslims ruled Syria, Palestine, and Iraq in the name of Allah. In 642, the Byzantine army abandoned Alexandria, marking the Muslim conquest of Lower (northern) Egypt. In 651, the successors of Muhammad ended more than 400 years of Sasanian rule in Iran (see Chapter 2). All of North Africa was under Muslim control by 710. A victory at Jerez de la Frontera in southern Spain in 711 seemed to open all of western Europe to the Muslims. By 732, they had advanced north to Poitiers in France, but an army of Franks under Charles Martel, the grandfather of Charlemagne, opposed them successfully (see Chapter 16), halting Muslim expansion at the Pyrenees. In Spain, in contrast, the Islamic rulers of Córdoba flourished until 1031, and not until 1492 did Muslim influence and power end in the Iberian Peninsula. That year the army of King Ferdinand and Queen Isabella, the sponsors of Columbus's voyage to the New World, overthrew the caliphs of Granada. In the East, the Muslims reached the Indus River by 751, and only in Anatolia could stubborn Byzantine resistance slow their advance. Relentless Muslim pressure against the shrinking Byzantine Empire eventually caused its collapse in 1453, when the Ottoman Turks entered Constantinople (see Chapter 12).

Military might alone, however, cannot account for the relentless and far-ranging sweep of Islam from Arabia to India to North Africa and Spain (MAP 13-1). That Islam endured in the conquered lands for centuries after the initial victories can be explained only by the nature of the Islamic faith and its appeal to millions of converts. Islam remains today one of the world's great religions, with adherents on all

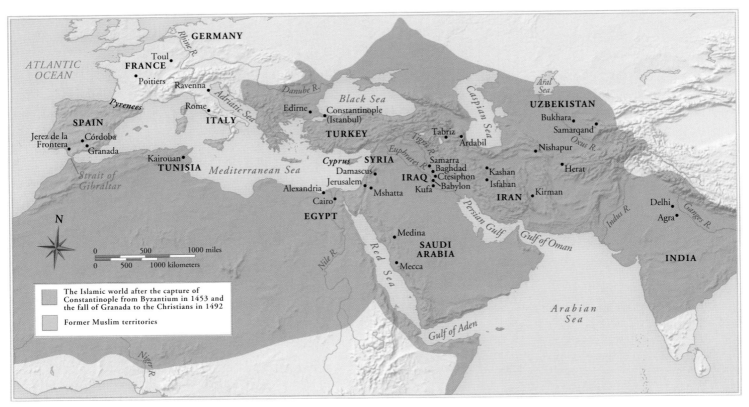

MAP 13-1 The Islamic world around 1500.

continents. Its sophisticated culture has had a profound impact around the globe. Arab scholars laid the foundations of arithmetic and algebra and made significant contributions to astronomy, medicine, and the natural sciences. Christian scholars in the West during the 12th and 13th centuries eagerly studied Arabic translations of Aristotle and other Greek writers of antiquity. Arabic love lyrics and poetic descriptions of nature inspired the early French troubadours.

The triumph of Islam also brought a new and compelling tradition to the history of world art and architecture. Like Islam itself, Islamic art spread quickly both eastward and westward from the land once inhabited by the peoples of the ancient Near East. In the Middle East and North Africa, Islamic art largely replaced Late Antique art. From a foothold in the Iberian Peninsula, Islamic art influenced Western medieval art. Islamic artists and architects also brought their distinctive style to South Asia, where a Muslim sultanate was established at Delhi in India in the early 13th century (see Chapter 26). In fact, perhaps the most famous building in Asia, the Taj Mahal (FIGS. 26-1 and 26-6) at Agra, is an Islamic mausoleum.

EARLY ISLAMIC ART

During the early centuries of Islamic history, the Muslim world's political and cultural center was the Fertile Crescent of ancient Mesopotamia (see Chapter 2). The caliphs of Damascus (capital of modern Syria) and Baghdad (capital of Iraq) appointed provincial governors to rule the vast territories they controlled. These governors eventually gained relative independence by setting up dynasties in various territories and provinces: the Umayyads in Syria (661–750) and in Spain (756–1031), the Abbasids in Iraq (750–1258, largely nominal after 945), the Fatimids in Egypt (909–1171), and so on.

Architecture

Like other potentates before and after, the Muslim caliphs were builders on a grand scale. The first Islamic buildings, both religious and secular, are in the Middle East, but important early examples of Islamic architecture still stand also in North Africa, Spain, and Central Asia.

DOME OF THE ROCK The first great Islamic building is the Dome of the Rock (FIG. **13-2**) in Jerusalem. The Muslims had taken the city from the Byzantines in 638, and the Umayyad caliph Abd al-Malik (r. 685–705) erected the monumental shrine between 687 and 692 as an architectural tribute to the triumph of Islam. The Dome of the Rock marked the coming of the new religion to the city that was—and still is—sacred to both Jews and Christians. The structure rises from a huge platform known as the Noble Enclosure, where in ancient times the Hebrews built the Temple of Solomon that the Roman emperor Titus destroyed in 70 (see Chapter 10). In time, the site took on additional significance as the reputed place where Adam was buried and where Abraham prepared to sacrifice Isaac. The rock that gives the building its name also later came to be identified with the spot from which Muhammad miraculously journeyed to Heaven and then, in the same night, returned to his home in Mecca.

As Islam took much of its teaching from Judaism and Christianity, so, too, its architects and artists borrowed and transformed design, construction, and ornamentation principles long applied in Byzantium and the Middle East. The Dome of the Rock is a domed octagon resembling San Vitale (FIG. **12-6**) in Ravenna in its basic design. In all likelihood, a neighboring Christian monument, Constantine's Church of the Holy Sepulchre, a domed rotunda, inspired the Dome of the Rock's designers. That fourth-century rotunda bore a family resemblance to the roughly contemporary Constantinian

Muhammad and Islam

Muhammad, founder of Islam and revered as its Final Prophet, was a native of Mecca on the west coast of Arabia. Born around 570 into a family of merchants in the great Arabian caravan trade, Muhammad was inspired to prophesy. Critical of the polytheistic religion of his fellow Arabs, he preached a religion of the one and only God ("Allah" in Arabic), whose revelations Muhammad received beginning in 610 and for the rest of his life. Opposition to Muhammad's message among the Arabs was strong enough to prompt the Prophet and his followers to flee from Mecca to a desert oasis eventually called Medina ("City of the Prophet"). Islam dates its beginnings from this flight in 622, known as the *Hijra* ("emigration").* Barely eight years later, in 630, Muhammad returned to Mecca with 10,000 soldiers. He took control of the city, converted the population to Islam, and destroyed all the idols. But he preserved as the Islamic world's symbolic center the small cubical building that had housed the idols, the *Kaaba* (from the Arabic for "cube"). The Arabs associated the Kaaba with the era of Abraham and Ishmael, the common ancestors of Jews and Arabs. Muhammad died in Medina in 632.

The essential meaning of Islam is acceptance of and submission to Allah's will. Believers in Islam are called Muslims ("those who submit"). Islam requires them to live according to the rules laid down in the collected revelations communicated through Muhammad during his lifetime. The *Koran,* Islam's sacred book, codified by the Muslim ruler Uthman (r. 644–656), records Muhammad's revelations. The word "Koran" means "recitations"—a reference to the archangel Gabriel's instructions to Muhammad in 610 to "recite in the name of Allah." The Koran is composed of 114 *surahs* ("chapters") divided into verses.

The profession of faith in the one God, Allah, is the first of five obligations binding all Muslims. In addition, the faithful must worship five times daily facing in Mecca's direction, give alms to the poor, fast during the month of Ramadan, and once in a lifetime—if possible—make a pilgrimage to Mecca. The revelations in the Koran are not the only guide for Muslims. Muhammad's exemplary ways and customs, collected in the *Sunnah,* offer models to the faithful on ethical problems of everyday life. The reward for the Muslim faithful is Paradise.

Islam has much in common with Judaism and Christianity. Its adherents think of it as a continuation, completion, and in some sense a reformation of those other great monotheisms. Islam incorporates many of the Old Testament teachings, with their sober ethical standards and rejection of idol worship, and those of the New Testament Gospels. Muslims acknowledge Adam, Abraham, Moses, and Jesus as the prophetic predecessors of Muhammad, the final and greatest of the prophets. Muhammad did not claim to be divine, as did Jesus. Rather, he was God's messenger, the purifier and perfecter of the common faith of Jews, Christians, and Muslims in one God. Islam also differs from Judaism and Christianity in its simpler organization. Muslims worship God directly, without a hierarchy of rabbis, priests, or saints acting as intermediaries.

In Islam, as Muhammad defined it, religious and secular authority were united even more completely than in Byzantium. Muhammad established a new social order, replacing the Arabs' old decentralized tribal one, and took complete charge of his community's temporal as well as spiritual affairs. After Muhammad's death, the *caliphs* (from the Arabic for "successor") continued this practice of uniting religious and political leadership in one ruler.

*Muslims date events beginning with the Hijra in the same way Christians reckon events from Christ's birth, and the Romans before them began their calendar with Rome's foundi ng by Romulus and Remus in 753 BCE. The Muslim year, however, is a 354-day year of 12 lunar months, and dates cannot be converted by simply subtracting 622 from Christian-era dates.

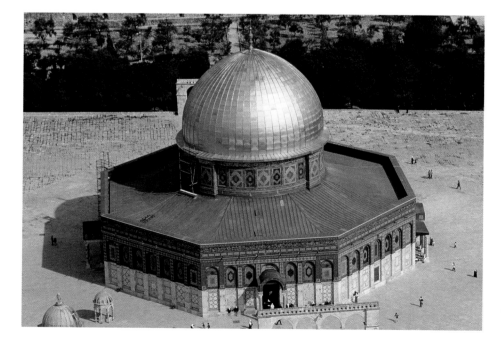

13-2 Aerial view of the Dome of the Rock, Jerusalem, 687–692.

Abd al-Malik erected the Dome of the Rock to mark the triumph of Islam in Jerusalem on a site sacred to Muslims, Christians, and Jews. The shrine takes the form of an octagon with a towering dome.

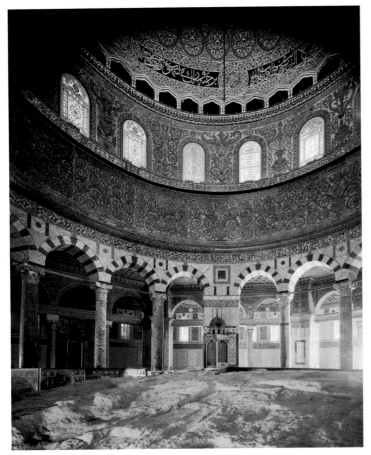

13-3 Interior of the Dome of the Rock, Jerusalem, 687–692.

Tiles from the 16th century adorn the exterior of the Dome of the Rock, but the interior's original mosaic ornament is preserved. The mosaics conjure the imagery of Paradise awaiting Muslims.

mausoleum later dedicated as Santa Costanza (FIGS. 11-11 and 11-12) in Rome. The Dome of the Rock is a member of the same extended family. Its double-shelled wooden dome, however, some 60 feet across and 75 feet high, so dominates the elevation as to reduce the octagon to function merely as its base. This soaring, majestic unit creates a decidedly more commanding effect than that produced by Late Roman and Byzantine domical structures (FIGS. 12-2 and 12-6). The silhouettes of those domes are comparatively insignificant when seen from the outside.

The building's exterior has been much restored. Tiling from the 16th century and later has replaced the original mosaic. Yet the vivid, colorful patterning that wraps the walls like a textile is typical of Islamic ornamentation. It contrasts markedly with Byzantine brickwork and Greco-Roman sculptured decoration. The interior's rich mosaic ornament (FIG. 13-3) has been preserved and suggests the original appearance of the exterior walls. Islamic practice does not significantly distinguish interior and exterior decor.

GREAT MOSQUE, DAMASCUS The Umayyads transferred their capital from Mecca to Damascus in 661. There, Abd al-Malik's son, the caliph al-Walid (r. 705–715), purchased a Byzantine church (formerly a Roman temple) and built an imposing new mosque for the expanding Muslim population (see "The Mosque," page 345). The Umayyads demolished the church, but they used the Roman precinct walls as a foundation for their own construction. Like the Dome of

the Rock, Damascus's Great Mosque (FIGS. 13-4 and 13-5) owes much to Roman and Early Christian architecture. The Islamic builders incorporated stone blocks, columns, and capitals salvaged from the earlier structures on the land al-Walid acquired for his mosque. Pier *arcades* reminiscent of Roman aqueducts frame the courtyard (FIG. 13-5). The minarets, two at the southern corners and one at the northern side of the enclosure—the earliest in the Islamic world—are modifications of the preexisting Roman square towers. The grand prayer hall, taller than the rest of the complex, is on the south side of the courtyard (facing Mecca). Its main entrance is distinguished by a facade with a pediment and arches, recalling Roman and Byzantine models. The facade faces into the courtyard, like a Roman forum temple (FIG. 10-12), a plan maintained throughout the long history of mosque architecture. The Damascus mosque synthesizes elements received from other cultures into a novel architectural unity, which includes the distinctive Islamic elements of mihrab, mihrab dome, minbar, and minaret.

An extensive cycle of mosaics once covered the walls of the Great Mosque. In one of the surviving sections (FIG. 13-4), a conch-shell niche "supports" an arcaded pavilion with a flowering rooftop flanked by structures shown in classical perspective. Like the architectural design, the mosaics owe much to Roman, Early Christian, and Byzantine art. Indeed, some evidence indicates that the Great Mosque mosaics were the work of Byzantine mosaicists. Characteristically, temples, clusters of houses, trees, and rivers compose the

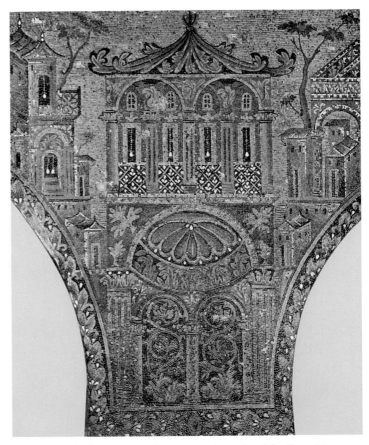

13-4 Detail of a mosaic in the courtyard arcade of the Great Mosque, Damascus, Syria, 706–715.

The mosaics of the Great Mosque at Damascus are probably the work of Byzantine artists and include buildings and landscape elements common in Late Antique art, but exclude any zoomorphic forms.

The Mosque

Islamic religious architecture is closely related to Muslim prayer, an obligation laid down in the Koran for all Muslims. In Islam, worshiping can be a private act and requires neither prescribed ceremony nor a special locale. Only the *qibla*—the direction (toward Mecca) Muslims face while praying—is important. But worship also became a communal act when the first Muslim community established a simple ritual for it. To celebrate the Muslim sabbath, which occurs on Friday, the community convened each Friday at noon, probably in the Prophet's house in Medina. The main feature of Muhammad's house was a large square court with rows of palm trunks supporting thatched roofs along the north and south sides. The southern side, which faced Mecca, was wider and had a double row of trunks. The *imam,* or leader of collective worship, stood on a stepped pulpit, or *minbar,* set up in front of the southern (qibla) wall.

These features became standard in the Islamic house of worship, the *mosque* (from Arabic "masjid," a place of prostration), where the faithful gathered for the five daily prayers. The *congregational mosque* (also called the *Friday mosque* or *great mosque*) was ideally large enough to accommodate a community's entire population for the Friday noon prayer. A very important feature both of ordinary mosques and of congregational mosques is the *mihrab* (FIG. 13-8, no. 2), a semicircular niche usually set into the qibla wall. Often a dome over the bay in front of it marked its position (FIGS. 13-5 and 13-8, no. 3). The niche was a familiar Greco-Roman architectural feature, generally enclosing a statue. Scholars still debate its origin, purpose, and meaning in Islamic architecture. The mihrab originally

may have honored the place where the Prophet stood in his house at Medina when he led communal worship.

In some mosques, a *maqsura* precedes the mihrab. The maqsura is the area generally reserved for the ruler or his representative and can be quite elaborate in form (FIG. 13-12). Many mosques also have one or more *minarets* (FIGS. 13-5, 13-9, AND 13-20), towers used to call the faithful to worship. When buildings of other faiths were converted into mosques, the Muslims clearly signaled the change on the exterior by the erection of minarets (FIG.12-2). *Hypostyle halls,* communal worship halls with roofs held up by a multitude of columns (FIGS. 13-8, no. 4, and 13-11), are characteristic features of early mosques. Later variations include mosques with four *iwans* (vaulted rectangular recesses), one on each side of the courtyard (FIGS. 13-22 and 13-23), and *central-plan* mosques with a single large dome-covered interior space (FIGS. 13-20 and 13-21), as in Byzantine churches, some of which later became mosques (FIG. 12-4).

The mosque's origin is still in dispute, although one prototype may well have been the Prophet's house in Medina. Today, despite many variations in design and detail (an adobe-and-wood mosque in Mali, FIGS. 15-1 and 15-8, is discussed later in the context of African architecture) and the employment of modern building techniques and materials unknown in Muhammad's day, the mosque's essential features are unchanged. All mosques, wherever they are built and whatever their plan, are oriented toward Mecca, and the faithful worship facing the qibla wall.

13-5 Aerial view of the Great Mosque, Damascus, Syria, 706–715. ◼◀

The hypostyle type of mosque most closely recalls the layout of Muhammad's house in Medina. Damascus's Great Mosque also owes a debt to Roman and Early Christian architecture in its plan and decoration.

pictorial fields, bounded by stylized vegetal designs also found in Roman, Early Christian, and Byzantine ornament. No zoomorphic forms, human or animal, appear in either the pictorial or ornamental spaces. This is true of all the mosaics in the Great Mosque as well as the mosaics in the earlier Dome of the Rock (FIG. 13-3). Islamic tradition shuns the representation of fauna of any kind in sacred

places. Accompanying (but now lost) inscriptions explained the world shown in the Damascus mosaics, suspended miragelike in a featureless field of gold, as an image of Paradise. Many passages from the Koran describe the gorgeous places of Paradise awaiting the faithful—gardens, groves of trees, flowing streams, and "lofty chambers."

UMAYYAD PALACE, MSHATTA

The Umayyad rulers of Damascus constructed numerous palatial residences throughout their domains. The urban palaces are lost, but some rural palaces survive. The latter were not merely idyllic residences removed from the congestion, noise, and disease of the cities. They seem to have served as nuclei for the agricultural development of acquired territories and possibly as hunting lodges. In addition, the Islamic palaces were symbols of authority over new lands as well as expressions of their owners' wealth.

One of the most impressive Umayyad palaces, despite the fact that it was never completed, is at Mshatta in the Jordanian desert. Its plan (FIG. 13-6) resembles that of Diocletian's palace (FIG. 10-74) at Split, which in turn reflects the layout of a Roman fortified camp. The high walls of the Mshatta palace incorporate 25 towers but lack parapet walkways for patrolling guards. The walls, nonetheless, offered safety from marauding nomadic tribes and provided privacy for the caliph and his entourage. Visitors entered the palace through a large portal on the south side. To the right was a mosque (FIG. 13-6, no. 2; the plan shows the mihrab niche in the qibla wall), in which the rulers and their guests could fulfill their obligation to pray five times a day. A small ceremonial area and an immense open courtyard separated the mosque from the palace's residential wing and official audience hall. Most Umayyad palaces also boasted fairly elaborate bathing facilities that displayed technical features, such as heating systems, adopted from Roman baths. Just as under the Roman Empire, these baths probably served more than merely hygienic purposes. Indeed, in several Umayyad palaces, excavators have uncovered in the baths paintings and sculptures of hunting and other secular themes, including depictions of dancing women—themes traditionally associated with royalty in the Near East. Large halls frequently attached to many of these baths seem to have been used as places of entertainment, as was the case in Roman times. Thus, the bath-spa as social center, a characteristic amenity of Roman urban culture that died out in the Christian world, survived in Islamic culture.

A richly carved stone frieze (FIG. 13-7) more than 16 feet high enlivens the facade of the Mshatta palace. Triangles contain large rosettes projecting from a field densely covered with curvilinear,

13-6 Plan of the Umayyad palace, Mshatta, Jordan, ca. 740–750 (after Alberto Berengo Gardin).

The fortified palace at Mshatta resembled Diocletian's palace (FIG. 10-74) at Split and incorporated the amenities of Roman baths but also housed a mosque in which the caliph could worship five times daily.

0 25 50 75 100 feet
0 10 20 30 meters

N

1. Entrance gate
2. Mosque
3. Small courtyard
4. Large courtyard
5. Audience hall

vegetal designs. No two triangles are exactly alike. Animals appear in some of them. Similar compositions of birds, felines, and vegetal scrolls can be found in Roman, Byzantine, and Sasanian art. The Mshatta frieze, however, in keeping with Islam's disavowal of representing living things in sacred contexts, has no animal figures to the right of the entrance portal—that is, on the part of the facade corresponding to the mosque's qibla wall.

BAGHDAD In 750, after years of civil war, the Abbasids, who claimed descent from Abbas, an uncle of Muhammad, overthrew the Umayyad caliphs. The new rulers moved the capital from Damascus to a site in Iraq near the old Sasanian capital of Ctesiphon (FIG. 2-27). There the caliph al-Mansur (r. 754–775) established a new capital, Baghdad, which he called Madina al-salam, the City of Peace. The city was laid out in 762 at a time astrologers determined as favorable. It

13-7 Frieze of the Umayyad palace, Mshatta, Jordan, ca. 740–750. Limestone, 16′ 7″ high. Museum für Islamische Kunst, Staatliche Museen, Berlin.

A long stone frieze richly carved with geometric, plant, and animal motifs decorated the facade of the Mshatta palace. No animals appear, however, on the exterior wall of the palace's mosque.

13-8 Aerial view (*left*) and plan (*right*) of the Great Mosque, Kairouan, Tunisia, ca. 836–875. ■◀

The arcaded forecourt in front of the hypostyle hall of the Kairouan mosque resembles a Roman forum (FIG. 10-43), but it incorporates the distinctive Islamic elements of mihrab, mihrab dome, minbar, and minaret.

1. Qibla wall
2. Mihrab
3. Mihrab dome
4. Hypostyle prayer hall
5. Nave
6. Entrance dome
7. Forecourt
8. Minaret

0   25   50   75   100 feet
0   10   20   30 meters

was round in plan, about a mile and a half in diameter. The shape signified that the new capital was the center of the universe. At the city's center was the caliph's palace, oriented to the four compass points. For almost 300 years Baghdad was the hub of Arab power and of a brilliant Islamic culture. The Abbasid caliphs were renowned throughout the world and even established diplomatic relations with Charlemagne in Germany. The Abbasids lavished their wealth on art, literature, and science and were responsible for the translation of numerous Greek texts that otherwise would have been lost. Many of these works were introduced to the medieval West through their Arabic versions.

GREAT MOSQUE, KAIROUAN Of all the variations in mosque plans, the hypostyle mosque most closely reflects the mosque's supposed origin, Muhammad's house in Medina (see "The Mosque," page 345). One of the finest hypostyle mosques, still in use today, is the mid-eighth-century Great Mosque (FIG. 13-8) at Kairouan in Abbasid Tunisia. It still houses its carved wooden minbar of 862, the oldest known. The precinct takes the form of a slightly askew parallelogram of huge scale, some 450 × 260 feet. Built of stone, its walls have sturdy buttresses, square in profile. A series of lateral entrances on the east and west lead to an arcaded forecourt (FIG. 13-8, no. 7) resembling a Roman forum (FIG. 10-43), oriented north-south on axis with the mosque's impressive minaret (no. 8) and the two domes of the hypostyle prayer hall (no. 4). The first dome (no. 6) is over the entrance bay, the second (no. 3) over the bay that fronts the mihrab (no. 2) set into the qibla wall (no. 1). A raised nave connects the domed spaces and prolongs the north-south axis of the minaret and courtyard. Eight columned aisles flank the nave on either side, providing space for a large congregation.

MALWIYA MINARET, SAMARRA The three-story minaret of the Kairouan mosque is square in plan, and scholars believe it is a near copy of a Roman lighthouse, but minarets can take a variety of forms. Perhaps the most striking and novel is that of the immense (more than 45,000 square yards) Great Mosque at Samarra, Iraq, the largest mosque in the world. The Abbasid caliph al-Mutawakkil (r. 847–861) erected it between 848 and 852. Known as the Malwiya ("snail shell" in Arabic) Minaret (FIG. 13-9) and more than 165 feet

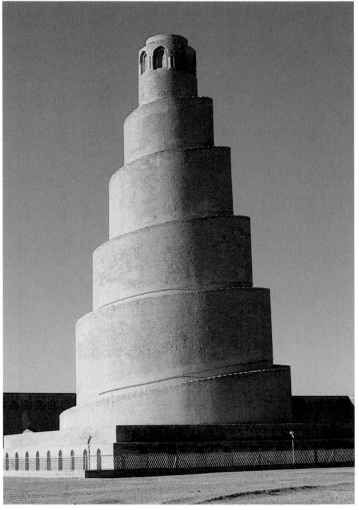

13-9 Malwiya Minaret, Great Mosque, Samarra, Iraq, 848–852.

The unique spiral Malwiya (snail shell) Minaret of Samarra's Great Mosque is more than 165 feet tall and can be seen from afar. It served to announce the presence of Islam in the Tigris Valley.

Early Islamic Art **347**

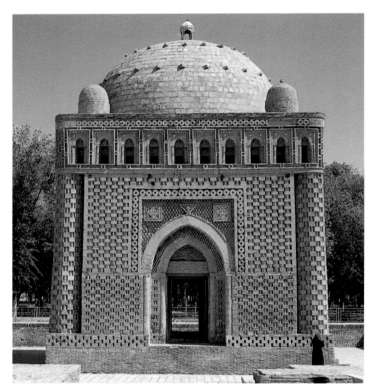

13-10 Mausoleum of the Samanids, Bukhara, Uzbekistan, early 10th century.

Monumental tombs were virtually unknown in the early Islamic period. The Samanid mausoleum at Bukhara is one of the oldest. Its dome-on-cube form had a long afterlife in Islamic funerary architecture.

Babel (Babylon's ziggurat; see "Babylon, City of Wonders," Chapter 2, page 48). Too tall to have been used to call Muslims to prayer, the Malwiya Minaret, visible from a considerable distance in the flat plain around Samarra, was probably intended to announce the presence of Islam in the Tigris Valley. Unfortunately, in 2005 the minaret suffered some damage during the Iraqi insurgency.

SAMANID MAUSOLEUM, BUKHARA Dynasties of governors who exercised considerable independence while recognizing the ultimate authority of the Baghdad caliphs oversaw the eastern realms of the Abbasid Empire. One of these dynasties, the Samanids (r. 819–1005), presided over the eastern frontier beyond the Oxus River (Transoxiana) on the border with India. In the early 10th century, they erected an impressive domed brick mausoleum (FIG. **13-10**) at Bukhara in modern Uzbekistan. Monumental tombs were virtually unknown in the early Islamic period. Muhammad opposed elaborate burials and instructed his followers to bury him in a simple unmarked grave. In time, however, the Prophet's resting place in Medina acquired a wooden screen and a dome. By the ninth century, Abbasid caliphs were laid to rest in dynastic mausoleums.

The Samanid mausoleum at Bukhara is one of the earliest preserved tombs in the Islamic world. Constructed of baked bricks, it takes the form of a dome-capped cube with slightly sloping sides. With exceptional skill, the builders painstakingly shaped the bricks to create a vivid and varied surface pattern. Some of the bricks form *engaged columns* (half-round, attached columns) at the corners. A brick *blind arcade* (a series of arches in relief, with blocked openings) runs around all four sides. Inside, the walls are as elaborate as the exterior. The brick dome rests on arcuated brick *squinches* (see "Pendentives and Squinches," Chapter 12, page 315) framed by engaged *colonnettes* (thin columns). The dome-on-cube form had a long and distinguished future in Islamic funerary architecture (FIGS. **13-18** and **26-1**).

tall, it now stands alone, but originally a bridge linked it to the mosque. The distinguishing feature of the brick tower is its stepped spiral ramp, which increases in slope from bottom to top. Once thought to be an ancient Mesopotamian *ziggurat,* the Samarra minaret inspired some European depictions of the biblical Tower of

GREAT MOSQUE, CÓRDOBA At the opposite end of the Muslim world, Abd al-Rahman I, the only eminent Umayyad to escape the Abbasid massacre of his clan in Syria, fled to Spain in 750. There, the Arabs had overthrown the Christian kingdom of the Visigoths in 711. The Arab military governors of the peninsula accepted the fugitive as their overlord, and he founded the Spanish Umayyad dynasty, which lasted almost three centuries. The capital of the Spanish Umayyads was Córdoba, which became the center of a brilliant culture rivaling that of the Abbasids at Baghdad and exerting major influence on the civilization of the Christian West.

The jewel of the capital at Córdoba was its Great Mosque, begun in 784 and enlarged several times during the 9th and 10th centuries. It eventually became one of the largest mosques in the Islamic West. The hypostyle prayer hall (FIG. **13-11**) has 36

13-11 Prayer hall of the Great Mosque, Córdoba, Spain, 8th to 10th centuries.

Córdoba was the capital of the Umayyad dynasty in Spain. In the Great Mosque's hypostyle prayer hall, 36 piers and 514 columns support a unique series of double-tiered horseshoe-shaped arches.

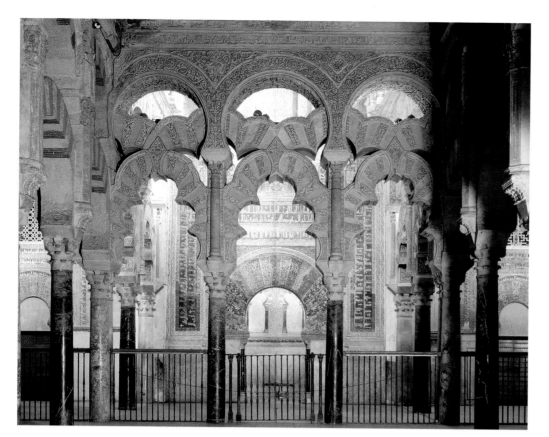

13-12 Maqsura of the Great Mosque, Córdoba, Spain, 961–965.

The maqsura of the Córdoba mosque was reserved for the caliph and connected to his palace. Its design is a prime example of Islamic experimentation with highly decorative multi-lobed arches.

piers and 514 columns topped by a unique system of double-tiered arches that carried a wooden roof (later replaced by vaults). The two-story system was the builders' response to the need to raise the roof to an acceptable height using short columns that had been employed earlier in other structures. The lower arches are horseshoe-shaped, a form perhaps adapted from earlier Near Eastern architecture or of Visigothic origin (FIG. 16-10). In the West, the horseshoe arch quickly became closely associated with Muslim architecture. Visually, these arches seem to billow out like windblown sails, and they contribute greatly to the light and airy effect of the Córdoba mosque's interior.

The caliph al-Hakam II (r. 961–976) undertook major renovations to the mosque. His builders expanded the prayer hall and added a series of domes. They also erected the elaborate maqsura (FIG. 13-12), the area reserved for the caliph and connected to his palace by a corridor in the qibla wall. The Córdoba maqsura is a prime example of Islamic experimentation with highly decorative, multilobed arches. The builders created rich and varied abstract patterns and further enhanced the magnificent effect of the complex arches by sheathing the walls with marbles and mosaics. The mosaicists and even the tesserae were brought to Spain from Constantinople by al-Hakam II, who wished to emulate the great mosaic-clad monuments his Umayyad predecessors had erected in Jerusalem (FIG. 13-3) and Damascus (FIG. 13-4).

The same desire for decorative effect also inspired the design of the dome (FIG. 13-13) that covers the area in front of the mihrab. One of the four domes built during the 10th century to emphasize the axis leading to the mihrab, the dome rests on an octagonal base of arcuated squinches. Crisscrossing ribs form an intricate pattern centered on two squares set at 45-degree angles to each other. The mosaics are the work of the same Byzantine artists responsible for the maqsura's decoration.

13-13 Dome in front of the mihrab of the Great Mosque, Córdoba, Spain, 961–965.

The dome in front of the Córdoba mihrab rests on an octagonal base of arcuated squinches. Crisscrossing ribs form an intricate decorative pattern. Byzantine artists fashioned the mosaic ornament.

Early Islamic Art **349**

Luxury Arts

The furnishings of Islamic mosques and palaces reflect a love of sumptuous materials and rich decorative patterns. Muslim artisans skillfully worked metal, wood, glass, and ivory into a great variety of objects for sacred spaces or the home. Glass workers used colored glass with striking effect in mosque lamps. Artisans produced numerous ornate ceramics of high quality and created basins, ewers, jewel cases, writing boxes, and other decorative items from bronze or brass, often engraving these pieces and adding silver inlays. Artists employed silk and wool to fashion textiles featuring both abstract and pictorial motifs. Because wood is scarce in most of the Islamic world, the kinds of furniture used in the West—beds, tables, and chairs—are rare in Muslim buildings. Movable furnishings, therefore, do not define Islamic architectural spaces. A room's function (eating or sleeping, for example) can be changed simply by rearranging the carpets and cushions.

SILK Silk textiles are among the glories of Islamic art. Unfortunately, because of their fragile nature, early Islamic textiles are rare today and often fragmentary. Silk thread was also very expensive. Silkworms, which can flourish only in certain temperate regions, produce silk. Silk textiles were manufactured first in China in the third millennium BCE. They were shipped over what came to be called the Silk Road through Asia to the Middle East and Europe (see "Silk and the Silk Road," Chapter 7, page 188).

One of the earliest Islamic silks (FIG. **13-14**) is today in Nancy, France, and probably dates to the eighth century. Unfortunately, the textile is fragmentary, and its colors, once rich blues, greens, and oranges, faded long ago. Said to come from Zandana near Bukhara, the precious fabric survives because of its association with the relics of Saint Amon housed in Toul Cathedral. It may have been used to wrap the treasures when they were transported to France in 820. The design, perhaps based on Sasanian models, consists of repeated medallions with confronting lions flanking a palm tree. Other animals scamper across the silk between the *roundels* (*tondi*, or circular frames). Such zoomorphic motifs are foreign to the decorative vocabulary of mosque architecture, but they could be found in Muslim households—even in Muhammad's in Medina. The Prophet, however, objected to curtains decorated with human or animal figures and permitted only cushions adorned with animals or birds.

METALWORK One of the most striking examples of Islamic metalwork is the cast brass ewer (FIG. **13-15**) in the form of a bird signed by SULAYMAN and dated 796. Some 15 inches tall, the ewer is nothing less than a freestanding statuette, although the holes between the eyes and beak function as a spout and betray its utilitarian purpose. The decoration on the body, which bears traces of silver and copper inlay, takes a variety of forms. In places, the incised lines seem to suggest natural feathers, but the rosettes on the neck, the large

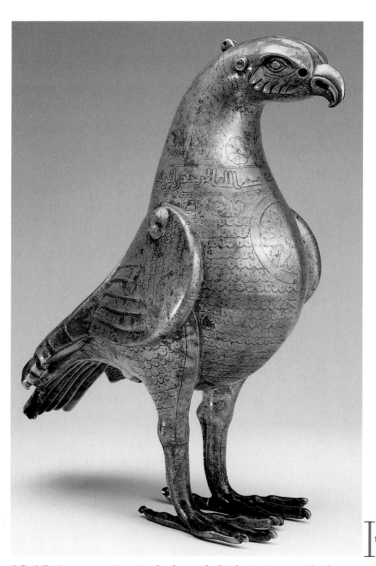

13-14 Confronting lions and palm tree, fragment of a textile said to be from Zandana, near Bukhara, Uzbekistan, eighth century. Silk compound twill, 2′ 11″ × 2′ 9½″. Musée Historique de Lorraine, Nancy.

Early examples of Islamic silk textiles are rare because of their fragile nature. This fragmentary fabric from Uzbekistan features animal motifs that were common in secular contexts but shunned for mosques.

13-15 SULAYMAN, Ewer in the form of a bird, 796. Brass with silver and copper inlay, 1′ 3″ high. Hermitage, Saint Petersburg.

Signed and dated by its maker, this utilitarian bird ewer resembles a freestanding statuette. The engraved decoration of the body combines natural feathers with abstract motifs and Arabic calligraphy.

13-16 Koran page with the beginning of surah 18, "Al-Kahf" (The Cave), 9th or early 10th century. Ink and gold on vellum, $7\frac{1}{4}'' \times 10\frac{1}{4}''$. Chester Beatty Library and Oriental Art Gallery, Dublin.

The stately rectilinear Kufic script was used in the oldest known Korans. This page has five text lines and a palm-tree finial but characteristically does not include any depictions of animals or humans.

1 in.

medallions on the breast, and the inscribed collar have no basis in anatomy. Similar motifs appear in Islamic textiles, pottery, and architectural tiles. The ready adaptability of motifs to various scales and techniques illustrates both the flexibility of Islamic design and the relative independence of the motifs from the surfaces they decorate.

CALLIGRAPHY In the Islamic world, the art of *calligraphy*, ornamental writing, held a place of honor even higher than the art of textiles. The faithful wanted to reproduce the Koran's sacred words in as beautiful a script as human hands could contrive. Passages from the Koran appeared not only on the fragile pages of books but also on the walls of buildings, for example, in the mosaic band above the outer ring of columns inside the Dome of the Rock (FIG. **13-3**). The practice of calligraphy was itself a holy task and required long and arduous training. The scribe had to possess exceptional spiritual refinement, as attested by an ancient Arabic proverb that proclaims "Purity of writing is purity of soul." Only in China does calligraphy hold as elevated a position among the arts (see "Calligraphy and Inscriptions on Chinese Paintings," Chapter 27, page 726).

Arabic script predates Islam. It is written from right to left with certain characters connected by a baseline. Although the chief

Islamic book, the sacred Koran, was codified in the mid-seventh century, the earliest preserved Korans are datable to the ninth century. Koran pages were either bound into books or stored as loose sheets in boxes. Most of the early examples feature texts written in the script form called *Kufic*, after the city of Kufa, one of the renowned centers of Arabic calligraphy. Kufic script is quite angular, with the uprights forming almost right angles with the baseline. As with Hebrew and other Semitic languages, the usual practice was to write in consonants only. But to facilitate recitation of the Koran, scribes often indicated vowels by red or yellow symbols above or below the line.

13-16A Dish with Arabic proverb, 10th century.

All of these features can be seen on a 9th- or early-10th-century page (FIG. **13-16**) now in Dublin that carries the heading and opening lines of surah 18 of the Koran. Five text lines in black ink with red vowels appear below a decorative band incorporating the chapter title in gold and ending in a palm-tree *finial* (a crowning ornament). This approach to page design has parallels at the extreme northwestern corner of the then-known world—in the early medieval manuscripts of the British Isles, where text and ornament are similarly united (FIG. **16-8**). But the stylized human and animal forms that populate those Christian books never appear in Korans.

13-16B *Blue Koran*, ninth to mid-10th century.

LATER ISLAMIC ART

The great centers of early Islamic art and architecture continued to flourish in the second millennium, but important new regional artistic centers emerged, especially in Turkey and South Asia. The discussion here centers on the later art and architecture of the Islamic Middle East, Spain, and Turkey. Developments in India are treated in Chapter 26.

Architecture

In the early years of the 11th century, the Umayyad caliphs' power in Spain unraveled, and their palaces fell prey to Berber soldiers from North Africa. The Berbers ruled southern Spain for several generations but could not resist the pressure of Christian forces from the north. Córdoba fell to the Christians in 1236. From then until the final Christian triumph in 1492, the Nasrids, an Arab dynasty that had established its capital at Granada in 1230, ruled the remaining Muslim territories in Spain.

ALHAMBRA On a rocky spur at Granada, the Nasrids constructed a huge palace-fortress called the Alhambra ("the Red" in Arabic) because of the rose color of the stone used for its walls and 23 towers. By the end of the 14th century, the complex, a veritable city with a population of 40,000, included at least a half dozen royal residences. Only two of these fared well over the centuries. Paradoxically, they owe their preservation to the Christian victors, who maintained a few of the buildings as trophies commemorating the expulsion of the Nasrids. The two palaces present a vivid picture of court life in Islamic Spain before the Christian reconquest.

The Palace of the Lions takes its name from its courtyard (FIG. **13-1**) that boasts a fountain with marble lions carrying a water basin on their backs. Colonnaded courtyards with fountains and statues have a long history in the Mediterranean world, especially in the houses and villas of the Roman Empire (see Chapter 10). The Alhambra's lion fountain is an unusual instance of freestanding stone sculpture in the Islamic world, unthinkable in a sacred setting. But the design of the courtyard is distinctly Islamic and features many multilobed pointed arches and lavish stuccoed walls in which calligraphy and abstract motifs are interwoven. The palace was the residence of Muhammad V (r. 1354–1391), and its courtyards, lush gardens, and luxurious carpets and other furnishings served to conjure the image of Paradise.

The Palace of the Lions is noteworthy also for its elaborate stucco ceilings. A spectacular example is the dome (FIG. **13-17**) of the so-called Hall of the Abencerrajes. The dome rests on an octagonal drum supported by squinches and pierced by eight pairs of windows, but its structure is difficult to discern because of the intricate carved stucco decoration. The ceiling is covered with some 5,000 *muqarnas*—tier after tier of stalactite-like prismatic forms that seem aimed at denying the structure's solidity. The muqarnas ceiling was intended to catch and reflect sunlight as well as form beautiful

13-17 Muqarnas dome, Hall of the Abencerrajes, Palace of the Lions, Alhambra, Granada, Spain, 1354–1391.

The structure of this dome on an octagonal drum is difficult to discern because of the intricately carved stucco muqarnas decoration. The prismatic forms catch and reflect sunlight, creating the effect of a starry sky.

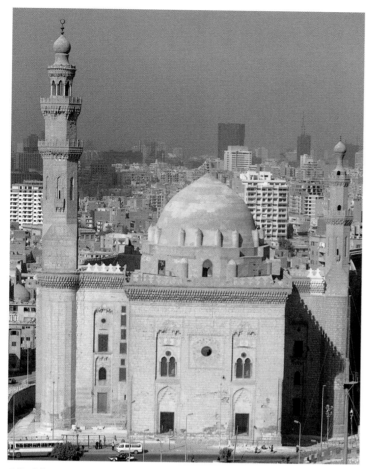

13-18 Madrasa-mosque-mausoleum complex of Sultan Hasan (looking northwest with the mausoleum in the foreground), Cairo, Egypt, begun 1356.

Hasan's mausoleum is a gigantic version of the much earlier Samanid mausoleum (FIG. 13-10). Because of its location directly south of the complex's mosque, praying Muslims faced the Mamluk sultan's tomb.

1. Mausoleum
2. Mosque (southern iwan)
3. Iwans
4. Madrasas
5. Courtyard with fountain

13-19 Plan of the madrasa-mosque-mausoleum complex of Sultan Hasan, Cairo, Egypt, begun 1356.

Sultan Hasan's complex comprised four madrasas as well as a mosque, his tomb, and various other buildings. The plan with four iwans opening onto a central courtyard derives from that of Iranian mosques.

abstract patterns. The lofty vault in this hall and others in the palace symbolized the dome of Heaven. The flickering light and shadows create the effect of a starry sky as the sun's rays glide from window to window during the day. To underscore the symbolism, the palace walls bear inscriptions with verses by the court poet Ibn Zamrak (1333–1393), who compared the Alhambra's lacelike muqarnas ceilings to "the heavenly spheres whose orbits revolve."

MAUSOLEUM OF SULTAN HASAN In the mid-13th century, under the leadership of Genghis Khan, the Mongols from east-central Asia (see Chapter 27) conquered much of the eastern Islamic world. The center of Islamic power moved from Baghdad to Egypt. The lords of Egypt at the time were former Turkish slaves ("mamluks" in Arabic) who converted to Islam. The capital of the Mamluk *sultans* (rulers) was Cairo, which became the largest Muslim city of the late Middle Ages. The Mamluks were prolific builders, and Sultan Hasan, although not an important figure in Islamic history, was the most ambitious of all. He ruled briefly as a child and was deposed, but regained the sultanate in 1354. He was assassinated in 1361.

Hasan's major building project in Cairo was a huge madrasa complex (FIGS. **13-18** and **13-19**) on a plot of land about 8,000 square yards in area. A *madrasa* ("place of study" in Arabic) is a theological college devoted to the teaching of Islamic law. Hasan's complex was so large that it housed not only four such colleges for the study of the four major schools of Islamic law but also a mosque,

mausoleum, orphanage, and hospital, as well as shops and baths. Like all Islamic building complexes incorporating religious, educational, and charitable functions, this one was supported by an endowment funded by rental properties. The income from these paid the salaries of attendants and faculty, provided furnishings and supplies such as oil for the lamps or free food for the poor, and supported scholarships for needy students.

The grandiose structure has a large central courtyard (FIG. **13-19**, no. 5) with a monumental fountain in the center and four vaulted iwans opening onto it, a design used earlier for Iranian mosques (see "The Mosque," page 345). In each corner of the main courtyard, between the iwans (FIG. **13-19**, no. 3), is a madrasa (no. 4) with its own courtyard and four or five stories of rooms for the students. The largest iwan (no. 2) in the complex, on the southern side, served as a mosque. Contemporaries believed the soaring vault that covered this iwan was taller than the arch of the Sasanian palace (FIG. **2-27**) at Ctesiphon, which was then one of the most admired engineering feats in the world. Behind the qibla wall stands the sultan's mausoleum (FIGS. **13-18** and **13-19**, no. 1), a gigantic version of the type of the Samanid tomb (FIG. **13-10**) at Bukhara. The builders intentionally placed the dome-covered cube south of the mosque so that the prayers of the faithful facing Mecca would be directed toward Hasan's tomb. (Only the sultan's two sons are buried there, however. Hasan's body was not returned when he was killed.)

A muqarnas cornice crowns the exterior walls of the complex, and marble plaques of several colors cover the mihrab in the mosque and the walls of Hasan's mausoleum. But the complex as a whole is relatively austere, characterized by its massiveness and geometric clarity. It presents a striking contrast to the filigreed elegance of the contemporary Alhambra (FIGS. **13-1** and **13-17**) and testifies to the diversity of regional styles within the Islamic world, especially after the end of the Umayyad and Abbasid dynasties.

Sinan the Great and the Mosque of Selim II

Sinan (ca. 1491–1588), called Sinan the Great, was truly the greatest Ottoman architect. Born a Christian, he was recruited for service in the Ottoman government, converted to Islam, and was trained in engineering and the art of building while in the Ottoman army. Officials quickly recognized his talent and entrusted him with increasing responsibility until, in 1538, he was appointed the chief court architect for Suleyman the Magnificent (r. 1520–1566), a generous patron of art and architecture. Architectural historians have attributed to Sinan hundreds of building projects, both sacred and secular, although he could not have been involved with all that bear his name.

The capstone of Sinan's distinguished career was the Edirne mosque (FIGS. 13-20 and 13-21) of Suleyman's son, Selim II, which Sinan designed when he was almost 80 years old. In this masterwork, he sought to surpass the greatest achievements of Byzantine architects, just as Sultan Hasan's builders in Cairo attempted to rival and exceed the Sasanian architects of antiquity. Sa'i Mustafa Çelebi, Sinan's biographer, recorded the architect's accomplishment in his own words:

Sultan Selim Khan ordered the erection of a mosque in Edirne. . . .
His humble servant [I, Sinan] prepared for him a drawing depicting,

on a dominating site in the city, four minarets on the four corners of a dome. . . . Those who consider themselves architects among Christians say that in the realm of Islam no dome can equal that of the Hagia Sophia; they claim that no Muslim architect would be able to build such a large dome. In this mosque, with the help of God and the support of Sultan Selim Khan, I erected a dome six cubits higher and four cubits wider than the dome of the Hagia Sophia.*

The Edirne dome is, in fact, higher than Hagia Sophia's (FIG. 12-4) when measured from its base, but its crown is not as far above the pavement. Nonetheless, Sinan's feat won universal acclaim as a triumph. The Ottomans considered the Mosque of Selim II proof that they finally had outshone the Christian emperors of Byzantium in the realm of architecture.

*Aptullah Kuran, *Sinan: The Grand Old Master of Ottoman Architecture* (Washington, D.C.: Institute of Turkish Studies, 1987), 168–169.

13-20A Tughra of Suleyman the Magnificent, ca. 1555–1560.

13-21 SINAN, interior of the Mosque of Selim II, Edirne, Turkey, 1568–1575.

The interior of Sinan's Edirne mosque is a fusion of an octagon and a dome-covered square with four half-domes at the corners. The plan features geometric clarity and precise numerical ratios.

13-20 SINAN, Mosque of Selim II, Edirne, Turkey, 1568–1575. ◼◣

The Ottomans developed a new type of mosque with a square prayer hall covered by a dome. Sinan's Mosque of Selim II has a taller dome than Hagia Sophia's (FIG. 12-4) and is an engineering triumph.

OTTOMAN EMPIRE During the course of the 9th to 11th centuries, the Turkic people, of central Asian origin, largely converted to Islam. They moved into Iran and the Near East in the 11th century, and by 1055 the Seljuk Turkish dynasty had built an extensive, although short-lived, empire that stretched from India to western Anatolia. By the end of the 12th century, this empire had broken up into regional states, and in the early 13th century it came under the sway of the Mongols, led by Genghis Khan (see Chapter 27). After the downfall of the Seljuks, several local dynasties established themselves in Anatolia, among them the Ottomans, founded by Osman I (r. 1281–1326). Under Osman's successors, the Ottoman state expanded for two and a half centuries throughout vast areas of Asia, Europe, and North Africa to become, by the middle of the 15th century, one of the great world powers.

The Ottoman emperors were lavish patrons of architecture. Ottoman builders developed a new type of mosque with a square prayer hall covered by a dome as its core. In fact, the dome-covered square, which had been a dominant form in Iran and was employed for the 10th-century Samanid mausoleum (FIG. 13-10), became the nucleus of all Ottoman architecture. The combination had an appealing geometric clarity. At first used singly, the domed units came to be used in multiples, a turning point in Ottoman architecture.

After the Ottoman Turks conquered Constantinople (Istanbul) in 1453, they firmly established their architectural code. The new lords of Constantinople were impressed by Hagia Sophia (FIGS. 12-2 to 12-4), which, in some respects, conformed to their own ideals. They converted the Byzantine church into a mosque with minarets. But the longitudinal orientation of Hagia Sophia's interior never satisfied Ottoman builders, and Anatolian development moved instead toward the central-plan mosque.

SINAN THE GREAT The first examples of the central-plan mosque were built in the 1520s, eclipsed later only by the works of the most famous Ottoman architect, SINAN (ca. 1491–1588). A contemporary of the great Italian Renaissance sculptor, painter, and architect Michelangelo (see Chapter 22), and with equal aspirations to immortality, Sinan perfected the Ottoman architectural style. By his time, Ottoman builders almost universally were using the basic domed unit, which they could multiply, enlarge, contract, or combine as needed. Thus, the typical Ottoman building of Sinan's time was a creative assemblage of domical units and artfully juxtaposed geometric spaces.

Builders usually erected domes with an extravagant margin of structural safety that has since served them well in earthquake-prone Istanbul and other Ottoman cities. (Vivid demonstration of the sound construction of Ottoman mosques came in August 1999 when a powerful earthquake centered 65 miles east of Istanbul toppled hundreds of modern buildings and killed thousands of people but caused no damage to the centuries-old mosques.) Working within this architectural tradition, Sinan searched for solutions to the problems of unifying the additive elements and of creating a monumental centralized space with harmonious proportions.

Sinan's vision found ultimate expression in the Mosque of Selim II (FIG. 13-20) at Edirne, which had been the capital of the Ottoman Empire from 1367 to 1472 and where Selim II (r. 1566–1574) maintained a palace. There, Sinan designed a mosque with a massive dome set off by four slender pencil-shaped minarets (each more than 200 feet high, among the tallest ever constructed). The dome's height surpasses that of Hagia Sophia (see "Sinan the Great and the Mosque of Selim II," page 354). But it is the organization of the Edirne mosque's interior space (FIG. 13-21) that reveals the genius of its builder. The mihrab is recessed into an apselike alcove deep enough to permit window illumination from three sides, making the brilliantly colored tile panels of its lower walls sparkle as if with their own glowing light. The plan of the main hall is an ingenious fusion of an octagon with the dome-covered square. The octagon, formed by the eight massive dome supports, is pierced by the four half-dome-covered corners of the square. The result is a fluid interpenetration of several geometric volumes that represents the culminating solution to Sinan's lifelong search for a monumental unified interior space. Sinan's forms are clear and legible, like mathematical equations. Height, width, and masses are related to one another in a simple but effective ratio of 1:2, and precise numerical ratios also characterize the complex as a whole. The forecourt of the building, for example, covers an area equal to that of the mosque proper. The Mosque of Selim II is generally regarded as the climax of Ottoman architecture. Sinan proudly proclaimed it his masterpiece.

GREAT MOSQUE, ISFAHAN The Mosque of Selim II at Edirne was erected during a single building campaign under the direction of a single master architect, but the construction of many other major Islamic architectural projects extended over several centuries. A case in point is the Great Mosque (FIG. 13-22) at Isfahan

13-22 Aerial view (looking southwest) of the Great Mosque, Isfahan, Iran, 11th to 17th centuries. ◼◀

The typical Iranian mosque plan with four vaulted iwans and a courtyard may have been employed for the first time in the mosque Sultan Malik Shah I built in the late 11th century at his capital of Isfahan.

0 25 50 75 100 feet

0 10 20 30 meters

1. Iwan
2. Courtyard
3. Qibla iwan
4. Domed maqsura

13-23 Plan of the Great Mosque, Isfahan, Iran, 11th to 17th centuries.

In the Great Mosque at Isfahan, as in other four-iwan mosques, the qibla iwan is the largest. Its size and the dome-covered maqsura in front of it indicated the proper direction for Muslim prayer.

in Iran. The earliest mosque on the site, of the hypostyle type, dates to the eighth century, during the Abbasid caliphate. But Sultan Malik Shah I (r. 1072–1092), whose capital was at Isfahan, transformed the structure in the 11th century. Later remodeling further altered the mosque's appearance. The present mosque, which retains its basic 11th-century plan (FIG. 13-23), consists of a large courtyard bordered by a two-story arcade on each side. As in the 14th-century complex (FIG. 13-19) of Sultan Hasan in Cairo, four iwans open onto the courtyard, one at the center of each side. The southwestern iwan (FIG. 13-23, no. 3) leads into a dome-covered room (no. 4) in front of the mihrab. It functioned as a maqsura reserved for the sultan and his attendants. It is uncertain whether this plan, with four iwans and a dome in front of the mihrab, was employed for the first time in the Great Mosque at Isfahan, but it became standard in Iranian mosque design. In four-iwan mosques, the qibla iwan is always the largest. Its size (and the dome that often accompanied it) immediately indicated to worshipers the proper direction for prayer.

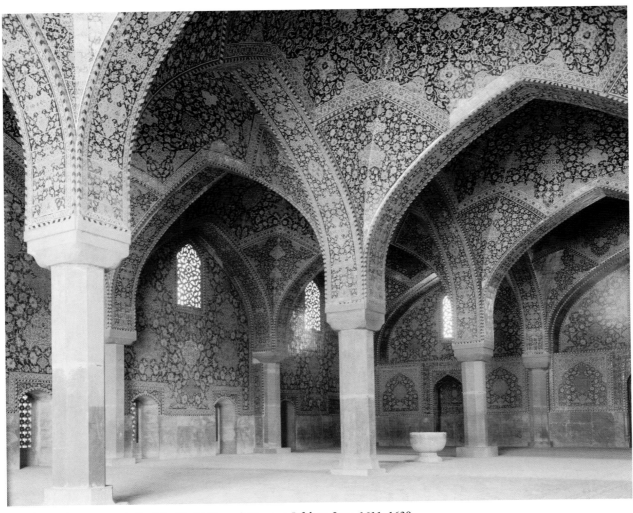

13-24 Winter prayer hall of the Shahi (Imam) Mosque, Isfahan, Iran, 1611–1638.

The ceramists who produced the cuerda seca tiles of this Isfahan mosque's winter prayer hall had to manufacture a wide variety of shapes with curved surfaces to cover the hall's arches and vaults.

Islamic Tilework

From the Dome of the Rock (FIGS. 13-2 and 13-3), the earliest major Islamic building, to the present day, architects have used mosaics or ceramic tiles to decorate the walls and vaults of mosques, madrasas, palaces, and tombs. The golden age of Islamic tilework was the 16th and 17th centuries. At that time, Islamic artists used two basic techniques to enliven building interiors with brightly colored tiled walls and to sheathe their exteriors with gleaming tiles that reflected the sun's rays.

In *mosaic tilework* (for example, FIG. 13-25), large ceramic panels of single colors are fired in the potter's kiln and then cut into smaller pieces and set in plaster in a manner similar to the laying of mosaic tesserae of stone or glass (see "Mosaics," Chapter 11, page 303).

Cuerda seca (dry cord) tilework was introduced in Umayyad Spain during the 10th century—hence its Spanish name even in Middle Eastern and Central Asian contexts. Cuerda seca tiles (for example, FIG. 13-24) are polychrome and can more easily bear complex geometric and vegetal patterns as well as Arabic script. They are more economical to use because vast surfaces can be covered with large tiles much more quickly than they can with thousands of smaller mosaic tiles. But when such tiles are used to sheathe curved surfaces, the ceramists must fire the tiles in the exact shape required. Polychrome tiles have other drawbacks. Because all the glazes are fired at the same temperature, cuerda seca tiles are not as brilliant in color as mosaic tiles and do not reflect light the way the more irregular surfaces of tile mosaics do. The preparation of the multicolored tiles also requires greater care. To prevent the colors from running together during firing, the potters must outline the motifs on cuerda seca tiles with greased cords containing manganese, which leaves a matte black line between the colors after firing.

13-25 Mihrab from the Madrasa Imami, Isfahan, Iran, ca. 1354. Glazed mosaic tilework, 11′ 3″ × 7′ 6″. Metropolitan Museum of Art, New York.

1 ft.

The Madrasa Imami mihrab is a masterpiece of mosaic tilework. Every piece had to be cut to fit its specific place in the design. It exemplifies the perfect aesthetic union between Islamic calligraphy and ornament.

IRANIAN TILEWORK The iwans of the Isfahan mosque feature soaring pointed arches framing tile-sheathed muqarnas vaults. The muqarnas ceilings probably date to the 14th century, and the ceramic-tile revetment on the walls and vaults is the work of the 17th-century Safavid rulers of Iran. The use of glazed tiles has a long history in the Middle East. Even in ancient Mesopotamia, builders sometimes covered gates and walls with colorful baked bricks (FIG. 2-24). In the Islamic world, the art of ceramic tilework reached its peak in the 16th and 17th centuries in Iran and Turkey (see "Islamic Tilework," above). Employed as a veneer over a brick core, tiles could sheathe entire buildings, including domes and minarets.

SHAHI MOSQUE, ISFAHAN The Shahi (or Royal) Mosque in Isfahan, now known as the Imam Mosque, which dates from the early 17th century, is widely recognized as one of the masterpieces of Islamic tilework. Its dome is a prime example of tile mosaic, and its winter prayer hall (FIG. 13-24) houses one of the finest ensembles of cuerda seca tiles in the world. Covering the walls, arches, and vaults of the prayer hall presented a special challenge to the Isfahan ceramists. They had to manufacture a wide variety of shapes with curved surfaces to sheathe the complex forms of the hall. The result was a technological triumph as well as a dazzling display of abstract ornament.

MADRASA IMAMI, ISFAHAN As already noted, verses from the Koran appeared in the mosaics of the Dome of the Rock (FIG. 13-3) in Jerusalem and in mosaics and other media on the walls of countless later Islamic structures. Indeed, some of the masterworks of Arabic calligraphy are not in manuscripts but on walls. A 14th-century mihrab (FIG. 13-25) from the Madrasa Imami in Isfahan exemplifies the perfect aesthetic union between the Islamic calligrapher's art and abstract ornament. The pointed arch that immediately frames the mihrab niche bears an inscription from the Koran in Kufic, the stately rectilinear script used in the ninth-century Koran (FIG. 13-16) discussed earlier. Many supple cursive styles also make up the repertoire of Islamic calligraphy. One of these styles, known as *Muhaqqaq,* fills the mihrab's outer rectangular frame. The mosaic tile ornament on the curving surface of the niche and the area above the pointed arch are composed of tighter and looser networks of geometric and abstract floral motifs. The mosaic technique is masterful. Every piece had to be cut to fit its specific place in the mihrab—even the tile inscriptions. The framed inscription in the center of the niche—proclaiming that the mosque is the domicile of the pious believer—is smoothly integrated with the subtly varied patterns. The mihrab's outermost inscription—detailing the five pillars of Islamic faith—serves as a fringelike extension, as well as a boundary, for the entire design. The calligraphic and geometric elements are so completely unified that only the practiced eye can distinguish them. The artist transformed the architectural surface into a textile surface—the three-dimensional wall into a two-dimensional hanging—weaving the calligraphy into it as another cluster of motifs within the total pattern.

Luxury Arts

The tile-covered mosques of Isfahan, Sultan Hasan's madrasa complex in Cairo, and the architecture of Sinan the Great in Edirne are enduring testaments to the brilliant artistic culture of the Safavid,

Mamluk, and Ottoman rulers of the Muslim world. Yet these are only some of the most conspicuous public manifestations of the greatness of later Islamic art and architecture (see Chapter 26 for the achievements of the Muslim rulers of India). In the smaller-scale, and often private, realm of the luxury arts, Muslim artists also excelled. From the vast array of manuscript paintings, ceramics, textiles, and metalwork, six masterpieces may serve to suggest both the range and the quality of the inappropriately dubbed Islamic "minor arts" of the 13th to 16th centuries.

TIMURID *BUSTAN* In the late 14th century, a new Islamic empire arose in Central Asia under the leadership of Timur (r. 1370–1405), known in the Western world as Tamerlane. Timur, a successor of the Mongol Genghis Khan, quickly extended his dominions to include Iran and parts of Anatolia. The Timurids ruled until 1501 and were great patrons of art and architecture in cities such as Herat, Bukhara, and Samarqand. Herat in particular became a leading center for the production of luxurious books under the patronage of the Timurid sultan Husayn Mayqara (r. 1470–1506).

The most famous Persian painter of his age was BIHZAD, who worked at the Herat court and illustrated the sultan's copy of Sadi's *Bustan* (*Orchard*). One page (FIG. **13-26**) represents a story in both the Bible and the Koran—the seduction of Yusuf (Joseph) by

13-26 BIHZAD, *Seduction of Yusuf,* folio 52 verso of the *Bustan* of Sultan Husayn Mayqara, from Herat, Afghanistan, 1488. Ink and color on paper, $11\frac{7}{8}'' \times 8\frac{5}{8}''$. National Library, Cairo.

The most famous Timurid manuscript painter was Bihzad. This page displays vivid color, intricate decorative detailing, and a brilliant balance between two-dimensional patterning and perspective.

1 in.

Potiphar's wife Zulaykha. Sadi's text is dispersed throughout the page in elegant Arabic script in a series of beige panels. According to the tale as told by Jami (1414–1492), an influential mystic theologian and poet whose Persian text appears in blue in the white pointed arch at the lower center of the composition, Zulaykha lured Yusuf into her palace and led him through seven rooms, locking each door behind him. In the last room she threw herself at Yusuf, but he resisted and was able to flee when the seven doors opened miraculously. Bihzad's painting of the story is characterized by vivid color, intricate decorative detailing suggesting luxurious textiles and tiled walls, and a brilliant balance between two-dimensional patterning and perspectival depictions of balconies and staircases.

SAFAVID *SHAHNAMA* The successors of the Timurids in Iran were the Safavids. Shah Tahmasp (r. 1524–1576) was a great patron of books. Around 1525 he commissioned an ambitious decade-long project to produce an illustrated 742-page copy of the *Shahnama* (*Book of Kings*). The *Shahnama* is the Persian national epic poem by Firdawsi (940–1025). It recounts the history of Iran from the Creation until the Muslim conquest. Tahmasp's *Shahnama* contains 258 illustrations by many artists, including some of the most renowned painters of the day. It was eventually presented as a gift to Selim II, the Ottoman sultan who was the patron of Sinan's

mosque (FIGS. **13-20** and **13-21**) at Edirne. The manuscript later entered a private collection in the West and ultimately was auctioned as a series of individual pages, destroying the work's integrity but underscoring that Western collectors viewed each page as a masterpiece.

The page reproduced here (FIG. **13-27**) is the work of SULTAN-MUHAMMAD and depicts Gayumars, the legendary first king of Iran, and his court. According to tradition, Gayumars ruled from a mountaintop when humans first learned to cook food and clothe themselves in leopard skins. In Sultan-Muhammad's representation of the story, Gayumars presides over his court (all the figures wear leopard skins) from his mountain throne. The king is surrounded by light amid a golden sky. His son and grandson perch on multicolored rocky outcroppings to the viewer's left and right, respectively. The court encircles the ruler and his heirs. Dozens of human faces appear within the rocks themselves. Many species of animals populate the lush landscape. According to the *Shahnama*, wild beasts became instantly tame in the presence of Gayumars. Sultan-Muhammad rendered the figures, animals, trees, rocks, and sky with an extraordinarily delicate touch. The sense of lightness and airiness that permeate the painting is enhanced by its placement on the page—floating, off center, on a speckled background of gold leaf. The painter gave his royal patron a singular vision of Iran's fabled past.

13-27 SULTAN-MUHAMMAD, *Court of Gayumars,* folio 20 verso of the *Shahnama* of Shah Tahmasp, from Tabriz, Iran, ca. 1525–1535. Ink, watercolor, and gold on paper, 1′ 1″ × 9″. Prince Sadruddin Aga Khan Collection, Geneva.

Sultan-Muhammad painted the story of the legendary king Gayumars for the Safavid ruler Shah Tahmasp. The off-center placement on the page enhances the sense of lightness that permeates the painting.

1 in.

13-28 Maqsud of Kashan, carpet from the funerary mosque of Shaykh Safi al-Din, Ardabil, Iran, 1540. Knotted pile of wool and silk, 34′ 6″ × 17′ 7″. Victoria & Albert Museum, London.

Maqsud of Kashan's enormous Ardabil carpet required roughly 25 million knots. It presents the illusion of a heavenly dome with mosque lamps reflected in a pool of water with floating lotus blossoms.

1 ft.

ARDABIL CARPETS Tahmasp also elevated carpet weaving to a national industry and set up royal factories at Isfahan, Kashan, Kirman, and Tabriz. Two of the masterworks of carpet weaving that date to his reign are the pair of carpets from the two-centuries older funerary mosque of Shaykh Safi al-Din (1252–1334), the founder of the Safavid line. The name Maqsud of Kashan is woven into the design of the carpet illustrated here (FIG. **13-28**). He must have been the designer who supplied the master pattern to two teams of royal weavers (one for each of the two carpets). The carpet, almost 35 × 18 feet, consists of roughly 25 million knots, some 340 to the square inch. (Its twin has even more knots.)

The design consists of a central sunburst medallion, representing the inside of a dome, surrounded by 16 pendants. Mosque lamps (appropriate motifs for the Ardabil funerary mosque) are suspended from two pendants on the long axis of the carpet. The lamps are of different sizes. This may be an optical device to make the two appear equal in size when viewed from the end of the carpet at the room's threshold (the bottom end in FIG. **13-28**). The rich blue background is covered with leaves and flowers attached to delicate stems that spread over the whole field. The entire composition presents the illusion of a heavenly dome with lamps reflected in a pool of water full of floating lotus blossoms. No human or animal figures appear, as befits a carpet intended for a mosque, although they can be found on other Islamic textiles used in secular contexts, both earlier (FIG. **13-14**) and later.

MOSQUE LAMPS Mosque lamps were often made of glass and highly decorated. Islamic artists perfected this art form and fortunately, despite their exceptionally fragile nature, many examples survive, in large part because the lamps were revered by those who handled them. One of the finest is the mosque lamp (FIG. **13-29**) made for Sayf al-Din Tuquztimur (d. 1345), an official in the court of the Mamluk sultan al-Nasir Muhammad. The glass lamps hung on chains from the mosque's ceilings. The shape of Tuquztimur's lamp

13-29 Mosque lamp of Sayf al-Din Tuquztimur, from Egypt, 1340. Glass with enamel decoration, 1′ 1″ high. British Museum, London.

The enamel decoration of this glass mosque lamp includes a quotation from the Koran comparing God's light to the light in a lamp. The burning wick dramatically illuminated the sacred verse.

1 in.

is typical of the period, consisting of a conical neck, wide body with six vertical handles, and a tall foot. Inside, a small glass container held the oil and wick. The *enamel* decoration (colors fused to the surfaces) includes Tuquztimur's emblem—an eagle over a cup (Tuquztimur served as the sultan's cup-bearer). Cursive Arabic calligraphy, also in enamel, gives the official's name and titles as well as a quotation of the Koranic verse (24:35) comparing God's light to the light in a lamp. When the lamp was lit, the verse (and Tuquztimur's name) would have been dramatically illuminated.

BAPTISTÈRE DE SAINT LOUIS Metalwork was another early Islamic art form (FIG. 13-15) that continued to play an important role in the later period. An example of the highest quality is a brass basin (FIG. 13-30) from Egypt inlaid with gold and silver and signed—six times—by the Mamluk artist MUHAMMAD IBN AL-ZAYN. The basin, used for washing hands at official ceremonies, must have been fashioned for a specific Mamluk patron. Some scholars think a court official named Salar ordered the piece as a gift for his sultan, but no inscription identifies him. The central band depicts Mamluk hunters and Mongol enemies. Running animals fill the friezes above and below. Stylized vegetal forms of inlaid silver fill the background of all the bands and roundels. Figures and animals also decorate the inside and underside of the basin. This Mamluk basin has long been

1 in.

13-30 MUHAMMAD IBN AL-ZAYN, basin (*Baptistère de Saint Louis*), from Egypt, ca. 1300. Brass, inlaid with gold and silver, 8¾″ high. Louvre, Paris.

Muhammad ibn al-Zayn proudly signed (six times) this basin used for washing hands at official ceremonies. The central band, inlaid with gold and silver, depicts Mamluk hunters and Mongol enemies.

Christian Patronage of Islamic Art

During the 11th, 12th, and 13th centuries, large numbers of Christians traveled to Islamic lands, especially to the Christian holy sites in Jerusalem and Bethlehem, either as pilgrims (see "Pilgrimages," Chapter 17, page 432) or as Crusaders (see "The Crusades," Chapter 17, page 442). Many returned with mementos of their journey, usually in the form of inexpensive mass-produced souvenirs. But some wealthy individuals commissioned local Muslim artists to produce custom-made pieces using costly materials.

A unique brass canteen (FIG. 13-31) inlaid with silver and decorated with scenes of the life of Christ appears to be the work of a 13th-century Ayyubid metalsmith in the employ of a Christian patron. The canteen is a luxurious version of the "pilgrim flasks" Christian visitors to the Holy Land often brought back to Europe. Four inscriptions in Arabic promise eternal glory, secure life, perfect prosperity, and increasing good luck to the canteen's owner, who is unfortunately not named. That the owner was a Christian is sug-

gested not only by the type of object but also by the choice of scenes engraved into the canteen. The Madonna and Christ Child appear enthroned in the central medallion, and three panels depicting New Testament events (see "The Life of Jesus in Art," Chapter 11, pages 296–297) fill most of the band around the medallion. The narrative unfolds in a counterclockwise sequence (Arabic is read from right to left), beginning with the Nativity (at 2 o'clock) and continuing with the Presentation in the Temple (10 o'clock) and the Entry into Jerusalem (6 o'clock). The scenes may have been chosen because the patron had visited their locales (Bethlehem and Jerusalem). Most scholars believe that the artist used Syrian Christian manuscripts as the source for the canteen's Christian iconography. Many of the decorative details, however, are common in contemporary Islamic metalwork inscribed with the names of Muslim patrons. Whoever the owner was, the canteen testifies to the fruitful artistic interaction between Christians and Muslims in 13th-century Syria.

13-31 Canteen with episodes from the life of Christ, from Syria, ca. 1240–1250. Brass, inlaid with silver, 1′ 2½″ high. Freer Gallery of Art, Washington, D.C.

This unique canteen is the work of an Ayyubid metalsmith in the employ of a Christian pilgrim to the Holy Land. The three scenes from the life of Jesus appear in counterclockwise sequence.

1 in.

known as the *Baptistère de Saint Louis,* but the association with the famous French king (see "Louis IX, the Saintly King," Chapter 18, page 482) is a myth. Louis died before the piece was made. Nonetheless, the *Baptistère,* brought to France long ago, was used in the baptismal rites of newborns of the French royal family as early as the

17th century. Like the Zandana silk (FIG. 13-14) from Toul Cathedral and a canteen (FIG. 13-31) adorned with scenes of the life of Christ (see "Christian Patronage of Islamic Art," above), Muhammad ibn al-Zayn's basin testifies to the prestige of Islamic art well outside the boundaries of the Islamic world.

THE ISLAMIC WORLD

UMAYYAD SYRIA AND ABBASID IRAQ, 661–1258

- The Umayyads (r. 661–750) were the first Islamic dynasty and ruled from their capital at Damascus in Syria until they were overthrown by the Abbasids (r. 750–1258), who established their capital at Baghdad in Iraq.

- The first great Islamic building is the Dome of the Rock. The domed octagon commemorated the triumph of Islam in Jerusalem, which the Muslims captured from the Byzantines in 638.

- Umayyad and Abbasid mosques, for example, those in Damascus and in Kairouan (Tunisia), are of the hypostyle-hall type and incorporate arcaded courtyards and minarets. The mosaic decoration of early mosques was often the work of Byzantine artists but excludes zoomorphic forms.

- The earliest preserved Korans date to the 9th century and feature Kufic calligraphy and decorative motifs but no figural illustrations.

Dome of the Rock, Jerusalem, 687–692

ISLAMIC SPAIN, 756–1492

- Abd-al-Rahman I established the Umayyad dynasty (r. 756–1031) in Spain after he escaped the Abbasid massacre of his clan in 750.

- The Umayyad capital was at Córdoba, where the caliphs erected and expanded the Great Mosque between the 8th and 10th centuries. The mosque features horseshoe and multilobed arches and mosaic-clad domes that rest on arcuated squinches.

- The last Spanish Muslim dynasty was the Nasrid (r. 1230–1492), whose capital was at Granada. The Alhambra is the best surviving example of Islamic palace architecture. It is famous for its stuccoed walls and arches and its muqarnas vaults and domes.

Great Mosque, Córdoba, 8th to 10th centuries

ISLAMIC EGYPT, 909–1517

- The Fatimids (r. 909–1171) established their caliphate in Egypt in 909 and ruled from their capital in Cairo. They were succeeded by the Ayyubids (r. 1171–1250) and the Mamluks (r. 1250–1517).

- The most ambitious Mamluk builder was Sultan Hasan, whose madrasa-mosque-mausoleum complex in Cairo is based on Iranian four-iwan mosque designs.

- Among the greatest works of the Islamic metalsmith's art is Muhammad ibn al-Zayn's brass basin inlaid with gold and silver and engraved with figures of Mamluk hunters and Mongol enemies.

Muhammad ibn al-Zayn, brass basin, ca. 1300

TIMURID AND SAFAVID IRAN AND CENTRAL ASIA, 1370–1732

- The Timurid (r. 1370–1501) and Safavid (r. 1501–1732) dynasties ruled Iran and Central Asia for almost four centuries and were great patrons of art and architecture.

- The Timurid court at Herat, Afghanistan, employed the most famous painters of the day, who specialized in illustrating books.

- Persian painting also flourished in Safavid Iran under Shah Tahmasp (r. 1524–1576), who in addition set up royal carpet factories in several cities.

- The art of tilework reached its peak under the patronage of the Safavid dynasty, when builders frequently used mosaic and cuerda seca tiles to cover the walls and vaults of mosques, madrasas, palaces, and tombs.

Sultan-Muhammad, *Court of Gayumars*, ca. 1525–1535

OTTOMAN TURKEY, 1281–1924

- Osman I (r. 1281–1326) founded the Ottoman dynasty in Turkey. By the middle of the 15th century, the Ottomans had become a fearsome power and captured Byzantine Constantinople in 1453.

- The greatest Ottoman architect was Sinan (ca. 1491–1588), who perfected the design of the domed central-plan mosque. His Mosque of Selim II at Edirne is also an engineering triumph. It has a dome taller than that of Hagia Sophia.

Sinan, Mosque of Selim II, Edirne, 1568–1575

1 ft.

14-1 Shield Jaguar and Lady Xoc, Maya, lintel 24 of temple 23, Yaxchilán, Mexico, ca. 725 CE. Limestone, 3′ 7″ × 2′ 6½″. British Museum, London.

The Maya built vast complexes of temples, palaces, and plazas and decorated many with painted reliefs. This carved lintel documents the central role that elite Maya women played in religious bloodletting rituals.

NATIVE ARTS OF THE AMERICAS BEFORE 1300

The origins of the indigenous peoples of the Americas are still uncertain. Sometime no later than 30,000 to 10,000 BCE, these first Americans probably crossed the now-submerged land bridge called Beringia, which connected the shores of the Bering Strait between Asia and North America. Some migrants may have reached the Western Hemisphere via boats traveling along the Pacific coast of North America. These Stone Age nomads were hunter-gatherers. They made tools only of bone, pressure-flaked stone, and wood. They had no knowledge of agriculture but possibly some of basketry. They could control fire and probably build simple shelters. For many centuries, they spread out until they occupied the two American continents. But they were always few in number. When the first Europeans arrived at the end of the 15th century (see Chapter 32), the total population of the Western Hemisphere probably did not exceed 40 million.

Between 8000 and 2000 BCE, a number of the migrants learned to fish, farm cotton, and domesticate plants such as squash and maize (corn). The nomads settled in villages and learned to make ceramic utensils and figurines. Metal technology, although extremely sophisticated when it existed, developed only in the Andean region of South America (eventually spreading north into present-day Mexico) and generally met only the need for ornamentation, not for tools. With these skills as a base, many cultures rose and fell over long periods.

Several of the peoples of North, Central, and South America had already reached a high level of social complexity and technological achievement by the early centuries CE. Although most relied on stone tools, did not use the wheel (except for toys), and had no pack animals but the llama (in South America), the early Americans developed complex agricultural techniques and excelled in the engineering arts associated with the planning and construction of cities, civic and domestic buildings, roads and bridges, and irrigation and drainage systems. They carved monumental stone statues and reliefs, painted extensive murals, and mastered the arts of weaving, pottery, and metalwork. In Mesoamerica, the Maya and other cultural groups even had a highly developed writing system and knowledge of mathematical calculation that allowed them to keep precise records and create a sophisticated calendar and a highly accurate astronomy.

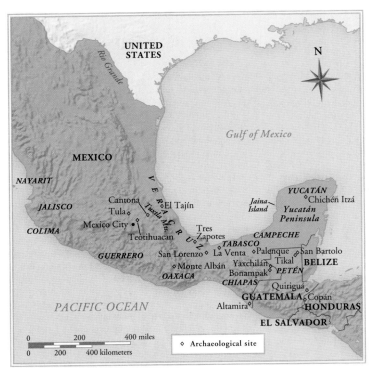

MAP 14-1 Early sites in Mesoamerica.

maize and other crops wherever water is available, lie between heavily forested mountain slopes, which at some places rise to a perpetual snow level. The moist tropical rain forests of the coastal plains yield rich crops, when the land can be cleared. In Yucatán, a subsoil of limestone furnishes abundant material for both building and carving. This limestone tableland merges with the vast Petén region of Guatemala, which separates Mexico from Honduras. Yucatán and the Petén, where dense rain forest alternates with broad stretches of grassland, host some of the most spectacular Maya ruins. The great mountain chains of Mexico and Guatemala extend into Honduras and slope sharply down to tropical coasts. Highlands and mountain valleys, with their chill and temperate climates, alternate dramatically with the humid climate of tropical rain forest and coastlines.

The variegated landscape of Mesoamerica may have much to do with the diversity of languages its native populations speak. Numerous languages are distributed among no fewer than 14 linguistic families. Many of the languages spoken in the pre–Spanish conquest period survive to this day. Various Mayan languages linger in Guatemala and southern Mexico. The Náhuatl of the Aztecs endures in the Mexican highlands. The Zapotec and Mixtec languages persist in Oaxaca and its environs. Diverse as the languages of these peoples were, their cultures otherwise had much in common. The Mesoamerican peoples shared maize cultivation, religious beliefs and rites, myths, social structures, customs, and arts.

Archaeologists, with ever-increasing refinement of technique, have been uncovering, describing, and classifying Mesoamerican monuments for more than a century. In the 1950s, linguists made important breakthroughs in deciphering the Maya hieroglyphic script, and epigraphers have made further progress in recent decades. Scholars can now list many Maya rulers by name and fix the dates of their reigns with precision. Other writing systems, such as that of the Zapotec, who began to record dates at a very early time, are less well understood, but researchers are making rapid progress in their interpretation. The general Mesoamerican chronology is now well established and widely accepted. The standard chronology, divided into three epochs, involves some overlapping of subperiods. The Preclassic (Formative) extends from 2000 BCE to about 300 CE. The Classic period runs from about 300 to 900. The Postclassic begins approximately 900 and ends with the Spanish conquest of 1521.

These advanced civilizations went into rapid decline, however, in the 16th century when the Europeans introduced new diseases to the Western Hemisphere, and Hernán Cortés, Francisco Pizarro, and their armies conquered the Aztec and Inka empires. Some native elites survived and adapted to the Spanish presence, but most of the once-glorious American cities were destroyed in the conquerors' zeal to obliterate all traces of pagan beliefs. Other sites were abandoned to the forces of nature—erosion and the encroachment of tropical forests. But despite the ruined state of the pre-Hispanic cities today, archaeologists and art historians have been able to reconstruct much of the history of art and architecture of ancient America. This chapter examines in turn the artistic achievements of the native peoples of Mesoamerica, South America, and North America before 1300. Chapter 32 treats the art and architecture of the Americas from 1300 to the present.

MESOAMERICA

The term *Mesoamerica* names the region that comprises part of present-day Mexico, Guatemala, Belize, Honduras, and the Pacific coast of El Salvador (MAP 14-1). Mesoamerica was the homeland of several of the great *pre-Columbian* civilizations—those that flourished before the arrival of Christopher Columbus and the subsequent European invasion.

The principal regions of pre-Columbian Mesoamerica are the Gulf Coast region (Olmec and Classic Veracruz cultures); the states of Jalisco, Colima, and Nayarit, collectively known as West Mexico; Chiapas, Yucatán, Quintana Roo, and Campeche states in Mexico, the Petén area of Guatemala, Belize, and Honduras (Maya culture); southwestern Mexico and the state of Oaxaca (Zapotec and Mixtec cultures); and the central plateau surrounding modern Mexico City (Teotihuacan, Toltec, and Aztec cultures). These cultures were often influential over extensive areas.

The Mexican highlands are a volcanic and seismic region. In highland Mexico, great reaches of arid plateau land, fertile for

Olmec and Preclassic West Mexico

The Olmec culture of the present-day Mexican states of Veracruz and Tabasco has often been called the "mother culture" of Mesoamerica, because many distinctive Mesoamerican religious, social, and artistic traditions can be traced to it. Recent archaeological discoveries, however, have revealed other important centers during the Preclassic period. The notion of a linear evolution of all Mesoamerican art and architecture from the Olmec is giving way to a more complex multicenter picture of early Mesoamerica. Settling in the tropical lowlands of the Gulf of Mexico, the Olmec peoples cultivated a terrain of rain forest and alluvial lowland washed by numerous rivers flowing into the gulf. Here, between approximately 1500 and 400 BCE, social organization assumed the form that later Mesoamerican cultures adapted and developed. The mass of the population—food-producing farmers scattered in hinterland villages—provided the sustenance and labor that maintained a hereditary caste of rulers, hierarchies of priests, functionaries, and artisans. The nonfarming population presumably lived, arranged by rank, within precincts that served ceremonial, administrative, and resi-

1 ft.

14-2 Colossal head, Olmec, La Venta, Mexico, ca. 900–400 BCE. Basalt, 9′ 4″ high. Museo-Parque La Venta, Villahermosa.

The identities of the Olmec colossi are uncertain, but their individualized features and distinctive headgear, as well as later Maya practice, suggest that these heads portray rulers rather than deities.

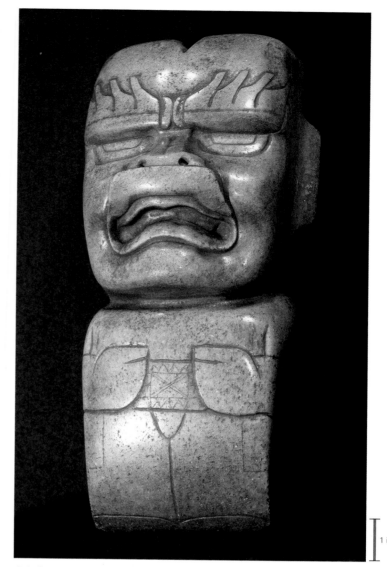

1 in.

14-3 Ceremonial ax in the form of a were-jaguar, Olmec, from La Venta, Mexico, ca. 900–400 BCE. Jadeite, $11\frac{1}{2}$″ high. British Museum, London.

Olmec celts were votive offerings to the gods. The composite human-animal representations may reflect the belief that religious practitioners underwent dangerous transformations on behalf of the community.

dential functions, and perhaps also as marketplaces. At regular intervals, the whole community convened for ritual observances at the religious-civic centers of towns such as San Lorenzo and La Venta. These centers were the formative architectural expressions of the structure and ideals of Olmec society.

OLMEC RULER PORTRAITS At La Venta, low clay-and-earthen platforms and stone fences enclosed two great courtyards. At one end of the larger area was a mound almost 100 feet high. Although now very eroded, this early pyramid, built of earth and adorned with colored clays, may have been intended to mimic a mountain, held sacred by Mesoamerican peoples as both a life-giving source of water and a feared destructive force. (Volcanic eruptions and earthquakes still wreak havoc in this region.) The La Venta layout is an early form of the temple-pyramid-plaza complex aligned on a north-south axis that characterized later Mesoamerican ceremonial center design.

Four colossal basalt heads (FIG. **14-2**), weighing about 10 tons each and standing between 6 and 10 feet high, face out from the plaza. More than a dozen similar heads have been found at San Lorenzo and Tres Zapotes. Almost as much of an achievement as the carving of these huge stones with stone tools was their transportation across the 60 miles of swampland from the nearest known basalt source, the Tuxtla Mountains. Although the identities of the colossi are uncertain, their individualized features and distinctive headgear and ear ornaments, as well as the later Maya practice of carving monumental ruler portraits, suggest that the Olmec heads portray rulers rather than deities. The sheer size of the heads and their intensity of expression evoke great power, whether mortal or divine.

JADE CELTS The Olmec also made paintings in caves, fashioned ceramic figurines, and carved sculptures in jade, a prized, extremely hard, dark-green stone they acquired from unknown sources far from their homeland. Sometimes the Olmec carved jade into ax-shaped polished forms art historians call *celts*, which they then buried as votive offerings under their ceremonial courtyards or platforms. The celt shape could be modified into a figural form, combining relief carving with incising. Olmec sculptors used stone-tipped drills and abrasive materials, such as sand, to carve jade. Subjects represented include crying babies (of unknown significance) and figures combining human and animal features and postures, such as the *were-jaguar* illustrated here (FIG. **14-3**). The Olmec human-animal representations may refer to the belief that religious practitioners underwent dangerous transformations to wrest power from supernatural forces and harness it for the good of the community.

1 in.

14-4 Drinker (seated figure with raised arms), from Colima, Mexico, ca. 200 BCE–500 CE. Clay with orange and red slip, 1′ 1″ high. Los Angeles County Museum of Art (Proctor Stafford Collection, purchased with funds provided by Mr. and Mrs. Allan C. Balch).

Preclassic West Mexico is famous for its ceramic sculptures. This one may depict a religious practitioner with a horn on his forehead or a political leader wearing a shell ornament—or someone serving both roles.

WEST MEXICO Far to the west of the tropical heartland of the Olmec are the Preclassic sites along Mexico's Pacific coast. Scholars long thought the ancient peoples of the modern West Mexican states of Nayarit, Jalisco, and Colima existed at Mesoamerica's geographic and cultural fringes. Recent archaeological discoveries, however, have revealed that although the West Mexicans did not produce large-scale stone sculpture, they did build permanent structures. These included tiered platforms and ball courts (see "The Meso-american Ball Game," page 372), architectural features found in nearly all Mesoamerican cultures. Yet West Mexico is best known for its rich tradition of clay sculpture. The sculptures come from tombs consisting of shafts as deep as 50 feet with chambers at their base. Because scientific excavations began only 20–30 years ago, much of what is known about West Mexican tomb contents derives primarily from the artifacts grave robbers found and sold. Researchers believe, however, that the West Mexicans built most of these tombs and filled them with elaborate offerings during the late Preclassic period, the half millennium before 300 CE.

The large ceramic figures found in the Colima tombs are consistently a highly burnished red-orange, instead of the distinctive polychrome surfaces of the majority of other West Mexican ceramics. The area also is noted for small-scale clay narrative scenes that include modeled houses and temples and numerous solid figurines shown in a variety of lively activities. These sculptures, which may provide informal glimpses of daily life, are not found in any other ancient Mesoamerican culture. Although archaeologists often describe the subjects of the sculptures as anecdotal and secular rather than religious, the Mesoamerican belief system did not recognize such a division. Consequently, scholars are unsure whether the figure illustrated here (FIG. **14-4**) is a religious practitioner with a horn on his forehead (a common indigenous symbol of special powers) or a political leader wearing a shell ornament (often a Mesoamerican emblem of rulership)—or a person serving both roles.

Teotihuacan

At Olmec sites, the characteristic later Mesoamerican temple-pyramid-plaza layout appeared in embryonic form. At Teotihuacan (FIG. **14-5**), northeast of modern Mexico City, the Preclassic scheme underwent a monumental expansion into a genuine city. Teotihuacan was a large, densely populated metropolis that fulfilled a central civic, economic, and religious role for the region and indeed for much of Mesoamerica. Built up between about 100 BCE and 600 CE, when fire ravaged the city, the site's major monuments were constructed between 50 and 250 CE, during the late Preclassic period. Teotihuacan covers nine square miles, laid out in a grid pattern with the axes oriented by sophisticated surveying. Astronomical phenomena apparently dictated not only the city's orientation but also the placement of some of its key pyramids.

At its peak, around 600 CE, Teotihuacan may have had as many as 125,000–200,000 residents, which would have made it the sixth-largest city in the world at that time. Divided into numerous ward-like sectors, this metropolis must have had a uniquely cosmopolitan character, with Zapotec peoples located in the city's western wards, and merchants from Veracruz living in the eastern wards, importing their own pottery and building their houses and tombs in the style of their homelands. The city's urbanization did nothing to detract from its sacred nature. In fact, it vastly augmented Teotihuacan's importance as a religious center. The Aztecs, who visited Teotihuacan regularly and reverently long after it had been abandoned, gave it its current name, which means "the place of the gods." Because the city's inhabitants left only a handful of undeciphered hieroglyphs, and linguists do not know what language they spoke, the names of many major features of the site are unknown. The Avenue of the Dead and the Pyramids of the Sun and Moon are later Aztec designations that do not necessarily reflect the original names of these entities.

North-south and east-west axes, each four miles in length, divide the grid plan into quarters. The rational scheme recalls Hellenistic and Roman urban planning (FIGS. **5-76** and **10-42**) and is an unusual feature in Mesoamerica before the Aztecs. The main north-south axis, the Avenue of the Dead (FIG. **14-5**), is 130 feet wide and connects the Pyramid of the Moon complex with the Citadel and its Temple of Quetzalcoatl. This two-mile stretch is not a continuously flat street but is broken by sets of stairs, giving pedestrians a constantly changing view of the surrounding buildings and landscape.

PYRAMIDS The Pyramid of the Sun (FIG. **14-5**, *top left*), facing west on the east side of the Avenue of the Dead, dates to the first century CE during the late Preclassic period. It is the city's centerpiece and its largest structure, rising to a height of more than 200 feet in its restored state, which may not accurately reflect the pyramid's original appearance. The Pyramid of the Moon (FIG. **14-5**,

14-5 Aerial view of Teotihuacan (looking south), Mexico. Pyramid of the Moon (*foreground*), Pyramid of the Sun (*top left*), and the Citadel (*background*), all connected by the Avenue of the Dead; main structures ca. 50–250 CE. ◼◀

At its peak around 600 CE, Teotihuacan was the sixth-largest city in the world. It featured a rational grid plan and a two-mile-long main avenue. Its monumental pyramids echo the shapes of surrounding mountains.

foreground) is a century or more later, about 150–250 CE. The shapes of the monumental structures at Teotihuacan echo the surrounding mountains. Their imposing mass and scale surpass those of all other Mesoamerican sites. Rubble-filled and faced with the local volcanic stone, the pyramids consist of stacked squared platforms diminishing in perimeter from the base to the top, much like the Stepped Pyramid (FIG. 3-5) of Djoser in Egyptian Saqqara. Ramped stairways led to crowning temples constructed of perishable materials such as wood and thatch, no longer preserved. A distinctive feature of Teotihuacan construction is the alternation of sloping (*talud*) and vertical (*tablero*) rubble layers. The employment of *talud-tablero construction* at other sites is a sure sign of Teotihuacan influence.

The Teotihuacanos built the Pyramid of the Sun over a cave, which they reshaped and filled with ceramic offerings. The pyramid may have been constructed to honor a sacred spring within the now-dry cave. Excavators found children buried at the four corners of each of the pyramid's tiers. The later Aztecs sacrificed children to bring rainfall, and Teotihuacan art abounds with references to water, so the Teotihuacanos may have shared the Aztec preoccupation with rain and agricultural fertility. The city's inhabitants rebuilt the Pyramid of the Moon (currently being excavated) at least five times in Teotihuacan's early history. The Teotihuacanos may have positioned it to mimic the shape of Cerro Gordo, the volcanic mountain behind it, undoubtedly an important source of life-sustaining streams.

The stone heads of Quetzalcoatl decorating this pyramid are the earliest representations of the feathered-serpent god. Beneath and around the pyramid excavators found remains of sacrificial victims.

14-7A Bloodletting rite, Teotihuacan, ca. 600–700 CE.

QUETZALCOATL At the south end of the Avenue of the Dead is the great quadrangle of the Citadel (FIG. **14-5**, *background*). It encloses a smaller pyramidal shrine datable to the third century CE, the Temple of Quetzalcoatl (FIG. **14-6**). Quetzalcoatl, the "feathered serpent," was a major god in the Mesoamerican pantheon at the time of the Spanish conquest, hundreds of years after the fall of Teotihuacan. The later Aztecs associated him with wind, rain clouds, and life. Beneath the temple, archaeologists found a tomb looted in antiquity, perhaps that of a Teotihuacan ruler. The discovery has led them to speculate that not only the Maya but the Teotihuacanos as well buried their elite in or under pyramids. Surrounding the tomb both beneath and around the pyramid were the remains of at least a hundred sacrificial victims. Some were adorned with necklaces made of strings of human jaws, both real and sculpted from shell. Like most other Mesoamerican groups, the Teotihuacanos invoked and appeased their gods through human sacrifice. The presence of such a large number of victims also may reflect Teotihuacan's militaristic expansion—throughout Mesoamerica, the victors often sacrificed captured warriors.

The temple's sculptured panels, which feature projecting stone heads of Quetzalcoatl alternating with heads of a long-snouted scaly creature with rings on its forehead, decorate each of the temple's six terraces. This is the first unambiguous representation of the feathered serpent in Mesoamerica. The scaly creature's identity is unclear. Linking these alternating heads are low-relief carvings of feathered-serpent bodies and seashells. The latter reflect Teotihuacan contact with the peoples of the Mexican coasts and also symbolize water, an essential ingredient for the sustenance of an agricultural economy.

MURAL PAINTING Like those of most ancient Mesoamerican cities, Teotihuacan's buildings and streets were once stuccoed over and brightly painted. Elaborate murals also covered the walls of the rooms of its elite residential compounds. The paintings chiefly depict deities, ritual activities, and processions of priests, warriors, and even animals. Experimenting with a variety of surfaces, materials, and techniques over the centuries, Teotihuacan muralists finally settled on applying pigments to a smooth lime-plaster surface coated with clay. They then polished the surface to a high sheen. Although some Teotihuacan paintings have a restricted palette of varying tones of red (largely derived from the mineral hematite), creating subtle contrasts between figure and ground, most employ vivid hues arranged in flat, carefully outlined patterns. One mural (FIG. **14-7**) depicts an earth or nature goddess who some scholars think was the city's principal deity. Always shown frontally with her face covered by a jade mask, she is dwarfed by her large feathered headdress and reduced to a bust placed upon a stylized pyramid. She stretches her hands out to provide liquid streams filled with bounty, but the stylized human hearts that flank the frontal bird mask in her headdress reflect her dual nature. They remind viewers that the ancient Mesoamericans saw human sacrifice as essential to agricultural renewal.

The influence of Teotihuacan was all-pervasive in Mesoamerica. The Teotihuacanos established colonies as far away as the southern borders of Maya civilization, in the highlands of Guatemala, some 800 miles from Teotihuacan.

Classic Maya

Strong cultural influences stemming from the Olmec tradition and from Teotihuacan contributed to the development of Classic Maya culture. As was true of Teotihuacan, the foundations of Maya civilization were laid in the Preclassic period, perhaps by 600 BCE or even earlier. At that time, the Maya, who occupied the moist lowland areas of Belize, southern Mexico, Guatemala, and Honduras, seem to have abandoned their early, somewhat egalitarian pattern of village life and adopted a hierarchical autocratic society. This system evolved into the typical Maya city-state governed by hereditary

14-7 Goddess, mural painting from the Tetitla apartment complex at Teotihuacan, Mexico, 650–750 CE. Pigments over clay and plaster.

Elaborate mural paintings adorned Teotihuacan's elite residential compound. This example may depict the city's principal deity, a goddess wearing a jade mask and a large feathered headdress.

rulers and ranked nobility. How and why this happened are still unknown.

Stupendous building projects signaled the change. Vast complexes of terraced temple-pyramids, palaces, plazas, ball courts (see "The Mesoamerican Ball Game," page 372), and residences of the governing elite dotted the Maya area. Unlike at Teotihuacan, no single Maya site ever achieved complete dominance as the center of power. The new architecture, and the art embellishing it, advertised the power of the rulers, who appropriated cosmic symbolism and stressed their descent from gods to reinforce their claims to legitimate rulership. The unified institutions of religion and kingship were established so firmly, their hold on life and custom was so tenacious, and their meaning was so fixed in the symbolism and imagery of art that the rigidly conservative system of the Classic Maya lasted 600 years. Maya civilization began to decline in the eighth century. By 900, it had vanished.

Although the causes of the beginning and end of Classic Maya civilization are obscure, researchers are gradually revealing its history, beliefs, ceremonies, conventions, and patterns of daily life through scientific excavation and progress made in decoding Mayan script. Two important breakthroughs have radically altered the understanding of both Mayan writing and the Maya worldview. The first was the realization that the Maya depicted their rulers (rather than gods or anonymous priests) in their art and noted their rulers' achievements in their texts. The second was that Mayan writing is largely phonetic—that is, the hieroglyphs are composed of signs representing sounds in the Mayan language. Fortunately, the Spaniards recorded the various Mayan languages in colonial texts and dictionaries, and most are still spoken today. Although perhaps only half of the ancient Mayan script can be translated accurately into spoken Mayan, today experts can at least grasp the general meaning of many more hieroglyphs.

The Maya possessed a highly developed knowledge of mathematical calculation and the ability to observe and record the movements of the sun, the moon, and numerous planets. They contrived an intricate but astonishingly accurate calendar with a fixed-zero date, and although this structuring of time was radically different in form from the Western calendar used today, it was just as precise and efficient. With their calendar, the Maya established the all-important genealogical lines of their rulers, which certified their claim to rule, and created the only true written history in ancient America. Although other ancient Mesoamerican societies, even in the Preclassic period, also possessed calendars, only the Maya calendar can be translated directly into today's calendrical system.

ARCHITECTURE AND RITUAL The Maya erected their most sacred and majestic buildings in enclosed, centrally located precincts within their cities. The religious-civic transactions that guaranteed the order of the state and the cosmos occurred in these settings. The Maya held dramatic rituals within a sculptured and painted environment, where huge symbols and images proclaimed the nature and necessity of that order. Maya builders designed spacious plazas for vast audiences who were exposed to overwhelming propaganda. The programmers of that propaganda, the ruling families and troops of priests, nobles, and retainers, incorporated its symbolism in their costumes. In Maya paintings and sculptures, the Maya elite wear extravagant costumery of vividly colorful cotton textiles, feathers, jaguar skins, and jade, all emblematic of their rank and wealth. On the different levels of the painted and polished temple platforms, the ruling classes performed the offices of their rites in clouds of incense to the music of maracas, flutes, and drums. The Maya transformed the architectural complex at each city's center into a theater of religion and statecraft. In the stagelike layout of a characteristic Maya city center, its principal group, or "site core," was the religious and administrative nucleus for a population of dispersed farmers settled throughout a suburban area of many square miles.

The Mesoamerican Ball Game

After witnessing the native ball game of Mexico soon after their arrival, the 16th-century Spanish conquerors took Aztec ball players back to Europe to demonstrate the novel sport. Their chronicles remark on the athletes' great skill, the heavy wagering that accompanied the competition, and the ball itself, made of rubber, a substance the Spaniards had never seen before.

The game was played throughout Mesoamerica and into the southwestern United States, beginning at least 3,400 years ago, the date of the earliest known ball court. The Olmec were apparently avid players. Their very name—a modern invention in Náhuatl, the Aztec language—means "rubber people," after the latex-growing region they inhabited. Not only do ball players appear in Olmec art, but archaeologists have found remnants of sunken earthen ball courts and even rubber balls at Olmec sites.

The Olmec earthen playing field evolved in other Mesoamerican cultures into a plastered masonry surface, I- or T-shaped in plan, flanked by two parallel sloping or straight walls. Sometimes the walls were wide enough to support small structures on top, as at Copán (FIG. 14-8). At other sites, temples stood at either end of the ball court. These structures were common features of Mesoamerican cities. At Cantona in the Mexican state of Puebla, for example, archaeologists have uncovered 22 ball courts even though only a small portion of the site has been excavated. Teotihuacan (FIG. 14-5) is an exception. Excavators have not yet found a ball court there, but mural paintings at the site illustrate people playing the game with portable markers and sticks. Most ball courts were adjacent to the important civic structures of Mesoamerican cities, such as palaces and temple-pyramids, as at Copán.

Surprisingly little is known about the rules of the ball game itself—how many players were on the field, how goals were scored and tallied, and how competitions were arranged. Unlike a modern soccer field with its standard dimensions, Mesoamerican ball courts vary widely in size. The largest known—at Chichén Itzá—is nearly 500 feet long. Copán's is about 93 feet long. Some have stone rings set high up on the walls at right angles to the ground, which a player conceivably could toss a ball through, but many courts lack this feature. Alternatively, players may have bounced the ball against the walls and into the end zones. As in soccer, the players could not touch the ball with their hands but used their heads, elbows, hips, and legs. They wore thick leather belts, and sometimes even helmets, and padded their knees and arms against the blows of the fast-moving solid rubber ball. Typically, the Maya portrayed ball players wearing heavy protective clothing and kneeling, poised to deflect the ball (FIG. 14-11).

Although widely enjoyed as a competitive spectator sport, the ball game did not serve solely for entertainment. The ball, for example, may have represented a celestial body such as the sun, its movements over the court imitating the sun's daily passage through the sky. Reliefs on the walls of ball courts at certain sites make clear that the game sometimes culminated in human sacrifice, probably of captives taken in battle and then forced to participate in a game they were predestined to lose.

Ball playing also had a role in Mesoamerican mythology. In the Maya epic known as the *Popol Vuh* (*Council Book*), first written down in Spanish in the colonial period, the evil lords of the Underworld force a legendary pair of twins to play ball. The brothers lose and are sacrificed. The sons of one twin eventually travel to the Underworld and, after a series of trials including a ball game, outwit the lords and kill them. They revive their father, buried in the ball court after his earlier defeat at the hands of the Underworld gods. The younger twins rise to the heavens to become the sun and the moon, and the father becomes the god of maize, principal sustenance of all Mesoamerican peoples. The ball game and its aftermath, then, were a metaphor for the cycle of life, death, and regeneration that permeated Mesoamerican religion.

14-8 Ball court (view looking north), Maya, Middle Plaza, Copán, Honduras, 738 CE.

Ball courts were common in Mesoamerican cities. Copán's is 93 feet long. The rules of the ball game itself are unknown, but games sometimes ended in human sacrifice, probably of captives taken in battle.

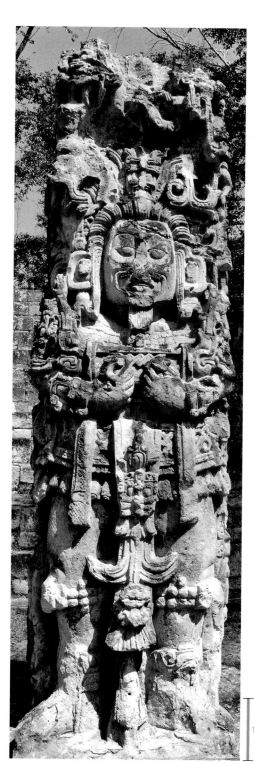

14-9 Stele D portraying Ruler 13 (Waxaklajuun-Ub'aah-K'awiil), Maya, Great Plaza, Copán, Honduras, 736 CE. Stone, 11′ 9″ high.

Ruler 13 reigned during the heyday of Copán. On this stele he wears an elaborate headdress and holds a double-headed serpent bar, symbol of the sky and of his absolute power.

1 ft.

tions of the god K'awiil." Scholars often call him Ruler 13 in the Copán dynastic sequence of 16 rulers. During his long reign, Copán may have reached its greatest physical extent and range of political influence. On Stele D, Ruler 13 wears an elaborate headdress and ornamented kilt and sandals. He holds across his chest a double-headed serpent bar, symbol of the sky and of his absolute power. His features are distinctly Maya, although highly idealized. The Maya elite tended to have themselves portrayed in a conventionalized manner and as eternally youthful. The dense, deeply carved ornamental details that frame the face and figure in florid profusion stand almost clear of the block and wrap around the sides of the stele. The high relief, originally painted, gives the impression of a freestanding statue, although a hieroglyphic text is carved on the flat back side of the stele. Ruler 13 erected many stelae and buildings at Copán, but the king of neighboring Quiriguá eventually captured and beheaded the powerful Copán ruler.

TIKAL Another great Maya site of the Classic period is Tikal in Guatemala, some 150 miles north of Copán. Tikal is one of the oldest and largest of the Maya cities. Together with its suburbs, Tikal originally covered some 75 square miles and served as the ceremonial center of a population of perhaps 75,000. The Maya did not lay out central Tikal on a grid plan as did the designers of contemporaneous Teotihuacan. Instead, causeways connected irregular groupings. Modern surveys have uncovered the remains of as many as 3,000 separate structures in an area of about six square miles. The site's nucleus, the Great Plaza, is studded with stelae and defined by numerous architectural complexes. The most prominent monuments are the two soaring pyramids, taller than the surrounding rain forest, that face each other across an open square. The larger pyramid (FIG. **14-10**), Temple I (also called the Temple of the Giant Jaguar after a motif on one of its carved wooden lintels), reaches a height of about 150 feet. It is the temple-mausoleum of a great Tikal ruler, Hasaw Chan K'awiil, who died in 732 CE. His body rested in a

14-10A Temple of the Inscriptions, Palenque, ca. 675–690 CE.

14-10 Temple I (Temple of the Giant Jaguar), Maya, Tikal, Guatemala, ca. 732 CE.

Temple I at Tikal is a 150-foot-tall pyramid that was the temple-mausoleum of Hasaw Chan K'awiil, who died in 732 CE. The nine tiers of the pyramid probably symbolize the nine levels of the Underworld.

COPÁN Because Copán, on the western border of Honduras, has more hieroglyphic inscriptions and well-preserved carved monuments than any other site in the Americas, it was one of the first Maya sites excavated. It also has proved one of the richest in the trove of architecture, sculpture, and artifacts recovered, and boasts one of Mesoamerica's best-preserved (and carefully restored) ball courts (FIG. **14-8**; see "The Mesoamerican Ball Game," page 372).

Conspicuous plazas dominated the heart of Copán. In the city's Great Plaza, the Maya set up tall, sculpted stone stelae. Carved with the portraits of the rulers who erected them, these stelae also recorded their names, dates of reign, and notable achievements in glyphs on the front, sides, or back. Stele D (FIG. **14-9**), erected in 736 CE, represents one of the city's foremost rulers, Waxaklajuun-Ub'aah-K'awiil (r. 695–738), whose name means "18 are the appari-

14-11 Ball player, Maya, from Jaina Island, Mexico, 700–900 CE. Painted clay, 6¼" high. Museo Nacional de Antropología, Mexico City.

Maya ceramic figurines represent a wide range of human types and activities. This kneeling ball player wears a thick leather belt and arm- and kneepads to protect him from the hard rubber ball.

vaulted chamber under the pyramid's base. The towering structure consists of nine sharply inclining platforms, probably a reference to the nine levels of the Underworld. A narrow stairway leads up to a three-chambered temple. Surmounting the temple is an elaborately sculpted *roof comb,* a vertical architectural projection that once bore the ruler's giant portrait modeled in stucco. The entire structure exhibits most concisely the ancient Mesoamerican formula for the stepped temple-pyramid and the compelling aesthetic and psychological power of Maya architecture.

JAINA The almost unlimited variety of figural attitude and gesture permitted in the modeling of clay explains the profusion of Maya ceramic figurines that, like their West Mexican predecessors (FIG. 14-4), may illustrate aspects of everyday life. Small-scale freestanding figures in the round, they are remarkably lifelike, carefully descriptive, and even comic at times. They represent a wider range of human types and activities than is commonly depicted on Maya stelae. Ball players (FIG. **14-11**), women weaving, older men, dwarfs, supernatural beings, and amorous couples, as well as elaborately attired rulers and warriors, make up the figurine repertory. Many of the hollow figurines are also whistles. They were made in ceramic workshops on the mainland, often with molds, but graves in the island cemetery of Jaina, off the western coast of Yucatán, yielded hundreds of these figures, including the ball player illustrated here. Traces of blue remain on the figure's belt—remnants of the vivid pigments that once covered many of these figurines. The Maya used "Maya blue," a combination of a particular kind of clay and indigo, a vegetable dye, to paint both ceramics and murals. This pigment has proved virtually indestructible, unlike the other colors that largely

have disappeared over time. Like the larger terracotta figures of West Mexico, these figurines accompanied the dead on their inevitable voyage to the Underworld. The excavations at Jaina, however, have revealed nothing more that might clarify the meaning and function of the figures. Male figurines do not come exclusively from burials of male individuals, for example.

BONAMPAK The vivacity of the Jaina figurines and their variety of pose, costume, and occupation have parallels in the mural paintings of Bonampak (Mayan for "painted walls") in southeastern Mexico. Three chambers in one Bonampak structure contain murals that record important aspects of Maya court life. The example reproduced here (FIG. **14-12**) shows warriors surrounding captives on a terraced platform. The figures have naturalistic proportions and overlap, twist, turn, and gesture. The artists used fluid and calligraphic line to outline the forms, working with color to indicate both texture and volume. The Bonampak painters combined their pigments—both mineral and organic—with a mixture of water, crushed limestone, and vegetable gums and applied them to their stucco walls in a technique best described as a cross between *fresco* and *tempera.*

14-12A Enthroned Maya lord, cylinder vase ca. 672–830 CE

The Bonampak murals are filled with circumstantial detail. The information given is comprehensive, explicit, and presented with the fidelity of an eyewitness report. The royal personages are identifiable by both their physical features and their costumes, and accompanying inscriptions provide the precise day, month, and year for the events recorded. All the scenes at Bonampak relate the events and ceremonies that welcome a new royal heir (shown as a toddler in some scenes). They include presentations, preparations for a royal fete, dancing, battle, and the taking and sacrificing of prisoners. On all occasions of state, public bloodletting was an integral part of Maya ritual. The ruler, his consort, and certain members of the nobility drew blood from their own bodies and sought union with the supernatural world. The slaughter of captives taken in war regularly accompanied this ceremony. Indeed, Mesoamerican cultures undertook warfare largely to provide victims for sacrifice. The torture and eventual execution of prisoners served both to nourish the gods and to strike fear into enemies and the general populace.

The scene (FIG. **14-12**) in room 2 of structure 1, depicts the presentation of prisoners to Lord Chan Muwan. The painter arranged the figures in registers that may represent a pyramid's steps. On the uppermost step, against a blue background, is a file of gorgeously appareled nobles wearing animal headgear. Conspicuous among them on the right are retainers clad in jaguar pelts and jaguar headdresses. Also present is Chan Muwan's wife (third from right). The ruler himself, in jaguar jerkin and high-backed sandals, stands at the center, facing a crouching victim who appears to beg for mercy. Naked captives, anticipating death, crowd the middle level. One of them, already dead, sprawls at the ruler's feet. Others dumbly contemplate the blood dripping from their mutilated hands. The lower zone, cut through by a doorway into the structure housing the murals, shows clusters of attendants who are doubtless of inferior rank to the lords of the upper zone. The stiff formality of the victors contrasts graphically with the supple imploring attitudes and gestures of the hapless victims. The Bonampak victory was short-lived. The artists never finished the murals, and shortly after the dates written on the walls, the Maya seem to have abandoned the site.

The Bonampak murals are the most famous Maya wall paintings, but they are not unique. In 2001 at San Bartolo in northeastern Guatemala, archaeologists discovered the earliest examples yet found. They date to about 100 BCE, almost a millennium before the Bonampak murals.

14-12 Presentation of captives to Lord Chan Muwan, Maya, room 2 of structure 1, Bonampak, Mexico, ca. 790 CE. Mural, 17′ × 15′; watercolor copy by Antonio Tejeda. Peabody Museum of Archaeology and Ethnology, Harvard University, Cambridge.

The figures in this mural—a cross between fresco and tempera—may be standing on a pyramid's steps. At the top, the richly attired Chan Muwan reviews naked captives with mutilated hands awaiting their death.

YAXCHILÁN Elite women played an important role in Maya society, and some surviving artworks document their high status. The painted reliefs on the lintels of temple 23 at Yaxchilán represent a woman as a central figure in Maya ritual. Lintel 24 (FIG. **14-1**) depicts the ruler Itzamna Balam II (r. 681–742 CE), known as Shield Jaguar, and his principal wife, Lady Xoc. Lady Xoc is magnificently outfitted in an elaborate woven garment, headdress, and jewels. She pierces her tongue with a barbed cord in a bloodletting ceremony that, according to accompanying inscriptions, celebrated the birth of a son to one of the ruler's other wives as well as an alignment between the planets Saturn and Jupiter. The celebration must have been held in a dark chamber or at night because Shield Jaguar provides illumination with a blazing torch. The purpose of these ceremonies was to produce hallucinations. (Lintel 25 depicts Lady Xoc and her vision of an ancestor emerging from the mouth of a serpent.)

Classic Veracruz

Although the Maya is the most famous Classic Mesoamerican culture today and its remains are the most abundant, other cultures also flourished, and some of their surviving monuments rival those of the Maya in size and sophistication. In the Veracruz plain, for example, the heir to the Olmec culture was a civilization that archaeologists call Classic Veracruz. The name of the people that occupied the area at the time is unknown.

14-13 Pyramid of the Niches, Classic Veracruz, El Tajín, Mexico, sixth century CE.

The Pyramid of the Niches, although only 66 feet tall, has 365 niches on its four sides, one for each day of the solar year. It is one of many Mesoamerican monuments connected with astronomy and the calendar.

EL TAJÍN The major Classic Veracruz site is El Tajín, which was discovered in the dense rain forest of the Gulf of Mexico coast in 1785. At its peak, El Tajín was a thriving city of hundreds of acres and tens of thousands of inhabitants. Its excavated portion has already revealed 17 ball courts. The building that dominates the ceremonial center of El Tajín is the so-called Pyramid of the Niches (FIG. **14-13**), a sixth-century CE structure of unusual form. In spite of its small size (only 66 feet tall), the Pyramid of the Niches encases an earlier smaller pyramid. The later structure has a steep staircase on its east side and six stories, each one incorporating a row of niches on each of the four sides, 365 in all. The number of niches, which corresponds to the number of days in a solar year, is unlikely to be coincidental. The Pyramid of the Niches is one of many examples of the close connection between the form of Mesoamerican monuments and astronomical observations and the measurement of time.

Postclassic Mexico

Throughout Mesoamerica, the Classic period ended at different times with the disintegration of the great civilizations. Teotihuacan's political and cultural empire, for example, was disrupted around 600, and its influence waned. About 600, fire destroyed the center of the great city, but the cause is still unknown. Within a century, however, Teotihuacan was deserted. Around 900, many of the great Maya sites were abandoned to the jungle, leaving a few northern Maya cities to flourish for another century or two before they, too, became depopulated. The Classic culture of the Zapotecs, centered at Monte Albán in the state of Oaxaca, came to an end around 700, and the neighboring Mixtec peoples assumed supremacy in this area during the Postclassic period. Classic El Tajín survived the general crisis that

afflicted the others but burned sometime in the 12th century. The war and confusion that followed the collapse of the Classic civilizations fractured the great states into small, local political entities isolated in fortified sites. The collapse encouraged even more warlike regimes and chronic aggression. The militant city-state of Chichén Itzá dominated Yucatán, while in central Mexico the Toltec and the later Aztec peoples, both ambitious migrants from the north, forged empires by force of arms.

CHICHÉN ITZÁ Yucatán, a flat, low, limestone peninsula covered with scrub vegetation, lies north of the rolling and densely forested region of the Guatemalan Petén. During the Classic period, Mayan-speaking peoples sparsely inhabited this northern region. For reasons scholars still debate, when the southern Classic Maya sites were abandoned after 900, the northern Maya continued to build many new temples in this area. They also experimented with building construction and materials to a much greater extent than their cousins farther south. Piers and columns appeared in doorways, and stone mosaics enlivened outer facades. The northern groups also invented a new type of construction, a solid core of coarse rubble faced on both sides with a veneer of square limestone plates.

Dominating the main plaza of Chichén Itzá today is the 98-foot-high pyramid (FIG. **14-14**) that the Spaniards nicknamed the Castillo (Castle). As at Tikal (FIG. **14-10**), this pyramid has nine levels. Atop the structure is a temple dedicated to Kukulkan, the Maya equivalent of Quetzalcoatl, and, as at El Tajín (FIG. **14-13**), the design of the Castillo is tied to the solar year. The north side has 92 steps and the other three sides 91 steps each for a total of 365. At the winter and summer equinoxes, the sun casts a shadow along the north-

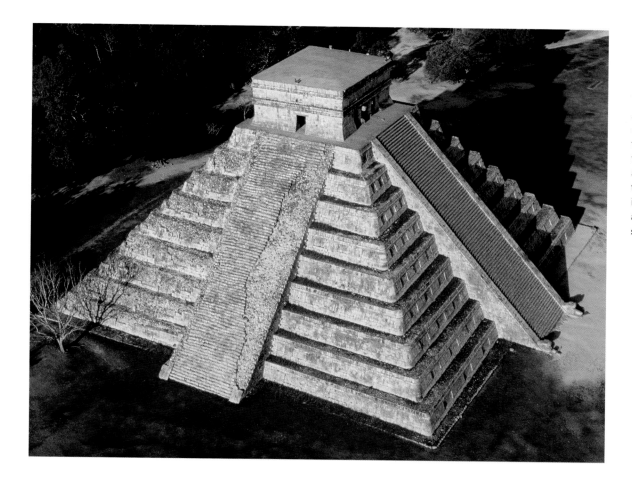

ern staircase of the pyramid. Because of the pyramid's silhouette and the angle of the sun, the shadow takes the shape of a serpent that slithers along the pyramid's face as the sun moves across the sky.

Excavations inside the Castillo in 1937 revealed an earlier nine-level pyramid within the later and larger structure. Inside was a royal burial chamber with a throne in the form of a red jaguar and a stone figure of a type called a *chacmool* depicting a fallen warrior. Chacmools (for example, FIG. **14-15,** found near the Castillo) recline on their backs and have receptacles on their chests to receive sacrificial offerings, probably of defeated enemies. The distinctive forms of the Mesoamerican chacmools made a deep impression upon 20th-century sculptors (FIG. **35-59**).

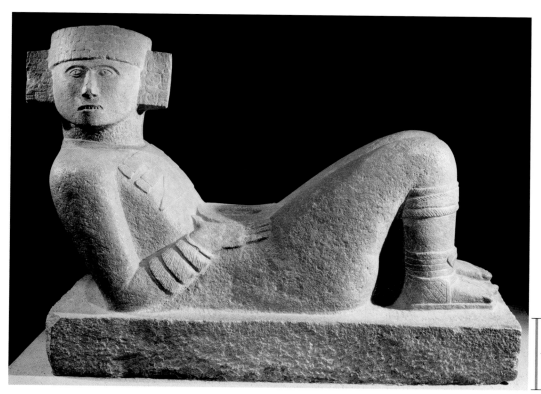

14-15 Chacmool, Maya, from the Platform of the Eagles, Chichén Itzá, Mexico, ca. 800–900 CE. Stone, 4′ 10½″ high. Museo Nacional de Antropología, Mexico City.

Chacmools represent fallen warriors reclining on their backs with receptacles on their chests to receive sacrificial offerings. Excavators discovered one in the burial chamber inside the Castillo (FIG. 14-14).

1 ft.

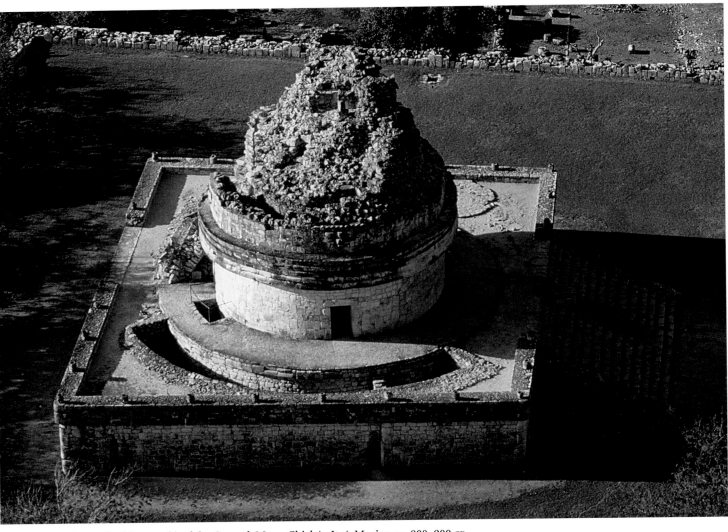

14-16 Aerial view (looking south) of the Caracol, Maya, Chichén Itzá, Mexico, ca. 800–900 CE.

Caracol means "snail shell," and this unusual round northern Maya structure encloses a circular staircase. The building may have been a temple to Kukulkan with an astronomical observatory at its summit.

The Caracol (FIG. **14-16**) at Chichén Itzá establishes that the northern Maya were as inventive with architectural form as they were experimental with construction and materials. A cylindrical tower rests on a broad terrace that is in turn supported by a larger rectangular platform measuring 169 × 232 feet. The tower, composed of two concentric walls, encloses a circular staircase that leads to a small chamber near the top of the structure. In plan, the building recalls the cross-section of a conch shell. (Caracol means "snail" in Spanish.) The conch shell was an attribute of the feathered serpent, and round temples were dedicated to him in central Mexico. This building may therefore also have been a temple to Kukulkan. Windows along the Caracol's staircase and an opening at the summit probably were used for astronomical observation.

TULA The name Toltec, which signifies "makers of things," generally refers to a powerful tribe of invaders from the north, whose arrival in central Mexico coincided with the great disturbances that must have contributed to the fall of the Classic civilizations. The Toltec capital at Tula flourished from about 900 to 1200. The Toltecs were expert political organizers and military strategists, dominating large parts of north and central Mexico. They also were master artisans and farmers, and later peoples such as the Aztecs looked back on the Toltecs admiringly, proud to claim descent from them.

Archaeologists have noted many similarities between the sites of Tula and Chichén Itzá.

At Tula, four colossal *atlantids* (male statue-columns; FIG. **14-17**) portraying armed warriors reflect the grim, warlike regime of the Toltecs. These images of brutal authority stand eternally at attention, warding off all hostile threats. Built up of four stone drums each, the sculptures stand atop pyramid B. They wear feathered headdresses and, as breastplates, stylized butterflies, heraldic symbols of the Toltec. In one hand they clutch a bundle of darts and in the other an *atlatl* (spear-thrower), typical weapons of highland Mexico. The figures originally supported a temple roof, now missing. Such an architectural function requires rigidity of pose, compactness, and strict simplicity of contour. The unity and regularity of architectural mass and silhouette here combine perfectly with abstraction of form.

By 1180 the last Toltec ruler abandoned Tula, and most of his people followed. Some years later, the city was catastrophically destroyed, its ceremonial buildings burned to their foundations, its walls demolished, and the straggling remainder of its population scattered. The exact reasons for the Toltecs' departure and for their city's destruction are unknown. Although the Toltec demise set the stage for the rise of the last great civilization of Mesoamerica, the Aztecs (see Chapter 32), that culture did not reach the height of its power for another 300 years.

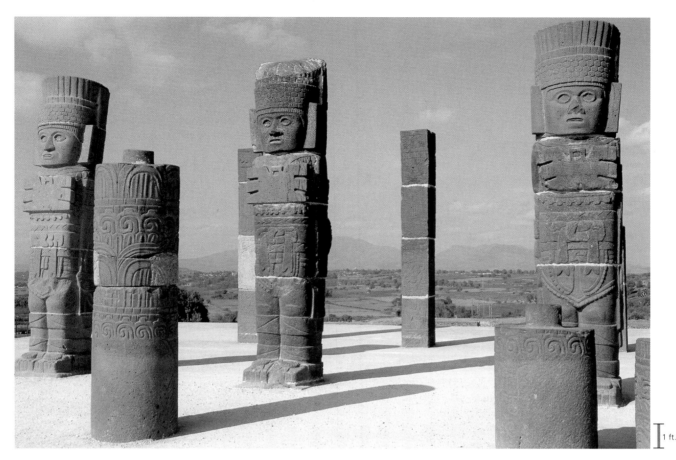

14-17 Colossal atlantids, pyramid B, Toltec, Tula, Mexico, ca. 900–1180 CE. Stone, each 16′ high.

The colossal statue-columns of Tula portraying warriors armed with darts and spear-throwers reflect the military regime of the Toltecs, whose arrival in central Mexico coincided with the decline of the Maya.

INTERMEDIATE AREA

Between the highly developed civilizations of Mesoamerica and the South American Andes lies a region archaeologists have dubbed the "Intermediate Area." Comprising parts of El Salvador, Honduras, Ecuador, and Venezuela, and all of Panama, Costa Rica, Nicaragua, and Colombia, at the time of the European invasion it was by no means a unified political territory but rather was divided among many small rival chiefdoms. Although the people of the Intermediate Area did not produce monumental architecture on the scale of their neighbors to the north and south and, unlike the Mesoamericans, left no written records, they too were consummate artists. Potters in the Intermediate Area made some of the earliest ceramics of the Americas, and they continued to create an astonishing variety of terracotta vessels and figures until the time of the Spanish conquest. Among the other arts practiced in the Intermediate Area were stone sculpture and jade carving. Inhabitants throughout the region prized goldworking, and the first Europeans to make contact here were astonished to see the natives nearly naked but covered in gold jewelry. The legend of El Dorado, a Colombian chief who coated himself in gold as part of his accession rites, was largely responsible for the Spanish invaders' ruthless plunder of the region.

TAIRONA In northern Colombia (MAP 14-2), the Sierra Nevada de Santa Marta rises above the Caribbean. The topography of lofty mountains and river valleys provided considerable isolation and fostered the independent development of various groups. The inhabitants of this region after about 1000 CE included a group known as the Tairona, whose metalwork is among the finest of all the ancient American goldworking styles.

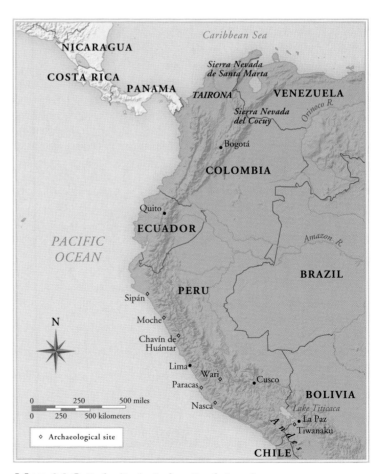

MAP 14-2 Early sites in Andean South America.

14-18 Pendant in the form of a bat-faced man, Tairona, from northeastern Colombia, after 1000 CE. Gold, $5\frac{1}{4}''$ high. Metropolitan Museum of Art, New York (Jan Mitchell and Sons Collection).

The peoples of the Intermediate Area between Mesoamerica and Andean South America were expert goldsmiths. This pendant depicting a bat-faced man with a large headdress served as an amulet.

Goldsmiths in Peru, Ecuador, and southern Colombia produced technologically advanced and aesthetically sophisticated work in gold mostly by cutting and hammering thin gold sheets. The Tairona smiths, however, who had to obtain gold by trade, used the *lost-wax process* in part to preserve the scarce amount of the precious metal available to them. Tairona pendants were not meant to be worn simply as rich accessories for costumes but as amulets or talismans representing powerful beings who gave the wearer protection and status. The pendant shown here (FIG. **14-18**) represents a bat-faced man—perhaps a masked man rather than a composite being, or a man in the process of spiritual transformation. In local mythology, the first animal created was the bat. This bat-man wears an immense headdress composed of two birds in the round, two great beaked heads, and a series of spirals crowned by two overarching stalks. The harmony of repeated curvilinear motifs, the rhythmic play of their contours, and the precise delineation of minute detail attest to the artist's technical control and aesthetic sensitivity.

SOUTH AMERICA

As in Mesoamerica, the indigenous civilizations of Andean South America (MAP **14-2**) jarred against and stimulated one another, produced towering monuments and sophisticated paintings, sculptures, ceramics, and textiles, and were crushed in violent confrontations with the Spanish conquistadors. Although less well studied than the ancient Mesoamerican cultures, those of South America are actually older, and in some ways they surpassed the accomplishments of their northern counterparts. Andean peoples, for example, mastered metalworking much earlier, and their monumental architecture predates that of the earliest Mesoamerican culture, the Olmec, by more than a millennium. The peoples of northern Chile even began to mummify their dead at least 500 years before the Egyptians.

The Central Andean region of South America lies between Ecuador and northern Chile, with its western border the Pacific Ocean. It consists of three well-defined geographic zones, running north and south and roughly parallel to one another. The narrow western coastal plain is a hot desert crossed by rivers, which create habitable fertile valleys. Next, the high peaks of the great Cordillera of the Andes hem in plateaus of a temperate climate. The region's inland border, the eastern slopes of the Andes, is a hot and humid jungle.

Andean civilizations flourished both in the highlands and on the coast. Highland cave dwellers fashioned the first rudimentary art objects by 8800 BCE. Artisans started producing sophisticated textiles as early as 2500 BCE, and the firing of clay began in Peru before 1800 BCE. Beginning about 800 BCE, Andean chronology alternates between periods known as "horizons," when a single culture appears to have dominated a broad geographic area for a relatively long period, and "intermediate periods" characterized by more independent regional development. The Chavín culture (ca. 800–200 BCE) represents the first period, Early Horizon; the Tiwanaku and Wari cultures (ca. 600–1000 CE) the Middle Horizon; and the Inka Empire (see Chapter 32) the Late Horizon. Among the many regional styles that flourished between these horizons, the most important are the Early Intermediate period (ca. 200 BCE–700 CE) Paracas and Nasca cultures of the south coast of Peru, and the Moche in the north.

The discovery of complex ancient communities documented by radiocarbon dating is changing the picture of early South American cultures. Planned communities boasting organized labor systems and monumental architecture dot the narrow river valleys that drop from the Andes to the Pacific Ocean. In the Central Andes, these early sites began to develop around 3000 BCE, about a millennium before the invention of pottery there. Carved gourds and some fragmentary cotton textiles survive from this early period. They depict composite creatures, such as crabs turning into snakes, as well as doubled and then reversed images, both hallmarks of later Andean art.

The architecture of the early coastal sites typically consists of large U-shaped, flat-topped platforms—some as high as a 10-story building—around sunken courtyards. Many had numerous small chambers on top. Construction materials included both uncut fieldstones and handmade *adobes* (sun-dried mud bricks) in the shape of cones, laid point to point in coarse mud plaster to form walls and platforms. These complexes almost always faced toward the Andes mountains, source of the life-giving rivers on which these communities depended for survival. Mountain worship, which continues in the Andean region to this day, was probably the focus of early religious practices as well. In the highlands, archaeologists also have discovered large ceremonial complexes. In place of the numerous interconnecting rooms found atop many coastal mounds, the highland examples have a single small chamber at the top, often with a stone-lined firepit in the center. These pits probably played a role in ancient fire rituals. Excavators have found burnt offerings in the pits, often of exotic objects such as marine shells and tropical bird feathers.

Chavín

Named after the ceremonial center of Chavín de Huántar, located in the northern highlands of Peru, the Chavín culture of the Early Horizon period developed and spread throughout much of the coastal region and the highlands during the first millennium BCE. Once thought to be the "mother culture" of the Andean region, the Chavín culture is now seen as the culmination of developments that began elsewhere some 2,000 years earlier.

14-19 *Raimondi Stele,* from the main temple, Chavín de Huántar, Peru, ca. 800–200 BCE. Incised green diorite, 6′ high. Instituto Nacional de Cultura, Lima.

The *Raimondi Stele* staff god wears a headdress of faces and snakes. Seen upside down, the god's face becomes two faces. The ability of the gods to transform themselves is a core aspect of Andean religion.

1 ft.

The Old Temple of Chavín de Huántar, dated to the first millennium BCE, resembles some of the sacred complexes of the earliest Andean cultures. It is a U-shaped, stone-faced structure between two rivers, with wings up to 83 yards long. Although at first glance its three stories appear to be a solid stepped platform, in fact narrow passageways, small chambers, and stairways penetrate the temple in a labyrinthine pattern. No windows, however, light the interior spaces. The few members of Chavín society with access to these rooms must have witnessed secret and sacred torch-lit ceremonies. The temple is fronted by sunken courts, an arrangement also adopted from earlier coastal sites.

The temple complex at Chavín de Huántar is famous for its extensive stone carvings. The most common subjects are composite creatures that combine feline, avian, reptilian, and human features. Consisting largely of low relief on panels, cornices, and columns, and some rarer instances of freestanding sculpture, Chavín carving is essentially shallow, linear incision. An immense oracular cult image once stood in the center of the temple's oldest part. Other examples of sculpture in the round include heads of mythological creatures, which were pegged into the exterior walls.

RAIMONDI STELE Found in the main temple at Chavín de Huántar and named after its discoverer, the *Raimondi Stele* (FIG. **14-19**), represents a figure called the "staff god." He appears in various versions from Colombia to northern Bolivia but always holds staffs. Seldom, however, do the representations have the degree of elaboration found at Chavín. The Chavín god gazes upward, frowns, and bares his teeth. His elaborate headdress dominates the upper two-thirds of the slab. Inverting the image reveals that the headdress is composed of a series of fanged jawless faces, each emerging from the mouth of the one above it. Snakes abound. They extend from the deity's belt, make up part of the staffs, serve as whiskers and hair for the deity and the headdress creatures, and form a braid at the apex of the composition. The *Raimondi Stele* clearly illustrates the Andean artistic tendency toward both multiplicity and dual readings. Upside down, the god's face turns into not one but two faces. The ability of gods to transform before the viewer's eyes is a core aspect of Andean religion.

Chavín iconography spread widely throughout the Andean region via portable media such as goldwork, textiles, and ceramics. For example, more than 300 miles from Chavín on the south coast of Peru, archaeologists have discovered cotton textiles with imagery recalling Chavín sculpture. Painted staff-bearing female deities, apparently local manifestations or consorts of the highland staff god, decorate these large cloths, which may have served as wall hangings in temples. Ceramic vessels found on the north coast of Peru also carry motifs much like those found on Chavín stone carvings.

Paracas, Nasca, and Moche

Several coastal traditions developed during the millennium from ca. 400 BCE to 700 CE. The most prominent were the Paracas (ca. 400 BCE–200 CE), Nasca (ca. 200 BCE–600 CE), and Moche (ca. 1–700 CE). Together they exemplify the great variations within Peruvian art styles.

PARACAS The Paracas culture occupied a desert peninsula and a nearby river valley on the south coast of Peru. Outstanding among the Paracas arts are the funerary textiles used to wrap the bodies of the dead in multiple layers. The dry desert climate preserved the textiles, buried in shaft tombs beneath the sands. These textiles are among the enduring masterpieces of Andean art (see "Andean Weaving," page 382). Most are of woven cotton with designs embroidered onto the fabric in alpaca or vicuña wool imported from the highlands. The weavers used more than 150 vivid colors, the majority derived from

Andean Weaving

When the Inka first encountered the Spanish conquistadors, they were puzzled by the Europeans' fixation on gold and silver. The Inka valued finely woven cloth just as highly as precious metal. Textiles and clothing dominated every aspect of their existence. Storing textiles in great warehouses, their leaders demanded cloth as tribute, gave it as gifts, exchanged it during diplomatic negotiations, and even burned it as a sacrificial offering. Although both men and women participated in cloth production, the Inka rulers selected the best women weavers from around the empire and sequestered them for life to produce textiles exclusively for the elite.

Andean weavers manufactured their textiles by spinning into yarn the cotton grown in five different shades on the warm coast and the fur sheared from highland llamas, alpacas, vicuñas, or guanacos, and then weaving the yarn into cloth. Rare tropical bird feathers and small plaques of gold and silver were sometimes sewn onto cloth destined for the nobility. Andean weavers mastered nearly every textile technique known today, many executed with a simple device known as a *backstrap loom*. Similar looms are still in use in the Andes. The weavers stretch the long *warp* (vertical) threads between two wooden bars. The top bar is tied to an upright. A belt or backstrap, attached to the bottom bar, encircles the waist of the seated weaver, who maintains the tension of the warp threads by leaning back. The weaver passes the *weft* (horizontal) threads over and under the warps and pushes them tightly against each other to produce the finished cloth. In ancient textiles, the sturdy cotton often formed the warp, and the wool, which can be dyed brighter colors, served to

create complex designs in the weft. *Embroidery,* the sewing of threads onto a finished ground cloth to form contrasting designs, was the specialty of the Paracas culture (FIG. **14-20**).

The dry deserts of coastal Peru have preserved not only numerous textiles from different periods but also hundreds of finely worked baskets containing spinning and weaving implements. These tools are invaluable sources of information about Andean textile production processes. The baskets found in documented contexts came from women's graves, attesting to the close identity between weaving and women, the reverence for the cloth-making process, and the Andean belief that textiles were necessary in the afterlife.

A special problem all weavers confront is that they must visualize the entire design in advance and cannot easily change it during the weaving process. No records exist of how Andean weavers learned, retained, and passed on the elaborate patterns they wove into cloth, but some painted ceramics depict weavers at work, apparently copying designs from finished models. However, the inventiveness of individual weavers is evident in the endless variety of colors and patterns in surviving Andean textiles. This creativity often led Andean artists to design textiles that are highly abstract and geometric. Paracas embroideries (FIG. **14-20**), for example, may depict humans, down to the patterns on the tunics they wear, yet the figures are reduced to their essentials in order to focus on their otherworldly role. The culmination of this tendency toward abstraction may be seen in the Wari compositions (FIG. **14-26**) in which figural motifs become stunning blocks of color that overwhelm the subject matter itself.

1 ft.

14-20 Embroidered funerary mantle, Paracas, from the southern coast of Peru, first century CE. Plain-weave camelid fiber with stem-stitch embroidery of camelid wool, 4′ 7⅞″ × 7′ 10⅞″. Museum of Fine Arts, Boston (William A. Paine Fund).

Outstanding among the Paracas arts are the woven mantles used to wrap the bodies of the dead. The flying or floating figure repeated endlessly on this mantle is probably either the deceased or a religious practitioner.

plants. Feline, bird, and serpent motifs appear on many of the textiles, but the human figure, real or mythological, predominates. Humans dressed up as or changing into animals are common motifs on the grave mantles—consistent with the Andean transformation theme noted on the *Raimondi Stele* (FIG. 14-19). On one well-preserved mantle (FIG. 14-20), a figure with prominent eyes appears scores of times over the surface. The flowing hair and the slow kicking motion of the legs suggest airy, hovering movement. The flying or floating figure carries batons and fans, or, according to some scholars, knives and hallucinogenic mushrooms. On other mantles the figures carry the skulls or severed heads of enemies. Art historians have interpreted the flying figures either as Paracas religious practitioners dancing or flying during an ecstatic trance or as images of the deceased. Despite endless repetitions of the motif, variations of detail occur throughout each textile, notably in the figures' positions and in subtle color changes.

NASCA The Nasca culture takes its name from the Nasca River valley south of Paracas. The early centuries of the Nasca civilization ran concurrently with the closing centuries of the Paracas culture, and Nasca style emulated Paracas style. The Nasca won renown for their pottery, and thousands of their ceramic vessels survive. The vases usually have round bottoms, double spouts connected by bridges, and smoothly burnished polychrome surfaces. The subjects vary greatly, but plants, animals, and composite mythological creatures, part human and part animal, are most common. Nasca painters often represented ritual impersonators, some of whom, like the Paracas flying figures, hold trophy heads and weapons. On the vessel illustrated here (FIG. 14-21) are two costumed flying figures. The painter reduced their bodies and limbs to abstract appendages and focused on the heads. The figures wear a multicolored necklace, a whiskered gold mouthpiece, circular disks hanging from the ears, and a rayed crown on the forehead. Masks or heads with streaming hair, possibly more trophy heads, flow over the impersonators' backs, increasing the sense of motion.

Nasca artists also depicted figures on a gigantic scale. Some 800 miles of lines drawn in complex networks on the dry surface of the Nasca plain have long attracted world attention because of their

1 in.

14-21 Bridge-spouted vessel with flying figures, Nasca, from Nasca River valley, Peru, ca. 50–200 CE. Painted ceramic, $5\frac{1}{2}''$ high. Art Institute of Chicago, Chicago (Kate S. Buckingham Endowment).

The Nasca were masters of pottery painting. The painter of this bridge-spouted vessel depicted two crowned and bejeweled flying figures, probably ritual impersonators with trophy heads.

colossal size, which defies human perception from the ground. Preserved today are about three dozen images of birds, fish, and plants, including a hummingbird (FIG. 14-22) several hundred feet long. The Nasca artists also drew geometric forms, such as trapezoids, spirals, and straight lines running for miles. Artists produced these Nasca Lines, as the immense earth drawings are called, by selectively

14-22 Hummingbird, Nasca, Nasca plain, Peru, ca. 500 CE. Dark layer of pebbles scraped aside to reveal lighter clay and calcite beneath.

The earth drawings known as Nasca Lines represent birds, fish, plants, and geometric forms. They may have marked pilgrimage routes leading to religious shrines, but their function is uncertain.

removing the dark top layer of stones to expose the light clay and calcite below. The Nasca created the lines quite easily from available materials and using rudimentary geometry. Small groups of workers have made modern reproductions of them with relative ease. The lines seem to be paths laid out using simple stone-and-string methods. Some lead in traceable directions across the deserts of the Nasca River drainage. Others are punctuated by many shrinelike nodes, like the knots on a cord. Some lines converge at central places usually situated close to water sources and seem to be associated with water supply and irrigation. They may have marked pilgrimage routes for those who journeyed to local or regional shrines on foot. Altogether, the vast arrangement of the Nasca Lines is a system—not a meaningless maze but a map that plotted the whole terrain of Nasca material and spiritual concerns. Remarkably, until quite recently, the peoples of highland Bolivia made and used similar ritual pathways in association with shrines, demonstrating the tenacity of the Andean indigenous belief systems.

MOCHE Among the most famous art objects the ancient Peruvians produced are the painted clay vessels of the Moche, who occupied a series of river valleys on the northern coast of Peru around the same time the Nasca flourished to the south. Among ancient civilizations, only the Greeks and the Maya surpassed the Moche in the information recorded on their ceramics. Moche pots illustrate architecture, metallurgy, weaving, the brewing of chicha (fermented maize beer), human deformities and diseases, and even sexual acts. Moche

vessels are predominantly flat-bottomed, stirrup-spouted jars derived from Chavín prototypes. The potters generally decorated them with a *bichrome* (two-color) slip. Although the Moche made early vessels by hand without the aid of a potter's wheel, they fashioned later ones in two-piece molds. Thus, numerous near-duplicates survive. Moche ceramists continued to refine the stirrup spout, making it an elegant slender tube, much narrower than the Chavín examples. The portrait vessel illustrated here (FIG. **14-23**) is an elaborate example of a common Moche type. It may depict the face of a warrior, a ruler, or even a royal retainer whose image may have been buried with many other pots to accompany his dead master. The realistic rendering of the physiognomy is particularly striking.

SIPÁN Elite men, along with retinues of sacrificial victims, appear to be the occupants of several rich Moche tombs excavated near the village of Sipán on the arid northwest coast of Peru. The Sipán burial sites have yielded a treasure of golden artifacts and more than a thousand ceramic vessels. The discovery of the tombs in the late 1980s created a great stir in the archaeological world, contributing significantly to the knowledge of Moche culture. Beneath a large adobe platform adjacent to two high but greatly eroded pyramids, excavators found several lavish graves, including the tomb of a man known today as the Lord of Sipán, or the Warrior Priest. The splendor of the funeral trappings that adorned his body, the quantity and quality of the sumptuous accessories, and the bodies of the retainers buried with him indicate that he was a personage of the highest rank. Indeed, he may have been one of the warrior priests so often depicted on Moche ceramic wares and murals (and in this tomb on a golden pyramid-shaped rattle) assaulting his enemies and participating in sacrificial ceremonies.

An ear ornament (FIG. **14-24**) of turquoise and gold found in one Sipán tomb shows a warrior priest clad much like the Lord of Sipán. Two retainers appear in profile to the left and right of the central figure. Represented frontally, he carries a war club and shield and

14-23 Vessel in the shape of a portrait head, Moche, from the northern coast of Peru, fifth to sixth century CE. Painted clay, 1′ ½″ high. Museo Arqueológico Rafael Larco Herrera, Lima.

The Moche culture produced an extraordinary variety of painted vessels. This one in the shape of a head may depict a warrior, ruler, or royal retainer. The realistic rendering of the face is particularly striking.

14-24 Ear ornament, Moche, from a tomb at Sipán, Peru, ca. 300 CE. Gold and turquoise, 4⅘″. Bruning Archaeological Museum, Lambayeque.

This ear ornament from a Sipán tomb depicts a Moche warrior priest and two retainers. The priest carries a war club and shield and wears a necklace of owl-head beads. The costume corresponds to actual finds.

14-25 Gateway of the Sun, Tiwanaku, Bolivia, ca. 375–700 CE. Stone, 9′ 10″ high.

The Gateway of the Sun probably led into a sacred area at Tiwanaku. The central figure is a version of the Chavín staff god (FIG. **14-19**). The relief was once painted, inlaid with turquoise, and covered with gold.

wears a necklace of owl-head beads. The figure's bladelike crescent-shaped helmet is a replica of the large golden one buried with the Sipán lord. The war club and shield also match finds in the Warrior Priest's tomb. The ear ornament of the jewelry image is a simplified version of the piece itself. Other details also correspond to actual finds—for example, the removable nose ring that hangs down over the mouth. The value of the Sipán find is incalculable for what it reveals about elite Moche culture and for its confirmation of the accuracy of the iconography of Moche artworks.

Tiwanaku and Wari

The bleak highland country of southeastern Peru and southwestern Bolivia contrasts markedly with the warm valleys of the coast. In the Bolivian mountains, the Tiwanaku culture (ca. 100–1000 CE) developed beginning in the second century CE. North of Paracas in Peru, the Wari culture (ca. 500–800 CE) dominated parts of the dry coast.

TIWANAKU Named after its principal archaeological site on the southern shore of Lake Titicaca, the Tiwanaku culture flourished for nearly a millennium. It spread to the adjacent coastal area as well as to other highland regions, eventually extending from southern Peru to northern Chile. Tiwanaku was an important ceremonial center. Its inhabitants constructed grand buildings using the region's fine sandstone, andesite, and diorite. Tiwanaku's imposing Gateway of the Sun (FIG. **14-25**) is a huge monolithic block of andesite pierced by a single doorway. Moved in ancient times from its original loca-

tion within the site, the gateway now forms part of an enormous walled platform. Relief sculpture crowns the gate. The central figure is a Tiwanaku version of the Chavín staff god (FIG. **14-19**). Larger than all the other figures and presented frontally, he dominates the composition and presides over the passageway. Rays project from his head. Many terminate in puma heads, representing the power of the highlands' fiercest predator. The staff god—possibly a sky and weather deity rather than the sun deity the rayed head suggests—appears in art throughout the Tiwanaku horizon, associated with smaller attendant figures. Those of the Gateway of the Sun are winged and have human or condor heads. Like the puma, the condor is an impressive carnivore, the largest raptor in the world. Sky and earth beings thus converge on the gate, which probably served as the doorway to a sacred area, a place of transformation. The reliefs were once colorfully painted. Artists apparently also inlaid the figures' eyes with turquoise and covered the surfaces with gold, producing a dazzling effect.

WARI The flat, abstract, and repetitive figures surrounding the central figure on the Gateway of the Sun recall woven textile designs. Indeed, the people of the Tiwanaku culture, like those of Paracas, were consummate weavers, although far fewer textiles survive from the damp highlands. However, excavators have recovered many examples of weaving, especially tunics, from the contemporaneous Wari culture in Peru.

Although Wari weavers fashioned cloth from both wool and cotton fibers, as did earlier Paracas weavers (FIG. **14-20**), the resemblance

1 ft.

14-26 *Lima Tapestry* (tunic), Wari, from Peru, ca. 500–800 CE. 3′ 3⅜″ × 2′ 11⅜″. Museo Nacional de Antropología Arqueología e Historia del Perú, Lima.

Whereas Paracas mantles (FIG. 14-20) are embroideries, Wari textiles are tapestries with the motifs woven directly into the fabric. The figures on this Wari tunic are so abstract as to be nearly unrecognizable.

between the two textile styles ends there. Whereas Paracas artists embroidered motifs onto the plain woven surface, Wari artists wove designs directly into the fabric, the weft threads packed densely over the warp threads in a technique known as *tapestry*. Some particularly fine pieces have more than 200 weft threads per inch. Furthermore, unlike the relatively naturalistic individual figures depicted on Paracas mantles, those appearing on Wari textiles are so closely connected and so abstract as to be nearly unrecognizable. In the tunic shown here, the so-called *Lima Tapestry* (FIG. **14-26**), the Wari designer expanded or compressed each figure in a different way and placed the figures in vertical rows pressed between narrow red bands of plain cloth. Elegant tunics like this one must have been prestige garments made for the elite. Clothing and status were closely connected in many ancient American societies, especially in the Inka Empire that eventually came to dominate Andean South America (see Chapter 32).

MAP 14-3 Early Native American sites in North America.

NORTH AMERICA

In many parts of the United States and Canada, archaeologists have identified indigenous cultures that date back as far as 12,000 years ago. Most of the surviving art objects, however, come from the past 2,000 years. Scholars divide the vast and varied territory of North America (MAP 14-3) into cultural regions based on the relative homogeneity of language and social and artistic patterns. Native lifestyles varied widely over the continent, ranging from small bands of migratory hunters to settled—at times even urban—agriculturalists. Among the art-producing peoples who inhabited the continent before the arrival of Europeans are the Eskimo of Alaska and the Inuit of Canada, who hunted and fished across the Arctic from Greenland to Siberia, and the maize farmers of the American Southwest, who wrested water from their arid environment and built effective irrigation systems as well as roads and spectacular cliff dwellings. Farmers also settled in the vast, temperate Eastern Woodlands—ranging from eastern Canada to Florida and from the Atlantic to the Great Plains west of the Mississippi. Some of them left behind great earthen mounds that once functioned as their elite residences or burial places.

Eskimo

The Eskimoan peoples originally migrated to North America across the Bering Strait. During the early first millennium CE, a community of Eskimo sea mammal hunters and tool makers occupied parts of Alaska during the Norton, or Old Bering Sea, culture that began around 500 BCE.

IPIUTAK MASK Archaeologists have uncovered major works of Eskimo art at the Ipiutak site at Point Hope. The finds include a variety of burial goods as well as tools. A burial mask (FIG. 14-27) datable to ca. 100 CE is of special interest. The artist fashioned the mask out of walrus ivory, the material used for most Arctic artworks because of the scarcity of wood in the region. The mask consists of nine carefully shaped parts that are interrelated to produce several faces, both human and animal, echoing the transformation theme noted in other ancient American cultures. The confident, subtle composition in shallow relief is a tribute to the artist's imaginative control over the material. The mask's abstract circles and curved lines are common motifs on the decorated tools discovered at Point Hope. For centuries, the Eskimo also carved human and animal figures, always at small scale, reflecting a nomadic lifestyle that required the creation of portable objects.

Woodlands

Early Native American artists also excelled in working stone into a variety of utilitarian and ceremonial objects. Some early cultures, such as those of the woodlands east of the Mississippi River, also established great urban centers with populations sometimes exceeding 20,000.

1 in.

14-27 Burial mask, Ipiutak, from Point Hope, Alaska, ca. 100 CE. Ivory, greatest width 9½″. American Museum of Natural History, New York.

Carved out of walrus ivory, this mask consists of nine parts that can be combined to produce several faces, both human and animal, echoing the transformation theme common in ancient American art.

14-28 Pipe, Adena, from a mound in Ohio, ca. 500–1 BCE. Stone, 8″ high. Ohio Historical Society, Columbus.

Smoking was an important ritual in ancient North America, and the Adena often buried pipes with men for use in the afterlife. This example resembles some Mesoamerican sculptures in form and costume.

1 in.

ADENA The Adena culture of Ohio is documented at about 500 sites in the Central Woodlands. An Adena pipe (FIG. **14-28**) in the shape of a man, carved between 500 BCE and the end of the millennium, is related in form and costume (note the prominent ear spools) to some Mesoamerican sculptures. The Adena buried their elite in great earthen mounds and often placed ceremonial pipes such as this one in the graves. Smoking was an important social and religious ritual in many Native American cultures, and pipes were treasured status symbols that men took with them into the afterlife. The standing figure on the pipe in FIG. **14-28** has naturalistic joint articulations and musculature, a lively flexed-leg pose, and an alert facial expression—all combining to suggest movement.

MISSISSIPPIAN The Adena were the first great mound builders of North America, but the Mississippian culture, which emerged around 800 CE and eventually encompassed much of the eastern United States, surpassed all earlier Woodlands peoples in the size and complexity of their communities. One Mississippian mound site, Cahokia in southern Illinois, was the largest city in North America in the early second millennium CE, with a population of at least 20,000 and an area of more than six square miles. There were approximately 120 mounds at Cahokia. The grandest, 100 feet tall and built in stages between about 900 and 1200 CE, was Monk's Mound. It is aligned with the position of the sun at the equinoxes and may have served as an astronomical observatory as well as the site of agricultural ceremonies. Each stage was topped by wooden structures that then were destroyed in preparation for the building of a new layer.

The Mississippians also constructed *effigy mounds* (mounds built in the form of animals or birds). One of the best preserved is Serpent Mound (FIG. **14-29**), a twisting earthwork on a bluff overlooking a creek in Ohio. It measures nearly a quarter mile from its open jaw (FIG. **14-29**, *top right*), which seems to clasp an oval-shaped mound in its mouth, to its tightly coiled tail (*far left*). Both its date and meaning are controversial (see "Serpent Mound," page 389).

The Mississippian peoples, like their predecessors in North America, also manufactured small portable art objects. The shell *gorget*, or neck pendant, was a favorite item. One example (FIG. **14-30**), found at a site in Tennessee, dates from about 1250 to 1300 CE and depicts a running warrior, shown in the same kind of composite profile and frontal view with bent arms and legs used to suggest motion in other ancient cultures (FIG. **5-17**). The Tennessee warrior wears an elaborate headdress incorporating an arrow. He carries a mace in his left hand and a severed human head in his right. On his face is the painted forked eye of a falcon. Most Mississippian gorgets come from burial and temple mounds, and archaeologists believe they were gifts to the dead to ensure their safe arrival and prosperity in the land of the spirits. Other art objects found in similar contexts include fine mica cutouts and embossed copper cutouts of hands, bodies, snakes, birds, and other presumably symbolic forms.

14-29A Monk's Mound, Cahokia, ca. 1050–1200 CE.

Serpent Mound

Serpent Mound (FIG. **14-29**) is one of the largest and best known of the Woodlands effigy mounds, but it is the subject of considerable controversy. The mound was first excavated in the 1880s and represents one of the first efforts at preserving a Native American site from destruction at the hands of pot hunters and farmers. For a long time after its exploration, archaeologists attributed its construction to the Adena culture, which flourished in the Ohio area during the last several centuries BCE. Radiocarbon dates taken from the mound, however, indicate that the people known as Mississippians built it much later. Unlike most other ancient mounds, Serpent Mound contained no evidence of burials or temples. Serpents, however, were important in Mississippian iconography, appearing, for example, etched on shell gorgets similar to the one illustrated in FIG. 14-30. These Native Americans strongly associated snakes with the earth and the fertility of crops. A stone figurine found at one Mississippian site, for example, depicts a woman digging her hoe into the back of a large serpentine creature whose tail turns into a vine of gourds.

Some researchers have proposed another possible meaning for the construction of Serpent Mound. The date suggested for it is 1070, not long after the brightest appearance in recorded history of Halley's Comet in 1066. Could Serpent Mound have been built in response to this important astronomical event? Scholars have even suggested that the serpentine form of the mound replicates the comet itself streaking across the night sky. Whatever its meaning, such a large and elaborate earthwork could have been built only by a large labor force under the firm direction of powerful elites eager to leave their mark on the landscape forever.

14-29 Serpent Mound, Mississippian, Ohio, ca. 1070 CE. 1,200′ long, 20′ wide, 5′ high.

The Mississippians constructed effigy mounds in the form of animals and birds. This well-preserved example seems to depict a serpent. Some scholars, however, think it replicates the path of Halley's Comet in 1066.

1 in.

Southwest

In the Southwest, Native Americans have been producing pottery since the late first millennium BCE, but the most impressive examples of decorated pottery date after 1000 CE.

MIMBRES The Mimbres culture of southwestern New Mexico, which flourished between approximately 1000 and 1250 CE, is renowned for its black-on-white painted bowls. Mimbres bowls have been found in burials under house floors, inverted over the head of the deceased and ritually "killed" by puncturing a small hole at the base, perhaps to allow the spirits of the deceased to join their ancestors in the sky (which contemporary Southwestern peoples view as a dome). The

14-30 Incised gorget with running warrior, Mississippian, from Sumner County, Tennessee, ca. 1250–1300 CE. Shell, 4″ wide. National Museum of the American Indian, Smithsonian Institution, Washington, D.C.

This neck pendant was probably a gift to the dead to ensure safe passage to the afterlife. It represents a Mississippian warrior running. He holds a mace in one hand and a severed human head in the other.

1 in.

14-31 Bowl with two cranes and geometric forms, Mimbres, from New Mexico, ca. 1250 CE. Ceramic, black-on-white, 1' ½" diameter. Art Institute of Chicago, Chicago (Hugh L. and Mary T. Adams Fund).

Native Americans have been producing pottery for more than 2,000 years, long before the introduction of the potter's wheel. Mimbres bowls feature black-and-white animals and abstract patterns.

bowl illustrated here (FIG. **14-31**) dates to about 1250 and features an animated graphic rendering of two black cranes on a white ground. The contrast between the bowl's abstract border designs and the birds creates a dynamic tension. Thousands of different compositions appear on Mimbres pottery. They range from lively and complex geometric patterns to abstract pictures of humans, animals, and composite mythological beings. Almost all are imaginative creations by artists who seem to have been bent on not repeating themselves. Their designs emphasize linear rhythms balanced and controlled within a clearly defined border. Because the potter's wheel was unknown in the Americas, the artists constructed their pots out of coils of clay, creating countless

sophisticated shapes of varied size, always characterized by technical excellence. Although historians have no direct knowledge about the potters' identities, the fact that pottery making was usually women's work in the Southwest during the historical period (see "Gender Roles in Native American Art," Chapter 32, page 863) suggests that the Mimbres potters also may have been women.

ANCESTRAL PUEBLOANS The Ancestral Puebloans, formerly known as the Anasazi, northern neighbors of the Mimbres, emerged as an identifiable culture around 200 CE, but the culture did not reach its peak until about 1000. (Anasazi, Navajo for "enemy ancestors," is a name that the descendants of these early Native Americans dislike, hence the new designation.) The many ruined *pueblos* (urban settlements) scattered throughout the Southwest reveal the masterful building skills of the Ancestral Puebloans. In Chaco Canyon, New Mexico, they built a great semicircle of 800 rooms reaching to five stepped-back stories, the largest of several such sites in and around the canyon. Chaco Canyon was the center of a wide trade network extending as far as Mexico.

14-32A Pueblo Bonito, Chaco Canyon, mid-9 to mid-11th centuries CE.

Sometime in the late 12th century, a drought occurred, and the Ancestral Puebloans largely abandoned their open canyon-floor dwelling sites to move farther north to the steep-sided canyons and lusher environment of Mesa Verde in southwestern Colorado. Cliff Palace (FIG. **14-32**) is wedged into a sheltered ledge above a valley floor. It contains about 200 rectangular rooms (mostly communal dwellings) of carefully laid stone and timber, once plastered inside and out with adobe. The location for Cliff Palace was not accidental. The Ancestral Puebloans designed it to take advantage of the sun to heat the pueblo in winter and shade it during the hot summer months. Scattered in the foreground of FIG. **14-32** are two dozen large circular semisubterranean structures, called *kivas*, which once were roofed over and entered with a ladder through a hole in the flat roof. These chambers were the spiritual centers of native Southwest life, male council houses where ritual regalia were stored and private rituals and preparations for public ceremonies took place—and still do.

The Ancestral Puebloans did not disappear but gradually evolved into the various Pueblo peoples who still live in Arizona, New Mexico, Colorado, and Utah. They continue to speak their native languages, practice deeply rooted rituals, and make pottery in the traditional manner. Their art is discussed in Chapter 32.

14-32 Cliff Palace, Ancestral Puebloan, Mesa Verde National Park, Colorado, ca. 1150–1300 CE.

Cliff Palace is wedged into a sheltered ledge to heat the pueblo in winter and shade it during the hot summer months. It contains about 200 stone-and-timber rooms plastered inside and out with adobe.

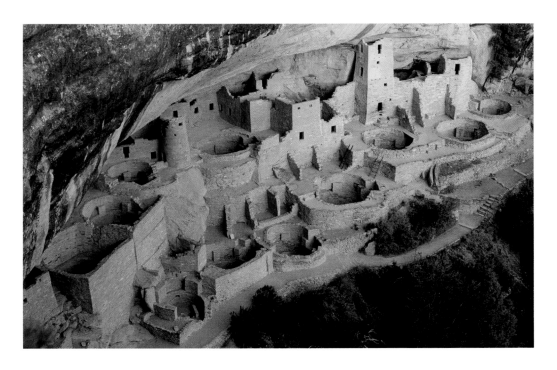

NATIVE ARTS OF THE AMERICAS BEFORE 1300

MESOAMERICA

▌ The Olmec (ca. 1200–400 BCE) is often called the "mother culture" of Mesoamerica. At La Venta and elsewhere, the Olmec built pyramids and ball courts and carved colossal basalt portraits of their rulers during the Preclassic period.

▌ In contrast to the embryonic civic centers of the Olmec, Teotihuacan in the Valley of Mexico was a huge metropolis laid out on a strict grid plan. Its major pyramids and plazas date to the late Preclassic period, ca. 50–250 CE.

▌ The Maya occupied parts of Mexico, Belize, Guatemala, and Honduras. During the Classic period (ca. 300–900 CE), they built vast complexes of temple-pyramids, palaces, plazas, and ball courts and decorated them with monumental sculptures and mural paintings glorifying their rulers and gods. The Maya also left extensive written records and possessed a sophisticated knowledge of astronomy and mathematical calculation.

Colossal head, La Venta, Olmec, ca. 900–400 BCE

Castillo, Chichén Itzá, Maya, ca. 800–900 CE

SOUTH AMERICA

▌ The ancient civilizations of South America are even older than those of Mesoamerica. The earliest Andean sites began to develop around 3000 BCE.

▌ Between ca. 800 and 200 BCE, during the Early Horizon period, U-shaped temple complexes were erected at Chavín de Huántar in Peru, where archaeologists have also uncovered monumental statues and reliefs.

▌ The Paracas (ca. 400 BCE–200 CE), Nasca (ca. 200 BCE–600 CE), and Moche (ca. 1–700 CE) cultures of the Early Intermediate period in Peru produced extraordinary textiles, distinctive painted ceramics, and turquoise-inlaid goldwork. The subjects range from composite human-animals to ruler portraits.

▌ The Tiwanaku (ca. 100–1000 CE) and Wari (ca. 500–800 CE) cultures of northern Bolivia and southern Peru flourished during the Middle Horizon period. The Tiwanaku culture is noteworthy for its monumental stone architecture. The Wari produced magnificent tapestries.

Ear ornament, from Sipán, Moche, ca. 300 CE

Gateway of the Sun, Tiwanaku, ca. 375–700 CE

NORTH AMERICA

▌ The indigenous cultures of the United States and Canada date as far back as 10,000 BCE, but most of the surviving art objects date from the past 2,000 years.

▌ The Eskimo produced small-scale artworks in ivory beginning in the early first millennium CE, reflecting a nomadic lifestyle that required portable objects.

▌ The peoples of the Mississippian culture (ca. 800–1500 CE) were great mound builders. Cahokia in Illinois encompassed about 120 mounds and was the largest city in North America during the early second millennium CE.

▌ In the Southwest, Native Americans have been producing pottery for more than 2,000 years. The black-and-white painted bowls of the Mimbres (ca. 1000–1250 CE) are among the finest.

▌ The Ancestral Puebloans were master builders of pueblos. The pueblo at Chaco Canyon, New Mexico, had about 800 rooms. Cliff Palace, Colorado, is noteworthy for its sophisticated design, wedged into a sheltered ledge to take advantage of the winter sun and the summer shade.

Cliff Palace, Colorado, Ancestral Puebloan, ca. 1150–1300 CE

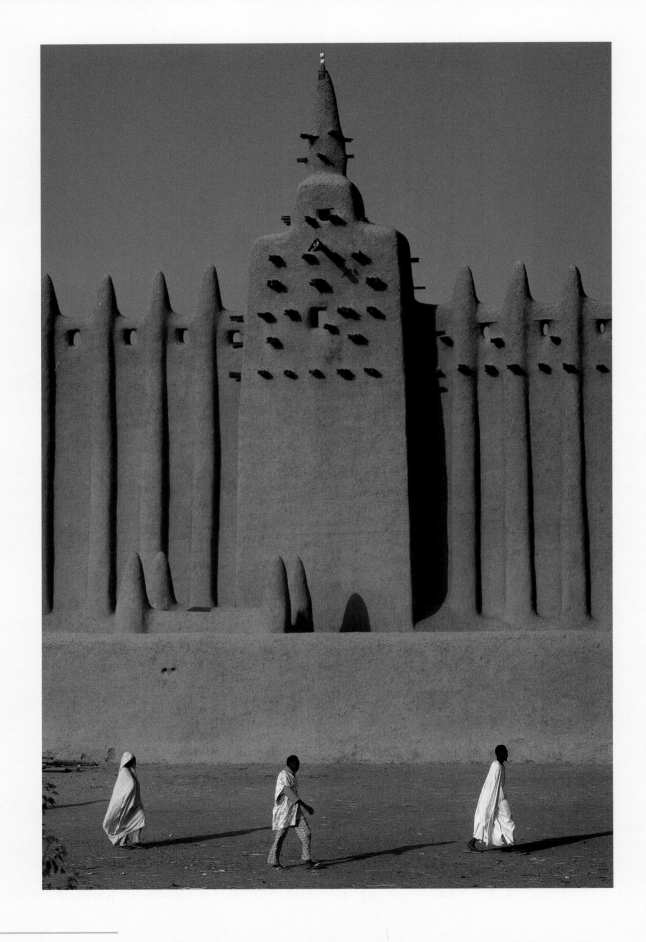

15-1 Detail of the eastern facade of the Great Mosque (FIG. 15-8), Djenne, Mali, begun 13th century, rebuilt 1906–1907.

Africa is a vast continent with a diverse population and myriad art forms. Native forms exist side by side with imported ones, such as this mosque marking the arrival of Islam in Mali.

15

AFRICA BEFORE 1800

Africa (MAP 15-1) is a vast continent of 52 nations comprising more than one-fifth of the world's land mass and many distinct topographical and ecological zones. Parched deserts occupy northern and southern regions, high mountains rise in the east, and three great rivers—the Niger, the Congo, and the Nile—and their lush valleys support agriculture and large settled populations. More than 2,000 distinct ethnic, cultural, and linguistic groups, often but inaccurately called "tribes," long have inhabited this enormous continent. These population groups historically have ranged in size from a few hundred, in hunting and gathering bands, to 10 to 20 million or more. Councils of elders often governed smaller groups, whereas larger populations sometimes formed a centralized state under a king.

Despite this great variety, African peoples share many core beliefs and practices. These include honoring ancestors, worshiping nature deities, and elevating rulers to sacred status. Most peoples also consult diviners or fortune tellers. These beliefs have given rise to many richly expressive art traditions, including rock engraving and painting, body decoration, masquerades and other lavish festivals, figural sculpture, and sacred and secular architecture. Given the size of the African continent and the diversity of ethnic groups, it is not surprising that African art varies enormously in subject, materials, and function. Nomadic and seminomadic peoples excelled in the arts of personal adornment and also produced rock engravings and paintings depicting animals and rituals. Farmers, in contrast, often created figural sculpture in terracotta, wood, and metal for display in shrines to legendary ancestors or nature deities held responsible for the health of crops and the well-being of the people. The regalia, art, and architecture of kings and their courts, as elsewhere in the world, celebrated the wealth and power of the rulers themselves. Nearly all African peoples lavished artistic energy on the decoration of their own bodies to express their identity and status, and many communities mounted richly layered festivals, including masquerades, to celebrate harvests and the New Year and to commemorate the deaths of leaders.

This chapter surveys the art and architecture of sub-Saharan Africa from prehistoric times through the 18th century (see "Dating African Art and Identifying African Artists," page 395), including the first contacts with Europeans, which began along the seacoasts in the late 15th century. Chapter 34 treats the art of the past two centuries, from the beginning of European colonization to the present. The art and architecture of Egypt and of Roman and Islamic North Africa were examined in Chapters 3, 10, and 13, respectively.

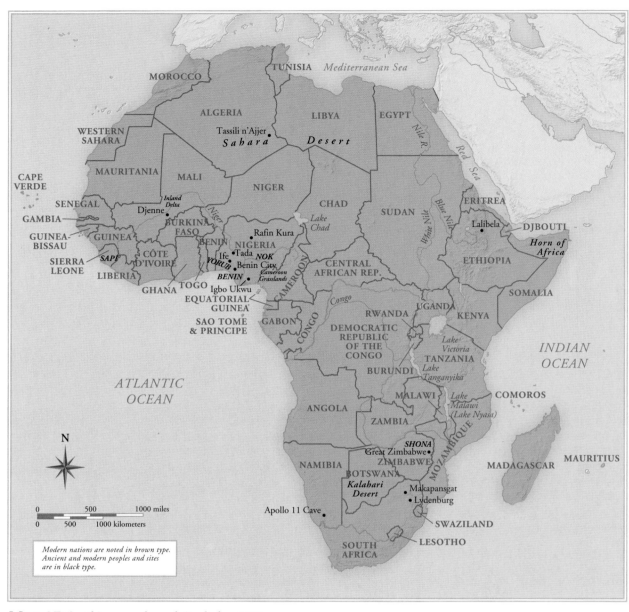

MAP 15-1 African peoples and sites before 1800.

PREHISTORY AND EARLY CULTURES

Thousands of rock engravings and paintings found at hundreds of sites across the continent constitute the earliest known African art. Some painted animals (FIG. 1-3) from the Apollo 11 Cave in southwestern Africa date to perhaps as long ago as 25,000 years, earlier than all but the oldest Paleolithic art of Europe (see Chapter 1). As humankind apparently originated in Africa, archaeologists may yet discover the world's earliest art there as well.

Rock Art

The greatest concentrations of rock art are in the Sahara Desert to the north, the Horn of Africa in the east, and the Kalahari Desert to the south, as well as in caves and on rock outcroppings in southern Africa. Accurately naturalistic renderings as well as stylized images on rock surfaces show animals and humans in many different positions and activities, singly or in groups, stationary or in motion. Most of these works date to within the past 4,000 to 6,000 years, but some may have

been created as early as 8000 BCE. They provide a rich record of the environment, human activities, and animal species in prehistoric times.

TASSILI N'AJJER A 7,000-year-old painting (FIG. 15-2) from Tassili n'Ajjer in southeastern Algeria in the central Sahara (at that time a verdant savanna) is one of the earliest and finest surviving examples of rock art. The painter depicted a running woman with convincing animation and significant detail. The dotted marks on her shoulders, legs, and torso probably indicate that she is wearing body paint applied for a ritual. Her face, however, is featureless, a common trait in the earliest art (see Chapter 1). The white parallel patterns attached to her arms and waist appear to represent flowing raffia decorations and a raffia skirt. Horns—shown in the *twisted perspective*, or *composite* view, typical of prehistoric art (see Chapter 1)—are also part of her ceremonial attire. Notably, the artist painted this detailed image over a field of much smaller painted human beings, an indication of why it is often so difficult to date and interpret art on rock surfaces, as subsequent superimpositions are frequent. Nonetheless, scholars have been able to establish a rough chronology for African rock art, an art form that continues to this day.

Dating African Art and Identifying African Artists

Most African objects bear neither labels nor signatures, and consequently it is nearly impossible to date them precisely or to identify their makers definitively. Early collectors did not bother to ask the names of artists or when the works were made. Although a firm chronology is currently beyond reach, broad historical trends are reasonably clear. But until archaeologists conduct more extensive fieldwork in sub-Saharan Africa, many artworks will remain difficult to date and interpret, and even whole cultures will continue to be poorly documented. Some African peoples, however, have left written documents that help date their artworks, even when their methods of measuring time differ from those used today. Other cultures, such as the Benin kingdom (FIGS. 15-12 and 15-13), have preserved complex oral records of past events. Historians can check these against the accounts of European travelers and traders who visited the kingdom.

When artists are members of craft or occupational guilds—such as blacksmiths and brass casters in the western Sudan—commissions for artwork go to the head of the guild, and the specific artist who worked on the commission may never be known. Nevertheless, art historians can identify individual hands if their work is distinctive. Documentation now exists for several hundred individual artists, even if their names are lost. For some sculptors who worked in the late 19th or early 20th centuries, scholars have been able to compile fairly detailed biographies (see "African Artists," Chapter 34, page 897).

Where documentation on authorship or dating is fragmentary or unavailable, art historians sometimes try to establish chronology from an object's style, although, as discussed in the Introduction, stylistic analysis is a subjective tool. Scientific techniques such as *radiocarbon dating* (measuring the decay rate of carbon isotopes in organic matter to provide dates for wood, fiber, and ivory) and *thermoluminescence* (dating the amounts of radiation found in fired clay objects) have proved useful but cannot provide precise dates. Nonetheless, art historians are slowly writing the history of African art, even if there are still large gaps to fill.

One of the major problems impeding compilation of an accurate history is illegal and uncontrolled excavation. By removing artworks from the ground, treasure hunters disturb or ruin their original contexts and reduce or eliminate the possibility of establishing accurate chronologies. This phenomenon is not unique to Africa, however (see "Archaeology, Art History, and the Art Market," Chapter 4, page 83). Archaeologists on all continents have to confront the problem of looting and the consequent loss of knowledge about the provenance and original function of objects that collectors wish to acquire. That is the unfortunate result of the worldwide appreciation of African art that began in the early 20th century, when many European artists looked to "primitive art" for inspiration (see "Primitivism," Chapter 35, page 920).

Although the precise meaning of most African rock art also remains uncertain, a considerable literature exists that describes, analyzes, and interprets the varied human and animal activities shown, as well as the evidently symbolic, more abstract patterns. The human and humanlike figures may include representations of supernatural beings as well as mortals. Some scholars have, in fact, interpreted the woman from Tassili n'Ajjer as a horned deity instead of a human wearing ceremonial headgear.

Nok and Lydenburg

Outside Egypt and neighboring Nubia (see Chapter 3), the earliest African sculptures in the round have been found at several sites in central Nigeria that archaeologists collectively call the Nok culture. Scholars disagree on whether the Nok sites were unified politically or socially. Named after the site where these sculptures were first discovered in 1928, Nok art dates between 500 BCE and 200 CE. Hundreds of Nok-style human and animal heads, body parts, and figures have been found accidentally during tin-mining operations but not in their original context.

15-2 Running horned woman, rock painting, from Tassili n'Ajjer, Algeria, ca. 6000–4000 BCE.

This early rock painting is thousands of years older than the first African sculptures. It represents a running woman with body paint, raffia skirt, and horned headgear, apparently in a ritual context.

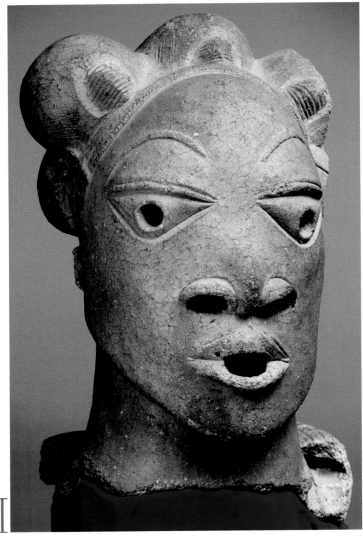

1 in.

15-3 Nok head, from Rafin Kura, Nigeria, ca. 500 BCE–200 CE. Terracotta, 1′ 2 3/16″ high. National Museum, Lagos.

The earliest African sculptures in the round come from Nigeria. The Nok culture produced expressive terracotta heads with large eyes, mouths, and ears. Piercing equalized the heat during the firing process.

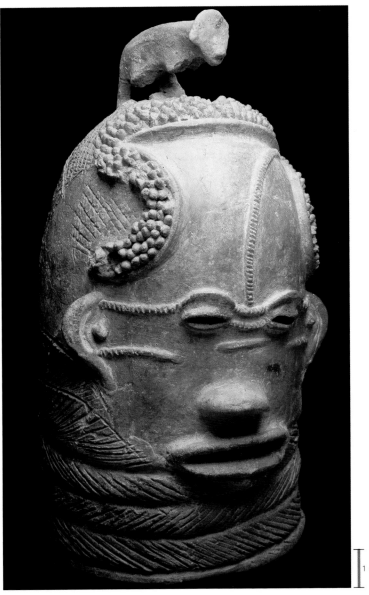

1 in.

15-4 Head, from Lydenburg, South Africa, ca. 500 CE. Terracotta, 1′ 2 15/16″ high. South African Museum, Iziko Museums of Cape Town, Cape Town.

This Lydenburg head resembles an inverted terracotta pot and may have been a helmet mask. The sculptor depicted the features by applying thin clay fillets. The scarification marks are signs of beauty in Africa.

RAFIN KURA HEAD A representative Nok terracotta head (FIG. **15-3**), found at Rafin Kura, is a fragment of what was originally a full figure. Preserved fragments of other Nok statues indicate that sculptors fashioned standing, seated, and kneeling figures. The heads are disproportionately large compared with the bodies. The head shown here has an expressive face with large alert eyes, flaring nostrils, and parted lips. The pierced eyes, mouth, and ear holes are characteristic of Nok sculpture and probably helped to equalize the heating of the hollow clay head during the firing process. The coiffure with incised grooves, the raised eyebrows, the perforated triangular eyes, and the sharp jaw line suggest that the sculptor carved some details of the head while modeling the rest. Researchers are unclear about the function of the Nok terracottas, but the broken tube around the neck of the Rafin Kura figure may be a bead necklace, an indication that the person portrayed held an elevated position in Nok society. The gender of the Nok artists is unknown. Because the primary ceramists and clay sculptors across the continent are women, Nok sculptors may have been as well (see "Gender Roles in African Art Production," Chapter 34, page 896).

LYDENBURG HEAD Later than the Nok examples are the seven life-size terracotta heads discovered carefully buried in a pit outside the town of Lydenburg in present-day South Africa. Radiocarbon evidence indicates the heads date to about 500 CE. One of the Lydenburg heads (FIG. **15-4**), reconstructed from fragments, has a humanlike form, although its inverted pot shape differs markedly from the more naturalistic Nok heads. The artist created the eyes, ears, nose, and mouth, as well as the hairline, by applying thin clay fillets onto the head. The same method produced what are probably *scarification* marks (scars intentionally created to form patterns on the flesh) on the forehead, temples, and between the eyes. Incised linear patterns also adorn the back of the head. The horizontal neck bands, with their incised surfaces, resemble the ringed or banded necks that are considered signs of beauty in many parts of the continent. A small, unidentifiable animal sits atop the head (compare

Art and Leadership in Africa

The relationships between leaders and art forms are strong, complex, and universal in Africa. Political, spiritual, and social leaders—kings, chiefs, titled people, and religious specialists—have the power and wealth to command the best artists and to require the most expensive and durable materials to adorn themselves, furnish their homes, and make visible the cultural and religious organizations they lead. Leaders also possess the power to dispense art or the prerogative to use it.

Several formal or structural principles characterize leaders' arts and thus set them off from the popular arts of ordinary Africans. Leaders' arts—for example, the sumptuous and layered regalia of chiefs and kings—tend to be durable and are often made of costly materials, such as ivory, beads, copper alloys, and other luxurious metals. Some of the objects made specifically for African leaders, such as stools or chairs (FIG. 34-5), ornate clothing (FIG. 34-21), and special weaponry, draw attention to their superior status. Handheld objects—for example, staffs, spears, knives, scepters, pipes, and fly whisks (FIG. 15-5)—extend a leader's reach and magnify his or her gestures. Other objects associated with leaders, such as fans (FIG. I-15), shields, and umbrellas, protect the leaders both physically and spiritually. Sometimes the regalia and implements of an important person are so heavy that they render the leader virtually immobile (FIG. 34-21), suggesting that the temporary holder of an office is less significant than the eternal office itself.

Although leaders' arts are easy to recognize in centralized, hierarchical societies, such as the Benin (FIGS. I-15, 15-12, and 15-13) and Bamum (FIG. 34-5) kingdoms, leaders among less centralized peoples are just as conversant with the power of art to move people and effect change. For example, African leaders often establish and run religious cults in which they may be less visible than the forms they commission and manipulate: shrines, altars, festivals, and rites of passage such as funerals, the last being especially elaborate and

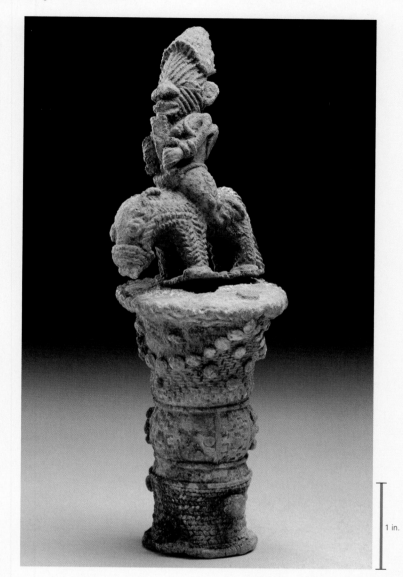

15-5 Equestrian figure on fly-whisk hilt, from Igbo Ukwu, Nigeria, 9th to 10th century CE. Copper-alloy bronze, figure $6\frac{3}{16}''$ high. National Museum, Lagos. ◼◃

The oldest known African lost-wax cast bronze is this fly-whisk hilt, which a leader used to extend his reach and magnify his gestures. The artist exaggerated the size of the ruler compared with his steed.

1 in.

festive in many parts of Africa. The arts that leaders control thus help create pageantry, mystery, and spectacle, enriching and changing the lives of the people.

FIG. 4-12). In the absence of contemporaneous written documents, scholars can only guess at the use and meaning of a head like this one, but it is noteworthy that animals appear only on those Lydenburg heads large enough to have served as helmet masks. The head, therefore, probably had a ceremonial function.

Igbo Ukwu

By the 9th or 10th century CE, a West African bronze-casting tradition of great sophistication had developed in the Lower Niger area, just east of that great river. Dozens of refined, varied objects in an extremely intricate style have been unearthed at Igbo Ukwu. The ceramic, copper, bronze, and iron artifacts include basins, bowls, altar

stands, staffs, swords, scabbards, knives, and pendants. One grave held numerous prestige objects—copper anklets, armlets, spiral ornaments, a fan handle, and more than 100,000 beads, which may have been used as a form of currency. The tomb also contained three elephant tusks, a crown, and a bronze leopard's skull. These items, doubtless the regalia of a leader (see "Art and Leadership in Africa," above), whether secular or religious, are the earliest cast-metal objects known from regions south of the Sahara.

EQUESTRIAN FLY WHISK A lost-wax cast bronze (FIG. 15-5), the earliest yet found in Africa, came from the same grave at Igbo Ukwu. It depicts an equestrian figure on a fly-whisk handle. The African artist made the handle using a casting method similar to

15-5A Igbo-Ukwu roped water pot, 9th to 10th century.

Idealized Naturalism at Ile-Ife

15-6 King, from Ita Yemoo (Ife), Nigeria, 11th to 12th century. Zinc-brass, 1′ 6½″ high. Museum of Ife Antiquities, Ife. ▮◀

Unlike most African sculptures, this royal figure has a naturalistically modeled torso and facial features that approach portraiture. The head, however, the locus of wisdom, is disproportionately large.

Just after the turn of the 19th century, the German anthropologist Leo Frobenius "discovered" the sculpture of Ile-Ife in the Lower Niger River region. Because of the refinement and naturalism of Ile-Ife statuary, he could not believe that these works were locally made. Rather, he ascribed authorship to ancient Greece, where similarly lifelike art was well known. Other scholars traced these works to ancient Egypt, along with patterns of sacred kingship that they also believed originated several thousand miles away in the Nile Valley. But excavations in and around Ile-Ife, especially near the king's palace, have established that local sculptors were indeed the artists who made the extraordinary sculptures in stone, terracotta, and copper alloys found at Ile-Ife. Radiocarbon dating places these works as early as the 11th or 12th century. A number of these sculptures served the kings in ceremonies of installation, in funerals, and probably in annual festivals that reaffirmed the sacred power of the ruler and the allegiance of his people.

As is the case with the figure of the king illustrated here (FIG. **15-6**), Ife sculptors modeled most heads and figures with focused attention on naturalistic detail, apart from blemishes or signs of age, which they intentionally omitted. Thus Ife style is lifelike but at the same time idealized. The artists portrayed most people as young adults in the prime of life and without any disfiguring warts or wrinkles. Some life-size heads, although still idealized, take naturalism to the point that they give the impression of being individual portraits. This is especially true of a group of 19 heads cast in copper alloys that scholars are quite certain record the features of specific persons, although nearly all their names are lost. Among the most convincing portraits, however, is a mask of almost pure copper that has long carried the name of a famous early king, Obalufon. Now in the Ife museum, the mask resided for centuries in the oni's palace. Several very naturalistic heads have small holes above the forehead and around the lips and jaw, where black beads were found. These suggest that some heads were fitted with beaded crowns with veils, such as those known among Yoruba kings today, and perhaps human hair as well. Elaborate beadwork, a Yoruba royal prerogative, is also present on the Ife king's image in FIG. **15-6**.

The hundreds of terracotta and copper-alloy heads, body parts and fragments, animals, and ritual vessels from Ile-Ife attest to a remarkable period in African art history, a period during which sensitive, meticulously rendered, idealized naturalism prevailed. To this day, works in this style stand in contrast to the vast majority of African objects, which show the human figure in many different, quite strongly conventionalized styles. Diversity of style in the art of a continent as vast and ancient as Africa, however, should surprise no one.

that documented much earlier in the Mediterranean and Near East (see "Hollow-Casting," Chapter 5, page 122). The sculpture's upper section consists of a figure seated on a horse, and the lower is an elaborately embellished handle with beaded and threadlike patterns.

The rider's head is of exaggerated size, a common trait in the art of many early cultures. The prominent facial stripes probably represent marks of titled status, as can still be found among Igbo-speaking peoples today.

11TH TO 18TH CENTURIES*

Although kings ruled some African population groups from an early date, the best evidence for royal arts in Africa comes from the several centuries between about 1000 and the beginning of European colonization in the 19th century. This period also brought the construction of major houses of worship for the religions of Christianity and Islam, both of which originated in the Middle East but quickly gained adherents in Africa.

Ile-Ife

15-6A Head of an Ife king, 12th to 13th century.

Africans have long considered Ile-Ife, about 200 miles west of Igbo Ukwu in southwestern Nigeria, the cradle of Yoruba civilization, the place where the gods Oduduwa and Obatala created earth and its peoples. Tradition also names Oduduwa the first *oni* (ruler) of Ile-Ife and the ancestor of all Yoruba kings.

IFE KING Ife artists often portrayed their sacred kings in sculpture. One of the most impressive examples is a statuette (FIG. **15-6**), cast in a zinc-brass alloy, datable to the 11th or 12th century. This and many similar representations of Ife rulers are exceptional in Africa because of their naturalism in recording facial features and fleshy anatomy (see "Idealized Naturalism at Ile-Ife," page 398). The naturalism does not extend to body proportions, however. The head of the statue, for example, is disproportionately large. For modern Yoruba, the head is the locus of wisdom, destiny, and the essence of being, and these ideas probably developed at least 800 years ago, accounting for the emphasis on the head in Ife statuary. Indicating that the man portrayed was a sacred ruler was also a priority, and the sculptor of the statue illustrated here accurately recorded the precise details of the heavily beaded costume, crown, and jewelry.

15-6B Seated man, Tada, 13th to 14th century.

Djenne and Lalibela

The inland floodplain of the Niger River was for the African continent a kind of "fertile crescent," analogous to that of ancient Mesopotamia (see Chapter 2). By about 800, a walled town, Djenne in present-day Mali, had been built on high ground left dry during the flooding season. Archaeologists have uncovered evidence of many specialist workshops of blacksmiths, sculptors, potters, and other artisans.

DJENNE TERRACOTTAS Hundreds of accomplished, confidently modeled terracotta sculptures, most dating to between 1100 and 1500, have been found at numerous sites in the Djenne region. Production tapered off sharply with the arrival of Islam. Unfortunately, as is true of the Nok terracottas, the vast majority of these sculptures came from illegal excavations, and contextual information about them has been destroyed. The subject matter includes equestrians, male and female couples, people with what some scholars interpret as lesions and swellings, and snake-entwined figures. There are seated, reclining, kneeling, and standing human figures. Some wear elaborate jewelry, but many are without adornment. The range of subjects and postures is extraordinary at this date.

The terracotta figure illustrated here (FIG. **15-7**) dates to the 13th to 15th centuries and represents a Djenne warrior with a quiver of arrows on his back and knives strapped to his left arm. The proportions of the figure present a striking contrast to those from Ile-Ife (FIG. **15-6**). The Djenne archer is thin and tall with tubular limbs and an elongated head with a prominent chin, bulging eyes, and large nose—characteristic features of Djenne style.

*From this point on, all dates in this chapter are CE unless otherwise stated.

1 in.

15-7 Archer, from Djenne, Mali, 13th to 15th century. Terracotta, 2′ 3/8″ high. National Museum of African Art, Washington, D.C.

Djenne terracottas present a striking contrast to the statues from Ile-Ife (FIG. 15-6). This archer is thin with tubular limbs and an elongated head featuring a prominent chin, bulging eyes, and large nose.

15-8 Aerial view (looking northwest) of the Great Mosque, Djenne, Mali, begun 13th century, rebuilt 1906–1907.

The Great Mosque at Djenne resembles Middle Eastern mosques in plan (large courtyard next to a roofed prayer hall), but the construction materials—adobe and wood—are distinctly African.

GREAT MOSQUE, DJENNE Djenne is also the site of one of the most ambitious examples of adobe architecture in the world, the city's Great Mosque (FIG. **15-8**), first built in the 13th century and reconstructed in 1906–1907 after a fire destroyed the earlier building in 1830. The mosque has a large courtyard and a roofed prayer hall, emulating the plan of many of the oldest mosques known (see "The Mosque," Chapter 13, page 345). The facade (FIG. **15-1**), however, is unlike any in the Middle East and features soaring adobe towers and vertical buttresses resembling engaged columns that produce a majestic rhythm. The many rows of protruding wooden beams further enliven the walls but also serve a practical function as perches for workers undertaking the essential recoating of sacred clay on the exterior that occurs during an annual festival.

BETA GIORGHIS, LALIBELA Many of the early African cultures maintained trade networks that sometimes extended well beyond the continent. The exchange of goods also brought an exchange of artistic ideas and forms. One of the most striking examples is found at Lalibela in the rugged highlands of present-day Ethiopia, where land travel is difficult. Christianity arrived in Ethiopia in the early fourth century, when the region was part of the indigenous Aksum Empire. In the early 13th century, Lalibela, a ruler of the Zagwe dynasty, commissioned 11 churches to be cut from the bedrock at his capital, which still bears his name.

Not the largest but in many ways the most interesting of these rock-cut churches is Beta Giorghis (FIG. **15-9**), the Church of Saint George, which was cut out of the tufa in the form of a Greek cross, revealing that the architect was familiar with contemporary Byzantine architecture (see Chapter 12). The roof of the structure has a Greek cross sculpted in relief, underscoring the sacred shape of the church. Inside are a carved dome and frescoes. Rock-cut buildings are rare worldwide, but they are documented in Egypt, India, and Jordan (see Chapters 3, 6, and 10). Some of the most complex designs are at Lalibela. Carving from the bedrock a complex building such as Beta Giorghis, with all its details, required careful planning and highly skilled labor. The bedrock tufa is soft and easily worked, but the designer had to visualize all aspects of the complete structure before the work began because there was no possibility of revision or correction.

15-9 Beta Giorghis (Church of Saint George), Lalibela, Ethiopia, 13th century.

During the 13th century, the Christian kingdom of Lalibela cut many churches out of the Ethiopian bedrock. This one emulates Byzantine models and has a Greek-cross plan and interior frescoes.

The Great Zimbabwe empire in southern Africa had a trade network that extended to the Near East and China. The royal residence was surrounded by 30-foot-high stone walls and conical towers.

Great Zimbabwe

Many of the earliest artworks found in Africa come from the southern part of the continent (for example, FIG. 1-3). The most famous southern African site is a complex of stone ruins at the large southeastern political center called Great Zimbabwe. First occupied in the 11th century, the site features walled enclosures and towers that date from about the late 13th century to the middle of the 15th century. At that time, the Great Zimbabwe empire had a wide trade network. Finds of beads and pottery from the Near East and China, along with copper and gold objects, underscore that Great Zimbabwe was a prosperous trade center well before Europeans began their coastal voyaging in the late 15th century.

GREAT ENCLOSURE Most scholars agree that Great Zimbabwe was a royal residence with special areas for the ruler (the royal hill complex), his wives, and nobles, including an open court for ceremonial gatherings. At the zenith of the empire's power, as many as 18,000 people may have lived in the surrounding area, with most of the commoners living outside the enclosed structures reserved for royalty. Although the actual habitations do not survive, the remaining enclosures are unusual for their size and the excellence of their stonework. Some perimeter walls reach heights of 30 feet. One of these, known as the Great Enclosure (FIG. **15-10**), houses one large and several small conical towerlike stone structures, which have been interpreted symbolically as masculine (large) and feminine (small) forms, but their precise significance is unknown. The form of the large tower suggests a granary. Grain bins were symbols of royal power and generosity, as the ruler received tribute in grain and dispensed it to the people in times of need.

SOAPSTONE MONOLITHS Explorations at Great Zimbabwe have yielded eight soapstone *monoliths* (sculptures carved from a single block of stone). Seven came from the royal hill complex and probably were set up as part of shrines to ancestors. The eighth monolith (FIG. **15-11**), found in an area now considered the ancestral

15-11 Monolith with bird and crocodile, from Great Zimbabwe, Zimbabwe, 15th century. Soapstone, bird image 1' 2½" high. Great Zimbabwe Site Museum, Great Zimbabwe.

This soapstone monolith stood in the ancestral shrine of a Great Zimbabwe ruler's wife. The bird and crocodile may symbolize previous rulers who act as messengers between the living and dead.

1 in.

shrine of the ruler's first wife, stands several feet tall. Some scholars have interpreted the bird at the top as symbolizing the first wife's ancestors, but most think it refers to the King or his ancestors. (Ancestral spirits among the present-day Shona-speaking peoples of the area take the form of birds, especially eagles, believed to communicate between the sky and the earth.) The crocodile on the front of the monolith may represent the wife's elder male ancestors. The circles beneath the bird are called the "eyes of the crocodile" in Shona and may symbolically represent elder female ancestors. The double- and single-chevron motifs may represent young male and young female ancestors, respectively. The bird perhaps signifies some form of bird of prey, such as an eagle, although this and other bird sculptures from the site have feet with five humanlike toes rather than an eagle's three-toed talons. In fact, experts cannot identify the species of the birds. Some researchers have speculated that the bird and crocodile symbolize previous rulers who would have acted as messengers between the living and the dead, as well as between the sky and the earth.

Benin

The Benin kingdom (not to be confused with the modern Republic of Benin; see MAP 15-1) was established before 1400, most likely in the 13th century, just west of the lower reaches of the Niger River in what is today Nigeria. According to oral tradition, the first king of the new dynasty was the grandson of a Yoruba king of Ile-Ife. Benin reached its greatest power and geographical extent in the 16th century. The kingdom's vicissitudes and slow decline thereafter culminated in 1897, when the British burned and sacked the Benin palace and city. Benin City thrives today, however, and the palace, where the Benin king continues to live, has been partially rebuilt. Benin artists have produced many complex, finely cast copper-alloy sculptures, as well as artworks in ivory, wood, ceramic, and wrought iron. The hereditary *oba*, or sacred king, and his court still use and dispense art objects as royal favors to title holders and other chiefs (see "Art and Leadership," page 397).

15-12A Head of a Benin Queen Mother, ca. 1520–1550.

QUEEN MOTHER IVORY One of the masterworks of Benin ivory carving is a woman's head (FIG. 15-12) in the Metropolitan Museum of Art, which a Benin king almost certainly wore at his waist. A nearly identical pendant, fashioned from the same piece of ivory, is in the British Museum. Oba Esigie (r. ca. 1504–1550), under whom, with the help of the Portuguese, the Benin kingdom flourished and expanded, probably commissioned the pair. Esigie's mother, Idia, helped him in warfare, and in return he created for her the title of Queen Mother, Iy'oba, and built her a separate palace and court. The pendant, remarkable for its sensitive naturalism, most likely represents Idia. On its crown are alternating Portuguese heads and mudfish, symbolic allusions, respectively, to Benin's trade and diplomatic relationships with the Portuguese and to Olokun, god of the sea, wealth, and creativity. Another series of Portuguese heads also adorns the lower part of the carving. In the late 15th and 16th centuries, Benin people probably associated the Portuguese, with their large ships from across the sea, their powerful weapons, and their wealth in metals, cloth, and other goods, with Olokun, the deity they deemed responsible for abundance and prosperity.

ALTAR TO THE HAND AND ARM The centrality of the sacred oba in Benin culture is well demonstrated by his depiction twice on a cast-brass royal shrine called an *ikegobo* (FIG. 15-13). It features symmetrical hierarchical compositions centered on the dominant king, probably Oba Eresonyen (r. 1735–1750). At the

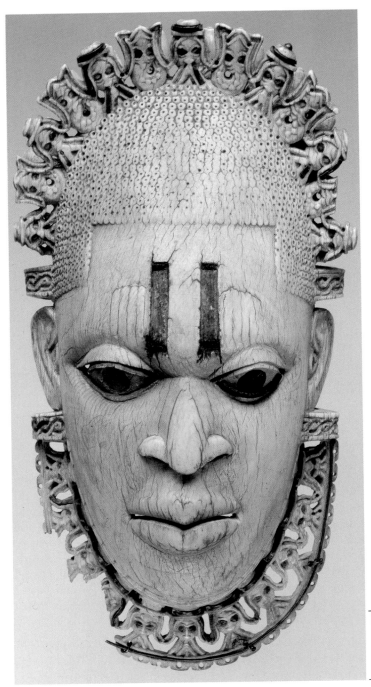

15-12 Waist pendant of a Queen Mother, from Benin, Nigeria, ca. 1520. Ivory and iron, $9\frac{3}{8}''$ high. Metropolitan Museum of Art, New York (Michael C. Rockefeller Memorial Collection, gift of Nelson A. Rockefeller, 1972).

This ivory head probably portrays Idia, mother of Oba Esigie, who wore it on his waist. Above Idia's head are Portuguese heads and mudfish, symbols, respectively, of trade and of Olokun, god of the sea.

top, flanking and supporting the king, are smaller, lesser members of the court, usually identified as priests, and in front, a pair of leopards, animals the sacred king sacrificed and symbolic of his power over all creatures. Similar compositions are common in Benin arts, as exemplified by the royal plaque (FIG. I-15) discussed in the Introduction. Notably, too, the artist distorted the king's proportions to emphasize his head, the seat of his will and power. Benin men celebrate a festival of the head called Igue. One of the king's praise

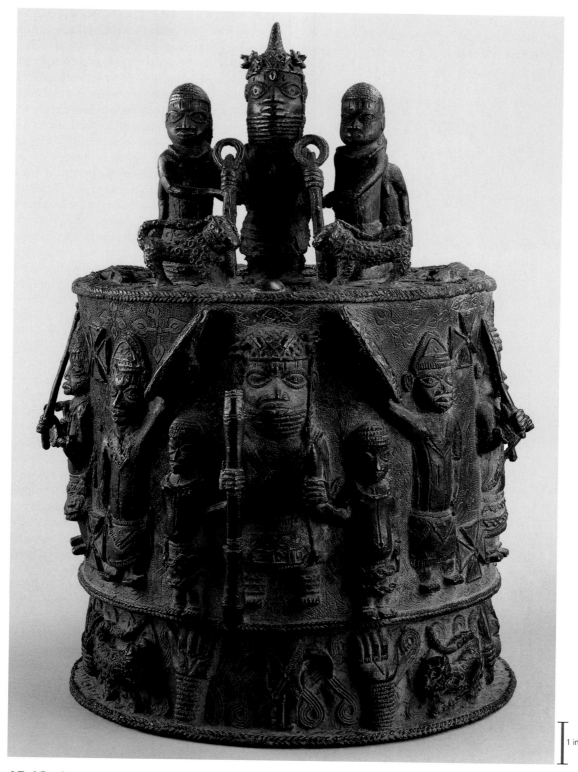

1 in.

15-13 Altar to the Hand and Arm (*ikegobo*), from Benin, Nigeria, 17th to 18th century. Bronze, 1′ 5½″ high. British Museum, London. 📹

One of the Benin king's praise names is "great head," and on this cast-bronze royal shrine, he is represented larger than all other figures and his proportions are distorted to emphasize his head.

names is "great head." At such personal altars, the king and other high-ranking officials made sacrifices to their own power and accomplishments—symbolized by the hand and arm. The inclusion of leopards on the top and around the base, along with ram and elephant heads and crocodiles (not all visible in FIG. 15-13), reiterates royal power.

Sapi

Between 1490 and 1540, some peoples on the Atlantic coast of Africa in present-day Sierra Leone, whom the Portuguese collectively called the Sapi, created art not only for themselves but also for Portuguese explorers and traders, who took the objects back to Europe.

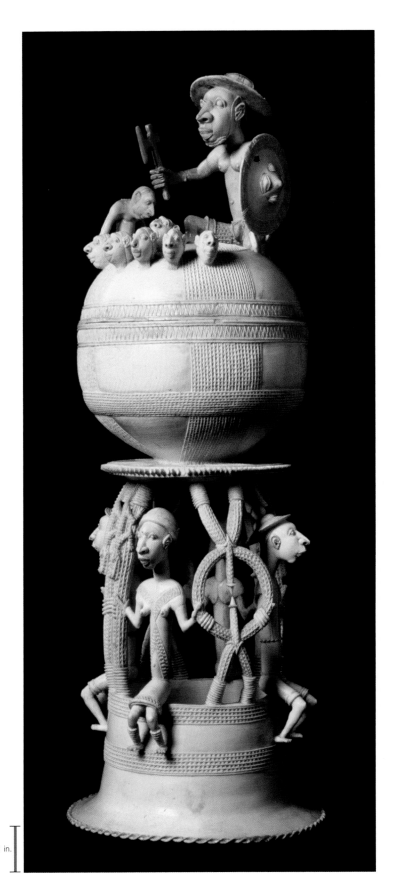

1 in.

SAPI SALTCELLARS The Portuguese commissions included delicate spoons, forks, and elaborate containers usually referred to as saltcellars, as well as boxes, hunting horns, and knife handles. Salt was a valuable commodity, used not only as a flavoring but also to keep food from spoiling. Costly saltcellars were prestige items that graced the tables of the European elite (for example, FIG. 22-51). The Sapi export items were all meticulously carved from elephant tusk ivory with refined detail and careful finish. Ivory was plentiful in those early days and was one of the coveted exports in early West and Central African trade with Europe. The Sapi export ivories, the earliest examples of African tourist art, are a fascinating hybrid art form.

Art historians have attributed the saltcellar shown here (FIG. 15-14), almost 17 inches high, to the MASTER OF THE SYMBOLIC EXECUTION, one of the three major Sapi ivory carvers during the period. This saltcellar, which depicts an execution scene, is one of his best pieces and the source of his modern name. A kneeling figure with a shield in one hand holds an ax (restored) in the other hand over another seated figure about to lose his head. On the ground before the executioner, six severed heads (FIG. 15-14) grimly testify to the executioner's power. A double zigzag line separates the lid of the globular container from the rest of the vessel. This vessel rests in turn on a circular platform held up by slender rods adorned with crocodile images. Two male and two female figures sit between these rods, grasping them. The men wear European-style pants and have long, straight hair. The women wear skirts, and the elaborate raised patterns on their upper chests surely represent decorative scars.

The European components of this saltcellar are the overall design of a spherical container on a pedestal and some of the geometric patterning on the base and the sphere, as well as certain elements of dress, such as the shirts and hats. Distinctly African are the style of the human heads and figures and their proportions, the latter skewed here to emphasize the head, as so often seen in African art. Identical large noses with flaring nostrils, as well as the conventions for rendering eyes and lips, characterize Sapi stone figures from the same region and period. Scholars cannot be sure whether the African carver or the European patron specified the subject matter and the configurations of various parts, but the Sapi works testify to a fruitful artistic interaction between Africans and Europeans during the early 16th century.

The impact of European art became much more pronounced in the late 19th and especially the 20th centuries. These developments and the continuing vitality of the native arts in Africa are examined in Chapter 34.

15-14 MASTER OF THE SYMBOLIC EXECUTION, saltcellar, Sapi-Portuguese, from Sierra Leone, ca. 1490–1540. Ivory, 1′ 4 $\frac{7}{8}$″ high. Museo Nazionale Preistorico e Etnografico Luigi Pigorini, Rome.

The Sapi saltcellars made for export combine African and Portuguese traits. This one represents an execution scene with an African-featured man, who wears European pants, seated among severed heads.

AFRICA BEFORE 1800

PREHISTORY AND EARLY CULTURES, ca. 25,000 BCE–1000 CE

■ Humankind apparently originated in Africa, and some of the oldest known artworks come from the Apollo 11 Cave (FIG. 1-3) in southwestern Africa. Most African rock art, however, is no earlier than about 6000 BCE.

■ The Nok culture of central Nigeria produced the oldest African examples of sculpture in the round between 500 BCE and 200 CE. The pierced eyes, noses, and mouths helped equalize the heat during the firing process.

■ Bronze-casting using the lost-wax method is first documented in Africa in the 9th or 10th century CE at Igbo Ukwu (Nigeria).

Running woman, Tassili n'Ajjer, ca. 6000–4000 BCE

Nok terracotta head, ca. 500 BCE–200 CE

11TH TO 15TH CENTURIES

■ The sculptors of Ile-Ife (Nigeria) fashioned images of their kings in an unusually naturalistic style during the 11th and 12th centuries, but the heads of the figures are disproportionately large, as in most African artworks.

■ The terracotta sculptures of Djenne (Mali), datable ca. 1100–1500, encompass an extraordinary variety of subjects and display a distinctive style with tubular limbs and elongated heads.

■ This period brought the construction of major shrines for Islamic and Christian worship that emulate foreign models but employ African building methods. Examples include the adobe Great Mosque at Djenne and the rock-cut church of Beta Giorghis at Lalibela (Ethiopia).

■ In southern Africa, the Great Zimbabwe empire conducted prosperous trade with the Near East and China well before the first contact with Europeans. Impressive stone walls and towers enclosed the royal palace complex.

Ife king, 11th to 12th century

Great Mosque, Djenne, 13th century

16TH TO 18TH CENTURIES

■ The Benin kingdom in the Lower Niger region was probably founded in the 13th century but reached its zenith in the 16th century. Benin sculptors excelled in ivory carving and bronze-casting, producing artworks that glorified the royal family.

■ An early example of the interaction between African artists and European patrons is the series of Sapi ivory saltcellars from Sierra Leone datable between 1490 and 1540.

Benin ivory waist pendant, ca. 1520

16-1 Cross-inscribed carpet page, folio 26 verso of the *Lindisfarne Gospels,* from Northumbria, England, ca. 698–721. Tempera on vellum, 1′ 1½″ × 9¼″. British Library, London.

Missionaries brought Christianity to the British Isles. The greatest examples of Hiberno-Saxon art are the Gospel books in which illuminators married Christian imagery with the native animal-interlace style.

EARLY MEDIEVAL EUROPE

The half millennium between 500 and 1000 was the great formative period of western medieval art,* a time of great innovation that produced some of the most extraordinary artworks in world history. Early medieval art in western Europe (MAP 16-1) was the result of a unique fusion of the Greco-Roman heritage of the former northwestern provinces of the Roman Empire, the cultures of the non-Roman peoples north of the Alps, and Christianity. Although the Romans called everyone who lived beyond the classical world's frontiers "barbarians," many northerners had risen to prominent positions within the Roman army and government during the later Roman Empire. Others established their own areas of rule, sometimes with Rome's approval, sometimes in opposition to imperial authority. Over the centuries the various population groups merged, and a new order gradually replaced what had been the Roman Empire, resulting eventually in the foundation of today's European nations.

ART OF THE WARRIOR LORDS

As Rome's power waned in Late Antiquity, armed conflicts and competition for political authority became commonplace among the Huns, Vandals, Merovingians, Franks, Goths, and other non-Roman peoples of Europe. As soon as one group established itself in Italy or in one of Rome's European provinces, another often pressed in behind and compelled it to move on. The Visigoths, for example, who at one time controlled part of Italy and formed a kingdom in what is today southern France, were forced southward into Spain under pressure from the Franks, who had crossed the lower Rhine River and established themselves firmly in France, Switzerland, the Netherlands, and parts of Germany. The Ostrogoths moved from Pannonia (at the junction of modern Hungary, Austria, and the former Yugoslavia) to Italy. Under Theodoric, they established their kingdom there, only to have it fall less than a century later to the Lombards, the last of the early Germanic powers to occupy land within the limits of the old Roman Empire

---

*The adjective *medieval* and the noun *Middle Ages* are very old terms stemming from an outmoded view of the roughly 1,000 years between the adoption of Christianity as the Roman Empire's official religion and the rebirth (Renaissance) of interest in classical antiquity. Earlier historians, following the lead of the humanist scholars of Renaissance Italy, viewed this period as a long and artistically crude interval between (in the middle of) two great civilizations. The force of tradition dictates the retention of both terms to describe this period and its art, although scholars long ago ceased to see medieval art as unsophisticated or inferior.

(see Chapter 12). Anglo-Saxons controlled what had been Roman Britain. Celts inhabited France and parts of the British Isles, including Ireland. In Scandinavia, the seafaring Vikings held sway.

Art historians do not know the full range of art and architecture these non-Roman peoples produced. What has survived is not truly representative and consists almost exclusively of small portable "status symbols"—weapons and lavish items of personal adornment such as bracelets, pendants, and belt buckles that archaeologists have discovered buried with the dead. Earlier scholars, who viewed medieval art through a Renaissance lens, ignored these "minor arts" because of their small scale, seeming utilitarian nature, and abstract ornament, and because the people who made them rejected the classical notion that the representation of organic nature should be the focus of artistic endeavor. In their own time, people regarded these objects, which often display a high degree of technical and stylistic sophistication, as treasures. They enhanced the prestige of their owners and testified to the stature of those buried with them. In the great early (possibly seventh-century) Anglo-Saxon epic *Beowulf*, his comrades cremate the hero and place his ashes in a huge *tumulus* (burial mound) overlooking the sea. As an everlasting tribute to Beowulf's greatness, they "buried rings and brooches in the barrow, all those adornments that brave men had brought out from the hoard after Beowulf died. They bequeathed the gleaming gold, treasure of men, to the earth."[1]

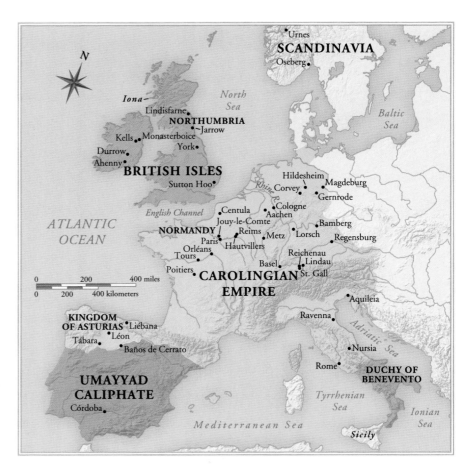

MAP 16-1 The Carolingian Empire at the death of Charlemagne in 814.

MEROVINGIAN FIBULAE Most characteristic, perhaps, of the prestige adornments was the *fibula,* a decorative pin the Romans wore (and the Etruscans before them; FIG. 9-2). Men and women alike used fibulae to fasten their garments. Made of bronze, silver, or gold, the pins often feature profuse decoration, sometimes incorporating inlaid precious or semiprecious stones. The pair of fibulae illustrated here (FIG. 16-2) is part of a larger find of jewelry of the mid-sixth century, when Merovingian kings (r. 482–751) ruled large parts of what is France today. The pins once must have been the proud possession of a wealthy Merovingian woman and seem to have been buried with her. They resemble, in general form, the roughly contemporaneous but plain fibulae used to fasten the outer garments of some of the attendants flanking the Byzantine emperor Justinian in the apse mosaic (FIG. 12-10) of San Vitale in Ravenna. (Note how much more elaborate is the emperor's clasp. In Rome, Byzantium, and early medieval Europe alike, these fibulae were emblems of office and of prestige.)

Covering almost the entire surface of each of the Merovingian fibulae are decorative patterns adjusted carefully to the basic shape of the object. They thus describe and amplify the fibula's form and structure, becoming an organic part of the pin itself. Often the early medieval metalworkers so successfully integrated zoomorphic elements into this type of highly disciplined, abstract decorative design that the animal forms became almost unrecognizable. For example, the fibulae in FIG. 16-2 incorporate a fish just above the center of each pin. The looped forms around the edges are stylized eagles' heads with red garnets forming the eyes.

SUTTON HOO SHIP BURIAL The *Beowulf* saga also recounts the funeral of the warrior lord Scyld, who was laid to rest in a

16-2 Pair of Merovingian looped fibulae, from Jouy-le-Comte, France, mid-sixth century. Silver gilt worked in filigree, with inlays of garnets and other stones, 4″ high. Musée d'Archéologie nationale, Saint-Germain-en-Laye.

Jeweled fibulae were status symbols among the warlords of the early Middle Ages. This pair belonged to a Merovingian woman and features eagle heads and fish integrated into a highly decorative design.

16-3 Purse cover, from the Sutton Hoo ship burial in Suffolk, England, ca. 625. Gold, glass, and cloisonné garnets, $7\frac{1}{2}$″ long. British Museum, London.

This purse cover is one of many treasures found in a ship beneath a royal burial mound. The combination of abstract interlace ornament with animal figures is the hallmark of early medieval art in western Europe.

ship set adrift in the North Sea overflowing with arms and armor and costly adornments:

> They laid their dear lord, the giver of rings, deep within the ship by the mast in majesty; many treasures and adornments from far and wide were gathered there. I have never heard of a ship equipped more handsomely with weapons and war-gear, swords and corselets; on his breast lay countless treasures that were to travel far with him into the waves' domain.[2]

In 1939, archaeologists uncovered a treasure-laden ship in a burial mound at Sutton Hoo, near the sea, in Suffolk, England. Although the Sutton Hoo ship was not sent out to sea, it epitomizes the early medieval tradition of burying great lords in ships with rich furnishings, as recorded in *Beowulf*. Among the many precious finds were a gold belt buckle, 10 silver bowls, a silver plate with the imperial stamp of the Byzantine emperor Anastasius I (r. 491–518), and 40 gold coins (perhaps to pay the 40 oarsmen who would row the deceased across the sea on his final voyage). Also placed in the ship were two silver spoons inscribed "Saulos" and "Paulos," Saint Paul's names in Greek before and after his baptism. They may allude to a conversion to Christianity. Some historians have associated the site with the East Anglian king Raedwald (r. 599?–625), who was baptized a Christian before his death in 625, but the identity of the king buried at Sutton Hoo is uncertain.

Most extraordinary of all the Sutton Hoo finds is a purse cover (FIG. **16-3**) decorated with *cloisonné* plaques. The cloisonné technique, a favorite of the early medieval "treasure givers," is documented at least as early as the New Kingdom in Egypt. Metalworkers produced cloisonné jewelry by soldering small metal strips, or *cloisons* (French for "partitions"), edge up, to a metal background, and then filling the

compartments with semiprecious stones, pieces of colored glass, or glass paste fired to resemble sparkling jewels. The edges of the cloisons are an important part of the design. Cloisonné is a cross between mosaic (see "Mosaics," Chapter 11, page 303) and stained glass (see "Stained-Glass Windows," Chapter 18, page 472), but medieval artists used it only on a miniature scale.

On the Sutton Hoo purse cover, four symmetrically arranged groups of figures make up the lower row. The end groups consist of a man standing between two beasts. He faces front, and they appear in profile. This heraldic type of grouping has a venerable heritage in the ancient world (FIG. **2-10**, *right*), but must have delivered a powerful contemporary message. It is a pictorial parallel to the epic sagas of the era in which heroes like Beowulf battle and conquer horrific monsters. The two center groups represent eagles attacking ducks. The animal figures are cunningly composed. For example, the convex beaks of the eagles (compare the Merovingian fibulae, FIG. **16-2**) fit against the concave beaks of the ducks. The two figures fit together so snugly that they seem at first to be a single dense abstract design. This is true also of the man-animals motif.

Above these figures are three geometric designs. The outer ones are purely linear, although they also rely on color contrasts for their effect. In the central design, an interlace pattern, the interlacements evolve into writhing animal figures. Elaborate intertwining linear patterns are characteristic of many times and places, notably in the art of the Islamic world (see Chapter 13). But the combination of interlace with animal figures was uncommon outside the realm of the early medieval warlords. In fact, metalcraft with interlace patterns and other motifs beautifully integrated with the animal form was, without doubt, the premier art of the early Middle Ages in western Europe. Interest in it was so great that artists imitated the colorful effects of jewelry designs in the painted decorations of manuscripts, in the masonry of churches, and in sculpture in stone and in wood, the last an especially important medium of Viking art.

VIKINGS In 793 the pre-Christian traders and pirates of Scandinavia known as Vikings (named after the *viks*—coves or "trading places"—of the Norwegian shoreline) landed in the British Isles. They destroyed the Christian monastic community on Lindisfarne Island off the Northumbrian (northeastern) coast of England. Shortly after, these Norsemen (North men) attacked the monastery at Jarrow in England as well as that on Iona Island, off the west coast of Scotland. From this time until the mid-11th century, the Vikings were the terror of western Europe. From their great ships they seasonally harried and plundered European coasts, harbors, and river settlements. Their fast, seaworthy longboats took them on wide-ranging voyages, from Ireland eastward to Russia and westward to Iceland and Greenland and even, briefly, to Newfoundland in North America, long before Columbus arrived in the "New World."

The Vikings were not intent merely on a hit-and-run strategy of destruction but on colonizing the lands they occupied by conquest. Their exceptional talent for organization and administration, as well as for war, enabled them to take and govern large territories in Ireland, England, and France, as well as in the Baltic regions and Russia. For a while, in the early 11th century, the whole of England was part of a Danish empire. When Vikings settled in northern France in the early 10th century, their territory came to be called Normandy—home of the Norsemen who became Normans. (Later, a Norman duke, William the Conqueror, sailed across the English Channel and invaded and became the master of Anglo-Saxon England; FIG. 17-35.)

16-4A Viking ship burial, Oseberg, ca. 815–820.

OSEBERG SHIP BURIAL Much of the preserved art of the Viking sea rovers consists of decoration of their great wooden ships. Striking examples of Viking woodcarving come from a ship burial near the sea at Oseberg, Norway. The ship, discovered beneath an earthen mound as was the earlier Sutton Hoo burial, was more than 70 feet long. The vessel contained the remains of two women. The size of the burial alone and the lavishly carved wooden ornament of the sleek ship attest to the importance of those laid to rest there. The vessel also once must have carried many precious objects that robbers removed long before its modern discovery.

An animal-head post (FIG. **16-4**) is characteristic of the masterfully carved wood ornamentation of the Oseberg ship. It combines in one composition the image of a roaring beast with protruding eyes and flaring nostrils and the deftly carved, controlled, and contained pattern of tightly interwoven animals that writhe, gripping and snapping, in serpentine fashion. The Oseberg animal head is a powerfully expressive example of the union of two fundamental motifs of warrior-lord art on the northern frontiers of the former Roman Empire—the animal form and the interlace pattern.

CHRISTIAN ART: SCANDINAVIA, BRITISH ISLES, SPAIN

At the same time that powerful warlords were amassing artworks dominated by abstract and animal motifs, elsewhere in northern Europe Christian missionaries were establishing monasteries and sponsoring artworks of Christian content. The early medieval art of northern Europe, however, is dramatically different in character from contemporaneous works produced in Italy and the Byzantine Empire. These Christian artworks are among the most distinctive ever created and testify to the fruitful fusion of native and imported artistic traditions.

STAVE CHURCH, URNES By the 11th century, much of Scandinavia had become Christian, but Viking artistic traditions persisted. Nowhere is this more evident than in the decoration of the portal (FIG. **16-5**) of the stave church (*staves* are wedge-shaped timbers placed vertically) at Urnes, Norway. The portal and a few staves are almost all that remain from a mid-11th-century church whose fragments were incorporated in the walls of a 12th-century church. Gracefully elongated animal forms intertwine with flexible plant stalks and tendrils in spiraling rhythm. The effect of natural growth is astonishing, yet the designer subjected it to a highly refined abstract sensibility. This intricate Urnes style was the culmination of three centuries of Viking inventiveness.

HIBERNO-SAXON ART In Ireland, the Christianization of the Celts began in the fifth century. The new converts, although nominally subject to the popes of Rome, quickly developed a form of monastic organization that differed from the Church of Rome. The relative independence of the Irish monasteries was due in part to their isolation. The monks often selected inaccessible and inhospitable places where they could carry on their duties far from worldly temptations and distractions. Before long, Irish monks, filled with missionary zeal, set up monastic establishments in Britain and Scotland. In 563, Saint Columba founded an important monastery on the Scottish island of Iona, where he successfully converted the native Picts to Christianity. Iona monks established the monastery at Lindisfarne off the northern coast of Britain in 635. These foundations became great centers of learning as well as the most important centers of artistic production of the early medieval period in northern Europe.

A style that art historians designate as *Hiberno-Saxon* (Hibernia was the Roman name of Ireland), or sometimes as *Insular* to denote

1 in.

16-4 Animal-head post, from the Viking ship burial, Oseberg, Norway, ca. 834. Wood, head 5″ high. Viking Ship Museum, University of Oslo, Bygdoy, Norway.

The Vikings were master wood carvers. This post from a Viking ship combines in one composition the head of a roaring beast with surface ornamentation in the form of tightly interwoven writhing animals.

Medieval Books

The central role books played in the medieval Christian Church led to the development of a large number of specialized types for priests, monks and nuns, and laypersons.

The primary sacred text came to be called the Bible ("the Book"), consisting of the Old Testament of the Jews, originally written in Hebrew, and the Christian New Testament, written in Greek. In the late fourth century, Saint Jerome produced the canonical Latin, or Vulgate (vulgar, or common tongue), version of the Bible, which incorporates 46 Old and 27 New Testament books. Before the invention of the printing press in the 15th century, all books were written by hand ("manuscripts," from the Latin *manu scriptus*). Bibles were extremely difficult to produce, and few early medieval monasteries possessed a complete Bible. Instead, scribes often gathered several biblical books in separate volumes.

The *Pentateuch* contains the first five books of the Old Testament, beginning with the Creation of Adam and Eve (Genesis). The *Gospels* ("good news") are the New Testament works of Saints Matthew, Mark, Luke, and John (see "The Four Evangelists," page 412) and tell the story of the life of Christ (see "The Life of Jesus in Art," Chapter 11, pages 296–297). Medieval Gospel books often contained *canon tables*—a concordance, or matching, of the corresponding passages of the four Gospels that Eusebius of Caesarea compiled in the fourth century. *Psalters* contained the 150 psalms of King David, written in Hebrew and translated into both Greek and Latin.

The Church also frequently employed other types of books. The *lectionary* contains passages from the Gospels reordered to appear in the sequence that priests read them during the celebration of Mass throughout the year. *Breviaries* include the texts required for the monks' daily recitations. *Sacramentaries* incorporate the prayers priests recite during Mass. *Benedictionals* contain bishops' blessings. In the later Middle Ages, scribes developed books for the private devotions of the laity, patterned after monks' readers. The most popular was the *Book of Hours,* so called because it contains the prayers to be read at specified times of the day.

Scribes produced many other types of books in the Middle Ages—theological treatises, secular texts on history and science, and even some classics of Greco-Roman literature—but these contained illustrations less frequently than the various sacred texts.

the Irish-English islands where it was produced, flourished within the monasteries of the British Isles. Its most distinctive products were the illuminated manuscripts of the Christian Church (see "Medieval Books," above). Books were the primary vehicles in the effort to Christianize the British Isles. They literally brought the Word of God to a predominantly illiterate population who regarded the monks' sumptuous volumes with awe. Books were scarce and jealously guarded treasures of the libraries and *scriptoria* (writing studios) of monasteries and major churches. Illuminated books are the most important extant monuments of the brilliant artistic culture that flourished in Ireland and Northumbria during the seventh and eighth centuries.

BOOK OF DURROW Among the earliest Hiberno-Saxon illuminated manuscripts is the *Book of Durrow,* a Gospel book that may have been written and decorated in the monastic scriptorium at Iona, although its provenance is not documented. In the late Middle Ages it was in the monastery in Durrow, Ireland—hence its modern name. The Durrow Gospels already display one of the most characteristic features of Insular book illumination: full pages devoted neither to text nor to illustration but to pure embellishment. The Hiberno-Saxon painters must have felt that such ornament lent prestige to books just as ornamental jewelry lent status to those who wore it. Interspersed between the Durrow text pages are so-called *carpet pages,* resembling textiles, made up of decorative panels of abstract and zoomorphic forms (compare FIG. 16-1). The *Book of Durrow*

16-5 Wooden portal of the stave church at Urnes, Norway, ca. 1050–1070.

By the 11th century, Scandinavia had become mostly Christian, but Viking artistic traditions persisted, as seen in the intertwining animal-and-plant decoration of the portal of this Norwegian church.

The Four Evangelists

The English word *evangelist* derives from the Greek word for "one who announces good news," namely the Gospel of Christ. The authors of the Gospels, the first four books of the New Testament, are Saints Matthew, Mark, Luke, and John, collectively known as the Four Evangelists. The Gospel books provide the authoritative account of the life of Jesus, differing in some details but together constituting the literary basis for the iconography of Christian art (see "The Life of Jesus in Art," Chapter 11, pages 296–297). Each evangelist has a unique symbol derived from passages in Ezekiel (1:5–14) and the Apocalypse (4:6–8).

▌ *Matthew* was a tax collector in Capernaum before Jesus called him to become one of his apostles. Little else is known about him, and there are differing accounts as to how he became a martyr. Matthew's symbol is the winged man or angel, because his Gospel opens with a description of the human ancestry of Christ.

▌ *Mark* was the first bishop of Alexandria in Egypt, where he suffered martyrdom. He was a companion of both Saint Peter and Saint Paul. One tradition says that Peter dictated the Gospel to Mark, or at least inspired him to write it. Because Mark's Gospel begins with a voice crying in the wilderness, his symbol is the lion, the king of the desert.

▌ *Luke* was a disciple of Saint Paul, who refers to him as a physician. A later tradition says that Luke painted a portrait of the Virgin Mary and the Christ Child. Consequently, late-medieval painters' guilds often chose Luke as their patron saint. Luke's symbol is the ox, because his Gospel opens with a description of the priest Zacharias sacrificing an ox.

▌ *John* was one of the most important apostles. He sat next to Jesus at the Last Supper and was present at the Crucifixion, Lamentation, and Transfiguration. John was also the author of the Apocalypse, the last book of the New Testament, which he wrote in exile on the Greek island of Patmos. The Apocalypse records John's visions of the end of the world, the Last Judgment, and the Second Coming. John's symbol is the eagle, the soaring bird connected with his apocalyptic visions.

The Four Evangelists appear frequently in medieval art, especially in illuminated Gospel books where they regularly serve as frontispieces to their respective Gospels. Often, artists represented them as seated authors, with or without their symbols (FIGS. I-7, 16-7,

16-6 Man (symbol of Saint Matthew), folio 21 verso of the *Book of Durrow*, possibly from Iona, Scotland, ca. 660–680. Ink and tempera on parchment, $9\frac{5}{8}"$ × $6\frac{1}{8}"$. Trinity College Library, Dublin.

The early Hiberno-Saxon *Book of Durrow* includes four pages devoted to the symbols of the Four Evangelists. The cloak of Saint Matthew's man resembles a cloisonné brooch filled with abstract ornament.

16-13, and 16-14). In some instances, all Four Evangelists appear together (FIG. I-7). Frequently, both in painting and in sculpture, artists represented only the symbols (FIGS. 12-17, 16-6, 17-1, 17-7, 17-17, and 18-6).

also contains pages where the illuminator enormously enlarged the initial letters of an important passage of sacred text and transformed those letters into elaborate decorative patterns (compare FIG. 16-8). These kinds of manuscript pages have no precedents in classical art. They reveal the striking independence of Insular artists from the classical tradition.

In the *Book of Durrow*, each of the four Gospel books has a carpet page facing a page dedicated to the symbol of the evangelist who wrote that Gospel. An elaborate interlace design like those found on contemporaneous belt buckles and brooches frames each symbol. These pages served to highlight the major divisions of the text. The

symbol of Saint Matthew (FIG. 16-6) is a man (more commonly represented later as winged; see "The Four Evangelists," above), but the only human parts that the artist, a seventh-century monk, chose to render are a schematic frontal head and two profile feet. A cloak of yellow, red, and green squares resembling cloisons filled with intricate abstract designs and outlined in dark brown or black envelops the rest of the "body." The *Book of Durrow* weds the abstraction of early medieval personal adornment with Early Christian pictorial imagery. The vehicle for the transmission of those Mediterranean forms was the illustrated book itself, which Christian missionaries brought to northern Europe.

LINDISFARNE GOSPELS The marriage between Christian imagery and the animal-interlace style of the northern warlords is evident in the cross-inscribed carpet page (FIG. **16-1**) of the *Lindisfarne Gospels*. Produced in the Northumbrian monastery on Lindisfarne Island, the book contains several ornamental pages and exemplifies Hiberno-Saxon art at its best. According to a later *colophon* (an inscription, usually on the last page, providing information regarding a book's manufacture), Eadfrith, bishop of Lindisfarne between 698 and his death in 721, wrote the *Lindisfarne Gospels* "for God and Saint Cuthbert." Cuthbert's relics (see "Pilgrimages and the Cult of Relics," Chapter 17, page 432) recently had been deposited in the Lindisfarne church.

The patterning and detail of the Lindisfarne ornamental page are much more intricate than those of the *Book of Durrow*. Serpentine interlacements of fantastic animals devour each other, curling over and returning on their writhing, elastic shapes. The rhythm of expanding and contracting forms produces a most vivid effect of motion and change, but the painter held it in check by the regularity of the design and by the dominating motif of the inscribed cross. The cross—the all-important symbol of the imported religion—stabilizes the rhythms of the serpentines and, perhaps by contrast with its heavy immobility, seems to heighten the effect of motion. The illuminator placed the motifs in detailed symmetries, with inversions, reversals, and repetitions that the viewer must study closely to appreciate not so much their variety as their mazelike complexity. The zoomorphic forms intermingle with clusters and knots of line, and the whole design vibrates with energy. The color is rich yet cool. The painter adroitly adjusted shape and color to achieve a smooth and perfectly even surface.

Like most Hiberno-Saxon artworks, the Lindisfarne cross page displays the artist's preference for small, infinitely complex, and painstaking designs. Even the Matthew symbol (FIG. **16-6**) in the *Book of Durrow* reveals that the illuminator's concern was abstract design, not the depiction of the natural world. But exceptions exist. In some Insular manuscripts, the northern artists based their compositions on classical pictures in imported Mediterranean books. This is the case with the author portrait of Saint Matthew (FIG. **16-7**) in the *Lindisfarne Gospels*. The Hiberno-Saxon illuminator's model must have been one of the illustrated Gospel books a Christian missionary brought from Italy to England. Author portraits were familiar features of Greek and Latin books, and similar representations of seated philosophers or poets writing or reading (FIGS. **10-71** and **11-6**) abound in ancient art. The Lindisfarne Matthew sits in his study composing his account of the life of Christ. A curtain sets the scene indoors, as in classical art (FIG. **5-58**), and the evangelist's seat is at an angle, which also suggests a Mediterranean model employing classical perspective. The painter (or the scribe) labeled Matthew in a curious combination of Greek (*O Agios*, saint—written, however, using Latin rather than Greek letters) and Latin (*Mattheus*), perhaps to lend the prestige of two classical languages to the page. The former was the language of the New Testament, the latter that of the Church of Rome. Accompanying Matthew is his symbol, the winged man (labeled *imago hominis*, image of the man). The identity of the figure—actually just a disembodied head and shoulders—behind the curtain is uncertain. Among the possibilities are Christ, Saint Cuthbert, and Moses holding the closed book of the Old Testament in contrast with the open book of Matthew's New Testament, a common juxtaposition in medieval Christian art and thought.

Although a southern manuscript inspired the Lindisfarne composition, the Northumbrian painter's goal was not to copy the model faithfully. Instead, uninterested in the emphasis on volume, shading, and perspective that are the hallmarks of the pictorial illusionism of Greco-Roman painting, the Lindisfarne illuminator conceived his subject in terms of line and color exclusively. In the Hiberno-Saxon manuscript, the drapery folds are a series of sharp, regularly spaced, curving lines filled in with flat colors. The painter converted fully modeled forms bathed in light into the linear idiom of northern art. The result is a vivid new vision of Saint Matthew.

BOOK OF KELLS The greatest achievement of Hiberno-Saxon art is the *Book of Kells*, which boasts an unprecedented number of full-page illuminations, including carpet pages, evangelist symbols, portrayals of the Virgin Mary and of Christ, New Testament narrative scenes, canon tables, and several instances of monumentalized and embellished words from the Bible. One medieval commentator described the *Book of Kells* in the *Annals of Ulster* for the year 1003 as "the chief relic of the western world." The manuscript (named after the monastery in central Ireland that owned it) was written and decorated either at Iona or a closely related Irish monastery. From an early date, the book was housed in an elaborate metalwork box, befitting a greatly revered "relic." The monks probably displayed the book on a church altar.

1 in.

16-7 Saint Matthew, folio 25 verso of the *Lindisfarne Gospels*, from Northumbria, England, ca. 698–721. Tempera on vellum, $1' \frac{1}{2}'' \times 9\frac{1}{4}''$. British Library, London. 🎥

The inspiration for this author portrait may have been a Mediterranean book. The illuminator converted the model's fully rounded forms into the linear flat-color idiom of northern European art.

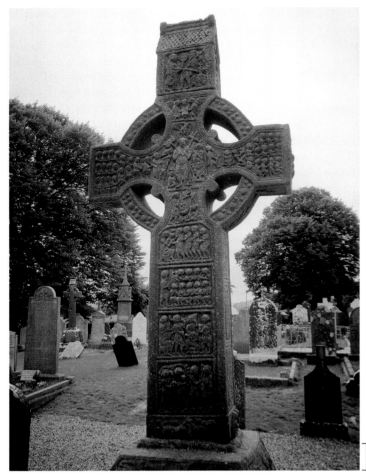

16-8 Chi-rho-iota (XPI) page, folio 34 recto of the *Book of Kells*, probably from Iona, Scotland, late eighth or early ninth century. Tempera on vellum, 1′ 1″ × 9½″. Trinity College Library, Dublin.

In this opening page to the Gospel of Saint Matthew, the painter transformed the biblical text into abstract pattern, literally making God's words beautiful. The intricate design recalls early medieval metalwork.

16-9 *High Cross of Muiredach* (east face), Monasterboice, Ireland, 923. Sandstone, 18′ high.

Early medieval Irish high crosses are exceptional in size. Muiredach's cross marked his grave and bears reliefs depicting the Crucifixion and Last Judgment, themes suited to a Christian funerary monument.

The page reproduced here (FIG. **16-8**) opens the account of the nativity of Jesus in the Gospel of Saint Matthew. The initial letters of Christ in Greek (XPI, *chi-rho-iota*) occupy nearly the entire page, although two words—*autem* (abbreviated simply as *h*) and *generatio*—appear at the lower right. Together they read: "Now this is how the birth of Christ came about." The page corresponds to the opening of Matthew's Gospel, the passage read in church on Christmas Day. The illuminator transformed the holy words into extraordinarily intricate abstract designs that recall Celtic and Anglo-Saxon metalwork. But the cloisonné-like interlace is not purely abstract pattern. The letter *rho*, for example, ends in a male head, and animals are at its base to the left of *h generatio*. Half-figures of winged angels appear to the left of *chi*, accompanying the monogram as if accompanying Christ himself. Close observation reveals many other figures, human and animal. When the priest Giraldus Cambrensis visited Ireland in 1185, he described a manuscript he saw that, if not the *Book of Kells* itself, must have been very similar:

> Fine craftsmanship is all about you, but you might not notice it. Look more keenly at it and you . . . will make out intricacies, so delicate and subtle, so exact and compact, so full of knots and links, with colors so fresh and vivid, that you might say that all this was the work of an angel, and not of a man. For my part, the oftener I see the book, the more carefully I study it, the more I am lost in ever fresh amazement, and I see more and more wonders in the book.[3]

HIGH CROSS OF MUIREDACH As noted, the preserved art of the early Middle Ages consists almost exclusively of small and portable works. The high crosses of Ireland and northern England, erected between the 8th and 10th centuries, are exceptional in their mass and scale. These majestic monuments, some more than 20 feet in height, preside over burial grounds adjoining monasteries. Free-standing and unattached to any architectural fabric, the high crosses have the imposing unity, weight, and presence of both building and statue—architecture and sculpture combined.

16-9A South Cross, Ahen late eighth century.

The *High Cross of Muiredach* (FIG. **16-9**) at Monasterboice, Ireland, is one of the largest and finest early medieval crosses. An inscription on the bottom of the west face of the shaft asks a prayer for a man named Muiredach. Most scholars identify him as the influential Irish cleric of the same name who was abbot of Monasterboice and died in 923. The monastery he headed was one of Ireland's oldest, founded in the late fifth century. The cross probably marked the abbot's grave. The concave arms of Muiredach's cross are looped by four arcs that form a circle. The arms expand into squared terminals (compare FIG. 16-1). The circle intersecting the cross identifies the type as Celtic. At the center of the west side is a depiction of the crucified Christ. On the east side (FIG. 16-9) the risen Christ stands as judge of the world, the hope of the dead. Below him the souls of the dead are being weighed on scales—a theme that sculptors of 12th-century church portals (FIGS. I-6 and 17-12) pursued with extraordinary intensity.

16-10 San Juan Bautista, Baños de Cerrato, Spain, 661.

This three-aisled basilican church dedicated to Saint John the Baptist is typical of Visigothic architecture in Spain. It features three square apses and an entrance portal crowned by a horseshoe arch.

VISIGOTHIC SPAIN When Muslim armies crossed into Spain from North Africa in 711 (see Chapter 13), they brought Islam to a land the Romans had ruled for centuries. Roman sovereignty had brought new roads to the Iberian Peninsula and new cities with Roman temples, forums, theaters, and aqueducts. But in the early fifth century, the Roman cities fell to Germanic invaders, most notably the Visigoths, who had converted to Christianity. Many of the stone churches the Visigoths built in the sixth and seventh centuries still stand. An outstanding example is the church of San Juan Bautista (Saint John the Baptist, FIG. **16-10**) at Baños de Cerrato, which the Visigothic king Recceswinth (r. 649–672) erected in 661 in thanksgiving for a cure after bathing in the waters there. The Visigothic churches are basilican in form but often have multiple square apses. (The Baños de Cerrato church has three.) They also regularly incorporate horseshoe arches, a form usually associated with Islamic architecture (FIG. **13-11**) but that in Spain predates the Muslim conquest.

MOZARABIC SPAIN Although the Islamic caliphs of Córdoba swept the Visigoths from power, they never succeeded in gaining control of the northernmost parts of the peninsula. There, the Christian culture called *Mozarabic* (referring to Christians living in Arab territories) continued to flourish. One northern Spanish monk, Beatus, abbot of San Martín at Liébana, wrote *Commentary on the Apocalypse* around 776. This influential work was widely copied and illustrated in the monastic scriptoria of medieval Europe. One copy was produced at the monastery of San Salvador at Tábara in the kingdom of Léon in 970. The colophon (FIG. **16-11**) to the illustrated *Commentary* presents the earliest known depiction of a medieval scriptorium. Because the artist provided a composite of exterior and interior views of the building, it is especially informative. At the left is a great bell tower with a monk on the ground floor ringing the bells. The painter carefully recorded the Islamic-style glazed-tile walls of the tower, its interior ladders, and its elegant windows with their horseshoe arches, the legacy of the Visigoths. To the right, in the scriptorium proper, three monks perform their respective specialized duties. The colophon identifies the two monks in the main room as the scribe Senior and the painter EMETERIUS. To the right, a third monk uses shears to cut sheets of parchment. The colophon also pays tribute to Magius, "the worthy master

1 in.

16-11 EMETERIUS, the tower and scriptorium of San Salvador de Tábara, colophon (folio 168) of the *Commentary on the Apocalypse* by Beatus, from Tábara, Spain, 970. Tempera on parchment, $1' \, 2\frac{1}{8}'' \times 10''$. Archivo Histórico Nacional, Madrid.

In this earliest known depiction of a medieval scriptorium, the painter carefully recorded the Islamic-style glazed-tile walls of the tower and its elegant windows with their horseshoe arches, a legacy of the Visigoths.

painter . . . May he deserve to be crowned with Christ,"[4] who died before he could complete his work on the book. His pupil Emeterius took his place and brought the project to fruition. He must be the painter of the colophon.

CAROLINGIAN ART

On Christmas Day of the year 800, Pope Leo III crowned Charles the Great (Charlemagne), king of the Franks since 768, as emperor of Rome (r. 800–814). In time, Charlemagne came to be seen as the first Holy (that is, Christian) Roman Emperor, a title his successors did not formally adopt until the 12th century. The setting for Charlemagne's coronation, fittingly, was Saint Peter's basilica (FIG. **11-9**) in Rome, built by Constantine, the first Roman emperor to embrace Christianity. Born in 742, when northern Europe was still in chaos, Charlemagne consolidated the Frankish kingdom his father and grandfather bequeathed him and defeated the Lombards in Italy (MAP **16-1**). He thus united Europe and laid claim to reviving the glory of the ancient Roman Empire. He gave his name (Carolus Magnus in Latin) to an entire era, the *Carolingian* period.

Charlemagne's
Renovatio Imperii Romani

Charlemagne's official seal bore the words *renovatio imperii Romani* (renewal of the Roman Empire). As the papally designated Roman emperor, Charlemagne sought to revive the glory of Early Christian Rome. He accomplished this in part through artistic patronage, commissioning imperial portrait statues (FIG. 16-12) and large numbers of illustrated manuscripts (FIG. 16-13), but also by fostering a general revival of learning.

To make his empire as splendid as Rome's, Charlemagne invited to his court at Aachen the best minds and the finest artisans of western Europe and the Byzantine East. Among them were Paulinus of Aquileia (ca. 726–804), Theodulf of Orléans (ca. 750–821), and Alcuin (ca. 735–804), master of the cathedral school at York, the center of Northumbrian learning. Alcuin brought Anglo-Saxon scholarship to the Carolingian court.

Charlemagne himself, according to Einhard, his biographer, could read and speak Latin fluently, in addition to Frankish, his native tongue. He also could understand Greek, and he studied rhetoric and mathematics with the learned men he gathered around him. But he never learned to write properly. That was a task best left to professional scribes. In fact, one of Charlemagne's dearest projects was the recovery of the true text of the Bible, which, through centuries of errors in copying, had become quite corrupt. Various scholars undertook the great project, but Alcuin of York's revision of the Bible, prepared at the new monastery at Tours, became the most widely used.

Charlemagne's scribes also were responsible for the development of a new, more compact, and more easily written and legible version of Latin script called *Caroline minuscule*. The letters on this page are descendants of the alphabet Carolingian scribes perfected. Later generations also owe to Charlemagne's patronage the restoration and copying of important classical texts. The earliest known manuscripts of many Greek and Roman authors are Carolingian in date.

1 in.

16-12 Equestrian portrait of Charlemagne or Charles the Bald, from Metz, France, ninth century. Bronze, originally gilt, $9\frac{1}{2}$" high. Louvre, Paris.

The Carolingian emperors sought to revive the glory and imagery of the ancient Roman Empire. This equestrian portrait depicts a crowned emperor holding a globe, the symbol of world dominion.

The "Carolingian Renaissance" was a remarkable historical phenomenon, an energetic, brilliant emulation of the art, culture, and political ideals of Early Christian Rome (see "Charlemagne's *Renovatio Imperii Romani*," above). Charlemagne's (Holy) Roman Empire, waxing and waning for a thousand years and with many hiatuses, existed in central Europe until Napoleon destroyed it in 1806.

Sculpture and Painting

When Charlemagne returned home from his coronation in Rome, he ordered the transfer of an equestrian statue of the Ostrogothic king Theodoric from Ravenna to the Carolingian palace complex at Aachen. That portrait is lost, as is the grand gilded-bronze statue of the Byzantine emperor Justinian that once crowned a column in Constantinople (see "The Emperors of New Rome," Chapter 12, page 323). But in the early Middle Ages, both statues stood as reminders of ancient Rome's glory and of the pretensions and aspirations of the medieval successors of Rome's Christian emperors.

EQUESTRIAN STATUETTE The portrait of Theodoric may have been the inspiration for a ninth-century bronze statuette (FIG. 16-12) of a Carolingian emperor on horseback. Charlemagne greatly admired Theodoric, the first Germanic ruler of Rome. Many scholars have identified the small bronze figure as Charlemagne himself, although others think it portrays his grandson, Charles the Bald (r. 840–877). The ultimate model for the statuette was the equestrian portrait (FIG. 10-59) of Marcus Aurelius in Rome. In the Middle Ages, people mistakenly thought the bronze statue represented Constantine, another revered predecessor of Charlemagne and his Carolingian successors. Both the Roman and the medieval sculptor portrayed their emperor as overly large so that the ruler, not the horse, is the center of attention. But unlike Marcus Aurelius, who extends his right arm in a gesture of clemency to a foe who once cowered beneath the raised foreleg of his horse, Charlemagne (or Charles the Bald) is on parade. He wears imperial robes rather than a general's cloak, although his sheathed sword is visible. On his head is a crown, and in his outstretched left hand he holds a globe, symbol of world domin-

1 in.

16-13 Saint Matthew, folio 15 recto of the *Coronation Gospels* (*Gospel Book of Charlemagne*), from Aachen, Germany, ca. 800–810. Ink and tempera on vellum, $1' \frac{3}{4}'' \times 10''$. Schatzkammer, Kunsthistorisches Museum, Vienna. ◼◀

The painted manuscripts produced for Charlemagne's court reveal the legacy of classical art. The Carolingian painter used light and shade and perspective to create the illusion of three-dimensional form.

1 in.

16-14 Saint Matthew, folio 18 verso of the *Ebbo Gospels* (*Gospel Book of Archbishop Ebbo of Reims*), from Hautvillers (near Reims), France, ca. 816–835. Ink and tempera on vellum, $10\frac{1}{4}'' \times 8\frac{3}{4}''$. Bibliothèque Municipale, Épernay. ◼◀

Saint Matthew writes frantically, and the folds of his drapery writhe and vibrate. Even the landscape behind him rears up alive. The painter merged classical illusionism with the northern linear tradition.

ion. The portrait proclaimed the *renovatio* of the Roman Empire's power and trappings.

3A Christ nroned, *escalc tionary*, –783.

CORONATION GOSPELS Charlemagne was a sincere admirer of learning, the arts, and classical culture. He, his successors, and the scholars under their patronage placed high value on books, both sacred and secular, importing many and producing far more. One of these is the purple vellum *Coronation Gospels* (also known as the *Gospel Book of Charlemagne*), which has a text written in handsome gold letters. The major full-page illuminations show the four Gospel authors at work. The page depicting Saint Matthew (FIG. **16-13**) reveals that the Carolingian painter's technique differs markedly from that of the Northumbrian painter of the Matthew portrait (FIG. **16-7**) in the *Lindisfarne Gospels*. Deft, illusionistic brushwork defines the massive drapery folds wrapped around the body beneath. The Carolingian illuminator used color and modulation of light and shade, not line, to create shapes. The cross-legged chair, the lectern, and the saint's toga are familiar Roman accessories. The landscape background has many parallels in Roman painting, and the frame consists of the kind of acanthus leaves found in Roman temple capitals and friezes (FIG. **10-32**). Almost nothing is known in the Hiberno-Saxon British Isles or Frankish Europe that could have prepared the way for this portrayal of Saint Matthew. If a Frank, rather than an Italian or a Byzantine, painted the Saint Matthew and the other evangelist portraits of the *Coronation Gospels*, the Carolingian artist had fully absorbed the classical manner. Classical painting style was one of the many components of Charlemagne's program to establish Aachen as the capital of a renewed Christian Roman Empire.

EBBO GOSPELS The classical-revival style evident in the *Coronation Gospels* was by no means the only one that appeared suddenly in the Carolingian world. Court schools and monasteries employed a wide variety of styles derived from Late Antique prototypes. Another Saint Matthew (FIG. **16-14**), in a Gospel book made for Archbishop Ebbo of Reims, France, may be an interpretation of an author portrait very similar to the one the *Coronation Gospels* master used as a model. The *Ebbo Gospels* illuminator, however, replaced the classical calm and solidity of the *Coronation Gospels* evangelist with an energy that amounts to frenzy. Matthew (the winged man in the upper right corner identifies him) writes in frantic haste. His hair stands on end, his eyes open wide, the folds of his drapery writhe and vibrate, the landscape behind him rears up alive. The painter even set the page's leaf border in motion. Matthew's face, hands, inkhorn, pen, and book are the focus of the composition. This presentation contrasts strongly with the settled pose of the Saint Matthew of the *Coronation Gospels* with its even stress so that no part of the composition jumps out at viewers to seize their attention. Just as the painter of the *Lindisfarne Gospels* Matthew (FIG. **16-7**) transformed an imported model into an original Hiberno-Saxon idiom, so the *Ebbo Gospels* artist translated a classical prototype into a new Carolingian vernacular. This master painter brilliantly merged classical illusionism and the northern linear tradition.

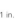

The drawings in the *Utrecht Psalter* are rich in anecdotal detail and show figures acting out—literally—King David's psalms. The vivid animation resembles that of the *Ebbo Gospels* Saint Matthew (FIG. 16-14).

16-15A Psalm 57, *Utrecht Psalter,* ca. 820–835.

UTRECHT PSALTER One of the most extraordinary medieval manuscripts is the *Utrecht Psalter.* The text reproduces the Psalms of David in three columns of Latin capital letters emulating the script and page organization of ancient books. The artist illustrated each psalm with a pen-and-ink drawing stretching across the entire width of the page. Some scholars have argued that the costumes and other details indicate that the artist followed one or more manuscripts compiled 400 years before. Even if the *Utrecht Psalter* is not a copy, the artist's intention was to evoke earlier artworks and to make the book appear "ancient."

The painter of the *Utrecht Psalter* displays a genius for anecdotal detail throughout the manuscript. On one page (FIG. 16-15) the figures act out—literally—Psalm 44 (Psalm 43 of the Vulgate text of the Carolingian era), in which the psalmist laments the plight of the oppressed Israelites. Where the text says, "we are counted as sheep for slaughter," the artist drew some slain sheep fallen to the ground in front of a walled city reminiscent of cities on the Column of Trajan (FIG. 10-44) in Rome and in Early Christian mosaics and manuscripts (FIG. 11-20). At the left, the faithful grovel on the ground before a temple because the psalm reads "our soul is bowed down to the dust; our belly cleaveth unto the earth." The artist's response to "Awake, why sleepest thou, O Lord" was to depict the Lord (as Christ instead of the Hebrew God, complete with cruciform halo), flanked by six pleading angels, reclining in a canopied bed overlooking the slaughter below. The drawing shows a vivid animation of much the same kind as in the Saint Matthew of the *Ebbo Gospels* (FIG. 16-14). The bodies of the *Utrecht Psalter* figures are tense, shoulders hunched, heads thrust forward. As in the *Ebbo Gospels,* even the earth heaves up around the figures. The rapid, sketchy techniques used to render the figures convey the same nervous vitality as the *Ebbo* evangelists.

LINDAU GOSPELS The taste for sumptuously wrought and portable objects, shown previously in the art of the early medieval warlords, persisted under Charlemagne and his successors. They commissioned numerous works employing costly materials, including book covers made of gold and jewels and sometimes also ivory or pearls. Gold and gems not only glorified the Word of God but also evoked the heavenly Jerusalem. One of the most luxurious Carolingian book covers (FIG. 16-16) is the one later added to the *Lindau Gospels.* The gold cover, fashioned in one of the workshops of Charles the Bald's court, is monumental in conception. A youthful Christ in the Early Christian tradition, nailed to the cross, is the central motif.

Surrounding Christ are pearls and jewels (raised on golden claw feet so that they can catch and reflect the light even more brilliantly and protect the delicate metal relief from denting). The statuesque open-eyed figure, rendered in *repoussé* (hammered or pressed relief), brings to mind the beardless unsuffering Christ of the fifth-century

16-16 Crucifixion, front cover of the *Lindau Gospels,* from Saint Gall, Switzerland, ca. 870. Gold, precious stones, and pearls, $1'\ 1\frac{3}{8}'' \times 10\frac{3}{8}''$. Pierpont Morgan Library, New York. ◼◄

This sumptuous Carolingian book cover revives the Early Christian imagery of the youthful Christ. The statuesque figure of the crucified Savior, heedless of pain, is classical in both conception and execution.

ivory plaque (FIG. 11-22) from Italy in the British Museum. In contrast, the four angels and the personifications of the Moon and the Sun above and the crouching figures of the Virgin Mary and Saint John (and two other figures of uncertain identity) in the quadrants below display the vivacity and nervous energy of the *Utrecht Psalter* figures. This eclectic work highlights the stylistic diversity of early medieval art in Europe. Here, however, the translated figural style of the Mediterranean prevails, in keeping with the classical tastes and imperial aspirations of the Frankish "emperors of Rome."

Architecture

In his eagerness to reestablish the imperial past, Charlemagne also encouraged the use of Roman building techniques. In architecture, as in sculpture and painting, innovations made in the reinterpretation of earlier Roman Christian sources became fundamental to the subsequent development of northern European architecture. For his models, Charlemagne went to Rome and Ravenna. One was the former heart of the Roman Empire, which he wanted to "renew." The other was the long-term western outpost of Byzantine might and splendor, which he wanted to emulate in his capital at Aachen, a site chosen because of its renowned hot springs.

AACHEN Charlemagne often visited Ravenna, and the equestrian statue of Theodoric he brought from there to display in his palace complex at Aachen served as a model for Carolingian equestrian portraits (FIG. 16-12). Charlemagne also imported porphyry (purple marble) columns from Ravenna to adorn his Palatine Chapel, and historians long have thought he chose one of Ravenna's churches as the model for the new structure. The plan (FIG. 16-17) of the Aachen chapel resembles that of San Vitale (FIG. 12-7), and a direct relationship very likely exists between the two.

A comparison between the Carolingian chapel, the first vaulted structure of the Middle Ages north of the Alps, and its southern counterpart is instructive. The Aachen plan is simpler. Omitted were San Vitale's apselike extensions reaching from the central octagon into the ambulatory. At Aachen, the two main units stand in greater independence of each other. This solution may lack the subtle sophis-

tication of the Byzantine building, but the Palatine Chapel gains geometric clarity. A view of the interior (FIG. 16-18) of the Palatine Chapel shows that the architect converted the "floating" quality of San Vitale (FIG. 12-8) into massive geometric form.

The Carolingian conversion of a complex, subtle Byzantine prototype into a building that expresses robust strength and clear structural articulation foreshadows the architecture of the 11th and 12th centuries and the style called Romanesque (see Chapter 17). So, too, does the treatment of the Palatine Chapel's exterior, where two cylindrical towers with spiral staircases flank the entrance portal (FIG. 16-17). This was a first step toward the great dual-tower facades of western European churches from the 10th century to the present. Above the portal, Charlemagne could appear in a large framing arch and be seen by those gathered in the atrium in front of the chapel. (The plan includes only part of the atrium.) Directly behind that second-story arch was Charlemagne's marble throne. From there he could peer down at the altar in the apse. Charlemagne's imperial gallery followed the model of the imperial gallery at Hagia Sophia (FIGS. 12-3 and 12-4) in Constantinople. The Palatine Chapel was in every sense a royal chapel. The coronation of Charlemagne's son, Louis the Pious (r. 814–840), took place there when he succeeded his father as emperor.

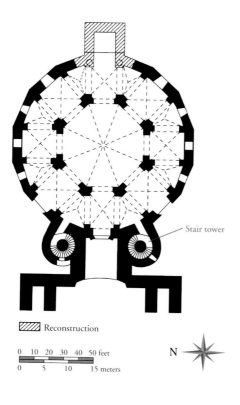

16-17

Restored plan of the Palatine Chapel of Charlemagne, Aachen, Germany, 792–805.

Charlemagne often visited Ravenna and sought to emulate Byzantine splendor in Germany. The plan of his Aachen palace chapel is based on that of San Vitale (FIG. 12-7), but the Carolingian plan is simpler.

Stair tower

⧄ Reconstruction

0 10 20 30 40 50 feet
0   5   10   15 meters

N

16-18 Interior of the Palatine Chapel of Charlemagne, Aachen, Germany, 792–805.

Charlemagne's palace chapel is the first vaulted structure of the Middle Ages north of the Alps. The architect transformed the complex, glittering interior of San Vitale (FIG. 12-8) into simple and massive geometric form.

Medieval Monasteries and Benedictine Rule

Monastic foundations appeared in western Europe beginning in Early Christian times. The monks who established monasteries also made the rules that governed them. The most significant of these monks was Benedict of Nursia (Saint Benedict), who founded the Benedictine order in 529. By the ninth century, the "Rule" Benedict wrote (*Regula Sancti Benedicti*) had become standard for all European monastic establishments, in part because Charlemagne had encouraged its adoption throughout the Frankish territories.

Saint Benedict believed the corruption of the clergy that accompanied the increasing worldliness of the Christian Church had is roots in the lack of firm organization and regulation. As he saw it, idleness and selfishness had led to neglect of the commandments of God and of the Church. The cure for this was communal association in an *abbey* under the absolute rule of an *abbot* the monks elected (or an *abbess* the nuns chose), who would see to it that the monks spent each hour of the day in useful work and in sacred reading. The emphasis on work and study and not on meditation and austerity is of great historical significance. Since antiquity, manual labor had been considered disgraceful, the business of the lowborn or of slaves. Benedict raised it to the dignity of religion. The core idea of what many people today call the "work ethic" found early expression here as an essential feature of spiritual life. By thus exalting the virtue of manual labor, Benedict not only rescued it from its age-old association with slavery but also recognized it as the way to self-sufficiency for the entire religious community.

16-19 Schematic plan for a monastery at Saint Gall, Switzerland, ca. 819. Red ink on parchment, 2′ 4″ × 3′ 8⅛″. Stiftsbibliothek, Saint Gall.

The purpose of this plan for an ideal, self-sufficient Benedictine monastery was to separate the monks from the laity. Near the center stands the church with its cloister, an earthly paradise reserved for the monks.

Whereas some of Saint Benedict's followers emphasized spiritual "work" over manual labor, others, most notably the Cistercians (see "Bernard of Clairvaux," Chapter 17, page 420), put his teachings about the value of physical work into practice. These monks reached into their surroundings and helped reduce the vast areas of daunting wilderness of early medieval Europe. They cleared dense forest teeming with wolves, bear, and wild boar; drained swamps and cultivated wastelands; and built roads, bridges, and dams as well as monastic churches and their associated living and service quarters.

The ideal monastery (FIG. **16-19**) provided all the facilities necessary for the conduct of daily life—a mill, bakery, infirmary, vegetable garden, and even a brewery—so that the monks felt no need to wander outside its protective walls. These religious communities were centrally important to the revival of learning. The clergy, who were also often scribes and scholars, had a monopoly on the skills of reading and writing in an age of almost universal illiteracy. The monastic libraries and scriptoria (FIG. **16-11**), where the monks read, copied, illuminated, and bound books with ornamented covers, became centers of study. Monasteries were almost the sole repositories of what remained of the literary culture of the Greco-Roman world and early Christianity. Saint Benedict's requirements of manual labor and sacred reading came to include writing and copying books, studying music for chanting the day's offices, and—of great significance—teaching. The monasteries were the schools of the early Middle Ages as well as self-sufficient communities and production centers.

SAINT GALL The construction and expansion of many monasteries also characterized the Carolingian period. A unique document, the ideal plan (FIG. **16-19**) for a Benedictine monastery (see "Medieval Monasteries and Benedictine Rule," above) at Saint Gall in Switzerland, provides precious information about the design of Carolingian monastic communities. Haito, the abbot of Reichenau and bishop of Basel, commissioned the drawing and sent it to the abbot of Saint Gall around 819 as a guide for the rebuilding of the Saint Gall monastery. The design's fundamental purpose was to separate the monks from the laity (nonclergy) who also inhabited the community. Variations of the scheme may be seen in later monasteries all across western Europe. Near the center, dominating everything, was the church with its *cloister*, a colonnaded courtyard not unlike the Early Christian atrium (FIG. **11-9**) but situated to the side of the church rather than in front of its main portal. Reserved for the monks alone, the cloister, a kind of earthly paradise removed from the world at large, provided the peace and quiet necessary for contemplation. Clustered around the cloister were the most essential buildings: dormitory, refectory, kitchen, and storage rooms. Other structures, including an infirmary, school, guest house, bakery, brewery, and workshops, were grouped around this central core of church and cloister.

Haito invited the abbot of Saint Gall to adapt the monastery plan as he saw fit, and, indeed, the Saint Gall builders did not follow the Reichenau model exactly. Nonetheless, if the abbot had wished, Haito's plan could have served as a practical guide for the Saint Gall masons because it was laid out using a *module* (standard unit) of two and a half feet. Parts or multiples of this module were employed consistently throughout the plan. For example, the nave's width, indicated on the plan as 40 feet, was equal to 16 modules; the length of each monk's bed to two and a half modules; and the width of paths in the vegetable garden to one and a quarter modules.

The models that carried the greatest authority for Charlemagne and his builders were those from the Christian phase of the Late Roman Empire. The widespread adoption of the Early Christian basilica, at Saint Gall and elsewhere, rather than the domed central plan of Byzantine churches, was crucial to the subsequent development of western European church architecture. Unfortunately, no Carolingian basilica has survived in anything approaching its original form. Nevertheless, it is possible to reconstruct the appearance of some of the structures with fair accuracy. Several appear to have followed their Early Christian models quite closely. But in other instances, Carolingian builders significantly modified the basilica plan, converting it into a much more complex form. The monastery church at Saint Gall, for example, was essentially a traditional basilica, but it had features not found in any Early Christian church. Most obvious is the addition of a second apse on the west end of the building, perhaps to accommodate additional altars and relics (see "Pilgrimages and the Cult of Relics," Chapter 17, page 432). Whatever its purpose, this feature remained a characteristic regional element of German churches until the 11th century.

Not quite as evident but much more important to the subsequent development of church architecture north of the Alps was the presence of a transept at Saint Gall, a very rare feature but one that characterized the two greatest Early Christian basilicas in Rome, Saint Peter's (FIG. 11-9) and Saint Paul's. The Saint Gall transept is as wide as the nave on the plan and was probably the same height. Early Christian builders had not been concerned with proportional relationships. On the Saint Gall plan, however, the various parts of the building relate to one another by a geometric scheme that ties them together into a tight and cohesive unit. Equalizing the widths of nave and transept automatically makes the area where they cross (the *crossing*) a square. Most Carolingian churches shared this feature. But Haito's planner also used the *crossing square* as the unit of measurement for the remainder of the church plan. The transept arms are equal to one crossing square, the distance between transept and apse is one crossing square, and the nave is four and a half crossing squares long. The fact that the two aisles are half as wide as the nave integrates all parts of the church in a rational and orderly plan.

The Saint Gall plan also reveals another important feature of many Carolingian basilicas: towers framing the end(s) of the church. Haito's plan shows only two towers, both cylindrical and on the west side of the church, as at Charlemagne's Palatine Chapel (FIG. 16-17), but they stand apart from the church facade. If a tower existed above the crossing, the silhouette of Saint Gall would have shown three towers altering the horizontal profile of the traditional basilica and identifying the church even from afar.

CORVEY Other Carolingian basilicas had towers incorporated in the fabric of the west end of the building, thereby creating a unified monumental facade that greeted all who entered the church. Architectural historians call this feature of Carolingian and some later churches the *westwork* (German *Westwerck*, "western entrance structure"). In contemporaneous documents, writers refer to it as a *castellum* (Latin, "castle" or "fortress") or *turris* ("tower"). The sole surviving example is the abbey church (FIG. 16-20) at Corvey. The uppermost parts are 12th-century additions (easily distinguishable from the original westwork by the differing masonry technique). Stairs in each tower provided access to the upper stories of the westwork. On the second floor was a two-story chapel with an aisle and a gallery on three sides. As at Aachen, the chapel opened onto the nave, and from it, on occasion, the emperor and his entourage could watch and participate in the service below. Not all Carolingian westworks, however, served as seats for the visiting emperor. They also functioned as churches within churches, housing a second altar for special celebrations on major feast days. Boys' choirs stationed in the westwork chapel participated from above in the services conducted in the church's nave.

16-20A Torhalle, Lorsch, late eighth or ninth century.

16-20 Westwork of the abbey church, Corvey, Germany, 873–885.

An important new feature of Carolingian church architecture is the westwork, a monumental western facade incorporating two towers. The sole surviving example is the abbey church at Corvey.

6-19A Saint-iquier, Centula, 90–799.

OTTONIAN ART

Charlemagne was buried in the Palatine Chapel at Aachen. His empire survived him by fewer than 30 years. When his son Louis the Pious died in 840, Louis's sons—Charles the Bald, Lothair, and Louis the German—divided the Carolingian Empire among themselves. After bloody conflicts, the brothers signed a treaty at Verdun in 843 partitioning the Frankish lands into western, central, and eastern areas, very roughly foreshadowing the later nations of France and Germany and a third realm corresponding to a long strip of land stretching from the Netherlands and Belgium to Rome. Intensified Viking incursions helped bring about the collapse of the Carolingians. The empire's breakup into weak kingdoms, ineffectual against the invasions, brought a time of confusion to Europe. Complementing the Viking scourge in Europe were the invasions of the Magyars in the Byzantine East and the plundering and piracy of the Saracens (Muslims) in the Mediterranean.

Only in the mid-10th century did the eastern part of the former empire consolidate under the rule of a new Saxon line of German emperors called, after the names of the three most illustrious family members, the *Ottonians*. The pope crowned the first Otto (r. 936–973) in Rome in 962, and Otto assumed the title of emperor of Rome that Charlemagne's weak successors held during most of the previous century. The three Ottos made headway against the invaders from the East, remained free from Viking attacks, and not only preserved but also enriched the culture and tradition of the Carolingian period. The Christian Church, which had become corrupt and disorganized, recovered in the 10th century under the influence of a great monastic reform that the Ottonians encouraged and sanctioned. The new German emperors also cemented ties with Italy and the papacy. By the time the last of the Ottonian line, Henry II, died in the early 11th century, the pagan marauders had become Christianized and settled, and the monastic reforms had been highly successful.

Architecture

Ottonian architects followed the course of their Carolingian predecessors, building basilican churches with towering spires and imposing westworks, but they also introduced new features that would have a long future in western European church architecture.

GERNRODE The best preserved 10th-century Ottonian basilica is Saint Cyriakus at Gernrode. The church was the centerpiece of a convent founded in 961. Construction of the church began the same year. In the 12th century, a large apse replaced the western entrance, but the upper parts of the westwork, including the two cylindrical towers, were left intact. The interior (FIG. **16-21**), although heavily restored in the 19th century, retains its 10th-century character. Saint Cyriakus reveals how Ottonian architects enriched the form of the Early Christian basilica. The church has a transept at the east with a square choir in front of the apse. The nave is one of the first in western Europe to incorporate a gallery between the ground-floor arcade and the clerestory, a design that became very popular in the succeeding Romanesque era (see Chapter 17). Scholars have reached no consensus on the function of these galleries in Ottonian churches. They cannot have been reserved for women, as some think they were in Byzantium, because Saint Cyriakus is a nuns' church. One suggestion is that the galleries housed additional altars, as in the westwork at Corvey. They may also have been where the choirs sang. The Gernrode builders also transformed the nave arcade itself by adopting the *alternate-support system,* in which heavy square piers alternate with columns, dividing the nave into vertical units. The division continues into the gallery level, breaking the smooth rhythm of the

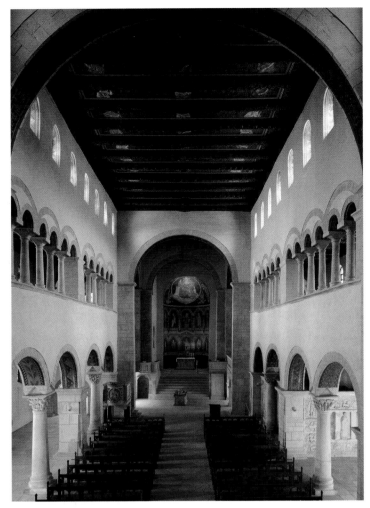

16-21 Nave of the church of Saint Cyriakus, Gernrode, Germany, 961–973.

Ottonian builders modified the interior elevation of the Early Christian basilica. The Gernrode designer added a gallery above the nave arcade and adopted an alternate-support system of piers and columns.

all-column arcades of Early Christian and Carolingian basilicas and leading the eye upward. Later architects would carry this "verticalization" of the basilican nave much further (FIG. **18-19**).

HILDESHEIM One of the great patrons of Ottonian art and architecture was Bishop Bernward of Hildesheim, Germany. He was the tutor of Otto III (r. 983–1002) and builder of the abbey church of Saint Michael (FIG. **16-22**) at Hildesheim. Bernward, who made Hildesheim a center of learning, was an eager scholar, a lover of the arts, and, according to Thangmar of Heidelberg, his biographer, an expert craftsman and bronze caster. In 1001, Bernward traveled to Rome as the guest of Otto III. During this stay, he studied at first hand the monuments of the empire the Carolingian and Ottonian emperors revered.

Constructed between 1001 and 1031 (and rebuilt after being bombed during World War II), Saint Michael's has a double-transept plan (FIG. **16-23**, *bottom*), tower groupings, and a westwork. The two transepts create eastern and western centers of gravity. The nave merely seems to be a hall that connects them. Lateral entrances leading into the aisles from the north and south additionally make for an almost complete loss of the traditional basilican orientation toward the east. Some ancient Roman basilicas, such as the Basilica Ulpia (FIG. **10-43**, no. 4) in Trajan's Forum, also had two apses and

16-22 Saint Michael's, Hildesheim, Germany, 1001–1031. ◼◂

Built by Bishop Bernward, a great art patron, Saint Michael's is a masterpiece of Ottonian basilica design. The church's two apses, two transepts, and multiple towers give it a distinctive profile.

16-23 Longitudinal section (*top*) and plan (*bottom*) of the abbey church of Saint Michael's, Hildesheim, Germany, 1001–1031.

Saint Michael's entrances are on the side. Alternating piers and columns divide the space in the nave into vertical units. These features transformed the tunnel-like horizontality of Early Christian basilicas.

16-23A Nave, Saint Michael's, Hildesheim, 1001–1031.

Entrances

Entrances

```
0   10  20  30  40  50 feet
0      5       10      15 meters
```

N

entrances on the side, and Bernward probably was familiar with this variant basilican plan.

At Hildesheim, as in the plan of the monastery at Saint Gall (FIG. 16-19), the builders adopted a modular approach. The crossing squares, for example, are the basis for the nave's dimensions—three crossing squares long and one square wide. The placement of heavy piers at the corners of each square gives visual emphasis to the three units. These piers alternate with pairs of columns (FIG. 16-23, *top*) as wall supports in a design similar to that of Saint Cyriakus (FIG. 16-21) at Gernrode.

Sculpture and Painting

In 1001, when Bishop Bernward was in Rome visiting the young Otto III, he resided in Otto's palace on the Aventine Hill in the neighborhood of Santa Sabina (FIG. 11-10), an Early Christian church renowned for its carved wooden doors. Those doors, decorated with episodes from both the Old and New Testaments, may have inspired the remarkable bronze doors the bishop had cast for his new church in Germany.

HILDESHEIM DOORS The colossal doors (FIG. **16-24**) for Saint Michael's, dated by inscription to 1015, are more than 16 feet tall. Each was cast in a single piece with the figural sculpture, a technological marvel. Carolingian sculpture, like most sculpture since Late Antiquity, consisted primarily of small-scale art executed in ivory and precious metals, often for book covers (FIG. **16-16**). The Hildesheim doors are huge in comparison, but the 16 individual panels stem from this tradition.

16-24A Otto I presenting Magdeburg Cathedral to Christ, 962–968.

Bernward placed the bronze doors at the entrance to Saint Michael's from the cloister, where the monks would see them each time they walked into the church. The panels of the left door illustrate highlights from the biblical book of Genesis, beginning with the creation of Eve (at the top) and ending with the murder of Adam and Eve's son Abel by his brother Cain (at the bottom). The right door recounts the life of Christ (reading from the bottom up), starting with the Annunciation and terminating with the appearance to Mary Magdalene of Christ after the Resurrection (see "The Life of Jesus in Art," Chapter 11, pages 296–297). Together, the doors tell the story of Original Sin and ultimate redemption, showing the expulsion from the Garden of Eden and the path back to Paradise through the Christian Church. As in Early Christian times, the Old Testament was interpreted as prefiguring the New Testament (see "Jewish Subjects in Christian Art," Chapter 11, page 293). The panel depicting the Fall of Adam and Eve, for example, is juxtaposed with the Crucifixion on the other door. Eve nursing the infant Cain is opposite Mary with the Christ Child in her lap.

The composition of many of the scenes on the doors derives from Carolingian manuscript illumination, and the style of the figures has an expressive strength that brings to mind the illustrations in the *Utrecht Psalter* (FIG. **16-15**). For example, in the fourth panel from the top on the left door, God, portrayed as a man, accuses Adam and Eve after their fall from grace. He jabs his finger at them with the force of his whole body. The force is concentrated in the gesture, which becomes the psychic focus of the whole composition. The frightened pair crouch, not only to hide their shame but also to escape the lightning bolt of divine wrath. Each passes the blame—Adam pointing backward to Eve and Eve pointing downward to the deceitful serpent. The starkly flat setting throws into relief the gestures and attitudes of rage, accusation, guilt, and fear. The sculptor presented the story with simplicity, although with great emotional impact, as well as a flair for anecdotal detail. Adam and Eve both struggle to point with one arm while attempting to shield their bodies from sight with the other. With an instinct for expressive pose and gesture, the artist brilliantly communicated their newfound embarrassment at their nakedness and their unconvincing denials of wrongdoing.

16-24 Doors with relief panels (Genesis, left door; life of Christ, right door), commissioned by Bishop Bernward for Saint Michael's, Hildesheim, Germany, 1015. Bronze, 16′ 6″ high. Dom-Museum, Hildesheim. ◼

Bernward's doors vividly tell the story of Original Sin and ultimate redemption, and draw parallels between the Old and New Testaments, as in the expulsion from Paradise and the infancy and suffering of Christ.

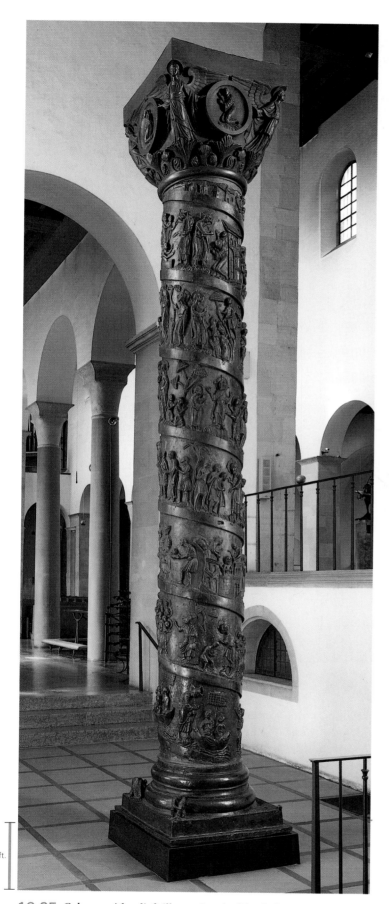

16-25 Column with reliefs illustrating the life of Christ, commissioned by Bishop Bernward for Saint Michael's, Hildesheim, Germany, ca. 1015–1022. Bronze, 12′ 6″ tall. Dom-Museum, Hildesheim. ▣◀

Modeled on the Column of Trajan (FIG. 10-44) in Rome, the seven spiral bands of the Hildesheim column relate the life of Jesus from his baptism to his entry into Jerusalem, episodes Bernward's doors omitted.

16-26 Crucifix commissioned by Archbishop Gero for Cologne Cathedral, Cologne, Germany, ca. 970. Painted wood, height of figure 6′ 2″. Cathedral, Cologne. ▣

In this early example of the revival of monumental sculpture in the Middle Ages, an Ottonian sculptor depicted with unprecedented emotional power the intense agony of Christ's ordeal on the cross.

HILDESHEIM COLUMN The great doors of Saint Michael's were not the only large-scale examples of bronze-casting Bernward commissioned. Within the church stood a bronze spiral column (FIG. 16-25) that survives intact, save for its later capital and missing surmounting cross. The seven spiral bands of relief tell the story of Jesus' life in 24 scenes, beginning with his baptism and concluding with his entry into Jerusalem. These are the missing episodes from the story told on the church's doors. The narrative reads from bottom to top, exactly as on the Column of Trajan (FIG. 10-44) in Rome. That triumphal column was unmistakably the model for the Hildesheim column, even though the Ottonian narrative unfolds from right to left instead of from left to right. Once again, a monument in Rome provided the inspiration for the Ottonian artists working under Bernward's direction. Both the doors and the column of Saint Michael's lend credence to the Ottonian emperors' claim to be the heirs to Charlemagne's *renovatio imperii Romani*.

GERO CRUCIFIX Nowhere was the revival of interest in monumental sculpture more evident than in the crucifix (FIG. 16-26) Archbishop Gero commissioned and presented to Cologne Cathedral

Abbess Uta dedicating her codex to the Virgin, folio 2 recto of the *Uta Codex,* from Regensburg, Germany, ca. 1025. Tempera on parchment, $9\frac{5}{8}'' \times 5\frac{1}{8}''$. Bayerische Staatsbibliothek, Munich.

The *Uta Codex* illustrates the important role that women could play both in religious life and as patrons of the arts. The dedicatory page shows Uta presenting her codex to the Virgin Mary.

1 in.

in 970. Carved in oak and then painted and gilded, the six-foot-tall image of Christ nailed to the cross is both statue and *reliquary* (a shrine for sacred relics; see "Pilgrimages and the Cult of Relics," Chapter 17, page 432). A compartment in the back of the head held the Host. A later story tells how a crack developed in the wood of Gero's crucifix but miraculously healed. Similar tales of miracles are attached to many sacred Christian objects, for example, some Byzantine icons (see "Icons and Iconoclasm," Chapter 12, page 326).

The Gero crucifix presents a dramatically different conception of the Savior from that seen on the *Lindau Gospels* cover (FIG. 16-16), with its Early Christian imagery of the youthful Christ triumphant over death. The bearded Christ of the Cologne crucifix is more akin to Byzantine representations (FIG. 12-23) of the suffering Jesus, but the emotional power of the Ottonian work is greater still. The sculptor depicted Christ as an all-too-human martyr. Blood streaks down his forehead from the (missing) crown of thorns. His eyelids are closed, and his face is contorted in pain. Christ's body sags under its own weight. The muscles stretch to their limit—those of his right shoulder and chest seem almost to rip apart. The halo behind Christ's head may foretell his subsequent Resurrection, but all the worshiper can sense is his pain. Gero's crucifix is the most powerful characterization of intense agony of the early Middle Ages.

UTA CODEX Ottonian artists carried on the Carolingian tradition of producing sumptuous books for the clergy and royalty alike. One of the finest is the lectionary produced at Regensburg, Germany, for Uta, abbess of Niedermünster. The *Uta Codex* illustrates the important role that women could play both in religious life and as patrons of the arts during the early Middle Ages. Uta was instrumental in bringing Benedictine reforms to the Niedermünster convent, whose nuns were usually the daughters of the local nobility. Uta herself was well known in Ottonian royal circles. Near the end of her life, she presented the nunnery with a luxurious codex containing many full-page illuminations interspersed with Gospel readings. The lectionary's gold, jewel, and enamel case also survives, underscoring the

The golden background of the illuminations in the *Lectionary of Henry II* reveals Byzantine influence on Ottonian art, which received added impetus when Otto II married the Byzantine princess Theophanu.

1 in.

full-page illumination (FIG. **16-28**) of the Annunciation of Christ's birth to the shepherds, the angel has just alighted on a hill, his wings still beating, and the wind of his landing agitates his robes. The angel looms immense above the startled and terrified shepherds, filling the golden sky, as he extends his hand in a gesture of authority and instruction. Emphasized more than the message itself are the power and majesty of God's authority. The painting is a highly successful fusion of the Carolingian-Ottonian anecdotal narrative tradition, elements derived from Late Antique painting—for example, the rocky landscape setting with grazing animals (FIG. **11-16**)—and the golden background of Byzantine book illumination and mosaic decoration. Byzantine influence on Ottonian art had received added impetus when Otto II (r. 973–983) married a Byzantine princess (see "Theophanu: A Byzantine Princess in Ottonian Germany," page 428).

nature of medieval books as sacred objects to be venerated in their own right as well as embodiments of the eternal Word of God.

The dedicatory page (FIG. **16-27**) at the front of the *Uta Codex* depicts the Virgin Mary with the Christ Child in her lap in the central medallion. Labeled *Virgo Virginum* (Virgin of Virgins), Mary is the model for Uta and the Niedermünster nuns. Uta is the full-length figure presenting a new book—*this* book—to the Virgin. An inscription accompanies the dedicatory image: "Virgin Mother of God, happy because of the divine Child, receive the votive offerings of your Uta of ready service."[5] The artist painted Uta last, superimposing her figure upon the design and carefully placing it so that Uta's head touches the Virgin's medallion but does not penetrate it, suggesting the interplay between, but also the separation of, the divine and human realms.

LECTIONARY OF HENRY II Uta presented her codex to the Niedermünster convent about the time the last Ottonian emperor, Henry II (r. 1002–1024), died. The *Lectionary of Henry II*, a book of Gospel readings for the Mass, was a gift to Bamberg Cathedral. In the

GOSPEL BOOK OF OTTO III Henry II's predecessor was his cousin, Otto III, son of Otto II and Theophanu. Of the three Ottos, the last dreamed the most of a revived Christian Roman Empire. Indeed, it was his life's obsession. Otto III was keenly aware of his descent from both German and Byzantine imperial lines. It is said that he was prouder of his Constantinopolitan than his German roots. He moved his court, with its Byzantine rituals, to Rome and there set up theatrically the symbols and trappings of Roman imperialism. Otto's romantic dream of imperial unity for Europe never materialized. He died prematurely, at age 21, and, at his own request, was buried beside Charlemagne at Aachen.

Theophanu, a Byzantine Princess in Ottonian Germany

The bishop of Mainz crowned Otto I king of the Saxons at Aachen in 936, but it was not until 962 that Pope John XII conferred the title of emperor of Rome upon him in Saint Peter's basilica. Otto, known as the Great, had ambitions to restore the glory of Charlemagne's Christian Roman Empire and to enlarge the territory under his rule. In 951 he defeated a Roman noble who had taken prisoner Adelaide, the widow of the Lombard king Lothar. Otto then married Adelaide, assumed the title of king of the Lombards, and extended his power south of the Alps. Looking eastward, in 972 he arranged the marriage of his son, Otto II, to Theophanu (ca. 955–991), the niece of the Byzantine emperor Nikephoros II Phokas. Otto was 17, Theophanu 16. They wed in Saint Peter's, with Pope John XIII presiding. When Otto the Great died the next year, Otto II succeeded him. The second Otto died in Italy in 983 and was buried in the atrium of Saint Peter's. His son, Otto III, only three years old at the time, nominally became king, but it was his mother, Theophanu, co-regent with Adelaide until 985 and sole regent thereafter, who wielded power in the Ottonian Empire until her own death in 991. Adelaide then served as regent until Otto III was old enough to rule on his own. He became emperor of Rome in 996.

Theophanu brought not only the prestige of Byzantium to Germany but also Byzantine culture and art. The Ottonian court emulated much of the splendor and pomp of Constantinople and imported Byzantine luxury goods in great quantities. One surviving ivory panel, probably carved in the West but of Byzantine style and labeled in Greek, depicts Christ simultaneously blessing Otto II and Theophanu. The impact of Byzantine art in Ottonian Germany can also be seen in manuscript illumination (FIG. 16-28).

16-28A Christ blessing Otto and Theopha 972–973.

1 in.

16-29 Otto III enthroned, folio 24 recto of the *Gospel Book of Otto III*, from Reichenau, Germany, 997–1000. Tempera on vellum, $1' 1'' \times 9\frac{3}{8}''$. Bayerische Staatsbibliothek, Munich.

Emperor Otto III, descended from both German and Byzantine imperial lines, appears in this Gospel book enthroned and holding the scepter and cross-inscribed orb that signify his universal authority.

Otto III is portrayed in a Gospel book (FIG. 16-29) that takes his name. The illuminator represented the emperor enthroned, holding the scepter and cross-inscribed orb that represent his universal authority, conforming to a Christian imperial iconographic tradition that went back to Constantine (FIG. 10-81, *right*). At his sides are the clergy and the barons (the Christian Church and the state), both aligned in his support. On the facing page (not illustrated), also derived from ancient Roman sources, female personifications of Slavinia, Germany, Gaul, and Rome—the provinces of the Ottonian Empire—bring tribute to the young emperor.

The ideal of a Christian Roman Empire gave partial unity to western Europe from the 9th through early 11th centuries. To this extent, ancient Rome lived on to the millennium, culminating in the frustrated ambition of Otto III. But with the death of Henry II in 1024, a new age began, and Rome ceased to be the deciding influence. Romanesque Europe instead found unity in a common religious heritage (see Chapter 17).

16-29A Jesus washing Pete feet, *Gospel Book of Otto I* 997–1000.

EARLY MEDIEVAL EUROPE

ART OF THE WARRIOR LORDS, 5th to 10th Centuries

▮ After the fall of Rome in 410, the Huns, Vandals, Merovingians, Franks, Goths, and other non-Roman peoples competed for power and territory in the former northwestern provinces of the Roman Empire.

▮ The surviving art of this period consists almost exclusively of small-scale status symbols, especially portable items of personal adornment such as bracelets, pins, and belt buckles, often featuring cloisonné ornament. The decoration of these early medieval objects displays a variety of abstract and zoomorphic motifs. Especially characteristic are intertwined animal and interlace patterns.

Sutton Hoo purse cover, ca. 625

CHRISTIAN ART: SCANDINAVIA, BRITISH ISLES, SPAIN, 6th to 10th Centuries

▮ The Christian art of the early medieval British Isles is called Hiberno-Saxon (or Insular). The most important extant artworks are the illuminated manuscripts produced in the monastic scriptoria of Ireland and Northumbria. The most distinctive features of these Insular books are the full pages devoted neither to text nor to illustration but to pure embellishment in the form of carpet pages made up of decorative panels of abstract and zoomorphic motifs. Some Hiberno-Saxon books also have full pages depicting each of the Four Evangelists or their symbols. Text pages often feature enlarged initial letters of important passages transformed into elaborate decorative patterns.

▮ In Spain, Visigothic churches of the sixth and seventh centuries were basilican in plan but had square apses and often incorporated horseshoe arches, a form usually associated with Islamic architecture.

▮ Scandinavian churches of the 11th century are notable for their carved wooden decoration recalling the pre-Christian art of the Vikings.

Lindisfarne Gospels, ca. 698–721

CAROLINGIAN ART, 768–877

▮ Charlemagne, king of the Franks since 768, expanded the territories he inherited from his father, and in 800, Pope Leo III crowned him emperor of Rome (r. 800–814). Charlemagne reunited much of western Europe and initiated a revival of the art and culture of Early Christian Rome.

▮ Carolingian illuminators merged the illusionism of classical painting with the northern linear tradition, replacing the calm and solid figures of their models with figures that leap from the page with frenzied energy.

▮ Carolingian sculptors revived the imperial Roman tradition of equestrian ruler portraiture and the Early Christian tradition of depicting Christ as a statuesque youth.

▮ Carolingian architects looked to Ravenna and Early Christian Rome for models, but transformed their sources, introducing, for example, the twin-tower western facade for basilicas and employing strict modular plans in their buildings.

Charlemagne or Charles the Bald, ninth century

OTTONIAN ART, 919–1024

▮ In the mid-10th century, a new line of emperors, the Ottonians, consolidated the eastern part of Charlemagne's former empire and sought to preserve and enrich the culture and tradition of the Carolingian period.

▮ Ottonian architects built basilican churches with the towering spires and imposing westworks of their Carolingian models but introduced the alternate-support system and galleries into the interior elevation of the nave.

▮ Ottonian sculptors also began to revive the art of monumental sculpture in works such as the Gero crucifix and the colossal bronze doors of Saint Michael's at Hildesheim.

▮ Ottonian painting combines motifs and landscape elements from Late Antique art with the golden backgrounds of Byzantine art. Byzantine influence on Ottonian art became especially pronounced after Otto II married Theophanu in 972.

Saint Michael's, Hildesheim, 1001–1031

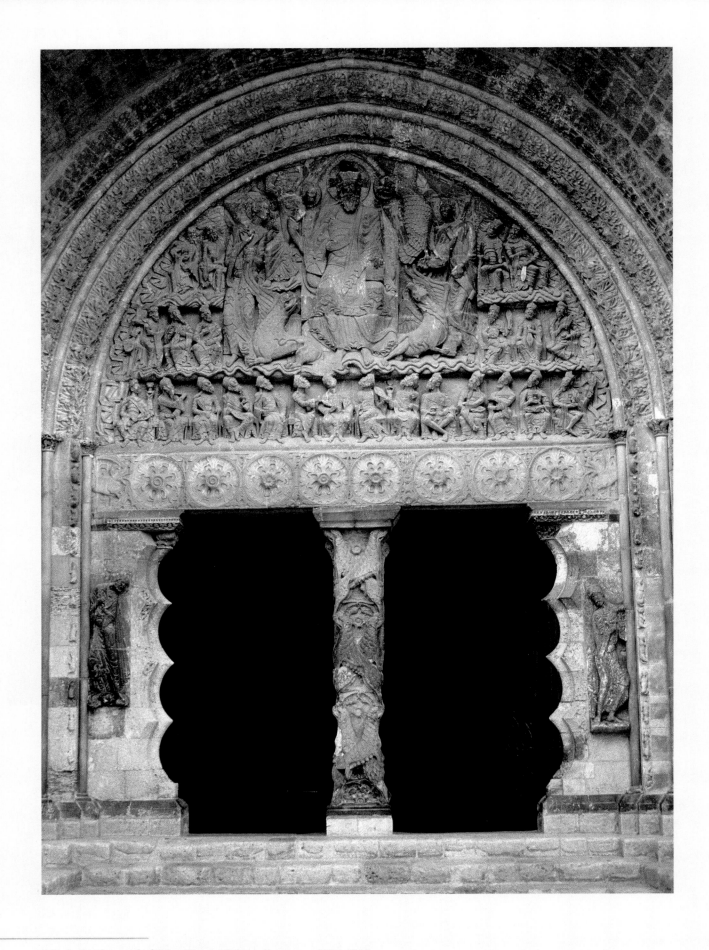

17-1 South portal of Saint-Pierre, Moissac, France, ca. 1115–1135.

Art historians first used the term *Romanesque* (Roman-like) to describe stone-vaulted churches of the 11th and 12th centuries, but the adjective also applies to the revival of monumental stone sculpture.

ROMANESQUE
EUROPE

The Romanesque era is the first since Archaic and Classical Greece to take its name from an artistic style rather than from politics or geography. Unlike Carolingian and Ottonian art, named for emperors, or Hiberno-Saxon art, a regional term, *Romanesque* is a title art historians invented to describe medieval art that appeared "Roman-like." Architectural historians first employed the adjective in the early 19th century to describe European architecture of the 11th and 12th centuries. Scholars noted that certain architectural elements of this period, principally barrel and groin vaults based on the round arch, resembled those of ancient Roman architecture. Thus, the word distinguished most Romanesque buildings from earlier medieval timber-roofed structures, as well as from later Gothic churches with vaults resting on pointed arches (see Chapter 18). Scholars in other fields quickly borrowed the term. Today "Romanesque" broadly designates the history and culture of western Europe between about 1050 and 1200 (MAP **17-1**).

In the early Middle Ages, the focus of life was the *manor,* or estate, of a landholding *liege lord,* who might grant rights to a portion of his land to *vassals.* The vassals swore allegiance to their liege and rendered him military service in return for use of the land and the promise of protection. But in the Romanesque period, a sharp increase in trade encouraged the growth of towns and cities, gradually displacing *feudalism* as the governing political, social, and economic system of late medieval Europe. Feudal lords granted independence to the new towns in the form of charters, which enumerated the communities' rights, privileges, immunities, and exemptions beyond the feudal obligations the vassals owed the lords. Often located on navigable rivers, the new urban centers naturally became the nuclei of networks of maritime and overland commerce.

Separated by design from the busy secular life of Romanesque towns were the monasteries (see "Medieval Monasteries," Chapter 16, page 420) and their churches. During the 11th and 12th centuries, thousands of ecclesiastical buildings were remodeled or newly constructed. This immense building enterprise was in part a natural by-product of the rise of independent cities and the prosperity they enjoyed. But it also was an expression of the widely felt relief and thanksgiving that the conclusion of the first Christian millennium in the year 1000 had not brought an end to the world, as many had feared. In the Romanesque age, the construction of churches became almost an obsession. Raoul Glaber (ca. 985–ca. 1046), a monk

Pilgrimages and the Cult of Relics

The cult of *relics* was not new in the Romanesque era. For centuries, Christians had traveled to sacred shrines that housed the body parts of, or objects associated with, the holy family or the saints. The faithful had long believed that bones, clothing, instruments of martyrdom, and the like had the power to heal body and soul. The veneration of relics reached a high point in the 11th and 12th centuries.

In Romanesque times, pilgrimage was the most conspicuous feature of public devotion, proclaiming the pilgrim's faith in the power of saints and hope for their special favor. The major shrines—Saint Peter's and Saint Paul's in Rome and the Church of the Holy Sepulchre in Jerusalem—drew pilgrims from all over Europe, just as Muslims journeyed from afar to Mecca (see "Muhammad and Islam," Chapter 13, page 343). To achieve salvation, Christian pilgrims braved bad roads and hostile wildernesses infested with robbers who preyed on innocent travelers. The journeys could take more than a year to complete—when they were successful. People often undertook pilgrimage as an act of repentance or as a last resort in their search for a cure for some physical disability. Hardship and austerity were means of increasing pilgrims' chances for the remission of sin or of disease. The distance and peril of the pilgrimage were measures of pilgrims' sincerity of repentance or of the reward they sought.

For those with insufficient time or money to make a pilgrimage to Rome or Jerusalem (in short, for most people at the time), holy destinations could be found closer to home. In France, for example, the church at Vézelay housed the bones of Mary Magdalene. Pilgrims could also view Saint Foy's remains at Conques, Lazarus's at Autun, Saint Martin's at Tours, and Saint Saturninus's at Toulouse. Each of these great shrines was also an important way station en route to the most venerated Christian shrine in western Europe, the tomb of Saint James at Santiago de Compostela in northwestern Spain.

Large crowds of pilgrims paying homage to saints placed a great burden on the churches that stored their relics and led to changes in church design, principally longer and wider naves and aisles, transepts and ambulatories with additional chapels (FIG. 17-5), and second-story galleries (FIG. 17-6). Pilgrim traffic also established the routes that later became the major avenues of commerce and communication in western Europe. The popularity of pilgrimages gave rise to travel guides akin to modern guidebooks. These provided pilgrims with information about saints and shrines and also about roads, accommodations, food, and drink. How widely circulated these handwritten books were is a matter of debate, but the information they provide modern scholars is still invaluable. The most famous Romanesque guidebook described the four roads leading to Santiago de Compostela through Arles and Toulouse, Conques and Moissac, Vézelay and Périgueux, and Tours and Bordeaux (MAP 17-1). Saint James was the symbol of Christian resistance to Muslim expansion in western Europe, and his relics, discovered in the ninth century, drew pilgrims to Santiago de Compostela from far and wide. The guidebook's anonymous 12th-century author, possibly Aimery Picaud, a Cluniac

MAP 17-1 Western Europe around 1100.

monk, was himself a well-traveled pilgrim. According to the guide, the author wrote it "in Rome, in the lands of Jerusalem, in France, in Italy, in Germany, in Frisia and mainly in Cluny."*

Pilgrims reading the guidebook learned about the saints and their shrines at each stop along the way to Spain. Saint Saturninus of Toulouse, for example, endured a martyr's death at the hands of pagans when he

> was tied to some furious and wild bulls and then precipitated from the height of the citadel. . . . His head crushed, his brains knocked out, his whole body torn to pieces, he rendered his worthy soul to Christ. He is buried in an excellent location close to the city of Toulouse where a large basilica [FIGS. 17-4 to 17-6] was erected by the faithful in his honor.†

Given the competition among monasteries and cities for the possession of saints' relics, the *Pilgrim's Guide to Santiago de Compostela* also included comments on authenticity. For example, about Saint James's tomb, the author stated:

> May therefore the imitators from beyond the mountains blush who claim to possess some portion of him or even his entire relic. In fact, the body of the Apostle is here in its entirety, divinely lit by paradisiacal carbuncles, incessantly honored with immaculate and soft perfumes, decorated with dazzling celestial candles, and diligently worshipped by attentive angels.‡

---

* William Melczer, *The Pilgrim's Guide to Santiago de Compostela* (New York: Italica Press, 1993), 133.

† Ibid., 103.

‡ Ibid., 127.

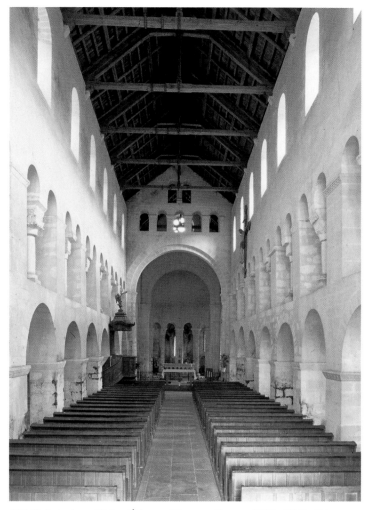

17-2 Interior of Saint-Étienne, Vignory, France, 1050–1057. ■◄

The timber-roofed abbey church of Saint Stephen at Vignory reveals a kinship with the three-story naves of Ottonian churches (FIG. 16-21), which also feature an alternate-support system of piers and columns.

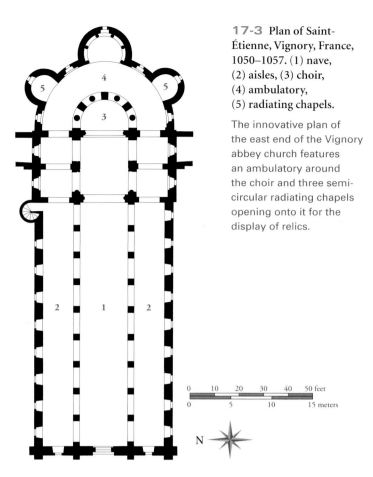

17-3 Plan of Saint-Étienne, Vignory, France, 1050–1057. (1) nave, (2) aisles, (3) choir, (4) ambulatory, (5) radiating chapels.

The innovative plan of the east end of the Vignory abbey church features an ambulatory around the choir and three semicircular radiating chapels opening onto it for the display of relics.

who witnessed the coming of the new millennium, described the sudden boom in church building:

> [After the] year of the millennium, which is now about three years past, there occurred, throughout the world, especially in Italy and Gaul, a rebuilding of church basilicas. Notwithstanding, the greater number were already well established and not in the least in need, nevertheless each Christian people strove against the others to erect nobler ones. It was as if the whole earth, having cast off the old by shaking itself, were clothing itself everywhere in the white robe of the church.[1]

The enormous investment in ecclesiastical buildings and furnishings also reflected a significant increase in pilgrimage traffic in Romanesque Europe (see "Pilgrimages and the Cult of Relics," page 432). Pilgrims, along with wealthy landowners, were important sources of funding for monasteries that possessed the relics of venerated saints. The clergy of these monasteries vied with one another to provide magnificent settings for the display of their relics. Justification for such heavy investment in buildings and furnishings could be found in the Bible itself, for example in Psalm 26:8, "Lord, I have loved the beauty of your house, and the place where your glory dwells." Traveling pilgrims fostered the growth of towns as well as monasteries. Pilgrimages were, in fact, a major economic as well as conceptual catalyst for the art and architecture of the Romanesque period.

FRANCE AND NORTHERN SPAIN

Although art historians use the adjective "Romanesque" to describe 11th- and 12th-century art and architecture throughout Europe, pronounced regional differences exist. The discussion in this chapter deals in turn with Romanesque France and Spain, the Holy Roman Empire, Italy, and Normandy and England. To a certain extent, Romanesque art and architecture parallel European Romance languages, which vary regionally but have a common core in Latin, the language of the Romans.

Architecture and Architectural Sculpture

The regional diversity of the Romanesque period is very evident in architecture. For example, some Romanesque churches, especially in Italy, retained the wooden roofs of their Early Christian predecessors long after stone vaulting had become commonplace elsewhere. Even in France and northern Spain, home of many of the most innovative instances of stone vaulting, some Romanesque architects still built timber-roofed churches.

17-2A Saint-Philibert, Tournus, ca. 1060.

SAINT-ÉTIENNE, VIGNORY The mid-11th-century church of Saint-Étienne (Saint Stephen) at Vignory in the Champagne region of central France has strong ties to Carolingian-Ottonian architecture but already incorporates features that became widely adopted only in later Romanesque architecture. The interior (FIG. **17-2**) reveals a kinship with the three-story wooden-roofed churches of the Ottonian era, for example, Saint Cyriakus (FIG. **16-21**) at Gernrode. At Vignory, however, the second story is not a true *tribune* (upper gallery over the aisle opening onto the nave) but rather a screen with alternating piers and columns opening onto very tall flanking aisles. The east end of the church, in contrast, has an innovative plan (FIG. **17-3**) with an

17-2B Sant Vicenç, Cardona, ca. 1029–1040.

Pilgrimages were a major economic catalyst for the art and architecture of the Romanesque period. The clergy vied with one another to provide magnificent settings for the display of holy relics.

ambulatory around the choir and three semicircular chapels opening onto it. These *radiating chapels* probably housed the church's relics, which the faithful could view without having to enter the choir where the main altar stood.

Saint-Étienne is also an early example of the introduction of stone sculpture into Romanesque ecclesiastical architecture, one of the period's defining features. At Vignory, however, the only sculpture is the relief decoration of the capitals of the ambulatory and false tribunes where abstract and vegetal ornament, lions, and other quadrupeds are the exclusive motifs.

17-4A Sainte-Foy, Conques, mid-11th to early 12th century.

SAINT-SERNIN, TOULOUSE One of the earliest Romanesque examples of stone vaulting is the church of Saint-Sernin (Saint Saturninus; FIGS. **17-4** to **17-6**) at Toulouse. Construction began

17-5 Plan of Saint-Sernin, Toulouse, France, ca. 1070–1120 (after Kenneth John Conant).

Increased traffic led to changes in church design. "Pilgrimage churches" such as Saint-Sernin have longer and wider naves and aisles, as well as transepts and ambulatories with radiating chapels for viewing relics.

17-6 Interior of Saint-Sernin, Toulouse, France, ca. 1070–1120. ▥◀

Saint-Sernin's groin-vaulted tribune galleries housed overflow crowds and buttressed the stone barrel vault over the nave. The transverse arches continue the lines of the compound piers.

Timber Roofs and Stone Vaults

The perils of wooden construction were the subject of frequent commentary among chroniclers of medieval ecclesiastical history. In some cases, churches burned repeatedly in the course of a single century and often had to be extensively repaired or completely rebuilt. In September 1174, for example, Canterbury Cathedral, which had been dedicated only 44 years earlier, was accidentally set ablaze and destroyed. Gervase of Canterbury (1141–1210), who entered the monastery at Canterbury in 1163 and wrote a history of the archbishopric from 1100 to 1199, provided a vivid eyewitness account of the disastrous fire in his *Chronica:*

[D]uring an extraordinarily violent south wind, a fire broke out before the gate of the church, and outside the walls of the monastery, by which three cottages were half destroyed. From thence, while the citizens were assembling and subduing the fire, cinders and sparks carried aloft by the high wind, were deposited upon the church, and being driven by the fury of the wind between the joints of the lead, remained there amongst the half-rotten planks, and shortly glowing with increased heat, set fire to the rotten rafters; from these the fire was communicated to the larger beams and their braces, no one yet perceiving or helping. For the well-painted ceiling below, and the sheet-lead covering above, concealed between them the fire that had arisen within. . . . But beams and braces burning, the flames arose to the slopes of the roof; and the sheets of lead yielded to the increasing heat and began to melt. Thus the raging wind, finding a freer entrance, increased the fury of the fire. . . . And now that the fire had loosened the beams from the pegs that bound them together, the half-burnt timbers fell into the choir below upon the seats of the monks; the seats, consisting of a great mass of woodwork, caught fire, and thus the mischief grew worse and worse. And it was marvellous, though sad, to behold how that glorious choir itself fed and assisted the fire that was destroying it. For the flames multiplied by this mass

of timber, and extending upwards full fifteen cubits [about twenty-five feet], scorched and burnt the walls, and more especially injured the columns of the church. . . . In this manner the house of God, hitherto delightful as a paradise of pleasures, was now made a despicable heap of ashes, reduced to a dreary wilderness.*

After the fire, the Canterbury monks summoned a master builder from Sens, a French city 75 miles southeast of Paris, to supervise the construction of their new church. Gervase reported that the first task William of Sens tackled was "the procuring of stone from beyond the sea."

A quest for fireproof structures, however, seems not to have been the primary rationale for stone vaulting. Although protection from devastating conflagrations was no doubt one of the attractions of building stone roofs in an age when candles provided interior illumination, other factors probably played a greater role in the decision to make the enormous investment that stone masonry required. The rapid spread of stone vaulting throughout Romanesque Europe is most likely the result of the clergy's desire to provide a suitably majestic setting for the display of relics as well as enhanced acoustics for the Christian liturgy and the music that accompanied it. Some contemporaneous texts, in fact, comment on the visual impact of costly stone vaults. For example, in 1150 at Angers in northwestern France, a church chronicler explained what the bishop sought to achieve by replacing the timber roof of his cathedral with stone vaults: "[He] took down the timber beams of the nave of the church, threatening to fall from sheer old age, and began to build stone vaults of wondrous effect."†

* Translated by Robert Willis. Quoted in Elizabeth Gilmore Holt, *A Documentary History of Art,* 2d ed. (Princeton, N.J.: Princeton University Press, 1981), 1:52–54.
† Translated by John Hooper Harvey, *The Medieval Architect* (London: Waylan, 1972), 39.

6A
nt James,
ntiago de
mpostela,
1075–1120.

around 1070 to honor the city's first bishop, a martyr saint of the middle of the third century. Toulouse was an important stop on the pilgrimage road through southwestern France to Santiago de Compostela (MAP 17-1). Large congregations were common at the shrines along the great pilgrimage routes, and the unknown architect designed Saint-Sernin to accommodate them. The grand scale of the building is apparent in the aerial view (FIG. 17-4), which includes automobiles, trucks, and nearly invisible pedestrians. The church's 12th-century exterior is still largely intact, although the two towers of the western facade (at the left in FIG. 17-4) were never completed, and the prominent crossing tower dates to the Gothic and later periods. Saint-Sernin's plan (FIG. 17-5) closely resembles those of the churches of Saint James at Santiago de Compostela and Saint Martin at Tours, and exemplifies the building type that has come to be called the "pilgrimage church." At Toulouse, the designer increased the length of the nave, doubled the side aisles, and added a transept, ambulatory, and radiating chapels to provide additional space for pilgrims and the clergy. Radiating chapels opening onto an ambulatory already were a feature of Vignory's abbey church (FIG. 17-3), but at Toulouse the chapels are greater in number and attached to the transept as well as to the ambulatory.

The Saint-Sernin plan is extremely regular and geometrically precise. The crossing square, flanked by massive piers and marked off by heavy arches, served as the module for the entire church. Each nave bay, for example, measures exactly one-half of the crossing square, and each aisle bay measures exactly one-quarter. The builders employed similar simple ratios throughout the church. The first suggestion of this kind of planning scheme in medieval Europe was the Saint Gall monastery plan (FIG. 16-19), almost three centuries earlier. The Toulouse solution was a crisply rational and highly refined realization of an idea first seen in Carolingian architecture. This approach to design became increasingly common in the Romanesque period.

Another telling feature of Saint-Sernin's design is the insertion of tribunes over the inner aisle and opening onto the nave (FIG. 17-6). These galleries housed overflow crowds on special occasions and played an important role in buttressing the continuous semicircular cut-stone *barrel vault* that covers Saint-Sernin's nave, in contrast to the timber roof over the nave (FIG. 17-2) of the smaller abbey church at Vignory (see "Timber Roofs and Stone Vaults," above). *Groin vaults* (indicated by Xs on the plan, FIG. 17-5) in the tribunes as well as in the ground-floor aisles absorbed the pressure exerted by the barrel vault along the entire length of the nave and transferred the main thrust to the thick outer walls.

The builders of Saint-Sernin were not content with just buttressing the massive nave vault. They also carefully coordinated the design of the vault with that of the nave arcade below and with the modular plan of the building as a whole. The geometric floor plan (FIG. 17-5) is fully reflected in the nave walls (FIG. 17-6), where *engaged columns* (attached half-columns) embellish the piers marking the corners of the bays. Architectural historians refer to piers with columns or pilasters attached to their rectangular cores as *compound piers.* At Saint-Sernin the engaged columns rise from the bottom of the compound piers to the vault's *springing* (the lowest stone of an arch) and continue across the nave as *transverse arches.* As a result, the Saint-Sernin nave seems to be composed of numerous identical vertical volumes of space placed one behind the other, marching down the building's length in orderly procession. Saint-Sernin's spatial organization corresponds to and renders visually the plan's geometric organization. The articulation of the building's exterior walls (FIG. 17-4), where buttresses frame each bay, also reflects the segmentation of the nave. This rationally integrated scheme, with repeated units decorated and separated by moldings, had a long future in later church architecture in the West.

17-7A Christ in Majesty, Saint-Genis-des-Fontaines, 1019–1020.

CHRIST IN MAJESTY Saint-Sernin also features one of the earliest precisely dated series of large Romanesque figure reliefs—a group of seven marble slabs representing angels, apostles, and Christ. An inscription states that the reliefs date to the year 1096 and that the artist was BERNARDUS GELDUINUS. Today the plaques are affixed to the church's ambulatory wall. Their original location is uncertain. Some scholars have suggested they once formed part of a shrine dedicated to Saint Saturninus that stood in the *crypt* (a vaulted underground chamber) of the grand pilgrimage church. Others believe the reliefs once decorated a choir screen or an exterior portal. The relief illustrated here (FIG. 17-7), the centerpiece of the group, depicts Christ in Majesty seated in a mandorla, his right hand raised in blessing, his left hand resting on an open book inscribed with the words *Pax vobis* ("peace be unto you"). The signs of the four evangelists (see "The Four Evangelists," Chapter 16, page 412) occupy the corners of the slab. Art historians debate the sources of Bernardus's style, but such a composition could have been used earlier for a Carolingian or Ottonian work in metal or ivory, perhaps a book cover. The polished marble has the gloss of both materials, and the sharply incised lines and ornamentation of Christ's aureole are characteristic of pre-Romanesque metalwork.

Stone sculpture, with some notable exceptions, such as the great crosses (FIG. 16-9) of the British Isles, had almost disappeared from the art of western Europe during the early Middle Ages. The revival of stonecarving is a hallmark of the Romanesque age—and one reason the period is aptly named. The inspiration for stone sculpture no doubt came, at least in part, from the abundant remains of ancient statues and reliefs throughout Rome's northwestern provinces. Yet these models had been available for centuries, so their presence cannot explain the sudden proliferation of stone sculpture in Romanesque churches. Many art historians have noted that the reemergence of monumental stone sculpture coincided with the introduction of stone vaulting in Romanesque churches. But medieval builders had erected stone-walled churches and monumental westworks for centuries, even if the structures bore timber ceilings and roofs. The earliest Romanesque sculptures, in fact, appear in timber-roofed churches, such as Saint-Étienne (FIG. 17-2) at Vignory. Therefore, the addition of stone vaults to basilican churches cannot explain the resurgence of

17-7 BERNARDUS GELDUINUS, Christ in Majesty, relief in the ambulatory of Saint-Sernin, Toulouse, France, ca. 1096. Marble, 4′ 2″ high.

One of the earliest series of large Romanesque figure reliefs decorated the pilgrimage church of Saint-Sernin. The models were probably Carolingian and Ottonian book covers in metal or ivory.

stonecarving in the Romanesque period. But just as stone vaulting reflects the greater prosperity of the age, so too does decorating churches with large-scale sculptures. Both are consistent with the widespread desire in the Romanesque period to beautify the house of God and make it, in the words of Gervase of Canterbury, "a paradise of pleasures."

The popularity of stone sculpture in the 12th century also reflects the changing role of many churches in western Europe. In the early Middle Ages, most churches served small monastic communities, and the worshipers were primarily or exclusively clergy. With the rise of towns in the Romanesque period, churches, especially those on the major pilgrimage routes, increasingly served the lay public. The display of sculpture both inside and outside Romanesque churches was a means of impressing—and educating—a new and largely illiterate audience.

CLUNY III The primary patrons of Romanesque sculpture were the monks of the Cluniac order. In 909 William the Pious, duke of Aquitaine (r. 893–918), donated land near Cluny in Burgundy to a community of reform-minded Benedictine monks under the leadership of Berno of Baume (d. 927). Because William waived his feudal rights to the land, the abbot of Cluny was subject only to the pope in Rome, a unique privilege. Berno founded a new order at Cluny according to the rules of Saint Benedict (see "Medieval Monasteries and Benedictine Rule," Chapter 16, page 420). Under Berno's successors, the Cluniac monks became famous for their scholarship,

17-8 Restored cutaway view of the third abbey church (Cluny III), Cluny, France, 1088–1130 (John Burge).

Cluny III was the largest church in Europe for 500 years. It had a 500-foot-long, three-story (arcade-tribune-clerestory) nave, four aisles, radiating chapels, and slightly pointed stone barrel vaults.

music, and art. Their influence and wealth grew rapidly, and they built a series of increasingly elaborate monastic churches at Cluny.

Abbot Hugh of Semur (1024–1109) began construction of the third church at Cluny in 1088. Called Cluny III by art historians, the building is, unfortunately, largely destroyed today, although scholars have reconstructed it on paper (FIG. **17-8**). At the time of its erection, Cluny III was the largest church in Europe, and it retained that distinction for almost 500 years until the completion of the new Saint Peter's (FIG. 24-4) in Rome in the early 17th century. Contemporaries considered Cluny III a place worthy for angels to dwell if they lived on earth. The church had a bold and influential design, with a barrel-vaulted nave, four aisles, and radiating chapels, as at Saint-Sernin, but with a three-story nave elevation (arcade-tribune-clerestory) and slightly pointed nave vaults. With a nave more than 500 feet long and more than 100 feet high (both dimensions are about 50 percent greater than at Saint-Sernin), Cluny III epitomized the grandiose scale of the new stone-vaulted Romanesque churches and was a symbol of the power and prestige of the Cluniac order.

SAINT-PIERRE, MOISSAC Moissac, an important stop in southwestern France along the pilgrimage route to Saint James's tomb at Santiago de Compostela, boasts the most extensive preserved ensemble of early Romanesque sculpture. The monks of the Moissac abbey had joined the Cluniac order in 1047. Enriched by the gifts of pilgrims and noble benefactors, they adorned their church with an elaborate series of relief sculptures, the oldest of which are in the cloister (FIG. **17-9**). "Cloister" (from the Latin *claustrum*, "enclosed place") connotes being shut away from the world. Architecturally, the medieval church cloister embodied the seclusion of the spiritual life, the *vita contemplativa*. At Moissac, as elsewhere, the cloister provided the monks (and nuns) with a foretaste of Paradise. In its garden or the timber-roofed columnar walkway that framed the garden (FIG. **17-9**, *left*), they could read their devotions, pray, and meditate in an atmosphere of calm serenity, each monk withdrawn into the private world where the soul communes only with God. The physical silence of the cloister matched the vow of silence that the more austere monastic communities required of their members.

Bernard of Clairvaux on Cloister Sculpture

The most influential theologian of the Romanesque era was Bernard of Clairvaux (1090–1153). A Cistercian monk and abbot of the monastery he founded at Clairvaux in northern Burgundy, he embodied not only the reforming spirit of the Cistercian order but also the new religious fervor awakening in western Europe. Bernard's impassioned eloquence made him a European celebrity and drew him into the stormy politics of the Romanesque era. He intervened in high ecclesiastical and secular matters, defended and sheltered embattled popes, counseled kings, denounced heretics, and preached Crusades against the Muslims (see "The Crusades," page 442)—all in defense of papal Christianity and spiritual values. The Church declared Bernard a saint in 1174, barely two decades after his death.

In a letter Bernard wrote in 1127 to William, abbot of Saint-Thierry, he complained about the rich outfitting of non-Cistercian churches in general and the sculptural adornment of monastic cloisters in particular:

> I will overlook the immense heights of the places of prayer, their immoderate lengths, their superfluous widths, the costly refinements, and painstaking representations which deflect the attention . . . of those who pray and thus hinder their devotion. . . . But so be it, let these things be made for the honor of God . . . . [But] in the cloisters, before the eyes of the brothers while they read—what . . . are the filthy apes doing there? The fierce lions? The monstrous centaurs? The creatures, part man and part beast? . . . You may see many bodies under one head, and conversely many heads on one body. On one side the tail of a serpent is seen on a quadruped, on the other side the head of a quadruped is on the body of a fish. Over there an animal has a horse for the front half and a goat for the back . . . . Everywhere so plentiful and astonishing a variety of contradictory forms is seen that one would rather read in the marble than in books, and spend the whole day wondering at every single one of them than in meditating on the law of God. Good God! If one is not ashamed of the absurdity, why is one not at least troubled at the expense?*

* *Apologia* 12.28–29. Translated by Conrad Rudolph, *The "Things of Greater Importance": Bernard of Clairvaux's* Apologia *and the Medieval Attitude toward Art* (Philadelphia: University of Pennsylvania Press, 1990), 279, 283.

17-9A Doubt
Thomas, Sar
Domingo, Si
ca. 1090–11C

1 ft.

17-9 General view of the cloister (*left*) and detail of the pier with the relief of Abbot Durandus (*right*), Saint-Pierre, Moissac, France, ca. 1100–1115. Relief: limestone, 6′ high.

The revived tradition of stonecarving seems to have begun with decorating capitals with reliefs. The most extensive preserved ensemble of sculptured early Romanesque capitals is in the Moissac cloister.

The monastery cloisters of the 12th century are monuments to the vitality, popularity, and influence of monasticism at its peak.

Moissac's cloister sculpture program consists of large figural reliefs on the piers as well as *historiated* (ornamented with figures) capitals on the columns. The pier reliefs (FIG. **17-9**, *right*) portray the 12 apostles and the first Cluniac abbot of Moissac, Durandus (1047–1072), who was buried in the cloister. The 76 capitals alternately crown single and paired column shafts. They are variously decorated, some with abstract patterns, many with biblical scenes or the lives of saints, others with fantastic monsters of all sorts—basilisks, griffins, lizards, gargoyles, and more. *Bestiaries*—collections of illustrations of real and imaginary animals—became very

The Romanesque Church Portal

One of the most significant and distinctive features of Romanesque art is the revival of monumental sculpture in stone. Large-scale carved Old and New Testament figures were extremely rare in Christian art before the Romanesque period. But in the late 11th and early 12th centuries, rich ensembles of figural reliefs began to appear again, most often in the grand stone portals (FIG. 17-1) through which the faithful had to pass. The clergy had placed sculpture in church doorways before. For example, carved wooden doors greeted Early Christian worshipers as they entered Santa Sabina in Rome, and Ottonian bronze doors (FIG. 16-24) decorated with Old and New Testament scenes marked the entrance to Saint Michael's at Hildesheim. But these were exceptions, and in the Romanesque era (and during the Gothic period that followed), sculpture usually appeared in the area surrounding the doors, not on them.

Shown in FIG. 17-10 are the parts of church portals that Romanesque sculptors regularly decorated with figural reliefs:

▌ *Tympanum* (FIGS. 17-1, 17-12, and 17-13), the prominent semicircular *lunette* above the doorway proper, comparable in importance to the triangular pediment of a Greco-Roman temple.

▌ *Voussoirs* (FIG. 17-13), the wedge-shaped blocks that together form the *archivolts* of the arch framing the tympanum.

▌ *Lintel* (FIGS. 17-12 and 17-13), the horizontal beam above the doorway.

▌ *Trumeau* (FIGS. 17-1 and 17-11), the center post supporting the lintel in the middle of the doorway.

▌ *Jambs* (FIG. 17-1), the side posts of the doorway.

17-10 **The Romanesque church portal.**

The clergy considered the church doorway the beginning of the path to salvation through Christ. Many Romanesque churches feature didactic sculptural reliefs above and beside the entrance portals.

popular in the Romanesque age. The monstrous forms were reminders of the chaos and deformity of a world without God's order. Medieval artists delighted in inventing composite beasts, often with multiple heads, and other fantastic creations. Historiated capitals were also a feature of Moissac's mother church, Cluny III, and were common in Cluniac monasteries.

Not everyone shared the enthusiasm of the Cluniac monks for stone sculpture. One group of Benedictine monks founded a new order at Cîteaux in eastern France in 1098. The Cistercians (so called from the Latin name for Cîteaux) split from the Cluniac order to return to the strict observance of the Rule of Saint Benedict, changing the color of their habits from Cluniac black to unbleached white. These so-called White Monks emphasized productive manual labor, and their systematic farming techniques stimulated the agricultural transformation of Europe. The Cistercian movement expanded with astonishing rapidity. Within a half century, more than 500 Cistercian monasteries had been established. The Cistercians rejected figural sculpture as a distraction from their devotions. The most outspoken Cistercian critic of church sculpture was Abbot Bernard of Clairvaux (see "Bernard of Clairvaux on Cloister Sculpture," page 438).

SOUTH PORTAL, MOISSAC Bernard directed his tirade against figural sculpture primarily at monks who allowed the carvings to distract them from their meditations. But at Moissac and other Cluniac churches, sculpture also appears outside the cloister. Saint-Pierre's south portal (FIG. 17-1), facing the town square, fea-

tured even more lavish decoration than did its cloister. The portal's vast tympanum (see "The Romanesque Church Portal," above) depicts the Second Coming of Christ as King and Judge of the world in its last days. As befits his majesty, the enthroned Christ is at the center, reflecting a compositional rule followed since Early Christian times. The signs of the four evangelists flank him. To one side of each pair of signs is an attendant angel holding scrolls to record human deeds for judgment. The figures of crowned musicians, which complete the design, are the 24 elders who accompany Christ as the kings of this world and make music in his praise. Each turns to face him, much as would the courtiers of a Romanesque monarch in attendance on their lord. Two courses of wavy lines symbolizing the clouds of Heaven divide the elders into three tiers.

Christ was the most common central motif in sculptured Romanesque portals. The pictorial programs of Romanesque church facades reflect the idea—one that dates to Early Christian times—that Christ is the door to salvation ("I am the door; who enters through me will be saved"—John 10:9). An inscription on the tympanum of the late 11th-century monastic church of Santa Cruz de la Serós in Spain made this message explicit: "I am the eternal door. Pass through me faithful. I am the source of life."[2]

Many variations exist within the general style of Romanesque sculpture, as within Romanesque architecture. The figures of the Moissac tympanum (FIG. 17-1) contrast sharply with those of the Saint-Sernin ambulatory reliefs (FIG. 17-7). The extremely elongated bodies of the recording angels, the cross-legged dancing pose of

17-11 Lions and Old Testament prophet (Jeremiah or Isaiah?), trumeau of the south portal of Saint-Pierre, Moissac, France, ca. 1115–1130.

This animated prophet displays the scroll recounting his vision. His position below the apparition of Christ as Last Judge is in keeping with the tradition of pairing Old and New Testament themes.

step. The animation of the body reveals the passionate nature of the soul within. The flowing lines of the drapery folds ultimately derive from manuscript illumination and here play gracefully around the elegant figure. The long, serpentine locks of hair and beard frame an arresting image of the dreaming mystic. The prophet seems entranced by his vision of what is to come, the light of ordinary day unseen by his wide eyes.

Six roaring interlaced lions fill the trumeau's outer face (FIG. 17-1). The animal world was never far from the medieval mind, and people often associated the most fiercely courageous animals with kings and barons—for example, Richard the Lionhearted, Henry the Lion, and Henry the Bear. Lions were the church's ideal protectors. In the Middle Ages, people believed lions slept with their eyes open. But the notion of placing fearsome images at the gateways to important places is of ancient origin. Ancestors of the interlaced lions at Moissac include the lions and composite monsters that guarded the palaces of Near Eastern and Mycenaean kings (FIGS. 2-18, 2-21, and 4-19) and the panthers and leopards in Greek temple pediments (FIG. 5-17) and Etruscan tombs (FIG. 9-9).

SAINT-LAZARE, AUTUN In 1132, the Cluniac bishop Étienne de Bage consecrated the Burgundian cathedral of Saint-Lazare (Saint Lazarus) at Autun. For its tympanum (FIG. **17-12**), he commissioned the sculptor GISLEBERTUS to carve a dramatic vision of the Last Judgment, which four trumpet-blowing angels announce. In the tympanum's center, far larger than any other figure, is Christ, enthroned in a mandorla. He dispassionately presides over the separation of the Blessed from the Damned. At the left, an obliging angel boosts one of the Blessed into the heavenly city. Below, the souls of the dead line up to await their fate. Two of the men near the center of the lintel carry bags emblazoned with a cross and a shell. These are the symbols of pilgrims to Jerusalem and Santiago de Compostela. Those who had made the difficult journey would be judged favorably. To their right, three small figures beg an angel to intercede on their behalf. The angel responds by pointing to the Judge above. On the right side (FIG. I-6) are those who will be condemned to Hell. Giant hands pluck one poor soul from the earth. Directly above, in the tympanum, is one of the most unforgettable renditions of the weighing of souls in the history of art (compare FIG. 16-9). Angels and devils compete at the scales, each trying to manipulate the balance for or against a soul. Hideous demons guffaw and roar. Their gaunt, lined bodies, with legs ending in sharp claws, writhe and bend like long, loathsome insects. A devil, leaning from the dragon mouth of Hell, drags souls in, while above him a howling demon crams souls headfirst into a furnace. The resources of the Romanesque imagination conjured an appalling scene.

The Autun tympanum must have inspired terror in the believers who passed beneath it as they entered the cathedral. Even those who could not read could, in the words of Bernard of Clairvaux, "read in the marble." For the literate, the Autun clergy composed explicit written warnings to reinforce the pictorial message and had the words engraved in Latin on the tympanum. For example, beneath the weighing of souls (FIG. I-6), the inscription reads, "May this terror terrify those whom earthly error binds, for the horror of these images here in this manner truly depicts what will be."[3] The admonition echoes the sentiment expressed in the colophon of a mid-10th-century illustrated copy of Beatus of Liébana's *Commentary on the Apocalypse*. There, the painter Magius (teacher of Emeterius; see FIG. 16-11) explained the purpose of his work: "I have painted a series of pictures for the wonderful words of [the Apocalypse] stories, so that the wise may fear the coming of the future judgment of the world's end."[4]

17-12A GISLEBERTUS, *Suicide of Judas,* ca. 1120–113

17-12B GISLEBERTUS, ca. 1120–113

Saint Matthew's angel, and the jerky, hinged movement of the elders' heads are characteristic of the nameless Moissac master's style of representing the human figure. The zigzag and dovetail lines of the draperies, the bandlike folds of the torsos, the bending back of the hands against the body, and the wide cheekbones are also common features of this distinctive style. The animation of the individual figures, however, contrasts with the stately monumentality of the composition as a whole, producing a dynamic tension in the tympanum.

Below the tympanum are a richly decorated trumeau (FIG. **17-11**) and elaborate door jambs with scalloped contours (FIG. 17-1), the latter a borrowing from Islamic architecture (FIG. 13-12). On the trumeau's right face is a prophet identified as Jeremiah by some scholars, as Isaiah by others. Whoever the prophet is, he displays the scroll where his prophetic vision is written. His position below the apparition of Christ as the apocalyptic Judge is yet another instance of the pairing of Old and New Testament themes. This is in keeping with an iconographic tradition established in Early Christian times (see "Jewish Subjects in Christian Art," Chapter 11, page 293). The prophet's figure is very tall and thin, in the manner of the tympanum angels, and, like Matthew's angel, he executes a cross-legged

17-12 GISLEBERTUS, *Last Judgment*, west tympanum of Saint-Lazare, Autun, France, ca. 1120–1135. Marble, 21′ wide at base. 📹

Christ in a mandorla presides over the separation of the Blessed from the Damned in this dramatic vision of the Last Judgment, designed to terrify those guilty of sin and beckon them into the church.

LA MADELEINE, VÉZELAY While Gislebertus was at work at Autun, nearby at the church of La Madeleine (Mary Magdalene) at Vézelay an unnamed sculptor was busy carving an even more elaborate tympanum (FIG. 17-13) over the central portal to the church's narthex. Vézelay is more closely associated with the Cru-sades (see "The Crusades," page 442) than any other church in Eu-rope. Pope Urban II had intended to preach the launching of the First Crusade at Vézelay in 1095, although he delivered the sermon at Clermont instead. In 1147, Bernard of Clairvaux called for the Second Crusade at Vézelay, and King Louis VII of France took up the

17-13 *Pentecost and Mission of the Apostles*, tympanum of the center portal of the narthex of La Madeleine, Vézelay, France, 1120–1132.

The light rays emanating from Christ's hands represent the instilling of the Holy Spirit in the apostles. On the lintel and in eight compartments around the tympanum, the heathen wait to be converted.

The Crusades

In 1095, Pope Urban II (r. 1088–1099) delivered a stirring sermon at the Council of Clermont in which he called for an assault on the Holy Land:

> [Y]our brethren who live in the East are in urgent need of your help . . . [because] the Turks and Arabs have attacked them . . . They have killed and captured many, and have destroyed the churches . . . I, or rather the Lord, beseech you as Christ's heralds . . . to persuade all people of whatever rank, foot-soldiers and knights, poor and rich, to carry aid promptly to those Christians and to destroy that vile race from the lands of our friends. . . . All who die by the way . . . shall have immediate remission of sins. . . . Let those who go not put off the journey, but rent their lands and collect money for their expenses . . . [and] eagerly set out on the way with God as their guide.*

Between 1095 and 1190, Christians launched three great Crusades from France. The *Crusades* ("taking of the Cross") were mass armed pilgrimages whose stated purpose was to wrest the Christian shrines of the Holy Land from Muslim control. Similar vows bound Crusaders and pilgrims. They hoped not only to atone for sins and win salvation but also to glorify God and extend the power of the Christian Church. The joint action of the papacy and the mostly French feudal lords in this type of holy war strengthened papal authority over the long run and created an image of Christian solidarity.

The symbolic embodiment of the joining of religious and secular forces in the Crusades was the Christian warrior, the fighting priest, or the priestly fighter. From the early medieval warrior evolved the Christian knight, who fought for the honor of God rather than in defense of his chieftain. The first and most typical of the crusading knights were the Knights Templar. After the Christian conquest of Jerusalem in 1099, they stationed themselves next to the Dome of the Rock (FIG. 13-2), that is, on the site of Solomon's Temple, the source of their name. Their mission was to protect pilgrims visiting the recovered Christian shrines. Formally founded in 1118, the Knights Templar order received the blessing of Bernard of Clairvaux, who gave them a rule of organization based on that of his own Cistercians. Bernard justified their militancy by declaring that "the knight of Christ" is "glorified in slaying the infidel . . . because thereby Christ is glorified," and the Christian knight then wins salvation. The Cistercian abbot saw the Crusades as part of the general reform of the Church and as the defense of the supremacy of Christendom. He himself called for the Second Crusade in 1147. For the Muslims, however, the Crusaders were nothing more than violent invaders who slaughtered the population of Jerusalem (Jewish as well as Muslim) when they took the city in July 1099.

In the end, the Muslims expelled the Christian armies. The Crusaders failed miserably in their attempt to regain the Holy Land. But in western Europe, the Crusades had much greater impact by increasing the power and prestige of the towns. Italian maritime cities such as Pisa (FIG. 17-25) thrived on the commercial opportunities presented by the transportation of Crusaders overseas. Many communities purchased their charters from the barons who owned their land when the latter needed to finance their campaigns in the Holy Land, and a middle class of merchants and artisans arose to rival the power of the feudal lords and the great monasteries.

* As recorded by Fulcher of Chartres (1059–ca. 1127). Translated by O. J. Thatcher and E. H. McNeal, quoted in Roberta Anderson and Dominic Aidan Bellenger, eds., *Medieval Worlds: A Sourcebook* (New York: Routledge, 2003), 88–90.

---

cross there. Finally, the Vézelay church was the site where King Richard the Lionhearted of England and King Philip Augustus of France set out on the Third Crusade in 1190.

The Vézelay tympanum depicts the Pentecost and the Mission of the Apostles. As related in Acts 1:4–9, Christ foretold that the 12 apostles would receive the power of the Holy Spirit and become the witnesses of the truth of the Gospels throughout the world. The light rays emanating from Christ's hands represent the instilling of the Holy Spirit in the apostles (Acts 2:1–42) at the Pentecost (the seventh Sunday after Easter). The apostles, holding the Gospel books, receive their spiritual assignment to preach the Gospel to all nations. The Christ figure is a splendid essay in calligraphic line. The drapery lines shoot out in rays, break into quick zigzag rhythms, and spin into whorls, wonderfully conveying the spiritual light and energy that flow from Christ over and into the equally animated apostles. The overall composition, as well as the detailed treatment of the figures, contrasts with the much more sedate representation of the Second Coming (FIG. 17-1) at Moissac, where a grid of horizontal and vertical lines contains almost all the figures. The sharp differences between the two tympana once again highlight the regional diversity of Romanesque art.

The world's heathen peoples, the objects of the apostles' mission, appear on the lintel below and in eight compartments around the tympanum. The portrayals of the yet-to-be-converted constitute a medieval anthropological encyclopedia. Present are the legendary giant-eared Panotii of India, Pygmies (who require ladders to mount horses), and a host of other races, some characterized by a dog's head, others by a pig's snout, and still others by flaming hair. The assembly of agitated figures also includes hunchbacks, mutes, blind men, and lame men. Humanity, still suffering, awaits the salvation to come. As at Moissac and Autun, as worshipers entered the building, the tympanum established God's omnipotence and presented the Church as the road to salvation.

17-13A Sain Trophîme, A mid-12th century.

NOTRE-DAME, FONTENAY Although the costly decoration of Cluniac churches like those at Moissac, Autun, and Vézelay appalled Bernard of Clairvaux, Cistercian monks were themselves great builders. Some of their churches were among the largest erected in Romanesque Europe. Nonetheless, the austerity of their buildings reflects the Cistercians' rejection of worldly extravagance and their emphasis on poverty, labor, and prayer. The abbey at Cîteaux itself no longer stands, but at nearby Fontenay, the church of Notre-Dame (FIG. 17-14) does. It is representative of the Cistercian approach to architectural design. The church has a square east end without an ambulatory or chapels. The walls are devoid of ornament, and the column capitals are plain. The nave has a single-story elevation with neither clerestory nor gallery. Light, however, reaches the nave

17-13B Notre Dame-la-Grande, Poitiers, ca. 1130–1150.

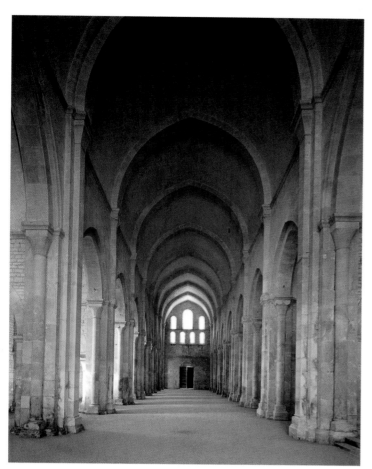

17-14 Interior of the abbey church of Notre-Dame, Fontenay, France, 1139–1147.

The Cistercians were great builders but rejected sculptural ornament. The Fontenay church is typically austere, with its single-story nave and square east end lacking ambulatory or chapels.

through the large windows in the flat east wall and because the aisle bays have *transverse barrel vaults* (tunnel-like vaults perpendicular to the nave) that channel light from outside to the center of the building. The architect used *pointed arches*—a feature of Cluny III (FIG. 17-8)—both in the nave arcade and in the barrel vaults. Romanesque builders may have thought this feature gave churches the look and feel of the architecture of the Holy Land, but pointed arches also brought structural advantages. Pointed arches transfer the thrust of the vaults more directly downward to the piers and require less buttressing on the sides than do round arches. This forward-looking structural device would permit Gothic architects to increase the height of the nave dramatically (see Chapter 18).

Painting and Other Arts

Unlike the practices of placing vaults over naves and aisles and decorating building facades with monumental stone reliefs, the art of painting did not need to be "revived" in the Romanesque period. Monasteries produced illuminated manuscripts in large numbers in the early Middle Ages, and even the Roman tradition of mural painting had never died. But the quantity of preserved frescoes and illustrated books from the Romanesque era is unprecedented.

MORALIA IN JOB One of the major Romanesque scriptoria was at the abbey of Cîteaux, mother church of the Cistercian order. Just

before Bernard joined the monastery in 1112, the monks completed work on an illuminated copy of Saint Gregory's (Pope Gregory the Great, r. 590–604) *Moralia in Job.* It is an example of Cistercian illumination before Bernard's passionate opposition to figural art in monasteries led in 1134 to a Cistercian ban on elaborate paintings in manuscripts as well as sculptural ornamentation in monasteries. After 1134 the Cistercian order prohibited full-page illustrations, and even initial letters had to be nonfigurative and of a single color. The historiated initial reproduced here (FIG. 17-15) clearly would have been in violation of Bernard's ban had it not been painted before his prohibitions took effect. A knight, his squire, and two roaring dragons form an intricate letter *R*, the initial letter of the salutation *Reverentissimo.* This page is the opening of Gregory's letter to "the very reverent" Leander (ca. 534–600), bishop of Seville, Spain. The knight is a slender, regal figure who raises his shield and sword against the dragons while the squire, crouching beneath him, runs a lance through one of the monsters. Although the clergy viewed the duel between knight and dragons as an allegory of the spiritual struggle of monks against the devil for the salvation of souls, Bernard opposed this kind of illumination, just as he condemned carvings of monstrous creatures and "fighting knights" on contemporary cloister capitals (see "Bernard of Clairvaux on Cloister Sculpture," page 438).

Ornamented initials date to the Hiberno-Saxon period (FIG. 16-8), but in the *Moralia in Job* the artist translated the theme into

17-15A Initial L, *Codex Colbertinus,* ca. 1100.

17-15 Initial *R* with knight fighting dragons, folio 4 verso of the *Moralia in Job,* from Cîteaux, France, ca. 1115–1125. Ink and tempera on vellum, $1' 1\frac{3}{4}'' \times 9\frac{1}{4}''$. Bibliothèque Municipale, Dijon.

Ornamented initials date to the Hiberno-Saxon era (FIG. 16-8), but this artist translated the theme into Romanesque terms. The duel between knight and dragons symbolized a monk's spiritual struggle.

17-16 Nave (*left*) and painted nave vault (*right*) of the abbey church, Saint-Savin-sur-Gartempe, France, ca. 1100.

Saint-Savin is a hall church with aisles approximately the same height as the nave. The tall aisle windows provide ample illumination for the biblical paintings on the nave's continuous barrel vault.

17-15B Saint Mark, *Corbie Gospels,* ca. 1120.

Romanesque terms. The page with the initial *R* may be a reliable picture of a medieval baron's costume. The typically French Romanesque banding of the torso and partitioning of the folds are evident (compare FIG. **17-11**), but the master painter deftly avoided stiffness and angularity. The partitioning actually accentuates the knight's verticality and elegance and the thrusting action of his servant. The flowing sleeves add a spirited flourish to the swordsman's gesture. The knight, handsomely garbed, cavalierly wears no armor and calmly aims a single stroke, unmoved by the ferocious dragons lunging at him.

SAINT-SAVIN-SUR-GARTEMPE Although the art of fresco painting never died in early medieval Europe, the murals (not true frescoes, however) of the Benedictine abbey church of Saint-Savin-sur-Gartempe have no Carolingian or Ottonian parallels, because the murals decorate the church's stone-vaulted nave (FIG. **17-16**). Saint-Savin is a *hall church* (from German *Hallenkirche*), a church where the aisles are approximately the same height as the nave. The tall windows in the aisles provided more illumination to the nave than in churches that had low aisles and tribunes. The abundant light coming into the church may explain why the monks chose to decorate the nave's continuous barrel vault with paintings. (They also painted the nave piers to imitate rich veined marble.) The subjects of Saint-Savin's nave paintings all come from the Pentateuch, the opening five books of the Old Testament, but New Testament themes appear in the transept, ambulatory, and chapels, where the painters also depicted the lives of Saint Savin and another local saint. The elongated, agitated cross-legged figures have stylistic affinities both to the reliefs of southern French portals and to illuminated manuscripts such as the *Moralia in Job*.

SANTA MARÍA DE MUR In the Romanesque period, northern Spain, home to the great pilgrimage church of Saint James at Santiago de Compostela, was an important regional artistic center. In fact, Catalonia in northeastern Spain has more Romanesque mural paintings today than anywhere else. One of the most

17-17 Christ in Majesty, apse, Santa María de Mur, near Lérida, Spain, mid-12th century. Fresco, 24′ × 22′. Museum of Fine Arts, Boston.

The Apocalypse fresco of the Santa María de Mur apse resembles the reliefs of French and Spanish Romanesque tympana. Christ appears in a mandorla between the signs of the four evangelists.

1 ft.

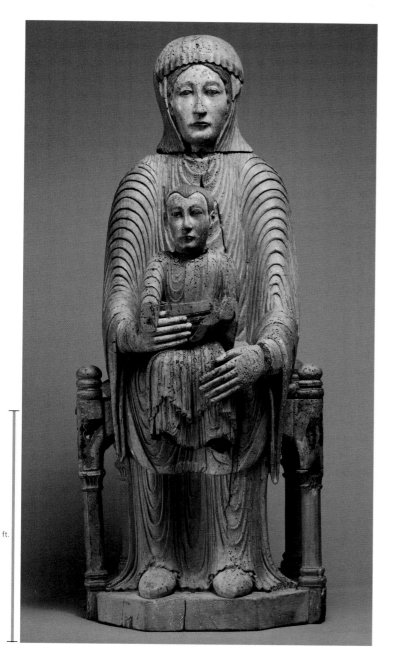

munities where Saint John addressed his revelation (the Apocalypse) at the beginning of his book (Rev. 1:4, 12, 20). Below stand apostles, paired off in formal frontality, as in the Monreale Cathedral apse (FIG. 12-25). The Spanish painter rendered the principal figures with partitioning of the drapery into volumes, here and there made tubular by local shading, and stiffened the irregular shapes of actual cloth into geometric patterns. The effect overall is one of simple, strong, and even blunt directness of statement, reinforced by harsh, bright color, appropriate for a powerful icon.

MORGAN MADONNA Despite the widespread use of stone relief sculptures to adorn Romanesque church portals, resistance to the creation of statues in the round—in any material—continued. The avoidance of creating anything that might be construed as an idol was still the rule, in keeping with the Second Commandment. Two centuries after Archbishop Gero commissioned a monumental wooden image of the crucified Christ (FIG. 16-26) for Cologne Cathedral, freestanding statues of Christ, the Virgin Mary, and the saints were still quite rare. The veneration of relics, however, brought with it a demand for small-scale images of the holy family and saints to be placed on the chapel altars of churches along the pilgrimage roads. Artisans began producing reliquaries in the form of saints (or parts of saints), tabletop crucifixes, and small wooden devotional images in great numbers.

One popular type, a specialty of the workshops of Auvergne, France, was a wooden statuette depicting the Virgin Mary with the Christ Child in her lap. The *Morgan Madonna* (FIG. **17-18**), so named because it once belonged to the American financier and art collector J. Pierpont Morgan, is one example. The type, known as the Throne of Wisdom—*sedes sapientiae* in Latin—is a western European freestanding version of the Byzantine Theotokos theme popular in icons and mosaics (FIGS. 12-18 and 12-19). Christ holds a Bible in his left hand and raises his right arm in blessing (both hands are broken off). He is the embodiment of the divine wisdom contained in the Holy Scriptures. His mother, seated on a wooden chair, is in turn the Throne of Wisdom because her lap is the Christ Child's throne. As in Byzantine art, both Mother and Child sit rigidly upright and are strictly frontal, emotionless figures. But the intimate scale, the gesture of benediction, the once-bright coloring of the garments, and the soft modeling of the Virgin's face make the group seem much less remote than its Byzantine counterparts.

17-18A Reliquary of Sainte-Foy, late 10th to early 11th century.

17-18 Virgin and Child (*Morgan Madonna*), from Auvergne, France, second half of 12th century. Painted wood, 2′ 7″ high. Metropolitan Museum of Art, New York (gift of J. Pierpont Morgan, 1916).

The veneration of relics brought with it a demand for small-scale images of the holy family and saints to be placed on chapel altars. This wooden statuette depicts the Virgin as the Throne of Wisdom.

impressive is the fresco (FIG. **17-17**), now in Boston, that once filled the apse of Santa María de Mur, a monastery church not far from Lérida. The formality, symmetry, and placement of the figures are Byzantine (compare FIGS. 12-13 and 12-25). But the Spanish artist rejected Byzantine mosaic in favor of direct painting on plaster-coated walls.

The iconographic scheme in the semidome of the apse echoes the designs of contemporary French and Spanish Romanesque church tympana (FIG. 17-1). The signs of the four evangelists flank Christ in a star-strewn mandorla—the Apocalypse theme that so fascinated the Romanesque imagination. Seven lamps between Christ and the evangelists' signs symbolize the seven Christian com-

HOLY ROMAN EMPIRE

The Romanesque successors of the Ottonians were the Salians (r. 1027–1125), a dynasty of Franks of the Salian tribe. They ruled an empire that corresponds roughly to present-day Germany and the Lombard region of northern Italy (MAP 17-1). Like their predecessors, the Salian emperors were important patrons of art and architecture, although, as elsewhere in Romanesque Europe, the monasteries remained great centers of artistic production.

Architecture

The continuous barrel-vaulted naves of Saint James at Santiago de Compostela, Cluny III (FIG. 17-8), Saint-Sernin (FIG. 17-6) at Toulouse, and Notre-Dame (FIG. 17-14) at Fontenay admirably met the goals that northern Spanish and French Romanesque architects had of making the house of the Lord beautiful and providing excellent acoustics for church services. In addition, the churches were relatively fireproof compared with timber-roofed structures such as Saint-Étienne (FIG. 17-2) at Vignory. But the barrel vaults often failed in one critical

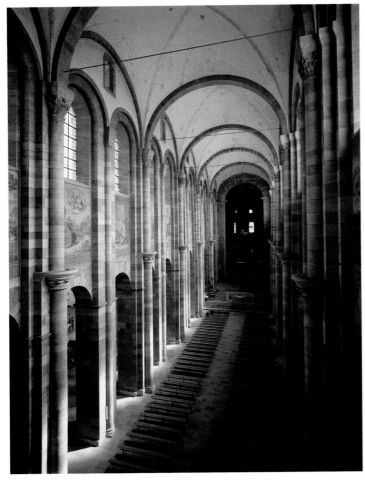

17-19 Interior of Speyer Cathedral, Speyer, Germany, begun 1030; nave vaults, ca. 1082–1105.

The imperial cathedral at Speyer is one of the earliest examples of the use of groin vaulting in a nave. Groin vaults made possible the insertion of large clerestory windows above the nave arcade.

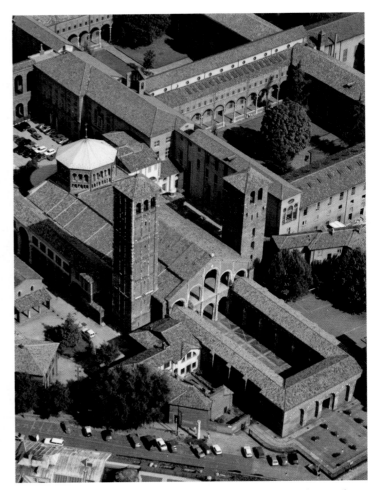

17-20 Aerial view of Sant'Ambrogio, Milan, Italy, late 11th to early 12th century.

With its atrium and low, broad proportions, Sant'Ambrogio recalls Early Christian basilicas. Over the nave's east end, however, is an octagonal tower that resembles Ottonian crossing towers.

requirement—lighting. Due to the great outward thrust barrel vaults exert along their full length, even when pointed instead of semicircular, a clerestory is difficult to construct. (The Santiago de Compostela, Toulouse, and Fontenay designers did not even attempt to introduce a clerestory, although their counterparts at Cluny III did and succeeded.) Structurally, the central aim of northern Romanesque architects was to develop a masonry vault system that admitted light and was also aesthetically pleasing.

Covering the nave with groin vaults instead of barrel vaults became the solution. Ancient Roman builders had used the groin vault widely, because they realized that its concentration of thrusts at four supporting points permitted clerestory windows (FIGS. 10-6*b–c*, 10-67, and 10-78). The great Roman vaults were made possible by the use of concrete, which could be poured into forms, where it solidified into a homogeneous mass (see "Roman Concrete Construction," Chapter 10, page 241). But the technique of mixing concrete had not survived into the Middle Ages. The technical problems of building groin vaults of cut stone and heavy rubble, which had very little cohesive quality, at first limited their use to the covering of small areas, such as the individual bays of the aisles of Saint-Sernin (FIG. 17-5). But during the 11th century, masons in the Holy Roman Empire, using cut-stone blocks joined by mortar, developed a groin vault of monumental dimensions.

SPEYER CATHEDRAL Construction of Speyer Cathedral (FIG. 17-19) in the German Rhineland, far from the pilgrimage routes of southern France and northern Spain, began in 1030. The church was the burial place of the Holy Roman emperors until the beginning of the 12th century, and funding for the building campaign came from imperial patrons, not traveling pilgrims and local landowners. Like all *cathedrals*, Speyer was also the seat (*cathedra* in Latin) of the powerful local bishop. In its earliest form, Speyer Cathedral was a timber-roofed structure. When the emperor Henry IV (r. 1084–1105) rebuilt it between 1082 and 1105, his masons covered the nave with stone groin vaults. The large clerestory windows above the nave arcade provided ample light to the interior. Scholars disagree about where the first comprehensive use of groin vaulting occurred in Romanesque times, and nationalistic concerns sometimes color the debate. But no one doubts that the large groin vaults covering the nave of Speyer Cathedral represent one of the most daring and successful engineering experiments of the time. The nave is 45 feet wide, and the crowns of the vaults are 107 feet above the floor.

Speyer Cathedral employs an alternate-support system in the nave, as in the Ottonian churches of Saint Cyriakus (FIG. 16-21) at Gernrode and Saint Michael's (FIG. 16-23) at Hildesheim. At Speyer, however, the alternation continues all the way up into the vaults, with the nave's more richly molded compound piers marking the

17-21 Interior of Sant'Ambrogio, Milan, Italy, late 11th to early 12th century.

Sant'Ambrogio's nave reveals the northern character of Lombard architecture. Each groin-vaulted nave bay corresponds to two aisle bays. The alternate-support system complements this modular plan.

corners of the groin vaults. Speyer's interior shows the same striving for height and the same compartmentalized effect seen in Saint-Sernin (FIG. 17-6), but by virtue of the alternate-support system, the rhythm of the Speyer nave is more complex. Because each compartment is individually vaulted, the effect of a sequence of vertical spatial blocks is even more convincing.

SANT'AMBROGIO, MILAN After Charlemagne crushed the Lombards in 773, German kings held sway over Lombardy, and the Rhineland and northern Italy cross-fertilized each other artistically. No agreement exists as to which source of artistic influence was dominant in the Romanesque age, the northern or the southern. The question, no doubt, will remain the subject of controversy until the construction date of Sant'Ambrogio (FIG. 17-20) in Milan can be established unequivocally. The church, erected in honor of Saint Ambrose, Milan's first bishop (d. 397), is the central monument of Lombard Romanesque architecture. Some scholars think the church was a prototype for Speyer Cathedral, but Sant'Ambrogio is a remarkable structure even if it wasn't a model for Speyer's builders. The Milanese church has an atrium in the Early Christian tradition (FIG. 11-9)—one of the last to be built—and a two-story narthex pierced by arches on both levels. Two bell towers (*campaniles*) join the building on the west. The shorter one dates to the 10th century, and the taller north campanile is a 12th-century addition. Over the nave's east end is an octagonal tower that recalls the crossing towers of Ottonian churches (FIG. 16-22).

Sant'Ambrogio has a nave (FIG. 17-21) and two aisles but no transept. Each bay consists of a full square in the nave flanked by two small squares in each aisle, all covered with groin vaults. The main vaults are slightly domical, rising higher than the transverse arches. The windows in the octagonal dome over the last bay—probably here, as elsewhere, a reference to the Dome of Heaven—provide the major light source (the building lacks a clerestory) for the otherwise rather dark interior. The emphatic alternate-support system perfectly reflects the geometric regularity of the plan. The lightest pier moldings are interrupted at the gallery level, and the heavier ones rise to support the main vaults. At Sant'Ambrogio, the compound piers even continue into the ponderous vaults, which have supporting arches, or *ribs*, along their groins. This is one of the first instances of rib vaulting, a salient characteristic of mature Romanesque and of later Gothic architecture (see "The Gothic Rib Vault," Chapter 18, page 464).

The regional diversity of Romanesque architecture becomes evident by comparing the proportions of Sant'Ambrogio with those of both Speyer Cathedral (FIG. 17-19) and Saint-Sernin (FIGS. 17-4 to 17-6) at Toulouse. The Milanese building does not aspire to the soaring height of the French and German churches. Save for the later of the two towers, Sant'Ambrogio's proportions are low and broad and remain close to those of Early Christian basilicas. Italian architects, even those working within the orbit of the Holy Roman Empire, had firm roots in the venerable Early Christian style and never accepted the verticality found in northern architecture, not even during the Gothic period.

Romanesque Countesses, Queens, and Nuns

Romanesque Europe was still a man's world, but women could and did have power and influence. Countess Matilda of Canossa (1046–1115), who ruled Tuscany after 1069, was sole heiress of vast holdings in northern Italy. She was a key figure in the political struggle between the popes and the German emperors who controlled Lombardy. With unflagging resolution, she defended Pope Gregory's reforms and at her death willed most of her lands to the papacy.

More famous and more powerful was Eleanor of Aquitaine (1122–1204), wife of Henry II of England. She married Henry after the annulment of her marriage to Louis VII, king of France. She was queen of France for 15 years and queen of England for 35 years. During that time she bore three daughters and five sons. Two became kings—Richard I (the Lionhearted) and John. She prompted her sons to rebel against their father, so Henry imprisoned her. Released at Henry's death, she lived on as dowager queen, managing England's government and King John's holdings in France.

Of quite different stamp was Hildegard of Bingen (1098–1179), the most prominent nun of the 12th century and one of the greatest religious figures of the Middle Ages. Hildegard was born into an aristocratic family that owned large estates in the German Rhineland. At a very early age she began to have visions. When she was eight, her parents placed her in the Benedictine *double monastery* (for both monks and nuns) at Disibodenberg. She became a nun at 15. In 1141, God instructed Hildegard to disclose her visions to the world. Before then she had revealed them only to close confidants at the monastery. One of these was the monk Volmar, and Hildegard chose to dictate her visions to him (FIG. **17-22**) for posterity. No less a figure than Bernard of Clairvaux certified in 1147 that her visions were authentic, and Archbishop Heinrich of Mainz joined in the endorsement. In 1148 the Cistercian pope Eugenius III (r. 1145–1153) formally authorized Hildegard "in the name of Christ and Saint Peter to publish all that she had learned from the Holy Spirit." At this time Hildegard became the abbess of a new convent built for her near Bingen. As reports of Hildegard's visions spread, kings, popes, barons, and prelates sought her counsel. All of them were attracted by her spiritual insight into the truth of the mysteries of the Christian faith. In addition to her visionary works—the most important is

17-22 Hildegard receives her visions, detail of a facsimile of a lost folio in the Rupertsberger *Scivias* by Hildegard of Bingen, from Trier or Bingen, Germany, ca. 1150–1179. Abbey of St. Hildegard, Rüdesheim/ Eibingen.

Hildegard of Bingen, the most prominent nun of her time, experienced divine visions, shown here as five tongues of fire entering her brain. She also composed music and wrote scientific treatises.

the *Scivias* (FIG. **17-22**)—Hildegard wrote two scientific treatises. *Physica* is a study of the natural world, and *Causae et curae* (*Causes and Cures*) is a medical encyclopedia. Hildegard also composed the music and wrote the lyrics of 77 songs, which appeared under the title *Symphonia*.

Hildegard was the most famous Romanesque nun, but she was by no means the only learned woman of her age. A younger contemporary, the abbess Herrad (d. 1195) of Hohenberg, Austria, was also the author of an important medieval encyclopedia. Herrad's *Hortus deliciarum* (*Garden of Delights*) is a history of the world intended for instructing the nuns under her supervision, but it reached a much wider audience.

Painting and Other Arts

The number and variety of illuminated manuscripts dating to the Romanesque era attest to the great demand for illustrated religious tomes in the abbeys of western Europe. The extraordinarily productive scribes and painters who created these books were almost exclusively monks and nuns working in the scriptoria of those same isolated religious communities.

HILDEGARD OF BINGEN One of the most interesting of these religious manuscripts is the *Scivias* (*Know the Ways [Scite vias] of God*) of Hildegard of Bingen. Hildegard was a German nun and eventually the abbess of the convent at Disibodenberg in the Rhineland (see "Romanesque Countesses, Queens, and Nuns," above). The manuscript, lost in 1945, exists today only in a facsimile. The original probably was written and illuminated at the monastery of Saint

Matthias at Trier between 1150 and Hildegard's death in 1179, but it is possible that Hildegard supervised production of the book at Bingen. The *Scivias* contains a record of Hildegard's vision of the divine order of the cosmos and of humankind's place in it. The vision came to her as a fiery light that poured into her brain from the open vault of Heaven.

On the opening page (FIG. **17-22**) of the Trier manuscript, Hildegard sits within the monastery walls, her feet resting on a footstool, in much the same way the painters of the *Coronation* and *Ebbo Gospels* (FIGS. **16-13** and **16-14**) represented the evangelists. This Romanesque page is a link in a chain of author portraits with roots in classical antiquity. The artist showed Hildegard experiencing her divine vision by depicting five long tongues of fire emanating from above and entering her brain, just as she describes the experience in the accompanying text. Hildegard immediately sets down what has been revealed to her on a wax tablet resting on her left knee. Nearby, the monk Volmar, Hildegard's confessor, copies into a book all she has written. Here, in a singularly dramatic context, is a picture of the essential nature of ancient and medieval book manufacture—individual scribes copying and recopying texts by hand (compare FIG. **16-11**).

RAINER OF HUY In the Holy Roman Empire, as in France, the names of some Romanesque sculptors are known. One is RAINER OF HUY, a bronzeworker from the Meuse River valley in Belgium, an area renowned for its metalwork. Art historians have attributed an 1118 bronze baptismal font (FIG. **17-23**) to him. Made for Notre-Dame-des-Fonts in Liège, the bronze basin rests on the foreparts of a dozen oxen. The oxen refer to the "molten sea . . . on twelve oxen" cast in bronze for King Solomon's Temple (1 Kings 7:23–25). The Old Testament story prefigured Christ's baptism (medieval scholars equated the oxen with the 12 apostles), which is the central scene on the Romanesque font. Rainer's work, as that of so many earlier artists in the Holy Roman Empire beginning in Carolingian times, revived the classical style and the classical spirit. The figures are softly rounded, with idealized bodies and faces and heavy clinging drapery. One figure (at the left in FIG. **17-23**) is even shown in a three-quarter view from the rear, a popular motif in classical art, and some of Rainer's figures, including Christ himself, are naked. Nudity is very rare in the art of the Middle Ages. Adam and Eve (FIGS. **11-7** and **16-24**) are exceptions, but medieval artists represented the first man and woman as embarrassed by their nudity, the opposite of the value the classical world placed on the beauty of the human body.

RELIQUARY OF SAINT ALEXANDER As noted, Romanesque church officials competed with one another in the display of relics and often expended large sums on elaborate containers to house them. The reliquary of Saint Alexander (FIG. **17-24**), made in 1145 for Abbot Wibald of Stavelot in Belgium to house the hallowed

1 ft.

17-23 RAINER OF HUY, baptism of Christ, baptismal font from Notre-Dame-des-Fonts, Liège, Belgium, 1118. Bronze, 2′ 1″ high. Saint-Barthélémy, Liège.

In the work of Rainer of Huy, the classical style and the classical spirit lived on in the Holy Roman Empire. His baptismal font at Liège features idealized figures and even a nude representation of Christ.

1 in.

17-24 Head reliquary of Saint Alexander, from Stavelot Abbey, Belgium, 1145. Silver repoussé (partly gilt), gilt bronze, gems, pearls, and enamel, 1′ 5½″ high. Musées Royaux d'Art et d'Histoire, Brussels.

Saint Alexander's reliquary is typical in the use of costly materials. The combination of an idealized classical head with Byzantine-style enamels underscores the stylistic diversity of Romanesque art.

pope's relics, is one of the finest examples. The almost life-size head, fashioned in repoussé silver with bronze gilding for the hair, gives worshipers the impression that the saint is alive and present. The idealized head resembles portraits of youthful Roman emperors such as Augustus (FIG. I-9) and Constantine (FIG. 10-77), and the Romanesque metalworker may have used an ancient sculpture as a model. The saint wears a collar of jewels and enamel plaques around his neck. Enamels and gems also adorn the box on which the head is mounted. The reliquary rests on four bronze dragons—mythical animals of the kind that populated Romanesque cloister capitals. Not surprisingly, Bernard of Clairvaux was as critical of lavish church furnishings like the Alexander reliquary as he was of Romanesque cloister sculpture:

> [Men's] eyes are fixed on relics covered with gold and purses are opened. The thoroughly beautiful image of some male or female saint is exhibited and that saint is believed to be the more holy the more highly colored the image is. People rush to kiss it, they are invited to donate, and they admire the beautiful more than they venerate the sacred. . . . O vanity of vanities, but no more vain than insane! The Church . . . dresses its stones in gold and it abandons its children naked. It serves the eyes of the rich at the expense of the poor.[5]

The central plaque on the front of the Stavelot reliquary depicts Pope Alexander II (r. 1061–1073). Saints Eventius and Theodolus flank him. The nine plaques on the other three sides represent female allegorical figures—Wisdom, Piety, and Humility among them. Although a local artist produced these enamels in the Meuse River region, the models were surely Byzantine. Saint Alexander's reliquary underscores the multiple sources of Romanesque art as well as its stylistic diversity. Not since antiquity had people journeyed as exten-

sively as they did in the Romanesque period, and artists regularly saw works of wide geographic origin. Abbot Wibald himself epitomized the well-traveled 12th-century clergyman. He was abbot of Montecassino in southern Italy and participated in the Second Crusade. Frederick Barbarossa (Holy Roman Emperor, r. 1152–1190) sent him to Constantinople to arrange Frederick's wedding to the niece of the Byzantine emperor Manuel Comnenus. (Two centuries before, another German emperor, Otto II, married the Byzantine princess Theophanu, which also served to promote Byzantine style in the Holy Roman Empire; see "Theophanu," Chapter 16, page 428.)

ITALY

Nowhere is the regional diversity of Romanesque art and architecture more readily apparent than in Italy, where the ancient Roman and Early Christian heritage was strongest. Although Tuscany, the ancient Etruscan heartland (see Chapter 9), and other regions south of Lombardy were part of the territory of the Salian emperors, Italy south of Milan represents a distinct artistic zone during the Romanesque period.

Architecture and Architectural Sculpture

Italian Romanesque architects designed buildings that were for the most part structurally less experimental than those erected in Germany and Lombardy. Italian builders adhered closely to the Early Christian basilican type of church.

PISA CATHEDRAL COMPLEX The cathedral complex (FIG. 17-25) at Pisa dramatically testifies to the prosperity that busy maritime city enjoyed. The spoils of a naval victory over the

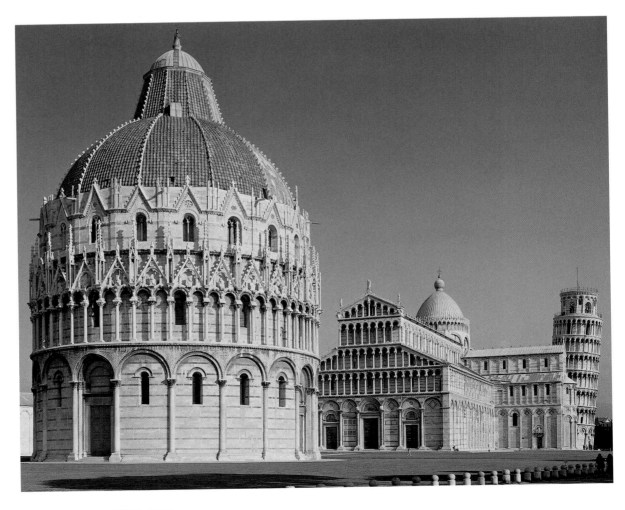

17-25 Cathedral complex, Pisa, Italy; cathedral begun 1063; baptistery begun 1153; campanile begun 1174.

Pisa's cathedral more closely resembles Early Christian basilicas than the structurally more experimental northern Romanesque churches. Separate bell towers and baptisteries are characteristically Italian.

17-26 Baptistery of San Giovanni, Florence, Italy, dedicated 1059.

The Florentine baptistery is a domed octagon descended from Roman and Early Christian central-plan buildings. The distinctive Tuscan Romanesque marble paneling stems from Roman wall designs.

began a daring project to remove soil from beneath the north side of the tower. The soil extraction has already moved the tower more than an inch closer to vertical and ensured the stability of the structure for at least 300 years. (Because of the touristic appeal of the Leaning Tower, there are no plans to restore the campanile to its original upright position.)

BAPTISTERY, FLORENCE The public always associates Florence with the Renaissance of the 15th and 16th centuries, but Florence was already an important independent city-state in the Romanesque period. The gem of Florentine Romanesque architecture is the baptistery (FIG. **17-26**) of San Giovanni (Saint John), the city's patron saint. Pope Nicholas II dedicated the building in 1059. It thus predates Pisa's baptistery (FIG. **17-25**, *left*), but construction of the Florentine baptistery continued into the next century. Both baptisteries face their city's cathedral. These freestanding Italian baptisteries are unusual and reflect the great significance the Florentines and Pisans attached to baptisms. On the day of a newborn child's anointment, the citizenry gathered in the baptistery to welcome a new member into the community. The Tuscan baptisteries therefore were important civic as well as religious structures. Some of the most renowned artists of the late Middle Ages and the Renaissance provided the Florentine and Pisan baptisteries with pulpits (FIG. **19-2**), bronze doors (FIGS. **21-2, 21-3,** and **21-10**), and mosaics.

The simple and serene classicism of San Giovanni's design recalls ancient Roman architecture. The baptistery stands in a direct line of descent from the Pantheon (FIG. **10-49**) and imperial mausoleums such as Diocletian's (FIG. **10-74**), the Early Christian Santa Costanza (FIG. **11-11**), the Byzantine San Vitale (FIG. **12-6**), and other central-plan structures, pagan or Christian, including Charlemagne's Palatine Chapel (FIG. **16-18**) at Aachen. The distinctive Tuscan Romanesque marble incrustation that patterns the walls stems ultimately from Roman wall designs (FIGS. **10-17** and **10-51**). The simple oblong and arcuated panels assert the building's structural lines and its elevation levels. In plan, San Giovanni is a domed octagon, wrapped on the exterior by an elegant arcade, three arches to a bay. It has three entrances, one each on the north, south, and east sides. On the west side an oblong sanctuary replaces the original semicircular apse. The domical vault is some 90 feet in diameter, its construction a remarkable feat for its time.

Muslims off Palermo in Sicily in 1062 provided the funds for the Pisan building program. The cathedral, its freestanding bell tower, and the baptistery, where infants and converts were initiated into the Christian community, present a rare opportunity to study a coherent group of three Romanesque buildings. Save for the upper portion of the baptistery, with its remodeled Gothic exterior, the three structures are stylistically homogeneous.

Construction of Pisa Cathedral began first—in 1063, the same year work began on Saint Mark's (FIG. **12-24**) in Venice, another powerful maritime city. Pisa Cathedral is large, with a nave and four aisles, and is one of the most impressive and majestic of all Romanesque churches. According to a document of the time, the Pisans wanted their bishop's church not only to be a monument to the glory of God but also to bring credit to the city. At first glance, the cathedral resembles an Early Christian basilica with a timber roof, columnar arcade, and clerestory. But the broadly projecting transept with apses, the crossing dome, and the facade's multiple arcaded galleries distinguish it as Romanesque. So too does the rich marble *incrustation* (wall decoration consisting of bright panels of different colors, as in the Pantheon's interior, FIG. **10-51**). The cathedral's campanile, detached in the standard Italian fashion, is Pisa's famous Leaning Tower (FIG. **17-25**, *right*). Graceful arcaded galleries mark the tower's stages and repeat the cathedral's facade motif, effectively relating the round campanile to its mother building. The tilted vertical axis of the tower is the result of a settling foundation. The tower began to "lean" even while under construction and by the late 20th century had inclined some 5.5 degrees (about 15 feet) out of plumb at the top. In 1999 an international team of scientists

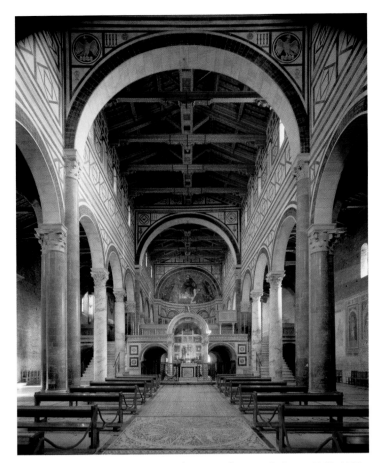

17-27 Interior of San Miniato al Monte, Florence, Italy, ca. 1062–1090.

The design of San Miniato is close to that of Early Christian basilicas, but diaphragm arches divide the nave into three equal compartments, and compound piers alternate with columns in the arcade.

17-27A *Entombment of Christ, Sant'Angelo in Formis, ca. 1085.*

SAN MINIATO AL MONTE Contemporaneous with the San Giovanni baptistery and also featuring elaborate marble incrustation is the Benedictine abbey church of San Miniato al Monte (FIG. **17-27**). It sits, as its name implies, on a hillside overlooking the Arno River and the heart of Florence. The builders completed the body of the church by 1090, its facade not until the early 13th century. Even more than Pisa Cathedral, the structure recalls the Early Christian basilica, but *diaphragm arches* divide its nave into

three equal compartments. The arches rise from compound piers and brace the rather high, thin walls. They also provide firebreaks beneath the wooden roof and compartmentalize the basilican interior in the manner so popular with most Romanesque builders. The compound piers alternate with pairs of simple columns with Roman-revival Composite capitals.

MODENA CATHEDRAL Despite the pronounced structural differences between Italian Romanesque churches and those of France, Spain, and the Holy Roman Empire, Italian church officials also frequently employed sculptors to adorn the facades of their buildings. In fact, one of the first examples of fully developed narrative relief sculpture in Romanesque art is the marble frieze (FIG. **17-28**) on the facade of Modena Cathedral in northern Italy. Carved around 1110, it represents scenes from Genesis set against an architectural backdrop of a type common on Roman and Early Christian sarcophagi, which were plentiful in the area. The segment in FIG. **17-28** illustrates the creation and temptation of Adam and Eve (Gen. 2, 3:1–8), the theme employed almost exactly a century earlier on Bishop Bernward's bronze doors (FIG. **16-24**) at Hildesheim. At Modena, as at Saint Michael's, the faithful entered the Lord's house with a reminder of Original Sin and the suggestion that the only path to salvation is through the Christian Church.

On the Modena frieze, Christ is at the far left, framed by a mandorla held up by angels—a variation on the motif of the Saint-Sernin ambulatory relief (FIG. **17-7**). The creation of Adam, then Eve, and the serpent's temptation of Eve are to the right. The relief carving is high, and some parts are almost entirely in the round. The frieze is the work of a master craftsman whose name, WILIGELMO, is given in an inscription on another relief on the facade. There he boasts, "Among sculptors, your work shines forth, Wiligelmo." The inscription is also an indication of the pride Wiligelmo's patrons had in obtaining the services of such an accomplished sculptor for their city's cathedral.

BENEDETTO ANTELAMI The reawakening of interest in stone sculpture in the round also may be seen in northern Italy, where the sculptor BENEDETTO ANTELAMI was active in the last quarter of the 12th century. Several reliefs by his hand exist, including Parma Cathedral's pulpit and the portals of that city's baptistery. But his most unusual works are the monumental marble statues of two Old Testament figures he carved for the west facade of Fidenza Cathedral. Benedetto's King David (FIG. **17-29**) seems confined within his niche, and he holds his elbows close to his body. Absent is

17-28 WILIGELMO, creation and temptation of Adam and Eve, detail of the frieze on the west facade, Modena Cathedral, Modena, Italy, ca. 1110. Marble, 3′ high.

For Modena's cathedral, Wiligelmo represented scenes from Genesis against an architectural backdrop of a type common on Roman and Early Christian sarcophagi, which were plentiful in the area.

1 ft.

17-29 BENEDETTO ANTELAMI, King David, statue in a niche on the west facade of Fidenza Cathedral, Fidenza, Italy, ca. 1180–1190. Marble, life-size.

Benedetto Antelami's King David on the facade of Fidenza Cathedral is a rare example of life-size statuary in the Romanesque period. The style is unmistakably rooted in Greco-Roman art.

the weight shift that is the hallmark of classical statuary. Yet the sculptor's conception of this prophet is unmistakably rooted in Greco-Roman art. Comparison of the Fidenza David with the prophet on the Moissac trumeau (FIG. 17-11), who also displays an unfurled scroll, reveals how much the Italian sculptor freed his figure from its architectural setting. Other sculptors did not immediately emulate Antelami's classical approach to portraying biblical figures in stone. But the idea of placing freestanding statues in niches would be taken up again in Italy by Early Renaissance sculptors (FIGS. 21-4 to 21-6).

17-30 West facade of Saint-Étienne, Caen, France, begun 1067.

The division of Saint-Étienne's facade into three parts corresponding to the nave and aisles reflects the methodical planning of the entire structure. The towers also have a tripartite design.

NORMANDY AND ENGLAND

After their conversion to Christianity in the early 10th century, the Vikings (see Chapter 16) settled on the northern coast of France in present-day Normandy. Almost at once, they proved themselves not only aggressive warriors but also skilled administrators and builders, active in Sicily (FIG. 12-25) as well as in northern Europe.

Architecture

The Normans quickly developed a distinctive Romanesque architectural style that became the major source of French Gothic architecture.

SAINT-ÉTIENNE, CAEN Most critics consider the abbey church of Saint-Étienne at Caen the masterpiece of Norman Romanesque architecture. Begun by William of Normandy (William the Conqueror; see page 455) in 1067, work must have advanced rapidly, because he was buried there in 1087. Saint-Étienne's west facade (FIG. 17-30) is a striking design rooted in the tradition of Carolingian and Ottonian westworks, but it reveals a new unified

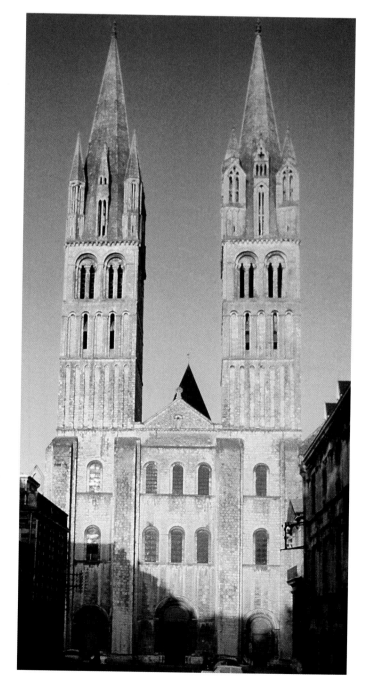

17-31 Interior of Saint-Étienne, Caen, France, vaulted ca. 1115–1120.

The groin vaults of Saint-Étienne made possible an efficient clerestory. The three-story elevation with its large arched openings provides ample light and makes the nave appear taller than it is.

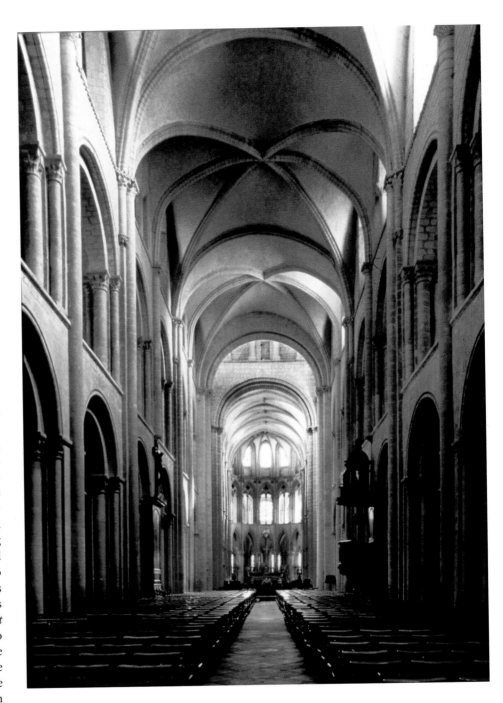

design. Four large buttresses divide the facade into three bays that correspond to the nave and aisles. Above the buttresses, the towers also display a triple division and a progressively greater piercing of their walls from lower to upper stages. (The culminating spires are a Gothic addition.) The tripartite division extends throughout the facade, both vertically and horizontally, organizing it into a close-knit, well-integrated design that reflects the careful and methodical planning of the entire structure.

The original design of Saint-Étienne called for a wooden roof, as originally at Speyer Cathedral. But the Caen nave (FIG. **17-31**) had compound piers with simple engaged half-columns alternating with piers with half-columns attached to pilasters. When the builders decided to install groin vaults around 1115, the existing alternating compound piers in the nave proved a good match. Those piers soar all the way to the vaults' springing. Their branching ribs divide the large square-vault compartments into six sections, making a *sexpartite vault* (FIG. **17-32**). The vaults rise high enough to provide room for an efficient clerestory. The resulting three-story elevation, with its large arched openings, admits more light to the interior. It also makes the nave appear even taller than it is. As in the Milanese church of Sant'Ambrogio (FIG. **17-21**), the Norman building has rib vaults. The diagonal and transverse ribs compose a structural skeleton that partially supports the still fairly massive paneling between them. Despite the heavy masonry, the large windows and reduced interior wall surface give Saint-Étienne's nave a light and airy quality that is unusual in the Romanesque period.

DURHAM CATHEDRAL William of Normandy's conquest of Anglo-Saxon England in 1066 began a new epoch in English history. In architecture, it signaled the importation of Norman Romanesque building and design methods. Durham Cathedral (FIGS. **17-33** and **17-34**) sits majestically on a cliff overlooking the Wear River in northern England, the centerpiece of a monastery, cathedral, and fortified-castle complex on the Scottish frontier. Unlike Speyer Cathedral and Saint-Étienne, Durham Cathedral, begun around 1093—earlier than the remodeled Caen church—was a vaulted structure from the very beginning. Consequently, the pattern of the ribs of the nave's groin vaults corresponds perfectly to the design of the arcade below. Each seven-part nave vault covers two bays. Large,

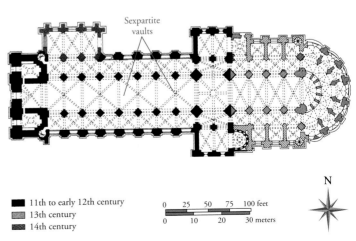

11th to early 12th century
13th century
14th century

0 25 50 75 100 feet
0 10 20 30 meters

N

17-32 Plan of Saint-Étienne, Caen, France.

The early-12th-century nave vaults of Saint-Étienne spring from compound piers with alternating half-columns and pilasters. The diagonal and transverse ribs divide the vaults into six compartments.

17-33 Interior (*left*) and lateral section (*right*) of Durham Cathedral, England, begun ca. 1093.

Durham Cathedral is the first example of a ribbed groin vault placed over a three-story nave. Quadrant arches were used in place of groin vaults in the tribune to buttress the nave vaults.

simple pillars ornamented with abstract designs (diamond, chevron, and cable patterns, all originally painted) alternate with compound piers that carry the transverse arches of the vaults. The pier-vault relationship scarcely could be more visible or the building's structural rationale better expressed.

The bold surface patterning of the Durham nave is a reminder that the raising of imposing stone edifices such as the Romanesque churches of England and Normandy required more than just the talents of master designers. A corps of expert masons had to transform rough stone blocks into the precise shapes necessary for their specific place in the church's fabric. Although thousands of simple quadrangular blocks make up the great walls of these buildings, the builders needed large numbers of blocks in much more complex shapes. To cover the nave and aisles, the stonecutters had to carve blocks with concave faces to conform to the curve of the vault. Also required were blocks with projecting moldings for the ribs, blocks with convex surfaces for the pillars or with multiple profiles for the compound piers, and so forth. It was an immense undertaking, and it is no wonder that medieval building campaigns often lasted for decades.

The plan (FIG. 17-34) of Durham Cathedral is typically English with its long, slender proportions. It does not employ the modular scheme with the same care and logic seen at Caen. But in other ways this English church is even more innovative than the French church. It is the earliest example known of a ribbed groin vault placed over a three-story nave. And in the nave's western parts, completed before 1130, the rib vaults have slightly pointed arches, bringing together for the first time two of the key elements that determined the struc-

17-34 Plan of Durham Cathedral, England (after Kenneth John Conant).

Durham Cathedral is typically English in its long, slender proportions. In the nave, simple pillars alternate with compound piers that support the transverse arches of the seven-part groin vaults.

tural evolution of Gothic architecture. Also of great significance is the way the English builders buttressed the nave vaults. The lateral section (FIG. 17-33, *right*) reveals that simple *quadrant arches* (arches whose curve extends for one quarter of a circle's circumference) take the place of groin vaults in the tribune. The structural descendants of these quadrant arches are the flying buttresses that epitomize the mature Gothic solution to church construction (see "The Gothic Cathedral," Chapter 18, page 469).

Embroidery and Tapestry

The most famous embroidery of the Middle Ages is, ironically, known as the *Bayeux Tapestry* (FIG. 17-35). Embroidery and tapestry are related but different means of decorating textiles. *Tapestry* designs are woven on a loom as part of the fabric. *Embroidery* patterns are sewn onto fabric with threads.

The needleworkers who fashioned the *Bayeux Tapestry* were either Norman or English women. They employed eight colors of dyed wool—two varieties of blue, three shades of green, yellow, buff, and terracotta red—and two kinds of stitches. In *stem stitching*, short overlapping strands of thread form jagged lines. *Laid-and-*

couched work creates solid blocks of color. In the latter technique, the needleworker first lays down a series of parallel and then a series of cross stitches. Finally, the stitcher tacks down the cross-hatched threads using couching (knotting). On the *Bayeux Tapestry*, the embroiderers left the natural linen color exposed for the background, human flesh, building walls, and other "colorless" design elements. Stem stitches define the contours of figures and buildings and delineate interior details, such as facial features, body armor, and roof tiles. The clothing, animal bodies, and other solid areas are laid-and-couched work.

17-35 Funeral procession to Westminster Abbey (*top*) and Battle of Hastings (*bottom*), details of the *Bayeux Tapestry*, from Bayeux Cathedral, Bayeux, France, ca. 1070–1080. Embroidered wool on linen, 1′ 8″ high (entire length of fabric 229′ 8″). Centre Guillaume le Conquérant, Bayeux. 🎞

The *Bayeux Tapestry* is unique in medieval art. Like historical narratives in ancient Roman art, it depicts contemporaneous events in full detail, as in the scroll-like frieze of Trajan's Column (FIG. 10-44).

Painting and Other Arts

Many of the finest illustrated manuscripts of the Romanesque age were the work of monks in English scriptoria, following in the tradition of Hiberno-Saxon book production (see Chapter 16). But the most famous work of English Romanesque art is neither a book nor Christian in subject.

BAYEUX TAPESTRY The so-called *Bayeux Tapestry* (FIG. **17-35**) is unique in medieval art. It is an embroidered fabric—not, in fact, a woven tapestry—made of wool sewn on linen (see "Embroidery and Tapestry," page 456). Closely related to Romanesque manuscript illumination, its borders contain the kinds of real and imaginary animals found in contemporaneous books, and an explanatory Latin text sewn in thread accompanies many of the pictures. Some 20 inches high and about 230 feet long, the *Bayeux Tapestry* is a continuous, friezelike, pictorial narrative of a crucial moment in England's history and of the events that led up to it. The Norman defeat of the Anglo-Saxons at Hastings in 1066 brought England under the control of the Normans, uniting all of England and much of France under one rule. The dukes of Normandy became the kings of England. Commissioned by Bishop Odo, the half brother of the conquering Duke William, the embroidery may have been sewn by women at the Norman court. Many art historians, however, believe it was the work of English stitchers in Kent, where Odo was earl after the Norman conquest. Odo donated the work to Bayeux Cathedral (hence its nickname), but it is uncertain whether it was originally intended for display in the church's nave, where the theme would have been a curious choice.

The circumstances leading to the Norman invasion of England are well documented. In 1066, Edward the Confessor, the Anglo-Saxon king of England, died. The Normans believed Edward had recognized William of Normandy as his rightful heir. But the crown went to Harold, earl of Wessex, the king's Anglo-Saxon brother-in-law, who had sworn allegiance to William. The betrayed Normans, descendants of the seafaring Vikings, boarded their ships, crossed the English Channel, and crushed Harold's forces.

Illustrated here are two episodes of the epic tale as represented in the *Bayeux Tapestry*. The first detail (FIG. 17-35, *top*) depicts King Edward's funeral procession. The hand of God points the way to the church in London where he was buried—Westminster Abbey, consecrated December 28, 1065, just a few days before Edward's death. The church was one of the first Romanesque buildings erected in England, and the embroiderers took pains to record its main features, including the imposing crossing tower and the long nave with tribunes. Here William was crowned king of England on Christmas Day, 1066. (The coronation of every English monarch since then also has occurred in Westminster Abbey.) The second detail (FIG. 17-35, *bottom*) shows the Battle of Hastings in progress. The Norman cavalry cuts down the English defenders. The lower border is filled with the dead and wounded, although the upper register continues the animal motifs of the rest of the embroidery. The Romanesque artist co-opted some of the characteristic motifs of Greco-Roman battle scenes, for example, the horses with twisted necks and contorted bodies (compare FIG. 5-70). But the artists rendered the figures in the Romanesque manner. Linear patterning and flat color replaced classical three-dimensional volume and modeling in light and dark hues.

The *Bayeux Tapestry* stands apart from all other Romanesque artworks in that it depicts an event in full detail at a time shortly after it occurred, recalling the historical narratives of ancient Roman art. Art historians have often likened the Norman embroidery to the scroll-like frieze of the Column of Trajan (FIG. 10-44). Like the Roman account, the story told on the *Bayeux Tapestry* is the conqueror's version of history, a proclamation of national pride. And as in the ancient frieze, the narrative is not confined to battlefield successes. It is a complete chronicle of events. Included are the preparations for war, with scenes depicting the felling and splitting of trees for ship construction, the loading of equipment onto the vessels, the cooking and serving of meals, and so forth. In this respect, the *Bayeux Tapestry* is the most *Roman*-esque work of Romanesque art.

BURY BIBLE The *Bury Bible* (FIG. **17-36**), produced at the Bury Saint Edmunds abbey in England around 1135, exemplifies the sumptuous illustration common to the large Bibles produced in wealthy Romanesque abbeys not subject to the Cistercian ban on luxurious illuminated manuscripts. These costly books lent prestige to monasteries that could afford them (see "Medieval Books," Chapter 16, page 411). The artist responsible for the *Bury Bible* is known: MASTER HUGO, who was also a sculptor and metalworker. With Bernardus Gelduinus (FIG. 17-7), Gislebertus (FIG. 17-12), Rainer of Huy (FIG. 17-23), Wiligelmo (FIG. 17-28), and Benedetto Antelami (FIG. 17-29),

17-36A *Mouth of Hell, Winchester Psalter,* ca. 1145–1155.

17-36 MASTER HUGO, *Moses expounding the Law,* folio 94 recto of the *Bury Bible,* from Bury Saint Edmunds, England, ca. 1135. Ink and tempera on vellum, 1′ 8″ × 1′ 2″. Corpus Christi College, Cambridge.

Master Hugo was a rare Romanesque lay artist, one of the emerging class of professional artists and artisans who depended for their livelihood on commissions from well-endowed monasteries.

Hugo is one of the small but growing number of Romanesque artists who signed their works or whose names were recorded. In the 12th century, artists, illuminators as well as sculptors, increasingly began to identify themselves. Although most medieval artists remained anonymous, the contrast of the Romanesque period with the early Middle Ages is striking. Hugo seems to have been a secular artist, one of the emerging class of professional artists and artisans who depended for their livelihood on commissions from well-endowed monasteries. These artists resided in towns rather than within secluded abbey walls, and they traveled frequently to find work. They were the exception, however, and the typical Romanesque scribes and illuminators continued to be monks and nuns working anonymously in the service of God. The Benedictine Rule, for example, specified that "artisans in the monastery . . . are to practice their craft with all humility, but only with the abbot's permission."[6]

One page (FIG. 17-36) of the *Bury Bible* shows two scenes from Deuteronomy framed by symmetrical leaf motifs in softly glowing harmonized colors. The upper register depicts Moses and Aaron proclaiming the Law to the Israelites. Master Hugo represented Moses with horns, consistent with Saint Jerome's translation of the Hebrew word that also means "rays" (compare Michelangelo's similar conception of the Hebrew prophet, FIG. 22-15). The lower panel portrays Moses pointing out the clean and unclean beasts. The slow, gentle gestures convey quiet dignity. The figures of Moses and Aaron seem to glide. This presentation is quite different from the abrupt emphasis and spastic movement seen in earlier Romanesque paintings. The movements of the figures appear more integrated and smooth. Yet patterning remains in the multiple divisions of the draped limbs, the lightly shaded volumes connected with sinuous lines and ladderlike folds. Hugo still thought of the drapery and body as somehow the same. The frame has a quite definite limiting function, and the painter carefully fit the figures within it.

EADWINE PSALTER The *Eadwine Psalter* is the masterpiece of an English monk known as EADWINE THE SCRIBE. It contains 166 illustrations, many of which are variations of those in the Carolingian *Utrecht Psalter* (FIG. 16-15). The last page (FIG. 17-37), however, presents a rare picture of a Romanesque artist at work. The style of the Eadwine portrait resembles that of the *Bury Bible*, but although the patterning is still firm (notably in the cowl and the thigh), the drapery falls more softly and follows the movements of the body beneath it. Here, the abstract patterning of many Romanesque painted and sculpted garments yielded slightly, but clearly, to the requirements of more naturalistic representation. The Romanesque artist's instinct for decorating the surface remained, as is apparent in the gown's whorls and spirals. Significantly, however, the artist painted in those interior lines very lightly so that they would not conflict with the functional lines that contain them.

The "portrait" of Eadwine—it is probably a generic type and not a specific likeness—is in the long tradition of author portraits in ancient and medieval manuscripts (FIGS. 16-7, 16-13, 16-14, and 17-22), although the true author of the *Eadwine Psalter* is King David. Eadwine

17-37 EADWINE THE SCRIBE, Eadwine the Scribe at work, folio 283 verso of the *Eadwine Psalter*, ca. 1160–1170. Ink and tempera on vellum. Trinity College, Cambridge. ◼◀

Although he humbly offered his book as a gift to God, the English monk Eadwine added an inscription to his portrait declaring himself a "prince among scribes" whose fame would endure forever.

exaggerated his importance by likening his image to that of an evangelist writing his gospel and by including an inscription within the inner frame that identifies him and proclaims himself a "prince among scribes." He declares that, due to the excellence of his work, his fame will endure forever and that he can offer his book as an acceptable gift to God. Eadwine, like other Romanesque sculptors and painters who signed their works, may have been concerned for his fame, but these artists, whether monks or laity, were not yet aware of the concepts of fine art and fine artist. To them, their work existed not for its own sake but for God's. Nonetheless, works such as this one are an early sign of a new attitude toward the role of the artist in society that presages the emergence of the notion of individual artistic genius in the Renaissance.

ROMANESQUE EUROPE

FRANCE AND NORTHERN SPAIN

▌ *Romanesque* takes its name from the Roman-like barrel and groin vaults based on round arches employed in many European churches built between 1050 and 1200. Romanesque vaults, however, are made of stone, not concrete.

▌ Numerous churches sprang up along the pilgrimage roads leading to the shrine of Saint James at Santiago de Compostela. These churches were large enough to accommodate crowds of pilgrims who came to view the relics displayed in radiating chapels off the ambulatory and transept.

▌ The Romanesque period also brought the revival of monumental stone relief sculpture, especially on church facades, where scenes of Christ as Last Judge often greeted the faithful as they entered the doorway to salvation.

▌ The leading patrons of Romanesque sculpture and painting were the monks of the Cluniac order. The Cistercians, under the leadership of Bernard of Clairvaux, condemned figural art in churches and religious books.

Saint-Sernin, Toulouse, ca. 1070–1120

Saint-Pierre, Moissac, ca. 1115–1135

HOLY ROMAN EMPIRE

▌ In the Romanesque period, the Salian dynasty (r. 1027–1125) ruled an empire that corresponds roughly to present-day Germany and northern Italy.

▌ Architects in the Holy Roman Empire built structurally innovative churches. Speyer Cathedral and Sant'Ambrogio in Milan are two of the earliest examples of the use of groin vaults in naves.

▌ In Belgium, sculptors excelled in metalwork, producing costly reliquaries of silver, jewels, and enamel. Rainer of Huy, one of several Romanesque artists whose name is known, cast a baptismal font in a single piece.

Rainer of Huy, baptismal font, 1118

ITALY

▌ The regional diversity of Romanesque art and architecture is especially evident in Italy, where the ancient Roman and Early Christian heritage was strongest.

▌ Romanesque churches in Pisa and Florence have wooden roofs in contrast to the vaulted interiors of northern buildings. The exteriors often feature marble paneling of different colors. Church campaniles were usually freestanding, and baptisteries were independent central-plan buildings facing the cathedral.

Cathedral complex, Pisa, 11th–12th centuries

NORMANDY AND ENGLAND

▌ After their conversion to Christianity in the early 10th century, the Vikings settled on the northern coast of France. From there, Duke William of Normandy crossed the channel and conquered England in 1066. The *Bayeux Tapestry* chronicles that war—a unique example of contemporaneous historical narrative art in the Middle Ages.

▌ Norman and English Romanesque architects introduced new features to church design that greatly influenced French Gothic architecture. Saint-Étienne at Caen and Durham Cathedral are the earliest examples of the use of rib groin vaults over a three-story nave elevation (arcade-tribune-clerestory). The Durham builders also experimented with quadrant arches in the tribune to buttress the nave vaults.

Bayeux Tapestry, ca. 1070–1080

10 ft.

18-1 Rose window and lancets, north transept, Chartres Cathedral, Chartres, France, ca. 1220. Stained glass, rose window 43′ in diameter.

The use of flying buttresses in Gothic cathedrals made possible the replacement of stone walls with immense stained-glass windows, which transformed natural sunlight into Abbot Suger's divine *lux nova*.

18

GOTHIC EUROPE

In 1550, Giorgio Vasari (1511–1574), the "father of art history," first used *Gothic* as a term of ridicule to describe late medieval art and architecture, which he attributed to the Goths and regarded as "monstrous and barbarous."[1] With the publication in that year of his influential *Introduction to the Three Arts of Design,* Vasari codified for all time the notion the early Renaissance artist Lorenzo Ghiberti (1378–1455) had already advanced in his *Commentarii,* namely, that the Middle Ages was a period of decline. The humanists of the Italian Renaissance, who placed Greco-Roman art on a pedestal, believed that the uncouth Goths were responsible for both the downfall of Rome and the destruction of the classical style in art and architecture. They regarded "Gothic" art with contempt and considered it ugly and crude. In the 13th and 14th centuries, however, when the Gothic style was the rage in most of Europe, contemporaries admired Gothic buildings as *opus modernum* ("modern work"). The clergy and the lay public alike recognized that the great cathedrals towering over their towns displayed an exciting new style. For them, Gothic cathedrals were not distortions of the classical style but images of the City of God, the Heavenly Jerusalem, which they were privileged to build on earth.

As in the Romanesque period, the great artistic innovations of the Gothic age were in part the outgrowth of widespread prosperity, but the era was also a time of turmoil in Europe (MAP **18-1**). In 1337 the Hundred Years' War began, shattering the peace between France and England. In the 14th century, a great plague, the Black Death, swept over western Europe and killed at least a quarter of its people. From 1378 to 1417, opposing popes resided in Rome and in Avignon in southern France during the political-religious crisis known as the Great Schism (see "The Great Schism," Chapter 19, page 501). Above all, the Gothic age was a time of profound change in European society. The focus of both intellectual and religious life shifted definitively from monasteries in the countryside to rapidly expanding secular cities. In these new Gothic urban centers, prosperous merchants made their homes and *guilds* (professional associations) of scholars founded the first modern universities. Although the papacy was at the height of its power, and knights throughout Europe still gathered to wage Crusades against the Muslims, the independent secular nations of modern Europe were beginning to take shape. Foremost among them was France.

MAP 18-1 Europe around 1200.

FRENCH GOTHIC

The Gothic style first appeared in northern France around 1140, and some late medieval writers called Gothic art in general *opus francigenum* ("French work"). By the 13th century, the *opus modernum* of the region around Paris had spread throughout western Europe, and in the next century it expanded still farther. Saint Vitus Cathedral in Prague (Czech Republic), for example, begun in 1344, closely emulates French Gothic architecture. Today, Gothic architecture lives on in the chapels, academic buildings, and dormitories of college campuses throughout North America. But although the Gothic style achieved international acclaim, it was a regional phenomenon. To the east and south of Europe, the Byzantine and Islamic styles still held sway. And many regional variants existed within European Gothic, just as distinct regional styles characterized the Romanesque period.

Architecture and Architectural Decoration

Art historians generally agree that the birthplace of Gothic architecture was at Saint-Denis, a few miles north of Paris. Saint Dionysius (Denis in French) was the apostle who brought Christianity to Gaul and who died a martyr's death there in the third century. The Benedictine order founded the abbey at Saint-Denis in the seventh century on the site of the saint's burial. In the ninth century, the monks constructed a basilica at Saint-Denis, which housed the saint's tomb and those of almost all of the French kings dating back to the sixth century, as well as the crimson military banner said to have belonged to Charlemagne. The Carolingian basilica became France's royal church, the very symbol of the monarchy (just as Speyer Cathedral, FIG. 17-19, was the burial place of the German rulers of the Holy Roman Empire).

SUGER AND SAINT-DENIS By 1122, when a monk named Suger became abbot of Saint-Denis, the old church was in disrepair and had become too small to accommodate the growing number of pilgrims. Suger also believed the basilica was of insufficient grandeur to serve as the official church of the French kings (see "Abbot Suger

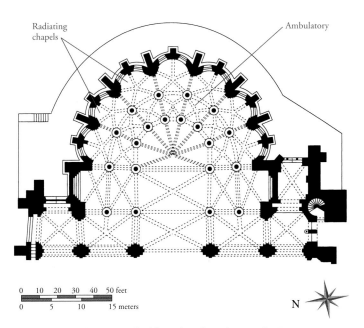

18-2 Plan of the east end, abbey church, Saint-Denis, France, 1140–1144 (after Sumner Crosby).

The innovative plan of the east end of Saint-Denis dates to Abbot Suger's lifetime. By using lightweight rib vaults, the builders were able to eliminate the walls between the radiating chapels.

Abbot Suger and
the Rebuilding of Saint-Denis

Abbot Suger of Saint-Denis (1081–1151) rose from humble parentage to become the right-hand man of both Louis VI (r. 1108–1137) and Louis VII (r. 1137–1180). When the latter, accompanied by his queen, Eleanor of Aquitaine, left to join the Second Crusade (1147–1149), Suger served as regent of France. From his youth, Suger wrote, he had dreamed of the possibility of embellishing the church in which most French monarchs had been buried for nearly 500 years. Within 15 years of becoming abbot of Saint-Denis, Suger began rebuilding its Carolingian basilica. In Suger's time, the power of the French kings, except for scattered holdings, extended over an area not much larger than the Île-de-France, the region centered on Paris. But the kings had pretensions to rule all of France. Suger aimed to increase the prestige both of his abbey and of the monarchy by rebuilding France's royal church in grand fashion.

Suger wrote three detailed treatises about his activities as abbot of Saint-Denis. He recorded that he summoned masons and artists

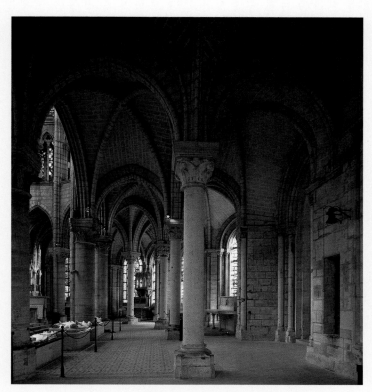

18-3 Ambulatory and radiating chapels, abbey church, Saint-Denis, France, 1140–1144.

Abbot Suger's remodeling of Saint-Denis marked the beginning of Gothic architecture. Rib vaults with pointed arches spring from slender columns. The radiating chapels have stained-glass windows.

from many regions to help design and construct his new church. In one important passage, he described the special qualities of the new east end (FIGS. 18-2 and 18-3) dedicated in 1144:

> [I]t was cunningly provided that—through the upper columns and central arches which were to be placed upon the lower ones built in the crypt—the central nave of the old [Carolingian church] should be equalized, by means of geometrical and arithmetical instruments, with the central nave of the new addition; and, likewise, that the dimensions of the old side-aisles should be equalized with the dimensions of the new side-aisles, except for that elegant and praiseworthy extension in [the form of] a circular string of chapels, by virtue of which the whole [church] would shine with the wonderful and uninterrupted light of most sacred windows, pervading the interior beauty.*

The abbot's brief discussion of Saint Denis's new ambulatory and chapels is key to the understanding of Early Gothic architecture. But he wrote at much greater length about his church's glorious golden and gem-studded furnishings. Here, for example, is Suger's description of the *altar frontal* (the decorative panel on the front of the altar) in the choir:

> Into this panel, which stands in front of [Saint Denis's] most sacred body, we have put . . . about forty-two marks of gold [and] a multifarious wealth of precious gems, hyacinths, rubies, sapphires, emeralds and topazes, and also an array of different large pearls.†

The costly furnishings and the light-filled space caused Suger to "delight in the beauty of the house of God" and "called [him] away from external cares." The new church made him feel as if he were "dwelling . . . in some strange region of the universe which neither exists entirely in the slime of the earth nor entirely in the purity of Heaven." In Suger's eyes, then, his splendid new church, permeated with light and outfitted with gold and precious gems, was a way station on the road to Paradise, which "transported [him] from this inferior to that higher world."‡ He regarded a lavish investment in art as a spiritual aid, not as an undesirable distraction for the pious monk, as did Bernard of Clairvaux (see "Bernard of Clairvaux," Chapter 17, page 438). Suger's forceful justification of art in the church set the stage for the proliferation of costly stained-glass windows and sculptures in the cathedrals of the Gothic age.

---

* Translated by Erwin Panofsky, *Abbot Suger on the Abbey Church of Saint-Denis and Its Art Treasures,* 2d ed. (Princeton: Princeton University Press, 1979), 101.
† Ibid., 55.
‡ Ibid., 65.

and the Rebuilding of Saint-Denis," above). Thus, Suger began to rebuild the church in 1135 by erecting a new west facade with sculptured portals. In 1140 work began on the east end (FIGS. **18-2** and **18-3**). Suger died before he could remodel the nave, but he attended the dedication of the new choir, ambulatory, and radiating

chapels on June 11, 1144. Also in attendance were King Louis VII of France, Queen Eleanor of Aquitaine, and five archbishops.

Because the French considered the old church a relic in its own right, the new east end had to conform to the dimensions of the crypt below it. Nevertheless, the remodeled portion of Saint-Denis

The Gothic Rib Vault

The ancestors of the Gothic *rib vault* are the Romanesque vaults found at Caen (FIG. 17-31), Durham (FIG. 17-33), and elsewhere. The rib vault's distinguishing feature is the crossed, or diagonal, arches under its groins, as seen in the Saint-Denis ambulatory and chapels (FIG. 18-3; compare FIG. 18-20). These arches form the *armature*, or skeletal framework, for constructing the vault. Gothic vaults generally have more thinly vaulted *webs* (the masonry between the ribs) than found in Romanesque vaults. But the chief difference between the two styles of rib vaults is the *pointed arch,* an integral part of the Gothic skeletal armature. The first wide use of pointed arches was in Sasanian architecture (FIG. 2-27), and Islamic builders later adopted them. French Romanesque architects (FIGS. 17-1 and 17-14) borrowed the form from Muslim Spain and passed it to their Gothic successors. Pointed arches allowed Gothic builders to make the crowns of all the vault's arches approximately the same level, regardless of the space to be vaulted. The Romanesque architects could not achieve this with their semicircular arches.

The drawings here (FIG. 18-4) illustrate this key difference. In FIG. 18-4*a,* the rectangle *ABCD* is an oblong nave bay to be vaulted. *AC* and *DB* are the diagonal ribs; *AB* and *DC,* the transverse arches; and *AD* and *BC,* the nave arcade's arches. If the architect uses semi-circular arches (*AFB, BJC,* and *DHC*), their radii and, therefore, their heights (*EF, IJ,* and *GH*) will be different, because the width of a semicircular arch determines its height. The result will be a vault (FIG. 18-4*b*) with higher transverse arches (*DHC*) than the arcade's arches (*CJB*). The vault's crown (*F*) will be still higher. If the builder uses pointed arches (FIG. 18-4*c*), the transverse (*DLC*) and arcade (*BKC*) arches can have the same heights (*GL* and *IK* in FIG. 18-4*a*). The result will be a Gothic rib vault where the points of the arches (*L* and *K*) are at the same level as the vault's crown (*F*).

A major advantage of the Gothic vault is its flexibility, which permits the vaulting of compartments of varying shapes, as may be seen at Saint-Denis (FIG. 18-2). Pointed arches also channel the weight of the vaults more directly downward than do semicircular arches. The vaults therefore require less buttressing to hold them in place, in turn permitting builders to open up the walls and place large windows beneath the arches. Because pointed arches also lead the eye upward, they make the vaults appear taller than they are. In FIG. 18-4, the crown (*F*) of both the Romanesque (*b*) and Gothic (*c*) vaults is the same height from the pavement, but the Gothic vault seems taller. Both the physical and visual properties of rib vaults with pointed arches aided Gothic builders in their quest for soaring height in church interiors.

18-4 Diagram (*a*) and drawings of rib vaults with semicircular (*b*) and pointed (*c*) arches.

Pointed arches channel the weight of the rib vaults more directly downward than do semicircular arches, requiring less buttressing. Pointed arches also make the vaults appear taller than they are.

represented a sharp break from past practice. Innovative rib vaults resting on pointed, or *ogival,* arches (see "The Gothic Rib Vault," above, and FIG. 18-4) cover the ambulatory and chapels (FIG. 18-3). These pioneering, exceptionally lightweight vaults spring from slender columns in the ambulatory and from the thin masonry walls framing the chapels. The lightness of the vaults enabled the builders to eliminate the walls between the chapels (FIG. 18-2) and open up the outer walls and fill them with stained-glass windows (see "Stained-Glass Windows," page 472). Suger and his contemporaries marveled at the "wonderful and uninterrupted light" that poured in through the "most sacred windows." The abbot called the colored light *lux nova,* "new light." The multicolored rays coming through the windows shone on the walls and columns, almost dissolving them. Both the new type of vaulting and the use of stained glass became hallmarks of French Gothic architecture.

Saint-Denis is also the key monument of Early Gothic sculpture. Little of the sculpture that Suger commissioned for the west facade of the abbey church survived the French Revolution of the late 18th century (see Chapter 29), but much of the mid-12th-century structure is intact. It consists of a double-tower westwork, as at Saint-Étienne (FIG. 17-30) at Caen, and has massive walls in the Romanesque tradition. A restored large central *rose window* (a circular stained-glass window), a new feature that became standard in French Gothic architecture, punctuates the facade's upper story. For the three portals, Suger imported sculptors to carry on the rich Romanesque heritage of southern France (see Chapter 17). But at Saint-Denis, the sculptors introduced statues of Old Testament kings, queens, and prophets attached to columns, which screened the jambs of all three doorways.

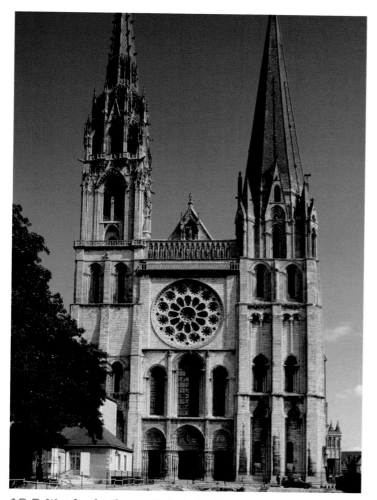

18-5 West facade, Chartres Cathedral, Chartres, France, ca. 1145–1155. ■◀

The Early Gothic west facade was all that remained of Chartres Cathedral after the fire of 1194. The design still has much in common with Romanesque facades. The rose window is an example of plate tracery.

ROYAL PORTAL, CHARTRES This innovative treatment of the portals of Suger's church appeared immediately afterward at Chartres, also in the Île-de-France, in the new cathedral dedicated to Notre Dame ("Our Lady," that is, the Virgin Mary). Work on the west facade (FIG. 18-5) began around 1145. The lower parts of the massive west towers at Chartres and the portals between them are all that remain of the cathedral destroyed by fire in 1194 before it had been completed. Reconstruction of the church began immediately but in the High Gothic style (discussed later). The west entrance, the Royal Portal (FIG. 18-6; so named because of the statue-columns of kings and queens flanking its three doorways) constitutes the most complete surviving ensemble of Early Gothic sculpture. Thierry of Chartres, chancellor of the Cathedral School of Chartres from 1141 until his death 10 years later, may have conceived the complex iconographical program. The archivolts of the right portal, for example, depict the seven female Liberal Arts and their male champions. The figures represent the core of medieval learning and symbolize human knowledge, which Thierry and other "Schoolmen" believed led to true faith (see "Scholasticism and Gothic Art and Architecture," page 466).

The sculptures of the Royal Portal (FIG. 18-6) proclaim the majesty and power of Christ. To unite the three doorways iconographically and visually, the sculptors carved episodes from Christ's life on the capitals, which form a kind of frieze linking one entrance to the next. In the tympanum of the right portal, Christ appears in the lap of the Virgin Mary (Notre Dame). Scenes of his birth and early life fill the lintel below. The tympanum's theme and composition recall Byzantine representations of the Theotokos (FIGS. 12-18 and 12-19), as well as the Romanesque Throne of Wisdom (FIG. 17-18). But Mary's prominence on the Chartres facade has no parallel in the decoration of Romanesque church portals. At Chartres the designers gave her a central role in the sculptural program, a position she maintained throughout the Gothic period. The cult of the Virgin Mary reached a high point in the Gothic age. As the Mother of Christ, she stood compassionately between the Last Judge and the horrors of Hell, interceding for all her faithful. Worshipers in the later 12th and 13th centuries

18-6 Royal Portal, west facade, Chartres Cathedral, Chartres, France, ca. 1145–1155. ■◀

The sculptures of the Royal Portal proclaim the majesty and power of Christ. The tympana depict, from left to right, Christ's Ascension, the Second Coming, and Jesus in the lap of the Virgin Mary.

Scholasticism and Gothic Art
and Architecture

A few years before the formal consecration of the church altar at Notre-Dame (FIG. 18-11) in Paris, Philip II Augustus (r. 1180–1223) succeeded to the French throne. Philip brought the feudal barons under his control and expanded the royal domains to include Normandy in the north and most of Languedoc in the south, laying the foundations for the modern nation of France. Renowned as "the maker of Paris," he gave the city its walls, paved its streets, and built the palace of the Louvre (now one of the world's great museums) to house the royal family. Although Rome remained the religious center of Western Christendom, Paris became its intellectual capital. The University of Paris attracted the best minds from all over Europe. Virtually every thinker of note in the Gothic world at some point studied or taught at Paris.

Even in the Romanesque period, Paris was a center of learning. Its Cathedral School professors, known as Schoolmen, developed the philosophy called *Scholasticism*. The greatest of the early Schoolmen was Peter Abelard (1079–1142), a champion of logical reasoning. Abelard and his contemporaries had been introduced to the writings of the Greek philosopher Aristotle through the Arabic scholars of Islamic Spain. Abelard applied Aristotle's system of rational inquiry to the interpretation of religious belief. Until the 12th century, both clergy and laymen considered truth the exclusive property of divine revelation as given in the Holy Scriptures. But the Schoolmen, using Aristotle's method, sought to demonstrate that reason alone could lead to certain truths. Their goal was to prove the central articles of Christian faith by argument (*disputatio*). A person using Scholastic argument first states a possibility, then cites an authoritative view in objection, next reconciles the positions, and, finally, offers a reply to each of the rejected original arguments.

One of Abelard's greatest critics was Bernard of Clairvaux (see "Bernard of Clairvaux," Chapter 17, page 438), who believed Scholasticism was equivalent to questioning Christian dogma. Although Bernard succeeded in 1140 in having the Catholic Church officially condemn Abelard's doctrines, the Schoolmen's philosophy developed systematically until it became the dominant Western philosophy of the late Middle Ages. By the 13th century, the Schoolmen of Paris already had organized as a professional guild of master scholars, separate from the numerous Church schools the bishop of Paris oversaw. The structure of the Parisian guild served as the model for many other European universities.

The greatest exponent of Abelard's Scholasticism was Thomas Aquinas (1225–1274), an Italian monk who became a saint in 1323. Aquinas settled in Paris in 1244. There, the German theologian Albertus Magnus instructed him in Aristotelian philosophy. Aquinas went on to become an influential teacher at the University of Paris. His most famous work, *Summa Theologica* (left unfinished at his death), is a model of the Scholastic approach to knowledge. Aquinas divided his treatise into books, the books into questions, the questions into articles, each article into objections with contradictions and responses, and, finally, answers to the objections. He set forth five ways to prove the existence of God by rational argument. Aquinas's work remains the foundation of contemporary Catholic teaching.

The earliest manifestations of the Gothic spirit in art and architecture—the sculptured portals and vaulted east end of Suger's Saint-Denis (FIGS. 18-2 and 18-3)—appeared concurrently with the first stages of Scholastic philosophy. Both originated in Paris and its environs. Many art historians have noted the parallels between them—how the logical thrust and counterthrust of Gothic construction, the geometric relationships of building parts, and the systematic organization of the iconographical programs of Gothic church portals coincide with Scholastic principles and methods. No documents exist, however, linking the scholars, builders, and sculptors.

---

sang hymns to her, put her image everywhere, and dedicated great cathedrals to her. Soldiers carried the Virgin's image into battle on banners, and her name joined that of Saint Denis as part of the French king's battle cry. Mary became the spiritual lady of chivalry, and the Christian knight dedicated his life to her. The severity of Romanesque themes stressing the Last Judgment yielded to the gentleness of Gothic art, in which Mary is the kindly Queen of Heaven.

Christ's Ascension into Heaven appears in the tympanum of the left portal. All around, in the archivolts, are the signs of the zodiac and scenes representing the various labors of the months of the year. They are symbols of the cosmic and earthly worlds. The Second Coming is the subject of the central tympanum. The signs of the four evangelists, the 24 elders of the Apocalypse, and the 12 apostles appear around Christ or on the lintel. The Second Coming—in essence, the Last Judgment theme—was still of central importance, as it was in Romanesque portals. But at Early Gothic Chartres, the theme became a symbol of salvation rather than damnation.

Statues of Old Testament kings and queens decorate the jambs flanking each doorway of the Royal Portal (FIGS. 18-6 and 18-7). They are the royal ancestors of Christ and, both figuratively and literally, support the New Testament figures above the doorways. They wear 12th-century clothes, and medieval observers also regarded them as images of the kings and queens of France. (This was the motivation for vandalizing the comparable figures at Saint-Denis during the French Revolution.) The figures stand rigidly upright with their elbows held close against their hips. The linear folds of their garments—inherited from the Romanesque style, along with the elongated proportions—generally echo the vertical lines of the columns behind them. (In this respect, Gothic jamb statues differ significantly from classical caryatids; FIG. 5-54. The Gothic figures are *attached* to columns; the classical statues *replaced* the columns.) And yet, within and despite this architectural straitjacket, the statues display the first signs of a new naturalism. The sculptors conceived and treated the figures as three-dimensional volumes, not reliefs, and they stand out from the plane of the wall. As was true of all stone sculpture on church facades, artists originally painted the Royal Portal statues in vivid colors, enhancing their lifelike appearance. The new naturalism is noticeable particularly in the statues' heads, where kindly human faces replace the masklike features of most Romanesque figures. At Chartres, a personalization of appearance began that led first to idealized portraits of the perfect Christian and finally, by 1400, into the portraiture of specific individuals. The sculptors of the Royal Portal statues initiated an era of artistic concern with personality and individuality.

18-7 Old Testament kings and queen, jamb statues, central doorway of Royal Portal, Chartres Cathedral, Chartres, France, ca. 1145–1155.

The biblical kings and queens of the Royal Portal are the royal ancestors of Christ. These Early Gothic statue-columns display the first signs of a new naturalism in European sculpture.

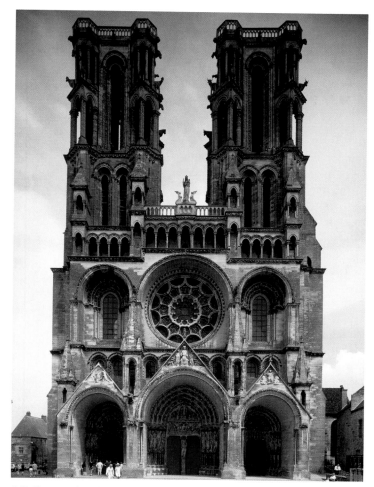

18-8 West facade of Laon Cathedral, Laon, France, begun ca. 1190.

The huge central rose window, the deep porches in front of the doorways, and the open structure of the towers distinguish Laon's Early Gothic facade from Romanesque church facades.

LAON CATHEDRAL Both Chartres Cathedral and the abbey church of Saint-Denis had long construction histories, and only small portions of the structures date to the Early Gothic period. Laon Cathedral (FIGS. **18-8** and **18-9**), however, completed shortly after 1200, provides a comprehensive picture of French church architecture of the second half of the 12th century. Although the Laon builders retained many Romanesque features in their design, they combined them with the rib vault resting on pointed arches, the essential element of Early Gothic architecture.

Among the Laon plan's Romanesque features are the nave bays with their large sexpartite rib vaults, flanked by two small groin-vaulted squares in each aisle. The vaulting system (except for the pointed arches), as well as the vaulted gallery above the aisles, derived from Norman Romanesque churches such as Saint-Étienne (FIG. **17-31**) at Caen. The Laon architect also employed the Romanesque alternate-support system of compound and simple piers in the nave arcade. Above, alternating bundles of three and five shafts frame the aisle bays. A new feature found in the Laon interior, however, is the *triforium*, the band of arcades below the clerestory

18-9 Interior of Laon Cathedral (looking northeast), Laon, France, begun ca. 1190.

The insertion of a triforium at Laon broke up the nave wall and produced the characteristic four-story Early Gothic interior elevation: nave arcade, vaulted gallery, triforium, and clerestory.

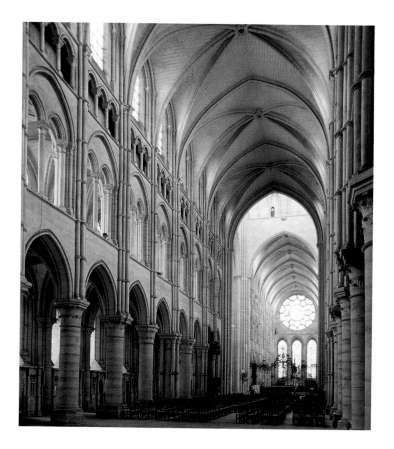

18-10 Nave elevations of four French Gothic cathedrals at the same scale (after Louis Grodecki).

Gothic nave designs evolved from the Early Gothic four-story elevation to the High Gothic three-story elevation (arcade, triforium, and clerestory). The height of the vaults also increased from 80 to 144 feet.

a Laon   **b** Paris   **c** Chartres   **d** Amiens

(FIGS. 18-9 and **18-10a**). The triforium occupies the space corresponding to the exterior strip of wall covered by the sloping timber roof above the galleries. The insertion of the triforium into the Romanesque three-story nave elevation reflected a growing desire to break up all continuous wall surfaces. The new horizontal zone produced the characteristic four-story Early Gothic interior elevation: nave arcade, vaulted gallery, triforium, and clerestory with single *lancets* (tall, narrow windows ending in pointed arches). Shown in FIG. 18-10 is a comparison of the Laon nave elevation with that of another four-story Early Gothic cathedral (FIG. **18-10b**) and with elevations of two three-story High Gothic cathedrals (FIGS. **18-10c** and **18-10d**).

Laon Cathedral's west facade (FIG. **18-8**) signals an even more pronounced departure from the Romanesque style still lingering at Saint-Denis and the Chartres Royal Portal. Typically Gothic are the huge central rose window, the deep porches in front of the doorways, and the open structure of the towers. A comparison of the facades of Laon Cathedral and Saint-Étienne (FIG. **17-30**) at Caen reveals a much deeper penetration of the wall mass in the later building. At Laon, as in Gothic architecture generally, the guiding principle was to reduce sheer mass and replace it with intricately framed voids.

NOTRE-DAME, PARIS About 1130, Louis VI moved his official residence to Paris, spurring much commercial activity and a great building boom. Paris soon became the leading city of France, indeed of all northern Europe, making a new cathedral a necessity. Notre-Dame (FIG. **18-11**) occupies a picturesque site on an island in the Seine River called the Île-de-la-Cité. The Gothic church, which replaced a large Merovingian basilica, has a complicated building history. The choir and transept were completed by 1182, the nave by about 1225, and the facade not until around 1250–1260. Sexpartite vaults cover the nave, as at Laon. The original elevation (the builders modified the design as work progressed) had four stories, but the scheme (FIG. **18-10b**) differed from Laon's (FIG. **18-10a**). In place of the triforium over the gallery, stained-glass *oculi* (singular *oculus*, a small round window) open up the wall below the clerestory lancets. As a result, windows fill two of the four stories, further reducing the

masonry area. (This four-story nave elevation can be seen in only one bay in FIG. 18-11, immediately to the right of the south transept and partially hidden by it.)

To hold the much thinner—and taller (compare FIGS. **18-10a** and **18-10b**)—walls of Notre-Dame in place, the unknown architect introduced *flying buttresses*, exterior arches that spring from the lower roofs over the aisles and ambulatory (FIG. **18-11**) and counter the outward thrust of the nave vaults. Gothic builders employed flying buttresses as early as 1150 in a few smaller churches, but at Notre-Dame in Paris they circle a great urban cathedral. At Durham, the internal quadrant arches (FIG. **17-33**, *right*) beneath the aisle roofs, also employed at Laon, perform a similar function and may be regarded as precedents for exposed Gothic flying buttresses. The combination of precisely positioned flying buttresses and rib vaults with pointed arches was the ideal solution to the problem of constructing towering naves with huge windows. The flying buttresses, like slender extended fingers holding up the walls, are key components of the distinctive "look" of Gothic cathedrals (see "The Gothic Cathedral," page 469, and FIG. **18-12**).

18-11 Notre-Dame (looking north), Paris, France, begun 1163; nave and flying buttresses, ca. 1180–1200; remodeled after 1225.

Architects first used flying buttresses on a grand scale in the Cathedral of Notre-Dame in Paris. The buttresses countered the outward thrust of the nave vaults and held up the towering nave walls.

The Gothic Cathedral

The great cathedrals erected throughout Europe in the later 12th and 13th centuries are the enduring symbols of the Gothic age. These towering structures are eloquent testimonies to the extraordinary skill of the architects, engineers, carpenters, masons, sculptors, glassworkers, and metalsmiths who constructed and decorated the buildings. Most of the architectural components of Gothic cathedrals appeared in earlier structures, but the way Gothic architects combined the elements made the buildings unique expressions of medieval faith. The essential ingredients of the Gothic "recipe" were rib vaults with pointed arches (see "The Gothic Rib Vault," page 464), flying buttresses, and huge colored-glass windows (see "Stained-Glass Windows," page 472). These and the other important Gothic architectural terms listed here are illustrated in FIG. 18-12.

- **Pinnacle** A sharply pointed ornament capping the piers or flying buttresses; also used on cathedral facades.

- **Flying buttresses** Masonry struts that transfer the thrust of the nave vaults across the roofs of the side aisles and ambulatory to a tall pier rising above the church's exterior wall. (Compare FIG. I-18, right.)

- **Vaulting web** The masonry blocks that fill the area between the ribs of a groin vault.

- **Diagonal rib** In plan, one of the ribs that form the X of a groin vault. In FIG. 18-4, the diagonal ribs are the lines AC and DB.

- **Transverse rib** A rib that crosses the nave or aisle at a 90-degree angle (lines AB and DC in FIG. 18-4).

- **Springing** The lowest stone of an arch; in Gothic vaulting, the lowest stone of a diagonal or transverse rib.

- **Clerestory** The windows below the vaults that form the nave elevation's uppermost level. By using flying buttresses and rib vaults on pointed arches, Gothic architects could build huge clerestory windows and

fill them with *stained glass* held in place by ornamental stonework called *tracery*.

- **Oculus** A small round window.

- **Lancet** A tall, narrow window crowned by a pointed arch.

- **Triforium** The story in the nave elevation consisting of arcades, usually *blind arcades* (FIG. 18-9), but occasionally filled with stained glass (FIG. I-2).

- **Nave arcade** The series of arches supported by piers separating the nave from the side aisles.

- **Compound pier with shafts (responds)** Also called the *cluster pier*, a pier with a group, or cluster, of attached shafts, or *responds*, extending to the springing of the vaults.

18-12 Cutaway view of a typical French Gothic cathedral (John Burge). (1) pinnacle, (2) flying buttress, (3) vaulting web, (4) diagonal rib, (5) transverse rib, (6) springing, (7) clerestory, (8) oculus, (9) lancet, (10) triforium, (11) nave arcade, (12) compound pier with responds. ◼◖

Rib vaults with pointed arches, flying buttresses, and stained-glass windows are the major ingredients in the "recipe" for constructing Gothic cathedrals, but other elements also contributed to the distinctive "look" of these churches.

18-13 Aerial view of Chartres Cathedral (looking north), Chartres, France, as rebuilt after 1194.

Architectural historians consider the rebuilt Chartres Cathedral the first great monument of High Gothic architecture. It is the first church to have been planned from the beginning with flying buttresses.

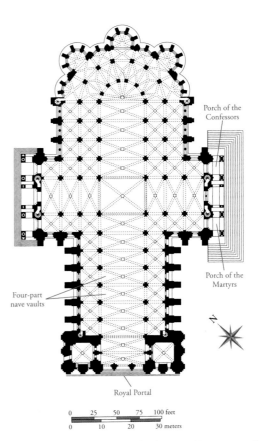

18-14 Plan of Chartres Cathedral, Chartres, France, as rebuilt after 1194 (after Paul Frankl).

The Chartres plan, in which a single square in each aisle (rather than two squares) flanks a single rectangular unit in the nave with a four-part vault, became the norm for High Gothic church architecture.

CHARTRES AFTER 1194 Churches burned frequently in the Middle Ages (see "Timber Roofs," Chapter 17, page 435), and church officials often had to raise money suddenly for new building campaigns. In contrast to monastic churches, which usually were small and completed fairly quickly, construction of urban cathedrals often extended over decades and sometimes over centuries. Their financing depended largely on collections and public contributions (not always voluntary), and a lack of funds often interrupted building programs. Unforeseen events, such as wars, famines, or plagues, or friction between the town and cathedral authorities would often stop construction, which then might not resume for years. At Reims (FIG. 18-23), the clergy offered *indulgences* (pardons for sins committed) to those who helped underwrite the enormous cost of erecting the cathedral. The rebuilding of Chartres Cathedral (FIG. **18-13**) after the devastating fire of 1194 took a relatively short 27 years, but at one point the townspeople revolted against the prospect of a heavier tax burden. They stormed the bishop's residence and drove him into exile for four years.

Chartres Cathedral's mid-12th-century west facade (FIG. 18-5) and the masonry of the crypt to the east were the only sections left standing after the 1194 conflagration. The crypt housed the most precious relic of Chartres—the mantle of the Virgin, which miraculously survived the fire. For reasons of piety and economy, the builders used the crypt for the foundation of the new structure. The retention of the crypt and west facade determined the new church's dimensions, but not its plan or elevation. Architectural historians usually consider the post-1194 Chartres Cathedral the first High Gothic building.

The Chartres plan (FIG. **18-14**) reveals a new kind of organization. Rectangular nave bays replaced the square bays with sexpartite vaults and the alternate-support system, still present in Early Gothic churches such as Laon Cathedral (FIG. 18-9). The new system, in which a single square in each aisle (rather than two, as before) flanks a single rectangular unit in the nave, became the High Gothic norm.

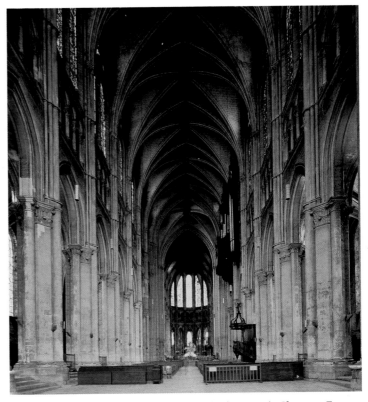

18-15 Interior of Chartres Cathedral (looking east), Chartres, France, begun 1194.

Chartres Cathedral became the model for High Gothic churches also in its tripartite elevation consisting of nave arcade, triforium, and clerestory with stained-glass windows almost as tall as the main arcade.

A change in vault design and the abandonment of the alternate-support system usually accompanied this new bay arrangement. The High Gothic nave vault, which covered just one bay and therefore could be braced more easily than its Early Gothic predecessor, had only four parts. The visual effect of these changes was to unify the interior (FIG. 18-15). The High Gothic architect aligned identical units so that viewers saw them in too rapid a sequence to perceive them as individual volumes of space. The level crowns of the successive nave vaults, which pointed arches made possible, enhanced this effect. The nave became a vast, continuous hall.

The 1194 Chartres Cathedral was also the first church to have been planned from the beginning with flying buttresses, another key High Gothic feature. The flying buttresses allowed the builders to eliminate the tribune above the aisle, which had partially braced Romanesque and Early Gothic naves (compare FIG. 18-10c with FIGS. 18-10a and 18-10b). The new High Gothic tripartite nave elevation consisted of arcade, triforium, and clerestory with greatly enlarged windows. The Chartres windows are almost as tall as the main arcade and consist of double lancets with a single crowning oculus. The strategic placement of flying buttresses permitted the construction of nave walls with so many voids that heavy masonry played a minor role.

CHARTRES STAINED GLASS Despite the vastly increased size of the clerestory windows, the Chartres nave (FIG. 18-15) is relatively dark. The explanation for this seeming contradiction is that light-suppressing colored glass fills the windows. The purpose of these windows was not to illuminate the interior with bright sunlight but to transform natural light into Suger's mystical lux nova (see "Stained-Glass Windows," page 472). Chartres retains almost the full complement of its original stained glass, which, although it has a dimming effect, transforms the character of the interior in dramatic fashion. Gothic churches that have lost their original stained-glass windows give a false impression of what their designers intended.

One Chartres window that survived the fire of 1194 and was subsequently reused in the High Gothic cathedral is the tall single lancet the French call *Notre Dame de la Belle Verrière* (Our Lady of the Beautiful Window, FIG. 18-16). The central section, depicting against a red background the Virgin Mary enthroned with the Christ Child in her lap, dates to about 1170. Glaziers added the framing angels seen against a blue ground when they reinstalled the window in the 13th-century choir. The frontal composition is traditional, but Mary is now the beautiful, young, rather worldly Queen of Heaven, haloed, crowned, and accompanied by the dove of the Holy Spirit. Comparing this Virgin and Child with the Theotokos and Child (FIG. 12-19) of Hagia Sophia highlights not only the greater severity and aloofness of the Byzantine image but also the sharp difference between the light-reflecting mosaic medium and Gothic light-filtering stained glass. Gothic and Byzantine builders used light to transform the material world into the spiritual, but in opposite ways. In Gothic architecture, light entered from outside the building through a screen of stone-set colored glass. In Byzantine architecture, light reflected off myriad glass tesserae set into the thick masonry wall.

Chartres's 13th-century Gothic windows are even more spectacular than the *Belle Verrière* because, thanks to the introduction of flying buttresses, the builders could plan from the outset to fill entire walls with stained glass. The immense rose window (approximately 43 feet in diameter) and tall lancets of Chartres Cathedral's north transept (FIG. 18-1) were the gift of the French queen Blanche of Castile, around 1220. The royal motifs of yellow castles on a red ground and yellow *fleurs-de-lis*—three-petaled iris flowers—on a blue ground fill the eight narrow windows in the rose's lower spandrels. The iconography is also fitting for a queen. The enthroned Virgin and Child appear in the

18-16 Virgin and Child and angels (*Notre Dame de la Belle Verrière*), detail of a window in the choir of Chartres Cathedral, Chartres, France, ca. 1170, with 13th-century side panels. Stained glass, full height 16′.

This stained-glass window miraculously survived the devastating Chartres fire of 1194. It has an armature of iron bands that forms a grid over the whole design, an Early Gothic characteristic.

roundel at the center of the rose, which resembles a gem-studded book cover or cloisonné brooch. Around her are four doves of the Holy Spirit and eight angels. Twelve square panels contain images of Old Testament kings, including David and Solomon (at the 12 and 1 o'clock positions respectively). These are the royal ancestors of Christ. Isaiah (11:1–3) had prophesied that the Messiah would come from the family of the patriarch Jesse, father of David. The genealogical "tree of Jesse" is a familiar motif in medieval art. Below, in the lancets, are Saint Anne and the baby Virgin. Flanking them are four of Christ's Old Testament ancestors, Melchizedek, David, Solomon, and Aaron, echoing the royal genealogy of the rose but at a larger scale. Many Gothic stained-glass windows also present narrative scenes, and their iconographical programs are sometimes as complex as those of the sculptured church portals.

The rose and lancets change in hue and intensity with the hours, turning solid architecture into a floating vision of the celestial heavens. Almost the entire mass of wall opens up into stained glass, held in place by an intricate stone armature of bar tracery. Here, the

Stained-Glass Windows

Although not a Gothic invention, *stained-glass* windows are almost synonymous with Gothic architecture. No other age produced windows of such rich color and beauty. The technology of manufacturing colored glass is very old, however. Egyptian artists excelled at fashioning colorful glass objects for both home and tomb, and archaeologists have also uncovered thousands of colored-glass artifacts at classical sites. But Gothic artists used stained glass in new ways. In earlier eras, the clergy introduced color and religious iconography into church interiors with mural paintings and mosaics, often with magnificent effect. Stained-glass windows differ from those techniques in one all-important respect. They do not conceal walls. They replace them. And they transmit rather than reflect light, filtering and transforming the natural sunlight.

Abbot Suger called this colored light *lux nova* (see "Abbot Suger," page 463). Suger's contemporary, Hugh of Saint-Victor (1096–1142), a prominent Parisian theologian, also commented on the special mystical quality of stained-glass windows: "Stained-glass windows are the Holy Scriptures . . . and since their brilliance lets the splendor of the True Light pass into the church, they enlighten those inside." * William Durandus, bishop of Mende, expressed a similar sentiment at the end of the 13th century: "The glass windows in a church are Holy Scriptures, which expel the wind and the rain, that is, all things hurtful, but transmit the light of the True Sun, that is, God, into the hearts of the faithful." † As early as the fourth century, architects used colored glass for church windows, and the stained-glass windows of Saint-Denis (FIG. 18-3) already show a high degree of skill. According to Suger, they were "painted by the exquisite hands of many masters from different regions," ‡ proving that the art was well established at that time. In fact, several fine Romanesque examples survive.

The manufacture of stained-glass windows was costly and labor-intensive. A Benedictine monk named Theophilus recorded the full process around 1100. First, the master designer drew the exact composition of the planned window on a wooden panel, indicating all the linear details and noting the colors for each section. Glassblowers provided flat sheets of glass of different colors to *glaziers* (glassworkers), who cut the windowpanes to the required size and shape with special iron shears. Glaziers produced an even greater range of colors by *flashing* (fusing one layer of colored glass to another). Next, painters added details such as faces, hands, hair, and clothing in enamel by tracing the master design on the wood panel through the colored glass. Then they heated the painted glass to fuse the enamel to the surface. At that point, the glaziers "leaded" the various fragments of glass—that is, they joined them by strips of lead called *cames*. The *leading* not only held the pieces together but also separated the colors to heighten the effect of the design as a whole. The

Detail of stained-glass rose window, north transept Chartres Cathedral, Chartres, France, ca. 1220 (see FIG. 18-1).

distinctive character of Gothic stained-glass windows is largely the result of this combination of fine linear details with broad flat expanses of color framed by black lead. Finally, the glassworkers strengthened the completed window with an armature of iron bands, which in the 12th century formed a grid over the whole design (FIG. 18-16). In the 13th century, the bands followed the outlines of the medallions and of the surrounding areas (FIGS. 18-1 and 18-25).

The form of the stone frames for the stained-glass windows also evolved. On Chartres Cathedral's 12th-century west facade (FIG. 18-5), *plate tracery* holds the rose window in place. The glass fills only the "punched holes" in the heavy ornamental stonework. *Bar tracery*, a later development, is much more slender. The 13th-century stained-glass windows (FIG. 18-1) of the Chartres transepts fill almost the entire opening, and the stonework is unobtrusive, more like delicate leading than masonry wall.

* Hugh of Saint-Victor, *Speculum de mysteriis ecclesiae*, Sermon 2.
† William Durandus, *Rationale divinorum officiorum*, 1.1.24. Translated by John Mason Neale and Benjamin Webb, *The Symbolism of Churches and Church Ornaments* (Leeds: T. W. Green, 1843), 28.
‡ Translated by Erwin Panofsky, *Abbot Suger*, 73.

Gothic passion for luminous colored light led to a most daring and successful attempt to subtract all superfluous material bulk just short of destabilizing the structure. That this vast, complex fabric of stone-set glass has maintained its structural integrity for almost 800 years attests to the Gothic builders' engineering genius.

CHARTRES SOUTH TRANSEPT The sculptures adorning the portals of the two new Chartres transepts erected after the 1194

fire are also prime examples of the new High Gothic spirit. As at Laon (FIG. 18-8) and Paris (FIG. 18-11), the Chartres transept portals project more forcefully from the church than do the Early Gothic portals of its west facade (compare FIGS. 18-5 and 18-13). Similarly, the statues of saints on the portal jambs are more independent of the architectural framework. Three figures (FIG. 18-17) from the Porch of the Confessors in the south transept reveal the great changes Gothic sculpture underwent since the Royal Portal statues (FIG. 18-7) of the

18-17 Saints Martin, Jerome, and Gregory, jamb statues, Porch of the Confessors (right doorway), south transept, Chartres Cathedral, Chartres, France, ca. 1220–1230.

In contrast to the Royal Portal statues (FIG. 18-7), the south-transept statues have individual personalities and turn slightly to left or right, breaking the rigid vertical lines of their 12th-century predecessors.

18-18 Saint Theodore, jamb statue, Porch of the Martyrs (left doorway), south transept, Chartres Cathedral, Chartres, France, ca. 1230.

Although the statue of Theodore is still attached to a column, the setting no longer determines its pose. The High Gothic sculptor portrayed the saint swinging out one hip, as in Greek statuary (FIG. 5-40).

mid-12th century. These changes recall in many ways the revolutionary developments in ancient Greek sculpture during the transition from the Archaic to the Classical style (see Chapter 5). The south-transept statues date from 1220 to 1230 and represent Saints Martin, Jerome, and Gregory. Although the figures are still attached to columns, the architectural setting does not determine their poses as much as it did on the west portals. The saints communicate quietly with one another, like waiting dignitaries. They turn slightly toward and away from each other, breaking the rigid vertical lines that fix the Royal Portal figures immovably. The drapery folds are not stiff and shallow vertical accents, as on the west facade. The fabric falls and laps over the bodies in soft, if still regular, folds.

The treatment of the faces is even more remarkable. The sculptor gave the figures individualized features and distinctive personalities and clothed them in the period's liturgical costumes. Saint Martin is a tall, intense priest with gaunt features (compare the spiritually moved but not particularized face of the Moissac prophet in FIG. 17-11). Saint Jerome appears as a kindly, practical administrator-scholar, holding his copy of the Scriptures. At the right, the introspective Saint Gregory seems lost in thought as he listens to the dove

of the Holy Ghost on his shoulder. Thus, the sculptor did not contrast the three men simply in terms of their poses, gestures, and attributes but as persons. Personality, revealed in human faces, makes the profound difference.

The south-transept figure of Saint Theodore (FIG. 18-18), the martyred warrior on the Porch of the Martyrs, presents an even sharper contrast with Early Gothic jamb statues. The sculptor portrayed Theodore as the ideal Christian knight and clothed him in the cloak and chain-mail armor of Gothic Crusaders. The handsome, long-haired youth holds his spear firmly in his right hand and rests his left hand on his shield. He turns his head to the left and swings out his hip to the right. The body's resulting torsion and pronounced sway call to mind Greek statuary, especially the contrapposto stance of Polykleitos's *Spear Bearer* (FIG. 5-40). The changes that occurred in 13th-century Gothic sculpture could appropriately be labeled a second "Classical revolution."

18-19 ROBERT DE LUZARCHES, THOMAS DE CORMONT, and RENAUD DE CORMONT, interior of Amiens Cathedral (looking east), Amiens, France, begun 1220. ▶

The concept of a self-sustaining skeletal architecture reached full maturity at Amiens Cathedral. The four-part High Gothic vaults on pointed arches rise an astounding 144 feet above the nave floor.

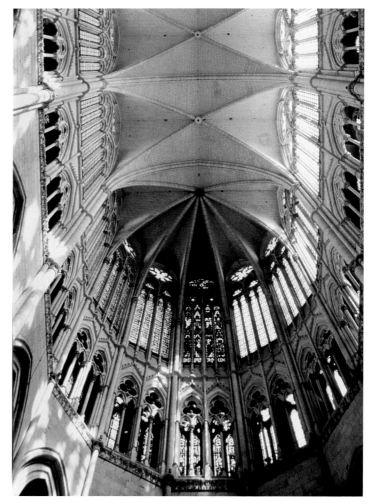

18-20 ROBERT DE LUZARCHES, THOMAS DE CORMONT, and RENAUD DE CORMONT, vaults, clerestory, and triforium of the choir of Amiens Cathedral, Amiens, France, begun 1220.

The Amiens choir vaults resemble a canopy suspended from bundled masts. The sunlight entering from the clerestory creates the effect of a buoyant lightness not normally associated with stone architecture.

AMIENS CATHEDRAL Chartres Cathedral was one of the most influential buildings in the history of architecture. Its builders set a pattern that many other Gothic architects followed, even if they refined the details. Construction of Amiens Cathedral (FIGS. **18-19** to **18-21**) began in 1220, while work was still in progress at Chartres. The architects were ROBERT DE LUZARCHES, THOMAS DE CORMONT, and RENAUD DE CORMONT. The builders finished the nave by 1236 and the radiating chapels by 1247, but work on the choir continued until almost 1270. The Amiens elevation (FIGS. **18-10***d* and **18-19**) derived from the High Gothic formula of Chartres (FIGS. **18-10***c* and **18-15**). But Amiens Cathedral's proportions are even more elegant, and the number and complexity of the lancet windows in both its clerestory and triforium are even greater. The whole design reflects the builders' confident use of the complete High Gothic structural vocabulary: the rectangular-bay system, the four-part rib vault, and a buttressing system that permitted almost complete dissolution of heavy masses and thick weight-bearing walls. At Amiens, the concept of a self-sustaining skeletal architecture reached full maturity. The remaining stretches of wall seem to serve no purpose other than to provide a weather screen for the interior (FIG. **18-20**).

Amiens Cathedral is one of the most impressive examples of the French Gothic obsession with constructing ever taller churches. Using their new skeletal frames of stone, French builders attempted goals almost beyond limit, pushing to new heights with increasingly slender supports. The nave vaults at Laon rise to a height of about 80 feet, at Paris 107 feet, and at Chartres 118 feet. Those at Amiens are 144 feet above the floor (FIG. **18-10**). The tense, strong lines of the Amiens vault ribs converge at the colonnettes and speed down the shell-like walls to the compound piers. Almost every part of the superstructure has its corresponding element below. The overall effect is of effortless strength, of a buoyant lightness not normally associated with stone architecture. Viewed directly from below, the choir vaults (FIG. **18-20**) seem like a canopy, tentlike and suspended from bundled masts. The light flooding in from the clerestory makes the vaults seem even more insubstantial. The effect recalls another great building, one utterly different from Amiens but where light also plays a defining role: Hagia Sophia (FIG. **12-4**) in Constantinople. Once again, the designers reduced the building's physical mass by structural ingenuity and daring, and light further dematerializes what remains. If Hagia Sophia is the perfect expression of Byzantine spirituality in architecture, Amiens, with its soaring vaults and giant windows admitting divine colored light, is its Gothic counterpart.

Work began on the Amiens west facade (FIG. **18-21**) at the same time as the nave (1220). Its lower parts reflect the influence of Laon

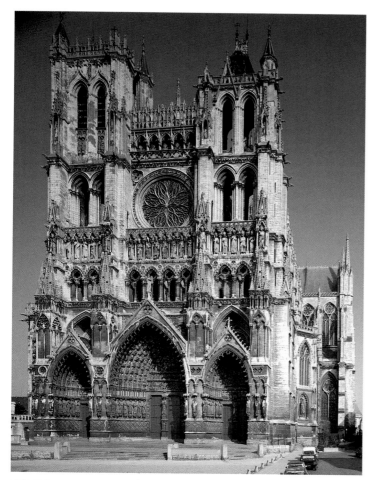

18-21 ROBERT DE LUZARCHES, THOMAS DE CORMONT, and RENAUD DE CORMONT, west facade of Amiens Cathedral, Amiens, France, begun 1220.

The deep piercing of the Amiens facade left few surfaces for decoration, but sculptors covered the remaining ones with colonnettes, pinnacles, and rosettes that nearly dissolve the structure's solid core.

18-22 Christ (*Beau Dieu*), trumeau statue of central doorway, west facade, Amiens Cathedral, Amiens, France, ca. 1220–1235.

The *Beau Dieu* is a kindly figure who blesses all who enter Amiens Cathedral. He tramples a lion and dragon symbolizing the evil forces in the world. The Gothic Christ gives humankind hope in salvation.

Cathedral (FIG. 18-8) in the spacing of the funnel-like and gable-covered portals. But the Amiens builders punctured the upper parts of the facade to an even greater degree than did the Laon designer. The deep piercing of walls and towers at Amiens left few surfaces for decoration, but sculptors covered the ones that remained with a network of colonnettes, arches, pinnacles, rosettes, and other decorative stonework that visually screens and nearly dissolves the structure's solid core. Sculpture also extends to the areas above the portals, especially the band of statues (the so-called kings' gallery) running the full width of the facade directly below the rose window (with 15th-century tracery). The uneven towers were later additions. The shorter one dates from the 14th century, the taller one from the 15th century.

BEAU DIEU The most prominent statue on the Amiens facade is the *Beau Dieu* (Beautiful God; FIG. **18-22**) on the central doorway's trumeau. The sculptor fully modeled Christ's figure, enveloping his body with massive drapery folds cascading from his waist. The statue stands freely and is as independent of its architectural setting as any Gothic facade statue ever was. Nonetheless, the sculptor still placed an architectural canopy over Christ's head. It is in the latest Gothic style, mimicking the east end of a 13th-century cathedral having a series of radiating chapels with elegant lancet windows. Above the canopy is the great central tympanum with the representation of Christ as Last Judge. The *Beau Dieu*, however, is a handsome, kindly

figure who does not strike terror into sinners. Instead he blesses those who enter the church and tramples a lion and a dragon symbolizing the evil forces in the world. This image of Christ gives humankind hope in salvation. The *Beau Dieu* epitomizes the bearded, benevolent Gothic image of Christ that replaced the youthful Early Christian Christ (FIG. 11-8) and the stern Byzantine Pantokrator (FIGS. 12-1 and 12-25) as the preferred representation of the Savior in later European art. The figure's quiet grace and grandeur also contrast sharply with the emotional intensity of the twisting Romanesque prophet (FIG. 17-11) carved in relief on the Moissac trumeau.

The facade of Reims Cathedral displays the High Gothic architect's desire to reduce sheer mass and replace it with intricately framed voids. Stained-glass windows, not stone reliefs, fill the tympana.

18-23A Nave, Reims Cathedral, begun 1211.

REIMS CATHEDRAL Construction of Reims Cathedral (FIG. **18-23**), where the coronations of the kings of France took place, began only a few years after work commenced at Amiens. The Reims builders carried the High Gothic style of the Amiens west facade still further, both architecturally and sculpturally. The two facades, although similar, display some significant differences. The kings' gallery of statues at Reims is above the great rose window, and the figures stand in taller and more ornate frames. In fact, the designer "stretched" every detail of the facade. The openings in the towers and those to the left and right of the rose window are taller, narrower, and more intricately decorated, and they more closely resemble the elegant lancets of the clerestory within. A pointed arch also frames the rose window itself, and the pinnacles over the portals are taller and more elaborate than those at Amiens. Most striking, however, is the treatment of the tympana over the doorways, where stained-glass windows replaced the stone relief sculpture of earlier facades. The contrast with Romanesque heavy masonry construction (FIG. 17-30) is extreme. But no less noteworthy is the rapid transformation of the Gothic facade since the 12th-century designs of Saint-Denis and Chartres (FIG. **18-5**) and even Laon (FIG. **18-8**).

Reims Cathedral is also a prime example of the High Gothic style in sculpture. The statues and reliefs of the west facade celebrate the Virgin Mary. Above the central gable, Mary is crowned as Queen of Heaven. On the trumeau, she appears in her role as the New Eve above reliefs depicting the Original Sin. The jamb statues relate episodes from the Infancy cycle (see "The Life of Jesus in Art," Chapter 11, pages 296–297), including the *Annunciation* and *Visitation* (FIG. **18-24**). All four illustrated statues appear to be completely detached from their architectural background. The sculptors shrank the supporting columns into insignificance so that they in no way restrict the free and easy movements of the full-bodied figures. These 13th-century statue-columns contrast strikingly with those of the Early Gothic Royal Portal (FIG. **18-7**), where the background columns occupy a volume equal to that of the figures.

The Reims statues also vividly illustrate that the sculptural ornamentation of Gothic cathedrals took decades to complete and required many sculptors often working in diverse styles. Art historians believe that three different sculptors carved the four statues in FIG. 18-24 at different times during the quarter century from 1230 to 1255. The *Visitation* group (FIG. 18-24, *right*) is the work of an artist who probably studied classical statuary. Reims was an ancient Roman city, and the heads of both Mary and Saint Elizabeth resemble Roman portraits. The Gothic statues are astonishing approximations of the classical naturalistic style and incorporate contrapposto postures that go far beyond the stance of the Chartres Saint Theodore (FIG. 18-18). The swaying of the hips is much more pronounced. The right legs bend, and the knees press through the rippling folds of the garments. The sculptor also set the figures' arms in motion. Mary and Elizabeth turn their faces toward each other, and they converse through gestures. In the Reims *Visitation* group, the formerly isolated Gothic jamb statues became actors in a biblical narrative.

The *Annunciation* group (FIG. 18-24, *left*) also features statues liberated from their architectural setting, but they are products of

18-24 *Annunciation* and *Visitation*, jamb statues of central doorway, west facade, Reims Cathedral, Reims, France, ca. 1230–1255.

Different sculptors working in diverse styles carved the Reims jamb statues, but all detached their figures from the columns and set the bodies and arms in motion. The figures converse through gestures.

different workshops and one—the angel Gabriel—was first set in the left portal and then moved to its present location, which explains the stylistic dichotomy of the pair. Mary is a slender figure with severe drapery. The artist preferred broad expanses of fabric to the multiplicity of folds of the *Visitation* Mary. Gabriel, the latest of the four statues, has a much more elongated body and is far more animated. He exhibits the elegant style of the Parisian court at the middle of the 13th century. He pivots gracefully, almost as if dancing, and smiles broadly. Like a courtier, he exudes charm. Mary, in contrast, is serious and introspective and does not respond overtly to the news the angel has brought.

SAINTE-CHAPELLE, PARIS The stained-glass windows inserted into the portal tympana of Reims Cathedral exemplify the wall-dissolving High Gothic architectural style. The architect of Sainte-Chapelle (FIG. 18-25) in Paris extended this style to an entire building. Louis IX built Sainte-Chapelle, joined to the royal palace, as a repository for the crown of thorns and other relics of Christ's Passion he had purchased in 1239 from his cousin Baldwin II (r. 1228–1261), the last Latin emperor of Constantinople. The chapel is a masterpiece of the so-called *Rayonnant* (radiant) style of the High Gothic age, which dominated the second half of the century. It was the preferred style of the royal Parisian court of Saint Louis (see "Louis IX, the Saintly King," page 482). Sainte-Chapelle's architect carried the dissolution of walls and the reduction of the bulk of the supports to the point that some 6,450 square feet of stained glass make up more

5A Santa
a, León,
in 1254.

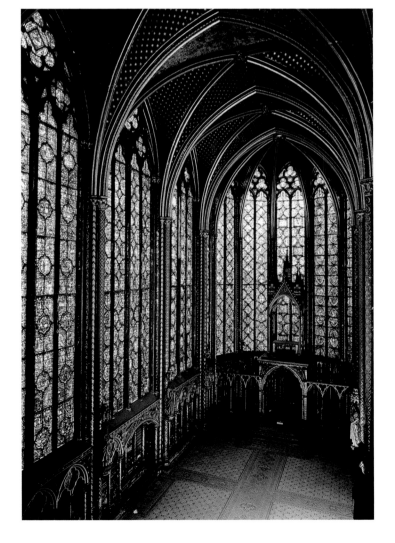

18-25 Interior of the upper chapel (looking northeast), Sainte-Chapelle, Paris, France, 1243–1248. ◼◀

At Louis IX's Sainte-Chapelle, the architect succeeded in dissolving the walls to such an extent that 6,450 square feet of stained glass account for more than three-quarters of the Rayonnant Gothic structure.

18-26 Virgin and Child (*Virgin of Paris*), Notre-Dame, Paris, France, early 14th century.

Late Gothic sculpture is elegant and mannered. Here, the solemnity of Early and High Gothic religious figures gave way to a tender and anecdotal portrayal of Mary and Jesus as royal mother and son.

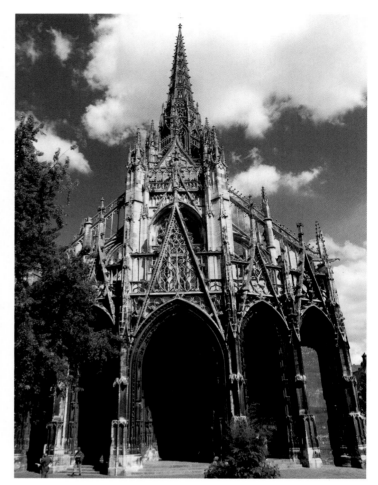

18-27 West facade of Saint-Maclou, Rouen, France, ca. 1500–1514.

Saint-Maclou is the masterpiece of Late Gothic Flamboyant architecture. Its ornate tracery features curves and countercurves that form brittle decorative webs masking the building's structure.

than three-quarters of the structure. The supporting elements are hardly more than large *mullions,* or vertical stone bars. The emphasis is on the extreme slenderness of the architectural forms and on linearity in general. Although the chapel required restoration in the 19th century (after suffering damage during the French Revolution), it retains most of its original 13th-century stained glass. Sainte-Chapelle's enormous windows filter the light and fill the interior with an unearthly rose-violet atmosphere. Approximately 49 feet high and 15 feet wide, they were the largest designed up to their time.

VIRGIN OF PARIS The "court style" of Sainte-Chapelle has its pictorial parallel in the mannered elegance of the roughly contemporaneous Gabriel of the Reims *Annunciation* group (FIG. 18-24, *left*), but the style long outlived Saint Louis and his royal artists and architects. The best example of the court style in Late Gothic sculpture is the early-14th-century statue nicknamed the *Virgin of Paris* (FIG. 18-26) because of its location in Paris at Notre-Dame. The sculptor portrayed Mary in an exaggerated **S**-curve posture typical of Late Gothic sculpture. She is a worldly queen, decked out in royal garments and wearing

a heavy gem-encrusted crown. The Christ Child is equally richly attired and is very much the infant prince in the arms of his young mother. The tender, anecdotal characterization of mother and son represents a further humanization of the portrayal of religious figures in Gothic sculpture. Late Gothic statuary is very different in tone from the solemnity of most High Gothic figures, just as Late Classical Greek statues of the Olympian gods (compare FIG. 18-26 with FIG. 5-63) differ from High Classical depictions.

SAINT-MACLOU, ROUEN Late French Gothic architecture also represents a departure from the norms of High Gothic. The change from Rayonnant architecture to the so-called *Flamboyant* style (named for the flamelike appearance of its pointed bar tracery) occurred in the 14th century. The style reached its florid maturity nearly a century later in Normandy in the church of Saint-Maclou (FIG. 18-27) in Rouen, its capital. The church is tiny (only about 75 feet high and 180 feet long) compared with the cathedrals of the High Gothic age. Its facade breaks sharply from the High Gothic style (FIGS. 18-21 and 18-23) of the 13th century. The five portals (two of them false doors) bend outward in an arc. Ornate gables crown the doorways, pierced through and filled with wiry, "flickering" Flamboyant tracery made up of curves and countercurves that form brittle decorative webs and mask the building's structure. The transparency of the pinnacles over the doorways permits visitors to see the central rose window and the flying buttresses, even though they are set well back from the facade. The overlapping of all features, pierced as they are, confuses the structural lines and produces

18-28 Aerial view of the fortified town of Carcassonne, France. Bastions and towers, 12th–13th centuries, restored by EUGÈNE VIOLLET-LE-DUC in the 19th century.

Carcassonne provides a rare glimpse of what was once a familiar sight in Gothic France: a tight complex of castle, cathedral, and town with a crenellated and towered wall circuit for defense.

a bewildering complexity of views that is the hallmark of the Flamboyant style.

CARCASSONNE The Gothic period has been called "the age of great cathedrals," but people, of course, also needed and architects also built secular structures such as town halls, palaces, and private residences. In an age of frequent warfare, the feudal barons often constructed fortified castles in places enemies could not easily reach. Sometimes thick defensive wall circuits, or *ramparts,* enclosed entire towns. In time, however, purely defensive wars became obsolete due to the invention of artillery and improvements in siege craft. The fortress era gradually passed, and throughout Europe once-mighty ramparts fell into ruin.

One of the most famous Gothic fortified towns is Carcassonne (FIG. **18-28**) in Languedoc in southern France. It was the regional center of resistance to the northern forces of royal France. Built on a hill bounded by the Aude River, Carcassonne had been fortified since Roman times. It had Visigothic walls dating from the 6th century, but in the 12th century masons reinforced them. *Battlements* (low parapets) with *crenellations* (composed of alternating solid *merlons* and open *crenels*) protected guards patrolling the stone ring surrounding the town. Carcassonne might be forced to surrender but could not easily be taken by storm. Within the town's double walls was a fortified castle (FIG. **18-28**, *left*) with a massive attached *keep,* a secure tower that could serve as a place of last refuge. Balancing that center of secular power was the bishop's seat, the Cathedral of Saint-Nazaire (FIG. **18-28**, *right*). The small church, built between 1269 and 1329, may have been the work of an architect brought in from northern France. In any case, Saint-Nazaire's builders were certainly familiar with the latest developments in architecture in the Île-de-France. Today, Carcassonne—as restored in the 19th century by EUGÈNE VIOLLET-LE-DUC (1814–1879)—provides a rare glimpse of what was once a familiar sight in Gothic France: a tightly contained complex of castle, cathedral, and town within towered walls.

GUILD HALL, BRUGES One of the many signs of the growing secularization of urban life in the late Middle Ages was the erection of monumental meeting halls and warehouses for the increasing number of craft guilds being formed throughout Europe. An early example is the imposing market and guild hall (FIG. **18-29**) of the

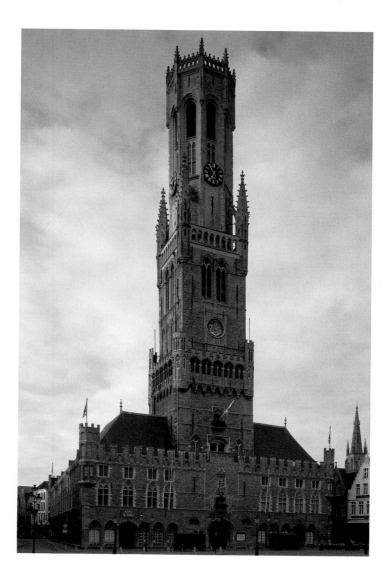

18-29 Hall of the cloth guild, Bruges, Belgium, begun 1230.

The Bruges cloth guild's meeting hall is an early example of a new type of secular architecture in the late Middle Ages. Its lofty tower competed for attention with the towers of the city's cathedral.

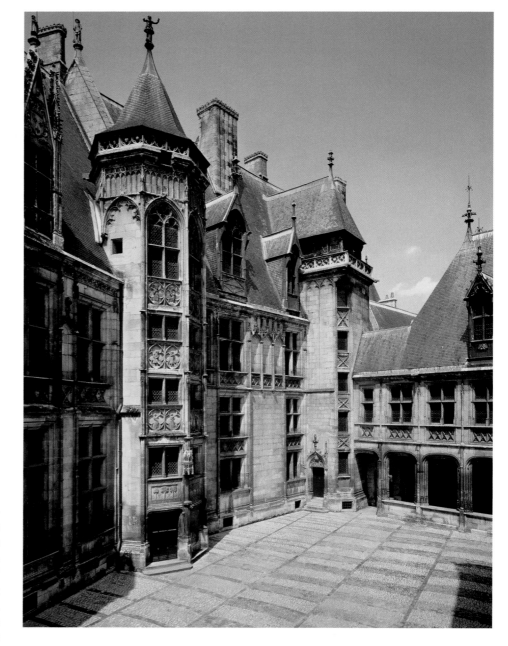

18-30 House of Jacques Coeur, Bourges, France, 1443–1451.

The house of the immensely wealthy Bourges financier Jacques Coeur is both a splendid example of Late Gothic architecture with elaborate tracery and a symbol of the period's new secular spirit.

clothmakers of Bruges, begun in 1230. Situated in the city's major square, it testifies to the important role of artisans and merchants in Gothic Europe. The design combines features of military (the corner "watchtowers" with their crenellations) and church (lancet windows with crowning oculi) architecture. The uppermost, octagonal portion of the tower with its flying buttresses and pinnacles dates to the 15th century, but even the original two-story tower is taller than the rest of the hall. Lofty towers were a common feature of late medieval guild and town halls, designed to compete for attention and prestige with the towers of city cathedrals.

HOUSE OF JACQUES COEUR The fortunes of the new class of wealthy merchants who rose to prominence throughout Europe in the late Middle Ages may not have equaled those of the hereditary royalty, but their power and influence were still enormous. The career of the French financier Jacques Coeur (1395–1456) illustrates how enterprising private citizens could win—and quickly lose— wealth and power. Coeur had banking houses in every city of France and many cities abroad. He employed more than 300 agents and competed with the great trading republics of Italy. His merchant ships filled the Mediterranean, and with the papacy's permission, he imported spices and textiles from the Muslim Near East. He was the treasurer of King Charles VII (r. 1422–1461) of France and a friend of Pope Nicholas V (r. 1447–1455). In 1451, however, his enemies framed him on an absurd charge of having poisoned Agnes Sorel, the king's mistress. The judges who sentenced Coeur to prison and confiscated his vast wealth and property were among those who

owed him money. Coeur escaped in 1454 and made his way to Rome, where the pope warmly received him. He died of fever while leading a fleet of papal war galleys in the eastern Mediterranean.

Jacques Coeur's great town house still stands in his native city of Bourges. Built between 1443 and 1451 (with special permission to encroach upon the town ramparts), it is the best-preserved example of Late Gothic domestic architecture. The house's plan is irregular, with the units arranged around an open courtyard (FIG. **18-30**). The service areas (maintenance shops, storage rooms, servants' quarters, and baths—a rare luxury in Gothic Europe) occupy the ground level. The upper stories house the great hall and auxiliary rooms used for offices and family living rooms. Over the main entrance is a private chapel. One of the towers served as a treasury. The exterior and interior facades have very steep pyramidal roofs of different heights. The decorative details include Flamboyant tracery and large pointed-arch stained-glass windows. An elegant canopied niche facing the street once housed a royal equestrian statue. A comparable statue of Coeur on horseback dominated the facade opening onto the interior courtyard. Jacques Coeur's house is both a splendid example of Late Gothic architecture and a monumental symbol of the period's new secular spirit.

Book Illumination and Luxury Arts

Paris's claim as the intellectual center of Gothic Europe (see "Scholasticism," page 466) did not rest solely on the stature of its university faculty and on the reputation of its architects, masons, sculptors, and stained-glass makers. The city was also a renowned center for the production of fine books. The famous Florentine poet Dante Alighieri (1265–1321), in fact, referred to Paris in his *Divine Comedy* of about 1310–1320 as the city famed for the art of illumination.[2] During the Gothic period, book manufacture shifted from monastic scriptoria shut off from the world to urban workshops of professional artists—and Paris had the most and best workshops. The owners of these new, for-profit secular businesses sold their products to the royal family, scholars, and prosperous merchants. The Parisian shops were the forerunners of modern publishing houses.

VILLARD DE HONNECOURT One of the most intriguing Parisian manuscripts preserved today was not, however, a book for sale but a personal sketchbook. Compiled by VILLARD DE HONNECOURT, an early-13th-century master mason, its pages contain details of buildings, plans of choirs with radiating chapels, church towers, lifting devices, a sawmill, stained-glass windows, and other subjects of obvious interest to architects and masons. But also sprinkled liberally throughout the pages are drawings depicting religious and worldly figures, as well as animals, some realistic and others purely fantastic. On the page reproduced here (FIG. 18-31), Villard demonstrated the value of the *ars de geometria* ("art of geometry") to artists. He showed that both natural forms and buildings are based on simple geometric shapes such as the square, circle, and triangle. Even where he claimed to have drawn his animals from nature, he composed his figures around a skeleton not of bones but of abstract geometric forms. Geometry was, in Villard's words, "strong help in drawing figures."

GOD AS ARCHITECT Geometry also played a symbolic role in Gothic art and architecture. Gothic artists, architects, and theologians alike thought the triangle, for example, embodied the idea of the Trinity of God the Father, Christ, and the Holy Spirit. The circle, which has neither a beginning nor an end, symbolized the eternity of the one God. When Gothic architects based their designs on the art of geometry, building their forms out of abstract shapes laden with symbolic meaning, they believed they were working according to the divinely established laws of nature.

A vivid illustration of this concept appears as the frontispiece (FIG. 18-32) of a moralized Bible produced in Paris during the

18-31 VILLARD DE HONNECOURT, figures based on geometric shapes, folio 18 verso of a sketchbook, from Paris, France, ca. 1220–1235. Ink on vellum, $9\frac{1}{4}" \times 6"$. Bibliothèque Nationale, Paris.

On this page from his private sketchbook, the master mason Villard de Honnecourt sought to demonstrate that simple geometric shapes are the basis of both natural forms and buildings.

18-32 God as architect of the world, folio 1 verso of a moralized Bible, from Paris, France, ca. 1220–1230. Ink, tempera, and gold leaf on vellum, $1' 1\frac{1}{2}" \times 8\frac{1}{4}"$. Österreichische Nationalbibliothek, Vienna.

Paris was the intellectual capital of Europe and the center of production of fine books. This artist portrayed God as an industrious architect creating the universe using the same tools as Gothic builders.

Louis IX, the Saintly King

The royal patron behind the Parisian Rayonnant "court style" of Gothic art and architecture was King Louis IX (1214–1270; r. 1226–1270), grandson of Philip Augustus. Louis inherited the throne when he was only 12 years old, so until he reached adulthood six years later, his mother, Blanche of Castile (FIG. 18-33), granddaughter of Eleanor of Aquitaine (see "Romanesque Countesses, Queens, and Nuns," Chapter 17, page 448), served as France's regent.

The French regarded Louis as the ideal king, and 27 years after Louis's death, in 1297, Pope Boniface VIII (r. 1294–1303) declared him a saint. In his own time, Louis was revered for his piety, justice, truthfulness, and charity. His almsgiving and his donations to religious foundations were extravagant. He especially favored the *mendicant* (begging) orders, the Dominicans and Franciscans. He admired their poverty, piety, and self-sacrificing disregard of material things.

Louis launched two unsuccessful Crusades, the Seventh (1248–1254, when, in her son's absence, Blanche was again French regent) and the Eighth (1270). He died in Tunisia during the latter. As a crusading knight who lost his life in the service of the Church, Louis personified the chivalric virtues of courage, loyalty, and self-sacrifice. Saint Louis united in his person the best qualities of the Christian knight, the benevolent monarch, and the holy man. He became the model of medieval Christian kingship.

Louis's political accomplishments were also noteworthy. He subdued the unruly French barons, and between 1243 and 1314 no one seriously challenged the crown. He negotiated a treaty with Henry III, king of France's traditional enemy, England. Such was his reputation for integrity and just dealing that he served as arbiter in at least a dozen international disputes. So successful was he as peacekeeper

18-33 Blanche of Castile, Louis IX, and two monks, dedication page (folio 8 recto) of a moralized Bible, from Paris, France, 1226–1234. Ink, tempera, and gold leaf on vellum, 1′ 3″ × 10½″. Pierpont Morgan Library, New York.

The costly gold-leaf dedication page of this royal book depicts Saint Louis, his mother Blanche of Castile, and two monks. The younger monk is at work on the paired illustrations of a moralized Bible.

1 in.

that despite civil wars through most of the 13th century, international peace prevailed. Under Saint Louis, medieval France was at its most prosperous, and its art and architecture were admired and imitated throughout Europe.

1220s. *Moralized Bibles* are heavily illustrated, each page pairing paintings of Old and New Testament episodes with explanations of their moral significance. (The page reproduced here does not conform to this formula because it is the introduction to all that follows.) Above the illustration, the scribe wrote (in French rather than Latin): "Here God creates heaven and earth, the sun and moon, and all the elements." God appears as the architect of the world, shaping the universe with the aid of a compass. Within the perfect circle already created are the spherical sun and moon and the unformed matter that will become the earth once God applies the same geometric principles to it. In contrast to the biblical account of Creation, in which God created the sun, moon, and stars after the earth had been formed, and made the world by sheer force of will and a simple "Let there be" command, on this page the Gothic artist portrayed God as an industrious architect, creating the universe with some of the same tools mortal builders used.

BLANCHE OF CASTILE Not surprisingly, most of the finest Gothic books known today belonged to the French monarchy. Saint Louis in particular was an avid collector of both secular and religious books. The vast library he and his royal predecessors and successors formed eventually became the core of France's national library, the Bibliothèque Nationale. One of the books the royal family commissioned is a moralized Bible now in the collection of New York's Pierpont Morgan Library. Louis's mother, Blanche of Castile, ordered the Bible during her regency (1226–1234) for her teenage son. The dedication page (FIG. 18-33) has a costly gold background and depicts Blanche and Louis enthroned beneath triple-lobed arches and miniature cityscapes. The latter are comparable to the architectural canopies above the heads of contemporaneous French portal statues (FIG. 18-22). Below, in similar architectural frames, are a monk and a scribe. The older clergyman dictates a sacred text to

18-34 Abraham and the three angels, folio 7 verso of the *Psalter of Saint Louis*, from Paris, France, 1253–1270. Ink, tempera, and gold leaf on vellum, 5″ × 3½″. Bibliothèque Nationale, Paris.

The architectural settings in the *Psalter of Saint Louis* reflect the screenlike lightness and transparency of royal buildings such as Sainte-Chapelle (FIG. 18-25). The colors emulate those of stained glass.

1 in.

can add initials and signs of division. Still another can arrange the leaves and attach the binding. Another of you can prepare the covers, the leather, the buckles and clasps. All sorts of assistance can be offered the scribe to help him pursue his work without interruption. He needs many things which can be prepared by others: parchment cut, flattened and ruled for script, ready ink and pens. You will always find something with which to help the scribe.[3]

The preparation of the illuminated pages also involved several hands. Some artists, for example, specialized in painting borders or initials. Only the workshop head or one of the most advanced assistants would paint the main figural scenes. Given this division of labor and the assembly-line nature of Gothic book production, it is astonishing how uniform the style is on a single page, as well as from page to page, in most illuminated manuscripts.

his young apprentice. The scribe already has divided his page into two columns of four roundels each, a format often used for the paired illustrations of moralized Bibles. The inspirations for such designs were probably the roundels of Gothic stained-glass windows (compare the borders of the *Belle Verrière* window, FIG. 18-16, at Chartres and the windows of Louis's own, later Sainte-Chapelle, FIG. 18-25).

The dedication page of Blanche of Castile's moralized Bible presents a very abbreviated portrayal of Gothic book production, similar to the view of a monastic scriptorium discussed earlier (FIG. 16-11). The manufacturing process used in the workshops of 13th-century Paris did not differ significantly from that of 10th-century Tábara. It involved many steps and numerous specialized artists, scribes, and assistants of varying skill levels. The Benedictine abbot Johannes Trithemius (1462–1516) described the way books were still made in his day in his treatise *In Praise of Scribes:*

If you do not know how to write, you still can assist the scribes in various ways. One of you can correct what another has written. Another can add the rubrics [headings] to the corrected text. A third

PSALTER OF SAINT LOUIS The golden background of Blanche's Bible is unusual and has no parallel in Gothic windows. But the radiance of stained glass probably inspired the glowing color of other 13th-century Parisian illuminated manuscripts. In some cases, masters in the same urban workshop produced both glass and books. Many art historians believe that the *Psalter of Saint Louis* (FIG. **18-34**) is one of several books produced in Paris for Louis IX by artists associated with those who made the stained glass for his Sainte-Chapelle. Certainly, the painted architectural setting in Louis's book of Psalms reflects the pierced screenlike lightness and transparency of royal Rayonnant buildings such as Sainte-Chapelle. The intense colors, especially the blues, emulate stained glass. The lines in the borders resemble leading. And the gables, pierced by rose windows with bar tracery, are standard Rayonnant architectural features.

The page from the *Psalter of Saint Louis* shown here (FIG. 18-34) represents Abraham and the three angels, the Old Testament story believed to prefigure the Christian Trinity (see "Jewish Subjects in Christian Art," Chapter 11, page 293). The Gothic artist included two episodes on the same page, separated by the tree of Mamre mentioned in the Bible. At the left, Abraham greets the three angels. In the other scene, he entertains them while his wife Sarah peers at them from a tent. The figures' delicate features and the linear wavy strands of their hair have parallels in Blanche of Castile's moralized Bible, as well as in Parisian stained glass. The elegant proportions, facial expressions, theatrical gestures, and swaying poses are characteristic of the Parisian court style admired throughout Europe. Compare, for example, the angel in the left foreground with the Gabriel statue (FIG. 18-24, *left*) of the Reims *Annunciation* group.

BREVIARY OF PHILIPPE LE BEL As in the Romanesque period, some Gothic manuscript illuminators signed their work. The names of others appear in royal accounts of payments made and similar official documents. One artist who produced books for the French court was MASTER HONORÉ, whose Parisian workshop was on the street known today as rue Boutebrie. Honoré illuminated a breviary (see "Medieval Books," Chapter 16, page 411) for Philippe le Bel (Philip the Fair, r. 1285–1314) in 1296. The page illustrated here (FIG. 18-35) features two Old Testament scenes involving David. In the upper panel, Samuel anoints the youthful David. Below, while King Saul looks on, David prepares to aim his slingshot at his most famous opponent, the giant Goliath (who already touches the wound on his forehead). Immediately to the right, David slays Goliath with his sword.

Master Honoré's linear treatment of hair, his figures' delicate hands and gestures, and their elegant swaying postures are typical of Parisian painting of the time. But this painter was much more interested than most of his colleagues in giving his figures sculptural volume and showing the play of light on their bodies. Honoré was not concerned with locating his figures in space, however. The Goliath panel in the *Breviary of Philippe le Bel* has a textilelike decorative background, and the feet of Honoré's figures frequently overlap the border. Compared with his contemporaries, Master Honoré pioneered naturalism in figure painting. But he still approached the art of book illumination as a decorator of two-dimensional pages. He did not embrace the classical notion that a painting should be an illusionistic window into a three-dimensional world.

18-36A PUCELLE, *Hours of Jeanne d'Evreux,* ca. 1325–1328.

BELLEVILLE BREVIARY David and Saul also are the subjects of a miniature painting at the top left of an elaborately decorated text page (FIG. 18-36) in the *Belleville Breviary,* which JEAN PUCELLE of Paris painted around 1325. Pucelle far exceeded Honoré and other French artists by placing his fully modeled figures in three-dimensional architectural settings rendered in convincing perspective. For example, he painted Saul as a weighty figure seated on a throne seen in a three-quarter view, and he meticulously depicted the receding coffers of the barrel vault over the young David's head. Such "stage sets" already had become commonplace in Italian painting, and scholars think Pucelle visited Italy and studied Duccio's work (FIGS. 19-10 and 19-11) in Siena. Pucelle's (or an assistant's) renditions of plants, a bird, butterflies, a dragonfly, a fish, a snail, and a monkey also reveal a keen interest in and close observation of the natural world. Nonetheless, in the *Belleville Breviary,* the text still dominates the figures, and the artist (and his patron) delighted in ornamental flourishes, fancy initial letters, and abstract patterns. In that respect, comparisons with monumental panel paintings are inappropriate. Pucelle's breviary remains firmly in the tradition of book illumination.

The *Belleville Breviary* is of special interest because Pucelle's name and those of some of his assistants appear at the end of the book, in a memorandum recording the payment they received for their work. Inscriptions in other Gothic illuminated books regularly state the production costs—the prices paid for materials, especially gold, and for the execution of initials, figures, flowery script, and

18-35 MASTER HONORÉ, David anointed by Samuel and battle of David and Goliath, folio 7 verso of the *Breviary of Philippe le Bel*, from Paris, France, 1296. Ink and tempera on vellum, $7\frac{7}{8}"\times 4\frac{7}{8}"$. Bibliothèque Nationale, Paris.

Master Honoré was one of the Parisian secular artists who produced books for the French monarchy. Notably, he gave his figures sculptural volume and showed the play of light on their bodies.

1 in.

other embellishments. By this time, illuminators were professional guild members, and their personal reputation, as with modern "brand names," guaranteed the quality of their work. Although the cost of materials was still the major factor determining a book's price, individual skill and reputation increasingly decided the value of the illuminator's services. The centuries-old monopoly of the Christian Church in book production had ended.

VIRGIN OF JEANNE D'EVREUX The royal family also patronized goldsmiths, silversmiths, and other artists specializing in the production of luxury works in metal and enamel for churches, palaces, and private homes. Especially popular were statuettes of sacred figures, which the wealthy purchased either for private devotion or as gifts to churches. The Virgin Mary was a favored subject, reflecting her new prominence in the iconography of Gothic portal sculpture.

1 in.

18-36 JEAN PUCELLE, *David before Saul,* folio 24 verso of the *Belleville Breviary,* from Paris, France, ca. 1325. Ink and tempera on vellum, $9\frac{1}{2}'' \times 6\frac{3}{4}''$. Bibliothèque Nationale, Paris.

Jean Pucelle's fully modeled figures in architectural settings rendered in convincing perspective reveal his study of contemporary painting in Italy. He was also a close observer of plants and fauna.

1 in.

18-37 *Virgin of Jeanne d'Evreux,* from the abbey church of Saint-Denis, France, 1339. Silver gilt and enamel, 2′ $3\frac{1}{2}''$ high. Louvre, Paris. ▣◀

Queen Jeanne d'Evreux donated this luxurious reliquary-statuette to the royal abbey church of Saint-Denis. The intimate human characterization of the holy figures recalls that of the *Virgin of Paris* (FIG. 18-26).

Perhaps the finest of these costly statuettes is the large silver-gilt figurine known as the *Virgin of Jeanne d'Evreux* (FIG. 18-37). The queen, wife of Charles IV (r. 1322–1328), donated the image of the Virgin and Child to the royal abbey church of Saint-Denis in 1339. Mary stands on a rectangular base decorated with enamel scenes of Christ's Passion. (Some art historians think the enamels are Jean Pucelle's work.) But no hint of grief appears in the beautiful young Mary's face. The Christ Child, also without a care in the world, playfully reaches for his mother. The elegant proportions of the two figures, Mary's emphatic swaying posture, the heavy drapery folds, and the intimate human characterization of mother and son are also features of the roughly contemporary *Virgin of Paris* (FIG. 18-26). The sculptor of large stone statues and the royal silversmith working at small scale approached the representation of the Virgin and Child in a similar fashion. In the *Virgin of Jeanne d'Evreux,* as in the *Virgin of Paris,* Mary appears not only as the Mother of Christ but also as the Queen of Heaven. The Saint-Denis Mary also originally had a crown on her head, and the scepter she holds is in the form of the fleur-de-lis, the French monarchy's floral emblem. The statuette also served

as a reliquary. The Virgin's scepter contained hairs believed to come from Mary's head.

THE CASTLE OF LOVE Gothic artists produced luxurious objects for secular as well as religious contexts. Sometimes they decorated these costly pieces with stories of courtly love inspired by the romantic literature of the day, such as the famous story of Lancelot and Queen Guinevere, wife of King Arthur of Camelot. The French poet Chrétien de Troyes recorded their love affair in the late 12th century.

18-38 The Castle of Love and knights jousting, lid of a jewelry casket, from Paris, France, ca. 1330–1350. Ivory and iron, $4\frac{1}{2}'' \times 9\frac{3}{4}''$. Walters Art Museum, Baltimore.

French Gothic artists also produced luxurious objects for secular use. This jewelry casket features ivory reliefs inspired by the romantic literature of the day in which knights joust and storm the Castle of Love.

1 in.

One of the most interesting objects of this type is a woman's jewelry box adorned with ivory relief panels. The theme of the panel illustrated here (FIG. 18-38) is related to the allegorical poem *Romance of the Rose* by Guillaume de Lorris, written about 1225–1235 and completed by Jean de Meung between 1275 and 1280. At the left the sculptor carved the allegory of the siege of the Castle of Love. Gothic knights attempt to capture love's fortress by shooting flowers from their bows and hurling baskets of roses over the walls from catapults. Among the castle's defenders is Cupid, who aims his arrow at one of the knights while a comrade scales the walls on a ladder. In the lid's two central sections, two knights joust on horseback. Several maidens survey the contest from a balcony and cheer the knights on, as trumpets blare. A youth in the crowd holds a hunting falcon. The sport was a favorite pastime of the leisure class in the late Middle Ages. At the right, the victorious knight receives his prize (a bouquet of roses) from a chastely dressed maiden on horseback. The scenes on the sides of the box include the famous medieval allegory of female virtue, the legend of the unicorn, a white horse with a single ivory horn. Only a virgin could attract the rare animal, and any woman who could do so thereby also demonstrated her moral purity. Religious themes may have monopolized artistic production for churches in the Gothic age, but secular themes figured prominently in private contexts. Unfortunately, very few examples of the latter survive.

GOTHIC OUTSIDE OF FRANCE

In 1269 the prior (deputy abbot) of the church of Saint Peter at Wimpfen-im-Tal in the German Rhineland hired "a very experienced architect who had recently come from the city of Paris" to rebuild his monastery church.[4] The architect reconstructed the church *opere francigeno* ("in the French manner")—that is, in the Gothic style, the *opus modernum* of the Île-de-France. The Parisian Gothic style had begun to spread even earlier, but in the second half of the 13th century, the new style became dominant throughout western Europe. European architecture did not turn Gothic all at once or even uniformly. Almost everywhere, patrons and builders modified the Rayonnant court style of the Île-de-France according to local preferences. Because the old Romanesque traditions lingered on in many places, each area, marrying its local Romanesque design to the new style, developed its own brand of Gothic architecture.

England

Beginning with the Norman conquest in 1066 (see Chapter 17), French architectural styles quickly made an impact in England, but in the Gothic period, as in the Romanesque, no one could have mistaken an English church for a French one.

SALISBURY CATHEDRAL Salisbury Cathedral (FIGS. **18-39** to **18-41**) embodies the essential characteristics of the English Gothic style. Begun in 1220, the same year work started on Amiens Cathedral (FIGS. **18-19** to **18-21**), construction of Salisbury Cathedral required about 40 years. The two cathedrals are therefore almost exactly contemporaneous, and the differences between them are very instructive. Although Salisbury's facade has lancet windows and blind arcades with pointed arches, as well as statuary, it presents a striking contrast to French High Gothic designs (FIGS. **18-21** and **18-23**). The English facade is a squat screen in front of the nave, wider than the building behind it. The soaring height of the French facades is absent. The Salisbury facade also does not correspond to

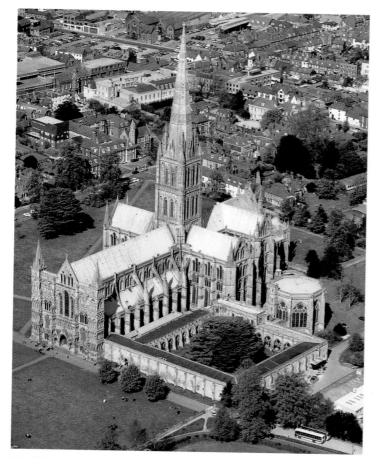

18-39 Aerial view of Salisbury Cathedral, Salisbury, England, 1220–1258; west facade completed 1265; spire ca. 1320–1330. �ణ◄

Exhibiting the distinctive regional features of English Gothic architecture, Salisbury Cathedral has a squat facade that is wider than the building behind it. The architects used flying buttresses sparingly.

18-41 Interior of Salisbury Cathedral (looking east), Salisbury, England, 1220–1258.

Salisbury Cathedral's interior differs from contemporaneous French Gothic designs in the strong horizontal emphasis of its three-story elevation and the use of dark Purbeck marble for moldings.

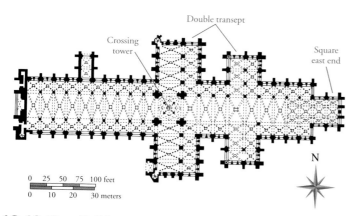

18-40 Plan of Salisbury Cathedral, Salisbury, England, 1220–1258.

The long rectilinear plan of Salisbury Cathedral, with its double transept and flat eastern end, is typically English. The four-part rib vaults of the nave follow the Chartres model (FIG. 18-14).

the three-part division of the interior (nave and two aisles). Different too is the emphasis on the great crossing tower (added about 1320–1330), which dominates the silhouette. Salisbury's height is modest compared with that of Amiens and Reims. And because height is not a decisive factor in the English building, the architect used the flying buttress sparingly and as a rigid prop, rather than as an integral part of the vaulting system within the church. In short, the English builders adopted some of the superficial motifs of French Gothic architecture but did not embrace its structural logic or emphasis on height.

Equally distinctive is the long rectilinear plan (FIG. 18-40) with its double transept and flat eastern end. The latter feature was characteristic of Cistercian (FIG. 17-14) and English churches since Romanesque times. The interior (FIG. 18-41), although Gothic in its three-story elevation, pointed arches, four-part rib vaults, compound piers, and the tracery of the triforium, conspicuously departs from the French Gothic style. The pier colonnettes stop at the springing of the nave arches and do not connect with the vault ribs (compare FIGS. 18-19 and 18-20). Instead, the vault ribs rise from corbels in the triforium, producing a strong horizontal emphasis. Underscoring this horizontality is the rich color contrast between the light stone of the walls and vaults and the dark Purbeck marble used for the triforium moldings and corbels, compound pier responds, and other details.

GLOUCESTER CATHEDRAL Early on, English architecture found its native language in the elaboration of architectural pattern for its own sake (for example, the decorative patterning of the Romanesque piers of Durham Cathedral; FIG. 17-33, *left*). The pier, wall, and vault elements, still relatively simple at Salisbury, became increasingly complex and decorative in the 14th century, culminating in what architectural historians call the *Perpendicular* style. This

18-42 Choir of Gloucester Cathedral (looking east), Gloucester, England, 1332–1357.

The Perpendicular style of English Late Gothic architecture takes its name from the pronounced verticality of its decorative details. The multiplication of ribs in the vaults is also a characteristic feature.

18-43 ROBERT and WILLIAM VERTUE, fan vaults of the chapel of Henry VII, Westminster Abbey, London, England, 1503–1519. ◼️◣

The chapel of Henry VII epitomizes the decorative and structure-disguising qualities of the Perpendicular style in the use of fan vaults with lacelike tracery and hanging pendants resembling stalactites.

late English Gothic style is on display in the choir (FIG. **18-42**) of Gloucester Cathedral, remodeled about a century after Salisbury. The Perpendicular style takes its name from the pronounced verticality of its decorative details, in contrast to the horizontal emphasis of Salisbury and Early English Gothic.

A single enormous window divided into tiers of small windows of like shape and proportion fills the characteristically flat east end of Gloucester Cathedral. At the top, two slender lancets flank a wider central section that also ends in a pointed arch. The design has much in common with the screen facade of Salisbury, but the proportions are different. Vertical, as opposed to horizontal, lines dominate. In the choir wall, the architect also erased Salisbury's strong horizontal accents, as the vertical wall elements lift directly from the floor to the vaulting, unifying the walls with the vaults in the French manner. The vault ribs, which designers had begun to multiply soon after Salisbury, are at Gloucester a dense thicket of entirely ornamental strands serving no structural purpose. The choir, in fact, does not have any rib vaults at all but a continuous Romanesque barrel vault with applied Gothic ornament. In the Gloucester choir, the taste for decorative surfaces triumphed over structural clarity.

CHAPEL OF HENRY VII The structure-disguising and decorative qualities of the Perpendicular style became even more pronounced in its late phases. A primary example is the early-16th-century ceiling (FIG. **18-43**) of the chapel of Henry VII (r. 1485–1509) adjoining Westminster Abbey in London. Here, ROBERT and WILLIAM VERTUE turned the earlier English linear play of ribs into a kind of ar-

chitectural embroidery. The architects pulled the ribs into uniquely English *fan vaults* (vaults with radiating ribs forming a fanlike pattern) with large hanging *pendants* resembling stalactites. The vault looks as if it had been some organic mass that hardened in the process of melting. Intricate tracery recalling lace overwhelms the cones hanging from the ceiling. The chapel represents the dissolution of structural Gothic into decorative fancy. The architects released the Gothic style's original lines from their function and multiplied them into the uninhibited architectural virtuosity and theatrics of the Perpendicular style. A contemporaneous phenomenon in France is the Flamboyant style of Saint-Maclou (FIG. **18-27**) at Rouen.

ROYAL TOMBS Henry VII's chapel also houses the king's tomb in the form of a large stone coffin with sculpted portraits of Henry and his queen, Elizabeth of York, lying on their backs. This type of tomb is a familiar feature of the churches of Late Gothic England— indeed, of Late Gothic Europe. Though not strictly part of the architectural fabric, as are tombs set into niches in the church walls, freestanding tombs with recumbent images of the deceased are permanent and immovable units of church furniture. They preserve both the remains and the memory of the person entombed and testify to the deceased's piety as well as prominence.

Services for the dead were a vital part of the Christian liturgy. The Christian hope for salvation in the hereafter prompted the dying faithful to request masses sung, sometimes in perpetuity, for

18-44 Tomb of Edward II, Gloucester Cathedral, Gloucester, England, ca. 1330–1335.

Edward II's tomb resembles a miniature Perpendicular English Gothic chapel with its forest of gables, ogee arches, and pinnacles. The shrinelike form suggests that the deceased is worthy of veneration.

the eternal repose of their souls. Toward that end, the highborn and wealthy endowed whole chapels for the chanting of masses (*chantries*), and made rich bequests of treasure and property to the Church. Many also required that their tombs be as near as possible to the choir or some other important location in the church. Sometimes, patrons built a chapel especially designed and endowed to house their tombs, such as Henry's chapel at Westminster Abbey. Freestanding tombs, accessible to church visitors, had a moral as well as a sepulchral and memorial purpose. The silent image of the deceased, cold and still, was a solemn reminder of human mortality, all the more effective because the remains of the person depicted were directly below the portrait. The tomb of an illustrious person could bring distinction, pilgrims, and patronage to a church, just as relics of saints attracted pilgrims from far and wide (see "Pilgrimages," Chapter 17, page 432).

An elaborate example of a freestanding tomb (FIG. **18-44**) is that of Edward II (r. 1307–1327), installed in Gloucester Cathedral several years after the king's murder. Edward III (r. 1327–1357) paid for the memorial to his father, who reposes in regal robes with his crown on his head. The sculptor portrayed the dead king as an idealized Christlike figure (compare FIG. **18-22**). On each side of Edward's head is an attentive angel tenderly touching his hair. At his feet is a guardian lion, emblem also of the king's strength and valor. An intricate Perpendicular Gothic canopy encases the coffin, forming a kind of miniature chapel protecting the deceased. It is a fine example of the English manner with its forest of delicate alabaster and

Purbeck marble gables, buttresses, and pinnacles. A distinctive feature is the use of *ogee arches* (arches made up of two double-curved lines meeting at a point), a characteristic Late Gothic form. Art historians often have compared tombs like Edward's to reliquaries. Indeed, the shrinelike frame and the church setting transform the deceased into a kind of saintly relic worthy of veneration.

Holy Roman Empire

The architecture of the Holy Roman Empire remained conservatively Romanesque well into the 13th century. In many German churches, the only Gothic feature was the rib vault, buttressed solely by the heavy masonry of the walls. By midcentury, though, the French Gothic style began to make a profound impact.

COLOGNE CATHEDRAL Cologne Cathedral (FIG. **18-45**), begun in 1248 under the direction of GERHARD OF COLOGNE, was not completed until more than 600 years later, making it one of the longest building projects on record. Work halted entirely from the mid-16th to the mid-19th centuries, when the 14th-century design for the facade was unexpectedly found. Gothic Revival architects (see Chapter 30) then completed the building according to the Gothic plans, adding the nave, towers, and facade to the east end that had stood alone for several centuries. The Gothic/Gothic

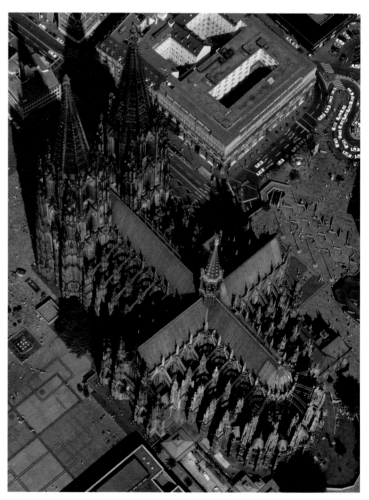

18-45 GERHARD OF COLOGNE, aerial view of Cologne Cathedral (looking northwest), Cologne, Germany, begun 1248; nave, facade, and towers completed 1880.

Cologne Cathedral, the largest church in northern Europe, took more than 600 years to build. Only the east end dates to the 13th century. The 19th-century portions follow the original Gothic plans.

18-46 GERHARD OF COLOGNE, interior of Cologne Cathedral (looking east), Cologne, Germany, choir completed 1322.

The nave of Cologne Cathedral is 422 feet long. The 150-foot-high choir, a taller variation on the Amiens Cathedral choir (FIG. 18-20), is a prime example of Gothic architects' quest for height.

Revival structure is the largest cathedral in northern Europe and boasts a giant (422-foot-long) nave (FIG. 18-46) with two aisles on each side.

The 150-foot-high 14th-century choir is a skillful variation of the Amiens Cathedral choir (FIGS. 18-19 and 18-20) design, with double lancets in the triforium and tall, slender single windows in the clerestory above and choir arcade below. Completed four decades after Gerhard's death but according to his plans, the choir expresses the Gothic quest for height even more emphatically than many French Gothic buildings. Despite the cathedral's seeming lack of substance, proof of its stability came during World War II, when the city of Cologne sustained extremely heavy aerial bombardments. The church survived the war by virtue of its Gothic skeletal design. Once the first few bomb blasts blew out all of its windows, subsequent explosions had no adverse effects, and the skeleton remained intact and structurally sound.

18-47A
Heiligkreuz-kirche, Schwäbisch Gmünd, begun 1351.

SAINT ELIZABETH, MARBURG A different type of design, also probably of French origin (FIG. 17-16, *left*) but developed especially in Germany, is the *Hallenkirche*, in which the aisles are the same height as the nave. Hall churches, consequently, have no tribune, triforium, or clerestory. An early German example of this type is the church of Saint Elizabeth (FIG. 18-47) at Marburg, built between 1235 and 1283. It incorporates French-inspired rib vaults with pointed arches and tall lancet windows. The facade has two spire-capped towers in the French manner but no tracery arcades or portal sculpture. Because the aisles provide much of the bracing for the nave vaults, the exterior of Saint Elizabeth is without the dramatic parade of flying buttresses that typically circles French Gothic churches. But the German interior, lighted by double rows of tall windows in the aisle walls, is more unified and free flowing, less narrow and divided, and more brightly illuminated than the interiors of French and English Gothic churches.

STRASBOURG CATHEDRAL In the German Rhineland, which the successors of the Carolingian and Ottonian emperors still ruled, work began in 1176 on a new cathedral for Strasbourg, today a French city. The apse, choir, and transepts were in place by around 1240. Stylistically, these sections of the new church are Romanesque. But the reliefs of the two south-transept portals are fully Gothic and reveal the impact of contemporary French sculpture, especially that of Reims.

18-47 Interior of Saint Elizabeth (looking west), Marburg, Germany, 1235–1283.

This German church is an early example of a Hallenkirche, in which the aisles are the same height as the nave. Because of the tall windows in the aisle walls, sunlight brightly illuminates the interior.

The subject of the left tympanum (FIG. 18-48) is the death of the Virgin Mary. A comparison of the Strasbourg Mary on her deathbed with the Mary of the Reims *Visitation* group (FIG. 18-24, *right*) suggests that the German master had studied the recently installed French jamb statues. The 12 apostles gather around the

Stylistically akin to the *Visitation* group (FIG. 18-24, *right*) of Reims Cathedral, the figures in Strasbourg's south-transept tympanum express profound sorrow through dramatic poses and gestures.

Virgin, forming an arc of mourners well suited to the semicircular frame. The sculptor adjusted the heights of the figures to fit the available space (the apostles at the right are the shortest), and, as in many depictions of crowds throughout history, some of the figures have no legs or feet. At the center, Christ receives his mother's soul (the doll-like figure he holds in his left hand). Mary Magdalene, wringing her hands in grief, crouches beside the deathbed. The sorrowing figures express emotion in varying degrees of intensity, from serene resignation to gesturing agitation. The sculptor organized the group by dramatic pose and gesture but also by the rippling flow of deeply incised drapery that passes among the figures like a rhythmic electric pulse. The sculptor's objective was to imbue the sacred figures with human emotions and to stir emotional responses in observers. In Gothic France, as already noted, art became increasingly humanized and natural. In Gothic Germany, artists carried this humanizing trend even further by emphasizing passionate drama.

EKKEHARD AND UTA The Strasbourg style, with its feverish emotionalism, was particularly appropriate for narrating dramatic events in relief. The sculptor entrusted with the decoration of the west choir of Naumburg Cathedral faced a very different challenge. The task was to carve statues of the 12 benefactors of the original 11th-century church on the occasion of a new fundraising campaign. The vivid gestures and agitated faces in the Strasbourg tympanum contrast with the quiet solemnity of the Naumburg statues. Two of the figures (FIG. 18-49) stand out from the group because of their exceptional quality. They represent the margrave (military governor) Ekkehard II of Meissen and his wife Uta. The statues are attached to columns and stand beneath architectural canopies, following the pattern of French Gothic portal statuary. Their location indoors accounts for the preservation of much of the original paint. Ekkehard and Uta suggest the original appearance of the facade and transept sculptures of Gothic cathedrals.

18-49 Ekkehard and Uta, statues in the west choir, Naumburg Cathedral, Naumburg, Germany, ca. 1249–1255. Painted limestone, Ekkehard 6′ 2″ high.

The period costumes and individualized features of these donor portraits give the impression that Ekkehard and Uta posed for their statues, but they lived long before the Naumburg sculptor's time.

1 ft.

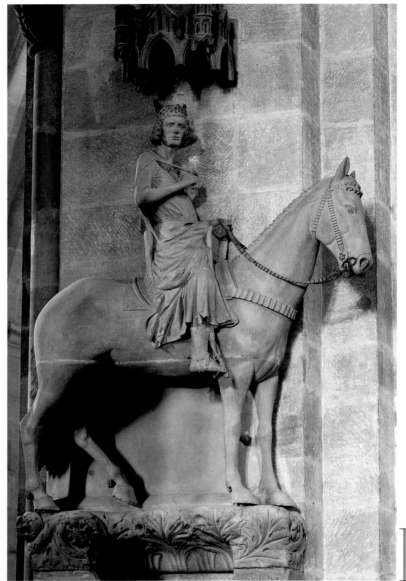

18-50 Equestrian portrait (*Bamberg Rider*), statue in the east choir, Bamberg Cathedral, Germany, ca. 1235–1240. Sandstone, 7′ 9″ high.

Probably a portrait of a German emperor, perhaps Frederick II, the *Bamberg Rider* revives the imagery of the Carolingian Empire. The French-style architectural canopy cannot contain the entire statue.

1 ft.

The period costumes and the individualized features and personalities of the margrave and his wife give the impression that they posed for their own portraits, although the subjects lived well before the sculptor's time. Ekkehard, the intense knight, contrasts with the beautiful and aloof Uta. With a wonderfully graceful gesture, she draws the collar of her gown partly across her face while she gathers up a soft fold of drapery with a jeweled, delicate hand. The sculptor subtly revealed the shape of Uta's right arm beneath her cloak and rendered the fall of drapery folds with an accuracy that indicates the use of a model. The two statues are arresting images of real people, even if they bear the names of aristocrats the artist never met. By the mid-13th century, in the Holy Roman Empire as well as in England (FIG. 18-44) and elsewhere, life-size images of secular personages had found their way into churches.

BAMBERG RIDER Somewhat earlier in date than the Naumburg "portraits" is the equestrian statue known as the *Bamberg Rider* (FIG. 18-50). For centuries this statue has been mounted against a pier in Bamberg Cathedral beneath an architectural canopy that frames the rider's body but not his horse. Scholars debate whether the statue was made for this location or moved there, perhaps from the church's exterior. Whatever the statue's original location, it revives the imagery of the Carolingian Empire (FIG. 16-12), derived in turn from that of ancient Rome (FIG. 10-59).

Like Ekkehard and Uta, the *Bamberg Rider* seems to be a true portrait. Some believe it represents a Holy Roman emperor, perhaps Frederick II (r. 1220–1250), who was a benefactor of Bamberg Cathedral. The many other identifications include Saint George and one of the three magi, but a historical personality is most likely the subject. The presence of a Holy Roman emperor in the cathedral would have underscored the unity of church and state in 13th-century Germany. The artist carefully represented the rider's costume, the high saddle, and the horse's trappings. The proportions of horse and rider are correct, although the sculptor did not quite understand the animal's anatomy, so its shape is rather stiffly schematic. The rider turns toward the observer, as if presiding at a review of troops. The torsion of this figure seems to reflect the same impatience with subordination to architecture found in the Reims portal statues (FIG. 18-24).

RÖTTGEN PIETÀ The confident 13th-century figures at Naumburg and Bamberg stand in marked contrast to a haunting 14th-century German painted wooden statuette (FIG. 18-51) of the Virgin Mary holding the dead Christ in her lap. The widespread troubles of the 14th century—war, plague, famine, and social strife—brought on an ever more acute awareness of suffering. This sensibility found its way readily into religious art. The Dance of Death, Christ as the Man of Sorrow, and the Seven Sorrows of the Virgin Mary became favorite themes. A fevered and fearful piety sought comfort and reassurance in the reflection that Christ and the Virgin Mother shared humanity's woes. To represent this, artists emphasized the traits of human suffering in powerful, expressive exaggeration. In the illustrated group, a *Pietà* ("pity" or "compassion" in Italian), the sculptor portrayed Christ as a stunted, distorted human wreck, stiffened in death and covered with streams of blood gushing from a huge wound. The Virgin Mother, who cradles him like a child in her lap, is the very image of maternal anguish, her oversized face twisted in an expression of unbearable grief. This statue expresses nothing of the serenity of Romanesque and earlier Gothic depictions of Mary (FIGS. 17-18 and 18-16). Nor does the *Röttgen Pietà* (named after a collector) have anything in common with the aloof, iconic images of the Theotokos with the infant Jesus in her lap common in Byzantine art (FIGS. 12-18 and 12-19). Here the artist forcibly confronts the devout with an appalling icon of agony, death, and sorrow that humanizes, lmost to the point of heresy, the sacred personages. The work calls out to the horrified believer, "What is your suffering compared to this?"

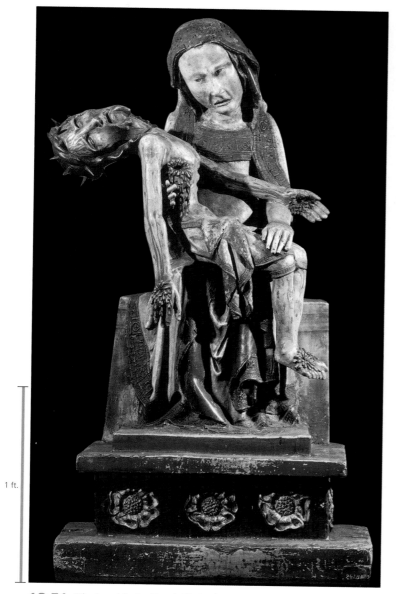

18-51 Virgin with the Dead Christ (*Röttgen Pietà*), from the Rhineland, Germany, ca. 1300–1325. Painted wood, 2′ 10½″ high. Rheinisches Landemuseum, Bonn.

This statuette of the Virgin grieving over the distorted dead body of Christ in her lap reflects the widespread troubles of the 14th century and the German interest in emotional imagery.

18-52 NICHOLAS OF VERDUN, sacrifice of Isaac, detail of the *Klosterneuburg Altar,* from the abbey church at Klosterneuburg, Austria, 1181. Gilded copper and enamel, 5½″ high. Stiftsmuseum, Klosterneuburg.

Nicholas of Verdun was the leading artist of the Meuse valley region, renowned for its metal- and enamelwork. His emotionally charged gold figures stand out vividly from the blue enamel background.

Throughout Europe, the humanizing of religious themes and religious images accelerated steadily from the 12th century. By the 14th century, art addressed the private person (often in a private place) in a direct appeal to the emotions. The expression of feeling accompanied the representation of the human body in motion. As the figures of the church portals began to twist on their columns, then move within their niches, and then stand independently, their details became more outwardly related to the human audience as expressions of recognizable human emotions.

NICHOLAS OF VERDUN As part of his plan to make his new church at Saint-Denis an earthly introduction to the splendors of Paradise (see "Abbot Suger," page 463), Suger selected artists from the Meuse River valley to fashion a magnificent crucifix for the choir. This region long had been famous for the quality of its metalworkers and enamelers (FIGS. 17-23 and 17-24). Suger described the Saint-Denis cross as standing on a sumptuous base decorated with 68

enamel scenes pairing Old and New Testament episodes. The enamel work of the leading Meuse valley artist of the late 12th and early 13th centuries, NICHOLAS OF VERDUN, suggests the appearance of the biblical enamels on Suger's lost crucifix.

In 1181, Nicholas completed work on a gilded-copper and enamel *ambo* (a pulpit for biblical readings) for the Benedictine abbey church at Klosterneuburg, near Vienna in Austria. After a fire damaged the pulpit in 1330, the church hired artists to convert the pulpit into an *altarpiece* (a decorative panel above and behind the altar). The pulpit's sides became the wings of a *triptych* (three-part altarpiece). The 14th-century artists also added six scenes to Nicholas's original 45. The *Klosterneuburg Altar* in its final form has a central row of enamels depicting New Testament episodes, beginning with the Annunciation, and bearing the label *sub gracia*, or the world "under grace," that is, after the coming of Christ. The upper and lower registers contain Old Testament scenes labeled, respectively, *ante legem*, "before the law" Moses received on Mount Sinai, and *sub lege*, "under the law" of the Ten Commandments. In this scheme, prophetic Old Testament events appear above and below the New Testament episodes they prefigure. For example, framing the Annunciation to Mary of the coming birth of Jesus are enamels of angels announcing the births of Isaac and Samson. In the central section of the triptych, the Old Testament counterpart of Christ's Crucifixion is Abraham's sacrifice of Isaac (FIG. 18-52), a parallel already established in Early Christian times in both art (FIG. 11-7)

18-52A
Klosterneuburg Altar, refashioned after 1330.

18-53 NICHOLAS OF VERDUN, *Shrine of the Three Kings,* from Cologne Cathedral, Cologne, Germany, begun ca. 1190. Silver, bronze, enamel, and gemstones, 5′ 8″ × 6′ × 3′ 8″. Cathedral Treasury, Cologne.

Cologne's archbishop commissioned this huge reliquary in the shape of a church to house relics of the three magi. The figures are sculpted versions of those on the *Klosterneuburg Altar* (FIG. 18-52).

and literature (see "Jewish Subjects in Christian Art," Chapter 11, page 293). Nicholas of Verdun's gold figures stand out vividly from the blue enamel background. The biblical actors twist and turn, make emphatic gestures, and wear garments that are almost overwhelmed by the intricate linear patterns of their folds. In the Abraham and Isaac panel, the angel flies in at the very last moment to grab the blade of Abraham's sword before he can kill the bound Isaac on the altar. The intense emotionalism of the representation and the linear complexity of the garments foreshadowed the tone and style of the Strasbourg tympanum depicting the death of the Virgin (FIG. 18-48).

Sculpted versions of the Klosterneuburg figures appear on the *Shrine of the Three Kings* (FIG. 18-53) in Cologne Cathedral. Nicholas of Verdun probably began work on the huge reliquary (six feet long and almost as tall) in 1190. Philip von Heinsberg, archbishop of Cologne from 1167 to 1191, commissioned the shrine to contain relics of the three magi. The Holy Roman Emperor Frederick Barbarossa acquired them in the conquest of Milan in 1164 and

donated them to the German cathedral. Possession of the magi's relics gave the Cologne archbishops the right to crown German kings. Nicholas's reliquary, made of silver and bronze with ornamentation in enamel and gemstones, is one of the most luxurious ever fashioned, especially considering its size. The shape resembles that of a basilican church. Repoussé figures of the Virgin Mary, the three magi, Old Testament prophets, and New Testament apostles in arcuated frames are variations of those on the Klosterneuburg pulpit. The deep channels and tight bunches of the drapery folds are hallmarks of Nicholas's style.

Nicholas of Verdun's *Klosterneuburg Altar* and his *Shrine of the Three Kings,* together with Suger's treatises on the furnishings of Saint-Denis, are welcome reminders of how magnificently outfitted medieval church interiors were. The so-called minor arts played a defining role in creating a special otherworldly atmosphere for Christian ritual. These Gothic examples continued a tradition that dates to the Roman emperor Constantine and the first imperial patronage of Christianity (see Chapter 11).

GOTHIC EUROPE

FRANCE

▍ The birthplace of Gothic art and architecture was Saint-Denis, where Abbot Suger used rib vaults with pointed arches and stained-glass windows to rebuild the Carolingian royal church. The west facade of Suger's church also introduced statue-columns on the portal jambs, which appeared shortly later on the Royal Portal of Chartres Cathedral. Laon Cathedral is another important example of Early Gothic (1140–1194) architecture.

▍ After a fire in 1194, Chartres Cathedral was rebuilt with flying buttresses, four-part nave vaults, and a three-story elevation of nave arcade, triforium, and clerestory, setting the pattern for High Gothic (1194–1300) cathedrals, including Amiens with its 144-foot-high vaults.

▍ Flying buttresses made possible huge stained-glass windows. High Gothic windows employ delicate lead cames and bar tracery. The divine colored light (*lux nova*) they admitted transformed the character of church interiors.

▍ High Gothic statue-columns broke out of the architectural straitjacket of their Early Gothic predecessors. At Chartres, Reims, and elsewhere, the sculpted figures move freely and sometimes converse with their neighbors.

▍ The High Gothic Rayonnant court style of Louis IX gave way in the Late Gothic (1300–1500) period to the Flamboyant style seen at Saint-Maclou at Rouen.

▍ Several important examples of secular architecture survive from the Gothic period, including the bastions and towers of Carcassonne, the hall of the cloth guild in Bruges, and the house of Jacques Coeur in Bourges.

▍ In the 13th century, Paris was the center of production of costly moralized Bibles and other illuminated manuscripts in urban workshops of professional artists, which usurped the role of monastic scriptoria.

Royal Portal, Chartres Cathedral, ca. 1145–1155

Amiens Cathedral, begun 1220

God as architect of the world, ca. 1220–1230

ENGLAND

▍ The Parisian Gothic style became the rage in most of Europe during the 13th century, but many regional styles developed, as in the Romanesque period. English Gothic churches like Salisbury Cathedral differ from their French counterparts in their wider and shorter facades, flat east ends, double transepts, and sparing use of flying buttresses.

▍ Especially characteristic of English Gothic architecture is the elaboration of architectural patterns, which often disguise the underlying structure of the buildings. Constructed in the Late Gothic Perpendicular style, the fan vaults of the chapel of Henry VII transform the logical rib vaults of French buildings into decorative fancy.

Salisbury Cathedral, Salisbury, 1220–1258

HOLY ROMAN EMPIRE

▍ German architects eagerly embraced the French Gothic architectural style at Cologne Cathedral and elsewhere. German originality manifested itself most clearly in the Gothic period in sculpture, which often features emotionally charged figures in dramatic poses.

▍ Statues of secular historical figures decorate the interiors of Naumburg and Bamberg cathedrals, signaling a revival of interest in the art of portraiture.

▍ Nicholas of Verdun was the leading artist of the Meuse River valley, an area renowned for metal- and enamelwork. Nicholas's altars and shrines provide an idea of how sumptuous were the furnishings of Gothic churches.

Nicholas of Verdun, *Shrine of the Three Kings*, ca. 1190

19-1 GIOTTO DI BONDONE, Arena Chapel (Cappella Scrovegni; interior looking west), Padua, Italy, 1305–1306.

Giotto, widely regarded as the first Renaissance painter, was a pioneer in pursuing a naturalistic approach to representation based on observation. The frescoes in the Arena Chapel show his art at its finest.

ITALY, 1200 TO 1400

When the Italian humanists of the 16th century condemned the art of the late Middle Ages in northern Europe as "*Gothic*" (see Chapter 18), they did so by comparing it with the contemporary art of Italy, which was a conscious revival of *classical** art. Italian artists and scholars regarded medieval artworks as distortions of the noble art of the Greeks and Romans. But interest in the art of classical antiquity was not entirely absent during the medieval period, even in France, the center of the Gothic style. For example, on the west front of Reims Cathedral, the statues of Christian *saints* and angels (FIG. **18-24**) reveal the unmistakable influence of Roman art on French sculptors. However, the classical revival that took root in Italy during the 13th and 14th centuries (MAP **19-1**) was much more pervasive and long-lasting.

THE 13TH CENTURY

Italian admiration for classical art surfaced early on at the court of Frederick II, king of Sicily (r. 1197–1250) and Holy Roman Emperor (r. 1220–1250). Frederick's nostalgia for the past grandeur of Rome fostered a revival of Roman sculpture in Sicily and southern Italy not unlike the neoclassical *renovatio* (renewal) that Charlemagne encouraged in Germany four centuries earlier (see Chapter 16).

Sculpture

NICOLA PISANO The sculptor Nicola d'Apulia (Nicholas of Apulia), better known as NICOLA PISANO (active ca. 1258–1278) after his adopted city (see "Italian Artists' Names," page 498), received his early training in southern Italy under Frederick's rule. In 1250, Nicola traveled northward and eventually settled in Pisa. Then at the height of its political and economic power, Pisa was a magnet for artists seeking lucrative commissions. Nicola specialized in carving marble reliefs and ornamentation for large *pulpits* (raised platforms from which priests lead church services), completing the first (FIG. **19-2**) in 1260 for Pisa's baptistery (FIG. **17-25**, *left*). Some elements of the pulpit's design carried on medieval traditions (for example, the *trefoil arches* and the lions supporting some of the *columns*), but Nicola also incorporated

---

* In *Art through the Ages* the adjective "Classical," with uppercase *C,* refers specifically to the Classical period of ancient Greece, 480–323 BCE. Lowercase "classical" refers to Greco-Roman antiquity in general, that is, the period treated in Chapters 5, 9, and 10.

Italian Artists' Names

In contemporary societies, people have become accustomed to a standardized method of identifying individuals, in part because of the proliferation of official documents such as driver's licenses, passports, and student identification cards. Given names are coupled with family names, although the order of the two (or more) names varies from country to country. This kind of regularity in names was not, however, the norm in premodern Italy. Many individuals were known by their place of birth or adopted hometown. Nicola Pisano was known as "Nicholas the Pisan," Giulio Romano was "Julius the Roman," and Domenico Veneziano was "the Venetian." Leonardo da Vinci ("Leonard from Vinci") hailed from the small town of Vinci.

Art historians therefore refer to these artists by their given name, not the name of their town: "Leonardo," not "da Vinci."

Nicknames were also common. Giorgione was "Big George." People usually referred to Tommaso di Cristoforo Fini as Masolino ("Little Thomas") to distinguish him from his more famous pupil Masaccio ("Brutish Thomas"). Guido di Pietro was called Fra Angelico (the Angelic Friar). Cenni di Pepo is remembered as Cimabue ("bull's head"). Names were also impermanent and could be changed at will. This flexibility has resulted in significant challenges for historians, who often must deal with archival documents and records that refer to the same artist by different names.

---

classical elements. The large, bushy *capitals* are a Gothic variation of the highly ornate *Corinthian capital.* The arches are round, as in Roman architecture, rather than pointed (*ogival*) as in Gothic buildings. And each of the large rectangular relief panels resembles the sculptured front of a Roman *sarcophagus,* or coffin (for example, FIG. 10-70).

The densely packed large-scale figures of the individual panels also seem to derive from the compositions found on Roman sarcophagi. One of these panels (FIG. 19-3) depicts scenes from the Infancy cycle of Christ (see "The Life of Jesus in Art," Chapter 11, pages 296–297, or xxvi–xxvii in Volume II), including the *Annunciation* (*top left*), the *Nativity* (*center* and *lower half*), and the *Adoration of the Shepherds* (*top right*). Mary appears twice, and her size varies. The focus of the composition is the reclining Virgin of the *Nativity,* whose posture and drapery are reminiscent of those of the lid figures on Etruscan (FIGS. 9-5 and 9-15) and Roman (FIG. 10-61) sarcophagi. The face types, beards, and coiffures as well as the bulk and weight of Nicola's figures also reveal the influence of classical relief sculpture. Scholars have even been able to pinpoint the models of some of the pulpit figures on Roman sarcophagi in Pisa.

MAP 19-1 Italy around 1400.

19-2 NICOLA PISANO, pulpit of the baptistery, Pisa, Italy, 1259–1260. Marble, 15' high.

Nicola Pisano's baptistery pulpit at Pisa retains many medieval design elements, for example, the trefoil arches and the lions supporting columns, but the panels draw on ancient Roman sarcophagus reliefs.

GIOVANNI PISANO Nicola Pisano's son, GIOVANNI PISANO (ca. 1250–1320), likewise became a sought-after sculptor of church pulpits. Giovanni's pulpit in Sant'Andrea at Pistoia also has a panel (FIG. **19-4**) featuring the Nativity and related scenes. The son's version of the subject is in striking contrast to his father's thick carving and placid, almost stolid, presentation of the religious narrative. Giovanni arranged the figures loosely and dynamically. They twist and bend in excited animation, and the spaces that open deeply between them suggest their motion. In the *Annunciation* episode (*top left*), the Virgin shrinks from the angel's sudden appearance in a posture of alarm touched with humility. The same spasm of apprehension contracts her supple body as she reclines in the *Nativity* scene (*center*). The drama's principals share in a peculiar nervous agitation, as if they all suddenly are moved by spiritual passion. Only the shepherds and the sheep (*right*) do not yet experience the miraculous event. The swiftly turning, sinuous draperies, the slender figures they enfold, and the general emotionalism of the scene are features not found in Nicola Pisano's interpretation. The father worked in the classical tradition, the son in a style derived from French Gothic. Both styles were important ingredients in the formation of the distinctive and original art of 14th-century Italy.

Painting and Architecture

A third contributing component of 14th-century Italian art was the Byzantine tradition (see Chapter 12). Throughout the Middle Ages, the Byzantine style dominated Italian painting, but its influence was especially strong after the fall of Constantinople in 1204, which precipitated a migration of Byzantine artists to Italy.

19-3 NICOLA PISANO, *Annunciation, Nativity, and Adoration of the Shepherds,* relief panel on the baptistery pulpit, Pisa, Italy, 1259–1260. Marble, 2' 10" × 3' 9".

Classical sculpture inspired the face types, beards, coiffures, and draperies, as well as the bulk and weight of Nicola's figures. The Madonna of the *Nativity* resembles lid figures on Roman sarcophagi.

19-4 GIOVANNI PISANO, *Annunciation, Nativity, and Adoration of the Shepherds,* relief panel on the pulpit of Sant'Andrea, Pistoia, Italy, 1297–1301. Marble, 2' 10" × 3' 4".

The French Gothic style had a greater influence on Giovanni Pisano, Nicola's son. Giovanni arranged his figures loosely and dynamically. They display a nervous agitation, as if moved by spiritual passion.

19-5 Bonaventura Berlinghieri, panel from the *Saint Francis Altarpiece*, San Francesco, Pescia, Italy, 1235. Tempera on wood, 5' × 3' × 6'.

Berlinghieri was one of the leading painters working in the Italo-Byzantine style, or *maniera greca*. The frontal pose of Saint Francis and the use of gold leaf reveal the painter's Byzantine sources.

BONAVENTURA BERLINGHIERI

One of the leading painters working in the Italo-Byzantine style, or *maniera greca* (Greek style), was BONAVENTURA BERLINGHIERI (active ca. 1235–1244) of Lucca. He created the *Saint Francis Altarpiece* (FIG. 19-5) for the church of San Francesco (Saint Francis) in Pescia in 1235. Painted in *tempera* on wood panel (see "Tempera and Oil Painting," Chapter 20, page 523), the *altarpiece* honors Saint Francis of Assisi (ca. 1181–1226). Francis wears the coarse clerical robe, tied at the waist with a rope, which became the costume of Franciscan monks. The saint displays the *stigmata*—marks resembling Christ's wounds—that appeared on his hands and feet. Flanking Francis are two angels, whose frontal poses, prominent halos, and lack of modeling reveal the Byzantine roots of Berlinghieri's style. So too does his use of *gold leaf* (gold beaten into tissue-paper-thin sheets, then applied to surfaces), which emphasizes the image's flatness and spiritual nature. The narrative scenes that run along the sides of the panel provide an active contrast to the stiff formality of the large central image of Francis. At the upper left, taking pride of place at the saint's right, Francis miraculously acquires the stigmata. Directly below, the saint preaches to the birds. These and the scenes depicting Francis's miracle cures strongly suggest that Berlinghieri's source was one or more Byzantine *illuminated manuscripts* (compare FIG. 12-17) having biblical narrative scenes.

Berlinghieri's *Saint Francis Altarpiece* also highlights the increasingly prominent role of religious orders in late medieval Italy (see "The Great Schism, Mendicant Orders, and Confraternities," page 501). Saint Francis's Franciscan order worked diligently to impress on the public the saint's valuable example and to demonstrate its monks' commitment to teaching and to alleviating suffering. Berlinghieri's Pescia altarpiece, painted nine years after Francis's death, is the earliest known signed and dated representation of the saint. Appropriately, the panel focuses on the aspects of the saint's life that the Franciscans wanted to promote, thereby making visible (and thus more credible) the legendary life of this holy man. Saint Francis believed he could get closer to God by rejecting worldly

19-5A San Francesco, Assisi, 1228–1253.

19-5B *Saint Francis Preaching to the Birds,* Assisi, ca. 1290–1300.

goods, and to achieve this he stripped himself bare in a public square and committed himself to a strict life of fasting, prayer, and meditation. The appearance of stigmata on his hands and feet (clearly visible in the saint's frontal image, which resembles an *icon*) was perceived as God's blessing and led some followers to see Francis as a second Christ. Fittingly, four of the six narrative scenes on the altarpiece depict miraculous healings, connecting him more emphatically to Christ.

SANTA MARIA NOVELLA The increased importance of the mendicant orders during the 13th century led to the construction of large churches in Florence by the Franciscans (Santa Croce; FIG. I-3) and the Dominicans. The Florentine government and contributions from private citizens subsidized the commissioning of the Dominicans' Santa Maria Novella (FIG. 19-6) around 1246. The large congregations these orders attracted necessitated the expansive scale of this church. Small *oculi* (round windows) and marble striping along

The Great Schism, Mendicant Orders, and Confraternities

In 1305 the College of Cardinals (the collective body of all cardinals) elected a French pope, Clement V, who settled in Avignon. Subsequent French popes remained in Avignon, despite their announced intentions to return to Rome. Understandably, this did not please the Italians, who saw Rome as the rightful capital of the universal church. The conflict between the French and Italians resulted in the election in 1378 of two popes— Clement VII, who resided in Avignon (and who does not appear in the Catholic Church's official list of popes), and Urban VI (r. 1378–1389), who remained in Rome. Thus began what became known as the Great Schism. After 40 years, the Holy Roman Emperor Sigismund (r. 1410–1437) convened a council that managed to resolve this crisis by electing a new Roman pope, Martin V (r. 1417–1431), who was acceptable to all.

The pope's absence from Italy during much of the 14th century (the Avignon papacy) contributed to an increase in prominence of *monastic orders*. The Augustinians, Carmelites, and Servites became very active, ensuring a constant religious presence in the daily life of Italians, but the largest and most influential monastic orders were the *mendicants* (begging friars)—the Franciscans, founded by Francis of Assisi (FIG. 19-5), and the Dominicans, founded by the Spaniard Dominic de Guzman (ca. 1170–1221). These mendicants renounced all worldly goods and committed themselves to spreading God's word, performing good deeds, and ministering to the sick and dying. The Dominicans, in particular, contributed significantly to establishing urban educational institutions. The Franciscans and Dominicans became very popular among Italian citizens because of their devotion to their faith and the more personal relationship with God they encouraged. Although both mendicant orders were working for the same purpose—the glory of God—a degree of rivalry nevertheless existed between the two. They established their churches on opposite sides of Florence—Santa Croce (FIG. I-3), the Franciscan church, on the eastern side, and the Dominicans' Santa Maria Novella (FIG. 19-6) on the western (MAP 21-1).

Confraternities, organizations consisting of laypersons who dedicated themselves to strict religious observance, also grew in popularity during the 14th and 15th centuries. The mission of confraternities included tending the sick, burying the dead, singing hymns, and performing other good works. The confraternities as well as the mendicant orders continued to play an important role in Italian religious life through the 16th century. Further, the numerous artworks and monastic churches they commissioned ensured their enduring legacy.

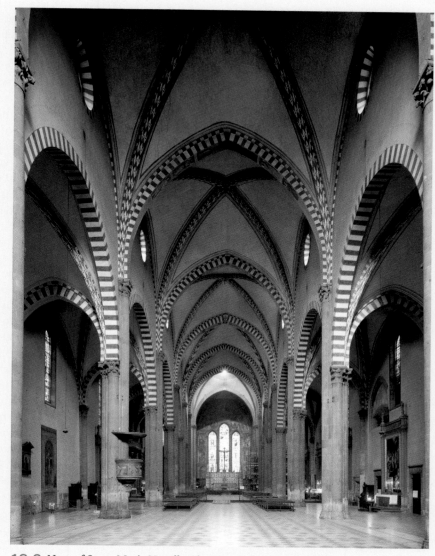

19-6 Nave of Santa Maria Novella, Florence, Italy, ca. 1246–1470.

The basilicas of Santa Maria Novella and Santa Croce (FIG. I-3) testify to the growing influence of the Dominican and Franciscan mendicant orders, respectively, in 13th-century Florence.

the ogival arches punctuate the *nave*, or central *aisle*. (For the nomenclature of *basilican* church architecture, see FIG. 11-9 or pages xxxii–xxxiii in Volume II.) Originally, a screen (*tramezzo*) placed across the nave separated the friars from the lay audience. The priests performed the *Mass* at separate altars on each side of the screen. Church officials removed this screen in the mid-16th century to encourage greater lay participation in the Mass.

CIMABUE One of the first artists to begin to break away from the Italo-Byzantine style that dominated 13th-century Italian painting was Cenni di Pepo, better known as CIMABUE (ca. 1240–1302). Although his works reveal the unmistakable influence of Gothic sculpture, Cimabue challenged some of the conventions that dominated late medieval art in pursuit of a new *naturalism*, the close observation of the natural world that was at the core of the classical

THE 14TH CENTURY

In the 14th century, Italy consisted of numerous independent *city-states,* each corresponding to a geographic region centered on a major city (MAP 19-1). Most of the city-states, such as Venice, Florence, Lucca, and Siena, were republics. These republics were constitutional oligarchies—governed by executive bodies, advisory councils, and special commissions. Other powerful 14th-century states included the Papal States, the Kingdom of Naples, and the Duchies of Milan, Modena, Ferrara, and Savoy. As their names indicate, these states were politically distinct from the republics, but all the states shared in the prosperity of the period. The sources of wealth varied from state to state. Italy's port cities expanded maritime trade, whereas the economies of other cities depended on banking or the manufacture of arms or textiles.

The eruption of the Black Death (bubonic plague) in the late 1340s threatened this prosperity, however. Originating in China, the Black Death swept across the entire European continent. The most devastating natural disaster in European history, the plague killed between 25 and 50 percent of Europe's population in about five years. Italy was particularly hard hit. In large cities, where people lived in relatively close proximity, the death tolls climbed as high as 50 or 60 percent of the population. The Black Death had a significant effect on art. It stimulated religious bequests and encouraged the commissioning of devotional images. The focus on sickness and death also led to a burgeoning in hospital construction.

Another significant development in 14th-century Italy was the blossoming of a vernacular (commonly spoken) literature, which dramatically affected Italy's intellectual and cultural life. Latin remained the official language of church liturgy and state documents. However, the creation of an Italian vernacular literature (based on the Tuscan dialect common in Florence) expanded the audience for philosophical and intellectual concepts because of its greater accessibility. Dante Alighieri (1265–1321; author of *The Divine Comedy*), poet and scholar Francesco Petrarch (1304–1374), and Giovanni Boccaccio (1313–1375; author of *Decameron*) were among those most responsible for establishing this vernacular literature.

RENAISSANCE HUMANISM The development of a vernacular literature was one important sign that the essentially religious view of the world that dominated medieval Europe was about to change dramatically in what historians call the *Renaissance.* Although religion continued to occupy a primary position in the lives of Europeans, a growing concern with the natural world, the individual, and humanity's worldly existence characterized the Renaissance period—the 14th through the 16th centuries. The word *renaissance* in French and English (*rinascità* in Italian) refers to a "rebirth" of art and culture. A revived interest in classical cultures—indeed, the veneration of classical antiquity as a model—was central to this rebirth. The notion that the Renaissance represented the restoration of the glorious past of Greece and Rome gave rise to the concept of the "Middle Ages" as the era spanning the time between antiquity and the Renaissance. The transition from the medieval to the Renaissance, though dramatic, did not come about abruptly, however. In fact, much that is medieval persisted in the Renaissance and in later periods.

Fundamental to the development of the Italian Renaissance was *humanism,* a concept that emerged during the 14th century and became a central component of Italian art and culture in the 15th and 16th centuries. Humanism was more a code of civil conduct, a theory of education, and a scholarly discipline than a philosophical system. As their name suggests, Italian humanists were concerned chiefly with human values and interests as distinct from—but not opposed to—religion's otherworldly values. Humanists pointed to

1 ft.

19-7 CIMABUE, *Madonna Enthroned with Angels and Prophets,* from Santa Trinità, Florence, Italy, ca. 1280–1290. Tempera and gold leaf on wood, 12′ 7″ × 7′ 4″. Galleria degli Uffizi, Florence. ◼️▶

Cimabue was one of the first artists to break away from the Italo-Byzantine style. Although he relied on Byzantine models, Cimabue depicted the Madonna's massive throne as receding into space.

tradition. Cimabue's *Madonna Enthroned with Angels and Prophets* (FIG. 19-7), created for the church of Santa Trinità (Holy Trinity) in Florence, nonetheless reveals the painter's reliance on Byzantine models for the composition as well as the gold background (compare FIG. 12-18). Cimabue used the gold embellishments common to Byzantine art for the folds of the Madonna's robe, but they are no longer merely decorative patterns. Here they enhance the three-dimensionality of the drapery. Cimabue also constructed a deeper space for the Madonna and the surrounding figures to inhabit than is common in Byzantine art. The Virgin's throne, for example, is a massive structure that Cimabue convincingly depicted as receding into space. The overlapping bodies of the angels on each side of the throne and the half-length prophets who look outward or upward from beneath it reinforce the sense of depth.

lives of the saints. Petrarch wrote a book on illustrious men, and his colleague Boccaccio complemented it with biographies of famous women—from Eve to his contemporary, Joanna, queen of Naples. Both Petrarch and Boccaccio were famous in their own day as poets, scholars, and men of letters—their achievements equivalent in honor to those of the heroes of civic virtue. In 1341 in Rome, Petrarch received the laurel wreath crown, the ancient symbol of victory and merit. The humanist cult of fame emphasized the importance of creative individuals and their role in contributing to the renown of the city-state and of all Italy.

Giotto

GIOTTO DI BONDONE (ca. 1266–1337) of Florence made a much more radical break with the past than did Cimabue. Art historians from Giorgio Vasari[†] to the present day have regarded Giotto as the first Renaissance painter, a pioneer in pursuing a naturalistic approach to representation based on observation. Scholars still debate the sources of Giotto's style, however. One formative influence must have been the work of the man Vasari said was his teacher, Cimabue, although Vasari lauded Giotto as having eclipsed Cimabue by abandoning the "crude *maniera greca*." Some late-13th-century *murals* in Rome with fully modeled figures of saints may also have influenced the young Giotto. French Gothic sculpture (which Giotto may have seen, but certainly familiar to him from the work of Giovanni Pisano, who had spent time in Paris) and ancient Roman art must also have contributed to Giotto's artistic education. Yet no mere synthesis of these varied influences could have produced the significant shift in artistic approach that has led some scholars to describe Giotto as the father of Western pictorial art. Renowned in his own day, he established a reputation that has never faltered. Regardless of the other influences on his artistic style, his true teacher was nature—the world of visible things.

19-8A PIETRO CAVALLINI, *Last Judgment,* ca. 1290–1295.

Giotto's revolution in painting did not consist only of displacing the Byzantine style, establishing painting as a major art form for the next seven centuries, and restoring the naturalistic approach the ancients developed and medieval artists largely abandoned. He also inaugurated a method of pictorial expression based on observation and initiated an age that might be called "early scientific." By stressing the preeminence of sight for gaining knowledge of the world, Giotto and his successors contributed to the foundation of empirical science. They recognized that the visual world must be observed before it can be analyzed and understood. Praised in his own and later times for his fidelity to nature, Giotto was more than a mere imitator of it. He revealed nature while observing it and divining its visible order. In fact, he showed his generation a new way of seeing. With Giotto, Western artists turned resolutely toward the visible world as their source of knowledge of nature.

MADONNA ENTHRONED On nearly the same great scale as Cimabue's enthroned Madonna (FIG. 19-7) is Giotto's panel (FIG. 19-8) depicting the same subject, painted for the high altar of the Ognissanti (All Saints) church in Florence. Although still seen against the traditional gold background, Giotto's Madonna rests within her Gothic throne with the unshakable stability of an ancient

19-8 GIOTTO DI BONDONE, *Madonna Enthroned,* from the Church of Ognissanti, Florence, Italy, ca. 1310. Tempera and gold leaf on wood, 10′ 8″ × 6′ 8″. Galleria degli Uffizi, Florence.

Giotto displaced the Byzantine style in Italian painting and revived the naturalism of classical art. His figures have substance, dimensionality, and bulk and give the illusion that they could throw shadows.

1 ft.

classical cultures as particularly praiseworthy. This enthusiasm for antiquity, represented by the elegant Latin of Cicero (106–43 BCE) and the Augustan age, involved study of Latin literature and a conscious emulation of what proponents thought were the Roman civic virtues. These included self-sacrificing service to the state, participation in government, defense of state institutions (especially the administration of justice), and stoic indifference to personal misfortune in the performance of duty. With the help of a new interest in and knowledge of Greek, the humanists of the late 14th and 15th centuries recovered a large part of the Greek as well as the Roman literature and philosophy that had been lost, left unnoticed, or cast aside in the Middle Ages. Indeed, classical cultures provided humanists with a model for living in this world, a model primarily of human focus that derived not from an authoritative and traditional religious dogma but from reason.

Ideally, humanists sought no material reward for services rendered. The sole reward for heroes of civic virtue was fame, just as the reward for leaders of the holy life was sainthood. For the educated, the lives of heroes and heroines of the past became as edifying as the

[†]Giorgio Vasari (1511–1574) established himself as both a painter and architect during the 16th century. However, people today usually associate him with his landmark book *Lives of the Most Eminent Painters, Sculptors, and Architects,* first published in 1550. Scholars long have considered this book a major source of information about Italian art and artists, although many of the details have proven inaccurate. Regardless, Vasari's *Lives* remains a tour de force—an ambitious, comprehensive book dedicated to recording the biographies of artists.

Fresco Painting

Fresco painting has a long history, particularly in the Mediterranean region, where the Minoans (FIGS. 4-7 to 4-9) used it as early as 1650 BCE. *Fresco* (Italian for "fresh") is a mural-painting technique that involves applying permanent limeproof pigments, diluted in water, on freshly laid lime plaster. Because the surface of the wall absorbs the pigments as the plaster dries, fresco is one of the most permanent painting techniques. The stable condition of frescoes such as those in the Arena Chapel (FIGS. 19-1 and 19-9) and in the Sistine Chapel (FIGS. 22-1, 22-18, and 22-19), now hundreds of years old, attest to the longevity of this painting method. The colors have remained vivid (although dirt and soot have necessitated cleaning) because of the chemically inert pigments the artists used. In addition to this *buon fresco* ("true" fresco) technique, artists used *fresco secco* (dry fresco). Fresco secco involves painting on dried lime plaster. Although the finished product visually approximates buon fresco, the plaster wall does not absorb the pigments, which simply adhere to the surface. Thus fresco secco does not have buon fresco's longevity.

The buon fresco process is time-consuming and demanding and requires several layers of plaster. Although buon fresco methods vary, generally the artist prepares the wall with a rough layer of lime plaster called the *arriccio* (brown coat). The artist then transfers the composition to the wall, usually by drawing directly on the arriccio with a burnt-orange pigment called *sinopia* (most popular during the 14th century) or by transferring a *cartoon* (a full-sized preparatory drawing). Cartoons increased in usage in the 15th and 16th centuries, largely replacing sinopia underdrawings. Finally, the painter lays the *intonaco* (painting coat) smoothly over the drawing in sections (called *giornate*, Italian for "days") only as large as the artist expects to complete in that session. The buon fresco painter must apply the colors fairly quickly, because once the plaster is dry, it will no longer absorb the pigment. Any areas of the intonaco that remain unpainted after a session must be cut away so that fresh plaster can be applied for the next giornata.

In areas of high humidity, such as Venice, fresco was less appropriate because moisture is an obstacle to the drying process. Over the centuries, fresco became less popular, although it did experience a revival in the 1930s with the Mexican muralists (FIGS. 35-67 and 35-68).

1 ft.

19-9 GIOTTO DI BONDONE, *Lamentation*, Arena Chapel (Cappella Scrovegni), Padua, Italy, ca. 1305. Fresco, 6' 6¾" × 6' 3¾".

In this fresco painted in several sections, Giotto used the diagonal slope of the rocky landscape to direct the viewer's attention toward the head of the sculpturesque figure of the dead Christ.

marble goddess. Giotto replaced Cimabue's slender Virgin, fragile beneath the thin ripplings of her drapery, with a weighty, queenly mother. In Giotto's painting, the Madonna's body is not lost. It is asserted. Giotto even shows Mary's breasts pressing through the thin fabric of her white undergarment. Gold highlights have disappeared from her heavy robe. Giotto aimed, before all else, to construct a figure that has substance, dimensionality, and bulk—qualities suppressed in favor of a spiritual immateriality in Byzantine and Italo-Byzantine art. Works painted in the new style portray sculpturesque figures—projecting into the light and giving the illusion that they could throw shadows. Giotto's *Madonna Enthroned* marks the end of medieval painting in Italy and the beginning of a new naturalistic approach to art.

ARENA CHAPEL, PADUA To project onto a flat surface the illusion of solid bodies moving through space presents a double challenge. Constructing the illusion of a body also requires constructing the illusion of a space sufficiently ample to contain that body. In his *fresco* cycles (see "Fresco Painting," above), Giotto constantly strove to reconcile these two aspects of illusionistic painting. His murals in the Arena Chapel (Cappella Scrovegni; FIG. 19-1) at Padua show his art at its finest. Enrico Scrovegni, a wealthy Paduan banker, built the chapel on a site adjacent to his now-razed palace. Consecrated in 1305, the Arena Chapel takes its name from an ancient Roman amphitheater nearby. Scrovegni erected the chapel, which he intended for his family's private use, in part to expiate the bankers' sin of usury. Some scholars have suggested that Giotto himself may have been the chapel's architect because its design is so perfectly suited to its interior decoration.

The rectangular *barrel-vaulted* hall has six narrow windows only in its south wall (FIG. 19-1, *left*), which left the entire north wall an unbroken and well-illuminated surface for painting. The building seems to have been designed to provide Giotto with as much flat surface as possible for presenting one of the most impressive and complete Christian pictorial cycles ever rendered. In 38 framed pictures, arranged on three levels, the artist related the most poignant incidents from the lives of the Virgin and her parents, Joachim and Anna (top level), the life and mission of Christ (middle level), and his Passion, Crucifixion, and Resurrection (bottom level). These three pictorial levels rest on a coloristically neutral base. Imitation marble veneer—reminiscent of ancient Roman decoration (FIG. 10-51), which Giotto may have seen—alternates with the Virtues and Vices painted in *grisaille* (monochrome grays, often used for modeling in paintings) to resemble sculpture. The climactic event of the cycle of human salvation, the Last Judgment, covers most of the west wall above the chapel's entrance (FIG. 19-1).

The hall's vaulted ceiling is blue, an azure sky dotted with golden stars symbolic of Heaven. Medallions bearing images of Christ, Mary, and various prophets also appear on the vault. Giotto painted the same blue in the backgrounds of the narrative panels on the walls below. The color thereby functions as a unifying agent for the entire decorative scheme and renders the scenes more realistic.

A GIOTTO,
*y into
salem*,
305.

Decorative borders frame the individual panels. They offer a striking contrast to the sparse simplicity of the images they surround. Subtly scaled to the chapel's space (only about half life-size), Giotto's stately and slow-moving actors present their dramas convincingly and with great restraint. *Lamentation* (FIG. 19-9) reveals the essentials of his style. In the presence of boldly *foreshortened* angels, seen head-on with their bodies receding into the background and darting about in hysterical grief, a congregation mourns over the dead body of the Savior just before its entombment. Mary cradles her son's body, while Mary Magdalene looks solemnly at the wounds in Christ's feet and Saint John the Evangelist throws his arms back dramatically. Giotto arranged a shallow stage for the figures, bounded by a thick diagonal rock incline that defines a horizontal ledge in the foreground. Though narrow, the ledge provides firm visual support for the figures, and the steep slope indicates the picture's dramatic focal point at the lower left. The rocky setting, which recalls that of a 12th-century Byzantine mural (FIG. 12-27), also links this scene with the adjoining one. Giotto connected the framed scenes throughout the fresco cycle with such formal elements. The figures are sculpturesque, simple, and weighty, but this mass did not preclude motion and emotion. Postures and gestures that might have been only rhetorical and mechanical convey, in *Lamentation*, a broad spectrum of grief. They range from Mary's almost fierce despair to the passionate outbursts of Mary Magdalene and John to the philosophical resignation of the two disciples at the right and the mute sorrow of the two hooded mourners in the foreground. Giotto constructed a kind of stage that served as a model for artists who depicted human dramas in many subsequent paintings. His style broke sharply from the isolated episodes and figures seen in art until the late 13th century. In *Lamentation*, a single event provokes an intense response. Painters before Giotto rarely attempted, let alone achieved, this combination of compositional complexity and emotional resonance.

B GIOTTO,
*ayal of
us*, ca. 1305.

The formal design of the *Lamentation* fresco—the way the figures are grouped within the constructed space—is worth close study. Each group has its own definition, and each contributes to the rhythmic order of the composition. The strong diagonal of the rocky ledge, with its single dead tree (the tree of knowledge of good and evil, which withered at the fall of Adam), concentrates the viewer's attention on the group around the head of Christ, whose positioning is dynamically off center. The massive bulk of the seated mourner in the painting's left corner arrests and contains all movement beyond this group. The seated mourner to the right establishes a relation with the center figures, who, by gazes and gestures, draw the viewer's attention back to Christ's head. Figures seen from the back, which are frequent in Giotto's compositions, represent an innovation in the development away from the formal Italo-Byzantine style. These figures emphasize the foreground, aiding the visual placement of the intermediate figures farther back in space. This device, the very contradiction of the old frontality, in effect puts viewers behind the "observer figures," who, facing the action as spectators, reinforce the sense of stagecraft as a model for painting.

Giotto's new devices for depicting spatial depth and body mass could not, of course, have been possible without his management of light and shade. He shaded his figures to indicate both the direction of the light that illuminates them and the shadows (the diminished light), giving the figures volume. In *Lamentation*, light falls upon the upper surfaces of the figures (especially the two central bending figures) and passes down to dark in their draperies, separating the volumes one from the other and pushing one to the fore, the other to the rear. The graded continuum of light and shade, directed by an even, neutral light from a single steady source—not shown in the picture—was the first step toward the development of *chiaroscuro* (the use of contrasts of dark and light to produce modeling) in later Renaissance painting.

The stagelike settings made possible by Giotto's innovations in *perspective* (the depiction of three-dimensional objects in space on a two-dimensional surface) and lighting suited perfectly the dramatic narrative the Franciscans emphasized then as a principal method for educating the faithful in their religion. In the age of humanism, the old stylized presentations of the holy mysteries had evolved into what were called *mystery plays*. The drama of the Mass was extended into one- and two-act tableaus and scenes and then into simple narratives offered at church portals and in city squares. (Eventually, confraternities also presented more elaborate religious dramas called *sacre rappresentazioni*—holy representations.) The great increase in popular sermons addressed to huge city audiences prompted a public taste for narrative, recited as dramatically as possible. The arts of illusionistic painting, of drama, and of sermon rhetoric with all their theatrical flourishes developed simultaneously and were mutually influential. Giotto's art masterfully synthesized dramatic narrative, holy lesson, and truth to human experience in a visual idiom of his own invention, accessible to all. Not surprisingly, Giotto's frescoes served as textbooks for generations of Renaissance painters.

Siena

Among 14th-century Italian city-states, the Republics of Siena and Florence were the most powerful. Both Siena and Florence (the major cities of these two republics) were urban centers of bankers and merchants with widespread international contacts and large sums available for the commissioning of artworks (see "Artists' Guilds, Commissions, and Contracts," page 506).

DUCCIO The works of DUCCIO DI BUONINSEGNA (active ca. 1278–1318) represent Sienese art in its supreme achievement. His most famous painting, the immense altarpiece called the *Maestà*

Artists' Guilds, Commissions, and Contracts

The structured organization of economic activity during the 14th century, when Italy had established a thriving international trade and held a commanding position in the Mediterranean world, extended to many trades and professions. *Guilds* (associations of master craftspeople, apprentices, and tradespeople), which had emerged during the 12th century, became prominent. These associations not only protected members' common economic interests against external pressures, such as taxation, but also provided them with the means to regulate their internal operations (for example, work quality and membership training).

Because of today's international open art market, the notion of an "artists' union" may seem strange. The general public tends to see art as the creative expression of an individual artist. However, artists did not always enjoy this degree of freedom. Historically, artists rarely undertook major artworks without a patron's concrete commission. The patron could be a civic group, religious entity, private individual, or even the artists' guild itself. Guilds, although primarily economic commercial organizations, contributed to their city's religious and artistic life by subsidizing the building and decoration of numerous churches and hospitals. For example, the Arte della Lana (wool manufacturers' guild) oversaw the start of Florence Cathedral (FIGS. 19-18 and 19-19) in 1296, and the Arte di Calimala (wool merchants' guild) supervised the completion of its dome.

Monastic orders, confraternities, and the popes were also major art patrons. In addition, wealthy families and individuals commissioned artworks for a variety of reasons. Besides the aesthetic pleasure these patrons derived from art, the images often served as testaments to the patron's wealth, status, power, and knowledge. Because artworks during this period were the product of what was, in effect, a service contract, a patron's needs or wishes played a crucial role in the final form of any painting, sculpture, or building. Some contracts between patrons and artists are preserved in European municipal and church archives. The patrons normally asked artists to submit drawings or models for approval, and they expected the artists they hired to adhere to the approved designs fairly closely. These contracts usually stipulated certain conditions, such as the insistence on the artist's own hand in the production of the work, the quality of pigment and amount of gold or other precious items to be used, completion date, payment terms, and penalties for failure to meet the contract's terms.

A few extant 13th- and 14th-century painting contracts are especially illuminating. Although they may specify the subject to be represented, the focus of these binding legal documents is always the financial aspects of the commission and the responsibilities of the painter to the patron (and vice versa). In a contract dated November 1, 1301, between Cimabue and another artist and the Hospital of Santa Chiara in Pisa, the artists agree to supply an altarpiece

> with colonnettes, tabernacles, and predella, painted with histories of the divine majesty of the Blessed Virgin Mary, of the apostles, of

the angels, and with other figures and pictures, as shall be seen fit and shall please the said master of or other legitimate persons for the hospital.*

Other contract terms specify the size of the panel and require that gold and silver gilding be used for parts of the altarpiece.

The contract for the construction of an altarpiece was usually a separate document, for that required the services of a master carpenter. For example, Duccio's April 15, 1285, contract with the rectors of the Confraternity of the Laudesi, the lay group associated with the Dominican church of Santa Maria Novella (FIG. 19-6) in Florence, specifies only that he is to provide the painting, not its frame—and it imposes conditions that he must meet if he is to be paid.

> [The rectors] promise . . . to pay the same Duccio . . . as the payment and price of the painting of the said panel that is to be painted and done by him in the way described below . . . 150 lire of the small florins. . . . [Duccio, in turn, promises] to paint and embellish the panel with the image of the blessed Virgin Mary and of her omnipotent Son and other figures, according to the wishes and pleasure of the lessors, and to gild [the panel] and do everything that will enhance the beauty of the panel, his being all the expenses and the costs. . . . If the said panel is not beautifully painted and it is not embellished according to the wishes and desires of the same lessors, they are in no way bound to pay him the price or any part of it.†

Sometimes patrons furnished the materials and paid artists by the day instead of a fixed amount. That was the arrangement Duccio made on October 9, 1308, when he agreed to paint the *Maestà* (FIG. 19-10) for the high altar of Siena Cathedral.

> Duccio has promised to paint and make the said panel as well as he can and knows how, and he further agreed not to accept or receive any other work until the said panel is done and completed. . . . [The church officials promise] to pay the said Duccio sixteen solidi of the Sienese denari as his salary for the said work and labor for each day that the said Duccio works with his own hands on the said panel . . . [and] to provide and give everything that will be necessary for working on the said panel so that the said Duccio need contribute nothing to the work save his person and his effort.‡

In all cases, the artists worked for their patrons and could count on being compensated for their talents and efforts only if the work they delivered met the standards of those who ordered it.

---

* Translated by John White, *Duccio: Tuscan Art and the Medieval Workshop* (London: Thames & Hudson, 1979), 34.
† Translated by James H. Stubblebine, *Duccio di Buoninsegna and His School* (Princeton, N.J.: Princeton University Press, 1979), 1: 192.
‡ Stubblebine, *Duccio*, 1: 201.

19-10 Duccio di Buoninsegna, *Virgin and Child Enthroned with Saints*, principal panel of the *Maestà* altarpiece, from Siena Cathedral, Siena, Italy, 1308–1311. Tempera and gold leaf on wood, 7′ × 13′ (center panel). Museo dell'Opera del Duomo, Siena. ◼◀

Duccio derived the formality and symmetry of his composition from Byzantine tradition, but relaxed the rigidity and frontality of the figures, softened the drapery, and individualized the faces.

10A Duccio, ck of the *Maestà*, 08–1311.

(*Virgin Enthroned in Majesty*; FIG. **19-10**), replaced a much smaller painting of the Virgin Mary on the high altar of Siena Cathedral. The Sienese believed the Virgin had brought them their victory over the Florentines at the battle of Monteperti in 1260, and she was the focus of the religious life of the republic. Duccio and his assistants began work on the prestigious commission in 1308 and completed the *Maestà* in 1311. As originally executed, it consisted of a seven-foot-high central panel (FIG. **19-10**), surmounted by seven *pinnacles* above, and a *predella*, or raised shelf, of panels at the base, altogether some 13 feet high. Painted in tempera front and back, the work unfortunately is no longer viewable in its entirety because of its dismantling in subsequent centuries. Many of Duccio's panels are now scattered as single masterpieces among the world's museums.

The main panel of the front side represents the Virgin enthroned as Queen of Heaven amid choruses of angels and saints. Duccio derived the composition's formality and symmetry, along with the figures and facial types of the principal angels and saints, from Byzantine tradition. But the artist relaxed the strict frontality and rigidity of the figures. They turn to each other in quiet conversation. Further, Duccio individualized the faces of the four saints kneeling in the foreground, who perform their ceremonial gestures without stiffness. Similarly, he softened the usual Byzantine hard body outlines and drapery patterning. The drapery, particularly that of the female saints at both ends of the panel, falls and curves loosely. This is a feature familiar in northern Gothic works (FIG. **18-37**) and is a mark of the artistic dialogue between Italy and the north in the 14th century.

Despite these changes that reveal Duccio's interest in the new naturalism, he respected the age-old requirement that as an altarpiece, the *Maestà* would be the focus of worship in Siena's largest

and most important church, its *cathedral,* the seat of the bishop of Siena. As such, Duccio knew the *Maestà* should be an object holy in itself—a work of splendor to the eyes, precious in its message and its materials. Duccio thus recognized that he could not be too radical—that the function of this work naturally limited experimentation with depicting narrative action and producing illusionistic effects (such as Giotto's) by modeling forms and adjusting their placement in pictorial space.

Instead, the Queen of Heaven panel is a miracle of color composition and *texture* manipulation, unfortunately not apparent in a photograph. Close inspection of the original reveals what the Sienese artist learned from other sources. In the 13th and 14th centuries, Italy was the distribution center for the great silk trade from China and the Middle East (see "Silk and the Silk Road," Chapter 7, page 188). After processing the silk in city-states such as Lucca and Florence, the Italians exported the precious fabric throughout Europe to satisfy an immense market for sumptuous dress. (Dante, Petrarch, and many of the humanists decried the appetite for luxury in costume, which to them represented a decline in civic and moral virtue.) People throughout Europe (Duccio and other artists among them) prized fabrics from China, Persia, Byzantium, and the Islamic realms. In the *Maestà* panel, Duccio created the glistening and shimmering effects of textiles, adapting the motifs and design patterns of exotic materials. Complementing the luxurious fabrics and the (lost) gilded wood frame are the gold haloes of the holy figures, which feature tooled decorative designs in gold leaf (*punchwork*). But Duccio, like Giotto (FIG. **19-8**), eliminated almost all the gold patterning of the figures' garments in favor of creating three-dimensional volume. Traces remain only in the Virgin's red dress.

19-11 DUCCIO DI BUONINSEGNA, *Betrayal of Jesus,* detail from the back of the *Maestà* altarpiece, from Siena Cathedral, Siena, Italy, 1309–1311. Tempera and gold leaf on wood, detail 1′ $10\frac{1}{2}$″ × 3′ 4″. Museo dell'Opera del Duomo, Siena.

On the back of the *Maestà,* Duccio painted a religious drama in which the actors display a variety of individual emotions. Duccio here took a decisive step toward the humanization of religious subject matter.

19-11A DUCCIO, *Entry into Jerusalem,* 1308–1311.

On the front panel of the *Maestà,* Duccio showed himself as the great master of the formal altarpiece. However, he allowed himself greater latitude for experimentation in the small accompanying panels, front and back. (Both sides of the altarpiece were always on view because the high altar stood at the very center of the sanctuary.) These images reveal Duccio's powers as a narrative painter. In the numerous panels on the back, he illustrated the later life of Christ—his ministry (on the *predella*), his Passion (on the main panel), and his Resurrection and appearances to the disciples (on the pinnacles). On one of the small panels, *Betrayal of Jesus* (FIG. **19-11**), the artist represented several episodes of the event—the betrayal of Jesus by Judas's false kiss, the disciples fleeing in terror, and Peter cutting off the ear of the high priest's servant. Although the background, with its golden sky and rock formations, remains traditional, the style of the figures before it has changed quite radically. The bodies are not the flat frontal shapes of Italo-Byzantine art. Duccio imbued them with mass, modeled them with a range from light to dark, and arranged their draperies around them convincingly. Even more novel and striking is the way the figures seem to react to the central event. Through posture, gesture, and even facial expression, they display a variety of emotions. Duccio carefully differentiated among the anger of Peter, the malice of Judas (echoed in the faces of the throng about Jesus), and the apprehension and timidity of the fleeing disciples. These figures are actors in a religious drama that the artist interpreted in terms of thoroughly human actions and reactions. In this and similar narrative panels, Duccio took a decisive step toward the humanization of religious subject matter.

ORVIETO CATHEDRAL While Duccio was working on the *Maestà* for Siena Cathedral, a Sienese architect, LORENZO MAITANI, was called to Orvieto to design that city's cathedral (FIG. **19-12**). The Orvieto *facade* imitates some elements of the French Gothic

architectural vocabulary (see Chapter 18), especially the pointed gables over the three doorways, the *rose window* and statues in niches in the upper zone, and the four large *pinnacles* that divide the facade into three bays. The outer pinnacles serve as miniature substitutes for the large northern European west-front towers. Maitani's facade, however, is merely a Gothic overlay masking a marble-revetted basil-

19-12 LORENZO MAITANI, west facade of Orvieto Cathedral, Orvieto, Italy, begun 1310.

The pointed gables over the doorways, the rose window, and the large pinnacles derive from French architecture, but the facade of Orvieto Cathedral is merely a Gothic overlay masking a timber-roofed basilica.

A pupil of Duccio, Martini was instrumental in the creation of the International Style. Its hallmarks are elegant shapes, radiant color, flowing line, and weightless figures in golden, spaceless settings.

2A Siena edral, un ca. 1226.

ican structure in the Tuscan Romanesque tradition, as the three-quarter view of the cathedral in FIG. 19-12 reveals. Few Italian architects fully accepted the northern Gothic style. Some architectural historians even have questioned whether it is proper to speak of late medieval Italian buildings as Gothic structures. The Orvieto facade resembles a great altar screen, its single plane covered with carefully placed carved and painted ornament. In principle, Orvieto belongs with Pisa Cathedral (FIG. 17-25) and other Italian buildings rather than with the French cathedrals at Amiens (FIG. 18-21) and Reims (FIG. 18-23). Inside, Orvieto Cathedral has a timber-roofed nave with a two-story elevation (columnar *arcade* and *clerestory*) in the Early Christian manner. Both the *chancel arch* framing the semicircular *apse* and the nave arcade's arches are round as opposed to pointed.

SIMONE MARTINI Duccio's successors in the Sienese school also produced innovative works. Simone Martini (ca. 1285–1344) was a pupil of Duccio and may have assisted him in painting the *Maestà*. Martini was a close friend of Petrarch, and the poet praised him highly for his portrait of "Laura" (the woman to whom Petrarch dedicated his sonnets). Martini worked for the French kings in Naples and Sicily and, in his last years, produced paintings for the papal court at Avignon, where he came in contact with Northern European painters. By adapting the insubstantial but luxuriant patterns of the French Gothic manner to Sienese art and, in turn, by acquainting painters north of the Alps with the Sienese style, Martini was instrumental in creating the so-called *International Style*. This new style swept Europe during the late 14th and early 15th centuries because it appealed to the aristocratic taste for brilliant colors, lavish costumes, intricate ornamentation, and themes involving splendid processions.

Martini's *Annunciation* altarpiece (FIG. 19-13) features elegant shapes and radiant color, fluttering line, and weightless figures in a spaceless setting—all hallmarks of the artist's style. The complex etiquette of the European chivalric courts probably dictated the presentation. The angel Gabriel has just alighted, the breeze of his passage lifting his mantle, his iridescent wings still beating. The gold of his sumptuous gown is representative of the celestial realm from which he has descended to deliver his message. The Virgin, putting down her book of devotions, shrinks demurely from Gabriel's reverent genuflection, an appropriate gesture in the presence of royalty. She draws about her the deep blue, golden-hemmed mantle, the heraldic colors she wears as Queen of Heaven. Between the two figures is a vase of white lilies, symbolic of the Virgin's purity. Despite the Virgin's modesty and diffidence and the tremendous import of the angel's message, the scene subordinates drama to court ritual, and structural experimentation to surface splendor. The intricate *tracery* of the richly tooled (reconstructed) French Gothic–inspired frame and the elaborate punchwork halos, now a characteristic feature of Sienese panel painting, enhance the tactile magnificence of the *Annunciation*.

Simone Martini and his student and assistant, Lippo Memmi (active ca. 1317–1350), signed the altarpiece and dated it (1333). The latter's contribution to the *Annunciation* is still a matter of debate, but art historians now generally agree he painted the two lateral saints. These figures, which are reminiscent of the jamb statues of Gothic church portals, have greater solidity and lack the linear elegance of Martini's central pair. Given the nature of medieval and Renaissance workshop practices, it is often next to impossible to distinguish the master's hand from that of an assistant, especially if the master corrected or redid part of the latter's work (see "Artistic Training in Renaissance Italy," page 510).

Artistic Training in Renaissance Italy

In 14th- through 16th-century Italy, training to become a professional artist (earning membership in the appropriate guild) was a laborious and lengthy process. Because Italians perceived art as a trade, they expected artists to be trained as they would be in any other profession. Accordingly, aspiring artists started their training at an early age, anywhere from 7 to 15 years old. Their fathers would negotiate arrangements with specific master artists whereby each youth lived with a master for a specified number of years, usually five or six. During that time, they served as apprentices to the masters in the workshop, learning the trade. (This living arrangement served as a major obstacle for aspiring female artists, as it was considered inappropriate for young girls to live in a master's household.)

The skills apprentices learned varied with the type of studio they joined. Those apprenticed to painters learned to grind pigments, draw, prepare wood panels for painting, gild, and lay plaster for fresco. Sculptors in training learned to manipulate different materials (for example, wood, stone, *terracotta* [baked clay], wax, bronze, or stucco), although many sculpture workshops specialized in only one or two of these materials. For stone carving, apprentices learned their craft by blocking out the master's designs for statues.

The guilds supervised this rigorous training. They wanted not only to ensure their professional reputations by admitting only the most talented members but also to control the number of artists (to limit undue competition). Toward this end they frequently tried to regulate the number of apprentices working under a single master. Surely, the quality of the apprentices a master trained reflected the master's competence. When encouraging a prospective apprentice to join his studio, the Paduan painter Francesco Squarcione (1397–1468) boasted he could teach "the true art of perspective and everything necessary to the art of painting. . . . I made a man of Andrea Mantegna [see Chapter 21] who stayed with me and I will also do the same to you."*

As their skills developed, apprentices took on increasingly difficult tasks. After completing their apprenticeships, artists entered the appropriate guilds. For example, painters, who ground pigments, joined the guild of apothecaries; sculptors were members of the guild of stoneworkers; and goldsmiths entered the silk guild, because gold often was stretched into threads wound around silk for weaving. Such memberships served as certification of the artists' competence. Once "certified," artists often affiliated themselves with established workshops, as assistants to master artists. This was largely for practical reasons. New artists could not expect to receive many commissions, and the cost of establishing their own workshops was high. In any case, this arrangement was not permanent, and workshops were not necessarily static enterprises. Although well-established and respected studios existed, workshops could be organized around individual masters (with no set studio locations) or organized for a specific project, especially an extensive decoration program.

Generally, assistants were responsible for gilding frames and backgrounds, completing decorative work, and, occasionally, rendering architectural settings. Artists regarded figures, especially those central to the represented subject, as the most important and difficult parts of a painting, and the master therefore reserved these for himself. Sometimes assistants painted secondary or marginal figures, but only under the master's close supervision.

Eventually, of course, artists hoped to attract patrons and establish themselves as masters. Artists, who were largely anonymous during the medieval period, began to enjoy greater emancipation during the 15th and 16th centuries, when they rose in rank from artisan to artist-scientist. The value of their individual skills—and their reputations—became increasingly important to their patrons and clients.

* Quoted in Giuseppe Fiocco, *Mantegna: La cappella Ovetari nella chiesa degli Eremitani* (Milan: A. Pizzi, 1974), 7.

PIETRO LORENZETTI One of Duccio's students, Pietro Lorenzetti (active 1320–1348), contributed significantly to the general experiments in pictorial realism that characterized the 14th century. Going well beyond his master, Lorenzetti achieved a remarkable degree of spatial illusionism in his large *triptych* (three-part panel painting) *Birth of the Virgin* (FIG. 19-14), created for the altar of Saint Savinus in Siena Cathedral. Lorenzetti painted the wooden architectural members that divide the panel as though they extend back into the painted space. Viewers seem to look through the wooden frame (apparently added later) into a boxlike stage, where the event takes place. That one of the vertical members cuts across one of the figures, blocking part of it from view, strengthens the illusion. In subsequent centuries, artists exploited this use of architectural elements to enhance the pictorial illusion that the painted figures are acting out a drama just a few feet away. This kind of pictorial illusionism characterized ancient Roman mural painting (FIGS. 10-18 and 10-19, *right*), but had not been practiced in Italy for a thousand years.

Lorenzetti's setting for his holy subject also represented a marked step in the advance of worldly realism. Saint Anne—who, like Nicola Pisano's Virgin of the *Nativity* (FIG. 19-3), resembles a reclining figure on the lid of a Roman sarcophagus (FIG. 10-61)—props herself up

wearily as the midwives wash the child and the women bring gifts. She is the center of an episode that occurs in an upper-class Italian house of the period. A number of carefully observed domestic details and the scene at the left, where Joachim eagerly awaits the news of the delivery, place the event in an actual household, as if viewers had moved the panels of the walls back and peered inside. Lorenzetti joined structural innovation in illusionistic space with the new curiosity that led to careful inspection and recording of what lay directly before the artist's eye in the everyday world.

PALAZZO PUBBLICO Not all Sienese painting of the early 14th century was religious in character. One of the most important fresco cycles of the period (discussed next) was a civic commission for Siena's Palazzo Pubblico ("public palace" or city hall). Siena was a proud commercial and political rival of Florence. As the secular center of the community, the civic meeting hall in the main square (the Campo, or Field; FIG. 19-15) was almost as great an object of civic pride as the city's cathedral. The Palazzo Pubblico has a slightly concave facade (to conform to the irregular shape of the Campo) and a gigantic tower visible from miles around. The imposing building and tower must have earned the admiration of Siena's citizens as well as of

19-14 PIETRO LORENZETTI, *Birth of the Virgin,* from the altar of Saint Savinus, Siena Cathedral, Siena, Italy, 1342. Tempera on wood, 6′ 1″ × 5′ 11″. Museo dell'Opera del Duomo, Siena.

In this triptych, Pietro Lorenzetti revived the pictorial illusionism of ancient Roman murals and painted the architectural members that divide the panel as though they extend back into the painted space.

1 ft.

19-15 Aerial view of the Campo with the Palazzo Pubblico, Siena, Italy, 1288–1309.

Siena's Palazzo Pubblico has a slightly concave facade and a gigantic tower visible from miles around. The tower served both as a defensive lookout over the countryside and a symbol of the city-state's power.

visitors to the city, inspiring in them respect for the republic's power and success. The tower served as lookout over the city and the countryside around it and as a bell tower (*campanile*) for ringing signals of all sorts to the populace. Siena, like other Italian city-states, had to defend itself against neighboring cities and often against kings and emperors. In addition, it had to be secure against the internal upheavals common in the history of the Italian city-republics. Class struggle, feuds between rich and powerful families, and even uprisings of the whole populace against the city governors were constant threats. The heavy walls and *battlements* (fortified *parapets*) of the Italian town hall eloquently express how frequently the city governors needed to defend themselves against their own citizens. The Sienese tower, out

19-16 Ambrogio Lorenzetti, *Peaceful City,* detail from *Effects of Good Government in the City and in the Country,* Sala della Pace, Palazzo Pubblico, Siena, Italy, 1338–1339. Fresco.

In the Hall of Peace of Siena's city hall, Ambrogio Lorenzetti painted an illusionistic panorama of the bustling city. The fresco served as an allegory of good government in the Sienese republic.

of reach of most missiles, includes *machicolated galleries* (galleries with holes in their floors to allow the dumping of stones or hot liquids on enemies below) built out on *corbels* (projecting supporting architectural members) for defense of the tower's base.

AMBROGIO LORENZETTI The painter entrusted with the vast fresco program in Siena's Palazzo Pubblico was Pietro Lorenzetti's brother, Ambrogio Lorenzetti (active 1319–1348), who both elaborated Pietro's advances in illusionistic representation in spectacular fashion and gave visual form to Sienese civic concerns. Ambrogio produced three frescoes for the walls of the Sala della Pace (Hall of Peace) in the Palazzo Pubblico: *Allegory of Good Government, Bad Government and the Effects of Bad Government in the City,* and *Effects of Good Government in the City and in the Country.* The turbulent politics of the Italian cities—the violent party struggles, the overthrow and reinstatement of governments—certainly would have called for solemn

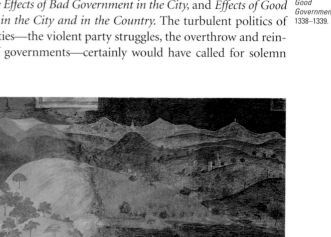

19-16A Ambrogio Lorenzetti, *Good Government,* 1338–1339.

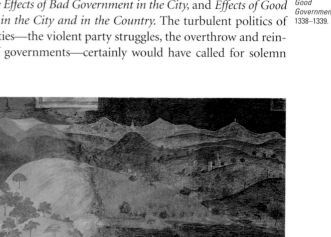

19-17 Ambrogio Lorenzetti, *Peaceful Country,* detail from *Effects of Good Government in the City and in the Country,* Sala della Pace, Palazzo Pubblico, Siena, Italy, 1338–1339. Fresco.

This sweeping view of the Sienese countryside is one of the first appearances of landscape in Western art since antiquity. An allegorical figure of winged Security promises safety to all who live under the rule of law.

reminders of fair and just administration. And the city hall was just the place for paintings such as Ambrogio Lorenzetti's. Indeed, the leaders of the Sienese government who commissioned this fresco series had undertaken the "ordering and reformation of the whole city and countryside of Siena."

In *Effects of Good Government in the City and in the Country,* the artist depicted the urban and rural effects of good government. *Peaceful City* (FIG. 19-16) is a panoramic view of Siena, with its clustering palaces, markets, towers, churches, streets, and walls, reminiscent of the townscapes of ancient Roman murals (FIG. 10-19, *left*). The city's traffic moves peacefully, guild members ply their trades and crafts, and several radiant maidens, hand in hand, perform a graceful circling dance. Dancers were regular features of festive springtime rituals. Here, their presence also serves as a metaphor for a peaceful commonwealth. The artist fondly observed the life of his city, and its architecture gave him an opportunity to apply Sienese artists' rapidly growing knowledge of perspective.

As an entourage passes through the city gate to the countryside beyond its walls, Ambrogio Lorenzetti's *Peaceful Country* (FIG. 19-17) presents a bird's-eye view of the undulating Tuscan countryside—its villas, castles, plowed farmlands, and peasants going about their seasonal occupations. An allegorical figure of Security hovers above the landscape, unfurling a scroll that promises safety to all who live under the rule of law. In this sweeping view of an actual countryside, *Peaceful Country* represents one of the first appearances of *landscape* in Western art since antiquity (FIG. 10-20). Whereas earlier depictions were fairly generic, Lorenzetti particularized the landscape—as well as the city view—by careful observation and endowed the painting with the character of a specific place and environment.

The Black Death may have ended the careers of both Lorenzettis. They disappear from historical records in 1348, the year that brought so much horror to defenseless Europe.

Florence

Like Siena, the Republic of Florence was a dominant city-state during the 14th century. The historian Giovanni Villani (ca. 1270–1348), for example, described Florence as "the daughter and the creature of Rome," suggesting a preeminence inherited from the Roman Empire. Florentines were fiercely proud of what they perceived as their economic and cultural superiority. Florence controlled the textile industry in Italy, and the republic's gold *florin* was the standard coin of exchange everywhere in Europe.

FLORENCE CATHEDRAL Florentines translated their pride in their predominance into landmark buildings, such as Florence Cathedral (FIG. 19-18), recognized as the center for the most important religious observances in the city. ARNOLFO DI CAMBIO (ca. 1245–1302) began work on the cathedral in 1296. Intended as the "most beautiful and honorable church in Tuscany," this structure reveals the competitiveness Florentines felt with cities such as Siena and Pisa. Cathedral authorities planned for the church to hold the city's entire population, and although it holds only about 30,000 (Florence's population at the time was slightly less than 100,000), it seemed so large that even the noted architect Leon Battista Alberti (see Chapter 21) commented that it seemed to cover "all of Tuscany with its shade." The builders ornamented the church's surfaces, in the old Tuscan fashion, with marble-encrusted geometric designs, matching the cathedral's *revetment* (decorative wall paneling) to that

19-18A ARNOLFO DI CAMBIO, Palazzo della Signoria, 1299–1310.

19-18 ARNOLFO DI CAMBIO and others, Florence Cathedral (aerial view looking northeast), Florence, Italy, begun 1296.

This basilican church with its marble-encrusted walls carries on the Tuscan Romanesque architectural tradition, linking Florence Cathedral more closely to Early Christian Italy than to contemporaneous France.

eye ever-upward and never permit it to rest until it reaches the sky. The Italian tower is entirely different. Neatly subdivided into cubic sections, Giotto's tower is the sum of its component parts. Not only could this tower be removed from the building without adverse effects, but also each of the parts—cleanly separated from each other by continuous moldings—seems capable of existing independently as an object of considerable aesthetic appeal. This compartmentalization is reminiscent of the Romanesque style, but it also forecasts the ideals of Renaissance architecture. Artists hoped to express structure in the clear, logical relationships of the component parts and to produce self-sufficient works that could exist in complete independence. Compared with Cologne's towers, Giotto's campanile has a cool and rational quality that appeals more to the intellect than to the emotions.

In Florence Cathedral's plan, the nave (FIG. 19-19) appears to have been added to the *crossing* complex almost as an afterthought. In fact, the nave was the first section to be built, mostly according to Arnolfo di Cambio's original plans (except for the vaulting). Midway through the 14th century, the Florentines redesigned the crossing to increase the cathedral's interior space. In its present form, the area beneath the *dome* is the design's focal point, and the nave leads to it. To visitors from north of the Alps, the nave may have seemed as strange as the plan. Neither has a northern European counterpart. The Florence nave *bays* are twice as deep as those of Amiens (FIG. 18-19), and the wide arcades permit the shallow aisles to become part of the central nave. The result is an interior of unmatched spaciousness. The accent here, as it is on the exterior, is on the horizontal elements. The substantial capitals of the *piers* prevent them from soaring into the vaults and emphasize their function as supports.

The facade of Florence Cathedral was not completed until the 19th century and then in a form much altered from its original design. In fact, until the 17th century, Italian builders exhibited little concern for the facades of their churches, and dozens remain unfinished to this day. One reason for this may be that Italian architects did not conceive the facades as integral parts of the structures but, as in the case of Orvieto Cathedral (FIG. 19-12), as screens that could be added to the church exterior at any time.

19-19A ANDREA PISANO, south doors, Baptistery, Florence, 1330–1336.

19-19B ANDREA ORCAGNA, tabernacle, Or San Michele, 1355–1359.

19-19 ARNOLFO DI CAMBIO and others, interior of Florence Cathedral (looking east), Florence, Italy, begun 1296.

Designed to hold 30,000 worshipers, Florence Cathedral has fewer but wider and deeper nave and aisle bays than do northern Gothic cathedrals. The result is an interior of unmatched spaciousness.

of the neighboring 11th-century Romanesque baptistery of San Giovanni (FIGS. 17-26 and 19-18, *bottom left*).

The vast gulf that separates Florence Cathedral from its northern European counterparts becomes evident in a comparison between the Italian church and a full-blown German representative of the High Gothic style, such as Cologne Cathedral (FIG. 18-45). Cologne Cathedral's emphatic stress on the vertical produces an awe-inspiring upward rush of almost unmatched vigor and intensity. The building has the character of an organic growth shooting heavenward, its toothed upper portions engaging the sky. The pierced, translucent stone tracery of the spires merges with the atmosphere. Florence Cathedral, in contrast, clings to the ground and has no aspirations toward flight. All emphasis is on the horizontal elements of the design, and the building rests firmly and massively earthbound. The clearly defined simple geometric volumes of the cathedral show no tendency to merge either into each other or into the sky.

Giotto di Bondone designed the cathedral's campanile in 1334. In keeping with Italian tradition (FIGS. 17-20 and 17-25), it stands apart from the church. In fact, it is essentially self-sufficient and could stand anywhere else in Florence without looking out of place. The same hardly can be said of the Cologne towers. They are essential elements of the building behind them, and it would be unthinkable to detach one of them and place it elsewhere. No individual element in the Cologne grouping seems capable of an independent existence. One form merges into the next in a series of rising movements that pull the

Pisa, Venice, and Milan

Italy's port cities—Genoa, Pisa, and Venice—controlled the ever busier and more extended avenues of maritime commerce that connected the West with the lands of Islam, with Byzantium and Russia, and overland with China. As a port city, Pisa established itself as a major shipping power and thus as a dominant Italian city-state. Yet Pisa was not immune from the disruption that the Black Death wreaked across all of Italy and Europe in the late 1340s. Concern with death was a significant theme in art even before the onset of the plague and became more prominent in the years after midcentury.

CAMPOSANTO, PISA *Triumph of Death* (FIG. 19-20) is a tour de force of death imagery. The creator of this large-scale (over 18 × 49 feet) fresco remains disputed. Some attribute the work to FRANCESCO TRAINI (active ca. 1321–1363), while others argue for BUONAMICO BUFFALMACCO (active 1320–1336). Painted on the wall of the Camposanto (Holy Field), the enclosed burial ground adjacent to Pisa's cathedral (FIG. 17-25), the fresco captures the horrors of death and forces viewers to confront their mortality. In the left foreground (FIG. 19-20, *left*), young aristocrats, mounted in a stylish cavalcade, encounter three coffin-encased corpses in differing stages of decomposition. As the horror of the confrontation with death strikes them, the ladies turn away with delicate disgust, while a gentleman holds his nose (the animals, horses and dogs, sniff excitedly). At the far left, the hermit Saint Macarius unrolls a scroll bearing an inscription commenting on

1 ft.

1 ft.

19-20 FRANCESCO TRAINI or BUONAMICO BUFFALMACCO, two details of *Triumph of Death*, 1330s. Full fresco, 18′ 6″ × 49′ 2″. Camposanto, Pisa.

Befitting its location on a wall in Pisa's Camposanto, the enclosed burial ground adjacent to the city's cathedral, this fresco captures the horrors of death and forces viewers to confront their mortality.

the folly of pleasure and the inevitability of death. On the far right (FIG. 19-20, *right*), ladies and gentlemen ignore dreadful realities, occupying themselves in an orange grove with music and amusements while all around them angels and demons struggle for the souls of the corpses heaped in the foreground.

In addition to these direct and straightforward scenes, the mural contains details that convey more subtle messages. For example, the painter depicted those who appear unprepared for death—and thus unlikely to achieve salvation—as wealthy and reveling in luxury. Given that the Dominicans—an order committed to a life of poverty—participated in the design for this fresco program, the imagery surely was a warning against greed and lust. Although *Triumph of Death* is a compilation of disparate scenes, the artist rendered each scene with natural-

ism and emotive power. It is an irony of history that as Western humanity drew both itself and the world into ever sharper visual focus, it perceived ever more clearly that corporeal things were perishable.

DOGE'S PALACE, VENICE One of the wealthiest cities of late medieval Italy—and of Europe—was Venice, renowned for its streets of water. Situated on a lagoon on the northeastern coast of Italy, Venice was secure from land attack and could rely on a powerful navy for protection against invasion from the sea. Internally, Venice was a tight corporation of ruling families who, for centuries, provided stable rule and fostered economic growth. The Venetian republic's seat of government was the Doge's (Duke's) Palace (FIG. 19-21). Begun around 1340–1345 and significantly remodeled

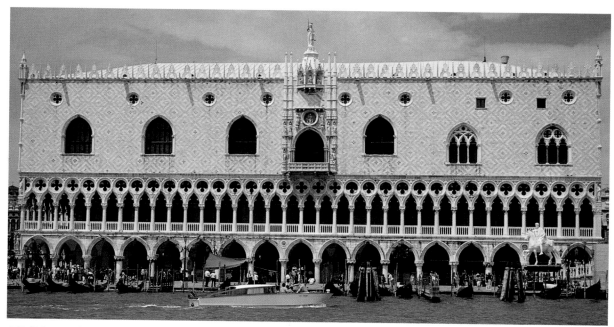

19-21 Doge's Palace, Venice, Italy, begun ca. 1340–1345; expanded and remodeled, 1424–1438.

The delicate patterning in cream- and rose-colored marbles, the pointed and ogee arches, and the quatrefoil medallions of the Doge's Palace constitute a distinctive Venetian variation of northern Gothic architecture.

The 14th Century   **515**

19-22 Milan Cathedral, Milan, Italy, begun 1386. ▶

Milan Cathedral's elaborate facade is a confused mixture of Late Gothic pinnacles and tracery and Renaissance pediment-capped rectilinear portals. It marks the waning of the Gothic style.

after 1424, it was the most ornate public building in medieval Italy. In a stately march, the first level's short and heavy columns support rather severe pointed arches that look strong enough to carry the weight of the upper structure. Their rhythm doubles in the upper arcades, where slimmer columns carry *ogee arches* (made up of double-curving lines), which terminate in flamelike tips between medallions pierced with *quatrefoils* (cloverleaf-shaped). Each story is taller than the one beneath it, the topmost as high as the two lower arcades combined. Yet the building does not look top-heavy. This is due in part to the complete absence of articulation in the top story and in part to the walls' delicate patterning, in cream- and rose-colored marbles, which makes them appear paper-thin. The Doge's Palace represents a delightful and charming variant of Late Gothic architecture. Colorful, decorative, light and airy in appearance, the Venetian Gothic is ideally suited to Venice, which floats between water and air.

MILAN CATHEDRAL Since Romanesque times, northern European influences had been felt more strongly in Lombardy than in the rest of Italy. When Milan's citizens decided to build their own cathedral (FIG. **19-22**) in 1386, they invited experts from France, Germany, and England, as well as from Italy. These masters argued among themselves and with the city council, and no single architect ever played a dominant role. The result of this attempt at "architecture by committee" was, not surprisingly, a compromise. The building's proportions, particularly the nave's, became Italian (that is, wide in relation to height), and the surface decorations and details remained Gothic. Clearly derived from France are the cathedral's multitude of pinnacles and the elaborate tracery on the facade, flank, and *transept*. But long before the completion of the building, the new classical style of the Italian Renaissance had been well launched (see Chapter 21), and the Gothic design had become outdated. Thus, Milan Cathedral's elaborate facade represents a confused mixture of Late Gothic and Renaissance elements. With its pediment-capped rectilinear portals amid Gothic pinnacles, the cathedral stands as a symbol of the waning of the Gothic style and the advent of the Renaissance.

ITALY, 1200 TO 1400

THE 13TH CENTURY

▌ Diversity of style characterizes the art of 13th-century Italy, with some artists working in the newly revived classical tradition, some in the mode of Gothic France, and others in the *maniera greca,* or Italo-Byzantine style.

▌ Trained in southern Italy in the court style of Frederick II (r. 1197–1250), Nicola Pisano was a master sculptor who settled in Pisa and carved pulpits incorporating marble panels that, both stylistically and in individual motifs, depend on ancient Roman sarcophagi.

▌ Nicola's son, Giovanni Pisano, also was a sculptor of church pulpits, but his work more closely reflects the Gothic sculpture of France.

▌ The leading painters working in the Italo-Byzantine style were Bonaventura Berlinghieri and Cimabue. Both artists drew inspiration from Byzantine icons and illuminated manuscripts. Berlinghieri's *Saint Francis Altarpiece* is the earliest dated portrayal of Saint Francis of Assisi, who died in 1226.

Nicola Pisano, Pisa baptistery pulpit, 1259–1260

Berlinghieri,
Saint Francis Altarpiece, 1235

THE 14TH CENTURY

▌ During the 14th century, Italy suffered the most devastating natural disaster in European history—the Black Death that swept through Europe—but it was also the time when Renaissance humanism took root. Although religion continued to occupy a primary position in Italian life, scholars and artists became much more concerned with the natural world.

▌ Giotto di Bondone of Florence, widely regarded as the first Renaissance painter, was a pioneer in pursuing a naturalistic approach to representation based on observation, which was at the core of the classical tradition in art. The Renaissance marked the rebirth of classical values in art and society.

▌ The greatest master of the Sienese school of painting was Duccio di Buoninsegna, whose *Maestà* still incorporates many elements of the *maniera greca.* He relaxed the frontality and rigidity of his figures, however, and in narrative scenes took a decisive step toward humanizing religious subject matter by depicting actors displaying individual emotions.

▌ Secular themes also came to the fore in 14th-century Italy, most notably in Ambrogio Lorenzetti's frescoes for Siena's Palazzo Pubblico. His depictions of the city and its surrounding countryside are among the first landscapes in Western art since antiquity.

▌ The 14th-century architecture of Italy underscores the regional character of late medieval art. Some architectural historians even have questioned whether it is proper to speak of Italian buildings of this period as Gothic structures. Orvieto Cathedral's facade, for example, imitates some elements of the French Gothic vocabulary, but it is merely an overlay masking a traditional timber-roofed structure with round arches in the nave arcade.

Giotto, Arena Chapel, Padua,
ca. 1305

Duccio, *Maestà,* Siena Cathedral,
1308–1311

Orvieto Cathedral,
begun 1310

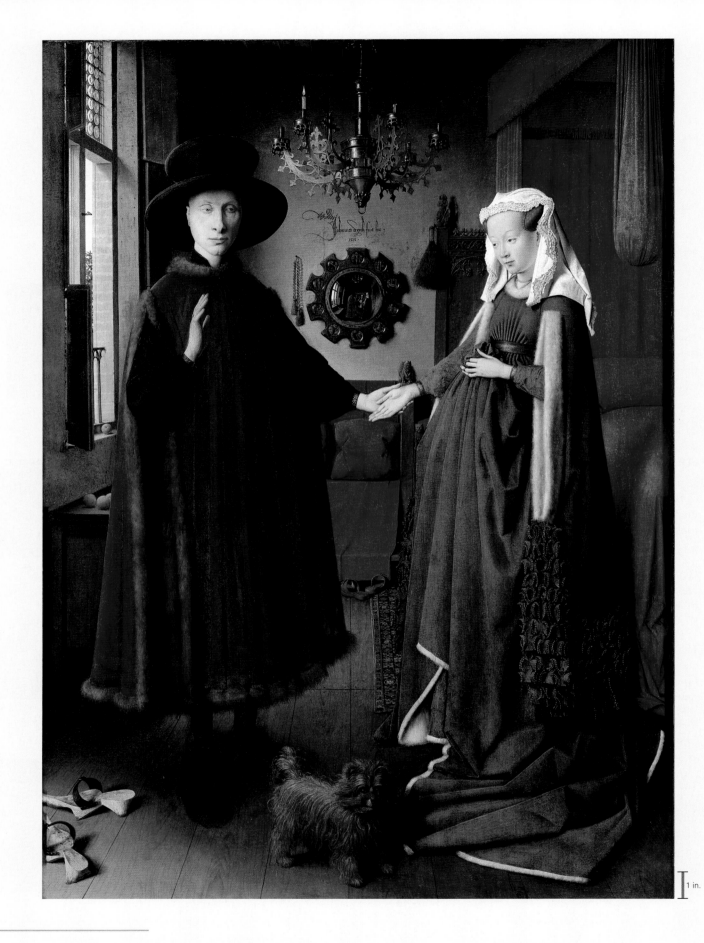

20-1 JAN VAN EYCK, *Giovanni Arnolfini and His Bride*, 1434. Oil on wood, 2′ 9″ × 1′ 10½″. National Gallery, London. ◼◀

Van Eyck played a major role in popularizing oil painting and in establishing portraiture as an important art form. In this portrait of an Italian financier and his wife, he also portrayed himself in the mirror.

1 in.

20

NORTHERN EUROPE, 1400 TO 1500

As the 15th century opened, two competing popes still resided in Rome and Avignon during the Great Schism (1378–1417), and France and England still fought each other in the Hundred Years' War (1337–1453). Social turmoil accompanied dying *feudalism* as the widespread European movement toward centralized royal governments, begun in the 12th century, continued apace. But out of conflict and turmoil also emerged a new economic system—the early stage of European capitalism. In response to the financial requirements of trade, new credit and exchange systems created an economic network of enterprising European cities. Trade in money accompanied trade in commodities, and the former financed industry. Both were in the hands of international trading companies such as those of Jacques Coeur in Bourges (see Chapter 18) and the Medici in Florence (see Chapter 21). In 1460 the Flemish established the first international commercial stock exchange in Antwerp. In fact, the French word for stock market (*bourse*) comes from the name of the van der Beurse family of Bruges, the wealthiest city in 15th-century Flanders—a region corresponding to what is today Belgium, the Netherlands, Luxembourg, and part of northern France (MAP **20-1**).

Art also thrived in Northern Europe during this time under royal, ducal, church, and private patronage. Two developments in particular were of special significance: the adoption of oil-based pigment as the leading medium for painting and the blossoming of printmaking as a major art form, which followed the invention of movable type. These new media had a dramatic impact on artistic production worldwide.

BURGUNDY AND FLANDERS

In the 15th century, Flanders was not an independent state but a region under the control of the duke of Burgundy, the ruler of the fertile east-central region of France still famous for its wines. Duke Philip the Bold (r. 1363–1404) was one of four sons of King John II (r. 1350–1364) of France. In 1369, Philip married Margaret of Mâle, the daughter of the count of Flanders, and acquired territory in the Netherlands. Thereafter, the major source of Burgundian wealth was Bruges, the city that made Burgundy a dangerous rival of France, which then, as in the Gothic age, was a smaller kingdom geographically than the modern nation-state. Bruges initially derived its wealth from the wool trade and soon expanded into banking, becoming the financial clearinghouse for all of Northern Europe. Indeed, Bruges so dominated Flanders that the duke of Burgundy eventually chose to make the city his capital and moved his court there from Dijon in the early 15th century.

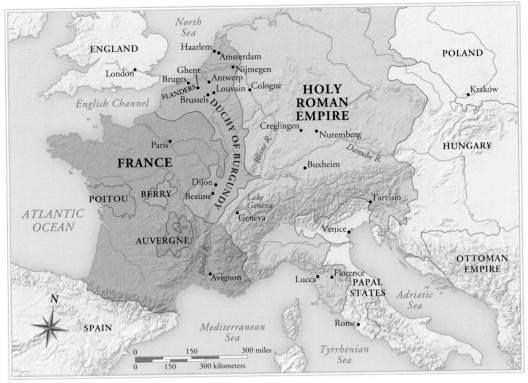

MAP 20-1 France, the duchy of Burgundy, and the Holy Roman Empire in 1477.

spouted water, because the Carthusian commitment to silence and prayer would have precluded anything that produced sound. Although the sculptor died before completing the entire fountain, he did finish *Well of Moses* (FIG. 20-2). Moses and five other prophets (David, Daniel, Isaiah, Jeremiah, and Zachariah) surround a base that once supported a 25-foot-tall group of Christ on the Cross, the Virgin Mary, John the Evangelist, and Mary Magdalene. The *Well of Moses* is a modern name. The Carthusians called it a *fons vitae,* a fountain of everlasting life. The blood of the crucified Christ symbolically flowed down over the grieving angels and Old Testament prophets, spilling into the well below, washing over Christ's prophetic predecessors and redeeming anyone who would drink water from the well. The inspiration for the well may have come in part from contemporaneous *mystery plays* in which actors portraying prophets frequently delivered commentaries on events in Christ's life.

Due to the expanded territory and the prosperity of the duchy of Burgundy, Philip the Bold and his successors were probably the most powerful rulers in Northern Europe during the first three-quarters of the 15th century. Although members of the French royal family, they usually supported England (on which they relied for the raw materials used in their wool industry) during the Hundred Years' War and, at times, controlled much of northern France, including Paris, the seat of the French monarchy. At the height of Burgundian power, the reigning duke's lands stretched from the Rhône River to the North Sea.

Chartreuse de Champmol

20-2A SLUTER, portal of the Chartreuse de Champmol, 1385–1393.

The dukes of Burgundy were major patrons of the arts and understood how art could support their dynastic and political goals as well as adorn their castles and town houses. Philip the Bold's grandest artistic enterprise was the building of the Chartreuse de Champmol, near Dijon. A *chartreuse* ("charter house" in English) is a Carthusian *monastery*. The Carthusian order, founded by Saint Bruno in the late 11th century at Chartreuse, near Grenoble in southeastern France, consisted of monks who devoted their lives to solitary living and prayer. Unlike monastic orders that earned income from farming and other work, the Carthusians generated no revenues. Philip's generous endowment at Champmol was therefore the sole funding for an ambitious artistic program. Inspired by Saint-Denis, the royal abbey of France and burial site of the French kings (see Chapter 18), Philip intended the Dijon chartreuse to become a ducal *mausoleum* and serve both as a means of securing salvation in perpetuity for the Burgundian dukes (the monks prayed continuously for the souls of the ducal family) and as a dynastic symbol of Burgundian power.

CLAUS SLUTER In 1389, Philip the Bold placed the Haarlem (Netherlands) sculptor CLAUS SLUTER (active ca. 1380–1406) in charge of the sculptural program for the Chartreuse de Champmol. For the cloister of the Carthusian monastery, Sluter designed a large sculptural fountain located in a well. The well served as a water source for the monastery. It seems improbable, however, that the fountain actually

Although the six figures recall the jamb statues (FIGS. 18-17 and 18-24) of Gothic portals, they are much more realistically rendered, and the prophets have almost portraitlike features and distinct individual personalities and costumes. David is an elegantly garbed Gothic king, Moses an elderly horned prophet (compare FIG. 17-36) with a waist-length beard. Sluter's intense observation of natural appearance provided him with the information necessary to sculpt the figures in minute detail. Heavy draperies with voluminous folds swathe the life-size figures. The artist succeeded in making their difficult, complex surfaces seem remarkably naturalistic. He enhanced this effect by skillfully differentiating textures, from coarse drapery to smooth flesh and silky hair. Originally, paint, much of which has flaked off, further augmented the naturalism of the figures. (The painter was Jean Malouel [ca. 1365–1415], another Netherlandish master.) This fascination with the specific and tangible in the visible world became one of the chief characteristics of 15th-century Flemish art.

MELCHIOR BROEDERLAM Philip the Bold also commissioned a major altarpiece for the main altar in the chapel of the Chartreuse. A collaborative project between two Flemish artists, this altarpiece consisted of a large sculptured shrine by Jacques de Baerze (active ca. 1384–1399) and a pair of exterior panels painted by MELCHIOR BROEDERLAM (active ca. 1387–1409).

Altarpieces were a major art form north of the Alps in the late 14th and 15th centuries. From their position behind the altar, they served as backdrops for the Mass. The Mass represents a ritual celebration of the Holy *Eucharist*. At the Last Supper, Christ commanded that his act of giving to his apostles his body to eat and his blood to drink be repeated in memory of him. This act serves as the nucleus of the Mass. The ritual of the Mass involves prayer, contemplation of the Word of God, and the reenactment of the Eucharistic sacrament. Because the Mass involves not only a memorial rite but complex Christian doctrinal tenets as well, art has traditionally played an important role in giving visual form to these often intricate theological concepts for the Christian faithful. Like sculpted

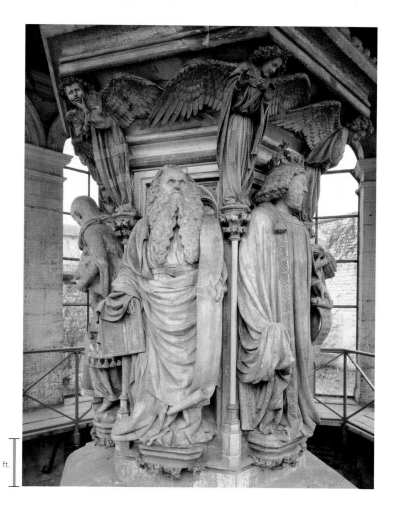

The *Well of Moses,* a symbolic fountain of life made for the duke of Burgundy, originally supported a Crucifixion group. Sluter's figures recall the jamb statues of French Gothic portals but are far more realistic.

1 ft.

medieval church portals, these altarpieces had a didactic role, especially for the illiterate. They also reinforced Church doctrines for viewers and stimulated devotion.

Given their function as backdrops to the Mass, it is not surprising that many altarpieces depict scenes directly related to Christ's sacrifice. The Champmol altarpiece, or *retable,* for example, features sculpted Passion scenes on the interior. These public altarpieces most often took the form of *polyptychs* (hinged multipaneled paintings) or carved relief panels. The hinges allowed the clergy to close the polyptych's side wings over the central panel(s). Artists decorated both the exterior and interior of the altarpieces. This multi-image format provided artists the opportunity to construct narratives through a sequence of images, somewhat as in manuscript illustration. Although scholars do not have concrete information about when the clergy opened and closed these altarpieces, evidence suggests they remained closed on regular days and were opened on Sundays and feast days. This schedule would have allowed viewers to see both the interior and exterior—diverse imagery at various times according to the liturgical calendar. Over time, however, differing Protestant conceptions of the Eucharist (see Chapter 23) ultimately led to a decline of the altarpiece as a dominant art form in Northern Europe.

The painted wings of the *Retable de Champmol* (FIG. 20-3) depict the *Annunciation* and *Visitation* on the left panel and the

1 ft.

20-3 MELCHIOR BROEDERLAM, *Retable de Champmol,* from the chapel of the Chartreuse de Champmol, Dijon, France, installed 1399. Oil on wood, each wing 5' 5¾" × 4' 1¼". Musée des Beaux-Arts, Dijon.

This early example of oil painting reveals an attempt to represent the three-dimensional world on a two-dimensional surface, but the gold background and flat halos recall medieval pictorial conventions.

Presentation in the Temple and *Flight into Egypt* on the right panel (see "The Life of Jesus in Art," Chapter 11, pages 296–297, or xxvi–xxvii in Volume II). Broederlam's painted images on the altarpiece's exterior deal with Christ's birth and infancy and set the stage for de Baerze's interior sculpted Passion scenes (not illustrated). The exterior panels are an unusual amalgam of different styles, locales, and religious symbolism. The two paintings include both landscape and interior scenes. The style of the buildings Broederlam depicted varies from Romanesque to Gothic (see Chapters 17 and 18). Scholars have suggested that the juxtaposition of different architectural styles in the left panel is symbolic. The *rotunda* (round building, usually with a dome) refers to the Old Testament, whereas the Gothic porch relates to the New Testament. In the right panel, a statue of a pagan god falls from the top of a column as the Holy Family approaches. These and other details symbolically announce the coming of the new order under Christ. Stylistically, Broederlam's representation of parts of the landscape and architecture reveals an attempt to render the three-dimensional world on a two-dimensional surface. Yet the gold background and the flat halos of the figures, regardless of the positions of their heads, recall medieval pictorial conventions. Despite this interplay of various styles and diverse imagery, the altarpiece was a precursor of many of the artistic developments (such as the illusionistic depiction of three-dimensional objects and the representation of landscape) that preoccupied European artists throughout the 15th century.

Robert Campin, Jan van Eyck, and Rogier van der Weyden

Melchior Broederlam's Champmol retable also foreshadowed another significant development in 15th-century art—the widespread adoption of *oil paints*. Oil paints facilitated the exactitude in rendering details so characteristic of Northern European painting. Although the Italian biographer Giorgio Vasari and other 16th-century commentators credited Jan van Eyck with the invention of oil painting, recent evidence has revealed that oil paints had been known for some time, well before Melchior Broederlam used oils in his work for Philip the Bold. Flemish painters built up their pictures by superimposing translucent paint layers on a layer of underpainting, which in turn had been built up from a carefully planned drawing made on a panel prepared with a white ground. With the oil medium, artists created richer colors than previously had been possible, giving their paintings an intense tonality, the illusion of glowing light, and enamel-like surfaces. These traits differed significantly from the high-keyed color, sharp light, and rather *matte* (dull) surface of *tempera* (see "Tempera and Oil Painting," page 523). The brilliant and versatile oil medium suited perfectly the formal intentions of the generation of Flemish painters after Broederlam, including Robert Campin, Jan van Eyck, and Rogier van der Weyden, who aimed for sharply focused clarity of detail in their representation of thousands of objects ranging in scale from large to almost invisible.

ROBERT CAMPIN One of the earliest masters of oil painting was the artist known as the "Master of Flémalle," who scholars generally agree was ROBERT CAMPIN (ca. 1378–1444), the leading painter of the city of Tournai. His most famous work is the *Mérode Altarpiece* (FIG. **20-4**). Similar in format to, but much smaller than, the Champmol retable, the *Mérode Altarpiece* was a private commission for household prayer. It was not unusual in that respect. Based on an accounting of extant Flemish religious paintings, lay patrons outnumbered clerical patrons by a ratio of two to one. At the time, various reform movements advocated personal devotion, and in the

years leading up to the Protestant Reformation in the early 16th century, private devotional exercises and prayer grew in popularity. One of the more prominent features of these images commissioned for private use is the integration of religious and secular concerns. For example, artists often presented biblical scenes as taking place in a Flemish house. Although this might seem inappropriate or even sacrilegious today, religion was such an integral part of Flemish life that separating the sacred from the secular became virtually impossible. Moreover, the presentation in religious art of familiar settings and objects no doubt strengthened the direct bond the patron or viewer felt with biblical figures.

The popular *Annunciation* theme, as prophesied in Isaiah 7:14, occupies the Mérode triptych's central panel. The archangel Gabriel approaches Mary, who sits reading. The artist depicted a well-kept middle-class Flemish home as the site of the event. The carefully rendered architectural scene in the background of the right wing confirms this identification of the locale. The depicted accessories, furniture, and utensils contribute to the identification of the setting as Flemish. However, the objects represented are not merely decorative. They also function as religious symbols. The book, extinguished candle, and lilies on the table, the copper basin in the corner niche, the towels, fire screen, and bench all symbolize, in different ways, the Virgin's purity and her divine mission. In the right panel, Joseph has made a mousetrap, symbolic of the theological tradition that Christ is bait set in the trap of the world to catch the Devil. Campin completely inventoried a carpenter's shop. The ax, saw, and rod in the foreground not only are tools of the carpenter's trade but also are mentioned in Isaiah 10:15.

In the left panel, the closed garden is symbolic of Mary's purity, and the flowers depicted all relate to Mary's virtues, especially humility. The altarpiece's donor, Peter Inghelbrecht, a wealthy merchant, and his wife kneel in the garden and witness the momentous event through an open door. *Donor portraits*—portraits of the individual(s) who commissioned (or "donated") the work—became very popular in the 15th century. In this instance, in addition to asking to be represented in their altarpiece, the Inghelbrechts probably specified the subject. Inghelbrecht means "angel bringer," a reference to the *Annunciation* theme of the central panel. The wife's name, Scrynmakers, means "cabinet- or shrine-makers," referring to the workshop scene in the right panel.

JAN VAN EYCK The first Netherlandish painter to achieve international fame was JAN VAN EYCK (ca. 1390–1441), who in 1425 became the court painter of Philip the Good, duke of Burgundy (r. 1419–1467). The artist moved his studio to Bruges, where the duke maintained his official residence, in 1432, the year he completed the *Ghent Altarpiece* (FIGS. **20-5** and **20-6**). This retable is one of the largest (nearly 12 feet tall) of the 15th century. Jodocus Vyd, diplomat-retainer of Philip the Good, and his wife Isabel Borluut commissioned this polyptych as the centerpiece of the chapel Vyd built in the church originally dedicated to Saint John the Baptist (since 1540 Saint Bavo Cathedral). Vyd's largesse and the political and social connections that the *Ghent Altarpiece* revealed to its audience contributed to Vyd's appointment as burgomeister (chief magistrate) of Ghent shortly after the unveiling of the work. Two of the exterior panels (FIG. **20-5**) depict the donors. The husband and wife, painted in illusionistically rendered niches, kneel with their hands clasped in prayer. They gaze piously at illusionistic stone sculptures of Ghent's patron saints, Saint John the Baptist and Saint John the Evangelist (who was probably also Vyd's patron saint). An *Annunciation* scene appears on the upper register, with a careful representation of a Flemish town outside the painted window of the center

20-5A VAN EYCK, *Madonna in a Church*, ca. 1425–1430.

Tempera and Oil Painting

The generic words "paint" and "pigment" encompass a wide range of substances artists have used over the years. Fresco aside (see "Fresco Painting," Chapter 19, page 504), during the 14th century, egg *tempera* was the material of choice for most painters, both in Italy and Northern Europe.

Tempera consists of egg combined with a wet paste of ground pigment. In his influential guidebook *Il libro dell'arte* (*The Artist's Handbook,* 1437), Cennino Cennini mentioned that artists mixed only the egg yolk with the ground pigment, but analyses of paintings from this period have revealed that some artists used the whole egg. Images painted with tempera have a velvety sheen. Artists usually applied tempera to the painting surface with a light touch because thick application of the pigment mixture results in premature cracking and flaking.

Scholars have discovered that artists used oil paints as far back as the 8th century, but not until the early 15th century did oil painting become widespread. Flemish artists such as Melchior Broederlam (FIG. 20-3) were among the first to employ oils extensively (often mixing them with tempera), and Italian painters quickly followed suit. The discovery of better drying components in the early 15th century enhanced the setting capabilities of oils. Rather than apply these oils in the light, flecked brushstrokes that tempera encouraged, artists laid the oils down in transparent layers, or *glazes,* over opaque or semiopaque underlayers. In this manner, painters could build up deep tones through repeated glazing. Unlike tempera, whose surface dries quickly due to water evaporation, oils dry more uniformly and slowly, providing the artist time to rework areas. This flexibility must have been particularly appealing to artists who worked very deliberately, such as Robert Campin (FIG. 20-4), Jan van Eyck (FIGS. 20-1, 20-5 to 20-7), and other Flemish masters discussed in this chapter and the Italian Leonardo da Vinci (see Chapter 22). Leonardo also preferred oil paint because its gradual drying process and consistency permitted him to blend the pigments, thereby creating the impressive *sfumato* (smoky effect) that contributed to his fame.

Both tempera and oils can be applied to various surfaces. Through the early 16th century, wooden panels served as the foundation for most paintings. Italians painted on poplar. Northern European artists used oak, lime, beech, chestnut, cherry, pine, and silver fir. Availability of these timbers determined the choice of wood. Linen canvas became increasingly popular in the late 16th century. Although evidence suggests that artists did not intend permanency for their early images on canvas, the material proved particularly useful in areas such as Venice where high humidity warped wood panels and made fresco unfeasible. Further, until artists began to use wooden bars to stretch the canvas to form a taut surface, canvas paintings were more portable than wood panels.

1 ft.

20-4 ROBERT CAMPIN (MASTER OF FLÉMALLE), *Mérode Altarpiece* (open), ca. 1425–1428. Oil on wood, center panel 2′ 1⅜″ × 2′ ⅞″, each wing 2′ 1⅜″ × 10⅞″. Metropolitan Museum of Art, New York (The Cloisters Collection, 1956).

Campin set the *Annunciation* in a Flemish merchant's home in which the everyday objects represented have symbolic significance. Oil paints permitted Campin to depict all the details with loving fidelity.

panel. In the uppermost arched panels, van Eyck depicted images of the Old Testament prophets Zachariah and Micah, along with *sibyls,* Greco-Roman mythological prophetesses whose writings the Christian Church interpreted as prophecies of Christ.

When opened (FIG. 20-6), the altarpiece reveals a sumptuous, superbly colored painting of humanity's redemption through Christ. In the upper register, God the Father—wearing the pope's triple tiara, with a worldly crown at his feet, and resplendent in a deep-scarlet mantle—presides in majesty. To God's right is the Virgin, represented, as in the Gothic age, as the Queen of Heaven, with a crown of 12 stars upon her head. Saint John the Baptist sits to God's left. To either side is a choir of angels, with an angel playing an organ on the right. Adam and Eve appear in the far panels. The inscriptions in the arches above Mary and Saint John extol the Virgin's virtue and purity and Saint John's greatness as the forerunner of Christ. The inscription above the Lord's head translates as "This is God, all-powerful in his divine majesty; of all the best, by the gentleness of his goodness; the most liberal giver, because of his infinite generosity." The step behind the crown at the Lord's feet bears the inscription "On his head, life without death. On his brow, youth without age. On his right, joy without sadness. On his left, security without fear." The entire altarpiece amplifies the central theme of salvation. Even though humans, symbolized by Adam and Eve, are sinful, they will be saved because God, in his infinite love, will sacrifice his own son for this purpose.

The panels of the lower register extend the symbolism of the upper. In the central panel, the community of saints comes from the four corners of the earth through an opulent, flower-spangled landscape. They proceed toward the altar of the Lamb and the octagonal fountain of life (compare FIG. 20-2). The Revelation passage recounting the Adoration of the Lamb is the main reading on All Saints' Day (November 1). The Lamb symbolizes the sacrificed Son of God, whose heart bleeds into a chalice, while into the fountain spills the "pure river of water of life, clear as crystal, proceeding out of the throne of God and of the Lamb" (Rev. 22:1). On the right, the 12 apostles and a group of martyrs in red robes advance. On the left appear prophets. In the right background come the virgin martyrs, and in the left background the holy confessors approach. On the lower wings, hermits, pilgrims, knights, and judges approach from left and right. They symbolize the four cardinal virtues: Temperance, Prudence, Fortitude, and Justice, respectively. The altarpiece celebrates the whole Christian cycle from the Fall to the Redemption, presenting the Church triumphant in heavenly Jerusalem.

Van Eyck used oil paints to render the entire altarpiece in a shimmering splendor of color that defies reproduction. No small detail escaped the painter. With pristine specificity, he revealed the beauty of the most insignificant object as if it were a work of piety as much as a work of art. He captured the soft texture of hair, the glitter of gold in the heavy brocades, the luster of pearls, and the flashing of gems, all with loving fidelity to appearance. This kind of meticulous attention to recording the exact surface appearance of humans, animals, objects, and landscapes, already evident in the *Mérode Altarpiece* (FIG. 20-4), became the hallmark of Flemish panel painting in the 15th century.

GIOVANNI ARNOLFINI

Emerging capitalism led to an urban prosperity that fueled the growing bourgeois market for art objects, particularly in Bruges, Antwerp, and, later, Amsterdam. This prosperity contributed to a growing interest in secular art in addition to

20-5 JAN VAN EYCK, *Ghent Altarpiece* (closed), Saint Bavo Cathedral, Ghent, Belgium, completed 1432. Oil on wood, 11′ 5″ × 7′ 6″.

Monumental painted altarpieces were popular in 15th-century Flemish churches. Artists decorated both the interiors and exteriors of these hinged polyptychs, which often, as here, included donor portraits.

religious artworks. Both the *Mérode Altarpiece* and the *Ghent Altarpiece* include painted portraits of their donors. These paintings marked a significant revival of portraiture, a genre that had languished since antiquity.

A purely secular portrait, but one with religious overtones, is Jan van Eyck's oil painting *Giovanni Arnolfini and His Bride* (FIG. 20-1). Van Eyck depicted the Lucca financier (who had established himself in Bruges as an agent of the Medici family) and his betrothed in a Flemish bedchamber that is simultaneously mundane and charged with the spiritual. As in the *Mérode Altarpiece,* almost every object portrayed conveys the sanctity of the event, specifically, the holiness of matrimony. Arnolfini and his bride, Giovanna Cenami, hand in hand, take the marriage vows. The cast-aside clogs indicate that this event is taking place on holy ground. The little dog symbolizes fidelity (the common canine name Fido originated from the Latin *fido,* "to trust"). Behind the pair, the curtains of the marriage bed have been opened. The bedpost's *finial* (crowning ornament) is a tiny statue of Saint Margaret, patron saint of childbirth. (Giovanna is not yet pregnant, although the fashionable costume she wears makes her appear so.) From the finial hangs a whisk broom, symbolic of domestic care. The oranges on the chest below the window may refer to fertility. The single

20-6 Jan van Eyck, *Ghent Altarpiece* (open), Saint Bavo Cathedral, Ghent, Belgium, completed 1432. Oil on wood, 11′ 5″ × 15′ 1″.

In this sumptuous painting of salvation from the Original Sin of Adam and Eve, God the Father presides in majesty. Van Eyck rendered every figure, garment, and object with loving fidelity to appearance.

candle burning in the left rear holder of the ornate chandelier and the mirror, in which the viewer sees the entire room reflected, symbolize the all-seeing eye of God. The small medallions set into the mirror frame show tiny scenes from the Passion of Christ and represent God's promise of salvation for the figures reflected on the mirror's convex surface. Flemish viewers would have been familiar with many of the objects included in the painting because of traditional Flemish customs. Husbands traditionally presented brides with clogs, and the solitary lit candle in the chandelier was part of Flemish marriage practices. Van Eyck's placement of the two figures suggests conventional gender roles—the woman stands near the bed and well into the room, whereas the man stands near the open window, symbolic of the outside world.

Van Eyck enhanced the documentary nature of this scene by exquisitely painting each object. He carefully distinguished textures and depicted the light from the window on the left reflecting off various surfaces. He augmented the scene's credibility by including the convex mirror (complete with its spatial distortion, brilliantly recorded), because viewers can see not only the principals, Arnolfini and his wife, but also two persons who look into the room through the door. (Arnolfini's raised right hand may be a gesture of greeting to the two men.) One of these must be the artist himself, as the florid inscription above the mirror, "Johannes de Eyck fuit hic" (Jan van Eyck was here),

announces he was present. The picture's purpose, then, seems to have been to record and sanctify this marriage. However, some scholars have taken issue with this traditional reading of the painting, suggesting instead that Arnolfini is conferring legal privileges on his wife to conduct business in his absence. In either case, the artist functions as a witness. The self-portrait of van Eyck in the mirror also underscores the painter's self-consciousness as a professional artist whose role deserves to be recorded and remembered. (Compare the 12th-century monk Eadwine's self-portrait as "prince of scribes" [FIG. **17-37**], a very early instance of an artist engaging in "self-promotion.")

MAN IN A RED TURBAN In 15th-century Flanders, artists also painted secular portraits without the layer of religious interpretation present in the Arnolfini double portrait. These private commissions began to multiply as both artists and patrons became interested in the reality (both physical and psychological) that portraits could reveal. For various reasons, great patrons embraced the opportunity to have their likenesses painted. They wanted to memorialize themselves in their dynastic lines and to establish their identities, ranks, and stations with images far more concrete than heraldic coats of arms. Portraits also served to represent state officials at events they could not attend. Sometimes, royalty, nobility, and the very rich would send artists to

Framed Paintings

Until recent decades, when painters began to be content with simply affixing canvas to wooden *stretcher bars* to provide a taut painting surface devoid of any ornamentation, artists considered the frame an integral part of the painting. Frames served a number of functions, some visual, others conceptual. For paintings such as large-scale altarpieces that were part of a larger environment, frames often served to integrate the painting with its surroundings. Frames could also be used to reinforce the illusionistic nature of the painted image. For example, the Italian painter Giovanni Bellini duplicated the carved pilasters of the architectural frame in his *San Zaccaria Altarpiece* (FIG. 22-33) in the painting itself, thereby enhancing the illusion of space and giving the painted figures an enhanced physical presence. In Jan van Eyck's *Ghent Altarpiece*, the frame seems to cast shadows on the floor between the angel and Mary in the *Annunciation* scene (FIG. 20-5, *top*.) More commonly, artists used frames specifically to distance the viewer from the (often otherworldly) scene by calling attention to the separation of the image from the viewer's space.

Most 15th- and 16th-century paintings included elaborate frames that the artists themselves helped design and construct. Frequently, the artists painted or gilded the frames, adding to the expense. Surviving contracts reveal that the frame accounted for as much as half the cost of an altarpiece. For small works, artists sometimes affixed the frames to the panels before painting, creating an insistent visual presence as they worked. Occasionally, a single piece of wood served as both panel and frame, and the artist carved the painting surface from the wood, leaving the edges as a frame. Larger images with elaborate frames, such as altarpieces, required the services of a woodcarver or stonemason. The painter worked closely with the individual constructing the frame to ensure its appropriateness for the image(s) produced.

Unfortunately, over time, many frames have been removed from their paintings. For instance, in 1566 church officials dismantled the *Ghent Altarpiece* and detached its elaborately carved frame in order to protect the sacred work from Protestant *iconoclasts* (see "Protes-

20-7 JAN VAN EYCK, *Man in a Red Turban*, 1433. Oil on wood, $1' 1\frac{1}{8}'' \times 10\frac{1}{4}''$. National Gallery, London.

Man in a Red Turban seems to be the first Western painted portrait in a thousand years in which the sitter looks directly at the viewer. The inscribed frame suggests it is a self-portrait of Jan van Eyck.

1 in.

tantism and Iconoclasm," Chapter 23, page 632). As ill luck would have it, when the panels were reinstalled in 1587, no one could find the frame. Sadly, the absence of many of the original frames of old paintings deprives viewers today of the complete artistic vision of the artists. Conversely, when the original frames exist, they sometimes provide essential information, such as the subject, name of the painter, and date. For example, the inscriptions on the frame of Jan van Eyck's *Man in a Red Turban* (FIG. 20-7) state that he painted it on October 21, 1433, and the inclusion of "As I can" and the omission of the sitter's name suggest that the painting is a self-portrait.

paint the likeness of a prospective bride or groom. When young King Charles VI (r. 1380–1422) of France sought a bride, a painter journeyed to three different royal courts to make portraits of the candidates for the king to use in making his choice.

In *Man in a Red Turban* (FIG. 20-7), the man van Eyck portrayed looks directly at the viewer. This seems to be the first Western painted portrait in a thousand years where the sitter does so. The level, composed gaze, directed from a true three-quarter head pose, must have impressed observers deeply. The painter created the illusion that from whatever angle a viewer observes the face, the eyes return that gaze. Van Eyck, with his considerable observational skill and controlled painting style, injected a heightened sense of speci-

ficity into this portrait by including beard stubble, veins in the bloodshot left eye, and weathered and aged skin. Although a definitive identification of the sitter has yet to be made, most scholars consider *Man in a Red Turban* to be a self-portrait, which van Eyck painted by looking at his image in a mirror (as he depicted himself in the mirror in the Arnolfinis' bedroom). The inscriptions on the frame (see "Framed Paintings," above) reinforce this identification. Across the top, van Eyck wrote "As I can" in Flemish using Greek letters, and across the bottom in Latin appears the statement "Jan van Eyck made me" and the date. The use of both Greek and Latin suggests the artist's view of himself as a successor to the fabled painters of antiquity.

20-8 ROGIER VAN DER WEYDEN, *Deposition,* center panel of a triptych from Notre-Dame hors-les-murs, Louvain, Belgium, ca. 1435. Oil on wood, s7′ 2⅝″ × 8′ 7⅛″. Museo del Prado, Madrid.

Deposition resembles a relief carving in which the biblical figures act out a drama of passionate sorrow as if on a shallow theatrical stage. The emotional impact of the painting is unforgettable.

ROGIER VAN DER WEYDEN When Jan van Eyck received the commission for the *Ghent Altarpiece,* ROGIER VAN DER WEYDEN (ca. 1400–1464) was an assistant in the workshop of Robert Campin, but the younger painter's fame eventually rivaled van Eyck's. Rogier soon became renowned for his dynamic compositions stressing human action and drama. He concentrated on Christian themes such as the Crucifixion and the *Pietà* (the Virgin Mary cradling the dead body of her son), moving observers emotionally by relating the sufferings of Christ.

An early masterwork is his 1435 *Deposition* (FIG. 20-8), the center panel of a triptych the Archers Guild of Louvain commissioned for the church of Notre-Dame hors-les-murs (Notre-Dame "outside the [town] walls") in Louvain. Rogier acknowledged the patrons of this large painting by incorporating the crossbow (the guild's symbol) into the decorative tracery in the corners. Instead of creating a deep landscape setting, as van Eyck might have, Rogier compressed the figures and action onto a shallow stage, imitating the large sculptured shrines so popular in the 15th century, especially in

the Holy Roman Empire (FIGS. 20-18 and 20-19). The device admirably served his purpose of expressing maximum action within a limited space. The painting, with the artist's crisp drawing and precise modeling of forms, resembles a stratified relief carving. A series of lateral undulating movements gives the group a compositional unity, a formal cohesion the artist strengthened by depicting the desolating anguish that many of the figures share. The similar poses of Christ and the Virgin Mary further unify the composition.

Few painters have equaled Rogier van der Weyden in the rendering of passionate sorrow as it vibrates through a figure or distorts a tearstained face. His depiction of the agony of loss is among the most authentic in religious art. The emotional impact on the viewer is immediate and unforgettable. It was probably Rogier van der Weyden that Michelangelo had in mind when, according to the Portuguese painter Francisco de Hollanda (1517–1584), the Italian master observed that "Flemish painting [will] please the devout better than any painting of Italy, which will never cause him to shed a tear, whereas that of Flanders will cause him to shed many."[1]

The Artist's Profession in Flanders

As in Italy (see "Artistic Training," Chapter 19, page 510), guilds controlled the Flemish artist's profession. To pursue a craft, individuals had to belong to the guild controlling that craft. Painters, for example, sought admission to the Guild of Saint Luke, the patron saint of painters (FIG. 20-9), as well as saddlers, glassworkers, and mirror-workers. The path to eventual membership in the guild began, for men, at an early age, when the father apprenticed his son in boyhood to a master, with whom the young aspiring painter lived. The master taught the fundamentals of his craft—how to make implements, prepare panels with *gesso* (plaster mixed with a binding material), and mix colors, oils, and varnishes. Once the youth mastered these procedures and learned to work in the master's traditional manner, he usually spent several years working as a journeyman in various cities, observing and absorbing ideas from other masters. He then was eligible to become a master and to apply for admission to the guild. Through the guild, he obtained commissions. The guild inspected his paintings to ensure that he used quality materials and to evaluate workmanship. It also secured him adequate payment for his labor. As a result of this quality control, Flemish artists soon gained a favorable reputation for their solid artisanship.

Women clearly had many fewer opportunities than men to train as artists, in large part because of social and moral constraints that would have forbidden women's apprenticeship in the homes of male masters. Moreover, from the 16th century, when academic training courses supplemented and then replaced guild training, until the 20th century, women would not as a rule expect or be permitted instruction in figure painting, insofar as it involved dissection of cadavers and study of the nude male model. Flemish women interested in pursuing art as a career, for example, Caterina van Hemessen (FIG. 23-17), most often received tutoring from fathers and husbands who were professionals and whom the women assisted in all the technical procedures of the craft. Despite these obstacles, membership records of the art guilds of cities such as Bruges reveal that a substantial number of

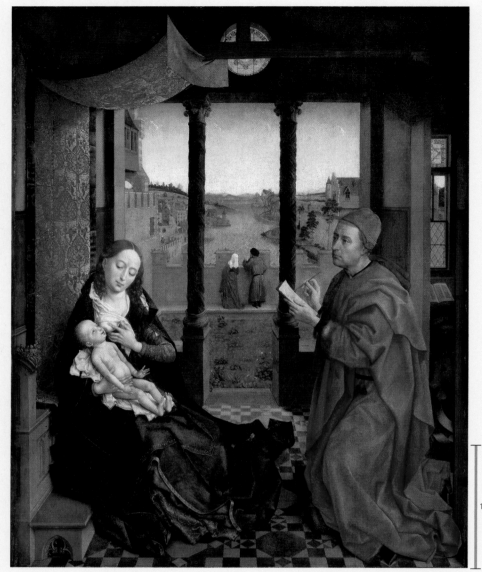

20-9 ROGIER VAN DER WEYDEN, *Saint Luke Drawing the Virgin*, ca. 1435–1440. Oil and tempera on wood, 4′ 6$\frac{1}{8}$″ × 3′ 7$\frac{5}{8}$″. Museum of Fine Arts, Boston. (Gift of Mr. and Mrs. Henry Lee Higginson)

Probably commissioned by the painters guild in Brussels, this panel honors the first Christian artist and the profession of painting. Saint Luke may be a self-portrait of Rogier van der Weyden.

Flemish women in the 15th century were able to establish themselves as artists. That they succeeded in negotiating the difficult path to acceptance as professionals is a testament to both their tenacity and their artistic skill.

SAINT LUKE Slightly later in date is Rogier's *Saint Luke Drawing the Virgin* (FIG. 20-9), probably painted for the Guild of Saint Luke, the artists guild in Brussels. The panel depicts the patron saint of painters drawing the Virgin Mary using a *silverpoint* (a sharp *stylus* that creates a fine line). The theme paid tribute to the profession of painting in Flanders (see "The Artist's Profession in Flanders," above) by drawing attention to the venerable history of the painter's craft. Many scholars believe that Rogier's *Saint Luke* is a self-portrait, identifying the Flemish painter with the first Christian artist and underscoring the holy nature of painting. Here, Rogier shares with Jan van Eyck the aim of recording every detail of the scene with loving fidelity to optical appearance, from the rich fabrics to the floor pattern to the landscape seen through the window. And, like Campin and van Eyck, Rogier imbued much of the representation with symbolic significance. At the right, the ox identifies the figure recording the Virgin's features as Saint Luke (see "The Four Evangelists," Chapter 16,

20-10 ROGIER VAN DER WEYDEN, *Portrait of a Lady,* ca. 1460. Oil on panel, 1′ 1$\frac{3}{8}$″ × 10$\frac{1}{16}$″. National Gallery, Washington, D.C. (Andrew W. Mellon Collection).

Rogier van der Weyden won renown for his penetrating portrayals of character. The lowered eyes, tightly locked thin fingers, and fragile physique convey this unnamed lady's reserved demeanor.

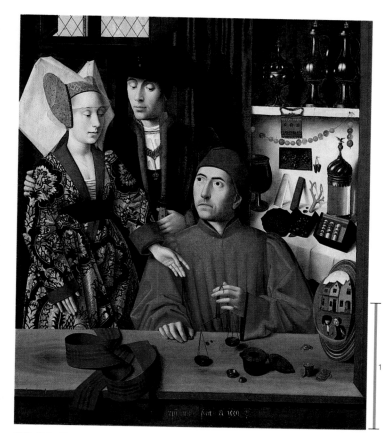

20-11 PETRUS CHRISTUS, *A Goldsmith in His Shop,* 1449. Oil on wood, 3′ 3″ × 2′ 10″. Metropolitan Museum of Art, New York (Robert Lehman Collection, 1975).

Once thought to depict Eligius, the patron saint of goldsmiths, Christus's painting, made for the Bruges goldsmiths' guild chapel, is more likely a generic scene of a couple shopping for a wedding ring.

page 412). The carved armrest of the Virgin's bench depicts Adam, Eve, and the serpent, reminding the viewer that Mary is the new Eve and Christ the new Adam who will redeem humanity from the Original Sin.

PORTRAIT OF A LADY Rogier, like van Eyck, also painted private portraits. The identity of the young woman he portrayed in FIG. **20-10** is unknown. Her dress and bearing imply noble rank. The portrait also reveals the lady's individual character. Her lowered eyes, tightly locked thin fingers, and fragile physique bespeak a reserved and pious demeanor. This style contrasted with the formal Italian approach (FIG. **21-25**), derived from the profiles common to coins and medallions, which was sterner and conveyed little of the sitter's personality. Rogier was perhaps chief among the Flemish in his penetrating readings of his subjects. As a great pictorial composer, he made beautiful use here of flat, sharply pointed angular shapes that so powerfully suggest this subject's composure. In this portrait, unlike in his *Saint Luke,* the artist placed little emphasis on minute description of surface detail. Instead, he defined large, simple planes and volumes and focused on capturing the woman's dignity and elegance.

Later Flemish Panel Painters

Robert Campin, Jan van Eyck, and Rogier van der Weyden were the leading figures of the first generation of "Northern Renaissance" painters. (Art historians usually transfer to Northern Europe, with less validity than in its original usage, the term "Renaissance," coined to describe the conscious revival of classical art in Italy.) The second generation of Flemish masters, active during the latter half of the 15th century, shared many of the concerns of their illustrious predecessors, especially the use of oil paints to create naturalistic representations, often, although not always, of traditional Christian subjects for installation in churches.

PETRUS CHRISTUS One work of uncertain Christian content is *A Goldsmith in His Shop* (FIG. **20-11**) by PETRUS CHRISTUS (ca. 1410–1472), who settled in Bruges in 1444. According to the traditional interpretation, *A Goldsmith in His Shop* portrays Saint Eligius (who was initially a master goldsmith before committing his life to God) sitting in his stall, showing an elegantly attired couple a selection of rings. The bride's betrothal girdle lies on the table as a symbol of chastity, and the woman reaches for the ring the goldsmith weighs. The artist's inclusion of a crystal container for Eucharistic wafers (on the lower shelf to the right of Saint Eligius) and the scales (a reference to the Last Judgment) supports a religious interpretation of this painting and continues the Flemish habit of imbuing everyday objects with symbolic significance. A halo once circled the goldsmith's head, seemingly confirming the religious nature of this scene, but when scientific analysis revealed that the halo was a later addition by an artist other than Christus, restorers removed it.

DIRK BOUTS A different means of suggesting spatial recession is evident in *Last Supper* (FIG. **20-12**) by DIRK BOUTS (ca. 1415–1475), who became the official painter of Louvain in 1468. The painting is the central panel of *Altarpiece of the Holy Sacrament,* which the Louvain Confraternity of the Holy Sacrament commissioned in 1464. It is one of the earliest Northern European paintings to demonstrate the use of a single *vanishing point* (see "Renaissance Perspectival Systems," Chapter 21, page 547) for creating *perspective.* All of the central room's *orthogonals* (converging diagonal lines imagined to be behind and perpendicular to the picture plane) lead to a single vanishing point in the center of the mantelpiece above Christ's head. However, the small side room has its own vanishing point, and neither it nor the vanishing point of the main room falls on the horizon of the landscape seen through the windows, as in Italian Renaissance paintings.

20-12A BOUTS *Justice of Otto III,* ca. 1470–1475.

In *Last Supper,* Bouts did not focus on the biblical narrative itself but instead presented Christ in the role of a priest performing a ritual from the liturgy of the Christian Church—the consecration of the Eucharistic wafer. This contrasts strongly with other Last Supper depictions, which often focused on Judas's betrayal or on Christ's comforting of John. Bouts also added to the complexity of this image by including four servants (two in the pass-through window and two standing), all dressed in Flemish attire. These servants are most likely portraits of the confraternity's members responsible for commissioning the altarpiece, continuing the Flemish tradition of inserting into biblical representations portraits of the painting's patrons, first noted in the *Mérode Altarpiece* (FIG. **20-4**).

HUGO VAN DER GOES By the mid-15th century, Flemish art had achieved renown throughout Europe. The *Portinari Altarpiece* (FIG. **20-13**), for example, is a large-scale Flemish work in a family chapel in Florence, Italy. The artist who received the commission was HUGO VAN DER GOES (ca. 1440–1482), the dean of the painters guild of Ghent from 1468 to 1475. Hugo painted the triptych for Tommaso Portinari, an Italian shipowner and agent for the powerful Medici family of Florence. Portinari appears on the wings of the altarpiece with his family and their patron saints. The central panel depicts the *Adoration of the Shepherds.* On this large surface, Hugo displayed a scene of solemn grandeur, muting the high drama of the joyous occasion. The Virgin, Joseph, and the angels seem to brood on the suffering to come rather than to meditate on the Nativity miracle. Mary kneels, somber and monumental, on a tilted ground that has the expressive function of centering the main actors. The composition may also reflect the tilted stage floors of contemporary mystery plays. From the right rear enter three shepherds, represented with powerful realism in attitudes of wonder, piety, and gaping curiosity. Their lined faces, work-worn hands, and uncouth dress and manner seem immediately familiar.

The symbolic architecture and a continuous wintry northern landscape unify the three panels. Symbols surface throughout the altarpiece. Iris and columbine flowers symbolize the Sorrows of the Virgin. The 15 angels represent the Fifteen Joys of Mary. A sheaf of wheat stands for Bethlehem (the "house of bread" in Hebrew), a reference to the Eucharist. The harp of David, emblazoned over the building's portal in the middle distance (just to the right of the Virgin's head), signifies the ancestry of Christ. To stress the meaning and significance of the depicted event, Hugo revived medieval pictorial devices. Small scenes shown in the background of the altarpiece represent (from left to right) the flight into Egypt, the annunciation to the shepherds, and the arrival of the magi. Hugo's variation in the scale of his figures to differentiate them by their importance to the central event also reflects older traditions. Still, he put a vigorous, penetrating realism to work in a new direction, characterizing human beings according to their social level while showing their common humanity.

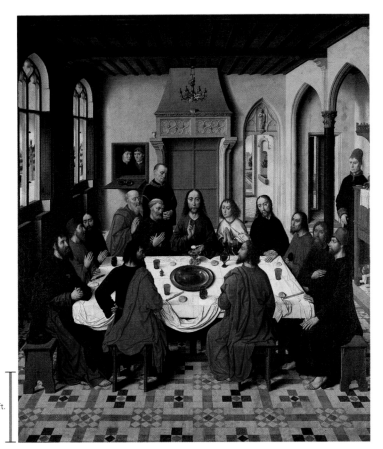

20-12 DIRK BOUTS, *Last Supper,* center panel of the *Altarpiece of the Holy Sacrament,* Saint Peter's, Louvain, Belgium, 1464–1468. Oil on wood, 6′ × 5′. ◧◀

One of the earliest Northern European paintings to employ single-vanishing-point perspective, this *Last Supper* includes four servants in Flemish attire, probably portraits of the altarpiece's patrons.

More recent scholarship has argued that this painting, although not devoid of religious content, should be seen in the context of the tradition of vocational paintings produced for installation in guild chapels. Although the couple's presence suggests a marriage portrait, most scholars now believe that the goldsmiths' guild in Bruges commissioned this painting. Saint Eligius was the patron saint of gold- and silversmiths, blacksmiths, and metalworkers, all of whom shared a chapel in a building adjacent to their meetinghouse. The reconsecration of this chapel took place in 1449, the same date as this painting. Therefore, it seems probable that Christus painted *A Goldsmith in His Shop,* which depicts an economic transaction and focuses on the goldsmith's profession, specifically for the guild chapel.

Christus went to great lengths to produce a historically credible image. For example, the variety of objects depicted in the painting serves as advertisement for the goldsmiths guild. Included are the profession's raw materials—precious stones, beads, crystal, coral, and seed pearls—scattered among finished products—rings, buckles, and brooches. The pewter vessels on the upper shelves are donation pitchers, which town leaders gave to distinguished guests. All these meticulously painted objects attest to the centrality and importance of the goldsmiths to both the secular and sacred communities as well as enhance the naturalism of the painting. The convex mirror in the foreground showing another couple and a street with houses serves to extend the painting's space into the viewer's space, further creating the illusion of reality.

20-13 Hugo van der Goes, *Portinari Altarpiece* (open), from Sant'Egidio, Florence, Italy, ca. 1476. Tempera and oil on wood, center panel 8′ 3½″ × 10′, each wing 8′ 3½″ × 4′ 7½″. Galleria degli Uffizi, Florence.

This altarpiece is a rare instance of the awarding of a major commission in Florence to a Flemish painter. The Italians admired the incredibly realistic details and Hugo's brilliant portrayal of human character.

After Portinari placed his altarpiece in the family chapel in the Florentine church of Sant'Egidio, it created a considerable stir among Italian artists. Although the painting as a whole may have seemed unstructured to them, Hugo's masterful technique and what the Florentines regarded as extraordinary realism in representing drapery, flowers, animals, and, above all, human character and emotion made a deep impression on them. At least one Florentine artist, Domenico Ghirlandaio (see Chapter 21), paid tribute to the Northern European master by using Hugo's most striking motif, the adoring shepherds, in one of his own Nativity paintings.

HANS MEMLING A contemporary of Hugo van der Goes was Hans Memling (ca. 1430–1494), who became a citizen of Bruges in 1465 and received numerous commissions from the city's wealthy merchants, Flemish and foreign alike. Memling specialized in portraits and images of the Madonna. The many that survive depict young, slight, pretty princesses, each holding a doll-like infant Christ. The center panel of the *Saint John Altarpiece* depicts the *Virgin with Saints and Angels* (FIG. 20-14). The patrons of this altarpiece—two brothers and two sisters of the order of the Hospital of Saint John in Bruges—appear on the exterior side panels (not illustrated). In the central panel, two

20-14A Memling, *Tommaso Portinari and Maria Baroncelli*, ca. 1470.

20-14B Memling, *Diptych of Martin van Nieuwenhove*, 1487.

20-14 Hans Memling, *Virgin with Saints and Angels*, center panel of the *Saint John Altarpiece*, Hospitaal Sint Jan, Bruges, Belgium, 1479. Oil on wood, 5′ 7¾″ × 5′ 7¾″ (center panel), 5′ 7¾″ × 2′ 7⅛″ (each wing).

Memling specialized in images of the Madonna. His *Saint John Altarpiece* exudes an opulence that results from the sparkling and luminous colors and the realistic depiction of rich tapestries and brocades.

Burgundy and Flanders **531**

angels, one playing a musical instrument and the other holding a book, flank the Virgin. To the sides of Mary's throne stand Saint John the Baptist on the left and Saint John the Evangelist on the right, and seated in the foreground are Saints Catherine and Barbara. This gathering celebrates the *mystic marriage* of Saint Catherine of Alexandria, one of many virgin saints who were believed to have entered into a special spiritual marriage with Christ. As one of the most revered virgins of Christ, Saint Catherine provided a model of devotion especially resonant with women viewers (particularly nuns). The altarpiece exudes an opulence that results from the rich colors, carefully depicted tapestries and brocades, and the serenity of the figures. The composition is balanced and serene, the color sparkling and luminous, and the execution of the highest technical quality—all characteristics of 15th-century Flemish painting in general.

FRANCE

In contrast to the prosperity and peace Flanders enjoyed during the 15th century, in France the Hundred Years' War crippled economic enterprise and brought political instability. The anarchy of war and the weakness of the kings gave rise to a group of duchies, each with significant power. The strongest and wealthiest of these was the duchy of Burgundy, which controlled Flanders and where artists prospered. But the dukes of Berry, Bourbon, and Nemours, as well as members of the French royal court, were also major art patrons.

Manuscript Painting

During the 15th century, French artists built on the achievements of Gothic painters (see Chapter 18) and produced exquisitely refined *illuminated manuscripts*. Among the most significant developments in French manuscript painting was a new conception and presentation of space. Paintings in manuscripts took on more pronounced characteristics as illusionistic scenes. Increased contact with Italy, where Renaissance artists had revived the pictorial principles of classical antiquity, may have influenced French painters' interest in illusionism.

LIMBOURG BROTHERS Among the early-15th-century artists who furthered the maturation of manuscript painting were the three LIMBOURG BROTHERS—POL, HERMAN, and JEAN—from Nijmegen in the Netherlands. They were nephews of Jean Malouel, the court artist of Philip the Bold. Following in the footsteps of earlier illustrators such as Jean Pucelle (FIG. 18-36), the Limbourg brothers expanded the illusionistic capabilities of illumination. Trained in the Netherlands, the brothers moved to Paris no later than 1402, and between 1405 and their death in 1416, probably from the plague, they worked in Paris and Bourges for Jean, duke of Berry (r. 1360–1416)

20-15 LIMBOURG BROTHERS (POL, JEAN, HERMAN), *January,* from *Les Très Riches Heures du Duc de Berry,* 1413–1416. Ink on vellum, $8\frac{7}{8}'' \times 5\frac{3}{8}''$. Musée Condé, Chantilly.

The sumptuous pictures in *Les Très Riches Heures* depict characteristic activities of each month and give unusual prominence to genre subjects, reflecting the increasing integration of religious and secular art.

and brother of King Charles V (r. 1364–1380) of France and of Philip the Bold of Burgundy. The duke ruled the western French regions of Berry, Poitou, and Auvergne. He was an avid art patron and focused much of his collecting energy on manuscripts, jewels, and rare artifacts. An inventory of the duke's libraries revealed that he owned more than 300 manuscripts, including Pucelle's *Belleville Breviary* (FIG. 18-36) and the *Hours of Jeanne d'Évreux.* For Jean, the Limbourg brothers produced a gorgeously illustrated Book of Hours, *Les Très Riches Heures du Duc de Berry* (*The Very Sumptuous*

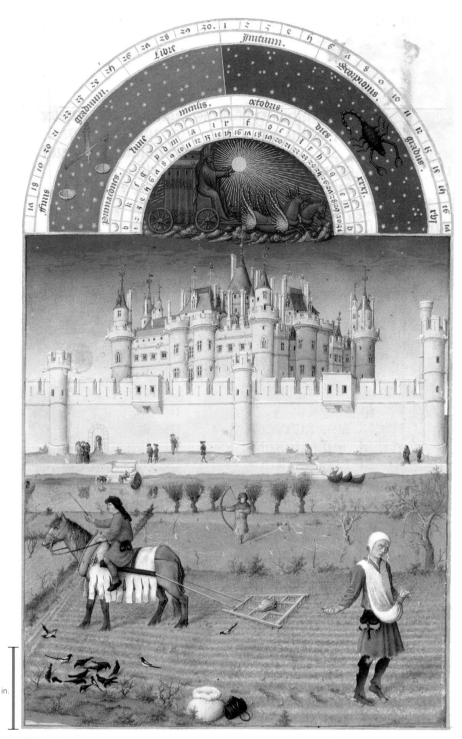

20-16 Limbourg brothers (Pol, Jean, Herman), *October*, from *Les Très Riches Heures du Duc de Berry,* 1413–1416. Ink on vellum, $8\frac{7}{8}''\times 5\frac{3}{8}''$. Musée Condé, Chantilly. ▸◂

The Limbourg brothers expanded the illusionistic capabilities of manuscript painting with their care in rendering architectural detail and convincing depiction of shadows cast by people and objects.

days usually preceded the Office of the Blessed Virgin. Penitential Psalms, devotional prayers, litanies to the saints, and other prayers, including those of the dead and of the Holy Cross, followed the centerpiece. Such books became favorite possessions of the Northern European aristocracy during the 14th and 15th centuries. They eventually became available to affluent burghers and contributed to the decentralization of religious practice that was one factor in the Protestant Reformation in the early 16th century (see Chapter 23).

The calendar pictures of *Les Très Riches Heures* are perhaps the most famous in the history of manuscript illumination. They represent the 12 months in terms of the associated seasonal tasks, alternating scenes of nobility and peasantry. Above each picture is a *lunette* (semicircular frame) in which the Limbourgs depicted the chariot of the sun as it makes its yearly cycle through the 12 months and zodiac signs. Beyond its function as a religious book, *Les Très Riches Heures* also visually captures the power of the duke and his relationship to the peasants. The colorful calendar picture for January (FIG. **20-15**) depicts a New Year's reception at court. The duke appears as magnanimous host, his head circled by the fire screen, almost halolike, behind him. His chamberlain stands next to him, urging the guests forward with the words "aproche, aproche." The lavish spread of food on the table and the large tapestry on the back wall augment the richness and extravagance of the setting and the occasion.

In contrast, the illustration for October (FIG. **20-16**) focuses on the peasantry. Here, the Limbourg brothers depicted a sower, a harrower on horseback, and washerwomen, along with city dwellers, who promenade in front of the Louvre (the French king's residence at the time, now one of the world's great art museums). The peasants do not appear particularly disgruntled as they go about their tasks. Surely, this imagery flattered the duke's sense of himself as a compassionate master. The growing artistic interest in naturalism is evident here in the careful way the brothers recorded the architectural details of the Louvre and in their convincing depiction of the shadows of the people and objects (such as the archer scarecrow and the horse) in the scene.

As a whole, *Les Très Riches Heures* reinforced the image of the duke of Berry as a devout man, cultured bibliophile, sophisticated art patron, and powerful and magnanimous leader. Further, the expanded range of subject matter, especially the prominence of *genre* subjects in a religious book, reflected the increasing integration of religious and secular concerns in both art and life at the time. Although all three Limbourg brothers worked on *Les Très Riches Heures,* art historians have never been able to ascertain definitively which brother painted which images. Given the common practice of collaboration on artistic projects at this time, this determination of specific authorship is not very important. The Limbourg brothers died before completing this Book of Hours, and another court illustrator finished the manuscript about 70 years later.

6A *Hours* *Mary of* *gundy,* 1480.

Hours of the Duke of Berry). A *Book of Hours,* like a *breviary,* was a book used for reciting prayers (see "Medieval Books," Chapter 16, page 411). As prayer books, they replaced the traditional *psalters* (book of Psalms), which were the only liturgical books in private hands until the mid-13th century. The centerpiece of a Book of Hours was the "Office [prayer] of the Blessed Virgin," which contained liturgical passages to be read privately at set times during the day, from *matins* (dawn prayers) to *compline* (the last of the prayers recited daily). An illustrated calendar listing local religious feast

1 ft.

20-17 Jean Fouquet, *Melun Diptych. Étienne Chevalier and Saint Stephen* (left wing), ca. 1450. Oil on wood, 3′ $\frac{1}{2}$″ × 2′ 9$\frac{1}{2}$″. Gemäldegalerie, Staatliche Museen, Berlin. *Virgin and Child* (right wing), ca. 1451. Oil on wood, 3′ 1$\frac{1}{4}$″ × 2′ 9$\frac{1}{2}$″. Koninklijk Museum voor Schone Kunsten, Antwerp.

Fouquet's meticulous representation of a pious kneeling donor with a standing patron saint recalls Flemish painting, as do the three-quarter stances and the sharp focus of the portraits.

Panel Painting

Images for private devotional use were popular in France, as in Flanders, and the preferred medium was oil paint on wooden panels.

JEAN FOUQUET Among the French artists whose paintings were in demand was JEAN FOUQUET (ca. 1420–1481), who worked for King Charles VII (r. 1422–1461, the patron and client of Jacques Coeur; FIG. 18-30) and for the duke of Nemours. Fouquet painted a *diptych* (two-paneled painting; FIG. 20-17) for Étienne Chevalier, who, despite his lowly origins, became Charles VII's treasurer in 1452. In the left panel, Chevalier appears with his patron saint, Saint Stephen (Étienne in French). Appropriately, Fouquet's donor portrait of Chevalier depicts his prominent patron as devout—kneeling, with hands clasped in prayer. The representation of the pious donor with his standing saint recalls Flemish art, as do the three-quarter stances and the sharp, clear focus of the portraits. The artist depicted Saint Stephen holding the stone of his martyrdom (death by stoning) atop a volume of the Scriptures, thereby ensuring that viewers properly identify the saint. Fouquet rendered the entire image in meticulous detail and included a highly ornamented architectural setting.

In its original diptych form (the two panels are now in different museums), the viewer would follow the gaze of Chevalier and Saint Stephen over to the right panel, which depicts the Virgin Mary and Christ Child. The juxtaposition of these two images allowed the patron to bear witness to the sacred. The integration of sacred and secular (especially the political or personal) prevalent in other Northern European artworks also emerges here, complicating the reading of this diptych. Agnès Sorel, the mistress of King Charles VII, was Fouquet's model for the Virgin Mary. Sorel was a pious individual,

and according to an inscription, Chevalier commissioned this painting to fulfill a vow he made after Sorel's death in 1450. Thus, in addition to the religious interpretation of this diptych, there is surely a personal narrative here as well.

HOLY ROMAN EMPIRE

Because the Holy Roman Empire (whose core was Germany) did not participate in the long, drawn-out saga of the Hundred Years' War, its economy remained stable and prosperous. Without a dominant court culture to commission artworks, wealthy merchants and clergy became the primary German patrons during the 15th century.

Sculpture

The art of the early "Northern Renaissance" in the Holy Roman Empire displays a pronounced stylistic diversity. Although some artists followed developments in Flemish painting, the works of artists who specialized in carving large wooden retables reveal most forcefully the power of the lingering Late Gothic style.

VEIT STOSS The sculptor VEIT STOSS (1447–1533) trained in the Upper Rhine region but settled in Kraków (in present-day Poland) in 1477. In that year, he began work on a great altarpiece (FIG. 20-18) for the church of Saint Mary in Kraków. In the central boxlike shrine, huge carved and painted figures, some nine feet high, represent *Death and Assumption of the Virgin*. On the wings, Stoss portrayed scenes from the lives of Christ and Mary. The altar expresses the intense piety of Gothic culture in its late phase, when artists used every figural and ornamental design resource from the vocabulary of Gothic art to heighten the emotion and to glorify the

10 ft.

sacred event. In the Kraków altarpiece, the disciples of Christ congregate around the Virgin, who sinks down in death. One of them supports her, while another, just above her, wrings his hands in grief. Stoss posed others in attitudes of woe and psychic shock, striving for realism in every minute detail. Moreover, he engulfed the figures in restless, twisting, and curving swaths of drapery whose broken and writhing lines unite the whole tableau in a vision of agitated emotion. The artist's massing of sharp, broken, and pierced forms that dart flamelike through the composition—at once unifying and animating it—recalls the design principles of Late Gothic architecture (FIG. 18-27). Indeed, in the Kraków altarpiece, Stoss merged sculpture and architecture, enhancing their union with paint and gilding.

TILMAN RIEMENSCHNEIDER The Virgin's Assumption also appears in the center panel (FIG. 20-19) of the *Creglingen Altarpiece,* created by TILMAN RIEMENSCHNEIDER (ca. 1460–1531) of Würzburg for a parish church in Creglingen, Germany. He also incorporated intricate Gothic forms, especially in the altarpiece's elaborate canopy, but unlike Stoss, he did not paint the figures or the background. By employing an endless and restless line that runs through the garments of the figures, Riemenschneider succeeded in setting the whole design into fluid motion, and no individual element functions without the rest. The draperies float and flow around bodies lost within them, serving not as descriptions but as design elements that tie the figures to one another and to the framework. A look of psychic strain, a facial expression common in Riemenschneider's work, heightens the spirituality of the figures, immaterial and weightless as they appear.

20-19 TILMAN RIEMENSCHNEIDER, *The Assumption of the Virgin,* center panel of the *Creglingen Altarpiece,* Herrgottskirche, Creglingen, Germany, ca. 1495–1499. Lindenwood, 6′ 1″ wide.

Tilman Riemenschneider specialized in carving large wooden retables. His works feature intricate Gothic tracery and religious figures whose bodies are almost lost within their swirling garments.

1 ft.

20-20 KONRAD WITZ, *Miraculous Draught of Fish,* from the *Altarpiece of Saint Peter,* from the Chapel of Notre-Dame des Maccabées, Cathedral of Saint Peter, Geneva, Switzerland, 1444. Oil on wood, 4′ 3″ × 5′ 1″. Musée d'Art et d'Histoire, Geneva.

Konrad Witz set this Gospel episode on Lake Geneva. The painting is one of the first 15th-century works depicting a specific landscape and is noteworthy for the painter's skill in rendering water effects.

1 ft.

Panel Painting

As in Flanders, large-scale altarpieces featuring naturalistically painted biblical themes were familiar sights in the Holy Roman Empire.

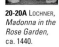

20-20A LOCHNER, *Madonna in the Rose Garden,* ca. 1440.

KONRAD WITZ Among the most notable 15th-century German altarpieces is the *Altarpiece of Saint Peter,* painted in 1444 for the chapel of Notre-Dame des Maccabées in the Cathedral of Saint Peter in Geneva, Switzerland. KONRAD WITZ (ca. 1400–1446), whose studio was in Basel, painted one exterior wing of this triptych with a representation of the *Miraculous Draught of Fish* (FIG. 20-20). The other exterior wing (not illustrated) depicts the release of Saint Peter from prison. The central panel is lost. On the interior wings, Witz painted scenes of the adoration of the magi and of Saint Peter's presentation of the donor (Bishop François de Mies) to the Virgin and Child. *Miraculous Draught of Fish* shows Peter, the first pope, unsuccessfully trying to emulate Christ walking on water. Some scholars think the detail is a subtle commentary on the limited power of the pope in Rome on the part of the Swiss cardinal who commissioned the work. The painting is particularly significant because of the landscape's prominence. Witz showed precocious skill in the study of water effects—the sky glaze on the slowly moving lake surface, the mirrored reflections of the figures in the boat, and the transparency of the shallow water in the foreground. He observed and depicted the landscape so carefully that art historians have determined the exact location shown. Witz presented a view of the shores of Lake Geneva, with the town of Geneva on the right and Le Môle Mountain in the distance behind Christ's head. This painting is one of the first 15th-century works depicting a specific site.

Graphic Arts

A new age blossomed in the 15th century with a sudden technological advance that had widespread effects—the invention by Johannes Gutenberg (ca. 1400–1468) of movable type around 1450 and the development of the printing press. Printing had been known in China centuries before but had never fostered, as it did in 15th-century Europe, a revolution in written communication and in the generation and management of information. Printing provided new and challenging media for artists, and the earliest form was the *woodcut* (see "Woodcuts, Engravings, and Etchings," page 537). Using a gouging instrument, artists remove sections of wood blocks, sawing along the grain. They ink the ridges that carry the designs, and the hollows remain dry of ink and do not print. Artists produced woodcuts well before the development of movable-type printing. But when a rise in literacy and the improved economy necessitated production of illustrated books on a grand scale, artists met the challenge of bringing the woodcut picture onto the same page as the letterpress.

20-21A *Buxheim Saint Christopher,* 1423.

MICHEL WOLGEMUT The so-called *Nuremberg Chronicle,* a history of the world produced in Nuremberg by ANTON KOBERGER (ca. 1445–1513) with more than 650 illustrations by the workshop of MICHEL WOLGEMUT (1434–1519), documents this achievement. The hand-colored page illustrated here (FIG. 20-21) represents Tarvisium (modern Tarvisio), a town in the extreme northeast of Italy, as it was in the "fourth age of the world" according to the Latin inscription at the top. The blunt, simple lines of the woodcut technique give a detailed perspective of Tarvisium, its harbor and shipping, its walls and towers, its churches and municipal buildings, and the baronial

Woodcuts, Engravings, and Etchings

With the invention of movable type in the 15th century and the new widespread availability of paper from commercial mills, the art of printmaking developed rapidly in Europe. A *print* is an artwork on paper, usually produced in multiple impressions. The set of prints an artist creates from a single print surface is called an *edition*. (The same term is used to describe a single printed version of a book. This is the 13th edition of *Art through the Ages*.) As with books manufactured on a press, the printmaking process involves the transfer of ink from a printing surface to paper. This can be accomplished in several ways. During the 15th and 16th centuries, artists most commonly used the *relief* and *intaglio* methods of printmaking.

Artists produce relief prints, the oldest and simplest of the printing methods, by carving into a surface, usually wood. Relief printing requires artists to conceptualize their images negatively—that is, they remove the surface areas around the images. Thus, when the printmaker inks the surface, the carved-out areas remain clean, and a positive image results when the artist presses the printing block against paper. Because artists produce *woodcuts* through a subtractive process (removing parts of the material), it is difficult to create very thin, fluid, and closely spaced lines. As a result, woodcut prints (for example, FIG. 20-21) tend to exhibit stark contrasts and sharp edges.

In contrast to the production of relief prints, the intaglio method involves a positive process. The artist *incises* (cuts) an image on a metal plate, often copper. The image can be created on the plate manually (*engraving* or *drypoint*; for example, FIG. 20-22) using a tool (a *burin* or *stylus*) or chemically (*etching*; for example, FIG. 25-16). In the latter process, an acid bath eats into the exposed parts of the plate where the artist has drawn through an acid-resistant coating. When the artist inks the surface of the intaglio plate and wipes it clean, the ink is forced into the incisions. Then the artist runs the plate and paper through a roller press, and the paper absorbs the remaining ink, creating the print. Because the artist "draws" the image onto the plate, intaglio prints differ in character from relief prints. Engravings, drypoints, and etchings generally present a wider variety of linear effects. They also often reveal to a greater extent evidence of the artist's touch, the result of the hand's changing pressure and shifting directions.

The paper and inks artists use also affect the finished look of the printed image. During the 15th and 16th centuries, European printmakers used papers produced from cotton and linen rags that papermakers mashed with water into a pulp. The papermakers then applied a thin layer of this pulp to a wire screen and allowed it to dry to create the paper. As contact with Asia increased, printmakers made greater use of what was called Japan paper (of mulberry fibers) and China paper. Artists, then as now, could select from a wide variety of inks. The type and proportion of the ink ingredients affect the consistency, color, and oiliness of inks, which various papers absorb differently. Paper is lightweight, and the portability of prints has appealed to artists over the years. The opportunity to produce multiple impressions from the same print surface also made printmaking attractive to 15th- and 16th-century artists. In addition, prints can be sold at cheaper prices than paintings or sculptures. Consequently, prints can reach a much wider audience than one-of-a-kind artworks can. The number and quality of existing 15th- and 16th-century European prints attest to the importance of the new print medium.

1 in.

20-21 MICHEL WOLGEMUT and shop, *Tarvisium*, page from the *Nuremberg Chronicle*, 1493. Woodcut, 1′ 2″ × 9″. Printed by ANTON KOBERGER.

The *Nuremberg Chronicle* is an early example of woodcut illustrations in printed books. The more than 650 pictures include detailed views of towns, but they are generic rather than specific portrayals.

Martin Schongauer was the most skilled of the early masters of metal engraving. By using a burin to incise lines in a copper plate, he was able to create a marvelous variety of tonal values and textures.

1 in.

castle on the hill. Despite the numerous architectural structures, historians cannot determine whether this illustration represents the artist's accurate depiction of the city or his fanciful imagination. Artists often reprinted the same image as illustrations of different cities, and this depiction of Tarvisium is very likely a generic view. Regardless, the work is a monument to a new craft, which expanded in concert with the art of the printed book.

MARTIN SCHONGAUER The woodcut medium hardly had matured when the technique of *engraving* (inscribing on a hard surface), begun in the 1430s and well developed by 1450, proved much more flexible. Predictably, in the second half of the century, engraving began to replace the woodcut process, for making both book illustrations and widely popular single prints. Metal engraving produces an *intaglio* (incised) surface for printing. The incised lines (hollows) of the design, rather than the ridges, take the ink. It is the reverse of the woodcut technique.

MARTIN SCHONGAUER (ca. 1430–1491) was the most skilled and subtle Northern European master of metal engraving. His *Saint Anthony Tormented by Demons* (FIG. **20-22**) shows both the versatility of the medium and the artist's mastery of it. The stoic saint is caught in a revolving thornbush of spiky demons, who claw and tear at him

furiously. With unsurpassed skill and subtlety, Schongauer created marvelous distinctions of tonal values and textures—from smooth skin to rough cloth, from the furry and feathery to the hairy and scaly. The use of *cross-hatching* to describe forms, which Schongauer probably developed, became standard among German graphic artists. The Italians preferred *parallel hatching* (FIG. **21-29**) and rarely adopted cross-hatching, which, in keeping with the general Northern European approach to art, tends to describe the surfaces of things rather than their underlying structures.

Schongauer probably engraved *Saint Anthony* between 1480 and 1490. By then, the political geography of Europe had changed dramatically. Charles the Bold, who had assumed the title of duke of Burgundy in 1467, died in 1477, bringing to an end the Burgundian dream of forming a strong middle kingdom between France and the Holy Roman Empire. After Charles's death at the battle of Nancy, the French monarchy reabsorbed the southern Burgundian lands, and the Netherlands passed to the Holy Roman Empire by virtue of the dynastic marriage of Charles's daughter, Mary of Burgundy, to Maximilian of Habsburg. Thus was inaugurated a new political and artistic era in Northern Europe (see Chapter 23). The next two chapters, however, explore Italian developments in painting, sculpture, and architecture during the 15th and 16th centuries.

NORTHERN EUROPE, 1400 TO 1500

BURGUNDY AND FLANDERS

■ The most powerful rulers north of the Alps during the first three-quarters of the 15th century were the dukes of Burgundy. They controlled Flanders, which derived its wealth from wool and banking.

■ Duke Philip the Bold (r. 1363–1404) was the great patron of the Carthusian monastery at Champmol, near Dijon. He employed Claus Sluter, whose *Well of Moses* features innovative statues of prophets with portraitlike features and realistic costumes.

■ Flemish painters popularized the use of oil paints on wooden panels. By superimposing translucent glazes, they created richer colors than possible using tempera or fresco. One of the earliest examples of oil paintng is Melchior Broederlam's *Retable de Champmol* (1399).

■ A major art form in churches and private homes alike was the altarpiece with folding wings. Robert Campin's *Mérode Altarpiece* is an early example painted in oils, in which the *Annunciation* takes place in a Flemish home. The work's donors are present as witnesses to the sacred event. Typical of "Northern Renaissance" painting, the everyday objects depicted often have symbolic significance.

■ Jan van Eyck, Rogier van der Weyden, and others established portraiture as an important art form in 15th-century Flanders. Van Eyck's self-portrait, *Man in a Red Turban,* and Rogier's *Saint Luke Drawing the Virgin* reveal the growing self-awareness of Renaissance artists.

■ Among the other major Flemish painters were Petrus Christus, Dirk Bouts, Hans Memling, and Hugo van der Goes. Hugo achieved such renown that he won a commission to paint an altarpiece for a church in Florence. The Italians marveled at the Flemish painter's masterful technique and extraordinary realism.

Sluter, *Well of Moses*, 1395–1406

Campin, *Mérode Altarpiece*, ca. 1425–1428

van Eyck, *Man in a Red Turban*, 1433

FRANCE

■ During the 15th century, the Hundred Years' War crippled the French economy, but dukes and members of the royal court still commissioned some notable artworks.

■ The Limbourg brothers expanded the illusionistic capabilities of manuscript illumination in the Book of Hours they produced for Jean, duke of Berry (r. 1360–1416) and brother of King Charles V (r. 1364–1380). Their full-page calendar pictures alternately represent the nobility and the peasantry, always in naturalistic settings with realistically painted figures.

■ French court art—for example, Jean Fouquet's *Melun Diptych*—owes a large debt to Flemish painting in style and technique as well as in the integration of sacred and secular themes.

Limbourg brothers, *Les Très Riches Heures du Duc de Berry*, 1413–1416

HOLY ROMAN EMPIRE

■ The Late Gothic style remained popular in 15th-century Germany for large carved wooden retables featuring highly emotive figures amid Gothic tracery.

■ The major German innovation of the 15th century was the development of the printing press, which soon was used to produce books with woodcut illustrations. Woodcuts are relief prints in which the artist carves out the areas around the printed lines, a method that requires the images to be conceptualized negatively.

■ German artists such as Martin Schongauer were also the earliest masters of engraving. This intaglio technique allows for a wider variety of linear effects because the artist incises the image directly onto a metal plate.

Schongauer, *Saint Anthony Tormented by Demons*, ca. 1480–1490

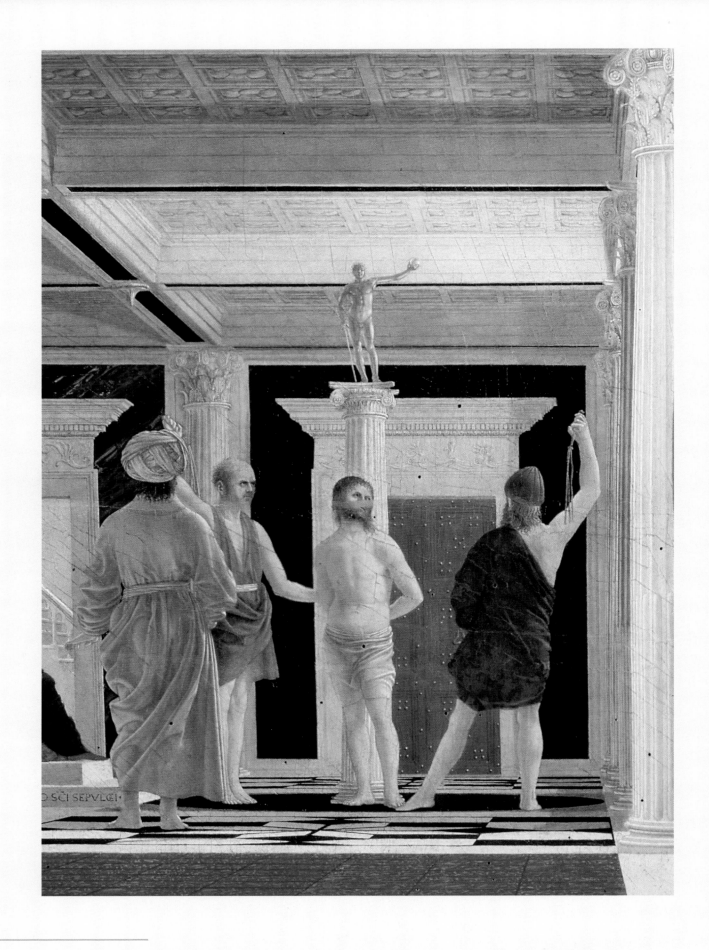

21-1 Piero della Francesca, detail of *Flagellation of Christ* (fig. 21-43), ca. 1455–1465. Galleria Nazionale delle Marche, Urbino.

One hallmark of Italian Renaissance painting is the representation of architecture using the new mathematically based science of linear perspective. Piero della Francesca was a master of perspective painting.

ITALY, 1400 TO 1500

The humanism that Petrarch and Boccaccio promoted during the 14th century (see Chapter 19) fully blossomed in the 15th century. Increasingly, Italians in elite circles embraced the tenets underlying humanism—an emphasis on education and on expanding knowledge (especially of classical antiquity), the exploration of individual potential and a desire to excel, and a commitment to civic responsibility and moral duty. Italy in the 1400s also enjoyed an abundance of artistic talent. The fortunate congruence of artistic genius, the spread of humanism, and economic prosperity nourished a significantly new and expanded artistic culture—the Renaissance. Artistic developments in 15th-century Italy forever changed the direction and perception of art in the Western world.

For the Italian humanists, the quest for knowledge began with the legacy of the Greeks and Romans—the writings of Socrates, Plato, Aristotle, Ovid, and others. The development of a literature based on the commonly spoken Tuscan dialect expanded the audience for humanist writings. Further, the invention of movable metal type in Germany around 1450 (see Chapter 20) facilitated the printing and widespread distribution of books. Italians enthusiastically embraced this new printing process. By 1464 Subiaco (near Rome) boasted a press, and by 1469 Venice had established one as well. Among the first books printed in Italy using this new press was Dante's vernacular epic about Heaven, Purgatory, and Hell, *Divine Comedy*. The production of editions in Foligno (1472), Mantua (1472), Venice (1472), Naples (1477 and 1478–1479), and Milan (1478) testifies to the extensive popularity of Dante's work.

The humanists also avidly acquired information in a wide range of subjects, including botany, geology, geography, optics, medicine, and engineering. Leonardo da Vinci's phenomenal expertise in many fields—from art and architecture to geology, aerodynamics, hydraulics, botany, and military science, among others—still defines the modern notion of a "Renaissance man." Humanism also fostered a belief in individual potential and encouraged individual achievement as well as civic responsibility. Whereas people in medieval society accorded great power to divine will in determining the events that affected lives, those in Renaissance Italy adopted a more secular stance. Humanists not only encouraged individual improvement but also rewarded excellence with fame and honor. Achieving and excelling through hard work became moral imperatives.

21-1A
ROSSELLINO,
Tomb of
Leonardo Bruni,
ca. 1444–1450.

Fifteenth-century Italy witnessed constant fluctuations in its political and economic spheres, including shifting power relations among the numerous city-states and the rise of princely courts (see "Italian Princely Courts and Artistic Patronage," page 569). *Condottieri* (military leaders) with large numbers of mercenary

MAP 21-1
Renaissance Florence.

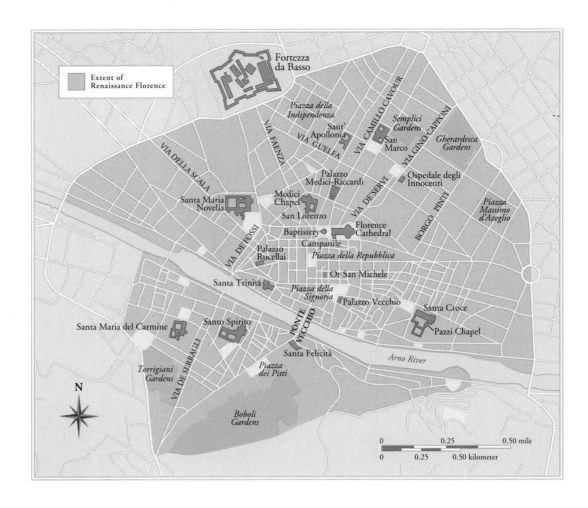

troops at their disposal played a major role in the ongoing struggle for power. Princely courts, such as those in Urbino and Mantua, emerged as cultural and artistic centers alongside the great art centers of the 14th century, especially the Republic of Florence. The association of humanism with education and culture appealed to accomplished individuals of high status, and humanism had its greatest impact among the elite and powerful, whether in the republics or the princely courts. These individuals were in the best position to commission art. As a result, humanist ideas permeate Italian Renaissance art. The intersection of art with humanist doctrines during the Renaissance is evident in the popularity of subjects selected from classical history or mythology; the increased concern with developing perspectival systems and depicting anatomy accurately; the revival of portraiture and other self-aggrandizing forms of patronage; and citizens' extensive participation in civic and religious art commissions.

FLORENCE

Because high-level patronage required significant accumulated wealth, the individuals and families who had managed to prosper economically, whether princes or merchants, came to the fore in artistic circles. The best-known Italian Renaissance art patrons were the Medici of the Republic of Florence (MAP **21-1**). Early in the 15th century, the banker Giovanni de' Medici (ca. 1360–1429) had established the family fortune. His son Cosimo (1389–1464) expanded his family's dominance in financial circles, which led to considerable political power as well. This consolidation of power in a city that prided itself on its republicanism did not go unchallenged. In the early 1430s, a power struggle with other elite families led to the family's expulsion from Florence. In 1434 the Medici returned and used their tremendous wealth to commission art and architecture on a scale rarely seen.

The Medici were avid humanists. Cosimo began the first public library since the ancient world, and historians estimate that in some 30 years he and his descendants expended the equivalent of more than $20 million for manuscripts and books. Scarcely a great architect, painter, sculptor, philosopher, or humanist scholar escaped the family's notice. Cosimo was the very model of the cultivated humanist. His grandson Lorenzo (1449–1492), called "the Magnificent," was a talented poet himself and gathered about him a galaxy of artists and gifted men in all fields, extending the library Cosimo had begun and revitalizing his academy for instructing artists. Lorenzo also participated in what some have called the Platonic Academy of Philosophy (most likely an informal reading group), and lavished funds (often the city's own) on splendid buildings, festivals, and pageants. The Medici were such grand patrons of art and learning that, to this day, a generous benefactor of the fine arts is often called "a Medici."

Sculpture

The earliest important artistic commission in 15th-century Florence was not, however, a Medici project, but a guild-sponsored competition in 1401 for a design for the east doors of the city's baptistery (FIG. **17-26**). Artists and public alike considered this commission particularly prestigious because of the intended placement of the doors on the building's east side, facing Florence Cathedral (FIG. **19-18**). Several traits associated with mature Renaissance art already characterized the baptistery competition: patronage as both a civic imperative and a form of self-promotion, the esteem accorded to individual artists, and the development of a new pictorial illusionism.

SACRIFICE OF ISAAC Andrea Pisano (ca. 1290–1348), unrelated to the two 13th-century Pisan sculptors Nicola and Giovanni discussed in Chapter 19, had designed the south doors of Florence's baptistery between 1330 and 1335. The wool merchants' guild sponsored the 1401 competition for the second set of doors, requiring each entrant to submit a relief panel depicting the sacrifice of Isaac. This biblical event centers on God's order to Abraham that he sacrifice his son Isaac as a demonstration of Abraham's devotion to God (see "Jewish Subjects in Christian Art," Chapter 11, page 293). Just as Abraham is about to comply, an angel intervenes and stops him from plunging the knife into his son's throat. Because of the parallel between Abraham's willingness to sacrifice Isaac and God's sacrifice of his son Jesus to redeem mankind, the sacrifice of Isaac was often linked to the Crucifixion. Both refer to covenants, and given that the sacrament of baptism initiates the newborn or the convert into the possibilities of these covenants, Isaac's sacrifice was certainly appropriate for representation on a baptistery.

Contemporary events, however, may have been an important factor in the selection of this theme. In the late 1390s, Giangaleazzo Visconti, the first duke of Milan (r. 1378–1395), began a military campaign to take over the Italian peninsula. By 1401, when the cathedral's art directors initiated the baptistery competition, Visconti's troops had surrounded Florence, and its independence was in serious jeopardy. Despite dwindling water and food supplies, Florentine officials exhorted the public to defend the city's freedom. For example, the humanist chancellor Coluccio Salutati (1331–1406) urged his fellow citizens to adopt the republican ideal of civil and political liberty associated with ancient Rome and to identify themselves with its spirit. To be Florentine was to be Roman. Freedom was the distinguishing virtue of both republics. The story of Abraham and Isaac, with its

theme of sacrifice, paralleled the message city officials had conveyed to inhabitants. It is certainly plausible that the wool merchants, asserting both their preeminence among Florentine guilds and their civic duty, selected the subject with this in mind. The Florentines' reward for their faith and sacrifice came in 1402 when Visconti died suddenly, ending the invasion threat.

BRUNELLESCHI AND GHIBERTI The jury selected seven semifinalists from among the many who entered the widely advertised competition for the baptistery commission. Only the panels of the two finalists, FILIPPO BRUNELLESCHI (1377–1446) and LORENZO GHIBERTI (1378–1455), have survived. As instructed, both artists used the same French Gothic *quatrefoil* frames Andrea Pisano had used for the baptistery's south doors and depicted the same moment of the narrative— the angel's halting of the action. Brunelleschi's panel (FIG. **21-2**) shows a sturdy and vigorous interpretation of the theme, with something of the emotional agitation of Giovanni Pisano's relief sculptures (FIG. **19-4**). Abraham seems suddenly to have summoned the dreadful courage needed to kill his son at God's command. He lunges forward, robes flying, exposing Isaac's throat to the knife. Matching Abraham's energy, the saving angel darts in from the left, grabbing Abraham's arm to stop the killing. Brunelleschi's figures demonstrate his ability to observe carefully and represent faithfully all the elements in the biblical narrative.

Whereas Brunelleschi imbued his image with dramatic emotion, Ghiberti, the youngest artist in the competition, emphasized grace and smoothness. In Ghiberti's panel (FIG. **21-3**), Abraham

21-2 FILIPPO BRUNELLESCHI, *Sacrifice of Isaac,* competition panel for east doors of the baptistery, Florence, Italy, 1401–1402. Gilded bronze, 1′ 9″ × 1′ 5½″. Museo Nazionale del Bargello, Florence.

Brunelleschi's entry in the competition to create new bronze doors for the Florentine baptistery shows a frantic angel about to halt an emotional, lunging Abraham clothed in swirling Gothic robes.

21-3 LORENZO GHIBERTI, *Sacrifice of Isaac,* competition panel for east doors of the baptistery, Florence, Italy, 1401–1402. Gilded bronze, 1′ 9″ × 1′ 5½″. Museo Nazionale del Bargello, Florence.

In contrast to Brunelleschi's panel (FIG. 21-2), Ghiberti's entry in the baptistery competition features gracefully posed figures that recall classical statuary. Even Isaac's altar has a Roman acanthus frieze.

appears in a typically Gothic pose with outthrust hip (compare FIG. 18-26) and seems to contemplate the act he is about to perform, even as he draws his arm back to strike. The figure of Isaac, beautifully posed and rendered, recalls Greco-Roman statuary and could be regarded as the first classical nude since antiquity. (Compare, for example, the torsion of Isaac's body and the dramatic turn of his head with those of the Hellenistic statue of a Gaul plunging a sword into his own chest, FIG. 5-80). Unlike his medieval predecessors, Ghiberti revealed a genuine appreciation of the nude male form and a deep interest in how the muscular system and skeletal structure move the human body. Even the altar on which Isaac kneels displays Ghiberti's emulation of antique models. Decorating it are acanthus scrolls of a type that commonly adorned Roman temple friezes in Italy and throughout the former Roman Empire (for example, FIG. 10-32). These classical references reflect the increasing influence of humanism in the 15th century. Ghiberti's entry in the baptistery competition is also noteworthy for the artist's interest in spatial illusion. The rocky landscape seems to emerge from the blank panel toward the viewer, as does the strongly foreshortened angel. Brunelleschi's image, in contrast, emphasizes the planar orientation of the surface.

Ghiberti's training included both painting and metalwork. His careful treatment of the gilded bronze surfaces, with their sharply and accurately incised detail, proves his skill as a goldsmith. That Ghiberti cast his panel in only two pieces (thereby reducing the amount of bronze needed) no doubt impressed the selection committee. Brunelleschi's panel consists of several cast pieces. Thus, not only would Ghiberti's doors, as proposed, be lighter and more impervious to the elements, but they also represented a significant cost savings. The younger artist's submission clearly had much to recommend it, both stylistically and technically, and the judges awarded the commission to him. Ghiberti's pride in winning is evident in his description of the award, which also reveals the fame and glory increasingly accorded to individual achievement during the Early Renaissance:

> To me was conceded the palm of the victory by all the experts and by all who had competed with me. To me the honor was conceded universally and with no exception. To all it seemed that I had at that time surpassed the others without exception, as was recognized by a great council and an investigation of learned men. . . . There were thirty-four judges from the city and the other surrounding countries. The testimonial of the victory was given in my favor by all.[1]

OR SAN MICHELE A second major Florentine sculptural project of the early 1400s was the decoration of Or San Michele, an early-14th-century building prominently located on the main street connecting the Palazzo della Signoria (seat of the *signoria*, Florence's governing body) and the cathedral (MAP 21-1). At various times Or San Michele housed a church, a granary, and the headquarters of Florence's guilds. After construction of the building, city officials assigned each of the niches on the exterior to a specific guild for decoration with a sculpture of its patron saint. By 1406 the guilds had placed statues in only 5 of the 14 niches, so the officials issued a dictum requiring the guilds to comply with the original plan and fill their assigned niches. A few years later, Florence was once again under siege, this time by King Ladislaus (r. 1399–1414) of Naples. Ladislaus had marched north, occupied Rome and the Papal States (MAP 19-1) by 1409, and threatened to overrun Florence. As they had previously, Florentine officials urged citizens to stand firm and defend their city-state from tyranny. Once again,

21-4 NANNI DI BANCO, *Four Crowned Saints*, Or San Michele, Florence, Italy, ca. 1410–1416. Marble, figures 6′ high. Modern copy in exterior niche. Original sculpture in museum on second floor of Or San Michele, Florence.

Nanni's group representing the four martyred patron saints of Florence's sculptors' guild is an early example of Renaissance artists' attempt to liberate statuary from its architectural setting.

Florence escaped unscathed. Ladislaus, on the verge of military success in 1414, fortuitously died. The guilds may well have viewed this new threat as an opportunity to perform their civic duty by rallying their fellow Florentines while also promoting their own importance and position in Florentine society. By 1423 statues by Ghiberti and other leading Florentine artists filled the nine remaining niches of Or San Michele.

NANNI DI BANCO Among the niches filled during the Neapolitan king's attempted siege was that assigned to the Florentine guild

21-5 Donatello, *Saint Mark,* Or San Michele, Florence, Italy, ca. 1411–1413. Marble, 7′ 9″ high. Modern copy in exterior niche. Original sculpture in museum on second floor of Or San Michele, Florence.

In this statue carved for the guild of linen drapers, Donatello introduced the classical principle of contrapposto into Early Renaissance sculpture. The drapery falls naturally and moves with the body.

them put to death. Because they placed their faith above all else, these saints were perfect role models for the 15th-century Florentines whom city leaders exhorted to stand fast in the face of the armies of Ladislaus.

Nanni's sculptural group, *Four Crowned Saints* (FIG. **21-4**), is an early attempt to solve the problem of integrating figures and space on a monumental scale. The artist's positioning of the figures, which stand in a niche that is *in* but confers some separation *from* the architecture, furthered the gradual emergence of sculpture from its architectural setting. This process began with works such as the 13th-century jamb statues (FIG. **18-24**) on the west front of Reims Cathedral. At Or San Michele, the niche's spatial recess permitted a new and dramatic possibility for the interrelationship of the figures. By placing them in a semicircle within their deep niche and relating them to one another by their postures and gestures, as well as by the arrangement of robes, Nanni arrived at a unified spatial composition. A remarkable psychological unity also connects these unyielding figures, whose bearing expresses the discipline and integrity necessary to face adversity. As the figure on the right speaks, pointing to his right, the two men opposite listen, and the one next to him looks out into space, pondering the meaning of the words and reinforcing the formal unity of the figural group with psychological cross-references.

In *Four Crowned Saints,* Nanni also displayed a deep respect for and close study of Roman portrait statues. The emotional intensity of the faces of the two inner saints owes much to the extraordinarily moving portrayals in stone of third-century Roman emperors (FIG. **10-68**), and the bearded heads of the outer saints reveal a familiarity with second-century imperial portraiture (FIG. **10-59**). Often, when Renaissance artists sought to portray individual personalities, they turned to ancient Roman models for inspiration, but they did not simply copy them. Rather, they strove to interpret or offer commentary on their classical models in the manner of humanist scholars dealing with classical texts.

DONATELLO Another sculptor who carved statues for Or San Michele's facade was Donato di Niccolo Bardi, or DONATELLO (ca. 1386–1466), who incorporated Greco-Roman sculptural principles in his *Saint Mark* (FIG. **21-5**), executed for the guild of linen drapers. In this sculpture, Donatello took a fundamental step toward depicting motion in the human figure by recognizing the principle of weight shift, or *contrapposto.* Greek sculptors of the fifth century BCE were the first to grasp that the act of standing requires balancing the position and weight of the different parts of the human body, as they demonstrated in works such as the *Kritios Boy* (FIG. **5-34**) and the *Doryphoros* (FIG. **5-40**). In contrast to earlier sculptors, they recognized that the human body is not a rigid mass but a flexible structure that moves by continuously shifting its weight from one supporting leg to the other, its constituent parts moving in consonance. Donatello reintroduced this concept into Renaissance statuary. As the saint's body "moves," his garment "moves" with it, hanging and folding naturally from and around different body parts so that the viewer senses the figure as a clothed nude human, not a stone statue with arbitrarily incised drapery. Donatello's *Saint Mark* is the first Renaissance statue whose voluminous cloth garment (the pride of the Florentine guild that paid for the statue) does not conceal but accentuates the movement of the arms, legs, shoulders, and hips. This development further contributed to the sculpted figure's independence from its architectural setting. Saint Mark's stirring limbs, shifting weight, and mobile drapery suggest impending movement out of the niche.

of stone- and woodworkers. They chose one of their members, NANNI DI BANCO (ca. 1380–1421), to create four life-size marble statues of the guild's martyred patron saints. These four Christian sculptors had defied an order from the Roman emperor Diocletian to carve a statue of a pagan deity. In response, the emperor ordered

21-6 DONATELLO, *Saint George*, Or San Michele, Florence, Italy, ca. 1410–1415. Marble, 6' 10" high. Museo Nazionale del Bargello, Florence.

Donatello's statue for the armorers' guild once had a bronze sword and helmet. The warrior saint stands defiantly, ready to spring from his niche to defend Florence, his sword pointed at the spectator.

SAINT GEORGE For the Or San Michele niche of the armorers' and swordmakers' guild, Donatello made a statue of *Saint George* (FIG. **21-6**). The saintly knight stands proudly with his shield in front of him. He once held a bronze sword in his right hand and wore a bronze helmet on his head, both fashioned by the sponsoring guild. The statue continues the Gothic tradition of depicting warrior saints on church facades, as seen in the statue of Saint Theodore (FIG. **18-18**) on the south-transept portal of Chartres Cathedral, but here it has a civic role to play. Saint George stands in a defiant manner—ready to spring out of his niche to defend Florence against attack from another Visconti or Ladislaus, his sword jutting out threateningly at all passersby. The saint's body is taut, and Donatello has given him a face filled with nervous energy.

Directly below the statue's base is Donatello's marble relief representing *Saint George and the Dragon* (FIG. **21-7**). Commissioned about two years after he installed the statue in its niche, the relief marks a turning point in Renaissance sculpture. Even the landscapes

21-8 DONATELLO, *Feast of Herod*, panel on the baptismal font of Siena Cathedral, Siena, Italy, 1423–1427. Gilded bronze, 1' 11½" × 1' 11½".

Donatello's *Feast of Herod* marked the advent of rationalized perspective space in Renaissance relief sculpture. Two arched courtyards of diminishing size open the space of the action well into the distance.

in the baptistery competition reliefs (FIGS. **21-2** and **21-3**) are modeled forms seen against a blank background. In *Saint George and the Dragon*, Donatello took a painterly approach to representation, creating an atmospheric effect by using incised lines. It is impossible to talk about a background plane in this work. The landscape recedes into distant space. The depth of that space cannot be measured. The relief is a window onto an infinite vista.

FEAST OF HEROD Donatello's mastery of relief sculpture is also evident in *Feast of Herod* (FIG. **21-8**), a bronze relief on the baptismal font in Siena Cathedral. Some of the figures, especially the dancing Salome (to the right), derive from classical reliefs, but nothing in Greco-Roman art can match the illusionism of Donatello's rendition of this New Testament scene. In Donatello's relief, Salome has already delivered the severed head of John the Baptist, which the kneeling executioner offers to King Herod. The other figures recoil in horror in two groups. At the right, one man covers his face with his

21-7 DONATELLO, *Saint George and the Dragon*, relief below the statue of Saint George (FIG. 21-6), Or San Michele, Florence, Italy, ca. 1417. Marble, 1' 3¼" × 3' 11¼". Museo Nazionale del Bargello, Florence.

Donatello's relief marked a turning point in Renaissance sculpture. He took a painterly approach, creating an atmospheric effect by using incised lines. The depth of the background cannot be measured.

Renaissance Perspectival Systems

Scholars long have noted the Renaissance fascination with perspective. In essence, portraying perspective involves constructing a convincing illusion of space in two-dimensional imagery while unifying all objects within a single spatial system. Renaissance artists were not the first to focus on depicting illusionistic space. Both the Greeks and the Romans were well versed in perspectival rendering. Many frescoes of buildings and colonnades (for example, FIG. 10-19, *right*) using a Renaissance-like system of converging lines survive on the walls of Roman houses. However, the Renaissance rediscovery of and interest in perspective contrasted sharply with the portrayal of space during the Middle Ages, when spiritual concerns superseded the desire to depict objects illusionistically.

Renaissance perspectival systems included both linear perspective and atmospheric perspective. Developed by Filippo Brunelleschi, *linear perspective* allows artists to determine mathematically the relative size of rendered objects to correlate them with the visual recession into space. Linear perspective can be either one-point or two-point.

■ In one-point linear perspective (FIG. 21-9*a*), the artist first must identify a horizontal line that marks, in the image, the horizon in the distance (hence the term *horizon line*). The artist then selects a *vanishing point* on that horizon line (often located at the exact center of the line). By drawing *orthogonals* (diagonal lines) from the edges of the picture to the vanishing point, the artist creates a structural grid that organizes the image and determines the size of objects within the image's illusionistic space. Among the works that provide clear examples of one-point linear perspective are Masaccio's *Holy Trinity* (FIG. 21-20), Leonardo da Vinci's *Last Supper* (FIG. 22-4), and Raphael's *School of Athens* (FIG. 22-9). All of these are representations of figures in architectural settings, but linear perspective can also be applied to single figures. An especially dramatic example of the use of one-point perspective to depict a body receding into the background is Andrea Mantegna's *Foreshortened Christ* (FIG. 21-49).

■ Two-point linear perspective (FIG. 21-9*b*) also involves the establishment of a horizon line. Rather than using a single vanishing point along this horizon line, the artist identifies two of them. The orthogonals that result from drawing lines from an object to each of the vanishing points create, as in one-point perspective, a grid that indicates the relative size of objects receding into space. An example of two-point perspective is Titian's *Madonna of the Pesaro Family* (FIG. 22-38).

■ Unlike linear perspective, which relies on a structured mathematical system, *atmospheric perspective* involves optical phenomena. Artists using atmospheric (sometimes called *aerial*) perspective exploit the principle that the farther back the object is in space, the blurrier, less detailed, and bluer it appears. Further, color saturation and value contrast diminish as the image recedes into the distance. Leonardo da Vinci used atmospheric perspective to great effect, as seen in works such as *Madonna of the Rocks* (FIG. 22-2) and *Mona Lisa* (FIG. 22-5).

These two methods of creating the illusion of space in pictures are not exclusive, and Renaissance artists often used both linear and atmospheric perspective in the same work to heighten the sensation of three-dimensional space, as in Raphael's *Marriage of the Virgin* (FIG. 22-7).

21-9 One-point (a) and two-point (b) linear perspective.

Linear perspective reflected the emergence of modern science itself. With its mathematical certitude, perspective also elevated the stature of painting by making pictures rational and measurable.

hand. At the left, Herod and two terrified children shrink back in dismay. The psychic explosion drives the human elements apart, leaving a gap across which the emotional electricity crackles. This masterful stagecraft obscures another drama Donatello was playing out on the stage itself. His *Feast of Herod* marks the advent of rationalized perspective space, long prepared for in 14th-century Italian art. As in *Saint George and the Dragon* (FIG. 21-7), Donatello opened the space of the action well into the distance. But here he employed the new mathematically based science of linear perspective to depict two arched courtyards and the groups of attendants in the background.

RENAISSANCE PERSPECTIVE In the 14th century, Italian artists, such as Duccio and the Lorenzetti brothers, had used several devices to indicate distance, but with the development of *linear perspective* (FIG. 21-9), Early Renaissance artists acquired a way to make the illusion of distance certain and consistent (see "Renaissance Perspectival Systems," above). In effect, they conceived the picture plane as a transparent window through which the observer looks to see the constructed pictorial world. This discovery was enormously important, for it made possible what has been called the "rationalization of sight." It brought all random and infinitely various visual

1 ft.

21-10 LORENZO GHIBERTI, east doors (*Gates of Paradise*), baptistery, Florence, Italy, 1425–1452. Gilded bronze, 17′ high. Modern copy, ca. 1980. Original panels in Museo dell'Opera del Duomo, Florence.

In Ghiberti's later doors for the Florentine baptistery, the sculptor abandoned the Gothic quatrefoil frames for the biblical scenes (compare FIG. 21-3) and employed painterly illusionistic devices.

1 ft.

21-11 LORENZO GHIBERTI, *Isaac and His Sons* (detail of FIG. 21-10), east doors (*Gates of Paradise*), baptistery, Florence, Italy, 1425–1452. Gilded bronze, 2′ 7½″ × 2′ 7½″. Museo dell'Opera del Duomo, Florence.

In this relief, Ghiberti employed linear perspective to create the illusion of distance, but he also used sculptural aerial perspective, with forms appearing less distinct the deeper they are in space.

sance paintings and made possible scale drawings, maps, charts, graphs, and diagrams—means of exact representation that laid the foundation for modern science and technology. Mathematical truth and formal beauty united in the minds of Renaissance artists.

GATES OF PARADISE Ghiberti was among the first Italian artists in the 15th century to embrace a unified system for representing space. His enthusiasm for perspectival illusion is particularly evident in the famous east doors (FIG. 21-10) that in 1425 church officials commissioned him to make for the Florentine baptistery (FIG. 17-26). Michelangelo later declared these as "so beautiful that they would do well for the gates of Paradise."[2] Three sets of doors provide access to the building. Andrea Pisano created the first set, on the south side, between 1330 and 1335. Ghiberti made his first pair of doors (1403–1424), the result of the competition, for the east portal, but church officials moved those doors to the north entrance so that his second pair of doors (1425–1452) could be placed on the east side. In the *Gates of Paradise*, Ghiberti abandoned the quatrefoil pattern that frames the reliefs on the south and north doors and reduced the number of panels from 28 to 10. Each panel contains a relief set in plain moldings and depicts a scene from the Old Testament. The complete gilding of the reliefs creates an effect of great splendor and elegance.

The individual panels, such as *Isaac and His Sons* (FIG. 21-11), clearly recall painting techniques in their depiction of space as well as in their treatment of the narrative. Some exemplify more fully than painting many of the principles the architect and theorist Leon Battista Alberti formulated in his 1435 treatise, *On Painting*. In his relief, Ghiberti created the illusion of space partly through the use of pictorial perspective and partly by sculptural means. He represented buildings according to a painter's one-point perspective construction, but the figures (in the bottom section of the relief, which

sensations under a simple rule that could be expressed mathematically. Indeed, Renaissance artists' interest in perspective reflects the emergence at this time of modern science itself. Of course, 15th-century artists were not primarily scientists. They simply found perspective an effective way to order and clarify their compositions. Nonetheless, there can be little doubt that perspective, with its new mathematical certitude, conferred a kind of aesthetic legitimacy on painting by making the picture measurable and exact. According to Plato, measure is the basis of beauty, and Classical Greek art reflects this belief (see "Polykleitos," Chapter 5, page 124). In the Renaissance, when humanists rediscovered Plato and eagerly read his works, artists once again exalted the principle of measure as the foundation of the beautiful in the fine arts. The projection of measurable objects on flat surfaces influenced the character of Renaisactually projects slightly toward the viewer) appear almost fully in the round, some of their heads standing completely free. As the eye progresses upward, the relief increasingly flattens, concluding with the architecture in the background, which Ghiberti depicted in barely raised lines. In this manner, the artist created a sort of sculptor's aerial perspective, with forms appearing less distinct the deeper they are in space. Ghiberti described the east doors as follows:

> I strove to imitate nature as closely as I could, and with all the perspective I could produce [to have] excellent compositions rich with many figures. In some scenes I placed about a hundred figures, in some less, and in some more. . . . There were ten stories, all [sunk] in frames because the eye from a distance measures and interprets the scenes in such a way that they appear round. The scenes are in the lowest relief and the figures are seen in the planes; those that are near appear large, those in the distance small, as they do in reality. I executed this entire work with these principles.[3]

In these panels, Ghiberti achieved a greater sense of depth than had previously seemed possible in a relief. His principal figures do not occupy the architectural space he created for them. Rather, the artist arranged them along a parallel plane in front of the grandiose architecture. (According to Leon Battista Alberti, in his *On the Art of Building,* the grandeur of the architecture reflects the dignity of the events shown in the foreground.) Ghiberti's figure style mixes a Gothic patterning of rhythmic line, classical poses and motifs, and a new realism in characterization, movement, and surface detail. Ghiberti retained the medieval narrative method of presenting several episodes within a single frame. In *Isaac and His Sons,* the women in the left foreground attend the birth of Esau and Jacob in the left background. In the central foreground, Isaac sends Esau and his dogs to hunt game. In the right foreground, Isaac blesses the kneeling Jacob as Rebecca looks on. Yet viewers experience little confusion because of Ghiberti's careful and subtle placement of each scene. The figures, in varying degrees of projection, gracefully twist and turn, appearing to occupy and move through a convincing stage space, which Ghiberti deepened by showing some figures from behind. The classicism derives from the artist's close study of ancient art. Ghiberti admired and collected classical sculpture, bronzes, and coins. Their influence appears throughout the panel, particularly in the figure of Rebecca, which Ghiberti based on a popular Greco-Roman statuary type. The emerging practice of collecting classical art in the 15th century had much to do with the incorporation of classical motifs and the emulation of classical style in Renaissance art.

DONATELLO, *DAVID* The use of perspectival systems in relief sculpture and painting represents only one aspect of the Renaissance revival of classical principles and values in the arts. Another was the revival of the freestanding nude statue. The first Renaissance sculptor to portray the nude male figure in statuary was Donatello. The date of his bronze *David* (FIG. **21-12**) is unknown, but he probably cast it sometime between 1440 and 1460 for display in the courtyard (FIG. **21-37**) of the Medici palace in Florence. In the Middle Ages, the clergy regarded nude statues as both indecent and idolatrous, and nudity in general appeared only rarely in art—and then only in biblical or moralizing contexts, such as the story of Adam and Eve or depictions of sinners in Hell. With *David,* Donatello reinvented the classical nude. His subject, however, was not a pagan god, hero, or athlete but the youthful biblical slayer of Goliath who had become the symbol of the independent Florentine republic—and therefore an ideal choice of subject for the residence of the most powerful family in Florence. The Medici were aware of Donatello's earlier *David* in the Palazzo della Signoria, Florence's town hall. The artist had pro-

duced it during the threat of invasion by King Ladislaus. Their selection of the same subject suggests that the Medici identified themselves with Florence or, at the very least, saw themselves as responsible for Florence's prosperity and freedom. The invoking of classical poses and formats also appealed to the humanist Medici. Donatello's *David* possesses both the relaxed classical contrapposto stance and the proportions and sensuous beauty of the gods (FIG. **5-63**) of Praxiteles, a famous Greek sculptor. These qualities were, not surprisingly, absent from medieval figures.

VERROCCHIO Another *David* (FIG. **21-13**), by ANDREA DEL VERROCCHIO (1435–1488), one of the most important sculptors during the second half of the century, reaffirms the Medici family's identification with Florence. A painter as well as a sculptor, Verrocchio

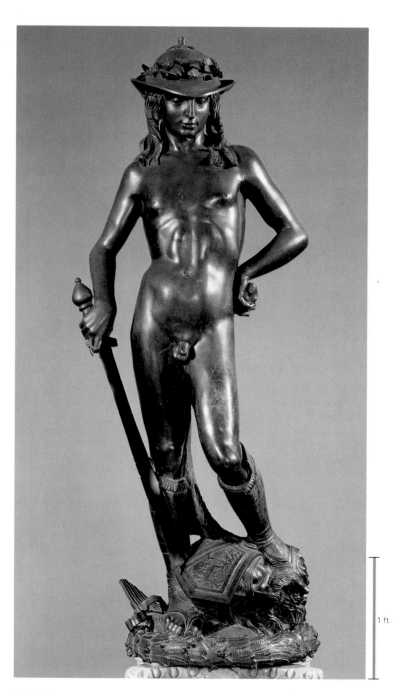

21-12 DONATELLO, *David,* ca. 1440–1460. Bronze, 5′ 2$\frac{1}{4}$″ high. Museo Nazionale del Bargello, Florence. ▪◀

Donatello's *David* possesses both the relaxed contrapposto and the sensuous beauty of nude Greek gods (FIG. **5-60**). The revival of classical statuary style appealed to the sculptor's patrons, the Medici.

Florence **549**

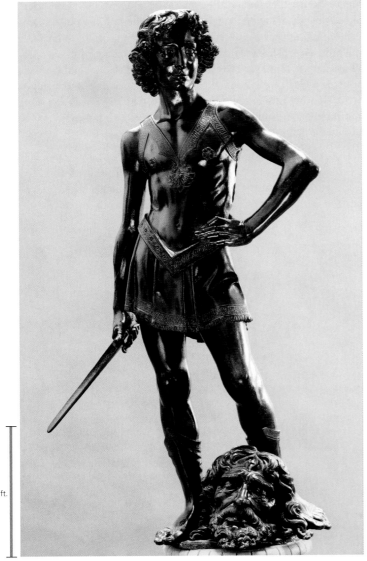

1 ft.

21-13 ANDREA DEL VERROCCHIO, *David*, ca. 1465–1470. Bronze, 4′ 1½″ high. Museo Nazionale del Bargello, Florence.

Verrocchio's *David*, also made for the Medici, displays a brash confidence. The statue's narrative realism contrasts strongly with the quiet classicism of Donatello's *David* (FIG. 21-12).

1 in.

21-14 ANTONIO DEL POLLAIUOLO, *Hercules and Antaeus*, ca. 1470–1475. Bronze, 1′ 6″ high with base. Museo Nazionale del Bargello, Florence.

The Renaissance interest in classical culture led to the revival of Greco-Roman mythological themes in art. *Hercules and Antaeus* exhibits the stress and strain of the human figure in violent action.

directed a flourishing *bottega* (studio-shop) in Florence that attracted many students, among them Leonardo da Vinci. Verrocchio, like Donatello, also had a broad repertoire. His *David* contrasts strongly in its narrative realism with the quiet classicism of Donatello's *David*. Verrocchio's *David* is a sturdy, wiry, young apprentice clad in a leathern doublet who stands with a jaunty pride. As in Donatello's version, Goliath's head lies at David's feet. He poses like a hunter with his kill. The easy balance of the weight and the lithe, still thinly adolescent musculature, with prominent veins, show how closely Verrocchio read the biblical text and how clearly he knew the psychology of brash young men. The Medici eventually sold Verrocchio's bronze *David* to the Florentine government for placement in the Palazzo della Signoria. After the expulsion of the Medici from Florence, officials appropriated Donatello's *David* for civic use and moved it to the city hall as well.

POLLAIUOLO The Renaissance interest in classical culture naturally also led to the revival of Greco-Roman mythological themes in art. The Medici were leading patrons in this sphere as well. Around 1470, ANTONIO DEL POLLAIUOLO (ca. 1431–1498), who was also important as a painter and engraver (FIG. 21-29), received a Medici com-

mission to produce a small-scale sculpture, *Hercules and Antaeus* (FIG. 21-14). The subject matter, derived from Greek mythology, and the emphasis on human anatomy reflect the Medici preference for humanist imagery. Even more specifically, the state seal of Florence had featured Hercules since the end of the 13th century. As commissions such as the two *David* sculptures demonstrate, the Medici clearly embraced every opportunity to associate themselves with the glory of the Florentine Republic, surely claiming much of the credit for it.

In contrast to the placid presentation of Donatello's *David* (FIG. 21-12), Pollaiuolo's *Hercules and Antaeus* exhibits the stress and strain of the human figure in violent action. This sculpture departs dramatically from the convention of frontality that had dominated statuary during the Middle Ages and the Early Renaissance. Only 18 inches high, *Hercules and Antaeus* embodies the ferocity and vitality of elemental physical conflict. The group illustrates the wrestling match between Antaeus (Antaios), a giant and son of the goddess Earth, and Hercules (Herakles), a theme the Greek painter Euphronios had represented on an ancient Greek vase (FIG. 5-23) 2,000 years before. According to the Greek myth, each time Hercules threw him down, Antaeus sprang up again, his strength renewed by contact with the earth. Finally, Hercules held him aloft so that he could not touch the ground, and strangled him around the waist. Pollaiuolo strove to convey the final excruciating moments of the struggle—the straining and cracking of sinews, the clenched teeth of Hercules, and the kicking and screaming of Antaeus. The figures intertwine and interlock as they fight, and the flickering reflections of light on the dark gouged bronze surface contribute to a fluid play of planes and the effect of agitated movement.

GATTAMELATA Given the increased emphasis on individual achievement and recognition that humanism fostered, it is not surprising that portraiture enjoyed a revival in the 15th century. Commemorative portraits of the deceased were common, and patrons also commissioned portraits of themselves. In 1443, Donatello left Florence for northern Italy to accept a rewarding commission from the Republic of Venice to create a commemorative monument in honor of the recently deceased Venetian condottiere Erasmo da Narni (1370–1443), nicknamed Gattamelata ("honeyed cat," a wordplay on his mother's name, Melania Gattelli). Although Gattamelata's family paid for the general's portrait (FIG. 21-15), the Venetian senate formally authorized its erection in the square in front of the church of Sant'Antonio in Padua, the condottiere's birthplace. Equestrian statues occasionally had been set up in Italy in the late Middle Ages, but Donatello's *Gattamelata* was the first to rival the grandeur of the mounted portraits of antiquity, such as that of Marcus Aurelius (FIG. 10-59), which the artist must have seen in Rome. Donatello's contemporaries, one of whom described Gattamelata as sitting "there with great magnificence like a triumphant Caesar,"[4] recognized this reference to antiquity. The statue stands on a lofty elliptical base, set apart from its surroundings, and almost celebrates sculpture's liberation from architecture. Massive and majestic, the great horse bears the armored general easily, for, unlike the sculptor of Marcus Aurelius, Donatello did not represent the Venetian commander as superhuman and more than life-size. Gattamelata dominates his mighty steed by force of character rather than sheer size. The Italian rider, his face set in a mask of dauntless resolution and unshakable will, is the very portrait of the Renaissance individualist. Such a man—intelligent, courageous, ambitious, and frequently of humble origin—could, by his own resourcefulness and on his own merits, rise to a commanding position in the world. Together, man and horse convey an overwhelming image of irresistible strength and unlimited power—an impression Donatello reinforced visually by placing the left forehoof of the horse on an orb, reviving a venerable ancient symbol for hegemony over the earth (compare FIG. 16-12). The imperial imagery is all the more remarkable because Erasmo da Narni was not a head of state.

BARTOLOMMEO COLLEONI Verrocchio also received a commission to make an equestrian statue of a Venetian condottiere, Bartolommeo Colleoni (1400–1475). His portrait (FIG. 21-16) provides a counterpoint to Donatello's statue. Eager to garner the same fame

1 ft.

21-15 DONATELLO, *Gattamelata* (equestrian statue of Erasmo da Narni), Piazza del Santo, Padua, Italy, ca. 1445–1453. Bronze, 12′ 2″ high.

Donatello based his giant portrait of a Venetian general on equestrian statues of ancient Roman emperors (FIG. 10-59). Together, man and horse convey an overwhelming image of irresistible strength.

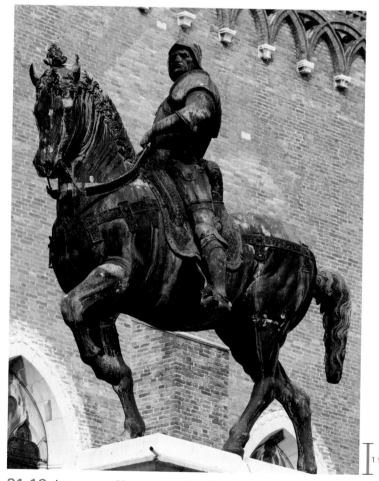

1 ft.

21-16 ANDREA DEL VERROCCHIO, *Bartolommeo Colleoni* (equestrian statue), Campo dei Santi Giovanni e Paolo, Venice, Italy, ca. 1481–1496. Bronze, 13′ high.

Eager to compete with Donatello's *Gattamelata* (FIG. 21-15), Colleoni provided the funds for his own equestrian statue in his will. The statue stands on a pedestal even taller than Gattamelata's.

21-17 Gentile da Fabriano, *Adoration of the Magi,* altarpiece from Strozzi Chapel, Santa Trinità, Florence, Italy, 1423. Tempera on wood, 9′ 11″ × 9′ 3″. Galleria degli Uffizi, Florence.

Gentile was the leading Florentine painter working in the International Style, but he successfully blended naturalistic details with Late Gothic splendor in color, costume, and framing ornament.

1 ft.

the *Gattamelata* portrait achieved, Colleoni provided funds in his will for his own statue. Since both Donatello and Verrocchio executed their statues after the deaths of their subjects, neither artist knew personally the individual he portrayed. The result is a fascinating difference of interpretation (like that between their two *Davids*) as to the demeanor of a professional captain of armies. Verrocchio placed the statue of the bold equestrian general on a pedestal even higher than that Donatello used for *Gattamelata* so that viewers could see the dominating, aggressive figure from all major approaches to the piazza (the Campo dei Santi Giovanni e Paolo). In contrast to the near repose of the *Gattamelata* steed and rider, the *Colleoni* horse moves in a prancing stride, arching and curving its powerful neck, while the commander seems suddenly to shift his whole weight to the stirrups and rise from the saddle with a violent twist of his body. The artist depicted the figures with an exaggerated tautness—the animal's bulging muscles and the man's fiercely erect and rigid body together convey brute strength. In *Gattamelata*, Donatello created a portrait of grim sagacity. Verroc-

chio's *Bartolommeo Colleoni* is a portrait of merciless might. Niccolò Machiavelli wrote in his famous political treatise of 1513, *The Prince*, that the successful ruler must combine the traits of the lion and the fox. Donatello's *Gattamelata* approaches the latter, whereas Verrocchio's *Bartolommeo Colleoni* tilts toward the former.

Painting

In 15th-century Italy, humanism and the celebration of classical artistic values also characterized panel and mural painting. The new Renaissance style did not, however, immediately displace all vestiges of the Late Gothic style. In particular, the International Style, the dominant mode in painting around 1400 (see Chapter 19) persisted well into the century.

GENTILE DA FABRIANO The leading Florentine master of the International Style was GENTILE DA FABRIANO (ca. 1370–1427), who in 1423 painted *Adoration of the Magi* (FIG. **21-17**) as the

Cennino Cennini on Imitation and Emulation in Renaissance Art

The familiar premium that contemporary Western society places on artistic originality is actually a fairly recent phenomenon. Among the concepts Renaissance artists most valued were imitation and emulation. Although many Renaissance artists did develop unique, recognizable styles, convention, in terms of both subject matter and representational practices, predominated. In a review of Italian Renaissance art, certain themes, motifs, and compositions surface with great regularity, and the traditional training practices reveal the importance of imitation and emulation to aspiring Renaissance artists.

▌ **Imitation** Imitation was the starting point in a young artist's training (see "Artistic Training in Renaissance Italy," Chapter 19, page 510). Italian Renaissance artists believed that the best way to learn was to copy the works of masters. Accordingly, much of an apprentice's training consisted of copying exemplary artworks. Leonardo da Vinci filled his sketchbooks with drawings of well-known sculptures and frescoes, and Michelangelo spent days sketching artworks in churches around Florence and Rome.

▌ **Emulation** The next step was emulation, which involved modeling one's art after that of another artist. Although imitation still provided the foundation for this practice, an artist used features of another's art only as a springboard for improvements or innovations. Thus, developing artists went beyond previous artists and attempted to prove their own competence and skill by improving on established and recognized masters. Comparison and a degree of competition were integral to emulation. To evaluate the "improved" artwork, viewers had to know the original "model."

Renaissance artists believed that developing artists would ultimately arrive at their own unique style through this process of imitation and emulation. Cennino Cennini (ca. 1370–1440) explained the value of this training procedure in a book he published in 1400, *Il Libro dell'Arte* (*The Artist's Handbook*), which served as a practical guide to producing art:

> Having first practiced drawing for a while, . . . take pains and pleasure in constantly copying the best things which you can find done by the hand of great masters. And if you are in a place where many good masters have been, so much the better for you. But I give you this advice: take care to select the best one every time, and the one who has the greatest reputation. And, as you go on from day to day, it will be against nature if you do not get some grasp of his style and of his spirit. For if you undertake to copy after one master today and after another one tomorrow, you will not acquire the style of either one or the other, and you will inevitably, through enthusiasm, become capricious, because each style will be distracting your mind. You will try to work in this man's way today, and in the other's tomorrow, and so you will not get either of them right. If you follow the course of one man through constant practice, your intelligence would have to be crude indeed for you not to get some nourishment from it. Then you will find, if nature has granted you any imagination at all, that you will eventually acquire a style individual to yourself, and it cannot help being good; because your hand and your mind, being always accustomed to gather flowers, would ill know how to pluck thorns.*

* Translated by Daniel V. Thompson Jr., *Cennino Cennini, The Artist's Handbook* (*Il Libro dell'Arte*), (New York: Dover Publications, 1960; reprint of 1933 ed.), 14–15.

altarpiece for the family chapel of Palla Strozzi (1372–1462) in the church of Santa Trinità in Florence. At the beginning of the 15th century, the Strozzi family was the wealthiest in Florence. The altarpiece, with its elaborate gilded Gothic frame, is testimony to Strozzi's lavish tastes. So too is the painting itself, with its gorgeous surface and sumptuously costumed kings, courtiers, captains, and retainers accompanied by a menagerie of exotic animals. Gentile portrayed all these elements in a rainbow of color with extensive use of gold. The painting presents all the pomp and ceremony of chivalric etiquette in a scene that sanctifies the aristocracy in the presence of the Madonna and Child. Although the style is fundamentally Late Gothic, Gentile inserted striking naturalistic details. For example, the artist depicted animals from a variety of angles and foreshortened the forms convincingly, most notably the horse at the far right seen in a three-quarter rear view. Gentile did the same with human figures, such as the kneeling man removing the spurs from the standing *magus* in the center foreground. In the left panel of the predella, Gentile painted what may have been the very first nighttime Nativity with the central light source—the radiant Christ Child—introduced into the picture itself. Although predominantly conservative, Gentile demonstrated that he was not oblivious to contemporary experimental trends and that he could blend naturalistic and inventive elements skillfully and subtly into a traditional composition without sacrificing Late Gothic splendor in color, costume, and framing ornament.

MASACCIO The artist who epitomizes the innovative spirit of early-15th-century Florentine painting was Tommaso di ser Giovanni di Mone Cassai, known as MASACCIO (1401–1428). Although his presumed teacher, Masolino da Panicale (see "Italian Artists' Names," Chapter 19, page 498), had worked in the International Style, Masaccio broke sharply from the normal practice of imitating his master's style (see "Imitation and Emulation in Renaissance Italy," above). He moved suddenly, within the short span of six years, into unexplored territory. Most art historians recognize no other painter in history to have contributed so much to the development of a new style in so short a time as Masaccio, whose untimely death at age 27 cut short his brilliant career. Masaccio was the artistic descendant of Giotto (see Chapter 19), whose calm, monumental style he revolutionized with a whole new repertoire of representational devices that generations of Renaissance painters later studied and developed. Masaccio also knew and understood the innovations of his great contemporaries, Ghiberti, Brunelleschi, and Donatello, and he introduced new possibilities for both form and content.

21-18 Masaccio, *Tribute Money*, Brancacci Chapel, Santa Maria del Carmine, Florence, Italy, ca. 1424–1427. Fresco, 8′ 4⅛″ × 19′ 7⅛″.

Masaccio's figures recall Giotto's in their simple grandeur, but they convey a greater psychological and physical credibility. He modeled his figures with light coming from a source outside the picture.

BRANCACCI CHAPEL The frescoes Masaccio painted in the Brancacci family chapel of Santa Maria del Carmine in Florence provide excellent examples of his innovations. In *Tribute Money* (FIG. **21-18**), painted shortly before his death, Masaccio depicted a seldom-represented narrative from the Gospel of Matthew (17:24–27). As the tax collector confronts Christ at the entrance to the Roman town of Capernaum, Christ directs Saint Peter to the shore of Lake Galilee. There, as Christ foresaw, Peter finds the tribute coin in the mouth of a fish and returns to pay the tax. Art historians have debated why Felice Brancacci (1382–1447), the chapel's patron, selected this obscure biblical narrative. Some scholars have suggested that *Tribute Money*, in which Christ condones taxation, served as a commentary on the income tax the Florentine republic was considering implementing at the time. However, Brancacci's considerable wealth makes it unlikely he would have supported a tax on income. Moreover, this fresco's placement in a private family chapel meant that the public had only limited access. Therefore, because this fresco lacked the general audience enjoyed by, for example, the Or San Michele niche sculptures, it seems ill-suited for public statements.

Whatever the reason for the choice of subject, Masaccio decided to divide the story into three episodes within the fresco. In the center, Christ, surrounded by his disciples, tells Saint Peter to retrieve the coin from the fish, while the tax collector stands in the foreground, his back to spectators and hand extended, awaiting payment. At the left, in the middle distance, Saint Peter extracts the coin from the fish's mouth, and, at the right, he thrusts the coin into the tax collector's hand. Masaccio's figures recall Giotto's in their simple grandeur, but they convey a greater psychological and physical credibility. Masaccio created the bulk of the figures by modeling not with a flat, neutral light lacking an identifiable source but with a light coming from a specific source outside the picture. The light comes from the right and strikes the figures at an angle, illuminating the parts of the solids that obstruct its path and leaving the rest in shadow, producing the illusion of deep sculptural relief. Between the extremes of light and dark, the light appears as a constantly active but fluctuating force highlighting the scene in varying degrees, almost a tangible substance independent of the figures. In his frescoes, Giotto used light only to model the masses. In Masaccio's works, light has its own nature, and the masses are visible only because of its direction and intensity. The viewer can imagine the light as playing over forms—revealing some and concealing others, as the artist directs it. The individual figures in *Tribute Money* are solemn and weighty, but they also move freely and reveal body structure, as do Donatello's statues. Masaccio's representations adeptly suggest bones, muscles, and the pressures and tensions of joints. Each figure conveys a maximum of contained energy. *Tribute Money* helps the viewer understand Giorgio Vasari's comment: "[T]he works made before his [Masaccio's] day can be said to be painted, while his are living, real, and natural."[5]

Masaccio's arrangement of the figures is equally inventive. They do not appear as a stiff screen in the foreground. Instead, the artist grouped them in circular depth around Christ, and he placed the whole group in a spacious landscape, rather than in the confined stage space of earlier frescoes. The group itself generates the foreground space that the architecture on the right amplifies. Masaccio depicted the building in one-point perspective, locating the vanishing point, where all the orthogonals converge, at Christ's head. Atmospheric perspective—the diminishing of light and the blurring of outlines as the distance increases (see "Renaissance Perspectival Systems," page 547)—unites the foreground with the background. Although ancient Roman painters used atmospheric perspective (FIG. **10-20**), medieval artists had abandoned it. Thus, it virtually disappeared from art until Masaccio and his contemporaries rediscovered it. They came to realize that the light and air interposed between viewers and what they see are two parts of the visual experience called "distance."

In an awkwardly narrow space at the entrance to the Brancacci Chapel, Masaccio painted *Expulsion of Adam and Eve from Eden* (FIG. **21-19**), another fresco displaying the representational innovations of *Tribute Money*. For example, the sharply slanted light from an outside source creates deep relief, with lights placed alongside darks, and acts as a strong unifying agent. Masaccio also presented the figures

1 ft.

21-19 Masaccio, *Expulsion of Adam and Eve from Eden*, Brancacci Chapel, Santa Maria del Carmine, Florence, Italy, ca. 1424–1427. Fresco, 7′ × 2′ 11″.

Adam and Eve, expelled from Eden, stumble on blindly, driven by the angel's will and their own despair. The hazy background specifies no locale but suggests a space around and beyond the figures.

1 ft.

21-20 Masaccio, *Holy Trinity*, Santa Maria Novella, Florence, Italy, ca. 1424–1427. Fresco, 21′ $10\frac{5}{8}$″ × 10′ $4\frac{3}{4}$″.

Masaccio's *Holy Trinity* is the premier early-15th-century example of the application of mathematics to pictorial organization in Brunelleschi's new science of perspective. The illusionism is breathtaking.

with convincing structural accuracy, thereby suggesting substantial body weight. Further, the hazy background specifies no locale but suggests a space around and beyond the figures. Adam's feet, clearly in contact with the ground, mark the human presence on earth, and the cry issuing from Eve's mouth voices her anguish. The angel does not force them physically from Eden. Rather, they stumble on blindly, the angel's will and their own despair driving them. The composition is starkly simple, its message incomparably eloquent.

HOLY TRINITY Masaccio's *Holy Trinity* fresco (FIG. **21-20**) in Santa Maria Novella is another of the young artist's masterworks and the premier early-15th-century example of the application of mathematics to the depiction of space. Masaccio painted the composition on two levels of unequal height. Above, in a *coffered* barrel-vaulted chapel reminiscent of a Roman *triumphal arch*

21-21 Fra Angelico, *Annunciation*, San Marco, Florence, Italy, ca. 1438–1447. Fresco, 7′ 1″ × 10′ 6″.

Painted for the Dominican monks of San Marco, Fra Angelico's fresco is simple and direct. Its figures and architecture have a pristine clarity that befits the fresco's function as a devotional image.

1 ft.

(FIG. 10-39), the Virgin Mary and Saint John appear on either side of the crucified Christ. God the Father emerges from behind Christ, supporting the arms of the cross and presenting his Son to the worshiper as a devotional object. The dove of the Holy Spirit hovers between God's head and Christ's head. Masaccio also included portraits of the donors of the painting, Lorenzo Lenzi and his wife, who kneel just in front of the *pilasters* that frame the chapel's entrance. Below, the artist painted a tomb containing a skeleton. An inscription in Italian painted above the skeleton reminds the spectator that "I was once what you are, and what I am you will become."

The illusionism of *Holy Trinity* is breathtaking. In this fresco, Masaccio brilliantly demonstrated the principles and potential of Brunelleschi's new science of perspective. Indeed, some historians have suggested Brunelleschi may have collaborated with Masaccio. The vanishing point of the composition is at the foot of the cross. With this point at eye level, spectators look up at the Trinity and down at the tomb. About five feet above the floor level, the vanishing point pulls the two views together, creating the illusion of an actual structure that transects the wall's vertical plane. Whereas the tomb appears to project forward into the church, the chapel recedes visually behind the wall and appears as an extension of the spectator's space. This adjustment of the pictured space to the viewer's position was an important innovation in illusionistic painting that other artists of the Renaissance and the later Baroque period would develop further. Masaccio was so exact in his metrical proportions that it is possible to calculate the dimensions of the chapel (for example, the span of the painted vault is seven feet and the depth of the chapel is nine feet). Thus, he achieved not only a successful illusion but also a rational measured coherence that is responsible for the unity and harmony of the fresco. *Holy Trinity* is, however, much more than a demonstration of Brunelleschi's perspective or of the painter's ability to represent fully modeled figures bathed in light. In this painting, Masaccio also powerfully conveyed one of the central tenets of Christian faith. The ascending pyramid of figures leads viewers from the despair of death to the hope of resurrection and eternal life through Christ's crucifixion.

FRA ANGELICO As Masaccio's *Holy Trinity* clearly demonstrates, humanism and religion were not mutually exclusive, but for many 15th-century Italian artists, humanist concerns were not a primary consideration. The art of Fra Angelico (ca. 1400–1455) focused on serving the Roman Catholic Church. In the late 1430s, the abbot of the Dominican monastery of San Marco (Saint Mark) in Florence asked Fra Angelico to produce a series of frescoes for the monastery. The Dominicans (see "The Great Schism," Chapter 19, page 501) of San Marco had dedicated themselves to lives of prayer

and work, and the religious compound was mostly spare and austere to encourage the monks to immerse themselves in their devotional lives. Fra Angelico's *Annunciation* (FIG. 21-21) appears at the top of the stairs leading to the friars' cells. Appropriately, Fra Angelico presented the scene of the Virgin Mary and the Archangel Gabriel with simplicity and serenity. The two figures appear in a plain *loggia* resembling San Marco's *portico*, and the artist painted all the fresco elements with a pristine clarity. As an admonition to heed the devotional function of the images, Fra Angelico included a small inscription at the base of the image: "As you venerate, while passing before it, this figure of the intact Virgin, beware lest you omit to say a Hail Mary." Like most of Fra Angelico's paintings, *Annunciation*'s simplicity and directness still have an almost universal appeal and fully reflect the artist's simple, humble character.

ANDREA DEL CASTAGNO Like Fra Angelico, Andrea del Castagno (ca. 1421–1457) accepted a commission to produce a series of frescoes for a religious establishment. His *Last Supper* (FIG. 21-22) in the *refectory* (dining hall) of Sant'Apollonia in Florence, a convent for Benedictine nuns, manifests both a commitment to the biblical narrative and an interest in perspective. The lavishly painted room that Christ and his 12 disciples occupy suggests Castagno's absorption with creating the illusion of three-dimensional space. However, close scrutiny reveals inconsistencies, such as the fact that Renaissance perspectival systems make it impossible to see both the ceiling from inside and the roof from outside, as Castagno depicted. The two side walls also do not appear parallel. The artist chose a conventional compositional format, with the figures seated at a horizontally placed table. Castagno derived the apparent self-absorption of most of the disciples and the malevolent features of Judas (who sits alone on the outside of the table) from the Gospel of Saint John, rather than the more familiar version of the Last Supper recounted in the Gospel of Saint Luke. Castagno's dramatic and spatially convincing depiction of the event no doubt was a powerful presence for the nuns during their daily meals.

FRA FILIPPO LIPPI A younger contemporary of Fra Angelico, Fra Filippo Lippi (ca. 1406–1469), was also a friar—but there all resemblance ends. Fra Filippo seems to have been unsuited for

21-22 ANDREA DEL CASTAGNO, *Last Supper,* the refectory, convent of Sant'Apollonia, Florence, Italy, 1447. Fresco, 15′ 5″ × 32′. ◼

Judas sits isolated in this *Last Supper* fresco based on the Gospel of Saint John. The figures are small compared to the setting, reflecting Castagno's preoccupation with the new science of perspective.

monastic life. He indulged in misdemeanors ranging from forgery and embezzlement to the abduction of a pretty nun, Lucretia, who became his mistress and the mother of his son, the painter Filippino Lippi (1457–1504). Only the intervention of the Medici on his behalf at the papal court saved Fra Filippo from severe punishment and total disgrace. An orphan, Fra Filippo spent his youth in a monastery adjacent to the church of Santa Maria del Carmine. When he was still in his teens, he must have met Masaccio there and witnessed the decoration of the Brancacci Chapel. Fra Filippo's early work survives only in fragments, but these show that he tried to work with Masaccio's massive forms. Later, probably under the influence of Ghiberti's and Donatello's relief sculptures, he developed a linear style that emphasized the contours of his figures and permitted him to suggest movement through flying and swirling draperies.

A painting from Fra Filippo's later years, *Madonna and Child with Angels* (FIG. **21-23**), shows his skill in employing a wonderfully fluid line, which unifies the composition and contributes to the precise and smooth delineation of forms. Fra Filippo interpreted his subject in a surprisingly worldly manner. The Madonna, a beautiful young mother, is not at all spiritual or fragile, and neither is the Christ Child, whom two angels hold up. One of the angels turns with the mischievous, puckish grin of a boy refusing to behave for the pious occasion. Significantly, all figures reflect the use of live models (perhaps even Lucretia for the Madonna). Fra Filippo plainly relished the charm of youth and beauty as he found it in this world. He

21-23 FRA FILIPPO LIPPI, *Madonna and Child with Angels,* ca. 1455. Tempera on wood, 2′ 11½″ × 2′ 1″. Galleria degli Uffizi, Florence.

Fra Filippo, a monk guilty of many misdemeanors, represented the Virgin and Christ Child in a distinctly worldly manner, carrying the humanization of the holy family further than ever before.

21-24 DOMENICO GHIRLANDAIO, *Birth of the Virgin*, Cappella Maggiore, Santa Maria Novella, Florence, Italy, ca. 1485–1490. Fresco, 24' 4" × 14' 9".

Ludovica Tornabuoni holds as prominent a place in Ghirlandaio's fresco as she must have held in Florentine society—evidence of the secularization of sacred themes in 15th-century Italian painting.

1 ft.

preferred the real in landscape also. The background, seen through the window, incorporates recognizable features of the Arno River valley. Compared with the earlier Madonnas by Giotto (FIG. **19-8**) and Duccio (FIG. **19-10**), this work shows how far artists had carried the humanization of the religious theme. Whatever the ideals of spiritual perfection may have meant to artists in past centuries, Renaissance artists realized those ideals in terms of the sensuous beauty of this world.

DOMENICO GHIRLANDAIO Toward the end of the 15th century, DOMENICO GHIRLANDAIO (1449–1494) received an important commission from Giovanni Tornabuoni, one of the wealthiest Florentines of his day. Tornabuoni asked Ghirlandaio to paint a cycle of frescoes depicting scenes from the lives of the Virgin and Saint John the Baptist for the choir of Santa Maria Novella, the Dominican church where Masaccio had earlier painted his revolutionary *Holy Trinity* (FIG. **21-20**). In *Birth of the Virgin* (FIG. **21-24**), Mary's mother, Saint Anne, reclines in a palatial Renaissance room embellished with fine wood inlay and sculpture, while midwives prepare the infant's bath. From the left comes a grave procession of women led by a young Tornabuoni family member, probably Ludovica, Giovanni's daughter. Ghirlandaio's composition epitomizes the achievements of 15th-century Florentine painting: clear spatial representation, statuesque figures, and rational order and logical relations among all figures and objects. If anything of earlier artistic traits remains here, it is the arrangement of the figures, who still cling somewhat rigidly to layers parallel to the picture plane. New, however, and in striking contrast to the dignity and austerity of Fra Angelico's frescoes (FIG. **21-21**) for the Dominican monastery of San Marco, is the dominating presence of the donor's family in the religious tableau. Ludovica holds as prominent a place in the composition (close to the central axis) as she must have held in Florentine society.

21-25 DOMENICO GHIRLANDAIO, *Giovanna Tornabuoni*(?), 1488. Oil and tempera on wood, 2' 6" × 1' 8". Museo Thyssen-Bornemisza, Madrid.

Renaissance artists revived the ancient art of portraiture. This portrait reveals the great wealth, courtly manners, and humanistic interest in classical literature that lie behind much 15th-century Florentine art.

1 in.

1 ft.

Her appearance in the painting (a different female member of the house appears in each fresco) is conspicuous evidence of the secularization of sacred themes. Artists depicted living persons of high rank not only as being present at biblical dramas (as Masaccio did in *Holy Trinity*) but also as even stealing the show—as here, where the Florentine women upstage the Virgin and Child. The display of patrician elegance tempers the biblical narrative and subordinates the fresco's devotional nature.

Ghirlandaio also painted individual portraits of wealthy Florentines. His 1488 panel painting (FIG. 21-25) of an aristocratic young woman is probably a portrait of Giovanna Tornabuoni (1468–1488), a member of the powerful Albizzi family and wife of Lorenzo Tornabuoni. Although artists at this time were beginning to employ three-quarter and full-face views for portraits in place of the more traditional profile pose, Ghirlandaio used the conventional format. This did not prevent him from conveying a character reading of the sitter. His portrait reveals the proud bearing of a sensitive and beautiful young woman. It also tells viewers much about the advanced state of culture in Florence, the value and careful cultivation of beauty in life and art, the breeding of courtly manners, and the great wealth behind it all. In addition, the painting shows the powerful attraction classical literature held for Italian humanists. In the background, an epitaph (Giovanna Tornabuoni died in childbirth) quotes the ancient Roman poet Martial.

PAOLO UCCELLO This secular side of Florentine art is on display in *Battle of San Romano* (FIG. 21-26) by PAOLO UCCELLO (1397–1475), a Florentine painter trained in the International Style. The panel painting is one of a series of three that Lorenzo de' Medici acquired for his bedchamber in the palatial family residence (FIGS. 21-36 and 21-37) in Florence. There is some controversy about the date of the painting because recently discovered documents suggest that Lorenzo may have purchased at least two of the paintings from a previous owner instead of commissioning the full series himself. The scenes commemorate the Florentine victory over the Sienese in 1432 and must have been painted no earlier than the mid-1430s if

not around 1455, the traditional date assigned to the commission. In the panel illustrated, Niccolò da Tolentino (ca. 1350–1435), a friend and supporter of Cosimo de' Medici, leads the charge against the Sienese. Although the painting focuses on Tolentino's military exploits, it also acknowledges the Medici, albeit in symbolic form. The bright orange fruit (appropriately placed) behind the unbroken and sturdy lances on the left were known as "mela medica" (Italian, "medicinal apples"). Given that the name Medici means "doctors," this fruit was a fitting symbol (one of many) of the family. It also suggests that at least this panel was a Medici commission.

Uccello was one of many 15th-century painters (and patrons) obsessed with the new science of perspective. The development of perspectival systems intrigued the humanists, because perspective represented the rationalization of vision. As staunch humanists, the Medici pursued all facets of expanding knowledge. In *Battle of San Romano*, Uccello created a composition that recalls the International Style processional splendor of Gentile's *Adoration of the Magi* (FIG. 21-17). But in contrast with Gentile, who emphasized surface decoration, Uccello painted immobilized solid forms. He foreshortened broken spears, lances, and a fallen soldier and carefully placed them along the converging orthogonals of the perspectival system to create a base plane like a checkerboard, on which he then placed the larger volumes in measured intervals. This diligently created space recedes to a landscape that resembles the low cultivated hillsides between Florence and Lucca. The rendering of three-dimensional form, used by other painters for representational or expressive purposes, became for Uccello a preoccupation. For him, it had a magic of its own, which he exploited to satisfy his inventive and original imagination.

SANDRO BOTTICELLI Of all the Florentine painters the Medici employed, perhaps the most famous today is SANDRO BOTTICELLI (1444–1510), a pupil of Fra Filippo Lippi (FIG. 21-23), who must have taught him the method of using firm, pure outlines with light shading within the contours. Art historians universally recognize Botticelli as one of the great masters of line. He was, however, a

21-27 Sandro Botticelli, *Primavera*, ca. 1482. Tempera on wood, 6′ 8″ × 10′ 4″. Galleria degli Uffizi, Florence. ◼◀

Probably intended to commemorate the May 1482 wedding of Lorenzo di Pierfrancesco de' Medici, Botticelli's lyrical painting celebrates love in spring, with Venus and Cupid at the center of the composition.

1 ft.

brilliant colorist as well, as is evident in *Primavera* (*Spring*; FIG. **21-27**), one of the most popular paintings among a host of other extraordinary works in the collection of the Uffizi Gallery in Florence. The precise meaning of this painting continues to elude scholars. Created for Lorenzo di Pierfrancesco de' Medici, one of Lorenzo the Magnificent's cousins, it features a friezelike series of classically inspired figures in the foreground and a lush backdrop of orange trees in honor of the patron (compare FIG. 21-26). Venus stands just to the right of center with her son Cupid hovering above her head. Botticelli drew attention to the goddess of love by opening the landscape behind her to reveal a portion of sky that forms a kind of halo around her head. To Venus's right, seemingly the target of Cupid's arrow, are the dancing Three Graces, based closely on ancient prototypes but clothed, albeit in thin, transparent garments. At the right, the blue ice-cold Zephyrus, the west wind, is about to carry off and then marry the nymph Chloris, whom he transforms into Flora, goddess of spring, appropriately shown wearing a rich floral gown. At the far left, the enigmatic figure of Mercury turns away from all the others and reaches up with his distinctive staff, the *caduceus,* perhaps to dispel storm clouds. The sensuality of the representation, the appearance of Venus in springtime, and the abduction and marriage of Chloris all suggest that the painting was commissioned on the occasion of young Lorenzo's May 1482 wedding.

BIRTH OF VENUS Rivaling *Primavera* in fame is Botticelli's tempera on canvas *Birth of Venus* (FIG. **21-28**), which the painter also created for the Medici family. The theme was the subject of a poem by Angelo Poliziano (1454–1494), a leading humanist of the day. In Botticelli's lyrical painting of the poet's retelling of the Greek myth, Zephyrus, carrying Chloris, blows Venus, born of sea foam and carried on a cockle shell, to her sacred island, Cyprus. There, the nymph Pomona runs to meet her with a brocaded mantle. The lightness and bodilessness of the winds propel all the figures without effort. Draperies undulate easily in the gentle gusts, perfumed by rose petals that fall on the whitecaps. In this painting, unlike *Primavera*, Botticelli depicted Venus as nude. As noted earlier, the nude, especially the female nude, was exceedingly rare during the Middle Ages. The artist's

use (particularly on such a large scale) of an ancient Venus statue (a Hellenistic variant of Praxiteles' famous *Aphrodite of Knidos,* FIG. 5-62) as a model could have drawn the charge of paganism. But in the more accommodating Renaissance culture and under the protection of the powerful Medici, the depiction went unchallenged.

Botticelli's style is clearly distinct from the earnest search many other artists pursued to comprehend humanity and the natural world through a rational, empirical order. Indeed, Botticelli's elegant and beautiful style seems to have ignored all of the scientific knowledge 15th-century artists had gained in the areas of perspective and anatomy. For example, the seascape in *Birth of Venus* is a flat backdrop devoid of atmospheric perspective. Botticelli's style paralleled the Florentine allegorical pageants that were chivalric tournaments structured around allusions to classical mythology. The same trend is evident in the poetry of the 1470s and 1480s. Artists and poets at this time did not directly imitate classical antiquity but used the myths, with delicate perception of their charm, in a way still tinged with medieval romance. Ultimately, Botticelli created a style of visual poetry parallel to the love poetry of Lorenzo de' Medici. His paintings possess a lyricism and courtliness that appealed to cultured Florentine patrons.

MEDICI PATRONAGE The wide range of Medici commissions illustrated in this chapter makes clear that the Florentine banking family did not restrict its collecting to any specific style or artist. Medici acquisitions ranged from mythological to biblical to contemporary historical subject matter and included both paintings and sculptures. Collectively, the art of the Medici reveals their wide and eclectic tastes and sincere love of art and learning and makes a statement about the patrons themselves as well. Careful businessmen that they were, the Medici were not sentimental about their endowment of art and scholarship. Cosimo acknowledged that his good works were not only for the honor of God but also to construct his own legacy. Fortunately, the Medici desired to promote their own fame, and this led to the creation of many of the most cherished masterpieces in the history of Western art.

21-27A Botticelli, *Young Man Holding a Me...* ca. 1474–1475

21-28 SANDRO BOTTICELLI, *Birth of Venus*, ca. 1484–1486. Tempera on canvas, 5′ 9″ × 9′ 2″. Galleria degli Uffizi, Florence.

Inspired by an Angelo Poliziano poem and classical statues of Aphrodite (FIG. 5-62), Botticelli revived the theme of the female nude in this elegant and romantic representation of Venus born of sea foam.

ENGRAVING Although the most prestigious commissions in 15th-century Florence were for large-scale panel paintings and frescoes and for monumental statues and reliefs, some artists also produced important small-scale works, such as Pollaiuolo's *Hercules and Antaeus* (FIG. 21-14). Pollaiuolo also experimented with the new medium of engraving, which Northern European artists had pioneered around the middle of the century. But whereas German graphic artists, such as Martin Schongauer (FIG. 20-22), used cross hatching that followed the forms, Italian engravers, such as Pollaiuolo, preferred parallel hatching. The former method was in keeping with the general Northern European approach to art, which tended to describe surfaces of forms rather than their underlying structures, whereas the latter better suited the anatomical studies that preoccupied Pollaiuolo and his Italian contemporaries.

Pollaiuolo's *Battle of the Ten Nudes* (FIG. **21-29**), like his *Hercules and Antaeus*, reveals the artist's interest in the realistic presentation of human figures in action. Earlier artists, such as Donatello and Masaccio, had dealt effectively with the problem of rendering human anatomy, but they usually depicted their figures at rest or in restrained motion. As is evident in his engraving as well as in his sculpture, Pollaiuolo took delight in showing violent action. He conceived the body as a powerful machine and liked to display its mechanisms, such as knotted muscles and taut sinews that activate the skeleton as ropes pull levers. To show this to best effect, Pollaiuolo developed a figure so lean and muscular that it appears *écorché* (as if without skin), with strongly accentuated delineations at the wrists, elbows, shoulders, and knees. *Battle of the Ten Nudes* shows this figure type in a variety of poses and from numerous

21-29 ANTONIO DEL POLLAIUOLO, *Battle of the Ten Nudes*, ca. 1465. Engraving, 1′ 3⅛″ × 1′ 11¼″. Metropolitan Museum of Art, New York (bequest of Joseph Pulitzer, 1917).

Pollaiuolo was fascinated by how muscles and sinews activate the human skeleton. He delighted in showing nude figures in violent action and from numerous foreshortened viewpoints.

viewpoints, allowing Pollaiuolo to demonstrate his prowess in rendering the nude male figure. In this, he was a kindred spirit of late-sixth-century Greek vase painters, such as Euthymides (FIG. 5-24), who had experimented with foreshortening for the first time in history. Even though Pollaiuolo's figures hack and slash at each other without mercy, they nevertheless seem somewhat stiff and frozen, because Pollaiuolo depicted *all* the muscle groups at maximum tension. Not until several decades later did an even greater anatomist, Leonardo da Vinci, observe that only part of the body's muscle groups participate in any one action, while the others remain relaxed.

Architecture

Filippo Brunelleschi's ability to codify a system of linear perspective derived in part from his skill as an architect. Although in a biography of him written around 1480, Antonio Manetti (1423–1497) reported that Brunelleschi turned to architecture out of disappointment over the loss of the commission for Florence's baptistery doors, he continued to work as a sculptor for several years and received commissions for sculpture as late as 1416. It is true, however, that as the 15th century progressed, Brunelleschi's interest turned increasingly toward architecture. Several trips to Rome (the first in 1402, probably with his friend Donatello), where the ruins of the ancient city captivated him, heightened his fascination with architecture. His close study of Roman monuments and his effort to make an accurate record of what he saw may well have been the catalyst that led Brunelleschi to develop his revolutionary system of geometric linear perspective.

FLORENCE CATHEDRAL Brunelleschi's broad knowledge of Roman construction principles, combined with an analytical and inventive mind, permitted him to solve an engineering problem that no other 15th-century architect could tackle. The challenge was the design and construction of a *dome* for the huge *crossing* of the unfinished Florence Cathedral (FIG. 19-18). The problem was staggering. The space to be spanned (140 feet) was much too wide to permit construction with the aid of traditional wooden centering. Nor was it possible (because of the crossing plan) to support the dome with *buttressed* walls. Brunelleschi began work on the problem about 1417. In 1420 the officials overseeing cathedral projects awarded Brunelleschi and Ghiberti a joint commission. The latter, however, soon retired from the project.

With exceptional ingenuity, Brunelleschi not only discarded traditional building methods and devised new ones but also invented much of the machinery necessary for the job. Although he might have preferred the hemispheric shape of Roman domes, Brunelleschi raised the center of his dome and designed it around an *ogival* (pointed arch) section (FIG. 21-30), which is inherently more stable because it reduces the outward *thrust* around the dome's base. To minimize the structure's weight, he designed a relatively thin double shell (the first in history) around a skeleton of 24 *ribs*. The eight most important are visible on the exterior. Finally, in almost paradoxical fashion, Brunelleschi anchored the structure at the top with a heavy lantern, built after his death but from his design. Despite Brunelleschi's knowledge of and admiration for Roman building techniques, and even though Florence Cathedral's dome was his most outstanding engineering achievement, he solved this critical structural problem through what were essentially Gothic building principles. Thus, the dome, which also had to harmonize in formal terms with the century-old building, does not express Brunelleschi's Renaissance architectural style.

SANTO SPIRITO Santo Spirito (FIGS. 21-31 and 21-32), begun around 1436 and completed, with some changes, after Brunel-

21-30 FILIPPO BRUNELLESCHI, cutaway view of the dome of Florence Cathedral, Florence, Italy, 1420–1436 (after Piero Sanpaolesi).

Brunelleschi solved the problem of placing a dome over the 140-foot-wide crossing of Florence Cathedral by designing a thin double shell that was ogival in section. A heavy lantern anchors the dome at the top.

leschi's death, is one of two *basilican* churches the architect built in Florence. It showcases the clarity and classically inspired rationality that characterize Brunelleschi's mature designs. Brunelleschi laid out this *cruciform* building in either multiples or segments of the dome-covered *crossing square*. The aisles, subdivided into small squares covered by shallow, saucer-shaped vaults, run all the way around the flat-roofed central space. They have the visual effect of compressing the longitudinal design into one comparable to a *central plan*, because the various aspects of the interior resemble one another, no matter where an observer stands. Originally, this centralization effect would have been even stronger. Brunelleschi had planned to extend the aisles across the front of the nave as well, as shown on the plan (FIG. 21-32, *left*). However, adherence to that design would have required four entrances in the facade, instead of the traditional and symbolic three, a feature hotly debated during Brunelleschi's lifetime and changed after his death. Successor builders later also modified the appearance of the exterior walls (compare the two plans in FIG. 21-32) by filling in the recesses between the projecting semicircular chapels to convert the original highly sculpted wall surface into a flat one.

The major features of Santo Spirito's interior (FIG. 21-31), however, are much as Brunelleschi designed them. In this *modular* scheme, a mathematical unit served to determine the dimensions of every aspect of the church. This unit, repeated throughout the interior, creates a rhythmic harmony. For example, the nave is twice as high as it is wide, and the arcade and clerestory are of equal height, which means that the height of the arcade equals the nave's width.

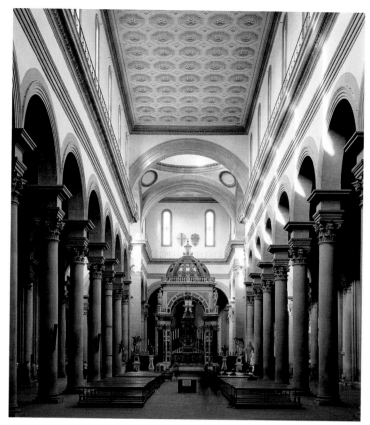

21-31 FILIPPO BRUNELLESCHI, interior of Santo Spirito (looking northeast), Florence, Italy, designed 1434–1436; begun 1446.

The austerity of the decor and the mathematical clarity of the interior of Santo Spirito contrast sharply with the soaring drama and spirituality of the nave arcades and vaults of Gothic churches.

Dome-covered crossing square

Four entrances

Three entrances

N

| 0 | | 50 | | 100 feet |
| 0 | 10 | 20 | 30 meters | |

21-32 FILIPPO BRUNELLESCHI, early plan (*left*) and plan as constructed (*right*) of Santo Spirito, Florence, Italy, designed 1434–1436; begun 1446.

Santo Spirito displays the classically inspired rationality of Brunelleschi's mature architectural style in its all-encompassing modular scheme based on the dimensions of the dome-covered crossing square.

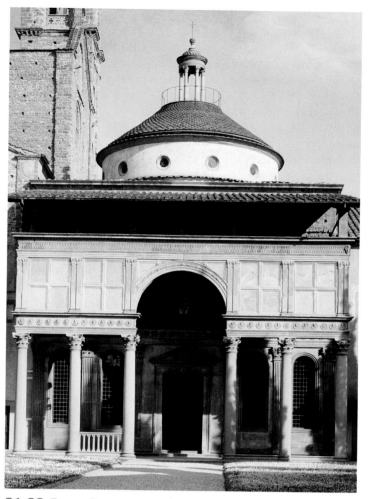

21-33 FILIPPO BRUNELLESCHI, facade of the Pazzi Chapel, Santa Croce, Florence, Italy, designed ca. 1423, begun 1442.

The Pazzi family erected this chapel as a gift to the Franciscan church of Santa Croce. One of the first independent Renaissance central-plan buildings, it served as the monks' chapter house.

Astute observers can read the proportional relationships among the interior's parts as a series of mathematical equations. The austerity of the decor enhances the rationality of the design and produces a restful and tranquil atmosphere. Brunelleschi left no space for expansive wall frescoes that only would interrupt the clarity of his architectural scheme. The calculated logic of the design echoes that of ancient Roman buildings, such as the Pantheon (FIG. 10-50, *right*). The rationality of Santo Spirito contrasts sharply, however, with the soaring drama and spirituality of the nave arcades and vaults of Gothic churches (for example, FIGS. 18-19 and 18-20). It even deviates from the design of Florence Cathedral's nave (FIG. 19-19), whose verticality is restrained compared with its Northern European counterparts. Santo Spirito fully expresses the new Renaissance spirit that placed its faith in reason rather than in the emotions.

PAZZI CHAPEL Brunelleschi's apparent effort to impart a centralized effect to the interior of Santo Spirito suggests that the compact and self-contained qualities of earlier central-plan buildings, such as the Roman Pantheon (FIGS. 10-49 to 10-51), intrigued him. The Pazzi Chapel (FIG. 21-33) presented Brunelleschi with the opportunity to explore this interest, in a structure much better suited to a centralized design than a basilican church. The chapel was the Pazzi family's gift to the Franciscan church of Santa Croce in Florence (see "Renaissance Family Chapel Endowments," page 564) and served as

Renaissance Family Chapel Endowments

During the 14th through 16th centuries in Italy, wealthy families regularly endowed chapels in or adjacent to major churches. These family chapels were usually on either side of the choir near the altar at the church's east end. Particularly wealthy families endowed chapels in the form of separate buildings constructed adjacent to churches. For example, the Medici Chapel (Old Sacristy) abuts San Lorenzo in Florence. Powerful banking families, such as the Baroncelli, Bardi, and Peruzzi, each sponsored chapels in the Florentine church of Santa Croce. The Pazzi commissioned a chapel (FIGS. 21-33 to 21-35) adjacent to Santa Croce, and the Brancacci family sponsored the decorative program (FIGS. 21-18 and 21-19) of their chapel in Santa Maria del Carmine.

These families endowed chapels to ensure the well-being of the souls of individual family members and ancestors. The chapels served as burial sites and as spaces for liturgical celebrations and commemorative services. Chapel owners sponsored Masses for the dead, praying to the Virgin Mary and the saints for intercession on behalf of their deceased loved ones. Changes in Christian doctrine

prompted these concerted efforts to improve donors' chances for eternal salvation. Until the 13th century, Christians believed that after death, souls went either to Heaven or to Hell. After that time, the concept of Purgatory—a way station between Heaven and Hell where souls could atone for sins before Judgment Day—increasingly won favor. Pope Innocent III (1198–1216) recognized the existence of such a place in 1215. Because Purgatory represented an opportunity for the faithful to improve their chances of eventually gaining admission to Heaven, they eagerly embraced this opportunity. When they extended this idea to improving their chances while alive, charitable work, good deeds, and devotional practices proliferated. Family chapels provided the space necessary for the performance of devotional rituals. Most chapels included altars as well as chalices, vestments, candlesticks, and other objects used in the Mass. Most patrons also commissioned decorations, such as painted altarpieces, frescoes on the walls, and sculptural objects. The chapels were therefore expressions of piety and devotion but also opportunities for the donors to burnish their images in the larger community.

the monk's *chapter house* (meeting hall). Brunelleschi began to design the Pazzi Chapel around 1423, but work continued until the 1460s, long after his death. The exterior (FIG. 21-33) probably does not reflect Brunelleschi's original design. The loggia, admirable as it is, seems to have been added as an afterthought, perhaps by the sculptor-architect Giuliano da Maiano (1432–1490). Historians have

21-34 FILIPPO BRUNELLESCHI, plan of the Pazzi Chapel, Santa Croce, Florence, Italy, designed ca. 1423, begun 1442.

Although the Pazzi Chapel is rectangular, rather than square or round, Brunelleschi created a central plan by placing all emphasis on the dome-covered space at the heart of the building.

21-35 FILIPPO BRUNELLESCHI, interior of the Pazzi Chapel (looking northeast), Santa Croce, Florence, Italy, designed ca. 1423, begun 1442, with glazed terracotta roundels by LUCA DELLA ROBBIA.

The interior trim of the Pazzi Chapel is gray pietra serena, which stands out against the white stuccoed walls and crisply defines the modular relationships of Brunelleschi's plan and elevation.

21-36 MICHELOZZO DI BARTOLOMMEO, facade of the Palazzo Medici-Riccardi, Florence, Italy, begun 1445. ■◀

The Medici palace, with its combination of dressed and rusticated masonry and classical moldings, draws heavily on ancient Roman architecture, but Michelozzo creatively reinterpreted his models.

suggested that the local chapter of Franciscan monks who held meetings in the chapel needed the expansion. Behind the loggia stands one of the first independent Renaissance buildings conceived basically as a central-plan structure. Although the plan (FIG. **21-34**) is rectangular, rather than square or round, the architect placed all emphasis on the central dome-covered space. The short barrel-vaulted sections that brace the dome on two sides appear to be incidental appendages. The interior trim (FIG. **21-35**) is gray pietra serena ("serene stone"), which stands out against the white stuccoed walls and crisply defines the modular relationships of plan and elevation. As he did in his design for Santo Spirito, Brunelleschi used a basic unit that allowed him to construct a balanced, harmonious, and regularly proportioned space.

Circular medallions, or *tondi,* in the dome's *pendentives* (see "Pendentives and Squinches," Chapter 12, page 315) consist of *glazed terracotta* reliefs representing the four evangelists. The technique for manufacturing these baked clay reliefs was of recent invention. Around 1430, LUCA DELLA ROBBIA (1400–1482) perfected the application of vitrified (heat-fused) colored potters' glazes to sculpture. Inexpensive and durable, these colorful sculptures became extremely popular and provided the basis for a flourishing family business. Luca's nephew Andrea della Robbia (1435–1525) and Andrea's sons, Giovanni della Robbia (1469–1529) and Girolamo della Robbia (1488–1566), carried on this tradition well into the 16th century. Most of the *roundels* in the Pazzi Chapel are the work of Luca della Robbia himself. Together with the images of the 12 apostles on the pilaster-framed wall panels, they add striking color accents to the tranquil interior.

PALAZZO MEDICI It seems curious that Brunelleschi, the most renowned architect of his time, did not participate in the upsurge of palace building that Florence experienced in the 1430s and 1440s. This proliferation of palazzi testified to the stability of the Florentine economy and to the affluence and confidence of the city's leading citizens. Brunelleschi, however, confined his efforts in this field to work on the Palazzo di Parte Guelfa (headquarters of Florence's then-ruling "party") and to a rejected model for a new palace that Cosimo de' Medici intended to build. When the Medici returned to Florence in 1434 after their short-lived exile, Cosimo, aware of the importance of public perception, attempted to maintain a lower profile and to wield his power from behind the scenes. In all probability, this attitude accounted for his rejection of Brunelleschi's design for the Medici residence, which he evidently found

too imposing and ostentatious to be politically wise. Cosimo eventually awarded the commission to MICHELOZZO DI BARTOLOMMEO (1396–1472), a young architect who had collaborated with Donatello in several sculptural enterprises. Although Cosimo passed over Brunelleschi, his architectural style in fact deeply influenced Michelozzo. To a limited extent, the Palazzo Medici (FIG. **21-36**) reflects Brunelleschian principles.

Later bought by the Riccardi family (hence the name Palazzo Medici-Riccardi), who almost doubled the facade's length in the 18th century, the palace, both in its original and extended form, is a simple, massive structure. Heavy *rustication* (rough unfinished masonry) on the ground floor accentuates its strength. Michelozzo divided the building block into stories of decreasing height by using long, unbroken *stringcourses* (horizontal bands), which give it coherence. *Dressed* (smooth, finished) *masonry* on the second level and an even smoother surface on the top story modify the severity of the ground floor and make the building appear progressively lighter as the eye moves upward. The extremely heavy *cornice,* which Michelozzo related not to the top story but to the building as a whole, dramatically reverses this effect. Like the ancient Roman cornices that served as

21-37 MICHELOZZO DI BARTOLOMMEO, interior court of the Palazzo Medici-Riccardi, Florence, Italy, begun 1445.

The Medici palace's interior court surrounded by a round-arched colonnade was the first of its kind, but the austere design clearly reveals Michelozzo's debt to Brunelleschi (FIG. 21-31).

Michelozzo's models (compare FIGS. 10-32, 10-39, and 10-47), the Palazzo Medici-Riccardi cornice is an effective lid for the structure, clearly and emphatically defining its proportions. Michelozzo also may have drawn inspiration from the many extant examples of Roman rusticated masonry, and Roman precedents even existed for the juxtaposition of rusticated and dressed stone masonry on the same facade (FIG. 10-34). However, nothing in the ancient world precisely compares to Michelozzo's design. The Palazzo Medici exemplifies the simultaneous respect for and independence from the antique that characterize the Early Renaissance in Italy.

The heart of the Palazzo Medici is an open colonnaded court (FIG. 21-37) that clearly shows Michelozzo's debt to Brunelleschi. The round-arched colonnade, although more massive in its proportions, closely resembles other buildings Brunelleschi designed. This internal court surrounded by an arcade was the first of its kind and influenced a long line of descendants in Renaissance domestic architecture.

LEON BATTISTA ALBERTI Although he entered the profession of architecture rather late in life, LEON BATTISTA ALBERTI (1404–1472) nevertheless made a remarkable contribution to architectural design. He was the first to study seriously the ancient Roman architectural treatise of Vitruvius, and his knowledge of it, combined with his own archaeological investigations, made him the first Renaissance architect to understand classical architecture in depth. Alberti's most influential theoretical work, *On the Art of Building* (written about 1450, published 1486), although inspired by Vitruvius, contains much original material. Alberti advocated a system of ideal proportions and believed that the central plan was the ideal form for a Christian church. He also considered incongruous the combination of column and arch, which had persisted since Roman times and throughout the Middle Ages. He argued that the arch is a wall opening that should be supported only by a section of wall (a pier), not by an independent sculptural element (a column) as in Brunelleschi's and Michelozzo's buildings (FIGS. 21-31, 21-33, and 21-37).

PALAZZO RUCELLAI Alberti's own architectural style represents a scholarly application of classical elements to contemporary buildings. He designed the Palazzo Rucellai (FIG. 21-38) in Flor-

21-38 LEON BATTISTA ALBERTI and BERNARDO ROSSELLINO, Palazzo Rucellai, Florence, Italy, ca. 1452–1470.

Alberti was an ardent student of classical architecture. He created the illusion that the Palazzo Rucellai becomes lighter toward its top by adapting the Roman manner of using different capitals for each story.

21-39 Leon Battista Alberti, west facade of Santa Maria Novella, Florence, Italy, 1456–1470.

Alberti's design for the facade of this Gothic church features a pediment-capped temple front and pilaster-framed arcades. Numerical ratios are the basis of the proportions of all parts of the facade.

his cue from a *Romanesque* design—that of the Florentine church of San Miniato al Monte (FIG. 17-27). Following his medieval model, he designed a small, pseudoclassical, *pediment*-capped temple front for the facade's upper part and supported it with a pilaster-framed arcade that incorporates the six tombs and three doorways of the Gothic building. But in the organization of these elements, Alberti applied Renaissance principles. The height of Santa Maria Novella (to the pediment tip) equals its width so that the entire facade can be inscribed in a square. Throughout the facade, Alberti defined areas and related them to one another in terms of proportions that can be expressed in simple numerical ratios. For example, the upper structure can be encased in a square one-fourth the size of the main square. The cornice separating the two levels divides the major square in half so that the lower portion of the building is a rectangle twice as wide as it is high. In his treatise,

ence, although his pupil and collaborator, Bernardo Rossellino (1409–1464), actually constructed the building using Alberti's plans and sketches. The facade of the palace is much more severe than that of the Palazzo Medici-Riccardi (FIG. 21-36). Pilasters define each story, and a classical cornice crowns the whole. Between the smooth pilasters are subdued and uniform wall surfaces. Alberti created the sense that the structure becomes lighter in weight toward its top by adapting the ancient Roman manner of using different capitals for each story. He chose *Tuscan* (the Etruscan variant of the Greek *Doric order;* FIG. 5-14 or page xxviii in Volume II) for the ground floor, *Composite* (the Roman combination of *Ionic volutes* with the acanthus leaves of the *Corinthian;* FIG. 5-73 or page xxviii in Volume II) for the second story, and Corinthian for the third floor. Alberti modeled his facade on the most imposing Roman ruin of all, the Colosseum (FIG. 10-1), but he was no slavish copyist. On the Colosseum's facade, the capitals employed are, from the bottom up, Tuscan, Ionic, and Corinthian. Moreover, Alberti adapted the Colosseum's varied surface to a flat facade, which does not allow the deep penetration of the building's mass that is so effective in the Roman structure. By converting his ancient model's *engaged columns* (half-round columns attached to a wall) into shallow pilasters that barely project from the wall, Alberti created a large-meshed linear net. Stretched tightly across the front of his building, it not only unifies the three levels but also emphasizes the wall's flat, two-dimensional qualities.

SANTA MARIA NOVELLA The Rucellai family also commissioned Alberti to design the facade (FIG. 21-39) of the 13th-century Gothic church of Santa Maria Novella in Florence. Here, Alberti took

Alberti wrote at length about the necessity of employing harmonic proportions to achieve beautiful buildings. Alberti shared this conviction with Brunelleschi, and this fundamental dependence on classically derived mathematics distinguished their architectural work from that of their medieval predecessors. They believed in the eternal and universal validity of numerical ratios as the source of beauty. In this respect, Alberti and Brunelleschi revived the true spirit of the High Classical age of ancient Greece, as epitomized by the sculptor Polykleitos and the architect Iktinos, who produced canons of proportions for the perfect statue and the perfect temple (see Chapter 5). But it was not only a desire to emulate Vitruvius and the Greek masters that motivated Alberti to turn to mathematics in his quest for beauty. His contemporary, the Florentine humanist Giannozzo Manetti (1396–1459), had argued that Christianity itself possessed the order and logic of mathematics. In his 1452 treatise, *On the Dignity and Excellence of Man,* Manetti stated that Christian religious truths were as self-evident as mathematical axioms.

The Santa Maria Novella facade was an ingenious solution to a difficult design problem. On the one hand, it adequately expressed the organization of the structure attached to it. On the other hand, it subjected preexisting and quintessentially medieval features, such as the large round window on the second level, to a rigid geometrical order that instilled a quality of classical calm and reason. This facade also introduced a feature of great historical consequence—the scrolls that simultaneously unite the broad lower and narrow upper level and screen the sloping roofs over the aisles. With variations, similar spirals appeared in literally hundreds of church facades throughout the Renaissance and Baroque periods.

GIROLAMO SAVONAROLA In the 1490s, Florence underwent a political, cultural, and religious upheaval. Florentine artists and their fellow citizens responded then not only to humanist ideas but also to the incursion of French armies and especially to the preaching of the Dominican monk Girolamo Savonarola (1452–1498), the reforming priest-dictator who denounced the paganism of the Medici and their artists, philosophers, and poets. Savonarola exhorted the people of Florence to repent their sins, and when Lorenzo de' Medici died in 1492, he prophesied the downfall of the city and of Italy and assumed absolute control of the state. Together with a large number of citizens, Savonarola believed that the Medici's political, social, and religious power had corrupted Florence and had invited the scourge of foreign invasion. Savonarola denounced humanism and encouraged citizens to burn their classical texts, scientific treatises, and philosophical publications. The Medici fled in 1494. Scholars still debate the significance of Savonarola's brief span of power. Apologists for the undoubtedly sincere monk deny that his actions played a role in the decline of Florentine culture at the end of the 15th century. But the puritanical spirit that moved Savonarola must have dampened considerably the neopagan enthusiasm of the Florentine Early Renaissance. Certainly, his condemnation of humanism as heretical nonsense, and his banishing of the Medici, Tornabuoni, and other wealthy families from Florence, deprived local artists of some of their major patrons. There were, however, abundant commissions for artists elsewhere in Italy.

THE PRINCELY COURTS

Although Florentine artists led the way in creating the Renaissance in art and architecture, art production flourished throughout Italy in the 15th century. The papacy in Rome and the princely courts in Urbino, Mantua, and elsewhere also deserve credit for nurturing Renaissance art (see "Italian Princely Courts and Artistic Patronage," page 569). These princely courts consisted of the prince (whose title varied from city to city), his consort and children, courtiers, household staff, and administrators. The considerable wealth these princes possessed, coupled with their desire for recognition, fame, and power, resulted in major art commissions.

Rome and the Papal States

Although not a secular ruler, the pope in Rome was the head of a court with enormous wealth at his disposal. In the 16th and 17th centuries, the popes became the major patrons of art and architecture in Italy (see Chapters 22 and 24), but even in the 15th century, the papacy was the source of some significant artistic commissions.

21-40A MELOZ DA FORLÌ, *Sixt IV Confirming Platina,* ca. 1477–148

PERUGINO Between 1481 and 1483, Pope Sixtus IV (r. 1414–1484) summoned a group of artists, including Botticelli and Ghirlandaio, to Rome to decorate the walls of the newly completed Sistine Chapel (MAP 24-1). Pietro Vannucci of Perugia in Umbria, who was known as PERUGINO (ca. 1450–1523), was among the painters the pope em-

21-40 PERUGINO, *Christ Delivering the Keys of the Kingdom to Saint Peter,* Sistine Chapel, Vatican, Rome, Italy, 1481–1483. Fresco, 11′ 5½″ × 18′ 8½″.

Painted for the Vatican, this fresco depicts the event on which the papacy bases its authority. The converging lines of the pavement connect the action in the foreground with the background.

Italian Princely Courts and Artistic Patronage

The absence of a single sovereign ruling all of Italy and the fragmented nature of the independent city-states (MAP 19-1) provided a fertile breeding ground for the ambitions of the power-hungry. In the 15th century, Italian society witnessed the expansion of princely courts throughout the peninsula. A prince was in essence the lord of a territory, and despite this generic title, he could have been a duke, marquis, tyrant, cardinal, pope, or papal vicar. At this time, major princely courts emerged in papal Rome, Milan, Naples, Ferrara, Savoy, Urbino, and Mantua. Rather than denoting a specific organizational structure or physical entity, the term "princely court" refers to a power relationship between the prince and the territory's inhabitants based on imperial models. Each prince worked tirelessly to preserve and extend his control and authority, seeking to establish a societal framework of people who looked to him for jobs, favors, protection, prestige, and leadership. The importance of these princely courts derived from their role as centers of power and culture.

The efficient functioning of a princely court required a sophisticated administrative structure. Each prince employed an extensive household staff, ranging from counts, nobles, cooks, waiters, stewards, footmen, stable hands, and ladies-in-waiting to dog handlers, leopard keepers, pages, and runners. The duke of Milan had more than 40 chamberlains to attend to his personal needs alone. Each prince also needed an elaborate bureaucracy to oversee political, economic, and military operations and to ensure his continued control. These officials included secretaries, lawyers, captains, ambassadors, and condottieri. Burgeoning international diplomacy and trade made each prince the center of an active and privileged sphere. The princes' domains extended to the realm of culture, for they saw themselves as more than political, military, and economic leaders. They felt responsible for the vitality of cultural life in their territories, and art was a major component for developing a cultured populace. Visual imagery also appealed to them as effective propaganda for reinforcing their control. As the wealthiest individuals in their regions, princes possessed the means to commission numerous artworks and buildings. Thus, art functioned in several capacities—as evidence of princely sophistication and culture, as a form of prestige or commemoration, as public education and propaganda, as a demonstration of wealth, and as a source of visual pleasure.

Princes often researched in advance the reputations and styles of the artists and architects they commissioned. Such assurances of excellence were necessary, because the quality of the work reflected not just on the artist but on the patron as well. Yet despite the importance of individual style, princes sought artists who also were willing, at times, to subordinate their personal styles to work collaboratively on large-scale projects.

Princes bestowed on selected individuals the title of "court artist." Serving as a court artist had its benefits, among them a guaranteed salary (not always forthcoming), living quarters in the palace, liberation from guild restrictions, and, on occasion, status as a member of the prince's inner circle, perhaps even a knighthood. For artists struggling to elevate their profession from the ranks of craftspeople, working for a prince presented a marvelous opportunity. Until the 16th century, artists had limited status and were in the same class as small shopkeepers and petty merchants. Indeed, at court dinners, artists most often sat with the other members of the salaried household: tailors, cobblers, barbers, and upholsterers. Thus, the possibility of advancement was a powerful and constant incentive.

Princes demanded a great deal from court artists. Artists not only created the frescoes, portraits, and sculptures that have become their legacies but also designed tapestries, seat covers, costumes, masks, and decorations for various court festivities. Because princes constantly entertained, received ambassadors and dignitaries, and needed to maintain a high profile to reinforce their authority, lavish social functions were the norm. Artists often created gifts for visiting nobles and potentates. Recipients judged such gifts on the quality of both the work and the materials. By using expensive materials—gold leaf, silver leaf, lapis lazuli (a rich azure-blue stone imported from Afghanistan), silk, and velvet brocade—princes could impress others with their wealth and good taste.

---

ployed. His contribution to the fresco cycle of the Sistine Chapel was *Christ Delivering the Keys of the Kingdom to Saint Peter* (FIG. 21-40). The papacy had, from the beginning, based its claim to infallible and total authority over the Roman Catholic Church on this biblical event, and therefore the subject was one of obvious appeal to Sixtus IV. In Perugino's version, Christ hands the keys to Saint Peter, who stands amid an imaginary gathering of the 12 apostles and Renaissance contemporaries. These figures occupy the apron of a great stage space that extends into the distance to a point of convergence in the doorway of a central-plan temple. (Perugino used parallel and converging lines in the pavement to mark off the intervening space.) Figures in the middle distance complement the near group, emphasizing its density and order by their scattered arrangement. At the corners of the great piazza, duplicate triumphal arches serve as the base angles of a distant compositional triangle whose apex is in the central building. Perugino modeled the arches very closely on the Arch of Constantine (FIG. 10-75) in Rome. Although an anachronism in a painting depicting a scene from Christ's life, the arches served to underscore the close ties between Saint Peter and Constantine, the first Christian emperor and the builder of the great basilica (FIG. 11-9) over Saint Peter's tomb in Rome. Christ and Peter flank the triangle's central axis, which runs through the temple's doorway, the perspective's vanishing point. Thus, the composition interlocks both two-dimensional and three-dimensional space, and the placement of central actors emphasizes the axial center. This spatial science allowed the artist to organize the action systematically. Perugino, in this single picture, incorporated the learning of generations.

LUCA SIGNORELLI Another Umbrian artist that Sixtus IV employed for the decoration of the Sistine Chapel was LUCA SIGNORELLI (ca. 1445–1523), in whose work the fiery passion of the sermons of Savonarola found its pictorial equal. Signorelli further developed Pollaiuolo's interest in the depiction of muscular bodies in violent action in a wide variety of poses and foreshortenings. In the San Brizio Chapel in the cathedral of the papal state of Orvieto (MAP 19-1), Signorelli painted for Pope Alexander VI (r. 1492–1503)

PROPHETARVMLAVDABILISNVMERVS

1 ft.

21-41 Luca Signorelli, *Damned Cast into Hell,* San Brizio Chapel, Orvieto Cathedral, Orvieto, Italy, 1499–1504. Fresco, 23′ wide.

Few figure compositions of the 15th century have the same psychic impact as Luca Signorelli's Orvieto Cathedral fresco of writhing, foreshortened muscular bodies tortured by demons in Hell.

scenes depicting the end of the world, including *Damned Cast into Hell* (FIG. **21-41**). Few figure compositions of the 15th century have the same psychic impact. Saint Michael and the hosts of Heaven hurl the damned into Hell, where, in a dense, writhing mass, they are vigorously tortured by demons. The horrible consequences of a sinful life had not been so graphically depicted since Gislebertus carved his vision of the Last Judgment (FIGS. **I-6** and **17-12**) in the west *tympanum* of Saint-Lazare at Autun around 1130. The figures—nude, lean, and muscular—assume every conceivable posture of anguish. Signorelli's skill at foreshortening the human figure was equaled by his mastery of its action, and although each figure is clearly a study from a model, he fit his theme to the figures in an entirely convincing manner. Terror and rage explode like storms through the wrenched and twisted bodies. The fiends, their hair flaming and their bodies the color of putrefying flesh, lunge at their victims in ferocious frenzy.

Urbino

Under the patronage of Federico da Montefeltro (1422–1482), Urbino, southeast of Florence across the Appennines (MAP **19-1**), became an important center of Renaissance art and culture. In fact, the humanist writer Paolo Cortese (1465–1540) described Federico as

one of the two greatest artistic patrons of the 15th century (the other was Cosimo de' Medici). Federico was a condottiere so renowned for his military expertise that he was in demand by popes and kings, and soldiers came from across Europe to study under his direction.

PIERO DELLA FRANCESCA One artist who received several commissions from Federico was PIERO DELLA FRANCESCA (ca. 1420–1492) of San Sepolcro in Tuscany, who had earlier painted for the Medici, among others. One of Piero's major works at the Urbino court was *Enthroned Madonna and Saints Adored by Federico da Montefeltro,* also called the *Brera Altarpiece* (FIG. **21-42**). Federico, clad in armor, kneels piously at the Virgin's feet. Directly behind him stands Saint John the Evangelist, his patron saint. Where the viewer would expect to see Federico's wife, Battista Sforza (on the lower left, kneeling and facing her husband), no figure is present. Battista had died in 1472, shortly before Federico commissioned this painting. Thus, her absence clearly announces his loss. Piero further called attention to it by depicting Saint John the Baptist, Battista's patron saint, at the far left. The ostrich egg that hangs suspended from a shell over the Virgin's head was common over altars dedicated to Mary. The figures appear in an illusionistically painted, coffered barrel vault, which may have resembled part of the interior of the church of

21-42A Piero DELLA FRANCES Battista Sfor and Federico da Montefelt ca. 1472–1474

21-42 PIERO DELLA FRANCESCA, *Enthroned Madonna and Saints Adored by Federico da Montefeltro* (*Brera Altarpiece*), ca. 1472–1474. Oil on wood, 8′ 2″ × 5′ 7″. Pinacoteca di Brera, Milan.

The illusionism of Piero's *Brera Altarpiece* is so convincing that the viewer is compelled to believe in Federico da Montefeltro's presence before the Virgin Mary, Christ Child, and saints.

1 ft.

San Bernadino degli Zoccolanti near Urbino, the painting's intended location. If so, the viewer would be compelled to believe in Federico's presence in the church before the Virgin, Christ Child, and saints. That Piero depicted Federico in left profile was undoubtedly a concession to his patron. The right side of Federico's face had sustained severe injury in a tournament, and the resulting deformity made him reluctant to show that side.

The *Brera Altarpiece* reveals Piero's deep interest in the properties of light and color. In his effort to make the clearest possible distinction among forms, he flooded his pictures with light, imparting a silver-blue tonality. To avoid heavy shadows, he illuminated the dark sides of his forms with reflected light. By moving the darkest tones of his modeling toward the centers of his volumes, he separated them from their backgrounds. Because of this technique, Piero's paintings lack some of Masaccio's relieflike qualities but gain in spatial clarity, as each shape forms an independent unit surrounded by an atmospheric envelope and movable to any desired position, like a figure on a chessboard.

21-43 Piero della Francesca, *Flagellation of Christ*, ca. 1455–1465. Oil and tempera on wood, 1′ 11$\frac{1}{8}$″ × 2′ 8$\frac{1}{4}$″. Galleria Nazionale delle Marche, Urbino.

The identification of the foreground figures continues to elude scholars. They appear to discuss the biblical tragedy that takes place in Pilate's palace (FIG. 21-1), which Piero rendered in perfect perspective.

21-43A Piero della Francesca, *Resurrection*, ca. 1463–1465.

FLAGELLATION Piero's most enigmatic painting is *Flagellation of Christ* (FIG. 21-43), a small panel painting perhaps also produced for Federico da Montefeltro. The setting for the New Testament drama is the portico of Pontius Pilate's palace in Jerusalem. Curiously, the focus of the composition is not Christ but the group of three large figures in the foreground, whose identity scholars still debate. Some have identified the bearded figure as a Turk and interpreted the painting as a commentary on the capture in 1453 of Christian Constantinople by the Muslims (see Chapter 12). Other scholars, however, identify the three men as biblical figures, including the Old Testament's King David, one of whose psalms theologians believed predicted the conspiracy against Christ. In any case, the three men appear to discuss the event in the background. As Pilate, the seated judge, watches, Christ, bound to a column topped by a classical statue, is about to be whipped (FIG. 21-1). Piero's perspective is so meticulous that the floor pattern can be reconstructed perfectly as a central porphyry (purple marble) circle with surrounding squares composed of various geometric shapes. Whatever the solution is to the iconographical puzzle of Piero's *Flagellation,* the panel reveals a mind cultivated by mathematics. The careful delineation of the setting suggests an architect's vision, certainly that of a man entirely familiar with compass and straightedge.

Piero planned his compositions almost entirely by his sense of the exact and lucid structures defined by mathematics. He believed that the highest beauty resides in forms that have the clarity and purity of geometric figures. Toward the end of his long career, Piero, a skilled geometrician, wrote the first theoretical treatise on systematic perspective, after having practiced the art with supreme mastery for almost a lifetime. His association with the architect Alberti at Ferrara and at Rimini around 1450–1451 probably turned his attention fully to perspective (a science in which Alberti was an influential pioneer) and helped determine his later, characteristically architectonic compositions. This approach appealed to Federico, a patron fascinated by architectural space and its depiction.

21-43B Piero della Francesca, *Legend of the True Cross*, ca. 1450–1455.

Mantua

Marquis Ludovico Gonzaga (1412–1478) ruled the court of Mantua in northeastern Italy (MAP 19-1). A famed condottiere like Federico da Montefeltro, Gonzaga established his reputation as a fierce military general while commanding the Milanese armies. The visit of Pope Pius II (r. 1458–1464) to Mantua in 1459 stimulated the marquis's determination to transform Mantua into a city that all Italy would envy.

Alberti's design for Sant'Andrea reflects his study of ancient Roman architecture. Employing a colossal order, the architect locked together a triumphal arch and a Roman temple front with pediment.

SANT'ANDREA One of the major projects Gonzaga instituted was the redesigning of the church of Sant'Andrea to replace an 11th-century church. Gonzaga turned to the renowned architect Leon Battista Alberti for this important commission. The facade (FIG. 21-44) Alberti designed locked together two complete ancient Roman architectural motifs—the temple front and the triumphal arch. The combination was already a familiar feature of Roman buildings still standing in Italy. For example, many triumphal arches incorporated a pediment over the arcuated passageway and engaged columns, but there is no close parallel in antiquity for Alberti's eclectic and inge-

nious design. The Renaissance architect's concern for proportion led him to equalize the vertical and horizontal dimensions of the facade, which left it considerably shorter than the church behind it. Because of the primary importance of visual appeal, many Renaissance architects made this concession not only to the demands of a purely visual proportionality in the facade but also to the facade's relation to the small square in front of it, even at the expense of continuity with the body of the building. Yet structural correspondences to the building do exist in Sant'Andrea's facade. The pilasters are the same height as those on the nave's interior walls, and the central barrel vault over the main exterior entrance, with smaller barrel vaults branching off at right angles, introduces on a smaller scale the arrangement of the nave and aisles (FIG. 21-45). The facade pilasters, as part of the wall, run uninterrupted through three stories in an early application of the *colossal* or *giant order* that became a favorite motif of Michelangelo.

21-45 LEON BATTISTA ALBERTI, plan of Sant'Andrea, Mantua, Italy, designed 1470, begun 1472.

In his architectural treatise, Alberti criticized the traditional basilican plan as impractical and designed Sant'Andrea as a single huge hall with independent chapels branching off at right angles.

21-46 LEON BATTISTA ALBERTI, interior of Sant'Andrea (looking northeast), Mantua, Italy, designed 1470, begun 1472.

Alberti abandoned the medieval columnar arcade for the nave of Sant'Andrea. The tremendous vaults suggest that he may have been inspired by Constantine's Basilica Nova (FIG. 10-78) in Rome.

21-46A
Ca d'Oro,
Venice,
1421–1437.

The tremendous vaults in the interior of Sant'Andrea suggest that Alberti's model may have been Constantine's Basilica Nova (FIG. 10-78) in Rome—erroneously thought in the Middle Ages and Renaissance to be a Roman temple. Consistent with his belief that arches should not be used with freestanding columns, Alberti abandoned the medieval columned arcade Brunelleschi still used in Santo Spirito (FIG. 21-31). Thick walls alternating with vaulted chapels, interrupted by a massive dome over the crossing, support the huge coffered barrel vault. Because Filippo Juvara (1678–1736) added the present dome in the 18th century, the effect may be somewhat different from what Alberti planned. Regardless, the vault calls to mind the vast interior spaces and dense enclosing masses of Roman architecture. In his treatise, Alberti criticized the traditional basilican plan (with continuous aisles flanking the central nave) as impractical because the colonnades conceal the ceremonies from the faithful in the aisles. For this reason, he designed a single huge hall (FIG. 21-46) with independent chapels branching off at right angles. This break with a Christian building tradition that had endured for a thousand years was extremely influential in later Renaissance and Baroque church planning.

ANDREA MANTEGNA Like other princes, Ludovico Gonzaga believed an impressive palace was an important visual expression of his authority. One of the most spectacular rooms in the Palazzo Ducale (Ducal Palace) is the duke's bedchamber and audience hall, the so-called Camera degli Sposi (Room of the Newlyweds), originally the Camera Picta (Painted Room; FIGS. **21-47** and **21-48**). ANDREA MANTEGNA (ca. 1431–1506) of Padua, near Venice, took almost nine years to complete the extensive fresco program in which he sought to aggrandize Ludovico Gonzaga and his family. The particulars of each scene are still a matter of scholarly debate, but any viewer standing in the Camera Picta surrounded by the spectacle and majesty of courtly life cannot help but be thoroughly impressed by both the commanding presence and elevated status of the patron and the dazzling artistic skills of Mantegna.

In the Camera Picta, Mantegna performed a triumphant feat by producing the first completely consistent illusionistic decoration of an entire room. By integrating real and painted architectural elements, Mantegna dissolved the room's walls in a manner that foretold later Baroque decoration (see Chapter 24). It recalls the efforts of Italian painters more than 15 centuries earlier at Pompeii and elsewhere to merge mural painting and architecture in frescoes of the so-called Second Style of Roman painting (FIGS. 10-18 and 10-19). Mantegna's *trompe l'oeil* (French, "deceives the eye") design, however, went far beyond anything preserved from ancient Italy.

21-47 Andrea Mantegna, interior of the Camera Picta (Painted Chamber), Palazzo Ducale, Mantua, Italy, 1465–1474.

Working for Ludovico Gonzaga, who established Mantua as a great art city, Mantegna produced for the duke's palace the first completely consistent illusionistic fresco decoration of an entire room.

1 ft.

The Renaissance painter's daring experimentalism led him to complete the room's decoration with the first perspective of a ceiling (FIG. 21-48) seen from below (called, in Italian, *di sotto in sù*, "from below upward"). Baroque ceiling decorators later broadly developed this technique. Inside the Camera Picta, the viewer becomes the viewed as figures look down into the room from the painted *oculus* ("eye"). Seen against the convincing illusion of a cloud-filled blue sky, several *putti* (cupids), strongly foreshortened, set the amorous mood of the Room of the Newlyweds, as the painted spectators (who are not identified) smile down on the scene. The prominent peacock is an attribute of Juno, Jupiter's bride, who oversees lawful marriages. This brilliant feat of illusionism climaxes almost a century of experimentation with perspective.

21-48 Andrea Mantegna, ceiling of the Camera Picta (Painted Chamber), Palazzo Ducale, Mantua, Italy, 1465–1474. Fresco, 8′ 9″ in diameter.

Inside the Camera Picta, the viewer becomes the viewed as figures look down into the room from a painted oculus opening onto a blue sky. This is the first perspectival view of a ceiling from below.

21-49 ANDREA MANTEGNA, *Foreshortened Christ*, ca. 1500. Tempera on canvas, 2′ 2¾″ × 2′ 7⅞″. Pinacoteca di Brera, Milan.

In this work of overwhelming emotional power, Mantegna presented both a harrowing study of a strongly foreshortened cadaver and an intensely poignant depiction of a biblical tragedy.

FORESHORTENED CHRIST One of Mantegna's later paintings (FIG. **21-49**) is another example of the artist's mastery of perspective. In fact, Mantegna seems to have set up for himself difficult problems in perspective simply for the joy in solving them. The painting popularly known as *Dead Christ,* but recorded under the name *Foreshortened Christ* at the time of Mantegna's death, is a work of overwhelming power. At first glance, as its 16th-century title implies, this painting seems to be a strikingly realistic study in foreshortening. Careful scrutiny, however, reveals that Mantegna reduced

the size of the figure's feet, which, as he must have known, would cover much of the body if properly represented. Thus, tempering naturalism with artistic license, Mantegna presented both a harrowing study of a strongly foreshortened cadaver and an intensely poignant depiction of a biblical tragedy. The painter's harsh, sharp line seems to cut the surface as if it were metal and conveys, by its grinding edge, the theme's corrosive emotion. Remarkably, in the hands of Andrea Mantegna all the scientific learning of the 15th century serves the purpose of devotion.

21-49A
MANTEGNA,
*Saint James
to Martyrdom*
1454–1457.

ITALY, 1400 TO 1500

FLORENCE

■ The fortunate congruence of artistic genius, the spread of humanism, and economic prosperity nourished the flowering of the new artistic culture that historians call the Renaissance—the rebirth of classical values in art and life. The greatest center of Renaissance art in the 15th century was Florence, home of the powerful Medici, who were among the most ambitious art patrons in history.

■ Some of the earliest examples of the new Renaissance style in sculpture are the statues Nanni di Banco and Donatello made for the facade niches of Or San Michele. Donatello's *Saint Mark* reintroduced the classical concept of contrapposto into Renaissance statuary. His later *David* was the first nude male statue since antiquity. Donatello was also a pioneer in relief sculpture, the first to incorporate the principles of linear and atmospheric perspective, devices also employed brilliantly by Lorenzo Ghiberti in his *Gates of Paradise* for the Florence baptistery.

Donatello, *Saint Mark,* ca. 1411–1413

■ The Renaissance interest in classical culture naturally also led to the revival of Greco-Roman mythological themes in art, for example, Antonio del Pollaiuolo's *Hercules and Antaeus,* and to the revival of equestrian portraits, such as Donatello's *Gattamelata* and Andrea del Verrocchio's *Bartolommeo Colleoni.*

■ Although some painters continued to work in the Late Gothic International Style, others broke fresh ground by exploring new modes of representation. Masaccio's figures recall Giotto's but have a greater psychological and physical credibility, and the light shining on Masaccio's figures comes from a source outside the picture. His *Holy Trinity* epitomizes Early Renaissance painting in its convincing illusionism, achieved through Filippo Brunelleschi's new science of linear perspective, yet it remains effective as a devotional painting in a church setting.

Masaccio, *Holy Trinity,* ca. 1424–1427

■ The secular side of 15th-century Italian painting is on display in historical works, such as Paolo Uccello's *Battle of San Romano* and Domenico Ghirlandaio's portrait *Giovanna Tornabuoni.* The humanist love of classical themes comes to the fore in the works of Sandro Botticelli, whose lyrical *Primavera* and *Birth of Venus* were inspired by contemporaneous poetry and scholarship.

■ Italian architects also revived the classical style. Brunelleschi's Santo Spirito showcases the clarity and Roman-inspired rationality of 15th-century Florentine architecture. The model for Leon Battista Alberti's influential treatise *On the Art of Building* was a similar work by the ancient Roman architect Vitruvius.

Brunelleschi, Santo Spirito, Florence, designed 1434–1436

THE PRINCELY COURTS

■ Although Florentine artists led the way in creating the Renaissance in art and architecture, the papacy in Rome and the princely courts in Urbino, Mantua, and elsewhere also were major art patrons.

■ Among the important papal commissions of the 15th century was the decoration of the walls of the Sistine Chapel with frescoes, including Perugino's *Christ Delivering the Keys of the Kingdom to Saint Peter,* a prime example of linear perspective.

Perugino, *Christ Delivering the Keys to Saint Peter,* 1481–1483

■ Under the patronage of Federico da Montefeltro, Urbino became a major center of Renaissance art and culture. The leading painter in Federico's employ was Piero della Francesca, a master of color and light and the author of the first theoretical treatise on perspective.

■ Mantua became an important art center under Marquis Ludovico Gonzaga, who brought in Alberti to rebuild the church of Sant'Andrea. Alberti applied the principles he developed in his architectural treatise to the project and freely adapted forms from Roman religious, triumphal, and civic architecture.

■ Gonzaga hired Andrea Mantegna to decorate the Camera Picta of his Ducal Palace, in which the painter produced the first completely consistent illusionistic decoration of an entire room.

Alberti, Sant'Andrea, Mantua, designed 1470

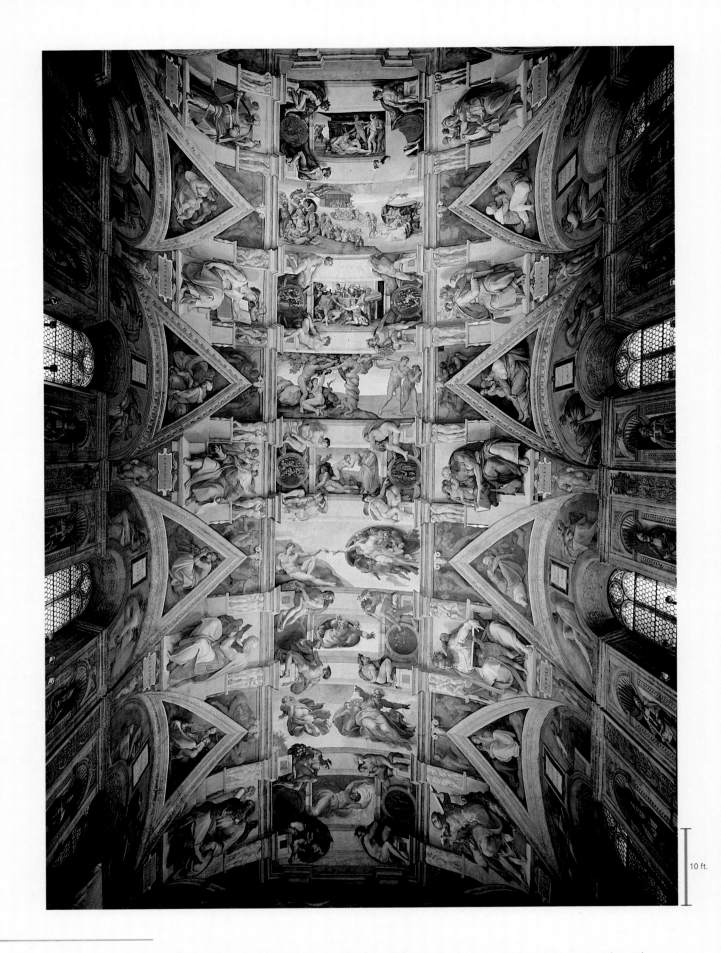

10 ft.

22-1 MICHELANGELO BUONARROTI, ceiling of the Sistine Chapel, Vatican City, Rome, Italy, 1508–1512. Fresco, 128' × 45'.

Michelangelo, the Renaissance genius who was also a sculptor and architect, labored almost four years in the Sistine Chapel painting more than 300 biblical figures illustrating the creation and fall of humankind.

ITALY, 1500 TO 1600

The 15th-century artistic developments in Italy (for example, the interest in perspective, anatomy, and classical cultures) matured during the early 16th century in the brief era that art historians call the High Renaissance—the period between 1495 and the deaths of Leonardo da Vinci in 1519 and Raphael in 1520. The Renaissance style, however, dominated the remainder of the 16th century (the Late Renaissance), although a new style, called Mannerism, challenged it almost as soon as Raphael had been laid to rest (in the ancient Roman Pantheon, FIG. 10-51). Thus, no singular artistic style characterizes 16th-century Italy. Nonetheless, Italian art of this period uniformly exhibits an astounding mastery, both technical and aesthetic.

HIGH AND LATE RENAISSANCE

The High Renaissance produced a cluster of extraordinary geniuses and found in divine inspiration the rationale for the exaltation of the artist-genius. The Neo-Platonists read in Plato's *Ion* his famous praise of the poet: "All good poets . . . compose their beautiful poems not by art, but because they are inspired and possessed. . . . For not by art does the poet sing, but by power divine."[1] And what the poet could claim, the Renaissance claimed also, raising visual art to the status formerly held only by poetry. Thus, painters, sculptors, and architects came into their own, successfully advocating for their work a high place among the fine arts. During the High Renaissance, the masters in essence created a new profession, one having its own rights of expression, its own venerable character, and its own claims to recognition by the great. The "fine" artist today lives, often without realizing it, on the accumulated prestige won by preceding artists, beginning with those who made the first great gains of the High Renaissance.

As in many other artistic eras, regional differences abounded in the 16th century, not only between Northern Europe (discussed in Chapter 23) and Italy but within Italy itself. The leading artistic centers of Central Italy were Florence and Rome, where three of the greatest artists who ever lived—Leonardo da Vinci, Raphael, and Michelangelo—created works whose appeal has endured for 500 years.

Leonardo da Vinci

Born in the small town of Vinci, near Florence, LEONARDO DA VINCI (1452–1519) trained in the studio of Andrea del Verrocchio (FIG. 21-13). The quintessential "Renaissance man," Leonardo had prodigious talent and an unbridled imagination. Art was but one of his innumerable interests. The scope and depth of these interests were without precedent—so great as to frustrate any hopes Leonardo might have had of realizing all that his extraordinarily inventive mind could conceive. Still, he succeeded in mapping the routes that both art and science were to take for generations. Although the discussion here focuses on Leonardo as an artist, exploring his art in conjunction with his other pursuits considerably enhances an understanding of his artistic production. Leonardo revealed his unquenchable curiosity in his voluminous notes, liberally interspersed with sketches dealing with botany, geology, geography, cartography, zoology, military engineering, animal lore, anatomy, and aspects of physical science, including hydraulics and mechanics. These studies informed his art. In his notes, he stated repeatedly that all his scientific investigations made him a better painter. For example, Leonardo's in-depth exploration of optics gave him an understanding of perspective, light, and color. His scientific drawings (FIG. 22-6) are themselves artworks.

Leonardo's great ambition in his painting, as well as in his scientific endeavors, was to discover the laws underlying the processes and flux of nature. With this end in mind, he also studied the human body and contributed immeasurably to the fields of physiology and psychology. Leonardo believed that reality in an absolute sense was inaccessible and that humans could know it only through its changing images. He considered the eyes the most vital organs and sight the most essential function. Better to be deaf than blind, he argued, because through the eyes individuals could grasp reality most directly and profoundly.

Around 1481, Leonardo left Florence after offering his services to Ludovico Sforza (1451–1508), the son and heir apparent of the ruler of Milan. The political situation in Florence was uncertain, and Leonardo may have felt that his particular skills would be in greater demand in Milan, providing him with the opportunity for increased financial security. He devoted most of a letter to Ludovico to advertising his competence and his qualifications as a military engineer, mentioning only at the end his abilities as a painter and sculptor. The letter illustrates the relationship between Renaissance artists and their patrons, as well as Leonardo's breadth of competence. That he should select expertise in military engineering as his primary attraction to the Sforzas is an index of the period's instability.

> And in short, according to the variety of cases, I can contrive various and endless means of offence and defence. . . . In time of peace I believe I can give perfect satisfaction and to the equal of any other in architecture and the composition of buildings, public and private; and in guiding water from one place to another. . . . I can carry out sculpture in marble, bronze, or clay, and also I can do in painting whatever may be done, as well as any other, be he whom he may.[2]

Ludovico accepted Leonardo's offer, and the Florentine artist remained in Milan for almost 20 years.

MADONNA OF THE ROCKS Shortly after settling in Milan, Leonardo painted *Madonna of the Rocks* (FIG. 22-2) as the central panel of an altarpiece for the chapel of the Confraternity of the Immaculate Conception in San Francesco Grande. The painting builds on Masaccio's understanding and usage of chiaroscuro, the subtle play of light and dark. Modeling with light and shadow and expressing emotional states were, for Leonardo, the heart of painting:

22-2 LEONARDO DA VINCI, *Madonna of the Rocks,* from San Francesco Grande, Milan, Italy, begun 1483. Oil on wood (transferred to canvas), 6′ 6½″ × 4′. Louvre, Paris.

In this groundbreaking work, Leonardo used gestures and a pyramidal composition to unite the Virgin, Saint John the Baptist, the Christ Child, and an angel. The figures share the same light-infused environment.

> A good painter has two chief objects to paint—man and the intention of his soul. The former is easy, the latter hard, for it must be expressed by gestures and the movement of the limbs. . . . A painting will only be wonderful for the beholder by making that which is not so appear raised and detached from the wall.[3]

Leonardo presented the figures in *Madonna of the Rocks* in a pyramidal grouping and, more notably, as sharing the same environment. This groundbreaking achievement—the unified representation of objects in an atmospheric setting—was a manifestation of his scientific curiosity about the invisible substance surrounding things. The Madonna, Christ Child, infant John the Baptist, and angel emerge through nuances of light and shade from the half-light of the cavernous visionary landscape. Light simultaneously veils and reveals the forms, immersing them in a layer of atmosphere. Leonardo's

Renaissance Drawings

In the 16th century in Italy, drawing (or *disegno*) assumed a position of greater prominence than ever before in artistic production. Until the late 15th century, the expense of drawing surfaces and their lack of availability limited the production of preparatory sketches. Most artists drew on *parchment* (prepared from the skins of calves, sheep, and goats) or on *vellum* (made from the skins of young animals and therefore very expensive). Because of the cost of these materials, drawings in the 14th and 15th centuries tended to be extremely detailed and meticulously executed. Artists often drew using *silverpoint* (a *stylus* made of silver) because of the fine line it produced and the sharp point it maintained. The introduction in the late 15th century of less expensive paper made of fibrous pulp produced for the developing printing industry (see "Woodcuts, Engravings, and Etchings," Chapter 20, page 537) allowed artists to experiment more and to draw with greater freedom. As a result, sketches abounded. Artists executed these drawings in pen and ink (FIG. 22-6), chalk, charcoal (FIG. 22-3), brush, and graphite or lead.

The importance of drawing transcended the mechanical or technical possibilities it afforded artists, however. The term *disegno* referred also to design, an integral component of good art. Design was the foundation of art, and drawing was the fundamental element of design. The painter Federico Zuccaro (1542–1609) summed up this philosophy when he stated that drawing is the external physical manifestation (*disegno esterno*) of an internal intellectual idea or design (*disegno interno*).

The design dimension of art production became increasingly important as artists cultivated their own styles. The early stages of artistic training largely focused on imitation and emulation (see "Cennino Cennini on Imitation and Emulation," Chapter 21, page 553), but to achieve widespread recognition, artists had to develop their own styles. Although the artistic community and public at large acknowledged technical skill, the conceptualization of the artwork—its theoretical and formal development—was paramount. Disegno—or design in this case—represented an artist's conception and intention. In the literature of the period, the terms writers and critics often invoked to praise esteemed artists included *invenzione* (invention), *ingegno* (innate talent), *fantasia* (imagination), and *capriccio* (originality).

1 ft.

22-3 LEONARDO DA VINCI, cartoon for *Madonna and Child with Saint Anne and the Infant Saint John*, ca. 1505–1507. Charcoal heightened with white on brown paper, 4′ 6″ × 3′ 3″. National Gallery, London.

The introduction of less expensive paper in the late 15th century allowed artists to draw more frequently. In this cartoon, Leonardo depicted monumental figures in a scene of tranquil grandeur and balance.

effective use of atmospheric perspective is the result in large part of his mastery of the relatively new medium of oil painting, which had previously been used mostly by Northern European painters (see "Tempera and Oil Painting," Chapter 20, page 523). The figures pray, point, and bless, and these acts and gestures, although their meanings are not certain, visually unite the individuals portrayed. The angel points to the infant John and, through his outward glance, involves the viewer in the tableau. John prays to the Christ Child, who blesses him in return. The Virgin herself completes the series of interlocking gestures, her left hand reaching toward the Christ Child and her right hand resting protectively on John's shoulder. The melting mood of tenderness, which the caressing light enhances, suffuses the entire composition. By creating an emotionally compelling, visually unified, and spatially convincing image, Leonardo succeeded in expressing "the intention of his soul."

MADONNA AND CHILD CARTOON Leonardo's style fully emerges in *Madonna and Child with Saint Anne and the Infant Saint John* (FIG. 22-3), a preliminary drawing for a painting (see "Renaissance Drawings," above) he made in 1505 or shortly thereafter. Here, the glowing light falls gently on the majestic forms in a scene of tranquil grandeur and balance. Leonardo ordered every part of his cartoon with an intellectual pictorial logic that results in an appealing visual unity. The figures are robust and monumental, the stately grace of their movements reminiscent of the Greek statues of goddesses (FIG. 5-49) in the pediments of the Parthenon. Leonardo's infusion of the principles of classical art into his designs, however, cannot be attributed to specific knowledge of Greek monuments. He and his contemporaries never visited Greece. Their acquaintance with classical art extended only to Etruscan and Roman monuments and Roman copies of Greek statues in Italy.

22-3A LEONARDO, *Vitruvian Man*, ca. 1485–1490.

22-4 LEONARDO DA VINCI, *Last Supper,* ca. 1495–1498. Oil and tempera on plaster, 13′ 9″ × 29′ 10″. Refectory, Santa Maria delle Grazie, Milan. ▪◀

Christ has just announced that one of his disciples will betray him, and each one reacts. Christ is both the psychological focus of Leonardo's fresco and the focal point of all the converging perspective lines.

LAST SUPPER For the refectory of the church of Santa Maria delle Grazie in Milan, Leonardo painted *Last Supper* (FIG. **22-4**). Cleaned and restored in 1999, the mural is still in a poor state, in part because of the painter's unfortunate experiments with his materials (see "Restoring Renaissance Paintings," page 595). Nonetheless, the painting is both formally and emotionally Leonardo's most impressive work. Christ and his 12 disciples sit at a long table placed parallel to the picture plane in a simple, spacious room. The austere setting amplifies the painting's highly dramatic action. Christ, with outstretched hands, has just said, "One of you is about to betray me" (Matt. 26:21). A wave of intense excitement passes through the group as each disciple asks himself and, in some cases, his neighbor, "Is it I?" (Matt. 26:22). Leonardo visualized a sophisticated conjunction of the dramatic "One of you is about to betray me" with the initiation of the ancient liturgical ceremony of the Eucharist, when Christ, blessing bread and wine, said, "This is my body, which is given for you. Do this for a commemoration of me. . . . This is the chalice, the new testament in my blood, which shall be shed for you" (Luke 22:19–20).

In the center, Christ appears isolated from the disciples and in perfect repose, the calm eye of the stormy emotion swirling around him. The central window at the back, whose curved pediment arches above his head, frames his figure. The pediment is the only curve in the architectural framework, and it serves here, along with the diffused light, as a halo. Christ's head is the focal point of all converging perspective lines in the composition. Thus, the still, psychological

focus and cause of the action is also the perspectival focus, as well as the center of the two-dimensional surface. The two-dimensional, the three-dimensional, and the psychodimensional focuses are the same.

Leonardo presented the agitated disciples in four groups of three, united among and within themselves by the figures' gestures and postures. The artist sacrificed traditional iconography to pictorial and dramatic consistency by placing Judas on the same side of the table as Jesus and the other disciples (compare FIG. **21-22**). The light source in the painting corresponds to the windows in the Milanese refectory. Judas's face is in shadow and he clutches a money bag in his right hand as he reaches his left forward to fulfill the Master's declaration: "But yet behold, the hand of him that betrayeth me is with me on the table" (Luke 22:21). The two disciples at the table ends are quieter than the others, as if to bracket the energy of the composition, which is more intense closer to Christ, whose serenity both halts and intensifies it. The disciples register a broad range of emotional responses, including fear, doubt, protestation, rage, and love. Leonardo's numerous preparatory studies—using live models—suggest that he thought of each figure as carrying a particular charge and type of emotion. Like a stage director, he read the Gospel story carefully, and scrupulously cast his actors as the New Testament described their roles. In this work, as in his other religious paintings, Leonardo revealed his extraordinary ability to apply his voluminous knowledge about the observable world to the pictorial representation of a religious scene, resulting in a psychologically complex and compelling painting.

22-5 LEONARDO DA VINCI, *Mona Lisa*, ca. 1503–1505. Oil on wood, 2′ 6¼″ × 1′ 9″. Louvre, Paris.

Leonardo's skill with chiaroscuro and atmospheric perspective is on display in this new kind of portrait depicting the sitter as an individual personality who engages the viewer psychologically.

MONA LISA Leonardo's *Mona Lisa* (FIG. **22-5**) is probably the world's most famous portrait. The sitter's identity is still the subject of scholarly debate, but in his biography of Leonardo, Giorgio Vasari asserted she was Lisa di Antonio Maria Gherardini, the wife of Francesco del Giocondo, a wealthy Florentine—hence, "Mona (an Italian contraction of *ma donna*, "my lady") Lisa." Despite the uncertainty of this identification, Leonardo's portrait is a convincing representation of an individual. Unlike earlier portraits, it does not serve solely as an icon of status. Indeed, Mona Lisa neither wears jewelry nor holds any attribute associated with wealth. She sits quietly, her hands folded, her mouth forming a gentle smile, and her gaze directed at the viewer. Renaissance etiquette dictated that a woman should not look directly into a man's eyes. Leonardo's portrayal of this self-assured young woman without the trappings of power but engaging the audience psychologically is thus quite remarkable. The painting is darker today than 500 years ago, and the colors are less vivid, but *Mona Lisa* still reveals the artist's fascination and skill with chiaroscuro and atmospheric perspective. *Mona Lisa* is a prime example of Leonardo's famous smoky *sfumato* (misty haziness)—his subtle adjustment of light and blurring of precise planes.

The lingering appeal of *Mona Lisa* derives in large part from Leonardo's decision to set his subject against the backdrop of a mysterious uninhabited landscape. This landscape, with roads and bridges that seem to lead nowhere, recalls his *Madonna of the Rocks* (FIG. 22-2). The composition also resembles Fra Filippo Lippi's *Madonna and Child with Angels* (FIG. 21-23) with figures seated in front of a window through which the viewer sees a distant landscape. Originally, the artist represented Mona Lisa in a *loggia* (columnar gallery). When the painting was trimmed (not by Leonardo), these columns were eliminated, but the remains of the column bases may still be seen to the left and right of Mona Lisa's shoulders.

ANATOMICAL STUDIES Leonardo completed very few paintings. His perfectionism, relentless experimentation, and far-ranging curiosity diffused his efforts. However, the drawings in his notebooks preserve an extensive record of his ideas. His interests focused increasingly on science in his later years, and he embraced knowledge of all facets of the natural world. His investigations in anatomy yielded drawings of great precision and beauty of execution. *The Fetus and Lining of the Uterus* (FIG. **22-6**), although it does not meet 21st-century standards for accuracy (for example, Leonardo regularized the uterus's shape to a sphere, and his characterization of the

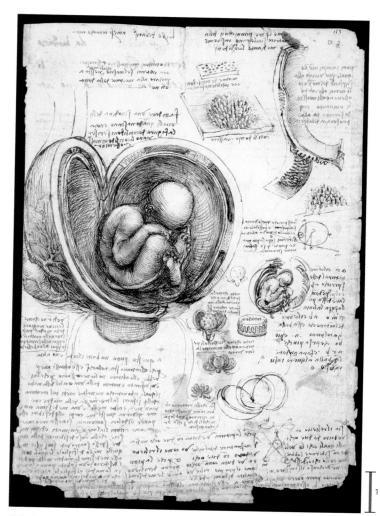

22-6 LEONARDO DA VINCI, *The Fetus and Lining of the Uterus*, ca. 1511–1513. Pen and ink with wash, over red chalk and traces of black chalk on paper, 1′ × 8⅝″. Royal Library, Windsor Castle.

Leonardo's analytical anatomical studies epitomize the scientific spirit of the Renaissance, establishing that era as a prelude to the modern world and setting it in sharp contrast to the preceding Middle Ages.

22-7 RAPHAEL, *Marriage of the Virgin,* from the Chapel of Saint Joseph, San Francesco, Città di Castello, Italy, 1504. Oil on wood, 5′ 7″ × 3′ 10½″. Pinacoteca di Brera, Milan.

In this early work depicting the marriage of the Virgin to Saint Joseph, Raphael demonstrated his mastery of foreshortening and of the perspective system he learned from his teacher, Perugino (FIG. **21-40**).

neer for Cesare Borgia (1476–1507), who, with the support of his father, Pope Alexander VI (r. 1492–1503), tried to conquer the cities of the Romagna region in north-central Italy and create a Borgia duchy. Leonardo eventually returned to Milan in the service of the French. At the invitation of King Francis I (FIG. **23-10**), he then went to France, where he died at the château of Cloux in 1519.

Raphael

Alexander VI's successor was Julius II (r. 1503–1513). In addition to his responsibility as the spiritual leader of Christendom, the new pope extended his quest for authority to the temporal realm, as other medieval and Renaissance popes had done. An immensely ambitious man, Julius II indulged his enthusiasm for engaging in battle, which earned him a designation as the "warrior-pope." Further, his selection of the name Julius, after Julius Caesar, reinforced the perception that the Roman Empire served as his governmental model. Julius II's 10-year papacy, however, was most notable for his contributions to the arts. He was an avid art patron and understood well the propagandistic value of visual imagery. After his election, he immediately commissioned artworks that would present an authoritative image of his rule and reinforce the primacy of the Catholic Church. Among the many projects he commissioned were a new design for Saint Peter's basilica (FIGS. **22-23** and **22-24**), the painting of the Sistine Chapel ceiling (FIG. **22-1**), the decoration of the papal apartments (FIG. **22-9**), and the construction of his tomb (FIGS. **22-15** and **22-16**).

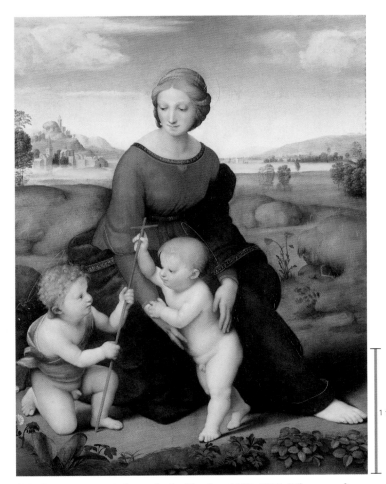

22-8 RAPHAEL, *Madonna in the Meadow,* 1505–1506. Oil on wood, 3′ 8½″ × 2′ 10¼″. Kunsthistorisches Museum, Vienna.

Emulating Leonardo's pyramidal composition (FIG. **22-2**) but rejecting his dusky modeling and mystery, Raphael set his Madonna in a well-lit landscape and imbued her with grace, dignity, and beauty.

lining is incorrect), was an astounding achievement in its day. Analytical anatomical studies such as this epitomize the scientific spirit of the Renaissance, establishing that era as a prelude to the modern world and setting it in sharp contrast to the preceding Middle Ages. Although Leonardo may not have been the first scientist of the modern world (at least not in the modern sense of the term), he certainly originated a method of scientific illustration, especially *cutaway* views. Scholars have long recognized the importance of these drawings for the development of anatomy as a science, especially in an age predating photographic methods such as X-rays.

Leonardo also won renown in his time as both architect and sculptor, although no surviving buildings or sculptures can be definitively attributed to him. From his many drawings of central-plan buildings, it appears he shared the interest of other Renaissance architects in this building type. As for sculpture, Leonardo left numerous drawings of monumental equestrian statues, and also made a full-scale model for a monument to Francesco Sforza (1401–1466; Ludovico's father). The French used the statue as a target and shot it to pieces when they occupied Milan in 1499. Due to the French presence, Leonardo left Milan and served for a while as a military engi-

22-6A LEONARDO, Central-plan church, ca. 1487–1490.

22-9 RAPHAEL, *Philosophy* (*School of Athens*), Stanza della Segnatura, Vatican Palace, Rome, Italy, 1509–1511. Fresco, 19′ × 27′.

Raphael included himself in this gathering of great philosophers and scientists whose self-assurance conveys calm reason. The setting resembles the interior of the new Saint Peter's (FIG. 24-5).

In 1508, Julius II called Raffaello Santi (or Sanzio), known as RAPHAEL (1483–1520) in English, to the papal court in Rome. Born in a small town in Umbria near Urbino, Raphael probably learned the rudiments of his art from his father, Giovanni Santi, a painter connected with the ducal court of Federico da Montefeltro (see Chapter 21), before entering the studio of Perugino in Perugia. Although strongly influenced by Perugino, Leonardo, and others, Raphael developed an individual style that exemplifies the ideals of High Renaissance art.

MARRIAGE OF THE VIRGIN Among Raphael's early works is *Marriage of the Virgin* (FIG. 22-7), which he painted for the Chapel of Saint Joseph in the church of San Francesco in Città di Castello, southeast of Florence. The subject is a fitting one for a chapel dedicated to Saint Joseph. According to the *Golden Legend* (a 13th-century collection of stories about the lives of the saints), Joseph competed with other suitors for Mary's hand. The high priest was to give the Virgin to whichever suitor presented to him a rod that had miraculously bloomed. Raphael depicted Joseph with his flowering rod in his left hand. In his right hand Joseph holds the wedding ring he is about to place on Mary's finger. Other virgins congregate at the left, and the unsuccessful suitors stand on the right. One of them breaks his rod in half over his knee in frustration, giving Raphael an opportunity to demonstrate his mastery of foreshortening. The perspective system he used is the one he learned from Perugino (FIG. 21-40). The temple in the background is Raphael's version of a centrally planned building (FIG. 22-22), featuring Brunelleschian arcades (FIG. 21-31).

MADONNA IN THE MEADOW Raphael spent the four years from 1504 to 1508 in Florence. There, still in his early 20s, he discovered that the painting style he had learned so painstakingly from Perugino was already outmoded (as was Brunelleschi's architectural style). Florentine crowds flocked to the church of Santissima Annunziata to see Leonardo's recently unveiled cartoon of the Virgin, Christ Child, Saint Anne, and Saint John (probably an earlier version of FIG. 22-3). Under Leonardo's influence, Raphael began to modify the Madonna compositions he had learned in Umbria. In *Madonna in the Meadow* (FIG. 22-8) of 1505–1506, Raphael adopted Leonardo's pyramidal composition and modeling of faces and figures in subtle chiaroscuro. Yet the Umbrian artist placed the large, substantial figures in a Peruginesque landscape, with his former master's typical feathery trees in the middle ground. Although Raphael experimented with Leonardo's dusky modeling, he tended to return to Perugino's lighter tonalities and blue skies. Raphael preferred clarity to obscurity, not fascinated, as Leonardo was, with mystery.

22-8A ANDREA DEL SARTO, *Madonna of the Harpies*, 1517.

SCHOOL OF ATHENS Three years after completing *Madonna in the Meadow*, Raphael received one of the most important painting commissions (FIG. 22-9) Julius II awarded—the decoration of

1 ft.

the papal apartments in the Apostolic Palace of the Vatican (MAP 24-1). Of the suite's several rooms (*stanze*), Raphael painted the Stanza della Segnatura (Room of the Signature—the papal library, where Julius II signed official documents) and the Stanza d'Eliodoro (Room of Heliodorus—the pope's private audience room, named for one of the paintings). His pupils completed the others, following his sketches. On the four walls of the Stanza della Segnatura, under the headings *Theology, Law* (*Justice*), *Poetry,* and *Philosophy,* Raphael presented images that symbolized and summed up Western learning as Renaissance society understood it. The frescoes refer to the four branches of human knowledge and wisdom while pointing out the virtues and the learning appropriate to a pope. Given Julius II's desire for recognition as both a spiritual and temporal leader, it is appropriate that the *Theology* and *Philosophy* frescoes face each other. The two images present a balanced picture of the pope—as a cultured, knowledgeable individual and as a wise, divinely ordained religious authority.

In Raphael's *Philosophy* mural (commonly known as *School of Athens,* FIG. 22-9) the setting is not a "school" but a congregation of the great philosophers and scientists of the ancient world. Raphael depicted these luminaries, revered by Renaissance humanists, conversing and explaining their various theories and ideas. The setting is a vast hall covered by massive vaults that recall ancient Roman architecture—and approximate the appearance of the new Saint Peter's (FIG. 24-5) in 1509, when Raphael began the fresco. Colossal statues of Apollo and Athena, patron deities of the arts and of wisdom, oversee the interactions. Plato and Aristotle serve as the central figures around whom Raphael carefully arranged the others. Plato holds his book *Timaeus* and points to Heaven, the source of his inspiration, while Aristotle carries his book *Nicomachean Ethics* and gestures toward the earth, from which his observations of reality sprang. Appropriately, ancient philosophers, men concerned with the ultimate mysteries that transcend this world, stand on Plato's side. On Aristotle's side are the philosophers and scientists interested in nature and human affairs. At the lower left, Pythagoras writes as a servant holds up the harmonic scale. In the foreground, Heraclitus (probably a portrait of Raphael's great contemporary, Michelangelo) broods alone. Diogenes sprawls on the steps. At the right, students surround Euclid, who demonstrates a theorem. Euclid may be a portrait of the architect Bramante, whom Julius II had recently commissioned to design a new Saint Peter's (FIGS. 22-23 and 22-24) to replace the Constantinian basilica (FIG. 11-9). At the extreme right, just to the right of the astronomers Zoroaster and Ptolemy, both holding globes, Raphael included his own portrait.

The groups appear to move easily and clearly, with eloquent poses and gestures that symbolize their doctrines and present an engaging variety of figural positions. Their self-assurance and natural dignity convey the very nature of calm reason, that balance and measure the great Renaissance minds so admired as the heart of philosophy. Significantly, in this work Raphael placed himself among the mathematicians and scientists rather than the humanists. Certainly the evolution of pictorial science came to its perfection in *School of Athens*. Raphael's convincing depiction of a vast perspectival space on a two-dimensional surface was the consequence of the union of mathematics with pictorial science, here mastered completely.

The artist's psychological insight matured along with his mastery of the problems of physical representation. All the characters in Raphael's *School of Athens,* like those in Leonardo's *Last Supper* (FIG. 22-4), communicate moods that reflect their beliefs, and the artist's placement of each figure tied these moods together. Raphael carefully considered his design devices for relating individuals and groups to one another and to the whole. These compositional elements demand close study. From the center, where Plato and Aristotle stand, Raphael arranged the groups of figures in an ellipse with a wide opening in the foreground. Moving along the floor's perspectival pattern, the viewer's eye penetrates the assembly of philosophers and continues, by way of the reclining Diogenes, up to the here-reconciled leaders of the two great opposing camps of Renaissance philosophy. The perspectival vanishing point falls on Plato's left hand, drawing attention to *Timaeus*. In the Stanza della Segnatura, Raphael reconciled and harmonized not only the Platonists and Aristotelians but also paganism and Christianity, surely a major factor in his appeal to Julius II.

GALATEA Pope Leo X (r. 1513–1521), the second son of Lorenzo de' Medici, succeeded Julius II as Raphael's patron. Leo was a worldly, pleasure-loving prince who, as a true Medici, spent huge sums on the arts. Raphael moved in the highest circles of the papal court, the star of a brilliant society. He was young, handsome, wealthy, and admired, not only by his followers but also by Rome and all of Italy. Genial, even-tempered, generous, and high-minded, Raphael had a personality that contrasted strikingly with that of the aloof, mysterious Leonardo or the tormented and obstinate Michelangelo (so depicted in *School of Athens*).

The pope was not Raphael's sole patron. Agostino Chigi (1465–1520), an immensely wealthy banker who managed the papal state's financial affairs, commissioned Raphael to decorate his palace on the Tiber River with scenes from classical mythology. Outstanding among the frescoes Raphael painted in the small but splendid Villa Farnesina is *Galatea* (FIG. 22-10), which Raphael based on *Stanzas for the Joust of Giuliano de' Medici* by the poet Angelo Poliziano (1454–1494). In Raphael's fresco, Galatea flees on a shell drawn by leaping dolphins as she escapes from her uncouth lover, the Cyclops Polyphemus (painted on another wall by a different artist). Sea creatures and playful cupids surround her. The painting erupts in unrestrained pagan joy and exuberance, an exultant song in praise of human beauty and zestful love. Compositionally, Raphael enhanced the liveliness of the image by arranging the sturdy figures around Galatea in bounding and dashing movements that always return to her as the energetic center. The cupids, skillfully foreshortened, repeat the circling motion. Raphael conceived his figures sculpturally, and Galatea's body—supple, strong, and vigorously in motion—contrasts with Botticelli's delicate, hovering, almost dematerialized Venus (FIG. 21-28) while suggesting the spiraling compositions of Hellenistic statuary (FIG. 5-80). In *Galatea*, pagan myth—presented here in monumental form, in vivacious movement, and in

a spirit of passionate delight—resurrects the naturalistic art and poetry of the classical world.

BALDASSARE CASTIGLIONE Raphael also excelled at portraiture. His subjects were the illustrious scholars and courtiers who surrounded Leo X, among them the pope's close friend Count Baldassare Castiglione (1478–1529), the author of a handbook on genteel behavior. In *Book of the Courtier*, Castiglione enumerated the attributes of the perfect Renaissance courtier: impeccable character, noble birth, military achievement, classical education, and knowledge of the arts. Castiglione then described a way of life based on cultivated rationality in imitation of the ancients. In Raphael's portrait of the count (FIG. 22-11), Castiglione, splendidly yet soberly garbed, looks directly at the viewer with a philosopher's grave and benign expression, clear-eyed and thoughtful. The figure is in half-length (the lower part with the hands was later cut off) and three-quarter view, a pose Leonardo made popular with *Mona Lisa* (FIG. 22-5). Both portraits exhibit the increasing attention High Renaissance artists paid to the subject's personality and psychic state. The muted and low-keyed tones befit the temper and mood of this reflective middle-aged man—the background is entirely neutral, without the usual landscape or architecture. The head and the hands wonderfully reveal the man, who himself had written so eloquently in *Courtier* of enlightenment through the love of beauty. This kind of love animated Raphael, Castiglione, and other artists and writers of their age, and Michelangelo's poetry suggests he shared in the widespread appreciation for the beauty found in the natural world.

1 in.

22-11 RAPHAEL, *Baldassare Castiglione,* ca. 1514. Oil on canvas, 2′ 6¼″ × 2′ 2½″. Louvre, Paris.

Raphael's painting of the famed courtier Count Baldassare Castiglione typifies High Renaissance portraiture in the increasing attention the artist paid to the subject's personality and psychic state.

Leonardo and Michelangelo
on Painting versus Sculpture

Leonardo da Vinci and Michelangelo each produced work in a variety of artistic media, earning enviable reputations not just as painters and sculptors but as architects and draftsmen as well. The two disagreed, however, on the relative merits of the different media. In particular, Leonardo, with his intellectual and analytical mind, preferred painting to sculpture, which he denigrated as manual labor. In contrast, Michelangelo, who worked in a more intuitive manner, regarded himself primarily as a sculptor. Two excerpts from their writings reveal their positions on the relationship between the two media.

Leonardo da Vinci wrote the following in his so-called *Treatise on Painting:*

> Painting is a matter of greater mental analysis, of greater skill, and more marvelous than sculpture, since necessity compels the mind of the painter to transform itself into the very mind of nature, to become an interpreter between nature and art. Painting justifies by reference to nature the reasons of the pictures which follow its laws: in what ways the images of objects before the eye come together in the pupil of the eye; which, among objects equal in size, looks larger to the eye; which, among equal colors, will look more or less dark or more or less bright; which, among things at the same depth, looks more or less low; which, among those objects placed at equal height, will look more or less high, and why, among objects placed at various distances, one will appear less clear than the other.

> This art comprises and includes within itself all visible things such as colors and their diminution which the poverty of sculpture cannot include. Painting represents transparent objects but the sculptor will show you the shapes of natural objects without artifice. The painter will show you things at different distances with variation of color due to the air lying between the objects and the eye; he shows you mists through which visual images penetrate with difficulty; he shows you rain which discloses within it clouds with mountains

and valleys; he shows the dust which discloses within it and beyond it the combatants who stirred it up; he shows streams of greater or lesser density; he shows fish playing between the surface of the water and its bottom; he shows the polished pebbles of various colors lying on the washed sand at the bottom of rivers, surrounded by green plants; he shows the stars at various heights above us, and thus he achieves innumerable effects which sculpture cannot attain.*

In response, although decades later, Michelangelo wrote these excerpts in a letter to Benedetto Varchi (1502–1565), a Florentine poet best known for his 16-volume history of Florence:

> I believe that painting is considered excellent in proportion as it approaches the effect of relief, while relief is considered bad in proportion as it approaches the effect of painting.

> I used to consider that sculpture was the lantern of painting and that between the two things there was the same difference as that between the sun and the moon. But . . . I now consider that painting and sculpture are one and the same thing.

> Suffice that, since one and the other (that is to say, both painting and sculpture) proceed from the same faculty, it would be an easy matter to establish harmony between them and to let such disputes alone, for they occupy more time than the execution of the figures themselves. As to that man [Leonardo] who wrote saying that painting was more noble than sculpture, if he had known as much about the other subjects on which he has written, why, my serving-maid would have written better![†]

* Leonardo da Vinci, *Treatise on Painting*, 51, in Robert Klein and Henri Zerner, *Italian Art 1500–1600: Sources and Documents* (Evanston, Ill.: Northwestern University Press, 1966), 7–8.
[†] Michelangelo to Benedetto Varchi, Rome, 1549; in Klein and Zerner, 13–14.

Michelangelo

Pope Julius II had a keen eye for talent and during his decade-long papacy also entrusted highly coveted commissions to MICHELANGELO BUONARROTI (1475–1564). Although Michelangelo was an architect, sculptor, painter, poet, and engineer, he thought of himself first as a sculptor, regarding that calling as superior to that of a painter because the sculptor shares in something like the divine power to "make man" (see "Leonardo and Michelangelo on Painting versus Sculpture," above). Drawing a conceptual parallel to Plato's ideas, Michelangelo believed that the image the artist's hand produces must come from the idea in the artist's mind. The idea, then, is the reality that the artist's genius has to bring forth. But artists are not the creators of the ideas they conceive. Rather, they find their ideas in the natural world, reflecting the absolute idea, which, for the artist, is beauty. One of Michelangelo's best-known observations about sculpture is that the artist must proceed by finding the idea—the image locked in the stone. By removing the excess stone, the sculptor extricates the idea from the block (FIG. I-16), bringing forth the living form. The artist, Michelangelo felt, works many years at this unceasing process of revelation and "arrives late at novel and lofty things."[4]

Michelangelo did indeed arrive "at novel and lofty things," for he broke sharply from the lessons of his predecessors and contemporaries in one important respect. He mistrusted the application of mathematical methods as guarantees of beauty in proportion. Measure and proportion, he believed, should be "kept in the eyes." Vasari quoted Michelangelo as declaring that "it was necessary to have the compasses in the eyes and not in the hand, because the hands work and the eye judges."[5] Thus, Michelangelo set aside the ancient Roman architect Vitruvius, Alberti, Leonardo, and others who tirelessly sought the perfect measure, asserting that the artist's inspired judgment could identify other pleasing proportions. In addition, Michelangelo argued that the artist must not be bound, except by the demands made by realizing the idea. This insistence on the artist's own authority was typical of Michelangelo and anticipated the modern concept of the right to a self-expression of talent limited only by the artist's judgment. The artistic license to aspire far beyond the "rules" was, in part, a manifestation of the pursuit of fame and success that humanism fostered. In this context, Michelangelo created works in architecture, sculpture, and painting that departed from High Renaissance regularity. He put in its stead a style of vast, expressive

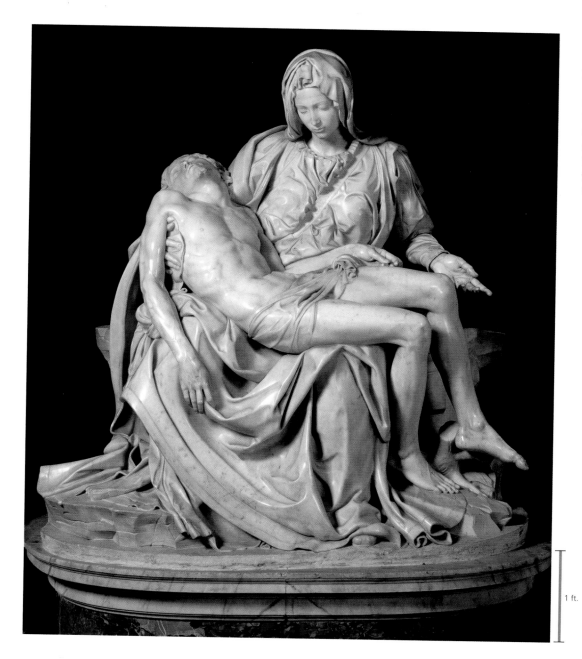

1 ft.

strength conveyed through complex, eccentric, and often titanic forms that loom before the viewer in tragic grandeur. Michelangelo's self-imposed isolation, creative furies, proud independence, and daring innovations led Italians to speak of the dominating quality of the man and his works in one word—*terribilità*, the sublime shadowed by the awesome and the fearful.

As a youth, Michelangelo was an apprentice in the studio of the painter Domenico Ghirlandaio, whom he left before completing his training. Although Michelangelo later claimed that in his art he owed nothing to anyone, he made detailed drawings in the manner of the great Florentines Giotto and Masaccio. Early on, he came to the attention of Lorenzo the Magnificent and studied sculpture under one of Lorenzo's favorite artists, Bertoldo di Giovanni (ca. 1420–1491), a former collaborator of Donatello. When the Medici fell in 1494, Michelangelo fled from Florence to Bologna, where the sculptures of the Sienese artist Jacopo della Quercia (1367–1438) impressed him.

PIETÀ Michelangelo's wanderings took him to Rome, where, around 1498, still in his early 20s, he produced his first masterpiece, a *Pietà* (FIG. 22-12), for the French cardinal Jean de Bilhères La-

graulas (1439–1499). The cardinal commissioned the statue to adorn the chapel in Old Saint Peter's (FIG. 11-9) in which he was to be buried. (The work is now on view in the new church that replaced the fourth-century basilica.) The theme—Mary cradling the dead body of Christ in her lap—was a staple in the repertoire of French and German artists (FIG. 18-51), and Michelangelo's French patron doubtless chose the subject. The Italian, however, rendered the Northern theme in an unforgettable manner. Michelangelo transformed marble into flesh, hair, and fabric with a sensitivity for texture that is almost without parallel. The polish and luminosity of the exquisite marble surface cannot be captured fully in photographs and can be appreciated only in the presence of the original. Breathtaking too is the tender sadness of the beautiful and youthful Mary as she mourns the death of her son. In fact, her age—seemingly less than that of Christ—was a subject of controversy from the moment of the unveiling of the statue. Michelangelo explained Mary's ageless beauty as an integral part of her purity and virginity. Beautiful too is the son whom she holds. Christ seems less to have died than to have drifted off into peaceful sleep in Mary's maternal arms. His wounds are barely visible.

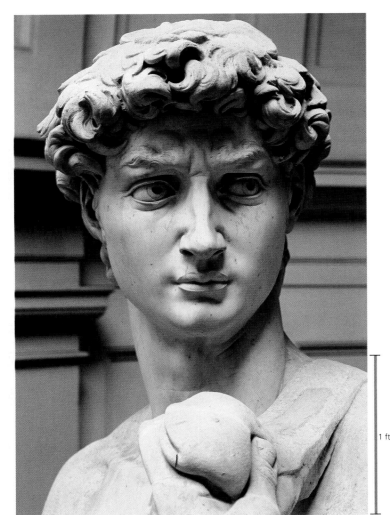

22-14 Michelangelo Buonarroti, head of *David* (detail of FIG. 22-13), 1501–1504. Galleria dell'Accademia, Florence. ◼◀

In contrast to earlier Renaissance depictions (FIGS. 21-12 and 21-13) of this Old Testament drama, Michelangelo portrayed David *before* the battle with Goliath, as he sternly watches his gigantic foe.

22-13 Michelangelo Buonarroti, *David*, from Piazza della Signoria, Florence, Italy, 1501–1504. Marble, 17′ high. Galleria dell'Accademia, Florence. ◼◀

In this colossal statue, Michelangelo represented David in heroic classical nudity, capturing the tension of Lysippan athletes (FIG. 5-65) and the emotionalism of Hellenistic statuary (FIGS. 5-80 and 5-81).

DAVID Michelangelo returned to Florence in 1501, seven years after the exile of the Medici (see Chapter 21). In 1495 the Florentine Republic had ordered the transfer of Donatello's *David* (FIG. 21-12) from the Medici palace to the Palazzo della Signoria to join Verrocchio's *David* (FIG. 21-13) there. The importance of David as a civic symbol led the Florence Cathedral building committee to invite Michelangelo to work a great block of marble left over from an earlier aborted commission into still another statue of *David* (FIG. 22-13). The colossal statue—Florentines referred to it as "the Giant"— Michelangelo created from that block assured his reputation then and now as an extraordinary talent. Only 40 years after *David*'s completion, Vasari extolled the work, which had been set up near the

west door of the Palazzo della Signoria, and claimed that "without any doubt the figure has put in the shade every other statue, ancient or modern, Greek or Roman—this was intended as a symbol of liberty for the Palace, signifying that just as David had protected his people and governed them justly, so whoever ruled Florence should vigorously defend the city and govern it with justice."[6]

Despite the traditional association of David with heroism, Michelangelo chose to represent the young biblical warrior not after his victory, with Goliath's head at his feet, but turning his head (FIG. 22-14) to his left, sternly watchful of the approaching foe. *David* exhibits the characteristic representation of energy in reserve that imbues Michelangelo's later figures with the tension of a coiled spring. The anatomy of David's body plays an important part in this prelude to action. His rugged torso, sturdy limbs, and large hands and feet alert viewers to the strength to come. The swelling veins and tightening sinews amplify the psychological energy of David's pose.

Michelangelo doubtless had the classical nude in mind when he conceived his *David*. Like many of his colleagues, he greatly admired Greco-Roman statues, in particular the skillful and precise rendering of heroic physique. Without strictly imitating the antique style, the Renaissance sculptor captured in his portrayal of the biblical hero the tension of Lysippan athletes (FIG. 5-65) and the psychological

22-15 MICHELANGELO BUONARROTI, *Moses,* from the tomb of Pope Julius II, Rome, Italy, ca. 1513–1515. Marble, 7' 8½" high. San Pietro in Vincoli, Rome.

Not since Hellenistic times had a sculptor captured as much pent-up energy, both emotional and physical, in a seated statue as Michelangelo did in the over-life-size *Moses* he carved for Julius II's tomb.

22-16 MICHELANGELO BUONARROTI, *Bound Slave* (*Rebellious Captive*), from the tomb of Pope Julius II, Rome, Italy, ca. 1513–1516. Marble, 7' ⅝" high. Louvre, Paris.

For Pope Julius II's grandiose tomb, Michelangelo planned a series of statues of captives or slaves in various attitudes of revolt and exhaustion. This defiant figure exhibits a violent contrapposto.

insight and emotionalism of Hellenistic statuary (FIGS. 5-80 and 5-81). His *David* differs from those of Donatello and Verrocchio in much the same way later Hellenistic statues departed from their Classical predecessors (see Chapter 5). Michelangelo abandoned the self-contained compositions of the 15th-century *David* statues by abruptly turning the hero's head (FIG. 22-14) toward his gigantic adversary. This *David* is compositionally and emotionally connected to an unseen presence beyond the statue, a feature also of Hellenistic sculpture (FIG. 5-85). As early as 1501, then, Michelangelo invested his efforts in presenting towering, pent-up emotion rather than calm, ideal beauty. He transferred his own doubts, frustrations, and passions into the great figures he created or planned.

TOMB OF JULIUS II The formal references to classical antiquity in *David* surely appealed to Julius II, who associated himself with the humanists and with Roman emperors. Thus, this sculpture and the fame that accrued to Michelangelo on its completion called the artist to the pope's attention, leading shortly thereafter to major papal commissions. The first project Julius II commissioned from Michelangelo was the pontiff's own tomb, to be placed in Old Saint Peter's. The original 1505 design called for a freestanding two-story structure with some 28 statues (FIGS. 22-15 and 22-16). This colossal monument would have given Michelangelo the latitude to sculpt numerous human figures while providing Julius II with a grandiose memorial that would associate the 16th-century pope with the first pope, Peter himself. Shortly after Michelangelo began work on this project, the pope, for unknown reasons, interrupted the commission, possibly because funds had to be diverted to the rebuilding of Saint Peter's. After Julius II's death in 1513, Michelangelo reluctantly reduced the scale of the project step-by-step until, in 1542, a final contract specified a simple wall tomb with fewer than one-third of the originally planned figures. Michelangelo completed the tomb in

1545 and saw it placed in San Pietro in Vincoli, Rome, where Julius II had served as a cardinal before his accession to the papacy. Given Julius's ambitions, it is safe to say that had he seen the final design of his tomb, or known where it would eventually be located, he would have been bitterly disappointed.

The spirit of the tomb may be summed up in *Moses* (FIG. 22-15), which Michelangelo completed during one of his sporadic resumptions of the work. Meant to be seen from below and to be balanced with seven other massive forms related to it in spirit, *Moses* in its final comparatively paltry setting does not convey the impact originally intended. Michelangelo depicted the Old Testament prophet seated, the Tablets of the Law under one arm and his hands gathering his voluminous beard. The horns that appear on Moses's head were a convention in Christian art (based on a mistranslation of the Hebrew word for "rays") and helped Renaissance viewers identify the prophet (compare FIGS. 17-36 and 20-2). Here again, Michelangelo used the turned head, which concentrates the expression of awful wrath that stirs in the mighty frame and eyes. The muscles bulge, the veins swell, and the great legs seem to begin slowly to move. Not since Hellenistic times had a sculptor captured so much pent-up energy—both emotional and physical—in a seated statue (FIG. 5-85).

Originally, Michelangelo intended the tomb to have some 20 statues of captives, popularly known as slaves, in various attitudes of revolt and exhaustion. One is *Bound Slave*, or *Rebellious Captive* (FIG. 22-16). Another is shown in FIG. I-16. Considerable scholarly uncertainty exists about these statues. Although art historians have traditionally connected them with Julius's tomb, some now doubt the association. Some scholars even reject their identification as "slaves" or "captives." Despite these unanswered questions, the statues, like *David* and *Moses*, represent definitive statements. Michelangelo created figures that do not so much represent an abstract concept, as in medieval allegory, as they embody powerful emotional states associated with oppression. Indeed, Michelangelo communicated his expansive imagination through every plane and hollow of the stone. In *Bound Slave*, the defiant figure's violent contrapposto is the image of frantic but impotent struggle. Michelangelo based his whole art on his conviction that whatever can be said greatly through sculpture and painting must be said through the human figure.

TOMB OF GIULIANO DE' MEDICI Following the death of Julius II, Michelangelo, like Raphael, went into the service of the Medici popes, Leo X and his successor Clement VII (r. 1523–1534). These Medici chose not to perpetuate their predecessor's fame by let-

ting Michelangelo complete Julius's tomb. Instead, they (Pope Leo X and the then-cardinal Giulio de' Medici) commissioned him in 1519 to build a funerary chapel, the New Sacristy, in San Lorenzo in Florence. At opposite sides of the New Sacristy stand Michelangelo's sculpted tombs of Giuliano (1478–1516), duke of Nemours (south of Paris), and Lorenzo (1492–1519), duke of Urbino, son and grandson of Lorenzo the Magnificent. Giuliano's tomb (FIG. 22-17) is compositionally the twin of Lorenzo's. Michelangelo finished neither tomb. Most scholars believe he intended to place pairs of recumbent river gods at the bottom of the sarcophagi, balancing the pairs of figures that rest on the sloping sides, but Michelangelo's grand design for the tombs remains a puzzle.

The traditional interpretation is that the arrangement Michelangelo planned, but never completed, mirrors the soul's ascent through the levels of the Neo-Platonic universe. Neo-Platonism, a school of thought based on Plato's idealistic, spiritualistic philosophy, experienced a renewed popularity in the 16th-century humanist community. The lowest level of the tomb, which the river gods represent, would have signified the Underworld of brute matter, the source of evil. The two statues on the sarcophagi would symbolize the realm of time—the specifically human world of the cycles of dawn, day, evening, and night. Humanity's state in this world of time was one of pain and anxiety, of frustration and exhaustion. At left, the female figure of Night and, at right, the male figure of Day ap-

22-17 MICHELANGELO BUONARROTI, tomb of Giuliano de' Medici, New Sacristy (Medici Chapel), San Lorenzo, Florence, Italy, 1519–1534. Marble, central figure 5′ 11″ high.

Michelangelo's portrait of Giuliano de' Medici clad in ancient Roman armor depicts the deceased as the model of the active and decisive man. Below are the anguished and twisting figures of Night and Day.

1 ft.

pear to be chained into never-relaxing tensions. Both exhibit that anguished twisting of the body's masses in contrary directions, seen also in Michelangelo's *Bound Slave* (FIG. 22-16) and in his Sistine Chapel paintings (FIG. 22-19). This contortion is a staple of Michelangelo's figural art. Day, with a body the thickness of a great tree and the anatomy of Hercules (or of a reclining Greco-Roman river god that may have inspired Michelangelo's statue), strains his huge limbs against each other, his unfinished visage rising menacingly above his shoulder. Night, the symbol of rest, twists as if in troubled sleep, her posture wrenched and feverish. The artist surrounded her with an owl, poppies, and a hideous mask symbolic of nightmares. Some scholars argue, however, that the personifications Night and Day allude not to humanity's pain but to the life cycle and the passage of time leading ultimately to death.

On their respective tombs, sculptures of Lorenzo and Giuliano appear in niches at the apex of the structures. Transcending worldly existence, they represent the two ideal human types—the contemplative man (Lorenzo) and the active man (Giuliano). Giuliano (FIG. 22-17) sits clad in the armor of a Roman emperor and holds a commander's baton, his head turned alertly as if in council (he looks toward the statue of the Virgin at one end of the chapel). Across the room, Lorenzo appears wrapped in thought, his face in deep shadow. Together, they symbolize the two ways human beings might achieve union with God—through meditation or through the active

life fashioned after that of Christ. In this sense, they are not individual portraits. Indeed, Michelangelo declined to make likenesses of Lorenzo and Giuliano. Who, he asked, would care what the two dukes looked like in a thousand years? This attitude is consistent with Michelangelo's interests. Throughout his career he demonstrated less concern for facial features and expressions than for the overall human form. The rather generic visages of the two Medici captains of the Church attest to this. For the artist, more important was the contemplation of what lies beyond the corrosion of time.

SISTINE CHAPEL CEILING When Julius II suspended work on his tomb, the pope gave the bitter Michelangelo the commission to paint the ceiling (FIG. 22-1) of the Sistine Chapel (FIG. 22-18) in 1508. The artist, insisting that painting was not his profession (a protest that rings hollow after the fact, but Michelangelo's major works until then had been in sculpture, and painting was of secondary interest to him), assented in the hope that the tomb project could be revived. Michelangelo faced enormous difficulties in painting the Sistine ceiling. He had to address the ceiling's dimensions (some 5,800 square feet), its height above the pavement (almost 70 feet), and the complicated perspective problems the vault's height and curve presented, as well as his inexperience in the fresco technique. (The first section Michelangelo completed had to be redone because of faulty preparation of the intonaco; see "Fresco Painting," Chapter 19, page 504.) Yet, in less than four years, Michelangelo produced an unprecedented work—a monumental fresco incorporating his patron's agenda, Church doctrine, and the artist's interests. Depicting the most august and solemn themes of all, the creation, fall, and redemption of humanity—themes most likely selected by Julius II with input from Michelangelo and a theological adviser, probably Cardinal Marco Vigerio della Rovere (1446–1516)—Michelangelo spread a colossal decorative scheme across the vast surface. He succeeded in weaving together more than 300 figures in an ultimate grand drama of the human race.

A long sequence of narrative panels describing the creation, as recorded in Genesis, runs along the crown of the vault, from *God's Separation of Light and Darkness* (above the altar) to *Drunkenness of Noah* (nearest the entrance to the chapel). Thus, as viewers enter the chapel, look up, and walk toward the altar, they review, in reverse order, the history of the fall of humankind. The Hebrew prophets and pagan sibyls who foretold the coming of Christ appear seated in large thrones on both sides of the central row of scenes

22-18 Interior of the Sistine Chapel (looking east), Vatican City, Rome, Italy, built 1473. ■◄

Michelangelo reluctantly agreed to paint the ceiling (FIG. 22-1) of the Sistine Chapel for Pope Julius II. He had to overcome the complicated perspective problems that the height and curve of the vault presented.

22-19 MICHELANGELO BUONARROTI, *Creation of Adam,* detail of the ceiling (FIG. 22-1) of the Sistine Chapel, Vatican City, Rome, Italy, 1511–1512. Fresco, 9′ 2″ × 18′ 8″.

Life leaps to Adam like a spark from the extended hand of God in this fresco, which recalls the communication between gods and heroes in the classical myths Renaissance humanists admired so much.

from Genesis, where the vault curves down. In the four corner *pendentives,* Michelangelo placed four Old Testament scenes with David, Judith, Haman, and Moses and the Brazen Serpent. Scores of lesser figures also appear. The ancestors of Christ fill the triangular compartments above the windows, nude youths punctuate the corners of the central panels, and small pairs of putti in *grisaille* (monochrome painting using shades of gray to imitate sculpture) support the painted cornice surrounding the entire central corridor. The overall conceptualization of the ceiling's design and narrative structure not only presents a sweeping chronology of Christianity but also is in keeping with Renaissance ideas about Christian history. These ideas included interest in the conflict between good and evil and between the energy of youth and the wisdom of age. The conception of the entire ceiling was astounding in itself, and the articulation of it in its thousands of details was a superhuman achievement.

Unlike Andrea Mantegna's decoration of the Camera Picta (FIGS. 21-47 and 21-48) in Mantua, the strongly marked unifying architectural framework in the Sistine Chapel does not produce "picture windows" enframing illusions just within. Rather, the viewer focuses on figure after figure, each sharply outlined against the neutral tone of the architectural setting or the plain background of the panels. Here, as in his sculpture, Michelangelo relentlessly concentrated his expressive purpose on the human figure. To him, the body was beautiful not only in its natural form but also in its spiritual and philosophical significance. The body was the manifestation of the soul or of a state of mind and character. Michelangelo represented the body in its most simple, elemental aspect—in the nude or simply draped, with no background and no ornamental embellishment. He always painted with a sculptor's eye for how light and shadow communicate volume and surface. It is no coincidence that many of the figures seem to be tinted reliefs or freestanding statues.

CREATION OF ADAM One of the ceiling's central panels is *Creation of Adam* (FIG. 22-19). Michelangelo did not paint the traditional representation but instead produced a bold humanistic interpretation of the momentous event. God and Adam confront each other in a primordial unformed landscape of which Adam is still a material part, heavy as earth. The Lord transcends the earth, wrapped in a billowing cloud of drapery and borne up by his powers. Life leaps to Adam as if a spark flashed from the extended, mighty hand of God. The communication between gods and heroes, so familiar in classical myth, is here concrete. This blunt depiction of the Lord as ruler of Heaven in the Olympian pagan sense indicates how easily High Renaissance thought joined classical and Christian traditions. Yet the classical trappings do not obscure the essential Christian message.

22-19A
MICHELANGELO
Fall of Man,
ca. 1510.

Beneath the Lord's sheltering left arm is a female figure, apprehensively curious but as yet uncreated. Scholars traditionally believed her to represent Eve, but many now think she is the Virgin Mary (with the Christ Child at her knee). If the second identification is correct, it suggests that Michelangelo incorporated into his fresco one of the essential tenets of Christian faith—the belief that Adam's Original Sin eventually led to the sacrifice of Christ, which in turn made possible the redemption of all humankind.

As God reaches out to Adam, the viewer's eye follows the motion from right to left, but Adam's extended left arm leads the eye back to the right, along the Lord's right arm, shoulders, and left arm to his left forefinger, which points to the Christ Child's face. The focal point of this right-to-left-to-right movement—the fingertips of Adam and the Lord—is dramatically off-center. Michelangelo replaced the straight architectural axes found in Leonardo's compositions with curves and diagonals. For example, the bodies of the two great figures are complementary—the concave body of Adam fitting the convex body and billowing "cloak" of God. Thus, motion directs

Restoring Renaissance Paintings

The year 1989 marked the culmination of a 12-year project to clean the Sistine Chapel ceiling (FIG. 22-1). Cleaning of Michelangelo's *Last Judgment* (FIG. 22-21) behind the altar followed during the next five years. Restorers removed centuries of accumulated grime, overpainting, and protective glue, uncovering much of Michelangelo's original form, color, style, and procedure.

The before-and-after details (FIG. 22-20) of one of the lunettes over the windows reveal the stark contrast in the appearance of the frescoes in 1977 and today. In these semicircular spaces, Michelangelo painted figures representing the ancestors of Christ (Matt. 1:1–17). After computer assessment of the damage (including use of infrared and ultraviolet lights), the restorers worked carefully and slowly to clean the fresco of soot, dirt, dissolved salts, and various types of gums and varnishes made of animal glues. Over the centuries, restorers had used various varnishes to brighten the darkening fresco. Unfortunately, over time the varnishes deteriorated, darkening the painting even more. For the latest cleaning effort, the restorers first wet a small section of the fresco with distilled, deionized water. The application of a cleaning solution made of bicarbonates of sodium and ammonium and supplemented with an antibacterial, antifungal agent followed. Adding carboxymethyl cellulose and water to this solution created a gel that clung to the ceiling fresco. After three minutes, restorers removed the gel.

Michelangelo's figures, once thought purposefully dark, now show brilliant colors of high intensity, brushed on with an astonishing freedom and verve. The fresh, luminous hues, boldly joined in unexpected harmonies, seemed uncharacteristically dissonant to some experts when first revealed and aroused brisk controversy. Some scholars believed that the restorers removed Michelangelo's

work along with the accumulated layers and that the apparently strident coloration could not possibly be his. Most art historians, however, now agree that the restoration effort has revealed to modern eyes the artist's real intentions and effects—and that in the Sistine Chapel, Michelangelo already had paved the way for the Mannerist reaction to the High Renaissance, examined later in this chapter.

The restoration of Leonardo's *Last Supper* (FIG. 22-4), which took more than two decades, presented conservators with an even greater challenge. Leonardo had mixed oil and tempera, applying much of it *a secco* (to dried, rather than wet, plaster) in order to create a mural that more closely approximated oil painting on canvas or wood instead of fresco. But because the wall did not absorb the pigment as in the *buon fresco* technique, the paint quickly began to flake (see "Fresco Painting," Chapter 19, page 504). Milan's humidity further accelerated the deterioration. Restoration efforts, completed in May 1999, were painstaking and slow, as were those in the Sistine Chapel, and involved extensive scholarly, chemical, and computer analysis. Like other restorations, this one was not without controversy. One scholar has claimed that 80 percent of what is visible today is the work of the modern restorers, not Leonardo. The controversies surrounding the cleanings of the Sistine Chapel ceiling and Santa Maria delle Grazie have not put a damper on other restoration projects. After the cleaning of *Last Judgment,* the Vatican continued the restoration of the remaining frescoes in the Sistine Chapel (FIG. 22-18), including Perugino's *Christ Delivering the Keys of the Kingdom to Saint Peter* (FIG. 21-40), completing the project in December 1999. Restorers have also cleaned the frescoes in the Stanza della Segnatura in the Vatican Apartments in Rome, including Raphael's *School of Athens* (FIG. 22-9).

22-20 Detail of the Azor-Sadoch lunette over one of the Sistine Chapel windows (FIG. 22-18) at the beginning (*left*) and final stage (*right*) of the restoration process.

The 1977–1989 restoration of the frescoes on the Sistine Chapel ceiling removed centuries of accumulated grime and revealed the original bright and luminous colors of Michelangelo's figures.

not only the figures but also the whole composition. The reclining positions of the figures, the heavy musculature, and the twisting poses are all intrinsic parts of Michelangelo's style.

The photographs of the Sistine Chapel reproduced here record the appearance of Michelangelo's frescoes after the completion of a 12-year cleaning project (1977–1989). The painstaking restoration

(FIG. 22-20) elicited considerable controversy because it revealed vivid colors that initially shocked art historians, producing accusations that the restorers were destroying Michelangelo's masterpieces (see "Restoring Renaissance Paintings," above). That reaction, however, was largely attributable to the fact that for centuries no one had ever seen Michelangelo's frescoes except covered with soot and grime.

Religious Art in Counter-Reformation Italy

Both Catholics and Protestants took seriously the role of devotional imagery in religious life. However, their views differed dramatically. Whereas Catholics deemed art as valuable for cultivating piety, Protestants believed visual imagery could produce idolatry and could distract the faithful from their goal—developing a personal relationship with God (see "Protestantism and Iconoclasm," Chapter 23, page 632). As part of the Counter-Reformation effort, Pope Paul III convened the Council of Trent in 1545 to review controversial Church doctrines. At its conclusion in 1563, the Council issued the following edict:

> The holy council commands all bishops and others who hold the office of teaching and have charge of the *cura animarum* [literally, "cure of souls"—the responsibility of laboring for the salvation of souls], that in accordance with the usage of the Catholic and Apostolic Church, received from the primitive times of the Christian religion, and with the unanimous teaching of the holy Fathers and the decrees of sacred councils, they above all instruct the faithful diligently in matters relating to intercession and invocation of the saints, the veneration of relics, and the legitimate use of images. . . . Moreover, that the images of Christ, of the Virgin Mother of God, and of the other saints are to be placed and retained especially in the churches, and that due honor and veneration is to be given them; . . . because the honor which is shown them is referred to the prototypes which they represent, so that by means of the images which we kiss

and before which we uncover the head and prostrate ourselves, we adore Christ and venerate the saints whose likeness they bear. That is what was defined by the decrees of the councils, especially of the Second Council of Nicaea, against the opponents of images.

> Moreover, let the bishops diligently teach that by means of the stories of the mysteries of our redemption portrayed in paintings and other representations the people are instructed and confirmed in the articles of faith, which ought to be borne in mind and constantly reflected upon; also that great profit is derived from all holy images, not only because the people are thereby reminded of the benefits and gifts bestowed on them by Christ, but also because through the saints the miracles of God and salutary examples are set before the eyes of the faithful, so that they may give God thanks for those things, may fashion their own life and conduct in imitation of the saints and be moved to adore and love God and cultivate piety. . . .

> That these things may be the more faithfully observed, the holy council decrees that no one is permitted to erect or cause to be erected in any place or church, howsoever exempt, any unusual image unless it has been approved by the bishop.*

* *Canons and Decrees of the Council of Trent*, December 3–4, 1563, in Robert Klein and Henri Zerner, *Italian Art 1500–1600: Sources and Documents* (Evanston, Ill.: Northwestern University Press, 1966), 120–121.

THE COUNTER-REFORMATION Paul III (r. 1534–1549) succeeded Clement VII as pope in 1534 at a time of widespread dissatisfaction with the leadership and policies of the Roman Catholic Church. Led by clerics such as Martin Luther (1483–1546) and John Calvin (1509–1564) in the Holy Roman Empire, early-16th-century reformers directly challenged papal authority, especially regarding secular issues. Disgruntled Catholics voiced concerns about the sale of *indulgences* (pardons for sins, reducing the time a soul spent in Purgatory), about nepotism (the appointment of relatives to important positions), and about how high Church officials were pursuing personal wealth. This Reformation movement resulted in the establishment of Protestantism, with sects such as Lutheranism and Calvinism (see Chapter 23). Central to Protestantism was a belief in personal faith rather than adherence to decreed Church practices and doctrines. Because the Protestants believed that the only true religious relationship was the personal relationship between an individual and God, they were, in essence, eliminating the need for Church intercession, which is central to Catholicism.

The Catholic Church, in response, mounted a full-fledged campaign to counteract the defection of its members to Protestantism. Led by Paul III, this response, the Counter-Reformation, consisted of numerous initiatives. The Council of Trent, which met intermittently from 1545 through 1563, was a major element of this effort. Composed of cardinals, archbishops, bishops, abbots, and theologians, the Council of Trent dealt with issues of Church doctrine, including many the Protestants contested. Many papal commissions during this period can be viewed as an integral part of the Counter-Reformation effort. Popes long had been aware of the power of visual imagery to

construct and reinforce ideological claims, and 16th-century popes exploited this capability (see "Religious Art in Counter-Reformation Italy," above).

LAST JUDGMENT Among Paul III's first papal commissions was an enormous (48 feet tall) fresco for the Sistine Chapel. Michelangelo agreed to paint the *Last Judgment* fresco (FIG. **22-21**) on the chapel's altar wall. Here, the artist depicted Christ as the stern judge of the world—a giant who raises his mighty right arm in a gesture of damnation so broad and universal as to suggest he will destroy all creation. The choirs of Heaven surrounding him pulse with anxiety and awe. Crowded into the space below are trumpeting angels, the ascending figures of the just, and the downward-hurtling figures of the damned. On the left, the dead awake and assume flesh. On the right, demons, whose gargoyle masks and burning eyes revive the demons of Romanesque tympana (FIG. I-6), torment the damned.

Michelangelo's terrifying vision of the fate that awaits sinners goes far beyond even Signorelli's gruesome images (FIG. **21-41**). Martyrs who suffered especially agonizing deaths crouch below the Judge. One of them, Saint Bartholomew, who was skinned alive, holds the flaying knife and the skin, its face a grotesque self-portrait of Michelangelo. The figures are huge and violently twisted, with small heads and contorted features. Although this immense fresco impresses on viewers Christ's wrath on Judgment Day, it also holds out hope. A group of saved souls—the elect—crowd around Christ, and on the far right appears a figure with a cross, most likely the Good Thief (crucified with Christ) or a saint martyred by crucifixion, such as Saint Andrew.

22-21 MICHELANGELO BUONARROTI, *Last Judgment,* altar wall of the Sistine Chapel (FIG. 22-18), Vatican City, Rome, Italy, 1536–1541. Fresco, 48′ × 44′. ◼◀

Michelangelo completed his fresco cycle in the Sistine Chapel with this terrifying vision of the fate that awaits sinners. Near the center, he placed his own portrait on the flayed skin Saint Bartholomew holds.

10 ft.

Architecture: Rome

The Sistine Chapel was but a small part of the vast Vatican palace complex on the west side of the Tiber River (MAPS 22-1 and 24-1), construction of which began under Constantine with the erection of a church over the site of Saint Peter's burial place (Old Saint Peter's, FIG. 11-9). By the 15th century, it was obvious that the millennium-old basilica was insufficient for the needs and aspirations of the Renaissance papacy. Rebuilding the fourth-century church would occupy some of the leading architects of Italy for more than a century.

BRAMANTE The first in the distinguished line of architects of the new Saint Peter's was DONATO D'ANGELO BRAMANTE (1444–1514). Born in Urbino and trained as a painter (perhaps by Piero della Francesca), Bramante went to Milan in 1481 and, like Leonardo, stayed there until the French arrived in 1499. In Milan, he abandoned painting to become one of his generation's most renowned architects. Under the influence of Filippo Brunelleschi, Leon Battista Alberti, and perhaps Leonardo, all of whom strongly favored the art and architecture of classical antiquity, Bramante developed the High Renaissance form of the central-plan church.

TEMPIETTO The architectural style Bramante championed was, consistent with the humanistic values of the day, based on ancient Roman models. This style is on display in the small architectural gem known as the Tempietto (FIG. 22-22) on the Janiculum hill overlooking the Vatican. The building received its name because, to contemporaries, it had the look of a small ancient temple. "Little Temple" is, in fact, a perfect nickname for the structure, because the round temples of Roman Italy (FIG. 10-4) directly inspired Bramante's design. King Ferdinand and Queen Isabella of Spain commissioned the Tempietto to mark the presumed location of Saint Peter's crucifixion. The patrons asked Bramante to undertake the project in 1502, but work may not have commenced until the end of the decade. Today the Tempietto stands inside the rectangular cloister alongside the church of San Pietro in Montorio, but Bramante planned, although never executed, a circular colonnaded courtyard

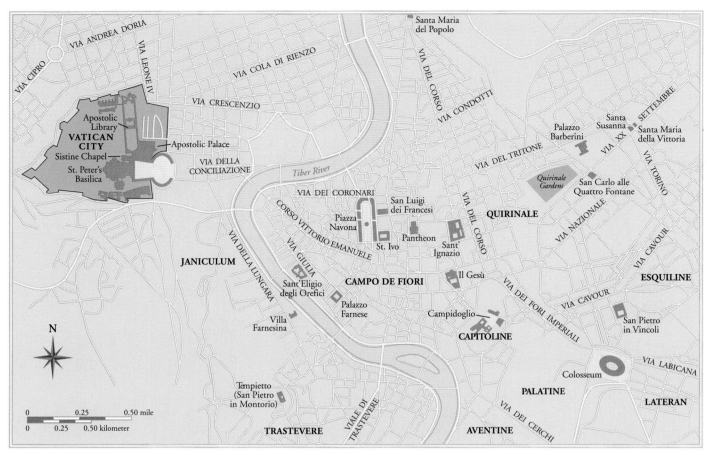

MAP 22-1 Rome with Renaissance and Baroque monuments.

to frame the "temple." His intent was to coordinate the Tempietto and its surrounding portico by aligning the columns of the two structures.

At first glance, the Tempietto (FIG. 22-22) may seem severely rational with its sober circular *stylobate* (stepped temple platform) and the austere *Tuscan* style of the *colonnade,* neither feature giving any indication of the placement of an interior altar or of the entrance. However, Bramante achieved a truly wonderful balance and harmony in the relationship of the parts (dome, drum, and base) to one another and to the whole. Conceived as a tall, domed cylinder projecting from the lower, wider cylinder of its colonnade, this small building incorporates all the qualities of a sculptured monument. Bramante's sculptural eye is most evident in the rhythmical play of light and shadow seen around the columns and balustrade and across the deep-set rectangular windows alternating with shallow shell-capped niches in the *cella* (central room of a temple), walls, and drum. Although the Tempietto, superficially at least, may resemble a Greek *tholos* (a circular shrine; FIG. 5-72), and although antique models provided the inspiration for all its details, the combination of parts and details was new and original. (Classical tholoi, for instance, had neither drum nor balustrade.)

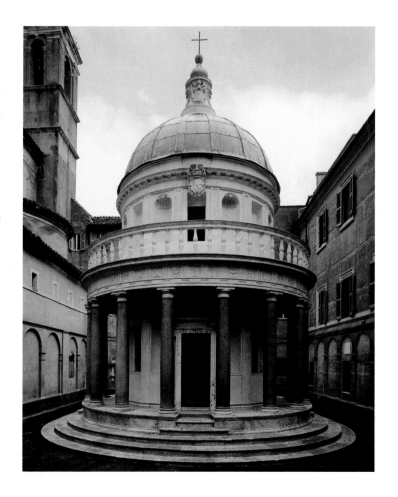

22-22 DONATO D'ANGELO BRAMANTE, Tempietto, San Pietro in Montorio, Rome, Italy, 1502(?).

Contemporaries celebrated Bramante as the first to revive the classical style in architecture. Roman round temples (FIG. 10-4) inspired this "little temple," but Bramante combined the classical parts in new ways.

One of the main differences between the Early and High Renaissance styles of architecture is the former's emphasis on detailing flat wall surfaces versus the latter's sculptural handling of architectural masses. Bramante's Tempietto initiated the High Renaissance era. Andrea Palladio, a brilliant theorist as well as a major later 16th-century architect (FIGS. 22-29 and 22-32), included the Tempietto in his survey of ancient temples because Bramante was "the first to bring back to light the good and beautiful architecture that from antiquity to that time had been hidden."[7] Round in plan and elevated on a base that isolates it from its surroundings, the Tempietto conforms to Alberti's and Palladio's strictest demands for an ideal church.

NEW SAINT PETER'S As noted, Bramante was the architect Julius II selected to design a replacement for the Constantinian basilican church of Old Saint Peter's (FIG. 11-9). The earlier building had fallen into considerable disrepair and, in any event, did not suit this ambitious pope's taste for the colossal. Julius wanted to gain control over the whole of Italy and to make the Rome of the popes reminiscent of (if not more splendid than) the Rome of the caesars. As the symbolic seat of the papacy, Saint Peter's represented the history of the Church.

Bramante originally designed the new Saint Peter's (FIG. 22-23) to consist of a cross with arms of equal length, each terminating in an apse. Julius II intended the new building to serve as a *martyrium* to mark Saint Peter's grave and also hoped to have his own tomb in it. A large dome would have covered the crossing, and smaller domes over subsidiary chapels would have covered the diagonal axes of the roughly square plan. Thus, Bramante's ambitious design called for a boldly sculptural treatment of the walls and piers under the dome. His organization of the interior space was complex in the extreme, with the intricate symmetries of a crystal. It is possible to detect in the plan some nine interlocking crosses, five of them supporting domes. The scale was titanic. According to sources, Bramante boasted he would place the dome of the Pantheon (FIGS. 10-49 to 10-51) over the Basilica Nova (FIG. 10-78).

A commemorative medal (FIG. 22-24) by CRISTOFORO FOPPA CARADOSSO (ca. 1452–1526) shows how Bramante's scheme would have attempted to do just that. The dome is hemispherical, as is that of the Pantheon, but the massive unity of that building is broken up here by two towers and a medley of domes and porticos. In light of Julius II's interest in the Roman Empire, using the Pantheon as a model was entirely appropriate. That Bramante's design for the new Saint Peter's was commemorated on a medal is in itself significant. Such medals proliferated in the 15th century, reviving the ancient Roman practice of placing images of important imperial building projects on the reverses of Roman coins and portraits of the emperors who commissioned them on the coins' fronts. Julius II appears on the front of the Caradosso medal.

During Bramante's lifetime, the actual construction of the new Saint Peter's did not advance beyond the building of the crossing piers and the lower choir walls. After his death, the work passed from one architect to another and, in 1546, to Michelangelo. With the Church facing challenges to its supremacy, Pope Paul III surely felt a sense of urgency about the completion of this project. Michelangelo's work on Saint Peter's became a long-term show of dedication, thankless and without pay. Among Michelangelo's difficulties was his struggle to preserve and carry through Bramante's original plan

22-23 DONATO D'ANGELO BRAMANTE, plan for the new Saint Peter's, the Vatican, Rome, Italy, 1505. (1) dome, (2) apse.

Bramante's design for the new church to replace the Constantinian basilica of Saint Peter's (FIG. 11-9) featured a central plan consisting of a cross with arms of equal length, each terminating in an apse.

1 in.

22-24 CRISTOFORO FOPPA CARADOSSO, medal showing Bramante's design for the new Saint Peter's, 1506. Bronze, $2\frac{1}{4}''$ diameter. British Museum, London.

Bramante's unexecuted 1506 design for Saint Peter's called for a large dome over the crossing, smaller domes over the subsidiary chapels, and a boldly sculptural treatment of the walls and piers.

units symmetrically around a central and unique axis, as the arms relate to the body or the eyes to the nose. "For it is an established fact," he wrote, "that the members of architecture resemble the members of man. Whoever neither has been nor is a master at figures, and especially at anatomy, cannot really understand architecture."[8]

In his modification of Bramante's plan, Michelangelo reduced the central component from a number of interlocking crosses to a compact domed *Greek cross* inscribed in a square and fronted with a double-columned portico. Without destroying the centralizing features of Bramante's plan, Michelangelo, with a few strokes of the pen, converted its snowflake complexity into massive, cohesive unity. His treatment of the building's exterior further reveals his interest in creating a unified and cohesive design. Because of later changes to the front of the church, the west (apse) end (FIG. **22-26**) offers the best view of his style and intention. Michelangelo's design incorporated the colossal order, the two-story pilasters first seen in more reserved fashion in Alberti's Mantuan church of Sant'Andrea (FIG. **21-44**). The giant pilasters seem to march around the undulating wall surfaces, confining the movement without interrupting it. The architectural sculpturing here extends up from the ground through the attic stories and into the *drum* and the dome (FIG. **24-4**), unifying the whole building from base to summit. Baroque architects later learned much from this kind of integral design, which Michelangelo based on his conviction that architecture is one with the organic beauty of the human form.

The domed west end—as majestic as it is today and as influential as it has been on architecture throughout the centuries—is not quite as Michelangelo intended it. Originally, he had planned a dome with an ogival section, like that of Florence Cathedral (FIG. **19-18**). But in his final version he decided on a hemispherical dome to temper the verticality of the design of the lower stories and to establish a balance between dynamic and static elements. However, when GIACOMO DELLA PORTA (ca. 1533–1602) executed the dome (FIG. **24-4**) after Michelangelo's death, he restored the earlier high design, ignoring Michelangelo's later version. Giacomo's reasons were probably the same ones that had impelled Brunelleschi to use an ogival section for his Florentine dome—greater stability and ease of construction. The result is that the dome seems to rise from its base, rather than rest firmly on it—an effect Michelangelo might not have approved. Nevertheless, Saint Peter's dome is probably the most impressive in the world.

22-25 MICHELANGELO BUONARROTI, plan for Saint Peter's, Vatican City, Rome, Italy, 1546. (1) dome, (2) apse, (3) portico.

In his modification of Bramante's plan (FIG. 22-23), Michelangelo reduced the central component from a number of interlocking crosses to a compact domed Greek cross inscribed in a square.

(FIG. 22-23), which he praised and chose to retain as the basis for his own design (FIG. **22-25**). Michelangelo shared Bramante's conviction that a central plan was the ideal form for a church. Always a sculptor first and foremost, Michelangelo carried his obsession with human form over to architecture and reasoned that buildings should follow the form of the human body. This meant organizing their

22-26 MICHELANGELO BUONARROTI, Saint Peter's (looking northeast), Vatican City, Rome, Italy, 1546–1564. Dome completed by GIACOMO DELLA PORTA, 1590.

The west end of Saint Peter's offers the best view of Michelangelo's intentions. The giant pilasters of his colossal order march around the undulating wall surfaces of the central-plan building.

PALAZZO FARNESE Another architectural project Michelangelo took over at the request of Paul III was the construction of the lavish private palace the pope had commissioned when he was still Cardinal Alessandro Farnese. The future pope had selected ANTONIO DA SANGALLO THE YOUNGER (1483–1546) to design the Palazzo Farnese (FIG. **22-27**) in Rome. (At Antonio's death in 1546, Michelangelo assumed control of the building's completion.) Antonio, the youngest of a family of architects, went to Rome around 1503 and became Bramante's draftsman and assistant. He is the perfect example of the professional architect. Indeed, his family constituted an architectural firm, often planning and drafting for other architects.

The broad, majestic front of the Palazzo Farnese asserts to the public the exalted station of a great family. This impressive facade encapsulates the aristocratic epoch that followed the stifling of the nascent middle-class democracy of European cities (especially the Italian cities) by powerful rulers heading centralized states. It is thus significant that Paul chose to enlarge greatly the original rather modest palace to its present form after his accession to the papacy in 1534, reflecting his ambitions both for his family and for the papacy. Facing a spacious paved square, the facade is the very essence of princely dignity in architecture. The *quoins* (rusticated building corners) and cornice firmly anchor the rectangle of the smooth front, and lines of windows (the central row with alternating triangular and segmental pediments, in Bramante's fashion) mark a majestic beat across it. The window frames are not flush with the wall, as in the Palazzo Medici-Riccardi (FIG. 21-36), but project from its surface, so instead of being a flat, thin plane, the facade is a spatially active three-dimensional mass. The rusticated doorway and second-story balcony, surmounted by the Farnese coat of arms, emphasize the central axis and bring the design's horizontal and vertical forces into harmony. This centralizing feature, absent from the palaces of Michelozzo (FIG. 21-36) and Alberti (FIG. 21-38), is the external opening of a central corridor axis that runs through the entire building and continues in the garden beyond. Around this axis, Antonio arranged the rooms with strict regularity.

The interior courtyard (FIG. **22-28**) displays stately column-enframed arches on the first two levels, as in the Roman Colosseum (FIG. 10-1). On the third level, Michelangelo incorporated his sophisticated variation on that theme (based in part on the Colosseum's fourth-story Corinthian pilasters), with overlapping pilasters replacing the weighty columns of Antonio's design. The Palazzo Farnese set the standard for Italian Renaissance palaces and fully expresses the classical order, regularity, simplicity, and dignity of the High Renaissance.

Andrea Palladio's Villa Rotonda has four identical facades, each one resembling a Roman temple with a columnar porch. In the center is a great dome-covered rotunda modeled on the Pantheon (FIG. 10-49).

Architecture: Venice

Venice long had been a major Mediterranean coastal port and served as the gateway to the Orient. Reaching the height of its commercial and political power during the 15th century, the city saw its fortunes decline in the 16th century. Even so, Venice and the Papal States were the only Italian sovereignties to retain their independence during the century of strife. Either France or Spain dominated all others. Although the discoveries in the New World and the economic shift from Italy to areas such as the Netherlands were largely responsible for the decline of Venice, even more immediate and pressing events drained its wealth and power. After their conquest of Constantinople, the Turks began to vie with the Venetians for control of the eastern Mediterranean. The Ottoman Empire evolved into a constant threat to Venice. Early in the century, the European powers of the League of Cambrai also attacked the Italian port city. Formed and led by Pope Julius II, who coveted Venetian holdings on Italy's mainland, the league included Spain, France, and the Holy Roman Empire, in addition to the Papal States. Despite these challenges, Venice developed a flourishing, independent, and influential school of artists.

ANDREA PALLADIO The chief architect of the Venetian Republic from 1570 until his death a decade later was Andrea di Pietro, known as ANDREA PALLADIO (1508–1580). (The surname derives from Pallas Athena, Greek goddess of wisdom, an appropriate reference for an architect schooled in the classical tradition of Alberti and Bramante.) Palladio began his career as a stonemason and decorative sculptor in Vicenza, but at age 30 he turned to architecture, the ancient literature on architecture, engineering, topography, and military science. In order to study the ancient buildings firsthand, Palladio made several trips to Rome. In 1556 he illustrated Daniele Barbaro's edition of Vitruvius's *De architectura* and later wrote his own treatise on architecture, *I quattro libri dell'architettura* (*The Four Books of Architecture*), originally published in 1570. That work had a wide-ranging influence on succeeding generations of architects throughout Europe. Palladio's influence outside Italy, most significantly in England and in colonial America (see Chapter 29), was stronger and more lasting than that of any other architect.

Palladio accrued his significant reputation from his many designs for villas, built on the Venetian mainland. Nineteen still stand, and they especially influenced later architects. The same spirit that prompted the

22-30 ANDREA PALLADIO, plan of the Villa Rotonda (formerly Villa Capra), near Vicenza, Italy, ca. 1550–1570. (1) dome, (2) porch.

Palladio published an influential treatise on architecture in 1570. Consistent with his design theories, all the parts of the Villa Rotonda relate to one another in terms of calculated mathematical ratios.

ancient Romans to build villas in the countryside motivated a similar villa-building boom in 16th-century Venice, which, with its very limited space, was highly congested. But a longing for the countryside was not the only motive. Declining fortunes prompted the Venetians to develop their mainland possessions with new land investment and reclamation projects. Citizens who could afford it set themselves up as aristocratic farmers and developed swamps into productive agricultural land. Wealthy families could look on their villas as providential investments. The villas were thus aristocratic farms surrounded by service outbuildings (like the much later American plantations, which emulated many aspects of Palladio's architectural style). Palladio generally arranged the outbuildings in long, low wings branching out from the main building and enclosing a large rectangular court area.

VILLA ROTONDA Palladio's most famous villa, Villa Rotonda (FIG. 22-29), near Vicenza, is exceptional because the architect did not build it for an aspiring gentleman farmer but for a retired monsignor who wanted a villa for social events. Palladio planned and designed Villa Rotonda, located on a hilltop, as a kind of *belvedere* (literally "beautiful view"; in architecture, a structure with a view of the countryside or the sea), without the usual wings of secondary buildings. It has a central plan (FIG. 22-30) with four identical facades and projecting porches oriented to the four compass points. Each facade of the Villa Rotonda resembles a Roman Ionic temple. In placing a traditional temple porch in front of a dome-covered interior, Palladio doubtless had the Pantheon (FIG. 10-49) in mind as a model. But, as Bramante did in his Tempietto (FIG. 22-22), Palladio transformed his model into a new design that has no parallel in antiquity. Each of the villa's four porches can be used as a platform for enjoying a different

view of the surrounding landscape. In this design, the central dome-covered rotunda logically functions as a kind of circular platform from which visitors may turn in any direction for the preferred view. The result is a building with functional parts systematically related to one another in terms of calculated mathematical relationships. Villa Rotonda embodies all the qualities of self-sufficiency and formal completeness most Renaissance architects sought.

SAN GIORGIO MAGGIORE One of the most dramatically placed buildings in Venice is San Giorgio Maggiore (FIG. 22-31), directly across the Grand Canal from Piazza San Marco. Dissatisfied with earlier solutions to the problem of integrating a high central nave and lower aisles into a unified facade design, Palladio solved it by superimposing a tall and narrow classical porch on a low broad one. This solution reflects the building's interior arrangement (FIG. 22-32) and in that sense is strictly logical, but the intersection of two temple facades is irrational and ambiguous, consistent with contemporaneous developments in Mannerist architecture, discussed

22-31A SANSOVINO, Mint and Library, Venice, begun 1536.

22-31 ANDREA PALLADIO, aerial view of San Giorgio Maggiore, Venice, Italy, begun 1566.

Dissatisfied with earlier solutions to the problem of integrating a high central nave and lower aisles into a unified facade, Palladio superimposed a tall and narrow classical porch on a low broad one.

22-32 ANDREA PALLADIO, interior of San Giorgio Maggiore, Venice, Italy, begun 1566.

In contrast to the somewhat irrational intersection of two temple facades on the exterior of San Giorgio Maggiore, Palladio's interior is strictly logical, consistent with classical architectural theory.

later. Palladio's design also created the illusion of three-dimensional depth, an effect intensified by the strong projection of the central columns and the shadows they cast. The play of shadow across the building's surfaces, its reflection in the water, and its gleaming white against sea and sky create a remarkably colorful effect. The interior of the church lacks the ambiguity of the facade and exhibits strong roots in High Renaissance architectural style. Light floods the interior and crisply defines the contours of the rich wall decorations, all beautifully and "correctly" profiled—the exemplar of what classical architectural theory meant by "rational" organization.

Venetian Painting

In the 16th century the Venetians developed a distinctive painting style. Artists in the maritime republic showed a special interest in recording the effect of Venice's soft-colored light on figures and landscapes, and Venetian paintings of the High and Late Renaissance are easy to distinguish from contemporaneous works in Florence and Rome.

GIOVANNI BELLINI One artist who contributed significantly to creating the High Renaissance painting style in Venice was GIOVANNI BELLINI (ca. 1430–1516). Trained in the International Style (see Chapter 19) by his father Jacopo, a student of Gentile da Fabriano, Bellini worked in the family shop and did not develop his own style until after his father's death in 1470. His early independent works show the dominant influence of his brother-in-law Andrea Mantegna. But in the late 1470s, he came into contact with the work of the Sicilian-born painter Antonello da Messina (ca. 1430–1479). Antonello received his early training in Naples, where he must have become familiar with Flemish painting and mastered using mixed oil (see "Tempera and Oil Painting," Chapter 20, page 523). This more flexible medium is wider in coloristic range than either tempera or fresco. Antonello arrived in Venice in 1475 and during his two-year stay introduced his Venetian colleagues to the possibilities the new oil technique offered. As a direct result of contact with Antonello, Bellini abandoned Mantegna's harsh linear style and developed a sensuous coloristic manner that was to characterize Venetian painting for a century.

SAN ZACCARIA ALTARPIECE Bellini earned great recognition for his many Madonnas, which he painted both in half-length (with or without accompanying saints) on small devotional panels and in full-length on large, monumental altarpieces of the *sacra conversazione* (holy conversation) type. In the sacra conversazione, which gained great popularity as a theme for religious paintings from the middle of the 15th century on, saints from different epochs occupy the same space and seem to converse either with each other or with the audience. (Raphael employed much the same conceit in his *School of Athens,* FIG. 22-9, where he gathered Greek philosophers of different eras.) Bellini carried on the tradition in one of his earliest major commissions, the *San Zaccaria Altarpiece* (FIG. **22-33**). As was conventional, the Virgin Mary sits enthroned, holding the Christ Child, with saints flanking her. Bellini placed the group in a carefully painted shrine. Attributes aid the identification of all the saints: Saint Lucy holding a tray with her plucked-out eyes displayed on it; Saint Peter with his key and book; Saint Catherine with the palm of martyrdom and the broken wheel; and Saint Jerome with a book (representing his translation of the Bible into Latin). At the foot of the throne sits an angel playing a viol. The painting radiates a feeling of serenity and spiritual calm. Viewers derive this sense less from the figures (no interaction occurs among them) than from Bellini's harmonious and balanced presentation of color and light. Line is not the chief agent of form, as it generally is in paintings produced in Rome and Florence. Indeed, outlines dissolve in light and shadow. Glowing color produces a soft radiance that envelops the forms with an atmospheric haze and enhances their majestic serenity.

22-33A BELLINI, *Saint Franci. in the Deser* ca. 1470–148

22-33 GIOVANNI BELLINI, *San Zaccaria Altarpiece,* 1505. Oil on wood transferred to canvas, 16′ 5$\frac{1}{2}$″ × 7′ 9″. San Zaccaria, Venice.

In this *sacra conversazione* uniting saints from different eras, Bellini created a feeling of serenity and spiritual calm through the harmonious and balanced presentation of color and light.

22-34 GIOVANNI BELLINI and TITIAN, *Feast of the Gods,* from the Camerino d'Alabastro, Palazzo Ducale, Ferrara, Italy, 1529. Oil on canvas, 5′ 7″ × 6′ 2″. National Gallery of Art, Washington, D.C. (Widener Collection).

In *Feast of the Gods,* based on Ovid's *Fasti,* Bellini developed a new kind of mythological painting in which the Olympian deities appear as peasants enjoying a picnic in the soft afternoon light.

FEAST OF THE GODS In painting *Feast of the Gods* (FIG. **22-34**), Bellini drew from the work of one of his students, Giorgione da Castelfranco (discussed next), who developed his master's landscape backgrounds into poetic Arcadian reveries. Derived from Arcadia, a region in southern Greece, the term *Arcadian* referred, by the time of the Renaissance, to an idyllic place of rural, rustic peace and simplicity. After Giorgione's premature death, Bellini embraced his student's interests and, in *Feast of the Gods,* developed a new kind of mythological painting. The duke of Ferrara, Alfonso d'Este, commissioned this work for a room in the Palazzo Ducale. Although Bellini drew some of the figures from the standard repertoire of Greco-Roman art—most notably, the nymph carrying a vase on her head and the sleeping nymph in the lower right corner—the Olympian gods appear as peasants enjoying a picnic in a shady glade. Bellini's source was Ovid's *Fasti,* which describes a banquet of the gods. The artist spread the figures across the foreground. Satyrs attend the gods, nymphs bring jugs of wine, a child draws from a keg, couples engage in love play, and the sleeping nymph with exposed breast receives amorous attention. The mellow light of a long afternoon glows softly around the gathering, caressing the surfaces of colorful fabrics, smooth flesh, and polished metal. Here, Bellini communicated the delight the Venetian school took in the beauty of texture revealed by the full resources of gently and subtly harmonized color. Behind the warm, lush tones of the figures, a background of cool green tree-filled glades extends into the distance. At the right, a screen of trees creates a verdant shelter. The atmosphere is idyllic, a lush countryside providing a setting for the never-ending pleasure of the immortal gods.

With Bellini, Venetian art became the great complement of the schools of Florence and Rome. The Venetians' instrument was color, that of the Florentines and Romans sculpturesque form. Scholars often distill the contrast between these two approaches down to *colorito* (colored or painted) versus *disegno* (drawing and design). Whereas most central Italian artists emphasized careful design preparation based on preliminary drawing (see "Renaissance Drawings," page 581), Venetian artists focused on color and the process of paint application. In addition, the general thematic focus of their work differed. Venetian artists painted the poetry of the senses and delighted in nature's beauty and the pleasures of humanity. Artists in Florence and

22-35 GIORGIONE DA CASTELFRANCO (and/or TITIAN), *Pastoral Symphony,* ca. 1508–1510. Oil on canvas, 3′ 7¼″ × 4′ 6¼″. Louvre, Paris.

Venetian art is often described as poetic. In this painting, Giorgione so eloquently evoked the pastoral mood that the uncertainty about the picture's meaning is not distressing. The mood and rich color are enough.

1 ft.

22-36 GIORGIONE DA CASTELFRANCO, *The Tempest,* ca. 1510. Oil on canvas, 2′ 8¼″ × 2′ 4¾″. Galleria dell'Accademia, Venice.

The subject of this painting set in a lush landscape beneath a stormy sky has never been identified. The uncertainty contributes to the painting's enigmatic quality and intriguing air and may have been intentional.

1 ft.

Rome gravitated toward more intellectual themes—the epic of humanity, the masculine virtues, the grandeur of the ideal, and the lofty conceptions of religion involving the heroic and sublime. Much of the history of later Western art involves a dialogue between these two traditions.

Describing Venetian art as "poetic" is particularly appropriate, given the development of *poesia,* or painting meant to evoke moods in a manner similar to poetry. Both classical and Renaissance poetry inspired Venetian artists, and their paintings focused on the lyrical and sensual. Thus, in many Venetian artworks, discerning concrete narratives or subjects (in the traditional sense) is virtually impossible.

GIORGIONE The Venetian artist who deserves much of the credit for developing this poetic manner of painting was GIORGIONE DA CASTELFRANCO (ca. 1477–1510). Giorgione's so-called *Pastoral Symphony* (FIG. **22-35**; many scholars believe it is an early work of his student Titian) exemplifies poesia and surely inspired the late Arcadian scenes by Bellini, his teacher. Out of dense shadow emerge the soft forms of figures and landscape. Giorgione cast a mood of tranquil reverie and dreaminess over the entire scene, evoking the landscape of a lost but never-forgotten paradise. The theme is as enigmatic as the lighting. Two nude women, accompanied by two clothed young men, occupy the rich, abundant landscape through which a shepherd passes. In the distance, a villa crowns a hill. The artist so eloquently evoked the pastoral mood that the viewer does not find the uncertainty about the picture's precise meaning distressing. The mood is enough. The shepherd symbolizes the poet. The pipes and lute symbolize his poetry. The two women accompanying the young men may be thought of as their invisible inspiration, their muses. One turns to lift water from the sacred well of poetic inspiration. The voluptuous bodies of the women, softly modulated by the smoky shadow, became the standard in Venetian art. The fullness of their figures contributes to their effect as poetic personifications of nature's abundance. As a pastoral poet in the pictorial medium and one of the greatest masters in the handling of light and color, Giorgione praised the beauty of nature, music, women, and pleasure. Vasari reported that Giorgione was an accomplished lutenist and singer, and adjectives from poetry and music seem well suited for describing the pastoral air and muted chords of his painting.

The Tempest (FIG. **22-36**) displays this same interest in the poetic qualities of the natural landscape inhabited by humans. Dominating the scene is a lush landscape. Stormy skies and lightning in the middle background threaten the tranquility of the pastoral setting. Pushed off to both sides are the human figures—a young woman nursing a baby in the right foreground and a man carrying a *halberd* (a combination spear and battle-ax) on the left. Although the attribution of this work to Giorgione seems secure, much scholarly debate has centered on the painting's subject, fueled by the fact that X-rays of the canvas have revealed that a nude woman originally stood where Giorgione subsequently placed the man. This flexibility in subject has led many art historians to believe that Giorgione did not intend the painting to have a definitive narrative, which is appropriate for a Venetian poetic rendering. Other scholars have suggested mythological and biblical narratives. This uncertainty about the subject contributes to the painting's enigmatic quality and intriguing air.

TITIAN Giorgione's Arcadianism passed not only to his much older yet constantly inquisitive master, Bellini, but also to Tiziano Vecelli, called TITIAN (ca. 1490–1576) in English. Titian was a supreme colorist and the most extraordinary and prolific of the great Venetian painters. His remarkable coloristic sense and ability

22-37 TITIAN, *Assumption of the Virgin,* 1516–1518. Oil on wood, 22′ 7½″ × 11′ 10″. Santa Maria Gloriosa dei Frari, Venice.

Titian won renown for his ability to convey light through color. In this dramatic depiction of the Virgin Mary's ascent to Heaven, the golden clouds seem to glow and radiate light into the church.

to convey light through color emerge in a major altarpiece, *Assumption of the Virgin* (FIG. **22-37**), painted in oils for the main altar of Santa Maria Gloriosa dei Frari in Venice. Commissioned by the prior of this Franciscan basilica, the monumental altarpiece (close to 23 feet high) depicts the glorious ascent of the Virgin's body to Heaven on a great white cloud borne aloft by putti. Above, golden clouds, so luminous they seem to glow and radiate light into the church, envelop the Virgin. God the Father appears above, awaiting Mary with open arms. Below, apostles gesticulate wildly as they witness this momentous event. Through vibrant color, Titian infused the image with a drama and intensity that assured his lofty reputation, then and now.

22-38 TITIAN, *Madonna of the Pesaro Family,* 1519–1526. Oil on canvas, 15' 11" × 8' 10". Pesaro Chapel, Santa Maria dei Frari, Venice.

In this dynamic composition presaging a new kind of pictorial design, Titian placed the figures on a steep diagonal, positioning the Madonna, the focus of the composition, well off the central axis.

1 ft.

PESARO MADONNA Trained by both Bellini and Giorgione, Titian learned so well from them that even today scholars cannot concur about the degree of his participation in their later works. However, it is clear that Titian completed several of Bellini's and Giorgione's unfinished paintings, including the background of Bellini's *Feast of the Gods* (FIG. 22-34). On Bellini's death in 1516, the Republic of Venice appointed Titian its official painter. Shortly thereafter, Bishop Jacopo Pesaro commissioned him to paint *Madonna of the Pesaro Family* (FIG. 22-38) and presented it to the church of the Frari, which already housed Titian's *Assumption of the Virgin.* This new work, with its rich surface textures and dazzling display of color in all its nuances, furthered Titian's reputation and established his personal style.

Pesaro, bishop of Paphos in Cyprus and commander of the papal fleet, had led a successful expedition in 1502 against the Turks during the Venetian-Turkish war and commissioned this painting in gratitude. In a stately sunlit setting in what may be the Madonna's palace in Heaven, Mary receives the commander, who kneels dutifully at the foot of her throne. A soldier (Saint George?) behind the commander carries a banner with the *escutcheons* (shields with coats of arms) of the Borgia (Pope Alexander VI) and of Pesaro. Behind him is a turbaned Turk, a prisoner of war of the Christian forces. Saint Peter appears seated on the steps of the throne, and Saint Francis introduces other Pesaro family members (all male—Italian depictions of donors in this era typically excluded women and children), who kneel solemnly in the right foreground. Thus, Titian entwined the human and the heavenly, depicting the Madonna and saints honoring the achievements of a specific man in this particular world. A quite worldly transaction takes place (albeit beneath a heavenly cloud bearing angels) between a queen and her court and loyal servants. Titian constructed this tableau in terms of Renaissance protocol and courtly splendor.

A prime characteristic of High Renaissance painting is the massing of monumental figures, singly and in groups, within a weighty and majestic architecture. But here Titian did not compose a horizontal and symmetrical arrangement, as did Leonardo in *Last Supper* (FIG. 22-4) and Raphael in *School of Athens* (FIG. 22-9). Rather, he placed the figures on a steep diagonal, positioning the Madonna, the focus of the composition, well off the central axis. Titian drew attention to her with the perspective lines, the inclination of the figures, and the directional lines of gaze and gesture. The banner inclining toward the left beautifully brings the design into equilibrium, balancing the rightward and upward tendencies of its main direction. This kind of composition is more dynamic than most High Renaissance examples and presaged a new kind of pictorial design—one built on movement rather than repose.

BACCHUS AND ARIADNE In 1511 the duke of Ferrara, Alfonso d'Este (r. 1505–1534), asked Titian to produce a painting for his Camerino d'Alabastro (small room of alabaster). The patron had requested one bacchanalian scene each from Titian, Bellini, Raphael, and Fra Bartolommeo. Both Raphael and Fra Bartolommeo died before fulfilling the commission, and Bellini painted only one scene (FIG. 22-34), leaving Titian to produce three. One of these three paintings is *Meeting of Bacchus and Ariadne* (FIG. 22-39). Bacchus, accompanied by a boisterous and noisy group, arrives in a leopard-drawn chariot to save Ariadne, whom Theseus abandoned on the island of Naxos. In this scene, Titian revealed his debt to classical art. He derived one of the figures, entwined with snakes, from the recently unearthed *Laocoön* (FIG. 5-88), which also made an indelible impression on Michelangelo and many others. Titian's rich and luminous colors (see "Palma il Giovane on Titian," page 609) add greatly to the sensuous appeal of this painting, making it perfect for Alfonso's "pleasure chamber."

Palma il Giovane on Titian

An important change occurring in Titian's time was the almost universal adoption of canvas, with its rough-textured surface, in place of wood panels for paintings. Titian's works (FIGS. 22-38 to 22-41) established oil color on canvas as the typical medium of the Western pictorial tradition thereafter. One of Titian's students and collaborators was Jacopo Negretti, known as Palma il Giovane (ca. 1548–1628), or "Palma the Younger." He wrote a valuable account of his teacher's working methods and described how he used the new medium to great advantage:

> Titian [employed] a great mass of colors, which served . . . as a base for the compositions. . . . I too have seen some of these, formed with bold strokes made with brushes laden with colors, sometimes of a pure red earth, which he used, so to speak, for a middle tone, and at other times of white lead; and with the same brush tinted with red, black and yellow he formed a highlight; and observing these princi-

ples he made the promise of an exceptional figure appear in four brushstrokes. . . . Having constructed these precious foundations he used to turn his pictures to the wall and leave them there without looking at them, sometimes for several months. When he wanted to apply his brush again he would examine them with the utmost rigor . . . to see if he could find any faults. . . . In this way, working on the figures and revising them, he brought them to the most perfect symmetry that the beauty of art and nature can reveal. . . . [T]hus he gradually covered those quintessential forms with living flesh, bringing them by many stages to a state in which they lacked only the breath of life. He never painted a figure all at once and . . . in the last stages he painted more with his fingers than his brushes.*

* Quoted in Francesco Valcanover, "An Introduction to Titian," in Susanna Biadene and Mary Yakush, eds., *Titian: Prince of Painters* (Venice: Marsilio Editori, 1990), 23–24.

1 ft.

22-39 TITIAN, *Meeting of Bacchus and Ariadne,* from the Camerino d'Alabastro, Palazzo Ducale, Ferrara, Italy, 1522–1523. Oil on canvas, 5′ 9″ × 6′ 3″. National Gallery, London.

Titian's rich and luminous colors add greatly to the sensuous appeal of this mythological painting in which he based one of the figures on the recently unearthed ancient statue of *Laocoön* (FIG. 5-88).

22-40 TITIAN, *Venus of Urbino*, 1538. Oil on canvas, 3′ 11″ × 5′ 5″. Galleria degli Uffizi, Florence. ▮◀

Titian established oil-based pigments on canvas as the preferred painting medium in Western art. Here, he also set the standard for representations of the reclining female nude, whether divine or mortal.

VENUS OF URBINO In 1538, at the height of his powers, Titian painted the so-called *Venus of Urbino* (FIG. **22-40**) for Guidobaldo II, who became the duke of Urbino the following year (r. 1539–1574). The title (given to the painting later) elevates to the status of classical mythology what is actually a representation of an Italian woman in her bedchamber. Indeed, no evidence suggests that Guidobaldo intended the commission as anything more than a female nude for his private enjoyment—the embodiment of womanly beauty and of the qualities he sought in a bride. Whether the subject is divine or mortal, Titian based his version on an earlier (and pioneering) painting of Venus (not illustrated) by Giorgione. Here, Titian established the compositional elements and the standard for paintings of the reclining female nude, regardless of the many variations that ensued. This "Venus" reclines on the gentle slope of her luxurious pillowed couch, the linear play of the draperies contrasting with her body's sleek continuous volume. At her feet is a pendant (balancing) figure—in this case, a slumbering lapdog. Behind her, a simple drape both places her figure emphatically in the foreground and indicates a vista into the background at the right half of the picture. Two servants bend over a chest, apparently searching for garments (Renaissance households stored clothing in carved wooden chests called *cassoni*) to clothe "Venus." Beyond them, a smaller vista opens into a landscape. Titian masterfully constructed the view backward into space and the division of the space into progressively smaller units.

As in other Venetian paintings, color plays a prominent role in *Venus of Urbino*. The red tones of the matron's skirt and the muted reds of the tapestries against the neutral whites of the matron's sleeves and the kneeling girl's gown echo the deep Venetian reds set off against the pale neutral whites of the linen and the warm ivory gold of the flesh. The viewer must study the picture carefully to realize the subtlety of color planning. For instance, the two deep reds (in the foreground cushions and in the background skirt) play a critical role in the composition as a gauge of distance and as indicators of an implied diagonal opposed to the real one of the reclining figure. Here, Titian used color not simply to record surface appearance but also to organize his placement of forms.

ISABELLA D'ESTE Titian was also a highly esteemed portraitist and in great demand. More than 50 portraits by his hand survive. Among the best is *Isabella d'Este* (FIG. **22-41**), Titian's portrait of one of the most prominent women of the Renaissance (see "Women in the Renaissance Art World," page 611). Isabella was the daughter of the duke of Ferrara. At 16, she married Francesco Gonzaga, marquis of Mantua, and through her patronage of art and music, she was instrumental in developing the Mantuan court into an important cultural center. Portraits by Titian generally emphasize his psychological reading of the subject's head and hands. Thus, Titian sharply highlighted Isabella's face, whereas her black dress fades into the undefined darkness of the background. The unseen light source also illuminates Isabella's hands, and Titian painted her sleeves with incredible detail to further draw viewers' attention to her hands. This portrait reveals not only Titian's skill but the patron's wish as well. Painted when Isabella was 60 years old, at her request it depicts her in her 20s. Titian used an earlier portrait of her as his guide, but his portrait is no copy. Rather, it is a distinctive portrayal of his poised and self-assured patron that owes little to its model.

Women in the Renaissance Art World

The Renaissance art world was decidedly male-dominated. Few women could become professional artists because of the obstacles they faced. In particular, for centuries, art-training practices mandating residence at a master's house (see "Artists' Guilds," Chapter 19, page 506) precluded women from acquiring the necessary experience. In addition, social proscriptions, such as those preventing women from drawing from nude models, further hampered an aspiring female artist's advancement through the accepted avenues of artistic training.

Still, there were determined women who surmounted these barriers and were able to develop not only considerable bodies of work but enviable reputations as well. One was Sofonisba Anguissola (FIG. 22-46), who was so accomplished that she can be considered the first Italian woman to have ascended to the level of international art celebrity. Lavinia Fontana (1552–1614) also achieved notable success, and her paintings constitute the largest surviving body of work by any woman artist before 1700. Fontana learned her craft from her father, a leading Bolognese painter. (Paternal training was the norm for aspiring women artists.) She was in demand as a portraitist and received commissions from important patrons, including members of the dominant Habsburg family. She even spent time as an official painter to the papal court in Rome.

22-41A FONTANA, Portrait of a Noblewoman, 1580.

Perhaps more challenging for women than the road to becoming a professional painter was the mastery of sculpture, made more difficult by the physical demands of the medium. Yet Properzia de' Rossi (ca. 1490–1530) established herself as a professional sculptor and was the only woman artist that Giorgio Vasari included in his comprehensive publication, *Lives of the Most Eminent Painters, Sculptors, and Architects*. Active in the early 16th century, she died of the plague in 1530, bringing her promising career to an early end.

Beyond the realm of art production, Renaissance women had a significant impact as art patrons. Scholars only recently have begun to explore systematically the role of women as patrons. As a result, current knowledge is sketchy at best but suggests that women played a much more extensive role than previously acknowledged. Among the problems researchers face in their quest to clarify women's participation as patrons is that women often wielded their influence and decision-making power behind the scenes. Many of them acquired their positions through marriage. Their power was thus indirect and provisional, based on their husbands' wealth and status. Thus, documentation of the networks within which women patrons operated and of the processes they used to exert power in a male-dominated society is less substantive than that available for male patrons.

One of the most important Renaissance patrons, male or female, was Isabella d'Este (1474–1539), marchioness of Mantua. Brought up in the cultured princely court of Ferrara (southwest of Venice), Isabella married Francesco Gonzaga (1466–1519), marquis of Mantua, in 1490. The marriage gave Isabella access to the position and wealth necessary to pursue her interest in becoming a major art patron. An avid collector, she enlisted the aid of agents who scoured Italy for appealing objects. Isabella did not limit her collection to painting and sculpture but included ceramics, glassware, gems, cameos, medals, classical texts, musical manuscripts, and musical instruments.

Isabella was undoubtedly a proud and ambitious woman well aware of how art could boost her fame and reputation. Accordingly, she commissioned several portraits of herself from the most esteemed artists of her day—Leonardo da Vinci, Andrea Mantegna, and Titian

1 in.

22-41 TITIAN, *Isabella d'Este*, 1534–1536. Oil on canvas, 3' 4$\frac{1}{8}$" × 2' 1$\frac{3}{16}$". Kunsthistorisches Museum, Vienna.

Isabella d'Este was one of the most powerful women of the Renaissance era. When, at age 60, she commissioned Titian to paint her portrait, she insisted that the artist depict her in her 20s.

(FIG. 22-41). The detail and complexity of many of her contracts with artists reveal her insistence on control over the artworks.

Other Renaissance women positioned themselves as serious art patrons. One was Caterina Sforza (1462–1509), daughter of Galeazzo Maria Sforza (heir to the duchy of Milan), who married Girolamo Riario in 1484. The death in 1488 of her husband, lord of Imola and count of Forlì, gave Caterina Sforza access to power denied most women. Another female art patron was Lucrezia Tornabuoni (married to Piero di Cosimo de' Medici), one of many Medici, both men and women, who earned reputations as unparalleled art patrons. Further archival investigation of women's roles in Renaissance Italy undoubtedly will produce more evidence of how women established themselves as patrons and artists and the extent to which they contributed to the flourishing of Renaissance art.

22-42 JACOPO DA PONTORMO, *Entombment of Christ*, Capponi Chapel, Santa Felicità, Florence, Italy, 1525–1528. Oil on wood, 10′ 3″ × 6′ 4″.

Mannerist paintings such as this one represent a departure from the compositions of the earlier Renaissance. Instead of concentrating masses in the center of the painting, Pontormo left a void.

MANNERISM

The Renaissance style of Rome, Florence, and Venice dominated Italian painting, sculpture, and architecture for most of the 16th century, but already in the 1520s another style—Mannerism—emerged in reaction to it. *Mannerism* is a term derived from the Italian word *maniera,* meaning "style" or "manner." In the field of art history, the term *style* usually refers to a characteristic or representative mode, especially of an artist or period (for example, Leonardo's style or Gothic style). Style also can refer to an absolute quality of fashion (for example, someone has "style"). Mannerism's style (or representative mode) is characterized by style (being stylish, cultured, elegant).

Painting

Among the features most closely associated with Mannerism is artifice. Of course, all art involves artifice, in the sense that art is not

22-43 PARMIGIANINO, *Madonna with the Long Neck,* from the Baiardi Chapel, Santa Maria dei Servi, Parma, Italy, 1534–1540. Oil on wood, 7′ 1″ × 4′ 4″. Galleria degli Uffizi, Florence.

Parmigianino's Madonna displays the stylish elegance that was a principal aim of Mannerism. Mary has a small oval head, a long slender neck, attenuated hands, and a sinuous body.

"natural"—it is a representation of a scene or idea. But many artists, including High Renaissance painters such as Leonardo and Raphael, chose to conceal that artifice by using such devices as perspective and shading to make their art look natural. In contrast, Mannerist painters consciously revealed the constructed nature of their art. In other words, Renaissance artists generally strove to create art that appeared natural, whereas Mannerist artists were less inclined to disguise the contrived nature of art production. This is why artifice is a central feature of discussions about Mannerism, and why Mannerist works can seem, appropriately, "mannered." The conscious display of artifice in Mannerism often reveals itself in imbalanced compositions and unusual complexities, both visual and conceptual. Ambiguous space, departures from expected conventions, and unique presentations of traditional themes also surface frequently in Mannerist art.

PONTORMO *Entombment of Christ* (FIG. 22-42) by JACOPO DA PONTORMO (1494–1557) exhibits almost all the stylistic features char-

22-44 BRONZINO, *Venus, Cupid, Folly, and Time*, ca. 1546. Oil on wood, 5′ 1″ × 4′ 8¼″. National Gallery, London.

In this painting of Cupid fondling his mother Venus, Bronzino demonstrated a fondness for learned allegories with lascivious undertones. As in many Mannerist paintings, the meaning here is ambiguous.

1 ft.

tions (for example, the torso of the foreground figure bends in an anatomically impossible way), elastic elongation of the limbs, and heads rendered as uniformly small and oval. The contrasting colors, primarily light blues and pinks, add to the dynamism and complexity of the work. The painting represents a departure from the balanced, harmoniously structured compositions of the High Renaissance.

PARMIGIANINO Girolamo Francesco Maria Mazzola of Parma, known as PARMIGIANINO (1503–1540), achieved in his best-known work, *Madonna with the Long Neck* (FIG. **22-43**), the elegant stylishness that was a principal aim of Mannerism. In Parmigianino's hands, this traditional, usually sedate, religious subject became a picture of exquisite grace and precious sweetness. The Madonna's small oval head, her long and slender neck, the otherworldly attenuation and delicacy of her hand, and the sinuous, swaying elongation of her frame—all are marks of the aristocratic, sumptuously courtly taste of a later phase of Mannerism. Parmigianino amplified this elegance by expanding the Madonna's form as viewed from head to toe. On the left stands a bevy of angelic creatures, melting with emotions as soft and smooth as their limbs. On the right, the artist included a line of columns without capitals and an enigmatic figure with a scroll, whose distance from the foreground is immeasurable and ambiguous—the antithesis of rational Renaissance perspectival diminution of size with distance.

22-43A PARMIGIANINO, *Self-Portrait in a Convex Mirror*, 1524.

Although the elegance and sophisticated beauty of the painting are due in large part to the Madonna's attenuated limbs, that exaggeration is not solely decorative in purpose. *Madonna with the Long Neck* takes its subject from a simile in medieval hymns that compared the Virgin's neck to a great ivory tower or column, such as that which Parmigianino depicted to the right of the Madonna. Thus, the work contains religious meaning in addition to the power derived from its beauty alone.

42A BECCA-
*I, Fall of the
bel Angels,*
1524.

acteristic of Mannerism's early phase in painting. Christ's descent from the cross and subsequent entombment had frequently been depicted in art (see "The Life of Jesus in Art," Chapter 11, pages 296–297, or pages xxvi–xxvii in Volume II), and Pontormo exploited the familiarity that 16th-century viewers would have had by playing off their expectations. For example, he omitted from the painting both the cross and Christ's tomb, so that scholars continue to debate whether he meant to represent the *Descent from the Cross* or the *Entombment*. And instead of presenting the action as occurring across the perpendicular picture plane, as artists such as Raphael and Rogier van der Weyden (FIG. **20-8**) had done in their paintings of these episodes from Christ's Passion, Pontormo rotated the conventional figural groups along a vertical axis. As a result, the Virgin Mary falls back (away from the viewer) as she releases her dead son's hand. Unlike High Renaissance artists, who had concentrated their masses in the center of the painting, Pontormo left a void. This emptiness accentuates the grouping of hands that fill that hole, calling attention to the void—symbolic of loss and grief. The artist enhanced the painting's ambiguity with the curiously anxious glances the figures cast in all directions. (The bearded young man at the upper right who looks out at the viewer is probably a self-portrait of Pontormo.) Athletic bending and twisting characterize many of the figures, with distor-

BRONZINO *Venus, Cupid, Folly, and Time* (FIG. **22-44**), by Agnolo di Cosimo, called BRONZINO (1503–1572), also displays all the chief features of Mannerist painting. A pupil of Pontormo, Bronzino was a Florentine and painter to the first grand duke of Tuscany, Cosimo I de' Medici (r. 1537–1574). In this painting, which Cosimo I commissioned as a gift for King Francis I of France,

22-45 Bronzino, *Portrait of a Young Man*, ca. 1530–1545. Oil on wood, 3′ 1½″ × 2′ 5½″. Metropolitan Museum of Art, New York (H. O. Havemeyer Collection, bequest of Mrs. H. O. Havemeyer, 1929).

This depiction of a young intellectual with a calculated attitude of nonchalance is typical of Mannerist portraiture. Bronzino recorded the rank and station but not the personality of his subject.

Bronzino demonstrated the Mannerists' fondness for learned allegories that often had lascivious undertones, a shift from the simple and monumental statements and forms of the High Renaissance. Bronzino depicted Cupid fondling his mother Venus, while Folly prepares to shower them with rose petals. Time, who appears in the upper right corner, draws back the curtain to reveal the playful incest in progress. Other figures in the painting represent other human qualities and emotions, including Envy. The masks, a favorite device of the Mannerists, symbolize deceit. The picture seems to suggest that love—accompanied by envy and plagued by inconstancy—is foolish and that lovers will discover its folly in time. But as in many Mannerist paintings, the meaning here is ambiguous, and interpretations of the painting vary. Compositionally, Bronzino placed the figures around the front plane, and they almost entirely block the space. The contours are strong and sculptural, the surfaces of enamel smoothness. Of special interest are the heads, hands, and feet, for the Mannerists considered the extremities the carriers of grace, and the clever depiction of them as evidence of artistic skill.

22-45A Bronzino, *Eleanora of Toledo and Giovanni de' Medici*, ca. 1546.

Mannerist painters most often achieved in portraiture the sophisticated elegance they sought. Bronzino's *Portrait of a Young Man* (FIG. **22-45**) exemplifies Mannerist portraiture. The subject is a

22-46

Sofonisba Anguissola, *Portrait of the Artist's Sisters and Brother*, ca. 1555. Oil on panel, 2′ 5¼″ × 3′ 1½″. Methuen Collection, Corsham Court, Wiltshire.

Anguissola was the leading female artist of her time. Her contemporaries greatly admired her use of relaxed poses and expressions in intimate and informal group portraits like this one of her own family.

22-47 TINTORETTO, *Last Supper*, 1594. Oil on canvas, 12′ × 18′ 8″. San Giorgio Maggiore, Venice. ◼◀

Tintoretto adopted many Mannerist pictorial devices to produce oil paintings imbued with emotional power, depth of spiritual vision, glowing Venetian color schemes, and dramatic lighting.

1 ft.

proud youth—a man of books and intellectual society, rather than a merchant or lowly laborer. His cool demeanor seems carefully affected, a calculated attitude of nonchalance. This staid and reserved formality is a standard component of Mannerist portraits. It asserts the rank and station but not the personality of the subject. In Bronzino's portrait, the haughty poise, the graceful long-fingered hands, the book, the carved faces of the furniture, and the severe architecture all suggest the traits and environment of the highbred, disdainful patrician. The somber black of the young man's Spanish doublet and cap and the room's slightly acid, olive-green walls make for a deeply restrained color scheme. Bronzino created a muted background for the man's sharply defined, asymmetrical silhouette that contradicts his impassive pose.

SOFONISBA ANGUISSOLA The aloof formality of Bronzino's portrait is much relaxed in the portraiture of SOFONISBA ANGUIS-SOLA (ca. 1532–1625). A northern Italian from Cremona, Anguissola introduced a new kind of group portrait of irresistible charm, characterized by an informal intimacy and subjects that are often moving, conversing, or engaged in activities. Like many of the other works she did before moving to Spain in 1559, the portrait illustrated here (FIG. **22-46**) represents members of her family. Against a neutral ground, Anguissola placed her two sisters and brother in an affectionate pose meant not for official display but for private showing. The sisters, wearing matching striped gowns, flank their brother, who caresses a lapdog. The older sister (at the left) summons the dignity required

for the occasion, while the boy looks quizzically at the portraitist with an expression of naive curiosity, and the other girl diverts her attention toward something or someone to the painter's left.

Anguissola's use of relaxed poses and expressions, her sympathetic personal presentation, and her graceful treatment of the forms did not escape the attention of her contemporaries, who praised her highly (see "Women in the Renaissance Art World," page 611). Her recognized talents allowed her to consort with esteemed individuals. She knew and learned from the aged Michelangelo, was court painter to Philip II (r. 1556–1598) of Spain, and, at the end of her life, gave advice on art to a young admirer of her work, Anthony Van Dyck, the great Flemish master (see Chapter 25).

TINTORETTO Venetian painting of the later 16th century built on established High Renaissance ideas but incorporated many elements of the Mannerist style. Jacopo Robusti, known as TINTORETTO (1518–1594), claimed to be a student of Titian and aspired to combine Titian's color with Michelangelo's drawing, but art historians consider Tintoretto the outstanding Venetian representative of Mannerism. He adopted many Mannerist pictorial devices, which he employed to produce works imbued with dramatic power, depth of spiritual vision, and glowing Venetian color schemes.

Toward the end of Tintoretto's life, his art became spiritual, even visionary, as solid forms melted away into swirling clouds of dark shot through with fitful light. In Tintoretto's *Last Supper* (FIG. **22-47**), painted for the right wall next to the high altar in Andrea Palladio's

22-48 Paolo Veronese, *Christ in the House of Levi,* from the refectory of Santi Giovanni e Paolo, Venice, Italy, 1573. Oil on canvas, 18′ 3″ × 42′. Galleria dell'Accademia, Venice.

Veronese's paintings feature superb color and majestic classical settings. The Catholic Church accused him of impiety for including dogs and dwarfs near Christ in this work originally titled *Last Supper.*

church of San Giorgio Maggiore (FIG. 22-32), the figures appear in a dark interior illuminated by a single light in the upper left of the image. The shimmering halos establish the biblical nature of the scene. The ability of this dramatic scene to engage viewers was well in keeping with Counter-Reformation ideals (see "Religious Art in Counter-Reformation Italy," page 596) and the Catholic Church's belief in the didactic nature of religious art.

Last Supper incorporates many Mannerist elements, including an imbalanced composition and visual complexity. In terms of design, the contrast with Leonardo's *Last Supper* (FIG. 22-4) is both extreme and instructive. Leonardo's composition, balanced and symmetrical, parallels the picture plane in a geometrically organized and closed space. The figure of Christ is the tranquil center of the drama and the perspectival focus. In Tintoretto's painting, Christ is above and beyond the converging perspective lines that race diagonally away from the picture surface, creating disturbing effects of limitless depth and motion. The viewer locates Tintoretto's Christ via the light flaring, beaconlike, out of darkness. The contrast of the two works reflects the direction Renaissance painting took in the 16th century, as it moved away from architectonic clarity of space and neutral lighting toward the dynamic perspectives and dramatic chiaroscuro of the coming Baroque.

VERONESE Among the great Venetian masters was Paolo Caliari of Verona, called Paolo Veronese (1528–1588). Whereas Tintoretto gloried in monumental drama and deep perspectives, Veronese specialized in splendid pageantry painted in superb color and set within majestic classical architecture. Like Tintoretto, Veronese painted on a huge scale and often produced canvases as large as 20 by 30 feet or more for the refectories of wealthy monasteries. He painted *Christ in*

the House of Levi (FIG. 22-48), originally called *Last Supper,* for the dining hall of Santi Giovanni e Paolo in Venice. In a great open loggia framed by three monumental arches, Christ sits at the center of the splendidly garbed elite of Venice. In the foreground, with a courtly gesture, the very image of gracious grandeur, the chief steward welcomes guests. Robed lords, their colorful retainers, dogs, and dwarfs crowd into the spacious loggia. Painted during the Counter-Reformation, this depiction prompted criticism from the Catholic Church. The Holy Office of the Inquisition accused Veronese of impiety for painting such creatures so close to the Lord, and it ordered him to make changes at his own expense. Reluctant to do so, he simply changed the painting's title, converting the subject to a less solemn one. As Palladio looked to the example of classically inspired High Renaissance architecture, so Veronese returned to High Renaissance composition, its symmetrical balance, and its ordered architectonics. His shimmering colors span the whole spectrum, although he avoided solid colors for half shades (light blues, sea greens, lemon yellows, roses, and violets), creating veritable flower beds of tone.

The Venetian Republic employed both Tintoretto and Veronese to decorate the grand chambers and council rooms of the Doge's Palace (FIG. 19-21). A great and popular decorator, Veronese revealed himself a master of imposing illusionistic ceiling compositions, such as *Triumph of Venice* (FIG. 22-49). Here, within an oval frame, he presented Venice, crowned by Fame, enthroned between two great twisted columns in a balustraded loggia, garlanded with clouds, and attended by figures symbolic of its glories. Unlike Mantegna's *di sotto in sù* (FIG. 21-48) perspective, Veronese's projection is not directly up from below but at a 45-degree angle to spectators, a technique many later Baroque decorators used (see Chapter 24).

1 ft.

22-49 PAOLO VERONESE, *Triumph of Venice,* ca. 1585. Oil on canvas, 29' 8" × 19'. Ceiling of the Hall of the Grand Council, Doge's Palace, Venice.

Within an immense oval frame, Veronese presented an illusionistic tableau of Venice crowned by Fame amid columns, clouds, and personifications. Baroque painters adopted this 45-degree view from the ground.

22-50 CORREGGIO, *Assumption of the Virgin*, 1526–1530. Fresco, 35′ 10″ × 37′ 11″. Parma Cathedral, Parma.

Working long before Veronese, Correggio, the teacher of Parmigianino, won little fame in his day, but his illusionistic ceiling designs, like this one in Parma Cathedral, inspired many 17th-century painters.

10 ft.

CORREGGIO One painter who developed a unique personal style that is almost impossible to classify was Antonio Allegri, known as CORREGGIO (ca. 1489–1534) from his birthplace, near Parma. The teacher of Parmigianino, Correggio, working more than a half century before Veronese, pulled together many stylistic trends, including those of Leonardo, Raphael, and the Venetians. Correggio's most enduring artistic contribution was his development of illusionistic ceiling perspectives. In Parma Cathedral, he painted away the entire dome with his *Assumption of the Virgin* (FIG. 22-50). Opening up the *cupola*, Correggio showed worshipers a view of the sky, with concentric rings of clouds where hundreds of soaring figures perform a wildly pirouetting dance in celebration of the Assumption. Versions of these angelic creatures became permanent tenants of numerous Baroque churches in later centuries. Correggio was also an influential painter of religious panels, anticipating in them many other Baroque compositional devices. Correggio's contemporaries expressed little appreciation for his art. Later, during the 17th century, Baroque painters recognized him as a kindred spirit.

Sculpture

Mannerism extended beyond painting. Artists translated its principles into sculpture and architecture as well.

22-51A CELLINI, *Genius of Fontainebleau*, 1542–1543.

BENVENUTO CELLINI Among those who made their mark as Mannerist sculptors was BENVENUTO CELLINI (1500–1571), the author of a fascinating autobiography. It is difficult to imagine a medieval artist composing an autobiography. Only in the Renaissance, with the birth of the notion of individual artistic genius, could a work such as Cellini's (or Vasari's *Lives*) have been conceived and written. Cellini's literary self-portrait presents him not only as a highly accomplished artist, but also as a statesman, soldier, and lover, among many other roles. He was, first of all, a goldsmith, but only one of his major

works in that medium survives, the saltcellar (FIG. 22-51) he made for Francis I (FIG. 23-10), who had hired Cellini with a retainer of an annual salary, supplemented by fees for the works he produced. The price paid for this luxurious gold-and-*enamel* item destined for the French royal table was almost 50 percent greater than Cellini's salary for the year. Neptune and Tellus (or, as Cellini named them, the Sea—the source of salt—and the Land) recline atop an ebony base decorated with relief figures of Dawn, Day, Twilight, Night, and the four winds—some based on Michelangelo's statues in the Medici Chapel (FIG. 22-17) in San Lorenzo. The boat next to Neptune's right leg contained the salt, and the triumphal arch (compare FIG. 10-75) next to the right leg of the earth goddess, the pepper. The elongated proportions of the figures, especially the slim, small-breasted figure of Tellus, whom ancient artists always represented as a matronly woman (FIG. 10-30), reveal Cellini's Mannerist approach to form.

GIOVANNI DA BOLOGNA The lure of Italy drew a brilliant young Flemish sculptor, Jean de Boulogne, to Italy, where he practiced his art under the equivalent Italian name of GIOVANNI DA BOLOGNA (1529–1608). Giovanni's *Abduction of the Sabine Women*

Famed as a master goldsmith, Cellini fashioned this costly saltcellar for the table of Francis I of France. The elongated proportions of the figures clearly reveal Cellini's Mannerist approach to form.

1 in.

(FIG. **22-52**) exemplifies Mannerist principles of figure composition. Drawn from the legendary history of early Rome, the group received its present title—relating how the Romans abducted wives for themselves from the neighboring Sabines—only after its exhibition. Earlier, it was *Paris Abducting Helen,* among other mythological titles. In fact, Giovanni had no interest in depicting any particular subject. He created the group as a demonstration piece. His goal was to achieve a dynamic spiral figural composition involving an old man, a young man, and a woman, all nude in the tradition of ancient statues portraying mythological figures. Although Giovanni would have known Antonio Pollaiuolo's *Hercules and Antaeus* (FIG. **21-14**), whose Greek hero lifts his opponent off the ground, he turned directly to ancient sculpture for inspiration. *Abduction of the Sabine Women* includes references to *Laocoön* (FIG. **5-88**)—once in the crouching old man and again in the woman's up-flung arm. The three bodies interlock on a vertical axis, creating an ascending spiral movement.

To appreciate the sculpture fully, the viewer must walk around it, because the work changes radically according to the viewing point. One factor contributing to the shifting imagery is the prominence of open spaces that pass through the masses (for example, the space between an arm and a body), giving the spaces an effect equal to that of the solids. This sculpture was the first large-scale group since classical antiquity designed to be seen from multiple viewpoints, in striking contrast to Pollaiuolo's group, which the artist intended to be seen from the angle shown in FIG. **21-14**. Giovanni's figures do not break out of this spiral vortex but remain as if contained within a cylinder. Nonetheless, they display athletic flexibility and Michelangelesque potential for action.

22-52 Giovanni da Bologna, *Abduction of the Sabine Women,* Loggia dei Lanzi, Piazza della Signoria, Florence, Italy, 1579–1583. Marble, 13' $5\frac{1}{2}''$ high.

This sculpture was the first large-scale group since classical antiquity designed to be seen from multiple viewpoints. The three bodies interlock to create a vertical spiral movement.

1 ft.

22-53 GIULIO ROMANO, interior courtyard facade of the Palazzo del Tè, Mantua, Italy, 1525–1535.

The Mannerist divergences from architectural convention, for example, the slipping triglyphs, are so pronounced in the Palazzo del Tè that they constitute a parody of Bramante's classical style.

Architecture

Mannerist architects used classical architectural elements in a highly personal and unorthodox manner, rejecting the balance, order, and stability that were the hallmarks of the High Renaissance style with the specific aim of revealing the contrived nature of architectural design.

22-53A GIULIO ROMANO, *Fall of the Giants*, 1530–1532.

GIULIO ROMANO Applying that anticlassical principle was the goal of GIULIO ROMANO (ca. 1499–1546) when he designed the Palazzo del Tè (FIG. **22-53**) in Mantua and, with it, formulated almost the entire architectural vocabulary of Mannerism. Giulio became Raphael's chief assistant in decorating the Vatican stanze. After Raphael's premature death in 1520, Giulio served as his master's artistic executor, completing Raphael's unfinished frescoes and panel paintings. In 1524, he went to Mantua, where he found a patron in Duke Federigo Gonzaga (r. 1530–1540), for whom Giulio built and decorated the Palazzo del Tè between 1525 and 1535. Gonzaga intended the Palazzo del Tè to serve as both suburban summer palace and stud farm for the duke's famous stables. Originally planned as a relatively modest country villa, Giulio's building so pleased his patron that Gonzaga soon commissioned the architect to enlarge the structure. In a second building campaign, Giulio expanded the villa to a palatial scale by adding three wings, which he placed around a square central court. This once-paved court, which functions both as a passage and as the focal point of the design, has a nearly urban character. Its surrounding buildings form a self-enclosed unit with a large garden, flanked by a stable, attached to it on the east side.

Giulio exhibited his Mannerist style in the facades that face the palace's interior courtyard (FIG. **22-53**), where the divergences from architectural convention are quite pronounced. Indeed, they consti-

tute an enormous parody of Bramante's classical style, thereby announcing the artifice of the palace design. In a building laden with structural surprises and contradictions, the design of these facades is the most unconventional of all. The *keystones* (central *voussoirs*), for example, either have not fully settled or seem to be slipping from the arches—and, more eccentric still, Giulio even placed voussoirs in the pediments over the rectangular niches, where no arches exist. The massive Tuscan columns that flank these niches carry incongruously narrow *architraves*. That these architraves break midway between the columns stresses their apparent structural insufficiency, and they seem unable to support the weight of the *triglyphs* of the *Doric frieze* above (see "Doric and Ionic Orders," Chapter 5, page 110, or page xxviii in Volume II), which threaten to crash down on the head of anyone foolish enough to stand below them. To be sure, appreciating Giulio's witticism requires a highly sophisticated audience, and recognizing some quite subtle departures from the norm presupposes a thorough familiarity with the established rules of classical architecture. It speaks well for the duke's sophistication that he accepted Giulio's form of architectural inventiveness.

LAURENTIAN LIBRARY Although he personifies the High Renaissance artist, Michelangelo, like Giulio Romano, also experimented with architectural designs that flouted most of the classical rules of order and stability. Michelangelo's restless genius is on display in the vestibule (FIG. **22-54**) he designed for the Medici library adjoining the Florentine church of San Lorenzo. The Laurentian Library had two contrasting spaces that Michelangelo had to unite: the long horizontal of the library proper and the vertical of the vestibule. The need to place the vestibule windows up high (at the level of

NORTHERN EUROPE AND SPAIN, 1500 TO 1600

The dissolution of the Burgundian Netherlands in 1477 led in the early 16th century to a realignment in the European geopolitical landscape (MAP 23-1). France and the Holy Roman Empire absorbed the former Burgundian territories and increased their power. But by the end of the century, through calculated marriages, military exploits, and ambitious territorial expansion, Spain was the dominant European state. Throughout the continent, monarchs gained additional prestige and cultivated a stronger sense of cultural and political unity among their subjects, thereby laying the foundation for today's European nations. Yet a momentous crisis in the Christian Church overshadowed these power shifts. Concerted attempts to reform the Church led to the Reformation and the establishment of Protestantism (as distinct from Catholicism), which in turn prompted the Catholic Church's response, the Counter-Reformation (see Chapter 22). Ultimately, the Reformation split Christendom in half and produced a hundred years of civil war between Protestants and Catholics.

Despite the tumultuous religious conflict engulfing 16th-century Europe, the exchange of intellectual and artistic ideas continued to thrive. Catholic Italy and the (mostly) Protestant Holy Roman Empire shared in a lively commerce—economic and cultural—and 16th-century art throughout Europe was a major beneficiary of that exchange. Humanism filtered up from Italy and spread throughout Northern Europe. Northern humanists, like their southern counterparts, cultivated a knowledge of classical cultures and literature. Because they focused more on reconciling humanism with Christianity, later scholars applied the general label "Christian humanists" to describe them.

Among the most influential Christian humanists were the Dutch-born Desiderius Erasmus (1466–1536) and the Englishman Thomas More (1478–1535). Erasmus demonstrated his interest in both Italian humanism and religion with his "philosophy of Christ," emphasizing education and scriptural knowledge. Both an ordained priest and avid scholar, Erasmus published his most famous essay, *The Praise of Folly*, in 1509. In this widely read work, he satirized not just the Church but various social classes as well. His ideas were to play an important role in the development of the Reformation, but he consistently declined to join any of the Reformation sects. Equally well educated was Thomas More, who served King Henry VIII (r. 1509–1547). Henry eventually ordered More executed because of his

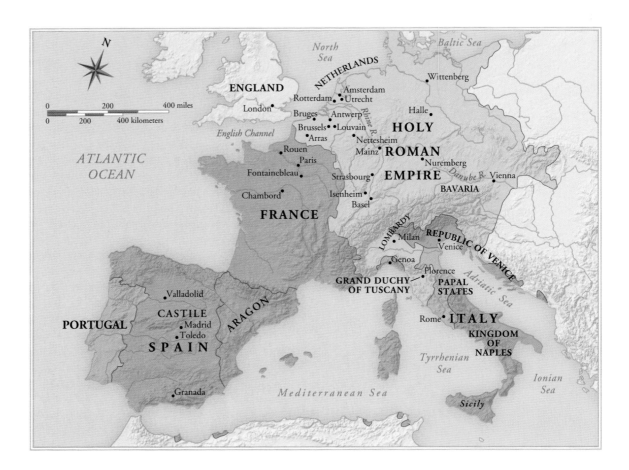

MAP 23-1 Europe in the early 16th century.

opposition to England's break with the Catholic Church. In France, François Rabelais (ca. 1494–1553), a former monk who advocated rejecting stagnant religious dogmatism, disseminated the humanist spirit.

The turmoil emerging during the 16th century lasted well into the 17th century and permanently affected the face of Europe. The concerted challenges to established authority and the persistent philosophical inquiry eventually led to the rise of new political systems (for example, the nation-state) and new economic systems (such as capitalism).

HOLY ROMAN EMPIRE

Although at the opening of the 16th century many in the Holy Roman Empire were expressing dissatisfaction with the Church in Rome, Martin Luther had not yet posted the *Ninety-five Theses* that launched the Protestant Reformation. The Catholic clergy in Germany still offered artists important commissions to adorn churches and other religious institutions.

MATTHIAS GRÜNEWALD Matthias Neithardt, known conventionally as MATTHIAS GRÜNEWALD (ca. 1480–1528), worked for the archbishops of Mainz from 1511 on in several capacities, from court painter and decorator to architect, hydraulic engineer, and superintendent of works. Grünewald eventually moved to northern Germany, where he settled at Halle in Saxony. Around 1510, he began work on the *Isenheim Altarpiece* (FIG. **23-2**), a complex and fascinating monument that reflects Catholic beliefs and incorporates several references to Catholic doctrines, such as the lamb (symbol of the Son of God), whose wound spurts blood into a chalice in the *Crucifixion* scene (FIG. 23-2, *top*) on the exterior of the altarpiece.

Created for the monastic hospital order Saint Anthony of Isenheim, the *Isenheim Altarpiece* consists of a wooden shrine (carved by

NIKOLAUS HAGENAUER in 1490) that includes gilded and polychromed statues of Saints Anthony Abbot, Augustine, and Jerome (FIG. **23-2**, *bottom*) in addition to Grünewald's two pairs of movable wings that open at the center. Hinged together at the sides, one pair stands directly behind the other. Grünewald painted the exterior panels of the first pair (visible when the altarpiece is closed, FIG. **23-2**, *top*) between 1510 and 1515: *Crucifixion* in the center, *Saint Sebastian* on the left, *Saint Anthony* on the right, and *Lamentation* in the predella. When these exterior wings are open, four additional scenes (not illustrated)—*Annunciation, Angelic Concert, Madonna and Child*, and *Resurrection*—appear. Opening this second pair of wings exposes Hagenauer's interior shrine, flanked by Grünewald's panels depicting *Meeting of Saints Anthony and Paul* and *Temptation of Saint Anthony* (FIG. **23-2**, *bottom*).

The placement of this altarpiece in the choir of a church adjacent to the monastery hospital dictated much of the imagery. Saints associated with the plague and other diseases and with miraculous cures, such as Saints Anthony and Sebastian, appear prominently in the *Isenheim Altarpiece*. Grünewald's panels specifically address the themes of dire illness and miraculous healing and accordingly emphasize the suffering of the order's patron saint, Anthony. The painted images served as warnings, encouraging increased devotion from monks and hospital patients. They also functioned therapeutically by offering some hope to the afflicted. Indeed, Saint Anthony's legend encompassed his role as both vengeful dispenser of justice (by inflicting disease) and benevolent healer. Grünewald brilliantly used color to enhance the impact of the altarpiece. He intensified the contrast of horror and hope by playing subtle tones and soft harmonies against shocking dissonance of color.

One of the most memorable scenes is *Temptation of Saint Anthony* (FIG. **23-2**, *bottom right*). It is a terrifying image of the five temptations, depicted as an assortment of ghoulish and bestial creatures in a dark landscape, attacking the saint. In the foreground, Grünewald

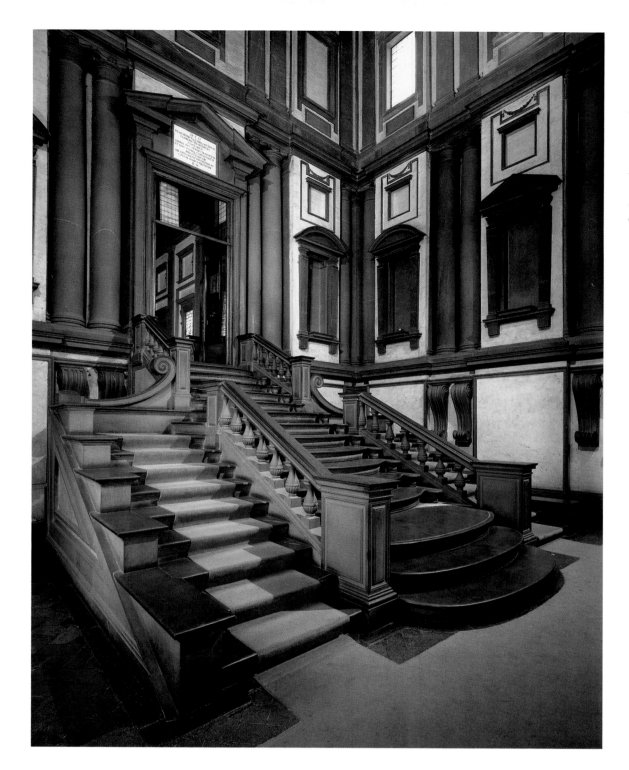

22-54 MICHELANGELO BUONARROTI, vestibule of the Laurentian Library, Florence, Italy, 1524–1534; staircase, 1558–1559.

With his customary independence of spirit, Michelangelo, working in a Mannerist mode in the vestibule of the Laurentian Library, disposed willfully of almost all the rules of classical architecture.

the reading room) determined the narrow verticality of the vestibule's elevation and proportions. Much taller than it is wide, the vestibule gives the impression of a vertically compressed, shaftlike space. Anyone schooled exclusively in the classical architecture of Bramante and the High Renaissance would have been appalled by Michelangelo's indifference here to classical norms in the use of the orders and in proportion. He used columns in pairs and sank them into the walls, where they perform no supporting function. He also split columns in halves around corners. Elsewhere, he placed scroll corbels on the walls beneath columns. They seem to hang from the moldings, holding up nothing. He arbitrarily broke through pediments as well as through cornices and stringcourses. He sculpted pilasters that taper downward instead of upward. In short, the High Renaissance master, working in a Mannerist mode, disposed willfully and abruptly of classical architecture. Moreover, in the vast, flowing stairway (the latest element of the vestibule) that protrudes tonguelike into the room from the "mouth" of the doorway to the library, Michelangelo foreshadowed the dramatic movement of Baroque architecture (see Chapter 24). With his customary trailblazing independence of spirit, Michelangelo created an interior space that conveyed all the strains and tensions found in his statuary and in his painted figures. Michelangelo's art began in the style of the 15th century, developed into the epitome of High Renaissance art, and, at the end, moved toward Mannerism. He was 89 when he died in 1564, still hard at work on Saint Peter's and other projects. Few artists, then or since, could escape his influence.

22-55 GIACOMO DELLA PORTA, facade of Il Gesù, Rome, Italy, ca. 1575–1584.

In Giacomo della Porta's innovative design, the march of pilasters and columns builds to a dramatic climax at the central bay. Many 17th-century Roman church facades are architectural variations of Il Gesù.

22-56 GIACOMO DA VIGNOLA, plan of Il Gesù, Rome, Italy, 1568. (1) dome, (2) nave, (3) chapel.

Giacomo da Vignola's plan for Il Gesù, with its exceptionally wide nave with side chapels instead of aisles, won wide acceptance in the Catholic world. It is an ideal space for grand processions.

IL GESÙ Probably the most influential building of the second half of the 16th century was the mother church of the Jesuit order. The activity of the Society of Jesus, known as the Jesuits, was an important component of the Counter-Reformation. Ignatius of Loyola (1491–1556), a Spanish nobleman who dedicated his life to the service of God, founded the Jesuit order. He attracted a group of followers, and in 1540 Pope Paul III formally recognized this group as a religious order. The Jesuits were the papacy's invaluable allies in its quest to reassert the supremacy of the Catholic Church. Particularly successful in the field of education, the order established numerous schools. In addition, its members were effective missionaries and carried the message of Catholicism to the Americas, Asia, and Africa.

As a major participant in the Counter-Reformation, the Jesuit order needed a church appropriate to its new prominence. Because Michelangelo was late in providing the plans for this church, called Il Gesù, or Church of Jesus, in 1568 the Jesuits turned to Giacomo della Porta, who was responsible for the facade (FIG. **22-55**)—and later designed the dome of Saint Peter's (FIG. 24-3)—and GIACOMO DA VIGNOLA (1507–1573), who designed the ground plan (FIG. **22-56**).

The plan of Il Gesù reveals a monumental expansion of Alberti's scheme for Sant'Andrea (FIGS. 21-45 and 21-46) in Mantua. In the new Jesuit church, the nave takes over the main volume of space, making the structure a great hall with side chapels. A dome empha-

sizes the approach to the altar. The wide acceptance of the Gesù plan in the Catholic world, even until modern times, speaks to its ritual efficacy. The opening of the church building into a single great hall provides an almost theatrical setting for large promenades and processions (which seemed to combine social with priestly functions). Above all, the space is adequate to accommodate the great crowds that gathered to hear the eloquent preaching of the Jesuits.

The facade of Il Gesù was also not entirely original, but it too had an enormous impact on later church design. The union of the lower and upper stories, effected by scroll buttresses, harks back to Alberti's Santa Maria Novella (FIG. 21-39). Its classical pediment is familiar in Alberti's work (FIG. 21-44) as well as in that of Palladio (FIGS. 22-29 and 22-31). The paired pilasters appear in Michelangelo's design for Saint Peter's (FIG. 22-26). Giacomo della Porta skillfully synthesized these existing motifs and unified the two stories. The horizontal march of the pilasters and columns builds to a dramatic climax at the central bay, and the bays of the facade snugly fit the nave-chapel system behind them. Many Roman church facades of the 17th century are architectural variations on Giacomo della Porta's design. Chronologically and stylistically, Il Gesù belongs to the Late Renaissance, but its enormous influence on later churches marks it as a significant monument for the development of Italian Baroque church architecture, discussed in Chapter 24.

ITALY, 1500 TO 1600

HIGH AND LATE RENAISSANCE, 1495–1600

▌ During the High (1500–1520) and Late (1520–1600) Renaissance periods in Italy, artists, often in the employ of the papacy, further developed the interest in perspective, anatomy, and classical cultures that had characterized 15th-century Italian art.

▌ The major regional artistic centers were Florence and Rome in central Italy and Venice in the north. Whereas most Florentine and Roman artists emphasized careful design preparation based on preliminary drawing (*disegno*), Venetian artists focused on color and the process of paint application (*colorito*).

▌ Leonardo da Vinci was a master of chiaroscuro and atmospheric perspective. He was famous for his hazy sfumato and for his psychological insight in depicting biblical narrative (*Last Supper*) and contemporary personalities (*Mona Lisa*). His anatomical drawings are the first modern scientific illustrations.

▌ Raphael favored lighter tonalities than Leonardo and clarity over obscurity. His sculpturesque figures appear in landscapes under blue skies (*Madonna of the Meadows*) or in grandiose architectural settings rendered in perfect perspective (*School of Athens*).

▌ Michelangelo, a temperamental genius, was a pioneer in several media, including architecture, but his first love was sculpture. His carved (*David, Moses*) and painted (*Creation of Adam*) figures have heroic physiques and great emotional impact. He preferred pent-up energy to Raphael's calm, ideal beauty.

▌ The leading architect of the early 16th century was Bramante, who championed the classical style of the ancients. He based his pioneering design for the Tempietto on antique models, but the combination of parts was new and original.

▌ Andrea Palladio, an important theorist as well as architect, carried on Bramante's classical style during the Late Renaissance. Famed for his villa designs, he had a lasting impact upon later European and American architecture.

▌ One of the great masters of the Venetian painting school was Giorgione, who developed the concept of *poesia,* poetical painting. The subjects of his paintings (*Pastoral Symphony, The Tempest*) are often impossible to identify. His primary goal was to evoke a pastoral mood.

▌ Titian, the official painter of the Venetian Republic, won renown for his rich surface textures and dazzling display of color in all its nuances. In paintings such as *Venus of Urbino,* he established oil color on canvas as the typical medium of the Western pictorial tradition.

MANNERISM, 1520–1600

▌ Mannerism emerged in the 1520s in reaction to the High Renaissance style. A prime feature of Mannerist art is artifice. Renaissance artists generally strove to create art that appeared natural, whereas Mannerist artists were less inclined to disguise the contrived nature of art production. Ambiguous space, departures from expected conventions, and unique presentations of traditional themes are common features of Mannerist art.

▌ Parmigianino's *Madonna with the Long Neck* epitomizes the elegant stylishness of Mannerist painting. The elongated proportions of the figures, the enigmatic line of columns without capitals, and the ambiguous position of the figure with a scroll are the antithesis of High Renaissance classical proportions, clarity of meaning, and rational perspective.

▌ Mannerism was also a sculptural style. Giovanni da Bologna's *Abduction of the Sabine Women*, which does not really have a subject, is typical. The sculptor's goal was to depict elegant nude figures in a dynamic spiral composition that presaged the movement of Baroque sculpture.

▌ The leading Mannerist architect was Giulio Romano, who rejected the balance, order, and stability that were hallmarks of the High Renaissance style. In the Palazzo del Tè in Mantua, the divergences from architectural convention parody Bramante's classical style and include triglyphs that slip out of the Doric frieze.

Michelangelo, *David*, 1501–1504

Bramante, Tempietto, Rome, 1502(?)

Titian, *Venus of Urbino*, 1538

Parmigianino, *Madonna with the Long Neck*, 1534-1540

Giulio Romano, Palazzo del Tè, Mantua, 1525–1535

1 in.

23-1 ALBRECHT DÜRER, *Fall of Man* (*Adam and Eve*), 1504. Engraving, $9\frac{7}{8}'' \times 7\frac{5}{8}''$. Museum of Fine Arts, Boston (centennial gift of Landon T. Clay).

Albrecht Dürer was the first Northern European artist to become an international celebrity. *Fall of Man,* with two figures based on ancient statues, reflects his studies of the Vitruvian theory of human proportions.

23-2 Matthias Grünewald, *Isenheim Altarpiece* (closed, *top;* open, *bottom*), from the chapel of the Hospital of Saint Anthony, Isenheim, Germany, ca. 1510–1515. Oil on wood, 9′ 9½″ × 10′ 9″ (center panel), 8′ 2½″ × 3′ ½″ (each wing), 2′ 5½″ × 11′ 2″ (predella). Shrine carved by Nikolaus Hagenauer in 1490. Painted and gilt limewood, 9′ 9½″ × 10′ 9″. Musée d'Unterlinden, Colmar.

Befitting its setting in a monastic hospital, Matthias Grünewald's *Isenheim Altarpiece* includes painted panels depicting suffering and disease but also miraculous healing, hope, and salvation.

painted a grotesque image of a man, whose oozing boils, withered arm, and distended stomach all suggest a horrible disease. Medical experts have connected these symptoms with ergotism (a disease caused by ergot, a fungus that grows especially on rye). Although doctors did not discover the cause of ergotism until about 1600, people lived in fear of its recognizable symptoms (convulsions and gangrene). The public referred to this illness as "Saint Anthony's Fire," and it was one of the major diseases treated at the Isenheim hospital. The gangrene often compelled amputation, and scholars have noted that the two movable halves of the altarpiece's predella (FIG. 23-2, *top*), if slid apart, make it appear as if Christ's legs have been amputated. The same observation can be made with regard to the two main exterior panels. Due to the off-center placement of the cross, opening the left panel "severs" one arm from the crucified figure.

Thus, Grünewald carefully selected and presented his altarpiece's iconography to be particularly meaningful for viewers at this hospital. In the interior shrine, the artist balanced the horrors of the disease and the punishments that awaited those who did not repent with scenes such as *Meeting of Saints Anthony and Paul*, depicting the two saints, healthy and aged, conversing peacefully. Even the exterior panels (the closed altarpiece; FIG. 23-2, *top*) convey these same concerns. *Crucifixion* emphasizes Christ's pain and suffering, but the knowledge that this act redeemed humanity tempers the misery. In addition, Saint Anthony appears in the right wing as a devout follower of Christ who, like Christ and for Christ, endured intense suffering for his faith. Saint Anthony's presence on the exterior thus reinforces the themes Grünewald intertwined throughout this entire altarpiece—themes of pain, illness, and death, as well as those of hope, comfort, and salvation.

HANS BALDUNG GRIEN Very different in size, technique, and subject, but equally dramatic, is *Witches' Sabbath* (FIG. 23-3), a *chiaroscuro woodcut* that HANS BALDUNG GRIEN (ca. 1484–1545) produced in 1510. Chiaroscuro woodcuts were a recent German innovation. The technique requires the use of two blocks of wood instead of one. The printmaker carves and inks one block in the usual way in order to produce a traditional black-and-white print (see "Woodcuts, Engravings, and Etchings," Chapter 20, page 537). Then the artist cuts a second block consisting of broad highlights that can be inked in gray or color and printed over the first block's impression. Chiaroscuro woodcuts therefore incorporate some of the qualities of painting and feature tonal subtleties absent in traditional woodcuts.

Witchcraft was a counter-religion in the 15th and 16th centuries that involved magical rituals, secret potions, and devil worship. Witches prepared brews that they inhaled or rubbed into their skin, sending them into hallucinogenic trances in which they allegedly flew through the night sky on broomsticks or goats. The popes condemned all witches, and Church inquisitors vigorously pursued these demonic heretics and subjected them to torture to wrest confessions from them. Witchcraft fascinated Baldung, and he turned to the subject repeatedly. For him and his contemporaries, witches were evil forces in the world, threats to man—as was Eve herself, whom Baldung also frequently depicted as a temptress responsible for Original Sin.

In *Witches' Sabbath*, Baldung depicted a night scene in a forest in which a coven of nude witches—both young seductresses and old hags—gathers around a covered jar from which a fuming concoction escapes into the air. One young witch rides through the night sky on a goat. She sits backward—Baldung's way of suggesting that witchcraft is the inversion of the true religion, Christianity.

ALBRECHT DÜRER The dominant artist of the early 16th century in the Holy Roman Empire was ALBRECHT DÜRER (1471–1528) of Nuremberg. Dürer was the first artist outside Italy to become an

23-3 HANS BALDUNG GRIEN, *Witches' Sabbath*, 1510. Chiaroscuro woodcut, $1' 2\frac{7}{8}'' \times 10\frac{1}{4}''$. British Museum, London.

Baldung's chiaroscuro woodcut depicts witches gathered around a secret potion. One witch on a goat flies through the night sky mounted backward—suggesting witchcraft is the inversion of Christianity.

international celebrity. He traveled extensively, visiting and studying in Colmar, Basel, Strasbourg, Venice, Antwerp, and Brussels, among other locales. As a result of these travels, Dürer met many of the leading humanists and artists of his time, including Erasmus of Rotterdam and the Venetian master Giovanni Bellini (FIGS. 22-33 and 22-34). A man of exceptional talents and tremendous energy, Dürer achieved widespread fame in his own time and has enjoyed a lofty reputation ever since.

Fascinated with classical ideas as passed along by Italian Renaissance artists, Dürer was among the first Northern European artists to travel to Italy expressly to study Italian art and its underlying theories at their source. After his first journey in 1494–1495 (the second was in 1505–1506), he incorporated many Italian Renaissance developments into his art. Art historians have acclaimed Dürer as the first Northern European artist to understand fully the basic aims of the Renaissance in Italy. Like Leonardo da Vinci, Dürer wrote theoretical treatises on a variety of subjects, such as perspective, fortification, and the ideal in human proportions. Unlike Leonardo, he both finished and published his writings. Dürer also was the first Northern European artist to leave a record of his life and career through several self-portraits, through his correspondence, and through a carefully kept, quite detailed, and eminently readable diary.

23-4 ALBRECHT DÜRER, *Great Piece of Turf,* 1503. Watercolor, $1' 3\frac{3}{4}'' \times 1' \frac{3}{8}''$. Albertina, Vienna.

Albrecht Dürer, who visited Italy twice, shared Leonardo da Vinci's belief that sight reveals scientific truth. Botanists have been able to identify each plant and grass variety in this watercolor.

GREAT PIECE OF TURF Dürer allied himself with Leonardo's scientific studies when he painted an extremely precise watercolor study of a piece of turf (FIG. 23-4). For both artists, observation yielded truth. Sight, sanctified by mystics such as Nicholas of Cusa (1401–1464) and artists such as Jan van Eyck (see Chapter 20), became the secularized instrument of modern knowledge. Dürer agreed with Aristotle (and Leonardo) that "sight is the noblest sense of man."[1] Nature holds the beautiful, Dürer said, for the artist who has the insight to extract it. Thus, beauty lies even in humble, perhaps ugly, things, and the ideal, which bypasses or improves on nature, may not be truly beautiful in the end. Disordered and ordinary nature might be a reasonable object of an artist's interest, quite as much as its composed and measured aspect. The remarkable *Great Piece of Turf* is as scientifically accurate as it is poetic. Botanists can distinguish each plant and grass variety—dandelions, great plantain, yarrow, meadow grass, and heath rush. "[D]epart not from nature according to your fancy," Dürer said, "imagining to find aught better by yourself; . . . For verily 'art' is embedded in nature; he who can extract it, has it."[2]

FALL OF MAN Dürer's fame in his own day, as today, rested more on his achievements as a printmaker than as a painter. Trained as a goldsmith by his father before he took up painting and printmaking, he developed an extraordinary proficiency in handling the burin, the engraving tool. This technical ability, combined with a feeling for the form-creating possibilities of line, enabled him to produce a body of graphic work in woodcut (FIG. I-8) and engraving (FIGS. 23-1 and 23-5) that few artists have rivaled for quality and number. Dürer created numerous book illustrations. He also circulated and sold prints in single sheets, which people of ordinary means could buy, expanding his audience considerably. Aggressively marketing his prints with the aid of an agent, Dürer became a wealthy man from the sale of these works. His wife, who served as his manager, and his mother also sold his prints at markets. Through his graphic works, he exerted strong influence throughout Europe (Hans Baldung Grien trained in Dürer's workshop), especially in Flanders but also in Italy. The lawsuit Dürer brought in 1506 against an Italian artist for copying his prints reveals his business acumen. Scholars generally regard this lawsuit as the first in history over artistic copyright.

23-5A DÜRER, *Melencolia I,* 1514.

An engraving, *Fall of Man* (*Adam and Eve;* FIG. 23-1), one of Dürer's early masterpieces, represents the first distillation of his studies of the Vitruvian theory of human proportions, a theory based on arithmetic ratios. Clearly outlined against the dark background of a northern forest, the two idealized figures of Adam and Eve stand in poses reminiscent of specific classical statues probably known to Dürer through graphic representations. Preceded by numerous geometric drawings in which the artist attempted to systematize sets of ideal human proportions in balanced contrapposto poses, the final print presents Dürer's concept of the "perfect" male and female figures. Yet he tempered this idealization with naturalism, demonstrating his well-honed observational skills in his rendering of the background foliage and animals. The gnarled bark of the trees and the feathery leaves authenticate the scene, as do the various creatures skulking underfoot. The animals populating the print are symbolic. The choleric cat, the melancholic elk, the sanguine rabbit, and the phlegmatic ox represent humanity's temperaments based on the "four humors," body fluids that were the basis of theories of the human body's function developed by the ancient Greek physician Hippocrates and practiced in medieval physiology. The tension between cat and mouse in the foreground symbolizes the relation between Adam and Eve at the crucial moment in *Fall of Man.*

KNIGHT, DEATH, AND THE DEVIL Dürer's lifelong interest in both idealization and naturalism surfaces again in *Knight, Death, and the Devil* (FIG. 23-5), in which he carried the art of engraving to the highest degree of excellence. Dürer used his burin to render differences in texture and tonal values that would be difficult to match even in the much more flexible medium of etching, which artists developed later in the century (see "Woodcuts, Engravings, and Etchings," Chapter 20, page 537). *Knight, Death, and the Devil* depicts a mounted armored knight who rides fearlessly through a foreboding landscape. Accompanied by his faithful retriever, the knight represents a Christian knight—a soldier of God. Armed with his faith, this warrior can repel the threats of Death, who appears as a crowned decaying cadaver wreathed with snakes and shaking an hourglass as a reminder of time and mortality. The knight is equally impervious to the Devil, a pathetically hideous horned creature who follows him. The knight triumphs because he has "put on the whole armor of God that [he] may be able to stand against the wiles of the devil," as urged in Saint Paul's Epistle to the Ephesians (Eph. 6:11).

The monumental knight and his mount display the strength, movement, and proportions of the Italian Renaissance equestrian statue. Dürer was familiar with Donatello's *Gattamelata* (FIG. 21-15) and Verrocchio's *Bartolommeo Colleoni* (FIG. 21-16) and had copied a number of Leonardo's sketches of horses. Dürer based the engraving on his observation of the real world, however, not other artworks, as seen in his meticulous rendering of myriad details—the knight's armor and weapons, the horse's anatomy, the textures of the

23-5 ALBRECHT DÜRER, *Knight, Death, and the Devil,* 1513. Engraving, $9\frac{5}{8}'' \times 7\frac{3}{8}''$. Metropolitan Museum of Art, New York.

Dürer's Christian knight, armed with his faith, rides fearlessly through a meticulously rendered landscape, challenging both Death and the Devil. The engraving rivals the tonal range of painting.

23-6 ALBRECHT DÜRER, *Four Apostles,* 1526. Oil on wood, each panel 7′ 1″ × 2′ 6″. Alte Pinakothek, Munich.

Dürer's support for Lutheranism surfaces in his portraitlike depictions of four saints on two painted panels. Peter, representative of the pope in Rome, plays a secondary role behind John the Evangelist.

loathsome features of Death and the Devil, the rock forms and rugged foliage. Dürer realized this great variety of imagery with the dense hatching of fluidly engraved lines that rival the tonal range of painting. Erasmus appropriately praised Dürer as the "Apelles [the famous ancient Greek painter] of black lines."[3]

FOUR APOSTLES Dürer was a phenomenally gifted artist. His impressive technical facility with different media extended also to oil painting. *Four Apostles* (FIG. **23-6**) is a two-panel oil painting he produced without commission and presented to the city fathers of Nuremberg in 1526 to be hung in the city hall. Saints John and Peter appear on the left panel, Mark and Paul on the right. In addition to showcasing Dürer's mastery of the oil technique, of his brilliant use of color and light and shade, and of his ability to imbue the four saints with individual personalities and portraitlike features, *Four Apostles* documents Dürer's support for the German theologian Martin Luther (1483–1546), who sparked the Protestant Reformation. Dürer conveyed his Lutheran sympathies by his positioning of the figures. He relegated Saint Peter (as representative of the pope in Rome) to a secondary role by placing him behind John the Evangelist. John assumed particular prominence for Luther because of the evangelist's focus on Christ's person in his Gospel. In addition, Peter and John both read from the Bible, the single authoritative source of religious truth, according to Luther. Dürer emphasized the Bible's centrality by depicting it open to the passage "In the beginning was the Word, and

the Word was with God, and the Word was God" (John 1:1). At the bottom of the panels, Dürer included quotations from each of the four apostles' books, using Luther's German translation. The excerpts warn against the coming of perilous times and the preaching of false prophets who will distort God's word.

LUTHER AND THE REFORMATION The Protestant Reformation, which came to fruition in the early 16th century, had its roots in long-term, growing dissatisfaction with Church leadership. The deteriorating relationship between the faithful and the Church hierarchy stood as an obstacle for the millions who sought a meaningful religious experience. Particularly damaging was the perception that the Roman popes concerned themselves more with temporal power and material wealth than with the salvation of Church members. The fact that many 15th-century popes and cardinals came from wealthy families, such as the Medici, intensified this perception. It was not only those at the highest levels who seemed to ignore their spiritual duties. Upper-level clergy (such as archbishops, bishops, and abbots) began to accumulate numerous offices, thereby increasing their revenues but also making it more difficult for them to fulfill all of their responsibilities. By 1517 dissatisfaction with the Church had grown so widespread that Luther felt free to challenge papal authority openly by posting in Wittenberg his *Ninety-five Theses,* in which he enumerated his objections to Church practices, especially the sale of indulgences. *Indulgences* were Church-sanctioned remittances (or reductions) of

Catholic and Protestant Views of Salvation

A central concern of the Protestant reformers was the question of how Christians achieve salvation. Martin Luther did not perceive salvation as something for which weak and sinful humans must constantly strive through good deeds performed under the watchful eye of a punitive God. Instead, he argued, faithful individuals attained redemption solely by God's bestowal of his grace. Therefore, people cannot earn salvation. Further, no ecclesiastical machinery with all its miraculous rites and indulgent forgivenesses could save sinners face-to-face with God. Only absolute faith in Christ could justify sinners and ensure salvation. Justification by faith alone, with the guidance of scripture, was the fundamental doctrine of Protestantism.

In *Allegory of Law and Grace* (FIG. **23-7**), Lucas Cranach the Elder gave pictorial form to these doctrinal differences between Protestantism and Catholicism. Cranach was a follower and close friend of Martin Luther. (They were godfathers to each other's children.) Many scholars, in fact, call Cranach "the painter of the Reformation." Cranach produced his allegorical woodcut about a dozen years after

Luther set the Reformation in motion with his *Ninety-five Theses*. In *Allegory of Law and Grace*, Cranach depicted the differences between Catholicism (based on Old Testament law, according to Luther) and Protestantism (based on a belief in God's grace) in two images separated by a centrally placed tree. On the left half, Judgment Day has arrived, as represented by Christ's appearance at the top of the scene, hovering amid a cloud halo and accompanied by angels and saints. Christ raises his left hand in the traditional gesture of damnation, and, below, a skeleton drives off a terrified person to burn for eternity in Hell. This person tried to live a good and honorable life, but despite his efforts, he fell short. Moses stands to the side, holding the Tablets of the Law—the commandments Catholics follow in their attempt to attain salvation. In contrast to this Catholic reliance on good works and clean living, Protestants emphasized God's grace as the source of redemption. Accordingly, God showers the sinner in the right half of the print with grace, as streams of blood flow from the crucified Christ. On the far right, Christ emerges from the tomb and promises salvation to all who believe in him.

23-7 LUCAS CRANACH THE ELDER, *Allegory of Law and Grace*, ca. 1530. Woodcut, $10\frac{5}{8}$" × 1' $\frac{3}{4}$". British Museum, London.

Lucas Cranach was a close friend of Martin Luther, whose *Ninety-five Theses* launched the Reformation in 1517. In this woodcut Cranach contrasted Catholic and Protestant views of how to achieve salvation.

time spent in Purgatory. The increasing frequency of their sale suggested that people were buying their way into Heaven.

Luther's goal was significant reform and clarification of major spiritual issues, but his ideas ultimately led to the splitting of Christendom. According to Luther, the Catholic Church's extensive ecclesiastical structure needed to be cast out, for it had no basis in scripture. Only the Bible—nothing else—could serve as the foundation

for Christianity. Luther declared the pope the Antichrist (for which the pope excommunicated him), called the Church the "whore of Babylon," and denounced ordained priests. He also rejected most of Catholicism's sacraments, decrying them as pagan obstacles to salvation (see "Catholic and Protestant Views of Salvation," above, and FIG. **23-7**). Luther maintained that for Christianity to be restored to its original purity, the Church must be cleansed of all the doctrinal

Protestantism and Iconoclasm

The Protestant concern over the role of religious imagery at times progressed to outright *iconoclasm*—the objection to and destruction of religious imagery (see "Icons and Iconoclasm," Chapter 12, page 326). In encouraging a more personal relationship with God, Protestant leaders spoke out against much of the religious art being produced. In his 1525 tract *Against the Heavenly Prophets in the Matter of Images and Sacraments,* Martin Luther explained his attitude toward religious imagery:

> I approached the task of destroying images by first tearing them out of the heart through God's Word and making them worthless and despised. . . . For when they are no longer in the heart, they can do no harm when seen with the eyes. . . . I have allowed and not forbidden the outward removal of images. . . . And I say at the outset that according to the law of Moses no other images are forbidden than an image of God which one worships. A crucifix, on the other hand, or any other holy image is not forbidden.*

Ulrich Zwingli (1484–1531), leader of the Zwinglians (a Protestant sect based in Switzerland), concurred with Luther and cautioned his followers about the potentially dangerous nature of religious imagery. Although Zwingli's ideas had much in common with those of Luther, he was more intent than Luther on simplifying religious belief and practices and rejected all sacraments (unlike Luther, who accepted both baptism and communion).

The Protestant Ten Commandments, which, although also excerpted from the Bible, differ slightly from those of the Catholic Church, further reinforced the Protestant condemnation of possibly idolatrous religious imagery. For Protestants, this is the Second Commandment:

> Thou shalt not make unto thee any graven image, or any likeness of any thing that is in heaven above, or that is in the earth beneath, or that is in the water under the earth. Thou shalt not bow down thyself to them, nor serve them, for I the Lord thy God am a jealous God, visiting the iniquity of the fathers upon the children unto the third and fourth generation of them that hate me. And showing mercy unto thousands of them that love me, and keep my commandments.

These many Protestant proscriptions against religious imagery often led to eruptions of iconoclasm. Particularly violent waves of iconoclastic fervor swept Basel, Zurich, Strasbourg, and Wittenberg in the 1520s. In an episode known as the Great Iconoclasm, bands of Calvinists visited Catholic churches in the Netherlands in 1566, shattering stained-glass windows, smashing statues, and destroying paintings and other artworks that they perceived as idolatrous. These strong reactions to art not only reflect the religious fervor of the time but also serve as dramatic demonstrations of the power of art—and of how much art mattered.

* Translated by Bernhard Erling, in Wolfgang Stechow, *Northern Renaissance Art 1400–1600: Sources and Documents* (Englewood Cliffs, N.J.: Prentice Hall, 1966), 129–130.

23-7A CRANACH THE ELDER, *Judgment of Paris,* 1530.

impurities that had collected through the ages. Luther advocated the Bible as the source of all religious truth. The Bible—the sole scriptural authority—was the word of God, and the Church's councils, law, and rituals carried no weight. Luther facilitated the lay public's access to biblical truths by producing the first translation of the Bible in a vernacular language. Luther's teachings found visual expression in *Allegory of Law and Grace* (FIG. 23-7) by LUCAS CRANACH THE ELDER (1472–1553).

VISUAL IMAGERY AND THE REFORMATION In addition to doctrinal differences, Catholics and Protestants took divergent stances on the role of visual imagery in religion. Catholics embraced church decoration as an aid to communicating with God, as seen in Italian ceiling frescoes (FIG. 22-1; see "Religious Art in Counter-Reformation Italy," Chapter 22, page 596) and German and Polish altarpieces (FIGS. 20-18, 20-19, and 23-2). In contrast, Protestants believed such imagery could lead to idolatry and would distract viewers from focusing on the real reason for their presence in church—to communicate directly with God (see "Protestantism and Iconoclasm," above). Because of this belief, Protestant churches were relatively austere and unadorned, and the extensive church decoration programs found especially in Italy were not as prominent in Protestant churches. This does not suggest that Protestants had no use for visual images. Art, especially prints (which were inexpensive and easily circulated), was a useful and effective teaching tool and facilitated the private devotional exercises that were fundamental to Protestantism. The popularity of prints both contributed to and received impetus from the transition from handwritten manuscripts to print media in Northern Europe during the 16th century.

ALBRECHT ALTDORFER Some 16th-century artists in the Holy Roman Empire addressed historical and political issues in their work. ALBRECHT ALTDORFER (ca. 1480–1538), for example, painted *Battle of Issus* (FIG. 23-8) in 1529, a depiction of Alexander the Great's defeat of King Darius III of Persia in 333 BCE at a town called Issus on the Pinarus River. Altdorfer announced the subject (which the Greek painter Philoxenos of Eretria [FIG. 5-70] had represented two millennia before) in the Latin inscription that hangs in the sky. The duke of Bavaria, Wilhelm IV (r. 1508–1550), commissioned *Battle of Issus* at the commencement of his military campaign against the invading Turks. The parallels between the historical and contemporary conflicts were no doubt significant to the duke. Both involved societies that deemed themselves progressive as being engaged in battles against infidels—the Persians in antiquity and the Turks in 1528. Altdorfer reinforced this connection by attiring the figures in 16th-century armor and depicting them embroiled in contemporary military alignments.

The scene also reveals Altdorfer's love of landscape. The battle takes place in an almost cosmological setting. From a bird's-eye view, the clashing armies swarm in the foreground. In the distance, craggy mountain peaks rise next to still bodies of water. Amid swirling clouds, a blazing sun descends. Although the spectacular topography may appear imaginary or invented, Altdorfer derived his depiction of the landscape from maps. Specifically, he set the scene

Interweaving history and 16th-century politics, Albrecht Altdorfer painted Alexander the Great's defeat of the Persians for a patron who had just embarked on a military campaign against the Turks.

1 ft.

in the eastern Mediterranean with a view from Greece to the Nile in Egypt. In addition, Altdorfer may have acquired his information about this battle from the German scholar Johannes Aventinus (1477–1534). In his account, Aventinus described the bloody day-long battle and Alexander's ultimate victory. Appropriately, given Alexander's designation as the "sun god," the sun sets over the victorious Greeks on the right, while a small crescent moon (a symbol of the Near East) hovers in the upper left corner over the retreating Persians.

HANS HOLBEIN Choosing less dramatic scenes, HANS HOLBEIN THE YOUNGER (ca. 1497–1543) excelled as a portraitist. Trained by his father, Holbein produced portraits reflecting the Northern European tradition of close realism that had emerged in 15th-century Flemish art (see Chapter 20). Yet he also incorporated Italian ideas about monumental composition and sculpturesque form. The surfaces of his paintings are as lustrous as enamel, his detail is exact and exquisitely drawn, and his contrasts of light and dark are never heavy.

Holbein began his artistic career in Basel, where he knew Erasmus of Rotterdam. Because of the immediate threat of a religious civil war in Basel, Erasmus suggested that Holbein leave for England and gave him a recommendation to Thomas More, chancellor of England under Henry VIII. Holbein did move and became painter to the English court. While there, he produced a superb double portrait of the French

23-9 Hans Holbein the Younger, *The French Ambassadors*, 1533. Oil and tempera on wood, 6′ 8″ × 6′ 9½″. National Gallery, London.

In this double portrait, Holbein depicted two humanists with a collection of objects reflective of their worldliness and learning, but he also included an anamorphic skull, a reminder of death.

1 ft.

ambassadors to England, Jean de Dinteville (at *left*) and Georges de Selve. *The French Ambassadors* (FIG. **23-9**) exhibits Holbein's considerable talents—his strong sense of composition, his subtle linear patterning, his gift for portraiture, his marvelous sensitivity to color, and his faultlessly firm technique. The two men, both ardent humanists, stand at opposite ends of a side table covered with an oriental rug and a collection of objects reflective of their worldliness and their interest in learning and the arts. These include mathematical and astronomical models and implements, a lute with a broken string, compasses, a sundial, flutes, globes, and an open hymnbook with Luther's translation of *Veni, Creator Spiritus* and of the Ten Commandments.

Of particular interest is the long gray shape that slashes diagonally across the picture plane and interrupts the stable, balanced, and serene composition. This form is an *anamorphic image*, a distorted image recognizable only when viewed with a special device, such as a cylindrical mirror, or by looking at the painting at an acute angle. In this case, if the viewer stands off to the right, the gray slash becomes a skull. Although scholars do not agree on the skull's meaning, at the very least it certainly refers to death. Artists commonly incorporated skulls into paintings as reminders of mortality. Indeed, Holbein depicted a skull on the metal medallion on Jean de Dinteville's hat. Holbein may have intended the skulls, in conjunction with the cruci-

fix that appears half hidden behind the curtain in the upper left corner, to encourage viewers to ponder death and resurrection.

This painting may also allude to the growing tension between secular and religious authorities. Jean de Dinteville was a titled landowner, Georges de Selve a bishop. The inclusion of Luther's translations next to the lute with the broken string (a symbol of discord) may subtly refer to this religious strife. Despite scholars' uncertainty about the precise meaning of *The French Ambassadors*, it is a painting of supreme artistic achievement. Holbein rendered the still-life objects with the same meticulous care as the men themselves, the woven design of the deep emerald curtain behind them, and the floor tiles, constructed in faultless perspective. He surely hoped this painting's elegance and virtuosity of skill (produced shortly after Holbein arrived in England) would impress Henry VIII.

23-9A Holbein the Younger, *Henry VIII*, 15

FRANCE

As *The French Ambassadors* illustrates, France in the early 16th century continued its efforts to secure widespread recognition as a political power and cultural force. The French kings were major patrons of art and architecture.

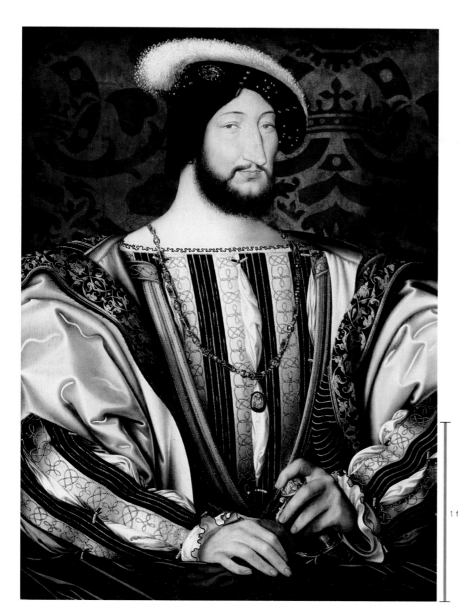

23-10 Jean Clouet, *Francis I,* ca. 1525–1530. Tempera and oil on wood, 3′ 2″ × 2′ 5″. Louvre, Paris.

Clouet's portrait of Francis I in elegant garb reveals the artist's attention to detail but also the flattening of features and disproportion between head and body, giving the painting a formalized quality.

1 ft.

FRANCIS I Under the rule of Francis I (r. 1515–1547), the French established a firm foothold in Milan and its environs. Francis waged a campaign (known as the Habsburg-Valois Wars) against Charles V (the Spanish king and Holy Roman Emperor; r. 1516–1558), which occupied him from 1521 to 1544. These wars involved disputed territories—southern France, the Netherlands, the Rhinelands, northern Spain, and Italy—and reflected France's central role in the shifting geopolitical landscape.

The French king also took a strong position in the religious controversies of his day. By the mid-16th century, the split between Catholics and Protestants had become so pronounced that subjects often felt compelled either to accept the religion of their sovereign or to emigrate to a territory where the sovereign's religion corresponded with their own. France was predominantly Catholic, and in 1534 Francis declared Protestantism illegal. The state persecuted its Protestants, the Huguenots, and drove them underground. The Huguenots' commitment to Protestantism eventually led to one of the bloodiest religious massacres in European history when the Protestants and Catholics clashed in Paris on August 24, 1572, with the violence quickly spreading throughout France.

Francis I also endeavored to elevate his country's cultural profile. To that end, he invited several esteemed Italian artists, including Leonardo da Vinci, to his court. Francis's attempt to glorify the state and himself meant the religious art that dominated the Middle Ages no longer prevailed, for the king and not the Christian Church held the power.

The portrait (FIG. **23-10**) Jean Clouet (ca. 1485–1541) painted of Francis I about a decade after he became king shows a worldly ruler magnificently bedecked in silks and brocades, wearing a gold chain with a medallion of the Order of Saint Michael, a French order Louis XI founded in 1469. Legend has it that the "merry monarch" was a great lover and the hero of hundreds of "gallant" deeds. Appropriately, he appears suave and confident, with his hand resting on the pommel of a dagger. Despite the careful detail, the portrait also exhibits an elegantly formalized quality, the result of Clouet's suppression of modeling, which flattens features, seen particularly in Francis's neck. The disproportion between the king's small head and his broad body, swathed in heavy layers of fabric, adds to the formalized nature.

Francis and his court favored art that was at once elegant, erotic, and unorthodox. Appropriately, Mannerism appealed to them most, and Francis thus brought Benvenuto Cellini (FIG. **22-51**) to France with the promise of a lucrative retainer (see Chapter 22). He also put two prominent Florentine Mannerists—Rosso Fiorentino and Francesco Primaticcio—in charge of decorating the new royal palace at Fontainebleau.

23-11 Château de Chambord, Chambord, France, begun 1519.

French Renaissance châteaux, which developed from medieval castles, served as country houses for royalty. King Francis I's Château de Chambord reflects Italian palazzo design but features a Gothic roof.

CHÂTEAU DE CHAMBORD Francis I indulged his passion for building by commissioning several large *châteaux*, among them the Château de Chambord (FIG. **23-11**). Reflecting more peaceful times, these châteaux, developed from medieval castles, served as country houses for royalty, who usually built them near forests for use as hunting lodges. Construction of Chambord began in 1519, but Francis I never saw its completion. Chambord's plan, originally drawn by a pupil of Giuliano da Sangallo, includes a central square block with four corridors, in the shape of a cross, and a broad, central staircase that gives access to groups of rooms—ancestors of the modern suite of rooms or apartments. At each of the four corners, a round tower punctuates the square plan, and a moat surrounds the whole. From the exterior, Chambord presents a carefully contrived horizontal accent on three levels, with continuous moldings separating its floors. Windows align precisely, one exactly over another. The Italian Renaissance palazzo served as the model for this matching of horizontal and vertical features, but above the third level the structure's lines break chaotically into a jumble of high dormers, chimneys, and lanterns that recall soaring ragged Gothic silhouettes on the skyline.

LOUVRE, PARIS Chambord essentially retains French architectural characteristics. During the reign of Francis's successor, Henry II (r. 1547–1559), however, translations of Italian architectural treatises appeared, and Italian architects themselves came to work in France.

Moreover, the French turned to Italy for study and travel. These exchanges caused a more extensive revolution in style than earlier, although certain French elements derived from the Gothic tradition persisted. This incorporation of Italian architectural ideas characterizes the redesigned Louvre in Paris, originally a medieval palace and fortress (FIG. **20-16**). Since Charles V's renovation of the Louvre in the mid-14th century, the castle had languished relatively empty and fallen into a state of disrepair. Francis I initiated the project to update and expand the royal palace, but he died before the work was well under way. His architect, PIERRE LESCOT (1510–1578), continued under Henry II and produced the classical style later associated with 16th-century French architecture.

Although Chambord incorporated the formal vocabulary of the Early Renaissance, particularly from Lombardy, Lescot and his associates were familiar with the architectural style of Bramante and his school. In the west wing of the Cour Carré (Square Court; FIG. **23-12**)

23-12 PIERRE LESCOT, west wing of the Cour Carré (Square Court) of the Louvre, Paris, France, begun 1546.

Lescot's design for the Louvre palace reflects the Italian Renaissance classicism of Bramante, but the decreasing height of the stories, large scale of the windows, and steep roof are Northern European features.

of the Louvre, each of the stories forms a complete order, and the cornices project enough to furnish a strong horizontal accent. The arcading on the ground story reflects the ancient Roman use of arches and produces more shadow than in the upper stories due to its recessed placement, thereby strengthening the design's visual base. On the second story, the pilasters rising from bases and the alternating curved and angular pediments supported by consoles have direct antecedents in several High Renaissance palaces (for example, FIG. 22-27). Yet the decreasing height of the stories, the scale of the windows (proportionately much larger than in Italian Renaissance buildings), and the steep roof suggest Northern European models. Especially French are the pavilions jutting from the wall. A feature the French long favored—double columns framing a niche—punctuates the pavilions. The building's vertical lines assert themselves. Openings deeply penetrate the wall, and sculptures by Jean Goujon (ca. 1510–1565) abound. Other Northern European countries imitated this French classical manner—its double-columned pavilions, tall and wide windows, profuse statuary, and steep roofs—although with local variations. The modified classicism the French produced was the only classicism to serve as a model for Northern European architects through most of the 16th century.

THE NETHERLANDS

With the demise of the Duchy of Burgundy in 1477 and the division of that territory between France and the Holy Roman Empire, the Netherlands at the beginning of the 16th century consisted of 17 provinces (corresponding to modern Holland, Belgium, and Luxembourg). The Netherlands was among the most commercially advanced and prosperous European countries. Its extensive network of rivers and easy access to the Atlantic Ocean provided a setting conducive to overseas trade, and shipbuilding was one of the most profitable businesses. The region's commercial center shifted geographically toward the end of the 15th century, partly because of buildup of silt in the Bruges estuary. Traffic relocated to Antwerp, which became the hub of economic activity in the Netherlands after 1510. As many as 500 ships a day passed through Antwerp's harbor, and large trading companies from England, the Holy Roman Empire, Italy, Portugal, and Spain established themselves in the city.

During the second half of the 16th century, the Netherlands was under the political control of Philip II of Spain (r. 1556–1598), who had inherited the region from his father Charles V. The economic prosperity of the Netherlands served as a potent incentive for Philip II to strengthen his control over the territory. However, his heavy-handed tactics and repressive measures led in 1579 to revolt, resulting in the formation of two federations. The Union of Arras, a Catholic confederation of southern Netherlandish provinces, remained under Spanish dominion, and the Union of Utrecht, consisting of Protestant northern provinces, became the Dutch Republic (MAP 25-1).

The increasing number of Netherlandish citizens converting to Protestantism affected the arts and resulted in a corresponding decrease in large-scale altarpieces and religious works (although grand works continued to be commissioned for Catholic churches). Much of Netherlandish art of this period provides a wonderful glimpse into the lives of various strata of society, from nobility to peasantry, capturing their activities, environment, and values.

HIERONYMUS BOSCH The most famous Netherlandish painter at the turn of the 16th century was HIERONYMUS BOSCH (ca. 1450–1516), whose most famous work is *Garden of Earthly Delights* (FIG. 23-13). Bosch is one of the most fascinating and puzzling

23-13 HIERONYMUS BOSCH, *Garden of Earthly Delights,* 1505–1510. Oil on wood, center panel 7′ 2$\frac{5}{8}$″ × 6′ 4$\frac{3}{4}$″, each wing 7′ 2$\frac{5}{8}$″ × 3′ 2$\frac{1}{4}$″. Museo del Prado, Madrid.

Bosch was the most imaginative and enigmatic painter of his era. In this triptych, which may commemorate a wedding, he created a fantasy world filled with nude men and women and bizarre creatures and objects.

23-14 JAN GOSSAERT, *Neptune and Amphitrite*, ca. 1516. Oil on wood, 6′ 2″ × 4′ $\frac{3}{4}$″. Gemälde-galerie, Staatliche Museen, Berlin.

Dürer's *Fall of Man* (FIG. 23-1) inspired the poses of Gossaert's classical deities, but the architectural setting is probably based on sketches of ancient buildings Gossaert made during his trip to Rome.

1 ft.

painters in history. Interpretations of Bosch differ widely. Scholars debate whether he was a satirist, an irreligious mocker, or a pornographer, a heretic or an orthodox fanatic like Girolamo Savonarola, his Italian contemporary (see Chapter 21).

Garden of Earthly Delights is Bosch's most enigmatic, and no interpretation has ever won universal acceptance. This large-scale work takes the familiar form of a monumental triptych. The format suggests a religious function for Bosch's painting, but *Garden of Earthly Delights* resided in the palace of Henry III of Nassau, regent of the Netherlands, seven years after its completion. This location suggests a secular commission for private use. Some scholars have proposed that, given the work's central themes of marriage, sex, and procreation, the painting probably commemorates a wedding, a theme seen earlier in *Giovanni Arnolfini and His Bride* (FIG. 20-1) and in *A Goldsmith in His Shop* (FIG. 20-11). Any similarity to these paintings ends there, however. Whereas Jan van Eyck and Petrus Christus grounded their depictions of betrothed couples in 15th-century life and custom, Bosch's image portrays a visionary world of fantasy and intrigue.

In the left panel, God presents Eve to Adam in a landscape, presumably the Garden of Eden. Bosch placed the event in a wildly imaginative setting that includes an odd pink fountainlike structure in a body of water and an array of fanciful and unusual animals. These details may hint at an interpretation involving *alchemy*—the medieval study of seemingly magical changes, especially chemical changes. (Witchcraft also involved alchemy.) The right panel, in contrast, bombards viewers with the horrors of Hell. Beastly creatures devour people, while others are impaled or strung on musical instruments, as if on a medieval rack. A gambler is nailed to his own table. A spidery monster embraces a girl while toads bite her. A sea of inky darkness envelops all of these horrific scenes. Observers must search through the hideous enclosure of Bosch's Hell to take in its fascinating though repulsive details.

Sandwiched between Paradise and Hell is the huge central panel, in which nude people blithely cavort in a landscape dotted with bizarre creatures and unidentifiable objects. The numerous

23-15 Quinten Massys, *Money-Changer and His Wife*, 1514. Oil on wood, $2' 3\frac{3}{4}'' \times 2' 2\frac{3}{8}''$. Louvre, Paris.

Massys's painting depicting a secular financial transaction is also a commentary on 16th-century Netherlandish values. The banker's wife shows more interest in the money-weighing than in her prayer book.

14A Gossaert, *nt Luke wing Virgin*, 1520–1525.

fruits and birds (fertility symbols) in the scene suggest procreation, and, indeed, many of the figures are paired off as couples. The orgiastic overtones of this panel, in conjunction with the terrifying image of Hell, have led some scholars to interpret this triptych as they have other Last Judgment images—as a warning to viewers of the fate awaiting the sinful, decadent, and immoral.

JAN GOSSAERT As in the Holy Roman Empire and France, developments in Italian Renaissance art interested many Netherlandish artists. JAN GOSSAERT (ca. 1478–1535) associated with humanist scholars and visited Italy, where he became fascinated with classical antiquity and its mythological subjects. Giorgio Vasari, the Italian artist and biographer and Gossaert's contemporary, wrote about him: "Jean Gossart [*sic*] of Mabuse was almost the first who took from Italy into Flanders the true method of making scenes full of nude figures and poetical inventions,"[4] although it is obvious Gossaert derived much of his classicism from Dürer.

Indeed, Dürer's *Fall of Man* (FIG. 23-1) inspired the composition and poses in Gossaert's *Neptune and Amphitrite* (FIG. 23-14). However, unlike Dürer's exquisitely small engraving, Gossaert's painting is more than six feet tall and four feet wide. The artist executed the painting with expected Netherlandish polish, skillfully drawing and carefully modeling the figures. Gossaert depicted the sea god with his

traditional attribute, the trident, and wearing a laurel wreath and an ornate conch shell rather than Dürer's fig leaf. Amphitrite is fleshy and, like Neptune, stands in a contrapposto stance. The architectural frame, which resembles the cella of a classical temple (FIG. 5-46), is an unusual mix of Doric and Ionic elements, including *bucrania* (ox skull decorations), a common motif in ancient architectural ornament. Gossaert likely based the classical setting on sketches he had made of ancient buildings while in Rome. He had traveled to Italy with Philip, bastard of Burgundy, this painting's patron. A Burgundian admiral (hence the Neptune reference), Philip became a bishop and kept this work in the innermost room of his castle.

QUINTEN MASSYS Antwerp's growth and prosperity, along with its wealthy merchants' propensity for collecting and purchasing art, attracted artists to the city. Among them was QUINTEN MASSYS (ca. 1466–1530), who became Antwerp's leading master after 1510. Son of a Louvain blacksmith, Massys demonstrated a willingness to explore the styles and modes of a variety of models, from Jan van Eyck to Bosch and from Rogier van der Weyden to Dürer and Leonardo. Yet his eclecticism was subtle and discriminating, enriched by an inventiveness that gave a personal stamp to his paintings.

In *Money-Changer and His Wife* (FIG. 23-15), Massys presented a professional man transacting business. He holds scales,

23-16 PIETER AERTSEN, *Butcher's Stall*, 1551. Oil on wood, 4' $\frac{3}{8}$" × 6' 5$\frac{3}{4}$". Uppsala University Art Collection, Uppsala.

At first glance *Butcher's Stall* appears to be a genre painting, but in the background Joseph leads a donkey carrying Mary and the Christ Child. Aertsen balanced images of gluttony with allusions to salvation.

checking the weight of coins on the table. The artist's detailed rendering of the figures, setting, and objects suggests a fidelity to observable fact. Thus, this work provides the viewer with insight into developing commercial practices. But *Money-Changer and His Wife* is also a commentary on Netherlandish values and mores. The painting highlights the financial transactions that were an increasingly prominent part of secular life in the 16th-century Netherlands and that distracted Christians from their religious duties. The banker's wife, for example, shows more interest in watching her husband weigh money than in reading her prayer book. Massys incorporated into his painting numerous references to the importance of a moral, righteous, and spiritual life, including a carafe with water and a candlestick, traditional religious symbols. The couple ignores them, focusing solely on money. On the right, through a window, an old man talks with another man, suggesting idleness and gossip. The reflected image in the convex mirror on the counter offsets this image of sloth and foolish chatter. There, a man reads what is most likely a Bible or prayer book. Behind him is a church steeple. An inscription on the original frame (now lost) read, "Let the balance be just and the weights equal" (Lev. 19:36), a caution that applies both to the money-changer's professional conduct and the eventual Last

Judgment. The couple in this painting, however, have tipped the balance in favor of the pursuit of wealth.

PIETER AERTSEN This tendency to inject reminders about spiritual well-being emerges in *Butcher's Stall* (FIG. 23-16) by PIETER AERTSEN (ca. 1507–1575), who worked in Antwerp for more than three decades. At first glance, this painting appears to be a descriptive *genre* scene (one from everyday life). On display is an array of meat products—a side of a hog, chickens, sausages, a stuffed intestine, pig's feet, meat pies, a cow's head, a hog's head, and hanging entrails. Also visible are fish, pretzels, cheese, and butter. Like Massys, Aertsen embedded strategically placed religious images in his painting. In the background, Joseph leads a donkey carrying Mary and the Christ Child. The Holy Family stops to offer alms to a beggar and his son, while the people behind the Holy Family wend their way toward a church. Furthermore, the crossed fishes on the platter and the pretzels and wine in the rafters on the upper left all refer to "spiritual food" (pretzels often served as bread during Lent). Aertsen accentuated these allusions to salvation through Christ by contrasting them to their opposite—a life of gluttony, lust, and sloth. He represented this degeneracy with the oyster and mussel shells

23-17 CATERINA VAN HEMESSEN, *Self-Portrait*, 1548. Oil on panel, $1' \frac{3}{4}'' \times 9 \frac{7}{8}''$. Kunstmuseum, Öffentliche Kunstsammlung Basel. ◼◀

In this first known Northern European self-portrait by a woman, Caterina van Hemessen represented herself as a confident artist momentarily interrupting her work to look out at the viewer.

23-18 Attributed to LEVINA TEERLINC, *Elizabeth I as a Princess*, ca. 1559. Oil on wood, $3' 6 \frac{3}{4}'' \times 2' 8 \frac{1}{4}''$. The Royal Collection, Windsor Castle, Windsor. ◼◀

Teerlinc received greater compensation for her work for the English court than did her male contemporaries. Her considerable skill is evident in this life-size portrait of Elizabeth I as a young princess.

(which Netherlanders believed possessed aphrodisiacal properties) scattered on the ground on the painting's right side, along with the people seen eating and carousing nearby under the roof.

CATERINA VAN HEMESSEN With the accumulation of wealth in the Netherlands, portraits increased in popularity. The self-portrait (FIG. **23-17**) by CATERINA VAN HEMESSEN (1528–1587) is the first known Northern European self-portrait by a woman. Here, she confidently presented herself as an artist who interrupts her work to look toward the viewer. She holds brushes, a palette, and a *maulstick* (a stick used to steady the hand while painting) in her left hand and delicately applies pigment to the canvas with her right hand. Van Hemessen's father, Jan Sanders van Hemessen, a well-known painter, trained her. Caterina ensured proper identification (and credit) through the inscription in the painting: "Caterina van Hemessen painted me / 1548 / her age 20."

LEVINA TEERLINC Another female painter, LEVINA TEERLINC (1515–1576) of Bruges, established herself as such a respected artist that Henry VIII and his successors invited her to England to paint miniatures for them. There, she was a formidable rival of some of her male contemporaries at the court, such as Hans Holbein, and received greater compensation for her work than they did for theirs. Teerlinc's considerable skill is evident in a life-size portrait (FIG. **23-18**) attributed to her, which depicts Elizabeth I (1533–1603, r. 1558–1603) as a

composed, youthful princess. Daughter of Henry VIII and Anne Boleyn, Elizabeth was probably in her late 20s when she sat for this portrait. Appropriate to her station in life, she wears an elegant brocaded gown, extravagant jewelry, and a headdress based on a style her mother popularized.

That female artists such as van Hemessen and Teerlinc were able to achieve such success is a testament to their determination and skill. Despite the difficulties for women in obtaining artistic training (see "The Artist's Profession in Flanders," Chapter 20, page 528), women contributed significantly to the lofty reputation Flemish artists enjoyed. In addition to participating as artists, women also played an important role as patrons in the 16th-century art world. Politically powerful women such as Margaret of Austria (regent of the Netherlands during the early 16th century; 1480–1530) and Mary of Hungary (queen consort of Hungary; 1505–1558) were avid collectors and patrons, and contributed substantially to the thriving state of the arts. Like other art patrons, these women collected and commissioned art not only for the aesthetic pleasure it provided but also for the status it bestowed on them and the cultural sophistication it represented.

JOACHIM PATINIR Landscape painting also flourished in the Netherlands. Particularly well known for his landscapes was JOACHIM PATINIR (d. 1524). According to one scholar, the word

23-19 Joachim Patinir, *Landscape with Saint Jerome*, ca. 1520–1524. Oil on wood, 2′ 5$\frac{1}{8}$″ × 2′ 11$\frac{7}{8}$″. Museo del Prado, Madrid.

Joachim Patinir, a renowned Netherlandish landscape painter, subordinated the story of Saint Jerome to the depiction of craggy rock formations, verdant rolling fields, and expansive bodies of water.

Landschaft (landscape) first emerged in German literature as a characterization of an artistic *genre* (category of art) when Dürer described Patinir as a "good land-scape painter." In *Landscape with Saint Jerome* (FIG. **23-19**), Patinir subordinated the saint, who removes a thorn from a lion's paw in the foreground, to the exotic and detailed landscape. Craggy rock formations, verdant rolling fields, villages with church steeples, expansive bodies of water, and a dramatic sky fill most of the panel. Patinir amplified the sense of distance by masterfully using color to enhance the visual effect of recession and advance.

PIETER BRUEGEL THE ELDER The greatest Netherlandish painter of the mid-16th century was PIETER BRUEGEL THE ELDER (ca. 1528–1569), whose works reveal both an interest in the interrelationship of human beings and nature and Patinir's influence. But in Bruegel's paintings, no matter how huge a slice of the world the artist shows, human activities remain the dominant theme. Like many of his contemporaries, Bruegel traveled to Italy, where he seems to have spent almost two years, venturing as far south as Sicily. Unlike other artists, however, Bruegel chose not to incorporate classical elements into his paintings.

23-20A BRUEGEL THE ELDER, *Fall of Icarus*, ca. 1555–1556.

23-20 PIETER BRUEGEL THE ELDER, *Netherlandish Proverbs*, 1559. Oil on wood, 3′ 10″ × 5′ 4$\frac{1}{8}$″. Gemäldegalerie, Staatliche Museen, Berlin. ◼◀

In this painting of a crowded Netherlandish village, Bruegel indulged his audience's obsession with proverbs and passion for clever imagery, and demonstrated his deep understanding of human nature.

23-21 PIETER BRUEGEL THE ELDER, *Hunters in the Snow*, 1565. Oil on wood, $3' \, 10\frac{1}{8}'' \times 5' \, 3\frac{3}{4}''$. Kunsthistorisches Museum, Vienna.

In *Hunters in the Snow*, one of a series of paintings illustrating annual seasonal changes, Bruegel draws the viewer diagonally deep into the landscape by his mastery of line, shape, and composition.

1 ft.

Bruegel's *Netherlandish Proverbs* (FIG. **23-20**) depicts a Netherlandish village populated by a wide range of people (nobility, peasants, and clerics). From a bird's-eye view, the spectator encounters a mesmerizing array of activities reminiscent of the topsy-turvy scenes of Bosch (FIG. **23-13**), but the purpose and meaning of Bruegel's anecdotal details are clear. By illustrating more than a hundred proverbs in this one painting, the artist indulged his Netherlandish audience's obsession with proverbs and passion for detailed and clever imagery. As the viewer scrutinizes the myriad vignettes within the painting, Bruegel's close observation and deep understanding of human nature become apparent. The proverbs depicted include, on the far left, a man in blue gnawing on a pillar ("He bites the column"—an image of hypocrisy). To his right, a man "beats his head against a wall" (an ambitious idiot). On the roof a man "shoots one arrow after the other, but hits nothing" (a shortsighted fool). In the far distance, the "blind lead the blind"—a subject to which Bruegel returned several years later in one of his most famous paintings.

In contrast to Patinir's Saint Jerome, lost in the landscape, the myriad, raucous characters of Bruegel's *Netherlandish Proverbs* fill the panel, so much so that the artist almost shut out the sky. *Hunters in the Snow* (FIG. **23-21**) is very different in character and illustrates the dynamic variety of Bruegel's work. One of a series of six paintings (some scholars think there were originally 12) illustrating seasonal changes in the year, *Hunters* refers back to older traditions of depicting seasons and peasants in Books of Hours (FIGS. **20-15** and **20-16**). The painting shows human figures and landscape locked in winter cold, reflecting the particularly severe winter of 1565, when Bruegel produced the painting. The weary hunters return with their hounds, women build fires, skaters skim the frozen pond, and the town and its church huddle in their mantle of snow. Bruegel rendered the landscape in an optically accurate manner. It develops smoothly from foreground to background and draws the viewer diagonally into its depths. The painter's consummate skill in using line and shape and his subtlety in tonal harmony make this one of the great landscape paintings and an occidental counterpart of the masterworks of classical Chinese landscape (see Chapters 7 and 27).

SPAIN

Spain's ascent to power in Europe began in the mid-15th century with the marriage of Isabella of Castile (1451–1504) and Ferdinand of Aragon (1452–1516) in 1469. By the end of the 16th century, Spain had emerged as the dominant European power. Under the Habsburg rulers Charles V and Philip II, the Spanish Empire controlled a territory greater in extent than any ever known—a large part of Europe, the western Mediterranean, a strip of North Africa, and vast expanses in the New World. Spain acquired many of its New World colonies through aggressive overseas exploration. Among the most notable conquistadors sailing under the Spanish flag were Christopher Columbus (1451–1506), Vasco Nuñez de Balboa (ca. 1475–1517), Ferdinand Magellan (1480–1521), Hernán Cortés (1485–1547), and Francisco Pizarro (ca. 1470–1541). The Habsburg Empire, enriched by New World plunder, supported the most powerful military force in Europe. Spain defended and then promoted the interests of the Catholic Church in its battle against the inroads of the Protestant Reformation. Indeed, Philip II earned the title "Most Catholic King." Spain's crusading spirit, nourished by centuries of war with Islam, engaged body and soul in forming the most Catholic civilization of Europe and the Americas. In the 16th century, for good or for ill, Spain left the mark of Spanish power, religion, language, and culture on two hemispheres.

23-22 Portal, Colegio de San Gregorio, Valladolid, Spain, ca. 1498.

The Plateresque architectural style takes its name from *platero* ("silversmith" in Spanish). At the center of this Valladolid portal's Late Gothic tracery is the coat of arms of King Ferdinand and Queen Isabella.

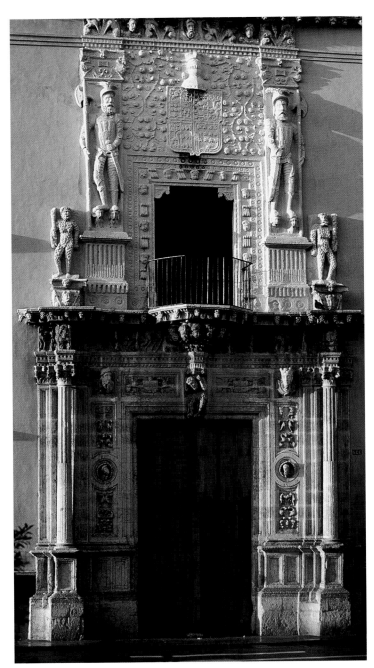

23-23 Portal, Casa de Montejo, Mérida, Mexico, 1549.

Spanish expansion brought the Plateresque style to the New World. The portal decoration of the home of the Yucatán's conqueror includes Spanish soldiers standing on the severed heads of Maya natives.

COLEGIO DE SAN GREGORIO During the 15th century and well into the 16th, a Late Gothic style of architecture, the Plateresque, prevailed in Spain. *Plateresque* derives from the Spanish word *platero,* meaning "silversmith," and the Plateresque style in architecture is characterized by the delicate execution of its ornamentation, which resembles elegant metalwork. The Colegio de San Gregorio (Seminary of Saint Gregory; FIG. 23-22) in the Castilian city of Valladolid handsomely exemplifies the Plateresque manner. Great carved retables, like the German altarpieces that influenced them (FIGS. 20-18, 20-19, and 23-2, *bottom*), appealed to church patrons and architects in Spain. They thus made such retables a conspicuous decorative feature of their exterior architecture, dramatizing a portal set into an otherwise blank wall. The Plateresque entrance of San Gregorio is a lofty sculptured stone screen that bears no functional relation to the architecture behind it. On the entrance level, lacelike tracery reminiscent of Moorish design hems the flamboyant ogival arches. A great screen, paneled into sculptured compartments, rises above the tracery. In the center, the branches of a huge pomegranate

tree (symbolizing Granada, the Moorish capital of Spain the Habsburgs captured in 1492) wreathe the coat of arms of King Ferdinand and Queen Isabella. Cupids play among the tree branches, and, flanking the central panel, niches frame armed pages of the court, heraldic wild men symbolizing aggression, and armored soldiers, attesting to Spain's proud new militancy. In typical Plateresque and Late Gothic fashion, the activity of a thousand intertwined motifs unifies the whole design, which, in sum, creates an exquisitely carved panel greatly expanded in scale from the retables that inspired it.

NEW SPAIN Spanish expansion into the Western Hemisphere brought the Plateresque style to "New Spain" as well. A mid-16th-century gem of Plateresque architecture is the portal (FIG. 23-23) of the Casa de Montejo in Mérida, Mexico. The house, built in 1549,

23-24 JUAN DE HERRERA and JUAN BAUTISTA DE TOLEDO, El Escorial, near Madrid, Spain, 1563–1584 (detail of an anonymous 18th-century painting).

Conceived by Charles V and built by Philip II, El Escorial is a combined royal mausoleum, church, monastery, and palace. The complex is classical in style with severely plain walls and massive towers.

was the palatial residence of Francisco de Montejo the Younger (1508–1565), the Spanish conqueror of the Yucatán who founded Mérida in 1542. The lower story features engaged classical columns on projecting pedestals and sculptured portrait busts of Montejo and his wife in roundels. The upper story is much more fanciful and fully Plateresque in style with a central coat of arms, as at Valladolid. The four statues of the second level are of special interest. The larger pair depicts bearded and armored Spanish soldiers standing on the severed heads of the Maya natives they conquered. Smaller in scale are two sheepskin-clad wild men holding clubs (also seen at Valladolid), probably personifications of the defeated indigenous population. The triumphal imagery is, ironically, the work of Maya sculptors from nearby Maní. In fact, the very stones used to build the Montejo house were taken from dismantled Maya temples in the area.

EL ESCORIAL In Spain itself, the Plateresque style gave way under Philip II to an Italian-derived classicism. The Italian style is on display in the expansive complex called El Escorial (FIG. **23-24**), which JUAN BAUTISTA DE TOLEDO (d. 1567) and JUAN DE HERRERA (ca. 1530–1597), principally the latter, constructed for Philip II. In his will, Charles V stipulated that a "dynastic pantheon" be constructed to house the remains of past and future monarchs of Spain. Philip II, obedient to his father's wishes, chose a site some 30 miles northwest of Madrid in rugged terrain with barren mountains. There he built El Escorial, not only a royal mausoleum but also a church, a monastery, and a palace. Legend has it that the gridlike plan for the enormous complex, 625 feet wide and 520 feet deep,

symbolized the gridiron on which Saint Lawrence, El Escorial's patron saint, suffered his martyrdom.

The vast structure is in keeping with Philip's austere and conscientious character, his passionate Catholic religiosity, his proud reverence for his dynasty, and his stern determination to impose his will worldwide. He insisted that in designing El Escorial, the architects focus on simplicity of form, severity in the whole, nobility without arrogance, and majesty without ostentation. The result is a classicism of Doric severity, ultimately derived from Italian architecture and with the grandeur of Saint Peter's (FIG. **24-4**) implicit in the scheme, but unique in Spanish and European architecture.

Only the three entrances, with the dominant central portal framed by superimposed orders and topped by a pediment in the Italian fashion, break the long sweep of the structure's severely plain walls. Massive square towers punctuate the four corners. The stress on the central axis, with its subdued echoes in the two flanking portals, anticipates the three-part organization of later Baroque facades (see Chapter 24). The construction material for the entire complex (including the church)—granite, a difficult stone to work—conveys a feeling of starkness and gravity. The church's massive facade and the austere geometry of the interior complex, with its blocky walls and ponderous arches, produce an effect of overwhelming strength and weight. The entire complex is a monument to the collaboration of a great king and remarkably understanding architects. El Escorial stands as the overpowering architectural expression of Spain's spirit in its heroic epoch and of the character of Philip II, the extraordinary ruler who directed it.

23-25 El Greco, *Burial of Count Orgaz*, 1586. Oil on canvas, 16' × 12'. Santo Tomé, Toledo.

El Greco's art is a blend of Byzantine and Italian Mannerist elements. His intense emotional content captured the fervor of Spanish Catholicism, and his dramatic use of light foreshadowed the Baroque style.

23-25A El Greco, *View of Toledo*, ca. 1610.

1 ft.

EL GRECO Doménikos Theotokópoulos, called El Greco (ca. 1547–1614), was born on Crete but emigrated to Italy as a young man. In his youth, he absorbed the traditions of Late Byzantine frescoes and mosaics. While still young, El Greco went to Venice, where he worked in Titian's studio, although Tintoretto's painting apparently made a stronger impression on him. A brief trip to Rome explains the influences of Roman and Florentine Mannerism on his work. By 1577 he had left for Spain to spend the rest of his life in Toledo.

El Greco's art is a strong personal blending of Byzantine and Mannerist elements. The intense emotionalism of his paintings, which naturally appealed to Spanish piety, and a great reliance on and mastery of color bound him to 16th-century Venetian art and to Mannerism. El Greco's art was not strictly Spanish (although it appealed to certain sectors of that society), for it had no Spanish antecedents and little effect on later Spanish painters. Nevertheless, El Greco's hybrid style captured the fervor of Spanish Catholicism.

A vivid expression of this fervor is the artist's masterpiece, *Burial of Count Orgaz* (FIG. **23-25**), painted in 1586 for the church of Santo Tomé in Toledo. El Greco based the painting on the legend that the count of Orgaz, who had died some three centuries before and who had been a great benefactor of Santo Tomé, was buried in the church by Saints Stephen and Augustine, who miraculously descended from Heaven to lower the count's body into its sepulcher. In the painting, El Greco carefully distinguished the terrestrial and celestial spheres. The brilliant Heaven that opens above irradiates the earthly scene. The painter represented the terrestrial realm with a firm realism, whereas he depicted the celestial, in his quite personal manner, with elongated undulating figures, fluttering draperies, and a visionary swirling cloud. Below, the two saints lovingly lower the count's armor-clad body, the armor and heavy robes painted with all the rich sensuousness of the Venetian school. A solemn chorus of black-clad Spanish personages fills the background. In the carefully individualized features of these figures, El Greco demonstrated that he was also a great portraitist. These men call to mind both the conquistadors of the early 16th century and the Spanish naval officers who, two years after the completion of this painting, led the Great Armada against both Protestant England and the Netherlands.

The upward glances of some of the figures below and the flight of an angel above link the painting's lower and upper spheres. The action of the angel, who carries the count's soul in his arms as Saint John and the Virgin intercede for it before the throne of Christ, reinforces this connection. El Greco's deliberate change in style to distinguish between the two levels of reality gives the viewer an opportunity to see the artist's early and late manners in the same work, one below the other. His relatively sumptuous and realistic presentation of the earthly sphere still has strong roots in Venetian art, but the abstractions and distortions El Greco used to show the immaterial nature of the heavenly realm characterized his later style. His elongated figures existing in undefined spaces, bathed in a cool light of uncertain origin, explain El Greco's usual classification as a Mannerist, but it is difficult to apply that label to him without reservations. Although he used Mannerist formal devices, El Greco's primary concerns were emotion and conveying his religious passion or arousing that of observers. The forcefulness of his paintings is the result of his unique, highly developed expressive style. His strong sense of movement and use of light prefigured the Baroque style of the 17th century, examined next in Chapter 24.

NORTHERN EUROPE AND SPAIN, 1500 TO 1600

HOLY ROMAN EMPIRE

▪ Widespread dissatisfaction with the Church in Rome led to the Protestant Reformation, splitting Christendom in half. Protestants objected to the sale of indulgences and rejected most of the sacraments of the Catholic Church. They also condemned ostentatious church decoration as a form of idolatry that distracted the faithful from communication with God.

▪ As a result, Protestant churches were relatively bare, but art, especially prints, still played a role in Protestantism. Lucas Cranach, for example, effectively used visual imagery to contrast Catholic and Protestant views of salvation in his woodcut *Allegory of Law and Grace*.

▪ The greatest printmaker of the Holy Roman Empire was Albrecht Dürer, who was also a painter. Dürer was the first artist outside Italy to become an international celebrity. His work ranged from biblical subjects to botanical studies. *Fall of Man* reflects Dürer's studies of the Vitruvian theory of human proportions and of classical statuary. Dürer's engravings rival painting in tonal quality.

▪ Other German artists, such as Albrecht Altdorfer, achieved fame as landscape painters. Hans Holbein was a renowned portraitist who became court painter in England. Holbein's *The French Ambassadors* portrays two worldly humanists and includes a masterfully rendered anamorphic skull.

Dürer, *Fall of Man*, 1504

Holbein, *The French Ambassadors*, 1533

FRANCE

▪ King Francis I fought against the Holy Roman Emperor Charles V and declared Protestantism illegal in France. An admirer of Italian art, he invited several prominent Mannerists to work at his court and decorate his palace at Fontainebleau.

▪ French architecture of the 16th century is an eclectic mix of Italian and Northern European elements, as seen in Pierre Lescot's design of the renovated Louvre palace in Paris and Francis's château at Chambord. The château combines classical motifs derived from Italian palazzi with a Gothic roof silhouette.

Château de Chambord, Chambord, begun 1519

THE NETHERLANDS

▪ The Netherlands was one of the most commercially advanced and prosperous countries in 16th-century Europe. Much of Netherlandish art of this period provides a picture of contemporary life and values.

▪ Pieter Aertsen of Antwerp, for example, painted *Butcher's Stall,* which seems to be a straightforward genre scene but includes the Holy Family offering alms to a beggar in the background. The painting provides a stark contrast between gluttony and religious piety.

▪ Landscapes were the specialty of Joachim Patinir. Pieter Bruegel's repertory also included landscape painting. His *Hunters in the Snow* is one of a series of paintings depicting the seasonal changes of the year and the activities associated with them, as in traditional Books of Hours.

▪ Prominent female artists of the period include Caterina van Hemessen, who painted the first known Northern European self-portrait of a woman, and Levina Teerlinc, who painted portraits for the English court.

Aertsen, *Butcher's Stall*, 1551

SPAIN

▪ At the end of the 16th century, Spain was the dominant power in Europe and ruled an empire greater in extent than any ever known, including vast territories in the New World.

▪ The Spanish Plateresque style of architecture takes its name from *platero* ("silversmith") and features delicate ornamentation resembling metalwork.

▪ Under Philip II the Plateresque style gave way to an Italian-derived classicism, seen at its best in El Escorial, a royal mausoleum, monastery, and palace complex near Madrid.

▪ The leading painter of 16th-century Spain was the Greek-born El Greco, who combined Byzantine style, Italian Mannerism, and the religious fervor of Catholic Spain in works such as *Burial of Count Orgaz*.

El Greco, *Burial of Count Orgaz*, 1586

24-1 GIANLORENZO BERNINI, interior of the Cornaro Chapel, Santa Maria della Vittoria, Rome, Italy, 1645–1652.

Bernini was the quintessential Baroque artist. For the Cornaro Chapel, he drew on the full capabilities of architecture, sculpture, and painting to create an intensely emotional experience for worshipers.

ITALY AND SPAIN, 1600 TO 1700

Art historians traditionally describe 17th-century European art as *Baroque*, but the term is problematic because the period encompasses a broad range of styles and genres. Although its origin is unclear, "Baroque" may have come from the Portuguese word *barroco,* meaning an irregularly shaped pearl. Use of the term emerged in the late 18th and early 19th centuries, when critics disparaged the Baroque period's artistic production, in large part because of perceived deficiencies in comparison with the art of the Italian Renaissance. Over time, this negative connotation faded, but the term is still useful to describe the distinctive new style that emerged during the 17th century—a style of complexity and drama seen especially in Italian art of this period. Whereas Renaissance artists reveled in the precise, orderly rationality of classical models, Baroque artists embraced dynamism, theatricality, and elaborate ornamentation, all used to spectacular effect, often on a grandiose scale.

ITALY

Although in the 16th century the Catholic Church launched the Counter-Reformation in response to—and as a challenge to—the Protestant Reformation, the considerable appeal of Protestantism continued to preoccupy the popes throughout the 17th century. The Treaty of Westphalia (see Chapter 25) in 1648 had formally recognized the principle of religious freedom, serving to validate Protestantism (predominantly in the German states). With the Church in Rome as the leading art patron in 17th-century Italy, the aim of much of Italian Baroque art was to restore Catholicism's predominance and centrality. The Council of Trent, one 16th-century Counter-Reformation initiative, firmly resisted Protestant objections to using images in religious worship, insisting on their necessity for teaching the laity (see "Religious Art in Counter-Reformation Italy," Chapter 22, page 596). Baroque art in Italy was therefore often overtly didactic.

Architecture and Sculpture

Italian 17th-century art and architecture, especially in Rome, embodied the renewed energy of the Catholic Counter-Reformation and communicated it to the populace. At the end of the 16th century, Pope Sixtus V (r. 1585–1590) had played a key role in the Roman Catholic Church's lengthy campaign to

24-2 CARLO MADERNO, facade of Santa Susanna, Rome, Italy, 1597–1603.

Maderno's facade of Santa Susanna is one of the earliest manifestations of the Baroque spirit. The rhythm of the columns and pilasters mounts dramatically toward the emphatically stressed vertical axis.

24-3 CARLO MADERNO, facade of Saint Peter's, Vatican City, Rome, Italy, 1606–1612.

For the facade of Saint Peter's, Maderno elaborated on his design for Santa Susanna (FIG. 24-2), but the two outer bays with bell towers were not part of his plan and detract from the verticality he sought.

reestablish its preeminence. He augmented the papal treasury and intended to rebuild Rome as an even more magnificent showcase of Church power. Between 1606 and 1667, several strong and ambitious popes—Paul V, Urban VIII, Innocent X, and Alexander VII—brought many of Sixtus V's dreams to fruition. Rome still bears the marks of their patronage everywhere.

SANTA SUSANNA The facade (FIG. 24-2) that CARLO MADERNO (1556–1629) designed at the turn of the century for the Roman church of Santa Susanna stands as one of the earliest manifestations of the Baroque artistic spirit. In its general appearance, Maderno's facade resembles Giacomo della Porta's immensely influential design for Il Gesù (FIG. 22-55). But Maderno's later facade has a greater verticality that concentrates and dramatizes the major features of its model. The tall central section projects forward from the horizontal lower story, and the scroll buttresses that connect the two levels are narrower and set at a sharper angle. The elimination of an arch framing the pediment over the doorway further enhances the design's vertical thrust. The rhythm of Santa Susanna's vigorously projecting columns and pilasters mounts dramatically toward the emphatically stressed central axis. The recessed niches, which contain statues and create pockets of shadow, heighten the sculptural effect.

MADERNO AND SAINT PETER'S The drama inherent in Santa Susanna's facade appealed to Pope Paul V (r. 1605–1621), who commissioned Maderno in 1606 to complete Saint Peter's in Rome. As the symbolic seat of the papacy, the church Constantine originally built over the first pope's tomb (see Chapter 11) radiated enormous symbolic presence. In light of Counter-Reformation concerns, the Baroque popes wanted to conclude the already century-long rebuilding project and reestablish the force embodied in the mammoth structure. In many ways Maderno's facade (FIG. 24-3) is a gigantic expansion of the elements of Santa Susanna's first level. But the compactness and verticality of the smaller church's facade are not as prominent because Saint Peter's enormous breadth counterbalances them. Mitigating circumstances must be considered when assessing this design, however. The preexisting core of an incomplete building restricted Maderno, so he did not have the luxury of formulating a

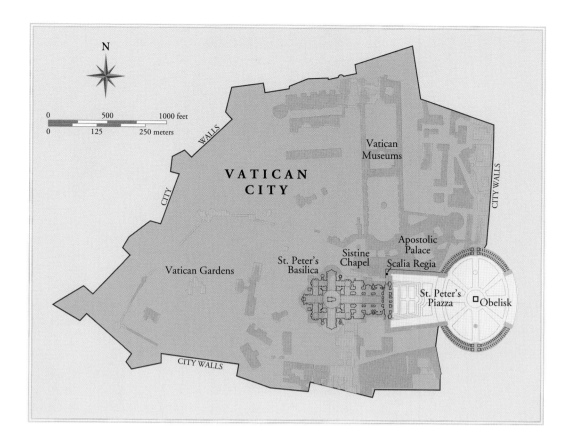

MAP 24-1 Vatican City.

longitudinal basilican plan used for the original fourth-century church (FIG. 11-9) reinforced the symbolic distinction between clergy and laity and provided a space for the processions of ever-growing assemblies. Lengthening the nave, unfortunately, pushed the dome farther back from the facade and all but destroyed the effect Michelangelo had planned—a structure pulled together and dominated by its dome. When viewed at close range, the dome barely emerges above the facade's soaring frontal plane. Seen from farther back (FIG. 24-3), it appears to have no drum. Visitors must move back quite a distance from the front (or fly over the church, FIG. 24-4) to see the dome and drum together. Today, viewers can appreciate the effect Michelangelo intended only by observing the church from the back (FIG. 22-26).

totally new concept for Saint Peter's. Moreover, the two outer bays with bell towers were not part of his original concept. Hence, had the facade been constructed according to the architect's initial design, the result would have been greater verticality and visual coherence.

Maderno's plan for Saint Peter's (MAP 24-1) also departed from the central plans designed for it during the Renaissance by Bramante (FIG. 22-23) and, later, by Michelangelo (FIG. 22-25). Paul V commissioned Maderno to add three nave bays to the earlier nucleus because Church officials had decided the central plan was too closely associated with pagan buildings, such as the Pantheon (FIG. 10-51). Moreover, the

BERNINI AND SAINT PETER'S Old Saint Peter's had a large forecourt, or *atrium* (FIG. 11-9, no. 6), in front of the church proper, and in the mid-17th century, GIANLORENZO BERNINI (1598–1680) received the prestigious commission to construct a monumental colonnade-framed *piazza* (plaza; FIG. 24-4) in front of Maderno's facade. Architect, painter, and sculptor, Bernini was one of the most important and imaginative artists of the Italian Baroque era and its most characteristic, sustaining spirit. Bernini's design had to accommodate two preexisting structures on the site—an ancient obelisk the Romans brought from Egypt (which

24-4A BERNINI, Four Rivers Fountain, 1648–1651.

Pope Sixtus V had moved to its present location in 1585 as part of his vision of Christian triumph in Rome) and a fountain Maderno designed. Bernini co-opted these features to define the long axis of a vast oval embraced by two colonnades joined to Maderno's facade. Four rows of huge Tuscan columns make up the two colonnades, which terminate in classical temple fronts. The colonnades extend a dramatic gesture of embrace to all who enter the piazza, symbolizing the welcome the Roman Catholic Church gave its members

24-4 Aerial view of Saint Peter's, Vatican City, Rome, Italy. Piazza designed by GIANLORENZO BERNINI, 1656–1667.

The dramatic gesture of embrace that Bernini's colonnade makes as worshipers enter Saint Peter's piazza symbolizes the welcome the Roman Catholic Church extended its members during the Counter-Reformation.

Italy   **651**

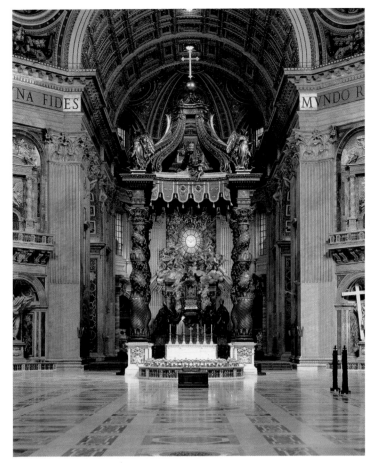

24-5 GIANLORENZO BERNINI, baldacchino, Saint Peter's, Vatican City, Rome, Italy, 1624–1633. Gilded bronze, 100′ high.

Bernini's baldacchino serves both functional and symbolic purposes. It marks Saint Peter's tomb and the high altar of the church, and it visually bridges human scale to the lofty vaults and dome above.

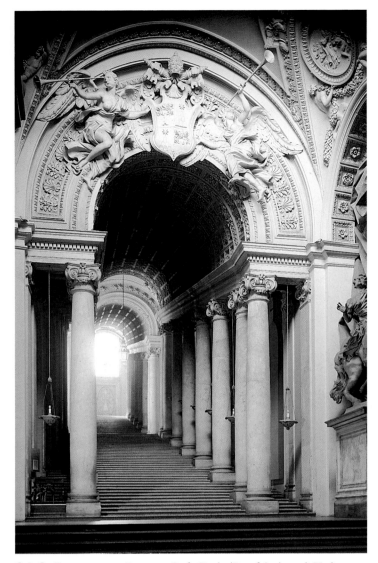

24-6 GIANLORENZO BERNINI, Scala Regia (Royal Stairway), Vatican City, Rome, Italy, 1663–1666.

By gradually reducing the distance between the columns and walls as the stairway ascends, Bernini created the illusion that the Scala Regia is of uniform width and that the aisles continue for its full length.

during the Counter-Reformation. Bernini himself referred to his colonnades as the welcoming arms of the church. Beyond their symbolic resonance, the colonnades served visually to counteract the natural perspective and bring the facade closer to the viewer. By emphasizing the facade's height in this manner, Bernini subtly and effectively compensated for its extensive width. Thus, a Baroque transformation expanded the compact central designs of Bramante and Michelangelo into a dynamic complex of axially ordered elements that reach out and enclose spaces of vast dimension. By its sheer scale and theatricality, the completed Saint Peter's fulfilled the desire of the Counter-Reformation Catholic Church to present an awe-inspiring, authoritative vision of itself.

BALDACCHINO, SAINT PETER'S Long before being invited to design the piazza, Bernini had been at work decorating the interior of Saint Peter's. His first commission, completed between 1624 and 1633, called for the design and erection of a gigantic bronze *baldacchino* (FIG. **24-5**) under the great dome. The canopy-like structure (*baldacco* is Italian for "silk from Baghdad," such as for a cloth canopy) stands 100 feet high (the height of an average eight-story building). The baldacchino serves both functional and symbolic purposes. It marks the high altar and the tomb of Saint Peter, and it visually bridges human scale to the lofty vaults and dome above. Further, for worshipers entering the nave of the huge church, it provides a dramatic, compelling presence at the crossing. Its columns also create a visual frame for the elaborate sculpture representing the throne of Saint Peter (the Cathedra Petri) at the far end of Saint Peter's (FIG. **24-5**,

rear). On a symbolic level, the structure's decorative elements speak to the power of the Catholic Church and of Pope Urban VIII (r. 1623–1644). Partially fluted and wreathed with vines, the baldacchino's four spiral columns recall those of the ancient baldacchino over the same spot in Old Saint Peter's, thereby invoking the past to reinforce the primacy of the Roman Catholic Church in the l7th century. At the top of the columns, four colossal angels stand guard at the upper corners of the canopy. Forming the canopy's apex are four serpentine brackets that elevate the orb and the cross. Since the time of Constantine (FIG. **10-81**, *right*), the orb and the cross had served as symbols of the Church's triumph. The baldacchino also features numerous bees, symbols of Urban VIII's family, the Barberini. The structure effectively gives visual form to the triumph of Christianity and the papal claim to doctrinal supremacy.

The construction of the baldacchino was itself a remarkable feat. Each of the bronze columns consists of five sections cast from wooden models using the *lost-wax process* (see "Hollow-Casting Life-Size Bronze Statues," Chapter 5, page 122). Although Bernini did some of the hands-on work himself, for example, cleaning and repairing the wax molds and doing the final *chasing* (engraving and embossing) of the bronze casts, he contracted out much of the work for the project to experienced bronzecasters and sculptors. The superstructure is predominantly cast bronze, although some of the sculptural elements are brass or wood. The enormous scale of the baldacchino required a considerable amount of bronze. On Urban VIII's orders, workers dismantled the portico of the Pantheon (FIG. 10-49) to acquire the bronze for the baldacchino—ideologically appropriate, given the Church's rejection of paganism.

The concepts of triumph and grandeur permeate every aspect of the 17th-century design of Saint Peter's. Suggesting a great and solemn procession, the main axis of the complex traverses the piazza (marked by the central obelisk) and enters Maderno's nave. It comes to a temporary halt at the altar beneath Bernini's baldacchino, but it continues on toward its climactic destination at another great altar in the apse.

SCALA REGIA Bernini demonstrated his impressive skill at transforming space in another project he undertook for the papacy, the Scala Regia (Royal Stairway; FIG. 24-6), that connects the papal apartments to Saint Peter's. Because the original passageway was irregular, dark, and dangerous to descend, Pope Alexander VII (r. 1655–1667) commissioned Bernini to replace it. A sculptural group of trumpeting angels and the papal arms crowns the entrance to the stairway, where columns carrying a barrel vault (built in two sections) form aisles flanking the central corridor. By gradually reducing the distance between the columns and walls as the stairway ascends, Bernini eliminated the aisles on the upper levels while creating the illusion that the whole stairway is of uniform width and that the aisles continue for its entire length. Likewise, the space between the colonnades narrows with ascent, reinforcing the natural perspective and making the stairs appear longer than they are. To minimize this effect, Bernini brightened the lighting at the top of the stairs, exploiting the natural human inclination to move from darkness toward light. To make the long ascent more tolerable, he inserted an illuminated landing that provides a midway resting point. The result is a highly sophisticated design, both dynamic and dramatic, that repeats on a smaller scale, perhaps even more effectively, the processional sequence found inside Saint Peter's. The challenge of this difficult assignment must have intrigued Bernini. The biographer Filippo Baldinucci (1625–1696) reported that Bernini "said the highest merit lay not in making beautiful and commodious buildings, but in being able to make do with little, to make use of a deficit in such a way that if it had not existed one would have to invent it."[1]

BERNINI, *DAVID* Although Bernini was a great and influential Baroque architect, his fame rests primarily on his sculpture, which also energetically expresses the Italian Baroque spirit. Baldinucci asserted: "[T]here was perhaps never anyone who manipulated marble with more facility and boldness. He gave his works a marvelous softness . . . making the marble, so to say, flexible."[2] Bernini's sculpture is expansive and theatrical, and the element of time usually plays an important role in it. A sculpture that predates his work on Saint Peter's is his *David* (FIG. 24-7). Bernini surely knew the Renaissance statues by Donatello (FIG. 21-12), Verrocchio (FIG. 21-13), and Michelangelo (FIG. 22-13) portraying the young biblical hero. Bernini's *David* fundamentally differs from those earlier masterpieces, however. Donatello and Verrocchio depicted David after his triumph over Goliath. Michelangelo portrayed David before his encounter with his gigantic adversary. Bernini chose to represent the combat itself. Unlike his Renaissance predecessors, the Baroque sculptor aimed to catch the split-second of maximum action. Bernini's *David*, his muscular legs widely and firmly planted, begins the violent, pivoting motion that will launch the stone from his sling. (A bag full of stones is

24-7 GIANLORENZO BERNINI, *David*, 1623. Marble, 5′ 7″ high. Galleria Borghese, Rome. ▣◀

Bernini's sculptures are expansive and theatrical, and the element of time plays an important role in them. His emotion-packed *David* seems to be moving through both time and space.

at David's left hip, suggesting that he thought the fight would be tough and long.) Unlike Myron, the fifth-century BCE Greek sculptor who froze his *Diskobolos* (FIG. 5-39) at a fleeting moment of inaction, Bernini selected the most dramatic of an implied sequence of poses, so that the viewer has to think simultaneously of the continuum and of this tiny fraction of it. The suggested continuum imparts a dynamic quality to the statue that conveys a bursting forth of the energy seen confined in Michelangelo's figures (FIGS. 22-15 and 22-16). Bernini's *David* seems to be moving through time and through space. This kind of sculpture cannot be inscribed in a cylinder or confined in a niche. Its dynamic action demands space around it. Nor is the statue self-sufficient in the Renaissance sense, as its pose and attitude direct attention beyond it to the unseen Goliath. Bernini's sculpted figure moves out into the space that surrounds it. Further, the expression of intense concentration on David's face contrasts vividly with the classically placid visages of Donatello's and

1 ft.

24-8 GIANLORENZO BERNINI, *Ecstasy of Saint Teresa*, Cornaro Chapel, Santa Maria della Vittoria, Rome, Italy, 1645–1652. Marble, height of group 11′ 6″.

The passionate drama of Bernini's depiction of Saint Teresa correlated with the ideas of Ignatius Loyola, who argued that the re-creation of spiritual experience would do much to increase devotion and piety.

24-9 FRANCESCO BORROMINI, facade of San Carlo alle Quattro Fontane, Rome, Italy, 1665–1667.

Borromini rejected the traditional notion that a building's facade should be a flat frontispiece. He set San Carlo's facade in undulating motion, creating a dynamic counterpoint of concave and convex elements.

Verrocchio's Davids and is more emotionally charged even than Michelangelo's (FIG. 22-14). The tension in David's face augments the dramatic impact of Bernini's sculpture.

ECSTASY OF SAINT TERESA Another work that displays the motion and emotion of Italian Baroque art and exemplifies Bernini's refusal to limit his statues to firmly defined spatial settings is *Ecstasy of Saint Teresa* in the Cornaro Chapel (FIG. 24-1) of the Roman church of Santa Maria della Vittoria. For this chapel, Bernini marshaled the full capabilities of architecture, sculpture, and painting to charge the entire area with palpable tension. He accomplished this by drawing on the considerable knowledge of the theater he absorbed from writing plays and producing stage designs. The marble sculpture (FIG. 24-8) that serves as the chapel's focus depicts Saint Teresa, a nun of the Carmelite order and one of the great mystical saints of the Spanish Counter-Reformation. Her conversion occurred after the death of her father, when she fell into a series of trances, saw visions, and heard voices. Feeling a persistent pain, she attributed it to the fire-tipped arrow of divine love that an angel had thrust repeatedly into her heart. In her writings, Saint Teresa described this experience as making her swoon in delightful anguish. In Bernini's hands, the entire Cornaro Chapel became a theater for the production of this mystical drama. The niche in which it takes place appears as a shallow

proscenium (the part of the stage in front of the curtain) crowned with a broken Baroque pediment and ornamented with polychrome marble. On either side of the chapel, sculpted portraits of the family of Cardinal Federico Cornaro (1579–1673) watch the heavenly drama unfold from choice balcony seats. Bernini depicted the saint in ecstasy, unmistakably a mingling of spiritual and physical passion, swooning back on a cloud, while the smiling angel aims his arrow. The sculptor's supreme technical virtuosity is evident in the visual differentiation in texture among the clouds, rough monk's cloth, gauzy material, smooth flesh, and feathery wings—all carved from the same white marble. Light from a hidden window of yellow glass pours down on golden rays that suggest the radiance of Heaven, whose painted representation covers the vault.

The passionate drama of Bernini's *Ecstasy of Saint Teresa* correlated with the ideas disseminated earlier by Ignatius Loyola (1491–1556), who founded the Jesuit order in 1534 and whom the Church canonized as Saint Ignatius in 1622. In his book *Spiritual Exercises,* Ignatius argued that the re-creation of spiritual experiences in artworks would do much to increase devotion and piety. Thus,

24-10 Francesco Borromini, plan of San Carlo alle Quattro Fontane, Rome, Italy, 1638–1641.

The plan of San Carlo is a hybrid of a Greek cross and an oval. The side walls pulsate in a way that reverses the facade's movement. The molded, dramatically lit space appears to flow from entrance to altar.

24-11 Francesco Borromini, San Carlo alle Quattro Fontane (view into dome), Rome, Italy, 1638–1641.

In place of a traditional round dome, Borromini capped the interior of San Carlo with a deeply coffered oval dome that seems to float on the light entering through windows hidden in its base.

theatricality and sensory impact were useful vehicles for achieving Counter-Reformation goals. Bernini was a devout Catholic, which undoubtedly contributed to his understanding of those goals. His inventiveness, technical skill, sensitivity to his patrons' needs, and energy account for his position as the quintessential Italian Baroque artist.

SAN CARLO ALLE QUATTRO FONTANE As gifted as Bernini was as an architect, FRANCESCO BORROMINI (1599–1667) took Italian Baroque architecture to even greater dramatic heights. In the little church of San Carlo alle Quattro Fontane (Saint Charles at the Four Fountains; FIG. **24-9**), Borromini went well beyond any of his predecessors or contemporaries in emphasizing a building's sculptural qualities. Although Maderno incorporated sculptural elements in his designs for the facades of Santa Susanna (FIG. **24-2**) and Saint Peter's (FIG. **24-3**), they still develop along relatively lateral planes. Borromini set his facade in undulating motion, creating a dynamic counterpoint of concave and convex elements on two levels (for example, the sway of the cornices). He emphasized the three-dimensional effect with deeply recessed niches. This facade is not the traditional flat frontispiece that defines a building's outer limits. It is a pulsating, engaging component inserted between interior and exterior space, designed not to separate but to provide a fluid transi-

tion between the two. Underscoring this functional interrelation of the building and its environment is the curious fact that the church has not one but two facades. The second, a narrow bay crowned with its own small tower, turns away from the main facade and, tracking the curve of the street, faces an intersection. (The upper facade dates seven years after Borromini's death, and it is uncertain to what degree the present design reflects his original intention.)

The interior is not only an ingenious response to an awkward site but also a provocative variation on the theme of the centrally planned church. In plan (FIG. **24-10**), San Carlo is a hybrid of a *Greek cross* (a cross with four arms of equal length) and an oval, with a long axis between entrance and apse. The side walls move in an undulating flow that reverses the facade's motion. Vigorously projecting columns define the space into which they protrude just as much as they accent the walls attached to them. Capping this molded interior space is a deeply coffered oval dome (FIG. **24-11**) that seems to float on the light entering through windows hidden in its base. Rich variations on the basic theme of the oval, dynamic relative to the static circle, create an interior that flows from entrance to altar, unimpeded by the segmentation so characteristic of Renaissance buildings.

Italy **655**

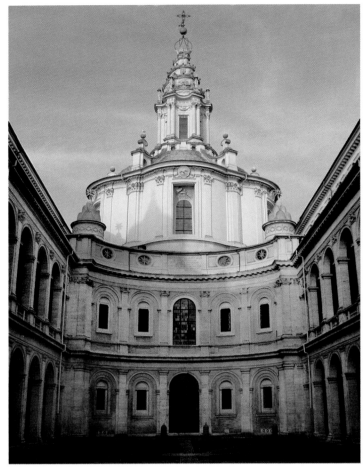

24-12 FRANCESCO BORROMINI, Chapel of Saint Ivo, College of the Sapienza, Rome, Italy, begun 1642.

In characteristic fashion, Borromini played concave against convex forms on the upper level of the Roman Chapel of Saint Ivo. Pilasters restrain the forces that seem to push the bulging forms outward.

24-13 FRANCESCO BORROMINI, plan of the Chapel of Saint Ivo, College of the Sapienza, Rome, Italy, begun 1642.

The interior elevation fully reflects all the elements of the highly complex plan of Borromini's chapel in the College of the Sapienza, which is star-shaped with rounded points and apses on all sides.

CHAPEL OF SAINT IVO Borromini carried the unification of interior space even further in the Chapel of Saint Ivo (FIG. **24-12**) in the courtyard of the College of the Sapienza (Wisdom) in Rome. In his characteristic manner, Borromini played concave against convex forms on the upper level of this chapel's exterior. The lower stories of the court, which frame the bottom facade, had already been constructed when Borromini began work. Above the facade's inward curve—its design adjusted to the earlier arcades of the court—rises a convex drumlike structure that supports the dome's lower parts.

24-14 FRANCESCO BORROMINI, Chapel of Saint Ivo (view into dome), College of the Sapienza, Rome, Italy, begun 1642.

Unlike Renaissance domes, Borromini's Saint Ivo dome is an organic part that evolves out of and shares the qualities of the supporting walls, and it cannot be separated from them.

Powerful pilasters restrain the forces that seem to push the bulging forms outward. Buttresses above the pilasters curve upward to brace a tall, ornate lantern topped by a spiral that, screwlike, seems to fasten the structure to the sky.

The centralized plan (FIG. 24-13) of the Saint Ivo chapel is that of a star having rounded points and apses on all sides. Indentations and projections along the angled curving walls create a highly complex plan, with all the elements fully reflected in the interior elevation. From floor to lantern, the wall panels rise in a continuously tapering sweep halted only momentarily by a single horizontal cornice (FIG. 24-14). Thus, the dome is not a separate unit placed on a supporting block, as in Renaissance buildings. It is an organic part that evolves out of and shares the qualities of the supporting walls, and it cannot be separated from them. This carefully designed progression up through the lantern creates a dynamic and cohesive shell that encloses and energetically molds a scalloped fragment of space. Few architects have matched Borromini's ability to translate extremely complicated designs into such masterfully unified structures as Saint Ivo.

Painting

Although architecture and sculpture provided the most obvious vehicles for manipulating space and creating theatrical effects, painting continued to be an important art form, as it was in previous centuries. Among the most noted Italian Baroque painters were Annibale Carracci and Caravaggio, whose styles, although different, were both thoroughly in accord with the period.

ANNIBALE CARRACCI A native of Bologna, ANNIBALE CARRACCI (1560–1609) received much of his training at an academy of art founded cooperatively by his family members, among them his cousin Ludovico Carracci (1555–1619) and brother Agostino Carracci (1557–1602). The Bolognese academy was the first significant institution of its kind in the history of Western art. The Carracci founded it on the premises that art can be taught—the basis of any academic philosophy of art—and that its instruction must include the classical and Renaissance traditions in addition to the study of anatomy and life drawing.

In *Flight into Egypt* (FIG. 24-15), based on the biblical narrative from Matthew 2:13–14, Annibale Carracci created the "ideal" or "classical" landscape, in which nature appears ordered by divine law and human reason. Tranquil hills and fields, quietly gliding streams, serene skies, unruffled foliage, shepherds with their flocks—all the props of the pastoral scene and mood familiar in Venetian Renaissance paintings (FIG. 22-35)—expand to fill the picture space in *Flight into Egypt* and similar paintings. Carracci regularly included screens of trees in the foreground, dark against the sky's even light. In contrast to many Renaissance artists, he did not create the sense of deep space by employing linear perspective but rather by varying light and shadow to suggest expansive atmosphere. In *Flight into Egypt,* streams or terraces, carefully placed one above the other and narrowed, zigzag through the terrain, leading the viewer's eye back to the middle ground. There, many Venetian Renaissance landscape artists depicted architectural structures (as Carracci did in *Flight into Egypt*)—walled towns or citadels, towers, temples, monumental tombs, and villas. These constructed environments captured idealized antiquity and the idyllic life. Although the artists often took the subjects for these classically rendered scenes from religious or heroic stories, they favored the pastoral landscapes over the narratives. Here, the painter greatly diminished the size of Mary, the Christ Child, and Saint Joseph, who simply become part of the landscape as they wend their way slowly to Egypt after having been ferried across a stream.

24-15 ANNIBALE CARRACCI, *Flight into Egypt,* 1603–1604. Oil on canvas, 4′ × 7′ 6″. Galleria Doria Pamphili, Rome.

Carracci's landscapes idealize antiquity and the idyllic life. Here, the pastoral setting takes precedence over the narrative of Mary, the Christ Child, and Saint Joseph wending their way slowly to Egypt.

24-16 Annibale Carracci, *Loves of the Gods,* ceiling frescoes in the gallery, Palazzo Farnese, Rome, Italy, 1597–1601.

On the shallow curved vault of this gallery in the Palazzo Farnese, Carracci arranged the mythological scenes in a *quadro riportato* format—a fresco resembling easel paintings on a wall.

24-16 Annibale Carracci, *Loves of the Gods,* ceiling frescoes in the gallery, Palazzo Farnese, Rome, Italy, 1597–1601.

LOVES OF THE GODS Among Carracci's most notable works is his decoration of the Palazzo Farnese gallery (FIG. 24-16) in Rome. Cardinal Odoardo Farnese (1573–1626), a wealthy descendant of Pope Paul III, commissioned this ceiling fresco to celebrate the wedding of the cardinal's brother. Appropriately, the title of its iconographic program is *Loves of the Gods*—interpretations of the varieties of earthly and divine love in classical mythology.

Carracci arranged the scenes in a format resembling framed easel paintings on a wall, but here he painted them on the surfaces of a shallow curved vault. This type of simulation of easel painting for ceiling design is called *quadro riportato* (transferred framed painting). By adapting the Northern European and Venetian tradition of oil painting to the central Italian fresco tradition, Carracci reoriented the direction of painting in Florence and Rome. His great influence made quadro riportato fashionable for more than a century.

Flanking the framed pictures are polychrome seated nude youths, who turn their heads to gaze at the scenes around them, and standing Atlas figures painted to resemble marble statues. Carracci derived these motifs from the Sistine Chapel ceiling (FIG. 22-1), but he did not copy Michelangelo's figures. Notably, the chiaroscuro of

the Farnese gallery frescoes differs for the pictures and the figures surrounding them. Carracci modeled the figures inside the quadri in an even light. In contrast, light from beneath seems to illuminate the outside figures, as if they were tangible, three-dimensional beings or statues lit by torches in the gallery below. This interest in illusion, already manifest in the Renaissance, continued in the grand ceiling compositions (FIGS. 24-21 to 24-24) of the 17th century. In the crown of the vault, a long panel representing the *Triumph of Bacchus* is an ingenious mixture of Raphael's drawing style and lighting and Titian's more sensuous and animated figures. It reflects Carracci's adroitness in adjusting their authoritative styles to create something of his own.

CARAVAGGIO Michelangelo Merisi, known as CARAVAGGIO (1573–1610) after the northern Italian town from which he came, developed a unique style that had tremendous influence throughout Europe. His outspoken disdain for the classical masters (probably more vocal than real) drew bitter criticism from many painters, one of whom denounced him as the "anti-Christ of painting." Giovanni Pietro Bellori, the most influential critic of the age and an admirer of

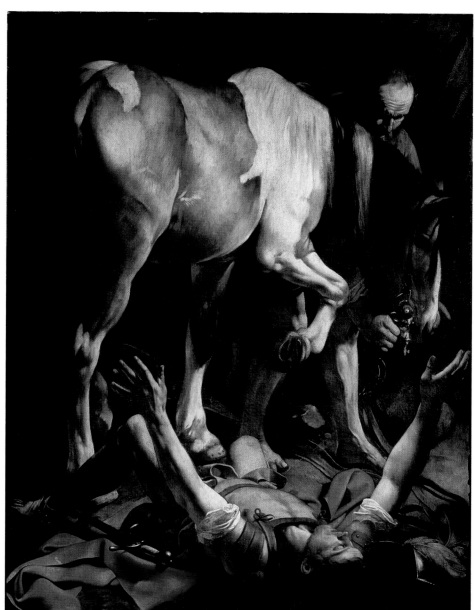

24-17 CARAVAGGIO, *Conversion of Saint Paul,* ca. 1601. Oil on canvas, 7′ 6″ × 5′ 9″. Cerasi Chapel, Santa Maria del Popolo, Rome.

Caravaggio used perspective, chiaroscuro, and dramatic lighting to bring viewers into this painting's space and action, almost as if they were participants in Saint Paul's conversion to Christianity.

1 ft.

Annibale Carracci, felt that Caravaggio's refusal to emulate the models of his distinguished predecessors threatened the whole classical tradition of Italian painting that had reached its zenith in Raphael's work (see "Giovanni Pietro Bellori on Annibale Carracci and Caravaggio," page 660). Yet despite this criticism and the problems in Caravaggio's troubled life (reconstructed from documents such as police records), Caravaggio received many commissions, both public and private, and numerous artists paid him the supreme compliment of borrowing from his innovations. His influence on later artists, as much outside Italy as within, was immense. In his art, Caravaggio injected a naturalism into both religion and the classics, reducing them to human dramas played out in the harsh and dingy settings of his time and place. His unidealized figures selected from the fields and the streets of Italy, however, were effective precisely because of their familiarity.

CONVERSION OF SAINT PAUL Caravaggio painted *Conversion of Saint Paul* (FIG. **24-17**) for the Cerasi Chapel in the Roman church of Santa Maria del Popolo. He depicted the saint-to-be at the moment of his conversion, flat on his back with his arms thrown up. In the background, an old hostler seems preoccupied with caring for the horse. At first inspection, little here suggests the momentous significance of the spiritual event in progress. The viewer of the painting could well be witnessing a mere stable accident, not a man overcome by a great miracle. Although many of his contemporaries criticized Caravaggio for departing from traditional depictions of religious scenes, the eloquence and humanity with which he imbued his paintings impressed many others.

To compel interest and involvement in Paul's conversion, Caravaggio employed a variety of formal devices. Here, as elsewhere, he used a perspective and a chiaroscuro intended to bring viewers as close as possible to the scene's space and action, almost as if they were participating in them. The low horizon line augments the sense of inclusion. Caravaggio designed *Conversion of Saint Paul* for its location on the chapel wall, positioned at the line of sight of an average-height person standing at the chapel entrance. The sharply lit figures emerge from the dark background as if lit by the light from the chapel's windows. The lighting resembles that of a stage production and is analogous to the rays in Bernini's *Ecstasy of Saint Teresa* (FIG. **24-8**).

Giovanni Pietro Bellori
on Annibale Carracci and Caravaggio

The written sources to which art historians turn as aids in understanding the art of the past are invaluable, but they reflect the personal preferences and prejudices of the writers. Pliny the Elder, for example, writing in the first century CE, reported that "art ceased"* after the death of Alexander the Great—a remark usually interpreted as expressing his disapproval of Hellenistic art in contrast to Classical art (see Chapter 5). Giorgio Vasari, the biographer and champion of Italian Renaissance artists, condemned Gothic art as "monstrous and barbarous,"† and considered medieval art in general as a distortion of the noble art of the Greeks and Romans (see Chapter 18). Giovanni Pietro Bellori (1613–1696), the leading biographer of Baroque artists, similarly recorded his admiration for Renaissance classicism as well as his distaste for Mannerism and realism in his opposing evaluations of Annibale Carracci and Caravaggio.

In the opening lines of his *Vita* of Carracci, Bellori praised "the divine Raphael . . . [whose art] raised its beauty to the summit, restoring it to the ancient majesty of . . . the Greeks and the Romans" and lamented that soon after, "artists, abandoning the study of nature, corrupted art with the *maniera,* that is to say, with the fantastic idea based on practice and not on imitation." But fortunately, Bellori observed, just "when painting was drawing to its end," Annibale Carraccci rescued "the declining and extinguished art."‡

Belloiri especially lauded Carracci's Palazzo Farnese frescoes (FIG. 24-16):

> No one could imagine seeing anywhere else a more noble and magnificent style of ornamentation, obtaining supreme excellence in the compartmentalization and in the figures and executed with the grandest manner in the design with the just proportion and the great strength of chiaroscuro. . . . Among modern works they have no comparison.§

In contrast, Bellori characterized Caravaggio as talented and widely imitated but misguided in his rejection of classicism in favor of realism.

> [Caravaggio] began to paint according to his own inclinations; not only ignoring but even despising the superb statuary of antiquity and the famous paintings of Raphael, he considered nature to be the only subject fit for his brush. As a result, when he was shown the most famous statues of [the ancient Greek masters] Phidias and Glykon in order that he might use them as models, his only answer was to point toward a crowd of people, saying that nature had given him an abundance of masters. . . . [W]hen he came upon someone in town who pleased him he made no attempt to improve on the creations of nature.**

> [Caravaggio] claimed that he imitated his models so closely that he never made a single brushstroke that he called his own, but said rather that it was nature's. Repudiating all other rules, he considered the highest achievement not to be bound to art. For this innovation he was greatly acclaimed, and many talented and educated artists seemed compelled to follow him. . . . Nevertheless he lacked *invenzione,* decorum, *disegno,* or any knowledge of the science of painting. The moment the model was taken from him, his hand and his mind became empty. . . . Thus, as Caravaggio suppressed the dignity of art, everybody did as he pleased, and what followed was contempt for beautiful things, the authority of antiquity and Raphael destroyed. . . . Now began the imitation of common and vulgar things, seeking out filth and deformity.#

---

* Pliny, *Natural History,* 25.52.
† Giorgio Vasari, *Introduzione alle tre arti del disegno* (1550), ch. 3.
‡ Giovanni Pietro Bellori, *Le vite de' pittori, scultori e architetti moderni* (Rome, 1672). Translated by Catherine Enggass, *The Lives of Annibale and Agostino Carracci by Giovanni Pietro Bellori* (University Park: Pennsylvania University Press, 1968), 5–6.
§ Ibid., 33.
** Translated by Howard Hibbard, *Caravaggio* (New York: Harper & Row, 1983), 362.
# Ibid., 371–372.

Caravaggio's figures are still heroic with powerful bodies and clearly delineated contours in the Renaissance tradition, but the stark and dramatic contrast of light and dark, which at first shocked and then fascinated his contemporaries, obscures the more traditional aspects of his style. Art historians call Caravaggio's use of dark settings enveloping their occupants—which profoundly influenced European art, especially in Spain and the Netherlands—*tenebrism,* from the Italian word *tenebroso,* or "shadowy" manner. In Caravaggio's work, tenebrism also contributed greatly to the essential meaning of his pictures. In *Conversion of Saint Paul,* the dramatic spotlight shining down upon the fallen Paul is the light of divine revelation converting him to Christianity.

24-18A CARAVAGGIO, *Musicians,* ca. 1595.

CALLING OF SAINT MATTHEW A piercing ray of light illuminating a world of darkness and bearing a spiritual message is also a central feature of one of Caravaggio's early masterpieces, *Calling of Saint Matthew* (FIG. 24-18). It is one of two large canvases honoring Saint Matthew that the artist painted for the side walls of the Contarelli Chapel in San Luigi dei Francesi in Rome. The commonplace setting of the painting—a tavern with unadorned walls—is typical of Caravag-

gio. Into this mundane environment, cloaked in mysterious shadow and almost unseen, Christ, identifiable initially only by his indistinct halo, enters from the right. With a commanding gesture that recalls the Lord's hand in Michelangelo's *Creation of Adam* (FIG. 22-19), he summons Levi, the Roman tax collector, to a higher calling. The astonished Levi—his face highlighted for the viewer by the beam of light emanating from an unspecified source above Christ's head and outside the picture—points to himself in disbelief. Although Christ's extended arm is reminiscent of the Lord's in *Creation of Adam,* the position of Christ's hand and wrist is similar to that of Adam's. This reference was highly appropriate, because the Church considered Christ to be the second Adam. Whereas Adam was responsible for the Fall of Man, Christ is responsible for human redemption. The conversion of Levi (who became Matthew) brought his salvation.

ENTOMBMENT In 1603, Caravaggio produced a large-scale painting, *Entombment* (FIG. 24-19), for the Chapel of Pietro Vittrice at Santa Maria in Vallicella in Rome. This work includes all the hallmarks of Caravaggio's distinctive style: the plebeian figure types (particularly visible in the scruffy, worn face of Nicodemus, who

The stark contrast of light and dark was a key feature of Caravaggio's style. Here, Christ, cloaked in mysterious shadow and almost unseen, summons Levi the tax collector (Saint Matthew) to a higher calling.

1 ft.

1 ft.

here holds Christ's legs in the foreground), the stark use of darks and lights, and the invitation to the viewer to participate in the scene. As in *Conversion of Saint Paul,* the action takes place in the foreground. Caravaggio positioned the figures on a stone slab the corner of which appears to extend into the viewer's space. This suggests that Christ's body will be laid directly in front of the viewer.

Beyond its ability to move its audience, Caravaggio's composition also had theological implications. In light of the ongoing Counter-Reformation efforts at that time, these implications cannot be overlooked. To viewers in the chapel, the men seem to be laying Christ's body on the altar, which stands in front of the painting. This serves to give visual form to the doctrine of *transubstantiation* (the transformation of the Eucharistic bread and wine into the body and blood of Christ)—a doctrine central to Catholicism that Protestants rejected. By depicting Christ's body as though it were physically present during the Mass, Caravaggio visually articulated an abstract theological precept. Unfortunately, because this painting is now in a museum, viewers no longer can experience this effect.

ARTEMISIA GENTILESCHI Caravaggio's combination of naturalism and drama appealed both to patrons and artists, and he had many followers. One of the most accomplished was ARTEMISIA GENTILESCHI (ca. 1593–1653), whose father Orazio (1563–1639), her teacher, was himself strongly influenced by Caravaggio. The daughter's successful career, pursued in Florence, Venice, Naples, and

24-19 Caravaggio, *Entombment,* from the Chapel of Pietro Vittrice, Santa Maria in Vallicella, Rome, Italy, ca. 1603. Oil on canvas, 9′ 10⅛″ × 6′ 7¹⁵⁄₁₆″. Pinacoteca, Musei Vaticani, Rome.

In *Entombment,* Caravaggio gave visual form to the doctrine of transubstantiation. The jutting painted stone slab makes it seem as if Christ's body will be laid on the actual altar of the chapel.

The Letters of Artemisia Gentileschi

Artemisia Gentileschi (FIG. 24-20) was the most renowned woman painter in Europe during the first half of the 17th century and the first woman ever admitted to membership in Florence's Accademia del Disegno. Like other women who could not become apprentices in all-male studios (see "The Artist's Profession," Chapter 20, page 528), she learned her craft from her father. Never forgotten in subsequent centuries, Artemisia's modern fame stems from the seminal 1976 exhibition *Women Artists: 1550–1950,** which opened a new chapter in feminist art history.

24-20A GENTILESCHI, *Self-Portrait*, ca. 1638–1639.

In addition to scores of paintings created for wealthy patrons that included the King of England and the Grand Duke of Tuscany, Gentileschi left behind 28 letters, some of which reveal that she believed patrons treated her differently because of her gender. Three 1649 letters written in Naples to Don Antonio Ruffo (1610–1678) in Messina make her feelings explicit.

I fear that before you saw the painting you must have thought me arrogant and presumptuous. . . . [I]f it were not for Your Most Illustrious Lordship . . . I would not have been induced to give it for one hundred and sixty, because everywhere else I have been I was paid one hundred *scudi* [Italian coins] per figure. . . . You think me pitiful, because a woman's name raises doubts until her work is seen.[†]

I was mortified to hear that you want to deduct one third from the already very low price that I had asked. . . . It must be that in your heart Your Most Illustrious Lordship finds little merit in me.[‡]

As for my doing a drawing and sending it, [tell the gentleman who wishes to know the price for a painting that] I have made a solemn vow never to send my drawings because people have cheated me. In particular, just today I found myself [in the situation] that, having done a drawing of souls in purgatory for the Bishop of St. Gata, he, in order to spend less, commissioned another painter to do the painting using my work. If I were a man, I can't imagine it would

24-20 ARTEMISIA GENTILESCHI, *Judith Slaying Holofernes*, ca. 1614–1620. Oil on canvas, 6′ 6⅓″ × 5′ 4″. Galleria degli Uffizi, Florence. ◼◀

Narratives involving heroic women were a favorite theme of Gentileschi. In *Judith Slaying Holofernes,* the controlled highlights on the action in the foreground recall Caravaggio's paintings and heighten the drama.

1 ft.

have turned out this way, because when the concept has been realized and defined with lights and darks, and established by means of planes, the rest is a trifle.[§]

* Ann Sutherland Harris and Linda Nochlin, *Women Artists: 1550–1950* (Los Angeles, Calif.: Los Angeles County Museum of Art, 1976), 118–124.
[†] Letter dated January 30, 1649. Translated by Mary D. Garrard, *Artemisia Gentileschi: The Image of the Female Hero in Italian Baroque Art* (Princeton, N.J.: Princeton University Press, 1989), 390.
[‡] Letter dated October 23, 1649. Ibid., 395–396.
[§] Letter dated November 13, 1649. Ibid., 397–398.

Rome, helped disseminate Caravaggio's style throughout the peninsula (see "The Letters of Artemisia Gentileschi," above).

In her *Judith Slaying Holofernes* (FIG. 24-20), Gentileschi used the tenebrism and what might be called the "dark" subject matter Caravaggio favored. Significantly, she chose a narrative involving a heroic female, a favorite theme of hers. The story, from the Old Testament Book of Judith, relates the delivery of Israel from its enemy, Holofernes. Having succumbed to Judith's charms, the Assyrian general Holofernes invited her to his tent for the night. When he fell asleep, Judith cut off his head. In this version of the scene (Gentileschi produced more than one painting of the subject), Judith and her maidservant behead Holofernes. Blood spurts everywhere as the two women summon all their strength to wield the heavy sword. The tension and strain are palpable. The controlled highlights on the

action in the foreground recall Caravaggio's work and heighten the drama here as well.

GUIDO RENI Caravaggio was not the only early-17th-century painter to win a devoted following. GUIDO RENI (1575–1642), known to his many admirers as "the divine Guido," trained in the Bolognese art academy founded by the Carracci family. The influence of Annibale Carracci and Raphael is evident in Reni's *Aurora* (FIG. 24-21), a ceiling fresco in the Casino Rospigliosi in Rome. Aurora (Dawn) leads Apollo's chariot, while the Hours dance about it. The artist conceived *Aurora* as a quadro riportato, like the paintings in Carracci's *Loves of the Gods* (FIG. 24-16), and painted a complex and convincing illusionistic frame. The fresco exhibits a fluid motion, soft modeling, and sure composition, although without Raphael's sculpturesque strength. It is

24-21 GUIDO RENI, *Aurora,* ceiling fresco in the Casino Rospigliosi, Rome, Italy, 1613–1614.

The "divine Guido" conceived *Aurora* as a quadro riportato, reflecting his training in the Bolognese art academy. The scene of Dawn leading Apollo's chariot derives from ancient Roman reliefs.

an intelligent interpretation of the Renaissance master's style. Reni, consistent with the precepts of the Bolognese academy, also looked to antiquity for his models. The ultimate sources for the *Aurora* composition were Roman reliefs (FIG. 10-41) and coins depicting emperors in triumphal chariots accompanied by flying Victories and other personifications.

PIETRO DA CORTONA The experience of looking up at a painting is different from simply seeing a painting hanging on a wall. The considerable height and the expansive scale of most ceiling frescoes induce a feeling of awe. Patrons who wanted to burnish their public image or control their legacy found monumental ceiling frescoes to be perfect vehicles for such statements. In 1633, Pope Urban VIII commissioned a ceiling fresco for the Gran Salone of the Palazzo Barberini in Rome. The most important decorative commission of the 1630s, the job went to PIETRO DA COR-TONA (1596–1669), a Tuscan architect and painter who had moved to Rome in about 1612. The grandiose and spectacular *Triumph of the Barberini* (FIG. 24-22) overwhelms spectators with the glory of the Barberini family (and Urban VIII

24-22 PIETRO DA CORTONA, *Triumph of the Barberini,* ceiling fresco in the Gran Salone, Palazzo Barberini, Rome, Italy, 1633–1639.

In this dramatic ceiling fresco, Divine Providence appears in a halo of radiant light directing Immortality, holding a crown of stars, to bestow eternal life on the family of Pope Urban VIII.

In the nave of Il Gesù, gilded architecture opens up to offer the faithful a glimpse of Heaven. To heighten the illusion, Gaulli painted figures on stucco extensions that project outside the painting's frame.

in particular). The iconographic program for this fresco, designed by the poet Francesco Bracciolini (1566–1645), centered on the accomplishments of the Barberini. Divine Providence appears in a halo of radiant light directing Immortality, holding a crown of stars, to bestow eternal life on the Barberini family. The virtues Faith, Hope, and Charity hold aloft a gigantic laurel wreath (also a symbol of immortality), which frames three bees (the family's symbols, which also appeared in Bernini's baldacchino, FIG. **24-5**). Also present are the papal tiara and keys announcing the personal triumphs of Urban VIII.

GIOVANNI BATTISTA GAULLI The dazzling spectacle of ceiling frescoes also proved very effective for commissions illustrating religious themes. Church authorities realized that such paintings, high above the ground, offered perfect opportunities to impress on worshipers the glory and power of the Catholic Church. In conjunction with the theatricality of Italian Baroque architecture and sculpture, frescoes spanning church ceilings contributed to creating transcendent spiritual environments well suited to the Church's needs in Counter-Reformation Rome.

24-24 Fra Andrea Pozzo, *Glorification of Saint Ignatius*, ceiling fresco in the nave of Sant'Ignazio, Rome, Italy, 1691–1694.

Pozzo created the illusion that Heaven is opening up above the viewer's head by continuing the church's architecture into the painted vault. The fresco gives the appearance that the roof has been lifted off.

Triumph of the Name of Jesus (FIG. **24-23**) in the nave of Il Gesù (FIGS. **22-55** and **22-56**) in Rome vividly demonstrates the dramatic impact Baroque ceiling frescoes could have. As the mother church of the Jesuit order, Il Gesù played a prominent role in Counter-Reformation efforts. In this immense fresco by GIOVANNI BATTISTA GAULLI (1639–1709), gilded architecture opens up in the center of the ceiling to offer the faithful a stunning glimpse of Heaven. Gaulli represented Jesus as a barely visible monogram (IHS) in a blinding radiant light that floats heavenward. In contrast, sinners experience a violent descent back to Earth. The painter glazed the gilded architecture to suggest shadows, thereby enhancing the scene's illusionistic quality. To further heighten the effect, Gaulli painted many of the sinners on three-dimensional stucco extensions that project outside the painting's frame.

FRA ANDREA POZZO Another master of ceiling decoration was FRA ANDREA POZZO (1642–1709), a lay brother of the Jesuit order and a master of perspective, on which he wrote an influential treatise. Pozzo designed and executed the vast ceiling fresco *Glorification of Saint Ignatius* (FIG. **24-24**) for the church of Sant'Ignazio in Rome. Like Il Gesù, Sant'Ignazio was a prominent church in Baroque Rome because of its dedication to the founder of the Jesuit order. The Jesuits played a major role in Counter-Reformation education and sent legions of missionaries to the New World and the Far East. As Gaulli did in Il Gesù, Pozzo created the illusion that Heaven

is opening up above the congregation. To accomplish this, the artist painted an extension of the church's architecture into the vault so that the roof seems to be lifted off. As Heaven and Earth commingle, Christ receives Saint Ignatius in the presence of figures personifying the four corners of the world. A disk in the nave floor marks the spot the viewer should stand to gain the whole perspectival illusion. For worshipers looking up from this point, the vision is complete. They find themselves in the presence of the heavenly and spiritual.

The effectiveness of Italian Baroque religious art depended on the drama and theatricality of individual images, as well as on the interaction and fusion of architecture, sculpture, and painting. Sound enhanced this experience. Architects designed churches with acoustical effect in mind, and, in an Italian Baroque church filled with music, the power of both image and sound must have been immensely moving. Through simultaneous stimulation of both the visual and auditory senses, the faithful might well have been transported into a trancelike state that would, indeed, as the great English poet John Milton (1608–1674) eloquently stated in *Il Penseroso* (1631), "bring all Heaven before [their] eyes."[3]

SPAIN

During the 16th century, Spain had established itself as an international power. The Habsburg kings had built a dynastic state that encompassed Portugal, part of Italy, the Netherlands, and extensive

24-25 José de Ribera, *Martyrdom of Saint Philip*, ca. 1639. Oil on canvas, 7′ 8″ × 7′ 8″. Museo del Prado, Madrid.

Martyrdom scenes were popular in Counter-Reformation Spain. Scorning idealization of any kind, Ribera represented Philip's executioners hoisting him into position to die on a cross.

1 ft.

areas of the New World (see Chapters 23 and 32). By the beginning of the 17th century, however, the Habsburg Empire was struggling, and although Spain mounted an aggressive effort during the Thirty Years' War (see Chapter 25), by 1660 the imperial age of the Spanish Habsburgs was over. In part, the demise of the Spanish empire was due to economic woes. The military campaigns Philip III (r. 1598–1621) and his son Philip IV (r. 1621–1665) waged during the Thirty Years' War were costly and led to higher taxes. The increasing tax burden placed on Spanish subjects in turn incited revolts and civil war in Catalonia and Portugal in the 1640s, further straining an already fragile economy. Thus, the dawn of the Baroque period in Spain found the country's leaders struggling to maintain control of their dwindling empire. But realizing the prestige that great artworks brought and the value of visual imagery in communicating to a wide audience, both Philip III and Philip IV continued to spend lavishly on art.

Painting

24-25A Murillo, *Immaculate Conception*, ca. 1661–1670.

In the 17th century, Spain maintained its passionate commitment to Catholic orthodoxy, and as in Counter-Reformation Italy, Spanish Baroque artists sought ways to move viewers and to encourage greater devotion and piety. Particularly appealing in this regard were scenes of death and martyrdom, which provided Spanish artists with opportunities both to depict extreme feelings and to instill those feelings in viewers. Spain prided itself on its saints—Saint Teresa of Avila (FIG. 24-8) and Saint Ignatius Loyola (FIG. 24-24) were both Spanish-born—and martyrdom scenes surfaced frequently in Spanish Baroque art.

JOSÉ DE RIBERA As a young man, José (Jusepe) de Ribera (ca. 1588–1652) emigrated to Naples and fell under the spell of Caravaggio, whose innovative style he introduced to Spain. Emulating

24-26 Francisco de Zurbarán, *Saint Serapion,* 1628. Oil on canvas, 3′ 11½″ × 3′ 4¾″. Wadsworth Atheneum, Hartford (The Ella Gallup Sumner and Mary Catlin Sumner Collection Fund).

The light shining on Serapion calls attention to his tragic death and increases the painting's dramatic impact. The Spanish monk's coarse features label him as common, evoking empathy from a wide audience.

1 ft.

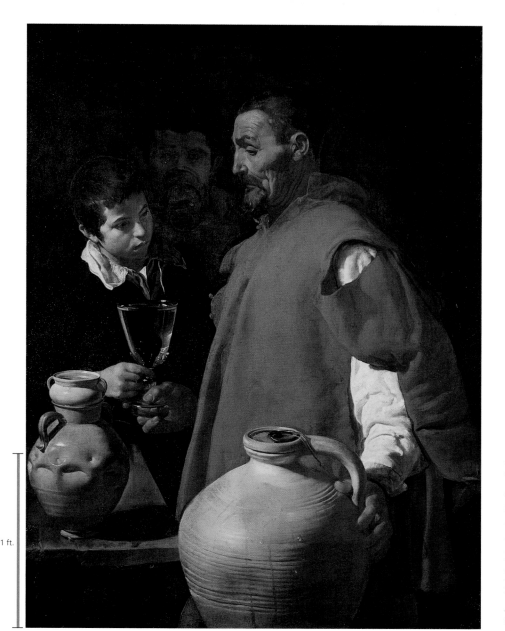

24-27 Diego Velázquez, *Water Carrier of Seville*, ca. 1619. Oil on canvas, 3' 5½" × 2' 7½". Victoria & Albert Museum, London.

In this early work—a genre scene that seems to convey a deeper significance—the contrast of darks and lights and the plebeian nature of the figures reveal Velázquez's indebtedness to Caravaggio.

1 ft.

chapel of the monastic Order of Mercy in Seville. The saint, who participated in the Third Crusade of 1196, suffered martyrdom while preaching the Gospel to Muslims. According to one account, the monk's captors tied him to a tree and then tortured and decapitated him. The Order of Mercy dedicated itself to self-sacrifice, and Serapion's membership in this order amplified the resonance of Zurbarán's painting. In *Saint Serapion* the monk emerges from a dark background and fills the foreground. The bright light shining on him calls attention to the saint's tragic death and increases the dramatic impact of the image. In the background are two barely visible tree branches. A small note next to the saint identifies him for viewers. The coarse features of the Spanish monk label him as common, no doubt evoking empathy from a wide audience.

Caravaggio, Ribera made naturalism and compelling drama primary ingredients of his paintings, which often embraced brutal themes, reflecting the harsh times of the Counter-Reformation and the Spanish taste for stories showcasing courage and devotion. Ribera's *Martyrdom of Saint Philip* (FIG. **24-25**) is grim and dark in subject and form. Scorning idealization of any kind, Ribera represented Philip's executioners hoisting him into position after tying him to a cross, the instrument of Christ's own martyrdom. The saint's rough, heavy body and swarthy, plebeian features reveal a kinship between him and his tormentors, who are similar to the types of figures found in Caravaggio's paintings. The patron of this painting is unknown, but it is possible that Philip IV commissioned the work, because Saint Philip was the king's patron saint.

FRANCISCO DE ZURBARÁN Another prominent Spanish painter of dramatic works was FRANCISCO DE ZURBARÁN (1598–1664), whose primary patrons throughout his career were rich Spanish monastic orders. Many of his paintings are quiet and contemplative, appropriate for prayer and devotional purposes. Zurbarán painted *Saint Serapion* (FIG. **24-26**) as a devotional image for the funerary

DIEGO VELÁZQUEZ The greatest Spanish painter of the Baroque age was DIEGO VELÁZQUEZ (1599–1660). An early work, *Water Carrier of Seville* (FIG. **24-27**), painted when Velázquez was only about 20, already reveals his impressive command of the painter's craft. Velázquez rendered the figures with clarity and dignity, and his careful and convincing depiction of the water jugs in the foreground, complete with droplets of water, adds to the credibility of the scene. The plebeian nature of the figures and the contrast of darks and lights again reveal the influence of Caravaggio, whose work Velázquez had studied.

SURRENDER OF BREDA Velázquez, like many other Spanish artists, produced religious pictures as well as genre scenes, but his renown in his day rested primarily on the works he painted for his major patron, King Philip IV (see "Velázquez and Philip IV," page 668). After the king appointed Velázquez as court painter, the artist largely abandoned both religious and genre subjects in favor of royal

24-27A Velázquez, *Christ on the Cross*, ca. 1631–1632.

Velázquez and Philip IV

Trained in Seville, Diego Velázquez was quite young when he came to the attention of Philip IV. The painter's immense talent impressed Philip, and the king named him chief court artist and palace chamberlain, a position that also involved curating the king's rapidly growing art collection and advising him regarding acquisitions and display. Among the works in Philip IV's possession were paintings by Titian, Annibale Carracci, Guido Reni, Albrecht Dürer, and Velázquez's famous Flemish contemporary, Peter Paul Rubens (see Chapter 25).

With the exception of two extended trips to Italy and a few excursions, Velázquez remained in Madrid for the rest of his life. His close relationship with Philip IV and his high office as chamberlain gave him prestige and a rare opportunity to fulfill the promise of his genius. One sign of Velázquez's fertile imagination as well as mastery of the brush is that he was able to create timeless artworks out of routine assignments to commemorate the achievements of his patron, as he did in his record of the Spanish victory over the Dutch in 1625 (*Surrender of Breda,* FIG. **24-29**).

Velázquez also painted dozens of portraits of Philip IV. One of the best is *King Philip IV of Spain* (FIG. **24-28**), also known as the *Fraga Philip* because it was painted during the Aragonese campaign in the town of Fraga. Velázquez accompanied the king and his troops in their attempt to reconquer the territory, and during a three-month stay in Fraga, Philip ordered the artist to produce this portrait. In it, Philip IV appears as a military leader, arrayed in salmon and silver campaign dress but without military accoutrements except his baton of command and sword. Because the king was not a commanding presence and because he had inherited the large Habsburg jaw, Velázquez had to find creative ways to "ennoble" the monarch. He succeeded by focusing attention on the exquisite attire Philip wears, particularly the elabo-

24-28 DIEGO VELÁZQUEZ, *King Philip IV of Spain* (*Fraga Philip*), 1644. Oil on canvas, 4′ 3⅛″ × 3′ 3⅛″. Frick Collection, New York.

Velázquez painted Philip IV during the king's campaign to reconquer Aragonese territory. The portrait is noteworthy for its faithful reproduction of the attire the king wore when reviewing troops.

1 ft.

rately embroidered cloak and *baldric* (the sashlike belt worn over one shoulder and across the chest to support a sword). Velázquez managed to make the silver needlework on these vestments shimmer. Detailed written accounts attest that this is the costume the king wore when reviewing the troops, and the artist's fidelity in depicting Philip's elegant attire no doubt added to the authority of the image.

portraits (FIG. **24-28**) and canvases recording historical events. In 1635 he painted *Surrender of Breda* (FIG. **24-29**) as part of an extensive program of decoration for the Hall of Realms in Philip IV's Palace of Buen Retiro in Madrid. The huge canvas (more than 12 feet long and almost as tall) was one of 10 paintings celebrating recent Spanish military successes around the globe. It commemorates the Spanish victory over the Dutch at Breda in 1625. Among the most troublesome situations for Spain was the conflict in the Netherlands. Determined to escape Spanish control, the northern Netherlands broke from the Spanish empire in the late 16th century. Skirmishes continued to flare up along the border between the northern (Dutch) and southern (Spanish) Netherlands, and in 1625 Philip IV sent General Ambrogio di Spínola to Breda to reclaim the town for Spain. Velázquez depicted the victorious Spanish troops, organized and well armed, on the right side of the painting. In sharp contrast, the defeated Dutch on the left appear bedraggled and disorganized. In the

center foreground, the mayor of Breda, Justinus of Nassau, hands the city's keys to the Spanish general—although no encounter of this kind ever occurred. Velázquez's fictional record of the event glorifies not only the strength of the Spanish military but the benevolence of Spínola as well. Velázquez portrayed the general standing and magnanimously stopping Justinus from kneeling, rather than astride his horse, lording over the vanquished Dutch. Indeed, the terms of surrender were notably lenient, and the Spaniards allowed the Dutch to retain their arms—which they used to recapture the city in 1637.

LAS MENINAS After an extended visit to Rome from 1648 to 1651, Velázquez returned to Spain and painted his greatest masterpiece, *Las Meninas* (*The Maids of Honor;* FIG. **24-30**). In it, Velázquez showed his mastery of both form and content. The painter represented himself in his studio standing before a large canvas. The young Infanta (Princess) Margarita appears in the foreground with her two

24-29 DIEGO VELÁZQUEZ, *Surrender of Breda*, 1634–1635. Oil on canvas, 10′ 1″ × 12′ $\frac{1}{2}$″. Museo del Prado, Madrid.

As Philip IV's court artist, Velázquez produced many history paintings, including fictional representations like this one depicting the Dutch mayor of Breda surrendering to the Spanish general.

1 ft.

maids-in-waiting, her favorite dwarfs, and a large dog. In the middle ground are a woman in widow's attire and a male escort. In the background, a chamberlain stands in a brightly lit open doorway. Scholars have been able to identify everyone in the room, including the two meninas and the dwarfs. The room was the artist's studio in the palace of the Alcázar in Madrid. After the death of Prince Baltasar Carlos in 1646, Philip IV ordered part of the prince's chambers converted into a studio for Velázquez.

Las Meninas is noteworthy for its visual and narrative complexity. Indeed, art historians have yet to agree on any particular reading or interpretation. A central issue preoccupying scholars has been what, exactly, is taking place in *Las Meninas*. What is Velázquez depicting on the huge canvas in front of him? He may be painting this very picture—an informal image of the infanta and her entourage. Alternately, Velázquez may be painting a portrait of King Philip IV and Queen Mariana, whose reflections appear in the mirror on the far wall. If so, that would suggest the presence of the king and queen in the viewer's space, outside the confines of the picture. Other scholars have proposed that the mirror image reflects not the physical appearance of the royal couple in Velázquez's studio but the image that he is in the process of painting on the canvas before him. This question has never been definitively resolved.

More generally, *Las Meninas* is Velázquez's attempt to elevate both himself and his profession. As first painter to the king and as chamberlain of the palace, Velázquez was conscious not only of the importance of his court office but also of the honor and dignity belonging to his profession as a painter. Throughout his career, Velázquez hoped to be ennobled by royal appointment to membership in the ancient and illustrious Order of Santiago. Because he lacked a sufficiently noble background, he gained entrance only with difficulty at the very end of his life, and then only through the pope's dispensation. In the painting, he wears the order's red cross on his doublet, painted there, legend says, by the king himself. In all likelihood, the artist painted it. In Velázquez's mind, *Las Meninas* might have embodied the idea of the great king visiting his studio, as Alexander the Great visited the studio of the painter Apelles in ancient times. The figures in the painting all appear to acknowledge the royal presence. Placed among them in equal dignity is Velázquez, face-to-face with his sovereign. The location of the completed painting reinforced this act of looking—of seeing and being seen. *Las Meninas* hung in the personal office of Philip IV in another part of the palace. Thus, although occasional visitors admitted to the king's private quarters may have seen this painting, Philip IV was the primary audience. Each time he stood before the canvas, he again participated in the work as the probable subject of the painting within the painting and as the object of the figures' gazes. In *Las Meninas*, Velázquez elevated the art of painting, in the person of the painter, to the highest status. The king's presence enhanced this status—either in person as the viewer of *Las Meninas* or as a reflected image in the painting itself. The paintings that appear in *Las Meninas* further reinforced this celebration of the painter's craft. On the wall above the doorway and mirror, two faintly recognizable pictures have been identified as copies made by Velázquez's son-in-law, Juan del Mazo (ca. 1612–1667), of paintings by Peter Paul Rubens. The paintings depict the immortal gods as the source of art. Ultimately, Velázquez sought ennoblement not for himself alone but for his art.

Velázquez intended this huge
and visually complex work,
with its cunning contrasts of
true spaces, mirrored spaces,
and picture spaces, to elevate
both himself and the pro-
fession of painting.

1 ft.

24-30A Sánchez
Cotán, *Still Life*
ca. 1600–1603.

Las Meninas is extraordinarily complex visually. Velázquez's optical report of the event, authentic in every detail, pictorially summarizes the various kinds of images in their different levels and degrees of reality. He portrayed the realities of image on canvas, of mirror image, of optical image, and of the two painted images. This work—with its cunning contrasts of mirrored spaces, "real" spaces, picture spaces, and pictures within pictures—itself appears to have been taken from a large mirror reflecting the whole scene. This would mean that the artist did not paint the princess and her suite as the main subjects of *Las Meninas* but himself in the process of painting them. *Las Meninas* is a pictorial summary and a commentary on the essential mystery of the visual world, as well as on the ambiguity that results when different states or levels interact or are juxtaposed.

Velázquez achieved these results in several ways. The extension of the composition's pictorial depth in both directions is noteworthy. The open doorway and its ascending staircase lead the eye beyond the artist's studio, and the mirror device and the outward glances of several

of the figures incorporate the viewer's space into the picture as well. (Compare how the mirror in Jan van Eyck's *Giovanni Arnolfini and His Bride*, FIG. **20-1**, similarly incorporates the area in front of the canvas into the picture, although less obviously and without a comparable extension of space beyond the rear wall of the room.) Velázquez also masterfully observed and represented form and shadow. Instead of putting lights abruptly beside darks, following Caravaggio, Velázquez allowed a great number of intermediate values of gray to come between the two extremes. His matching of tonal gradations approached effects that were later discovered in the photography age.

The inclusion of the copies of two Rubens paintings hanging on the wall in Velázquez's studio is the Spanish master's tribute to the great Flemish painter, one of the towering figures who made the 17th century so important in the history of art in Northern Europe. The works of Rubens, Rembrandt, and the other leading Baroque painters, sculptors, and architects of Flanders, the Dutch Republic, France, and England are the subject of Chapter 25.

ITALY AND SPAIN,
1600 TO 1700

ITALY

■ Art historians call the art of 17th-century Italy and Spain "Baroque," a term that probably derives from the Portuguese word for an irregularly shaped pearl. In contrast to the precision and orderly rationality of Italian Renaissance classicism, Baroque art and architecture are dynamic, theatrical, and highly ornate.

Borromini, San Carlo alle
Quattro Fontane, Rome, 1665–1667

■ Baroque architects emphatically rejected the classical style. Francesco Borromini emphasized the sculptural qualities of buildings. The facades of his churches, for example, San Carlo alle Quattro Fontane, are not flat frontispieces but undulating surfaces that provide a fluid transition from exterior to interior space. The interiors of his buildings pulsate with energy and feature complex domes that grow organically from curving walls.

■ The greatest Italian Baroque sculptor was Gianlorenzo Bernini, who was also an important architect. In *Ecstasy of Saint Teresa,* he marshaled the full capabilities of architecture, sculpture, and painting to create an intensely emotional experience for worshipers, consistent with the Catholic Counter-Reformation principle of using artworks to inspire devotion and piety.

Bernini, *Ecstasy of Saint Teresa,*
1645–1652

■ In painting, Caravaggio broke new ground by employing stark and dramatic contrasts of light and dark (tenebrism) and by setting religious scenes in everyday locales filled with rough-looking common people. An early masterpiece, *Calling of Saint Matthew,* for example, takes place in an ordinary tavern.

■ Caravaggio's combination of drama and realism attracted both loyal followers and harsh critics. The biographer Giovanni Pietro Bellori, for example, deplored Caravaggio's abandonment of the noble style of Raphael and the ancients and his "suppression of the dignity of art." He preferred the more classical style of Annibale Carracci and the Bolognese art academy.

Caravaggio, *Calling of Saint Matthew,*
ca. 1597–1601

■ Illusionistic ceiling paintings were very popular in Baroque Italy. In Sant'Ignazio in Rome, Fra Andrea Pozzo created the illusion that Heaven is opening up above the viewer's head by continuing the church's architecture into the painted nave vault.

Pozzo, *Glorification of Saint Ignatius,*
1691–1694

SPAIN

■ Although the power of the Habsburg kings of Spain declined over the course of the 17th century, the royal family, which was devoutly Catholic, continued to spend lavishly on art. Spanish artists eagerly embraced the drama and emotionalism of Italian Baroque art. Scenes of death and martyrdom were popular in Spain during the Counter-Reformation. Painters such as José de Ribera and Francisco de Zurbarán produced moving images of martyred saints that incorporated the lighting and realism of Caravaggio.

Velázquez, *Las Meninas,* 1656

■ The greatest Spanish Baroque painter was Diego Velázquez, court painter to Philip IV (r. 1621–1665). Velázquez painted a wide variety of themes ranging from religious subjects to royal portraits and historical events. His masterwork, *Las Meninas,* is extraordinarily complex visually and mixes true spaces, mirrored spaces, picture spaces, and pictures within pictures. It is a celebration of the art of painting itself.

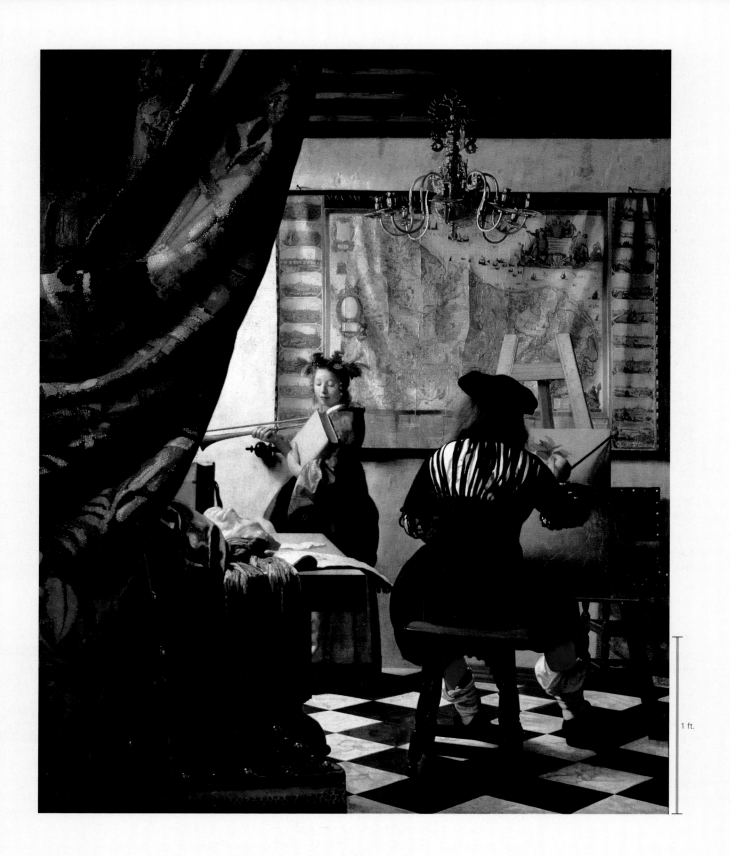

1 ft.

25-1 Jan Vermeer, *Allegory of the Art of Painting*, 1670–1675. Oil on canvas, 4′ 4″ × 3′ 8″. Kunsthistorisches Museum, Vienna.

Dutch painters often specialized in domestic scenes, but Vermeer's mother-in-law described this work as "the Art of Painting." Vermeer's tribute to his craft includes a model holding the attributes of Clio.

NORTHERN EUROPE, 1600 TO 1700

During the 17th and early 18th centuries, numerous geopolitical shifts occurred in Europe as the fortunes of the individual countries waxed and waned. Pronounced political and religious friction resulted in widespread unrest and warfare. Indeed, between 1562 and 1721, all of Europe was at peace for a mere four years. The major conflict of this period was the Thirty Years' War (1618–1648), which ensnared Spain, France, Sweden, Denmark, the Netherlands, Germany, Austria, Poland, the Ottoman Empire, and the Holy Roman Empire. Although the outbreak of the war had its roots in the conflict between militant Catholics and militant Protestants, the driving force quickly shifted to secular, dynastic, and nationalistic concerns. Among the major political entities vying for expanded power and authority in Europe were the Bourbon dynasty of France and the Habsburg dynasties of Spain and the Holy Roman Empire. The war, which concluded with the Treaty of Westphalia in 1648, was largely responsible for the political restructuring of Europe (MAP **25-1**). As a result, the United Provinces of the Netherlands (the Dutch Republic), Sweden, and France expanded their authority. Spanish and Danish power diminished. In addition to reconfiguring territorial boundaries, the Treaty of Westphalia in essence granted freedom of religious choice throughout Europe. This treaty thus marked the abandonment of the idea of a united Christian Europe and accepted the practical realities of secular political systems. The building of today's nation-states was emphatically under way.

The 17th century also brought heightened economic competition to Europe. Much of the foundation for worldwide mercantilism—extensive voyaging and geographic exploration, improved cartography, and advances in shipbuilding—had been laid in the previous century. In the 17th century, however, changes in financial systems, lifestyles, and trading patterns, along with expanding colonialism, fueled the creation of a worldwide marketplace. The Dutch founded the Bank of Amsterdam in 1609, which eventually became the center of European transfer banking. By establishing a system in which merchant firms held money on account, the bank relieved traders of having to transport precious metals as payment. Trading practices became more complex. Rather than simple reciprocal trading, triangular trade (trade among three parties) allowed for a larger pool of desirable goods. Exposure to an ever-growing array of goods affected European diets and lifestyles. Coffee (from island colonies) and tea (from China)

MAP 25-1 Europe in 1648 after the Treaty of Westphalia.

became popular beverages during the early 17th century. Equally explosive was the growth of sugar use. Sugar, tobacco, and rice were slave crops, and the slave trade expanded to meet the demand for these goods. Traders captured and enslaved Africans and shipped them to European colonies and the Americas to provide the requisite labor force for producing these commodities.

The resulting worldwide mercantile system permanently changed the face of Europe. The prosperity international trade generated affected social and political relationships, necessitating new rules of etiquette and careful diplomacy. With increased disposable income, more of the newly wealthy spent money on art, expanding the number of possible sources of patronage.

FLANDERS

In the 16th century, the Netherlands had come under the crown of Habsburg Spain when the emperor Charles V retired, leaving the Spanish kingdoms, their Italian and American possessions, and the Netherlandish provinces to his only legitimate son, Philip II (r. 1556–1598). (Charles bestowed the imperial title and the German lands on his brother.) Philip's repressive measures against the Protestants led the northern provinces to break from Spain and to set up the Dutch Republic. The southern provinces remained under Spanish control, and they retained Catholicism as their official religion. The political distinction between modern Holland and Belgium more or less reflects this original separation, which in the 17th century signaled not only religious but also artistic differences.

Painting

The leading art of 17th-century Flanders (the Spanish Netherlands) was painting. Flemish Baroque painters retained close connections to the Baroque art of Catholic Europe, whereas the Dutch schools of painting developed their own subjects and styles. This was consistent with their reformed religion and the new political, social, and economic structure of the Dutch Republic.

PETER PAUL RUBENS The renowned Flemish master PETER PAUL RUBENS (1577–1640) drew together the main contributions of the Italian Renaissance and Baroque masters to formulate the first truly pan-European painting style. Rubens's art is an original and powerful synthesis of the manners of many painters, especially Michelangelo, Titian, Carracci, and Caravaggio. His style had wide appeal, and his influence was international. Among the most learned individuals of his time, Rubens possessed an aristocratic education and a courtier's manner, diplomacy, and tact, which, with his facility for language, made him the associate of princes and scholars. He became court painter to the dukes of Mantua (descended from Mantegna's patrons), friend of King Philip IV (r. 1621–1665) of Spain and his adviser on art collecting, painter to Charles I (r. 1625–1649) of England and Marie de' Medici (1573–1642) of France, and permanent court painter to the Spanish governors of Flanders. Rubens

25-2 PETER PAUL RUBENS, *Elevation of the Cross,* from Saint Walburga, Antwerp, 1610. Oil on wood, 15′ 1$\frac{7}{8}$″ × 11′ 1$\frac{1}{2}$″ (center panel), 15′ 1$\frac{7}{8}$″ × 4′ 11″ (each wing). Antwerp Cathedral, Antwerp.

In this triptych, Rubens explored foreshortened anatomy and violent action. The composition seethes with a power that comes from heroic exertion. The tension is emotional as well as physical.

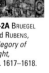

-2A BRUEGEL d RUBENS, legory of ght, . 1617–1618.

also won the confidence of his royal patrons in matters of state, and they often entrusted him with diplomatic missions of the highest importance. In the practice of his art, scores of associates and apprentices assisted Rubens, turning out numerous paintings for an international clientele. In addition, he functioned as an art dealer, buying and selling contemporary artworks and classical antiquities. His many enterprises made him a rich man, with a magnificent town house and a castle in the countryside. Rubens, like Raphael, was a successful and renowned artist, a consort of kings, a shrewd man of the world, and a learned philosopher.

ELEVATION OF THE CROSS Rubens became a master in 1598 and departed for Italy two years later, where he remained until 1608. During these years, he formulated the foundations of his style. Shortly after returning home, he painted *Elevation of the Cross* (FIG. **25-2**) for the church of Saint Walburga in Antwerp. Later moved to the city's cathedral, the altarpiece is but one of many commissions for religious works that Rubens received at this time. By investing in sacred art, churches sought to affirm their allegiance to Catholicism and Spanish Habsburg rule after a period of Protestant iconoclastic fervor in the region.

The Saint Walburga triptych also reveals Rubens's interest in Italian art, especially the works of Michelangelo and Caravaggio. The scene brings together tremendous straining forces and counterforces

as heavily muscled men labor to lift the cross. Here, as in his *Lion Hunt* (FIG. I-13), Rubens used the subject as an opportunity to show foreshortened anatomy and the contortions of violent action reminiscent of the twisted figures that Michelangelo sculpted and painted. Rubens placed the body of Christ on the cross as a diagonal that cuts dynamically across the picture while inclining back into it. The whole composition seethes with a power that comes from genuine exertion, from elastic human sinew taut with effort. The tension is emotional as well as physical, as reflected not only in Christ's face but also in the features of his followers. Strong modeling in dark and light, which heightens the drama, marks Rubens's work at this stage of his career.

Although Rubens later developed a much subtler coloristic style, the human body in action, draped or undraped, male or female, remained the focus of his art. This interest, combined with his voracious intellect, led Rubens to copy the works of classical antiquity and of the Italian masters. When he was in Rome in 1606 to 1608, he made many black-chalk drawings of great artworks, including figures in Michelangelo's Sistine Chapel frescoes (FIG. 22-1) and the ancient marble group of Laocoön and his two sons (FIG. 5-88). In a Latin treatise he wrote titled *De imitatione statuarum* (*On the Imitation of Statues*), Rubens stated: "I am convinced that in order to achieve the highest perfection one needs a full understanding of the [ancient] statues, indeed a complete absorption in them; but one must make judicious use of them and before all avoid the effect of stone."[1]

25-3 PETER PAUL RUBENS, *Arrival of Marie de' Medici at Marseilles*, 1622–1625. Oil on canvas, 12' 11½" × 9' 7". Louvre, Paris.

Marie de' Medici asked Rubens to paint 21 large canvases glorifying her career. In this historical-allegorical picture of robust figures in an opulent setting, the sea and sky rejoice at the queen's arrival in France.

25-3A RUBENS, *Garden of Lov* 1630–1632.

MARIE DE' MEDICI Rubens's interaction with royalty and aristocrats provided him with an understanding of the ostentation and spectacle of Baroque (particularly Italian) art that appealed to the wealthy and privileged. Rubens, the born courtier, reveled in the pomp and majesty of royalty. Likewise, those in power embraced the lavish spectacle that served the Catholic Church so well in Italy. The magnificence and splendor of Baroque imagery reinforced the authority and right to rule of the highborn. Among Rubens's royal patrons was Marie de' Medici, a member of the famous Florentine house and widow of Henry IV (r. 1589–1610), the first Bourbon king of France. She commissioned Rubens to paint a series memorializing and glorifying her career. Between 1622 and 1626, Rubens, working with amazing creative energy, produced 21 huge historical-allegorical pictures designed to hang in the queen's new palace, the Luxembourg, in Paris.

In *Arrival of Marie de' Medici at Marseilles* (FIG. 25-3), Marie disembarks in France after her sea voyage from Italy. An allegorical personification of France, draped in a cloak decorated with the *fleur-de-lis* (the floral symbol of French royalty), welcomes her. The sea and sky rejoice at her safe arrival. Neptune and the Nereids (daughters of the sea god Nereus) salute her, and a winged, trumpeting Fame hovers overhead. Conspicuous in the galley's opulently carved stern-castle, under the Medici coat of arms, stands the imperious commander of the vessel, the only immobile figure in the composi-

tion. In black and silver, this figure makes a sharp accent amid the swirling tonality of ivory, gold, and red. Rubens enriched the surfaces with a decorative splendor that pulls the whole composition together. The audacious vigor that customarily enlivens the artist's figures, beginning with the monumental, twisting sea creatures, vibrates through the entire design.

CONSEQUENCES OF WAR Rubens's diplomatic missions gave him great insight into European politics, and he never ceased to promote peace. Throughout most of his career, war was constant. When commissioned in 1638 to produce a painting (FIG. 25-4) for Ferdinando II de' Medici, the grand duke of Tuscany (r. 1621–1670), Rubens took the opportunity to express his attitude toward the Thirty Years' War (see "Rubens on *Consequences of War*," page 677). The fluid articulation of human forms in this work and the energy that emanates from the chaotic scene are reminiscent of Rubens's other paintings.

Rubens on *Consequences of War*

In the ancient and medieval worlds, artists rarely wrote commentaries on the works they produced. Beginning with the Renaissance, however, the increased celebrity artists enjoyed and the ready availability of paper encouraged artists to record their intentions in letters to friends and patrons.

In March 1638, Peter Paul Rubens wrote a letter to Justus Sustermans (1597–1681), court painter to Grand Duke Ferdinando II de' Medici of Tuscany, explaining his *Consequences of War* (FIG. **25-4**) and his attitude toward the European military conflicts of his day.

The principal figure is Mars, who has left the open temple of Janus (which in time of peace, according to Roman custom, remained closed) and rushes forth with shield and blood-stained sword, threatening the people with great disaster. He pays little heed to Venus, his mistress, who, accompanied by Amors and Cupids, strives with caresses and embraces to hold him. From the other side, Mars is dragged forward by the Fury Alekto, with a torch in her hand. Near by are monsters personifying Pestilence and Famine, those inseparable partners of War. On the ground, turning her back, lies a woman with a broken lute, representing Harmony, which is incompatible with the discord of War. There is also a mother with her child in her arms, indicating that fecundity, procreation and charity are thwarted by War, which corrupts and destroys everything. In addition, one sees an architect thrown on his back, with his instruments in his hand, to show that which in time of peace is constructed for the use and ornamentation of the City, is hurled to the ground by the force of arms and falls to ruin. I believe, if I remember rightly, that you will find on the ground, under the feet of Mars a book and a drawing on paper, to imply that he treads underfoot all the arts and letters. There ought also to be a bundle of darts or arrows, with the band which held them together undone; these when bound form the symbol of Concord. Beside them is the caduceus and an olive branch, attribute of Peace; these are also cast aside. That grief-stricken woman clothed in black, with torn veil, robbed of all her jewels and other ornaments, is the unfortunate Europe who, for so many years now, has suffered plunder, outrage, and misery, which are so injurious to everyone that it is unnecessary to go into detail. Europe's attribute is the globe, borne by a small angel or genius, and surmounted by the cross, to symbolize the Christian world.*

* Translated by Kristin Lohse Belkin, *Rubens* (London: Phaidon, 1998), 288–289.

1 ft.

25-4 PETER PAUL RUBENS, *Consequences of War*, 1638–1639. Oil on canvas, 6′ 9″ × 11′ 3$\frac{7}{8}$″. Palazzo Pitti, Florence.

Beginning with the Renaissance, artists have left behind many writings shedding light on their life and work. In a 1638 letter, Rubens explained the meaning of each figure in this allegorical painting.

25-5 Anthony Van Dyck, *Charles I Dismounted,* ca. 1635. Oil on canvas, 8′ 11″ × 6′ 11½″. Louvre, Paris.

Van Dyck specialized in court portraiture. In this painting, he depicted the absolutist monarch Charles I at a sharp angle so that the king, a short man, appears to be looking down at the viewer.

ANTHONY VAN DYCK Most of Rubens's successors in Flanders were at one time his assistants. The most famous of these was ANTHONY VAN DYCK (1599–1641). Early on, the younger man, unwilling to be overshadowed by the master's undisputed stature, left his native Antwerp for Genoa and then London, where he became court portraitist to Charles I. Although Van Dyck created dramatic compositions of high quality, his specialty became the portrait. He developed a courtly manner of great elegance that was influential internationally. In one of his finest works, *Charles I Dismounted* (FIG. 25-5), the ill-fated Stuart king stands in a landscape with the Thames River in the background. An equerry and a page attend him. The portrait is a stylish image of relaxed authority, as if the king is out for a casual ride in his park, but no one can mistake the regal poise and the air of absolute authority that his Parliament resented and was soon to rise against. Here, King Charles turns his back on his attendants as he surveys his domain. The king's placement in the composition is exceedingly artful. He stands off-center but balances the picture with a single keen glance at the viewer. Van Dyck even managed to portray Charles I in a position to look down on the observer. In reality, the monarch's short stature forced him to exert his

25-6 CLARA PEETERS, *Still Life with Flowers, Goblet, Dried Fruit, and Pretzels,* 1611. Oil on panel, 1′ 7¾″ × 2′ 1¼″. Museo del Prado, Madrid.

Clara Peeters was a pioneer of still-life painting. Although a Flemish artist, she spent time in Holland and laid the groundwork for many Dutch artists (FIGS. 25-21 to 25-23).

power in ways other than physical. Van Dyck's elegant style resounded in English portrait painting well into the 19th century.

CLARA PEETERS Some Flemish Baroque artists also explored *still-life* painting (inanimate objects artfully arranged). A pioneer of this genre was CLARA PEETERS (1594–ca. 1657), a Flemish artist who spent time in Holland and laid the groundwork for the Dutch artists Pieter Claesz (FIG. 25-21), William Kalf (FIG. 25-22), and Rachel Ruysch (FIG. 25-23). Peeters won renown for her depictions of food and flowers together, and for still lifes that included bread and fruit. Such still lifes became known as *breakfast pieces.* In the breakfast piece *Still Life with Flowers, Goblet, Dried Fruit, and Pretzels* (FIG. 25-6), Peeters's considerable skills are on full display. One of a series of four paintings, each of which depicts a typical early-17th-century meal, *Still Life* reveals Peeters's virtuosity in painting a wide variety of objects convincingly, from the smooth, reflective surfaces of the glass and silver goblets to the soft petals of the blooms in the vase. Although Peeters often depicted the objects in her still lifes against a dark background, thereby negating any sense of deep space, in this painting she presented the leaves of the flower on the stone ledge as though they were encroaching into the viewer's space.

DUTCH REPUBLIC

The Dutch succeeded in securing their independence from the Spanish in the late 16th century. Not until 1648, however, after years of continual border skirmishes with the Spanish (as depicted in Diego Velázquez's *Surrender of Breda*, FIG. 24-29), did the northern Netherlands achieve official recognition as the United Provinces of the Netherlands (the Dutch Republic; MAP 25-1). The Dutch Republic owed its ascendance during the 17th century largely to its economic prosperity. With the founding of the Bank of Amsterdam in 1609, Amsterdam emerged as the financial center of the Continent. In the 17th century, the city had the highest per capita income in Europe. The Dutch economy also benefited enormously from the

country's expertise on the open seas, which facilitated establishing far-flung colonies. By 1650, Dutch trade routes extended to North America, South America, the west coast of Africa, China, Japan, Southeast Asia, and much of the Pacific. Due to this prosperity and in the absence of an absolute ruler, political power increasingly passed into the hands of an urban patrician class of merchants and manufacturers, especially in cities such as Amsterdam, Haarlem, and Delft. That all these bustling cities were located in Holland (the largest of the seven United Provinces) perhaps explains why historians informally use the name "Holland" to refer to the entire country.

Ter Brugghen, van Honthorst, Hals, Leyster

Religious differences were a major consideration during the northern Netherlands' insistent quest for independence during the 16th and early 17th centuries. Whereas Spain and the southern Netherlands were Catholic, the people of the northern Netherlands were predominantly Protestant. The prevailing Calvinism demanded a puritanical rejection of art in churches, and thus artists produced relatively little religious art in the Dutch Republic at this time (especially in comparison with that created in the wake of the Counter-Reformation in areas dominated by Catholicism; see Chapter 24).

HENDRICK TER BRUGGHEN Religious art was not unknown in the Dutch Republic, however. HENDRICK TER BRUGGHEN (1588–1629), for example, painted *Calling of Saint Matthew* (FIG. 25-7) in 1621, after returning from a trip to Italy, selecting as his subject a theme Caravaggio had painted (FIG. 24-18). The moment of the narrative depicted and the naturalistic presentation of the figures echo Caravaggio's work. But although ter Brugghen was an admirer of the Italian master, he dispensed with Caravaggio's stark contrasts of dark and light and instead presented the viewer with a more colorful palette of soft tints. Further, the Dutch painter compressed the figures into a small but well-lit space, creating an intimate effect that differs from Caravaggio's more spacious setting.

25-7 HENDRICK TER BRUGGHEN, *Calling of Saint Matthew*, 1621. Oil on canvas, 3′ 4″ × 4′ 6″. The Hague.

Although middle-class patrons in the Protestant Dutch Republic preferred genre scenes, still lifes, and portraits, some artists, including Hendrick ter Brugghen, also painted religious scenes.

1 ft.

Middle-Class Patronage and
the Art Market in the Dutch Republic

Throughout history, the wealthy have been the most avid art collectors. Indeed, the money necessary to commission major artworks from esteemed artists can be considerable. During the 17th century in the Dutch Republic, however, the widespread prosperity a large proportion of the population enjoyed significantly expanded the range of art patrons. As a result, one of the distinguishing hallmarks of Dutch art production during the Baroque period was how it catered to the tastes of a middle-class audience. The term "middle class" is used broadly here. An aristocracy and an upper class of large-ship owners, rich businesspeople, high-ranking officers, and directors of large companies still existed. These groups continued to be major patrons of the arts. But with the expansion of the Dutch economy, traders, craftspeople, bureaucrats, and soldiers also commissioned and collected art.

Although steeped in the morality and propriety central to the Calvinist ethic, members of the Dutch middle class sought ways to announce their success and newly acquired status. House furnishings, paintings, tapestries, and porcelain were among the items they collected and displayed in their homes. The Dutch disdain for excessive ostentation, however, attributable to Calvinism, led these collectors to favor small, low-key works—portraits, still lifes, genre scenes, and landscapes. This contrasted with the Italian Baroque penchant for large-scale, dazzling ceiling frescoes and opulent room decoration (see Chapter 24).

Although it is risky to generalize about the spending and collecting habits of the Dutch middle class, probate records, contracts, and archived inventories reveal some interesting facts. These records suggest that an individual earning between 1,500 and 3,000 guilders a year would have been living comfortably. This individual might have spent 1,000 guilders for a house and another 1,000 guilders on furnishings, which would have included a significant amount of art, particularly paintings. Although there was, of course, considerable

variation in the prices of artworks, a great deal of art was very affordable. Prints were extremely cheap because of the quantity in which artists produced them. In terms of paintings, interior and genre scenes were relatively inexpensive, perhaps costing one or two guilders. Small landscapes fetched between three and four guilders. Commissioned portraits were the most costly. The size of the work and quality of the frame, as well as the reputation of the artist, were other factors in determining the price.

With the exception of portraits, Dutch artists produced most of their paintings for an anonymous market, hoping to appeal to a wide audience. To ensure success, artists in the United Provinces adapted to the changed conditions of art production and sales. They marketed their paintings in many ways, selling their works directly to buyers who visited their studios and through art dealers, exhibitions, fairs, auctions, and even lotteries. Because of the uncertainty of these sales mechanisms (as opposed to the certainty of an ironclad contract for a commission from a church or king), artists became more responsive to market demands. Specialization became common among Dutch artists. For example, painters might limit their practice to painting portraits, still lifes, or landscapes—the most popular genres among middle-class patrons.

Artists did not always sell their paintings. Frequently they used their work to pay off loans or debts. Tavern debts, in particular, could be settled with paintings, which may explain why many art dealers (such as Jan Vermeer and his father before him) were also innkeepers. This connection between art dealing and other businesses eventually solidified, and innkeepers, for example, often would mount art exhibitions in their taverns, hoping to make a sale. The institutions of today's open art market—dealers, galleries, auctions, and estate sales—owe their establishment to the emergence in the 17th century of a prosperous middle class in the Dutch Republic.

MERCANTILIST PATRONAGE Given the absence of an authoritative ruler and the Calvinist concern for the potential misuse of religious art, commissions from royalty or the Catholic Church, prominent in the art of other countries, were uncommon in the United Provinces. With the new prosperity, however, an expanding class of merchant patrons emerged, and this shift led to an emphasis on different pictorial content. Dutch Baroque art centered on genre scenes, landscapes, portraits, and still lifes, all of which appealed to the prosperous middle class (see "Middle-Class Patronage and the Art Market in the Dutch Republic," above).

GERRIT VAN HONTHORST Typical of 17th-century Dutch genre scenes is *Supper Party* (FIG. **25-8**) by GERRIT VAN HONTHORST (1590–1656) of Utrecht. In this painting, van Honthorst presented an informal gathering of nonidealized human figures. While a musician serenades the group, his companions delight in watching a young woman feeding a piece of chicken to a man whose hands are both occupied—one holds a jug and the other a glass. Van Honthorst spent several years in Italy, and while there he carefully studied Caravaggio's work. The Italian artist's influence surfaces in the mun-

dane tavern setting and the nocturnal lighting. Fascinated by nighttime effects, van Honthorst frequently placed a hidden light source in his pictures and used it as a pretext to work with dramatic and starkly contrasting dark and light effects. Seemingly lighthearted genre scenes such as *Supper Party* were popular in Baroque Holland, but Dutch viewers could also interpret them moralistically. For example, *Supper Party* can be read as a warning against the sins of gluttony (represented by the man on the right) and lust (the woman feeding the glutton is, in all likelihood, a prostitute with her aged procuress at her side). Or perhaps the painting represents the loose companions of the Prodigal Son (Luke 15:13)—panderers and prostitutes drinking, singing, strumming, and laughing. Strict Dutch Calvinists no doubt approved of such interpretations. Others simply took delight in the immediacy of the scenes and the skill of the artists.

FRANS HALS Dutch artists also excelled in portraiture. FRANS HALS (ca. 1581–1666), the leading painter in Haarlem, made portraits his specialty. Portrait artists traditionally had relied heavily on convention—for example, specific poses, settings, attire, and accou-

25-8 GERRIT VAN HONTHORST, *Supper Party,* 1620. Oil on canvas, 4′ 8″ × 7′. Galleria degli Uffizi, Florence.

Gerrit van Honthorst spent several years in Italy and studied the paintings of Caravaggio, whose influence is evident in the mundane tavern setting and the nocturnal light of *Supper Party.*

1 ft.

trements—to convey a sense of the sitter. Because the subject was usually someone of status or note, such as a pope, king, duchess, or wealthy banker, the artist's goal was to produce an image appropriate to the subject's station in life. With the increasing number of Dutch middle-class patrons, the tasks for portraitists became more challenging. The Calvinists shunned ostentation, instead wearing subdued and dark clothing with little variation or decoration, and the traditional conventions became inappropriate and thus unusable. Despite these difficulties, or perhaps because of them, Hals produced lively portraits that seem far more relaxed than traditional formulaic portraiture. He injected an engaging spontaneity into his images and conveyed the individuality of his sitters as well. His manner of execution intensified the casualness, immediacy, and intimacy in his paint-

ings. Because the touch of Hals's brush was as light and fleeting as the moment he captured the pose, the figure, the highlights on clothing, and the facial expression all seem instantaneously created.

ARCHERS OF SAINT HADRIAN Hals's group portraits reflect the widespread popularity in the Dutch Republic of vast canvases commemorating the participation of Dutch burghers in civic organizations. These commissions presented a far greater challenge to the painter than requests to depict a single sitter. Hals rose to the challenge and achieved great success with this new portrait genre. His *Archers of Saint Hadrian* (FIG. 25-9) is typical in that the subject is one of the many Dutch civic militia groups that claimed credit for liberating the Dutch Republic from Spain. Like other companies, the

25-9 FRANS HALS, *Archers of Saint Hadrian,* ca. 1633. Oil on canvas, 6′ 9″ × 11′. Frans Halsmuseum, Haarlem.

In this brilliant composition, Hals succeeded in solving the problem of adequately representing each individual in a group portrait while retaining action and variety in the painting as a whole.

1 ft.

Dutch Republic **681**

25-10 Frans Hals, *The Women Regents of the Old Men's Home at Haarlem,* 1664. Oil on canvas, 5′ 7″ × 8′ 2″. Frans Halsmuseum, Haarlem.

Dutch women played a major role in public life as regents of charitable institutions. A stern puritanical sensibility suffuses Hals's group portrait of the regents of Haarlem's old men's home.

1 ft.

Archers met on their saint's feast day in dress uniform for a grand banquet. The celebrations sometimes lasted an entire week, prompting an ordinance limiting them to three or four days. These events often involved a group portrait.

In *Archers of Saint Hadrian,* Hals attacked the problem of how to represent each militia member adequately yet retain action and variety in the composition. Whereas earlier group portraits in the Netherlands were rather ordered, regimented images, Hals sought to enliven his depictions.

In the *Archers* portrait, for example, each man is both a troop member and an individual with a distinct physiognomy. The sitters' movements and moods vary enormously. Some engage the viewer directly. Others look away or at a companion. Whereas one is stern, another is animated. Each man is equally visible and clearly recognizable. The uniformity of attire—black military dress, white ruffs, and sashes—did not deter Hals from injecting spontaneity into the work. Indeed, he used those elements to create a lively rhythm that extends throughout the composition and energizes the portrait. The impromptu effect—the preservation of every detail and fleeting facial expression—is, of course, the result of careful planning. Yet Hals's vivacious brush appears to have moved instinctively, directed by a plan in his mind but not traceable in any preparatory scheme on the canvas.

WOMEN REGENTS OF HAARLEM In *The Women Regents of the Old Men's Home at Haarlem* (FIG. **25-10**), Hals produced a group portrait of Calvinist women engaged in charitable work. Although Dutch women had primary responsibility for the welfare of the family and the orderly operation of the home, they also populated the labor force in the cities. Among the more prominent roles that educated women played in public life were regents of orphanages, hospitals, old-age homes, and houses of correction. In Hals's portrait, the regents sit quietly in a manner becoming of devout

25-11 Judith Leyster, *Self-Portrait,* ca. 1630. Oil on canvas, 2′ 5$\frac{3}{8}$″ × 2′ 1$\frac{5}{8}$″. National Gallery of Art, Washington, D.C. (gift of Mr. and Mrs. Robert Woods Bliss).

Although presenting herself as an artist specializing in genre scenes, Leyster wears elegant attire instead of a painter's smock, placing her socially as a member of a well-to-do family.

1 ft.

Calvinists. Unlike the more relaxed, seemingly informal character of his other group portraits, a stern, puritanical, and composed sensibility suffuses Hals's portrayal of the Haarlem regents. The women—all carefully distinguished as individuals—gaze out from the painting with expressions ranging from dour disinterest to kindly concern. The somber and virtually *monochromatic* (one-color) palette, punctuated only by the white accents of the clothing, contributes to the painting's restraint. Both the coloration and the mood of Hals's portrait are appropriate for this commission. Portraying the Haarlem regents called for a very different kind of portrait from those Hals made of men at festive militia banquets.

JUDITH LEYSTER Some of Hals's students developed thriving careers of their own as portraitists. One was JUDITH LEYSTER (1609–1660), whose *Self-Portrait* (FIG. 25-11) suggests the strong training she received. The picture is detailed, precise, and accurate but also imbued with the spontaneity found in Hals's works. In this self-portrait, Leyster succeeded at communicating a great deal about herself. She depicted herself as an artist, seated in front of a painting resting on an easel. The palette in her left hand and brush in her right announce that the painting is her creation. She thus allows the viewer to evaluate her skill, which both the fiddler on the canvas and the image of herself demonstrate as considerable. Although she produced a wide range of paintings, including still lifes and floral pieces, her specialty was genre scenes such as the comic image seen on the easel. Her self-assurance is reflected in her quick smile and her relaxed pose as she stops her work to meet the viewer's gaze. Although presenting herself as an artist, Leyster did not portray herself wearing the traditional artist's smock, as Rembrandt did in his self-portrait (FIG. 25-15). Her elegant attire distinguishes her socially as a member of a well-to-do family, another important aspect of Leyster's identity.

Rembrandt

REMBRANDT VAN RIJN (1606–1669), Hals's younger contemporary, was an artist of great versatility, a master of light and shadow, and a unique interpreter of the Protestant conception of scripture. The leading Dutch painter of his time, Rembrandt was an undisputed genius. Born in Leiden, he moved to Amsterdam around 1631, which provided him with a more extensive clientele than possible in his native city. Rembrandt had trained as a history painter in Leiden, but in Amsterdam he immediately entered the lucrative market for portrait painting and soon became renowned for that genre.

ANATOMY LESSON OF DR. TULP In a painting he created shortly after he arrived in Amsterdam, *Anatomy Lesson of Dr. Tulp* (FIG. 25-12), Rembrandt deviated even further from the traditional staid group portrait than had Hals. Despite Hals's determination to enliven his portraits, he still evenly spread his subjects across the canvas. In contrast, Rembrandt chose to portray the members of the surgeons' guild (who commissioned this group portrait) clustered together on the painting's left side. In the foreground appears the corpse that Dr. Tulp, a noted physician, is in the act of dissecting. Rembrandt diagonally placed and foreshortened the corpse, activating the space by disrupting the strict horizontal, planar orientation found in traditional portraiture. He depicted each of the "students" specifically, and although they wear virtually identical attire, their poses and facial expressions suggest the varying degrees of intensity with which they watch Dr. Tulp's demonstration—or ignore it. One, at the apex of Rembrandt's triangular composition of bodies, looks out at the viewer instead of at the operating table. Another directs his attention at the open book (a manual of anatomy) at the corpse's feet. Rembrandt produced this painting when he was 26 and just beginning his career, a fact that makes his innovative approach to group portraiture all the more remarkable.

25-12 REMBRANDT VAN RIJN, *Anatomy Lesson of Dr. Tulp*, 1632. Oil on canvas, 5′ 3¾″ × 7′ 1¼″. Mauritshuis, The Hague. ◼◀

In this early work, Rembrandt used an unusual composition, portraying members of Amsterdam's surgeons' guild clustered together on one side of the painting as they watch Dr. Tulp dissect a corpse.

1 ft.

25-13 REMBRANDT VAN RIJN, *The Company of Captain Frans Banning Cocq* (*Night Watch*), 1642. Oil on canvas, 11′ 11″ × 14′ 4″ (cropped from original size). Rijksmuseum, Amsterdam.

Rembrandt's dramatic use of light contributes to the animation of this militia group portrait in which the artist showed the company rushing about as they organize themselves for a parade.

1 ft.

NIGHT WATCH Rembrandt amplified the complexity and energy of the group portrait in *The Company of Captain Frans Banning Cocq* (FIG. **25-13**), better known as *Night Watch*. This more commonly used title is a misnomer, however—the painting is not of a nocturnal scene. Rembrandt used light in a masterful way, and dramatic lighting certainly enhances the image. Still, the painting's darkness (which explains the commonly used title) is due more to the varnish the artist used, which darkened considerably over time, than to the subject depicted.

This painting was one of many civic-guard group portraits produced during this period. From the limited information available about the commission, it appears that the two officers, Captain Frans Banning Cocq and his lieutenant, Willem van Ruytenburch, along with 16 members of their militia, contributed to Rembrandt's fee. (Despite the prominence of the girl just to the left of center, scholars have yet to ascertain her identity.) *Night Watch* was one of six paintings by different artists that various groups commissioned around 1640 for the assembly and banquet room of Amsterdam's new Musketeers Hall, the largest and most prestigious interior space in the city. Unfortunately, in 1715, when city officials moved Rembrandt's painting to Amsterdam's town hall, they cropped it on all sides, leaving an incomplete record of the artist's final resolution of the challenge of portraying this group.

Even in its truncated form, *The Company of Captain Frans Banning Cocq* succeeds in capturing the excitement and frenetic activity of the men preparing for the parade. A comparison of this militia group portrait with Hals's *Archers of Saint Hadrian* (FIG. **25-9**) reveals Rembrandt's inventiveness in enlivening what was, by then, becoming a conventional portrait format. Rather than present assembled men, posed in orderly fashion, the younger artist chose to portray the company scurrying about in the act of organizing themselves, thereby animating the image considerably. At the same time, he managed to record the three most important stages of using a musket—loading, firing, and readying the weapon for reloading—details that must have pleased his patrons.

RETURN OF THE PRODIGAL SON The Calvinist injunctions against religious art did not prevent Rembrandt from making a

series of religious paintings and prints. In the Dutch Republic, paintings depicting biblical themes were not objects of devotion, but they still brought great prestige, and Rembrandt and other artists vied to demonstrate their ability to narrate holy scripture in dramatic new ways. The Dutch images, however, are unlike the opulent, overwhelming art of Baroque Italy. Rather, Rembrandt's religious art is that of a committed Christian who desired to interpret biblical narratives in human (as opposed to lofty theological) terms. Rembrandt had a special interest in probing the states of the human soul. The spiritual stillness of his religious paintings is that of inward-turning contemplation, far from the choirs and trumpets and the heavenly tumult of Bernini (FIG. **24-1**) or Pozzo (FIG. **24-24**). The Dutch artist's psychological insight and his profound sympathy for human affliction produced, at the very end of his life, one of the most moving pictures in all religious art, *Return of the Prodigal Son* (FIG. **25-14**). Tenderly embraced by his forgiving father, the son crouches before him in weeping contrition, while three figures, immersed to varying degrees in the soft shadows, note the lesson of mercy. The light, everywhere mingled with shadow, directs the viewer's attention by illuminating the father and son and largely veiling the witnesses. Its focus is the beautiful, spiritual face of the old man. Secondarily, the light touches the contrasting stern face of the foremost witness. The painting demonstrates the degree to which Rembrandt developed a personal style completely in tune with the simple eloquence of the biblical passage.

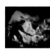

25-14A REMBRANDT, *Blinding of Samson*, 1636.

REMBRANDT'S LIGHT From the few paintings by Rembrandt discussed thus far, it should be clear that the artist's use of light is among the hallmarks of his style. Rembrandt's pictorial method involved refining light and shade into finer and finer nuances until they blended with one another. Earlier painters' use of abrupt lights and darks gave way to gradation in the work of artists

25-14 Rembrandt van Rijn, *Return of the Prodigal Son*, ca. 1665. Oil on canvas, 8′ 8″ × 6′ 9″. Hermitage Museum, Saint Petersburg.

The spiritual stillness of Rembrandt's religious paintings is that of inward-turning contemplation, far from the choirs and trumpets and heavenly tumult of Italian Baroque Counter-Reformation works.

such as Rembrandt and Velázquez (see Chapter 24). Although these later artists may have sacrificed some of the dramatic effects of sharp chiaroscuro, a greater fidelity to actual appearances offset those sacrifices. This technique is closer to reality because the eyes perceive light and dark not as static but as always subtly changing.

In general, Renaissance artists represented forms and faces in a flat, neutral modeling light (even Leonardo's shading is of a standard kind). They represented the *idea* of light, rather than the real look of it. Artists such as Rembrandt discovered degrees of light and dark, degrees of differences in pose, in the movements of facial features, and in psychic states. They arrived at these differences optically, not conceptually or in terms of some ideal. Rembrandt found that by manipulating the direction, intensity, distance, and surface texture of light and shadow, he could render the most subtle nuances of character and mood, both in persons and in whole scenes. He discovered for the modern world that variation of light and shade, subtly modulated, can be read as emotional differences. In the visible world, light, dark, and the wide spectrum of values between the two are charged with meanings and feelings that sometimes are independent of the shapes and figures they modify. The theater and the photographic arts have used these discoveries to great dramatic effect.

REMBRANDT'S SELF-PORTRAITS Rembrandt carried over the spiritual quality of his religious works into his later portraits by the same means—what could be called the "psychology of

light." Light and dark are not in conflict in his portraits. They are reconciled, merging softly and subtly to produce the visual equivalent of quietness. Their prevailing mood is that of tranquil meditation, of philosophical resignation, of musing recollection—indeed, a whole cluster of emotional tones heard only in silence.

In a self-portrait (FIG. 25-15) produced late in Rembrandt's life, the light that shines from the upper left of the painting bathes the painter's face in soft highlights, leaving the lower part of his body in shadow. The artist depicted himself here as possessing dignity and strength, and the portrait serves as a summary of the many stylistic and professional concerns that occupied him throughout his career. Rembrandt's distinctive use of light is evident, as is the assertive brushwork that suggests a quiet confidence and self-assurance. He presented himself as a working artist holding his brushes, palette, and maulstick (compare FIG. 23-17) and wearing his studio garb—a smock and painter's turban. The circles on the wall behind him (the subject of much scholarly debate) may allude to a legendary sign of artistic virtuosity—the ability to draw a perfect circle freehand. Ultimately, Rembrandt's abiding interest in revealing the human soul emerged here in his careful focus on his expressive visage. His controlled use of light and the nonspecific setting contribute to this focus. Further, X-rays of the painting have revealed that Rembrandt originally depicted himself in the act of painting. His final resolution, with the viewer's attention drawn to his face, produced a portrait not just of the artist but of the man as well. Indeed, Rembrandt's nearly 70 self-portraits in various media have no parallel in sheer quantity. They reflect the artist's deeply personal connection to his craft.

25-15A Rembrandt, *Self-Portrait*, 1658.

25-15 Rembrandt van Rijn, *Self-Portrait*, ca. 1659–1660. Oil on canvas, 3′ 8¾″ × 3′ 1″. Kenwood House, London (Iveagh Bequest).

In this late self-portrait, Rembrandt's interest in revealing the human soul is evident in the attention given to his expressive face. The controlled use of light and the nonspecific setting contribute to this focus.

25-16 REMBRANDT VAN RIJN, *Christ with the Sick around Him, Receiving the Children* (*Hundred-Guilder Print*), ca. 1649. Etching, $11'' \times 1' 3\frac{1}{4}''$. Pierpont Morgan Library, New York.

Rembrandt's mastery of the new printmaking medium of etching is evident in his expert use of light and dark to draw attention to Christ as he preaches compassionately to the blind and lame.

1 in.

REMBRANDT'S ETCHINGS

Rembrandt's virtuosity also extended to the graphic media—in particular, to etching (see "Woodcuts, Engravings, and Etchings," Chapter 20, page 537). Many artists took up etching after its perfection early in the 17th century, because etching allowed greater freedom than engraving in drawing the design. For etching, the printmaker covers a copper plate with a layer of wax or varnish. The artist incises the design into this surface with a pointed tool, exposing the metal below but not cutting into its surface. The printer then immerses the plate in acid, which etches, or eats away, the exposed parts of the metal, acting the same as the burin in engraving. The medium's softness gives etchers greater carving freedom than woodcutters and engravers have working directly in their more resistant media of wood and metal. If Rembrandt had never painted, he still would be renowned, as he principally was in his lifetime, for his prints. Prints were a major source of income for Rembrandt, as they were for Albrecht Dürer (see Chapter 23), and he often reworked the plates so that they could be used to produce a new issue or edition. This constant reworking was unusual within the context of 17th-century printmaking practices.

HUNDRED-GUILDER PRINT One of Rembrandt's most celebrated etchings is *Christ with the Sick around Him, Receiving the Children* (FIG. 25-16). Indeed, the title by which this work has been known since the early 18th century, *Hundred-Guilder Print*, refers to the high price it brought during Rembrandt's lifetime. *Christ with the Sick* demonstrates the artist's mastery of all aspects of the printmaker's craft, for Rembrandt used both engraving and etching to depict the figures and the setting. As in his other religious works, Rembrandt suffused this print with a deep and abiding piety, presenting the viewer not the celestial triumph of the Catholic Church but the humanity and humility of Jesus. Christ appears in the center preaching compassionately to, and simultaneously blessing, the blind, the lame, and the young who are spread throughout the composition in a dazzling array of standing, kneeling, and lying positions. Also present is a young man in elegant garments with his head in his hand, lamenting Christ's insistence that the wealthy need to give their possessions to the poor in order to gain entrance to Heaven. The tonal range of the print is remarkable. At the right, the figures near the city gate are in deep shadow. At the left, the figures, some rendered almost exclusively in outline, are in bright light—not the light of day but the illumination radiating from Christ himself. A second, unseen source of light comes from the right and casts the shadow of the praying man's arms and head onto Christ's tunic. Technically and in terms of its humanity, the *Hundred-Guilder Print* is Rembrandt's supreme achievement as a printmaker.

Landscape and Interior Painting

Landscape scenes abound in 17th-century Dutch art. Due to topography and politics, the Dutch had a unique relationship to the terrain, one that differed from those of other European countries. After gaining independence from Spain, the Dutch undertook an extensive land reclamation project that lasted almost a century. Dikes and drainage systems cropped up across the countryside. Because of the effort expended on these endeavors, people developed a very direct relationship to the land. Further, the reclamation affected Dutch social and economic life. The marshy and swampy nature of much of the land made it less desirable for large-scale exploitation, so the extensive feudal landowning system that existed elsewhere in Europe never developed in the United Provinces. Most Dutch families owned and worked their own farms, cultivating a feeling of closeness to the terrain.

AELBERT CUYP One Dutch artist who established his reputation as a specialist in landscape painting was AELBERT CUYP (ca. 1620–1691). His works were the products of careful observation and a deep respect for and understanding of the Dutch terrain. *Distant View of Dordrecht, with a Milkmaid and Four Cows, and Other Figures* (FIG. 25-17) reveals Cuyp's substantial skills. Unlike the idealized classical landscapes that appear in many Italian Renaissance paintings, this landscape is particularized. In fact, the church in the background can be identified as the Grote Kerk in Dordrecht. The dairy cows, shepherds, and milkmaid in the foreground refer to a cornerstone of Dutch agriculture—the demand for dairy products such as butter and cheese, which increased with the development of urban centers. The credibility of this and similar paintings rests on Cuyp's pristine rendering of each detail.

JACOB VAN RUISDAEL Depicting the Dutch landscape with precision and sensitivity was also a specialty of JACOB VAN RUISDAEL (ca. 1628–1682). In *View of Haarlem from the Dunes at Overveen* (FIG. 25-18), van Ruisdael provided an overarching view of this major Dutch city. The specificity of the artist's image—the Saint Bavo church in the background, the numerous windmills that refer to the land reclamation efforts, and the figures in the foreground stretching linen

25-18A RUISDAEL *Jewish Cemetery,* ca. 1655–1660.

25-17 AELBERT CUYP, *Distant View of Dordrecht, with a Milkmaid and Four Cows, and Other Figures*, late 1640s. Oil on canvas, 5′ 1″ × 6′ 4$\frac{7}{8}$″. National Gallery, London.

Unlike idealized Italian Renaissance classical landscapes, Cuyp's painting portrays a particular locale. The cows, shepherds, and milkmaid refer to the Dutch Republic's important dairy industry.

1 ft.

25-18 JACOB VAN RUISDAEL, *View of Haarlem from the Dunes at Overveen*, ca. 1670. Oil on canvas, 1′ 10″ × 2′ 1″. Mauritshuis, The Hague.

In this painting, van Ruisdael succeeded in capturing a specific view of Haarlem, its windmills, and Saint Bavo church, but he also imbued the landscape with a quiet serenity that approaches the spiritual.

1 in.

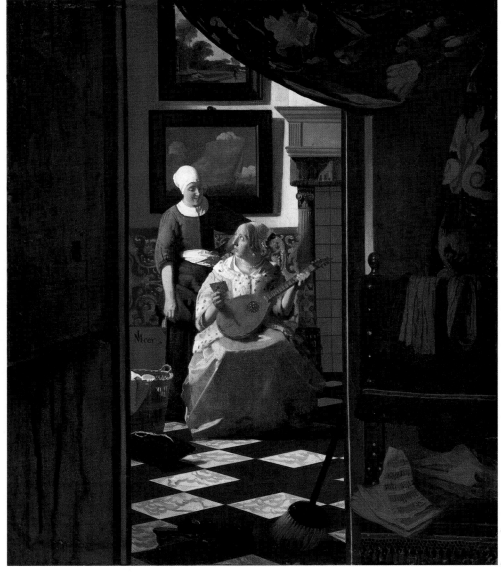

Vermeer used both mirrors and the camera obscura to depict opulent 17th-century Dutch domestic interiors so convincingly. He was also far ahead of his time in understanding the science of color.

to be bleached (a major industry in Haarlem)—reflects the pride Dutch painters took in recording their homeland and the activities of their fellow citizens. Nonetheless, in this painting the inhabitants and dwellings are so minuscule that they blend into the land itself, unlike the figures in Cuyp's view of Dordrecht (FIG. 25-17). Further, the horizon line is low, so the sky fills almost three-quarters of the picture space, and the sun illuminates the landscape only in patches, where it has broken through the clouds above. In *View of Haarlem,* as in his other landscape paintings, van Ruisdael not only captured the appearance of a specific locale but also succeeded in imbuing the work with a quiet serenity that becomes almost spiritual.

25-19A VERMEER, *View of Delft,* ca. 1661.

JAN VERMEER The sense of peace, familiarity, and comfort that Dutch landscape paintings exude also emerges in interior scenes, another popular subject among middle-class patrons. These paintings offer the viewer glimpses into the lives of prosperous, responsible, and cultured citizens of the United Provinces. The foremost Dutch painter of interior scenes was JAN VERMEER (1632–1675) of Delft. Vermeer derived much of his income from his work as an innkeeper and art dealer (see "Middle-Class Patronage and the Art Market," page 680), and he painted no more than 35 paintings that can be definitively attributed to him. He began his career as a painter of biblical and historical themes but soon abandoned those traditional subjects in favor of domestic scenes. Flemish artists of the 15th century also had painted domestic interiors, but persons of sacred significance often occupied those scenes (FIG. 20-4). In contrast, Vermeer and his contemporaries composed neat, quietly opulent interiors of Dutch middle-class dwellings with men, women, and children engaging in household tasks or some little recreation. Women are the primary occupants of Vermeer's homes, and his paintings are highly idealized depictions of the social values of Dutch burghers.

THE LETTER A room of a well-appointed Dutch house is the scene of Vermeer's *The Letter* (FIG. 25-19). The drawn curtain and open doorway through which viewers must peer reinforce their status as outsiders getting a glimpse of a private scene. The painting features two women. One wears elegant attire, suggesting that she is

a woman of considerable means. A maid interrupts her lute playing to deliver a letter. The 17th-century Dutch audience would immediately recognize that it is a love letter, because the lute was a traditional symbol of the music of love, and the painting of a ship on a calm (as opposed to rough) sea on the back wall was a symbol of love requited. In Jan Harmensz Krul's book *Love Emblems,* published in Amsterdam in 1634, the author wrote, "Love may rightly be compared to the sea, considering its changeableness . . . just so does it go with a lover as with a skipper embarking on the sea, one day good weather, another day storm and howling wind."[2]

25-19B VERMEER, *Woman Holding a Balance,* ca. 1664.

Vermeer was a master of pictorial light and used it with immense virtuosity. He could render space so convincingly through his depiction of light that in his works, the picture surface functions as an invisible glass pane through which the viewer looks into the constructed illusion. Historians are confident that Vermeer used as tools both mirrors and the *camera obscura,* an ancestor of the modern camera based on passing light through a tiny pinhole or lens to project an image on a screen or the wall of a room. (In later versions, artists projected the image on a ground-glass wall of a box whose opposite wall contained the pinhole or lens.) This does not mean that Vermeer merely copied the image. Instead, these aids helped him obtain results he reworked compositionally, placing his figures and the furniture of a room in a beautiful stability of quadrilateral shapes. His designs have a matchless classical serenity. Enhancing

25-20 JAN STEEN, *Feast of Saint Nicholas,* ca. 1660–1665. Oil on canvas, 2′ 8$\frac{1}{4}$″ × 2′ 3$\frac{3}{4}$″. Rijksmuseum, Amsterdam.

Steen's lively scene of Dutch children discovering their Christmas gifts may also have an allegorical dimension. *Feast of Saint Nicholas* probably alludes to selfishness, pettiness, and jealousy.

1 in.

in *The Letter*, the viewer is outside the space of the action, looking in through the drawn curtain that separates the artist in his studio from the rest of the house—and from the viewer. Some art historians have suggested that the light radiating from an unseen window on the left that illuminates both the model and the canvas being painted alludes to the light of artistic inspiration. Accordingly, many art historians have interpreted this painting as an allegory—a reference to painting inspired by history. Vermeer's mother-in-law confirmed this allegorical reading in 1677 when she sought to retain the painting after the artist's death, when 26 of his works were scheduled to be sold to pay his widow's debts. She listed the painting in her written claim as "the piece . . . wherein the Art of Painting is portrayed."[3]

this quality are colors so true to the optical facts and so subtly modulated that they suggest Vermeer was far ahead of his time in color science. Close examination of his paintings shows that Vermeer realized shadows are not colorless and dark, that adjoining colors affect each other, and that light is composed of colors. Thus, he painted reflections off of surfaces in colors modified by others nearby. Some experts have suggested that Vermeer also perceived the phenomenon modern photographers call "circles of confusion," which appear on out-of-focus negatives. Vermeer could have seen them in images projected by the camera obscura's primitive lenses. He approximated these effects with light dabs that, in close view, give the impression of an image slightly "out of focus." When the observer draws back a step, however, as if adjusting the lens, the color spots cohere, giving an astonishingly accurate illusion of a third dimension.

THE ART OF PAINTING Vermeer's stylistic precision and commitment to his profession surface in *Allegory of the Art of Painting* (FIG. **25-1**). The artist himself appears in the painting, with his back to the viewer and dressed in "historical" clothing (reminiscent of Burgundian attire). He is hard at work on a painting of the model who stands before him wearing a laurel wreath and holding a trumpet and book, traditional attributes of Clio, the muse of history. The map of the provinces (an increasingly common adornment in Dutch homes) on the back wall serves as yet another reference to history. As

JAN STEEN Whereas Vermeer's paintings reveal the charm and beauty of Dutch domesticity, the works of JAN STEEN (ca. 1625–1679) provide a counterpoint. In *Feast of Saint Nicholas* (FIG. **25-20**), Steen rejected painting a tidy, calm Dutch household and opted instead for a scene of chaos and disruption. Saint Nicholas has just visited this residence, and the children are in an uproar as they search their shoes for the Christmas gifts he has left. Some children are delighted. The little girl in the center clutches her gifts, clearly unwilling to share with the other children despite her mother's pleas. Others are disappointed. The boy on the left is in tears because he has received only a birch rod. An appropriately festive atmosphere reigns, which contrasts sharply with the decorum that prevails in Vermeer's works. Like the paintings of other Dutch artists, Steen's lively scenes often take on an allegorical dimension and moralistic tone. Steen frequently used children's activities as satirical comments on foolish adult behavior, and *Feast of Saint Nicholas* is not his only allusion to selfishness, pettiness, and jealousy.

Still-Life Painting

The prosperous Dutch were justifiably proud of their accomplishments, and the popularity of still-life paintings—particularly images of accumulated goods—reflected this pride. These still lifes, like Vermeer's interior scenes, are beautifully crafted images that are both scientific in their optical accuracy and poetic in their beauty and lyricism.

Vanitas still lifes reflect the pride Dutch citizens had in their material possessions, but Calvinist morality and humanity tempered that pride. The skull and timepiece remind the viewer of life's transience.

1 in.

PIETER CLAESZ Many Dutch still-life paintings, such as *Vanitas Still Life* (FIG. **25-21**) by PIETER CLAESZ (1597/98–1660), celebrate material possessions, here presented as if strewn across a tabletop or dresser. The ever-present morality and humility central to the Calvinist faith tempered Dutch pride in worldly goods, however. Thus, while Claesz fostered the appreciation and enjoyment of the beauty and value of the objects he depicted, he also reminded the viewer of life's transience by incorporating references to death. Paintings with such features are called *vanitas* (vanity) *paintings*. Each feature is referred to as a *memento mori* (reminder of death). In *Vanitas Still Life*, references to mortality include the skull, timepiece, tipped glass, and cracked walnut. All suggest the passage of time or a presence that has disappeared. Something or someone was here—and now is gone. Claesz emphasized this element of time (and demonstrated his technical virtuosity) by including a self-portrait, reflected in the glass ball on the left side of the table. He appears to be painting this still life. But in an apparent challenge to the message of inevitable mortality that vanitas paintings convey, the portrait serves to immortalize the subject—in this case, the artist himself.

WILLEM KALF As Dutch prosperity increased, precious objects and luxury items made their way into still-life paintings. *Still Life with a Late Ming Ginger Jar* (FIG. **25-22**) by WILLEM KALF (1619–1693) reveals both the wealth Dutch citizens had accrued and the painter's exquisite skills, both technical and aesthetic. Kalf highlighted the breadth of Dutch maritime trade through his depiction of the Indian floral carpet and the Chinese jar used to store ginger (a luxury item). He delighted in recording the lustrous sheen of fabric and the light glinting off reflective surfaces. As is evident in this image, Kalf's works present an array of ornamental objects, such as the Venetian

and Dutch glassware and the silver dish. The inclusion of the watch, Mediterranean peach, and peeled lemon suggests that this work is also a vanitas painting.

RACHEL RUYSCH As living objects that soon die, flowers, particularly cut blossoms, appeared frequently in vanitas paintings. However, floral painting as a distinct genre also flourished in the Dutch Republic. Among the leading practitioners of this art was RACHEL RUYSCH (1663–1750). Ruysch's father was a professor of botany and anatomy, which may account for her interest in and knowledge of plants and insects. She acquired an international reputation for lush paintings such as *Flower Still Life* (FIG. **25-23**). In this image, the lav-

25-22 WILLEM KALF, *Still Life with a Late Ming Ginger Jar*, 1669. Oil on canvas, 2′ 6″ × 2′ 1¾″. Indianapolis Museum of Art, Indianapolis (gift in commemoration of the 60th anniversary of the Art Association of Indianapolis, in memory of Daniel W. and Elizabeth C. Marmon).

The opulent objects, especially the Indian carpet and Chinese jar, attest to the prosperous Dutch maritime trade. Kalf's inclusion of a watch suggests that this painting may also be a vanitas still life.

1 ft.

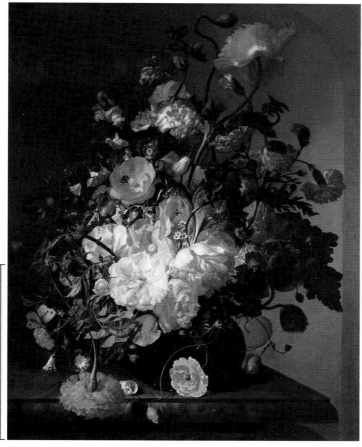

1 ft.

25-23 RACHEL RUYSCH, *Flower Still Life,* after 1700. Oil on canvas, 2′ 5¾″ × 1′ 11⅞″. Toledo Museum of Art, Toledo (purchased with funds from the Libbey Endowment, gift of Edward Drummond Libbey).

Flower paintings were very popular in the Dutch Republic. Rachel Ruysch achieved international renown for her lush paintings of floral arrangements, noted also for their careful compositions.

ish floral arrangement is so full that many of the blossoms seem to be spilling out of the vase. Ruysch carefully constructed her paintings. Here, for example, she positioned the flowers to create a diagonal that runs from the lower left of the painting to the upper right corner and that offsets the opposing diagonal of the table edge. Ruysch became famous for her floral paintings and still lifes, and from 1708 to 1716 she served as court painter to the elector Palatine (the ruler of the Palatinate, a former division of Bavaria) in Düsseldorf, Germany.

FRANCE

In France, monarchical authority had been increasing for centuries, culminating in the reign of Louis XIV (r. 1661–1715), who sought to determine the direction of French society and culture. Although its economy was not as expansive as that of the Dutch Republic, France became Europe's largest and most powerful country in the 17th century. Against this backdrop, the arts flourished.

Painting and Graphic Art

NICOLAS POUSSIN Rome's ancient and Renaissance monuments enticed many French artists to study there. Normandy-born NICOLAS POUSSIN (1594–1665), for example, spent most of his life in Rome, where he produced grandly severe paintings modeled on those of Titian and Raphael. He also carefully worked out a theoretical explanation of his method and was ultimately responsible for establishing classical painting as an important ingredient of 17th-century French art (see "Poussin's Notes for a Treatise on Painting," page 692). His classical style presents a striking contrast to the contemporaneous Baroque style of his Italian counterparts in Rome (see Chapter 24), underscoring the multifaceted character of the art of 17th-century Europe.

ET IN ARCADIA EGO Poussin's *Et in Arcadia Ego* (*I, Too, in Arcadia,* or *Even in Arcadia, I* [am present]; FIG. **25-24**) draws on the rational order and stability of Raphael's paintings and on antique

25-24 NICOLAS POUSSIN, *Et in Arcadia Ego,* ca. 1655. Oil on canvas, 2′ 10″ × 4′. Louvre, Paris.

Poussin was the leading proponent of classicism in 17th-century Rome. His works incorporate the rational order and stability of Raphael's compositions as well as figures inspired by ancient statuary.

1 ft.

Poussin's Notes for a Treatise on Painting

As the leading exponent of classical painting in 17th-century Rome, Nicolas Poussin (FIGS. 25-24 and 25-25) outlined the principles of classicism in notes for an intended treatise on painting, left incomplete at his death. In those notes, Poussin described the essential ingredients necessary to produce a beautiful painting in "the grand manner":

> The grand manner consists of four things: subject-matter or theme, thought, structure, and style. The first thing that, as the foundation of all others, is required, is that the subject-matter shall be grand, as are battles, heroic actions, and divine things. But assuming that the subject on which the painter is laboring is grand, his next consideration is to keep away from minutiae . . . [and paint only] things magnificent and grand . . . . Those who elect mean subjects take refuge in them because of the weakness of their talents.*

The idea of beauty does not descend into matter unless [a painting] is prepared as carefully as possible. This preparation consists of three things: arrangement, measure, and aspect or form. Arrangement means the relative position of the parts; measure refers to their size; and form consists of lines and colors. Arrangement and relative position of the parts and making every limb of the body hold its natural place are not sufficient unless measure is added, which gives to each limb its correct size, proportionate to that of the whole body [compare "Polykleitos's Prescription for the Perfect Statue," Chapter 5, page 124], and unless form joins in, so that the lines will be drawn with grace and with a harmonious juxtaposition of light and shadow.†

* Translated by Robert Goldwater and Marco Treves, eds., *Artists on Art*, 3d ed. (New York: Pantheon Books, 1958), 155.
† Ibid., 156.

25-25 NICOLAS POUSSIN, *Burial of Phocion*, 1648. Oil on canvas, 3' 11" × 5' 10". Louvre, Paris.

Poussin's landscapes do not represent a particular place and time but are idealized settings for noble themes, like this one based on Plutarch's biography of the Athenian general Phocion.

1 ft.

25-25A POUSSIN, *Saint John on Patmos*, 1640.

statuary. Landscape, of which Poussin became increasingly fond, provides the setting for the picture. Dominating the foreground, however, are three shepherds, living in the idyllic land of Arcadia, who study an inscription on a tomb as a statuesque female figure quietly places her hand on the shoulder of one of them. She may be the spirit of death, reminding these mortals, as does the inscription, that death is found even in Arcadia, supposedly a spot of paradisiacal bliss. The countless draped female statues surviving in Italy from Roman times supplied the models for this figure, and the posture of the youth with one foot resting on a boulder derives from Greco-Roman statues of Neptune, the sea god, leaning on his trident. The classically compact and balanced grouping of the figures, the even light, and the thoughtful and reserved mood complement Poussin's classical figure types.

BURIAL OF PHOCION Among Poussin's finest works is *Burial of Phocion* (FIG. 25-25), a subject the artist characteristically chose from the literature of antiquity. Poussin's source was Plutarch's *Life of Phocion*, a biography of the distinguished Athenian general whom his compatriots unjustly put to death for treason. Eventually, the state gave Phocion a public funeral and memorialized him. In the foreground of Poussin's painting, the hero's body is being taken away, his burial on Athenian soil initially forbidden. The two massive bearers and the bier are starkly isolated in a great landscape that throws them into solitary relief, eloquently expressive of the hero abandoned in death. The landscape's interlocking planes slope upward to the lighted sky at the left. Its carefully arranged terraces bear slowly moving streams, shepherds and their flocks, and, in the dis-

25-26 CLAUDE LORRAIN, *Landscape with Cattle and Peasants*, 1629. Oil on canvas, 3′ 6″ × 4′ 10½″. Philadelphia Museum of Art, Philadelphia (George W. Elkins Collection).

Claude used atmospheric and linear perspective to transform the rustic Roman countryside filled with peasants and animals into an idealized classical landscape bathed in sunlight in infinite space.

tance, whole assemblies of solid geometric structures (temples, towers, walls, villas, and a central grand sarcophagus). The skies are untroubled, and the light is even and revealing of form. The trees are few and carefully arranged, like curtains lightly drawn back to reveal a natural setting carefully cultivated for a single human action. Unlike van Ruisdael in *View of Haarlem* (FIG. 25-18), Poussin did not intend this scene to represent a particular place and time. It was the French artist's construction of an idea of a noble landscape to frame a noble theme, much like Annibale Carracci's classical landscape (FIG. 24-15). The *Phocion* landscape is nature subordinated to a rational plan.

CLAUDE LORRAIN Claude Gellée, called CLAUDE LORRAIN (1600–1682) after his birthplace in the duchy of Lorraine, which was technically independent from the French monarchy during this period, rivaled Poussin in fame. Claude modulated in a softer style the disciplined rational art of Poussin, with its sophisticated revelation of the geometry of landscape. Unlike the figures in Poussin's pictures, those in Claude's landscapes tell no dramatic story, point out no moral, and praise no hero. Indeed, they often appear to be added as mere excuses for the radiant landscape itself. For Claude, painting

involved essentially one theme—the beauty of a broad sky suffused with the golden light of dawn or sunset glowing through a hazy atmosphere and reflecting brilliantly off rippling water.

In *Landscape with Cattle and Peasants* (FIG. 25-26), the figures in the right foreground chat in animated fashion. In the left foreground, cattle relax contentedly. In the middle ground, cattle amble slowly away. The well-defined foreground, distinct middle ground, and dim background recede in serene orderliness, until all form dissolves in a luminous mist. Atmospheric and linear perspective reinforce each other to turn a vista into a typical Claudian vision, an ideal classical world bathed in sunlight in infinite space (compare FIG. I-11).

Claude's formalizing of nature with balanced groups of architectural masses, screens of trees, and sheets of water followed the great tradition of classical landscape. It began with the backgrounds of Venetian painting (FIGS. 22-34 and 22-35) and continued in the art of Annibale Carracci (FIG. 24-15) and Poussin (FIG. 25-25). Yet Claude, like the Dutch painters, studied the light and the atmospheric nuances of nature, making a unique contribution. He recorded carefully in hundreds of sketches the look of the Roman countryside, its gentle terrain accented by stone-pines, cypresses, and poplars and by the ever-present ruins of ancient aqueducts,

25-27 Louis Le Nain, *Family of Country People,* ca. 1640. Oil on canvas, 3′ 8″ × 5′ 2″. Louvre, Paris.

Le Nain's painting expresses the grave dignity of a peasant family made stoic by hardship. It reflects 17th-century French social theory, which celebrated the natural virtue of those who worked the soil.

tombs, and towers. He made these the fundamental elements of his compositions. Travelers could understand the picturesque beauties of the outskirts of Rome in Claude's landscapes.

The artist achieved his marvelous effects of light by painstakingly placing tiny value gradations, which imitated, though on a very small scale, the range of values of outdoor light and shade. Avoiding the problem of high-noon sunlight overhead, Claude preferred, and convincingly represented, the sun's rays as they gradually illuminated the morning sky or, with their dying glow, set the pensive mood of evening. Thus, he matched the moods of nature with those of human subjects. Claude's infusion of nature with human feeling and his recomposition of nature in a calm equilibrium greatly appealed to the landscape painters of the 18th and early 19th centuries.

LOUIS LE NAIN Although classicism was an important presence in French art during the 17th and early 18th centuries, not all artists pursued this direction. Louis Le Nain (ca. 1593–1648) bears comparison to the Dutch. Subjects that in Dutch painting were opportunities for boisterous good humor, the French treated with somber stillness. *Family of Country People* (FIG. **25-27**) reflects the thinking of 17th-century French social theorists who celebrated the natural virtue of peasants who worked the soil. Le Nain's painting expresses the grave dignity of one peasant family made stoic and resigned by hardship. These drab country folk surely had little reason for merriment. The peasant's lot, never easy, was miserable during the Thirty Years' War. The anguish and frustration of the peasantry, suffering from the cruel depredations of unruly armies living off the

countryside, often broke out in violent revolts that the same armies savagely suppressed. This family, however, is pious, docile, and calm. Because Le Nain depicted peasants as dignified and subservient despite their harsh living conditions, some scholars have suggested he intended to please wealthy urban patrons with these paintings.

JACQUES CALLOT Two other prominent artists from Lorraine were Jacques Callot and Georges de La Tour. Jacques Callot (ca. 1592–1635) conveyed a sense of military life during these troubled times in a series of etchings called *Miseries of War.* Callot confined himself almost exclusively to the art of etching and was widely influential in his own time and since. (Rembrandt was among those who knew and learned from his work.) Callot perfected the medium and the technique of etching, developing a very hard surface for the copper plate to permit fine and precise delineation with the needle. His quick, vivid touch and faultless drawing produced panoramas sparkling with sharp details of life—and death. In the *Miseries of War* series, he observed these details coolly, presenting without comment images based on events he himself must have seen in the wars in Lorraine.

In *Hanging Tree* (FIG. **25-28**), Callot depicted a mass execution of thieves (identified in the text at the bottom of the etching). The event takes place in the presence of a disciplined army, drawn up on parade with banners, muskets, and lances, their tents in the background. Hanged men sway in clusters from the branches of a huge cross-shaped tree. A monk climbs a ladder, holding up a crucifix to a man while the executioner adjusts the noose around the man's neck. At the foot of the ladder, another victim kneels to receive absolution.

25-28 JACQUES CALLOT, *Hanging Tree,* from the *Miseries of War* series, 1629–1633. Etching, $3\frac{3}{4}'' \times 7\frac{1}{4}''$. Private collection.

Callot's *Miseries of War* etchings were among the first realistic pictorial records of the human disaster of military conflict. *Hanging Tree* depicts a mass execution of thieves in the presence of an army.

Under the crucifix tree, men roll dice on a drumhead for the belongings of the executed. (This may be an allusion to the soldiers who cast lots for the garments of the crucified Christ.) In the right foreground, a hooded priest consoles a bound man. Callot's *Miseries of War* etchings are among the first realistic pictorial records of the human disaster of armed conflict.

GEORGES DE LA TOUR France, unlike Flanders and the Dutch Republic, was a Catholic country, and religious themes, al-

though not as common as in Italian Baroque art, occupied some 17th-century French painters. Among the artists well known for their religious imagery was GEORGES DE LA TOUR (1593–1652). His work, particularly his use of light, suggests a familiarity with Caravaggio's art. La Tour may have learned about Caravaggio from the Dutch school of Utrecht. Although La Tour used the devices of Caravaggio's northern followers, his effects are strikingly different from theirs. His *Adoration of the Shepherds* (FIG. **25-29**) makes use of the night setting favored by that school, much as van Honthorst

25-29 GEORGES DE LA TOUR, *Adoration of the Shepherds,* 1645–1650. Oil on canvas, 3′ 6″ × 4′ 6″. Louvre, Paris.

Without the aid of the title, Georges de la Tour's painting could be a genre piece instead of a biblical narrative. The French painter did not even paint halos around the heads of the holy figures.

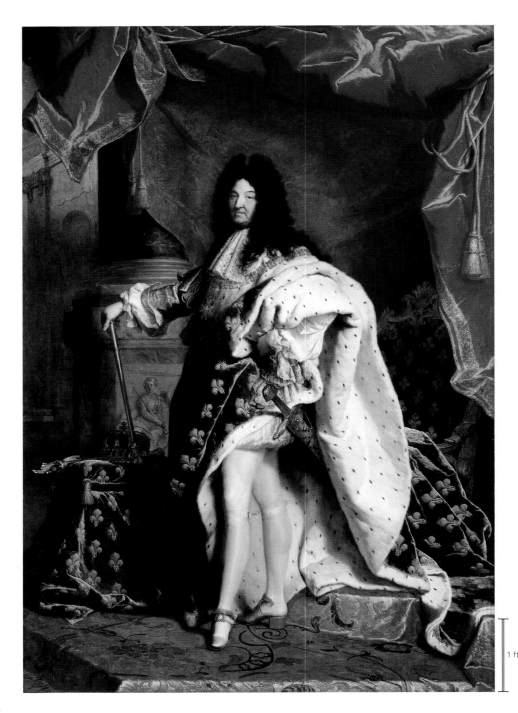

25-30 Hyacinthe Rigaud, *Louis XIV*, 1701. Oil on canvas, 9′ 2″ × 6′ 3″. Louvre, Paris.

In this portrait set against a stately backdrop, Rigaud portrayed the 5′ 4″ Sun King wearing red high-heeled shoes and with his ermine-lined coronation robes thrown over his left shoulder.

1 ft.

portrayed it (FIG. **25-8**). But here, the light, its source shaded by an old man's hand, falls upon a very different company in a very different mood. A group of humble men and women, coarsely clad, gather in prayerful vigil around a luminous baby Jesus. Without the aid of the title, this might be construed as a genre piece, a narrative of some event from peasant life. Nothing in the environment, placement, poses, dress, or attributes of the figures distinguishes them as the scriptural Virgin Mary, Joseph, Christ Child, or shepherds. The artist did not even paint halos. The light is not spiritual but material: It comes from a candle. La Tour's scientific scrutiny of the effects of light, as it throws precise shadows on surfaces that intercept it, nevertheless had religious intention and consequence. The light illuminates a group of ordinary people held in a mystic trance induced by their witnessing the miracle of the Incarnation. In this timeless tableau of simple people, La Tour eliminated the dogmatic significance and traditional iconography of the Incarnation. Still, these people reverently contemplate something they regard as holy. The devout of any religious persuasion can read this painting, regardless of their familiarity with the New Testament.

The supernatural calm that pervades *Adoration of the Shepherds* is characteristic of the mood of Georges de La Tour's art. He achieved this tone by eliminating motion and emotive gesture (only the light is dramatic), by suppressing surface detail, and by simplifying body volumes. These stylistic traits are among those associated with classical and Renaissance art. Thus, several apparently contradictory elements meet in the work of La Tour: classical composure, fervent spirituality, and genre realism.

LOUIS XIV The preeminent French art patron of the 17th century was King Louis XIV. Determined to consolidate and expand his power, Louis was a master of political strategy and propaganda. He established a carefully crafted and nuanced relationship with the nobility, granting them sufficient benefits to keep them pacified but simultaneously maintaining rigorous control to avoid insurrection or rebellion. He also ensured subservience by anchoring his rule in divine right (a belief in a king's absolute power as God's will), rendering Louis's authority incontestable. So convinced was Louis of his importance and centrality to the French kingdom that he eagerly adopted the title "le Roi Soleil" ("the Sun King"). Like the sun, Louis XIV was the center of the universe.

Louis's desire for control extended to all realms of French life, including art. The king and his principal adviser, Jean-Baptiste Colbert (1619–1683), strove to organize art and architecture in the service of the state. They understood well the power of art as propaganda and the value of visual imagery for cultivating a public persona, and they spared no pains to raise great symbols and monuments to the king's absolute power. Louis and Colbert sought to regularize taste and establish the classical style as the preferred French manner. The founding of the Royal Academy of Painting and Sculpture in 1648 served to advance this goal.

Louis XIV maintained a workshop of artists, each with a specialization—faces, fabric, architecture, landscapes, armor, or fur. Thus, many of the king's portraits were a group effort, but the finest is the work of one artist. The portrait of Louis XIV (FIG. 25-30) by Hyacinthe Rigaud (1659–1743) successfully conveys the image of an absolute monarch. The king, age 63 when Rigaud painted this work, looks out at the viewer with directness. He stands with his left hand on his hip and with his elegant ermine-lined fleur-de-lis coronation robes (compare FIG. 25-3) thrown over his shoulder, suggesting an air of haughtiness. Louis also draws his garment back to expose his legs. (The king was a ballet dancer in his youth and was proud of his well-toned legs.) The portrait's majesty derives in large part from the composition. The Sun King is the unmistakable focal point of the image, and Rigaud placed him so that he seems to look down on the viewer. Given that Louis XIV was very short in stature—only five feet, four inches, a fact that drove him to invent the red-heeled shoes he wears in the portrait—the artist apparently catered to his patron's wishes. The carefully detailed environment in which the king stands also contributes to the painting's stateliness and grandiosity. Indeed,

when the king was not present, Rigaud's portrait, which hung over the throne, served in his place, and courtiers were not permitted to turn their backs on the painting.

Architecture and Sculpture

THE LOUVRE The first great architectural project Louis XIV and his adviser Colbert undertook was the closing of the east side of the Louvre's Cour Carré (FIG. 23-12), left incomplete by Pierre Lescot in the 16th century. The king summoned Gianlorenzo Bernini, as the most renowned architect of his day, from Rome to submit plans, but Bernini envisioned an Italian palace on a monumental scale that would have involved the demolition of all previous work. His plan rejected, Bernini indignantly returned to Rome. Louis then turned to three French architects—Claude Perrault (1613–1688), Louis Le Vau (1612–1670), and Charles Le Brun (1619–1690)—for the Louvre's east facade (FIG. 25-31). The design is a brilliant synthesis of French and Italian classical elements, culminating in a new and definitive formula. The facade has a central and two corner projecting columnar pavilions. The central pavilion is in the form of a classical temple front. To either side is a giant colonnade of paired columns, resembling the columned flanks of a temple folded out like wings. The whole rests on a stately podium. The designers favored an even roofline, balustraded and broken only by the central pediment, over the traditional French pyramidal roof of the Louvre's west wing

25-31 Claude Perrault, Louis Le Vau, and Charles Le Brun, east facade of the Louvre, Paris, France, 1667–1670.

The design of the Louvre's east facade is a brilliant synthesis of French and Italian classical elements, including a central pavilion that resembles an ancient temple front with a pediment.

25-32 Aerial view (looking west) of the palace and gardens, Versailles, France, begun 1669.

Louis XIV ordered his architects to convert a royal hunting lodge at Versailles into a gigantic palace and park with a satellite city whose three radial avenues intersect in the king's bedroom.

(FIG. 23-12). The emphatically horizontal sweep of the 17th-century facade brushed aside all memory of Gothic verticality. Its stately proportions and monumentality were both an expression of the new official French taste and a symbol of centrally organized authority.

VERSAILLES PALACE Work on the Louvre had barely begun when Louis XIV decided to convert a royal hunting lodge at Versailles, a few miles outside Paris, into a great palace. He assembled a veritable army of architects, decorators, sculptors, painters, and landscape architects under the general management of Charles Le Brun. In their hands, the conversion of a simple lodge into the palace of Versailles (FIG. 25-32) became the greatest architectural project of the age—a defining statement of French Baroque style and an undeniable symbol of Louis XIV's power and ambition.

Planned on a gigantic scale, the project called not only for a large palace flanking a vast park but also for the construction of a satellite city to house court and government officials, military and guard detachments, courtiers, and servants (undoubtedly to keep them all under the king's close supervision). Le Brun laid out this town to the east of the palace along three radial avenues that converge on the palace structure. Their axes, in a symbolic assertion of the ruler's absolute power over his domains, intersected in the king's spacious bedroom, which served as an official audience chamber. The palace itself, more than a quarter mile long, is perpendicular to the dominant east-west axis that runs through the associated city and park.

Every detail of the extremely rich decoration of the palace's interior received careful attention. The architects and decorators designed everything from wall paintings to doorknobs in order to reinforce the splendor of Versailles and to exhibit the very finest sense of artisanship. Of the literally hundreds of rooms within the palace, the most famous is the Galerie des Glaces, or Hall of Mirrors (FIG. 25-33), designed by JULES HARDOUIN-MANSART (1646–1708) and Le Brun. This hall overlooks the park from the second floor and extends along most of the width of the central block. Although deprived of its original sumptuous furniture, which included gold and silver chairs and bejeweled trees, the Galerie des Glaces retains much of its splendor today. Hundreds of mirrors, set into the wall opposite the windows, alleviate the hall's tunnel-like quality and illusionistically extend the width of the room. The mirror, that ultimate source of illusion, was a favorite element of Baroque interior design. Here, it also enhanced the dazzling extravagance of the great festivals Louis XIV was so fond of hosting.

VERSAILLES PARK The enormous palace might appear unbearably ostentatious were it not for its extraordinary setting in the vast park that makes it almost an adjunct. From the Galerie des Glaces, the king and his guests could gaze out on a sweeping vista down the park's tree-lined central axis and across terraces, lawns, pools, and lakes to the horizon. The park of Versailles (FIG. 25-32), designed by ANDRÉ LE NÔTRE (1613–1700), must rank among the world's greatest artworks in both size and concept. Here, the French architect transformed an entire forest into a park. Although its geometric plan may appear stiff and formal, the park in fact offers an almost unlimited assortment of vistas, as Le Nôtre used not only the multiplicity of natural forms but also the terrain's slightly rolling contours with stunning effectiveness.

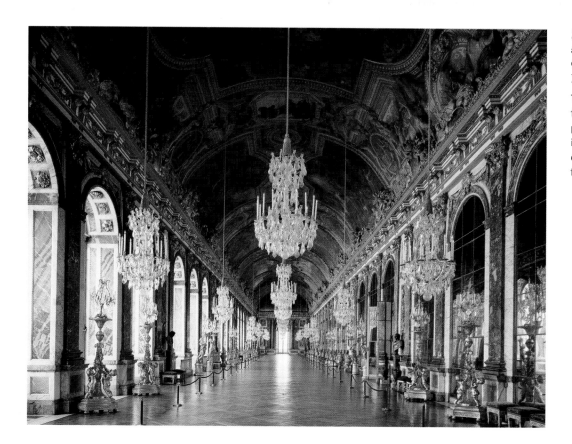

25-33 Jules Hardouin-Mansart and Charles Le Brun, Galerie des Glaces (Hall of Mirrors), palace of Louis XIV, Versailles, France, ca. 1680.

This hall overlooks the Versailles park from the second floor of Louis XIV's palace. Hundreds of mirrors illusionistically extend the room's width and once reflected gilded and jeweled furnishings.

The formal gardens near the palace provide a rational transition from the frozen architectural forms to the natural living ones. Here, the elegant shapes of trimmed shrubs and hedges define the tightly designed geometric units. Each unit is different from its neighbor and has a focal point in the form of a sculptured group, a pavilion, a reflecting pool, or perhaps a fountain. Farther away from the palace, the design loosens as trees, in shadowy masses, screen or frame views of open countryside. Le Nôtre carefully composed all vistas for maximum effect. Light and shadow, formal and informal, dense growth and open meadows—all play against one another in unending combinations and variations. No photograph or series of photographs can reveal the design's full richness. The park unfolds itself only to people who actually walk through it. In this respect, it is a temporal artwork. Its aspects change with the time of day, the seasons, and the relative position of the observer.

For the Grotto of Thetis above a dramatic waterfall in the gardens of Versailles, François Girardon (1628–1715) designed *Apollo Attended by the Nymphs* (FIG. **25-34**). Both stately and graceful, the

25-34 François Girardon and Thomas Regnaudin, *Apollo Attended by the Nymphs*, Grotto of Thetis, Versailles, France, ca. 1666–1672. Marble, life-size.

Girardon's study of ancient sculpture and Poussin's figure compositions influenced the design of this mythological group in a grotto above a dramatic waterfall in the gardens of Versailles.

25-35 JULES HARDOUIN-MANSART, Royal Chapel, with ceiling decorations by ANTOINE COYPEL, palace of Louis XIV, Versailles, France, 1698–1710.

Because the apse is as high as the nave, the central space of the Royal Chapel at Versailles has a curved Baroque quality. Louis XIV could reach the royal pew directly from his apartments.

25-36 JULES HARDOUIN-MANSART, Église du Dôme, Church of the Invalides, Paris, France, 1676–1706.

Hardouin-Mansart's church marries the Italian and French architectural styles. The grouping of the orders is similar to the Italian Baroque manner but without the dramatic play of curved surfaces.

nymphs display a compelling charm as they minister to the god Apollo at the end of the day. (The three nymphs in the background are the work of THOMAS REGNAUDIN, 1622–1706.) Girardon's close study of Greco-Roman sculpture heavily influenced his design of the figures, and Poussin's figure compositions (FIG. **25-24**) inspired their arrangement. Since Apollo was often equated with the sun god, the group refers obliquely to Louis XIV as the "god of the sun." This was bound to assure the work's success at court. Girardon's classical style and mythological symbolism were well suited to France's glorification of royal majesty.

VERSAILLES CHAPEL In 1698, Jules Hardouin-Mansart received the commission to add a Royal Chapel to the Versailles palace complex. The chapel's interior (FIG. **25-35**) is essentially rectangular, but because its apse is as high as the nave, the fluid central space takes on a curved Baroque quality. However, the light entering through the large clerestory windows lacks the directed dramatic effect of the Italian Baroque, instead illuminating the interior's precisely chiseled details brightly and evenly. Pier-supported arcades carry a majestic row of Corinthian columns that define the royal gallery. The royal pew occupies its rear, accessible directly from the king's apartments. Amid the restrained decoration, only the illusionistic ceiling paintings, added in 1708–1709 by ANTOINE COYPEL (1661–1722), suggest the drama and complexity of Italian Baroque art.

As a symbol of the power of absolutism, Versailles has no equal. It also expresses, in the most monumental terms of its age, the ratio-

nalistic creed—based on scientific advances, such as the physics of Sir Isaac Newton (1642–1727) and the mathematical philosophy of René Descartes (1596–1650)—that all knowledge must be systematic and all science must be the consequence of the intellect imposed on matter. The whole spectacular design of Versailles proudly proclaims the mastery of human intelligence (and the mastery of Louis XIV) over the disorderliness of nature.

ÉGLISE DU DÔME, PARIS Another of Hardouin-Mansart's masterworks, the Église du Dôme (FIG. **25-36**), or Church of the Invalides, in Paris, also marries the Italian Baroque and French classical architectural styles. An intricately composed domed square of great scale, the church adjoins the veterans hospital Louis XIV established for the disabled soldiers of his many wars. Two firmly separated levels, the upper one pedimented, compose the frontispiece. The grouping of the orders and of the bays they frame is not unlike that in Italian Baroque architecture but without the dramatic play of curved surfaces characteristic of many 17th-century Italian churches (FIG. **24-9**). The compact facade is low and narrow in relation to the vast drum and dome, seeming to serve simply as a base for them. The overpowering dome, conspicuous on the Parisian skyline, is itself expressive of the Italian Baroque love for dramatic magnitude, as is the way that its designer aimed for theatrical effects of light and space. The dome consists of three shells, the lowest cut off so that a visitor to the interior looks up through it to the one above, which is filled with light from hidden windows in the third, outermost dome. Charles de La Fosse (1636–1716) painted the interior of the second dome in 1705 with an Italian-inspired representation of the heavens opening up to receive Saint Louis, patron of France.

ENGLAND

In England, in sharp distinction to France, the common law and the Parliament kept royal power in check. England also differed from France (and Europe in general) in other significant ways. Although an important part of English life, religion was not the contentious issue it was on the Continent. The religious affiliations of the English included Catholicism, Anglicanism, Protestantism, and Puritanism (the English version of Calvinism). In the economic realm, England was the one country (other than the Dutch Republic) to take advantage of the opportunities overseas trade offered. As an island country, Britain (which after 1603 consisted of England, Wales, and Scotland), like the Dutch Republic, possessed a large and powerful navy as well as excellent maritime capabilities.

Architecture

In the realm of art, the most important English achievements were in the field of architecture, much of it, as in France, incorporating classical elements.

INIGO JONES The most notable English architect of the first half of the 17th century was INIGO JONES (1573–1652), architect to Kings James I (r. 1603–1625) and Charles I (FIG. 25-5). Jones spent considerable time in Italy. He greatly admired the classical authority and restraint of Andrea Palladio's structures and studied with great care his treatise on architecture (see Chapter 22). Jones took many motifs from Palladio's villas and palaces, and he adopted Palladio's basic design principles for his own architecture. The nature of his achievement is evident in the buildings he designed for his royal patrons, among them the Banqueting House (FIG. 25-37) at Whitehall in London. For this structure, a symmetrical block of great clarity and dignity, Jones superimposed two orders, using columns in the center and pilasters near the ends. The balustraded roofline, uninterrupted in its horizontal sweep, predates the Louvre's facade (FIG. 25-31) by more than 40 years. Palladio would have recognized and approved all of the design elements, but the building as a whole is not a copy of his work. Although relying on the revered Italian's architectural vocabulary and syntax, Jones retained his own independence as a designer. For two centuries his influence was almost as authoritative in English architecture as that of Palladio.

25-37 INIGO JONES, Banqueting House at Whitehall, London, England, 1619–1622.

Jones was a great admirer of the classical architecture of Palladio, and he adopted motifs from the Italian Renaissance architect's villas and palaces for the buildings he designed for his royal patrons.

25-38 SIR CHRISTOPHER WREN, Saint Paul's Cathedral, London, England, 1675–1710.

Wren's cathedral replaced an old Gothic church. The facade design owes much to Palladio (FIG. 22-31) and Borromini (FIG. 24-12). The great dome recalls Saint Peter's in Rome (FIGS. 24-3 and 24-4).

CHRISTOPHER WREN London's majestic Saint Paul's Cathedral (FIG. 25-38) is the work of England's most renowned architect, CHRISTOPHER WREN (1632–1723). A mathematical genius and skilled engineer whose work won Isaac Newton's praise, Wren became professor of astronomy in London at age 25. Mathematics led to architecture, and Charles II (r. 1649–1685) asked Wren to prepare a plan for restoring the old Gothic church of Saint Paul. Wren proposed to remodel the building based on Roman structures. Within a few months, the Great Fire of London, which destroyed the old structure and many churches in the city in 1666, gave Wren his opportunity. Although Jones's work strongly influenced him, Wren also traveled in France, where the splendid palaces and state buildings being created in and around Paris at the time of the competition for the Louvre design must have impressed him. Wren also closely studied prints illustrating Baroque architecture in Italy. In Saint Paul's, he harmonized Palladian, French, and Italian Baroque features.

In view of its size, the cathedral was built with remarkable speed—in little more than 30 years—and Wren lived to see it completed. The building's form underwent constant refinement during construction, and Wren did not determine the final appearance of the towers until after 1700.

In the splendid skyline composition, two foreground towers act effectively as foils to the great dome. Wren must have known similar schemes that Italian architects devised for Saint Peter's (FIG. 24-4) in Rome to solve the problem of the relationship between the facade and dome. Certainly, the influence of Borromini (FIG. 24-12) appears in the upper levels and lanterns of the towers and that of Palladio (FIG. 22-31) in the lower levels. Further, the superposed paired columnar porticos recall the Louvre facade (FIG. 25-31). Wren's skillful eclecticism brought all these foreign features into a monumental unity.

Wren designed many other London churches after the Great Fire. Even today, his towers and domes punctuate the skyline of London. Saint Paul's dome is the tallest of all. Wren's legacy was significant and long-lasting, in both England and colonial America (see Chapter 29).

NORTHERN EUROPE,
1600 TO 1700

FLANDERS

▐ In the 17th century, Flanders remained Catholic and under Spanish control. Flemish Baroque art is more closely tied to the Baroque art of Italy than is the art of much of the rest of northern Europe.

▐ The leading Flemish painter of this era was Peter Paul Rubens, whose work and influence were international in scope. A diplomat as well as an artist, he counted kings and queens among his patrons and friends. His paintings of the career of Marie de' Medici exhibit Baroque splendor in color and ornament, and feature Rubens's characteristic robust and foreshortened figures in swirling motion.

Rubens, *Arrival of Marie de' Medici*, 1622–1625

DUTCH REPUBLIC

▐ The Dutch Republic received official recognition of its independence from Spain in the Treaty of Westphalia of 1648. Worldwide trade and banking brought prosperity to its predominantly Protestant citizenry, which largely rejected church art in favor of private commissions of portraits, genre scenes, landscapes, and still lifes.

▐ Frans Hals produced innovative portraits of middle-class patrons in which a lively informality replaced the formulaic patterns of traditional portraiture. Aelbert Cuyp and Jacob van Ruisdael specialized in landscapes depicting specific places, not idealized Renaissance settings. Pieter Claesz, Willem Kalf, and others painted vanitas still lifes featuring meticulous depictions of worldly goods and reminders of death.

Rembrandt, *Anatomy Lesson of Dr. Tulp*, 1632

▐ Rembrandt van Rijn, the greatest Dutch artist of the age, treated a broad range of subjects, including religious themes and portraits. His oil paintings are notable for their dramatic impact and subtle gradations of light and shade as well as the artist's ability to convey human emotions. Rembrandt was also a master printmaker renowned for his etchings.

▐ Jan Vermeer specialized in painting Dutch families in serenely opulent homes. Vermeer's convincing representation of interior spaces depended in part on his employment of the camera obscura. He was also a master of light and color and understood that shadows are not colorless.

Vermeer, *The Letter*, 1666

FRANCE AND ENGLAND

▐ The major art patron in 17th-century France was the Sun King, the absolutist monarch Louis XIV, who expanded the Louvre and built a gigantic palace-and-garden complex at Versailles featuring sumptuous furnishings and sweeping vistas. Among the architects Louis employed were Charles Le Brun and Jules Hardouin-Mansart, who succeeded in marrying Italian Baroque and French classical styles.

Rigaud, *Louis XIV*, 1701

▐ The leading French proponent of classical painting was Nicolas Poussin, who spent most of his life in Rome and championed the "grand manner" of painting, which called for heroic or divine subjects and classical compositions with figures often modeled on ancient statues.

▐ Claude Lorrain, whose fame rivaled Poussin's, specialized in classical landscapes rendered in linear and atmospheric perspective. His compositions often incorporated ancient ruins.

▐ In 17th-century England, architecture was the most important art form. Two architects who achieved international fame were Inigo Jones and Christopher Wren, who harmonized the architectural principles of Andrea Palladio with the Italian Baroque and French classical styles.

Wren, *Saint Paul's, London*, 1675–1710

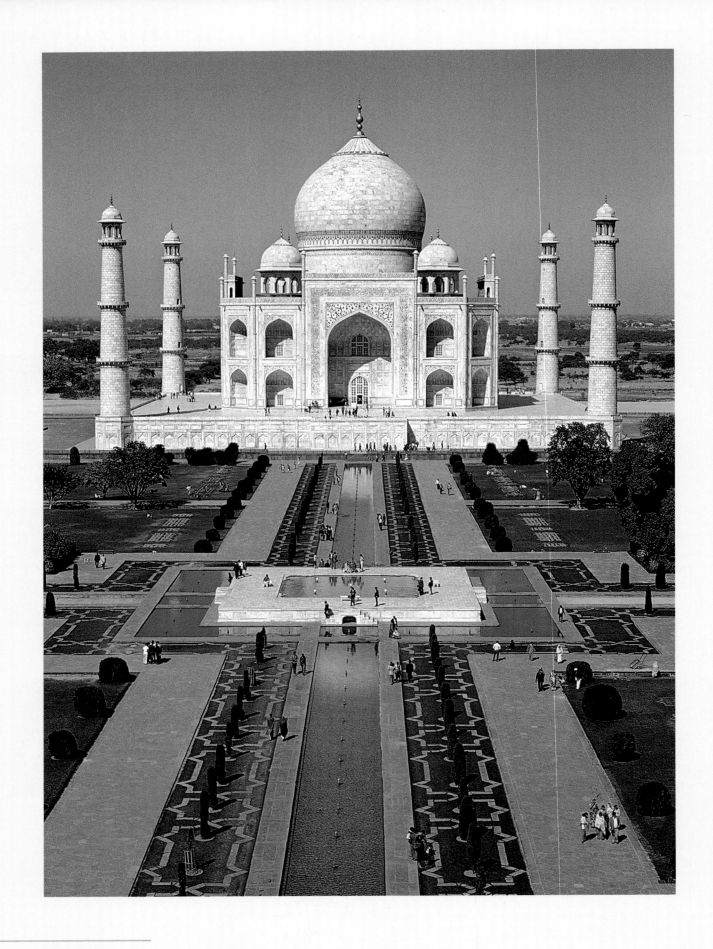

26-1 Taj Mahal, Agra, India, 1632–1647.

The first Islamic dynasty in South Asia was the 13th-century sultanate of Delhi, but the greatest was the Mughal Empire. The Taj Mahal, the most famous building in Asia, is a Mughal mausoleum.

SOUTH AND SOUTHEAST ASIA AFTER 1200

Buddhism, which originated in South Asia in the mid-first millennium BCE, gradually declined in the medieval period in favor of Hinduism, although Buddhism continued as the dominant religion in Southeast Asia (see Chapter 6). After 1200, Hinduism remained strong in South Asia, as did Buddhism in Southeast Asia, but a newer faith—Islam—also rose to prominence. Under a succession of Hindu, Buddhist, *Muslim,* and secular rulers, the arts continued to flourish in South and Southeast Asia from the early 13th century through the British colonial period to the present.

INDIA

Arab armies first appeared in South Asia (MAP **26-1**)—at Sindh in present-day Pakistan—in 712. With them came Islam, the new religion that had already spread with astonishing speed from the Arabian Peninsula to Syria, Iraq, Iran, Egypt, North Africa, and even southern Spain (see Chapter 13). At first, the Muslims established trading settlements but did not press deeper into the subcontinent. At the Battle of Tarain in 1192, however, Muhammad of Ghor (Afghanistan) defeated the armies of a confederation of South Asian states. The Ghorids and other Islamic rulers gradually transformed South Asian society, religion, and art.

Sultanate of Delhi

In 1206, Qutb al-Din Aybak, Muhammad of Ghor's general, established the sultanate of Delhi (1206–1526). On his death in 1211, he passed power to his son Iltutmish (r. 1211–1236), who extended Ghorid rule across northern India.

QUTB MINAR To mark the triumph of Islam, Qutb al-Din Aybak built a great *congregational mosque* (see "The Mosque," Chapter 13, page 345) at Delhi, in part with pillars taken from Hindu and other temples. He named Delhi's first mosque the Quwwat al-Islam (Might of Islam) Mosque. During the course of the next century, as the Islamic population of Delhi grew, the *sultans* (Muslim rulers) enlarged

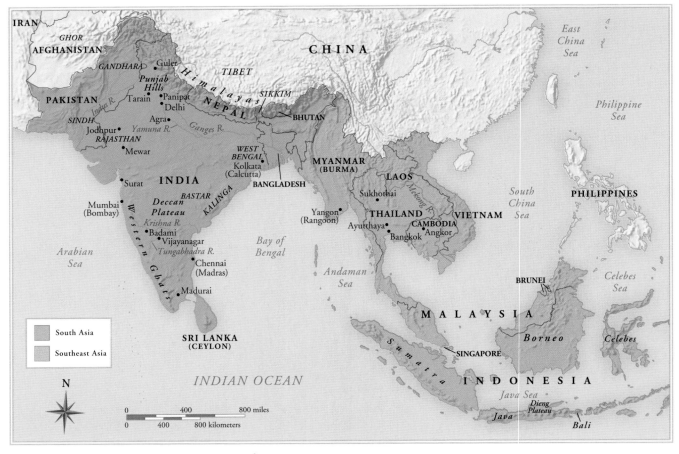

MAP 26-1 South and Southeast Asia, 1200 to the present.

the mosque to more than triple its original size. Iltutmish erected the mosque's 238-foot tapering sandstone *minaret,* the Qutb Minar (FIG. **26-2**, *left*)—the tallest extant minaret in the world. It is too tall, in fact, to serve the principal function of a minaret—to provide a platform from which to call the Islamic faithful to prayer. Rather, it is a towering monument to the victory of Islam, engraved with inscriptions in Arabic and Persian proclaiming that the minaret casts the shadow of Allah over the conquered Hindu city. Added in 1311, the Alai Darvaza, the entrance pavilion (FIG. **26-2**, *right*), is a mix of architectural traditions, combining Islamic pointed arches, decorative grills over the windows, and a hemispherical dome with a crowning *finial* that recalls the motifs at the top of many Hindu temple towers (see Chapter 6).

Vijayanagar Empire

While Muslim sultans from Central Asia ruled much of northern India from Delhi, Hindu rulers controlled most of central and southern India. The most powerful of the Hindu kingdoms of the era was the Vijayanagar. Established in 1336 by Harihara, a local king, the Vijayanagar Empire (1336–1565) took its name from Vijayanagara ("City of Victory") on the Tungabhadra River. Under the patronage of the royal family, Vijayanagara, located at the junction of several trade

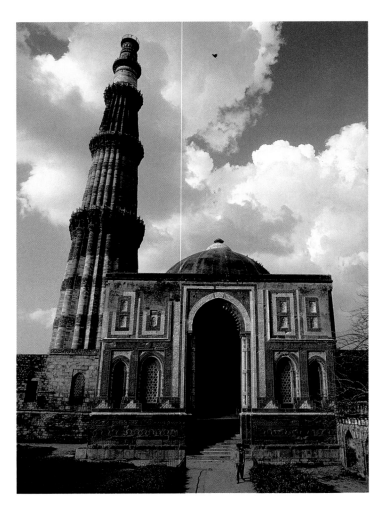

26-2 Qutb Minar, begun early 13th century, and Alai Darvaza, 1311, Delhi, India.

Qutb al-Din Aybak established the sultanate of Delhi in 1206 and built the city's first mosque to mark the triumph of Islam in northern India. The 238-foot-high Qutb Minar is the tallest minaret in the world.

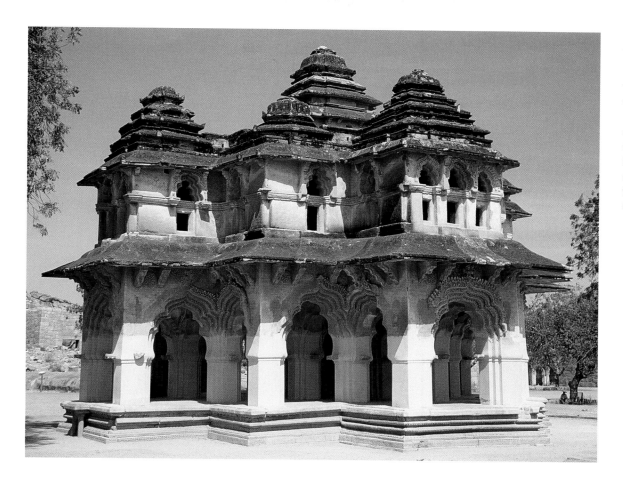

26-3 Lotus Mahal, Vijayanagara, India, 15th or early 16th century.

The Vijayanagar Empire was the most powerful Hindu kingdom in southern India during the 14th to 16th centuries. The Lotus Mahal is an eclectic mix of Hindu temple features and Islamic architectural elements.

routes through Asia, became one of the most magnificent cities in the East. Although the capital lies in ruins today, in its heyday ambassadors and travelers from as far away as Italy and Portugal marveled at Vijayanagara's riches. Under its greatest king, Krishnadevaraya (r. 1509–1529), who was also a renowned poet, the Vijayanagar kingdom was a magnet for the learned and cultured from all corners of India.

LOTUS MAHAL Vijayanagara's sacred center, built up over two centuries, boasts imposing temples to the Hindu gods in the Dravida style of southern India with tall pyramidal *vimanas* (towers) over the *garbha griha,* the inner sanctuary (see "Hindu Temples," Chapter 6, page 172). The buildings of the so-called Royal Enclave are more eclectic in character. One example in this prosperous royal city is the two-story monument of uncertain function known as the Lotus Mahal (FIG. **26-3**). The stepped towers crowning the vaulted second-story rooms resemble the pyramidal roofs of Dravida temple *mandapas* (pillared halls; FIG. **6-22**). But the windows of the upper level as well as the arches of the ground-floor piers have the distinctive multilobed contours of Islamic architecture (FIGS. **13-1** and **13-12**). The Lotus Mahal, like the entrance pavilion of Delhi's first mosque (FIG. **26-2**, *right*), exemplifies the stylistic crosscurrents that typify much of South Asian art and architecture of the second millennium.

Mughal Empire

The 16th century was a time of upheaval in South Asia. In 1565, only a generation after the poet-king Krishnadevaraya, a confederacy of sultanates in the Deccan plateau of central India brought the Vijayanagar Empire of the south to an end. Even earlier, a Muslim prince named Babur had defeated the last of the Ghorid sultans of northern India at the Battle of Panipat. Declaring himself the ruler of India, Babur established the Mughal Empire (1526–1857) at Delhi. *Mughal,* originally a Western term, means "descended from the Mongols,"

although the Mughals considered themselves descendants of Timur (r. 1370–1405), the Muslim ruler whose capital was at Samarkand in Uzbekistan. In 1527, Babur vanquished the Rajput Hindu kings of Mewar (see page 711). By the time of his death in 1530, Babur headed a vast new empire in India.

AKBAR THE GREAT The first great flowering of Mughal art and architecture occurred during the long reign of Babur's grandson, Akbar (r. 1556–1605), called the Great, who ascended the throne at age 14. Like his father Humayun (r. 1530–1556), Akbar was a great admirer of the narrative paintings (FIG. **13-27**) produced at the court of Shah Tahmasp in Iran. Just before he died, Humayun had persuaded two Persian masters to move to Delhi and train local artists in the art of painting. When Akbar succeeded his father, he already oversaw an imperial workshop of Indian painters under the direction of the two Iranians. The young ruler enlarged their number to about a hundred and kept them busy working on a series of ambitious projects. One of these was to illustrate the text of the *Hamzanama*—the story of Hamza, Muhammad's uncle—in some 1,400 large paintings on cloth. The assignment took 15 years to complete.

26-4A BANU, *Shah Tahmasp,* early 17th century.

The illustrated books and engravings that traders, diplomats, and Christian missionaries brought from Europe to India also fascinated Akbar. In 1580, Portuguese Jesuits brought one particularly important source, the eight-volume *Royal Polyglot Bible,* as a gift to Akbar. This massive set of books, printed in Antwerp, contained engravings by several Flemish artists. Akbar immediately set his painters to copying the illustrations.

AKBARNAMA Akbar also commissioned Abul Fazl (1551–1602), a member of his court and close friend, to chronicle his life in a great biography, the *Akbarnama* (*History of Akbar*), which the emperor's painters illustrated. One of the full-page miniatures (see "Indian

Indian Miniature Painting

Although India had a tradition of mural painting dating to ancient times (see "The Painted Caves of Ajanta," Chapter 6, page 167, and FIG. 6-14), the most popular form of painting under the Mughal emperors (FIGS. 26-4 and 26-5) and Rajput kings (FIG. 26-7) was miniature painting. Art historians now call these paintings *miniatures* because of their small size (about the size of a page in this book) compared with that of paintings on walls, wooden panels, or canvas, but the original terminology derives from the fact that the earliest examples in the West employed red lead (*miniatum*) as a pigment. The artists who painted the Indian miniatures designed them to be held in the hands, either as illustrations in books or as loose-leaf pages in albums. Owners did not place Indian miniatures in frames and only rarely hung them on walls.

Indian artists used opaque watercolors and paper (occasionally cotton cloth) to produce their miniatures. The manufacturing and painting of miniatures were complicated processes and required years of apprenticeship training in a workshop. The painters' assistants created pigments by grinding natural materials—minerals such as malachite for green and lapis lazuli for blue; earth ochers for red and yellow; and metallic foil for gold, silver, and copper. They fashioned brushes from bird quills and kitten or baby squirrel hairs.

The artist began the painting process by making a full-size sketch of the composition. The next step was to transfer the sketch onto paper by *pouncing,* or tracing, using thin, transparent gazelle skin placed on top of the drawing and pricking the contours of the design with a pin. Then, with the skin laid on a fresh sheet of fine paper, the painter forced black pigment through the tiny holes, reproducing the outlines of the composition. Painting proper started with the darkening of the outlines with black or reddish-brown ink. Painters of miniatures sat on the ground, resting their painting boards on one raised knee. The paintings usually required several layers of color, with gold always applied

26-4 BASAWAN and CHATAR MUNI, *Akbar and the Elephant Hawai,* folio 22 from the *Akbarnama* (*History of Akbar*) by Abul Fazl, ca. 1590. Opaque watercolor on paper, 1′ 1$\frac{7}{8}$″ × 8$\frac{3}{4}$″. Victoria & Albert Museum, London.

The Mughal rulers of India were great patrons of miniature painting. This example, showing the young emperor Akbar bringing the elephant Hawai under control, is also an allegory of his ability to rule.

1 in.

last. The final step was to burnish the painted surface. The artists accomplished this by placing the miniature, painted side down, on a hard, smooth surface and stroking the paper with polished agate or crystal.

Miniature Painting," above) in the emperor's personal copy of the *Akbarnama* was a collaborative effort between the painter BASAWAN, who designed and drew the composition, and CHATAR MUNI, who colored it. The painting (FIG. **26-4**) depicts the episode of Akbar and Hawai, a wild elephant the 19-year-old ruler mounted and pitted against another ferocious elephant. When the second animal fled in defeat, Hawai, still carrying Akbar, chased it to a pontoon bridge. The enormous weight of the elephants capsized the boats, but Akbar managed to bring Hawai under control and dismount safely. The young ruler viewed the episode as an allegory of his ability to govern—that is, to take charge of an unruly state.

For his pictorial record of that frightening day, Basawan chose the moment of maximum chaos and danger—when the elephants crossed the pontoon bridge, sending boatmen flying into the water. The composition is a bold one, with a very high horizon and two strong diagonal lines formed by the bridge and the shore. Together these devices tend to flatten out the vista, yet at the same time Basawan created a sense of depth by diminishing the size of the figures in the background. He was also a master of vivid gestures and anecdotal detail. Note especially the bare-chested figure in the foreground clinging to the end of a boat, the figure near the lower-right corner with outstretched arms sliding into the water as the bridge sinks, and

26-5 Bichitr, *Jahangir Preferring a Sufi Shaykh to Kings*, ca. 1615–1618. Opaque watercolor on paper, 1′ 6$\frac{7}{8}$″ × 1′ 1″. Freer Gallery of Art, Washington, D.C.

The impact of European art on Mughal painting is evident in this allegorical portrait of the haloed emperor Jahangir on an hourglass throne, seated above time, favoring spiritual power over worldly power.

26-5A Abul Hasan and Manohar, *Darbar of Jahangir*, ca. 1620.

father, acquired many luxury goods from Europe, including globes, hourglasses, prints, and portraits.

The influence of European as well as Persian styles on Mughal painting under Jahangir is evident in Bichitr's allegorical portrait (FIG. 26-5) of Jahangir seated on an hourglass throne, a miniature from an album made for the emperor around 1615–1618. As the sands of time run out, two cupids (clothed, unlike their European models more closely copied at the top of the painting) inscribe the throne with the wish that Jahangir would live a thousand years. Bichitr portrayed his patron as an emperor above time and also placed behind Jahangir's head a radiant halo combining a golden sun and a white crescent moon, indicating that Jahangir is the center of the universe and its light source. One of the inscriptions on the painting gives the emperor's title as "Light of the Faith."

At the left are four figures. The lowest, both spatially and in the social hierarchy, is the Hindu painter Bichitr himself, wearing a red turban. He holds a miniature representing two horses and an elephant, costly gifts from Jahangir, and another self-portrait. In the miniature-within-the-miniature, Bichitr bows deeply before the emperor. In the larger painting, the artist signed his name across the top of the footstool Jahangir uses to step up to his hourglass throne. Thus, the ruler steps on Bichitr's name, further indicating the painter's inferior status.

Above Bichitr is a portrait in full European style (compare FIGS. 23-9 and 23-10) of King James I of England (r. 1603–1625), copied from a painting by John de Critz (ca. 1552–1642) that the English ambassador to the Mughal court had given Jahangir as a gift. Above the king is a Turkish sultan, a convincing study of physiognomy but probably not a specific portrait. The highest member of the foursome is an elderly Muslim Sufi *shaykh* (mystic saint). Jahangir's father, Akbar, had visited the mystic to pray for an heir. The current emperor, the answer to Akbar's prayers, presents the holy man with a sumptuous book as a gift. An inscription explains that "although to all appearances kings stand before him, Jahangir looks inwardly toward the dervishes [Islamic holy men]" for guidance. Bichitr's allegorical painting portrays his emperor in both words and pictures as favoring spiritual over worldly power.

the oarsman just beyond the bridge who strains to steady his vessel while his three passengers stand up or lean overboard in reaction to the surrounding commotion.

JAHANGIR That the names Basawan and Chatar Muni are known is significant in itself. In contrast to the anonymity of pre-Mughal artists in India, many of those whom the Mughal emperors employed signed their artworks. Another of these was BICHITR, whom Akbar's son and successor, Jahangir (r. 1605–1627), employed in the imperial workshop. The Mughals presided over a cosmopolitan court with refined tastes. After the establishment of the East India Company (see page 712), British ambassadors and merchants were frequent visitors to the Mughal capital, and Jahangir, like his

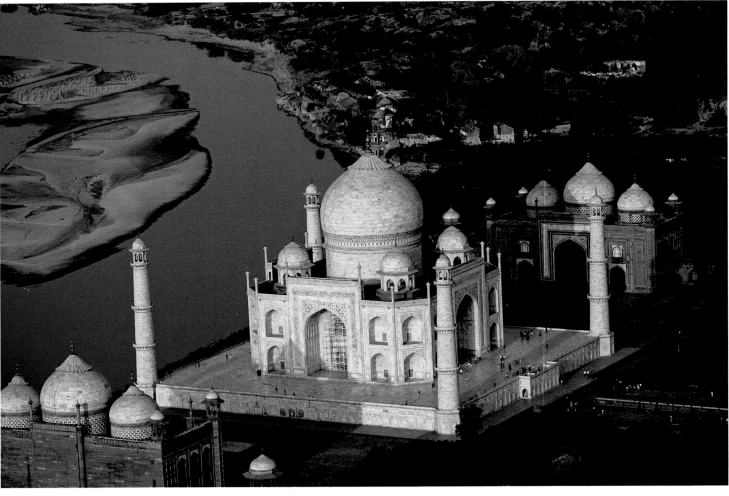

26-6 Aerial view of the Taj Mahal, Agra, India, 1632–1647. ◼◀

This Mughal mausoleum seems to float magically over reflecting pools in a vast garden (FIG. 26-1). The tomb may have been conceived as the Throne of God perched above the gardens of Paradise on Judgment Day.

TAJ MAHAL Monumental tombs were not part of either the Hindu or Buddhist traditions but had a long history in Islamic architecture. The Delhi sultans had erected tombs in India, but none could compare in grandeur to the fabled Taj Mahal (FIGS. **26-1** and **26-6**) at Agra. Shah Jahan (r. 1628–1658), Jahangir's son, built the immense *mausoleum* as a memorial to his favorite wife, Mumtaz Mahal, although it eventually became the ruler's tomb as well. The dome-on-cube shape of the central block has antecedents in earlier Islamic mausoleums (FIGS. **13-10** and **13-18**) and other Islamic buildings such as the Alai Darvaza (FIG. **26-2**, *right*) at Delhi, but modifications and refinements in the design of the Agra tomb have converted the earlier massive structures into an almost weightless vision of glistening white marble. The Agra mausoleum seems to float magically above the tree-lined reflecting pools (FIG. **26-1**) that punctuate the garden leading to it. Reinforcing the illusion that the marble tomb is suspended above the water is the absence of any visible means of ascent to the upper platform. A stairway does exist, but the architect intentionally hid it from the view of anyone who approaches the memorial.

The Taj Mahal follows the plan of Iranian garden pavilions, except that the building stands at one end rather than in the center of the formal garden. The tomb is octagonal in plan and has typically Iranian arcuated niches (FIG. **13-25**) on each side. The interplay of shadowy voids with light-reflecting marble walls that seem paper-thin creates an impression of translucency. The pointed arches lead

the eye in a sweeping upward movement toward the climactic dome, shaped like a crown (*taj*). Four carefully related minarets and two flanking triple-domed pavilions (FIG. **26-6**) enhance and stabilize the soaring form of the mausoleum. The architect achieved this delicate balance between verticality and horizontality by strictly applying an all-encompassing system of proportions. The Taj Mahal (excluding the minarets) is exactly as wide as it is tall, and the height of its dome is equal to the height of the facade.

Abd al-Hamid Lahori (d. 1654), a court historian who witnessed the construction of the Taj Mahal, compared its minarets to ladders reaching toward Heaven and its surrounding gardens to Paradise. In fact, inscribed on the gateway to the gardens and the walls of the mausoleum are carefully selected excerpts from the Koran that confirm the historian's interpretation of the tomb's symbolism. The designer of the Taj Mahal may have conceived the mausoleum as the Throne of God perched above the gardens of Paradise on Judgment Day. The minarets hold up the canopy of that throne. In Islam, the most revered place of burial is beneath the Throne of God.

Hindu Rajput Kingdoms

The Mughal emperors ruled vast territories, but much of northwestern India (present-day Rajasthan) remained under the control of Hindu Rajput (literally "sons of kings") rulers. These small kingdoms, some claiming to have originated well before 1500, had stub-

1 in.

26-7 *Krishna and Radha in a Pavilion,* ca. 1760. Opaque watercolor on paper, $11\frac{1}{8}'' \times 7\frac{3}{4}''$. National Museum, New Delhi.

The love of Krishna (the "Blue God") for Radha is the subject of this colorful, lyrical, and sensual Pahari watercolor. Krishna's love was a model of the devotion paid to the Hindu god Vishnu.

bornly resisted Mughal expansion, but even the strongest of them, Mewar, eventually submitted to the Mughal emperors. When Jahangir defeated the Mewari forces in 1615, the Mewari maharana (great king), like the other Rajput rulers, maintained a degree of independence but had to pay tribute to the Mughal Empire until it collapsed in 1857.

Rajput painting resembles Mughal (and Persian) painting in format and material, but it differs sharply in other respects. Most Rajput artists, for example, worked in anonymity, never inserting self-portraits into their paintings as the Mughal painter Bichitr did in his miniature (FIG. 26-5) of Jahangir on an hourglass throne.

7A Krishna d the Gopis, . 1550.

KRISHNA AND RADHA One of the most popular subjects for Rajput paintings was the amorous adventures of Krishna, the "Blue God," the most popular of the *avatars,* or incarnations, of the Hindu god Vishnu, who descends to earth to aid mortals (see "Hinduism," Chapter 6, page 168, or page xxv in Volume II). Krishna was a herdsman who spent an idyllic existence tending his cows, fluting, and sporting with beautiful herdswomen. His favorite lover was Radha. The 12th-century poet Jayadeva related the story of Krishna and Radha in the *Gita Govinda* (*Song of the Cowherd*). Their love was a model of the devotion, or *bhakti,* paid to Vishnu. Jayadeva's poem was the source for hundreds of later paintings, including *Krishna and Radha in a Pavilion* (FIG. 26-7), a miniature painted in the Pun-

jab Hills, probably for Raja Govardhan Chand (r. 1741–1773) of Guler. The painters that the rulers of the Punjab Hill states employed, referred to collectively as the Pahari School, had a distinctive style. Although Pahari painting owed much to Mughal drawing style, its coloration, lyricism, and sensuality are readily recognizable. In *Krishna and Radha in a Pavilion,* the lovers sit naked on a bed beneath a jeweled pavilion in a lush garden of ripe mangoes and flowering shrubs. Krishna gently touches Radha's breast while gazing directly into her face. Radha shyly averts her gaze. It is night, the time of illicit trysts, and the dark monsoon sky momentarily lights up with a lightning flash indicating the moment's electric passion. Lightning is a standard element used in Rajput and Pahari miniatures to symbolize sexual excitement.

Nayak Dynasty

The Nayakas, governors under the Vijayanagar kings, declared their independence in 1529, and after their former overlords' defeat in 1565 at the hands of the Deccan sultanates, they continued Hindu rule in the far south of India for two centuries (1529–1736).

GREAT TEMPLE, MADURAI Construction of some of the largest temple complexes in India occurred under Nayak patronage. The most striking features of these huge complexes are their gateway towers called *gopuras* (FIG. 26-8), decorated from top to bottom with painted sculptures. After erecting the gopuras, the builders

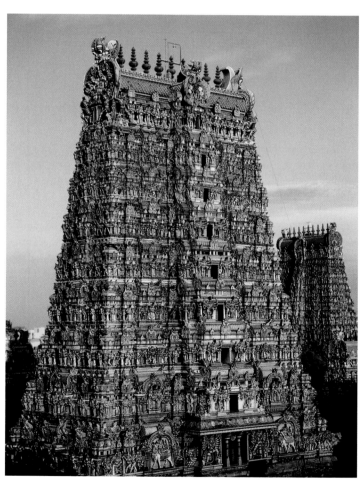

26-8 Outermost gopuras of the Great Temple, Madurai, India, completed 17th century.

The colossal gateway towers erected during the Nayak dynasty at the Great Temple at Madurai feature brightly painted stucco sculptures representing the vast pantheon of Hindu deities.

26-9 Frederick W. Stevens, *Victoria Terminus* (Chhatrapati Shivaji Terminus), Mumbai (Bombay), India, 1878–1887.

Victoria Terminus, named after Queen Victoria of England, is a monument to colonial rule. Designed by a British architect, it is a European transplant to India, modeled on late medieval Venetian architecture.

constructed walls to connect them and then built more gopuras, always expanding outward from the center. Each set of gopuras was taller than those of the previous wall circuit. The outermost towers reached colossal size, dwarfing the temples at the heart of the complexes. The tallest gopuras of the Great Temple at Madurai, dedicated to Shiva (under his local name, Sundareshvara, the Handsome One) and his consort Minakshi (the Fish-Eyed One), stand about 150 feet tall. Rising in a series of tiers of diminishing size, they culminate in a barrel-vaulted roof with finials. The ornamentation is extremely rich, consisting of row after row of brightly painted stucco sculptures representing the vast pantheon of Hindu deities and a host of attendant figures. Reconsecration of the temple occurs at 12-year intervals, at which time the gopura sculptures receive a new coat of paint, which accounts for the vibrancy of their colors today. The Madurai Nayak temple complex also contains large and numerous mandapas, as well as great water tanks the worshipers use for ritual bathing. These temples were, and continue to be, almost independent cities, with thousands of pilgrims, merchants, and priests flocking from far and near to the many yearly festivals the temples host.

The British in India

English merchants first arrived in India toward the end of the 16th century, attracted by the land's spices, gems, and other riches. On December 31, 1599, Queen Elizabeth I (r. 1558–1603) granted a charter to the East India Company, which sought to compete with the Portuguese and Dutch in the lucrative trade with South Asia. The company estab-

lished a "factory" (trading post) at the port of Surat, approximately 150 miles from Mumbai (Bombay) in western India in 1613. After securing trade privileges with the Mughal emperor Jahangir, the British expanded their factories to Chennai (Madras), Kolkata (Calcutta), and Bombay by 1661. These outposts gradually spread throughout India, especially after the British defeated the ruler of Bengal in 1757. By the opening of the 19th century, the East India Company effectively ruled large portions of the subcontinent, and in 1835, the British declared English India's official language. A great rebellion in 1857 persuaded the British Parliament that the East India Company could no longer be the agent of British rule. The next year Parliament abolished the company and replaced its governor-general with a viceroy of the crown. Two decades later, in 1877, Queen Victoria (r. 1837–1901) assumed the title Empress of India with sovereignty over all the former Indian states.

VICTORIA TERMINUS The British brought the Industrial Revolution and railways to India. One of the most enduring monuments of British rule, still used by millions of travelers, is Victoria Terminus (FIG. **26-9**) in Mumbai, named for the new empress of India (but now called Chhatrapati Shivaji Terminus). A British architect, Frederick W. Stevens (1847–1900), was the designer. Construction of the giant railway station began in 1878 and took a decade to complete. Although built of the same local sandstone used for temples and statues throughout India's long history, Victoria Terminus is a European transplant to the subcontinent, the architectural counterpart of colonial rule. Conceived as a cathedral to modernization, the terminus fittingly has an allegorical statue of Progress heritage of the wealth and splendor of his family's rule. The other, a wide gold band with a cameo, is the Order of the Star of India, a high honor his British overlords bestowed on him.

The painter of this portrait worked on the same scale and employed the same materials—opaque watercolor on paper—that Indian miniature painters had used for centuries, but the artist copied the ruler's likeness from a photograph. This accounts in large part for the realism of the portrait. Indian artists sometimes even painted directly on top of photographs. Photography arrived in India at an early date. In 1840, just one year after its invention in Paris, the *daguerreotype* (FIG. 30-50) was introduced in Calcutta. Indian artists readily adopted the new medium, not just to produce portraits but also to record landscapes and monuments.

In 19th-century India, however, admiration of Western art and culture was by no means universal. During the half century after Jaswant Singh's death, calls for Indian self-government grew ever louder. Under the leadership of Mahatma Gandhi (1869–1948) and others, India achieved independence in 1947—not, however, as a unified state but as the two present-day nations of India and Pakistan. The contemporary art of South Asia is the subject of the last section of this chapter.

26-10 *Maharaja Jaswant Singh of Marwar,* ca. 1880. Opaque watercolor on paper, 1′ 3½″ × 11⅝″. Brooklyn Museum, Brooklyn (gift of Mr. and Mrs. Robert L. Poster).

Jaswant Singh, the ruler of Jodhpur, had himself portrayed as if he were a British gentleman in his sitting room, but the artist employed the same materials that Indian miniature painters had used for centuries.

SOUTHEAST ASIA

India was not alone in experiencing major shifts in political power and religious preferences during the past 800 years. The Khmer of Angkor (see Chapter 6), after reaching the height of their power at the beginning of the 13th century, lost one of their outposts in northern Thailand to their Thai vassals at midcentury. The newly founded Thai kingdoms quickly replaced Angkor as the region's major powers, while Theravada Buddhism (see "Buddhism and Buddhist Iconography," Chapter 6, page 161, or page xxiv in Volume II) became the religion of the entire mainland except Vietnam. The Vietnamese, restricted to the northern region of today's Vietnam, gained independence in the 10th century after a thousand years of Chinese political and cultural domination. They pushed to the south, ultimately destroying the indigenous Cham culture, which had dominated there for more than a millennium. A similar Burmese drive southward in Myanmar matched the Thai and Vietnamese expansions. All these movements resulted in demographic changes during the second millennium that led to the cultural, political, and artistic transformation of mainland Southeast Asia. A religious shift also occurred in Indonesia. With Islam growing in importance, all of Indonesia except the island of Bali became predominantly Muslim by the 16th century.

Thailand

Southeast Asians practiced both Buddhism and Hinduism, but by the 13th century, in contrast to developments in India, Hinduism was in decline and Buddhism dominated much of the mainland. Two prominent Buddhist kingdoms came to power in Thailand during the 13th and early 14th centuries. Historians date the beginning of the Sukhothai kingdom to 1292, the year King Ramkhamhaeng (r. 1279–1299) erected a four-sided stele bearing the first inscription written in the Thai language. Sukhothai's political dominance proved short-lived, however. Ayutthaya, a city founded in central Thailand in 1350, quickly became the more powerful kingdom and warred sporadically with other states in Southeast Asia until the mid-18th century. Scholars nonetheless regard the Sukhothai period as the golden age of Thai art. In the inscription on his stele, Ramkhamhaeng ("Rama the Strong") described Sukhothai as a city of monasteries and many images of the Buddha.

crowning its tallest dome. Nonetheless, the building's design looks backward, not forward. Inside, passengers gaze up at groin-vaulted ceilings and *stained-glass* windows, and the exterior of the station resembles a Western church with a gabled facade and flanking towers. Stevens modeled Victoria Terminus, with its tiers of screened windows, on the architecture of late medieval Venice (FIG. 19-21).

JASWANT SINGH With British rulers and modern railways also came British or, more generally, European ideas, but Western culture and religion never supplanted India's own rich traditions. Many Indians, however, readily adopted the trappings of European society. When Jaswant Singh (r. 1873–1895), the ruler of Jodhpur in Rajasthan, sat for his portrait (FIG. 26-10), he chose to sit in an ordinary chair rather than on a throne, with his arm resting on a simple table with a bouquet and a book on it. In other words, he posed as an ordinary British gentleman in his sitting room. Nevertheless, the painter, an anonymous local artist who had embraced Western style, left no question about Jaswant Singh's regal presence and pride. The ruler's powerful chest and arms, along with the sword and his leather riding boots, indicate his abilities as a warrior and hunter. The curled beard signified fierceness to Indians of that time. The unflinching gaze records the ruler's confidence. Perhaps the two necklaces Jaswant Singh wears best exemplify the combination of his two worlds. One necklace is a bib of huge emeralds and diamonds, the

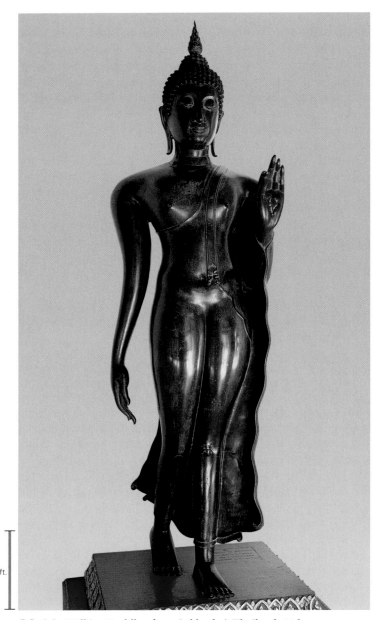

26-11 Walking Buddha, from Sukhothai, Thailand, 14th century. Bronze, 7' 2½" high. Wat Bechamabopit, Bangkok. ■◀

The walking-Buddha statuary type is unique to Thailand and displays a distinctive approach to body form. The Buddha's body is soft and elastic, and the right arm hangs loosely, like an elephant trunk.

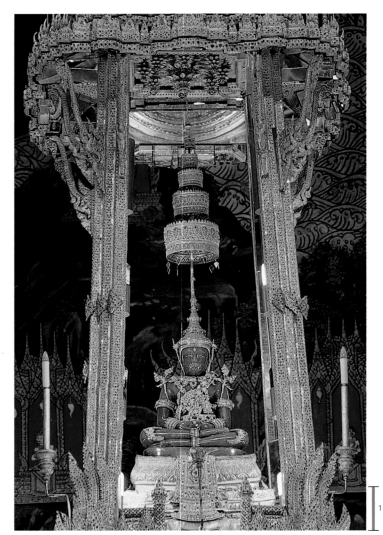

26-12 Emerald Buddha, Emerald Temple, Bangkok, Thailand, 15th century. Jade or jasper, 2' 6" high.

The Thai king dresses the Emerald Buddha, carved from green jade or jasper, in a monk's robe and a king's robe at different times of the year, underscoring the image's symbolic role as both Buddha and king.

WALKING BUDDHA Theravada Buddhism came to Sukhothai from Sri Lanka (see Chapter 6). At the center of the city stood Wat Mahathat, Sukhothai's most important Buddhist monastery. Its *stupa* (mound-shaped Buddhist shrine; see "The Stupa," Chapter 6, page 163) housed a *relic* of the Buddha (Wat Mahathat means "Monastery of the Great Relic") and attracted crowds of pilgrims. Sukhothai's crowning artistic achievement was the development of a type of walking-Buddha statue (FIG. 26-11) displaying a distinctively Thai approach to body form. The bronze Buddha has broad shoulders and a narrow waist and wears a clinging monk's robe. He strides forward, his right heel off the ground and his left arm raised with the hand held in the gesture that in Buddhist art signifies "do not fear" to encourage worshipers to come forward in reverence. A flame leaps from the top of the Buddha's head, and a sharp nose projects from his rounded face. The right arm hangs loosely, seemingly without muscles or joints, like an elephant's trunk. The Sukhothai artists intended the body type to suggest a supernatural being and to ex-

press the Buddha's beauty and perfection. Although images in stone exist, the Sukhothai artists handled bronze best, a material well suited to their conception of the Buddha's body as elastic. The Sukhothai walking-Buddha statuary type does not occur elsewhere in Buddhist art.

EMERALD BUDDHA A second distinctive Buddha image from northern Thailand is the *Emerald Buddha* (FIG. 26-12), housed in Bangkok in the Emerald Temple on the Royal Palace grounds. The sculpture is small, only 30 inches tall, and conforms to the ancient type of the Buddha seated in meditation in a yogic posture with his legs crossed and his hands in his lap, palms upward (FIG. 6-10). It first appears in historical records in 1434 in northern Thailand, where Buddhist chronicles record its story. The chronicles describe the Buddha image as plaster-encased, and thus no one knew the statue was green stone. A lightning bolt caused some of the plaster to flake off, disclosing its gemlike nature. Taken by various rulers to a series of cities in northern Thailand and in Laos over the course of more than 300 years, the small image finally reached Bangkok in 1778 in the possession of the founder of the present Thai royal dynasty.

The *Emerald Buddha* is not, in fact, emerald but probably green jade. Nonetheless, its nature as a gemstone gives it a special aura. The

Thai believe the gem enables the universal king, or *chakravartin*, possessing the statue to bring the rains. The historical Buddha renounced his secular destiny for the spiritual life, yet his likeness carved from the gem of a universal king allows fulfillment of the Buddha's royal destiny as well. The Buddha can also be regarded as the universal king. Thus, the combination of the sacred and the secular in the small image explains its symbolic power. The Thai king dresses the *Emerald Buddha* at different times of the year in a monk's robe and a king's robe (in FIG. 26-12 the Buddha wears the royal garment), reflecting the image's dual nature and accentuating its symbolic role as both Buddha and king. The Thai king possessing the image therefore has both religious and secular authority.

Myanmar

Myanmar, like Thailand, is overwhelmingly a Theravada Buddhist country today. Important Buddhist monasteries and monuments dot the countryside.

SCHWEDAGON PAGODA In Rangoon, an enormous complex of buildings, including shrines filled with Buddha images, has as its centerpiece one of the largest stupas in the world, the Schwedagon Pagoda (FIG. 26-13). (*Pagoda* derives from the Portuguese version of a word for stupa.) The Rangoon pagoda houses two of the Buddha's hairs, traditionally said to have been brought to Myanmar by merchants who received them from the Buddha himself. Rebuilt several times, this highly revered stupa is famous for the gold, silver, and jewels encrusting its surface. The Schwedagon Pagoda stands 344 feet high. Covering its upper part are 13,153 plates of gold, each about a foot square. At the very top is a seven-tiered umbrella crowned with a gold ball inlaid with 4,351 diamonds, one of which weighs 76 carats. This great wealth was a gift to the Buddha from the laypeople of Myanmar to produce merit.

Vietnam

The history of Vietnam is particularly complex, as it reveals both an Indian-related art and culture, broadly similar to those of the rest of Southeast Asia, and a unique and intense relationship with China's art and culture. Vietnam's tradition of fine ceramics is of special interest. The oldest Vietnamese ceramics date to the Han period (206 BCE–220 CE), when the Chinese began to govern the northern area of Vietnam. China directly controlled Vietnam for a thousand years, and early Vietnamese ceramics closely reflected Chinese wares. But during the Ly (1009–1225) and Tran (1225–1400) dynasties, when Vietnam had regained its independence, Vietnamese potters developed an array of ceramic shapes, designs, and *glazes* that brought their wares to the highest levels of quality and creativity.

UNDERGLAZE CERAMICS In the 14th century, the Vietnamese began exporting *underglaze* wares modeled on the blue-and-white ceramics first produced in China (see "Chinese Porcelain," Chapter 27, page 722). During the 15th and 16th centuries, the ceramic industry in Vietnam became the supplier of pottery of varied shapes to an international market extending throughout Southeast Asia and to the Middle East. A 16th-century Vietnamese dish (FIG. 26-14) with two mynah birds on a flowering branch reveals both the potter's debt to China and how the spontaneity, power, and playfulness of Vietnamese painting contrast with the formality of Chinese

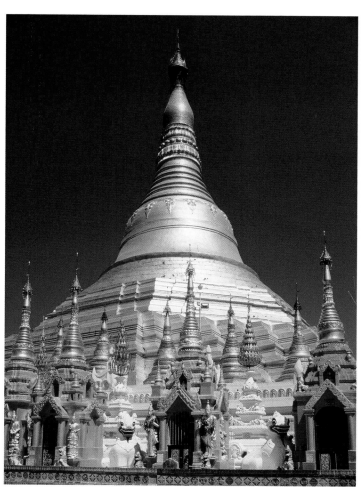

26-13 Schwedagon Pagoda, Rangoon (Yangon), Myanmar (Burma), 14th century or earlier (rebuilt several times).

The 344-foot-tall Schwedagon Pagoda houses two of the Buddha's hairs. Silver and jewels and 13,153 gold plates sheathe its exterior. The gold ball at the top is inlaid with 4,351 diamonds.

1 in.

26-14 Dish with two mynah birds on a flowering branch, from Vietnam, 16th century. Stoneware painted with underglaze cobalt, 1′ 2½″ in diameter. Pacific Asia Museum, Pasadena.

Vietnamese ceramists exported underglaze pottery throughout Southeast Asia and beyond. The spontaneity of the depiction of mynah birds on this dish contrasts with the formality of Chinese porcelains.

wares (FIG. 27-5). The artist suggested the foliage with curving and looped lines executed in almost one continuous movement of the brush over the surface. This technique—very different from the more deliberate Chinese habit of lifting the brush after painting a single motif in order to separate the shapes more sharply—facilitated rapid production. Combined with the painter's control, it created a fresh and unique design that made Vietnamese pottery attractive to a wide export market.

CONTEMPORARY ART

Contemporary art in India and Southeast Asia is as multifaceted a phenomenon as contemporary art elsewhere in the world. In India, for example, many traditional artists work at the village level, making images of deities out of inexpensive materials, such as clay, plaster, and papier-mâché, for local use. Some urban artists use these same materials to produce elaborate religious tableaux, such as depictions of the goddess Durga killing the buffalo demon that are used during the annual 10-day Durga Festival in Calcutta. Participants in the festival often ornament the tableaux with thousands of colored electric lights. The most popular art form for religious imagery, however, is the brightly colored print, sold for only a few rupees each. In the Buddhist countries of Southeast Asia (Thailand, Cambodia, Myanmar, and Laos), some artists continue to produce traditional images of the Buddha, primarily in bronze, for worship in homes, businesses, and temples.

Many contemporary artists, in contrast, create works for the international market. Although many of them received their training in South or Southeast Asia or Japan, others attended schools in Europe or the United States, and some artists now work outside their home countries. They face one of the fundamental quandaries of many contemporary Asian artists—how to identify themselves and situate their work between local and international, traditional and modern, and non-Western and Western cultures.

MEERA MUKHERJEE One Indian artist who successfully bridged these two poles of modern Asian art was MEERA MUKHERJEE (1923–1998). Mukherjee studied with European masters in Germany, but when she returned to India, she rejected much of what she had learned in favor of the techniques long employed by traditional sculptors of the Bastar tribe in central India. Mukherjee went to live with Bastar bronze-casters, who had perfected a variation on the classic *lost-wax process* (see "Hollow-Casting Life-Size Bronze Statues," Chapter 5, page 122). Beginning with a rough core of clay, the Bastar sculptors build up what will be the final shape of the statue by placing long threads of beeswax over the core. Then they apply a coat of clay paste to the beeswax and tie up the mold with metal wire. After heating the mold over a charcoal fire, which melts the wax, they pour liquid bronze into the space once occupied by the wax threads. Large sculptures require many separate molds. The Bastar artists complete their statues by welding together the separately cast sections, usually leaving the seams visible.

Many scholars regard *Ashoka at Kalinga* (FIG. 26-15) as Mukherjee's greatest work. Twice life-size and assembled from 26 cast-bronze sections, the towering statue combines the intricate surface textures of traditional Bastar work with the expressively swelling abstract forms of some 20th-century European sculpture (FIG. 35-59). Mukherjee chose as her subject the third-century BCE Maurya emperor Ashoka standing on the battlefield at Kalinga. There, Ashoka

26-15 MEERA MUKHERJEE, *Ashoka at Kalinga*, 1972. Bronze, 11′ 6¾″ high. Maurya Sheraton Hotel, New Delhi.

Mukherjee combined the bronze-casting techniques of the Bastar tribe with the swelling forms of 20th-century European sculpture in this statue of King Ashoka meant to be a pacifist's protest against violence.

witnessed more than 100,000 deaths and, shocked by the horrors of the war he had unleashed, rejected violence and adopted Buddhism as the official religion of his empire (see "Ashoka's Conversion to Buddhism," Chapter 6, page 162). Mukherjee conceived her statue as a pacifist protest against political violence in late-20th-century India. By reaching into India's remote history to make a contemporary political statement and by employing the bronze-casting methods of tribal sculptors while molding her forms in a modern idiom, she united her native land's past and present in a single work of great emotive power.

SOUTH AND SOUTHEAST ASIA AFTER 1200

SULTANATE OF DELHI, 1206–1526

▍ Qutb al-Din Aybak (r. 1206–1211) established the sultanate of Delhi in 1206, bringing Muslim rule to northern India.

▍ To mark the triumph of Islam, he built Delhi's first mosque and its 238-foot minaret, the tallest in the world.

Qutb Minar, Delhi,
begun early 13th century

VIJAYANAGAR EMPIRE, 1336–1565

▍ The most powerful Hindu kingdom in southern India when Muslim sultans ruled the north was the Vijayanagar Empire.

▍ Vijayanagar buildings like the Lotus Mahal display an eclectic mix of Hindu and Islamic architectural motifs.

Lotus Mahal, Vijayanagara,
15th or early 16th century

MUGHAL EMPIRE, 1526–1857

▍ Babur (r. 1526–1530) defeated the Delhi sultans in 1526 and established the Mughal Empire.

▍ The first great flowering of Mughal art and architecture occurred under Akbar the Great (r. 1556–1605), who sponsored a series of important painting projects, including his illustrated biography, the *Akbarnama.*

▍ Shah Jahan (r. 1628–1658) built the Taj Mahal as a memorial to his favorite wife. The mausoleum may symbolize the Throne of God above the gardens of Paradise.

Basawan and Chatar Muni,
Akbar and the Elephant Hawai, ca. 1590

OTHER SOUTH AND SOUTHEAST ASIAN KINGDOMS,
15th to 19th Centuries

▍ During the Mughal Empire, Hindu Rajput kings ruled much of northwestern India. The coloration and sensuality of Rajput painting distinguish it from the contemporaneous Mughal style.

▍ Between 1529 and 1736 the Hindu Nayak dynasty controlled southern India and erected temple complexes with immense gateway towers (gopuras) decorated with painted stucco sculptures of Hindu deities.

▍ In Thailand, Theravada Buddhism was the dominant religion. The Sukhothai walking-Buddha statuary type displays a unique approach to body form, for example, the Buddha's trunklike right arm.

▍ Myanmar's Schwedagon Pagoda in Rangoon is one of the largest stupas in the world and is encrusted with gold, silver, and jewels.

Walking Buddha, from Sukhothai,
14th century

BRITISH COLONIAL PERIOD (1600–1947) TO THE PRESENT

▍ Queen Elizabeth I (r. 1558–1603) established the East India Company, which eventually effectively ruled large portions of the subcontinent. In 1877, Queen Victoria I (r. 1837–1901) assumed the title Empress of India.

▍ Victoria Terminus is an architectural symbol of colonial rule, a European transplant to India capped by an allegorical statue of Progress.

▍ Under the leadership of Mahatma Gandhi (1869–1948), India and Pakistan achieved independence from England in 1947.

▍ Contemporary South Asian art ranges from the traditional to the modern and embraces both native and Western styles.

Frederick W. Stevens, Victoria Terminus,
Mumbai, 1878–1887

27-1 Throne room, Hall of Supreme Harmony, Forbidden City, Beijing, China, Ming dynasty, 15th century and later.

The Ming emperors—the Sons of Heaven—ruled China for almost three centuries from the Forbidden City (FIG. 27-6) in Beijing. Few ever entered the palace's magnificent throne room.

CHINA AND KOREA AFTER 1279

The 13th century was a time of profound political upheaval in Asia. The opening decade brought the establishment of a Muslim sultanate at Delhi (see Chapter 26) after the Islamic armies of Muhammad of Ghor wrested power from India's Hindu kings. Momentous changes followed immediately in China.

CHINA

In 1210, the Mongols invaded northern China from Central Asia (MAP **27-1**), opening a new chapter in the history and art of that ancient land. Under the dynamic leadership of Genghis Khan (1167–1230), the Mongol armies made an extraordinarily swift advance into China. By 1215 the Mongols had destroyed the Jin dynasty's capital at Beijing and had taken control of northern China. Two decades later, they attacked the Song dynasty in southern China. It was not until 1279, however, that the last Song emperor fell at the hands of Genghis Khan's grandson, Kublai Khan (1215–1294). Kublai proclaimed himself the new emperor of China (r. 1279–1294) and founded the Yuan dynasty.

Yuan Dynasty

During the relatively brief tenure of the Yuan (r. 1279–1368), trade between Europe and Asia increased dramatically. It was no coincidence that the most famous early European visitor to China, Marco Polo (1254–1324), arrived during the reign of Kublai Khan. Part fact and part fable, Marco Polo's chronicle of his travels to and within China was the only eyewitness description of East Asia available in Europe for several centuries. Marco Polo's account makes clear that the Venetian had a profound admiration for Yuan China. He marveled not only at Kublai Khan's opulent lifestyle and palaces but also at the volume of commercial traffic on the Yangtze River, the splendors of Hangzhou, the use of paper currency, porcelain, and coal, the efficiency of the Chinese postal system, and the hygiene of the Chinese people. In the early second millennium, China was richer and technologically more advanced than late medieval Europe.

MAP 27-1 China during the Ming dynasty.

27-2A ZHAO MENGFU, *Sheep and Goat*, ca. 1300.

ZHAO MENGFU AND GUAN DAOSHENG The Mongols were great admirers of Chinese art and culture, but they were very selective in admitting former Southern Song subjects into their administration. In addition, many Chinese loyal to the former emperors refused to collaborate with their new foreign overlords, whom they considered barbarian usurpers. One who did accept an official post under Kublai Khan was Zhao Mengfu (1254–1322), a descendant of the first Song emperor. A learned man, skilled in both calligraphy and poetry, he won renown as a painter of horses and of landscapes.

Zhao's wife, GUAN DAOSHENG (1262–1319), was also a successful painter, calligrapher, and poet. Although she painted a variety of subjects, including Buddhist murals in Yuan temples, Guan became famous for her paintings of bamboo. The plant was a popular subject because it was a symbol of the ideal Chinese gentleman, who bends in adversity but does not break, and because depicting bamboo branches and leaves approximated the cherished art of calligraphy (see "Calligraphy and Inscriptions on Chinese Paintings," page 726). *Bamboo Groves in Mist and Rain* (FIG. 27-2), a *handscroll* (see

27-2 GUAN DAOSHENG, *Bamboo Groves in Mist and Rain* (detail), Yuan dynasty, 1308. Section of a handscroll, ink on paper, $9\frac{1}{8}'' \times 3' 8\frac{7}{8}''$. National Palace Museum, Tabei.

Guan Daosheng was a calligrapher, poet, and painter. She achieved the misty atmosphere in this landscape by restricting the ink tones to a narrow range and by blurring the bamboo thickets in the distance.

27-3 Wu Zhen, *Stalks of Bamboo by a Rock,* Yuan dynasty, 1347. Hanging scroll, ink on paper, $2' 11\frac{1}{2}'' \times 1' 4\frac{5}{8}''$. National Palace Museum, Tabei. 📹

Wu Shen was one of the leading Yuan literati (scholar-artists). The bamboo plants in his hanging scroll are perfect complements to the prominently featured black Chinese calligraphic characters.

"Chinese Painting Materials and Formats," Chapter 7, page 190), is one of her best paintings. Guan achieved the misty atmosphere by restricting the ink tones to a narrow range and by blurring the bamboo thickets in the distance, suggesting not only the receding landscape but fog as well.

WU ZHEN The Yuan painter Wu Zhen (1280–1354), in stark contrast to Zhao Mengfu and Guan Daosheng, shunned the Mongol court and lived as a hermit, far from the luxurious milieu of the Yuan emperors. He was among the *literati,* or scholar-artists, who emerged during the Song dynasty. The literati painted primarily for a small audience of their educational and social peers. Highly educated and steeped in traditional Chinese culture, these men and women came from prominent families. They cultivated calligraphy, poetry, painting, and other arts as a sign of social status and refined taste. Literati art is usually personal in nature and often shows nostalgia for the past.

Wu Zhen's treatment of the bamboo theme, *Stalks of Bamboo by a Rock* (FIG. **27-3**), differs sharply from Guan's. The artist clearly differentiated among the individual bamboo plants and reveled in the abstract patterns the stalks and leaves form. The bamboo plants in his *hanging scroll* are perfect complements to the calligraphic beauty of the Chinese black characters and red seals so prominently featured on the scroll (see "Calligraphy and Inscriptions," page 726). Both the bamboo and the inscriptions gave Wu Zhen the opportunity to display his proficiency with the brush.

HUANG GONGWANG One of the great works of Yuan literati painting is *Dwelling in the Fuchun Mountains* (FIG. **27-4**) by Huang Gongwang (1269–1354), a former civil servant and a teacher of Daoist philosophy. According to the artist's explanatory inscription at the end of the long handscroll, he sketched the full composition in one burst of inspiration, but then added to and modified his painting whenever he felt moved to do so over a period of years. In the

27-4 Huang Gongwang, *Dwelling in the Fuchun Mountains,* Yuan dynasty, 1347–1350. Section of a handscroll, ink on paper, $1' \frac{7}{8}'' \times 20' 9''$ (full scroll). National Palace Museum, Tabei.

In this Yuan handscroll, the painter built up the textured mountains with richly layered wet and dry brush strokes and ink-wash accents that capture the landscape's inner structure and momentum.

Chinese Porcelain

No other Chinese art form has achieved such worldwide admiration, inspired such imitation, or penetrated so deeply into everyday life as *porcelain* (FIGS. **27-5** and **27-16**). Long imported by neighboring countries as luxury goods and treasures, Chinese porcelains later captured great attention in the West, where potters did not succeed in mastering the production process until the early 18th century.

In China, primitive porcelains emerged during the Tang dynasty (618–906), and mature forms developed in the Song (960–1279). Like *stoneware* (see "Chinese Earthenwares and Stonewares," Chapter 7, page 196), porcelain objects are fired at an extremely high temperature (well over 2,000°F) in a kiln until the clay fully fuses into a dense, hard substance resembling stone or glass. Unlike stoneware, however, porcelain is made from a fine white clay called kaolin mixed with ground petuntse (a type of feldspar). True porcelain is translucent and rings when struck. Its rich, shiny surface resembles that of jade, a luxurious natural material the Chinese long admired (see "Chinese Jade," Chapter 7, page 185).

Chinese ceramists often decorate porcelains with colored designs or pictures, working with finely ground minerals suspended in water and a binding agent (such as glue). The minerals change color dramatically in the kiln. The painters apply some mineral colors to the clay surface before the main firing and then apply a clear *glaze* over them. The *underglaze* decoration fully bonds to the piece in the kiln, but only a few colors are possible because the raw materials must withstand intense heat. The most stable and widely used coloring agents for porcelains are cobalt compounds, which fire to an intense blue (FIG. **27-5**). Rarely, potters use copper compounds to produce stunning reds by carefully manipulating the kiln's temperature and oxygen content. To obtain a wider palette, ceramic decorators must paint on top of the glaze after firing the work (FIG. **27-16**). The *overglaze* colors, or *enamels*, then fuse to the glazed surface in an additional firing at a much lower temperature. Enamels also offer glaze

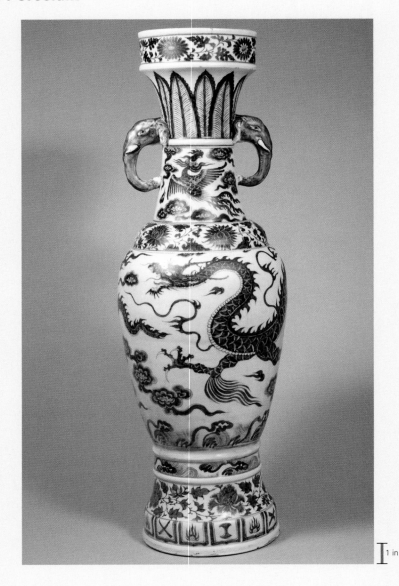

27-5 Temple vase, Yuan dynasty, 1351. White porcelain with cobalt-blue underglaze, 2′ 1″ × 8⅛″. Percival David Foundation of Chinese Art, London.

This vase is an early example of porcelain with cobalt-blue underglaze decoration. Dragons and phoenixes, symbols of male and female energy, respectively, are the major painted motifs.

decorators a much brighter palette, with colors ranging from deep browns to brilliant reds and greens, but they do not have the durability of underglaze decoration.

detail shown in FIG. **27-4**, the painter built up the textured mountains with richly layered brush strokes, at times interweaving dry brush strokes and at other times placing dry strokes over wet ones, darker strokes over lighter ones, often with ink-wash accents. The rhythmic play of brush and ink captures the landscape's inner structure and momentum.

JINGDEZHEN PORCELAIN By the Yuan period, Chinese potters had extended their mastery to fully developed porcelains, a very technically demanding medium (see "Chinese Porcelain," above). A tall temple vase (FIG. **27-5**) from the Jingdezhen kilns, which during the Ming dynasty became the official source of porcelains for the court, is one of a nearly identical pair dated by inscription to 1351. The inscription also says the vases, together with an incense burner, made up an

altar set donated to a Buddhist temple as a prayer for peace, protection, and prosperity for the donor's family. The vase is one of the earliest dated examples of fine porcelain with cobalt-blue underglaze decoration. The painted decoration consists of bands of floral motifs between broader zones containing auspicious symbols, including phoenixes in the lower part of the neck and dragons (compare FIG. **7-5**) on the main body of the vessel, both among clouds. These motifs may suggest the donor's high status or invoke prosperity blessings. Because of their vast power and associations with nobility and prosperity, the dragon and the phoenix also symbolize the emperor and empress, respectively, and often appear on objects made for the imperial household. The dragon also may represent *yang*, the Chinese principle of active masculine energy, while the phoenix may represent *yin*, the principle of passive feminine energy.

27-6 Aerial view (looking north) of the Forbidden City, Beijing, China, Ming dynasty, 15th century and later.

The layout of the Forbidden City provided the perfect setting for the elaborate ritual surrounding the Ming emperor. Successive gates regulated access to the Hall of Supreme Harmony (FIG. 27-1).

Ming Dynasty

In 1368, Zhu Yuanzhong led a popular uprising that drove the last Mongol emperor from Beijing. After expelling the foreigners from China, he founded the native Chinese Ming dynasty (r. 1368–1644), proclaiming himself its first emperor under the official name of Hongwu (r. 1368–1398). The new emperor built his capital at Nanjing, but the third Ming emperor, Yongle (r. 1403–1424), moved the capital back to Beijing. Although Beijing had been home to the Yuan dynasty, Ming architects designed much of the city as well as the imperial palace at its core.

THE FORBIDDEN CITY The Ming builders laid out Beijing as three nested walled cities. The outer perimeter wall was 15 miles long and enclosed the walled Imperial City, with a perimeter of 6 miles, and the vast imperial palace compound, the moated Forbidden City (FIG. 27-6), so named because of the highly restricted access to it. There resided the Ming emperor, the Son of Heaven. The layout of the Forbidden City provided the perfect setting for the elaborate ritual

of the imperial court. For example, the entrance gateway, the Noon Gate (in the foreground in the aerial view) has five portals. Only the emperor could walk through the central doorway. The two entrances to its left and right were reserved for the imperial family and high officials. Others had to use the outermost passageways. More gates and a series of courtyards and imposing buildings, all erected using the traditional Chinese bracketing system (see "Chinese Wooden Construction," Chapter 7, page 189), led eventually to the Hall of Supreme Harmony, perched on an immense platform above marble staircases, the climax of a long north-south axis. Within the hall, the emperor sat on his throne on another high stepped platform (FIG. **27-1**).

SUZHOU GARDENS At the opposite architectural pole from the formality and rigid axiality of palace architecture is the Chinese pleasure garden. Several Ming gardens at Suzhou have been meticulously restored, including the huge (almost 54,000 square feet) Wangshi Yuan (Garden of the Master of the Fishing Nets; FIG. **27-7**). Designing a Ming garden was not a matter of cultivating plants in rows

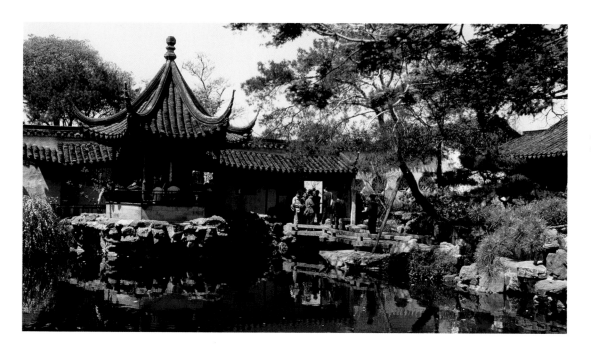

27-7 Wangshi Yuan (Garden of the Master of the Fishing Nets), Suzhou, China, Ming dynasty, 16th century and later.

Ming gardens are arrangements of natural and artificial elements intended to reproduce the irregularities of nature. This approach to design is the opposite of the formality and axiality of the Ming palace.

27-8 Liu Yuan (Lingering Garden), Suzhou, China, Ming dynasty, 16th century and later.

A favorite element of Chinese gardens was fantastic rockwork. For the Lingering Garden, workmen dredged the stones from a nearby lake and sculptors shaped them to produce an even more natural look.

MATERIALS AND TECHNIQUES

Lacquered Wood

From ancient times the Chinese used lacquer to cover wood. Lacquer is produced from the sap of the Asiatic sumac tree, native to central and southern China. When it dries, it cures to great hardness and prevents the wood from decaying. Often colored with mineral pigments, lacquered objects have a lustrous surface that transforms the appearance of natural wood. The earliest examples of lacquered wood to survive in quantity date to the Eastern Zhou period (770–256 BCE).

The first step in producing a lacquered object is to heat and purify the sap. Then the lacquer worker mixes the minerals—carbon black and cinnabar red are the most common—into the sap. To apply the lacquer, the artisan uses a hair brush similar to a calligrapher's or painter's brush, applying the lacquer one layer at a time. Each coat must dry and be sanded before another coat can be applied. If a sufficient number of layers is built up, the lacquer can be carved as if it were the wood itself (FIG. 27-9).

Other techniques for decorating lacquer include inlaying metals and lustrous materials, such as mother-of-pearl, and sprinkling gold powder into the still-wet lacquer. These techniques also flourished in both Korea and Japan (FIG. 28-10).

1 ft.

27-9 Table with drawers, Ming dynasty, ca. 1426–1435. Carved red lacquer on a wood core, 3′ 11″ long. Victoria & Albert Museum, London.

The Orchard Factory was the leading Ming workshop for lacquered wood furniture. The lacquer on this table was thick enough to be carved with floral motifs and the imperial dragon and phoenix.

27-10 SHANG XI, *Guan Yu Captures General Pang De,* Ming dynasty, ca. 1430. Hanging scroll, ink and colors on silk, 6′ 5″ × 7′ 7″. Palace Museum, Beijing.

The official painters of the Ming court lived in the Forbidden City and specialized in portraiture and history painting. This very large scroll celebrates a famed general of the third century.

or of laying out terraces, flower beds, and avenues in geometric fashion, as was the case in many other cultures (compare, for example, the 17th-century French gardens at Versailles, FIG. 25-32). Instead, Ming gardens are often scenic arrangements of natural and artificial elements intended to reproduce the irregularities of uncultivated nature. Verandas and pavilions rise on pillars above the water, and stone bridges, paths, and causeways encourage wandering through ever-changing vistas of trees, flowers, rocks, and their reflections in the ponds. The typical design is a sequence of carefully contrived visual surprises.

A favorite garden element, fantastic rockwork, is a prominent feature of Liu Yuan (Lingering Garden; FIG. 27-8) in Suzhou. Workmen dredged the stones from nearby Lake Tai, and sculptors shaped them to create an even more natural look. The one at the center of FIG. 27-8 is about 20 feet tall and weighs about five tons. The Ming gardens of Suzhou were the pleasure retreats of high officials and the landed gentry, sanctuaries where the wealthy could commune with nature in all its representative forms and as an ever-changing and boundless presence. Chinese poets never cease to sing of the restorative effect of gardens on mind and spirit.

ORCHARD FACTORY The Ming court's appetite for luxury goods gave new impetus to brilliant technical achievement in the decorative arts. Like the Yuan rulers, the Ming emperors turned to the Jingdezhen kilns for fine porcelains. For objects in lacquered wood (see "Lacquered Wood," page 724), their patronage went to a large workshop known today as the Orchard Factory. A table with drawers (FIG. 27-9), made between 1426 and 1435, is one of the workshop's masterpieces. The artist carved floral motifs, along with the dragon and phoenix imperial emblems, into the thick cinnabar-colored lacquer, which had to be built up in numerous layers.

SHANG XI At the Ming court, the official painters lived in the Forbidden City itself, and portraiture of the imperial family was their major subject. The court artists also depicted historical figures as exemplars of virtue, wisdom, or heroism. An exceptionally large example of Ming history painting is a hanging scroll that SHANG XI (active in the second quarter of the 15th century) painted around 1430. *Guan Yu Captures General Pang De* (FIG. 27-10) represents an episode from the tumultuous third century (Period of Disunity; see Chapter 7), whose wars inspired one of the first great Chinese novels, *The Romance of the Three Kingdoms*. Guan Yu was a famed general of the Wei dynasty (220–280) and a fictional hero in the novel. The painting depicts the historical Guan Yu, renowned for his loyalty to his emperor and his military valor, being presented with the captured enemy general Pang De. In his painting, Shang Xi used color to focus attention on Guan Yu and his attendants, who stand out sharply from the ink landscape. He also contrasted the victors' armor and bright garments with the vulnerability of the captive, who has been stripped almost naked, further heightening his humiliation.

Calligraphy and Inscriptions
on Chinese Paintings

Many Chinese paintings (FIGS. 7-21, 7-24, 27-3, and 27-11 to 27-13) bear inscriptions, texts written on the same surface as the picture, or *colophons,* texts written on attached pieces of paper or silk. Throughout history, the Chinese have held *calligraphy* (Greek, "beautiful writing") in very high esteem—higher, in fact, than painting. Inscriptions appear almost everywhere in China—on buildings and in gardens, on furniture and sculpture. Chinese calligraphy and painting have always been closely connected. Even the primary implements and materials for writing and drawing are the same—a round tapered brush, soot-based ink, and paper or silk. Calligraphy depends for its effects on the controlled vitality of individual brush strokes and on the dynamic relationships of strokes within a *character* (an elaborate Chinese sign that by itself can represent several words) and among the characters themselves. Training in calligraphy was a fundamental part of the education and self-cultivation of Chinese scholars and officials, and inscriptions are especially common on literati paintings. Many stylistic variations exist in Chinese calligraphy. At the most formal extreme, each character consists of distinct straight and angular strokes and is separate from the next character. At the other extreme, the characters flow together as cursive abbreviations with many rounded forms.

A long tradition in China links pictures and poetry. Famous poems frequently provided subjects for paintings, and poets composed poems inspired by paintings. Either practice might prompt inscriptions on art, some addressing painted subjects, some praising the painting's quality or the character of the painter or another individual. In praise of a beloved teacher, Shen Zhou added a long poem in beautiful Chinese characters to his painting of Mount Lu (FIG. 27-11). Sometimes inscriptions explain the circumstances of the work. Guan Daosheng's *Bamboo Groves in Mist and Rain* (FIG. 27-2) has two inscriptions (not included in the detail reproduced here). One is a dedication to another noblewoman. The other is a statement that she painted the handscroll "in a boat on the green waves of the lake." Later admirers and owners of paintings frequently inscribed their own appreciative words. The inscriptions are often quite prominent and sometimes compete for the viewer's attention with the painted motifs (FIG. 27-3).

Painters, inscribers, and even owners usually also added *seal* impressions in red ink (FIGS. 27-2 to 27-4 and 27-11 to 27-15) to identify themselves. With all these textual additions, some paintings that have passed through many collections may seem cluttered to Western eyes. However, the historical importance given to these inscriptions and the works' ownership history has been and remains a critical aspect of painting appreciation in China.

27-11 SHEN ZHOU, *Lofty Mount Lu,* Ming dynasty, 1467. Hanging scroll, ink and color on paper, $6' 4\frac{1}{4}'' \times 3' 2\frac{5}{8}''$. National Palace Museum, Tabei.

The inscriptions and seals are essential elements in this scroll, in which Shen Zhou used the lofty peaks of Mount Lu to express visually the grandeur of a beloved teacher's virtue and character.

1 ft.

SHEN ZHOU The work of Shang Xi and other professional court painters, designed to promote the official Ming ideology, differs sharply in both form and content from the venerable tradition of literati painting, which also flourished during the Ming dynasty. As under the Yuan emperors, the Ming literati worked largely independently of court patronage. One of the leading figures was SHEN ZHOU (1427–1509), a master of the Wu School of painting, so called because of the ancient name (Wu) of the city of Suzhou. Shen Zhou came from a family of scholars and painters and turned down an offer to serve in the Ming bureaucracy in order to devote himself to poetry and painting. His hanging scroll *Lofty Mount Lu* (FIG. **27-11**), a birthday gift to one of his teachers, bears a long poem he wrote in the teacher's honor (see "Calligraphy and Inscriptions on Chinese Paintings," page 726). Shen Zhou had never seen Mount Lu, but he chose the subject because he wished the lofty mountain peaks to express the grandeur of his teacher's virtue and character. The artist suggested the immense scale of Mount Lu by placing a tiny figure at the bottom center of the painting, sketched in lightly and partly obscured by a rocky outcropping. The composition owes a great deal to early masters like Fan Kuan (FIG. **7-1**). But, characteristic of literati painting in general, the scroll is in the end a very personal conversation—in pictures and words—between Shen Zhou and the teacher for whom he painted it.

DONG QICHANG One of the most intriguing and influential literati of the late Ming dynasty was DONG QICHANG (1555–1636), a wealthy landowner and high official who was a poet, calligrapher, and painter. He also amassed a vast collection of Chinese art and achieved great fame as an art critic. In Dong Qichang's view, most Chinese landscape painters could be classified as belonging to either the Northern School of precise, academic painting or the Southern School of more subjective, freer painting. "Northern" and "Southern" were therefore not geographic but stylistic labels. Dong Qichang chose these names for the two schools because he determined that their characteristic styles had parallels in the northern and southern schools of *Chan* Buddhism (see "Chan Buddhism," Chapter 7, page 201). Northern Chan Buddhists were "gradualists" and believed that enlightenment could be achieved only after long training. The Southern Chan Buddhists believed that enlightenment could come suddenly. The professional, highly trained court painters belonged to the Northern School. The leading painters of the Southern School were the literati, whose freer and more expressive style Dong Qichang judged to be far superior.

Dong Qichang's own work—for example, *Dwelling in the Qingbian Mountains* (FIG. **27-12**), painted in 1617—belongs to the Southern School he admired so much. Subject and style, as well as the incorporation of a long inscription at the top, immediately reveal his debt to earlier literati painters. But Dong Qichang was also an innovator, especially in his treatment of the towering mountains, where shaded masses of rocks alternate with flat, blank bands, flattening the composition and creating highly expressive and abstract patterns. Some critics have called Dong Qichang the first *modernist* painter, because his work foreshadows developments in 19th-century European landscape painting (FIG. **31-20**).

1 ft.

27-12 DONG QICHANG, *Dwelling in the Qingbian Mountains,* Ming dynasty, 1617. Hanging scroll, ink on paper, 7′ 3½″ × 2′ 2½″. Cleveland Museum of Art, Cleveland (Leonard C. Hanna Jr. bequest). ▪◀

Dong Qichang, the "first modernist painter," conceived his landscapes as shaded masses of rocks alternating with blank bands, flattening the composition and creating expressive, abstract patterns.

27-13 WEN SHU, *Carnations and Garden Rock*, Ming dynasty, 1627. Fan, ink and colors on gold paper, $6\frac{3}{8}'' \times 1' 9\frac{1}{4}''$. Honolulu Academy of Arts, Honolulu (gift of Mr. Robert Allerton).

Flower painting was the specialty of Ming women artists, as was fan painting, a format imported from Japan. Wen Shu's depiction of a rock formation and three flower sprays is an example of both genres.

WEN SHU Landscape painting was the most prestigious artistic subject in Ming China, and it was the preferred theme of male literati. Ming women artists usually painted other subjects, especially flowers. WEN SHU (1595–1634), the daughter of an aristocratic Suzhou family and the wife of Zhao Jun, descended from Zhao Mengfu and the Song imperial house, was probably the finest flower painter of the Ming era. Her *Carnations and Garden Rock* (FIG. **27-13**) is also an example of Chinese arc-shaped fan painting, a format imported from Japan. In this genre, the artist paints on flat paper, but then folds the completed painting and mounts it on sticks to form a fan. The best fan paintings were probably never used as fans. Collectors purchased them to store in albums. As in her other flower paintings, Wen Shu focused on a few essential elements, in this instance a central rock formation and three sprays of flowers, and presented them against a plain background. Using delicate brush strokes and a restricted palette, she brilliantly communicated the fragility of the red flowers, con-

trasting them with the solidity of the brown rock. The spare composition creates a quiet mood of contemplation.

Qing Dynasty

The Ming bureaucracy's internal decay permitted another group of invaders, the Manchus of Manchuria, to overrun China in the 17th century. The Qing dynasty (r. 1644–1911) the Manchus established quickly restored effective imperial rule in the north. Southern China remained rebellious until the second Qing emperor, Kangxi (r. 1662–1722), succeeded in pacifying all of China. The Manchus adapted themselves to Chinese life and cultivated knowledge of China's arts.

SHITAO Traditional literati painting continued to be fashionable among conservative Qing artists, but other painters experimented with extreme effects of massed ink or individualized brushwork patterns. Bold and freely manipulated compositions with a new, expres-

27-14 SHITAO, *Man in a House beneath a Cliff*, Qing dynasty, late 17th century. Album leaf, ink and colors on paper, $9\frac{1}{2}'' \times 11''$. C. C. Wang Collection, New York.

Shitao experimented with extreme effects of massed ink and individualized brushwork patterns. In this album leaf, he surrounded a hut with vibrant, free-floating colored dots and sinuous contour lines.

sive force began to appear. A prominent painter in this mode was SHITAO (DAOJI, 1642–1707), a descendant of the Ming imperial family who became a Chan Buddhist monk at age 20. His theoretical writings, most notably his *Sayings on Painting from Monk Bitter Gourd* (his adopted name), called for use of the "single brush stroke" or "primordial line" as the root of all phenomena and representation. Although he carefully studied classical paintings, Shitao opposed mimicking earlier works and believed he could not learn anything from them unless he changed them. In *Man in a House beneath a Cliff* (FIG. 27-14), Shitao surrounded the figure in a hut with vibrant, free-floating colored dots and multiple sinuous contour lines. Unlike traditional literati, Shitao did not so much depict the landscape's appearance in his *album leaf* painting as animate it, molding the forces running through it.

LANG SHINING During the Qing dynasty, European Jesuit missionaries were familiar figures at the imperial court. Many of the missionaries were also artists, and they were instrumental in introducing modern European (that is, High Renaissance and Baroque)

painting styles to China. The Chinese, while admiring the Europeans' technical virtuosity, found Western style unsatisfactory. Those Jesuit painters who were successful in China adapted their styles to Chinese tastes. The most prominent European artist at the Qing court was GIUSEPPE CASTIGLIONE (1688–1768), who went by the name LANG SHINING in China. His hybrid Italian-Chinese painting style is on display in *Auspicious Objects* (FIG. 27-15), which he painted in 1724 in honor of the Yongzheng (r. 1723–1735) emperor's birthday. Castiglione's emphasis on a single source of light that creates consistent shadows, and his interest in three-dimensional volume, are unmistakably European. But the influence of Chinese literati painting on the Italian artist is equally clear, especially in the composition of the branches and leaves of the overhanging pine tree. Above all, the subject is purely Chinese. The white eagle, the pine tree, the rocks, and the red mushroomlike plants (lingzhi) are traditional Chinese symbols. The eagle connotes imperial status, courage, and military achievement. The evergreen pines and the rocks connote longevity, which eating lingzhi will promote, according to Chinese belief. All are fitting motifs with which to celebrate the birthday of an emperor.

QING PORCELAIN Qing potters at the imperial kilns at Jingdezhen continued to expand on the Yuan and Ming achievements in developing fine porcelain pieces with underglaze and overglaze decoration, and this art form gained wide admiration in Europe. A dish (FIG. 27-16) with a lobed rim exemplifies the overglaze technique. All of its colors—black, green, brown, yellow, and even blue—come from applying enamels (see "Chinese Porcelain," page 722). The decoration reflects important social changes in China. Economic prosperity and the possibility of advancement through success on civil service examinations made it realistic for many more families to hope that their sons could achieve wealth and higher social standing. In the

27-15 GIUSEPPE CASTIGLIONE (LANG SHINING), *Auspicious Objects,* Qing dynasty, 1724. Hanging scroll, ink and colors on silk, 7' 11$\frac{3}{8}$″ × 5' 1$\frac{7}{8}$″. Palace Museum, Beijing.

Castiglione was a Jesuit painter in Qing China who successfully combined European lighting techniques and three-dimensional volume with traditional Chinese literati subjects and compositions.

27-16 Dish with lobed rim, Qing dynasty, ca. 1700. White porcelain with overglaze, 1' 1$\frac{5}{8}$″ diameter. Percival David Foundation of Chinese Art, London.

This dish featuring the three star gods of happiness, success, and longevity exemplifies the overglaze porcelain technique in which all the colors come from applying enamels on top of the glaze surface.

27-17 Yᴇ Yᴜsʜᴀɴ and others, *Rent Collection Courtyard* (detail of larger tableau), Dayi, China, 1965. Clay, 100 yards long with life-size figures.

In this propagandistic tableau incorporating 114 figures, sculptors depicted the exploitation of peasants by their merciless landlords during the grim times before the Communists' takeover of China.

center of the dish are Fu, Lu, and Shou, the three celestial star gods of happiness, success, and longevity. The cranes and spotted deer, believed to live to advanced ages, and the pine trees around the rim are all symbols of long life. Artists represented similar themes in the inexpensive woodblock prints produced in great quantities during the Qing era. They were the commoners' equivalent of Castiglione's imperial painting of auspicious symbols (FIG. 27-15).

Modern China

The overthrow of the Qing dynasty and the establishment of the Republic of China under the Nationalist Party in 1912 did not bring an end to the traditional themes and modes of Chinese art. But the Marxism that triumphed in 1949, when the Communists took control of China and founded the People's Republic, inspired a social realism that broke drastically with the past. The intended purpose of Communist art was to serve the people in the struggle to liberate and elevate the masses.

YE YUSHAN In *Rent Collection Courtyard* (FIG. 27-17), a 1965 tableau 100 yards long and incorporating 114 life-size figures, Yᴇ Yᴜsʜᴀɴ (b. 1935) and a team of sculptors grimly represented the old times before the People's Republic. Peasants, worn and bent by toil, bring their taxes (in produce) to the courtyard of their merciless, plundering landlord. The message is clear—this kind of exploitation must not occur again. Initially, the authorities did not

reveal the artists' names. The anonymity of those who depicted the event was significant in itself. The secondary message was that only collective action could effect the transformations the People's Republic sought.

XU BING In the late 1980s and 1990s, Chinese artists began to make a mark on the *postmodern* international scene (see Chapter 36). One of them was Xᴜ Bɪɴɢ (b. 1955), who created a large installation called *A Book from the Sky* (FIG. 27-18) in 1988. First exhibited in China and then in Japan, the United States, and Hong Kong, the work presents an enormous number of woodblock-printed texts in characters that resemble Chinese writing but that the artist invented. Producing them required both an intimate knowledge of real Chinese characters and extensive training in block carving. Xu's work, however, is no hymn to tradition. Critics have interpreted it both as a stinging critique of the meaninglessness of contemporary political language and as a commentary on the unintelligibility of the past. Like many works of art, past and present, Eastern and Western, this piece can be read on many levels.

27-18A Wᴜ
Gᴜᴀɴᴢʜᴏɴɢ,
Wild Vines wi
Flowers Like
Pearls, 1997.

KOREA

The great political, social, religious, and artistic changes that occurred in China from the time of the Mongols to the People's Republic find parallels elsewhere in East Asia, especially in Korea.

27-18 Xᴜ Bɪɴɢ, *A Book from the Sky,* 1988. Installation at Chazen Museum of Art, University of Wisconsin, Madison, 1991. Movable-type prints and books.

Xu Bing is a leader of the postmodern movement in China. *A Book from the Sky,* with its invented Chinese characters, may be a stinging critique of the meaninglessness of contemporary political language.

dynasty, however, the Ming emperors of China attempted to take control of northeastern Korea. General Yi Song-gye repelled them and founded the last Korean dynasty, the Choson in 1392. The long rule of the Choson kings ended only in 1910, when Japan annexed Korea.

NAMDAEMUN, SEOUL Public building projects helped give the new Korean state an image of dignity and power. One impressive early monument, built for the new Choson capital of Seoul, is the city's south gate, or Namdaemun (FIG. **27-19**). It combines the imposing strength of its impressive stone foundations with the sophistication of its intricately bracketed wooden superstructure. In East Asia, elaborate gateways, often in a processional series, are a standard element in city designs as well as royal and sacred compounds, all usually surrounded by walls, as at Beijing's Forbidden City (FIG. **27-6**). These gateways served as magnificent symbols of the ruler's authority, as did the triumphal arches of imperial Rome (see Chapter 10).

Choson Dynasty

At the time the Yuan overthrew the Song dynasty in China, the Koryo dynasty (918–1392), which had ruled Korea since the downfall of China's Tang dynasty, was still in power (see Chapter 7). The Koryo kings outlasted the Yuan as well. Toward the end of the Koryo

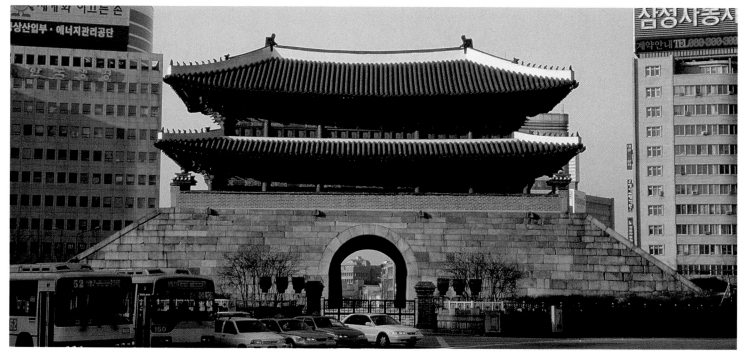

27-19 Namdaemun, Seoul, South Korea, Choson dynasty, first built in 1398.

The new Choson dynasty leaders constructed the south gate to their new capital of Seoul as a symbol of their authority. Namdaemun combines stone foundations with Chinese-style bracketed wooden construction.

CHONG SON Over the long course of the Choson dynasty, Korean painters worked in many different modes and treated the same wide range of subjects seen in Ming and Qing China. One of Korea's most renowned painters was CHONG SON (1676–1759), a great admirer of Chinese Southern School painting who brought his own unique vision to the traditional theme of the mountainous landscape. In his *Kumgang (Diamond) Mountains* (FIG. **27-20**), Chong Son evoked a real scene, an approach known in Korea as "true view" painting. He used sharper, darker versions of the fibrous brush strokes that most Chinese literati favored in order to represent the bright crystalline appearance of the mountains and to emphasize their spiky forms.

Modern Korea

After its annexation in 1910, Korea remained part of Japan until 1945, when the Western Allies and the Soviet Union took control of the peninsula nation at the end of World War II. Korea was divided into the Democratic People's Republic of Korea (North Korea) and the Republic of Korea (South Korea) in 1948. South Korea has emerged as a fully industrialized nation, and its artists have had a wide exposure to art styles from around the globe. While some Korean artists continue to work in a traditional East Asian manner, others have embraced developments in contemporary Europe and America.

SONG SU-NAM One painter who has very successfully combined native and international traditions is SONG SU-NAM (b. 1938), a professor at Hongik University in Seoul and one of the founders of the Oriental Ink Movement of the 1980s. His *Summer Trees* (FIG. **27-21**), painted in 1983, owes a great deal to the *Post-Painterly Abstraction* movement of the 20th century and to the work of American painters such as Morris Louis (FIG. **36-13**). But in place of Louis's acrylic resin on canvas, Song used ink on paper, the preferred medium of East Asian literati. He forsook, however, the traditional emphasis on brush strokes to explore the subtle tonal variations that broad stretches of ink wash made possible. Nonetheless, the painting's name recalls the landscapes of earlier Korean and Chinese masters. This simultaneous respect for tradition and innovation has been a hallmark of both Chinese and Korean art through their long histories.

27-20 CHONG SON, *Kumgang Mountains*, Choson dynasty, 1734. Hanging scroll, ink and colors on paper, $4' 3\frac{1}{2}'' \times 1' 11\frac{1}{4}''$. Hoam Art Museum, Kyunggi-Do.

In a variation on Chinese literati painting, Chong Son used sharp, dark brush strokes to represent the bright crystalline appearance of the Diamond Mountains and to emphasize their spiky forms.

27-21 SONG SU-NAM, *Summer Trees*, 1983. Ink on paper, $2' 1\frac{5}{8}''$ high. British Museum, London.

Song Su-nam combined native and international traditions in *Summer Trees,* an ink painting that evokes Asian landscape painting but owes a great deal to American Post-Painterly Abstraction.

CHINA AND KOREA
AFTER 1279

YUAN DYNASTY, 1279–1368

▮ The Mongols invaded northern China in 1210 and defeated the last Song emperor in 1279. Under the first Yuan emperor, Kublai Khan, and his successors, China was richer and technologically more advanced than Europe.

▮ The Mongols admired Chinese art and culture, and traditional landscape painting and calligraphy in particular continued to flourish during the century of Yuan rule.

▮ The Jingdezhen kilns gained renown for porcelain pottery with cobalt-blue underglaze decoration.

Temple vase, Yuan dynasty, 1351

MING DYNASTY, 1368–1644

▮ A popular uprising in 1368 drove the last Mongol emperor from Beijing. The new native Ming dynasty expanded the capital and constructed a vast new imperial palace compound, the Forbidden City. Surrounded by a moat and featuring an axial plan, it was the ideal setting for court ritual.

▮ At the opposite architectural pole are the gardens of Suzhou. The Ming designers employed pavilions, bridges, ponds, winding paths, and sculpted rocks to reproduce the irregularities of uncultivated nature.

▮ Ming painting is also diverse, ranging from formal official portrait and history painting to literati painting. Male painters favored landscapes, and female artists specialized in flowers, sometimes painted on fans.

▮ The Orchard Factory satisfied the Ming court's appetite for luxury goods with furniture and other objects in lacquered wood.

Forbidden City, Beijing, 15th century and later

QING DYNASTY, 1644–1911

▮ In 1644 the Ming dynasty fell to the Manchus, northern invaders who, like the Yuan, embraced Chinese art.

▮ Traditional painting styles remained fashionable, but some Qing painters, such as Shitao, experimented with extreme effects of massed ink and free brushwork patterns.

▮ Increased contact with Europe brought many Jesuit missionaries to the Qing court. The most prominent Jesuit artist was Giuseppe Castiglione, who developed a hybrid Italian-Chinese painting style.

▮ The Jingdezhen imperial potters developed multicolor porcelains using the overglaze enamel technique.

Shitao, *Man in a House beneath a Cliff*, late 17th century

MODERN CHINA, 1912–Present

▮ The overthrow of the Qing dynasty did not bring a dramatic change in Chinese art, but when the Communists gained control in 1949, state art focused on promoting Marxist ideals. Teams of sculptors produced vast propaganda pieces like *Rent Collection Courtyard*.

▮ Contemporary art in China is multifaceted. Some artists, for example, Xu Bing, have made their mark on the postmodern international art scene.

Ye Yushan, *Rent Collection Courtyard*, 1965

KOREA, 1392–Present

▮ The last Korean dynasty was the Choson (r. 1392–1910), which established its capital at Seoul and erected impressive public monuments like the Namdaemun gate to serve as symbols of imperial authority.

▮ After the division of Korea into two republics following World War II, South Korea emerged as a modern industrial nation. Some of its artists have successfully combined native and international traditions. Song Su-nam's landscapes owe a great deal to American Post-Painterly Abstraction.

Song Su-nam, *Summer Trees*, 1983

1 ft.

28-1 OGATA KORIN, *Red Plum Blossoms,* Edo period, ca. 1710–1716. Detail of one of a pair of two-panel folding screens (FIG. I-12). Ink, color, and gold leaf on paper, each screen 5′ 1$\frac{5}{8}$″ × 5′ 7$\frac{7}{8}$″. MOA Art Museum, Shizuoka-ken.

Ogata Korin was one of the leading painters of the 18th-century Rinpa School. In this work he reduced the landscape motifs to a minimum to offer a dramatic contrast of forms and visual textures.

JAPAN AFTER 1336

Early Japanese cultural history (see Chapter 8) reveals the dialogue that occurred between the Japanese islands and continental eastern Asia and the indebtedness of Japanese art and architecture to the paintings, sculptures, buildings, and crafts of China and Korea. Nonetheless, the Japanese developed a rich variety and unique identity in their art. This ability to incorporate foreign elements yet maintain a consciousness of their own heritage and traditions became more apparent in the arts of Japan as time progressed. It is especially evident from the 14th century to the present.

JAPAN, 1336 TO 1868

In 1185 the Japanese emperor in Kyoto appointed the first *shogun* (military governor) in Kamakura in eastern Japan (MAP **28-1**). Although the imperial family retained its right to reign and, in theory, the shogun managed the country on the ruling emperor's behalf, in reality the emperor lost all governing authority. The Japanese *shogunate* was a political and economic arrangement in which *daimyo* (local lords), the leaders of powerful warrior bands composed of *samurai* (warriors), paid obeisance to the shogun. These local lords had considerable power over affairs within their domains. The Kamakura shogunate ruled Japan for more than a century but collapsed in 1332. Several years of civil war followed, ending only when Ashikaga Takauji (1305–1358) succeeded in establishing domination of his clan over all Japan and became the new imperially recognized shogun.

Muromachi Period

The rise of the Ashikaga clan marked the beginning of the Muromachi period (1336–1573), named after the district in Kyoto in which the Ashikaga shoguns maintained their headquarters. During the Muromachi period, Zen Buddhism (see "Zen Buddhism," page 736) rose to prominence alongside the older traditions, such as Pure Land and Esoteric Buddhism. Unlike the Pure Land faith, which stressed reliance on the saving power of Amida, the Buddha of the West, Zen emphasized rigorous discipline and personal

Zen Buddhism

Zen (*Chan* in Chinese), as a fully developed Buddhist tradition, began filtering into Japan in the 12th century and had its most pervasive impact on Japanese culture starting in the 14th century during the Muromachi period. As in other forms of Buddhism, Zen followers hoped to achieve enlightenment. Zen teachings assert that everyone has the potential for enlightenment, but worldly knowledge and mundane thought patterns suppress it. Thus, to achieve enlightenment, followers must break through the boundaries of everyday perception and logic. This is most often achieved through meditation. Indeed, the word *zen* means "meditation." Some Zen schools stress meditation as a long-term practice eventually leading to enlightenment, whereas others emphasize the benefits of sudden shocks to the worldly mind. One of these shocks is the subject of Kano Motonobu's *Zen Patriarch Xiangyen Zhixian Sweeping with a Broom* (FIG. 28-4), in which the shattering of a fallen roof tile opens the monk's mind. Beyond personal commitment, the guidance of an enlightened Zen teacher is essential to arriving at enlightenment. Years of strict training that involve manual labor under the tutelage of this master coupled with meditation provide the foundation for a receptive mind. According to Zen beliefs, by cultivating discipline and intense concentration, Buddhists can transcend their ego and release themselves from the shackles of the mundane world.

Although Zen is not primarily devotional, followers do pray to specific deities. In general, Zen teachings view mental calm, lack of fear, and spontaneity as signs of a person's advancement on the path to enlightenment.

Zen training for monks takes place at temples, some of which have gardens designed in accord with Zen principles, such as the dry-landscape garden of Kyoto's Saihoji temple (FIG. 28-2). Zen temples also sometimes served as centers of Chinese learning and handled funeral rites. Zen temples even embraced many traditional Buddhist observances, such as devotional rituals before images, which had little to do with meditation per se.

As the teachings spread, Zen ideals reverberated throughout Japanese culture. Lay followers as well as Zen monks painted pictures and produced other artworks that appear to reach toward Zen ideals through their subjects and their means of expression. Other cultural practices reflected the widespread appeal of Zen. For example, the tea ceremony (see "The Japanese Tea Ceremony," page 740), or ritual drinking of tea, as it developed in the 15th and 16th centuries, offered a temporary respite from everyday concerns, a brief visit to a quiet retreat with a meditative atmosphere, such as the Taian teahouse (FIG. 28-7).

28-2 Dry cascade and pools, upper garden, Saihoji temple, Kyoto, Japan, modified in Muromachi period, 14th century.

Zen temples often incorporated gardens to facilitate meditation. The dry cascade and pools of the upper garden of the Saihoji temple in Kyoto are an early example of Muromachi dry-landscape gardening (karesansui).

responsibility. For this reason, Zen held a special attraction for the upper echelons of samurai, whose behavioral codes placed high values on loyalty, courage, and self-control. Further, familiarity with Chinese Zen culture (see "Chan Buddhism," Chapter 7, page 201) carried implications of superior knowledge and refinement, thereby legitimizing the elevated status of the warrior elite.

Zen, however, was not simply the religion of Zen monks and highly placed warriors. Aristocrats, merchants, and others studied at and supported Zen temples. Furthermore, those who embraced Zen, including samurai, also generally accepted other Buddhist teachings, especially the ideas of the Pure Land sects. These sects gave much greater attention to the issues of death and salvation. Zen temples mundane reality. The dry landscape, or rock garden, became very popular in Japan in the Muromachi period and afterward, especially at Zen temples. In its extreme form, a karesansui garden consists purely of artfully arranged rocks on a raked bed of sand.

SESSHU TOYO As was common in earlier eras of Japanese history, Muromachi painters usually closely followed Chinese precedents (often arriving by way of Korea). Muromachi painting nonetheless displays great variety in both style and subject matter. Indeed, individual masters often worked in different styles, as did the most celebrated Muromachi priest-painter, SESSHU TOYO (1420–1506), one of the very few Japanese painters who traveled to China and studied contemporaneous Ming painting. His most dramatic works are in the *splashed-ink* (*haboku*) style, a technique with Chinese roots. The painter of a haboku picture paused to visualize the image, loaded the brush with ink, and then applied primarily broad, rapid strokes, sometimes even dripping the ink onto the paper. The result often hovers at the edge of legibility, without dissolving into sheer abstraction. This balance between spontaneity and a thorough knowledge of the painting tradition gives the pictures their artistic strength. In the haboku landscape illustrated here (FIG. **28-3**), images of mountains, trees, and buildings emerge from the ink-washed surface. Two figures appear in a boat (to the lower right), and the two swift strokes nearby represent the pole and banner of a wine shop.

stood out not only as religious institutions but also as centers of secular culture, where people could study Chinese art, literature, and learning, which the Japanese imported along with Zen Buddhism. Some Zen monasteries accumulated considerable wealth overseeing trade missions to China.

SAIHOJI GARDENS The Saihoji temple gardens in Kyoto bear witness to both the continuities and changes that marked religious art in the Muromachi period. In the 14th century, this Pure Land temple with its extensive gardens became a Zen institution. However, Zen leaders did not attempt to erase other religious traditions, and the Saihoji gardens in their totality originally included some Pure Land elements even as they served the Zen faith's more meditative needs. In this way, they perfectly echoed the complementary roles of these two Buddhist traditions in the Muromachi period, with Pure Land providing a promise of salvation and Zen promoting study and meditation.

Saihoji's lower gardens center on a pond in the shape of the Japanese character for "mind" or "spirit" and are thus the perfect setting for monks to meditate. Today those gardens are famous for their iridescently green mosses, whose beauty is almost otherworldly. In contrast, arrangements of rocks and sand on the hillsides of the upper garden, especially the dry cascade and pools (FIG. **28-2**), are treasured early examples of Muromachi *karesansui* (dry-landscape gardening). The designers stacked the rocks to suggest a swift mountain stream rushing over the stones to form pools below. In eastern Asia, people long considered gazing at dramatic natural scenery highly beneficial to the human spirit. These activities refreshed people after too much contact with daily affairs and helped them reach beyond

-2A
aresansui
rden,
oanji Temple,
. 1488.

28-3 SESSHU TOYO, splashed-ink (haboku) landscape, detail of the lower part of a hanging scroll, Muromachi period, 1495. Ink on paper, full scroll 4′ 10$\frac{1}{4}$″ × 1′ $\frac{7}{8}$″; detail 4′ $\frac{1}{2}$″ high. Tokyo National Museum, Tokyo.

In this splashed-ink landscape, the artist applied primarily broad, rapid strokes, sometimes even dripping the ink on the paper. The result hovers at the edge of legibility, without dissolving into sheer abstraction.

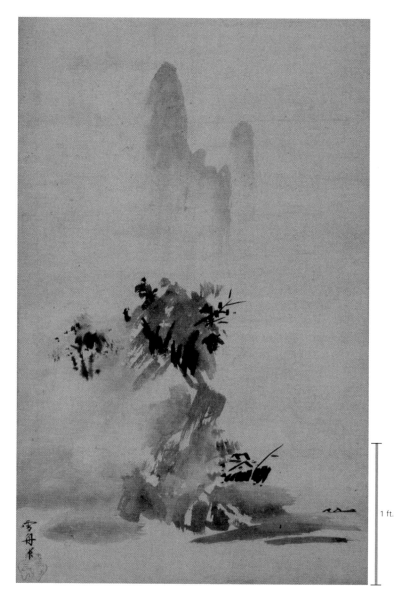

1 ft.

KANO MOTONOBU The opposite pole of Muromachi painting style is represented by the Kano School, which by the 17th century had become a virtual national painting academy. The school flourished until the late 19th century. KANO MOTONOBU (1476–1559) was largely responsible for establishing the Kano style during the Muromachi period. His *Zen Patriarch Xiangyen Zhixian Sweeping with a Broom* (FIG. **28-4**) is one of six panels depicting Zen patriarchs that Motonobu designed as sliding door paintings (*fusuma*) for the abbot's room in the Zen temple complex of Daitokuji in Kyoto. Later refashioned as a hanging scroll, the painting represents the Zen patriarch Xiangyen Zhixian (d. 898) at the moment he achieved enlightenment. Motonobu depicted the patriarch sweeping the ground near his rustic retreat as a roof tile falls at his feet and shatters. His Zen training is so deep that the resonant sound propels the patriarch into an awakening. In contrast to Muromachi splashed-ink painting, Motonobu's work displays exacting precision in applying ink in bold outlines by holding the brush perpendicular to the paper. Thick clouds obscure the mountainous setting and focus the viewer's attention on the sharp, angular rocks, bamboo branches, and modest hut that frame the patriarch. Lightly applied colors also draw attention to Xiangyen Zhixian, whom Motonobu portrayed as having let go of his broom with his right hand as he recoils in astonishment. Although very different in style, the Japanese painting recalls the subject of Liang Kai's Song hanging scroll (FIG. **7-25**).

Momoyama Period

Despite the hierarchical nature of Japanese society during the Muromachi period, the control the Ashikaga shoguns exerted was tenuous and precarious. Ambitious daimyo often seized opportunities to expand their power, sometimes aspiring to become shoguns themselves. By the late 15th century, Japan was experiencing violent confrontations over territory and dominance. In fact, scholars refer to the last century of the Muromachi period as the Era of Warring States, intentionally borrowing the terminology used to describe a much earlier tumultuous period in Chinese history (see Chapter 7). Finally, three successive warlords seized power, and the last succeeded in restoring order and establishing a new and long-lasting shogunate. In 1573, Oda Nobunaga (1534–1582) overthrew the Ashikaga shogunate in Kyoto but was later killed by one of his generals. Toyotomi Hideyoshi (1536–1598) took control of the government after Nobunaga's assassination and ruled until he died of natural causes in 1598. In the struggle following Hideyoshi's death, Tokugawa Ieyasu (1542–1616) emerged victorious and assumed the title of shogun in 1603. Ieyasu continued to face challenges, but by 1615 he had eliminated his last rival and established his clan as the rulers of Japan for two and a half centuries. To reinforce their power, these warlords constructed huge castles with palatial residences—partly as symbols of their authority and partly as fortresses. The new era's designation, Momoyama (Peach Blossom Hill), derives from the scenic foliage at one

28-4 KANO MOTONOBU, *Zen Patriarch Xiangyen Zhixian Sweeping with a Broom*, from Daitokuji, Kyoto, Japan, Muromachi period, ca. 1513. Hanging scroll, ink and color on paper, $5' 7\frac{3}{8}'' \times 2' 10\frac{3}{4}''$. Tokyo National Museum, Tokyo.

The Kano School represents the opposite pole of Muromachi style from splashed-ink painting. In this scroll depicting a Zen patriarch experiencing enlightenment, Motonobu used bold outlines to define the forms.

of Hideyoshi's castles southeast of Kyoto. The Momoyama period (1573–1615), although only a brief interlude between two major shogunates, produced many outstanding artworks.

KANO EITOKU Each Momoyama warlord commissioned lavish decorations for the interior of his castle, including paintings, sliding doors, and folding screens (*byobu*) in ink, color, and gold leaf. Gold screens had existed since Muromachi times, but Momoyama painters made them even bolder, reducing the number of motifs and often greatly enlarging them against flat, shimmering fields of gold leaf.

The grandson of Motonobu, KANO EITOKU (1543–1590), was the leading painter of murals and screens and received numerous commissions from the powerful warlords. So extensive were these commissions (in both scale and number) that Eitoku used a painting system developed by his grandfather that relied on a team of specialized painters to assist him. Unfortunately, little of Eitoku's elaborate work remains because of the subsequent destruction of the ostenta-

28-5A Himeji Castle, Osaka, begun 1581.

28-5 KANO EITOKU, *Chinese Lions,* Momoyama period, late 16th century. Six-panel screen, color, ink, and gold leaf on paper, 7' 4" × 14' 10". Imperial Household Agency, Tokyo.

Chinese lions were fitting imagery for the castle of a Momoyama warlord because they exemplified power and bravery. Eitoku's huge screen features boldly outlined forms on a gold ground.

tious castles he helped decorate—not surprising in an era marked by power struggles. However, a painting of Chinese lions on a six-panel screen (FIG. **28-5**) offers a glimpse of his work's grandeur. Possibly created for Toyotomi Hideyoshi, the second of the three great warlords of the Momoyama period, this screen, originally one of a pair, appropriately speaks to the emphasis on militarism so prevalent at the time. The lions Eitoku depicted are mythological beasts that have their origin in ancient Chinese legends. Appearing in both religious and secular contexts, the lions came to be associated with power and bravery and are thus fitting imagery for a military leader. Indeed, Chinese lions became an important symbolic motif during the Momoyama period. In Eitoku's painting, the colorful beasts' powerfully muscled bodies, defined and flattened by broad contour lines, stride

forward within a gold field and minimal setting elements. The dramatic impact of this work derives in part from its scale—it is more than 7 feet tall and nearly 15 feet long.

HASEGAWA TOHAKU Momoyama painters did not work exclusively in the colorful style exemplified by Eitoku's *Chinese Lions.* HASEGAWA TOHAKU (1539–1610) was a leading painter who became familiar with the aesthetics and techniques of Chinese Chan and Japanese Zen painters such as Sesshu Toyo (FIG. **28-3**) by studying the art collections of the Daitokuji temple in Kyoto. Tohaku sometimes painted in ink monochrome using loose brushwork with brilliant success, as seen in *Pine Forest* (FIG. **28-6**), one of a pair of six-panel byobu. His wet brush strokes—long and slow, short and quick,

28-6 HASEGAWA TOHAKU, *Pine Forest,* Momoyama period, late 16th century. One of a pair of six-panel screens, ink on paper, 5' 1¾" × 11' 4". Tokyo National Museum, Tokyo.

Tohaku used wet brush strokes to paint a grove of great pines shrouded in mist. In Zen terms, the six-panel screen suggests the illusory nature of mundane reality while evoking a calm, meditative mood.

The Japanese Tea Ceremony

The Japanese tea ceremony involves the ritual preparation, serving, and drinking of green tea. The fundamental practices began in China, but they developed in Japan to a much higher degree of sophistication, peaking in the Momoyama period. Simple forms of the tea ceremony started in Japan in Zen temples as a symbolic withdrawal from the ordinary world to cultivate the mind and spirit. The practices spread to other social groups, especially samurai and, by the late 16th century, wealthy merchants. Until the late Muromachi period, grand tea ceremonies in warrior residences served primarily as an excuse to display treasured collections of Chinese objects, such as porcelains, lacquers, and paintings.

Initially, the Japanese held tea ceremonies in a room or section of a house. As the popularity of the ceremonies increased, freestanding teahouses (FIG. 28-7) became common. The ceremony involves a sequence of rituals in which both host and guests participate. The host's responsibilities include serving the guests; selecting special utensils, such as water jars (FIG. 28-8) and tea bowls; and determining the tearoom's decoration, which changes according to occasion and season. Acknowledged as having superior aesthetic sensibilities, individuals recognized as master tea ceremony practitioners (tea masters) advise patrons on the ceremony and acquire students. Tea masters even direct or influence the design of teahouses and of tearooms within larger structures (including interiors and gardens) as well as the design of tea utensils. They often make simple bamboo implements and occasionally even ceramic vessels.

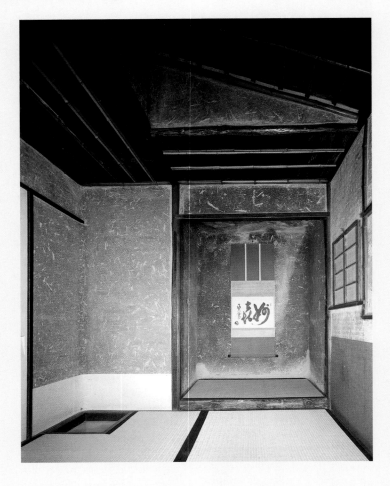

28-7 SEN NO RIKYU, Taian teahouse (interior view), Myokian Temple, Kyoto, Japan, Momoyama period, ca. 1582.

The dimness and tiny size of Rikyu's Taian tearoom and its alcove produce a cavelike feel and encourage intimacy among the host and guests, who must crawl through a small sliding door to enter.

dark and pale—present a grove of great pines shrouded in mist. His trees emerge from and recede into the heavy atmosphere, as if the landscape hovers at the edge of formlessness. In Zen terms, the picture suggests the illusory nature of mundane reality while evoking a calm, meditative mood.

SEN NO RIKYU A favorite exercise of cultivation and refinement in the Momoyama period was the tea ceremony (see "The Japanese Tea Ceremony," above). In Japan, this important practice eventually came to carry various political and ideological implications. For example, it provided a means for individuals relatively new to political or economic power to assert authority in the cultural realm. For instance, upon returning from a major military campaign, Toyotomi Hideyoshi held an immense tea ceremony that lasted 10 days and was open to everyone in Kyoto. The ceremony's political associations became so serious that warlords granted or refused their vassals the right to practice it.

The most venerated tea master of the Momoyama period was SEN NO RIKYU (1522–1591), who was instrumental in establishing the rituals and aesthetics of the tea ceremony, for example, the manner of entry into a teahouse (crawling on one's hands and knees). Rikyu believed this behavior fostered humility and created the impression, however unrealistic, that there was no rank in a teahouse. Rikyu was the designer of the first Japanese teahouse built as an independent structure as opposed to being part of a house. The Taian teahouse (FIG. 28-7) at the

Myokian Temple in Kyoto, also attributed to Rikyu, is the oldest in Japan. The interior displays two standard features of Japanese residential architecture of the late Muromachi period—very thick, rigid straw mats called *tatami* (a Heian innovation) and an alcove called a *tokonoma*. The tatami accommodate the traditional Japanese customs of not wearing shoes indoors and of sitting on the floor. They can still be found in Japanese homes today. Less common in contemporary houses are tokonoma, which developed as places to hang scrolls of painting or calligraphy and to display other prized objects.

The Taian tokonoma and the tearoom as a whole have unusually dark walls, with earthen plaster covering even some of the square corner posts. The room's dimness and tiny size (about six feet square, the size of two tatami mats) produce a cavelike feel and encourage intimacy among the tea host and guests. The guests enter from the garden outside through a small sliding door that forces them humbly to crawl inside. The means of entrance emphasizes a guest's passage into a ceremonial space set apart from the ordinary world.

SHINO CERAMICS Sen no Rikyu also was influential in determining the aesthetics of tea ceremony utensils. He maintained that value and refinement lay in character and ability and not in bloodline or rank, and he therefore encouraged the use of tea items whose value was their inherent beauty rather than their monetary worth. Even before Rikyu, in the late 15th century during the Muromachi

28-8 Kogan, tea ceremony water jar, Momoyama period, late 16th century. Shino ware with underglaze design, 7″ high. Hatakeyama Memorial Museum, Tokyo.

The vessels used in the Japanese tea ceremony reflect the concepts of wabi, the aesthetic of refined rusticity, and sabi, the value found in weathered objects. These qualities suggest the tranquility achieved in old age.

period, admiration of the technical brilliance of Chinese objects had begun to give way to ever greater appreciation of the virtues of rustic Korean and Japanese wares. This new aesthetic of refined rusticity, or *wabi*, was consistent with Zen concepts. Wabi suggests austerity and simplicity. Related to wabi and also important as a philosophical and aesthetic principle was *sabi*—the value found in the old and weathered, suggesting the tranquility reached in old age.

Wabi and sabi aesthetics underlie the ceramic vessels produced for the tea ceremony, such as the Shino water jar named *kogan* (FIG. **28-8**). The name, which means "ancient stream bank," comes

from the painted design on the jar's surface as well as from its coarse texture and rough form, both reminiscent of earth cut by water. The term *Shino* generally refers to ceramic wares produced during the late 16th and early 17th centuries in kilns in Mino. Shino vessels typically have rough surfaces and feature heavy glazes containing feldspar. These glazes are predominantly white when fired but can include pinkish red or gray hues. The kogans' coarse stoneware body and seemingly casual decoration offer the same sorts of aesthetic and interpretive challenges and opportunities as dry-landscape gardens (FIG. **28-2**). The kogan illustrated here, for example, has a prominent crack in one side and sagging contours (both intentional) to suggest the accidental and natural, qualities essential to the values of wabi and sabi.

Edo Period

When Tokugawa Ieyasu consolidated his power in 1615, he abandoned Kyoto, the official capital, and set up his headquarters in Edo (modern Tokyo), initiating the Edo period (1615–1868) of Japanese history and art. The new regime instituted many policies designed to limit severely the pace of social and cultural change in Japan. Fearing destabilization of the social order, the Tokugawa rulers banned Christianity and expelled all Western foreigners except the Dutch. The Tokugawa also transformed Confucian ideas of social stratification and civic responsibility into public policy, and they tried to control the social influence of urban merchants, some of whose wealth far outstripped that of most warrior leaders. However, the population's great expansion in urban centers, the spread of literacy in the cities and beyond, and a growing thirst for knowledge and diversion made for a very lively popular culture not easily subject to tight control.

KATSURA IMPERIAL VILLA In the Edo period, the imperial court's power remained as it had been for centuries, symbolic and ceremonial, but the court continued to wield influence in matters of taste and culture. For example, for a 50-year period in the 17th century, a princely family developed a modest country retreat into a villa that became the standard for Japanese domestic architecture. Since the early 20th century, it has inspired architects worldwide (FIG. **35-77**), even as ordinary living environments in Japan became increasingly Westernized in structure and decor. The Katsura Imperial Villa (FIG. **28-9**), built between 1620 and 1663 on the

28-9 Eastern facade of the Katsura Imperial Villa, Kyoto, Japan, Edo period, 1620–1663.

This princely villa on the Katsura River has long been the standard for Japanese residential architecture. The design relies on subtleties of proportion, color, and texture instead of ornament for its aesthetic appeal.

Katsura River southwest of Kyoto, has many features that derive from earlier teahouses, such as Rikyu's Taian (FIG. 28-7). However, tea ceremony aesthetics later moved away from Rikyu's wabi extremes, and the Katsura Villa's designers and carpenters incorporated elements of courtly gracefulness as well.

Ornament that disguises structural forms has little place in this architecture's appeal, which relies instead on subtleties of proportion, color, and texture. A variety of textures (stone, wood, tile, and plaster) and subdued colors and tonal values enrich the villa's lines, planes, and volumes. Artisans painstakingly rubbed and burnished all surfaces to bring out the natural beauty of their grains and textures. The rooms are not large, but parting or removing the sliding doors between them can create broad rectangular spaces. Perhaps most important, the residents can open the doors to the outside to achieve a harmonious integration of building and garden—one of the primary ideals of Japanese residential architecture.

THE RINPA SCHOOL In painting, the Kano School enjoyed official governmental sponsorship during the Edo period, and its workshops provided paintings to the Tokugawa and their major vassals. By the mid-18th century, Kano masters also served as the primary painting teachers for nearly everyone aspiring to a career in the field. Even so, individualist painters and other schools emerged and flourished, working in quite distinct styles.

28-10A SOTATSU, *Waves at Matsushima,* ca. 1630.

The earliest major alternative school to emerge in the Edo period, Rinpa, was quite different in nature from the Kano School. It did not have a similar continuity of lineage and training through father and son, master and pupil. Instead, over time, Rinpa aesthetics and principles attracted a variety of individuals as practitioners and champions. Stylistically, Rinpa works feature vivid color and extensive use of gold and silver and often incorporate decorative patterns. The Rinpa School traced its roots to Tawaraya Sotatsu, an artist who emerged as an important figure during the late Momoyama period, but Rinpa takes its first syllable from the last syllable in the name of Ogata Korin. Both Sotatsu and Korin were scions of wealthy merchant families with close connections to the Japanese court. Many Rinpa works incorporate literary themes the nobility favored.

HONAMI KOETSU One of the earliest Rinpa masters was HONAMI KOETSU (1558–1637), the heir of an important family in the ancient capital of Kyoto and a greatly admired calligrapher. He also participated in and produced ceramics for the tea ceremony. Many scholars credit him with overseeing the design of wooden objects with lacquer decoration (see "Lacquered Wood," Chapter 27, page 724), perhaps with the aid of Sotatsu, the proprietor of a fan-painting shop. Scholars do know that together the two artists drew on ancient traditions of painting and craft decoration to develop a style that collapsed boundaries between the two arts. Paintings, the lacquered surfaces of writing boxes, and ceramics shared motifs and compositions.

In typical Rinpa fashion, Koetsu's *Boat Bridge* writing box (FIG. 28-10) exhibits motifs drawn from a 10th-century poem about the boat bridge at Sano, in the eastern provinces. The lid presents a subtle, gold-on-gold scene of small boats lined up side by side in the water to support the planks of a temporary bridge. The bridge itself, a lead overlay, forms a band across the lid's convex surface. The raised metallic lines on the water, boats, and bridge are a few Japanese characters from the poem, which describes the experience of crossing a bridge as evoking reflection on life's insecurities. The box also shows the dramatic contrasts of form, texture, and color that mark Rinpa aesthetics, especially the juxtaposition of the bridge's dark metal and the box's brilliant gold surface. The gold decoration comes from careful sprinkling of gold dust in wet lacquer. Whatever Koetsu's contribution to the design process, specialists well versed in the demanding techniques of metalworking and lacquering produced the writing box.

OGATA KORIN The son of an important textile merchant, OGATA KORIN (1658–1716) was primarily a painter, but he also designed lacquers in Koetsu's manner. One of Korin's painted masterpieces is a pair of two-panel folding screens depicting red and white blossoming plum trees separated by a stream (FIGS. I-12 and 28-1). As Koetsu did with his writing box, Korin reduced the motifs to a minimum to offer a dramatic contrast of forms and visual textures. The landscape consists solely of delicate, slender branches, gnarled, aged tree trunks, and an undulating stream. Korin mixed viewpoints (he depicted the stream as seen from above but the trees from the ground)

28-10 HONAMI KOETSU, *Boat Bridge,* writing box, Edo period, early 17th century. Lacquered wood with sprinkled gold and lead overlay, $9\frac{1}{2}'' \times 9'' \times 4\frac{3}{8}''$. Tokyo National Museum, Tokyo.

Koetsu's writing box is an early work of the Rinpa School, which drew on ancient traditions of painting and craft decoration to develop a style that collapsed boundaries between the two arts.

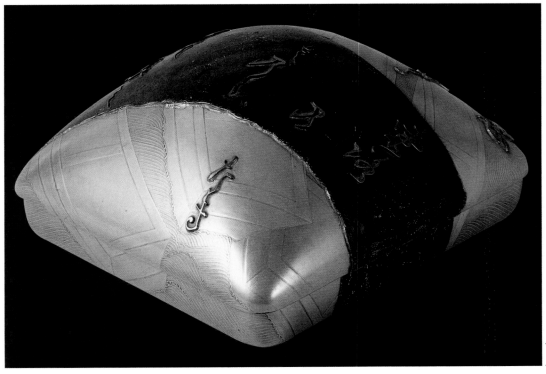

1 in.

to produce a striking two-dimensional pattern of dark forms on a gold ground. He even created a contrast between the dark motifs of stream and trees by varying painting techniques. The mottling of the trees comes from a signature Rinpa technique called *tarashikomi,* the dropping of ink and pigments onto surfaces still wet with previously applied ink and pigments. In sharp contrast, the pattern in the stream has the precision and elegant stylization of a textile design, produced by applying pigment through the forms cut in a paper stencil.

LITERATI PAINTING In the 17th and 18th centuries, Japan's increasingly urban, educated population spurred a cultural and social restlessness among commoners and samurai of lesser rank that the policies of the restrictive Tokugawa could not suppress. People eagerly sought new ideas and images, directing their attention primarily to China, as had happened throughout Japanese history, but also to the West. From each direction, dramatically new ideas about painting emerged.

Starting in the late 17th century, illustrations in printed books and imported paintings of lesser quality brought limited knowledge of Chinese literati painting (see Chapter 27) into Japan. As a result, some Japanese painters began to emulate Chinese models, although the difference in context resulted in variations. In China, literati were cultured intellectuals whose education and upbringing as landed gentry afforded them positions in the bureaucracy that governed the country. Chinese literati artists were predominantly amateurs and pursued painting as one of the proper functions of an educated and cultivated person. In contrast, although Japanese literati artists acquired a familiarity with and appreciation for Chinese literature, they were mostly professionals, painting to earn a living. Because of the diffused infiltration of Chinese literati painting into Japan, the resulting character of Japanese literati painting was less stylistically defined than in China. Despite the inevitable changes as Chinese ideas disseminated throughout Japan, the newly seen Chinese models were valuable in supporting emerging ideals of self-expression in painting by offering a worthy alternative to the Kano School's standardized repertoire.

YOSA BUSON One of the outstanding early representatives of Japanese literati painting was YOSA BUSON (1716–1783). A master writer of *haiku* (the 17-syllable Japanese poetic form that became popular from the 17th century on), Buson had a command of literati painting that extended beyond a knowledge of Chinese models. His poetic abilities gave rise to a lyricism that pervaded both his haiku and his painting. *Cuckoo Flying over New Verdure* (FIG. **28-11**) reveals his fully mature style. He incorporated in this work basic elements of Chinese literati painting by rounding the landscape forms and rendering their soft texture in fine fibrous brush strokes, and by including dense foliage patterns, but the cuckoo is a motif specific to Japanese poetry and literati painting. Moreover, although Buson imitated the vocabulary of brush strokes associated with the Chinese literati, his touch was bolder and more abstract, and the gentle palette of pale colors was very much his own.

UKIYO-E The growing urbanization in cities such as Osaka, Kyoto, and Edo led to an increase in the pursuit of sensual pleasure and entertainment in the brash popular theaters and the pleasure houses found in certain locales, including Edo's Yoshiwara brothel district. The Tokugawa tried to hold these activities in check, but their efforts were largely in vain, in part because of demographics. The population of Edo during this period included significant numbers of merchants and samurai (whose families remained in their home territories), and both groups were eager to enjoy secular city life. Those of lesser means could partake in these pleasures and amusements vicariously. Rapid developments in the printing industry led to the availability of numerous books and

28-11 YOSA BUSON, *Cuckoo Flying over New Verdure,* Edo period, late 18th century. Hanging scroll, ink and color on silk, $5' \frac{1}{2}'' \times 2' 7\frac{1}{4}''$. Hiraki Ukiyo-e Museum, Yokohama.

Buson, a master of haiku poetry, was a leading Japanese literati painter. Although inspired by Chinese works, he used a distinctive palette of pale colors and bolder, more abstract brush strokes.

printed images (see "Japanese Woodblock Prints," page 744), and these could convey the city's delights for a fraction of the cost of actual participation. Taking part in the emerging urban culture involved more than simple physical satisfactions and rowdy entertainments. Many participants were also admirers of literature, music, and art. The best-known products of this sophisticated counterculture were known as *ukiyo-e*—"pictures of the floating world," a term that suggests the transience of human life and the ephemerality of the material world. The main subjects of these paintings and especially prints came from the realms of pleasure, such as the Yoshiwara brothels and the popular theater, but Edo printmakers also frequently depicted beautiful young women in domestic settings (FIG. **28-12**) and landscapes (FIG. **28-13**).

Japanese Woodblock Prints

During the Edo period, *ukiyo-e* (pictures of the floating world) woodblock prints became enormously popular. Sold in small shops and on the street, an ordinary print went for the price of a bowl of noodles. People of very modest income could therefore collect prints in albums or paste them on their walls. A highly efficient production system made this wide distribution of Japanese graphic art possible.

Ukiyo-e artists were generally painters who did not participate in the making of the prints that made them so famous both in their own day and today. As the designers, they sold drawings to publishers, who in turn oversaw their printing. The publishers also played a role in creating ukiyo-e prints by commissioning specific designs or adapting them before printing. Certainly, the names of both designer and publisher appeared on the final prints.

Unacknowledged in nearly all cases were the individuals who made the prints, the block carvers and printers. Using skills honed since childhood, they worked with both speed and precision for relatively low wages and thus made ukiyo-e prints affordable. The master ukiyo-e printmakers were primarily men. Women, especially wives and daughters, often assisted painters and other artists, but few gained separate recognition. Among the exceptions was the daughter of Katsushika Hokusai (FIG. 28-13), Katsushika Oi (1818–1854), who became well known as a painter and probably helped her father with his print designs.

Stylistically, Japanese prints during the Edo period tend to have black outlines separating distinct color areas (FIG. 28-12). This format is a result of the printing process. A master carver pasted painted designs face down on a wooden block. Wetting and gently scraping the thin paper revealed the reversed image to guide the cutting of the block. After the carving, only the outlines of the forms and other elements that would be black in the final print remained raised in relief. The master printer then coated the block with black ink and printed several initial outline prints. These master prints became the guides for carving the other blocks, one for each color used. On each color block, the carver left in relief only the areas to be printed in that color. Even ordinary prints sometimes required up to 20 colors and thus 20 blocks. To print a color, a printer applied the appropriate pigment to a block's raised surface, laid a sheet of paper on it, and rubbed the back of the paper with a smooth flat object. Then another printer would print a different color on the same sheet of paper. Perfect alignment of the paper in each step was critical to prevent overlapping of colors, so the block carvers included printing guides—an L-shaped ridge in one corner and a straight ridge on one side—in their blocks. The printers could cover small alignment errors with a final printing of the black outlines from the last block.

The materials used in printing varied over time but by the mid-18th century had reached a level of standardization. The blocks were planks of fine-grained hardwood, usually cherry. The best paper came from the white layer beneath the bark of mulberry trees,

28-12 SUZUKI HARUNOBU, *Evening Bell at the Clock,* from *Eight Views of the Parlor,* Edo period, ca. 1765. Woodblock print, $11\frac{1}{4}'' \times 8\frac{1}{2}''$. Art Institute of Chicago, Chicago (Clarence Buckingham Collection). ◼◀

Harunobu's nishiki-e (brocade pictures) took their name from their costly pigments and paper. The rich color and flatness of the objects, women, and setting in this print are characteristic of the artist's style.

because its long fibers helped the paper stand up to repeated rubbing on the blocks. The printers used a few mineral pigments but favored inexpensive dyes made from plants for most colors. As a result, the colors of ukiyo-e prints were and are highly susceptible to fading, especially when exposed to strong light. In the early 19th century, more permanent European synthetic dyes began to enter Japan. The first, Prussian blue, can be seen in Hokusai's *The Great Wave off Kanagawa* (FIG. 28-13).

The popularity of ukiyo-e prints extended to the Western world as well. Their affordability and portability facilitated the dissemination of the prints, especially throughout Europe. Ukiyo-e prints appear in the backgrounds of a number of Impressionist and Post-Impressionist paintings, attesting to the appeal these works held for Westerners (see "Japonisme," Chapter 31, page 829).

SUZUKI HARUNOBU The urban appetite for ukiyo pleasures and for their depiction in ukiyo-e provided fertile ground for many print designers to flourish. Consequently, competition among publishing houses led to ever-greater refinement and experimentation in printmaking. One of the most admired and emulated 18th-century designers, SUZUKI HARUNOBU (ca. 1725–1770), played a key role in developing multicolored prints. Called *nishiki-e* (brocade pictures) because of their sumptuous and brilliant color, these prints employed only the highest-quality paper and costly pigments. Harunobu gained a tremendous advantage over his fellow designers when he received commissions from members of a poetry club to design limited-edition nishiki-e prints. He transferred much of the knowledge he derived from nishiki-e to his design of more commercial prints. Harunobu even issued some of the private designs later under his own name for popular consumption.

The sophistication of Harunobu's work is evident in *Evening Bell at the Clock* (FIG. 28-12), from a series called *Eight Views of the Parlor*. This series draws upon a Chinese series usually titled *Eight Views of the Xiao and Xiang Rivers*, in which each image focuses on a particular time of day or year. In Harunobu's adaptation, beautiful young women and the activities that occupy their daily lives became the subject. In *Evening Bell at the Clock*, two young women seen from the typically Japanese elevated viewpoint (compare FIG. 8-14) sit on a veranda. One appears to be drying herself after a bath, while the other turns to face the chiming clock. Here, the artist has playfully transformed the great temple bell that rings over the waters in the Chinese series into a modern Japanese clock. This image incorporates the refined techniques characteristic of nishiki-e. Further, the flatness of the depicted objects and the rich color recall the traditions of court painting, a comparison many nishiki-e artists openly sought.

KATSUSHIKA HOKUSAI Woodblock prints afforded artists great opportunity for experimentation. For example, in producing landscapes, Japanese artists often incorporated Western perspective techniques. One of the most famous designers in this genre was KATSUSHIKA HOKUSAI (1760–1849). In *The Great Wave off Kanagawa* (FIG. 28-13), part of a woodblock series called *Thirty-six Views of Mount Fuji*, the huge foreground wave dwarfs the artist's representation of a distant Fuji. This contrast and the whitecaps' ominous fingers magnify the wave's threatening aspect. The men in the trading boats bend low to dig their oars against the rough sea and drive their long low vessels past the danger. Although Hokusai's print draws on Western techniques and incorporates the distinctive European color called Prussian blue, it also engages the Japanese pictorial tradition. Against a background with the low horizon typical of Western painting, Hokusai placed in the foreground the traditionally flat wave and its powerfully graphic forms.

28-13A
HIROSHIGE,
*Plum Estate,
Kameido,* 1857.

12A UTAMARO,
*isa of the
kashima
a Shop,
82–1793.*

28-13 KATSUSHIKA HOKUSAI, *The Great Wave off Kanagawa,* from *Thirty-six Views of Mount Fuji,* Edo period, ca. 1826–1833. Woodblock print, ink and colors on paper, $9\frac{7}{8}'' \times 1' 2\frac{3}{4}''$. Museum of Fine Arts, Boston (Bigelow Collection). ■◀

Against a background with the low horizon line typical of Western painting, Hokusai placed a threatening wave in the foreground, painted using the traditional flat and powerful graphic forms of Japanese art.

MODERN JAPAN

The Edo period and the rule of the shoguns ended in 1868, when rebellious samurai from provinces far removed from Edo toppled the Tokugawa. Facilitating this revolution was the shogunate's inability to handle increasing pressure from Western nations for Japan to open itself to the outside world. Although the rebellion restored direct sovereignty to the imperial throne, real power rested with the emperor's cabinet. As a symbol of imperial authority, however, the official name of this new period was Meiji ("Enlightened Rule"), after the emperor's chosen reign name.

Meiji Period

Oil painting became a major genre in Japan in the late 19th century during the Meiji period (1868–1912). Ambitious students studied with Westerners at government schools and during trips abroad.

TAKAHASHI YUICHI One oil painting highlighting the cultural ferment of the early Meiji period is *Oiran* (*Grand Courtesan;* FIG. **28-14**), by TAKAHASHI YUICHI (1828–1894). The artist created it for a client nostalgic for vanishing elements of Japanese culture. Ukiyo-e printmakers frequently represented similar grand courte-

28-14 TAKAHASHI YUICHI, *Oiran* (*Grand Courtesan*), Meiji period, 1872. Oil on canvas, 2′ 6½″ × 1′ 9⅝″. Tokyo National University of Fine Arts and Music, Tokyo.

The subject of Takahashi's *Oiran* and the abstract rendering of the courtesan's garment derive from the repertory of ukiyo-e printmakers and traditional Japanese art, but the oil technique is a Western import.

sans of the pleasure quarters. In this painting, however, Takahashi (historical figures from the Meiji period onward are usually referred to by their family names, which come first, in contrast to earlier eras, when the second, given, name was used) did not portray the courtesan's features in the idealizing manner of ukiyo-e artists but in the more analytical manner of Western portraiture. Yet Takahashi's more abstract rendering of the garments reflects a very old practice in East Asian portraiture.

YOKOYAMA TAIKAN Unbridled enthusiasm for Westernization in some quarters led to resistance and concern over a loss of distinctive Japanese identity in other quarters. Ironically, one of those most eager to preserve "Japaneseness" in the arts was Ernest Fenollosa (1853–1908), an American professor of philosophy and political economy at Tokyo Imperial University. He and a former student named Okakura Kakuzo (1862–1913) joined with others in a movement that eventually led to the founding of an arts university dedicated to Japanese arts under Okakura's direction. Their goal for Japanese painting was to make it viable in the modern age rather than preserve it as a relic. To this end, they encouraged artists to incorporate some Western techniques such as chiaroscuro, perspective, and bright hues in Japanese-style paintings. The name given to the resulting style was *nihonga* (Japanese painting), as opposed to *yoga* (Western painting).

Kutsugen (FIG. **28-15**), a silk scroll by YOKOYAMA TAIKAN (1868–1958), is an example of nihonga. It combines a low horizon line and subtle shading effects taken from Western painting with East Asian techniques, such as anchoring a composition in one corner (FIGS. **7-24** and **27-14**), employing strong ink brushwork to define contours, applying washes of water-and-glue-based pigments, and using applications of heavy mineral pigments. The painting's subject, a Chinese poet who fell out of the emperor's favor and subsequently committed suicide, no doubt resonated with the artist and his associates. It provided a nice analogy to a real-life situation. At the time, Okakura was locked in a battle over his artistic principles with the Ministry of Education. Whether intended or not, this painting, in which the poet stands his ground, staunchly defying the strong winds that agitate the foliage behind him, was perceived as a comment on the friction between Okakura and authorities.

Showa Period

During the 20th century, Japan became increasingly prominent on the world stage in economics, politics, and culture. Among the events that propelled Japan into the spotlight was its participation in World War II during the Showa period (1926–1989). The most tragic consequences of that involvement were the widespread devastation and loss of life resulting from the atomic bombings of Hiroshima and Nagasaki in 1945. During the succeeding occupation period, the United States imposed new democratic institutions on Japan, with the emperor serving as only a ceremonial head of state. Japan's economy rebounded with remarkable speed, and during the ensuing half century Japan also assumed a positive and productive place in the international art world. As they did in earlier times with the art and culture of China and Korea, Japanese artists internalized Western lessons and transformed them into a part of Japan's own vital culture.

TANGE KENZO In the 20th century, Japanese architecture, especially public and commercial building, underwent rapid transformation along Western lines. In fact, architecture may be the art form providing Japanese practitioners the most substantial presence on

28-15 Yokoyama Taikan, *Kutsugen,* Itsukushima Shrine, Hiroshima Prefecture, Japan, Meiji period, 1898. Hanging scroll, color on silk, 4′ 4″ × 9′ 6″.

This Meiji silk scroll combines a low horizon line and subtle shading effects taken from Western painting with Asian features, such as strong ink brushwork and anchoring of the composition in one corner.

1 ft.

the world scene today. Japanese architects have made major contributions to both modern and postmodern developments (see Chapter 36). One of the most daringly experimental architects of the post–World War II period was Tange Kenzo (1913–2005). In the design of the stadiums (FIG. **28-16**) for the 1964 Olympics, he employed a cable suspension system that allowed him to shape steel and concrete into remarkably graceful structures. His attention to both the sculptural qualities of each building's raw concrete form and the fluidity of its spaces allied him with architects worldwide who carried on the legacy of the late style of Le Corbusier (FIG. **36-56**) in France. His stadiums thus bear comparison with Joern Utzon's Sydney Opera House (FIG. **36-59**).

28-16 Tange Kenzo, national indoor Olympic stadiums, Tokyo, Japan, Showa period, 1961–1964.

Tange was one of the most daring architects of post–World War II Japan. His Olympic stadiums employ a cable suspension system that allowed him to shape steel and concrete into remarkably graceful structures.

1 ft.

28-17 HAMADA SHOJI, dish, Showa period, 1962. Black trails on translucent glaze, 1′ 10½″ diameter. National Museum of Modern Art, Kyoto.

Hamada was a leading figure in the modern folk art movement in Japan and gained international fame. His unsigned stoneware features casual slip designs and a coarser, darker texture than porcelain.

1 ft.

28-18 TSUCHIYA KIMIO, *Symptom,* Showa period, 1987. Branches, 13′ 1½″ × 14′ 9⅛″ × 3′ 11¼″. Installation view, *Jeune Sculpture '87,* Paris 1987.

Tsuchiya's sculptures are constructed of branches or driftwood and despite their abstract nature assert the life forces found in natural materials. His approach to sculpture reflects ancient Shinto beliefs.

HAMADA SHOJI Another modern Japanese art form attracting great attention worldwide is ceramics. Many contemporary admirers of folk art are avid collectors of traditional Japanese pottery. A formative figure in Japan's folk art movement, the philosopher Yanagi Soetsu (1889–1961), promoted an ideal of beauty inspired by the Japanese tea ceremony. He argued that true beauty could be achieved only in functional objects made of natural materials by anonymous craftspeople. Among the ceramists who produced this type of folk pottery, known as *mingei,* was HAMADA SHOJI (1894–1978). Although Hamada did espouse Yanagi's selfless ideals, he still gained international fame and in 1955 received official recognition in Japan as a Living National Treasure. Works such as his dish (FIG. **28-17**) with casual slip designs are unsigned, but connoisseurs easily recognize them as his. This kind of stoneware is coarser, darker, and heavier than porcelain and lacks the latter's fine decoration. To those who appreciate simpler, earthier beauty, however, this dish holds great attraction. Hamada's artistic influence extended beyond the production of pots. He traveled to England in 1920 and, along with English potter Bernard Leach (1887–1978), established a community of ceramists committed to the mingei aesthetic. Together, Hamada and Leach expanded international knowledge of Japanese ceramics, and even now, the "Hamada-Leach aesthetic" is part of potters' education worldwide.

TSUCHIYA KIMIO Although no one style, medium, or subject dominates contemporary Japanese art, much of it does spring from ideas or beliefs that have been integral to Japanese culture over the

years. For example, the Shinto belief in the generative forces in nature and in humankind's position as part of the totality of nature (see "Shinto," Chapter 8, page 211) holds great appeal for contemporary artists, including TSUCHIYA KIMIO (b. 1955), who produces large-scale sculptures (FIG. **28-18**) constructed of branches or driftwood. Despite their relatively abstract nature, his works assert the life forces found in natural materials, thereby engaging viewers in a consideration of their own relationship to nature. Tsuchiya does not specifically invoke Shinto when speaking about his art, but it is clear that he has internalized Shinto principles. He identifies as his goal "to bring out and present the life of nature emanating from this energy of trees. . . . It is as though the wood is part of myself, as though the wood has the same kind of life force."[1]

Tsuchiya is but one of many artists working in Japan today who have attracted international attention. Contemporary art in Japan, as elsewhere in the world, is multifaceted and ever-changing, and the traditional and the modern flourish side by side.

JAPAN AFTER 1336

MUROMACHI PERIOD, 1336–1573

■ The period takes its name from the Kyoto district in which the Ashikaga shoguns maintained their headquarters.

■ During the Muromachi period, Zen Buddhism rose to prominence in Japan. Zen temples often featured gardens of the karesansui (dry-landscape) type, which promoted meditation.

■ Muromachi painting displays great variety in both subject matter and style. One characteristic technique is the haboku (splashed-ink) style, which has Chinese roots. An early haboku master was Sesshu Toyo.

Sesshu Toyo, splashed-ink landscape, 1495

MOMOYAMA PERIOD, 1573–1615

■ This brief interlude between two long-lasting shogunates was dominated by three successive warlords. The period takes its name from one of their castles (Momoyama, Peach Blossom Hill) outside Kyoto.

■ Many of the finest works of this period were commissions from those warlords, including *Chinese Lions* by Kano Eitoku, a six-part folding screen featuring animals considered to be symbols of power and bravery.

■ The Momoyama period also saw the Japanese tea ceremony become an important social ritual. The tea master Sen no Rikyu designed the first teahouse built as an independent structure. The favored tea utensils were rustic Shino wares.

Kano Eitoku, *Chinese Lions*, late 16th century

EDO PERIOD, 1615–1868

■ The Edo period began when the Momoyama shogun Tokugawa Ieyasu (1542–1616) moved his headquarters from Kyoto to Edo (modern Tokyo).

■ The Rinpa School, named for Ogata Korin, emerged as a major alternative school of painting to the Kano School, which became a virtual national art academy. Rinpa works, both paintings and crafts, feature vivid colors and extensive use of gold, as in the *Boat Bridge* writing box by Honami Koetsu.

■ Growing urbanization in the major Japanese cities fostered a lively popular culture focused on sensual pleasure and theatrical entertainment. The best-known products of this sophisticated counterculture are the ukiyo-e woodblock prints of Edo's "floating world" by Suzuki Harunobu and others, which feature scenes from brothels and the theater as well as beautiful women in domestic settings.

■ The Katsura Imperial Villa, which relies on subtleties of proportion, color, and texture instead of ornament for its aesthetic appeal, set the standard for all later Japanese domestic architecture.

Honami Koetsu, *Boat Bridge*, early 17th century

Suzuki Harunobu, *Evening Bell at the Clock*, ca. 1765

MODERN JAPAN, 1868–Present

■ The Tokugawa shogunate toppled in 1868, opening the modern era of Japanese history. In art, Western styles and techniques had great influence, and many Japanese artists incorporated shading and perspective in their works and even produced oil paintings.

■ In the post–World War II period, Japanese architects achieved worldwide reputations. Tange Kenzo was a master of creating dramatic shapes using a cable suspension system for his concrete-and-steel buildings.

■ Contemporary art in Japan is multifaceted, and the traditional and the modern flourish side by side.

Tange Kenzo, Olympic stadiums, Tokyo, 1961–1964

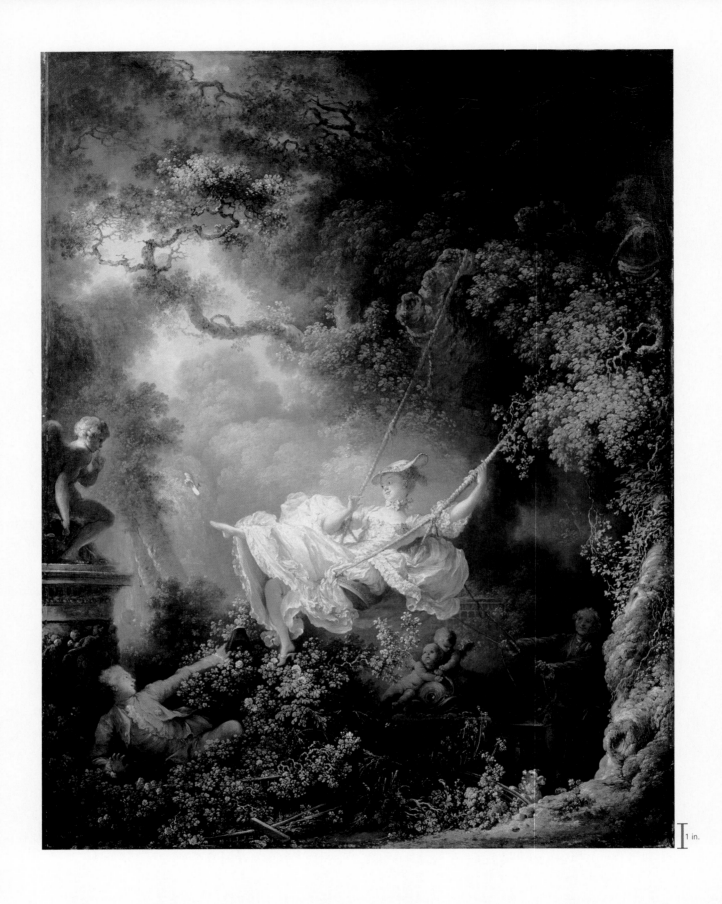

1 in.

29-1 Jean-Honoré Fragonard, *The Swing*, 1766. Oil on canvas, 2′ 8⅝″ × 2′ 2″. Wallace Collection, London.

In this painting epitomizing Rococo style, pastel colors and soft light complement a sensuous scene in which a young lady flirtatiously kicks off her shoe at a statue of Cupid while her lover watches.

EUROPE
AND AMERICA,
1700 TO 1800

In 1700, Louis XIV still ruled as the Sun King of France, presiding over his realm and French culture from his palatial residence at Versailles (FIG. 25-32). By 1800, revolutions had overthrown the monarchy in France and achieved independence for the British colonies in America (MAP 29-1). The 18th century also gave birth to a revolution of a different kind—the Industrial Revolution, which began in England and soon transformed the economies of continental Europe and North America and eventually the world. Against this backdrop of revolutionary change, social as well as political, economic, and technological, came major transformations in the arts. Indeed, *Pilgrimage to Cythera* (FIG. 29-6), painted in 1717 and set in a lush landscape, celebrates the romantic dalliances of the moneyed elite. In contrast, the 1784 *Oath of the Horatii* (FIG. 29-23) takes place in an austere Doric hall and glorifies the civic virtue and heroism of an ancient Roman family. The two works have little in common other than that both are French oil paintings. In the 18th century, shifts in style and subject matter were both rapid and significant.

ROCOCO

The death of Louis XIV in 1715 brought many changes in French high society. The elite quickly abandoned the court of Versailles for the pleasures of town life. Although French citizens still owed allegiance to a monarch, the early 18th century brought a resurgence of aristocratic social, political, and economic power. Members of the nobility not only exercised their traditional privileges (for example, exemption from certain taxes and from forced labor on public works) but also sought to expand their power. In the cultural realm, aristocrats reestablished their predominance as art patrons. The *hôtels* (town houses) of Paris soon became the centers of a new, softer style called *Rococo*. Associated with the regency (1715–1723) that followed the death of Louis XIV and with the reign of Louis XV (r. 1723–1774), the Rococo style in art and architecture was the perfect expression of the sparkling gaiety the wealthy cultivated in their elegant homes (see "Femmes Savantes and Salon Culture," page 753).

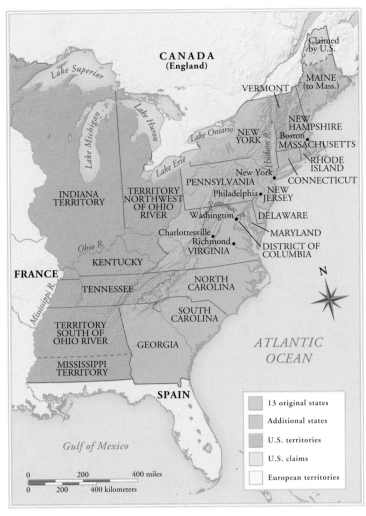

MAP 29-1 The United States in 1800.

Legend:
- 13 original states
- Additional states
- U.S. territories
- U.S. claims
- European territories

Architecture

29-2A VANBRUGH and HAWKSMOOR, Blenheim Palace, 1705–1725.

Rococo appeared in France in about 1700, primarily as a style of interior design. The French Rococo exterior was most often simple, or even plain, but Rococo exuberance took over the interior. The term derived from the French word *rocaille* (literally, "pebble"), but it referred especially to the small stones and shells used to decorate grotto interiors. Shells or shell forms were the principal motifs in Rococo ornament.

SALON DE LA PRINCESSE A typical French Rococo room is the Salon de la Princesse (FIG. 29-2) in the Hôtel de Soubise in Paris, designed by GERMAIN BOFFRAND (1667–1754). Parisian salons of this sort were the center of Rococo social life. They usurped the role that Louis XIV's Versailles palace (FIG. 25-32) played in the 17th century, when the Sun King set the tone for French culture. In the early 18th century, the centralized and grandiose palace-based culture of Baroque France gave way to a much more intimate and decentralized culture based in private homes. The new architectural style mirrored this social and cultural shift. A comparison between the Salon de la Princesse and the Galerie des Glaces (FIG. 25-33) at Versailles reveals how Boffrand softened the strong architectural lines and panels of the earlier style into flexible, sinuous curves luxuriantly multiplied in mirror reflections. The walls melt into the vault. Irregular painted shapes, surmounted by sculpture and separated by the typical rocaille shells, replace the hall's cornices. Painting, architecture, and sculpture combine to form a single ensemble. The profusion of curving tendrils and sprays of foliage blends with the shell forms to give an effect of freely growing nature, suggesting that the designer permanently decked the Rococo room for a festival.

French Rococo interiors were lively total works of art. Exquisitely wrought furniture, enchanting small sculptures, ornamented mirror frames, delightful ceramics and silver, small paintings, and decorative *tapestries* complemented the architecture, relief sculptures, and mural paintings. The Salon de la Princesse no longer has most of the movable furnishings and decor that once contributed so much to its total ambience. Visitors can imagine, however, how this and similar Rococo rooms—with their alternating gilded moldings, vivacious relief sculptures, luxurious furniture, and daintily colored ornamentation of flowers and garlands—must have harmonized with the chamber music played in them, with the elaborate costumes of satin and brocade, and with the equally elegant etiquette and sparkling wit of the people who graced them.

AMALIENBURG The French Rococo style quickly spread beyond Paris. The Amalienburg, a small lodge the French architect FRANÇOIS DE CUVILLIÉS (1695–1768) built in the park of the Nymphenburg Palace in Munich, is a prime example of Germany's adoption of the Parisian style. The most spectacular room in the lodge is the circular Hall of Mirrors (FIG. 29-3), a silver-and-blue ensemble of architecture, stucco relief, silvered bronze mirrors, and crystal that represents the Rococo style at its zenith. The hall dazzles the eye with myriad scintillating motifs, forms, and figurations the designer borrowed from the full Rococo ornamental repertoire. Silvery light, reflected and amplified by windows and mirrors, bathes the room and creates shapes and contours that weave rhythmically around the upper walls and the ceiling coves. Everything seems organic, growing, and in motion, an ultimate refinement of illusion that the architect, artists, and artisans, all magically in command of their varied media, created with virtuoso flourishes.

29-2 GERMAIN BOFFRAND, Salon de la Princesse, with painting by CHARLES-JOSEPH NATOIRE and sculpture by J. B. LEMOINE, Hôtel de Soubise, Paris, France, 1737–1740.

Elegant Rococo rooms such as this salon, featuring sinuous curves, gilded moldings and mirrors, small sculptures and paintings, and floral ornament, were the center of Parisian social and intellectual life.

Femmes Savantes and Salon Culture

The feminine look of the Rococo style suggests that the taste and social initiative of women dominated the age—and, to a large extent, they did. Women—for example, Madame de Pompadour (1721–1764), mistress of Louis XV of France; Maria Theresa (1717–1780), archduchess of Austria and queen of Hungary and Bohemia; and Empresses Elizabeth (r. 1741–1762) and Catherine the Great (r. 1762–1796) of Russia—held some of the most influential positions in Europe. Female taste also had an impact in numerous smaller courts as well as in the private sphere.

In the early 18th century, Paris was the social capital of Europe, and the Rococo salon (FIG. 29-2) was the center of Parisian society. Wealthy, ambitious, and clever society hostesses competed to attract the most famous and the most accomplished people to their salons, whether in Paris or elsewhere in Europe (FIG. 29-3). The medium of social intercourse was conversation spiced with wit, repartee as quick and deft as a fencing match. Artifice reigned supreme, and participants considered enthusiasm or sincerity in bad taste.

The women who hosted these salons referred to themselves as *femmes savantes,* or learned women. Among them was Julie de Lespinasse (1732–1776), one of the most articulate, urbane, and intelligent French women of the time. She held daily salons from five o'clock until nine in the evening. The book *Memoirs of Marmontel* documented the liveliness of these gatherings and the remarkable nature of this hostess.

The circle was formed of persons who were not bound together. She had taken them here and there in society, but so well assorted were they that once there they fell into harmony like the strings of an instrument touched by an able hand. Following out that comparison, I may say that she played the instrument with an art that came of genius; she seemed to know what tone each string would yield before she touched it; I mean to say that our minds and our natures were so well known to her that in order to bring them into play she had but to say a word. Nowhere was conversation more lively, more brilliant, or better regulated than at her house. It was a rare phenomenon indeed, the degree of tempered, equable heat which she knew so well how to maintain, sometimes by moderating it, sometimes by quickening it. The continual activity of her soul was communicated to our souls, but measurably; her imagination was the mainspring, her reason the regulator. Remark that the brains she stirred at will were neither feeble nor frivolous. . . . Her talent for casting out a thought and giving it for discussion to men of that class, her own talent in discussing it with precision, sometimes with eloquence, her talent for bringing forward new ideas and varying the topic—always with the facility and ease of a fairy . . . these talents, I say, were not those of an ordinary woman. It was not with the follies of fashion and vanity that daily, during four hours of conversation, without languor and without vacuum, she knew how to make herself interesting to a wide circle of strong minds.*

* Jean François Marmontel, *Memoirs of Marmontel,* translated by Brigit Patmore (London: Routledge, 1930), 270.

29-3 FRANÇOIS DE CUVILLIÉS, **Hall of Mirrors, the Amalienburg, Nymphenburg Palace park, Munich, Germany, early 18th century.**

Designed by a French architect, this circular hall in a German lodge displays the Rococo architectural style at its zenith, dazzling the eye with the organic interplay of mirrors, crystal, and stucco relief.

designed. The interior (FIG. 29-4, *top*) exhibits a vivacious play of architectural fantasy that retains the dynamic energy of Italian Baroque architecture (see Chapter 24) but not its drama. Numerous large windows in the richly decorated but continuous walls of Vierzehnheiligen flood the interior with an even, bright, and cheerful light. The feeling is one of lightness and delicacy.

29-4A NEUMANN, Kaisersaal, Würzburg, 1719–1744.

29-4B ZIMMERMANN, Wieskirche, Füssen, 1745–1754.

Vierzehnheiligen's plan (FIG. 29-4, *bottom*) reveals the influence of Borromini (FIGS. 24-10 and 24-13) but is even more complex. Neumann seems deliberately to have banished all straight lines. The composition, made up of tangent ovals and circles, achieves a quite different interior effect within the essential outlines of a traditional rectilinear basilican church with a nave, transept, and apse. Undulating space is in continuous motion, creating unlimited vistas bewildering in their variety and surprise effects. The structural features pulse, flow, and commingle as if they were ceaselessly in the process of being molded. The design's fluidity of line, the floating and hovering surfaces, the interwoven spaces, and the dematerialized masses combine to suggest a "frozen" counterpart to the intricacy of voices in a Bach fugue. The church is a brilliant ensemble of architecture, painting, sculpture, and music that dissolves the boundaries of the arts in a visionary unity.

Painting and Sculpture

ANTOINE WATTEAU The painter whom scholars most associate with French Rococo is ANTOINE WATTEAU (1684–1721). The differences between the Baroque age in France and the Rococo age can be

29-4 BALTHASAR NEUMANN, interior (*top*) and plan (*bottom*) of the pilgrimage church of Vierzehnheiligen, near Staffelstein, Germany, 1743–1772.

The Rococo style also appeared in ecclesiastical architecture. Vierzehnheiligen's interior is light and delicate. Its plan features undulating lines and a dynamic interplay of ovals and circles.

VIERZEHNHEILIGEN Rococo style was not exclusively a domestic phenomenon, however. One of the most splendid examples of Rococo ecclesiastical architecture is the pilgrimage church of Vierzehnheiligen (Fourteen Saints; FIG. 29-4) near Staffelstein (MAP 25-1), which the German architect BALTHASAR NEUMANN (1687–1753)

29-5 ANTOINE WATTEAU, *L'Indifférent*, ca. 1716. Oil on canvas, 10″ × 7″. Louvre, Paris.

This small Rococo painting of a languid, gliding dancer exhibits lightness and delicacy in both color and tone. It contrasts sharply with Rigaud's majestic portrait (FIG. 25-30) of the pompous Louis XIV.

29-6 Antoine Watteau, *Pilgrimage to Cythera*, 1717. Oil on canvas, 4′ 3″ × 6′ 4½″. Louvre, Paris.

Watteau's *fête galante* paintings depict the outdoor amusements of French upper-class society. The haze of color, subtly modeled shapes, gliding motion, and air of suave gentility match Rococo taste.

seen clearly by contrasting Rigaud's portrait of Louis XIV (FIG. **25-30**) with one of Watteau's paintings, *L'Indifférent* (*The Indifferent One;* FIG. **29-5**). Rigaud portrayed pompous majesty in supreme glory, as if the French monarch were reviewing throngs of bowing courtiers at Versailles. Watteau's painting, in contrast, is more delicate and lighter in both color and tone. The artist presented a languid, gliding dancer whose stilted minuet could be a parody of the monarch's solemnity if the paintings were hung together. In Rigaud's portrait, stout architecture, bannerlike curtains, flowing ermine, and fleur-de-lis exalt the king. In Watteau's painting, the dancer moves in a rainbow shimmer of color, emerging onto the stage of the intimate comic opera to the silken sounds of strings. As in architecture, this contrast of paintings also highlights the different patronage of the eras. Whereas royal patronage, particularly that of Louis XIV, dominated the French Baroque period, Rococo was the culture of a wider aristocracy in which private patrons dictated taste.

PILGRIMAGE TO CYTHERA Watteau was largely responsible for creating a specific type of Rococo painting, called a *fête galante* (amorous festival) painting. These works depicted the outdoor entertainment or amusements of French high society. An example of a fête galante painting is Watteau's masterpiece (painted in two versions), *Pilgrimage to Cythera* (FIG. **29-6**). The painting was the artist's entry for admission to the French Royal Academy of Painting and Sculpture (see "Academic Salons," Chapter 31, page 823). In 1717 the fête galante

was not an acceptable category for submission, but rather than reject Watteau's candidacy, the academy created a new category to accommodate his entry. At the turn of the century, two competing doctrines sharply divided the membership of the French academy. Many members followed Nicolas Poussin in teaching that form was the most important element in painting, whereas "colors in painting are as allurements for persuading the eyes"—additions for effect and not really essential.[1] The other group took Peter Paul Rubens as its model and proclaimed the natural supremacy of color and the coloristic style as the artist's proper guide. Depending on which doctrine they supported, academy members were either *Poussinistes* or *Rubénistes*. Watteau was Flemish, and Rubens's coloristic style heavily influenced his work. With Watteau in their ranks, the Rubénistes carried the day, establishing Rococo painting as the preferred style of the early 18th century.

Watteau's *Pilgrimage to Cythera* (FIG. **29-6**) portrays luxuriously costumed lovers who have made a "pilgrimage" to Cythera, the island of eternal youth and love, sacred to Aphrodite. The elegant figures move gracefully from the protective shade of a woodland park filled with amorous cupids and voluptuous statuary. Watteau's figural poses blend elegance and sweetness. He composed his generally quite small paintings from albums of superb drawings in which he sought to capture slow movement from difficult and unusual angles, obviously intending to find the smoothest, most poised, and most refined attitudes. As he experimented with nuances of posture and movement, Watteau also strove for the most exquisite shades of

1 ft.

29-7 FRANÇOIS BOUCHER, *Cupid a Captive*, 1754. Oil on canvas, 5′ 6″ × 2′ 10″. Wallace Collection, London. ◼◂

In this Rococo canvas, François Boucher, painter for Madame de Pompadour, portrayed a rosy pyramid of infant and female flesh and fluttering draperies set off against a cool, leafy background.

color difference, defining in a single stroke the shimmer of silk at a bent knee or the iridescence that touches a glossy surface as it emerges from shadow. The haze of color, the subtly modeled shapes, the gliding motion, and the air of suave gentility appealed greatly to the Rococo artist's wealthy patrons.

FRANÇOIS BOUCHER After Watteau's early death at 37, his follower, FRANÇOIS BOUCHER (1703–1770), rose to dominance in French painting, in large part because of Madame de Pompadour's patronage. Although he was an excellent portraitist, Boucher's fame rested primarily on his graceful canvases depicting Arcadian shep-

29-8 GIAMBATTISTA TIEPOLO, *Apotheosis of the Pisani Family,* ceiling fresco in the Villa Pisani, Stra, Italy, 1761–1762. Fresco, 77′ 1″ × 44′ 3″.

A master of illusionistic ceiling painting in the Baroque tradition, Tiepolo adopted the bright, cheerful colors and weightless figures of Rococo easel paintings for huge frescoes.

herds, nymphs, and goddesses cavorting in shady glens engulfed in pink and sky-blue light. *Cupid a Captive* (FIG. 29-7) presents a rosy pyramid of infant and female flesh set off against a cool, leafy background, with fluttering draperies both hiding and revealing the nudity of the figures. Boucher used the full range of Italian and French Baroque devices—the dynamic play of crisscrossing diagonals, curvilinear forms, and slanting recessions—to create his masterly composition. But in his work he dissected powerful Baroque curves into a multiplicity of decorative flourishes, dissipating Baroque drama into sensual playfulness. Lively and lighthearted, Boucher's artful Rococo fantasies became mirrors for his patrons, the wealthy French, to behold the ornamental reflections of their cherished pastimes.

JEAN-HONORÉ FRAGONARD Boucher's greatest student, JEAN-HONORÉ FRAGONARD (1732–1806), was an outstanding colorist whose decorative skill almost surpassed his master's. An example of his manner can stand as characteristic not only of his work but also of the later Rococo style in general. In *The Swing* (FIG. 29-1), a young gentleman has managed an arrangement whereby an unsuspecting old bishop swings the young man's pretty sweetheart higher

29-9 CLODION, *Satyr Crowning a Bacchante*, 1770. Terracotta, 1′ 5/8″ high. Louvre, Paris.

The erotic playfulness of Boucher's and Fragonard's paintings is evident in Clodion's tabletop terracotta sculptures representing sensuous fantasies often involving satyrs and bacchantes, the followers of Bacchus.

and higher, while her lover (and the work's patron), in the lower left corner, stretches out to admire her ardently from a strategic position on the ground. The young lady flirtatiously and boldly kicks off her shoe toward the little statue of Cupid. The infant love god holds his finger to his lips. The landscape setting is out of Watteau—a luxuriant perfumed bower in a park that very much resembles a stage scene for comic opera. The glowing pastel colors and soft light convey, almost by themselves, the theme's sensuality.

GIAMBATTISTA TIEPOLO *The Swing* is less than three feet in height, and Watteau's *L'Indifférent* (FIG. 29-5) barely 10 inches tall. But the intimate Rococo style could also be adopted for paintings of huge size, as the work of GIAMBATTISTA TIEPOLO (1696–1770) demonstrates. Of Venetian origin, Tiepolo worked for patrons in Austria, Germany, and Spain as well as in Italy. A master of illusionistic ceiling decoration in the Baroque tradition, Tiepolo favored the bright, cheerful colors and relaxed compositions of Rococo easel paintings. *Apotheosis of the Pisani Family* (FIG. 29-8), a ceiling fresco in the Villa Pisani at Stra in northern Italy (MAP 25-1), shows airy figures fluttering through vast sunlit skies and fleecy clouds, their forms casting dark accents against the brilliant light of high noon. Tiepolo here elevated the Pisani family members to the rank of gods in a heavenly scene that recalls the ceiling paintings of Pozzo (FIG. 24-24). But while retaining 17th-century illusionism, Tiepolo softened the rhetoric and created pictorial schemes of great elegance and grace, unsurpassed for their sheer effectiveness as decor.

CLODION Rococo was nonetheless a style best suited for small-scale works that projected a mood of sensual intimacy in elegant salons. Artists such as Claude Michel, called CLODION (1738–1814), specialized in small, lively sculptures representing sensuous Rococo

fantasies. Clodion lived in Rome for several years, and his work incorporates echoes of Italian Mannerist sculpture. His small group *Satyr Crowning a Bacchante* (FIG. 29-9) depicts two mythological followers of Bacchus, the Roman god of wine. The languorous bacchante being crowned by the satyr with a floral wreath is reminiscent of the nude female personification in Benvenuto Cellini's *Saltcellar of Francis I* (FIG. 22-51). The erotic playfulness of Boucher's and Fragonard's paintings is also evident in Clodion's sculpture. He captured the sensual exhilaration of the Rococo style in diminutive scale and inexpensive terracotta. As is true of so many Rococo artifacts, the artist designed this group for a tabletop.

THE ENLIGHTENMENT

The aristocratic culture celebrated in Rococo art did not go unchallenged during the 18th century. Indeed, the feudal system that served as the foundation of social and economic life in Europe dissolved, and the rigid social hierarchies that provided the basis for Rococo art and patronage relaxed. By the end of the 18th century, revolutions had erupted in France and America. A major factor in these political, social, and economic changes was the Enlightenment.

Philosophy and Science

The *Enlightenment* was in essence a new way of thinking critically about the world and about humankind, independently of religion, myth, or tradition. The basis of Enlightenment thought was empirical evidence. Enlightenment thinkers promoted the scientific questioning of all assertions and rejected unfounded beliefs about the nature of humankind and of the world. Thus, the Enlightenment encouraged and stimulated the habit and application of mind known as the scientific method.

This new approach to the acquisition of knowledge had its roots in the 17th century, with the mathematical and scientific achievements of René Descartes (1596–1650), Blaise Pascal (1623–1662), Isaac Newton (1642–1727), and Gottfried Wilhelm von Leibniz (1646–1716). England and France were the principal centers of the Enlightenment, though its dictums influenced the thinking of intellectuals throughout Europe and in the American colonies. Benjamin Franklin (1706–1790), Thomas Jefferson (1743–1826), and other American notables embraced its principles.

NEWTON AND LOCKE Of particular importance for Enlightenment thought was the work of Great Britain's Isaac Newton and John Locke (1632–1704). In his scientific studies, Newton insisted on empirical proof of his theories and encouraged others to avoid metaphysics and the supernatural—realms that extended beyond the natural physical world. This emphasis on both tangible data and concrete experience became a cornerstone of Enlightenment thought. In addition, Newton's experiments revealed a rationality in the physical world, and Enlightenment thinkers transferred that concept to the sociopolitical world by promoting a rationally organized society. Locke, whose works acquired the status of Enlightenment gospel, developed these ideas further. According to Locke's "doctrine of empiricism," knowledge comes to people through their sense perception of the material world. From these perceptions alone people form ideas. Locke asserted that human beings are born good, not cursed by Original Sin. The laws of Nature grant them the natural rights of life, liberty, and property as well as the right to freedom of conscience. Government is by contract, and its purpose is to protect these rights. If and when government abuses these rights, the citizenry has the further natural right of revolution. Locke's ideas empowered people to take control of their own destinies.

PHILOSOPHES The work of Newton and Locke also inspired many French intellectuals, or *philosophes*. These thinkers conceived of individuals and societies at large as parts of physical nature. They shared the conviction that the ills of humanity could be remedied by applying reason and common sense to human problems. They criticized the powers of church and state as irrational limits placed on political and intellectual freedom. They believed that by the accumulation and propagation of knowledge, humanity could advance by degrees to a happier state than it had ever known. This conviction matured into the "doctrine of progress" and its corollary doctrine of the "perfectibility of humankind." Previous societies, for the most part, perceived the future as inevitable—the cycle of life and death. Religious beliefs determined fate. The notion of progress—the systematic and planned improvement of society—first developed during the 18th century and continues to influence 21st-century thought.

DIDEROT Animated by their belief in human progress and perfectibility, the philosophes took on the task of gathering knowledge and making it accessible to all who could read. Their program was, in effect, the democratization of knowledge. Denis Diderot (1713–1784) greatly influenced the Enlightenment's rationalistic and materialistic thinking. He became editor of the pioneering *Encyclopédie,* a compilation of articles written by more than a hundred contributors, including all the leading philosophes. The *Encyclopédie* was truly comprehensive (its formal title was *Systematic Dictionary of the Sciences, Arts, and Crafts*) and included all available knowledge—historical, scientific, and technical as well as religious and moral—and political theory. The first volume appeared in 1751 and the last of the 35 volumes of text and illustrations in 1780. Other Enlightenment authors produced different compilations of knowledge. Diderot's contemporary, Comte de Buffon (1707–1788), undertook a kind of encyclopedia of the natural sciences. His *Natural History,* a monumental work of 44 volumes, was especially valuable for its zoological study. Buffon's contemporary, the Swedish botanist Carolus Linnaeus (1707–1778), established a system of plant classification.

The political, economic, and social consequences of this increase in knowledge and the doctrine of progress were explosive. It is no coincidence that the French Revolution, the American Revolution, and the Industrial Revolution in England all occurred during this period. These upheavals precipitated yet other major changes, including the growth of cities, the emergence of an urban working class, and the expansion of colonialism as the demand for cheap labor and raw materials increased. This enthusiasm for growth gave birth to the doctrine of Manifest Destiny—the ideological justification for continued territorial expansion. Thus, the Age of Enlightenment ushered in a new way of thinking and affected historical developments worldwide.

VOLTAIRE François Marie Arouet, better known as Voltaire (1694–1778), became, and still is, the most representative figure—almost the personification—of the Enlightenment spirit. Voltaire was instrumental in introducing Newton and Locke to the French intelligentsia. He hated, and attacked through his writings, the arbitrary despotic rule of kings, the selfish privileges of the nobility and the church, religious intolerance, and, above all, the injustice of the *ancien régime* (the "old order"). In his numerous books and pamphlets, which the authorities regularly condemned and burned, he protested against government persecution of the freedoms of thought and religion. Voltaire believed humankind could never be happy until an enlightened society removed the traditional obstructions to the progress of the human mind. His personal and public involvement in the struggle against established political and religious authority gave authenticity to his ideas. It converted a whole generation to the conviction that fundamental changes were necessary. This conviction paved the way for a revolution in France that Voltaire never intended, and he probably would never have approved of it. He was not convinced that "all men are created equal," the credo of Jean-Jacques Rousseau, Thomas Jefferson, and the American Declaration of Independence.

29-10 JOSEPH WRIGHT OF DERBY, *A Philosopher Giving a Lecture at the Orrery,* ca. 1763–1765. Oil on canvas, 4′ 10″ × 6′ 8″. Derby Museums and Art Gallery, Derby.

Wright's celebration of the inventions of the Industrial Revolution was in tune with the Enlightenment doctrine of progress. In this dramatically lit scene, the wonders of science mesmerize everyone present.

1 ft.

INDUSTRIAL REVOLUTION The Enlightenment's emphasis on scientific investigation and technological invention opened up new possibilities for human understanding of the world and for control of its material forces. Research into the phenomena of electricity and combustion, along with the discovery of oxygen and the power of steam, had enormous consequences. Steam power as an adjunct to, or replacement for, human labor began a new era in world history, beginning with the Industrial Revolution in England. These technological advances, coupled with the celebration of "progress," gave rise to industrialization. Most scholars mark the beginning of the Industrial Revolution with the invention of steam engines in England for industrial production and, later, their use for transportation in the 1740s. By 1850, England had a manufacturing economy—a revolutionary development because for the first time in history, societies were capable of producing a seemingly limitless supply of goods and services. Within a century, the harnessed power of steam, coal, oil, iron, steel, and electricity working in concert transformed Europe. These scientific and technological developments also affected the arts, particularly the use of new materials for constructing buildings (FIG. **29-11**) and the invention of photography (see Chapter 30).

JOSEPH WRIGHT Technological advance fueled a new enthusiasm for mechanical explanations about the wonders of the universe. The fascination science held for ordinary people as well as for the learned is the subject of *A Philosopher Giving a Lecture at the Orrery* (FIG. **29-10**) by the English painter JOSEPH WRIGHT OF DERBY (1734–1797). Wright specialized in painting dramatic candlelit and moonlit scenes. He loved subjects such as the orrery demonstration, which could be illuminated by a single light from within the picture. In the painting, a scholar demonstrates a mechanical model of the solar system called an *orrery,* in which each planet (represented by a metal orb) revolves around the sun (a lamp) at the correct relative velocity. Light from the lamp pours forth from in front of the boy silhouetted in the foreground to create dramatic light and shadows that heighten the drama of the scene. Awed children crowd close to the tiny orbs that represent the planets within the arcing bands that symbolize their orbits. An earnest listener makes notes, while the lone woman seated at the left and the two gentlemen at the right look on with rapt attention. The wonders of scientific knowledge mesmerize everyone in Wright's painting. The artist visually reinforced the fascination with the orrery by composing his image in a circular fashion, echoing the device's orbital design. The postures and gazes of all the participants and observers focus attention on the cosmic model. Wright scrupulously rendered with careful accuracy every detail of the figures, the mechanisms of the orrery, and even the books and curtain in the shadowy background.

Wright's realism appealed to the great industrialists of his day. Scientific-industrial innovators, such as Josiah Wedgwood, who pioneered many techniques of mass-produced pottery, and Sir Richard Arkwright, whose spinning frame revolutionized the textile industry, often purchased works such as *Orrery.* To them, Wright's elevation of the theories and inventions of the Industrial Revolution to the plane of history painting was exciting and appropriately in tune with the future.

COALBROOKDALE BRIDGE Advances in engineering and the development of new industrial materials during the 18th century had a profound impact on the history of architecture, leading eventually to the steel-and-glass skyscrapers of cities all over the world today. The first use of iron in bridge design was in the cast-iron bridge (FIG. **29-11**) built over the Severn River, near Coalbrookdale in England (MAP **30-1**), where ABRAHAM DARBY III (1750–1789), one of the bridge's two designers, ran his family's cast-iron business. The Darby family had spearheaded the evolution of the iron industry in England, and they vigorously supported the investigation of new uses for the material. The fabrication of cast-iron rails and bridge elements inspired Darby to work with architect THOMAS F. PRITCHARD (1723–1777) in designing the Coalbrookdale Bridge. The cast-iron armature that supports the roadbed springs from stone pier to stone pier until it leaps the final 100 feet across the Severn River gorge. The style of the graceful center arc echoes the grand arches of Roman aqueducts (FIG. **10-33**). At the same time, the exposed structure of the bridge's cast-iron parts prefigured the skeletal use of iron and steel in the 19th century. Visible structural armatures became expressive factors in the design of buildings such as the Crystal Palace (FIG. **30-48**) in England and the Eiffel Tower (FIG. **31-1**) in France.

29-11 ABRAHAM DARBY III and THOMAS F. PRITCHARD, iron bridge, Coalbrookdale, England, 1776–1779.

The first use of iron in bridge design was in this bridge over the Severn River. The Industrial Revolution brought engineering advances and new materials that revolutionized architectural construction.

Diderot on Chardin and Naturalism

Denis Diderot was a pioneer in the field of art criticism as well as in the encyclopedic compilation of human knowledge. Between 1759 and 1781 he contributed reviews of the biennial Salon of the French Royal Academy of Painting and Sculpture (see "Academic Salons," Chapter 31, page 823) to the Parisian journal *Correspondence littéraire.* In his review of the 1763 Salon, Diderot, a great admirer of Jean-Baptiste-Siméon Chardin (FIG. 29-12), had the following praise for that painter's still lifes and for naturalism in painting.

> There are many small pictures by Chardin at the Salon, almost all of them depicting fruit with the accoutrements for a meal. This is nature itself. The objects stand out from the canvas and they are so real that my eyes are fooled by them. . . . In order to look at other people's paintings, I feel as though I need different eyes; but to look at Chardin's, I need only keep the ones nature gave me and use them properly. If I had painting in mind as a career for my child, I'd buy this one [and have him copy it]. . . . Yet nature itself may be no more difficult to copy. . . . O Chardin, it's not white, red or black pigment that you grind on your palette but rather the very substance of objects; it's real air and light that you take onto the tip of your brush and transfer onto the canvas. . . . It's magic, one can't understand how it's done: thick layers of colour, applied one on top of the other, each one filtering through from underneath to create the effect. . . . Close up, everything blurs, goes flat and disappears. From a distance, everything comes back to life and reappears.*

* Translated by Kate Tunstall, in Charles Harrison, Paul Wood, and Jason Gaiger, eds., *Art in Theory 1648–1815: An Anthology of Changing Ideas* (Oxford: Blackwell, 2000), 604.

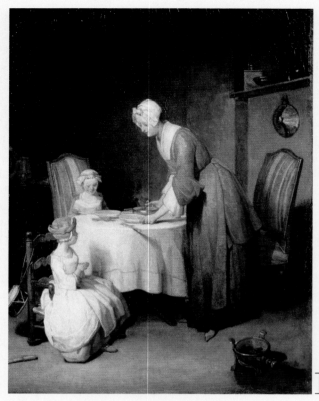

1 in.

29-12 JEAN-BAPTISTE-SIMÉON CHARDIN, *Saying Grace,* 1740. Oil on canvas, 1′ 7″ × 1′ 3″. Louvre, Paris.

Chardin embraced naturalism and celebrated the simple goodness of ordinary people, especially mothers and children, who lived in a world far from the frivolous Rococo salons of Paris.

"Natural" Art

ROUSSEAU The second key figure of the French Enlightenment, who was also instrumental in preparing the way ideologically for the French Revolution, was Jean-Jacques Rousseau (1712–1778). Voltaire believed the salvation of humanity was in the advancement of science and in the rational improvement of society. In contrast, Rousseau declared that the arts, sciences, society, and civilization in general had corrupted "natural man"—people in their primitive state—and that humanity's only salvation lay in a return to something like "the ignorance, innocence and happiness" of its original condition. According to Rousseau, human capacity for feeling, sensibility, and emotions came before reason: "To exist is to feel; our feeling is undoubtedly earlier than our intelligence, and we had feelings before we had ideas." Nature alone must be the guide: "All our natural inclinations are right." Fundamental to Rousseau's thinking was the notion that "Man by nature is good . . . he is depraved and perverted by society." He rejected the idea of progress, insisting that "Our minds have been corrupted in proportion as the arts and sciences have improved."[2] Rousseau's elevation of feelings above reason as the most primitive—and hence the most "natural"—of human expressions led him to exalt as the ideal the peasant's simple life, with its honest and unsullied emotions.

CHARDIN Rousseau's views, popular and widely read, were largely responsible for the turning away from the Rococo sensibility and the formation of a taste for the "natural," as opposed to the artificial and frivolous. Reflecting Rousseau's values, JEAN-BAPTISTE-SIMÉON CHARDIN (1699–1779) painted quiet scenes of domestic life, which offered the opportunity to praise the simple goodness of ordinary people, especially mothers and young children, who in spirit, occupation, and environment lived far from corrupt society. In *Saying Grace* (FIG. 29-12), Chardin ushers the viewer into a modest room where a mother and her small daughters are about to dine. The mood of quiet attention is at one with the hushed lighting and mellow color and with the closely studied still-life accessories whose worn surfaces tell their own humble domestic history. The viewer witnesses a moment of social instruction, when mother and older sister supervise the younger sister in the simple, pious ritual of giving thanks to God before a meal. The simplicity of the composition reinforces the subdued charm of this scene, with the three figures highlighted against the dark background. Chardin was the poet of the commonplace and the master of its nuances. A gentle sentiment prevails in all his pictures, an emotion not contrived and artificial but born of the painter's honesty, insight, and sympathy. Chardin's paintings had wide appeal, even in unexpected places. Louis XV, the royal personification of the Rococo in his life and tastes, once owned *Saying Grace.* The painter was also a favorite of Diderot, the leading art critic of the day as well as the editor of the *Encylopédie* (see "Diderot on Chardin and Naturalism," above).

Greuze was a master of sentimental narrative, which appealed to a new audience that admired "natural" virtue. Here, in an unadorned room, a father blesses his daughter and her husband-to-be.

1 ft.

JEAN-BAPTISTE GREUZE

The sentimental narrative in art became the specialty of French artist Jᴇᴀɴ-Bᴀᴘᴛɪsᴛᴇ Gʀᴇᴜᴢᴇ (1725–1805), whose most popular work, *Village Bride* (FIG. **29-13**), sums up the characteristics of the genre. The setting is an unadorned room in a rustic dwelling. In a notary's presence, the elderly father has passed his daughter's dowry to her youthful husband-to-be and blesses the pair, who gently take each other's arms. The old mother tearfully gives her daughter's arm a farewell caress, while the youngest sister melts in tears on the shoulder of the demure bride. An envious older sister broods behind her father's chair. Rosy-faced, healthy children play around the scene. The picture's story is simple—the happy climax of a rural romance. The painting's moral is just as clear—happiness is the reward of "natural" virtue.

Greuze produced this work at a time when the audience for art was expanding. The strict social hierarchy that provided the foundation for Rococo art and patronage gave way to a bourgeois economic and social system. Members of this bourgeois class increasingly embraced art, and paintings such as *Village Bride* particularly appealed to them. They carefully analyzed each gesture and each nuance of sentiment and reacted enthusiastically. At the 1761 Salon of the Royal Academy, Greuze's picture received enormous attention. Diderot, who reviewed the exhibition for *Correspondence littéraire,* declared that it was difficult to get near it because of the throngs of admirers.

Vigée-Lebrun was one of the few women admitted to France's Royal Academy of Painting and Sculpture. In this self-portrait, she depicted herself confidently painting the likeness of Queen Marie Antoinette.

VIGÉE-LEBRUN *Self-Portrait* (FIG. **29-14**) by Éʟɪsᴀʙᴇᴛʜ Lᴏᴜɪsᴇ Vɪɢéᴇ-Lᴇʙʀᴜɴ (1755–1842) is another variation of the "naturalistic" impulse in 18th-century French art. In this new mode of portraiture, Vigée-Lebrun looks directly at viewers and pauses in her work to return their gaze. Although her mood is lighthearted and her costume's details echo the serpentine curve Rococo artists and wealthy patrons loved, nothing about Vigée-Lebrun's pose or her mood speaks of Rococo frivolity. Hers is the self-confident stance of a woman whose art has won her an independent role in her society. She portrayed herself in a close-up, intimate view at work on one of the portraits that won her renown, that of Queen Marie Antoinette (1755–1793). Like many of her contemporaries, Vigée-Lebrun lived a life of extraordinary personal and economic independence, working for the nobility throughout Europe. She was famous for the force and grace of her portraits, especially those of highborn ladies and royalty. She was successful during the age of the late monarchy in France and was one of the few women admitted to the Royal Academy. After the French

29-15 WILLIAM HOGARTH, *Breakfast Scene,* from *Marriage à la Mode,* ca. 1745. Oil on canvas, 2′ 4″ × 3′. National Gallery, London.

Hogarth won fame for his paintings and prints satirizing 18th-century English life with comic zest. This is one of a series of six paintings in which he chronicled the marital immoralities of the moneyed class.

1 ft.

29-14B
LABILLE-GUIARD, *Self-Portrait,* 1785.

Revolution, however, the Academy rescinded her membership, because women were no longer welcome, but she enjoyed continued success owing to her talent, wit, and ability to forge connections with those in power in the postrevolutionary period.

WILLIAM HOGARTH Across the Channel, a truly English style of painting emerged with WILLIAM HOGARTH (1697–1764), who satirized the lifestyle of the newly prosperous middle class with comic zest. Traditionally, the British imported painters from the Continent—Holbein, Rubens, and Van Dyck among them. Hogarth waged a lively campaign throughout his career against the English feeling of dependence on, and inferiority to, these artists. Although Hogarth would have been the last to admit it, his own painting owed much to the work of his contemporaries in France, the Rococo artists. Yet his subject matter, frequently moral in tone, was distinctively English. It was the great age of English satirical writing, and Hogarth—who knew and admired this genre and included Henry Fielding (1701–1754), the author of *Tom Jones,* among his closest friends—clearly saw himself as translating satire into the visual arts.

Hogarth's favorite device was to make a series of narrative paintings and prints, in a sequence like chapters in a book or scenes in a play, following a character or group of characters in their encounters with some social evil. *Breakfast Scene* (FIG. **29-15**), from *Marriage à la Mode,* is one in a sequence of six paintings that satirize the marital immoralities of the moneyed classes in England. In it, the marriage of a young viscount is just beginning to founder. The husband and wife are tired after a long night spent in separate pursuits. While the wife stayed home for an evening of cards and music-making, her young husband had been away from the house for a night of suspicious business. He thrusts his hands deep into the empty money-pockets of his breeches, while his wife's small dog sniffs inquiringly at a woman's lacy cap protruding from his coat pocket. A steward, his hands full of unpaid bills, raises his eyes to Heaven in despair at the actions of his no-

ble master and mistress. The house is palatial, but Hogarth filled it with witty clues to the dubious taste of its occupants. For example, the row of pious religious paintings on the upper wall of the distant room concludes with a curtain-shielded work that undoubtedly depicts an erotic subject. According to the custom of the day, ladies could not view this discretely hidden painting, but at the pull of a cord, the master and his male guests could gaze at the cavorting figures. In *Breakfast Scene,* as in all his work, Hogarth proceeded as a novelist might, elaborating on his subject with carefully chosen detail, whose discovery heightens the comedy.

Hogarth designed the marriage series to be published as a set of engravings. The prints of this and his other moral narratives were so popular that unscrupulous entrepreneurs produced unauthorized versions almost as fast as the artist created his originals. The popularity of these prints speaks not only to the appeal of their subjects but also to the democratization of knowledge and culture the Enlightenment fostered and to the exploitation of new printing technologies that produced a more affordable and widely disseminated visual culture.

THOMAS GAINSBOROUGH A contrasting blend of "naturalistic" representation and Rococo setting is found in the portrait *Mrs. Richard Brinsley Sheridan* (FIG. **29-16**) by the British painter THOMAS GAINSBOROUGH (1727–1788). This painting shows a lovely woman, dressed informally, seated in a rustic landscape faintly reminiscent of Watteau (FIG. **29-6**) in its soft-hued light and feathery brushwork. Gainsborough intended to match the natural, unspoiled beauty of the landscape with that of his sitter. Mrs. Sheridan's dark brown hair blows freely in the slight wind, and her clear "English" complexion and air of ingenuous sweetness contrast sharply with the pert sophistication of those that Continental Rococo artists portrayed. Gainsborough originally had planned to give the picture a more pastoral air by adding several sheep, but he did not live long enough to paint them. Even without this element, the painting

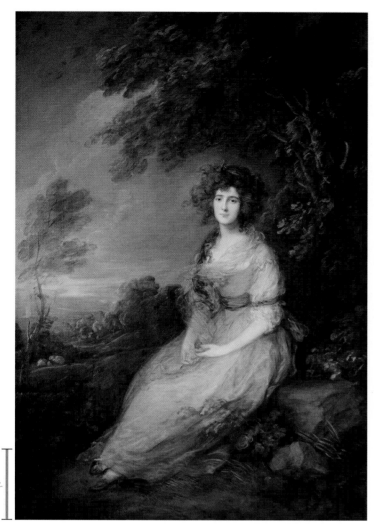

29-16 THOMAS GAINSBOROUGH, *Mrs. Richard Brinsley Sheridan*, 1787. Oil on canvas, 7′ 2⅝″ × 5′ ⅝″. National Gallery of Art, Washington, D.C. (Andrew W. Mellon Collection).

In this life-size portrait, Gainsborough sought to match the natural beauty of Mrs. Sheridan with that of the landscape. The rustic setting, soft-hued light, and feathery brushwork recall Rococo painting.

clearly expresses the artist's deep interest in the landscape setting. Although he won greater fame in his time for his portraits, he had begun as a landscape painter and always preferred painting scenes of nature to depicting human likenesses.

JOSHUA REYNOLDS Morality of a more heroic tone than that found in the work of Greuze, yet in harmony with "naturalness," included the virtues of honor, valor, and love of country. According to 18th-century Western thought, these virtues produced great people and exemplary deeds. The concept of "nobility," especially as discussed by Rousseau, referred to character, not to aristocratic birth. As the century progressed and people felt the tremors of coming revolutions, these virtues of courage and resolution, patriotism, and self-sacrifice assumed greater importance. Having risen from humble origins, the modern military hero, not the decadent aristocrat, brought the tumult of war into the company of the "natural" emotions.

SIR JOSHUA REYNOLDS (1723–1792) specialized in what became known as *Grand Manner portraiture* and often depicted contemporaries who participated in the great events of the latter part of the 18th century. Although clearly showing individualized people, Grand Manner portraiture also elevated the sitter by conveying refinement and elegance. Painters communicated a person's grace and class through

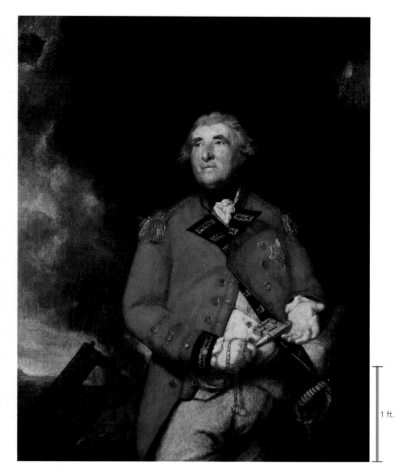

29-17 SIR JOSHUA REYNOLDS, *Lord Heathfield*, 1787. Oil on canvas, 4′ 8″ × 3′ 9″. National Gallery, London.

In this Grand Manner portrait, Reynolds depicted the English commander who defended Gibraltar. Typical of this genre, Heathfield is large in relation to the canvas size and stands in a dramatic pose.

certain standardized conventions, such as the large scale of the figure relative to the canvas, the controlled pose, the landscape setting, and the low horizon line. Reynolds painted his portrait of *Lord Heathfield* (FIG. **29-17**) in 1787. This burly, ruddy English officer, commandant of the fortress at Gibraltar, was a perfect subject for a Grand Manner portrait. Heathfield had doggedly defended the British fortress against the Spanish and the French, and later received the honorary title Baron Heathfield of Gibraltar. Here, he holds the huge key to the fortress, the symbol of his victory. He stands in front of a curtain of dark smoke rising from the battleground, flanked by one cannon that points ineffectively downward and another whose tilted barrel indicates that it lies uselessly on its back. Reynolds portrayed the features of the general's heavy, honest face and his uniform with unidealized realism. But Lord Heathfield's posture and the setting dramatically suggest the heroic themes of battle and refer to the revolutions (American and French) then taking shape in deadly earnest, as the old regimes faded into the past.

BENJAMIN WEST Some American artists also became well known in England. BENJAMIN WEST (1738–1820), born in Pennsylvania on what was then the colonial frontier, traveled to Europe early in life to study art and then went to England, where he met with almost immediate success. A cofounder of the Royal Academy of Arts, West succeeded Reynolds as its president. He became official painter to King George III (r. 1760–1801) and retained that position during the strained period of the American Revolution.

West's great innovation was to blend contemporary subject matter and costumes with the grand tradition of history painting. Here, West likened General Wolfe's death to that of a martyred saint.

In *Death of General Wolfe* (FIG. **29-18**), West depicted the mortally wounded young English commander just after his defeat of the French in the decisive battle of Quebec in 1759, which gave Canada to Great Britain. In portraying a contemporary historical subject, he put his characters in contemporary costume (although the military uniforms are not completely accurate in all details). However, West blended this realism of detail with the grand tradition of history painting by arranging his figures in a complex, theatrically ordered composition. His modern hero dies among grieving officers on the field of victorious battle in a way that suggests the death of a great saint. West wanted to present this hero's death in the service of the state as a martyrdom charged with religious emotions. His innovative combination of the conventions of traditional heroic painting with a look of modern realism was so effective that it won viewers' hearts in his own day and continued to influence history painting well into the 19th century.

JOHN SINGLETON COPLEY American artist JOHN SINGLETON COPLEY (1738–1815) matured as a painter in the Massachusetts Bay Colony. Like West, Copley later emigrated to England, where he absorbed the fashionable English portrait style. But unlike Grand Manner portraiture, Copley's *Portrait of Paul Revere* (FIG. **29-19**), painted before Copley left Boston, conveys a sense of directness and faithfulness to visual fact that marked the taste for honesty and plainness many visitors to America noticed during the 18th and 19th centuries. When Copley painted his portrait, Revere was not yet the familiar hero of the American Revolution. In the picture, he is working at his profession of silversmithing. The setting is plain, the lighting clear and revealing. Revere sits in his shirtsleeves, bent over a teapot in progress. He pauses and turns his head to look the observer straight in the eye. Copley treated the reflections in the polished wood of the tabletop with as much care as Revere's figure, his tools, and the teapot resting on its leather graver's pillow. Copley gave special prominence to Revere's eyes by reflecting intense reddish light onto the darkened side of his face and hands. The informality and the sense of the moment link this

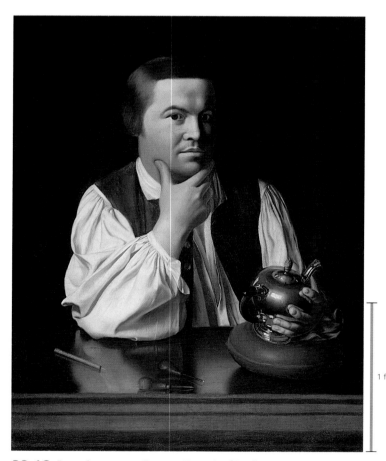

29-19 JOHN SINGLETON COPLEY, *Portrait of Paul Revere,* ca. 1768–1770. Oil on canvas, $2'\ 11\frac{1}{8}'' \times 2'\ 4''$. Museum of Fine Arts, Boston (gift of Joseph W., William B., and Edward H. R. Revere).

In contrast to Grand Manner portraiture, Copley's *Paul Revere* emphasizes his subject's down-to-earth character, differentiating this American work from its European counterparts.

The Grand Tour and Veduta Painting

Although travel throughout Europe was common-place in the 18th century, Italy became a particularly popular destination. This "pilgrimage" of aristocrats, the wealthy, politicians, and diplomats from France, England, Germany, Flanders, Sweden, the United States, Russia, Poland, and Hungary came to be known as the Grand Tour. Italy's allure fueled the revival of classicism, and the popularity of Neoclassical art drove this fascination with Italy. One British observer noted: "All our religion, all our arts, almost all that sets us above savages, has come from the shores of the Mediterranean."*

The Grand Tour was not simply leisure travel. The education available in Italy to the inquisitive mind made the trip an indispensable experience for anyone who wished to make a mark in society. The Enlightenment had made knowledge of ancient Rome and Greece imperative, and a steady stream of Europeans and Americans traveled to Italy in the late 18th and early 19th centuries. These tourists aimed to increase their knowledge of literature, the visual arts, architecture, theater, music, history, customs, and folklore. Given this extensive agenda, it is not surprising that a Grand Tour could take a number of years to complete, and most travelers moved from location to location, following an established itinerary.

The British were the most avid travelers, and they conceived the initial "tour code," including important destinations and required itineraries. Although they designated Rome early on as the primary destination, visitors traveled as far north as Venice and as far south as Naples. Eventually, Paestum, Sicily, Florence, Genoa, Milan, Siena, Pisa, Bologna, and Parma (MAP 25-1) all appeared in guidebooks and in paintings. Joseph Wright of Derby (FIG. 29-10) and Joseph Mallord William Turner (FIG. 30-23) were among the many British artists to undertake a Grand Tour.

Many of those who completed a Grand Tour returned home with a painting by Antonio Canaletto, the leading painter of scenic views (*vedute*) of Venice. It must have been very cheering on a gray winter afternoon in England to look up and see a sunny, panoramic view such as that in Canaletto's *Riva degli Schiavoni, Venice* (FIG. 29-20), with its cloud-studded sky, picturesque water traffic, and well-known Venetian landmarks (the Doge's Palace, FIG. 19-21, is at the left in *Riva degli Schiavoni*) painted in scrupulous perspective and minute detail. Canaletto usually made drawings "on location" to take back to his studio and use as sources for paintings. To help make the on-site drawings true to life, he often used a camera obscura, as Vermeer (FIGS. 25-1 and 25-19) did before him. These instruments were darkened chambers (some of them virtually portable closets) with optical lenses fitted into a hole in one wall through which light entered to project an inverted image of the subject onto the chamber's opposite wall. The artist could trace the main details from this image for later reworking and refinement. The camera obscura allowed artists to create visually convincing paintings that included variable focus of objects at different distances. Canaletto's paintings give the impression of capturing every detail, with no omissions. In fact, he presented each site within Renaissance perspectival rules and exercised great selectivity about which details to include and which to omit to make a coherent and engagingly attractive veduta.

29-20 ANTONIO CANALETTO, *Riva degli Schiavoni, Venice,* ca. 1735–1740. Oil on canvas, $1' 6\frac{1}{2}'' \times 2' \frac{7}{8}''$. Toledo Museum of Art, Toledo.

Canaletto was the leading painter of Venetian *vedute*, which were treasured souvenirs for 18th-century travelers visiting Italy on a Grand Tour. He used a camera obscura for his on-site drawings.

* Cesare de Seta, "Grand Tour: The Lure of Italy in the Eighteenth Century," in Andrew Wilton and Ilaria Bignamini, eds., *Grand Tour: The Lure of Italy in the Eighteenth Century* (London: Tate Gallery, 1996), 13.

painting to contemporaneous English and European portraits. But the spare style and the emphasis on the sitter's down-to-earth character differentiate this American work from its European counterparts.

THE GRAND TOUR The 18th-century public also sought "naturalness" in artists' depictions of landscapes. Documentation of particular places became popular, in part due to growing travel opportunities and expanding colonialism. These depictions of geographic settings also served the needs of the many scientific expeditions mounted during the century and satisfied the desires of genteel tourists for mementos of their journeys. By this time, a "Grand Tour" of the major sites of Europe was an essential part of every well-bred person's education (see "The Grand Tour," above). Naturally, those on tour wished to return with items that would help them remember their experiences and impress those at home with the wonders they had seen. The English were especially eager collectors of pictorial souvenirs. Certain artists in Venice specialized in painting the most characteristic scenes, or *vedute* (views), of that city to sell to British visitors. Chief among the Venetian painters was ANTONIO CANALETTO (1697–1768), whose works, for example *Riva degli Schiavoni, Venice* (FIG. 29-20), English tourists avidly acquired as evidence of their visit to the city of the Grand Canal.

The Excavations of Herculaneum and Pompeii

Among the events that fueled the European fascination with classical antiquity were the excavations of two ancient Roman cities on the Bay of Naples—Herculaneum and Pompeii. The violent eruption of Mount Vesuvius in August 79 CE had buried both cities under volcanic ash and mud (see "An Eyewitness Account of the Eruption of Mount Vesuvius," Chapter 10, page 245). Although each city was "rediscovered" at various times during the ensuing centuries, systematic exploration of both sites did not begin until the mid-1700s. Because Vesuvius buried these cities under volcanic ash and lava, the excavations produced unusually rich evidence for reconstructing Roman art and life. The 18th-century excavators uncovered paintings, sculptures, furniture, vases, and silverware in addition to buildings. As a result, European interest in ancient Rome expanded tremendously. European collectors acquired many of the newly discovered objects. For example, Sir William Hamilton, British consul in Naples from 1764 to 1800, purchased numerous vases and small objects, which he sold to the British Museum in 1772. The finds at Pompeii and Herculaneum, therefore, quickly became available to a wide public.

"Pompeian" style soon became all the rage in England, as evident in the interior designs of Robert Adam, which were inspired by the slim, straight-lined, elegant frescoes of the Third and early Fourth Styles of Roman mural painting (FIGS. 10-21 and 10-22). The new Neoclassical style almost entirely displaced the curvilinear Rococo (FIGS. 29-2 and 29-3) after midcentury. In the Etruscan Room (FIG. 29-21) at Osterley Park House, Adam took decorative motifs (medallions, urns, vine scrolls, sphinxes, and tripods) from Roman art and arranged them sparsely within broad, neutral spaces and slender margins, as in his ancient models. Adam was an archaeologist as well, and he had explored and written accounts of the ruins of Diocletian's palace (FIG. 10-74) at Split. Kedleston House in Derbyshire, Adelphi Terrace in London, and a great many other structures he designed show the influence of the Split palace on his work.

29-21 ROBERT ADAM, Etruscan Room, from Osterley Park House, Middlesex, England, begun 1761. Victoria & Albert Museum, London.

Inspired by the recent discoveries at Herculaneum and Pompeii, Adam incorporated classical decorative motifs into his Etruscan Room, which he based on Roman mural painting.

The archaeological finds from Herculaneum and Pompeii also affected garden and landscape design, fashion, and tableware. Clothing based on classical garb became popular, and Emma Hamilton, wife of Sir William Hamilton, often gave lavish parties dressed in floating and delicate Greek-style drapery. Neoclassical taste also determined the pottery designs of John Flaxman (1755–1826) and Josiah Wedgwood (1730–1795). Wedgwood established his reputation in the 1760s with his creamware inspired by ancient art. He eventually produced vases based on what were thought to be Etruscan designs (actually Greek vases found in Etruscan tombs) and expanded his business by producing small busts of classical figures as well as cameos and medallions adorned with copies of antique reliefs and statues.

NEOCLASSICISM

One of the defining characteristics of the late 18th century was a renewed admiration for classical antiquity, which the Grand Tour was instrumental in fueling. This interest gave rise to the artistic movement known as *Neoclassicism,* which incorporated the subjects and styles of ancient art. Painting, sculpture, and architecture, however, were only the most prominent manifestations of Neoclassicism. Fascination with Greek and Roman culture was widespread and extended to the public culture of fashion and home decor. The Enlightenment's emphasis on rationality in part explains this classical focus, because the geometric harmony of classical art and architecture embodied Enlightenment ideals. In addition, classical cultures represented the pinnacle of civilized society, and Greece and Rome served as models of enlightened political organization. These cultures, with their traditions of liberty, civic virtue, morality, and sacrifice, were ideal models during a period of great political upheaval. Given these traditional associations, it is not coincidental that Neoclassicism was particularly appealing during the French and American Revolutions. Further whetting the public appetite for classicism were the excavations of Herculaneum (begun in 1738) and Pompeii (1748), which the volcanic eruption of Mount Vesuvius had buried (see "The Excavations of Herculaneum and Pompeii," page 766). Soon, murals based on artwork unearthed in the excavations began to appear on the walls of rooms in European town houses, such as the "Etruscan Room" (FIG. 29-21) by ROBERT ADAM (1728–1792) in Osterley Park House in Middlesex, begun in 1761.

WINCKELMANN The enthusiasm for classical antiquity also permeated much of the scholarship of the time. In the late 18th century, the ancient world increasingly became the focus of scholarly attention. A visit to Rome stimulated Edward Gibbon (1737–1794) to begin his monumental *Decline and Fall of the Roman Empire,* which appeared between 1776 and 1788. Earlier, in 1755, Johann Joachim Winckelmann (1717–1768), the first modern art historian, published *Reflections on the Imitation of Greek Works in Painting and Sculpture,* uncompromisingly designating Greek art as the most perfect to come from human hands—and far preferable to "natural" art.

> Good taste, which is becoming more prevalent throughout the world, had its origins under the skies of Greece. . . . The only way for us to become great . . . is to imitate the ancients. . . . In the masterpieces of Greek art, connoisseurs and imitators find not only nature at its most beautiful but also something beyond nature, namely certain ideal forms of its beauty. . . . A person enlightened enough to penetrate the innermost secrets of art will find beauties hitherto seldom revealed when he compares the total structure of Greek figures with most modern ones, especially those modelled more on nature than on Greek taste.[3]

In his *History of Ancient Art* (1764), Winckelmann described each monument and positioned it within a huge inventory of works organized by subject matter, style, and period. Before Winckelmann, art historians had focused on biography, as did Giorgio Vasari and

Giovanni Pietro Bellori in the 16th and 17th centuries. Winckelmann thus initiated one modern art historical method thoroughly in accord with Enlightenment ideas of ordering knowledge—a system of description and classification that provided a pioneering model for the understanding of stylistic evolution. His familiarity with classical art derived predominantly (as was the norm) from Roman works and Roman copies of Greek art in Italy. Yet he was instrumental in bringing to scholarly attention the distinctions between Greek and Roman art. Thus, he paved the way for more thorough study of the distinct characteristics of the art and architecture of these two cultures. Winckelmann's writings also laid a theoretical and historical foundation for the enormously widespread taste for Neoclassicism that lasted well into the 19th century.

29-22A MENGS, *Parnassus,* 1761.

Painting

ANGELICA KAUFFMANN One of the pioneers of Neoclassical painting was ANGELICA KAUFFMANN (1741–1807). Born in Switzerland and trained in Italy, Kauffmann spent many of her productive years in England. A student of Reynolds, and an interior decorator of many houses built by Adam, she was a founding member of the British Royal Academy of Arts and enjoyed an enviable reputation. Her *Cornelia Presenting Her Children as Her Treasures,* or *Mother of the Gracchi* (FIG. 29-22), is an *exemplum virtutis* (example or model of virtue) drawn from Greek and Roman history and literature. The moralizing pictures of Greuze (FIG. 29-13) and Hogarth (FIG. 29-15) already had marked a change in taste, but Kauffmann replaced the modern setting and character of their works. She clothed her actors in ancient Roman garb and posed them in statuesque attitudes within Roman interiors. The theme in this painting is the virtue of Cornelia, mother of the future political leaders Tiberius and Gaius Gracchus, who, in the second century BCE, attempted to reform the Roman Republic. Cornelia reveals her character in this scene, which takes place after the seated visitor showed off her fine jewelry and then insisted haughtily that Cornelia show hers. Instead of rushing to get her own precious adornments, Cornelia brought her sons forward, presenting them as her jewels. The architectural setting is severely Roman, with no Rococo motif in evidence, and the composition and drawing have the simplicity and firmness of low-relief carving.

1 ft.

29-22 ANGELICA KAUFFMANN, *Cornelia Presenting Her Children as Her Treasures,* or *Mother of the Gracchi,* ca. 1785. Oil on canvas, 3′ 4″ × 4′ 2″. Virginia Museum of Fine Arts, Richmond (the Adolph D. and Wilkins C. Williams Fund).

Kauffmann's painting of a virtuous Roman mother who presented her children to a visitor as her jewels exemplifies the Enlightenment fascination with classical antiquity and with classical art.

David on Greek Style and Public Art

Jacques-Louis David was the leading Neoclassical painter in France at the end of the 18th century. He championed a return to Greek style and the painting of inspiring heroic and patriotic subjects. In 1796 he made the following statement to his pupils:

> I want to work in a pure Greek style. I feed my eyes on antique statues, I even have the intention of imitating some of them. The Greeks had no scruples about copying a composition, a gesture, a type that had already been accepted and used. They put all their attention and all their art on perfecting an idea that had been already conceived. They thought, and they were right, that in the arts the way in which an idea is rendered, and the manner in which it is expressed, is much more important than the idea itself. To give a body and a perfect form to one's thought, this—and only this—is to be an artist.*

David also strongly believed that paintings depicting noble events in ancient history, such as *Oath of the Horatii* (FIG. **29-23**),

would instill patriotism and civic virtue in the public at large in postrevolutionary France. In November 1793 he wrote:

> [The arts] should help to spread the progress of the human spirit, and to propagate and transmit to posterity the striking examples of the efforts of a tremendous people who, guided by reason and philosophy, are bringing back to earth the reign of liberty, equality, and law. The arts must therefore contribute forcefully to the education of the public. . . . The arts are the imitation of nature in her most beautiful and perfect form. . . . [T]hose marks of heroism and civic virtue offered the eyes of the people [will] electrify the soul, and plant the seeds of glory and devotion to the fatherland.[†]

* Translated by Robert Goldwater and Marco Treves, eds., *Artists on Art*, 3d ed. (New York: Pantheon Books, 1958), 206.
[†] Ibid., 205.

29-23 Jacques-Louis David, *Oath of the Horatii*, 1784. Oil on canvas, 10′ 10″ × 13′ 11″. Louvre, Paris. ▣◀

David was the Neoclassical painter-ideologist of the French Revolution. This huge canvas celebrating ancient Roman patriotism and sacrifice features statuesque figures and classical architecture.

1 ft.

JACQUES-LOUIS DAVID The Enlightenment idea of a participatory and knowledgeable citizenry lay behind the revolt against the French monarchy in 1789, but the immediate causes of the French Revolution were the country's economic crisis and the clash between the Third Estate (bourgeoisie, peasantry, and urban and rural workers) and the First and Second Estates (the clergy and nobility, respectively). They fought over the issue of representation in the legislative body, the Estates-General, which had been convened to discuss taxation as a possible solution to the economic problem. However, the ensuing revolution revealed the instability of the monarchy and of French society's traditional structure and resulted in a succession of republics and empires as France struggled to find a way to adjust to these decisive changes.

JACQUES-LOUIS DAVID (1748–1825) became the Neoclassical painter-ideologist of the French Revolution. A distant relative of Boucher, he followed the Rococo painter's style until a period of study in Rome won the younger man over to the classical art tradition. David favored the academic teachings about using the art of the ancients and of the great Renaissance masters as models. He rebelled against Rococo style as an "artificial taste" and exalted the "perfect form" of Greek art (see "David on Greek Style and Public Art," page 768).

OATH OF THE HORATII David concurred with the Enlightenment belief that subject matter should have a moral and should be presented so that noble deeds in the past could inspire virtue in the present. A milestone painting in David's career, *Oath of the Horatii* (FIG. 29-23), depicts a story from pre-Republican Rome, the heroic phase of Roman history. The topic was not too arcane for David's audience. Pierre Corneille (1606–1684) had retold this story of conflict between love and patriotism, first recounted by the ancient Roman historian Livy, in a play performed in Paris several years earlier, making it familiar to David's viewing public. According to the story, the leaders of the warring cities of Rome and Alba decided to resolve their conflicts in a series of encounters waged by three representatives from each side. The Romans chose as their champions the three Horatius brothers, who had to face the three sons of the Curatius family from Alba. A sister of the Horatii, Camilla, was the bride-to-be of one of the Curatius sons, and the wife of the youngest Horatius was the sister of the Curatii.

David's painting shows the Horatii as they swear on their swords, held high by their father, to win or die for Rome, oblivious to the anguish and sorrow of their female relatives. In its form, *Oath of the Horatii* is a paragon of the Neoclassical style. Not only does the subject matter deal with a narrative of patriotism and sacrifice excerpted from Roman history, but the painter presented the image with force and clarity. David depicted the scene in a shallow space much like a stage setting, defined by a severely simple architectural framework. He deployed his statuesque and carefully modeled figures across the space, close to the foreground, in a manner reminiscent of ancient relief sculpture. The rigid, angular, and virile forms of the men on the left effectively contrast with the soft curvilinear shapes of the distraught women on the right. This pattern visually pits virtues the Enlightenment leaders ascribed to men (such as courage, patriotism, and unwavering loyalty to a cause) against the emotions of love, sorrow, and despair that the women in the painting express. The French viewing audience perceived such emotionalism as characteristic of the female nature. The message was clear and of a type readily identifiable to the prerevolutionary French public. The picture created a sensation at its first exhibition in Paris in 1785, and although David had painted it under royal patronage and did not intend the painting as a revolutionary statement, the Neoclassical style of *Oath of the Horatii* soon became the semiofficial voice of the French Revolution. David may have painted in the academic tradition, but he brought new impetus to it. He created a program for arousing his audience to patriotic zeal.

DEATH OF MARAT When the French Revolution broke out in 1789, David threw in his lot with the Jacobins, the radical and militant revolutionary faction. He accepted the role of de facto minister of propaganda, organizing political pageants and ceremonies that included floats, costumes, and sculptural props. David believed that art could play an important role in educating the public and that dramatic paintings emphasizing patriotism and civic virtue would prove

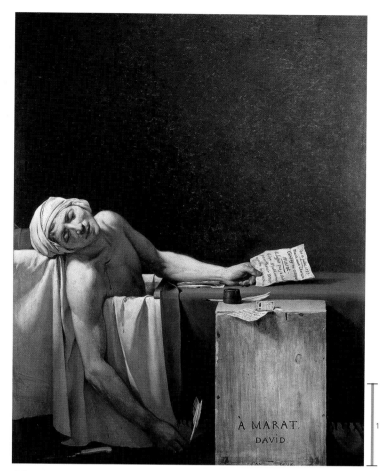

29-24 JACQUES-LOUIS DAVID, *Death of Marat*, 1793. Oil on canvas, 5′ 5″ × 4′ 2½″. Musées Royaux des Beaux-Arts de Belgique, Brussels.

David depicted the revolutionary Marat as a tragic martyr, stabbed to death in his bath. Although the painting displays severe Neoclassical spareness, its convincing realism conveys pain and outrage.

effective as rallying calls. However, rather than continuing to create artworks focused on scenes from antiquity, David began to portray scenes from the French Revolution itself. He intended *Death of Marat* (FIG. 29-24) not only to serve as a record of an important event in the struggle to overthrow the monarchy but also to provide inspiration and encouragement to the revolutionary forces. Jean-Paul Marat (1743–1793), a writer and David's friend, was tragically assassinated in 1793. David depicted the martyred revolutionary after Charlotte Corday (1768–1793), a member of a rival political faction, stabbed him to death in his medicinal bath. (Marat suffered from a painful skin disease.) David presented the scene with directness and clarity. The cold neutral space above Marat's figure slumped in the tub produces a chilling oppressiveness. The painter vividly placed narrative details—the knife, the wound, the blood, the letter with which the young woman gained entrance—to sharpen the sense of pain and outrage and to confront viewers with the scene itself. *Death of Marat* is convincingly real, yet David masterfully composed the painting to present Marat as a tragic martyr who died in the service of the revolution. David based the figure of Marat on Christ in Michelangelo's *Pietà* (FIG. 22-12) in Saint Peter's in Rome. The reference to Christ's martyrdom made the painting a kind of "altarpiece" for the new civic "religion," inspiring the French people with the saintly dedication of their slain leader.

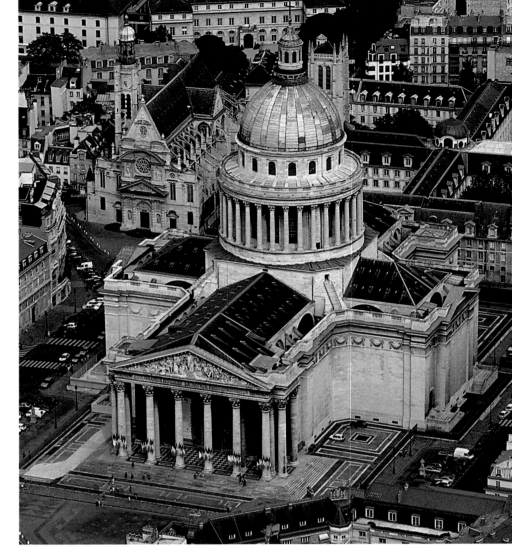

29-25 JACQUES-GERMAIN SOUFFLOT, Panthéon (Sainte-Geneviève), Paris, France, 1755–1792.

Soufflot's Panthéon is a testament to the Enlightenment admiration for Greece and Rome. It combines a portico based on an ancient Roman temple with a colonnaded dome and a Greek-cross plan.

Architecture and Sculpture

Architecture in the Enlightenment era also exhibits a dependence on classical models. Early in the 18th century, architects began to turn away from the theatricality and ostentation of Baroque and Rococo design and embraced a more streamlined antique look.

29-25A FISCHER VON ERLACH, Karlskirche, Vienna, 1716–1737.

PANTHÉON The portico of the Parisian church of Sainte-Geneviève, now the Panthéon (FIG. 29-25), by JACQUES-GERMAIN SOUFFLOT (1713–1780), stands as testament to the revived interest in Greek and Roman cultures. The Roman ruins at Baalbek in Lebanon, especially the titanic colonnade of the temple of Jupiter, provided much of the inspiration for Soufflot's design. The columns, reproduced with studied archaeological precision, stand out from walls that are severely blank, except for a repeated garland motif near the top. The colonnaded dome, a Neoclassical version of the domes of Saint Peter's (FIGS. 24-3 and 24-4) in Rome, the Église du Dôme (FIG. 25-36) in Paris, and Saint Paul's (FIG. 25-38) in London, rises above a Greek-cross plan. Both the dome and the vaults rest on an interior grid of splendid freestanding Corinthian columns, as if the portico's colonnade continued within. Although the overall effect, inside and out, is Roman, the structural principles employed are essentially Gothic. Soufflot was one of the first 18th-century builders to suggest that the logical engineering of Gothic cathedrals (see "The Gothic Cathedral," Chapter 18, page 469) could be applied to modern buildings. In his work, the curious, but not unreasonable, conjunction of Gothic and classical has a structural integration that laid the foundation for the 19th-century admiration of Gothic building principles.

CHISWICK HOUSE The appeal of classical antiquity extended well beyond French borders. The popularity of Greek and Roman cultures was due not only to their association with morality, rationality, and integrity but also to their connection to political systems ranging from Athenian democracy to Roman imperial rule. Thus, parliamentary England joined revolutionary France in embracing Neoclassicism. In England, Neoclassicism's appeal also was due to its clarity and simplicity. These characteristics provided a stark contrast to the complexity and opulence of Baroque art, then associated with the flamboyant rule of absolute monarchy. In English architecture, the preference for a simple style derived indirectly from the authority of the classical Roman architect Vitruvius, through Andrea Palladio's work (FIGS. 22-29 to 22-32), and on through that of Inigo Jones (FIG. 25-37).

RICHARD BOYLE (1695–1753), earl of Burlington, strongly restated Jones's Palladian doctrine in a new style in Chiswick House (FIG. 29-26), which he built on London's outskirts with the help of WILLIAM KENT (ca. 1686–1748). The way had been paved for this shift in style by, among other things, the publication of Colin Campbell's *Vitruvius Britannicus* (1715), three volumes of engravings of ancient buildings, prefaced by a denunciation of Italian Baroque and high praise for Palladio and Jones. Chiswick House is a free variation on the theme of Palladio's Villa Rotonda (FIG. 22-29). The exterior design provided a clear alternative to the colorful splendors of Versailles (FIG. 25-32). In its simple symmetry, unadorned planes, right

29-26 RICHARD BOYLE and WILLIAM KENT, Chiswick House, near London, England, begun 1725.

For this British villa, Boyle and Kent emulated the simple symmetry and unadorned planes of the Palladian architectural style. Chiswick House is a free variation on the Villa Rotonda (FIG. 22-29).

29-27 JAMES STUART, Doric portico, Hagley Park, Worcestershire, England, 1758.

Most Neoclassical architects used Roman buildings in Italy and France as models. Stuart, who spent four years in Greece, based his Doric portico on a fifth-century BCE temple in Athens.

angles, and precise proportions, Chiswick looks very classical and "rational." But the Palladian-style villa's setting within informal gardens, where a charming irregularity of layout and freely growing uncropped foliage dominate the scene, mitigates the classical severity and rationality. Just as the owners of English villas cultivated irregularity in the landscaping surrounding their homes, they sometimes preferred interiors ornamented in a style more closely related to Rococo decoration. At Chiswick, the interior design creates a luxurious Baroque foil to the stern symmetry of the exterior and the plan. Palladian classicism prevailed in English architecture until about 1760, when it began to evolve into Neoclassicism.

29-26A WALPOLE, Strawberry Hill, Twickenham, 1749–1777.

STUART AND REVETT British painters and architects JAMES STUART (1713–1788) and NICHOLAS REVETT (1720–1804) introduced to Europe the splendor and originality of Greek art in their enormously influential *Antiquities of Athens*, the first volume of which appeared in 1762. These volumes firmly distinguished Greek art from the "derivative" Roman style that had served as the model for classicism since the Renaissance. Stuart and Revett fostered a new preference for Greek art and architecture over Roman antiquities, despite the fact that in the 18th century, familiarity with Greek art continued to be based primarily on Roman copies of Greek originals. Notwithstanding the popularity of the Grand Tour (see "The Grand Tour," page 765), travel to Greece was hazardous, making firsthand inspection of Greek monuments difficult. Stuart and Revett spent four years visiting Greece in the early 1750s, where they formed their preference for Greek art. When Stuart received the commission to design a portico (FIG. 29-27) for Hagley Park in Worcestershire, he used as his model the fifth-century BCE Doric temple in Athens known as the Theseion. His Doric portico is consequently much more severe (and authentic) than any contemporaneous Neoclassical building in Europe based on Roman or Renaissance designs.

29-27A FLITCROFT and HOARE, Stourhead, 1743–1765.

29-28 THOMAS JEFFERSON, Monticello, Charlottesville, Virginia, 1770–1806. 🎞◀

Jefferson led the movement to adopt Neoclassicism as the architectural style of the United States. Although built of local materials, his Palladian Virginia home recalls Chiswick House (FIG. 29-26).

29-29 THOMAS JEFFERSON, Rotunda and Lawn, University of Virginia, Charlottesville, Virginia, 1819–1826.

Modeled on the Pantheon (FIG. 10-49), Jefferson's Rotunda, like a temple in a Roman forum, sits on an elevated platform overlooking the colonnaded Lawn of the University of Virginia.

THOMAS JEFFERSON Part of the appeal of Neoclassicism was due to the values with which it was connected—morality, idealism, patriotism, and civic virtue. Thus, it is not surprising that in the new American republic (MAP 29-1), THOMAS JEFFERSON (1743–1826)—scholar, economist, educational theorist, statesman, and gifted amateur architect—spearheaded a movement to adopt Neoclassicism as the national architectural style. Jefferson admired Palladio immensely and read carefully the Italian architect's *Four Books of Architecture.* Later, while minister to France, he studied French 18th-century classical architecture and city planning and visited the Maison Carrée (FIG. 10-32), a Roman temple at Nîmes. After his European trip, Jefferson completely remodeled his own home, Monticello (FIG. 29-28), near Charlottesville, Virginia, which he first had designed in a different style. The final version of Monticello is somewhat reminiscent of Palladio's Villa Rotonda (FIG. 22-29) and of Chiswick House (FIG. 29-26), but its materials are the local wood and brick used in Virginia.

UNIVERSITY OF VIRGINIA Jefferson's Neoclassicism was an extension of the Enlightenment belief in the perfectibility of human beings and in the power of art to help achieve that perfection. When he became president, he selected Benjamin Latrobe (1764–1820) to build the United States Capitol in Washington, D.C., specifying that Latrobe use a Roman style. Jefferson's choice in part reflected his admiration for the beauty of the Roman buildings he had seen in Europe and in part his association of those buildings with an idealized Roman republican government and, through that, with the democracy of ancient Greece.

In his own designs for public buildings, Jefferson also looked to Rome for models. He modeled the State Capitol in Richmond, Virginia, on the Maison Carrée (FIG. 10-32). For the University of Virginia, which he founded, Jefferson turned to the Pantheon (FIG. 10-49). The Rotunda (FIG. 29-29) is the centerpiece of Jefferson's "academical village" in Charlottesville. It sits on an elevated platform at one end of a grassy quadrangle ("the Lawn"), framed by Neoclassical pavilions and colonnades—just as temples in Roman forums (FIGS. 10-12 and 10-43) stood at one short end of a colonnaded square. Each of the ten pavilions (five on each side) resembles a small classical temple. No two are exactly alike. Jefferson experimented with variations of all the different classical orders in their designs. Jefferson was no mere copyist. He had absorbed all the principles of classical architecture and clearly delighted in borrowing from major buildings in his own designs, which were nonetheless highly original—and, in turn, frequently emulated.

JEAN-ANTOINE HOUDON Neoclassicism also became the preferred style for public sculptural commissions in the new American republic. When the Virginia legislature wanted to erect a life-size marble statue of Virginia-born George Washington, the commission turned to the leading French Neoclassical sculptor of the late 18th century, JEAN-ANTOINE HOUDON (1741–1828). Houdon had already carved a bust portrait of Benjamin Franklin when he was U.S. ambassador to France. His portrait of Washington (FIG. 29-30) is the sculptural equivalent of a painted Grand Manner portrait (FIG. 29-18). But although both Washington and West's General Wolfe (FIG. 29-18) wear contemporary garb, the Houdon statue makes overt reference to the Roman Republic. The "column" on which Washington leans is a bundle of rods with an ax attached—the ancient Roman *fasces,* an emblem of authority (used much later as the emblem of Mussolini's Fascist—the term derives from "fasces"—government in 20th-century Italy). The 13 rods symbolize the 13 original states. The plow behind Washington and the fasces alludes to Cincinnatus, a patrician of the early Roman Republic who was elected dictator during a time of war and resigned his position as soon as victory had been achieved in order to return to his farm. Washington wears the badge of the Society of the Cincinnati (visible beneath the bottom of his waistcoat), an association founded in 1783 for officers in the revolutionary army who had resumed their peacetime roles. Tellingly, Washington no longer holds his sword in Houdon's statue.

1 ft.

29-30 JEAN-ANTOINE HOUDON, *George Washington,* 1788–1792. Marble, 6′ 2″ high. State Capitol, Richmond.

Houdon portrayed Washington in contemporary garb, but he incorporated the Roman *fasces* and Cincinnatus's plow in the statue, because Washington had returned to his farm after his war service.

29-31 HORATIO
GREENOUGH, *George
Washington,* 1840. Marble,
11′ 4″ high. Smithsonian
American Art Museum,
Washington, D.C.

In this posthumous por-
trait, Greenough likened
Washington to a god by
depicting him seminude
and enthroned in the
manner of Phidias's
Olympian statue of Zeus,
king of the Greek gods.

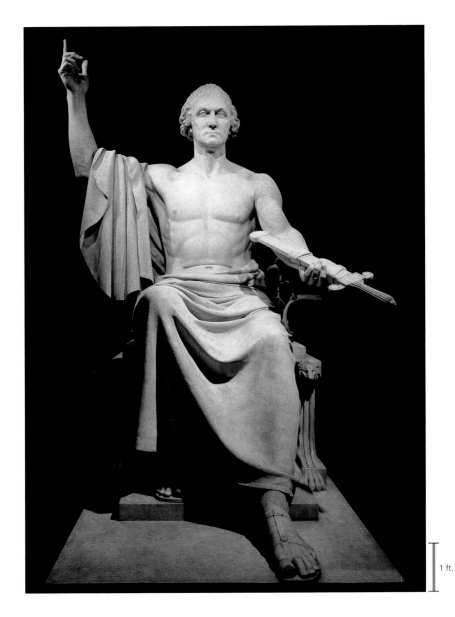

1 ft.

HORATIO GREENOUGH After his death, Washington gradually acquired almost godlike stature as the "father of his country."
In 1840 the United States Congress commissioned the American
sculptor HORATIO GREENOUGH (1805–1852) to make a statue (FIG.
29-31) of the country's first president for the Capitol. Greenough
used Houdon's portrait as his model for the head, but he portrayed
Washington as seminude and enthroned, like the famous lost statue
of Zeus that Phidias made for the god's temple at Olympia in ancient
Greece. The statue, which epitomizes the Neoclassical style, did not,
however, win favor with either the Congress that commissioned it or
the public. Although no one ever threw Greenough's statue into the
Potomac River, as one congressman suggested, the legislators never
placed it in its intended site beneath the Capitol dome. In fact, by
1840 the Neoclassical style itself was no longer in vogue. The leading
artists of Europe and America had embraced a new style, Romanticism, examined in the next chapter.

EUROPE AND AMERICA, 1700 TO 1800

ROCOCO

▌ In the early 18th century, the centralized and grandiose palace-based culture of Baroque France gave way to the much more intimate Rococo culture based in the town houses of Paris. There, aristocrats and intellectuals gathered for witty conversation in salons featuring delicate colors, sinuous lines, gilded mirrors, elegant furniture, and small paintings and sculptures.

▌ The leading Rococo painter was Antoine Watteau, whose usually small canvases feature light colors and elegant figures in ornate costumes moving gracefully through lush landscapes. His *fête galante* paintings depict the outdoor amusements of French high society.

▌ Watteau's successors included François Boucher and Jean-Honoré Fragonard, who carried on the Rococo style late into the 18th century. In Italy, Giambattista Tiepolo adapted the Rococo manner to huge ceiling frescoes in the Baroque tradition.

Watteau, *Pilgrimage to Cythera*, 1717

THE ENLIGHTENMENT

▌ By the end of the 18th century, revolutions had overthrown the monarchy in France and achieved independence for the British colonies in America. A major factor was the Enlightenment, a new way of thinking critically about the world independently of religion and tradition.

▌ The Enlightenment promoted scientific questioning of all assertions and embraced the doctrine of progress. The first modern encyclopedias appeared during the 18th century. The Industrial Revolution began in England in the 1740s. Engineers and architects developed new building materials. Iron was first used in bridge construction at Coalbrookdale, England, in 1776.

▌ The Enlightenment also made knowledge of ancient Rome imperative for the cultured elite, and Europeans and Americans in large numbers undertook a Grand Tour of Italy. Among the most popular souvenirs of the Grand Tour were Antonio Canaletto's *vedute* of Venice rendered in precise Renaissance perspective with the aid of a camera obscura.

▌ Rejecting the idea of progress, Rousseau, one of the leading French *philosophes,* argued for a return to natural values and exalted the simple, honest life of peasants. His ideas had a profound impact on artists such as Jean-Baptiste-Siméon Chardin and Jean-Baptiste Greuze, who painted sentimental narratives about rural families.

▌ The taste for naturalism also led to the popularity of portrait paintings set against landscape backgrounds, a specialty of Thomas Gainsborough, among others, and to a reawakening of an interest in realism. Benjamin West represented the protagonists in his history paintings wearing contemporary costumes.

Canaletto, *Riva degli Schiavoni, Venice,* ca. 1735–1740

Greuze, *Village Bride,* 1761

NEOCLASSICISM

▌ The Enlightenment revival of interest in Greece and Rome, which spurred systematic excavations at Herculaneum and Pompeii, also gave rise in the late 18th century to the artistic movement known as Neoclassicism, which incorporated the subjects and styles of ancient art.

▌ One pioneer of the new style was Angelica Kauffmann, who often chose subjects drawn from Roman history for her paintings. Jacques-Louis David, who exalted classical art as "the imitation of nature in her most beautiful and perfect form," also favored ancient Roman themes. Painted on the eve of the French Revolution, *Oath of the Horatii,* set in a severe classical hall, served as an example of patriotism and sacrifice.

▌ The Neoclassical style also became the rage in interior decoration, fashion, and architecture. Roman and Italian Renaissance structures inspired Jacques-Germain Soufflot's Panthéon in Paris and Richard Boyle's Chiswick House near London. A Greek temple in Athens was the model for James Stuart's Doric portico in Worcestershire.

▌ In the United States, Thomas Jefferson adopted the Neoclassical style in his designs for Monticello, the Virginia Capitol, and the University of Virginia. He championed Neoclassicism as the official architectural style of the new American republic because it represented for him idealism, patriotism, and civic virtue.

David, *Oath of the Horatii,* 1784

Jefferson, Monticello, Charlottesville, 1770–1806

1 in.

30-1 Nadar, *Eugène Delacroix*, ca. 1855. Modern print, $8\frac{1}{2}'' \times 6\frac{2}{3}''$, from the original negative. Bibliothèque Nationale, Paris.

Eugène Delacroix, the great Romantic painter, was one of many 19th-century artists intrigued by how photography presented reality. Here, he sat for Nadar, one of the earliest portrait photographers.

EUROPE AND AMERICA, 1800 TO 1870

The revolution of 1789 initiated a new era in France, but the overthrow of the monarchy also opened the door for Corsican-born Napoleon Bonaparte (1769–1821) to exploit the resulting disarray and establish a different kind of monarchy with himself at its head. In 1799, after serving in various French army commands, including leading major campaigns in Italy and Egypt, Napoleon became first consul of the French Republic, a title with clear and intentional links to the ancient Roman Republic (see Chapter 10). During the next 15 years, the ambitious general gained control of almost all of continental Europe in name or through alliances (MAP 30-1). In May 1804, for example, he became king of Italy. Later that year, the pope journeyed to Paris for Napoleon's coronation as Emperor of the French (FIG. 30-2). But in 1812, Napoleon launched a disastrous invasion of Russia that ended in retreat, and in 1815 he suffered a devastating loss at the hands of the British at Waterloo in present-day Belgium. Forced to abdicate the imperial throne, Napoleon went into exile on the island of Saint Helena in the South Atlantic, dying there six years later.

Following Napoleon's exile, the political geography of Europe changed dramatically (MAP 30-2), but in many ways the more significant changes during the first half of the 19th century were technological and economic. The Industrial Revolution caused a population boom in European cities, and railroads spread to many parts of the Continent, facilitating the transportation of both goods and people. During this period, the arts also underwent important changes. The century opened with Neoclassicism still supreme, but by 1870 Romanticism and Realism in turn had captured the imagination of artists and public alike. New construction techniques had a major impact on architectural design, and the invention of photography revolutionized picture making of all kinds.

ART UNDER NAPOLEON

At the fall of the French revolutionary Maximilien Robespierre (1758–1794) and his party in 1794, Jacques-Louis David, who had aligned himself personally and through his work with the revolutionary forces (see Chapter 29), barely escaped with his life. He stood trial and went to prison. After his release in

MAP 30-1
The Napoleonic
Empire in 1815.

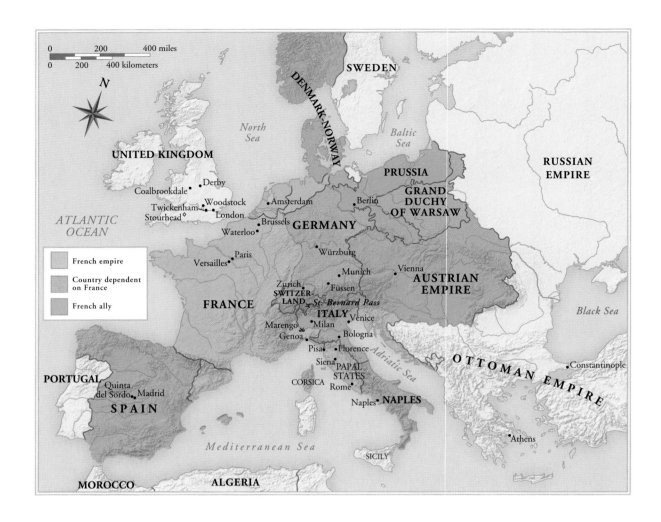

MAP 30-2
Europe around 1850.

30-2 Jacques-Louis David, *Coronation of Napoleon*, 1805–1808. Oil on canvas, 20′ 4½″ × 32′ 1¾″. Louvre, Paris.

As First Painter of the Empire, David recorded Napoleon at his December 1804 coronation crowning his wife with the pope as witness, thus underscoring the authority of the state over the church.

2A David, *Napoleon crossing Saint-Bernard,* 1800–1801.

1795, he worked hard to resurrect his career. When Napoleon Bonaparte approached David in 1804 and offered him the position of First Painter of the Empire, David seized the opportunity. It was not just the artist's personal skill but Neoclassicism in general that appealed to Napoleon. The emperor embraced all links with the classical past as symbolic sources of authority. Classical associations, particularly connections to the Roman Empire, served Napoleon well, since he aspired to rule an empire that might one day rival ancient Rome's.

CORONATION OF NAPOLEON One of the major paintings David produced for Napoleon was *Coronation of Napoleon* (FIG. **30-2**), a monumental painting (20 by 32 feet) that documented the pomp and pageantry of the new emperor's coronation in December 1804. Napoleon was well aware of the power of art for constructing a public image and of David's ability to produce inspiring patriotic images. To a large extent, David adhered to historical fact regarding the coronation, duly recording the appearance of the interior of Paris's Notre-Dame Cathedral as Napoleon's architects, Charles Percier (1764–1838) and Pierre-François-Léonard Fontaine (1762–1853), had decorated it for the occasion. David also faithfully portrayed those in attendance. In addition to Napoleon, his wife Josephine (1763–1814; kneeling to receive her crown), and Pope Pius VII (r. 1800–1823; seated behind Napoleon), others present at the occasion and in the painting included Joseph (1768–1814) and Louis (1778–1846) Bonaparte, Napoleon's ministers, the retinues of the emperor and empress, and a representative group of the clergy, as well as David himself, seated among the rows of spectators in the balconies. Despite the

artist's apparent fidelity to historical fact, preliminary studies and drawings reveal that David made changes at Napoleon's request. For example, Napoleon insisted that the painter depict the pope with his hand raised in blessing. Further, Napoleon's mother appears prominently in the center background, yet she had refused to attend the coronation.

Although David had to incorporate numerous figures and lavish pageantry in his painting, he retained the structured composition central to the Neoclassical style. As in his *Oath of the Horatii* (FIG. **29-23**), David presented the action as if on a theater stage—which in this instance was literally the case, even if the stage Percier and Fontaine constructed was inside a church. In addition, as he did in his arrangement of the men and women in *Oath of the Horatii*, David conceptually divided the painting to reveal polarities. The pope, prelates, and priests representing the Catholic Church appear on the right, contrasting with members of Napoleon's imperial court on the left. The relationship between church and state was one of this period's most contentious issues. Napoleon's decision to crown himself, rather than to allow the pope to perform the coronation, as was traditional, reflected Napoleon's concern about the power relationship between church and state. For the painting commemorating the occasion, the emperor insisted that David depict the moment when, having already crowned himself, Napoleon places a crown on his wife's head, further underscoring his authority. Thus, although this painting represents an important visual document in the tradition of history painting, it is also a more complex statement about the changing politics in Napoleonic France.

30-2B Ingres, *Napoleon on His Throne,* 1806.

Napoleon constructed La Madeleine as a "temple of glory" for his armies. Based on ancient temples (FIG. 10-32) and Neoclassical in style, Vignon's design linked the Napoleonic and Roman empires.

LA MADELEINE Napoleon also embraced Neoclassical architecture as an ideal vehicle for expressing his imperial authority. For example, the emperor resumed construction of the church of La Madeleine (FIG. 30-3) in Paris, which had begun in 1764 but ceased in 1790. However, he converted the building to a "temple of glory" for France's imperial armies. The structure reverted again to a church after Napoleon's defeat and long before its completion in 1842. Designed by PIERRE VIGNON (1763–1828), the grandiose Napoleonic temple includes a high podium and broad flight of stairs leading to a deep porch in the front. These architectural features, coupled with the Corinthian columns, recall Roman temples in France, such as the Maison Carrée (FIG. 10-32) at Nîmes, making La Madeleine a symbolic link between the Napoleonic and Roman empires. Curiously, the building's classical shell surrounds an interior covered by a sequence of three domes, a feature found in Byzantine and Romanesque churches. It is as though Vignon clothed a traditional church in the costume of pagan Rome.

30-4A CANOVA, Cupid and Psyche, 1787–1793.

ANTONIO CANOVA Neoclassical sculpture also was in vogue under Napoleon. His favorite sculptor was ANTONIO CANOVA (1757–1822), who somewhat reluctantly left a successful career in Italy to settle in Paris and serve the emperor. Once in France, Canova became Napoleon's admirer and made numerous portraits, all in the Neoclassical style, of the emperor and his family. Perhaps the best known of these works is the marble portrait (FIG. 30-4) of Napoleon's sister, Pauline Borghese, as Venus. Initially, Canova had suggested depicting Borghese as Diana, goddess of the hunt. Pauline, however, demanded to be shown as Venus, the goddess of love. Thus, she appears reclining on a divan and gracefully holding the golden apple, the symbol of the goddess's triumph in the judgment of Paris. Canova clearly based his work on Greek statuary—the sensuous pose and seminude body recall Hellenistic works such as *Venus de Milo* (FIG. 5-83)—and the reclining figure has parallels on Roman sarcophagus lids (FIG. 10-61; compare FIG. 9-5).

30-4 ANTONIO CANOVA, *Pauline Borghese as Venus*, 1808. Marble, 6′ 7″ long. Galleria Borghese, Rome.

Canova was Napoleon's favorite sculptor. Here, the artist depicted the emperor's sister nude—at her request—as the Roman goddess of love in a marble statue inspired by classical models.

The French public never got to admire Canova's portrait, however. Napoleon had arranged the marriage of his sister to an heir of the noble Roman Borghese family. Once Pauline was in Rome, her behavior was less than dignified, and the public gossiped extensively about her affairs. Her insistence on being portrayed as the goddess of love reflected her self-perception. Due to his wife's questionable reputation, Prince Camillo Borghese (1775–1832), the work's official patron, kept the sculpture sequestered in the Villa Borghese in Rome, where it remains today. Borghese allowed relatively few people to see it (and then only by torchlight). Still, knowledge of the existence of the sculpture was widespread and increased the notoriety of both artist and subject.

ANTOINE-JEAN GROS, *Napoleon at the Pesthouse at Jaffa,* 1804. Oil on canvas, 17′ 5″ × 23′ 7″. Louvre, Paris.

Gros's huge painting glorifies Napoleon as possessing the miraculous power to heal and reflects David's compositional principles, but Gros's fascination with the exotic Near East presaged Romanticism.

1 ft.

DAVID'S STUDENTS Given Jacques-Louis David's stature and prominence as an artist in Napoleonic France, along with the popularity of Neoclassicism, it is not surprising that he attracted numerous students and developed an active and flourishing teaching studio. David gave practical instruction to and deeply influenced many important artists of the period. So strong was David's commitment to classicism that he encouraged all his students to learn Latin, the better to immerse themselves in and understand classical culture. David even initially demanded that his pupils select their subjects from Plutarch, the ancient author of *Lives of the Great Greeks and Romans* and a principal source of Neoclassical subject matter. Due to this thorough classical foundation, David's students produced work that at its core retains Neoclassical elements. Yet David was open-minded and far from authoritarian in his teaching, and he encouraged his students to find their own artistic identities. The work of three of David's pupils—Antoine-Jean Gros, Anne-Louis Girodet-Trioson, and Jean-Auguste-Dominique Ingres—represents a departure from the structured confines of Neoclassicism. These artists laid the foundation for the Romantic movement, discussed in detail later. They explored the realm of the exotic and the erotic, and often turned to fictional narratives for the subjects of their paintings, as Romantic artists also did.

GROS Like his teacher David, ANTOINE-JEAN GROS (1771–1835) was aware of the benefits that could accrue to artists whom the powerful favored. Following David's lead, Gros produced several paintings that contributed to the growing mythic status of Napoleon Bonaparte in the early 1800s. In *Napoleon at the Pesthouse at Jaffa* (FIG. 30-5), the artist, at Napoleon's request, recorded an incident during an outbreak of the bubonic plague that erupted in the course of the Near

Eastern campaigns of 1799. This fearsome disease struck Muslim and French forces alike, and in March 1799, Napoleon himself visited the pesthouse at Jaffa to quell the growing panic and hysteria. Gros depicted Napoleon's staff officers covering their noses against the stench of the place, whereas Napoleon, amid the dead and dying, is fearless and in control. He comforts those still alive, who are clearly awed by his presence and authority. Indeed, by depicting the French leader touching the sores of a plague victim, Gros implied that Napoleon possessed the miraculous power to heal. This exaltation of the French leader was necessary to counteract the negative publicity he was subject to at the time. Apparently, two months after his visit to the pesthouse, Napoleon ordered all plague-stricken French soldiers poisoned so as to relieve him of having to return them to Cairo or abandon them to the Turks. Some of the soldiers survived, and from their accounts highly critical stories about Napoleon began to circulate. Gros's painting was an attempt at damage control—to resurrect the event and rehabilitate Napoleon's compromised public image.

Gros structured his composition in a manner reminiscent of David's major paintings, with the horseshoe arches and Moorish arcades of the mosque courtyard providing a backdrop for the unfolding action. In addition, Gros's placement of Muslim doctors ministering to plague-stricken Muslims on the left contrasts them with Napoleon and his soldiers on the right, bathed in radiant light. David had used this polarized compositional scheme to great effect in works such as *Oath of the Horatii* (FIG. 29-23). However, Gros's fascination with the exoticism of the Near East, as is evident in his attention to the unique architecture, attire, and terrain, represented a departure from Neoclassicism. This interest in the exotic, along with the artist's emphasis on death, suffering, and an emotional rendering of the scene, foreshadowed prominent aspects of Romanticism.

Girodet's depiction of Native American lovers in the Louisiana wilderness appealed to the French public's fascination with what it perceived as the passion and primitivism of tribal life in the New World.

1 ft.

30-6A GIRODET-TRIOSON, *Jean-Baptiste Belley*, 1797.

GIRODET-TRIOSON Another of David's students, ANNE-LOUIS GIRODET-TRIOSON (1767–1824), also produced paintings that conjured images of exotic locales and cultures. He moved further into the domain of Romanticism with *Burial of Atala* (FIG. **30-6**), based on *The Genius of Christianity*, a novel by French writer François René de Chateaubriand (1768–1848). The section of the novel dealing with Atala appeared as an excerpt a year before the publication of the entire book in 1802. Both the excerpt and the novel were enormously successful, and as a result, Atala became almost a cult figure. The exoticism and eroticism integral to the narrative accounted in large part for the public's interest in *The Genius of Christianity*. Set in Louisiana, Chateaubriand's work focuses on two young Native Americans, Atala and Chactas. The two, from different tribes, fall in love and run away together through the wilderness. Erotic passion permeates the story, and Atala, sworn to lifelong virginity, finally commits suicide rather than break her oath. Girodet's painting depicts this tragedy. Atala's grief-stricken lover, Chactas, buries the heroine in the shadow of a cross. Assisting in the burial is a cloaked priest, whose presence is appropriate given Chateaubriand's emphasis on the revival of Christianity (and the Christianization of the New World) in his novel. Like Gros's depiction of the foreign Muslim world, Girodet's representation of American Indian lovers in the Louisiana wilderness appealed to the public's fascination (whetted by the Louisiana Purchase in 1803) with what it perceived as the passion and primitivism of Native American tribal life. *Burial of Atala* speaks here to emotions, rather than inviting philosophical meditation or revealing some grand order of nature and form. Unlike David's appeal in *Oath of the Horatii* (FIG. **29-23**) to feelings that manifest themselves in public action, the appeal here is to the viewer's private world of fantasy and emotion.

INGRES JEAN-AUGUSTE-DOMINIQUE INGRES (1780–1867) arrived at David's studio in the late 1790s after Girodet-Trioson had left to establish an independent career. Ingres's study there was to be short-

Inspired by *School of Athens* (FIG. **22-9**) by Ingres's favorite painter, Raphael, this monumental canvas is a Neoclassical celebration of Homer and other ancient worthies, Dante, and select French authors.

1 ft.

30-8 Jean-Auguste-Dominique Ingres, *Grande Odalisque*, 1814. Oil on canvas, 2′ 11 $\frac{7}{8}$″ × 5′ 4″. Louvre, Paris. ◼◀

The reclining female nude was a Greco-Roman subject, but Ingres converted his Neoclassical figure into an odalisque in a Turkish harem, consistent with the new Romantic taste for the exotic.

lived, however, as he soon broke with David on matters of style. This difference of opinion involved Ingres's embrace of what he believed to be a truer and purer Greek style than what David employed. The younger artist adopted flat and linear forms approximating those found in Greek vase painting (see Chapter 5). In many of his works, Ingres placed the figure in the foreground, much like a piece of low-relief sculpture.

Ingres exhibited his huge composition *Apotheosis of Homer* (FIG. 30-7) at the Salon of 1827 (see "Academic Salons," Chapter 31, page 823). The painting presented in a single statement the doctrines of ideal form and of Neoclassical taste, and generations of academic painters remained loyal to that style. Raphael's *School of Athens* (FIG. 22-9) served as the inspiration for *Apotheosis of Homer*. Enthroned before an Ionic temple, the epic poet Homer receives a crown from Fame or Victory. At the poet's feet are two statuesque women, who personify the *Iliad* and the *Odyssey,* the offspring of his imagination. Symmetrically grouped about him is a company of the "sovereign geniuses"—as Ingres called them—who expressed humanity's highest ideals in philosophy, poetry, music, and art. To Homer's left are the Greek poet Anacreon with his lyre, Phidias with his sculptor's hammer, the philosophers Plato and Socrates, and other ancient worthies. To his far right are the Roman poets Horace and Vergil, and two Italian greats: Dante and, conspicuously, Raphael, the painter Ingres most admired. Among the forward group on the painting's left side are Poussin (pointing) and Shakespeare (half concealed), and at the right are French writers Jean Baptiste Racine, Molière, Voltaire, and François de Salignac de la Mothe Fénelon. Ingres had planned a much larger and more inclusive group, but he never completed the project. For years he agonized over whom to choose for this select company of heroes in various humanistic disciplines.

GRANDE ODALISQUE As a true Neoclassical painter, Ingres condemned "modern" styles such as Romanticism. But despite his commitment to ideal form and careful compositional structure, Ingres also produced works that, like those of Gros and Girodet, his contemporaries saw as departures from Neoclassicism. One of those paintings was *Grande Odalisque* (FIG. 30-8). Ingres's subject, the reclining nude figure, followed the tradition of Giorgione and Titian (FIG. 22-40). The work also shows Ingres's admiration for Raphael in his borrowing of that master's type of female head (FIGS. 22-7 and 22-8). The figure's languid pose, small head and elongated limbs, and the generally cool color scheme reveal his debt to Parmigianino (FIG. 22-43) and the Italian Mannerists. However, by converting the figure to an *odalisque* (woman in a Turkish harem), the artist made a strong concession to the contemporary Romantic taste for the exotic.

This rather strange mixture of artistic allegiances—the combination of precise classical form and Romantic themes—prompted confusion, and when Ingres first exhibited *Grande Odalisque* in 1814, the painting drew acid criticism. Critics initially saw Ingres as a rebel in terms of both the form and content of his works. They did not cease their attacks until the mid-1820s, when another enemy of the official style, Eugène Delacroix, appeared on the scene. Then they suddenly perceived that Ingres's art, despite its innovations and deviations, still contained many elements that adhered to the official Neoclassicism—the taste for the ideal. Ingres soon led the academic forces in their battle against the "barbarism" of Delacroix, Théodore Géricault, and the Romantic movement. Gradually, Ingres warmed to the role his critics had cast for him, and he came to see himself as the conservator of good and true art, a protector of its principles against its would-be destroyers.

30-9 Henry Fuseli, *The Nightmare*, 1781. Oil on canvas, 3′ 3$\frac{3}{4}$″ × 4′ 1$\frac{1}{2}$″. Detroit Institute of the Arts (Founders Society Purchase with funds from Mr. and Mrs. Bert L. Smokler and Mr. and Mrs. Lawrence A. Fleishman).

The transition from Neoclassicism to Romanticism marked a shift in emphasis from reason to feeling. Fuseli was among the first painters to depict the dark terrain of the human subconscious.

ROMANTICISM

Whereas Neoclassicism's rationality reinforced Enlightenment thought (see Chapter 29), particularly Voltaire's views, Rousseau's ideas contributed to the rise of *Romanticism*. Rousseau's exclamation "Man is born free, but is everywhere in chains!"—the opening line of his *Social Contract* (1762)—summarizes a fundamental Romantic premise. Romanticism emerged from a desire for freedom—not only political freedom but also freedom of thought, of feeling, of action, of worship, of speech, and of taste. Romantics asserted that freedom was the right and property of all. They believed the path to freedom was through imagination rather than reason and functioned through feeling rather than through thinking.

The allure of the Romantic spirit grew dramatically during the late 18th century. The term originated toward the end of that century among German literary critics, who aimed to distinguish peculiarly "modern" traits from the Neoclassical traits that already had displaced Baroque and Rococo design elements. Consequently, many scholars refer to Romanticism as a phenomenon that began around 1750 and ended about 1850, but most use the term more narrowly to denote a movement that flourished from about 1800 to 1840, between Neoclassicism and Realism.

Roots of Romanticism

The transition from Neoclassicism to Romanticism represented a shift in emphasis from reason to feeling, from calculation to intuition, and from objective nature to subjective emotion. Among Romanticism's manifestations were the interests in the medieval period and in the sublime. For people living in the 18th century, the Middle Ages were the "dark ages," a time of barbarism, superstition, dark mystery, and miracle. The Romantic imagination stretched its perception of the Middle Ages into all the worlds of fantasy open to it, including the ghoulish, the infernal, the terrible, the nightmarish, the grotesque, the sadistic, and all the imagery that emerges from the chamber of horrors when reason sleeps. Related to the imaginative sensibility was the period's notion of the sublime. Among the individuals most involved in studying the sublime was the British politician and philosopher Edmund Burke (1729–1797). In his 1757 publication *A Philosophical Enquiry into the Origins of Our Ideas of the Sublime and Beautiful*, Burke articulated his definition of the sublime—feelings of awe mixed with terror. Burke observed that pain or fear evoked the most intense human emotions and that these emotions could also be thrilling. Thus, raging rivers and great storms at sea could be sublime to their viewers. Accompanying this taste for

1 in.

30-10 William Blake, *Ancient of Days,* frontispiece of *Europe: A Prophecy,* 1794. Metal relief etching, hand colored, $9\frac{1}{2}'' \times 6\frac{3}{4}''$. Pierpont Morgan Library, New York.

Although art historians classify Blake as a Romantic artist, he incorporated classical references in his works. Here, ideal classical anatomy merges with the inner dark dreams of Romanticism.

to depict the dark terrain of the human subconscious that became fertile ground for later artists to sow.

WILLIAM BLAKE In their images of the sublime and the terrible, Romantic artists often combined Baroque dynamism with naturalistic details in their quest for grippingly moving visions. These preferences became the mainstay of Romantic art and contrasted with the more intellectual, rational Neoclassical themes and presentations. The two were not mutually exclusive, however. Gros, Girodet-Trioson, and Ingres effectively integrated elements of Neoclassicism with Romanticism. So too did the visionary English poet, painter, and engraver WILLIAM BLAKE (1757–1827). Blake greatly admired ancient Greek art because it exemplified for him the mathematical and thus the eternal, and his work often incorporated classical references. Yet Blake did not align himself with prominent Enlightenment figures. Like many other Romantic artists, he also found the art of the Middle Ages appealing. Blake derived the inspiration for many of his paintings and poems from his dreams. The importance he attached to these nocturnal experiences led him to believe that the rationalist search for material explanations of the world stifled the spiritual side of human nature. He also believed that the stringent rules of behavior imposed by orthodox religions killed the individual's creative impulse.

the sublime was the taste for the fantastic, the occult, and the macabre—for the adventures of the soul voyaging into the dangerous reaches of consciousness.

HENRY FUSELI The concept of the nightmare is the subject of a 1781 painting (FIG. 30-9) by HENRY FUSELI (1741–1825). Swiss by birth, Fuseli settled in England and eventually became a member of the Royal Academy and an instructor there. Largely self-taught, he contrived a distinctive manner to express the fantasies of his vivid imagination. Fuseli specialized in night moods of horror and in dark fantasies—in the demonic, in the macabre, and often in the sadistic. In *The Nightmare,* a beautiful young woman lies asleep, draped across the bed with her limp arm dangling over the side. An *incubus,* a demon believed in medieval times to prey, often sexually, on sleeping women, squats ominously on her body. In the background, a ghostly horse with flaming eyes bursts into the scene from beyond the curtain. Despite the temptation to see the painting's title as a pun because of this horse, the word "nightmare" actually derives from "night" and "Mara." Mara was a spirit in Northern European mythology that people thought tormented and suffocated sleepers. Fuseli was among the first to attempt

Blake's vision of the Almighty in *Ancient of Days* (FIG. 30-10) combines his ideas and interests in a highly individual way. For Blake, this figure united the concept of the Creator with that of wisdom as a part of God. He chose *Ancient of Days* as the frontispiece for his book *Europe: A Prophecy,* and juxtaposed it with a quotation ("When he set a compass upon the face of the deep") from Proverbs 8:27 in the Old Testament. The speaker in that Bible chapter is Wisdom, who tells the reader how she was with the Lord through all the time of the Creation (Prov. 8:22–23, 27–30). Energy fills Blake's composition. The Almighty leans forward from a fiery orb, peering toward earth and unleashing power through his outstretched left arm into twin rays of light. These emerge between his spread fingers as might an architect's measuring instrument. A strong wind surges through his thick hair and beard. Only the strength of his Michelangelesque physique keeps him firmly planted on his heavenly perch. Here, ideal classical anatomy merges with the inner dark dreams of Romanticism.

Spain and France

From its roots in the work of Fuseli, Blake, and other late-18th-century artists, Romanticism gradually displaced Neoclassicism as the dominant painting style of the first half of the 19th century. Romantic artists, including Francisco Goya in Spain and Théodore Géricault and Eugène Delacroix in France, explored the exotic, erotic, and fantastic in their paintings.

FRANCISCO GOYA The Spaniard Francisco José de Goya y Lucientes (1746–1828) was David's contemporary, but their work has little in common. Goya did not arrive at his general dismissal of Neoclassicism without considerable thought about the Enlightenment and the Neoclassical penchant for rationality and order. This reflection emerges in such works as *The Sleep of Reason Produces Monsters* (FIG. 30-11) from a series titled *Los Caprichos* (*The Caprices*). In this print, Goya depicted himself asleep, slumped onto a table or writing stand, while threatening creatures converge on him. Seemingly poised to attack the artist are owls (symbols of folly) and bats (symbols of ignorance). The viewer might read this as a portrayal of what emerges when reason is suppressed and, therefore, as an espousal of Enlightenment ideals. However, it also can be interpreted as Goya's commitment to the creative process and the Romantic spirit—the unleashing of imagination, emotions, and even nightmares.

FAMILY OF CHARLES IV The emotional art Goya produced during his long career stands as testimony not only to the allure of the Romantic vision but also to the turmoil in Spain and to the conflicts in Goya's life. His art is multifaceted in character, however, and many of his works deal with traditional religious subjects. Others are royal portraits painted after 1786, when Goya became Pintor del Rey (Painter to the King). Charles IV (r. 1788–1808) promoted him to First Court Painter in 1799. In his official capacity, Goya produced paintings very different in character from his *Caprichos*, such as *Family of Charles IV* (FIG. 30-12). Goya greatly admired the achievements of his predecessor Diego Velázquez, and Velázquez's *Las Meninas* (FIG. 24-30) was the inspiration for this image of the king and his queen, Maria Luisa, surrounded by their children. As in *Las Meninas*, the royal family appears facing the viewer in an interior space while the artist included himself on the left, dimly visible, in the act of painting on a large canvas. Goya's portrait of the royal family has been subjected to intense scholarly scrutiny, resulting in a variety of interpretations. Some scholars see this painting as a naturalistic depiction of Spanish royalty. Others believe it to be a pointed commentary in a time of Spanish turmoil. It is clear that his patrons authorized the painting's basic elements—the king and his family, their attire, and Goya's inclusion. Little evidence exists as to how the royal family reacted to this painting. Although some scholars have argued that they disliked the portrait, others have suggested that the painting confirmed the Spanish monarchy's continuing presence and strength and thus elicited a positive response from the patrons.

As dissatisfaction with the rule of Charles IV and Maria Luisa increased, the political situation grew more tenuous. The Spanish people eventually threw their support behind Ferdinand VII, son of the royal couple, in the hope that he would initiate reform. To overthrow his father and mother, Ferdinand VII enlisted the aid of Napoleon Bonaparte, who possessed uncontested authority and military expertise at that time. Napoleon had designs on the Spanish throne and thus willingly sent French troops to Spain. Not surprisingly, as soon as he ousted Charles IV, Napoleon revealed his plan to rule Spain himself by installing his brother Joseph Bonaparte (r. 1808–1813) on the Spanish throne.

30-11 Francisco Goya, *The Sleep of Reason Produces Monsters,* from *Los Caprichos,* ca. 1798. Etching and aquatint, $8\frac{1}{2}'' \times 5\frac{7}{8}''$. Metropolitan Museum of Art, New York (gift of M. Knoedler & Co., 1918).

In this print, Goya depicted himself asleep while threatening creatures converge on him, revealing his commitment to the Romantic spirit—the unleashing of imagination, emotions, and nightmares.

THIRD OF MAY, 1808 The Spanish people, finally recognizing the French as invaders, sought a way to expel the foreign troops. On May 2, 1808, in frustration, the Spanish attacked Napoleon's soldiers in a chaotic and violent clash. In retaliation and as a show of force, the French responded the next day by executing numerous Spanish citizens. This tragic event is the subject of Goya's most famous painting, *Third of May, 1808* (FIG. 30-13). In emotional fashion, Goya depicted the anonymous murderous wall of French soldiers ruthlessly executing the unarmed and terrified Spanish peasants. The artist encouraged empathy for the Spanish by portraying horrified expressions and anguish on their faces, endowing them with a humanity absent from the firing squad. Moreover, the peasant about to be shot throws his arms out in a cruciform gesture reminiscent of Christ's position on the cross. Goya enhanced the emotional drama of this tragic event through his stark use of darks and lights and by extending the time frame depicted. Although Goya captured the specific moment when one man is about to be executed, he also

30-12 Francisco Goya, *Family of Charles IV,* 1800. Oil on canvas, 9′ 2″ × 11′. Museo del Prado, Madrid.

Goya painted the family of the Spanish king Charles IV while serving as Pintor del Rey. Goya's model for the portrait was Velázquez's *Las Meninas* (FIG. 24-30), which also included the artist in the painting.

1 ft.

30-13 Francisco Goya, *Third of May, 1808,* 1814–1815. Oil on canvas, 8′ 9″ × 13′ 4″. Museo del Prado, Madrid.

Goya encouraged empathy for the massacred Spanish peasants by portraying horrified expressions and anguish on their faces, endowing them with a humanity lacking in the French firing squad.

1 ft.

depicted the bloody bodies of others already lying dead on the ground. Still others have been herded together to be shot in a few moments. Its depiction of the resistance and patriotism of the Spanish people notwithstanding, *Third of May, 1808*, was a royal commission, painted in 1814 for Ferdinand VII (r. 1813–1833), who had reclaimed the throne after the ouster of the French.

SATURN Over time, Goya became increasingly disillusioned and pessimistic, and his declining health only contributed to this state of mind. Among his later works are the Black Paintings, frescoes he painted on the walls of his farmhouse in Quinta del Sordo, outside Madrid. Because Goya created these works solely on his terms and for his private viewing, they provide great insight into the artist's outlook, which is terrifying and disturbing. *Saturn Devouring One of His Children* (FIG. **30-14**) depicts the raw carnage and violence of Saturn (the Greek god Kronos; see "The Gods and Goddesses of Mount Olympus," Chapter 5, page 101, or page xxiii in Volume II), wild-eyed and monstrous, as he consumes one of his children. Because of the similarity of Kronos and *khronos* (Greek for "time"), Saturn has come to be associated with time. This has led some scholars to interpret Goya's painting as an expression of the artist's despair over the passage of time. Despite the simplicity of the image, it conveys a wildness, boldness, and brutality that cannot help but evoke an elemental response from any viewer. Goya's work, rooted both in personal and national history, presents darkly emotional images well in keeping with Romanticism.

30-15A
GÉRICAULT,
*Charging
Chasseur,* 1812.

THÉODORE GÉRICAULT In France one of the artists most closely associated with the Romantic movement was THÉODORE GÉRICAULT (1791–1824), who studied with an admirer of David, P. N. Guérin (1774–1833). Although Géricault retained an interest in the heroic and the epic and was well trained in classical drawing, he chafed at the rigidity of the Neoclassical style, instead producing works that captivate the viewer with their drama, visual complexity, and emotional force.

Géricault's most ambitious project was a gigantic canvas (approximately 16 by 23 feet) titled *Raft of the Medusa* (FIG. **30-15**). In this depiction of a historical event, the artist abandoned the idealism of Neoclassicism and instead invoked the theatricality of Romanticism. The painting's subject is a shipwreck that occurred in 1816 off the African coast. The French frigate *Medusa* ran aground on a reef due to the incompetence of the captain, a political appointee. In an attempt to survive, 150 remaining passengers built a makeshift raft from pieces of the disintegrating ship. The raft drifted for 12 days, and the number of survivors dwindled to 15. Finally, a ship spotted the raft and rescued the emaciated survivors. This horrendous event was political dynamite once it became public knowledge.

In *Raft of the Medusa,* which Géricault took eight months to complete, the artist sought to capture the horror, chaos, and emotion of the tragedy yet invoke the grandeur and impact of large-scale history painting. Géricault went to great lengths to ensure the accuracy of his representation. He visited hospitals and morgues to examine corpses, interviewed the survivors, and had a model of the raft constructed in his studio. In the painting, the few despairing survivors summon what little strength they have left to flag down the passing ship far on the horizon. Géricault departed from the straightforward organization of Neoclassical compositions and instead presented a jumble of writhing bodies. He arranged the survivors and several corpses in a powerful X-shaped composition, and piled one body on another in every attitude of suffering, despair, and death (recalling the plague-stricken bodies in Gros's *Napoleon at Jaffa,* FIG. **30-5**). One light-filled diagonal axis stretches from bodies

1 ft.

30-14 FRANCISCO GOYA, *Saturn Devouring One of His Children,* 1819–1823. Detached fresco mounted on canvas, 4' 9$\frac{1}{8}$" × 2' 8$\frac{5}{8}$". Museo del Prado, Madrid.

This disturbing fresco in Goya's farmhouse uses a mythological tale perhaps to express the aging artist's despair over the passage of time. Saturn's Greek name Kronos is similar to the Greek word for time.

at the lower left up to the black man raised on his comrades' shoulders and waving a piece of cloth toward the horizon. The cross axis descends from the storm clouds and the dark, billowing sail at the upper left to the shadowed upper torso of the body trailing in the open sea. Géricault's decision to place the raft at a diagonal so that a corner juts outward further compels viewers' participation in this scene. Indeed, it seems as though some of the corpses are sliding off the raft into the viewing space. The subdued palette and prominent shadows lend an ominous pall to the scene.

Géricault also took this opportunity to insert a comment on the practice of slavery. The artist was a member of an abolitionist group that sought ways to end the slave trade in the colonies. Given his

30-15 Théodore Géricault, *Raft of the Medusa*, 1818–1819. Oil on canvas, 16′ 1″ × 23′ 6″. Louvre, Paris.

In this gigantic history painting, Géricault rejected Neoclassical compositional principles and, in the Romantic spirit, presented a jumble of writhing bodies in every attitude of suffering, despair, and death.

antipathy to slavery, it is appropriate that Géricault placed Jean Charles, a black soldier and one of the few survivors, at the top of the pyramidal heap of bodies.

INSANE WOMAN Mental aberration and irrational states of mind could not fail to interest the rebels against Enlightenment rationality. Géricault, like many of his contemporaries, examined the influence of mental states on the human face and believed, as others did, that a face accurately revealed character, especially in madness and at the moment of death. He made many studies of the inmates of hospitals and institutions for the criminally insane, and he studied the severed heads of guillotine victims. Scientific and artistic curiosity often accompanied the morbidity of the Romantic interest in derangement and death. Géricault's *Insane Woman* (FIG. **30-16**)—her mouth tense, her eyes red-rimmed with suffering—is one of several of his portraits of the insane that have a peculiar hypnotic power. These portraits present the psychic facts with astonishing authenticity, especially in contrast to earlier idealized commissioned portraiture.

30-16 Théodore Géricault, *Insane Woman*, 1822–1823. Oil on canvas, 2′ 4″ × 1′ 9″. Musée des Beaux-Arts, Lyons.

The insane and the influence of aberrant states of mind on the appearance of the human face fascinated Géricault and other Romantic artists, who rebelled against Enlightenment rationality.

The Romantic Spirit in Art, Music, and Literature

The appeal of Romanticism, with its emphasis on freedom and feeling, extended well beyond the realm of the visual arts. The imagination and vision that characterized Romantic paintings and sculptures were equally moving and riveting in musical or written form. In European music, literature, and poetry, the Romantic spirit was a dominant presence during the late 18th and early 19th centuries. These artistic endeavors rejected classicism's structured order in favor of the emotive and expressive. In music, the compositions of Franz Schubert (1797–1828), Franz Liszt (1811–1886), Frédéric Chopin (1810–1849), and Johannes Brahms (1833–1897) all emphasized the melodic or lyrical. For these composers, music had the power to express the unspeakable and to communicate the subtlest and most powerful human emotions.

In literature, Romantic poets such as John Keats (1795–1821), William Wordsworth (1770–1850), and Samuel Taylor Coleridge (1772–1834) published volumes of poetry that serve as manifestations of the Romantic interest in lyrical drama. *Ozymandias*, by Percy Bysshe Shelley (1792–1822), speaks of faraway, exotic locales. The setting of Lord Byron's *Sardanapalus* is the ancient Assyrian Empire (see Chapter 2). Byron's poem conjures images of eroticism and fury unleashed—images that appear in Delacroix's painting *Death of Sardanapalus* (FIG. 30-17). One of the best examples of the Romantic spirit is the engrossing novel *Frankenstein,* written in 1818 by Shelley's wife, Mary Wollstonecraft Shelley (1797–1851). This tale of a monstrous creature run amok remains popular to the present day. As was true of many Romantic artworks, the novel not only embraced the emotional but also rejected the rationalism that underlay Enlightenment thought. Dr. Frankenstein's monster was a product of science, and the novel is an indictment of the tenacious belief in science that Enlightenment thinkers such as Voltaire promoted. *Frankenstein* served as a cautionary tale of the havoc that could result from unrestrained scientific experimentation and from the arrogance of scientists like Dr. Frankenstein.

30-17 Eugène Delacroix, *Death of Sardanapalus,* 1827. Oil on canvas, 12′ 1½″ × 16′ 2⅞″. Louvre, Paris. ▶

Inspired by Byron's 1821 poem, Delacroix painted the Romantic spectacle of an Assyrian king on his funeral pyre. The richly colored and emotionally charged canvas is filled with exotic figures.

1 ft.

EUGÈNE DELACROIX Art historians often present the history of painting during the first half of the 19th century as a contest between two major artists—Ingres, the Neoclassical draftsman, and EUGÈNE DELACROIX (1798–1863), the Romantic colorist. Their dialogue recalls the quarrel between the Poussinistes and the Rubénistes at the end of the 17th century and into the 18th (see Chapter 29). The Poussinistes were conservative defenders of academism who regarded drawing as superior to color, whereas the Rubénistes proclaimed the importance of color over line (line quality being more intellectual and thus more restrictive than color). Delacroix's works were products of his view that the artist's powers of imagination would in turn capture and inflame the viewer's imagination. Literature of imaginative power served Delacroix (and many of his contemporaries) as a useful source of subject matter. Théophile Gautier (1811–1872), the prominent Romantic critic and novelist, recalled:

> In those days painting and poetry fraternized. The artists read the poets, and the poets visited the artists. We found Shakespeare, Dante, Goethe, Lord Byron and Walter Scott in the studio as well as in the study. There were as many splashes of color as there were blots of ink in the margins of those beautiful books which we endlessly perused. Imagination, already excited, was further fired by reading those foreign works, so rich in color, so free and powerful in fantasy.[1]

DEATH OF SARDANAPALUS Delacroix's *Death of Sardanapalus* (FIG. 30-17) is grand Romantic pictorial drama. Although inspired by the 1821 narrative poem *Sardanapalus* by Lord Byron (1788–1824), the painting does not illustrate that text (see "The Romantic Spirit in Art, Music, and Literature," page 790). Instead, Delacroix depicted the last hour of the Assyrian king (who had just received news of his armies' defeat and the enemies' entry into his city) in a much more tempestuous and crowded setting than Byron described. Here, orgiastic destruction replaces the sacrificial suicide found in the poem. In the painting, the king reclines on his funeral pyre, soon to be set alight, and gloomily watches the destruction of all of his most precious possessions—his women, slaves, horses, and treasure. Sardanapalus's favorite concubine throws herself on the bed, determined to go up in flames with her master. The king presides like a genius of evil over the tragic scene. Most conspicuous are the tortured and dying bodies of the harem women. In the foreground, a muscular slave plunges his knife into the neck of one woman. Delacroix filled this awful spectacle of suffering and death with the most daringly difficult and tortuous poses, and chose the richest intensities of hue. With its exotic and erotic overtones, *Death of Sardanapalus* tapped into the Romantic fantasies of 19th-century viewers.

LIBERTY LEADING THE PEOPLE Although *Death of Sardanapalus* is a seventh-century BCE drama, Delacroix, like Géricault, also turned to current events, particularly tragic or sensational ones, for his subject matter. For example, he produced several images based on the Greek war for independence (1821–1829). Certainly, the French perception of the Greeks locked in a brutal struggle for freedom from the cruel and exotic Ottoman Turks generated great interest in Romantic circles. Closer to home, Delacroix captured the passion and energy of the 1830 revolution in France in his painting *Liberty Leading the People* (FIG. 30-18). Based on the Parisian uprising against Charles X (r. 1824–1830) at the end of July 1830, it depicts the allegorical personification of Liberty defiantly thrusting forth the republic's tricolor banner as she urges the masses to fight on. The scarlet Phrygian cap (the symbol of a freed slave in antiquity) she wears reinforces the urgency of this struggle. Arrayed around Liberty are bold Parisian types—the street boy brandishing his pistols, the menacing worker with a cutlass, and the intellectual dandy in top hat with sawed-off musket. As in Géricault's *Raft of the Medusa* (FIG. 30-15), dead bodies lie all around. In the background, the towers of Notre-Dame rise through the smoke and haze. The painter's inclusion of this recognizable Parisian landmark announces the specificity of locale and event, balancing contemporary historical fact with poetic allegory.

30-18A DELACROIX, *Massacre at Chios,* 1822–1824.

30-18 EUGÈNE DELACROIX, *Liberty Leading the People,* 1830. Oil on canvas, 8′ 6″ × 10′ 8″. Louvre, Paris.

Balancing contemporaneous historical fact with poetic allegory, Delacroix captured the passion and energy of the 1830 revolution in this painting of Liberty leading the Parisian uprising against Charles X.

1 ft.

Delacroix in Morocco

Romantic painters often depicted exotic faraway places they had never seen, but Eugène Delacroix journeyed to Morocco in 1832 and discovered in the sun-drenched landscape—and in the hardy and colorful Moroccans dressed in robes reminiscent of the Roman toga—new insights into a culture built on proud virtues. He found there a culture more classical than anything European Neoclassicism could conceive. In a letter to his friend Fréderic Villot dated February 29, 1832, he wrote:

> This place is made for painters. . . . [B]eauty abounds here; not the over-praised beauty of fashionable paintings. The heroes of David and Co. with their rose-pink limbs would cut a sorry figure beside these children of the sun, who moreover wear the dress of classical antiquity with a nobler air, I dare assert.*

In a second letter, written June 4, 1832, he reported to Auguste Jal:

> You have seen Algiers and you can imagine what the natives of these regions are like. Here there is something even simpler and more primitive; there is less of the Turkish alloy; I have Romans and Greeks on my doorstep: it makes me laugh heartily at David's Greeks, apart, of course, from his sublime skill as a painter. I know now what they were really like; . . . If painting schools persist in [depicting classical subjects], I am convinced, and you will agree with me, that they would gain far more from being shipped off as cabin boys on the first boat bound for the Barbary coast than from

spending any more time wearing out the classical soil of Rome. Rome is no longer to be found in Rome.†

The gallantry, valor, and fierce love of liberty of the Moroccans made them, in Delacroix's eyes, unspoiled heroes uncontaminated by European decadence. The Moroccan journey renewed Delacroix's Romantic conviction that beauty exists in the fierceness of nature, natural processes, and natural beings, especially animals. After Morocco, more and more of Delacroix's subjects involved combats between beasts and between beasts and men. He painted snarling tangles of lions and tigers, battles between horses, and clashes of Muslims with great cats in swirling hunting scenes using compositions reminiscent of those of Rubens (FIG. I-13), as in his 1854 painting *Tiger Hunt* (FIG. 30-19), which clearly speaks to the Romantic interest in faraway lands and exotic cultures.

* Translated by Jean Stewart, in Charles Harrison, Paul Wood, and Jason Gaiger, eds., *Art in Theory 1815–1900: An Anthology of Changing Ideas* (Oxford: Blackwell, 1998), 87.
† Ibid., 88.

30-19 EUGÈNE DELACROIX, *Tiger Hunt*, 1854. Oil on canvas, 2′ 5″ × 3′. Musée d'Orsay, Paris.

Tiger Hunt reflects Delacroix's 1832 trip to Morocco, which had a lasting impact on his art. His paintings of men battling ferocious beasts are consistent with the Romantic interest in exotic places.

1 ft.

30-19A
DELACROIX, *Women of Algiers*, 1834.

TIGER HUNT An enormously influential event in Delacroix's life that affected his art in both subject and form was his visit to North Africa in 1832 (see "Delacroix in Morocco," above). Things he saw there shocked his imagination with fresh impressions that lasted throughout his life and resulted in paintings such as *Tiger Hunt* (FIG. 30-19), which he completed more than two decades after his trip.

Delacroix's African experience also further heightened his already considerable awareness of the expressive power of color and light. What Delacroix knew about color he passed on to later painters of the 19th century, particularly the Impressionists (see Chapter 31). He observed that pure colors are as rare in nature as lines and that color appears only in an infinitely varied scale of different tones, shadings, and reflections, which he tried to re-create in his paintings. He recorded his observations in his journal, which became for later painters and scholars a veritable handbook of pre-Impressionist color theory. Delacroix anticipated the later development of Impressionist color science. But that art-science had to await the discoveries by Michel Eugène Chevreul (1786–1889) and Hermann von Helmholtz (1821–1894) of the laws of light decomposition and the properties of complementary colors before the problems of color perception and juxtaposition in painting could be properly formulated (see "19th-Century Color Theory," Chapter 31, page 832). Nevertheless, Delacroix's observations were significant, and he advised other artists not to fuse their brush strokes, as those strokes would appear to fuse naturally from a distance.

No other painter of the time explored the domain of Romantic subject and mood as thoroughly and definitively as Delacroix. His technique was impetuous, improvisational, and instinctive, rather than deliberate, studious, and cold. It epitomized Romantic colorist painting, catching the impression quickly and developing it in the execution process. His contemporaries commented on how furiously Delacroix worked once he had an idea, keeping the whole painting progressing at once. The fury of his attack matched the fury of his imagination and his subjects.

10 ft.

30-20 François Rude, *Departure of the Volunteers of 1792* (*La Marseillaise*), Arc de Triomphe, Paris, France, 1833–1836. Limestone, 41′ 8″ high.

In this historical-allegorical sculpture, the figures wear classical costumes, but the violent motion, jagged contours, and densely packed masses relate more closely to the compositions of Romantic paintings.

FRANÇOIS RUDE The Romantic spirit pervaded all media during the early 19th century. Many sculptors, like the painters of the period, produced work that incorporated both Neoclassical and Romantic elements. The colossal sculptural group *Departure of the Volunteers of 1792* (FIG. **30-20**), also called *La Marseillaise*, is one example. The limestone relief by François Rude (1784–1855) decorates one of the gigantic piers of the Arc de Triomphe in Paris. This French landmark was commissioned by Napoleon in 1806 and designed by Jean François Thérèse Chalgrin (1739–1811) on the model of the triumphal arches of ancient Rome (FIGS. **10-39**, **10-47**, and **10-75**). Work on the arch stopped after Napoleon's defeat but resumed in 1833. Three years later, workers inserted Rude's group (and three similar ones by other sculptors) into the completed arch. The sculpture depicts the volunteers of 1792 departing to defend France's borders against the foreign enemies of the revolution. The Roman goddess of war, Bellona (who here personifies Liberty as well as the "Marseillaise," the revolutionary hymn that is now France's national anthem), soars above patriots of all ages, exhorting them forward with her thundering battle cry. The figures recall David's classically armored (FIG. **29-23**) or nude heroes, as do the rhetorical gestures of the wide-flung arms and the striding poses. Yet the violent motion, the jagged contours, and the densely packed, overlapping masses relate more closely to the compositional method of dramatic Romanticism, as found in Géricault (FIG. **30-15**) and Delacroix (FIG. **30-18**), whose Liberty is the spiritual sister of the allegorical figure in *La Marseillaise*. Rude's stone figure shares the same Phrygian cap, the badge of liberty, with Delacroix's earlier painted figure, but Rude's soldiers wear classical costumes or are heroically nude, whereas those in Delacroix's painting appear in modern Parisian dress. Both works are allegorical, but one looks to the past and the other to the present.

Landscape Painting

Landscape painting came into its own in the 19th century as a fully independent and respected genre. Briefly eclipsed at the century's beginning by the taste for ideal form, which favored figural composition and history, landscape painting flourished as leading painters made it their profession. Increasing tourism, which came courtesy of improved and expanded railway systems both in Europe (MAP **30-2**) and America, contributed to the popularity of landscape painting.

The notion of the picturesque became particularly resonant in the Romantic era. Already in the 18th century, artists had regarded the pleasurable, aesthetic mood that natural landscape inspired as making the landscape itself "picturesque"—that is, worthy of being painted. Rather than simply describe nature, Romantic poets and artists often used nature as allegory. In this manner, artists commented on spiritual, moral, historical, or philosophical issues. Landscape painting was a particularly effective vehicle for such commentary.

In the early 19th century, most Northern European (especially German) landscape painting to some degree expressed the Romantic view (first extolled by Rousseau) of nature as a "being" that included the totality of existence in organic unity and harmony. In nature— "the living garment of God," as German poet and dramatist Johann Wolfgang von Goethe (1749–1832) called it—artists found an ideal subject to express the Romantic theme of the soul unified with the natural world. As all nature was mysteriously permeated by "being," landscape artists had the task of interpreting the signs, symbols, and emblems of universal spirit disguised within visible material things. Artists no longer merely beheld a landscape but rather participated in its spirit, becoming translators of nature's transcendent meanings.

30-21 CASPAR DAVID FRIEDRICH, *Abbey in the Oak Forest*, 1810. Oil on canvas, 3' 7½" × 5' 7¼". Nationalgalerie, Staatliche Museen zu Berlin, Berlin. ◼◀

Friedrich was a master of the Romantic transcendental landscape. The reverential mood of this winter scene with the ruins of a Gothic church and cemetery demands the silence appropriate to sacred places.

1 ft.

30-21A FRIEDRICH, *Wanderer above a Sea of Mist*, 1817–1818.

CASPAR DAVID FRIEDRICH Among the first Northern European artists to depict the Romantic transcendental landscape was CASPAR DAVID FRIEDRICH (1774–1840). For Friedrich, landscapes were temples and his paintings were altarpieces. The reverential mood of his works demands from the viewer the silence appropriate to sacred places filled with a divine presence. *Abbey in the Oak Forest* (FIG. 30-21) serves as a solemn requiem. Under a winter sky, through the leafless oaks of a snow-covered cemetery, a funeral procession bears a coffin into the ruins of a Gothic church that Friedrich based on the remains of Eldana Abbey in Greifswald. The emblems of death are everywhere—the season's desolation, the leaning crosses and tombstones, the black of mourning that the grieving wear, the skeletal trees, the destruction time has wrought on the church. The painting is a meditation on human mortality. As Friedrich himself remarked: "Why, it has often occurred to me to ask myself, do I so frequently choose death, transience, and the grave as subjects for my paintings? One must submit oneself many times to death in order some day to attain life everlasting."[2] The artist's sharp-focused rendering of details demonstrates his keen perception of everything in the physical environment relevant to his message. Friedrich's work balances inner and outer experience. "The artist," he wrote, "should not only paint what he sees before him, but also what he sees within him. If he does not see anything within him, he should give up painting what he sees before him."[3] Although Friedrich's works may not have the theatrical energy of the paintings of Géricault or Delacroix, a resonant and deep emotion pervades them.

JOHN CONSTABLE One of the most momentous developments in Western history—the Industrial Revolution—influenced the evolution of Romantic landscape painting in England. Although discussion of the Industrial Revolution invariably focuses on technological advances, factory development, and growth of urban centers, its effect on the countryside and the land itself was no less severe. The detrimental economic impact industrialization had on prices for agrarian products produced significant unrest in the English countryside. In particular, increasing numbers of displaced farmers could no longer afford to farm their small land plots.

JOHN CONSTABLE (1776–1837) addressed the agrarian situation in his landscape paintings. *The Haywain* (FIG. 30-22) is representative of Constable's art and reveals much about his outlook. A small cottage sits on the left of this placid, picturesque scene of the countryside, and in the center foreground a man leads a horse and wagon across the stream. Billowy clouds float lazily across the sky. The muted greens and golds and the delicacy of Constable's brush strokes augment the scene's tranquility. The artist portrayed the oneness with nature that the Romantic poets sought. The relaxed figures are not observers but participants in the landscape's being.

Constable made countless studies from nature for each of his canvases, which helped him produce in his paintings the convincing sense of reality that won so much praise from his contemporaries. In his quest for the authentic landscape, Constable studied it as a meteorologist (which he was by avocation). His special gift was for capturing the texture that the atmosphere (the climate and the weather, which delicately veil what is seen) gave to landscape. Constable's use of tiny dabs of local color, stippled with white, created a sparkling shimmer of light and hue across the canvas surface—the vibration itself suggestive of movement and process.

The Haywain is also significant for precisely what it does not show—the civil unrest of the agrarian working class and the outbreaks of violence and arson that resulted. The people who populate Constable's landscapes blend into the scenes and are at one with nature. Rarely does the viewer see workers engaged in tedious labor. Indeed, this painting has a nostalgic, wistful air to it, and reflects Constable's memories of a disappearing rural pastoralism. The artist's father was a rural landowner of considerable wealth, and many of the scenes Constable painted (*The Haywain* included) depict his family's property near East Bergholt in Suffolk, East Anglia. This nostalgia, presented in such naturalistic terms, renders Constable's works Romantic in tone. That Constable felt a kindred spirit with the Romantic artists is revealed by his comment "painting is but another word for feeling."[4]

J.M.W. TURNER Constable's contemporary in the English school of landscape painting, JOSEPH MALLORD WILLIAM TURNER (1775–1851), produced work that also responded to encroaching in-

30-22 JOHN CONSTABLE, *The Haywain*, 1821. Oil on canvas, 4′ 3″ × 6′ 2″. National Gallery, London.

The Haywain is a nostalgic view of the disappearing English country-side during the Industrial Revolution. Constable had a special gift for capturing the texture that climate and weather give to landscape.

1 ft.

dustrialization. However, where Constable's paintings are serene and precisely painted, Turner's feature turbulent swirls of frothy pigment. The passion and energy of Turner's works reveal the Romantic sensibility that was the foundation for his art and also clearly illustrate Edmund Burke's concept of the sublime—awe mixed with terror.

Among Turner's most notable works is *The Slave Ship* (FIG. 30-23). Its subject is a 1783 incident reported in an extensively read book titled *The History of the Abolition of the Slave Trade,* by Thomas Clarkson. Because the book had just been reprinted in

1839, Clarkson's account probably prompted Turner's choice of subject for this 1840 painting. The incident involved the captain of a slave ship who, on realizing that his insurance company would reimburse him only for slaves lost at sea but not for those who died en route, ordered the sick and dying slaves thrown overboard. Appropriately, the painting's full title is *The Slave Ship* (*Slavers Throwing Overboard the Dead and Dying, Typhoon Coming On*). Turner's frenzied emotional depiction of this act matches its barbaric nature. The artist transformed the sun into an incandescent comet amid flying

30-23 JOSEPH MALLORD WILLIAM TURNER, *The Slave Ship* (*Slavers Throwing Overboard the Dead and Dying, Typhoon Coming On*), 1840. Oil on canvas, 2′ $11\frac{11}{16}$″ × 4′ $\frac{5}{16}$″. Museum of Fine Arts, Boston (Henry Lillie Pierce Fund).

The essence of Turner's innovative style is the emotive power of color. He released color from any defining outlines to express both the forces of nature and the painter's emotional response to them.

1 ft.

1 ft.

scarlet clouds. The slave ship moves into the distance, leaving in its wake a turbulent sea choked with the bodies of slaves sinking to their deaths. The relative scale of the minuscule human forms compared with the vast sea and overarching sky reinforces the sense of the sublime, especially the immense power of nature over humans. Almost lost in the boiling colors are the event's particulars, but on close inspection, the viewer can discern the iron shackles and manacles around the wrists and ankles of the drowning slaves, cruelly denying them any chance of saving themselves.

A key ingredient of Turner's highly personal style is the emotive power of pure color. The haziness of the painter's forms and the indistinctness of his compositions intensify the colors and energetic brush strokes. Turner's innovation in works such as *The Slave Ship* was to release color from any defining outlines so as to express both the forces of nature and the painter's emotional response to them. In his paintings, the reality of color is at one with the reality of feeling. Turner's methods had an incalculable effect on the later development of painting. His discovery of the aesthetic and emotive power of pure color and his pushing of the medium's fluidity to a point where the paint itself is almost the subject were important steps toward 20th-century abstract art, which dispensed with shape and form altogether (see Chapter 36).

THOMAS COLE In America, landscape painting was the specialty of a group of artists known as the Hudson River School, so named because its members drew their subjects primarily from the uncultivated regions of New York State's Hudson River Valley, although many of these painters depicted scenes from across the country. Like the early-19th-century landscape painters in Germany and England, the artists of the Hudson River School not only presented Romantic panoramic landscape views but also participated in the ongoing exploration of the individual's and the country's relationship to the land. American landscape painters frequently focused on identifying qualities that made America unique. One American painter of

English birth, THOMAS COLE (1801–1848), often referred to as the leader of the Hudson River School, articulated this idea:

> Whether he [an American] beholds the Hudson mingling waters with the Atlantic—explores the central wilds of this vast continent, or stands on the margin of the distant Oregon, he is still in the midst of American scenery—it is his own land; its beauty, its magnificence, its sublimity—all are his; and how undeserving of such a birthright, if he can turn towards it an unobserving eye, an unaffected heart![5]

Another issue that surfaced frequently in Hudson River School paintings was the moral question of America's direction as a civilization. Cole addressed this question in *The Oxbow (View from Mount Holyoke, Northampton, Massachusetts, after a Thunderstorm;* FIG. **30-24**). A splendid scene opens before the viewer, dominated by the lazy oxbow-shaped curve of the Connecticut River. Cole divided the composition in two, with the dark, stormy wilderness on the left and the more developed civilization on the right. The minuscule artist in the bottom center of the painting (wearing a top hat), dwarfed by the landscape's scale, turns to the viewer as if to ask for input in deciding the country's future course. Cole's depictions of expansive wilderness incorporated reflections and moods romantically appealing to the public.

ALBERT BIERSTADT Other Hudson River artists used the landscape genre as an allegorical vehicle to address moral and spiritual concerns. ALBERT BIERSTADT (1830–1902) traveled west in 1858 and produced many paintings depicting the Rocky Mountains, Yosemite Valley, and other dramatic sites. His works, such as *Among the Sierra Nevada Mountains, California* (FIG. **30-25**), present breathtaking scenery and natural beauty. This panoramic view (the painting is 10 feet wide) is awe-inspiring. Deer and waterfowl appear at the edge of a placid lake, and steep and rugged mountains soar skyward on the left and in the distance. A stand of trees, uncultivated and wild, frames the lake on the right. To underscore the almost transcendental nature of this scene, Bierstadt depicted the sun's rays

30-25 ALBERT BIERSTADT, *Among the Sierra Nevada Mountains, California,* 1868. Oil on canvas, 6′ × 10′. National Museum of American Art, Smithsonian Institution, Washington, D.C.

Bierstadt's panoramic landscape presents the breathtaking natural beauty of the American West. His paintings reinforced the 19th-century doctrine of Manifest Destiny, which justified western expansion.

breaking through the clouds overhead, which suggests a heavenly consecration of the land. That Bierstadt focused attention on the West is not insignificant. By calling national attention to the splendor and uniqueness of the regions beyond the Rocky Mountains, Bierstadt's paintings reinforced the idea of Manifest Destiny. This popular 19th-century doctrine held that westward expansion across the continent was the logical destiny of the United States. As John L. O'Sullivan (1813–1895) expounded in the earliest known use of the term in 1845, "Our manifest destiny [is] to overspread the continent allotted by Providence for the free development of our yearly multiplying millions."[6] Paintings of the scenic splendor of the American West helped to mute growing concerns about the realities of conquest, the displacement of the Native Americans, and the exploitation of the environment. It should come as no surprise that among those most eager to purchase Bierstadt's work were mail-service magnates and railroad builders—the very entrepreneurs and financiers involved in westward expansion.

FREDERIC CHURCH Another painter usually associated with the Hudson River School was FREDERIC EDWIN CHURCH (1826–1900), but his interest in landscape scenes extended beyond America. During his life he traveled to South America, Mexico, Europe, the Middle East, Newfoundland, and Labrador. Church's paintings are firmly in the idiom of the Romantic sublime, yet they also reveal contradictions and conflicts in the constructed mythology of American providence and character. *Twilight in the Wilderness* (FIG. 30-26) presents a panoramic view of the sun setting over the majestic landscape. Beyond Church's precise depiction of the awe-inspiring spectacle of nature, the painting is remarkable for what it does not depict. Like Constable, Church and the other Hudson River

30-26 FREDERIC EDWIN CHURCH, *Twilight in the Wilderness,* 1860s. Oil on canvas, 3′ 4″ × 5′ 4″. Cleveland Museum of Art, Cleveland (Mr. and Mrs. William H. Marlatt Fund, 1965.233).

Church's paintings eloquently express the Romantic notion of the sublime. Painted during the Civil War, this wilderness landscape presents an idealistic view of America free of conflict.

School painters worked in a time of great upheaval. *Twilight in the Wilderness* dates to the 1860s, when the Civil War was tearing apart the country. Yet this painting does not display evidence of turbulence or discord. Indeed, it does not include even a trace of humanity. By constructing such an idealistic and comforting view, Church contributed to the national mythology of righteousness and divine providence—a mythology that had become increasingly difficult to maintain in the face of conflict.

Landscape painting was immensely popular in the late 18th and early 19th centuries, in large part because it provided viewers with breathtaking and sublime spectacles of nature. Artists also could allegorize nature, and it was rare for a landscape painting not to touch on spiritual, moral, historical, or philosophical issues. Landscape painting became the perfect vehicle for artists (and the viewing public) to "naturalize" conditions, rendering debate about contentious issues moot and eliminating any hint of conflict.

REALISM

Realism was a movement that developed in France around midcentury against the backdrop of an increasing emphasis on science. Advances in industrial technology during the early 19th century reinforced the Enlightenment's foundation of rationalism. The connection between science and progress seemed obvious to many, both in intellectual circles and among the general public, and people increasingly embraced *empiricism* (the search for knowledge based on observation and direct experience). Indicative of the widespread faith in science was the influence of *positivism,* a Western philosophical model developed by the French philosopher Auguste Comte (1798–1857). Positivists promoted science as the mind's highest achievement and advocated a purely empirical approach to nature and society. Comte believed that scientific laws governed the environment and human activity and could be revealed through careful recording and analysis of observable data. Like the empiricists and positivists, Realist artists argued that only the things of one's own time—what people could see for themselves—were "real." Accordingly, Realists focused their attention on the experiences and sights of everyday contemporary life and disapproved of historical and fictional subjects on the grounds that they were neither real and visible nor of the present.

France

GUSTAVE COURBET The leading figure of the Realist movement in 19th-century art was GUSTAVE COURBET (1819–1877). In fact, Courbet used the term *Realism* when exhibiting his works, even though he shunned labels (see "Courbet on Realism," page 799). The Realists' sincerity about scrutinizing their environment led them to portray objects and images that in recent centuries artists had deemed unworthy of depiction—the mundane and trivial, working-class laborers and peasants, and so forth. Moreover, the Realists depicted these scenes on a scale and with an earnestness and seriousness previously reserved for grand history painting.

STONE BREAKERS Courbet presented a glimpse into the life of rural menial laborers in *The Stone Breakers* (FIG. **30-27**), capturing on canvas in a straightforward manner two men—one about 70, the other quite young—in the act of breaking stones, traditionally the lot of the lowest in French society. By juxtaposing youth and age, Courbet suggested that those born to poverty remain poor their entire lives. The artist neither romanticized nor idealized the men's work but depicted their thankless toil with directness and accuracy. Courbet's palette of dirty browns and grays conveys the dreary and dismal nature of the task, while the angular positioning of the older stone breaker's limbs suggests a mechanical monotony.

This interest in the working poor as subject matter had special meaning for the mid-19th-century French audience. In 1848 laborers rebelled against the bourgeois leaders of the newly formed Second Republic and against the rest of the nation, demanding better working conditions and a redistribution of property. The army quelled the revolution in three days, but not without long-lasting trauma and significant loss of life. That uprising thus raised the issue of labor as a national concern and placed workers center stage, both literally and symbolically. Courbet's depiction of stone breakers in 1849 was very timely and populist.

BURIAL AT ORNANS Also representative of Courbet's work is *Burial at Ornans* (FIG. **30-28**), which depicts a funeral set in a bleak provincial landscape outside his home town. Attending the funeral are the types of ordinary people Honoré de Balzac (1799–1850) and Gustave Flaubert (1821–1880) presented in their novels. While an officious clergyman reads the Office of the Dead, those attending

30-27 GUSTAVE COURBET, *The Stone Breakers,* 1849. Oil on canvas, 5′ 3″ × 8′ 6″. Formerly Gemäldegalerie, Dresden (destroyed in 1945).

Courbet was the leading figure in the Realist movement. Using a palette of dirty browns and grays, he conveyed the dreary and dismal nature of menial labor in mid-19th-century France.

1 ft.

Courbet on Realism

The Parisian academic jury selecting work for the 1855 Salon (part of the Exposition Universelle in that year) rejected two paintings by Gustave Courbet on the grounds that his subjects and figures were too coarse (so much so as to be plainly "socialistic") and too large (*Burial at Ornans*, FIG. 30-28, is almost 22 feet long). In response, Courbet withdrew all of his works and set up his own exhibition outside the grounds, calling it the Pavilion of Realism. Courbet was the first artist ever to stage a private exhibition of his own work. His pavilion and the statement he issued to explain the paintings shown there amounted to the new movement's manifestos. Although Courbet maintained that he founded no school and was of no school, he did, as the name of his pavilion suggests, accept the term *Realism* as descriptive of his art. The statement Courbet distributed at his pavilion reads in part:

> The title of "realist" has been imposed upon me . . . . Titles have never given a just idea of things; were it otherwise, the work would be superfluous. . . . I have studied the art of the moderns, avoiding any preconceived system and without prejudice. I have no more wanted to imitate the former than to copy the latter; nor have I thought of achieving the idle aim of "art for art's sake." No! I have simply wanted to draw from a thorough knowledge of tradition the reasoned and free sense of my own individuality. . . . To be able to translate the customs, ideas, and appearances of my time as I see them—in a word, to create a living art—this has been my aim.*

Six years later, on Christmas Day, 1861, Courbet wrote an open letter, published a few days later in the *Courier du dimanche*, addressed to prospective students. In the letter, the painter reflected on the nature of his art.

> [An artist must apply] his personal faculties to the ideas and the events of the times in which he lives. . . . [A]rt in painting should consist only of the representation of things that are visible and tangible to the artist. Every age should be represented only by its own artists, that is to say, by the artists who have lived in it. I also maintain that painting is an essentially concrete art form and can consist only of the representation of both real and existing things. . . . An abstract object, not visible, nonexistent, is not within the domain of painting.†

Courbet's most famous statement, however, is his blunt dismissal of academic painting, in which he concisely summed up the core principle of Realist painting:

> I have never seen an angel. Show me an angel, and I'll paint one.‡

* Translated by Robert Goldwater and Marco Treves, eds., *Artists on Art from the XIV to the XX Century*, 3d ed. (New York: Pantheon, 1958), 295.
† Translated by Petra ten-Doesschate Chu, *Letters of Gustave Courbet* (Chicago: University of Chicago Press, 1992), 203–204.
‡ Quoted by Vincent van Gogh in a July 1885 letter to his brother Theo. Ronald de Leeuw, *The Letters of Vincent van Gogh* (New York: Penguin, 1996), 302.

1 ft.

30-28 GUSTAVE COURBET, *Burial at Ornans*, 1849. Oil on canvas, 10′ 3½″ × 21′ 9½″. Musée d'Orsay, Paris.

Although as monumental in scale as a traditional history painting, *Burial at Ornans* horrified critics because of the ordinary nature of the subject and Courbet's starkly antiheroic composition.

cluster around the excavated grave site, their faces registering all degrees of response to the situation. Although the painting has the monumental scale of a traditional history painting, the subject's ordinariness and the starkly antiheroic composition horrified contemporaneous critics. Arranged in a wavering line extending across the broad horizontal width of the canvas are three groups—the somberly clad women at the back right, a semicircle of similarly clad men by the open grave, and assorted churchmen at the left. This wall of

30-29 Jean-François Millet, *The Gleaners*, 1857. Oil on canvas, 2′ 9″ × 3′ 8″. Musée d'Orsay, Paris.

Millet and the Barbizon School painters specialized in depictions of French country life. Here, Millet portrayed three impoverished women gathering the remainders left in the field after a harvest.

1 ft.

figures, seen at eye level in person, blocks any view into deep space. The faces are portraits. Some of the models were Courbet's sisters (three of the women in the front row, toward the right) and friends. Behind and above the figures are bands of overcast sky and barren cliffs. The dark pit of the grave opens into the viewer's space in the center foreground. Despite the unposed look of the figures, Courbet controlled the composition in a masterful way by his sparing use of bright color. In place of the heroic, the sublime, and the dramatic, Courbet aggressively presents the viewer with the mundane realities of daily life and death. In 1857, Jules-François-Félix Husson Champfleury (1821–1889), one of the first critics to recognize and appreciate Courbet's work, wrote of *Burial at Ornans*, "[I]t represents a small-town funeral and yet reproduces the funerals of *all* small towns."[7] Unlike the theatricality of Romanticism, Realism captured the ordinary rhythms of daily existence.

Of great importance for the later history of art, Realism also involved a reconsideration of the painter's primary goals and departed from the established priority on illusionism. Accordingly, Realists called attention to painting as a pictorial construction by the ways they applied pigment or manipulated composition. Courbet's intentionally simple and direct methods of expression in composition and technique seemed unbearably crude to many of his more traditional contemporaries, who called him a primitive. Although his bold, somber palette was essentially traditional, Courbet often used the *palette knife* for quickly placing and unifying large daubs of paint, producing a roughly wrought surface. His example inspired the young artists who worked for him (and later Impressionists such as Claude Monet and Auguste Renoir; see Chapter 31), but the public accused him of carelessness and critics wrote of his "brutalities."

JEAN-FRANÇOIS MILLET Like Courbet, Jean-François Millet (1814–1878) found his subjects in the people and occupations of the everyday world. Millet was one of a group of French painters of country life who, to be close to their rural subjects, settled near the village of Barbizon in the forest of Fontainebleau. This Barbizon School specialized in detailed pictures of forest and countryside. Millet, perhaps their most prominent member, was of peasant stock and identified with the hard lot of the country poor. In *The Gleaners* (FIG. **30-29**), he depicted three peasant women performing the backbreaking task of gleaning the last wheat scraps. These impoverished women were members of the lowest level of peasant society. Landowning nobles traditionally permitted them to glean— to pick up the remainders left in the field after the harvest. Millet characteristically placed his monumental figures in the foreground, against a broad sky. Although the field stretches back to a rim of haystacks, cottages, trees, and distant workers and a flat horizon, the gleaners quietly doing their tedious and time-consuming work dominate the canvas.

Although Millet's works have a sentimentality absent from those of Courbet, the French public still reacted to his paintings with disdain and suspicion. In the aftermath of the 1848 revolution, for Millet to invest the poor with solemn grandeur did not meet with the approval of the prosperous classes. In particular, middle-class landowners resisted granting gleaning rights, and thus Millet's relatively dignified depiction of gleaning did not gain their favor. The middle class also linked the poor with the dangerous, newly defined working class, which was finding outspoken champions in men such as Karl Marx (1818–1883), Friedrich Engels (1820–1895), and the novelists Émile Zola (1840–1902) and Charles Dickens (1812–1870).

Lithography

In 1798 the German printmaker Alois Senefelder (1771–1834) created the first prints using stone instead of metal plates or wooden blocks. In contrast to earlier printing techniques (see "Woodcuts, Engravings, and Etchings," Chapter 20, page 537) in which the artist applied ink to either a raised or incised surface, in *lithography* (Greek, "stone writing") the printing and nonprinting areas of the plate are on the same plane.

The chemical phenomenon fundamental to lithography is the repellence of oil and water. The lithographer uses a greasy, oil-based crayon to draw directly on a stone plate and then wipes water onto the stone, which clings only to the areas the drawing does not cover. Next, the artist rolls oil-based ink onto the stone, which adheres to the drawing but is repelled by the water. When the artist presses the stone against paper, only the inked areas—the drawing—transfer to the paper. Color lithography requires multiple plates, one for each color, and the printmaker must take special care to make sure that each impression lines up perfectly with the previous one so that each color prints in its proper place.

One of the earliest masters of this new printmaking process was Honoré Daumier (FIG. 30-30), whose politically biting lithographs published in a widely read French journal reached an audience of unprecedented size.

1 in.

30-30 Honoré Daumier, *Rue Transnonain*, 1834. Lithograph, $1' \times 1' 5\frac{1}{2}''$. Philadelphia Museum of Art, Philadelphia (bequest of Fiske and Marie Kimball).

Daumier used the recent invention of lithography to reach a wide audience for his social criticism and political protest. This print records the horrific 1834 massacre in a workers' housing block.

Socialism was a growing movement, and both its views on property and its call for social justice, even economic equality, frightened the bourgeoisie. In Millet's sympathetic portrayal of the poor, many saw a political manifesto.

HONORÉ DAUMIER Because people widely recognized the power of art to serve political means, the political and social agitation accompanying the violent revolutions in France and the rest of Europe in the later 18th and early 19th centuries prompted the French people to suspect artists of subversive intention. A person could be jailed for too bold a statement in the press, in literature, in art—even in music and drama. Realist artist HONORÉ DAUMIER (1808–1879) was a defender of the urban working classes, and in his art he boldly confronted authority with social criticism and political protest. In response, the authorities imprisoned the artist. A painter, sculptor, and, like Dürer, Rembrandt, and Goya, one of the world's great printmakers, Daumier produced *lithographs* (see "Lithography," above) that allowed him to create an unprecedented number of prints, thereby reaching a broader audience. In addition to producing individual lithographs for sale, Daumier also contributed satirical lithographs to the widely read, liberal French Republican journal *Caricature*. In these prints, he mercilessly lampooned the foibles and misbehavior of politicians, lawyers, doctors, and the rich bourgeoisie in general. His in-depth knowledge of the acute political and social unrest in Paris during the revolutions of 1830 and 1848 endowed his work with truthfulness and, therefore, with power.

RUE TRANSNONAIN Daumier's lithograph *Rue Transnonain* (FIG. 30-30) depicts an atrocity with the same shocking impact as Goya's *Third of May, 1808* (FIG. 30-13). The title refers to a street in Paris where an unknown sniper killed a civil guard, part of a government force trying to repress a worker demonstration. Because the fatal shot had come from a workers' housing block, the remaining guards immediately stormed the building and massacred all of its inhabitants. With Goya's power, Daumier created a view of the slaughter from a sharp, realistic angle of vision. He depicted not the dramatic moment of execution but the terrible, quiet aftermath. The broken, scattered forms lie amid violent disorder, as if newly found. The print's significance lies in its factualness. It is an example of the period's increasing artistic bias toward using facts as subject, and not always illusionistically. Daumier's pictorial manner is rough and spontaneous. How it carries expressive exaggeration is part of its remarkable force. Daumier's work is true to life in content, but his style is uniquely personal.

Daumier frequently depicted the plight of the disinherited masses of 19th-century industrialism. Here, he portrayed the anonymous poor cramped together in a grimy third-class railway carriage.

1 ft.

THIRD-CLASS CARRIAGE Daumier brought the same convictions exhibited in his graphic work to his paintings as well, especially after 1848. His unfinished *Third-Class Carriage* (FIG. 30-31) provides a glimpse into the cramped and grimy railway carriage of the 1860s. The riders are poor and can afford only third-class tickets. While first- and second-class carriages had closed compartments, third-class passengers were crammed together on hard benches that filled the carriage. The disinherited masses of 19th-century industrialism were Daumier's indignant concern, and he made them his subject repeatedly. He showed them in the unposed attitudes and unplanned arrangements of the millions thronging the modern cities—anonymous, insignificant, dumbly patient with a lot they could not change. Daumier saw people as they ordinarily appeared, their faces vague, impersonal, and blank—unprepared for any observers. He tried to achieve the real by isolating a random collection of the unrehearsed details of human existence from the continuum of ordinary life. Daumier's vision anticipated the spontaneity and candor of scenes captured with the camera by the end of the century.

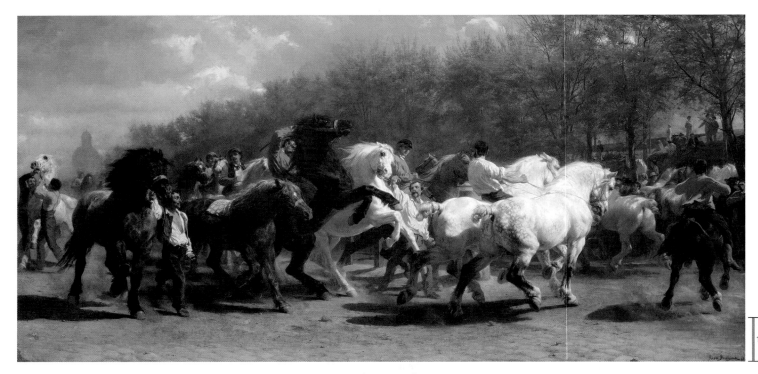

1 ft.

30-32 ROSA BONHEUR, *The Horse Fair*, 1853–1855. Oil on canvas, 8′ ¼″ × 16′ 7½″. Metropolitan Museum of Art, New York (gift of Cornelius Vanderbilt, 1887).

Bonheur was the most celebrated woman artist of the 19th century. A Realist, she went to great lengths to record accurately the anatomy of living horses, even studying carcasses in slaughterhouses.

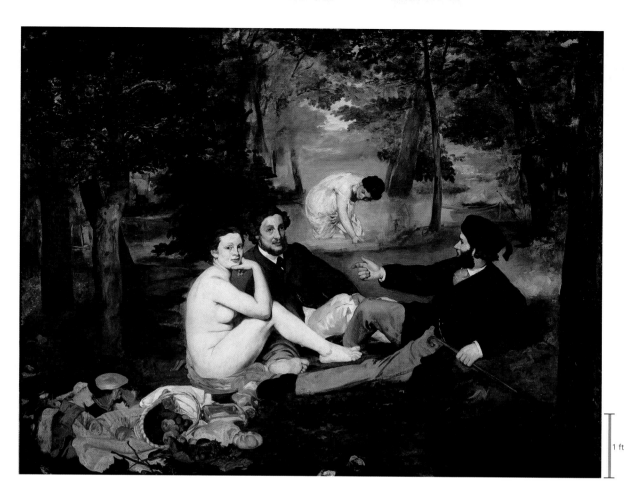

30-33 ÉDOUARD
MANET, *Le Déjeuner
sur l'Herbe* (*Luncheon
on the Grass*), 1863. Oil
on canvas, 7′ × 8′ 8″.
Musée d'Orsay, Paris.

Manet was widely crit-
icized for both his shocking subject matter and
his manner of painting.
Moving away from
illusionism, he used
colors to flatten form
and to draw attention to
the painting surface.

1 ft.

ROSA BONHEUR The most celebrated woman artist of the 19th century was MARIE-ROSALIE (ROSA) BONHEUR (1822–1899). The winner of the gold medal at the Salon of 1848, Bonheur became in 1894 the first woman officer in the French Legion of Honor. Bonheur received her artistic training from her father, who was a proponent of *Saint-Simonianism,* an early-19th-century utopian socialist movement that championed the education and enfranchisement of women. As a result of her father's influence, Bonheur launched her career believing that as a woman and an artist, she had a special role to play in creating a new and perfect society. A Realist passion for accuracy in painting drove Bonheur, but she resisted depicting the problematic social and political situations seen in the work of Courbet, Millet, Daumier, and other Realists. Rather, she turned to the animal world—not, however, to the exotic wild animals that so fascinated Delacroix (FIG. 30-19), but to animals common in the French countryside, especially horses, but also rabbits, cows, and sheep. She went to great lengths to observe the anatomy of living horses at the great Parisian horse fair and spent long hours studying the anatomy of carcasses in the Paris slaughterhouses. For her best-known work, *The Horse Fair* (FIG. **30-32**), she adopted a panoramic composition similar to that in Courbet's *Burial at Ornans* (FIG. 30-28). Bonheur filled her broad canvas with the sturdy farm Percherons and their grooms seen on parade at the annual Parisian horse sale. Some horses, not quite broken, rear up. Others plod or trot, guided on foot or ridden by their keepers. Bonheur recorded the Percherons' uneven line of march, their thunderous pounding, and their seemingly overwhelming power based on her close observation of living animals, even though she acknowledged some inspiration from the Parthenon frieze (FIG. 5-50, *top*). The dramatic lighting, loose brushwork, and rolling sky also reveal her admiration of the style of Géricault (FIG. **30-15**). The equine drama in *The Horse Fair* captivated viewers, who eagerly bought engraved reproductions of Bonheur's painting, making it one of the best-known artworks of the century.

ÉDOUARD MANET Like Gustave Courbet, ÉDOUARD MANET (1832–1883) was a pivotal artist during the 19th century. Not only was his work critical for the articulation of Realist principles, but his art also played an important role in the development of Impressionism in the 1870s (see Chapter 31). Manet's masterpiece, *Le Déjeuner sur l'Herbe* (*Luncheon on the Grass;* FIG. **30-33**), depicts two women, one nude, and two clothed men enjoying a picnic of sorts. Consistent with Realist principles, Manet based all of the foreground figures on living people. The seated nude is Victorine Meurend (Manet's favorite model at the time), and the gentlemen are his brother Eugène (with cane) and probably the sculptor Ferdinand Leenhof, although scholars have suggested other identifications. The two men wear fashionable Parisian attire of the 1860s, and the foreground nude not only is a distressingly unidealized figure type but also seems disturbingly unabashed and at ease, gazing directly at the viewer without shame or flirtatiousness.

This audacious painting outraged the public—rather than a traditional pastoral scene, like the Renaissance *Pastoral Symphony* (FIG. 22-35), which featured anonymous idealized figures in an idyllic setting, *Le Déjeuner* seemed merely to represent ordinary men and promiscuous women in a Parisian park. One hostile critic, no doubt voicing public opinion, said: "A commonplace woman of the demimonde, as naked as can be, shamelessly lolls between two dandies dressed to the teeth. These latter look like schoolboys on a holiday, perpetrating an outrage to play the man. . . . This is a young man's practical joke—a shameful, open sore."[8] Manet surely anticipated criticism of his painting, but shocking the public was not his primary aim. His goal was more complex and involved a reassessment of the entire range of

30-34 ÉDOUARD MANET, *Olympia*, 1863. Oil on canvas, 4′ 3″ × 6′ 2¼″. Musée d'Orsay, Paris. ◼◀

Manet scandalized the public with this painting of a nude prostitute and her black maid carrying a bouquet from a client. Critics also faulted him for using rough brush strokes and abruptly shifting tonality.

art. *Le Déjeuner* contains sophisticated references and allusions to many painting genres—history painting, portraiture, pastoral scenes, nudes, and even religious scenes. What *Le Déjeuner* thus represents is an impressive synthesis and critique of the history of painting.

The negative response to this painting by public and critics alike extended beyond subject matter. Manet's manner of presenting his figures also prompted severe criticism. He rendered them in soft focus and broadly painted the landscape, including the pool in which the second woman bathes. The loose manner of painting contrasts with the clear forms of the harshly lit foreground trio and the pile of discarded female attire and picnic foods at the lower left. The lighting creates strong contrasts between darks and highlighted areas. In the main figures, many values are summed up in one or two lights or darks. The effect is both to flatten the forms and to give them a hard snapping presence. Form, rather than a matter of line, is only a function of paint and light. Manet himself declared that the chief actor in the painting is the light. Manet used art to call attention to art. In other words, he was moving away from illusionism and toward open acknowledgment of painting's properties, such as the flatness of the painting surface, which would become a core principle of many later 19th- and 20th-century painters. The public, however, saw only a crude sketch without the customary finish. The style of the painting, coupled with the unorthodox subject matter, made this work exceptionally controversial.

OLYMPIA Even more scandalous to the French viewing public was Manet's 1863 painting *Olympia* (FIG. **30-34**). This work depicts

a young white prostitute (Olympia was a common "professional" name for prostitutes in the 19th century) reclining on a bed that extends across the foreground. Entirely nude except for a thin black ribbon tied around her neck, a bracelet on her arm, an orchid in her hair, and fashionable mule slippers on her feet, Olympia meets the viewer's eyes with a look of cool indifference. Behind her appears a black maid, who presents her a bouquet of flowers from a client.

Olympia horrified public and critics alike. Although images of prostitutes were not unheard of during this period, the shamelessness of Olympia and her look that verges on defiance shocked viewers. The depiction of a black woman was also not new to painting, but the viewing public perceived Manet's inclusion of both a black maid and a nude prostitute as evoking moral depravity, inferiority, and animalistic sexuality. The contrast of the black servant with the fair-skinned courtesan also made reference to racial divisions. One critic described Olympia as "a courtesan with dirty hands and wrinkled feet . . . her body has the livid tint of a cadaver displayed in the morgue; her outlines are drawn in charcoal and her greenish, bloodshot eyes appear to be provoking the public, protected all the while by a hideous Negress."[9] From this statement, it is clear that viewers were responding not just to the subject matter but to Manet's artistic style as well. Manet's brush strokes are rougher and the shifts in tonality are more abrupt than those found in traditional academic painting. This departure from accepted practice exacerbated the audacity of the subject matter.

ADOLPHE-WILLIAM BOUGUEREAU To understand better the public's reaction to Manet's radically new painting style, it is in-empiricism and positivism appealed to artists in many European countries and in the United States.

WILHELM LEIBL *Three Women in a Village Church* (FIG. 30-36) by WILHELM LEIBL (1844–1900) demonstrates the German artist's commitment to Realist principles and his mastery of the quaint and quiet details of country life. His painting records a sacred moment—the moment of prayer—in the life of three country women of different generations. Dressed in rustic costume, their Sunday best, they pursue their devotions unself-consciously, their prayer books held in large hands roughened by work. Their manners and dress reflect their unaffected nature, untouched by the refinements of urban life. Leibl highlighted their natural virtues: simplicity, honesty, steadfastness, patience.

Leibl spent three years working on this image of peasants in their village church, often under impossible conditions of lighting and temperature. Despite the meticulous application of paint and sharpness of focus, *Three Women* is a moving expression of the German artist's compassionate view of his subjects, a reading of character without sentimentality.

30-35 ADOLPHE-WILLIAM BOUGUEREAU, *Nymphs and a Satyr,* 1873. Oil on canvas, 9′ $\frac{3}{8}$″ × 5′ 10$\frac{7}{8}$″. Sterling and Francine Clark Art Institute, Williamstown.

More renowned than Manet in his own day, Bouguereau was an artist in the French academic tradition who specialized in depicting subjects from classical mythology with polished naturalism.

structive to compare *Olympia* with a work by a highly acclaimed French academic artist of the time, ADOLPHE-WILLIAM BOUGUEREAU (1825–1905). In *Nymphs and a Satyr* (FIG. 30-35), Bouguereau characteristically depicted a classical mythological subject with polished illusionism. The flirtatious and ideally beautiful nymphs strike graceful poses yet seem based as closely on nature as are the details of their leafy surroundings. They playfully pull in different directions the *satyr,* the mythical Greek beast-man, with a goat's hindquarters and horns, a horse's ears and tail, and a man's upper body. Although Bouguereau arguably depicted this scene in a very naturalistic manner, it is emphatically not Realist. His choice of a fictional theme and adherence to established painting conventions were staunchly traditional. In contrast to the daring and pioneering—and underappreciated—Manet, Bouguereau was immensely popular during the later 19th century, enjoying the favor of state patronage throughout his career.

Germany and the United States

Although French artists took the lead in promoting Realism and the notion that artists should depict the realities of modern life, this movement was not exclusively French. The Realist foundation in

30-36 WILHELM LEIBL, *Three Women in a Village Church,* 1878–1882. Oil on canvas, 2′ 5″ × 2′ 1″. Kunsthalle, Hamburg.

French Realism spread quickly to Germany, where Leibl painted this moving depiction of simple peasant women of different generations holding their prayer books in hands roughened by work.

This veteran's productive work implies a smooth transition to peace after the Civil War, but Homer placed a single-bladed scythe in his hands, a symbol of the deaths of soldiers and of Abraham Lincoln.

WINSLOW HOMER Realism received an especially warm reception in the United States. One of the leading American Realist painters was WINSLOW HOMER (1836–1910) of Boston. Homer experienced at first hand the most momentous event of his lifetime—the Civil War. In 1860 he joined the Union campaign as an artist-reporter for *Harper's Weekly*. At the end of the war, he painted *Veteran in a New Field* (FIG. 30-37). Although it is fairly simple and direct, this painting provides significant commentary on the effects and aftermath of America's catastrophic national conflict. The painting depicts a man with his back to the viewer, harvesting wheat. Homer identified him as a veteran by the uniform and canteen carelessly thrown on the ground in the lower right corner, but the man's current occupation is as a farmer, and he has cast aside his former role as a soldier. The veteran's involvement in meaningful, productive work implies a smooth transition from war to peace. This postwar transition to work and the fate of disbanded soldiers were national concerns. Echoing the sentiments that lay behind Houdon's portrayal of George Washington as the new Cincinnatus (FIG. 29-30), the *New York Weekly Tribune* commented: "Rome took her great man from the plow, and made him a dictator—we must now take our soldiers from the camp and make them farmers."[10] America's ability to effect a smooth transition was seen as evidence of its national strength. "The peaceful and harmonious disbanding of the armies in the summer of 1865," poet Walt Whitman wrote, was one of the "immortal proofs of democracy, unequall'd in all the history of the past."[11] Homer's painting thus reinforced the perception of the country's greatness.

Veteran in a New Field also comments symbolically about death. By the 1860s, farmers used cradled scythes to harvest wheat. In this instance, however, Homer rejected realism in favor of symbolism. He painted a single-bladed scythe, thereby transforming the veteran into a symbol of Death—the Grim Reaper himself—and the painting into an elegy to the thousands of soldiers who died in the Civil War and into a lamentation on the death of recently assassinated President Abraham Lincoln.

THOMAS EAKINS Even more resolutely a Realist than Homer was Philadelphia-born THOMAS EAKINS (1844–1916), who possessed a dedicated appetite for showing the realities of the human experience. Eakins studied both painting and medical anatomy in Philadelphia before undertaking further study under French artist Jean-Léon Gérôme (1824–1904). Eakins aimed to paint things as he saw them rather than as the public might wish them portrayed. This attitude was very much in tune with 19th-century American taste, combining an admiration for accurate depiction with a hunger for truth.

The too-brutal Realism of Eakins's early masterpiece, *Gross Clinic* (FIG. 30-38), prompted the art jury to reject it for the Philadelphia exhibition that celebrated the American independence centennial in 1876. The work presents the renowned surgeon Dr. Samuel Gross in the operating amphitheater of the Jefferson Medical

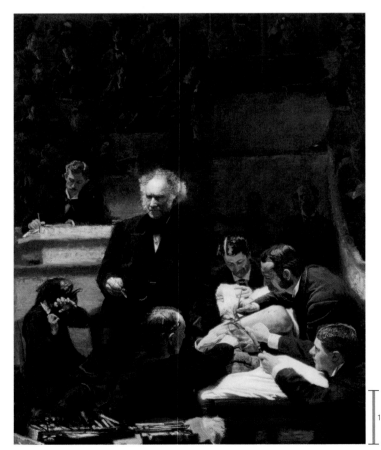

30-38 THOMAS EAKINS, *The Gross Clinic*, 1875. Oil on canvas, 8′ × 6′ 6″. Philadelphia Museum of Art, Philadelphia. ◼◀

The too-brutal realism of Eakins's unsparing depiction of a medical college operating amphitheater caused rejection of this painting from the Philadelphia exhibition celebrating America's centennial.

College in Philadelphia, where the painting hung until its sale in 2006. That Eakins chose to depict this event testifies to the public's increasing faith in scientific and medical progress. Dr. Gross, with bloody fingers and scalpel, lectures about his surgery on a young man's leg. The patient suffered from osteomyelitis, a bone infection. Watching the surgeon, acclaimed for his skill in this particular operation, are several colleagues, all of whom historians have identified, and the patient's mother, who covers her face. Indicative of the contemporaneity of this scene is the anesthetist in the background holding the cloth over the patient's face. Anesthetics had been introduced in 1846, and their development eliminated a major obstacle to extensive surgery. The painting is an unsparing description of an unfolding event, with a good deal more reality than many viewers could endure. "It is a picture," one critic said, "that even strong men find difficult to look at long, if they can look at it at all."[12]

Eakins believed that knowledge—and where relevant, scientific knowledge—was a prerequisite to his art. As a scientist (in his anatomical studies), Eakins preferred a slow, deliberate method of careful invention based on his observations of the perspective, the anatomy, and the details of his subject. This insistence on scientific fact corresponded to the dominance of empiricism during the latter half of the 19th century. Eakins's concern for anatomical correctness led him to investigate the human form and humans in motion, both with regular photographic apparatuses and with a special camera devised by the French kinesiologist (a person who studies the physiology of body movement) Étienne-Jules Marey (1830–1904). Eakins's later collaboration with Eadweard Muybridge (FIG. 30-54) in the photographic study of animal and human action of all types anticipated the motion picture.

JOHN SINGER SARGENT The expatriate American artist JOHN SINGER SARGENT (1856–1925), born in Florence, Italy, was a younger contemporary of Eakins. Sargent developed a looser, more dashing Realist portrait style, in contrast to Eakins's carefully rendered details. Sargent studied art in Paris before settling in London, where he won renown both as a cultivated and cosmopolitan gentleman and as a facile and fashionable portrait painter. He learned his adept brushing of paint in thin layers and his effortless achievement of quick and lively illusion from his study of Velázquez, whose masterpiece, *Las Meninas* (FIG. 24-30), may have influenced Sargent's portrait *The Daughters of Edward Darley Boit* (FIG. 30-39). The four girls (the children of one of Sargent's close friends) appear in a hall and small drawing room in their Paris home. The informal, eccentric arrangement of their slight figures suggests how much at ease they are within this familiar space and with objects such as the monumental Japanese vases, the red screen, and the fringed rug, whose scale subtly emphasizes the children's diminutive stature. Sargent must have known the Boit daughters well and liked them. Relaxed and trustful, they gave the artist an opportunity to record a gradation of young innocence. He sensitively captured the naive, wondering openness of the little girl in the foreground, the grave artlessness of the 10-year-old child, and the slightly self-conscious poise of the adolescents. Sargent's casual positioning of the figures and seemingly random choice of the setting communicate a sense of spontaneity. The children seem to be attending momentarily to an adult who has asked them to interrupt their activity. The painting embodies the Realist belief that the artist's business is to record modern people in modern contexts.

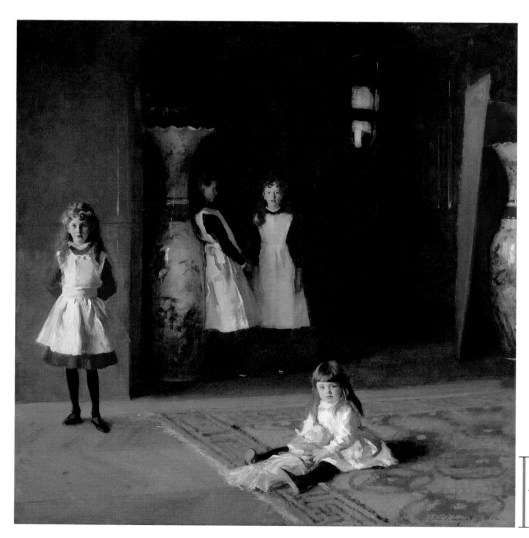

30-39 JOHN SINGER SARGENT, *The Daughters of Edward Darley Boit,* 1882. Oil on canvas, 7′ 3⅜″ × 7′ 3⅝″. Museum of Fine Arts, Boston (gift of Mary Louisa Boit, Florence D. Boit, Jane Hubbard Boit, and Julia Overing Boit, in memory of their father, Edward Darley Boit).

Sargent's casual positioning of the Boit sisters creates a sense of the momentary and spontaneous, consistent with Realist painters' interest in recording modern people in modern contexts.

1 ft.

30-40 Henry Ossawa Tanner, *The Thankful Poor,* 1894. Oil on canvas, 2′ 11½″ × 3′ 8¼″. Collection of William H. and Camille Cosby.

Tanner combined the Realists' belief in careful study from nature with a desire to portray with dignity the life of African American families. Expressive lighting reinforces the painting's reverent spirit.

HENRY OSSAWA TANNER Typical of the Realist painter's desire to depict the lives of ordinary people is the early work of the American artist HENRY OSSAWA TANNER (1859–1937). Tanner studied art with Eakins before moving to Paris. There he combined Eakins's belief in careful study from nature with a desire to portray with dignity the life of the ordinary people he had been raised among as the son of an African American minister in Pennsylvania. The mood in *The Thankful Poor* (FIG. **30-40**) is one of quiet devotion not far removed from the Realism of Millet (FIG. **30-29**). Tanner painted the grandfather, grandchild, and main objects in the room with the greatest detail, while everything else dissolves into loose strokes of color and light. Expressive lighting reinforces the painting's reverent spirit, with deep shadows intensifying the man's devout concentration and golden light pouring in the window to illuminate the quiet expression of thanksgiving on the younger face. The deep sense of sanctity expressed here in terms of everyday experience became increasingly important for Tanner. Within a few years of completing *The Thankful Poor,* he began painting biblical subjects grounded in direct study from nature and in the love of Rembrandt that had inspired him from his days as a Philadelphia art student.

EDMONIA LEWIS About 15 years older than Tanner, the sculptor EDMONIA LEWIS (ca. 1845–after 1909) produced work that was stylistically indebted to Neoclassicism but depicted contemporary Realist themes. *Forever Free* (FIG. **30-41**) is a marble sculpture

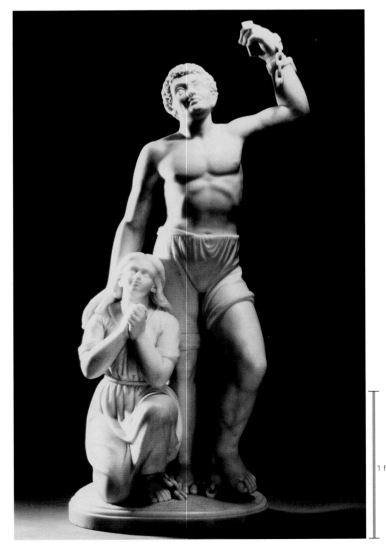

30-41 Edmonia Lewis, *Forever Free,* 1867. Marble, 3′ 5¼″ high. James A. Porter Gallery of Afro-American Art, Howard University, Washington, D.C.

Lewis was a sculptor whose work owes a stylistic debt to Neoclassicism but depicts contemporary Realist themes. She carved *Forever Free* four years after Lincoln's Emancipation Proclamation.

Lewis carved while living in Rome, surrounded by examples of both classical and Renaissance art. It represents two freed African American slaves. The man stands heroically in a contrapposto stance reminiscent of classical statues. His right hand rests on the shoulder of the kneeling woman, and his left hand holds aloft a broken manacle and chain as literal and symbolic references to his former servitude. Produced four years after President Lincoln's issuance of the Emancipation Proclamation, *Forever Free* (originally titled *The Morning of Liberty*) was widely perceived as an abolitionist statement. However, other factors caution against an overly simplistic reading. Because Lewis was female, African American, and Native American (she was the daughter of a Chippewa mother and African American father), scholars have debated the degree to which the sculptor attempted to inject a statement about African American gender relationships into this statue. For example, does the kneeling position of the woman represent Lewis's acceptance of female subordination?

Lewis's accomplishments as a sculptor speak to the increasing access to training that was available to women in the 19th century. Educated at Oberlin College (the first American college to grant degrees to women), Lewis financed her trip to Rome with the sale of medallions and marble busts. Her success in a field dominated by white male artists is a testament to both her skill and her determination.

Pre-Raphaelite Brotherhood

Realism did not appeal to all artists, however. In England a group of painters who called themselves the Pre-Raphaelite Brotherhood refused to be limited to the contemporary scenes strict Realists portrayed. These artists chose instead to represent fictional, historical, and fanciful subjects but with a significant degree of convincing illusion.

JOHN EVERETT MILLAIS One of the founders of the Pre-Raphaelite Brotherhood was JOHN EVERETT MILLAIS (1829–1896). So painstakingly careful was Millais in his study of visual facts

closely observed from nature that Charles Baudelaire (1821–1867) called him "the poet of meticulous detail." The Pre-Raphaelite Brotherhood, organized in 1848, wished to create fresh and sincere art, free from what its members considered the tired and artificial manner propagated in the academies by the successors of Raphael. Influenced by the well-known critic, artist, and writer John Ruskin (1819–1900), the Pre-Raphaelites agreed with his distaste for the materialism and ugliness of the contemporary industrializing world. They also expressed appreciation for the spirituality and idealism (as well as the art and artisanship) of past times, especially the Middle Ages and the Early Renaissance.

Millais's *Ophelia* (FIG. 30-42) garnered enthusiastic praise when he exhibited it in the Exposition Universelle in Paris in 1855, where Courbet set up his Pavilion of Realism. The subject, from Shakespeare's *Hamlet* (4.7.176–179), is the drowning of Ophelia, who, in her madness, is unaware of her plight:

> Her clothes spread wide,
> And mermaidlike awhile they bore her up—
> Which time she chanted snatches of old tunes,
> As one incapable of her own distress.

To make the pathos of the scene visible, Millais became a faithful and feeling witness of its every detail, reconstructing it with a lyricism worthy of the original poetry. Although the scene is fictitious, Millais worked diligently to present it with unswerving fidelity to visual fact. He painted the background on-site at a spot along the Hogsmill River in Surrey. For the figure of Ophelia, Millais had a friend lie in a heated bathtub full of water for hours at a stretch.

DANTE GABRIEL ROSSETTI Another founder of the Pre-Raphaelite Brotherhood was DANTE GABRIEL ROSSETTI (1828–1882), who established an enviable reputation as both a painter and poet. Like other members of the group, Rossetti focused on literary and biblical themes in his art. He also produced numerous portraits of

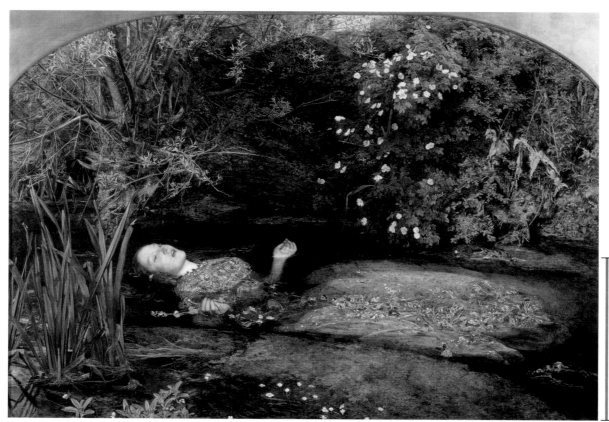

30-42 JOHN EVERETT MILLAIS, *Ophelia,* 1852. Oil on canvas, 2′ 6″ × 3′ 8″. Tate Gallery, London.

Millais was a founder of the Pre-Raphaelite Brotherhood, whose members refused to be limited to the contemporary scenes strict Realists portrayed. The drowning of Ophelia is a Shakespearean subject.

1 ft.

women that projected an image of ethereal beauty and melded apparent opposites—a Victorian prettiness with sensual allure. His *Beata Beatrix* (FIG. 30-43) is ostensibly a portrait of a literary figure—Beatrice, from Dante's *Vita Nuova*—as she overlooks Florence in a trance after being mystically transported to Heaven. Yet the portrait also had personal resonance for Rossetti. It served as a memorial to his wife, Elizabeth Siddal (the model for Millais's *Ophelia*), who had died shortly before Rossetti began this painting in 1862. In the image, the woman (Siddal-Beatrice) sits in a trancelike state, while a red dove (a messenger of both love and death) deposits a poppy (symbolic of sleep and death) in her hands. Because Siddal died of an opium overdose, the presence of the poppy assumes greater significance.

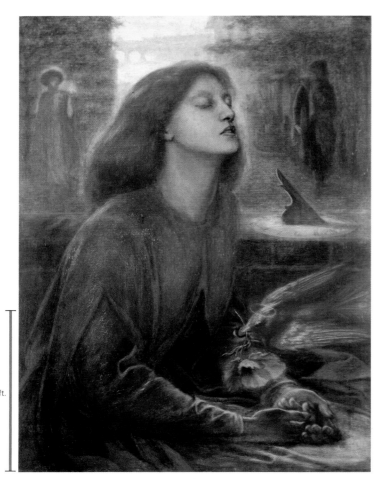

30-43 DANTE GABRIEL ROSSETTI, *Beata Beatrix,* ca. 1863. Oil on canvas, 2′ 10″ × 2′ 2″. Tate Gallery, London.

This painting of a beautiful and sensuous woman is ostensibly a literary portrait of Dante's Beatrice, but the work also served as a memorial to Rossetti's wife, who died of an opium overdose.

ARCHITECTURE

As 19th-century scholars gathered the documentary materials of European history in extensive historiographic enterprises, each nation came to value its past as evidence of the validity of its ambitions and claims to greatness. Intellectuals appreciated the art of the remote past as a product of cultural and national genius. Italy, of course, had its Roman ruins, which had long inspired later architects. In France, Napoleon had co-opted the classical tradition, but even at the height of his power a reawakening of interest in Gothic architecture also surfaced. In 1802 the eminent French writer François-René de Chateaubriand (1768–1848) published his influential *Genius of Christianity,* which defended religion on the grounds of its beauty and mystery rather than on the grounds of truth. Gothic cathedrals, according to Chateaubriand, were translations of the sacred groves of the ancient Gauls into stone and should be cherished as manifestations of France's holy history. One result of this new nationalistic respect for the Gothic style was that Eugène Emmanuel Viollet-le-Duc (1814–1879) received a commission in 1845 to restore the inte-

30-44A SCHINKEL, Altes Museum, Berlin, 1822–1830.

30-44 CHARLES BARRY and A.W.N. PUGIN, Houses of Parliament, London, England, designed 1835. ▣◀

The 19th century brought the revival of many architectural styles, often reflecting nationalistic pride. The Houses of Parliament have an exterior veneer and towers that recall late English Gothic style.

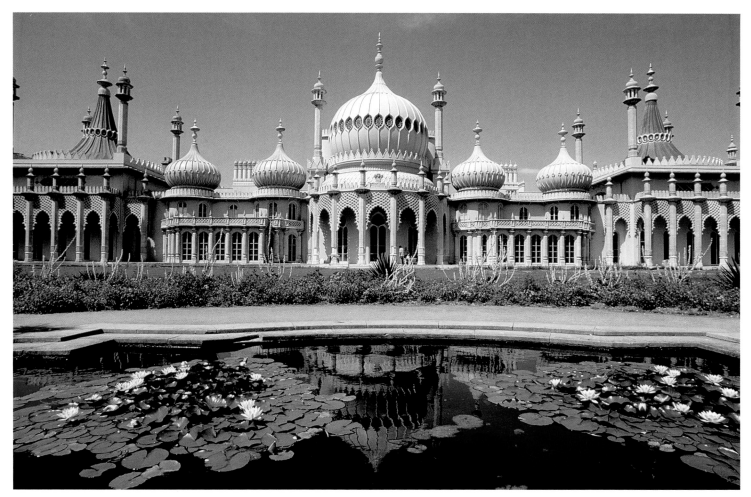

30-45 JOHN NASH, Royal Pavilion, Brighton, England, 1815–1818.

British territorial expansion brought a familiarity with many exotic styles. This palatial "Indian Gothic" seaside pavilion is a conglomeration of Islamic domes, minarets, and screens.

44B UPJOHN,
nity Church,
w York,
41–1852.

rior of Paris's Notre-Dame to its Gothic splendor after removing the Baroque and Napoleonic (FIG. 30-2) alterations.

HOUSES OF PARLIAMENT England also celebrated its medieval heritage with *Neo-Gothic* buildings. In London, after the old Houses of Parliament burned in 1834, the Parliamentary Commission decreed that designs for the new building be either Gothic or Elizabethan. CHARLES BARRY (1795–1860), with the assistance of A.W.N. PUGIN (1812–1852), submitted the winning design (FIG. 30-44) in 1835. By this time, style had become a matter of selection from the historical past. Barry had traveled widely in Europe, Greece, Turkey, Egypt, and Palestine, studying the architecture of each place. He preferred the classical Renaissance styles, but he had designed some earlier Neo-Gothic buildings, and Pugin successfully influenced him in the direction of English Late Gothic. Pugin was one of a group of English artists and critics who saw moral purity and spiritual authenticity in the religious architecture of the Middle Ages. They also glorified the careful medieval artisans who built the great cathedrals. The Industrial Revolution was flooding the market with cheaply made and ill-designed commodities, and machine work was replacing handicraft. Many, such as Pugin, believed in the necessity of restoring the old artisanship, which had honesty and quality. The design of the Houses of Parliament, however, is not genuinely Gothic, despite its picturesque tower groupings (the Clock Tower, containing Big Ben, at one end, and the Victoria Tower at the other). The building has a formal axial plan and a kind of Pal-

ladian regularity beneath its Neo-Gothic detail. Pugin himself said of it, "All Grecian, Sir. Tudor [late English Gothic] details on a classical body."[13]

ROYAL PAVILION Although the Neoclassical and Neo-Gothic styles dominated early-19th-century architecture, exotic new styles of all types soon began to appear, due in part to European imperialism and in part to the Romantic spirit that permeated all the arts. Great Britain's forays throughout the world, particularly India, had exposed English culture to a broad range of non-Western artistic styles. The Royal Pavilion (FIG. 30-45), designed by JOHN NASH (1752–1835), exhibits a wide variety of these styles. Nash was an established architect, known for Neoclassical buildings in London, when he was asked to design a royal pleasure palace in the seaside resort of Brighton for the prince regent (later King George IV). The structure's fantastic exterior is a conglomeration of Islamic domes, minarets, and screens that historians have called "Indian Gothic," and sources ranging from Greece and Egypt to China influenced the interior decor. Underlying the exotic facade is a cast-iron skeleton, an early (if hidden) use of this material in noncommercial building. Nash also put this metal to fanciful use, creating life-size palm-tree columns in cast iron to support the Royal Pavilion's kitchen ceiling. The building, an appropriate enough backdrop for gala throngs pursuing pleasure by the seaside, served as the prototype for numerous playful architectural exaggerations still found in European and American resorts.

PARIS OPÉRA The Baroque style also found favor in 19th-century architecture because it was well suited to conveying a grandeur worthy of the riches the European elite acquired during this age of expansion. The Paris Opéra (FIG. 30-46), designed by CHARLES GARNIER (1825–1898), mirrored the opulence that permeated the lives of these privileged few. The opera house has a festive and spectacularly theatrical Neo-Baroque front and two wings resembling Baroque domed central-plan churches. Inside, intricate arrangements of corridors, vestibules, stairways, balconies, alcoves, entrances, and exits facilitate easy passage throughout the building and provide space for entertainment and socializing at intermissions. The Baroque grandeur of the layout and of the building's ornamental appointments is characteristic of an architectural style called *Beaux-Arts,* which flourished in the late 19th and early 20th centuries in France. Based on ideas taught at the dominant École des Beaux-Arts (School of Fine Arts) in Paris, the Beaux-Arts style incorporated classical principles (such as symmetry in design, including interior spaces that extended radially from a central core or axis) and included extensive exterior ornamentation. As an example of a Beaux-Arts building, Garnier's Opéra proclaims, through its majesty and lavishness, its function as a gathering place for fashionable audiences in an era of conspicuous wealth. The style was so attractive to the moneyed classes who supported the arts that theaters and opera houses continued to reflect the Paris Opéra's design until World War I transformed society.

CAST-IRON CONSTRUCTION Work on Garnier's Opéra began in 1861, but by the middle of the 19th century, many architects had already abandoned sentimental and Romantic designs from the past. They turned to honest expressions of a building's purpose. Since the 18th century, bridges had been built of cast iron (FIG. 29-11), and most other utilitarian architecture—factories, warehouses, dockyard structures, mills, and the like—long had been built

simply and without historical ornamentation. Iron, along with other industrial materials, permitted engineering advancements in the construction of larger, stronger, and more fire-resistant structures than before. The tensile strength of iron (and especially of steel, available after 1860) permitted architects to create new designs involving vast enclosed spaces, as in the great train sheds of railroad stations and in exposition halls.

SAINTE-GENEVIÈVE LIBRARY The Bibliothèque Sainte-Geneviève (1843–1850), built by HENRI LABROUSTE (1801–1875), is an interesting mix of Renaissance revival style and modern cast-iron construction. Its two-story facade with arched windows recalls Renaissance palazzo designs, but Labrouste exposed the structure's metal skeleton on the interior. The lower story of the library housed the book stacks. The upper floor featured a spacious reading room (FIG. 30-47) consisting essentially of two barrel-vaulted halls, roofed in terracotta and separated by a row of slender cast-iron columns on concrete pedestals. The columns, recognizably Corinthian, support the iron roof arches pierced with intricate vine-scroll ornament out of the Renaissance architectural vocabulary. Labrouste's design highlights how the peculiarities of the new structural material aesthetically altered the forms of traditional masonry architecture. But it also makes clear how reluctant the 19th-century architect was to surrender traditional forms, even when fully aware of new possibilities for design and construction. Architects scoffed at "engineers' architecture" for many years and continued to clothe their steel-and-concrete structures in the Romantic "drapery" of a historical style.

CRYSTAL PALACE Completely "undraped" construction first became popular in the conservatories (greenhouses) of English country estates. JOSEPH PAXTON (1801–1865) built several such structures for his patron, the duke of Devonshire. In the largest—

30-47 HENRI LABROUSTE, reading room of the Bibliothèque Sainte-Geneviève, Paris, France, 1843–1850.

The exterior of this Parisian library looks like a Renaissance palazzo, but the interior has an exposed cast-iron skeleton, which still incorporates classical Corinthian capitals and Renaissance scrolls.

30-48A ROEBLING, Brooklyn Bridge, 1867–1883.

300 feet long—he used an experimental system of glass-and-metal roof construction. Encouraged by the success of this system, Paxton submitted a winning glass-and-iron building plan to the design competition for the hall to house the Great Exhibition of 1851, organized to present "works of industry of all nations" in London. Paxton constructed the exhibition building, the Crystal Palace (FIG. **30-48**), with prefabricated parts. This allowed the vast structure to be erected in the then-unheard-of time of six months and dismantled at the exhibition's closing to avoid permanent obstruction of the park. The plan borrowed much from ancient Roman and Christian basilicas, with a central flat-roofed "nave" and a barrel-vaulted crossing "transept." The design provided ample interior space to contain displays of huge machines as well as to accommodate decorative touches in the form of large working fountains and giant trees. The public admired the building so much that the workers who dismantled it erected an enlarged version of the Crystal Palace at a new location on the outskirts of London at Sydenham, where it remained until fire destroyed it in 1936. A few old black-and-white photographs and several color lithographs (FIG. **30-48**) preserve a record of the Crystal Palace's appearance.

30-48 JOSEPH PAXTON, Crystal Palace, London, England, 1850–1851; enlarged and relocated at Sydenham, England, 1852–1854. Detail of a color lithograph by ACHILLE-LOUIS MARTINET, ca. 1862. Private collection.

The tensile strength of iron permitted Paxton to experiment with a new system of glass-and-metal roof construction. Built with prefabricated parts, the vast Crystal Palace required only six months to erect.

Daguerreotype, Calotype, and Wet-Plate Photography

The earliest photographic processes were the *daguerreotype*, named after L.J.M. Daguerre (FIG. 30-50), and the *calotype*. Daguerre was an architect and theatrical set painter and designer. This background led Daguerre and a partner to open a popular entertainment called the Diorama. Audiences witnessed performances of "living paintings" created by changing the lighting effects on a "sandwich" composed of a painted backdrop and several layers of painted translucent front curtains. Daguerre used a camera obscura for the Diorama, but he wanted to find a more efficient and effective procedure. Through a mutual acquaintance, he met Joseph Nicéphore Niépce (1765–1833), who in 1826 had successfully made a permanent picture of the cityscape outside his upper-story window by exposing, in a camera obscura, a metal plate covered with a light-sensitive coating. Niépce's process, however, had the significant drawback that it required an eight-hour exposure time. After Niépce died in 1833, Daguerre continued his work, making two important discoveries. Latent development—that is, bringing out the image through treatment in chemical solutions—considerably shortened the length of time needed for exposure. Daguerre also discovered a better way to "fix" the image by chemically stopping the action of light on the photographic plate, which otherwise would continue to darken until the image turned solid black.

The daguerreotype reigned supreme in photography until the 1850s, but the second major photographic invention, the ancestor of the modern negative-print system, eventually replaced it. On January 31, 1839, less than three weeks after Daguerre unveiled his method in Paris, William Henry Fox Talbot presented a paper on his "photogenic drawings" to the Royal Institution in London. As early as 1835, Talbot made "negative" images by placing objects on sensitized paper and exposing the arrangement to light. This created a design of light-colored silhouettes recording the places where opaque or translucent objects had blocked light from darkening the paper's emulsion. In his experiments, Talbot next exposed sensitized papers inside simple cameras and, with a second sheet, created "positive" images. He further improved the process with more light-sensitive chemicals and a chemical development of the negative image. This technique allowed multiple prints. However, in Talbot's process, which he named the calotype (from the Greek word *kalos*, "beautiful"), the photographic images incorporated the texture of the paper. This produced a slightly blurred, grainy effect very different from the crisp detail and wide tonal range available with the daguerreotype. Also discouraging widespread adoption of the calotype were the stiff licensing and equipment fees charged for many years after Talbot patented his new process in 1841.

An early master of an improved kind of calotype photography was the multitalented Frenchman known as Nadar. He used glass negatives and albumen printing paper (prepared with egg white), which could record finer detail and a wider range of light and shadow than Talbot's calotype process. The new *wet-plate* technology (so named because the photographic plate was exposed, developed, and fixed while wet) almost at once became the universal way of making negatives until 1880. However, wet-plate photography had drawbacks. The plates had to be prepared and processed on the spot. Working outdoors

NADAR élevant la Photographie à la hauteur de l'Art

1 in.

30-49 HONORÉ DAUMIER, *Nadar Raising Photography to the Height of Art*, 1862. Lithograph, $10\frac{3}{4}'' \times 8\frac{3}{4}''$. Museum of Fine Arts, Boston.

Daumier's lithograph commemorates a court decision acknowledging photography as an art form protected by copyright law. Nadar (FIG. 30-1) was one of photography's early masters.

meant taking along a portable darkroom of some sort—a wagon, tent, or box with light-tight sleeves for the photographer's arms.

Nadar achieved so much fame for his wet-plate photographic portraits (FIG. 30-1) that he became the subject of a Daumier lithograph (FIG. 30-49) that provides incisive and amusing commentary about the struggle of photography to be recognized as a fine art. Daumier made his print in response to an 1862 court decision acknowledging that photography was indeed an art and therefore entitled to protection under copyright law. In the lithograph, Nadar energetically takes pictures with his camera as his balloon rises over Parisian rooftops—Daumier's literal representation of the elevation of photography's status that the court decision reaffirmed. The image also refers to the fact that Nadar was a staunch advocate of balloon transportation and aerial reconnaissance. He produced the first aerial photographs of Paris in 1858 from his balloon Le Géant (The Giant).

PHOTOGRAPHY

A technological device of immense consequence for the modern experience was invented shortly before the mid-19th century: the camera, with its attendant art of photography. Ever since Frenchman LOUIS-JACQUES-MANDÉ DAGUERRE (1789–1851) and Briton William Henry Fox Talbot (1800–1877) announced the first practical photographic processes in 1839, people have celebrated photography as a revelation of visible things. The relative ease of the process, even in its earliest and most primitive form, seemed a dream come true for 19th-century scientists and artists, who for centuries had grappled with less satisfying methods of capturing accurate images of their subjects. Photography also perfectly suited an age that saw artistic patronage continue to shift away from the elite few toward a broader base of support. The growing and increasingly powerful middle class embraced both the comprehensible images of the new medium and its lower cost.

For the traditional artist, photography suggested new answers to the great debate about what was real and how to represent the real in art. It also challenged the place of traditional modes of pictorial representation originating in the Renaissance. Artists as diverse as Delacroix, Ingres, Courbet, and the Impressionist Edgar Degas (see Chapter 31) welcomed photography as a helpful auxiliary to painting. In a memorable lithograph (FIG. 30-49), Daumier celebrated the new medium as a genuine art form, and many artists marveled at the ability of photography to translate three-dimensional objects onto a two-dimensional surface. Other artists, however, saw photography as a mechanism capable of displacing the painstaking work of skilled painters dedicated to representing the optical truth of chosen subjects. Photography's challenge to painting, both historically and technologically, seemed to some artists an expropriation of the realistic image, until then the exclusive property of painting. But just as some painters looked to the new medium of photography for an-

swers on how best to render an image in paint, so too some photographers looked to painting for suggestions about ways to imbue the photographic image with qualities beyond simple reproduction.

Artists themselves were instrumental in the development of this new technology. The camera obscura was familiar to 18th-century artists. In 1807 the invention of the *camera lucida* (lighted room) replaced the enclosed chamber of the camera obscura. Now the photographer aimed a small prism lens, hung on a stand, downward at an object. The lens projected the image of the object onto a sheet of paper. Artists using either of these devices found the process long and arduous, no matter how accurate the resulting work. All yearned for a more direct way to capture a subject's image. Two very different scientific inventions that accomplished this—the *daguerreotype* (FIG. 30-50) and the *calotype* (see "Daguerreotype, Calotype, and Wet-Plate Photography," page 814)—were announced almost simultaneously in France and England in 1839.

DAGUERREOTYPES The French government presented the new daguerreotype process at the Academy of Science in Paris on January 7, 1839, with the understanding that its details would be made available to all interested parties without charge (although the inventor received a large annuity in appreciation). Soon, people worldwide began taking pictures with the daguerreotype "camera" (a name shortened from camera obscura) in a process almost immediately christened "photography," from the Greek *photos* ("light") and *graphos* ("writing"). From the start, the possibilities of the process as a new art medium intrigued painters. Paul Delaroche (1797–1856), a leading academic painter of the day, wrote in an official report to the French government:

> Daguerre's process completely satisfies all the demands of art, carrying certain essential principles of art to such perfection that it must become a subject of observation and study even to the most

30-50 LOUIS-JACQUES-MANDÉ DAGUERRE, *Still Life in Studio*, 1837. Daguerreotype, $6\frac{1}{4}'' \times 8\frac{1}{4}''$. Société Française de Photographie, Paris. ◾◀

One of the first plates Daguerre produced after perfecting his new photographic process was this still life, in which he was able to capture amazing detail and finely graduated tones from black to white.

1 in.

30-51 JOSIAH JOHNSON HAWES and ALBERT SANDS SOUTHWORTH, *Early Operation under Ether, Massachusetts General Hospital*, ca. 1847. Daguerreotype, $6\frac{1}{2}'' \times 8\frac{1}{2}''$. Massachusetts General Hospital Archives and Special Collections, Boston. ◀

In this early daguerreotype, which predates Eakins's *Gross Clinic* FIG. 30-38) by almost 30 years, Hawes and Southworth demonstrated the documentary power of the new medium of photography.

1 in.

accomplished painters. The pictures obtained by this method are as remarkable for the perfection of the details as for the richness and harmony of the general effect. Nature is reproduced in them not only with truth, but also with art.[14]

Each daguerreotype is a unique work with amazing detail and finely graduated tones from black to white. *Still Life in Studio* (FIG. 30-50) is one of the first successful plates Daguerre produced after perfecting his method. The process captured every detail—the subtle forms, the varied textures, the diverse tones of light and shadow—in Daguerre's carefully constructed tableau. The three-dimensional forms of the sculptures, the basket, and the bits of cloth spring into high relief and are convincingly represented. The inspiration for the composition came from 17th-century Dutch vanitas still lifes, such as those of Claesz (FIG. 25-21). Like Claesz, Daguerre arranged his objects to reveal their textures and shapes clearly. Unlike a painter, Daguerre could not alter anything within his arrangement to effect a stronger image. However, he could suggest a symbolic meaning through his choice of objects. Like the skull and timepiece in Claesz's painting, Daguerre's sculptural and architectural fragments and the framed print of an embrace suggest that even art is vanitas and will not endure forever.

HAWES AND SOUTHWORTH In the United States, photographers began to make daguerreotypes within two months of Daguerre's presentation in Paris. Two particularly avid and resourceful advocates of the new medium were JOSIAH JOHNSON HAWES (1808–1901), a painter, and ALBERT SANDS SOUTHWORTH (1811–1894), a pharmacist and teacher. Together, they ran a daguerreotype studio in Boston that specialized in portraiture, then popular due to the shortened exposure time required for the process (although it was still long enough to require head braces to help subjects remain motionless while photographers recorded their images).

The partners also took their equipment outside the studio to record places and events of particular interest to them. One resultant image is *Early Operation under Ether, Massachusetts General Hospital* (FIG. 30-51). This daguerreotype, taken from the gallery of a hospital operating room, put the viewer in the position of medical students looking down on a lecture-demonstration typical throughout the 19th century. An image of historical record, this early daguerreotype, which predates Eakins's *Gross Clinic* (FIG. 30-38) by almost three decades, gives the viewer a glimpse into the whole of Western medical practice. The focus of attention in *Early Operation* is the white-draped patient surrounded by a circle of darkly clad doctors. The details of the figures and the room's furnishings are in sharp focus, but the slight blurring of several of the figures betrays motion during the exposure. The elevated viewpoint flattens the spatial perspective and emphasizes the relationships of the figures in ways that the Impressionists, especially Degas, found intriguing.

NADAR Portraiture was one of the first photography genres to use a technology that improved the calotype. Making portraits was an important economic opportunity for most photographers, as Southworth and Hawes proved, but the greatest of the early portrait photographers was undoubtedly Gaspar-Félix Tournachon, known simply as NADAR (1828–1910), a French novelist, journalist, enthusiastic balloonist, caricaturist, and, later, photographer (see "Daguerreotype," page 814). Photographic studies for his caricatures led Nadar to open a portrait studio. So talented was he at capturing the essence of his subjects that the most important people in France, including Delacroix, Daumier, Courbet, and Manet, flocked to his studio to have their portraits made. Nadar said he sought in his work "that instant of understanding that puts you in touch with the model—helps you sum him up, guides you to his habits, his ideas,

30-52 JULIA MARGARET CAMERON, *Ophelia, Study No. 2,* 1867. Albumen print, 1′ 1″ × 10⅔″. George Eastman House, Rochester (gift of Eastman Kodak Company; formerly Gabriel Cromer Collection).

Cameron was a prominent 19th-century photographer who often depicted her female subjects as characters in literary or biblical narratives. The slightly blurred focus is a distinctive feature of her work.

and character and enables you to produce . . . a really convincing and sympathetic likeness, an intimate portrait."[15]

Nadar's *Eugène Delacroix* (FIG. **30-1**) shows the painter at the height of his career. In this photograph, the artist imparts remarkable

presence. Even in half-length, his gesture and expression create a mood that seems to reveal much about him. Perhaps Delacroix responded to Nadar's famous gift for putting his clients at ease by assuming the pose that best expressed his personality. The new photographic materials made possible the rich range of tones in Nadar's images.

JULIA MARGARET CAMERON Among the most famous portrait photographers in 19th-century England was JULIA MARGARET CAMERON (1815–1879), who did not take up photography seriously until age 48. Although she produced images of many well-known men of the period, including Charles Darwin, Alfred Tennyson, and Thomas Carlyle, she photographed more women than men, as was true of many women photographers. *Ophelia, Study No. 2* (FIG. **30-52**) typifies her portrait style. Cameron often depicted her female subjects as characters in literary or biblical narratives. The slightly blurred focus also became a distinctive feature of her work— the byproduct of photographing with a lens having a short focal length, which allowed only a small area of sharp focus. The blurriness adds an ethereal, dreamlike tone to the photographs, appropriate for Cameron's fictional "characters." Her photograph of Ophelia has a mysterious, fragile quality reminiscent of Pre-Raphaelite paintings (FIG. **30-43**) of literary heroines.

TIMOTHY O'SULLIVAN Photographers were quick to realize the documentary power of their new medium. Thus began the story of photography's influence on modern life and of the immense changes it brought to communication and information management. Historical events could be recorded in permanent form on the spot for the first time. The photographs taken of the Crimean War (1856) by Roger Fenton (1819–1869) and of the American Civil War by Mathew B. Brady (1823–1896), Alexander Gardner (1821–1882), and TIMOTHY O'SULLIVAN (1840–1882) remain unsurpassed as incisive accounts of military life, unsparing in their truthful detail and poignant as expressions of human experience.

Of the Civil War photographs, the most moving are the inhumanly objective records of combat deaths. Perhaps the most reproduced of these photographs is O'Sullivan's *A Harvest of Death, Gettysburg, Pennsylvania, July 1863* (FIG. **30-53**). Although viewers

30-53 TIMOTHY O'SULLIVAN, *A Harvest of Death, Gettysburg, Pennsylvania, July 1863,* 1863. Negative by Timothy O'Sullivan. Albumen print by ALEXANDER GARDNER, 6¾″ × 8¾″. New York Public Library (Astor, Lenox and Tilden Foundations, Rare Books and Manuscript Division), New York. ◼◄

Wet-plate technology enabled photographers to record historical events on the spot— and to comment on the high price of war, as in this photograph of dead Union soldiers at Gettysburg in 1863.

30-54 EADWEARD MUYBRIDGE, *Horse Galloping,* 1878. Calotype print, 9″ × 12″. George Eastman House, Rochester. ◼◀

Muybridge specialized in photographic studies of the successive stages in human and animal motion—details too quick for the human eye to capture. Modern cinema owes a great deal to his work.

1 in.

could regard this image as simple news reportage, it also functions to impress on people the high price of the Civil War. Corpses litter the battlefield as far as the eye can see. O'Sullivan presented a scene stretching far to the horizon. As the photograph modulates from the precise clarity of the bodies of Union soldiers in the foreground, boots stolen and pockets picked, to the almost indistinguishable corpses in the distance, the suggestion of innumerable other dead soldiers is unavoidable. This "harvest" is far more sobering and depressing than that in Winslow Homer's Civil War painting, *Veteran in a New Field* (FIG. **30-37**). Though it would be many years before photolithography could reproduce photographs like this in newspapers, photographers exhibited them publicly. They made an impression that newsprint engravings never could.

EADWEARD MUYBRIDGE The Realist photographer and scientist EADWEARD MUYBRIDGE (1830–1904) came to the United States from England in the 1850s and settled in San Francisco, where he established a prominent international reputation for his photographs of the western United States. In 1872 the governor of California, Leland Stanford (1824–1893), sought Muybridge's assistance in settling a bet about whether, at any point in a stride, all four feet of a horse galloping at top speed were off the ground. Through his sequential photography, as seen in *Horse Galloping* (FIG. **30-54**), Muybridge proved they were. This experience was the beginning of Muybridge's photographic studies of the successive stages in human

and animal motion—details too quick for the human eye to capture. These investigations culminated in 1885 at the University of Pennsylvania with a series of multiple-camera motion studies that recorded separate photographs of progressive moments in a single action. Muybridge's discoveries received extensive publicity through the book *Animal Locomotion* (1887), and his motion photographs earned him a place in the history of science as well as art. These sequential motion studies, along with those of Eakins and Marey, influenced many other artists, including their contemporary, the painter and sculptor Edgar Degas (FIG. **31-10**), and 20th-century artists such as Marcel Duchamp (FIG. **35-1**).

Muybridge presented his work to scientists and general audiences with a device called the *zoopraxiscope,* which he invented to project his sequences of images (mounted on special glass plates) onto a screen. The result was so lifelike that one viewer said it "threw upon the screen apparently the living, moving animals. Nothing was wanting but the clatter of hoofs upon the turf."[16] The illusion of motion here was the result of an aspect of human eyesight called "persistence of vision." Stated simply, it means that the brain retains whatever the eye sees for a fraction of a second after the eye stops seeing it. Thus, viewers saw a rapid succession of different images merging one into the next, producing the illusion of continuous change. This illusion lies at the heart of the motion-picture industry that debuted in the 20th century, and thus was born cinema as a new art form.

EUROPE AND AMERICA, 1800 TO 1870

ART UNDER NAPOLEON

▮ As Emperor of the French from 1804 to 1815, Napoleon embraced the Neoclassical style in order to associate his regime with the empire of ancient Rome. Napoleon chose Jacques-Louis David as First Painter of the Empire. Roman temples were the models for La Madeleine in Paris, which Pierre Vignon built as a temple of glory for France's imperial armies.

▮ Napoleon's favorite sculptor was Antonio Canova, who carved marble Neoclassical portraits of the imperial family, including Napoleon's sister, Pauline Borghese, in the guise of Venus.

▮ The beginning of a break from Neoclassicism can already be seen in the work of some of David's students, including Gros, Girodet-Trioson, and Ingres, all of whom painted some exotic subjects that reflect Romantic taste.

Canova, *Pauline Borghese as Venus*, 1808

ROMANTICISM

▮ The roots of Romanticism are in the 18th century, but usually the term more narrowly denotes the artistic movement that flourished from 1800 to 1840, between Neoclassicism and Realism. Romantic artists gave precedence to feeling and imagination over Enlightenment reason. Romantic painters explored the exotic, erotic, and fantastic in their art. In Spain, Francisco Goya's *Caprichos* series celebrated the unleashing of imagination, emotions, and even nightmares.

▮ In France, Eugène Delacroix led the way in depicting Romantic narratives set in faraway places and distant times. He set his colorful *Death of Sardanapalus* in ancient Assyria.

▮ Romantic painters often chose landscapes as an ideal subject to express the Romantic theme of the soul unified with the natural world. Masters of the transcendental landscape include Friedrich in Germany, Constable and Turner in England, and Cole, Bierstadt, and Church in the United States.

Delacroix, *Death of Sardanapalus*, 1827

REALISM

▮ Realism developed as an artistic movement in mid-19th-century France. Its leading proponent was Gustave Courbet, whose paintings of menial labor and ordinary people exemplify his belief that painters should depict only their own time and place. Honoré Daumier boldly confronted authority with his satirical lithographs commenting on the plight of the working classes. Édouard Manet shocked the public with his paintings featuring promiscuous women and rough brush strokes, which emphasized the flatness of the painting surface, paving the way for modern abstract art.

Courbet, *The Stone Breakers*, 1849

▮ American Realists include Winslow Homer, Thomas Eakins, and John Singer Sargent. Eakins's painting of surgery in progress was too brutally realistic for the Philadelphia art jury that rejected it.

ARCHITECTURE

▮ Territorial expansion, the Romantic interest in exotic locales and earlier eras, and nationalistic pride led to the revival in the 19th century of older architectural styles, especially the Gothic.

▮ By the middle of the century, many architects had already abandoned sentimental and Romantic designs from the past in favor of exploring the possibilities of cast-iron construction, as in Henri Labrouste's Sainte-Geneviève Library in Paris and Joseph Paxton's Crystal Palace in London.

Labrouste, Bibliothèque Sainte-Geneviève, Paris, 1843–1850

PHOTOGRAPHY

▮ In 1839, Daguerre in Paris and Talbot in London invented the first practical photographic processes. In 1862, a French court formally recognized photography as an art form subject to copyright protection. Many of the earliest photographers, including Nadar and Cameron, specialized in portrait photography, but others, including Hawes, Southworth, and O'Sullivan in the United States, quickly realized the documentary power of the new medium. Muybridge's sequential photos of human and animal motion were the forerunners of the modern cinema.

O'Sullivan, *A Harvest of Death*, 1863

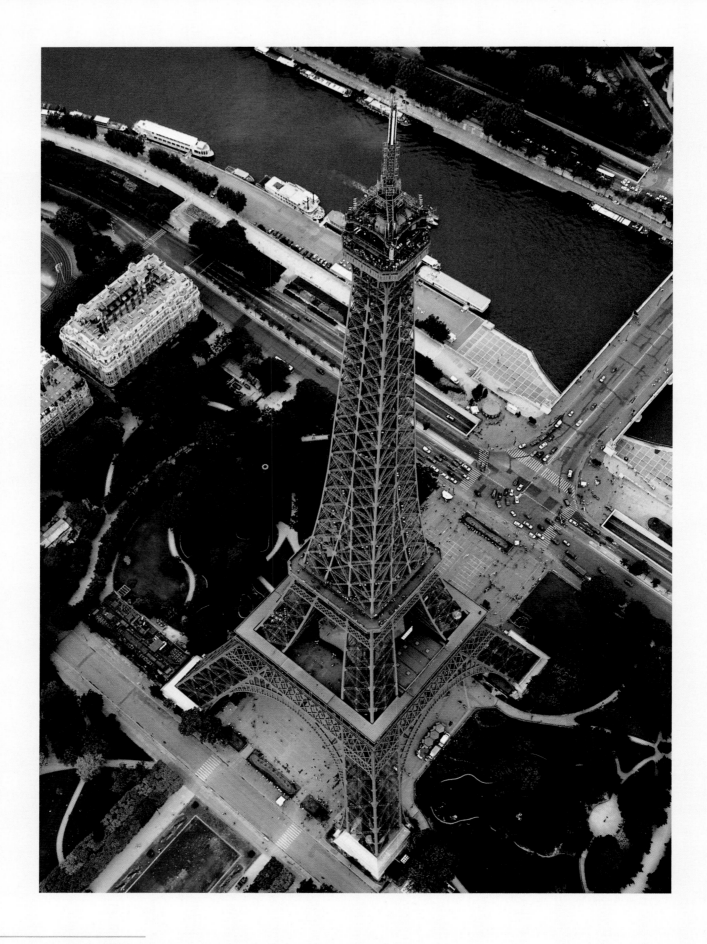

31-1 ALEXANDRE-GUSTAVE EIFFEL, Eiffel Tower, Paris, France, 1889.

New materials and technologies and the modernist aesthetic fueled radically new architectural designs in the late 19th century. Eiffel jolted the world with the exposed iron skeleton of his tower.

31

EUROPE
AND AMERICA,
1870 TO 1900

The momentous Western developments of the early 19th century—industrialization, urbanization, and increased economic and political interaction worldwide—matured quickly during the latter half of the century. The Industrial Revolution in England spread to France (MAP 31-1) and the rest of Europe and to the United States. Because of this dramatic expansion, historians often refer to the third quarter of the 19th century as the second Industrial Revolution. Whereas the first Industrial Revolution centered on textiles, steam, and iron, the second focused on steel, electricity, chemicals, and oil. The discoveries in these fields provided the foundation for developments in plastics, machinery, building construction, and automobile manufacturing and paved the way for the invention of the radio, electric light, telephone, and electric streetcar.

One of the most significant consequences of industrialization was urbanization. The number and size of Western cities grew dramatically during the later 19th century, largely due to migration from rural regions. Rural dwellers relocated to urban centers because expanded agricultural enterprises squeezed the smaller property owners from the land. The widely available work opportunities in the cities, especially in the factories, were also a major factor in this migration. In addition, improving health and living conditions in the cities contributed to their explosive growth.

MARXISM AND DARWINISM The rise of the urban working class was fundamental to the ideas of Karl Marx (1818–1883), one of the era's dominant figures. Born in Trier, Marx received a doctorate in philosophy from the University of Berlin. After moving to Paris, he met fellow German Friedrich Engels (1820–1895), who became his lifelong collaborator. Together they wrote *The Communist Manifesto* (1848), which called for the working class to overthrow the capitalist system. Like other 19th-century empiricists, Marx believed that scientific, rational law governed nature and, indeed, all human history. For Marx, economic forces based on class struggle induced historical change. Throughout history, insisted Marx, those who controlled the means of production conflicted with those whose labor they exploited for their own enrichment. This constant opposition—a dynamic he called "dialectical materialism"—generated change. Marxism's ultimate goal was to create a socialist state in which the working class seized power and destroyed capitalism. Marxism held great appeal for the oppressed as well as many intellectuals.

Equally influential was the English naturalist Charles Darwin (1809–1882), whose theory of natural selection did much to increase interest in science. Darwin and his compatriot Alfred Russel Wallace (1823–1913), working independently, proposed a model for the process of evolution based on mechanistic laws, rather than attributing evolution to random chance or God's plan. They postulated a competitive system in which only the fittest survived. Darwin's controversial ideas, as presented in *On the Origin of Species by Means of Natural Selection* (1859), sharply contrasted with the biblical narrative of creation. By challenging traditional Christian beliefs, Darwinism contributed to a growing secular attitude.

Other theorists and social thinkers, most notably British philosopher Herbert Spencer (1820–1903), applied Darwin's principles to the rapidly changing socioeconomic realm. As in the biological world, they asserted, industrialization's intense competition led to the survival of the most economically fit companies, enterprises, and countries. The social Darwinists provided Western leaders with justification for the colonization of peoples and cultures that they deemed less advanced. By 1900 the major economic and political powers had divided up much of the world. The French had colonized most of North Africa and Indochina, while the British occupied India, Australia, and large areas of Africa, including Nigeria, Egypt, Sudan, Rhodesia, and the Union of South Africa. The Dutch were a major presence in the Pacific, and the Germans, Portuguese, Spanish, and Italians all established themselves in various areas of Africa.

MAP 31-1 France around 1870.

MODERNISM The combination of extensive technological changes and increased exposure to other cultures, coupled with the rapidity of these changes, led to an acute sense in Western cultures of the world's impermanence. Darwin's ideas of evolution and Marx's emphasis on a continuing sequence of economic conflicts reinforced this awareness of a constantly shifting reality. These societal changes in turn fostered a new and multifaceted artistic approach that historians call *modernism*. Modernist artists seek to capture the images and sensibilities of their age, but modernism transcends the simple present to involve the artist's critical examination of or reflection on the premises of art itself. Modernism thus implies certain concerns about art and aesthetics that are internal to art production, regardless of whether the artist is producing scenes from contemporary social life. Clement Greenberg (1909–1994), an influential American art critic, explained:

> The essence of Modernism lies . . . in the use of the characteristic methods of a discipline to criticize the discipline itself—not in order to subvert it, but to entrench it more firmly in its area of competence. . . . Realistic, illusionist art had dissembled the medium, using art to conceal art. Modernism used art to call attention to art. The limitations that constitute the medium of painting—the flat surface, the shape of the support, the properties of pigment—were treated by the Old Masters as negative factors that could be acknowledged only implicitly or indirectly. Modernist painting has come to regard these same limitations as positive factors that are to be acknowledged openly.[1]

The work of Gustave Courbet and the Realists (see Chapter 30) already expressed this modernist viewpoint, but modernism emerged even more forcefully in the late-19th-century movements that art historians call Impressionism, Post-Impressionism, and Symbolism.

IMPRESSIONISM

Impressionism, both in content and in style, was an art of industrialized, urbanized Paris, a reaction to the sometimes brutal and chaotic transformation of French life that occurred during the latter half of the 19th century. The rapidity of these changes made the world seem unstable and insubstantial. As the poet and critic Charles Baudelaire (1821–1867) observed in 1860 in his essay "The Painter of Modern Life": "[M]odernity is the transitory, the fugitive, the contingent."[2] Accordingly, Impressionist works represent an attempt to capture a fleeting moment—not in the absolutely fixed, precise sense of a Realist painting but by conveying the elusiveness and impermanence of images and conditions.

CLAUDE MONET A hostile critic applied the term "Impressionism" in response to the painting *Impression: Sunrise* (FIG. 31-2) that CLAUDE MONET (1840–1926) exhibited in the first Impressionist show in 1874 (see "Academic Salons and Independent Art Exhibitions," page 823). Although the critic intended the label to be derogatory, by the third Impressionist show in 1878 the artists had embraced it and were calling themselves Impressionists. Artists and

Academic Salons and Independent Art Exhibitions

For both artists and art historians, modernist art stands in marked contrast—indeed in forceful opposition—to academic art, that is, to the art the established art schools such as the Royal Academy of Painting and Sculpture in France (founded 1648) and the Royal Academy of Arts in Britain (founded 1768) promoted. These academies provided instruction for art students and sponsored exhibitions, exerting tight control over the art scene. The annual exhibitions, called "Salons" in France, were highly competitive, as was membership in these academies. Subsidized by the government, the French Royal Academy supported a limited range of artistic expression, focusing on traditional subjects and highly polished technique. Because of the challenges modernist art presented to established artistic conventions, the juries for the Salons and other exhibitions often rejected the works more adventurous artists wished to display. As noted in the previous chapter, Gustave Courbet's reaction to the rejection of some of his paintings was to set up his own Pavilion of Realism in 1855 (see "Courbet on Realism," Chapter 30, page 799). Years later, he wrote:

> [I]t is high time that someone have the courage to be an honest man and that he say that the Academy is a harmful, all-consuming institution, incapable of fulfilling the goal of its so-called mission.*

Growing dissatisfaction with the decisions of the French Academy's jurors prompted Napoleon III (r. 1852–1870) in 1863 to establish the Salon des Refusés (Salon of the Rejected) to show all of the works not accepted for exhibition in the regular Salon. Manet's *Le Déjeuner sur l'Herbe* (FIG. 30-33) was among them. The public greeted it and the entire exhibition with derision. One reviewer of the rejected works summed up the prevailing attitude:

> This exhibition, at once sad and grotesque, . . . offers abundant proof . . . that the jury always displays an unbelievable leniency. Save for one or two questionable exceptions there is not a painting which deserves the honor of the official galleries . . . . There is even something cruel about this exhibition; people laugh as they do at a farce.†

In 1867, after further rejections, Manet, following Courbet, mounted a private exhibition of 50 of his paintings outside the Paris World's Fair. Six years later, the Impressionists (FIG. 31-2) formed their own society and began mounting shows of their works in Paris. This decision gave the Impressionists much more freedom, for they did not have to contend with the Academy's authoritative and confining viewpoint, and thereafter they held exhibitions at one- or two-year intervals from 1874 until 1886.

Another group of artists unhappy with the Salon's conservative nature adopted the same renegade approach. In 1884 these artists formed the Société des Artistes Indépendants (Society of Independent Artists) and held annual Salons des Indépendants. Georges Seurat's *A Sunday on La Grande Jatte* (FIG. 31-15) was one of the paintings in the Independents' 1886 Salon.

As the art market expanded, venues for the exhibition of art increased. Art circles and societies sponsored private shows in which both amateurs and professionals participated. Dealers became more aggressive in promoting the artists they represented by mounting exhibitions in a variety of spaces, some fairly intimate and small, others large and grandiose. All of these proliferating opportunities for exhibition gave artists alternatives to the traditional constraints of the Salon and provided fertile breeding ground for the development of radically new art forms and styles.

* Letter to Jules-Antoine Castagnary, October 17, 1868. Translated by Petra ten-Doesschate Chu, *Letters of Gustave Courbet* (Chicago: University of Chicago Press, 1992), 346.
† Maxime du Camp, in *Revue des deux mondes*, 1863, quoted in George Heard Hamilton, *Manet and His Critics* (New Haven: Yale University Press, 1986), 42–43.

1 in.

31-2 CLAUDE MONET, *Impression: Sunrise*, 1872. Oil on canvas, 1' 7$\frac{1}{2}$" × 2' 1$\frac{1}{2}$". Musée Marmottan, Paris.

A hostile critic applied the derogatory term "Impressionism" to this painting because of its sketchy quality and clearly evident brush strokes. Monet and his circle embraced the label for their movement.

critics had used the term before, but only in relation to sketches. Impressionist paintings do incorporate the qualities of sketches—abbreviation, speed, and spontaneity. This is apparent in *Impression: Sunrise*, in which Monet made no attempt to disguise the brush strokes or blend the pigment to create smooth tonal gradations and an optically accurate scene. This concern with acknowledging the paint and the canvas surface continued the modernist exploration that the Realists began. Beyond this connection to the sketch, Impressionism operated at the intersection of what the artists saw and what they felt. In other words, the "impressions" these artists recorded in their paintings were neither purely objective descriptions of the exterior world nor solely subjective responses but the interaction between the two. They were sensations—the artists' subjective and personal responses to nature.

31-2A MONET, *Bank of the Seine, Bennecourt,* 1868.

In sharp contrast to traditional studio artists, Monet painted outdoors, which sharpened his focus on the roles light and color play in capturing an instantaneous representation of atmosphere and climate. Monet carried the systematic investigation of light and color further than any other Impressionist, but all of them recognized the importance of carefully observing and understanding how light and color operate. This thorough study permitted the Impressionists to present images that truly conveyed a sense of the momentary and transitory. Lila Cabot Perry (1848–1933), a student of Monet's late in his career, gave this description of Monet's approach:

31-2B MONET, *Monet in His Studio Boat,* 1874.

> I remember his once saying to me: "When you go out to paint, try to forget what objects you have before you—a tree, a house, a field, or whatever. Merely think, here is a little square of blue, here an oblong of pink, here a streak of yellow, and paint it just as it looks to you, the exact color and shape, until it gives your own naïve impression of the scene before you."[3]

Scientific studies of light and the invention of chemically synthesized pigments increased artists' sensitivity to the multiplicity of colors in nature and gave them new colors for their work. After scrutinizing the effects of light and color on forms, the Impressionists concluded that *local color*—an object's true color in white light—becomes modified by the quality of the light shining on it, by reflections from other objects, and by the effects juxtaposed colors produce. Shadows do not appear gray or black, as many earlier painters thought, but are composed of colors modified by reflections or other conditions. If artists use complementary colors (see "19th-Century Color Theory," page 832) side by side over large enough areas, the colors intensify each other, unlike the effect of small quantities of adjoining mixed pigments, which blend into neutral tones. Furthermore, the "mixing" of colors by juxtaposing them on a canvas produces a more intense hue than the same colors mixed on the palette. It is not strictly true that the Impressionists used only primary hues, placing them side by side to create secondary colors (blue and yellow, for example, to create green). But they did achieve remarkably brilliant effects with their characteristic short, choppy brush strokes, which so accurately caught the vibrating quality of light. The fact that their canvas surfaces look incomprehensible at close range and their forms and objects appear only when the eye fuses the strokes at a certain distance accounts for much of the early adverse criticism leveled at their work. Some critics even accused the Impressionists of firing their paint at the canvas with pistols.

ROUEN CATHEDRAL Monet's intensive study of the phenomena of light and color is especially evident in several series of paintings he made of the same subject. In one series he painted some 40 views of Rouen Cathedral, northwest of Paris (MAP **31-1**). For each canvas in the series, Monet observed the cathedral from nearly

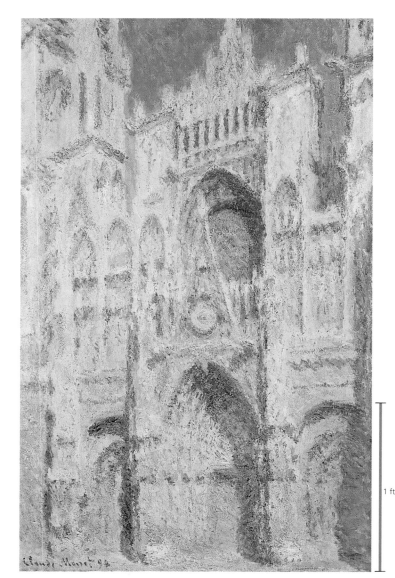

1 ft.

31-3 CLAUDE MONET, *Rouen Cathedral: The Portal (in Sun)*, 1894. Oil on canvas, 3′ 3$\frac{1}{4}$″ × 2′ 1$\frac{7}{8}$″. Metropolitan Museum of Art, New York (Theodore M. Davis Collection, bequest of Theodore M. Davis, 1915).

Monet painted some 40 views of Rouen Cathedral at different times of day and under various climatic conditions. The real subject of this painting is not the building but the sunlight shining on it.

the same viewpoint but at different times of the day or under various climatic conditions. In the painting illustrated here (FIG. **31-3**), Monet depicted the church bathed in bright light. With scientific precision, he created an unparalleled record of the passing of time as seen in the movement of light over identical forms. In fact, the real subject of Monet's painting—as the title *Rouen Cathedral: The Portal (in Sun)* implies—is not the cathedral, which he shows only in part, but the sunlight on the building's main portal. Later critics accused Monet and his companions of destroying form and order for fleeting atmospheric effects, but Monet focused on light and color precisely to reach a greater understanding of the appearance of form.

SAINT-LAZARE Most of the Impressionists depicted scenes in and around Paris, the heart of modern life in France. Monet's *Saint-Lazare Train Station* (FIG. **31-4**) shows a dominant aspect of the contemporary urban scene. The expanding railway network had made travel more convenient, bringing throngs of people into Paris. In this painting, Monet captured the energy and vitality of Paris's modern transportation hub. The train, emerging from the steam

31-4 CLAUDE MONET, *Saint-Lazare Train Station*, 1877. Oil on canvas, 2′ 5¾″ × 3′ 5″. Musée d'Orsay, Paris.

Impressionist canvas surfaces are incomprehensible at close range, but the eye fuses the brush strokes at a distance. Monet's agitated application of paint contributes to the sense of energy in this urban scene.

smoke, which lashes the glass roof of the main hall. . . . We see the vast and manic movements at the station where the ground shakes with every turn of the wheel. The platforms are sticky with soot, and the air is full of that bitter scent exuded by burning coal. As we look at this magnificent picture, we are overcome by the same feelings as if we were really there, and these feelings are perhaps even more powerful, because in the picture the artist has conveyed his own feelings as well.[4]

and smoke it emits, rumbles into the station. In the background haze are the tall buildings that were becoming a major component of the Parisian landscape. Monet's agitated paint application contributes to the sense of energy and conveys the atmosphere of urban life.

Georges Rivière (1855–1943), a critic and friend of some of the Impressionists, saw this painting in the third Impressionist exhibition and recorded the essence of what Monet had tried to achieve:

> Like a fiery steed, stimulated rather than exhausted by the long trek that it has only just finished, [the locomotive] tosses its mane of

GUSTAVE CAILLEBOTTE Other Impressionists also represented facets of city life, although not always using Monet's impressionistic brush strokes. The setting of *Paris: A Rainy Day* (FIG. **31-5**) by GUSTAVE CAILLEBOTTE (1849–1893) is a junction of spacious boulevards that resulted from the redesigning of Paris that began in 1852. The city's population had reached nearly 1.5 million by midcentury. To accommodate this congregation of humanity—and to facilitate the movement of troops in the event of another revolution—Napoleon III ordered Paris rebuilt. The emperor named Baron Georges Haussmann (1809–1891), a city superintendent, to oversee the entire project. In addition to new water and sewer systems, street lighting, and new residential and commercial buildings, a major component of the new Paris was the creation of the wide, open boulevards seen in Caillebotte's painting. These great avenues, whose construction caused the demolition of thousands of old buildings and streets, transformed medieval Paris into the present modern city, with its superb vistas and wide uninterrupted arteries for the flow of vehicular and pedestrian traffic. Caillebotte chose to focus on these markers of the city's rapid urbanization.

31-5 GUSTAVE CAILLEBOTTE, *Paris: A Rainy Day,* 1877. Oil on canvas, 6′ 9″ × 9′ 9″. Art Institute of Chicago, Chicago (Worcester Fund).

Although Caillebotte did not use Impressionistic broken brush strokes, the seemingly randomly placed figures and the arbitrary cropping of the vista suggest the transitory nature of modern life.

Impressionism   **825**

This Impressionist view of a crowded Paris square seen from several stories above street level has much in common with photographs, especially the flattening spatial effect resulting from the high viewpoint.

1 ft.

Although Caillebotte did not dissolve his image into the broken color and brushwork characteristic of Impressionism, he did use an informal and asymmetrical composition. The figures seem randomly placed, with the frame cropping them arbitrarily, suggesting the transitory nature of the street scene. Well-dressed Parisians of the leisure class share the viewer's space. Despite the sharp focus of *Paris: A Rainy Day*, the picture captures the artist's "impression" of urban life.

CAMILLE PISSARRO Other Impressionists also found the spacious boulevards and avenues that were the product of "Haussmannization" attractive subjects for paintings. *La Place du Théâtre Français* (FIG. 31-6) is one of many panoramic scenes of Paris that CAMILLE PISSARRO (1830–1903) painted. The artist recorded the blurred dark accents against a light ground that constituted his visual sensations of a crowded Paris square viewed from several stories above street level. The moment Pissarro captured in this painting is not so much of fugitive light effects as it is of street life, achieved through a deliberate casualness in the arrangement of figures. To accomplish this sense of spontaneity, Pissarro, like many of his fellow Impressionists, sometimes used photography to record the places he wished to paint. Scholars have been quick to point out the visual parallels between Impressionist paintings and photographs. These parallels include, here, the arbitrary cutting off of figures at the frame's edge and the curious flattening spatial effect produced by the high viewpoint.

BERTHE MORISOT Many Impressionist paintings depict scenes from resort areas on the seashore or along the Seine River, such as Argenteuil, Bougival, and Chatou. The railway line that carried people to and from Saint-Lazare Station connected Argenteuil to Paris, so transportation was not an obstacle. Parisians often would take the train out to these resort areas for a day of sailing, picnicking, and strolling along the Seine. BERTHE MORISOT (1841–1895), Édouard Manet's sister-in-law, regularly exhibited with the Impres-

31-7A MORIS
Summer's C
1879.

In this informal view of a woman and child enjoying their leisure time at a fashionable seashore resort, Berthe Morisot used swift, sketchy strokes of light colors to convey a feeling of airiness.

1 in.

Renoir on the Art of Painting

Many 19th-century artists were concerned with the theoretical basis of picture making. One of the most cogent statements on this subject is Pierre-Auguste Renoir's concise summary of how he, as an Impressionist, painted pictures (for example, FIG. 31-8) and what he hoped to achieve as an artist.

I arrange my subject as I want it, then I go ahead and paint it, like a child. I want a red to be sonorous, to sound like a bell; if it doesn't turn out that way, I add more reds and other colors until I get it. I am no cleverer than that. I have no rules and no methods; . . . I have no secrets. I look at a nude; there are myriads of tiny tints. I must find the ones that will make the flesh on my canvas live and quiver. . . .

[If viewers] could explain a picture, it wouldn't be art. Shall I tell you what I think are the two qualities of art? It must be indescribable and it must be inimitable. . . . The work of art must seize upon you, wrap you up in itself, carry you away. It is the means by which the artist conveys his passions. . . . I want people to feel that neither the setting nor the figures are dull and lifeless.*

* Quoted in Eric Protter, ed., *Painters on Painting* (New York: Grosset & Dunlap, 1971), 145.

31-8 PIERRE-AUGUSTE RENOIR, *Le Moulin de la Galette*, 1876. Oil on canvas, 4′ 3″ × 5′ 8″. Musée d'Orsay, Paris.

Renoir's painting of this popular Parisian dance hall is dappled by sunlight and shade, artfully blurred into the figures to produce the effect of floating and fleeting light that the Impressionists cultivated.

sionists. Most of her paintings focus on domestic subjects, the one realm of Parisian life where society allowed an upper-class woman such as Morisot free access, but she also produced many outdoor scenes. Morisot's considerable skills are evident in *Villa at the Seaside* (FIG. 31-7). Both the subject and style correlate well with Impressionist concerns. The setting is the shaded veranda of a summer hotel at a fashionable seashore resort. A woman elegantly but not ostentatiously dressed sits gazing out across the railing to a sunlit beach with its umbrellas and bathing cabins. Her child, its discarded toy boat a splash of red, is attentive to the passing sails on the placid sea. The mood is of relaxed leisure. Morisot used the open brushwork and the *plein air* (outdoor) lighting characteristic of Impressionism. Sketchy brush strokes record her quick perceptions. Nowhere did Morisot linger on contours or enclosed details. She presented the scene in a slightly filmy soft focus that conveys a feeling of airiness. The composition also recalls the work of other Impressionists. The figures fall informally into place, as someone who shared their intimate space would perceive them. Morisot was both immensely ambitious and talented, as her ability to catch the pictorial moment demonstrates. She escaped the hostile criticism directed at most of the other Impressionists. People praised her work for its sensibility, grace, and delicacy.

PIERRE-AUGUSTE RENOIR Another facet of the new industrialized Paris that drew the Impressionists' attention was the leisure activities of its inhabitants. Scenes of dining, dancing, the café-concerts, the opera, the ballet, and other forms of urban recreation were mainstays of Impressionism. Although seemingly unrelated, industrialization facilitated these pursuits. With the advent of set working hours, people's schedules became more regimented, allowing them to plan their favorite pastimes. *Le Moulin de la Galette* (FIG. 31-8) by PIERRE-AUGUSTE RENOIR (1841–1919) depicts throngs of people gathered in a popular Parisian dance hall. Some crowd the tables and chatter, while others dance energetically. So lively is the atmosphere that the viewer can virtually hear the sounds of music, laughter, and tinkling glasses. The painter dappled the whole scene with sunlight and shade, artfully blurred into the figures to produce just the effect of floating and fleeting light the Impressionists so cultivated. Renoir's casual, unposed placement of the figures and the suggested continuity of space, spreading in all directions and only accidentally limited by the frame, position the viewer as a participant rather than as an outsider. Whereas classical art sought to express universal and timeless qualities, Impressionism attempted to depict just the opposite—the incidental, momentary, and passing aspects of reality (see "Renoir on the Art of Painting," above).

Impressionism **827**

ÉDOUARD MANET Another artist who depicted Parisian nightlife was Édouard Manet, whose career bridged Realism (see Chapter 30) and Impressionism. One of his later paintings in the Impressionist mode is *Bar at the Folies-Bergère* (FIG. 31-9). The Folies-Bergère was a popular café with music-hall performances, one of the fashionable gathering places for Parisian revelers that many Impressionists frequented. In Manet's 1882 painting, a barmaid, centrally placed, looks out from the canvas but seems disinterested or lost in thought, divorced from her patrons as well as from the viewer. Manet blurred and roughly applied the brush strokes, particularly those in the background, and the effects of modeling and perspective are minimal. This painting method further calls attention to the surface by forcing the viewer to scrutinize the work to make sense of the scene. On such scrutiny, visual discrepancies emerge. For example, what initially seems easily recognizable as a mirror behind the barmaid creates confusion throughout the rest of the painting. Is the woman on the right the barmaid's reflection? If so, it is impossible to reconcile the spatial relationship among the barmaid, the mirror, the bar's frontal horizontality, and the barmaid's seemingly displaced reflection. These visual contradictions reveal Manet's insistence on calling attention to the pictorial structure of his painting, in keeping with his modernist interest in examining the basic premises of the medium.

EDGAR DEGAS Impressionists also depicted more formal leisure activities. The fascination EDGAR DEGAS (1834–1917) had with patterns of motion brought him to the Paris Opéra (FIG. 30-46) and its ballet school. There, his great observational power took in the formalized movements of classical ballet, one of his favorite subjects. In *The Rehearsal* (FIG. 31-10), Degas used several devices to bring the observer into the pictorial space. The frame cuts off the spiral stair, the windows in the background, and the group of figures in the right foreground. The figures are not at the center of a classically balanced composition. Instead, Degas arranged them in a seemingly random manner. The prominent diagonals of the wall bases and floorboards carry the viewer into and along the directional lines of the dancers. Finally, as is customary in Degas's ballet pictures, a large, off-center, empty space creates the illusion of a continuous floor that connects the observer with the pictured figures.

The often arbitrarily cut-off figures, the patterns of light splotches, and the blurriness of the images in this and other Degas works indicate the artist's interest in reproducing single moments. Further, they reveal his fascination with photography. Degas not only studied the photography of others but also used the camera to make preliminary studies for his works, particularly photographing figures in interiors. Japanese woodblock prints (see "Japonisme," page 829) were another inspirational source for paintings such as *The Rehearsal*. The cunning spatial projections in Degas's paintings probably derived in part from Japanese prints, such as those by Suzuki Harunobu (FIG. 28-12). Japanese artists used diverging lines

Japonisme

Despite Europe's and America's extensive colonization during the 19th century, Japan avoided Western intrusion until 1853–1854, when Commodore Matthew Perry (1794–1858) and American naval forces exacted trading and diplomatic privileges from Japan. From the increased contact, Westerners became familiar with Japanese culture. So intrigued were the French with Japanese art and culture that they introduced a specific label—*Japonisme*—to describe the Japanese aesthetic, which, because of both its beauty and exoticism, greatly appealed to the fashionable segment of Parisian society. In 1867 at the Exposition Universelle in Paris, the Japanese pavilion garnered more attention than any other. Soon, Japanese kimonos, fans, lacquer cabinets, tea caddies, folding screens, tea services, and jewelry flooded Paris. Japanese-themed novels and travel books were immensely popular as well. As demand for Japanese merchandise grew in the West, the Japanese began to develop import-export businesses, and the foreign currency that flowed into Japan helped to finance much of its industrialization.

Artists in particular were great admirers of Japanese art. Among those the Japanese aesthetic influenced were the Impressionists and Post-Impressionists, especially Édouard Manet, Edgar Degas, Mary Cassatt, James Abbott McNeill Whistler, Henri de Toulouse-Lautrec, Vincent van Gogh, and Paul Gauguin. For the most part, the Japanese presentation of space in woodblock prints (FIGS. 28-12 and 28-13),

which were more readily available in the West than any other art form, intrigued these artists. Because of the simplicity of the woodblock printing process (see "Japanese Woodblock Prints," Chapter 28, page 744), these prints feature broad areas of flat color with a limited amount of modulation or gradation. This flatness interested modernist painters, who sought ways to call attention to the picture surface. The right side of Degas's *The Tub* (FIG. 31-11, *left*), for example, has this two-dimensional quality. Degas, in fact, owned a print by Japanese artist TORII KIYONAGA (1752–1815) depicting eight women at a bath in various poses and states of undress. That print inspired Degas's painting. A comparison between Degas's bather and a detail (FIG. 31-11, *right*) of a bather from another of Kiyonaga's prints is striking, although Degas did not closely copy any of the Japanese artist's figures. Instead, he absorbed the essence of Japanese compositional style and the distinctive angles employed in representing human figures, and he translated them into the Impressionist mode.

The decorative quality of Japanese images also appealed to the artists associated with the Arts and Crafts movement in England. Artists such as William Morris (FIG. 31-34) and Charles Rennie Mackintosh (FIG. 31-35) found Japanese prints attractive because those artworks intersected nicely with two fundamental Arts and Crafts principles: Art should be available to the masses, and functional objects should be artistically designed.

1 ft.   1 in.

31-11 *Left:* EDGAR DEGAS, *The Tub*, 1886. Pastel, $1' 11\frac{1}{2}'' \times 2' 8\frac{3}{8}''$. Musée d'Orsay, Paris. *Right:* TORII KIYONAGA, detail of *Two Women at the Bath*, ca. 1780. Color woodblock, full print $10\frac{1}{2}'' \times 7\frac{1}{2}''$, detail $3\frac{3}{4}'' \times 3\frac{1}{2}''$. Musée Guimet, Paris.

The Tub reveals the influence of Japanese prints, especially the distinctive angles artists such as Torii Kiyonaga used in representing figures. Degas translated his Japanese model into the Impressionist mode.

A VAN
*Flowering
Tree,* 1887.

not only to organize the flat shapes of figures but also to direct the viewer's attention into the picture space. The Impressionists, acquainted with these prints as early as the 1860s, greatly admired their spatial organization, familiar and intimate themes, and flat unmodeled color areas, and drew much instruction from them.

THE TUB Although color and light were major components of the Impressionist quest to capture fleeting sensations, these artists considered other formal elements as well. Degas, for example, became a

superb master of line, so much so that his works often differ significantly from those of Monet and Renoir. Degas specialized in studies of figures in rapid and informal action, recording the quick impression of arrested motion, as is evident in *The Rehearsal* (FIG. 31-10). He often employed lines to convey this sense of movement. In *The Tub* (FIG. 31-11, *left*), inspired by a Japanese print similar to the one illustrated here (FIG. 31-11, *right*), a young woman crouches in a washing tub. The artist outlined the major objects in the painting—the woman, tub, and pitchers—and covered all surfaces with linear

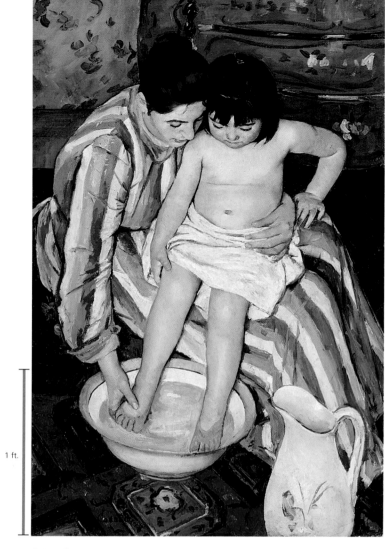

1 ft.

31-12 MARY CASSATT, *The Bath*, ca. 1892. Oil on canvas, 3′ 3″ × 2′ 2″. Art Institute of Chicago, Chicago (Robert A. Walker Fund). ■◄

Cassatt's style owed much to the compositional devices of Degas and of Japanese prints, but her subjects differed from those of most Impressionists, in part because, as a woman, she could not frequent cafés.

hatch marks. Degas achieved this leaner quality with *pastels*, his favorite medium. Using these dry sticks of powdered pigment, Degas drew directly on the paper, as one would with a piece of chalk, thus accounting for the linear basis of his work. Although the applied pastel is subject to smudging, the colors tend to retain their autonomy, so they appear fresh and bright.

The Tub also reveals how Degas's work, like that of the other Impressionists, continued the modernist exploration of the premises of painting by acknowledging the artwork's surface. Although the viewer clearly perceives the woman as a depiction of a three-dimensional form in space, the tabletop or shelf on the right of the image appears so severely tilted that it seems to parallel the picture plane. The two pitchers on the table complicate this visual conflict between the table's flatness and the illusion of the bathing woman's three-dimensional volume. The limited foreshortening of the pitchers and their shared edge, in conjunction with the rest of the image, create a visual perplexity for the viewer.

MARY CASSATT In the Salon of 1874, Degas admired a painting by a young American artist, MARY CASSATT (1844–1926), the

daughter of a Philadelphia banker. Degas befriended and influenced Cassatt, who exhibited regularly with the Impressionists. She had trained as a painter before moving to Europe to study masterworks in France and Italy. As a woman, she could not easily frequent the cafés with her male artist friends, and she had the responsibility of caring for her aging parents, who had moved to Paris to join her. Because of these restrictions, Cassatt's subjects, like Morisot's (FIG. 31-7), were principally women and children, whom she presented with a combination of objectivity and genuine sentiment. Works such as *The Bath* (FIG. 31-12) show the tender relationship between a mother and child. As in Degas's *The Tub*, the visual solidity of the mother and child contrasts with the flattened patterning of the wallpaper and rug. Cassatt's style in this work owed much to the compositional devices of Degas and of Japanese prints, but the painting's design has an originality and strength all its own.

JAMES WHISTLER Another American expatriate artist in Europe was JAMES ABBOTT MCNEILL WHISTLER (1834–1903), who spent time in Paris before settling finally in London. He met many of the French Impressionists, and his art is a unique combination of some of their concerns and his own. Whistler shared the Impressionists' interests in the subject of contemporary life and the sensations color produces on the eye. To these influences he added his own desire to create harmonies paralleling those achieved in music.

1 in.

31-13 JAMES ABBOTT MCNEILL WHISTLER, *Nocturne in Black and Gold (The Falling Rocket)*, ca. 1875. Oil on panel, 1′ 11⅝″ × 1′ 6½″. Detroit Institute of Arts, Detroit (gift of Dexter M. Ferry Jr.).

In this painting, Whistler displayed an Impressionist's interest in conveying the atmospheric effects of fireworks at night, but he also emphasized the abstract arrangement of shapes and colors.

Nature contains the elements, in color and form, of all pictures, as the keyboard contains the notes of all music. But the artist is born to pick, and choose, and group with science, these elements, that the result may be beautiful—as the musician gathers his notes, and forms his chords, until he brings forth from chaos glorious harmony.[5]

To underscore his artistic intentions, Whistler began calling his paintings "arrangements" or "nocturnes." *Nocturne in Black and Gold*, or *The Falling Rocket* (FIG. **31-13**), is a daring painting with gold flecks and splatters that represent the exploded firework punctuating the darkness of the night sky. More interested in conveying the atmospheric effects than in providing details of the scene, Whistler emphasized creating a harmonious arrangement of shapes and colors on the rectangle of his canvas, an approach that appealed to many 20th-century artists. These works angered many 19th-century viewers, however. The British critic John Ruskin (1819–1900) responded to this painting with a scathing review accusing Whistler of "flinging a pot of paint in the public's face" with his style. In reply, Whistler sued Ruskin for libel. During the trial, Ruskin's attorney asked Whistler about the subject of *Nocturne:*

> What is your definition of a Nocturne?
>
> It is an arrangement of line, form, and colour first; . . . Among my works are some night pieces; and I have chosen the word Nocturne because it generalizes and amplifies the whole set of them. . . . The nocturne in black and gold is a night piece and represents the fireworks at Cremorne [Gardens in London].
>
> Not a view of Cremorne?
>
> If it were a view of Cremorne, it would certainly bring about nothing but disappointment on the part of the beholders. It is an artistic arrangement.[6]

The court transcript notes that the spectators in the courtroom laughed at that response, but Whistler won the case. However, his victory had sadly ironic consequences for him. The judge in the case,

showing where his—and the public's—sympathies lay, awarded the artist only one farthing (less than a penny) in damages and required him to pay all of the court costs, which ruined him financially.

POST-IMPRESSIONISM

By 1886 most critics and a large segment of the public accepted the Impressionists as serious artists. Just when their images of contemporary life no longer seemed crude and unfinished, however, some of these painters and a group of younger followers came to feel that the Impressionists were neglecting too many of the traditional elements of picture making in their attempts to capture momentary sensations of light and color on canvas. In a conversation with the influential art dealer Ambroise Vollard (1866–1939) in about 1883, Renoir commented: "I had wrung impressionism dry, and I finally came to the conclusion that I knew neither how to paint nor how to draw. In a word, impressionism was a blind alley, as far as I was concerned."[7] By the 1880s, some artists were more systematically examining the properties and the expressive qualities of line, pattern, form, and color. Among them were Dutch-born Vincent van Gogh and the French painter Paul Gauguin, who focused their artistic efforts on exploring the expressive capabilities of formal elements, and Georges Seurat and Paul Cézanne, also from France, who were more analytical in orientation. Because their art had its roots in Impressionist precepts and methods, but is not stylistically homogeneous, these artists and others have become known as the *Post-Impressionists.*

HENRI DE TOULOUSE-LAUTREC Closest to the Impressionists in many ways was the French artist HENRI DE TOULOUSE-LAUTREC (1864–1901), who deeply admired Degas and shared the Impressionists' interest in capturing the sensibility of modern life. His work, however, has an added satirical edge to it and often borders on caricature. Genetic defects that stunted his growth and in part crippled him led to Toulouse-Lautrec's self-exile from the high society his ancient aristocratic name entitled him to enter. He became a denizen of the night world of Paris, consorting with a tawdry population of entertainers, prostitutes, and other social outcasts. He reveled in the energy of cheap music halls, cafés, and bordellos. *At the Moulin Rouge* (FIG. **31-14**) reveals the influences of Degas, of the Japanese print, and of photography in the oblique and asymmetrical composition, the spatial diagonals, and the strong line patterns with added dissonant colors. But although Toulouse-Lautrec closely studied such scenes in real life and they were already familiar to viewers in the work of the earlier Impressionists, he so emphasized or exaggerated each element that

31-14A TOULOUSE-LAUTREC, *Jane Avril*, 1893.

1 ft.

31-14 HENRI DE TOULOUSE-LAUTREC, *At the Moulin Rouge*, 1892–1895. Oil on canvas, 4′ × 4′ 7″. Art Institute of Chicago, Chicago (Helen Birch Bartlett Memorial Collection).

The influences of Degas, Japanese prints, and photography show in this painting's oblique composition, but the glaring lighting, masklike faces, and dissonant colors are Toulouse-Lautrec's.

19th-Century Color Theory

In the 19th century, advances in the sciences contributed to changing theories about color and how people perceive it. Many physicists and chemists immersed themselves in studying optical reception and the behavior of the human eye in response to light of differing wavelengths. They also investigated the psychological dimension of color. These new ideas about color and its perception provided a framework within which artists such as Georges Seurat worked. Although historians do not know which publications on color Seurat himself read, he no doubt relied on aspects of these evolving theories to develop pointillism (FIG. 31-15).

Discussions of color often focus on *hue* (for example, red, yellow, and blue), but it is important to consider the other facets of color—*saturation* (the hue's brightness or dullness) and *value* (the hue's lightness or darkness). Most artists during the 19th century understood the concepts of *primary colors* (red, yellow, and blue), *secondary colors* (orange, purple, and green), and *complementary colors* (red and green, yellow and purple, blue and orange; see Introduction, page 7). Chemist Michel-Eugène Chevreul (1786–1889) extended artists' understanding of color dynamics by formulating the law of *simultaneous contrasts* of colors. Chevreul asserted that juxtaposed colors affect the eye's reception of each, making the two colors as dissimilar as possible, both in hue and in value. For example, placing light green next to dark green has the effect of making the light green look even lighter and the dark green darker. Chevreul further provided an explanation of *successive contrasts*—the phenomenon of colored afterimages. When a person looks intently at a color (green, for example) and then shifts to a white area, the fatigued eye momentarily perceives the complementary color (red).

Charles Blanc (1813–1882), who coined the term *optical mixture* to describe the visual effect of juxtaposed complementary colors, asserted that the smaller the areas of adjoining complementary colors, the greater the tendency for the eye to "mix" the colors, so that the viewer perceives a grayish or neutral tint. Seurat used this principle frequently in his paintings.

Also influential for Seurat was the work of physicist Ogden Rood (1831–1902), who published his ideas in *Modern Chromatics, with Applications to Art and Industry* in 1879. Expanding on the ideas of Chevreul and Blanc, Rood constructed an accurate and understandable diagram of contrasting colors. Further (and particularly significant to Seurat), Rood explored representing color gradation. He suggested that artists could achieve gradation by placing small dots or lines of color side by side, which he observed would blend in the eye of the beholder when viewed from a distance.

The color experiments of Seurat and other late-19th-century artists were also part of a larger discourse about human vision and how people see and understand the world. The theories of physicist Ernst Mach (1838–1916) focused on the psychological experience of sensation. He believed humans perceive their environments in isolated units of sensation that the brain then recomposes into a comprehensible world. Another scientist, Charles Henry (1859–1926), also pursued research into the psychological dimension of color—how colors affect people, and under what conditions. He went even further to explore the physiological effects of perception. Seurat's work, though characterized by a systematic and scientifically minded approach, also incorporated his concerns about the emotional tone of the images.

---

the tone is new. Compare, for instance, this painting's mood with the relaxed and casual atmosphere of Renoir's *Le Moulin de la Galette* (FIG. 31-8). Toulouse-Lautrec's scene is nightlife, with its glaring artificial light, brassy music, and assortment of corrupt, cruel, and masklike faces. (He included himself in the background—the tiny man with the derby accompanying the very tall man, his cousin.) Such distortions by simplification of the figures and faces anticipated Expressionism (see Chapter 35), when artists' use of formal elements—for example, brighter colors and bolder lines than ever before—increased the impact of the images on observers.

GEORGES SEURAT The themes Georges Seurat (1859–1891) addressed in his paintings were also Impressionist subjects, but he depicted them in a resolutely intellectual way. He devised a disciplined and painstaking system of painting that focused on color analysis. Seurat was less concerned with the recording of immediate color sensations than he was with their careful and systematic organization into a new kind of pictorial order. He disciplined the free and fluent play of color that characterized Impressionism into a calculated arrangement based on scientific color theory (see "19th-Century Color Theory," above). Seurat's system, known as *pointillism* or *divisionism,* involves carefully observing color and separating it into its component parts. The artist then applies these pure component colors to the canvas in tiny dots (points) or daubs. Thus, the shapes, figures, and spaces in the image become totally comprehensible only from a distance, when the viewer's eye blends the many pigment dots.

Pointillism was on view at the eighth and last Impressionist exhibition in 1886, when Seurat showed his *A Sunday on La Grande Jatte* (FIG. 31-15). The subject of the painting is consistent with Impressionist recreational themes, and Seurat also shared the Impressionists' interest in analyzing light and color. But Seurat's rendition is strangely rigid and remote, unlike the spontaneous representations of most Impressionists. Seurat applied pointillism to produce a carefully composed and painted image. By using meticulously calculated values, the painter carved out a deep rectangular space. He played on repeated motifs both to create flat patterns and to suggest spatial depth. Reiterating the profile of the female form, the parasol, and the cylindrical forms of the figures, Seurat placed each in space to set up a rhythmic movement in depth as well as from side to side. Sunshine fills the picture, but the painter did not break the light into transient patches of color. Light, air, people, and landscape are formal elements in an abstract design in which line, color, value, and shape cohere in a precise and tightly controlled organization. Seurat's orchestration of the many forms across the monumental (almost 7-by-10-foot) canvas created a rhythmic cadence that harmonizes the entire composition.

Seurat once stated: "They see poetry in what I have done. No, I apply my method, and that is all there is to it."[8] Despite this claim,

31-15 GEORGES SEURAT, *A Sunday on La Grande Jatte,* 1884–1886. Oil on canvas, 6′ 9″ × 10′. Art Institute of Chicago, Chicago (Helen Birch Bartlett Memorial Collection, 1926).

Seurat's color system—pointillism—involved dividing colors into their component parts and applying those colors to the canvas in tiny dots. The forms become comprehensible only from a distance.

his art is much more than a scientifically based system. *La Grande Jatte* reveals Seurat's recognition of the tenuous and shifting social and class relationships at the time. La Grande Jatte (The Big Bowl) is an island in the Seine River near Asnières, one of Paris's rapidly growing industrial suburbs. Seurat's painting captures public life on a Sunday—a congregation of people from various classes, from the sleeveless worker lounging in the left foreground to the middle-class man and woman seated next to him. Most of the people wear their Sunday best, making class distinctions less obvious.

VINCENT VAN GOGH In marked contrast to Seurat, VIN-CENT VAN GOGH (1853–1890) explored the capabilities of colors and distorted forms to express his emotions as he confronted nature. The son of a Dutch Protestant pastor, van Gogh believed he had a religious calling and did missionary work in the coal-mining area of Belgium. Repeated professional and personal failures brought him close to despair. Only after he turned to painting did he find a way to communicate his experiences. When van Gogh died of a self-inflicted gunshot wound at age 37, he considered himself a failure as an artist. He felt himself an outcast not only from artistic circles but also from society at large. The hostile reception to his work, both from fellow artists and the general public, no doubt reinforced this

perception. He sold only one painting during his lifetime. Since his death, however, his reputation and the appreciation of his art have grown dramatically. Subsequent painters, especially the Fauves and German Expressionists (see Chapter 35), built on the use of color and the expressiveness of van Gogh's art. This kind of influence is an important factor in determining artistic significance, and it is no exaggeration to state that today van Gogh is one of the most revered artists in history.

NIGHT CAFÉ After relocating to Arles in southern France in 1888, van Gogh painted *Night Café* (FIG. **31-16**). Although the subject is apparently benign, van Gogh invested it with a charged energy. As he stated in a letter to his brother Theo (see "The Letters of Vincent van Gogh," page 834), he wanted the painting to convey an oppressive atmosphere—"a place where one can ruin oneself, go mad, or commit a crime."[9] The proprietor rises like a specter from the edge of the billiard table, which the painter depicted in such a steeply tilted perspective that it threatens to slide out of the painting into the viewer's space. Van Gogh communicated the "madness" of the place by selecting vivid hues whose juxtaposition augmented their intensity. His insistence on the expressive values of color led him to develop a corresponding expressiveness in his paint application. The

The Letters of Vincent van Gogh

Throughout his life, Vincent van Gogh wrote letters to his brother Theo van Gogh (1857–1891), a Parisian art dealer, on matters both mundane and philosophical. The letters are precious documents of the vicissitudes of the painter's life and reveal his emotional anguish. In many of the letters, van Gogh also forcefully stated his views about art. In one letter, he told Theo: "In both my life and in my painting, I can very well do without God but I cannot, ill as I am, do without something which is greater than I, . . . the power to create."* For van Gogh, the power to create involved the expressive use of color. "Instead of trying to reproduce exactly what I have before my eyes, I use color more arbitrarily so as to express myself forcibly."† Color in painting, he argued, is "not locally true from the point of view of the delusive realist, but color suggesting some emotion of an ardent temperament."‡

Some of van Gogh's letters contain vivid descriptions of his paintings, which are invaluable to art historians in gauging his intentions and judging his success. For example, about *Night Café* (FIG. **31-16**), he wrote:

> I have tried to express the terrible passions of humanity by means of red and green. The room is blood red and dark yellow with a green billiard table in the middle; there are four citron-yellow lamps with a glow of orange and green. Everywhere there is a clash and contrast of the most disparate reds and greens in the figures of little sleeping hooligans, in the empty, dreary room, in violet and blue. The blood-red and the yellow-green of the billiard table, for instance, contrast with the soft, tender Louis XV green of the counter, on which there is a pink nosegay. The white coat of the landlord, awake in a corner of that furnace, turns citron-yellow, or pale luminous green.§

31-16 VINCENT VAN GOGH, *Night Café*, 1888. Oil on canvas, 2′ 4½″ × 3′. Yale University Art Gallery, New Haven (bequest of Stephen Carlton Clark).

In *Night Café*, van Gogh explored the abilities of colors and distorted forms to express emotions. The thickness, shape, and direction of his brush strokes create a tactile counterpart to the intense colors.

* Vincent van Gogh to Theo van Gogh, September 3, 1888, in W. H. Auden, ed., *Van Gogh: A Self-Portrait. Letters Revealing His Life as a Painter* (New York: Dutton, 1963), 319.
† August 11, 1888. Ibid., 313.
‡ September 8, 1888. Ibid., 321.
§ September 8, 1888. Ibid., 320.

thickness, shape, and direction of his brush strokes created a tactile counterpart to his intense color schemes. He often moved the brush vehemently back and forth or at right angles, giving a textilelike effect, even squeezing dots or streaks directly onto his canvas from his paint tube. This bold, almost slapdash attack enhanced the intensity of his colors.

STARRY NIGHT Similarly illustrative of van Gogh's "expressionist" method is *Starry Night* (FIG. **31-17**), which the artist painted in 1889, the year before his death. At this time, van Gogh was living at Saint-Paul-de-Mausole, an asylum in Saint-Rémy, near Arles, where he had committed himself. In *Starry Night*, the artist did not represent the sky's appearance. Rather, he communicated his feelings about the electrifying vastness of the universe, filled with whirling and exploding stars and galaxies of stars, the earth and humanity huddling beneath it. The church nestled in the center of the village is perhaps van Gogh's attempt to express or reconcile his conflicted views about religion. Although the style in *Starry Night* suggests a very personal vision, this work does correspond in many ways to the view available to the painter from the window of his room in Saint-Paul-de-Mausole. The existence of cypress trees and the placement of the constellations have been confirmed as matching the view van Gogh would have had during his stay in the asylum. Still, the artist translated any visible objects into his unique vision. Given van Gogh's determination to "use color . . . to express [him]self forcibly," the dark, deep blue that suffuses the entire painting cannot be overlooked. Together with the turbulent brush strokes, the color suggests a quiet but pervasive depression. Van Gogh's written observation to his brother reveals his contemplative state of mind:

> Perhaps death is not the hardest thing in a painter's life. . . . [L]ooking at the stars always makes me dream, as simply as I dream over the black dots representing towns and villages on a map. Why, I ask myself, shouldn't the shining dots of the sky be as accessible as the black dots on the map of France? Just as we take the train to get to Tarascon or Rouen, we take death to reach a star.[10]

31-17 VINCENT VAN GOGH, *Starry Night*, 1889. Oil on canvas, 2′ 5″ × 3′ $\frac{1}{4}$″. Museum of Modern Art, New York (acquired through the Lillie P. Bliss Bequest).

In this late work, van Gogh painted the vast night sky filled with whirling and exploding stars, the earth huddled beneath it. The painting is an almost abstract pattern of expressive line, shape, and color.

1 ft.

PAUL GAUGUIN After painting as an amateur, PAUL GAUGUIN (1848–1903) took lessons with Pissarro and then resigned from his prosperous brokerage business in 1883 to devote his time entirely to painting. Like van Gogh, he rejected objective representation in favor of subjective expression. He also broke with the Impressionists' studies of minutely contrasted hues because he believed that color above all must be expressive and that the artist's power to determine

the colors in a painting was a central element of creativity. However, whereas van Gogh's heavy, thick brush strokes were an important component of his expressive style, Gauguin's color areas appear flatter, often visually dissolving into abstract patches or patterns.

In 1886, attracted by Brittany's unspoiled culture, its ancient Celtic folkways, and the still-medieval Catholic piety of its people, Gauguin moved to Pont-Aven. Although in the 1870s and 1880s Brittany had been transformed into a profitable market economy, Gauguin still viewed the Bretons as "natural" men and women, perfectly at ease in their unspoiled peasant environment. At Pont-Aven, he painted *Vision after the Sermon*, or *Jacob Wrestling with the Angel* (FIG. 31-18), a work that decisively rejects both Realism and Impressionism. The painting shows Breton women, wearing their starched white Sunday caps and black dresses, visualizing the sermon they have just heard at church on Jacob's encounter with the Holy

1 ft.

31-18 PAUL GAUGUIN, *Vision after the Sermon*, or *Jacob Wrestling with the Angel*, 1888. Oil on canvas, 2′ 4$\frac{3}{4}$″ × 3′ $\frac{1}{2}$″. National Gallery of Scotland, Edinburgh.

Gauguin admired Japanese prints, stained glass, and cloisonné enamels. Their influences are evident in this painting of Breton women, in which firm outlines enclose large areas of unmodulated color.

Spirit (Gen. 32:24–30). The women pray devoutly before the apparition, as they would have before the roadside crucifix shrines that were familiar features of the Breton countryside. Gauguin departed from optical realism and composed the picture elements to focus the viewer's attention on the idea and intensify its message. The images are not what the Impressionist eye would have seen and replicated but what memory would have recalled and imagination would have modified. Thus the artist twisted the perspective and allotted the space to emphasize the innocent faith of the unquestioning women, and he shrank Jacob and the angel, wrestling in a ring enclosed by a Breton stone fence, to the size of fighting cocks. Wrestling matches were regular features at the entertainment held after high mass, so Gauguin's women are spectators at a contest that was, for them, a familiar part of their culture.

Gauguin did not unify the picture with a horizon perspective, light and shade, or a naturalistic use of color. Instead, he abstracted the scene into a pattern. Pure unmodulated color fills flat planes and shapes bounded by firm lines: white caps, black dresses, and the red field of combat. The shapes are angular, even harsh. The caps, the sharp fingers and profiles, and the hard contours suggest the austerity of peasant life and ritual. Gauguin admired Japanese prints, stained glass, and *cloisonné* metalwork (FIGS. **16-2** and **16-3**). These art forms contributed to his own daring experiment to transform traditional painting and Impressionism into abstract, expressive patterns of line, shape, and pure color. His revolutionary method found its first authoritative expression in *Vision after the Sermon.*

WHERE DO WE COME FROM? After a brief period of association with van Gogh in Arles in 1888, Gauguin, in his restless search for provocative subjects and for an economical place to live, settled in Tahiti (MAP **33-1**). The South Pacific island attracted Gauguin because it offered him a life far removed from materialistic Europe and an opportunity to reconnect with nature. Upon his arrival, he discovered that Tahiti, under French control since 1842, had been extensively colonized. Disappointed, Gauguin tried to maintain his vision of an untamed paradise by moving to the Tahitian countryside, where he expressed his fascination with primitive life and brilliant color in a series of striking decorative canvases. Gauguin often based the design, although indirectly, on native motifs, and the color owed its peculiar harmonies of lilac, pink, and lemon to the tropical flora of the island.

Despite the allure of the South Pacific, Gauguin continued to struggle with life. His health suffered, and his art had a hostile reception. In 1897, worn down by these obstacles, Gauguin decided to take his own life, but not before painting a large canvas titled *Where Do We Come From? What Are We? Where Are We Going?* (FIG. **31-19**). This painting can be read as a summary of Gauguin's artistic methods and of his views on life. The scene is a tropical landscape, populated with native women and children. Despite the setting, most of the canvas surface, other than the figures, consists of broad areas of flat color, which convey a lushness and intensity.

In a letter to his friend Charles Morice, Gauguin shed light on the meaning of this painting:

> Where are we going? Near to death an old woman. . . . What are we? Day to day existence. . . . Where do we come from? Source. Child. Life begins. . . . Behind a tree two sinister figures, cloaked in garments of sombre colour, introduce, near the tree of knowledge, their note of anguish caused by that very knowledge in contrast to some simple beings in a virgin nature, which might be paradise as conceived by humanity, who give themselves up to the happiness of living.[11]

Where Do We Come From? is, therefore, a sobering, pessimistic image of the life cycle's inevitability. Gauguin's attempt to commit suicide in Tahiti was unsuccessful, but he died a few years later, in 1903, in the Marquesas Islands, his artistic genius still unrecognized.

PAUL CÉZANNE Although a lifelong admirer of Eugène Delacroix, PAUL CÉZANNE (1839–1906) allied himself early in his career with the Impressionists, especially Pissarro. He at first accepted their color theories and their faith in subjects chosen from everyday life, but his studies of the Old Masters in the Louvre persuaded him that Impressionism lacked form and structure. Cézanne declared he wanted to "make of Impressionism something solid and durable like the art of the museums."[12]

1 ft.

31-19 PAUL GAUGUIN, *Where Do We Come From? What Are We? Where Are We Going?* 1897. Oil on canvas, 4' 6¾" × 12' 3". Museum of Fine Arts, Boston (Tompkins Collection).

In search of a place far removed from European materialism, Gauguin moved to Tahiti, where he used native women and tropical colors to present a pessimistic view of the inevitability of the life cycle.

31-20 PAUL CÉZANNE, *Mont Sainte-Victoire*, 1902–1904. Oil on canvas, 2′ 3½″ × 2′ 11¼″. Philadelphia Museum of Art, Philadelphia (The George W. Elkins Collection). ▣◀

In his landscapes, Cézanne replaced the transitory visual effects of changing atmospheric conditions, a focus for the Impressionists, with careful analysis of the lines, planes, and colors of nature.

1 ft.

20A CÉZANNE, *ge Bathers*, 6.

The basis of Cézanne's art was his unique way of studying nature in works such as *Mont Sainte-Victoire* (FIG. 31-20), one of many views he painted of this mountain near his home in Aix-en-Provence. His aim was not truth in appearance, especially not photographic truth, nor was it the "truth" of Impressionism. Rather, he sought a lasting structure behind the formless and fleeting visual information the eye absorbs. Instead of employing the Impressionists' random approach when he was face-to-face with nature, Cézanne developed a more analytical style. He sought to order the lines, planes, and colors that comprised nature. He constantly and painstakingly checked his painting against the part of the real scene—he called it the "motif"—he was studying at the moment. Cézanne wrote in March 1904 that his goal was "[to do] Poussin over entirely from nature . . . in the open air, with color and light, instead of one of those works imagined in a studio, where everything has the brown coloring of feeble daylight without reflections from the sky and sun."[13] He sought to achieve Poussin's effects of distance, depth, structure, and solidity not by using traditional perspective and chiaroscuro but by recording the color patterns an optical analysis of nature provides.

With special care, Cézanne explored the properties of line, plane, and color and their interrelationships. He studied the effect of every kind of linear direction, the capacity of planes to create the sensation of depth, the intrinsic qualities of color, and the power of colors to modify the direction and depth of lines and planes. To create the illusion of three-dimensional form and space, Cézanne focused on carefully selecting colors. He understood that the visual properties—hue, saturation, and value—of different colors vary (see "19th-Century Color Theory," page 832). Cool colors tend to recede, whereas warm ones advance. By applying to the canvas small patches of juxtaposed colors, some advancing and some receding, Cézanne

created volume and depth in his works. On occasion, the artist depicted objects chiefly in one hue and achieved convincing solidity by modulating the intensity (or saturation). At other times, he juxtaposed contrasting colors—for example, green, yellow, and red—of like saturation (usually in the middle range rather than the highest intensity) to compose specific objects, such as fruit or bowls.

In *Mont Sainte-Victoire*, he replaced the transitory visual effects of changing atmospheric conditions, effects that occupied Monet, with a more concentrated, lengthier analysis of the colors in large lighted spaces. The main space stretches out behind and beyond the canvas plane and includes numerous small elements, such as roads, fields, houses, and the viaduct at the far right, each seen from a slightly different viewpoint. Above this shifting, receding perspective rises the largest mass of all, the mountain, with an effect—achieved by equally stressing background and foreground contours—of being simultaneously near and far away. This portrayal approximates the real experience a person has when viewing a landscape's forms piecemeal. The relative proportions of objects vary rather than being fixed by a strict one- or two-point perspective, such as that normally found in a photograph. Cézanne immobilized the shifting colors of Impressionism into an array of clearly defined planes that compose the objects and spaces in his scene. Describing his method in a letter to a fellow painter, he wrote:

> [T]reat nature by the cylinder, the sphere, the cone, everything in proper perspective so that each side of an object or a plane is directed towards a central point. Lines parallel to the horizon give breadth . . . Lines perpendicular to this horizon give depth. But nature for us men is more depth than surface, whence the need of introducing into our light vibrations, represented by reds and yellows, a sufficient amount of blue to give the impression of air.[14]

31-21 PAUL CÉZANNE, *Basket of Apples*, ca. 1895. Oil on canvas, 2' $\frac{3}{8}$" × 2' 7". Art Institute of Chicago, Chicago (Helen Birch Bartlett Memorial Collection, 1926). ◼◀

Cézanne's analytical approach to painting is evident in his still lifes. He captured the solidity of bottles and fruit by juxtaposing color patches, but the resulting abstract shapes are not optically realistic.

BASKET OF APPLES Still life was another good vehicle for Cézanne's experiments, as he could arrange a limited number of selected objects to provide a well-ordered point of departure. So analytical was Cézanne in preparing, observing, and painting still lifes (in contrast to the Impressionist emphasis on the concept of spontaneity) that he had to abandon using real fruit and flowers because they tended to rot. In *Basket of Apples* (FIG. **31-21**), the objects have lost something of their individual character as bottles and fruit and almost become cylinders and spheres. Cézanne captured the solidity of each object by juxtaposing color patches. His interest in the study of volume and solidity is evident from the disjunctures in the painting—the table edges are discontinuous, and various objects seem to be depicted from different vantage points. In his zeal to understand three-dimensionality and to convey the placement of forms relative to the space around them, Cézanne explored his still-life arrangements from different viewpoints. This resulted in paintings that, although conceptually coherent, do not appear optically realistic. Cézanne created what might be called, paradoxically, an architecture of color.

In keeping with the modernist concern with the integrity of the painting surface, Cézanne's methods never allow the viewer to disregard the two-dimensionality of the picture plane. In this manner, Cézanne achieved a remarkable feat—presenting the viewer with two-dimensional and three-dimensional images simultaneously.

SYMBOLISM

The Impressionists and Post-Impressionists believed their emotions and sensations were important elements for interpreting nature, but the depiction of nature remained a primary focus of their efforts. By

31-22 PIERRE PUVIS DE CHAVANNES, *Sacred Grove*, 1884. Oil on canvas, 2' $11\frac{1}{2}$" × 6' 10". Art Institute of Chicago, Chicago (Potter Palmer Collection).

The Symbolists revered Puvis de Chavannes for his rejection of Realism. His statuesque figures in timeless poses inhabit a tranquil landscape, their gestures suggesting a symbolic ritual significance.

the end of the 19th century, the representation of nature became completely subjective. Artists no longer sought to imitate nature but created free interpretations of it, concerned solely with expressing their individual spirit. They rejected the optical world as observed in favor of a fantasy world, of forms they conjured in their free imagination, with or without reference to things conventionally seen. Color, line, and shape, divorced from conformity to the optical image, became symbols of personal emotions in response to the world. Deliberately choosing to stand outside of convention and tradition, artists spoke like prophets, in signs and symbols.

Many of the artists following this path adopted an approach to subject and form that associated them with a general European movement called *Symbolism*. Symbolists, whether painters or writers, disdained Realism as trivial. The task of Symbolist visual and verbal artists was not to see things but to see through them to a significance and reality far deeper than what superficial appearance gave. In this function, as the poet Arthur Rimbaud (1854–1891) insisted, artists became beings of extraordinary insight. (One group of Symbolist painters called itself the *Nabis*, the Hebrew word for "prophet.") Rimbaud, whose poems had great influence on the artistic community, went so far as to say, in his *Letter from a Seer* (1871), that to achieve the seer's insight, artists must become deranged. In effect, they must systematically unhinge and confuse the everyday faculties of sense and reason, which served only to blur artistic vision. The artists' mystical vision must convert the objects of the commonsense world into symbols of a reality beyond that world and, ultimately, a reality from within the individual. Elements of Symbolism appeared in the works of van Gogh and Gauguin, but their art differed from mainstream Symbolism in their insistence on showing unseen powers as linked to a physical reality, instead of attempting to depict an alternate, wholly interior life.

The extreme subjectivism of the Symbolists led them to cultivate all the resources of fantasy and imagination, no matter how deeply buried or obscure. Moreover, they urged artists to stand against the vulgar materialism and conventional mores of industrial and middle-class society. Above all, the Symbolists wished to purge literature and art of anything utilitarian, to cultivate an exquisite aesthetic sensitivity, and to make the slogan "art for art's sake" into a doctrine and a way of life. The subjects of the Symbolists, conditioned by this reverent attitude toward art and exaggerated aesthetic sensation, became increasingly esoteric and exotic, mysterious, visionary, dreamlike, and fantastic. Perhaps not coincidentally, contemporary with the Symbolists, Sigmund Freud (1856–1939), the founder of psychoanalysis, began the age of psychiatry with his *Interpretation of Dreams* (1900), an introduction to the concept and the world of unconscious experience.

PIERRE PUVIS DE CHAVANNES Although he never formally identified himself with the Symbolists, the French painter PIERRE PUVIS DE CHAVANNES (1824–1898) became the "prophet" of those artists. Puvis rejected Realism and Impressionism and went his own way in the 19th century, serenely unaffected by these movements. He produced an ornamental and reflective art—a dramatic rejection of Realism's noisy everyday world. In *Sacred Grove* (FIG. 31-22), which may have influenced Seurat's *Grande Jatte* (FIG. 31-15), he deployed statuesque figures in a tranquil landscape with a classical shrine. Suspended in timeless poses, the figures' contours are simple and sharp, and their modeling is as shallow as *bas-relief*. The calm and still atmosphere suggests some consecrated place, where all movements and gestures have a permanent ritual significance. The stillness and simplicity of the forms, the linear patterns their rhythmic contours create, and the suggestion of their symbolic weight constitute a type of anti-Realism. Puvis garnered support from a wide range of artists. The conservative French Academy and the government applauded his classicism. The Symbolists revered Puvis for his vindication of imagination and his independence from the capitalist world of materialism and the machine.

GUSTAVE MOREAU In keeping with Symbolist tenets, GUSTAVE MOREAU (1826–1898) gravitated toward subjects inspired by dreaming, which was as remote as possible from the everyday world. Moreau presented these subjects sumptuously, and his natural love of sensuous design led him to incorporate gorgeous color, intricate line, and richly detailed shape. *Jupiter and Semele* (FIG. 31-23) is one of the artist's rare finished works. The mortal girl Semele, one of Jupiter's loves, begged the god to appear to her in all his majesty. When he did, the sight was so powerful that she died from it.

31-23A MOREAU, *The Apparition,* 1874–1876.

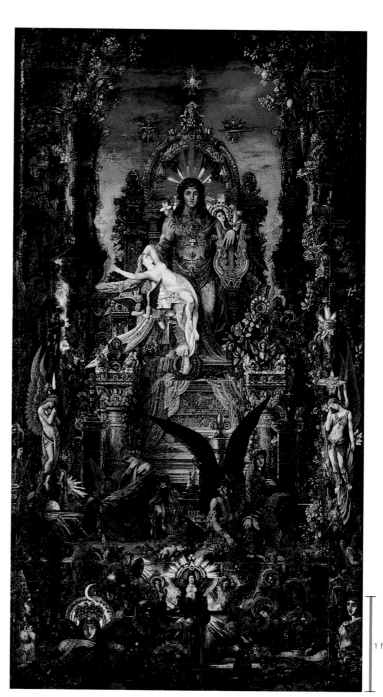

1 ft.

31-23 GUSTAVE MOREAU, *Jupiter and Semele,* ca. 1875. Oil on canvas, 7′ × 3′ 4″. Musée Gustave Moreau, Paris.

Moreau favored subjects inspired by dreaming. In this painting, the apparition of Jupiter with his halo of thunderbolts overwhelms the mortal Semele, who dies upon seeing so powerful a sight.

Moreau presented the theme within an operalike setting, a towering opulent architecture. (Moreau loved the music of Richard Wagner [1813–1883] and, like that great composer, dreamed of a grand synthesis of the arts.) The painter depicted the royal hall of Olympus as shimmering in iridescent color, with tabernacles filled with the glowing shapes that enclose Jupiter like an encrustation of gems. In *Jupiter and Semele,* the rich color harmonizes with the exotic hues of Byzantine *mosaics,* medieval *enamels,* Indian *miniatures,* and the designs of exotic wares then influencing modern artists. The apparition of the god with his halo of thunderbolts overwhelms Semele, who sits in Jupiter's lap. Her languorous swoon and the suspended motion of all the entranced figures show the "beautiful inertia" that Moreau said he wished to render with all "necessary richness."

ODILON REDON Like Moreau, ODILON REDON (1840–1916) was a visionary. He had been aware of an intense inner world since childhood and later wrote of "imaginary things" that haunted him. Redon adapted the Impressionist palette and stippling brush stroke for a very different purpose. In *The Cyclops* (FIG. **31-24**), Redon projected a figment of the imagination as if it were visible, coloring it whimsically with a rich profusion of fresh saturated hues that harmonized with the mood he felt fitted the subject. The fetal head of the shy, simpering Polyphemus, with its single huge loving eye, rises balloonlike above the sleeping Galatea. The image born of the dreaming world and the color analyzed and disassociated from the waking world come together here at the artist's will. The contrast with Raphael's representation of the same subject (FIG. **22-10**) could hardly be more striking. As Redon himself observed: "All my originality consists . . . in making unreal creatures live humanly by putting, as much as possible, the logic of the visible at the service of the invisible."[15]

31-25A ROUSSEAU, *The Dream,* 1910.

HENRI ROUSSEAU The imagination of the French artist HENRI ROUSSEAU (1844–1910) engaged a different but equally powerful world of personal fantasy. Gauguin had journeyed to the South Seas in search of primitive innocence. Rousseau was a "primitive" without leaving Paris—an untrained amateur painter. Rousseau produced an art of dream and fantasy in a style that had its own sophistication and made its own departure from the artistic currency of the time. He compensated for his apparent visual, conceptual, and technical naïveté with a natural talent for design and an imagination teeming with exotic images of mysterious tropical landscapes. In

31-24 ODILON REDON, *The Cyclops,* 1898. Oil on canvas, 2′ 1″ × 1′ 8″. Kröller-Müller Foundation, Otterlo.

In *The Cyclops,* the Symbolist painter Odilon Redon projected a figment of the imagination as if it were visible, coloring it whimsically with a rich profusion of hues adapted from the Impressionist palette.

Sleeping Gypsy (FIG. **31-25**), the recumbent figure occupies a desert world, silent and secret, and dreams beneath a pale, perfectly round moon. In the foreground, a lion that resembles a stuffed, but somehow menacing, animal doll sniffs at the gypsy. A critical encounter

31-25 HENRI ROUSSEAU, *Sleeping Gypsy,* 1897. Oil on canvas, 4′ 3″ × 6′ 7″. Museum of Modern Art, New York (gift of Mrs. Simon Guggenheim).

In *Sleeping Gypsy,* Henri Rousseau depicted a doll-like but menacing lion sniffing at a recumbent dreaming figure in a mysterious landscape. The painting conjures the vulnerable subconscious during sleep.

31-26 AUBREY BEARDSLEY, *The Peacock Skirt,* 1894. Pen-and-ink illustration for Oscar Wilde's *Salomé,* $9'' \times 6\frac{5}{8}''$. Fogg Art Museum, Harvard University, Cambridge (bequest of Grenville L. Winthrop).

Banishing the Impressionist and Post-Impressionist emphasis on color, Aubrey Beardsley, a master of calligraphic line and curvilinear shapes, confined himself to patterns of black and white without shading.

impends—an encounter of the type that recalls the uneasiness of a person's vulnerable subconscious self during sleep.

AUBREY BEARDSLEY Not all Symbolist artists were French. AUBREY BEARDSLEY (1872–1898) was one of a circle of English artists whose work was at the intersection of Symbolism and Art Nouveau (see page 846). For *Salomé,* an illustration for a book by Oscar Wilde (1854–1900), Beardsley drew *The Peacock Skirt* (FIG. **31-26**), a dazzlingly decorative composition perfectly characteristic of his style. The Japanese print influence is obvious, although Beardsley assimilated it into his unique manner. Banishing Realism as well as the Impressionists' and Post-Impressionists' emphasis on color, he confined himself to lines and to patterns of black and white, eliminating all shading. His tense, elastic line encloses sweeping curvilinear shapes that lie flat on the surface—some left almost vacant, others filled with swirling complexes of mostly organic motifs. Beardsley's unfailing sense of linear rhythms and harmonies supports his mastery of calligraphic line.

EDVARD MUNCH Also linked in spirit to the Symbolists was the Norwegian painter and graphic artist EDVARD MUNCH (1863–1944). Munch felt deeply the pain of human life. His belief that humans were powerless before the great natural forces of death and love and the emotions associated with them—jealousy, loneli-

ness, fear, desire, despair—became the theme of most of his art. Because Munch's goal was to describe the conditions of "modern psychic life," as he put it, Realist and Impressionist techniques were inappropriate, focusing as they did on the tangible world. In the spirit of Symbolism, Munch developed a style of putting color, line, and figural distortion to expressive ends. Influenced by Gauguin, Munch produced both paintings and prints whose high emotional charge was a major source of inspiration for the German Expressionists in the early 20th century (see Chapter 35).

Munch's *The Scream* (FIG. **31-27**) exemplifies his style. The image—a man standing on a bridge or jetty in a landscape—comes from the real world, but Munch's treatment of the image departs significantly from visual reality. *The Scream* evokes a visceral, emotional response from the viewer because of the painter's dramatic presentation. The man in the foreground, simplified to almost skeletal form, emits a primal scream. The landscape's sweeping curvilinear lines reiterate the curvilinear shape of the mouth and head, almost like an echo, as the cry seems to reverberate through the setting. The fiery red and yellow stripes that give the sky an eerie glow also contribute to this work's resonance. Munch wrote a revealing epigraph to accompany the painting: "I stopped and leaned against the balustrade, almost dead with fatigue. Above the blue-black fjord hung the clouds, red as blood and tongues of fire. My friends had left me, and alone, trembling with anguish, I became aware of the vast, infinite cry of nature."[16] Appropriately, the original title of this work was *Despair.*

31-27 EDVARD MUNCH, *The Scream,* 1893. Tempera and pastels on cardboard, $2'\ 11\frac{3}{4}'' \times 2'\ 5''$. National Gallery, Oslo.

Although grounded in the real world, *The Scream* departs significantly from visual reality. Munch used color, line, and figural distortion to evoke a strong emotional response from the viewer.

-26A ENSOR, *Christ's Entry into Brussels,* 1888.

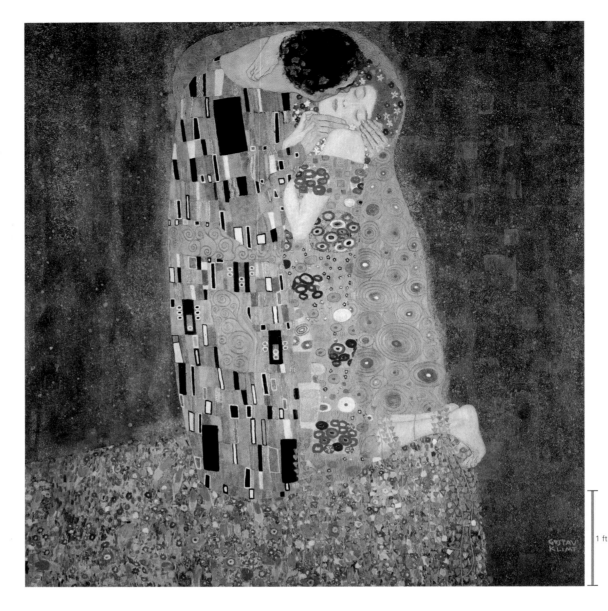

31-28 GUSTAV KLIMT, *The Kiss*, 1907–1908. Oil on canvas, 5′ 10¾″ × 5′ 10¾″. Österreichische Galerie Belvedere, Vienna. ◼◀

In this opulent Viennese fin-de-siècle painting, Gustav Klimt revealed only a small segment of each lover's body. The rest of his painting dissolves into shimmering, extravagant flat patterning.

1 ft.

FIN-DE-SIÈCLE Historians have adopted the term *fin-de-siècle*, which means "end of the century," to describe the culture of the late 1800s. This designation is not merely chronological but also refers to a certain sensibility. The increasingly large and prosperous middle classes aspired to the advantages the aristocracy traditionally enjoyed. They too strove to live "the good life," which evolved into a culture of decadence and indulgence. Characteristic of the fin-de-siècle period was an intense preoccupation with sexual drives, powers, and perversions. People at the end of the century also immersed themselves in an exploration of the unconscious. This culture was unrestrained and freewheeling, but the determination to enjoy life masked an anxiety prompted by significant political upheaval and an uncertain future. The country most closely associated with fin-de-siècle culture was Austria.

GUSTAV KLIMT The Viennese artist GUSTAV KLIMT (1863–1918) captured this period's flamboyance in his work but tempered it with unsettling undertones. In *The Kiss* (FIG. **31-28**), Klimt depicted a couple locked in an embrace. All that is visible of the couple, however, is a small segment of each person's body. The rest of the painting dissolves into shimmering, extravagant flat patterning. This patterning has clear ties to Art Nouveau and to the Arts and Crafts movement (see page 846) and also evokes the conflict between two- and three-dimensionality intrinsic to the work of Degas and other modernists.

Paintings such as *The Kiss* were visual manifestations of fin-de-siècle spirit because they captured a decadence conveyed by opulent and sensuous images.

GERTRUDE KÄSEBIER Photography, which during the 19th century most people regarded as the ultimate form of Realism, could also be manipulated by artists to produce effects more akin to painting than to factual records of contemporary life. After the first great breakthroughs, which bluntly showed what was before the eye, some photographers began to pursue new ways of using the medium as a vehicle of artistic expression. One of the leading practitioners of what might be called the pictorial style in photography was the American GERTRUDE KÄSEBIER (1852–1934). Käsebier took up photography in 1897 after raising a family and working as a portrait painter. She soon became famous for photographs with symbolic themes, such as *Blessed Art Thou among Women* (FIG. **31-29**). The title repeats the phrase the angel Gabriel used in the New Testament to announce to the Virgin Mary that she will be the mother of Jesus. In the context of Käsebier's photography, the words suggest a parallel between the biblical "Mother of God" and the modern mother in the image, who both protects and sends forth her daughter. The white setting and the mother's pale gown shimmer in soft focus behind the serious girl, who is dressed in darker tones and captured

31-29 GERTRUDE KÄSEBIER, *Blessed Art Thou among Women,* 1899. Platinum print on Japanese tissue, $9\frac{3}{8}'' \times 5\frac{1}{2}''$. Museum of Modern Art, New York (gift of Mrs. Hermine M. Turner).

Gertrude Käsebier was able to inject a sense of the spiritual and the divine into scenes from everyday life. The soft focus of this photograph invests the whole scene with an aura of otherworldly peace.

31-30 AUGUSTUS SAINT-GAUDENS, Adams Memorial, Rock Creek Cemetery, Washington, 1891. Bronze, 5′ 10″ high. Smithsonian American Art Museum, Washington, D.C.

For the Adams Memorial, Augustus Saint-Gaudens chose a classical mode of representation. A woman of majestic bearing sits in mourning. The gesture of her right arm derives from ancient Roman statuary.

with sharper focus. Käsebier deliberately combined an out-of-focus background with a sharp or almost-sharp foreground in order to achieve an expressive effect by blurring the entire image slightly. In *Blessed Art Thou,* the soft focus invests the whole scene with an aura of otherworldly peace. The photograph showcases Käsebier's ability to inject a sense of the spiritual and the divine into scenes from everyday life.

SCULPTURE

The three-dimensional art of sculpture was not suited to capturing the optical sensations many painters favored in the later 19th century. Its very nature—its tangibility and solidity—suggests permanence. Consequently, the sculptors of this period pursued artistic

goals markedly different from those of contemporaneous painters and photographers.

AUGUSTUS SAINT-GAUDENS One artist who used sculpture to express timeless ideals rather than to depict transitory moments was the American AUGUSTUS SAINT-GAUDENS (1848–1907), who trained in France. When Saint-Gaudens received the commission to produce a memorial monument honoring Mrs. Henry Adams (FIG. 31-30), he chose a classical mode of representation, sculpting a woman of majestic bearing sitting in mourning. The voluminous garment that enfolds her body also partly shadows her classically beautiful face. The gesture of the woman's right arm, which reproduces a common motif in ancient Roman portraits of women, only slightly stirs the immobility of her form, set in an attitude of eternal vigilance.

31-31 Jean-Baptiste Carpeaux, *Ugolino and His Children*, 1865–1867. Marble, 6′ 5″ high. Metropolitan Museum of Art, New York (Josephine Bay Paul and C. Michael Paul Foundation, Inc., and the Charles Ulrich and Josephine Bay Foundation, Inc., gifts, 1967).

Based on Dante's *Inferno*, this group represents Ugolino biting his hands in despair as he and his sons await death by starvation. The twisted forms suggest the self-devouring torment of frustration.

31-31A Carpeaux, *The Dance*, 1867–1869.

JEAN-BAPTISTE CARPEAUX In France, Jean-Baptiste Carpeaux (1827–1875) combined an interest in Realism with a love of ancient, Renaissance, and Baroque sculpture. He based his group *Ugolino and His Children* (FIG. **31-31**) on a passage in Dante's *Inferno* (33.58–75) in which Count Ugolino and his four sons starve to death while shut up in a tower. In Hell, Ugolino relates to Dante how, in a moment of extreme despair, he bit both his hands in grief. His children, thinking he did it because of his hunger, offered him their own flesh as food. In Carpeaux's statuary group, the powerful forms—twisted, intertwined, and densely concentrated—suggest the self-devouring torment of frustration and despair that wracks the unfortunate Ugolino. A careful student of Michelangelo's male figures, Carpeaux also said he had the *Laocoön* group (FIG. 5-88) in mind. Certainly, the storm and stress of *Ugolino and His Children* recall similar characteristics of that ancient work. Regardless of these influences, the sense of vivid reality in the anatomy of Carpeaux's figures shows the artist's interest in study from life.

31-32A Rodin, *Gates of Hell*, 1880–1900.

AUGUSTE RODIN The leading French sculptor of the later 19th century was Auguste Rodin (1840–1917), who conceived and executed his sculptures with a Realist sensibility. Like Muybridge and Eakins (see Chapter 30), Rodin was fascinated by the human body in motion (see "Rodin on Movement in Art and Photography," page 845). He was also well aware of the innovations of the Impressionists. Although color was not a significant factor in Rodin's work, the influence of Impressionism is evident in the artist's abiding concern for the effect of light on the three-dimensional surface. When focusing on the human form, he joined his profound knowledge of anatomy and movement with special attention to the body's exterior, saying, "The sculptor must learn to reproduce the surface, which means all that vibrates on the surface, soul, love, passion, life. . . . Sculpture is thus the art of hollows and mounds, not of smoothness, or even polished planes."[17] Primarily a modeler of pliable material rather than a carver of hard wood or stone, Rodin worked his surfaces with fingers sensitive to the subtlest variations of surface, catching the fugitive play of constantly shifting light on the body. In his studio, he often would have a model move around in front of him while he modeled sketches with coils of clay.

In *Walking Man* (FIG. **31-32**), a preliminary study for the sculptor's *Saint John the Baptist Preaching*, Rodin succeeded in representing the momentary in cast bronze. He portrayed the headless and armless figure in midstride at the moment when weight is transferred across the pelvis from the back leg to the front. In addition to capturing the sense of the transitory, Rodin demonstrated his mastery of realistic detail in his meticulous rendition of muscle, bone, and tendon.

BURGHERS OF CALAIS Rodin also made many nude and draped studies for each of the figures in one of his most ambitious works—the life-size group *Burghers of Calais* (FIG. **31-33**). This cast bronze monument commemorated a heroic episode in the Hundred Years' War. During the English siege of Calais, France, in 1347, six of the city's leading citizens agreed to offer their lives in return for the English king's promise to lift the siege and spare the rest of the populace. Each of the bedraggled-looking figures is a convincing study of despair, resignation, or quiet defiance. Rodin enhanced the psychic effects through his choreographic placement of the group members. Rather than clustering in a tightly formal composition, the *burghers* (middle-class citizens) seem to wander aimlessly. The roughly textured surfaces add to the pathos of the figures and compel the viewer's continued interest. Rodin designed the monument without the traditional high base in the hope that the citizens of Calais would be inspired by the sculptural representation of their ancestors stand-

1 ft.

Rodin on Movement in Art and Photography

Photography had a profound effect on 19th-century art, and many artists used photographs as an aid in capturing "reality" on canvas or in stone. Eadweard Muybridge's photographs of a galloping horse (FIG. 30-54), for example, definitively established that at certain times all four hooves of the animal are in the air. But not all artists believed that photography was "true to life." The sculptor Auguste Rodin (FIGS. 31-32 and 31-33) was one of the "doubters."

I have always sought to give some indication of movement [in my statues]. I have very rarely represented complete repose. I have always endeavoured to express the inner feelings by the mobility of the muscles. . . . The illusion of life is obtained in our art by good modelling and by movement. . . . [M]ovement is the transition from one attitude to another. . . . Have you ever attentively examined instantaneous photographs of walking figures? . . . [Photographs] present the odd appearance of a man suddenly stricken with paralysis and petrified in his pose. . . . If, in fact, in instantaneous photographs, the figures, though taken while moving, seem suddenly fixed in mid-air, it is because, all parts of the body being reproduced exactly at the same twentieth or fortieth of a second, there is no progressive development of movement as there is in art. . . . [I]t is the artist who is truthful and it is photography which lies, for in reality time does not stop.*

* Translated by Robin Fedden, in Elizabeth Gilmore Holt, ed., *From the Classicists to the Impressionists: Art and Architecture in the 19th Century* (New Haven: Yale University Press, 1966; reprint 1986), 406–409.

31-32 AUGUSTE RODIN, *Walking Man,* 1905. Bronze, 6′ 11¾″ high. Musée d'Orsay, Paris.

In this study for a statue of Saint John the Baptist, Rodin depicted a headless and armless figure in mid-stride. *Walking Man* demonstrates Rodin's mastery of anatomy and his ability to capture transitory motion.

1 ft.

1 ft.

ing eye-level in the city center and preparing eternally to set off on their sacrificial journey. However, the city officials who commissioned the group found Rodin's Realist vision so offensive that they banished the monument to a remote site and modified the work's impact by placing it high on an isolating pedestal.

Rodin's ability to capture the quality of the transitory through his highly textured surfaces while revealing larger themes and deeper, lasting sensibilities is one of the reasons he had a strong influence on 20th-century artists. Because many of his works, such as *Walking Man,* were deliberate fragments, he was also instrumental in creating a taste for the incomplete, an aesthetic that many later sculptors embraced enthusiastically.

31-33 AUGUSTE RODIN, *Burghers of Calais,* 1884–1889. Bronze, 6′ 10½″ high, 7′ 11″ long, 6′ 6″ deep. Musée Rodin, Paris.

Rodin's bronze group commemorates an episode during the Hundred Years' War, when six Calais citizens offered their lives to save their city. Each highly textured figure is a convincing character study.

Sculpture   **845**

ARCHITECTURE
AND DECORATIVE ARTS

The decisive effects of industrialization were impossible to ignore, and although many artists embraced this manifestation of "modern life" or at least explored its effects, other artists decried the impact of rampant industrialism. The latter response came from the Arts and Crafts movement in England. This movement, which developed during the last decades of the 19th century, was shaped by the ideas of John Ruskin, the critic who skewered Whistler's *Nocturne* (FIG. 31-13), and the artist William Morris. Both men shared a distrust of machines and industrial capitalism, which they believed alienated workers from their own nature. Accordingly, they advocated an art "made by the people for the people as a joy for the maker and the user."[18] This condemnation of capitalism and support for manual laborers were compatible with socialism, and many artists in the Arts and Crafts movement, especially in England, considered themselves socialists and participated in the labor movement.

This democratic, or at least populist, attitude carried over to the art they produced as well. Members of the Arts and Crafts movement dedicated themselves to producing functional objects with high aesthetic value for a wide public. The style they advocated was based on natural, rather than artificial, forms and often consisted of repeated designs of floral or geometric patterns. For Ruskin, Morris, and others in the Arts and Crafts movement, high-quality artisanship and honest labor were crucial.

WILLIAM MORRIS In order to promote these ideals, WILLIAM MORRIS (1834–1896) formed a decorating firm dedicated to Arts and Crafts principles: Morris, Marshall, Faulkner, and Company, Fine Arts Workmen in Painting, Carving, Furniture, and Metals. His company did a flourishing business producing wallpaper, textiles, tiles, furniture, books, rugs, stained glass, and pottery. In 1867, Morris received the commission to decorate the Green Dining Room (FIG. 31-34) at London's South Kensington Museum (now the Victoria & Albert Museum), the center of public art education and home of decorative art collections. The range of room features—windows, lights, and *wainscoting* (paneling on the lower part of interior walls)—that Morris decorated to create this unified, beautiful, and functional environment is all-encompassing. Nothing escaped his eye. Morris's design for this room also reveals the penchant of Arts and Crafts designers for intricate patterning.

CHARLES RENNIE MACKINTOSH Numerous Arts and Crafts societies in America, England, and Germany carried on this ideal of artisanship. In Scotland, CHARLES RENNIE MACKINTOSH (1868–1929) designed a number of tearooms, including the Ladies Luncheon Room (FIG. 31-35) located in the Ingram Street Tea Room in Glasgow. The room decor is consistent with Morris's vision of a functional, exquisitely designed art. The chairs, stained-glass windows, and large panels of colored gesso with twine, glass beads, thread, mother-of-pearl, and tin leaf (made by MARGARET MACDONALD MACKINTOSH [1864–1933], an artist-designer and Mackintosh's wife, who collaborated with him on many projects) are all pristinely geometric and rhythmical in design.

ART NOUVEAU An important international architectural and design movement that developed out of the ideas the Arts and Crafts movement promoted was *Art Nouveau* (New Art), which took its name from a shop in Paris called L'Art Nouveau. Known by that name in France, Belgium, Holland, England, and the United States, the style had other names elsewhere: *Jugendstil* in Austria and Germany (after the magazine *Der Jugend*, "youth"), *Modernismo* in Spain, and *Floreale* in Italy. Proponents of this movement tried to

31-34 WILLIAM MORRIS, Green Dining Room, South Kensington Museum (now Victoria & Albert Museum), London, England, 1867.

William Morris was a founder of the Arts and Crafts movement. His Green Dining Room exemplifies the group's dedication to creating intricately patterned yet unified and functional environments.

31-35 CHARLES RENNIE MACKINTOSH and MARGARET MACDONALD MACKINTOSH, reconstruction (1992–1995) of Ladies Luncheon Room, Ingram Street Tea Room, Glasgow, Scotland, 1900–1912. Glasgow Art Galleries and Museum, Glasgow.

Charles Mackintosh's Ladies Luncheon Room features functional and exquisitely designed decor, including stained-glass windows and pristinely geometric furnishings by Margaret Macdonald Mackintosh.

synthesize all the arts in a determined attempt to create art based on natural forms that could be mass-produced for a large audience. The Art Nouveau style adapted the twining-plant form to the needs of architecture, painting, sculpture, and all of the decorative arts.

VICTOR HORTA The mature Art Nouveau style of the 1890s appears in the houses the Belgian architect VICTOR HORTA (1861–1947) designed. The staircase (FIG. 31-36) in the Van Eetvelde House, which Horta built in Brussels in 1895, is a characteristic example. Every detail functions as part of a living whole. Furniture, drapery folds, veining in the lavish stone paneling, and the patterning of the door moldings join with real plants to provide graceful counterpoints for the twining-plant theme. Metallic tendrils curl around the railings and posts, delicate metal tracery fills the glass dome, and floral and leaf motifs spread across the fabric panels of the screen.

31-36A HORTA, Tassel House, Brussels, 1892–1893.

The Art Nouveau style reflects several influences. In addition to the rich, foliated two-dimensional ornament of Arts and Crafts design and that movement's respect for materials, the sinuous whiplash curve of Japanese print designs (FIG. 28-13) inspired Art Nouveau artists. Art Nouveau also borrowed from the expressively patterned styles of van Gogh (FIGS. 31-16 and 31-17), Gauguin (FIGS. 31-18 and 31-19), and their Post-Impressionist and Symbolist contemporaries.

31-36 VICTOR HORTA, staircase in the Van Eetvelde House, Brussels, Belgium, 1895.

The Art Nouveau movement was an attempt to create art and architecture based on natural forms. In this room, every detail conforms to the theme of the twining plant and functions as part of a living whole.

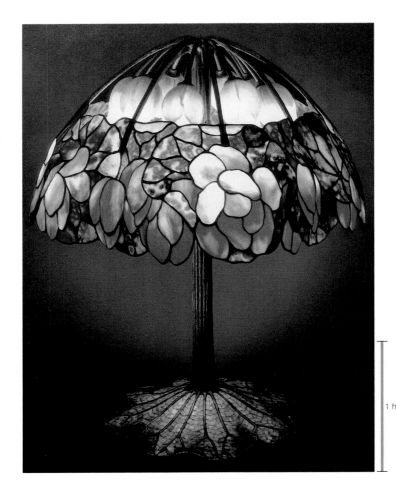

Tiffany's lamps of leaded Favrile stained glass (a patented Tiffany technique), mosaic, and bronze, based on the curvilinear floral forms of the lotus, exemplify the sensuous opulence of the Art Nouveau style.

LOUIS COMFORT TIFFANY The sensuous opulence of Art Nouveau is also on display in the stained-glass lamps of LOUIS COMFORT TIFFANY (1848–1933). His lotus table lamp (FIG. 31-37), constructed of leaded glass (often *Favrile,* a type of glass Tiffany patented), mosaic, and bronze, is based on the curvilinear floral forms of the lotus. Intended for wealthy buyers, this was the most expensive lamp Tiffany Studios produced in 1906. Because of the careful attention to detail required to produce lamps of this type, Tiffany's workshop could make only one at a time. This ensured the high-quality artisanship the Arts and Crafts movement so prized.

ANTONIO GAUDI Art Nouveau achieved its most personal expression in the work of the Spanish architect ANTONIO GAUDI (1852–1926). Before becoming an architect, Gaudi had trained as an ironworker. Like many young artists of his time, he longed to create a style that was both modern and appropriate to his country. Taking inspiration from Moorish-Spanish architecture and from the simple architecture of his native Catalonia, Gaudi developed a personal aesthetic. He conceived a building as a whole and molded it almost as a sculptor might shape a figure from clay. Although work on his designs proceeded slowly under the guidance of his intuition and imagination, Gaudi was a master who invented many new structural techniques that facilitated construction of his visions. His Barcelona apartment house, Casa Milá (FIG. 31-38), is a wondrously free-form mass wrapped around a street corner. Lacy iron railings enliven the swelling curves of the cut-stone facade. Dormer windows peep from the undulating tiled roof, on which fantastically writhing chimneys poke energetically into the air above. The rough surfaces of the stone walls suggest naturally worn rock. The entrance portals look like eroded sea caves, but their design also may reflect the excitement that swept Spain following the 1879 discovery of Paleolithic cave paintings (FIG. 1-9) at Altamira. Gaudi felt that each of his buildings was symbolically a living thing. The passionate naturalism of his Casa Milá is the spiritual kin of early-20th-century Expressionist painting and sculpture (see Chapter 35).

31-38 ANTONIO GAUDI, Casa Milá, Barcelona, Spain, 1907.

The Spanish Art Nouveau architect Antonio Gaudi conceived this apartment house as if it were a gigantic sculpture to be molded from clay. Twisting chimneys cap the undulating roof and walls.

ALEXANDRE-GUSTAVE EIFFEL In the later 19th century, new technologies and the changing needs of urbanized, industrialized society affected architecture throughout the Western world. Since the 18th century, bridges had been built of cast iron (FIG. 29-11), which permitted engineering advancements in the construction of larger, stronger, and more fire-resistant structures. Steel, available after 1860, allowed architects to enclose ever larger spaces, such as those found in railroad stations (FIG. 31-4) and exposition halls. The Realist impulse also encouraged architectural designs that honestly expressed a building's purpose, rather than elaborately disguising its function. The elegant metal skeleton structures of the French engineer-architect ALEXANDRE-GUSTAVE EIFFEL (1832–1923) constituted responses to this idea and were an important contribution to the development of the 20th-century skyscraper. A native of Burgundy, Eiffel trained in Paris before beginning a distinguished career designing exhibition halls, bridges, and the interior armature for France's anniversary gift to the United States—Frédéric Auguste Bartholdi's *Statue of Liberty*.

Eiffel designed his best-known work, the Eiffel Tower (FIG. 31-1), for a great exhibition in Paris in 1889. Originally seen as a symbol of modern Paris and still considered a symbol of 19th-century civilization, the elegant iron tower thrusts its needle shaft 984 feet above the city, making it at the time of its construction (and for some time thereafter) the world's tallest structure. The tower rests on four giant supports connected by gracefully arching open-frame skirts that provide a pleasing mask for the heavy horizontal girders needed to strengthen the legs. Visitors can take two elevators to the top, or they can use the internal staircase. Either way, the view of Paris and the Seine from the tower is incomparable, as is the design of the tower itself. The transparency of Eiffel's structure blurs the distinction between interior and exterior to an extent never before achieved or even attempted. This interpenetration of inner and outer space became a hallmark of 20th-century art and architecture. Eiffel's tower and the earlier iron skeletal frames designed by Labrouste (FIG. 30-47) and Paxton (FIG. 30-48) jolted the architectural profession into a realization that modern materials and processes could germinate a completely new style and a radically innovative approach to architectural design.

AMERICAN SKYSCRAPERS The desire for greater speed and economy in building, as well as for a reduction in fire hazards, prompted the use of cast and wrought iron for many building programs, especially commercial ones. Designers in both England and the United States enthusiastically developed cast-iron architecture until a series of disastrous fires in the early 1870s in New York, Boston, and Chicago demonstrated that cast iron by itself was far from impervious to fire. This discovery led to encasing the metal in masonry, combining the first material's strength with the second's fire resistance.

In cities, convenience required closely grouped buildings, and increased property values forced architects literally to raise the roof. Even an attic could command high rentals if the builders installed one of the new elevators, used for the first time in the Equitable Building in New York (1868–1871). Metal, which could support these towering structures, gave birth to the American skyscraper.

HENRY HOBSON RICHARDSON One of the pioneers in designing these modern commercial structures was HENRY HOBSON RICHARDSON (1838–1886), but he also had profound respect for earlier architectural styles. Because Richardson had a special fondness for the Romanesque architecture of the Auvergne area in France, he frequently used heavy round arches and massive masonry walls. Architectural historians sometimes consider his work to constitute a

31-39 HENRY HOBSON RICHARDSON, Marshall Field wholesale store, Chicago, 1885–1887 (demolished 1930).

Richardson was a pioneer in designing commercial structures using a cast-iron skeleton encased in fire-resistant masonry. This construction technique permitted him to open up the walls with large windows.

Romanesque revival related to the Neo-Gothic style (FIG. 30-44), but this designation does not do credit to the originality and quality of most of the buildings Richardson designed during his brief 18-year practice. Trinity Church in Boston and his smaller public libraries, residences, railroad stations, and courthouses in New England and elsewhere best demonstrate his vivid imagination and the solidity (the sense of enclosure and permanence) so characteristic of his style. However, his most important and influential building was the Marshall Field wholesale store (FIG. 31-39) in Chicago, begun in 1885 and later demolished. This vast building, occupying a city block and designed for the most practical of purposes, recalled historical styles without imitating them at all. The tripartite elevation of a Renaissance palace (FIG. 21-36) or of the Roman aqueduct (FIG. 10-33) near Nîmes, France, may have been close to Richardson's mind. Yet he used no classical ornament, made much of the massive courses of masonry, and, in the strong horizontality of the windowsills and the interrupted courses that defined the levels, stressed the long sweep of the building's lines as well as its ponderous weight. Although the structural frame still lay behind and in conjunction with the masonry screen, the great glazed arcades opened up the walls of the monumental store. They pointed the way to the modern total penetration of walls and the transformation of them into mere screens or curtains that serve both to echo the underlying structural grid and to protect it from the weather.

LOUIS HENRY SULLIVAN As skyscrapers proliferated, architects refined the visual vocabulary of these buildings. LOUIS HENRY SULLIVAN (1856–1924), whom many architectural historians call the first truly modern architect, arrived at a synthesis of industrial structure and ornamentation that perfectly expressed the spirit

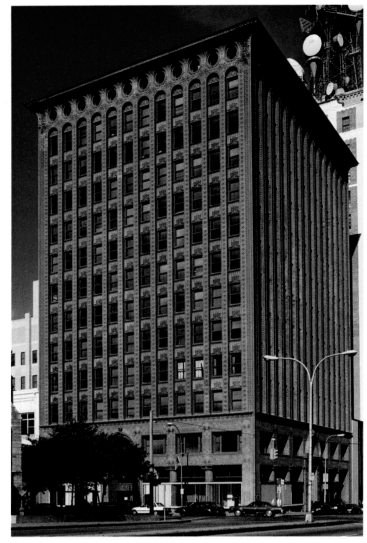

31-40 LOUIS HENRY SULLIVAN, Guaranty (Prudential) Building, Buffalo, New York, 1894–1896.

Louis Sullivan used the latest technologies to create this light-filled, well-ventilated Buffalo office building. He added ornate surface embellishments to impart a sense of refinement and taste.

31-41 LOUIS HENRY SULLIVAN, Carson, Pirie, Scott Building, Chicago, 1899–1904.

Sullivan's slogan was "form follows function." He tailored the design of this steel, glass, and stone Chicago department store to meet the needs of its employees and customers.

31-40A SULLIVAN, Wainwright Building, St. Louis, 1890–1891.

of late-19th-century commerce. To achieve this, he employed the latest technological developments to create light-filled, well-ventilated office buildings and adorned both exteriors and interiors with ornate embellishments. Such decoration served to connect commerce and culture and imbued these white-collar workspaces with a sense of refinement and taste. These characteristics are evident in the Guaranty (Prudential) Building (FIG. **31-40**) in Buffalo, New York, built between 1894 and 1896. The structure is steel, sheathed with terracotta. The imposing scale of the building and the regularity of the window placements served as an expression of the large-scale, refined, and orderly office work that took place within. Sullivan tempered the severity of the structure with lively ornamentation, both on the piers and cornice on the exterior of the building and on the stairway balustrades, elevator cages, and ceiling in the interior. The

Guaranty Building illustrates Sullivan's famous dictum that "form follows function," which became the slogan of many early-20th-century architects. Still, Sullivan did not advocate a rigid and doctrinaire correspondence between exterior and interior design. Rather, he espoused a free and flexible relationship—one his pupil Frank Lloyd Wright (see Chapter 35) later described as similar to that between the hand's bones and tissue.

Sullivan also designed the Carson, Pirie, Scott Building (FIG. **31-41**) in Chicago. Built between 1899 and 1904, this department store required broad, open, well-illuminated display spaces. Sullivan again used a minimal structural steel skeleton to achieve this goal. The architect gave over the lowest two levels of the building to an ornament in cast iron (of his invention) made of wildly fantastic motifs. He regarded the display windows as pictures and as such felt they merited elaborate frames. As in the Guaranty Building, Sullivan revealed his profound understanding of the maturing consumer economy and tailored the Chicago department store to meet the functional and symbolic needs of its users.

Thus, in architecture as well as in the pictorial arts, the late 19th century was a period during which artists challenged traditional modes of expression, often emphatically rejecting the past. Architects and painters as different as Sullivan, Monet, van Gogh, and Cézanne, each in his own way, contributed significantly to the entrenchment of modernism as the new cultural orthodoxy of the early 20th century (see Chapter 35).

EUROPE AND AMERICA, 1870 TO 1900

IMPRESSIONISM

❚ A hostile critic applied the term *Impressionism* to the paintings of Claude Monet because of their sketchy quality. The Impressionists—Monet, Pierre-Auguste Renoir, Edgar Degas, and others—strove to capture fleeting moments and transient effects of light and climate on canvas. Monet, for example, repeatedly painted Rouen Cathedral at different times of day.

❚ The Impressionists also focused on recording the contemporary urban scene in Paris. They frequently painted bars, dance halls, the ballet, wide boulevards, and railroad stations.

❚ Complementing the Impressionists' sketchy, seemingly spontaneous brush strokes are the compositions of their paintings. Reflecting the influence of Japanese prints and photography, Impressionist works often have arbitrarily cut-off figures and settings seen at sharply oblique angles.

Monet, *Rouen Cathedral*, 1894

POST-IMPRESSIONISM

❚ Post-Impressionism is not a unified style. The term refers to the group of late-19th-century artists who followed the Impressionists and took painting in new directions.

❚ Georges Seurat refined the Impressionist approach to color and light into pointillism—the disciplined application of pure color in tiny daubs that become recognizable forms only when seen from a distance. Vincent van Gogh explored the capabilities of colors and distorted forms to express emotions, as in his dramatic depiction of the sky in *Starry Night*. Paul Gauguin, another admirer of Japanese prints, moved away from Impressionism in favor of large areas of flat color bounded by firm lines. Paul Cézanne replaced the transitory visual effects of the Impressionists with a rigorous analysis of the lines, planes, and colors that make up landscapes and still lifes.

Van Gogh,
Starry Night, 1889

SYMBOLISM

❚ The Symbolists disdained Realism as trivial and sought to depict a reality beyond that of the everyday world. They rejected materialism and celebrated fantasy and imagination. Their subjects were often mysterious, exotic, and sensuous.

❚ Gustave Moreau, Odilon Redon, and Henri Rousseau were the leading French Symbolists. Rousseau's *Sleeping Gypsy,* which depicts the world of the subconscious during sleep, is a characteristic example of Symbolist painting.

Rousseau, *Sleeping Gypsy*, 1897

SCULPTURE

❚ Sculpture is not suited to capturing transitory optical effects or exploring the properties of color and line, and late-19th-century sculptors pursued goals different from those of the Impressionists and Post-Impressionists. The leading figure of the era was Auguste Rodin, who explored Realist themes and the representation of movement, as in his moving portrayal of six leading citizens of Calais who sacrificed their lives for their countrymen. He also made statues that were deliberate fragments, creating a taste for the incomplete that appealed to many later sculptors.

Rodin, *Burghers of Calais*,
1884–1889

ARCHITECTURE AND DECORATIVE ARTS

❚ Not all artists embraced the industrialization that transformed daily life during the 19th century. The Arts and Crafts movement in England and the international Art Nouveau style formed in opposition to modern mass production. Both schools advocated natural forms and high-quality craftsmanship.

❚ New technologies and the changing needs of industrialized society transformed Western architecture in the late 19th century. The exposed iron skeleton of the Eiffel Tower, which blurs the distinction between interior and exterior, jolted architects into a realization that modern materials and processes could revolutionize architectural design. In the United States, Henry Hobson Richardson and Louis Sullivan were pioneers in designing the first metal, stone, and glass skyscrapers.

Eiffel, Eiffel Tower, Paris, 1889

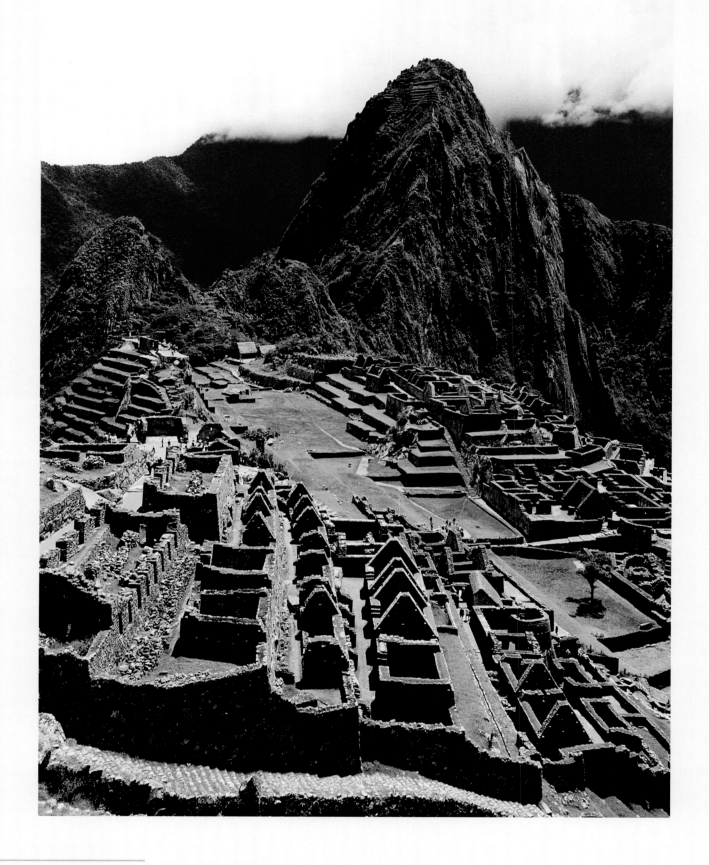

32-1 Machu Picchu (view from adjacent peak), Inka, Peru, 15th century.

Inka architects designed Machu Picchu so that the windows and doors frame spectacular views. Inka masons cut large upright stones in shapes that echo the contours of nearby sacred peaks.

32

NATIVE ARTS OF THE AMERICAS AFTER 1300

In the years following the arrival of Christopher Columbus (1451–1506) in the New World in 1492, the Spanish monarchs poured money into expeditions that probed the coasts of North and South America, but the Spaniards had little luck in finding the wealth they sought. When brief stops on the coast of Yucatán, Mexico, yielded a small but still impressive amount of gold and other precious artifacts, the Spanish governor of Cuba outfitted yet another expedition. Headed by Hernán Cortés (1485–1547), this contingent of explorers was the first to make contact with the great Aztec emperor Moctezuma II (r. 1502–1521). In only two years, with the help of guns, horses, native allies revolting against their Aztec overlords, and perhaps also a smallpox epidemic that had swept across the Caribbean and already thinned the Aztec ranks, Cortés managed to overthrow the vast and rich Aztec Empire. His victory in 1521 opened the door to hordes of Spanish conquistadors seeking their fortunes and to missionaries eager for new converts to Christianity. The ensuing clash of cultures led to a century of turmoil throughout the Spanish king's new domains.

The Aztec Empire that the Spaniards defeated was but the latest of a series of highly sophisticated indigenous art-producing cultures in the Americas. Their predecessors have been treated in Chapter 14. This chapter examines in turn the artistic achievements of the native peoples of *Mesoamerica*, Andean South America, and North America after 1300.

MESOAMERICA

After the fall and destruction of the great central Mexican city of Teotihuacan in the eighth century and the abandonment of the southern Maya sites around 900, new cities arose to take their places. Notable were the Maya city of Chichén Itzá in Yucatán and the Toltec capital of Tula, not far from modern Mexico City (see Chapter 14). Their dominance was relatively short-lived, however. For the early Postclassic period (ca. 900–1250) in Mesoamerica, scholars have less information than for Classic Mesoamerica, but much more evidence exists for the cultures of the late Postclassic period.

Mixteca-Puebla

One of the most impressive art-producing peoples of the Postclassic period in Mesoamerica was the Mixtecs, who succeeded the Zapotecs at Monte Albán in southern Mexico (MAP **32-1**) after 700. They extended their political sway in Oaxaca by dynastic intermarriage as well as by war. The treasures found in the tombs at Monte Albán bear witness to Mixtec wealth, and the quality of these works demonstrates the high level of Mixtec artistic achievement. The Mixtecs were highly skilled goldsmiths and won renown for their work in *mosaic* using turquoise obtained from distant regions such as present-day New Mexico.

BORGIA CODEX The peoples of Mesoamerica prized illustrated books. Miraculously, some manuscripts survived the depredations of the Spanish invasion. The Postclassic Maya were preeminent in the art of writing. Their books were precious vehicles for recording history, rituals, astronomical tables, calendrical calculations, maps, and trade and tribute accounts. The texts consisted of *hieroglyphic* columns read from left to right and top to bottom. Unfortunately, only three Maya books exist today. Bishop Diego de Landa (1524–1579), the author of an invaluable treatise on the Maya of Yucatán, described how the "Indians" made their books and why so few remain:

> They wrote their books on a long sheet doubled in folds, which was then enclosed between two boards finely ornamented; the writing was on one side and the other, according to the folds. . . . We found a great number of books in these [Indian] letters and, since they contained nothing but superstitions and falsehoods of the devil, we burned them all, which they took most grievously, and which gave them great pain.[1]

In contrast, 10 non-Maya books survive, five from Mixtec Oaxaca and five from the Puebla region (MAP **32-1**). Art historians have named the style they represent Mixteca-Puebla, an interesting example of a Mesoamerican style that crossed both ethnic and regional boundaries. The Mixteca-Puebla artists painted on long sheets of deerskin, which they first coated with fine white lime plaster and folded into accordion-like pleats. Some of the manuscripts are *codices* (singular, *codex*) and resemble modern books with covers of wood, mosaic, or feathers.

One extensively illustrated book that escaped the Spanish destruction is the *Borgia Codex*, from somewhere in central highland Mexico (possibly the states of Puebla or Tlaxcala). It is the largest and most elaborate of several manuscripts known as the Borgia Group. One illustration (FIG. **32-2**) in the codex shows two richly attired, vividly gesticulating gods rendered predominantly in reds and yellows with black outlines. The god of life, the black Quetzalcoatl (depicted here as a masked human rather than in the usual form of a feathered serpent), sits back-to-back with the god of death, the white Mictlantecuhtli. Below them is an inverted skull with a double keyboard of teeth, a symbol of the Underworld (Mictlan), which could be entered through the mouth of a great earth monster. Both figures hold scepters in one hand and gesticulate with the other. The image conveys the inevitable relationship of life and death, an important theme in Mesoamerican art. Some scholars believe the image may also be a kind of writing conveying a specific divinatory meaning. Symbols of the 13 divisions of 20 days in the 260-day Mesoamerican ritual calendar appear in panels in the margins. The origins of this calendar, used even today in remote parts of Mexico and Central America, are unknown. Except for the Mixtec genealogical codices, most books painted before and immediately after the Spanish conquest deal with astronomy, calendrics, divination, and ritual.

Aztec

The greatest Mesoamerican culture at the time of the European conquest was that of the Aztecs, a Nahuatl-speaking people who left behind a history of their rise to power. Scholars have begun to question the accuracy of the Aztec account, and some think it is a mythic construct. According to the traditional history, the destruction of Toltec

32-2 Mictlantecuhtli and Quetzalcoatl, from the *Borgia Codex,* Mixteca-Puebla, possibly from Puebla or Tlaxcala, Mexico, ca. 1400–1500. Mineral and vegetable pigments on deerskin, $10\frac{5}{8}'' \times 10\frac{3}{8}''$. Biblioteca Apostolica Vaticana, Rome.

One of the rare surviving Mesoamerican books, the Mixteca-Puebla *Borgia Codex* includes this painting of the gods of life and death above an inverted skull symbolizing the Underworld.

1 in.

MAP 32-1 Mixteca-Puebla and Aztec sites in Mesoamerica.

Tula about 1200 (see Chapter 14) brought a century of anarchy to the Valley of Mexico, the vast highland valley 7,000 feet above sea level that now contains sprawling Mexico City (MAP 32-1). Waves of northern invaders established warring city-states and wrought destruction in the valley. The Aztecs were the last of these conquerors. With astonishing rapidity, they transformed themselves within a few generations from migratory outcasts and serfs to mercenaries for local rulers and then to masters in their own right of the Valley of Mexico's small kingdoms. They began to call themselves Mexica, and, following a legendary prophecy that they would build a city where they saw an eagle perched on a cactus with a serpent in its mouth, they settled on an island in Lake Texcoco (Lake of the Moon). Their settlement grew into the magnificent city of Tenochtitlán, which in 1519 amazed Cortés and his small band of adventurers.

Recognized by those they subdued as fierce in war and cruel in peace, the Aztecs indeed seemed to glory in battle and in military prowess. They radically changed the social and political structure in Mexico. Subservient groups not only had to submit to Aztec military power but also had to provide victims to be sacrificed to Huitzilopochtli, the hummingbird god of war, and to other Aztec deities (see "Aztec Religion," page 856). The Aztecs practiced bloodletting and human sacrifice—which had a long history in Mesoamerica (see Chapter 14)—to please the gods and sustain the great cycles of the universe. But the Aztecs engaged in human sacrifice on a greater scale than any of their predecessors, even waging special battles, called the "flowery wars," expressly to obtain captives for future sacrifice. This cruelty is one reason Cortés found ready allies among the peoples the Aztecs had subjugated.

TENOCHTITLÁN The ruins of the Aztec capital, Tenochtitlán, lie directly beneath the center of Mexico City. In the late 1970s, Mexican archaeologists identified the exact location of many of the most important structures within the Aztec sacred precinct, and extensive excavations near the cathedral in Mexico City continue. The principal building is the Great Temple (FIG. 32-3), a temple-pyramid honoring the Aztec god Huitzilopochtli and the local rain god

Tlaloc. Two great staircases originally swept upward from the plaza level to the double sanctuaries at the summit. The Great Temple is a remarkable example of *superimposition,* a common trait in Mesoamerican architecture. The excavated structure, composed of seven shells, indicates how the earlier walls nested within the later ones. (Today, only two of the inner structures remain. The Spaniards destroyed the later ones in the 16th century.) The sacred precinct also contained the temples of other deities, a ball court (see "The Mesoamerican Ball Game," Chapter 14, page 372), a skull rack for the exhibition of the heads of victims killed in sacrificial rites, and a school for children of the nobility.

The Aztecs laid out Tenochtitlán on a grid plan that divided the city into quarters and wards, reminiscent of Teotihuacan (FIG. 14-5), which, long abandoned, had become a pilgrimage site for the Aztecs. Tenochtitlán's island location required conducting communication and transport via canals and other waterways. Many of the Spaniards thought of Venice in Italy when they saw the city rising from the waters like a radiant vision. Crowded with buildings, plazas, and courtyards, the city also boasted a vast and ever-busy marketplace. In the words of Bernal Díaz del Castillo, "Some of the soldiers among us who had been in many parts of the world, in Constantinople, and all over Italy, and in Rome, said that so large a marketplace and so full of people, and so well regulated and arranged, they had never beheld before."[2] The city proper had a population of more than 100,000. (The total population of the area of Mexico the Aztecs dominated at the time of the conquest was approximately 11 million.)

32-3A Founding of Tenochtitlán, *Codez Mendoza,* 1541–1542.

32-3 Reconstruction drawing with cutaway view of various rebuildings of the Great Temple, Aztec, Tenochtitlán, Mexico City, Mexico, ca. 1400–1500. C = Coyolxauhqui disk (FIG. 32-4).

The Great Temple in the Aztec capital encased successive earlier structures. The latest temple honored the gods Huitzilopochtli and Tlaloc, whose sanctuaries were at the top of a stepped pyramid.

Aztec Religion

The Aztecs saw their world as a flat disk resting on the back of a monstrous earth deity. Tenochtitlán, their capital, was at its center, with the Great Temple (FIG. 32-3) representing a sacred mountain and forming the axis passing up to the heavens and down through the Underworld—a concept with parallels in other cultures (see, for example, "The Stupa," Chapter 6, page 163). Each of the four cardinal points had its own god, color, tree, and calendrical symbol. The sky consisted of 13 layers, whereas the Underworld had nine. The Aztec Underworld was an unpleasant place where the dead gradually ceased to exist.

The Aztecs often adopted the gods of conquered peoples, and their pantheon was complex and varied. When the Aztecs arrived in the Valley of Mexico, their own patron, Huitzilopochtli, a war and sun deity, joined such well-established Mesoamerican gods as Tlaloc and Quetzalcoatl (the latter the feathered serpent who was a benevolent god of life, wind, and learning and culture, as well as the patron of priests). As the Aztecs went on to conquer much of Mesoamerica, they appropriated the gods of their subjects, such as Xipe Totec, a god of early spring and patron of gold workers imported from the Gulf Coast and Oaxaca. Images of the various gods made of stone (FIG. 32-5), terracotta, wood, and even dough (eaten at the end of rituals) stood in and around their temples. Reliefs (FIG. 32-4) depicting Aztec deities, often with political overtones, also adorned the temple complexes.

The Aztec ritual cycle was very full, given that they celebrated events in two calendars—the sacred calendar (260 days) and the solar one (360 days plus 5 unlucky and nameless days). The Spanish friars of the 16th century noted that the solar calendar dealt largely with agricultural matters. The two Mesoamerican calendars functioned simultaneously, requiring 52 years for the same date to recur in both. A ritual called the New Fire Ceremony commemorated this rare event. The Aztecs broke pots and made new ones for the next period, hid their pregnant women, and extinguished all fires. At midnight on a mountaintop, fire priests took out the heart of a sacrificial victim and with a fire drill renewed the flame in the exposed cavity. Then they set ablaze bundles of sticks representing the 52 years that had just passed, ensuring that the sun would rise in the morning and that another cycle would begin.

Most Aztec ceremonies involved the burning of incense (made from copal, resin from conifer trees). Colorfully attired dancers and actors performed, and musicians played conch shell trumpets, drums, rattles, rasps, bells, and whistles. Almost every Aztec festival also included human sacrifice. To Tlaloc, the rain god, the priests offered small children, because their tears brought the rains.

Rituals also marked the completion of important religious structures. The dedication of the last major rebuilding of the Great Temple at Tenochtitlán in 1487, for example, reportedly involved the sacrifice of thousands of captives from recent wars in the Gulf Coast region. Varied offerings have been found within earlier layers of the temple, many representing tribute from subjugated peoples. These include blue-painted stone and ceramic vessels, conch shells, a

1 ft.

32-4 Coyolxauhqui (She of the Golden Bells), Aztec, from the Great Temple of Tenochtitlán, Mexico City, Mexico, ca. 1469. Stone, diameter 10′ 10″. Museo del Templo Mayor, Mexico City.

The bodies of sacrificed foes that the Aztecs hurled down the stairs of the Great Temple landed on this disk depicting the murdered, segmented body of the moon goddess Coyolxauhqui, Huitzilopochtli's sister.

jaguar skeleton, flint and obsidian knives, and even Mesoamerican "antiques"—carved stone Olmec and Teotihuacan masks made hundreds of years before the Aztec ascendancy.

Thousands of priests served in Aztec temples. Distinctive hairstyles, clothing, and black body paint identified the priests. Women served as priestesses, particularly in temples dedicated to various earth-mother cults. Bernal Díaz del Castillo (1492–1581), a soldier who accompanied Cortés when the Spaniards first entered Tenochtitlán, recorded his shock upon seeing a group of foul-smelling priests with uncut fingernails, long hair matted with blood, and ears covered in cuts, not realizing they were performing rites in honor of the deities they served, including piercing their skin with cactus spines to draw blood. These priests were the opposite of the "barbarians" the European conquistadors considered them to be. They were, in fact, the most highly educated Aztecs. The Spanish reaction to the customs they encountered in the New World has colored popular opinion about Aztec culture ever since. The religious practices that horrified their European conquerors, however, were not unique to the Aztecs but were deeply rooted in earlier Mesoamerican society (see Chapter 14).

COYOLXAUHQUI The Temple of Huitzilopochtli at Tenochtitlán commemorated the god's victory over his sister and 400 brothers, who had plotted to kill their mother, Coatlicue (She of the Serpent Skirt). The myth signifies the birth of the sun at dawn, a role

Huitzilopochtli sometimes assumed, and the sun's battle with the forces of darkness, the stars and moon. Huitzilopochtli chased away his brothers and dismembered the body of his sister, the moon goddess Coyolxauhqui (She of the Golden Bells, referring to the bells on her cheeks), at a hill near Tula (represented by the pyramid itself). The mythical event is depicted on a huge stone disk (FIG. 32-4), whose discovery in 1971 set off the ongoing archaeological investigations near the main plaza in Mexico City. The relief had been placed at the foot of the staircase leading up to one of Huitzilopochtli's earlier temples on the site. (Cortés and his army never saw it because it lay within the outermost shell of the Great Temple.) Carved on the disk is an image of the murdered and segmented body of Coyolxauhqui. The mythological theme also carried a contemporary political message. The Aztecs sacrificed their conquered enemies at the top of the Great Temple and then hurled their bodies down the temple stairs to land on this stone. The victors thus forced their foes to reenact the horrible fate of the goddess that Huitzilopochtli dismembered. The Coyolxauhqui disk is a superb example of art in the service of state ideology. The unforgettable image of the fragmented goddess proclaimed the power of the Mexica over their enemies and the inevitable fate that must befall them when defeated. Marvelously composed, the relief has a kind of dreadful yet formal beauty. Within the circular space, the design's carefully balanced, richly detailed components have a slow turning rhythm reminiscent of a revolving galaxy. The carving is in low relief, a smoothly even, flat surface raised from a flat ground. It is the sculptural equivalent of the line and flat tone, the figure and neutral ground, characteristic of Mesoamerican painting.

COATLICUE In addition to relief carving, the Aztecs produced freestanding statuary. Perhaps the most impressive is the colossal statue (FIG. 32-5) of the beheaded Coatlicue discovered in 1790 near Mexico City's cathedral. The sculpture's original setting is unknown, but some scholars believe it was one of a group set up at the Great Temple. The main forms are in high relief, the details executed either in low relief or by incising. The overall aspect is of an enormous blocky mass, its ponderous weight looming over awed viewers. From the beheaded goddess's neck writhe two serpents whose heads meet to form a tusked mask. Coatlicue wears a necklace of severed human hands and excised human hearts. The pendant of the necklace is a skull. Entwined snakes form her skirt. From between her legs emerges another serpent, symbolic perhaps of both menses and the male member. Like most Aztec deities, Coatlicue has both masculine and feminine traits. Her hands and feet have great claws, which she used to tear the human flesh she consumed. All her attributes symbolize sacrificial death. Yet, in Aztec thought, this mother of the gods combined savagery and tenderness, for out of destruction arose new life, a theme seen earlier at Teotihuacan (FIG. 14-7).

Given the Aztecs' almost meteoric rise from obscurity to their role as the dominant culture of Mesoamerica, the quality of the art they sponsored is astonishing. Granted, they swiftly appropriated the best artworks and most talented artists of conquered territories, bringing both back to Tenochtitlán. Thus, craftspeople from other areas, such as the Mixtecs of Oaxaca, may have created much of the exquisite pottery, goldwork, and turquoise mosaics the Aztec elite used. Gulf Coast artists probably made the life-size terracotta sculptures of eagle warriors found at the Great Temple. Nonetheless, the Aztecs' own sculptural style, developed at the height of their power in the late 15th century, is unique.

AZTECS AND SPANIARDS Unfortunately, much of Aztec and Aztec-sponsored art did not survive the Spanish conquest and the subsequent period of evangelization. The conquerors took Aztec gold artifacts back to Spain and melted them down, zealous friars destroyed "idols" and illustrated books, and perishable materials such as textiles and wood largely disappeared. Aztec artisans also fashioned beautifully worked feathered objects and even created mosaic-like

32-5 Coatlicue (She of the Serpent Skirt), Aztec, from Tenochtitlán, Mexico City, Mexico, ca. 1487–1520. Andesite, 11′ 6″ high. Museo Nacional de Antropología, Mexico City.

This colossal statue may have stood in the Great Temple complex. The beheaded goddess wears a necklace of human hands and hearts. Entwined snakes form her skirt. All her attributes symbolize sacrificial death.

images with feathers, an art they put to service for the Catholic Church for a brief time after the Spanish conquest, creating religious pictures and decorating ecclesiastical clothing with the bright feathers of tropical birds.

The Spanish conquerors found it impossible to reconcile the beauty of the great city of Tenochtitlán with what they regarded as its hideous cults. They admired its splendid buildings ablaze with color, its luxuriant and spacious gardens, its sparkling waterways, its teeming markets, and its grandees resplendent in exotic bird feathers. But when the emperor Moctezuma II brought Cortés and his entourage into the shrine of Huitzilopochtli's temple, the newcomers started back in horror and disgust from the huge statues clotted with dried blood. Cortés was furious. Denouncing Huitzilopochtli as a devil, he proposed to put a high cross above the pyramid and a statue of the Virgin in the sanctuary to exorcise its evil. This proposal came to symbolize the avowed purpose and the historical result of the Spanish conquest of Mesoamerica. The conquistadors venerated the cross and the Virgin, triumphant, in new shrines raised on the ruins of the plundered temples of the ancient American gods. The banner of the Most Catholic King of Spain waved over new atrocities of a European kind.

SOUTH AMERICA

Late Horizon is the name of the period in the Andes Mountains of Peru and Bolivia (MAP 32-2) that corresponds to the end of the late Postclassic period in Mesoamerica. The dominant power in the region at that time was the Inka.

Inka

The Inka were a small highland group who established themselves in the Cuzco Valley around 1000. In the 15th century, however, they rapidly extended their power until their empire stretched from modern Quito, Ecuador, to central Chile, a distance of more than 3,000 miles. Perhaps 12 million subjects inhabited the area the Inka ruled. At the time of the Spanish conquest, the Inka Empire, although barely a century old, was the largest in the world. Expertise in mining and metalwork enabled the Inka to accumulate enormous wealth and to amass the fabled troves of gold and silver the Spaniards so coveted. An empire as vast and rich as the Inka's required skillful organizational and administrative control. The Inka had rare talent for both. They divided their Andean empire, which they called Tawantinsuyu, the Land of the Four Quarters, into sections and subsections, provinces and communities, whose boundaries all converged on, or radiated from, the capital city of Cuzco.

The engineering prowess of the Inka matched their organizational talent. They mastered the difficult problems of Andean agriculture with expert terracing and irrigation and knitted together the fabric of their empire with networks of roads and bridges. Shunning wheeled vehicles and horses, they used their highway system to move goods by llama herds and armies by foot throughout their territories. The Inka upgraded or built more than 14,000 miles of roads, one main highway running through the highlands and another along the coast, with connecting roads linking the two regions. They also established a highly efficient, swift communication system of relay runners who carried messages the length of the empire. The Inka emperor in Cuzco could get fresh fish from the coast in only three days. Where the terrain was too steep for a paved flat surface, the Inka built stone steps, and their rope bridges crossed canyons high over impassable rivers. They placed small settlements along the roads no more than a day apart where travelers could rest and obtain supplies for the journey.

The Inka aimed at imposing not only political and economic control but also their art style throughout their realm, subjugating local traditions to those of the empire. Control extended even to clothing, which communicated the social status of the person wearing the garment. The Inka wove bands of small squares of various repeated abstract designs into their fabrics. Scholars believe the patterns had political meaning, connoting membership in particular social groups. The Inka ruler's tunics displayed a full range of abstract motifs, perhaps to indicate his control over all groups. Those the Inka conquered had to wear their characteristic local dress at all times, a practice reflected in the distinctive and varied clothing of today's indigenous Andean peoples.

The Inka never developed a writing system, but they employed a remarkably sophisticated record-keeping system using a device known as the *khipu,* with which they recorded calendrical and astronomical information, census and tribute totals, and inventories. For example, the Spaniards noted that Inka officials always knew exactly how much maize or cloth was in any storeroom in their empire. Not a book or a tablet, the khipu consisted of a main fiber cord and other knotted threads hanging perpendicularly off it. The color and position of each thread, as well as the kind of knot and its location, signified numbers and categories of things, whether people, llamas, or crops. Studies of khipus have demonstrated that the Inka used the

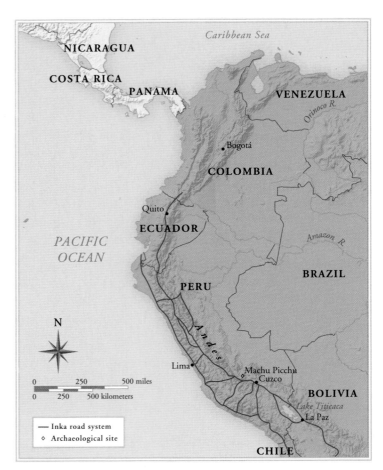

MAP 32-2 Inka sites in Andean South America.

decimal system, were familiar with the zero concept, and could record numbers up to five digits. The Inka census taker or tax collector could easily roll up and carry the khipu, one of the most lightweight and portable "computers" ever invented.

MACHU PICCHU The imperial Inka were great architects. Although they also worked with adobe, the Inka were supreme masters of shaping and fitting stone. As a militant people, they selected breathtaking, naturally fortified sites and further strengthened them by building various defensive structures. Inka city planning reveals an almost instinctive grasp of the proper relation of architecture to site.

One of the world's most awe-inspiring sights is the Inka city of Machu Picchu (FIGS. 32-1 and 32-6), which perches on a ridge between two jagged peaks 9,000 feet above sea level. Completely invisible from the Urubamba River Valley some 1,600 feet below, the site remained unknown to the outside world until Hiram Bingham (1875–1956), an American explorer, discovered it in 1911. In the very heart of the Andes, Machu Picchu is about 50 miles north of Cuzco and, like some of the region's other cities, was the estate of a powerful mid-15th-century Inka ruler. Though relatively small and insignificant compared with its neighbors (it had a resident population of little more than a thousand), the city is of great archaeological importance as a rare site left undisturbed since Inka times. The accommodation of its architecture to the landscape is so complete that Machu Picchu seems a natural part of the mountain ranges that surround it on all sides. The Inka even cut large stones to echo the shapes of the mountain beyond (FIG. 32-1). Terraces spill down the mountainsides (FIG. 32-6) and extend even up to the very peak of Huayna Picchu, the great hill just beyond the city's main plaza. The Inka carefully sited buildings so that windows and doors framed spectacular views of sacred peaks and facilitated the recording of important astronomical events.

Machu Picchu was the estate of an Inka ruler. Stone terraces spill down the Peruvian mountainsides. Precisely placed windows and doors facilitated astronomical observations.

CUZCO In the 16th century, the Spanish conquistadors largely destroyed the Inka capital at Cuzco. Consequently, most of the information about the city has been gleaned from often contradictory Spanish sources rather than from archaeology. Some descriptions state that Cuzco's plan was in the shape of a puma, with a great shrine-fortress on a hill above the city representing its head and the southeastern convergence of two rivers forming its tail. Cuzco residents still refer to the river area as "the puma's tail." A great plaza, still the hub of the modern city, nestled below the animal's stomach. The puma referred to Inka royal power.

One Inka building at Cuzco that survives in small part is the Temple of the Sun (FIG. 32-7), built of *ashlar masonry* (fitting stone blocks together without mortar), an ancient construction technique the Inka mastered. Inka masons laid the stones with perfectly joined faces so that the lines of separation between blocks and courses were almost undectable. Remarkably, the Inka produced the close joints of their masonry by abrasion alone, grinding the surfaces to a perfect fit. The stonemasons usually laid the blocks in regular horizontal courses (FIG. 32-7, *right*). Inka builders were so skilled that they could fashion walls with curved surfaces (FIG. 32-7, *left*), their planes as level and

32-7 Remains of the Temple of the Sun (surmounted by the church of Santo Domingo), Inka, Cuzco, Peru, 15th century. Exterior (*left*); interior (*right*).

Perfectly constructed ashlar masonry walls are all that remain of the Temple of the Sun, the most important shrine in the Inka capital. Gold, silver, and emeralds covered the temple's interior walls.

continuous as if they were a single form. The surviving walls of the Temple of the Sun are a prime example of this single-form effect. On the exterior, for example, the stones, precisely fitted and polished, form a curving semi-parabola. The Inka set the ashlar blocks for flexibility in earthquakes, allowing for a temporary dislocation of the courses, which then would return to their original position.

Known to the Spanish as Coricancha (Golden Enclosure), the Temple of the Sun was the most magnificent of all Inka shrines. The 16th-century Spanish chroniclers wrote in awe of Coricancha's splendor, its interior veneered with sheets of gold, silver, and emeralds. Built on the site of the home of Manco Capac, son of the sun god and founder of the Inka dynasty, the temple housed mummies of some of the early rulers. Dedicated to the worship of several Inka deities, including the creator god Viracocha and the gods of the sun, moon, stars, and the elements, the temple was the center point of a network of radiating sight lines leading to some 350 shrines, which had both calendrical and astronomical significance.

Smallpox spreading south from Spanish-occupied Mesoamerica killed the last Inka emperor and his heir before they ever laid eyes on a Spaniard. The deaths of the emperor and his named successor unleashed a struggle among competing elite families that only aided the Europeans in their conquest. In 1532, Francisco Pizarro (1471–1541), the Spanish explorer of the Andes, ambushed the would-be emperor

Atawalpa on his way to be crowned at Cuzco after vanquishing his rival half-brother. Although Atawalpa paid a huge ransom of gold and silver, the Spaniards killed him and took control of his vast domain, only a decade after Cortés had defeated the Aztecs in Mexico. Following the murder of Atawalpa, the Spanish erected the church of Santo Domingo (FIG. **32-7**, *left*), in an imported European style, on what remained of the Golden Enclosure. A curved section of Inka wall serves to this day as the foundation for Santo Domingo's *apse*. A violent earthquake in 1950 seriously damaged the colonial building, but the Peruvians rebuilt the church. The two contrasting structures remain standing one atop the other. The Coricancha is therefore of more than architectural and archaeological interest. It is a symbol of the Spanish conquest of the Americas and serves as a composite monument to it.

NORTH AMERICA

In North America during the centuries preceding the arrival of Europeans, power was much more widely dispersed and the native art and architecture more varied than in Mesoamerica and Andean South America. Three major regions of the United States and Canada are of special interest: the American Southwest, the Northwest Coast (Washington and British Columbia) and Alaska, and the Great Plains (MAP **32-3**).

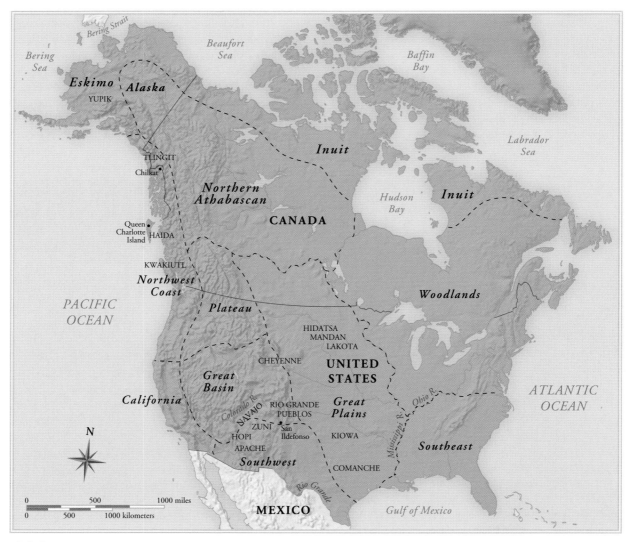

MAP 32-3 Later Native American sites in North America.

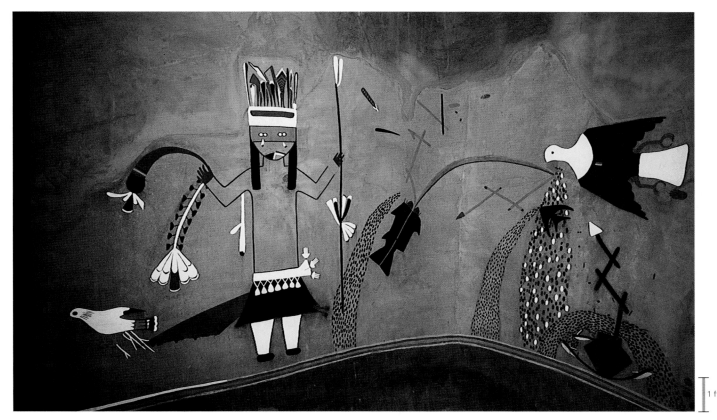

32-8 Detail of a kiva mural from Kuaua Pueblo (Coronado State Monument), Ancestral Puebloan, New Mexico, late 15th to early 16th century. Interior of the kiva, 18′ × 18′. Museum of New Mexico, Santa Fe.

The kiva, or male council house, was the spiritual center of Puebloan life. Kivas were decorated with mural paintings associated with agricultural fertility. This one depicts a lightning man, fish, birds, and seeds.

Southwest

The dominant culture of the American Southwest between 1300 and 1500 was the Ancestral Puebloan (formerly called the Anasazi), the builders of great architectural complexes such as Chaco Canyon and Cliff Palace (FIG. 14-32). The spiritual center of Puebloan life was the *kiva*, or male council house, decorated with elaborate mural paintings representing deities associated with agricultural fertility. According to their descendants, the present-day Hopi and Zuni, the detail of the Kuaua Pueblo (*pueblo* is Spanish for "urban settlement") mural shown here (FIG. 32-8) depicts a "lightning man" on the left side. Fish and eagle images (associated with rain) appear on the right side. Seeds, a lightning bolt, and a rainbow stream from the eagle's mouth. All these figures are associated with the fertility of the earth and the life-giving properties of the seasonal rains, a constant preoccupation of Southwest farmers. The Ancestral Puebloan painter depicted the figures with great economy, using thick black lines, dots, and a restricted palette of black, brown, yellow, and white. The frontal figure of the lightning man seen against a neutral ground makes an immediate visual impact.

NAVAJO PAINTING AND WEAVING When the first Europeans came into contact with the ancient peoples of the Southwest, they called them "Pueblo Indians." The successors of the Ancestral Puebloans and other Southwest groups, the Pueblo Indians include linguistically diverse but culturally similar peoples such as the Hopi of northern Arizona and the Rio Grande Pueblos of New Mexico. Living among them are the descendants of nomadic hunters who arrived in the Southwest from their homelands in northwestern Canada sometime between 1200 and 1500. These

are the Apache and Navajo, who, although culturally quite distinct from the original inhabitants of the Southwest, adopted many features of Pueblo life.

Among these borrowed elements is *sand painting*, which the Navajo learned from the Pueblos but transformed into an extraordinarily complex ritual art form. The temporary sand paintings (also known as *dry paintings*), constructed to the accompaniment of prayers and chants, are an essential part of ceremonies for curing disease. (Because of the sacred nature of sand paintings, the Navajo do not permit photographing them.) In the healing ceremony, the patient sits in the painting's center to absorb the life-giving powers of the gods and their representations. The Navajo perform similar rites to assure success in hunting and to promote fertility in human beings and nature alike. The artists who supervise the making of these complex images are religious leaders or "medicine men" (rarely women), thought to have direct contact with the powers of the supernatural world, which they use to help both individuals and the community.

The natural materials used—sand, varicolored powdered stones, corn pollen, and charcoal—play a symbolic role that reflects the Native Americans' preoccupation with the forces of nature. The paintings depict the gods and mythological heroes whose help the Navajo seek. As part of the ritual, the participants destroy the sand paintings, so no models exist. However, the traditional prototypes, passed on from artist to artist, must be adhered to as closely as possible. Mistakes can render the ceremony ineffective. Navajo dry painting is therefore highly stylized. Simple curves, straight lines, right angles, and serial repetition characterize most sand paintings.

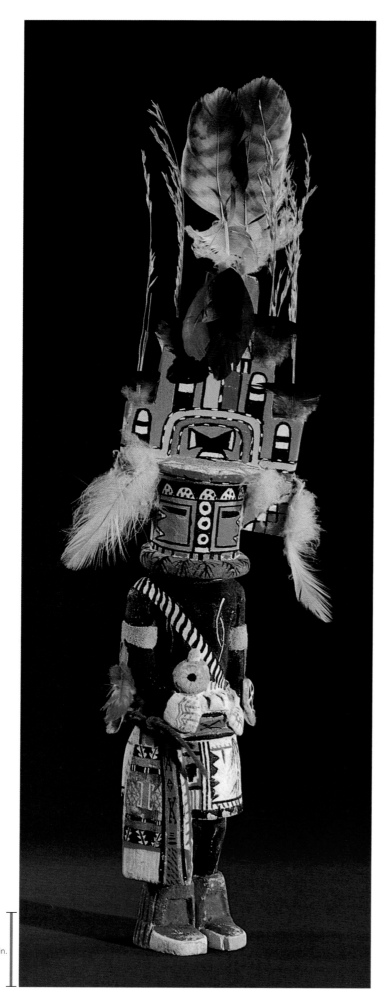

1 in.

By the mid-17th century, the Navajo had also learned how to weave from their Hopi and other Pueblo neighbors, quickly adapting to new materials such as sheep wool and synthetic dyes introduced by Spanish settlers and, later, by Anglo-Americans. They rapidly transformed blankets they wore into handsome rugs in response to the new market created by the arrival of the railroad and early tourists in the 1880s. Other tribes, including those of the Great Plains, also purchased Navajo textiles, which became famous for their quality (the thread count in a typical Navajo rug is extraordinarily high) as well as the sophistication of their designs. Navajo rugs often incorporate vivid abstract motifs known as "eye dazzlers" and copies of sand paintings (altered slightly to preserve the sacred quality of the impermanent ritual images).

HOPI KATSINAS Another art form from the Southwest, the *katsina* figurine, also has deep roots in the area. Katsinas are benevolent supernatural spirits personifying ancestors and natural elements living in mountains and water sources. Humans join their world after death. Among contemporary Pueblo groups, masked dancers ritually impersonate katsinas during yearly festivals dedicated to rain, fertility, and good hunting. To educate young girls in ritual lore, the Hopi traditionally give them miniature representations of the masked dancers. The Hopi katsina illustrated here (FIG. 32-9), carved in cottonwood root with added feathers, is the work of OTTO PENTEWA (d. 1963). It represents a rain-bringing deity who wears a mask painted in geometric patterns symbolic of water and agricultural fertility. Topping the mask is a stepped shape signifying thunderclouds and feathers to carry the Hopis' airborne prayers. The origins of the katsina figurines have been lost in time (they even may have developed from carved saints the Spaniards introduced during the colonial period). However, the cult is probably very ancient.

PUEBLO POTTERY The Southwest has also provided the finest examples of North American pottery. Originally producing utilitarian forms, Southwest potters worked without the potter's wheel and instead coiled clay shapes that they then slipped, polished, and fired. Decorative motifs, often abstract and conventionalized, dealt largely with forces of nature—clouds, wind, and rain. The efforts of San Ildefonso Pueblo potter MARÍA MONTOYA MARTÍNEZ (1887–1980) and her husband Julian Martínez (see "Gender Roles in Native American Art," page 863) in the early decades of the 20th century revived old techniques to produce forms of striking shape, proportion, and texture. Her black-on-black pieces (FIG. 32-10) feature matte designs on highly polished surfaces achieved by extensive polishing and special firing in an oxygen-poor atmosphere.

Northwest Coast and Alaska

The Native Americans of the coasts and islands of northern Washington state, the province of British Columbia in Canada, and southern Alaska have long enjoyed a rich and reliable environment. They fished, hunted sea mammals and game, gathered edible plants, and made their homes, utensils, ritual objects, and even clothing from the region's great cedar forests. Among the numerous groups who make up

32-9 OTTO PENTEWA, Katsina figurine, Hopi, New Oraibi, Arizona, carved before 1959. Cottonwood root and feathers, 1′ high. Arizona State Museum, University of Arizona, Tucson.

Katsinas are benevolent spirits living in mountains and water sources. This Hopi katsina represents a rain-bringing deity who wears a mask painted in geometric patterns symbolic of water and agricultural fertility.

Gender Roles in Native American Art

Although both Native American women and men have created art objects for centuries, they have traditionally worked in different media or at different tasks. Among the Navajo, for example, weavers tend to be women, whereas among the neighboring Hopi the men weave. According to Navajo myth, long ago Spider Woman's husband built her a loom for weaving. In turn, she taught Navajo women how to spin and weave so that they might have clothing to wear. Today, young girls learn from their mothers how to work the loom, just as Spider Woman instructed their ancestors, passing along the techniques and designs from one generation to the next.

Among the Pueblos, pottery making normally has been the domain of women. But in response to heavy demand for her wares, María Montoya Martínez, of San Ildefonso Pueblo in New Mexico, coiled, slipped, and burnished her pots, and her husband Julian painted the designs. Although they worked in many styles, some based on prehistoric ceramics, around 1918 they invented the black-on-black ware (FIG. 32-10) that made María, and indeed the whole pueblo, famous. The elegant shapes of the pots, as well as the traditional but abstract designs, had affinities with the contemporary Art Deco style in architecture (FIG. 35-76) and interior design, and collectors avidly sought (and continue to seek) them. When nonnative buyers suggested she sign her pots to increase their value, María obliged, but, in the communal spirit typical of the Pueblos, she also signed her neighbors' names so that they might share in her good fortune. Though María died in 1980, her descendants continue to garner awards as outstanding potters.

Women also produced the elaborately decorated skin and, later, the trade-cloth clothing of the Woodlands and Great Plains regions using moose hair, dyed porcupine quills, and imported beads. Among the Cheyenne, quillworking was a sacred art, and young women worked at learning both proper ritual and correct techniques to obtain membership in the prestigious quillworkers' guild. Women gained the same honor and dignity from creating finely worked utilitarian objects that men earned from warfare. Both women and men painted on tipis and clothing (FIGS. 32-16 and 32-17), with women creating abstract designs (FIG. 32-16) and men working in a more realistic narrative style, often celebrating their exploits in war or recording the cultural changes resulting from the transfer to reservations.

In the far north, women tended to work with soft materials such as animal skins, whereas men were sculptors of wood masks among the Alaskan Eskimos and of walrus ivory pieces (FIG. 14-27) through-

32-10 MARÍA MONTOYA MARTÍNEZ, jar, San Ildefonso Pueblo, New Mexico, ca. 1939. Blackware, $11\frac{1}{8}''$ × 1' 1''. National Museum of Women in the Arts, Washington, D.C. (gift of Wallace and Wilhelmina Hollachy).

Pottery is traditionally a Native American woman's art form. María Montoya Martínez won renown for her black-on-black vessels of striking shapes with matte designs on highly polished surfaces.

out the Arctic. The introduction of printmaking, a foreign medium with no established gender associations, to some Canadian Inuit communities in the 1950s provided both native women and men with a new creative outlet. Printmaking became an important source of economic independence vital to these isolated and once-impoverished settlements. Today, both Inuit women and men make prints, but men still dominate in carving stone sculpture, another new medium also produced for and sold to outsiders.

Throughout North America, indigenous artists continue to work in traditional media, such as ceramics, beadwork, and basketry, marketing their wares through museum shops, galleries, regional art fairs, and, most recently, the Internet. Many also obtain degrees in art and express themselves in European media such as oil painting and mixed-media sculpture (FIG. 36-66).

the Northwest Coast area are the Kwakiutl of southern British Columbia; the Haida, who live on Queen Charlotte Island off the coast of the province; and the Tlingit of southern Alaska (MAP 32-3). In the Northwest, a class of professional artists developed, in contrast to the more typical Native American pattern of part-time artists. Working in a

highly formalized, subtle style, Northwest Coast artists have produced a wide variety of art objects for centuries: totem poles, masks, rattles, chests, bowls, clothing, charms, and decorated houses and canoes. Some artistic traditions originated as early as 500 BCE, although others developed only after the arrival of Europeans in North America.

Eagle transformation mask, closed (*top*) and open (*bottom*) views, Kwakiutl, Alert Bay, Canada, late 19th century. Wood, feathers, and string, 1′ 10″ × 11″. American Museum of Natural History, New York.

The wearer of this Kwakiutl mask could open and close it rapidly by manipulating hidden strings, magically transforming himself from human to eagle and back again as he danced.

1 ft.

1 ft.

KWAKIUTL AND TLINGIT MASKS Northwest Coast religious specialists used masks in their healing rituals. Men also wore masks in dramatic public performances during the winter ceremonial season. The animals and mythological creatures represented in masks and a host of other carvings derive from the Northwest Coast's rich oral tradition and celebrate the mythological origins and inherited privileges of high-ranking families. The artist who made the Kwakiutl mask illustrated here (FIG. 32-11) meant it to be seen in flickering firelight, and ingeniously constructed it to open and close rapidly when the wearer manipulated hidden strings. He could thus magically transform himself from human to eagle and back again as he danced. The transformation theme, in myriad forms, is a central aspect of the art and religion of the Americas. The Kwakiutl mask's

human aspect also owes its dramatic character to the exaggeration and distortion of facial parts—such as the hooked beaklike nose and flat flaring nostrils—and to the deeply undercut curvilinear depressions, which form strong shadows. In contrast to the carved human face, but painted in the same colors, is the two-dimensional abstract image of the eagle painted on the inside of the outer mask.

The Kwakiutl mask is a refined yet forceful carving typical of the area's more dramatic styles. Others are more subdued, and some, such as a wooden Tlingit war helmet (FIG. 32-12), are exceedingly naturalistic. Although the helmet mask may be a portrait, it might also represent a supernatural being whose powers enhance the wearer's strength. In either case, the artist surely created its grimacing expression to intimidate the enemy.

This naturalistic wood war helmet mask may be a portrait of a Tlingit warrior or a representation of a supernatural being. The carver intended the face's grimacing expression to intimidate enemies.

3A REID, *The*
ven and the
t Men,
8–1980.

1 in.

HAIDA TOTEM POLES Although Northwest Coast arts have a spiritual dimension, they are often more important as expressions of social status. Haida house frontal poles, displaying totemic emblems of clan groups, strikingly express this interest in prestige and family history. Totem poles emerged as a major art form about 300 years ago. The examples in FIG. **32-13** date to the 19th century. They stand today in a reconstructed Haida village that BILL REID (1920–1998, Haida) and his assistant DOUG CRANMER (b. 1927, Kwakiutl) completed in 1962. Each of the superimposed forms carved on these poles represents a crest, an animal, or a supernatural being that figures in the clan's origin story.

Additional crests could also be obtained through marriage and trade. The Haida so jealously guarded the right to own and display crests that even warfare could erupt over the disputed ownership of a valued crest. In the poles shown, the crests represented include an upside-down dogfish (a small shark), an eagle with a downturned beak, and a killer whale with a crouching human between its snout and its upturned tail flukes. During the 19th century, the Haida erected more poles and made them larger in response to greater competitiveness and the availability of metal tools. The artists carved poles up to 60 feet tall from the trunks of single cedar trees.

32-13 BILL REID (Haida), assisted by DOUG CRANMER (Nāmgīs), 19th-century-style Haida houses and totem poles, 1962. Courtesy University of British Columbia, Museum of Anthropology, Vancouver, Canada.

Each of the superimposed forms carved on Haida totem poles represents a crest, an animal, or a supernatural being who figures in the clan's origin story. Some Haida poles are 60 feet tall.

32-14 Chilkat blanket with stylized animal motifs, Tlingit, Canada, early 20th century. Mountain goat wool and cedar bark, 2′ 11″ × 6′. Southwest Museum of the American Indian, Los Angeles.

Chilkat blankets were collaborations between male designers and female weavers. Decorated with animal and abstract motifs, they were worn over the shoulder and were items of ceremonial dress.

CHILKAT BLANKETS Another characteristic Northwest Coast art form is the Chilkat blanket (FIG. **32-14**), named for an Alaskan Tlingit village. Male designers provided the templates for these blankets in the form of wooden pattern boards for female weavers. Woven of shredded cedar bark and mountain goat wool on an upright loom, the Tlingit blankets took at least six months to complete. These blankets, which served as robes worn over the shoulders, became widespread prestige items of ceremonial dress during the 19th century. They display several characteristics of the Northwest Coast style recurrent in all media: symmetry and rhythmic repetition, schematic abstraction of animal motifs (in the robe illustrated, a bear), eye designs, a regularly swelling and thinning line, and a tendency to round off corners.

YUPIK MASKS Farther north, the 19th-century Yupik Eskimos living around the Bering Strait of Alaska had a highly developed ceremonial life focused on game animals, particularly seal. Their religious specialists wore highly imaginative masks with moving parts. The Yupik generally made these masks for single occasions and then abandoned them. Consequently, many masks have ended up in museums and private collections. The example shown here (FIG. **32-15**) represents the spirit of the north wind, its face surrounded by a hoop signifying the universe, its voice mimicked by the rattling appendages. The paired human hands commonly found on these masks refer to the wearer's power to attract animals for hunting. The painted white spots represent snowflakes.

The devastating effects of 19th-century epidemics, coupled with government and missionary repression of Native American ritual and social activities, threatened to eradicate the traditional arts of the Northwest Coast and the Eskimos. In the past half century, however, there has been an impressive revival of traditional art forms, some created for collectors and the tourist trade, as well as the development of new ones, such as printmaking. Canadian Eskimos, known as the Inuit, have set up cooperatives to produce and market stone carvings and prints. With these new media, artists generally depict themes from the rapidly vanishing traditional Inuit way of life.

Great Plains

After colonial governments disrupted settled indigenous communities on the East Coast and the Europeans introduced the horse to North America, a new mobile Native American culture flourished for a short time on the Great Plains. Artists of the Great Plains worked in materials and styles quite different from those of the Northwest Coast and Eskimo/Inuit peoples. Much artistic energy went into the decoration of leather garments, pouches, and horse trappings, first with compactly sewn quill designs and later with beadwork patterns. Artists painted tipis, tipi linings, and buffalo-skin robes with geometric and stiff figural designs prior to about 1830. After that, they gradually introduced naturalistic scenes, often of war exploits, in styles adapted from those of visiting European artists.

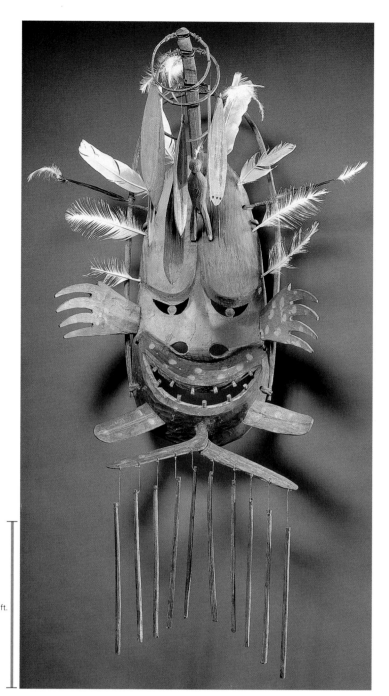

32-15 Mask, Yupik Eskimo, Alaska, early 20th century. Wood and feathers, 3′ 9″ high. Metropolitan Museum of Art, New York (Michael C. Rockefeller Memorial Collection, gift of Nelson Rockefeller).

This Yupik mask represents the spirit of the north wind, its face surrounded by a hoop signifying the universe, its voice mimicked by the rattling appendages. The white spots represent snowflakes.

32-16 KARL BODMER, *Hidatsa Warrior Pehriska-Ruhpa* (*Two Ravens*), 1833. Watercolor, 1′ 3$\frac{7}{8}$″ × 11$\frac{1}{2}$″. Joslyn Art Museum, Omaha (gift of the Enron Art Foundation). 📹◀

The personal regalia of a Hidatsa warrior included his pipe, painted buffalo robe, bear-claw necklace, and feather decorations, all symbols of his affiliations and military accomplishments.

2-16A Mandan
uffalo-hide
be, ca. 1800.

HIDATSA REGALIA Because most Plains peoples were nomadic, they focused their aesthetic attention largely on their clothing and bodies and on other portable objects, such as shields, clubs, pipes, tomahawks, and various containers. Transient but important Plains art forms can sometimes be found in the paintings and drawings of visiting American and European artists. The Swiss painter KARL BODMER (1809–1893), for example, portrayed the personal decoration of Two Ravens, a Hidatsa warrior, in an 1833 watercolor (FIG. 32-16). The painting depicts his pipe, painted buffalo robe,

bear-claw necklace, and feather decorations, all symbolic of his affiliations and military accomplishments. These items represent his "biography"—a composite artistic statement in several media that neighboring Native Americans could have "read" easily. The concentric circle design over his left shoulder, for example, is an abstract rendering of an eagle-feather war bonnet.

Plains peoples also made shields and shield covers that were both artworks and "power images." Shield paintings often derived from personal religious visions. The owners believed that the symbolism, the pigments themselves, and added materials, such as feathers, provided them with magical protection and supernatural power.

LEDGER PAINTINGS Plains warriors battled incursions into their territory throughout the 19th century. The pursuit of Plains natives culminated in the 1890 slaughter of Lakota participants who had gathered for a ritual known as the Ghost Dance at Wounded Knee Creek, South Dakota. Indeed, from the 1830s on, U.S. troops forcibly removed Native Americans from their homelands and resettled them in other parts of the country. Toward the end of the century, governments confined them to reservations in both the United States and Canada.

32-17 Honoring song at painted tipi, in Julian Scott Ledger, Kiowa, 1880. Pencil, ink, and colored pencil, $7\frac{1}{2}'' \times 1'$. Mr. and Mrs. Charles Diker Collection. ◼◀

During the reservation period, some Plains artists recorded their traditional lifestyle in ledger books. This one depicts men and women dancing an honoring song in front of three painted tipis.

During the reservation period, some Plains arts continued to flourish, notably beadwork for the women and painting in ledger books for the men. Traders, the army, and Indian agents had for years provided Plains peoples with pencils and new or discarded ledger books. They, in turn, used them to draw their personal exploits for themselves or for interested Anglo buyers. Sometimes warriors carried them into battle, where U.S. Army opponents retook the ledgers. After confinement to reservations, Plains artists began to record not only their heroic past and vanished lifestyle but also their reactions to their new surroundings, frequently in a state far from home. These images, often poignant and sometimes humorous, are important native documents of a time of great turmoil and change. In the example shown here (FIG. 32-17), the work of an unknown Kiowa artist, a group of men and women, possibly Comanches (allies of the Kiowa), appear to dance an honoring song be-

fore three tipis, the left forward one painted with red stone pipes and a dismembered leg and arm. The women (at the center and right) wear the mixture of clothing typical of the late 19th century among the Plains Indians—traditional high leather moccasins, dresses made from calico trade cloth, and (on the right) a red Hudson's Bay blanket with a black stripe. Although the Plains peoples no longer paint ledger books, beadwork has never completely died out. The ancient art of creating quilled, beaded, and painted clothing has evolved into the elaborate costumes displayed today at competitive dances called *powwows*.

Whether secular and decorative or spiritual and highly symbolic, the diverse styles and forms of Native American art in the United States and Canada reflect the indigenous peoples' reliance on and reverence toward the environment they considered it their privilege to inhabit.

NATIVE ARTS OF THE AMERICAS AFTER 1300

MESOAMERICA

▌ When the first Europeans arrived in the New World, they encountered native peoples with sophisticated civilizations and a long history of art production, including illustrated books. The few books that survive provide precious insight into Mesoamerican rituals, science, mythology, and painting style.

▌ The dominant power in Mesoamerica in the centuries before Cortés overthrew it was the Aztec Empire. The Aztec capital was Tenochtitlán (Mexico City), a magnificent island city laid out on a grid plan with a population of more than 100,000.

▌ The Great Temple at Tenochtitlán was a towering pyramid encasing several earlier pyramids. Dedicated to the worship of Huitzilopochtli and Tlaloc, it was also the place where enemies were sacrificed and their battered bodies thrown down the stone staircase to land on a huge disk bearing a representation in relief of the dismembered body of the goddess Coyolxauhqui.

▌ In addition to relief carving, Aztec sculptors produced stone statues, some of colossal size, for example, the 11' 6" image of the beheaded Coatlicue from Tenochtitlán.

Borgia Codex, ca. 1400–1500

Coyolxauhqui, Great Temple, Tenochtitlán, ca. 1469

SOUTH AMERICA

▌ In the 15th century, the Inka Empire, with its capital at Cuzco in modern Peru, extended from Ecuador to Chile. The Inka were superb engineers and constructed 14,000 miles of roads to exert control over their vast empire. They kept track of inventories, census and tribute totals, and astronomical information using a "computer of strings" called a khipu.

▌ Master architects, the Inka were experts in ashlar masonry construction. The most impressive preserved Inka site is Machu Picchu, the estate of an Inka ruler. Stone terraces spill down the mountainsides, and the buildings have windows and doors designed to frame views of sacred peaks and facilitate the recording of important astronomical events.

Machu Picchu, 15th century

NORTH AMERICA

▌ In North America, power was much more widely dispersed and the native art and architecture more varied than in Mesoamerica and Andean South America.

▌ In the American Southwest, the Ancestral Puebloans built urban settlements (pueblos) and decorated their council houses (kivas) with mural paintings. The Navajo produced magnificent textiles and created temporary sand paintings as part of complex rituals. The Hopi carved katsina figurines representing benevolent supernatural spirits. The Pueblo Indian pottery produced by artists like María Montoya Martínez is among the finest in the world.

Martínez, San Ildefonso Pueblo jar, ca. 1939

▌ On the Northwest Coast, masks played an important role in religious rituals. Some examples can open and close rapidly so that the wearer can magically transform himself from human to animal and back again. Haida totem poles sometimes reach 60 feet in height and are carved with superimposed forms representing clan crests, animals, and supernatural beings. Chilkat blankets are the result of a fruitful collaboration between male designers and female weavers.

▌ The peoples of the Great Plains won renown for their magnificent painted buffalo robes, bead necklaces, feather headdresses, and shields. Native American art lived on even after the U.S. government forcibly relocated the Plains peoples to reservations. Painted ledger books record their vanished lifestyle, but the production of fine crafts continues to the present day.

Kwakiutl eagle transformation mask, late 19th century

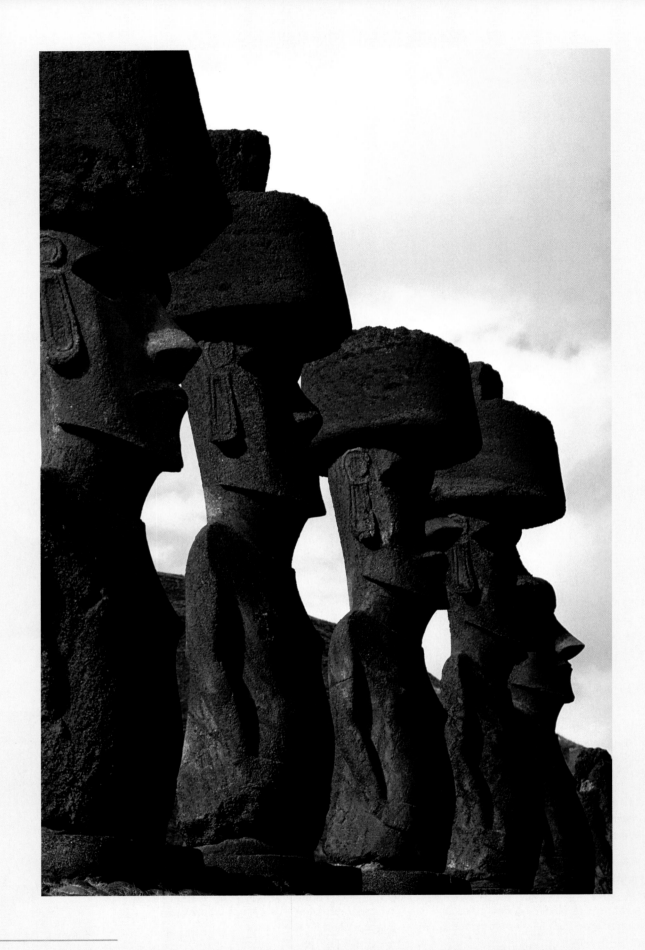

33-1 Moai, Anakena, Rapa Nui (Easter Island), Polynesia, 10th to 12th centuries. Volcanic tuff and red scoria.

The colossal stone sculptures of Easter Island predate the arrival of Europeans in Oceania by several centuries. Almost 900 moai are known, even though each statue took 30 men a full year to carve.

OCEANIA

When people think of the South Pacific, images of balmy tropical islands usually come to mind. But the islands of the Pacific Ocean encompass a wide range of habitats. Environments range from the arid deserts of the Australian outback to the tropical rain forests of inland New Guinea to the coral atolls of the Marshall Islands. In all, more than 25,000 islands dot Oceania (MAP 33-1), and the region is not only geographically varied but also politically, linguistically, culturally, and artistically diverse. In 1831 the French explorer Jules Sébastien César Dumont d'Urville (1790–1842) proposed dividing the Pacific into major regions based on general geographical, racial, and linguistic distinctions. Despite its limitations, his division of Oceania into the areas of Melanesia ("black islands"), Micronesia ("small islands"), and Polynesia ("many islands") continues in use today. Melanesia includes New Guinea, New Ireland, New Britain, New Caledonia, the Admiralty Islands, and the Solomon Islands, along with other smaller island groups. Micronesia consists primarily of the Caroline, Mariana, Gilbert, and Marshall Islands in the western Pacific. Polynesia covers much of the eastern Pacific and consists of a triangular area defined by the Hawaiian Islands in the north, Rapa Nui (Easter Island) in the east, and New Zealand in the southwest.

Although documentary evidence does not exist for Oceanic cultures until the arrival of seafaring Europeans in the early 16th century, archaeologists have determined that the islands have been inhabited for tens of thousands of years. Their research has revealed that different parts of the Pacific experienced distinct migratory waves. The first group arrived during the last Ice Age, at least 40,000 and perhaps as many as 75,000 years ago, when a large continental shelf extended from Southeast Asia and gave land access to Australia and New Guinea. After the end of the Ice Age, descendants of these first settlers dispersed to other islands in Melanesia. The most recent migratory wave occurred sometime after 3000 BCE and involved peoples of Asian ancestry moving to areas of Micronesia and Polynesia. The last Pacific islands to be settled were those of Polynesia, but habitation on its most far-flung islands—Hawaii, New Zealand, and Easter Island—began no later than 500 to 1000 CE. Because of the lengthy chronological span of these migrations, Pacific cultures vary widely. For example, the Aboriginal peoples of Australia speak a language unrelated to those of New Guinea, whose languages fall into a distinct but diverse group. In contrast, most of the rest of the Pacific islanders speak languages derived from the Austronesian language family.

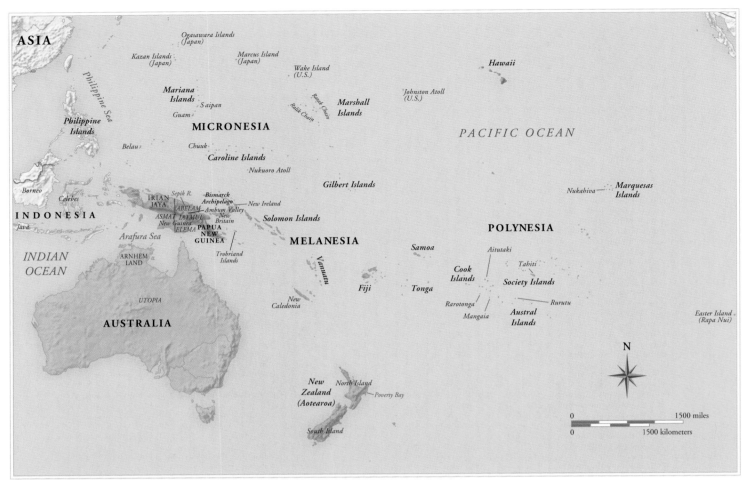

MAP 33-1 Oceania.

These island groups came to Western attention as a result of the extensive exploration and colonization that began in the 16th century and reached its peak in the 19th century. Virtually all of the major Western nations—including Great Britain, France, Spain, Holland, Germany, and the United States—established a presence in the Pacific. Much of the history of Oceania in the 20th century revolved around indigenous peoples' struggles for independence from these colonial powers. Yet colonialism also facilitated an exchange of ideas—not solely the one-way transfer of Western cultural values and technology to the Pacific. Oceanic art, for example, had a strong impact on many Western artists, including, as already noted, Paul Gauguin (FIG. 31-19). The "primitive" art of Oceania also influenced many early-20th-century artists (see "Primitivism," Chapter 35, page 920).

This chapter focuses on Oceanic art from the European discovery of the islands in the 16th century until the present, although the colossal stone statues of Easter Island (FIG. 33-1) predate the arrival of Europeans by several centuries. Knowledge of early Oceanic art and the history of the Pacific islands in general is unfortunately very incomplete. Traditionally, the transmission of information from one generation to the next in Pacific societies was largely oral, rather than written, and little archival documentation exists. Nonetheless, archaeologists, linguists, anthropologists, ethnologists, and art historians continue to make progress in illuminating the Oceanic past.

AUSTRALIA AND MELANESIA

The westernmost Oceanic islands are the continent-nation of Australia and New Guinea in Melanesia. Together they dwarf the area of all the other Pacific islands combined.

Australia

Over the past 40,000 years, the Aboriginal peoples of Australia spread out over the entire continent and adapted to a variety of ecological conditions, ranging from those of tropical and subtropical areas in the north to desert regions in the interior and to more temperate locales in the south. European explorers reaching the region in the late 18th and early 19th centuries found that the Aborigines had a special relationship with the land they lived on. The Aboriginal perception of the world centers on a concept known as the Dreamings, ancestral beings whose spirits pervade the present. All Aborigines identify certain Dreamings as totemic ancestors, and those who share the same Dreamings have social links. The Aborigines call the spiritual domain that the Dreamings occupy Dreamtime, which is both a physical space within which the ancestral beings moved in creating the landscape and a psychic space that provides Aborigines with cultural, religious, and moral direction. Because of the importance of Dreamings to all aspects of Aboriginal life, native Australian art symbolically links Aborigines with these ancestral spirits. The Aborigines recite creation myths in concert with songs and dances, and many art forms—body painting, carved figures, sacred objects, decorated stones, and rock and bark painting—serve as essential props in these dramatic re-creations. Most Aboriginal art is relatively small and portable. As hunters and gatherers in difficult terrain, the Aborigines were generally nomadic peoples. Monumental art was impractical.

BARK PAINTING Bark, widely available in Australia, is portable and lightweight, and bark painting became a mainstay of Aboriginal art. Dreamings, mythic narratives (often tracing the movement of var-

33-2 Auuenau, from Western Arnhem Land, Australia, 1913. Ochre on bark, 4′ 10⅔″ × 1′ 1″. South Australian Museum, Adelaide.

Aboriginal painters frequently depicted Dreamings, ancestral beings whose spirits pervade the present, using the "X-ray style" that shows both the figure's internal organs and external appearance.

1 ft.

EMILY KAME KNGWARREYE Aboriginal artists today retain close ties to the land and the spirits that inhabit it, but some contemporary painters have eliminated figures from their work and produced canvases that, superficially at least, resemble American *Abstract Expressionist* paintings (FIG. 36-5). EMILY KAME KNGWARREYE (1910–1996) began painting late in life after cofounding a communal women's *batik* group in Utopia. Her canvases (FIG. 33-3) clearly reveal her background as a fabric artist, but they draw their inspiration from the landscape of her native land. Using thousands of color dots that sometimes join to form thick curvilinear bands, she conjured the image of arid land, seeds, and plants. The often huge size of her paintings further suggests the vastness of the Australian countryside.

ious ancestral spirits through the landscape), and sacred places were common subjects. Ancestral spirits pervade the lives of the Aborigines, and these paintings served to give visual form to that presence. Traditionally, an Aborigine could depict only a Dreaming with which the artist had a connection. Thus, specific Aboriginal lineages, clans, or regional groups "owned" individual designs. The bark painting illustrated here (FIG. 33-2) depicts a Dreaming known as Auuenau and comes from Arnhem Land in northern Australia. The artist represented the elongated figure in a style known as "X-ray," which Aboriginal painters used to depict both animal and human forms. In this style, the artist simultaneously portrays the subject's internal organs and exterior appearance. The painting possesses a fluid and dynamic quality, with the X-ray-like figure clearly defined against a solid background.

New Guinea

Because of its sheer size, New Guinea dominates Melanesia. This 309,000-square-mile island consists today of parts of two countries—Irian Jaya, a province of nearby Indonesia, on the island's western end, and Papua New Guinea on the eastern end. New Guinea's inhabitants together speak nearly 800 different languages, almost one quarter of the world's known tongues. Among the Melanesian cultures discussed in this chapter, the Asmat, Iatmul, Elema, and Abelam peoples of New Guinea all speak Papuan-derived languages. Scholars believe they are descendants of the early settlers who came to the island in the remote past. In contrast, the people of New Ireland and the Trobriand Islands are Austronesian speakers and probably descendants of a later wave of Pacific migrants.

33-4A *Ambum Stone*, Papua New Guinea, ca. 1500 BCE.

Typical Melanesian societies are fairly democratic and relatively unstratified. What political power exists belongs to groups of elder men and, in some areas, elder women. The elders handle the people's affairs in a communal fashion. Within some of these groups, persons of local distinction, known as "Big Men," renowned for their political, economic, and, historically, warrior skills, have accrued power. Because power and position in Melanesia can be earned (within limits), many cultural practices (such as rituals and cults) revolve around the acquisition of knowledge that allows advancement in society. To represent and acknowledge this advancement in rank, Melanesian societies mount elaborate festivals, construct communal meetinghouses, and produce art objects. These cultural products serve to reinforce the social order and maintain social stability.

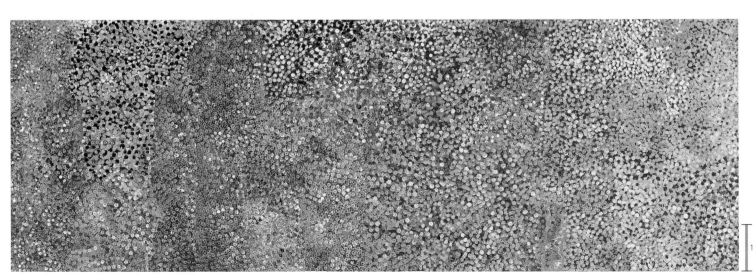

1 ft.

33-3 EMILY KAME KNGWARREYE, Untitled, 1992. Synthetic polymer paint on canvas, 5′ 5″ × 15′ 9″. Art Gallery of New South Wales, Sydney.

Aboriginal painter Kngwarreye's canvases reveal her background as a batik artist. Her abstract paintings draw their inspiration from the seeds and plants of the arid Australian landscape.

33-4 *Left:* Asmat bisj poles, Buepis village, Fajit River, Casuarina Coast, Irian Jaya, Melanesia, early to mid-20th century. *Above:* Detail of a bisj pole. Painted wood. Asmat Museum, Agats.

The Asmat carved bisj poles from mangrove tree trunks and erected them before undertaking a headhunting raid. The carved figures represent the relatives whose deaths the hunters must avenge.

Given the wide diversity in environments and languages, it is no surprise that hundreds of art styles are found on New Guinea alone. Only a sample can be presented here.

ASMAT Living along the southwestern coast of New Guinea, the Asmat people of Irian Jaya eke out their existence by hunting and gathering the varied flora and fauna found in the mangrove swamps, rivers, and tropical forests. Each Asmat community is in constant competition for limited resources. Historically, the Asmat extended this competitive spirit beyond food and materials to energy and power as well. To increase one's personal energy or spiritual power required taking it forcibly from someone else. As a result, warfare and headhunting became central to Asmat culture and art. The Asmat did not believe any death was natural. Death could result only from a direct assault (headhunting or warfare) or sorcery, and it diminished ancestral power.

Thus, to restore a balance of spirit power, an enemy's head had to be taken to avenge a death and to add to one's communal spirit power. Headhunting was still common in the 1930s when Europeans established an administrative and missionary presence among the Asmat, but as a result of European efforts, the custom ceased by the 1960s.

When they still practiced headhunting, the Asmat erected *bisj poles* (FIG. **33-4**) that served as a pledge to avenge a relative's death. A man would set up a bisj pole when he could command the support of enough men to undertake a headhunting raid. Carved from the trunk of the mangrove tree, bisj poles include superimposed figures of dead individuals. At the top, extending flangelike from the bisj pole, was one of the tree's buttress roots carved into an openwork pattern. All of the decorative elements on the pole related to headhunting and foretold a successful raid. The many animals carved on bisj poles (and in Asmat art in general) are symbols of headhunting.

uninitiated boys cannot enter the men's house. In this manner, the Iatmul men control access to knowledge and therefore to power. Given its important political and cultural role, the men's house is appropriately monumental, physically dominating Iatmul villages and dwarfing family houses. Although men's houses are common in New Guinea, those of the Iatmul are the most lavishly decorated.

Traditionally, the house symbolizes the protective mantle of the ancestors and represents an enormous female ancestor. The Iatmul house and its female ancestral figures symbolize a reenacted death and rebirth when a clan member scales a ladder and enters and then exits the second story of the house. The gable ends of men's houses are usually covered and include a giant female gable mask, making the ancestral symbolism visible. The interior carvings, however, are normally hidden from view. The Iatmul placed carved images of clan ancestors on the central ridge-support posts and on the roof-support posts on both sides of the house. They capped each roof-support post with large faces representing mythical spirits of the clans. At the top of the two raised spires at each end, birds symbolizing the war spirit of the village men sit above carvings of headhunting victims (on occasion, male ancestors).

The subdivision of the house's interior into parts for each clan reflects the social demographic of the village. Many meetinghouses have three parts—a front, middle, and end—representing the three major clans who built it. These parts have additional subclan divisions, which also have support posts carved with images of mythical male and female ancestors. Beneath the house, each clan keeps large carved slit-gongs to serve as both instruments of communication (for sending drum messages within and between villages) and the voices of ancestral spirits. On the second level of the house, above the horizontal crossbeam beneath the gable, the Iatmul placed carved wooden figures symbolizing female clan ancestors, depicted in a birthing position. The Iatmul also keep various types of portable art in their ceremonial houses. These include ancestors' skulls overmodeled with clay in a likeness of the deceased, ceremonial chairs, sacred flutes, hooks for hanging sacred items and food, and several types of masks.

ELEMA Central to the culture of the Elema people of Orokolo Bay in the Papuan Gulf was *Hevehe,* an elaborate cycle of ceremonial activities. Conceptualized as the mythical visitation of the water spirits (*ma-hevehe*), the Hevehe cycle involved the production and presentation of large, ornate masks (also called hevehe). The Elema last practiced Hevehe in the 1930s. Primarily organized by the male elders of the village, the cycle was a communal undertaking, completion of which normally took from 10 to 20 years. The duration of the Hevehe and the resources and human labor required reinforced cultural and economic relations and maintained the social structure in which elder male authority dominated.

Throughout the cycle, the Elema held ceremonies to initiate male youths into higher ranks. These ceremonies involved the exchange of wealth (such as pigs and shell ornaments), thereby serving an economic purpose as well. The cycle culminated in the display of the finished hevehe masks. Each mask consisted of painted bark-cloth (see "Barkcloth," page 881) wrapped around a cane-and-wood frame that fit over the wearer's body. A hevehe mask was normally 9 to 10 feet tall, although extensions often raised the height to as much as 25 feet. Because of its size and intricate design, a hevehe mask required great skill to construct, and only trained men would participate in mask making. Designs were specific to particular clans, and elder men passed them down to the next generation from memory. Each mask represented a female sea spirit, but the decoration of the mask often incorporated designs from local flora and fauna as well.

33-5 Iatmul ceremonial men's house, East Sepik, Papua New Guinea, Melanesia, mid- to late 20th century.

The men's house is the center of Iatmul life. Its distinctive saddle-shaped roof symbolizes the protective mantle of ancestors. The carved ornament includes female ancestors in the birthing position.

The Asmat see the human body as a tree—the feet as the roots, the arms as the branches, and the head as the fruit. Thus any fruit-eating bird or animal (such as the black king cockatoo, the hornbill, or the flying fox) was symbolic of the headhunter and appeared frequently on bisj poles. Asmat art also often includes representations of the praying mantis. The Asmat consider the female praying mantis's practice of beheading her mate after copulation and then eating him as another form of headhunting. The curvilinear or spiral patterns that fill the pierced openwork at the top of the bisj poles can be related to the characteristic curved tail of the cuscus (a fruit-eating mammal) or the tusk of a boar (related to hunting and virility). Once the Asmat carved the bisj poles, they placed them on a rack near the community's men's house. After the success of the headhunting expedition, the men discarded the bisj poles and allowed them to rot, because they had served their purpose.

IATMUL The Iatmul people live along the middle Sepik River in Papua New Guinea in communities based on kinship. Villages include extended families as well as different clans. The social center of every Iatmul village is a massive saddle-shaped men's ceremonial house (FIG. **33-5**). In terms of both function and form, the men's house reveals the primacy of the kinship network. The meetinghouse reinforces kinship links by serving as the locale for initiation of local youths for advancement in rank, for men's discussions of community issues, and for ceremonies linked to the Iatmul's ancestors. Because only men can advance in Iatmul society, women and

The Hevehe was a cycle of ceremonial activities spanning 10 to 20 years, culminating in the dramatic appearance of hevehe masks from the Elema men's house. The masks represent female sea spirits.

The final stage of the cycle (FIG. **33-6**) focused on the dramatic appearance of the masks from the *eravo* (men's house). After a procession, men wearing the hevehe mingled with relatives. Upon conclusion of related dancing (often lasting about one month), the Elema ritually killed the masks and then dumped them in piles and burned them. This destruction allowed the sea spirits to return to their mythic domain and provided a pretext for commencing the cycle again.

ABELAM The art of the Abelam people highlights that Oceanic art relates not only to fundamental spiritual beliefs but also to basic subsistence. The Abelam are agriculturists living in the hilly regions north of the Sepik River. Relatively isolated, the Abelam received only sporadic visits from foreigners until the 1930s, and thus little is known about early Abelam history. The principal crop is the yam. Because of the importance of yams to the survival of Abelam society, those who can grow the largest yams achieve power and prestige. Indeed, the Abelam developed a complex yam cult, which involves a series of rites and activities intended to promote the growth of the tubers. Special plantations focus on yam cultivation. Only initiated men who observe strict rules of conduct, including sexual abstinence, can work these fields. The Abelam believe that ancestors aid in the growth of yams, and they hold ceremonies to honor these ancestors. Special long yams (distinct from the short yams cultivated for consumption) are on display during these festivities, and the largest bear the names of important ancestors. Yam masks (FIG. **33-7**) with cane or wood frames, usually painted red, white, yellow, and black, are an integral part of the ceremonies. The most elaborate masks also incorporate sculpted faces, cassowary feathers, and shell ornaments. The Abelam use the same designs to decorate their bodies for dances, revealing how closely they identify with their principal food source.

33-7 Abelam yam mask, from Maprik district, Papua New Guinea, Melanesia. Painted cane, 1' 6$\frac{9}{10}$" high. Musée Barbier-Mueller, Geneva.

The Abelam believe their ancestors aid in the growth of their principal crop, the yam. Painted cane yam masks are an important part of the elaborate ceremonies honoring these ancestors.

New Ireland and the Trobriand Islands

East of New Guinea but part of the modern nation of Papua New Guinea are New Ireland and the Trobriand Islands, two important Melanesian art centers.

NEW IRELAND Mortuary rites and memorial festivals are a central concern of the Austronesian-speaking peoples who live in the northern section of New Ireland. The term *malanggan* refers to both the festivals held in honor of the deceased and the carvings and objects produced for these festivals. One of the first references to malanggan appears in an 1883 publication, and these rituals continue today. Malanggan rites are part of an ancestor cult and are critical in facilitating the transition of the soul from the world of the living to the realm of the dead. In addition to the religious function of malanggan, the extended ceremonies also promote social solidarity and stimulate the economy (as a result of the resources necessary to mount impressive festivities). To educate the younger generation about these practices, malanggan ceremonies also include the initiation of young men.

Among the many malanggan carvings produced—masks, figures, poles, friezes, and ornaments—are tatanua masks (FIG. 33-8). *Tatanua* represent the spirits of specific deceased people. The materials used to make New Ireland tatanua masks are primarily soft wood, vegetable fiber, and rattan. The crested hair, made of fiber, duplicates a hairstyle formerly common among the men. For the eyes, the mask makers insert sea snail opercula (the operculum is the plate that closes the shell). Traditionally, artists paint the masks black, white, yellow, and red—colors the people of New Ireland associate with warfare, magic spells, and violence. Although some masks are display pieces, dancers wear most of them. Rather than destroying their ritual masks after the conclusion of the ceremonies, as some other cultures do, the New Irelanders store them for future use.

TROBRIAND ISLANDS The various rituals of Oceanic cultures discussed thus far often involve exchanges that cement social relationships and reinforce or stimulate the economy. Further, these rituals usually have a spiritual dimension. All of these aspects apply to the practices of the Trobriand Islanders, who live off the coast of the southeastern corner of New Guinea. *Kula*—an exchange of white conus-shell arm ornaments for red chama-shell necklaces—is a char-

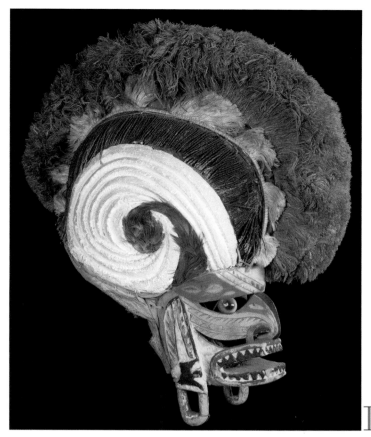

33-8 Tatanua mask, from New Ireland, Papua New Guinea, Melanesia, 19th to 20th centuries. Wood, fiber, shell, lime, and feathers, 1′ 5½″ high. Otago Museum, Dunedin.

In New Ireland, malanggan rites facilitate the transition of the soul from this world to that of the dead. Dancers wearing tatanua masks representing the deceased play a key role in these ceremonies.

acteristic practice of the Trobriand Islanders. Possibly originating some 500 years ago, kula came to Western attention through the extensive documentation of anthropologist Bronislaw Malinowski (1884–1942), published in 1920 and 1922. Kula exchanges can be complex, and there is great competition for valuable shell ornaments (determined by aesthetic appeal and exchange history). Because of the isolation imposed by their island existence, the Trobriand Islanders had to undertake potentially dangerous voyages to participate in kula trading. Appropriately, the Trobrianders lavish a great deal of effort on decorating their large and elaborately carved canoes, which feature ornate prows and splashboards (FIG. 33-9). To ensure a successful kula expedition, the Trobrianders invoke spells when attaching these prows to the canoes. Human, bird, and serpent motifs—references to sea spirits, ancestors, and totemic animals—appear on the prows and splashboards.

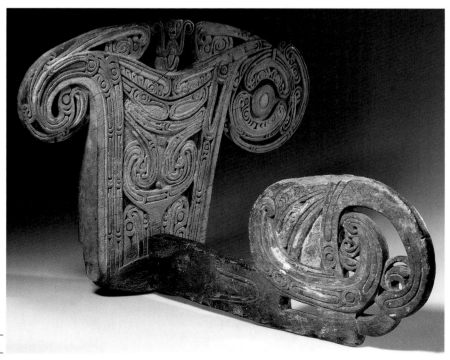

33-9 Canoe prow and splashboard, from Trobriand Islands, Papua New Guinea, Melanesia, 19th to 20th centuries. Wood and paint, 1′ 3½″ high, 1′ 11″ long. Musée du quai Branly, Paris.

To participate in kula exchanges, the Trobriand Islanders had to undertake dangerous sea voyages. They decorated their canoes with abstract human, bird, and serpent motifs referring to sea spirits.

Because the sculptors use highly stylized motifs in intricate, intertwined curvilinear designs, identification of the specific representations is difficult. In recent decades, the Trobrianders have adapted kula to modern circumstances, largely abandoning canoes for motorboats. The exchanges now facilitate business and political networking.

MICRONESIA

The Austronesian-speaking cultures of Micronesia tend to be more socially stratified than those found in New Guinea and other Melanesian areas. Micronesian cultures frequently center on chieftainships with craft and ritual specializations, and their religions include named deities as well as honored ancestors. Life in virtually all Micronesian cultures focuses on seafaring activities—fishing, trading, and long-distance travel in large oceangoing vessels. For this reason, much of the artistic imagery of Micronesia relates to the sea.

Caroline Islands

The Caroline Islands are the largest island group in Micronesia. The arts of the Caroline Islands include the carving of canoes and the fashioning of charms and images of spirits to protect travelers at sea and for fishing and fertility magic.

CHUUK Given the importance of seafaring, it is not surprising that many of the most highly skilled artists in the Caroline Islands were master canoe builders. The canoe prow ornament illustrated here (FIG. **33-10**) comes from Chuuk. Carved from a single plank of wood and fastened to a large, paddled war canoe, the prow ornament provided protection on arduous or long voyages. That this and similar prow ornaments are not permanent parts of the canoes reflects their function. When approaching another vessel, the Micronesian seafarers lowered these ornaments as a signal that their voyage was in peace. The seemingly abstract design of the Chuuk prow may represent, at the top, two facing sandpipers. Some scholars, however, think the entire piece represents a stylized human figure, with the "birds" constituting the arms.

BELAU On Belau (formerly Palau) in the Caroline Islands, the islanders put much effort into creating and maintaining elaborately painted men's ceremonial clubhouses called *bai*. Whereas the Iatmul make their ceremonial houses (FIG. **33-5**) by tying, lashing, and weaving different-size posts, trees, saplings, and grasses, the Belau people construct the main structure of the bai entirely of worked, fitted, joined, and pegged wooden elements, which allows them to assemble it easily. The Belau bai (FIG. **33-11**) have steep overhanging roofs decorated with geometric patterns along the roof boards. Skilled artists carve the gable in low relief and paint it with narrative scenes as well as various abstracted forms of the shell money used traditionally on Belau as currency. These decorated storyboards illustrate important historical events and myths related to the clan who built the bai. Similar carved and painted crossbeams are inside the house. The rooster images along the base of the facade symbolize the rising sun, while the multiple frontal human faces carved and painted above the entrance and on the vertical elements above the

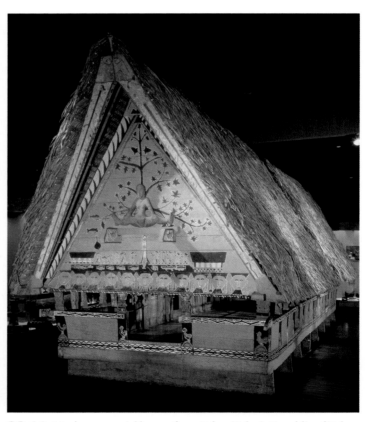

1 in.

33-10 Canoe prow ornament, from Chuuk, Caroline Islands, late 19th century. Painted wood, birds $11'' \times 10\frac{5}{8}''$. British Museum, London.

Prow ornaments protected canoe paddlers and could be lowered to signal a peaceful voyage. This Micronesian example may represent facing sandpipers or perhaps a stylized human figure.

33-11 Men's ceremonial house, from Belau (Palau), Republic of Belau, Micronesia, 20th century. Ethnologisches Museum, Staatliche Museen zu Berlin, Berlin.

The Belau men's clubhouses (bai) have extensive carved and painted decorations illustrating important events and myths related to the clan who built the bai. The central motif is a Dilukai (FIG. 33-12).

Women's Roles in Oceania

Given the prominence of men's houses and the importance of male initiation in so many Oceanic societies, one might conclude that women are peripheral members of these cultures. Much of the extant material culture—ancestor masks, shields, clubs—seems to corroborate this. In reality, however, women play crucial roles in most Pacific cultures, although those functions may be less ostentatious or public than those of men. In addition to their significant contributions through exchange and ritual activities to the maintenance and perpetuation of the social network upon which the stability of village life depends, women are important producers of art.

Historically, Oceanic women's artistic production has been restricted mainly to forms such as barkcloth, weaving, and pottery. In some cultures in New Guinea, potters were primarily female. Throughout much of Polynesia, women produced barkcloth (see "Tongan Barkcloth," page 881), which they often dyed and stenciled and sometimes even perfumed. Women in the Trobriand Islands still make brilliantly dyed skirts of shredded banana fiber that not only are aesthetically beautiful but also serve as a form of wealth, presented symbolically during mortuary rituals.

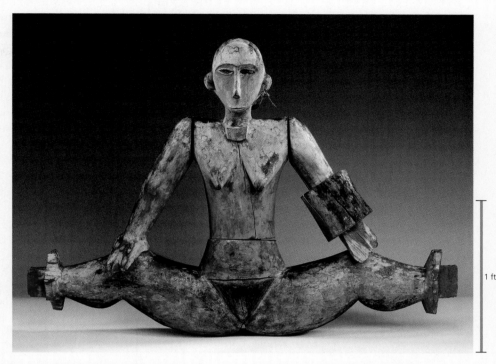

33-12 Dilukai, from Belau (Palau). Wood, pigment, and fiber, 1′ 11⅝″ high. Linden Museum, Stuttgart.

Sculpted wooden figures of a splayed female, or Dilukai, commonly appear over the entrance to a Belau bai (FIG. 33-11). The figures served as symbols of fertility and protected the men's house.

In most Oceanic cultures, women cannot use specialized tools and work in hard materials, such as wood, stone, bone, or ivory, or produce images that have religious or spiritual powers or that confer status on their users. Scholars investigating the role of the artist in Oceania have concluded that the reason for these restrictions is a perceived difference in innate power. Because women have the natural power to create and control life, male-dominated societies developed elaborate ritual practices that served to counteract this female power. By excluding women from participating in these rituals and denying them access to knowledge about specific practices, men derived a political authority that could be perpetuated. It is important to note, however, that even in rituals or activities restricted to men, women often participate. For example, in the now-defunct Hevehe ceremonial cycle (FIG. 33-5) in Papua New Guinea, women helped to construct the masks but feigned ignorance about these sacred objects, because such knowledge was the exclusive privilege of initiated men.

Pacific cultures often acknowledged the innate power of women in the depictions of them in Oceanic art. For example, the splayed Dilukai female sculpture (FIG. 33-12) that appears regularly on Belau bai (men's houses; FIG. 33-11) celebrates women's procreative powers. The Dilukai figure also confers protection upon visitors to the bai, another symbolic acknowledgment of female power. Similar concepts underlie the design of the Iatmul men's house (FIG. 33-5). Conceived as a giant female ancestor, the men's house incorporates women's natural power into the conceptualization of what is normally the most important architectural structure of an Iatmul village. In addition, the Iatmul associate entrance and departure from the men's house with death and rebirth, thereby reinforcing the primacy of fertility and the perception of the men's house as representing a woman's body.

One reason scholars have tended to overlook the active participation of women in all aspects of Oceanic life is that until recently the objects visitors to the Pacific collected were primarily those that suggest aggressive, warring societies. That the majority of these Western travelers were men and therefore had contact predominantly with men no doubt accounts for this pattern of collecting. Recent scholarship has done a great deal to rectify this misperception, thereby revealing the richness of social, artistic, and political activity in the Pacific.

rooster images represent a deity called Blellek. He warns women to stay away from the ocean and the bai or he will molest them.

Although the bai was the domain of men, women figured prominently in the imagery that covered it, consistent with the important symbolic and social positions that women held in Belau culture (see "Women's Roles in Oceania," above). A common element surmounting the main bai entrance was a simple, symmetrical wooden sculpture (on occasion, a painting) of a splayed female figure, known as *Dilukai* (FIGS. 33-11 and 33-12). Serving as a symbol of both protection and fertility, the Dilukai faces east to absorb the sun's life-giving rays.

POLYNESIA

Polynesia was one of the last areas in the world that humans settled. Habitation in the western Polynesian islands did not begin until about the end of the first millennium BCE, and in the south not until the first millennium CE. The settlers brought complex sociopolitical and religious institutions with them. Whereas Melanesian societies are fairly egalitarian and advancement in rank is possible, Polynesian societies typically are highly stratified, with power determined by heredity. Indeed, rulers often trace their genealogies directly to the gods of creation. Most Polynesian societies possess elaborate political organizations headed by chiefs and ritual specialists. By the 1800s, some Polynesian cultures (Hawaii and the Society Islands, for example) evolved into kingdoms. Because of this social hierarchy, historically most Polynesian art belonged to persons of noble or high religious background and served to reinforce their power and prestige. These objects, like their eminent owners, often possessed *mana*, or spiritual power.

Easter Island

MOAI Some of the earliest datable artworks in Oceania are also the largest. The *moai* (FIG. **33-13**) found on Easter Island are monumental sculptures as much as 40 feet tall. They stand as silent sentinels on stone platforms (*ahu*) marking burial or sacred sites used for religious ceremonies. Most of the moai consist of huge, blocky figures with planar facial features—large staring eyes, strong jaws, straight noses with carefully articulated nostrils, and elongated earlobes. A number of the moai have *pukao*—small red scoria cylinders that serve as a sort of topknot or hat—placed on their heads (FIG. **33-1**). Although debate continues, many scholars believe that lineage heads or their sons erected the moai and that the sculptures depict ancestral chiefs. The moai, however, are not individual portraits but generic images that the Easter Islanders believed had the ability to accommodate spirits or gods. The statues thus mediate between chiefs and gods, and between the natural and cosmic worlds.

Archaeological surveys have documented nearly 900 moai. Most of the stones are soft volcanic tuff and came from the same quarry. Some of the sculptures are red scoria, basalt, or trachyte. After quarrying and carving the moai, the Easter Islanders dragged them to the particular ahu site and then positioned them vertically. Given the extraordinary size of these *monoliths*, their production and placement serve as testaments to the achievements of this Polynesian culture. Each statue weighs up to 100 tons. According to one scholar, it would have taken 30 men one year to carve a moai, 90 men two months to move it from the quarry, and 90 men three months to position it vertically on the platform.

33-13 Row of moai on a stone platform, Rapa Nui (Easter Island), Polynesia, 10th to 12th centuries. Volcanic tuff and red scoria. ◼◀

The moai of Easter Island are monoliths as much as 40 feet tall. Most scholars believe they portray ancestral chiefs. They stand on platforms marking burials or sites for religious ceremonies.

Tongan Barkcloth

Tongan barkcloth provides an instructive example of the labor-intensive process of tapa production. At the time of early contact between Europeans and Polynesians in the late 18th and early 19th centuries, ranking women in Tonga made decorated barkcloth (*ngatu*). Today, organizations called *kautaha*—groups of women not of noble birth—produce it, although high-ranking women are often sponsors of the kautaha. In Tonga men plant the paper mulberry tree and harvest it in two to three years. They cut the trees into about 10-foot lengths and allow them to dry for several days. Then the women strip off the outer bark and soak the inner bark in water to prepare it for further processing. They place these soaked inner bark strips over a wooden anvil and repeatedly strike them with a wooden beater until they spread out and flatten. Folding and layering the strips while beating them, a type of felting process, results in a wider

piece of ngatu than the original strips. Afterward, the beaten barkcloth dries and bleaches in the sun.

The next stage of ngatu production involves the placement of the thin, beaten sheets over semicircular boards. The women then fasten embroidered design tablets (*kupesi*—usually produced by men) of low-relief leaf, coconut leaf midribs, and string patterns to the boards. They transfer the patterns on the design tablets to the barkcloth by rubbing. Then the women fill in the lines and patterns by painting, covering the large white spaces with painted figures. The Tongans use brown, red, and black pigments derived from various types of bark, clay, fruits, and soot to create the colored patterns on ngatu. Sheets, rolls, and strips of ngatu play an important role in weddings, funerals, and ceremonial presentations for ranking persons.

33-14 MELE SITANI, ngatu with manulua designs, Tonga, Polynesia, 1967. Barkcloth.

In Tonga, the production of decorated barkcloth, or ngatu, involves dyeing, painting, stenciling, and perfuming. Mele Sitani made this one with a two-bird design for the coronation of Tupou IV.

Tonga

Tonga is the westernmost island in Polynesia. Its arts are varied, but one of its most distinctive products is barkcloth, which women have traditionally produced throughout Polynesia.

BARKCLOTH Artists produce barkcloth from the inner bark of the paper mulberry tree. The finished product goes by various names in Polynesia, but during the 19th century, when the production of barkcloth reached its zenith, *tapa* became the most widely used term. Although the primary use of tapa in Polynesia was for clothing and bedding, in Tonga large sheets (FIG. **33-14**) were (and still are) produced for exchange (see "Tongan Barkcloth," above). In addition, barkcloth has a spiritual dimension in that it can confer sanctity upon an object wrapped in it. Appropriately, the Polyne-

sians traditionally wrapped the bodies of high-ranking deceased chiefs in barkcloth.

The use and decoration of tapa have varied over the years. In the 19th century, tapa used for everyday clothing was normally unadorned, whereas tapa intended for ceremonial or ritual purposes was dyed, painted, stenciled, and sometimes even perfumed. The designs applied to the tapa differed depending upon the particular island group producing it and the function of the cloth. The production process was complex and time-consuming. Indeed, some Oceanic cultures, such as those of Tahiti and Hawaii, constructed buildings specifically for the beating stage in the production of barkcloth. Tapa production reached its peak in the early 19th century, partly as a result of the interest expressed by Western whalers and missionaries. By the late 19th century, the use of tapa for cloth had been abandoned throughout much of eastern Polynesia, although its use in rituals (for example, as a wrap for corpses of deceased chiefs or as a marker of tabooed sites) continued. Even today, tapa exchanges are still an integral part of funerals and marriage ceremonies and even the coronation of kings.

The decorated barkcloth, or *ngatu,* shown in FIG. 33-14 clearly shows the richness of pattern, subtlety of theme, and variation of geometric forms that characterize Tongan royal barkcloth. MELE SITANI made this ngatu for the accession ceremony of King Tupou IV (r. 1965–2006) of Tonga. She kneels in the middle of the ngatu, which features triangular patterns known as *manulua.* This pattern results from the intersection of three or four triangular points. "Manulua" means "two birds," and the design gives the illusion of two birds flying together. The motif symbolizes chieftain status derived from both parents.

Cook and Marquesas Islands

Even though the Polynesians were skillful navigators, various island groups remained isolated from one another for centuries by the vast distances they would have had to cover in open outriggers. This geographical separation allowed distinct regional styles to develop within a recognizable general Polynesian style.

RAROTONGA Deity images with multiple figures attached to their bodies are characteristic of Rarotonga and Mangaia in the Cook Islands and Rurutu in the Austral Islands. These carvings probably represented clan and district ancestors, revered for their protective and procreative powers. Ultimately, the images refer to the creator deities the Polynesians venerate for their central role in human fertility.

33-15A A'a, Rurutu, late 18th or early 19th century.

33-15 Staff god (Tangaroa?), from Rarotonga, Cook Islands, Polynesia. Wood, 2′ 4½″ high. Cambridge University Museum of Archaeology and Anthropology, Cambridge.

The "body" of the Polynesian god Tangaroa consists of seven figures that probably represent generations of his human offspring. Several of the figures have erect penises, a reference to procreation.

1 in.

The residents of the central Polynesian island of Rarotonga used various types of carved deity figures well into the early decades of the 19th century, when Christians converted the islanders and destroyed their deities as part of the process. These included carved wooden fishermen's gods, large naturalistic deity images, and at least three types of staff gods (also called district gods), some more than 20 feet long.

One of the smaller but best-preserved examples (FIG. 33-15) may depict the Polynesian creator god Tangaroa. His head, with its enormous eyes, is about a third of the height of the sculpture. The "body" of the god resembles a spinal column and consists of seven figures with alternating frontal and profile heads. They probably represent the successive generations of humans Tangaroa created. The imagery suggests that these humans come from the body of the god. Several of the figures have erect penises, an unmistakable reference to sexual reproduction and the continuation of the race for many generations to come.

MARQUESAS ISLANDS Although Marquesan chiefs trace their right to rule genealogically, the political system before European contact allowed for the acquisition of power by force. As a result, warfare was widespread through the late 19th century. Among the items produced by Marquesan artists were ornaments (FIG. 33-16) that often adorned the hair of warriors. The hollow, cylindrical bone or ivory ornaments (*ivi p'o*) functioned as protective amulets. Warriors wore them until they avenged the death of a kinsman. The ornaments are in the form of *tiki*—carvings of exalted, deified ancestor figures. The large, rounded eyes and wide mouths of the tiki are typically Marquesan.

Another important art form for Marquesan warriors during the 19th century was *tattoo,* which, like the hair ornaments, protected the individual, serving in essence as a form of spiritual armor. Body decoration in general is among the most pervasive art forms found throughout Oceania. Polynesians developed the painful but prestigious art of tattoo more fully than many other Oceanic peoples (see "Tattoo in Polynesia," page 883), although tattooing was also common in Micronesia. In Polynesia, with its hierarchical social structure, nobles and warriors in particular accumulated various tattoo patterns over the years to enhance their status, mana, and personal beauty. Largely as a result of missionary pressure in the 19th century,

33-16 Hair ornaments from the Marquesas Islands, Polynesia, collected in the 1870s. Bone, 1½″ high (*left*), 1⅖″ high (*right*). University of Pennsylvania Museum of Archaeology and Anthropology, Philadelphia.

These hollow cylindrical bone ornaments representing deified ancestors adorned the hair of Marquesan warriors during the 19th century. The warriors wore them until they avenged the death of a kinsman.

Tattoo in Polynesia

Throughout Oceanic cultures, body decoration was an important means of representing cultural and personal identity. In addition to clothing and ornaments, body adornment most often took the form of tattoo. Tattooing was common among Micronesian cultures, but it was even more extensively practiced in Polynesia. Indeed, the English term *tattoo* is Polynesian in origin, related to the Tahitian, Samoan, and Tongan word *tatau* or *tatu*. In New Zealand, the markings are called *moko*. Within Polynesian cultures, tattooing reached its zenith in the highly stratified societies—New Zealand, the Marquesas Islands, Tahiti, Tonga, Samoa, and Hawaii. Both sexes displayed tattoos. In general, men had more tattoos than did women, and the location of tattoos on the body differed. For instance, in New Zealand, the face and buttocks were the primary areas of male tattooing, whereas tattoos appeared on the lips and chin of women.

Historically, tattooing served a variety of functions in Polynesia beyond personal beautification. It indicated status, because the quantity and quality of tattoos often reflected rank. In the Marquesas Islands, for example, tattoos completely covered the bodies of men of high status (FIG. 33-17). Certain patterns could be applied only to ranking individuals, but commoners also had tattoos, generally on a less extensive scale than elite individuals. For identification purposes, slaves had tattoos on their foreheads in Hawaii and on their backs in New Zealand. There are also accounts of defeated warriors being tattooed. In some Polynesian societies, tattoos identified clan or familial connections. The markings could also serve a protective function by in essence wrapping the body in a spiritual armor. On occasion, tattoos marked significant events. In Hawaii, for example, a tattooed tongue was a sign of grief. The pain the tattooed person endured was a sign of respect for the deceased.

Priests who were specially trained in the art form usually applied the tattoos. Rituals, chants, or ceremonies often accompanied the procedure, which took place in a special structure. Tattooing involves the introduction of black, carbon-based pigment under the skin with the use of a bird-bone tattooing comb or chisel and a mallet. In New Zealand, a distinctive technique emerged for tattooing the face. In a manner similar to Maori woodcarving, a serrated chisel created a groove in the skin to receive pigment, thereby producing a colored line.

Polynesian tattoo designs were predominantly geometric, and affinities with other forms of Polynesian art are evident. For example, the curvilinear patterns that predominate in Maori facial moko recall the patterns found on *poupou*, decorated wall panels in Maori meetinghouses (FIG. 33-20). Depending on their specific purpose, many tattoos could be "read" or deciphered. For facial tattoos, the Maori generally divided the face into four major symmetrical zones: the left and right forehead down to the eyes, the left lower face, and the right lower face. The right-hand side conveyed information on the father's rank, tribal affiliations, and social position, while the

33-17 Tattooed warrior with war club, Nukahiva, Marquesas Islands, Polynesia, early 19th century. Color engraving in Carl Bertuch, *Bilderbuch für Kinder* (Weimar, 1813).

In Polynesia, with its hierarchical social structure, nobles and warriors accumulated tattoo patterns to enhance their status and beauty. Tattoos wrapped a warrior's body in spiritual armor.

left-hand side provided matrilineal information. Smaller secondary facial zones imparted information about the tattooed individual's profession and position in society. Te Pehi Kupe (FIG. I-19) was the chief of the Ngato Toa in the early 19th century. The upward and downward *koru* (unrolled spirals) in the middle of his forehead connote his descent from two paramount tribes. The small design in the center of his forehead documents the extent of his domain—north, south, east, and west. The five double koru in front of his left ear indicate that the supreme chief (the highest rank in Maori society) was part of his matrilineal line. The designs on his lower jaw and the anchor-shaped koru nearby reveal that Te Pehi Kupe was not only a master carver but descended from master carvers as well.

tattooing virtually disappeared in many Oceanic societies, but some Pacific peoples have revived tattooing as an expression of cultural pride.

An 1813 engraving (FIG. 33-17) depicts a Marquesan warrior from Nukahiva Island covered with elaborate tattoo patterns. The warrior holds a large wooden war club over his right shoulder and carries a decorated water gourd in his left hand. The various tattoo patterns marking his entire body seem to subdivide his body parts into zones on both sides of a line down the center. Some tattoos accentuate joint areas, whereas others separate muscle masses into horizontal and vertical geometric shapes. The warrior also covered his face, hands, and feet with tattoos.

33-18 Feather cloak, from Hawaii, Polynesia, ca. 1824–1843. Feathers and fiber netting, 4' 8$\frac{1}{3}$" × 8'. Bishop Museum, Honolulu.

Costly Hawaiian feather cloaks ('ahu 'ula) like this one, which belonged to King Kamehameha III, provided the protection of the gods. Each cloak required the feathers of thousands of birds.

Hawaii

The Hawaiians developed the most highly stratified social structure in the Pacific. By 1795 the chief Kamehameha unified the major islands of the Hawaiian archipelago and ascended to the pinnacle of power as King Kamehameha I (r. 1810–1819). This kingdom did not endure, however, and Hawaii soon came under American control. The United States annexed Hawaii as a territory in 1898 and eventually conferred statehood on the island group in 1959.

FEATHER CLOAKS Because perpetuation of the social structure was crucial to social stability, most of the Hawaiian art forms produced before American control served to visualize and reinforce the hierarchy. Regalia for chieftains and other elite individuals were a prominent part of artistic production. For example, elegant feather cloaks ('ahu 'ula) such as the early-19th-century example shown here (FIG. 33-18) belonged to men of high rank. Every aspect of the 'ahu 'ula reflected the status of its wearer. The materials were exceedingly precious, particularly the red and yellow feathers from the 'i 'iwi, 'apapane, 'o 'o, and mamo birds. Some of these birds yield only six or seven suitable feathers, and given that a full-length cloak could require up to 500,000 feathers, extraordinary resources and labor went into producing the garment. The cloak also linked its owner to the gods. The Polynesians associated the sennit (plaited fiber or cord) base for the feathers with deities. Not only did these cloaks confer the protection of the gods on their wearers, but their dense fiber base and feather matting also provided physical protection. The cloak in FIG. 33-18 originally belonged to King Kamehameha III (r. 1824–1854), who gave it to Commodore Lawrence Kearny of the U.S. frigate *Constellation* in 1843 in gratitude for Kearny's assistance during a temporary occupation of Hawaii.

KUKA'ILIMOKU The gods were a pervasive presence in Hawaiian society and were part of every person's life, regardless of status. Chiefs in particular invoked them regularly and publicized their own genealogical links to the gods to reinforce their right to rule. One prominent Hawaiian deity was Kuka'ilimoku, the war god. As chiefs in the prekingdom years struggled to maintain and expand their control, warfare was endemic, hence Kuka'ilimoku's importance. Indeed, Kuka'ilimoku served as Kamehameha I's special tutelary deity, and the

33-18A Head of Lono, Hawaii, ca. 1775–1780.

33-19 Kuka'ilimoku, from Hawaii, Polynesia, late 18th or early 19th century. Wood, 2' 5$\frac{3}{4}$" high (figure only). British Museum, London.

This wooden statue of the Hawaiian war god comes from a temple. His muscular body is flexed to attack, and his wide mouth and bared teeth set in a large head convey aggression and defiance.

Kuka'ilimoku sculpture illustrated here (FIG. 33-19) stood in a *heiau* (temple) on the island of Hawaii, where Kamehameha I originally ruled before expanding his authority to the entire Hawaiian chain. This late-18th- or early-19th-century Hawaiian wooden temple image, more than four feet tall, confronts its audience with a ferocious expression. The war god's head comprises nearly a third of his entire body. His enlarged, angled eyes and wide-open figure-eight-shaped mouth, with its rows of teeth, convey aggression and defiance. His muscular body appears to stand slightly flexed, as if ready to act. The artist realized this Hawaiian war god's overall athleticism through the full-volume, faceted treatment of his arms, legs, and the pectoral area of the chest. In addition to sculptures of deities such as this, Hawaiians placed smaller versions of lesser deities and ancestral images in the heiau. Differing styles have surfaced in the various islands of the Hawaiian chain, but the sculptured figures share a tendency toward athleticism and expressive defiance.

New Zealand

The Maori of New Zealand (Aotearoa) share many cultural practices with other Polynesian societies. As in other cultures, ancestors and lineage play an important role.

MEETINGHOUSES The Maori meetinghouses demonstrate the primacy of ancestral connections. The Maori conceptualize the entire building as the body of an ancestor. The central beam across the roof is the spine, the rafters are ribs, and the barge boards (the angled boards that outline the house gables) in front represent arms. Construction of the Mataatua meetinghouse (FIG. 33-20) at Whakatane began in 1871 and took four years to complete. The lead sculptor was WEPIHA APANUI of the Ngati Awa clan. On the inside of the meetinghouse, ancestors constitute a potent presence through their appearance on *poupou* (the relief panels along the walls). The panels depict specific ancestors, each of which appears frontally with hands across the stomach. The elaborate curvilinear patterns covering the entire poupou may represent tattoos. Decoration appears on virtually every surface of the meetinghouse. In the spaces between the poupou are *tukutuku* (stitched lattice panels). Above, intricate painted shapes cover the rafters. In the center of the meetinghouse stand *pou tokomanawa,* sculptures of ancestors that support the building's ridgepoles (not visible in FIG. 33-20). The composite presence of all of these ancestral images and of the energetic, persistent patterning creates a charged space for the initiation of collective action.

33-20A Te Hau-ki-Turanga meeting house, 1842–1845.

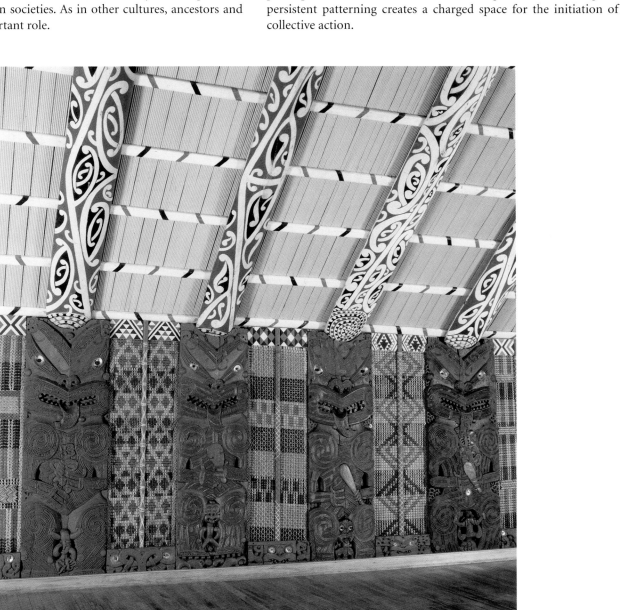

33-20 WEPIHA APANUI, Mataatua meetinghouse (view of interior), Maori, Whakatane, New Zealand, Polynesia, 1871–1875.

Maori meetinghouses feature elaborate decoration. In this late-19th-century example, Wepiha Apanui carved figures of ancestors along the interior walls. The patterns on their bodies may be tattoos.

1 ft.

33-21 Cliff Whiting (Te Whanau-A-Apanui), *Tawhiri-Matea* (*God of the Winds*), Maori, Polynesia, 1984. Oil on wood and fiberboard, 6′ 4⅜″ × 11′ 10¾″. Meteorological Service of New Zealand, Wellington.

In this carved wooden mural depicting the Maori creation myth, Cliff Whiting revived native formal and iconographic traditions and techniques. The abstract curvilinear design suggests wind turbulence.

CLIFF WHITING Largely as a result of colonial and missionary intervention in the 18th through 20th centuries, many Oceanic cultures abandoned traditional practices, and production of many of the art forms illustrated in this chapter ceased. In recent years, however, a new, confident cultural awareness has led some Pacific artists to assert their inherited values with pride and to express them in a resurgence of traditional arts, such as weaving, painting, tattooing, and carving. Today's thriving tourist trade has also contributed to a resurgence of traditional art production.

One example that represents the many cases of cultural renewal in native Oceanic art is the vigorously productive school of New Zealand artists who draw on their Maori heritage for formal and iconographic inspiration. The historical Maori woodcarving craft (FIG. 33-20) brilliantly reemerges in what the artist CLIFF WHITING (Te Whanau-A-Apanui, b. 1936) calls a "carved mural" (FIG. 33-21). Whiting's *Tawhiri-Matea* is a masterpiece of woodcrafting designed for the very modern environment of an exhibition gallery. The artist suggested the wind turbulence with the restless curvature of the main motif and its myriad serrated edges. The 1984 mural depicts events in the Maori creation myth. The central figure, Tawhiri-Matea, god of the winds, wrestles to control the children of the four winds, seen as blue spiral forms. Ra, the sun, energizes the scene from the top left, complemented by Marama, the moon, in the opposite corner. The top right image refers to the primal separation of Ranginui, the Sky Father, and Papatuanuku, the Earth Mother. Spiral koru motifs symbolizing growth and energy flow through the composition. Blue waves and green fronds around Tawhiri suggest his brothers Tangaroa and Tane, gods of the sea and forest.

Whiting is securely at home with the native tradition of form and technique, as well as with the worldwide aesthetic of modern design. Out of the seamless fabric made by uniting both, he feels something new can develop that loses nothing of the power of the old. The artist champions not only the renewal of Maori cultural life and its continuity in art but also the education of the young in the values that made that culture great—values he asks them to perpetuate. The salvation of the native identity of the next generation of New Zealanders will depend on their success in making the Maori culture once again their own.

OCEANIA

AUSTRALIA AND MELANESIA

▮ The westernmost Oceanic islands have been populated for at least 40,000 years, but most of the preserved art dates to the past several centuries.

▮ The Aboriginal art of Australia focuses on ancestral spirits called Dreamings, whom artists represented in an X-ray style showing the internal organs.

▮ The Asmat of New Guinea avenged a relative's death by headhunting. Before embarking on a raid, they erected bisj poles bearing carved and painted figures of ancestors and animals.

▮ The center of every Iatmul village was a saddle-shaped ceremonial men's house representing a woman. Images of clan ancestors decorated the interior.

▮ Masks figured prominently in many Melanesian cultures. The Elema celebrated water spirits in the festive cycle called Hevehe, which involved ornate masks up to 25 feet tall. The Abelam fashioned yam masks for rituals revolving around their principal crop. In New Ireland, dancers wore tatanua masks representing the spirits of the deceased.

▮ Seafaring was also a major theme of much Melanesian art. The Trobriand Islanders decorated their canoes with elaborately carved prows and splashboards.

Auuenau, Western Arnhem Land, Australia, 1913

Canoe prow and splashboard, Trobriand Islands, 19th to 20th centuries

MICRONESIA

▮ The major themes of Melanesian art are also found in Micronesia. For example, the people of the Caroline Islands produced carved and painted prow ornaments for their canoes.

▮ The Micronesian peoples also erected ceremonial men's houses. The bai of Belau are distinctive in having Dilukai figures in the gable of the eastern entrance. The Dilukai is a woman with splayed legs who faces the sun and serves as a symbol of procreation and as a guardian of the house.

Men's ceremonial house, Belau, 20th century

POLYNESIA

▮ Polynesia was one of the last areas of the world that humans settled, but the oldest monumental art of Oceania is the series of moai on Easter Island. These colossal monolithic sculptures, which stood in rows on stone platforms, probably represent ancestors.

▮ Barkcloth is an important art form in Polynesia even today. The decorated barkcloth, or ngatu, of Tonga was used to wrap the corpses of deceased chiefs and for other ritual purposes, including the coronation of kings.

▮ Body adornment in the form of tattooing was widespread in Polynesia, especially in the Marquesas Islands and New Zealand. In addition to personal beautification, tattoos served to distinguish rank and provided warriors with a kind of spiritual armor.

▮ Meetinghouses played an important role in Polynesian societies, as elsewhere in the Pacific islands. The meetinghouses of the Maori of New Zealand are notable for their elaborate ornament featuring carved relief panels depicting ancestors.

▮ Images of named gods are common in Polynesia. Wood sculptures from Rarotonga represent the creator god Tangaroa. The Hawaiians erected statues of the war god Kuka'ilimoku in their temples. The tradition continues today in the work of sculptors such as Cliff Whiting of New Zealand.

Moai, Easter Island, 10th to 12th centuries

Tattooed warrior, Marquesas Islands, early 19th century

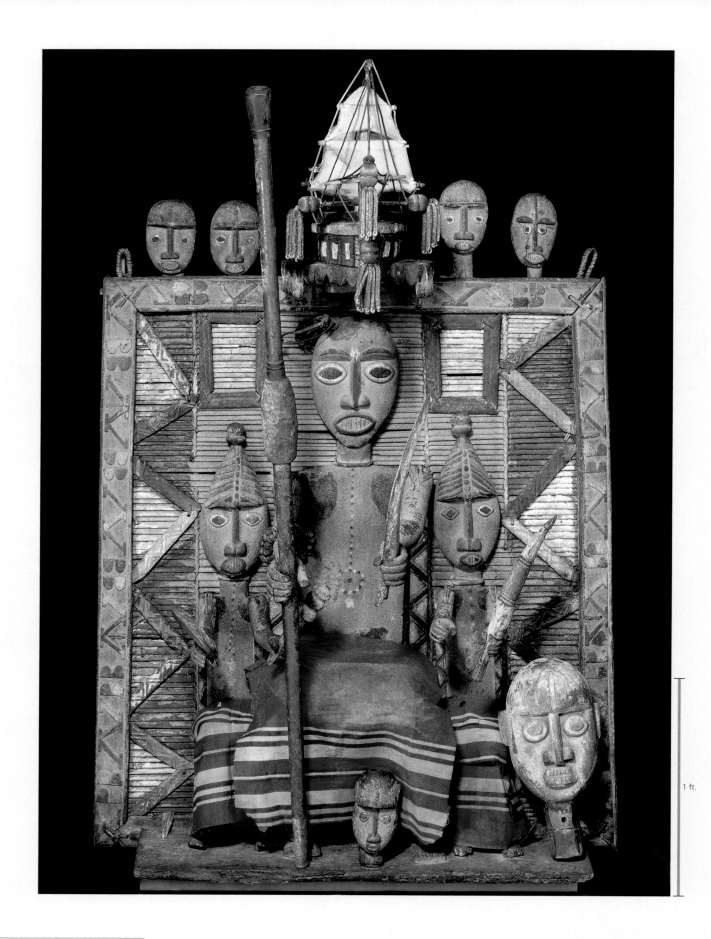

34-1 Ancestral screen (nduen fobara), Kalabari Ijaw, Nigeria, late 19th century. Wood, fiber, and cloth, 3′ 9½″ high. British Museum, London.

The hierarchical composition and the stylized human anatomy and facial features in this Kalabari ancestral screen are common in African art, but the shrine's complexity is exceptional.

AFRICA AFTER 1800

Africa (MAP **34-1**) was one of the first art-producing regions of the world (see Chapters 1 and 15), but its early history remains largely undocumented. In fact, a mere generation ago, scholars still often presented African art as if it had no history. For the period treated in this chapter, however, art historians are on firmer ground. Information gleaned from archaeology and field research in Africa (mainly interviews with local people) provides much more detail on the use, function, and meaning of art objects produced during the past two centuries than for the period before 1800. As in earlier eras, the arts in Africa exist in greatly varied human situations, and knowledge of these contexts is essential for understanding the artworks. In Africa, art is nearly always an active agent in the lives of its diverse peoples. This chapter presents a sample of characteristic works from different regions of the continent from the early 19th century to the present.

19TH CENTURY

Rock paintings are among the most ancient arts of Africa (FIGS. **1-3** and **15-2**). Yet the tradition also continued well into the historical period. The latest examples date as recently as the 19th century, and some of these depict events involving Europeans. Many examples have been found in South Africa.

San

Scholars use the generic name San to describe the peoples who occupied the southeastern coast of Africa at the time of the earliest European colonization. The San were hunters and gatherers, and their art often centered on the animals they pursued.

BAMBOO MOUNTAIN One of the most impressive preserved San rock paintings (FIG. **34-2**), originally about eight feet long but now regrettably in fragments, comes from near the source of the Mzimkhulu River at Bamboo Mountain and dates to the mid-19th century. At that time, the increasing development of colonial ranches and the settlements of African agriculturists had greatly affected the lifestyle

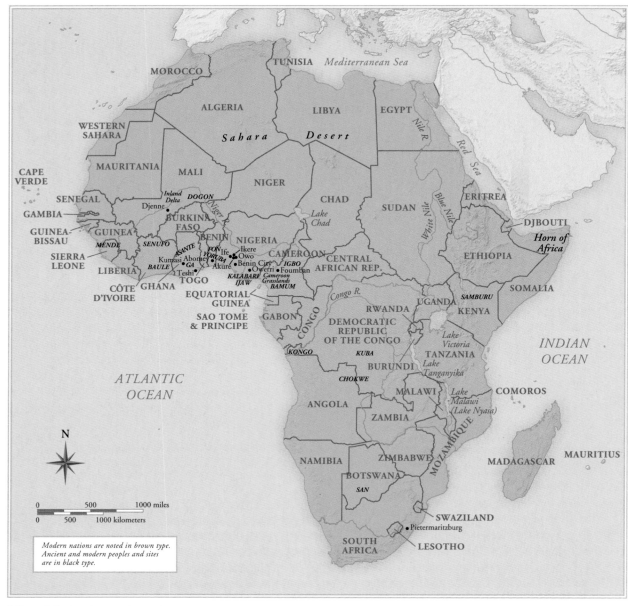

MAP 34-1 Africa in the early 21st century.

and movement patterns of San hunters and gatherers, often displacing them from their ancestral lands. In some regions, they began to raid local ranches for livestock and horses as an alternate food source. The Bamboo Mountain rock painting was probably made after a series of stock raids over a period from about 1838 to 1848. Various South African military and police forces unsuccessfully pursued the San raiders. Poor weather, including frequent rains and fog, added to the difficulty of capturing a people who had lived in the region for many generations and knew its terrain intimately.

On the right side of the composition (not illustrated), two San riders on horses laden with meat drive a large herd of cattle and horses toward a San encampment located left of center and encircled by an outline (FIG. 34-2, *bottom*). Within the camp are various women and children. To the far left (FIG. 34-2, *top*), a single figure (perhaps a diviner or rainmaker) leads an eland, an animal the San considered effective in rainmaking and ancestor rituals, toward the encampment. The similarity of this scene to other rock paintings with spiritual interpretations (a human leading an animal) suggests that this motif

may represent a ritual leader in a trance state. The leader calls on rain—brought by the intervention of the sacred eland—to foil the attempts of the government soldiers and police to locate and punish the San raiders. The close correspondence between the painting's imagery and the events of 1838–1848 adds to the likelihood that the San created this work to record government action as well as to facilitate rainmaking.

Fang and Kota

Although African works of art are often difficult to date precisely, art historians have been able to assign to the 19th century with some confidence a number of objects that lack historical references. These include the *reliquary* guardian figures made by the Fang and several other migratory peoples living just south of the equator in Gabon and Cameroon. Throughout the continent, Africans venerate ancestors for the continuing aid they believe they provide the living, including help in maintaining the productivity of the earth for bountiful crop pro-

34-2 Stock raid with cattle, horses, encampment, and magical "rain animal," rock painting (two details), San, Bamboo Mountain, South Africa, mid-19th century. Pigments on rock, full painting 8′ long. Natal Museum, Pietermaritzburg.

Rock paintings are among the most ancient arts in Africa, and the tradition continued into the 19th century. This example depicts events of 1838–1848 and San rainmaking rituals in South Africa.

1 in.

34-3 Reliquary guardian figure (bieri), Fang, Gabon, late 19th century. Wood, 1′ 8⅜″ high. Philadelphia Museum of Art, Philadelphia.

Fang bieri guard cylindrical bark boxes of ancestor bones (reliquaries). The figures have the bodies of infants and the muscularity of adults, a combination of traits suggesting the cycle of life.

duction. The reliquary figures play an important role in ancestor worship. Among both the Fang and the peoples scholars usually refer to as Kota in neighboring areas, ancestor veneration takes material form as collections of cranial and other bones (*relics*) gathered in special containers. These portable reliquaries were ideal for African nomadic population groups such as the Fang and the Kota.

FANG BIERI Stylized wooden human figures (FIG. **34-3**), or in some cases, simply heads protected the Fang relic containers. The sculptors of these Fang guardian figures, or *bieri*, designed them to sit on the edge of cylindrical bark boxes of ancestral bones, ensuring that no harm would befall the ancestral spirits. The wood figures are symmetrical, with proportions that greatly emphasize the head, and they feature a rhythmic buildup of forms that suggests contained

power. Particularly striking are the proportions of the bodies of the bieri, which resemble those of an infant, although the muscularity of the figures implies an adult. Scholars believe the sculptor chose this combination of traits to suggest the cycle of life, appropriate for an art form connected with the cult of ancestors.

34-4 Reliquary guardian figure (mbulu ngulu), Kota, Gabon, 19th or early 20th century. Wood, copper, iron, and brass, 1′ 9 1/16″ high. Musée Barbier-Mueller, Geneva.

Kota guardian figures have bodies in the form of an open lozenge and large heads. Polished copper and brass sheets cover the wood forms. The Kota believe that gleaming surfaces repel evil.

1 in.

1 ft.

34-5 Throne and footstool of King Nsangu, Bamum, Cameroon, ca. 1870. Wood, textile, glass beads, and cowrie shells, 5′ 9″ high. Museum für Völkerkunde, Staatliche Museen zu Berlin, Berlin.

King Nsangu's throne features luminous beads and shells and richly colored textiles. The decoration includes intertwining serpents, male and female retainers, and bodyguards with European rifles.

KOTA MBULU NGULU The Kota of Gabon also have reliquary guardian figures, called *mbulu ngulu* (FIG. 34-4). These figures have severely stylized bodies in the form of an open diamond below a wooden head covered with strips and sheets of polished copper and brass. The Kota believe the gleaming surfaces repel evil. The simplified heads have hairstyles flattened out laterally above and beside the face. Geometric ridges, borders, and subdivisions add a textured elegance to the shiny forms. The copper alloy on most of these images is reworked sheet brass (or copper wire) taken from brass basins originating in Europe and traded into this area of equatorial Africa in the 18th and 19th centuries. The Kota insert the lower portion of the image into a basket or box of ancestral relics.

Kalabari Ijaw

The Kalabari Ijaw peoples have hunted and fished in the eastern delta of the Niger River in present-day Nigeria for several centuries. A cornerstone of this economy, however, has long been trade, and trading organizations known locally as canoe houses play a central role in Kalabari society

ANCESTRAL SCREENS As in so many other African cultures, Kalabari artists and patrons have lavished attention on shrines in honor of ancestors. The Kalabari shrines take a unique form and feature elaborate screens of wood, fiber, textiles, and other materials.

An especially elaborate example (FIG. 34-1) is the almost four-foot-tall *nduen fobara* honoring a deceased chief of a trading corporation. Displayed in the house in which the chief lived, the screen represents the chief himself at the center holding a long silver-tipped staff in his right hand and a curved knife in his left hand. His chest is bare, and drapery covers the lower part of his body. His impressive headdress is in the form of a 19th-century European sailing ship, a reference to the chief's successful trading business. Flanking him are his attendants, smaller in size as appropriate for their lower rank. The heads of his slaves are at the top of the screen and those of his conquered rivals are at the bottom. The hierarchical composition and the stylized rendition of human anatomy and facial features are common in African art, but the richness and complexity of this shrine are exceptional.

Bamum

In addition to celebrating ancestors, much African art glorifies living rulers (see "Art and Leadership in Africa," Chapter 15, page 397). In the kingdom of Bamum in present-day Cameroon, the ruler lived in a palace compound at the capital city of Foumban until its destruction in 1910. Some items of the royal regalia survive.

THRONE OF NSANGU The royal arts of Bamum make extensive use of richly colored textiles and luminous materials, such as glass beads and cowrie shells. The ultimate status symbol was the

34-6 AKATI AKPELE KENDO, Warrior figure (Gu?), from the palace of King Glele, Abomey, Fon, Republic of Benin, 1858–1859. Iron, 5' 5" high. Musée du quai Branly, Paris.

This bocio, or empowerment figure, probably representing the war god Gu, was the centerpiece of a circle of iron swords. The Fon believed it protected their king, and they set it up on the battlefield.

1 ft.

34-7 Yombe mother and child (pfemba), Kongo, Democratic Republic of Congo, late 19th century. Wood, glass, glass beads, brass tacks, and pigment, $10\frac{1}{8}$" high. National Museum of African Art, Washington, D.C.

The mother in this Yombe group wears a royal cap and jewelry and displays her chest scarification. The image may commemorate an ancestor or, more likely, a legendary founding clan mother.

1 in.

king's throne. The throne (FIG. **34-5**) that belonged to King Nsangu (r. 1865–1872 and 1885–1887) is a masterpiece of Bamum art. Intertwining blue and black serpents decorate the cylindrical seat. Above are the figures of two of the king's retainers, perpetually at his service. One, a man, holds the royal drinking horn. The other is a woman carrying a serving bowl in her hands. Below are two of the king's bodyguards wielding European rifles. Decorating the rectangular footstool are dancing figures. When the king sat on this throne, his rich garments complemented the bright colors of his seat, advertising his wealth and power to all who were admitted to his palace.

Fon

The foundation of the Fon kingdom in the present-day Republic of Benin dates to around 1600. Under King Guezo (r. 1818–1858), the Fon became a regional power with an economy based on the trade in palm oil. In 1900 the French dismantled the kingdom and brought many artworks to Paris, where they inspired several prominent early-20th-century Western artists (see "Primitivism," Chapter 35, page 920).

KING GLELE After his first military victory, Guezo's son Glele (r. 1858–1889) commissioned a prisoner of war, AKATI AKPELE KENDO, to make a life-size iron statue (FIG. **34-6**) of a warrior, probably Gu, god of war and iron, for a battle shrine in Glele's palace at Abomey. This *bocio*, or empowerment figure, was the centerpiece of a circle of iron

swords and other weapons set vertically into the ground. The warrior strides forward with swords in both hands, ready to do battle. He wears a crown of miniature weapons and tools on his head. The form of the crown echoes the circle of swords around the statue. The Fon believed that the bocio protected their king, and they transported it to the battlefield whenever they set out to fight an enemy force. King Glele's iron warrior is remarkable for its size and for the fact that not only is the patron's name known but so too is the artist's name—a rare instance in Africa before the 20th century (see "African Artists," page 897).

Kongo

The Congo River formed the principal transportation route for the peoples of Central Africa during the 19th century, fostering cultural exchanges as well as trade, both among Africans and with Europeans.

YOMBE PFEMBA Some scholars have suggested that the mother-and-child groups (*pfemba*) of the Yombe in the Democratic Republic of Congo may reflect the influence of Christian Madonna-and-Child imagery. The Yombe pfemba are not deities, however, but images of Kongo royalty. One 19th-century example (FIG. **34-7**) represents a woman with a royal cap, chest scarification, and jewelry. The image may commemorate an ancestor or, more likely, a legendary founding clan mother. The Kongo call some of these figures "white chalk," a reference to the medicinal power of white kaolin clay. Diviners own some time they inserted a nail or blade, as if to prod the spirit to do its work. People invoked other spirits by repeating certain chants, by rubbing them, or by applying special powders. The roles of power figures varied enormously, from curing minor ailments to stimulating crop growth, from punishing thieves to weakening an enemy. Very large Kongo figures, such as this one, had exceptional ascribed powers and aided entire communities. Although benevolent for their owners, the figures stood at the boundary between life and death, and most villagers held them in awe. As is true of the pfemba group (FIG. 34-7), compared with the sculptures of other African peoples, this Kongo figure is relatively naturalistic, although the carver simplified the facial features and magnified the size of the head for emphasis.

Dogon

The Dogon live in the Bandiagara escarpment south of the inland delta region of the great Niger River in what is today Mali. Numbering almost 300,000, spread among hundreds of small villages, the Dogon practice farming as their principal occupation.

LINKED MAN AND WOMAN One of the most common themes in African art is the human couple. A characteristic Dogon linked-man-and-woman group (FIG. 34-9) of the early 19th century is probably a shrine or altar, although contextual information is lacking. Interpretations vary, but the image vividly documents primary gender roles in traditional African society. The man wears a quiver on his back, and the woman carries a child on hers. Thus, the man assumes a protective role as hunter or warrior, the woman a nurturing role. The slightly larger man reaches behind his mate's neck and touches her breast, as if to protect her. His left hand points to his genitalia. Four stylized figures support the stool upon which they sit. They are probably either spirits or ancestors, but the identity of the larger figures is uncertain.

The strong stylization of Dogon sculptures contrasts sharply with the organic, relatively realistic treatment of the human body in Kongo art (FIG. 34-7). The artist who carved the Dogon couple (FIG. 34-9) based the forms more on the idea or concept of the human body than on observation of individual heads, torsos, and limbs. The linked body parts are tubes and columns articulated inorganically. The carver reinforced the almost abstract geometry of the overall composition by incising rectilinear and diagonal patterns on the surfaces. The Dogon artist also understood the importance of space, and charged the voids, as well as the sculptural forms, with rhythm and tension.

Baule

The Baule of present-day Côte d'Ivoire do not have kings, and their societies are relatively egalitarian compared to others in Africa, but Baule art encompasses some of the same basic themes seen elsewhere on the continent.

BUSH SPIRITS The wooden Baule statues (FIG. 34-10) of a man and woman probably portray bush spirits (*asye usu*). The sculptor most likely carved them for a trance diviner, a religious specialist who consulted the spirits symbolized by the figures on behalf of clients either sick or in some way troubled. In Baule thought, bush spirits are short, horrible-looking, and sometimes deformed creatures, yet Baule sculptors represent them in the form of beautiful, ideal human beings, because ugly figures would offend the spirits and would refuse to work for the diviner. Among the Baule, as among many West African peoples, bush or wilderness spirits both cause difficulties in life and, if properly addressed and placated, may solve problems or cure sickness. In dance and trance performances—with wooden figures and other objects displayed nearby—the diviner can

1 ft.

34-8 Nail figure (nkisi n'kondi), Kongo, from Shiloango River area, Democratic Republic of Congo, ca. 1875–1900. Wood, nails, blades, medicinal materials, and cowrie shell, 3′ 10¾″ high. Detroit Institute of Arts, Detroit.

Only priests using ritual formulas could consecrate Kongo power figures, which embody spirits that can heal or inflict harm. The statue has simplified anatomical forms and a very large head.

of them, and others have been used by women's organizations to treat infertility, but the function of this 19th-century pfemba is uncertain.

NKISI N'KONDI The large standing statue (FIG. 34-8) of a man bristling with nails and blades is a Kongo power figure (*nkisi n'kondi*) that a trained priest consecrated using precise ritual formulas. These images embodied spirits believed to heal and give life or sometimes inflict harm, disease, or even death. Each figure had its specific role, just as it wore particular medicines—here protruding from the abdomen and featuring a large cowrie shell. The Kongo also activated every image differently. Owners appealed to a figure's forces every

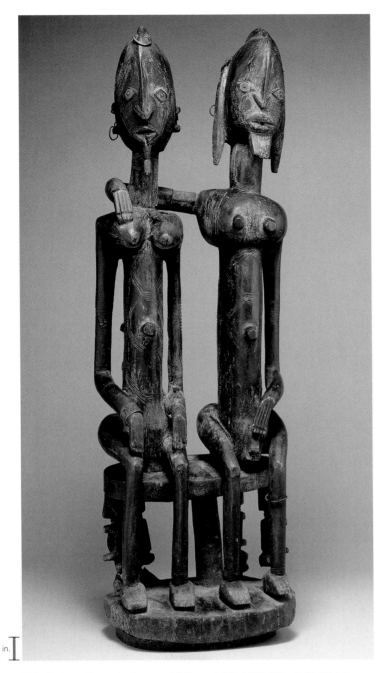

1 in.

34-9 Seated couple, Dogon, Mali, ca. 1800–1850. Wood, 2′ 4″ high. Metropolitan Museum of Art, New York (gift of Lester Wunderman).

This Dogon carving of a linked man and woman documents gender roles in traditional African society. The protective man wears a quiver on his back. The nurturing woman carries a child on hers.

1 in.

34-10 Male and female figures, probably bush spirits (asye usu), Baule, Côte d'Ivoire, late 19th or early 20th century. Wood, beads, and kaolin, man 1′ 9$\frac{3}{4}$″ high, woman 1′ 8$\frac{5}{8}$″ high. Metropolitan Museum of Art, New York (Michael C. Rockefeller Memorial Collection, gift of Nelson A. Rockefeller).

In contrast to the Dogon couple (FIG. 34-9), this pair includes many naturalistic aspects of human anatomy, but the sculptor enlarged the necks, calves, and heads, a form of idealization in Baule culture.

divine, or understand, the will of unseen spirits as well as their needs or prophecies, which the diviner passes on to clients. When not set up outdoors for a performance, the figures and other objects remain in the diviner's house or shrine, where more private consultations take place. In striking contrast to the Dogon sculptor of the seated man and woman (FIG. 34-9), the artist who created this matched pair of Baule male and female images recorded many naturalistic aspects of human anatomy, skillfully translating them into finished sculptural form. At the same time, the sculptor was well aware of creating *waka sran* (people of wood) rather than living beings. Thus, the artist freely exaggerated the length of the figures' necks and the size of their heads and calf muscles, all of which are forms of idealization in Baule culture.

20TH CENTURY

The art of Africa during the past 100 years ranges from traditional works depicting age-old African themes to modern works that are international in both content and style. Both men and women have long been active in African art production, usually specializing in different types of objects (see "Gender Roles in African Art Production," page 896).

Benin

Some of the most important 20th-century African artworks come from areas with strong earlier artistic traditions. The kingdom of Benin (see Chapter 15) in present-day Nigeria is a prime example.

Gender Roles in African Art Production

Until the past decade or two, art production in Africa has been quite rigidly gender-specific. Men have been, and largely still are, iron smiths and gold and copper-alloy casters. Men were architects, builders, and carvers of both wood and ivory. Women were, and for the most part remain, wall and body painters, calabash decorators, potters, and often clay sculptors, although men make clay figures in some areas. Both men and women work with beads and weave baskets and textiles, with men executing narrow strips (later sewn together) on horizontal looms and women working wider pieces of cloth on vertical looms.

Much African art, however, is collaborative. Men may build a clay wall, for example, but women will normally decorate it. The Igbo people build *mbari* houses (FIG. 34-23)—for ceremonies to honor the earth goddess—that are truly collaborative despite the fact that professional male artists model the figures displayed in the houses. Festivals, invoking virtually all the arts, are also collaborative. Masquerades (see "African Masquerades," page 899) are largely the province of men, yet in some cases women are asked to con-

tribute costume elements such as skirts, wrappers, and scarves. And even though women dance masks among the Mende and related peoples (see "Mende Women," page 901), men have always carved the masks themselves.

In late colonial and especially in postcolonial times, earlier gender distinctions in art production began breaking down. Women, as well as men, now weave kente cloth, and a number of women are now sculptors in wood, metal, stone, and composite materials. Men are making pottery, once the exclusive prerogative of women. Both women and men make international art forms in urban and university settings, although male artists are more numerous. One well-known Nigerian woman artist, Sokari Douglas Camp (b. 1958), produces welded metal sculptures, sometimes of masqueraders. Douglas Camp is thus doubly unusual. She might find it difficult to do this work in her traditional home in the Niger River delta, but as she lives and works in London, she encounters no adverse response. In the future there will undoubtedly be a further breaking down of restrictive barriers and greater mobility for artists.

SHRINE OF EWEKA II In 1897, when the British sacked Benin City, there were still 17 shrines to ancestors in the Benin royal palace. Today only one 20th-century altar (FIG. 34-11) remains. According to oral history, it is similar to centuries-earlier versions. With a base of sacred riverbank clay, it is an assemblage of varied materials, objects, and symbols: a central copper-alloy altarpiece depicting a sacred king flanked by members of his entourage, plus copper-alloy heads, each fitted on top with an ivory tusk carved in relief. Behind are wood staffs and metal bells. The heads represent both the kings themselves and, through the durability of their material, the enduring nature of kingship. Their glistening surfaces, seen as red and signaling danger, repel evil forces that might adversely affect the shrine and thus the king and kingdom. Elephant-tusk relief carvings atop

the heads commemorate important events and personages in Benin history. Their bleached white color signifies purity and goodness (probably of royal ancestors), and the tusks themselves represent male physical power. The carved wood rattle-staffs standing at the back refer to generations of dynastic ancestors by their bamboolike, segmented forms. The rattle-staffs and the pyramidal copper-alloy bells serve the important function of calling royal ancestral spirits to rituals performed at the altar.

The Benin king's head stands for wisdom, good judgment, and divine guidance for the kingdom. The several heads in the ancestral altar multiply these qualities. By means of animal sacrifices at this site, the living king annually purifies his own head (and being) by invoking the collective strength of his ancestors. Thus, the varied

34-11 Royal ancestral altar of Benin King Eweka II, in the palace in Benin City, Nigeria, photographed in 1970. Clay, copper alloy, wood, and ivory.

This shrine to the heads of royal ancestors is an assemblage of varied materials, objects, and symbols. By sacrificing animals at this site, the Benin king annually invokes the collective strength of his ancestors.

African Artists and Apprentices

Traditionally, Africans have tended not to exalt artistic individuality as much as Westerners have. Many people, in fact, consider African art as anonymous, but that is primarily because early researchers rarely asked for artists' names. Nonetheless, art historians can recognize many individual hands or styles even when an artist's name has not been recorded. During the past century, art historians and anthropologists have been systematically noting the names and life histories of specific individual artists, many of whom have strong regional reputations. One of the earliest recorded names is that of the mid-19th-century Fon sculptor and metalsmith Akati Akpele Kendo (FIG. 34-6). Two 20th-century artists, renowned even from one kingdom to another, were Osei Bonsu (FIGS. 34-12 and 34-13), based in the Asante capital of Kumasi, and the Yoruba sculptor called Olowe of Ise (FIG. 34-14) because he came from the town of Ise. Both artists were master carvers, producing sculptures for kings and commoners alike.

Like other great artists in other places and times, both Bonsu and Olowe had apprentices to assist them for several years while learning their trade. Although there are various kinds of apprenticeship in Africa, novices typically lived with their masters and were household servants as well as assistant carvers. They helped fell trees, carry logs, and rough out basic shapes that the master later transformed into finished work. African sculptors typically worked on commission. Sometimes, as in Bonsu's case, patrons traveled to the home of the artist. But other times, even Bonsu moved to the home of a patron for weeks or months while working on a commission. Masters, and in some instances also apprentices, lived and ate in the patron's compound. Olowe, for example, resided with different kings for many months at a time while he carved doors, veranda posts (FIG. 34-14), and other works for royal families.

34-12 Osei Bonsu, Akua'ba (Akua's child), Asante, Ghana, ca. 1935. Wood, beads, and pigment, $10\frac{1}{4}$″ high. Private collection.

Osei Bonsu was one of Africa's leading sculptors. This figure, carried by women hoping to conceive a child, has a flattened face and crosshatched eyebrows, typical of the artist's style.

1 in.

objects, symbols, colors, and materials comprising this shrine contribute both visually and ritually to the imaging of royal power, as well as to its history, renewal, and perpetuation. The composition of the shrine, like that of the altar at its center and the Altar to the Hand and Arm (FIG. 15-13), is hierarchical. At the center of all Benin hierarchies stands the king (FIG. I-15).

Asante

The Asante of modern Ghana formed a strong confederacy around 1700. They are one of several peoples, including the Baule of Côte d'Ivoire, who speak an Akan dialect.

OSEI BONSU A common stylistic characteristic of Asante figural art is the preference for conventionalized, flattened heads. Many

Akan peoples considered long, slightly flattened foreheads to be emblems of beauty, and mothers gently molded their children's cranial bones to reflect this value. These anatomical features appear in a wooden image of a young girl (FIG. 34-12), or *akua'ba* (Akua's child), by one of the 20th century's leading African sculptors, Osei Bonsu (1900–1976). After consecrating a simplified wood akua'ba sculpture at a shrine, a young woman hoping to conceive carried it with her. Once pregnant, she continued to carry the figure to ensure the safe delivery of a healthy and handsome child—among these matrilineal people, preferably a girl. Compared with traditional sculptures of this type, the more naturalistic rendering of the face and crosshatched eyebrows in Osei Bonsu's sculpture are distinctive features of his personal style (see "African Artists and Apprentices," above).

-12A Asante
blemen in
nte cloth
es, 1972.

34-13 Osei Bonsu, linguist's staff of two men sitting at a table of food, Asante, Ghana, mid-20th century. Wood and gold leaf, section shown 10″ high. Collection of the Paramount Chief of Offinso, Asante.

Osei Bonsu carved this gold-covered wooden linguist's staff for someone who could speak for the Asante king. At the top are two men sitting at a table of food—a metaphor for the office of the king.

34-14 Olowe of Ise, veranda post, from Akure, Yoruba, Nigeria, 1920s. Wood and pigment, 14′ 6″ high. Denver Art Museum, Denver.

Olowe carved this post when Europeans had already become familiar among Yoruba peoples. He subtly recorded this colonialism in the European cap of one of the men supporting the equestrian warrior.

LINGUIST'S STAFF Bonsu also carved the gold-covered wood sculpture (FIG. **34-13**) that depicts two men sitting at a table of food. This object, commonly called a *linguist's staff* because its carrier often speaks for a king or chief, has a related proverb: "Food is for its rightful owner, not for the one who happens to be hungry." Food is a metaphor for the office the king or chief rightfully holds. The "hungry" man lusts for the office. The linguist, who is an important counselor and adviser to the king, might carry this staff to a meeting at which a rival contests the king's title to the stool (his throne, the office). Many hundreds of sculptures from this region have proverbs or other sayings associated with them, which has created a rich verbal tradition relating to the visual arts of the Akan peoples.

Yoruba

The Yoruba have a long history in southwestern Nigeria and the southern Republic of Benin dating to the founding of Ile-Ife in the 11th century (see Chapter 15). In the 20th century, Yoruba artists were among the most skilled on the continent. One who achieved international recognition was OLOWE OF ISE (ca. 1873–1938).

OLOWE OF ISE Olowe was the leading Yoruba sculptor of the early 20th century, and kings throughout Yorubaland sought his services. The king of Ikere, for example, employed Olowe for four years starting in 1910. A tall veranda post (FIG. **34-14**) that Olowe

carved in the 1920s for the house of Chief Elefoshan of Akure is typical of his style. To achieve greater height, Olowe stacked his weapon-carrying equestrian warrior on top of a platform supported on the heads and upraised arms of four attenuated figures, two men and two women, with long necks and enlarged heads. The latter trait is common among most Yoruba sculptors, but elongated bodies are an Olowe characteristic, along with finely textured detail, seen in the warrior's tunic. The post dates to a time when Europeans had already become a colonial presence among Yoruba peoples. Olowe subtly recorded this presence by placing a European-style billed cap on one of the male supporting figures. The overall design, more complex and with more open space than most posts by other carvers, signals Olowe's virtuosity.

34-14A OLOWE OF ISE, palace doors, Ikere, 1910–1914.

African Masquerades

The art of masquerade has long been a quintessential African expressive form, replete with meaning and cultural importance. This is so today, but was even more critically true in colonial times and earlier, when African masking societies boasted extensive regulatory and judicial powers. In stateless societies, such as those of the Senufo (FIGS. 34-15 and 34-16), Dogon (FIG. 34-17), and Mende (FIG. 34-18), masks sometimes became so influential they had their own priests and served as power sources or as oracles. Societies empowered maskers to levy fines and to apprehend witches (usually defined as socially destructive people) and criminals, and to judge and punish them. Normally, however—especially today—masks are less threatening and more secular and educational, and they serve as diversions from the humdrum of daily life. Masked dancers usually embody either ancestors, seen as briefly returning to the human realm, or various nature spirits called upon for their special powers.

The mask, a costume ensemble's focal point, combines with held objects, music, and dance gestures to invoke a specific named character, almost always considered a spirit. A few masked spirits appear by themselves, but more often several characters come out together or in turn. Maskers enact a broad range of human, animal, and fantastic otherworldly behavior that is usually both stimulating and didactic. Masquerades, in fact, vary in function or effect along a continuum from weak spirit power and strong entertainment value to those rarely seen but possessing vast executive powers backed by powerful shrines. Most operate between these extremes, crystallizing varieties of human and animal behavior—caricatured, ordinary, comic, bizarre, serious, or threatening. These actions inform and affect audience members because of their dramatic staging. It is the purpose of most masquerades to move people, to affect them, to effect change.

Thus, masks and masquerades are mediators—between men and women, youths and elders, initiated and uninitiated, powers of nature and those of human agency, and even life and death. For many groups in West and Central Africa, masking plays (or once played) an active role in the socialization process, especially for men, who control most masks. Maskers carry boys (and, more rarely, girls) away from their mothers to bush initiation camps, put them through ordeals and schooling, and welcome them back to society as men months or even years later. A second major role is in aiding the transformation of important deceased persons into productive ancestors who, in their new roles, can bring benefits to the living community. Because most masking cultures are agricultural, it is not surprising that Africans often invoke masquerades to increase the productivity of the fields, to stimulate the growth of crops, and later to celebrate the harvest.

34-15 Senufo masquerader, Côte d'Ivoire, photographed ca. 1980–1990. ◼◀

Senufo masqueraders are always men. Their masks often represent composite creatures that incarnate both ancestors and bush powers. They fight malevolent spirits with their aggressively powerful forms.

Senufo

The Senufo peoples of the western Sudan region in what is now northern Côte d'Ivoire have a population today of more than a million. They speak several different languages, sometimes even in the same village. Not surprisingly, there are many different Senufo art forms, all closely tied to community life.

MASQUERADES Senufo men dance many masks (see "African Masquerades," above), mostly in the context of Poro, the primary men's association for socialization and initiation, a protracted process

that takes nearly 20 years to complete. Maskers also perform at funerals and other public spectacles. Large Senufo masks (for example, FIG. 34-15) are composite creatures, combining characteristics of antelope, crocodile, warthog, hyena, and human: sweeping horns, a head, and an open-jawed snout with sharp teeth. These masks incarnate both ancestors and bush powers that combat witchcraft and sorcery, malevolent spirits, and the wandering dead. They are protectors who fight evil with their aggressively powerful forms and their medicines.

At funerals, Senufo maskers attend the corpse and help expel the deceased from the village. This is the deceased individual's final

Dogon

The Dogon (FIG. 34-9) continue to excel at carving wood figures, but many Dogon artists are specialists in fashioning large masks for elaborate cyclical masquerades.

SATIMBE MASKS Dogon masqueraders dramatize creation legends. These stories say that women were the first ancestors to imitate spirit maskers and thus the first human masqueraders. Men later took over the masks, forever barring women from direct involvement with masking processes. A mask called *Satimbe* (FIG. 34-17), that is, "sister on the head," seems to represent all women and commemo-

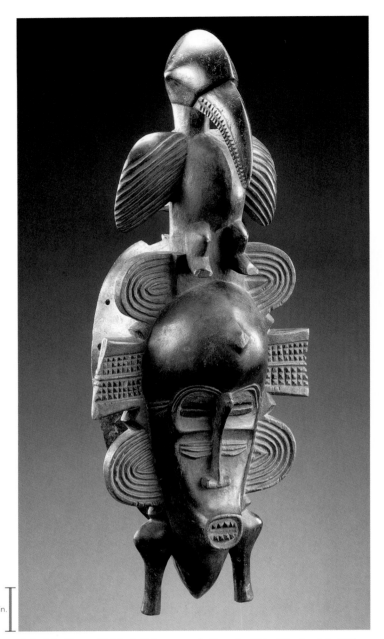

34-16 "Beautiful Lady" dance mask, Senufo, Côte d'Ivoire, late 20th century. Wood, 1′ ½″ high. Musée Barbier-Mueller, Geneva.

Some Senufo men dance female masks like this one with a hornbill bird rising from the forehead. The female characters are sometimes the wives of the terrorizing male masks (FIG. 34-15).

34-16A Ancient Mother, Senufo, early 20th century.

transition, a rite of passage parallel to that undergone by all men during their years of Poro socialization. When an important person dies, the convergence of several masking groups, as well as the music, dancing, costuming, and feasting of many people, constitute a festive and complex work of art that transcends any one mask or character.

Some men also dance female masks. The most recurrent type has a small face with fine features, several extensions, and varied motifs—a hornbill bird in the illustrated example (FIG. 34-16)—rising from the forehead. The men who dance these feminine characters also wear knitted body suits or trade-cloth costumes to indicate their beauty and their ties with the order and civilization of the village. They may be called "pretty young girl," "beautiful lady," or "wife" of one of the heavy, terrorizing masculine masks (FIG. 34-15) that appear before or after them.

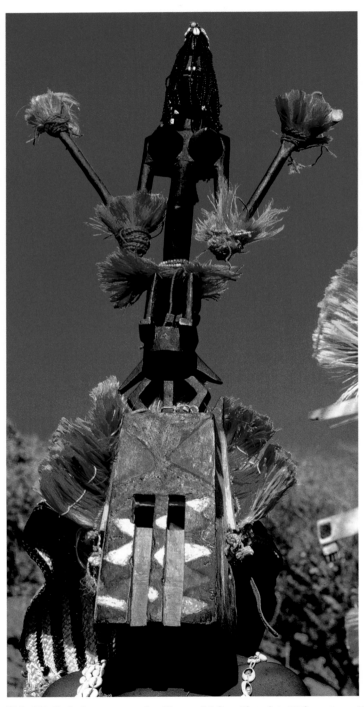

34-17 Satimbe masquerader, Dogon, Mali, mid- to late 20th century.

Satimbe ("sister on the head") masks commemorate the legend describing women as the first masqueraders. The mask's crown is a woman with large breasts and sticklike bent arms.

Mende Women as Maskers

The Mende and neighboring peoples of Sierra Leone, Liberia, and Guinea are unique in Africa in that women rather than men are the masqueraders. The masks (FIG. 34-18) and costumes they wear conceal the women's bodies from the audience attending their performance. The Sande society of the Mende is the women's counterpart to its Poro society for men. These associations control the initiation, education, and acculturation of female and male youth, respectively. Women leaders who dance the Sande masks serve as priestesses and judges during the three years the women's society controls the ritual calendar (alternating with the men's society in this role), thus serving the community as a whole. Women maskers, also initiators, teachers, and mentors, help girl novices with their transformation into educated and marriageable women. Sande women associate their Sowie masks with water spirits and the color black, which the society, in turn, connects with human skin color and the civilized world. The women wear these helmet masks on top of their heads as headdresses, with black raffia and cloth costumes to hide the wearers' identity during public performances. Elaborate coiffures, shiny black color, dainty triangular-shaped faces with slit eyes, rolls around the neck, and actual and carved versions of amulets and various emblems on the top commonly characterize Sowie masks (FIG. 34-18). These symbolize the adult women's roles as wives, mothers, providers for the family, and keepers of medicines for use within the Sande association and the society at large.

Sande members commission the masks from male carvers, with the carver and patron together determining the type of mask needed for a particular societal purpose. The Mende often keep, repair, and reuse masks for many decades, thereby preserving them as models for subsequent generations of carvers.

34-18 Female mask, Mende, Sierra Leone, 20th century. Wood and pigment, 1' 2$\frac{1}{2}$" high. Fowler Museum of Cultural History, University of California, Los Angeles (gift of the Wellcome Trust).

This Mende mask refers to ideals of female beauty, morality, and behavior. The large forehead signifies wisdom, the neck design beauty and health, and the plaited hair the order of ideal households.

1 in.

---

rates this legend. Satimbe masks consist of a roughly rectangular covering for the head with narrow rectangular openings for the eyes and a crowning element, much larger than the mask proper, depicting a schematic woman with large protruding breasts and sticklike bent arms. In ceremonies called Dama, held every several years to honor the lives of people who have died since the last Dama, Satimbe is among the dozens of different masked spirit characters that escort dead souls away from the village. The deceased are sent off to the land of the dead where, as ancestors, they will be enjoined to benefit their living descendants and stimulate agricultural productivity.

Mende

The Mende are farmers who occupy the Atlantic coast of Africa in Sierra Leone. Although men own and perform most masks in Africa, in Mende society the women control and dance the masks (see "Mende Women as Maskers," above).

SOWIE MASKS The glistening black surface of Mende Sowie masks (FIG. 34-18) evokes female water spirits newly emergent from their underwater homes (also symbolized by the turtle on top). The mask and its parts refer to ideals of female beauty, morality, and behavior. A high, broad forehead signifies wisdom and success. The neck ridges have multiple meanings. They are signs of beauty, good health, and prosperity and also refer to the ripples in the water from which the water spirits emerge. Intricately woven or plaited hair is the essence of harmony and order found in ideal households. A small closed mouth and downcast eyes indicate the silent, serious demeanor expected of recent initiates.

Kuba

The Kuba have been well established in the Democratic Republic of Congo since at least the 16th century. They represent almost 20 different ethnic groups who all recognize the authority of a single king.

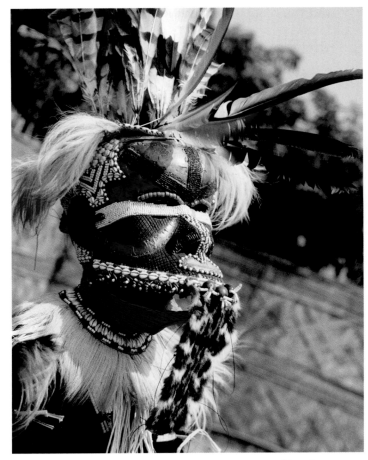

34-19 Bwoom masquerader, Kuba, Democratic Republic of Congo, photographed ca. 1950.

At Kuba festivals, masqueraders reenact creation legends involving Bwoom, Mwashamboy, and Ngady Amwaash. The first two are males who vie for the attention of Ngady, the first female ancestor.

34-20 Ngady Amwaash mask, Kuba, Democratic Republic of Congo, late 19th or early 20th century. Peabody Museum, Harvard University, Cambridge. ◼◀

Ngady's mask incorporates beads, shells, and feathers in geometric patterns. The stripes on her cheeks are tears from the pain of childbirth after incest with her father, represented by the Mwashamboy mask.

BWOOM AND NGADY AMWAASH At the court of Kuba kings, three masks, known as Mwashamboy, Bwoom, and Ngady Amwaash, represent legendary royal ancestors. Mwashamboy symbolizes the founding ancestor, Woot, and embodies the king's supernatural and political powers. Bwoom (FIG. 34-19), with its bulging forehead, represents a legendary dwarf or pygmy who signifies the indigenous peoples on whom kingship was imposed. Bwoom also vies with Mwashamboy for the attention of the beautiful female ancestor, Ngady Amwaash (FIG. 34-20), who symbolizes both the first woman and all women. On her cheeks are striped tears from the pain of childbirth, and because to procreate, Ngady must commit incest with her father, Woot. These three characters reenact creation stories during royal initiation ceremonies. The masks and their costumes, with elaborate beads, feathers, animal pelts, cowrie shells, cut-pile cloth, and ornamental trappings, as well as geometric patterning, make for a sumptuous display at Kuba festivals.

KING KOT A-MBWEEKY III Throughout history, African costumes have been laden with meaning and have projected messages that all members of the society could read. A photograph (FIG. 34-21) taken in 1970 shows Kuba King Kot a-Mbweeky III (r. 1969–) seated in state before his court, bedecked in a dazzling multimedia costume with many symbolic elements. The king commissioned the costume he wears and now has become art himself. Eagle feathers, leopard skin, cowrie shells, imported beads, raffia, and other materials combine to overload and expand the image of the man, making him larger than life and most

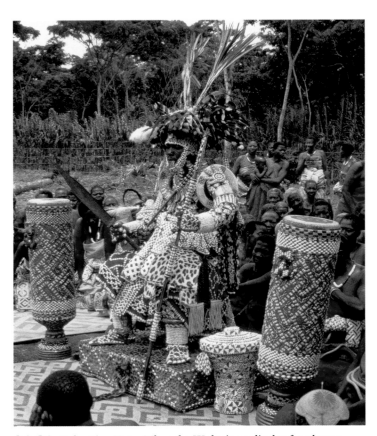

34-21 Kuba King Kot a-Mbweeky III during a display for photographer and filmmaker Eliot Elisofon in 1970, Mushenge, Democratic Republic of Congo.

Eagle feathers, leopard skin, cowrie shells, imported beads, raffia, and other materials combine to make the Kuba king larger than life. He is a collage of wealth, dignity, and military might.

Men and women in many rural areas of Africa embellish themselves with elaborate hairstyles, painted bodies, and beaded jewelry. This personal decoration reveals age, marital status, and parentage.

certainly a work of art. He is a *collage,* an assemblage. He holds not one but two weapons, symbolic of his military might and underscoring his wealth, dignity, and grandeur. The man, with his regalia, embodies the office of sacred kingship. He is a superior being actually and figuratively, raised upon a dais, flanked by ornate drums, with a treasure basket of sacred relics by his left foot. The geometric patterns on the king's costume and nearby objects, and the abundance and redundancy of rich materials, epitomize the opulent style of Kuba court arts.

Samburu

In addition to wearing masks and costumes on special occasions, people in many rural areas of eastern Africa, including the Samburu in northern Kenya, continue to embellish their bodies.

BODY ADORNMENT The Samburu men and women shown in FIG. 34-22 at a spontaneous dance have distinct styles of personal decoration. Men, particularly warriors who are not yet married, expend hours creating elaborate hairstyles for one another. They paint their bodies with red ocher, and wear bracelets, necklaces, and other bands of beaded jewelry young women make for them. For themselves, women fashion more lavish constellations of beaded collars, which they mass around their necks. As if to help separate the genders, women shave their heads and adorn them with beaded headbands. Personal decoration begins in childhood, increasing to become lavish and highly self-conscious in young adulthood, and diminishing as people age. Much of the decoration contains coded information—age, marital or initiation status, parentage of a warrior son—that can be read by those who know the codes. Dress ensembles have evolved over time. Different colors and sizes of beads became available, as did plastics and aluminum, and specific fashions have changed, but the overall concept of fine personal adornment—that is, dress raised to the level of art—remains much the same today as it was centuries ago.

Igbo

The Igbo of the Lower Niger region in present-day Nigeria have a distinguished artistic tradition dating back more than a thousand years (see Chapter 15). The arts still play a vital role in Igbo society today.

MBARI HOUSES The powerful nature gods of the Igbo demand about every 50 years that a community build an *mbari* house. The Igbo construct these houses from mud as sacrifices to major

deities, often Ala, goddess of the earth. The houses are elaborate unified artistic complexes that incorporate numerous unfired clay sculptures and paintings—occasionally more than a hundred in a single mbari house. In an mbari house at Umugote Orishaeze, near Owerri, two of the sculptures (FIG. 34-23) depict Ala and her consort, the thunder god Amadioha. The god wears modern clothing, whereas Ala appears with traditional body paint and a fancy hairstyle. These differing modes of dress relate to Igbo concepts of modernity and tradition, both viewed as positive by the men who control the ritual and art. They allow themselves modern attire but want their women to remain traditional. The artist enlarged and extended both figures' torsos, necks, and heads to express their aloofness, dignity, and power. More informally

34-23 Ala and Amadioha, painted clay sculptures in an mbari, Igbo, Umugote Orishaeze, Nigeria, photographed in 1966.

The Igbo erect mud mbari houses to the earth goddess Ala. The painted statues inside this one represent Ala in traditional dress with body paint and the thunder god Amadioha in modern dress.

34-24 Togu na (men's house of words), Dogon, Mali, photographed in 1989. Wood and pigment.

Dogon men hold their communal deliberations in togu na. The posts of this one are of varied date. The oldest have traditional carvings, and the newest feature polychrome narrative or topical paintings.

posed figures and groups appear on the other sides of the house, including beautiful, amusing, or frightening figures of animals, humans, and spirits taken from mythology, history, dreams, and everyday life—a kaleidoscope of subjects and meanings. The mbari construction process, veiled in secrecy behind a fence, is a stylized world-renewal ritual. Ceremonies for unveiling the house to public view indicate that Ala accepted the sacrificial offering (of the mbari) and, for a time at least, will be benevolent. An mbari house never undergoes repair. Instead, the Igbo allow it to disintegrate and return to its source, the earth.

of legendary female ancestors, similar to stylized ancestral couples (FIG. 34-9) or masked figures (FIG. 34-17). Recent replacement posts feature narrative and topical scenes of varied subjects, such as horsemen or hunters or women preparing food, and these artworks include abundant descriptive detail, bright polychrome painting in enamels, and even some writing. Unlike earlier traditional sculptors, the contemporary artists who made these posts want to be recognized and are eager to sell their work (other than these posts) to tourists.

CONTEMPORARY ART

The art forms of contemporary Africa are immensely varied and defy easy classification. Four examples, however, can give a sense of the variety and vitality of African art today.

DOGON TOGU NA Traditionalism and modernism unite in the contemporary Dogon *togu na*, or "men's house of words." The togu na is so called because men's deliberations vital to community welfare take place under its sheltering roof. It is considered the "head" and the most important part of the community, which the Dogon characterize with human attributes. The Dogon build the men's houses over time. Earlier posts, such as the central one in the illustrated togu na (FIG. 34-24), show schematic renderings

34-25 TRIGO PIULA, *Ta Tele*, Democratic Republic of Congo, 1988. Oil on canvas, 3′ 3$\frac{3}{8}$″ × 3′ 4$\frac{3}{8}$″. Collection of the artist. ◼️

Ta Tele is a commentary on modern life showing Congolese citizens transfixed by television pictures of the world outside Africa. Even the traditional power figure at the center has a TV screen for a chest.

1 ft.

TRIGO PIULA The Democratic Republic of Congo's TRIGO PIULA (b. ca. 1950) is a painter trained in Western artistic techniques and styles whose works fuse Western and Congolese images and objects in a pictorial blend that provides social commentary on present-day Congolese culture. *Ta Tele* (FIG. **34-25**) depicts a group of Congolese citizens staring transfixed at colorful pictures of life beyond Africa displayed on 14 television screens. The TV images include references to travel to exotic places (such as Paris with the Eiffel Tower, FIG. **31-1**), sports events, love, the earth seen from a satellite, and Western worldly goods. A traditional Kongo power figure (compare FIG. **34-8**) associated with warfare and divination stands at the composition's center as a visual mediator between the anonymous foreground viewers and the multiple TV images. In traditional Kongo contexts, this figure's feather headdress links it to supernatural and magical powers from the sky, such as lightning and storms. In Piula's rendition, the headdress perhaps refers to the power of airborne televised pictures. In the stomach area, where Kongo power figures often have glass in front of a medicine packet, Piula painted a television screen showing a second power figure, as if to double the figure's power. The artist shows most of the television viewers with a small white image of a foreign object—for example, a car, shoe, or bottle—on the backs of their heads. One meaning of this picture appears to be that television messages have deadened the minds of Congolese peoples to anything but modern thoughts or commodities. The

power figure stands squarely on brown earth. Two speaker cabinets set against the back wall beneath the TV screens have wires leading to the figure, which in the past could inflict harm. In traditional Kongo thinking and color symbolism, the color white and earth tones are associated with spirits and the land of the dead. Perhaps Piula suggests that like earlier power figures, the contemporary world's new television-induced consumerism is poisoning the minds and souls of Congolese people as if by magic or sorcery.

WILLIE BESTER Social and political issues also figure in contemporary South African art. For example, artists first helped protest against apartheid (government-sponsored racial separation), then celebrated its demise and the subsequent democratically elected government under the first president, Nelson Mandela, in 1994. WILLIE BESTER (b. 1956) was among the critics of the apartheid system. His 1992 *Homage to Steve Biko* (FIG. **34-26**) is a tribute to the gentle and heroic leader of the South African Black Liberation Movement whom the authorities killed while he was in detention. The exoneration of the two white doctors in charge of him sparked protests around the world. Bester packed his picture with references to death and injustice. Biko's portrait, at the center, is near another of the police minister, James Kruger, who had Biko transported 1,100 miles to Pretoria in the yellow Land Rover ambulance seen left of center and again beneath Biko's portrait. Bester portrayed Biko

34-26 WILLIE BESTER, *Homage to Steve Biko,* South Africa, 1992. Mixed media, 3′ 7⅚″ × 3′ 7⅚″. Collection of the artist.

Homage to Steve Biko is a tribute to a leader of the Black Liberation Movement that protested apartheid in South Africa. References to the injustice of Biko's death fill this complex painting.

1 ft.

The wood caskets of Paa Joe take many forms, including animals, airplanes, and automobiles. When commissioned, the form always relates to the deceased, but many collectors buy the caskets as art objects.

with his chained fists raised in the recurrent protest gesture. This portrait memorializes both Biko and the many other antiapartheid activists indicated by the white graveyard crosses above a blue sea of skulls beside Biko's head. The crosses stand out against a red background that recalls the inferno of burned townships. The stop sign (lower left) seems to mean "stop Kruger" or perhaps "stop apartheid." The tagged foot, as if in a morgue, above the ambulance (to the left) also refers to Biko's death. The red crosses on the ambulance door and on Kruger's reflective dark glasses echo, with sad irony, the graveyard crosses.

Blood red and ambulance yellow are in fact unifying colors dripped or painted on many parts of the work. Writing and numbers, found fragments and signs, both stenciled and painted—favorite Cubist motifs (FIGS. 35-14 and 35-16)—also appear throughout the composition. Numbers refer to dehumanized life under apartheid. Found objects—wire, sticks, cardboard, sheet metal, cans, and other discards—from which the poor construct fragile, impermanent township dwellings, remind viewers of the degraded lives of most South African people of color. The oil-can guitar (bottom center), another recurrent Bester symbol, refers both to the social harmony and joy provided by music and to the control imposed by apartheid policies. The whole composition is rich in texture and dense in its collage combinations of objects, photographs, signs, symbols, and painting. *Homage to Steve Biko* is a radical and powerful critique of an oppressive sociopolitical system, and it exemplifies the extent to which art can be invoked in the political process.

KANE KWEI AND PAA JOE Some contemporary African artists specialize in the most traditional African art form, wood sculpture, but have pioneered new forms. Kane Kwei (1922–1992) of the Ga people in urban coastal Ghana created a new kind of wooden casket that brought him both critical acclaim and commercial success. Beginning around 1970, Kwei, trained as a carpenter, created figurative coffins intended to reflect the deceased's life, occupation, or major accomplishments. On commission he made such diverse shapes as a cow, a whale, a bird, a Mercedes-Benz, and various local food crops, such as onions and cocoa pods, all pieced together using nails and glue rather than carved. Kwei also created coffins in traditional leaders' symbolic forms, such as an eagle, an

elephant, a leopard, and a stool. Kwei's sons and his cousin PAA JOE (b. 1944) have carried on his legacy. In a 2000 photograph (FIG. 34-27) of Joe's showroom in Teshi, prospective customers view the caskets on display, including an airplane and a cow. Only some of the coffins made by Kwei and Joe were ever buried. Many are in museum galleries and the homes of private collectors today. Their popularity in the Western world is due in part to the affinities between the coffins and the European and American Pop Art movement (see Chapter 36).

AFRICAN ART TODAY During the past two centuries and especially in recent decades, the encroachments of Christianity, Islam, Western education, and market economies have led to increasing secularization in all the arts of Africa. Many figures and masks earlier commissioned for shrines or as incarnations of ancestors or spirits are now made mostly for sale to outsiders, essentially as tourist arts. They are sold in art galleries abroad as collector's items for display. In towns and cities, painted murals and cement sculptures appear frequently, often making implicit comments about modern life. Nonetheless, despite the growing importance of urbanism, most African people still live in rural communities. Traditional values, although under pressure, hold considerable force in villages especially, and some people adhere to spiritual beliefs that uphold traditional art forms. African art remains as varied as the vast continent itself and continues to evolve.

AFRICA AFTER 1800

19TH CENTURY

▮ Most of the traditional forms of African art continued into the 19th century. Among these are sculptures and shrines connected with the veneration of ancestors. Wooden or metal-covered figures guarded Fang and Kota reliquaries. Especially elaborate are some Kalabari Ijaw screens with figures of a deceased chief, his retainers, and the heads of his slaves and conquered rivals.

▮ The royal arts also flourished in the 19th century. The ultimate status symbol was the king's throne. That of Nsangu of Bamum makes extensive use of richly colored textiles and luminous materials like glass beads and cowrie shells.

▮ One of the earliest African artists whose name survives is Akati Akpele Kendo, who worked for the Fon king Glele around 1858, but most African art remains anonymous.

▮ Throughout history, African artists have been masters of woodcarving. Especially impressive examples are the Kongo power figures bristling with nails and blades, and the Dogon and Baule sculptures of male and female couples. Although stylistically diverse, most African sculpture exhibits hierarchy of scale, both among figures and within the human body, and enlarged heads are common.

Kalabari Ijaw ancestral screen, late 19th century

Throne of King Nsangu, Bamum, ca. 1870

20TH CENTURY

▮ As in the 19th century, traditional arts flourished in 20th-century Africa, but the names of many more individual artists are known. Two of the most famous are the Asante sculptor Osei Bonsu and the Yoruba sculptor Olowe of Ise.

▮ Osei Bonsu worked for kings and commoners alike, carving both single figures and groups, sometimes for the linguist's staff of a leader's spokesman. The distinctive features of his style are the flattened faces and crosshatched eyebrows of his figures.

▮ Olowe of Ise won renown for the multifigure veranda posts that he carved for houses and palaces. Elongated bodies are an Olowe characteristic, along with finely textured detail.

▮ In Africa, art is nearly always an active agent in the lives of its peoples. A major African art form is the fashioning of masks for festive performances. Masqueraders are almost always men, even when the masks they dance are female, as among the Senufo, Dogon, and Kuba, but in Mende society, women are the masqueraders.

Bonsu, linguist's staff, mid-20th century

Senufo dance mask, late 20th century

CONTEMPORARY ART

▮ The art forms of contemporary Africa range from the traditional to works of international character using Western techniques and motifs. Among the former are the sculpted wooden posts of Dogon men's houses.

▮ Two contemporary painters whose works often incorporate social and political commentary are Trigo Piula of the Democratic Republic of Congo and Willie Bester of South Africa.

Bester, *Homage to Steve Biko*, 1992

1 ft.

35-1 Marcel Duchamp, *Nude Descending a Staircase, No. 2,* 1912. Oil on canvas, 4′ 10″ × 2′ 11″. Philadelphia Museum of Art, Philadelphia (Louise and Walter Arensberg Collection).

The Armory Show of 1913 introduced European avant-garde art to America. Duchamp's figure in motion down a staircase in a time continuum reveals the artist's indebtedness to Cubism and Futurism.

EUROPE
AND AMERICA,
1900 TO 1945

The first half of the 20th century was a period of significant upheaval worldwide. Between 1900 and 1945, the major industrial powers expanded their colonial empires, fought two global wars, witnessed the rise of Communism, Fascism, and Nazism, and suffered the Great Depression. These decades were also a time of radical change in the arts when painters and sculptors challenged some of the most basic assumptions about the purpose of art and what form an artwork should take.

During the 19th century, the development of modern nation-states and advanced industrial societies in Europe and America had led to frenzied imperialist expansion. By the beginning of the 20th century (MAP 35-1), Britain, France, Germany, Belgium, Italy, Spain, and Portugal all had footholds in Africa. In Asia, Britain ruled India, the Dutch controlled Indonesia's vast archipelago, the French held power in Indochina, and the Russians ruled Central Asia and Siberia. Japan began rising as a new and formidable Pacific power that would stake its claims to empire in the 1930s. This imperialism was capitalist and expansionist, establishing colonies as raw-material sources, as manufacturing markets, and as territorial acquisitions. Early-20th-century colonialism also often had the missionary dimension of bringing the "light" of Christianity and civilization to "backward peoples" and educating "inferior races."

Nationalism and rampant imperialism also led to competition. Eventually, countries negotiated alliances to protect their individual state interests. The conflicts between the two major blocs—the Triple Alliance (Germany, Austria-Hungary, and Italy) and the Triple Entente (Russia, France, and Great Britain)—led to World War I, which began in 1914. The slaughter and devastation of the Great War lasted until 1918. Not only were more than nine million soldiers killed in battle, but the introduction of poison gas in 1915 added to the horror of humankind's inhumanity to itself. Although the United States tried to remain neutral, it finally felt compelled to enter the war in 1917. In 1919, the 27 Allied nations negotiated the official end of World War I, whose legacy was widespread misery, social disruption, and economic collapse—the ultimate effects of nationalism, imperialism, and expansionist goals.

The Russian Revolution exacerbated the global chaos when it erupted in 1917. Dissatisfaction with the regime of Tsar Nicholas II (r. 1894–1917) had led workers to stage a general strike, and the monarchy's rule ended with the tsar's abdication in March. In late 1917 the Bolsheviks wrested control of the country

MAP 35-1 Colonial empires around 1900.

Legend:
- Belgian Empire
- British Empire
- Danish Empire
- Dutch Controlled
- French Empire
- German Empire
- Italian Controlled
- Japanese Empire
- Ottoman Empire
- Portuguese Empire
- Russian Empire
- Spanish Controlled
- United States Controlled
- Independent Nations

from the ruling provisional government. The Bolsheviks, a faction of Russian Social Democrats led by Vladimir Lenin (1870–1924), promoted violent revolution. Once in power, Lenin nationalized the land and turned it over to the local rural soviets (councils of workers and soldiers' deputies). After extensive civil war, the Communists, as they now called themselves, succeeded in retaining control of Russia and taking over an assortment of satellite countries in Eastern Europe. This new state took the official name the Union of Soviet Socialist Republics (USSR, or Soviet Union) in 1923.

Economic upheaval followed on the heels of war and revolution. The Great Depression of the 1930s dealt a serious blow to the stability of Western countries. Largely due to the international scope of banking and industrial capitalism, the economic depression deeply affected the United States and many European countries. By 1932 unemployment in the British workforce stood at 25 percent, and 40 percent of German workers were without jobs. Production in the United States plummeted by 50 percent.

This economic disaster, along with the failure of postwar treaties and the League of Nations to keep the peace, provided a fertile breeding ground for destabilizing forces to emerge once again. In the 1920s and 1930s, totalitarian regimes came to the fore in several European countries. Benito Mussolini (1883–1945) headed the nationalistic Fascist regime in Italy. Joseph Stalin (1879–1953) consolidated his control of the Soviet Union by 1929. Concurrently, in Germany Adolf Hitler (1889–1945) built the National Socialist German Workers Party (also known as the Nazi Party) into a mass political movement and eliminated all opposition.

These ruthless seizures of power led to the many conflicts that evolved into World War II. This catastrophic struggle erupted in 1939 when Germany invaded Poland, and Britain and France declared war on Germany. Eventually, the conflict earned its designation as a world war. While Germany and Italy fought most of Europe and the Soviet Union, Japan invaded China and occupied Indochina. After the Japanese bombing of Pearl Harbor in Hawaii in 1941, the United States declared war on Japan. Germany, in loose alliance with Japan, declared war on the United States, which joined the conflict in Europe on the side of Britain and France. Although most of the concerns of individual countries participating in World War II were territorial and nationalistic, other agendas surfaced as well. The Nazis, propelled by Hitler's staunch anti-Semitism, sought to build a racially exclusive Aryan state. This resolve led to the horror of the Holocaust, the killing of nearly two out of every three European Jews.

World War II drew to an end in 1945, when the Allied forces defeated Germany, and the United States dropped atomic bombs on Hiroshima and Nagasaki in Japan. The shock of the war's physical, economic, and psychological devastation immediately tempered the elation people felt at the conclusion of these global hostilities.

EUROPE, 1900 TO 1920

Like other members of society, artists deeply felt the effects of the political and economic disruptions of the early 20th century. As the old social orders collapsed and new ones, from communism to corporate capitalism, took their places, artists searched for new definitions of and uses for art in a changed world.

Already in the 19th century, each successive modernist movement—Realism, Impressionism, and Post-Impressionism—had challenged artistic conventions with ever-greater intensity. This relentless challenge gave rise to the *avant-garde* ("front guard"), a term derived from 19th-century French military usage. The avant-garde were soldiers sent ahead of the army's main body to reconnoiter and make occasional raids on the enemy. Politicians who deemed themselves visionary and forward-thinking subsequently adopted the term. It then migrated to the art world in the 1880s, where it referred to artists who were ahead of their time and who transgressed the limits of established art forms.

These artists were the vanguard, or trailblazers. The avant-garde rejected the classical, academic, and traditional, and zealously explored the premises and formal qualities of painting, sculpture, and other media. The Post-Impressionists were the first artists labeled avant-garde. Although the general public found avant-garde art incomprehensible, the principles underlying late-19th-century modernism appealed to increasing numbers of artists as the 20th century dawned. Avant-garde artists in all their diversity became a major force during the first half of the 20th century and beyond.

Avant-garde principles emerged forcefully in European art of the early 1900s in the general movement that art historians call *Expressionism,* a term used over the years in connection with a wide range of art. At its essence, Expressionism refers to art that is the result of the artist's unique inner or personal vision and that often has an emotional dimension. This contrasts strongly with most Western art produced since the Renaissance that focused on visually describing the empirical world. The term "Expressionism" first gained currency after *Der Sturm,* an avant-garde periodical initially published in Munich, popularized it.

Fauvism

One of the first movements to tap into this pervasive desire for expression was *Fauvism.* In 1905, at the third Salon d'Automne in Paris, a group of young painters exhibited canvases so simplified in design and so shockingly bright in color that a startled critic, Louis Vauxcelles (1870–1943), described the artists as *fauves* (wild beasts). The Fauves were totally independent of the French Academy and the "official" Salon (see "Academic Salons and Independent Art Exhibitions," Chapter 31, page 823). Driving the Fauve movement was a desire to develop an art having the directness of Impressionism but also embracing intense color juxtapositions and their emotional capabilities.

Building on the legacy of artists such as van Gogh and Gauguin (see Chapter 31), Fauve artists went even further in liberating color from its descriptive function and using it for both expressive and structural ends. They produced portraits, landscapes, still lifes, and nudes of spontaneity and verve, with rich surface textures, lively linear patterns, and, above all, bold colors. The Fauves employed startling contrasts of vermilion and emerald green and of cerulean blue and vivid orange held together by sweeping brush strokes and bold patterns. Thus, these artists explored both facets of Expressionism. They combined outward expression, in the form of a bold release of internal feelings through wild color and powerful, even brutal, brushwork, and inward expression, awakening the viewer's emotions by these very devices.

The Fauve painters never officially organized, and the looseness of both personal connections and stylistic affinities caused the Fauve

movement to begin to disintegrate almost as soon as it emerged. Within five years, most of the artists had departed from a strict adherence to Fauve principles and developed their own, more personal styles. During the brief existence of the movement, however, the Fauve artists made a remarkable contribution to the direction of painting by demonstrating color's structural, expressive, and aesthetic capabilities.

HENRI MATISSE The dominant figure of the Fauve group was HENRI MATISSE (1869–1954), who believed that color could play a primary role in conveying meaning and focused his efforts on developing this premise. In an early painting, *Woman with the Hat* (FIG. 35-2), Matisse depicted his wife Amélie in a rather conventional manner compositionally, but the seemingly arbitrary colors immediately startle the viewer, as does the sketchiness of the forms. The entire image—the woman's face, clothes, hat, and background—consists of patches and splotches of color juxtaposed in ways that sometimes produce jarring contrasts. Matisse explained his approach: "What characterized fauvism was that we rejected imitative colors, and that with pure colors we obtained stronger reactions."[1] For Matisse and the Fauves, therefore, color became the formal element most responsible for pictorial coherence and the primary conveyor of meaning (see "Matisse on Color," page 912).

35-2A MATISSE, *Le Bonheur de Vivre,* 1905–1906.

35-2 HENRI MATISSE, *Woman with the Hat,* 1905. Oil on canvas, $2' 7\frac{3}{4}'' \times 1' 11\frac{1}{2}''$. San Francisco Museum of Modern Art, San Francisco (bequest of Elise S. Haas).

Matisse portrayed his wife Amélie using patches and splotches of seemingly arbitrary colors. He and the other Fauve painters used color not to imitate nature but to produce a reaction in the viewer.

Matisse on Color

In an essay entitled "Notes of a Painter," published in the Parisian journal *La Grande Revue* on Christmas Day, 1908, Henri Matisse responded to his critics and set forth his principles and goals as a painter. The excerpts that follow help explain what Matisse was trying to achieve in paintings such as *Harmony in Red* (FIG. 35-3).

What I am after, above all, is expression. . . . Expression, for me, does not reside in passions glowing in a human face or manifested by violent movement. The entire arrangement of my picture is expressive: the place occupied by the figures, the empty spaces around them, the proportions, everything has its share. Composition is the art of arranging in a decorative manner the diverse elements at the painter's command to express his feelings. . . .

Both harmonies and dissonances of colour can produce agreeable effects. . . . Suppose I have to paint an interior: I have before me a cupboard; it gives me a sensation of vivid red, and I put down a red which satisfies me. A relation is established between this red and the white of the canvas. Let me put a green near the red, and make the floor yellow; and again there will be relationships between the green or yellow and the white of the canvas which will satisfy me. . . . A new combination of colours will succeed the first and render the totality of my representation. I am forced to transpose until finally my picture may seem completely changed when, after successive modifications, the red has succeeded the green as the dominant colour. I cannot copy nature in a servile way; I am forced to interpret nature and submit it to the spirit of the picture. From the relationship I have found in all the tones there must result a living harmony of colours, a harmony analogous to that of a musical composition. . . .

The chief function of colour should be to serve expression as well as possible. . . . My choice of colours does not rest on any scientific theory; it is based on observation, on sensitivity, on felt experiences. . . . I simply try to put down colours which render my sensation. There is an impelling proportion of tones that may lead me to change the shape of a figure or to transform my composition. Until I have achieved this proportion in all parts of the composition I strive towards it and keep on working. Then a moment comes when all the parts have found their definite relationships, and from then on it would be impossible for me to add a stroke to my picture without having to repaint it entirely.*

* Translated by Jack D. Flam, *Matisse on Art* (London: Phaidon, 1973), 32–40.

35-3 HENRI MATISSE, *Red Room* (*Harmony in Red*), 1908–1909. Oil on canvas, 5′ 11″ × 8′ 1″. State Hermitage Museum, Saint Petersburg.

Matisse believed painters should choose compositions and colors that express their feelings. Here, the table and wall seem to merge because they are the same color and have identical patterning.

Derain worked closely with Matisse, but the tropical setting and the bold colors of *The Dance* also reflect Derain's study of Gauguin's paintings (FIGS. 31-18 and 31-19), as does the flattened perspective.

HARMONY IN RED The maturation of Matisse's color discoveries coalesced in his *Red Room* (*Harmony in Red;* FIG. 35-3). The subject is the interior of a comfortable, prosperous household with a maid placing fruit and wine on the table, but Matisse's canvas is radically different from traditional paintings of domestic interiors (FIG. 25-19). The Fauve painter depicted objects in simplified and schematized fashion and flattened out the forms. For example, Matisse eliminated the front edge of the table, making the table, with its identical patterning, as flat as the wall behind it. The window at the upper left could also be a painting on the wall, further flattening the space. Everywhere, the colors contrast richly and intensely. Matisse's process of overpainting reveals the importance of color for striking the right chord in the viewer. Initially, this work was predominantly green, and then he repainted it blue. Neither seemed appropriate to Matisse, and not until he repainted this work in red did he feel he had found the right color for the "harmony" he wished to compose.

ANDRÉ DERAIN Another Fauve painter was ANDRÉ DERAIN (1880–1954), who worked closely with Matisse. Like Matisse, Derain worked to use color to its fullest potential—to produce aesthetic and compositional coherence, to increase luminosity, and to elicit emotional responses from the viewer. *The Dance* (FIG. 35-4), in which several figures, some nude, others clothed, frolic in a lush landscape, is typical of Derain's art. The tropical setting and the bold colors reflect in part Derain's study of Paul Gauguin's paintings (FIGS. 31-18 and 31-19), as does the flattened perspective. Color delineates space, and Derain indicated light and shadow not by differences in value but by contrasts of hue. For the Fauves, as for Gauguin and van Gogh, color does not describe the local tones of objects but expresses the picture's content.

German Expressionism

The immediacy and boldness of the Fauve images appealed to many artists, including the German Expressionists. However, although color plays a prominent role in contemporaneous German painting, the expressiveness of the German images is due as much to wrenching distortions of form, ragged outline, and agitated brush strokes. This approach resulted in savagely powerful, emotional canvases in the years leading to World War I.

ERNST LUDWIG KIRCHNER The first group of German artists to explore Expressionist ideas gathered in Dresden in 1905 under the leadership of ERNST LUDWIG KIRCHNER (1880–1938). The group members thought of themselves as paving the way for a more perfect age by bridging the old age and the new. They derived their name, *Die Brücke* (The Bridge), from this concept. Kirchner's early studies in architecture, painting, and the graphic arts had instilled in him a deep admiration for German medieval art. Like the British artists associated with the Arts and Crafts movement, such as William Morris (FIG. 31-34), members of Die Brücke modeled themselves on their ideas of medieval craft guilds by living together and practicing all the arts equally. Kirchner described their lofty goals in a ringing statement published in the form of a woodcut in 1913 and titled *Chronik der Brücke:*

> With faith in progress and in a new generation of creators and spectators we call together all youth. As youth, we carry the future and want to create for ourselves freedom of life and of movement against the long-established older forces. Everyone who reproduces that which drives him to creation with directness and authenticity belongs to us.[2]

These artists protested the hypocrisy and materialistic decadence of those in power. Kirchner, in particular, focused much of his attention on the detrimental effects of industrialization, such as the alienation of individuals in cities, which he felt fostered a mechanized and impersonal society. The tensions leading to World War I further exacerbated the discomfort and anxiety evidenced in the works of Die Brücke artists.

35-5 ERNST LUDWIG KIRCHNER, *Street, Dresden*, 1908 (dated 1907). Oil on canvas, 4′ 11¼″ × 6′ 6⅞″. Museum of Modern Art, New York. ◼◀

Kirchner's perspectival distortions, disquieting figures, and color choices reflect the influence of the Fauves and of Edvard Munch (FIG. 31-27), who made similar expressive use of formal elements.

Kirchner's *Street, Dresden* (FIG. 35-5) provides a glimpse into the frenzied urban activity of a bustling German city before World War I. Rather than offering the distant, panoramic urban view of the Impressionists (FIG. 31-5), Kirchner's street scene is jarring and dissonant in both composition and color. The women in the foreground loom large, approaching somewhat menacingly. The steep perspective of the street, which threatens to push the women directly into the viewer's space, increases their confrontational nature. Harshly rendered, the women's features make them appear ghoulish, and the garish, clashing colors—juxtapositions of bright orange, emerald green, chartreuse, and pink—add to the expressive impact of the image. Kirchner's perspectival distortions, disquieting figures, and color choices reflect the influence of the work of Edvard Munch, who made similar expressive use of formal elements in *The Scream* (FIG. 31-27).

35-6A NOLDE, *Masks*, 1911.

EMIL NOLDE Much older than most Die Brücke artists was EMIL NOLDE (1867–1956), but because he pursued similar ideas in his work, the younger artists invited him to join their group in 1906. (Die Brücke dissolved by 1913, and each member continued to work independently.) The content of Nolde's work centered, for the most part, on religious imagery. In contrast to the quiet spirituality and restraint of traditional religious images, however, Nolde's paintings, for example, *Saint Mary of Egypt among Sinners* (FIG. 35-6), are visceral and forceful. Mary, before her conversion, entertains lechers whose lust magnifies their brutal ugliness. The distortions of form and color (especially the jolting juxtaposition of blue and orange) and the rawness of the brush strokes amplify the harshness of the leering faces.

Borrowing ideas from van Gogh, Munch, the Fauves, and African and Oceanic art (see "Primitivism and Colonialism," page 920), Nolde and the other Die Brücke artists created images that derive much of their power from a dissonance and seeming lack of finesse. The harsh colors, aggressively brushed paint, and distorted forms expressed the artists' feelings about the injustices of society and their belief in a healthful union of human beings and nature. Their use of these diverse sources reflects the expanding scope of global contact brought about by colonialism and international capitalism.

35-6 EMIL NOLDE, *Saint Mary of Egypt among Sinners*, 1912. Left panel of a triptych, oil on canvas, 2′ 10″ × 3′ 3″. Hamburger Kunsthalle, Hamburg.

In contrast to the quiet spirituality of traditional religious images, Nolde's paintings produce visceral emotions and feature distortions of form, jarring juxtapositions of color, and raw brush strokes.

Science and Art in the Early 20th Century

In the early 20th century, societies worldwide contended with discoveries and new ways of thinking in a wide variety of fields, including science. These new ideas forced people to revise radically how they understood their world. In particular, the values and ideals that were the legacy of the Enlightenment (see Chapter 29) began to yield to innovative views. Thus, intellectuals countered 18th- and 19th-century assumptions about progress and reason with ideas challenging traditional notions about the physical universe, the structure of society, and human nature. Artists participated in this reassessment. Modernist artists, in particular, often acknowledged these new discoveries and shifting theoretical bases in their work. Accordingly, much of the history of early-20th-century Western art is a history of the rejection of traditional limitations and definitions both of art and of the universe.

One of the fundamental Enlightenment beliefs was faith in science. Because of its basis in empirical, or observable, fact, science provided a

35-7 VASSILY KANDINSKY, *Improvisation 28* (second version), 1912. Oil on canvas, $3' 7\frac{7}{8}'' \times 5' 3\frac{7}{8}''$. Solomon R. Guggenheim Museum, New York (gift of Solomon R. Guggenheim, 1937).

The scientific theories of Einstein and Rutherford convinced Kandinsky that material objects had no real substance. He was one of the first painters to explore complete abstraction in his canvases.

mechanistic conception of the universe, which reassured a populace that was finding traditional religions less certain. As promoted in the classic physics of Isaac Newton (1642–1727), the universe was a huge machine consisting of time, space, and matter. The early 20th century witnessed an astounding burst of scientific activity challenging this model of the universe. It amounted to what has been called "the second scientific and technological revolution." Particularly noteworthy was the work of various physicists: Max Planck (1858–1947), Albert Einstein (1879–1955), Ernest Rutherford (1871–1937), and Niels Bohr (1885–1962). With their discoveries, each of these scientists shattered the existing faith in the objective reality of matter and, in so doing, paved the way for a new model of the universe. Planck's quantum theory (1900) raised questions about the emission of atomic energy. In his 1905 paper, "The Electrodynamics of Moving Bodies," Einstein carried

Planck's work further by introducing his theory of relativity. He argued that space and time are not absolute, as postulated in Newtonian physics. Rather, Einstein explained, time and space are relative to the observer and linked in what he called a four-dimensional space-time continuum. He also concluded that matter, rather than a solid, tangible reality, was actually another form of energy. Einstein's famous equation $E = mc^2$, where E stands for energy, m for mass, and c for the speed of light, provided a formula for understanding atomic energy. Rutherford's and Bohr's exploration of atomic structure between 1906 and 1913 contributed to this new perception of matter and energy. Together, all these scientific discoveries constituted a changed view of physical nature and contributed to the growing interest in abstraction, as opposed to the mimetic representation of the world, among early-20th-century artists like Vassily Kandinsky (FIG. **35-7**).

VASSILY KANDINSKY A second major German Expressionist group, *Der Blaue Reiter* (The Blue Rider), formed in Munich in 1911. The two founding members, Vassily Kandinsky and Franz Marc, whimsically selected this name because of their mutual interest in the color blue and horses. Like Die Brücke, this group produced paintings that captured their feelings in visual form while also eliciting intense visceral responses from viewers.

Born in Russia, VASSILY KANDINSKY (1866–1944) moved to Munich in 1896 and soon developed a spontaneous and aggressively avant-garde expressive style. Indeed, Kandinsky was one of the first artists to explore complete abstraction, as in *Improvisation 28* (FIG. **35-7**), painted in 1912. Kandinsky fueled his elimination of repre-

sentational elements with his interest in theosophy (a religious and philosophical belief system incorporating a wide range of tenets from, among other sources, Buddhism and mysticism) and the occult, as well as with advances in the sciences. A true intellectual, widely read in philosophy, religion, history, and the other arts, especially music, Kandinsky was also one of the few early modernists to read with some comprehension the new scientific theories of the era (see "Science and Art in the Early 20th Century," above). Scientists' exploration of atomic structure, for example, convinced Kandinsky that material objects had no real substance, thereby shattering his faith in a world of tangible things. The painter articulated his ideas in an influential treatise, *Concerning the Spiritual in Art*, published in

35-8 Franz Marc, *Fate of the Animals*, 1913. Oil on canvas, 6′ 4¾″ × 8′ 9½″. Kunstmuseum, Basel.

Marc developed a system of correspondences between specific colors and feelings or ideas. In this apocalyptic scene of animals trapped in a forest, the colors of severity and brutality dominate.

1 ft.

1912. Artists, Kandinsky believed, must express the spirit and their innermost feelings by orchestrating color, form, line, and space. He produced numerous works like *Improvisation 28,* conveying feelings with color juxtapositions, intersecting linear elements, and implied spatial relationships. Ultimately, Kandinsky saw these abstractions as evolving blueprints for a more enlightened and liberated society emphasizing spirituality.

FRANZ MARC Like many of the other German Expressionists, Franz Marc (1880–1916), the cofounder of Der Blaue Reiter, grew increasingly pessimistic about the state of humanity, especially as World War I loomed on the horizon. His perception of human beings as deeply flawed led him to turn to the animal world for his subjects. Animals, he believed, were more pure than humanity and thus more appropriate as a vehicle to express an inner truth. In his quest to imbue his paintings with greater emotional intensity, Marc focused on color and developed a system of correspondences between specific colors and feelings or ideas. In a letter to a fellow Blaue Reiter, Marc explained: "Blue is the *male* principle, severe and spiritual. Yellow is the *female* principle, gentle, happy and sensual. Red is *matter,* brutal and heavy."[3] Marc's attempts to create, in a sense, an iconography (or representational system) of color linked him to other avant-garde artists struggling to redefine the practice of art.

Fate of the Animals (FIG. **35-8**) represents the culmination of Marc's color explorations. Painted in 1913, when the tension of impending cataclysm had pervaded society, the animals appear trapped in a forest amid falling trees, some apocalyptic event destroying both the forest and the animals inhabiting it. The painter distorted the entire scene and shattered it into fragments. Significantly, the lighter and brighter colors—the passive, gentle, and cheerful ones—are absent, and the colors of severity and brutality dominate the work. On the back of the canvas Marc wrote "All being is flaming suffering." The artist discovered just how well his painting portended war's anguish and tragedy when he ended up at the front the following year.

His experiences in battle prompted him to write to his wife that *Fate of the Animals* "is like a premonition of this war—horrible and shattering. I can hardly conceive that I painted it."[4] His contempt for people's inhumanity and his attempt to express that through his art ended, with tragic irony, in his death in action in 1916.

KÄTHE KOLLWITZ The emotional range of German Expressionism extends from passionate protest and satirical bitterness to the poignantly expressed pity for the poor in the prints of KÄTHE KOLLWITZ (1867–1945), who had no formal association with any Expressionist group. The graphic art of Gauguin and Munch stimulated a revival of the print medium in Germany, especially the woodcut, and these proved inspiring models. Kollwitz worked in a variety of printmaking techniques, including woodcut, lithography, and etching, and explored a range of issues from the overtly political to the deeply personal. One image she explored in depth, producing a number of print variations, was that of a mother with her dead child. Although she initially derived the theme from the Christian *Pietà,* she transformed it into a universal statement of maternal loss and grief. In *Woman with Dead Child* (FIG. **35-9**), an etching and lithograph, she disavowed the reverence and grace that pervaded most Christian depictions of Mary holding the dead Christ (FIG. **22-12**) and replaced those attributes with an animalistic passion, shown in the way the mother ferociously grips the body of her dead child. The primal nature of the image is in keeping with the aims of the Expressionists, and the scratchy lines the etching needle produced serve as evidence of Kollwitz's very personal touch. The impact of this image is undeniably powerful. Not since the Gothic age in Germany (FIG. **18-51**) had any artist produced a mother-and-son group of comparable emotional power. That Kollwitz used her son Peter as the model for the dead child no doubt made the image all the more personal to her. The image stands as a poignant premonition. Peter died fighting in World War I at age 21.

35-9A Modersohn-Becker, *Self-Portrait,* 1906.

WILHELM LEHMBRUCK The Great War also deeply affected Wilhelm Lehmbruck (1881–1919). His figurative sculptures exude

The theme of the mother mourning over her dead child comes from images of the *Pietà* in Christian art, but Kollwitz transformed it into a powerful universal statement of maternal loss and grief.

a quiet mood but still possess a compelling emotional sensibility. Lehmbruck studied sculpture, painting, and the graphic arts in Düsseldorf before moving to Paris in 1910, where he developed the style of his *Seated Youth* (FIG. **35-10**). His sculpture combines the expressive qualities he much admired in the work of fellow sculptors, especially the psychological energies of Rodin (FIGS. **31-32** and **31-33**). In *Seated Youth*, the poignant elongation of human proportions, the slumped shoulders, and the hands that hang uselessly all impart an undertone of anguish to the rather classical figure. Lehmbruck's figure communicates by pose and gesture alone. Although its extreme proportions may recall Mannerist attenuation (FIG. **22-43**), its distortions announce a new freedom in interpreting the human figure. For Lehmbruck, as for Rodin, the human figure could express every human condition and emotion. The quiet, contemplative nature of this sculpture serves both as a personal expression of Lehmbruck's increasing depression and as a powerful characterization of the general sensibility in the wake of World War I. Appropriately, the original title of *Seated Youth* was *The Friend*, in reference to the artist's many friends who lost their lives in the war. After Lehmbruck's tragic suicide in 1919, officials placed this sculpture as a memorial in the soldiers' cemetery in Lehmbruck's native city of Duisburg.

35-10A SCHIELE, *Self-Portrait, Grimacing*, 1910.

35-10 Wilhelm Lehmbruck, *Seated Youth*, 1917. Composite tinted plaster, 3' 4⅝" × 2' 6" × 3' 9". National Gallery of Art, Washington, D.C. (Andrew W. Mellon Fund).

The poignant elongation of human proportions, the slumped shoulders, and the hands that hang uselessly all impart an undertone of anguish to Lehmbruck's rather classical figure.

Gertrude and Leo Stein and the Avant-Garde

One of the many unexpected developments in the history of art is that two Americans—Gertrude (1874–1946) and Leo (1872–1947) Stein—played pivotal roles in the history of the European avant-garde because they provided a hospitable environment in their Paris home. Artists, writers, musicians, collectors, and critics interested in progressive art and ideas could meet there to talk and socialize. Born in Pennsylvania, the Stein siblings moved to 27 rue de Fleurus in Paris in 1903. Gertrude's experimental writing stimulated her interest in the latest developments in the arts. Conversely, the avant-garde ideas discussed at the Steins' house influenced her unique poetry, plays, and other works. She is perhaps best known for *The Autobiography of Alice B. Toklas* (1933), a unique memoir written in the persona of her longtime lesbian companion.

The Steins' interest in the exciting, invigorating debates taking place in avant-garde circles led them to welcome visitors to their Saturday salons, which included lectures, thoughtful discussions, and spirited arguments. Often, these gatherings lasted until dawn and included not only their French friends but also visiting Americans, Britons, Swedes, Germans, Hungarians, Spaniards, Poles, and Russians. Among the hundreds who welcomed the opportunity to visit the Steins were artists Henri Matisse, Pablo Picasso, Georges Braque, Mary Cassatt, Marcel Duchamp, Alfred Stieglitz, and Arthur B. Davis; writers Ernest Hemingway, F. Scott Fitzgerald, John dos Passos, Jean Cocteau, and Guillaume Apollinaire; art dealers Daniel Kahnweiler and Ambroise Vollard; critics Roger Fry and Clive Bell; and collectors Sergei Shchukin and Ivan Morosov.

The Steins were avid art collectors, and the works decorating their walls attracted many visitors. One of the first paintings Leo purchased was Matisse's notorious *Woman with the Hat* (FIG. 35-2), and he subsequently bought numerous important paintings by Matisse and Picasso, along with works by Gauguin, Cézanne, Renoir, and Braque. Picasso, who developed a close friendship with Gertrude, painted her portrait (FIG. 35-11) in 1907. Gertrude loved the painting so much that she kept it by her all her life and donated it to the Metropolitan Museum of Art only upon her death in 1946.

35-11 Pablo Picasso, *Gertrude Stein,* 1906–1907. Oil on canvas, 3′ 3¾″ × 2′ 8″. Metropolitan Museum of Art, New York (bequest of Gertrude Stein, 1947). ■◀

Picasso had left this portrait of his friend and patron unfinished until he decided to incorporate the planar simplicity of ancient Iberian stone sculptures into his depiction of her face.

Primitivism and Cubism

The Expressionist departure from any strict adherence to illusionism in art was a path that other artists followed. Among those who most radically challenged prevailing artistic conventions and moved most aggressively into the realm of abstraction was Pablo Picasso.

PABLO PICASSO Born in Spain four years after Gustave Courbet's death, PABLO PICASSO (1881–1973) mastered all aspects of late-19th-century Realist technique by the time he entered the Barcelona Academy of Fine Art in the late 1890s. His prodigious talent led him to experiment with a wide range of visual expression, first in Spain and then in Paris, where he settled in 1904. An artist whose importance to the history of art is uncontested, Picasso made staggering contributions to new ways of representing the surrounding world. Perhaps the most prolific artist in history, he explored virtually every artistic medium during his lengthy career, but remained a traditional artist in making careful preparatory studies for each major work. Picasso epitomized modernism, however, in his enduring quest for innovation, which resulted in sudden shifts from one

style to another. By the time he settled permanently in Paris, Picasso's work had evolved from Spanish painting's sober Realism through an Impressionistic phase to the so-called Blue Period (1901–1904), when, in a melancholy state of mind, he used primarily blue colors to depict worn, pathetic, and alienated figures.

35-11A Picasso, *Family of Saltimbanques,* 1905.

GERTRUDE STEIN By 1906, Picasso was searching restlessly for new ways to depict form. He found clues in the ancient Iberian sculpture of his homeland and other "primitive" cultures. Inspired by these sources, Picasso returned to a portrait of *Gertrude Stein* (FIG. 35-11), his friend and patron (see "Gertrude and Leo Stein and the Avant-Garde," above). Picasso had begun the painting earlier that year but left it unfinished after more than 80 sittings. When he resumed work on the portrait, Picasso painted Stein's head as a simplified planar form, incorporating aspects derived from Iberian stone heads. Although the disparity between the style of the face and the rest of Stein's image is striking, together they provide an insightful portrait of a forceful, vivacious woman. More important, Picasso had discovered a new approach to the representation of the human form.

35-12 PABLO PICASSO, *Les Demoiselles d'Avignon*, 1907. Oil on canvas, 8' × 7' 8". Museum of Modern Art, New York (acquired through the Lillie P. Bliss Bequest). ◼◀

African and ancient Iberian sculpture and the late paintings of Cézanne influenced this pivotal work, with which Picasso opened the door to a radically new method of representing forms in space.

DEMOISELLES D'AVIGNON The influence of "primitive" art also surfaces in *Les Demoiselles d'Avignon* (*The Young Ladies of Avignon*; FIG. 35-12), which opened the door to a radically new method of representing form in space. Picasso began the work as a symbolic picture to be titled *Philosophical Bordello*, portraying two male clients (who, based on surviving drawings, had features resembling Picasso's) intermingling with women in the reception room of a brothel on Avignon Street in Barcelona. One was a sailor. The other carried a skull, an obvious reference to death. By the time the artist finished, he had eliminated the male figures and simplified the room's details to a suggestion of drapery and a schematic foreground still life. Picasso had become wholly absorbed in the problem of finding a new way to represent the five female figures in their interior space. Instead of depicting the figures as continuous volumes, he fractured their shapes and interwove them with the equally jagged planes that represent drapery and empty

space. Indeed, the space, so entwined with the bodies, is virtually illegible. Here Picasso pushed Cézanne's treatment of form and space (FIGS. 31-20 and 31-21) to a new level. The tension between Picasso's representation of three-dimensional space and his conviction that a painting is a two-dimensional design lying flat on the surface of a stretched canvas is a tension between representation and abstraction.

The artist extended the radical nature of *Les Demoiselles d'Avignon* even further by depicting the figures inconsistently. Ancient Iberian sculptures inspired the calm, ideal features of the three young women at the left, as they had the head of Gertrude Stein (FIG. 35-11). The energetic, violently striated features of the two heads to the right emerged late in Picasso's production of the work and grew directly from his increasing fascination with the power of African sculpture (see "Primitivism and Colonialism," page 920), which the artist studied in Paris's Trocadéro ethnography museum as well as collected and kept in his

Primitivism and Colonialism

Many scholars have noted that one major source for much of early-20th-century art is non-Western culture. Many modernist artists incorporated stylistic elements from the artifacts of Africa, Oceania, and the native peoples of the Americas—a phenomenon art historians call *primitivism*. Some of them, for example, Henri Matisse and Pablo Picasso (FIG. 35-13), were enthusiastic collectors of "primitive art," but all of them could view the numerous non-Western objects displayed in European and American collections and museums. During the second half of the 19th century, anthropological and ethnographic museums began to proliferate. In 1882, the Musée d'Ethnographie du Trocadéro (now the Musée du quai Branly) in Paris opened its doors to the public. The Musée Permanent des Colonies (now the Musée National des Arts d'Afrique et d'Océanie) in Paris also provided the public with a wide array of objects—weapons, tools, basketwork, headdresses—from colonial territories, as did the Musée Africain in Marseilles. In Berlin, the Museum für Völkerkunde housed close to 10,000 African objects by 1886, when it opened for public viewing. The Expositions Universelles, regularly scheduled exhibitions in France designed to celebrate industrial progress, included products from Oceania and Africa after 1851, familiarizing the public with these cultures. By the beginning of the 20th century, significant non-Western collections were on view in museums in Liverpool, Glasgow, Edinburgh, London, Hamburg, Stuttgart, Vienna, Berlin, Munich, Leiden, Copenhagen, and Chicago.

The formation of these collections was a by-product of the rampant colonialism central to the geopolitical dynamics of the 19th century and much of the 20th century. Most of the Western powers maintained colonies (MAP 35-1). For example, the United States, Holland, and France all kept a colonial presence in the Pacific. Britain, France, Germany, Belgium, Holland, Spain, and Portugal divided up the African continent. People often perceived these colonial cultures as "primitive" and referred to many of the non-Western artifacts displayed in museums as "artificial curiosities" or "fetish objects." Indeed, the exhibition of these objects collected during expeditions to the colonies served to reinforce the perceived "need" for a colonial presence in these countries. These objects, which often seemed to depict strange gods or creatures, bolstered the view that these peoples were "barbarians" who needed to be "civilized" or "saved," and this perception thereby justified colonialism—including its missionary dimension—worldwide.

Whether avant-garde artists were aware of the imperialistic implications of their appropriation of non-Western culture is unclear. Certainly, however, many artists reveled in the energy and freshness of non-Western images and forms. These different cultural products provided Western artists with new ways of looking at their own art. Matisse always maintained he saw African sculptures as simply "good sculptures . . . like any other."* Picasso, in contrast, believed "the masks weren't just like any other pieces of sculpture. Not at all.

35-13 FRANK GELETT BURGESS, Pablo Picasso in his studio, Paris, France, 1908. Collection of the Musée Picasso, Paris. ◼◀

Picasso was familiar with ancient Iberian art from his homeland and studied African and other "primitive" art in Paris's Trocadéro museum. He kept his own collection of primitive art in his studio.

They were magic things. . . . mediators" between humans and the forces of evil, and he sought to capture their power as well as their forms in his paintings. "[In the Trocadéro] I understood why I was a painter. . . . All alone in that awful museum, with masks, dolls . . . *Les Demoiselles d'Avignon* [FIG. 35-12)] must have come to me that day."† Further, "primitive" art seemed to embody a directness, closeness to nature, and honesty that appealed to modernist artists determined to reject conventional models. Non-Western art served as an important revitalizing and energizing force in Western art.

* Jean-Louis Paudrat, "From Africa," in William Rubin, ed., *"Primitivism" in 20th Century Art: Affinity of the Tribal and the Modern* (New York: Museum of Modern Art, 1984), 1:141.
† Ibid.

Paris studio (FIG. 35-13). Perhaps responding to the energy of these two new heads, Picasso also revised their bodies. He broke them into more ambiguous planes suggesting a combination of views, as if the observer sees the figures from more than one place in space at once. The woman seated at the lower right shows these multiple angles most clearly, seeming to present the viewer simultaneously with a three-quarter back view from the left, another from the right, and a front view of the head that suggests seeing the figure frontally as well. Gone is the traditional concept of an orderly, constructed, and unified pictorial space that mirrors the world. In its place are the rudimentary beginnings of a new representation of the world as a dynamic interplay of time and space. Clearly, *Les Demoiselles d'Avignon* represents a dramatic departure from the careful presentation of a visual reality. Explained Picasso: "I paint forms as I think them, not as I see them."[5]

GEORGES BRAQUE AND CUBISM For many years, Picasso showed *Les Demoiselles* only to other painters. One of the first to see it was GEORGES BRAQUE (1882–1963), a Fauve painter who found it so challenging that he began to rethink his own painting style. Using the painting's revolutionary ideas as a point of departure, together Braque and Picasso formulated *Cubism* around 1908. Cubism represented a radical turning point in the history of art, nothing less than a dismissal of the pictorial illusionism that had dominated Western art since the Renaissance. The Cubists rejected naturalistic depictions, preferring compositions of shapes and forms abstracted from the conventionally perceived world. These artists pursued the analysis of form central to Cézanne's artistic explorations, and they dissected life's continuous optical spread into its many constituent features, which they then recomposed, by a new logic of design, into a coherent aesthetic object. For the Cubists, the art of painting had to move far beyond the description of visual reality. This rejection of accepted artistic practice illustrates both the period's aggressive avant-garde critique of pictorial convention and the public's dwindling faith in a safe, concrete Newtonian world in the face of the physics of Einstein and others (see "Science and Art," page 915).

The new style received its name after Matisse described some of Braque's work to the critic Louis Vauxcelles as having been painted "with little cubes." In his review, Vauxcelles described the new paintings as "cubic oddities."[6] The French writer and theorist Guillaume Apollinaire (1880–1918) summarized well the central concepts of Cubism in 1913:

> Authentic cubism [is] the art of depicting new wholes with formal elements borrowed not from the reality of vision, but from that of conception. This tendency leads to a poetic kind of painting which stands outside the world of observation; for, even in a simple cubism, the geometrical surfaces of an object must be opened out in order to give a complete representation of it. . . . Everyone must agree that a chair, from whichever side it is viewed, never ceases to have four legs, a seat and a back, and that, if it is robbed of one of these elements, it is robbed of an important part.[7]

Art historians refer to the first phase of Cubism, developed jointly by Picasso and Braque, as *Analytic Cubism.* Because Cubists could not achieve Apollinaire's total view through the traditional method of drawing or painting models from one position, these artists began to dissect the forms of their subjects. They presented that dissection for the viewer to inspect across the canvas surface. In simplistic terms, Analytic Cubism involves analyzing the structure of forms.

THE PORTUGUESE Georges Braque's painting *The Portuguese* (FIG. **35-14**) exemplifies Analytic Cubism. The artist derived the subject from his memories of a Portuguese musician seen years earlier in a bar in Marseilles. Braque concentrated his attention on dissecting the form and placing it in dynamic interaction with the space around it. Unlike the Fauves and German Expressionists, who used vibrant colors, the Cubists chose subdued hues—here solely brown tones—in order to focus the viewer's attention on form. In *The Portuguese,* the artist carried his analysis so far that the viewer must work diligently to discover clues to the subject. The construction of large intersecting planes suggests the forms of a man and a guitar. Smaller shapes interpenetrate and hover in the large planes. The way Braque treated light and shadow reveals his departure from conventional artistic practice. Light and dark passages suggest both chiaroscuro modeling and transparent planes that allow the viewer to see through one level to another. As the observer looks, solid forms emerge only to be canceled almost immediately by a different reading of the subject.

35-14 GEORGES BRAQUE, *The Portuguese,* 1911. Oil on canvas, 3′ 10 1/8″ × 2′ 8″. Kunstmuseum, Basel (gift of Raoul La Roche, 1952). ◼◀

The Cubists rejected the pictorial illusionism that had dominated Western art for centuries. In this painting, Braque concentrated on dissecting form and placing it in dynamic interaction with space.

The stenciled letters and numbers add to the painting's complexity. Letters and numbers are flat shapes, but as elements of a Cubist painting such as *The Portuguese,* they allow the artist to play with the viewer's perception of two- and three-dimensional space. The letters and numbers lie flat on the painted canvas surface, yet the image's shading and shapes seem to flow behind and underneath them, pushing the letters and numbers forward into the viewing space. Occasionally, they seem attached to the surface of some object within the painting. Ultimately, the constantly shifting imagery makes it impossible to arrive at any definitive or final reading of the image. Examining this kind of painting is a disconcerting excursion into ambiguity and doubt, especially since the letters and numbers seem to anchor the painting in the world of representation, thereby exacerbating the tension between representation and abstraction. Analytical Cubist paintings radically disrupt expectations about the representation of space and time.

ROBERT DELAUNAY Artists and art historians generally have regarded the suppression of color as crucial to Cubism's success, but ROBERT DELAUNAY (1885–1941), a contemporary of Picasso and Braque, worked toward a kind of color Cubism. Apollinaire called this art style *Orphism,* after Orpheus, the Greek god with magical powers of music-making. Apollinaire believed art, like music, was

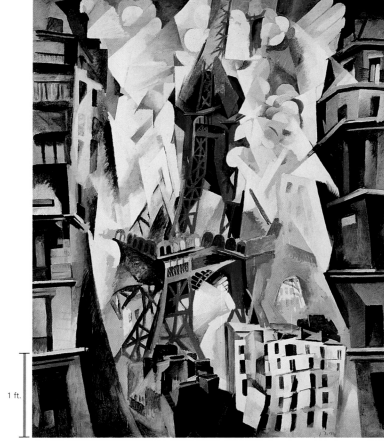

35-15 ROBERT DELAUNAY, *Champs de Mars,* or *The Red Tower,* 1911. Oil on canvas, 5′ 3″ × 4′ 3″. Art Institute of Chicago, Chicago.

Orphism is a kind of color Cubism. Delaunay broke the Eiffel Tower into a kaleidoscopic array of colored pieces. Some scholars have interpreted the painting as a commentary on the collapse of society.

1 ft.

distinct from the representation of the visible world. Delaunay developed his ideas about color use in dialogue with his Russian-born wife, Sonia (1885–1974), also an artist. She created paintings, quilts, other textile arts, and book covers that exploited the expressive capabilities of color. As a result of their artistic explorations, both Delaunays became convinced that the rhythms of modern life could best be expressed through color harmonies and dissonances. *Champs de Mars,* or *The Red Tower* (FIG. **35-15**), is one of many paintings Delaunay produced between 1909 and 1912 depicting the Eiffel Tower (FIG. **31-1**). The title *Champs de Mars* refers to the Parisian field on which the Eiffel Tower stands, named after the Campus Martius (Field of Mars) located outside the walls of Republican Rome.

The artist broke Eiffel's tower into a kaleidoscopic array of colored pieces, which variously leap forward or pull back according to the relative hues and values of the broken shapes. The structure ambiguously rises and collapses. Delaunay's experiments with color dynamics strongly influenced the Futurists (discussed later) and the German Expressionists (he exhibited with Der Blaue Reiter as well as with Cubists). These artists found in his art a means for intensifying expression by suggesting violent motion through shape and color.

Some scholars have interpreted Delaunay's fragmentation of the Eiffel Tower in *Champs de Mars* in political terms as a commentary on societal collapse in the years leading to World War I. Delaunay himself described the collapsing-tower imagery as "the synthesis of a period of destruction; likewise a prophetic vision with social repercussions: war, and the base crumbles."[8] This statement encapsulates well the social and artistic climate during these years—the destruction of old world

1 in.

35-16 PABLO PICASSO, *Still Life with Chair-Caning,* 1912. Oil and oilcloth on canvas, 10⅝″ × 1′ 1¾″. Musée Picasso, Paris. ▣◀

This painting includes a piece of oilcloth imprinted with the photolithographed pattern of a cane chair seat. Framed with a piece of rope, the still life challenges the viewer's understanding of reality.

orders and of artistic practices deemed obsolete, as well as the avant-garde's prophetic nature and its determination to subvert tradition.

SYNTHETIC CUBISM In 1912, Cubism entered a new phase called *Synthetic Cubism,* in which artists constructed paintings and drawings from objects and shapes cut from paper or other materials to represent parts of a subject. The work marking the point of departure for this new style was Picasso's *Still Life with Chair-Caning* (FIG. **35-16**), a painting in which the artist imprinted a photolithographed pattern of a cane chair seat on the canvas and then pasted a piece of oilcloth on it. Framed with a piece of rope, this work challenges the viewer's understanding of reality. The photographically replicated chair-caning seems so "real" that one expects the holes to break any brush strokes laid upon it. But the chair-caning, although optically suggestive of the real, is only an illusion or representation of an object. In contrast, the painted abstract areas do not refer to tangible objects in the real world. Yet the fact they do not imitate anything makes them more "real" than the chair-caning. No pretense exists. Picasso extended the visual play by making the letter *U* escape from the space of the accompanying *J* and *O* and partially covering it with a cylindrical shape that pushes across its left side. The letters *JOU* appear in many Cubist paintings. These letters formed part of the masthead of the daily French newspapers (*journaux*) often found among the objects represented. Picasso and Braque especially delighted in the punning references to *jouer* and *jouir*—the French verbs meaning "to play" and "to enjoy."

COLLAGE After *Still Life with Chair-Caning,* both Picasso and Braque continued to explore the medium of *collage* introduced into the realm of high art in that work. From the French word "coller" ("to stick"), a collage is a composition of bits of objects, such as newspaper or cloth, glued to a surface. Its possibilities can be seen in Braque's *Bottle, Newspaper, Pipe, and Glass* (FIG. **35-17**), done in a variant of collage called *papier collé* ("stuck paper")—gluing assorted paper shapes to a drawing or painting. Here, charcoal lines and shadows provide clues to the Cubist multiple views of various surfaces and objects. Roughly rectangular strips of variously printed and colored paper dominate the composition. The paper imprinted with wood grain and

This Cubist collage of glued paper is a visual game to be deciphered. The pipe in the foreground, for example, seems to lie on the newspaper, but it is actually cut through the printed paper.

1 in.

ety. Many artists and writers of the period allied themselves with various anarchist groups whose social critiques and utopian visions appealed to progressive thinkers. It was, therefore, not a far leap to see radical art, like Cubism, as having political ramifications. Indeed, many critics in the French press consistently equated Cubism with anarchism, revolution, and disdain for tradition. Picasso himself, however, never viewed Cubism as a protest movement or even different in kind from traditional painting (see "Picasso on Cubism," page 924).

moldings provides an illusion whose concreteness contrasts with the lightly rendered objects on the right. Five pieces of paper overlap each other in the center of the composition to create a layering of flat planes that both echo the space the lines suggest and establish the flatness of the work's surface. All shapes in the image seem to oscillate, pushing forward and dropping back in space. Shading carves space into flat planes in some places and turns planes into transparent surfaces in others. The pipe in the foreground illustrates this complex visual interplay especially well. Although it appears to lie on the newspaper, it is in fact a form cut through the printed paper to reveal the canvas surface, which Braque lightly modeled with charcoal. The artist thus kept his audience aware that *Bottle, Newspaper, Pipe, and Glass* is an artwork, a visual game to be deciphered, and not an attempt to reproduce nature. Picasso explained the goals of Cubist collage:

> Not only did we try to displace reality; reality was no longer in the object. . . . [In] the *papier collé* . . . [w]e didn't any longer want to fool the eye; we wanted to fool the mind. . . . If a piece of newspaper can be a bottle, that gives us something to think about in connection with both newspapers and bottles, too.[9]

Like all collage, the papier collé technique was modern in its medium—mass-produced materials never before found in "high" art—and modern in the way the artist embedded the art's "message" in the imagery and in the nature of these everyday materials.

Although most discussions of Cubism and collage focus on the formal innovations they represented, it is important to note that the public also viewed the revolutionary and subversive nature of Cubism in sociopolitical terms. The public saw Cubism's challenge to artistic convention and tradition as an attack on 20th-century soci-

PICASSO, GUITAR Cubism did not just open new avenues for representing form on two-dimensional surfaces. It also inspired new approaches to sculpture. Picasso explored Cubism's possibilities in sculpture throughout the years he and Braque developed the style. Picasso created *Guitar* (FIG. 35-18) in 1912. As in his Cubist paintings, this sculpture operates at the intersection of two- and three-dimensionality. Picasso took the form of a guitar (an image that

35-18A PICASSO, *Three Musicians,* 1921.

35-18 PABLO PICASSO, maquette for *Guitar,* 1912. Cardboard, string, and wire (restored), $2' 1\frac{1}{4}'' \times 1' 1'' \times 7\frac{1}{2}''$. Museum of Modern Art, New York.

In this model for a sculpture of sheet metal, Picasso presented what is essentially a cutaway view of a guitar, allowing the viewer to examine both surface and interior space, both mass and void.

1 in.

Picasso on Cubism

In 1923, Picasso granted an interview to the Mexican-born painter and critic Marius de Zayas (1880–1961), who had settled in New York City in 1907 and in 1911 had been instrumental in putting together the first exhibition in the United States of Picasso's paintings. In their conversation, the approved English translation of which appeared in the journal *The Arts* under the title "Picasso Speaks," the artist set forth his views about Cubism and the nature of art in general.

> We all know that Art is not truth. Art is a lie that makes us realize truth, at least the truth that is given us to understand. The artist must know the manner whereby to convince others of the truthfulness of his lies. . . . They speak of naturalism in opposition to modern painting. I would like to know if anyone has ever seen a natural work of art. Nature and art, being two different things, cannot be the same thing. Through art we express our conception of what nature is not. . . .

> Cubism is no different from any other school of painting. The same principles and the same elements are common to all. . . . Many think that Cubism is an art of transition, an experiment which is to bring ulterior results. Those who think that way have not understood it. Cubism is not either a seed or a foetus, but an art dealing primarily with forms, and when a form is realized it is there to live its own life. . . . Mathematics, trigonometry, chemistry, psychoanalysis, music, and whatnot, have been related to Cubism to give it an easier interpretation. All this has been pure literature, not to say nonsense, . . . Cubism has kept itself within the limits and limitations of painting, never pretending to go beyond it. Drawing, design, and color are understood and practiced in Cubism in the spirit and manner that they are understood and practiced in all other schools. Our subjects might be different, as we have introduced into painting objects and forms that were formerly ignored. . . . [I]n our subjects, we keep the joy of discovery, the pleasure of the unexpected; our subject itself must be a source of interest.*

* Marius de Zayas, "Picasso Speaks," *The Arts* (May 1923), 315–326. Reprinted in Herschel B. Chipp, *Theories of Modern Art: A Source Book by Artists and Critics* (Berkeley and Los Angeles: University of California Press, 1968), 263–266.

surfaces in many of his paintings as well) and explored its volume via flat planar cardboard surfaces. (FIG. 35-18 reproduces the maquette, or model. The finished sculpture was to be made of sheet metal.) By presenting what is essentially a cutaway view of a guitar, Picasso allowed the viewer to examine both surface and interior space, both mass and void. This approach, of course, was completely in keeping with the Cubist program. Some scholars have suggested that Picasso derived the cylindrical form that serves as the sound hole on the guitar from the eyes on masks from the Ivory Coast of Africa. African masks were a continuing and persistent source of inspiration for the artist (see "Primitivism," page 920). Here, however, Picasso seems to have transformed the anatomical features of African masks into a part of a musical instrument—dramatic evidence of his unique, innovative artistic vision. Ironically—and intentionally—the sound hole, the central void in a real guitar, is, in Picasso's guitar, the only solid form.

JACQUES LIPCHITZ One of the most successful sculptors to adapt into three dimensions the planar, fragmented dissolution of form central to Analytic Cubist painting was JACQUES LIPCHITZ (1891–1973). Born in Lithuania, Lipchitz resided for many years in France and the United States. He worked out his ideas for many of his sculptures in clay before creating them in bronze or in stone. *Bather* (FIG. 35-19) is typical of his Cubist style. Lipchitz broke the continuous form of the human body into cubic volumes and planes. The interlocking and gracefully intersecting irregular facets and curves recall the paintings of Picasso and Braque and represent a parallel analysis of dynamic form in space. Lipchitz later produced less volumetric sculptures that included empty spaces outlined by metal shapes. In these sculptures, Lipchitz pursued even further the Cubist notion of spatial ambiguity and the relationship between solid forms and space.

ALEKSANDR ARCHIPENKO The Russian sculptor ALEKSANDR ARCHIPENKO (1887–1964) explored similar ideas, as seen in *Woman Combing Her Hair* (FIG. 35-20). In this statuette Archipenko introduced, in place of the head, a void with a shape of its

35-19 JACQUES LIPCHITZ, *Bather*, 1917. Bronze, $2' 10\frac{3}{4}'' \times 1' 1\frac{1}{4}'' \times 1' 1''$. Nelson-Atkins Museum of Art, Kansas City (gift of the Friends of Art).

The interlocking and gracefully intersecting irregular facets and curves of Lipchitz's *Bather* recall the Cubist paintings of Picasso and Braque and represent a parallel analysis of dynamic form in space.

1 in.

1 in.

35-20 ALEKSANDR ARCHIPENKO, *Woman Combing Her Hair*, 1915. Bronze, 1′ 1¾″ × 3¼″ × 3⅛″. Museum of Modern Art, New York (acquired through the Lillie P. Bliss Bequest).

In this statuette Archipenko introduced, in place of the head, a void with a shape of its own that figures importantly in the whole design. The void is not simply the negative counterpart of the volume.

1 ft.

35-21 JULIO GONZÁLEZ, *Woman Combing Her Hair*, 1936. Iron, 4′ 4″ × 1′ 11½″ × 2′ ⅝″. Museum of Modern Art, New York (Mrs. Simon Guggenheim Fund).

Using prefabricated metal pieces, González reduced his figure to an interplay of curves, lines, and planes—virtually a complete abstraction without any vestiges of traditional representational art.

own that figures importantly in the whole design. Enclosed spaces have always existed in figurative sculpture—for example, the space between the arm and the body when the hand rests on the hip (FIG. 21-13). But here the space penetrates the figure's continuous mass and is a defined form equal in importance to the mass of the bronze. It is not simply the negative counterpart to the volume. Archipenko's figure shows the same fluid intersecting planes seen in Cubist painting, and the relation of the planes to each other is similarly complex. Thus, in both painting and sculpture, the Cubists broke through traditional limits and transformed the medium.

JULIO GONZÁLEZ A friend of Picasso, JULIO GONZÁLEZ (1876–1942) shared his interest in the artistic possibilities of new materials and new methods borrowed from both industrial technology and traditional metalworking. Born into a family of metalworkers in Barcelona, González helped Picasso construct a number of welded sculptures. This contact with Picasso in turn allowed González

to refine his own sculptural vocabulary. Using prefabricated bars, sheets, or rods of welded or wrought iron and bronze, González created dynamic sculptures with both linear elements and volumetric forms. A comparison between his *Woman Combing Her Hair* (FIG. 35-21) and Archipenko's version of the same subject (FIG. 35-20) is instructive. Archipenko's figure still incorporates the basic shapes of a woman's body. González reduced his figure to an interplay of curves, lines, and planes—virtually a complete abstraction without any vestiges of traditional representational art. Although González's sculpture received limited exposure during his lifetime, his work had a great impact on later abstract artists working in welded metal.

FERNAND LÉGER AND PURISM Le Corbusier is today best known as one of the most important modernist architects (FIG. 35-75), but he was also a painter. In 1918 he founded a movement called *Purism,* which opposed Synthetic Cubism on the grounds that it was becoming merely an esoteric, decorative art out of touch with

35-22 FERNAND LÉGER, *The City*, 1919. Oil on canvas, 7' 7" × 9' 9½". Philadelphia Museum of Art, Philadelphia (A. E. Gallatin Collection).

Léger was a champion of the "machine aesthetic." In *The City*, he depicted the mechanical commotion of urban life, incorporating the effects of billboard advertisements, flashing lights, and noisy traffic.

35-22A LÉGER, *Three Women*, 1921.

the machine age. Purists maintained that machinery's clean functional lines and the pure forms of its parts should direct the artist's experiments in design, whether in painting, architecture, or industrially produced objects. This "machine aesthetic" inspired FERNAND LÉGER (1881–1955), a French painter who early on had painted with the Cubists. He devised an effective compromise of tastes, bringing together meticulous Cubist analysis of form with Purism's broad simplification and machinelike finish of the design components. He retained from his Cubist practice a preference for cylindrical and tube-shaped motifs, suggestive of machined parts such as pistons and cylinders.

Léger's works have the sharp precision of the machine, whose beauty and quality he was one of the first artists to discover. For example, in his film *Ballet Mécanique* (1924), Léger contrasted inanimate objects such as functioning machines with humans in dancelike variations. Preeminently the painter of modern urban life, Léger incorporated into his work the massive effects of modern posters and billboard advertisements, the harsh flashing of electric lights, the noise of traffic, and the robotic movements of mechanized people. These effects appear in *The City* (FIG. **35-22**), an early work that incorporates the aesthetic of Synthetic Cubism. Its monumental scale suggests that Léger, had he been given the opportunity, would have been one of the great mural painters of his age. In a definitive way, he depicted the mechanical commotion of urban life.

Futurism

Artists associated with another major early-20th-century movement, *Futurism*, pursued many of the ideas the Cubists explored. Equally important to the Futurists, however, was their well-defined sociopolitical agenda. Inaugurated and given its name by the charismatic Italian poet and playwright Filippo Tommaso Marinetti (1876–1944) in 1909, Futurism began as a literary movement but soon encompassed the visual arts, cinema, theater, music, and architecture. Indignant over the political and cultural decline of Italy, the Futurists published numerous

manifestos in which they aggressively advocated revolution, both in society and in art. Like Die Brücke and other avant-garde artists, the Futurists aimed at ushering in a new, more enlightened era.

In their quest to launch Italian society toward a glorious future, the Futurists championed war as a means of washing away the stagnant past. Indeed, they saw war as a cleansing agent. Marinetti declared: "We will glorify war—the only true hygiene of the world."[10] The Futurists agitated for the destruction of museums, libraries, and

35-23 GIACOMO BALLA, *Dynamism of a Dog on a Leash*, 1912. Oil on canvas, 2' 11⅜" × 3' 7¼". Albright-Knox Art Gallery, Buffalo (bequest of A. Conger Goodyear, gift of George F. Goodyear, 1964). ◼◀

The Futurists' interest in motion and in the Cubist dissection of form is evident in Balla's painting of a passing dog and its owner. Simultaneity of views was central to the Futurist program.

Futurist Manifestos

On April 11, 1910, a group of young Italian artists published *Futurist Painting: Technical Manifesto* in Milan in an attempt to apply the writer Filippo Tommaso Marinetti's views on literature to the visual arts. Signed jointly by Umberto Boccioni (FIG. 35-24), Carlo Carrà, Luigi Russolo, Giacomo Balla (FIG. 35-23), and Gino Severini (FIG. 34-25), the manifesto also appeared in an English translation supervised by Marinetti himself. It states in part:

> On account of the persistency of an image on the retina, moving objects constantly multiply themselves [and] their form changes. . . . Thus a running horse has not four legs, but twenty. . . .

> What was true for the painters of yesterday is but a falsehood today. . . . To paint a human figure you must not paint it; you must render the whole of its surrounding atmosphere. . . . [T]he vivifying current of science [must] soon deliver painting from academic tradition. . . . The shadows which we shall paint shall be more luminous than the highlights of our predecessors, and our pictures, next to those of the museums, will shine like blinding daylight compared with deepest night. . . .

> We declare . . . that all forms of imitation must be despised, all forms of originality glorified . . . that all subjects previously used must be swept aside in order to express our whirling life of steel, of pride, of fever and of speed . . . that movement and light destroy the materiality of bodies.*

Two years later, Boccioni published a *Technical Manifesto of Futurist Sculpture,* in which he argued that traditional sculpture was "a monstrous anachronism" and that modern sculpture should be

> a translation, in plaster, bronze, glass, wood or any other material, of those atmospheric planes which bind and intersect things. . . . Let's . . . proclaim the absolute and complete abolition of finite lines and the contained statue. Let's split open our figures and place the environment inside them. We declare that the environment must form part of the plastic whole.†

Boccioni's own work (FIG. 35-24) is the perfect expression of these principles and goals.

1 ft.

35-24 UMBERTO BOCCIONI, *Unique Forms of Continuity in Space,* 1913 (cast 1931). Bronze, 3′ 7$\frac{7}{8}$″ × 2′ 10$\frac{7}{8}$″ × 1′ 3$\frac{3}{4}$″. Museum of Modern Art, New York (acquired through the Lillie P. Bliss Bequest). ◼◀

Boccioni's Futurist manifesto for sculpture advocated abolishing the enclosed statue. This running figure is so expanded and interrupted that it almost disappears behind the blur of its movement.

* *Futurist Painting: Technical Manifesto* (*Poesia,* April 11, 1910). Translated by Filippo Tommaso Marinetti, in Umbro Apollonio, ed., *Futurist Manifestos* (Boston: Museum of Fine Arts, 1970), 27–31.

† Translated by Robert Brain, in ibid., 51–65.

similar repositories of accumulated culture, which they described as mausoleums. They also called for radical innovation in the arts. Of particular interest to the Futurists were the speed and dynamism of modern technology. Marinetti insisted that a racing "automobile adorned with great pipes like serpents with explosive breath . . . is more beautiful than the *Victory of Samothrace*" (FIG. 5-82, by then representative of classicism and the glories of past civilizations).[11] Appropriately, Futurist art often focuses on motion in time and space, incorporating the Cubist discoveries derived from the analysis of form.

GIACOMO BALLA The Futurists' interest in motion and in the Cubist dissection of form is evident in *Dynamism of a Dog on a Leash* (FIG. 35-23) by GIACOMO BALLA (1871–1958). Here, observers focus their gaze on a passing dog and its owner, whose skirts the artist placed just within visual range. Balla achieved the effect of motion by repeating shapes, as in the dog's legs and tail and in the swinging line of the leash. Simultaneity of views, as demonstrated here, was central to the Futurist program (see "Futurist Manifestos," above).

UMBERTO BOCCIONI One of the artists who cosigned the Futurist manifesto was UMBERTO BOCCIONI (1882–1916), who produced what is perhaps the definitive work of Futurist sculpture, *Unique Forms of Continuity in Space* (FIG. 35-24). This piece highlights the formal and spatial effects of motion rather than their source, the striding human figure. The figure is so expanded, interrupted, and broken in plane and contour that it almost disappears behind the blur of its movement. Boccioni's search for sculptural means for expressing dynamic action reached majestic expression here. In its power and sense of vital activity, this sculpture surpasses similar efforts in Futurist painting to create images symbolic of the dynamic quality of modern life. To be convinced by it, people need only reflect on how details of an adjacent landscape appear in their peripheral vision when they are traveling at great speed on a highway or in a low-flying airplane. Although Boccioni's figure bears a curious resemblance to the ancient *Nike of Samothrace* (FIG. 5-82), even a cursory comparison reveals how far the modern work departs from the ancient one.

35-25 GINO SEVERINI, *Armored Train*, 1915. Oil on canvas, 3′ 10″ × 2′ 10⅛″. Collection of Richard S. Zeisler, New York.

Severini's glistening armored train with protruding cannon reflects the Futurist faith in the cleansing action of war. The painting captures the dynamism and motion central to the Futurist manifesto.

This Futurist representation of motion in sculpture has its limitations. The eventual development of the motion picture, based on the rapid sequential projection of fixed images, produced more convincing illusions of movement. And several decades later in sculpture, Alexander Calder (FIG. **35-61**) pioneered the development of kinetic sculpture—with parts that really move. However, in the early 20th century, Boccioni's sculpture was notable for its ability to capture the sensation of motion.

GINO SEVERINI The painting *Armored Train* (FIG. **35-25**) by GINO SEVERINI (1883–1966) nicely encapsulates the Futurist program, both artistically and politically. The artist depicted a high-tech armored train with its rivets glistening and a huge booming cannon protruding from the top. Submerged in the bowels of the train, a row of soldiers train guns at an unseen target. Severini's painting reflects the Futurist faith in the cleansing action of war. Not only are the colors predominantly light and bright, but the artist also omitted death and destruction—the tragic consequences of war—from the image. This sanitized depiction of war contrasts sharply with Francisco Goya's *Third of May, 1808* (FIG. **30-13**), which also depicts a uniform row of anonymous soldiers in the act of shooting. Goya, however, graphically presented the dead and those about to be shot, and the dark tones of the work cast a dramatic and sobering pall. *Armored Train* captures the dynamism and motion central to Futurism.

In Cubist fashion, Severini depicted all of the objects, from the soldiers to the smoke emanating from the cannon, broken into facets and planes, suggesting action and movement. Once World War I broke out, the Futurist group began to disintegrate, largely because so many of them felt compelled (given the Futurist support for the war) to join the Italian army. Some of them, including Umberto Boccioni, died in the war. The ideas the Futurists promoted became integral to the Fascism that emerged in Italy shortly thereafter.

Dada

Although the Futurists celebrated World War I and the changes they hoped it would effect, the mass destruction and chaos that conflict unleashed horrified other artists. Humanity had never before witnessed such wholesale slaughter on so grand a scale over such an extended period. Millions died or sustained grievous wounds in great battles. For example, in 1916, the battle of Verdun (lasting five months) left 500,000 casualties. On another day in 1916, the British lost 60,000 men in the opening battle of the Somme. The new technology of armaments, bred of the age of steel, made it a "war of the guns" (as in Severini's *Armored Train;* FIG. **35-25**). In the face of massed artillery hurling millions of tons of high explosives and gas shells and in the sheets of fire from thousands of machine guns, attack was suicidal, and battle movement congealed into the stalemate of trench warfare, stretching from the English Channel almost to Switzerland. The mud, filth, and blood of the trenches, the pounding and shattering of incessant shell fire, and the terrible deaths and mutilations were a devastating psychological, as well as physical, experience for a generation brought up with the doctrine of progress and a belief in the fundamental values of civilization.

With the war as a backdrop, many artists contributed to an artistic and literary movement that became known as *Dada*. This movement emerged, in large part, in reaction to what many of these artists saw as nothing more than an insane spectacle of collective homicide. Although Dada began independently in New York and Zurich, it also emerged in Paris, Berlin, and Cologne, among other cities. Dada was more a mind-set or attitude than a single identifiable style. As André Breton (1896–1966), founder of the slightly later Surrealist movement, explained: "Cubism was a school of painting, futurism a political movement: DADA is a state of mind."[12] The Dadaists believed reason and logic had been responsible for the unmitigated disaster of global warfare, and they concluded that the only route to salvation was through political anarchy, the irrational, and the intuitive. Thus, an element of absurdity is a cornerstone of Dada, even reflected in the movement's name. There are many explanations for the choice of "Dada," but according to an often repeated anecdote, the Dadaists chose the word at random from a French-German dictionary. Dada is French for a child's hobbyhorse. The word satisfied the Dadaists' desire for something irrational and nonsensical.

The Dadaists' pessimism and disgust surfaced in their disdain for convention and tradition. These artists made a concerted and sustained attempt to undermine cherished notions and assumptions about art. Because of this destructive dimension, art historians often describe Dada as a nihilistic enterprise. Dada's nihilism and its derisive iconoclasm can be read at random from the Dadaists' numerous manifestos and declarations of intent:

> Dada knows everything. Dada spits on everything. Dada says
> "knowthing," Dada has no fixed ideas. Dada does not catch flies.
> Dada is bitterness laughing at everything that has been accomplished,
> sanctified. . . . Dada is never right. . . . No more painters, no more
> writers, no more religions, no more royalists, no more anarchists,
> no more socialists, no more police, no more airplanes, no more uri-
> nary passages. . . . Like everything in life, Dada is useless, everything

happens in a completely idiotic way.... We are incapable of treating seriously any subject whatsoever, let alone this subject: ourselves.[13]

Although cynicism and pessimism inspired the Dadaists, the movement they developed was phenomenally influential and powerful. By attacking convention and logic, the Dada artists unlocked new avenues for creative invention, thereby fostering a more serious examination of the basic premises of art than had prior movements. But the Dadaists could also be lighthearted in their subversiveness. Although horror and disgust about the war initially prompted Dada, an undercurrent of humor and whimsy—sometimes sardonic or irreverent—runs through much of the art. For example, Marcel Duchamp (see page 930) painted a mustache and goatee on a reproduction of Leonardo da Vinci's *Mona Lisa*. The French painter Francis Picabia (1879–1953), Duchamp's collaborator in setting up Dada in New York, nailed a toy monkey to a board and labeled it *Portrait of Cézanne.*

In its emphasis on the spontaneous and intuitive, Dada paralleled the views of Sigmund Freud (1856–1939) and Carl Jung (1875–1961). Freud was a Viennese doctor who developed the fundamental principles for what became known as psychoanalysis. In his book *The Interpretation of Dreams* (1900), Freud argued that the unconscious and inner drives (of which people are largely unaware) control human behavior. Jung, a Swiss psychiatrist who developed Freud's theories further, believed that the unconscious is composed of two facets, a personal unconscious and a collective unconscious. The collective unconscious comprises memories and associations all humans share, such as archetypes and mental constructions. According to Jung, the collective unconscious accounts for the development of myths, religions, and philosophies.

Particularly interested in the exploration of the unconscious as Freud advocated, the Dada artists believed that art was a powerfully practical means of self-revelation and catharsis, and that the images arising out of the subconscious mind had a truth of their own, independent of conventional vision. A Dada filmmaker, Hans Richter (1888–1976), summarized the attitude of the Dadaists:

> Possessed, as we were, of the ability to entrust ourselves to "chance," to our conscious as well as our unconscious minds, we became a sort of public secret society.... We laughed at everything.... But laughter was only the expression of our new discoveries, not their essence and not their purpose. Pandemonium, destruction, anarchy, anti-everything of the World War? How could Dada have been anything but destructive, aggressive, insolent, on principle and with gusto?[14]

JEAN ARP A Dada artist whose works illustrate Richter's element of chance was Zurich-based JEAN (HANS) ARP (1887–1966). Arp pioneered the use of chance in composing his images. Tiring of the look of some Cubist-related collages he was making, he took some sheets of paper, tore them into roughly shaped squares, haphazardly dropped them onto a sheet of paper on the floor, and glued them into the resulting arrangement. The rectilinearity of the shapes guaranteed a somewhat regular design (which Arp no doubt enhanced by adjusting the random arrangement into a quasi-grid), but chance had introduced an imbalance that seemed to Arp to restore to his work a special mysterious vitality he wanted to preserve. *Collage Arranged According to the Laws of Chance* (FIG. 35-26) is a work he created by this method. The operations of chance were for Dadaists a crucial part of this kind of improvisation. As Richter stated: "For us chance was the 'unconscious mind' that Freud had discovered in 1900.... Adoption of chance had another purpose, a secret one. This was to restore to the work of art its primeval magic power and to find a way back to the immediacy it had lost through contact with ... classicism."[15] Arp's renunciation of artis-

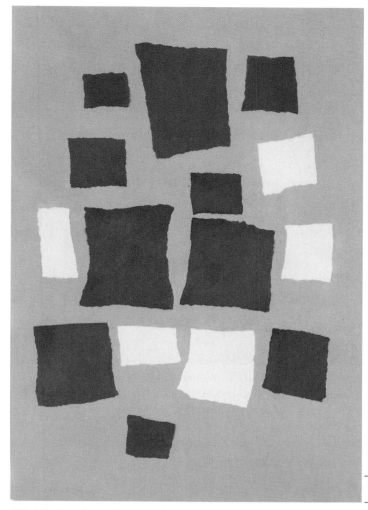

35-26 JEAN (HANS) ARP, *Collage Arranged According to the Laws of Chance*, 1916–1917. Torn and pasted paper, $1' 7\frac{1}{8}'' \times 1' 1\frac{5}{8}''$. Museum of Modern Art, New York.

In this collage, Arp dropped torn paper squares onto a sheet of paper and then glued them into the resulting arrangement. His reliance on chance in composing images reinforced the anarchy inherent in Dada.

tic control and reliance on chance when creating his compositions reinforced the anarchy and subversiveness inherent in Dada.

CABARET VOLTAIRE Among the manifestations of Dada that matured in 1916 in Zurich were the performances presented at the Cabaret Voltaire, founded by Dadaist Hugo Ball (1886–1927), a poet, musician, and theatrical producer. The first Dada performances were fairly tame, consisting of musical presentations and poetry readings. In keeping with Dada thought, however, they quickly became more aggressive, anarchic, and illogical. Tristan Tzara (1896–1963) described one of these performances in characteristically absurd Dadaist language:

> Boxing resumed: Cubist dance, costumes by Janco, each man his own big drum on his head, noise, Negro music/trabatgea bonooooooo oo ooooo/5 literary experiments; Tzara in tails stands before the curtain, stone sober for the animals, and explains the new aesthetic: gymnastic poem, concert of vowels, bruitist poem, static poem chemical arrangement of ideas, 'Biriboom biriboom' saust der Ochs im Kreis herum (the ox dashes round in a ring) (Huelsenbeck), vowel poem a a ò, i e o, a i ï, new interpretation of subjective folly of the arteries the dance of the heart on burning buildings and acrobatics in the audience.[16]

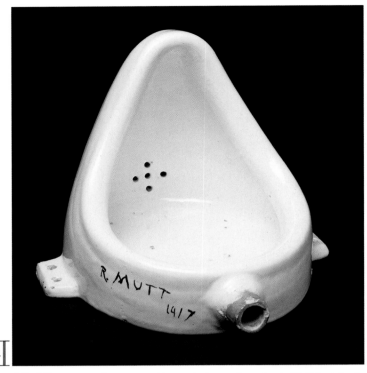

35-27 MARCEL DUCHAMP, *Fountain* (second version), 1950 (original version produced 1917). Readymade glazed sanitary china with black paint, 1′ high. Philadelphia Museum of Art, Philadelphia.

Duchamp's "readymade" sculptures were mass-produced objects that the Dada artist modified. In *Fountain*, he conferred the status of art on a urinal and forced people to see the object in a new light.

35-27A DUCHAMP, *L.H.O.O.Q.*, 1919.

MARCEL DUCHAMP Perhaps the most influential Dadaist was MARCEL DUCHAMP (1887–1968), a Frenchman who became the central artist of New York Dada but was also active in Paris. In 1913 he exhibited his first "readymade" sculptures, which were mass-produced common objects—"found objects" the artist selected and sometimes "rectified" by modifying their substance or combining them with another object. The creation of readymades, he insisted, was free from any consideration of either good or bad taste, qualities shaped by a society he and other Dada artists found aesthetically bankrupt. Perhaps his most outrageous readymade was *Fountain* (FIG. **35-27**), a porcelain urinal presented on its back, signed "R. Mutt," and dated. The "artist's signature" was, in fact, a witty pseudonym derived from the Mott plumbing company's name and that of the short half of the then-popular Mutt and Jeff comic-strip team. As with Duchamp's other readymades, he did not select this object for exhibition because of its aesthetic qualities. The "art" of this "artwork" lies in the artist's choice of object, which has the effect of conferring the status of art on it and forces the viewer to see the object in a new light. As he wrote in a "defense" published in 1917, after an exhibition committee rejected *Fountain* for display: "Whether Mr. Mutt with his own hands made the fountain or not has no importance. He CHOSE it. He took an ordinary article of life, placed it so that its useful significance disappeared under the new title and point of view—created a new thought for that object."[17] It is hard to imagine a more aggressively avant-garde approach to art. Dada persistently presented staggering challenges to artistic conventions.

THE LARGE GLASS Among the most visually and conceptually challenging of Duchamp's works is *The Bride Stripped Bare by Her Bachelors, Even* (FIG. **35-28**), often referred to as *The Large Glass*. Begun in 1915 and abandoned by Duchamp as unfinished in 1923,

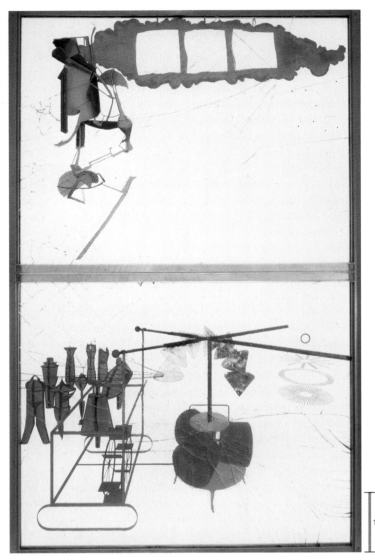

35-28 MARCEL DUCHAMP, *The Bride Stripped Bare by Her Bachelors, Even* (*The Large Glass*), 1915–1923. Oil, lead, wire, foil, dust, and varnish on glass, 9′ 1½″ × 5′ 9⅛″. Philadelphia Museum of Art, Philadelphia (Katherine S. Dreier Bequest).

The Large Glass is a simultaneously playful and serious examination of humans as machines. The bride is a motor fueled by "love gasoline," and the male figures in the lower half also move mechanically.

The Large Glass is a simultaneously playful and serious examination of humans as machines. Consisting of oil paint, wire, and lead foil sandwiched in between two large glass panels, the artwork presents the viewer with an array of images, some apparently mechanical, others diagrammatic, and yet others seemingly abstract in nature. Duchamp provided some clues to the intriguing imagery in a series of notes that accompanied the work. The top half of the work represents "the bride," whom Duchamp has depicted as "basically a motor" fueled by "love gasoline." In contrast, the bachelors appear as uniformed male figures in the lower half of the work. They too move mechanically. The chocolate grinder in the center of the lower glass pane represents masturbation ("the bachelor grinds his own chocolate"). In *The Large Glass*, Duchamp provided his own whimsical but insightful ruminations into the ever-confounding realm of desire and sexuality. In true Dadaist fashion, chance completed the work. During the transportation of *The Large Glass* from an exhibition in 1927, the glass panes shattered. Rather than replace the broken glass, Duchamp painstakingly pieced together the glass fragments. After encasing the recon-

35-29 Hannah Höch, *Cut with the Kitchen Knife Dada through the Last Weimar Beer Belly Cultural Epoch of Germany,* 1919–1920. Photomontage, 3′ 9″ × 2′ 11½″. Neue Nationalgalerie, Staatliche Museen zu Berlin, Berlin. ◼◄

In Höch's photomontage, photographs of some of her fellow Dadaists appear among images of Marx and Lenin, and the artist juxtaposed herself with a map of Europe showing the progress of women.

1 ft.

sity a technique that had been used in private and popular arts long before the 20th century to create a composition by pasting together pieces of paper. A few years earlier, the Cubists had named the process "collage." The Berliners christened their version of the technique *photomontage.* Unlike Cubist collage (FIGS. 35-16 and 35-17), the parts of a Dada collage consisted almost entirely of "found" details, such as pieces of magazine photographs, usually combined into deliberately antilogical compositions. Collage lent itself well to the Dada desire to use chance when creating art and antiart, but not all Dada collage was as savagely aggressive as that of the Berlin photomontagists.

structed work, broken panes and all, between two heavier panes of glass, Duchamp declared the work completed "by chance."

Duchamp (and the generations of later artists who were profoundly influenced by his art and especially his attitude) considered life and art matters of chance and choice freed from the conventions of society and tradition. Within his approach to art and life, each act was individual and unique. Every person's choice of found objects would be different, for example, and each person's throw of the dice would be at a different instant and probably would yield a different number. This philosophy of utter freedom for artists was fundamental to the history of art in the 20th century. Duchamp spent much of World War I in New York, inspiring a group of American artists and collectors with his radical rethinking of the role of artists and of the nature of art.

HANNAH HÖCH Dada spread throughout much of western Europe, arriving as early as 1917 in Berlin, where it soon took on an activist political edge, partially in response to the economic, social, and political chaos in that city in the years at the end of and immediately after World War I. The Berlin Dadaists developed to a new inten-

One of the Berlin Dadaists who perfected the photomontage technique was Hannah Höch (1889–1978). Höch's photomontages advanced the absurd illogic of Dada by presenting the viewer with chaotic, contradictory, and satiric compositions. They also provided insightful and scathing commentary on two of the most dramatic developments during the Weimar Republic (1918–1933) in Germany— the redefinition of women's social roles and the explosive growth of mass print media. She revealed these combined themes in *Cut with the Kitchen Knife Dada through the Last Weimar Beer Belly Cultural Epoch of Germany* (FIG. 35-29). In this work Höch arranged an eclectic mixture of cutout photos in seemingly haphazard fashion. On closer inspection, however, the viewer can see that the artist carefully placed photographs of some of her fellow Dadaists among images of Marx, Lenin, and other revolutionary figures in the lower right section, aligning this movement with other revolutionary forces. She promoted Dada in prominently placed cutout lettering— "Die grosse Welt dada" (the great Dada world). Certainly, juxtaposing the heads of German military leaders with exotic dancers' bodies provided the wickedly humorous critique central to much of Dada. Höch also positioned herself in this topsy-turvy world she created.

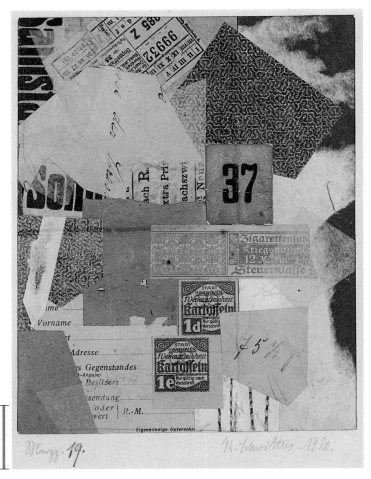

1 in.

35-30 KURT SCHWITTERS, *Merz 19*, 1920. Paper collage, $7\frac{1}{4}'' \times 5\frac{7}{8}''$. Yale University Art Gallery, New Haven (gift of Collection Société Anonyme).

Inspired by Cubist collage but working nonobjectively, Schwitters found visual poetry in the cast-off junk of modern society, which he pasted and nailed together into striking Dada compositions.

A photograph of her head appears in the lower right corner, juxtaposed with a map of Europe showing the progress of women's enfranchisement. Aware of the power both women and Dada had to destabilize society, Höch made forceful visual manifestations of that belief.

KURT SCHWITTERS The Hanover Dada artist KURT SCHWITTERS (1887–1948) followed a gentler muse. Inspired by Cubist collage but working nonobjectively, Schwitters found visual poetry in the cast-off junk of modern society and scavenged in trash bins for materials, which he pasted and nailed together into designs such as *Merz 19* (FIG. **35-30**). The term "Merz," which Schwitters used as a generic title for a whole series of collages, derived nonsensically from the German word Kommerzbank (commerce bank) and appeared as a word fragment in one of his compositions. Although nonobjective, his collages still resonate with the meaning of the fragmented found objects they contain. The recycled elements of Schwitters's collages, like Duchamp's readymades, acquire new meanings through their new uses and locations. Elevating objects that are essentially trash to the status of high art certainly fits within the parameters of the Dada program and parallels the absurd dimension of much of Dada art. Contradiction, paradox, irony, and even blasphemy are Dada's bequest. They are, in the view of Dada and its successors, the free and defiant artist's weapons in what has been called the hundred years' war with the public.

AMERICA, 1900 TO 1930

Avant-garde experiments in the arts were not limited to Europe. A wide range of artists engaged in a lively exchange of artistic ideas and significant transatlantic travel. In the latter part of the 19th century, American artists such as John Singer Sargent (see Chapter 30), James Abbott McNeil Whistler, and Mary Cassatt (see Chapter 31) spent much of their productive careers in Europe, whereas many European artists ended their careers in America, especially in anticipation of and, later, in the wake of World War I. Visionary patrons sup-

35-31 JOHN SLOAN, *Sixth Avenue and Thirtieth Street, New York City*, 1907. Oil on canvas, $2' \frac{1}{4}'' \times$ 2′ 8″. Philadelphia Museum of Art, Philadelphia (gift of Meyer P. Potamkin and Vivian O. Potamkin, 2000).

A prominent member of the American Realist group called The Eight, Sloan captured in his paintings the bleak and seedy aspects of the rapidly changing urban landscape of New York City.

1 in.

Art "Matronage" in America

Until the 20th century, the dearth of women artists was often due to professional institutions that restricted women's access to artistic training. For example, the proscription against women participating in life-drawing classes, a staple of academic artistic training, in effect denied women the opportunity to become professional artists. Further, the absence of women from the art historical canon is also partly because art historians have not considered as "high art" many of the art objects women have traditionally produced (for example, quilts or basketry).

By the early 20th century, many of the impediments to women becoming recognized artists had been removed. Today, women are a major presence in the art world. One development in the early 20th century that laid the groundwork for this change was the prominent role women played as art patrons. These "art matrons" provided financial, moral, and political support to cultivate the advancement of the arts in America. Among these women were Gertrude Vanderbilt Whitney, Lillie P. Bliss, Mary Quinn Sullivan, Abby Aldrich Rockefeller, Isabella Stewart Gardner, Peggy Guggenheim, and Jane Stanford.*

Gertrude Vanderbilt Whitney (1875–1942) was a practicing sculptor and enthusiastic collector. To assist young American artists such as Robert Henri and John Sloan (FIG. 35-31) to exhibit their work, she opened the Whitney Studio in 1914. By 1929, dissatisfied with the recognition accorded young, progressive American artists, she offered her entire collection of 500 works to the Metropolitan Museum of Art. Her offer rejected, she founded her own museum, the Whitney Museum of American Art in New York City. She chose as the first director a visionary and energetic woman, Juliana Force (1876–1948), who inaugurated a pioneering series of monographs on living American artists and organized lecture series by influential art historians and critics. Through the efforts of these two women, the Whitney Museum became a major force in American art.

A trip to Paris in 1920 whetted the interest of Peggy Guggenheim (1898–1979) in avant-garde art. Like Whitney, she collected art and eventually opened a gallery in England to exhibit the work of in-novative artists. She continued her support for avant-garde art after her return to the United States. Guggenheim's New York gallery, called Art of This Century, was instrumental in advancing the careers of many artists, including her husband, Max Ernst (FIG. 35-47). She eventually moved her art collection to a lavish Venetian palace, where the public can still view these important artworks.

Other women contributed significantly to the arts, including Lillie P. Bliss (1864–1931), Mary Quinn Sullivan (1877–1939), and Abby Aldrich Rockefeller (1874–1948). Philanthropists, art collectors, and educators, these visionary and influential women saw the need for a museum to collect and exhibit modernist art. Together they established the Museum of Modern Art in New York City in 1929, which became (and continues to be) the most influential museum of modern art in the world (see "The Museum of Modern Art," page 954).

Isabella Stewart Gardner (1840–1924) and Jane Stanford (1828–1905) also undertook the ambitious project of founding museums. The Isabella Stewart Gardner Museum in Boston, established in 1903, contains an impressive collection of art that is comprehensive in scope. The Stanford Museum, the first American museum west of the Mississippi, got its start in 1905 on the grounds of Stanford University, which Leland Stanford Sr. and Jane Stanford founded after the tragic death of their son. The Stanford Museum houses a wide range of objects, including archaeological and ethnographic artifacts. These two driven women committed much of their time, energy, and financial resources to ensure the success of these museums. Both were intimately involved in the day-to-day operations of their institutions.

The museums these women established flourish today, attesting to the extraordinary vision of these "art matrons" and the remarkable contributions they made to the advancement of art in the United States.

* Art historian Wanda Corn coined the term "art matronage" in the catalog *Cultural Leadership in America: Art Matronage and Patronage* (Boston: Isabella Stewart Gardner Museum, 1997).

---

ported the efforts of American artists to pursue modernist ideas (see "Art 'Matronage' in America," above).

Painting and Sculpture

The art scene in America before the establishment of a significant and consistent dialogue with European modernists was, of course, quite varied. However, many American artists active in the early 20th century were committed to presenting what they considered to be a realistic, unvarnished look at life. In this regard, their work parallels that of the French Realists in the mid-19th century (see Chapter 30).

JOHN SLOAN AND THE EIGHT One group of American Realist artists, The Eight, consisted of eight painters who gravitated into the circle of the influential and evangelical artist and teacher Robert Henri (1865–1929). Henri urged his followers to make "pictures from life,"[18] and accordingly, these artists pursued with zeal the production of images depicting the rapidly changing urban landscape of New York City. Because these vignettes often captured the bleak and seedy aspects of city life, The Eight eventually became known as the Ash Can School. Some critics referred to them as "the apostles of ugliness."

A prominent member of The Eight was JOHN SLOAN (1871–1951). A self-described "incorrigible window watcher,"[19] Sloan constantly wandered the streets of New York, observing human drama. He focused much of his attention on the working class, which he perceived as embodying the realities of life. So sympathetic was Sloan to the working class that he joined the Socialist Party in 1909 and eventually ran for public office on the Socialist ticket. In paintings such as *Sixth Avenue and Thirtieth Street* (FIG. 35-31), Sloan revealed his ability to capture both the visual and social realities of American urban life shortly after the turn of the century. When he painted this image in 1907, Sloan was living on West 23rd Street, on the outskirts

The Armory Show

From February 17 to March 15, 1913, the American public flocked in large numbers to view the International Exhibition of Modern Art (FIG. 35-32) at the 69th Regiment Armory in New York City. The "Armory Show," as it came universally to be called, was an ambitious endeavor organized primarily by two artists, Walt Kuhn (1877–1949) and Arthur B. Davies (1862–1928). The show contained more than 1,600 artworks by American and European artists. Among the European artists represented were Matisse, Derain, Picasso, Braque, Duchamp, Kandinsky, Kirchner, Lehmbruck, and Brancusi. In addition to exposing American artists and the public to the latest in European artistic developments, this show also provided American artists with a prime showcase for their work. The foreword to the exhibition catalogue spelled out the goals of the organizers:

> The American artists exhibiting here consider the exhibition of equal importance for themselves as for the public. The less they find their work showing signs of the developments indicated in the Europeans, the more reason they will have to consider whether or not painters or sculptors here have fallen behind . . . the forces that have manifested themselves on the other side of the Atlantic.*

On its opening, this provocative exhibition served as a lightning rod for commentary, immediately attracting heated controversy. The *New York Times* described the show as "pathological" and called the modernist artists "cousins to the anarchists," while the magazine *Art and Progress* compared them to "bomb throwers, lunatics, depravers."[†] Other critics demanded the exhibition be closed as a menace to public morality. The *New York Herald*, for example, asserted: "The United States is invaded by aliens, thousands of whom constitute so many perils to the health of the body politic. Modernism is of precisely the same heterogeneous alien origin and is imperiling the republic of art in the same way."[‡]

35-32 Installation photo of the Armory Show, New York National Guard's 69th Regiment, New York, 1913. Museum of Modern Art, New York.

The groundbreaking Armory Show introduced European modernism to the American public. Works like Duchamp's *Nude Descending a Staircase* (FIG. 35-1) received a hostile reception in the press.

Nonetheless, the exhibition was an important milestone in the history of art in the United States. The Armory Show traveled to Chicago and Boston after it closed in New York and was a significant catalyst for the reevaluation of the nature and purpose of American art.

* Quoted in Herschel B. Chipp, *Theories of Modern Art: A Source Book by Artists and Critics* (Berkeley and Los Angeles: University of California Press, 1968), 503.
[†] Quoted in Sam Hunter, John Jacobus, and Daniel Wheeler, *Modern Art*, rev. 3d ed. (Upper Saddle Hill, N.J.: Prentice Hall, 2005), 250.
[‡] Quoted in Francis K. Pohl, *Framing America: A Social History of American Art* (New York: Thames & Hudson, 2002), 321.

---

of the Tenderloin District, an area cluttered with brothels, dance halls, saloons, gambling dens, and cheap hotels. *Sixth Avenue* depicts a bustling intersection. Bracketing the throngs of people filling the intersection are elevated train tracks on the left and a row of storefronts and apartment buildings on the right side of the painting. These two defining elements of city life converge in the far center background. Sloan's paintings also capture a slice of American urban life in the cross-section of people depicted. In the foreground of *Sixth Avenue*, Sloan prominently placed three women. One, in a shabby white dress, is a drunkard, stumbling along with her pail of beer. Two streetwalkers stare at her. In turn, two well-dressed men gaze at the prostitutes. Sloan's depiction of the women allied him with reformers of the time, who saw streetwalkers not as immoral but as victims of an unfair social and economic system. At a time

when traditional art centered on genteel and proper society, Sloan's forthright depiction of prostitutes was categorically "Realist."

ARMORY SHOW One of the major vehicles for disseminating information about European artistic developments in the United States was the Armory Show (FIG. **35-32**), held in early 1913 (see "The Armory Show," above). The exhibition received a hostile response from the press. The work the journalists and critics most maligned was Marcel Duchamp's *Nude Descending a Staircase, No. 2* (FIG. **35-1**). The painting, a single figure in motion down a staircase in a time continuum, suggests the effect of a sequence of overlaid film stills. Unlike Duchamp's contributions to the Dada movement (FIGS. **35-27** and **35-28**), *Nude Descending a Staircase* has much in common with the work of the Cubists and the Futurists.

The monochromatic palette is reminiscent of Analytic Cubism, as is Duchamp's faceted presentation of the human form. The artist's interest in depicting the figure in motion reveals an affinity for the Futurists' ideas. One critic described this work as "an explosion in a shingle factory,"[20] and newspaper cartoonists had a field day lampooning the painting.

MAN RAY One American artist to incorporate the latest European trends in his work was Emmanuel Radnitzky, known as MAN RAY (1890–1976), who was a close associate of Duchamp in the 1920s. Man Ray produced art with a decidedly Dada spirit, often incorporating found objects in his paintings, sculptures, movies, and photographs. Trained as an architectural draftsman and engineer, Man Ray earned his living as a graphic designer and portrait photographer. He brought to his personal work an interest in mass-produced objects and technology, as well as a dedication to exploring the psychological realm of human perception of the exterior world. Like Schwitters, Man Ray used chance and the dislocation of ordinary things from their everyday settings to surprise his viewers into new awareness. His displacement of found objects was particularly effective in works such as *Cadeau* (*Gift;* FIG. **35-33**). For this sculpture, Man Ray—with characteristic Dada humor—equipped a laundry iron with a row of wicked-looking spikes, subverting its proper function of smoothing and pressing.

MARSDEN HARTLEY Other American artists developed personal styles that intersected with movements such as Cubism. MARSDEN HARTLEY (1877–1943) traveled to Europe in 1912, visiting Paris, where he became acquainted with the work of the Cubists, and Munich, where he gravitated to the Blaue Reiter circle. Kandinsky's work particularly impressed Hartley, and he developed a style he called "Cosmic Cubism." He took these influences with him when he landed in Berlin in 1913. With the heightened militarism in Germany and the eventual outbreak of World War I, Hartley immersed himself in military imagery. Among his most famous paintings of this period is *Portrait of a German Officer* (FIG. **35-34**). It depicts an array of military-related images: German imperial flags, regimental insignia, badges, and emblems such as the Iron Cross. Although this image resonates in the general context of wartime militarism, elements in the painting did have personal significance for Hartley. In particular, the painting includes references to his lover, Lieutenant Karl von Freyberg, who lost his life in battle a few months before Hartley painted this work. Von Freyberg's initials appear in the lower

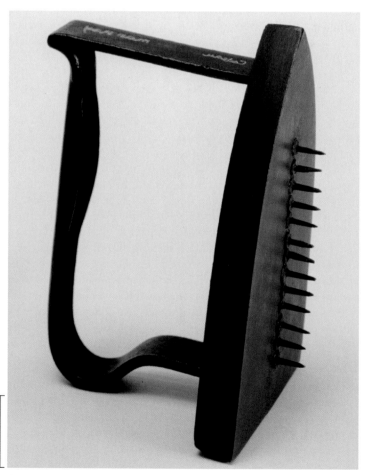

35-33 MAN RAY, *Cadeau* (*Gift*), ca. 1958 (replica of 1921 original). Painted flatiron with row of 13 tacks with heads glued to the bottom, $6\frac{1}{8}'' \times 3\frac{5}{8}'' \times 4\frac{1}{2}''$. Museum of Modern Art, New York (James Thrall Soby Fund).

With characteristic Dada humor, the American artist Man Ray equipped a laundry iron with a row of wicked-looking spikes, subverting its proper function of smoothing and pressing.

35-34 MARSDEN HARTLEY, *Portrait of a German Officer,* 1914. Oil on canvas, $5' 8\frac{1}{4}'' \times 3' 5\frac{3}{8}''$. Metropolitan Museum of Art, New York (Alfred Stieglitz Collection).

In this elegy to a lover killed in battle, Hartley arranged military-related images against a somber black background. The flattened, planar presentation reveals the influence of Synthetic Cubism.

left corner. His age when he died (24) appears in the lower right corner, and his regiment number (4) appears in the center of the painting. Also incorporated is the letter *E* for von Freyberg's regiment, the Bavarian Eisenbahn. The influence of Synthetic Cubism is evident in the flattened, planar presentation of the elements, which almost appear as abstract patterns. The somber black background against which the artist placed the colorful stripes, patches, and shapes casts an elegiac pall over the painting.

STUART DAVIS Philadelphia-born STUART DAVIS (1894–1964) created what he believed was a modern American art style by combining the flat shapes of Synthetic Cubism with his sense of jazz tempos and his perception of the energy of fast-paced American culture.

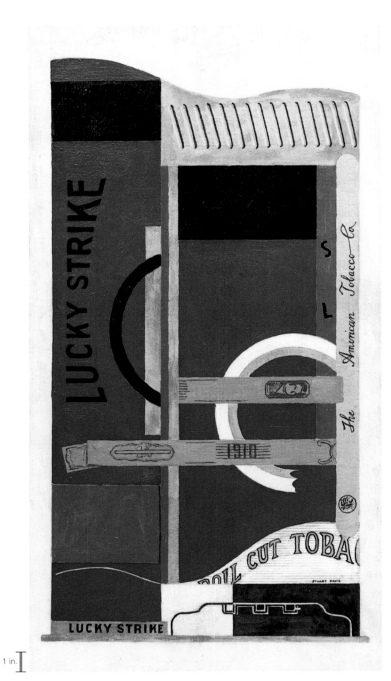

1 in.

35-35 STUART DAVIS, *Lucky Strike,* 1921. Oil on canvas, 2′ 9¼″ × 1′ 6″. Museum of Modern Art, New York (gift of the American Tobacco Company, Inc.). Art © Estate of Stuart Davis/Licensed by VAGA, New York.

Tobacco products fascinated Davis, a heavy smoker. In *Lucky Strike,* he depicted a cigarette package in fragmented form, reminiscent of Cubism, and imbued his painting with an American jazz rhythm.

Lucky Strike (FIG. **35-35**) is one of several tobacco still lifes Davis began in 1921. Davis was a heavy smoker, and tobacco products and their packaging fascinated him. He insisted that the late-19th-century introduction of packaging was evidence of high civilization and therefore, he concluded, of the progressiveness of American culture. Davis depicted the Lucky Strike package in fragmented form, reminiscent of Synthetic Cubist collages. However, although the work does incorporate flat printed elements, these are illusionistically painted rather than glued onto the canvas surface. The discontinuities and the interlocking planes imbue *Lucky Strike* with a dynamism and rhythm not unlike American jazz or the pace of life in a lively American metropolis. This work is both resolutely American and modern.

AARON DOUGLAS Also deriving his personal style from Synthetic Cubism was African American artist AARON DOUGLAS (1898–1979), who used the style to represent symbolically the historical and cultural memories of African Americans. Born in Kansas, Douglas studied in Nebraska and Paris before settling in New York City, where he became part of the flowering of art and literature in the 1920s known as the Harlem Renaissance. Spearheaded by writers and editors Alain Locke and Charles Johnson, the Harlem Renaissance was a manifestation of the desire of African Americans to promote their cultural accomplishments. They also aimed to cultivate pride among fellow African Americans and to foster racial tolerance across the United States. Expansive and diverse, the fruits of the Harlem Renaissance included the writings of authors such as Langston Hughes, Countee Cullen, and Zora Neale Hurston; the jazz and blues of Duke Ellington, Bessie Smith, Eubie Blake, Fats Waller, and Louis Armstrong; the photographs of James Van Der Zee and Prentice H. Polk; and the paintings and sculptures of Meta Warrick Fuller and Augusta Savage.

35-36A DOUGLAS, *Slavery through Reconstruction,* 1934.

Aaron Douglas arrived in New York City in 1924 and became one of the most sought-after graphic artists in the African American community. Encouraged to create art that would express the cultural history of his race, Douglas incorporated motifs from African sculpture into compositions painted in a version of Synthetic Cubism that stressed transparent angular planes. *Noah's Ark* (FIG. **35-36**) was one of seven paintings based on a book of poems by James Weldon Johnson (1871–1938) called *God's Trombones: Seven Negro Sermons in Verse.* Douglas used flat planes to evoke a sense of mystical space and miraculous happenings. In *Noah's Ark,* lightning strikes and rays of light crisscross the pairs of animals entering the ark, while men load supplies in preparation for departure. The artist suggested deep space by differentiating the size of the large human head and shoulders of the worker at the bottom and the small person at work on the far deck of the ship. Yet the composition's unmodulated color shapes create a pattern on the Masonite surface that cancels any illusion of three-dimensional depth. Here, Douglas used Cubism's formal language to express a powerful religious vision.

PRECISIONISM It is obvious from viewing American art in the period immediately after the Armory Show that the latest European avant-garde art, from Cubism to Dada, intrigued American artists. However, the Americans did not just passively absorb the ideas transported across the Atlantic. The challenge was to understand the ideas modernist European art presented and then filter them through an American sensibility. Ultimately, many American artists, including a group that became known as Precisionists, set as their goal the development of a uniquely American art.

Precisionism was not an organized movement, but the Precisionists did share certain thematic and stylistic traits in their art, which developed in the 1920s out of a fascination with the machine's precision and importance in modern life. Although many European

35-36 AARON DOUGLAS, *Noah's Ark,* ca. 1927. Oil on Masonite, 4′ × 3′. Fisk University Galleries, University of Tennessee, Nashville.

In *Noah's Ark* and other paintings of the cultural history of African Americans, Douglas incorporated motifs from African sculpture and the transparent angular planes characteristic of Synthetic Cubism.

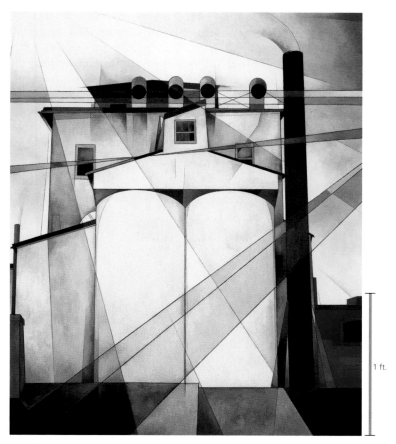

35-37 CHARLES DEMUTH, *My Egypt,* 1927. Oil on composition board, 2′ 11¾″ × 2′ 6″. Collection of Whitney Museum of American Art, New York (purchased with funds from Gertrude Vanderbilt Whitney).

Demuth was one of the leading Precisionists—American artists who extolled the machine age. This painting depicts grain elevators reduced to geometric forms amid Cubist transparent diagonal planes.

artists, especially the Futurists, had demonstrated interest in burgeoning technology, Americans generally seemed more enamored by the prospects of a mechanized society than did Europeans. Even the Frenchman Francis Picabia, Duchamp's collaborator, noted: "Since machinery is the soul of the modern world, and since the genius of machinery attains its highest expression in America, why is it not reasonable to believe that in America the art of the future will flower most brilliantly?"[21] Precisionism, however, expanded beyond the exploration of machine imagery. Many artists associated with this group gravitated toward Synthetic Cubism's flat, sharply delineated planes as an appropriate visual idiom for their imagery, adding to the clarity and precision of their work. Eventually, Precisionism came to be characterized by a merging of a familiar native style in American architecture and artifacts with a modernist vocabulary derived largely from Synthetic Cubism.

CHARLES DEMUTH One of the leading Precisionists was CHARLES DEMUTH (1883–1935), who spent the years 1912–1914 in Paris and thus had firsthand exposure to Cubism and other avant-garde directions in art. He incorporated the spatial discontinuities characteristic of Cubism into his work, focusing much of it on industrial sites near his native Lancaster, Pennsylvania. *My Egypt* (FIG. 35-37) is a prime example of Precisionist painting. Demuth depicted the John W. Eshelman and Sons grain elevators, which he

reduced to simple geometric forms. The grain elevators remain insistently recognizable and solid. However, the "beams" of transparent planes and the diagonal force lines threaten to destabilize the image and correspond to Cubist fragmentation of space. The degree to which Demuth intended to extol the American industrial scene is unclear. The title, *My Egypt,* is sufficiently ambiguous in tone to accommodate differing readings. On the one hand, Demuth could have been suggesting a favorable comparison between the Egyptian pyramids and American grain elevators as cultural icons. On the other hand, the title could be read cynically, as a negative comment on the limitations of American culture.

GEORGIA O'KEEFFE The work of Wisconsin-born GEORGIA O'KEEFFE (1887–1986), like that of many artists, changed stylistically throughout her career. During the 1920s, O'Keeffe was a Precisionist. She had moved from the tiny town of Canyon to New York City in 1918, and although she had visited the city before, what she found there excited her. "You have to live in today," she told a friend. "Today the city is something bigger, more complex than ever before in history. And nothing can be gained from running away. I couldn't even if I could."[22] While in New York, O'Keeffe met Alfred Stieglitz (FIG. 35-39), who played a major role in promoting the avant-garde in the United States. Stieglitz had established an art gallery at 291 Fifth Avenue in New York. In "291," as the gallery came to be called, he exhibited the latest in both European and American art. Thus, 291, like the Armory Show, played an important role in the history of early-20th-century art in America. Stieglitz had seen and exhibited some of O'Keeffe's earlier

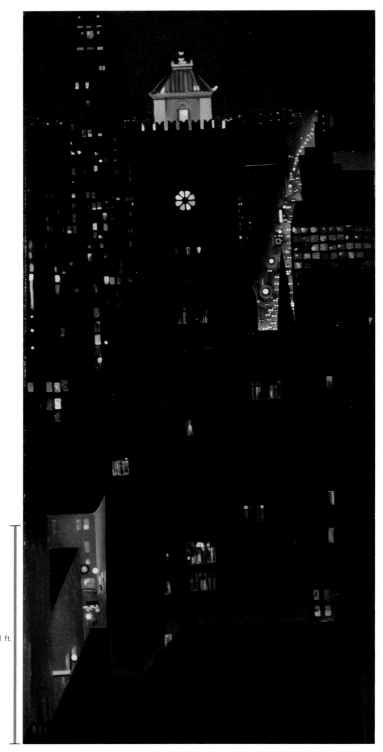

35-38 GEORGIA O'KEEFFE, *New York, Night,* 1929. Oil on canvas, 3′ 4$\frac{1}{8}$″ × 1′ 7$\frac{1}{8}$″. Sheldon Memorial Art Gallery, Lincoln (Nebraska Art Association, Thomas C. Woods Memorial Collection).

O'Keeffe's Precisionist representation of New York's soaring skyscrapers reduces the buildings to large, simple, dark planes punctuated by small windows that add rhythm and energy to the image.

work and drew her into his circle of avant-garde painters and photographers. Stieglitz became one of O'Keeffe's staunchest supporters and, eventually, her husband. The interest of Stieglitz and his circle in capturing the sensibility of the machine age intersected with O'Keeffe's fascination with the fast pace of city life, and she produced paintings during this period, such as *New York, Night* (FIG. **35-38**), that depict the soaring skyscrapers dominating the city. Like other Precisionists,

O'Keeffe reduced her images to simple planes, here punctuated by small rectangular windows that add rhythm and energy to the image, countering the monolithic darkness of the looming buildings.

Despite O'Keeffe's affiliation with the Precisionist movement and New York, she is probably best known for her paintings of cow skulls and of flowers, for example, *Jack in the Pulpit No. 4* (FIG. I-4), which reveals her interest in stripping subjects to their purest forms and colors to heighten their expressive power. In this work, O'Keeffe reduced the incredible details of a flower to a symphony of basic colors, shapes, textures, and vital rhythms. Exhibiting the natural flow of curved planes and contour, O'Keeffe simplified the form almost to the point of complete abstraction. The fluid planes unfold like undulant petals from a subtly placed axis—the white jetlike streak—in a vision of the slow, controlled motion of growing life. O'Keeffe's painting, in its graceful, quiet poetry, reveals the organic reality of the object by strengthening its characteristic features.

Photography

35-39A STIEGLITZ, *Equivalent,* 1923.

ALFRED STIEGLITZ As an artist, ALFRED STIEGLITZ (1864–1946) is best known for his photographs. Taking his camera everywhere he went, he photographed whatever he saw around him, from the bustling streets of New York City to cloudscapes in upstate New York and the faces of friends and relatives. He believed in making only "straight, unmanipulated" photographs. Thus, he exposed and printed them using basic photographic processes, without resorting to techniques such as double-exposure or double-printing that would add information not present in the subject when he released the shutter. Stieglitz said he wanted the photographs he made with this direct technique "to hold a moment, to record something so completely that those who see it would relive an equivalent of what has been expressed."[23]

Stieglitz began a lifelong campaign to win a place for photography among the fine arts while he was a student of photochemistry in Germany. Returning to New York, he founded the Photo-Secession group, which mounted traveling exhibitions in the United States and sent loan collections abroad, and he also published an influential journal titled *Camera Work*. In his own works, Stieglitz specialized in photographs of his environment and saw these subjects in terms of arrangements of forms and of the "colors" of his black-and-white materials. His aesthetic approach crystallized during the making of *The Steerage* (FIG. **35-39**), taken during a voyage to Europe with his first wife and daughter in 1907. Traveling first class, Stieglitz rapidly grew bored with the company of the prosperous passengers in that section of the ship. He walked as far forward on the first-class level as he could, when the rail around the opening onto the lower deck brought him up short. This level was for the steerage passengers the government sent back to Europe after refusing them entrance into the United States. Later, Stieglitz described what happened next:

> The scene fascinated me: A round hat; the funnel leaning left, the stairway leaning right; the white drawbridge, its railing made of chain; white suspenders crossed on the back of a man below; circular iron machinery; a mast that cut into the sky, completing a triangle. I stood spellbound. I saw shapes related to one another—a picture of shapes, and underlying it, a new vision that held me: simple people; the feeling of ship, ocean, sky; a sense of release that I was away from the mob called rich. Rembrandt came into my mind and I wondered would he have felt as I did. . . . I had only one plate holder with one unexposed plate. Could I catch what I saw and felt? I released the shutter. If I had captured what I wanted, the photograph would go far beyond any of my previous prints. It would be a picture based on related shapes and deepest human feeling—a step in my own evolution, a spontaneous discovery.[24]

1 in.

This description reveals Stieglitz's abiding interest in the formal elements of the photograph—an insistently modernist focus. The finished print fulfilled Stieglitz's vision so well that it shaped his future photographic work, and its haunting mixture of found patterns and human activity has continued to stir viewers' emotions to this day.

EDWARD WESTON Stieglitz's concern for positioning photography as an art form with the same fine-art status as painting and sculpture was also the aim of EDWARD WESTON (1886–1958). In addition to making "straight" photographs, like those of Stieglitz, Weston experimented with photographs that moved toward greater abstraction, paralleling developments in other media. *Nude* (FIG. 35-40) is an example of the latter photographic style. The image's simplicity and the selection of a small segment of the human body as the subject result in a lyrical photograph of dark and light areas that at first glance suggests a landscape. Further inspection reveals the fluid curves and underlying skeletal armature of the human form. This photograph, in its reductiveness, formally expresses a study of the body that verges on the abstract.

35-40A WESTON, *Pepper No. 30*, 1930.

1 in.

EUROPE, 1920 TO 1945

Because World War I was fought entirely on European soil, European artists experienced its devastating effects to a much greater degree than did their American counterparts. The war had a profound impact on Europe's geopolitical terrain, on individual and national psyches, and on the art of the 1920s and 1930s.

Picasso in the 1930s

The previous discussion of Pablo Picasso focused on his immersion in aesthetic issues, but he was acutely aware of politics throughout his life. As Picasso watched his homeland descend into civil war in the late 1930s, his involvement in political issues grew even stronger. He declared: "[P]ainting is not made to decorate apartments. It is an instrument for offensive and defensive war against the enemy."[25]

GUERNICA In January 1937, the Spanish Republican government-in-exile in Paris asked Picasso to produce a major work for the Spanish Pavilion at the Paris International Exposition that summer. Picasso was well aware of the immense visibility and large international audience this opportunity afforded him, but he did not formally accept this invitation until he received word that Guernica, capital of the Basque region (an area in southern France and northern Spain populated by Basque speakers), had been almost totally destroyed in an air raid on April 26 by Nazi bombers acting on behalf of the rebel general Francisco Franco (1892–1975). Not only did the Germans attack the city itself, but because they dropped their bombs at the busiest hour of a market day, they also killed or wounded many of Guernica's 7,000 citizens. The event jolted Picasso into action. By the end of June, he had completed *Guernica* (FIG. **35-41**), a mural-sized canvas of immense power.

Despite the painting's title, Picasso made no specific reference to the event in *Guernica*—no bombs, no German planes. Rather, the collected images in *Guernica* combine to create a visceral outcry of human grief. In the center, along the lower edge of the painting, lies a slain warrior clutching a broken and useless sword. A gored horse tramples him and rears back in fright as it dies. On the left, a shrieking, anguished woman cradles her dead child. On the far right, a woman on fire runs screaming from a burning building, while another woman flees mindlessly. In the upper right corner, a woman, represented by only a head, emerges from the burning building, thrusting forth a light to illuminate the horror. Overlooking the destruction is a bull, which, according to the artist, represents "brutality and darkness."[26]

Picasso used aspects of his Cubist discoveries to expressive effect in *Guernica*, particularly the fragmentation of objects and the dislocation of anatomical features. This Cubist fragmentation gave visual form to the horror. What happened to these figures in the artist's act of painting—the dissections and contortions of the human form—paralleled what happened to them in real life. To emphasize the scene's severity and starkness, Picasso reduced his palette to black, white, and shades of gray.

Revealing his political commitment and his awareness of the power of art, Picasso refused to allow exhibition of *Guernica* in Spain while Generalissimo Franco was in power. At the artist's request, *Guernica* hung in the Museum of Modern Art in New York City after the 1937 World's Fair concluded. Not until after Franco's death in 1975 did Picasso allow the mural to be exhibited in his homeland. It hangs today in the Centro de Arte Reina Sofia in Madrid as a testament to a tragic chapter in Spanish history.

Neue Sachlichkeit

In Germany, World War I gave rise to an artistic movement called *Neue Sachlichkeit* (New Objectivity). The artists associated with Neue Sachlichkeit served, at some point, in the German army, and their military experiences deeply influenced their worldviews and informed their art. "New Objectivity" captures the group's aim—to present a clear-eyed, direct, and honest image of the war and its effects.

GEORGE GROSZ One of the Neue Sachlichkeit artists was GEORGE GROSZ (1893–1958), who was, for a time, associated with the Dada group in Berlin. Grosz observed the onset of World War I with horrified fascination, but that feeling soon turned to anger and frustration. He reported:

35-41 PABLO PICASSO, *Guernica,* 1937. Oil on canvas, 11′ 5½″ × 25′ 5¾″. Museo Nacional Centro de Arte Reina Sofia, Madrid.

Picasso used Cubist techniques, especially the fragmentation of objects and dislocation of anatomical features, to expressive effect in this condemnation of the Nazi bombing of the Basque capital.

35-42 GEORGE GROSZ, *Fit for Active Service*, 1916–1917. Pen and brush and ink on paper, 1′ 8″ × 1′ 2⅜″. Museum of Modern Art, New York (gift of the American Tobacco Company, Inc.). Art © Estate of George Grosz/Licensed by VAGA, New York.

In a drawing that is an indictment of the German army and based on Grosz's personal experience, a doctor proclaims the skeleton before him "fit for service," and no one disputes his evaluation.

1 in.

Of course, there was a kind of mass enthusiasm at the start. But this intoxication soon evaporated, leaving a huge vacuum. . . . And then after a few years when everything bogged down, when we were defeated, when everything went to pieces, all that remained, at least for me and most of my friends, were disgust and horror.[27]

Grosz produced numerous paintings and drawings, such as *Fit for Active Service* (FIG. **35-42**), that were caustic indictments of the military. In these works, he often depicted army officers as heartless or incompetent. This particular drawing may relate to Grosz's personal experience. On the verge of a nervous breakdown in 1917, he was sent to a sanatorium where doctors examined him and, much to his horror, declared him "fit for service." In this biting and sarcastic drawing, an army doctor proclaims the skeleton before him "fit for service." The other officers or doctors attending do not dispute this evaluation. The spectacles perched on the skeleton's face, very similar to the gold-rimmed glasses Grosz wore, further suggest he based this scene on his experiences. Grosz's searing wit is all the more evident upon comparing *Fit for Active Service* with Marsden Hartley's *Portrait of a German Officer* (FIG. **35-34**). Although Hartley's painting deals with the death of his lover in battle, the incorporation of colorful German military insignia and emblems imbues the painting with a more heroic, celebratory tone. In contrast, the simplicity of Grosz's line drawing contributes to the directness and immediacy of the work, which scathingly portrays the German army.

MAX BECKMANN Like Grosz, MAX BECKMANN (1884–1950) enlisted in the German army and initially rationalized the war. He believed the chaos would lead to a better society, but over time the massive death and destruction increasingly disillusioned him. Soon his work began to emphasize the horrors of war and of a society he saw descending into madness. His disturbing view of society is evident in *Night* (FIG. **35-43**), which depicts a cramped room three intruders have forcibly invaded. A bound woman, apparently raped, is splayed across the foreground of the painting. Her husband appears on the left. One of the intruders hangs him, while another one twists his left arm out of its socket. An unidentified woman cowers in the background. On the far right, the third intruder prepares to flee with the child.

Although this image does not depict a war scene, the violence and wrenching brutality pervading the home are a searing and horrifying comment on society's condition. Beckmann also injected a personal

1 ft.

35-43 MAX BECKMANN, *Night*, 1918–1919. Oil on canvas, 4′ 4⅜″ × 5′ ¼″. Kunstsammlung Nordrhein-Westfalen, Düsseldorf.

Beckmann's treatment of forms and space in *Night* matched his view of the brutality of early-20th-century society. Objects seem dislocated and contorted, and the space appears buckled and illogical.

35-44 OTTO DIX, *Der Krieg* (*The War*), 1929–1932. Oil and tempera on wood, 6' 8$\frac{1}{3}$" × 13' 4$\frac{3}{4}$". Staatliche Kunstsammlungen, Gemäldegalerie Neue Meister, Dresden.

In this triptych recalling earlier altarpieces, Dix captured the panoramic devastation that war inflicts on the terrain and on humans. He depicted himself as a soldier dragging a comrade to safety.

reference by using himself, his wife, and his son as the models for the three family members. The stilted angularity of the figures and the roughness of the paint surface contribute to the image's savageness. In addition, the artist's treatment of forms and space reflects the world's violence. Objects seem dislocated and contorted, and the space appears buckled and illogical. For example, the woman's hands are bound to the window that opens from the room's back wall, but her body appears to hang vertically, rather than lying across the plane of the intervening table.

OTTO DIX The third artist most closely associated with Neue Sachlichkeit was OTTO DIX (1891–1959). Having served as both a machine gunner and an aerial observer, Dix was well acquainted with war's effects. Like Grosz, he initially tried to find redeeming value in the apocalyptic event: "The war was a horrible thing, but there was something tremendous about it, too. . . . You have to have seen human beings in this unleashed state to know what human nature is. . . . I need to experience all the depths of life for myself, that's why I go out, and that's why I volunteered."[28] This idea of experiencing the "depths of life" stemmed from Dix's interest in the philosophy of Friedrich Nietzsche (1844–1900). In particular, Dix avidly read Nietzsche's *The Joyous Science,* deriving from it a belief in life's cyclical nature—procreation and death, building up and tearing down, and growth and decay.

As the war progressed, however, Dix's faith in the potential improvement of society dissipated, and he began to produce unflinch-

ingly direct and provocative artworks. His *Der Krieg* (*The War;* FIG. 35-44) vividly captures the panoramic devastation that war inflicts, both on the terrain and on humans. In the left panel, armed and uniformed soldiers march off into the distance. Dix graphically displayed the horrific results in the center and right panels, where mangled bodies, many riddled with bullet holes, are scattered throughout the eerily lit apocalyptic landscape. As if to emphasize the intensely personal nature of this scene, the artist painted himself into the right panel as the ghostly but determined soldier who drags a comrade to safety. In the bottom panel, in a coffinlike bunker, lie soldiers asleep—or perhaps dead. Dix significantly chose to present this sequence of images in a triptych format, and the work recalls triptychs such as Matthias Grünewald's *Isenheim Altarpiece* (FIG. 23-2). However, Dix's work presents a bleaker outlook than that piece: The hope of salvation extended to viewers of the *Isenheim Altarpiece* through Christ's eventual Resurrection is absent from *Der Krieg*. Like his fellow Neue Sachlichkeit artists, Dix felt compelled to lay bare the realities of his time, which the war's violence dominated. Even years later, Dix still maintained:

> You have to see things the way they are. You have to be able to say yes to the human manifestations that exist and will always exist. That doesn't mean saying yes to war, but to a fate that approaches you under certain conditions and in which you have to prove yourself. Abnormal situations bring out all the depravity, the bestiality of human beings. . . . I portrayed states, states that the war brought about, and the results of war, as states.[29]

ERNST BARLACH A work more spiritual in its expression is the *War Monument* (FIG. 35-45), which the German sculptor ERNST BARLACH (1870–1938) created for the cathedral in his hometown of Güstrow in 1927. Working often in wood, Barlach sculpted single figures usually dressed in flowing robes and portrayed in strong, simple poses that embody deep human emotions and experiences such as grief, vigilance, or self-comfort. Barlach's works combine sharp, smoothly planed forms with intense expression. The cast-bronze hovering figure of his *War Monument* is one of the most poignant memorials of World War I. Unlike traditional war memorials depicting heroic military figures, often engaged in battle, the hauntingly symbolic figure that Barlach created speaks to the experience of all caught in the conflict of war. The floating human form, suspended above a tomb inscribed with the dates 1914–1918 (and later also 1939–1945), suggests a dying soul at the moment when it is about to awaken to everlasting life—the theme of death and transfiguration. The rigid economy of surfaces concentrates attention on the simple but expressive head. So powerful was this sculpture that the Nazis had it removed from the cathedral in 1937 and melted down for ammunition. Luckily, a friend hid another version Barlach made. A Protestant parish in Cologne purchased this surviving cast, from which bronzeworkers made a new cast for the Güstrow cathedral.

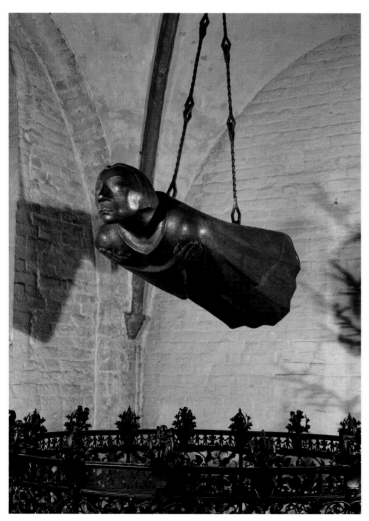

35-45 ERNST BARLACH, *War Monument*, Cathedral, Güstrow, Germany, 1927. Bronze.

In this World War I memorial, a human form floating above a tomb suggests a dying soul at the moment when it is about to awaken to everlasting life. The Nazis melted down the piece for ammunition.

Surrealism

The exuberantly aggressive momentum of the Dada movement that emerged during World War I was of short duration. By 1924, with the publication in France of the *First Surrealist Manifesto,* most of the artists associated with Dada joined the *Surrealism* movement and its determined exploration of ways to express in art the world of dreams and the unconscious. Not surprisingly, the Surrealists incorporated many of the Dadaists' improvisational techniques. They believed these methods important for engaging the elements of fantasy and activating the unconscious forces that lie deep within every human being. The Surrealists sought to explore the inner world of the psyche, the realm of fantasy and the unconscious. Inspired in part by the ideas of the psychoanalysts Sigmund Freud and Carl Jung, the Surrealists had a special interest in the nature of dreams. They viewed dreams as occurring at the level connecting all human consciousness and as constituting the arena in which people could move beyond their environment's constricting forces to reengage with the deeper selves society had long suppressed. In the words of André Breton, one of the leading Surrealist thinkers:

> Surrealism is based on the belief in the superior reality of certain forms of association heretofore neglected, in the omnipotence of dreams, in the undirected play of thought. . . . I believe in the future resolution of the states of dream and reality, in appearance so contradictory, in a sort of absolute reality, or surreality.[30]

Thus, the Surrealists' dominant motivation was to bring the aspects of outer and inner "reality" together into a single position, in much the same way life's seemingly unrelated fragments combine in the vivid world of dreams. The projection in visible form of this new conception required new techniques of pictorial construction. The Surrealists adapted some Dada devices and invented new methods such as automatic writing (spontaneous writing using free association), not so much to reveal a world without meaning as to provoke reactions closely related to subconscious experience.

Surrealism developed along two lines. In *Naturalistic Surrealism,* artists present recognizable scenes that seem to have metamorphosed into a dream or nightmare image. The artists Salvador Dalí (FIG. 35-49) and René Magritte (FIG. 35-50) were the most famous practitioners of this variant of Surrealism. In contrast, some artists gravitated toward an interest in *Biomorphic Surrealism.* In Biomorphic (life forms) Surrealism, *automatism*—the creation of art without conscious control—predominated. Biomorphic Surrealists such as Joan Miró (FIG. 35-52) produced largely abstract compositions, although the imagery sometimes suggests organisms or natural forms.

GIORGIO DE CHIRICO The Italian painter GIORGIO DE CHIRICO (1888–1978) produced emphatically ambiguous works that position him as a precursor of Surrealism. De Chirico's paintings of cityscapes and shop windows were part of a movement called *Pittura Metafisica,* or Metaphysical Painting. Returning to Italy after study in Munich, de Chirico found hidden reality revealed through strange juxtapositions, such as those seen on late autumn afternoons in the city of Turin, when the long shadows of the setting sun transformed vast open squares and silent public monuments into what the painter called "metaphysical towns." De Chirico translated this vision into paint in works such as *Melancholy and Mystery of a Street* (FIG. 35-46), where the spaces and buildings evoke a disquieting sense of foreboding. The choice of the term "metaphysical" to describe de Chirico's paintings suggests that these images transcend their physical appearances. *Melancholy and Mystery of a Street,* for all of its clarity and simplicity, takes on a rather sinister air. Only a few inexplicable and incongruous elements punctuate the scene's solitude—a small

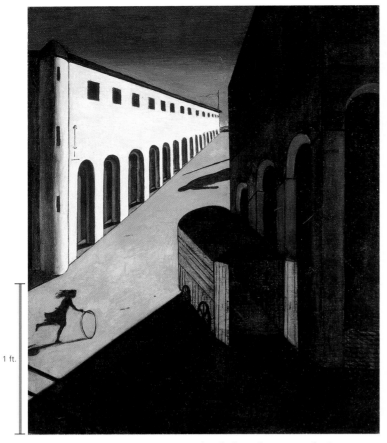

35-46 Giorgio de Chirico, *Melancholy and Mystery of a Street*, 1914. Oil on canvas, 2′ 10$\frac{1}{4}$″ × 2′ 4$\frac{1}{2}$″. Private collection.

De Chirico's Metaphysical Painting movement was a precursor of Surrealism. In this street scene, filled with mysterious forms and shadows, the painter evoked a disquieting sense of foreboding.

35-47 Max Ernst, *Two Children Are Threatened by a Nightingale*, 1924. Oil on wood with wood construction, 2′ 3$\frac{1}{2}$″ × 1′ 10$\frac{1}{2}$″ × 4$\frac{1}{2}$″. Museum of Modern Art, New York.

In this early Surrealist painting with an intentionally ambiguous title, Ernst used traditional perspective to represent the setting, but the three sketchily rendered figures belong to a dream world.

girl with her hoop in the foreground, the empty van, and the ominous shadow of a man emerging from behind the building. The sense of strangeness de Chirico could conjure with familiar objects and scenes recalls Nietzsche's "foreboding that underneath this reality in which we live and have our being, another and altogether different reality lies concealed."[31]

De Chirico's paintings were reproduced in periodicals almost as soon as he completed them, and his works quickly influenced artists outside Italy, including both the Dadaists and, later, the Surrealists. The incongruities in his work intrigued the Dadaists, whereas the eerie mood and visionary quality of paintings such as *Melancholy and Mystery of a Street* excited and inspired Surrealist artists who sought to portray the world of dreams.

MAX ERNST Originally a Dada activist in Germany, Max Ernst (1891–1976) became one of the early adherents of the Surrealist circle that André Breton anchored. As a child living in a small community near Cologne, Ernst had found his existence fantastic and filled with marvels. In autobiographical notes, written mostly in the third person, he said of his birth: "Max Ernst had his first contact with the world of sense on the 2nd April 1891 at 9:45 A.M., when he emerged from the egg which his mother had laid in an eagle's nest and which the bird had incubated for seven years."[32] Ernst's service in the German army during World War I swept away his early success as an Expressionist. In his own words:

> Max Ernst died on 1st August 1914. He returned to life on 11th November 1918, a young man who wanted to become a magician and

find the central myth of his age. From time to time he consulted the eagle which had guarded the egg of his prenatal existence. The bird's advice can be detected in his work.[33]

Before joining the Surrealists, Ernst explored every means to achieve the sense of the psychic in his art. Like other Dadaists, he set out to incorporate found objects and chance into his works. Using a process called *frottage,* he created some works by combining the patterns achieved by rubbing a crayon or another medium across a sheet of paper placed over a surface having a strong, evocative textural pattern. In other works, Ernst joined fragments of images he had cut from old books, magazines, and prints to form one hallucinatory collage.

Ernst soon began making paintings that shared the mysterious dreamlike effect of his collages. In 1920 his works brought him into contact with Breton, who instantly recognized Ernst's affinity with the Surrealist group. In 1922, Ernst moved to Paris. His *Two Children Are Threatened by a Nightingale* (FIG. **35-47**) manifests many of the creative bases of Surrealism. Here, Ernst displayed a private dream that challenged the post-Renaissance idea that a painting should resemble a window looking into a "real" scene rendered illusionistically three-dimensional through mathematical perspective. In *Two Children,* the artist painted the landscape, the distant city, and the tiny flying bird in conventional fashion, following all the established rules of linear and atmospheric perspective. The three sketchily rendered figures, however, clearly belong to a dream world, and the literally three-dimensional miniature gate, the odd button knob, and the strange

Degenerate Art

Although avant-garde artists often had to endure public ridicule both in Europe and America (see "The Armory Show," page 934), they suffered outright political persecution in Germany in the 1930s and 1940s. The most dramatic example of this abuse was the infamous *Entartete Kunst* (Degenerate Art) exhibition that Adolf Hitler (1889–1945) and the Nazis mounted in 1937.

Hitler aspired to become an artist himself and produced numerous drawings and paintings. These works reflected his firm belief that 19th-century realistic genre painting represented the zenith of Aryan art development. Accordingly, he denigrated anything that did not conform to that standard—in particular, avant-garde art. Turning his criticism into action, Hitler ordered the confiscation of more than 16,000 artworks he considered "degenerate." To publicize his condemnation of this art, he directed his minister for public enlightenment and propaganda, Joseph Goebbels (1897–1945), to organize a massive exhibition of this "degenerate art." Hitler defined it as works that "insult German feeling, or destroy or confuse natural form, or simply reveal an absence of adequate manual and artistic skill."* The term "degenerate" also had other specific connotations at the time. The Nazis used it to designate supposedly inferior racial, sexual, and moral types. Hitler's order to Goebbels to target 20th-century avant-garde art for inclusion in this exhibition aimed to impress on viewers the general inferiority of the artists producing this work. To make this point even more dramatically, Hitler mandated the organization of another exhibition, the *Grosse Deutsche Kunstausstellung* (Great German Art Exhibition), which ran concurrently and presented an extensive array of Nazi-approved conservative art.

Entartete Kunst opened in Munich on July 19, 1937, and included more than 650 paintings, sculptures, prints, and books. The exhibition was immensely popular. Roughly 20,000 viewers visited the show daily. By the end of its four-month run, it had attracted more than two million viewers, and nearly a million more viewed it as it traveled through Germany and Austria. Among the 112 artists whose works the Nazis presented for ridicule were Ernst Barlach, Max Beckmann, Otto Dix, Max Ernst, George Grosz, Vassily Kandinsky, Ernst Kirchner, Paul Klee, Wilhelm Lehmbruck, Franz Marc, Emil Nolde, and Kurt Schwitters. A memorable photograph (FIG. **35-48**) recorded Hitler visiting the exhibition, pausing in front of the Dada wall where the organizers initially deliberately hung askew works by Schwitters, Klee, and Kandinsky. No avant-garde or even modernist artist was safe from Hitler's attack. (Only six of the artists in the exhibition were Jewish.) Indeed, despite his status as a charter member of the Nazi Party, Emil Nolde received particularly harsh treatment. The Nazis confiscated more than 1,000 of Nolde's works from German

35-48 Adolf Hitler, accompanied by Nazi commission members, including photographer Heinrich Hoffmann, Wolfgang Willrich, Walter Hansen, and painter Adolf Ziegler, viewing the *Entartete Kunst* show on July 16, 1937.

For Hitler's visit, the curators deliberately hung askew the works of Kandinsky, Klee, and Schwitters (although they subsequently straightened them for the duration of the exhibition).

museums and included 27 of them in the exhibition, more than for almost any other artist.

Clearly, artists needed considerable courage to defy tradition and produce avant-garde art. Especially in Germany in the 1930s and 1940s, in the face of Nazi persecution, commitment to the avant-garde demanded a resoluteness that extended beyond issues of aesthetics and beyond the confines of the art world. This persecution exacted an immense toll on these artists. Kirchner, for example, responded to the stress of Nazi pressure by destroying all his woodblocks and burning many of his works. A year later, in 1938, he committed suicide. Beckmann and his wife fled to Amsterdam on the exhibit's opening day, never to return to their homeland. Although *Entartete Kunst* was just a fragment of the tremendous destruction of life and spirit Hitler and the Nazis wrought, Hitler's insistence on suppressing and discrediting this art dramatically demonstrates art's power to affect viewers.

* Stephanie Barron, *"Degenerate Art": The Fate of the Avant-Garde in Nazi Germany* (Los Angeles: Los Angeles County Museum of Art, 1991), 19.

closed building "violate" the bulky frame's space. Additional dislocation occurs in the traditional museum identification label, which Ernst displaced into a cutaway part of the frame. Handwritten, it announces the work's title (taken from a poem Ernst wrote before he painted this), adding another note of irrational mystery.

As is true of many Surrealist works, the title, *Two Children Are Threatened by a Nightingale*, is ambiguous and relates uneasily to what the spectator sees. The viewer must struggle to decipher connections between the image and words. When Surrealists (and

Dadaists and Metaphysical artists before them) used such titles, they intended the seeming contradiction between title and picture to throw the spectator off balance with all expectations challenged. Much of the impact of Surrealist works begins with the viewer's sudden awareness of the incongruity and absurdity of what the artist pictured. These were precisely the qualities that subjected the Dadaists and Surrealists to public condemnation and, in Germany under Adolf Hitler (FIG. **35-48**), to governmental persecution (see "Degenerate Art," above).

35-49 Salvador Dalí, *The Persistence of Memory*, 1931. Oil on canvas, $9\frac{1}{2}''\times$ 1' 1''. Museum of Modern Art, New York. ▶

Dalí aimed to paint "images of concrete irrationality." In this realistically rendered landscape featuring three "decaying" watches, he created a haunting allegory of empty space where time has ended.

SALVADOR DALÍ The Surrealists' exploration of the human psyche and dreams reached new heights in the works of Spain's Salvador Dalí (1904–1989). In his paintings, sculptures, jewelry, and designs for furniture and movies, Dalí probed a deeply erotic dimension, studying the writings of Richard von Krafft-Ebing (1840–1902) and Sigmund Freud and inventing what he called the "paranoiac-critical method" to assist his creative process. As he described it, in his painting he aimed "to materialize the images of concrete irrationality with the most imperialistic fury of precision . . . in order that the world of imagination and of concrete irrationality may be as objectively evident . . . as that of the exterior world of phenomenal reality."[34]

All these aspects of Dalí's style appear in *The Persistence of Memory* (FIG. **35-49**), a haunting allegory of empty space where time has ended. In the painting, an eerie, never-setting sun illuminates the barren landscape. An amorphous creature draped with a limp pocket watch sleeps in the foreground. Another watch hangs from the branch of a dead tree that springs unexpectedly from a blocky architectural form. A third watch hangs half over the edge of the rectangular form, beside a small timepiece resting face down on the block's surface. Ants swarm mysteriously over the small watch, while a fly walks along the face of its large neighbor, almost as if this assembly of watches were decaying organic life—soft and sticky. Dalí rendered every detail of this dreamscape with precise control, striving to make the world of his paintings as convincingly real as the most meticulously rendered landscape based on a real scene from nature.

35-50A Magritte, *The False Mirror*, 1928.

RENÉ MAGRITTE The Belgian painter René Magritte (1898–1967) also expressed in exemplary fashion the Surrealist idea and method—the dreamlike dissociation of image and meaning. His works administer disruptive shocks because they subvert the viewer's expectations based on logic and common sense. The danger of relying on rationality when viewing a Surrealist work is glaringly apparent in Magritte's *The Treachery (or Perfidy) of Images* (FIG. **35-50**). Magritte presented a meticulously rendered *trompe l'oeil* depiction of a briar pipe. The caption beneath the image, however, contradicts what seems obvious: "Ceci n'est pas une pipe" ("This is not a pipe"). The discrepancy between image and caption clearly challenges the assumptions underlying the reading of visual art. Like the other Surrealists' work, this painting wreaks havoc on the viewer's reliance on the conscious and the rational.

MERET OPPENHEIM Sculpture especially appealed to the Surrealists because its concrete tangibility made their art all the more disquieting. *Object* (FIG. **35-51**), also called *Le Déjeuner en fourrure* (*Luncheon in Fur*), by Swiss artist Meret Oppenheim (1913–1985) captures the incongruity, humor, visual appeal, and, often, eroticism characterizing Surrealism. The artist presented a fur-lined teacup inspired by a conversation she had with Picasso. After admiring a bracelet Oppenheim had made from a piece of brass covered with fur, Picasso noted that anything might be covered with fur. When her tea grew cold, Oppenheim responded to Picasso's com-

35-50 René Magritte, *The Treachery (or Perfidy) of Images*, 1928–1929. Oil on canvas, 1' $11\frac{5}{8}''\times$ 3' 1''. Los Angeles County Museum of Art, Los Angeles (purchased with funds provided by the Mr. and Mrs. William Preston Harrison Collection).

The discrepancy between Magritte's meticulously painted briar pipe and his caption, "This is not a pipe," challenges the viewer's reliance on the conscious and the rational in the reading of visual art.

35-51 MERET OPPENHEIM, *Object (Le Déjeuner en fourrure)*, 1936. Fur-covered cup, $4\frac{3}{8}''$ diameter; saucer, $9\frac{3}{8}''$ diameter; spoon, 8″ long. Museum of Modern Art, New York.

The Surrealists loved the concrete tangibility of sculpture, which made their art even more disquieting. Oppenheim's functional fur-covered object captures the Surrealist flair for magical transformation.

porates a sensuality and eroticism (seen here in the seductively soft, tactile fur lining the concave form) that are also components of much of Surrealist art.

JOAN MIRÓ Like the Dadaists, the Surrealists used many methods to free the creative process from reliance on the kind of conscious control they believed society had shaped too much. Dalí used his paranoiac-critical approach to encourage the free play of association as he worked. Other Surrealists used automatism and various types of planned "accidents" to provoke reactions closely related to subconscious experience. The Spanish artist JOAN MIRÓ (1893–1983) was a master of this approach. Although Miró resisted formal association with any movement or group, including the Surrealists, André Breton identified him as "the most Surrealist of us all."[35] From the beginning, Miró's work contained an element of fantasy and hallucination. After Surrealist poets in Paris introduced him to the use of chance to create art, the young Spaniard devised a new painting method that allowed him to create works such as *Painting* (FIG. **35-52**). Miró began this painting by making a scattered collage composition with assembled fragments cut from a catalogue for machinery. The shapes in the collage became motifs the artist freely reshaped to create black silhouettes—solid or in outline, with dramatic accents of white and vermilion. They suggest, in the painting, a host of amoebic organisms or constellations in outer space floating in an immaterial background space filled with soft reds, blues, and greens.

ment by ordering "un peu plus de fourrure" (a little more fur), and the sculpture had its genesis. *Object* takes on an anthropomorphic quality, animated by the quirky combination of the fur with a functional object. Further, the sculpture captures the Surrealist flair for alchemical, seemingly magical or mystical, transformation. It incor-

Miró described his creative process as a back-and-forth switch between unconscious and conscious image-making: "Rather than setting out to paint something, I begin painting and as I paint the picture begins to assert itself, or suggest itself under my brush. The form becomes a sign for a woman or a bird as I work.... The first stage is free, unconscious.... The second stage is carefully calculated."[36] Even the artist could not always explain the meanings of pictures such as *Painting*. They are, in the truest sense, spontaneous and intuitive expressions of the little-understood, submerged unconscious part of life.

35-52 JOAN MIRÓ, *Painting*, 1933. Oil on canvas, 5′ 8″ × 6′ 5″. Museum of Modern Art, New York (Loula D. Lasker Bequest by exchange). ◼◂

Miró promoted automatism, the creation of art without conscious control. He began this painting with a scattered collage and then added forms suggesting floating amoebic organisms.

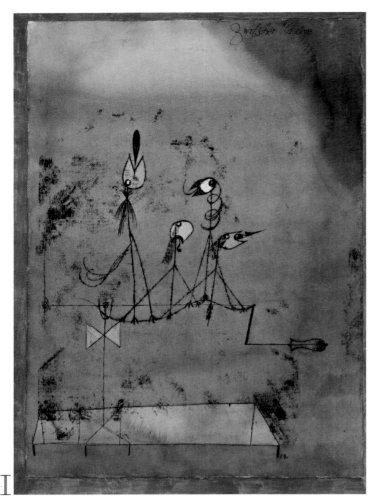

1 in.

35-53 PAUL KLEE, *Twittering Machine*, 1922. Watercolor and pen and ink, on oil transfer drawing on paper, mounted on cardboard, 2′ 1″ × 1′ 7″. Museum of Modern Art, New York.

Although based on forms in the tangible world easily read as birds, Klee's *Twittering Machine* is a fanciful vision of a mysterious world presented in a simplified, almost childlike manner.

PAUL KLEE Perhaps the most inventive artist using fantasy images to represent the nonvisible world was the Swiss-German painter PAUL KLEE (1879–1940). Like Miró, he shunned formal association with groups such as the Dadaists and Surrealists but pursued their interest in the subconscious. Klee sought clues to humanity's deeper nature in primitive shapes and symbols. Like Jung, Klee seems to have accepted the existence of a collective unconscious that reveals itself in archaic signs and patterns and that is everywhere evident in the art of "primitive" cultures (see "Primitivism," page 920). The son of a professional musician and himself an accomplished violinist, Klee thought of painting as similar to music in its ability to express emotions through color, form, and line. In 1920, Klee set down his *Creative Credo*, which reads in part:

> Art does not reproduce the visible; rather it makes visible. . . . The formal elements of graphic art are dot, line, plane, and space— the last three charged with energy of various kinds. . . . Formerly we used to represent things visible on earth, things we either liked to look at or would have liked to see. Today we reveal the reality that is behind visible things.[37]

To penetrate the reality behind visible things, Klee studied nature avidly, taking special interest in analyzing processes of growth and change. He coded these studies in diagrammatic form in notebooks. The root of his work was thus nature, but nature filtered through his mind. Upon starting an image, he would allow the pencil or brush to lead him until an image emerged, to which he would then respond to complete the idea.

Twittering Machine (FIG. **35-53**) reveals Klee's fanciful vision. The painting, although based on forms in the tangible world easily read as birds, is far from illusionistic. Klee presented the scene in a simplified, almost childlike manner, imbuing the work with a poetic lyricism. The small size of Klee's works enhanced their impact. A viewer must draw near to decipher the delicately rendered forms and enter this mysterious dream world. The inclusion of a crank-driven mechanism adds a touch of whimsy. Perhaps no other artist of the 20th century matched Klee's subtlety as he deftly created a world of ambiguity and understatement that draws each viewer into finding a unique interpretation of the work.

Suprematism, Constructivism, and De Stijl

The pessimism and cynicism of movements such as Dada reflect the historical circumstances of the early 20th century. However, not all artists reacted to the profound turmoil of the times by retreating from society. Some avant-garde artists promoted utopian ideals, believing staunchly in art's ability to contribute to improving society and all humankind. These efforts often surfaced in the face of significant political upheaval, illustrating the link established early on between revolution in politics and revolution in art. Among the art movements espousing utopian notions were Suprematism and Constructivism in Russia and De Stijl in Holland.

KAZIMIR MALEVICH Despite Russia's distance from Paris, the center of the international art world in the early 20th century, Russians had a long history of cultural contact and interaction with western Europe. Wealthy Russians, such as Ivan Morozov (1871–1921) and Sergei Shchukin (1854–1936), amassed extensive collections of Impressionist, Post-Impressionist, and avant-garde paintings. Shchukin became particularly enamored with the work of both Picasso and Matisse. By the mid-1910s, he had acquired 37 paintings by Matisse and 51 by Picasso. Because of their access to collections such as these, Russian artists were familiar with early-20th-century artistic developments, especially Fauvism, Cubism, and Futurism.

Among the Russian artists who pursued the avant-garde direction Cubism introduced was KAZIMIR MALEVICH (1878–1935). Malevich developed an abstract style to convey his belief that the supreme reality in the world is pure feeling, which attaches to no object. Thus, this belief called for new, nonobjective forms in art—shapes not related to objects in the visible world. Malevich had studied painting, sculpture, and architecture and had worked his way through most of the avant-garde styles of his youth before deciding none could express the subject he found most important—"pure feeling." He christened his new artistic approach *Suprematism*, explaining: "Under Suprematism I understand the supremacy of pure feeling in creative art. To the Suprematist, the visual phenomena of the objective world are, in themselves, meaningless; the significant thing is feeling, as such, quite apart from the environment in which it is called forth."[38]

The basic form of Malevich's new Suprematist nonobjective art was the square. Combined with its relatives, the straight line and the rectangle, the square soon filled his paintings, such as *Suprematist Composition: Airplane Flying* (FIG. **35-54**). In this work, the brightly colored shapes float against and within a white space, and the artist placed them in dynamic relationship to one another. Malevich believed all people would easily understand his new art because of the universality of its symbols. It used the pure language of shape and color, to which everyone could respond intuitively.

35-54A POPOVA, *Architectonic Painting*, 1916–1917.

35-54 Kazimir Malevich, *Suprematist Composition: Airplane Flying*, 1915 (dated 1914). Oil on canvas, 1′ 10$\frac{7}{8}$″ × 1′ 7″. Museum of Modern Art, New York. ◼◀

Malevich developed an abstract style he called Suprematism to convey that the supreme reality in the world is pure feeling. In this work, the brightly colored rectilinear shapes float against white space.

Having formulated his artistic approach, Malevich welcomed the Russian Revolution, which broke out in 1917, as a political act that would wipe out past traditions and begin a new culture. He believed his art could play a major role because of its universal accessibility. In actuality, after a short period when the new regime heralded avant-garde art, the political leaders of the postrevolution Soviet Union decided the new society needed a more "practical" art. Soviet authorities promoted a "realistic," illusionistic art that they believed a wide public could understand and that they hoped would teach citizens about their new government. This horrified Malevich. To him, true art could never have a practical connection with life. As he explained, "Every social idea, however great and important it may be, stems from the sensation of hunger; every art work, regardless of how small and insignificant it may seem, originates in pictorial or plastic feeling. It is high time for us to realize that the problems of art lie far apart from those of the stomach or the intellect."[39] Disappointed and unappreciated in his own country, Malevich eventually gravitated toward other disciplines, such as mathematical theory and geometry, logical fields given his interest in pure abstraction.

NAUM GABO Like Malevich, the Russian-born sculptor Naum Gabo (1890–1977) wanted to create an innovative art to express a new reality, and, also like Malevich, Gabo believed art should spring from sources separate from the everyday world. For Gabo, the new reality was the space-time world described by early-20th-century scientists (see "Science and Art," page 915). As he wrote in *The Realistic Manifesto*, published with his brother Anton Pevsner (1886–1962) in 1920:

35-55 Naum Gabo, *Column*, ca. 1923 (reconstructed 1937). Perspex, wood, metal, glass, 3′ 5″ × 2′ 5″ × 2′ 5″. Solomon R. Guggenheim Museum, New York.

Gabo's Constructivist sculptures rely on the relationship of mass and space to suggest the nature of space-time. Space seems to flow through as well as around the transparent materials he used.

Space and time are the only forms on which life is built and hence art must be constructed. . . . The realization of our perceptions of the world in the forms of space and time is the only aim of our pictorial and plastic art. . . . We renounce the thousand-year-old delusion in art that held the static rhythms as the only elements of the plastic and pictorial arts. We affirm in these arts a new element, the kinetic rhythms, as the basic forms of our perception of real time.[40]

Gabo was one of the Russian sculptors known as Constructivists. The name *Constructivism* may have come originally from the title *Construction,* which the Russian artist Vladimir Tatlin (FIG. **35-70**) used for some relief sculptures he made in 1913 and 1914. Gabo explained that he called himself a Constructivist partly because he built up his sculptures piece by piece in space, instead of carving or modeling them in the traditional way. Although Gabo experimented briefly with real motion in his work, most of his sculptures relied on the relationship of mass and space to suggest the nature of space-time. To indicate the volumes of mass and space more clearly in his sculpture, Gabo used some of the new synthetic plastic materials, including celluloid, nylon, and Lucite, to create constructions whose space seems to flow through as well as around the transparent materials. In works such as *Column* (FIG. **35-55**), the sculptor opened up the column's circular mass so that the viewer can experience the volume of space it occupies. Two transparent planes extend through its diameter, crossing at right angles at the center of the implied cylindrical column shape. The opaque colored planes at the base and the inclined open ring set up counter-rhythms to the crossed upright planes. They establish the sense of dynamic kinetic movement that Gabo always sought to express as an essential part of reality.

DE STIJL The utopian spirit and ideals of the Suprematists and Constructivists extended beyond Russia. In Holland, a group of young artists formed a new movement in 1917 and began publishing a magazine, calling both movement and magazine *De Stijl* (The Style). The group's cofounders were the painters PIET MONDRIAN (1872–1944) and Theo van Doesburg (1883–1931). In addition to promoting utopian ideals, De Stijl artists believed in the birth of a new age in the wake of World War I. They felt it was a time of balance between individual and universal values, when the machine would assure ease of living. In their first manifesto of De Stijl, the artists declared: "There is an old and a new consciousness of time. The old is connected with the individual. The new is connected with the universal."[41] The goal, according to van Doesburg and architect Cor van Eesteren (1897–1988), was a total integration of art and life:

> We must realize that life and art are no longer separate domains. That is why the "idea" of "art" as an illusion separate from real life must disappear. The word "Art" no longer means anything to us. In its place we demand the construction of our environment in accordance with creative laws based upon a fixed principle. These laws, following those of economics, mathematics, technique, sanitation, etc., are leading to a new, plastic unity.[42]

PIET MONDRIAN Toward this goal of integration, Mondrian created a new style based on a single ideal principle. The choice of the term "De Stijl" reflected Mondrian's confidence that this style—*the* style—revealed the underlying eternal structure of existence. Accordingly, De Stijl artists reduced their artistic vocabulary to simple geometric elements. Time spent in Paris, just before World War I, introduced Mondrian to modes of abstraction such as Cubism. However, as his attraction to contemporary theological writings grew, Mondrian sought to purge his art of every overt reference to individual objects in the external world. He initially favored the teachings of theosophy, a tradition basing knowledge of nature and the human condition on knowledge of the divine nature or spiritual powers. (His fellow theosophist, Vassily Kandinsky [FIG. **35-7**], pursued a similar path.) Mondrian, however, quickly abandoned the strictures of theosophy and turned toward a conception of nonobjective design—"pure plastic art"—that he believed expressed universal reality. He articulated his credo with great eloquence in 1914:

> What first captivated us does not captivate us afterward (like toys). If one has loved the surface of things for a long time, later on one will look for something more. . . . The interior of things shows through the surface; thus as we look at the surface the inner image is formed in our soul. It is this inner image that should be represented. For the natural surface of things is beautiful, but the imitation of it is without life. . . . Art is higher than reality and has no direct relation to reality. . . . To approach the spiritual in art, one will make as little use as possible of reality, because reality is opposed to the spiritual. . . . [W]e find ourselves in the presence of an abstract art. Art should be above reality, otherwise it would have no value for man.[43]

Mondrian soon moved beyond Cubism because he felt "Cubism did not accept the logical consequences of its own discoveries; it was not developing towards its own goal, the expression of pure plastics."[44] Caught by the outbreak of hostilities while on a visit to

35-56 PIET MONDRIAN, *Composition with Red, Blue and Yellow,* 1930. Oil on canvas, $1' 6\frac{1}{8}'' \times 1' 6\frac{1}{8}''$. Kunsthaus, Zürich. © 2008 Mondrian/Holtzman Trust c/o HCR International, VA, USA.

Mondrian created numerous "pure plastic" paintings in which he locked primary colors into a grid of intersecting vertical and horizontal lines. By altering the grid patterns, he created a dynamic tension.

Holland, Mondrian remained there during World War I, developing his theories for what he called *Neoplasticism*—the new "pure plastic art." He believed all great art had polar but coexistent goals, the attempt to create "universal beauty" and the desire for "aesthetic expression of oneself."[45] The first goal is objective in nature, whereas the second is subjective, existing within the individual's mind and heart. To create such a universal expression, an artist must communicate "a real equation of the universal and the individual."[46]

To express this vision, Mondrian eventually limited his formal vocabulary to the three primary colors (red, yellow, and blue), the three primary values (black, white, and gray), and the two primary directions (horizontal and vertical). Basing his ideas on a combination of teachings, he concluded that primary colors and values are the purest colors and therefore are the perfect tools to help an artist construct a harmonious composition. Using this system, he created numerous paintings locking color planes into a grid of intersecting vertical and horizontal lines, as in *Composition with Red, Blue, and Yellow* (FIG. **35-56**). In each of these paintings, Mondrian altered the grid patterns and the size and placement of the color planes to create an internal cohesion and harmony. This did not mean inertia. Rather, Mondrian worked to maintain a dynamic tension in his paintings from the size and position of lines, shapes, and colors.

Sculpture

It was impossible for early-20th-century artists to ignore the increasingly intrusive expansion of mechanization and growth of technology. However, not all artists embraced these developments, as had the Futurists. In contrast, many artists attempted to overcome the

Brancusi, Hepworth, and Moore on Abstract Sculpture

Many early-20th-century sculptors rejected the notion that reproducing the physical world of nature was the purpose of sculpture. Instead, they championed abstraction as the sculptor's proper goal. Among those who not only produced enduring masterpieces of abstract sculpture but also wrote eloquently about the theoretical basis of their work were Constantin Brancusi (FIG. 35-57), Barbara Hepworth (FIG. 35-58), and Henry Moore (FIG. 35-59). Some excerpts from their writings on sculpture illustrate their commitment to abstraction as their guiding principle.

▌ *Constantin Brancusi* Simplicity is not an objective in art, but one achieves simplicity despite oneself by entering into the real sense of things.* What is real is not the external form but the essence of things. Starting from this truth it is impossible for anyone to express anything essentially real by imitating its exterior surface.†

▌ *Barbara Hepworth* The forms which have had special meaning for me since childhood have been the standing form (which is the translation of my feeling towards the human being standing in landscape); the two forms (which is the tender relationship of one living thing beside another); and the closed form, such as the oval, spherical, or pierced form (sometimes incorporating colour) which translates for me the association and meaning of gesture in the landscape. . . . In all these shapes the translation of what one feels about man and nature must be conveyed by the sculptor in terms of mass, inner tension, and rhythm, scale in relation to our human size, and the quality of surface which speaks through our hands and eyes.‡

▌ *Henry Moore* Since the Gothic, European sculpture had become overgrown with moss, weeds—all sorts of surface excrescences which completely concealed shape. It has been Brancusi's special mission to get rid of this overgrowth, and to make us once more shape-conscious. To do this he has had to concentrate on very simple direct shapes. . . . Abstract qualities of design are essential to the value of a work. . . . Because a work does not aim at reproducing natural appearances, it is not, therefore, an escape from life—but may be a penetration into reality. . . . My sculpture is becoming

less representational, less an outward visual copy . . . but only because I believe that in this way I can present the human psychological content of my work with greatest directness and intensity.§

* Quoted in Herschel B. Chipp, *Theories of Modern Art: A Source Book by Artists and Critics* (Berkeley and Los Angeles: University of California Press, 1968), 364–365.
† Quoted in George Heard Hamilton, *Painting and Sculpture in Europe, 1880–1940,* 6th ed. (New Haven: Yale University Press, 1993), 426.
‡ Barbara Hepworth, *A Pictorial Autobiography* (London: Tate Gallery, 1978), 9, 53.
§ Quoted in Robert L. Herbert, *Modern Artists on Art,* 2d ed. (Mineola, N.Y.: Dover, 2000), 173–179.

35-57 Constantin Brancusi, *Bird in Space,* 1924. Bronze, 4′ 2$\frac{5}{16}$″ high. Philadelphia Museum of Art, Philadelphia (Louise and Walter Arensberg Collection, 1950).

Although not a literal depiction of a bird, Brancusi's softly curving, light-reflecting abstract sculpture in polished bronze suggests a bird about to soar in free flight through the heavens.

1 ft.

---

predominance of mechanization in society by immersing themselves in a search for the organic and natural.

57A
ANCUSI,
e Newborn,
5.

CONSTANTIN BRANCUSI Romanian artist CONSTANTIN BRANCUSI (1876–1957) was one of many sculptors eager to produce works emphasizing the natural or organic. Often composed of softly curving surfaces and ovoid forms, his sculptures refer, directly or indirectly, to the cycle of life. Brancusi sought to move beyond surface appearances to capture the essence or spirit of the object depicted (see "Brancusi, Hepworth, and Moore on Abstract Sculpture," above). Brancusi's ability to design rhythmic, elegant sculptures conveying the essence of his subjects is evident in *Bird in Space* (FIG. 35-57). Clearly not a literal depiction of a bird, the work is the final result of a long process. Brancusi started with the image of a bird at rest with its wings folded at its sides and ended with an abstract columnar form sharply tapered at each end. Despite the abstraction, the sculpture retains the suggestion of a bird about to soar in free flight

through the heavens. The highly reflective surface of the polished bronze does not allow the eye to linger on the sculpture itself (as do, for example, Rodin's agitated and textured surfaces; FIGS. **31-32** and **31-33**). Instead, the viewer's eye follows the gleaming reflection along the delicate curves to glide right off the tip of the work, thereby inducing a feeling of flight. Brancusi stated, "All my life I have sought the essence of flight. Don't look for mysteries. I give you pure joy. Look at the sculptures until you see them. Those nearest to God have seen them."[47]

BARBARA HEPWORTH British artist BARBARA HEPWORTH (1903–1975) developed her own kind of essential sculptural form, combining pristine shape with a sense of organic vitality. She sought a sculptural idiom that would express her sense both of nature and the landscape and of the person who is in and observes nature (see "Brancusi, Hepworth, and Moore," above). By 1929, Hepworth arrived at a breakthrough that evolved into an enduring and commanding

1 in.

35-58 Barbara Hepworth, *Oval Sculpture (No. 2),* 1943. Plaster cast, $11\frac{1}{4}'' \times 1' \, 4\frac{1}{4}'' \times 10''$. Tate Gallery, London.

Hepworth's major contribution to the history of sculpture was the introduction of the hole, or negative space, as an abstract element that is as integral and important to the sculpture as its mass.

HENRY MOORE British sculptor Henry Moore (1898–1986) shared Hepworth's interest in the hole, or void, and Brancusi's profound love of nature and knowledge of organic forms and materials. Moore maintained that every "material has its own individual qualities" and that these qualities could play a role in the creative process: "It is only when the sculptor works direct, when there is an active relationship with his material, that the material can take its part in the shaping of an idea."[48] Accordingly, the forms and lines of Moore's lead and stone sculptures tend to emphasize the material's hardness and solidity, whereas his fluid wood sculptures draw attention to the flow of the wood grain. One major recurring theme in Moore's work is the reclining female figure with simplified and massive forms. A tiny photograph of a Chacmool (FIG. 14-15) from ancient Mexico originally inspired this motif.

Although viewers can recognize a human figure in most of Moore's works, the artist simplified and abstracted the figure, attempting to express a universal truth beyond the physical world (see "Brancusi, Hepworth, and Moore," page 951). *Reclining Figure* (FIG. 35-59) reveals Moore's expressive handling of the human form and his responsiveness to his chosen material—here, elm wood. The contours of the sculpture follow the grain of the wood. The figure's massive shapes suggest Surrealist biomorphic forms (FIG. 35-52), but Moore's recumbent woman is also a powerful earth mother whose undulant forms and hollows suggest nurturing human energy. Similarly, they evoke the contours of the Yorkshire hills of Moore's childhood and the wind-polished surfaces of weathered wood and stone. The sculptor heightened the allusions to landscape and to Surrealist organic forms in his work by interplaying mass and void, based on the intriguing qualities of cavities in nature. As he explained, "The hole connects one side to the other, making it immediately more three-dimensional. . . . The mystery of the hole—the mysterious fascination of caves in hillsides and cliffs."[49] The concern with the void—the holes—recalls the sculpture of artists such as Barbara Hepworth (FIG. 35-58), whose work influenced him, and Aleksandr Archipenko (FIG. 35-20). Above all, *Reclining Figure* combines the organic vocabulary central to Moore's philosophy—bone shapes, eroded rocks, and geologic formations—to communicate the human form's fluidity, dynamism, and evocative nature.

element in her work from that point forward, and that represents her major contribution to the history of sculpture: the use of the hole, or void. Particularly noteworthy is that Hepworth introduced the hole, or negative space, in her sculpture as an abstract element—it does not represent anything specific—and one that is as integral and important to the sculpture as its mass. *Oval Sculpture (No. 2)* is a plaster cast (FIG. 35-58) of an earlier wooden sculpture Hepworth carved in 1943. Pierced in four places, *Oval Sculpture* is as much defined by the smooth, curving holes as by the volume of white plaster. Like the forms in all of Hepworth's mature works, those in *Oval Sculpture* are basic and universal, expressing a sense of eternity's timelessness.

1 ft.

35-59 Henry Moore, *Reclining Figure,* 1939. Elm wood, $3' \, 1'' \times 6' \, 7'' \times 2' \, 6''$. Detroit Institute of Arts, Detroit (Founders Society purchase with funds from the Dexter M. Ferry Jr. Trustee Corporation).

The reclining female figure was a major theme in Moore's sculptures. He simplified and abstracted the massive form in a way that recalls Biomorphic Surrealism. The contours follow the grain of the wood.

10 ft.

35-60 VERA MUKHINA, *The Worker and the Collective Farm Worker*, Soviet Pavilion, Paris Exposition, 1937. Stainless steel, 78′ high. Art © Estate of Vera Mukhina/RAO, Moscow/VAGA, New York.

In contrast to contemporaneous abstract sculpture, Mukhina's realistic representation of a male factory worker and a female farm worker glorifies the communal labor of the Soviet people.

VERA MUKHINA Not all sculptors of this period pursued abstraction, however. *The Worker and the Collective Farm Worker* (FIG. **35-60**) by Russian artist VERA MUKHINA (1889–1963) presents a vivid contrast to the work of Brancusi, Hepworth, and Moore. Produced in 1937 for the International Exposition in Paris—the same venue in which Picasso displayed *Guernica* (FIG. **35-41**)—Mukhina's monumental stainless-steel sculpture glorifies the communal labor of the Soviet people. Whereas Picasso employed Cubist abstraction to convey the horror of wartime bombing, Mukhina relied on realism to represent exemplars of the Soviet citizenry. Her sculpture, which stood atop the Soviet Pavilion at the exposition, depicts a male factory worker holding aloft the tool of his trade, the hammer. Alongside him is a female farm worker raising her sickle to the sky. The juxtaposed hammer and sickle, appearing as they do at the apex of the sculpture, replicate their appearance on the Soviet flag, thereby celebrating the Soviet system. The artist augmented the heroic tenor of this sculpture by emphasizing the solidity of the figures, who stride forward with their clothes billowing dramatically behind them. Mukhina had studied in Paris and was familiar with abstraction, especially Cubism, but felt that a commitment to real-

ism produced the most powerful sculpture. The Soviet government officially approved this realist style, and Mukhina earned high praise for her sculpture. Indeed, Russian citizens celebrated the work as a national symbol for decades.

AMERICA, 1930 TO 1945

The Armory Show of 1913 (see "The Armory Show," page 934) was an important vehicle for exposing American artists to modernist European art. Equally significant was the emigration of European artists across the Atlantic Ocean. The havoc Hitler and the National Socialists wreaked in the early 1930s (see "Degenerate Art," page 945) forced artists to flee. The United States, among other countries, offered both survival and a more hospitable environment for producing their art. Léger, Lipchitz, Beckmann, Grosz, Ernst, and Dalí, among many others, all made their way to American cities.

Museums in the United States, wanting to demonstrate their familiarity and connection with the most progressive European art, mounted exhibitions centered on the latest European artistic developments. In 1938, for example, the City Art Museum of Saint Louis presented an exhibition of Beckmann's work, and the Art Institute of Chicago organized *George Grosz: A Survey of His Art from 1918–1938.* This interest in exhibiting the work of persecuted artists driven from their homelands also had political overtones. In the highly charged atmosphere of the late 1930s leading to the onset of World War II, people often perceived support for these artists and their work as support for freedom and democracy. In 1942, Alfred H. Barr Jr. (1902–1981), director of the Museum of Modern Art, stated:

> Among the freedoms which the Nazis have destroyed, none has been more cynically perverted, more brutally stamped upon, than the Freedom of Art. For not only must the artist of Nazi Germany bow to political tyranny, he must also conform to the personal taste of that great art connoisseur, Adolf Hitler. . . . But German artists of spirit and integrity have refused to conform. They have gone into exile or slipped into anxious obscurity. . . . Their paintings and sculptures, too, have been hidden or exiled. . . . But in free countries they can still be seen, can still bear witness to the survival of a free German culture.[50]

Despite this moral support for exiled artists, once the United States formally entered the war, Germany officially became the enemy. Then it was much more difficult for the American art world to promote German artists, however persecuted. Many émigré artists, including Léger, Grosz, Ernst, and Dalí, returned to Europe after the war ended. Their collective presence in the United States until then, however, was critical for the development of American art and contributed to the burgeoning interest in the avant-garde among American artists.

Sculpture and Photography

ALEXANDER CALDER One American artist who rose to international prominence at this time was ALEXANDER CALDER (1898–1976). Both the artist's father and grandfather were sculptors, but Calder initially studied mechanical engineering. Fascinated all his life by motion, he explored that phenomenon and its relationship to three-dimensional form in much of his sculpture. As a young artist in Paris in the late 1920s, Calder invented a circus filled with wire-based miniature performers that he activated into realistic analogues of their real-life counterparts' motion. After a visit to Mondrian's studio in the early 1930s, Calder set out to put the Dutch painter's brightly colored rectangular shapes (FIG. **35-56**) into motion. (Marcel Duchamp, intrigued by Calder's early motorized and hand-cranked examples of moving abstract pieces, named them *mobiles*.) Calder's

The Museum of Modern Art and the Avant-Garde

Established in 1929, the Museum of Modern Art (often called MoMA) in New York City owes its existence to a trio of women—Lillie P. Bliss, Mary Quinn Sullivan, and Abby Aldrich Rockefeller (see "Art 'Matronage' in America," page 933). These women saw the need for a museum to collect and exhibit modernist art. Together they founded what quickly became the most influential museum of modern art in the world. Their success was extraordinary considering the skepticism and hostility greeting much of modernist art at the time of the museum's inception. Indeed, at that time, few American museums exhibited late-19th- and 20th-century art at all.

In its quest to expose the public to the energy and challenge of modernist, particularly avant-garde, art, MoMA developed unique and progressive exhibitions. Among those the museum mounted during the early years of its existence were *Cubism and Abstract Art* and *Fantastic Art, Dada, Surrealism* (1936). Two other noteworthy shows were *American Sources of Modern Art (Aztec, Maya, Inca)* in 1933 and *African Negro Art* in 1935, among the first exhibitions to deal with "primitive" artifacts in artistic rather than anthropological terms (see "Primitivism," page 920).

The organization of MoMA's administrative structure and the scope of the museum's early activities were also remarkable. MoMA's first director, Alfred H. Barr Jr., insisted on establishing departments not only for painting and sculpture but also for photography, prints and drawing, architecture, and the decorative arts. He developed a library of books on modern art and a film library, both of which have become world-class collections, as well as an extensive publishing program.

It is the museum's art collection, however, that has drawn the most attention. By cultivating an influential group of patrons, MoMA has developed an extensive and enviable collection of late-19th- and

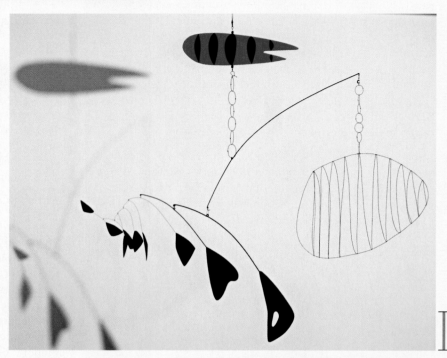

35-61 ALEXANDER CALDER, *Lobster Trap and Fish Tail*, 1939. Painted sheet aluminum and steel wire, 8' 6" × 9' 6". Museum of Modern Art, New York.

Using his thorough knowledge of engineering to combine nonobjective organic forms and motion, Calder created a new kind of sculpture—the mobile—that expressed reality's innate dynamism.

20th-century art. Its collection includes such important works as van Gogh's *Starry Night* (FIG. 31-17), Picasso's *Les Demoiselles d'Avignon* (FIG. 35-12), and Dalí's *The Persistence of Memory* (FIG. 35-49), as well as many others illustrated in this book, including 19 in this chapter alone. MoMA has also served as an art patron itself, commissioning works like Calder's *Lobster Trap and Fish Tail* (FIG. 35-61) in 1939, just a decade after the institution's founding.

---

engineering skills soon helped him to fashion a series of balanced structures hanging from rods, wires, and colored, organically shaped plates. This new kind of sculpture, which combined nonobjective organic forms and motion, succeeded in expressing the innate dynamism of the natural world.

An early Calder mobile is *Lobster Trap and Fish Tail* (FIG. 35-61), which the artist created in 1939 under a commission from the Museum of Modern Art in New York City for the stairwell of the museum's new building on 53rd Street (see "The Museum of Modern Art and the Avant-Garde," above). Calder carefully planned each nonmechanized mobile so that any air current would set the parts moving to create a constantly shifting dance in space. Mondrian's work may have provided the initial inspiration for the mobiles, but their organic

shapes resemble those in Joan Miró's Surrealist paintings (FIG. 35-52). Indeed, a viewer can read Calder's forms as either geometric or organic. Geometrically, the lines suggest circuitry and rigging, and the shapes derive from circles and ovoid forms. Organically, the lines suggest nerve axons, and the shapes resemble cells, leaves, fins, wings, and other bioforms.

GREAT DEPRESSION In the 1930s much of the Western world plunged into the Great Depression, which had particularly acute ramifications in the United States. The decade following the catastrophic stock market crash of October 1929 dramatically changed the nation, and artists were among the many economic victims. The limited art market virtually disappeared, and museums curtailed both their purchases and exhibition schedules. Many artists sought financial support from the federal government, which established numerous programs to provide relief, assist recovery, and promote reform. Among the programs supporting artists were the Treasury Relief Art Project, founded in 1934 to commission art for federal buildings, and the Works Progress Administration (WPA), founded in 1935 to relieve widespread unemployment. Under the WPA, varied activities of the Federal Art Project paid artists, writers, and theater people a regular wage in exchange for work in their professions. Another important program was the Resettlement Administration (RA), better known by its later name, the Farm Security Administration. The RA oversaw emergency aid programs for farm families caught in the Depression.

DOROTHEA LANGE The RA hired American photographer DOROTHEA LANGE (1895–1965) in 1936 and dispatched her to photograph the rural poor attempting to survive the desperate conditions wrought by the Great Depression. At the end of an assignment to document the lives of migratory pea pickers in California, Lange stopped at a camp in Nipomo and found the migrant workers there starving because the crops had frozen in the fields. Among the pictures Lange made on this occasion was *Migrant Mother, Nipomo Valley* (FIG. **35-62**), in which she captured the mixture of strength and worry in the raised hand and careworn face of a young mother, who holds a baby on her lap. Two older children cling to their

1 in.

35-62 DOROTHEA LANGE, *Migrant Mother, Nipomo Valley,* 1935. Gelatin silver print, 1′ 1″ × 9″. Oakland Museum of California, Oakland (gift of Paul S. Taylor). ◼◀

While documenting the lives of migratory farm workers during the Depression, Lange made this unforgettable photograph of a mother in which she captured the woman's strength and worry.

mother trustingly while shunning the camera. Lange described how she got the picture:

> [I] saw and approached the hungry and desperate mother, as if drawn by a magnet. I do not remember how I explained my presence or my camera to her, but I remember she asked me no questions. I made five exposures, working closer and closer from the same direction. . . . There she sat in that lean-to tent with her children huddled around her, and she seemed to know that my pictures might help her, and so she helped me.[51]

Within days after Lange's photograph appeared in a San Francisco newspaper, people rushed food to Nipomo to feed the hungry workers.

Painting

The political, social, and economic developments of the 1930s and 1940s also had a profound effect on American painters.

BEN SHAHN Born in Lithuania, BEN SHAHN (1898–1969) came to the United States in 1906 and trained as a lithographer before broadening the media in which he worked to include easel painting, photography, and murals. He focused on the lives of ordinary people and the injustices often done to them by the structure of an impersonal, bureaucratic society. In the early 1930s, he completed a cycle of 23 paintings and prints inspired by the trial and execution of the two Italian anarchists Nicola Sacco and Bartolomeo Vanzetti. Accused of killing two men in a holdup in 1920 in South Braintree, Massachusetts, the Italians were convicted in a trial that many people thought resulted in a grave miscarriage of justice. Shahn felt he had found in this story a subject the equal of any in Western art history: "Suddenly I realized . . . I was living through another crucifixion."[52] Basing many of the works in this cycle on newspaper photographs of the events, Shahn devised a style that adapted his knowledge of Synthetic Cubism and his training in commercial art to an emotionally expressive use of flat, intense color in figural compositions filled with sharp, dry, angular forms. He called the major work in the series *The Passion of Sacco and Vanzetti* (FIG. **I-5**), drawing a parallel to Christ's Passion. This tall, narrow painting condenses the narrative in terms of both time and space. The two executed men lie in coffins at the bottom of the composition. Presiding over them are the three members of the commission chaired by Harvard University president A. Laurence Lowell, who declared the original trial fair and cleared the way for the executions to take place. A framed portrait of Judge Webster Thayer, who handed down the initial sentence, hangs on the wall of a simplified government building. The gray pallor of the dead men, the stylized mask-faces of the mock-pious mourning commissioners, and the sanctimonious, distant judge all contribute to the mood of anguished commentary that makes this image one of Shahn's most powerful works.

EDWARD HOPPER Trained as a commercial artist, EDWARD HOPPER (1882–1967) studied painting and printmaking in New York and then in Paris. When he returned to the United States, he concentrated on scenes of contemporary American city and country life. His paintings depict buildings, streets, and landscapes that are curiously muted, still, and filled with empty spaces, evoking the national mind-set during the Depression era. Hopper did not paint historically specific scenes. He took as his subject the more generalized theme of the overwhelming loneliness and echoing isolation of modern life in the United States. In his paintings, motion is stopped

35-63 EDWARD HOPPER, *Nighthawks,* 1942. Oil on canvas, 2′ 6″ × 4′ 8 11/16″. Art Institute of Chicago, Chicago (Friends of American Art Collection).

The seeming indifference of Hopper's characters to one another, and the echoing spaces that surround them, evoke the overwhelming loneliness and isolation of Depression-era life in the United States.

and time suspended, as if the artist recorded the major details of a poignant personal memory. From the darkened streets outside a restaurant in *Nighthawks* (FIG. **35-63**), the viewer glimpses the lighted interior through huge plate-glass windows, which lend the inner space the paradoxical sense of being both a safe refuge and a vulnerable place for the three customers and the counterman. The seeming indifference of Hopper's characters to one another and the echoing spaces that surround them suggest the pervasive loneliness of modern humans. In *Nighthawks* and other works, Hopper created a Realist vision recalling that of 19th-century artists such as Thomas Eakins (FIG. **30-38**) and Henry Ossawa Tanner (FIG. **30-40**), but, consistent with more recent trends in painting, he simplified the shapes in a move toward abstraction.

JACOB LAWRENCE African American artist JACOB LAWRENCE (1917–2000) found his subjects in modern history, concentrating on the culture and history of his own people. Lawrence moved to Harlem, New York, in 1927 at about age 10. There, he came under the spell of the African art and the African American history he found in lectures and exhibitions and in the special programs sponsored by the 135th Street New York Public Library, which had outstanding collections of African American art and archival data. Inspired by the politically oriented art of Goya (FIG. **30-13**), Daumier (FIG. **30-30**), and Orozco (FIG. **35-67**), and influenced by the many artists and writers of the Harlem Renaissance whom he met, including Aaron Douglas (FIG. **35-36**), Lawrence found his subjects in the everyday life of Harlem and in African American history.

In 1941, Lawrence began a 60-painting series titled *The Migration of the Negro,* in which he defined his own vision of the continuing African American struggle against discrimination. Unlike his earlier historical paintings depicting important figures in American history,

such as the abolitionists Frederick Douglass and Harriet Tubman, this series called attention to a contemporaneous event—the ongoing exodus of black labor from the southern United States. Disillusioned with their lives in the South, hundreds of thousands of African Americans migrated north in the years following World War I, seeking improved economic opportunities and more hospitable political and social conditions. This subject had personal relevance to Lawrence:

> I was part of the migration, as was my family, my mother, my sister, and my brother. . . . I grew up hearing tales about people "coming up," another family arriving. . . . I didn't realize what was happening until about the middle of the 1930s, and that's when the *Migration* series began to take form in my mind.[53]

The "documentation" of the period, such as the RA program, ignored African Americans, and thus this major demographic shift remained largely invisible to most Americans. Of course, the conditions African Americans encountered both during their migration and in the North were often as difficult and discriminatory as those they had left behind in the South.

Lawrence's series provides numerous vignettes capturing the experiences of these migrating people. Often, a sense of bleakness and of the degradation of African American life dominates the images. *No. 49* (FIG. **35-64**) of this series bears the caption "They also found discrimination in the North although it was much different from that which they had known in the South." The artist depicted a blatantly segregated dining room with a barrier running down the room's center separating the whites on the left from the African Americans on the right. To ensure a continuity and visual integrity among all 60 paintings, Lawrence interpreted his themes systematically in rhythmic arrangements of bold, flat, and strongly colored shapes. His style drew equally from his interest in the push-pull

35-64 JACOB LAWRENCE, *No. 49* from *The Migration of the Negro,* 1940–1941. Tempera on Masonite, 1′ 6″ × 1′. Phillips Collection, Washington, D.C.

The 49th in a series of 60 paintings documenting African American life in the North, Lawrence's depiction of a segregated dining room underscored that the migrants had not left discrimination behind.

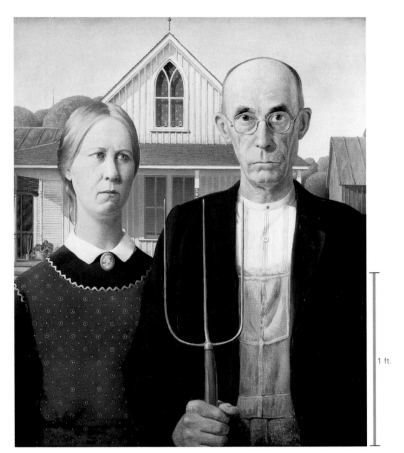

35-65 GRANT WOOD, *American Gothic,* 1930. Oil on beaverboard, 2′ 5$\frac{7}{8}$″ × 2′ $\frac{7}{8}$″. Art Institute of Chicago, Chicago (Friends of American Art Collection). Art © Estate of Grant Wood/Licensed by VAGA, New York. ◼◀

In reaction to modernist abstract painting, the Midwestern Regionalism movement focused on American subjects. Wood's painting of an Iowa farmer and his daughter is an American icon.

effects of Cubist space and his memories of the patterns made by the colored scatter rugs brightening the floors of his childhood homes. He unified the narrative with a consistent palette of bluish green, orange, yellow, and grayish brown throughout the entire series.

GRANT WOOD Although many American artists, such as the Precisionists (FIGS. 35-37 and 35-38), preferred to depict the city or rapidly developing technological advances, others avoided subjects tied to modern life. At a 1931 arts conference, GRANT WOOD (1891–1942) announced a new movement developing in the Midwest, known as *Regionalism,* which he described as focused on American subjects and as standing in reaction to the modernist abstraction of Europe and New York. Four years later, Wood published an essay "Revolt against the City" that underscored this new focus. Wood and the Regionalists, sometimes referred to as the American Scene Painters, turned their attention instead to rural life as America's cultural backbone. Wood's paintings, for example, focus on rural Iowa, where he was born and raised.

The work that catapulted Wood to national prominence was *American Gothic* (FIG. 35-65), which became an American icon. The artist depicted a farmer and his spinster daughter standing in front of a

neat house with a small *lancet* window, typically found on Gothic cathedrals. The man and woman wear traditional attire. He appears in worn overalls, and she in an apron trimmed with rickrack. The dour expression on both faces gives the painting a severe quality, which Wood enhanced with his meticulous brushwork. The public and professional critics agreed that *American Gothic* was "quaint, humorous, and AMERICAN" and embodied "strength, dignity, fortitude, resoluteness, integrity," qualities that represented the true spirit of America.[54]

Wood's Regionalist vision involved more than his subjects. It extended to a rejection of avant-garde styles in favor of a clearly readable, Realist style. Surely this approach appealed to many people alienated by the increasing presence of abstraction in art. Interestingly enough, despite the accolades this painting received, it also attracted criticism. Not everyone saw the painting as a sympathetic portrayal of Midwestern life. Indeed, some in Iowa considered the depiction insulting. In addition, despite the seemingly reportorial nature of *American Gothic,* some viewed it as a political statement—one of staunch nationalism. In light of the problematic nationalism in Germany at the time, many observers found Wood's nationalistic attitude disturbing. Nonetheless, during the Great Depression, Regionalist paintings had a popular appeal because they often projected a reassuring image of America's heartland. The public saw Regionalism as a means of coping with the national crisis through a search for cultural roots. Thus, people deemed acceptable any nostalgia implicit in Regionalist paintings or mythologies these works perpetuated because they served a larger purpose.

Benton's mural for Missouri's State Capitol is one of the major Regionalist artworks. Part documentary and part invention, the images include both positive and negative aspects of state history.

THOMAS HART BENTON Another major Regionalist artist was THOMAS HART BENTON (1889–1975). Whereas Wood focused his attention on Iowa, Benton turned to scenes from his native Missouri. He produced one of his major works, a series of murals titled *A Social History of the State of Missouri,* in 1936 for the Missouri State Capitol. The murals depict a collection of images from the state's true and legendary history, such as primitive agriculture, horse trading, a vigilante lynching, and an old-fashioned political meeting. Other scenes portray the mining industry, grain elevators, Native Americans, and family life. One segment, *Pioneer Days and Early Settlers* (FIG. **35-66**), shows a white man using whiskey as a bartering tool with a Native American (at left), along with scenes documenting the building of Missouri. Part documentary and part invention, Benton's images include both positive and negative aspects of Missouri's history, as these examples illustrate. Although the public perceived the Regionalists as dedicated to glorifying Midwest-ern life, that belief distorted their aims. Indeed, Grant Wood observed, "your true regionalist is not a mere eulogist; he may even be a severe critic."[55] Benton, like Wood, championed a visually accessible style, but he developed a highly personal aesthetic that included complex compositions, a fluidity of imagery, and simplified figures depicted with a rubbery distortion.

JOSÉ CLEMENTE OROZCO During the period between the two world wars, three Mexican painters achieved international renown for their work both in Mexico and in the United States. The eldest of the three was JOSÉ CLEMENTE OROZCO (1883–1949), one of a group of Mexican artists determined to base their art on the indigenous history and culture existing in Mexico before Europeans arrived. The movement these artists formed was part of the idealistic rethinking of society that occurred in conjunction with the Mexican Revolution (1910–1920) and the lingering political turmoil of the 1920s.

One of 24 panels depicting the history of Mexico from ancient times, this scene focuses on a heroic peasant soldier of the Mexican Revolution surrounded by symbolic figures of his oppressors.

Rivera on Art for the People

Diego Rivera was an avid proponent of a social and political role for art in the lives of common people and wrote passionately about the proper goals for an artist—goals he fully met in his murals depicting Mexican history (FIG. 35-68). Rivera's views stand in sharp contrast to the growing interest in abstraction on the part of many early-20th-century painters and sculptors.

> Art has always been employed by the different social classes who hold the balance of power as one instrument of domination—hence, as a political instrument. One can analyze epoch after epoch—from the stone age to our own day—and see that there is no form of art which does not also play an essential political role. . . . What is it then that we really need? . . . An art with revolution as its subject: because the principal interest in the worker's life has to be touched first. It is necessary that he find aesthetic satisfaction and the highest pleasure appareled in the essential interest of his life. . . . The subject is to the painter what the rails are to a locomotive. He cannot do without it. In fact, when he refuses to seek or accept a subject, his own plastic methods and his own aesthetic theories become his subject instead. . . . [H]e himself becomes the subject of his work. He becomes nothing but an illustrator of his own state of mind . . . That is the deception practiced under the name of "Pure Art."*

35-68 DIEGO RIVERA, *Ancient Mexico,* from the *History of Mexico,* Palacio Nacional, Mexico City, 1929–1935. Fresco.

A staunch Marxist, Rivera painted vast mural cycles in public buildings to dramatize the history of his native land. This fresco depicts the conflicts between indigenous Mexicans and the Spanish colonizers.

* Quoted in Robert Goldwater and Marco Treves, eds., *Artists on Art from the XIV to the XX Century* (New York: Pantheon, 1945), 475–477.

Among the projects these politically motivated artists undertook were vast mural cycles placed in public buildings to dramatize and validate the history of Mexico's native peoples. Orozco worked on one of the first major cycles, painted in 1922 on the walls of the National Training School in Mexico City. He carried the ideas of this mural revolution to the United States, completing many commissions for wall paintings between 1927 and 1934. From 1932 to 1934, he worked on one of his finest mural cycles in Baker Library at Dartmouth College in New Hampshire, partly in honor of its superb collection of books in Spanish. The college let him choose the subject. Orozco depicted, in 14 large panels and 10 smaller ones, a panoramic and symbolic history of ancient and modern Mexico, from the early mythic days of the feathered-serpent god Quetzalcoatl (see Chapters 14 and 32) to a contemporary and bitterly satiric vision of modern education.

The imagery in panel 16, *Epic of American Civilization: Hispano-America* (FIG. 35-67), revolves around the monumental figure of a heroic Mexican peasant armed to participate in the Mexican Revolution. Looming on either side of him are mounds crammed with symbolic figures of his oppressors—bankers, government soldiers, officials, gangsters, and the rich. Money-grubbers pour hoards of gold at the incorruptible peon's feet, cannons threaten him, and a bemedaled general raises a dagger to stab him in the back. Orozco's training as an architect gave him a sense of the framed wall surface, which he easily commanded, projecting his clearly defined figures onto the solid mural plane in monumental scale. In addition, Orozco's early training as a maker of political prints and as a newspaper artist had taught him the rhetorical strength of graphic brevity, which he used here to assure that his allegory could be read easily. His special merging of the graphic and mural media effects gives his work an originality and force rarely seen in mural painting after the Renaissance and Baroque periods.

DIEGO RIVERA Like his countryman, DIEGO RIVERA (1886–1957) received great acclaim for his murals, both in Mexico and in the United States. A staunch Marxist, Rivera strove to develop an art that served his people's needs (see "Rivera on Art for the People," above). Toward that end, he sought to create a national Mexican style focusing on Mexico's history and incorporating a popular, generally accessible aesthetic in keeping with the socialist spirit of the Mexican Revolution. Rivera produced numerous large murals in public buildings, among them a series lining the staircase of the National Palace in Mexico City. In these images, painted between 1929 and 1935, he depicted scenes from Mexico's history, of which *Ancient Mexico* (FIG. 35-68) is one. This section of the mural represents the

Kahlo's deeply personal paintings touch sensual and psychological memories in her audience. Here, twin self-portraits linked by clasped hands and a common artery suggest different sides of her personality.

conflicts between the indigenous people and the Spanish colonizers. Rivera included portraits of important figures in Mexican history and, in particular, in the struggle for Mexican independence. Although complex, the decorative, animated murals retain the legibility of folklore, and the figures consist of simple monumental shapes and areas of bold color.

FRIDA KAHLO Born to a Mexican mother and German father, the painter FRIDA KAHLO (1907–1954), who married Diego Rivera, used the details of her life as powerful symbols for the psychological pain of human existence. Art historians often consider Kahlo a Surrealist due to the psychic and autobiographical issues she dealt with in her art. Indeed, André Breton deemed her a Natural Surrealist, although Kahlo herself rejected any association with Surrealism. Kahlo began painting seriously as a young student, during convalescence from an accident that tragically left her in constant pain. Her life became a heroic and tumultuous battle for survival against illness and stormy personal relationships.

Typical of her long series of unflinching self-portraits is *The Two Fridas* (FIG. **35-69**), one of the few large-scale canvases Kahlo ever produced. The twin figures sit side by side on a low bench in a barren landscape under a stormy sky. The figures suggest different sides of the artist's personality, inextricably linked by the clasped hands and by the thin artery that stretches between them, joining their exposed hearts. The artery ends on one side in surgical forceps and on the other in a miniature portrait of her husband as a child. Her deeply personal paintings touch sensual and psychological memories in her audience.

However, to read Kahlo's paintings solely as autobiographical overlooks the powerful political dimension of her art. Kahlo was deeply nationalistic and committed to her Mexican heritage. Politically active, she joined the Communist Party in 1920 and participated in public political protests. *The Two Fridas* incorporates Kahlo's commentary on the struggle facing Mexicans in the early 20th century in defining their national cultural identity. The Frida on the right (representing indigenous culture) appears in a Tehuana dress, the traditional costume of Zapotec women from the Isthmus of Tehuantepec, whereas the Frida on the left (representing imperialist forces) wears a European-style white lace dress. The heart, depicted here in such dramatic fashion, was an important symbol in the art of the Aztecs, whom Mexican nationalists idealized as the last independent rulers of an indigenous political unit. Thus, *The Two Fridas* represents both Kahlo's personal struggles and the struggles of her homeland.

ARCHITECTURE

The first half of the 20th century was a time of great innovation in architecture too. As in painting, sculpture, and photography, new ideas came from both sides of the Atlantic.

Europe

In the years immediately following the Russian Revolution, a new art movement called *Productivism* emerged in the Soviet Union as an offshoot of the Constructivist movement. The Productivists devoted their talents to designing a better environment for human beings.

VLADIMIR TATLIN One of the most gifted leaders of the Productivism movement was VLADIMIR TATLIN (1885–1953). The revolution was the signal to Tatlin and other avant-garde artists in Russia that the hated old order was about to end. In utopian fashion, these artists aspired to play a significant role in creating a new world, one that would fully use the power of industrialization to benefit all the people. Initially, like Malevich (FIG. 35-54) and Gabo (FIG. 35-55), Tatlin believed that nonobjective art was ideal for the new society, free as such art was from any past symbolism. But after the 1917 revolution, Tatlin enthusiastically abandoned abstract art for "functional art" by designing products such as an efficient stove and a set of worker's clothing.

Tatlin's most famous work is his design for *Monument to the Third International* (FIG. **35-70**), commissioned by the Department of Artistic Work of the People's Commissariat for Enlightenment early in 1919 to honor the Russian Revolution. He envisioned a huge glass-and-iron building that—at 1,300 feet—would have been one-third taller than the Eiffel Tower (FIG. 31-1). Widely influential, "Tatlin's Tower," as it became known, served as a model for those seeking to encourage socially committed and functional art. On its

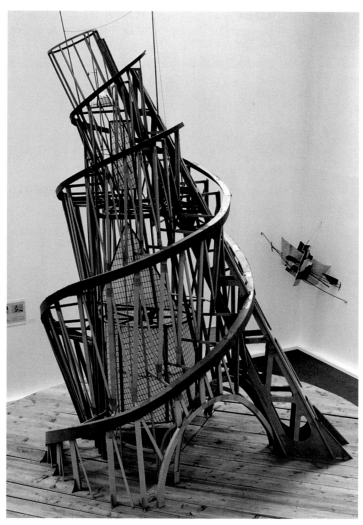

35-70 VLADIMIR TATLIN, *Monument to the Third International,* 1919–1920. Reconstruction of the lost model, 1992–1993. Kunsthalle, Düsseldorf.

"Tatlin's Tower" was an ambitious avant-garde design for a Soviet governmental building with three geometrically shaped chambers rotating at different speeds within a dynamically tilted spiral cage.

proposed site in the center of Moscow, it would have functioned as a propaganda and news center for the Soviet people. Within a dynamically tilted spiral cage, three geometrically shaped chambers were to rotate around a central axis, each chamber housing facilities for a different type of governmental activity and rotating at a different speed. The one at the bottom, a huge cylindrical glass structure for lectures and meetings, was to revolve once a year. Higher up was a cone-shaped chamber intended for administrative functions and monthly rotations. At the top, a cubic information center would have revolved daily, issuing news bulletins and proclamations via the most modern means of communication. These included an open-air news screen (illuminated at night) and a special instrument designed to project words on the clouds on any overcast day. The decreasing size of the chambers as visitors ascended the monument paralleled the decision-making hierarchy in the political system, with the most authoritative, smallest groups near the building's apex. The design thus served as a visual reinforcement of a social and political reality.

Tatlin envisioned the whole complex as a dynamic communications center perfectly suited to the exhilarating pace of the new age. In addition, the design's reductive geometry demonstrates the architect's connection to the artistic programs of the Suprematists and the Con-

structivists. Due to Russia's desperate economic situation during these years, however, Tatlin's ambitious design never materialized as a building. It existed only in metal and wood models exhibited on various official occasions before disappearing. The only records of the models are a few drawings, photographs, and recent reconstructions (FIG. 35-70).

GERRIT RIETVELD Some European architects explored the ideas Mondrian and De Stijl artists advanced. One of the masterpieces of De Stijl architecture is the Schröder House (FIG. 35-71) in Utrecht, built in 1924 by GERRIT THOMAS RIETVELD (1888–1964). Rietveld came to the group as a cabinetmaker and made De Stijl furnishings throughout his career. His architecture carries the same spirit into a larger integrated whole and perfectly expresses Theo van Doesburg's definition of De Stijl architecture:

> The new architecture is anti-cubic, i.e., it does not strive to contain the different functional space cells in a single closed cube, but it throws the functional space (as well as canopy planes, balcony volumes, etc.) out from the centre of the cube, so that height, width, and depth plus time become a completely new plastic expression in open spaces. . . . The plastic architect . . . has to construct in the new field, time-space.[56]

The main living rooms of the Schröder House are on the second floor, with more private rooms on the ground floor. However, Rietveld's house has an open plan and a relationship to nature more like the houses of his contemporary, the American architect Frank Lloyd Wright (FIGS. 35-77 and FIG. 35-79). Rietveld designed the entire second floor with sliding partitions that can be closed to define separate rooms or pushed back to create one open space broken into units only by the furniture arrangement. This shifting quality appears also on the outside, where railings, free-floating walls, and long rectangular windows give the effect of cubic units breaking up before the viewer's eyes. Rietveld's design clearly links all the arts. Rectangular planes seem to slide across each other on the Schröder House facade like movable panels, making this structure a kind of three-dimensional projection of the rigid but carefully proportioned flat color rectangles in Mondrian's paintings (FIG. 35-56).

35-71 GERRIT THOMAS RIETVELD, Schröder House, Utrecht, the Netherlands, 1924.

The De Stijl Schröder House has an open plan and an exterior that is a kind of three-dimensional projection of the carefully proportioned flat color rectangles in Mondrian's paintings (FIG. 35-56).

WALTER GROPIUS De Stijl architects not only developed an appealing simplified geometric style but also promoted the notion that art should be thoroughly incorporated into living environments. As Mondrian had insisted, "[A]rt and life are *one*; art and life are both expressions of truth."[57] In Germany, WALTER GROPIUS (1883–1969) developed a particular vision of "total architecture." He made this concept the foundation of not only his own work but also the work of generations of pupils under his influence at a school called the *Bauhaus*. In 1919, Gropius became the director of the Weimar School of Arts and Crafts in Germany, founded in 1906. Under Gropius, the school assumed a new name—Das Staatliche Bauhaus (roughly translated as "State School of Building"). Gropius's goal was to train artists, architects, and designers to accept and anticipate 20th-century needs. He developed an extensive curriculum based on certain principles. First, Gropius staunchly advocated the importance of strong basic design (including principles of composition, two- and three-dimensionality, and color theory) and craftsmanship as fundamental to good art and architecture. He declared: "Architects, sculptors, painters, we must all go back to the crafts. . . . There is no essential difference between the artist and the craftsman."[58] To achieve this integration of art and craft, both a technical instructor and a "teacher of form"—an artist—taught in each department. Among the teachers Gropius hired were Vassily Kandinsky (FIG. 35-7) and Paul Klee (FIG. 35-53).

Second, Gropius promoted the unity of art, architecture, and design. "Architects, painters, and sculptors," he insisted, "must recognize anew the composite character of a building as an entity."[59] To encourage the elimination of boundaries that traditionally separated art from architecture and art from craft, the Bauhaus offered courses in a wide range of artistic disciplines. These included weaving, pottery, bookbinding, carpentry, metalwork, stained glass, mural painting, stage design, and advertising and typography, in addition to painting, sculpture, and architecture.

Third, because Gropius wanted the Bauhaus to produce graduates who could design progressive environments that satisfied 20th-century needs, he emphasized thorough knowledge of machine-age technologies and materials. He felt that to produce truly successful designs, the artist-architect-craftsperson had to understand industry and mass production. Ultimately, Gropius hoped for a marriage between art and industry—a synthesis of design and production.

Like the De Stijl movement, the Bauhaus philosophy had its roots in utopian principles. Gropius's declaration reveals the idealism of the entire Bauhaus enterprise: "Together let us conceive and create the new building of the future, which will embrace architecture and sculpture and painting in one unity and which will rise one day toward heaven from the hands of a million workers like a crystal symbol of a new faith."[60] In its reference to a unity of workers, this statement also reveals the undercurrent of socialism present in Germany at the time.

BAUHAUS IN DESSAU After encountering increasing hostility from a new government elected in 1924, the Bauhaus moved north to Dessau in early 1925. By this time, the Bauhaus program had matured. In a statement, Walter Gropius listed the school's goals more clearly:

- A decidedly positive attitude to the living environment of vehicles and machines.

- The organic shaping of things in accordance with their own current laws, avoiding all romantic embellishment and whimsy.

- Restriction of basic forms and colors to what is typical and universally intelligible.

- Simplicity in complexity, economy in the use of space, materials, time, and money.[61]

35-72A LOOS, Steiner House, Vienna, 1910.

The building Gropius designed for the Bauhaus at Dessau visibly expressed these goals. It is, in fact, the Bauhaus's architectural manifesto. The Dessau Bauhaus consisted of workshop and class areas, a dining room, a theater, a gymnasium, a wing with studio apartments, and an enclosed two-story bridge housing administrative offices. Of the major wings, the most dramatic was the Shop Block (FIG. 35-72). Three stories tall, the Shop Block housed a printing shop and dye works facility, in addition to other work areas. The builders constructed the skeleton of reinforced concrete but set these supports well back, sheathing the entire structure in glass to create a streamlined and light effect. This design's simplicity followed Gropius's dictum that architecture should avoid "all romantic embellishment and whimsy." Further, he realized his principle of "economy in the use of space" in his interior layout of the Shop Block, which consisted of large areas of free-flowing undivided space. Gropius believed this kind of spatial organization encouraged interaction and the sharing of ideas.

MARCEL BREUER The interior decor of this Dessau building also reveals the comprehensiveness of the Bauhaus program. Because carpentry, furniture design, and weaving were all part of the Bauhaus curriculum, Gropius gave students and teachers the task of designing furniture and light fixtures for the building. One of the memorable furniture designs that emerged from the Bauhaus was the tubular steel "Wassily chair" (FIG. 35-73) crafted by Hungarian MARCEL BREUER (1902–1981) and named in honor of Bauhaus instructor Vassily

35-73A STÖLZL, Gobelin tapestry, 1927–1928.

35-72 WALTER GROPIUS, Shop Block, the Bauhaus, Dessau, Germany, 1925–1926.

Gropius constructed this Bauhaus building by sheathing a reinforced concrete skeleton in glass. The design followed his dictum that architecture should avoid "all romantic embellishment and whimsy."

1 ft.

35-73 MARCEL BREUER, Wassily chair, 1925. Chrome-plated tubular steel and canvas, $2' 4\frac{1}{4}'' \times 2' 6\frac{3}{4}'' \times 2' 4''$. Museum of Modern Art, New York (gift of Herbert Bayer).

The Bauhaus advocated a comprehensive approach to architecture, which included furniture design. Breuer's chair has a simple geometric look in keeping with Bauhaus aesthetics.

(sometimes spelled Wassily) Kandinsky. Breuer supposedly got the inspiration to use tubular steel while riding his bicycle and admiring the handlebars. In keeping with Bauhaus aesthetics, his chairs have a simplified, geometric look, and the leather or cloth supports add to the furniture's comfort and functionality. These chairs could also easily be mass produced and thus epitomize the goals of the Bauhaus.

LUDWIG MIES VAN DER ROHE In 1928, Gropius left the Bauhaus, and LUDWIG MIES VAN DER ROHE (1886–1969) eventually took over the directorship, moving the school to Berlin. Taking as his motto "less is more" and calling his architecture "skin and bones," the new Bauhaus director had already fully formed his aesthetic when he conceived the model (FIG. **35-74**) for a glass skyscraper building in 1921. In the glass model, which was on display at the first Bauhaus exhibition in 1923, three irregularly shaped towers flow outward from a central court designed to hold a lobby, a porter's room, and a community center. Two cylindrical entrance shafts rise at the ends of the court, each containing elevators, stairways, and toilets. Wholly transparent, the perimeter walls reveal the regular horizontal patterning of the cantilevered floor planes and their thin vertical supporting elements. The bold use of glass sheathing and inset supports was, at the time, technically and aesthetically adventurous. The weblike delicacy of the lines of the model, as well as the illusion of movement created by reflection and by light changes seen through the glass, appealed to many other architects. A few years later, Gropius pursued these principles in his design for the Bauhaus building (FIG. **35-72**) in Dessau. The glass-and-steel skyscrapers found in major cities throughout the world today are the enduring legacy of Mies van der Rohe's design.

END OF THE BAUHAUS One of Hitler's first acts after coming to power was to close the Bauhaus in 1933. During its 14-year existence, the beleaguered school graduated fewer than 500 students, yet it achieved legendary status. Its phenomenal impact extended beyond painting, sculpture, and architecture to interior design, graphic design, and advertising. Moreover, art schools everywhere began to structure their curricula in line with the program the

35-74 LUDWIG MIES VAN DER ROHE, model for a glass skyscraper, Berlin, Germany, 1922 (no longer extant).

In this technically and aesthetically adventurous design, the architect whose motto was "less is more" proposed a transparent building that revealed its cantilevered floor planes and thin supports.

Bauhaus pioneered. The numerous Bauhaus instructors who fled Nazi Germany disseminated the school's philosophy and aesthetic. Many Bauhaus members came to the United States. Gropius and Breuer ended up at Harvard University. Mies van der Rohe moved to Chicago and taught there.

LE CORBUSIER The simple geometric aesthetic that Gropius and Mies van der Rohe developed became known as the *International Style* because of its widespread popularity. The first and purest adherent of this style was the Swiss architect Charles-Edouard Jeanneret, who adopted his maternal grandfather's name—LE CORBUSIER (1887–1965). Trained in Paris and Berlin, he was also a painter, but Le Corbusier wielded greater influence as an architect and theorist on modern architecture. As such, he applied himself to designing a functional living space, which he described as a "machine for living."[62]

Le Corbusier maintained that the basic physical and psychological needs of every human being were sun, space, and vegetation combined with controlled temperature, good ventilation, and insulation

35-75 LE CORBUSIER, Villa Savoye, Poissy-sur-Seine, France, 1929.

Steel and ferroconcrete made it possible for Le Corbusier to invert the traditional practice of placing light architectural elements above heavy ones and to eliminate weight-bearing walls on the ground story.

against harmful and undesirable noise. He also advocated basing dwelling designs on human scale, because the house is humankind's assertion within nature. All these qualities characterize Le Corbusier's Villa Savoye (FIG. **35-75**), located at Poissy-sur-Seine near Paris. This country house sits conspicuously within its site, tending to dominate it, and has a broad view of the landscape. Several colors appear on the exterior—originally, a dark-green base, cream walls, and a rose-and-blue windscreen on top. They were a deliberate analogy for the colors in the contemporary machine-inspired Purist style of painting (FIG. **35-22**) Le Corbusier practiced.

A cube of lightly enclosed and deeply penetrated space, the Villa Savoye has an only partially confined ground floor (containing a three-car garage, bedrooms, a bathroom, and utility rooms). Much of the house's interior is open space, with the thin columns supporting the main living floor and the roof garden area. The major living rooms in the Villa Savoye are on the second floor, wrapping around an open central court. Strip windows that run along the membranelike exterior walls provide illumination to the rooms. From the second-floor court, a ramp leads up to a flat roof-terrace and garden protected by a curving windbreak along one side. The Villa Savoye has no traditional facade. The ostensible approach to the house does not define an entrance. People must walk around and through the house to comprehend its layout. Spaces and masses interpenetrate so fluidly that inside and outside space intermingle. The machine-planed smoothness of the unadorned surfaces, the slender ribbons of continuous windows, and the buoyant lightness of the whole fabric—all combine to reverse the effect of traditional country houses (FIG. **22-29**). By placing heavy elements above and light ones below, and by refusing to enclose the ground story of the Villa Savoye with masonry walls, Le Corbusier inverted traditional design practice. This openness, made possible by the use of steel and ferroconcrete as construction materials, makes the Villa Savoye's heavy upper stories appear to hover lightly on the slender column supports.

The Villa Savoye was a marvelous house for a single family, but like De Stijl architects, Le Corbusier dreamed of extending his ideas of the house as a "machine for living" to designs for efficient and humane cities. He saw great cities as spiritual workshops, and he proposed to correct the deficiencies in existing cities caused by poor traffic circulation, inadequate living units, and the lack of space for recreation and exercise. Le Corbusier suggested replacing traditional cities with three types of new communities. Vertical cities would house workers and the business and service industries. Linear-industrial cities would run as belts along the routes between the vertical cities and would serve as centers for the people and processes involved in manufacturing. Finally, separate centers would be constructed for people involved in intensive agricultural activity. Le Corbusier's cities would provide for human cultural needs in addition to serving every person's physical, mental, and emotional comfort needs.

Later in his career, Le Corbusier designed a few vertical cities, most notably the Unité d'Habitation in Marseilles (1945–1952). He also created the master plan for the entire city of Chandigarh, the capital city of Punjab, India (1950–1957). He ended his career with a personal expressive style in his design of the Chapel of Notre Dame du Haut (FIGS. **36-56** and **36-57**) at Ronchamp.

America

America also embraced the new European architecture, particularly the Bauhaus style, which rejected ornament of any kind. But other styles also won wide followings, some of which were reactions against the severity of Bauhaus design.

ART DECO According to Bauhaus principles, pure form emerged from functional structure and required no decoration. Yet popular taste still favored ornamentation, especially in public architecture. A movement in the 1920s and 1930s sought to upgrade industrial design as a "fine art." Proponents wanted to work new materials into decorative patterns that could be either machined or handcrafted and that could, to a degree, reflect the simplifying trend in architecture. A remote descendant of Art Nouveau, this movement became known as *Art Deco*, which acquired its name at the Exposition des Arts Décoratifs et Industriels Modernes (Exposition of Modern Decorative and Industrial Arts), held in Paris in 1925. Art Deco had universal application—to buildings, interiors, furniture, utensils, jewelry, fashions, illustration, and commercial products of every sort. Art Deco products have a "streamlined," elongated symmetrical aspect. Simple flat shapes alternate with shallow volumes in hard patterns. The concept of streamlining predominated in industrial-design circles in the 1930s and involved the use of organic, tapered shapes and forms. Derived from nature, these simple forms are inherently aerodynamic, making them technologically efficient (because of their reduced resistance as they move through air or water) as well as aesthetically pleasing. Designers adopted streamlined shapes for trains and cars, and the popular appeal of these designs led to their use in an array of objects, from machines to consumer products.

Art Deco's exemplary masterpiece is the stainless-steel spire of the Chrysler Building (FIG. **35-76**) in New York City, designed by WILLIAM VAN ALEN (1882–1954). The building and spire are monuments to the fabulous 1920s, when American millionaires and corporations competed with one another to raise the tallest skyscrapers in the biggest cities. Built up of diminishing fan shapes, the spire glitters triumphantly in the sky, a resplendent crown honoring the business achievements of the great auto manufacturer. As a temple of commerce, the Chrysler Building celebrated the principles and success of American business before the onset of the Great Depression.

35-76 WILLIAM VAN ALEN, Chrysler Building, New York, New York, 1928–1930.

The Chrysler Building's stainless steel spire epitomizes Art Deco architecture. The skyscraper's glittering crown of diminishing fan shapes has a streamlined form that was popular during the 1920s.

FRANK LLOYD WRIGHT One of the most striking personalities in the development of early-20th-century architecture was FRANK LLOYD WRIGHT (1867–1959). Born in Wisconsin, Wright moved to Chicago, where he eventually joined the firm headed by Louis Sullivan (FIGS. 31-40 and 31-41). Wright set out to create an "architecture of democracy."[63] Always a believer in architecture as "natural" and "organic," Wright saw it as serving free individuals who have the right to move within a "free" space, envisioned as a nonsymmetrical design interacting spatially with its natural surroundings. He sought to develop an organic unity of planning, structure, materials, and site. Wright identified the principle of continuity as fundamental to understanding his view of organic unity:

> Classic architecture was all fixation. . . . Now why not let walls, ceilings, floors become seen as component parts of each other? . . . You may see the appearance in the surface of your hand contrasted with the articulation of the bony structure itself. This ideal, profound in its architectural implications . . . I called . . . continuity.[64]

Wright manifested his vigorous originality early, and by 1900 he had arrived at a style entirely his own. In his work during the first decade of the 20th century, his cross-axial plan and his fabric of continuous roof planes and screens defined a new domestic architecture.

ROBIE HOUSE Wright fully expressed these elements and concepts in the Robie House (FIG. 35-77), built between 1907 and 1909. Like other buildings in the Chicago area he designed at about the same time, he called this home a "prairie house." Wright conceived the long, sweeping, ground-hugging lines, unconfined by abrupt wall limits, as reaching out toward and capturing the expansiveness of the Midwest's great flatlands. Abandoning all symmetry, the architect eliminated a facade, extended the roofs far beyond the walls, and all but concealed the entrance. Wright filled the house's "wandering" plan (FIG. 35-78) with intricately joined spaces (some large and open, others closed), grouped freely around a great central

35-77 FRANK LLOYD WRIGHT, Robie House, Chicago, Illinois, 1907–1909.

The Robie House is an example of Wright's "architecture of democracy," in which free individuals move within a "free" space—a nonsymmetrical design interacting spatially with its natural surroundings.

35-78 FRANK LLOYD WRIGHT, plan of the second (main) level of the Robie House, Chicago, Illinois, 1907–1909.

Typical of Wright's "prairie houses," the Robie House has a bold "wandering" asymmetrical plan with intricately joined open and closed spaces grouped freely around a great central fireplace.

Perched on a rocky hillside over a waterfall, Wright's Fallingwater has long sweeping lines, unconfined by abrupt wall limits, reaching out and capturing the expansiveness of the natural environment.

fireplace. (He believed strongly in the hearth's age-old domestic significance.) Wright designed enclosed patios, overhanging roofs, and strip windows to provide unexpected light sources and glimpses of the outdoors as the inhabitants moved through the interior space. These elements, together with the open ground plan, created a sense of space in motion, inside and out. Wright matched his new and fundamental interior spatial arrangement in his exterior treatment. The flow of interior space determined the sharp angular placement of exterior walls.

FALLINGWATER The Robie House is an example of Wright's "naturalism"—his adjustment of a building to its site. In this particular case, however, the confines of the city lot constrained the building-to-site relationship more than did the sites of some of Wright's more expansive suburban and country homes. The Kaufmann House, nicknamed "Fallingwater" (FIG. **35-79**) and designed as a weekend retreat at Bear Run, Pennsylvania, for Pittsburgh department store magnate Edgar Kaufmann Sr., is a prime example of the latter. Perched on a rocky hillside over a small waterfall, this structure, which has become an icon of modernist architectural design, extends the Robie House's blocky masses in all four directions. Ever since the completion of this residence, architects and the public alike have marveled at the fluid interplay between interior and exterior. In designing Fallingwater, Wright, in keeping with his commitment to an "architecture of democracy," sought to incorporate the structure more fully into the site, thereby ensuring a fluid, dynamic exchange between the interior of the house and the natural environment outside. Rather than build the house overlooking or next to the waterfall, Wright decided to build it over the waterfall, because he believed the inhabitants would become desensitized to the waterfall's presence and power if they merely overlooked it. To take advantage of the location, Wright designed a series of terraces that extend on three levels from a central core structure. The contrast in textures between concrete, painted metal, and natural stones in the house's terraces and walls enlivens its shapes, as does Wright's use of full-length strip windows to create a stunning interweaving of interior and exterior space.

The implied message of Wright's new architecture was space, not mass—a space designed to fit the patron's life and enclosed and divided as required. Wright took special pains to meet his clients' requirements, often designing all the accessories of a house (including, in at least one case, gowns for his client's wife). In the late 1930s, he acted on a cherished dream to provide good architectural design for less prosperous people by adapting the ideas of his prairie house to plans for smaller, less-expensive dwellings. These residences, known as Usonian houses, became templates for suburban housing developments in the post–World War II housing boom.

The publication of Wright's plans brought him a measure of fame in Europe, especially in Holland and Germany. The issuance in Berlin in 1910 of a portfolio of his work and an exhibition of his designs the following year stimulated younger architects to adopt some of his ideas about open plans that afforded clients freedom. Some 40 years before his career ended, his work was already of revolutionary significance. Mies van der Rohe wrote in 1940 that the "dynamic impulse from [Wright's] work invigorated a whole generation. His influence was strongly felt even when it was not actually visible."[65]

Frank Lloyd Wright's influence in Europe was exceptional, however, for any American artist before World War II. But in the decades following that global conflict, American painters, sculptors, and architects often took the lead in establishing new styles that artists elsewhere quickly emulated. This new preeminence of America in the arts is the subject of Chapter 36.

EUROPE AND AMERICA, 1900 TO 1945

EUROPE, 1900 to 1920

- During the early 20th century, avant-garde artists searched for new definitions of art in a changed world. Matisse and the Fauves used bold colors as the primary means of conveying feeling. German Expressionist paintings feature clashing colors, disquieting figures, and perspectival distortions.
- Pablo Picasso and Georges Braque radically challenged prevailing artistic conventions with Cubism, in which artists dissect forms and place them in interaction with the space around them.
- The Futurists focused on motion in time and space in their effort to create paintings and sculptures that captured the dynamic quality of modern life. The Dadaists celebrated the spontaneous and intuitive, often incorporating found objects in their artworks.

Picasso, *Les Demoiselles d'Avignon*, 1907

AMERICA, 1900 to 1930

- The Armory Show of 1913 introduced avant-garde European art to American artists. Man Ray, for example, embraced Dada's fondness for chance and the displacement of ordinary items, and Stuart Davis adopted the Cubist interest in fragmented form.
- The Harlem Renaissance brought African American artists to the forefront, including Aaron Douglas, whose paintings drew on Cubist principles. Charles Demuth, Georgia O'Keeffe, and the Precisionists used European modernist techniques to celebrate contemporary American subjects.
- Photography emerged as an important American art form in the work of Alfred Stieglitz, who emphasized the careful arrangement of forms and patterns of light and dark. Edward Weston experimented with photographs of segments of the human body that verge on abstraction.

Weston, *Nude*, 1925

EUROPE, 1920 to 1945

- World War I gave rise to the Neue Sachlichkeit movement in Germany. "New Objectivity" artists depicted the horrors of war and explored the themes of death and transfiguration.
- The Surrealists investigated ways to express in art the world of dreams and the unconscious. Natural Surrealists aimed for "concrete irrationality" in their naturalistic paintings of dreamlike scenes. Biomorphic Surrealists experimented with automatism and employed abstract imagery.
- Many European modernists pursued utopian ideals. The Suprematists developed an abstract style to express pure feeling. The Constructivists used nonobjective forms to suggest the nature of space-time. De Stijl artists employed simple geometric forms in their search for "pure plastic art."
- Sculptors, including Hepworth and Moore, also increasingly turned to abstraction and emphasized voids as well as masses in their work. Brancusi captured the essence of flight in *Bird in Space,* a glistening abstract sculpture that does not mimic the form of a bird.

Brancusi, *Bird in Space*, 1924

AMERICA, 1930 to 1945

- Although Calder created abstract works between the wars, other American artists favored figural art. Lange and Shahn chronicled social injustice. Hopper explored the loneliness of the Depression era. Lawrence recorded the struggle of African Americans. Wood depicted life in rural Iowa.
- Mexican artists Orozco and Rivera painted epic mural cycles of the history of Mexico. Kahlo's powerful and frequently autobiographical paintings explored the human psyche.

Kahlo, *The Two Fridas*, 1939

ARCHITECTURE

- Under Walter Gropius, the Bauhaus in Germany promoted the vision of "total architecture," which called for the integration of all the arts in constructing modern living environments. Bauhaus buildings were simple glass and steel designs devoid of "romantic embellishment and whimsy."
- In France, Le Corbusier used modern construction materials in his "machines for living"—simple houses with open plans and unadorned surfaces.
- The leading American architect of the first half of the 20th century was Frank Lloyd Wright, who promoted the "architecture of democracy," in which free individuals move in a "free" space. Fallingwater is a bold asymmetrical design integrating the building with the natural environment.

Wright, Fallingwater, 1936–1939

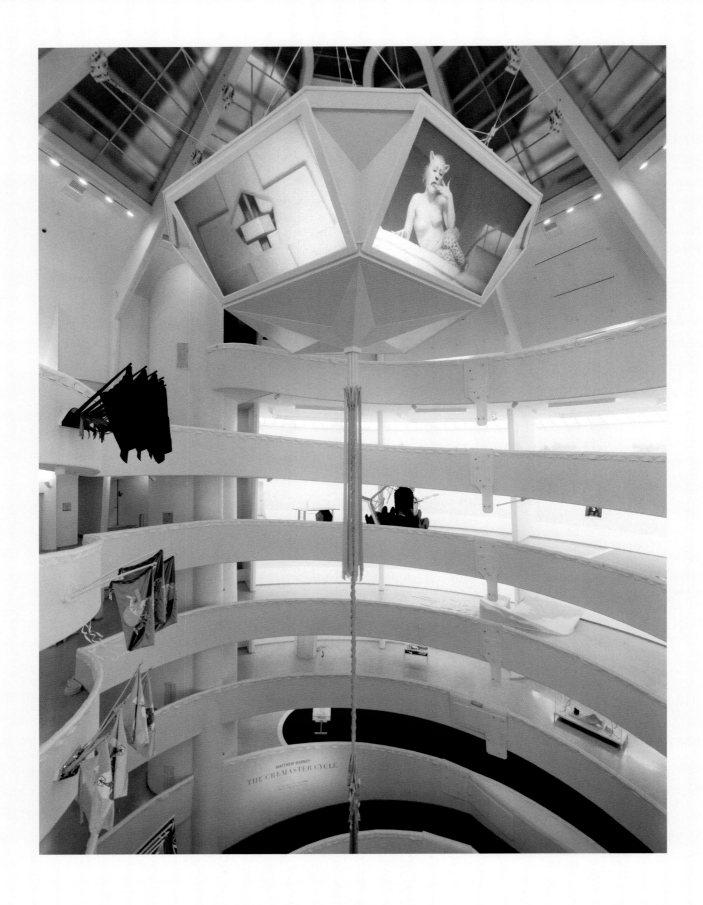

36-1 MATTHEW BARNEY, *Cremaster* cycle, installation at the Solomon R. Guggenheim Museum, New York, 2003.

Barney's vast multimedia installations of drawings, photographs, sculptures, and videos typify the relaxation at the opening of the 21st century of the traditional boundaries among artistic media.

36

EUROPE AND AMERICA AFTER 1945

World War II, with the global devastation it unleashed on all dimensions of life—psychological, political, physical, and economic—set the stage for the second half of the 20th century. The dropping of atomic bombs by the United States on the Japanese cities of Hiroshima and Nagasaki in 1945 signaled a turning point not only in the war but in the geopolitical balance and the nature of international conflict as well. For the rest of the century, nuclear war became a very real threat. Indeed, the two nuclear superpowers, the United States and the Soviet Union, divided the post–World War II world into spheres of influence, and each regularly intervened politically, economically, and militarily wherever and whenever it considered its interests to be at stake.

Persistent conflict throughout the world in the later 20th century resulted in widespread disruption and dislocation. In 1947 the British left India, dividing the subcontinent into the new, still hostile nations of India and Pakistan. After a catastrophic war, Communists came to power in China in 1949. North Korea invaded South Korea in 1950 and fought a grim war with the United States and its allies that ended in 1953. The Soviet Union brutally suppressed uprisings in its subject nations—East Germany, Poland, Hungary, and Czechoslovakia. The United States intervened in disputes in Central and South America. Almost as soon as many previously colonized nations of Africa—Kenya, Uganda, Nigeria, Angola, Mozambique, the Sudan, Rwanda, and the Congo—won their independence, civil wars devastated them. In Indonesia civil conflict left more than 100,000 dead. Algeria expelled France in 1962 after the French waged a prolonged, vicious war with Algeria's Muslim natives. After 15 years of bitter war in Southeast Asia, the United States suffered defeat in Vietnam. From 1979 to 1989 the Soviets unsuccessfully tried to occupy Afghanistan. Arab nations fought wars with Israel in 1967, 1973, and the early 1980s. The Palestinian conflict remains the subject of almost daily newspaper headlines. A revitalized Islam, which inspired a fundamentalist religious revolution in Iran, has encouraged "holy war" with the West, using a new weapon, international terrorism—most dramatically in the attacks on New York City and Washington, D.C., on September 11, 2001. In response, the United States and allied Western nations launched invasions of Afghanistan and Iraq. Conflict and unrest continue to plague large areas of the globe today.

Upheaval has also characterized the cultural sphere in the decades since the end of World War II. In the United States, for example, various groups forcefully questioned the status quo. During the 1960s and 1970s, the struggle for civil rights for African Americans, for free speech on university campuses, and for disengagement from the Vietnam War led to a rebellion of the young, who took to the streets in often raucous demonstrations, with violent repercussions. The prolonged ferment produced a new system of values, a "youth culture," expressed in the radical rejection not only of national policies but often also of the society generating them. Young Americans derided their elders' lifestyles and adopted unconventional dress, manners, habits, and morals deliberately subversive of mainstream social standards. The youth era witnessed the sexual revolution, the widespread use and abuse of drugs, and the development of rock music, then an exclusively youthful art form. Young people "dropped out" of regulated society, embraced alternative belief systems, and rejected Western university curricula as irrelevant.

This counterculture had considerable societal impact and widespread influence beyond its political phase. The civil rights movement of the 1960s and later the women's liberation movement of the 1970s reflected the spirit of rebellion, coupled with the rejection of racism and sexism. In keeping with the growing resistance to established authority, women systematically began to challenge the male-dominated culture, which they perceived as having limited their political power and economic opportunities for centuries. Feminists charged that the institutions of Western society, particularly the nuclear family headed by the patriarch, perpetuated male power and subordination of women. They further contended that monuments of Western culture—its arts and sciences as well as its political, social, and economic institutions—masked the realities of male power.

The central issue that fueled these rebellions and changes—from international political conflicts to the rise of feminism—was power. Increasingly, individuals and groups sought not just to uncover the dynamics of power, but to combat actively the inappropriate exercise of power or change the balance of power. For example, following patterns developed first in the civil rights movement and later in feminism, various ethnic groups and gays and lesbians all mounted challenges to discriminatory policies and attitudes. These groups fought for recognition, respect, and legal protection and battled discrimination with political action. In addition, the growing scrutiny in numerous academic fields—cultural studies, literary theory, and colonial and postcolonial studies—of the dynamics and exercise of power also contributed to the dialogue on these issues. As a result of this concern for the dynamics of power, identity (both individual and group) has emerged as a potent arena for discussion and action. Explorations into the politics of identity now aim to increase personal and public understanding of how self-identifications, along with imposed or inherited identities, affect lives.

As has been true since human beings first began to make sculptures and paintings and erect buildings, European and American art and architecture since 1945 have reflected the changing cultural world in which artists and architects live and work.

PAINTING AND SCULPTURE, 1945 TO 1970

The end of World War II in 1945 left devastated cities, ruptured economies, and governments in chaos throughout Europe. These factors, coupled with the massive loss of life and the indelible horror of the Holocaust and of Hiroshima and Nagasaki, resulted in a pervasive sense of despair, disillusionment, and skepticism. Although many groups (for example, the Futurists in Italy; see Chapter 35) had tried to find redemptive value in World War I, it was virtually impossible to do the same with World War II, coming as it did so soon after the war that was supposed to "end all wars." Additionally, World War I was largely a European conflict that left roughly 10 million people dead, whereas World War II was a truly global catastrophe that claimed 35 million lives.

Postwar Expressionism in Europe

The cynicism that emerged across Europe in the 1940s found voice in existentialism, a philosophy asserting the absurdity of human existence and the impossibility of achieving certitude. As existentialism gained widespread popularity, many adherents also promoted atheism and questioned the possibility of situating God within a systematic philosophy. Most scholars trace the roots of existentialism to the Danish theologian Søren Kierkegaard (1813–1855), but in the postwar period, the writings of French author Jean-Paul Sartre (1905–1980) most clearly captured the existentialist spirit. According to Sartre, if God does not exist, then individuals must constantly struggle in isolation with the anguish of making decisions in a world without absolutes or traditional values. This spirit of pessimism and despair emerged frequently in European art of the immediate postwar period.

1 ft.

36-2 ALBERTO GIACOMETTI, *Man Pointing* (no. 5 of 6), 1947. Bronze, 5′ 10″ × 3′ 1″ × 1′ 5$\frac{5}{8}$″. Des Moines Art Center, Des Moines (Nathan Emory Coffin Collection).

The writer Jean-Paul Sartre considered Giacometti's thin and virtually featureless sculpted figures as the epitome of existentialist humanity—alienated, solitary, and lost in the world's immensity.

A brutality or roughness appropriately expressing both the artist's state of mind and the larger cultural sensibility characterized the work of many European sculptors and painters.

ALBERTO GIACOMETTI The sculpture of Swiss artist ALBERTO GIACOMETTI (1901–1966) perhaps best expresses the spirit of existentialism. Although Giacometti never claimed he pursued existentialist ideas in his art, his works capture the essence of that philosophy. Indeed, Sartre, Giacometti's friend, saw the artist's figural sculptures as the epitome of existentialist humanity—alienated, solitary, and lost in the world's immensity. Giacometti's sculptures of the 1940s, such as *Man Pointing* (FIG. 36-2), are thin, virtually featureless figures with rough, agitated surfaces. Rather than conveying the solidity and mass of conventional bronze sculpture, these severely attenuated figures seem swallowed up by the space surrounding them, imparting a sense of isolation and fragility. Giacometti's sculptures are evocative and moving, speaking to the pervasive despair in the aftermath of world war.

FRANCIS BACON Created in the year after World War II ended, *Painting* (FIG. 36-3) by British artist FRANCIS BACON (1910–1992) is an indictment of humanity and a reflection of war's butchery. The painting is a compelling and revolting image of a powerful, stocky man with a gaping mouth and a vivid red stain on his upper lip, as if he were a carnivore devouring the raw meat sitting on the railing surrounding him. Bacon may have based his depiction of this central figure on news photos of similarly dressed European and American officials. The umbrella in particular recalls images of Neville Chamberlain (1869–1940), the wartime British prime minister who frequently appeared in photographs with an umbrella. Bacon added to the visceral impact of the painting by depicting the flayed carcass hanging behind the central figure as if it were a crucified human form. Although the specific sources for the imagery in *Painting* may not be entirely clear, the work is unmistakably "an attempt to remake the violence of reality itself," as Bacon often described his art, based on what he referred to as "the brutality of fact."[1]

36-3A BACON, *Figure with Meat*, 1954.

JEAN DUBUFFET Although less specific, the works of French artist JEAN DUBUFFET (1901–1985) also express a tortured vision of the world through manipulated materials. In works such as *Vie Inquiète* (*Uneasy Life*; FIG. 36-4), Dubuffet presented a scene incised into thickly encrusted, parched-looking surfaces. He first built up an *impasto* (a layer of thickly applied pigment) of plaster, glue, sand, asphalt, and other common materials. Over that he painted or incised crude images of the type produced by children, the insane, and graffiti scrawlers. Scribblings interspersed with the images heighten the impression of smeared and gashed surfaces of crumbling walls and worn pavements marked by random individuals.

36-3 FRANCIS BACON, *Painting*, 1946. Oil and pastel on linen, 6′ 5 7/8″ × 4′ 4″. Museum of Modern Art, New York.

Painted in the aftermath of World War II, this intentionally revolting image of a powerful figure presiding over a slaughter is Bacon's indictment of humanity and a reflection of war's butchery.

36-4 JEAN DUBUFFET, *Vie Inquiète* (*Uneasy Life*), 1953. Oil on canvas, 4′ 3″ × 6′ 4″. Tate Gallery, London.

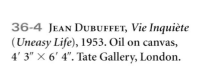

Dubuffet expressed a tortured vision of the world through thickly encrusted painted surfaces and crude images of the kind children and the insane produce. He called it "art brut"—untaught and coarse art.

Dubuffet believed the art of children, the mentally unbalanced, prisoners, and outcasts was more direct and genuine because those who created it did so unrestrained by conventional standards of art. He promoted "art brut"—untaught and coarse art.

Abstract Expressionism

36-5A GORKY, *Garden in Sochi,* ca. 1943.

In the 1940s, the center of the Western art world shifted from Paris to New York because of the devastation World War II had inflicted across Europe and the resulting influx of émigré artists escaping to the United States. American artists picked up the European avant-garde's energy, which movements such as Cubism and Dada had fostered, but in the postwar years, modernism increasingly became synonymous with a strict *formalism*—an emphasis on an artwork's visual elements rather than its subject. The most important champion of New York formalist painting was the American art critic Clement Greenberg (1909–1994), who wielded considerable influence from the 1940s through the 1970s. Greenberg helped redefine the parameters of modernism by advocating the rejection of illusionism and the exploration of the properties of each artistic medium. So dominant was Greenberg that scholars often refer to the general modernist tenets during this period as Greenbergian formalism.

Although Greenberg modified his complex ideas about art over the years, he consistently expounded certain basic concepts. In particular, he promoted the idea of purity in art. "Purity in art consists in the acceptance, willing acceptance, of the limitations of the medium of the specific art."[2] In other words, Greenberg believed artists should strive for a more explicit focus on the properties exclusive to each medium—for example, two-dimensionality or flatness in painting, and three-dimensionality in sculpture.

It follows that a modernist work of art must try, in principle, to avoid communication with any order of experience not inherent in the most literally and essentially construed nature of its medium. Among other things, this means renouncing illusion and explicit subject matter. The arts are to achieve concreteness, "purity," by dealing solely with their respective selves—that is, by becoming "abstract" or nonfigurative.[3]

Abstract Expressionism, the first major American avant-garde movement, emerged in New York in the 1940s. As the name suggests, the artists associated with the New York School of Abstract Expressionism produced paintings that are, for the most part, abstract but express the artist's state of mind with the goal also of striking emotional chords in the viewer. The Abstract Expressionists turned inward to create, and the resulting works convey a rough spontaneity and palpable energy. The New York School painters wanted the viewer to grasp the content of their art intuitively, in a state free from structured thinking. The artist Mark Rothko (FIG. **36-9**) eloquently wrote:

We assert man's absolute emotions. We don't need props or legends. We create images whose realities are self evident. Free ourselves from memory, association, nostalgia, legend, myth. Instead of making cathedrals out of Christ, man or life, we make it out of ourselves, out of our own feelings. The image we produce is understood by anyone who looks at it without nostalgic glasses of history.[4]

1 ft.

36-5 JACKSON POLLOCK, *Number 1, 1950* (*Lavender Mist*), 1950. Oil, enamel, and aluminum paint on canvas, 7' 3" × 9' 10". National Gallery of Art, Washington, D.C. (Ailsa Mellon Bruce Fund).

Pollock's paintings emphasize the creative process. His mural-size canvases consist of rhythmic drips, splatters, and dribbles of paint that envelop viewers, drawing them into a lacy spider web.

Jackson Pollock on Easel and Mural Painting

In two statements made in 1947, one as part of his application for a Guggenheim Fellowship and one in a published essay, Jackson Pollock explained the motivations for his new kind of "action painting" and described the manner in which he applied pigment to canvas (FIG. 36-6).

> I intend to paint large movable pictures which will function between the easel and mural. . . . I believe the easel picture to be a dying form, and the tendency of modern feeling is towards the wall picture or mural.*

My painting does not come from the easel. I hardly ever stretch my canvas before painting. I prefer to tack the unstretched canvas to the hard wall or the floor. I need the resistance of a hard surface. On the floor I am more at ease. I feel nearer, more a part of the painting, since this way I can walk around it, work from the four sides and literally be *in* the painting. This is akin to the method of the Indian sand painters of the West [see Chapter 32, page 861]. I continue to get further away from the usual painter's tools such as easel, palette, brushes, etc. I prefer sticks, trowels, knives and dripping fluid paint or a heavy impasto with sand, broken glass and other foreign matter added. When I am *in* my painting, I'm not aware of what I'm doing. . . . [T]he painting has a life of its own. I try to let it come through. . . . The source of my painting is the unconscious.†

* Quoted in Francis V. O'Connor, *Jackson Pollock* (New York: Museum of Modern Art, 1967), 39.
† Ibid., 39–40.

36-6 HANS NAMUTH, Jackson Pollock painting in his studio in Springs, Long Island, New York, 1950. Center for Creative Photography, University of Arizona, Tucson.

"Gestural abstraction" nicely describes Pollock's working technique. Using sticks or brushes, he flung, poured, and dripped paint onto a section of canvas he simply unrolled across his studio floor.

The Abstract Expressionist movement developed along two lines—*gestural abstraction* and *chromatic abstraction.* The gestural abstractionists relied on the expressiveness of energetically applied pigment. In contrast, the chromatic abstractionists focused on color's emotional resonance.

JACKSON POLLOCK The artist whose work best exemplifies gestural abstraction is JACKSON POLLOCK (1912–1956), who developed his signature style in the mid-1940s. By 1950, Pollock had refined his technique and was producing large-scale abstract paintings such as *Number 1, 1950* (*Lavender Mist;* FIG. 36-5). These works consist of rhythmic drips, splatters, and dribbles of paint. The mural-sized fields of energetic skeins of pigment envelop viewers, drawing them into a lacy spider web. Using sticks or brushes, Pollock flung, poured, and dripped paint (not only traditional oil paints but aluminum paints and household enamels as well) onto a section of canvas he simply unrolled across his studio floor (FIG. 36-6). This working method earned Pollock the derisive nickname "Jack the Dripper."

Responding to the image as it developed, he created art that was both spontaneous and choreographed. Pollock's painting technique highlights a particularly avant-garde aspect of gestural abstraction—its emphasis on the creative process. Indeed, Pollock literally immersed himself in the painting during its creation.

Art historians have linked Pollock's ideas about improvisation in the creative process to his interest in what psychiatrist Carl Jung called the collective unconscious. The improvisational nature of Pollock's work and his reliance on the subconscious also have parallels in the "psychic automatism" of Surrealism and the work of Vassily Kandinsky (FIG. 35-7), whom critics described as an "abstract expressionist" as early as 1919. In addition to Pollock's unique working methods and the expansive scale of his canvases, the lack of a well-defined compositional focus in his paintings significantly departed from conventional easel painting (see "Jackson Pollock on Easel and Mural Painting," above). A towering figure in 20th-century art, Pollock tragically died in a car accident at age 44, cutting short the development of his innovative artistic vision.

WILLEM DE KOONING Despite the public's skepticism about Pollock's art, other artists enthusiastically pursued similar avenues of expression. Dutch-born WILLEM DE KOONING (1904–1997) also developed a gestural abstractionist style. Even images such as *Woman I* (FIG. 36-7), although rooted in figuration, display the sweeping gestural brush strokes and energetic application of pigment typical of gestural abstraction. Out of the jumbled array of slashing lines and agitated patches of color appears a ferocious-looking woman with staring eyes and ponderous breasts. Her toothy smile, modeled on an ad for Camel cigarettes, becomes a grimace. Female models on advertising billboards partly inspired *Woman I*, one of a series of female images, but de Kooning's female forms also suggest fertility figures and a satiric inversion of the traditional image of Venus, goddess of love.

36-7A KLINE, *Mahoning*, 195

Process was important to de Kooning, as it was to Pollock. Continually working on *Woman I* for almost two years, de Kooning painted an image and then scraped it away the next day and began anew. His wife Elaine, also a painter, estimated that he painted approximately 200 scraped-away images of women on this canvas before settling on the final one.

In addition to this *Woman* series, de Kooning created nonrepresentational works dominated by huge swaths and splashes of pigment. His images suggest rawness and intensity. His dealer, Sidney Janis (1896–1989), confirmed this impression, recalling that de Kooning occasionally brought him paintings with ragged holes in them, the result of overly vigorous painting. Like Pollock, de Kooning was very much "in" his paintings. That kind of physical interaction between the painter and the canvas led the critic Harold Rosenberg (1906–1978) to describe the work of the New York School as *action painting*. In his influential 1952 article "The American Action Painters," Rosenberg described the attempts of Pollock, de Kooning, and others to get "inside the canvas."

At a certain moment the canvas began to appear to one American painter after another as an arena in which to act—rather than as a space in which to reproduce, re-design, analyze or "express" an

36-7 WILLEM DE KOONING, *Woman I,* 1950–1952. Oil on canvas, 6′ 3$\frac{7}{8}$″ × 4′ 10″. Museum of Modern Art, New York.

Although rooted in figuration, including pictures of female models on advertising billboards, de Kooning's *Woman I* displays the energetic application of pigment typical of gestural abstraction.

1 ft.

36-8 BARNETT NEWMAN, *Vir Heroicus Sublimis,* 1950–1951. Oil on canvas, 7′ 11$\frac{3}{8}$″ × 17′ 9$\frac{1}{4}$″. Museum of Modern Art, New York (gift of Mr. and Mrs. Ben Heller).

Newman's canvases consist of a single slightly modulated color field split by "zips" (narrow bands) running from one edge of the painting to the other, energizing the color field and giving it scale.

36-9 MARK ROTHKO, *No. 14,* 1960. Oil on canvas, 9′ 6″ × 8′ 9″. San Francisco Museum of Modern Art, San Francisco (Helen Crocker Russell Fund Purchase).

Rothko's chromatic abstractionist paintings—consisting of hazy rectangles of pure color hovering in front of a colored background—are compositionally simple but compelling visual experiences.

object, actual or imagined. What was to go on the canvas was not a picture but an event. The painter no longer approached his easel with an image in his mind; he went up to it with material in his hand to do something to that other piece of material in front of him. The image would be the result of this encounter.[5]

BARNETT NEWMAN In contrast to the aggressively energetic images of the gestural abstractionists, the work of the chromatic abstractionists exudes a quieter aesthetic, exemplified by the work of Barnett Newman and Mark Rothko. The emotional resonance of their works derives from their eloquent use of color. In his early paintings, BARNETT NEWMAN (1905–1970) presented organic abstractions inspired by his study of biology and his fascination with Native American art. He soon simplified his compositions so that each canvas, such as *Vir Heroicus Sublimis* (FIG. **36-8**)—Latin, "sublime heroic man"—consists of a single slightly modulated color field split by narrow bands the artist called "zips," which run from one edge of the painting to the other. As Newman explained it, "The streak was always going through an atmosphere; I kept trying to create a world around it."[6] He did not intend the viewer to perceive the zips as specific entities, separate from the ground, but as accents energizing the field and giving it scale. By simplifying his compositions, Newman increased color's capacity to communicate and to express his feelings about the tragic condition of modern life and the human struggle to survive. He claimed that "the artist's problem . . . [is] the idea-complex that makes contact with mystery—of life, of men, of nature, of the hard black chaos that is death, or the grayer, softer chaos that is tragedy."[7] Confronted by one of Newman's monumental colored canvases, viewers truly feel as if they are in the presence of the epic.

MARK ROTHKO The work of MARK ROTHKO (1903–1970) also deals with universal themes. Born in Russia, Rothko moved with

his family to the United States when he was 10. His early paintings were figural in orientation, but he soon arrived at the belief that references to anything specific in the physical world conflicted with the sublime idea of the universal, supernatural "spirit of myth," which he saw as the core of meaning in art. In a statement cowritten with Newman and artist Adolph Gottlieb (1903–1974), Rothko expressed his beliefs about art:

> We favor the simple expression of the complex thought. We are for the large shape because it has the impact of the unequivocal. . . . We assert that . . . only that subject matter is valid which is tragic and timeless. That is why we profess spiritual kinship with primitive and archaic art.[8]

Rothko's paintings became compositionally simple, and he increasingly focused on color as the primary conveyor of meaning. In works such as *No. 14* (FIG. **36-9**), Rothko created compelling visual experiences consisting of two or three large rectangles of pure color with hazy, brushy edges that seem to float on the canvas surface, hovering in front of a colored background. These paintings appear as shimmering veils of intensely luminous colors suspended in front of the canvases. Although the color juxtapositions are visually captivating, Rothko intended them as more than decorative. He saw color as a doorway to another reality, and insisted that color could express "basic human emotions—tragedy, ecstasy, doom. . . . The people who weep before my pictures are having the same religious experience I had when I painted them. And if you, as you say, are moved only by their color relationships, then you miss the point."[9] Like the other Abstract Expressionists, Rothko produced highly evocative, moving paintings that relied on formal elements rather than specific representational content to elicit emotional responses in the viewer.

Post-Painterly Abstraction

Post-Painterly Abstraction, another American art movement, developed out of Abstract Expressionism. Indeed, many of the artists associated with Post-Painterly Abstraction produced Abstract Expressionist work early in their careers. Yet Post-Painterly Abstraction, a term Clement Greenberg coined, manifests a radically different sensibility from Abstract Expressionism. Whereas Abstract Expressionism conveys a feeling of passion and visceral intensity, a cool, detached rationality emphasizing tighter pictorial control characterizes Post-Painterly Abstraction. Greenberg saw this art as contrasting with "painterly" art, characterized by loose, visible pigment application. Evidence of the artist's hand, so prominent in gestural abstraction, is conspicuously absent in Post-Painterly Abstraction. Greenberg championed this art form because it seemed to embody his idea of purity in art.

36-10 ELLSWORTH KELLY, *Red Blue Green*, 1963. Oil on canvas, 6′ 11⅝″ × 11′ 3⅞″. Museum of Contemporary Art, San Diego (gift of Dr. and Mrs. Jack M. Farris).

Hard-edge painting is one variant of Post-Painterly Abstraction. Kelly used razor-sharp edges and clearly delineated areas of color to distill painting to its essential two-dimensional elements.

1 ft.

ELLSWORTH KELLY Attempting to arrive at pure painting, the Post-Painterly Abstractionists distilled painting down to its essential elements, producing spare, elemental images. An example of one variant of Post-Painterly Abstraction, *hard-edge painting,* is *Red Blue Green* (FIG. **36-10**) by ELLSWORTH KELLY (b. 1923). With its razor-sharp edges and clearly delineated shapes, this work is completely abstract and extremely simple compositionally. Further, the painting contains no suggestion of the illusion of depth—the color shapes appear resolutely two-dimensional.

FRANK STELLA Another artist associated with the hard-edge painters of the 1960s is FRANK STELLA (b. 1936). In works such as *Mas o Menos* (*More or Less;* FIG. **36-11**), Stella eliminated many of

the variables associated with painting. His simplified images of thin, evenly spaced pinstripes on colored grounds have no central focus, no painterly or expressive elements, only limited surface modulation, and no tactile quality. Stella's systematic painting illustrates Greenberg's insistence on purity in art. The artist's famous comment on his work, "What you see is what you see," reinforces the notions that painters interested in producing advanced art must reduce their work to its essential elements and that the viewer must acknowledge that a painting is simply pigment on a flat surface.

36-11A RILEY, *Fission,* 1963.

HELEN FRANKENTHALER *Color-field painting,* another variant of Post-Painterly Abstraction, also emphasized painting's basic properties. However, rather than produce sharp, unmodulated

36-11 FRANK STELLA, *Mas o Menos* (*More or Less*), 1964. Metallic powder in acrylic emulsion on canvas, 9′ 10″ × 13′ 8½″. Musée National d'Art Moderne, Centre Georges Pompidou, Paris (purchase 1983 with participation of Scaler Foundation).

Stella tried to achieve purity in painting using evenly spaced pinstripes on colored grounds. His canvases have no central focus, no painterly or expressive elements, and no tactile quality.

1 ft.

Helen Frankenthaler
on Color-Field Painting

In 1965 the art critic Henry Geldzahler interviewed Helen Frankenthaler about her work as an abstract painter. In the following excerpt, Frankenthaler describes her approach to placing color on canvas (FIG. 36-12) and compares her method with the way earlier modernist artists used color in their paintings.

I will sometimes start a picture feeling "What will happen if I work with three blues and another color, and maybe more or less of the other color than the combined blues?" And very often midway through the picture I have to change the basis of the experience. . . .

When you first saw a Cubist or Impressionist picture there was a whole way of instructing the eye or the subconscious. Dabs of color had to stand for real things; it was an abstraction of a guitar or a hillside. The opposite is going on now. If you have bands of blue, green, and pink, the mind doesn't think sky, grass and flesh. These are colors and the question is what are they doing with themselves and with each other. Sentiment and nuance are being squeezed out.*

* Henry Geldzahler, "Interview with Helen Frankenthaler," *Artforum* 4, no. 2 (October 1965), 37–38.

36-12 HELEN FRANKENTHALER, *The Bay,* 1963. Acrylic on canvas, 6′ 8$\frac{7}{8}$″ × 6′ 9$\frac{7}{8}$″. Detroit Institute of Arts, Detroit.

Color-field painters like Frankenthaler poured paint onto unprimed canvas, allowing the pigments to soak into the fabric. Her works underscore that a painting is simply pigment on a flat surface.

1 ft.

---

shapes as the hard-edge artists had done, the color-field painters poured diluted paint onto unprimed canvas, allowing the pigments to soak in. It is hard to conceive of another painting method that results in such literal flatness. The images created, such as *The Bay* (FIG. 36-12) by HELEN FRANKENTHALER (b. 1928), appear spontaneous and almost accidental (see "Helen Frankenthaler on Color-Field Painting," above). These works differ from those of Rothko and Newman in that Frankenthaler subordinated the emotional component, so integral to Abstract Expressionism, to resolving formal problems.

MORRIS LOUIS Another artist who pursued color-field painting was MORRIS LOUIS (1912–1962). Clement Greenberg, an admirer of Frankenthaler's paintings, took Louis to her studio, and there she introduced him to the possibilities presented by the staining technique. Louis used this method of pouring diluted paint onto the surface of unprimed canvas in several series of paintings. *Saraband* (FIG. 36-13) is one of the works in Louis's *Veils* series. By holding up the canvas edges and pouring on diluted acrylic resin, Louis created billowy, fluid, transparent shapes that run down the length of the canvas. Like Frankenthaler, Louis reduced painting to the concrete fact of the paint-impregnated material.

1 ft.

36-13 MORRIS LOUIS, *Saraband,* 1959. Acrylic resin on canvas, 8′ 5$\frac{1}{8}$″ × 12′ 5″. Solomon R. Guggenheim Museum, New York.

Louis created his color-field paintings by holding up the canvas edges and pouring diluted acrylic resin to produce billowy, fluid, transparent shapes that run down the length of the fabric.

David Smith on Outdoor Sculpture

From ancient times, sculptors have frequently created statues for display in the open air, whether a portrait of a Roman emperor on horseback in a forum (FIG. 10-43, no. 6) or Michelangelo's *David* (FIG. 22-13) in Florence's Piazza della Signoria. But rarely have sculptors taken into consideration the effects of sunlight in the conception of their works. David Smith (FIG. 36-14) was an exception.

> I like outdoor sculpture and the most practical thing for outdoor sculpture is stainless steel, and I make them and I polish them in such a way that on a dull day, they take on the dull blue, or the color of the sky in the late afternoon sun, the glow, golden like the rays, the colors of nature. And in a particular sense, I have used atmosphere in a reflective way on the surfaces. They are colored by the sky and the surroundings, the green or blue of water. Some are down by the water and some are by the mountains. They reflect the colors. They are designed for the outdoors.*

* Quoted in Cleve Gray, ed., *David Smith by David Smith* (New York: Holt, Rinehart, and Winston, 1968), 133.

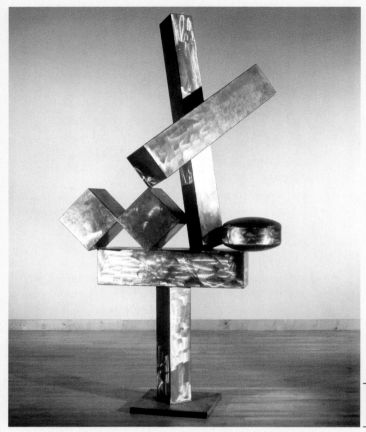

36-14 DAVID SMITH, *Cubi XIX*, 1964. Stainless steel, 9′ 4¾″ × 4′ 10¼″ × 3′ 4″. Tate Gallery, London. Art © Estate of David Smith/Licensed by VAGA, New York.

David Smith designed his abstract metal sculptures of simple geometric forms to reflect the natural light and color of their outdoor settings, not the sterile illumination of a museum gallery.

1 ft.

CLYFFORD STILL Another American painter whose work art historians usually classify as Post-Painterly Abstraction was CLYFFORD STILL (1904–1980), a pioneering abstract painter who produced a large series of canvases titled simply with their dates, underscoring his rejection of the very notion that the purpose of art is to represent places, people, or objects. Nonetheless, Still's paintings remind many viewers of vast landscapes seen from the air. But the artist's canvases make no reference to any forms in nature. His paintings, for example, *1948-C* (FIG. I-1), are pure exercises in the expressive use of color, shape, and texture.

Sculpture

Painters were not the only artists interested in Greenberg's formalist ideas. American sculptors also aimed for purity in their medium. While painters worked to emphasize flatness, sculptors, understandably, chose to focus on three-dimensionality as the unique characteristic and inherent limitation of the sculptural idiom.

DAVID SMITH American sculptor DAVID SMITH (1906–1965) produced metal sculptures that have affinities with the Abstract Expressionist movement in painting. Smith learned to weld in an automobile plant in 1925 and later applied to his art the technical expertise in handling metals he gained from that experience. In addition, working in large scale at the factories helped him visualize the possibilities for monumental metal sculpture. After experimenting with a variety of sculptural styles and materials, Smith created his *Cubi* series in the early 1960s. These works, for example *Cubi XIX* (FIG. 36-14), consist of simple geometric forms—cubes, cylinders, and rectangular bars. Made of stainless steel sections piled atop one another and then welded together, these large-scale sculptures make a striking visual statement. Smith added gestural elements reminiscent of Abstract

36-15 TONY SMITH, *Die*, 1962. Steel, 6′ × 6′ × 6′. Museum of Modern Art, New York (gift of Jane Smith in honor of Agnes Gund).

By rejecting illusionism and symbolism and reducing sculpture to basic geometric forms, Minimalist sculptors like Tony Smith emphasized their art's "objecthood" and concrete tangibility.

1 ft.

Donald Judd on Sculpture and Industrial Materials

In a 1965 essay entitled "Specific Objects," the Minimalist sculptor Donald Judd described the advantages of sculpture over painting and the attractions of using industrial materials for his works (FIG. 36-16).

> Three dimensions are real space. That gets rid of the problem of illusionism . . . one of the salient and most objectionable relics of European art. The several limits of painting are no longer present. A work can be as powerful as it can be thought to be. Actual space is intrinsically more powerful and specific than paint on a flat surface. . . . The use of three dimensions makes it possible to see all sorts of materials and colors. Most of [my] work involves new materials, either recent inventions or things not used before in art. Little was done until lately with the wide range of industrial products. . . . Materials vary greatly and are simply materials—formica, aluminum, cold-rolled steel, plexiglas, red and common brass, and so forth. They are specific. If they are used directly, they are more specific. Also, they are usually aggressive. There is an objectivity to the obdurate identity of a material. . . . The form of a work of art and its materials are closely related. In earlier work the structure and the imagery were executed in some neutral and homogeneous material.*

*Donald Judd, *Complete Writings 1959–1975* (New York: New York University Press, 1975), 181–189.

36-16 DONALD JUDD, *Untitled*, 1969. Brass and colored fluorescent Plexiglas on steel brackets, 10 units, $6\frac{1}{8}"$ × 2' × 2' 3" each, with 6" intervals. Hirshhorn Museum and Sculpture Garden, Smithsonian Institution, Washington, D.C. (gift of Joseph H. Hirshhorn, 1972). Art © Judd Foundation/Licensed by VAGA, New York.

Judd's Minimalist sculpture incorporates boxes fashioned from undisguised industrial materials. The artist used Plexiglas because its translucency gives the viewer access to the work's interior.

1 ft.

Expressionism by burnishing the metal with steel wool, producing swirling random-looking patterns that draw attention to the two-dimensionality of the sculptural surface. This treatment, which captures the light hitting the sculpture, activates the surface and imparts a texture to his pieces. Meant to be seen outdoors (see "David Smith on Outdoor Sculpture," page 978), Smith's sculptures unfortunately lose much of their character in the sterile lighting of a museum.

TONY SMITH A predominantly sculptural movement that emerged in the 1960s among artists seeking Greenbergian purity of form was *Minimalism*. One leading Minimalist was TONY SMITH (1912–1980), who created simple volumetric sculptures such as *Die* (FIG. 36-15). Difficult to describe other than as three-dimensional objects, Minimalist artworks often lack identifiable subjects, colors, surface textures, and narrative elements. By rejecting illusionism and reducing sculpture to basic geometric forms, Minimalists emphatically stress their art's "objecthood" and concrete tangibility. In so doing, they reduce experience to its most fundamental level, preventing viewers from drawing on assumptions or preconceptions when dealing with the art before them.

DONALD JUDD Another Minimalist sculptor, DONALD JUDD (1928–1994), embraced a spare, universal aesthetic corresponding to

the core tenets of the movement. Judd's determination to arrive at a visual vocabulary that avoided deception or ambiguity propelled him away from representation and toward precise and simple sculpture. For Judd, a work's power derived from its character as a whole and from the specificity of its materials (see "Donald Judd on Sculpture and Industrial Materials," above). *Untitled* (FIG. 36-16) presents basic geometric boxes constructed of brass and red Plexiglas, undisguised by paint or other materials. The artist did not intend the work to be metaphorical or symbolic but a straightforward declaration of sculpture's objecthood. Judd used Plexiglas because its translucency permits the viewer to access the interior, thereby rendering the sculpture both open and enclosed. This aspect of the design reflects Judd's desire to banish ambiguity or falseness from his works.

Interestingly, despite the ostensible connections between Minimalism and Greenbergian formalism, Greenberg did not embrace this direction in art. In his view,

> Minimal Art remains too much a feat of ideation [the mental formation of ideas], and not enough anything else. Its idea remains an idea, something deduced instead of felt and discovered. The geometrical and modular simplicity may announce and signify the artistically furthest-out, but the fact that the signals are understood for

what they want to mean betrays them artistically. There is hardly any aesthetic surprise in Minimal Art. . . . Aesthetic surprise hangs on forever—it is there in Raphael as it is in Pollock—and ideas alone cannot achieve it.[10]

LOUISE NEVELSON Although Minimalism was a dominant sculptural trend in the 1960s, many sculptors pursued other styles. Russian-born LOUISE NEVELSON (1899–1988) created sculpture that combines a sense of the architectural fragment with the power of Dada and Surrealist found objects to express her personal sense of life's underlying significance. Multiplicity of meaning was important to Nevelson. She sought "the in-between place. . . . The dawns and the dusks"[11]—the transitional realm between one state of being and another. Beginning in the late 1950s, she assembled sculptures of found wooden objects and forms, enclosing small sculptural compositions in boxes of varied sizes, and joined the boxes to one another to form "walls," which she then painted in a single hue—usually black, white, or gold. This monochromatic color scheme unifies the diverse parts of pieces such as *Tropical Garden II* (FIG. 36-17) and creates a mysterious field of shapes and shadows. The structures suggest magical environments resembling the treasured secret hideaways dimly remembered from childhood. Yet the boxy frames and the precision of the manufactured found objects create a rough geometric structure that the eye roams over freely, lingering on some details. The parts of a Nevelson sculpture and their interrelation recall the *Merz* constructions of Kurt Schwitters (FIG. 35-30). The effect is also rather like viewing the side of an apartment building from a moving elevated train or like looking down on a city from the air.

LOUISE BOURGEOIS In contrast to the architectural nature of Nevelson's work, a sensuous organic quality recalling the evocative Biomorphic Surrealist forms of Joan Miró (FIG. 35-52) pervades the work of French-American artist LOUISE BOURGEOIS (b. 1911). *Cumul I* (FIG. 36-18) is a collection of round-headed units huddled, with their heads protruding, within a collective cloak dotted with holes. The units differ in size, and their position within the group lends a distinctive personality to each. Although the shapes remain abstract, they refer strongly to human bodies. Bourgeois uses a wide variety of materials in her works, including wood, plaster, latex, and plastics, in addition to alabaster, marble, and bronze. She exploits each material's qualities to suit the expressiveness of the piece.

In *Cumul I,* the alternating high gloss and matte finish of the marble increases the sensuous distinction between the group of swelling forms and the soft folds swaddling them. Like Barbara Hepworth (FIG. 35-58), Bourgeois connects her sculpture with the body's multiple relationships to landscape: "[My pieces] are anthropomorphic and they are landscape also, since our body could be considered from a topographical point of view, as a land with mounds and valleys and caves and holes."[12] However, Bourgeois's sculptures are more personal and more openly sexual than those of Hepworth. *Cumul I* represents perfectly the allusions Bourgeois seeks: "There has always been sexual suggestiveness in my work. Sometimes I am totally concerned with female shapes—characters of breasts like clouds—but often I merge the activity—phallic breasts, male and female, active and passive."[13]

EVA HESSE A Minimalist in the early part of her career, EVA HESSE (1936–1970) later moved away from the severity characterizing much of Minimalist art. She created sculptures that, although spare and simple, have a compelling presence. Using nontraditional sculptural materials such as fiberglass, cord, and latex, Hesse produced sculptures whose pure Minimalist forms appear to crumble,

1 ft.

36-19 Eva Hesse, *Hang-Up,* 1965–1966. Acrylic on cloth over wood and steel, 6′ × 7′ × 6′ 6″. Art Institute of Chicago, Chicago (gift of Arthur Keating and Mr. and Mrs. Edward Morris by exchange).

Hesse created spare and simple sculptures with parts that extend into the room. She wanted her works to express the strangeness and absurdity that she considered the central conditions of modern life.

sag, and warp under the pressures of atmospheric force and gravity. Born Jewish in Hitler's Germany, the young Hesse hid with a Christian family when her parents and elder sister had to flee the Nazis. She did not reunite with them until the early 1940s, just before her parents divorced. Those extraordinary circumstances helped give her a lasting sense that the central conditions of modern life are strangeness and absurdity. Struggling to express these qualities in her art, she created informal sculptural arrangements with units often hung from the ceiling, propped against the walls, or spilled out along the floor. She said she wanted her pieces to be "non art, non connotative, non anthropomorphic, non geometric, non nothing, everything, but of another kind, vision, sort."[14]

Hang-Up (FIG. 36-19) fulfills these requirements. The piece looks like a carefully made empty frame sprouting a strange feeler that extends into the room and doubles back to the frame. Hesse wrote that in this work, for the first time, her "idea of absurdity or extreme feeling came through. . . . [*Hang-Up*] has a kind of depth I don't always achieve and that is the kind of depth or soul or absurdity of life or meaning or feeling or intellect that I want to get."[15] The sculpture possesses a disquieting and touching presence, suggesting the fragility and grandeur of life amid the pressures of the modern age. Hesse was herself a touching and fragile presence in the art world. She died of a brain tumor at age 34.

Pop Art

Despite their differences, the Abstract Expressionists, Post-Painterly Abstractionists, and Minimalists all adopted an artistic vocabulary of resolute abstraction. Other artists, however, observing that the insular and introspective attitude of the avant-garde had alienated the public, sought to harness the communicative power of art to reach a wide audience. However, they did not create reactionary or academic work. Their art still incorporated avant-garde elements, but their focus was not on the formalist issues characteristic of the modernist mindset.

The artists of the *Pop Art* movement reintroduced all of the devices the postwar avant-garde artists, in search of purity, had purged from their abstract and often reductive works. Thus, Pop artists revived the tools traditionally used to convey meaning in art, such as signs, symbols, metaphors, allusions, illusions, and figural imagery. They not only embraced representation but also produced an art firmly grounded in consumer culture and the mass media, thereby making it much more accessible and understandable to the average person. Indeed, the name "Pop Art" (credited to the British art critic Lawrence Alloway) is short for "popular art" and referred to the popular mass culture and familiar imagery of the contemporary urban environment. This was an art form rooted in the sensibilities and visual language of a late-20th-century mass audience.

RICHARD HAMILTON Art historians trace the roots of Pop Art to a group of young British artists, architects, and writers who formed the Independent Group at the Institute of Contemporary Art in London in the early 1950s. They sought to initiate fresh thinking in art, in part by sharing their fascination with the aesthetics and content of such facets of popular culture as advertising, comic books, and movies. In 1956 an Independent Group member, RICHARD HAMILTON (b. 1922), made a small collage, *Just What Is It That Makes Today's Homes So Different, So Appealing?* (FIG. 36-20), which exemplifies many of the attitudes of British Pop Art. Trained as an engineering draftsman, exhibition designer, and painter, Hamilton studied the way advertising shapes public attitudes. Long intrigued by

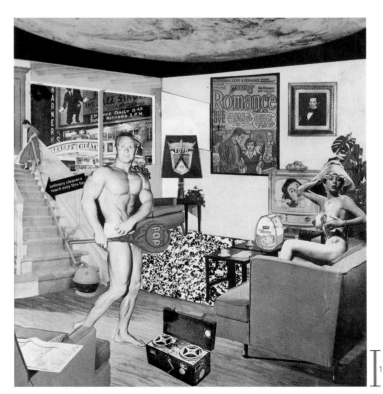

1 in.

36-20 RICHARD HAMILTON, *Just What Is It That Makes Today's Homes So Different, So Appealing?* 1956. Collage, 10¼″ × 9¾″. Kunsthalle Tübingen, Tübingen.

The fantasy interior in Hamilton's collage reflects the values of modern consumer culture through figures and objects cut from glossy magazines. Toying with mass-media imagery typifies British Pop Art.

36-21 JASPER JOHNS, *Flag*, 1954–1955, dated on reverse 1954. Encaustic, oil, and collage on fabric mounted on plywood, 3′ 6¼″ × 5′ ⅝″. Museum of Modern Art, New York (gift of Philip Johnson in honor of Alfred H. Barr Jr.). Art © Jasper Johns/Licensed by VAGA, New York.

American Pop artist Jasper Johns wanted to draw attention to common objects that people view frequently but rarely scrutinize. He made several series of paintings of targets, flags, numbers, and alphabets.

36-22 ROBERT RAUSCHENBERG, *Canyon*, 1959. Oil, pencil, paper, fabric, metal, cardboard box, printed paper, printed reproductions, photograph, wood, paint tube, and mirror on canvas, with oil on bald eagle, string, and pillow, 6′ 9¾″ × 5′ 10″ × 2′. Sonnabend Collection. Art © Robert Rauschenberg/Licensed by VAGA, New York.

Rauschenberg's "combines" intersperse painted passages with sculptural elements. *Canyon* incorporates pigment on canvas with pieces of printed paper, photographs, a pillow, and a stuffed eagle.

Duchamp's ideas, Hamilton consistently combined elements of popular art and fine art, seeing both as belonging to the whole world of visual communication. He created *Just What Is It?* for the poster and catalogue of one section of an exhibition titled *This Is Tomorrow*, which included images from Hollywood cinema, science fiction, the mass media, and one reproduction of a van Gogh painting (to represent popular fine artworks).

The fantasy interior in Hamilton's collage reflects the values of modern consumer culture through figures and objects cut from glossy magazines. *Just What Is It?* includes references to mass media (the television, the theater marquee outside the window, the newspaper), advertising (Hoover vacuums, Ford cars, Armour hams, Tootsie Pops), and popular culture (the girlie magazine, bodybuilder Charles Atlas, romance comic books). Scholars have written much about the possible deep message of this piece, and few would deny the work's sardonic effect, whether or not the artist intended to make a pointed comment. Artworks of this sort stimulated the viewer's wide-ranging speculation about society's values, and this kind of intellectual toying with mass-media meaning and imagery typified Pop Art in England and Europe.

JASPER JOHNS Although Pop Art originated in England, the movement found its greatest articulation and success in the United States, in large part because the more fully matured American consumer culture provided a fertile environment in which the movement flourished through the 1960s. Indeed, Independent Group members claimed their inspiration came from Hollywood, Detroit, and New York's Madison Avenue, paying homage to America's predominance in the realms of mass media, mass production, and advertising. One of the artists pivotal to the early development of American Pop was JASPER JOHNS (b. 1930), who sought to draw attention to common objects in the world—what he called things "seen but not looked at."[16] To this end, he created several series of paintings of targets, flags, numbers, and alphabets. For example, *Flag* (FIG. **36-21**) depicts an object people view frequently but rarely scrutinize. The highly textured surface of the work is the result of Johns's use of *encaustic*, an ancient method of painting with liquid

36-21A JOHNS, *Three Flags*, 1958.

wax and dissolved pigment (see "Encaustic Painting," Chapter 10, page 275). First, the artist embedded a collage of newspaper scraps or photographs in wax. He then painted over them with the encaustic. Because the wax hardened quickly, Johns could work rapidly, and the translucency of the wax allows the viewer to see the layered painting process.

ROBERT RAUSCHENBERG Johns's friend ROBERT RAUSCHENBERG (1925–2008) began using mass-media images in his work in the 1950s. Rauschenberg set out to create works that would be open and indeterminate, and he began by making *combines*, which intersperse painted passages with sculptural elements. Combines are, in a sense, Rauschenberg's personal variation on *assemblages*, artworks constructed from already existing objects. At times, these combines seem to be sculptures with painting incorporated into certain sections. Others seem to be paintings with three-dimensional objects attached to the surface. In the 1950s, assemblages usually contained an array of art reproductions, magazine and newspaper clippings, and passages painted in an Abstract Expressionist style. In the early 1960s, Rauschenberg adopted the commercial medium of *silk-screen printing*, first in black and white and then in color, and began filling entire canvases with appropriated news images and anonymous photographs of city scenes.

Canyon (FIG. **36-22**) is typical of Rauschenberg's combines. Pieces of printed paper and photographs cover parts of the canvas.

Roy Lichtenstein on Pop Art

In 1963, Roy Lichtenstein was one of eight painters interviewed for a profile on Pop Art in *Art News*. G. R. Swenson posed the questions. Part of Lichtenstein's response follows.

[Pop Art is] the use of commercial art as a subject matter in painting . . . . [Pop artists portray] what I think to be the most brazen and threatening characteristics of our culture, things we hate, but which are also so powerful in their impingement on us. . . . I paint directly . . . [without] perspective or shading. It doesn't look like a painting *of* something, it looks like the thing itself. Instead of looking like a painting *of* a billboard . . . Pop Art seems to be the actual thing. It is an intensification, a stylistic intensification of the excitement which the subject matter has for me; but the style is . . . cool. One of the things a cartoon does is to express violent emotion and passion in a completely mechanized and removed style. To express this thing in a painterly style would dilute it. . . . Everybody has called Pop Art "American" painting, but it's actually industrial painting. America was hit by industrialism and capitalism harder and sooner . . . I think the meaning of my work is that it's industrial, it's what all the world will soon become. Europe will be the same way, soon, so it won't be American; it will be universal.*

36-23 ROY LICHTENSTEIN, *Hopeless,* 1963. Oil on canvas, 3′ 8″ × 3′ 8″. Kunstmuseum, Basel. © Estate of Roy Lichtenstein.

1 ft.

Comic books appealed to Lichtenstein because they were a mainstay of American popular culture, meant to be read and discarded. The Pop artist immortalized their images on large canvases.

* Roy Lichtenstein quoted in G. R. Swenson, "What Is Pop Art? Interviews with Eight Painters," *Art News* 62, no. 7 (November 1963), 25, 64.

Much of the unevenly painted surface consists of pigment roughly applied in a manner reminiscent of de Kooning's work (FIG. 36-7). A stuffed bald eagle attached to the lower part of the combine spreads its wings as if lifting off in flight toward the viewer. Completing the combine, a pillow dangles from a string attached to a wood stick below the eagle. The artist presented the work's components in a jumbled fashion. He tilted or turned some of the images sideways, and each overlays part of another image. The compositional confusion may resemble that of a Dada collage, but the parts of Rauschenberg's combines maintain their individuality more than those in, for example, a Schwitters piece (FIG. 35-30). The eye scans a Rauschenberg canvas much as it might survey the environment on a walk through a city. The various recognizable images and objects seem unrelated and defy a consistent reading, although Rauschenberg chose all the elements of his combines with specific meanings in mind. For example, Rauschenberg based *Canyon* on a Rembrandt painting of Jupiter in the form of an eagle carrying the boy Ganymede heavenward. The photo in the combine is a reference to the Greek boy, and the hanging pillow is a visual pun on his buttocks.

ROY LICHTENSTEIN As the Pop movement matured, the images became more concrete and tightly controlled. American artist ROY LICHTENSTEIN (1923–1997) turned his attention to commercial art and especially to the comic book as a mainstay of popular culture (see "Roy Lichtenstein on Pop Art," above). In paintings such as *Hopeless* (FIG. 36-23), Lichtenstein excerpted an image from a comic book, a form of entertainment meant to be read and discarded, and immortalized the image on a large canvas. Aside from that modification, Lichtenstein remained remarkably faithful to the original comic strip image. His subject was one of the melodramatic scenes common to popular romance comic books of the time. Lichtenstein also used the visual vocabulary of the comic strip, with its dark black outlines and unmodulated color areas, and retained the familiar square dimensions. Moreover, his printing technique, *benday dots,* called attention to the mass-produced derivation of the image. Named after its inventor, the newspaper printer Benjamin Day (1810–1889), the benday dot system involves the modulation of colors through the placement and size of colored dots. Lichtenstein thus transferred the visual shorthand language of the comic book to the realm of monumental painting.

36-24 ANDY WARHOL, *Green Coca-Cola Bottles,* 1962. Oil on canvas, 6' 10½" × 4' 9". Whitney Museum of American Art, New York.

Warhol was the quintessential American Pop artist. Here, he selected an icon of mass-produced consumer culture and then multiplied it, reflecting Coke's omnipresence in American society.

ANDY WARHOL The quintessential American Pop artist was ANDY WARHOL (1928–1987). An early successful career as a commercial artist and illustrator grounded Warhol in the sensibility and visual rhetoric of advertising and the mass media, knowledge that proved useful for his Pop artworks. In paintings such as *Green Coca-Cola Bottles* (FIG. 36-24), Warhol selected an icon of mass-produced, consumer culture of the time. The reassuringly familiar curved Coke bottle especially appealed to Warhol:

> What's great about this country is that America started the tradition where the richest consumers buy essentially the same things as the poorest. You can be watching TV and see Coca-Cola, and you can know that the President drinks Coke, Liz Taylor drinks Coke, and just think, you can drink Coke, too. A Coke is a Coke and no amount of money can get you a better Coke.[17]

As did other Pop artists, Warhol used a visual vocabulary and a printing technique that reinforced the image's connections to consumer culture. The repetition and redundancy of the Coke bottle reflect the omnipresence and dominance of this product in American society. The silk-screen technique allowed Warhol to print the image endlessly (although he varied each bottle slightly). So immersed was Warhol in a culture of mass production that he not only produced numerous canvases of the same image but also named his studio "the Factory."

Warhol often produced images of Hollywood celebrities, such as Marilyn Monroe. Like his other paintings, these works emphasize the commodity status of the subjects depicted. Warhol created *Marilyn Diptych* (FIG. 36-25) in the weeks following the movie star's suicide in August 1962, capitalizing on the media frenzy her death prompted. Warhol selected a Hollywood publicity photo, one that provides no insight into the real Norma Jean Baker (the actress's name before she assumed the persona of Marilyn Monroe). Rather, the viewer sees only a mask—the image the Hollywood myth machine generated. The garish colors and the flat application of paint contribute to that image's masklike quality. The repetition of Monroe's face reinforces her status as a consumer product on a par with Coke bottles, her glamorous, haunting visage seemingly confronting the viewer endlessly, as it did the American public in the aftermath of her death. The right half of this work, with its poor registration of pigment, suggests a sequence of film stills, a reference to the realm from which Monroe derived her fame.

Warhol's ascendance to the rank of celebrity artist underscored his remarkable and astute understanding of the dynamics and visual language of mass culture. He predicted

36-24A SEGAL *The Gas Station,* 1963

36-25A MARIS *The Last Supp* 1982–1984.

36-25 ANDY WARHOL, *Marilyn Diptych,* 1962. Oil, acrylic, and silkscreen enamel on canvas, each panel 6' 8" × 4' 9". Tate Gallery, London.

Warhol's repetition of Monroe's face reinforced her status as a consumer product, her glamorous visage confronting the viewer endlessly, as it did the American public in the aftermath of her death.

that the age of mass media would enable everyone to become famous for 15 minutes. His own fame has lasted much longer.

CLAES OLDENBURG The Swedish-born Pop artist CLAES OLDENBURG (b. 1929) has produced sculptures that incisively comment on American consumer culture. His early works consisted of reliefs of food and clothing items. Oldenburg constructed these sculptures of plaster layered on chicken wire and muslin, painting them with cheap commercial house enamel. In later works, focused on the same subjects, he shifted to large-scale stuffed sculptures of sewn vinyl or canvas. Examples of both types of sculptures appear in the photograph (FIG. 36-26) of his one-person show at the Green Gallery in New York in 1962. Oldenburg had included many of the works in this exhibition in an earlier show he mounted titled *The Store*—an appropriate comment on the function of art as a commodity in a consumer society. Over the years, Oldenburg's sculpture has become increasingly monumental. In recent decades, he and his wife and collaborator, Dutch American Coosje van Bruggen (b. 1942), have become particularly well known for their mammoth outdoor sculptures of familiar, commonplace objects, such as cue balls, shuttlecocks, clothespins, and torn notebooks.

Superrealism

Like the Pop artists, the artists associated with *Superrealism* sought a form of artistic communication that was more accessible to the public than the remote, unfamiliar visual language of the Abstract Expressionists, Post-Painterly Abstractionists, and Minimalists. The Superrealists expanded Pop's iconography in both painting and sculpture by making images in the late 1960s and 1970s involving scrupulous fidelity to optical fact. Because many Superrealists used photographs as sources for their imagery, art historians also refer to this postwar art movement as *Photorealism*.

AUDREY FLACK American artist AUDREY FLACK (b. 1931) was one of Superrealism's pioneers. Her paintings, such as *Marilyn* (FIG. 36-27), were not simply technical exercises in recording objects in

minute detail but were also conceptual inquiries into the nature of photography and the extent to which photography constructs an understanding of reality. Flack observed that "[photography is] my whole life, I studied art history, it was always photographs, I never saw the paintings, they were in Europe. . . . Look at TV and at magazines

36-27 AUDREY FLACK, *Marilyn*, 1977. Oil over acrylic on canvas, 8′ × 8′. University of Arizona Museum, Tucson (museum purchase with funds provided by the Edward J. Gallagher Jr. Memorial Fund).

Flack's pioneering Photorealist still lifes record objects with great optical fidelity. *Marilyn* alludes to Dutch vanitas paintings (FIG. 25-21) and incorporates multiple references to the transience of life.

Chuck Close on Portrait Painting and Photography

In a 1970 interview, the art critic Cindy Nemser asked Chuck Close about the scale of his huge portraits (FIG. 36-28) and the relationship of his paintings to the photographs that lie behind them. He answered in part:

> The large scale allows me to deal with information that is overlooked in an eight-by-ten inch photograph ... My large scale forces the viewer to focus on one area at a time. In that way he is made aware of the blurred areas that are seen with peripheral vision. Normally we never take those peripheral areas into account. When we focus on an area it is sharp. As we turn our attention to adjacent areas they sharpen up too. In my work, the blurred areas don't come into focus, but they are too large to be ignored. ... In order to ... make [my painted] information stack up with photographic information, I tried to purge my work of as much of the baggage of traditional portrait painting as I could. To avoid a painterly brush stroke and surface, I use some pretty devious means, such as razor blades, electric drills and airbrushes. I also work as thinly as possible and I don't use white paint as it tends to build up and become chalky and opaque. In fact, in a nine-by-seven foot picture, I only use a couple of tablespoons of black paint to cover the entire canvas.*

* Cindy Nemser, "Chuck Close: Interview with Cindy Nemser," *Artforum* 8, no. 5 (January 1970), 51–55.

36-28 CHUCK CLOSE, *Big Self-Portrait*, 1967–1968. Acrylic on canvas, 8′ 11″ × 6′ 11″. Walker Art Center, Minneapolis (Art Center Acquisition Fund, 1969). ◼◀

Close's goal was to translate photographic information into painted information. In his portraits, he deliberately avoided creative compositions, flattering lighting effects, and revealing facial expressions.

1 ft.

---

and reproductions, they're all influenced by photo-vision."[18] The photograph's formal qualities also intrigued her, and she used photographic techniques by first projecting an image in slide form onto the canvas. By next using an *airbrush* (a device that uses compressed air to spray paint, originally designed as a photo-retouching tool), Flack could duplicate the smooth gradations of tone and color found in photographs. Most of her paintings are still lifes that present the viewer with a collection of familiar objects painted with great optical fidelity. *Marilyn* is a still life that incorporates photographs of the actress's face. Flack's commentary on Monroe's tragic death differs from that in Warhol's *Marilyn Diptych* (FIG. 36-25). Flack alludes to Dutch vanitas paintings (FIG. 25-21), and her still life includes multiple references to death. In addition to the black-and-white photographs of a youthful, smiling Monroe, fresh fruit, an hourglass, a burning candle, a watch, and a calendar all refer to the passage of time and the transience of life on earth.

CHUCK CLOSE Also usually considered a Superrealist is American artist CHUCK CLOSE (b. 1940), best known for his large-scale portraits, such as *Big Self-Portrait* (FIG. 36-28). However, Close felt his connection to the Photorealists was tenuous, because for him realism, rather than an end in itself, was the result of an intellectually rigorous, systematic approach to painting. He based his paintings of

the late 1960s and early 1970s on photographs, and his main goal was to translate photographic information into painted information. Because he aimed simply to record visual information about his subject's appearance, Close deliberately avoided creative compositions, flattering lighting effects, and revealing facial expressions. Not interested in providing great insight into the personalities of those portrayed, Close painted anonymous and generic people, mostly friends. By reducing the variables in his paintings (even their canvas size is a constant 9 by 7 feet), he could focus on employing his methodical presentations of faces, thereby encouraging the viewer to deal with the formal aspects of his works. Indeed, because of the large scale of Close paintings, careful scrutiny causes the images to dissolve into abstract patterns (see "Chuck Close on Portrait Painting and Photography," above).

DUANE HANSON Not surprisingly, many sculptors also were Superrealists, including DUANE HANSON (1925–1996), who perfected a casting technique that allowed him to create life-size figural sculptures that many viewers initially mistake for real people. Hanson first made plaster molds from live models and filled the molds with polyester resin. After the resin hardened, the artist removed the outer molds and cleaned, painted with an airbrush, and decorated the sculptures with wigs, clothes, and other accessories. These works,

36-29 Duane Hanson, *Supermarket Shopper,* 1970. Polyester resin and fiberglass polychromed in oil, with clothing, steel cart, and groceries, life-size. Nachfolgeinstitut, Neue Galerie, Sammlung Ludwig, Aachen. Art © Estate of Duane Hanson/Licensed by VAGA, New York.

Hanson used molds from live models to create his Superrealistic life-size painted plaster sculptures. His aim was to capture the emptiness and loneliness of average Americans in familiar settings.

1 ft.

such as *Supermarket Shopper* (FIG. 36-29), depict stereotypical average Americans, striking chords with the public precisely because of their familiarity. Hanson explained his choice of imagery: "The subject matter that I like best deals with the familiar lower and middle-class American types of today. To me, the resignation, emptiness and loneliness of their existence captures the true reality of life for these people. . . . I want to achieve a certain tough realism which speaks of the fascinating idiosyncrasies of our time."[19]

PAINTING AND SCULPTURE SINCE 1970

The Pop artists and Superrealists were not the only artists to challenge modernist formalist doctrine. By the 1970s, the range of art produced in both traditional and new media in reaction to Abstract Expressionism, Minimalism, and other formalist movements had become so diverse that only a broad general term can describe the phenomenon: *postmodernism.* There is no agreement about the definition of postmodern art. Some scholars, such as Fredric Jameson, assert that a major characteristic of postmodernism is the erosion of the boundaries between high culture and popular culture—a separation Clement Greenberg and the modernists had staunchly defended. With the appearance of Pop Art, that separation became more difficult to maintain. For Jameson, the intersection of high and mass culture is, in fact, a defining feature of the new postmodernism. He attributed the emergence of postmodernism to "a new type of social life and a new economic order—what is often euphemistically called modernization, postindustrial or consumer society, the society of the media or the spectacle, or multinational capitalism."[20]

For many recent artists, postmodernism involves examining the process by which meaning is generated and the negotiation or dialogue that transpires between viewers and artworks. This kind of examination of the nature of art parallels the literary field of study known as critical theory. Critical theorists view art and architecture, as well as literature and the other humanities, as a culture's intellectual products, or "constructs." These constructs unconsciously suppress or conceal the true premises that inform the culture, primarily the values of those politically in control. Thus, cultural products function in an ideological capacity, obscuring, for example, racist or sexist attitudes. When revealed by analysis, the facts behind these constructs, according to critical theorists, contribute to a more substantial understanding of artworks, buildings, books, and the overall culture.

Many critical theorists use an analytical strategy called *deconstruction,* after a method developed in the 1960s and 1970s by French intellectuals, notably Michel Foucault (1926–1984) and Jacques Derrida (1930–2004). For those employing deconstruction, all cultural constructs are "texts." Acknowledging the lack of fixed or uniform meanings in these texts, critical theorists accept a variety of interpretations as valid. Further, as cultural products, how texts signify and what they signify are entirely conventional. They can refer to nothing outside of themselves, only to other texts. Thus, no extratextual reality exists that people can reference. The enterprise of deconstruction is to reveal the contradictions and instabilities of these texts, or cultural language (written or visual).

With primarily political and social aims, deconstructive analysis has the ultimate goal of effecting political and social change. Accordingly, critical theorists who employ this approach seek to uncover—to deconstruct—the facts of power, privilege, and prejudice underlying the practices and institutions of any given culture. In the process, deconstruction reveals the precariousness of structures and systems, such as language and cultural practices, along with the assumptions underlying them. Yet because of the lack of fixed meaning in texts, many politically committed thinkers assert that deconstruction does not provide a sufficiently stable basis for dissent.

Critical theorists do not agree upon any philosophy or analytical method, because in principle they oppose firm definitions. They do share a healthy suspicion of all traditional truth claims and value standards, all hierarchical authority and institutions. For them, deconstruction means destabilizing established meanings, definitions, and interpretations while encouraging subjectivity and individual differences.

Certainly, one thing all postmodern artists have in common is a self-consciousness about their place in the historical continuum of art. Consequently, many of them resurrect artistic traditions to comment on and reinterpret those styles or idioms. However defined, postmodern art comprises a dizzying array of artworks in different media. Only a representative sample can be presented here.

Neo-Expressionism

One of the first coherent movements to emerge during the postmodern era was *Neo-Expressionism.* This movement's name reflects postmodern artists' interest in reexamining earlier art production and connects this art to the powerful, intense works of the German Expressionists (see Chapter 35) and the Abstract Expressionists, among other artists.

SUSAN ROTHENBERG In the 1970s, Susan Rothenberg (b. 1945) produced a major series of large paintings with the horse as the central image. The horse theme resonates with history and metaphor—from the Parthenon frieze and Roman and Renaissance equestrian portraits to the paintings of German Expressionist Franz

36-30 SUSAN ROTHENBERG, *Tattoo*, 1979. Acrylic paint on canvas, 5′ 7″ × 8′ 7″. Walker Art Center, Minneapolis (purchased with the aid of funds from Mr. and Mrs. Edmond R. Ruben, Mr. and Mrs. Julius E. Davis, the Art Center Acquisition Fund, and the National Endowment for the Arts, 1979).

Rothenberg's Neo-Expressionist paintings feature loose brush-work, agitated surfaces, and hazy, semiabstract forms. This work's title refers to the horse's head drawn within the outline of its leg.

1 ft.

Marc (FIG. 35-8). Like Marc, Rothenberg saw horses as metaphors for humanity: "The horse was a way of not doing people, yet it was a symbol of people, a self-portrait, really."[21] Rothenberg, however, distilled the image to a ghostly outline or hazy depiction that is more poetic than descriptive. As such, her works fall in the nebulous area between representation and abstraction. In paintings such as *Tattoo* (FIG. 36-30), the loose brushwork and agitated surface contribute to the expressiveness of the image and account for Rothenberg's cat-

egorization as a Neo-Expressionist. The title, *Tattoo*, refers to the horse's head drawn within the outline of its leg—"a tattoo or memory image," according to the artist.[22]

JULIAN SCHNABEL The work of another American artist, JULIAN SCHNABEL (b. 1951), forcefully restates the premises of Abstract Expressionism. When executing his artworks in the 1980s, however, Schnabel experimented widely with materials and sup-

1 ft.

36-31 JULIAN SCHNABEL, *The Walk Home*, 1984–1985. Oil, plates, copper, bronze, fiberglass, and Bondo on wood, 9′ 3″ × 19′ 4″. Broad Art Foundation and the Pace Gallery, New York. ◼◀

Schnabel's paintings recall the work of the gestural abstractionists, but he employs an amalgamation of media, bringing together painting, mosaic, and low-relief sculpture.

36-32 ANSELM KIEFER, *Nigredo,* 1984. Oil paint on photosensitized fabric, acrylic emulsion, straw, shellac, relief paint on paper pulled from painted wood, 11′ × 18′. Philadelphia Museum of Art, Philadelphia (gift of Friends of the Philadelphia Museum of Art).

Kiefer's paintings have thickly encrusted surfaces incorporating materials such as straw. Here, the German artist used perspective to pull the viewer into an incinerated landscape alluding to the Holocaust.

1 ft.

31A BASQUIAT, *n Players,* 3.

ports—from fragmented china plates bonded to wood, to paint on velvet and tarpaulin. He had a special interest in the physicality of the objects, and by attaching broken crockery, as in *The Walk Home* (FIG. 36-31), he found an extension of what paint could do. Superficially, the painting recalls the work of the gestural abstractionists—the spontaneous drips of Pollock (FIG. 36-5) and the energetic brush strokes of de Kooning (FIG. 36-7). The thick, mosaic-like texture, an amalgamation of media, brings together painting, mosaic, and low-relief sculpture. In effect, Schnabel reclaimed older media for his expressionistic method, which considerably amplifies his bold, distinctive statement.

ANSELM KIEFER Neo-Expressionism was by no means a solely American movement. German artist ANSELM KIEFER (b. 1945) has produced some of the most lyrical and engaging works of the contemporary period. Like Schnabel's, Kiefer's paintings, such as *Nigredo* (FIG. 36-32), are monumental in scale, recall Abstract Expressionist canvases, and draw the viewer to their textured surfaces, made more complex by the addition of materials such as straw and lead. It is not merely the impressive physicality of Kiefer's paintings that accounts for the impact of his work, however. His images function on a mythological or metaphorical level as well as on a historically specific one. Kiefer's works of the 1970s and 1980s often involve a reexamination of German history, particularly the painful Nazi era of 1933–1945, and evoke the feeling of despair. Kiefer believes that Germany's participation in World War II and the Holocaust left permanent scars on the souls of the German people and on the souls of all humanity.

Nigredo ("blackening") pulls the viewer into an expansive landscape depicted using Renaissance perspectival principles. This landscape, however, is far from pastoral or carefully cultivated. Rather, it is bleak and charred. Although it makes no specific reference to the Holocaust, this incinerated landscape indirectly alludes to the horrors of that event. More generally, the blackness of the landscape may refer to the notion of alchemical change or transformation, a concept of great interest to Kiefer. Black is one of the four symbolic colors of the alchemist—a color that refers both to death and to the

molten, chaotic state of substances broken down by fire. The alchemist, however, focuses on the transformation of substances, and thus the emphasis on blackness is not absolute but can also be perceived as part of a process of renewal and redemption. Kiefer thus imbued his work with a deep symbolic meaning that, when combined with the intriguing visual quality of his parched, congealed surfaces, results in paintings of enduring power.

Feminist Art

With the renewed interest in representation that the Pop artists and Superrealists introduced in the 1960s and 1970s, painters and sculptors once again began to embrace the persuasive powers of art to communicate with a wide audience. In recent decades, artists have investigated more insistently the dynamics of power and privilege, especially in relation to issues of gender, race, ethnicity, class, and sexual orientation.

In the 1970s, the feminist movement focused public attention on the history of women and their place in society. In art, two women—Judy Chicago and Miriam Schapiro—largely spearheaded the American feminist art movement. Chicago and a group of students at California State University, Fresno, founded the Feminist Art Program, and Chicago and Schapiro coordinated it at the California Institute of the Arts in Valencia. In 1972, as part of this program, teachers and students joined to create projects such as Womanhouse, an abandoned house in Los Angeles they completely converted into a suite of "environments," each based on a different aspect of women's lives and fantasies.

JUDY CHICAGO In her own work in the 1970s, JUDY CHICAGO (Judy Cohen, b. 1939) wanted to educate viewers about women's role in history and the fine arts. She aimed to establish a respect for women and their art, to forge a new kind of art expressing women's experiences, and to find a way to make that art accessible to a large audience. Inspired early in her career by the work of Barbara Hepworth (FIG. 35-58), Georgia O'Keeffe (FIGS. I-4 and 35-38), and Louise Nevelson (FIG. 36-17), Chicago developed a personal painting style that consciously included abstract organic vaginal images. In the early 1970s, Chicago began planning an ambitious piece, *The*

Judy Chicago on *The Dinner Party*

One of the acknowledged masterpieces of feminist art is Judy Chicago's *The Dinner Party* (FIG. 36-33), which required a team of nearly 400 to create and assemble. In 1979, Chicago published a book explaining the genesis and symbolism of the work.

[By 1974] I had discarded [my original] idea of painting a hundred abstract portraits on plates, each paying tribute to a different historic female figure. . . . In my research I realized over and over again that women's achievements had been left out of history . . . . My new idea was to try to symbolize this. . . . [I thought] about putting the plates on a table with silver, glasses, napkins, and tablecloths, and over the next year and a half the concept of *The Dinner Party* slowly evolved. I began to think about the piece as a reinterpretation of the Last Supper from the point of view of women, who, throughout history, had prepared the meals and set the table. In my "Last Supper," however, the women would be the honored guests. Their representation in the form of plates set on the table would express the way women had been confined, and the piece would thus reflect both women's achievements and their oppression. . . . My goal with *The Dinner Party* was . . . to forge a new kind of art expressing women's experience . . . . [It] seemed appropriate to relate our history through

36-33 JUDY CHICAGO, *The Dinner Party*, 1979. Multimedia, including ceramics and stitchery, 48′ long on each side. Brooklyn Museum, Brooklyn.

Chicago's *Dinner Party* honors 39 women from antiquity to 20th-century America. The triangular form and the materials—painted china and fabric—are traditionally associated with women.

art, particularly through techniques traditionally associated with women—china-painting and needlework.*

* Judy Chicago, *The Dinner Party: A Symbol of Our Heritage* (Garden City, N.Y.: Anchor Press, 1979) 11–12.

Dinner Party (FIG. 36-33), using craft techniques (such as china painting and needlework) traditionally practiced by women, to celebrate the achievements and contributions women made throughout history (see "Judy Chicago on *The Dinner Party*," above). She originally conceived the work as a feminist Last Supper for 13 "honored guests," as in the New Testament, but all women. There also are 13 women in a witches' coven, and Chicago's *Dinner Party* refers to witchcraft and the worship of the Mother Goddess. But because Chicago had uncovered so many worthy women in the course of her research, she expanded the number of guests threefold to 39 and placed them around a triangular table 48 feet long on each side. The triangular form refers to the ancient symbol for both woman and the Goddess. The notion of a dinner party also alludes to women's traditional role as homemakers.

The Dinner Party rests on a white tile floor inscribed with the names of 999 additional women of achievement to signify that the accomplishments of the 39 honored guests rest on a foundation other women laid. Among those with place settings at the table are O'Keeffe, the Egyptian pharaoh Hatshepsut (see "Hatshepsut," Chapter 3, page 68), the British writer Virginia Woolf, the Native American guide

Sacagawea, and the American suffragist Susan B. Anthony. Each woman's place has identical eating utensils and a goblet but a unique oversized porcelain plate and a long place mat or table runner covered with imagery that reflects significant facts about that woman's life and culture. The plates range from simple concave shapes with china-painted imagery to dishes whose sculptured three-dimensional designs almost seem to struggle to free themselves. The designs on each plate incorporate both butterfly and vulval motifs—the butterfly as the ancient symbol of liberation and the vulva as the symbol of female sexuality. Each table runner combines traditional needlework techniques, including needlepoint, embroidery, crochet, beading, patchwork, and appliqué. *The Dinner Party* is, however, more than the sum of its parts. It provides viewers with a powerful launching point for considering broad feminist concerns.

MIRIAM SCHAPIRO After enjoying a thriving career as a hard-edge painter in California in the late 1960s, MIRIAM SCHAPIRO (b. 1923) became fascinated with the hidden metaphors for womanhood she then saw in her abstract paintings. Intrigued by the materials

36-34 MIRIAM SCHAPIRO, *Anatomy of a Kimono* (section), 1976. Fabric and acrylic on canvas, 6′ 8″ high. Collection of Bruno Bishofberger, Zurich.

Schapiro calls her huge sewn collages *femmages* to make the point that women had been doing collages of fabric long before Picasso (FIG. 35-16). This femmage incorporates patterns from Japanese kimonos.

she had used to create a doll's house for her part in Womanhouse, in the 1970s Schapiro began to make huge sewn collages, assembled from fabrics, quilts, buttons, sequins, lace, and rickrack collected at antique shows. She called these works *femmages* to make the point that women had been doing collages using these materials long before Pablo Picasso (FIG. 35-16) introduced them to the art world. *Anatomy of a Kimono* (FIG. 36-34) is one of a series of monumental femmages based on the patterns of Japanese kimonos, fans, and robes. This vast composition repeats the kimono shape in a sumptuous array of fabric fragments.

CINDY SHERMAN Early attempts at dealing with feminist issues in art tended toward essentialism, emphasizing universal differences—either biological or experiential—between women and men. More recent discussions have gravitated toward the notion of gender as a socially constructed concept, and an extremely unstable one at that. Identity is multifaceted and changeable, making the discussion of feminist issues more challenging. Consideration of the many variables, however, results in a more complex understanding of gender roles.

American artist CINDY SHERMAN (b. 1954) addresses in her work the way much of Western art presents female beauty for the enjoyment of the "male gaze," a primary focus of contemporary feminist theory. Since 1977, Sherman has produced a series of more than 80 black-and-white photographs titled *Untitled Film Stills*. She got the idea for the series after examining soft-core pornography magazines and noting the stereotypical ways they depicted women. She decided to produce her own series of photographs, designing, acting in, directing, and photographing the works. In so doing, she took control of her own image and constructed her own identity, a primary feminist concern. In works from the series, such as *Untitled Film Still #35* (FIG. 36-35), Sherman appears, often in costume and wig, in a photograph that seems to be a film still. Most of the images in this series recall popular film genres but are sufficiently generic that the viewer cannot relate them to specific movies. Sherman often reveals the constructed nature of these images with the shutter release cable she holds in her hand to take the pictures. (The cord runs across the floor in *#35*.) Although the artist is still the object of the viewer's gaze in these images, the identity is one she alone chose to assume.

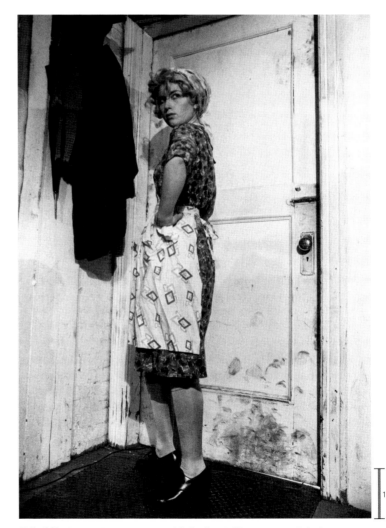

36-35 CINDY SHERMAN, *Untitled Film Still #35*, 1979. Gelatin silverprint, 10″ × 8″. Private collection. ◼◀

Sherman here assumed a role for one of a series of 80 photographs resembling film stills in which she addressed the way women have been presented in Western art for the enjoyment of the "male gaze."

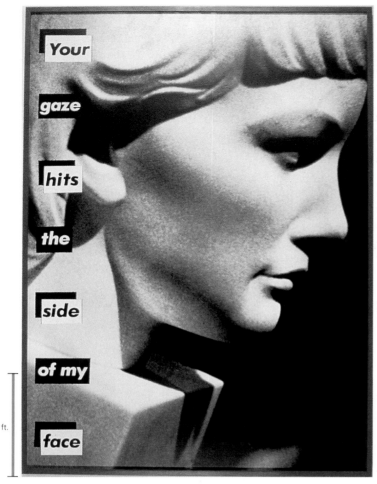

36-36 BARBARA KRUGER, *Untitled* (*Your Gaze Hits the Side of My Face*), 1981. Photograph, red painted frame, 4' 7" × 3' 5". Courtesy Mary Boone Gallery, New York. ◼◀

Kruger, like Sherman, has explored the male gaze in her art. Using the layout techniques of mass media, she constructed this word-and-photograph collage to challenge culturally constructed notions of gender.

BARBARA KRUGER   Another artist who has examined the male gaze and the culturally constructed notion of gender in her art is BARBARA KRUGER (b. 1945). Kruger's work explores the strategies and techniques of contemporary mass media and draws on her early training as a graphic designer who contributed to *Mademoiselle* magazine. *Untitled* (*Your Gaze Hits the Side of My Face*; FIG. 36-36) incorporates layout techniques the mass media use to sell consumer goods. Although Kruger favored the reassuringly familiar format and look of advertising, her goal was to subvert the typical use of such imagery. Rather, she aimed to expose the deceptiveness of the media messages the viewer complacently absorbs. Kruger wanted to undermine the myths—particularly those about women—the media constantly reinforce. Her huge (often 4 by 6 feet) word-and-photograph collages challenge the cultural attitudes embedded in commercial advertising.

In *Your Gaze,* Kruger overlaid a photograph of a classically beautiful sculpted head of a woman with a vertical row of text composed of eight words. The words cannot be taken in with a single glance, and reading them is a staccato exercise, with an overlaid cumulative quality that delays understanding and intensifies the meaning (rather like reading a series of roadside billboards from a speeding car). Kruger's use of text in her work is significant. Many cultural theorists have asserted that language is one of the most powerful vehicles for internalizing stereotypes and conditioned roles.

36-37 ANA MENDIETA, *Flowers on Body,* 1973. Color photograph of earth/body work with flowers, executed at El Yagul, Mexico. Courtesy of the Estate of Ana Mendieta and Galerie Lelong, New York.

In this earth/body sculpture, Mendieta appears covered with flowers in a womblike cavity to address issues of birth and death as well as the human connection to the earth.

ANA MENDIETA   Cuban-born artist ANA MENDIETA (1948–1985), like Sherman, used her body as a component in her artworks. Although gender issues concerned her, Mendieta's art also dealt with issues of spirituality and cultural heritage. The artist's best-known series, *Silueta* (*Silhouettes*), consists of approximately 200 earth/body works completed between 1973 and 1980. These works represented Mendieta's attempt to carry on, as she described, "a dialogue between the landscape and the female body (based on my own silhouette)."[23]

Flowers on Body (FIG. 36-37) is a documentary photograph of the first of the earth/body sculptures in the *Silueta* series. In this work, Mendieta appears covered with flowers in an earthen, womblike cavity. Executed at El Yagul, a Mexican archaeological site, the work speaks to the issues of birth and death, the female experience of childbirth, and the human connection to the earth. Objects and locations from nature play an important role in Mendieta's art. She explained the centrality of this connection to nature:

I believe this has been a direct result of my having been torn from my homeland during my adolescence. I am overwhelmed by the

1 ft.

36-38 HANNAH WILKE, *S.O.S.—Starification Object Series,* 1974. Ten black-and-white photographs with 15 chewing-gum sculptures in Plexiglas cases mounted on ragboard, from a series originally made for *S.O.S. Mastication Box* and used in an exhibition-performance at the Clocktower, January 1, 1975, 3′ 5″ × 5′ 8″. Courtesy Ronald Feldman Fine Arts, New York. Art © Marsie, Emanuelle, Damon and Andrew Scharlatt/Licensed by VAGA, New York.

In this photographic series, Wilke posed topless decorated with chewing-gum sculptures of vulvas that allude to female pleasure but also to pain, because they resemble scars.

feeling of having been cast from the womb (nature). My art is the way I re-establish the bonds that unite me to the universe. It is a return to the maternal source. Through my earth/body sculptures I become one with the earth.[24]

Beyond their sensual, moving presence, Mendieta's works also generate a palpable spiritual force. In longing for her homeland, she sought the cultural understanding and acceptance of the spiritual powers inherent in nature that modern Western societies often seem to reject in favor of scientific and technological developments. Mendieta's art is lyrical and passionate and operates at the intersection of cultural, spiritual, physical, and feminist concerns.

HANNAH WILKE Like Mendieta, HANNAH WILKE (1940–1993) used her own nude body as her artistic material. In her 1974–1982 series *S.O.S.—Starification Object Series* (FIG. 36-38), Wilke's images of herself trigger readings that are simultaneously metaphorical and real, stereotypical and unique, erotic and disconcerting, and that deal with both pleasure and pain. In these 10 black-and-white photographs documenting a performance, Wilke appears topless in a variety of poses, some seductive and others more confrontational. In each, pieces of chewed gum shaped into small vulvas decorate her body. While these tiny vaginal sculptures allude to female pleasure, they also appear as scars, suggesting pain. Ultimately, Wilke hoped that women would "take control of and have pride in the sensuality of their own bodies and create a sexuality in their own terms, without deferring to concepts degenerated by culture."[25]

GUERRILLA GIRLS Some feminist artists have taken the world of the woman artist as their subject, rather than women in society at large. The New York–based GUERRILLA GIRLS, formed in 1984, bill themselves as the "conscience of the art world." This group sees its duty as calling attention to injustice in the art world, especially what it perceives as the sexist and racist orientation of the major art institutions. The women who are members of the Guerrilla Girls have chosen to remain anonymous. To protect their identities, they wear

gorilla masks in public. The Guerrilla Girls employ guerrilla tactics by demonstrating in public, putting on performances, and placing posters and flyers in public locations. This distribution network expands the impact of their messages. One poster that reflects the Guerrilla Girls' agenda facetiously lists "the advantages of being a woman artist" (FIG. 36-39). In fact, the list itemizes the numerous obstacles women artists face in the contemporary art world. The Guerrilla Girls hope their publicizing of these obstacles will inspire improvements in the situation for women artists.

THE ADVANTAGES OF BEING A WOMAN ARTIST:

Working without the pressure of success
Not having to be in shows with men
Having an escape from the art world in your 4 free-lance jobs
Knowing your career might pick up after you're eighty
Being reassured that whatever kind of art you make it will be labeled feminine
Not being stuck in a tenured teaching position
Seeing your ideas live on in the work of others
Having the opportunity to choose between career and motherhood
Not having to choke on those big cigars or paint in Italian suits
Having more time to work when your mate dumps you for someone younger
Being included in revised versions of art history
Not having to undergo the embarrassment of being called a genius
Getting your picture in the art magazines wearing a gorilla suit

A PUBLIC SERVICE MESSAGE FROM **GUERRILLA GIRLS** CONSCIENCE OF THE ART WORLD

1 in.

36-39 GUERRILLA GIRLS, *The Advantages of Being a Woman Artist,* 1988. Offset print, 1′ 5″ × 1′ 10″. Collection of the artists.

The anonymous Guerrilla Girls wear gorilla masks in public performances and produce posters in which they call attention to injustice in the art world, especially what they perceive as sexist or racist treatment.

Other Social and Political Art

Feminist issues are by no means the only social and political concerns that contemporary artists have addressed in their work. Race, ethnicity, and sexual orientation are among the other pressing issues that have given rise to important artworks during the past few decades.

KIKI SMITH American sculptor KIKI SMITH (b. 1954) has explored the question of who controls the human body, an interest that grew out of her training as an emergency medical service technician in New York City. Smith, however, also wants to reveal the socially constructed nature of the body, and she encourages the viewer to consider how external forces shape people's perceptions of their bodies. In works such as *Untitled* (FIG. 36-40), the artist dramatically departed from conventional representations of the body, both in art and in the media. She suspended two life-size wax figures, one male and one female, both nude, from metal stands. Smith marked each of the sculptures with long white drips—body

1 ft.

36-40 KIKI SMITH, *Untitled,* 1990. Beeswax and microcrystalline wax figures on metal stands, female figure installed height 6′ 1½″; male figure 6′ 4¹⁵⁄₁₆″. Whitney Museum of American Art, New York (purchased with funds from the Painting and Sculpture Committee).

Asking "who controls the body?" Kiki Smith sculpted two life-size wax figures of a nude man and woman with body fluids running from the woman's breasts and down the man's leg.

fluids running from the woman's breasts and down the man's leg. She commented:

> Most of the functions of the body are hidden . . . from society. . . . [W]e separate our bodies from our lives. But, when people are dying, they are losing control of their bodies. That loss of function can seem humiliating and frightening. But, on the other hand, you can look at it as a kind of liberation of the body. It seems like a nice metaphor—a way to think about the social—that people lose control despite the many agendas of different ideologies in society, which are trying to control the body(ies) . . . medicine, religion, law, etc. Just thinking about control—who has control of the body? . . . Does the mind have control of the body? Does the social?[26]

FAITH RINGGOLD Other artists, reflecting their own identities and backgrounds, have used their art to address issues associated with African American women. Inspired by the civil rights movement, FAITH RINGGOLD (b. 1930) produced numerous works in the 1960s that provided incisive commentary on the realities of racial prejudice. She increasingly incorporated references to gender as well and, in the 1970s, turned to fabric as the predominant material in her art. Using fabric enabled her to make more pointed reference to the domestic sphere, traditionally associated with women, and to collaborate with her mother, Willi Posey, a fashion designer. After her mother's death in 1981, Ringgold created *Who's Afraid of Aunt Jemima?* (FIG. 36-41), a quilt composed of dyed, painted, and pieced fabric. A moving tribute to her mother, this work combines the personal and the political. The quilt includes a narrative—the witty story of the family of Aunt Jemima, most familiar as the stereotypical black "mammy" but here a successful African American businesswoman. Ringgold conveyed this

1 ft.

36-41 FAITH RINGGOLD, *Who's Afraid of Aunt Jemima?* 1983. Acrylic on canvas with fabric borders, quilted, 7′ 6″ × 6′ 8″. Private collection.

In this quilt, a medium associated with women, Ringgold presented a tribute to her mother that also addresses African American culture and the struggles of women to overcome oppression.

36-42 Lorna Simpson, *Stereo Styles,* 1988. 10 black-and-white Polaroid prints and 10 engraved plastic plaques, 5′ 4″ × 9′ 8″ overall. Private collection.

In *Stereo Styles,* Simpson presents photographs of African American hairstyles as racial symbols associated with personality traits. She also comments on those coiffures as fashion commodities.

narrative using both text (written in black dialect) and embroidered portraits interspersed with traditional patterned squares. This work, while resonating with autobiographical references, also speaks to the larger issues of the history of African American culture and the struggles of women to overcome oppression.

LORNA SIMPSON The issues of racism and sexism are also central to the work of Lorna Simpson (b. 1960). Simpson has spent much of her career producing photographs that explore feminist and African American strategies to reveal and subvert conventional representations of gender and race. Like Sherman (FIG. **36-35**), she deals with the issue of "the gaze," trying to counteract the process of objectification to which both women and African Americans are subject. In *Stereo Styles* (FIG. **36-42**), a series of Polaroid photographs and engravings, Simpson focuses on African American hairstyles, often used to symbolize the entire race. Hair is a physical code tied to issues of social status and position. Kobena Mercer, who has studied the cultural importance of hair, observed that "Hair is never a straightforward biological 'fact' because it is almost always groomed, ... cut, ... and generally 'worked upon' by human hands. Such practices socialize hair, making it the medium of significant 'statements' about self and society."[27] On the issue of race, Mercer argued, "where race structures social relations of power, hair—as visible as skin color, but also the most tangible sign of racial difference—takes on another forcefully symbolic dimension."[28] In *Stereo Styles,* Simpson also commented on the appropriation of African-derived hairstyles as a fashion commodity, and the personality traits listed correlate with specific hairstyles.

MELVIN EDWARDS American Melvin Edwards (b. 1937) also has sought to reveal a history of collective oppression through his art. One of Edwards's major sculptural series focused on the metaphor of lynching to provoke thought about the legacy of racism. This *Lynch Fragment* series encompassed more than 150 welded-steel sculptures produced in the years after 1963. Lynching

as an artistic theme prompts an immediate and visceral response, conjuring chilling and gruesome images from the past. Edwards sought to extend this emotional resonance further in his art. He constructed the series' relatively small welded sculptures, such as *Tambo* (FIG. **36-43**), from found metal objects—for example, chains, hooks, hammers, spikes, knife blades, and handcuffs. Although Edwards often intertwined or welded together the individual metal

36-43 Melvin Edwards, *Tambo,* 1993. Welded steel, 2′ 4$\frac{1}{8}$″ × 2′ 1$\frac{1}{4}$″. Smithsonian American Art Museum, Washington, D.C.

Edwards's welded sculptures of chains, spikes, knife blades, and other found objects allude to the lynching of African Americans and the continuing struggle for civil rights and an end to racism.

Public Funding of Controversial Art

Although art can be beautiful and uplifting, throughout history art has also challenged and offended. Since the early 1980s, a number of heated controversies about art have surfaced in the United States. There have been many calls to remove the "offensive" works from public view (see "Richard Serra's *Tilted Arc*," page 1016) and, in reaction, accusations of censorship. The central questions in all cases have been whether there are limits to what art can appropriately be exhibited, and whether governmental authorities have the right to monitor and pass judgment on creative endeavors. A related question is whether the acceptability of a work should be a criterion in determining the public funding of art.

Two exhibits in 1989 placed the National Endowment for the Arts (NEA), a government agency charged with distributing federal funds to support the arts, squarely in the middle of this debate. One of the exhibitions, devoted to recipients of the Awards for the Visual Arts (AVA), took place at the Southeastern Center for Contemporary Art in North Carolina. Among the award winners was Andres Serrano, whose *Piss Christ*, a photograph of a crucifix submerged in urine, sparked an uproar. Responding to this artwork, Reverend Donald Wildmon, an evangelical minister from Mississippi and head of the American Family Association, expressed outrage that such work was in an exhibition funded by the NEA and the Equitable Life Assurance Society (a sponsor of the AVA). He demanded that the work be removed and launched a letter-writing campaign that led Equitable Life to cancel its sponsorship of the awards. To Wildmon and other staunch conservatives, this exhibition, along with the *Robert Mapplethorpe: The Perfect Moment* show, served as evidence of cultural depravity and immorality, which they insisted should not be funded by government agencies such as the NEA. Mapplethorpe was a photographer well known for his elegant, spare photographs of flowers and vegetables as well as his erotic, homosexually oriented images. As a result of media furor over *The Perfect Moment*, the director of the Corcoran Museum of Art canceled the scheduled exhibition of this traveling show. But the director of the Contemporary Arts Center in Cincinnati decided to mount the show. The government indicted him on charges of obscenity, but a jury acquitted him six months later.

36-44A
MAPPLETHORPE, *Self-Portrait,* 1980.

These controversies intensified public criticism of the NEA and its funding practices. The next year, the head of the NEA, John Frohnmayer, vetoed grants for four lesbian, gay, or feminist performance artists—Karen Finley, John Fleck, Holly Hughes, and Tim Miller—who became known as the "NEA Four." Infuriated by what they perceived as overt censorship, the artists filed suit, eventually settling the case and winning reinstatement of their grants. Congress responded by dramatically reducing the NEA's budget, and the agency no longer awards grants or fellowships to individual artists.

Controversies have also erupted on the municipal level. In 1999, Rudolph Giuliani, then mayor of New York, joined a number of individuals and groups protesting the inclusion of several artworks in the exhibition *Sensation: Young British Artists from the Saatchi Collec-*

36-44 CHRIS OFILI, *The Holy Virgin Mary,* 1996. Paper collage, oil paint, glitter, polyester resin, map pins, elephant dung on linen, 7′ 11″ × 5′ 11$\frac{5}{16}$″. Saatchi Collection, London.

Ofili, a British-born Catholic of Nigerian descent, represented the Virgin Mary with African elephant dung on one breast and surrounded by genitalia and buttocks. The painting produced a public outcry.

tion at the Brooklyn Museum. Chris Ofili's *The Holy Virgin Mary* (FIG. 36-44), a collage of Mary incorporating cutouts from pornographic magazines and shellacked clumps of elephant dung, became the flashpoint for public furor. Denouncing the show as "sick stuff," the mayor threatened to cut off all city subsidies to the museum.

Art that seeks to unsettle and challenge is critical to the cultural, political, and psychological life of a society. The regularity with which such art raises controversy suggests that it operates at the intersection of two competing principles: free speech and artistic expression on the one hand and a reluctance to impose images upon an audience that finds them repugnant or offensive on the other. What these controversies do demonstrate, beyond doubt, is the enduring power of art.

components so as to diminish immediate identifiability, the sculptures still retain a haunting connection to the overall theme. These works refer to a historical act that evokes a collective memory of oppression, but they also speak to the continuing struggle for civil rights and an end to racism. While growing up in Los Angeles, Edwards experienced racial conflict firsthand. Among the metal objects incorporated into his *Lynch Fragments* sculptures are items he found in the streets in the aftermath of the Watts riots in 1965. The inclusion of these found objects imbued his disquieting, haunting works with an even greater intensity.

36-45 David Hammons, *Public Enemy,* installation at Museum of Modern Art, New York, 1991. Photographs, balloons, sandbags, guns, and other mixed media. ◼◀

Hammons intended this multimedia installation, with Theodore Roosevelt flanked by an African American and a Native American as servants, to reveal the racism embedded in America's cultural heritage.

CHRIS OFILI Another contemporary artist who has explored his ethnic and racial heritage in his art is CHRIS OFILI (b. 1968). One theme Ofili has treated is religion, interpreted through the eyes of a British-born Catholic of Nigerian descent. Ofili's *The Holy Virgin Mary* (FIG. 36-44) depicts Mary in a manner that departs radically from conventional Renaissance representations. Ofili's work presents the Virgin in simplified form, and she appears to float in an indeterminate space. The artist employed brightly colored pigments, applied to the canvas in multiple layers of beadlike dots (inspired by images from ancient caves in Zimbabwe). Surrounding the Virgin are tiny images of genitalia and buttocks cut from pornographic magazines, which, to the artist, parallel the putti that often surround Mary in Renaissance paintings. Another reference to Ofili's African heritage surfaces in the clumps of elephant dung—one attached to the Virgin's breast, and two more on which the canvas rests, serving as supports. The dung allowed Ofili to incorporate Africa into his work in a literal way. Still, he wants the viewer to move beyond the cultural associations of the materials and see those materials in new ways.

Not surprisingly, *The Holy Virgin Mary* has elicited strong reactions. Its inclusion in *Sensation* at the Brooklyn Museum in 1999 prompted indignant demands for cancellation of the show and countercharges of censorship (see "Public Funding of Controversial Art," page 996).

DAVID HAMMONS Nurturing viewer introspection is the driving force behind the art of DAVID HAMMONS (b. 1943). In his *installations* (artworks creating an artistic environment in a room or gallery), he combines sharp social commentary with beguiling sensory elements to push viewers to confront racism in American society. He created *Public Enemy* (FIG. 36-45) for an exhibition at the Museum of Modern Art in New York in 1991. Hammons enticed viewers to interact with the installation by scattering fragrant autumn leaves on the floor and positioning helium-filled balloons throughout the gallery. The leaves crunched underfoot, and the dangling strings of the balloons gently brushed spectators walking around the installation. Once drawn into the environment, viewers encountered the central element in *Public Enemy*—large black-and-white photographs of a public monument depicting President Theodore Roosevelt (1858–1919) triumphantly seated on a horse, flanked by an African American man and a Native American man, both appearing in the role of servants. Around the edge of the installation, circling the photographs of the monument, were piles of sandbags with both real and toy guns propped on top, aimed at the statue. By selecting evocative found objects and presenting them in a dynamic manner that encouraged viewer interaction, Hammons attracted an audience and then revealed the racism embedded in received cultural heritage. In this way, he prompted reexamination of American values and cultural emblems.

JAUNE QUICK-TO-SEE SMITH Another contemporary artist who has explored the politics of identity is JAUNE QUICK-TO-SEE SMITH (b. 1940), a Native American artist descended from the Shoshone, the Salish, and the Cree tribes and raised on the Flatrock Reservation in Montana. Quick-to-See Smith's native heritage has always informed her art, and her concern about the invisibility of Native American artists has led her to organize exhibitions of their art. Yet she has acknowledged a wide range of influences, including "pictogram forms from Europe, the Amur [the river between Russia and China], the Americas; color from beadwork, parfleches [hide cases], the landscape; paint application from Cobra art, New York expressionism, primitive art; composition from Kandinsky, Klee or Byzantine art."[29] She has even compared her use of tribal images to that of the Abstract Expressionists.

Despite the myriad references and visual material in Quick-to-See Smith's art, her work displays coherence and power, and, like many other artists who have explored issues associated with identity, she

1 ft.

challenges stereotypes and unacknowledged assumptions. *Trade (Gifts for Trading Land with White People;* FIG. **36-46**) is a large-scale painting with collage elements and attached objects, reminiscent of a Rauschenberg combine (FIG. **36-22**). The painting's central image, a canoe, appears in an expansive field painted in loose Abstract Expressionist fashion and covered with clippings from Native American newspapers. Above the painting, as if hung from a clothesline, is an array of objects. These include Native American artifacts, such as beaded belts and feather headdresses, and contemporary sports memorabilia from teams with American Indian–derived names—the Cleveland Indians, Atlanta Braves, and Washington Redskins. The inclusion of these contemporary objects immediately recalls the vocal opposition to these names and to acts such as the Braves' "tomahawk chop." Like Edwards, Quick-to-See Smith uses the past to comment on the present.

LEON GOLUB In his paintings, American artist Leon Golub (1922–2004) expressed a brutal vision of contemporary life through a sophisticated reading of the news media's raw data. His best-known work deals with violent events of recent decades—the narratives people have learned to extract from news photos of anonymous characters participating in atrocious street violence, terrorism, and torture. Paintings in Golub's *Assassins* and *Mercenaries* series suggest not specific stories but a condition of being. As the artist said,

> Through media we are under constant, invasive bombardment of images—from all over—and we often have to take evasive action to avoid discomforting recognitions. . . . The work [of art] should have an edge, veering between what is visually and cognitively acceptable and what might stretch these limits as we encounter or try to visualize the real products of the uses of power.[30]

Mercenaries IV (FIG. **36-47**), a huge canvas, represents a mysterious tableau of five tough freelance military professionals willing to fight, for a price, for any political cause. The three clustering at the right side of the canvas react with tense physical gestures to something one of the two other mercenaries standing at the far left is saying. The dark uniforms and skin tones of the four black fighters flatten their figures and make them stand out against the searing dark red background. The slightly modulated background seems to push their forms forward up against the picture plane and becomes an echoing void in the space between the two groups. Golub painted the mercenaries so that the viewer's eye is level with the menacing figures' knees. He placed the men so close to the front plane of the

1 ft.

When I put my hands on your body, on your flesh, I feel the history of that body. Not just the beginning of its forming in that distant lake but all the way beyond its ending. I feel the warmth and texture and simultaneously see the flesh unwrap from the layers of fat and disappear. I see the fat self-consumed. I see the muscle disappearing from around the organs and detaching itself from the bones. I see the organs gradually fade into transparency leaving a gleaming skeleton gleaming like ivory that slowly revolves until it becomes dust. I am consumed in the sense of your weight the way your flesh occupies momentary space the fullness of it beneath my palms. I am amazed at how perfectly your body fits to the curves of my hands. If I could attach our blood vessels so we could become each other I would. If I could attach our blood vessels in order to anchor you to the earth to this present time I would. If I could open up your body and slip inside your skin and look out your eyes and forever have my lips fused with yours I would. It makes me weep to feel the history of you of your flesh beneath my hands in a time of so much loss. It makes me weep to feel the movement of your flesh beneath my palms as you twist and turn over to one side to create a series of gestures to reach up around my neck to draw me nearer. All these memories will be lost in time like the spoke of a wheel.

36-48 David Wojnarowicz, *"When I put my hands on your body,"* 1990. Gelatin-silver print and silk-screened text on museum board, 2′ 2″ × 3′ 2″. Private collection.

In this disturbing yet eloquent print, Wojnarowicz overlaid typed commentary on a photograph of skeletal remains. He movingly communicated his feelings about watching a loved one die of AIDS.

1 ft.

work that the lower edge of the painting cuts off their feet, thereby trapping the viewer in the painting's compressed space. Golub emphasized both the scarred light tones of the white mercenary's skin and the weapons. Modeled with shadow and gleaming highlights, the guns contrast with the harshly scraped, flattened surfaces of the figures. The rawness of the canvas reinforces the rawness of the imagery. Golub often dissolved certain areas with solvent after applying pigment and scraped off applied paint with, among other tools, a meat cleaver. The feeling of peril confronts viewers mercilessly. They become one with all the victims caught in today's political battles.

DAVID WOJNAROWICZ As a gay activist and as someone who had lost many friends to AIDS (acquired immune deficiency syndrome), David Wojnarowicz (1955–1992) created disturbing yet eloquent works about the tragedy of this disease. (Wojnarowicz himself died of AIDS.) In *"When I put my hands on your body"* (FIG. **36-48**), he overlaid a photograph of a pile of skeletal remains with evenly spaced typed commentary that communicated his feelings about watching a loved one dying of AIDS. Wojnarowicz movingly described the effects of AIDS on the human body and soul. He juxtaposed text with imagery, which, like the works of Barbara Kruger (FIG. **36-36**) and Lorna Simpson (FIG. **36-42**), paralleled the use of both words and images in advertising. The public's familiarity with this format ensured greater receptivity to the artist's message.

KRZYSZTOF WODICZKO When working in Canada in 1980, Polish-born artist Krzysztof Wodiczko (b. 1943) developed artworks involving outdoor slide images. He projected photographs on specific buildings to expose how civic buildings embody, legitimize, and perpetuate power. When Wodiczko moved to New York City in 1983, the pervasive homelessness troubled him, and he resolved to use his art to publicize this problem. In 1987 he produced *The Homeless Projection* (FIG. **36-49**) as part of a New Year's celebration in Boston. The artist projected images of homeless people on all four sides of the Soldiers and Sailors Civil War Memorial on the Boston Common. In these photos, plastic bags filled with their few possessions flanked the people depicted. At the top of the monument, Wodiczko projected a local condominium construction site, which helped viewers make a connection between urban development and homelessness.

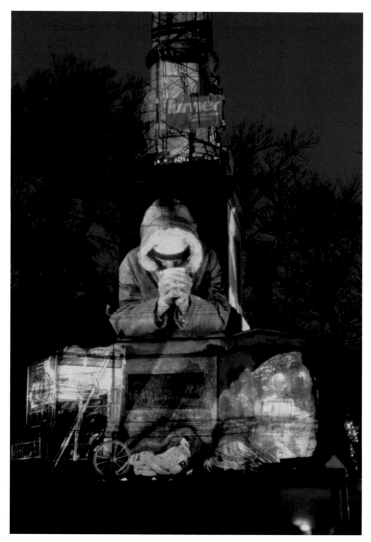

36-49 Krzysztof Wodiczko, *The Homeless Projection*, 1986. Outdoor slide projection at the Soldiers and Sailors Civil War Memorial, Boston. ◼◀

To publicize their plight, Wodiczko projected on the walls of a monument on the Boston Common images of homeless people and their plastic bags filled with their few possessions.

1 ft.

36-50 MAGDALENA ABAKANOWICZ, *80 Backs,* 1976–1980. Burlap and resin, each 2′ 3″ high. Museum of Modern Art, Dallas.

Polish fiber artist Abakanowicz explored the stoic, everyday toughness of the human spirit in this group of nearly identical sculptures that serve as symbols of distinctive individuals lost in the crowd.

MAGDALENA ABAKANOWICZ The stoic, everyday toughness of the human spirit has been the subject of Polish fiber artist MAGDALENA ABAKANOWICZ (b. 1930). A leader in the recent exploration in sculpture of the expressive powers of weaving techniques, Abakanowicz gained fame with experimental freestanding pieces in both abstract and figural modes. For Abakanowicz, fiber materials are deeply symbolic:

> I see fiber as the basic element constructing the organic world on our planet, as the greatest mystery of our environment. It is from fiber that all living organisms are built—the tissues of plants and ourselves. . . . Fabric is our covering and our attire. Made with our hands, it is a record of our souls.[31]

To all of her work, Abakanowicz brought the experiences of her early life as a member of an aristocratic family disturbed by the dislocations of World War II and its aftermath. Initially attracted to weaving as a medium that would adapt well to the small studio space she had available, Abakanowicz gradually developed huge abstract hangings she called Abakans that suggest organic spaces as well as giant pieces of clothing. She returned to a smaller scale with works based on human forms—*Heads, Seated Figures,* and *Backs*—multiplying each type for exhibition in groups as symbols for the individual in society lost in the crowd yet retaining some distinctiveness. This impression is especially powerful in an installation of *80 Backs* (FIG. 36-50). Abakanowicz made each piece by pressing layers of natural organic fibers into a plaster mold. Every sculpture depicts the slumping shoulders, back, and arms of a figure of indeterminate sex and rests legless directly on the floor. The repeated pose of the figures in *80 Backs* suggests meditation, submission, and anticipation. Although made from a single mold, the figures achieve a touch-

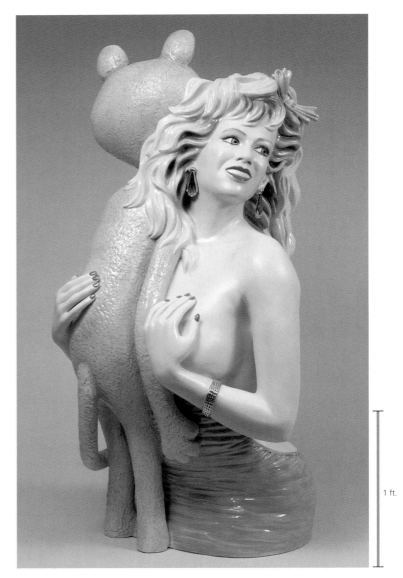

1 ft.

36-51 JEFF KOONS, *Pink Panther,* 1988. Porcelain, 3′ 5″ × 1′ 8½″ × 1′ 7″. Museum of Contemporary Art, Chicago (Gerald S. Elliot Collection). ◼◣

In the 1980s Koons created sculptures that highlight everything wrong with contemporary American consumer culture. In this work, he intertwined a centerfold nude and a cartoon character.

ing sense of individuality because each assumed a slightly different posture as the material dried and because the artist imprinted a different pattern of fiber texture on each.

JEFF KOONS While many contemporary artists have pursued personally meaningful agendas in their art, others have addressed society-wide concerns, for example, postmodern commodity culture. American JEFF KOONS (b. 1955), who was a commodities broker before turning to art, first became prominent in the art world for a series of works in the early 1980s that involved exhibiting common purchased objects such as vacuum cleaners. Clearly following in the footsteps of artists such as Marcel Duchamp (FIG. 35-27) and Andy Warhol (FIG. 36-24), Koons made no attempt to manipulate or alter the objects. More recently, he has produced porcelain sculptures, such as *Pink Panther* (FIG. 36-51), in which he continued his immersion in contemporary mass culture by intertwining a magazine centerfold nude with a famous cartoon character. Koons reinforced the trite and kitschy nature of this imagery by titling the exhibition of which this work was a part *The Banality Show.* Some art critics have argued that Koons and his work instruct viewers because both

Underscoring the
importance of art
critics in the con-
temporary art world,
Arneson produced
this self-portrait
incorporating all
the stereotypes a
New York Times
critic attributed to
California artists.

artist and work serve as the most visible symbols of everything that is wrong with contemporary American society. Whether or not this is true, Koons's prominence in the art world indicates that he, like Warhol before him, has developed an acute understanding of the dynamics of consumer culture.

ROBERT ARNESON During his career, ROBERT ARNESON (1930–1992) developed a body of work of predominantly figural ceramic sculpture, often satirical or amusing and sometimes biting. In 1981 the influential *New York Times* art critic Hilton Kramer (b. 1928) published a review of an exhibition that included a scathing assessment of the artist's work. Arneson, who spent his life in a small town north of San Francisco, created *California Artist* (FIG. 36-52) as a direct response to Kramer, particularly to the critic's derogatory comments on the provincialism of California art. This ceramic sculpture, a half-length self-portrait, incorporates all of the stereotypes Kramer perpetuated. The artist placed the top half of his likeness on a pedestal littered with beer bottles, cigarette butts, and marijuana plants. Arneson appears clad only in a denim jacket and sunglasses, looking very defiant with his arms crossed. Of course, by creating an artwork that responded directly to Kramer's comments, Arneson validated the importance of art critics in the contemporary art world.

MARK TANSEY This kind of interaction between artists and critics also underscores the self-consciousness on the part of contemporary artists about their place in the continuum of art history. For many postmodern artists, referencing the past is much more than incorporating elements from earlier works and styles in their own art. It involves a critique of or commentary on fundamental art historical premises. In short, their art is about making art.

In his humorous *A Short History of Modernist Painting* (FIG. 36-53), American artist MARK TANSEY (b. 1949) provides viewers with a tongue-in-cheek summary of the various approaches to painting artists have embraced over the years. Tansey presents a sequence of three images, each visualizing a way of looking at art. At the far left, a glass window encapsulates the Renaissance ideal of viewing art as though one were looking through a window. In the

36-53 MARK TANSEY, *A Short History of Modernist Painting*, 1982. Oil on canvas, three panels, each 4' 10" × 3' 4". Courtesy Gagosian Gallery, New York.

Tansey's tripartite history of painting includes the Renaissance window onto the world, the modernist insistence on a painting as a flat surface, and postmodern artists' reflections on their place in art history.

36-54 HANS HAACKE, *MetroMobiltan,* 1985. Fiberglass construction, three banners, and photomural, 11′ 8″ × 20′ × 5′. Musée National d'Art Moderne, Centre Georges Pompidou, Paris.

MetroMobiltan focuses attention on the connections between political and economic conditions in South Africa and the conflicted politics of corporate patronage of art exhibitions.

1 ft.

center image, a man pushing his head against a solid wall represents the thesis central to much of modernist formalism—that the painting should be acknowledged as an object in its own right. In the image on the right, Tansey summarizes the postmodern approach to art with a chicken pondering its reflection in the mirror. The chicken's action reveals postmodern artists' reflections on their place in the art historical continuum.

HANS HAACKE Along with a conscious reappraisal of the processes of art historical validation, postmodern artists have turned to assessing art institutions, such as museums and galleries, and their role in validating art. Many artists have also scrutinized the discriminatory policies and politics of these cultural institutions. German artist HANS HAACKE (b. 1936) has focused his attention on the politics of art museums and how acquisition and exhibition policies affect the public's understanding of art history. The specificity of his works, based on substantial research, makes them stinging indictments of the institutions whose practices he critiques. In *MetroMobiltan* (FIG. **36-54**), Haacke illustrated the connection between the realm of art (more specifically, the Metropolitan Museum of Art in New York) and the "real" world of political and economic interests. *MetroMobiltan* is a large sculptural work that includes a photomural of a funeral for South African black people. This photomural serves as the backdrop for a banner for the 1980 Mobil Oil–sponsored Metropolitan Museum show *Treasures of Ancient Nigeria.* In 1980, Mobil was a principal U.S. investor in South Africa, and Haacke's work suggests that one of the driving forces behind Mobil's sponsorship of this exhibition was the fact that Nigeria was one of the richest oil-producing countries in Africa. In 1981 the public pressured Mobil's board of directors to stop providing oil to the white South African military and police. Printed on the blue banners hanging on either side of *Metro-Mobiltan* is the official corporate response refusing to comply with this demand. Haacke set the entire tableau in a fiberglass replica of the Metropolitan Museum's entablature. By bringing together these disparate visual and textual elements that make reference to the mu-

seum, Mobil Oil, and Africa, the artist forced viewers to think about the connections among multinational corporations, political and economic conditions in South Africa, and the conflicted politics of corporate patronage of art exhibitions, thereby undermining the public's view that cultural institutions are exempt from political and economic concerns.

ARCHITECTURE AND SITE-SPECIFIC ART

Some of the leading architects of the first half of the 20th century, most notably Frank Lloyd Wright (FIGS. **35-77** to **35-79**), Le Corbusier (FIG. **35-75**), and Ludwig Mies van der Rohe (FIG. **35-74**), concluded their long and productive careers in the postwar period. At the same time, younger architects rose to international prominence, some working in the modernist idiom but others taking architectural design in new directions, including postmodernism and Deconstructivism. Still, one common denominator exists in the diversity of contemporary architectural design: the breaking down of national boundaries, with major architects pursuing projects on several continents (MAP **36-1**), often simultaneously.

Modernism

In parallel with the progressive movement toward formal abstraction in painting and sculpture in the decades following World War II, modernist architects became increasingly concerned with a formalism that stressed simplicity. They articulated this in buildings that retained intriguing organic sculptural qualities, as well as in buildings that adhered to a more rigid geometry.

FRANK LLOYD WRIGHT The last great building Frank Lloyd Wright designed was the Solomon R. Guggenheim Museum (FIG. **36-55**), built in New York City between 1943 and 1959. Using rein-

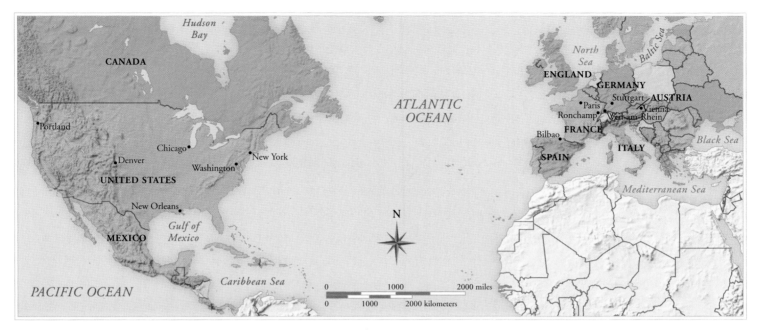

MAP 36-1 Modernist and postmodernist architecture in Europe and America.

forced concrete almost as a sculptor might use resilient clay, Wright, who often described his architecture as "organic," designed a structure inspired by the spiral of a snail's shell. Wright had introduced curves and circles into some of his plans in the 1930s, and, as the architectural historian Peter Blake noted, "The spiral was the next logical step; it is the circle brought into the third and fourth dimensions."[32] Inside the building (FIGS. 36-1 and 36-85), the shape of the shell expands toward the top, and a winding interior ramp spirals to

connect the gallery bays. A skylight strip embedded in the museum's outer wall provides illumination to the ramp, which visitors can stroll up (or down, if they first take an elevator to the top of the building), viewing the artworks displayed along the gently sloping pathway. Thick walls and the solid organic shape give the building, outside and inside, the sense of turning in on itself, and the long interior viewing area opening onto a 90-foot central well of space creates a sheltered environment, secure from the bustling city outside.

36-55 FRANK LLOYD WRIGHT, Solomon R. Guggenheim Museum (looking north), New York, 1943–1959.

Using reinforced concrete almost as a sculptor might use resilient clay, Wright designed a snail shell–shaped museum with a winding interior ramp for the display of artworks along its gently inclined path (FIGS. 36-1 and 36-85).

The organic forms of Le Corbusier's mountaintop chapel present a fusion of architecture and sculpture. The architect based the shapes on praying hands, a dove's wings, and a ship's prow.

LE CORBUSIER Compared with his pristine geometric design for Villa Savoye (FIG. 35-75), the organic forms of Le Corbusier's Notre-Dame-du-Haut (FIG. 36-56) come as a startling surprise. Completed in 1955 at Ronchamp, France, the chapel attests to the boundless creativity of this great architect. A fusion of architecture and sculpture, the small chapel, which replaced a building destroyed in World War II, occupies a pilgrimage site in the Vosges Mountains. The monumental impression of Notre-Dame-du-Haut seen from afar is somewhat deceptive. Although one massive exterior wall contains a pulpit facing a spacious outdoor area for large-scale open-air services on holy days, the interior (FIG. 36-57) holds at most 200 people. The intimate scale, stark and heavy walls, and mysterious illumination (jewel tones cast from the deeply recessed stained-glass windows) give this space an aura reminiscent of a sacred cave or a medieval monastery.

Notre-Dame-du-Haut's structure may look free-form to the untrained eye, but Le Corbusier based it, like the medieval cathedral, on an underlying mathematical system. The builders formed the fabric from a frame of steel and metal mesh, which they sprayed with concrete and painted white, except for two interior private chapel niches with colored walls and the roof, which Le Corbusier wished to have darken naturally with the passage of time. The roof appears to float freely above the sanctuary, intensifying the quality of mystery in the interior space. In reality, a series of nearly invisible blocks holds up the roof. The mystery of the roof's means of support recalls the reaction to Hagia Sophia's miraculously floating dome (FIG. 12-4) a millennium and a half before. Le Corbusier's preliminary sketches for the building indicate he linked the design with the shape of praying hands, with the wings of a dove (representing both peace and the Holy Spirit), and with the prow of a ship (a reminder that the Latin word used for the main gathering place in Christian churches is *nave*, meaning "ship"). The artist envisioned that in these powerful sculptural solids and voids, human beings could find new values—new interpretations of their sacred beliefs and of their natural environments.

EERO SAARINEN Dramatic, sweeping, curvilinear rooflines are characteristic features of the buildings designed by Finnish-born architect EERO SAARINEN (1910–1961). One of his signature buildings of the late 1950s is the former Trans World Airlines terminal (FIG. 36-58) at John F. Kennedy International Airport in New York, which Saarinen based on the theme of motion. The terminal consists of two immense concrete shells split down the middle and slightly rotated, giving the building a fluid curved outline that fits its corner site. The shells immediately suggest expansive wings and flight. Saarinen also designed everything on the interior, including the furniture, ventilation ducts, and signboards, with this same curvilinear vocabulary in mind.

36-57 LE CORBUSIER, interior of Notre-Dame-du-Haut, Ronchamp, France, 1950–1955.

Constructed of concrete sprayed on a frame of steel and metal mesh, the heavy walls of the Ronchamp chapel enclose an intimate and mysteriously lit interior that has the aura of a sacred cave.

36-58 EERO SAARINEN, Trans World Airlines terminal (terminal 5), John F. Kennedy International Airport, New York, 1956–1962.

Saarinen based the design for this airline terminal on the theme of motion. The concrete-and-glass building's dramatic, sweeping, curvilinear rooflines appropriately suggest expansive wings and flight.

JOERN UTZON Saarinen was responsible for selecting the Danish architect JOERN UTZON (b. 1918) to build the Sydney Opera House (FIG. 36-59) in Australia. Utzon's design is a bold composition of organic forms on a colossal scale. Utzon worked briefly with Frank Lloyd Wright at Taliesin (Wright's Wisconsin residence), and the style of the Sydney Opera House resonates distantly with the graceful curvature of Wright's Guggenheim Museum. Two clusters of immense concrete shells—the largest is 200 feet tall—rise from massive platforms and soar to delicate peaks. Recalling at first the ogival shapes of Gothic vaults, the shells also suggest both the buoyancy of seabird wings and the billowing sails of the tall ships that brought European settlers to Australia in the 18th and 19th centuries. These architectural metaphors are appropriate to the harbor surrounding Bennelong Point, whose bedrock foundations support the building. Utzon's matching of the structure with its site and atmosphere adds to the organic nature of the design.

Begun in 1959, completion of the opera house had to wait until 1972, primarily because Utzon's daring design required construc-

tion technology that had not yet been developed. Today the opera house is Sydney's defining symbol, a monument of civic pride that functions as the city's cultural center. In addition to the opera auditorium, the complex houses auxiliary halls and rooms for concerts, the performing arts, motion pictures, lectures, art exhibitions, and conventions.

MIES VAN DER ROHE Sculpturesque building design was not the only manifestation of postwar modernist architecture. From the mid-1950s through the 1970s, other architects created massive, sleek, and geometrically rigid buildings. They designed most of these structures following Bauhaus architect Mies van der Rohe's contention that "less is more." Many of these more "Minimalist" designs are powerful, heroic presences in the urban landscape that effectively symbolize the giant corporations that often inhabit them.

The "purest" example of these corporate skyscrapers is the mid-1950s rectilinear glass-and-bronze Seagram Building (FIG. 36-60) in Manhattan, designed by Mies van der Rohe and American architect

36-59 JOERN UTZON, Sydney Opera House, Sydney, Australia, 1959–1972.

The two soaring clusters of concrete shells of Utzon's opera house on an immense platform in Sydney's harbor suggest both the buoyancy of seabird wings and the billowing sails of tall ships.

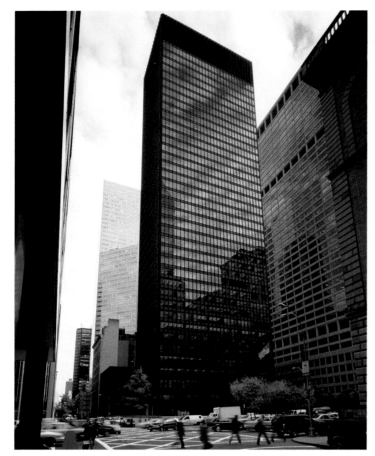

36-60 Ludwig Mies van der Rohe and Philip Johnson, Seagram Building, New York, 1956–1958.

Massive, sleek, and geometrically rigid, this modernist skyscraper has a bronze and glass skin that masks its concrete and steel frame. The giant corporate tower appears to rise from the pavement on stilts.

Philip Johnson (FIG. 36-64). By this time, the concrete-steel-and-glass towers pioneered by Louis Sullivan (FIGS. 31-40 and 31-41) and carried further by Mies van der Rohe (FIG. 35-74) had become a familiar sight in cities all over the world. Appealing in its structural logic and clarity, the style, easily imitated, quickly became the norm for postwar commercial high-rise buildings. The architects of the Seagram Building (FIG. 36-60) deliberately designed it as a thin shaft, leaving the front quarter of its midtown site as an open pedestrian plaza. The tower appears to rise from the pavement on stilts. Glass walls even surround the recessed lobby. The building's recessed structural elements make it appear to have a glass skin, interrupted only by the thin strips of bronze anchoring the windows. The bronze metal and the amber glass windows give the tower a richness found in few of its neighbors. Mies van der Rohe and Johnson carefully planned every detail of the Seagram Building, inside and out, to create an elegant whole. They even designed the interior and exterior lighting to make the edifice an impressive sight both day and night.

SKIDMORE, OWINGS, AND MERRILL The architectural firm SKIDMORE, OWINGS, AND MERRILL (SOM), perhaps the purest proponent of Miesian-inspired structures, designed a number of these simple rectilinear glass-sheathed buildings, and SOM's success indicates the popularity of this building type. By 1970 the company employed more than a thousand architects and had offices in New York, Chicago, San Francisco, Portland, and Washington, D.C. In 1974 the firm completed the Sears Tower (FIG. 36-61), a mammoth corporate building in Chicago. Consisting of nine clustered shafts

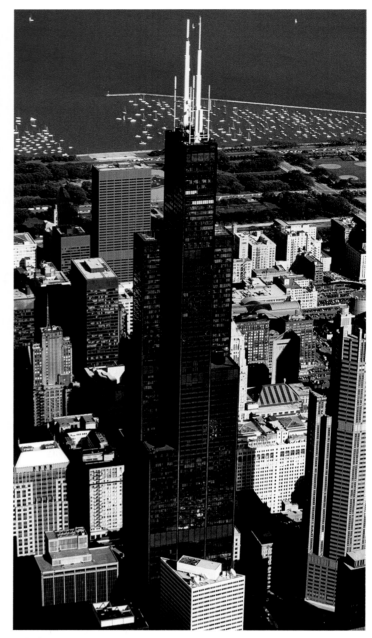

36-61 Skidmore, Owings and Merrill, Sears Tower, Chicago, 1974.

Consisting of nine black aluminum and smoked glass shafts soaring to 110 stories, the Sears Tower dominates Chicago's skyline. It was the tallest building in the world at the time of its erection.

soaring vertically, this 110-floor building houses more than 12,000 workers. Original plans called for 104 stories, but the architects acquiesced to Sears's insistence on making the building the tallest (measured to the structural top) in the world at the time. The tower's size, coupled with the black aluminum that sheathes it and the smoked glass, establish a dominant presence in a city of many corporate skyscrapers—exactly the image Sears executives wanted to project.

MAYA YING LIN Often classified as a work of Minimalist sculpture rather than architecture is the Vietnam Veterans Memorial (FIG. 36-62) in Washington, D.C., designed in 1981 by MAYA YING LIN (b. 1960) when she was only 21. The austere, simple memorial, a V-shaped wall constructed of polished black granite panels, begins at ground level at each end and gradually ascends to a height of 10 feet at the center of the V. Each wing is 246 feet long. Lin set the wall into the landscape, enhancing visitors' awareness of descent as they walk along the wall toward the center. The names of the Vietnam War's

36-62A Whiteread, Holocaust Memorial, Vienna, 2000.

Maya Lin's Vietnam Veterans Memorial

Maya Lin's design for the Vietnam Veterans Memorial (FIG. 36-62) is, like Minimalist sculptures (FIGS. 36-15 and 36-16), an unadorned geometric form. Yet the monument, despite its serene simplicity, actively engages viewers in a psychological dialogue, rather than standing mute. This dialogue gives visitors the opportunity to explore their feelings about the Vietnam War and perhaps arrive at some sense of closure.

The history of the Vietnam Veterans Memorial provides dramatic testimony to this monument's power. In 1981 a jury of architects, sculptors, and landscape architects selected Lin's design in a blind competition for a memorial to be placed in Constitution Gardens in Washington, D.C. Conceivably, the jury not only found her design compelling but also thought its simplicity would be the least likely to provoke controversy. But when the jury made its selection public, heated debate ensued. Even the wall's color came under attack. One veteran charged that black is "the universal color of shame, sorrow and degradation in all races, all societies worldwide."[*] But the sharpest protests concerned the form and siting of the monument. Because of the stark contrast between the massive white memorials (the Washington Monument and the Lincoln Memorial) bracketing Lin's sunken wall, some people saw her Minimalist design as minimizing the Vietnam War and, by extension, the efforts of those who fought in the conflict. Lin herself, however, described the wall as follows:

> The Vietnam Veterans Memorial is not an object inserted into the earth but a work formed from the act of cutting open the earth and polishing the earth's surface—dematerializing the stone to pure surface, creating an interface between the world of the light and the quieter world beyond the names.[†]

Due to the vocal opposition, a compromise was necessary to ensure the memorial's completion. The Commission of Fine Arts, the federal group overseeing the project, commissioned an additional memorial from artist Frederick Hart (1943–1999) in 1983. This larger-than-life-size realistic bronze sculpture of three soldiers, armed and in uniform, now stands approximately 120 feet from Lin's wall. Several years later, a group of nurses, organized as the Vietnam Women's Memorial Project, gained approval for a sculpture honoring women's service in the Vietnam War. The seven-foot-tall bronze statue by Glenna Goodacre (b. 1939) depicts three female figures, one cradling a wounded soldier in her arms. Unveiled in 1993, the work occupies a site about 300 feet south of the Lin memorial.

Whether celebrated or condemned, the Vietnam Veterans Memorial generates dramatic responses. Commonly, visitors react very emotionally, even those who know none of the soldiers named on the monument. The polished granite surface prompts individual soul-searching—viewers see themselves reflected among the names. Many visitors leave mementos at the foot of the wall in memory of loved ones they lost in the Vietnam War or make rubbings from the incised names. Arguably, much of this memorial's power derives from its Minimalist simplicity. Like Minimalist sculpture, it does not dictate response and therefore successfully encourages personal exploration.

[*] Elizabeth Hess, "A Tale of Two Memorials," *Art in America* 71, no. 4 (April 1983), 122.
[†] Excerpt from an unpublished 1995 lecture, quoted in Kristine Stiles and Peter Selz, *Theories and Documents of Contemporary Art: A Sourcebook of Artists' Writings* (Berkeley and Los Angeles: University of California Press, 1996), 525.

36-62 MAYA YING LIN, Vietnam Veterans Memorial (looking southwest), Washington, D.C., 1981–1983.

Like Minimalist sculpture, Lin's memorial to the veterans of Vietnam is a simple geometric form. Its inscribed polished walls actively engage the viewer in a psychological dialogue about the war.

57,939 casualties (and those still missing) incised on the memorial's walls, in the order of their deaths, contribute to the monument's dramatic effect.

When Lin designed this pristinely simple monument, she gave a great deal of thought to the purpose of war memorials. She concluded that a memorial

> should be honest about the reality of war and be for the people who gave their lives. . . . [I] didn't want a static object that people would just look at, but something they could relate to as on a journey, or passage, that would bring each to his own conclusions. . . . I wanted to work with the land and not dominate it. I had an impulse to cut open the earth . . . an initial violence that in time would heal. The grass would grow back, but the cut would remain.[33]

In light of the tragedy of the war, this unpretentious memorial's allusion to a wound and long-lasting scar contributes to its communicative ability (see "Maya Lin's Vietnam Veterans Memorial," page 1007).

Postmodernism

The restrictiveness of modernist architecture and the impersonality and sterility of many modernist structures eventually led to a rejection of modernism's authority in architecture. Along with the apparent lack of responsiveness to the unique character of the cities and neighborhoods in which modernist architects erected their buildings, these reactions ushered in postmodernism, one of the most dramatic developments in later-20th-century architecture as in contemporary painting and sculpture. Postmodernism in architecture is also not a unified style. It is a widespread cultural phenomenon that is far more encompassing and accepting than the more rigid confines of modernist practice. In contrast to the simplicity of modernist architecture, the terms most often invoked to describe postmodern architecture are pluralism, complexity, and eclecticism. Whereas the modernist program was reductive, the postmodern vocabulary of the 1970s and 1980s was expansive and inclusive.

Among the first to explore this new direction in architecture were Jane Jacobs (1916–2006) and Robert Venturi (FIG. 36-66). In their influential books *The Death and Life of Great American Cities* (Jacobs, 1961) and *Complexity and Contradiction in Architecture* (Venturi, 1966), Jacobs and Venturi argued that the uniformity and anonymity of modernist architecture (in particular, the corporate skyscrapers dominating many urban skylines) were unsuited to human social interaction and that diversity was the great advantage of urban life. Postmodern architects accepted, indeed embraced, the messy and chaotic nature of urban life.

When designing these varied buildings, many postmodern architects consciously selected past architectural elements or references and juxtaposed them with contemporary elements or fashioned them of high-tech materials, thereby creating a dialogue between past and present. Postmodern architecture incorporates not only traditional architectural references but references to mass culture and popular imagery as well. This was precisely the "complexity and contradiction" Venturi referred to in the title of his book.

36-63A STIRLING, Neue Staatsgalerie, Stuttgart, 1977–1983.

CHARLES MOORE A clear example of the eclecticism and the dialogue between traditional and contemporary elements found in postmodern architecture is the Piazza d'Italia (FIG. 36-63) by American architect CHARLES MOORE (1925–1993). Designed in the late 1970s in New Orleans, the Piazza d'Italia is an open plaza dedicated to the city's Italian-American community. Appropriately, Moore selected elements relating specifically to Italian history, dating all the way back to ancient Roman culture.

36-63B PEI, Grand Louvre Pyramide, Paris, 1988.

Backed up against a contemporary high-rise and set off from urban traffic patterns, the Piazza d'Italia can be reached on foot from three sides through gateways of varied design. The approaches lead to an open circular area partially formed by short segments of colonnades arranged in staggered concentric arcs, which direct the eye to the focal point of the composition—an *exedra*. This recessed area on a raised platform serves as a *rostrum* (speaker's platform) during the annual festivities of Saint Joseph's Day. Moore inlaid the piazza's pavement with a map of Italy centered on Sicily, from which the majority of the city's Italian families originated. From there, the map's Italian "boot" moves in the direction of the steps that ascend the rostrum and correspond to the Alps.

36-63 CHARLES MOORE, Piazza d'Italia, New Orleans, Louisiana, 1976–1980.

Moore's circular postmodern Italian plaza incorporates elements drawn from ancient Roman architecture with the instability of Mannerist designs and modern stainless-steel columns with neon collars.

Philip Johnson
on Postmodern Architecture

Philip Johnson, who died in 2005 at age 98, had a distinguished career that spanned almost the entire 20th century, during which he transformed himself from a modernist closely associated with Mies van der Rohe (FIG. 36-60) into one of the leading postmodernists, whose AT&T Building (FIG. 36-64) in New York City remains an early icon of postmodernism. The following remarks illustrate Johnson's thoughts about his early "Miesian" style and about the incorporation of various historical styles in postmodernist buildings.

> My eyes are set by the Miesian tradition . . . . The continuity with my Miesian approach also shows through in my classicism. . . . [But in] 1952, about the same time that my whole generation did, I became very restless. . . . In the last decade there has been such a violent switch that it is almost embarrassing. But it isn't a switch, so much as a centrifugal splintering of architecture, to a degree that I don't think has been seen in the past few hundred years. Perfectly responsible architects build, even in one year, buildings that you cannot believe are done by the same person.*

> Structural honesty seems to me one of the bugaboos that we should free ourselves from very quickly. The Greeks with their marble columns imitating wood, and covering up the roofs inside! The Gothic designers with their wooden roofs above to protect their delicate vaulting. And Michelangelo, the greatest architect in history, with his Mannerist column! There is only one absolute today and this is change. There are no rules, surely no certainties in any of the arts. There is only the feeling of a wonderful freedom, of endless possibilities to investigate, of endless past years of historically great buildings to enjoy.†

* Quoted in Paul Heyer, *Architects on Architecture: New Directions in America* (New York: Van Nostrand Reinhold, 1993), 285–286.
† Ibid., 279.

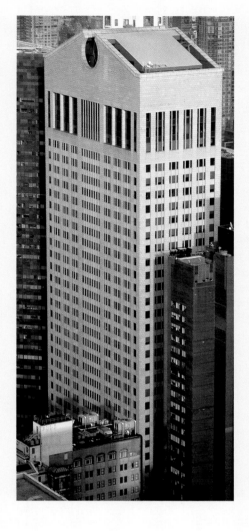

36-64 PHILIP JOHNSON and JOHN BURGEE (with SIMMONS ARCHITECTS), AT&T (now Sony) Building, New York, 1978–1984.

In a startling shift of style, modernist Johnson (FIG. 36-60) designed this postmodernist skyscraper with more granite than glass and with a variation on a classical pediment as the crowning motif.

The piazza's most immediate historical reference is to the Roman forum (FIGS. 10-12 and 10-43). However, its circular form alludes to the ideal geometric figure of the Renaissance (FIG. 22-22). The irregular placement of the concentrically arranged colonnade fragments inserts a note of instability into the design reminiscent of Mannerism (FIG. 22-54). Illusionistic devices, such as the continuation of the piazza's pavement design (apparently through a building and out into the street), are Baroque in character (FIG. 24-4). Moore incorporated all of the classical orders—most with whimsical modifications. Nevertheless, challenging the piazza's historical character are modern features, such as the stainless-steel columns and capitals, neon collars around the column necks, and neon lights that frame various parts of the exedra.

In sum, Moore designed the Piazza d'Italia as a complex conglomeration of symbolic, historical, and geographic allusions—some overt and others obscure. Although the piazza's specific purpose was to honor the Italian community of New Orleans, its more general purpose was to revitalize an urban area by becoming a focal point and an architectural setting for the social activities of neighborhood residents. Unfortunately, the piazza suffered extensive damage during Hurricane Katrina in 2005.

PHILIP JOHNSON Even architects instrumental in the proliferation of the modernist idiom embraced postmodernism. Early in his career, PHILIP JOHNSON (1906–2005), for example, had been a leading proponent of modernism and worked with Mies van der Rohe on the design of the Seagram Building (FIG. 36-60). Johnson had even served as the director of the Department of Architecture at New York's Museum of Modern Art, the bastion of modernism, from 1930 to 1934 and from 1946 to 1954. Yet he made one of the most startling shifts of style in 20th-century architecture, eventually moving away from the severe geometric formalism exemplified by the Seagram Building to a classicizing transformation of it in his AT&T (American Telephone and Telegraph) Building (FIG. 36-64)—now the Sony Building—in New York City. Architect JOHN BURGEE (b. 1933) codesigned it with assistance from the firm SIMMONS ARCHITECTS. This structure was influential in turning architectural taste and practice away from modernism and toward postmodernism—from organic "concrete sculpture" and the rigid "glass box" to elaborate shapes, motifs, and silhouettes freely adapted from historical styles (see "Philip Johnson on Postmodernist Architecture," above).

The 660-foot-high slab of the AT&T Building is mostly granite. Johnson reduced the window space to some 30 percent of the building, in contrast to modernist glass-sheathed skyscrapers. His design of its exterior elevation is classically tripartite, having an arcaded base and arched portal; a tall, shaftlike body segmented by slender *mullions* (vertical elements dividing a window); and a crowning pediment broken by an *orbiculum* (a disklike opening). The arrangement refers to the base, column, and entablature system of classical architecture (FIG. 5-14). More specifically, the pediment, indented by the circular space, resembles the crown of a typical 18th-century Chippendale high chest of drawers. It rises among the monotonously flat-topped glass towers of the New York skyline as an ironic rebuke to the rigid uniformity of modernist architecture.

MICHAEL GRAVES Philip Johnson at first endorsed, then disapproved of, a building that rode considerably farther on the wave of postmodernism than did his AT&T tower. The Portland Building (FIG. 36-65) by American architect MICHAEL GRAVES (b. 1934) reasserts the wall's horizontality against the verticality of the tall, fenestrated shaft. Graves favored the square's solidity and stability, making it the main body of his composition (echoed in the windows), which rests upon a wider base and carries a set-back penthouse crown. Narrow vertical windows tying together seven stories open two paired facades. These support capital-like large hoods on one pair of opposite facades and a frieze of stylized Baroque roundels tied by bands on the other pair. A huge painted keystone motif joins five upper levels on one facade pair, and painted surfaces further define the building's base, body, and penthouse levels.

The modernist purist surely would not welcome the ornamental wall, color painting, or symbolic reference. These features, taken together, raised an even greater storm of criticism than that which greeted the Sydney Opera House or the AT&T Building. Various critics denounced Graves's Portland Building as "an enlarged jukebox," an "oversized Christmas package," a "marzipan monstrosity," a "histrionic masquerade," and a kind of "pop surrealism." Yet others approvingly noted its classical references as constituting a "symbolic temple" and praised the building as a courageous architectural adventure. Whatever will be history's verdict, the Portland Building, like the AT&T tower, is an early marker of postmodernist innovation that borrowed from the lively, if more-or-less garish, language of pop culture. The night-lit dazzle of entertainment sites such as Las Vegas, and the carnival colors, costumes, and fantasy of theme park props, all lie behind the Portland Building design, which many critics regard as a vindication of architectural populism against the pretension of modernist elitism.

36-65 MICHAEL GRAVES, Portland Building, Portland, 1980.

In this early example of postmodern architecture, Graves reasserted the horizontality and solidity of the wall. He drew attention to the mural surfaces through polychromy and ornamental motifs.

ROBERT VENTURI As a coauthor of *Learning from Las Vegas* (1972), ROBERT VENTURI (b. 1925) codified these ideas about populism and postmodernism, and in his designs for houses he adapted historical as well as contemporary styles to suit his symbolic and expressive purpose. A fundamental axiom of modernism is that a building's form must arise directly and logically from its function and structure. Against this rule, Venturi asserted that the form should be separate from function and structure and that decorative and symbolic forms of everyday life should enwrap the structural core. Thus, for a Delaware residence (FIG. 36-66) designed in 1978 with JOHN RAUCH (b. 1930) and DENISE SCOTT BROWN (b. 1931), Venturi respected the countryside setting and its 18th-century history by recalling the stone-based barnlike, low-profile farm dwellings with their shingled roofs and double-hung multipaned windows. He fronted the house with an amusingly cut-out and asymmetrical parody of a Neoclassical portico.

36-66 ROBERT VENTURI, JOHN RAUCH, and DENISE SCOTT BROWN, house in eastern Delaware, 1978–1983.

Venturi asserted that form should be separate from function and structure. This rural home has the low profile of a farmhouse, but its facade is an asymmetrical parody of a Neoclassical portico.

with visitors since it opened. The flexible interior spaces and the colorful structural body provide a festive environment for the crowds flowing through the building and enjoying its art galleries, industrial design center, library, science and music centers, conference rooms, research and archival facilities, movie theaters, rest areas, and restaurant (which looks down and through the building to the terraces outside). The sloping plaza in front of the main entrance has become part of the local scene. Peddlers, street performers, Parisians, and tourists fill this square at almost all hours of the day and night. The kind of secular activity that once occurred in the open spaces in front of cathedral entrances now takes place next to a center for culture and popular entertainment.

ROGERS AND PIANO During their short-lived partnership, British architect RICHARD ROGERS (b. 1933) and Italian architect RENZO PIANO (b. 1937) used motifs and techniques from ordinary industrial buildings in their design for the Georges Pompidou National Center of Art and Culture in Paris, known popularly as the "Beaubourg" (FIG. 36-67). The architects fully exposed the anatomy of this six-level building, which is a kind of updated version of the Crystal Palace (FIG. 30-48), and made its "metabolism" visible. They color-coded pipes, ducts, tubes, and corridors according to function (red for the movement of people, green for water, blue for air-conditioning, and yellow for electricity), much as in a sophisticated factory.

Critics who deplore the Beaubourg's vernacular qualities disparagingly refer to the complex as a "cultural supermarket" and point out that its exposed entrails require excessive maintenance to protect them from the elements. Nevertheless, the building has been popular

Deconstructivism

In architecture, as in painting and sculpture, deconstruction as an analytical and design strategy emerged in the 1970s. Architectural *Deconstructivism* seeks to disorient the observer. To this end, Deconstructivist architects attempt to disrupt the conventional categories of architecture and to rupture the viewer's expectations based on them. Destabilization plays a major role in Deconstructivist architecture. Disorder, dissonance, imbalance, asymmetry, unconformity, and irregularity replace their opposites—order, consistency, balance, symmetry, regularity, and clarity, as well as harmony, continuity, and completeness. The haphazardly presented volumes, masses, planes, borders, lighting, locations, directions, spatial relations, as well as the disguised structural facts, challenge the viewer's assumptions about architectural form as it relates to function. According to Deconstructivist principles, the very absence of the stability of traditional categories of architecture in a structure announces a "deconstructed" building.

GÜNTER BEHNISCH Audacious in its dissolution of form, and well along on the path of deconstruction, is the Hysolar Institute (FIG. 36-68) at the University of Stuttgart, Germany. GÜNTER BEHNISCH (b. 1922)

Frank Gehry on Architectural Design and Materials

Frank Gehry has been designing buildings since the 1950s, but it was only in the 1970s that he began to break away from the rectilinearity of modernist architecture and develop the dramatic sculptural style seen in buildings like the Guggenheim Museum (FIGS. 36-69 and 36-70) in Bilbao. In 1999 the Deconstructivist architect reflected on his career and his many projects in a book titled *Gehry Talks.*

> My early work was rectilinear because you take baby steps. I guess the work has become a kind of sculpture as architecture. . . . I'm a strict modernist in the sense of believing in purity, that you shouldn't decorate. And yet buildings need decoration, because they need scaling elements. They need to be human scale, in my opinion. They can't just be faceless things. That's how some modernism failed.*

36-69 FRANK GEHRY, Guggenheim Bilbao Museo, Bilbao, Spain, 1997.

Gehry's limestone-and-titanium Bilbao museum is an immensely dramatic building. Its disorder and seeming randomness of design epitomize Deconstructivist architectural principles.

They teach materials and methods in architecture school, as a separate course. I'm a craftsman. . . . It seems to me that when you're doing architecture, you're building something out of something. There are social issues, there's context, and then there's how do you make the enclosure and what do you make it with? . . . I explored metal: how it dealt with the light . . . . It does beautiful things with light. . . . Flat was a fetish, and everybody was doing that. I found out that I could use metal if I didn't worry about it being flat; I could do it cheaper. It was intuitive. I just went with it. I liked it. Then when I saw it on the building, I loved it. . . . Bilbao . . . [is] titanium. . . . [I] prefer titanium because it's stronger; it's an element, a pure element, and it doesn't oxidize. It stays the same forever. They give a hundred-year guarantee!†

* Milton Friedman, ed., *Gehry Talks: Architecture + Process,* rev. ed. (New York: Universe, 2002), 47–48.
† Ibid., 44, 47.

designed it as part of a joint German–Saudi Arabian research project on the technology of solar energy. The architect intended to deny here the possibility of spatial enclosure altogether, and his apparently chaotic arrangement of the units defies easy analysis. The shapes of the Hysolar Institute's roof, walls, and windows seem to explode, avoiding any suggestion of clear, stable masses. Behnisch aggressively played with the whole concept of architecture and the viewer's relationship to it. The disordered architectural elements seem precarious and visually threaten to collapse, frustrating the observer's expectations of what a building should look like.

FRANK GEHRY The architect most closely identified with Deconstructivist architecture is the Canadian-born FRANK GEHRY (b. 1929). Trained in sculpture, and at different times a collaborator with Donald Judd (FIG. 36-16) and Claes Oldenburg (FIG. 36-26), Gehry works up his designs by constructing models and then cutting them up and arranging them until he has a satisfying composition. Among Gehry's most notable projects is the Guggenheim Museum (FIG. 36-69) in Bilbao, Spain. The immensely dramatic building appears as a mass of asymmetrical and imbalanced forms, and the irregularity of the main masses—whose profiles change dramatically with every shift of a visitor's position—suggests a collapsed or collapsing aggregate of units. The scaled limestone- and titanium-clad exterior lends a space-age character to the building and highlights further the unique cluster effect of the many forms (see "Frank Gehry on Architectural Design and Materials," above). A group of organic forms that Gehry refers to as a "metallic flower" tops the museum. In the center of the museum, an enormous glass-walled

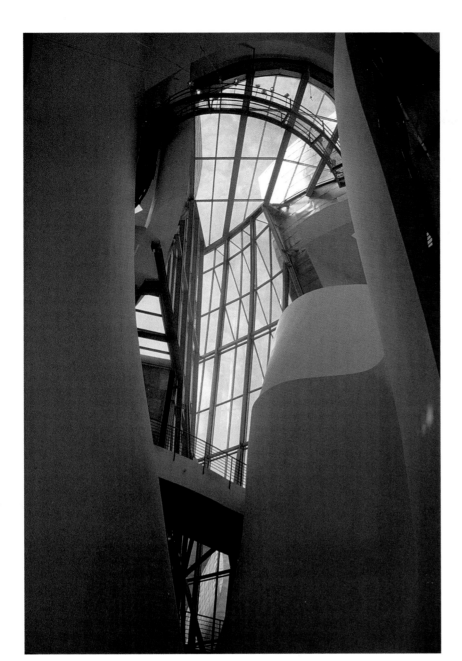

The glass-walled atrium of the Guggenheim Bilbao Museum soars to 165 feet in height. The asymmetrical and imbalanced screens and vaults flow into one another, creating a sense of disequilibrium.

atrium (FIG. 36-70) soars to 165 feet in height, serving as the focal point for the three levels of galleries radiating from it. The seemingly weightless screens, vaults, and volumes of the interior float and flow into one another, guided only by light and dark cues. Overall, the Guggenheim in Bilbao is a profoundly compelling structure. Its disorder, its seeming randomness of design, and the disequilibrium it prompts in viewers epitomize Deconstructivist principles.

DANIEL LIBESKIND Deconstructivist architecture remains very much in vogue today. One of the leading practitioners is Polish-born DANIEL LIBESKIND (b. 1946), whose studio is in Berlin, Germany, but who has, like other successful contemporary architects, erected buildings in several countries, including the United States. Libeskind achieved instant international fame with his design for the reconstructed World Trade Center complex in New York City. More recently, his 146,000-square-foot expansion of the Denver Art Museum (FIG. 36-71) created a sensation when it opened to the public in October 2006. Libeskind has stated that he drew his inspiration for the design from the jagged peaks of Colorado's Rocky Mountains, and the stone-and-titanium structure, despite its kinship with Gehry's Bilbao museum (FIG. 36-69), presents a striking contrast with that building's swelling curves. Tilted walls, asymmetrical shapes, and surprising sequences of spaces engender a sense of disorientation in visitors to the galleries, which, appropriately, house the museum's collection of modern and contemporary art.

36-71A HADID, Vitra Fire Station, Weil-am-Rhein, 1989–1993.

36-71 DANIEL LIBESKIND, Denver Art Museum, Denver, Colorado, 2006.

Inspired by the jagged peaks of the Rocky Mountains, Libeskind's expansion of the Denver Art Museum features tilted walls, asymmetrical shapes, and a disorienting sequence of spaces.

Environmental and Site-Specific Art

Like Maya Lin's Vietnam Veterans Memorial (FIG. 36-62), works of *Environmental Art*, sometimes called *earthworks*, exist at the intersection of architecture and sculpture. The Environmental Art movement emerged in the 1960s and included a wide range of artworks, most *site-specific* (created for only one location) and existing outdoors. Many artists associated with these sculptural projects also used natural or organic materials, including the land itself. It is no coincidence that this art form developed during a period of increased concern for the American environment. The ecology movement of the 1960s and 1970s aimed to publicize and combat escalating pollution, depletion of natural resources, and the dangers of toxic waste. The problems of public aesthetics (for example, litter, urban sprawl, and compromised scenic areas) were also at issue. Widespread concern about the environment led to the passage of the U.S. National Environmental Policy Act in 1969 and the creation of the federal Environmental Protection Agency. Environmental artists used their art to call attention to the landscape and, in so doing, were part of this national dialogue.

As an innovative art form that challenged traditional assumptions about art making and artistic models, Environmental Art clearly had an avant-garde, progressive dimension. But like Pop artists, Environmental artists insisted on moving art out of the rarefied atmosphere of museums and galleries and into the public sphere. Most encouraged spectator interaction with their works. Ironically, the remote locations of many earthworks have limited public access.

ROBERT SMITHSON A leading American Environmental artist was ROBERT SMITHSON (1938–1973), who used industrial construction equipment to manipulate vast quantities of earth and rock on isolated sites. One of Smithson's best-known projects is *Spiral Jetty* (FIG. 36-72), a mammoth 1,500-foot-long coil of black basalt, limestone rocks, and earth that extends out into the Great Salt Lake in Utah. As he was driving by the lake one day, Smithson came across some abandoned mining equipment, left there by a company that had tried and failed to extract oil from the site. Smithson saw this as a testament to the enduring power of nature and to humankind's inability to conquer it. He decided to create an artwork in the lake that ultimately became a monumental spiral curving out from the shoreline and running 1,500 linear feet into the water. Smithson insisted on designing his work in response to the location itself. He wanted to avoid the arrogance of an artist merely imposing an unrelated concept on the site. The spiral idea grew from Smithson's first impression of the location. Then, while researching the Great Salt Lake, Smithson discovered that the molecular structure of the salt crystals coating the rocks at the water's edge was spiral in form.

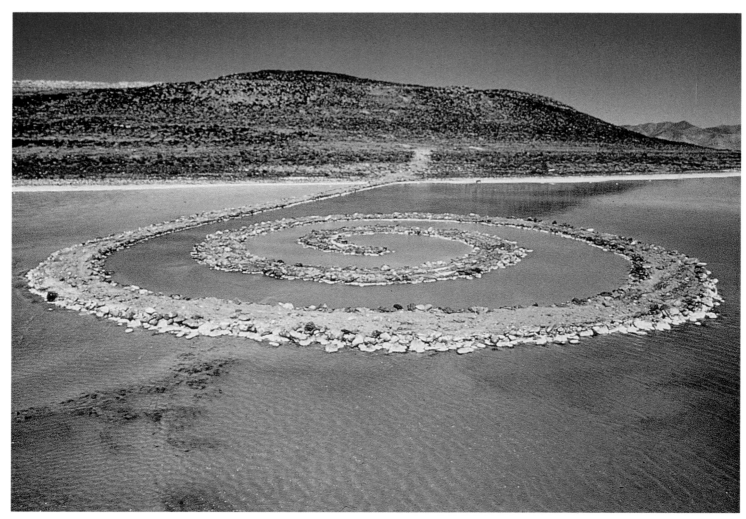

36-72 ROBERT SMITHSON, *Spiral Jetty,* Great Salt Lake, Utah, 1970. Art © Estate of Robert Smithson/Licensed by VAGA, New York.

Smithson used industrial equipment to create Environmental artworks by manipulating earth and rock. *Spiral Jetty* is a mammoth coil of black basalt, limestone, and earth extending into the Great Salt Lake.

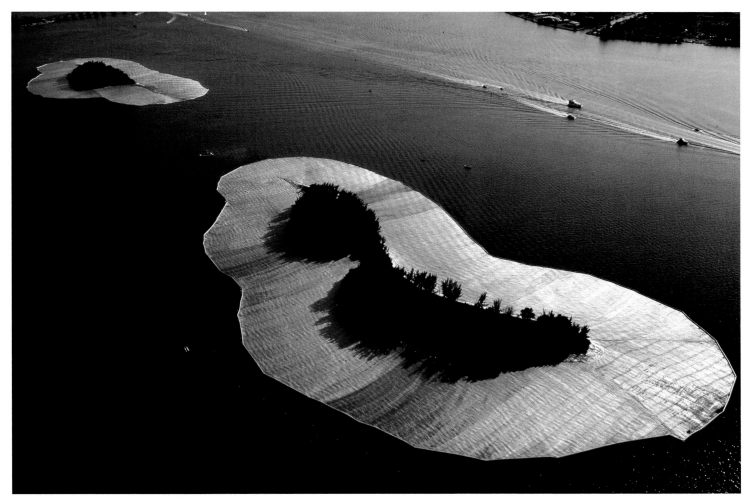

36-73 CHRISTO and JEANNE-CLAUDE, *Surrounded Islands 1980–83, Biscayne Bay, Miami, Florida,* 1980–1983. ◼◀

Christo and Jeanne-Claude created this Environmental artwork by surrounding 11 small islands with 6.5 million square feet of pink fabric. Characteristically, the work existed for only two weeks.

As I looked at the site, it reverberated out to the horizons only to suggest an immobile cyclone while flickering light made the entire landscape appear to quake. A dormant earthquake spread into the fluttering stillness, into a spinning sensation without movement. The site was a rotary that enclosed itself in an immense roundness. From that gyrating space emerged the possibility of the Spiral Jetty.[34]

Smithson not only recorded *Spiral Jetty* in photographs but also filmed its construction in a movie that describes the forms and life of the whole site. The photographs and film have become increasingly important references, because fluctuations in the Great Salt Lake's water level often place *Spiral Jetty* underwater.

CHRISTO AND JEANNE-CLAUDE Like Smithson, CHRISTO and JEANNE-CLAUDE (both b. 1935) seek to intensify the viewer's awareness of the space and features of rural and urban sites. However, rather than physically alter the land itself, as Smithson often did, Christo and Jeanne-Claude prompt this awareness by temporarily modifying the landscape with cloth. Christo studied art in his native Bulgaria and in Vienna. After a move to Paris, he began to encase objects in clumsy wrappings, thereby appropriating bits of the real world into the mysterious world of the unopened package whose contents can be dimly seen in silhouette under the wrap.

Starting in 1961, Christo and Jeanne-Claude, husband and wife, began to collaborate on large-scale projects that normally deal with the environment itself. For example, in 1969 the couple wrapped a million square feet of Australian coast and in 1972 hung a vast curtain across a valley at Rifle Gap, Colorado. Their works of art require years of preparation and research and scores of meetings with local authorities and interested groups of local citizens. These temporary works are usually on view for only a few weeks.

Surrounded Islands 1980–83 (FIG. **36-73**), created in Biscayne Bay in Miami, Florida, for two weeks in May 1983, typifies Christo and Jeanne-Claude's work. For this project, they surrounded 11 small human-made islands in the bay (from a dredging project) with 6.5 million square feet of specially fabricated pink polypropylene floating fabric. This Environmental artwork required three years of preparation to obtain the necessary permits and to assemble the labor force and obtain the $3.2 million needed to complete the project. The artists raised the money by selling preparatory drawings, collages, models, and works they created in the 1950s and 1960s. Huge crowds watched as crews removed accumulated trash from the 11 islands (to assure maximum contrast between their dark colors, the pink of the cloth, and the blue of the bay) and then unfurled the fabric "cocoons" to form magical floating "skirts" around each tiny bit of land. Despite the brevity of its existence, *Surrounded Islands 1980–83* lives on in the host of photographs, films, and books documenting the project.

Richard Serra's *Tilted Arc*

When Richard Serra installed *Tilted Arc* (FIG. 36-74) in the plaza in front of the Javits Federal Building in New York City in 1981, much of the public immediately responded with hostile criticism. Prompting the chorus of complaints was the uncompromising presence of a Minimalist sculpture bisecting the plaza. Many argued that *Tilted Arc* was ugly, that it attracted graffiti, that it interfered with the view across the plaza, and that it prevented using the plaza for performances or concerts. Due to the sustained barrage of protests and petitions demanding the removal of *Tilted Arc,* the GSA held a series of public hearings. Afterward, the agency decided to remove the sculpture despite its prior approval of Serra's maquette. This, understandably, infuriated Serra, who had a legally binding contract acknowledging the site-specific nature of *Tilted Arc.* "To remove the work is to destroy the work," the artist stated.*

This episode raised intriguing issues about the nature of public art, including the public reception of experimental art, the artist's responsibilities and rights when executing public commissions, censorship in the arts, and the purpose of public art. If an artwork is on display in a public space outside the relatively private confines of a museum or gallery, do different guidelines apply? As one participant in the *Tilted Arc* saga asked, "Should an artist have the right to impose his values and taste on a public that now rejects his taste and values?"† One of the express functions of the historical avant-garde was to challenge convention by rejecting tradition and disrupting the complacency of the viewer. Will placing experimental art in a public place always cause controversy? From Serra's statements, it is clear he intended the sculpture to challenge the public.

Another issue *Tilted Arc* presented involved the rights of the artist, who in this case accused the GSA of censorship. Serra filed a lawsuit against the government for infringement of his First Amendment rights and insisted that "the artist's work must be uncensored, respected, and tolerated, although deemed abhorrent, or perceived as

36-74 RICHARD SERRA, *Tilted Arc,* Jacob K. Javits Federal Plaza, New York City, 1981.

Serra intended his Minimalist *Tilted Arc* to alter the character of an existing public space. He succeeded but unleashed a storm of protest that caused the government to remove the work.

challenging, or experienced as threatening."‡ Did removal of the work constitute censorship? A federal district court held that it did not.

Ultimately, who should decide what artworks are appropriate for the public arena? One artist argued, "we cannot have public art by plebiscite [popular vote]."§ But to avoid recurrences of the *Tilted Arc* controversy, the GSA changed its procedures and now solicits input from a wide range of civic and neighborhood groups before commissioning public artworks. Despite the removal of *Tilted Arc* (now languishing in storage), the sculpture maintains a powerful presence in all discussions of the aesthetics, politics, and dynamics of public art.

* Grace Glueck, "What Part Should the Public Play in Choosing Public Art?" *New York Times,* February 3, 1985, 27.
† Calvin Tomkins, "The Art World: *Tilted Arc,*" *New Yorker,* May 20, 1985, 98.
‡ Ibid., 98–99.
§ Ibid., 98.

RICHARD SERRA Other artists have created site-specific works that are not set in nature but in the built environment. Their purpose is to focus attention on art's role in public spaces. One work that sparked national discussion about public art was *Tilted Arc* (FIG. 36-74) by American artist RICHARD SERRA (b. 1939). The General Services Administration (GSA), the federal agency responsible for, among other tasks, overseeing the selection and installation of artworks for government buildings, commissioned *Tilted Arc.* This enormous 120-foot-long, 12-foot-high curved wall of Cor-Ten steel bisected the plaza in front of the Jacob K. Javits Federal Building in

lower Manhattan. Serra situated the sculpture in a way that significantly altered the space of the open plaza and the traffic flow across the square. He intended *Tilted Arc* to "dislocate or alter the decorative function of the plaza and actively bring people into the sculpture's context."35

By creating such a monumental presence in this large public space, Serra succeeded in forcing viewers to reconsider the plaza's physical space as a sculptural form—but only temporarily, because the public forced the sculpture to be removed (see "Richard Serra's *Tilted Arc,*" above).

PERFORMANCE AND CONCEPTUAL ART AND NEW MEDIA

Among the most significant developments in the art world after World War II has been the expansion of the range of works considered "art." Some of the new types of artworks are the result of the invention of new media, such as computers and video cameras. But the new art forms also reflect avant-garde artists' continued questioning of the status quo. For example, in keeping with the modernist critique of artistic principles, some artists, in a spirit reminiscent of Dada and Surrealism (see Chapter 35), developed the fourth dimension—time—as an integral element of their artwork. The term that art historians use to describe these temporal works is *Performance Art*.

Performance Art

Performance artists replace traditional stationary artworks with movements, gestures, and sounds carried out before an audience, whose members may or may not participate in the performance. Generally, documentary photographs taken contemporaneously are the only evidence remaining after these performances. The informal and spontaneous events Performance artists initially staged anticipated the rebellion and youthful exuberance of the 1960s and at first pushed art outside the confines of mainstream art institutions (museums and galleries). Performance Art also served as an antidote to the affectation of most traditional art objects and challenged art's function as a commodity. In the later 1960s, however, museums commissioned performances with increasing frequency, thereby neutralizing much of the subversiveness that characterized this new art form.

JOHN CAGE Many of the artists instrumental in the development of Performance Art were students or associates of the charismatic American teacher and composer John Cage (1912–1992). Cage encouraged his students at both the New School for Social Research in New York and Black Mountain College in North Carolina to link their art directly with life. He brought to music composition some of the ideas of Duchamp and of Eastern philosophy. Cage used methods such as chance to avoid the closed structures marking traditional music and, in his view, separating it from the unpredictable and multilayered qualities of daily existence. For example, the score for one of Cage's piano compositions instructs the performer to appear, sit down at the piano, raise the keyboard cover to mark the beginning of the piece, remain motionless at the instrument for 4 minutes and 33 seconds, and then close the keyboard cover, rise, and bow to signal the end of the work. The "music" would be the unplanned sounds and noises (such as coughs and whispers) emanating from the audience during the "performance."

ALLAN KAPROW One of Cage's students in the 1950s was Allan Kaprow (b. 1927). Schooled in art history as well as music composition, Kaprow sought to explore the intersection of art and life. He believed, for example, that Jackson Pollock's actions when producing a painting (FIG. 36-6) were more important than the finished painting. This led Kaprow to develop a type of event known as a *Happening*. He described a Happening as

> an assemblage of events performed or perceived in more than one time and place. Its material environments may be constructed, taken over directly from what is available, or altered slightly: just as its activities may be invented or commonplace. A Happening, unlike a stage play, may occur at a supermarket, driving along a highway, under a pile of rags, and in a friend's kitchen, either at once or sequentially. If sequentially, time may extend to more than a year.

The Happening is performed according to plan but without rehearsal, audience, or repetition. It is art but seems closer to life.[36]

Happenings were often participatory. One Happening consisted of a constructed setting with partitions on which viewers wrote phrases, while another involved spectators walking on a pile of tires. One of Kaprow's first Happenings, titled *18 Happenings in Six Parts,* took place in 1959 at the Reuben Gallery in New York City. For the event, he divided the gallery space into three sections with translucent plastic sheets. Over the course of the 90-minute piece, performers, including Kaprow's artist friends, bounced balls, read from placards, extended their arms like wings, and played records as slides and lights flashed on and off in programmed sequences.

FLUXUS Other Cage students interested in the composer's search to find aesthetic potential in the nontraditional and commonplace formed the *Fluxus* group. Eventually expanding to include European and Japanese artists, this group's performances were more theatrical than Happenings. To distinguish their performances from Happenings, the artists associated with Fluxus coined the term *Events* to describe their work. Events focused on single actions, such as turning a light on and off or watching falling snow—what Fluxus artist La Monte Young (b. 1935) called "the theater of the single event."[37] The Events usually took place on a stage separating the performers from the audience but without costumes or added decor. Events were not spontaneous. They followed a compositional "score," which, given the restricted nature of these performances, was short.

KAZUO SHIRAGA Some artists produced works that involved both painting and performance. Gutai Bijutsu Kyokai (Concrete Art Association), a group of 18 Japanese artists in Osaka, expanded the action of painting into the realm of performance—in a sense, taking Jackson Pollock's painting methods into a public arena. Led by Jiro Yoshihara (1905–1972), Gutai, founded in 1954, devoted itself to art that combined Japanese traditional practices such as Zen (see "Zen Buddhism," Chapter 28, page 736) with a renewed appreciation for materials. In the *Gutai Art Manifesto*, Yoshihara explained: "Gutai does not alter the material. Gutai imparts life to the material. . . . [T]he human spirit and the material shake hands with each other, but keep their distance."[38] Accordingly, Gutai works, for example, *Making a Work with His Own Body* (FIG. 36-75), by KAZUO SHIRAGA

36-75 KAZUO SHIRAGA, *Making a Work with His Own Body,* 1955. Mud.

The Performance artists of the Japanese Gutai Bijutsu Kyokai (Concrete Art Association) expanded action painting into the realm of performance. Shiraga used his body to "paint" with mud.

Carolee Schneemann on Painting, Performance Art, and Art History

Carolee Schneemann (FIG. 36-76), one of the pioneering Performance artists of the 1960s, also produced works in other media. In notes she wrote in 1962–1963, Schneemann contrasted her Performance works with more traditional art forms.

Environments, happenings—concretions—are an extension of my painting-constructions which often have moving (motorized) sections. . . . [But, the] steady exploration and repeated viewing which the eye is required to make with my painting-constructions is reversed in the performance situation where the spectator is overwhelmed with changing recognitions, carried emotionally by a flux of evocative actions and led or held by the specified time sequence which marks the duration of a performance. In this way the audience is actually *visually* more *passive* than when confronting a . . . "still" work . . . . With paintings, constructions and sculptures the viewers are able to carry out repeated examinations of the work, to select and vary viewing positions (to walk with the eye), to touch surfaces and to freely indulge responses to areas of color and texture at their chosen speed.*

Readers of this book will also take special interest in Schneemann's 1975 essay entitled "Woman in the Year 2000," in which she envisioned what introductory art history courses would be like at the beginning of the 21st century:

By the year 2000 [every] young woman will study Art Istory [sic] courses enriched by the inclusion, discovery, and re-evaluation of works by women artists: works (and lives) until recently buried away, willfully destroyed, [or] ignored.†

A comparison between this 13th edition of *Art through the Ages* and editions published in the 1960s and 1970s will immediately reveal the accuracy of Schneemann's prediction.

* Quoted in Bruce McPherson, ed., *More Than Meat Joy: Complete Performance Works and Selected Writings* (New Paltz, N.Y.: Documentext, 1979), 10–11.
† Ibid., 198.

36-76 Carolee Schneemann, *Meat Joy,* 1964. Performance at Judson Church, New York City.

In her performances, Schneemann transformed the nature of Performance art by introducing a feminist dimension through the use of her body (often nude) to challenge traditional gender roles.

(b. 1924), involved such actions as throwing paint balls at blank canvases or wallowing in mud as a means of shaping it. In *Making a Work,* Shiraga used his body to "paint" with mud. The Gutai group dissolved upon Yoshihara's death in 1972.

CAROLEE SCHNEEMANN Like Gutai, Carolee Schneemann (b. 1939) integrated painting and performance in her artworks (see "Carolee Schneemann on Painting, Performance Art, and Art History," above). Her self-described "kinetic theater" radically transformed the nature of Performance Art by introducing a feminist dimension through the use of her body (often nude) to challenge "the psychic territorial power lines by which women were admitted to the Art Stud Club."[39] In her 1964 performance *Meat Joy* (FIG. 36-76), Schneemann reveled in the taste, smell, and feel of raw sausages, chickens, and fish.

JOSEPH BEUYS The leftist politics of the Fluxus group in the early 1960s strongly influenced German artist Joseph Beuys (1921–1986). Drawing on Happenings and Fluxus, Beuys created actions aimed at illuminating the condition of modern humanity. He wanted to make a new kind of sculptural object that would include "Thinking Forms: how we mould our thoughts or Spoken Forms: how we shape our thoughts into words or Social Sculpture: how we mould and shape the world in which we live."[40]

Beuys's commitment to artworks stimulating thought about art and life derived in part from his experiences as a pilot during World War II. After the enemy shot down his plane over the Crimea, nomadic Tatars nursed him back to health by swaddling his body in fat and felt to warm him. Fat and felt thus symbolized healing and regeneration to Beuys, and he incorporated these materials into many of his sculptures and actions, such as *How to Explain Pictures to a*

36-77 JOSEPH BEUYS, *How to Explain Pictures to a Dead Hare,* 1965. Performance at the Schmela Gallery, Düsseldorf. ◼◀

In this one-person event, Beuys coated his head with honey and gold leaf. Assuming the role of a shaman, he used stylized actions to evoke a sense of mystery and sacred ritual.

Dead Hare (FIG. 36-77). This one-person event consisted of stylized actions evoking a sense of mystery and sacred ritual. Beuys appeared in a room hung with his drawings, cradling a dead hare to which he spoke softly. Beuys coated his head with honey covered with gold leaf, creating a shimmering mask. In this manner, he took on the role of the shaman, an individual with special spiritual powers. As a shaman, Beuys believed he was acting to help revolutionize human thought so that each human being could become a truly free and creative person.

JEAN TINGUELY The paradoxical notion of destruction as an act of creation surfaces in a number of kinetic artworks, most notably in the sculpture of JEAN TINGUELY (1925–1991). Trained as a painter in his native Switzerland, Tinguely gravitated to motion sculpture. In the 1950s, he made a series of *metamatics,* motor-driven devices that produced instant abstract paintings. He programmed these metamatics electronically to act with an antimechanical unpredictability when viewers inserted felt-tipped marking pens into a pincer and pressed a button to initiate the pen's motion across a small sheet of paper clipped to an "easel." Viewers could use different-colored markers in succession and could stop and start the device to achieve some degree of control over the final image. These operations created a series of small works resembling Abstract Expressionist paintings.

In 1960, Tinguely expanded the scale of his work with a kinetic piece designed to "perform" and then destroy itself in the sculpture garden of the Museum of Modern Art in New York City. He created *Homage to New York* (FIG. 36-78) with the aid of engineer Billy Klüver (1927–2004), who helped him scrounge wheels and other moving objects from a dump near Manhattan. The completed structure, painted white for visibility against the dark night sky, included a player piano modified into a metamatic painting machine, a weather balloon that inflated during the performance, vials of colored smoke, and a host of gears, pulleys, wheels, and other found machine parts.

This work premiered (and instantly self-destructed) on March 17, 1960, with New York Governor Nelson Rockefeller, an array of distinguished guests, and three television crews in attendance. Once

36-78 JEAN TINGUELY, *Homage to New York,* 1960, just prior to its self-destruction in the garden of the Museum of Modern Art, New York.

Tinguely produced motor-driven devices programmed to make instant abstract paintings. To explore the notion of destruction as an act of creation, he designed this one to perform and then destroy itself.

Tinguely turned on the machine, smoke poured from its interior and the piano caught fire. Various parts of the machine broke off and rambled away, while one of the metamatics tried but failed to produce an abstract painting. Finally, Tinguely summoned a firefighter to extinguish the blaze and ensure the demise of *Homage to New York* with his ax. Like the artist's other kinetic sculptures, *Homage to New York* recalls the satiric Dadaist spirit and the droll import of Klee's *Twittering Machine* (FIG. 35-53). But Tinguely deliberately made the wacky behavior of *Homage to New York* more playful and more endearing. Having been given a freedom of eccentric behavior unprecedented in the mechanical world, Tinguely's creations often seemed to behave with the whimsical individuality of human actors.

Conceptual Art

The relentless challenges to artistic convention fundamental to the historical avant-garde reached a logical conclusion with *Conceptual Art* in the late 1960s. Conceptual artists asserted that the "artfulness" of art lay in the artist's idea rather than in its final expression. These artists regarded the idea, or concept, as the defining component of the artwork. Indeed, some Conceptual artists eliminated the object altogether.

JOSEPH KOSUTH American artist JOSEPH KOSUTH (b. 1945) was a major proponent of Conceptual Art.

> Like everyone else I inherited the idea of art as a set of *formal* problems. So when I began to re-think my ideas of art, I had to re-think that thinking process. . . . [T]he radical shift was in changing the idea of art itself. . . . It meant you could have an art work which was that *idea* of an art work, and its formal components weren't important. I felt I had found a way to make art without formal components being confused for an expressionist composition. The expression was in the idea, not the form—the forms were only a device in the service of the idea.[41]

Kosuth's work operates at the intersection of language and vision, dealing with the relationship between the abstract and the concrete. For example, in *One and Three Chairs* (FIG. 36-79), Kosuth juxtaposed a real chair, a full-scale photograph of the chair, and an enlarged reproduction of a dictionary definition of the word "chair." By so doing, the Conceptual artist asked the viewer to ponder the notion of what constitutes "chairness."

BRUCE NAUMAN In the mid-1960s, BRUCE NAUMAN (b. 1941) made his artistic presence known when he abandoned painting and turned to object-making. Since then, his work has been amazingly varied. In addition to sculptural pieces constructed from different materials, including rubber, fiberglass, and cardboard, he has also produced photographs, films, videos, books, and large room installations, as well as Performance Art. Nauman's work of the 1960s intersected with that of the Conceptual artists, especially in terms of the philosophical exploration that was the foundation of much of his art, and in his interest in language and wordplay. *The True Artist Helps the World by Revealing Mystic Truths* (FIG. 36-80) was the first of Nauman's many neon sculptures. He selected neon because he wanted to find a medium that would be identified with a nonartistic function. Determined to discover a way to connect objects with words, he used the method outlined in *Philosophical Investigations,* in which the Austrian philosopher Ludwig Wittgenstein (1889–1951) encouraged contradictory and nonsensical arguments. Nauman's neon sculpture spins out an emphatic assertion, but as Nauman explained, "It was kind of a test—like when you say something out loud to see if you believe it. . . . [I]t was on the one hand a totally silly idea and yet, on the other hand, I believed it."[42]

36-80A NAUMAN *Self-Portrait a a Fountain,* 1966–1967.

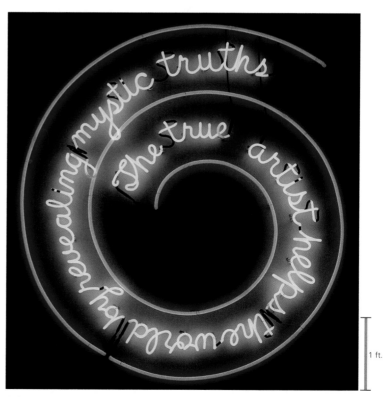

36-79 JOSEPH KOSUTH, *One and Three Chairs,* 1965. Wooden folding chair, photographic copy of a chair, and photographic enlargement of a dictionary definition of a chair; chair, 2′ 8 3/8″ × 1′ 2 7/8″ × 1′ 8 7/8″; photo panel, 3′ × 2′ 1/8″; text panel, 2′ × 2′ 1/8″. Museum of Modern Art, New York (Larry Aldrich Foundation Fund).

Conceptual artists regard the concept as an artwork's defining component. To portray "chairness," Kosuth juxtaposed a chair, a photograph of the chair, and a dictionary definition of "chair."

36-80 BRUCE NAUMAN, *The True Artist Helps the World by Revealing Mystic Truths,* 1967. Neon with glass tubing suspension frame, 4′ 11″ × 4′ 7″ × 2″. Private collection.

Nauman, like other Conceptual artists, explores his interest in language and wordplay in his art. He described this neon sculpture's emphatic assertion as "a totally silly idea," but one that he believed.

36-81 Nam June Paik, Video still from *Global Groove,* 1973. Color videotape, sound, 30 minutes. Collection of the artist.

Korean-born video artist Paik's best-known work is a cascade of fragmented sequences of performances and commercials intended as a sample of the rich worldwide television menu of the future.

Other Conceptual artists pursued the notion that the idea is a work of art itself by creating works involving invisible materials, such as inert gases, radioactive isotopes, or radio waves. In each case, viewers must base their understanding of the artwork on what they know about the properties of these materials, rather than on any visible empirical data, and must depend on the artist's linguistic description of the work. Ultimately, the Conceptual artists challenged the very premises of artistic production, pushing art's boundaries to a point where no concrete definition of "art" is possible.

New Media

During the past half century, many avant-garde artists have eagerly embraced new technologies in their attempt to find fresh avenues of artistic expression. Among the most popular new media are video recording and computer graphics.

VIDEO Initially, only commercial television studios possessed video equipment, but in the 1960s, with the development of relatively inexpensive portable video recorders and of electronic devices allowing manipulation of recorded video material, artists began to explore in earnest the expressive possibilities of this new technology. In its basic form, video recording involves a special motion-picture camera that captures visible images and translates them into electronic data that can be displayed on a video monitor or television screen. Video pictures resemble photographs in the amount of detail they contain, but, like computer graphics, a video image consists of a series of points of light on a grid, giving the impression of soft focus. Viewers looking at television or video art are not aware of the monitor's surface. Instead, fulfilling the Renaissance ideal, they concentrate on the image and look through the glass surface, as through a window, into the "space" beyond. Video images combine the optical realism of photography with the sense that the subjects move in real time in a deep space "inside" the monitor.

NAM JUNE PAIK When video introduced the possibility of manipulating subjects in real time, artists such as Korean-born NAM

JUNE PAIK (1932–2006) were eager to work with the medium. Inspired by the ideas of John Cage and after studying music performance, art history, and Eastern philosophy in Korea and Japan, Paik worked with electronic music in Germany in the late 1950s. In 1965, after relocating to New York City, Paik acquired the first inexpensive video recorder sold in Manhattan (the Sony Porta-Pak) and immediately recorded everything he saw out the window of his taxi on the return trip to his studio downtown. Experience acquired as artist-in-residence at television stations WGBH in Boston and WNET in New York allowed him to experiment with the most advanced broadcast video technology.

A grant permitted Paik to collaborate with the gifted Japanese engineer-inventor Shuya Abe in developing a video synthesizer. This instrument allows artists to manipulate and change the electronic video information in various ways, causing images or parts of images to stretch, shrink, change color, or break up. With the synthesizer, artists can also layer images, inset one image into another, or merge images from various cameras with those from video recorders to make a single visual kaleidoscopic "time-collage." This kind of compositional freedom permitted Paik to combine his interests in painting, music, Eastern philosophy, global politics for survival, humanized technology, and cybernetics. Paik called his video works "physical music" and said that his musical background enabled him to understand time better than could video artists trained in painting or sculpture.

Paik's best-known video work, *Global Groove* (FIG. 36-81), combines in quick succession fragmented sequences of female tap dancers, beat-generation poet Allen Ginsberg (1926–1997) reading his work, a performance by Fluxus artist and cellist Charlotte Moorman (1933–1991) using a man's back as her instrument, Pepsi commercials from Japanese television, Korean drummers, and a shot of the Living Theatre group performing a controversial piece called *Paradise Now.* Commissioned originally for broadcast over the United Nations satellite, the cascade of imagery in *Global Groove* gives viewers a glimpse of the rich worldwide television menu Paik predicted would be available in the future.

36-82 ADRIAN PIPER, *Cornered*, 1988. Mixed-media installation of variable size; video monitor, table, and birth certificates. Museum of Contemporary Art, Chicago. ■◀

In this installation, Piper, a light-skinned African American, appeared on a video monitor, "cornered" behind an overturned table, and made provocative comments about overt racism and more subtle bigotry.

ADRIAN PIPER One video artist committed to using her art to effect social change—in particular, to combat pervasive racism—is ADRIAN PIPER (b. 1948). Appropriately, her art, such as the installation *Cornered* (FIG. **36-82**), is provocative and confrontational. This piece included a video monitor placed behind an overturned table. Piper appeared on the video monitor, literally cornered behind the table, as she spoke to viewers. Her comments sprang from her experiences as a light-skinned African American woman and from her belief that although overt racism had diminished, subtle and equally damaging forms of bigotry were still rampant. "I'm black," she announces on the 16-minute videotape. "Now let's deal with this social fact and the fact of my stating it together. . . . If you feel that my letting people know that I'm not white is making an unnecessary fuss, you must feel that the right and proper course of action for me to take is to pass for white. Now this kind of thinking presupposes a belief that it's inherently better to be identified as white," she continues. The directness of Piper's art forces viewers to examine their own behaviors and values.

BILL VIOLA For much of his artistic career, BILL VIOLA (b. 1951) has also explored the capabilities of digitized imagery, producing many video installations and single-channel works. Often focused on sensory perception, the pieces not only heighten viewer awareness of the senses but also suggest an exploration into the spiritual realm. Viola, an American, spent years seriously studying Buddhist, Christian, Sufi, and Zen mysticism. Because he fervently believes in art's transformative power and in a spiritual view of human nature, Viola designs works encouraging spectator introspection. His recent video projects involve using techniques such as extreme slow motion, contrasts in scale, shifts in focus, mirrored reflections, staccato editing, and multiple or layered screens to achieve dramatic effects.

The power of Viola's work is evident in *The Crossing* (FIG. **36-83**), an installation piece involving two color video channels projected on 16-foot-high screens. The artist either shows the two projections on the front and back of the same screen or on two separate screens in the same installation. In these two companion videos, shown simultaneously on the two screens, a man surrounded

36-83 BILL VIOLA, *The Crossing*, 1996. Video/sound installation with two channels of color video projection onto screens 16′ high. Private collection. ■◀

Viola's video projects use extreme slow motion, contrasts in scale, shifts in focus, mirrored reflections, and staccato editing to create dramatic sensory experiences rooted in tangible reality.

in darkness appears, moving closer until he fills the screen. On one screen, drops of water fall from above onto the man's head, while on the other screen, a small fire breaks out at the man's feet. Over the next few minutes, the water and fire increase in intensity until the man disappears in a torrent of water on one screen (FIG. **36-83**) and flames consume the man on the other screen. The deafening roar of a raging fire and a torrential downpour accompany these visual images. Eventually, everything subsides and fades into darkness. This installation's elemental nature and its presentation in a dark space immerse viewers in a pure sensory experience very much rooted in tangible reality.

COMPUTER GRAPHICS Perhaps the most promising new medium for creating and manipulating illusionistic three-dimensional forms is computer graphics. This new medium uses light to make images and, like photography, can incorporate specially recorded camera images. Unlike video recording, computer graphic art allows artists to work with wholly invented forms, as painters can. Developed during the 1960s and 1970s, this technology opened up new possibilities for both abstract and figurative art. It involves electronic programs dividing the surface of the computer monitor's cathode-ray tube into a grid of tiny boxes called "picture elements," or *pixels*. Artists can electronically address pixels individually to create a design, much as knitting or weaving patterns have a grid matrix as a guide for making a design in fabric. Once created, parts of a com-

36-84 David Em, *Nora*, 1979.
Computer-generated color photograph,
1' 5" × 1' 11". Private collection. ◼◀

Unlike video recording, computer
graphic art allows the creation of
wholly invented forms, as in painting.
Em builds fantastic digital images of
imaginary landscapes out of tiny boxes
called pixels.

1 in.

Institute of Technology's Jet Propulsion Laboratory, Em created brilliantly colored scenes of alien worlds using the laboratory's advanced computer graphics equipment. He also had access to software programs developed to create computer graphics simulations of NASA's missions in outer space. Creating images with the computer gave Em great flexibility in manipulating simple geometric shapes—shrinking or enlarging them, stretching or reversing them, repeating them, adding texture to their surfaces, and creating the illusion of light and shadow. In images such as *Nora* (FIG. **36-84**), Em created futuristic geometric versions of Surrealistic dreamscapes whose forms seem familiar and strange at the same time. The illusion of space in these works is immensely vivid and seductive. It almost seems possible to wander through the tubelike foreground "frame" and up the inclined foreground plane or to hop aboard the hovering globe at the lower left for a journey through the strange patterns and textures of this mysterious labyrinthine setting.

puter graphic design can be changed quickly through an electronic program, allowing artists to revise or duplicate shapes in the design and to manipulate at will the color, texture, size, number, and position of any desired detail. Computer graphics pictures appear in luminous color on the cathode-ray tube. The effect suggests a view into a vast world existing inside the tube.

DAVID EM One of the best-known artists working in this electronic painting mode, DAVID EM (b. 1952) uses what he terms "computer imaging" to fashion fantastic imaginary landscapes. These have an eerily believable existence within the "window" of the computer monitor. When he was artist-in-residence at the California

JENNY HOLZER Another contemporary artist who has harnessed new technology for artistic purposes is JENNY HOLZER (b. 1950), who created several series of artworks using electronic signs, most involving light-emitting diode (LED) technology. In 1989, Holzer did a major installation at the Guggenheim Museum in New York that included elements from her previous series and consisted of a large continuous LED display spiraling around the museum's interior ramp (FIG. **36-85**). Holzer's installation focused specifically on text, and she invented sayings with an authoritative tone for her LED displays. Statements included "Protect me from what I want," "Abuse of power comes as no

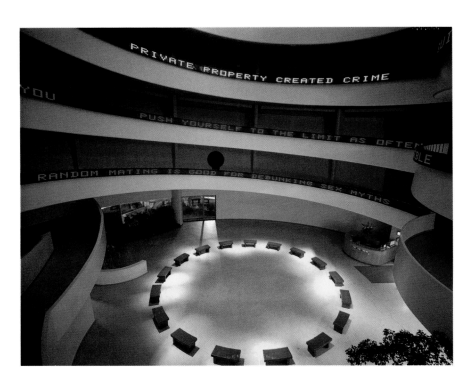

36-85 JENNY HOLZER, *Untitled* (selections from *Truisms, Inflammatory Essays, The Living Series, The Survival Series, Under a Rock, Laments,* and *Child Text*), 1989. Extended helical tricolor LED electronic display signboard, 16' × 162' × 6'. Solomon R. Guggenheim Museum, New York, December 1989–February 1990 (partial gift of the artist, 1989).

Holzer's 1989 installation consisted of electronic signs created using light-emitting diode (LED) technology. The continuous display of texts spiraled around the Guggenheim Museum's interior ramp.

36-86

Tony Oursler, *Mansheshe*, 1997. Ceramic, glass, video player, videocassette, CPJ-200 video projector, sound, 11″ × 7″ × 8″ each. Private collection.

Video artist Oursler projects his digital images onto sculptural objects, insinuating them into the "real" world. Here, he projected talking heads onto egg-shaped forms suspended from poles.

1 in.

surprise," and "Romantic love was invented to manipulate women." The statements, which people could read from a distance, were intentionally vague and, in some cases, contradictory.

TONY OURSLER While many artists present video and digital imagery to the audience on familiar flat screens, thus reproducing the format in which we most often come into contact with such images, Tony Oursler (b. 1957) manipulates his images, projecting them onto sculptural objects. This has the effect of taking such images out of the digital world and insinuating them into the "real" world. Accompanied by sound tapes, Oursler's installations, such as *Mansheshe* (FIG. 36-86), not only engage but often challenge the viewer. In this example, Oursler projected talking heads onto egg-shaped forms suspended from poles. Because the projected images of people look directly at the viewer, the statements they make about religious beliefs, sexual identity, and interpersonal relationships cannot be easily dismissed.

MATTHEW BARNEY One of the major trends in the art world of the opening decade of the 21st century is the relaxation of the traditional boundaries between and among artistic media. In fact, many artists today are creating vast and complex multimedia installations combining new and traditional media. One of these artists is Matthew Barney (b. 1967). The 2003 installation (FIG. 36-1) of his epic *Cremaster* cycle (1994–2002) at the Solomon R. Guggenheim Museum in New York typifies the expansive scale of many contemporary works. A multimedia extravaganza involving drawings, photographs, sculptures, videos, films, and performances (presented in videos), the

Cremaster cycle is a lengthy narrative that takes place in a self-enclosed universe Barney created. The title of the work refers to the cremaster muscle, which controls testicular contractions in response to external stimuli. Barney uses the development of this muscle in the embryonic process of sexual differentiation as the conceptual springboard for the entire *Cremaster* project, in which he explores the notion of creation in expansive and complicated ways. The cycle's narrative, revealed in the five 35-mm feature-length films and the artworks, makes reference to, among other things, a musical revue in Boise, Idaho (Barney's hometown), the life cycle of bees, the execution of convicted murderer Gary Gilmore, the construction of the Chrysler Building (FIG. 35-76), Celtic mythology, Masonic rituals, a motorcycle race, and a lyric opera set in late-19th-century Budapest. In the installation, Barney tied the artworks together conceptually by a five-channel video piece that is projected on screens hanging in the Guggenheim's rotunda. Immersion in Barney's constructed world is disorienting and overwhelming and has a force that competes with the immense scale and often frenzied pace of contemporary life.

No one knows what the next years and decades will bring, but given the expansive scope of postmodernism, it is likely that no single approach to or style of art will dominate. But new technologies will certainly continue to redefine what constitutes a "work of art." The universally expanding presence of computers, digital technology, and the Internet may well erode what few conceptual and geographical boundaries remain and make art and information about art available to virtually everyone, thereby creating a truly global artistic community.

EUROPE AND AMERICA AFTER 1945

PAINTING AND SCULPTURE

■ The art of the second half of the 20th century reflects cultural upheaval: the rejection of traditional values, the civil rights and feminist movements, and the new consumer society.

■ The first major postwar avant-garde art movement was Abstract Expressionism, which championed an artwork's formal elements rather than its subject. Gestural abstractionists, such as Pollock and de Kooning, sought expressiveness through energetically applied pigment. Chromatic abstractionists, such as Rothko, struck emotional chords through large areas of pure color.

■ Post-Painterly Abstraction promoted a cool rationality in contrast to Abstract Expressionism's passion. Both hard-edge painters, such as Kelly and Stella, and color-field painters, such as Frankenthaler and Louis, pursued purity in art by emphasizing the flatness of pigment on canvas.

■ Pop artists, such as Johns, Lichtenstein, and Warhol, turned away from abstraction to the representation of subjects grounded in popular culture—flags, comic strips, movie stars.

■ Superrealists, such as Flack, Close, and Hanson—kindred spirits to Pop artists in many ways— created paintings and sculptures featuring scrupulous fidelity to optical fact.

■ The leading sculptural movement was Minimalism. Tony Smith and Judd created artworks consisting of simple unadorned geometric shapes to underscore the "objecthood" of their sculptures.

■ Much of the art since 1970 addresses pressing social issues. Leading feminist artists include Chicago, whose *Dinner Party* honors important women throughout history and features crafts traditionally associated with women; Sherman and Kruger, who explored the "male gaze" in their art; and Mendieta and Wilke, whose bodies are their subjects.

■ Other artists explored race, ethnicity, class, and sexual orientation. Ringgold and Simpson addressed issues important to African American women, Edwards civil rights themes, and Quick-to-See Smith Native American heritage. Wodiczko's art has documented the plight of the homeless. Wojnarowicz recorded the devastating effect of AIDS on the gay community.

Pollock, *Lavender Mist*, 1950

Warhol, *Marilyn Diptych*, 1962

Chicago, *The Dinner Party*, 1979

ARCHITECTURE AND SITE-SPECIFIC ART

■ Some of the leading early-20th-century modernist architects were also active after 1945. Wright built the snail-shell Guggenheim Museum, Le Corbusier the sculpturesque Notre-Dame-du-Haut, and Mies van der Rohe the Minimalist Seagram skyscraper. Later modernists Saarinen and Utzon designed structures having dramatic curvilinear rooflines.

■ In contrast to modernist architecture, postmodernist architecture is complex and eclectic and often incorporates references to historical styles. Among the best-known postmodern projects are Moore's Piazza d'Italia and Graves's Portland Building, both of which echo classical motifs.

■ Deconstructivist architects seek to disorient the viewer with asymmetrical and irregular shapes. Among the most prominent practicing today are Gehry and Libeskind.

■ Site-specific art exists at the intersection of architecture and sculpture and is sometimes temporary in nature, as was Christo and Jeanne-Claude's *Surrounded Islands*.

Gehry, Guggenheim Museum, Bilbao, 1997

PERFORMANCE AND CONCEPTUAL ART AND NEW MEDIA

■ Among the most significant developments in the art world after World War II has been the expansion of the range of works considered "art."

■ Performance artists, notably Schneemann and Beuys, replace traditional stationary artworks with movements and sounds carried out before an audience. Their Performance Art often addresses the same social and political issues that contemporary painters and sculptors explore.

■ Conceptual artists, including Kosuth and Nauman, believe that the "artfulness" of art is in the artist's idea, not in the work resulting from the idea.

■ Paik, Piper, Viola, and others have embraced video recording technology to produce artworks that combine images and sounds, sometimes viewed on small monitors, other times on huge screens.

■ Em, Holzer, Oursler, and Barney have explored computer graphics and other new media, often in vast and complex museum installations.

Oursler, *Mansheshe*, 1997

NOTES

Introduction

1. Quoted in George Heard Hamilton, *Painting and Sculpture in Europe, 1880–1940,* 6th ed. (New Haven, Conn.: Yale University Press, 1993), 345.
2. Quoted in *Josef Albers: Homage to the Square* (New York: Museum of Modern Art, 1964), n.p.

Chapter 2

1. Translated by Françoise Tallon, in Prudence O. Harper et al., *The Royal City of Susa* (New York: Metropolitan Museum of Art, 1992), 132.

Chapter 3

1. Herodotus, *Histories,* 2.35.
2. The chronology adopted in this chapter is that of John Baines and Jaromír Malék, *Atlas of Ancient Egypt* (Oxford: Oxford University Press, 1980), 36–37. The division of kingdoms is that of, among others, Mark Lehner, *The Complete Pyramids* (New York: Thames & Hudson, 1997), 8–9, and David P. Silverman, ed., *Ancient Egypt* (New York: Oxford University Press, 1997), 20–39.

Chapter 4

1. Homer, *Iliad,* 2.466–649.

Chapter 5

1. Plutarch, *Life of Pericles,* 12.
2. Pliny, *Natural History,* 34.74.
3. Ibid., 36.20.
4. Lucian, *Amores,* 13–14; *Imagines,* 6.
5. Plutarch, *Moralia,* 335A–B. Translated by J. J. Pollitt, *The Art of Ancient Greece: Sources and Documents* (New York: Cambridge University Press, 1990), 99.
6. Pliny, *Natural History,* 35.110.

Chapter 10

1. Livy, *History of Rome,* 25.40.1–3.
2. Recorded by the Venerable Bede, the great English scholar, monk, and saint, who died in 735. Translated by Lord Byron in *Childe Harold's Pilgrimage* (1817), 4.145.
3. Juvenal, *Satires,* 3.225, 232.

Chapter 11

1. Translated by Raymond Davis, *The Book of Pontiffs* (Liverpool: Liverpool University Press, 1989), 18–19.

Chapter 12

1. Paulus Silentarius, *Descriptio Sanctae Sophiae,* 617–646. Translated by Cyril Mango, *The Art of the Byzantine Empire, 312–1453: Sources and Documents* (reprint of 1972 ed., Toronto: University of Toronto Press, 1986), 85–86.
2. Procopius, *De aedificiis,* 1.1.23ff. Translated by Mango, 74.
3. Paulus Silentarius, 489, 668. Translated by Mango, 83, 86.
4. Translated by Colin Luibheid, *Pseudo-Dionysius: The Complete Works* (New York: Paulist, 1987), 68ff.

5. Procopius, 1.1.23ff. Translated by Mango, 75.
6. *Libri Carolini* 4.2. Translated by Herbert L. Kessler, *Spiritual Seeing: Picturing God's Invisibility in Medieval Art* (Philadelphia: University of Pennsylvania Press, 2000), 119.
7. Nina G. Garsoïan, "Later Byzantium," in John A. Garraty and Peter Gay, eds., *The Columbia History of the World* (New York: Harper & Row, 1972), 453.
8. Ibid., 460.

Chapter 16

1. *Beowulf,* 3162–3164, translated by Kevin Crossley-Holland (New York: Farrar, Straus & Giroux, 1968), 119.
2. *Beowulf,* 33.
3. Translated by Françoise Henry, *The Book of Kells* (New York: Knopf, 1974), 165.
4. Translated by John W. Williams, in *The Art of Medieval Spain A.D. 500–1200* (New York: Metropolitan Museum of Art, 1993), 156.
5. Translated by Adam S. Cohen, *The Uta Codex* (University Park: Pennsylvania State University Press, 2000), 11, 41.

Chapter 17

1. Translated by Charles P. Parkhurst Jr., in Elizabeth G. Holt, *A Documentary History of Art,* 2d ed. (Princeton, N.J.: Princeton University Press, 1981), 1: 18.
2. Translated by Giovanna De Appolonia, Boston University.
3. Translated by Calvin B. Kendall, *The Allegory of the Church: Romanesque Portals and Their Verse Inscriptions* (Toronto: University of Toronto Press, 1998), 207.
4. Translated by John Williams, *A Spanish Apocalypse: The Morgan Beatus Manuscript* (New York: Braziller, 1991), 223.
5. Bernard of Clairvaux, *Apologia* 12.28. Translated by Conrad Rudolph, *The "Things of Greater Importance": Bernard of Clairvaux's* Apologia *and the Medieval Attitude toward Art* (Philadelphia: University of Pennsylvania Press, 1990), 281, 283.
6. *Rule of Saint Benedict,* 57.1. Translated by Timothy Fry, *The Rule of St. Benedict* (Collegeville, Minn.: Liturgical, 1981), 265.

Chapter 18

1. Giorgio Vasari, *Introduzione alle tre arti del disegno* (1550), ch. 3. Translated by Paul Frankl, *The Gothic: Literary Sources and Interpretation through Eight Centuries* (Princeton, N.J.: Princeton University Press, 1960), 290–291, 859–860.
2. Dante, *Divine Comedy,* Purgatory, 11.81.
3. Translated by Roland Behrendt, *Johannes Trithemius, in Praise of Scribes: De laude scriptorum* (Lawrence, Kans.: Coronado, 1974), 71.
4. Frankl, 55.

Chapter 20

1. Francisco de Hollanda, *De pintura antigua* (1548). Robert Klein and Henri Zerner, *Italian Art, 1500–1600: Sources and Documents* (Englewood Cliffs, N.J.: Prentice Hall, 1966), 33.

Chapter 21

1. Ghiberti, *I commentarii,* II. Quoted in Elizabeth Gilmore Holt, ed., *A Documentary History of Art, I: The Middle Ages and the Renaissance* (Princeton, N.J.: Princeton University Press, 1981), 157–158.

2. Giorgio Vasari, *Lives of the Painters, Sculptors, and Architects,* translated by Gaston du C. de Vere (New York: Knopf, 1996), 1: 304.

3. Ghiberti, *I commentarii,* II. Quoted in Holt, 161.

4. Quoted in H. W. Janson, *The Sculpture of Donatello* (Princeton, N.J.: Princeton University Press, 1965), 154.

5. Vasari, 1: 318.

Chapter 22

1. Plato, *Ion,* 534. Translated by Benjamin Jowett, *The Dialogues of Plato,* 4th ed., vol. 1 (Oxford: Clarendon, 1953), 107–108.

2. Leonardo to Ludovico Sforza, ca. 1480–1481. In Elizabeth Gilmore Holt, ed., *A Documentary History of Art* (Princeton, N.J.: Princeton University Press, 1981), I: 274–275.

3. Quoted in Anthony Blunt, *Artistic Theory in Italy, 1450–1600* (London: Oxford University Press, 1964), 34.

4. Quoted in James M. Saslow, *The Poetry of Michelangelo: An Annotated Translation* (New Haven, Conn.: Yale University Press, 1991), 407.

5. Giorgio Vasari, *Lives of the Painters, Sculptors, and Architects,* translated by Gaston du C. de Vere (New York: Knopf, 1996), 2: 736.

6. Quoted in A. Richard Turner, *Renaissance Florence: The Invention of a New Art* (New York: Abrams, 1997), 163.

7. Quoted in Bruce Boucher, *Andrea Palladio: The Architect in His Time* (New York: Abbeville, 1998), 229.

8. Quoted in Robert J. Clements, *Michelangelo's Theory of Art* (New York: New York University Press, 1961), 320.

Chapter 23

1. Translated by William Martin Conway, in Wolfgang Stechow, *Northern Renaissance Art, 1400–1600: Sources and Documents* (Evanston, Ill.: Northwestern University Press, 1989), 111.

2. Ibid., 118.

3. Translated by Erwin Panofsky, in Stechow, 123.

4. Giorgio Vasari, *Lives of the Painters, Sculptors, and Architects,* translated by Gaston du C. de Vere (New York: Knopf, 1996), 2: 863.

Chapter 24

1. Filippo Baldinucci, *Vita del Cavaliere Giovanni Lorenzo Bernini* (1681). Translated by Robert Enggass, in Robert Enggass and Jonathan Brown, *Italian and Spanish Art 1600–1750: Sources and Documents* (Evanston, Ill.: Northwestern University Press, 1992), 119.

2. Ibid., 116.

3. John Milton, *Il Penseroso* (1631, published 1645), 166.

Chapter 25

1. Translated by Kristin Lohse Belkin, *Rubens* (London: Phaidon, 1998), 47.

2. Jan Harmensz Krul, *Minne-beeldn* (Amsterdam 1634). Translated by Bob Haak, *The Golden Age: Dutch Painters of the Seventeenth Century* (New York: Abrams, 1984), 75.

3. Albert Blankert, *Johannes Vermeer van Delft 1632–1675* (Utrecht: Spectrum, 1975), 133, no. 51. Translated by Haak, 450.

Chapter 28

1. Quoted in Junichi Shiota, *Kimio Tsuchiya, Sculpture 1984–1988* (Tokyo: Morris Gallery, 1988), 3.

Chapter 29

1. Translated by Robert Goldwater and Marco Treves, eds., *Artists on Art,* 3d ed. (New York: Pantheon, 1958), 157.

2. Quoted in Thomas A. Bailey, *The American Pageant: A History of the Republic,* 2d ed. (Boston: Heath, 1961), 280.

3. Translated by Elfriede Heyer and Roger C. Norton, in Charles Harrison, Paul Wood, and Jason Gaiger, eds., *Art in Theory, 1648–1815: An Anthology of Changing Ideas* (Oxford: Blackwell, 2000), 451–453.

Chapter 30

1. Théophile Gautier, *Histoire de Romantisme* (Paris: Charpentier, 1874), 204.

2. Quoted in Helmut Borsch-Supan, *Caspar David Friedrich* (New York: Braziller, 1974), 7.

3. Translated by Jason Gaiger, in Charles Harrison, Paul Wood, and Jason Gaiger, eds., *Art in Theory, 1815–1900: An Anthology of Changing Ideas* (Oxford: Blackwell, 1998), 54.

4. Quoted by Brian Lukacher, in Stephen F. Eisenman, ed., *Nineteenth Century Art: A Critical History,* 2d ed. (New York: Thames & Hudson, 2002), 125.

5. Quoted in John W. McCoubrey, *American Art, 1700–1960: Sources and Documents* (Upper Saddle River, N.J.: Prentice Hall, 1965), 98.

6. Quoted in Thomas A. Bailey, *The American Pageant: A History of the Republic,* 2d ed. (Boston: Heath, 1961), 280.

7. Quoted in Linda Nochlin, *Realism and Tradition in Art, 1848–1900* (Upper Saddle River, N.J.: Prentice Hall, 1966), 42.

8. Quoted in George Heard Hamilton, *Manet and His Critics* (New Haven, Conn.: Yale University Press, 1954), 45.

9. Quoted in Eisenman, 286.

10. *New York Weekly Tribune,* September 30, 1865.

11. Quoted in Nikolai Cikovsky Jr. and Franklin Kelly, *Winslow Homer* (Washington, D.C.: National Gallery of Art, 1995), 26.

12. Quoted in Lloyd Goodrich, *Thomas Eakins, His Life and Work* (New York: Whitney Museum of American Art, 1933), 51–52.

13. Quoted in Nicholas Pevsner, *An Outline of European Architecture* (Baltimore: Penguin, 1960), 627.

14. Letter from Delaroche to François Arao, quoted in Helmut Gernsheim, *Creative Photography* (New York: Bonanza, 1962), 24.

15. Quoted in Naomi Rosenblum, *A World History of Photography* (New York: Abbeville, 1984), 69.

16. Quoted in Kenneth MacGowan, *Behind the Screen* (New York: Delta, 1965), 49.

Chapter 31

1. Clement Greenberg, "Modernist Painting," *Art and Literature,* no. 4 (Spring 1965): 193–194.

2. Quoted in Linda Nochlin, *Realism* (Harmondsworth: Penguin, 1971), 28.

3. Quoted in Linda Nochlin, *Impressionism and Post-Impressionism 1874–1904: Sources and Documents* (Englewood Cliffs, N.J.: Prentice Hall, 1966), 35.

4. Translated by Carola Hicks, in Charles Harrison, Paul Wood, and Jason Gaiger, eds., *Art in Theory, 1815–1900: An Anthology of Changing Ideas* (Oxford: Blackwell, 1998), 595.

5. Quoted in John McCoubrey, *American Art, 1700–1960: Sources and Documents* (Englewood Cliffs, N.J.: Prentice Hall, 1965), 184.

6. Quoted in Harrison et al., 835–836.

7. Quoted in Robert Goldwater and Marco Treves, eds., *Artists on Art, from the XIV to the XX Century* (New York: Pantheon, 1945), 322.

8. Ibid., 375.

9. Vincent van Gogh to Theo van Gogh, September 1888, in J. van Gogh–Bonger and V. W. van Gogh, eds., *The Complete Letters of Vincent van Gogh* (Greenwich, Conn.: New York Graphic Society, 1979), 3: 534.

10. Vincent van Gogh to Theo van Gogh, July 16, 1888, in W. H. Auden, ed., *Van Gogh: A Self-Portrait: Letters Revealing His Life as a Painter* (New York: Dutton, 1963), 299.

11. Quoted in Belinda Thompson, ed., *Gauguin by Himself* (Boston: Little, Brown, 1993), 270–271.

12. Quoted in Sam Hunter, John Jacobus, and Daniel Wheeler, *Modern Art,* 3d ed. (Upper Saddle River, N.J.: Prentice Hall, 2004), 28.

13. Cézanne to Émile Bernard, March 1904. Quoted in Goldwater and Treves, 363.

14. Cézanne to Émile Bernard, April 15, 1904, in ibid., 363.

15. Translated by Akane Kawakami, in Harrison et al., 1066.

16. Quoted in George Heard Hamilton, *Painting and Sculpture in Europe, 1880–1940,* 6th ed. (New Haven, Conn.: Yale University Press, 1993), 124.

17. Quoted in V. Frisch and J. T. Shipley, *Auguste Rodin* (New York: Stokes, 1939), 203.

18. Quoted in Eileen Boris, *Art and Labor: Ruskin, Morris, and the Craftsman Ideal in America* (Philadelphia: Temple University Press, 1986), 7.

Chapter 32

1. Diego de Landa, *Yucatan before and after the Conquest,* translated by William Gates (Mineola, N.Y.: Dover, 1978), 13, 82.

2. Bernal Díaz del Castillo, *The Discovery and Conquest of Mexico,* translated by A. P. Maudslay (New York: Farrar, Straus & Giroux, 1956), 218–219.

Chapter 35

1. Quoted in John Elderfield, *The "Wild Beasts": Fauvism and Its Affinities* (New York: Museum of Modern Art, 1976), 29.

2. Translated by Charles Harrison and Paul Wood, eds., *Art in Theory, 1900–2000: An Anthology of Changing Ideas* (Oxford: Blackwell, 2003), 65.

3. Quoted in Frederick S. Levine, *The Apocalyptic Vision: The Art of Franz Marc as German Expressionism* (New York: Harper & Row, 1979), 57.

4. Quoted in Sam Hunter, John Jacobus, and Daniel Wheeler, *Modern Art,* rev. 3d ed. (Upper Saddle Hill, N.J.: Prentice Hall, 2004), 121.

5. Quoted in George Heard Hamilton, *Painting and Sculpture in Europe, 1880–1940,* 6th ed. (New Haven, Conn.: Yale University Press, 1993), 246.

6. Ibid., 238.

7. Quoted in Edward Fry, ed., *Cubism* (London: Thames & Hudson, 1966), 112–113.

8. Quoted in Michael Hoog, *R. Delaunay* (New York: Crown, 1976), 49.

9. Quoted in Françoise Gilot and Carlton Lake, *Life with Picasso* (New York: McGraw-Hill, 1964), 77.

10. Filippo Tommaso Marinetti, *The Foundation and Manifesto of Futurism* (*Le Figaro*, February 20, 1909). Translated by Joshua C. Taylor, in Herschel B. Chipp, *Theories of Modern Art: A Source Book by Artists and Critics* (Berkeley and Los Angeles: University of California Press, 1968), 284.

11. Ibid., 286.

12. Quoted in Robert Short, *Dada and Surrealism* (London: Octopus, 1980), 18.

13. Quoted in Robert Motherwell, ed., *The Dada Painters and Poets: An Anthology*, 2d ed. (Cambridge, Mass.: Belknap Press of Harvard University, 1989).

14. Hans Richter, *Dada: Art and Anti-Art* (London: Thames & Hudson, 1961), 64–65.

15. Ibid., 57.

16. Tristan Tzara, "Chronique Zurichoise," translated by Ralph Manheim, in Motherwell, *Dada Painters*, 236.

17. Quoted in Arturo Schwarz, *The Complete Works of Marcel Duchamp* (London: Thames & Hudson, 1965), 466.

18. Quoted in Sam Hunter, *American Art of the 20th Century* (New York: Abrams, 1972), 30.

19. Ibid., 37.

20. Charles C. Eldredge, "The Arrival of European Modernism," *Art in America* 61 (July–August 1973), 35.

21. Quoted in Gail Stavitsky, "Reordering Reality: Precisionist Directions in American Art, 1915–1941," in Diana Murphy, ed., *Precisionism in America 1915–1941: Reordering Reality* (New York: Abrams, 1994), 12.

22. Quoted in Karen Tsujimoto, *Images of America: Precisionist Painting and Modern Photography* (Seattle: University of Washington Press, 1982), 70.

23. Dorothy Norman, *Alfred Stieglitz: An American Seer* (Millerton, N.Y.: Aperture, 1973), 9–10.

24. Ibid., 161.

25. Pablo Picasso, "Statement to Simone Téry," in Harrison and Wood, *Art in Theory, 1900–2000*, 649.

26. Quoted in Roland Penrose, *Picasso: His Life and Work*, rev. ed. (New York: Harper & Row, 1971), 311.

27. Quoted in Matthias Eberle, *World War I and the Weimar Artists: Dix, Grosz, Beckmann, Schlemmer* (New Haven, Conn.: Yale University Press, 1985), 54.

28. Ibid., 22.

29. Ibid., 42.

30. Quoted in William S. Rubin, *Dada, Surrealism, and Their Heritage* (New York: Museum of Modern Art, 1968), 64.

31. Quoted in Hamilton, *Painting and Sculpture*, 392.

32. Quoted in Richter, *Dada*, 155.

33. Ibid., 159.

34. Quoted in Rubin, *Dada, Surrealism*, 111.

35. Quoted in Hunter, Jacobus, and Wheeler, *Modern Art*, 179.

36. Quoted in William S. Rubin, *Miró in the Collection of the Museum of Modern Art* (New York: Museum of Modern Art, 1973), 32.

37. Translated by Norbert Guterman, quoted in Chipp, *Theories of Modern Art*, 182–186.

38. Translated by Howard Dearstyne, in Robert L. Herbert, *Modern Artists on Art*, 2d ed. (Mineola, N.Y.: Dover, 2000), 117.

39. Ibid., 124.

40. Translated by Herbert Read and Leslie Martin, quoted in Chipp, *Theories of Modern Art*, 325–330.

41. Translated by Nicholas Bullock, quoted in Harrison and Wood, *Art in Theory, 1900–2000*, 281.

42. Quoted in Kenneth Frampton, *Modern Architecture: A Critical History*, 3d ed. (New York: Thames & Hudson, 1992), 147.

43. Quoted in Michel Seuphor, *Piet Mondrian: Life and Work* (New York: Abrams, 1956), 117.

44. Piet Mondrian, *Plastic Art and Pure Plastic Art* (1937), quoted in Hamilton, *Painting and Sculpture*, 319.

45. Mondrian, quoted in Chipp, *Theories of Modern Art*, 349.

46. Ibid., 350.

47. Quoted in H. H. Arnason and Peter Kalb, *History of Modern Art*, 5th ed. (Upper Saddle River, N.J.: Prentice Hall, 2004), 154.

48. Quoted in Robert L. Herbert, *Modern Artists on Art*, 2d ed. (Mineola, N.Y.: Dover, 2000), 173.

49. Ibid., 177.

50. Quoted in Vivian Endicott Barnett, "Banned German Art: Reception and Institutional Support of Modern German Art in the United States, 1933–45," in Stephanie Barron, *Exiles and Emigrés: The Flight of European Artists from Hitler* (Los Angeles: Los Angeles County Museum of Art, 1997), 283.

51. Quoted in Milton Meltzer, *Dorothea Lange: A Photographer's Life* (New York: Farrar, Straus & Giroux, 1978), 133, 220.

52. Quoted in Frances K. Pohl, *Ben Shahn: New Deal Artist in a Cold War Climate, 1947–1954* (Austin: University of Texas Press, 1989), 159.

53. Quoted in Henry Louis Gates Jr., "New Negroes, Migration, and Cultural Exchange," in Elizabeth Hutton Turner, ed., *Jacob Lawrence: The Migration Series* (Washington, D.C.: Phillips Collection, 1993), 20.

54. Wanda M. Corn, *Grant Wood: The Regionalist Vision* (New Haven, Conn.: Yale University Press, 1983), 131.

55. Quoted in Matthew Baigell, *A Concise History of American Painting and Sculpture* (New York: Harper & Row, 1984), 264.

56. Quoted in Hans L. Jaffé, *De Stijl* (New York: Abrams, 1971), 185–188.

57. Piet Mondrian, *Dialogue on the New Plastic* (1919). Translated by Harry Holzman and Martin S. James, in Harrison and Wood, *Art in Theory, 1900–2000*, 285.

58. Walter Gropius, from *The Manifesto of the Bauhaus*, April 1919.

59. Ibid.

60. Ibid.

61. Quoted in John Willett, *Art and Politics in the Weimar Period: The New Sobriety, 1917–1933* (New York: Da Capo, 1978), 119.

62. Quoted in Wayne Craven, *American Art: History and Culture* (Madison, Wis.: Brown & Benchmark, 1994), 403.

63. Quoted in Vincent Scully Jr., *Frank Lloyd Wright* (New York: Braziller, 1960), 18.

64. Quoted in Edgar Kauffmann, ed., *Frank Lloyd Wright: An American Architect* (New York: Horizon, 1955), 205, 208.

65. Quoted in Philip Johnson, *Mies van der Rohe*, rev. ed. (New York: Museum of Modern Art, 1954), 200–201.

Chapter 36

1. Dawn Ades and Andrew Forge, *Francis Bacon* (London: Thames & Hudson, 1985), 8; and David Sylvester, *The Brutality of Fact: Interviews with Francis Bacon*, 3d ed. (London: Thames & Hudson, 1987), 182.

2. Clement Greenberg, "Toward a Newer Laocoon," *Partisan Review* 7, no. 4 (July–August 1940): 305.

3. Clement Greenberg, "Sculpture in Our Time," *Arts Magazine* 32, no. 9 (June 1956): 22.

4. Marcus Rothko and Adolph Gottlieb, quoted in Edward Alden Jewell, "The Realm of Art: A New Platform and Other Matters: 'Globalism' Pops into View," *New York Times*, June 13, 1943, 9.

5. Reprinted in Harold Rosenberg, *The Tradition of the New* (New York: Horizon, 1959), 25.

6. Quoted in Thomas Hess, *Barnett Newman* (New York: Walker and Company, 1969), 51.

7. Quoted in John P. O'Neill, ed., *Barnett Newman: Selected Writings and Interviews* (New York: Knopf, 1990), 108.

8. Rothko and Gottlieb, 9.

9. Quoted in Selden Rodman, *Conversations with Artists* (New York: Devin-Adair, 1957), 93–94.

10. Clement Greenberg, "Recentness of Sculpture," in Gregory Battcock, ed., *Minimal Art: A Critical Anthology* (New York: Dutton, 1968), 183–184.

11. Louise Nevelson, quoted in John Gordon, *Louise Nevelson* (New York: Praeger, 1967), 12.

12. Quoted in Deborah Wye, *Louise Bourgeois* (New York: Museum of Modern Art, 1982), 22.

13. Ibid., 25.

14. Quoted in Lucy Lippard, *Eva Hesse* (New York: New York University Press, 1976), 165.

15. Ibid., 56.

16. Quoted in Richard Francis, *Jasper Johns* (New York: Abbeville, 1984), 21.

17. Andy Warhol, *The Philosophy of Andy Warhol* (New York: Harcourt Brace Jovanovich, 1975), 100.

18. Quoted in Christine Lindey, *Superrealist Painting and Sculpture* (London: Orbis, 1980), 50.

19. Ibid., 130.

20. Fredric Jameson, "Postmodernism and Consumer Society," in Hal Foster, ed., *The Anti-Aesthetic: Essays on Postmodern Culture* (Port Townsend, Wash.: Bay, 1983), 113.

21. Quoted in Grace Glueck, "Susan Rothenberg: New Outlook for a Visionary Artist," *New York Times Magazine*, July 22, 1984, 20.

22. Quoted in *Walker Art Center: Painting and Sculpture from the Collection* (Minneapolis: Walker Art Center, 1990), 435.

23. Quoted in Susanna Torruella Leval, "Recapturing History: The (Un)official Story in Contemporary Latin American Art," *Art Journal* 51, no. 4 (Winter 1992): 74.

24. Ibid.

25. Hannah Wilke, "Visual Prejudice," in *Hannah Wilke: A Retrospective* (Columbia: University of Missouri Press, 1989), 141.

26. Quoted in Donald Hall, *Corporal Politics* (Cambridge: MIT List Visual Arts Center, 1993), 46.

27. Kobena Mercer, "Black Hair/Style Politics," in Russell Ferguson, Martha Gever, Trinh T. Minh-ha, and Cornel West, eds., *Out There: Marginalization and Contemporary Culture* (New York: New Museum of Contemporary Art, 1990), 248–249.

28. Ibid.

29. Jaune Quick-to-See Smith and Harmony Hammond, *Women of Sweetgrass: Cedar and Sage* (New York: American Indian Center, 1984), 97.

30. Quoted in Richard Marshall and Robert Mapplethorpe, *50 New York Artists* (San Francisco: Chronicle, 1986), 448–449.

31. Quoted in Mary Jane Jacob, *Magdalena Abakanowicz* (New York: Abbeville, 1982), 94.

32. Peter Blake, *Frank Lloyd Wright* (Harmondsworth: Penguin, 1960), 115.

33. Quoted in "Vietnam Memorial: America Remembers," *National Geographic* 167, no. 5 (May 1985): 557.

34. Quoted in Nancy Holt, ed., *The Writings of Robert Smithson* (New York: New York University Press, 1975), 111.

35. Quoted in Calvin Tomkins, "The Art World: *Tilted Arc*," *New Yorker*, May 20, 1985, 100.

36. Quoted in H. H. Arnason and Peter Kalb, *History of Modern Art*, 5th ed. (Upper Saddle River, N.J.: Prentice Hall, 2004), 489.

37. Quoted in Barbara Haskell, *Blam! The Explosion of Pop, Minimalism, and Performance 1958–1964* (New York: Whitney Museum of American Art, 1984), 53.

38. Jiro Yoshihara, "Gutai Art Manifesto" (1956), translated by Reiko Tomii, in Alexandra Munroe, *Japanese Art after 1945: Scream against the Sky* (New York: Abrams, 1994), 370.

39. Quoted in Bruce McPherson, ed., *More Than Meat Joy: Complete Performance Works and Selected Writings* (New Paltz, N.Y.: Documentext, 1979), 52.

40. Quoted in Caroline Tisdall, *Joseph Beuys* (New York: Thames & Hudson, 1979), 6.

41. Quoted in "Joseph Kosuth: Art as Idea as Idea," in Jeanne Siegel, ed., *Artwords: Discourse on the 60s and 70s* (Ann Arbor, Mich.: UMI Research Press, 1985), 221, 225.

42. Quoted in Brenda Richardson, *Bruce Nauman: Neons* (Baltimore: Baltimore Museum of Art, 1982), 20.

GLOSSARY

à la grecque—French, "in Greek style."

a secco—Italian, "dried." See *fresco*.

abacus—The uppermost portion of the *capital* of a *column*, usually a thin slab.

abbess—See *abbey*.

abbey—A religious community under the direction of an abbot (for monks) or an abbess (for nuns).

abbot—See *abbey*.

abhaya—See *mudra*.

abrasion—The rubbing or grinding of stone or another material to produce a smooth finish.

Abstract Expressionism—The first major American avant-garde movement, Abstract Expressionism emerged in New York City in the 1940s. The artists produced *abstract* paintings that expressed their state of mind and that they hoped would strike emotional chords in viewers. The movement developed along two lines: *gestural abstraction* and *chromatic abstraction*.

acropolis—Greek, "high city." In ancient Greece, usually the site of the city's most important temple(s).

action painting—Also called *gestural abstraction*. The kind of *Abstract Expressionism* practiced by Jackson Pollock, in which the emphasis was on the creation process, the artist's gesture in making art. Pollock poured liquid paint in linear webs on his canvases, which he laid out on the floor, thereby physically surrounding himself in the painting during its creation.

additive light—Natural light, or sunlight, the sum of all the wavelengths of the visible *spectrum*. See also *subtractive light*.

additive sculpture—A kind of sculpture *technique* in which materials (for example, clay) are built up or "added" to create form.

adobe—The clay used to make a kind of sun-dried mud brick of the same name; a building made of such brick.

aerial perspective—See *perspective*.

agora—An open square or space used for public meetings or business in ancient Greek cities.

ahu—A stone platform on which the *moai* of Easter Island stand. Ahu marked burial sites or served ceremonial purposes.

'ahu 'ula—A Hawaiian feather cloak.

airbrush—A tool that uses compressed air to spray paint onto a surface.

aisle—The portion of a *basilica* flanking the *nave* and separated from it by a row of *columns* or *piers*.

akua'ba—"Akua's child." A Ghanaian image of a young girl.

ala (pl. **alae**)—One of a pair of rectangular recesses at the back of the *atrium* of a Roman house.

album leaf—A painting on a single sheet of paper for a collection stored in an album.

alchemy—The medieval study of seemingly magical changes, especially chemical changes.

altar frontal—A decorative panel on the front of a church altar.

altarpiece—A panel, painted or sculpted, situated above and behind an altar. See also *retable*.

alternate-support system—In church architecture, the use of alternating wall supports in the *nave*, usually *piers* and *columns* or *compound piers* of alternating form.

amalaka—In Hindu temple design, the large flat disk with ribbed edges surmounting the beehive-shaped tower.

Amazonomachy—In Greek mythology, the battle between the Greeks and Amazons.

ambo—A church *pulpit* for biblical readings.

ambulatory—A covered walkway, outdoors (as in a church *cloister*) or indoors; especially the passageway around the *apse* and the *choir* of a church. In Buddhist architecture, the passageway leading around the *stupa* in a *chaitya hall*.

amphiprostyle—A *classical* temple *plan* in which the *columns* are placed across both the front and back but not along the sides.

amphitheater—Greek, "double theater." A Roman building type resembling two Greek theaters put together. The Roman amphitheater featured a continuous elliptical *cavea* around a central *arena*.

amphora—An ancient Greek two-handled jar used for general storage purposes, usually to hold wine or oil.

amulet—An object worn to ward off evil or to aid the wearer.

Analytic Cubism—The first phase of *Cubism*, developed jointly by Pablo Picasso and Georges Braque, in which the artists analyzed form from every possible vantage point to combine the various views into one pictorial whole.

anamorphic image—A distorted image that must be viewed by some special means (such as a mirror) to be recognized.

ancien régime—French, "old order." The term used to describe the political, social, and religious order in France before the Revolution at the end of the 18th century.

antae—The molded projecting ends of the walls forming the *pronaos* or *opisthodomos* of an ancient Greek temple.

ante legem—Latin, "before the law." In Christian thought, the period before Moses received the Ten Commandments. See also *sub lege*.

apadana—The great audience hall in ancient Persian palaces.

apostle—Greek, "messenger." One of the 12 disciples of Jesus.

apotheosis—Elevated to the rank of gods, or the ascent to heaven.

apoxyomenos—Greek, "athlete scraping oil from his body."

apse—A recess, usually semicircular, in the wall of a building, commonly found at the east end of a church.

apsidal—Rounded; *apse*-shaped.

arcade—A series of *arches* supported by *piers* or *columns*.

Arcadian (adj.)—In Renaissance and later art, depictions of an idyllic place of rural peace and simplicity. Derived from Arcadia, an ancient district of the central Peloponnesos in southern Greece.

arch—A curved structural member that spans an opening and is generally composed of wedge-shaped blocks (*voussoirs*) that transmit the downward pressure laterally. See also *thrust*.

Archaic—The artistic style of 600–480 BCE in Greece, characterized in part by the use of the *composite view* for painted and *relief* figures and of Egyptian stances for statues.

Archaic smile—The smile that appears on all *Archaic* Greek statues from about 570 to 480 BCE. The smile is the Archaic sculptor's way of indicating that the person portrayed is alive.

architrave—The *lintel* or lowest division of the *entablature;* also called the epistyle.

archivolt—The continuous molding framing an *arch.* In *Romanesque* and *Gothic* architecture, one of the series of concentric bands framing the *tympanum.*

arcuated—*Arch-*shaped.

arena—In a Roman *amphitheater,* the central area where bloody *gladiatorial* combats and other boisterous events took place.

armature—The crossed, or diagonal, *arches* that form the skeletal framework of a *Gothic rib vault.* In sculpture, the framework for a clay form.

arriccio—In *fresco* painting, the first layer of rough lime plaster applied to the wall.

Art Deco—Descended from *Art Nouveau,* this movement of the 1920s and 1930s sought to upgrade industrial design as a "fine art" and to work new materials into decorative patterns that could be either machined or handcrafted. Characterized by streamlined, elongated, and symmetrical design.

Art Nouveau—French, "new art." A late-19th- and early-20th-century art movement whose proponents tried to synthesize all the arts in an effort to create art based on natural forms that could be mass produced by technologies of the industrial age. The movement had other names in other countries: Jugendstil in Austria and Germany, Modernismo in Spain, and Floreale in Italy.

asceticism—Self-discipline and self-denial.

ashlar masonry—Carefully cut and regularly shaped blocks of stone used in construction, fitted together without mortar.

assemblage—An artwork constructed from already existing objects.

asye usu—Baule (Côte d'Ivoire) bush spirits.

atlantid—A male figure that functions as a supporting *column.* See also *caryatid.*

atlatl—Spear-thrower, the typical weapon of the Toltecs of ancient Mexico.

atmospheric perspective—See *perspective.*

atrium—The central reception room of a Roman house that is partly open to the sky. Also the open, *colonnaded* court in front of and attached to a Christian *basilica.*

attic—The uppermost story of a building, *triumphal arch,* or city gate.

attribute—(n.) The distinctive identifying aspect of a person, for example, an object held, an associated animal, or a mark on the body. (v.) To make an *attribution.*

attribution—Assignment of a work to a maker or makers.

automatism—In painting, the process of yielding oneself to instinctive motions of the hands after establishing a set of conditions (such as size of paper or medium) within which a work is to be created.

avant-garde—French, "advance guard" (in a platoon). Late-19th- and 20th-century artists who emphasized innovation and challenged established convention in their work. Also used as an adjective.

avatar—A manifestation of a deity incarnated in some visible form in which the deity performs a sacred function on earth. In Hinduism, an incarnation of a god.

axial plan—See *plan.*

axis mundi—Latin, "axis of the universe." In South Asia, a tall pillar planted deep in the ground, connecting earth and sky.

backstrap loom—A simple Andean loom featuring a belt or backstrap encircling the waist of the seated weaver.

bai—An elaborately painted men's ceremonial house on Belau (formerly Palau) in the Caroline Islands of Micronesia.

baldacchino—A canopy on *columns,* frequently built over an altar. The term derives from *baldacco.*

baldacco—Italian, "silk from Baghdad." See *baldacchino.*

baldric—A sashlike belt worn over one shoulder and across the chest to support a sword.

baptism—The Christian bathing ceremony in which an infant or a convert becomes a member of the Christian community.

baptistery—In Christian architecture, the building used for *baptism,* usually situated next to a church. Also, the designated area or hall within a church for baptismal rites.

bar tracery—See *tracery.*

baray—One of the large reservoirs laid out around Cambodian *wats* that served as means of transportation as well as irrigation. A network of canals connected the reservoirs.

Baroque—The traditional blanket designation for European art from 1600 to 1750. The stylistic term *Baroque,* which describes art that features dramatic theatricality and elaborate ornamentation in contrast to the simplicity and orderly rationality of *Renaissance art,* is most appropriately applied to Italian art of this period. The term derives from *barroco.*

barrel vault—See *vault.*

barroco—Portuguese, "irregularly shaped pearl." See *Baroque.*

base—In ancient Greek architecture, the molded projecting lowest part of *Ionic* and *Corinthian columns.* (*Doric* columns do not have bases.)

basilica—In Roman architecture, a public building for legal and other civic proceedings, rectangular in plan with an entrance usually on a long side. In Christian architecture, a church somewhat resembling the Roman basilica, usually entered from one end and with an *apse* at the other.

bas-relief—See *relief.*

batik—An Indonesian fabric-dyeing technique using melted wax to form patterns the dye cannot penetrate.

battlement—A low parapet at the top of a circuit wall in a fortification.

Bauhaus—A *school* of architecture in Germany in the 1920s under the aegis of Walter Gropius, who emphasized the unity of art, architecture, and design.

bay—The space between two columns, or one unit in the *nave arcade* of a church; also, the passageway in an *arcuated* gate.

beam—A horizontal structural member that carries the load of the superstructure of a building; a timber *lintel.*

Beaux-Arts—An architectural *style* of the late 19th and early 20th centuries in France. Based on ideas taught at the École des Beaux-Arts in Paris, the Beaux-Arts style incorporated classical principles, such as symmetry in design, and included extensive exterior ornamentation.

belvedere—Italian, "beautiful view." A building or other structure with a view of a *landscape* or seascape.

ben-ben—A pyramidal stone; a fetish of the Egyptian god Re.

benday dots—Named after the newspaper printer Benjamin Day, the benday dot system involves the modulation of *colors* through the placement and size of colored dots.

benedictional—A Christian religious book containing bishops' blessings.

bent-axis plan—A *plan* that incorporates two or more angular changes of direction, characteristic of Sumerian architecture.

bestiary—A collection of illustrations of real and imaginary animals.

bhakti—In Buddhist thought, the adoration of a personalized deity (*bodhisattva*) as a means of achieving unity with it; love felt by the devotee for the deity. In Hinduism, the devout, selfless direction of all tasks and activities of life to the service of one god.

Bharat Mata—Mother India; the female personification of India.

bhumisparsha—See *mudra.*

bi—In ancient China, jade disks carved as ritual objects for burial with the dead. They were often decorated with piercings that extended entirely through the object, as well as with surface carvings.

bichrome—Two-color.

bieri—The wooden *reliquary* guardian figures of the Fang in Gabon and Cameroon.

bilateral symmetry—Having the same *forms* on either side of a central axis.

bilingual vases—Experimental Greek vases produced for a short time in the late sixth century BCE; one side featured *black-figure* decoration, the other *red-figure.*

Biomorphic Surrealism—See *Surrealism.*

bisj pole—An elaborately carved pole constructed from the trunk of the mangrove tree. The Asmat people of southwestern New Guinea created bisj poles to indicate their intent to avenge a relative's death.

black-figure painting—In early Greek pottery, the silhouetting of dark figures against a light background of natural, reddish clay, with linear details *incised* through the silhouettes.

blind arcade—An *arcade* having no true openings, applied as decoration to a wall surface.

block statue—In ancient Egyptian sculpture, a cubic stone image with simplified body parts.

bocio—A Fon (Republic of Benin) empowerment figure.

bodhisattva—In Buddhist thought, a potential Buddha who chooses not to achieve enlightenment in order to help save humanity.

Book of Hours—A Christian religious book for private devotion containing prayers to be read at specified times of the day.

boshan—A Chinese incense burner.

boss—A circular knob.

bottega—An artist's studio-shop.

braccia—Italian, "arm." A unit of measurement; 1 braccia equals 23 inches.

breakfast piece—A *still life* that includes bread and fruit.

breviary—A Christian religious book of selected daily prayers and Psalms.

brocade—The weaving together of threads of different colors.

bucranium (pl. **bucrania**)—Latin, "bovine skull." A common motif in classical architectural ornament.

Buddha triad—A three-figure group with a central Buddha flanked on each side by a *bodhisattva.*

buon fresco—See *fresco.*

burgher—A middle-class citizen.

burin—A pointed tool used for *engraving* or *incising.*

buttress—An exterior masonry structure that opposes the lateral *thrust* of an *arch* or a *vault.* A pier buttress is a solid mass of masonry. A flying buttress consists typically of an inclined member carried on an arch or a series of arches and a solid buttress to which it transmits lateral thrust.

byobu—Japanese painted folding screens.

Byzantine—The art, territory, history, and culture of the Eastern Christian Empire and its capital of Constantinople (ancient Byzantium).

caduceus—In ancient Greek mythology, a magical rod entwined with serpents, the attribute of Hermes (Roman, Mercury), the messenger of the gods.

caldarium—The hot-bath section of a Roman bathing establishment.

caliph(s)—Islamic rulers, regarded as successors of Muhammad.

calligrapher—One who practices *calligraphy.*

calligraphy—Greek, "beautiful writing." Handwriting or penmanship, especially elegant writing as a decorative art.

calotype—From the Greek *kalos,* "beautiful." A photographic process in which a positive image is made by shining light through a negative image onto a sheet of sensitized paper.

came—A lead strip in a *stained-glass* window that joins separate pieces of colored glass.

camera lucida—Latin, "lighted room." A device in which a small lens projects the image of an object downward onto a sheet of paper.

camera obscura—Latin, "dark room." An ancestor of the modern camera in which a tiny pinhole, acting as a lens, projects an image on a screen, the wall of a room, or the ground-glass wall of a box; used by artists in the 17th, 18th, and early 19th centuries as an aid in drawing from nature.

campanile—A bell tower of a church, usually, but not always, freestanding.

canon—A rule, for example, of proportion. The ancient Greeks considered beauty to be a matter of "correct" proportion and sought a canon of proportion, for the human figure and for buildings. The fifth-century BCE sculptor Polykleitos wrote the *Canon,* a treatise incorporating his formula for the perfectly proportioned statue.

canon table—A concordance, or matching, of the corresponding passages of the four *Gospels* as compiled by Eusebius of Caesarea in the fourth century.

canopic jar—In ancient Egypt, the container in which the organs of the deceased were placed for later burial with the mummy.

capital—The uppermost member of a *column,* serving as a transition from the *shaft* to the *lintel.* In classical architecture, the form of the capital varies with the *order.*

Capitolium—An ancient Roman temple dedicated to the gods Jupiter, Juno, and Minerva.

capriccio—Italian, "originality." One of several terms used in Italian *Renaissance* literature to praise the originality and talent of artists.

cardo—The north-south street in a Roman town, intersecting the *decumanus* at right angles.

Caroline minuscule—The alphabet that *Carolingian* scribes perfected, from which the modern English alphabet was developed.

Carolingian (adj.)—Pertaining to the empire of Charlemagne (Latin, "Carolus Magnus") and his successors.

carpet page—In early medieval manuscripts, a decorative page resembling a textile.

cartography—The art of mapmaking.

cartoon—In painting, a full-size preliminary drawing from which a painting is made.

carving—A *technique* of sculpture in which the artist cuts away material (for example, from a stone block) in order to create a *statue* or a *relief.*

caryatid—A female figure that functions as a supporting *column.* See also *atlantid.*

cassone (pl. **cassoni**)—A carved chest, often painted or gilded, popular in Renaissance Italy for the storing of household clothing.

castellum—See *westwork.*

casting—A sculptural *technique* in which the artist pours liquid metal, plaster, clay or another material into a *mold.* When the material dries, the sculptor removes the cast piece from the mold.

castrum—A Roman military encampment.

catacombs—Subterranean networks of rock-cut galleries and chambers designed as cemeteries for the burial of the dead.

cathedra—Latin, "seat." See *cathedral.*

cathedral—A bishop's church. The word derives from *cathedra,* referring to the bishop's chair.

cavea—Latin, "hollow place or cavity." The seating area in ancient Greek and Roman theaters and *amphitheaters.*

celadon—A Chinese-Korean pottery *glaze,* fired in an oxygen-deprived kiln to a characteristic gray-green or pale blue color.

cella—The chamber at the center of an ancient temple; in a classical temple, the room (Greek, *naos*) in which the *cult statue* usually stood.

celt—In Olmec Mexico, an ax-shaped form made of polished jade; generally, a prehistoric metal or stone implement shaped like a chisel or ax head.

centaur—In ancient Greek mythology, a creature with the front or top half of a human and the back or bottom half of a horse.

centauromachy—In ancient Greek mythology, the battle between the Greeks and *centaurs.*

central plan—See *plan.*

cestrum—A small spatula used in *encaustic* painting.

chacmool—A Mesoamerican statuary type depicting a fallen warrior on his back with a receptacle on his chest for sacrificial offerings.

chaitya hall—A South Asian rock-cut temple hall having a votive *stupa* at one end.

chakra—The Buddha's wheel, set in motion at Sarnath.

chakravartin—In South Asia, the ideal king, the Universal Lord who ruled through goodness.

chamfer—The surface formed by cutting off a corner of a board or post; a bevel.

chancel arch—The arch separating the chancel (the *apse* or *choir*) or the *transept* from the *nave* of a basilica or church.

Chan—See *Zen.*

chantry—An endowed chapel for the chanting of the mass for the founder of the chapel.

chaplet—A metal pin used in hollow-casting to connect the *investment* with the clay core.

chapter house—The meeting hall in a *monastery.*

characters—In Chinese writing, signs that record spoken words.

chartreuse—A Carthusian *monastery.*

charun—An Etruscan death demon.

chasing—The engraving or embossing of metal.

château (pl. **châteaux**)—French, "castle." A luxurious country residence for French royalty, developed from medieval castles.

chatra—See *yasti.*

chiaroscuro—In drawing or painting, the treatment and use of light and dark, especially the gradations of light that produce the effect of *modeling.*

chiaroscuro woodcut—A *woodcut* technique using two blocks of wood instead of one. The printmaker carves and inks one block in the usual way in order to produce a traditional black-and-white print. Then the artist cuts a second block consisting of broad highlights that can be inked in gray or color and printed over the first block's impression.

chigi—Decorative extensions of the *rafters* at each end of the roof of a Japanese shrine.

chimera—A monster of Greek invention with the head and body of a lion and the tail of a serpent. A second head, that of a goat, grows out of one side of the body.

chisel—A tool with a straight blade at one end for cutting and shaping stone or wood.

chiton—A Greek tunic, the essential (and often only) garment of both men and women, the other being the *himation,* or mantle.

choir—The space reserved for the clergy and singers in the church, usually east of the *transept* but, in some instances, extending into the *nave.*

Christogram—The three initial letters (chi-rho-iota, or ☧) of Christ's name in Greek, which came to serve as a monogram for Christ.

chromatic abstraction—A kind of *Abstract Expressionism* that focuses on the emotional resonance of color, as exemplified by the work of Barnett Newman and Mark Rothko.

chronology—In art history, the dating of art objects and buildings.

chryselephantine—Fashioned of gold and ivory.

circumambulation—In Buddhist worship, walking around the *stupa* in a clockwise direction, a process intended to bring the worshiper into harmony with the cosmos.

cire perdue—See *lost-wax process.*

cista (pl. **cistae**)—An Etruscan cylindrical container made of sheet bronze with cast handles and feet, often with elaborately engraved bodies, used for women's toiletry articles.

city-state—An independent, self-governing city.

Classical—The art and culture of ancient Greece between 480 and 323 BCE. Lowercase *classical* refers more generally to Greco-Roman art and culture.

clerestory—The *fenestrated* part of a building that rises above the roofs of the other parts. The oldest known clerestories are Egyptian. In Roman *basilicas* and medieval churches, clerestories are the windows that form the *nave's* uppermost level below the timber ceiling or the *vaults.*

cloison—French, "partition." A cell made of metal wire or a narrow metal strip soldered edge-up to a metal base to hold *enamel,* semiprecious stones, pieces of colored glass, or glass paste fired to resemble sparkling jewels.

cloisonné—A decorative metalwork technique employing *cloisons;* also, decorative brickwork in later Byzantine architecture.

cloister—A *monastery* courtyard, usually with covered walks or *ambulatories* along its sides.

cluster pier—See *compound pier.*

codex (pl. **codices**)—Separate pages of *vellum* or *parchment* bound together at one side; the predecessor of the modern book. The codex superseded the *rotulus.* In *Mesoamerica,* a painted and inscribed book on long sheets of bark paper or deerskin coated with fine white plaster and folded into accordion-like pleats.

coffer—A sunken panel, often ornamental, in a *vault* or a ceiling.

collage—A composition made by combining on a flat surface various materials, such as newspaper, wallpaper, printed text and illustrations, photographs, and cloth.

colonnade—A series or row of *columns,* usually spanned by *lintels.*

colonnette—A thin *column.*

colophon—An inscription, usually on the last page, giving information about a book's manufacture. In Chinese painting, written texts on attached pieces of paper or silk.

color—The value, or tonality, of a color is the degree of its lightness or darkness. The intensity, or saturation, of a color is its purity, its brightness or dullness. See also *primary colors, secondary colors,* and *complementary colors.*

color-field painting—A variant of *Post-Painterly Abstraction* in which artists sought to reduce painting to its physical essence by pouring diluted paint onto unprimed canvas and letting these pigments soak into the fabric, as exemplified by the work of Helen Frankenthaler and Morris Louis.

colorito—Italian, "colored" or "painted." A term used to describe the application of paint. Characteristic of the work of 16th-century Venetian artists who emphasized the application of paint as an important element of the creative process. Central Italian artists, in contrast, largely emphasized *disegno*—the careful design preparation based on preliminary drawing.

colossal order—An architectural design in which the *columns* or *pilasters* are two or more stories tall. Also called a giant order.

column—A vertical, weight-carrying architectural member, circular in cross-*section* and consisting of a *base* (sometimes omitted), a *shaft,* and a *capital.*

combines—The name American artist Robert Rauschenberg gave to his *assemblages* of painted passages and sculptural elements.

commedia dell'arte—A traditional Italian comic play performed by actors and musicians.

complementary colors—Those pairs of *colors,* such as red and green, that together embrace the entire spectrum. The complement of one of the three *primary colors* is a mixture of the other two.

compline—The last prayer of the day in a *Book of Hours.*

compose—See *composition.*

Composite capital—A capital combining *Ionic* volutes and *Corinthian* acanthus leaves, first used by the ancient Romans.

composite view—A convention of representation in which part of a figure is shown in profile and another part of the same figure is shown frontally; also called twisted perspective.

composition—The way in which an artist organizes *forms* in an artwork, either by placing shapes on a flat surface or arranging forms in space.

compound pier—A *pier* with a group, or cluster, of attached *shafts,* or *responds,* especially characteristic of *Gothic* architecture.

Conceptual Art—An American *avant-garde* art movement of the 1960s whose premise was that the "artfulness" of art lay in the artist's idea rather than its final expression.

conceptual representation—The representation of the fundamental distinguishing properties of a person or object, not the way a figure or object appears in space and light at a specific moment. See *composite view.*

concrete—A building material invented by the Romans and consisting of various proportions of lime mortar, volcanic sand, water, and small stones.

condottiere (pl. **condottieri**)—An Italian mercenary general.

confraternity—In Late Antiquity, an association of Christian families pooling funds to purchase property for burial. In late medieval Europe, an organization founded by laypersons who dedicated themselves to strict religious observances.

congregational mosque—A city's main *mosque,* designed to accommodate the entire Muslim population for the Friday noonday prayer. Also called the great mosque or Friday mosque.

connoisseur—An expert in *attributing* artworks to one artist rather than another. More generally, an expert on artistic *style.*

Constructivism—An early-20th-century Russian art movement formulated by Naum Gabo, who built up his sculptures piece by piece in space instead of carving or *modeling* them. In this way the sculptor worked with "volume of mass" and "volume of space" as different materials.

consuls—In the Roman Republic, the two chief magistrates.

continuous narration—The depiction of the same figure more than once in the same space at different stages of a story.

contour line—In art, a continuous line defining the outer shape of an object.

contrapposto—The disposition of the human figure in which one part is turned in opposition to another part (usually hips and legs one way, shoulders and chest another), creating a counterpositioning of the body about its central axis. Sometimes called "weight shift" because the weight of the body tends to be thrown to one foot, creating tension on one side and relaxation on the other.

corbel—A projecting wall member used as a support for some element in the superstructure. Also, *courses* of stone or brick in which each course projects beyond the one beneath it. Two such walls, meeting at the topmost course, create a corbeled *arch* or corbeled *vault.*

corbeled arch—See *corbel.*

corbeled vault—A *vault* formed by the piling of stone blocks in horizontal *courses,* cantilevered inward until the two walls meet in an *arch.*

Corinthian capital—A more ornate form than *Doric* or *Ionic;* it consists of a double row of acanthus leaves from which tendrils and flowers grow, wrapped around a bell-shaped *echinus.* Although this *capital* form is often cited as the distinguishing feature of the Corinthian *order,* no such order exists, in strict terms, but only this type of capital used in the *Ionic* order.

cornice—The projecting, crowning member of the *entablature* framing the *pediment;* also, any crowning projection.

corona civica—Latin, "civic crown." A Roman honorary wreath worn on the head.

course—In masonry construction, a horizontal row of stone blocks.

crenel—See *crenellation.*

crenellation—Alternating solid merlons and open crenels in the notched tops of walls, as in *battlements.*

crossing—The space in a *cruciform* church formed by the intersection of the *nave* and the *transept.*

cross-hatching—See *hatching.*

cross vault—See *vault.*

crossing square—The area in a church formed by the intersection (*crossing*) of a *nave* and a *transept* of equal width, often used as a standard *module* of interior proportion.

crossing tower—The tower over the *crossing* of a church.

cruciform—Cross-shaped.

Crusades—In medieval Europe, armed pilgrimages aimed at recapturing the Holy Land from the *Muslims.*

crypt—A *vaulted* space under part of a building, wholly or partly underground; in churches, normally the portion under an *apse.*

cubiculum (pl. **cubicula**)—A small cubicle or bedroom that opened onto the *atrium* of a Roman house. Also, a chamber in an Early Christian *catacomb* that served as a mortuary chapel.

Cubism—An early-20th-century art movement that rejected *naturalistic* depictions, preferring *compositions* of shapes and forms abstracted from the conventionally perceived world. See also *Analytic Cubism* and *Synthetic Cubism.*

cuerda seca—A type of polychrome tilework used in decorating Islamic buildings.

cuirass—A military leather breastplate.

cult statue—The statue of the deity that stood in the *cella* of an ancient temple.

cuneiform—Latin, "wedge-shaped." A system of writing used in ancient Mesopotamia, in which wedge-shaped characters were produced by pressing a *stylus* into a soft clay tablet, which was then baked or otherwise allowed to harden.

cuneus (pl. **cunei**)—In ancient Greek and Roman theaters and *amphitheaters,* the wedge-shaped section of stone benches separated by stairs.

cupola—An exterior architectural feature composed of a *drum* with a shallow cap; a *dome.*

cutaway—An architectural drawing that combines an exterior view with an interior view of part of a building.

Cycladic—The prehistoric art of the Aegean Islands around Delos, excluding Crete.

Cyclopean masonry—A method of stone construction, named after the mythical *Cyclopes,* using massive, irregular blocks without mortar, characteristic of the Bronze Age fortifications of Tiryns and other *Mycenaean* sites.

Cyclops (pl. **Cyclopes**)—A mythical Greek one-eyed giant.

cylinder seal—A cylindrical piece of stone usually about an inch or so in height, decorated with an *incised* design, so that a raised pattern is left when the seal is rolled over soft clay. In the ancient Near East, documents, storage jars, and other important possessions were signed, sealed, and identified in this way. Stamp seals are an earlier, flat form of seal used for similar purposes.

Dada—An early-20th-century art movement prompted by a revulsion against the horror of World War I. Dada embraced political anarchy, the

irrational, and the intuitive. A disdain for convention, often enlivened by humor or whimsy, is characteristic of the art the Dadaists produced.

Daedalic—The Greek *Orientalizing* sculptural style of the seventh century BCE named after the legendary artist Daedalus.

daguerreotype—A photograph made by an early method on a plate of chemically treated metal; developed by Louis J. M. Daguerre.

daimyo—Local lords who controlled small regions and owed obeisance to the *shogun* in the Japanese *shogunate* system.

damnatio memoriae—The Roman decree condemning those who ran afoul of the Senate. Those who suffered damnatio memoriae had their memorials demolished and their names erased from public inscriptions.

darshan—In Hindu worship, seeing images of the divinity and being seen by the divinity.

De Stijl—Dutch, "the style." An early-20th-century art movement (and magazine), founded by Piet Mondrian and Theo van Doesburg, whose members promoted utopian ideals and developed a simplified geometric style.

deconstruction—An analytical strategy developed in the late 20th century according to which all cultural "constructs" (art, architecture, literature) are "texts." People can read these texts in a variety of ways, but they cannot arrive at fixed or uniform meanings. Any interpretation can be valid, and readings differ from time to time, place to place, and person to person. For those employing this approach, deconstruction means destabilizing established meanings and interpretations while encouraging subjectivity and individual differences.

Deconstructivism—An architectural *style* using *deconstruction* as an analytical strategy. Deconstructivist architects attempt to disorient the observer by disrupting the conventional categories of architecture. The haphazard presentation of volumes, masses, planes, lighting, and so forth challenges the viewer's assumptions about *form* as it relates to function.

decumanus—The east-west street in a Roman town, intersecting the *cardo* at right angles.

decursio—The ritual circling of a Roman funerary pyre.

Deësis—Greek, "supplication." An image of Christ flanked by the figures of the Virgin Mary and Saint John the Baptist, who intercede on behalf of humankind.

demos—Greek, "the people," from which the word *democracy* is derived.

demotic—Late Egyptian writing.

denarius—The standard Roman silver coin from which the word *penny* ultimately derives.

Der Blaue Reiter—German, "the blue rider." An early-20th-century German *Expressionist* art movement founded by Vassily Kandinsky and Franz Marc. The artists selected the whimsical name because of their mutual interest in the color blue and horses.

dharma—In Buddhism, moral law based on the Buddha's teaching.

dharmachakra—See *mudra*.

dhyana—See *mudra*.

di sotto in sù—Italian, "from below upward." A *perspectival* view seen from below.

diagonal rib—See *rib*.

diaphragm arch—A transverse, wall-bearing *arch* that divides a *vault* or a ceiling into compartments, providing a kind of firebreak.

dictator—In the Roman Republic, the supreme magistrate with extraordinary powers, appointed during a crisis for a specified period. Julius Caesar eventually became *dictator perpetuo*, dictator for life.

dictator perpetuo—See *dictator*.

Die Brücke—German, "the bridge." An early-20th-century German *Expressionist* art movement under the leadership of Ernst Ludwig Kirchner. The group thought of itself as the bridge between the old age and the new.

Dilukai—A female figure with splayed legs, a common motif over the entrance to a Belau *bai*, serving as both guardian and fertility symbol.

dipteral—See *peristyle*.

diptych—A two-paneled painting or *altarpiece*; also, an ancient Roman, Early Christian, or Byzantine hinged writing tablet, often of ivory and carved on the external sides.

disegno—Italian, "drawing" and "design." *Renaissance* artists considered drawing to be the external physical manifestation (*disegno esterno*) of an internal intellectual idea of design (*disegno interno*).

disputatio—Latin, "logical argument." The philosophical methodology used in *Scholasticism*.

divisionism—See *pointillism*.

documentary evidence—In art history, the examination of written sources in order to determine the date of an artwork, the circumstances of its creation, or the identity of the artist(s) who made it.

doge—Duke; a ruler of the Republic of Venice, Italy.

dome—A hemispherical *vault*; theoretically, an *arch* rotated on its vertical axis. In *Mycenaean* architecture, domes are beehive-shaped.

domus—A Roman private house.

donor portrait—A portrait of the individual(s) who commissioned (donated) a religious work, for example, an *altarpiece*, as evidence of devotion.

Doric—One of the two systems (or *orders*) invented in ancient Greece for articulating the three units of the elevation of a *classical* building—the platform, the *colonnade*, and the superstructure (*entablature*). The Doric order is characterized by, among other features, *capitals* with funnel-shaped *echinuses*, *columns* without *bases*, and a *frieze* of *triglyphs* and *metopes*. See also *Ionic*.

doryphoros—Greek, "spear bearer."

dotaku—Ancient Japanese bronze ceremonial bells, usually featuring raised decoration.

double monastery—A *monastery* for both monks and nuns.

dressed masonry—Stone blocks shaped to the exact dimensions required, with smooth faces for a perfect fit.

dromos—The passage leading to a *tholos tomb*.

drum—One of the stacked cylindrical stones that form the *shaft* of a *column*. Also, the cylindrical wall that supports a *dome*.

dry painting—See *sand painting*.

drypoint—An *engraving* in which the design, instead of being cut into the plate with a *burin*, is scratched into the surface with a hard steel "pencil." See also *etching, intaglio*.

earthenware—Pottery made of clay that is fired at low temperatures and is slightly porous. Also, clay figurines and statues produced in the same manner.

earthworks—See *Environmental Art*.

eaves—The lower part of a roof that overhangs the wall.

echinus—The convex element of a *capital* directly below the *abacus*.

écorché—The representation of a nude body as if without skin.

edition—A set of impressions taken from a single print surface.

effigy mounds—Ceremonial mounds built in the shape of animals or birds by native North American peoples.

elevation—In architecture, a head-on view of an external or internal wall, showing its features and often other elements that would be visible beyond or before the wall.

emblema—The central framed figural panel of a *mosaic* floor.

embroidery—The technique of sewing threads onto a finished ground to form contrasting designs. Stem stitching employs short overlapping strands of thread to form jagged lines. Laid-and-couched work creates solid blocks of color.

empiricism—The search for knowledge based on observation and direct experience.

enamel—A decorative coating, usually colored, fused onto the surface of metal, glass, or ceramics.

encaustic—A painting *technique* in which pigment is mixed with melted wax and applied to the surface while the mixture is hot.

engaged column—A half-round *column* attached to a wall. See also *pilaster*.

engraving—The process of *incising* a design in hard material, often a metal plate (usually copper); also, the *print* or impression made from such a plate.

Enlightenment—The Western philosophy based on empirical evidence that dominated the 18th century. The Enlightenment was a new way of thinking critically about the world and about humankind, independently of religion, myth, or tradition.

ensi—A Sumerian ruler.

entablature—The part of a building above the *columns* and below the roof. The entablature has three parts: *architrave, frieze,* and *pediment*.

entasis—The convex profile (an apparent swelling) in the *shaft* of a *column*.

Environmental Art—An American art form that emerged in the 1960s. Often using the land itself as their material, Environmental artists construct monuments of great scale and minimal form. Permanent or impermanent, these works transform some section of the environment, calling attention both to the land itself and to the hand of the artist. Sometimes referred to as earthworks.

eravo—A ceremonial men's meetinghouse constructed by the Elema people in New Guinea.

escutcheon—An emblem bearing a coat of arms.

etching—A kind of *engraving* in which the design is *incised* in a layer of wax or varnish on a metal plate. The parts of the plate left exposed are then etched (slightly eaten away) by the acid in which the plate is immersed after incising. See also *drypoint, intaglio*.

Eucharist—In Christianity, the partaking of the bread and wine, which believers hold to be either Christ himself or symbolic of him.

evangelist—One of the four authors (Matthew, Mark, Luke, John) of the New Testament *Gospels*.

Events—See *Fluxus*.

exedra—Recessed area, usually semicircular.

exemplum virtutis—Latin, "example or model of virtue."

Expressionism (adj. **Expressionist**)—Twentieth-century art that is the result of the artist's unique inner or personal vision and that often has an emotional dimension. Expressionism contrasts with art focused on visually describing the empirical world.

facade—Usually, the front of a building; also, the other sides when they are emphasized architecturally.

faience—A low-fired opaque glasslike silicate.

fan vault—See *vault*.

fantasia—Italian, "imagination." One of several terms used in Italian *Renaissance* literature to praise the originality and talent of artists.

fasces—A bundle of rods with an ax attached, representing an emblem of authority in ancient Rome.

fauces—Latin, "jaws." In a Roman house, the narrow foyer leading to the *atrium*.

Fauves—French, "wild beasts." See *Fauvism*.

Fauvism—An early-20th-century art movement led by Henri Matisse. For the Fauves, color became the formal element most responsible for pictorial coherence and the primary conveyor of meaning.

Favrile—A type of leaded stained glass patented by Louis Comfort Tiffany in the late 19th century.

femmages—The name American artist Miriam Schapiro gave to her sewn *collages,* assembled from fabrics, quilts, buttons, sequins, lace trim, and rickrack collected at antique shows and fairs.

femme fatale—French, "fatal woman." A destructive temptress of men.

femme savante—French, "learned woman." The term used to describe the cultured hostesses of *Rococo* salons.

fenestra coeli—Latin, "window to Heaven."

fenestrated—Having windows.

fenestration—The arrangement of the windows of a building.

fête galante—French, "amorous festival." A type of *Rococo* painting depicting the outdoor amusements of French upper-class society.

feudalism—The medieval political, social, and economic system held together by the relationship between landholding *liege lords* and the *vassals* who were granted tenure of a portion of their land and in turn swore allegiance to the liege lord.

fibula (pl. **fibulae**)—A decorative pin, usually used to fasten garments.

fin-de-siècle—French, "end of the century." A period in Western cultural history from the end of the 19th century until just before World War I, when decadence and indulgence masked anxiety about an uncertain future.

findspot—Place where an artifact was found; *provenance*.

finial—A crowning ornament.

First Style mural—The earliest style of Roman *mural* painting. Also called the Masonry Style, because the aim of the artist was to imitate, using painted stucco *relief,* the appearance of costly marble panels.

Flamboyant—A Late French *Gothic* style of architecture superseding the *Rayonnant* style and named for the flamelike appearance of its pointed bar *tracery*.

flashing—In making *stained-glass* windows, fusing one layer of colored glass to another to produce a greater range of *colors*.

fleur-de-lis—A three-petaled iris flower; the royal flower of France.

Floreale—See *Art Nouveau*.

florin—The denomination of gold coin of *Renaissance* Florence that became an international currency for trade.

flute or **fluting**—Vertical channeling, roughly semicircular in cross-*section* and used principally on *columns* and *pilasters*.

Fluxus—A group of American, European, and Japanese artists of the 1960s who created *Performance Art*. Their performances, or Events, often focused on single actions, such as turning a light on and off or watching falling snow, and were more theatrical than *Happenings*.

flying buttress—See *buttress*.

folio—A page of a manuscript or book.

fons vitae—Latin, "fountain of life." A symbolic fountain of everlasting life.

foreshortening—The use of *perspective* to represent in art the apparent visual contraction of an object that extends back in space at an angle to the perpendicular plane of sight.

form—In art, an object's shape and structure, either in two dimensions (for example, a figure painted on a surface) or in three dimensions (such as a *statue*).

formal analysis—The visual analysis of artistic *form*.

formalism—Strict adherence to, or dependence on, stylized shapes and methods of *composition*. An emphasis on an artwork's visual elements rather than its subject.

forum—The public square of an ancient Roman city.

Fourth Style mural—In Roman *mural* painting, the Fourth Style marks a return to architectural *illusionism,* but the architectural vistas of the Fourth Style are irrational fantasies.

freedmen, freedwomen—In ancient and medieval society, men and women who had been freed from servitude, as opposed to having been born free.

freestanding sculpture—See *sculpture in the round*.

fresco—Painting on lime plaster, either dry (dry fresco, or fresco secco) or wet (true, or buon, fresco). In the latter method, the pigments are mixed with water and become chemically bound to the freshly laid lime plaster. Also, a painting executed in either method.

fresco secco—See *fresco*.

Friday mosque—See *congregational mosque*.

frieze—The part of the *entablature* between the *architrave* and the *cornice;* also, any sculptured or painted band in a building. See *register*.

frigidarium—The cold-bath section of a Roman bathing establishment.

frottage—A *technique* in which the artist rubs a crayon or another medium across a sheet of paper placed over a surface having a strong textural pattern.

furta sacra—Latin, "holy theft."

fusuma—Japanese painted sliding-door panels.

Futurism—An early-20th-century Italian art movement that championed war as a cleansing agent and that celebrated the speed and dynamism of modern technology.

garbha griha—Hindi, "womb chamber." In Hindu temples, the *cella,* the holy inner sanctum often housing the god's image or *symbol*.

genius—Latin, "spirit." In art, the personified spirit of a person or place.

genre—A *style* or category of art; also, a kind of painting that realistically depicts scenes from everyday life.

Geometric—The *style* of Greek art during the ninth and eighth centuries BCE, characterized by *abstract* geometric ornament and schematic figures.

German Expressionism—An early-20th-century regional Expressionist movement.

gesso—Plaster mixed with a binding material, used as the base coat for paintings on wood panels.

gestural abstraction—Also known as *action painting*. A kind of *abstract* painting in which the gesture, or act of painting, is seen as the subject of art. Its most renowned proponent was Jackson Pollock. See also *Abstract Expressionism*.

giant order—See *colossal order*.

gigantomachy—In ancient Greek mythology, the battle between gods and giants.

giornata (pl. **giornate**)—Italian, "day." The section of plaster that a *fresco* painter expects to complete in one session.

gladiator—An ancient Roman professional fighter, usually a slave, who competed in an *amphitheater*.

glaze—A vitreous coating applied to pottery to seal and decorate the surface; it may be colored, transparent, or opaque, and glossy or *matte*. In oil painting, a thin, transparent, or semitransparent layer applied over a *color* to alter it slightly.

glazier—A glassworker.

Gobelin tapestry—A *tapestry* produced on a vertical loom using a weaving *technique* in which no *weft* threads extend the full width of the fabric.

gold leaf—Gold beaten into tissue-paper-thin sheets that then can be applied to surfaces.

gopis—South Asian herdswomen.

gopuras—The massive, ornamented entrance gateway towers of southern Indian temple compounds.

gorget—A neck pendant, usually made of shell.

gorgon—In ancient Greek mythology, a hideous female demon with snake hair. Medusa, the most famous gorgon, was capable of turning anyone who gazed at her into stone.

Gospels—The four New Testament books that relate the life and teachings of Jesus.

Gothic—Originally a derogatory term named after the Goths, used to describe the history, culture, and art of western Europe in the 12th to 14th centuries. Typically divided into periods designated Early (1140–1194), High (1194–1300), and Late (1300–1500).

Grand Manner portraiture—A type of 18th-century portrait painting designed to communicate a person's grace and class through certain standardized conventions, such as the large scale of the figure relative to the canvas, the controlled pose, the landscape setting, and the low *horizon line*.

granulation—A decorative technique in which tiny metal balls (granules) are fused to a metal surface.

graver—An *engraving* tool. See also *burin*.

great mosque—See *congregational mosque*.

Greek cross—A cross with four arms of equal length.

griffin—A mythical animal that is part lion and part bird.

grisaille—A monochrome painting done mainly in neutral grays to simulate sculpture.

groin—The edge formed by the intersection of two barrel *vaults*.

groin vault—See *vault*.

ground line—In paintings and *reliefs,* a painted or carved baseline on which figures appear to stand.

guang—An ancient Chinese covered vessel, often in animal form, holding wine, water, grain, or meat for sacrificial rites.

guild—An association of merchants, craftspersons, or scholars in medieval and *Renaissance* Europe.

haboku—In Japanese art, a loose and rapidly executed painting *style* in which the ink seems to have been applied by flinging or splashing it onto the paper.

haiku—A 17-syllable Japanese poetic form.

halberd—A combination spear and battle-ax.

hall church—See *Hallenkirche.*

Hallenkirche—German, "hall church." A church design favored in Germany, but also used elsewhere, in which the *aisles* rise to the same height as the *nave.*

handscroll—In Asian art, a horizontal painted scroll that is unrolled right to left, section by section, and often used to present illustrated religious texts or *landscapes.*

hanging scroll—In Asian art, a vertical scroll hung on a wall with pictures mounted or painted directly on it.

haniwa—Sculpted fired pottery cylinders, modeled in human, animal, or other forms and placed on Japanese *tumuli* of the Kofun period.

Happenings—A term coined by American artist Allan Kaprow in the 1960s to describe loosely structured performances, whose creators were trying to suggest the aesthetic and dynamic qualities of everyday life; as actions, rather than objects, Happenings incorporate the fourth dimension (time).

hard-edge painting—A variant of *Post-Painterly Abstraction* that rigidly excluded all reference to gesture and incorporated smooth knife-edge geometric forms to express the notion that painting should be reduced to its visual components.

harmika—In Buddhist architecture, a stone fence or railing that encloses an area surmounting the *dome* of a *stupa* that represents one of the Buddhist heavens; from the center arises the *yasti.*

harpies—Mythological creatures of the underworld.

haruspex (pl. **haruspices**)—An Etruscan priest who foretells events by studying animal livers.

hatching—A series of closely spaced drawn or *engraved* parallel lines. Cross-hatching employs sets of lines placed at right angles.

heiau—A Hawaiian temple.

Helladic—The prehistoric art of the Greek mainland (*Hellas* in Greek).

Hellas—The ancient name of Greece.

Hellenes (adj. **Hellenic**)—The name the ancient Greeks called themselves as the people of *Hellas.*

Hellenistic—The term given to the art and culture of the roughly three centuries between the death of Alexander the Great in 323 BCE and the death of Queen Cleopatra in 30 BCE, when Egypt became a Roman province.

henge—An arrangement of *megalithic* stones in a circle, often surrounded by a ditch.

heraldic composition—A *composition* that is symmetrical on either side of a central figure.

herm—A bust on a quadrangular *pillar.*

Hevehe—An elaborate cycle of ceremonial activities performed by the Elema people of the Papuan Gulf region of New Guinea. Also, the large, ornate masks produced for and presented during these ceremonies.

Hiberno-Saxon—An art *style* that flourished in the *monasteries* of the British Isles in the early Middle Ages. Also called Insular.

hierarchy of scale—An artistic convention in which greater size indicates greater importance.

hieroglyphic—A system of writing using symbols or pictures.

high relief—See *relief.*

High-Tech—A contemporary architectural *style* calling for buildings that incorporate the latest innovations in engineering and technology and expose the structures' component parts.

Hijra—The flight of Muhammad from Mecca to Medina in 622, the year from which Islam dates its beginnings.

himation—An ancient Greek mantle worn by men and women over the *chiton* and draped in various ways.

Hippodamian plan—A city *plan* devised by Hippodamos of Miletos ca. 466 BCE, in which a strict grid was imposed on a site, regardless of the terrain, so that all streets would meet at right angles.

hiragana—A phonetic cursive script developed in Japan from Chinese characters; it came to be the primary script for Japanese court poetry.

historiated—Ornamented with representations, such as plants, animals, or human figures, that have a narrative—as distinct from a purely decorative—function.

hokkyo—Japanese, "Bridge of the Law." The third highest rank among Buddhist monks.

hookah—A Moroccan water pipe.

horizon line—See *perspective.*

hôtel—French, "town house."

hubris—Greek, "arrogant pride."

hue—The name of a *color.* See also *primary colors, secondary colors,* and *complementary colors.*

humanism—In the *Renaissance,* an emphasis on education and on expanding knowledge (especially of *classical* antiquity), the exploration of individual potential and a desire to excel, and a commitment to civic responsibility and moral duty.

hydria—An ancient Greek three-handled water pitcher.

hypaethral—A building having no *pediment* or roof, open to the sky.

hypostyle hall—A hall with a roof supported by *columns.*

icon—A portrait or image; especially in Byzantine churches, a panel with a painting of sacred personages that are objects of veneration. In the visual arts, a painting, a piece of sculpture, or even a building regarded as an object of veneration.

iconoclasm—The destruction of religious or sacred images. In Byzantium, the period from 726 to 843 when there was an imperial ban on such images. The destroyers of images were known as iconoclasts. Those who opposed such a ban were known as iconophiles.

iconoclast—See *iconoclasm.*

iconography—Greek, the "writing of images." The term refers both to the content, or subject, of an artwork and to the study of content in art. It also includes the study of the symbolic, often religious, meaning of objects, persons, or events depicted in works of art.

iconophile—See *iconoclasm.*

iconostasis—Greek, "icon stand." In Byzantine churches, a screen or a partition, with doors and many tiers of *icons,* separating the sanctuary from the main body of the church.

ikegobo—A Benin royal shrine.

illuminated manuscript—A luxurious handmade book with painted illustrations and decorations.

illusionism (adj. **illusionistic**)—The representation of the three-dimensional world on a two-dimensional surface in a manner that creates the illusion that the person, object, or place represented is three-dimensional. See also *perspective.*

imagines—In ancient Rome, wax portraits of ancestors.

imam—In Islam, the leader of collective worship.

impasto—A layer of thickly applied pigment.

imperator—Latin, "commander in chief," from which the word *emperor* derives.

impluvium—In a Roman house, the basin located in the *atrium* that collected rainwater.

impost block—The uppermost block of a wall or *pier* beneath the *springing* of an arch.

Impressionism—A late-19th-century art movement that sought to capture a fleeting moment, thereby conveying the elusiveness and impermanence of images and conditions.

in antis—In ancient Greek architecture, the area between the *antae.*

incise—To cut into a surface with a sharp instrument; also, a method of decoration, especially on metal and pottery.

incrustation—Wall decoration consisting of bright panels of different *colors.*

incubus—A demon believed in medieval times to prey, often sexually, on sleeping women.

indulgence—A religious pardon for a sin committed.

ingegno—Italian, "innate talent." One of several terms used in Italian *Renaissance* literature to praise the originality and talent of artists.

installation—An artwork that creates an artistic environment in a room or gallery.

insula (pl. **insulae**)—In Roman architecture, a multistory apartment house, usually made of brick-faced *concrete;* also refers to an entire city block.

Insular—See *Hiberno-Saxon.*

intaglio—A graphic technique in which the design is *incised,* or scratched, on a metal plate, either manually (*engraving, drypoint*) or chemically (*etching*). The incised lines of the design take the ink, making this the reverse of the *woodcut* technique.

intensity—See *color.*

interaxial or **intercolumniation**—The distance between the center of the lowest *drum* of a *column* and the center of the next.

intercolumniation—See *interaxial.*

internal evidence—In art history, the examination of what an artwork represents (people, clothing, hairstyles, and so on) in order to determine its date. Also, the examination of the *style* of an artwork to identify the artist who created it.

International Style—A *style* of 14th- and 15th-century painting begun by Simone Martini, who adapted the French *Gothic* manner to Sienese art fused with influences from Northern Europe. This style appealed to the aristocracy because of its brilliant *color,* lavish costumes, intricate ornamentation, and themes involving splendid processions of knights and ladies. Also, a style of 20th-century architecture associated with Le Corbusier, whose elegance of design came to influence the look of modern office buildings and skyscrapers.

intonaco—In *fresco* painting, the last layer of smooth lime plaster applied to the wall; the painting layer.

invenzione—Italian, "invention." One of several terms used in Italian *Renaissance* literature to praise the originality and talent of artists.

investment—In hollow-casting, the final clay *mold* applied to the exterior of the wax model.

Ionic—One of the two systems (or *orders*) invented in ancient Greece for articulating the three units of the elevation of a *classical* building: the platform, the *colonnade,* and the superstructure (*entablature*). The Ionic order is characterized by, among other features, *volutes, capitals, columns* with *bases,* and an uninterrupted *frieze.*

iron-wire lines—In ancient Chinese painting, thin brush lines suggesting tensile strength.

ivi p'o—Hollow, cylindrical bone or ivory ornaments produced in the Marquesas Islands (Polynesia).

iwan—In Islamic architecture, a *vaulted* rectangular recess opening onto a courtyard.

jambs—In architecture, the side posts of a doorway.

Japonisme—The French fascination with all things Japanese. Japonisme emerged in the second half of the 19th century.

jataka—Tales of the past lives of the Buddha. See also *sutra.*

joined-wood technique—A Japanese sculptural *technique* in which a statue is assembled from multiple wood blocks, each hollowed out to make the pieces lighter.

jomon—Japanese, "cord markings." A type of Japanese ceramic technique characterized by ropelike markings.

Jugendstil—See *Art Nouveau.*

junzi—Chinese, "superior person" or "gentleman." A person who is a model of Confucian behavior.

ka—In ancient Egypt, the immortal human life force.

Kaaba—Arabic, "cube." A small cubical building in Mecca, the Islamic world's symbolic center.

kami—Shinto deities or spirits, believed in Japan to exist in nature (mountains, waterfalls) and in charismatic people.

karesansui—Japanese dry-landscape gardening.

karma—In Vedic religions (see *Veda*), the ethical consequences of a person's life, which determine his or her fate.

katsina—An art form of Native Americans of the Southwest, the katsina doll represents benevolent supernatural spirits (katsinas) living in mountains and water sources.

katsuogi—Wooden logs placed at right angles to the *ridgepole* of a Japanese shrine to hold the thatched roof in place.

kautaha—Women's organizations in Tonga (Polynesia) that produce barkcloth.

keep—A fortified tower in a castle that served as a place of last refuge.

kente—Brightly colored patterned cloth woven by Asante men on horizontal looms in long narrow strips sewn together to form *toga*-like robes.

keystone—See *voussoir.*

khan—An Ottoman lord, or *sultan.*

khipu—Andean record-keeping device consisting of numerous knotted strings hanging from a main cord; the strings signified, by position and *color,* numbers and categories of things.

kiva—A square or circular underground structure that is the spiritual and ceremonial center of Pueblo Indian life.

kline (pl. **klinai**)—A couch or funerary bed. A type of *sarcophagus* with a reclining portrait of the deceased on its lid.

kogan—A *Shino* water jar.

kondo—Japanese, "golden hall." The main hall for worship in a Japanese Buddhist temple complex. The

kondo contained *statues* of the Buddha and the *bodhisattvas* to whom the temple was dedicated.

Koran—Islam's sacred book, composed of *surahs* (chapters) divided into verses.

kore (pl. **korai**)—Greek, "young woman." An *Archaic* Greek *statue* of a young woman.

koru—An unrolled spiral design used by the Maori of New Zealand in their *tattoos.*

kouros (pl. **kouroi**)—Greek, "young man." An *Archaic* Greek *statue* of a young man.

krater—An ancient Greek wide-mouthed bowl for mixing wine and water.

Kufic—An early form of Arabic script, characterized by angularity, with the uprights forming almost right angles with the baseline.

kula—An exchange of white conus-shell arm ornaments and red chama-shell necklaces that takes place among the Trobriand Islanders of Papua New Guinea.

kupesi—Embroidered design tablets used by Tonga (Polynesia) women in the production of barkcloth.

kylix—An ancient Greek drinking cup with a wide bowl and two horizontal handles.

labyrinth—Maze. The English word derives from the mazelike plan of the *Minoan* palace at Knossos.

lacquer—A varnishlike substance made from the sap of the Asiatic sumac tree, used to decorate wood and other organic materials. Often colored with mineral pigments, lacquer cures to great hardness and has a lustrous surface.

laid-and-couched work—See *embroidery.*

lakshana—One of the distinguishing marks of the Buddha. The lakshanas include the *urna* and *ushnisha.*

lalitasana—In Buddhist iconography, the body pose with one leg folded and the other hanging down, indicating relaxation.

lamassu—Assyrian guardian in the form of a man-headed winged bull.

lancet—In *Gothic* architecture, a tall narrow window ending in a *pointed arch.*

landscape—A picture showing natural scenery, without narrative content.

Landschaft—German, "landscape."

lateral section—See *section.*

laudatio—Latin, "essay of praise."

leading—In the manufacture of *stained-glass* windows, the joining of colored glass pieces using lead *cames.*

lectionary—A book containing passages from the *Gospels,* arranged in the sequence that they are to be read during the celebration of religious services, including the *Mass,* throughout the year.

lekythos (pl. **lekythoi**)—A flask containing perfumed oil; lekythoi were often placed in Greek graves as offerings to the deceased.

liege lord—In *feudalism,* a landowner who grants tenure of a portion of his land to a *vassal.*

line—The extension of a point along a path, made concrete in art by drawing on or chiseling into a *plane.*

linear perspective—See *perspective.*

linga—In Hindu art, the depiction of Shiva as a phallus or cosmic *pillar.*

linguist's staff—In Africa, a staff carried by a person authorized to speak for a king or chief.

lintel—A horizontal *beam* used to span an opening.

literati—In China, talented amateur painters and scholars from the landed gentry.

lithograph—See *lithography.*

lithography—A printmaking technique in which the artist uses an oil-based crayon to draw directly on a stone plate and then wipes water onto the stone. When ink is rolled onto the plate, it adheres only to the drawing. The print produced by this method is a lithograph.

liturgy (adj. **liturgical**)—The official ritual of public worship.

local color—An object's true *color* in white light.

loculi—Openings in the walls of *catacombs* to receive the dead.

loggia—A gallery with an open *arcade* or a *colonnade* on one or both sides.

lohan—A Buddhist holy person who has achieved enlightenment and *nirvana* by suppression of all desire for earthly things.

longitudinal plan—See *plan.*

longitudinal section—See *section.*

lost-wax (cire perdue) process—A bronze-casting method in which a figure is modeled in wax and covered with clay; the whole is fired, melting away the wax (French, cire perdue) and hardening the clay, which then becomes a *mold* for molten metal.

low relief—See *relief.*

lunette—A semicircular area (with the flat side down) in a wall over a door, niche, or window; also, a painting or *relief* with a semicircular frame.

lux nova—Latin, "new light." Abbot Suger's term for the light that enters a *Gothic* church through *stained-glass* windows.

machicolated gallery—A gallery in a defensive tower with holes in the floor to allow stones or hot liquids to be dumped on enemies below.

madrasa—An Islamic theological college adjoining and often containing a *mosque.*

maebyong—A Korean vase similar to the Chinese *meiping.*

magus (pl. **magi**)—One of the three wise men from the East who presented gifts to the infant Jesus.

ma-hevehe—Mythical Oceanic water spirits. The Elema people of New Guinea believed these spirits visited their villages.

malanggan—Festivals held in honor of the deceased in New Ireland (Papua New Guinea). Also, the carvings and objects produced for these festivals.

mana—In Polynesia, spiritual power.

mandala—Sanskrit term for the sacred diagram of the universe; Japanese, mandara.

mandapa—*Pillared* hall of a Hindu temple.

mandara—See *mandala.*

mandorla—An almond-shaped *nimbus* surrounding the figure of Christ or other sacred figure. In Buddhist Japan, a lotus-petal-shaped nimbus.

maniera—Italian, "style" or "manner." See *Mannerism.*

maniera greca—Italian, "Greek manner." The Italo-*Byzantine* painting *style* of the 13th century.

Mannerism—A *style* of later *Renaissance* art that emphasized "artifice," often involving contrived imagery not derived directly from nature. Such artworks showed a self-conscious stylization involving complexity, caprice, fantasy, and polish. Mannerist architecture tended to flout the *classical* rules of order, stability, and symmetry, sometimes to the point of parody.

manor—In *feudalism,* the estate of a *liege lord.*

mantra—Sanskrit term for the ritual words or syllables recited in *Shingon* Buddhism.

manulua—Triangular patterns based on the form of two birds, common in Tongan *tapa* designs.

maqsura—In some *mosques,* a screened area in front of the *mihrab* reserved for a ruler.

Mara—A spirit in Northern European mythology that was thought to torment and suffocate sleepers.

martyr—A person who chooses to die rather than deny his or her religious belief. See also *saint.*

martyrium—A shrine to a Christian martyr *saint.*

Masonry Style—See *First Style* mural.

mass—The bulk, density, and weight of matter in *space.*

Mass—The Catholic and Orthodox ritual in which believers understand that Christ's redeeming sacrifice on the cross is repeated when the priest consecrates the bread and wine in the *Eucharist.*

mastaba—Arabic, "bench." An ancient Egyptian rectangular brick or stone structure with sloping sides erected over a subterranean tomb chamber connected with the outside by a shaft.

matins—The dawn prayer in a *Book of Hours.*

matte—In painting, pottery, and photography, a dull finish.

maulstick—A stick used to steady the hand while painting.

mausoleum—A monumental tomb. The name derives from the mid-fourth-century BCE tomb of Mausolos at Halikarnassos, one of the Seven Wonders of the ancient world.

mbari—A ceremonial Igbo (Nigeria) house built about every 50 years in honor of the earth goddess Ala.

mbulu ngulu—The wood-and-metal *reliquary* guardian figures of the Kota of Gabon.

meander—An ornament, usually in bands but also covering broad surfaces, consisting of interlocking geometric motifs. An ornamental pattern of contiguous straight lines joined usually at right angles.

medium (pl. **media**)—The material (for example, marble, bronze, clay, *fresco*) in which an artist works; also, in painting, the vehicle (usually liquid) that carries the pigment.

megalith (adj. **megalithic**)—Greek, "great stone." A large, roughly hewn stone used in the construction of monumental prehistoric structures.

megaron—The large reception hall and throne room in a *Mycenaean* palace, fronted by an open, two-*columned* porch.

meiping—A Chinese vase of a high-shouldered shape; the *sgraffito technique* was used in decorating such vases.

memento mori—Latin, "reminder of death." In painting, a reminder of human mortality, usually represented by a skull.

mendicants—In medieval Europe, friars belonging to the Franciscan and Dominican orders, who renounced all worldly goods, lived by contributions of laypersons (the word *mendicant* means "beggar"), and devoted themselves to preaching, teaching, and doing good works.

menorah—In antiquity, the Jewish sacred seven-branched candelabrum.

merlon—See *crenellation.*

Mesoamerica—The region that comprises Mexico, Guatemala, Belize, Honduras, and the Pacific coast of El Salvador.

Mesolithic—The "middle" Stone Age, between the *Paleolithic* and the *Neolithic* ages.

Messiah—The savior of the Jews prophesied in the Old Testament. Christians believe that Jesus of Nazareth was the Messiah.

metamatics—The name Swiss artist Jean Tinguely gave to the motor-driven devices he constructed to produce instant abstract paintings.

metope—The square panel between the *triglyphs* in a *Doric frieze,* often sculpted in *relief.*

mihrab—A semicircular niche set into the *qibla* wall of a *mosque.*

minaret—A distinctive feature of *mosque* architecture, a tower from which the faithful are called to worship.

minbar—In a *mosque,* the *pulpit* on which the *imam* stands.

mingei—A type of modern Japanese folk pottery.

miniatures—Small individual Indian paintings intended to be held in the hand and viewed by one or two individuals at one time.

Minimalism—A predominantly sculptural American trend of the 1960s characterized by works featuring a severe reduction of *form,* often to single, homogeneous units.

Minoan—The prehistoric art of Crete, named after the legendary King Minos of Knossos.

Minotaur—The mythical beast, half man and half bull, that inhabited the *labyrinth* of the *Minoan* palace at Knossos.

mithuna—In South Asian art, a male-female couple embracing or engaged in sexual intercourse.

moai—Large, blocky figural stone sculptures found on Rapa Nui (Easter Island) in Polynesia.

mobile—A kind of sculpture, invented by Alexander Calder, combining nonobjective organic forms and motion in balanced structures hanging from rods, wires, and colored, organically shaped plates.

modeling—The shaping or fashioning of three-dimensional forms in a soft material, such as clay; also, the gradations of light and shade reflected from the surfaces of matter in space, or the illusion of such gradations produced by alterations of value in a drawing, painting, or print.

modernism—A movement in Western art that developed in the second half of the 19th century and sought to capture the images and sensibilities of the age. Modernist art goes beyond simply dealing with the present and involves the artist's critical examination of the premises of art itself.

Modernismo—See *Art Nouveau.*

modernist formalism—See *formalism.*

module (adj. **modular**)—A basic unit of which the dimensions of the major parts of a work are multiples. The principle is used in sculpture and other art forms, but it is most often employed in architecture, where the module may be the dimensions of an important part of a building, such as the diameter of a *column.*

moko—The form of tattooing practiced by the Maori of New Zealand.

moksha—See *nirvana.*

mold—A hollow form for *casting.*

molding—In architecture, a continuous, narrow surface (projecting or recessed, plain or ornamented) designed to break up a surface, to accent, or to decorate.

monastery—A group of buildings in which monks live together, set apart from the secular community of a town.

monastic—Relating to life in a *monastery.*

monastic order—An organization of monks living according to the same rules, for example, the Benedictine, Franciscan, and Dominican orders.

monochrome (adj. **monochromatic**)—One color.

monolith (adj. **monolithic**)—A stone *column shaft* that is all in one piece (not composed of *drums*); a large, single block or piece of stone used in *megalithic* structures. Also, a colossal statue carved from a single piece of stone.

monotheism—The worship of one all-powerful god.

moralized Bible—A heavily illustrated Bible, each page pairing paintings of Old and New Testament episodes with explanations of their moral significance.

mortise-and-tenon system—See *tenon.*

mortuary temple—In Egyptian architecture, a temple erected for the worship of a deceased *pharaoh.*

mosaic—Patterns or pictures made by embedding small pieces (*tesserae*) of stone or glass in cement on surfaces such as walls and floors; also, the *technique* of making such works.

mosaic tilework—An Islamic decorative *technique* in which large ceramic panels are fired, cut into smaller pieces, and set in plaster.

moschophoros—Greek, "calf bearer."

mosque—The Islamic building for collective worship. From the Arabic word *masjid,* meaning a "place for bowing down."

Mozarabic—Referring to the Christian culture of northern Spain during the time Islamic *caliphs* ruled southern Spain.

mudra—In Buddhist and Hindu iconography, a stylized and symbolic hand gesture. The dhyana (meditation) mudra consists of the right hand over the left, palms upward, in the lap. In the bhumisparsha (earth-touching) mudra, the right hand reaches down to the ground, calling the earth to witness the Buddha's enlightenment. The dharmachakra (Wheel of the Law, or teaching) mudra is a two-handed gesture with right thumb and index finger forming a circle. The abhaya (do not fear) mudra, with the right hand up, palm outward, is a gesture of protection or blessing.

Mughal—"Descended from the Mongols." The Muslim rulers of India, 1526–1857.

Muhaqqaq—A cursive style of Islamic *calligraphy.*

mullion—A vertical member that divides a window or that separates one window from another.

mummification—A *technique* used by ancient Egyptians to preserve human bodies so that they may serve as the eternal home of the immortal *ka.*

muqarnas—Stucco decorations of Islamic buildings in which stalactite-like forms break a structure's solidity.

mural—A wall painting.

Muslim—A believer in Islam.

Mycenaean—The prehistoric art of the Late *Helladic* period in Greece, named after the citadel of Mycenae.

mystery play—A dramatic enactment of the holy mysteries of the Christian faith performed at church portals and in city squares.

mystic marriage—A spiritual marriage of a woman with Christ.

Nabis—Hebrew, "prophet." A group of *Symbolist* painters influenced by Paul Gauguin.

naos—See *cella.*

narthex—A porch or vestibule of a church, generally *colonnaded* or *arcaded* and preceding the *nave.*

natatio—The swimming pool in a Roman bathing establishment.

naturalism—The style of painted or sculptured representation based on close observation of the natural world that was at the core of the *classical* tradition.

Naturalistic Surrealism—See *Surrealism*.

nave—The central area of an ancient Roman *basilica* or of a church, demarcated from *aisles* by *piers* or *columns*.

nave arcade—In *basilica* architecture, the series of *arches* supported by *piers* or *columns* separating the *nave* from the *aisles*.

nduen fobara—A Kalabari Ijaw (Nigeria) ancestral screen in honor of a deceased chief of a trading house.

necropolis—Greek, "city of the dead." A large burial area or cemetery.

nembutsu—The six-syllable Japanese prayer professing faith in the compassion of Amida Buddha.

nemes—In ancient Egypt, the linen headdress worn by the *pharaoh*, with the *uraeus* cobra of kingship on the front.

Neoclassicism—A *style* of art and architecture that emerged in the late 18th century as part of a general revival of interest in *classical* cultures. Neoclassical artists adopted themes and styles from ancient Greece and Rome.

Neo-Expressionism—An art movement that emerged in the 1970s and that reflects artists' interest in the expressive capability of art, seen earlier in *German Expressionism* and *Abstract Expressionism*.

Neo-Gothic—The revival of the *Gothic style* in architecture, especially in the 19th century.

Neolithic—The "new" Stone Age.

Neoplasticism—The Dutch artist Piet Mondrian's theory of "pure plastic art," an ideal balance between the universal and the individual using an abstract formal vocabulary.

Neue Sachlichkeit—German, "new objectivity." An art movement that grew directly out of the World War I experiences of a group of German artists who sought to show the horrors of the war and its effects.

ngatu—Decorated *tapa* made by women in Tonga.

niello—A black metallic alloy.

nihonga—A 19th-century Japanese painting style that incorporated some Western techniques in Japanese-style painting, as opposed to *yoga* (Western painting).

nimbus—A halo or aureole appearing around the head of a holy figure to signify divinity.

nio—A Japanese guardian figure.

nipote—Italian, "nephew."

nirvana—In Buddhism and Hinduism, a blissful state brought about by absorption of the individual soul or consciousness into the supreme spirit. Also called moksha.

nishiki-e—Japanese, "brocade pictures." Japanese polychrome *woodcut prints* valued for their sumptuous colors.

nkisi n'kondi—A power figure carved by the Kongo people of the Democratic Republic of Congo. Such images embodied spirits believed to heal and give life or to be capable of inflicting harm or death.

nomarch—Egyptian, "great/overlord." A regional governor during the Middle Kingdom.

Nun—In ancient Egypt, the primeval waters from which the creator god emerged.

nymphs—In *classical* mythology, female divinities of springs, caves, and woods.

oba—An African sacred king.

oculus (pl. **oculi**)—Latin, "eye." The round central opening of a *dome*. Also, a small round window in a *Gothic cathedral*.

odalisque—A woman in a Turkish harem.

ogee arch—An *arch* composed of two double-curving lines meeting at a point.

ogive (adj. **ogival**)—The diagonal *rib* of a *Gothic vault;* a pointed, or Gothic, *arch*.

Ogoga—A Yoruba king.

oil painting—A painting *technique* using oil-based pigments that rose to prominence in Northern Europe in the 15th century and is now the standard medium for painting on canvas.

Olympiad—The four-year period defined by the staging of the Olympic Games in ancient Greece.

oni—An African ruler.

Op Art—An artistic movement of the 1960s in which painters sought to produce optical illusions of motion and depth using only geometric forms on two-dimensional surfaces.

opere francigeno—See *opus francigenum*.

opisthodomos—In ancient Greek architecture, a porch at the rear of a temple, set against the blank back wall of the *cella*.

optical mixture—The visual effect of juxtaposed *complementary colors*.

opus francigenum—Latin, "French work." Architecture in the *style* of *Gothic* France; *opere francigeno* (adj.), "in the French manner."

opus modernum—Latin, "modern work." The late medieval term for *Gothic* art and architecture. Also called *opus francigenum*.

opus reticulatum—An ancient Roman method of facing concrete walls with lozenge-shaped bricks or stones to achieve a netlike ornamental surface pattern.

orant—In Early Christian art, a figure with both arms raised in the ancient gesture of prayer.

oratory—The church of a Christian *monastery*.

orbiculum—A disklike opening.

orchestra—Greek, "dancing place." In ancient Greek theaters, the circular piece of earth with a hard and level surface on which the performance took place.

order—In *classical* architecture, a *style* represented by a characteristic design of the *columns* and *entablature*. See also *superimposed orders*.

Orientalizing—The early phase of *Archaic* Greek art (seventh century BCE), so named because of the adoption of forms and motifs from the ancient Near East and Egypt. See also *Daedalic*.

Orphism—A form of *Cubism* developed by the French painter Robert Delaunay in which color plays an important role.

orrery—A mechanical model of the solar system demonstrating how the planets revolve around the sun.

orthogonal—A line imagined to be behind and perpendicular to the picture plane; the orthogonals in a painting appear to recede toward a vanishing point on the horizon.

orthogonal plan—The imposition of a strict grid *plan* on a site, regardless of the terrain, so that all streets meet at right angles. See also *Hippodamian plan*.

Ottonian (adj.)—Pertaining to the empire of Otto I and his successors.

overglaze—In *porcelain* decoration, the technique of applying mineral colors over the *glaze* after the work has been fired. The overglaze colors, or

enamels, fuse to the glazed surface in a second firing at a much lower temperature than the main firing. See also *underglaze*.

oxidizing—The first phase of the ancient Greek ceramic firing process, which turned both the pot and the clay *slip* red. During the second (reducing) phase, the oxygen supply into the kiln was shut off, and both pot and slip turned black. In the final (reoxidizing) phase, the pot's coarser material reabsorbed oxygen and became red again, whereas the smoother slip did not and remained black.

pagoda—An East Asian tower, usually associated with a Buddhist temple, having a multiplicity of winged *eaves;* thought to be derived from the Indian *stupa*.

pala—A panel placed behind and over the altar in a church.

palaestra—An ancient Greek and Roman exercise area, usually framed by a *colonnade*. In Greece, the palaestra was an independent building; in Rome, palaestras were also frequently incorporated into a bathing complex.

Paleolithic—The "old" Stone Age, during which humankind produced the first sculptures and paintings.

palette—A thin board with a thumb hole at one end on which an artist lays and mixes *colors;* any surface so used. Also, the colors or kinds of colors characteristically used by an artist. In ancient Egypt, a slate slab used for preparing makeup.

palette knife—A flat tool used to scrape paint off the *palette*. Artists sometimes also use the palette knife in place of a brush to apply paint directly to the canvas.

Pantokrator—Greek, "ruler of all." Christ as ruler and judge of heaven and earth.

papier collé—French, "stuck paper." See *collage*.

papyrus—A plant native to Egypt and adjacent lands used to make paperlike writing material; also, the material or any writing on it.

parade helmet—A masklike helmet worn by Roman soldiers on special ceremonial occasions.

parallel hatching—See *hatching*.

parapet—A low, protective wall along the edge of a balcony, roof, or bastion.

parchment—Lambskin prepared as a surface for painting or writing.

parekklesion—The side chapel in a Byzantine church.

parinirvana—Image of the reclining Buddha, a position often interpreted as representing his death.

parthenos—Greek, "virgin." The epithet of Athena, the virgin goddess.

passage grave—A prehistoric tomb with a long stone corridor leading to a burial chamber covered by a great *tumulus*.

Passional—A Christian book containing the lives of *saints*.

pastel—A powdery paste of pigment and gum used for making crayons; also, the pastel crayons themselves.

paten—A large shallow bowl or plate for the bread used in the *Eucharist*.

patrician—A Roman freeborn landowner.

patron—The person or entity that pays an artist to produce individual artworks or employs an artist on a continuing basis.

pebble mosaic—A *mosaic* made of irregularly shaped stones of various *colors*.

pectoral—An ornament worn on the chest.

pediment—In *classical* architecture, the triangular space (gable) at the end of a building, formed by the ends of the sloping roof above the *colonnade;* also, an ornamental feature having this shape.

pendant—The large hanging terminal element of a *Gothic* fan *vault.*

pendentive—A concave, triangular section of a hemisphere, four of which provide the transition from a square area to the circular base of a covering *dome.* Although pendentives appear to be hanging (pendant) from the dome, they in fact support it.

Pentateuch—The first five books of the Old Testament.

peplos—A simple, long belted garment of wool worn by women in ancient Greece.

Performance Art—An American *avant-garde* art trend of the 1960s that made time an integral element of art. It produced works in which movements, gestures, and sounds of persons communicating with an audience replace physical objects. Documentary photographs are generally the only evidence remaining after these events. See also *Happenings.*

period style—See *style.*

peripteral—See *peristyle.*

peristyle—In *classical* architecture, a *colonnade* all around the *cella* and its porch(es). A peripteral colonnade consists of a single row of *columns* on all sides; a dipteral colonnade has a double row all around.

Perpendicular—A Late English *Gothic style* of architecture distinguished by the pronounced verticality of its decorative details.

personal style—See *style.*

personification—An *abstract* idea represented in bodily form.

perspective (adj. **perspectival**)—A method of presenting an illusion of the three-dimensional world on a two-dimensional surface. In linear perspective, the most common type, all parallel lines or surface edges converge on one, two, or three vanishing points located with reference to the eye level of the viewer (the horizon line of the picture), and associated objects are rendered smaller the farther from the viewer they are intended to seem. Atmospheric, or aerial, perspective creates the illusion of distance by the greater diminution of color intensity, the shift in color toward an almost neutral blue, and the blurring of contours as the intended distance between eye and object increases.

pfemba—A Yombe (Democratic Republic of Congo) mother-and-child group.

pharaoh (adj. **pharaonic**)—An ancient Egyptian king.

philosophe—French, "thinker, philosopher." The term applied to French intellectuals of the *Enlightenment.*

photomontage—A *composition* made by pasting together pictures or parts of pictures, especially photographs. See also *collage.*

Photorealism—See *Superrealism.*

physical evidence—In art history, the examination of the materials used to produce an artwork in order to determine its date.

piano nobile—Italian, "noble floor." The main (second) floor of a building.

piazza—Italian, "plaza."

pictograph—A picture, usually stylized, that represents an idea; also, writing using such means; also, painting on rock. See also *hieroglyphic.*

Picturesque garden—An "unordered" garden designed in accord with the *Enlightenment* taste for the natural.

pier—A vertical, freestanding masonry support.

Pietà—A painted or sculpted representation of the Virgin Mary mourning over the body of the dead Christ.

pilaster—A flat, rectangular, vertical member projecting from a wall of which it forms a part. It usually has a *base* and a *capital* and is often *fluted.*

pillar—Usually a weight-carrying member, such as a *pier* or a *column;* sometimes an isolated, freestanding structure used for commemorative purposes.

pinakotheke—Greek, "picture gallery." An ancient Greek building for the display of paintings on wood panels.

pinnacle—In *Gothic* churches, a sharply pointed ornament capping the *piers* or flying *buttresses;* also used on church *facades.*

Pittura Metafisica—Italian, "metaphysical painting." An early-20th-century Italian art movement led by Giorgio de Chirico, whose work conveys an eerie mood and visionary quality.

pixels—Shortened form of "picture elements." The tiny boxes that make up digital images displayed on a computer monitor.

plan—The horizontal arrangement of the parts of a building or of the buildings and streets of a city or town, or a drawing or diagram showing such an arrangement. In an axial plan, the parts of a building are organized longitudinally, or along a given axis; in a central plan, the parts of the structure are of equal or almost equal dimensions around the center.

plane—A flat surface.

plate tracery—See *tracery.*

Plateresque—A style of Spanish architecture characterized by elaborate decoration based on *Gothic,* Italian *Renaissance,* and Islamic sources; derived from the Spanish word *platero,* meaning "silversmith."

platero—See *Plateresque.*

plebeian—The Roman social class that included small farmers, merchants, and freed slaves.

plein air—An approach to painting much popular among the *Impressionists,* in which an artist sketches outdoors to achieve a quick impression of light, air, and color. The artist then takes the sketches to the studio for reworking into more finished works of art.

poesia—A term describing "poetic" art, notably Venetian *Renaissance* painting, which emphasizes the lyrical and sensual.

pointed arch—A narrow *arch* of pointed profile, in contrast to a semicircular arch.

pointillism—A system of painting devised by the 19th-century French painter Georges Seurat. The artist separates *color* into its component parts and then applies the component colors to the canvas in tiny dots (points). The image becomes comprehensible only from a distance, when the viewer's eyes optically blend the pigment dots. Sometimes referred to as divisionism.

polis (pl. **poleis**)—An independent *city-state* in ancient Greece.

polyptych—An *altarpiece* composed of more than three sections.

polytheism—The belief in multiple gods.

pontifex maximus—Latin, "chief priest." The high priest of the Roman state religion, often the emperor himself.

Pop Art—A term coined by British art critic Lawrence Alloway to refer to art, first appearing in the 1950s, that incorporated elements from consumer culture, the mass media, and popular culture, such as images from motion pictures and advertising.

porcelain—Extremely fine, hard, white ceramic. Unlike *stoneware,* porcelain is made from a fine white clay called kaolin mixed with ground petuntse, a type of feldspar. True porcelain is translucent and rings when struck.

portico—A roofed *colonnade;* also an entrance porch.

positivism—A Western philosophical model that promoted science as the mind's highest achievement.

post-and-lintel system—A system of construction in which two posts support a *lintel.*

Post-Impressionism—The term used to describe the stylistically heterogeneous work of the group of late-19th-century painters in France, including van Gogh, Gauguin, Seurat, and Cézanne, who more systematically examined the properties and expressive qualities of *line,* pattern, *form,* and *color* than the Impressionists did.

postmodernism—A reaction against *modernist formalism,* seen as elitist. Far more encompassing and accepting than the more rigid confines of modernist practice, postmodernism offers something for everyone by accommodating a wide range of *styles,* subjects, and formats, from traditional easel painting to *installation* and from *abstraction* to *illusionistic* scenes. Postmodern art often includes irony or reveals a self-conscious awareness on the part of the artist of art-making processes or the workings of the art world.

Post-Painterly Abstraction—An American art movement that emerged in the 1960s and was characterized by a cool, detached rationality emphasizing tighter pictorial control. See also *color-field painting* and *hard-edge painting.*

pou tokomanawa—A sculpture of an ancestor that supports a *ridgepole* of a Maori (New Zealand) meetinghouse.

pouncing—The method of transferring a sketch onto paper or a wall by tracing, using thin paper or transparent gazelle skin placed on top of the sketch, pricking the contours of the design into the skin or paper with a pin, placing the skin or paper on the surface to be painted, and forcing black pigment through the holes.

poupou—A decorated wall panel in a Maori (New Zealand) meetinghouse.

Poussiniste—A member of the French Royal Academy of Painting and Sculpture during the early 18th century who followed Nicolas Poussin in insisting that *form* was the most important element of painting. See also *Rubéniste.*

powwow—A traditional Native American ceremony featuring dancing in quilled, beaded, and painted costumes.

prasada—In Hindu worship, food that becomes sacred by first being given to a god.

Precisionism—An American art movement of the 1920s and 1930s. The Precisionists concentrated on portraying man-made environments in a clear and concise manner to express the beauty of perfect and precise machine forms.

pre-Columbian (adj.)—The cultures that flourished in the Western Hemisphere before the arrival of Christopher Columbus and the beginning of European contact and conquest.

predella—The narrow ledge on which an *altarpiece* rests on an altar.

prefiguration—In Early Christian art, the depiction of Old Testament persons and events as prophetic forerunners of Christ and New Testament events.

primary colors—Red, yellow, and blue—the *colors* from which all other colors may be derived.

primitivism—The incorporation in early-20th-century Western art of stylistic elements from the artifacts of Africa, Oceania, and the native peoples of the Americas.

princeps—Latin, "first citizen." The title Augustus and his successors as Roman emperor used to distinguish themselves from Hellenistic monarchs.

print—An artwork on paper, usually produced in multiple impressions.

Productivism—An art movement that emerged in the Soviet Union after the Russian Revolution; its members believed that artists must direct art toward creating products for the new society.

pronaos—The space, or porch, in front of the *cella,* or naos, of an ancient Greek temple.

proportion—The relationship in size of the parts of persons, buildings, or objects, often based on a *module.*

proscenium—The part of a theatrical stage in front of the curtain.

prostyle—A *classical* temple *plan* in which the *columns* are only in front of the *cella* and not on the sides or back.

protome—The head, forelegs, and part of the body of an animal.

provenance—Origin or source; *findspot.*

psalter—A book containing the Psalms.

pseudoperipteral—In Roman architecture, a pseudoperipteral temple has a series of engaged *columns* all around the sides and back of the *cella* to give the appearance of a *peripteral colonnade.*

pueblo—A communal multistoried dwelling made of stone or *adobe* brick by the Native Americans of the Southwest. Upper-case *Pueblo* refers to various groups that occupied such dwellings.

pukao—A small red scoria cylinder serving as a topknot or hat on Easter Island *moai.*

pulpit—A raised platform in a church or *mosque* on which a priest or *imam* stands while leading the religious service.

pulque—An intoxicating drink, similar to tequila, consumed during Mesoamerican religious rituals.

punchwork—Tooled decorative work in *gold leaf.*

Purism—An early-20th-century art movement that embraced the "machine aesthetic" and sought purity of *form* in the clean functional lines of industrial machinery.

purlins—Horizontal *beams* in a roof structure, parallel to the *ridgepoles,* resting on the main *rafters* and giving support to the secondary rafters.

putto (pl. **putti**)—A cherubic young boy.

pylon—The wide entrance gateway of an Egyptian temple, characterized by its sloping walls.

pyxis (pl. **pyxides**)—A cylindrical container with a hemispherical lid.

qibla—The direction (toward Mecca) Muslims face when praying.

quadrant arch—An *arch* whose curve extends for one quarter of a circle's circumference.

quadrifrons—Latin, "four-fronted." An *arch* with four equal *facades* and four *arcuated bays.*

quadro riportato—A ceiling design in which painted scenes are arranged in panels that resemble framed pictures transferred to the surface of a shallow, curved *vault.*

quatrefoil—A shape or plan in which the parts assume the form of a cloverleaf.

quoins—The large, sometimes *rusticated,* usually slightly projecting stones that often form the corners of the exterior walls of masonry buildings.

radiating chapels—In medieval churches, chapels for the display of *relics* that opened directly onto the *ambulatory* and the *transept.*

radiocarbon dating—A method of measuring the decay rate of carbon isotopes in organic matter to determine the age of organic materials such as wood and fiber.

rafters—The sloping supporting timber planks that run from the *ridgepole* of a roof to its edge.

raking cornice—The *cornice* on the sloping sides of a *pediment.*

ramparts—Defensive wall circuits.

ratha—Small, freestanding Hindu temple carved from a huge boulder.

Rayonnant—The "radiant" style of *Gothic* architecture, dominant in the second half of the 13th century and associated with the French royal court of Louis IX at Paris.

Realism—A movement that emerged in mid-19th-century France. Realist artists represented the subject matter of everyday life (especially subjects that previously had been considered inappropriate for depiction) in a relatively *naturalistic* mode.

red-figure painting—In later Greek pottery, the silhouetting of red figures against a black background, with painted linear details; the reverse of *black-figure painting.*

reducing—See *oxidizing.*

refectory—The dining hall of a Christian *monastery.*

regional style—See *style.*

Regionalism—A 20th-century American art movement that portrayed American rural life in a clearly readable, *realist* style. Major Regionalists include Grant Wood and Thomas Hart Benton.

register—One of a series of superimposed bands or *friezes* in a pictorial narrative, or the particular levels on which motifs are placed.

relics—The body parts, clothing, or objects associated with a holy figure, such as the Buddha or Christ or a Christian *saint.*

relief—In sculpture, figures projecting from a background of which they are part. The degree of relief is designated high, low (bas), or sunken. In the last, the artist cuts the design into the surface so that the highest projecting parts of the image are no higher than the surface itself. See also *repoussé.*

relief sculpture—See *relief.*

relieving triangle—In *Mycenaean* architecture, the triangular opening above the *lintel* that serves to lighten the weight to be carried by the lintel itself.

reliquary—A container for holding *relics.*

ren—Chinese, "human-heartedness." The quality that the ideal Confucian *junzi* possesses.

Renaissance—French, "rebirth." The term used to describe the history, culture, and art of 14th- through 16th-century western Europe during which artists consciously revived the *classical* style.

renovatio—Latin, "renewal." During the *Carolingian* period, Charlemagne sought to revive the culture of ancient Rome (renovatio imperi Romani).

reoxidizing—See *oxidizing.*

repoussé—Formed in *relief* by beating a metal plate from the back, leaving the impression on the face. The metal sheet is hammered into a hollow *mold* of wood or some other pliable material and finished with a *graver.* See also *relief.*

respond—An engaged *column, pilaster,* or similar element that either projects from a *compound pier* or some other supporting device or is bonded to a wall and carries one end of an *arch.*

retable—An architectural screen or wall above and behind an altar, usually containing painting, sculpture, carving, or other decorations. See also *altarpiece.*

revetment—In architecture, a wall covering or facing.

rhyton—A pouring vessel.

rib—A relatively slender, molded masonry *arch* that projects from a surface. In *Gothic* architecture, the ribs form the framework of the *vaulting.* A diagonal rib is one of the ribs that form the X of a *groin vault.* A transverse rib crosses the *nave* or *aisle* at a 90-degree angle.

rib vault—A *vault* in which the diagonal and transverse *ribs* compose a structural skeleton that partially supports the masonry *web* between them.

ridgepole—The *beam* running the length of a building below the peak of the gabled roof.

rocaille—See *Rococo.*

Rococo—A style, primarily of interior design, that appeared in France around 1700. Rococo interiors featured lavish decoration, including small sculptures, ornamental mirrors, easel paintings, *tapestries, reliefs,* wall paintings, and elegant furniture. The term Rococo derived from the French word *rocaille* ("pebble") and referred to the small stones and shells used to decorate grotto interiors.

Romanesque—"Roman-like." A term used to describe the history, culture, and art of medieval western Europe from ca. 1050 to ca. 1200.

Romanticism—A Western cultural phenomenon, beginning around 1750 and ending about 1850, that gave precedence to feeling and imagination over reason and thought. More narrowly, the art movement that flourished from about 1800 to 1840.

roof comb—The elaborately sculpted vertical projection surmounting a Maya temple-pyramid.

rose window—A circular *stained-glass* window.

rostrum—Speaker's platform.

rotulus—The manuscript scroll used by Egyptians, Greeks, Etruscans, and Romans; predecessor of the *codex.*

rotunda—The circular area under a *dome;* also a domed round building.

roundel—See *tondo.*

rubbing—An impression of a relief made by placing paper over the surface and rubbing with a pencil or crayon.

Rubéniste—A member of the French Royal Academy of Painting and Sculpture during the early 18th century who followed Peter Paul Rubens in insisting that *color* was the most important element of painting. See also *Poussiniste.*

rusticate (n. **rustication**)—To give a rustic appearance by roughening the surfaces and beveling the edges of stone blocks to emphasize the joints between them. Rustication is a technique employed in ancient Roman architecture, and was also popular during the *Renaissance,* especially for stone *courses* at the ground-floor level.

sabi—Japanese; the value found in the old and weathered, suggesting the tranquility reached in old age.

sacra conversazione—Italian, "holy conversation." A style of *altarpiece* painting popular after the middle of the 15th century, in which *saints* from different epochs are joined in a unified space and seem to be conversing either with one another or with the audience.

sacra rappresentazione (pl. **sacre rappresentazioni**)—Italian, "holy representation." A more elaborate version of a *mystery play* performed for a lay audience by a *confraternity.*

sacramentary—A Christian religious book incorporating the prayers priests recite during *Mass.*

saint—From the Latin word *sanctus,* meaning "made holy by God." Applied to persons who suffered and died for their Christian faith or who merited reverence for their Christian devotion while alive. In the Roman Catholic Church, a worthy deceased Catholic who is canonized by the pope.

Saint-Simonianism—An early-19th-century utopian movement that emphasized the education and enfranchisement of women.

sakkos—The tunic worn by a Byzantine priest.

saltimbanque—An itinerant circus performer.

Samarqand ware—A type of Islamic pottery produced in Samarqand and Nishapur in which the ceramists formed the shape of the vessel from dark pink clay and then immersed it in a tub of white slip, over which they painted ornamental or calligraphic decoration and which they sealed with a transparent glaze before firing.

sangha—The Buddhist monastic order.

samsara—In Hindu belief, the rebirth of the soul into a succession of lives.

samurai—Medieval Japanese warriors.

sand painting—A temporary painting *technique* using sand, varicolored powdered stones, corn pollen, and charcoal. Sand paintings, also called dry paintings, are integral parts of sacred Navajo rituals.

sarcophagus (pl. **sarcophagi**)—Latin, "consumer of flesh." A coffin, usually of stone.

Satimbe—"Sister on the head." A Dogon (Mali) mask representing all women.

saturation—See *color.*

satyr—A Greek mythological follower of Dionysos having a man's upper body, a goat's hindquarters and horns, and a horse's ears and tail.

saz—An Ottoman fabric design composed of sinuous curved leaves and complex blossoms.

scarab—An Egyptian gem in the shape of a beetle.

scarification—Decorative markings on the human body made by cutting or piercing the flesh to create scars.

Scholasticism—The *Gothic* school of philosophy in which scholars applied Aristotle's system of rational inquiry to the interpretation of religious belief.

school—A chronological and stylistic classification of works of art with a stipulation of place.

screen facade—A *facade* that does not correspond to the structure of the building behind it.

scriptorium (pl. **scriptoria**)—The writing studio of a *monastery.*

scudi—Italian, "shields." A coin denomination in 17th-century Italy.

sculpture in the round—Freestanding figures, carved or modeled in three dimensions.

seal—In Asian painting, a stamp affixed to a painting to identify the artist, the *calligrapher,* or the owner. See also *cylinder seals.*

secco—Italian, "dry." See also *fresco.*

Second Style mural—The style of Roman *mural* painting in which the aim was to dissolve the confining walls of a room and replace them with the illusion of a three-dimensional world constructed in the artist's imagination.

secondary colors—Orange, green, and purple, obtained by mixing pairs of *primary colors* (red, yellow, blue).

section—In architecture, a diagram or representation of a part of a structure or building along an imaginary plane that passes through it vertically. Drawings showing a theoretical slice across a structure's width are lateral sections. Those cutting through a building's length are longitudinal sections. See also *elevation* and *cutaway.*

sedes sapientiae—Latin, "throne of wisdom." A Romanesque sculptural type depicting the Virgin Mary with the Christ Child in her lap.

senate—Latin senatus, "council of elders." The Senate was the main legislative body in Roman constitutional government.

serdab—A small concealed chamber in an Egyptian *mastaba* for the statue of the deceased.

Severe Style—The Early *Classical* style of Greek sculpture, ca. 480–450 BCE.

sexpartite vault—See *vault.*

sfumato—Italian, "smoky." A smokelike haziness that subtly softens outlines in painting; particularly applied to the paintings of Leonardo da Vinci and Correggio.

sgraffito—A Chinese ceramic technique in which the design is *incised* through a colored *slip.*

shaft—The tall, cylindrical part of a *column* between the *capital* and the *base.*

shakti—In Hinduism, the female power of the deity Devi (or Goddess), which animates the matter of the cosmos.

shaykh—An Islamic mystic *saint.*

sherd—A fragmentary piece of a broken ceramic vessel.

shikara—The beehive-shaped tower of a northern-style Hindu temple.

Shingon—The primary form of Buddhism in Japan through the mid-10th century. Lowercase *shingon* is the Japanese term for the words or syllables recited in Buddhist ritual.

Shino—Japanese ceramic wares produced during the late 16th and early 17th centuries in kilns in Mino.

shogun—In 12th- through 19th-century Japan, a military governor who managed the country on behalf of a figurehead emperor.

shogunate—The Japanese military government of the 12th through 19th centuries.

sibyl—A Greco-Roman mythological prophetess.

signoria—The governing body in the Republic of Florence.

silk-screen printing—An industrial printing *technique* that creates a sharp-edged image by pressing ink through a design on silk or a similar tightly woven porous fabric stretched tight on a frame.

silverpoint—A *stylus* made of silver, used in drawing in the 14th and 15th centuries because of the fine line it produced and the sharp point it maintained.

Simultanéisme—Robert Delaunay's version of *Cubism* in which he created spatial effects and kaleidoscopic movement solely through color contrasts; also known as *Orphism.*

simultaneous contrasts—The phenomenon of juxtaposed *colors* affecting the eye's reception of each, as when a painter places dark green next to light green, making the former appear even darker and the latter even lighter. See also *successive contrasts.*

sinopia—A burnt-orange pigment used in *fresco* painting to transfer a *cartoon* to the *arriccio* before the artist paints the plaster.

siren—In ancient Greek mythology, a creature that was part bird and part woman.

site-specific art—Art created for a specific location. See also *Environmental Art.*

skene—Greek, "stage." The stage of a *classical* theater.

skenographia—Greek, "scene painting"; the Greek term for *perspective* painting.

skiagraphia—Greek, "shadow painting." The Greek term for shading, said to have been invented by Apollodoros, an Athenian painter of the fifth century BCE.

slip—A mixture of fine clay and water used in ceramic decoration.

space—In art history, both the actual area an object occupies or a building encloses, and the *illusionistic* representation of space in painting and sculpture.

spandrel—The roughly triangular space enclosed by the curves of adjacent *arches* and a horizontal member connecting their vertexes; also, the space enclosed by the curve of an *arch* and an enclosing right angle. The area between the arch proper and the framing *columns* and *entablature.*

spectrum—The range or band of visible colors in natural light.

sphinx—A mythical Egyptian beast with the body of a lion and the head of a human.

splashed-ink painting—See *haboku.*

springing—The lowest stone of an *arch,* resting on the *impost block.* In *Gothic vaulting,* the lowest stone of a diagonal or transverse *rib.*

squinch—An architectural device used as a transition from a square to a polygonal or circular base for a *dome.* It may be composed of *lintels, corbels,* or *arches.*

stained glass—In *Gothic* architecture, the colored glass used for windows.

stamp seal—See *cylinder seal.*

stanza (pl. **stanze**)—Italian, "room."

statue—A three-dimensional sculpture.

stave—A wedge-shaped timber; vertically placed staves embellish the architectural features of a building.

stele (pl. **stelae**)—A carved stone slab used to mark graves or to commemorate historical events.

stem stitching—See *embroidery.*

stigmata—In Christian art, the wounds Christ received at his crucifixion that miraculously appear on the body of a *saint.*

still life—A picture depicting an arrangement of inanimate objects.

stoa—In ancient Greek architecture, an open building with a roof supported by a row of *columns* parallel to the back wall. A covered *colonnade* or *portico.*

Stoic—A philosophical school of ancient Greece, named after the *stoas* in which the philosophers met.

stoneware—Pottery fired at high temperatures to produce a stonelike hardness and density.

strategos—Greek, "general."

stretcher bar—One of a set of wooden bars used to stretch canvas to provide a taut surface for painting.

strigil—A tool ancient Greek athletes used to scrape oil from their bodies after exercising.

stringcourse—A raised horizontal *molding,* or band, in masonry. Its principal use is ornamental but it usually reflects interior structure.

strut—A timber plank or other structural member used as a support in a building. Also a short section of marble used to support an arm or leg in a *statue.*

stucco—A type of plaster used as a coating on exterior and interior walls. Also used as a sculptural medium.

stupa—A large, mound-shaped Buddhist shrine.

style—A distinctive artistic manner. Period style is the characteristic style of a specific time. Regional style is the style of a particular geographical area. Personal style is an individual artist's unique manner.

stylistic evidence—In art history, the examination of the *style* of an artwork in order to determine its date or the identity of the artist.

stylobate—The uppermost course of the platform of a *classical* Greek temple, which supports the *columns.*

stylus—A needlelike tool used in *engraving* and *incising;* also, an ancient writing instrument used to inscribe clay or wax tablets.

sub gracia—Latin, "under grace." In Christian thought, the period after the coming of Christ.

sub lege—Latin, "under the law." In Christian thought, the period after Moses received the Ten Commandments and before the coming of Christ. See also *sub gracia.*

subtractive light—The painter's light in art; the light reflected from pigments and objects. See also *additive light.*

subtractive sculpture—A kind of sculpture technique in which materials are taken away from the original mass; carving.

successive contrasts—The phenomenon of colored afterimages. When a person looks intently at a *color* (green, for example) and then shifts to a white area, the fatigued eye momentarily perceives the *complementary color* (red). See also *simultaneous contrasts.*

sultan—A *Muslim* ruler.

sunken relief—See *relief.*

Sunnah—The collection of the Prophet Muhammad's moral sayings and descriptions of his deeds.

superimposed orders—*Orders* of architecture that are placed one above another in an *arcaded* or *colonnaded* building, usually in the following sequence: *Doric* (the first story), *Ionic,* and *Corinthian.* Superimposed orders are found in later Greek architecture and were used widely by Roman and *Renaissance* builders.

superimposition—In *Mesoamerican* architecture, the erection of a new structure on top of, and incorporating, an earlier structure; the nesting of a series of buildings inside each other.

Superrealism—A *school* of painting and sculpture of the 1960s and 1970s that emphasized producing artworks based on scrupulous fidelity to optical fact. The Superrealist painters were also called Photorealists because many used photographs as sources for their imagery.

Suprematism—A type of art formulated by Kazimir Malevich to convey his belief that the supreme reality in the world is pure feeling, which attaches to no object and thus calls for new, nonobjective forms in art—shapes not related to objects in the visible world.

surah—A chapter of the *Koran,* divided into verses.

Surrealism—A successor to *Dada,* Surrealism incorporated the improvisational nature of its predecessor into its exploration of the ways to express in art the world of dreams and the unconscious. Biomorphic Surrealists, such as Joan Miró, produced largely *abstract compositions. Naturalistic* Surrealists, notably Salvador Dalí, presented recognizable scenes transformed into a dream or nightmare image.

sutra—In Buddhism, an account of a sermon by or a dialogue involving the Buddha. A scriptural account of the Buddha. See also *jataka.*

symbol—An image that stands for another image or encapsulates an idea.

Symbolism—A late-19th-century movement based on the idea that the artist was not an imitator of nature but a creator who transformed the facts of nature into a *symbol* of the inner experience of that fact.

symmetria—Greek, "commensurability of parts." Polykleitos's treatise on his *canon* of proportions incorporated the principle of symmetria.

symposium—An ancient Greek banquet attended solely by men (and female servants and prostitutes).

Synthetic Cubism—A later phase of *Cubism,* in which paintings and drawings were constructed from objects and shapes cut from paper or other materials to represent parts of a subject, in order to engage the viewer with pictorial issues, such as figuration, realism, and abstraction.

taberna—In Roman architecture, a single-room shop usually covered by a barrel *vault.*

tablero—See *talud-tablero construction.*

tablinum—The study or office in a Roman house.

taj—Arabic and Persian, "crown."

talud-tablero construction—The alternation of sloping (talud) and vertical (tablero) rubble layers, characteristic of Teotihuacan architecture in Mesoamerica.

tapa—Barkcloth made particularly in Polynesia. Tapa is often dyed, painted, stenciled, and sometimes perfumed.

tapestry—A weaving *technique* in which the *weft* threads are packed densely over the *warp* threads so that the designs are woven directly into the fabric.

tarashikomi—In Japanese art, a painting *technique* involving the dropping of ink and pigments onto surfaces still wet with previously applied ink and pigments.

tatami—The traditional woven straw mat used for floor covering in Japanese architecture.

tatanua—In New Ireland (Papua New Guinea), the spirits of the dead.

tatau—See *tattoo.*

tattoo—A permanent design on the skin produced using indelible dyes. The term derives from the Tahitian, Samoan, and Tongan word tatau or tatu.

tatu—See *tattoo.*

technique—The processes artists employ to create *form,* as well as the distinctive, personal ways in which they handle their materials and tools.

tempera—A *technique* of painting using pigment mixed with egg yolk, glue, or casein; also, the *medium* itself.

templon—The columnar screen separating the sanctuary from the main body of a Byzantine church.

tenebrism—Painting in the "shadowy manner," using violent contrasts of light and dark, as in the work of Caravaggio. The term derives from *tenebroso.*

tenebroso—Italian, "shadowy." See *tenebrism.*

tenon—A projection on the end of a piece of wood that is inserted into a corresponding hole (mortise) in another piece of wood to form a joint.

tephra—The volcanic ash produced by the eruption on the *Cycladic* island of Thera.

tepidarium—The warm-bath section of a Roman bathing establishment.

terracotta—Hard-baked clay, used for sculpture and as a building material. It may be *glazed* or painted.

tessera (pl. **tesserae**)—Greek, "cube." A tiny stone or piece of glass cut to the desired shape and size for use in forming a *mosaic.*

tetrarch—One of four corulers.

tetrarchy—Greek, "rule by four." A type of Roman government established in the late third century CE by Diocletian in an attempt to foster order by sharing power with potential rivals.

texture—The quality of a surface (rough, smooth, hard, soft, shiny, dull) as revealed by light. In represented texture, a painter depicts an object as having a certain texture even though the paint is the actual texture.

theatron—Greek, "place for seeing." In ancient Greek theaters, the slope overlooking the *orchestra* on which the spectators sat.

Theotokos—Greek, "she who bore God." The Virgin Mary, the mother of Jesus.

thermoluminescence—A method of dating by measuring amounts of radiation found within the clay of ceramic or sculptural forms, as well as in the clay cores from metal castings.

Third Style mural—In Roman *mural* painting, the style in which delicate linear fantasies were sketched on predominantly *monochromatic* backgrounds.

tholos (pl. **tholoi**)—A temple with a circular plan. Also, the burial chamber of a *tholos tomb.*

tholos tomb—In *Mycenaean* architecture, a beehive-shaped tomb with a circular plan.

thrust—The outward force exerted by an *arch* or a *vault* that must be counterbalanced by a *buttress.*

tiki—A Marquesas Islands (Polynesia) three-dimensional carving of an exalted, deified ancestor figure.

toga—The garment worn by an ancient Roman male citizen.

togu na—"House of words." A Dogon (Mali) men's house, where deliberations vital to community welfare take place.

tokonoma—A shallow alcove in a Japanese room, which is used for decoration, such as a painting or stylized flower arrangement.

tonality—See *color.*

tondo (pl. **tondi**)—A circular painting or *relief* sculpture.

Torah—The Hebrew religious scroll containing the *Pentateuch.*

torana—Gateway in the stone fence around a *stupa,* located at the cardinal points of the compass.

torque—The distinctive necklace worn by the Gauls.

tracery—Ornamental stonework for holding *stained glass* in place, characteristic of *Gothic cathedrals.*

In plate tracery, the glass fills only the "punched holes" in the heavy ornamental stonework. In bar tracery, the stained-glass windows fill almost the entire opening, and the stonework is unobtrusive.

tramezzo—A screen placed across the *nave* of a church to separate the clergy from the lay audience.

transept—The part of a church with an axis that crosses the *nave* at a right angle.

transubstantiation—The transformation of the Eucharistic bread and wine into the body and blood of Christ.

transverse arch—An *arch* separating one *vaulted bay* from the next.

transverse barrel vault—In medieval architecture, a semicylindrical *vault* oriented at a 90-degree angle to the *nave* of a church.

transverse rib—See *rib.*

treasury—In ancient Greece, a small building set up for the safe storage of *votive offerings.*

trefoil—A cloverlike ornament or symbol with stylized leaves in groups of three.

tribune—In church architecture, a gallery over the inner *aisle* flanking the *nave.*

triclinium—The dining room of a Roman house.

trident—The three-pronged pitchfork associated with the ancient Greek sea god Poseidon (Roman, Neptune).

triforium—In a *Gothic cathedral,* the *blind arcaded* gallery below the *clerestory;* occasionally, the *arcades* are filled with *stained glass.*

triglyph—A triple projecting, grooved member of a *Doric frieze* that alternates with *metopes.*

trilithons—A pair of *monoliths* topped with a *lintel;* found in *megalithic* structures.

Trinity—In Christianity, God the Father, his son Jesus Christ, and the Holy Spirit.

tripod—An ancient Greek deep bowl on a tall three-legged stand.

triptych—A three-paneled painting, ivory plaque, or *altarpiece.* Also, a small, portable shrine with hinged wings used for private devotion.

triratna—A tripartite symbol of the three jewels of Buddhism—the Buddha himself, his *dharma,* and the *sangha.*

triumphal arch—In Roman architecture, a freestanding *arch* commemorating an important event, such as a military victory or the opening of a new road.

trompe l'oeil—French, "fools the eye." A form of *illusionistic* painting that aims to deceive viewers into believing they are seeing real objects rather than a representation of those objects.

trumeau—In church architecture, the *pillar* or center post supporting the *lintel* in the middle of the doorway.

tubicen—Latin, "trumpet player."

tughra—The official signature of an Ottoman emperor.

tukutuku—A stitched lattice panel found in a Maori (New Zealand) meetinghouse.

tumulus (pl. **tumuli**)—Latin, "burial mound." In Etruscan architecture, tumuli cover one or more subterranean multichambered tombs cut out of the local tufa (limestone). Also characteristic of the Japanese Kofun period of the third and fourth centuries.

tunnel vault—See *vault.*

turris—See *westwork.*

Tuscan column—The standard type of Etruscan *column.* It resembles ancient Greek *Doric* columns

but is made of wood, is unfluted, and has a *base.* Also a popular motif in *Renaissance* and *Baroque* architecture.

twisted perspective—See *composite view.*

tympanum (pl. **tympana**)—The space enclosed by a *lintel* and an *arch* over a doorway.

typology—In Christian theology, the recognition of concordances between events, especially between episodes in the Old and New Testaments.

ukiyo-e—Japanese, "pictures of the floating world." During the Edo period, *woodcut prints* depicting brothels, popular entertainment, and beautiful women.

underglaze—In *porcelain* decoration, the *technique* of applying mineral colors to the surface before the main firing, followed by an application of clear *glaze.* See also *overglaze.*

Upanishads—South Asian religious texts of ca. 800–500 BCE that introduced the concepts of *samsara, karma,* and *moksha.*

uraeus—An Egyptian cobra; one of the emblems of *pharaonic* kingship.

urna—A whorl of hair, represented as a dot, between the brows; one of the *lakshanas* of the Buddha.

ushabti—In ancient Egypt, a figurine placed in a tomb to act as a servant to the deceased in the afterlife.

ushnisha—A knot of hair on the top of the head; one of the *lakshanas* of the Buddha.

valley temple—The temple closest to the Nile River associated with each of the Great Pyramids at Gizeh in ancient Egypt.

value—See *color.*

vanishing point—See *perspective.*

vanitas—Latin, "vanity." A term describing paintings (particularly 17th-century Dutch *still lifes*) that include references to death.

vassal—In *feudalism,* a person who swears allegiance to a *liege lord* and renders him military service in return for tenure of a portion of the lord's land.

vault (adj. **vaulted**)—A masonry roof or ceiling constructed on the *arch* principle, or a concrete roof of the same shape. A barrel (or tunnel) vault, semicylindrical in cross-*section,* is in effect a deep arch or an uninterrupted series of arches, one behind the other, over an oblong space. A quadrant vault is a half-barrel vault. A groin (or cross) vault is formed at the point at which two barrel vaults intersect at right angles. In a ribbed vault, there is a framework of *ribs* or arches under the intersections of the vaulting sections. A sexpartite vault is one whose ribs divide the vault into six compartments. A fan vault is a vault characteristic of English *Perpendicular Gothic* architecture, in which radiating ribs form a fanlike pattern.

vaulting web—See *web.*

Veda—Sanskrit, "knowledge." One of four second-millennium BCE South Asian compilations of religious learning.

veduta (pl. **vedute**)—Italian, "scenic view."

velarium—In a Roman *amphitheater,* the cloth awning that could be rolled down from the top of the *cavea* to shield spectators from sun or rain.

vellum—Calfskin prepared as a surface for writing or painting.

venationes—Ancient Roman wild animal hunts staged in an *amphitheater.*

veristic—True to natural appearance; superrealistic.

vihara—A Buddhist *monastery,* often cut into a hill.

vimana—A pyramidal tower over the *garbha griha* of a Hindu temple of the southern, or Dravida, style.

vita—Italian, "life." Also, the title of a biography.

vita contemplativa—Latin, "contemplative life." The secluded spiritual life of monks and nuns.

volume—The *space* that *mass* organizes, divides, or encloses.

volute—A spiral, scroll-like form characteristic of the ancient Greek *Ionic* and the Roman *Composite capital.*

votive offering—A gift of gratitude to a deity.

voussoir—A wedge-shaped stone block used in the construction of a true *arch.* The central voussoir, which sets the arch, is called the keystone.

wabi—A 16th-century Japanese art style characterized by refined rusticity and an appreciation of simplicity and austerity.

wainscoting—Paneling on the lower part of interior walls.

waka sran—"People of wood." Baule (Côte d'Ivoire) wooden figural sculptures.

warp—The vertical threads of a loom or cloth.

wat—A Buddhist *monastery* in Cambodia.

web—The masonry blocks that fill the area between the *ribs* of a *groin vault.* Also called vaulting web.

wedjat—The eye of the Egyptian falcon-god Horus, a powerful *amulet.*

weft—The horizontal threads of a loom or cloth.

weld—To join metal parts by heating, as in assembling the separate parts of a *statue* made by *casting.*

were-jaguar—A composite human-jaguar; a common motif in Olmec art.

westwork—German, "western entrance structure." The *facade* and towers at the western end of a medieval church, principally in Germany. In contemporary documents the westwork is called a castellum (Latin, "castle" or "fortress") or turris ("tower").

wet-plate photography—An early photographic process in which the photographic plate is exposed, developed, and fixed while wet.

white-ground painting—An ancient Greek vase-painting *technique* in which the pot was first covered with a *slip* of very fine white clay, over which black *glaze* was used to outline figures, and diluted brown, purple, red, and white were used to color them.

woodcut—A wooden block on the surface of which those parts not intended to *print* are cut away to a slight depth, leaving the design raised; also, the printed impression made with such a block.

yaksha (m.), **yakshi** (f.)—Lesser local male and female Buddhist and Hindu divinities. Yakshis are goddesses associated with fertility and vegetation. Yakshas, the male equivalent of yakshis, are often represented as fleshy but powerful males.

yamato-e—Also known as native-style painting, a purely Japanese style that often involved colorful, decorative representations of Japanese narratives or *landscapes.*

yang—In Chinese cosmology, the principle of active masculine energy, which permeates the universe in varying proportions with yin, the principle of passive feminine energy.

yasti—In Buddhist architecture, the mast or pole that arises from the dome of the *stupa* and its *harmika* and symbolizes the axis of the universe; it is adorned with a series of chatras (stone disks).

yin—See *yang.*

yoga—A method for controlling the body and relaxing the mind used in later Indian religions to yoke, or unite, the practitioner to the divine.

yosegi—Japanese *joined-wood technique.*

zecca—Italian, "mint."

Zen—A Japanese Buddhist sect and its doctrine, emphasizing enlightenment through intuition and introspection rather than the study of scripture. In Chinese, Chan.

ziggurat—In ancient Mesopotamian architecture, a monumental platform for a temple.

zoopraxiscope—A device invented by Eadweard Muybridge in the 19th century to project sequences of still photographic images; a predecessor of the modern motion-picture projector.

BIBLIOGRAPHY

This list of books is very selective but comprehensive enough to satisfy the reading interests of the beginning art history student and general reader. The resources listed range from works that are valuable primarily for their reproductions to those that are scholarly surveys of schools and periods or monographs on individual artists. The emphasis is on recent in-print books and on books likely to be found in college and municipal libraries. No entries for periodical articles appear, but the bibliography begins with a list of some of the major journals that publish art historical scholarship in English.

SELECTED PERIODICALS

African Arts
American Art
American Indian Art
American Journal of Archaeology
Antiquity
Archaeology
Archives of American Art
Archives of Asian Art
Ars Orientalis
Art Bulletin
Art History
Art in America
Art Journal
Artforum International
Burlington Magazine
Gesta
History of Photography
Journal of Roman Archaeology
Journal of the Society of Architectural Historians
Journal of the Warburg and Courtauld Institutes
Latin American Antiquity
Oxford Art Journal
Women's Art Journal

GENERAL STUDIES

Baxandall, Michael. *Patterns of Intention: On the Historical Explanation of Pictures.* New Haven, Conn.: Yale University Press, 1985.

Bindman, David, ed. *The Thames & Hudson Encyclopedia of British Art.* London: Thames & Hudson, 1988.

Boström, Antonia. *The Encyclopedia of Sculpture.* 3 vols. London: Routledge, 2003.

Broude, Norma, and Mary D. Garrard, eds. *The Expanding Discourse: Feminism and Art History.* New York: Harper Collins, 1992.

Bryson, Norman. *Vision and Painting: The Logic of the Gaze.* New Haven, Conn.: Yale University Press, 1983.

Bryson, Norman, Michael Ann Holly, and Keith Moxey. *Visual Theory: Painting and Interpretation.* New York: Cambridge University Press, 1991.

Büttner, Nils. *Landscape Painting: A History.* New York: Abbeville, 2006.

Chadwick, Whitney. *Women, Art, and Society.* 4th ed. New York: Thames & Hudson, 2007.

Cheetham, Mark A., Michael Ann Holly, and Keith Moxey, eds. *The Subjects of Art History: Historical Objects in Contemporary Perspective.* New York: Cambridge University Press, 1998.

Chilvers, Ian, and Harold Osborne, eds. *The Oxford Dictionary of Art.* 3d ed. New York: Oxford University Press, 2004.

Corbin, George A. *Native Arts of North America, Africa, and the South Pacific: An Introduction.* New York: Harper Collins, 1988.

Crouch, Dora P., and June G. Johnson. *Traditions in Architecture: Africa, America, Asia, and Oceania.* New York: Oxford University Press, 2000.

Curl, James Stevens. *Oxford Dictionary of Architecture and Landscape Architecture.* 2d ed. New York: Oxford University Press, 2006.

Encyclopedia of World Art. 17 vols. New York: McGraw-Hill, 1959–1987.

Fielding, Mantle. *Dictionary of American Painters, Sculptors, and Engravers.* 2d ed. Poughkeepsie, N.Y.: Apollo, 1986.

Fine, Sylvia Honig. *Women and Art: A History of Women Painters and Sculptors from the Renaissance to the 20th Century.* Rev. ed. Montclair, N.J.: Alanheld & Schram, 1978.

Fleming, John, Hugh Honour, and Nikolaus Pevsner. *The Penguin Dictionary of Architecture and Landscape Architecture.* 5th ed. New York: Penguin, 2000.

Frazier, Nancy. *The Penguin Concise Dictionary of Art History.* New York: Penguin, 2000.

Freedberg, David. *The Power of Images: Studies in the History and Theory of Response.* Chicago: University of Chicago Press, 1989.

Gaze, Delia., ed. *Dictionary of Women Artists.* 2 vols. London: Routledge, 1997.

Hall, James. *Illustrated Dictionary of Subjects and Symbols in Eastern and Western Art.* New York: Icon Editions, 1994.

Harris, Anne Sutherland, and Linda Nochlin. *Women Artists: 1550–1950.* Los Angeles: Los Angeles County Museum of Art; New York: Knopf, 1977.

Hauser, Arnold. *The Sociology of Art.* Chicago: University of Chicago Press, 1982.

Hults, Linda C. *The Print in the Western World: An Introductory History.* Madison: University of Wisconsin Press, 1996.

Kemp, Martin. *The Science of Art: Optical Themes in Western Art from Brunelleschi to Seurat.* New Haven, Conn.: Yale University Press, 1990.

Kostof, Spiro, and Gregory Castillo. *A History of Architecture: Settings and Rituals.* 2d ed. Oxford: Oxford University Press, 1995.

Kultermann, Udo. *The History of Art History.* New York: Abaris, 1993.

Lucie-Smith, Edward. *The Thames & Hudson Dictionary of Art Terms.* 2d ed. New York: Thames & Hudson, 2004.

Moffett, Marian, Michael Fazio, and Lawrence Wadehouse. *A World History of Architecture.* Boston: McGraw-Hill, 2004.

Murray, Peter, and Linda Murray. *A Dictionary of Art and Artists.* 7th ed. New York: Penguin, 1998.

Nelson, Robert S., and Richard Shiff, eds. *Critical Terms for Art History.* Chicago: University of Chicago Press, 1996.

Penny, Nicholas. *The Materials of Sculpture.* New Haven, Conn.: Yale University Press, 1993.

Pevsner, Nikolaus. *A History of Building Types.* London: Thames & Hudson, 1987. Reprint of 1979 ed.

———. *An Outline of European Architecture.* 8th ed. Baltimore: Penguin, 1974.

Pierce, James Smith. *From Abacus to Zeus: A Handbook of Art History.* 7th ed. Upper Saddle River, N.J.: Pearson Prentice Hall, 1998.

Placzek, Adolf K., ed. *Macmillan Encyclopedia of Architects.* 4 vols. New York: Macmillan, 1982.

Podro, Michael. *The Critical Historians of Art.* New Haven, Conn.: Yale University Press, 1982.

Pollock, Griselda. *Vision and Difference: Femininity, Feminism, and Histories of Art.* London: Routledge, 1988.

Preziosi, Donald, ed. *The Art of Art History: A Critical Anthology.* New York: Oxford University Press, 1998.

Read, Herbert. *The Thames & Hudson Dictionary of Art and Artists.* Rev. ed. New York: Thames & Hudson, 1994.

Reid, Jane D. *The Oxford Guide to Classical Mythology in the Arts 1300–1990s.* 2 vols. New York: Oxford University Press, 1993.

Roth, Leland M. *Understanding Architecture: Its Elements, History, and Meaning.* 2d ed. Boulder, Colo.: Westview, 2006.

Schama, Simon. *The Power of Art.* New York: Ecco, 2006.

Slatkin, Wendy. *Women Artists in History: From Antiquity to the 20th Century.* 4th ed. Upper Saddle River, N.J.: Prentice Hall, 2000.

Steer, John, and Antony White. *Atlas of Western Art History: Artists, Sites, and Monuments from Ancient Greece to the Modern Age.* New York: Facts on File, 1994.

Stratton, Arthur. *The Orders of Architecture: Greek, Roman, and Renaissance.* London: Studio, 1986.

Sutton, Ian. *Western Architecture: From Ancient Greece to the Present.* New York: Thames & Hudson, 1999.

Trachtenberg, Marvin, and Isabelle Hyman. *Architecture, from Prehistory to Post-Modernism.* 2d ed. Upper Saddle River, N.J.: Prentice Hall, 2003.

Turner, Jane, ed. *The Dictionary of Art.* 34 vols. New ed. New York: Oxford University Press, 2003.

Wittkower, Rudolf. *Sculpture Processes and Principles.* New York: Harper & Row, 1977.

Wren, Linnea H., and Janine M. Carter, eds. *Perspectives on Western Art: Source Documents and Readings from the Ancient Near East through the Middle Ages.* New York: Harper & Row, 1987.

Ancient Art, General

Aruz, Joan, and Ronald Wallenfels, eds. *Art of the First Cities: The Third Millennium BC from the Mediterranean to the Indus.* New York: Metropolitan Museum of Art, 2003.

Beard, Mary, and John Henderson. *Classical Art: From Greece to Rome.* New York: Oxford University Press, 2001.

Boardman, John. *The World of Ancient Art.* London: Thames & Hudson, 2006.

———, ed. *The Oxford History of Classical Art.* New York: Oxford University Press, 1997.

Clayton, Peter A., and Martin J. Price, eds. *The Seven Wonders of the Ancient World.* New York: Routledge, 1988.

Connolly, Peter, and Hazel Dodge. *The Ancient City: Life in Classical Athens and Rome.* New York: Oxford University Press, 1998.

De Grummond, Nancy Thomson, ed. *An Encyclopedia of the History of Classical Archaeology.* 2 vols. Westport, Conn.: Greenwood, 1996.

Dunbabin, Katherine. *Mosaics of the Greek and Roman World.* New York: Cambridge University Press, 1999.

Gates, Charles. *Ancient Cities: The Archaeology of Urban Life in the Ancient Near East and Egypt, Greece, and Rome.* London: Routledge, 2003.

Kampen, Natalie B., ed. *Sexuality in Ancient Art.* New York: Cambridge University Press, 1996.

Lexicon Iconographicum Mythologiae Classicae. 10 vols. Zurich: Artemis, 1981–1999.

Ling, Roger. *Ancient Mosaics.* Princeton, N.J.: Princeton University Press, 1998.

Lloyd, Seton, and Hans Wolfgang Muller. *Ancient Architecture: Mesopotamia, Egypt, Crete.* New York: Electa/Rizzoli, 1980.

Oliphant, Margaret. *The Atlas of the Ancient World: Charting the Great Civilizations of the Past.* New York: Simon & Schuster, 1992.

Onians, John. *Classical Art and the Cultures of Greece and Rome.* New Haven, Conn.: Yale University Press, 1999.

Renfrew, Colin, and Paul G. Bahn. *Archaeology: Theories, Methods, and Practices.* London: Thames & Hudson, 1991.

Stillwell, Richard, William L. MacDonald, and Marian H. McAllister, eds. *The Princeton Encyclopedia of Classical Sites.* Princeton, N.J.: Princeton University Press, 1976.

Trigger, Bruce. *Understanding Early Civilizations: A Comparative Study.* New York: Cambridge University Press, 2003.

Ward-Perkins, John B. *Cities of Ancient Greece and Italy: Planning in Classical Antiquity.* Rev. ed. New York: Braziller, 1987.

Wolf, Walther. *The Origins of Western Art: Egypt, Mesopotamia, the Aegean.* New York: Universe, 1989.

Chapter 1: Art before History

Bahn, Paul G. *The Cambridge Illustrated History of Prehistoric Art.* New York: Cambridge University Press, 1998.

Bahn, Paul G., and Jean Vertut. *Journey through the Ice Age.* Berkeley: University of California Press, 1997.

Beltrán, Antonio, ed. *The Cave of Altamira.* New York: Abrams, 1999.

Burl, Aubrey. *Great Stone Circles.* New Haven, Conn.: Yale University Press, 1999.

Chauvet, Jean-Marie, Eliette Brunel Deschamps, and Christian Hillaire. *Dawn of Art: The Chauvet Cave.* New York: Abrams, 1996.

Chippindale, Christopher. *Stonehenge Complete.* New York: Thames & Hudson, 1994.

Cunliffe, Barry, ed. *The Oxford Illustrated Prehistory of Europe.* New York: Oxford University Press, 1994.

Hodder, Ian. *The Leopard's Tale: Revealing the Mysteries of Çatalhöyük.* London: Thames & Hudson, 2006.

Kenyon, Kathleen M. *Digging up Jericho.* New York: Praeger, 1974.

Leroi-Gourhan, André. *The Dawn of European Art: An Introduction to Paleolithic Cave Painting.* Cambridge: Cambridge University Press, 1982.

Marshack, Alexander. *The Roots of Civilization: The Cognitive Beginnings of Man's First Art, Symbol and Notation.* 2d ed. Wakefield, R.I.: Moyer Bell, 1991.

Pfeiffer, John E. *The Creative Explosion: An Inquiry into the Origins of Art and Religion.* New York: Harper & Row, 1982.

Renfrew, Colin, ed. *British Prehistory: A New Outline.* London: Noyes, 1975.

Ruspoli, Mario. *The Cave of Lascaux: The Final Photographs.* New York: Abrams, 1987.

Scarre, Chris. *Exploring Prehistoric Europe.* New York: Oxford University Press, 1998.

Wainwright, Geoffrey. *The Henge Monuments: Ceremony and Society in Prehistoric Britain.* London: Thames & Hudson, 1990.

White, Randall. *Prehistoric Art: The Symbolic Journey of Humankind.* New York: Abrams, 2003.

Chapter 2: The Ancient Near East

Akurgal, Ekrem. *Art of the Hittites.* New York: Abrams, 1962.

Allen, Lindsay. *The Persian Empire.* Chicago: University of Chicago Press, 2005.

Amiet, Pierre. *Art of the Ancient Near East.* New York: Abrams, 1980.

Bahrani, Zainab. *The Graven Image: Representation in Babylonia and Assyria.* Philadelphia: University of Pennsylvania Press, 2003.

Bienkowski, Piotr, and Alan Millard, eds. *Dictionary of the Ancient Near East.* Philadelphia: University of Pennsylvania Press, 2000.

Collon, Dominique. *Ancient Near Eastern Art.* Berkeley: University of California Press, 1995.

———. *First Impressions: Cylinder Seals in the Ancient Near East.* 2d ed. London: British Museum, 1993.

———. *Near Eastern Seals.* Berkeley: University of California Press, 1990.

Crawford, Harriet. *Sumer and the Sumerians.* New York: Cambridge University Press, 1991.

Curatola, Giovanni. *The Art and Architecture of Mesopotamia.* New York: Abbeville, 2007.

Curtis, John E. *Ancient Persia.* Cambridge, Mass.: Harvard University Press, 1990.

Curtis, John E., and Julian E. Reade. *Art and Empire: Treasures from Assyria in the British Museum.* New York: Metropolitan Museum of Art, 1995.

Curtis, John E., and Nigel Tallis. *Forgotten Empire: The World of Ancient Persia.* Berkeley: University of California Press, 2005.

Frankfort, Henri. *The Art and Architecture of the Ancient Orient.* 5th ed. New Haven, Conn.: Yale University Press, 1996.

Ghirshman, Roman. *The Arts of Ancient Iran: From Its Origins to the Time of Alexander the Great.* New York: Golden, 1964.

———. *Persian Art: The Parthian and Sassanian Dynasties, 249 BC–AD 651.* New York: Golden, 1962.

Gunter, Ann C., ed. *Investigating Artistic Environments in the Ancient Near East.* Washington, D.C.: Arthur M. Sackler Gallery, 1990.

Harper, Prudence O., Joan Aruz, and Françoise Tallon, eds. *The Royal City of Susa: Ancient Near Eastern Treasures in the Louvre.* New York: Metropolitan Museum of Art, 1992.

Lloyd, Seton. *The Archaeology of Mesopotamia: From the Old Stone Age to the Persian Conquest.* London: Thames & Hudson, 1984.

Macqueen, James G. *The Hittites and Their Contemporaries in Asia Minor.* Rev. ed. New York: Thames & Hudson, 1986.

Meyers, Eric M., ed. *The Oxford Encyclopedia of Archaeology in the Near East.* 5 vols. New York: Oxford University Press, 1997.

Moortgat, Anton. *The Art of Ancient Mesopotamia.* New York: Phaidon, 1969.

Oates, Joan. *Babylon.* Rev. ed. London: Thames & Hudson, 1986.

Parrot, André. *The Arts of Assyria.* New York: Golden, 1961.

———. *Sumer: The Dawn of Art.* New York: Golden, 1961.

Porada, Edith. *Man and Images in the Ancient Near East.* Wakefield, R.I.: Moyer Bell, 1995.

Porada, Edith, and Robert H. Dyson. *The Art of Ancient Iran: Pre-Islamic Cultures.* Rev. ed. New York: Greystone, 1969.

Postgate, J. Nicholas. *Early Mesopotamia: Society and Economy at the Dawn of History.* London: Routledge, 1992.

Potts, Daniel T. *The Archaeology of Elam: Formation and Transformation of an Ancient Iranian State.* New York: Cambridge University Press, 1999.

Reade, Julian E. *Assyrian Sculpture.* Cambridge, Mass.: Harvard University Press, 1999.

———. *Mesopotamia.* Cambridge, Mass.: Harvard University Press, 1991.

Roaf, Michael. *Cultural Atlas of Mesopotamia and the Ancient Near East.* New York: Facts on File, 1990.

Russell, John M. *Sennacherib's Palace without Rival at Nineveh.* Chicago: University of Chicago Press, 1991.

Saggs, H.W.F. *Babylonians.* London: British Museum, 1995.

Sasson, Jack M., ed. *Civilizations of the Ancient Near East.* 4 vols. New York: Scribner, 1995.

Snell, Daniel C. *Life in the Ancient Near East: 3100–332 BC.* New Haven, Conn.: Yale University Press, 1997.

Strommenger, Eva, and Max Hirmer. *5,000 Years of the Art of Mesopotamia.* New York: Abrams, 1964.

Zettler, Richard L., and Lee Horne. *Treasures from the Royal Tombs of Ur.* Philadelphia: University of Pennsylvania Museum of Archaeology and Anthropology, 1998.

Chapter 3: Egypt under the Pharaohs

Arnold, Dieter. *Building in Egypt: Pharaonic Stone Masonry.* New York: Oxford University Press, 1991.

Arnold, Dorothea. *The Royal Women of Amarna.* New York: Metropolitan Museum of Art, 1996.

———. *When the Pyramids Were Built: Egyptian Art of the Old Kingdom.* New York: Rizzoli, 1999.

Baines, John, and Jaromír Málek. *Atlas of Ancient Egypt.* New York: Facts on File, 1980.

Bard, Kathryn A. *An Introduction to the Archaeology of Ancient Egypt.* Oxford: Blackwell, 2007.

———, ed. *Encyclopedia of the Archaeology of Ancient Egypt.* London: Routledge, 1999.

Bianchi, Robert S. *Cleopatra's Egypt: Age of the Ptolemies.* Brooklyn: Brooklyn Museum, 1988.

———. *Splendors of Ancient Egypt from the Egyptian Museum, Cairo.* London: Booth-Clibborn, 1996.

Capel, Anne K., and Glenn E. Markoe, eds. *Mistress of the House, Mistress of Heaven: Women in Ancient Egypt.* New York: Hudson Hills, 1996.

D'Auria, Sue, Peter Lacovara, and Catharine H. Roehrig. *Mummies and Magic: The Funerary Arts of Ancient Egypt.* Boston: Museum of Fine Arts, 1988.

Davis, Whitney. *The Canonical Tradition in Ancient Egyptian Art.* New York: Cambridge University Press, 1989.

Egyptian Art in the Age of the Pyramids. New York: Abrams, 1999.

Hawass, Zahi. *Valley of the Golden Mummies.* New York: Abrams, 2000.

Ikram, Salima, and Aidan Dodson. *The Mummy in Ancient Egypt: Equipping the Dead for Eternity.* New York: Thames & Hudson, 1998.

Kemp, Barry J. *Ancient Egypt: Anatomy of a Civilization.* 2d ed. New York: Routledge, 2006.

Kozloff, Arielle P., and Betsy M. Bryan. *Egypt's Dazzling Sun: Amenhotep III and His World.* Cleveland: Cleveland Museum of Art, 1992.

Lange, Kurt, and Max Hirmer. *Egypt: Architecture, Sculpture, and Painting in Three Thousand Years.* 4th ed. London: Phaidon, 1968.

Lehner, Mark. *The Complete Pyramids: Solving the Ancient Mysteries.* New York: Thames & Hudson, 1997.

Mahdy, Christine, ed. *The World of the Pharaohs: A Complete Guide to Ancient Egypt.* London: Thames & Hudson, 1990.

Málek, Jaromír. *Egypt: 4,000 Years of Art.* New York: Phaidon, 2003.

———. *Egyptian Art.* London: Phaidon, 1999.

———, ed. *Egypt: Ancient Culture, Modern Land.* Norman: University of Oklahoma Press, 1993.

Redford, Donald B. *Akhenaton, the Heretic King.* Princeton, N.J.: Princeton University Press, 1984.

———, ed. *The Oxford Encyclopedia of Ancient Egypt.* 3 vols. New York: Oxford University Press, 2001.

Reeves, C. Nicholas. *The Complete Tutankhamun: The King, the Tomb, the Royal Treasure.* London: Thames & Hudson, 1990.

Robins, Gay. *The Art of Ancient Egypt.* Cambridge, Mass.: Harvard University Press, 1997.

———. *Egyptian Painting and Relief.* Aylesbury: Shire, 1986.

———. *Proportion and Style in Ancient Egyptian Art.* Austin: University of Texas Press, 1994.

———. *Women in Ancient Egypt.* London: British Museum, 1993.

Romer, John. *Valley of the Kings: Exploring the Tombs of the Pharaohs.* New York: Holt, 1994.

Russmann, Edna R. *Egyptian Sculpture: Cairo and Luxor.* Austin: University of Texas Press, 1989.

Schäfer, Heinrich. *Principles of Egyptian Art.* Rev. ed. Oxford: Clarendon, 1986.

Schulz, Regina, and Matthias Seidel, eds. *Egypt: The World of the Pharaohs.* Cologne: Könemann, 1999.

Shafer, Byron E., ed. *Temples of Ancient Egypt.* Ithaca, N.Y.: Cornell University Press, 1997.

Shaw, Ian, and Paul Nicholson. *The Dictionary of Ancient Egypt.* London: British Museum, 1995.

Silverman, David P., ed. *Ancient Egypt.* New York: Oxford University Press, 1997.

Smith, William Stevenson, and William Kelly Simpson. *The Art and Architecture of Ancient Egypt.* Rev. ed. New Haven, Conn.: Yale University Press, 1998.

Weeks, Kent R., ed. *Valley of the Kings.* Vercelli: White Star, 2001.

Wildung, Dietrich. *Egypt: From Prehistory to the Romans.* Cologne: Taschen, 1997.

CHAPTER 4:
THE PREHISTORIC AEGEAN

Barber, R. L. N. *The Cyclades in the Bronze Age.* Iowa City: University of Iowa Press, 1987.

Betancourt, Philip P. *A History of Minoan Pottery.* Princeton, N.J.: Princeton University Press, 1965.

Cadogan, Gerald. *Palaces of Minoan Crete.* London: Methuen, 1980.

Chadwick, John. *The Mycenaean World.* New York: Cambridge University Press, 1976.

Cullen, Tracey, ed. *Aegean Prehistory: A Review.* Boston: Archaeological Institute of America, 2001.

Demargne, Pierre. *The Birth of Greek Art.* New York: Golden, 1964.

Dickinson, Oliver P.T.K. *The Aegean Bronze Age.* New York: Cambridge University Press, 1994.

Doumas, Christos. *Thera, Pompeii of the Ancient Aegean: Excavations at Akrotiri, 1967–1979.* New York: Thames & Hudson, 1983.

———. *The Wall-Paintings of Thera.* Athens: Thera Foundation, 1992.

Fitton, J. Lesley. *Cycladic Art.* Cambridge, Mass.: Harvard University Press, 1989.

———. *The Discovery of the Greek Bronze Age.* London: British Museum, 1995.

Forsyth, Phyllis Young. *Thera in the Bronze Age.* New York: Peter Lang, 1997.

Getz-Preziosi, Patricia. *Sculptors of the Cyclades: Individual and Tradition in the Third Millennium BC.* Ann Arbor: University of Michigan Press, 1987.

Graham, James W. *The Palaces of Crete.* Princeton, N.J.: Princeton University Press, 1987.

Hampe, Roland, and Erika Simon. *The Birth of Greek Art: From the Mycenaean to the Archaic Period.* New York: Oxford University Press, 1981.

Higgins, Reynold. *Minoan and Mycenaean Art.* Rev. ed. New York: Thames & Hudson, 1997.

Hood, Sinclair. *The Arts in Prehistoric Greece.* New Haven, Conn.: Yale University Press, 1992.

Immerwahr, Sarah A. *Aegean Painting in the Bronze Age.* University Park: Pennsylvania State University Press, 1990.

MacGillivray, J. A. *Minotaur: Sir Arthur Evans and the Archaeology of the Minoan Myth.* New York: Hill and Wang, 2000.

Marinatos, Nanno. *Art and Religion in Thera: Reconstructing a Bronze Age Society.* Athens: Mathioulakis, 1984.

Marinatos, Spyridon, and Max Hirmer. *Crete and Mycenae.* London: Thames & Hudson, 1960.

McDonald, William A., and Carol G. Thomas. *Progress into the Past: The Rediscovery of Mycenaean Civilization.* 2d ed. Bloomington: Indiana University Press, 1990.

Preziosi, Donald, and Louise A. Hitchcock. *Aegean Art and Architecture.* New York: Oxford University Press, 1999.

Taylour, Lord William. *The Mycenaeans.* London: Thames & Hudson, 1990.

Vermeule, Emily. *Greece in the Bronze Age.* Chicago: University of Chicago Press, 1972.

Warren, Peter. *The Aegean Civilisations from Ancient Crete to Mycenae.* 2d ed. Oxford: Elsevier-Phaidon, 1989.

CHAPTER 5:
ANCIENT GREECE

Arias, Paolo. *A History of One Thousand Years of Greek Vase Painting.* New York: Abrams, 1962.

Ashmole, Bernard. *Architect and Sculptor in Classical Greece.* New York: New York University Press, 1972.

Berve, Helmut, Gottfried Gruben, and Max Hirmer. *Greek Temples, Theatres, and Shrines.* New York: Abrams, 1963.

Biers, William. *The Archaeology of Greece: An Introduction.* 2d ed. Ithaca, N.Y.: Cornell University Press, 1996.

Boardman, John. *Athenian Black Figure Vases.* Rev. ed. New York: Thames & Hudson, 1985.

———. *Athenian Red Figure Vases: The Archaic Period.* New York: Thames & Hudson, 1988.

———. *Athenian Red Figure Vases: The Classical Period.* New York: Thames & Hudson, 1989.

———. *Early Greek Vase Painting, 11th–6th Centuries BC.* New York: Thames & Hudson, 1998.

———. *Greek Sculpture: The Archaic Period.* Rev. ed. New York: Thames & Hudson, 1985.

———. *Greek Sculpture: The Classical Period.* New York: Thames & Hudson, 1987.

———. *Greek Sculpture: The Late Classical Period and Sculpture in Colonies and Overseas.* New York: Thames & Hudson, 1995.

———. *The Parthenon and Its Sculpture.* Austin: University of Texas Press, 1985.

Camp, John M. *The Archaeology of Athens.* New Haven, Conn.: Yale University Press, 2001.

Carpenter, Thomas H. *Art and Myth in Ancient Greece.* New York: Thames & Hudson, 1991.

Charbonneaux, Jean, Roland Martin, and François Villard. *Archaic Greek Art.* New York: Braziller, 1971.

———. *Classical Greek Art.* New York: Braziller, 1972.

———. *Hellenistic Art.* New York: Braziller, 1973.

Coldstream, J. Nicholas. *Geometric Greece.* New York: St. Martin's, 1977.

Coulton, J. J. *Ancient Greek Architects at Work.* Ithaca, N.Y.: Cornell University Press, 1982.

Fullerton, Mark D. *Greek Art.* New York: Cambridge University Press, 2000.

Haynes, Denys E. L. *The Technique of Greek Bronze Statuary.* Mainz: von Zabern, 1992.

Houser, Caroline. *Greek Monumental Bronze Sculpture.* New York: Vendome, 1983.

Hurwit, Jeffrey M. *The Art and Culture of Early Greece, 1100–480 BC.* Ithaca, N.Y.: Cornell University Press, 1985.

———. *The Athenian Acropolis: History, Mythology, and Archaeology from the Neolithic Era to the Present.* New York: Cambridge University Press, 1999.

Jenkins, Ian. *Greek Architecture and Its Sculpture.* Cambridge, Mass.: Harvard University Press, 2006.

———. *The Parthenon Frieze.* Austin: University of Texas Press, 1994.

Lawrence, Arnold W., and R. A. Tomlinson. *Greek Architecture.* Rev. ed. New Haven, Conn.: Yale University Press, 1996.

Martin, Roland. *Greek Architecture: Architecture of Crete, Greece, and the Greek World.* New York: Electa/Rizzoli, 1988.

Mattusch, Carol C. *Classical Bronzes: The Art and Craft of Greek and Roman Statuary.* Ithaca, N.Y.: Cornell University Press, 1996.

———. *Greek Bronze Statuary from the Beginnings through the Fifth Century BC.* Ithaca, N.Y.: Cornell University Press, 1988.

Mee, Christopher, and Tony Spawforth. *Greece: An Oxford Archaeological Guide.* New York: Oxford University Press, 2001.

Morris, Sarah P. *Daidalos and the Origins of Greek Art.* Princeton, N.J.: Princeton University Press, 1992.

Osborne, Robin. *Archaic and Classical Greek Art.* New York: Oxford University Press, 1998.

Palagia, Olga. *The Pediments of the Parthenon.* Leiden: E. J. Brill, 1993.

———, ed. *Greek Sculpture: Functions, Materials, and Techniques in the Archaic and Classical Periods.* New York: Cambridge University Press, 2006.

Palagia, Olga, and Jerome J. Pollitt. *Personal Styles in Greek Sculpture.* New York: Cambridge University Press, 1996.

Pedley, John Griffiths. *Greek Art and Archaeology.* 4th ed. Upper Saddle River, N.J.: Prentice Hall, 2007.

Pollitt, Jerome J. *Art and Experience in Classical Greece.* New York: Cambridge University Press, 1972.

———. *Art in the Hellenistic Age.* New York: Cambridge University Press, 1986.

———. *The Art of Ancient Greece: Sources and Documents.* 2d ed. New York: Cambridge University Press, 1990.

Pugliese Carratelli, G. *The Greek World: Art and Civilization in Magna Graecia and Sicily.* New York: Rizzoli, 1996.

Reeder, Ellen D., ed. *Pandora: Women in Classical Greece.* Baltimore: Walters Art Gallery, 1995.

Rhodes, Robin F. *Architecture and Meaning on the Athenian Acropolis.* New York: Cambridge University Press, 1995.

Richter, Gisela M. *The Portraits of the Greeks.* Rev. ed. by R.R.R. Smith. Ithaca, N.Y.: Cornell University Press, 1984.

Ridgway, Brunilde S. *The Archaic Style in Greek Sculpture.* 2d ed. Chicago: Ares, 1993.

———. *Fifth-Century Styles in Greek Sculpture.* Princeton, N.J.: Princeton University Press, 1981.

———. *Fourth-Century Styles in Greek Sculpture.* Madison: University of Wisconsin Press, 1997.

———. *Hellenistic Sculpture I: The Styles of ca. 331–200 BC.* Madison: University of Wisconsin Press, 1990.

———. *Hellenistic Sculpture II: The Styles of ca. 200–100 BC.* Madison: University of Wisconsin Press, 2000.

———. *Prayers in Stone: Greek Architectural Sculpture.* Berkeley: University of California Press, 1999.

———. *Roman Copies of Greek Sculpture: The Problem of the Originals.* Ann Arbor: University of Michigan Press, 1984.

———. *The Severe Style in Greek Sculpture.* Princeton, N.J.: Princeton University Press, 1970.

Robertson, Martin. *The Art of Vase-Painting in Classical Athens.* New York: Cambridge University Press, 1992.

———. *A History of Greek Art.* Rev. ed. 2 vols. New York: Cambridge University Press, 1986.

———. *A Shorter History of Greek Art.* New York: Cambridge University Press, 1981.

Shapiro, H. Alan. *Art and Cult in Athens under the Tyrants.* Mainz: von Zabern, 1989.

———. *Myth into Art: Poet and Painter in Classical Greece.* New York: Routledge, 1994.

Smith, R. R. R. *Hellenistic Sculpture.* New York: Thames & Hudson, 1991.

Spawforth, Tony. *The Complete Greek Temples.* London, Thames & Hudson, 2006.

Spivey, Nigel. *Greek Art.* London: Phaidon, 1997.

Stansbury-O'Donnell, Mark D. *Pictorial Narrative in Ancient Greek Art.* New York: Cambridge University Press, 1999.

Stewart, Andrew. *Art, Desire, and the Body in Ancient Greece.* New York: Cambridge University Press, 1997.

———. *Greek Sculpture: An Exploration.* 2 vols. New Haven, Conn.: Yale University Press, 1990.

Wycherley, Richard E. *How the Greeks Built Cities.* New York: Norton, 1976.

Asher, Frederick M. *The Art of Eastern India, 300–800.* Minneapolis: University of Minnesota Press, 1980.

Blurton, T. Richard. *Hindu Art.* Cambridge, Mass.: Harvard University Press, 1993.

Chaturachinda, Gwyneth, Sunanda Krishnamurty, and Pauline W. Tabtiang. *Dictionary of South and Southeast Asian Art.* Chiang Mai, Thailand: Silkworm Books, 2000.

Chihara, Daigoro. *Hindu-Buddhist Architecture in Southeast Asia.* Leiden: E. J. Brill, 1996.

Craven, Roy C. *Indian Art: A Concise History.* Rev. ed. London: Thames & Hudson, 1997.

Dehejia, Vidya. *Early Buddhist Rock Temples.* Ithaca, N.Y.: Cornell University Press, 1972.

———. *Indian Art.* London: Phaidon, 1997.

Desai, Vishakha N., and Darielle Mason. *Gods, Guardians, and Lovers: Temple Sculptures from North India AD 700–1200.* New York: Asia Society Galleries, 1993.

Encyclopedia of Indian Temple Architecture. 8 vols. New Delhi: American Institute of Indian Studies; Philadelphia: University of Pennsylvania Press, 1983–1996.

Fisher, Robert E. *Buddhist Art and Architecture.* New York: Thames & Hudson, 1993.

Frederic, Louis. *Borobudur.* New York: Abbeville, 1996.

Gopinatha Rao, T. A. *Elements of Hindu Iconography.* 2d ed. 4 vols. New York: Paragon, 1968.

Harle, James C. *The Art and Architecture of the Indian Subcontinent.* 2d ed. New Haven, Conn.: Yale University Press, 1994.

Huntington, Susan L., and John C. Huntington. *The Art of Ancient India: Buddhist, Hindu, Jain.* New York: Weatherhill, 1985.

Jacques, Claude, and Michael Freeman. *Angkor: Cities and Temples.* Bangkok: River Books, 1997.

Jessup, Helen Ibbitson, and Thierry Zephir, eds. *Sculpture of Angkor and Ancient Cambodia: Millennium of Glory.* Washington, D.C.: National Gallery of Art, 1997.

McIntosh, Jane R. *A Peaceful Realm: The Rise and Fall of the Indus Civilization.* Boulder, Colo.: Westview, 2002.

Michell, George. *Hindu Art and Architecture.* New York: Thames & Hudson, 2000.

———. *The Hindu Temple: An Introduction to Its Meaning and Forms.* Chicago: University of Chicago Press, 1988.

Mitter, Partha. *Indian Art.* New York: Oxford University Press, 2001.

Possehl, Gregory L. *The Indus Civilization: A Contemporary Perspective.* Lanham, Md.: AltaMira, 2002.

Rawson, Phillip. *The Art of Southeast Asia.* New York: Thames & Hudson, 1990.

Srinivasan, Doris Meth. *Many Heads, Arms, and Eyes: Origin, Meaning, and Form of Multiplicity in Indian Art.* Leiden: E. J. Brill, 1997.

Stierlin, Henri. *Hindu India from Khajuraho to the Temple City of Madurai.* Cologne: Taschen, 1998.

Williams, Joanna G. *The Art of Gupta India: Empire and Province.* Princeton, N.J.: Princeton University Press, 1982.

Bush, Susan, and Shio-yen Shih. *Early Chinese Texts on Painting.* Cambridge, Mass.: Harvard University Press, 1985.

Cahill, James. *The Painter's Practice: How Artists Lived and Worked in Traditional China.* New York: Columbia University Press, 1994.

Clunas, Craig. *Art in China.* New York: Oxford University Press, 1997.

Fahr-Becker, Gabriele, ed. *The Art of East Asia.* Cologne: Könemann, 1999.

Fisher, Robert E. *Buddhist Art and Architecture.* New York: Thames & Hudson, 1993.

Fong, Wen C. *Beyond Representation: Chinese Painting and Calligraphy, 8th–14th Century.* New Haven, Conn.: Yale University Press, 1992.

———. *The Great Bronze Age of China: An Exhibition from the People's Republic of China.* New York: Metropolitan Museum of Art, 1980.

Fong, Wen C., and James C. Y. Watt. *Preserving the Past: Treasures from the National Palace Museum, Taipei.* New York: Metropolitan Museum of Art, 1996.

Howard, Angela Falco, Li Song, Wu Hong, and Yang Hong. *Chinese Sculpture.* New Haven, Conn.: Yale University Press, 2006.

Li, Chu-tsing, ed. *Artists and Patrons: Some Social and Economic Aspects of Chinese Painting.* Lawrence, Kans.: Kress Department of Art History, in cooperation with Indiana University Press, 1989.

Little, Stephen, and Shawn Eichman. *Taoism and the Arts of China.* Chicago: Art Institute of Chicago, 2000.

Portal, Jane. *Korea: Art and Archaeology.* New York: Thames & Hudson, 2000.

Powers, Martin J. *Art and Political Expression in Early China.* New Haven, Conn.: Yale University Press, 1991.

Rawson, Jessica. *Ancient China: Art and Archaeology.* New York: Harper & Row, 1980.

———, ed. *The British Museum Book of Chinese Art.* New York: Thames & Hudson, 1992.

Sickman, Laurence, and Alexander C. Soper. *The Art and Architecture of China.* 3d ed. New Haven, Conn.: Yale University Press, 1992.

Silbergeld, Jerome. *Chinese Painting Style: Media, Methods, and Principles of Form.* Seattle and London: University of Washington Press, 1982.

Steinhardt, Nancy S., ed. *Chinese Architecture.* New Haven, Conn.: Yale University Press, 2002.

Sullivan, Michael. *The Arts of China.* 4th ed. Berkeley: University of California Press, 2000.

———. *The Birth of Landscape Painting.* Berkeley: University of California Press, 1962.

Thorp, Robert L., and Richard Ellis Vinograd. *Chinese Art and Culture.* New York: Abrams, 2001.

Vainker, S. J. *Chinese Pottery and Porcelain: From Prehistory to the Present.* New York: Braziller, 1991.

Watson, William. *The Arts of China to AD 900.* New Haven, Conn.: Yale University Press, 1995.

———. *The Arts of China 900–1620.* New Haven, Conn.: Yale University Press, 2000.

Weidner, Marsha, ed. *Flowering in the Shadows: Women in the History of Chinese and Japanese Painting.* Honolulu: University of Hawaii Press, 1990.

Whitfield, Roger, and Anne Farrer. *Caves of the Thousand Buddhas: Chinese Art of the Silk Route.* New York: Braziller, 1990.

Wu, Hung. *Monumentality in Early Chinese Art.* Stanford, Calif.: Stanford University Press, 1996.

———. *The Wu Liang Shrine: The Ideology of Early Chinese Pictorial Art.* Stanford, Calif.: Stanford University Press, 1989.

Xin, Yang, Nie Chongzheng, Lang Shaojun, Richard M. Barnhart, James Cahill, and Hung Wu. *Three Thousand Years of Chinese Painting.* New Haven, Conn.: Yale University Press, 1997.

Aikens, C. Melvin, and Takayama Higuchi. *Prehistory of Japan.* New York: Academic, 1982.

Coaldrake, William H. *Architecture and Authority in Japan.* London: Routledge, 1996.

Elisseeff, Danielle, and Vadime Elisseeff. *Art of Japan.* Translated by I. Mark Paris. New York: Abrams, 1985.

Kidder, J. Edward, Jr. *The Art of Japan.* New York: Park Lane, 1985.

Kurata, Bunsaku. *Horyu-ji: Temple of the Exalted Law.* Translated by W. Chie Ishibashi. New York: Japan Society, 1981.

Mason, Penelope. *History of Japanese Art.* New York: Abrams, 1993.

Nishi, Kazuo, and Kazuo Hozumi. *What Is Japanese Architecture?* Translated by H. Mack Horton. New York: Kodansha International, 1985.

Nishikawa, Kyotaro, and Emily Sano. *The Great Age of Japanese Buddhist Sculpture AD 600–1300.* Fort Worth, Tex.: Kimbell Art Museum, 1982.

Okudaira, Hideo. *Narrative Picture Scrolls.* Adapted by Elizabeth ten Grotenhuis. New York: Weatherhill, 1973.

Pearson, Richard J. *Ancient Japan.* New York: Braziller, 1992.

Pearson, Richard J., Gina Lee Barnes, and Karl L. Hutterer, eds. *Windows on the Japanese Past.* Ann Arbor: Center for Japanese Studies, University of Michigan, 1986.

Rosenfield, John M. *Japanese Art of the Heian Period, 794–1185.* New York: Asia Society, 1967.

Shimizu, Yoshiaki, ed. *The Shaping of Daimyo Culture 1185–1868.* Washington, D.C.: National Gallery of Art, 1988.

Stanley-Baker, Joan. *Japanese Art.* Rev. ed. New York: Thames & Hudson, 2000.

Suzuki, Kakichi. *Early Buddhist Architecture in Japan.* Translated and adapted by Mary Neighbor Parent and Nancy Shatzman Steinhardt. New York: Kodansha International, 1980.

Weidner, Marsha, ed. *Flowering in the Shadows: Women in the History of Chinese and Japanese Painting.* Honolulu: University of Hawaii Press, 1990.

Banti, Luisa. *The Etruscan Cities and Their Culture.* Berkeley: University of California Press, 1973.

Barker, Graeme, and Tom Rasmussen. *The Etruscans.* Oxford: Blackwell, 1998.

Boethius, Axel. *Etruscan and Early Roman Architecture.* 2d ed. New Haven, Conn.: Yale University Press, 1978.

Bonfante, Larissa, ed. *Etruscan Life and Afterlife: A Handbook of Etruscan Studies.* Detroit: Wayne State University Press, 1986.

Brendel, Otto J. *Etruscan Art.* 2d ed. New Haven, Conn.: Yale University Press, 1995.

Cristofani, Mauro. *The Etruscans: A New Investigation.* London: Orbis, 1979.

De Grummond, Nancy Thomson. *Etruscan Myth, Sacred History, and Legend.* Philadelphia: University of Pennsylvania Museum, 2006.

Haynes, Sybille. *Etruscan Civilization: A Cultural History.* Los Angeles: J. Paul Getty Museum, 2000.

Heurgon, Jacques. *Daily Life of the Etruscans.* London: Weidenfeld & Nicolson, 1964.

Pallottino, Massimo. *The Etruscans.* Harmondsworth: Penguin, 1978.

Richardson, Emeline. *The Etruscans: Their Art and Civilization.* Rev. ed. Chicago: University of Chicago Press, 1976.

Ridgway, David, and Francesca Ridgway, eds. *Italy before the Romans.* New York: Academic, 1979.

Spivey, Nigel. *Etruscan Art.* New York: Thames & Hudson, 1997.

Spivey, Nigel, and Simon Stoddart. *Etruscan Italy: An Archaeological History.* London: Batsford, 1990.

Sprenger, Maja, Gilda Bartoloni, and Max Hirmer. *The Etruscans: Their History, Art, and Architecture.* New York: Abrams, 1983.

Steingräber, Stephan. *Abundance of Life: Etruscan Wall Painting.* Los Angeles: J. Paul Getty Museum, 2006.

Torelli, Mario, ed. *The Etruscans.* New York: Rizzoli, 2001.

Anderson, James C., Jr. *Roman Architecture and Society.* Baltimore: Johns Hopkins University Press, 1997.

Andreae, Bernard. *The Art of Rome.* New York: Abrams, 1977.

Bianchi Bandinelli, Ranuccio. *Rome: The Center of Power: Roman Art to AD 200.* New York: Braziller, 1970.

———. *Rome: The Late Empire: Roman Art AD 200–400.* New York: Braziller, 1971.

Brendel, Otto J. *Prolegomena to the Study of Roman Art.* New Haven, Conn.: Yale University Press, 1979.

Claridge, Amanda. *Rome: An Oxford Archaeological Guide.* New York: Oxford University Press, 1998.

Clarke, John R. *The Houses of Roman Italy, 100 BC–AD 250.* Berkeley: University of California Press, 1991.

Cornell, Tim, and John Matthews. *Atlas of the Roman World.* New York: Facts on File, 1982.

D'Ambra, Eve. *Roman Art.* New York: Cambridge University Press, 1998.

———, ed. *Roman Art in Context.* Upper Saddle River, N.J.: Prentice Hall, 1994.

Dobbins, John J., and Pedar Foss, eds. *The World of Pompeii.* London: Routledge, 2007.

Gazda, Elaine K., ed. *Roman Art in the Private Sphere.* Ann Arbor: University of Michigan Press, 1991.

Grant, Michael. *Cities of Vesuvius: Pompeii and Herculaneum.* Harmondsworth: Penguin, 1976.

Hannestad, Niels. *Roman Art and Imperial Policy.* Aarhus: Aarhus University Press, 1986.

Henig, Martin, ed. *A Handbook of Roman Art.* Ithaca, N.Y.: Cornell University Press, 1983.

Kent, John P. C., and Max Hirmer. *Roman Coins.* New York: Abrams, 1978.

Kleiner, Diana E. E. *Roman Sculpture.* New Haven, Conn.: Yale University Press, 1992.

Kleiner, Diana E. E., and Susan B. Matheson, eds. *I Claudia: Women in Ancient Rome.* New Haven, Conn.: Yale University Art Gallery, 1996.

Kleiner, Fred S. *A History of Roman Art.* Belmont, Calif.: Wadsworth, 2007.

Kraus, Theodor. *Pompeii and Herculaneum: The Living Cities of the Dead.* New York: Abrams, 1975.

Lancaster, Lynne. *Concrete Vaulted Construction in Imperial Rome.* New York: Cambridge University Press, 2006.

Ling, Roger. *Roman Painting.* New York: Cambridge University Press, 1991.

L'Orange, Hans Peter. *The Roman Empire: Art Forms and Civic Life.* New York: Rizzoli, 1985.

MacCormack, Sabine G. *Art and Ceremony in Late Antiquity.* Berkeley: University of California Press, 1981.

MacDonald, William L. *The Architecture of the Roman Empire I: An Introductory Study.* Rev. ed. New Haven, Conn.: Yale University Press, 1982.

———. *The Architecture of the Roman Empire II: An Urban Appraisal.* New Haven, Conn.: Yale University Press, 1986.

———. *The Pantheon: Design, Meaning, and Progeny.* Cambridge, Mass.: Harvard University Press, 1976.

Mazzoleni, Donatella. *Domus: Wall Painting in the Roman House.* Los Angeles: J. Paul Getty Museum, 2004.

McKay, Alexander G. *Houses, Villas, and Palaces in the Roman World.* Ithaca, N.Y.: Cornell University Press, 1975.

Nash, Ernest. *Pictorial Dictionary of Ancient Rome.* 2d ed. 2 vols. New York: Praeger, 1962.

Pollitt, Jerome J. *The Art of Rome, 753 BC–AD 337: Sources and Documents.* Rev. ed. New York: Cambridge University Press, 1983.

Richardson, Lawrence, Jr. *A New Topographical Dictionary of Ancient Rome.* Baltimore: Johns Hopkins University Press, 1992.

———. *Pompeii: An Architectural History.* Baltimore: Johns Hopkins University Press, 1988.

Sear, Frank. *Roman Architecture.* Rev. ed. Ithaca, N.Y.: Cornell University Press, 1989.

Stambaugh, John E. *The Ancient Roman City.* Baltimore: Johns Hopkins University Press, 1988.

Taylor, Rabun. *Roman Builders.* New York: Cambridge University Press, 2003.

Toynbee, Jocelyn M. C. *Death and Burial in the Roman World.* London: Thames & Hudson, 1971.

Wallace-Hadrill, Andrew. *Houses and Society in Pompeii and Herculaneum.* Princeton, N.J.: Princeton University Press, 1994.

Ward-Perkins, John B. *Roman Architecture.* New York: Electa/Rizzoli, 1988.

———. *Roman Imperial Architecture.* 2d ed. New Haven, Conn.: Yale University Press, 1981.

Wilson-Jones, Mark. *Principles of Roman Architecture.* New Haven, Conn.: Yale University Press, 2000.

Wood, Susan. *Roman Portrait Sculpture AD 217–260.* Leiden: E. J. Brill, 1986.

Yegül, Fikret. *Baths and Bathing in Classical Antiquity.* Cambridge, Mass.: MIT Press, 1992.

Zanker, Paul. *Pompeii: Public and Private Life.* Cambridge, Mass.: Harvard University Press, 1998.

———. *The Power of Images in the Age of Augustus.* Ann Arbor: University of Michigan Press, 1988.

CHAPTER 11:
LATE ANTIQUITY

Bowersock, G. W., Peter Brown, and Oleg Grabar, eds. *Late Antiquity: A Guide to the Postclassical World.* Cambridge, Mass.: Harvard University Press, 1998.

Elsner, Jaś. *Art and the Roman Viewer: The Transformation of Art from the Pagan World to Christianity.* New York: Cambridge University Press, 1995.

———. *Imperial Rome and Christian Triumph.* New York: Oxford University Press, 1998.

Finney, Paul Corby. *The Invisible God: The Earliest Christians on Art.* New York: Oxford University Press, 1994.

Grabar, André. *The Beginnings of Christian Art, 200–395.* London: Thames & Hudson, 1967.

———. *Christian Iconography.* Princeton, N.J.: Princeton University Press, 1980.

Gutmann, Joseph. *Sacred Images: Studies in Jewish Art from Antiquity to the Middle Ages.* Northampton, Mass.: Variorum, 1989.

Janes, Dominic. *God and Gold in Late Antiquity.* New York: Cambridge University Press, 1998.

Jensen, Robin Margaret. *Understanding Early Christian Art.* New York: Routledge, 2000.

Koch, Guntram. *Early Christian Art and Architecture.* London: SCM, 1996.

Krautheimer, Richard. *Rome, Profile of a City: 312–1308.* Princeton, N.J.: Princeton University Press, 1980.

Krautheimer, Richard, and Slobodan Curcić. *Early Christian and Byzantine Architecture.* 4th ed. New Haven, Conn.: Yale University Press, 1986.

Lowden, John. *Early Christian and Byzantine Art.* London: Phaidon, 1997.

Mathews, Thomas P. *The Clash of Gods: A Reinterpretation of Early Christian Art.* Rev. ed. Princeton, N.J.: Princeton University Press, 1999.

Milburn, Robert. *Early Christian Art and Architecture.* Berkeley: University of California Press, 1988.

Nicolai, Vincenzo Fiocchi, Fabrizio Bisconti, and Danilo Mazzoleni. *The Christian Catacombs of Rome: History, Decoration, Inscriptions.* Regensburg: Schnell & Steiner, 2006.

Perkins, Ann Louise. *The Art of Dura-Europos.* Oxford: Clarendon, 1973.

Volbach, Wolfgang, and Max Hirmer. *Early Christian Art.* New York: Abrams, 1962.

Webster, Leslie, and Michelle Brown, eds. *The Transformation of the Roman World, AD 400–900.* Berkeley: University of California Press, 1997.

Weitzmann, Kurt. *Late Antique and Early Christian Book Illumination.* New York: Braziller, 1977.

———, ed. *Age of Spirituality: Late Antique and Early Christian Art, Third to Seventh Century.* New York: Metropolitan Museum of Art, 1979.

CHAPTER 12:
BYZANTIUM

Barber, Charles. *Figure and Likeness: On the Limits of Representation in Byzantine Iconoclasm.* Princeton, N.J.: Princeton University Press, 2002.

Borsook, Eve. *Messages in Mosaic: The Royal Programmes of Norman Sicily.* Oxford: Clarendon, 1990.

Cormack, Robin. *Byzantine Art.* New York: Oxford University Press, 2000.

———. *Painting the Soul: Icons, Death Masks, and Shrouds.* London: Reaktion, 1997.

———. *Writing in Gold: Byzantine Society and Its Icons.* New York: Oxford University Press, 1985.

Cutler, Anthony. *The Hand of the Master: Craftsmanship, Ivory, and Society in Byzantium, 9th–11th Centuries.* Princeton, N.J.: Princeton University Press, 1994.

Demus, Otto. *The Mosaic Decoration of San Marco, Venice.* Chicago: University of Chicago Press, 1990.

Evans, Helen C., and William D. Wixom, eds. *The Glory of Byzantium: Art and Culture of the Middle Byzantine Era AD 843–1261.* New York: Metropolitan Museum of Art, 1997.

Grabar, André. *The Golden Age of Justinian: From the Death of Theodosius to the Rise of Islam.* New York: Odyssey, 1967.

Grabar, André, and Manolis Chatzidakis. *Greek Mosaics of the Byzantine Period.* New York: New American Library, 1964.

Lowden, John. *Early Christian and Byzantine Art.* London: Phaidon, 1997.

Maguire, Henry. *Art and Eloquence in Byzantium.* Princeton, N.J.: Princeton University Press, 1981.

———. *The Icons of Their Bodies: Saints and Their Images in Byzantium.* Princeton, N.J.: Princeton University Press, 1996.

Mainstone, Rowland J. *Hagia Sophia: Architecture, Structure, and Liturgy of Justinian's Great Church.* London: Thames & Hudson, 1988.

Mango, Cyril. *Art of the Byzantine Empire, 312–1453: Sources and Documents.* Toronto: University of Toronto Press, 1986. Reprint of 1972 ed.

———. *Byzantine Architecture.* New York: Electa/Rizzoli, 1985.

Mark, Robert, and Ahmet S. Cakmak, eds. *Hagia Sophia from the Age of Justinian to the Present.* New York: Cambridge University Press, 1992.

Mathews, Thomas F. *Byzantium: From Antiquity to the Renaissance.* New York: Abrams, 1998.

Ousterhout, Robert. *Master Builders of Byzantium.* Princeton, N.J.: Princeton University Press, 2000.

Pelikan, Jaroslav. *Imago Dei: The Byzantine Apologia for Icons.* Princeton, N.J.: Princeton University Press, 1990.

Rodley, Lyn. *Byzantine Art and Architecture: An Introduction.* New York: Cambridge University Press, 1994.

Von Simson, Otto G. *Sacred Fortress: Byzantine Art and State-craft in Ravenna.* Princeton, N.J.: Princeton University Press, 1986.

Weitzmann, Kurt. *The Icon.* New York: Dorset, 1987.

———. *Illustrations in Roll and Codex.* Princeton, N.J.: Princeton University Press, 1970.

CHAPTER 13:
THE ISLAMIC WORLD

Allan, James, and Sheila R. Canby. *Hunt for Paradise: Court Arts of Safavid Iran 1501–76.* Geneva: Skira, 2004.

Atil, Esin. *The Age of Sultan Suleyman the Magnificent.* Washington, D.C.: National Gallery of Art, 1987.

Baker, Patricia L. *Islamic Textiles.* London: British Museum, 1995.

Blair, Sheila S., and Jonathan Bloom. *The Art and Architecture of Islam 1250–1800.* New Haven, Conn.: Yale University Press, 1994.

Bloom, Jonathan, and Sheila S. Blair. *Islamic Arts.* London: Phaidon, 1997.

Brend, Barbara. *Islamic Art.* Cambridge, Mass.: Harvard University Press, 1991.

Canby, Sheila R. *Persian Painting.* London: British Museum, 1993.

Dodds, Jerrilynn D., ed. *Al-Andalus: The Art of Islamic Spain.* New York: Metropolitan Museum of Art, 1992.

Ettinghausen, Richard, Oleg Grabar, and Marilyn Jenkins-Madina. *The Art and Architecture of Islam, 650–1250.* Rev. ed. New Haven, Conn.: Yale University Press, 2001.

Ferrier, Ronald W., ed. *The Arts of Persia.* New Haven, Conn.: Yale University Press, 1989.

Frishman, Martin, and Hasan-Uddin Khan. *The Mosque: History, Architectural Development, and Regional Diversity.* New York: Thames & Hudson, 1994.

Goodwin, Godfrey. *A History of Ottoman Architecture.* 2d ed. New York: Thames & Hudson, 1994.

Grabar, Oleg. *The Alhambra.* Cambridge, Mass.: Harvard University Press, 1978.

———. *The Formation of Islamic Art.* Rev. ed. New Haven, Conn.: Yale University Press, 1987.

Grube, Ernst J. *Architecture of the Islamic World: Its History and Social Meaning.* 2d ed. New York: Thames & Hudson, 1984.

Hattstein, Markus, and Peter Delius, eds. *Islam: Art and Architecture.* Cologne: Könemann, 2000.

Hillenbrand, Robert. *Islamic Architecture: Form, Function, Meaning.* Edinburgh: Edinburgh University Press, 1994.

——. *Islamic Art and Architecture.* New York: Thames & Hudson, 1999.

Irwin, Robert. *Islamic Art in Context: Art, Architecture, and the Literary World.* New York: Abrams, 1997.

Michell, George, ed. *Architecture of the Islamic World.* New York: Thames & Hudson, 1978.

Necipoglu, Gulru. *The Age of Sinan: Architectural Culture in the Ottoman Empire.* Princeton, N.J.: Princeton University Press, 2005.

Porter, Venetia. *Islamic Tiles.* London: British Museum, 1995.

Robinson, Frank. *Atlas of the Islamic World.* Oxford: Equinox, 1982.

Schimmel, Annemarie. *Calligraphy and Islamic Culture.* New York: New York University Press, 1984.

Stierlin, Henri. *Islam I: Early Architecture from Baghdad to Cordoba.* Cologne: Taschen, 1996.

——. *Islamic Art and Architecture from Isfahan to the Taj Mahal.* New York: Thames & Hudson, 2002.

Ward, Rachel M. *Islamic Metalwork.* New York: Thames & Hudson, 1993.

Welch, Anthony. *Calligraphy in the Arts of the Islamic World.* Austin: University of Texas Press, 1979.

CHAPTER 14:
NATIVE ARTS OF THE AMERICAS BEFORE 1300

Alva, Walter, and Christopher Donnan. *Royal Tombs of Sipán.* Los Angeles: Fowler Museum of Cultural History, 1993.

Benson, Elizabeth P., and Beatriz de la Fuente, eds. *Olmec Art of Ancient Mexico.* Washington, D.C.: National Gallery of Art, 1996.

Berlo, Janet Catherine, ed. *Art, Ideology, and the City of Teotihuacan.* Washington, D.C.: Dumbarton Oaks, 1992.

Berlo, Janet Catherine, and Ruth B. Phillips. *Native North American Art.* New York: Oxford University Press, 1998.

Berrin, Kathleen, ed. *The Spirit of Ancient Peru: Treasures from the Museo Arqueologico Rafael Larco Herrera.* San Francisco: Fine Arts Museums of San Francisco, 1997.

Brody, J. J., and Rina Swentzell. *To Touch the Past: The Painted Pottery of the Mimbres People.* New York: Hudson Hills, 1996.

Brose, David. *Ancient Art of the American Woodland Indians.* New York: Abrams, 1985.

Bruhns, Karen O. *Ancient South America.* New York: Cambridge University Press, 1994.

Burger, Richard. *Chavín and the Origins of Andean Civilization.* New York: Thames & Hudson, 1992.

Carrasco, David. *The Oxford Encyclopedia of Mesoamerican Cultures: The Civilizations of Mexico and Central America.* New York: Oxford University Press, 2001.

Clark, John E., and Mary E. Pye, eds. *Olmec Art and Archaeology in Mesoamerica.* Washington, D.C.: National Gallery of Art, 2000.

Coe, Michael D. *The Maya.* 7th ed. New York: Thames & Hudson, 2005.

——. *Mexico: From the Olmecs to the Aztecs.* 5th ed. New York: Thames & Hudson, 2002.

Cordell, Linda S. *Ancient Pueblo Peoples.* Washington, D.C.: Smithsonian Institution, 1994.

Fagan, Brian. *Ancient North America: The Archaeology of a Continent.* 4th ed. New York: Thames & Hudson, 2005.

Fash, William. *Scribes, Warriors, and Kings: The City of Copan and the Ancient Maya.* New York: Thames & Hudson, 1991.

Feest, Christian F. *Native Arts of North America.* 2d ed. New York: Thames & Hudson, 1992.

Foster, Michael S., and Shirley Gorenstein, eds. *Greater Mesoamerica: The Archaeology of West and Northwest Mexico.* Salt Lake City: University of Utah Press, 2000.

Grube, Nikolai, ed. *Maya: Divine Kings of the Rain Forest.* Cologne: Könemann, 2000.

Kolata, Alan. *The Tiwanaku: Portrait of an Andean Civilization.* Cambridge: Blackwell, 1993.

Kubler, George. *The Art and Architecture of Ancient America: The Mexican, Maya, and Andean Peoples.* 3d ed. New Haven, Conn.: Yale University Press, 1992.

Miller, Mary Ellen. *The Art of Mesoamerica, from Olmec to Aztec.* 4th ed. New York: Thames & Hudson, 2006.

——. *Maya Art and Architecture.* New York: Thames & Hudson, 1999.

Miller, Mary Ellen, and Karl Taube. *The Gods and Symbols of Ancient Mexico and the Maya: An Illustrated Dictionary of Mesoamerican Religion.* New York: Thames & Hudson, 1993.

Morris, Craig, and Adriana von Hagen. *The Inka Empire and Its Andean Origins.* New York: Abbeville, 1993.

Nabokov, Peter, and Robert Easton. *Native American Architecture.* New York: Oxford University Press, 1989.

Pasztory, Esther. *Pre-Columbian Art.* New York: Cambridge University Press, 1998.

Paul, Anne. *Paracas Ritual Attire: Symbols of Authority in Ancient Peru.* Norman: University of Oklahoma Press, 1990.

Penney, David, and George C. Longfish. *Native American Art.* Hong Kong: Hugh Lauter Levin and Associates, 1994.

Schele, Linda, and Peter Mathews. *The Code of Kings: The Language of Seven Sacred Maya Temples and Tombs.* New York: Scribner, 1998.

Schele, Linda, and Mary E. Miller. *The Blood of Kings: Dynasty and Ritual in Maya Art.* Fort Worth, Tex.: Kimbell Art Museum, 1986.

Schmidt, Peter, Mercedes de la Garza, and Enrique Nalda, eds. *Maya.* New York: Rizzoli, 1998.

Stone-Miller, Rebecca. *Art of the Andes from Chavín to Inca.* 2d ed. New York: Thames & Hudson, 2002.

Townsend, Richard F., ed. *Ancient West Mexico.* Chicago: Art Institute of Chicago, 1998.

Von Hagen, Adriana, and Craig Morris. *The Cities of the Ancient Andes.* New York: Thames & Hudson, 1998.

Wardwell, Allen. *Ancient Eskimo Ivories of the Bering Strait.* New York: Rizzoli, 1986.

Whiteford, Andrew H., Stewart Peckham, and Kate Peck Kent. *I Am Here: Two Thousand Years of Southwest Indian Arts and Crafts.* Santa Fe: Museum of New Mexico Press, 1989.

CHAPTER 15:
AFRICA BEFORE 1800

Bacquart, Jean-Baptiste. *The Tribal Arts of Africa.* New York: Thames & Hudson, 2002.

Bassani, Ezio. *Arts of Africa: 7,000 Years of African Art.* Milan: Skira, 2005.

Ben-Amos, Paula. *The Art of Benin.* New York: Thames & Hudson, 1980.

Blier, Suzanne P. *Royal Arts of Africa: The Majesty of Form.* New York: Abrams, 1998.

Campbell, Alec, and David Coulson. *African Rock Art: Paintings and Engravings on Stone.* New York: Abrams, 2001.

Connah, Graham. *African Civilizations.* 2d ed. Cambridge: Cambridge University Press, 2001.

Dewey, William J. *Legacies of Stone: Zimbabwe Past and Present.* Tervuren: Royal Museum for Central Africa, 1997.

Drewal, Henry J., John Pemberton, and Rowland Abiodun. *Yoruba: Nine Centuries of African Art and Thought.* New York: Center for African Art, in association with Abrams, 1989.

Eyo, Ekpo, and Frank Willett. *Treasures of Ancient Nigeria.* New York: Knopf, 1980.

Fagg, Bernard. *Nok Terracottas.* Lagos: Ethnographica, 1977.

Garlake, Peter. *Early Art and Architecture of Africa.* Oxford: Oxford University Press, 2002.

——. *Great Zimbabwe.* London: Thames & Hudson, 1973.

Huffman, Thomas N. *Snakes and Crocodiles: Power and Symbolism in Ancient Zimbabwe.* Johannesburg: Witwatersrand University Press, 1996.

Lajoux, Jean-Dominique. *The Rock Paintings of Tassili.* Cleveland: World Publishing, 1963.

Perani, Judith, and Fred T. Smith. *The Visual Arts of Africa: Gender, Power, and Life Cycle Rituals.* Upper Saddle River, N.J.: Prentice Hall, 1998.

Phillips, Tom, ed. *Africa, the Art of a Continent.* New York: Prestel, 1995.

Phillipson, D. W. *African Archaeology.* 2d ed. New York: Cambridge University Press, 1993.

——. *Ancient Ethiopia: Aksum, Its Antecedents and Successors.* London: British Museum, 1998.

Schädler, Karl-Ferdinand. *Earth and Ore: 2,500 Years of African Art in Terra-Cotta and Metal.* Munich: Panterra Verlag, 1997.

Shaw, Thurstan. *Nigeria: Its Archaeology and Early History.* London: Thames & Hudson, 1978.

——. *Unearthing Igbo-Ukwu: Archaeological Discoveries in Eastern Nigeria.* New York: Oxford University Press, 1977.

Visonà, Monica Blackmun, ed. *A History of Art in Africa.* Upper Saddle River, N.J.: Prentice Hall, 2003.

Willett, Frank. *Ife in the History of West African Sculpture.* New York: McGraw-Hill, 1967.

MEDIEVAL ART, GENERAL

Alexander, Jonathan J. G. *Medieval Illuminators and Their Methods of Work.* New Haven, Conn.: Yale University Press, 1992.

The Art of Medieval Spain, AD 500–1200. New York: Metropolitan Museum of Art, 1993.

Benton, Janetta Rebold. *Art of the Middle Ages.* New York: Thames & Hudson, 2002.

Binski, Paul. *Painters (Medieval Craftsmen).* Toronto: University of Toronto Press, 1991.

Calkins, Robert G. *Illuminated Books of the Middle Ages.* Ithaca, N.Y.: Cornell University Press, 1983.

——. *Medieval Architecture in Western Europe: From AD 300 to 1500.* New York: Oxford University Press, 1998.

Coldstream, Nicola. *Masons and Sculptors (Medieval Craftsmen).* Toronto: University of Toronto Press, 1991.

——. *Medieval Architecture.* New York: Oxford University Press, 2002.

Cross, Frank L., and Livingstone, Elizabeth A., eds. *The Oxford Dictionary of the Christian Church.* 3d ed. New York: Oxford University Press, 1997.

De Hamel, Christopher. *A History of Illuminated Manuscripts.* Oxford: Phaidon, 1986.

——. *Scribes and Illuminators (Medieval Craftsmen).* Toronto: University of Toronto Press, 1992.

Kessler, Herbert L. *Seeing Medieval Art.* Toronto: Broadview, 2004.

——. *Spiritual Seeing: Picturing God's Invisibility in Medieval Art.* Philadelphia: University of Pennsylvania Press, 2000.

Lasko, Peter. *Ars Sacra, 800–1200.* 2d ed. New Haven, Conn.: Yale University Press, 1994.

Murray, Peter, and Linda Murray. *The Oxford Companion to Christian Art and Architecture.* New York: Oxford University Press, 1996.

Pelikan, Jaroslav. *Mary through the Centuries: Her Place in the History of Culture.* New Haven, Conn.: Yale University Press, 1996.

Prache, Anne. *Cathedrals of Europe.* Ithaca, N.Y.: Cornell University Press, 1999.

Raguin, Virginia Chieffo. *Stained Glass from Its Origins to the Present.* New York: Abrams, 2003.

Ross, Leslie. *Medieval Art: A Topical Dictionary.* Westport, Conn.: Greenwood, 1996.

Schütz, Bernard. *Great Cathedrals.* New York: Abrams, 2002.

Sekules, Veronica. *Medieval Art.* New York: Oxford University Press, 2001.

Snyder, James, Henry Luttikhuizen, and Dorothy Verkerk. *Art of the Middle Ages.* 2d ed. Upper Saddle River, N.J.: Prentice Hall, 2006.

Stokstad, Marilyn. *Medieval Art.* 2d ed. Boulder, Colo.: Westview, 2004.

Tasker, Edward G. *Encyclopedia of Medieval Church Art.* London: Batsford, 1993.

CHAPTER 16:
EARLY MEDIEVAL EUROPE

Alexander, Jonathan J. G. *Insular Manuscripts, Sixth to the Ninth Century.* London: Miller, 1978.

The Art of Medieval Spain, AD 500–1200. New York: Metropolitan Museum of Art, 1993.

Backhouse, Janet, D. H. Turner, and Leslie Webster, eds. *The Golden Age of Anglo-Saxon Art, 966–1066.* Bloomington: Indiana University Press, 1984.

Barral i Altet, Xavier. *The Early Middle Ages: From Late Antiquity to AD 1000.* Cologne: Taschen, 1997.

Brown, Katharine Reynolds, Dafydd Kidd, and Charles T. Little, eds. *From Attila to Charlemagne.* New York: Metropolitan Museum of Art, 2000.

Collins, Roger. *Early Medieval Europe, 300–1000.* New York: St. Martin's, 1991.

Conant, Kenneth J. *Carolingian and Romanesque Architecture, 800–1200.* 4th ed. New Haven, Conn.: Yale University Press, 1992.

Davis-Weyer, Caecilia. *Early Medieval Art, 300–1150: Sources and Documents.* Toronto: University of Toronto Press, 1986. Reprint of 1971 ed.

Diebold, William J. *Word and Image: An Introduction to Early Medieval Art.* Boulder, Colo.: Westview Press, 2000.

Dodwell, Charles R. *Anglo-Saxon Art: A New Perspective.* Ithaca, N.Y.: Cornell University Press, 1982.

———. *The Pictorial Arts of the West, 800–1200.* New Haven, Conn.: Yale University Press, 1993.

Harbison, Peter. *The Golden Age of Irish Art: The Medieval Achievement 600–1200.* New York: Thames & Hudson, 1999.

Henderson, George. *From Durrow to Kells: The Insular Gospel-Books, 650–800.* London: Thames & Hudson, 1987.

Hubert, Jean, Jean Porcher, and Wolfgang Fritz Volbach. *The Carolingian Renaissance.* New York: Braziller, 1970.

———. *Europe of the Invasions.* New York: Braziller, 1969.

Klindt-Jensen, Ole, and David M. Wilson. *Viking Art.* 2d ed. Minneapolis: University of Minnesota Press, 1980.

Mayr-Harting, Henry. *Ottonian Book Illumination: An Historical Study.* 2 vols. London: Miller, 1991–1993.

McClendon, Charles. *The Origins of Medieval Architecture: Building in Europe, AD 600–900.* New Haven, Conn.: Yale University Press, 2005.

Megaw, Ruth, and John Vincent Megaw. *Celtic Art: From Its Beginning to the Book of Kells.* New York: Thames & Hudson, 1989.

Mütherich, Florentine, and Joachim E. Gaehde. *Carolingian Painting.* New York: Braziller, 1976.

Nees, Lawrence J. *Early Medieval Art.* New York: Oxford University Press, 2002.

Nordenfalk, Carl. *Celtic and Anglo-Saxon Painting: Book Illumination in the British Isles, 600–800.* New York: Braziller, 1977.

O'Brien, Jacqueline, and Peter Harbison. *Ancient Ireland: From Prehistory to the Middle Ages.* New York: Oxford University Press, 2000.

Richardson, Hilary, and John Scarry. *An Introduction to Irish High Crosses.* Dublin: Mercier, 1996.

Stalley, Roger. *Early Medieval Architecture.* New York: Oxford University Press, 1999.

Wilson, David M. *Anglo-Saxon Art: From the Seventh Century to the Norman Conquest.* London: Thames & Hudson, 1984.

Chapter 17:
Romanesque Europe

Armi, C. Edson. *Masons and Sculptors in Romanesque Burgundy: The New Aesthetics of Cluny III.* 2 vols. University Park: Pennsylvania State University Press, 1983.

Barral i Altet, Xavier. *The Romanesque: Towns, Cathedrals, and Monasteries.* Cologne: Taschen, 1998.

Cahn, Walter. *Romanesque Bible Illumination.* Ithaca, N.Y.: Cornell University Press, 1982.

———. *Romanesque Manuscripts: The Twelfth Century.* 2 vols. London: Miller, 1998.

Conant, Kenneth J. *Carolingian and Romanesque Architecture, 800–1200.* 4th ed. New Haven, Conn.: Yale University Press, 1992.

Demus, Otto. *Romanesque Mural Painting.* New York: Thames & Hudson, 1970.

Dodwell, Charles R. *The Pictorial Arts of the West, 800–1200.* New Haven, Conn.: Yale University Press, 1993.

Fergusson, Peter. *Architecture of Solitude: Cistercian Abbeys in Twelfth-Century Europe.* Princeton, N.J.: Princeton University Press, 1984.

Grape, Wolfgang. *The Bayeux Tapestry: Monument to a Norman Triumph.* New York: Prestel, 1994.

Hearn, Millard F. *Romanesque Sculpture: The Revival of Monumental Stone Sculpture in the Eleventh and Twelfth Centuries.* Ithaca, N.Y.: Cornell University Press, 1981.

Kahn, Deborah, ed. *The Romanesque Frieze and Its Spectator.* London: Miller, 1992.

Male, Émile. *Religious Art in France: The Twelfth Century.* Rev. ed. Princeton, N.J.: Princeton University Press, 1978.

Minne-Sève, Viviane, and Hervé Kergall. *Romanesque and Gothic France: Architecture and Sculpture.* New York: Abrams, 2000.

Nichols, Stephen G. *Romanesque Signs: Early Medieval Narrative and Iconography.* New Haven, Conn.: Yale University Press, 1983.

Nordenfalk, Carl. *Early Medieval Book Illumination.* New York: Rizzoli, 1988.

Petzold, Andreas. *Romanesque Art.* New York: Abrams, 1995.

Schapiro, Meyer. *The Sculpture of Moissac.* New York: Thames & Hudson, 1985.

Stalley, Roger. *Early Medieval Architecture.* New York: Oxford University Press, 1999.

Tate, Robert B., and Marcus Tate. *The Pilgrim Route to Santiago.* Oxford: Phaidon, 1987.

Toman, Rolf, ed. *Romanesque: Architecture, Sculpture, Painting.* Cologne: Könemann, 1997.

Zarnecki, George, Janet Holt, and Tristram Holland, eds. *English Romanesque Art, 1066–1200.* London: Weidenfeld & Nicolson, 1984.

Chapter 18:
Gothic Europe

Bony, Jean. *The English Decorated Style: Gothic Architecture Transformed, 1250–1350.* Ithaca, N.Y.: Cornell University Press, 1979.

———. *French Gothic Architecture of the Twelfth and Thirteenth Centuries.* Berkeley: University of California Press, 1983.

Branner, Robert. *Manuscript Painting in Paris during the Reign of St. Louis.* Berkeley: University of California Press, 1977.

———. *St. Louis and the Court Style in Gothic Architecture.* London: Zwemmer, 1965.

———, ed. *Chartres Cathedral.* New York: Norton, 1969.

Brown, Sarah, and David O'Connor. *Glass-Painters (Medieval Craftsmen).* Toronto: University of Toronto Press, 1991.

Camille, Michael. *Gothic Art: Glorious Visions.* New York: Abrams, 1996.

———. *The Gothic Idol: Ideology and Image-Making in Medieval Art.* New York: Cambridge University Press, 1989.

Courtenay, Lynn T., ed. *The Engineering of Medieval Cathedrals.* Aldershot: Scolar, 1997.

Erlande-Brandenburg, Alain. *The Cathedral: The Social and Architectural Dynamics of Construction.* New York: Cambridge University Press, 1994.

———. *Gothic Art.* New York: Abrams, 1989.

Favier, Jean. *The World of Chartres.* New York: Abrams, 1990.

Fitchen, John. *The Construction of Gothic Cathedrals: A Study of Medieval Vault Erection.* Chicago: University of Chicago Press, 1981.

Frankl, Paul, and Paul Crossley. *Gothic Architecture.* New Haven, Conn.: Yale University Press, 2000.

———. *The Gothic: Literary Sources and Interpretations through Eight Centuries.* Princeton, N.J.: Princeton University Press, 1960.

Frisch, Teresa G. *Gothic Art 1140–c. 1450: Sources and Documents.* Toronto: University of Toronto Press, 1998. Reprint of 1971 ed.

Gerson, Paula, ed. *Abbot Suger and Saint-Denis.* New York: Metropolitan Museum of Art, 1986.

Grodecki, Louis. *Gothic Architecture.* New York: Electa/Rizzoli, 1985.

Grodecki, Louis, and Catherine Brisac. *Gothic Stained Glass, 1200–1300.* Ithaca, N.Y.: Cornell University Press, 1985.

Jantzen, Hans. *High Gothic: The Classic Cathedrals of Chartres, Reims, Amiens.* Princeton, N.J.: Princeton University Press, 1984.

Male, Émile. *Religious Art in France: The Thirteenth Century.* Rev. ed. Princeton, N.J.: Princeton University Press, 1984.

Minne-Sève, Viviane, and Hervé Kergall. *Romanesque and Gothic France: Architecture and Sculpture.* New York: Abrams, 2000.

Nussbaum, Norbert. *German Gothic Church Architecture.* New Haven, Conn.: Yale University Press, 2000.

Panofsky, Erwin. *Abbot Suger on the Abbey Church of St. Denis and Its Art Treasures.* 2d ed. Princeton, N.J.: Princeton University Press, 1979.

Radding, Charles M., and William W. Clark. *Medieval Architecture, Medieval Learning.* New Haven, Conn.: Yale University Press, 1992.

Rudolph, Conrad. *Artistic Change at St-Denis: Abbot Suger's Program and the Early Twelfth-Century Controversy over Art.* Princeton, N.J.: Princeton University Press, 1990.

Sauerländer, Willibald, and Max Hirmer. *Gothic Sculpture in France, 1140–1270.* New York: Abrams, 1973.

Scott, Robert A. *The Gothic Enterprise: A Guide to Understanding the Medieval Cathedral.* Berkeley and Los Angeles: University of California Press, 2003.

Simson, Otto G. von. *The Gothic Cathedral: Origins of Gothic Architecture and the Medieval Concept of Order.* 3d ed. Princeton, N.J.: Princeton University Press, 1988.

Toman, Rolf, ed. *The Art of Gothic: Architecture, Sculpture, Painting.* Cologne: Könemann, 1999.

Williamson, Paul. *Gothic Sculpture, 1140–1300.* New Haven, Conn.: Yale University Press, 1995.

Wilson, Christopher. *The Gothic Cathedral: The Architecture of the Great Church, 1130–1530.* London: Thames & Hudson, 1990.

Renaissance Art, General

Adams, Laurie Schneider. *Italian Renaissance Art.* Boulder, Colo.: Westview, 2001.

Andrés, Glenn M., John M. Hunisak, and Richard Turner. *The Art of Florence.* 2 vols. New York: Abbeville, 1988.

Campbell, Gordon. *Renaissance Art and Architecture.* New York: Oxford University Press, 2005.

Campbell, Lorne. *Renaissance Portraits: European Portrait-Painting in the Fourteenth, Fifteenth, and Sixteenth Centuries.* New Haven, Conn.: Yale University Press, 1990.

Cole, Bruce. *Italian Art, 1250–1550: The Relation of Renaissance Art to Life and Society.* New York: Harper & Row, 1987.

———. *The Renaissance Artist at Work: From Pisano to Titian.* New York: Harper Collins, 1983.

Frommel, Christoph Luitpold. *The Architecture of the Italian Renaissance.* London: Thames & Hudson, 2007.

Hall, Marcia B. *Color and Meaning: Practice and Theory in Renaissance Painting.* Cambridge: Cambridge University Press, 1992.

Hartt, Frederick, and David G. Wilkins. *History of Italian Renaissance Art.* 6th ed. Upper Saddle River, N.J.: Prentice Hall, 2006.

Haskell, Francis, and Nicholas Penny. *Taste and the Antique: The Lure of Classical Sculpture 1500–1900.* New Haven, Conn.: Yale University Press, 1981.

Kent, F. W., and Patricia Simons, eds. *Patronage, Art, and Society in Renaissance Italy.* Canberra: Humanities Research Centre and Clarendon Press, 1987.

Levey, Michael. *Florence: A Portrait.* Cambridge, Mass.: Harvard University Press, 1998.

Lubbock, Jules. *Storytelling in Christian Art from Giotto to Donatello.* New Haven, Conn.: Yale University Press, 2006.

Paoletti, John T., and Gary M. Radke. *Art, Power, and Patronage in Renaissance Italy.* Upper Saddle River, N.J.: Prentice Hall, 2005.

Pope-Hennessy, John. *Introduction to Italian Sculpture.* 3d ed. 3 vols. New York: Phaidon, 1986.

Richardson, Carol M., Kim W. Woods, and Michael W. Franklin. *Renaissance Art Reconsidered: An Anthology of Primary Sources.* Oxford: Blackwell, 2007.

Smith, Jeffrey Chipps. *The Northern Renaissance.* New York: Phaidon, 2004.

Snyder, James, Larry Silver, and Henry Luttikhuizen. *Northern Renaissance Art: Painting, Sculpture, the Graphic Arts from 1350 to 1575*. Upper Saddle River, N.J.: Prentice Hall, 2005.

Thomson, David. *Renaissance Architecture: Critics, Patrons, and Luxury*. Manchester: Manchester University Press, 1993.

Wittkower, Rudolf. *Architectural Principles in the Age of Humanism*. 4th ed. London: Academy, 1988.

CHAPTER 19:
ITALY, 1200 TO 1400

Bomford, David. *Art in the Making: Italian Painting before 1400*. London: National Gallery, 1989.

Borsook, Eve, and Fiorelli Superbi Gioffredi. *Italian Altarpieces 1250–1550: Function and Design*. Oxford: Clarendon, 1994.

Cole, Bruce. *Sienese Painting: From Its Origins to the Fifteenth Century*. New York: Harper Collins, 1987.

Hills, Paul. *The Light of Early Italian Painting*. New Haven, Conn.: Yale University Press, 1987.

Maginnis, Hayden B. J. *Painting in the Age of Giotto: A Historical Reevaluation*. University Park: Pennsylvania State University Press, 1997.

———. *The World of the Early Sienese Painter*. University Park: Pennsylvania State University Press, 2001.

Meiss, Millard. *Painting in Florence and Siena after the Black Death*. Princeton, N.J.: Princeton University Press, 1976.

Moskowitz, Anita Fiderer. *Italian Gothic Sculpture, c. 1250–c. 1400*. Cambridge: Cambridge University Press, 2001.

Norman, Diana, ed. *Siena, Florence, and Padua: Art, Society, and Religion 1280–1400*. New Haven, Conn.: Yale University Press, 1995.

Pope-Hennessy, John. *Italian Gothic Sculpture*. 3d ed. Oxford: Phaidon, 1986.

Stubblebine, James H. *Duccio di Buoninsegna and His School*. Princeton, N.J.: Princeton University Press, 1979.

White, John. *Art and Architecture in Italy: 1250–1400*. 3d ed. New Haven, Conn.: Yale University Press, 1993.

———. *Duccio: Tuscan Art and the Medieval Workshop*. London: Thames & Hudson, 1979.

CHAPTER 20:
NORTHERN EUROPE, 1400 TO 1500

Baxandall, Michael. *The Limewood Sculptors of Renaissance Germany*. New Haven, Conn.: Yale University Press, 1980.

Campbell, Lorne. *The Fifteenth-Century Netherlandish Schools*. London: National Gallery Publications, 1998.

Châtelet, Albert. *Early Dutch Painting*. New York: Konecky, 1988.

Friedlander, Max J. *Early Netherlandish Painting*. 14 vols. New York: Praeger/Phaidon, 1967–1976.

———. *From Van Eyck to Bruegel*. 3d ed. Ithaca, N.Y.: Cornell University Press, 1981.

Harbison, Craig. *The Mirror of the Artist: Northern Renaissance Art in Its Historical Context*. New York: Abrams, 1995.

Jacobs, Lynn F. *Early Netherlandish Carved Altarpieces, 1380–1550: Medieval Tastes and Mass Marketing*. Cambridge: Cambridge University Press, 1998.

Lane, Barbara G. *The Altar and the Altarpiece: Sacramental Themes in Early Netherlandish Painting*. New York: Harper & Row, 1984.

Meiss, Millard. *French Painting in the Time of Jean de Berry: The Limbourgs and Their Contemporaries*. New York: Braziller, 1974.

Müller, Theodor. *Sculpture in the Netherlands, Germany, France, and Spain: 1400–1500*. New Haven, Conn.: Yale University Press, 1986.

Pächt, Otto. *Early Netherlandish Painting from Rogier van der Wayden to Gerard David*. New York: Harvey Miller, 1997.

Panofsky, Erwin. *Early Netherlandish Painting: Its Origins and Character*. 2 vols. Cambridge, Mass.: Harvard University Press, 1966.

Parshall, Peter, and Rainer Schoch. *Origins of European Printmaking: Fifteenth-Century Woodcuts and Their Public*. New Haven, Conn.: Yale University Press, 2005.

Prevenier, Walter, and Wim Blockmans. *The Burgundian Netherlands*. Cambridge: Cambridge University Press, 1986.

Wolfthal, Diane. *The Beginnings of Netherlandish Canvas Painting, 1400–1530*. New York: Cambridge University Press, 1989.

CHAPTER 21:
ITALY, 1400 TO 1500

Ames-Lewis, Francis. *Drawing in Early Renaissance Italy*. New Haven, Conn.: Yale University Press, 1981.

Baxandall, Michael. *Painting and Experience in Fifteenth-Century Italy: A Primer in the Social History of Pictorial Style*. 2d ed. New York: Oxford University Press, 1988.

Bober, Phyllis Pray, and Ruth Rubinstein. *Renaissance Artists and Antique Sculpture: A Handbook of Sources*. Oxford: Oxford University Press, 1986.

Borsook, Eve. *The Mural Painters of Tuscany*. New York: Oxford University Press, 1981.

Cole, Alison. *Virtue and Magnificence: Art of the Italian Renaissance Courts*. New York: Abrams, 1995.

Cole, Bruce. *Masaccio and the Art of Early Renaissance Florence*. Bloomington: Indiana University Press, 1980.

Dempsey, Charles. *The Portrayal of Love: Botticelli's Primavera and Humanist Culture at the Time of Lorenzo the Magnificent*. Princeton, N.J.: Princeton University Press, 1992.

Edgerton, Samuel Y., Jr. *The Heritage of Giotto's Geometry: Art and Science on the Eve of the Scientific Revolution*. Ithaca, N.Y.: Cornell University Press, 1991.

———. *The Renaissance Rediscovery of Linear Perspective*. New York: Harper & Row, 1976.

Gilbert, Creighton, ed. *Italian Art 1400–1500: Sources and Documents*. Evanston, Ill.: Northwestern University Press, 1992.

Goldthwaite, Richard A. *The Building of Renaissance Florence: An Economic and Social History*. Baltimore: Johns Hopkins University Press, 1980.

Heydenreich, Ludwig H. *Architecture in Italy, 1400–1500*. 2d ed. New Haven, Conn.: Yale University Press, 1996.

Hollingsworth, Mary. *Patronage in Renaissance Italy: From 1400 to the Early Sixteenth Century*. Baltimore: Johns Hopkins University Press, 1994.

Kemp, Martin. *Behind the Picture: Art and Evidence in the Italian Renaissance*. New Haven, Conn.: Yale University Press, 1997.

Kempers, Bram. *Painting, Power, and Patronage: The Rise of the Professional Artist in the Italian Renaissance*. London: Penguin, 1992.

Lieberman, Ralph. *Renaissance Architecture in Venice*. New York: Abbeville, 1982.

McAndrew, John. *Venetian Architecture of the Early Renaissance*. Cambridge, Mass.: MIT Press, 1980.

Murray, Peter. *Renaissance Architecture*. New York: Electa/Rizzoli, 1985.

Olson, Roberta J. M. *Italian Renaissance Sculpture*. London: Thames & Hudson, 1992.

Osborne, June. *Urbino: The Story of a Renaissance City*. Chicago: University of Chicago Press, 2003.

Seymour, Charles. *Sculpture in Italy: 1400–1500*. New Haven, Conn.: Yale University Press, 1992.

Turner, A. Richard. *Renaissance Florence: The Invention of a New Art*. New York: Abrams, 1997.

Wackernagel, Martin. *The World of the Florentine Renaissance Artist: Projects and Patrons, Workshops and Art Market*. Princeton, N.J.: Princeton University Press, 1981.

Welch, Evelyn. *Art and Society in Italy 1350–1500*. Oxford: Oxford University Press, 1997.

White, John. *The Birth and Rebirth of Pictorial Space*. 3d ed. Boston: Faber & Faber, 1987.

CHAPTER 22:
ITALY, 1500 TO 1600

Blunt, Anthony. *Artistic Theory in Italy, 1450–1600*. London: Oxford University Press, 1975.

Brown, David Alan, and Sylvia Ferino-Pagden. *Bellini, Giorgione, Titian, and the Renaissance of Venetian Painting*. New Haven, Conn.: Yale University Press, 2006.

Brown, Patricia Fortini. *Art and Life in Renaissance Venice*. New York: Abrams, 1997.

Franklin, David. *Painting in Renaissance Florence, 1500–1550*. New Haven, Conn.: Yale University Press, 2001.

Freedberg, Sydney J. *Painting in Italy: 1500–1600*. 3d ed. New Haven, Conn.: Yale University Press, 1993.

Goffen, Rona. *Piety and Patronage in Renaissance Venice: Bellini, Titian, and the Franciscans*. New Haven, Conn.: Yale University Press, 1986.

———. *Renaissance Rivals: Michelangelo, Leonardo, Raphael, Titian*. New Haven, Conn.: Yale University Press, 2002.

Hall, Marcia B. *After Raphael: Painting in Central Italy in the Sixteenth Century*. Cambridge: Cambridge University Press, 1999.

———, ed. *Rome*. Artistic Centers of the Italian Renaissance. New York: Cambridge University Press, 2005.

Holt, Elizabeth Gilmore, ed. *A Documentary History of Art. Vol. 2, Michelangelo and the Mannerists*. Rev. ed. Princeton, N.J.: Princeton University Press, 1982.

Humfry, Peter. *Painting in Renaissance Venice*. New Haven, Conn.: Yale University Press, 1995.

Huse, Norbert, and Wolfgang Wolters. *The Art of Renaissance Venice: Architecture, Sculpture, and Painting*. Chicago: University of Chicago Press, 1990.

Levey, Michael. *High Renaissance*. New York: Viking Penguin, 1978.

Lotz, Wolfgang. *Architecture in Italy, 1500–1600*. 2d ed. New Haven, Conn.: Yale University Press, 1995.

Partridge, Loren. *The Art of Renaissance Rome*. New York: Abrams, 1996.

Pietrangeli, Carlo, André Chastel, John Shearman, John O'Malley, S.J., Pierluigi de Vecchi, Michael Hirst, Fabrizio Mancinelli, Gianluigi Colalucci, and Franco Bernbei. *The Sistine Chapel: The Art, the History, and the Restoration*. New York: Harmony, 1986.

Pope-Hennessy, John. *Italian High Renaissance and Baroque Sculpture*. 3d ed. 3 vols. Oxford: Phaidon, 1986.

Rosand, David. *Painting in Cinquecento Venice: Titian, Veronese, Tintoretto*. New Haven, Conn.: Yale University Press, 1982.

Shearman, John K. G. *Mannerism*. Baltimore: Penguin, 1978.

———. *Only Connect . . . Art and the Spectator in the Italian Renaissance*. Princeton, N.J.: Princeton University Press, 1990.

Summers, David. *Michelangelo and the Language of Art*. Princeton, N.J.: Princeton University Press, 1981.

Wilde, Johannes. *Venetian Art from Bellini to Titian*. Oxford: Clarendon, 1981.

CHAPTER 23:
NORTHERN EUROPE AND SPAIN, 1500 TO 1600

Blunt, Anthony. *Art and Architecture in France, 1500–1700*. Rev. ed. New Haven, Conn.: Yale University Press, 1999.

Farago, Claire, ed. *Reframing the Renaissance: Visual Culture in Europe and Latin America, 1450–1650*. New Haven, Conn.: Yale University Press, 1995.

Gibson, W. S. *"Mirror of the Earth": The World Landscape in Sixteenth-Century Flemish Painting*. Princeton, N.J.: Princeton University Press, 1989.

Harbison, Craig. *The Mirror of the Artist: Northern Renaissance Art in Its Historical Context*. New York: Abrams, 1995.

Koerner, Joseph Leo. *The Reformation of the Image*. Chicago: University of Chicago Press, 2004.

Landau, David, and Peter Parshall. *The Renaissance Print: 1470–1550*. New Haven, Conn.: Yale University Press, 1994.

Smith, Jeffrey C. *German Sculpture of the Later Renaissance, c. 1520–1580: Art in an Age of Uncertainty*. Princeton, N.J.: Princeton University Press, 1993.

Stechow, Wolfgang. *Northern Renaissance Art, 1400–1600: Sources and Documents*. Evanston, Ill.: Northwestern University Press, 1989.

Zerner, Henri. *Renaissance Art in France: The Invention of Classicism*. Paris: Flammarion, 2003.

BAROQUE ART, GENERAL

Blunt, Anthony, ed. *Baroque and Rococo: Architecture and Decoration.* Cambridge: Harper & Row, 1982.

Harris, Ann Sutherland. *Seventeenth-Century Art & Architecture.* Upper Saddle River, N.J.: Prentice Hall, 2005.

Harrison, Charles, Paul Wood, and Jason Gaiger, eds. *Art in Theory, 1648–1815: An Anthology of Changing Ideas.* Oxford: Blackwell, 2000.

Held, Julius, and Donald Posner. *17th- and 18th-Century Art: Baroque Painting, Sculpture, Architecture.* New York: Abrams, 1971.

Minor, Vernon Hyde. *Baroque & Rococo: Art & Culture.* New York, Abrams, 1999.

Norberg-Schulz, Christian. *Baroque Architecture.* New York: Rizzoli, 1986.

———. *Late Baroque and Rococo Architecture.* New York: Electa/Rizzoli, 1985.

Toman, Rolf. *Baroque: Architecture, Sculpture, Painting.* Cologne: Könemann, 1998.

CHAPTER 24:
ITALY AND SPAIN, 1600 TO 1700

Brown, Jonathan. *The Golden Age of Painting in Spain.* New Haven, Conn.: Yale University Press, 1991.

———. *Velázquez: Painter and Courtier.* New Haven, Conn.: Yale University Press, 1988.

Enggass, Robert, and Jonathan Brown. *Italy and Spain, 1600–1750: Sources and Documents.* Upper Saddle River, N.J.: Prentice Hall, 1970.

Freedberg, Sydney J. *Circa 1600: A Revolution of Style in Italian Painting.* Cambridge, Mass.: Harvard University Press, 1983.

Haskell, Francis. *Patrons and Painters: A Study in the Relations between Italian Art and Society in the Age of the Baroque.* Rev. ed. New Haven, Conn.: Yale University Press, 1980.

Krautheimer, Richard. *The Rome of Alexander VII, 1655–1677.* Princeton, N.J.: Princeton University Press, 1985.

Lagerlöf, Margaretha R. *Ideal Landscape: Annibale Carracci, Nicolas Poussin, and Claude Lorrain.* New Haven, Conn.: Yale University Press, 1990.

Montagu, Jennifer. *Roman Baroque Sculpture: The Industry of Art.* New Haven, Conn.: Yale University Press, 1989.

Puglisi, Catherine. *Caravaggio.* London: Phaidon, 2000.

Varriano, John. *Italian Baroque and Rococo Architecture.* New York: Oxford University Press, 1986.

Wittkower, Rudolf. *Art and Architecture in Italy 1600–1750.* 6th ed. 3 vols. Revised by Joseph Connors and Jennifer Montagu. New Haven, Conn.: Yale University Press, 1999.

CHAPTER 25:
NORTHERN EUROPE, 1600 TO 1700

Alpers, Svetlana. *The Art of Describing: Dutch Art in the Seventeenth Century.* Chicago: University of Chicago Press, 1984.

———. *Rembrandt's Enterprise: The Studio and the Market.* Chicago: University of Chicago Press, 1988.

Belkin, Kristin Lohse. *Rubens.* London: Phaidon, 1998.

Blunt, Anthony. *Art and Architecture in France, 1500–1700.* Rev. ed. New Haven, Conn.: Yale University Press, 1999.

Brown, Christopher. *Scenes of Everyday Life: Dutch Genre Painting of the Seventeenth Century.* London: Faber & Faber, 1984.

Bryson, Norman. *Word and Image: French Painting of the Ancien Régime.* Cambridge: Cambridge University Press, 1981.

Chastel, André. *French Art: The Ancien Régime, 1620–1775.* New York: Flammarion, 1996.

Franits, Wayne. *Looking at Seventeenth-Century Dutch Art: Realism Reconsidered.* Cambridge: Cambridge University Press, 1997.

Haak, Bob. *The Golden Age: Dutch Painters of the Seventeenth Century.* New York: Abrams, 1984.

Mérot, Alain. *French Painting in the Seventeenth Century.* New Haven, Conn.: Yale University Press, 1995.

Muller, Sheila D., ed. *Dutch Art: An Encyclopedia.* New York: Garland, 1997.

North, Michael. *Art and Commerce in the Dutch Golden Age.* New Haven, Conn.: Yale University Press, 1997.

Rosenberg, Jakob, Seymour Slive, and E. H. ter Kuile. *Dutch Art and Architecture, 1600–1800.* New Haven, Conn.: Yale University Press, 1979.

Schama, Simon. *The Embarrassment of Riches: An Interpretation of Dutch Culture in the Golden Age.* Berkeley: University of California Press, 1988.

Stechow, Wolfgang. *Dutch Landscape Painting of the 17th Century.* 3d ed. Oxford: Phaidon, 1981.

Vlieghe, Hans. *Flemish Art and Architecture, 1585–1700.* New Haven, Conn.: Yale University Press, 1998.

Westermann, Mariët. *Rembrandt.* London: Phaidon, 2000.

———. *A Worldly Art: The Dutch Republic 1585–1718.* New Haven, Conn.: Yale University Press, 1996.

CHAPTER 26:
SOUTH AND SOUTHEAST ASIA AFTER 1200

Asher, Catherine B. *Architecture of Mughal India.* New York: Cambridge University Press, 1992.

Beach, Milo Cleveland. *Mughal and Rajput Painting.* Cambridge: Cambridge University Press, 1992.

Blurton, T. Richard. *Hindu Art.* Cambridge, Mass.: Harvard University Press, 1993.

Chaturachinda, Gwyneth, Sunanda Krishnamurty, and Pauline W. Tabtiang. *Dictionary of South and Southeast Asian Art.* Chiang Mai, Thailand: Silkworm Books, 2000.

Craven, Roy C. *Indian Art: A Concise History.* Rev. ed. London: Thames & Hudson, 1997.

Dallapiccola, Anna Libera, ed. *Vijayanagara: City and Empire.* 2 vols. Stuttgart: Steiner, 1985.

Dehejia, Vidya. *Indian Art.* London: Phaidon, 1997.

Encyclopedia of Indian Temple Architecture. 8 vols. New Delhi: American Institute of Indian Studies; Philadelphia: University of Pennsylvania Press, 1983–1996.

Girard-Geslan, Maud, ed. *Art of Southeast Asia.* New York: Abrams, 1998.

Harle, James C. *The Art and Architecture of the Indian Subcontinent.* 2d ed. New Haven, Conn.: Yale University Press, 1994.

Huntington, Susan L., and John C. Huntington. *The Art of Ancient India: Buddhist, Hindu, Jain.* New York: Weatherhill, 1985.

Michell, George. *Architecture and Art of Southern India: Vijayanagara and the Successor States, 1350–1750.* Cambridge: Cambridge University Press, 1995.

———. *Hindu Art and Architecture.* New York: Thames & Hudson, 2000.

———. *The Hindu Temple: An Introduction to Its Meaning and Forms.* Chicago: University of Chicago Press, 1988.

Mitter, Partha. *Indian Art.* New York: Oxford University Press, 2001.

Pal, Pratapaditya, ed. *Master Artists of the Imperial Mughal Court.* Mumbai: Marg, 1991.

Rawson, Phillip. *The Art of Southeast Asia.* New York: Thames & Hudson, 1990.

Stadtner, Donald M. *The Art of Burma: New Studies.* Mumbai: Marg, 1999.

Stevenson, John, and John Guy, eds. *Vietnamese Ceramics: A Separate Tradition.* Chicago: Art Media Resources, 1997.

Stierlin, Henri. *Hindu India from Khajuraho to the Temple City of Madurai.* Cologne: Taschen, 1998.

Welch, Stuart Cary. *Imperial Mughal Painting.* New York: Braziller, 1978.

———. *India: Art and Culture 1300–1900.* New York: Metropolitan Museum of Art, 1985.

CHAPTER 27:
CHINA AND KOREA AFTER 1279

Andrews, Julia Frances, and Kuiyi Shen. *A Century in Crisis: Modernity and Tradition in the Art of Twentieth-Century China.* New York: Guggenheim Museum, 1998.

Barnhart, Richard M. *Painters of the Great Ming: The Imperial Court and the Zhe School.* Dallas: Dallas Museum of Art, 1993.

Cahill, James. *The Painter's Practice: How Artists Lived and Worked in Traditional China.* New York: Columbia University Press, 1994.

Clunas, Craig. *Art in China.* New York: Oxford University Press, 1997.

Fahr-Becker, Gabriele, ed. *The Art of East Asia.* Cologne: Könemann, 1999.

Fisher, Robert E. *Buddhist Art and Architecture.* New York: Thames & Hudson, 1993.

Fong, Wen C., and James C. Y. Watt. *Preserving the Past: Treasures from the National Palace Museum, Taipei.* New York: Metropolitan Museum of Art, 1996.

Laing, Ellen Johnston. *The Winking Owl: Art in the People's Republic of China.* Berkeley: University of California Press, 1989.

Li, Chu-tsing, ed. *Artists and Patrons: Some Social and Economic Aspects of Chinese Painting.* Lawrence, Kans.: Kress Department of Art History in cooperation with Indiana University Press, 1989.

Nakata, Yujiro, ed. *Chinese Calligraphy.* New York: Weatherhill, 1983.

Portal, Jane. *Korea: Art and Archaeology.* New York: Thames & Hudson, 2000.

Rawson, Jessica, ed. *The British Museum Book of Chinese Art.* New York: Thames & Hudson, 1992.

Silbergeld, Jerome. *Chinese Painting Style: Media, Methods, and Principles of Form.* Seattle: University of Washington Press, 1982.

Steinhardt, Nancy S., ed. *Chinese Architecture.* New Haven, Conn.: Yale University Press, 2002.

Sullivan, Michael. *Art and Artists of Twentieth-Century China.* Berkeley: University of California Press, 1996.

———. *The Arts of China.* 4th ed. Berkeley: University of California Press, 1999.

Thorp, Robert L. *Son of Heaven: Imperial Arts of China.* Seattle: Son of Heaven, 1988.

Thorp, Robert L., and Richard Ellis Vinograd. *Chinese Art and Culture.* New York: Abrams, 2001.

Vainker, S. J. *Chinese Pottery and Porcelain: From Prehistory to the Present.* London: Braziller, 1991.

Watson, William. *The Arts of China 900–1260.* New Haven, Conn.: Yale University Press, 2000.

———. *The Arts of China after 1260.* New Haven, Conn.: Yale University Press, 2007.

Weidner, Marsha, ed. *Flowering in the Shadows: Women in the History of Chinese and Japanese Painting.* Honolulu: University of Hawaii Press, 1990.

———. *Views from Jade Terrace: Chinese Women Artists 1300–1912.* Indianapolis: Indianapolis Museum of Art, 1988.

Xin, Yang, Nie Chongzheng, Lang Shaojun, Richard M. Barnhart, James Cahill, and Wu Hung. *Three Thousand Years of Chinese Painting.* New Haven, Conn.: Yale University Press, 1997.

CHAPTER 28:
JAPAN AFTER 1336

Addiss, Stephen. *The Art of Zen.* New York: Abrams, 1989.

Baekeland, Frederick. *Imperial Japan: The Art of the Meiji Era (1868–1912).* Ithaca, N.Y.: Herbert F. Johnson Museum of Art, 1980.

Brown, Kendall. *The Politics of Reclusion: Painting and Power in Muromachi Japan.* Honolulu: University of Hawaii Press, 1997.

Cahill, James. *Scholar Painters of Japan.* New York: Asia Society, 1972.

Coaldrake, William H. *Architecture and Authority in Japan.* London: Routledge, 1996.

Fontein, Jan, and Money L. Hickman. *Zen Painting and Calligraphy.* Greenwich, Conn.: New York Graphic Society, 1970.

Guth, Christine. *Art of Edo Japan: The Artist and the City, 1615–1868.* New York: Abrams, 1996.

Hickman, Money L., John T. Carpenter, Bruce A. Coats, Christine Guth, Andrew J. Pekarik, John M. Rosenfield, and Nicole C. Rousmaniere. *Japan's Golden Age: Momoyama.* New Haven, Conn.: Yale University Press, 1996.

Kawakita, Michiaki. *Modern Currents in Japanese Art.* Translated by Charles E. Terry. New York: Weather-hill, 1974.

Kidder, J. Edward, Jr. *The Art of Japan.* New York: Park Lane, 1985.

Lane, Richard. *Images from the Floating World: The Japanese Print.* New York: Dorset, 1978.

Mason, Penelope. *History of Japanese Art.* New York: Abrams, 1993.

Munroe, Alexandra. *Japanese Art after 1945: Scream against the Sky.* New York: Abrams, 1994.

Nishi, Kazuo, and Kazuo Hozumi. *What Is Japanese Architecture?* Translated by H. Mack Horton. New York: Kodansha International, 1985.

Sanford, James H., William R. LaFleur, and Masatoshi Nagatomi. *Flowing Traces: Buddhism in the Literary and Visual Arts of Japan.* Princeton, N.J.: Princeton University Press, 1992.

Shimizu, Yoshiaki, ed. *Japan: The Shaping of Daimyo Culture, 1185–1868.* Washington, D.C.: National Gallery of Art, 1988.

Singer, Robert T. *Edo: Art in Japan 1615–1868.* Washington, D.C.: National Gallery of Art, 1998.

Stanley-Baker, Joan. *Japanese Art.* Rev. ed. New York: Thames & Hudson, 2000.

Stewart, David B. *The Making of a Modern Japanese Architecture, 1868 to the Present.* New York: Kodansha International, 1988.

CHAPTER 29:
EUROPE AND AMERICA, 1700 TO 1800

Bermingham, Ann. *Landscape and Ideology: The English Rustic Tradition, 1740–1850.* Berkeley: University of California Press, 1986.

Boime, Albert. *Art in the Age of Revolution, 1750–1800.* Chicago: University of Chicago Press, 1987.

Braham, Allan. *The Architecture of the French Enlightenment.* Berkeley: University of California Press, 1980.

Brion, Marcel. *Art of the Romantic Era: Romanticism, Classicism, Realism.* New York: Praeger, 1966.

Conisbee, Philip. *Painting in Eighteenth-Century France.* Ithaca, N.Y.: Phaidon/Cornell University Press, 1981.

Crow, Thomas E. *Painters and Public Life in Eighteenth-Century Paris.* New Haven, Conn.: Yale University Press, 1985.

Gaunt, W. *The Great Century of British Painting: Hogarth to Turner.* New York: Phaidon, 1971.

Harrison, Charles, Paul Wood, and Jason Gaiger, eds. *Art in Theory, 1648–1815: An Anthology of Changing Ideas.* Oxford: Blackwell, 2000.

Herrmann, Luke. *British Landscape Painting of the Eighteenth Century.* New York: Oxford University Press, 1974.

Honour, Hugh. *Neo-Classicism.* Harmondsworth: Penguin, 1968.

Irwin, David. *Neoclassicism.* London: Phaidon, 1997.

Kalnein, Wend Graf, and Michael Levey. *Art and Architecture of the Eighteenth Century in France.* New York: Viking/Pelican, 1973.

Lee, Simon. *David.* London: Phaidon, 1999.

Levey, Michael. *Rococo to Revolution: Major Trends in Eighteenth-Century Painting.* London: Thames & Hudson, 1966.

Rosenblum, Robert. *Transformations in Late Eighteenth-Century Art.* Princeton, N.J.: Princeton University Press, 1970.

Roston, Murray. *Changing Perspectives in Literature and the Visual Arts, 1650–1820.* Princeton, N.J.: Princeton University Press, 1990.

Rykwert, Joseph. *The First Moderns: Architects of the Eighteenth Century.* Cambridge, Mass.: MIT Press, 1983.

Stillman, Damie. *English Neo-Classical Architecture.* 2 vols. London: Zwemmer, 1988.

Waterhouse, Ellis Kirkham. *Painting in Britain: 1530–1790.* 4th ed. New Haven, Conn.: Yale University Press, 1979.

Wilton, Andrew. *The Swagger Portrait: Grand Manner Portraiture in Britain from Van Dyck to Augustus John, 1630–1930.* London: Tate Gallery, 1992.

19TH AND 20TH CENTURIES, GENERAL

Arnason, H. H., and Peter Kalb. *History of Modern Art: Painting, Sculpture, Architecture, Photography.* 5th ed. Upper Saddle River, N.J.: Prentice Hall, 2004.

Ashton, Dore. *Twentieth-Century Artists on Art.* New York: Pantheon Books, 1985.

Brown, Milton, Sam Hunter, and John Jacobus. *American Art: Painting, Sculpture, Architecture, Decorative Arts, Photography.* New York: Abrams, 1979.

Burnham, Jack. *Beyond Modern Sculpture: The Effects of Science and Technology on the Sculpture of This Century.* New York: Braziller, 1968.

Chipp, Herschel B. *Theories of Modern Art.* Berkeley: University of California Press, 1968.

Chu, Petra ten-Doesschate. *Nineteenth-Century European Art.* 2d ed. Upper Saddle River, N.J.: Prentice Hall, 2006.

Coke, Van Deren. *The Painter and the Photograph from Delacroix to Warhol.* Rev. ed. Albuquerque: University of New Mexico Press, 1972.

Colquhoun, Alan. *Modern Architecture.* New York: Oxford University Press, 2002.

Craven, Wayne. *American Art: History and Culture.* Madison, Wis.: Brown & Benchmark, 1994.

Doss, Erika. *Twentieth-Century American Art.* New York: Oxford University Press, 2002.

Driskell, David C. *Two Centuries of Black American Art.* Los Angeles: Los Angeles County Museum of Art; New York: Knopf, 1976.

Eisenman, Stephen F., ed. *Nineteenth-Century Art: A Critical History.* 3d ed. New York: Thames & Hudson, 2007.

Elsen, Albert. *Origins of Modern Sculpture.* New York: Braziller, 1974.

Foster, Hal, Rosalind Krauss, Yve-Alain Bois, and Benjamin H. D. Buchloh. *Art since 1900: Modernism, Antimodernism, Postmodernism.* New York: Thames & Hudson, 2004.

Frampton, Kenneth. *Modern Architecture: A Critical History.* 3d ed. London: Thames & Hudson, 1992.

Frascina, Francis, and Charles Harrison, eds. *Modern Art and Modernism: A Critical Anthology.* New York: Harper & Row, 1982.

Giedion, Siegfried. *Space, Time, and Architecture: The Growth of a New Tradition.* 4th ed. Cambridge, Mass.: Harvard University Press, 1965.

Goldwater, Robert, and Marco Treves, eds. *Artists on Art.* 3d ed. New York: Pantheon, 1958.

Greenough, Sarah, Joel Snyder, David Travis, and Colin Westerbeck. *On the Art of Fixing a Shadow: One Hundred and Fifty Years of Photography.* Washington, D.C.: National Gallery of Art; Chicago: Art Institute of Chicago, 1989.

Hamilton, George H. *Painting and Sculpture in Europe, 1880–1940.* 6th ed. New Haven, Conn.: Yale University Press, 1993.

Harrison, Charles, and Paul Wood. *Art in Theory, 1900–2000: An Anthology of Changing Ideas.* Oxford: Blackwell, 2003.

Herbert, Robert L., ed. *Modern Artists on Art.* Upper Saddle River, N.J.: Prentice Hall, 1971.

Hertz, Richard, and Norman M. Klein, eds. *Twentieth-Century Art Theory: Urbanism, Politics, and Mass Culture.* Englewood Cliffs, N.J.: Prentice Hall, 1990.

Heyer, Paul. *Architects on Architecture: New Directions in America.* New York: Van Nostrand Reinhold, 1993.

Hills, Patricia. *Modern Art in the USA: Issues and Controversies of the 20th Century.* Upper Saddle River, N.J.: Prentice Hall, 2000.

Hitchcock, Henry-Russell. *Architecture: Nineteenth and Twentieth Centuries.* 4th ed. New Haven, Conn.: Yale University Press, 1977.

Hunter, Sam, John Jacobus, and Daniel Wheeler. *Modern Art: Painting, Sculpture, Architecture, Photography.* Rev. 3d ed. Upper Saddle River, N.J.: Prentice Hall, 2004.

Jencks, Charles. *Modern Movements in Architecture.* Garden City, N.Y.: Anchor; Doubleday, 1973.

Kaufmann, Edgar, Jr., ed. *The Rise of an American Architecture.* New York: Metropolitan Museum of Art; Praeger, 1970.

Krauss, Rosalind E. *The Originality of the Avant-Garde and Other Modernist Myths.* Cambridge, Mass.: MIT Press, 1985.

———. *Passages in Modern Sculpture.* Cambridge, Mass.: MIT Press, 1981.

Lewis, Samella S. *African American Art and Artists.* Rev. ed. Berkeley: University of California Press, 1994.

Licht, Fred. *Sculpture, Nineteenth and Twentieth Centuries.* Greenwich, Conn.: New York Graphic Society, 1967.

Marien, Mary Warner. *Photography: A Cultural History.* 2d ed. Upper Saddle River, N.J.: Prentice Hall, 2006.

Mason, Jerry, ed. *International Center of Photography Encyclopedia of Photography.* New York: Crown, 1984.

McCoubrey, John W. *American Art, 1700–1960: Sources and Documents.* Englewood Cliffs, N.J.: Prentice Hall, 1965.

Newhall, Beaumont. *The History of Photography.* New York: Museum of Modern Art, 1982.

Osborne, Harold. *The Oxford Companion to Twentieth-Century Art.* New York: Oxford University Press, 1981.

Pohl, Francis K. *Framing America: A Social History of American Art.* New York: Thames & Hudson, 2002.

Rose, Barbara. *American Art since 1900.* Rev. ed. New York: Praeger, 1975.

Rosenblum, Naomi. *A World History of Photography.* 3d ed. New York: Abbeville, 1997.

Rosenblum, Robert. *Modern Painting and the Northern Romantic Tradition: Friedrich to Rothko.* New York: Harper & Row, 1975.

Rosenblum, Robert, and Horst W. Janson. *19th-Century Art.* Rev. ed. Upper Saddle River, N.J.: Prentice Hall, 2005.

Ross, Stephen David, ed. *Art and Its Significance: An Anthology of Aesthetic Theory.* Albany: State University of New York Press, 1987.

Russell, John. *The Meanings of Modern Art.* New York: Museum of Modern Art; Thames & Hudson, 1981.

Scully, Vincent. *Modern Architecture.* Rev. ed. New York: Braziller, 1974.

Spalding, Francis. *British Art since 1900.* London: Thames & Hudson, 1986.

Spencer, Harold. *American Art: Readings from the Colonial Era to the Present.* New York: Scribner, 1980.

Steinberg, Leo. *Other Criteria: Confrontations with 20th-Century Art.* New York: Oxford University Press, 1972.

Szarkowski, John. *Photography until Now.* New York: Museum of Modern Art, 1989.

Upton, Dell. *Architecture in the United States.* Oxford: Oxford University Press, 1998.

Weaver, Mike. *The Art of Photography: 1839–1989.* New Haven, Conn.: Yale University Press, 1989.

Whiffen, Marcus, and Frederick Koeper. *American Architecture, 1607–1976.* Cambridge, Mass.: MIT Press, 1983.

Wilmerding, John. *American Art.* Harmondsworth: Penguin, 1976.

Wilson, Simon. *Holbein to Hockney: A History of British Art.* London: Tate Gallery & Bodley Head, 1979.

CHAPTER 30:
EUROPE AND AMERICA, 1800 TO 1870

Bergdoll, Barry. *European Architecture 1750–1890.* New York: Oxford University Press, 2000.

Boime, Albert. *The Academy and French Painting in the 19th Century.* London: Phaidon, 1971.

———. *Art in the Age of Bonapartism, 1800–1815.* Chicago: University of Chicago Press, 1990.

Brown, David Blayney. *Romanticism.* London: Phaidon, 2001.

Bryson, Norman. *Tradition and Desire: From David to Delacroix.* New York: Cambridge University Press, 1984.

Clark, T. J. *The Absolute Bourgeois: Artists and Politics in France, 1848–1851.* London: Thames & Hudson, 1973.

———. *Image of the People: Gustave Courbet and the 1848 Revolution.* London: Thames & Hudson, 1973.

———. *The Painting of Modern Life: Paris in the Art of Manet and His Followers.* Princeton, N.J.: Princeton University Press, 1984.

Clay, Jean. *Romanticism.* New York: Phaidon, 1981.

Eitner, Lorenz. *Neoclassicism and Romanticism, 1750–1850: An Anthology of Sources and Documents.* New York: Harper & Row, 1989.

Fried, Michael. *Courbet's Realism.* Chicago: University of Chicago Press, 1982.

———. *Manet's Modernism, or, The Face of Painting in the 1860s.* Chicago: University of Chicago Press, 1996.

Hilton, Timothy. *The Pre-Raphaelites.* New York: Oxford University Press, 1970.

Holt, Elizabeth Gilmore, ed. *From the Classicists to the Impressionists: A Documentary History of Art and Architecture in the Nineteenth Century.* Garden City, N.J.: Anchor Books; Doubleday, 1966.

Honour, Hugh. *Romanticism.* New York: Harper & Row, 1979.

Janson, Horst W. *19th-Century Sculpture.* New York: Abrams, 1985.

Krell, Alain. *Manet and the Painters of Contemporary Life.* London: Thames & Hudson, 1996.

Kroeber, Karl. *British Romantic Art.* Berkeley: University of California Press, 1986.

Mainardi, Patricia. *Art and Politics of the Second Empire: The Universal Expositions of 1855 and 1867.* New Haven, Conn.: Yale University Press, 1987.

———. *The End of the Salon: Art and the State in the Early Third Republic.* Cambridge: Cambridge University Press, 1993.

Middleton, Robin. *Architecture of the Nineteenth Century.* London: Phaidon, 2003.

Middleton, Robin, and David Watkin. *Neoclassical and 19th-Century Architecture.* 2 vols. New York: Electa/Rizzoli, 1987.

Needham, Gerald. *19th-Century Realist Art.* New York: Harper & Row, 1988.

Nochlin, Linda. *Realism and Tradition in Art, 1848–1900: Sources and Documents.* Upper Saddle River, N.J.: Prentice Hall, 1966.

Novak, Barbara. *American Painting of the Nineteenth Century: Realism and the American Experience.* New York: Harper & Row, 1979.

Novotny, Fritz. *Painting and Sculpture in Europe, 1780–1880.* 3d ed. New Haven, Conn.: Yale University Press, 1988.

Porterfield, Todd. *The Allure of Empire: Art in the Service of French Imperialism 1798–1836.* Princeton, N.J.: Princeton University Press, 1998.

Rosen, Charles, and Henri Zerner. *Romanticism and Realism: The Mythology of Nineteenth-Century Art.* New York: Viking, 1984.

Rubin, James Henry. *Courbet.* London: Phaidon, 1997.

Sloane, Joseph C. *French Painting between the Past and the Present: Artists, Critics, and Traditions from 1848 to 1870.* Princeton, N.J.: Princeton University Press, 1973.

Symmons, Sarah. *Goya.* London: Phaidon, 1998.

Taylor, Joshua, ed. *Nineteenth-Century Theories of Art.* Berkeley: University of California Press, 1987.

Vaughn, William. *German Romantic Painting.* New Haven, Conn.: Yale University Press, 1980.

Wolf, Bryan Jay. *Romantic Revision: Culture and Consciousness in Nineteenth-Century American Painting and Literature.* Chicago: University of Chicago Press, 1986.

Wood, Christopher. *The Pre-Raphaelites.* New York: Viking, 1981.

CHAPTER 31:
EUROPE AND AMERICA, 1870 TO 1900

Adams, Steven. *The Barbizon School and the Origins of Impressionism.* London: Phaidon, 1994.

Broude, Norma. *Impressionism: A Feminist Reading.* New York: Rizzoli, 1991.

Duncan, Alastair. *Art Nouveau.* New York: Thames & Hudson, 1994.

Escritt, Stephen. *Art Nouveau.* London: Phaidon, 2000.

Garb, Tamar. *Bodies of Modernity: Figure and Flesh in Fin-de-Siècle France.* New York: Thames & Hudson, 1998.

Gerdts, William H. *American Impressionism.* New York: Abbeville, 1984.

Herbert, Robert L. *Impressionism: Art, Leisure, and Parisian Society.* New Haven, Conn.: Yale University Press, 1988.

Jensen, Robert. *Marketing Modernism in Fin-de-Siècle Europe.* Princeton, N.J.: Princeton University Press, 1994.

Lewis, Mary Tompkins. *Cézanne.* London: Phaidon, 2000.

Nochlin, Linda. *Impressionism and Post-Impressionism, 1874–1904: Sources and Documents.* Upper Saddle River, N.J.: Prentice Hall, 1966.

Pfeiffer, Ingrid, and Max Hollein, eds. *Women Impressionists.* Ostfildern, Germany: Hatje Cantz, 2008.

Rachman, Carla. *Monet.* London: Phaidon, 1997.

Rapetti, Rodolphe. *Symbolism.* Paris: Flammarion, 2006.

Rubin, James H. *Impressionism.* London: Phaidon, 1999.

Schorske, Carl E. *Fin-de-Siècle Vienna: Politics and Culture.* New York: Knopf, 1980.

Shiff, Richard. *Cézanne and the End of Impressionism: A Study of the Theory, Technique, and Critical Evaluation of Modern Art.* Chicago: University of Chicago Press, 1984.

Silverman, Debora L. *Art Nouveau in Fin-de-Siècle France: Politics, Psychology, and Style.* Berkeley: University of California Press, 1989.

Smith, Paul. *Impressionism: Beneath the Surface.* New York: Abrams, 1995.

Sund, Judy. *Van Gogh.* London: Phaidon, 2002.

CHAPTER 32:
NATIVE ARTS OF THE AMERICAS AFTER 1300

Bawden, Garth. *Moche.* Oxford: Blackwell, 1999.

Berlo, Janet Catherine, ed. *Plains Indian Drawings 1865–1935.* New York: Abrams, 1996.

Berlo, Janet Catherine, and Ruth B. Phillips. *Native North American Art.* New York: Oxford University Press, 1998.

Boone, Elizabeth. *The Aztec World.* Washington, D.C.: Smithsonian Institution Press, 1994.

Bruhns, Karen O. *Ancient South America.* New York: Cambridge University Press, 1994.

Coe, Michael D. *The Maya.* 7th ed. New York: Thames & Hudson, 2005.

———. *Mexico: From the Olmecs to the Aztecs.* 5th ed. New York: Thames & Hudson, 2002.

D'Altroy, Terence N. *The Incas.* New ed. Oxford: Blackwell, 2003.

Davies, Nigel. *The Ancient Kingdoms of Peru.* New York: Penguin, 1997.

Feest, Christian F. *Native Arts of North America.* 2d ed. New York: Thames & Hudson, 1992.

Fienup-Riordan, Ann. *The Living Tradition of Yup'ik Masks.* Seattle: University of Washington Press, 1996.

Fitzhugh, William W., and Aron Crowell, eds. *Crossroads of Continents: Cultures of Siberia and Alaska.* Washington, D.C.: Smithsonian Institution Press, 1988.

Gasparini, Graziano, and Luise Margolies. *Inca Architecture.* Bloomington: Indiana University Press, 1980.

Hill, Tom, and Richard W. Hill, Sr., eds. *Creation's Journey: Native American Identity and Belief.* Washington, D.C.: Smithsonian Institution Press, 1994.

Kubler, George. *The Art and Architecture of Ancient America: The Mexican, Maya, and Andean Peoples.* 3d ed. New Haven, Conn.: Yale University Press, 1992.

Malpass, Michael A. *Daily Life in the Inca Empire.* Westport, Conn.: Greenwood, 1996.

Mathews, Zena, and Aldona Jonaitis, eds. *Native North American Art History.* Palo Alto, Calif.: Peek, 1982.

Matos, Eduardo M. *The Great Temple of the Aztecs: Treasures of Tenochtitlan.* New York: Thames & Hudson, 1988.

Maurer, Evan M. *Visions of the People: A Pictorial History of Plains Indian Life.* Seattle: University of Washington Press, 1992.

McEwan, Gordon F. *The Incas: New Perspectives.* Santa Barbara, Calif.: ABC-CLIO, 2006.

Miller, Mary Ellen. *The Art of Mesoamerica, from Olmec to Aztec.* 4th ed. New York: Thames & Hudson, 2006.

Morris, Craig, and Adriana von Hagen. *The Inka Empire and Its Andean Origins.* New York: Abbeville, 1993.

Moseley, Michael E. *The Incas and Their Ancestors: The Archaeology of Peru.* Rev. ed. New York: Thames & Hudson, 2001.

Nabokov, Peter, and Robert Easton. *Native American Architecture.* New York: Oxford University Press, 1989.

Pasztory, Esther. *Aztec Art.* New York: Abrams, 1983.

———. *Pre-Columbian Art.* New York: Cambridge University Press, 1998.

Penney, David W. *North American Indian Art.* New York: Thames & Hudson, 2004.

Phillips, Ruth B. *Trading Identities: The Souvenir in Native North American Art.* Seattle: University of Washington Press, 1998.

Samuel, Cheryl. *The Chilkat Dancing Blanket.* Norman: University of Oklahoma Press, 1982.

Schaafsma, Polly, ed. *Kachinas in the Pueblo World.* Albuquerque: University of New Mexico Press, 1994.

Silverman, Helaine. *The Nasca.* Oxford: Blackwell, 2002.

———, ed. *Andean Archaeology.* Oxford: Blackwell, 2004.

Smith, Michael Ernest. *The Aztecs.* 2d ed. Oxford: Blackwell, 2002.

Stewart, Hilary. *Looking at Totem Poles.* Seattle: University of Washington Press, 1993.

Von Hagen, Adriana, and Craig Morris. *The Cities of the Ancient Andes.* New York: Thames & Hudson, 1998.

Wardwell, Allen. *Tangible Visions: Northwest Coast Indian Shamanism and Its Art.* New York: Monacelli, 1996.

Washburn, Dorothy. *Living in Balance: The Universe of the Hopi, Zuni, Navajo, and Apache.* Philadelphia: University Museum, 1995.

Weaver, Muriel Porter. *The Aztecs, Mayas, and Their Predecessors.* 3d ed. San Diego: Academic, 1993.

Wright, Robin K. *Northern Haida Master Carvers.* Seattle: University of Washington Press, 2001.

Wyman, Leland C. *Southwest Indian Drypainting.* Albuquerque: University of New Mexico Press, 1983.

CHAPTER 33:
OCEANIA

Caruana, Wally. *Aboriginal Art.* 2d ed. New York: Thames & Hudson, 2003.

Cox, J. Halley, and William H. Davenport. *Hawaiian Sculpture.* Rev. ed. Honolulu: University of Hawaii Press, 1988.

D'Alleva, Anne. *Arts of the Pacific Islands.* New York: Abrams, 1998.

Feldman, Jerome, and Donald H. Rubinstein. *The Art of Micronesia.* Honolulu: University of Hawaii Art Gallery, 1986.

Greub, Suzanne, ed. *Authority and Ornament: Art of the Sepik River, Papua New Guinea.* Basel: Tribal Art Centre, 1985.

Hanson, Allan, and Louise Hanson, eds. *Art and Identity in Oceania.* Honolulu: University of Hawaii Press, 1990.

Kaeppler, Adrienne L., Christian Kaufmann, and Douglas Newton. *Oceanic Art.* New York: Abrams, 1997.

Kooijman, Simon. *Tapa in Polynesia.* Honolulu: Bishop Museum Press, 1972.

Mead, Sidney Moko, ed. *Te Maori: Maori Art from New Zealand Collections.* New York: Abrams in association with the American Federation of Arts, 1984.

Morphy, Howard. *Aboriginal Art.* London: Phaidon, 1998.

Sayers, Andrew. *Australian Art.* New York: Oxford University Press, 2001.

Schneebaum, Tobias. *Embodied Spirits: Ritual Carvings of the Asmat.* Salem, Mass.: Peabody Museum of Salem, 1990.

Smidt, Dirk, ed. *Asmat Art: Woodcarvings of Southwest New Guinea.* New York: Braziller in association with Rijksmuseum voor Volkenkunde, Leiden, 1993.

Starzecka, Dorota, ed. *Maori Art and Culture.* Chicago: Art Media Resources, 1996.

Sutton, Peter, ed. *Dreamings: The Art of Aboriginal Australia.* New York: Braziller in association with the Asia Society Galleries, 1988.

Thomas, Nicholas. *Oceanic Art.* London: Thames & Hudson, 1995.

CHAPTER 34:
AFRICA AFTER 1800

Abiodun, Roland, Henry J. Drewal, and John Pemberton III, eds. *The Yoruba Artist: New Theoretical Perspectives on African Arts.* Washington, D.C.: Smithsonian Institution Press, 1994.

Bassani, Ezio. *Arts of Africa: 7,000 Years of African Art.* Milan: Skira, 2005.

Blier, Suzanne P. *The Royal Arts of Africa*. New York: Abrams, 1998.

Cole, Herbert M. *Icons: Ideals and Power in the Art of Africa*. Washington, D.C.: National Museum of African Art, Smithsonian Institution, 1989.

———, ed. *I Am Not Myself: The Art of African Masquerade*. Los Angeles: UCLA Fowler Museum of Cultural History, 1985.

Cole, Herbert M., and Chike C. Aniakor. *Igbo Art: Community and Cosmos*. Los Angeles: UCLA Fowler Museum of Cultural History, 1984.

Fraser, Douglas F., and Herbert M. Cole, eds. *African Art and Leadership*. Madison: University of Wisconsin Press, 1972.

Geary, Christraud M. *Things of the Palace: A Catalogue of the Bamum Palace Museum in Foumban (Cameroon)*. Weisbaden: Franz Steiner Verlag, 1983.

Glaze, Anita J. *Art and Death in a Senufo Village*. Bloomington: Indiana University Press, 1981.

Kasfir, Sidney L. *Contemporary African Art*. London: Thames & Hudson, 1999.

———. *West African Masks and Cultural Systems*. Tervuren: Musée Royal de l'Afrique Centrale, 1988.

Magnin, Andre, with Jacques Soulillou. *Contemporary Art of Africa*. New York: Abrams, 1996.

Nooter, Mary H. *Secrecy: African Art That Conceals and Reveals*. New York: Museum for African Art, 1993.

Oguibe, Olu, and Okwui Enwezor, eds. *Reading the Contemporary: African Art from Theory to the Marketplace*. London: Institute of International Visual Arts, 1999.

Perani, Judith, and Fred T. Smith. *The Visual Arts of Africa: Gender, Power, and Life Cycle Rituals*. Upper Saddle River, N.J.: Prentice Hall, 1998.

Phillips, Ruth B. *Representing Women: Sande Masquerades of the Mende of Sierra Leone*. Los Angeles: UCLA Fowler Museum of Cultural History, 1995.

Sieber, Roy, and Roslyn A. Walker. *African Art in the Cycle of Life*. Washington, D.C.: Smithsonian Institution Press, 1987.

Thompson, Robert F., and Joseph Cornet. *The Four Moments of the Sun: Kongo Art in Two Worlds*. Washington, D.C.: National Gallery of Art, 1981.

Vinnicombe, Patricia. *People of the Eland: Rock Paintings of the Drakensberg Bushmen as a Reflection of Their Life and Thought*. Pietermaritzburg: University of Natal Press, 1976.

Visonà, Monica Blackmun, ed. *A History of Art in Africa*. Upper Saddle River, N.J.: Prentice Hall, 2003.

Vogel, Susan M. *Baule: African Art, Western Eyes*. New Haven, Conn.: Yale University Press, 1997.

———, ed. *Africa Explores: Twentieth-Century African Art*. New York: Te Neues, 1990.

Walker, Roslyn A. *Olowe of Ise: A Yoruba Sculptor to Kings*. Washington, D.C.: National Museum of African Art, 1998.

CHAPTER 35:
EUROPE AND AMERICA, 1900 TO 1945

Antliff, Mark. *Cultural Politics and the Parisian Avant-Garde*. Princeton, N.J.: Princeton University Press, 1993.

Antliff, Mark, and Patricia Leighten. *Cubism and Culture*. New York: Thames & Hudson, 2001.

Baigell, Matthew. *The American Scene: American Painting of the 1930s*. New York: Praeger, 1974.

Barr, Alfred H., Jr. *Cubism and Abstract Art: Painting, Sculpture, Constructions, Photography, Architecture, Industrial Arts, Theatre, Films, Posters, Typography*. Cambridge, Mass.: Belknap, 1986.

Barron, Stephanie. *Exiles and Emigrés: The Flight of European Artists from Hitler*. Los Angeles: Los Angeles County Museum of Art, 1997.

———, ed. *Degenerate Art: The Fate of the Avant-Garde in Nazi Germany*. Los Angeles: Los Angeles County Museum of Art, 1991.

Bayer, Herbert, Walter Gropius, and Ise Gropius. *Bauhaus, 1919–1928*. New York: Museum of Modern Art, 1975.

Bearden, Romare, and Harry Henderson. *A History of African-American Artists from 1792 to the Present*. New York: Pantheon, 1993.

Breton, André. *Surrealism and Painting*. New York: Harper & Row, 1972.

Brown, Milton. *Story of the Armory Show: The 1913 Exhibition That Changed American Art*. 2d ed. New York: Abbeville, 1988.

Campbell, Mary Schmidt, David C. Driskell, David Lewis Levering, and Deborah Willis Ryan. *Harlem Renaissance: Art of Black America*. New York: Studio Museum in Harlem; Abrams, 1987.

Cox, Neil. *Cubism*. London: Phaidon, 2000.

Curtis, Penelope. *Sculpture 1900–1945*. New York: Oxford University Press, 1999.

Curtis, William J. R. *Modern Architecture since 1900*. Upper Saddle River, N.J.: Prentice Hall, 1996.

Davidson, Abraham A. *Early American Modernist Painting, 1910–1935*. New York: Harper & Row, 1981.

Eberle, Matthias. *World War I and the Weimar Artists: Dix, Grosz, Beckmann, Schlemmer*. New Haven, Conn.: Yale University Press, 1985.

Edwards, Steve, and Paul Wood, eds. *Art of the Avant-Gardes*. New Haven, Conn.: Yale University Press, 2004.

Elderfield, John. *The "Wild Beasts": Fauvism and Its Affinities*. New York: Museum of Modern Art, 1976.

Fer, Briony, David Batchelor, and Paul Wood. *Realism, Rationalism, Surrealism: Art between the Wars*. New Haven, Conn.: Yale University Press, 1993.

Friedman, Mildred, ed. *De Stijl, 1917–1931: Visions of Utopia*. Minneapolis: Walker Art Center; New York: Abbeville, 1982.

Gale, Matthew. *Dada and Surrealism*. London: Phaidon, 1997.

Goldberg, Rose Lee. *Performance: Live Art 1909 to the Present*. New York: Abrams, 1979.

Golding, John. *Cubism: A History and an Analysis, 1907–1914*. Cambridge, Mass.: Belknap, 1988.

Gordon, Donald E. *Expressionism: Art and Idea*. New Haven, Conn.: Yale University Press, 1987.

Harrison, Charles, Francis Frascina, and Gil Perry. *Primitivism, Cubism, Abstraction: The Early Twentieth Century*. New Haven, Conn.: Yale University Press, 1993.

Herbert, James D. *Fauve Painting: The Making of Cultural Politics*. New Haven, Conn.: Yale University Press, 1992.

Hitchcock, Henry-Russell, and Philip Johnson. *The International Style*. New York: Norton, 1995.

Hurlburt, Laurance P. *The Mexican Muralists in the United States*. Albuquerque: University of New Mexico Press, 1989.

Jaffé, Hans L. C. *De Stijl, 1917–1931: The Dutch Contribution to Modern Art*. Cambridge, Mass.: Belknap, 1986.

Krauss, Rosalind. *The Originality of the Avant-Garde and Other Modernist Myths*. Cambridge, Mass.: MIT Press, 1986.

Kuspit, Donald. *The Cult of the Avant-Garde Artist*. Cambridge: Cambridge University Press, 1993.

Lloyd, Jill. *German Expressionism: Primitivism and Modernity*. New Haven, Conn.: Yale University Press, 1991.

Lodder, Christina. *Russian Constructivism*. New Haven, Conn.: Yale University Press, 1983.

Martin, Marianne W. *Futurist Art and Theory*. Oxford: Clarendon, 1968.

Motherwell, Robert, ed. *The Dada Painters and Poets: An Anthology*. 2d ed. Boston: Hall, 1981.

Rhodes, Colin. *Primitivism and Modern Art*. New York: Thames & Hudson, 1994.

Richter, Hans. *Dada: Art and Anti-Art*. London: Thames & Hudson, 1961.

Rosenblum, Robert. *Cubism and Twentieth-Century Art*. Rev. ed. New York: Abrams, 1984.

Rubin, William S. *Dada and Surrealist Art*. New York: Abrams, 1968.

———, ed. *Pablo Picasso: A Retrospective*. New York: Museum of Modern Art; Boston: New York Graphic Society, 1980.

———, ed. *"Primitivism" in 20th-Century Art: Affinity of the Tribal and the Modern*. 2 vols. New York: Museum of Modern Art, 1984.

Selz, Peter. *German Expressionist Painting*. Berkeley: University of California Press, 1974. Reprint of 1957 edition.

Silver, Kenneth E. *Esprit de Corps: The Art of the Parisian Avant-Garde and the First World War, 1914–1925*. Princeton, N.J.: Princeton University Press, 1989.

Smith, Terry. *Making the Modern: Industry, Art, and Design in America*. Chicago: University of Chicago Press, 1993.

Stott, William. *Documentary Expression and Thirties America*. New York: Oxford University Press, 1973.

Taylor, Joshua C. *Futurism*. New York: Museum of Modern Art, 1961.

Tisdall, Caroline, and Angelo Bozzolla. *Futurism*. New York: Oxford University Press, 1978.

Trachtenberg, Alan. *Reading American Photographs: Images as History—Mathew Brady to Walker Evans*. New York: Hill and Wang, 1989.

Tsujimoto, Karen. *Images of America: Precisionist Painting and Modern Photography*. Seattle: University of Washington Press, 1982.

Tucker, William. *Early Modern Sculpture*. New York: Oxford University Press, 1974.

Vogt, Paul. *Expressionism: German Painting, 1905–1920*. New York: Abrams, 1980.

Weiss, Jeffrey S. *The Popular Culture of Modern Art: Picasso, Duchamp, and Avant-Gardism*. New Haven, Conn.: Yale University Press, 1994.

Whitford, Frank. *Bauhaus*. New York: Thames & Hudson, 1984.

CHAPTER 36:
EUROPE AND AMERICA AFTER 1945

Alloway, Lawrence. *American Pop Art*. New York: Whitney Museum of American Art; Macmillan, 1974.

———. *Topics in American Art since 1945*. New York: Norton, 1975.

Anfam, David. *Abstract Expressionism*. New York: Thames & Hudson, 1990.

Archer, Michael. *Art since 1960*. New ed. New York: Thames & Hudson, 2002.

Ashton, Dore. *American Art since 1945*. New York: Oxford University Press, 1983.

———. *The New York School: A Cultural Reckoning*. Harmondsworth: Penguin, 1979.

Battcock, Gregory, ed. *Idea Art: A Critical Anthology*. New York: Dutton, 1973.

———. *Minimal Art: A Critical Anthology*. New York: Studio Vista, 1969.

———. *The New Art: A Critical Anthology*. New York: Dutton, 1973.

———. *New Artists Video: A Critical Anthology*. New York: Dutton, 1978.

Battcock, Gregory, and Robert Nickas, eds. *The Art of Performance: A Critical Anthology*. New York: Dutton, 1984.

Beardsley, John, and Jane Livingston. *Hispanic Art in the United States: Thirty Contemporary Painters and Sculptors*. Houston: Museum of Fine Arts; New York: Abbeville, 1987.

Beardsley, Richard. *Earthworks and Beyond: Contemporary Art in the Landscape*. New York: Abbeville, 1984.

Broude, Norma, and Mary D. Garrard. *The Power of Feminist Art: The American Movement of the 1970s, History and Impact*. New York: Abrams, 1994.

Bürger, Peter. *Theory of the Avant-Garde*. Minneapolis: University of Minnesota Press, 1984.

Causey, Andrew. *Sculpture since 1945*. New York: Oxford University Press, 1998.

Cockcroft, Eva, John Weber, and James Cockcroft. *Toward a People's Art*. New York: Dutton, 1977.

Cook, Peter. *New Spirit in Architecture*. New York: Rizzoli, 1990.

Crow, Thomas. *The Rise of the Sixties: American and European Art in the Era of Dissent*. New Haven, Conn.: Yale University Press, 2005.

Cummings, P. *Dictionary of Contemporary American Artists*. 6th ed. New York: St. Martin's, 1994.

Deepwell, K., ed. *New Feminist Art*. Manchester: Manchester University Press, 1994.

Ferguson, Russell, ed. *Discourses: Conversations in Postmodern Art and Culture*. Cambridge, Mass.: MIT Press, 1990.

Fineberg, Jonathan. *Art since 1940: Strategies of Being.* 2d ed. Upper Saddle River, N.J.: Prentice Hall, 2000.

Frascina, Francis, ed. *Pollock and After: The Critical Debate.* New York: Harper & Row, 1985.

Geldzahler, Henry. *New York Painting and Sculpture, 1940–1970.* New York: Dutton, 1969.

Ghirardo, Diane. *Architecture after Modernism.* New York: Thames & Hudson, 1996.

Godfrey, Tony. *Conceptual Art.* London: Phaidon, 1998.

Goldberg, Rose Lee. *Performance Art: From Futurism to the Present.* Rev. ed. New York: Abrams, 1988.

Goldhagen, Sarah Williams, and Réjean Legault. *Anxious Modernisms: Experimentation in Postwar Architectural Culture.* Cambridge, Mass.: MIT Press, 2002.

Goodman, Cynthia. *Digital Visions: Computers and Art.* New York: Abrams, 1987.

Goodyear, Frank H., Jr. *Contemporary American Realism since 1960.* Boston: New York Graphic Society, 1981.

Green, Jonathan. *American Photography: A Critical History 1945 to the Present.* New York: Abrams, 1984.

Greenberg, Clement. *Clement Greenberg: The Collected Essays and Criticism.* Edited by J. O'Brien. 4 vols. Chicago: University of Chicago Press, 1986–1993.

Grundberg, Andy. *Photography and Art: Interactions since 1945.* New York: Abbeville, 1987.

Guilbaut, Serge. *How New York Stole the Idea of Modern Art.* Chicago: University of Chicago Press, 1983.

Hays, K. Michael, and Carol Burns, eds. *Thinking the Present: Recent American Architecture.* New York: Princeton Architectural, 1990.

Henri, Adrian. *Total Art: Environments, Happenings, and Performance.* New York: Oxford University Press, 1974.

Hertz, Richard, ed. *Theories of Contemporary Art.* 2d ed. Upper Saddle River, N.J.: Prentice Hall, 1993.

Hoffman, Katherine. *Explorations: The Visual Arts since 1945.* New York: Harper Collins, 1991.

Hopkins, David. *After Modern Art, 1945–2000.* New York: Oxford University Press, 2000.

Hughes, Robert. *The Shock of the New.* New York: Knopf, 1981.

Hunter, Sam. *An American Renaissance: Painting and Sculpture since 1940.* New York: Abbeville, 1986.

Jacobs, Jane. *The Death and Life of Great American Cities.* New York: Random House, 1961.

Jacobus, John. *Twentieth-Century Architecture: The Middle Years, 1940–1964.* New York: Praeger, 1966.

Jencks, Charles. *The Language of Post-Modern Architecture.* 6th ed. New York: Rizzoli, 1991.

———. *What Is Post-Modernism?* 3d ed. London: Academy Editions, 1989.

Johnson, Ellen H., ed. *American Artists on Art from 1940 to 1980.* Boulder, Colo.: Westview, 1982.

Joselit, David. *American Art since 1945.* New York: Thames & Hudson, 2003.

Kaprow, Allan. *Assemblage, Environments, and Happenings.* New York: Abrams, 1966.

Kirby, Michael. *Happenings.* New York: Dutton, 1966.

Kramer, Hilton. *The Age of the Avant-Garde: An Art Chronicle of 1956–1972.* New York: Farrar, Straus & Giroux, 1973.

Leja, Michael. *Reframing Abstract Expressionism: Subjectivity and Painting in the 1940s.* New Haven, Conn.: Yale University Press, 1993.

Lippard, Lucy R. *Mixed Blessings: New Art in a Multicultural America.* New York: Pantheon, 1990.

———. *Pop Art.* New York: Praeger, 1966.

———, ed. *From the Center: Feminist Essays on Women's Art.* New York: Dutton, 1976.

———. *Six Years: The Dematerialization of the Art Object from 1966 to 1972.* New York: Praeger, 1973.

Lovejoy, Margot. *Postmodern Currents: Art and Artists in the Age of the Electronic Media.* Ann Arbor, Mich.: UMI Research Press, 1989.

Lucie-Smith, Edward. *Art Now.* Edison, N.J.: Wellfleet, 1989.

———. *Movements in Art since 1945.* New ed. New York: Thames & Hudson, 2001.

Mamiya, Christin J. *Pop Art and Consumer Culture: American Super Market.* Austin: University of Texas Press, 1992.

Marder, Tod A. *The Critical Edge: Controversy in Recent American Architecture.* New Brunswick, N.J.: Rutgers University Press, 1980.

———. *An International Survey of Recent Painting and Sculpture.* New York: Museum of Modern Art, 1984.

Meyer, Ursula. *Conceptual Art.* New York: Dutton, 1972.

Mitchell, William J. *The Reconfigured Eye: Visual Truth in the Post-Photographic Era.* Cambridge, Mass.: MIT Press, 1992.

Norris, Christopher, and Andrew Benjamin. *What Is Deconstruction?* New York: St. Martin's, 1988.

Perry, Gill, and Paul Wood. *Themes in Contemporary Art.* New Haven, Conn.: Yale University Press, 2004.

Polcari, Stephen. *Abstract Expressionism and the Modern Experience.* Cambridge: Cambridge University Press, 1991.

Popper, Frank. *Origins and Development of Kinetic Art.* Translated by Stephen Bann. Greenwich, Conn.: New York Graphic Society, 1968.

Price, Jonathan. *Video Visions: A Medium Discovers Itself.* New York: New American Library, 1977.

Reichardt, Jasia, ed. *Cybernetics, Art, and Ideas.* Greenwich, Conn.: New York Graphics Society, 1971.

Risatti, Howard, ed. *Postmodern Perspectives: Issues in Contemporary Art.* Upper Saddle River, N.J.: Prentice Hall, 1990.

Robbins, Corinne. *The Pluralist Era: American Art, 1968–1981.* New York: Harper & Row, 1984.

Rosen, Randy, and Catherine C. Brawer, eds. *Making Their Mark: Women Artists Move into the Mainstream, 1970–1985.* New York: Abbeville, 1989.

Rosenberg, Harold. *The Tradition of the New.* New York: Horizon, 1959.

Rush, Michael. *New Media in Art.* 2d ed. New York: Thames & Hudson, 2005.

Russell, John, and Suzi Gablik. *Pop Art Redefined.* New York: Praeger, 1969.

Sandford, Mariellen R., ed. *Happenings and Other Acts.* New York: Routledge, 1995.

Sandler, Irving. *Art of the Postmodern Era.* New York: Harper Collins, 1996.

———. *The Triumph of American Painting: A History of Abstract Expressionism.* New York: Praeger, 1970.

Sayre, Henry M. *The Object of Performance: The American Avant-Garde since 1970.* Chicago: University of Chicago Press, 1989.

Schneider, Ira, and Beryl Korot. *Video Art: An Anthology.* New York: Harcourt Brace Jovanovich, 1976.

Shapiro, David, and Cecile Shapiro. *Abstract Expressionism: A Critical Record.* New York: Cambridge University Press, 1990.

Smagula, Howard. *Currents: Contemporary Directions in the Visual Arts.* 2d ed. Upper Saddle River, N.J.: Prentice Hall, 1989.

Sonfist, Alan, ed. *Art in the Landscape: A Critical Anthology of Environmental Art.* New York: Dutton, 1983.

Sontag, Susan. *On Photography.* New York: Farrar, Straus & Giroux, 1973.

Stiles, Kristine, and Peter Selz. *Theories and Documents of Contemporary Art: A Sourcebook of Artists' Writings.* Berkeley and Los Angeles: University of California Press, 1996.

Taylor, Brendon. *Contemporary Art: Art since 1970.* Upper Saddle River, N.J.: Prentice Hall, 2005.

Tuchman, Maurice. *American Sculpture of the Sixties.* Los Angeles: Los Angeles County Museum of Art, 1967.

Venturi, Robert. *Complexity and Contradiction in Architecture.* New York: Museum of Modern Art, 1966.

Venturi, Robert, Denise Scott-Brown, and Steven Isehour. *Learning from Las Vegas.* Cambridge, Mass.: MIT Press, 1972.

Waldman, Diane. *Collage, Assemblage, and the Found Object.* New York: Abrams, 1992.

Wallis, Brian, ed. *Art after Modernism: Rethinking Representation.* New York: New Museum of Contemporary Art in association with David R. Godine, 1984.

Wheeler, Daniel. *Art since Mid-Century: 1945 to the Present.* Upper Saddle River, N.J.: Prentice Hall, 1991.

Wood, Paul. *Modernism in Dispute: Art since the Forties.* New Haven, Conn.: Yale University Press, 1993.

CREDITS

The author and publisher are grateful to the proprietors and custodians of various works of art for photographs of these works and permission to reproduce them in this book. Sources not included in the captions are listed here.

Introduction—I-1: Clifford Still, 1948-C, PH-15, 80-7/8 x 70-3/4 inches, Oil on canvas, © The Clyfford Still Estate. Photo: akg images; **I-2:** © English Heritage; **I-3:** akg-images/Rabatti–Domingie; **I-4:** National Gallery of Art, Alfred Stieglitz Collection, Bequest of Georgia O'Keeffe; 1987.58.3. © 2007 The Georgia O'Keefe Foundation/Artist's Rights Society (ARS), NY; **I-5:** Art © Estate of Ben Shahn/Licensed by VAGA, NY, NY. Whitney Museum of American Art, NY. (gift of Edith and Milton Lowenthal in memory of Juliana Force); **I-6:** www.bednorz-photo.de; **I-7:** akg images; **I-8:** Metropolitan Museum of Art, Gift of Junius S. Morgan, 1919 (19.73.209) Image © The Metropolitan Museum of Art; **I-9:** Courtesy Saskia Ltd., © Dr. Ron Wiedenhoeft; **I-10:** Photo © Whitney Museum of American Art /© 2007 The Josef and Anni Albers Foundation/Artists Rights Society (ARS), NY; **I-11:** National Gallery, London. NG14. Bought, 1824; **I-12:** MOA Art Museum, Shizuoka-ken, Japan; **I-13:** Bayerische Staatsgemälde-sammlungen, Alte Pinakothek, Munich and Kunstdia-Archiv ARTOTHEK, Weilheim, Germany; **I-14:** Jürgen Liepe, Berlin; **I-15:** Metropolitan Museum of Art, Michael C. Rockefeller Memorial Collection, Gift of Nelson A. Rockefeller, 1965. (1987.412.309) Photograph © 1983 The Metropolitan Museum of Art; **I-16:** © Nimatallah/Art Resource, NY; **I-17:** © Scala/Art Resource, NY; **I-19 (left):** © National Library of Australia, Canberra, Australia/The Bridgeman Art Library, NY; **I-19 (right):** From *The Childhood of Man* by Leo Frobenius (New York: J.B. Lippincott, 1909).

Chapter 1—1-1: © Bob Krist/CORBIS; **1-2:** Photo: Paul G. Bahn; **1-3:** With permission: Namibia Archaeological Trust; **1-4:** © Ulmer Museum. Photo: Thomas Stephan; **1-5:** © Archivio Iconografico, S.A./CORBIS; **1-5A:** © Réunion des Musées Nationaux/Art Resource, NY; **1-6:** © Musee des Antiquites Nationales, St. Germain-en-Laye, France, Lauros/Giraudon/The Bridgeman Art Library, NY; **1-6A:** Louis de Seille/Courtesy Jean Clottes; **1-6B:** From *The Eternal Present, A Contribution on Constancy and Change* by S. Giedion © 1964 by Sigfried Giedion. Used by permission of Knopf Doubleday Publishing Group, a division of Random House, Inc.; **1-7:** Jean Vertut; **1-8:** © Réunion des Musées Nationaux/Art Resource, NY; **1-9:** Jean Vertut; **1-10:** Jean Vertut; **1-11:** Jean Vertut; **1-11A:** akg-images; **1-12:** French Ministry of Culture and Communication, Regional Direction for Cultural Affairs, Rhone-Alpes region, Regional Department of Archaeology; **1-13:** Jean Vertut; **1-14:** Archivio e Studio Folco Quilici, Roma; **1-14A:** The Art Archive/Archaeological Museum Amman Jordan/Gianni Dagli Orti/Picture Desk; **1-15:** ANCIENT STATUES FROM JORDAN. These life-size, human-form figures made of plaster and bitumen date from 6500 B.C. And were recovered in 1985 from the statue pit at Ain Ghazal the Neolithic site located on the outskirts of Amman the capital of Jordan. Courtesy of the Hashemite Kingdom of Jordan, Dept. of Antiquities Statues from Ain Ghazal; **1-16:** John Swogger/© Catalhoyuk Research Project; **1-17:** © Gianni Dagli Orti/CORBIS; **1-18:** James Mellaart; **1-19:** © Sandro Vannini/CORBIS; **1-19A:** © Adam Woolfitt/CORBIS; **1-20:** © Adam Woolfitt/CORBIS.

Chapter 2—2-1: © Réunion des Musées Nationaux/Art Resource, NY; **02-1A:** © Lauros/Giraudon/The Bridgeman Art Library International; **2-2:** © Robert Harding Picture Library; **2-4:** © Aladin Abdel Naby/Reuters/CORBIS; **2-5:** Erwin Bohm; **2-6:** © Erich Lessing/Art Resource, NY; **2-6A:** Hirmer Verlag GMBH; **2-7:** © Réunion des Musées Nationaux/Art Resource, NY; **2-8:** © British Museum, London, UK/The Bridgeman Art Library, NY; **2-9:** © British Museum, London, UK/The Bridgeman Art Library, NY; **2-10 both:** University of Pennsylvania Museum of Archaeology and Anthropology, Philadelphia; **2-11:** © Copyright the Trustees of The British Museum; **2-12:** © Joseph Scherschel/National Geographic Image Collection; **2-13:** © Réunion des Musées Nationaux/Art Resource, NY; **2-14:** University of Pennsylvania Museum of Archaeology and Anthropology, Philadelphia; **2-15:** Erwin Bohm; **2-16:** © Erich Lessing/Art Resource, NY; **2-16A:** © Erich Lessing/Art Resource, NY; **2-17:** © Réunion des Musées Nationaux/Art Resource, NY; **2-18:** © Borromeo/Art Resource, NY; **2-19:** © Réunion des Musées Nationaux/Art Resource, NY; **2-21:** Courtesy Saskia Ltd., © Dr. Ron Wiedenhoeft; **2-22:** © British Museum/HIP/Art Resource, NY; **2-22A:** © Courtesy of the Trustees of the British Museum, London; **2-23:** © Copyright the Trustees of The British Museum; **2-24:** © Bildarchiv Preussischer Kulturbesitz/Art Resource, NY; **2-25:** The Art Archive/Dagli Orti (A); **2-25A:** © age fotostock/SuperStock; **2-26:** © David Poole/Robert Harding Picture Library; **2-26A:** © Scala/Art Resource, NY; **2-27:** akg-images/Gérard Degeorge; **2-28:** Courtesy Saskia Ltd., © Dr. Ron Wiedenhoeft.

Chapter 3—3-1: © Robert Harding Picture Library; **3-2:** J. E. Quibell and F. W. Geen, Hierakonpolis vol. 2 (London 1902) p. 76; **3-3:** Hirmer Fotoarchiv, Munich; **3-5:** © Werner Forman/Art Resource, NY; **3-6A:** Ancient Art and Architecture Collection; **3-7:** © Erich Lessing/Art Resource, NY; **3-8:** © Yann Arthus-Bertrand/CORBIS; **3-10:** Courtesy of the Semitic Museum, Harvard University; **3-11:** © Robert Harding Picture Library; **3-12:** © Araldo de Luca; **3-12A:** akg-images/Andrea Jemolo; **3-12B:** © Erich Lessing/Art Resource, NY; **3-13:** Museum of Fine Arts, Boston. Harvard University—Boston Museum of Fine Arts Expedition, 11.1738. Photograph © 2008 Museum of Fine Arts, Boston; **3-14:** © Erich Lessing/Art Resource, NY; **3-14A:** Roemer- und Pelizaeus-Museum, Hildesheim; **3-14B:** Jürgen Liepe, Berlin; **3-15:** Jean Vertut; **3-16:** Maurice Babey; **3-17:** The Metropolitan Museum of Art, Purchase, Edward S. Harkness Gift, 1926 (26.7.1394) Photograph © 1979 The Metropolitan Museum of Art; **3-17A:** *Statue of Lady Sennuwy,* probably for Tomb of Djefaihapu, Asyut, Egypt, found in Royal Tumulus K III, Kerma, Nubia, Sudan, Middle Kingdom, reign of Senwosret I, 1971–26 BCE (grandiorite), Egyptian 12th Dynasty (1991–1786 BCE)/Museum of Fine Arts, Boston, Massachusetts, USA/Harvard University–Museum of Fine Arts Expedition. Photograph © 2009 Museum of Fine Arts, Boston; **3-18:** © Marburg/Art Resource, NY; **3-19:** akg-images/Francois Guenet; **3-20:** Getty Research Library, Wim Swaan Photograph Collection, 96.P.21; **3-20A:** © Scala/Art Resource, NY; **3-21:** The Metropolitan Museum of Art, Rogers Fund, 1929. (29.3.1) Photograph by Schecter Lee. Photograph © 1986 The Metropolitan Museum of Art; **3-22:** © Carmen Redondo/CORBIS; **3-23:** © Robert Harding Picture Library; **3-24:** Jean Claude Golvin; **3-24A:** © Yann Arthus-Bertrand/CORBIS; **3-25:** © Robert Harding Picture Library; **3-26:** Metropolitan Museum of Art, Levi Hale Willard Bequest, 1890 (90.35.1), and the Frank H. McClung Museum, The University of Tennessee; **3-27:** © Bildarchiv Preussischer Kulturbesitz/Art Resource, NY; **3-28:** © Archivo Iconografico, S.A./CORBIS ; **3-29:** © Werner Forman/CORBIS ; **3-30:** © Araldo de Luca; **3-31:** © Bildarchiv Preussischer Kulturbesitz/Art Resource, NY; **3-32:** © Bildarchiv Preussischer Kulturbesitz/Art Resource, NY; **3-33:** © Bildarchiv Preussischer Kulturbesitz/Art Resource, NY; **3-34:** © Boltin Picture Library/The Bridgeman Art Library, NY; **3-35:** © Robert Harding Picture Library; **3-36:** © British Museum/HIP/Art Resource, NY; **3-37:** © British Museum/HIP/Art Resource, NY; **3-37A:** Jürgen Liepe, Berlin; **3-38:** © Yann Arthus-Bertrand/CORBIS.

Chapter 4—4-1: © Pete Saloutos/zefa/CORBIS; **4-2:** © Erich Lessing/Art Resource, NY; **4-3:** The Art Archive/National Archaeological Museum Athens/Dagli Orti; **4-4:** © Yann Arthus-Bertrand/CORBIS; **4-6:** © Roger Wood/CORBIS; **4-7:** Courtesy Saskia Ltd., © Dr. Ron Wiedenhoeft; **4-8:** The Art Archive/Heraklion Museum/Dagli Orti; **4-8A:** © Nimatallah/Art Resource, NY; **4-9:** © Nimatallah/Art Resource, NY; **4-9A:** Photo, Henri Stierlin; **4-9B:** Ch. Doumas, "The Wall Paintings of Thera," Idryma Theras-Petros M. Nomikos, Athens, 1992; **4-10:** Hans Hinz; **4-11:** © Scala/Art Resource, NY; **4-12:** © Nimatallah/Art Resource, NY; **4-13:** © British School at Athens; **4-14:** © Roger Wood/CORBIS; **4-15:** Photo by Raymond V. Schoder, © 1987 by Bolchazy-Carducci Publishers, Inc.; **4-16:** © Paul Almasy/ CORBIS; **4-18A:** The Art Archive/Archaeological Museum Chora Greece/Gianni Dagli Orti/Picture Desk; **4-19:** Copyright © SIME s.a.s /eStock Photo—All rights reserved; **4-20:** © Vanni Archive/CORBIS; **4-21:** © Vanni Archive/CORBIS; **4-22:** © Archivo Iconografico, S.A./CORBIS; **4-23:** The Art Archive/National Archaeological Museum Athens/Dagli Orti; **4-23A:** © Erich Lessing/Art Resource, NY; **4-24:** The Art Archive/National Archaeological Museum Athens/Dagli Orti; **4-24A:** © Nimatallah/Art Resource, NY; **4-25:** akg-images.

Chapter 5—5-1: © Araldo de Luca/CORBIS; **5-2:** The Metropolitan Museum of Art, Rogers Fund, 1914. (14.130.14) Photograph © 1996 The Metropolitan Museum of Art; **5-2A:** © Nimatallah/Art Resource, NY; **5-3:** The Metropolitan Museum of Art, Gift of J. Pierpont Morgan, 1917. (17.190.2072). Photograph © 1996 The Metropolitan Museum of Art; **5-4:** © Museum of Fine Arts, Boston, MA, USA, Denman Waldo Ross Collection/The Bridgeman Art Library, NY; **5-5:** © Copyright the Trustees of The British Museum; **5-7:** © Réunion des Musées Nationaux/Art Resource, NY; **5-8:** The Metropolitan Museum of Art, Fletcher Fund, 1932 (32.11.1). Photograph © 1997 The Metropolitan Museum of Art; **5-9:** © Nimatallah/Art Resource, NY; **5-10:** © Gianni Dagli Orti/CORBIS; **5-11:** © Nimatallah/Art Resource, NY; **5-12:** Studio Kontos; **5-15:** © Vanni/Art Resource, NY; **5-17:** © Vanni/Art Resource, NY; **5-18A:**

Chapter 12—**12-1:** The Art Archive/Dagli Orti; **12-2:** © Yann Arthus-Bertrand/CORBIS; **12-4:** Photo, Henri Stierlin; **12-6:** Archivio e Studio Folco Quilici, Roma; **12-8:** Canali Photobank, Italy; **12-9:** © Scala/Art Resource, NY; **12-10:** Canali Photobank, Italy; **12-11:** Canali Photobank, Italy; **12-12:** © Scala/Art Resource, NY; **12-13:** © Ronald Sheraton/Ancient Art and Architecture Collection Ltd.; **12-14:** © Réunion des Musées Nationaux/Art Resource, NY; **12-15:** © British Museum/HIP/Art Resource, NY; **12-15A:** The Art Archive/Episcopal Museum Ravenna/Gianni Dagli Orti/Picture Desk; **12-16:** Österreichische Nationalbibliothek, Vienna, Bildarchiv, Cod.med.gr. 1, fol. 6v; **12-17:** Firenze, Biblioteca Medicea Laurenziana, Ms. Laur. Plut. 1.56, c. 13v; **12-17A:** © Scala/Art Resource, NY; **12-18:** © Ronald Sheraton/Ancient Art and Architecture Collection Ltd.; **12-18A:** © The Bridgeman Art Library International; **12-19:** © Erich Lessing/Art Resource, NY; **12-20:** © Scala/Art Resource, NY; **12-22:** © Vanni/Art Resource, NY; **12-22A:** © Kurt Scholz/SuperStock; **12-23:** Studio Kontos; **12-24:** © Alinari/Art Resource, NY; **12-24A:** © Cameraphoto Arte, Venice/Art Resource, NY; **12-24B:** © Werner Forman/Art Resource, NY; **12-25:** © Scala/Art Resource, NY; **12-25A:** © Mimmo Jodice/CORBIS Art/CORBIS; **12-26:** © Réunion des Musées Nationaux/Art Resource, NY; **12-27:** Josephine Powell; **12-28:** © Snark/Art Resource, NY; **12-29:** © Scala/Art Resource, NY; **12-30:** Kariye Camii, Istanbul, Turkey, © Held Collection/The Bridgeman Art Library, NY; **12-30A:** © Vanni/Art Resource, NY; **12-31:** Icon Gallery of Saint Clement, Ohrid; **12-32:** © Erich Lessing/Art Resource, NY; **12-33:** © Scala/Art Resource, NY; **12-33A:** State Historical Cultural Museum, Kremlin, Moscow.

Chapter 13—**13-1:** The Art Archive/Dagli Orti; **13-2:** © Moshe Shai/CORBIS; **13-3:** © Erich Lessing/Art Resource, NY; **13-4:** Photo Archives Skira, Geneva, Switzerland; **13-5:** Photo, Henri Stierlin; **13-7:** © Bildarchiv Preussischer Kulturbesitz/Art Resource, NY; **13-8 (left):** © Yann Arthus-Bertrand/CORBIS; **13-9:** Photo, Henri Stierlin; **13-10:** E. Simanor/Robert Harding Picture Library; **13-11:** www.bednorz-photo.de; **13-12:** www.bednorz-photo.de; **13-13:** © Adam Woolfit/Robert Harding Picture Library; **13-14:** © Musée Lorrain, Nancy, France/photo G. Mangin; **13-14A:** © Réunion des Musées Nationaux/Art Resource, NY; **13-15:** © The State Hermitage Museum, St. Petersburg; **13-16:** © The Trustees of the Chester Beatty Library, Dublin; **13-16A:** © Réunion des Musées Nationaux/Art Resource, NY; **13-16B:** Photo: Katya Kallsen © President and Fellows of Harvard College; **13-17:** © Toyohiro Yamada/Getty Images/Taxi; **13-18:** Photo, Henri Stierlin; **13-20:** Photo, Henri Stierlin; **13-20A:** © The Metropolitan Museum of Art/Art Resource, NY; **13-21:** Photo, Henri Stierlin; **13-22:** Photo Henri Stierlin; **13-24:** © SEF/Art Resource, NY; **13-25:** Metropolitan Museum of Art, Harris Brisbane Dick Fund, 1939 (39.20) Photograph © 1982 The Metropolitan Museum of Art; **13-26:** © Erich Lessing/Art Resource, NY; **13-27:** AKTC 2005.01 [M200] © Aga Khan Trust for Culture, formerly in the collection of Prince and Princess Sadruddin Aga Khan; **13-28:** © Victoria & Albert Museum, London/Art Resource, NY; **13-29:** © Copyright the Trustees of The British Museum; **13-30:** © Réunion des Musées Nationaux/Art Resource, NY; **13-31:** Freer Gallery of Art Washington, D.C., Purchase, F1941.10.

Chapter 14—**14-1:** © The British Museum/HIP/The Image Works; **14-2:** © Danny Lehman/CORBIS; **14-3:** © Werner Forman/Art Resource NY; **14-4:** Los Angeles County Museum of Art, The Proctor Stafford Collection, purchased with funds provided by Mr. and Mrs. Allan C. Balch. Photograph © 2006 Museum Associates/LACMA; **14-5:** © Georg Gerster/Photo Researchers, Inc.; **14-6:** Gianni Dagli Orti/CORBIS; **14-7:** The Art Archive/Dagli Orti; **14-7A:** Image © The Cleveland Museum of Art; **14-8:** © Philip Baird www.anthroarcheart.com; **14-9:** © Sean Sprague/The Image Works; **14-10:** © Enzo and Paolo Rogazzini/CORBIS; **14-10A:** © Charles & Josette Lenars/CORBIS; **14-11:** akg-images/François Guénet; **14-12:** © 2007 Peabody Museum of Archaeology and Ethnology, Harvard University, Cambridge. 48-63-20/17561 T1021.2 (detail); **14-12A:** Dumbarton Oaks Research Library and Collections, Washington, D.C.; **14-13:** © Danny Lehman/CORBIS; **14-14:** © Yann Arthus-Bertrand/CORBIS; **14-15:** © Scala/Art Resource, NY; **14-16:** © Yann Arthus-Bertrand/ CORBIS; **14-17:** © Jonathan Blair/CORBIS; **14-18:** Metropolitan Museum of Art, NY, Jan Mitchell and Sons Collection. Gift of Jan Mitchell, 1991 (1991.419.31) Photography by Justin Kerr. Photograph © 1984 The Metropolitan Museum of Art; **14-19:** © Instituto Nacional de Cultura, Lima, Peru; **14-20:** Museum of Fine Arts, Boston, William A. Paine Fund, 1931, 31.501. Photograph © 2008 Museum of Fine Arts, Boston; **14-21:** Peru, South Coast, Nazca Culture, Dome-shaped jar depicting ceremonial figure, 50–200 A.D., ceramic, 15 × 15 cm, Kate S. Buckingham Endowment, 1955.2128, The Art Institute of Chicago. Photography © The Art Institute of Chicago; **14-22:** © Charles & Josette Lenars/CORBIS; **14-23:** © Nathan Benn/ CORBIS; **14-24:** Museo Tumbas Reales de Sipan/Lambayeque, Peru; **14-25:** © Hubert Stadler/ CORBIS; **14-26:** © National Museum of Archaeology, Anthropology, and History of Peru; **14-27:** © Werner Forman/CORBIS; **14-28:** © Ohio Historical Society; **14-29:** © Tony Linck/ SuperStock; **14-29A:** © Michael S. Lewis/Encyclopedia/CORBIS; **14-30:** © Werner Forman/Art Resource, NY; **14-31:** Southwest, Mimbres Culture, Bowl, c. 1100–1250, ceramic, pigment, Purchased from Mr. George Teraski. Hugh L. and Mary T. Adams Fund income, 1976-306. Photography © The Art Institute of Chicago; **14-32:** © Kevin Fleming/CORBIS; **14-32A:** © Richard A. Cooke/Encyclopedia/CORBIS.

Chapter 15—**15-1:** © Charles & Josette Lenars/CORBIS; **15-2:** © Jean-Dominique Lajoux; **15-3:** Photograph © 1980 Dirk Bakker; **15-4:** IZIKO Museum of Cape Town; **15-5:** Photograph © 1980 Dirk Bakker; **15-5A:** Dirk Bakker; **15-6:** Photograph © 1980 Dirk Bakker; **15-6A:** © Ancient Art and Architecture Collection Ltd./The Bridgeman Art Library International; **15-6B:** © Scala/Art Resource, NY; **15-7:** Photograph by Franko Khoury, National Museum of African Art, Smithsonian Institution, Museum purchase, 86-12-1; **15-8:** © Yann Arthus-Bertrand/CORBIS; **15-9:** © Gavin Hellier/Getty Images/Robert Harding Picture Library; **15-10:** © I. Vanderharst/Getty Images/Robert Harding Picture Library; **15-11:** © Great Zimbabwe Site Museum, Great Zimbabwe; **15-12:** Metropolitan Museum of Art. The Michael C. Rockefeller Memorial Collection, Gift of Nelson A. Rockefeller, 1972. (1978.412.323) Photograph © 1995 The Metropolitan Museum of Art; **15-12A:** © Werner Forman/Art Resource, NY; **15-13:** © British Museum/HIP/Art Resource, NY; **15-14:** © Museo Nazionale Preistorico e Etnografico Luigi Pigorini, Rome.

Chapter 16—**16-1:** © British Library/HIP/Art Resource, NY; **16-2:** © Réunion des Musées Nationaux/Art Resource, NY; **16-3:** © British Museum/HIP/Art Resource, NY; **16-3A:** © The Trustees of The British Museum/Art Resource, NY; **16-4:** University Museum of National Antiquities, Oslo, Norway. Eirik Irgens Johnsen; **16-4A:** © Christophe Boisvieux/Terra/CORBIS;

16-5: © Erich Lessing/ Art Resource, NY; **16-6:** © The Board of Trinity College, Dublin, Ireland/The Bridgeman Art Library, NY; **16-7:** akg-images/British Library; **16-8:** © The Board of Trinity College, Dublin, Ireland/The Bridgeman Art Library, NY; **16-9:** Courtesy Saskia Ltd., © Dr. Ron Wiedenhoeft; **16-9A:** © Michael Jenner/Robert Harding; **16-10:** The Art Archive/Dagli Orti; **16-11:** Archivo Historico Nacional, Madrid; **16-12:** © Louvre, Paris, France, Lauros/Giraudon/The Bridgeman Art Library, NY; **16-13:** Kunsthistorisches Museums, Wien; **16-13A:** akg-images; **16-14:** © Erich Lessing/Art Resource, NY; **16-15:** University Library, Utrecht; **16-15A:** University Library, Utrecht; **16-16:** © The Pierpont Morgan Library/Art Resource, NY; **16-18:** © Aachen Cathedral, Aachen, Germany, Bildarchiv Steffens/The Bridgeman Art Library, NY; **16-19:** akg-images; **16-19A:** © Lauros/Giraudon/The Bridgeman Art Library; **16-20:** www.bednorz-photo.de; **16-20A:** Hirmer Verlag GMBH; **16-21:** www.bednorz-photo.de; **16-22:** www.bednorz-photo.de; **16-23A:** The Art Archive/Gianni Dagli Orti/Picture Desk; **16-24:** Photo: Dom-Museum, Hildesheim (Frank Tomio); **16-24A:** © The Metropolitan Museum of Art/Art Resource, NY; **16-25:** Photo: Dom-Museum, Hildesheim (Frank Tomio); **16-26:** Rheinisches Bildarchiv; **16-27:** Bayerische Staatsbibliothek, Munich; **16-28:** Bayerische Staatsbibliothek, Munich; **16-28A:** © Réunion des Musées Nationaux/Art Resource, NY; **16-29:** Bayerische Staatsbibliothek, Munich; **16-29A:** Bayerische Staatsbibliothek, Munich.

Chapter 17—**17-1:** © Vanni/Art Resource, NY; **17-2:** Claude Huber; **17-2A:** © Vanni/Art Resource, NY; **17-2B:** Photo © AISA/The Bridgeman Art Library; **17-4:** Jean Dieuzaide; **17-4A:** © Scala/Art Resource, NY; **17-6:** akg-images/Stefan Drechsel; **17-6A:** akg-images/Andrea Jemolo; **17-7:** The Art Archive /Dagli Orti; **17-7A:** Koenemann GmbH/Photo: Achim Bednorz/www.bednorz-photo.de; **17-9 (left):** © Michael Busselle/ Robert Harding Picture Library; **17-9 (right):** © St. Pierre, Moissac, France, Peter Willi/The Bridgeman Art Library, NY; **17-9A:** © John Bethell/The Bridgeman Art Library; **17-11:** akg-images/Elizabeth Disney; **17-12:** akg-images/Paul M.R. Maeyaert; **17-12A:** © Giraudon/Art Resource, NY; **17-12B:** © The Bridgeman Art Library International; **17-13:** Hervé Champollion/ akg-images; **17-13A:** www.bednorz-photo.de; **17-13B:** © Peter Willi/The Bridgeman Art Library International; **17-14:** www.bednorz-photo.de; **17-15:** © Erich Lessing/Art Resource, NY; **17-15A:** Bibliothèque Nationale, Paris; **17-15B:** © Giraudon/Art Resource, NY; **17-16 (left):** www.bednorz-photo.de; **17-16 (right):** © Vanni/Art Resource, NY; **17-17:** Museum of Fine Arts, Boston, Maria Antoinette Evans Fund, 21.1285. Photograph © 2008 Museum of Fine Arts, Boston; **17-18:** The Metropolitan Museum of Art, Gift of J. Pierpont Morgan, 1916. (16.32.194) Photograph © 1999 The Metropolitan Museum of Art; **17-18A:** The Art Archive/Abbaye de Saint Foy Conques/Gianni Dagli Orti/Picture Desk; **17-19:** © Florian Monheim, www.bildarchiv-monheim.de; **17-20:** Pubbli Aer Foto; **17-21:** Canali Photobank, Italy; **17-22:** Abtei St. Hildegard; **17-22A:** Fondation Martin Bodmer, Bibliothèque and Musée; **17-23:** © Scala/Art Resource, NY; **17-24:** Photograph Speldoorn © Musées royaux d'Art et d'Histoire - Brussels; **17-25:** © Scala/Art Resource, NY; **17-26:** akg-images/Rabatti–Domingie; **17-27:** © Massimo Listri/CORBIS; **17-27A:** Canali Photobank, Italy; **17-28:** www.bednorz-photo.de; **17-29:** www.bednorz-photo.de; **17-30:** Universal Art Images; **17-31:** © Anthony Scibilia/Art Resource, NY; **17-33 (left):** © Angelo Hornak/CORBIS; **17-35:** By special permission of the City of Bayeux; **17-36:** The Master and Fellows of Corpus Christi College, Cambridge; **17-36A:** © British Library Board. All Rights Reserved/The Bridgeman Art Library; **17-37:** Trinity College, Cambridge, England. MS R.17.1.f.283, Eadwine the Scribe.

Chapter 18—**18-1:** © Angelo Hornak/CORBIS; **18-2A:** The Art Archive/Gianni Dagli Orti/Picture Desk; **18-3:** www.bednorz-photo.de; **18-5:** © Vanni/Art Resource, NY; **18-6:** © Vanni/Art Resource, NY; **18-7:** © SuperStock, Inc./SuperStock; **18-8:** © Angelo Hornak/CORBIS; **18-9:** Courtesy Saskia Ltd., © Dr. Ron Wiedenhoeft; **18-11:** Hirmer Fotoarchiv, Munich; **18-13:** © Marc Garanger/CORBIS; **18-15:** © Chartres Cathedral, Chartres, France, Paul Maeyaert/The Bridgeman Art Library, NY; **18-16:** © Giraudon/ Art Resource, NY; **Page 472:** © Angelo Hornak/CORBIS; **18-17:** www.bednorz-photo.de; **18-18:** © Anthony Scibilia/Art Resource, NY; **18-19:** Hirmer Fotoarchiv, Munich; **18-20:** © Anthony Scibilia/Art Resource, NY; **18-21:** Hirmer Fotoarchiv, Munich; **18-22:** © Anthony Scibilia/ Art Resource, NY; **18-23:** www.bednorz-photo.de; **18-23A:** The Art Archive/Gianni Dagli Orti/Picture Desk; **18-24:** © Scala/Art Resource, NY; **18-25:** © Giraudon/Art Resource, NY; **18-25A:** akg-images/Schütze/Rodemann; **18-26:** www.bednorz-photo.de; **18-27:** Courtesy Saskia Ltd., © Dr. Ron Wiedenhoeft; **18-28:** © Adam Woolfitt/CORBIS; **18-29:** www.bednorz-photo.de; **18-30:** © Giraudon/Art Resource, NY; **18-32:** Österreichische Nationalbibliothek, Vienna. Bildarchiv. folio 1 verso of a moralized Bible; **18-31:** Bibliotheque Nationale, Paris, France; **18-33:** © The Pierpont Morgan Library/Art Resource, NY; **18-34:** Bibliotheque Nationale, Paris, France; **18-35:** Bibliotheque Nationale, Paris, France; **18-36:** © Snark/Art Resource, NY; **18-36A:** The Metropolitan Museum of Art, The Cloisters Collection, 1954 (54.1.2) Image © The Metropolitan Museum; **18-37:** © Réunion des Musées Nationaux/Art Resource, NY; **18-38:** Photo © The Walters Art Museum, Baltimore. Acquired by Henry Walters, 1923. Accession No. 71.264; **18-39:** © English Heritage; **18-41:** Archivo Iconografico, S.A./CORBIS; **18-42:** © Scala/Art Resource, NY; **18-43:** © Werner Forman/CORBIS; **18-44:** © Angelo Hornak/CORBIS; **18-44A:** The Dean and Chapters of Hereford/Hereford Mappa Mundi Trust; **18-45:** © Felix Zaska/CORBIS; **18-46:** © Svenja-Foto/zefa/CORBIS; **18-47:** www.bednorz-photo.de; **18-47A:** © 2005 Ken Phillips; **18-48:** www.bednorz-photo.de; **18-49:** www.bednorz-photo.de; **18-49A:** akg-images/Hilbich; **18-50:** © Erich Lessing/Art Resource, NY; **18-51:** © Erich Lessing/Art Resource, NY; **18-52:** © Erich Lessing/Art Resource, NY; **18-52A:** © Erich Lessing/Art Resource, NY; **18-53:** © Erich Lessing/Art Resource, NY.

Chapter 19—**19-1:** © Scala/Art Resource, NY; **19-2:** Canali Photobank, Italy; **19-3:** © Scala/Art Resource, NY; **19-4:** © Scala/Art Resource, NY; **19-5:** © Scala/Art Resource, NY; **19-5A:** © Alinari/Art Resource, NY; **19-5B:** © Erich Lessing/Art Resource, NY; **19-6:** Photo by Ralph Lieberman; **19-7:** © Scala/Art Resource, NY; **19-8:** © Summerfield Press/CORBIS; **19-8A:** © Scala/Art Resource, NY; **19-9:** © Scala/Art Resource, NY; **19-9A:** © Alinari/Art Resource, NY; **19-9B:** © Alinari/Art Resource, NY; **19-10:** © Scala/Art Resource, NY; **19-10A:** © Scala/Art Resource, NY; **19-11:** © Scala/Art Resource, NY; **19-11A:** © Scala/Art Resource, NY; **19-12:** Canali Photobank, Italy; **19-12A:** © Scala/Art Resource, NY; **19-13:** Canali Photobank, Italy; **19-14:** © Scala/Art Resource, NY; **19-15:** © MUZZI FABIO/CORBIS SYGMA; **19-16:** © Scala/ Art Resource, NY; **19-16A:** © Scala/Art Resource, NY; **19-17:** © Scala/Art Resource, NY; **19-18:** © MUZZI FABIO/CORBIS SYGMA; **19-18A:** © Atlantide Phototravel/

CORBIS; **19-19:** Photo by Ralph Lieberman; **19-19A:** © The Bridgeman Art Library International; **19-19B:** © Scala/Art Resource, NY; **19-20 both:** © Scala/Art Resource, NY; **19-21:** www.bednorz-photo.de; **19-22:** © Scala/Art Resource, NY.

Chapter 20—**20-1:** © Erich Lessing/Art Resource, NY; **20-2:** © Erich Lessing/Art Resource, NY; **20-2A:** © Paul Maeyaert/The Bridgeman Art Library International; **20-3:** Erich Lessing/Art Resource, NY; **20-4:** Image Copyright © The Metropolitan Museum of Art/Art Resource, NY; **20-5:** © Scala/Art Resource, NY; **20-5A:** © Bildarchiv Preussischer Kulturbesitz/Art Resource, NY; **20-6:** © Scala/Art Resource, NY; **20-7:** Copyright © National Gallery, London; **20-8:** © Erich Lessing/Art Resource, NY; **20-8A:** © Paul Maeyaert/The Bridgeman Art Library International; **20-9:** Photograph © 2008 Museum of Fine Arts, Boston; **20-10:** Copyright © 1999 Board of Trustees, National Gallery of Art, Washington, D.C.; **20-11:** Image copyright © The Metropolitan Museum of Art/Art Resource, NY; **20-12:** Paul Laes; **20-12A:** © Giraudon/Art Resource, NY; **20-12B:** © Scala/Art Resource, NY; **20-13:** © Scala/Art Resource, NY; **20-14:** © Erich Lessing/Art Resource, NY; **20-14A_1:** © The Metropolitan Museum of Art/Art Resource, NY; **20-14A_2:** © The Metropolitan Museum of Art/Art Resource, NY; **20-14B:** © Erich Lessing/Art Resource, NY; **20-15:** © Réunion des Musées Nationaux/Art Resource, NY; **20-16:** © Réunion des Musées Nationaux/Art Resource, NY; **20-16A:** The Art Archive/Osterreichisches National Bibliothek Vienna/Eileen Tweedy/Picture Desk; **20-17 (left):** Bildarchiv Preussischer Kulturbesitz/Art Resource, NY; **20-17 (right):** © Scala/Art Resource, NY; **20-18:** © Erich Lessing/Art Resource, NY; **20-19:** © Erich Lessing/Art Resource, NY; **20-20:** © Erich Lessing/Art Resource, NY; **20-20A:** © Erich Lessing/Art Resource, NY; **20-21:** Courtesy Luarine Tansey; **20-21A:** John Rylands University Library, University of Manchester, Manchester; **20-22:** © Scala/Art Resource.

Chapter 21—**21-1:** © Scala/Art Resource, NY; **21-2:** © Erich Lessing/Art Resource, NY; **21-3:** © Erich Lessing/Art Resource, NY; **21-4:** © Scala/Art Resource, NY; **21-5:** © Scala/ Art Resource, NY; **21-6:** © Scala/Art Resource, NY; **21-7:** © Scala/Art Resource, NY; **21-8:** © Scala/Art Resource, NY; **21-10:** © Scala/Art Resource, NY; **21-11:** © The Art Archive/Dagli Orti; **21-11A:** © Alinari/The Bridgeman Art Library International; **21-12:** © Scala/Art Resource, NY; **21-12A:** akg-images/Rabatti-Domingie; **21-13:** © Scala/Art Resource, NY; **21-14:** © Scala/Art Resource, NY; **21-15:** © Elio Ciol/CORBIS; **21-16:** © Erich Lessing/Art Resource, NY; **21-17:** © Erich Lessing/Art Resource; **21-18:** © Scala/Art Resource, NY; **21-19:** Canali Photobank, Italy; **21-20:** © Erich Lessing/Art Resource, NY; **21-21:** Canali Photobank, Italy; **21-22:** © Scala/Art Resource, NY; **21-23:** Canali Photobank, Italy; **21-24:** © Scala/Art Resource, NY; **21-25:** © The Bridgeman Art Library; **21-26:** © Erich Lessing/Art Resource, NY; **21-27:** © Scala/Art Resource, NY; **21-28:** © Summerfield Press Ltd.; **21-28A:** akg-images/Rabatti-Domingie; **21-29:** Image Copyright © The Metropolitan Museum of Art/Art Resource, NY; **21-30:** From *Architecture of the Italian Renaissance* by P. Murray, copyright © 1963 by Peter Murray. Used by permission of Schocken books, a division of Random House, Inc.; **21-30A:** © Alinari/Art Resource, NY; **21-31:** © Scala/Art Resource, NY; **21-31A:** The Bridgeman Art Library International; **21-33:** © Angelo Hornak/CORBIS; **21-35:** © Scala/Art Resource, NY; **21-35A:** © Scala/Art Resource, NY; **21-36:** © Scala/Art Resource, NY; **21-37** Scala/Art Resource, NY; **21-38:** © Scala/Art Resource, NY; **21-39:** © The Bridgeman Art Library; **21-40:** © 1987 M. Sarri/Photo Vatican Museums; **21-40A:** Scala/Art Resource, NY; **21-41:** © Scala/Art Resource, NY; **21-42:** © Scala/Art Resource, NY; **21-42A:** © Scala/Ministero per i Beni e le Attività culturali/Art Resource, NY; **21-43:** © Scala/Art Resource, NY; **21-43A:** © Scala/Art Resource; **21-43B:** © Nicolo Orsi Battaglini/Art Resource, NY; **21-44:** © Alinari/Art Resource, NY; **21-45:** From Nikolaus Pevsner, *An Outline of European Architecture*, 6th ed., 1960, Penguin Books Ltd., Copyright © Nikolaus Pevsner, 1943, 1960, 1963; **21-46:** Canali Photobank, Italy; **21-46A:** © Angelo Hornak/CORBIS Art/CORBIS; **21-47:** © Scala/Art Resource, NY; **21-48:** © Scala/Art Resource, NY; **21-49:** © Erich Lessing/Art Resource, NY; **21-49A:** © Alinari/The Bridgeman Art Library International.

Chapter 22—**22-1:** Photo Vatican Museums; **22-2:** © Erich Lessing/Art Resource, NY; **22-3:** © The Art Archive/National Gallery, London/Eileen Tweedy; **22-3A:** © Scala/Art Resource, NY; **22-4:** © Alinari/Art Resource, NY; **22-5:** © Réunion des Musées Nationaux/Art Resource, NY; **22-6:** The Royal Collection © 2005, Her Majesty Queen Elizabeth II; **22-6A:** © Bibliothèque de l'Institut de France/Réunion des Musées Nationaux/Art Resource, NY; **22-7:** © Erich Lessing/Art Resource, NY; **22-8:** © Erich Lessing/Art Resource, NY; **22-8A:** © Scala/Art Resource, NY; **22-9:** © M. Sarri 1983/Photo Vatican Museums; **22-10:** © Scala/Art Resource, NY; **22-11:** © Erich Lessing/Art Resource, NY; **22-11A:** © Scala/Ministero per i Beni e le Attività culturali/Art Resource, NY; **22-12:** © Araldo de Luca/CORBIS; **22-12A:** © Erich Lessing/Art Resource, NY; **22-13:** © Arte & Immagini/CORBIS; **22-14:** © Scala/Art Resource, NY; **22-15:** © Scala/Art Resource, NY; **22-16:** © Réunion des Musées Nationaux/Art Resource, NY; **22-17:** © Scala/Art Resource, NY; **22-18:** Copyright © Nippon Television Network Corporation, Tokyo; **22-19:** © Bracchietti-Zigrosi/Vatican Museums; **22-19A:** © Erich Lessing/Art Resource, NY; **22-20:** Copyright © Nippon Television Network Corporation, Tokyo; **22-21:** Copyright © Nippon Television Network Corporation, Tokyo; **22-22:** © Scala/Art Resource, NY; **22-24:** © HIP/Art Resource, NY; **22-26:** © Scala/Art Resource, NY; **22-27:** © Alinari/CORBIS; **22-27A:** Pubbli Aer Foto; **22-28:** © Alinari/CORBIS; **22-29:** © akg-images/Schütze/Rodemann; **22-31:** © Bill Ross/CORBIS; **22-31A:** © Scala/Art Resource, NY; **22-32:** © John Heseltine/ CORBIS; **22-33:** © Scala/Art Resource, NY; **22-33A:** Giovanni Bellini (c. 1430–1516) *St. Francis in the Desert*, 1480. Oil and tempera on poplar panel. 49 in. x 55 7/8 in. (124.46 cm x 141.92 cm) Henry Clay Frick Bequest. Accession number: 1915.1.03; **22-34:** © 1999 Board of Trustees, National Gallery of Art, Washington, D.C.; **22-35:** © Erich Lessing/Art Resource, NY; **22-36:** © Cameraphoto/Art Resource, NY; **22-37:** © Scala/Art Resource, NY; **22-38:** © Scala/Art Resource, NY; **22-39:** © National Gallery, London; **22-39A:** © Scala/Art Resource, NY; **22-40:** © Scala/Art Resource, NY; **22-41:** © Erich Lessing/Art Resource, NY; **22-41A:** National Museum of Women in the Arts; **22-42:** © Scala/Art Resource, NY; **22-42A:** The Art Archive/Pinacoteca Nazionale di Siena/Alfredo Dagli Orti/Picture Desk; **22-43:** © Scala/Art Resource, NY; **22-43A:** © Erich Lessing/Art Resource, NY; **22-44:** © National Gallery, London; **22-45:** Image Copyright © The Metropolitan Museum of Art/Art Resource, NY; **22-45A:** © The Bridgeman Art Library International; **22-46:** © The Bridgeman Art Library; **22-47:** © Scala/Art Resource, NY; **22-48:** © Scala/Art Resource, NY; **22-49:** Canali Photobank, Italy; **22-50:** © Alinari/Art Resource, NY; **22-51:** © Erich Lessing/Art Resource, NY; **22-51A:** © Lauros/Giraudon/The Bridgeman Art

Library International; **22-52:** © 2006 Fred S. Kleiner; **22-53:** © Erich Lessing/Art Resource, NY; **22-53A:** © Scala/Art Resource, NY; **22-54:** © akg-images/Rabatti-Domingie; **22-55:** © The Art Archive/Dagli Orti.

Chapter 23—**23-1:** Photograph © 2008 Museum of Fine Arts, Boston; **23-2 (top):** © Erich Lessing/Art Resource, NY; **23-2 (bottom):** © Musée d'Unterlinden Colmar, photo O. Zimmermann; **23-3:** HIP/Art Resource, NY; **23-3A:** © Erich Lessing/Art Resource, NY; **23-4:** © The Bridgeman Art Library; **23-4A:** akg-images; **23-5:** Image Copyright © The Metropolitan Museum of Art/Art Resource, NY; **23-5A:** © Victoria & Albert Museum, London/Art Resource, NY; **23-6:** © Scala/Art Resource, NY; **23-7:** © The British Museum; **23-7A:** Staatliche Kunsthalle, Karlsruhe; **23-8:** © Scala/Art Resource, NY; **23-9:** © National Gallery, London; **23-9A:** © Scala/Art Resource, NY; **23-10:** © Réunion des Musées Nationaux/Art Resource, NY; **23-11:** © Charles E. Rotkin/CORBIS; **23-12:** © 2009 Fred S. Kleiner; **23-12A:** The Art Archive/Dagli Orti; **23-13:** © Institut Amatller D'art Hispànic; **23-14:** © Bildarchiv Preussischer Kulturbesitz/Art Resource, NY; **23-14A:** © Erich Lessing/Art Resource, NY; **23-15:** © Réunion des Musées Nationaux/Art Resource, NY; **23-16:** Uppsala University Art Collection; **23-17:** Oeffentliche Kunstsammlung Basel, photo Martin Bühler; **23-18:** The Royal Collection © 2007 Her Majesty Queen Elizabeth II; **23-19:** © Erich Lessing/Art Resource, NY; **23-20:** © Bildarchiv Preussischer Kulturbesitz/Art Resource, NY; **23-20A:** © Scala/Art Resource, NY; **23-21:** © Kunsthistorisches Museum, Vienna; **23-22:** © Institut Amatller D'art Hispànic; **23-23:** © John Elk III; **23-24:** © Institut Amatller D'art Hispànic; **23-25:** © Scala/Art Resource, NY; **23-25A:** © The Metropolitan Museum of Art/Art Resource, NY.

Chapter 24—**24-1:** © akg-images/Pirozzi; **24-2:** © akg-images/Pirozzi; **24-3:** © Andrea Jemolo/CORBIS; **24-4:** © Alinari/CORBIS; **24-4A:** The Art Archive/Gianni Dagli Orti/Picture Desk; **24-5:** © akg-images/Joseph Martin; **24-6:** Canali Photobank. Italy; **24-7:** © Scala/Art Resource, NY; **24-7A:** © Araldo de Luca/CORBIS; **24-8:** © Araldo de Luca; **24-9A:** © Scala/Art Resource, NY; **24-11:** www.bednorz-photo.de; **24-12:** © 2006 Fred S. Kleiner; **24-14:** © Scala/Art Resource; **24-14A:** © Alinari/The Bridgeman Art Library International; **24-15:** © Alinari/Art Resource, NY; **24-16:** © Scala/Art Resource, NY; **24-17:** © Scala/Art Resource, NY; **24-18:** © Scala/Art Resource, NY; **24-18A:** © The Metropolitan Museum of Art/Art Resource, NY; **24-19:** © Scala/Art Resource, NY; **24-20:** © Alinari/Art Resource, NY; **24-20A:** The Royal Collection © 2009 Her Majesty Queen Elizabeth II; **24-21:** © Nimatallah/Art Resource, NY; **24-22:** © The Bridgeman Art Library; **24-23:** © Scala/Art Resource, NY; **24-24:** © Summerfield Press Ltd.; **24-25:** © The Art Archive/Museo del Prado; **24-25A:** © Erich Lessing/Art Resource, NY; **24-26:** Photograph © Wadsworth Atheneum Museum of Art; **24-27:** © Victoria & Albert Museum, London/Art Resource, NY; **24-27A:** © Scala/Art Resource, NY; **24-28:** © The Frick Collection, NY; **24-29:** © Scala/Art Resource, NY; **24-30:** © Erich Lessing/Art Resource, NY; **24-30A:** © Erich Lessing/Art Resource, NY.

Chapter 25—**25-1:** © Erich Lessing/Art Resource, NY; **25-2:** Copyright © IRPA-KIK, Brussels, www.kikirpa.be; **25-2A:** © Erich Lessing/Art Resource, NY; **25-3:** © Erich Lessing/Art Resource, NY; **25-3A:** © Erich Lessing/Art Resource, NY; **25-4:** © Scala/Art Resource, NY; **25-5:** © Réunion des Musées Nationaux/Art Resource, NY; **25-6:** © Scala/Art Resource, NY; **25-7:** © Centraal Museum, Utrecht, photo Ernst Moritz, The Hague; **25-8:** © Alinari/The Bridgeman Art Library; **25-9:** © Frans Halsmuseum. Haarlem; **25-10:** © Frans Halsmuseum, Haarlem; **25-11:** Image © 2007 Board of Trustees, National Gallery of Art, Washington, D.C.; **25-12:** © Erich Lessing/Art Resource, NY; **25-13:** © The Bridgeman Art Library; **25-14:** © The Bridgeman Art Library; **25-14A:** akg-images; **25-15:** © English Heritage Photographic Library; **25-15A:** Rembrandt Harmensz. van Rijn (1606–1669) Self-Portrait, 1658. Oil on canvas. 52-5/8 in. x 40-7/8 in. (133.67 cm x 103.82 cm) Henry Clay Frick Bequest. Accession number: 1906.1.97; **25-16:** © The Pierpont Morgan Library/Art Resource, NY; **25-17:** © National Gallery, London; **25-18:** © Mauritshuis. The Hague; **25-18A:** © Erich Lessing/Art Resource, NY; **25-19:** © Rijksmuseum, Amsterdam; **25-19A:** © Giraudon/The Bridgeman Art Library International; **25-19B:** © National Gallery of Art, Washington D.C., USA/The Bridgeman Art Library International; **25-20:** © Rijksmuseum, Amsterdam; **25-21:** © Germanisches Nationalmuseum; Nuremberg; **25-22:** Photo copyright © Indianapolis Museum of Art, Indianapolis; **25-23:** Photo Copyright © Toledo Museum of Art, Toledo, 1956.57; **25-24:** © Erich Lessing/Art Resource, NY; **25-25:** © Scala/Art Resource, NY; **25-25A:** Reproduction, The Art Institute of Chicago; **25-26:** Photo copyright © Philadelphia Museum of Art, Philadelphia; **25-27:** © Réunion des Musées Nationaux/Art Resource, NY; **25-28:** © Erich Lessing/Art Resource, NY; **25-29:** © Erich Lessing/Art Resource, NY; **25-30:** © Réunion des Musées Nationaux/Art Resource, NY; **25-31:** www.bednorz-photo.de; **25-32:** © Yann Arthus-Bertrand/ Altitude; **25-33:** © Massimo Listri/CORBIS; **25-34:** © Bernard Annebicque/CORBIS; **25-35:** © akg-images/Paul M. R. Maeyaert; **25-36:** Saskia; **25-37:** © Angelo Hornak/CORBIS; **25-38:** © Angelo Hornak/CORBIS.

Chapter 26—**26-1:** © Kevin R. Morris/CORBIS; **26-2:** © The Art Archive; **26-3:** © Geoffrey Taunton/Cordaiy Photo Library Ltd./CORBIS; **26-4:** © Victoria & Albert Museum, London/Art Resource, NY; **26-4A:** © Victoria & Albert Museum, London/Art Resource, NY; **26-5:** Freer Gallery of Art, Smithsonian Institution, Washington, D.C., Purchase, F1942.15a; **26-5A:** Photograph © 2009 Museum of Fine Arts, Boston; **26-6:** © Yann-Arthus Bertrand/CORBIS; **26-7:** National Museum, New Delhi; **26-7A:** Courtesy of the Trustees of the Chhatrapati Shivaji Maharaj Vastu Sangrahalaya formerly Prince of Wales Museum of Western India, Mumbai. Not to be reproduced without prior permission of the Trustees; **26-8:** © Christophe Boisvieux/CORBIS; **26-9:** © Tony Waltham/Robert Harding Picture Library; **26-10:** The Brooklyn Museum of Art, 87.234.6; **26-11:** © Stuart Westmorland; **26-12:** © Luca Tettoni Photography; **26-13:** © Ladislav Janicek/zefa/CORBIS; **26-14:** Pacific Asia Museum Collection, Gift of Hon. and Mrs. Jack Lydman, Museum No. 1991.47.34; **26-15:** © Benoy K. Behl.

Chapter 27—**27-1:** © Alfred Ko/CORBIS; **27-2:** Collection of the National Palace Museum, Taiwan, Republic of China; **27-2A:** Freer Gallery of Art, Smithsonian Institution, Washington, D.C.; **27-3:** Collection of the National Palace Museum, Taiwan, Republic of China; **27-4:** Collection of the National Palace Museum, Taiwan, Republic of China; **27-5:** Percival David Foundation of Chinese Art, B614; **27-6:** photos12.com, Panorama Stock; **27-7:** © Carl and Ann Purcell/CORBIS; **27-8:** © Werner Forman/Art Resource, NY; **27-9:** © Victoria & Albert Museum/Art Resource, NY; **27-10:** Cultural Relics Publishing House, Beijing; **27-11:** Collection of the National Palace Museum, Taiwan, Republic of China; **27-11A:** Nelson-Atkins Museum of Art, Kansas City;

INDEX

Boldface names refer to artists. Page numbers in *italics* refer to illustrations.
Figure numbers in **bold** refer to thumbnail images and related text on the book's premium website, ArtStudy Online.

Hagia Sophia, 313–314, *313*, 315, 324, 327–328, 329, 339, 354, 355, 363, 419, 471, 474, 1004; Ottoman Turks and, 311, 336, 339, 341, 355, 363; patriarch of, 320; Ravenna and, 316

Constantius Chlorus, 282, 285

Constitution Garden, 1007

Constructivism, 948–950, 961, 967

Contarelli Chapel, 660

Continuous narration, 265, **10-47A, 11-20A**

Contrapposto, 127, 155, 545, 549

Conversion of Saint Paul (Caravaggio), 659–660, *659*, 661

Cook Islands, art of, 882

Copán: ball court at, 372, *372*; Great Plaza, 373; Stele D, Ruler 13, 373, *373*

Copley, John Singleton: work of, 764–765, *764*

Corbie Gospels: folio from, **17-15B**

Córdoba, 352, 363, 415; Great Mosque, 348–349, *348, 349*, 363

Corfu, Temple of Artemis, 48, 112, *112*, 230

Corinthians, black-figure technique and, 104, 114

Cormont, Renaud de: work of, 474, *474, 475*

Cormont, Thomas de: work of, 474, *474, 475*

Cornaro Chapel (Bernini), 654; interior of, *648, 654*

Corneille, Pierre, 769

Cornelia Presenting Her Children as Her Treasures, or Mother of the Gracchi (Kauffmann), 767, *767*

Cornered (Piper), 1022, *1022*

Coronation Gospels, 417, 449; folio of, *417*

Coronation of Napoleon (David), 779, *779*

Correggio (Antonio Allegri): work of, 618, *618*

Correspondence littéraire: Diderot in, 760, 761

Cortés, Hernán, 366, 643, 855; Aztecs and, 860, 869; Moctezuma II and, 853, 857

Cortese, Paolo: on Federico da Montefeltro, 570

Corvey, 421; westwork of, *421*, 422

Cosmic Buddha, 214

Cosmic Cubism, 935

Council of Clermont, 442

Council of Ephesus, 301

Council of Nicaea, 282

Council of Trent, 596, 649

Counter-Reformation, 616, 649, 650, 651, 652, 654, 655, 661, 664, 665, 667, 679, 685; art and, 671; Catholic Church and, 625; Jesuits and, 622; martyrdom scenes and, 666; religious art of, 596

Courbet, Gustave, 803, 809, 816, 819, 822, 918; photography and, 815; on Realism, 799; rejection of, 823; work of, 798–800, *798*

Courier du dimanche: Courbet's letter in, 799

Court of Gayumars (Sultan-Muhammad), *359*

Coyolxauhqui, 856–857, *856*, 869

Coypel, Antoine: work of, 700, *700*

Cranach, Lucas, the Elder, 647; work of, 631, *631*, 632, **23-7A**

Cranmer, Doug: work of, 865, *865*

Creation of Adam (Michelangelo), 594–595, *594*, 623, 660

Creglingen Altarpiece (Riemenschneider), 535, *535*

Cremaster cycle (Barney), 968, 1024

Crete, palace sites on, 84

Crimean War, photographs of, 817

Crocus gatherers (Akrotiri), **4-9B**

Crossing, The (Viola), 1022, *1022*

Crossing square, 421, 562

Crossing towers, 302, 446, 447

Crucifixion, 294–295, 306, 308, 315, 330, 331, 412, 414, *418*, 424; art about, 297; mosaic of, *330;* representation of, 307; symbolism of, 5

Crucifixion (Naumburg Cathedral), **18-49A**

Crucifixion and Resurrection, Rabbula Gospels, **12-17A**

Crucifixion scene (Grünewald), 626, *627*, 628

Cruciform, 302, 331, 562

Crusades, 335, 339, 362, 438, 441, 442, 450, 463, 482

Crystal Palace (Paxton), 759, 812–813, *813*, 819, 1011, **16-67A**

Ctesiphon, 49, 347, 353; palace at, 50

Cubi XIX (D. Smith), 978, *978*

Cubiculum, 246, 247, 248, *249*, 270, 292, *292*

Cubiculum Leonis, Rome, **11-5B**

Cubism, 4, 906, 908, 918–926, 934, 948, 950, 953, 967, 972, 977, **31-20A, 35-34A, 35-54A;** Analytic, 921, 935; Cosmic, 935; Picasso on, 924; Synthetic, 922, 925–926, 935, 936, 937, 955

Cubism and Abstract Art (MoMA exhibition), 954

Cuckoo Flying over New Verdure (Buson), 743, *743*

Cult statues, 109, 295

Cumul I (Bourgeois), 980, *980*

Cuneiform, 32, 36, 39

Cupid (Eros, Amor), 255, 275, 486, 560, 677, 750, *756*, 757; Venus and, 613

Cupid a Captive (Boucher), 756

Cupid and Psyche (Canova), **30-4A**

Cut with the Kitchen Knife Dada through the Last Weimar Beer Belly Cultural Epoch of Germany (Höch), 931, *931*

Cutaways, 12

Cuthbert, Saint, 413

Cuvilliés, François de: work of, 752, *753*

Cuyp, Aelbert, 703; work of, 686, *687*

Cuzco, 858, 859–860, 869; Temple of the Sun, 859, *859*, 860

Cycladic figurines, 82–83, *83*, 84, 95, 97, **4-8A**

Cyclopean masonry, 91, 97

Cyclopes, 91, 92

Cyclops, The (Redon), 840, *840*

Cylindrical bone ornaments, 882, *882*

Dacian Wars, 264, 265

Dada, 928–932, 940, 972, 980, 983, 1017; pessimism of, 928, 948; Surrealism and, 943, 944

Dadaists, 931, 945, 948, 967, **35-27A, 36-80A;** manifestos of, 928–929

Daddi, Bernardo, 19-19B

Daedalus (legendary Greek artist), 105, 106, **23-20A**

Daggers, 94–95, *95*, 97

Daguerre, Louis-Jacques-Mandé, 814, 819; work of, 815, *815*

Daguerreotypes, 713, 814, 815–816

Daibutsuden, 214, *214*, 221

Dalí, Salvador, 943, 953, **35-50A;** work of, 946, *946*

Damascus, Great Mosque, 344–345, *344, 345*

Damned Cast into Hell (Signorelli), 570, *570*

Dance, The (Carpeaux), **31-31A**

Dance, The (Derain), 913, *913*

Dante Alighieri, 481, 502, 507, 541, 783, 791, 810, 844

Daodejing (The Way and Its Power) (Laozi), 186

Daoism, 184, 186, 205

Daoji. *See* Shitao

Daphni, Church of the Dormition, *310*, 330, *330*

Daphni Crucifixion, 330, *330*

Daphni Pantokrator, 330, **12-22A**

Daphnis of Miletos: work of, 145–146, *145*

Darbar of Jahangir (Abul Hasan and Manohar), **26-5A**

Darby, Abraham, III: work of, 759, *759*

Darius I, King, 48, 51

Darius III, King, 48, 98, 142, 632

Dark Ages, 96, 100, 784

Darwin, Charles, 817, 822

Darwinism, 821–822

Das Staatliche Bauhaus, 962

Daumier, Honoré, *802*, 803, 816, 819, 956; photography and, 815; printmaking and, 801; work of, 801–802, *801, 814*

David, Jacques-Louis, 775, 786, 788, 792, 793, **30-2B, 30-15A;** French Revolution and, 769; on Greek style/public art, 768; Napoleon and, 779, 819; Neoclassicism and, 781, 819; students of, 781–783; work of, 768–769, *768, 769*, 777, 779, *779*, **30-2A**

David (Bernini), 653–654, *653*, **24-7A**

David (Donatello), 549, *549*, 550, 577, 591, 653, **21-12A;** transfer of, 590

David (Michelangelo), 590–591, *590*, 592, 623, 653, 654, 978

David (Verrocchio), 549–550, *550*, 590, 591, 653, 654

David and Samuel, mural of, *291*, 304

David composing the Psalms, *334*

Davies, Arthur B., 918, 924

Davis, Stuart: work of, 936, *936*

"De," many names with "de," "del," "di" and the like are listed under next element of name, e.g. "Chirico, Giorgio de," 1222

De architectura (Vitruvius), 602

De Chirico, Giorgio, 35-50A; work of, 943–944, *944*

De imitatione statuarum (Rubens), 675

de Kooning, Willem, 983, 989, 1025, **36-7A;** work of, 974–975, *974*

de la Tour, Georges, 694; work of, 695–696, *695*

De Stijl, 948–950, 962, 964, 967; defining, 961

De Stijl (magazine), 950

de Zayas, Marius, 924

Dead Christ (Mantegna), 576

Death: personification of, 5; symbol of, 806

Death and Assumption of the Virgin (Stoss), 534, *535*

Death and Life of Great American Cities, The (Jacobs), 1008

Death and the Maiden (Baldung Grien), **23-3A**

Death of General Wolfe (West), 764, *764*

Death of Marat (David), 769, *769*

Death of Sardanapalus (Delacroix), 790, *790*, 791, 819

Death of the Virgin, Strasbourg, *491*

Decameron (Boccaccio), 502

Decline and Fall of the Roman Empire (Gibbon), 767

Deconstructivism, 987, 1002, 1011–1013, 1025, **36-71A**

Decorative arts, 846–850, 851

Decursio, 272, *272*, 273

Deer Park, 161, 165, 167

Degas, Edgar, 818, 842, **31-7A, 31-14A, 35-11A;** Impressionism and, 851; influence of, 831; Japanese art and, 829, **31-11A;** photography and, 815, 816, 828; work of, 828–830, *828, 829*

Degenerate art, 945, 953

Deir el-Bahri, Temple of Hatshepsut, 67–68, *67*

Déjeuner en fourrure, Le (Oppenheim), 946, *947*

Déjeuner sur l'Herbe, Le (Manet), 803–804, *803*, 823, **31-20A**

Del Monte, Cardinal, **24-18A**

Delacroix, Eugène, 776, 783, 794, 803, 816, 819, 836, **31-23A;** in Morocco, 792; Nadar and, 817; photography and, 815; Romanticism and, 790; work of, 790–793, *790, 791, 792*, **30-18A, 30-19A**

Delaroche, Paul, 815

Delaunay, Robert: work of, 921–922, *922*

Delaware residence (Venturi, Rauch, and Brown), 1010, *1010*

Delhi sultanate, 174, 342, 705–706, 717

Delian League, 125, 127, 129

Della Robbia, Andrea, 565, **21-30A**

Della Robbia, Luca, 564, 565; work of, **21-35A**

Delphi: sanctuary of Apollo, aerial view, **5-18A;** Siphnian Treasury, 113, *113*, 133, 148

Demoiselles d'Avignon, Les (Picasso), 919–920, *919*, 920, 921, 954, **31-20A, 35-2A, 35-11A**

Demosthenes (Polyeuktos), 152–153, *152*

Demuth, Charles, 967, **35-62A;** work of, 937, *937*

Denarius, *244*

Denver Art Museum (Libeskind), 1013, *1013*

Deogarh, Vishnu Temple, 170, *170*, 176, 179

Departure of the Volunteers of 1792 (Rude), 793, *793*

Deposition (Rogier van der Weyden), 527, *527*

Depth, illusion of, 9

Der Blaue Reiter, 915, 916, 922, 935

Der Jugend, 846

Der Krieg (The War) (Dix), 942, *942*

Der Sturm, 911

Derain, André, 934, **35-34A;** work of, 913, *913*, **35-4A**

Derrida, Jacques, 987

Descartes, René, 700, 757

Descent from the Cross (Pontormo), 613

Descent of the Ganges River (or *Penance of Arjuna*), rock-cut relief (Mamallapuram), **6-21A**

Dessau, Shop Block, 962, *962*

Devi, 168, 171, **6-21B**

Diamond World mandara, 215, 221

Díaz del Castillo, Bernal, 855, 856

Diderot, Denis, 761; on Chardin/Naturalism, 760; work of, 758

Didyma, Temple of Apollo, 145–146, *145*, 155

Die (Smith), 978, 979

Die Brücke, 913, 914, 915, 926, **35-6A**

Dijon, Chartreuse de Champmol, 520–522, 539

Dilukai, 878, 879, *879*, 887

Dinner Party, The (Chicago), 989–990, *990*, 1025; Chicago on, 990

Dio Cassius, 260; on Hadrian/Apollodorus, 269

Diocletian, 239, 287, 300, 311, 545, 766; abdication of, 282; Christianity and, 291; mausoleum of, 282, 451; palace of, 346, **11-18A;** tetrarchy and, 280–282

Diogenes, 586, 587

Dione, 101, 129, *129*

Dionysius, Saint, 462

Dionysius of Halicarnassus: on Tusci, 223

Dionysos (Bacchus), 101, 129, *129*, 136, *136*, 138, *138*, 143, 151, 248

Dioscurides, 275, 304

Dioskorides (Vienna), 324

Diptych of Martin van Nieuwenhove (Memling), **20-14B**

Diptych of the Symmachi, 308; leaf of, *308*

Dipylon cemetery, 102, 134

Dipylon Gate, 130